The Holy Bible

With Deuterocanonical & Apocryphal Books.

INTERNATIONAL
ENGLISH

BIBLE

Contents

Preface to the International English Bible

What is the Holy Bible?

The Holy Bible is a collection of books and letters written by many people who were inspired by the Holy Spirit of God. These books tell us how we can be saved from the evil of this world and gain eternal life that is truly worth living. Although the Holy Bible contains rules of conduct, it is not just a rule book. It reveals God's heart—a Father's heart, full of love and compassion. The Holy Bible tells you what you need to know and believe to be saved from sin and evil and how to live a life that is truly worth living, no matter what your current circumstances may be.

The Holy Bible consists of two main sections: the Old Testament (including Psalms and Proverbs) and the New Testament (Matthew through Revelation). The Old Testament records God's interaction with mankind before He sent His son to redeem us, while recording prophesy predicting that coming. The New Testament tells us of God's Son and Anointed One, Jesus, and the wonderful salvation that He purchased for us.

The same Holy Spirit who inspired the Holy Bible is living amongst us today, and He is happy to help you understand what He intended as you study His Word. Just ask Him, and He is more than happy to help you apply His message to your life.

The Old Testament was originally written mostly in Hebrew. The New Testament was originally written mostly in the common street Greek (not the formal Greek used for official legal matters). The Holy Bible is translated into many languages, and being translated into many more, so that everyone may have an opportunity to hear the Good News about Jesus Christ.[a]

Why was the International English Bible translated?

There are already many good translations of the Holy Bible into contemporary English. Unfortunately, almost all of them are restricted by copyright and copyright holder policy. This restricts publication and republication of God's Word in many ways, such as in downloadable files on the Internet, use of extensive quotations in books, etc. The International English Bible was commissioned by God in response to prayer about this subject.

Because the International English Bible is in the Public Domain (not copyrighted), it can be freely copied, distributed, and redistributed without any payment of royalties. You don't even have to ask permission to do so. You may publish the whole International English Bible in book form, bind it in leather and sell it. You may incorporate it into your Bible study software. You may make and distribute audio recordings of it. You may broadcast it. All you have to do is maintain the integrity of God's Word before God, and reserve the name "International English Bible" for faithful copies of this translation.

How was the International English Bible translated?

The International English Bible is an update of the American Standard Version (ASV) of the Holy Bible, published in 1901 and is derived from International English Bible (IEB). A custom computer program updated the archaic words and word forms to contemporary equivalents, and then a team of volunteers proofread and updated the grammar. The New Testament was updated to conform to the Majority Text reconstruction of the original Greek manuscripts, thus taking advantage of the superior access to manuscripts that we have now compared to when the original ASV was translated.

What is different about the International English Bible?

The style of the International English Bible, while fairly literally translated, is in informal, spoken English. The International English Bible is designed to sound good and be accurate when read aloud. It is not formal in its language, just as the original Greek of the New Testament was not formal. The IEB uses contractions rather freely.

The International English Bible doesn't capitalise pronouns pertaining to God. The original manuscripts made no such distinction. Hebrew has no such thing as upper and lower case, and the original Greek manuscripts were written in all upper case letters. Attempting to add in such a distinction raises some difficulties in translating dual-meaning Scriptures such as the coronation psalms.

The International English Bible main edition translates God's Proper Name in the Old Testament as "Yahweh." The Messianic Edition and the British Edition of the International English Bible translates the same name as "LORD" (all capital letters), or when used with "Lord" (mixed case, translated from "Adonai",) GOD. There are solid translational arguments for both traditions.

Because International English Bible uses the Majority Text as the basis for the New Testament, you may notice the following differences in comparing the IEB to other translations:

The order of Matthew 23:13 and 14 is reversed in some translations.

Luke 17:36 and Acts 15:34, which are not found in the majority of the Greek Manuscripts (and are relegated to footnotes in the IEB) may be included in some other translations.

Romans 14:24-26 in the IEB may appear as Romans 16:25-27 in other translations.

1 John 5:7-8 contains an addition in some translations, including the KJV. Erasmus admitted adding this text to his published Greek New Testament, even though he could at first find no Greek manuscript support for it, because he was being pressured by men to do so, and because he didn't see any doctrinal harm in it. Lots of things not written by John in this letter are true, but we decline to add them to what the Holy Spirit inspired through John.

With all of the above and some other places where lack of clarity in the original manuscripts has led to multiple possible readings, significant variants are listed in footnotes. The reading that in our prayerful judgement is best is in the main text. Overall, the International English Bible doesn't differ very much from several other good contemporary English translations of the Holy Bible. The message of Salvation through Jesus Christ is still the same. The point of this translation was not to be very different (except for legal status), but to update the ASV for readability while retaining or improving the accuracy of that well-respected translation and retaining the public domain status of the ASV.

Does the International English Bible include the Apocrypha?

The International English Bible is an ecumenical project that includes books included in Bibles in many denominations. The main 66 books of the Old and New Testaments are recognised as Scripture by all true Christians. There are also books considered to be part of, depending on which book and who you ask, Deuterocanon, Apocrypha, and Pseudepigrapha.

The following books and parts of books are recognised as Deuterocanonical Scripture by the Roman Catholic, Greek, and Russian Orthodox Churches: *Tobit, Judith, Esther from the Greek Septuagint, The Wisdom of Solomon, Ecclesiasticus* (also called *The Wisdom of Jesus Son of Sirach), Baruch, The Song of the Three Holy Children, Susanna,* and *Bel and the Dragon, 1 Maccabees, 2 Maccabees.* In this edition, *The Letter of Jeremiah* is included as chapter 6 of *Baruch.* Three of those books come from parts of Daniel found in the Greek Septuagint, but not the Hebrew Old Testament: *The Song of the Three Holy Children, Susanna,* and *Bel and the Dragon.* These three are included in *Daniel (Greek),* in context, as they make more sense that way.

The following books are recognised as Deuterocanonical Scripture by the Greek and Russian Orthodox Churches, but not the Roman Catholic Church: 1 Esdras, The Prayer of Manasseh, Psalm 151, and 3 Maccabees. Note that 1 Esdras and the Prayer of Manasseh are also in an appendix to the Latin Vulgate Bible.

The Slavonic Bible includes 2 Esdras, but calls it 3 Esdras. This same book is in the Appendix to the Latin Vulgate as 4 Esdras.

An appendix to the Greek Septuagint contains 4 Maccabees. It is included for its historical value.

Amongst Christian denominations and amongst individual Christians, opinions vary widely on the Deuterocanon / Apocrypha, as do the collective names they give them. Many regard them as useful in gaining additional understanding of the Old and New Testaments and the hand of God in history, even if they don't give them the same status as the 66 books of the Old and New Testaments. They are included here in support of the churches and individuals who read them and use them, as separate from, but frequently used with, the core canon of the 66 books of the Holy Bible.

What are MT, TR, and NU?

In the footnotes, MT refers to the Greek Majority Text New Testament, which is the authoritative basis for this translation. TR stands for Textus Receptus, which is the Greek Text from which the King James Version New Testament was translated. NU stands for the Nestle-Aland/UBS critical text of the Greek New Testament, which is used as a basis for some other Bible translations.

More Information

For answers to frequently asked questions about the International English Bible, please visit our IEB site at IEB.THEBIBLEUNLOCKED.ORG

---

[a] *1:0* "Christ" means "Anointed One".

The Old Testament

#1 - Genesis: Genesis, the first book of the Bible, narrates the creation of the world, the fall of human kind, and the early history of humanity, including the stories of Adam and Eve, Noah, and the Tower of Babel. It also details the patriarchal history of the Israelites, focusing on Abraham, Isaac, Jacob, and Joseph, ending with the Israelites in Egypt.

#2 - Exodus: The book of Exodus chronicles the story of Moses' leadership in freeing the Israelites from Egyptian bondage, including the Ten Plagues and the parting of the Red Sea. The book also details the journey of the Israelites to Mount Sinai, where Moses received the Ten Commandments and other laws from God.

#3 - Leviticus: In this third book of the Bible, the focus shifts to the laws and religious rituals given to the Israelites. It details a wide array of laws, including those related to rituals, moral conduct, and holiness, primarily communicated through Moses. The book emphasizes the importance of holiness and the procedures for offerings and festivals.

#4 - Numbers: Numbers recounts the Israelites' journey in the wilderness, led by Moses, from Mount Sinai to the border of Canaan. It includes a census of the people, various laws, and accounts of rebellion and faithlessness, highlighting the challenges and trials faced during their wanderings. The narrative also details God's guidance and provision for the Israelites throughout their journey.

#5 - Deuteronomy: Deuteronomy presents itself as a collection of Moses' discourses delivered to the Israelites on the brink of their entry into Canaan. Modern scholarship views these speeches as a retrospective compilation that emphasizes loyalty to God, centralization of worship, and social justice. This book acts as a theological bridge by underscoring the significance of obedience and communal responsibility.

#6 - Joshua: In this narrative, the Israelites, under the leadership of Joshua, enter and conquer the land of Canaan following Moses' death. The book details a series of military campaigns and the subsequent division of the land among the twelve tribes of Israel. It also emphasizes Joshua's role in reaffirming the covenant between the Israelites and God.

#7 - Judges: The Book of Judges depicts a cycle of Israelite leaders, known as judges, rising and falling in a period of instability after the conquest of Canaan. The narrative portrays a pattern of Israelite disobedience to God, leading to oppression by foreign powers, followed by a judge delivering them from these oppressors. Notable figures include Deborah, Gideon, and Samson, each illustrating the challenges and moral complexities of this era.

#8 - Ruth: A touching narrative of loyalty and love, Ruth, a Moabite, remains devoted to her Israelite mother-in-law, Naomi, after tragedy strikes. Her eventual marriage to Boaz not only highlights the theme of redemption but also positions her in the direct lineage of King David.

#9 - 1 Samuel: From the birth of the prophet Samuel to the tumultuous reign of Israel's first king, Saul, this book provides a look at the transition of Israel from a tribal confederation to a monarchy. It sets the stage for the rise of David, Israel's greatest king.

#10 - 2 Samuel: This sequel continues the story of David's reign, following his anointing as king of Israel. The book details his political and military achievements, personal struggles, and moral failings, including the story of David and Bathsheba. It concludes with David's consolidation of power and preparations for the building of the Temple thus setting the stage for the transition to his son Solomon's reign.

#11 - 1 Kings: 1 Kings chronicles the zenith and decline of Israel's united monarchy. From the glory days of Solomon's temple construction to the division of the kingdom into Israel and Judah, the narrative reveals how leaders can shape a nation's fate.

#12 - 2 Kings: With a succession of rulers, 2 Kings details the final chapters of both the northern and southern kingdoms. Despite intermittent revivals, rampant idolatry ultimately leads to Israel's exile by Assyria and Judah's devastation by Babylon.

#13 - 1 Chronicles: 1 Chronicles offers a genealogical retelling of Israel's history, with an emphasis on David's reign. It begins with a series of genealogies tracing the lineage from Adam to the Davidic line, emphasizing the continuity of God's promises. The latter part of the book details David's reign, his preparations for the construction of the Temple, and the organization of the priesthood and Levites, showcasing his role in establishing religious worship in Israel.

#14 - 2 Chronicles: Focusing on the reign of Solomon and subsequent kings of Judah, this narrative extends to the Babylonian exile. It highlights Solomon's construction of the Temple in Jerusalem and his wisdom, as well as the varying degrees of faithfulness of Judah's kings to their covenant with God. The book culminates with the Temple's destruction and the exile, presented as repercussions of the nation's unfaithfulness.

#15 - Ezra: This post-exilic book chronicles the return of the Jewish exiles from Babylon and their efforts to rebuild the Temple in Jerusalem under the leadership of Zerubbabel and the priestly guidance of Ezra. It focuses on the restoration of religious and communal life in Jerusalem, emphasizing the importance of adherence to the Law of Moses.

#16 - Nehemiah: As the walls of Jerusalem lay in ruins, Nehemiah, the cupbearer to the Persian king, takes on the daunting task of rebuilding. His leadership and the people's collaborative spirit exemplify restoration in the face of adversity.

#17 - Esther: Set in the Persian Empire, Esther, a Jewish queen, bravely intervenes to prevent the genocide of her people. With divine providence at play, the narrative celebrates the origins of the Jewish festival of Purim.

#18 - Job: The Book of Job delves into the themes of suffering and divine justice, narrating the story of Job, a righteous man whose faith is tested through extreme hardships. In this narrative, God allows Satan to test Job's faith, resulting in a series of catastrophic events that include the heartbreaking loss of his children. The book also presents a series of dialogues between Job and his friends about the nature of suffering. The book concludes with a poetic discourse on the power and wisdom of God, underscoring the limitations of human understanding.

#19 - Psalms: Comprising 150 songs and poems, this collection expresses a wide range of emotions and themes, from praise, worship, and thanksgiving to lament and supplication. The Psalms address the human experience of God, exploring themes like faith, suffering, and God's sovereignty. They are used extensively in Jewish, Christian, and Islamic liturgies, reflecting their enduring spiritual and cultural significance.

#20 - Proverbs: Traditionally attributed to King Solomon, Proverbs is a compilation of wise sayings and instructions on leading a righteous life. These bite-sized pearls of wisdom touch on topics like character, relationships, and personal integrity.

#21 - Ecclesiastes: Ecclesiastes presents a philosophical reflection on the meaning of life and the best way to live, voiced by a narrator called 'the Teacher.' It explores themes of vanity, the fleeting nature of earthly pursuits, and the limits of human wisdom, ultimately advocating for finding enjoyment in life's simple pleasures and fearing God.

#22 - Song of Solomon: Also known as the Song of Songs, this book is a collection of lyrical poems celebrating love and romantic desire. Within Judaism, it is often interpreted allegorically as symbolizing the relationship between God and Israel, while in Christian tradition, it is seen as a metaphor for the bond between Christ and the Church. The text vividly portrays the beauty and power of love through passionate dialogues between lovers.

#23 - Isaiah: Isaiah is a composite text, traditionally attributed to the prophet Isaiah, that addresses the political and social conditions of ancient Judah. The book spans pre-exilic warnings of judgment, reflections on exile, and post-exilic themes of restoration and hope, blending oracles, narratives, and prophetic discourses. Its messages focus on themes of justice, righteousness, and the consequences of both faithfulness and rebellion against God.

#24 - Jeremiah: Often referred to as the "weeping prophet", the book of Jeremiah persistently warns Judah of impending doom due to their idolatry and unfaithfulness. However, amid his dire predictions, he offers hope through the promise of a "new covenant."

#25 - Lamentations: Traditionally attributed to Jeremiah, this collection of poetic laments mourns the tragic fall of Jerusalem and the subsequent exile. The verses capture the deep sorrow, yet also contain glimmers of hope in God's enduring mercy.

#26 - Ezekiel: Traditionally attributed to the prophet of the same name, Ezekiel combines visions, prophecies, and parables to address the exile of the Judeans in Babylon. It emphasizes themes of judgment and restoration, with vivid imagery depicting the fall of Jerusalem and the eventual promise of the nation's spiritual renewal.

#27 - Daniel: The book of Daniel combines tales of Jewish heroism in a foreign court with apocalyptic visions, set during the Babylonian exile and early Persian period. The first half narrates stories of Daniel and his companions, who maintain their faith and integrity in the face of challenges. The latter half presents symbolic dreams and visions that offer hope for divine deliverance and the establishment of God's kingdom.

#28 - Hosea: Set in the turbulent final days of the Northern Kingdom of Israel, the book of Hosea combines prophecies of doom due to the people's unfaithfulness to God with promises of restoration. The book is distinguished by its symbolic use of Hosea's troubled marriage as a metaphor for the relationship between God and Israel, emphasizing themes of love, betrayal, and redemption.

#29 - Joel: Joel, set against the backdrop of a devastating locust plague, uses this natural disaster as a metaphor for an impending day of divine judgment. The book calls for repentance and portrays a future of divine restoration and blessings, including the outpouring of God's spirit on all people.

#30 - Amos: In this book, prophet Amos delivers a stern message of judgment to the Northern Kingdom for its societal injustices and idolatry. Amidst the warning, there's a glimmer of hope for restoration.

#31 - Obadiah: Traditionally attributed to Obadiah, this is the shortest book in the collection. However, many scholars disagree with that attribution. Regardless of its authorship, the text portrays Edom's impending downfall and Israel's eventual triumph in the "Day of the Lord".

#32 - Jonah: Unique among the prophetic books Jonah is a narrative about a reluctant prophet sent to warn the city of Nineveh of impending divine judgment. It explores themes of obedience, mercy, and God's compassion for all people, highlighted by Jonah's resistance to God's command and the eventual repentance of the Ninevites.

#33 - Micah: The book of Micah delivers a message of judgment and hope, addressing the social injustices and corrupt leadership of his time. The book combines dire warnings to both Israel and Judah with promises of restoration and future leadership from Bethlehem, emphasizing the themes of justice, mercy, and humility before God.

#34 - Nahum: Focusing on the impending downfall of Nineveh, the book of Nahum proclaims God's judgment on this oppressive Assyrian city, contrasting God's wrath and His goodness.

#35 - Habakkuk: In a dialogue with God, Habakkuk grapples with the problem of evil and why the wicked prosper. The answer, according to Habakkuk, lies in living by faith and trusting in God's sovereign plan.

#36 - Zephaniah: Warning of the impending "Day of the Lord," the book of Zephaniah calls for repentance. Amid the judgment pronouncements, there's the promise of joy and restoration for the faithful remnant.

#37 - Haggai: As post-exile Israel delays rebuilding the temple, the book of Haggai reminds them of their priorities and assures them of God's presence in their midst.

#38 - Zechariah: Composed post-exile, the book of Zechariah combines visions, prophecies, and oracles to encourage the rebuilding of the Jerusalem Temple and to offer hope for the restoration of Israel. The book blends apocalyptic elements with expectations of the coming of the future king who will restore peace and justice.

#39 - Malachi: The final book of the Old Testament prophets! It addresses issues of social justice, religious sincerity, and moral conduct in post-exilic Judah. It calls for faithfulness to God's covenant, warning of judgment while promising a future day of purification and renewal, symbolized by the coming of 'Elijah the prophet'.

The First Book of Moses, Commonly Called Genesis

1

1 In the beginning, God[a] created the heavens and the earth. 2 The earth was formless and empty. Darkness was on the surface of the deep and God's Spirit was hovering over the surface of the waters.

3 God said, "Let there be light," and there was light. 4 God saw the light, and saw that it was good. God divided the light from the darkness. 5 God called the light "day", and the darkness he called "night". There was evening and there was morning, the first day.

6 God said, "Let there be an expanse in the middle of the waters, and let it divide the waters from the waters." 7 God made the expanse, and divided the waters which were under the expanse from the waters which were above the expanse; and it was so. 8 God called the expanse "sky". There was evening and there was morning, a second day.

9 God said, "Let the waters under the sky be gathered together to one place, and let the dry land appear;" and it was so. 10 God called the dry land "earth", and the gathering together of the waters he called "seas". God saw that it was good. 11 God said, "Let the earth yield grass, herbs yielding seeds, and fruit trees bearing fruit after their kind, with their seeds in it, on the earth;" and it was so. 12 The earth yielded grass, herbs yielding seed after their kind, and trees bearing fruit, with their seeds in it, after their kind; and God saw that it was good. 13 There was evening and there was morning, a third day.

14 God said, "Let there be lights in the expanse of the sky to divide the day from the night; and let them be for signs to mark seasons, days, and years; 15 and let them be for lights in the expanse of the sky to give light on the earth;" and it was so. 16 God made the two great lights: the greater light to rule the day, and the lesser light to rule the night. He also made the stars. 17 God set them in the expanse of the sky to give light to the earth, 18 and to rule over the day and over the night, and to divide the light from the darkness. God saw that it was good. 19 There was evening and there was morning, a fourth day.

20 God said, "Let the waters abound with living creatures, and let birds fly above the earth in the open expanse of the sky." 21 God created the large sea creatures and every living creature that moves, with which the waters swarmed, after their kind, and every winged bird after its kind. God saw that it was good. 22 God blessed them, saying, "Be fruitful, and multiply, and fill the waters in the seas, and let birds multiply on the earth." 23 There was evening and there was morning, a fifth day.

24 God said, "Let the earth produce living creatures after their kind, livestock, creeping things, and animals of the earth after their kind;" and it was so. 25 God made the animals of the earth after their kind, and the livestock after their kind, and everything that creeps on the ground after its kind. God saw that it was good.

26 God said, "Let's make man in our image, after our likeness. Let them have dominion over the fish of the sea, and over the birds of the sky, and over the livestock, and over all the earth, and over every creeping thing that creeps on the earth." 27 God created man in his own image. In God's image he created him; male and female he created them. 28 God blessed them. God said to them, "Be fruitful, multiply, fill the earth, and subdue it. Have dominion over the fish of the sea, over the birds of the sky, and over every living thing that moves on the earth." 29 God said, "Behold,[b] I have given you every herb yielding seed, which is on the surface of all the earth, and every tree, which bears fruit yielding seed. It will be your food. 30 To every animal of the earth, and to every bird of the sky, and to everything that creeps on the earth, in which there is life, I have given every green herb for food;" and it was so.

31 God saw everything that he had made, and, behold, it was very good. There was evening and there was morning, a sixth day.

2

1 The heavens, the earth, and all their vast array were finished. 2 On the seventh day God finished his work which he had done; and he rested on the seventh day from all his work which he had done. 3 God blessed the seventh day, and made it holy, because he rested in it from all his work of creation which he had done.

4 This is the history of the generations of the heavens and of the earth when they were created, in the day that the LORD[c] God made the earth and the heavens. 5 No plant of the field was yet in the earth, and no herb of the field had yet sprung up; for the LORD God had not caused it to rain on the earth. There was not a man to till the ground, 6 but a mist went up from the earth, and watered the whole surface of the ground. 7 The LORD God formed man from the dust of the ground, and breathed into his nostrils the breath of life; and man became a living soul. 8 The LORD God planted a garden eastward, in Eden, and there he put the man whom he had formed. 9 Out of the ground the LORD God made every tree to grow that is pleasant to the sight, and good for food, including the tree of life in the middle of the garden and the tree of the knowledge of good and evil. 10 A river went out of Eden to water the garden; and from there it was parted, and became the source of four rivers. 11 The name of the first is Pishon: it flows through the whole land of Havilah, where there is gold; 12 and the gold of that land is

good. Bdellium[d] and onyx stone are also there. 13 The name of the second river is Gihon. It is the same river that flows through the whole land of Cush. 14 The name of the third river is Hiddekel. This is the one which flows in front of Assyria. The fourth river is the Euphrates. 15 The LORD God took the man, and put him into the garden of Eden to cultivate and keep it. 16 The LORD God commanded the man, saying, "You may freely eat of every tree of the garden; 17 but you shall not eat of the tree of the knowledge of good and evil; for in the day that you eat of it, you will surely die."

18 The LORD God said, "It is not good for the man to be alone. I will make him a helper comparable to[e] him." 19 Out of the ground the LORD God formed every animal of the field, and every bird of the sky, and brought them to the man to see what he would call them. Whatever the man called every living creature became its name. 20 The man gave names to all livestock, and to the birds of the sky, and to every animal of the field; but for man there was not found a helper comparable to him. 21 The LORD God caused the man to fall into a deep sleep. As the man slept, he took one of his ribs, and closed up the flesh in its place. 22 The LORD God made a woman from the rib which he had taken from the man, and brought her to the man. 23 The man said, "This is now bone of my bones, and flesh of my flesh. She will be called 'woman,' because she was taken out of Man." 24 Therefore a man will leave his father and his mother, and will join with his wife, and they will be one flesh. 25 The man and his wife were both naked, and they were not ashamed.

3

1 Now the serpent was more subtle than any animal of the field which the LORD God had made. He said to the woman, "Has God really said, 'You shall not eat of any tree of the garden'?"

2 The woman said to the serpent, "We may eat fruit from the trees of the garden, 3 but not the fruit of the tree which is in the middle of the garden. God has said, 'You shall not eat of it. You shall not touch it, lest you die.'"

4 The serpent said to the woman, "You won't really die, 5 for God knows that in the day you eat it, your eyes will be opened, and you will be like God, knowing good and evil."

6 When the woman saw that the tree was good for food, and that it was a delight to the eyes, and that the tree was to be desired to make one wise, she took some of its fruit, and ate. Then she gave some to her husband with her, and he ate it, too. 7 Their eyes were opened, and they both knew that they were naked. They sewed fig leaves together, and made coverings for themselves. 8 They heard the LORD God's voice walking in the garden in the cool of the day, and the man and his wife hid themselves from the presence of the LORD God amongst the trees of the garden.

9 The LORD God called to the man, and said to him, "Where are you?"

10 The man said, "I heard your voice in the garden, and I was afraid, because I was naked; so I hid myself."

11 God said, "Who told you that you were naked? Have you eaten from the tree that I commanded you not to eat from?"

12 The man said, "The woman whom you gave to be with me, she gave me fruit from the tree, and I ate it."

13 The LORD God said to the woman, "What have you done?"

The woman said, "The serpent deceived me, and I ate."

14 The LORD God said to the serpent,

"Because you have done this,
    you are cursed above all livestock,
    and above every animal of the field.
You shall go on your belly
    and you shall eat dust all the days of your life.
15 I will put hostility between you and the woman,
    and between your offspring and her offspring.
He will bruise your head,
    and you will bruise his heel."

16 To the woman he said,
"I will greatly multiply your pain in childbirth.
    You will bear children in pain.
Your desire will be for your husband,
    and he will rule over you."

17 To Adam he said,
"Because you have listened to your wife's voice,
    and have eaten from the tree,
    about which I commanded you, saying, 'You shall not eat of it,'
    the ground is cursed for your sake.
You will eat from it with much labour all the days of your life.
18 It will yield thorns and thistles to you;
    and you will eat the herb of the field.
19 You will eat bread by the sweat of your face until you return to the
        ground,
    for you were taken out of it.
For you are dust,
    and you shall return to dust."

20 The man called his wife Eve because she would be the mother of all the living. 21 The LORD God made garments of animal skins for Adam and for his wife, and clothed them.

---

a *1:1* The Hebrew word rendered "God" is "אֱלֹהִים" (Elohim).

b *1:29* "Behold", from "הִנֵּה", means look at, take notice, observe, see, or gaze at. It is often used as an interjection.

c *2:4* When rendered in ALL CAPITAL LETTERS, "LORD" or "GOD" is the translation of God's Proper Name.

d *2:12* or, aromatic resin

e *2:18* or, suitable for, or appropriate for.

22 The LORD God said, "Behold, the man has become like one of us, knowing good and evil. Now, lest he reach out his hand, and also take of the tree of life, and eat, and live forever—" 23 Therefore the LORD God sent him out from the garden of Eden, to till the ground from which he was taken. 24 So he drove out the man; and he placed cherubim[a] at the east of the garden of Eden, and a flaming sword which turned every way, to guard the way to the tree of life.

4

1 The man knew[b] Eve his wife. She conceived,[c] and gave birth to Cain, and said, "I have gotten a man with the LORD's help." 2 Again she gave birth, to Cain's brother Abel. Abel was a keeper of sheep, but Cain was a tiller of the ground. 3 As time passed, Cain brought an offering to the LORD from the fruit of the ground. 4 Abel also brought some of the firstborn of his flock and of its fat. The LORD respected Abel and his offering, 5 but he didn't respect Cain and his offering. Cain was very angry, and the expression on his face fell. 6 The LORD said to Cain, "Why are you angry? Why has the expression of your face fallen? 7 If you do well, won't it be lifted up? If you don't do well, sin crouches at the door. Its desire is for you, but you are to rule over it." 8 Cain said to Abel, his brother, "Let's go into the field." While they were in the field, Cain rose up against Abel, his brother, and killed him.

9 The LORD said to Cain, "Where is Abel, your brother?"

He said, "I don't know. Am I my brother's keeper?"

10 The LORD said, "What have you done? The voice of your brother's blood cries to me from the ground. 11 Now you are cursed because of the ground, which has opened its mouth to receive your brother's blood from your hand. 12 From now on, when you till the ground, it won't yield its strength to you. You will be a fugitive and a wanderer in the earth."

13 Cain said to the LORD, "My punishment is greater than I can bear. 14 Behold, you have driven me out today from the surface of the ground. I will be hidden from your face, and I will be a fugitive and a wanderer in the earth. Whoever finds me will kill me."

15 The LORD said to him, "Therefore whoever slays Cain, vengeance will be taken on him sevenfold." The LORD appointed a sign for Cain, so that anyone finding him would not strike him.

16 Cain left the LORD's presence, and lived in the land of Nod, east of Eden. 17 Cain knew his wife. She conceived, and gave birth to Enoch. He built a city, and named the city after the name of his son, Enoch. 18 Irad was born to Enoch. Irad became the father of Mehujael. Mehujael became the father of Methushael. Methushael became the father of Lamech. 19 Lamech took two wives: the name of the first one was Adah, and the name of the second one was Zillah. 20 Adah gave birth to Jabal, who was the father of those who dwell in tents and have livestock. 21 His brother's name was Jubal, who was the father of all who handle the harp and pipe. 22 Zillah also gave birth to Tubal Cain, the forger of every cutting instrument of bronze and iron. Tubal Cain's sister was Naamah. 23 Lamech said to his wives, "Adah and Zillah, hear my voice.

You wives of Lamech, listen to my speech,
for I have slain a man for wounding me,
   a young man for bruising me.
24 If Cain will be avenged seven times,
   truly Lamech seventy-seven times."

25 Adam knew his wife again. She gave birth to a son, and named him Seth, saying, "for God has given me another child instead of Abel, for Cain killed him." 26 A son was also born to Seth, and he named him Enosh. At that time men began to call on the LORD's name.

5

1 This is the book of the generations of Adam. In the day that God created man, he made him in God's likeness. 2 He created them male and female, and blessed them. On the day they were created, he named them Adam.[d] 3 Adam lived one hundred and thirty years, and became the father of a son in his own likeness, after his image, and named him Seth. 4 The days of Adam after he became the father of Seth were eight hundred years, and he became the father of other sons and daughters. 5 All the days that Adam lived were nine hundred and thirty years, then he died.

6 Seth lived one hundred and five years, then became the father of Enosh. 7 Seth lived after he became the father of Enosh eight hundred and seven years, and became the father of other sons and daughters. 8 All of the days of Seth were nine hundred and twelve years, then he died.

9 Enosh lived ninety years, and became the father of Kenan. 10 Enosh lived after he became the father of Kenan eight hundred and fifteen years, and became the father of other sons and daughters. 11 All of the days of Enosh were nine hundred and five years, then he died.

12 Kenan lived seventy years, then became the father of Mahalalel. 13 Kenan lived after he became the father of Mahalalel eight hundred and forty years, and became the father of other sons and daughters 14 and all of the days of Kenan were nine hundred and ten years, then he died.

15 Mahalalel lived sixty-five years, then became the father of Jared. 16 Mahalalel lived after he became the father of Jared eight hundred and thirty years, and became the father of other sons and daughters. 17 All of the days of Mahalalel were eight hundred and ninety-five years, then he died.

18 Jared lived one hundred and sixty-two years, then became the father of Enoch. 19 Jared lived after he became the father of Enoch eight hundred years, and became the father of other sons and daughters. 20 All of the days of Jared were nine hundred and sixty-two years, then he died.

21 Enoch lived sixty-five years, then became the father of Methuselah. 22 After Methuselah's birth, Enoch walked with God for three hundred years, and became the father of more sons and daughters. 23 All the days of Enoch were three hundred and sixty-five years. 24 Enoch walked with God, and he was not found, for God took him.

25 Methuselah lived one hundred and eighty-seven years, then became the father of Lamech. 26 Methuselah lived after he became the father of Lamech seven hundred and eighty-two years, and became the father of other sons and daughters. 27 All the days of Methuselah were nine hundred and sixty-nine years, then he died.

28 Lamech lived one hundred and eighty-two years, then became the father of a son. 29 He named him Noah, saying, "This one will comfort us in our work and in the toil of our hands, caused by the ground which the LORD has cursed." 30 Lamech lived after he became the father of Noah five hundred and ninety-five years, and became the father of other sons and daughters. 31 All the days of Lamech were seven hundred and seventy-seven years, then he died.

32 Noah was five hundred years old, then Noah became the father of Shem, Ham, and Japheth.

6

1 When men began to multiply on the surface of the ground, and daughters were born to them, 2 God's sons saw that men's daughters were beautiful, and they took any that they wanted for themselves as wives. 3 The LORD said, "My Spirit will not strive with man forever, because he also is flesh; so his days will be one hundred and twenty years." 4 The Nephilim[e] were in the earth in those days, and also after that, when God's sons came in to men's daughters and had children with them. Those were the mighty men who were of old, men of renown.

5 The LORD saw that the wickedness of man was great in the earth, and that every imagination of the thoughts of man's heart was continually only evil. 6 The LORD was sorry that he had made man on the earth, and it grieved him in his heart. 7 The LORD said, "I will destroy man whom I have created from the surface of the ground—man, along with animals, creeping things, and birds of the sky—for I am sorry that I have made them." 8 But Noah found favour in the LORD's eyes.

9 This is the history of the generations of Noah: Noah was a righteous man, blameless amongst the people of his time. Noah walked with God. 10 Noah became the father of three sons: Shem, Ham, and Japheth. 11 The earth was corrupt before God, and the earth was filled with violence. 12 God saw the earth, and saw that it was corrupt, for all flesh had corrupted their way on the earth.

13 God said to Noah, "I will bring an end to all flesh, for the earth is filled with violence through them. Behold, I will destroy them and the earth. 14 Make a ship of gopher wood. You shall make rooms in the ship, and shall seal it inside and outside with pitch. 15 This is how you shall make it. The length of the ship shall be three hundred cubits,[f] its width fifty cubits, and its height thirty cubits. 16 You shall make a roof in the ship, and you shall finish it to a cubit upward. You shall set the door of the ship in its side. You shall make it with lower, second, and third levels. 17 I, even I, will bring the flood of waters on this earth, to destroy all flesh having the breath of life from under the sky. Everything that is in the earth will die. 18 But I will establish my covenant with you. You shall come into the ship, you, your sons, your wife, and your sons' wives with you. 19 Of every living thing of all flesh, you shall bring two of every sort into the ship, to keep them alive with you. They shall be male and female. 20 Of the birds after their kind, of the livestock after their kind, of every creeping thing of the ground after its kind, two of every sort will come to you, to keep them alive. 21 Take with you some of all food that is eaten, and gather it to yourself; and it will be for food for you, and for them." 22 Thus Noah did. He did all that God commanded him.

7

1 The LORD said to Noah, "Come with all of your household into the ship, for I have seen your righteousness before me in this generation. 2 You shall take seven pairs of every clean animal with you, the male and his female. Of the animals that are not clean, take two, the male and his female. 3 Also of the birds of the sky, seven and seven, male and female, to keep seed alive on the surface of all the earth. 4 In seven days, I will cause it to rain on the earth for forty days and forty nights. I will destroy every living thing that I have made from the surface of the ground."

5 Noah did everything that the LORD commanded him.

6 Noah was six hundred years old when the flood of waters came on the earth. 7 Noah went into the ship with his sons, his wife, and his sons' wives, because of the floodwaters. 8 Clean animals, unclean animals, birds, and everything that creeps on the ground 9 went by pairs to Noah into the ship, male and female, as God commanded Noah. 10 After the seven days, the floodwaters came on the earth. 11 In the six hundredth year of Noah's life, in the second month, on the seventeenth day of the month, on that day

---

a 3:24 cherubim are powerful angelic creatures, messengers of God with wings. See Ezekiel 10.
b 4:1 or, lay with, or, had relations with
c 4:1 or, became pregnant

d 5:2 "Adam" and "Man" are spelled with the exact same consonants in Hebrew, so this can be correctly translated either way.
e 6:4 or, giants
f 6:15 A cubit is the length from the tip of the middle finger to the elbow on a man's arm, or about 18 inches or 46 centimetres.

all the fountains of the great deep burst open, and the sky's windows opened. 12 It rained on the earth forty days and forty nights. 13 In the same day Noah, and Shem, Ham, and Japheth—the sons of Noah—and Noah's wife and the three wives of his sons with them, entered into the ship— 14 they, and every animal after its kind, all the livestock after their kind, every creeping thing that creeps on the earth after its kind, and every bird after its kind, every bird of every sort. 15 Pairs from all flesh with the breath of life in them went into the ship to Noah. 16 Those who went in, went in male and female of all flesh, as God commanded him; then the LORD shut him in. 17 The flood was forty days on the earth. The waters increased, and lifted up the ship, and it was lifted up above the earth. 18 The waters rose, and increased greatly on the earth; and the ship floated on the surface of the waters. 19 The waters rose very high on the earth. All the high mountains that were under the whole sky were covered. 20 The waters rose fifteen cubits[a] higher, and the mountains were covered. 21 All flesh died that moved on the earth, including birds, livestock, animals, every creeping thing that creeps on the earth, and every man. 22 All on the dry land, in whose nostrils was the breath of the spirit of life, died. 23 Every living thing was destroyed that was on the surface of the ground, including man, livestock, creeping things, and birds of the sky. They were destroyed from the earth. Only Noah was left, and those who were with him in the ship. 24 The waters flooded the earth one hundred and fifty days.

8

1 God remembered Noah, all the animals, and all the livestock that were with him in the ship; and God made a wind to pass over the earth. The waters subsided. 2 The deep's fountains and the sky's windows were also stopped, and the rain from the sky was restrained. 3 The waters continually receded from the earth. After the end of one hundred and fifty days the waters receded. 4 The ship rested in the seventh month, on the seventeenth day of the month, on Ararat's mountains. 5 The waters receded continually until the tenth month. In the tenth month, on the first day of the month, the tops of the mountains were visible.

6 At the end of forty days, Noah opened the window of the ship which he had made, 7 and he sent out a raven. It went back and forth, until the waters were dried up from the earth. 8 He himself sent out a dove to see if the waters were abated from the surface of the ground, 9 but the dove found no place to rest her foot, and she returned into the ship to him, for the waters were on the surface of the whole earth. He put out his hand, and took her, and brought her to him into the ship. 10 He waited yet another seven days; and again he sent the dove out of the ship. 11 The dove came back to him at evening and, behold, in her mouth was a freshly plucked olive leaf. So Noah knew that the waters were abated from the earth. 12 He waited yet another seven days, and sent out the dove; and she didn't return to him any more.

13 In the six hundred first year, in the first month, the first day of the month, the waters were dried up from the earth. Noah removed the covering of the ship, and looked. He saw that the surface of the ground was dry. 14 In the second month, on the twenty-seventh day of the month, the earth was dry.

15 God spoke to Noah, saying, 16 "Go out of the ship, you, your wife, your sons, and your sons' wives with you. 17 Bring out with you every living thing that is with you of all flesh, including birds, livestock, and every creeping thing that creeps on the earth, that they may breed abundantly in the earth, and be fruitful, and multiply on the earth."

18 Noah went out, with his sons, his wife, and his sons' wives with him. 19 Every animal, every creeping thing, and every bird, whatever moves on the earth, after their families, went out of the ship.

20 Noah built an altar to the LORD, and took of every clean animal, and of every clean bird, and offered burnt offerings on the altar. 21 The LORD smelled the pleasant aroma. The LORD said in his heart, "I will not again curse the ground any more for man's sake because the imagination of man's heart is evil from his youth. I will never again strike every living thing, as I have done. 22 While the earth remains, seed time and harvest, and cold and heat, and summer and winter, and day and night will not cease."

9

1 God blessed Noah and his sons, and said to them, "Be fruitful, multiply, and replenish the earth. 2 The fear of you and the dread of you will be on every animal of the earth, and on every bird of the sky. Everything that moves along the ground, and all the fish of the sea, are delivered into your hand. 3 Every moving thing that lives will be food for you. As I gave you the green herb, I have given everything to you. 4 But flesh with its life, that is, its blood, you shall not eat. 5 I will surely require accounting for your life's blood. At the hand of every animal I will require it. At the hand of man, even at the hand of every man's brother, I will require the life of man. 6 Whoever sheds man's blood, his blood will be shed by man, for God made man in his own image. 7 Be fruitful and multiply. Increase abundantly in the earth, and multiply in it."

8 God spoke to Noah and to his sons with him, saying, 9 "As for me, behold, I establish my covenant with you, and with your offspring after you, 10 and with every living creature that is with you: the birds, the livestock, and every animal of the earth with you, of all that go out of the ship, even every animal of the earth. 11 I will establish my covenant with you: All flesh will not be cut off any more by the waters of the flood. There will never again be a flood to destroy the earth." 12 God said, "This is the token of the covenant which I make between me and you and every living creature that is with you, for perpetual generations: 13 I set my rainbow in the cloud, and it will be a sign of a covenant between me and the earth. 14 When I bring a cloud over the earth, that the rainbow will be seen in the cloud, 15 I will remember my covenant, which is between me and you and every living creature of all flesh, and the waters will no more become a flood to destroy all flesh. 16 The rainbow will be in the cloud. I will look at it, that I may remember the everlasting covenant between God and every living creature of all flesh that is on the earth." 17 God said to Noah, "This is the token of the covenant which I have established between me and all flesh that is on the earth."

18 The sons of Noah who went out from the ship were Shem, Ham, and Japheth. Ham is the father of Canaan. 19 These three were the sons of Noah, and from these the whole earth was populated.

20 Noah began to be a farmer, and planted a vineyard. 21 He drank of the wine and got drunk. He was uncovered within his tent. 22 Ham, the father of Canaan, saw the nakedness of his father, and told his two brothers outside. 23 Shem and Japheth took a garment, and laid it on both their shoulders, went in backwards, and covered the nakedness of their father. Their faces were backwards, and they didn't see their father's nakedness. 24 Noah awoke from his wine, and knew what his youngest son had done to him. 25 He said,

"Canaan is cursed.
  He will be a servant of servants to his brothers."

26 He said,

"Blessed be the LORD, the God of Shem.
  Let Canaan be his servant.
27 May God enlarge Japheth.
  Let him dwell in the tents of Shem.
  Let Canaan be his servant."

28 Noah lived three hundred and fifty years after the flood. 29 All the days of Noah were nine hundred and fifty years, and then he died.

10

1 Now this is the history of the generations of the sons of Noah and of Shem, Ham, and Japheth. Sons were born to them after the flood.

2 The sons of Japheth were: Gomer, Magog, Madai, Javan, Tubal, Meshech, and Tiras. 3 The sons of Gomer were: Ashkenaz, Riphath, and Togarmah. 4 The sons of Javan were: Elishah, Tarshish, Kittim, and Dodanim. 5 Of these were the islands of the nations divided in their lands, everyone after his language, after their families, in their nations.

6 The sons of Ham were: Cush, Mizraim, Put, and Canaan. 7 The sons of Cush were: Seba, Havilah, Sabtah, Raamah, and Sabteca. The sons of Raamah were: Sheba and Dedan. 8 Cush became the father of Nimrod. He began to be a mighty one in the earth. 9 He was a mighty hunter before the LORD. Therefore it is said, "like Nimrod, a mighty hunter before the LORD". 10 The beginning of his kingdom was Babel, Erech, Accad, and Calneh, in the land of Shinar. 11 Out of that land he went into Assyria, and built Nineveh, Rehoboth Ir, Calah, 12 and Resen between Nineveh and the great city Calah. 13 Mizraim became the father of Ludim, Anamim, Lehabim, Naphtuhim, 14 Pathrusim, Casluhim (which the Philistines descended from), and Caphtorim.

15 Canaan became the father of Sidon (his firstborn), Heth, 16 the Jebusites, the Amorites, the Girgashites, 17 the Hivites, the Arkites, the Sinites, 18 the Arvadites, the Zemarites, and the Hamathites. Afterward the families of the Canaanites were spread abroad. 19 The border of the Canaanites was from Sidon—as you go towards Gerar—to Gaza—as you go towards Sodom, Gomorrah, Admah, and Zeboiim—to Lasha. 20 These are the sons of Ham, after their families, according to their languages, in their lands and their nations.

21 Children were also born to Shem (the elder brother of Japheth), the father of all the children of Eber. 22 The sons of Shem were: Elam, Asshur, Arpachshad, Lud, and Aram. 23 The sons of Aram were: Uz, Hul, Gether, and Mash. 24 Arpachshad became the father of Shelah. Shelah became the father of Eber. 25 To Eber were born two sons. The name of the one was Peleg, for in his days the earth was divided. His brother's name was Joktan. 26 Joktan became the father of Almodad, Sheleph, Hazarmaveth, Jerah, 27 Hadoram, Uzal, Diklah, 28 Obal, Abimael, Sheba, 29 Ophir, Havilah, and Jobab. All these were the sons of Joktan. 30 Their dwelling extended from Mesha, as you go towards Sephar, the mountain of the east. 31 These are the sons of Shem, by their families, according to their languages, lands, and nations.

32 These are the families of the sons of Noah, by their generations, according to their nations. The nations divided from these in the earth after the flood.

11

1 The whole earth was of one language and of one speech. 2 As they travelled east,[b] they found a plain in the land of Shinar, and they lived there. 3 They said to one another, "Come, let's make bricks, and burn them thoroughly." They had brick for stone, and they used tar for mortar. 4 They said, "Come, let's build ourselves a city, and a tower whose top reaches to the sky, and let's make a name for ourselves, lest we be scattered abroad on the surface of the whole earth."

5 The LORD came down to see the city and the tower, which the children of men built. 6 The LORD said, "Behold, they are one people, and they all have one language, and this is what they begin to do. Now nothing

---

a *7:20* A cubit is the length from the tip of the middle finger to the elbow on a man's arm, or about 18 inches or 46 centimetres.

b *11:2* LXX reads "from the east".

will be withheld from them, which they intend to do. 7 Come, let's go down, and there confuse their language, that they may not understand one another's speech." 8 So the LORD scattered them abroad from there on the surface of all the earth. They stopped building the city. 9 Therefore its name was called Babel, because there the LORD confused the language of all the earth. From there, the LORD scattered them abroad on the surface of all the earth.

10 This is the history of the generations of Shem: Shem was one hundred years old when he became the father of Arpachshad two years after the flood. 11 Shem lived five hundred years after he became the father of Arpachshad, and became the father of more sons and daughters.

12 Arpachshad lived thirty-five years and became the father of Shelah. 13 Arpachshad lived four hundred and three after he became the father of Shelah, and became the father of more sons and daughters.

14 Shelah lived thirty years, and became the father of Eber. 15 Shelah lived four hundred and three years after he became the father of Eber, and became the father of more sons and daughters.

16 Eber lived thirty-four years, and became the father of Peleg. 17 Eber lived four hundred and thirty years after he became the father of Peleg, and became the father of more sons and daughters.

18 Peleg lived thirty years, and became the father of Reu. 19 Peleg lived two hundred and nine years after he became the father of Reu, and became the father of more sons and daughters.

20 Reu lived thirty-two years, and became the father of Serug. 21 Reu lived two hundred and seven years after he became the father of Serug, and became the father of more sons and daughters.

22 Serug lived thirty years, and became the father of Nahor. 23 Serug lived two hundred years after he became the father of Nahor, and became the father of more sons and daughters.

24 Nahor lived twenty-nine years, and became the father of Terah. 25 Nahor lived one hundred and nineteen years after he became the father of Terah, and became the father of more sons and daughters.

26 Terah lived seventy years, and became the father of Abram, Nahor, and Haran.

27 Now this is the history of the generations of Terah. Terah became the father of Abram, Nahor, and Haran. Haran became the father of Lot. 28 Haran died in the land of his birth, in Ur of the Chaldees, while his father Terah was still alive. 29 Abram and Nahor married wives. The name of Abram's wife was Sarai, and the name of Nahor's wife was Milcah, the daughter of Haran, who was also the father of Iscah. 30 Sarai was barren. She had no child. 31 Terah took Abram his son, Lot the son of Haran, his son's son, and Sarai his daughter-in-law, his son Abram's wife. They went from Ur of the Chaldees, to go into the land of Canaan. They came to Haran and lived there. 32 The days of Terah were two hundred and five years. Terah died in Haran.

12

1 Now the LORD said to Abram, "Leave your country, and your relatives, and your father's house, and go to the land that I will show you. 2 I will bless you and make your name great. You will be a blessing. 3 I will bless those who bless you, and I will curse him who treats you with contempt. All the families of the earth will be blessed through you."

4 So Abram went, as the LORD had told him. Lot went with him. Abram was seventy-five years old when he departed from Haran. 5 Abram took Sarai his wife, Lot his brother's son, all their possessions that they had gathered, and the people whom they had acquired in Haran, and they went to go into the land of Canaan. They entered into the land of Canaan. 6 Abram passed through the land to the place of Shechem, to the oak of Moreh. At that time, Canaanites were in the land.

7 The LORD appeared to Abram and said, "I will give this land to your offspring."[a]

He built an altar there to the LORD, who had appeared to him. 8 He left from there to go to the mountain on the east of Bethel and pitched his tent, having Bethel on the west, and Ai on the east. There he built an altar to the LORD and called on the LORD's name. 9 Abram travelled, still going on towards the South.

10 There was a famine in the land. Abram went down into Egypt to live as a foreigner there, for the famine was severe in the land. 11 When he had come near to enter Egypt, he said to Sarai his wife, "See now, I know that you are a beautiful woman to look at. 12 It will happen that when the Egyptians see you, they will say, 'This is his wife.' They will kill me, but they will save you alive. 13 Please say that you are my sister, that it may be well with me for your sake, and that my soul may live because of you."

14 When Abram had come into Egypt, Egyptians saw that the woman was very beautiful. 15 The princes of Pharaoh saw her, and praised her to Pharaoh; and the woman was taken into Pharaoh's house. 16 He dealt well with Abram for her sake. He had sheep, cattle, male donkeys, male servants, female servants, female donkeys, and camels. 17 The LORD afflicted Pharaoh and his house with great plagues because of Sarai, Abram's wife. 18 Pharaoh called Abram and said, "What is this that you have done to me? Why didn't you tell me that she was your wife? 19 Why did you say, 'She is my sister,' so that I took her to be my wife? Now therefore, see your wife, take her, and go your way."

20 Pharaoh commanded men concerning him, and they escorted him away with his wife and all that he had.

13

1 Abram went up out of Egypt—he, his wife, all that he had, and Lot with him—into the South. 2 Abram was very rich in livestock, in silver, and in gold. 3 He went on his journeys from the South as far as Bethel, to the place where his tent had been at the beginning, between Bethel and Ai, 4 to the place of the altar, which he had made there at the first. There Abram called on the LORD's name. 5 Lot also, who went with Abram, had flocks, herds, and tents. 6 The land was not able to bear them, that they might live together; for their possessions were so great that they couldn't live together. 7 There was strife between the herdsmen of Abram's livestock and the herdsmen of Lot's livestock. The Canaanites and the Perizzites lived in the land at that time. 8 Abram said to Lot, "Please, let there be no strife between you and me, and between your herdsmen and my herdsmen; for we are relatives. 9 Isn't the whole land before you? Please separate yourself from me. If you go to the left hand, then I will go to the right. Or if you go to the right hand, then I will go to the left."

10 Lot lifted up his eyes, and saw all the plain of the Jordan, that it was well-watered everywhere, before the LORD destroyed Sodom and Gomorrah, like the garden of the LORD, like the land of Egypt, as you go to Zoar. 11 So Lot chose the Plain of the Jordan for himself. Lot travelled east, and they separated themselves from one other. 12 Abram lived in the land of Canaan, and Lot lived in the cities of the plain, and moved his tent as far as Sodom. 13 Now the men of Sodom were exceedingly wicked and sinners against the LORD.

14 The LORD said to Abram, after Lot was separated from him, "Now, lift up your eyes, and look from the place where you are, northward and southward and eastward and westward, 15 for I will give all the land which you see to you and to your offspring forever. 16 I will make your offspring as the dust of the earth, so that if a man can count the dust of the earth, then your offspring may also be counted. 17 Arise, walk through the land in its length and in its width; for I will give it to you."

18 Abram moved his tent, and came and lived by the oaks of Mamre, which are in Hebron, and built an altar there to the LORD.

14

1 In the days of Amraphel, king of Shinar; Arioch, king of Ellasar; Chedorlaomer, king of Elam; and Tidal, king of Goiim, 2 they made war with Bera, king of Sodom; Birsha, king of Gomorrah; Shinab, king of Admah; Shemeber, king of Zeboiim; and the king of Bela (also called Zoar). 3 All these joined together in the valley of Siddim (also called the Salt Sea). 4 They served Chedorlaomer for twelve years, and in the thirteenth year they rebelled. 5 In the fourteenth year Chedorlaomer and the kings who were with him came and struck the Rephaim in Ashteroth Karnaim, the Zuzim in Ham, the Emim in Shaveh Kiriathaim, 6 and the Horites in their Mount Seir, to El Paran, which is by the wilderness. 7 They returned, and came to En Mishpat (also called Kadesh), and struck all the country of the Amalekites, and also the Amorites, that lived in Hazazon Tamar. 8 The king of Sodom, and the king of Gomorrah, the king of Admah, the king of Zeboiim, and the king of Bela (also called Zoar) went out; and they set the battle in array against them in the valley of Siddim 9 against Chedorlaomer king of Elam, Tidal king of Goiim, Amraphel king of Shinar, and Arioch king of Ellasar; four kings against the five. 10 Now the valley of Siddim was full of tar pits; and the kings of Sodom and Gomorrah fled, and some fell there. Those who remained fled to the hills. 11 They took all the goods of Sodom and Gomorrah, and all their food, and went their way. 12 They took Lot, Abram's brother's son, who lived in Sodom, and his goods, and departed.

13 One who had escaped came and told Abram, the Hebrew. At that time, he lived by the oaks of Mamre, the Amorite, brother of Eshcol and brother of Aner. They were allies of Abram. 14 When Abram heard that his relative was taken captive, he led out his three hundred and eighteen trained men, born in his house, and pursued as far as Dan. 15 He divided himself against them by night, he and his servants, and struck them, and pursued them to Hobah, which is on the left hand of Damascus. 16 He brought back all the goods, and also brought back his relative Lot and his goods, and the women also, and the other people.

17 The king of Sodom went out to meet him after his return from the slaughter of Chedorlaomer and the kings who were with him, at the valley of Shaveh (that is, the King's Valley). 18 Melchizedek king of Salem brought out bread and wine. He was priest of God Most High. 19 He blessed him, and said, "Blessed be Abram of God Most High, possessor of heaven and earth. 20 Blessed be God Most High, who has delivered your enemies into your hand."

Abram gave him a tenth of all.

21 The king of Sodom said to Abram, "Give me the people, and take the goods for yourself."

22 Abram said to the king of Sodom, "I have lifted up my hand to the LORD, God Most High, possessor of heaven and earth, 23 that I will not take a thread nor a sandal strap nor anything that is yours, lest you should say, 'I have made Abram rich.' 24 I will accept nothing from you except that which the young men have eaten, and the portion of the men who went with me: Aner, Eshcol, and Mamre. Let them take their portion."

15

1 After these things the LORD's word came to Abram in a vision, saying, "Don't be afraid, Abram. I am your shield, your exceedingly great reward."

---

a *12:7* or, seed

2 Abram said, "Lord[a] GOD, what will you give me, since I go childless, and he who will inherit my estate is Eliezer of Damascus?" 3 Abram said, "Behold, you have given no children to me: and, behold, one born in my house is my heir."

4 Behold, the LORD's word came to him, saying, "This man will not be your heir, but he who will come out of your own body will be your heir." 5 The LORD brought him outside, and said, "Look now towards the sky, and count the stars, if you are able to count them." He said to Abram, "So your offspring will be." 6 He believed in the LORD, who credited it to him for righteousness. 7 He said to Abram, "I am the LORD who brought you out of Ur of the Chaldees, to give you this land to inherit it."

8 He said, "Lord GOD, how will I know that I will inherit it?"

9 He said to him, "Bring me a heifer three years old, a female goat three years old, a ram three years old, a turtledove, and a young pigeon." 10 He brought him all these, and divided them in the middle, and laid each half opposite the other; but he didn't divide the birds. 11 The birds of prey came down on the carcasses, and Abram drove them away.

12 When the sun was going down, a deep sleep fell on Abram. Now terror and great darkness fell on him. 13 He said to Abram, "Know for sure that your offspring will live as foreigners in a land that is not theirs, and will serve them. They will afflict them four hundred years. 14 I will also judge that nation, whom they will serve. Afterward they will come out with great wealth; 15 but you will go to your fathers in peace. You will be buried at a good old age. 16 In the fourth generation they will come here again, for the iniquity of the Amorite is not yet full." 17 It came to pass that, when the sun went down, and it was dark, behold, a smoking furnace and a flaming torch passed between these pieces. 18 In that day the LORD made a covenant with Abram, saying, "I have given this land to your offspring, from the river of Egypt to the great river, the river Euphrates: 19 the land of the Kenites, the Kenizzites, the Kadmonites, 20 the Hittites, the Perizzites, the Rephaim, 21 the Amorites, the Canaanites, the Girgashites, and the Jebusites."

16

1 Now Sarai, Abram's wife, bore him no children. She had a servant, an Egyptian, whose name was Hagar. 2 Sarai said to Abram, "See now, the LORD has restrained me from bearing. Please go in to my servant. It may be that I will obtain children by her." Abram listened to the voice of Sarai. 3 Sarai, Abram's wife, took Hagar the Egyptian, her servant, after Abram had lived ten years in the land of Canaan, and gave her to Abram her husband to be his wife. 4 He went in to Hagar, and she conceived. When she saw that she had conceived, her mistress was despised in her eyes. 5 Sarai said to Abram, "This wrong is your fault. I gave my servant into your bosom, and when she saw that she had conceived, she despised me. May The LORD judge between me and you."

6 But Abram said to Sarai, "Behold, your maid is in your hand. Do to her whatever is good in your eyes." Sarai dealt harshly with her, and she fled from her face.

7 The LORD's angel found her by a fountain of water in the wilderness, by the fountain on the way to Shur. 8 He said, "Hagar, Sarai's servant, where did you come from? Where are you going?"

She said, "I am fleeing from the face of my mistress Sarai."

9 The LORD's angel said to her, "Return to your mistress, and submit yourself under her hands." 10 The LORD's angel said to her, "I will greatly multiply your offspring, that they will not be counted for multitude." 11 The LORD's angel said to her, "Behold, you are with child, and will bear a son. You shall call his name Ishmael, because the LORD has heard your affliction. 12 He will be like a wild donkey amongst men. His hand will be against every man, and every man's hand against him. He will live opposed to all of his brothers."

13 She called the name of the LORD who spoke to her, "You are a God who sees," for she said, "Have I even stayed alive after seeing him?" 14 Therefore the well was called Beer Lahai Roi.[b] Behold, it is between Kadesh and Bered.

15 Hagar bore a son for Abram. Abram called the name of his son, whom Hagar bore, Ishmael. 16 Abram was eighty-six years old when Hagar bore Ishmael to Abram.

17

1 When Abram was ninety-nine years old, the LORD appeared to Abram and said to him, "I am God Almighty. Walk before me and be blameless. 2 I will make my covenant between me and you, and will multiply you exceedingly."

3 Abram fell on his face. God talked with him, saying, 4 "As for me, behold, my covenant is with you. You will be the father of a multitude of nations. 5 Your name will no more be called Abram, but your name will be Abraham; for I have made you the father of a multitude of nations. 6 I will make you exceedingly fruitful, and I will make nations of you. Kings will come out of you. 7 I will establish my covenant between me and you and your offspring after you throughout their generations for an everlasting covenant, to be a God to you and to your offspring after you. 8 I will give to you, and to your offspring after you, the land where you are travelling, all the land of Canaan, for an everlasting possession. I will be their God."

9 God said to Abraham, "As for you, you shall keep my covenant, you and your offspring after you throughout their generations. 10 This is my covenant, which you shall keep, between me and you and your offspring after you. Every male amongst you shall be circumcised. 11 You shall be circumcised in the flesh of your foreskin. It will be a token of the covenant between me and you. 12 He who is eight days old shall be circumcised amongst you, every male throughout your generations, he who is born in the house, or bought with money from any foreigner who is not of your offspring. 13 He who is born in your house, and he who is bought with your money, must be circumcised. My covenant shall be in your flesh for an everlasting covenant. 14 The uncircumcised male who is not circumcised in the flesh of his foreskin, that soul shall be cut off from his people. He has broken my covenant."

15 God said to Abraham, "As for Sarai your wife, you shall not call her name Sarai, but her name shall be Sarah. 16 I will bless her, and moreover I will give you a son by her. Yes, I will bless her, and she will be a mother of nations. Kings of peoples will come from her."

17 Then Abraham fell on his face, and laughed, and said in his heart, "Will a child be born to him who is one hundred years old? Will Sarah, who is ninety years old, give birth?" 18 Abraham said to God, "Oh that Ishmael might live before you!"

19 God said, "No, but Sarah, your wife, will bear you a son. You shall call his name Isaac.[c] I will establish my covenant with him for an everlasting covenant for his offspring after him. 20 As for Ishmael, I have heard you. Behold, I have blessed him, and will make him fruitful, and will multiply him exceedingly. He will become the father of twelve princes, and I will make him a great nation. 21 But I will establish my covenant with Isaac, whom Sarah will bear to you at this set time next year."

22 When he finished talking with him, God went up from Abraham. 23 Abraham took Ishmael his son, all who were born in his house, and all who were bought with his money: every male amongst the men of Abraham's house, and circumcised the flesh of their foreskin in the same day, as God had said to him. 24 Abraham was ninety-nine years old when he was circumcised in the flesh of his foreskin. 25 Ishmael, his son, was thirteen years old when he was circumcised in the flesh of his foreskin. 26 In the same day both Abraham and Ishmael, his son, were circumcised. 27 All the men of his house, those born in the house, and those bought with money from a foreigner, were circumcised with him.

18

1 The LORD appeared to him by the oaks of Mamre, as he sat in the tent door in the heat of the day. 2 He lifted up his eyes and looked, and saw that three men stood near him. When he saw them, he ran to meet them from the tent door, and bowed himself to the earth, 3 and said, "My lord, if now I have found favour in your sight, please don't go away from your servant. 4 Now let a little water be fetched, wash your feet, and rest yourselves under the tree. 5 I will get a piece of bread so you can refresh your heart. After that you may go your way, now that you have come to your servant."

They said, "Very well, do as you have said."

6 Abraham hurried into the tent to Sarah, and said, "Quickly prepare three seahs[d] of fine meal, knead it, and make cakes." 7 Abraham ran to the herd, and fetched a tender and good calf, and gave it to the servant. He hurried to dress it. 8 He took butter, milk, and the calf which he had dressed, and set it before them. He stood by them under the tree, and they ate.

9 They asked him, "Where is Sarah, your wife?"

He said, "There, in the tent."

10 He said, "I will certainly return to you at about this time next year; and behold, Sarah your wife will have a son."

Sarah heard in the tent door, which was behind him. 11 Now Abraham and Sarah were old, well advanced in age. Sarah had passed the age of childbearing. 12 Sarah laughed within herself, saying, "After I have grown old will I have pleasure, my lord being old also?"

13 The LORD said to Abraham, "Why did Sarah laugh, saying, 'Will I really bear a child when I am old?' 14 Is anything too hard for the LORD? At the set time I will return to you, when the season comes around, and Sarah will have a son."

15 Then Sarah denied it, saying, "I didn't laugh," for she was afraid.

He said, "No, but you did laugh."

16 The men rose up from there, and looked towards Sodom. Abraham went with them to see them on their way. 17 The LORD said, "Will I hide from Abraham what I do, 18 since Abraham will surely become a great and mighty nation, and all the nations of the earth will be blessed in him? 19 For I have known him, to the end that he may command his children and his household after him, that they may keep the way of the LORD, to do righteousness and justice; to the end that the LORD may bring on Abraham that which he has spoken of him." 20 The LORD said, "Because the cry of Sodom and Gomorrah is great, and because their sin is very grievous, 21 I will go down now, and see whether their deeds are as bad as the reports which have come to me. If not, I will know."

22 The men turned from there, and went towards Sodom, but Abraham stood yet before the LORD. 23 Abraham came near, and said, "Will you consume the righteous with the wicked? 24 What if there are fifty righteous within the city? Will you consume and not spare the place for the fifty righteous who are in it? 25 May it be far from you to do things like that, to kill the righteous with the wicked, so that the righteous should be like the wicked. May that be far from you. Shouldn't the Judge of all the earth do right?"

26 The LORD said, "If I find in Sodom fifty righteous within the city, then I will spare the whole place for their sake." 27 Abraham answered, "See

---

a *15:2* The word translated "Lord" is "Adonai".
b *16:14* Beer Lahai Roi means "well of the one who lives and sees me".
c *17:19* Isaac means "he laughs".
d *18:6* 1 seah is about 7 litres or 1.9 gallons or 0.8 pecks

now, I have taken it on myself to speak to the Lord, although I am dust and ashes. 28 What if there will lack five of the fifty righteous? Will you destroy all the city for lack of five?"

He said, "I will not destroy it if I find forty-five there."

29 He spoke to him yet again, and said, "What if there are forty found there?"

He said, "I will not do it for the forty's sake."

30 He said, "Oh don't let the Lord be angry, and I will speak. What if there are thirty found there?"

He said, "I will not do it if I find thirty there."

31 He said, "See now, I have taken it on myself to speak to the Lord. What if there are twenty found there?"

He said, "I will not destroy it for the twenty's sake."

32 He said, "Oh don't let the Lord be angry, and I will speak just once more. What if ten are found there?"

He said, "I will not destroy it for the ten's sake."

33 The LORD went his way as soon as he had finished communing with Abraham, and Abraham returned to his place.

19

1 The two angels came to Sodom at evening. Lot sat in the gate of Sodom. Lot saw them, and rose up to meet them. He bowed himself with his face to the earth, 2 and he said, "See now, my lords, please come into your servant's house, stay all night, wash your feet, and you can rise up early, and go on your way."

They said, "No, but we will stay in the street all night."

3 He urged them greatly, and they came in with him, and entered into his house. He made them a feast, and baked unleavened bread, and they ate. 4 But before they lay down, the men of the city, the men of Sodom, surrounded the house, both young and old, all the people from every quarter. 5 They called to Lot, and said to him, "Where are the men who came in to you this night? Bring them out to us, that we may have sex with them."

6 Lot went out to them through the door, and shut the door after himself. 7 He said, "Please, my brothers, don't act so wickedly. 8 See now, I have two virgin daughters. Please let me bring them out to you, and you may do to them what seems good to you. Only don't do anything to these men, because they have come under the shadow of my roof."

9 They said, "Stand back!" Then they said, "This one fellow came in to live as a foreigner, and he appoints himself a judge. Now we will deal worse with you than with them!" They pressed hard on the man Lot, and came near to break the door. 10 But the men reached out their hand, and brought Lot into the house to them, and shut the door. 11 They struck the men who were at the door of the house with blindness, both small and great, so that they wearied themselves to find the door.

12 The men said to Lot, "Do you have anybody else here? Sons-in-law, your sons, your daughters, and whomever you have in the city, bring them out of the place: 13 for we will destroy this place, because the outcry against them has grown so great before the LORD that the LORD has sent us to destroy it."

14 Lot went out, and spoke to his sons-in-law, who were pledged to marry his daughters, and said, "Get up! Get out of this place, for the LORD will destroy the city!"

But he seemed to his sons-in-law to be joking. 15 When the morning came, then the angels hurried Lot, saying, "Get up! Take your wife and your two daughters who are here, lest you be consumed in the iniquity of the city." 16 But he lingered; and the men grabbed his hand, his wife's hand, and his two daughters' hands, the LORD being merciful to him; and they took him out, and set him outside of the city. 17 It came to pass, when they had taken them out, that he said, "Escape for your life! Don't look behind you, and don't stay anywhere in the plain. Escape to the mountains, lest you be consumed!"

18 Lot said to them, "Oh, not so, my lord. 19 See now, your servant has found favour in your sight, and you have magnified your loving kindness, which you have shown to me in saving my life. I can't escape to the mountain, lest evil overtake me, and I die. 20 See now, this city is near to flee to, and it is a little one. Oh let me escape there (isn't it a little one?), and my soul will live."

21 He said to him, "Behold, I have granted your request concerning this thing also, that I will not overthrow the city of which you have spoken. 22 Hurry, escape there, for I can't do anything until you get there." Therefore the name of the city was called Zoar.ª

23 The sun had risen on the earth when Lot came to Zoar. 24 Then the LORD rained on Sodom and on Gomorrah sulphur and fire from the LORD out of the sky. 25 He overthrew those cities, all the plain, all the inhabitants of the cities, and that which grew on the ground. 26 But Lot's wife looked back from behind him, and she became a pillar of salt.

27 Abraham went up early in the morning to the place where he had stood before the LORD. 28 He looked towards Sodom and Gomorrah, and towards all the land of the plain, and saw that the smoke of the land went up as the smoke of a furnace.

29 When God destroyed the cities of the plain, God remembered Abraham, and sent Lot out of the middle of the overthrow, when he overthrew the cities in which Lot lived.

30 Lot went up out of Zoar, and lived in the mountain, and his two daughters with him; for he was afraid to live in Zoar. He lived in a cave with his two daughters. 31 The firstborn said to the younger, "Our father is old,

and there is not a man in the earth to come in to us in the way of all the earth. 32 Come, let's make our father drink wine, and we will lie with him, that we may preserve our father's family line." 33 They made their father drink wine that night: and the firstborn went in, and lay with her father. He didn't know when she lay down, nor when she arose. 34 It came to pass on the next day, that the firstborn said to the younger, "Behold, I lay last night with my father. Let's make him drink wine again tonight. You go in, and lie with him, that we may preserve our father's family line." 35 They made their father drink wine that night also. The younger went and lay with him. He didn't know when she lay down, nor when she got up. 36 Thus both of Lot's daughters were with child by their father. 37 The firstborn bore a son, and named him Moab. He is the father of the Moabites to this day. 38 The younger also bore a son, and called his name Ben Ammi. He is the father of the children of Ammon to this day.

20

1 Abraham travelled from there towards the land of the South, and lived between Kadesh and Shur. He lived as a foreigner in Gerar. 2 Abraham said about Sarah his wife, "She is my sister." Abimelech king of Gerar sent, and took Sarah. 3 But God came to Abimelech in a dream of the night, and said to him, "Behold, you are a dead man, because of the woman whom you have taken; for she is a man's wife."

4 Now Abimelech had not come near her. He said, "Lord, will you kill even a righteous nation? 5 Didn't he tell me, 'She is my sister'? She, even she herself, said, 'He is my brother.' I have done this in the integrity of my heart and the innocence of my hands."

6 God said to him in the dream, "Yes, I know that in the integrity of your heart you have done this, and I also withheld you from sinning against me. Therefore I didn't allow you to touch her. 7 Now therefore, restore the man's wife. For he is a prophet, and he will pray for you, and you will live. If you don't restore her, know for sure that you will die, you, and all who are yours."

8 Abimelech rose early in the morning, and called all his servants, and told all these things in their ear. The men were very scared. 9 Then Abimelech called Abraham, and said to him, "What have you done to us? How have I sinned against you, that you have brought on me and on my kingdom a great sin? You have done deeds to me that ought not to be done!" 10 Abimelech said to Abraham, "What did you see, that you have done this thing?"

11 Abraham said, "Because I thought, 'Surely the fear of God is not in this place. They will kill me for my wife's sake.' 12 Besides, she is indeed my sister, the daughter of my father, but not the daughter of my mother; and she became my wife. 13 When God caused me to wander from my father's house, I said to her, 'This is your kindness which you shall show to me. Everywhere that we go, say of me, "He is my brother."'"

14 Abimelech took sheep and cattle, male servants and female servants, and gave them to Abraham, and restored Sarah, his wife, to him. 15 Abimelech said, "Behold, my land is before you. Dwell where it pleases you." 16 To Sarah he said, "Behold, I have given your brother a thousand pieces of silver. Behold, it is for you a covering of the eyes to all that are with you. In front of all you are vindicated."

17 Abraham prayed to God. So God healed Abimelech, his wife, and his female servants, and they bore children. 18 For the LORD had closed up tight all the wombs of the house of Abimelech, because of Sarah, Abraham's wife.

21

1 The LORD visited Sarah as he had said, and the LORD did to Sarah as he had spoken. 2 Sarah conceived, and bore Abraham a son in his old age, at the set time of which God had spoken to him. 3 Abraham called his son who was born to him, whom Sarah bore to him, Isaac.ᵇ 4 Abraham circumcised his son, Isaac, when he was eight days old, as God had commanded him. 5 Abraham was one hundred years old when his son, Isaac, was born to him. 6 Sarah said, "God has made me laugh. Everyone who hears will laugh with me." 7 She said, "Who would have said to Abraham that Sarah would nurse children? For I have borne him a son in his old age."

8 The child grew and was weaned. Abraham made a great feast on the day that Isaac was weaned. 9 Sarah saw the son of Hagar the Egyptian, whom she had borne to Abraham, mocking. 10 Therefore she said to Abraham, "Cast out this servant and her son! For the son of this servant will not be heir with my son, Isaac."

11 The thing was very grievous in Abraham's sight on account of his son. 12 God said to Abraham, "Don't let it be grievous in your sight because of the boy, and because of your servant. In all that Sarah says to you, listen to her voice. For your offspring will be named through Isaac. 13 I will also make a nation of the son of the servant, because he is your child." 14 Abraham rose up early in the morning, and took bread and a container of water, and gave it to Hagar, putting it on her shoulder; and gave her the child, and sent her away. She departed, and wandered in the wilderness of Beersheba. 15 The water in the container was spent, and she put the child under one of the shrubs. 16 She went and sat down opposite him, a good way off, about a bow shot away. For she said, "Don't let me see the death of the child." She sat opposite him, and lifted up her voice, and wept. 17 God heard the voice of the boy.

The angel of God called to Hagar out of the sky, and said to her, "What troubles you, Hagar? Don't be afraid. For God has heard the voice of the

---

ª 19:22 Zoar means "little".

ᵇ 21:3 Isaac means "He laughs".

boy where he is. 18 Get up, lift up the boy, and hold him with your hand. For I will make him a great nation."

19 God opened her eyes, and she saw a well of water. She went, filled the container with water, and gave the boy a drink.

20 God was with the boy, and he grew. He lived in the wilderness, and as he grew up, he became an archer. 21 He lived in the wilderness of Paran. His mother got a wife for him out of the land of Egypt.

22 At that time, Abimelech and Phicol the captain of his army spoke to Abraham, saying, "God is with you in all that you do. 23 Now, therefore, swear to me here by God that you will not deal falsely with me, nor with my son, nor with my son's son. But according to the kindness that I have done to you, you shall do to me, and to the land in which you have lived as a foreigner."

24 Abraham said, "I will swear." 25 Abraham complained to Abimelech because of a water well, which Abimelech's servants had violently taken away. 26 Abimelech said, "I don't know who has done this thing. You didn't tell me, and I didn't hear of it until today."

27 Abraham took sheep and cattle, and gave them to Abimelech. Those two made a covenant. 28 Abraham set seven ewe lambs of the flock by themselves. 29 Abimelech said to Abraham, "What do these seven ewe lambs, which you have set by themselves, mean?"

30 He said, "You shall take these seven ewe lambs from my hand, that it may be a witness to me, that I have dug this well." 31 Therefore he called that place Beersheba,ᵃ because they both swore an oath there. 32 So they made a covenant at Beersheba. Abimelech rose up with Phicol, the captain of his army, and they returned into the land of the Philistines. 33 Abraham planted a tamarisk tree in Beersheba, and there he called on the name of the LORD, the Everlasting God. 34 Abraham lived as a foreigner in the land of the Philistines many days.

22

1 After these things, God tested Abraham, and said to him, "Abraham!"

He said, "Here I am."

2 He said, "Now take your son, your only son, Isaac, whom you love, and go into the land of Moriah. Offer him there as a burnt offering on one of the mountains which I will tell you of."

3 Abraham rose early in the morning, and saddled his donkey; and took two of his young men with him, and Isaac his son. He split the wood for the burnt offering, and rose up, and went to the place of which God had told him. 4 On the third day Abraham lifted up his eyes, and saw the place far off. 5 Abraham said to his young men, "Stay here with the donkey. The boy and I will go over there. We will worship, and come back to you." 6 Abraham took the wood of the burnt offering and laid it on Isaac his son. He took in his hand the fire and the knife. They both went together. 7 Isaac spoke to Abraham his father, and said, "My father?"

He said, "Here I am, my son."

He said, "Here is the fire and the wood, but where is the lamb for a burnt offering?"

8 Abraham said, "God will provide himself the lamb for a burnt offering, my son." So they both went together. 9 They came to the place which God had told him of. Abraham built the altar there, and laid the wood in order, bound Isaac his son, and laid him on the altar, on the wood. 10 Abraham stretched out his hand, and took the knife to kill his son.

11 The LORD's angel called to him out of the sky, and said, "Abraham, Abraham!"

He said, "Here I am."

12 He said, "Don't lay your hand on the boy or do anything to him. For now I know that you fear God, since you have not withheld your son, your only son, from me."

13 Abraham lifted up his eyes, and looked, and saw that behind him was a ram caught in the thicket by his horns. Abraham went and took the ram, and offered him up for a burnt offering instead of his son. 14 Abraham called the name of that place "The LORD Will Provide".ᵇ As it is said to this day, "On the LORD's mountain, it will be provided."

15 The LORD's angel called to Abraham a second time out of the sky, 16 and said, "'I have sworn by myself,' says the LORD, 'because you have done this thing, and have not withheld your son, your only son, 17 that I will bless you greatly, and I will multiply your offspring greatly like the stars of the heavens, and like the sand which is on the seashore. Your offspring will possess the gate of his enemies. 18 All the nations of the earth will be blessed by your offspring, because you have obeyed my voice.'"

19 So Abraham returned to his young men, and they rose up and went together to Beersheba. Abraham lived at Beersheba.

20 After these things, Abraham was told, "Behold, Milcah, she also has borne children to your brother Nahor: 21 Uz his firstborn, Buz his brother, Kemuel the father of Aram, 22 Chesed, Hazo, Pildash, Jidlaph, and Bethuel." 23 Bethuel became the father of Rebekah. These eight Milcah bore to Nahor, Abraham's brother. 24 His concubine, whose name was Reumah, also bore Tebah, Gaham, Tahash, and Maacah.

23

1 Sarah lived one hundred and twenty-seven years. This was the length of Sarah's life. 2 Sarah died in Kiriath Arba (also called Hebron), in the land of Canaan. Abraham came to mourn for Sarah, and to weep for her. 3 Abraham rose up from before his dead and spoke to the children of Heth,

saying, 4 "I am a stranger and a foreigner living with you. Give me a possession of a burying-place with you, that I may bury my dead out of my sight."

5 The children of Heth answered Abraham, saying to him, 6 "Hear us, my lord. You are a prince of God amongst us. Bury your dead in the best of our tombs. None of us will withhold from you his tomb. Bury your dead."

7 Abraham rose up, and bowed himself to the people of the land, to the children of Heth. 8 He talked with them, saying, "If you agree that I should bury my dead out of my sight, hear me, and entreat for me to Ephron the son of Zohar, 9 that he may sell me the cave of Machpelah, which he has, which is in the end of his field. For the full price let him sell it to me amongst you as a possession for a burial place."

10 Now Ephron was sitting in the middle of the children of Heth. Ephron the Hittite answered Abraham in the hearing of the children of Heth, even of all who went in at the gate of his city, saying, 11 "No, my lord, hear me. I give you the field, and I give you the cave that is in it. In the presence of the children of my people I give it to you. Bury your dead."

12 Abraham bowed himself down before the people of the land. 13 He spoke to Ephron in the audience of the people of the land, saying, "But if you will, please hear me. I will give the price of the field. Take it from me, and I will bury my dead there."

14 Ephron answered Abraham, saying to him, 15 "My lord, listen to me. What is a piece of land worth four hundred shekels of silverᶜ between me and you? Therefore bury your dead."

16 Abraham listened to Ephron. Abraham weighed to Ephron the silver which he had named in the hearing of the children of Heth, four hundred shekels of silver, according to the current merchants' standard.

17 So the field of Ephron, which was in Machpelah, which was before Mamre, the field, the cave which was in it, and all the trees that were in the field, that were in all of its borders, were deeded 18 to Abraham for a possession in the presence of the children of Heth, before all who went in at the gate of his city. 19 After this, Abraham buried Sarah his wife in the cave of the field of Machpelah before Mamre (that is, Hebron), in the land of Canaan. 20 The field, and the cave that is in it, were deeded to Abraham by the children of Heth as a possession for a burial place.

24

1 Abraham was old, and well advanced in age. The LORD had blessed Abraham in all things. 2 Abraham said to his servant, the elder of his house, who ruled over all that he had, "Please put your hand under my thigh. 3 I will make you swear by the LORD, the God of heaven and the God of the earth, that you shall not take a wife for my son of the daughters of the Canaanites, amongst whom I live. 4 But you shall go to my country, and to my relatives, and take a wife for my son Isaac."

5 The servant said to him, "What if the woman isn't willing to follow me to this land? Must I bring your son again to the land you came from?"

6 Abraham said to him, "Beware that you don't bring my son there again. 7 The LORD, the God of heaven—who took me from my father's house, and from the land of my birth, who spoke to me, and who swore to me, saying, 'I will give this land to your offspring—he will send his angel before you, and you shall take a wife for my son from there. 8 If the woman isn't willing to follow you, then you shall be clear from this oath to me. Only you shall not bring my son there again."

9 The servant put his hand under the thigh of Abraham his master, and swore to him concerning this matter. 10 The servant took ten of his master's camels, and departed, having a variety of good things of his master's with him. He arose, and went to Mesopotamia, to the city of Nahor. 11 He made the camels kneel down outside the city by the well of water at the time of evening, the time that women go out to draw water. 12 He said, "LORD, the God of my master Abraham, please give me success today, and show kindness to my master Abraham. 13 Behold, I am standing by the spring of water. The daughters of the men of the city are coming out to draw water. 14 Let it happen, that the young lady to whom I will say, 'Please let down your pitcher, that I may drink,' then she says, 'Drink, and I will also give your camels a drink,'—let her be the one you have appointed for your servant Isaac. By this I will know that you have shown kindness to my master."

15 Before he had finished speaking, behold, Rebekah came out, who was born to Bethuel the son of Milcah, the wife of Nahor, Abraham's brother, with her pitcher on her shoulder. 16 The young lady was very beautiful to look at, a virgin. No man had known her. She went down to the spring, filled her pitcher, and came up. 17 The servant ran to meet her, and said, "Please give me a drink, a little water from your pitcher."

18 She said, "Drink, my lord." She hurried, and let down her pitcher on her hand, and gave him a drink. 19 When she had finished giving him a drink, she said, "I will also draw for your camels, until they have finished drinking." 20 She hurried, and emptied her pitcher into the trough, and ran again to the well to draw, and drew for all his camels.

21 The man looked steadfastly at her, remaining silent, to know whether the LORD had made his journey prosperous or not. 22 As the camels had done drinking, the man took a golden ring of half a shekelᵈ weight, and two bracelets for her hands of ten shekels weight of gold, 23 and said, "Whose daughter are you? Please tell me. Is there room in your father's house for us to stay?"

ᵃ *21:31* Beersheba can mean "well of the oath" or "well of seven".
ᵇ *22:14* or, the LORD Jireh, or, the LORD Seeing
ᶜ *23:15* A shekel is about 10 grams, so 400 shekels would be about 4 kg. or 8.8 pounds.
ᵈ *24:22* A shekel is about 10 grams or about 0.35 ounces.

24 She said to him, "I am the daughter of Bethuel the son of Milcah, whom she bore to Nahor." 25 She said moreover to him, "We have both straw and feed enough, and room to lodge in."

26 The man bowed his head, and worshipped the LORD. 27 He said, "Blessed be the LORD, the God of my master Abraham, who has not forsaken his loving kindness and his truth towards my master. As for me, the LORD has led me on the way to the house of my master's relatives."

28 The young lady ran, and told her mother's house about these words. 29 Rebekah had a brother, and his name was Laban. Laban ran out to the man, to the spring. 30 When he saw the ring, and the bracelets on his sister's hands, and when he heard the words of Rebekah his sister, saying, "This is what the man said to me," he came to the man. Behold, he was standing by the camels at the spring. 31 He said, "Come in, you blessed of the LORD. Why do you stand outside? For I have prepared the house, and room for the camels."

32 The man came into the house, and he unloaded the camels. He gave straw and feed for the camels, and water to wash his feet and the feet of the men who were with him. 33 Food was set before him to eat, but he said, "I will not eat until I have told my message."

Laban said, "Speak on."

34 He said, "I am Abraham's servant. 35 The LORD has blessed my master greatly. He has become great. The LORD has given him flocks and herds, silver and gold, male servants and female servants, and camels and donkeys. 36 Sarah, my master's wife, bore a son to my master when she was old. He has given all that he has to him. 37 My master made me swear, saying, 'You shall not take a wife for my son from the daughters of the Canaanites, in whose land I live, 38 but you shall go to my father's house, and to my relatives, and take a wife for my son.' 39 I asked my master, 'What if the woman will not follow me?' 40 He said to me, 'The LORD, before whom I walk, will send his angel with you, and prosper your way. You shall take a wife for my son from my relatives, and of my father's house. 41 Then you will be clear from my oath, when you come to my relatives. If they don't give her to you, you shall be clear from my oath.' 42 I came today to the spring, and said, 'The LORD, the God of my master Abraham, if now you do prosper my way which I go— 43 behold, I am standing by this spring of water. Let it happen, that the maiden who comes out to draw, to whom I will say, "Please give me a little water from your pitcher to drink," 44 then she tells me, "Drink, and I will also draw for your camels,"—let her be the woman whom the LORD has appointed for my master's son.' 45 Before I had finished speaking in my heart, behold, Rebekah came out with her pitcher on her shoulder. She went down to the spring, and drew. I said to her, 'Please let me drink.' 46 She hurried and let down her pitcher from her shoulder, and said, 'Drink, and I will also give your camels a drink.' So I drank, and she also gave the camels a drink. 47 I asked her, and said, 'Whose daughter are you?' She said, 'The daughter of Bethuel, Nahor's son, whom Milcah bore to him.' I put the ring on her nose, and the bracelets on her hands. 48 I bowed my head, and worshipped the LORD, and blessed the LORD, the God of my master Abraham, who had led me in the right way to take my master's brother's daughter for his son. 49 Now if you will deal kindly and truly with my master, tell me. If not, tell me, that I may turn to the right hand, or to the left."

50 Then Laban and Bethuel answered, "The thing proceeds from the LORD. We can't speak to you bad or good. 51 Behold, Rebekah is before you. Take her, and go, and let her be your master's son's wife, as the LORD has spoken."

52 When Abraham's servant heard their words, he bowed himself down to the earth to the LORD. 53 The servant brought out jewels of silver, and jewels of gold, and clothing, and gave them to Rebekah. He also gave precious things to her brother and her mother. 54 They ate and drank, he and the men who were with him, and stayed all night. They rose up in the morning, and he said, "Send me away to my master."

55 Her brother and her mother said, "Let the young lady stay with us a few days, at least ten. After that she will go."

56 He said to them, "Don't hinder me, since the LORD has prospered my way. Send me away that I may go to my master."

57 They said, "We will call the young lady, and ask her." 58 They called Rebekah, and said to her, "Will you go with this man?"

She said, "I will go."

59 They sent away Rebekah, their sister, with her nurse, Abraham's servant, and his men. 60 They blessed Rebekah, and said to her, "Our sister, may you be the mother of thousands of ten thousands, and let your offspring possess the gate of those who hate them."

61 Rebekah arose with her ladies. They rode on the camels, and followed the man. The servant took Rebekah, and went his way. 62 Isaac came from the way of Beer Lahai Roi, for he lived in the land of the South. 63 Isaac went out to meditate in the field at the evening. He lifted up his eyes and looked. Behold, there were camels coming. 64 Rebekah lifted up her eyes, and when she saw Isaac, she got off the camel. 65 She said to the servant, "Who is the man who is walking in the field to meet us?"

The servant said, "It is my master."

She took her veil, and covered herself. 66 The servant told Isaac all the things that he had done. 67 Isaac brought her into his mother Sarah's tent, and took Rebekah, and she became his wife. He loved her. So Isaac was comforted after his mother's death.

25

1 Abraham took another wife, and her name was Keturah. 2 She bore him Zimran, Jokshan, Medan, Midian, Ishbak, and Shuah. 3 Jokshan became the father of Sheba, and Dedan. The sons of Dedan were Asshurim, Letushim, and Leummim. 4 The sons of Midian were Ephah, Epher, Hanoch, Abida, and Eldaah. All these were the children of Keturah. 5 Abraham gave all that he had to Isaac, 6 but Abraham gave gifts to the sons of Abraham's concubines. While he still lived, he sent them away from Isaac his son, eastward, to the east country. 7 These are the days of the years of Abraham's life which he lived: one hundred and seventy-five years. 8 Abraham gave up his spirit, and died at a good old age, an old man, and full of years, and was gathered to his people. 9 Isaac and Ishmael, his sons, buried him in the cave of Machpelah, in the field of Ephron, the son of Zohar the Hittite, which is near Mamre, 10 the field which Abraham purchased from the children of Heth. Abraham was buried there with Sarah, his wife. 11 After the death of Abraham, God blessed Isaac, his son. Isaac lived by Beer Lahai Roi.

12 Now this is the history of the generations of Ishmael, Abraham's son, whom Hagar the Egyptian, Sarah's servant, bore to Abraham. 13 These are the names of the sons of Ishmael, by their names, according to the order of their birth: the firstborn of Ishmael, Nebaioth, then Kedar, Adbeel, Mibsam, 14 Mishma, Dumah, Massa, 15 Hadad, Tema, Jetur, Naphish, and Kedemah. 16 These are the sons of Ishmael, and these are their names, by their villages, and by their encampments: twelve princes, according to their nations. 17 These are the years of the life of Ishmael: one hundred and thirty-seven years. He gave up his spirit and died, and was gathered to his people. 18 They lived from Havilah to Shur that is before Egypt, as you go towards Assyria. He lived opposite all his relatives.

19 This is the history of the generations of Isaac, Abraham's son. Abraham became the father of Isaac. 20 Isaac was forty years old when he took Rebekah, the daughter of Bethuel the Syrian of Paddan Aram, the sister of Laban the Syrian, to be his wife. 21 Isaac entreated the LORD for his wife, because she was barren. The LORD was entreated by him, and Rebekah his wife conceived. 22 The children struggled together within her. She said, "If it is like this, why do I live?" She went to enquire of the LORD. 23 The LORD said to her,

"Two nations are in your womb.
Two peoples will be separated from your body.
The one people will be stronger than the other people.
The elder will serve the younger."

24 When her days to be delivered were fulfilled, behold, there were twins in her womb. 25 The first came out red all over, like a hairy garment. They named him Esau. 26 After that, his brother came out, and his hand had hold on Esau's heel. He was named Jacob. Isaac was sixty years old when she bore them.

27 The boys grew. Esau was a skilful hunter, a man of the field. Jacob was a quiet man, living in tents. 28 Now Isaac loved Esau, because he ate his venison. Rebekah loved Jacob. 29 Jacob boiled stew. Esau came in from the field, and he was famished. 30 Esau said to Jacob, "Please feed me with some of that red stew, for I am famished." Therefore his name was called Edom.a

31 Jacob said, "First, sell me your birthright."

32 Esau said, "Behold, I am about to die. What good is the birthright to me?"

33 Jacob said, "Swear to me first."

He swore to him. He sold his birthright to Jacob. 34 Jacob gave Esau bread and lentil stew. He ate and drank, rose up, and went his way. So Esau despised his birthright.

26

1 There was a famine in the land, in addition to the first famine that was in the days of Abraham. Isaac went to Abimelech king of the Philistines, to Gerar. 2 The LORD appeared to him, and said, "Don't go down into Egypt. Live in the land I will tell you about. 3 Live in this land, and I will be with you, and will bless you. For I will give to you, and to your offspring, all these lands, and I will establish the oath which I swore to Abraham your father. 4 I will multiply your offspring as the stars of the sky, and will give all these lands to your offspring. In your offspring all the nations of the earth will be blessed, 5 because Abraham obeyed my voice, and kept my requirements, my commandments, my statutes, and my laws."

6 Isaac lived in Gerar. 7 The men of the place asked him about his wife. He said, "She is my sister," for he was afraid to say, "My wife", lest, he thought, "the men of the place might kill me for Rebekah, because she is beautiful to look at." 8 When he had been there a long time, Abimelech king of the Philistines looked out at a window, and saw, and, behold, Isaac was caressing Rebekah, his wife. 9 Abimelech called Isaac, and said, "Behold, surely she is your wife. Why did you say, 'She is my sister'?"

Isaac said to him, "Because I said, 'Lest I die because of her.'"

10 Abimelech said, "What is this you have done to us? One of the people might easily have lain with your wife, and you would have brought guilt on us!"

11 Abimelech commanded all the people, saying, "He who touches this man or his wife will surely be put to death."

12 Isaac sowed in that land, and reaped in the same year one hundred times what he planted. The LORD blessed him. 13 The man grew great, and grew more and more until he became very great. 14 He had possessions of flocks, possessions of herds, and a great household. The Philistines envied

---

a 25:30 "Edom" means "red".

him. 15 Now all the wells which his father's servants had dug in the days of Abraham his father, the Philistines had stopped, and filled with earth. 16 Abimelech said to Isaac, "Go away from us, for you are much mightier than we."

17 Isaac departed from there, encamped in the valley of Gerar, and lived there.

18 Isaac dug again the wells of water, which they had dug in the days of Abraham his father, for the Philistines had stopped them after the death of Abraham. He called their names after the names by which his father had called them. 19 Isaac's servants dug in the valley, and found there a well of flowing^a water. 20 The herdsmen of Gerar argued with Isaac's herdsmen, saying, "The water is ours." So he called the name of the well Esek,^b because they contended with him. 21 They dug another well, and they argued over that, also. So he called its name Sitnah.^c 22 He left that place, and dug another well. They didn't argue over that one. So he called it Rehoboth.^d He said, "For now the LORD has made room for us, and we will be fruitful in the land."

23 He went up from there to Beersheba. 24 The LORD appeared to him the same night, and said, "I am the God of Abraham your father. Don't be afraid, for I am with you, and will bless you, and multiply your offspring for my servant Abraham's sake."

25 He built an altar there, and called on the LORD's name, and pitched his tent there. There Isaac's servants dug a well.

26 Then Abimelech went to him from Gerar with Ahuzzath his friend, and Phicol the captain of his army. 27 Isaac said to them, "Why have you come to me, since you hate me, and have sent me away from you?"

28 They said, "We saw plainly that the LORD was with you. We said, 'Let there now be an oath between us, even between us and you, and let's make a covenant with you, 29 that you will do us no harm, as we have not touched you, and as we have done to you nothing but good, and have sent you away in peace.' You are now the blessed of the LORD."

30 He made them a feast, and they ate and drank. 31 They rose up some time in the morning, and swore an oath to one another. Isaac sent them away, and they departed from him in peace. 32 The same day, Isaac's servants came, and told him concerning the well which they had dug, and said to him, "We have found water." 33 He called it "Shibah."^e Therefore the name of the city is "Beersheba"^f to this day.

34 When Esau was forty years old, he took as wife Judith, the daughter of Beeri the Hittite, and Basemath, the daughter of Elon the Hittite. 35 They grieved Isaac's and Rebekah's spirits.

27

1 When Isaac was old, and his eyes were dim, so that he could not see, he called Esau his elder son, and said to him, "My son?"

He said to him, "Here I am."

2 He said, "See now, I am old. I don't know the day of my death. 3 Now therefore, please take your weapons, your quiver and your bow, and go out to the field, and get me venison. 4 Make me savoury food, such as I love, and bring it to me, that I may eat, and that my soul may bless you before I die."

5 Rebekah heard when Isaac spoke to Esau his son. Esau went to the field to hunt for venison, and to bring it. 6 Rebekah spoke to Jacob her son, saying, "Behold, I heard your father speak to Esau your brother, saying, 7 'Bring me venison, and make me savoury food, that I may eat, and bless you before the LORD before my death.' 8 Now therefore, my son, obey my voice according to that which I command you. 9 Go now to the flock and get me two good young goats from there. I will make them savoury food for your father, such as he loves. 10 You shall bring it to your father, that he may eat, so that he may bless you before his death."

11 Jacob said to Rebekah his mother, "Behold, Esau my brother is a hairy man, and I am a smooth man. 12 What if my father touches me? I will seem to him as a deceiver, and I would bring a curse on myself, and not a blessing."

13 His mother said to him, "Let your curse be on me, my son. Only obey my voice, and go get them for me."

14 He went, and got them, and brought them to his mother. His mother made savoury food, such as his father loved. 15 Rebekah took the good clothes of Esau, her elder son, which were with her in the house, and put them on Jacob, her younger son. 16 She put the skins of the young goats on his hands, and on the smooth of his neck. 17 She gave the savoury food and the bread, which she had prepared, into the hand of her son Jacob.

18 He came to his father, and said, "My father?"

He said, "Here I am. Who are you, my son?"

19 Jacob said to his father, "I am Esau your firstborn. I have done what you asked me to do. Please arise, sit and eat of my venison, that your soul may bless me."

20 Isaac said to his son, "How is it that you have found it so quickly, my son?"

He said, "Because the LORD your God gave me success."

21 Isaac said to Jacob, "Please come near, that I may feel you, my son, whether you are really my son Esau or not."

22 Jacob went near to Isaac his father. He felt him, and said, "The voice is Jacob's voice, but the hands are the hands of Esau." 23 He didn't recognise him, because his hands were hairy, like his brother Esau's hands. So he blessed him. 24 He said, "Are you really my son Esau?"

He said, "I am."

25 He said, "Bring it near to me, and I will eat of my son's venison, that my soul may bless you."

He brought it near to him, and he ate. He brought him wine, and he drank. 26 His father Isaac said to him, "Come near now, and kiss me, my son." 27 He came near, and kissed him. He smelled the smell of his clothing, and blessed him, and said,
"Behold, the smell of my son
is as the smell of a field which the LORD has blessed.
28 God give you of the dew of the sky,
of the fatness of the earth,
and plenty of grain and new wine.
29 Let peoples serve you,
and nations bow down to you.
Be lord over your brothers.
Let your mother's sons bow down to you.
Cursed be everyone who curses you.
Blessed be everyone who blesses you."

30 As soon as Isaac had finished blessing Jacob, and Jacob had just gone out from the presence of Isaac his father, Esau his brother came in from his hunting. 31 He also made savoury food, and brought it to his father. He said to his father, "Let my father arise, and eat of his son's venison, that your soul may bless me."

32 Isaac his father said to him, "Who are you?"

He said, "I am your son, your firstborn, Esau."

33 Isaac trembled violently, and said, "Who, then, is he who has taken venison, and brought it to me, and I have eaten of all before you came, and have blessed him? Yes, he will be blessed."

34 When Esau heard the words of his father, he cried with an exceedingly great and bitter cry, and said to his father, "Bless me, even me also, my father."

35 He said, "Your brother came with deceit, and has taken away your blessing."

36 He said, "Isn't he rightly named Jacob? For he has supplanted me these two times. He took away my birthright. See, now he has taken away my blessing." He said, "Haven't you reserved a blessing for me?"

37 Isaac answered Esau, "Behold, I have made him your lord, and all his brothers I have given to him for servants. I have sustained him with grain and new wine. What then will I do for you, my son?"

38 Esau said to his father, "Do you have just one blessing, my father? Bless me, even me also, my father." Esau lifted up his voice, and wept.

39 Isaac his father answered him,
"Behold, your dwelling will be of the fatness of the earth,
and of the dew of the sky from above.
40 You will live by your sword, and you will serve your brother.
It will happen, when you will break loose,
that you will shake his yoke from off your neck."

41 Esau hated Jacob because of the blessing with which his father blessed him. Esau said in his heart, "The days of mourning for my father are at hand. Then I will kill my brother Jacob."

42 The words of Esau, her elder son, were told to Rebekah. She sent and called Jacob, her younger son, and said to him, "Behold, your brother Esau comforts himself about you by planning to kill you. 43 Now therefore, my son, obey my voice. Arise, flee to Laban, my brother, in Haran. 44 Stay with him a few days, until your brother's fury turns away— 45 until your brother's anger turns away from you, and he forgets what you have done to him. Then I will send, and get you from there. Why should I be bereaved of you both in one day?"

46 Rebekah said to Isaac, "I am weary of my life because of the daughters of Heth. If Jacob takes a wife of the daughters of Heth, such as these, of the daughters of the land, what good will my life do me?"

28

1 Isaac called Jacob, blessed him, and commanded him, "You shall not take a wife of the daughters of Canaan. 2 Arise, go to Paddan Aram, to the house of Bethuel your mother's father. Take a wife from there from the daughters of Laban, your mother's brother. 3 May God Almighty bless you, and make you fruitful, and multiply you, that you may be a company of peoples, 4 and give you the blessing of Abraham, to you and to your offspring with you, that you may inherit the land where you travel, which God gave to Abraham."

5 Isaac sent Jacob away. He went to Paddan Aram to Laban, son of Bethuel the Syrian, the brother of Rebekah, Jacob's and Esau's mother.

6 Now Esau saw that Isaac had blessed Jacob and sent him away to Paddan Aram, to take him a wife from there, and that as he blessed him he gave him a command, saying, "You shall not take a wife of the daughters of Canaan;" 7 and that Jacob obeyed his father and his mother, and was gone to Paddan Aram. 8 Esau saw that the daughters of Canaan didn't please Isaac, his father. 9 So Esau went to Ishmael, and took, in addition to the wives that he had, Mahalath the daughter of Ishmael, Abraham's son, the sister of Nebaioth, to be his wife.

10 Jacob went out from Beersheba, and went towards Haran. 11 He came to a certain place, and stayed there all night, because the sun had set. He took one of the stones of the place, and put it under his head, and lay down in that place to sleep. 12 He dreamt and saw a stairway set upon the

---

earth, and its top reached to heaven. Behold, the angels of God were ascending and descending on it. 13 Behold, the LORD stood above it, and said, "I am the LORD, the God of Abraham your father, and the God of Isaac. I will give the land you lie on to you and to your offspring. 14 Your offspring will be as the dust of the earth, and you will spread abroad to the west, and to the east, and to the north, and to the south. In you and in your offspring, all the families of the earth will be blessed. 15 Behold, I am with you, and will keep you, wherever you go, and will bring you again into this land. For I will not leave you until I have done that which I have spoken of to you."

16 Jacob awakened out of his sleep, and he said, "Surely the LORD is in this place, and I didn't know it." 17 He was afraid, and said, "How awesome this place is! This is none other than God's house, and this is the gate of heaven."

18 Jacob rose up early in the morning, and took the stone that he had put under his head, and set it up for a pillar, and poured oil on its top. 19 He called the name of that place Bethel, but the name of the city was Luz at the first. 20 Jacob vowed a vow, saying, "If God will be with me, and will keep me in this way that I go, and will give me bread to eat, and clothing to put on, 21 so that I come again to my father's house in peace, and the LORD will be my God, 22 then this stone, which I have set up for a pillar, will be God's house. Of all that you will give me I will surely give a tenth to you."

29

1 Then Jacob went on his journey, and came to the land of the children of the east. 2 He looked, and saw a well in the field, and saw three flocks of sheep lying there by it. For out of that well they watered the flocks. The stone on the well's mouth was large. 3 There all the flocks were gathered. They rolled the stone from the well's mouth, and watered the sheep, and put the stone back on the well's mouth in its place. 4 Jacob said to them, "My relatives, where are you from?"

They said, "We are from Haran."

5 He said to them, "Do you know Laban, the son of Nahor?"

They said, "We know him."

6 He said to them, "Is it well with him?"

They said, "It is well. See, Rachel, his daughter, is coming with the sheep."

7 He said, "Behold, it is still the middle of the day, not time to gather the livestock together. Water the sheep, and go and feed them."

8 They said, "We can't, until all the flocks are gathered together, and they roll the stone from the well's mouth. Then we will water the sheep."

9 While he was yet speaking with them, Rachel came with her father's sheep, for she kept them. 10 When Jacob saw Rachel the daughter of Laban, his mother's brother, and the sheep of Laban, his mother's brother, Jacob went near, and rolled the stone from the well's mouth, and watered the flock of Laban his mother's brother. 11 Jacob kissed Rachel, and lifted up his voice, and wept. 12 Jacob told Rachel that he was her father's relative, and that he was Rebekah's son. She ran and told her father.

13 When Laban heard the news of Jacob, his sister's son, he ran to meet Jacob, and embraced him, and kissed him, and brought him to his house. Jacob told Laban all these things. 14 Laban said to him, "Surely you are my bone and my flesh." Jacob stayed with him for a month. 15 Laban said to Jacob, "Because you are my relative, should you therefore serve me for nothing? Tell me, what will your wages be?"

16 Laban had two daughters. The name of the elder was Leah, and the name of the younger was Rachel. 17 Leah's eyes were weak, but Rachel was beautiful in form and attractive. 18 Jacob loved Rachel. He said, "I will serve you seven years for Rachel, your younger daughter."

19 Laban said, "It is better that I give her to you, than that I should give her to another man. Stay with me."

20 Jacob served seven years for Rachel. They seemed to him but a few days, for the love he had for her.

21 Jacob said to Laban, "Give me my wife, for my days are fulfilled, that I may go in to her."

22 Laban gathered together all the men of the place, and made a feast. 23 In the evening, he took Leah his daughter, and brought her to Jacob. He went in to her. 24 Laban gave Zilpah his servant to his daughter Leah for a servant. 25 In the morning, behold, it was Leah! He said to Laban, "What is this you have done to me? Didn't I serve with you for Rachel? Why then have you deceived me?"

26 Laban said, "It is not done so in our place, to give the younger before the firstborn. 27 Fulfil the week of this one, and we will give you the other also for the service which you will serve with me for seven more years."

28 Jacob did so, and fulfilled her week. He gave him Rachel his daughter as wife. 29 Laban gave Bilhah, his servant, to his daughter Rachel to be her servant. 30 He went in also to Rachel, and he loved also Rachel more than Leah, and served with him seven more years.

31 The LORD saw that Leah was hated, and he opened her womb, but Rachel was barren. 32 Leah conceived, and bore a son, and she named him Reuben. For she said, "Because the LORD has looked at my affliction; for now my husband will love me." 33 She conceived again, and bore a son, and said, "Because the LORD has heard that I am hated, he has therefore given me this son also." She named him Simeon. 34 She conceived again, and bore a son. She said, "Now this time my husband will be joined to me, because I have borne him three sons." Therefore his name was called Levi.

35 She conceived again, and bore a son. She said, "This time I will praise the LORD." Therefore she named him Judah. Then she stopped bearing.

30

1 When Rachel saw that she bore Jacob no children, Rachel envied her sister. She said to Jacob, "Give me children, or else I will die."

2 Jacob's anger burnt against Rachel, and he said, "Am I in God's place, who has withheld from you the fruit of the womb?"

3 She said, "Behold, my maid Bilhah. Go in to her, that she may bear on my knees, and I also may obtain children by her." 4 She gave him Bilhah her servant as wife, and Jacob went in to her. 5 Bilhah conceived, and bore Jacob a son. 6 Rachel said, "God has judged me, and has also heard my voice, and has given me a son." Therefore she called his name Dan. 7 Bilhah, Rachel's servant, conceived again, and bore Jacob a second son. 8 Rachel said, "I have wrestled with my sister with mighty wrestlings, and have prevailed." She named him Naphtali.

9 When Leah saw that she had finished bearing, she took Zilpah, her servant, and gave her to Jacob as a wife. 10 Zilpah, Leah's servant, bore Jacob a son. 11 Leah said, "How fortunate!" She named him Gad. 12 Zilpah, Leah's servant, bore Jacob a second son. 13 Leah said, "Happy am I, for the daughters will call me happy." She named him Asher.

14 Reuben went in the days of wheat harvest, and found mandrakes in the field, and brought them to his mother, Leah. Then Rachel said to Leah, "Please give me some of your son's mandrakes."

15 Leah said to her, "Is it a small matter that you have taken away my husband? Would you take away my son's mandrakes, also?"

Rachel said, "Therefore he will lie with you tonight for your son's mandrakes."

16 Jacob came from the field in the evening, and Leah went out to meet him, and said, "You must come in to me; for I have surely hired you with my son's mandrakes."

He lay with her that night. 17 God listened to Leah, and she conceived, and bore Jacob a fifth son. 18 Leah said, "God has given me my hire, because I gave my servant to my husband." She named him Issachar. 19 Leah conceived again, and bore a sixth son to Jacob. 20 Leah said, "God has endowed me with a good dowry. Now my husband will live with me, because I have borne him six sons." She named him Zebulun. 21 Afterwards, she bore a daughter, and named her Dinah.

22 God remembered Rachel, and God listened to her, and opened her womb. 23 She conceived, bore a son, and said, "God has taken away my reproach." 24 She named him Joseph,[a] saying, "May the LORD add another son to me."

25 When Rachel had borne Joseph, Jacob said to Laban, "Send me away, that I may go to my own place, and to my country. 26 Give me my wives and my children for whom I have served you, and let me go; for you know my service with which I have served you."

27 Laban said to him, "If now I have found favour in your eyes, stay here, for I have divined that the LORD has blessed me for your sake." 28 He said, "Appoint me your wages, and I will give it."

29 Jacob said to him, "You know how I have served you, and how your livestock have fared with me. 30 For it was little which you had before I came, and it has increased to a multitude. The LORD has blessed you wherever I turned. Now when will I provide for my own house also?"

31 Laban said, "What shall I give you?"

Jacob said, "You shall not give me anything. If you will do this thing for me, I will again feed your flock and keep it. 32 I will pass through all your flock today, removing from there every speckled and spotted one, and every black one amongst the sheep, and the spotted and speckled amongst the goats. This will be my hire. 33 So my righteousness will answer for me hereafter, when you come concerning my hire that is before you. Every one that is not speckled and spotted amongst the goats, and black amongst the sheep, that might be with me, will be considered stolen."

34 Laban said, "Behold, let it be according to your word."

35 That day, he removed the male goats that were streaked and spotted, and all the female goats that were speckled and spotted, every one that had white in it, and all the black ones amongst the sheep, and gave them into the hand of his sons. 36 He set three days' journey between himself and Jacob, and Jacob fed the rest of Laban's flocks.

37 Jacob took to himself rods of fresh poplar, almond, and plane tree, peeled white streaks in them, and made the white appear which was in the rods. 38 He set the rods which he had peeled opposite the flocks in the watering troughs where the flocks came to drink. They conceived when they came to drink. 39 The flocks conceived before the rods, and the flocks produced streaked, speckled, and spotted. 40 Jacob separated the lambs, and set the faces of the flocks towards the streaked and all the black in Laban's flock. He put his own droves apart, and didn't put them into Laban's flock. 41 Whenever the stronger of the flock conceived, Jacob laid the rods in front of the eyes of the flock in the watering troughs, that they might conceive amongst the rods; 42 but when the flock were feeble, he didn't put them in. So the feebler were Laban's, and the stronger Jacob's. 43 The man increased exceedingly, and had large flocks, female servants and male servants, and camels and donkeys.

31

1 Jacob heard Laban's sons' words, saying, "Jacob has taken away all that was our father's. He has obtained all this wealth from that which was our father's." 2 Jacob saw the expression on Laban's face, and, behold, it

---

a 30:24 Joseph means "may he add".

was not towards him as before. 3 The LORD said to Jacob, "Return to the land of your fathers, and to your relatives, and I will be with you."

4 Jacob sent and called Rachel and Leah to the field to his flock, 5 and said to them, "I see the expression on your father's face, that it is not towards me as before; but the God of my father has been with me. 6 You know that I have served your father with all of my strength. 7 Your father has deceived me, and changed my wages ten times, but God didn't allow him to hurt me. 8 If he said, 'The speckled will be your wages,' then all the flock bore speckled. If he said, 'The streaked will be your wages,' then all the flock bore streaked. 9 Thus God has taken away your father's livestock, and given them to me. 10 During mating season, I lifted up my eyes, and saw in a dream, and behold, the male goats which leapt on the flock were streaked, speckled, and grizzled. 11 The angel of God said to me in the dream, 'Jacob,' and I said, 'Here I am.' 12 He said, 'Now lift up your eyes, and behold, all the male goats which leap on the flock are streaked, speckled, and grizzled, for I have seen all that Laban does to you. 13 I am the God of Bethel, where you anointed a pillar, where you vowed a vow to me. Now arise, get out from this land, and return to the land of your birth.'"

14 Rachel and Leah answered him, "Is there yet any portion or inheritance for us in our father's house? 15 Aren't we considered as foreigners by him? For he has sold us, and has also used up our money. 16 For all the riches which God has taken away from our father are ours and our children's. Now then, whatever God has said to you, do."

17 Then Jacob rose up, and set his sons and his wives on the camels, 18 and he took away all his livestock, and all his possessions which he had gathered, including the livestock which he had gained in Paddan Aram, to go to Isaac his father, to the land of Canaan. 19 Now Laban had gone to shear his sheep; and Rachel stole the teraphim[a] that were her father's.

20 Jacob deceived Laban the Syrian, in that he didn't tell him that he was running away. 21 So he fled with all that he had. He rose up, passed over the River, and set his face towards the mountain of Gilead.

22 Laban was told on the third day that Jacob had fled. 23 He took his relatives with him, and pursued him seven days' journey. He overtook him in the mountain of Gilead. 24 God came to Laban the Syrian in a dream of the night, and said to him, "Be careful that you don't speak to Jacob either good or bad."

25 Laban caught up with Jacob. Now Jacob had pitched his tent in the mountain, and Laban with his relatives encamped in the mountain of Gilead. 26 Laban said to Jacob, "What have you done, that you have deceived me, and carried away my daughters like captives of the sword? 27 Why did you flee secretly, and deceive me, and didn't tell me, that I might have sent you away with mirth and with songs, with tambourine and with harp; 28 and didn't allow me to kiss my sons and my daughters? Now have you done foolishly. 29 It is in the power of my hand to hurt you, but the God of your father spoke to me last night, saying, 'Be careful that you don't speak to Jacob either good or bad.' 30 Now, you want to be gone, because you greatly longed for your father's house, but why have you stolen my gods?"

31 Jacob answered Laban, "Because I was afraid, for I said, 'Lest you should take your daughters from me by force.' 32 Anyone you find your gods with shall not live. Before our relatives, discern what is yours with me, and take it." For Jacob didn't know that Rachel had stolen them.

33 Laban went into Jacob's tent, into Leah's tent, and into the tent of the two female servants; but he didn't find them. He went out of Leah's tent, and entered into Rachel's tent. 34 Now Rachel had taken the teraphim, put them in the camel's saddle, and sat on them. Laban felt around all the tent, but didn't find them. 35 She said to her father, "Don't let my lord be angry that I can't rise up before you; for I'm having my period." He searched, but didn't find the teraphim.

36 Jacob was angry, and argued with Laban. Jacob answered Laban, "What is my trespass? What is my sin, that you have hotly pursued me? 37 Now that you have felt around in all my stuff, what have you found of all your household stuff? Set it here before my relatives and your relatives, that they may judge between us two.

38 "These twenty years I have been with you. Your ewes and your female goats have not cast their young, and I haven't eaten the rams of your flocks. 39 That which was torn of animals, I didn't bring to you. I bore its loss. Of my hand you required it, whether stolen by day or stolen by night. 40 This was my situation: in the day the drought consumed me, and the frost by night; and my sleep fled from my eyes. 41 These twenty years I have been in your house. I served you fourteen years for your two daughters, and six years for your flock, and you have changed my wages ten times. 42 Unless the God of my father, the God of Abraham, and the fear of Isaac, had been with me, surely now you would have sent me away empty. God has seen my affliction and the labour of my hands, and rebuked you last night."

43 Laban answered Jacob, "The daughters are my daughters, the children are my children, the flocks are my flocks, and all that you see is mine! What can I do today to these my daughters, or to their children whom they have borne? 44 Now come, let's make a covenant, you and I. Let it be for a witness between me and you."

45 Jacob took a stone, and set it up for a pillar. 46 Jacob said to his relatives, "Gather stones." They took stones, and made a heap. They ate there by the heap. 47 Laban called it Jegar Sahadutha,[b] but Jacob called it Galeed.[c] 48 Laban said, "This heap is witness between me and you today."

Therefore it was named Galeed 49 and Mizpah, for he said, "The LORD watch between me and you, when we are absent one from another. 50 If you afflict my daughters, or if you take wives in addition to my daughters, no man is with us; behold, God is witness between me and you." 51 Laban said to Jacob, "See this heap, and see the pillar, which I have set between me and you. 52 May this heap be a witness, and the pillar be a witness, that I will not pass over this heap to you, and that you will not pass over this heap and this pillar to me, for harm. 53 The God of Abraham, and the God of Nahor, the God of their father, judge between us." Then Jacob swore by the fear of his father, Isaac. 54 Jacob offered a sacrifice in the mountain, and called his relatives to eat bread. They ate bread, and stayed all night in the mountain. 55 Early in the morning, Laban rose up, and kissed his sons and his daughters, and blessed them. Laban departed and returned to his place.

32

1 Jacob went on his way, and the angels of God met him. 2 When he saw them, Jacob said, "This is God's army." He called the name of that place Mahanaim.[d]

3 Jacob sent messengers in front of him to Esau, his brother, to the land of Seir, the field of Edom. 4 He commanded them, saying, "This is what you shall tell my lord, Esau: 'This is what your servant, Jacob, says. I have lived as a foreigner with Laban, and stayed until now. 5 I have cattle, donkeys, flocks, male servants, and female servants. I have sent to tell my lord, that I may find favour in your sight.'" 6 The messengers returned to Jacob, saying, "We came to your brother Esau. He is coming to meet you, and four hundred men are with him." 7 Then Jacob was greatly afraid and was distressed. He divided the people who were with him, along with the flocks, the herds, and the camels, into two companies. 8 He said, "If Esau comes to the one company, and strikes it, then the company which is left will escape." 9 Jacob said, "God of my father Abraham, and God of my father Isaac, the LORD, who said to me, 'Return to your country, and to your relatives, and I will do you good,' 10 I am not worthy of the least of all the loving kindnesses, and of all the truth, which you have shown to your servant; for with just my staff I crossed over this Jordan; and now I have become two companies. 11 Please deliver me from the hand of my brother, from the hand of Esau; for I fear him, lest he come and strike me and the mothers with the children. 12 You said, 'I will surely do you good, and make your offspring as the sand of the sea, which can't be counted because there are so many.'"

13 He stayed there that night, and took from that which he had with him a present for Esau, his brother: 14 two hundred female goats and twenty male goats, two hundred ewes and twenty rams, 15 thirty milk camels and their colts, forty cows, ten bulls, twenty female donkeys and ten foals. 16 He delivered them into the hands of his servants, every herd by itself, and said to his servants, "Pass over before me, and put a space between herd and herd." 17 He commanded the foremost, saying, "When Esau, my brother, meets you, and asks you, saying, 'Whose are you? Where are you going? Whose are these before you?' 18 Then you shall say, 'They are your servant, Jacob's. It is a present sent to my lord, Esau. Behold, he also is behind us.'" 19 He commanded also the second, and the third, and all that followed the herds, saying, "This is how you shall speak to Esau, when you find him. 20 You shall say, 'Not only that, but behold, your servant, Jacob, is behind us.'" For, he said, "I will appease him with the present that goes before me, and afterward I will see his face. Perhaps he will accept me."

21 So the present passed over before him, and he himself stayed that night in the camp.

22 He rose up that night, and took his two wives, and his two servants, and his eleven sons, and crossed over the ford of the Jabbok. 23 He took them, and sent them over the stream, and sent over that which he had. 24 Jacob was left alone, and wrestled with a man there until the breaking of the day. 25 When he saw that he didn't prevail against him, the man touched the hollow of his thigh, and the hollow of Jacob's thigh was strained as he wrestled. 26 The man said, "Let me go, for the day breaks."

Jacob said, "I won't let you go unless you bless me."

27 He said to him, "What is your name?"

He said, "Jacob".

28 He said, "Your name will no longer be called Jacob, but Israel; for you have fought with God and with men, and have prevailed."

29 Jacob asked him, "Please tell me your name."

He said, "Why is it that you ask what my name is?" So he blessed him there.

30 Jacob called the name of the place Peniel;[e] for he said, "I have seen God face to face, and my life is preserved." 31 The sun rose on him as he passed over Peniel, and he limped because of his thigh. 32 Therefore the children of Israel don't eat the sinew of the hip, which is on the hollow of the thigh, to this day, because he touched the hollow of Jacob's thigh in the sinew of the hip.

33

1 Jacob lifted up his eyes, and looked, and, behold, Esau was coming, and with him four hundred men. He divided the children between Leah, Rachel, and the two servants. 2 He put the servants and their children in front, Leah and her children after, and Rachel and Joseph at the rear. 3 He himself passed over in front of them, and bowed himself to the ground seven times, until he came near to his brother.

---

a 31:19 teraphim were household idols that may have been associated with inheritance rights to the household property.
b 31:47 "Jegar Sahadutha" means "Witness Heap" in Aramaic.
c 31:47 "Galeed" means "Witness Heap" in Hebrew.
d 32:2 "Mahanaim" means "two camps".
e 32:30 Peniel means "face of God".

4 Esau ran to meet him, embraced him, fell on his neck, kissed him, and they wept. 5 He lifted up his eyes, and saw the women and the children; and said, "Who are these with you?"

He said, "The children whom God has graciously given your servant." 6 Then the servants came near with their children, and they bowed themselves. 7 Leah also and her children came near, and bowed themselves. After them, Joseph came near with Rachel, and they bowed themselves.

8 Esau said, "What do you mean by all this company which I met?" Jacob said, "To find favour in the sight of my lord."

9 Esau said, "I have enough, my brother; let that which you have be yours."

10 Jacob said, "Please, no, if I have now found favour in your sight, then receive my present at my hand, because I have seen your face, as one sees the face of God, and you were pleased with me. 11 Please take the gift that I brought to you, because God has dealt graciously with me, and because I have enough." He urged him, and he took it.

12 Esau said, "Let's take our journey, and let's go, and I will go before you."

13 Jacob said to him, "My lord knows that the children are tender, and that the flocks and herds with me have their young, and if they overdrive them one day, all the flocks will die. 14 Please let my lord pass over before his servant, and I will lead on gently, according to the pace of the livestock that are before me and according to the pace of the children, until I come to my lord to Seir."

15 Esau said, "Let me now leave with you some of the people who are with me."

He said, "Why? Let me find favour in the sight of my lord."

16 So Esau returned that day on his way to Seir. 17 Jacob travelled to Succoth, built himself a house, and made shelters for his livestock. Therefore the name of the place is called Succoth.[a]

18 Jacob came in peace to the city of Shechem, which is in the land of Canaan, when he came from Paddan Aram; and encamped before the city. 19 He bought the parcel of ground where he had spread his tent, at the hand of the children of Hamor, Shechem's father, for one hundred pieces of money. 20 He erected an altar there, and called it El Elohe Israel.[b]

34

1 Dinah, the daughter of Leah, whom she bore to Jacob, went out to see the daughters of the land. 2 Shechem the son of Hamor the Hivite, the prince of the land, saw her. He took her, lay with her, and humbled her. 3 His soul joined to Dinah, the daughter of Jacob, and he loved the young lady, and spoke kindly to the young lady. 4 Shechem spoke to his father, Hamor, saying, "Get me this young lady as a wife."

5 Now Jacob heard that he had defiled Dinah, his daughter; and his sons were with his livestock in the field. Jacob held his peace until they came. 6 Hamor the father of Shechem went out to Jacob to talk with him. 7 The sons of Jacob came in from the field when they heard it. The men were grieved, and they were very angry, because he had done folly in Israel in lying with Jacob's daughter, a thing that ought not to be done. 8 Hamor talked with them, saying, "The soul of my son, Shechem, longs for your daughter. Please give her to him as a wife. 9 Make marriages with us. Give your daughters to us, and take our daughters for yourselves. 10 You shall dwell with us, and the land will be before you. Live and trade in it, and get possessions in it."

11 Shechem said to her father and to her brothers, "Let me find favour in your eyes, and whatever you will tell me I will give. 12 Ask me a great amount for a dowry, and I will give whatever you ask of me, but give me the young lady as a wife."

13 The sons of Jacob answered Shechem and Hamor his father with deceit when they spoke, because he had defiled Dinah their sister, 14 and said to them, "We can't do this thing, to give our sister to one who is uncircumcised; for that is a reproach to us. 15 Only on this condition will we consent to you. If you will be as we are, that every male of you be circumcised, 16 then will we give our daughters to you; and we will take your daughters to us, and we will dwell with you, and we will become one people. 17 But if you will not listen to us and be circumcised, then we will take our sister,[c] and we will be gone."

18 Their words pleased Hamor and Shechem, Hamor's son. 19 The young man didn't wait to do this thing, because he had delight in Jacob's daughter, and he was honoured above all the house of his father. 20 Hamor and Shechem, his son, came to the gate of their city, and talked with the men of their city, saying, 21 "These men are peaceful with us. Therefore let them live in the land and trade in it. For behold, the land is large enough for them. Let's take their daughters to us for wives, and let's give them our daughters. 22 Only on this condition will the men consent to us to live with us, to become one people, if every male amongst us is circumcised, as they are circumcised. 23 Won't their livestock and their possessions and all their animals be ours? Only let's give our consent to them, and they will dwell with us."

24 All who went out of the gate of his city listened to Hamor, and to Shechem his son; and every male was circumcised, all who went out of the gate of his city. 25 On the third day, when they were sore, two of Jacob's sons, Simeon and Levi, Dinah's brothers, each took his sword, came upon the unsuspecting city, and killed all the males. 26 They killed Hamor and

Shechem, his son, with the edge of the sword, and took Dinah out of Shechem's house, and went away. 27 Jacob's sons came on the dead, and plundered the city, because they had defiled their sister. 28 They took their flocks, their herds, their donkeys, that which was in the city, that which was in the field, 29 and all their wealth. They took captive all their little ones and their wives, and took as plunder everything that was in the house. 30 Jacob said to Simeon and Levi, "You have troubled me, to make me odious to the inhabitants of the land, amongst the Canaanites and the Perizzites. I am few in number. They will gather themselves together against me and strike me, and I will be destroyed, I and my house."

31 They said, "Should he deal with our sister as with a prostitute?"

35

1 God said to Jacob, "Arise, go up to Bethel, and live there. Make there an altar to God, who appeared to you when you fled from the face of Esau your brother."

2 Then Jacob said to his household, and to all who were with him, "Put away the foreign gods that are amongst you, purify yourselves, and change your garments. 3 Let's arise, and go up to Bethel. I will make there an altar to God, who answered me in the day of my distress, and was with me on the way which I went."

4 They gave to Jacob all the foreign gods which were in their hands, and the rings which were in their ears; and Jacob hid them under the oak which was by Shechem. 5 They travelled, and a terror of God was on the cities that were around them, and they didn't pursue the sons of Jacob. 6 So Jacob came to Luz (that is, Bethel), which is in the land of Canaan, he and all the people who were with him. 7 He built an altar there, and called the place El Beth El; because there God was revealed to him, when he fled from the face of his brother. 8 Deborah, Rebekah's nurse, died, and she was buried below Bethel under the oak; and its name was called Allon Bacuth.

9 God appeared to Jacob again, when he came from Paddan Aram, and blessed him. 10 God said to him, "Your name is Jacob. Your name shall not be Jacob any more, but your name will be Israel." He named him Israel. 11 God said to him, "I am God Almighty. Be fruitful and multiply. A nation and a company of nations will be from you, and kings will come out of your body. 12 The land which I gave to Abraham and Isaac, I will give it to you, and to your offspring after you I will give the land."

13 God went up from him in the place where he spoke with him. 14 Jacob set up a pillar in the place where he spoke with him, a pillar of stone. He poured out a drink offering on it, and poured oil on it. 15 Jacob called the name of the place where God spoke with him "Bethel".

16 They travelled from Bethel. There was still some distance to come to Ephrath, and Rachel travailed. She had hard labour. 17 When she was in hard labour, the midwife said to her, "Don't be afraid, for now you will have another son."

18 As her soul was departing (for she died), she named him Benoni,[d] but his father named him Benjamin.[e] 19 Rachel died, and was buried on the way to Ephrath (also called Bethlehem). 20 Jacob set up a pillar on her grave. The same is the Pillar of Rachel's grave to this day. 21 Israel travelled, and spread his tent beyond the tower of Eder. 22 While Israel lived in that land, Reuben went and lay with Bilhah, his father's concubine, and Israel heard of it.

Now the sons of Jacob were twelve. 23 The sons of Leah: Reuben (Jacob's firstborn), Simeon, Levi, Judah, Issachar, and Zebulun. 24 The sons of Rachel: Joseph and Benjamin. 25 The sons of Bilhah (Rachel's servant): Dan and Naphtali. 26 The sons of Zilpah (Leah's servant): Gad and Asher. These are the sons of Jacob, who were born to him in Paddan Aram.

27 Jacob came to Isaac his father, to Mamre, to Kiriath Arba (which is Hebron), where Abraham and Isaac lived as foreigners. 28 The days of Isaac were one hundred and eighty years. 29 Isaac gave up the spirit and died, and was gathered to his people, old and full of days. Esau and Jacob, his sons, buried him.

36

1 Now this is the history of the generations of Esau (that is, Edom). 2 Esau took his wives from the daughters of Canaan: Adah the daughter of Elon, the Hittite; and Oholibamah the daughter of Anah, the daughter of Zibeon, the Hivite; 3 and Basemath, Ishmael's daughter, sister of Nebaioth. 4 Adah bore to Esau Eliphaz. Basemath bore Reuel. 5 Oholibamah bore Jeush, Jalam, and Korah. These are the sons of Esau, who were born to him in the land of Canaan. 6 Esau took his wives, his sons, his daughters, and all the members of his household, with his livestock, all his animals, and all his possessions, which he had gathered in the land of Canaan, and went into a land away from his brother Jacob. 7 For their substance was too great for them to dwell together, and the land of their travels couldn't bear them because of their livestock. 8 Esau lived in the hill country of Seir. Esau is Edom.

9 This is the history of the generations of Esau the father of the Edomites in the hill country of Seir: 10 these are the names of Esau's sons: Eliphaz, the son of Adah, the wife of Esau; and Reuel, the son of Basemath, the wife of Esau. 11 The sons of Eliphaz were Teman, Omar, Zepho, and Gatam, and Kenaz. 12 Timna was concubine to Eliphaz, Esau's son; and she bore to Eliphaz Amalek. These are the descendants of Adah, Esau's wife. 13 These are the sons of Reuel: Nahath, Zerah, Shammah, and Mizzah. These were the descendants of Basemath, Esau's wife. 14 These were the sons of

---

[a] *33:17* succoth means shelters or booths.

[b] *33:20* El Elohe Israel means "God, the God of Israel" or "The God of Israel is mighty".

[c] *34:17* Hebrew has, literally, "daughter"

[d] *35:18* "Benoni" means "son of my trouble".

[e] *35:18* "Benjamin" means "son of my right hand".

Oholibamah, the daughter of Anah, the daughter of Zibeon, Esau's wife: she bore to Esau Jeush, Jalam, and Korah.

15 These are the chiefs of the sons of Esau: the sons of Eliphaz the firstborn of Esau: chief Teman, chief Omar, chief Zepho, chief Kenaz, 16 chief Korah, chief Gatam, chief Amalek. These are the chiefs who came of Eliphaz in the land of Edom. These are the sons of Adah. 17 These are the sons of Reuel, Esau's son: chief Nahath, chief Zerah, chief Shammah, chief Mizzah. These are the chiefs who came of Reuel in the land of Edom. These are the sons of Basemath, Esau's wife. 18 These are the sons of Oholibamah, Esau's wife: chief Jeush, chief Jalam, chief Korah. These are the chiefs who came of Oholibamah the daughter of Anah, Esau's wife. 19 These are the sons of Esau (that is, Edom), and these are their chiefs.

20 These are the sons of Seir the Horite, the inhabitants of the land: Lotan, Shobal, Zibeon, Anah, 21 Dishon, Ezer, and Dishan. These are the chiefs who came of the Horites, the children of Seir in the land of Edom. 22 The children of Lotan were Hori and Heman. Lotan's sister was Timna. 23 These are the children of Shobal: Alvan, Manahath, Ebal, Shepho, and Onam. 24 These are the children of Zibeon: Aiah and Anah. This is Anah who found the hot springs in the wilderness, as he fed the donkeys of Zibeon his father. 25 These are the children of Anah: Dishon and Oholibamah, the daughter of Anah. 26 These are the children of Dishon: Hemdan, Eshban, Ithran, and Cheran. 27 These are the children of Ezer: Bilhan, Zaavan, and Akan. 28 These are the children of Dishan: Uz and Aran. 29 These are the chiefs who came of the Horites: chief Lotan, chief Shobal, chief Zibeon, chief Anah, 30 chief Dishon, chief Ezer, and chief Dishan. These are the chiefs who came of the Horites, according to their chiefs in the land of Seir.

31 These are the kings who reigned in the land of Edom, before any king reigned over the children of Israel. 32 Bela, the son of Beor, reigned in Edom. The name of his city was Dinhabah. 33 Bela died, and Jobab, the son of Zerah of Bozrah, reigned in his place. 34 Jobab died, and Husham of the land of the Temanites reigned in his place. 35 Husham died, and Hadad, the son of Bedad, who struck Midian in the field of Moab, reigned in his place. The name of his city was Avith. 36 Hadad died, and Samlah of Masrekah reigned in his place. 37 Samlah died, and Shaul of Rehoboth by the river, reigned in his place. 38 Shaul died, and Baal Hanan the son of Achbor reigned in his place. 39 Baal Hanan the son of Achbor died, and Hadar reigned in his place. The name of his city was Pau. His wife's name was Mehetabel, the daughter of Matred, the daughter of Mezahab.

40 These are the names of the chiefs who came from Esau, according to their families, after their places, and by their names: chief Timna, chief Alvah, chief Jetheth, 41 chief Oholibamah, chief Elah, chief Pinon, 42 chief Kenaz, chief Teman, chief Mibzar, 43 chief Magdiel, and chief Iram. These are the chiefs of Edom, according to their habitations in the land of their possession. This is Esau, the father of the Edomites.

37

1 Jacob lived in the land of his father's travels, in the land of Canaan. 2 This is the history of the generations of Jacob. Joseph, being seventeen years old, was feeding the flock with his brothers. He was a boy with the sons of Bilhah and Zilpah, his father's wives. Joseph brought an evil report of them to their father. 3 Now Israel loved Joseph more than all his children, because he was the son of his old age, and he made him a tunic of many colours. 4 His brothers saw that their father loved him more than all his brothers, and they hated him, and couldn't speak peaceably to him.

5 Joseph dreamt a dream, and he told it to his brothers, and they hated him all the more. 6 He said to them, "Please hear this dream which I have dreamt: 7 for behold, we were binding sheaves in the field, and behold, my sheaf arose and also stood upright; and behold, your sheaves came around, and bowed down to my sheaf."

8 His brothers asked him, "Will you indeed reign over us? Will you indeed have dominion over us?" They hated him all the more for his dreams and for his words. 9 He dreamt yet another dream, and told it to his brothers, and said, "Behold, I have dreamt yet another dream: and behold, the sun and the moon and eleven stars bowed down to me." 10 He told it to his father and to his brothers. His father rebuked him, and said to him, "What is this dream that you have dreamt? Will I and your mother and your brothers indeed come to bow ourselves down to the earth before you?" 11 His brothers envied him, but his father kept this saying in mind.

12 His brothers went to feed their father's flock in Shechem. 13 Israel said to Joseph, "Aren't your brothers feeding the flock in Shechem? Come, and I will send you to them." He said to him, "Here I am."

14 He said to him, "Go now, see whether it is well with your brothers, and well with the flock; and bring me word again." So he sent him out of the valley of Hebron, and he came to Shechem. 15 A certain man found him, and behold, he was wandering in the field. The man asked him, "What are you looking for?"

16 He said, "I am looking for my brothers. Tell me, please, where they are feeding the flock."

17 The man said, "They have left here, for I heard them say, 'Let's go to Dothan.'"

Joseph went after his brothers, and found them in Dothan. 18 They saw him afar off, and before he came near to them, they conspired against him to kill him. 19 They said to one another, "Behold, this dreamer comes. 20 Come now therefore, and let's kill him, and cast him into one of the pits, and we will say, 'An evil animal has devoured him.' We will see what will become of his dreams."

21 Reuben heard it, and delivered him out of their hand, and said, "Let's not take his life." 22 Reuben said to them, "Shed no blood. Throw him into this pit that is in the wilderness, but lay no hand on him"—that he might deliver him out of their hand, to restore him to his father. 23 When Joseph came to his brothers, they stripped Joseph of his tunic, the tunic of many colours that was on him; 24 and they took him, and threw him into the pit. The pit was empty. There was no water in it.

25 They sat down to eat bread, and they lifted up their eyes and looked, and saw a caravan of Ishmaelites was coming from Gilead, with their camels bearing spices and balm and myrrh, going to carry it down to Egypt. 26 Judah said to his brothers, "What profit is it if we kill our brother and conceal his blood? 27 Come, and let's sell him to the Ishmaelites, and not let our hand be on him; for he is our brother, our flesh." His brothers listened to him. 28 Midianites who were merchants passed by, and they drew and lifted up Joseph out of the pit, and sold Joseph to the Ishmaelites for twenty pieces of silver. The merchants brought Joseph into Egypt.

29 Reuben returned to the pit, and saw that Joseph wasn't in the pit; and he tore his clothes. 30 He returned to his brothers, and said, "The child is no more; and I, where will I go?" 31 They took Joseph's tunic, and killed a male goat, and dipped the tunic in the blood. 32 They took the tunic of many colours, and they brought it to their father, and said, "We have found this. Examine it, now, and see if it is your son's tunic or not."

33 He recognised it, and said, "It is my son's tunic. An evil animal has devoured him. Joseph is without doubt torn in pieces." 34 Jacob tore his clothes, and put sackcloth on his waist, and mourned for his son many days. 35 All his sons and all his daughters rose up to comfort him, but he refused to be comforted. He said, "For I will go down to Sheolᵃ to my son, mourning." His father wept for him. 36 The Midianites sold him into Egypt to Potiphar, an officer of Pharaoh's, the captain of the guard.

38

1 At that time, Judah went down from his brothers, and visited a certain Adullamite, whose name was Hirah. 2 There, Judah saw the daughter of a certain Canaanite man named Shua. He took her, and went in to her. 3 She conceived, and bore a son; and he named him Er. 4 She conceived again, and bore a son; and she named him Onan. 5 She yet again bore a son, and named him Shelah. He was at Chezib when she bore him. 6 Judah took a wife for Er, his firstborn, and her name was Tamar. 7 Er, Judah's firstborn, was wicked in the LORD's sight. So the LORD killed him.

8 Judah said to Onan, "Go in to your brother's wife, and perform the duty of a husband's brother to her, and raise up offspring for your brother." 9 Onan knew that the offspring wouldn't be his; and when he went in to his brother's wife, he spilled his semen on the ground, lest he should give offspring to his brother. 10 The thing which he did was evil in the LORD's sight, and he killed him also. 11 Then Judah said to Tamar, his daughter-in-law, "Remain a widow in your father's house, until Shelah, my son, is grown up;" for he said, "Lest he also die, like his brothers." Tamar went and lived in her father's house.

12 After many days, Shua's daughter, the wife of Judah, died. Judah was comforted, and went up to his sheep shearers to Timnah, he and his friend Hirah, the Adullamite. 13 Tamar was told, "Behold, your father-in-law is going up to Timnah to shear his sheep." 14 She took off the garments of her widowhood, and covered herself with her veil, and wrapped herself, and sat in the gate of Enaim, which is on the way to Timnah; for she saw that Shelah was grown up, and she wasn't given to him as a wife. 15 When Judah saw her, he thought that she was a prostitute, for she had covered her face. 16 He turned to her by the way, and said, "Please come, let me come in to you," for he didn't know that she was his daughter-in-law.

She said, "What will you give me, that you may come in to me?"

17 He said, "I will send you a young goat from the flock."

She said, "Will you give me a pledge, until you send it?"

18 He said, "What pledge will I give you?"

She said, "Your signet and your cord, and your staff that is in your hand."

He gave them to her, and came in to her, and she conceived by him. 19 She arose, and went away, and put off her veil from her, and put on the garments of her widowhood. 20 Judah sent the young goat by the hand of his friend, the Adullamite, to receive the pledge from the woman's hand, but he didn't find her. 21 Then he asked the men of her place, saying, "Where is the prostitute, that was at Enaim by the road?"

They said, "There has been no prostitute here."

22 He returned to Judah, and said, "I haven't found her; and also the men of the place said, 'There has been no prostitute here.'" 23 Judah said, "Let her keep it, lest we be shamed. Behold, I sent this young goat, and you haven't found her."

24 About three months later, Judah was told, "Tamar, your daughter-in-law, has played the prostitute. Moreover, behold, she is with child by prostitution."

Judah said, "Bring her out, and let her be burnt." 25 When she was brought out, she sent to her father-in-law, saying, "I am with child by the man who owns these." She also said, "Please discern whose these are—the signet, and the cords, and the staff."

26 Judah acknowledged them, and said, "She is more righteous than I, because I didn't give her to Shelah, my son."

He knew her again no more. 27 In the time of her travail, behold, twins were in her womb. 28 When she travailed, one put out a hand, and the midwife took and tied a scarlet thread on his hand, saying, "This came out

---

ᵃ *37:35* Sheol is the place of the dead.

first." 29 As he drew back his hand, behold, his brother came out, and she said, "Why have you made a breach for yourself?" Therefore his name was called Perez.[a] 30 Afterward his brother came out, who had the scarlet thread on his hand, and his name was called Zerah.[b]

39

1 Joseph was brought down to Egypt. Potiphar, an officer of Pharaoh's, the captain of the guard, an Egyptian, bought him from the hand of the Ishmaelites that had brought him down there. 2 The LORD was with Joseph, and he was a prosperous man. He was in the house of his master the Egyptian. 3 His master saw that the LORD was with him, and that the LORD made all that he did prosper in his hand. 4 Joseph found favour in his sight. He ministered to him, and Potiphar made him overseer over his house, and all that he had he put into his hand. 5 From the time that he made him overseer in his house, and over all that he had, the LORD blessed the Egyptian's house for Joseph's sake. The LORD's blessing was on all that he had, in the house and in the field. 6 He left all that he had in Joseph's hand. He didn't concern himself with anything, except for the food which he ate.

Joseph was well-built and handsome. 7 After these things, his master's wife set her eyes on Joseph; and she said, "Lie with me."

8 But he refused, and said to his master's wife, "Behold, my master doesn't know what is with me in the house, and he has put all that he has into my hand. 9 No one is greater in this house than I am, and he has not kept back anything from me but you, because you are his wife. How then can I do this great wickedness, and sin against God?"

10 As she spoke to Joseph day by day, he didn't listen to her, to lie by her, or to be with her. 11 About this time, he went into the house to do his work, and there were none of the men of the house inside. 12 She caught him by his garment, saying, "Lie with me!"

He left his garment in her hand, and ran outside. 13 When she saw that he had left his garment in her hand, and had run outside, 14 she called to the men of her house, and spoke to them, saying, "Behold, he has brought a Hebrew in to us to mock us. He came in to me to lie with me, and I cried with a loud voice. 15 When he heard that I lifted up my voice and cried, he left his garment by me, and ran outside." 16 She laid up his garment by her, until his master came home. 17 She spoke to him according to these words, saying, "The Hebrew servant, whom you have brought to us, came in to me to mock me, 18 and as I lifted up my voice and cried, he left his garment by me, and ran outside."

19 When his master heard the words of his wife, which she spoke to him, saying, "This is what your servant did to me," his wrath was kindled. 20 Joseph's master took him, and put him into the prison, the place where the king's prisoners were bound, and he was there in custody. 21 But the LORD was with Joseph, and showed kindness to him, and gave him favour in the sight of the keeper of the prison. 22 The keeper of the prison committed to Joseph's hand all the prisoners who were in the prison. Whatever they did there, he was responsible for it. 23 The keeper of the prison didn't look after anything that was under his hand, because the LORD was with him; and that which he did, the LORD made it prosper.

40

1 After these things, the butler of the king of Egypt and his baker offended their lord, the king of Egypt. 2 Pharaoh was angry with his two officers, the chief cup bearer and the chief baker. 3 He put them in custody in the house of the captain of the guard, into the prison, the place where Joseph was bound. 4 The captain of the guard assigned them to Joseph, and he took care of them. They stayed in prison many days. 5 They both dreamt a dream, each man his dream, in one night, each man according to the interpretation of his dream, the cup bearer and the baker of the king of Egypt, who were bound in the prison. 6 Joseph came in to them in the morning, and saw them, and saw that they were sad. 7 He asked Pharaoh's officers who were with him in custody in his master's house, saying, "Why do you look so sad today?"

8 They said to him, "We have dreamt a dream, and there is no one who can interpret it."

Joseph said to them, "Don't interpretations belong to God? Please tell it to me."

9 The chief cup bearer told his dream to Joseph, and said to him, "In my dream, behold, a vine was in front of me, 10 and in the vine were three branches. It was as though it budded, it blossomed, and its clusters produced ripe grapes. 11 Pharaoh's cup was in my hand; and I took the grapes, and pressed them into Pharaoh's cup, and I gave the cup into Pharaoh's hand."

12 Joseph said to him, "This is its interpretation: the three branches are three days. 13 Within three more days, Pharaoh will lift up your head, and restore you to your office. You will give Pharaoh's cup into his hand, the way you did when you were his cup bearer. 14 But remember me when it is well with you. Please show kindness to me, and make mention of me to Pharaoh, and bring me out of this house. 15 For indeed, I was stolen away out of the land of the Hebrews, and here also I have done nothing that they should put me into the dungeon."

16 When the chief baker saw that the interpretation was good, he said to Joseph, "I also was in my dream, and behold, three baskets of white bread were on my head. 17 In the uppermost basket there were all kinds of baked food for Pharaoh, and the birds ate them out of the basket on my head."

18 Joseph answered, "This is its interpretation. The three baskets are three days. 19 Within three more days, Pharaoh will lift up your head from off you, and will hang you on a tree; and the birds will eat your flesh from off you." 20 On the third day, which was Pharaoh's birthday, he made a feast for all his servants, and he lifted up the head of the chief cup bearer and the head of the chief baker amongst his servants. 21 He restored the chief cup bearer to his position again, and he gave the cup into Pharaoh's hand; 22 but he hanged the chief baker, as Joseph had interpreted to them. 23 Yet the chief cup bearer didn't remember Joseph, but forgot him.

41

1 At the end of two full years, Pharaoh dreamt, and behold, he stood by the river. 2 Behold, seven cattle came up out of the river. They were sleek and fat, and they fed in the marsh grass. 3 Behold, seven other cattle came up after them out of the river, ugly and thin, and stood by the other cattle on the brink of the river. 4 The ugly and thin cattle ate up the seven sleek and fat cattle. So Pharaoh awoke. 5 He slept and dreamt a second time; and behold, seven heads of grain came up on one stalk, healthy and good. 6 Behold, seven heads of grain, thin and blasted with the east wind, sprung up after them. 7 The thin heads of grain swallowed up the seven healthy and full ears. Pharaoh awoke, and behold, it was a dream. 8 In the morning, his spirit was troubled, and he sent and called for all of Egypt's magicians and wise men. Pharaoh told them his dreams, but there was no one who could interpret them to Pharaoh.

9 Then the chief cup bearer spoke to Pharaoh, saying, "I remember my faults today. 10 Pharaoh was angry with his servants, and put me in custody in the house of the captain of the guard, with the chief baker. 11 We dreamt a dream in one night, he and I. Each man dreamt according to the interpretation of his dream. 12 There was with us there a young man, a Hebrew, servant to the captain of the guard, and we told him, and he interpreted to us our dreams. He interpreted to each man according to his dream. 13 As he interpreted to us, so it was. He restored me to my office, and he hanged him."

14 Then Pharaoh sent and called Joseph, and they brought him hastily out of the dungeon. He shaved himself, changed his clothing, and came in to Pharaoh. 15 Pharaoh said to Joseph, "I have dreamt a dream, and there is no one who can interpret it. I have heard it said of you, that when you hear a dream you can interpret it."

16 Joseph answered Pharaoh, saying, "It isn't in me. God will give Pharaoh an answer of peace."

17 Pharaoh spoke to Joseph, "In my dream, behold, I stood on the brink of the river; 18 and behold, seven fat and sleek cattle came up out of the river. They fed in the marsh grass; 19 and behold, seven other cattle came up after them, poor and very ugly and thin, such as I never saw in all the land of Egypt for ugliness. 20 The thin and ugly cattle ate up the first seven fat cattle; 21 and when they had eaten them up, it couldn't be known that they had eaten them, but they were still ugly, as at the beginning. So I awoke. 22 I saw in my dream, and behold, seven heads of grain came up on one stalk, full and good; 23 and behold, seven heads of grain, withered, thin, and blasted with the east wind, sprung up after them. 24 The thin heads of grain swallowed up the seven good heads of grain. I told it to the magicians, but there was no one who could explain it to me."

25 Joseph said to Pharaoh, "The dream of Pharaoh is one. What God is about to do he has declared to Pharaoh. 26 The seven good cattle are seven years; and the seven good heads of grain are seven years. The dream is one. 27 The seven thin and ugly cattle that came up after them are seven years, and also the seven empty heads of grain blasted with the east wind; they will be seven years of famine. 28 That is the thing which I have spoken to Pharaoh. God has shown Pharaoh what he is about to do. 29 Behold, seven years of great plenty throughout all the land of Egypt are coming. 30 Seven years of famine will arise after them, and all the plenty will be forgotten in the land of Egypt. The famine will consume the land, 31 and the plenty will not be known in the land by reason of that famine which follows; for it will be very grievous. 32 The dream was doubled to Pharaoh, because the thing is established by God, and God will shortly bring it to pass.

33 "Now therefore let Pharaoh look for a discreet and wise man, and set him over the land of Egypt. 34 Let Pharaoh do this, and let him appoint overseers over the land, and take up the fifth part of the land of Egypt's produce in the seven plenteous years. 35 Let them gather all the food of these good years that come, and store grain under the hand of Pharaoh for food in the cities, and let them keep it. 36 The food will be to supply the land against the seven years of famine, which will be in the land of Egypt; so that the land will not perish through the famine."

37 The thing was good in the eyes of Pharaoh, and in the eyes of all his servants. 38 Pharaoh said to his servants, "Can we find such a one as this, a man in whom is the Spirit of God?" 39 Pharaoh said to Joseph, "Because God has shown you all of this, there is no one so discreet and wise as you. 40 You shall be over my house. All my people will be ruled according to your word. Only in the throne I will be greater than you." 41 Pharaoh said to Joseph, "Behold, I have set you over all the land of Egypt." 42 Pharaoh took off his signet ring from his hand, and put it on Joseph's hand, and arrayed him in robes of fine linen, and put a gold chain about his neck. 43 He made him ride in the second chariot which he had. They cried before him, "Bow the knee!" He set him over all the land of Egypt. 44 Pharaoh said to Joseph, "I am Pharaoh. Without you, no man shall lift up his hand or his foot in all the land of Egypt." 45 Pharaoh called Joseph's

---

[a] 38:29 Perez means "breaking out".

[b] 38:30 Zerah means "scarlet" or "brightness".

name Zaphenath-Paneah. He gave him Asenath, the daughter of Potiphera priest of On as a wife. Joseph went out over the land of Egypt.

₄₆ Joseph was thirty years old when he stood before Pharaoh king of Egypt. Joseph went out from the presence of Pharaoh, and went throughout all the land of Egypt. ₄₇ In the seven plenteous years the earth produced abundantly. ₄₈ He gathered up all the food of the seven years which were in the land of Egypt, and laid up the food in the cities. He stored food in each city from the fields around that city. ₄₉ Joseph laid up grain as the sand of the sea, very much, until he stopped counting, for it was without number. ₅₀ To Joseph were born two sons before the year of famine came, whom Asenath, the daughter of Potiphera priest of On, bore to him. ₅₁ Joseph called the name of the firstborn Manasseh,ᵃ "For", he said, "God has made me forget all my toil, and all my father's house." ₅₂ The name of the second, he called Ephraim:ᵇ "For God has made me fruitful in the land of my affliction."

₅₃ The seven years of plenty, that were in the land of Egypt, came to an end. ₅₄ The seven years of famine began to come, just as Joseph had said. There was famine in all lands, but in all the land of Egypt there was bread. ₅₅ When all the land of Egypt was famished, the people cried to Pharaoh for bread, and Pharaoh said to all the Egyptians, "Go to Joseph. What he says to you, do." ₅₆ The famine was over all the surface of the earth. Joseph opened all the store houses, and sold to the Egyptians. The famine was severe in the land of Egypt. ₅₇ All countries came into Egypt, to Joseph, to buy grain, because the famine was severe in all the earth.

42

₁ Now Jacob saw that there was grain in Egypt, and Jacob said to his sons, "Why do you look at one another?" ₂ He said, "Behold, I have heard that there is grain in Egypt. Go down there, and buy for us from there, so that we may live, and not die." ₃ Joseph's ten brothers went down to buy grain from Egypt. ₄ But Jacob didn't send Benjamin, Joseph's brother, with his brothers; for he said, "Lest perhaps harm happen to him." ₅ The sons of Israel came to buy amongst those who came, for the famine was in the land of Canaan. ₆ Joseph was the governor over the land. It was he who sold to all the people of the land. Joseph's brothers came, and bowed themselves down to him with their faces to the earth. ₇ Joseph saw his brothers, and he recognised them, but acted like a stranger to them, and spoke roughly with them. He said to them, "Where did you come from?"

They said, "From the land of Canaan, to buy food."

₈ Joseph recognised his brothers, but they didn't recognise him. ₉ Joseph remembered the dreams which he dreamt about them, and said to them, "You are spies! You have come to see the nakedness of the land."

₁₀ They said to him, "No, my lord, but your servants have come to buy food. ₁₁ We are all one man's sons; we are honest men. Your servants are not spies."

₁₂ He said to them, "No, but you have come to see the nakedness of the land!"

₁₃ They said, "We, your servants, are twelve brothers, the sons of one man in the land of Canaan; and behold, the youngest is today with our father, and one is no more."

₁₄ Joseph said to them, "It is like I told you, saying, 'You are spies!' ₁₅ By this you shall be tested. By the life of Pharaoh, you shall not go out from here, unless your youngest brother comes here. ₁₆ Send one of you, and let him get your brother, and you shall be bound, that your words may be tested, whether there is truth in you, or else by the life of Pharaoh surely you are spies." ₁₇ He put them all together into custody for three days.

₁₈ Joseph said to them the third day, "Do this, and live, for I fear God. ₁₉ If you are honest men, then let one of your brothers be bound in your prison; but you go, carry grain for the famine of your houses. ₂₀ Bring your youngest brother to me; so will your words be verified, and you won't die."

They did so. ₂₁ They said to one another, "We are certainly guilty concerning our brother, in that we saw the distress of his soul, when he begged us, and we wouldn't listen. Therefore this distress has come upon us." ₂₂ Reuben answered them, saying, "Didn't I tell you, saying, 'Don't sin against the child,' and you wouldn't listen? Therefore also, behold, his blood is required." ₂₃ They didn't know that Joseph understood them; for there was an interpreter between them. ₂₄ He turned himself away from them, and wept. Then he returned to them, and spoke to them, and took Simeon from amongst them, and bound him before their eyes. ₂₅ Then Joseph gave a command to fill their bags with grain, and to restore each man's money into his sack, and to give them food for the way. So it was done to them.

₂₆ They loaded their donkeys with their grain, and departed from there. ₂₇ As one of them opened his sack to give his donkey food in the lodging place, he saw his money. Behold, it was in the mouth of his sack. ₂₈ He said to his brothers, "My money is restored! Behold, it is in my sack!" Their hearts failed them, and they turned trembling to one another, saying, "What is this that God has done to us?" ₂₉ They came to Jacob their father, to the land of Canaan, and told him all that had happened to them, saying, ₃₀ "The man, the lord of the land, spoke roughly with us, and took us for spies of the country. ₃₁ We said to him, 'We are honest men. We are no spies. ₃₂ We are twelve brothers, sons of our father; one is no more, and the youngest is today with our father in the land of Canaan.' ₃₃ The man, the lord of the land, said to us, 'By this I will know that you are honest men: leave one of your brothers with me, and take grain for the famine of your houses, and go your way. ₃₄ Bring your youngest brother to me. Then I will know that you

are not spies, but that you are honest men. So I will deliver your brother to you, and you shall trade in the land.'"

₃₅ As they emptied their sacks, behold, each man's bundle of money was in his sack. When they and their father saw their bundles of money, they were afraid. ₃₆ Jacob, their father, said to them, "You have bereaved me of my children! Joseph is no more, Simeon is no more, and you want to take Benjamin away. All these things are against me."

₃₇ Reuben spoke to his father, saying, "Kill my two sons, if I don't bring him to you. Entrust him to my care, and I will bring him to you again." ₃₈ He said, "My son shall not go down with you; for his brother is dead, and he only is left. If harm happens to him along the way in which you go, then you will bring down my grey hairs with sorrow to Sheol."ᶜ

43

₁ The famine was severe in the land. ₂ When they had eaten up the grain which they had brought out of Egypt, their father said to them, "Go again, buy us a little more food."

₃ Judah spoke to him, saying, "The man solemnly warned us, saying, 'You shall not see my face, unless your brother is with you.' ₄ If you'll send our brother with us, we'll go down and buy you food; ₅ but if you don't send him, we won't go down, for the man said to us, 'You shall not see my face, unless your brother is with you.'"

₆ Israel said, "Why did you treat me so badly, telling the man that you had another brother?"

₇ They said, "The man asked directly concerning ourselves, and concerning our relatives, saying, 'Is your father still alive? Have you another brother?' We just answered his questions. Is there any way we could know that he would say, 'Bring your brother down'?"

₈ Judah said to Israel, his father, "Send the boy with me, and we'll get up and go, so that we may live, and not die, both we, and you, and also our little ones. ₉ I'll be collateral for him. From my hand will you require him. If I don't bring him to you, and set him before you, then let me bear the blame forever; ₁₀ for if we hadn't delayed, surely we would have returned a second time by now."

₁₁ Their father, Israel, said to them, "If it must be so, then do this: Take from the choice fruits of the land in your bags, and carry down a present for the man, a little balm, a little honey, spices and myrrh, nuts, and almonds; ₁₂ and take double money in your hand, and take back the money that was returned in the mouth of your sacks. Perhaps it was an oversight. ₁₃ Take your brother also, get up, and return to the man. ₁₄ May God Almighty give you mercy before the man, that he may release to you your other brother and Benjamin. If I am bereaved of my children, I am bereaved."

₁₅ The men took that present, and they took double money in their hand, and Benjamin; and got up, went down to Egypt, and stood before Joseph. ₁₆ When Joseph saw Benjamin with them, he said to the steward of his house, "Bring the men into the house, and butcher an animal, and prepare; for the men will dine with me at noon."

₁₇ The man did as Joseph commanded, and the man brought the men to Joseph's house. ₁₈ The men were afraid, because they were brought to Joseph's house; and they said, "Because of the money that was returned in our sacks the first time, we're brought in; that he may seek occasion against us, attack us, and seize us as slaves, along with our donkeys." ₁₉ They came near to the steward of Joseph's house, and they spoke to him at the door of the house, ₂₀ and said, "Oh, my lord, we indeed came down the first time to buy food. ₂₁ When we came to the lodging place, we opened our sacks, and behold, each man's money was in the mouth of his sack, our money in full weight. We have brought it back in our hand. ₂₂ We have brought down other money in our hand to buy food. We don't know who put our money in our sacks."

₂₃ He said, "Peace be to you. Don't be afraid. Your God, and the God of your father, has given you treasure in your sacks. I received your money." He brought Simeon out to them. ₂₄ The man brought the men into Joseph's house, and gave them water, and they washed their feet. He gave their donkeys fodder. ₂₅ They prepared the present for Joseph's coming at noon, for they heard that they should eat bread there.

₂₆ When Joseph came home, they brought him the present which was in their hand into the house, and bowed themselves down to the earth before him. ₂₇ He asked them of their welfare, and said, "Is your father well, the old man of whom you spoke? Is he yet alive?"

₂₈ They said, "Your servant, our father, is well. He is still alive." They bowed down humbly. ₂₉ He lifted up his eyes, and saw Benjamin, his brother, his mother's son, and said, "Is this your youngest brother, of whom you spoke to me?" He said, "God be gracious to you, my son." ₃₀ Joseph hurried, for his heart yearned over his brother; and he sought a place to weep. He entered into his room, and wept there. ₃₁ He washed his face, and came out. He controlled himself, and said, "Serve the meal."

₃₂ They served him by himself, and them by themselves, and the Egyptians who ate with him by themselves, because the Egyptians don't eat with the Hebrews, for that is an abomination to the Egyptians. ₃₃ They sat before him, the firstborn according to his birthright, and the youngest according to his youth, and the men marvelled with one another. ₃₄ He sent portions to them from before him, but Benjamin's portion was five times as much as any of theirs. They drank, and were merry with him.

44

₁ He commanded the steward of his house, saying, "Fill the men's sacks with food, as much as they can carry, and put each man's money in

---

his sack's mouth. 2 Put my cup, the silver cup, in the sack's mouth of the youngest, with his grain money." He did according to the word that Joseph had spoken. 3 As soon as the morning was light, the men were sent away, they and their donkeys. 4 When they had gone out of the city, and were not yet far off, Joseph said to his steward, "Up, follow after the men. When you overtake them, ask them, 'Why have you rewarded evil for good? 5 Isn't this that from which my lord drinks, and by which he indeed divines? You have done evil in so doing.'" 6 He overtook them, and he spoke these words to them.

7 They said to him, "Why does my lord speak such words as these? Far be it from your servants that they should do such a thing! 8 Behold, the money, which we found in our sacks' mouths, we brought again to you out of the land of Canaan. How then should we steal silver or gold out of your lord's house? 9 With whomever of your servants it is found, let him die, and we also will be my lord's slaves."

10 He said, "Now also let it be according to your words. He with whom it is found will be my slave; and you will be blameless."

11 Then they hurried, and each man took his sack down to the ground, and each man opened his sack. 12 He searched, beginning with the oldest, and ending at the youngest. The cup was found in Benjamin's sack. 13 Then they tore their clothes, and each man loaded his donkey, and returned to the city.

14 Judah and his brothers came to Joseph's house, and he was still there. They fell on the ground before him. 15 Joseph said to them, "What deed is this that you have done? Don't you know that such a man as I can indeed do divination?"

16 Judah said, "What will we tell my lord? What will we speak? How will we clear ourselves? God has found out the iniquity of your servants. Behold, we are my lord's slaves, both we and he also in whose hand the cup is found."

17 He said, "Far be it from me that I should do so. The man in whose hand the cup is found, he will be my slave; but as for you, go up in peace to your father."

18 Then Judah came near to him, and said, "Oh, my lord, please let your servant speak a word in my lord's ears, and don't let your anger burn against your servant; for you are even as Pharaoh. 19 My lord asked his servants, saying, 'Have you a father, or a brother?' 20 We said to my lord, 'We have a father, an old man, and a child of his old age, a little one; and his brother is dead, and he alone is left of his mother; and his father loves him.' 21 You said to your servants, 'Bring him down to me, that I may set my eyes on him.' 22 We said to my lord, 'The boy can't leave his father, for if he should leave his father, his father would die.' 23 You said to your servants, 'Unless your youngest brother comes down with you, you will see my face no more.' 24 When we came up to your servant my father, we told him the words of my lord. 25 Our father said, 'Go again and buy us a little food.' 26 We said, 'We can't go down. If our youngest brother is with us, then we will go down: for we may not see the man's face, unless our youngest brother is with us.' 27 Your servant, my father, said to us, 'You know that my wife bore me two sons. 28 One went out from me, and I said, "Surely he is torn in pieces;" and I haven't seen him since. 29 If you take this one also from me, and harm happens to him, you will bring down my grey hairs with sorrow to Sheol.'a 30 Now therefore when I come to your servant my father, and the boy is not with us; since his life is bound up in the boy's life; 31 it will happen, when he sees that the boy is no more, that he will die. Your servants will bring down the grey hairs of your servant, our father, with sorrow to Sheol.b 32 For your servant became collateral for the boy to my father, saying, 'If I don't bring him to you, then I will bear the blame to my father forever.' 33 Now therefore, please let your servant stay instead of the boy, my lord's slave; and let the boy go up with his brothers. 34 For how will I go up to my father, if the boy isn't with me?—lest I see the evil that will come on my father."

45

1 Then Joseph couldn't control himself before all those who stood before him, and he called out, "Cause everyone to go out from me!" No one else stood with him, while Joseph made himself known to his brothers. 2 He wept aloud. The Egyptians heard, and the house of Pharaoh heard. 3 Joseph said to his brothers, "I am Joseph! Does my father still live?"

His brothers couldn't answer him; for they were terrified at his presence. 4 Joseph said to his brothers, "Come near to me, please."

They came near. He said, "I am Joseph, your brother, whom you sold into Egypt. 5 Now don't be grieved, nor angry with yourselves, that you sold me here, for God sent me before you to preserve life. 6 For these two years the famine has been in the land, and there are yet five years, in which there will be no ploughing and no harvest. 7 God sent me before you to preserve for you a remnant in the earth, and to save you alive by a great deliverance. 8 So now it wasn't you who sent me here, but God, and he has made me a father to Pharaoh, lord of all his house, and ruler over all the land of Egypt. 9 Hurry, and go up to my father, and tell him, 'This is what your son Joseph says, "God has made me lord of all Egypt. Come down to me. Don't wait. 10 You shall dwell in the land of Goshen, and you will be near to me, you, your children, your children's children, your flocks, your herds, and all that you have. 11 There I will provide for you; for there are yet five years of famine; lest you come to poverty, you, and your household, and all that you have."' 12 Behold, your eyes see, and the eyes of my brother Benjamin, that it is my mouth that speaks to you. 13 You shall tell my father of all my glory in Egypt, and of all that you have seen. You shall

hurry and bring my father down here." 14 He fell on his brother Benjamin's neck and wept, and Benjamin wept on his neck. 15 He kissed all his brothers, and wept on them. After that his brothers talked with him.

16 The report of it was heard in Pharaoh's house, saying, "Joseph's brothers have come." It pleased Pharaoh well, and his servants. 17 Pharaoh said to Joseph, "Tell your brothers, 'Do this: Load your animals, and go, travel to the land of Canaan. 18 Take your father and your households, and come to me, and I will give you the good of the land of Egypt, and you will eat the fat of the land.' 19 Now you are commanded to do this: Take wagons out of the land of Egypt for your little ones, and for your wives, and bring your father, and come. 20 Also, don't concern yourselves about your belongings, for the good of all the land of Egypt is yours."

21 The sons of Israel did so. Joseph gave them wagons, according to the commandment of Pharaoh, and gave them provision for the way. 22 He gave each one of them changes of clothing, but to Benjamin he gave three hundred pieces of silver and five changes of clothing. 23 He sent the following to his father: ten donkeys loaded with the good things of Egypt, and ten female donkeys loaded with grain and bread and provision for his father by the way. 24 So he sent his brothers away, and they departed. He said to them, "See that you don't quarrel on the way."

25 They went up out of Egypt, and came into the land of Canaan, to Jacob their father. 26 They told him, saying, "Joseph is still alive, and he is ruler over all the land of Egypt." His heart fainted, for he didn't believe them. 27 They told him all the words of Joseph, which he had said to them. When he saw the wagons which Joseph had sent to carry him, the spirit of Jacob, their father, revived. 28 Israel said, "It is enough. Joseph my son is still alive. I will go and see him before I die."

46

1 Israel travelled with all that he had, and came to Beersheba, and offered sacrifices to the God of his father, Isaac. 2 God spoke to Israel in the visions of the night, and said, "Jacob, Jacob!"

He said, "Here I am."

3 He said, "I am God, the God of your father. Don't be afraid to go down into Egypt, for there I will make of you a great nation. 4 I will go down with you into Egypt. I will also surely bring you up again. Joseph's hand will close your eyes."

5 Jacob rose up from Beersheba, and the sons of Israel carried Jacob, their father, their little ones, and their wives, in the wagons which Pharaoh had sent to carry him. 6 They took their livestock, and their goods, which they had gotten in the land of Canaan, and came into Egypt—Jacob, and all his offspring with him, 7 his sons, and his sons' sons with him, his daughters, and his sons' daughters, and he brought all his offspring with him into Egypt.

8 These are the names of the children of Israel, who came into Egypt, Jacob and his sons: Reuben, Jacob's firstborn. 9 The sons of Reuben: Hanoch, Pallu, Hezron, and Carmi. 10 The sons of Simeon: Jemuel, Jamin, Ohad, Jachin, Zohar, and Shaul the son of a Canaanite woman. 11 The sons of Levi: Gershon, Kohath, and Merari. 12 The sons of Judah: Er, Onan, Shelah, Perez, and Zerah; but Er and Onan died in the land of Canaan. The sons of Perez were Hezron and Hamul. 13 The sons of Issachar: Tola, Puvah, Iob, and Shimron. 14 The sons of Zebulun: Sered, Elon, and Jahleel. 15 These are the sons of Leah, whom she bore to Jacob in Paddan Aram, with his daughter Dinah. All the souls of his sons and his daughters were thirty-three. 16 The sons of Gad: Ziphion, Haggi, Shuni, Ezbon, Eri, Arodi, and Areli. 17 The sons of Asher: Imnah, Ishvah, Ishvi, Beriah, and Serah their sister. The sons of Beriah: Heber and Malchiel. 18 These are the sons of Zilpah, whom Laban gave to Leah, his daughter, and these she bore to Jacob, even sixteen souls. 19 The sons of Rachel, Jacob's wife: Joseph and Benjamin. 20 To Joseph in the land of Egypt were born Manasseh and Ephraim, whom Asenath, the daughter of Potiphera, priest of On, bore to him. 21 The sons of Benjamin: Bela, Becher, Ashbel, Gera, Naaman, Ehi, Rosh, Muppim, Huppim, and Ard. 22 These are the sons of Rachel, who were born to Jacob: all the souls were fourteen. 23 The son of Dan: Hushim. 24 The sons of Naphtali: Jahzeel, Guni, Jezer, and Shillem. 25 These are the sons of Bilhah, whom Laban gave to Rachel, his daughter, and these she bore to Jacob: all the souls were seven. 26 All the souls who came with Jacob into Egypt, who were his direct offspring, in addition to Jacob's sons' wives, all the souls were sixty-six. 27 The sons of Joseph, who were born to him in Egypt, were two souls. All the souls of the house of Jacob, who came into Egypt, were seventy.

28 Jacob sent Judah before him to Joseph, to show the way before him to Goshen, and they came into the land of Goshen. 29 Joseph prepared his chariot, and went up to meet Israel, his father, in Goshen. He presented himself to him, and fell on his neck, and wept on his neck a good while. 30 Israel said to Joseph, "Now let me die, since I have seen your face, that you are still alive."

31 Joseph said to his brothers, and to his father's house, "I will go up, and speak with Pharaoh, and will tell him, 'My brothers, and my father's house, who were in the land of Canaan, have come to me. 32 These men are shepherds, for they have been keepers of livestock, and they have brought their flocks, and their herds, and all that they have.' 33 It will happen, when Pharaoh summons you, and will say, 'What is your occupation?' 34 that you shall say, 'Your servants have been keepers of livestock from our youth even until now, both we, and our fathers:' that you may dwell in the land of Goshen; for every shepherd is an abomination to the Egyptians."

---

a 44:29 Sheol is the place of the dead.

b 44:31 Sheol is the place of the dead.

1 Then Joseph went in and told Pharaoh, and said, "My father and my brothers, with their flocks, their herds, and all that they own, have come out of the land of Canaan; and behold, they are in the land of Goshen." 2 From amongst his brothers he took five men, and presented them to Pharaoh. 3 Pharaoh said to his brothers, "What is your occupation?"

They said to Pharaoh, "Your servants are shepherds, both we, and our fathers." 4 They also said to Pharaoh, "We have come to live as foreigners in the land, for there is no pasture for your servants' flocks. For the famine is severe in the land of Canaan. Now therefore, please let your servants dwell in the land of Goshen."

5 Pharaoh spoke to Joseph, saying, "Your father and your brothers have come to you. 6 The land of Egypt is before you. Make your father and your brothers dwell in the best of the land. Let them dwell in the land of Goshen. If you know any able men amongst them, then put them in charge of my livestock."

7 Joseph brought in Jacob, his father, and set him before Pharaoh; and Jacob blessed Pharaoh. 8 Pharaoh said to Jacob, "How old are you?"

9 Jacob said to Pharaoh, "The years of my pilgrimage are one hundred and thirty years. The days of the years of my life have been few and evil. They have not attained to the days of the years of the life of my fathers in the days of their pilgrimage." 10 Jacob blessed Pharaoh, and went out from the presence of Pharaoh.

11 Joseph placed his father and his brothers, and gave them a possession in the land of Egypt, in the best of the land, in the land of Rameses, as Pharaoh had commanded. 12 Joseph provided his father, his brothers, and all of his father's household with bread, according to the sizes of their families.

13 There was no bread in all the land; for the famine was very severe, so that the land of Egypt and the land of Canaan fainted by reason of the famine. 14 Joseph gathered up all the money that was found in the land of Egypt, and in the land of Canaan, for the grain which they bought: and Joseph brought the money into Pharaoh's house. 15 When the money was all spent in the land of Egypt, and in the land of Canaan, all the Egyptians came to Joseph, and said, "Give us bread, for why should we die in your presence? For our money fails."

16 Joseph said, "Give me your livestock; and I will give you food for your livestock, if your money is gone."

17 They brought their livestock to Joseph, and Joseph gave them bread in exchange for the horses, and for the flocks, and for the herds, and for the donkeys: and he fed them with bread in exchange for all their livestock for that year. 18 When that year was ended, they came to him the second year, and said to him, "We will not hide from my lord how our money is all spent, and the herds of livestock are my lord's. There is nothing left in the sight of my lord, but our bodies, and our lands. 19 Why should we die before your eyes, both we and our land? Buy us and our land for bread, and we and our land will be servants to Pharaoh. Give us seed, that we may live, and not die, and that the land won't be desolate."

20 So Joseph bought all the land of Egypt for Pharaoh, for every man of the Egyptians sold his field, because the famine was severe on them, and the land became Pharaoh's. 21 As for the people, he moved them to the cities from one end of the border of Egypt even to the other end of it. 22 Only he didn't buy the land of the priests, for the priests had a portion from Pharaoh, and ate their portion which Pharaoh gave them. That is why they didn't sell their land. 23 Then Joseph said to the people, "Behold, I have bought you and your land today for Pharaoh. Behold, here is seed for you, and you shall sow the land. 24 It will happen at the harvests, that you shall give a fifth to Pharaoh, and four parts will be your own, for seed of the field, for your food, for them of your households, and for food for your little ones."

25 They said, "You have saved our lives! Let us find favour in the sight of my lord, and we will be Pharaoh's servants."

26 Joseph made it a statute concerning the land of Egypt to this day, that Pharaoh should have the fifth. Only the land of the priests alone didn't become Pharaoh's.

27 Israel lived in the land of Egypt, in the land of Goshen; and they got themselves possessions therein, and were fruitful, and multiplied exceedingly. 28 Jacob lived in the land of Egypt seventeen years. So the days of Jacob, the years of his life, were one hundred and forty-seven years. 29 The time came near that Israel must die, and he called his son Joseph, and said to him, "If now I have found favour in your sight, please put your hand under my thigh, and deal kindly and truly with me. Please don't bury me in Egypt, 30 but when I sleep with my fathers, you shall carry me out of Egypt, and bury me in their burying place."

Joseph said, "I will do as you have said."

31 Israel said, "Swear to me," and he swore to him. Then Israel bowed himself on the bed's head.

48

1 After these things, someone said to Joseph, "Behold, your father is sick." He took with him his two sons, Manasseh and Ephraim. 2 Someone told Jacob, and said, "Behold, your son Joseph comes to you," and Israel strengthened himself, and sat on the bed. 3 Jacob said to Joseph, "God Almighty appeared to me at Luz in the land of Canaan, and blessed me, 4 and said to me, 'Behold, I will make you fruitful, and multiply you, and I will make of you a company of peoples, and will give this land to your offspring after you for an everlasting possession.' 5 Now your two sons, who were born to you in the land of Egypt before I came to you into Egypt, are mine; Ephraim and Manasseh, even as Reuben and Simeon, will be mine. 6 Your offspring, whom you become the father of after them, will be yours. They will be called after the name of their brothers in their inheritance. 7 As for me, when I came from Paddan, Rachel died beside me in the land of Canaan on the way, when there was still some distance to come to Ephrath, and I buried her there on the way to Ephrath (also called Bethlehem)."

8 Israel saw Joseph's sons, and said, "Who are these?"

9 Joseph said to his father, "They are my sons, whom God has given me here."

He said, "Please bring them to me, and I will bless them." 10 Now the eyes of Israel were dim for age, so that he couldn't see well. Joseph brought them near to him; and he kissed them, and embraced them. 11 Israel said to Joseph, "I didn't think I would see your face, and behold, God has let me see your offspring also." 12 Joseph brought them out from between his knees, and he bowed himself with his face to the earth. 13 Joseph took them both, Ephraim in his right hand towards Israel's left hand, and Manasseh in his left hand towards Israel's right hand, and brought them near to him. 14 Israel stretched out his right hand, and laid it on Ephraim's head, who was the younger, and his left hand on Manasseh's head, guiding his hands knowingly, for Manasseh was the firstborn. 15 He blessed Joseph, and said,

"The God before whom my fathers Abraham and Isaac walked,
the God who has fed me all my life long to this day,
16 the angel who has redeemed me from all evil, bless the lads,
and let my name be named on them,
and the name of my fathers Abraham and Isaac.
Let them grow into a multitude upon the earth."

17 When Joseph saw that his father laid his right hand on the head of Ephraim, it displeased him. He held up his father's hand, to remove it from Ephraim's head to Manasseh's head. 18 Joseph said to his father, "Not so, my father, for this is the firstborn. Put your right hand on his head."

19 His father refused, and said, "I know, my son, I know. He also will become a people, and he also will be great. However, his younger brother will be greater than he, and his offspring will become a multitude of nations." 20 He blessed them that day, saying, "Israel will bless in you, saying, 'God make you as Ephraim and as Manasseh'" He set Ephraim before Manasseh. 21 Israel said to Joseph, "Behold, I am dying, but God will be with you, and bring you again to the land of your fathers. 22 Moreover I have given to you one portion above your brothers, which I took out of the hand of the Amorite with my sword and with my bow."

49

1 Jacob called to his sons, and said: "Gather yourselves together, that I may tell you that which will happen to you in the days to come.
2 Assemble yourselves, and hear, you sons of Jacob.
    Listen to Israel, your father.

3 "Reuben, you are my firstborn, my might, and the beginning of my strength,
    excelling in dignity, and excelling in power.
4 Boiling over like water, you shall not excel,
    because you went up to your father's bed,
    then defiled it. He went up to my couch.

5 "Simeon and Levi are brothers.
    Their swords are weapons of violence.
6 My soul, don't come into their council.
    My glory, don't be united to their assembly;
for in their anger they killed men.
    In their self-will they hamstrung cattle.
7 Cursed be their anger, for it was fierce;
    and their wrath, for it was cruel.
I will divide them in Jacob,
    and scatter them in Israel.

8 "Judah, your brothers will praise you.
    Your hand will be on the neck of your enemies.
    Your father's sons will bow down before you.
9 Judah is a lion's cub.
    From the prey, my son, you have gone up.
He stooped down, he crouched as a lion,
    as a lioness.
    Who will rouse him up?
10 The sceptre will not depart from Judah,
    nor the ruler's staff from between his feet,
until he comes to whom it belongs.
    The obedience of the peoples will be to him.
11 Binding his foal to the vine,
    his donkey's colt to the choice vine,
he has washed his garments in wine,
    his robes in the blood of grapes.
12 His eyes will be red with wine,
    his teeth white with milk.

13 "Zebulun will dwell at the haven of the sea.
    He will be for a haven of ships.
    His border will be on Sidon.

14 "Issachar is a strong donkey,
    lying down between the saddlebags.
15 He saw a resting place, that it was good,

the land, that it was pleasant.
He bows his shoulder to the burden,
    and becomes a servant doing forced labour.

16 "Dan will judge his people,
    as one of the tribes of Israel.
17 Dan will be a serpent on the trail,
    an adder in the path,
that bites the horse's heels,
    so that his rider falls backward.
18 I have waited for your salvation, LORD.

19 "A troop will press on Gad,
    but he will press on their heel.

20 "Asher's food will be rich.
    He will produce royal dainties.

21 "Naphtali is a doe set free,
    who bears beautiful fawns.

22 "Joseph is a fruitful vine,
    a fruitful vine by a spring.
    His branches run over the wall.
23 The archers have severely grieved him,
    shot at him, and persecuted him:
24 But his bow remained strong.
    The arms of his hands were made strong,
    by the hands of the Mighty One of Jacob,
    (from there is the shepherd, the stone of Israel),
25 even by the God of your father, who will help you,
    by the Almighty, who will bless you,
with blessings of heaven above,
    blessings of the deep that lies below,
    blessings of the breasts, and of the womb.
26 The blessings of your father have prevailed above the blessings of my
        ancestors,
    above the boundaries of the ancient hills.
They will be on the head of Joseph,
    on the crown of the head of him who is separated from his brothers.

27 "Benjamin is a ravenous wolf.
    In the morning he will devour the prey.
    At evening he will divide the plunder."

28 All these are the twelve tribes of Israel, and this is what their father spoke to them, and blessed them. He blessed everyone according to his own blessing. 29 He instructed them, and said to them, "I am to be gathered to my people. Bury me with my fathers in the cave that is in the field of Ephron the Hittite, 30 in the cave that is in the field of Machpelah, which is before Mamre, in the land of Canaan, which Abraham bought with the field from Ephron the Hittite as a burial place. 31 There they buried Abraham and Sarah, his wife. There they buried Isaac and Rebekah, his wife, and there I buried Leah: 32 the field and the cave that is therein, which was purchased from the children of Heth." 33 When Jacob finished charging his sons, he gathered up his feet into the bed, breathed his last breath, and was gathered to his people.

50

1 Joseph fell on his father's face, wept on him, and kissed him. 2 Joseph commanded his servants, the physicians, to embalm his father; and the physicians embalmed Israel. 3 Forty days were used for him, for that is how many days it takes to embalm. The Egyptians wept for Israel for seventy days.

4 When the days of weeping for him were past, Joseph spoke to Pharaoh's staff, saying, "If now I have found favour in your eyes, please speak in the ears of Pharaoh, saying, 5 'My father made me swear, saying, "Behold, I am dying. Bury me in my grave which I have dug for myself in the land of Canaan." Now therefore, please let me go up and bury my father, and I will come again.'"

6 Pharaoh said, "Go up, and bury your father, just like he made you swear."

7 Joseph went up to bury his father; and with him went up all the servants of Pharaoh, the elders of his house, all the elders of the land of Egypt, 8 all the house of Joseph, his brothers, and his father's house. Only their little ones, their flocks, and their herds, they left in the land of Goshen. 9 Both chariots and horsemen went up with him. It was a very great company. 10 They came to the threshing floor of Atad, which is beyond the Jordan, and there they lamented with a very great and severe lamentation. He mourned for his father seven days. 11 When the inhabitants of the land, the Canaanites, saw the mourning in the floor of Atad, they said, "This is a grievous mourning by the Egyptians." Therefore its name was called Abel Mizraim, which is beyond the Jordan. 12 His sons did to him just as he commanded them, 13 for his sons carried him into the land of Canaan, and buried him in the cave of the field of Machpelah, which Abraham bought with the field, as a possession for a burial site, from Ephron the Hittite, near Mamre. 14 Joseph returned into Egypt—he, and his brothers, and all that went up with him to bury his father, after he had buried his father.

15 When Joseph's brothers saw that their father was dead, they said, "It may be that Joseph will hate us, and will fully pay us back for all the evil which we did to him." 16 They sent a message to Joseph, saying, "Your father commanded before he died, saying, 17 'You shall tell Joseph, "Now please forgive the disobedience of your brothers, and their sin, because they did evil to you."' Now, please forgive the disobedience of the servants of the God of your father." Joseph wept when they spoke to him. 18 His brothers also went and fell down before his face; and they said, "Behold, we are your servants." 19 Joseph said to them, "Don't be afraid, for am I in the place of God? 20 As for you, you meant evil against me, but God meant it for good, to save many people alive, as is happening today. 21 Now therefore don't be afraid. I will provide for you and your little ones." He comforted them, and spoke kindly to them.

22 Joseph lived in Egypt, he, and his father's house. Joseph lived one hundred and ten years. 23 Joseph saw Ephraim's children to the third generation. The children also of Machir, the son of Manasseh, were born on Joseph's knees. 24 Joseph said to his brothers, "I am dying, but God will surely visit you, and bring you up out of this land to the land which he swore to Abraham, to Isaac, and to Jacob." 25 Joseph took an oath from the children of Israel, saying, "God will surely visit you, and you shall carry up my bones from here." 26 So Joseph died, being one hundred and ten years old, and they embalmed him, and he was put in a coffin in Egypt.

The Second Book of Moses, Commonly Called Exodus

1

1 Now these are the names of the sons of Israel, who came into Egypt (every man and his household came with Jacob): 2 Reuben, Simeon, Levi, and Judah, 3 Issachar, Zebulun, and Benjamin, 4 Dan and Naphtali, Gad and Asher. 5 All the souls who came out of Jacob's body were seventy souls, and Joseph was in Egypt already. 6 Joseph died, as did all his brothers, and all that generation. 7 The children of Israel were fruitful, and increased abundantly, and multiplied, and grew exceedingly mighty; and the land was filled with them.

8 Now there arose a new king over Egypt, who didn't know Joseph. 9 He said to his people, "Behold,ᵃ the people of the children of Israel are more and mightier than we. 10 Come, let's deal wisely with them, lest they multiply, and it happen that when any war breaks out, they also join themselves to our enemies and fight against us, and escape out of the land." 11 Therefore they set taskmasters over them to afflict them with their burdens. They built storage cities for Pharaoh: Pithom and Raamses. 12 But the more they afflicted them, the more they multiplied and the more they spread out. They started to dread the children of Israel. 13 The Egyptians ruthlessly made the children of Israel serve, 14 and they made their lives bitter with hard service in mortar and in brick, and in all kinds of service in the field, all their service, in which they ruthlessly made them serve.

15 The king of Egypt spoke to the Hebrew midwives, of whom the name of the one was Shiphrah, and the name of the other Puah, 16 and he said, "When you perform the duty of a midwife to the Hebrew women, and see them on the birth stool, if it is a son, then you shall kill him; but if it is a daughter, then she shall live." 17 But the midwives feared God,ᵇ and didn't do what the king of Egypt commanded them, but saved the baby boys alive. 18 The king of Egypt called for the midwives, and said to them, "Why have you done this thing and saved the boys alive?"

19 The midwives said to Pharaoh, "Because the Hebrew women aren't like the Egyptian women; for they are vigorous and give birth before the midwife comes to them."

20 God dealt well with the midwives, and the people multiplied, and grew very mighty. 21 Because the midwives feared God, he gave them families. 22 Pharaoh commanded all his people, saying, "You shall cast every son who is born into the river, and every daughter you shall save alive."

2

1 A man of the house of Levi went and took a daughter of Levi as his wife. 2 The woman conceived and bore a son. When she saw that he was a fine child, she hid him three months. 3 When she could no longer hide him, she took a papyrus basket for him, and coated it with tar and with pitch. She put the child in it, and laid it in the reeds by the river's bank. 4 His sister stood far off, to see what would be done to him. 5 Pharaoh's daughter came down to bathe at the river. Her maidens walked along by the riverside. She saw the basket amongst the reeds, and sent her servant to get it. 6 She opened it, and saw the child, and behold, the baby cried. She had compassion on him, and said, "This is one of the Hebrews' children."

7 Then his sister said to Pharaoh's daughter, "Should I go and call a nurse for you from the Hebrew women, that she may nurse the child for you?"

8 Pharaoh's daughter said to her, "Go."

The young woman went and called the child's mother. 9 Pharaoh's daughter said to her, "Take this child away, and nurse him for me, and I will give you your wages."

The woman took the child, and nursed it. 10 The child grew, and she brought him to Pharaoh's daughter, and he became her son. She named him Moses,ᶜ and said, "Because I drew him out of the water."

11 In those days, when Moses had grown up, he went out to his brothers and saw their burdens. He saw an Egyptian striking a Hebrew, one of his brothers. 12 He looked this way and that way, and when he saw that there was no one, he killed the Egyptian, and hid him in the sand.

13 He went out the second day, and behold, two men of the Hebrews were fighting with each other. He said to him who did the wrong, "Why do you strike your fellow?"

14 He said, "Who made you a prince and a judge over us? Do you plan to kill me, as you killed the Egyptian?"

Moses was afraid, and said, "Surely this thing is known." 15 Now when Pharaoh heard this thing, he sought to kill Moses. But Moses fled from the face of Pharaoh, and lived in the land of Midian, and he sat down by a well.

16 Now the priest of Midian had seven daughters. They came and drew water, and filled the troughs to water their father's flock. 17 The shepherds came and drove them away; but Moses stood up and helped them, and watered their flock. 18 When they came to Reuel, their father, he said, "How is it that you have returned so early today?"

19 They said, "An Egyptian delivered us out of the hand of the shepherds, and moreover he drew water for us, and watered the flock."

20 He said to his daughters, "Where is he? Why is it that you have left the man? Call him, that he may eat bread."

21 Moses was content to dwell with the man. He gave Moses Zipporah, his daughter. 22 She bore a son, and he named him Gershom,ᵈ for he said, "I have lived as a foreigner in a foreign land."

23 In the course of those many days, the king of Egypt died, and the children of Israel sighed because of the bondage, and they cried, and their cry came up to God because of the bondage. 24 God heard their groaning, and God remembered his covenant with Abraham, with Isaac, and with Jacob. 25 God saw the children of Israel, and God understood.

3

1 Now Moses was keeping the flock of Jethro, his father-in-law, the priest of Midian, and he led the flock to the back of the wilderness, and came to God's mountain, to Horeb. 2 The LORD'sᵉ angel appeared to him in a flame of fire out of the middle of a bush. He looked, and behold, the bush burnt with fire, and the bush was not consumed. 3 Moses said, "I will go now, and see this great sight, why the bush is not burnt."

4 When the LORD saw that he came over to see, God called to him out of the middle of the bush, and said, "Moses! Moses!"

He said, "Here I am."

5 He said, "Don't come close. Take off your sandals, for the place you are standing on is holy ground." 6 Moreover he said, "I am the God of your father, the God of Abraham, the God of Isaac, and the God of Jacob."

Moses hid his face because he was afraid to look at God.

7 The LORD said, "I have surely seen the affliction of my people who are in Egypt, and have heard their cry because of their taskmasters, for I know their sorrows. 8 I have come down to deliver them out of the hand of the Egyptians, and to bring them up out of that land to a good and large land, to a land flowing with milk and honey; to the place of the Canaanite, the Hittite, the Amorite, the Perizzite, the Hivite, and the Jebusite. 9 Now, behold, the cry of the children of Israel has come to me. Moreover I have seen the oppression with which the Egyptians oppress them. 10 Come now therefore, and I will send you to Pharaoh, that you may bring my people, the children of Israel, out of Egypt."

11 Moses said to God, "Who am I, that I should go to Pharaoh, and that I should bring the children of Israel out of Egypt?"

12 He said, "Certainly I will be with you. This will be the token to you, that I have sent you: when you have brought the people out of Egypt, you shall serve God on this mountain."

13 Moses said to God, "Behold, when I come to the children of Israel, and tell them, 'The God of your fathers has sent me to you,' and they ask me, 'What is his name?' what should I tell them?"

14 God said to Moses, "I AM WHO I AM," and he said, "You shall tell the children of Israel this: 'I AM has sent me to you.'" 15 God said moreover to Moses, "You shall tell the children of Israel this, 'The LORD, the God of your fathers, the God of Abraham, the God of Isaac, and the God of Jacob, has sent me to you.' This is my name forever, and this is my memorial to all generations. 16 Go and gather the elders of Israel together, and tell them, 'The LORD, the God of your fathers, the God of Abraham, of Isaac, and of Jacob, has appeared to me, saying, "I have surely visited you, and seen that which is done to you in Egypt. 17 I have said, I will bring you up out of the affliction of Egypt to the land of the Canaanite, the Hittite, the Amorite, the Perizzite, the Hivite, and the Jebusite, to a land flowing with milk and honey."' 18 They will listen to your voice. You shall come, you and the elders of Israel, to the king of Egypt, and you shall tell him, 'The LORD, the God of the Hebrews, has met with us. Now please let us go three days' journey into the wilderness, that we may sacrifice to the LORD, our God.' 19 I know that the king of Egypt won't give you permission to go, no, not by a mighty hand. 20 I will reach out my hand and strike Egypt with all my wonders which I will do amongst them, and after that he will let you go. 21 I will give this people favour in the sight of the Egyptians, and it will happen that when you go, you shall not go empty-handed. 22 But every woman shall ask of her neighbour, and of her who visits her house, jewels of silver, jewels of gold, and clothing. You shall put them on your sons, and on your daughters. You shall plunder the Egyptians."

4

1 Moses answered, "But, behold, they will not believe me, nor listen to my voice; for they will say, 'The LORD has not appeared to you.'"

2 The LORD said to him, "What is that in your hand?"

He said, "A rod."

3 He said, "Throw it on the ground."

He threw it on the ground, and it became a snake; and Moses ran away from it.

4 The LORD said to Moses, "Stretch out your hand, and take it by the tail."

He stretched out his hand, and took hold of it, and it became a rod in his hand.

5 "This is so that they may believe that the LORD, the God of their fathers, the God of Abraham, the God of Isaac, and the God of Jacob, has appeared to you." 6 The LORD said furthermore to him, "Now put your hand inside your cloak."

He put his hand inside his cloak, and when he took it out, behold, his hand was leprous, as white as snow.

ᵃ *1:9* "Behold", from "הִנֵּה", means look at, take notice, observe, see, or gaze at. It is often used as an interjection.

ᵇ *1:17* The Hebrew word rendered "God" is "אֱלֹהִים" (Elohim).

ᶜ *2:10* "Moses" sounds like the Hebrew for "draw out".

ᵈ *2:22* "Gershom" sounds like the Hebrew for "an alien there".

ᵉ *3:2* When rendered in ALL CAPITAL LETTERS, "LORD" or "GOD" is the translation of God's Proper Name.

7 He said, "Put your hand inside your cloak again."

He put his hand inside his cloak again, and when he took it out of his cloak, behold, it had turned again as his other flesh.

8 "It will happen, if they will not believe you or listen to the voice of the first sign, that they will believe the voice of the latter sign. 9 It will happen, if they will not believe even these two signs or listen to your voice, that you shall take of the water of the river, and pour it on the dry land. The water which you take out of the river will become blood on the dry land."

10 Moses said to the LORD, "O Lord,ᵃ I am not eloquent, neither before now, nor since you have spoken to your servant; for I am slow of speech, and of a slow tongue."

11 The LORD said to him, "Who made man's mouth? Or who makes one mute, or deaf, or seeing, or blind? Isn't it I, the LORD? 12 Now therefore go, and I will be with your mouth, and teach you what you shall speak."

13 Moses said, "Oh, Lord, please send someone else."

14 The LORD's anger burnt against Moses, and he said, "What about Aaron, your brother, the Levite? I know that he can speak well. Also, behold, he is coming out to meet you. When he sees you, he will be glad in his heart. 15 You shall speak to him, and put the words in his mouth. I will be with your mouth, and with his mouth, and will teach you what you shall do. 16 He will be your spokesman to the people. It will happen that he will be to you a mouth, and you will be to him as God. 17 You shall take this rod in your hand, with which you shall do the signs."

18 Moses went and returned to Jethro his father-in-law, and said to him, "Please let me go and return to my brothers who are in Egypt, and see whether they are still alive."

Jethro said to Moses, "Go in peace."

19 The LORD said to Moses in Midian, "Go, return into Egypt; for all the men who sought your life are dead."

20 Moses took his wife and his sons, and set them on a donkey, and he returned to the land of Egypt. Moses took God's rod in his hand. 21 The LORD said to Moses, "When you go back into Egypt, see that you do before Pharaoh all the wonders which I have put in your hand, but I will harden his heart and he will not let the people go. 22 You shall tell Pharaoh, 'The LORD says, Israel is my son, my firstborn, 23 and I have said to you, "Let my son go, that he may serve me;" and you have refused to let him go. Behold, I will kill your firstborn son.'"

24 On the way at a lodging place, the LORD met Moses and wanted to kill him. 25 Then Zipporah took a flint, and cut off the foreskin of her son, and cast it at his feet; and she said, "Surely you are a bridegroom of blood to me."

26 So he let him alone. Then she said, "You are a bridegroom of blood," because of the circumcision.

27 The LORD said to Aaron, "Go into the wilderness to meet Moses."

He went, and met him on God's mountain, and kissed him. 28 Moses told Aaron all the LORD's words with which he had sent him, and all the signs with which he had instructed him. 29 Moses and Aaron went and gathered together all the elders of the children of Israel. 30 Aaron spoke all the words which the LORD had spoken to Moses, and did the signs in the sight of the people. 31 The people believed, and when they heard that the LORD had visited the children of Israel, and that he had seen their affliction, then they bowed their heads and worshipped.

5

1 Afterward Moses and Aaron came, and said to Pharaoh, "This is what the LORD, the God of Israel, says, 'Let my people go, that they may hold a feast to me in the wilderness.'"

2 Pharaoh said, "Who is the LORD, that I should listen to his voice to let Israel go? I don't know the LORD, and moreover I will not let Israel go."

3 They said, "The God of the Hebrews has met with us. Please let us go three days' journey into the wilderness, and sacrifice to the LORD, our God, lest he fall on us with pestilence, or with the sword."

4 The king of Egypt said to them, "Why do you, Moses and Aaron, take the people from their work? Get back to your burdens!" 5 Pharaoh said, "Behold, the people of the land are now many, and you make them rest from their burdens." 6 The same day Pharaoh commanded the taskmasters of the people and their officers, saying, 7 "You shall no longer give the people straw to make brick, as before. Let them go and gather straw for themselves. 8 You shall require from them the number of the bricks which they made before. You shall not diminish anything of it, for they are idle. Therefore they cry, saying, 'Let's go and sacrifice to our God.' 9 Let heavier work be laid on the men, that they may labour in it. Don't let them pay any attention to lying words."

10 The taskmasters of the people went out with their officers, and they spoke to the people, saying, "This is what Pharaoh says: 'I will not give you straw. 11 Go yourselves, get straw where you can find it, for nothing of your work shall be diminished.'" 12 So the people were scattered abroad throughout all the land of Egypt to gather stubble for straw. 13 The taskmasters were urgent saying, "Fulfil your work quota daily, as when there was straw!" 14 The officers of the children of Israel, whom Pharaoh's taskmasters had set over them, were beaten, and were asked, "Why haven't you fulfilled your quota both yesterday and today, in making brick as before?"

15 Then the officers of the children of Israel came and cried to Pharaoh, saying, "Why do you deal this way with your servants? 16 No straw is given to your servants, and they tell us, 'Make brick!' and behold, your servants are beaten; but the fault is in your own people."

17 But Pharaoh said, "You are idle! You are idle! Therefore you say, 'Let's go and sacrifice to the LORD.' 18 Go therefore now, and work; for no straw shall be given to you; yet you shall deliver the same number of bricks!"

19 The officers of the children of Israel saw that they were in trouble when it was said, "You shall not diminish anything from your daily quota of bricks!"

20 They met Moses and Aaron, who stood along the way, as they came out from Pharaoh. 21 They said to them, "May the LORD look at you and judge, because you have made us a stench to be abhorred in the eyes of Pharaoh, and in the eyes of his servants, to put a sword in their hand to kill us!"

22 Moses returned to the LORD, and said, "Lord, why have you brought trouble on this people? Why is it that you have sent me? 23 For since I came to Pharaoh to speak in your name, he has brought trouble on this people. You have not rescued your people at all!"

6

1 The LORD said to Moses, "Now you shall see what I will do to Pharaoh, for by a strong hand he shall let them go, and by a strong hand he shall drive them out of his land."

2 God spoke to Moses, and said to him, "I am the LORD. 3 I appeared to Abraham, to Isaac, and to Jacob, as God Almighty; but by my name the LORD I was not known to them. 4 I have also established my covenant with them, to give them the land of Canaan, the land of their travels, in which they lived as aliens. 5 Moreover I have heard the groaning of the children of Israel, whom the Egyptians keep in bondage, and I have remembered my covenant. 6 Therefore tell the children of Israel, 'I am the LORD, and I will bring you out from under the burdens of the Egyptians, and I will rid you out of their bondage, and I will redeem you with an outstretched arm, and with great judgements. 7 I will take you to myself for a people. I will be your God; and you shall know that I am the LORD your God, who brings you out from under the burdens of the Egyptians. 8 I will bring you into the land which I swore to give to Abraham, to Isaac, and to Jacob; and I will give it to you for a heritage: I am the LORD.'"

9 Moses spoke so to the children of Israel, but they didn't listen to Moses for anguish of spirit, and for cruel bondage.

10 The LORD spoke to Moses, saying, 11 "Go in, speak to Pharaoh king of Egypt, that he let the children of Israel go out of his land."

12 Moses spoke before the LORD, saying, "Behold, the children of Israel haven't listened to me. How then shall Pharaoh listen to me, when I have uncircumcised lips?" 13 The LORD spoke to Moses and to Aaron, and gave them a command to the children of Israel, and to Pharaoh king of Egypt, to bring the children of Israel out of the land of Egypt.

14 These are the heads of their fathers' houses. The sons of Reuben the firstborn of Israel: Hanoch, and Pallu, Hezron, and Carmi; these are the families of Reuben. 15 The sons of Simeon: Jemuel, and Jamin, and Ohad, and Jachin, and Zohar, and Shaul the son of a Canaanite woman; these are the families of Simeon. 16 These are the names of the sons of Levi according to their generations: Gershon, and Kohath, and Merari; and the years of the life of Levi were one hundred and thirty-seven years. 17 The sons of Gershon: Libni and Shimei, according to their families. 18 The sons of Kohath: Amram, and Izhar, and Hebron, and Uzziel; and the years of the life of Kohath were one hundred and thirty-three years. 19 The sons of Merari: Mahli and Mushi. These are the families of the Levites according to their generations. 20 Amram took Jochebed his father's sister to himself as wife; and she bore him Aaron and Moses. The years of the life of Amram were one hundred and thirty-seven years. 21 The sons of Izhar: Korah, and Nepheg, and Zichri. 22 The sons of Uzziel: Mishael, Elzaphan, and Sithri. 23 Aaron took Elisheba, the daughter of Amminadab, the sister of Nahshon, as his wife; and she bore him Nadab and Abihu, Eleazar and Ithamar. 24 The sons of Korah: Assir, Elkanah, and Abiasaph; these are the families of the Korahites. 25 Eleazar Aaron's son took one of the daughters of Putiel as his wife; and she bore him Phinehas. These are the heads of the fathers' houses of the Levites according to their families. 26 These are that Aaron and Moses to whom the LORD said, "Bring out the children of Israel from the land of Egypt according to their armies." 27 These are those who spoke to Pharaoh king of Egypt, to bring out the children of Israel from Egypt. These are that Moses and Aaron.

28 On the day when the LORD spoke to Moses in the land of Egypt, 29 The LORD said to Moses, "I am the LORD. Tell Pharaoh king of Egypt all that I tell you."

30 Moses said before the LORD, "Behold, I am of uncircumcised lips, and how shall Pharaoh listen to me?"

7

1 The LORD said to Moses, "Behold, I have made you as God to Pharaoh; and Aaron your brother shall be your prophet. 2 You shall speak all that I command you; and Aaron your brother shall speak to Pharaoh, that he let the children of Israel go out of his land. 3 I will harden Pharaoh's heart, and multiply my signs and my wonders in the land of Egypt. 4 But Pharaoh will not listen to you, so I will lay my hand on Egypt, and bring out my armies, my people the children of Israel, out of the land of Egypt by great judgements. 5 The Egyptians shall know that I am the LORD when I stretch out my hand on Egypt, and bring the children of Israel out from amongst them."

ᵃ *4:10* The word translated "Lord" is "Adonai".

6 Moses and Aaron did so. As the LORD commanded them, so they did. 7 Moses was eighty years old, and Aaron eighty-three years old, when they spoke to Pharaoh.

8 The LORD spoke to Moses and to Aaron, saying, 9 "When Pharaoh speaks to you, saying, 'Perform a miracle!' then you shall tell Aaron, 'Take your rod, and cast it down before Pharaoh, and it will become a serpent.'"

10 Moses and Aaron went in to Pharaoh, and they did so, as the LORD had commanded. Aaron cast down his rod before Pharaoh and before his servants, and it became a serpent. 11 Then Pharaoh also called for the wise men and the sorcerers. They also, the magicians of Egypt, did the same thing with their enchantments. 12 For they each cast down their rods, and they became serpents; but Aaron's rod swallowed up their rods. 13 Pharaoh's heart was hardened, and he didn't listen to them, as the LORD had spoken.

14 The LORD said to Moses, "Pharaoh's heart is stubborn. He refuses to let the people go. 15 Go to Pharaoh in the morning. Behold, he is going out to the water. You shall stand by the river's bank to meet him. You shall take the rod which was turned to a serpent in your hand. 16 You shall tell him, 'The LORD, the God of the Hebrews, has sent me to you, saying, "Let my people go, that they may serve me in the wilderness. Behold, until now you haven't listened." 17 The LORD says, "In this you shall know that I am the LORD. Behold, I will strike with the rod that is in my hand on the waters which are in the river, and they shall be turned to blood. 18 The fish that are in the river will die and the river will become foul. The Egyptians will loathe to drink water from the river."'" 19 The LORD said to Moses, "Tell Aaron, 'Take your rod, and stretch out your hand over the waters of Egypt, over their rivers, over their streams, and over their pools, and over all their ponds of water, that they may become blood. There will be blood throughout all the land of Egypt, both in vessels of wood and in vessels of stone.'"

20 Moses and Aaron did so, as the LORD commanded; and he lifted up the rod, and struck the waters that were in the river, in the sight of Pharaoh, and in the sight of his servants; and all the waters that were in the river were turned to blood. 21 The fish that were in the river died. The river became foul. The Egyptians couldn't drink water from the river. The blood was throughout all the land of Egypt. 22 The magicians of Egypt did the same thing with their enchantments. So Pharaoh's heart was hardened, and he didn't listen to them, as the LORD had spoken. 23 Pharaoh turned and went into his house, and he didn't even take this to heart. 24 All the Egyptians dug around the river for water to drink; for they couldn't drink the river water. 25 Seven days were fulfilled, after the LORD had struck the river.

8

1 The LORD spoke to Moses, "Go in to Pharaoh, and tell him, 'This is what the LORD says, "Let my people go, that they may serve me. 2 If you refuse to let them go, behold, I will plague all your borders with frogs. 3 The river will swarm with frogs, which will go up and come into your house, and into your bedroom, and on your bed, and into the house of your servants, and on your people, and into your ovens, and into your kneading troughs. 4 The frogs shall come up both on you, and on your people, and on all your servants."'" 5 The LORD said to Moses, "Tell Aaron, 'Stretch out your hand with your rod over the rivers, over the streams, and over the pools, and cause frogs to come up on the land of Egypt.'" 6 Aaron stretched out his hand over the waters of Egypt; and the frogs came up, and covered the land of Egypt. 7 The magicians did the same thing with their enchantments, and brought up frogs on the land of Egypt.

8 Then Pharaoh called for Moses and Aaron, and said, "Entreat the LORD, that he take away the frogs from me and from my people; and I will let the people go, that they may sacrifice to the LORD."

9 Moses said to Pharaoh, "I give you the honour of setting the time that I should pray for you, and for your servants, and for your people, that the frogs be destroyed from you and your houses, and remain in the river only."

10 Pharaoh said, "Tomorrow."

Moses said, "Let it be according to your word, that you may know that there is no one like the LORD our God. 11 The frogs shall depart from you, and from your houses, and from your servants, and from your people. They shall remain in the river only."

12 Moses and Aaron went out from Pharaoh, and Moses cried to the LORD concerning the frogs which he had brought on Pharaoh. 13 The LORD did according to the word of Moses, and the frogs died out of the houses, out of the courts, and out of the fields. 14 They gathered them together in heaps, and the land stank. 15 But when Pharaoh saw that there was a respite, he hardened his heart, and didn't listen to them, as the LORD had spoken.

16 The LORD said to Moses, "Tell Aaron, 'Stretch out your rod, and strike the dust of the earth, that it may become lice throughout all the land of Egypt.'" 17 They did so; and Aaron stretched out his hand with his rod, and struck the dust of the earth, and there were lice on man, and on animal; all the dust of the earth became lice throughout all the land of Egypt. 18 The magicians tried with their enchantments to produce lice, but they couldn't. There were lice on man, and on animal. 19 Then the magicians said to Pharaoh, "This is God's finger;" but Pharaoh's heart was hardened, and he didn't listen to them, as the LORD had spoken.

20 The LORD said to Moses, "Rise up early in the morning, and stand before Pharaoh; behold, he comes out to the water; and tell him, 'This is what the LORD says, "Let my people go, that they may serve me. 21 Else, if you will not let my people go, behold, I will send swarms of flies on you, and on your servants, and on your people, and into your houses. The houses of the Egyptians shall be full of swarms of flies, and also the

ground they are on. 22 I will set apart in that day the land of Goshen, in which my people dwell, that no swarms of flies shall be there, to the end you may know that I am the LORD on the earth. 23 I will put a division between my people and your people. This sign shall happen by tomorrow."'" 24 The LORD did so; and there came grievous swarms of flies into the house of Pharaoh, and into his servants' houses. In all the land of Egypt the land was corrupted by reason of the swarms of flies.

25 Pharaoh called for Moses and for Aaron, and said, "Go, sacrifice to your God in the land!"

26 Moses said, "It isn't appropriate to do so; for we shall sacrifice the abomination of the Egyptians to the LORD our God. Behold, if we sacrifice the abomination of the Egyptians before their eyes, won't they stone us? 27 We will go three days' journey into the wilderness, and sacrifice to the LORD our God, as he shall command us."

28 Pharaoh said, "I will let you go, that you may sacrifice to the LORD your God in the wilderness, only you shall not go very far away. Pray for me."

29 Moses said, "Behold, I am going out from you. I will pray to the LORD that the swarms of flies may depart from Pharaoh, from his servants, and from his people, tomorrow; only don't let Pharaoh deal deceitfully any more in not letting the people go to sacrifice to the LORD." 30 Moses went out from Pharaoh, and prayed to the LORD. 31 The LORD did according to the word of Moses, and he removed the swarms of flies from Pharaoh, from his servants, and from his people. There remained not one. 32 Pharaoh hardened his heart this time also, and he didn't let the people go.

9

1 Then the LORD said to Moses, "Go in to Pharaoh, and tell him, 'This is what the LORD, the God of the Hebrews, says: "Let my people go, that they may serve me. 2 For if you refuse to let them go, and hold them still, 3 behold, the LORD's hand is on your livestock which are in the field, on the horses, on the donkeys, on the camels, on the herds, and on the flocks with a very grievous pestilence. 4 The LORD will make a distinction between the livestock of Israel and the livestock of Egypt; and nothing shall die of all that belongs to the children of Israel."'" 5 The LORD appointed a set time, saying, "Tomorrow the LORD shall do this thing in the land." 6 The LORD did that thing on the next day; and all the livestock of Egypt died, but of the livestock of the children of Israel, not one died. 7 Pharaoh sent, and, behold, there was not so much as one of the livestock of the Israelites dead. But the heart of Pharaoh was stubborn, and he didn't let the people go.

8 The LORD said to Moses and to Aaron, "Take handfuls of ashes of the furnace, and let Moses sprinkle it towards the sky in the sight of Pharaoh. 9 It shall become small dust over all the land of Egypt, and shall be boils and blisters breaking out on man and on animal, throughout all the land of Egypt."

10 They took ashes of the furnace, and stood before Pharaoh; and Moses sprinkled it up towards the sky; and it became boils and blisters breaking out on man and on animal. 11 The magicians couldn't stand before Moses because of the boils; for the boils were on the magicians and on all the Egyptians. 12 The LORD hardened the heart of Pharaoh, and he didn't listen to them, as the LORD had spoken to Moses.

13 The LORD said to Moses, "Rise up early in the morning, and stand before Pharaoh, and tell him, 'This is what the LORD, the God of the Hebrews, says: "Let my people go, that they may serve me. 14 For this time I will send all my plagues against your heart, against your officials, and against your people; that you may know that there is no one like me in all the earth. 15 For now I would have stretched out my hand, and struck you and your people with pestilence, and you would have been cut off from the earth; 16 but indeed for this cause I have made you stand: to show you my power, and that my name may be declared throughout all the earth, 17 because you still exalt yourself against my people, that you won't let them go. 18 Behold, tomorrow about this time I will cause it to rain a very grievous hail, such as has not been in Egypt since the day it was founded even until now. 19 Now therefore command that all of your livestock and all that you have in the field be brought into shelter. The hail will come down on every man and animal that is found in the field, and isn't brought home, and they will die."'"

20 Those who feared the LORD's word amongst the servants of Pharaoh made their servants and their livestock flee into the houses. 21 Whoever didn't respect the LORD's word left his servants and his livestock in the field.

22 The LORD said to Moses, "Stretch out your hand towards the sky, that there may be hail in all the land of Egypt, on man, and on animal, and on every herb of the field, throughout the land of Egypt."

23 Moses stretched out his rod towards the heavens, and the LORD sent thunder and hail; and lightning flashed down to the earth. The LORD rained hail on the land of Egypt. 24 So there was very severe hail, and lightning mixed with the hail, such as had not been in all the land of Egypt since it became a nation. 25 The hail struck throughout all the land of Egypt all that was in the field, both man and animal; and the hail struck every herb of the field, and broke every tree of the field. 26 Only in the land of Goshen, where the children of Israel were, there was no hail.

27 Pharaoh sent and called for Moses and Aaron, and said to them, "I have sinned this time. The LORD is righteous, and I and my people are wicked. 28 Pray to the LORD; for there has been enough of mighty thunderings and hail. I will let you go, and you shall stay no longer."

29 Moses said to him, "As soon as I have gone out of the city, I will spread out my hands to the LORD. The thunders shall cease, and there will

not be any more hail; that you may know that the earth is the LORD's. 30 But as for you and your servants, I know that you don't yet fear the LORD God."

31 The flax and the barley were struck, for the barley had ripened and the flax was blooming. 32 But the wheat and the spelt were not struck, for they had not grown up. 33 Moses went out of the city from Pharaoh, and spread out his hands to the LORD; and the thunders and hail ceased, and the rain was not poured on the earth. 34 When Pharaoh saw that the rain and the hail and the thunders had ceased, he sinned yet more, and hardened his heart, he and his servants. 35 The heart of Pharaoh was hardened, and he didn't let the children of Israel go, just as the LORD had spoken through Moses.

10

1 The LORD said to Moses, "Go in to Pharaoh, for I have hardened his heart and the heart of his servants, that I may show these my signs amongst them; 2 and that you may tell in the hearing of your son, and of your son's son, what things I have done to Egypt, and my signs which I have done amongst them; that you may know that I am the LORD."

3 Moses and Aaron went in to Pharaoh, and said to him, "This is what the LORD, the God of the Hebrews, says: 'How long will you refuse to humble yourself before me? Let my people go, that they may serve me. 4 Or else, if you refuse to let my people go, behold, tomorrow I will bring locusts into your country, 5 and they shall cover the surface of the earth, so that one won't be able to see the earth. They shall eat the residue of that which has escaped, which remains to you from the hail, and shall eat every tree which grows for you out of the field. 6 Your houses shall be filled, and the houses of all your servants, and the houses of all the Egyptians, as neither your fathers nor your fathers' fathers have seen, since the day that they were on the earth to this day.'" He turned, and went out from Pharaoh.

7 Pharaoh's servants said to him, "How long will this man be a snare to us? Let the men go, that they may serve the LORD, their God. Don't you yet know that Egypt is destroyed?"

8 Moses and Aaron were brought again to Pharaoh, and he said to them, "Go, serve the LORD your God; but who are those who will go?"

9 Moses said, "We will go with our young and with our old. We will go with our sons and with our daughters, with our flocks and with our herds; for we must hold a feast to the LORD."

10 He said to them, "The LORD be with you if I let you go with your little ones! See, evil is clearly before your faces. 11 Not so! Go now you who are men, and serve the LORD; for that is what you desire!" Then they were driven out from Pharaoh's presence.

12 The LORD said to Moses, "Stretch out your hand over the land of Egypt for the locusts, that they may come up on the land of Egypt, and eat every herb of the land, even all that the hail has left." 13 Moses stretched out his rod over the land of Egypt, and the LORD brought an east wind on the land all that day, and all night; and when it was morning, the east wind brought the locusts. 14 The locusts went up over all the land of Egypt, and rested in all the borders of Egypt. They were very grievous. Before them there were no such locusts as they, nor will there ever be again. 15 For they covered the surface of the whole earth, so that the land was darkened, and they ate every herb of the land, and all the fruit of the trees which the hail had left. There remained nothing green, either tree or herb of the field, through all the land of Egypt. 16 Then Pharaoh called for Moses and Aaron in haste, and he said, "I have sinned against the LORD your God, and against you. 17 Now therefore please forgive my sin again, and pray to the LORD your God, that he may also take away from me this death."

18 Moses went out from Pharaoh, and prayed to the LORD. 19 The LORD sent an exceedingly strong west wind, which took up the locusts, and drove them into the Red Sea.ª There remained not one locust in all the borders of Egypt. 20 But the LORD hardened Pharaoh's heart, and he didn't let the children of Israel go.

21 The LORD said to Moses, "Stretch out your hand towards the sky, that there may be darkness over the land of Egypt, even darkness which may be felt." 22 Moses stretched out his hand towards the sky, and there was a thick darkness in all the land of Egypt for three days. 23 They didn't see one another, and nobody rose from his place for three days; but all the children of Israel had light in their dwellings.

24 Pharaoh called to Moses, and said, "Go, serve the LORD. Only let your flocks and your herds stay behind. Let your little ones also go with you."

25 Moses said, "You must also give into our hand sacrifices and burnt offerings, that we may sacrifice to the LORD our God. 26 Our livestock also shall go with us. Not a hoof shall be left behind, for of it we must take to serve the LORD our God; and we don't know with what we must serve the LORD, until we come there."

27 But the LORD hardened Pharaoh's heart, and he wouldn't let them go. 28 Pharaoh said to him, "Get away from me! Be careful to see my face no more; for in the day you see my face you shall die!"

29 Moses said, "You have spoken well. I will see your face again no more."

11

1 The LORD said to Moses, "I will bring yet one more plague on Pharaoh, and on Egypt; afterwards he will let you go. When he lets you go, he will surely thrust you out altogether. 2 Speak now in the ears of the people, and let every man ask of his neighbour, and every woman of her neighbour, jewels of silver, and jewels of gold." 3 The LORD gave the

people favour in the sight of the Egyptians. Moreover, the man Moses was very great in the land of Egypt, in the sight of Pharaoh's servants, and in the sight of the people.

4 Moses said, "This is what the LORD says: 'About midnight I will go out into the middle of Egypt, 5 and all the firstborn in the land of Egypt shall die, from the firstborn of Pharaoh who sits on his throne, even to the firstborn of the female servant who is behind the mill, and all the firstborn of livestock. 6 There will be a great cry throughout all the land of Egypt, such as there has not been, nor will be any more. 7 But against any of the children of Israel a dog won't even bark or move its tongue, against man or animal, that you may know that the LORD makes a distinction between the Egyptians and Israel. 8 All these servants of yours will come down to me, and bow down themselves to me, saying, "Get out, with all the people who follow you;" and after that I will go out.'" He went out from Pharaoh in hot anger.

9 The LORD said to Moses, "Pharaoh won't listen to you, that my wonders may be multiplied in the land of Egypt." 10 Moses and Aaron did all these wonders before Pharaoh, but the LORD hardened Pharaoh's heart, and he didn't let the children of Israel go out of his land.

12

1 The LORD spoke to Moses and Aaron in the land of Egypt, saying, 2 "This month shall be to you the beginning of months. It shall be the first month of the year to you. 3 Speak to all the congregation of Israel, saying, 'On the tenth day of this month, they shall take to them every man a lamb, according to their fathers' houses, a lamb for a household; 4 and if the household is too little for a lamb, then he and his neighbour next to his house shall take one according to the number of the souls. You shall make your count for the lamb according to what everyone can eat. 5 Your lamb shall be without defect, a male a year old. You shall take it from the sheep or from the goats. 6 You shall keep it until the fourteenth day of the same month; and the whole assembly of the congregation of Israel shall kill it at evening. 7 They shall take some of the blood, and put it on the two door posts and on the lintel, on the houses in which they shall eat it. 8 They shall eat the meat in that night, roasted with fire, with unleavened bread. They shall eat it with bitter herbs. 9 Don't eat it raw, nor boiled at all with water, but roasted with fire; with its head, its legs and its inner parts. 10 You shall let nothing of it remain until the morning; but that which remains of it until the morning you shall burn with fire. 11 This is how you shall eat it: with your belt on your waist, your sandals on your feet, and your staff in your hand; and you shall eat it in haste: it is the LORD's Passover. 12 For I will go through the land of Egypt in that night, and will strike all the firstborn in the land of Egypt, both man and animal. I will execute judgements against all the gods of Egypt. I am the LORD. 13 The blood shall be to you for a token on the houses where you are. When I see the blood, I will pass over you, and no plague will be on you to destroy you when I strike the land of Egypt. 14 This day shall be a memorial for you. You shall keep it as a feast to the LORD. You shall keep it as a feast throughout your generations by an ordinance forever.

15 "'Seven days you shall eat unleavened bread; even the first day you shall put away yeast out of your houses, for whoever eats leavened bread from the first day until the seventh day, that soul shall be cut off from Israel. 16 In the first day there shall be to you a holy convocation, and in the seventh day a holy convocation; no kind of work shall be done in them, except that which every man must eat, only that may be done by you. 17 You shall observe the feast of unleavened bread; for in this same day I have brought your armies out of the land of Egypt. Therefore you shall observe this day throughout your generations by an ordinance forever. 18 In the first month, on the fourteenth day of the month at evening, you shall eat unleavened bread, until the twenty first day of the month at evening. 19 There shall be no yeast found in your houses for seven days, for whoever eats that which is leavened, that soul shall be cut off from the congregation of Israel, whether he is a foreigner, or one who is born in the land. 20 You shall eat nothing leavened. In all your habitations you shall eat unleavened bread.'"

21 Then Moses called for all the elders of Israel, and said to them, "Draw out, and take lambs according to your families, and kill the Passover. 22 You shall take a bunch of hyssop, and dip it in the blood that is in the basin, and strike the lintel and the two door posts with the blood that is in the basin. None of you shall go out of the door of his house until the morning. 23 For the LORD will pass through to strike the Egyptians; and when he sees the blood on the lintel, and on the two door posts, the LORD will pass over the door, and will not allow the destroyer to come in to your houses to strike you. 24 You shall observe this thing for an ordinance to you and to your sons forever. 25 It shall happen when you have come to the land which the LORD will give you, as he has promised, that you shall keep this service. 26 It will happen, when your children ask you, 'What do you mean by this service?' 27 that you shall say, 'It is the sacrifice of the LORD's Passover, who passed over the houses of the children of Israel in Egypt, when he struck the Egyptians, and spared our houses.'"

The people bowed their heads and worshipped. 28 The children of Israel went and did so; as the LORD had commanded Moses and Aaron, so they did.

29 At midnight, the LORD struck all the firstborn in the land of Egypt, from the firstborn of Pharaoh who sat on his throne to the firstborn of the captive who was in the dungeon, and all the firstborn of livestock. 30

ª *10:19* "Red Sea" is the translation for the Hebrew "Yam Suf", which could be more literally translated "Sea of Reeds" or "Sea of Cattails". It refers to the body of water currently known as the Red Sea, or possibly to one of the bodies of water connected to it or near it.

Pharaoh rose up in the night, he, and all his servants, and all the Egyptians; and there was a great cry in Egypt, for there was not a house where there was not one dead. 31 He called for Moses and Aaron by night, and said, "Rise up, get out from amongst my people, both you and the children of Israel; and go, serve the LORD, as you have said! 32 Take both your flocks and your herds, as you have said, and be gone; and bless me also!"

33 The Egyptians were urgent with the people, to send them out of the land in haste, for they said, "We are all dead men." 34 The people took their dough before it was leavened, their kneading troughs being bound up in their clothes on their shoulders. 35 The children of Israel did according to the word of Moses; and they asked of the Egyptians jewels of silver, and jewels of gold, and clothing. 36 The LORD gave the people favour in the sight of the Egyptians, so that they let them have what they asked. They plundered the Egyptians.

37 The children of Israel travelled from Rameses to Succoth, about six hundred thousand on foot who were men, in addition to children. 38 A mixed multitude went up also with them, with flocks, herds, and even very much livestock. 39 They baked unleavened cakes of the dough which they brought out of Egypt; for it wasn't leavened, because they were thrust out of Egypt, and couldn't wait, and they had not prepared any food for themselves. 40 Now the time that the children of Israel lived in Egypt was four hundred and thirty years. 41 At the end of four hundred and thirty years, to the day, all of the LORD's armies went out from the land of Egypt. 42 It is a night to be much observed to the LORD for bringing them out from the land of Egypt. This is that night of the LORD, to be much observed by all the children of Israel throughout their generations.

43 The LORD said to Moses and Aaron, "This is the ordinance of the Passover. No foreigner shall eat of it, 44 but every man's servant who is bought for money, when you have circumcised him, then shall he eat of it. 45 A foreigner and a hired servant shall not eat of it. 46 It must be eaten in one house. You shall not carry any of the meat outside of the house. Do not break any of its bones. 47 All the congregation of Israel shall keep it. 48 When a stranger lives as a foreigner with you, and would like to keep the Passover to the LORD, let all his males be circumcised, and then let him come near and keep it. He shall be as one who is born in the land; but no uncircumcised person shall eat of it. 49 One law shall be to him who is born at home, and to the stranger who lives as a foreigner amongst you." 50 All the children of Israel did so. As the LORD commanded Moses and Aaron, so they did. 51 That same day, the LORD brought the children of Israel out of the land of Egypt by their armies.

13

1 The LORD spoke to Moses, saying, 2 "Sanctify to me all the firstborn, whatever opens the womb amongst the children of Israel, both of man and of animal. It is mine."

3 Moses said to the people, "Remember this day, in which you came out of Egypt, out of the house of bondage; for by strength of hand the LORD brought you out from this place. No leavened bread shall be eaten. 4 Today you go out in the month Abib. 5 It shall be, when the LORD brings you into the land of the Canaanite, and the Hittite, and the Amorite, and the Hivite, and the Jebusite, which he swore to your fathers to give you, a land flowing with milk and honey, that you shall keep this service in this month. 6 Seven days you shall eat unleavened bread, and in the seventh day shall be a feast to the LORD. 7 Unleavened bread shall be eaten throughout the seven days; and no leavened bread shall be seen with you. No yeast shall be seen with you, within all your borders. 8 You shall tell your son in that day, saying, 'It is because of that which the LORD did for me when I came out of Egypt.' 9 It shall be for a sign to you on your hand, and for a memorial between your eyes, that the LORD's law may be in your mouth; for with a strong hand the LORD has brought you out of Egypt. 10 You shall therefore keep this ordinance in its season from year to year.

11 "It shall be, when the LORD brings you into the land of the Canaanite, as he swore to you and to your fathers, and will give it to you, 12 that you shall set apart to the LORD all that opens the womb, and every firstborn that comes from an animal which you have. The males shall be the LORD's. 13 Every firstborn of a donkey you shall redeem with a lamb; and if you will not redeem it, then you shall break its neck; and you shall redeem all the firstborn of man amongst your sons. 14 It shall be, when your son asks you in time to come, saying, 'What is this?' that you shall tell him, 'By strength of hand the LORD brought us out from Egypt, from the house of bondage. 15 When Pharaoh stubbornly refused to let us go, the LORD killed all the firstborn in the land of Egypt, both the firstborn of man, and the firstborn of livestock. Therefore I sacrifice to the LORD all that opens the womb, being males; but all the firstborn of my sons I redeem.' 16 It shall be for a sign on your hand, and for symbols between your eyes; for by strength of hand the LORD brought us out of Egypt."

17 When Pharaoh had let the people go, God didn't lead them by the way of the land of the Philistines, although that was near; for God said, "Lest perhaps the people change their minds when they see war, and they return to Egypt"; 18 but God led the people around by the way of the wilderness by the Red Sea; and the children of Israel went up armed out of the land of Egypt. 19 Moses took the bones of Joseph with him, for he had made the children of Israel swear, saying, "God will surely visit you, and you shall carry up my bones away from here with you." 20 They took their journey from Succoth, and encamped in Etham, in the edge of the wilderness. 21 The LORD went before them by day in a pillar of cloud, to lead them on their way, and by night in a pillar of fire, to give them light, that they might go by day and by night: 22 the pillar of cloud by day, and the pillar of fire by night, didn't depart from before the people.

14

1 The LORD spoke to Moses, saying, 2 "Speak to the children of Israel, that they turn back and encamp before Pihahiroth, between Migdol and the sea, before Baal Zephon. You shall encamp opposite it by the sea. 3 Pharaoh will say of the children of Israel, 'They are entangled in the land. The wilderness has shut them in.' 4 I will harden Pharaoh's heart, and he will follow after them; and I will get honour over Pharaoh, and over all his armies; and the Egyptians shall know that I am the LORD." They did so.

5 The king of Egypt was told that the people had fled; and the heart of Pharaoh and of his servants was changed towards the people, and they said, "What is this we have done, that we have let Israel go from serving us?" 6 He prepared his chariot, and took his army with him; 7 and he took six hundred chosen chariots, and all the chariots of Egypt, with captains over all of them. 8 The LORD hardened the heart of Pharaoh king of Egypt, and he pursued the children of Israel; for the children of Israel went out with a high hand.[a] 9 The Egyptians pursued them. All the horses and chariots of Pharaoh, his horsemen, and his army overtook them encamping by the sea, beside Pihahiroth, before Baal Zephon.

10 When Pharaoh came near, the children of Israel lifted up their eyes, and behold, the Egyptians were marching after them; and they were very afraid. The children of Israel cried out to the LORD. 11 They said to Moses, "Because there were no graves in Egypt, have you taken us away to die in the wilderness? Why have you treated us this way, to bring us out of Egypt? 12 Isn't this the word that we spoke to you in Egypt, saying, 'Leave us alone, that we may serve the Egyptians'? For it would have been better for us to serve the Egyptians than to die in the wilderness."

13 Moses said to the people, "Don't be afraid. Stand still, and see the salvation of the LORD, which he will work for you today; for you will never again see the Egyptians whom you have seen today. 14 The LORD will fight for you, and you shall be still."

15 The LORD said to Moses, "Why do you cry to me? Speak to the children of Israel, that they go forward. 16 Lift up your rod, and stretch out your hand over the sea and divide it. Then the children of Israel shall go into the middle of the sea on dry ground. 17 Behold, I myself will harden the hearts of the Egyptians, and they will go in after them. I will get myself honour over Pharaoh, and over all his armies, over his chariots, and over his horsemen. 18 The Egyptians shall know that I am the LORD when I have gotten myself honour over Pharaoh, over his chariots, and over his horsemen." 19 The angel of God, who went before the camp of Israel, moved and went behind them; and the pillar of cloud moved from before them, and stood behind them. 20 It came between the camp of Egypt and the camp of Israel. There was the cloud and the darkness, yet it gave light by night. One didn't come near the other all night.

21 Moses stretched out his hand over the sea, and the LORD caused the sea to go back by a strong east wind all night, and made the sea dry land, and the waters were divided. 22 The children of Israel went into the middle of the sea on the dry ground, and the waters were a wall to them on their right hand and on their left. 23 The Egyptians pursued, and went in after them into the middle of the sea: all of Pharaoh's horses, his chariots, and his horsemen. 24 In the morning watch, the LORD looked out on the Egyptian army through the pillar of fire and of cloud, and confused the Egyptian army. 25 He took off their chariot wheels, and they drove them heavily; so that the Egyptians said, "Let's flee from the face of Israel, for the LORD fights for them against the Egyptians!"

26 The LORD said to Moses, "Stretch out your hand over the sea, that the waters may come again on the Egyptians, on their chariots, and on their horsemen." 27 Moses stretched out his hand over the sea, and the sea returned to its strength when the morning appeared; and the Egyptians fled against it. The LORD overthrew the Egyptians in the middle of the sea. 28 The waters returned, and covered the chariots and the horsemen, even all Pharaoh's army that went in after them into the sea. There remained not so much as one of them. 29 But the children of Israel walked on dry land in the middle of the sea, and the waters were a wall to them on their right hand and on their left. 30 Thus the LORD saved Israel that day out of the hand of the Egyptians; and Israel saw the Egyptians dead on the seashore. 31 Israel saw the great work which the LORD did to the Egyptians, and the people feared the LORD; and they believed in the LORD and in his servant Moses.

15

1 Then Moses and the children of Israel sang this song to the LORD, and said,
"I will sing to the LORD, for he has triumphed gloriously.
    He has thrown the horse and his rider into the sea.
2 The LORD is my strength and song.
    He has become my salvation.
This is my God, and I will praise him;
    my father's God, and I will exalt him.
3 The LORD is a man of war.
    The LORD is his name.
4 He has cast Pharaoh's chariots and his army into the sea.
    His chosen captains are sunk in the Red Sea.
5 The deeps cover them.
    They went down into the depths like a stone.
6 Your right hand, LORD, is glorious in power.
    Your right hand, LORD, dashes the enemy in pieces.

---

a 14:8 or, defiantly.

7 In the greatness of your excellency, you overthrow those who rise up against you.

You send out your wrath. It consumes them as stubble.

8 With the blast of your nostrils, the waters were piled up.

The floods stood upright as a heap.

The deeps were congealed in the heart of the sea.

9 The enemy said, 'I will pursue. I will overtake. I will divide the plunder.

My desire will be satisfied on them.

I will draw my sword. My hand will destroy them.'

10 You blew with your wind.

The sea covered them.

They sank like lead in the mighty waters.

11 Who is like you, LORD, amongst the gods?

Who is like you, glorious in holiness,

fearful in praises, doing wonders?

12 You stretched out your right hand.

The earth swallowed them.

13 "You, in your loving kindness, have led the people that you have redeemed.

You have guided them in your strength to your holy habitation.

14 The peoples have heard.

They tremble.

Pangs have taken hold of the inhabitants of Philistia.

15 Then the chiefs of Edom were dismayed.

Trembling takes hold of the mighty men of Moab.

All the inhabitants of Canaan have melted away.

16 Terror and dread falls on them.

By the greatness of your arm they are as still as a stone,

until your people pass over, LORD,

until the people you have purchased pass over.

17 You will bring them in, and plant them in the mountain of your inheritance,

the place, LORD, which you have made for yourself to dwell in:

the sanctuary, Lord, which your hands have established.

18 The LORD will reign forever and ever."

19 For the horses of Pharaoh went in with his chariots and with his horsemen into the sea, and the LORD brought back the waters of the sea on them; but the children of Israel walked on dry land in the middle of the sea. 20 Miriam the prophetess, the sister of Aaron, took a tambourine in her hand; and all the women went out after her with tambourines and with dances. 21 Miriam answered them,

"Sing to the LORD, for he has triumphed gloriously.

He has thrown the horse and his rider into the sea."

22 Moses led Israel onward from the Red Sea, and they went out into the wilderness of Shur; and they went three days in the wilderness, and found no water. 23 When they came to Marah, they couldn't drink from the waters of Marah, for they were bitter. Therefore its name was called Marah.ᵃ 24 The people murmured against Moses, saying, "What shall we drink?" 25 Then he cried to the LORD. The LORD showed him a tree, and he threw it into the waters, and the waters were made sweet. There he made a statute and an ordinance for them, and there he tested them. 26 He said, "If you will diligently listen to the LORD your God's voice, and will do that which is right in his eyes, and will pay attention to his commandments, and keep all his statutes, I will put none of the diseases on you which I have put on the Egyptians; for I am the LORD who heals you."

27 They came to Elim, where there were twelve springs of water and seventy palm trees. They encamped there by the waters.

16

1 They took their journey from Elim, and all the congregation of the children of Israel came to the wilderness of Sin, which is between Elim and Sinai, on the fifteenth day of the second month after their departing out of the land of Egypt. 2 The whole congregation of the children of Israel murmured against Moses and against Aaron in the wilderness; 3 and the children of Israel said to them, "We wish that we had died by the LORD's hand in the land of Egypt, when we sat by the meat pots, when we ate our fill of bread, for you have brought us out into this wilderness to kill this whole assembly with hunger."

4 Then the LORD said to Moses, "Behold, I will rain bread from the sky for you, and the people shall go out and gather a day's portion every day, that I may test them, whether they will walk in my law or not. 5 It shall come to pass on the sixth day, that they shall prepare that which they bring in, and it shall be twice as much as they gather daily."

6 Moses and Aaron said to all the children of Israel, "At evening, you shall know that the LORD has brought you out from the land of Egypt. 7 In the morning, you shall see the LORD's glory; because he hears your murmurings against the LORD. Who are we, that you murmur against us?" 8 Moses said, "Now the LORD will give you meat to eat in the evening, and in the morning bread to satisfy you, because the LORD hears your murmurings which you murmur against him. And who are we? Your murmurings are not against us, but against the LORD." 9 Moses said to Aaron, "Tell all the congregation of the children of Israel, 'Come close to the LORD, for he has heard your murmurings.'" 10 As Aaron spoke to the whole congregation of the children of Israel, they looked towards the wilderness, and behold, the LORD's glory appeared in the cloud. 11 The

LORD spoke to Moses, saying, 12 "I have heard the murmurings of the children of Israel. Speak to them, saying, 'At evening you shall eat meat, and in the morning you shall be filled with bread. Then you will know that I am the LORD your God.'"

13 In the evening, quail came up and covered the camp; and in the morning the dew lay around the camp. 14 When the dew that lay had gone, behold, on the surface of the wilderness was a small round thing, small as the frost on the ground. 15 When the children of Israel saw it, they said to one another, "What is it?" For they didn't know what it was. Moses said to them, "It is the bread which the LORD has given you to eat. 16 This is the thing which the LORD has commanded: 'Gather of it everyone according to his eating; an omerᵇ a head, according to the number of your persons, you shall take it, every man for those who are in his tent.'" 17 The children of Israel did so, and some gathered more, some less. 18 When they measured it with an omer, he who gathered much had nothing over, and he who gathered little had no lack. They each gathered according to his eating. 19 Moses said to them, "Let no one leave of it until the morning." 20 Notwithstanding they didn't listen to Moses, but some of them left of it until the morning, so it bred worms and became foul; and Moses was angry with them. 21 They gathered it morning by morning, everyone according to his eating. When the sun grew hot, it melted. 22 On the sixth day, they gathered twice as much bread, two omers for each one; and all the rulers of the congregation came and told Moses. 23 He said to them, "This is that which the LORD has spoken, 'Tomorrow is a solemn rest, a holy Sabbath to the LORD. Bake that which you want to bake, and boil that which you want to boil; and all that remains over lay up for yourselves to be kept until the morning.'" 24 They laid it up until the morning, as Moses ordered, and it didn't become foul, and there were no worms in it. 25 Moses said, "Eat that today, for today is a Sabbath to the LORD. Today you shall not find it in the field. 26 Six days you shall gather it, but on the seventh day is the Sabbath. In it there shall be none." 27 On the seventh day, some of the people went out to gather, and they found none. 28 The LORD said to Moses, "How long do you refuse to keep my commandments and my laws? 29 Behold, because the LORD has given you the Sabbath, therefore he gives you on the sixth day the bread of two days. Everyone stay in his place. Let no one go out of his place on the seventh day." 30 So the people rested on the seventh day.

31 The house of Israel called its name "Manna",ᶜ and it was like coriander seed, white; and its taste was like wafers with honey. 32 Moses said, "This is the thing which the LORD has commanded, 'Let an omer-full of it be kept throughout your generations, that they may see the bread with which I fed you in the wilderness, when I brought you out of the land of Egypt.'" 33 Moses said to Aaron, "Take a pot, and put an omer-full of manna in it, and lay it up before the LORD, to be kept throughout your generations." 34 As the LORD commanded Moses, so Aaron laid it up before the Testimony, to be kept. 35 The children of Israel ate the manna forty years, until they came to an inhabited land. They ate the manna until they came to the borders of the land of Canaan. 36 Now an omer is one tenth of an ephah.ᵈ

17

1 All the congregation of the children of Israel travelled from the wilderness of Sin, starting according to the LORD's commandment, and encamped in Rephidim; but there was no water for the people to drink. 2 Therefore the people quarrelled with Moses, and said, "Give us water to drink."

Moses said to them, "Why do you quarrel with me? Why do you test the LORD?"

3 The people were thirsty for water there; so the people murmured against Moses, and said, "Why have you brought us up out of Egypt, to kill us, our children, and our livestock with thirst?"

4 Moses cried to the LORD, saying, "What shall I do with these people? They are almost ready to stone me."

5 The LORD said to Moses, "Walk on before the people, and take the elders of Israel with you, and take the rod in your hand with which you struck the Nile, and go. 6 Behold, I will stand before you there on the rock in Horeb. You shall strike the rock, and water will come out of it, that the people may drink." Moses did so in the sight of the elders of Israel. 7 He called the name of the place Massah,ᵉ and Meribah,ᶠ because the children of Israel quarrelled, and because they tested the LORD, saying, "Is the LORD amongst us, or not?"

8 Then Amalek came and fought with Israel in Rephidim. 9 Moses said to Joshua, "Choose men for us, and go out to fight with Amalek. Tomorrow I will stand on the top of the hill with God's rod in my hand." 10 So Joshua did as Moses had told him, and fought with Amalek; and Moses, Aaron, and Hur went up to the top of the hill. 11 When Moses held up his hand, Israel prevailed. When he let down his hand, Amalek prevailed. 12 But Moses' hands were heavy; so they took a stone, and put it under him, and he sat on it. Aaron and Hur held up his hands, the one on the one side, and the other on the other side. His hands were steady until sunset. 13 Joshua defeated Amalek and his people with the edge of the sword. 14 The LORD said to Moses, "Write this for a memorial in a book, and rehearse it in the ears of Joshua: that I will utterly blot out the memory of Amalek from under the

---

ᵃ *15:23* Marah means bitter.

ᵇ *16:16* An omer is about 2.2 litres or about 2.3 quarts

ᶜ *16:31* "Manna" means "What is it?"

ᵈ *16:36* 1 ephah is about 22 litres or about 2/3 of a bushel

ᵉ *17:7* Massah means testing.

ᶠ *17:7* Meribah means quarrelling.

sky." 15 Moses built an altar, and called its name "The LORD our Banner".[a] 16 He said, "The LORD has sworn: 'The LORD will have war with Amalek from generation to generation.'"

18

1 Now Jethro, the priest of Midian, Moses' father-in-law, heard of all that God had done for Moses and for Israel his people, how the LORD had brought Israel out of Egypt. 2 Jethro, Moses' father-in-law, received Zipporah, Moses' wife, after he had sent her away, 3 and her two sons. The name of one son was Gershom,[b] for Moses said, "I have lived as a foreigner in a foreign land". 4 The name of the other was Eliezer,[c] for he said, "My father's God was my help and delivered me from Pharaoh's sword." 5 Jethro, Moses' father-in-law, came with Moses' sons and his wife to Moses into the wilderness where he was encamped, at the Mountain of God. 6 He said to Moses, "I, your father-in-law Jethro, have come to you with your wife, and her two sons with her."

7 Moses went out to meet his father-in-law, and bowed and kissed him. They asked each other of their welfare, and they came into the tent. 8 Moses told his father-in-law all that the LORD had done to Pharaoh and to the Egyptians for Israel's sake, all the hardships that had come on them on the way, and how the LORD delivered them. 9 Jethro rejoiced for all the goodness which the LORD had done to Israel, in that he had delivered them out of the hand of the Egyptians. 10 Jethro said, "Blessed be the LORD, who has delivered you out of the hand of the Egyptians, and out of the hand of Pharaoh; who has delivered the people from under the hand of the Egyptians. 11 Now I know that the LORD is greater than all gods because of the way that they treated people arrogantly." 12 Jethro, Moses' father-in-law, took a burnt offering and sacrifices for God. Aaron came with all the elders of Israel, to eat bread with Moses' father-in-law before God.

13 On the next day, Moses sat to judge the people, and the people stood around Moses from the morning to the evening. 14 When Moses' father-in-law saw all that he did to the people, he said, "What is this thing that you do for the people? Why do you sit alone, and all the people stand around you from morning to evening?"

15 Moses said to his father-in-law, "Because the people come to me to enquire of God. 16 When they have a matter, they come to me, and I judge between a man and his neighbour, and I make them know the statutes of God, and his laws." 17 Moses' father-in-law said to him, "The thing that you do is not good. 18 You will surely wear away, both you, and this people that is with you; for the thing is too heavy for you. You are not able to perform it yourself alone. 19 Listen now to my voice. I will give you counsel, and God be with you. You represent the people before God, and bring the causes to God. 20 You shall teach them the statutes and the laws, and shall show them the way in which they must walk, and the work that they must do. 21 Moreover you shall provide out of all the people able men which fear God: men of truth, hating unjust gain; and place such over them, to be rulers of thousands, rulers of hundreds, rulers of fifties, and rulers of tens. 22 Let them judge the people at all times. It shall be that every great matter they shall bring to you, but every small matter they shall judge themselves. So shall it be easier for you, and they shall share the load with you. 23 If you will do this thing, and God commands you so, then you will be able to endure, and all these people also will go to their place in peace."

24 So Moses listened to the voice of his father-in-law, and did all that he had said. 25 Moses chose able men out of all Israel, and made them heads over the people, rulers of thousands, rulers of hundreds, rulers of fifties, and rulers of tens. 26 They judged the people at all times. They brought the hard cases to Moses, but every small matter they judged themselves. 27 Moses let his father-in-law depart, and he went his way into his own land.

19

1 In the third month after the children of Israel had gone out of the land of Egypt, on that same day they came into the wilderness of Sinai. 2 When they had departed from Rephidim, and had come to the wilderness of Sinai, they encamped in the wilderness; and there Israel encamped before the mountain. 3 Moses went up to God, and the LORD called to him out of the mountain, saying, "This is what you shall tell the house of Jacob, and tell the children of Israel: 4 'You have seen what I did to the Egyptians, and how I bore you on eagles' wings, and brought you to myself. 5 Now therefore, if you will indeed obey my voice and keep my covenant, then you shall be my own possession from amongst all peoples; for all the earth is mine; 6 and you shall be to me a kingdom of priests and a holy nation.' These are the words which you shall speak to the children of Israel."

7 Moses came and called for the elders of the people, and set before them all these words which the LORD commanded him. 8 All the people answered together, and said, "All that the LORD has spoken we will do."

Moses reported the words of the people to the LORD. 9 The LORD said to Moses, "Behold, I come to you in a thick cloud, that the people may hear when I speak with you, and may also believe you forever." Moses told the words of the people to the LORD. 10 The LORD said to Moses, "Go to the people, and sanctify them today and tomorrow, and let them wash their garments, 11 and be ready for the third day; for on the third day the LORD will come down in the sight of all the people on Mount Sinai. 12 You shall set bounds to the people all around, saying, 'Be careful that you don't go up onto the mountain, or touch its border. Whoever touches the mountain shall be surely put to death. 13 No hand shall touch him, but he shall surely be

stoned or shot through; whether it is animal or man, he shall not live.' When the trumpet sounds long, they shall come up to the mountain."

14 Moses went down from the mountain to the people, and sanctified the people; and they washed their clothes. 15 He said to the people, "Be ready by the third day. Don't have sexual relations with a woman."

16 On the third day, when it was morning, there were thunders and lightnings, and a thick cloud on the mountain, and the sound of an exceedingly loud trumpet; and all the people who were in the camp trembled. 17 Moses led the people out of the camp to meet God; and they stood at the lower part of the mountain. 18 All of Mount Sinai smoked, because the LORD descended on it in fire; and its smoke ascended like the smoke of a furnace, and the whole mountain quaked greatly. 19 When the sound of the trumpet grew louder and louder, Moses spoke, and God answered him by a voice. 20 The LORD came down on Mount Sinai, to the top of the mountain. The LORD called Moses to the top of the mountain, and Moses went up.

21 The LORD said to Moses, "Go down, warn the people, lest they break through to the LORD to gaze, and many of them perish. 22 Let the priests also, who come near to the LORD, sanctify themselves, lest the LORD break out on them."

23 Moses said to the LORD, "The people can't come up to Mount Sinai, for you warned us, saying, 'Set bounds around the mountain, and sanctify it.'"

24 The LORD said to him, "Go down! You shall bring Aaron up with you, but don't let the priests and the people break through to come up to the LORD, lest he break out against them."

25 So Moses went down to the people, and told them.

20

1 God[d] spoke all these words, saying, 2 "I am the LORD your God, who brought you out of the land of Egypt, out of the house of bondage.

3 "You shall have no other gods before me.

4 "You shall not make for yourselves an idol, nor any image of anything that is in the heavens above, or that is in the earth beneath, or that is in the water under the earth: 5 you shall not bow yourself down to them, nor serve them, for I, the LORD your God, am a jealous God, visiting the iniquity of the fathers on the children, on the third and on the fourth generation of those who hate me, 6 and showing loving kindness to thousands of those who love me and keep my commandments.

7 "You shall not misuse the name of the LORD your God,[e] for the LORD will not hold him guiltless who misuses his name.

8 "Remember the Sabbath day, to keep it holy. 9 You shall labour six days, and do all your work, 10 but the seventh day is a Sabbath to the LORD your God. You shall not do any work in it, you, nor your son, nor your daughter, your male servant, nor your female servant, nor your livestock, nor your stranger who is within your gates; 11 for in six days the LORD made heaven and earth, the sea, and all that is in them, and rested the seventh day; therefore the LORD blessed the Sabbath day, and made it holy.

12 "Honour your father and your mother, that your days may be long in the land which the LORD your God gives you.

13 "You shall not murder.

14 "You shall not commit adultery.

15 "You shall not steal.

16 "You shall not give false testimony against your neighbour.

17 "You shall not covet your neighbour's house. You shall not covet your neighbour's wife, nor his male servant, nor his female servant, nor his ox, nor his donkey, nor anything that is your neighbour's."

18 All the people perceived the thunderings, the lightnings, the sound of the trumpet, and the mountain smoking. When the people saw it, they trembled, and stayed at a distance. 19 They said to Moses, "Speak with us yourself, and we will listen; but don't let God speak with us, lest we die."

20 Moses said to the people, "Don't be afraid, for God has come to test you, and that his fear may be before you, that you won't sin." 21 The people stayed at a distance, and Moses came near to the thick darkness where God was.

22 The LORD said to Moses, "This is what you shall tell the children of Israel: 'You yourselves have seen that I have talked with you from heaven. 23 You shall most certainly not make gods of silver or gods of gold for yourselves to be alongside me. 24 You shall make an altar of earth for me, and shall sacrifice on it your burnt offerings and your peace offerings, your sheep and your cattle. In every place where I record my name I will come to you and I will bless you. 25 If you make me an altar of stone, you shall not build it of cut stones; for if you lift up your tool on it, you have polluted it. 26 You shall not go up by steps to my altar, that your nakedness may not be exposed to it.'

21

1 "Now these are the ordinances which you shall set before them:

2 "If you buy a Hebrew servant, he shall serve six years, and in the seventh he shall go out free without paying anything. 3 If he comes in by himself, he shall go out by himself. If he is married, then his wife shall go out with him. 4 If his master gives him a wife and she bears him sons or daughters, the wife and her children shall be her master's, and he shall go out by himself. 5 But if the servant shall plainly say, 'I love my master, my wife, and my children. I will not go out free;' 6 then his master shall bring

---

a 17:15 Or, The LORD Nissi

b 18:3 "Gershom" sounds like the Hebrew for "an alien there".

c 18:4 Eliezer means "God is my helper".

d 20:1 After "God", the Hebrew has the two letters "Aleph Tav" (the first and last letters of the Hebrew alphabet), not as a word, but as a grammatical marker.

e 20:7 or, You shall not take the name of the LORD your God in vain him to God, and shall bring him to the door or to the doorpost, and his master shall bore his ear through with an awl, and he shall serve him forever.

7 "If a man sells his daughter to be a female servant, she shall not go out as the male servants do. 8 If she doesn't please her master, who has married her to himself, then he shall let her be redeemed. He shall have no right to sell her to a foreign people, since he has dealt deceitfully with her. 9 If he marries her to his son, he shall deal with her as a daughter. 10 If he takes another wife to himself, he shall not diminish her food, her clothing, and her marital rights. 11 If he doesn't do these three things for her, she may go free without paying any money.

12 "One who strikes a man so that he dies shall surely be put to death, 13 but not if it is unintentional, but God allows it to happen; then I will appoint you a place where he shall flee. 14 If a man schemes and comes presumptuously on his neighbour to kill him, you shall take him from my altar, that he may die.

15 "Anyone who attacks his father or his mother shall be surely put to death.

16 "Anyone who kidnaps someone and sells him, or if he is found in his hand, he shall surely be put to death.

17 "Anyone who curses his father or his mother shall surely be put to death.

18 "If men quarrel and one strikes the other with a stone, or with his fist, and he doesn't die, but is confined to bed; 19 if he rises again and walks around with his staff, then he who struck him shall be cleared; only he shall pay for the loss of his time, and shall provide for his healing until he is thoroughly healed.

20 "If a man strikes his servant or his maid with a rod, and he dies under his hand, the man shall surely be punished. 21 Notwithstanding, if his servant gets up after a day or two, he shall not be punished, for the servant is his property.

22 "If men fight and hurt a pregnant woman so that she gives birth prematurely, and yet no harm follows, he shall be surely fined as much as the woman's husband demands and the judges allow. 23 But if any harm follows, then you must take life for life, 24 eye for eye, tooth for tooth, hand for hand, foot for foot, 25 burning for burning, wound for wound, and bruise for bruise.

26 "If a man strikes his servant's eye, or his maid's eye, and destroys it, he shall let him go free for his eye's sake. 27 If he strikes out his male servant's tooth, or his female servant's tooth, he shall let the servant go free for his tooth's sake.

28 "If a bull gores a man or a woman to death, the bull shall surely be stoned, and its meat shall not be eaten; but the owner of the bull shall not be held responsible. 29 But if the bull had a habit of goring in the past, and this has been testified to its owner, and he has not kept it in, but it has killed a man or a woman, the bull shall be stoned, and its owner shall also be put to death. 30 If a ransom is imposed on him, then he shall give for the redemption of his life whatever is imposed. 31 Whether it has gored a son or has gored a daughter, according to this judgement it shall be done to him. 32 If the bull gores a male servant or a female servant, thirty shekels[a] of silver shall be given to their master, and the ox shall be stoned.

33 "If a man opens a pit, or if a man digs a pit and doesn't cover it, and a bull or a donkey falls into it, 34 the owner of the pit shall make it good. He shall give money to its owner, and the dead animal shall be his.

35 "If one man's bull injures another's, so that it dies, then they shall sell the live bull, and divide its price; and they shall also divide the dead animal. 36 Or if it is known that the bull was in the habit of goring in the past, and its owner has not kept it in, he shall surely pay bull for bull, and the dead animal shall be his own.

22

1 "If a man steals an ox or a sheep, and kills it or sells it, he shall pay five oxen for an ox, and four sheep for a sheep. 2 If the thief is found breaking in, and is struck so that he dies, there shall be no guilt of bloodshed for him. 3 If the sun has risen on him, he is guilty of bloodshed. He shall make restitution. If he has nothing, then he shall be sold for his theft. 4 If the stolen property is found in his hand alive, whether it is ox, donkey, or sheep, he shall pay double.

5 "If a man causes a field or vineyard to be eaten by letting his animal loose, and it grazes in another man's field, he shall make restitution from the best of his own field, and from the best of his own vineyard.

6 "If fire breaks out, and catches in thorns so that the shocks of grain, or the standing grain, or the field are consumed; he who kindled the fire shall surely make restitution.

7 "If a man delivers to his neighbour money or stuff to keep, and it is stolen out of the man's house, if the thief is found, he shall pay double. 8 If the thief isn't found, then the master of the house shall come near to God, to find out whether or not he has put his hand on his neighbour's goods. 9 For every matter of trespass, whether it is for ox, for donkey, for sheep, for clothing, or for any kind of lost thing, about which one says, 'This is mine,' the cause of both parties shall come before God. He whom God condemns shall pay double to his neighbour.

10 "If a man delivers to his neighbour a donkey, an ox, a sheep, or any animal to keep, and it dies or is injured, or driven away, no man seeing it; 11 the oath of the LORD shall be between them both, he has not put his hand on his neighbour's goods; and its owner shall accept it, and he shall not

make restitution. 12 But if it is stolen from him, the one who stole shall make restitution to its owner. 13 If it is torn in pieces, let him bring it for evidence. He shall not make good that which was torn.

14 "If a man borrows anything of his neighbour's, and it is injured, or dies, its owner not being with it, he shall surely make restitution. 15 If its owner is with it, he shall not make it good. If it is a leased thing, it came for its lease.

16 "If a man entices a virgin who isn't pledged to be married, and lies with her, he shall surely pay a dowry for her to be his wife. 17 If her father utterly refuses to give her to him, he shall pay money according to the dowry of virgins.

18 "You shall not allow a sorceress to live.

19 "Whoever has sex with an animal shall surely be put to death.

20 "He who sacrifices to any god, except to the LORD only, shall be utterly destroyed.

21 "You shall not wrong an alien or oppress him, for you were aliens in the land of Egypt.

22 "You shall not take advantage of any widow or fatherless child. 23 If you take advantage of them at all, and they cry at all to me, I will surely hear their cry; 24 and my wrath will grow hot, and I will kill you with the sword; and your wives shall be widows, and your children fatherless.

25 "If you lend money to any of my people with you who is poor, you shall not be to him as a creditor. You shall not charge him interest. 26 If you take your neighbour's garment as collateral, you shall restore it to him before the sun goes down, 27 for that is his only covering, it is his garment for his skin. What would he sleep in? It will happen, when he cries to me, that I will hear, for I am gracious.

28 "You shall not blaspheme God, nor curse a ruler of your people.

29 "You shall not delay to offer from your harvest and from the outflow of your presses.

"You shall give the firstborn of your sons to me. 30 You shall do likewise with your cattle and with your sheep. It shall be with its mother seven days, then on the eighth day you shall give it to me.

31 "You shall be holy men to me, therefore you shall not eat any meat that is torn by animals in the field. You shall cast it to the dogs.

23

1 "You shall not spread a false report. Don't join your hand with the wicked to be a malicious witness.

2 "You shall not follow a crowd to do evil. You shall not testify in court to side with a multitude to pervert justice. 3 You shall not favour a poor man in his cause.

4 "If you meet your enemy's ox or his donkey going astray, you shall surely bring it back to him again. 5 If you see the donkey of him who hates you fallen down under his burden, don't leave him. You shall surely help him with it.

6 "You shall not deny justice to your poor people in their lawsuits.

7 "Keep far from a false charge, and don't kill the innocent and righteous; for I will not justify the wicked.

8 "You shall take no bribe, for a bribe blinds those who have sight and perverts the words of the righteous.

9 "You shall not oppress an alien, for you know the heart of an alien, since you were aliens in the land of Egypt.

10 "For six years you shall sow your land, and shall gather in its increase, 11 but the seventh year you shall let it rest and lie fallow, that the poor of your people may eat; and what they leave the animal of the field shall eat. In the same way, you shall deal with your vineyard and with your olive grove.

12 "Six days you shall do your work, and on the seventh day you shall rest, that your ox and your donkey may have rest, and the son of your servant, and the alien may be refreshed.

13 "Be careful to do all things that I have said to you; and don't invoke the name of other gods or even let them be heard out of your mouth.

14 "You shall observe a feast to me three times a year. 15 You shall observe the feast of unleavened bread. Seven days you shall eat unleavened bread, as I commanded you, at the time appointed in the month Abib (for in it you came out of Egypt), and no one shall appear before me empty. 16 And the feast of harvest, the first fruits of your labours, which you sow in the field; and the feast of ingathering, at the end of the year, when you gather in your labours out of the field. 17 Three times in the year all your males shall appear before the Lord GOD.

18 "You shall not offer the blood of my sacrifice with leavened bread. The fat of my feast shall not remain all night until the morning.

19 You shall bring the first of the first fruits of your ground into the house of the LORD your God.

"You shall not boil a young goat in its mother's milk.

20 "Behold, I send an angel before you, to keep you by the way, and to bring you into the place which I have prepared. 21 Pay attention to him, and listen to his voice. Don't provoke him, for he will not pardon your disobedience, for my name is in him. 22 But if you indeed listen to his voice, and do all that I speak, then I will be an enemy to your enemies, and an adversary to your adversaries. 23 For my angel shall go before you, and bring you in to the Amorite, the Hittite, the Perizzite, the Canaanite, the Hivite, and the Jebusite; and I will cut them off. 24 You shall not bow down to their gods, nor serve them, nor follow their practices, but you shall utterly overthrow them and demolish their pillars. 25 You shall serve the

---

[a] 21:32 A shekel is about 10 grams or about 0.35 ounces, so 30 shekels is about 300 grams or about 10.6 ounces.

LORD your God, and he will bless your bread and your water, and I will take sickness away from amongst you. 26 No one will miscarry or be barren in your land. I will fulfil the number of your days. 27 I will send my terror before you, and will confuse all the people to whom you come, and I will make all your enemies turn their backs to you. 28 I will send the hornet before you, which will drive out the Hivite, the Canaanite, and the Hittite, from before you. 29 I will not drive them out from before you in one year, lest the land become desolate, and the animals of the field multiply against you. 30 Little by little I will drive them out from before you, until you have increased and inherit the land. 31 I will set your border from the Red Sea even to the sea of the Philistines, and from the wilderness to the River; for I will deliver the inhabitants of the land into your hand, and you shall drive them out before you. 32 You shall make no covenant with them, nor with their gods. 33 They shall not dwell in your land, lest they make you sin against me, for if you serve their gods, it will surely be a snare to you."

24

1 He said to Moses, "Come up to the LORD, you, and Aaron, Nadab, and Abihu, and seventy of the elders of Israel; and worship from a distance. 2 Moses alone shall come near to the LORD, but they shall not come near. The people shall not go up with him."

3 Moses came and told the people all the LORD's words, and all the ordinances; and all the people answered with one voice, and said, "All the words which the LORD has spoken will we do."

4 Moses wrote all the LORD's words, then rose up early in the morning and built an altar at the base of the mountain, with twelve pillars for the twelve tribes of Israel. 5 He sent young men of the children of Israel, who offered burnt offerings and sacrificed peace offerings of cattle to the LORD. 6 Moses took half of the blood and put it in basins, and half of the blood he sprinkled on the altar. 7 He took the book of the covenant and read it in the hearing of the people, and they said, "We will do all that the LORD has said, and be obedient."

8 Moses took the blood, and sprinkled it on the people, and said, "Look, this is the blood of the covenant, which the LORD has made with you concerning all these words."

9 Then Moses, Aaron, Nadab, Abihu, and seventy of the elders of Israel went up. 10 They saw the God of Israel. Under his feet was like a paved work of sapphire[a] stone, like the skies for clearness. 11 He didn't lay his hand on the nobles of the children of Israel. They saw God, and ate and drank.

12 The LORD said to Moses, "Come up to me on the mountain, and stay here, and I will give you the stone tablets with the law and the commands that I have written, that you may teach them."

13 Moses rose up with Joshua, his servant, and Moses went up onto God's Mountain. 14 He said to the elders, "Wait here for us, until we come again to you. Behold, Aaron and Hur are with you. Whoever is involved in a dispute can go to them."

15 Moses went up on the mountain, and the cloud covered the mountain. 16 The LORD's glory settled on Mount Sinai, and the cloud covered it six days. The seventh day he called to Moses out of the middle of the cloud. 17 The appearance of the LORD's glory was like devouring fire on the top of the mountain in the eyes of the children of Israel. 18 Moses entered into the middle of the cloud, and went up on the mountain; and Moses was on the mountain forty days and forty nights.

25

1 The LORD spoke to Moses, saying, 2 "Speak to the children of Israel, that they take an offering for me. From everyone whose heart makes him willing you shall take my offering. 3 This is the offering which you shall take from them: gold, silver, bronze, 4 blue, purple, scarlet, fine linen, goats' hair, 5 rams' skins dyed red, sea cow hides,[b] acacia wood, 6 oil for the light, spices for the anointing oil and for the sweet incense, 7 onyx stones, and stones to be set for the ephod and for the breastplate. 8 Let them make me a sanctuary, that I may dwell amongst them. 9 According to all that I show you, the pattern of the tabernacle, and the pattern of all of its furniture, even so you shall make it.

10 "They shall make an ark of acacia wood. Its length shall be two and a half cubits,[c] its width a cubit and a half, and a cubit and a half its height. 11 You shall overlay it with pure gold. You shall overlay it inside and outside, and you shall make a gold moulding around it. 12 You shall cast four rings of gold for it, and put them in its four feet. Two rings shall be on the one side of it, and two rings on the other side of it. 13 You shall make poles of acacia wood, and overlay them with gold. 14 You shall put the poles into the rings on the sides of the ark to carry the ark. 15 The poles shall be in the rings of the ark. They shall not be taken from it. 16 You shall put the covenant which I shall give you into the ark. 17 You shall make a mercy seat of pure gold. Two and a half cubits shall be its length, and a cubit and a half its width. 18 You shall make two cherubim of hammered gold. You shall make them at the two ends of the mercy seat. 19 Make one cherub at the one end, and one cherub at the other end. You shall make the cherubim on its two ends of one piece with the mercy seat. 20 The cherubim shall spread out their wings upward, covering the mercy seat with their wings, with their faces towards one another. The faces of the cherubim shall be towards the mercy seat. 21 You shall put the mercy seat on top of the ark, and in the ark you shall put the covenant that I will give you. 22

There I will meet with you, and I will tell you from above the mercy seat, from between the two cherubim which are on the ark of the covenant, all that I command you for the children of Israel.

23 "You shall make a table of acacia wood. Its length shall be two cubits, and its width a cubit, and its height one and a half cubits. 24 You shall overlay it with pure gold, and make a gold moulding around it. 25 You shall make a rim of a hand width around it. You shall make a golden moulding on its rim around it. 26 You shall make four rings of gold for it, and put the rings in the four corners that are on its four feet. 27 The rings shall be close to the rim, for places for the poles to carry the table. 28 You shall make the poles of acacia wood, and overlay them with gold, that the table may be carried with them. 29 You shall make its dishes, its spoons, its ladles, and its bowls with which to pour out offerings. You shall make them of pure gold. 30 You shall set bread of the presence on the table before me always.

31 "You shall make a lamp stand of pure gold. The lamp stand shall be made of hammered work. Its base, its shaft, its cups, its buds, and its flowers shall be of one piece with it. 32 There shall be six branches going out of its sides: three branches of the lamp stand out of its one side, and three branches of the lamp stand out of its other side; 33 three cups made like almond blossoms in one branch, a bud and a flower; and three cups made like almond blossoms in the other branch, a bud and a flower, so for the six branches going out of the lamp stand; 34 and in the lamp stand four cups made like almond blossoms, its buds and its flowers; 35 and a bud under two branches of one piece with it, and a bud under two branches of one piece with it, and a bud under two branches of one piece with it, for the six branches going out of the lamp stand. 36 Their buds and their branches shall be of one piece with it, all of it one beaten work of pure gold. 37 You shall make its lamps seven, and they shall light its lamps to give light to the space in front of it. 38 Its snuffers and its snuff dishes shall be of pure gold. 39 It shall be made of a talent[d] of pure gold, with all these accessories. 40 See that you make them after their pattern, which has been shown to you on the mountain.

26

1 "Moreover you shall make the tabernacle with ten curtains of fine twined linen, and blue, and purple, and scarlet, with cherubim. You shall make them with the work of a skilful workman. 2 The length of each curtain shall be twenty-eight cubits,[e] and the width of each curtain four cubits: all the curtains shall have one measure. 3 Five curtains shall be coupled together to one another, and the other five curtains shall be coupled to one another. 4 You shall make loops of blue on the edge of the one curtain from the edge in the coupling, and you shall do likewise on the edge of the curtain that is outermost in the second coupling. 5 You shall make fifty loops in the one curtain, and you shall make fifty loops in the edge of the curtain that is in the second coupling. The loops shall be opposite one another. 6 You shall make fifty clasps of gold, and couple the curtains to one another with the clasps. The tabernacle shall be a unit.

7 "You shall make curtains of goats' hair for a covering over the tabernacle. You shall make eleven curtains. 8 The length of each curtain shall be thirty cubits, and the width of each curtain four cubits: the eleven curtains shall have one measure. 9 You shall couple five curtains by themselves, and six curtains by themselves, and shall double over the sixth curtain in the forefront of the tent. 10 You shall make fifty loops on the edge of the one curtain that is outermost in the coupling, and fifty loops on the edge of the curtain which is outermost in the second coupling. 11 You shall make fifty clasps of bronze, and put the clasps into the loops, and couple the tent together, that it may be one. 12 The overhanging part that remains of the curtains of the tent—the half curtain that remains—shall hang over the back of the tabernacle. 13 The cubit on the one side and the cubit on the other side, of that which remains in the length of the curtains of the tent, shall hang over the sides of the tabernacle on this side and on that side, to cover it. 14 You shall make a covering for the tent of rams' skins dyed red, and a covering of sea cow hides above.

15 "You shall make the boards for the tabernacle of acacia wood, standing upright. 16 Ten cubits shall be the length of a board, and one and a half cubits the width of each board. 17 There shall be two tenons in each board, joined to one another: thus you shall make for all the boards of the tabernacle. 18 You shall make twenty boards for the tabernacle, for the south side southward. 19 You shall make forty sockets of silver under the twenty boards; two sockets under one board for its two tenons, and two sockets under another board for its two tenons. 20 For the second side of the tabernacle, on the north side, twenty boards, 21 and their forty sockets of silver; two sockets under one board, and two sockets under another board. 22 For the far side of the tabernacle westward you shall make six boards. 23 You shall make two boards for the corners of the tabernacle in the far side. 24 They shall be double beneath, and in the same way they shall be whole to its top to one ring: thus shall it be for them both; they shall be for the two corners. 25 There shall be eight boards, and their sockets of silver, sixteen sockets; two sockets under one board, and two sockets under another board.

26 "You shall make bars of acacia wood: five for the boards of the one side of the tabernacle, 27 and five bars for the boards of the other side of the tabernacle, and five bars for the boards of the side of the tabernacle, for

---

a 24:10 or, lapis lazuli
b 25:5 or, fine leather
c 25:10 A cubit is the length from the tip of the middle finger to the elbow on a man's arm, or about 18 inches or 46 centimetres.

d 25:39 A talent is about 30 kilograms or 66 pounds or 965 Troy ounces
e 26:2 A cubit is the length from the tip of the middle finger to the elbow on a man's arm, or about 18 inches or 46 centimetres.

the far side westward. 28 The middle bar in the middle of the boards shall pass through from end to end. 29 You shall overlay the boards with gold, and make their rings of gold for places for the bars. You shall overlay the bars with gold. 30 You shall set up the tabernacle according to the way that it was shown to you on the mountain.

31 "You shall make a veil of blue, and purple, and scarlet, and fine twined linen, with cherubim. It shall be the work of a skilful workman. 32 You shall hang it on four pillars of acacia overlaid with gold; their hooks shall be of gold, on four sockets of silver. 33 You shall hang up the veil under the clasps, and shall bring the ark of the covenant in there within the veil. The veil shall separate the holy place from the most holy for you. 34 You shall put the mercy seat on the ark of the covenant in the most holy place. 35 You shall set the table outside the veil, and the lamp stand opposite the table on the side of the tabernacle towards the south. You shall put the table on the north side.

36 "You shall make a screen for the door of the Tent, of blue, and purple, and scarlet, and fine twined linen, the work of the embroiderer. 37 You shall make for the screen five pillars of acacia, and overlay them with gold. Their hooks shall be of gold. You shall cast five sockets of bronze for them.

27

1 "You shall make the altar of acacia wood, five cubits[a] long, and five cubits wide. The altar shall be square. Its height shall be three cubits.[b] 2 You shall make its horns on its four corners. Its horns shall be of one piece with it. You shall overlay it with bronze. 3 You shall make its pots to take away its ashes; and its shovels, its basins, its meat hooks, and its fire pans. You shall make all its vessels of bronze. 4 You shall make a grating for it of network of bronze. On the net you shall make four bronze rings in its four corners. 5 You shall put it under the ledge around the altar beneath, that the net may reach halfway up the altar. 6 You shall make poles for the altar, poles of acacia wood, and overlay them with bronze. 7 Its poles shall be put into the rings, and the poles shall be on the two sides of the altar when carrying it. 8 You shall make it hollow with planks. They shall make it as it has been shown you on the mountain.

9 "You shall make the court of the tabernacle: for the south side southward there shall be hangings for the court of fine twined linen one hundred cubits long for one side. 10 Its pillars shall be twenty, and their sockets twenty, of bronze. The hooks of the pillars and their fillets shall be of silver. 11 Likewise for the length of the north side, there shall be hangings one hundred cubits long, and its pillars twenty, and their sockets twenty, of bronze; the hooks of the pillars, and their fillets, of silver. 12 For the width of the court on the west side shall be hangings of fifty cubits; their pillars ten, and their sockets ten. 13 The width of the court on the east side eastward shall be fifty cubits. 14 The hangings for the one side of the gate shall be fifteen cubits; their pillars three, and their sockets three. 15 For the other side shall be hangings of fifteen cubits; their pillars three, and their sockets three. 16 For the gate of the court shall be a screen of twenty cubits, of blue and purple, and scarlet, and fine twined linen, the work of the embroiderer; their pillars four, and their sockets four. 17 All the pillars of the court around shall be filleted with silver; their hooks of silver, and their sockets of bronze. 18 The length of the court shall be one hundred cubits, and the width fifty throughout, and the height five cubits, of fine twined linen, and their sockets of bronze. 19 All the instruments of the tabernacle in all its service, and all its pins, and all the pins of the court, shall be of bronze.

20 "You shall command the children of Israel, that they bring to you pure olive oil beaten for the light, to cause a lamp to burn continually. 21 In the Tent of Meeting, outside the veil which is before the covenant, Aaron and his sons shall keep it in order from evening to morning before the LORD: it shall be a statute forever throughout their generations on the behalf of the children of Israel.

28

1 "Bring Aaron your brother, and his sons with him, near to you from amongst the children of Israel, that he may minister to me in the priest's office: Aaron, with Nadab, Abihu, Eleazar, and Ithamar, Aaron's sons. 2 You shall make holy garments for Aaron your brother, for glory and for beauty. 3 You shall speak to all who are wise-hearted, whom I have filled with the spirit of wisdom, that they make Aaron's garments to sanctify him, that he may minister to me in the priest's office. 4 These are the garments which they shall make: a breastplate, an ephod, a robe, a fitted tunic, a turban, and a sash. They shall make holy garments for Aaron your brother and his sons, that he may minister to me in the priest's office. 5 They shall use the gold, and the blue, and the purple, and the scarlet, and the fine linen.

6 "They shall make the ephod of gold, blue, purple, scarlet, and fine twined linen, the work of the skilful workman. 7 It shall have two shoulder straps joined to the two ends of it, that it may be joined together. 8 The skilfully woven band, which is on it, shall be like its work and of the same piece; of gold, blue, purple, scarlet, and fine twined linen. 9 You shall take two onyx stones, and engrave on them the names of the children of Israel. 10 Six of their names on the one stone, and the names of the six that remain on the other stone, in the order of their birth. 11 With the work of an engraver in stone, like the engravings of a signet, you shall engrave the two stones, according to the names of the children of Israel. You shall make them to be enclosed in settings of gold. 12 You shall put the two stones on

the shoulder straps of the ephod, to be stones of memorial for the children of Israel. Aaron shall bear their names before the LORD on his two shoulders for a memorial. 13 You shall make settings of gold, 14 and two chains of pure gold; you shall make them like cords of braided work. You shall put the braided chains on the settings.

15 "You shall make a breastplate of judgement, the work of the skilful workman; like the work of the ephod you shall make it; of gold, of blue, and purple, and scarlet, and fine twined linen, you shall make it. 16 It shall be square and folded double; a span[c] shall be its length, and a span its width. 17 You shall set in it settings of stones, four rows of stones: a row of ruby, topaz, and beryl shall be the first row; 18 and the second row a turquoise, a sapphire,[d] and an emerald; 19 and the third row a jacinth, an agate, and an amethyst; 20 and the fourth row a chrysolite, an onyx, and a jasper. They shall be enclosed in gold in their settings. 21 The stones shall be according to the names of the children of Israel, twelve, according to their names; like the engravings of a signet, everyone according to his name, they shall be for the twelve tribes. 22 You shall make on the breastplate chains like cords, of braided work of pure gold. 23 You shall make on the breastplate two rings of gold, and shall put the two rings on the two ends of the breastplate. 24 You shall put the two braided chains of gold in the two rings at the ends of the breastplate. 25 The other two ends of the two braided chains you shall put on the two settings, and put them on the shoulder straps of the ephod in its forepart. 26 You shall make two rings of gold, and you shall put them on the two ends of the breastplate, on its edge, which is towards the side of the ephod inward. 27 You shall make two rings of gold, and shall put them on the two shoulder straps of the ephod underneath, in its forepart, close by its coupling, above the skilfully woven band of the ephod. 28 They shall bind the breastplate by its rings to the rings of the ephod with a lace of blue, that it may be on the skilfully woven band of the ephod, and that the breastplate may not swing out from the ephod. 29 Aaron shall bear the names of the children of Israel in the breastplate of judgement on his heart, when he goes in to the holy place, for a memorial before the LORD continually. 30 You shall put in the breastplate of judgement the Urim and the Thummim; and they shall be on Aaron's heart, when he goes in before the LORD. Aaron shall bear the judgement of the children of Israel on his heart before the LORD continually.

31 "You shall make the robe of the ephod all of blue. 32 It shall have a hole for the head in the middle of it. It shall have a binding of woven work around its hole, as it were the hole of a coat of mail, that it not be torn. 33 On its hem you shall make pomegranates of blue, and of purple, and of scarlet, all around its hem; with bells of gold between and around them: 34 a golden bell and a pomegranate, a golden bell and a pomegranate, around the hem of the robe. 35 It shall be on Aaron to minister: and its sound shall be heard when he goes in to the holy place before the LORD, and when he comes out, that he not die.

36 "You shall make a plate of pure gold, and engrave on it, like the engravings of a signet, 'HOLY TO THE LORD.' 37 You shall put it on a lace of blue, and it shall be on the sash. It shall be on the front of the sash. 38 It shall be on Aaron's forehead, and Aaron shall bear the iniquity of the holy things, which the children of Israel shall make holy in all their holy gifts; and it shall be always on his forehead, that they may be accepted before the LORD. 39 You shall weave the tunic with fine linen. You shall make a turban of fine linen. You shall make a sash, the work of the embroiderer.

40 "You shall make tunics for Aaron's sons. You shall make sashes for them. You shall make headbands for them, for glory and for beauty. 41 You shall put them on Aaron your brother, and on his sons with him, and shall anoint them, and consecrate them, and sanctify them, that they may minister to me in the priest's office. 42 You shall make them linen pants to cover their naked flesh. They shall reach from the waist even to the thighs. 43 They shall be on Aaron and on his sons, when they go in to the Tent of Meeting, or when they come near to the altar to minister in the holy place, that they don't bear iniquity, and die. This shall be a statute forever to him and to his offspring after him.

29

1 "This is the thing that you shall do to them to make them holy, to minister to me in the priest's office: take one young bull and two rams without defect, 2 unleavened bread, unleavened cakes mixed with oil, and unleavened wafers anointed with oil. You shall make them of fine wheat flour. 3 You shall put them into one basket, and bring them in the basket, with the bull and the two rams. 4 You shall bring Aaron and his sons to the door of the Tent of Meeting, and shall wash them with water. 5 You shall take the garments, and put on Aaron the tunic, the robe of the ephod, the ephod, and the breastplate, and clothe him with the skilfully woven band of the ephod. 6 You shall set the turban on his head, and put the holy crown on the turban. 7 Then you shall take the anointing oil, and pour it on his head, and anoint him. 8 You shall bring his sons, and put tunics on them. 9 You shall clothe them with belts, Aaron and his sons, and bind headbands on them. They shall have the priesthood by a perpetual statute. You shall consecrate Aaron and his sons.

10 "You shall bring the bull before the Tent of Meeting; and Aaron and his sons shall lay their hands on the head of the bull. 11 You shall kill the bull before the LORD at the door of the Tent of Meeting. 12 You shall take of the blood of the bull, and put it on the horns of the altar with your finger; and you shall pour out all the blood at the base of the altar. 13 You shall

---

a 27:1 A cubit is the length from the tip of the middle finger to the elbow on a man's arm, or about 18 inches or 46 centimetres.
b 27:1 The altar was to be about 2.3×2.3×1.4 metres or about 7½×7½×4½ feet.

c 28:16 A span is the length from the tip of a man's thumb to the tip of his little finger when his hand is stretched out (about half a cubit, or 9 inches, or 22.8 cm.)
d 28:18 or, lapis lazuli

take all the fat that covers the innards, the cover of the liver, the two kidneys, and the fat that is on them, and burn them on the altar. ₁₄ But the meat of the bull, and its skin, and its dung, you shall burn with fire outside of the camp. It is a sin offering.

₁₅ "You shall also take the one ram, and Aaron and his sons shall lay their hands on the head of the ram. ₁₆ You shall kill the ram, and you shall take its blood, and sprinkle it around on the altar. ₁₇ You shall cut the ram into its pieces, and wash its innards, and its legs, and put them with its pieces, and with its head. ₁₈ You shall burn the whole ram on the altar: it is a burnt offering to the LORD; it is a pleasant aroma, an offering made by fire to the LORD.

₁₉ "You shall take the other ram, and Aaron and his sons shall lay their hands on the head of the ram. ₂₀ Then you shall kill the ram, and take some of its blood, and put it on the tip of the right ear of Aaron, and on the tip of the right ear of his sons, and on the thumb of their right hand, and on the big toe of their right foot; and sprinkle the blood around on the altar. ₂₁ You shall take of the blood that is on the altar, and of the anointing oil, and sprinkle it on Aaron, and on his garments, and on his sons, and on the garments of his sons with him: and he shall be made holy, and his garments, and his sons, and his sons' garments with him. ₂₂ Also you shall take some of the ram's fat, the fat tail, the fat that covers the innards, the cover of the liver, the two kidneys, the fat that is on them, and the right thigh (for it is a ram of consecration), ₂₃ and one loaf of bread, one cake of oiled bread, and one wafer out of the basket of unleavened bread that is before the LORD. ₂₄ You shall put all of this in Aaron's hands, and in his sons' hands, and shall wave them for a wave offering before the LORD. ₂₅ You shall take them from their hands, and burn them on the altar on the burnt offering, for a pleasant aroma before the LORD: it is an offering made by fire to the LORD.

₂₆ "You shall take the breast of Aaron's ram of consecration, and wave it for a wave offering before the LORD. It shall be your portion. ₂₇ You shall sanctify the breast of the wave offering and the thigh of the wave offering, which is waved, and which is raised up, of the ram of consecration, even of that which is for Aaron, and of that which is for his sons. ₂₈ It shall be for Aaron and his sons as their portion forever from the children of Israel; for it is a wave offering. It shall be a wave offering from the children of Israel of the sacrifices of their peace offerings, even their wave offering to the LORD.

₂₉ "The holy garments of Aaron shall be for his sons after him, to be anointed in them, and to be consecrated in them. ₃₀ Seven days shall the son who is priest in his place put them on, when he comes into the Tent of Meeting to minister in the holy place.

₃₁ "You shall take the ram of consecration and boil its meat in a holy place. ₃₂ Aaron and his sons shall eat the meat of the ram, and the bread that is in the basket, at the door of the Tent of Meeting. ₃₃ They shall eat those things with which atonement was made, to consecrate and sanctify them; but a stranger shall not eat of it, because they are holy. ₃₄ If anything of the meat of the consecration, or of the bread, remains to the morning, then you shall burn the remainder with fire. It shall not be eaten, because it is holy.

₃₅ "You shall do so to Aaron and to his sons, according to all that I have commanded you. You shall consecrate them seven days. ₃₆ Every day you shall offer the bull of sin offering for atonement. You shall cleanse the altar when you make atonement for it. You shall anoint it, to sanctify it. ₃₇ Seven days you shall make atonement for the altar, and sanctify it; and the altar shall be most holy. Whatever touches the altar shall be holy.

₃₈ "Now this is that which you shall offer on the altar: two lambs a year old day by day continually. ₃₉ The one lamb you shall offer in the morning; and the other lamb you shall offer at evening; ₄₀ and with the one lamb a tenth part of an ephah[a] of fine flour mixed with the fourth part of a hin[b] of beaten oil, and the fourth part of a hin of wine for a drink offering. ₄₁ The other lamb you shall offer at evening, and shall do to it according to the meal offering of the morning and according to its drink offering, for a pleasant aroma, an offering made by fire to the LORD. ₄₂ It shall be a continual burnt offering throughout your generations at the door of the Tent of Meeting before the LORD, where I will meet with you, to speak there to you. ₄₃ There I will meet with the children of Israel; and the place shall be sanctified by my glory. ₄₄ I will sanctify the Tent of Meeting and the altar. I will also sanctify Aaron and his sons to minister to me in the priest's office. ₄₅ I will dwell amongst the children of Israel, and will be their God. ₄₆ They shall know that I am the LORD their God, who brought them out of the land of Egypt, that I might dwell amongst them: I am the LORD their God.

30

₁ "You shall make an altar to burn incense on. You shall make it of acacia wood. ₂ Its length shall be a cubit,[c] and its width a cubit. It shall be square, and its height shall be two cubits. Its horns shall be of one piece with it. ₃ You shall overlay it with pure gold, its top, its sides around it, and its horns; and you shall make a gold moulding around it. ₄ You shall make two golden rings for it under its moulding; on its two ribs, on its two sides you shall make them; and they shall be for places for poles with which to bear it. ₅ You shall make the poles of acacia wood, and overlay them with gold. ₆ You shall put it before the veil that is by the ark of the covenant,

before the mercy seat that is over the covenant, where I will meet with you. ₇ Aaron shall burn incense of sweet spices on it every morning. When he tends the lamps, he shall burn it. ₈ When Aaron lights the lamps at evening, he shall burn it, a perpetual incense before the LORD throughout your generations. ₉ You shall offer no strange incense on it, nor burnt offering, nor meal offering; and you shall pour no drink offering on it. ₁₀ Aaron shall make atonement on its horns once in the year; with the blood of the sin offering of atonement once in the year he shall make atonement for it throughout your generations. It is most holy to the LORD."

₁₁ The LORD spoke to Moses, saying, ₁₂ "When you take a census of the children of Israel, according to those who are counted amongst them, then each man shall give a ransom for his soul to the LORD when you count them, that there be no plague amongst them when you count them. ₁₃ They shall give this, everyone who passes over to those who are counted, half a shekel according to the shekel[d] of the sanctuary (the shekel is twenty gerahs[e]); half a shekel for an offering to the LORD. ₁₄ Everyone who passes over to those who are counted, from twenty years old and upward, shall give the offering to the LORD. ₁₅ The rich shall not give more, and the poor shall not give less, than the half shekel,[f] when they give the offering of the LORD, to make atonement for your souls. ₁₆ You shall take the atonement money from the children of Israel, and shall appoint it for the service of the Tent of Meeting; that it may be a memorial for the children of Israel before the LORD, to make atonement for your souls."

₁₇ The LORD spoke to Moses, saying, ₁₈ "You shall also make a basin of bronze, and its base of bronze, in which to wash. You shall put it between the Tent of Meeting and the altar, and you shall put water in it. ₁₉ Aaron and his sons shall wash their hands and their feet in it. ₂₀ When they go into the Tent of Meeting, they shall wash with water, that they not die; or when they come near to the altar to minister, to burn an offering made by fire to the LORD. ₂₁ So they shall wash their hands and their feet, that they not die. This shall be a statute forever to them, even to him and to his descendants throughout their generations."

₂₂ Moreover the LORD spoke to Moses, saying, ₂₃ "Also take fine spices: of liquid myrrh, five hundred shekels;[g] and of fragrant cinnamon half as much, even two hundred and fifty; and of fragrant cane, two hundred and fifty; ₂₄ and of cassia five hundred, according to the shekel of the sanctuary; and a hin[h] of olive oil. ₂₅ You shall make it into a holy anointing oil, a perfume compounded after the art of the perfumer: it shall be a holy anointing oil. ₂₆ You shall use it to anoint the Tent of Meeting, the ark of the covenant, ₂₇ the table and all its articles, the lamp stand and its accessories, the altar of incense, ₂₈ the altar of burnt offering with all its utensils, and the basin with its base. ₂₉ You shall sanctify them, that they may be most holy. Whatever touches them shall be holy. ₃₀ You shall anoint Aaron and his sons, and sanctify them, that they may minister to me in the priest's office. ₃₁ You shall speak to the children of Israel, saying, 'This shall be a holy anointing oil to me throughout your generations. ₃₂ It shall not be poured on man's flesh, and do not make any like it, according to its composition. It is holy. It shall be holy to you. ₃₃ Whoever compounds any like it, or whoever puts any of it on a stranger, he shall be cut off from his people.'"

₃₄ The LORD said to Moses, "Take to yourself sweet spices, gum resin, onycha, and galbanum: sweet spices with pure frankincense. There shall be an equal weight of each. ₃₅ You shall make incense of it, a perfume after the art of the perfumer, seasoned with salt, pure and holy. ₃₆ You shall beat some of it very small, and put some of it before the covenant in the Tent of Meeting, where I will meet with you. It shall be to you most holy. ₃₇ You shall not make this incense, according to its composition, for yourselves: it shall be to you holy for the LORD. ₃₈ Whoever shall make any like that, to smell of it, he shall be cut off from his people."

31

₁ The LORD spoke to Moses, saying, ₂ "Behold, I have called by name Bezalel the son of Uri, the son of Hur, of the tribe of Judah. ₃ I have filled him with the Spirit of God, in wisdom, and in understanding, and in knowledge, and in all kinds of workmanship, ₄ to devise skilful works, to work in gold, and in silver, and in bronze, ₅ and in cutting of stones for setting, and in carving of wood, to work in all kinds of workmanship. ₆ Behold, I myself have appointed with him Oholiab, the son of Ahisamach, of the tribe of Dan; and in the heart of all who are wise-hearted I have put wisdom, that they may make all that I have commanded you: ₇ the Tent of Meeting, the ark of the covenant, the mercy seat that is on it, all the furniture of the Tent, ₈ the table and its vessels, the pure lamp stand with all its vessels, the altar of incense, ₉ the altar of burnt offering with all its vessels, the basin and its base, ₁₀ the finely worked garments—the holy garments for Aaron the priest, the garments of his sons to minister in the priest's office— ₁₁ the anointing oil, and the incense of sweet spices for the holy place: according to all that I have commanded you they shall do."

₁₂ The LORD spoke to Moses, saying, ₁₃ "Speak also to the children of Israel, saying, 'Most certainly you shall keep my Sabbaths; for it is a sign between me and you throughout your generations, that you may know that I am the LORD who sanctifies you. ₁₄ You shall keep the Sabbath therefore, for it is holy to you. Everyone who profanes it shall surely be put to death;

---

a *29:40* 1 ephah is about 22 litres or about 2/3 of a bushel
b *29:40* A hin is about 6.5 litres or 1.7 gallons, so a fourth of a hin is about 1.6 litres.
c *30:2* A cubit is the length from the tip of the middle finger to the elbow on a man's arm, or about 18 inches or 46 centimetres.
d *30:13* A shekel is about 10 grams or about 0.35 ounces.

e *30:13* a gerah is about 0.5 grams or about 7.7 grains
f *30:15* A shekel is about 10 grams or about 0.35 ounces.
g *30:23* A shekel is about 10 grams or about 0.35 ounces, so 500 shekels is about 5 kilograms or about 11 pounds.
h *30:24* A hin is about 6.5 litres or 1.7 gallons.

for whoever does any work therein, that soul shall be cut off from amongst his people. 15 Six days shall work be done, but on the seventh day is a Sabbath of solemn rest, holy to the LORD. Whoever does any work on the Sabbath day shall surely be put to death. 16 Therefore the children of Israel shall keep the Sabbath, to observe the Sabbath throughout their generations, for a perpetual covenant. 17 It is a sign between me and the children of Israel forever; for in six days the LORD made heaven and earth, and on the seventh day he rested, and was refreshed.'"

18 When he finished speaking with him on Mount Sinai, he gave Moses the two tablets of the covenant, stone tablets, written with God's finger.

32

1 When the people saw that Moses delayed coming down from the mountain, the people gathered themselves together to Aaron, and said to him, "Come, make us gods, which shall go before us; for as for this Moses, the man who brought us up out of the land of Egypt, we don't know what has become of him."

2 Aaron said to them, "Take off the golden rings, which are in the ears of your wives, of your sons, and of your daughters, and bring them to me."

3 All the people took off the golden rings which were in their ears, and brought them to Aaron. 4 He received what they handed him, fashioned it with an engraving tool, and made it a moulded calf. Then they said, "These are your gods, Israel, which brought you up out of the land of Egypt."

5 When Aaron saw this, he built an altar before it; and Aaron made a proclamation, and said, "Tomorrow shall be a feast to the LORD."

6 They rose up early on the next day, and offered burnt offerings, and brought peace offerings; and the people sat down to eat and to drink, and rose up to play.

7 The LORD spoke to Moses, "Go, get down; for your people, whom you brought up out of the land of Egypt, have corrupted themselves! 8 They have turned away quickly out of the way which I commanded them. They have made themselves a moulded calf, and have worshipped it, and have sacrificed to it, and said, 'These are your gods, Israel, which brought you up out of the land of Egypt.'"

9 The LORD said to Moses, "I have seen these people, and behold, they are a stiff-necked people. 10 Now therefore leave me alone, that my wrath may burn hot against them, and that I may consume them; and I will make of you a great nation."

11 Moses begged the LORD his God, and said, "LORD, why does your wrath burn hot against your people, that you have brought out of the land of Egypt with great power and with a mighty hand? 12 Why should the Egyptians talk, saying, 'He brought them out for evil, to kill them in the mountains, and to consume them from the surface of the earth'? Turn from your fierce wrath, and turn away from this evil against your people. 13 Remember Abraham, Isaac, and Israel, your servants, to whom you swore by your own self, and said to them, 'I will multiply your offspring[a] as the stars of the sky, and all this land that I have spoken of I will give to your offspring, and they shall inherit it forever.'"

14 So The LORD turned away from the evil which he said he would do to his people.

15 Moses turned, and went down from the mountain, with the two tablets of the covenant in his hand; tablets that were written on both their sides. They were written on one side and on the other. 16 The tablets were the work of God, and the writing was the writing of God, engraved on the tablets.

17 When Joshua heard the noise of the people as they shouted, he said to Moses, "There is the noise of war in the camp."

18 He said, "It isn't the voice of those who shout for victory. It is not the voice of those who cry for being overcome; but the noise of those who sing that I hear." 19 As soon as he came near to the camp, he saw the calf and the dancing. Then Moses' anger grew hot, and he threw the tablets out of his hands, and broke them beneath the mountain. 20 He took the calf which they had made, and burnt it with fire, ground it to powder, and scattered it on the water, and made the children of Israel drink it.

21 Moses said to Aaron, "What did these people do to you, that you have brought a great sin on them?"

22 Aaron said, "Don't let the anger of my lord grow hot. You know the people, that they are set on evil. 23 For they said to me, 'Make us gods, which shall go before us. As for this Moses, the man who brought us up out of the land of Egypt, we don't know what has become of him.' 24 I said to them, 'Whoever has any gold, let them take it off.' So they gave it to me; and I threw it into the fire, and out came this calf."

25 When Moses saw that the people were out of control, (for Aaron had let them lose control, causing derision amongst their enemies), 26 then Moses stood in the gate of the camp, and said, "Whoever is on the LORD's side, come to me!"

All the sons of Levi gathered themselves together to him. 27 He said to them, "The LORD, the God of Israel, says, 'Every man put his sword on his thigh, and go back and forth from gate to gate throughout the camp, and every man kill his brother, and every man his companion, and every man his neighbour.'" 28 The sons of Levi did according to the word of Moses. About three thousand men fell of the people that day. 29 Moses said, "Consecrate yourselves today to the LORD, for every man was against his son and against his brother, that he may give you a blessing today."

30 On the next day, Moses said to the people, "You have sinned a great sin. Now I will go up to the LORD. Perhaps I shall make atonement for your sin."

31 Moses returned to the LORD, and said, "Oh, this people have sinned a great sin, and have made themselves gods of gold. 32 Yet now, if you will, forgive their sin—and if not, please blot me out of your book which you have written."

33 The LORD said to Moses, "Whoever has sinned against me, I will blot him out of my book. 34 Now go, lead the people to the place of which I have spoken to you. Behold, my angel shall go before you. Nevertheless, in the day when I punish, I will punish them for their sin." 35 The LORD struck the people, because of what they did with the calf, which Aaron made.

33

1 The LORD spoke to Moses, "Depart, go up from here, you and the people that you have brought up out of the land of Egypt, to the land of which I swore to Abraham, to Isaac, and to Jacob, saying, 'I will give it to your offspring.' 2 I will send an angel before you; and I will drive out the Canaanite, the Amorite, and the Hittite, and the Perizzite, the Hivite, and the Jebusite. 3 Go to a land flowing with milk and honey; but I will not go up amongst you, for you are a stiff-necked people, lest I consume you on the way."

4 When the people heard this evil news, they mourned; and no one put on his jewellery.

5 The LORD had said to Moses, "Tell the children of Israel, 'You are a stiff-necked people. If I were to go up amongst you for one moment, I would consume you. Therefore now take off your jewellery from you, that I may know what to do to you.'"

6 The children of Israel stripped themselves of their jewellery from Mount Horeb onward.

7 Now Moses used to take the tent and pitch it outside the camp, far away from the camp, and he called it "The Tent of Meeting." Everyone who sought the LORD went out to the Tent of Meeting, which was outside the camp. 8 When Moses went out to the Tent, all the people rose up, and stood, everyone at their tent door, and watched Moses, until he had gone into the Tent. 9 When Moses entered into the Tent, the pillar of cloud descended, stood at the door of the Tent, and the LORD spoke with Moses. 10 All the people saw the pillar of cloud stand at the door of the Tent, and all the people rose up and worshipped, everyone at their tent door. 11 The LORD spoke to Moses face to face, as a man speaks to his friend. He turned again into the camp, but his servant Joshua, the son of Nun, a young man, didn't depart from the Tent.

12 Moses said to the LORD, "Behold, you tell me, 'Bring up this people;' and you haven't let me know whom you will send with me. Yet you have said, 'I know you by name, and you have also found favour in my sight.' 13 Now therefore, if I have found favour in your sight, please show me your way, now, that I may know you, so that I may find favour in your sight; and consider that this nation is your people."

14 He said, "My presence will go with you, and I will give you rest."

15 Moses said to him, "If your presence doesn't go with me, don't carry us up from here. 16 For how would people know that I have found favour in your sight, I and your people? Isn't it that you go with us, so that we are separated, I and your people, from all the people who are on the surface of the earth?"

17 The LORD said to Moses, "I will do this thing also that you have spoken; for you have found favour in my sight, and I know you by name."

18 Moses said, "Please show me your glory."

19 He said, "I will make all my goodness pass before you, and will proclaim the LORD's name before you. I will be gracious to whom I will be gracious, and will show mercy on whom I will show mercy." 20 He said, "You cannot see my face, for man may not see me and live." 21 The LORD also said, "Behold, there is a place by me, and you shall stand on the rock. 22 It will happen, while my glory passes by, that I will put you in a cleft of the rock, and will cover you with my hand until I have passed by; 23 then I will take away my hand, and you will see my back; but my face shall not be seen."

34

1 The LORD said to Moses, "Chisel two stone tablets like the first. I will write on the tablets the words that were on the first tablets, which you broke. 2 Be ready by the morning, and come up in the morning to Mount Sinai, and present yourself there to me on the top of the mountain. 3 No one shall come up with you or be seen anywhere on the mountain. Do not let the flocks or herds graze in front of that mountain."

4 He chiselled two tablets of stone like the first; then Moses rose up early in the morning, and went up to Mount Sinai, as the LORD had commanded him, and took in his hand two stone tablets. 5 The LORD descended in the cloud, and stood with him there, and proclaimed the LORD's name. 6 The LORD passed by before him, and proclaimed, "The LORD! The LORD, a merciful and gracious God, slow to anger, and abundant in loving kindness and truth, 7 keeping loving kindness for thousands, forgiving iniquity and disobedience and sin; and who will by no means clear the guilty, visiting the iniquity of the fathers on the children, and on the children's children, on the third and on the fourth generation."

8 Moses hurried and bowed his head towards the earth, and worshipped. 9 He said, "If now I have found favour in your sight, Lord, please let the Lord go amongst us, even though this is a stiff-necked people; pardon our iniquity and our sin, and take us for your inheritance."

---

a *32:13* or, seed

10 He said, "Behold, I make a covenant: before all your people I will do marvels, such as have not been worked in all the earth, nor in any nation; and all the people amongst whom you are shall see the work of the LORD; for it is an awesome thing that I do with you. 11 Observe that which I command you today. Behold, I will drive out before you the Amorite, the Canaanite, the Hittite, the Perizzite, the Hivite, and the Jebusite. 12 Be careful, lest you make a covenant with the inhabitants of the land where you are going, lest it be for a snare amongst you; 13 but you shall break down their altars, and dash in pieces their pillars, and you shall cut down their Asherah poles; 14 for you shall worship no other god; for the LORD, whose name is Jealous, is a jealous God.

15 "Don't make a covenant with the inhabitants of the land, lest they play the prostitute after their gods, and sacrifice to their gods, and one call you and you eat of his sacrifice; 16 and you take of their daughters to your sons, and their daughters play the prostitute after their gods, and make your sons play the prostitute after their gods.

17 "You shall make no cast idols for yourselves.

18 "You shall keep the feast of unleavened bread. Seven days you shall eat unleavened bread, as I commanded you, at the time appointed in the month Abib; for in the month Abib you came out of Egypt.

19 "All that opens the womb is mine; and all your livestock that is male, the firstborn of cow and sheep. 20 You shall redeem the firstborn of a donkey with a lamb. If you will not redeem it, then you shall break its neck. You shall redeem all the firstborn of your sons. No one shall appear before me empty.

21 "Six days you shall work, but on the seventh day you shall rest: in ploughing time and in harvest you shall rest.

22 "You shall observe the feast of weeks with the first fruits of wheat harvest, and the feast of harvest at the year's end. 23 Three times in the year all your males shall appear before the Lord GOD, the God of Israel. 24 For I will drive out nations before you and enlarge your borders; neither shall any man desire your land when you go up to appear before the LORD, your God, three times in the year.

25 "You shall not offer the blood of my sacrifice with leavened bread. The sacrifice of the feast of the Passover shall not be left to the morning.

26 "You shall bring the first of the first fruits of your ground to the house of the LORD your God.

"You shall not boil a young goat in its mother's milk."

27 The LORD said to Moses, "Write these words; for in accordance with these words I have made a covenant with you and with Israel."

28 He was there with the LORD forty days and forty nights; he neither ate bread, nor drank water. He wrote on the tablets the words of the covenant, the ten commandments.

29 When Moses came down from Mount Sinai with the two tablets of the covenant in Moses' hand, when he came down from the mountain, Moses didn't know that the skin of his face shone by reason of his speaking with him. 30 When Aaron and all the children of Israel saw Moses, behold, the skin of his face shone; and they were afraid to come near him. 31 Moses called to them, and Aaron and all the rulers of the congregation returned to him; and Moses spoke to them. 32 Afterward all the children of Israel came near, and he gave them all the commandments that the LORD had spoken with him on Mount Sinai. 33 When Moses was done speaking with them, he put a veil on his face. 34 But when Moses went in before the LORD to speak with him, he took the veil off, until he came out; and he came out, and spoke to the children of Israel that which he was commanded. 35 The children of Israel saw Moses' face, that the skin of Moses' face shone; so Moses put the veil on his face again, until he went in to speak with him.

35

1 Moses assembled all the congregation of the children of Israel, and said to them, "These are the words which the LORD has commanded, that you should do them. 2 'Six days shall work be done, but on the seventh day there shall be a holy day for you, a Sabbath of solemn rest to the LORD: whoever does any work in it shall be put to death. 3 You shall kindle no fire throughout your habitations on the Sabbath day.'"

4 Moses spoke to all the congregation of the children of Israel, saying, "This is the thing which the LORD commanded, saying, 5 'Take from amongst you an offering to the LORD. Whoever is of a willing heart, let him bring it as the LORD's offering: gold, silver, bronze, 6 blue, purple, scarlet, fine linen, goats' hair, 7 rams' skins dyed red, sea cow hides, acacia wood, 8 oil for the light, spices for the anointing oil and for the sweet incense, 9 onyx stones, and stones to be set for the ephod and for the breastplate.

10 "'Let every wise-hearted man amongst you come, and make all that the LORD has commanded: 11 the tabernacle, its outer covering, its roof, its clasps, its boards, its bars, its pillars, and its sockets; 12 the ark, and its poles, the mercy seat, the veil of the screen; 13 the table with its poles and all its vessels, and the show bread; 14 the lamp stand also for the light, with its vessels, its lamps, and the oil for the light; 15 and the altar of incense with its poles, the anointing oil, the sweet incense, the screen for the door, at the door of the tabernacle; 16 the altar of burnt offering, with its grating of bronze, its poles, and all its vessels, the basin and its base; 17 the hangings of the court, its pillars, their sockets, and the screen for the gate of the court; 18 the pins of the tabernacle, the pins of the court, and their cords; 19 the finely worked garments for ministering in the holy place—the holy garments for Aaron the priest, and the garments of his sons—to minister in the priest's office.'"

20 All the congregation of the children of Israel departed from the presence of Moses. 21 They came, everyone whose heart stirred him up, and everyone whom his spirit made willing, and brought the LORD's offering for the work of the Tent of Meeting, and for all of its service, and for the holy garments. 22 They came, both men and women, as many as were willing-hearted, and brought brooches, earrings, signet rings, and armlets, all jewels of gold; even every man who offered an offering of gold to the LORD. 23 Everyone with whom was found blue, purple, scarlet, fine linen, goats' hair, rams' skins dyed red, and sea cow hides, brought them. 24 Everyone who offered an offering of silver and bronze brought the LORD's offering; and everyone with whom was found acacia wood for any work of the service, brought it. 25 All the women who were wise-hearted spun with their hands, and brought that which they had spun: the blue, the purple, the scarlet, and the fine linen. 26 All the women whose heart stirred them up in wisdom spun the goats' hair. 27 The rulers brought the onyx stones and the stones to be set for the ephod and for the breastplate; 28 with the spice and the oil for the light, for the anointing oil, and for the sweet incense. 29 The children of Israel brought a free will offering to the LORD; every man and woman whose heart made them willing to bring for all the work, which the LORD had commanded to be made by Moses.

30 Moses said to the children of Israel, "Behold, the LORD has called by name Bezalel the son of Uri, the son of Hur, of the tribe of Judah. 31 He has filled him with the Spirit of God, in wisdom, in understanding, in knowledge, and in all kinds of workmanship; 32 and to make skilful works, to work in gold, in silver, in bronze, 33 in cutting of stones for setting, and in carving of wood, to work in all kinds of skilful workmanship. 34 He has put in his heart that he may teach, both he and Oholiab, the son of Ahisamach, of the tribe of Dan. 35 He has filled them with wisdom of heart to work all kinds of workmanship, of the engraver, of the skilful workman, and of the embroiderer, in blue, in purple, in scarlet, and in fine linen, and of the weaver, even of those who do any workmanship, and of those who make skilful works.

36

1 "Bezalel and Oholiab shall work with every wise-hearted man, in whom the LORD has put wisdom and understanding to know how to do all the work for the service of the sanctuary, according to all that the LORD has commanded."

2 Moses called Bezalel and Oholiab, and every wise-hearted man, in whose heart the LORD had put wisdom, even everyone whose heart stirred him up to come to the work to do it. 3 They received from Moses all the offering which the children of Israel had brought for the work of the service of the sanctuary, with which to make it. They kept bringing free will offerings to him every morning. 4 All the wise men, who performed all the work of the sanctuary, each came from his work which he did. 5 They spoke to Moses, saying, "The people have brought much more than enough for the service of the work which the LORD commanded to make."

6 Moses gave a commandment, and they caused it to be proclaimed throughout the camp, saying, "Let neither man nor woman make anything else for the offering for the sanctuary." So the people were restrained from bringing. 7 For the stuff they had was sufficient to do all the work, and too much.

8 All the wise-hearted men amongst those who did the work made the tabernacle with ten curtains of fine twined linen, blue, purple, and scarlet. They made them with cherubim, the work of a skilful workman. 9 The length of each curtain was twenty-eight cubits,ª and the width of each curtain four cubits. All the curtains had one measure. 10 He coupled five curtains to one another, and the other five curtains he coupled to one another. 11 He made loops of blue on the edge of the one curtain from the edge in the coupling. Likewise he made in the edge of the curtain that was outermost in the second coupling. 12 He made fifty loops in the one curtain, and he made fifty loops in the edge of the curtain that was in the second coupling. The loops were opposite to one another. 13 He made fifty clasps of gold, and coupled the curtains to one another with the clasps: so the tabernacle was a unit.

14 He made curtains of goats' hair for a covering over the tabernacle. He made them eleven curtains. 15 The length of each curtain was thirty cubits, and four cubits the width of each curtain. The eleven curtains had one measure. 16 He coupled five curtains by themselves, and six curtains by themselves. 17 He made fifty loops on the edge of the curtain that was outermost in the coupling, and he made fifty loops on the edge of the curtain which was outermost in the second coupling. 18 He made fifty clasps of bronze to couple the tent together, that it might be a unit. 19 He made a covering for the tent of rams' skins dyed red, and a covering of sea cow hides above.

20 He made the boards for the tabernacle of acacia wood, standing up. 21 Ten cubits was the length of a board, and a cubit and a half the width of each board. 22 Each board had two tenons, joined to one another. He made all the boards of the tabernacle this way. 23 He made the boards for the tabernacle, twenty boards for the south side southward. 24 He made forty sockets of silver under the twenty boards: two sockets under one board for its two tenons, and two sockets under another board for its two tenons. 25 For the second side of the tabernacle, on the north side, he made twenty boards 26 and their forty sockets of silver: two sockets under one board, and two sockets under another board. 27 For the far part of the tabernacle westward he made six boards. 28 He made two boards for the corners of the

---

ª 36:9 A cubit is the length from the tip of the middle finger to the elbow on a man's arm, or about 18 inches or 46 centimetres.

tabernacle in the far part. 29 They were double beneath, and in the same way they were all the way to its top to one ring. He did this to both of them in the two corners. 30 There were eight boards and their sockets of silver, sixteen sockets—under every board two sockets.

31 He made bars of acacia wood: five for the boards of the one side of the tabernacle, 32 and five bars for the boards of the other side of the tabernacle, and five bars for the boards of the tabernacle for the hinder part westward. 33 He made the middle bar to pass through in the middle of the boards from the one end to the other. 34 He overlaid the boards with gold, and made their rings of gold as places for the bars, and overlaid the bars with gold.

35 He made the veil of blue, purple, scarlet, and fine twined linen, with cherubim. He made it the work of a skilful workman. 36 He made four pillars of acacia for it, and overlaid them with gold. Their hooks were of gold. He cast four sockets of silver for them. 37 He made a screen for the door of the tent, of blue, purple, scarlet, and fine twined linen, the work of an embroiderer; 38 and the five pillars of it with their hooks. He overlaid their capitals and their fillets with gold, and their five sockets were of bronze.

37

1 Bezalel made the ark of acacia wood. Its length was two and a half cubits,ᵃ and its width a cubit and a half, and a cubit and a half its height. 2 He overlaid it with pure gold inside and outside, and made a moulding of gold for it around it. 3 He cast four rings of gold for it in its four feet—two rings on its one side, and two rings on its other side. 4 He made poles of acacia wood and overlaid them with gold. 5 He put the poles into the rings on the sides of the ark, to bear the ark. 6 He made a mercy seat of pure gold. Its length was two and a half cubits, and a cubit and a half its width. 7 He made two cherubim of gold. He made them of beaten work, at the two ends of the mercy seat: 8 one cherub at the one end, and one cherub at the other end. He made the cherubim of one piece with the mercy seat at its two ends. 9 The cherubim spread out their wings above, covering the mercy seat with their wings, with their faces towards one another. The faces of the cherubim were towards the mercy seat.

10 He made the table of acacia wood. Its length was two cubits, and its width was a cubit, and its height was a cubit and a half. 11 He overlaid it with pure gold, and made a gold moulding around it. 12 He made a border of a hand's width around it, and made a golden moulding on its border around it. 13 He cast four rings of gold for it, and put the rings in the four corners that were on its four feet. 14 The rings were close by the border, the places for the poles to carry the table. 15 He made the poles of acacia wood, and overlaid them with gold, to carry the table. 16 He made the vessels which were on the table, its dishes, its spoons, its bowls, and its pitchers with which to pour out, of pure gold.

17 He made the lamp stand of pure gold. He made the lamp stand of beaten work. Its base, its shaft, its cups, its buds, and its flowers were of one piece with it. 18 There were six branches going out of its sides: three branches of the lamp stand out of its one side, and three branches of the lamp stand out of its other side: 19 three cups made like almond blossoms in one branch, a bud and a flower, and three cups made like almond blossoms in the other branch, a bud and a flower; so for the six branches going out of the lamp stand. 20 In the lamp stand were four cups made like almond blossoms, its buds and its flowers; 21 and a bud under two branches of one piece with it, and a bud under two branches of one piece with it, and a bud under two branches of one piece with it, for the six branches going out of it. 22 Their buds and their branches were of one piece with it. The whole thing was one beaten work of pure gold. 23 He made its seven lamps, and its snuffers, and its snuff dishes, of pure gold. 24 He made it of a talentᵇ of pure gold, with all its vessels.

25 He made the altar of incense of acacia wood. It was square: its length was a cubit, and its width a cubit. Its height was two cubits. Its horns were of one piece with it. 26 He overlaid it with pure gold: its top, its sides around it, and its horns. He made a gold moulding around it. 27 He made two golden rings for it under its moulding crown, on its two ribs, on its two sides, for places for poles with which to carry it. 28 He made the poles of acacia wood, and overlaid them with gold. 29 He made the holy anointing oil and the pure incense of sweet spices, after the art of the perfumer.

38

1 He made the altar of burnt offering of acacia wood. It was square. Its length was five cubits,ᶜ its width was five cubits, and its height was three cubits. 2 He made its horns on its four corners. Its horns were of one piece with it, and he overlaid it with bronze. 3 He made all the vessels of the altar: the pots, the shovels, the basins, the forks, and the fire pans. He made all its vessels of bronze. 4 He made for the altar a grating of a network of bronze, under the ledge around it beneath, reaching halfway up. 5 He cast four rings for the four corners of bronze grating, to be places for the poles. 6 He made the poles of acacia wood, and overlaid them with bronze. 7 He

put the poles into the rings on the sides of the altar, with which to carry it. He made it hollow with planks.

8 He made the basin of bronze, and its base of bronze, out of the mirrors of the ministering women who ministered at the door of the Tent of Meeting.

9 He made the court: for the south side southward the hangings of the court were of fine twined linen, one hundred cubits; 10 their pillars were twenty, and their sockets twenty, of bronze; the hooks of the pillars and their fillets were of silver. 11 For the north side one hundred cubits, their pillars twenty, and their sockets twenty, of bronze; the hooks of the pillars, and their fillets, of silver. 12 For the west side were hangings of fifty cubits, their pillars ten, and their sockets ten; the hooks of the pillars, and their fillets, of silver. 13 For the east side eastward fifty cubits, 14 the hangings for the one side were fifteen cubits; their pillars three, and their sockets three; 15 and so for the other side: on this hand and that hand by the gate of the court were hangings of fifteen cubits; their pillars three, and their sockets three. 16 All the hangings around the court were of fine twined linen. 17 The sockets for the pillars were of bronze. The hooks of the pillars and their fillets were of silver. Their capitals were overlaid with silver. All the pillars of the court had silver bands. 18 The screen for the gate of the court was the work of the embroiderer, of blue, purple, scarlet, and fine twined linen. Twenty cubits was the length, and the height along the width was five cubits, like the hangings of the court. 19 Their pillars were four, and their sockets four, of bronze; their hooks of silver, and the overlaying of their capitals, and their fillets, of silver. 20 All the pins of the tabernacle, and around the court, were of bronze.

21 These are the amounts of materials used for the tabernacle, even the Tabernacle of the Testimony, as they were counted, according to the commandment of Moses, for the service of the Levites, by the hand of Ithamar, the son of Aaron the priest. 22 Bezalel the son of Uri, the son of Hur, of the tribe of Judah, made all that the LORD commanded Moses. 23 With him was Oholiab, the son of Ahisamach, of the tribe of Dan, an engraver, and a skilful workman, and an embroiderer in blue, in purple, in scarlet, and in fine linen.

24 All the gold that was used for the work in all the work of the sanctuary, even the gold of the offering, was twenty-nine talentsᵈ and seven hundred and thirty shekels, according to the shekelᵉ of the sanctuary. 25 The silver of those who were counted of the congregation was one hundred talentsᶠ and one thousand and seven hundred and seventy-five shekels,ᵍ according to the shekel of the sanctuary: 26 a bekaʰ a head, that is, half a shekel, according to the shekelⁱ of the sanctuary, for everyone who passed over to those who were counted, from twenty years old and upward, for six hundred and three thousand and five hundred and fifty men. 27 The one hundred talentsʲ of silver were for casting the sockets of the sanctuary and the sockets of the veil: one hundred sockets for the one hundred talents, one talent per socket. 28 From the one thousand and seven hundred and seventy-five shekelsᵏ he made hooks for the pillars, overlaid their capitals, and made fillets for them. 29 The bronze of the offering was seventy talentsˡ and two thousand and four hundred shekels.ᵐ 30 With this he made the sockets to the door of the Tent of Meeting, the bronze altar, the bronze grating for it, all the vessels of the altar, 31 the sockets around the court, the sockets of the gate of the court, all the pins of the tabernacle, and all the pins around the court.

39

1 Of the blue, purple, and scarlet, they made finely worked garments for ministering in the holy place, and made the holy garments for Aaron, as the LORD commanded Moses.

2 He made the ephod of gold, blue, purple, scarlet, and fine twined linen. 3 They beat the gold into thin plates, and cut it into wires, to work it in with the blue, the purple, the scarlet, and the fine linen, the work of the skilful workman. 4 They made shoulder straps for it, joined together. It was joined together at the two ends. 5 The skilfully woven band that was on it, with which to fasten it on, was of the same piece, like its work: of gold, of blue, purple, scarlet, and fine twined linen, as the LORD commanded Moses.

6 They worked the onyx stones, enclosed in settings of gold, engraved with the engravings of a signet, according to the names of the children of Israel. 7 He put them on the shoulder straps of the ephod, to be stones of memorial for the children of Israel, as the LORD commanded Moses.

8 He made the breastplate, the work of a skilful workman, like the work of the ephod: of gold, of blue, purple, scarlet, and fine twined linen. 9 It was square. They made the breastplate double. Its length was a span,ⁿ and its width a span, being double. 10 They set in it four rows of stones. A row of ruby, topaz, and beryl was the first row; 11 and the second row, a turquoise, a sapphire,ᵒ and an emerald; 12 and the third row, a jacinth, an agate, and an amethyst; 13 and the fourth row, a chrysolite, an onyx, and a jasper. They

---

ᵃ *37:1* A cubit is the length from the tip of the middle finger to the elbow on a man's arm, or about 18 inches or 46 centimetres.
ᵇ *37:24* A talent is about 30 kilograms or 66 pounds or 965 Troy ounces
ᶜ *38:1* A cubit is the length from the tip of the middle finger to the elbow on a man's arm, or about 18 inches or 46 centimetres.
ᵈ *38:24* A talent is about 30 kilograms or 66 pounds or 965 Troy ounces.
ᵉ *38:24* A shekel is about 10 grams or about 0.32 Troy ounces.
ᶠ *38:25* A talent is about 30 kilograms or 66 pounds
ᵍ *38:25* A shekel is about 10 grams or about 0.35 ounces.
ʰ *38:26* a beka is about 5 grams or about 0.175 ounces

ⁱ *38:26* A shekel is about 10 grams or about 0.35 ounces.
ʲ *38:27* A talent is about 30 kilograms or 66 pounds.
ᵏ *38:28* A shekel is about 10 grams or about 0.35 ounces, so 1775 shekels is about 17.75 kilograms or about 39 pounds.
ˡ *38:29* A talent is about 30 kilograms or 66 pounds
ᵐ *38:29* 70 talents + 2400 shekels is about 2124 kilograms, or 2.124 metric tonnes.
ⁿ *39:9* A span is the length from the tip of a man's thumb to the tip of his little finger when his hand is stretched out (about half a cubit, or 9 inches, or 22.8 cm.)
ᵒ *39:11* or, lapis lazuli

were enclosed in gold settings. 14 The stones were according to the names of the children of Israel, twelve, according to their names; like the engravings of a signet, everyone according to his name, for the twelve tribes. 15 They made on the breastplate chains like cords, of braided work of pure gold. 16 They made two settings of gold, and two gold rings, and put the two rings on the two ends of the breastplate. 17 They put the two braided chains of gold in the two rings at the ends of the breastplate. 18 The other two ends of the two braided chains they put on the two settings, and put them on the shoulder straps of the ephod, in its front. 19 They made two rings of gold, and put them on the two ends of the breastplate, on its edge, which was towards the side of the ephod inward. 20 They made two more rings of gold, and put them on the two shoulder straps of the ephod underneath, in its front, close by its coupling, above the skilfully woven band of the ephod. 21 They bound the breastplate by its rings to the rings of the ephod with a lace of blue, that it might be on the skilfully woven band of the ephod, and that the breastplate might not come loose from the ephod, as the LORD commanded Moses.

22 He made the robe of the ephod of woven work, all of blue. 23 The opening of the robe in the middle of it was like the opening of a coat of mail, with a binding around its opening, that it should not be torn. 24 They made on the skirts of the robe pomegranates of blue, purple, scarlet, and twined linen. 25 They made bells of pure gold, and put the bells between the pomegranates around the skirts of the robe, between the pomegranates; 26 a bell and a pomegranate, a bell and a pomegranate, around the skirts of the robe, to minister in, as the LORD commanded Moses.

27 They made the tunics of fine linen of woven work for Aaron and for his sons, 28 the turban of fine linen, the linen headbands of fine linen, the linen trousers of fine twined linen, 29 the sash of fine twined linen, blue, purple, and scarlet, the work of the embroiderer, as the LORD commanded Moses.

30 They made the plate of the holy crown of pure gold, and wrote on it an inscription, like the engravings of a signet: "HOLY TO THE LORD". 31 They tied to it a lace of blue, to fasten it on the turban above, as the LORD commanded Moses.

32 Thus all the work of the tabernacle of the Tent of Meeting was finished. The children of Israel did according to all that the LORD commanded Moses; so they did. 33 They brought the tabernacle to Moses: the tent, with all its furniture, its clasps, its boards, its bars, its pillars, its sockets, 34 the covering of rams' skins dyed red, the covering of sea cow hides, the veil of the screen, 35 the ark of the covenant with its poles, the mercy seat, 36 the table, all its vessels, the show bread, 37 the pure lamp stand, its lamps, even the lamps to be set in order, all its vessels, the oil for the light, 38 the golden altar, the anointing oil, the sweet incense, the screen for the door of the Tent, 39 the bronze altar, its grating of bronze, its poles, all of its vessels, the basin and its base, 40 the hangings of the court, its pillars, its sockets, the screen for the gate of the court, its cords, its pins, and all the instruments of the service of the tabernacle, for the Tent of Meeting, 41 the finely worked garments for ministering in the holy place, the holy garments for Aaron the priest, and the garments of his sons, to minister in the priest's office. 42 According to all that the LORD commanded Moses, so the children of Israel did all the work. 43 Moses saw all the work, and behold, they had done it as the LORD had commanded. They had done so; and Moses blessed them.

40

1 The LORD spoke to Moses, saying, 2 "On the first day of the first month you shall raise up the tabernacle of the Tent of Meeting. 3 You shall put the ark of the covenant in it, and you shall screen the ark with the veil. 4 You shall bring in the table, and set in order the things that are on it. You shall bring in the lamp stand, and light its lamps. 5 You shall set the golden altar for incense before the ark of the covenant, and put the screen of the door to the tabernacle.

6 "You shall set the altar of burnt offering before the door of the tabernacle of the Tent of Meeting. 7 You shall set the basin between the Tent of Meeting and the altar, and shall put water therein. 8 You shall set up the court around it, and hang up the screen of the gate of the court.

9 "You shall take the anointing oil, and anoint the tabernacle and all that is in it, and shall make it holy, and all its furniture, and it will be holy. 10 You shall anoint the altar of burnt offering, with all its vessels, and sanctify the altar, and the altar will be most holy. 11 You shall anoint the basin and its base, and sanctify it.

12 "You shall bring Aaron and his sons to the door of the Tent of Meeting, and shall wash them with water. 13 You shall put on Aaron the holy garments; and you shall anoint him, and sanctify him, that he may minister to me in the priest's office. 14 You shall bring his sons, and put tunics on them. 15 You shall anoint them, as you anointed their father, that they may minister to me in the priest's office. Their anointing shall be to them for an everlasting priesthood throughout their generations." 16 Moses did so. According to all that the LORD commanded him, so he did.

17 In the first month in the second year, on the first day of the month, the tabernacle was raised up. 18 Moses raised up the tabernacle, and laid its sockets, and set up its boards, and put in its bars, and raised up its pillars. 19 He spread the covering over the tent, and put the roof of the tabernacle above on it, as the LORD commanded Moses. 20 He took and put the covenant into the ark, and set the poles on the ark, and put the mercy seat above on the ark. 21 He brought the ark into the tabernacle, and set up the veil of the screen, and screened the ark of the covenant, as the LORD commanded Moses. 22 He put the table in the Tent of Meeting, on the north side of the tabernacle, outside of the veil. 23 He set the bread in order on it before the LORD, as the LORD commanded Moses. 24 He put the lamp

stand in the Tent of Meeting, opposite the table, on the south side of the tabernacle. 25 He lit the lamps before the LORD, as the LORD commanded Moses. 26 He put the golden altar in the Tent of Meeting before the veil; 27 and he burnt incense of sweet spices on it, as the LORD commanded Moses. 28 He put up the screen of the door to the tabernacle. 29 He set the altar of burnt offering at the door of the tabernacle of the Tent of Meeting, and offered on it the burnt offering and the meal offering, as the LORD commanded Moses. 30 He set the basin between the Tent of Meeting and the altar, and put water therein, with which to wash. 31 Moses, Aaron, and his sons washed their hands and their feet there. 32 When they went into the Tent of Meeting, and when they came near to the altar, they washed, as the LORD commanded Moses. 33 He raised up the court around the tabernacle and the altar, and set up the screen of the gate of the court. So Moses finished the work.

34 Then the cloud covered the Tent of Meeting, and the LORD's glory filled the tabernacle. 35 Moses wasn't able to enter into the Tent of Meeting, because the cloud stayed on it, and the LORD's glory filled the tabernacle. 36 When the cloud was taken up from over the tabernacle, the children of Israel went onward, throughout all their journeys; 37 but if the cloud wasn't taken up, then they didn't travel until the day that it was taken up. 38 For the cloud of the LORD was on the tabernacle by day, and there was fire in the cloud by night, in the sight of all the house of Israel, throughout all their journeys.

The Third Book of Moses, Commonly Called Leviticus

1

1 The LORD[a] called to Moses, and spoke to him from the Tent of Meeting, saying, 2 "Speak to the children of Israel, and tell them, 'When anyone of you offers an offering to the LORD, you shall offer your offering of the livestock, from the herd and from the flock.

3 "'If his offering is a burnt offering from the herd, he shall offer a male without defect. He shall offer it at the door of the Tent of Meeting, that he may be accepted before the LORD. 4 He shall lay his hand on the head of the burnt offering, and it shall be accepted for him to make atonement for him. 5 He shall kill the bull before the LORD. Aaron's sons, the priests, shall present the blood and sprinkle the blood around on the altar that is at the door of the Tent of Meeting. 6 He shall skin the burnt offering and cut it into pieces. 7 The sons of Aaron the priest shall put fire on the altar, and lay wood in order on the fire; 8 and Aaron's sons, the priests, shall lay the pieces, the head, and the fat in order on the wood that is on the fire which is on the altar; 9 but he shall wash its innards and its legs with water. The priest shall burn all of it on the altar, for a burnt offering, an offering made by fire, of a pleasant aroma to the LORD.

10 "'If his offering is from the flock, from the sheep or from the goats, for a burnt offering, he shall offer a male without defect. 11 He shall kill it on the north side of the altar before the LORD. Aaron's sons, the priests, shall sprinkle its blood around on the altar. 12 He shall cut it into its pieces, with its head and its fat. The priest shall lay them in order on the wood that is on the fire which is on the altar, 13 but the innards and the legs he shall wash with water. The priest shall offer the whole, and burn it on the altar. It is a burnt offering, an offering made by fire, of a pleasant aroma to the LORD.

14 "'If his offering to the LORD is a burnt offering of birds, then he shall offer his offering from turtledoves or young pigeons. 15 The priest shall bring it to the altar, and wring off its head, and burn it on the altar; and its blood shall be drained out on the side of the altar; 16 and he shall take away its crop and its feathers, and cast it beside the altar on the east part, in the place of the ashes. 17 He shall tear it by its wings, but shall not divide it apart. The priest shall burn it on the altar, on the wood that is on the fire. It is a burnt offering, an offering made by fire, of a pleasant aroma to the LORD.

2

1 "'When anyone offers an offering of a meal offering to the LORD, his offering shall be of fine flour. He shall pour oil on it, and put frankincense on it. 2 He shall bring it to Aaron's sons, the priests. He shall take his handful of its fine flour, and of its oil, with all its frankincense, and the priest shall burn its memorial on the altar, an offering made by fire, of a pleasant aroma to the LORD. 3 That which is left of the meal offering shall be Aaron's and his sons'. It is a most holy part of the offerings of the LORD made by fire.

4 "'When you offer an offering of a meal offering baked in the oven, it shall be unleavened cakes of fine flour mixed with oil, or unleavened wafers anointed with oil. 5 If your offering is a meal offering made on a griddle, it shall be of unleavened fine flour, mixed with oil. 6 You shall cut it in pieces, and pour oil on it. It is a meal offering. 7 If your offering is a meal offering of the pan, it shall be made of fine flour with oil. 8 You shall bring the meal offering that is made of these things to the LORD. It shall be presented to the priest, and he shall bring it to the altar. 9 The priest shall take from the meal offering its memorial, and shall burn it on the altar, an offering made by fire, of a pleasant aroma to the LORD. 10 That which is left of the meal offering shall be Aaron's and his sons'. It is a most holy part of the offerings of the LORD made by fire.

11 "'No meal offering which you shall offer to the LORD shall be made with yeast; for you shall burn no yeast, nor any honey, as an offering made by fire to the LORD. 12 As an offering of first fruits you shall offer them to the LORD, but they shall not rise up as a pleasant aroma on the altar. 13 Every offering of your meal offering you shall season with salt. You shall not allow the salt of the covenant of your God[b] to be lacking from your meal offering. With all your offerings you shall offer salt.

14 "'If you offer a meal offering of first fruits to the LORD, you shall offer for the meal offering of your first fruits fresh heads of grain parched with fire and crushed. 15 You shall put oil on it and lay frankincense on it. It is a meal offering. 16 The priest shall burn as its memorial part of its crushed grain and part of its oil, along with all its frankincense. It is an offering made by fire to the LORD.

3

1 "'If his offering is a sacrifice of peace offerings, if he offers it from the herd, whether male or female, he shall offer it without defect before the LORD. 2 He shall lay his hand on the head of his offering, and kill it at the door of the Tent of Meeting. Aaron's sons, the priests, shall sprinkle the blood around on the altar. 3 He shall offer of the sacrifice of peace offerings an offering made by fire to the LORD. The fat that covers the innards, and all the fat that is on the innards, 4 and the two kidneys, and the fat that is on them, which is by the loins, and the cover on the liver, with the kidneys, he shall take away. 5 Aaron's sons shall burn it on the altar on the burnt

offering, which is on the wood that is on the fire: it is an offering made by fire, of a pleasant aroma to the LORD.

6 "'If his offering for a sacrifice of peace offerings to the LORD is from the flock, either male or female, he shall offer it without defect. 7 If he offers a lamb for his offering, then he shall offer it before the LORD; 8 and he shall lay his hand on the head of his offering, and kill it before the Tent of Meeting. Aaron's sons shall sprinkle its blood around on the altar. 9 He shall offer from the sacrifice of peace offerings an offering made by fire to the LORD; its fat, the entire tail fat, he shall take away close to the backbone; and the fat that covers the entrails, and all the fat that is on the entrails, 10 and the two kidneys, and the fat that is on them, which is by the loins, and the cover on the liver, with the kidneys, he shall take away. 11 The priest shall burn it on the altar: it is the food of the offering made by fire to the LORD.

12 "'If his offering is a goat, then he shall offer it before the LORD. 13 He shall lay his hand on its head, and kill it before the Tent of Meeting; and the sons of Aaron shall sprinkle its blood around on the altar. 14 He shall offer from it as his offering, an offering made by fire to the LORD; the fat that covers the innards, and all the fat that is on the innards, 15 and the two kidneys, and the fat that is on them, which is by the loins, and the cover on the liver, with the kidneys, he shall take away. 16 The priest shall burn them on the altar: it is the food of the offering made by fire, for a pleasant aroma; all the fat is the LORD's.

17 "'It shall be a perpetual statute throughout your generations in all your dwellings, that you shall eat neither fat nor blood.'"

4

1 The LORD spoke to Moses, saying, 2 "Speak to the children of Israel, saying, 'If anyone sins unintentionally, in any of the things which the LORD has commanded not to be done, and does any one of them, 3 if the anointed priest sins so as to bring guilt on the people, then let him offer for his sin which he has sinned a young bull without defect to the LORD for a sin offering. 4 He shall bring the bull to the door of the Tent of Meeting before the LORD; and he shall lay his hand on the head of the bull, and kill the bull before the LORD. 5 The anointed priest shall take some of the blood of the bull, and bring it to the Tent of Meeting. 6 The priest shall dip his finger in the blood, and sprinkle some of the blood seven times before the LORD, before the veil of the sanctuary. 7 The priest shall put some of the blood on the horns of the altar of sweet incense before the LORD, which is in the Tent of Meeting; and he shall pour out the rest of the blood of the bull at the base of the altar of burnt offering, which is at the door of the Tent of Meeting. 8 He shall take all the fat of the bull of the sin offering from it: the fat that covers the innards, and all the fat that is on the innards, 9 and the two kidneys, and the fat that is on them, which is by the loins, and the cover on the liver, with the kidneys, he shall remove, 10 as it is removed from the bull of the sacrifice of peace offerings. The priest shall burn them on the altar of burnt offering. 11 He shall carry the bull's skin, all its meat, with its head, and with its legs, its innards, and its dung 12—all the rest of the bull—outside of the camp to a clean place where the ashes are poured out, and burn it on wood with fire. It shall be burnt where the ashes are poured out.

13 "'If the whole congregation of Israel sins, and the thing is hidden from the eyes of the assembly, and they have done any of the things which the LORD has commanded not to be done, and are guilty; 14 when the sin in which they have sinned is known, then the assembly shall offer a young bull for a sin offering, and bring it before the Tent of Meeting. 15 The elders of the congregation shall lay their hands on the head of the bull before the LORD; and the bull shall be killed before the LORD. 16 The anointed priest shall bring some of the blood of the bull to the Tent of Meeting. 17 The priest shall dip his finger in the blood and sprinkle it seven times before the LORD, before the veil. 18 He shall put some of the blood on the horns of the altar which is before the LORD, that is in the Tent of Meeting; and the rest of the blood he shall pour out at the base of the altar of burnt offering, which is at the door of the Tent of Meeting. 19 All its fat he shall take from it, and burn it on the altar. 20 He shall do this with the bull; as he did with the bull of the sin offering, so he shall do with this; and the priest shall make atonement for them, and they shall be forgiven. 21 He shall carry the bull outside the camp, and burn it as he burnt the first bull. It is the sin offering for the assembly.

22 "'When a ruler sins, and unwittingly does any one of all the things which the LORD his God has commanded not to be done, and is guilty, 23 if his sin in which he has sinned is made known to him, he shall bring as his offering a goat, a male without defect. 24 He shall lay his hand on the head of the goat, and kill it in the place where they kill the burnt offering before the LORD. It is a sin offering. 25 The priest shall take some of the blood of the sin offering with his finger, and put it on the horns of the altar of burnt offering. He shall pour out the rest of its blood at the base of the altar of burnt offering. 26 All its fat he shall burn on the altar, like the fat of the sacrifice of peace offerings; and the priest shall make atonement for him concerning his sin, and he will be forgiven.

27 "'If anyone of the common people sins unwittingly, in doing any of the things which the LORD has commanded not to be done, and is guilty, 28 if his sin which he has sinned is made known to him, then he shall bring for his offering a goat, a female without defect, for his sin which he has sinned. 29 He shall lay his hand on the head of the sin offering, and kill the sin offering in the place of burnt offering. 30 The priest shall take some of its blood with his finger, and put it on the horns of the altar of burnt offering;

---

a *1:1* When rendered in ALL CAPITAL LETTERS, "LORD" or "GOD" is the translation of God's Proper Name.

b *2:13* The Hebrew word rendered "God" is "אֱלֹהִים" (Elohim).

and the rest of its blood he shall pour out at the base of the altar. 31 All its fat he shall take away, like the fat is taken away from the sacrifice of peace offerings; and the priest shall burn it on the altar for a pleasant aroma to the LORD; and the priest shall make atonement for him, and he will be forgiven.

32 "'If he brings a lamb as his offering for a sin offering, he shall bring a female without defect. 33 He shall lay his hand on the head of the sin offering, and kill it for a sin offering in the place where they kill the burnt offering. 34 The priest shall take some of the blood of the sin offering with his finger, and put it on the horns of the altar of burnt offering; and all the rest of its blood he shall pour out at the base of the altar. 35 He shall remove all its fat, like the fat of the lamb is removed from the sacrifice of peace offerings. The priest shall burn them on the altar, on the offerings of the LORD made by fire. The priest shall make atonement for him concerning his sin that he has sinned, and he will be forgiven.

5

1 "'If anyone sins, in that he hears a public adjuration to testify, he being a witness, whether he has seen or known, if he doesn't report it, then he shall bear his iniquity.

2 "'Or if anyone touches any unclean thing, whether it is the carcass of an unclean animal, or the carcass of unclean livestock, or the carcass of unclean creeping things, and it is hidden from him, and he is unclean, then he shall be guilty.

3 "'Or if he touches the uncleanness of man, whatever his uncleanness is with which he is unclean, and it is hidden from him; when he knows of it, then he shall be guilty.

4 "'Or if anyone swears rashly with his lips to do evil or to do good— whatever it is that a man might utter rashly with an oath, and it is hidden from him—when he knows of it, then he will be guilty of one of these. 5 It shall be, when he is guilty of one of these, he shall confess that in which he has sinned; 6 and he shall bring his trespass offering to the LORD for his sin which he has sinned: a female from the flock, a lamb or a goat, for a sin offering; and the priest shall make atonement for him concerning his sin.

7 "'If he can't afford a lamb, then he shall bring his trespass offering for that in which he has sinned, two turtledoves, or two young pigeons, to the LORD; one for a sin offering, and the other for a burnt offering. 8 He shall bring them to the priest, who shall first offer the one which is for the sin offering. He shall wring off its head from its neck, but shall not sever it completely. 9 He shall sprinkle some of the blood of the sin offering on the side of the altar; and the rest of the blood shall be drained out at the base of the altar. It is a sin offering. 10 He shall offer the second for a burnt offering, according to the ordinance; and the priest shall make atonement for him concerning his sin which he has sinned, and he shall be forgiven.

11 "'But if he can't afford two turtledoves or two young pigeons, then he shall bring as his offering for that in which he has sinned, one tenth of an ephah[a] of fine flour for a sin offering. He shall put no oil on it, and he shall not put any frankincense on it, for it is a sin offering. 12 He shall bring it to the priest, and the priest shall take his handful of it as the memorial portion, and burn it on the altar, on the offerings of the LORD made by fire. It is a sin offering. 13 The priest shall make atonement for him concerning his sin that he has sinned in any of these things, and he will be forgiven; and the rest shall be the priest's, as the meal offering.'"

14 The LORD spoke to Moses, saying, 15 "If anyone commits a trespass, and sins unwittingly regarding the LORD's holy things, then he shall bring his trespass offering to the LORD: a ram without defect from the flock, according to your estimation in silver by shekels, according to the shekel[b] of the sanctuary, for a trespass offering. 16 He shall make restitution for that which he has done wrong regarding the holy thing, and shall add a fifth part to it, and give it to the priest; and the priest shall make atonement for him with the ram of the trespass offering, and he will be forgiven.

17 "If anyone sins, doing any of the things which the LORD has commanded not to be done, though he didn't know it, he is still guilty, and shall bear his iniquity. 18 He shall bring a ram without defect from the flock, according to your estimation, for a trespass offering, to the priest; and the priest shall make atonement for him concerning the thing in which he sinned and didn't know it, and he will be forgiven. 19 It is a trespass offering. He is certainly guilty before the LORD."

6

1 The LORD spoke to Moses, saying, 2 "If anyone sins, and commits a trespass against the LORD, and deals falsely with his neighbour in a matter of deposit, or of bargain, or of robbery, or has oppressed his neighbour, 3 or has found that which was lost, and lied about it, and swearing to a lie—in any of these things that a man sins in his actions— 4 then it shall be, if he has sinned, and is guilty, he shall restore that which he took by robbery, or the thing which he has gotten by oppression, or the deposit which was committed to him, or the lost thing which he found, 5 or any thing about which he has sworn falsely: he shall restore it in full, and shall add a fifth part more to it. He shall return it to him to whom it belongs in the day of his being found guilty. 6 He shall bring his trespass offering to the LORD: a ram without defect from the flock, according to your estimation, for a trespass offering, to the priest. 7 The priest shall make atonement for him before the LORD, and he will be forgiven concerning whatever he does to become guilty."

8 The LORD spoke to Moses, saying, 9 "Command Aaron and his sons, saying, 'This is the law of the burnt offering: the burnt offering shall be on the hearth on the altar all night until the morning; and the fire of the altar shall be kept burning on it. 10 The priest shall put on his linen garment, and he shall put on his linen trousers upon his body; and he shall remove the ashes from where the fire has consumed the burnt offering on the altar, and he shall put them beside the altar. 11 He shall take off his garments, and put on other garments, and carry the ashes outside the camp to a clean place. 12 The fire on the altar shall be kept burning on it, it shall not go out; and the priest shall burn wood on it every morning. He shall lay the burnt offering in order upon it, and shall burn on it the fat of the peace offerings. 13 Fire shall be kept burning on the altar continually; it shall not go out.

14 "'This is the law of the meal offering: the sons of Aaron shall offer it before the LORD, before the altar. 15 He shall take from there his handful of the fine flour of the meal offering, and of its oil, and all the frankincense which is on the meal offering, and shall burn it on the altar for a pleasant aroma, as its memorial portion, to the LORD. 16 That which is left of it Aaron and his sons shall eat. It shall be eaten without yeast in a holy place. They shall eat it in the court of the Tent of Meeting. 17 It shall not be baked with yeast. I have given it as their portion of my offerings made by fire. It is most holy, as are the sin offering and the trespass offering. 18 Every male amongst the children of Aaron shall eat of it, as their portion forever throughout your generations, from the offerings of the LORD made by fire. Whoever touches them shall be holy.'"

19 The LORD spoke to Moses, saying, 20 "This is the offering of Aaron and of his sons, which they shall offer to the LORD in the day when he is anointed: one tenth of an ephah[c] of fine flour for a meal offering perpetually, half of it in the morning, and half of it in the evening. 21 It shall be made with oil in a griddle. When it is soaked, you shall bring it in. You shall offer the meal offering in baked pieces for a pleasant aroma to the LORD. 22 The anointed priest that will be in his place from amongst his sons shall offer it. By a statute forever, it shall be wholly burnt to the LORD. 23 Every meal offering of a priest shall be wholly burnt. It shall not be eaten."

24 The LORD spoke to Moses, saying, 25 "Speak to Aaron and to his sons, saying, 'This is the law of the sin offering: in the place where the burnt offering is killed, the sin offering shall be killed before the LORD. It is most holy. 26 The priest who offers it for sin shall eat it. It shall be eaten in a holy place, in the court of the Tent of Meeting. 27 Whatever shall touch its flesh shall be holy. When there is any of its blood sprinkled on a garment, you shall wash that on which it was sprinkled in a holy place. 28 But the earthen vessel in which it is boiled shall be broken; and if it is boiled in a bronze vessel, it shall be scoured, and rinsed in water. 29 Every male amongst the priests shall eat of it. It is most holy. 30 No sin offering, of which any of the blood is brought into the Tent of Meeting to make atonement in the Holy Place, shall be eaten. It shall be burnt with fire.

7

1 "'This is the law of the trespass offering: It is most holy. 2 In the place where they kill the burnt offering, he shall kill the trespass offering; and its blood he shall sprinkle around on the altar. 3 He shall offer all of its fat: the fat tail, and the fat that covers the innards, 4 and he shall take away the two kidneys, and the fat that is on them, which is by the loins, and the cover on the liver, with the kidneys; 5 and the priest shall burn them on the altar for an offering made by fire to the LORD: it is a trespass offering. 6 Every male amongst the priests may eat of it. It shall be eaten in a holy place. It is most holy.

7 "'As is the sin offering, so is the trespass offering; there is one law for them. The priest who makes atonement with them shall have it. 8 The priest who offers any man's burnt offering shall have for himself the skin of the burnt offering which he has offered. 9 Every meal offering that is baked in the oven, and all that is prepared in the pan and on the griddle, shall be the priest's who offers it. 10 Every meal offering, mixed with oil or dry, belongs to all the sons of Aaron, one as well as another.

11 "'This is the law of the sacrifice of peace offerings, which one shall offer to the LORD: 12 If he offers it for a thanksgiving, then he shall offer with the sacrifice of thanksgiving unleavened cakes mixed with oil, and unleavened wafers anointed with oil, and cakes mixed with oil. 13 He shall offer his offering with the sacrifice of his peace offerings for thanksgiving with cakes of leavened bread. 14 Of it he shall offer one out of each offering for a heave offering to the LORD. It shall be the priest's who sprinkles the blood of the peace offerings. 15 The flesh of the sacrifice of his peace offerings for thanksgiving shall be eaten on the day of his offering. He shall not leave any of it until the morning.

16 "'But if the sacrifice of his offering is a vow, or a free will offering, it shall be eaten on the day that he offers his sacrifice. On the next day what remains of it shall be eaten, 17 but what remains of the meat of the sacrifice on the third day shall be burnt with fire. 18 If any of the meat of the sacrifice of his peace offerings is eaten on the third day, it will not be accepted, and it shall not be credited to him who offers it. It will be an abomination, and the soul who eats any of it will bear his iniquity.

19 "'The meat that touches any unclean thing shall not be eaten. It shall be burnt with fire. As for the meat, everyone who is clean may eat it; 20 but the soul who eats of the meat of the sacrifice of peace offerings that belongs to the LORD, having his uncleanness on him, that soul shall be cut off from his people. 21 When anyone touches any unclean thing, the uncleanness of man, or an unclean animal, or any unclean abomination, and eats some of the meat of the sacrifice of peace offerings which belong to the LORD, that soul shall be cut off from his people.'"

---

a 5:11 1 ephah is about 22 litres or about 2/3 of a bushel
b 5:15 A shekel is about 10 grams or about 0.35 ounces.

c 6:20 1 ephah is about 22 litres or about 2/3 of a bushel

22 The LORD spoke to Moses, saying, 23 "Speak to the children of Israel, saying, 'You shall eat no fat, of bull, or sheep, or goat. 24 The fat of that which dies of itself, and the fat of that which is torn of animals, may be used for any other service, but you shall in no way eat of it. 25 For whoever eats the fat of the animal which men offer as an offering made by fire to the LORD, even the soul who eats it shall be cut off from his people. 26 You shall not eat any blood, whether it is of bird or of animal, in any of your dwellings. 27 Whoever it is who eats any blood, that soul shall be cut off from his people.'"

28 The LORD spoke to Moses, saying, 29 "Speak to the children of Israel, saying, 'He who offers the sacrifice of his peace offerings to the LORD shall bring his offering to the LORD out of the sacrifice of his peace offerings. 30 With his own hands he shall bring the offerings of the LORD made by fire. He shall bring the fat with the breast, that the breast may be waved for a wave offering before the LORD. 31 The priest shall burn the fat on the altar, but the breast shall be Aaron's and his sons'. 32 The right thigh you shall give to the priest for a heave offering out of the sacrifices of your peace offerings. 33 He amongst the sons of Aaron who offers the blood of the peace offerings, and the fat, shall have the right thigh for a portion. 34 For the waved breast and the heaved thigh I have taken from the children of Israel out of the sacrifices of their peace offerings, and have given them to Aaron the priest and to his sons as their portion forever from the children of Israel.'"

35 This is the consecrated portion of Aaron, and the consecrated portion of his sons, out of the offerings of the LORD made by fire, in the day when he presented them to minister to the LORD in the priest's office; 36 which the LORD commanded to be given them of the children of Israel, in the day that he anointed them. It is their portion forever throughout their generations. 37 This is the law of the burnt offering, the meal offering, the sin offering, the trespass offering, the consecration, and the sacrifice of peace offerings 38 which the LORD commanded Moses in Mount Sinai in the day that he commanded the children of Israel to offer their offerings to the LORD, in the wilderness of Sinai.

8

1 The LORD spoke to Moses, saying, 2 "Take Aaron and his sons with him, and the garments, and the anointing oil, and the bull of the sin offering, and the two rams, and the basket of unleavened bread; 3 and assemble all the congregation at the door of the Tent of Meeting."

4 Moses did as the LORD commanded him; and the congregation was assembled at the door of the Tent of Meeting. 5 Moses said to the congregation, "This is the thing which the LORD has commanded to be done." 6 Moses brought Aaron and his sons, and washed them with water. 7 He put the tunic on him, tied the sash on him, clothed him with the robe, put the ephod on him, and he tied the skilfully woven band of the ephod on him and fastened it to him with it. 8 He placed the breastplate on him. He put the Urim and Thummim in the breastplate. 9 He set the turban on his head. He set the golden plate, the holy crown, on the front of the turban, as the LORD commanded Moses. 10 Moses took the anointing oil, and anointed the tabernacle and all that was in it, and sanctified them. 11 He sprinkled it on the altar seven times, and anointed the altar and all its vessels, and the basin and its base, to sanctify them. 12 He poured some of the anointing oil on Aaron's head, and anointed him, to sanctify him. 13 Moses brought Aaron's sons, and clothed them with tunics, and tied sashes on them, and put headbands on them, as the LORD commanded Moses.

14 He brought the bull of the sin offering, and Aaron and his sons laid their hands on the head of the bull of the sin offering. 15 He killed it; and Moses took the blood, and put it around on the horns of the altar with his finger, and purified the altar, and poured out the blood at the base of the altar, and sanctified it, to make atonement for it. 16 He took all the fat that was on the innards, and the cover of the liver, and the two kidneys, and their fat; and Moses burnt it on the altar. 17 But the bull, and its skin, and its meat, and its dung, he burnt with fire outside the camp, as the LORD commanded Moses. 18 He presented the ram of the burnt offering. Aaron and his sons laid their hands on the head of the ram. 19 He killed it; and Moses sprinkled the blood around on the altar. 20 He cut the ram into its pieces; and Moses burnt the head, and the pieces, and the fat. 21 He washed the innards and the legs with water; and Moses burnt the whole ram on the altar. It was a burnt offering for a pleasant aroma. It was an offering made by fire to the LORD, as the LORD commanded Moses. 22 He presented the other ram, the ram of consecration. Aaron and his sons laid their hands on the head of the ram. 23 He killed it; and Moses took some of its blood, and put it on the tip of Aaron's right ear, and on the thumb of his right hand, and on the great toe of his right foot. 24 He brought Aaron's sons; and Moses put some of the blood on the tip of their right ear, and on the thumb of their right hand, and on the great toe of their right foot; and Moses sprinkled the blood around on the altar. 25 He took the fat, the fat tail, all the fat that was on the innards, the cover of the liver, the two kidneys and their fat, and the right thigh; 26 and out of the basket of unleavened bread that was before the LORD, he took one unleavened cake, one cake of oiled bread, and one wafer, and placed them on the fat and on the right thigh. 27 He put all these in Aaron's hands and in his sons' hands, and waved them for a wave offering before the LORD. 28 Moses took them from their hands, and burnt them on the altar on the burnt offering. They were a consecration offering for a pleasant aroma. It was an offering made by fire to the LORD. 29 Moses took the breast, and waved it for a wave offering before the LORD. It was Moses' portion of the ram of consecration, as the LORD commanded Moses. 30 Moses took some of the anointing oil, and some of the blood which was on the altar, and sprinkled it on Aaron, on his garments, and on

his sons, and on his sons' garments with him, and sanctified Aaron, his garments, and his sons, and his sons' garments with him.

31 Moses said to Aaron and to his sons, "Boil the meat at the door of the Tent of Meeting, and there eat it and the bread that is in the basket of consecration, as I commanded, saying, 'Aaron and his sons shall eat it.' 32 What remains of the meat and of the bread you shall burn with fire. 33 You shall not go out from the door of the Tent of Meeting for seven days, until the days of your consecration are fulfilled: for he shall consecrate you seven days. 34 What has been done today, so the LORD has commanded to do, to make atonement for you. 35 You shall stay at the door of the Tent of Meeting day and night seven days, and keep the LORD's command, that you don't die: for so I am commanded." 36 Aaron and his sons did all the things which the LORD commanded by Moses.

9

1 On the eighth day, Moses called Aaron and his sons, and the elders of Israel; 2 and he said to Aaron, "Take a calf from the herd for a sin offering, and a ram for a burnt offering, without defect, and offer them before the LORD. 3 You shall speak to the children of Israel, saying, 'Take a male goat for a sin offering; and a calf and a lamb, both a year old, without defect, for a burnt offering; 4 and a bull and a ram for peace offerings, to sacrifice before the LORD; and a meal offering mixed with oil: for today the LORD appears to you.'"

5 They brought what Moses commanded before the Tent of Meeting. All the congregation came near and stood before the LORD. 6 Moses said, "This is the thing which the LORD commanded that you should do; and the LORD's glory shall appear to you." 7 Moses said to Aaron, "Draw near to the altar, and offer your sin offering, and your burnt offering, and make atonement for yourself, and for the people; and offer the offering of the people, and make atonement for them, as the LORD commanded."

8 So Aaron came near to the altar, and killed the calf of the sin offering, which was for himself. 9 The sons of Aaron presented the blood to him; and he dipped his finger in the blood, and put it on the horns of the altar, and poured out the blood at the base of the altar; 10 but the fat, and the kidneys, and the cover from the liver of the sin offering, he burnt upon the altar, as the LORD commanded Moses. 11 The meat and the skin he burnt with fire outside the camp. 12 He killed the burnt offering; and Aaron's sons delivered the blood to him, and he sprinkled it around on the altar. 13 They delivered the burnt offering to him, piece by piece, and the head. He burnt them upon the altar. 14 He washed the innards and the legs, and burnt them on the burnt offering on the altar. 15 He presented the people's offering, and took the goat of the sin offering which was for the people, and killed it, and offered it for sin, like the first. 16 He presented the burnt offering, and offered it according to the ordinance. 17 He presented the meal offering, and filled his hand from there, and burnt it upon the altar, in addition to the burnt offering of the morning. 18 He also killed the bull and the ram, the sacrifice of peace offerings, which was for the people. Aaron's sons delivered to him the blood, which he sprinkled around on the altar; 19 and the fat of the bull and of the ram, the fat tail, and that which covers the innards, and the kidneys, and the cover of the liver; 20 and they put the fat upon the breasts, and he burnt the fat on the altar. 21 Aaron waved the breasts and the right thigh for a wave offering before the LORD, as Moses commanded. 22 Aaron lifted up his hands towards the people, and blessed them; and he came down from offering the sin offering, and the burnt offering, and the peace offerings.

23 Moses and Aaron went into the Tent of Meeting, and came out, and blessed the people; and the LORD's glory appeared to all the people. 24 Fire came out from before the LORD, and consumed the burnt offering and the fat upon the altar. When all the people saw it, they shouted, and fell on their faces.

10

1 Nadab and Abihu, the sons of Aaron, each took his censer, and put fire in it, and laid incense on it, and offered strange fire before the LORD, which he had not commanded them. 2 Fire came out from before the LORD, and devoured them, and they died before the LORD.

3 Then Moses said to Aaron, "This is what the LORD spoke of, saying, 'I will show myself holy to those who come near me,
and before all the people I will be glorified.'"
Aaron held his peace. 4 Moses called Mishael and Elzaphan, the sons of Uzziel the uncle of Aaron, and said to them, "Draw near, carry your brothers from before the sanctuary out of the camp." 5 So they came near, and carried them in their tunics out of the camp, as Moses had said.

6 Moses said to Aaron, and to Eleazar and to Ithamar, his sons, "Don't let the hair of your heads go loose, and don't tear your clothes, so that you don't die, and so that he will not be angry with all the congregation; but let your brothers, the whole house of Israel, bewail the burning which the LORD has kindled. 7 You shall not go out from the door of the Tent of Meeting, lest you die; for the anointing oil of the LORD is on you." They did according to the word of Moses. 8 Then The LORD said to Aaron, 9 "You and your sons are not to drink wine or strong drink whenever you go into the Tent of Meeting, or you will die. This shall be a statute forever throughout your generations. 10 You are to make a distinction between the holy and the common, and between the unclean and the clean. 11 You are to teach the children of Israel all the statutes which the LORD has spoken to them by Moses."

12 Moses spoke to Aaron, and to Eleazar and to Ithamar, his sons who were left, "Take the meal offering that remains of the offerings of the LORD made by fire, and eat it without yeast beside the altar; for it is most holy; 13 and you shall eat it in a holy place, because it is your portion, and your

sons' portion, of the offerings of the LORD made by fire; for so I am commanded. 14 The waved breast and the heaved thigh you shall eat in a clean place, you, and your sons, and your daughters with you: for they are given as your portion, and your sons' portion, out of the sacrifices of the peace offerings of the children of Israel. 15 They shall bring the heaved thigh and the waved breast with the offerings made by fire of the fat, to wave it for a wave offering before the LORD. It shall be yours, and your sons' with you, as a portion forever, as the LORD has commanded."

16 Moses diligently enquired about the goat of the sin offering, and, behold,[a] it was burnt. He was angry with Eleazar and with Ithamar, the sons of Aaron who were left, saying, 17 "Why haven't you eaten the sin offering in the place of the sanctuary, since it is most holy, and he has given it to you to bear the iniquity of the congregation, to make atonement for them before the LORD? 18 Behold, its blood was not brought into the inner part of the sanctuary. You certainly should have eaten it in the sanctuary, as I commanded."

19 Aaron spoke to Moses, "Behold, today they have offered their sin offering and their burnt offering before the LORD; and such things as these have happened to me. If I had eaten the sin offering today, would it have been pleasing in the LORD's sight?"

20 When Moses heard that, it was pleasing in his sight.

11

1 The LORD spoke to Moses and to Aaron, saying to them, 2 "Speak to the children of Israel, saying, 'These are the living things which you may eat amongst all the animals that are on the earth. 3 Whatever parts the hoof, and is cloven-footed, and chews the cud amongst the animals, that you may eat.

4 "'Nevertheless these you shall not eat of those that chew the cud, or of those who part the hoof: the camel, because it chews the cud but doesn't have a parted hoof, is unclean to you. 5 The hyrax,[b] because it chews the cud but doesn't have a parted hoof, is unclean to you. 6 The hare, because it chews the cud but doesn't have a parted hoof, is unclean to you. 7 The pig, because it has a split hoof, and is cloven-footed, but doesn't chew the cud, is unclean to you. 8 You shall not eat their meat. You shall not touch their carcasses. They are unclean to you.

9 "'You may eat of all these that are in the waters: whatever has fins and scales in the waters, in the seas, and in the rivers, that you may eat. 10 All that don't have fins and scales in the seas and rivers, all that move in the waters, and all the living creatures that are in the waters, they are an abomination to you, 11 and you shall detest them. You shall not eat of their meat, and you shall detest their carcasses. 12 Whatever has no fins nor scales in the waters is an abomination to you.

13 "'You shall detest these amongst the birds; they shall not be eaten because they are an abomination: the eagle, the vulture, the black vulture, 14 the red kite, any kind of black kite, 15 any kind of raven, 16 the horned owl, the screech owl, the gull, any kind of hawk, 17 the little owl, the cormorant, the great owl, 18 the white owl, the desert owl, the osprey, 19 the stork, any kind of heron, the hoopoe, and the bat.

20 "'All flying insects that walk on all fours are an abomination to you. 21 Yet you may eat these: of all winged creeping things that go on all fours, which have long, jointed legs for hopping on the earth. 22 Even of these you may eat: any kind of locust, any kind of katydid, any kind of cricket, and any kind of grasshopper. 23 But all winged creeping things which have four feet are an abomination to you.

24 "'By these you will become unclean: whoever touches their carcass shall be unclean until the evening. 25 Whoever carries any part of their carcass shall wash his clothes, and be unclean until the evening.

26 "'Every animal which has a split hoof that isn't completely divided, or doesn't chew the cud, is unclean to you. Everyone who touches them shall be unclean. 27 Whatever goes on its paws, amongst all animals that go on all fours, they are unclean to you. Whoever touches their carcass shall be unclean until the evening. 28 He who carries their carcass shall wash his clothes, and be unclean until the evening. They are unclean to you.

29 "'These are they which are unclean to you amongst the creeping things that creep on the earth: the weasel, the rat, any kind of great lizard, 30 the gecko, and the monitor lizard, the wall lizard, the skink, and the chameleon. 31 These are they which are unclean to you amongst all that creep. Whoever touches them when they are dead shall be unclean until the evening. 32 Anything they fall on when they are dead shall be unclean; whether it is any vessel of wood, or clothing, or skin, or sack, whatever vessel it is, with which any work is done, it must be put into water, and it shall be unclean until the evening. Then it will be clean. 33 Every earthen vessel into which any of them falls and all that is in it shall be unclean. You shall break it. 34 All food which may be eaten which is soaked in water shall be unclean. All drink that may be drunk in every such vessel shall be unclean. 35 Everything whereupon part of their carcass falls shall be unclean; whether oven, or range for pots, it shall be broken in pieces. They are unclean, and shall be unclean to you. 36 Nevertheless a spring or a cistern in which water is gathered shall be clean, but that which touches their carcass shall be unclean. 37 If part of their carcass falls on any sowing seed which is to be sown, it is clean. 38 But if water is put on the seed, and part of their carcass falls on it, it is unclean to you.

39 "'If any animal of which you may eat dies, he who touches its carcass shall be unclean until the evening. 40 He who eats of its carcass shall wash his clothes, and be unclean until the evening. He also who carries its carcass shall wash his clothes, and be unclean until the evening.

41 "'Every creeping thing that creeps on the earth is an abomination. It shall not be eaten. 42 Whatever goes on its belly, and whatever goes on all fours, or whatever has many feet, even all creeping things that creep on the earth, them you shall not eat; for they are an abomination. 43 You shall not make yourselves abominable with any creeping thing that creeps. You shall not make yourselves unclean with them, that you should be defiled by them. 44 For I am the LORD your God. Sanctify yourselves therefore, and be holy; for I am holy. You shall not defile yourselves with any kind of creeping thing that moves on the earth. 45 For I am the LORD who brought you up out of the land of Egypt, to be your God. You shall therefore be holy, for I am holy.

46 "'This is the law of the animal, and of the bird, and of every living creature that moves in the waters, and of every creature that creeps on the earth, 47 to make a distinction between the unclean and the clean, and between the living thing that may be eaten and the living thing that may not be eaten.'"

12

1 The LORD spoke to Moses, saying, 2 "Speak to the children of Israel, saying, 'If a woman conceives, and bears a male child, then she shall be unclean seven days; as in the days of her monthly period she shall be unclean. 3 In the eighth day the flesh of his foreskin shall be circumcised. 4 She shall continue in the blood of purification thirty-three days. She shall not touch any holy thing, nor come into the sanctuary, until the days of her purifying are completed. 5 But if she bears a female child, then she shall be unclean two weeks, as in her period; and she shall continue in the blood of purification sixty-six days.

6 "'When the days of her purification are completed for a son or for a daughter, she shall bring to the priest at the door of the Tent of Meeting, a year old lamb for a burnt offering, and a young pigeon or a turtledove, for a sin offering. 7 He shall offer it before the LORD, and make atonement for her; then she shall be cleansed from the fountain of her blood.

"'This is the law for her who bears, whether a male or a female. 8 If she cannot afford a lamb, then she shall take two turtledoves or two young pigeons: the one for a burnt offering, and the other for a sin offering. The priest shall make atonement for her, and she shall be clean.'"

13

1 The LORD spoke to Moses and to Aaron, saying, 2 "When a man shall have a swelling in his body's skin, or a scab, or a bright spot, and it becomes in the skin of his body the plague of leprosy, then he shall be brought to Aaron the priest or to one of his sons, the priests. 3 The priest shall examine the plague in the skin of the body. If the hair in the plague has turned white, and the appearance of the plague is deeper than the body's skin, it is the plague of leprosy; so the priest shall examine him and pronounce him unclean. 4 If the bright spot is white in the skin of his body, and its appearance isn't deeper than the skin, and its hair hasn't turned white, then the priest shall isolate the infected person for seven days. 5 The priest shall examine him on the seventh day. Behold, if in his eyes the plague is arrested and the plague hasn't spread in the skin, then the priest shall isolate him for seven more days. 6 The priest shall examine him again on the seventh day. Behold, if the plague has faded and the plague hasn't spread in the skin, then the priest shall pronounce him clean. It is a scab. He shall wash his clothes, and be clean. 7 But if the scab spreads on the skin after he has shown himself to the priest for his cleansing, he shall show himself to the priest again. 8 The priest shall examine him; and behold, if the scab has spread on the skin, then the priest shall pronounce him unclean. It is leprosy.

9 "When the plague of leprosy is in a man, then he shall be brought to the priest; 10 and the priest shall examine him. Behold, if there is a white swelling in the skin, and it has turned the hair white, and there is raw flesh in the swelling, 11 it is a chronic leprosy in the skin of his body, and the priest shall pronounce him unclean. He shall not isolate him, for he is already unclean.

12 "If the leprosy breaks out all over the skin, and the leprosy covers all the skin of the infected person from his head even to his feet, as far as it appears to the priest, 13 then the priest shall examine him. Behold, if the leprosy has covered all his flesh, he shall pronounce him clean of the plague. It has all turned white: he is clean. 14 But whenever raw flesh appears in him, he shall be unclean. 15 The priest shall examine the raw flesh, and pronounce him unclean: the raw flesh is unclean. It is leprosy. 16 Or if the raw flesh turns again, and is changed to white, then he shall come to the priest. 17 The priest shall examine him. Behold, if the plague has turned white, then the priest shall pronounce him clean of the plague. He is clean.

18 "When the body has a boil on its skin, and it has healed, 19 and in the place of the boil there is a white swelling, or a bright spot, reddish-white, then it shall be shown to the priest. 20 The priest shall examine it. Behold, if its appearance is deeper than the skin, and its hair has turned white, then the priest shall pronounce him unclean. It is the plague of leprosy. It has broken out in the boil. 21 But if the priest examines it, and behold, there are no white hairs in it, and it isn't deeper than the skin, but is dim, then the priest shall isolate him seven days. 22 If it spreads in the skin, then the priest shall pronounce him unclean. It is a plague. 23 But if the

---

bright spot stays in its place, and hasn't spread, it is the scar from the boil; and the priest shall pronounce him clean.

24 "Or when the body has a burn from fire on its skin, and the raw flesh of the burn becomes a bright spot, reddish-white, or white, 25 then the priest shall examine it; and behold, if the hair in the bright spot has turned white, and its appearance is deeper than the skin, it is leprosy. It has broken out in the burning, and the priest shall pronounce him unclean. It is the plague of leprosy. 26 But if the priest examines it, and behold, there is no white hair in the bright spot, and it isn't deeper than the skin, but has faded, then the priest shall isolate him seven days. 27 The priest shall examine him on the seventh day. If it has spread in the skin, then the priest shall pronounce him unclean. It is the plague of leprosy. 28 If the bright spot stays in its place, and hasn't spread in the skin, but is faded, it is the swelling from the burn, and the priest shall pronounce him clean, for it is the scar from the burn.

29 "When a man or woman has a plague on the head or on the beard, 30 then the priest shall examine the plague; and behold, if its appearance is deeper than the skin, and the hair in it is yellow and thin, then the priest shall pronounce him unclean. It is an itch. It is leprosy of the head or of the beard. 31 If the priest examines the plague of itching, and behold, its appearance isn't deeper than the skin, and there is no black hair in it, then the priest shall isolate the person infected with itching seven days. 32 On the seventh day the priest shall examine the plague; and behold, if the itch hasn't spread, and there is no yellow hair in it, and the appearance of the itch isn't deeper than the skin, 33 then he shall be shaved, but he shall not shave the itch. Then the priest shall isolate the one who has the itch seven more days. 34 On the seventh day, the priest shall examine the itch; and behold, if the itch hasn't spread in the skin, and its appearance isn't deeper than the skin, then the priest shall pronounce him clean. He shall wash his clothes and be clean. 35 But if the itch spreads in the skin after his cleansing, 36 then the priest shall examine him; and behold, if the itch has spread in the skin, the priest shall not look for the yellow hair; he is unclean. 37 But if in his eyes the itch is arrested and black hair has grown in it, then the itch is healed. He is clean. The priest shall pronounce him clean.

38 "When a man or a woman has bright spots in the skin of the body, even white bright spots, 39 then the priest shall examine them. Behold, if the bright spots on the skin of their body are a dull white, it is a harmless rash. It has broken out in the skin. He is clean.

40 "If a man's hair has fallen from his head, he is bald. He is clean. 41 If his hair has fallen off from the front part of his head, he is forehead bald. He is clean. 42 But if a reddish-white plague is in the bald head or the bald forehead, it is leprosy breaking out in his bald head or his bald forehead. 43 Then the priest shall examine him. Behold, if the swelling of the plague is reddish-white in his bald head, or in his bald forehead, like the appearance of leprosy in the skin of the body, 44 he is a leprous man. He is unclean. The priest shall surely pronounce him unclean. His plague is on his head.

45 "The leper in whom the plague is shall wear torn clothes, and the hair of his head shall hang loose. He shall cover his upper lip, and shall cry, 'Unclean! Unclean!' 46 All the days in which the plague is in him he shall be unclean. He is unclean. He shall dwell alone. His dwelling shall be outside of the camp.

47 "The garment also that the plague of leprosy is in, whether it is a woollen garment, or a linen garment; 48 whether it is in warp or woof;[a] of linen or of wool; whether in a leather, or in anything made of leather; 49 if the plague is greenish or reddish in the garment, or in the leather, or in the warp, or in the woof, or in anything made of leather; it is the plague of leprosy, and shall be shown to the priest. 50 The priest shall examine the plague, and isolate the plague seven days. 51 He shall examine the plague on the seventh day. If the plague has spread in the garment, either in the warp, or in the woof, or in the skin, whatever use the skin is used for, the plague is a destructive mildew. It is unclean. 52 He shall burn the garment, whether the warp or the woof, in wool or in linen, or anything of leather, in which the plague is, for it is a destructive mildew. It shall be burnt in the fire.

53 "If the priest examines it, and behold, the plague hasn't spread in the garment, either in the warp, or in the woof, or in anything of skin; 54 then the priest shall command that they wash the thing that the plague is in, and he shall isolate it seven more days. 55 Then the priest shall examine it, after the plague is washed; and behold, if the plague hasn't changed its colour, and the plague hasn't spread, it is unclean; you shall burn it in the fire. It is a mildewed spot, whether the bareness is inside or outside. 56 If the priest looks, and behold, the plague has faded after it is washed, then he shall tear it out of the garment, or out of the skin, or out of the warp, or out of the woof; 57 and if it appears again in the garment, either in the warp, or in the woof, or in anything of skin, it is spreading. You shall burn what the plague is in with fire. 58 The garment, either the warp, or the woof, or whatever thing of skin it is, which you shall wash, if the plague has departed from them, then it shall be washed the second time, and it will be clean."

59 This is the law of the plague of mildew in a garment of wool or linen, either in the warp, or the woof, or in anything of skin, to pronounce it clean, or to pronounce it unclean.

14

1 The LORD spoke to Moses, saying,

2 "This shall be the law of the leper in the day of his cleansing: He shall be brought to the priest, 3 and the priest shall go out of the camp. The priest shall examine him. Behold, if the plague of leprosy is healed in the leper, 4 then the priest shall command them to take for him who is to be cleansed two living clean birds, cedar wood, scarlet, and hyssop. 5 The priest shall command them to kill one of the birds in an earthen vessel over running water. 6 As for the living bird, he shall take it, the cedar wood, the scarlet, and the hyssop, and shall dip them and the living bird in the blood of the bird that was killed over the running water. 7 He shall sprinkle on him who is to be cleansed from the leprosy seven times, and shall pronounce him clean, and shall let the living bird go into the open field.

8 "He who is to be cleansed shall wash his clothes, and shave off all his hair, and bathe himself in water; and he shall be clean. After that he shall come into the camp, but shall dwell outside his tent seven days. 9 It shall be on the seventh day, that he shall shave all his hair off his head and his beard and his eyebrows. He shall shave off all his hair. He shall wash his clothes, and he shall bathe his body in water. Then he shall be clean.

10 "On the eighth day he shall take two male lambs without defect, one ewe lamb a year old without defect, three tenths of an ephah[b] of fine flour for a meal offering, mixed with oil, and one log[c] of oil. 11 The priest who cleanses him shall set the man who is to be cleansed, and those things, before the LORD, at the door of the Tent of Meeting.

12 "The priest shall take one of the male lambs, and offer him for a trespass offering, with the log of oil, and wave them for a wave offering before the LORD. 13 He shall kill the male lamb in the place where they kill the sin offering and the burnt offering, in the place of the sanctuary; for as the sin offering is the priest's, so is the trespass offering. It is most holy. 14 The priest shall take some of the blood of the trespass offering, and the priest shall put it on the tip of the right ear of him who is to be cleansed, and on the thumb of his right hand, and on the big toe of his right foot. 15 The priest shall take some of the log of oil, and pour it into the palm of his own left hand. 16 The priest shall dip his right finger in the oil that is in his left hand, and shall sprinkle some of the oil with his finger seven times before the LORD. 17 The priest shall put some of the rest of the oil that is in his hand on the tip of the right ear of him who is to be cleansed, and on the thumb of his right hand, and on the big toe of his right foot, upon the blood of the trespass offering. 18 The rest of the oil that is in the priest's hand he shall put on the head of him who is to be cleansed, and the priest shall make atonement for him before the LORD.

19 "The priest shall offer the sin offering, and make atonement for him who is to be cleansed because of his uncleanness. Afterward he shall kill the burnt offering; 20 then the priest shall offer the burnt offering and the meal offering on the altar. The priest shall make atonement for him, and he shall be clean.

21 "If he is poor, and can't afford so much, then he shall take one male lamb for a trespass offering to be waved, to make atonement for him, and one tenth of an ephah[d] of fine flour mixed with oil for a meal offering, and a log[e] of oil; 22 and two turtledoves, or two young pigeons, such as he is able to afford; and the one shall be a sin offering, and the other a burnt offering.

23 "On the eighth day he shall bring them for his cleansing to the priest, to the door of the Tent of Meeting, before the LORD. 24 The priest shall take the lamb of the trespass offering, and the log of oil, and the priest shall wave them for a wave offering before the LORD. 25 He shall kill the lamb of the trespass offering. The priest shall take some of the blood of the trespass offering and put it on the tip of the right ear of him who is to be cleansed, and on the thumb of his right hand, and on the big toe of his right foot. 26 The priest shall pour some of the oil into the palm of his own left hand; 27 and the priest shall sprinkle with his right finger some of the oil that is in his left hand seven times before the LORD. 28 Then the priest shall put some of the oil that is in his hand on the tip of the right ear of him who is to be cleansed, and on the thumb of his right hand, and on the big toe of his right foot, on the place of the blood of the trespass offering. 29 The rest of the oil that is in the priest's hand he shall put on the head of him who is to be cleansed, to make atonement for him before the LORD. 30 He shall offer one of the turtledoves, or of the young pigeons, which ever he is able to afford, 31 of the kind he is able to afford, the one for a sin offering, and the other for a burnt offering, with the meal offering. The priest shall make atonement for him who is to be cleansed before the LORD."

32 This is the law for him in whom is the plague of leprosy, who is not able to afford the sacrifice for his cleansing.

33 The LORD spoke to Moses and to Aaron, saying, 34 "When you have come into the land of Canaan, which I give to you for a possession, and I put a spreading mildew in a house in the land of your possession, 35 then he who owns the house shall come and tell the priest, saying, 'There seems to me to be some sort of plague in the house.' 36 The priest shall command that they empty the house, before the priest goes in to examine the plague, that all that is in the house not be made unclean. Afterward the priest shall go in to inspect the house. 37 He shall examine the plague; and behold, if the plague is in the walls of the house with hollow streaks, greenish or reddish, and it appears to be deeper than the wall, 38 then the priest shall go out of the house to the door of the house, and shut up the house seven days. 39 The priest shall come again on the seventh day, and look. If the plague has spread in the walls of the house, 40 then the priest shall command that they take out the stones in which is the plague, and cast them into an unclean place outside of the city. 41 He shall cause the inside

---

a 13:48 warp and woof are the vertical and horizontal threads in woven cloth
b 14:10 1 ephah is about 22 litres or about 2/3 of a bushel
c 14:10 a log is a liquid measure of about 300 ml or 10 ounces

d 14:21 1 ephah is about 22 litres or about 2/3 of a bushel
e 14:21 a log is a liquid measure of about 300 ml or 10 ounces

of the house to be scraped all over. They shall pour out the mortar that they scraped off outside of the city into an unclean place. 42 They shall take other stones, and put them in the place of those stones; and he shall take other mortar, and shall plaster the house.

43 "If the plague comes again, and breaks out in the house after he has taken out the stones, and after he has scraped the house, and after it was plastered, 44 then the priest shall come in and look; and behold, if the plague has spread in the house, it is a destructive mildew in the house. It is unclean. 45 He shall break down the house, its stones, and its timber, and all the house's mortar. He shall carry them out of the city into an unclean place.

46 "Moreover he who goes into the house while it is shut up shall be unclean until the evening. 47 He who lies down in the house shall wash his clothes; and he who eats in the house shall wash his clothes.

48 "If the priest shall come in, and examine it, and behold, the plague hasn't spread in the house, after the house was plastered, then the priest shall pronounce the house clean, because the plague is healed. 49 To cleanse the house he shall take two birds, cedar wood, scarlet, and hyssop. 50 He shall kill one of the birds in an earthen vessel over running water. 51 He shall take the cedar wood, the hyssop, the scarlet, and the living bird, and dip them in the blood of the slain bird, and in the running water, and sprinkle the house seven times. 52 He shall cleanse the house with the blood of the bird, and with the running water, with the living bird, with the cedar wood, with the hyssop, and with the scarlet; 53 but he shall let the living bird go out of the city into the open field. So shall he make atonement for the house; and it shall be clean."

54 This is the law for any plague of leprosy, and for an itch, 55 and for the destructive mildew of a garment, and for a house, 56 and for a swelling, and for a scab, and for a bright spot; 57 to teach when it is unclean, and when it is clean.

This is the law of leprosy.

15

1 The LORD spoke to Moses and to Aaron, saying, 2 "Speak to the children of Israel, and tell them, 'When any man has a discharge from his body, because of his discharge he is unclean. 3 This shall be his uncleanness in his discharge: whether his body runs with his discharge, or his body has stopped from his discharge, it is his uncleanness.

4 "'Every bed on which he who has the discharge lies shall be unclean; and everything he sits on shall be unclean. 5 Whoever touches his bed shall wash his clothes, and bathe himself in water, and be unclean until the evening. 6 He who sits on anything on which the man who has the discharge sat shall wash his clothes, and bathe himself in water, and be unclean until the evening.

7 "'He who touches the body of him who has the discharge shall wash his clothes, and bathe himself in water, and be unclean until the evening.

8 "'If he who has the discharge spits on him who is clean, then he shall wash his clothes, and bathe himself in water, and be unclean until the evening.

9 "'Whatever saddle he who has the discharge rides on shall be unclean. 10 Whoever touches anything that was under him shall be unclean until the evening. He who carries those things shall wash his clothes, and bathe himself in water, and be unclean until the evening.

11 "'Whomever he who has the discharge touches, without having rinsed his hands in water, he shall wash his clothes, and bathe himself in water, and be unclean until the evening.

12 "'The earthen vessel, which he who has the discharge touches, shall be broken; and every vessel of wood shall be rinsed in water.

13 "'When he who has a discharge is cleansed of his discharge, then he shall count to himself seven days for his cleansing, and wash his clothes; and he shall bathe his flesh in running water, and shall be clean. 14 "'On the eighth day he shall take two turtledoves, or two young pigeons, and come before the LORD to the door of the Tent of Meeting, and give them to the priest. 15 The priest shall offer them, the one for a sin offering, and the other for a burnt offering. The priest shall make atonement for him before the LORD for his discharge.

16 "'If any man has an emission of semen, then he shall bathe all his flesh in water, and be unclean until the evening. 17 Every garment and every skin which the semen is on shall be washed with water, and be unclean until the evening. 18 If a man lies with a woman and there is an emission of semen, they shall both bathe themselves in water, and be unclean until the evening.

19 "'If a woman has a discharge, and her discharge in her flesh is blood, she shall be in her impurity seven days. Whoever touches her shall be unclean until the evening.

20 "'Everything that she lies on in her impurity shall be unclean. Everything also that she sits on shall be unclean. 21 Whoever touches her bed shall wash his clothes, and bathe himself in water, and be unclean until the evening. 22 Whoever touches anything that she sits on shall wash his clothes, and bathe himself in water, and be unclean until the evening. 23 If it is on the bed, or on anything she sits on, when he touches it, he shall be unclean until the evening.

24 "'If any man lies with her, and her monthly flow is on him, he shall be unclean seven days; and every bed he lies on shall be unclean.

25 "'If a woman has a discharge of her blood many days not in the time of her period, or if she has a discharge beyond the time of her period, all the days of the discharge of her uncleanness shall be as in the days of her period. She is unclean. 26 Every bed she lies on all the days of her discharge shall be to her as the bed of her period. Everything she sits on shall be unclean, as the uncleanness of her period. 27 Whoever touches

these things shall be unclean, and shall wash his clothes and bathe himself in water, and be unclean until the evening.

28 "'But if she is cleansed of her discharge, then she shall count to herself seven days, and after that she shall be clean. 29 On the eighth day she shall take two turtledoves, or two young pigeons, and bring them to the priest, to the door of the Tent of Meeting. 30 The priest shall offer the one for a sin offering, and the other for a burnt offering; and the priest shall make atonement for her before the LORD for the uncleanness of her discharge.

31 "'Thus you shall separate the children of Israel from their uncleanness, so they will not die in their uncleanness when they defile my tabernacle that is amongst them.'"

32 This is the law of him who has a discharge, and of him who has an emission of semen, so that he is unclean by it; 33 and of her who has her period, and of a man or woman who has a discharge, and of him who lies with her who is unclean.

16

1 The LORD spoke to Moses after the death of the two sons of Aaron, when they came near before the LORD, and died; 2 and the LORD said to Moses, "Tell Aaron your brother not to come at just any time into the Most Holy Place within the veil, before the mercy seat which is on the ark; lest he die; for I will appear in the cloud on the mercy seat.

3 "Aaron shall come into the sanctuary with a young bull for a sin offering, and a ram for a burnt offering. 4 He shall put on the holy linen tunic. He shall have the linen trousers on his body, and shall put on the linen sash, and he shall be clothed with the linen turban. They are the holy garments. He shall bathe his body in water, and put them on. 5 He shall take from the congregation of the children of Israel two male goats for a sin offering, and one ram for a burnt offering.

6 "Aaron shall offer the bull of the sin offering, which is for himself, and make atonement for himself and for his house. 7 He shall take the two goats, and set them before the LORD at the door of the Tent of Meeting. 8 Aaron shall cast lots for the two goats: one lot for the LORD, and the other lot for the scapegoat. 9 Aaron shall present the goat on which the lot fell for the LORD, and offer him for a sin offering. 10 But the goat on which the lot fell for the scapegoat shall be presented alive before the LORD, to make atonement for him, to send him away as the scapegoat into the wilderness.

11 "Aaron shall present the bull of the sin offering, which is for himself, and shall make atonement for himself and for his house, and shall kill the bull of the sin offering which is for himself. 12 He shall take a censer full of coals of fire from off the altar before the LORD, and two handfuls of sweet incense beaten small, and bring it within the veil. 13 He shall put the incense on the fire before the LORD, that the cloud of the incense may cover the mercy seat that is on the covenant, so that he will not die. 14 He shall take some of the blood of the bull, and sprinkle it with his finger on the mercy seat on the east; and before the mercy seat he shall sprinkle some of the blood with his finger seven times.

15 "Then he shall kill the goat of the sin offering that is for the people, and bring his blood within the veil, and do with his blood as he did with the blood of the bull, and sprinkle it on the mercy seat and before the mercy seat. 16 He shall make atonement for the Holy Place, because of the uncleanness of the children of Israel, and because of their transgressions, even all their sins; and so he shall do for the Tent of Meeting that dwells with them in the middle of their uncleanness. 17 No one shall be in the Tent of Meeting when he enters to make atonement in the Holy Place, until he comes out, and has made atonement for himself and for his household, and for all the assembly of Israel.

18 "He shall go out to the altar that is before the LORD and make atonement for it, and shall take some of the bull's blood, and some of the goat's blood, and put it around on the horns of the altar. 19 He shall sprinkle some of the blood on it with his finger seven times, and cleanse it, and make it holy from the uncleanness of the children of Israel.

20 "When he has finished atoning for the Holy Place, the Tent of Meeting, and the altar, he shall present the live goat. 21 Aaron shall lay both his hands on the head of the live goat, and confess over him all the iniquities of the children of Israel, and all their transgressions, even all their sins; and he shall put them on the head of the goat, and shall send him away into the wilderness by the hand of a man who is ready. 22 The goat shall carry all their iniquities on himself to a solitary land, and he shall release the goat in the wilderness.

23 "Aaron shall come into the Tent of Meeting, and shall take off the linen garments which he put on when he went into the Holy Place, and shall leave them there. 24 Then he shall bathe himself in water in a holy place, put on his garments, and come out and offer his burnt offering and the burnt offering of the people, and make atonement for himself and for the people. 25 The fat of the sin offering he shall burn on the altar.

26 "He who lets the goat go as the scapegoat shall wash his clothes, and bathe his flesh in water, and afterward he shall come into the camp. 27 The bull for the sin offering, and the goat for the sin offering, whose blood was brought in to make atonement in the Holy Place, shall be carried outside the camp; and they shall burn their skins, their flesh, and their dung with fire. 28 He who burns them shall wash his clothes, and bathe his flesh in water, and afterward he shall come into the camp.

29 "It shall be a statute to you forever: in the seventh month, on the tenth day of the month, you shall afflict your souls, and shall do no kind of work, whether native-born or a stranger who lives as a foreigner amongst you; 30 for on this day shall atonement be made for you, to cleanse you. You shall be clean from all your sins before the LORD. 31 It is a Sabbath of solemn rest to you, and you shall afflict your souls. It is a statute forever. 32

The priest, who is anointed and who is consecrated to be priest in his father's place, shall make the atonement, and shall put on the linen garments, even the holy garments. 33 Then he shall make atonement for the Holy Sanctuary; and he shall make atonement for the Tent of Meeting and for the altar; and he shall make atonement for the priests and for all the people of the assembly.

34 "This shall be an everlasting statute for you, to make atonement for the children of Israel once in the year because of all their sins."

It was done as the LORD commanded Moses.

17

1 The LORD spoke to Moses, saying, 2 "Speak to Aaron, and to his sons, and to all the children of Israel, and say to them, 'This is the thing which the LORD has commanded: 3 Whatever man there is of the house of Israel who kills a bull, or lamb, or goat in the camp, or who kills it outside the camp, 4 and hasn't brought it to the door of the Tent of Meeting to offer it as an offering to the LORD before the LORD's tabernacle: blood shall be imputed to that man. He has shed blood. That man shall be cut off from amongst his people. 5 This is to the end that the children of Israel may bring their sacrifices, which they sacrifice in the open field, that they may bring them to the LORD, to the door of the Tent of Meeting, to the priest, and sacrifice them for sacrifices of peace offerings to the LORD. 6 The priest shall sprinkle the blood on the LORD's altar at the door of the Tent of Meeting, and burn the fat for a pleasant aroma to the LORD. 7 They shall no more sacrifice their sacrifices to the goat idols, after which they play the prostitute. This shall be a statute forever to them throughout their generations.'

8 "You shall say to them, 'Any man there is of the house of Israel, or of the strangers who live as foreigners amongst them, who offers a burnt offering or sacrifice, 9 and doesn't bring it to the door of the Tent of Meeting to sacrifice it to the LORD, that man shall be cut off from his people.

10 "'Any man of the house of Israel, or of the strangers who live as foreigners amongst them, who eats any kind of blood, I will set my face against that soul who eats blood, and will cut him off from amongst his people. 11 For the life of the flesh is in the blood. I have given it to you on the altar to make atonement for your souls; for it is the blood that makes atonement by reason of the life. 12 Therefore I have said to the children of Israel, "No person amongst you may eat blood, nor may any stranger who lives as a foreigner amongst you eat blood."

13 "'Whatever man there is of the children of Israel, or of the strangers who live as foreigners amongst them, who takes in hunting any animal or bird that may be eaten, he shall pour out its blood, and cover it with dust. 14 For as to the life of all flesh, its blood is with its life. Therefore I said to the children of Israel, "You shall not eat the blood of any kind of flesh; for the life of all flesh is its blood. Whoever eats it shall be cut off."

15 "'Every person that eats what dies of itself, or that which is torn by animals, whether he is native-born or a foreigner, shall wash his clothes, and bathe himself in water, and be unclean until the evening. Then he shall be clean. 16 But if he doesn't wash them, or bathe his flesh, then he shall bear his iniquity.'"

18

1 The LORD said to Moses, 2 "Speak to the children of Israel, and say to them, 'I am the LORD your God. 3 You shall not do as they do in the land of Egypt, where you lived. You shall not do as they do in the land of Canaan, where I am bringing you. You shall not follow their statutes. 4 You shall do my ordinances. You shall keep my statutes and walk in them. I am the LORD your God. 5 You shall therefore keep my statutes and my ordinances, which if a man does, he shall live in them. I am the LORD.

6 "'None of you shall approach any close relatives, to uncover their nakedness: I am the LORD.

7 "'You shall not uncover the nakedness of your father, nor the nakedness of your mother: she is your mother. You shall not uncover her nakedness.

8 "'You shall not uncover the nakedness of your father's wife. It is your father's nakedness.

9 "'You shall not uncover the nakedness of your sister, the daughter of your father, or the daughter of your mother, whether born at home or born abroad.

10 "'You shall not uncover the nakedness of your son's daughter, or of your daughter's daughter, even their nakedness; for theirs is your own nakedness.

11 "'You shall not uncover the nakedness of your father's wife's daughter, conceived by your father, since she is your sister.

12 "'You shall not uncover the nakedness of your father's sister. She is your father's near kinswoman.

13 "'You shall not uncover the nakedness of your mother's sister, for she is your mother's near kinswoman.

14 "'You shall not uncover the nakedness of your father's brother. You shall not approach his wife. She is your aunt.

15 "'You shall not uncover the nakedness of your daughter-in-law. She is your son's wife. You shall not uncover her nakedness.

16 "'You shall not uncover the nakedness of your brother's wife. It is your brother's nakedness.

17 "'You shall not uncover the nakedness of a woman and her daughter. You shall not take her son's daughter, or her daughter's daughter, to uncover her nakedness. They are near kinswomen. It is wickedness.

18 "'You shall not take a wife in addition to her sister, to be a rival, to uncover her nakedness, while her sister is still alive.

19 "'You shall not approach a woman to uncover her nakedness, as long as she is impure by her uncleanness.

20 "'You shall not lie carnally with your neighbour's wife, and defile yourself with her.

21 "'You shall not give any of your children as a sacrifice to Molech. You shall not profane the name of your God. I am the LORD.

22 "'You shall not lie with a man as with a woman. That is detestable.

23 "'You shall not lie with any animal to defile yourself with it. No woman may give herself to an animal, to lie down with it: it is a perversion.

24 "'Don't defile yourselves in any of these things; for in all these the nations which I am casting out before you were defiled. 25 The land was defiled. Therefore I punished its iniquity, and the land vomited out her inhabitants. 26 You therefore shall keep my statutes and my ordinances, and shall not do any of these abominations; neither the native-born, nor the stranger who lives as a foreigner amongst you 27 (for the men of the land that were before you had done all these abominations, and the land became defiled), 28 that the land not vomit you out also, when you defile it, as it vomited out the nation that was before you.

29 "'For whoever shall do any of these abominations, even the souls that do them shall be cut off from amongst their people. 30 Therefore you shall keep my requirements, that you do not practise any of these abominable customs which were practised before you, and that you do not defile yourselves with them. I am the LORD your God.'"

19

1 The LORD spoke to Moses, saying, 2 "Speak to all the congregation of the children of Israel, and tell them, 'You shall be holy; for I, the LORD your God, am holy.

3 "'Each one of you shall respect his mother and his father. You shall keep my Sabbaths. I am the LORD your God.

4 "'Don't turn to idols, nor make molten gods for yourselves. I am the LORD your God.

5 "'When you offer a sacrifice of peace offerings to the LORD, you shall offer it so that you may be accepted. 6 It shall be eaten the same day you offer it, and on the next day. If anything remains until the third day, it shall be burnt with fire. 7 If it is eaten at all on the third day, it is an abomination. It will not be accepted; 8 but everyone who eats it shall bear his iniquity, because he has profaned the holy thing of the LORD, and that soul shall be cut off from his people.

9 "'When you reap the harvest of your land, you shall not wholly reap the corners of your field, neither shall you gather the gleanings of your harvest. 10 You shall not glean your vineyard, neither shall you gather the fallen grapes of your vineyard. You shall leave them for the poor and for the foreigner. I am the LORD your God.

11 "'You shall not steal.

"'You shall not lie.

"'You shall not deceive one another.

12 "'You shall not swear by my name falsely, and profane the name of your God. I am the LORD.

13 "'You shall not oppress your neighbour, nor rob him.

"'The wages of a hired servant shall not remain with you all night until the morning.

14 "'You shall not curse the deaf, nor put a stumbling block before the blind; but you shall fear your God. I am the LORD.

15 "'You shall do no injustice in judgement. You shall not be partial to the poor, nor show favouritism to the great; but you shall judge your neighbour in righteousness.

16 "'You shall not go around as a slanderer amongst your people.

"'You shall not endanger the life[a] of your neighbour. I am the LORD.

17 "'You shall not hate your brother in your heart. You shall surely rebuke your neighbour, and not bear sin because of him.

18 "'You shall not take vengeance, nor bear any grudge against the children of your people; but you shall love your neighbour as yourself. I am the LORD.

19 "'You shall keep my statutes.

"'You shall not cross-breed different kinds of animals.

"'You shall not sow your field with two kinds of seed;

"'Don't wear a garment made of two kinds of material.

20 "'If a man lies carnally with a woman who is a slave girl, pledged to be married to another man, and not ransomed or given her freedom; they shall be punished. They shall not be put to death, because she was not free. 21 He shall bring his trespass offering to the LORD, to the door of the Tent of Meeting, even a ram for a trespass offering. 22 The priest shall make atonement for him with the ram of the trespass offering before the LORD for his sin which he has committed; and the sin which he has committed shall be forgiven him.

23 "'When you come into the land, and have planted all kinds of trees for food, then you shall count their fruit as forbidden.[b] For three years it shall be forbidden to you. It shall not be eaten. 24 But in the fourth year all its fruit shall be holy, for giving praise to the LORD. 25 In the fifth year you shall eat its fruit, that it may yield its increase to you. I am the LORD your God.

---

a 19:16 literally, "blood"

b 19:23 literally, "uncircumcised"

26 "'You shall not eat any meat with the blood still in it. You shall not use enchantments, nor practise sorcery.

27 "'You shall not cut the hair on the sides of your head or clip off the edge of your beard.

28 "'You shall not make any cuttings in your flesh for the dead, nor tattoo any marks on you. I am the LORD.

29 "'Don't profane your daughter, to make her a prostitute; lest the land fall to prostitution, and the land become full of wickedness.

30 "'You shall keep my Sabbaths, and reverence my sanctuary; I am the LORD.

31 "'Don't turn to those who are mediums, nor to the wizards. Don't seek them out, to be defiled by them. I am the LORD your God.

32 "'You shall rise up before the grey head and honour the face of the elderly; and you shall fear your God. I am the LORD.

33 "'If a stranger lives as a foreigner with you in your land, you shall not do him wrong. 34 The stranger who lives as a foreigner with you shall be to you as the native-born amongst you, and you shall love him as yourself; for you lived as foreigners in the land of Egypt. I am the LORD your God.

35 "'You shall do no unrighteousness in judgement, in measures of length, of weight, or of quantity. 36 You shall have just balances, just weights, a just ephah,ª and a just hin.ᵇ I am the LORD your God, who brought you out of the land of Egypt.

37 "'You shall observe all my statutes and all my ordinances, and do them. I am the LORD.'"

20

1 The LORD spoke to Moses, saying, 2 "Moreover, you shall tell the children of Israel, 'Anyone of the children of Israel, or of the strangers who live as foreigners in Israel, who gives any of his offspringᶜ to Molech shall surely be put to death. The people of the land shall stone that person with stones. 3 I also will set my face against that person, and will cut him off from amongst his people, because he has given of his offspring to Molech, to defile my sanctuary, and to profane my holy name. 4 If the people of the land all hide their eyes from that person when he gives of his offspring to Molech, and don't put him to death, 5 then I will set my face against that man and against his family, and will cut him off, and all who play the prostitute after him to play the prostitute with Molech, from amongst their people.

6 "'The person that turns to those who are mediums and wizards, to play the prostitute after them, I will even set my face against that person, and will cut him off from amongst his people.

7 "'Sanctify yourselves therefore, and be holy; for I am the LORD your God. 8 You shall keep my statutes, and do them. I am the LORD who sanctifies you.

9 "'For everyone who curses his father or his mother shall surely be put to death. He has cursed his father or his mother. His blood shall be upon himself.

10 "'The man who commits adultery with another man's wife, even he who commits adultery with his neighbour's wife, the adulterer and the adulteress shall surely be put to death.

11 "'The man who lies with his father's wife has uncovered his father's nakedness. Both of them shall surely be put to death. Their blood shall be upon themselves.

12 "'If a man lies with his daughter-in-law, both of them shall surely be put to death. They have committed a perversion. Their blood shall be upon themselves.

13 "'If a man lies with a male, as with a woman, both of them have committed an abomination. They shall surely be put to death. Their blood shall be upon themselves.

14 "'If a man takes a wife and her mother, it is wickedness. They shall be burnt with fire, both he and they, that there may be no wickedness amongst you.

15 "'If a man lies with an animal, he shall surely be put to death; and you shall kill the animal.

16 "'If a woman approaches any animal and lies with it, you shall kill the woman and the animal. They shall surely be put to death. Their blood shall be upon them.

17 "'If a man takes his sister—his father's daughter, or his mother's daughter—and sees her nakedness, and she sees his nakedness, it is a shameful thing. They shall be cut off in the sight of the children of their people. He has uncovered his sister's nakedness. He shall bear his iniquity.

18 "'If a man lies with a woman having her monthly period, and uncovers her nakedness, he has made her fountain naked, and she has uncovered the fountain of her blood. Both of them shall be cut off from amongst their people.

19 "'You shall not uncover the nakedness of your mother's sister, nor of your father's sister, for he has made his close relative naked. They shall bear their iniquity. 20 If a man lies with his uncle's wife, he has uncovered his uncle's nakedness. They shall bear their sin. They shall die childless.

21 "'If a man takes his brother's wife, it is an impurity. He has uncovered his brother's nakedness. They shall be childless.

22 "'You shall therefore keep all my statutes and all my ordinances, and do them, that the land where I am bringing you to dwell may not vomit you out. 23 You shall not walk in the customs of the nation which I am casting out before you; for they did all these things, and therefore I abhorred them. 24 But I have said to you, "You shall inherit their land, and I will give it to you to possess it, a land flowing with milk and honey." I am the LORD your God, who has separated you from the peoples.

25 "'You shall therefore make a distinction between the clean animal and the unclean, and between the unclean fowl and the clean. You shall not make yourselves abominable by animal, or by bird, or by anything with which the ground teems, which I have separated from you as unclean for you. 26 You shall be holy to me, for I, the LORD, am holy, and have set you apart from the peoples, that you should be mine.

27 "'A man or a woman that is a medium or is a wizard shall surely be put to death. They shall be stoned with stones. Their blood shall be upon themselves.'"

21

1 The LORD said to Moses, "Speak to the priests, the sons of Aaron, and say to them, 'A priest shall not defile himself for the dead amongst his people, 2 except for his relatives that are near to him: for his mother, for his father, for his son, for his daughter, for his brother, 3 and for his virgin sister who is near to him, who has had no husband; for her he may defile himself. 4 He shall not defile himself, being a chief man amongst his people, to profane himself.

5 "'They shall not shave their heads or shave off the corners of their beards or make any cuttings in their flesh. 6 They shall be holy to their God, and not profane the name of their God, for they offer the offerings of the LORD made by fire, the bread of their God. Therefore they shall be holy.

7 "'They shall not marry a woman who is a prostitute, or profane. A priest shall not marry a woman divorced from her husband; for he is holy to his God. 8 Therefore you shall sanctify him, for he offers the bread of your God. He shall be holy to you, for I the LORD, who sanctify you, am holy.

9 "'The daughter of any priest, if she profanes herself by playing the prostitute, she profanes her father. She shall be burnt with fire.

10 "'He who is the high priest amongst his brothers, upon whose head the anointing oil is poured, and who is consecrated to put on the garments, shall not let the hair of his head hang loose, or tear his clothes. 11 He must not go in to any dead body, or defile himself for his father or for his mother. 12 He shall not go out of the sanctuary, nor profane the sanctuary of his God; for the crown of the anointing oil of his God is upon him. I am the LORD.

13 "'He shall take a wife in her virginity. 14 He shall not marry a widow, or one divorced, or a woman who has been defiled, or a prostitute. He shall take a virgin of his own people as a wife. 15 He shall not profane his offspring amongst his people, for I am the LORD who sanctifies him.'"

16 The LORD spoke to Moses, saying, 17 "Say to Aaron, 'None of your offspring throughout their generations who has a defect may approach to offer the bread of his God. 18 For whatever man he is that has a defect, he shall not draw near: a blind man, or a lame, or he who has a flat nose, or any deformity, 19 or a man who has an injured foot, or an injured hand, 20 or hunchbacked, or a dwarf, or one who has a defect in his eye, or an itching disease, or scabs, or who has damaged testicles. 21 No man of the offspring of Aaron the priest who has a defect shall come near to offer the offerings of the LORD made by fire. Since he has a defect, he shall not come near to offer the bread of his God. 22 He shall eat the bread of his God, both of the most holy, and of the holy. 23 He shall not come near to the veil, nor come near to the altar, because he has a defect; that he may not profane my sanctuaries, for I am the LORD who sanctifies them.'"

24 So Moses spoke to Aaron, and to his sons, and to all the children of Israel.

22

1 The LORD spoke to Moses, saying, 2 "Tell Aaron and his sons to separate themselves from the holy things of the children of Israel, which they make holy to me, and that they not profane my holy name. I am the LORD.

3 "Tell them, 'If anyone of all your offspring throughout your generations approaches the holy things which the children of Israel make holy to the LORD, having his uncleanness on him, that soul shall be cut off from before me. I am the LORD.

4 "'Whoever of the offspring of Aaron is a leper or has a discharge shall not eat of the holy things until he is clean. Whoever touches anything that is unclean by the dead, or a man who has a seminal emission, 5 or whoever touches any creeping thing by which he may be made unclean, or a man from whom he may become unclean, whatever uncleanness he has— 6 the person that touches any such shall be unclean until the evening, and shall not eat of the holy things unless he bathes his body in water. 7 When the sun is down, he shall be clean; and afterward he shall eat of the holy things, because it is his bread. 8 He shall not eat that which dies of itself or is torn by animals, defiling himself by it. I am the LORD.

9 "'They shall therefore follow my commandment, lest they bear sin for it and die in it, if they profane it. I am the LORD who sanctifies them.

10 "'No stranger shall eat of the holy thing: a foreigner living with the priests, or a hired servant, shall not eat of the holy thing. 11 But if a priest buys a slave, purchased by his money, he shall eat of it; and those who are born in his house shall eat of his bread. 12 If a priest's daughter is married to an outsider, she shall not eat of the heave offering of the holy things. 13 But if a priest's daughter is a widow, or divorced, and has no child, and has returned to her father's house as in her youth, she may eat of her father's bread; but no stranger shall eat any of it.

ª *19:36* 1 ephah is about 22 litres or about 2/3 of a bushel
ᵇ *19:36* A hin is about 6.5 litres or 1.7 gallons.

ᶜ *20:2* or, seed

14 "'If a man eats something holy unwittingly, then he shall add the fifth part of its value to it, and shall give the holy thing to the priest. 15 The priests shall not profane the holy things of the children of Israel, which they offer to the LORD, 16 and so cause them to bear the iniquity that brings guilt when they eat their holy things; for I am the LORD who sanctifies them.'"

17 The LORD spoke to Moses, saying, 18 "Speak to Aaron, and to his sons, and to all the children of Israel, and say to them, 'Whoever is of the house of Israel, or of the foreigners in Israel, who offers his offering, whether it is any of their vows or any of their free will offerings, which they offer to the LORD for a burnt offering: 19 that you may be accepted, you shall offer a male without defect, of the bulls, of the sheep, or of the goats. 20 But you shall not offer whatever has a defect, for it shall not be acceptable for you. 21 Whoever offers a sacrifice of peace offerings to the LORD to accomplish a vow, or for a free will offering of the herd or of the flock, it shall be perfect to be accepted. It shall have no defect. 22 You shall not offer what is blind, is injured, is maimed, has a wart, is festering, or has a running sore to the LORD, nor make an offering by fire of them on the altar to the LORD. 23 Either a bull or a lamb that has any deformity or lacking in his parts, that you may offer for a free will offering; but for a vow it shall not be accepted. 24 You must not offer to the LORD that which has its testicles bruised, crushed, broken, or cut. You must not do this in your land. 25 You must not offer any of these as the bread of your God from the hand of a foreigner, because their corruption is in them. There is a defect in them. They shall not be accepted for you.'"

26 The LORD spoke to Moses, saying, 27 "When a bull, a sheep, or a goat is born, it shall remain seven days with its mother. From the eighth day on it shall be accepted for the offering of an offering made by fire to the LORD. 28 Whether it is a cow or ewe, you shall not kill it and its young both in one day.

29 "When you sacrifice a sacrifice of thanksgiving to the LORD, you shall sacrifice it so that you may be accepted. 30 It shall be eaten on the same day; you shall leave none of it until the morning. I am the LORD.

31 "Therefore you shall keep my commandments, and do them. I am the LORD. 32 You shall not profane my holy name, but I will be made holy amongst the children of Israel. I am the LORD who makes you holy, 33 who brought you out of the land of Egypt, to be your God. I am the LORD."

23

1 The LORD spoke to Moses, saying, 2 "Speak to the children of Israel, and tell them, 'The set feasts of the LORD, which you shall proclaim to be holy convocations, even these are my set feasts.

3 "'Six days shall work be done, but on the seventh day is a Sabbath of solemn rest, a holy convocation; you shall do no kind of work. It is a Sabbath to the LORD in all your dwellings.

4 "'These are the set feasts of the LORD, even holy convocations, which you shall proclaim in their appointed season. 5 In the first month, on the fourteenth day of the month in the evening, is the LORD's Passover. 6 On the fifteenth day of the same month is the feast of unleavened bread to the LORD. Seven days you shall eat unleavened bread. 7 In the first day you shall have a holy convocation. You shall do no regular work. 8 But you shall offer an offering made by fire to the LORD seven days. In the seventh day is a holy convocation. You shall do no regular work.'"

9 The LORD spoke to Moses, saying, 10 "Speak to the children of Israel, and tell them, 'When you have come into the land which I give to you, and shall reap its harvest, then you shall bring the sheaf of the first fruits of your harvest to the priest. 11 He shall wave the sheaf before the LORD, to be accepted for you. On the next day after the Sabbath the priest shall wave it. 12 On the day when you wave the sheaf, you shall offer a male lamb without defect a year old for a burnt offering to the LORD. 13 The meal offering with it shall be two tenths of an ephah[a] of fine flour mixed with oil, an offering made by fire to the LORD for a pleasant aroma; and the drink offering with it shall be of wine, the fourth part of a hin.[b] 14 You must not eat bread, or roasted grain, or fresh grain, until this same day, until you have brought the offering of your God. This is a statute forever throughout your generations in all your dwellings.

15 "'You shall count from the next day after the Sabbath, from the day that you brought the sheaf of the wave offering: seven Sabbaths shall be completed. 16 The next day after the seventh Sabbath you shall count fifty days; and you shall offer a new meal offering to the LORD. 17 You shall bring out of your habitations two loaves of bread for a wave offering made of two tenths of an ephah[c] of fine flour. They shall be baked with yeast, for first fruits to the LORD. 18 You shall present with the bread seven lambs without defect a year old, one young bull, and two rams. They shall be a burnt offering to the LORD, with their meal offering and their drink offerings, even an offering made by fire, of a sweet aroma to the LORD. 19 You shall offer one male goat for a sin offering, and two male lambs a year old for a sacrifice of peace offerings. 20 The priest shall wave them with the bread of the first fruits for a wave offering before the LORD, with the two lambs. They shall be holy to the LORD for the priest. 21 You shall make proclamation on the same day that there shall be a holy convocation to you. You shall do no regular work. This is a statute forever in all your dwellings throughout your generations.

22 "'When you reap the harvest of your land, you must not wholly reap into the corners of your field. You must not gather the gleanings of your harvest. You must leave them for the poor and for the foreigner. I am the LORD your God.'"

23 The LORD spoke to Moses, saying, 24 "Speak to the children of Israel, saying, 'In the seventh month, on the first day of the month, there shall be a solemn rest for you, a memorial of blowing of trumpets, a holy convocation. 25 You shall do no regular work. You shall offer an offering made by fire to the LORD.'"

26 The LORD spoke to Moses, saying, 27 "However on the tenth day of this seventh month is the day of atonement. It shall be a holy convocation to you. You shall afflict yourselves and you shall offer an offering made by fire to the LORD. 28 You shall do no kind of work in that same day, for it is a day of atonement, to make atonement for you before the LORD your God. 29 For whoever it is who shall not deny himself in that same day shall be cut off from his people. 30 Whoever does any kind of work in that same day, I will destroy that person from amongst his people. 31 You shall do no kind of work: it is a statute forever throughout your generations in all your dwellings. 32 It shall be a Sabbath of solemn rest for you, and you shall deny yourselves. In the ninth day of the month at evening, from evening to evening, you shall keep your Sabbath."

33 The LORD spoke to Moses, saying, 34 "Speak to the children of Israel, and say, 'On the fifteenth day of this seventh month is the feast of booths[d] for seven days to the LORD. 35 On the first day shall be a holy convocation. You shall do no regular work. 36 Seven days you shall offer an offering made by fire to the LORD. On the eighth day shall be a holy convocation to you. You shall offer an offering made by fire to the LORD. It is a solemn assembly; you shall do no regular work.

37 "'These are the appointed feasts of the LORD which you shall proclaim to be holy convocations, to offer an offering made by fire to the LORD, a burnt offering, a meal offering, a sacrifice, and drink offerings, each on its own day— 38 in addition to the Sabbaths of the LORD, and in addition to your gifts, and in addition to all your vows, and in addition to all your free will offerings, which you give to the LORD.

39 "'So on the fifteenth day of the seventh month, when you have gathered in the fruits of the land, you shall keep the feast of the LORD seven days. On the first day shall be a solemn rest, and on the eighth day shall be a solemn rest. 40 You shall take on the first day the fruit of majestic trees, branches of palm trees, and boughs of thick trees, and willows of the brook; and you shall rejoice before the LORD your God seven days. 41 You shall keep it as a feast to the LORD seven days in the year. It is a statute forever throughout your generations. You shall keep it in the seventh month. 42 You shall dwell in temporary shelters[e] for seven days. All who are native-born in Israel shall dwell in temporary shelters,[f] 43 that your generations may know that I made the children of Israel to dwell in temporary shelters[g] when I brought them out of the land of Egypt. I am the LORD your God.'"

44 So Moses declared to the children of Israel the appointed feasts of the LORD.

24

1 The LORD spoke to Moses, saying, 2 "Command the children of Israel, that they bring to you pure olive oil beaten for the light, to cause a lamp to burn continually. 3 Outside of the veil of the Testimony, in the Tent of Meeting, Aaron shall keep it in order from evening to morning before the LORD continually. It shall be a statute forever throughout your generations. 4 He shall keep in order the lamps on the pure gold lamp stand before the LORD continually.

5 "You shall take fine flour, and bake twelve cakes of it: two tenths of an ephah[h] shall be in one cake. 6 You shall set them in two rows, six on a row, on the pure gold table before the LORD. 7 You shall put pure frankincense on each row, that it may be to the bread for a memorial, even an offering made by fire to the LORD. 8 Every Sabbath day he shall set it in order before the LORD continually. It is an everlasting covenant on the behalf of the children of Israel. 9 It shall be for Aaron and his sons. They shall eat it in a holy place; for it is most holy to him of the offerings of the LORD made by fire by a perpetual statute."

10 The son of an Israelite woman, whose father was an Egyptian, went out amongst the children of Israel; and the son of the Israelite woman and a man of Israel strove together in the camp. 11 The son of the Israelite woman blasphemed the Name, and cursed; and they brought him to Moses. His mother's name was Shelomith, the daughter of Dibri, of the tribe of Dan. 12 They put him in custody until the LORD's will should be declared to them. 13 The LORD spoke to Moses, saying, 14 "Bring him who cursed out of the camp; and let all who heard him lay their hands on his head, and let all the congregation stone him. 15 You shall speak to the children of Israel, saying, 'Whoever curses his God shall bear his sin. 16 He who blasphemes the LORD's name, he shall surely be put to death. All the congregation shall certainly stone him. The foreigner as well as the native-born shall be put to death when he blasphemes the Name.

17 "'He who strikes any man mortally shall surely be put to death. 18 He who strikes an animal mortally shall make it good, life for life. 19 If anyone injures his neighbour, it shall be done to him as he has done: 20 fracture for fracture, eye for eye, tooth for tooth. It shall be done to him as he has injured someone. 21 He who kills an animal shall make it good; and he who

---

a 23:13 1 ephah is about 22 litres or about 2/3 of a bushel
b 23:13 A hin is about 6.5 litres or 1.7 gallons.
c 23:17 1 ephah is about 22 litres or about 2/3 of a bushel
d 23:34 or, feast of tents, or Succoth

e 23:42 or, booths
f 23:42 or, booths
g 23:43 or, booths
h 24:5 1 ephah is about 22 litres or about 2/3 of a bushel

kills a man shall be put to death. 22 You shall have one kind of law for the foreigner as well as the native-born; for I am the LORD your God.'"

23 Moses spoke to the children of Israel; and they brought him who had cursed out of the camp, and stoned him with stones. The children of Israel did as the LORD commanded Moses.

25

1 The LORD said to Moses on Mount Sinai, 2 "Speak to the children of Israel, and tell them, 'When you come into the land which I give you, then the land shall keep a Sabbath to the LORD. 3 You shall sow your field six years, and you shall prune your vineyard six years, and gather in its fruits; 4 but in the seventh year there shall be a Sabbath of solemn rest for the land, a Sabbath to the LORD. You shall not sow your field or prune your vineyard. 5 What grows of itself in your harvest you shall not reap, and you shall not gather the grapes of your undressed vine. It shall be a year of solemn rest for the land. 6 The Sabbath of the land shall be for food for you; for yourself, for your servant, for your maid, for your hired servant, and for your stranger, who lives as a foreigner with you. 7 For your livestock also, and for the animals that are in your land, shall all its increase be for food.

8 "'You shall count off seven Sabbaths of years, seven times seven years; and there shall be to you the days of seven Sabbaths of years, even forty-nine years. 9 Then you shall sound the loud trumpet on the tenth day of the seventh month. On the Day of Atonement you shall sound the trumpet throughout all your land. 10 You shall make the fiftieth year holy, and proclaim liberty throughout the land to all its inhabitants. It shall be a jubilee to you; and each of you shall return to his own property, and each of you shall return to his family. 11 That fiftieth year shall be a jubilee to you. In it you shall not sow, neither reap that which grows of itself, nor gather from the undressed vines. 12 For it is a jubilee; it shall be holy to you. You shall eat of its increase out of the field.

13 "'In this Year of Jubilee each of you shall return to his property.

14 "'If you sell anything to your neighbour, or buy from your neighbour, you shall not wrong one another. 15 According to the number of years after the Jubilee you shall buy from your neighbour. According to the number of years of the crops he shall sell to you. 16 According to the length of the years you shall increase its price, and according to the shortness of the years you shall diminish its price; for he is selling the number of the crops to you. 17 You shall not wrong one another, but you shall fear your God; for I am the LORD your God.

18 "'Therefore you shall do my statutes, and keep my ordinances and do them; and you shall dwell in the land in safety. 19 The land shall yield its fruit, and you shall eat your fill, and dwell therein in safety. 20 If you said, "What shall we eat the seventh year? Behold, we shall not sow, nor gather in our increase;" 21 then I will command my blessing on you in the sixth year, and it shall bear fruit for the three years. 22 You shall sow the eighth year, and eat of the fruits from the old store until the ninth year. Until its fruits come in, you shall eat the old store.

23 "'The land shall not be sold in perpetuity, for the land is mine; for you are strangers and live as foreigners with me. 24 In all the land of your possession you shall grant a redemption for the land.

25 "'If your brother becomes poor, and sells some of his possessions, then his kinsman who is next to him shall come, and redeem that which his brother has sold. 26 If a man has no one to redeem it, and he becomes prosperous and finds sufficient means to redeem it, 27 then let him reckon the years since its sale, and restore the surplus to the man to whom he sold it; and he shall return to his property. 28 But if he isn't able to get it back for himself, then what he has sold shall remain in the hand of him who has bought it until the Year of Jubilee. In the Jubilee it shall be released, and he shall return to his property.

29 "'If a man sells a dwelling house in a walled city, then he may redeem it within a whole year after it has been sold. For a full year he shall have the right of redemption. 30 If it isn't redeemed within the space of a full year, then the house that is in the walled city shall be made sure in perpetuity to him who bought it, throughout his generations. It shall not be released in the Jubilee. 31 But the houses of the villages which have no wall around them shall be accounted for with the fields of the country: they may be redeemed, and they shall be released in the Jubilee.

32 "'Nevertheless, in the cities of the Levites, the Levites may redeem the houses in the cities of their possession at any time. 33 The Levites may redeem the house that was sold, and the city of his possession, and it shall be released in the Jubilee; for the houses of the cities of the Levites are their possession amongst the children of Israel. 34 But the field of the pasture lands of their cities may not be sold, for it is their perpetual possession.

35 "'If your brother has become poor, and his hand can't support himself amongst you, then you shall uphold him. He shall live with you like an alien and a temporary resident. 36 Take no interest from him or profit; but fear your God; that your brother may live amongst you. 37 You shall not lend him your money at interest, nor give him your food for profit. 38 I am the LORD your God, who brought you out of the land of Egypt, to give you the land of Canaan, and to be your God.

39 "'If your brother has grown poor amongst you, and sells himself to you, you shall not make him to serve as a slave. 40 As a hired servant, and as a temporary resident, he shall be with you; he shall serve with you until the Year of Jubilee. 41 Then he shall go out from you, he and his children with him, and shall return to his own family, and to the possession of his fathers. 42 For they are my servants, whom I brought out of the land of Egypt. They shall not be sold as slaves. 43 You shall not rule over him with harshness, but shall fear your God.

44 "'As for your male and your female slaves, whom you may have from the nations that are around you, from them you may buy male and female slaves. 45 Moreover, of the children of the aliens who live amongst you, of them you may buy, and of their families who are with you, which they have conceived in your land; and they will be your property. 46 You may make them an inheritance for your children after you, to hold for a possession. Of them you may take your slaves forever, but over your brothers the children of Israel you shall not rule, one over another, with harshness.

47 "'If an alien or temporary resident with you becomes rich, and your brother beside him has grown poor, and sells himself to the stranger or foreigner living amongst you, or to a member of the stranger's family, 48 after he is sold he may be redeemed. One of his brothers may redeem him; 49 or his uncle, or his uncle's son, may redeem him, or any who is a close relative to him of his family may redeem him; or if he has grown rich, he may redeem himself. 50 He shall reckon with him who bought him from the year that he sold himself to him to the Year of Jubilee. The price of his sale shall be according to the number of years; he shall be with him according to the time of a hired servant. 51 If there are yet many years, according to them he shall give back the price of his redemption out of the money that he was bought for. 52 If there remain but a few years to the year of jubilee, then he shall reckon with him; according to his years of service he shall give back the price of his redemption. 53 As a servant hired year by year shall he be with him. He shall not rule with harshness over him in your sight. 54 If he isn't redeemed by these means, then he shall be released in the Year of Jubilee: he and his children with him. 55 For to me the children of Israel are servants; they are my servants whom I brought out of the land of Egypt. I am the LORD your God.

26

1 "'You shall make for yourselves no idols, and you shall not raise up a carved image or a pillar, and you shall not place any figured stone in your land, to bow down to it; for I am the LORD your God.

2 "'You shall keep my Sabbaths, and have reverence for my sanctuary. I am the LORD.

3 "'If you walk in my statutes and keep my commandments, and do them, 4 then I will give you your rains in their season, and the land shall yield its increase, and the trees of the field shall yield their fruit. 5 Your threshing shall continue until the vintage, and the vintage shall continue until the sowing time. You shall eat your bread to the full, and dwell in your land safely.

6 "'I will give peace in the land, and you shall lie down, and no one will make you afraid. I will remove evil animals out of the land, neither shall the sword go through your land. 7 You shall chase your enemies, and they shall fall before you by the sword. 8 Five of you shall chase a hundred, and a hundred of you shall chase ten thousand; and your enemies shall fall before you by the sword.

9 "'I will have respect for you, make you fruitful, multiply you, and will establish my covenant with you. 10 You shall eat old supplies long kept, and you shall move out the old because of the new. 11 I will set my tent amongst you, and my soul won't abhor you. 12 I will walk amongst you, and will be your God, and you will be my people. 13 I am the LORD your God, who brought you out of the land of Egypt, that you should not be their slaves. I have broken the bars of your yoke, and made you walk upright.

14 "'But if you will not listen to me, and will not do all these commandments, 15 and if you shall reject my statutes, and if your soul abhors my ordinances, so that you will not do all my commandments, but break my covenant, 16 I also will do this to you: I will appoint terror over you, even consumption and fever, that shall consume the eyes, and make the soul to pine away. You will sow your seed in vain, for your enemies will eat it. 17 I will set my face against you, and you will be struck before your enemies. Those who hate you will rule over you; and you will flee when no one pursues you.

18 "'If you in spite of these things will not listen to me, then I will chastise you seven times more for your sins. 19 I will break the pride of your power, and I will make your sky like iron, and your soil like bronze. 20 Your strength will be spent in vain; for your land won't yield its increase, neither will the trees of the land yield their fruit.

21 "'If you walk contrary to me, and won't listen to me, then I will bring seven times more plagues on you according to your sins. 22 I will send the wild animals amongst you, which will rob you of your children, destroy your livestock, and make you few in number. Your roads will become desolate.

23 "'If by these things you won't be turned back to me, but will walk contrary to me, 24 then I will also walk contrary to you; and I will strike you, even I, seven times for your sins. 25 I will bring a sword upon you that will execute the vengeance of the covenant. You will be gathered together within your cities, and I will send the pestilence amongst you. You will be delivered into the hand of the enemy. 26 When I break your staff of bread, ten women shall bake your bread in one oven, and they shall deliver your bread again by weight. You shall eat, and not be satisfied.

27 "'If you in spite of this won't listen to me, but walk contrary to me, 28 then I will walk contrary to you in wrath. I will also chastise you seven times for your sins. 29 You will eat the flesh of your sons, and you will eat the flesh of your daughters. 30 I will destroy your high places, and cut down your incense altars, and cast your dead bodies upon the bodies of your idols; and my soul will abhor you. 31 I will lay your cities waste, and will bring your sanctuaries to desolation. I will not take delight in the sweet fragrance of your offerings. 32 I will bring the land into desolation, and your enemies who dwell in it will be astonished at it. 33 I will scatter you amongst the nations, and I will draw out the sword after you. Your land will be a

desolation, and your cities shall be a waste. 34 Then the land will enjoy its Sabbaths as long as it lies desolate and you are in your enemies' land. Even then the land will rest and enjoy its Sabbaths. 35 As long as it lies desolate it shall have rest, even the rest which it didn't have in your Sabbaths when you lived on it.

36 "'As for those of you who are left, I will send a faintness into their hearts in the lands of their enemies. The sound of a driven leaf will put them to flight; and they shall flee, as one flees from the sword. They will fall when no one pursues. 37 They will stumble over one another, as it were before the sword, when no one pursues. You will have no power to stand before your enemies. 38 You will perish amongst the nations. The land of your enemies will eat you up. 39 Those of you who are left will pine away in their iniquity in your enemies' lands; and also in the iniquities of their fathers they shall pine away with them.

40 "'If they confess their iniquity and the iniquity of their fathers, in their trespass which they trespassed against me; and also that because they walked contrary to me, 41 I also walked contrary to them, and brought them into the land of their enemies; if then their uncircumcised heart is humbled, and they then accept the punishment of their iniquity, 42 then I will remember my covenant with Jacob, my covenant with Isaac, and also my covenant with Abraham; and I will remember the land. 43 The land also will be left by them, and will enjoy its Sabbaths while it lies desolate without them; and they will accept the punishment of their iniquity because they rejected my ordinances, and their soul abhorred my statutes. 44 Yet for all that, when they are in the land of their enemies, I will not reject them, neither will I abhor them, to destroy them utterly and to break my covenant with them; for I am the LORD their God. 45 But I will for their sake remember the covenant of their ancestors, whom I brought out of the land of Egypt in the sight of the nations, that I might be their God. I am the LORD.'"

46 These are the statutes, ordinances, and laws, which the LORD made between him and the children of Israel in Mount Sinai by Moses.

27

1 The LORD spoke to Moses, saying, 2 "Speak to the children of Israel, and say to them, 'When a man consecrates a person to the LORD in a vow, according to your valuation, 3 your valuation of a male from twenty years old to sixty years old shall be fifty shekels of silver, according to the shekel[a] of the sanctuary. 4 If she is a female, then your valuation shall be thirty shekels. 5 If the person is from five years old to twenty years old, then your valuation shall be for a male twenty shekels, and for a female ten shekels. 6 If the person is from a month old to five years old, then your valuation shall be for a male five shekels of silver, and for a female your valuation shall be three shekels of silver. 7 If the person is from sixty years old and upward; if he is a male, then your valuation shall be fifteen shekels, and for a female ten shekels. 8 But if he is poorer than your valuation, then he shall be set before the priest, and the priest shall assign a value to him. The priest shall assign a value according to his ability to pay.

9 "'If it is an animal of which men offer an offering to the LORD, all that any man gives of such to the LORD becomes holy. 10 He shall not alter it, nor exchange it, a good for a bad, or a bad for a good. If he shall at all exchange animal for animal, then both it and that for which it is exchanged shall be holy. 11 If it is any unclean animal, of which they do not offer as an offering to the LORD, then he shall set the animal before the priest; 12 and the priest shall evaluate it, whether it is good or bad. As the priest evaluates it, so it shall be. 13 But if he will indeed redeem it, then he shall add the fifth part of it to its valuation.

14 "'When a man dedicates his house to be holy to the LORD, then the priest shall evaluate it, whether it is good or bad. As the priest evaluates it, so it shall stand. 15 If he who dedicates it will redeem his house, then he shall add the fifth part of the money of your valuation to it, and it shall be his.

16 "'If a man dedicates to the LORD part of the field of his possession, then your valuation shall be according to the seed for it. The sowing of a homer[b] of barley shall be valued at fifty shekels[c] of silver. 17 If he dedicates his field from the Year of Jubilee, according to your valuation it shall stand. 18 But if he dedicates his field after the Jubilee, then the priest shall reckon to him the money according to the years that remain to the Year of Jubilee; and an abatement shall be made from your valuation. 19 If he who dedicated the field will indeed redeem it, then he shall add the fifth part of the money of your valuation to it, and it shall remain his. 20 If he will not redeem the field, or if he has sold the field to another man, it shall not be redeemed any more; 21 but the field, when it goes out in the Jubilee, shall be holy to the LORD, as a devoted field. It shall be owned by the priests.

22 "'If he dedicates a field to the LORD which he has bought, which is not of the field of his possession, 23 then the priest shall reckon to him the worth of your valuation up to the Year of Jubilee; and he shall give your valuation on that day, as a holy thing to the LORD. 24 In the Year of Jubilee the field shall return to him from whom it was bought, even to him to whom the possession of the land belongs. 25 All your valuations shall be according to the shekel of the sanctuary: twenty gerahs[d] to the shekel.[e]

26 "'However the firstborn amongst animals, which belongs to the LORD as a firstborn, no man may dedicate, whether an ox or a sheep. It is the LORD's. 27 If it is an unclean animal, then he shall buy it back according to your valuation, and shall add to it the fifth part of it; or if it isn't redeemed, then it shall be sold according to your valuation.

28 "'Notwithstanding, no devoted thing that a man devotes to the LORD of all that he has, whether of man or animal, or of the field of his possession, shall be sold or redeemed. Everything that is permanently devoted is most holy to the LORD.

29 "'No one devoted to destruction, who shall be devoted from amongst men, shall be ransomed. He shall surely be put to death.

30 "'All the tithe of the land, whether of the seed of the land or of the fruit of the trees, is the LORD's. It is holy to the LORD. 31 If a man redeems anything of his tithe, he shall add a fifth part to it. 32 All the tithe of the herds or the flocks, whatever passes under the rod, the tenth shall be holy to the LORD. 33 He shall not examine whether it is good or bad, neither shall he exchange it. If he exchanges it at all, then both it and that for which it is exchanged shall be holy. It shall not be redeemed.'"

34 These are the commandments which the LORD commanded Moses for the children of Israel on Mount Sinai.

---

[a] 27:3 A shekel is about 10 grams or about 0.35 ounces.
[b] 27:16 1 homer is about 220 litres or 6 bushels
[c] 27:16 A shekel is about 10 grams or about 0.35 ounces.
[d] 27:25 A gerah is about 0.5 grams or about 7.7 grains.
[e] 27:25 A shekel is about 10 grams or about 0.35 ounces.

The Fourth Book of Moses, Commonly Called Numbers

1

1 The LORD[a] spoke to Moses in the wilderness of Sinai, in the Tent of Meeting, on the first day of the second month, in the second year after they had come out of the land of Egypt, saying, 2 "Take a census of all the congregation of the children of Israel, by their families, by their fathers' houses, according to the number of the names, every male, one by one, 3 from twenty years old and upward, all who are able to go to war in Israel. You and Aaron shall count them by their divisions. 4 With you there shall be a man of every tribe, each one head of his fathers' house. 5 These are the names of the men who shall stand with you:

Of Reuben: Elizur the son of Shedeur.

6 Of Simeon: Shelumiel the son of Zurishaddai.

7 Of Judah: Nahshon the son of Amminadab.

8 Of Issachar: Nethanel the son of Zuar.

9 Of Zebulun: Eliab the son of Helon.

10 Of the children of Joseph: of Ephraim: Elishama the son of Ammihud; of Manasseh: Gamaliel the son of Pedahzur.

11 Of Benjamin: Abidan the son of Gideoni.

12 Of Dan: Ahiezer the son of Ammishaddai.

13 Of Asher: Pagiel the son of Ochran.

14 Of Gad: Eliasaph the son of Deuel.

15 Of Naphtali: Ahira the son of Enan."

16 These are those who were called of the congregation, the princes[b] of the tribes of their fathers; they were the heads of the thousands of Israel. 17 Moses and Aaron took these men who are mentioned by name. 18 They assembled all the congregation together on the first day of the second month; and they declared their ancestry by their families, by their fathers' houses, according to the number of the names, from twenty years old and upward, one by one. 19 As the LORD commanded Moses, so he counted them in the wilderness of Sinai.

20 The children of Reuben, Israel's firstborn, their generations, by their families, by their fathers' houses, according to the number of the names, one by one, every male from twenty years old and upward, all who were able to go out to war: 21 those who were counted of them, of the tribe of Reuben, were forty-six thousand and five hundred.

22 Of the children of Simeon, their generations, by their families, by their fathers' houses, those who were counted of it, according to the number of the names, one by one, every male from twenty years old and upward, all who were able to go out to war: 23 those who were counted of them, of the tribe of Simeon, were fifty-nine thousand and three hundred.

24 Of the children of Gad, their generations, by their families, by their fathers' houses, according to the number of the names, from twenty years old and upward, all who were able to go out to war: 25 those who were counted of them, of the tribe of Gad, were forty-five thousand and six hundred and fifty.

26 Of the children of Judah, their generations, by their families, by their fathers' houses, according to the number of the names, from twenty years old and upward, all who were able to go out to war: 27 those who were counted of them, of the tribe of Judah, were seventy-four thousand and six hundred.

28 Of the children of Issachar, their generations, by their families, by their fathers' houses, according to the number of the names, from twenty years old and upward, all who were able to go out to war: 29 those who were counted of them, of the tribe of Issachar, were fifty-four thousand and four hundred.

30 Of the children of Zebulun, their generations, by their families, by their fathers' houses, according to the number of the names, from twenty years old and upward, all who were able to go out to war: 31 those who were counted of them, of the tribe of Zebulun, were fifty-seven thousand and four hundred.

32 Of the children of Joseph: of the children of Ephraim, their generations, by their families, by their fathers' houses, according to the number of the names, from twenty years old and upward, all who were able to go out to war: 33 those who were counted of them, of the tribe of Ephraim, were forty thousand and five hundred.

34 Of the children of Manasseh, their generations, by their families, by their fathers' houses, according to the number of the names, from twenty years old and upward, all who were able to go out to war: 35 those who were counted of them, of the tribe of Manasseh, were thirty-two thousand and two hundred.

36 Of the children of Benjamin, their generations, by their families, by their fathers' houses, according to the number of the names, from twenty years old and upward, all who were able to go out to war: 37 those who were counted of them, of the tribe of Benjamin, were thirty-five thousand and four hundred.

38 Of the children of Dan, their generations, by their families, by their fathers' houses, according to the number of the names, from twenty years old and upward, all who were able to go out to war: 39 those who were counted of them, of the tribe of Dan, were sixty-two thousand and seven hundred.

40 Of the children of Asher, their generations, by their families, by their fathers' houses, according to the number of the names, from twenty years old and upward, all who were able to go out to war: 41 those who were counted of them, of the tribe of Asher, were forty-one thousand and five hundred.

42 Of the children of Naphtali, their generations, by their families, by their fathers' houses, according to the number of the names, from twenty years old and upward, all who were able to go out to war: 43 those who were counted of them, of the tribe of Naphtali, were fifty-three thousand and four hundred.

44 These are those who were counted, whom Moses and Aaron counted, and the twelve men who were princes of Israel, each one for his fathers' house. 45 So all those who were counted of the children of Israel by their fathers' houses, from twenty years old and upward, all who were able to go out to war in Israel— 46 all those who were counted were six hundred and three thousand and five hundred and fifty. 47 But the Levites after the tribe of their fathers were not counted amongst them. 48 For the LORD spoke to Moses, saying, 49 "Only the tribe of Levi you shall not count, neither shall you take a census of them amongst the children of Israel; 50 but appoint the Levites over the Tabernacle of the Testimony, and over all its furnishings, and over all that belongs to it. They shall carry the tabernacle and all its furnishings; and they shall take care of it, and shall encamp around it. 51 When the tabernacle is to move, the Levites shall take it down; and when the tabernacle is to be set up, the Levites shall set it up. The stranger who comes near shall be put to death. 52 The children of Israel shall pitch their tents, every man by his own camp, and every man by his own standard, according to their divisions. 53 But the Levites shall encamp around the Tabernacle of the Testimony, that there may be no wrath on the congregation of the children of Israel. The Levites shall be responsible for the Tabernacle of the Testimony."

54 Thus the children of Israel did. According to all that the LORD commanded Moses, so they did.

2

1 The LORD spoke to Moses and to Aaron, saying, 2 "The children of Israel shall encamp every man by his own standard, with the banners of their fathers' houses. They shall encamp around the Tent of Meeting at a distance from it.

3 "Those who encamp on the east side towards the sunrise shall be of the standard of the camp of Judah, according to their divisions. The prince of the children of Judah shall be Nahshon the son of Amminadab. 4 His division, and those who were counted of them, were seventy-four thousand and six hundred.

5 "Those who encamp next to him shall be the tribe of Issachar. The prince of the children of Issachar shall be Nethanel the son of Zuar. 6 His division, and those who were counted of it, were fifty-four thousand and four hundred.

7 "The tribe of Zebulun: the prince of the children of Zebulun shall be Eliab the son of Helon. 8 His division, and those who were counted of it, were fifty-seven thousand and four hundred.

9 "All who were counted of the camp of Judah were one hundred and eighty-six thousand and four hundred, according to their divisions. They shall set out first.

10 "On the south side shall be the standard of the camp of Reuben according to their divisions. The prince of the children of Reuben shall be Elizur the son of Shedeur. 11 His division, and those who were counted of it, were forty-six thousand and five hundred.

12 "Those who encamp next to him shall be the tribe of Simeon. The prince of the children of Simeon shall be Shelumiel the son of Zurishaddai. 13 His division, and those who were counted of them, were fifty-nine thousand and three hundred.

14 "The tribe of Gad: the prince of the children of Gad shall be Eliasaph the son of Reuel. 15 His division, and those who were counted of them, were forty-five thousand and six hundred and fifty.

16 "All who were counted of the camp of Reuben were one hundred and fifty-one thousand and four hundred and fifty, according to their armies. They shall set out second.

17 "Then the Tent of Meeting shall set out, with the camp of the Levites in the middle of the camps. As they encamp, so shall they set out, every man in his place, by their standards.

18 "On the west side shall be the standard of the camp of Ephraim according to their divisions. The prince of the children of Ephraim shall be Elishama the son of Ammihud. 19 His division, and those who were counted of them, were forty thousand and five hundred.

20 "Next to him shall be the tribe of Manasseh. The prince of the children of Manasseh shall be Gamaliel the son of Pedahzur. 21 His division, and those who were counted of them, were thirty-two thousand and two hundred.

22 "The tribe of Benjamin: the prince of the children of Benjamin shall be Abidan the son of Gideoni. 23 His army, and those who were counted of them, were thirty-five thousand and four hundred.

24 "All who were counted of the camp of Ephraim were one hundred and eight thousand and one hundred, according to their divisions. They shall set out third.

25 "On the north side shall be the standard of the camp of Dan according to their divisions. The prince of the children of Dan shall be

---

Ahiezer the son of Ammishaddai. 26 His division, and those who were counted of them, were sixty-two thousand and seven hundred.

27 "Those who encamp next to him shall be the tribe of Asher. The prince of the children of Asher shall be Pagiel the son of Ochran. 28 His division, and those who were counted of them, were forty-one thousand and five hundred.

29 "The tribe of Naphtali: the prince of the children of Naphtali shall be Ahira the son of Enan. 30 His division, and those who were counted of them, were fifty-three thousand and four hundred.

31 "All who were counted of the camp of Dan were one hundred and fifty-seven thousand and six hundred. They shall set out last by their standards."

32 These are those who were counted of the children of Israel by their fathers' houses. All who were counted of the camps according to their armies were six hundred and three thousand and five hundred and fifty. 33 But the Levites were not counted amongst the children of Israel, as the LORD commanded Moses.

34 Thus the children of Israel did. According to all that the LORD commanded Moses, so they encamped by their standards, and so they set out, everyone by their families, according to their fathers' houses.

3

1 Now this is the history of the generations of Aaron and Moses in the day that the LORD spoke with Moses in Mount Sinai. 2 These are the names of the sons of Aaron: Nadab the firstborn, and Abihu, Eleazar, and Ithamar.

3 These are the names of the sons of Aaron, the priests who were anointed, whom he consecrated to minister in the priest's office. 4 Nadab and Abihu died before the LORD when they offered strange fire before the LORD in the wilderness of Sinai, and they had no children. Eleazar and Ithamar ministered in the priest's office in the presence of Aaron their father.

5 The LORD spoke to Moses, saying, 6 "Bring the tribe of Levi near, and set them before Aaron the priest, that they may minister to him. 7 They shall keep his requirements, and the requirements of the whole congregation before the Tent of Meeting, to do the service of the tabernacle. 8 They shall keep all the furnishings of the Tent of Meeting, and the obligations of the children of Israel, to do the service of the tabernacle. 9 You shall give the Levites to Aaron and to his sons. They are wholly given to him on the behalf of the children of Israel. 10 You shall appoint Aaron and his sons, and they shall keep their priesthood, but the stranger who comes near shall be put to death."

11 The LORD spoke to Moses, saying, 12 "Behold,[a] I have taken the Levites from amongst the children of Israel instead of all the firstborn who open the womb amongst the children of Israel; and the Levites shall be mine, 13 for all the firstborn are mine. On the day that I struck down all the firstborn in the land of Egypt I made holy to me all the firstborn in Israel, both man and animal. They shall be mine. I am the LORD."

14 The LORD spoke to Moses in the wilderness of Sinai, saying, 15 "Count the children of Levi by their fathers' houses, by their families. You shall count every male from a month old and upward."

16 Moses counted them according to the LORD's word, as he was commanded.

17 These were the sons of Levi by their names: Gershon, Kohath, and Merari.

18 These are the names of the sons of Gershon by their families: Libni and Shimei.

19 The sons of Kohath by their families: Amram, Izhar, Hebron, and Uzziel.

20 The sons of Merari by their families: Mahli and Mushi.

These are the families of the Levites according to their fathers' houses.

21 Of Gershon was the family of the Libnites, and the family of the Shimeites. These are the families of the Gershonites.

22 Those who were counted of them, according to the number of all the males from a month old and upward, even those who were counted of them were seven thousand and five hundred.

23 The families of the Gershonites shall encamp behind the tabernacle westward.

24 Eliasaph the son of Lael shall be the prince of the fathers' house of the Gershonites. 25 The duty of the sons of Gershon in the Tent of Meeting shall be the tabernacle, the tent, its covering, the screen for the door of the Tent of Meeting, 26 the hangings of the court, the screen for the door of the court which is by the tabernacle and around the altar, and its cords for all of its service.

27 Of Kohath was the family of the Amramites, the family of the Izharites, the family of the Hebronites, and the family of the Uzzielites. These are the families of the Kohathites. 28 According to the number of all the males from a month old and upward, there were eight thousand and six hundred keeping the requirements of the sanctuary.

29 The families of the sons of Kohath shall encamp on the south side of the tabernacle. 30 The prince of the fathers' house of the families of the Kohathites shall be Elizaphan the son of Uzziel. 31 Their duty shall be the

ark, the table, the lamp stand, the altars, the vessels of the sanctuary with which they minister, the screen, and all its service. 32 Eleazar the son of Aaron the priest shall be prince of the princes of the Levites, with the oversight of those who keep the requirements of the sanctuary.

33 Of Merari was the family of the Mahlites and the family of the Mushites. These are the families of Merari. 34 Those who were counted of them, according to the number of all the males from a month old and upward, were six thousand and two hundred.[b]

35 The prince of the fathers' house of the families of Merari was Zuriel the son of Abihail. They shall encamp on the north side of the tabernacle. 36 The appointed duty of the sons of Merari shall be the tabernacle's boards, its bars, its pillars, its sockets, all its instruments, all its service, 37 the pillars of the court around it, their sockets, their pins, and their cords.

38 Those who encamp before the tabernacle eastward, in front of the Tent of Meeting towards the sunrise, shall be Moses, with Aaron and his sons, keeping the requirements of the sanctuary for the duty of the children of Israel. The outsider who comes near shall be put to death. 39 All who were counted of the Levites, whom Moses and Aaron counted at the commandment of the LORD, by their families, all the males from a month old and upward, were twenty-two thousand.

40 The LORD said to Moses, "Count all the firstborn males of the children of Israel from a month old and upward, and take the number of their names. 41 You shall take the Levites for me—I am the LORD—instead of all the firstborn amongst the children of Israel; and the livestock of the Levites instead of all the firstborn amongst the livestock of the children of Israel."

42 Moses counted, as the LORD commanded him, all the firstborn amongst the children of Israel. 43 All the firstborn males according to the number of names from a month old and upward, of those who were counted of them, were twenty-two thousand and two hundred and seventy-three.

44 The LORD spoke to Moses, saying, 45 "Take the Levites instead of all the firstborn amongst the children of Israel, and the livestock of the Levites instead of their livestock; and the Levites shall be mine. I am the LORD. 46 For the redemption of the two hundred and seventy-three of the firstborn of the children of Israel who exceed the number of the Levites, 47 you shall take five shekels apiece for each one; according to the shekel[c] of the sanctuary you shall take them (the shekel is twenty gerahs[d]); 48 and you shall give the money, with which their remainder is redeemed, to Aaron and to his sons."

49 Moses took the redemption money from those who exceeded the number of those who were redeemed by the Levites; 50 from the firstborn of the children of Israel he took the money, one thousand and three hundred and sixty-five shekels,[e] according to the shekel of the sanctuary; 51 and Moses gave the redemption money to Aaron and to his sons, according to the LORD's word, as the LORD commanded Moses.

4

1 The LORD spoke to Moses and to Aaron, saying, 2 "Take a census of the sons of Kohath from amongst the sons of Levi, by their families, by their fathers' houses, 3 from thirty years old and upward even until fifty years old, all who enter into the service to do the work in the Tent of Meeting.

4 "This is the service of the sons of Kohath in the Tent of Meeting, regarding the most holy things. 5 When the camp moves forward, Aaron shall go in with his sons; and they shall take down the veil of the screen, cover the ark of the Testimony with it, 6 put a covering of sealskin on it, spread a blue cloth over it, and put in its poles.

7 "On the table of show bread they shall spread a blue cloth, and put on it the dishes, the spoons, the bowls, and the cups with which to pour out; and the continual bread shall be on it. 8 They shall spread on them a scarlet cloth, and cover it with a covering of sealskin, and shall put in its poles.

9 "They shall take a blue cloth and cover the lamp stand of the light, its lamps, its snuffers, its snuff dishes, and all its oil vessels, with which they minister to it. 10 They shall put it and all its vessels within a covering of sealskin, and shall put it on the frame.

11 "On the golden altar they shall spread a blue cloth, and cover it with a covering of sealskin, and shall put in its poles.

12 "They shall take all the vessels of ministry with which they minister in the sanctuary, and put them in a blue cloth, cover them with a covering of sealskin, and shall put them on the frame.

13 "They shall take away the ashes from the altar, and spread a purple cloth on it. 14 They shall put on it all its vessels with which they minister about it, the fire pans, the meat hooks, the shovels, and the basins—all the vessels of the altar; and they shall spread on it a covering of sealskin, and put in its poles.

15 "When Aaron and his sons have finished covering the sanctuary and all the furniture of the sanctuary, as the camp moves forward; after that, the sons of Kohath shall come to carry it; but they shall not touch the sanctuary, lest they die. The sons of Kohath shall carry these things belonging to the Tent of Meeting.

---

a *3:12* "Behold", from "הָנֵּה", means look at, take notice, observe, see, or gaze at. It is often used as an interjection.

b *3:34* + 22,000 is the sum rounded to 2 significant digits. The sum of the Gershonites, Kohathites, and Merarites given above is 22,300, but the traditional Hebrew text has the number rounded to 2 significant digits, not 3 significant digits.

c *3:47* A shekel is about 10 grams or about 0.35 ounces.

d *3:47* A gerah is about 0.5 grams or about 7.7 grains.

e *3:50* A shekel is about 10 grams or about 0.35 ounces, so 1365 shekels is about 13.65 kilograms or about 30 pounds.

16 "The duty of Eleazar the son of Aaron the priest shall be the oil for the light, the sweet incense, the continual meal offering, and the anointing oil, the requirements of all the tabernacle, and of all that is in it, the sanctuary, and its furnishings."

17 The LORD spoke to Moses and to Aaron, saying, 18 "Don't cut off the tribe of the families of the Kohathites from amongst the Levites; 19 but do this to them, that they may live, and not die, when they approach the most holy things: Aaron and his sons shall go in and appoint everyone to his service and to his burden; 20 but they shall not go in to see the sanctuary even for a moment, lest they die."

21 The LORD spoke to Moses, saying, 22 "Take a census of the sons of Gershon also, by their fathers' houses, by their families; 23 you shall count them from thirty years old and upward until fifty years old: all who enter in to wait on the service, to do the work in the Tent of Meeting.

24 "This is the service of the families of the Gershonites, in serving and in bearing burdens: 25 they shall carry the curtains of the tabernacle and the Tent of Meeting, its covering, the covering of sealskin that is on it, the screen for the door of the Tent of Meeting, 26 the hangings of the court, the screen for the door of the gate of the court which is by the tabernacle and around the altar, their cords, and all the instruments of their service, and whatever shall be done with them. They shall serve in there. 27 At the commandment of Aaron and his sons shall be all the service of the sons of the Gershonites, in all their burden and in all their service; and you shall appoint their duty to them in all their responsibilities. 28 This is the service of the families of the sons of the Gershonites in the Tent of Meeting. Their duty shall be under the hand of Ithamar the son of Aaron the priest.

29 "As for the sons of Merari, you shall count them by their families, by their fathers' houses; 30 you shall count them from thirty years old and upward even to fifty years old—everyone who enters on the service, to do the work of the Tent of Meeting. 31 This is the duty of their burden, according to all their service in the Tent of Meeting: the tabernacle's boards, its bars, its pillars, its sockets, 32 the pillars of the court around it, their sockets, their pins, their cords, with all their instruments, and with all their service. You shall appoint the instruments of the duty of their burden to them by name. 33 This is the service of the families of the sons of Merari, according to all their service in the Tent of Meeting, under the hand of Ithamar the son of Aaron the priest."

34 Moses and Aaron and the princes of the congregation counted the sons of the Kohathites by their families, and by their fathers' houses, 35 from thirty years old and upward even to fifty years old, everyone who entered into the service for work in the Tent of Meeting. 36 Those who were counted of them by their families were two thousand and seven hundred and fifty. 37 These are those who were counted of the families of the Kohathites, all who served in the Tent of Meeting, whom Moses and Aaron counted according to the commandment of the LORD by Moses.

38 Those who were counted of the sons of Gershon, by their families, and by their fathers' houses, 39 from thirty years old and upward even to fifty years old—everyone who entered into the service for work in the Tent of Meeting, 40 even those who were counted of them, by their families, by their fathers' houses, were two thousand and six hundred and thirty. 41 These are those who were counted of the families of the sons of Gershon, all who served in the Tent of Meeting, whom Moses and Aaron counted according to the commandment of the LORD.

42 Those who were counted of the families of the sons of Merari, by their families, by their fathers' houses, 43 from thirty years old and upward even to fifty years old—everyone who entered into the service for work in the Tent of Meeting, 44 even those who were counted of them by their families, were three thousand and two hundred. 45 These are those who were counted of the families of the sons of Merari, whom Moses and Aaron counted according to the commandment of the LORD by Moses.

46 All those who were counted of the Levites whom Moses and Aaron and the princes of Israel counted, by their families and by their fathers' houses, 47 from thirty years old and upward even to fifty years old, everyone who entered in to do the work of service and the work of bearing burdens in the Tent of Meeting, 48 even those who were counted of them, were eight thousand and five hundred and eighty. 49 According to the commandment of the LORD they were counted by Moses, everyone according to his service and according to his burden. Thus they were counted by him, as the LORD commanded Moses.

5

1 The LORD spoke to Moses, saying, 2 "Command the children of Israel that they put out of the camp every leper, everyone who has a discharge, and whoever is unclean by a corpse. 3 You shall put both male and female outside of the camp so that they don't defile their camp, in the midst of which I dwell."

4 The children of Israel did so, and put them outside of the camp; as the LORD spoke to Moses, so the children of Israel did.

5 The LORD spoke to Moses, saying, 6 "Speak to the children of Israel: 'When a man or woman commits any sin that men commit, so as to trespass against the LORD, and that soul is guilty, 7 then he shall confess his sin which he has done; and he shall make restitution for his guilt in full, add to it the fifth part of it, and give it to him in respect of whom he has been guilty. 8 But if the man has no kinsman to whom restitution may be made for the guilt, the restitution for guilt which is made to the LORD shall be the priest's, in addition to the ram of the atonement, by which atonement shall be made for him. 9 Every heave offering of all the holy things of the children of Israel, which they present to the priest, shall be his. 10 Every man's holy things shall be his; whatever any man gives the priest, it shall be his.'"

11 The LORD spoke to Moses, saying, 12 "Speak to the children of Israel, and tell them: 'If any man's wife goes astray and is unfaithful to him, 13 and a man lies with her carnally, and it is hidden from the eyes of her husband and this is kept concealed, and she is defiled, there is no witness against her, and she isn't taken in the act; 14 and the spirit of jealousy comes on him, and he is jealous of his wife and she is defiled; or if the spirit of jealousy comes on him, and he is jealous of his wife and she isn't defiled; 15 then the man shall bring his wife to the priest, and shall bring her offering for her: one tenth of an ephah[a] of barley meal. He shall pour no oil on it, nor put frankincense on it, for it is a meal offering of jealousy, a meal offering of memorial, bringing iniquity to memory. 16 The priest shall bring her near, and set her before the LORD. 17 The priest shall take holy water in an earthen vessel; and the priest shall take some of the dust that is on the floor of the tabernacle and put it into the water. 18 The priest shall set the woman before the LORD, and let the hair of the woman's head go loose, and put the meal offering of memorial in her hands, which is the meal offering of jealousy. The priest shall have in his hand the water of bitterness that brings a curse. 19 The priest shall cause her to take an oath and shall tell the woman, "If no man has lain with you, and if you haven't gone aside to uncleanness, being under your husband's authority, be free from this water of bitterness that brings a curse. 20 But if you have gone astray, being under your husband's authority, and if you are defiled, and some man has lain with you besides your husband—" 21 then the priest shall cause the woman to swear with the oath of cursing, and the priest shall tell the woman, "May The LORD make you a curse and an oath amongst your people, when the LORD allows your thigh to fall away, and your body to swell; 22 and this water that brings a curse will go into your bowels, and make your body swell, and your thigh fall away." The woman shall say, "Amen, Amen."

23 "'The priest shall write these curses in a book, and he shall wipe them into the water of bitterness. 24 He shall make the woman drink the water of bitterness that causes the curse; and the water that causes the curse shall enter into her and become bitter. 25 The priest shall take the meal offering of jealousy out of the woman's hand, and shall wave the meal offering before the LORD, and bring it to the altar. 26 The priest shall take a handful of the meal offering, as its memorial portion, and burn it on the altar, and afterward shall make the woman drink the water. 27 When he has made her drink the water, then it shall happen, if she is defiled and has committed a trespass against her husband, that the water that causes the curse will enter into her and become bitter, and her body will swell, and her thigh will fall away; and the woman will be a curse amongst her people. 28 If the woman isn't defiled, but is clean; then she shall be free, and shall conceive offspring.[b]

29 "'This is the law of jealousy, when a wife, being under her husband, goes astray, and is defiled, 30 or when the spirit of jealousy comes on a man, and he is jealous of his wife; then he shall set the woman before the LORD, and the priest shall execute on her all this law. 31 The man shall be free from iniquity, and that woman shall bear her iniquity.'"

6

1 The LORD spoke to Moses, saying, 2 "Speak to the children of Israel, and tell them: 'When either man or woman shall make a special vow, the vow of a Nazirite, to separate himself to the LORD, 3 he shall separate himself from wine and strong drink. He shall drink no vinegar of wine, or vinegar of fermented drink, neither shall he drink any juice of grapes, nor eat fresh grapes or dried. 4 All the days of his separation he shall eat nothing that is made of the grapevine, from the seeds even to the skins.

5 "'All the days of his vow of separation no razor shall come on his head, until the days are fulfilled in which he separates himself to the LORD. He shall be holy. He shall let the locks of the hair of his head grow long.

6 "'All the days that he separates himself to the LORD he shall not go near a dead body. 7 He shall not make himself unclean for his father, or for his mother, for his brother, or for his sister, when they die, because his separation to God[c] is on his head. 8 All the days of his separation he is holy to the LORD.

9 "'If any man dies very suddenly beside him, and he defiles the head of his separation, then he shall shave his head in the day of his cleansing. On the seventh day he shall shave it. 10 On the eighth day he shall bring two turtledoves or two young pigeons to the priest, to the door of the Tent of Meeting. 11 The priest shall offer one for a sin offering, and the other for a burnt offering, and make atonement for him, because he sinned by reason of the dead, and shall make his head holy that same day. 12 He shall separate to the LORD the days of his separation, and shall bring a male lamb a year old for a trespass offering; but the former days shall be void, because his separation was defiled.

13 "'This is the law of the Nazirite: when the days of his separation are fulfilled, he shall be brought to the door of the Tent of Meeting, 14 and he shall offer his offering to the LORD: one male lamb a year old without defect for a burnt offering, one ewe lamb a year old without defect for a sin offering, one ram without defect for peace offerings, 15 a basket of unleavened bread, cakes of fine flour mixed with oil, and unleavened wafers anointed with oil with their meal offering and their drink offerings. 16 The

---

a 5:15 1 ephah is about 22 litres or about 2/3 of a bushel
b 5:28 or, seed

c 6:7 The Hebrew word rendered "God" is "אֱלֹהִים" (Elohim).

priest shall present them before the LORD, and shall offer his sin offering and his burnt offering. 17 He shall offer the ram for a sacrifice of peace offerings to the LORD, with the basket of unleavened bread. The priest shall offer also its meal offering and its drink offering. 18 The Nazirite shall shave the head of his separation at the door of the Tent of Meeting, take the hair of the head of his separation, and put it on the fire which is under the sacrifice of peace offerings. 19 The priest shall take the boiled shoulder of the ram, one unleavened cake out of the basket, and one unleavened wafer, and shall put them on the hands of the Nazirite after he has shaved the head of his separation; 20 and the priest shall wave them for a wave offering before the LORD. They are holy for the priest, together with the breast that is waved and the thigh that is offered. After that the Nazirite may drink wine.

21 "'This is the law of the Nazirite who vows and of his offering to the LORD for his separation, in addition to that which he is able to afford. According to his vow which he vows, so he must do after the law of his separation.'"

22 The LORD spoke to Moses, saying, 23 "Speak to Aaron and to his sons, saying, 'This is how you shall bless the children of Israel.' You shall tell them,

24 'The LORD bless you, and keep you.

25 The LORD make his face to shine on you,
and be gracious to you.

26 The LORD lift up his face towards you,
and give you peace.'

27 "So they shall put my name on the children of Israel; and I will bless them."

7

1 On the day that Moses had finished setting up the tabernacle, and had anointed it and sanctified it with all its furniture, and the altar with all its vessels, and had anointed and sanctified them; 2 the princes of Israel, the heads of their fathers' houses, gave offerings. These were the princes of the tribes. These are they who were over those who were counted; 3 and they brought their offering before the LORD, six covered wagons and twelve oxen; a wagon for every two of the princes, and for each one an ox. They presented them before the tabernacle. 4 The LORD spoke to Moses, saying, 5 "Accept these from them, that they may be used in doing the service of the Tent of Meeting; and you shall give them to the Levites, to every man according to his service."

6 Moses took the wagons and the oxen, and gave them to the Levites. 7 He gave two wagons and four oxen to the sons of Gershon, according to their service. 8 He gave four wagons and eight oxen to the sons of Merari, according to their service, under the direction of Ithamar the son of Aaron the priest. 9 But to the sons of Kohath he gave none, because the service of the sanctuary belonged to them; they carried it on their shoulders.

10 The princes gave offerings for the dedication of the altar in the day that it was anointed. The princes gave their offerings before the altar.

11 The LORD said to Moses, "They shall offer their offering, each prince on his day, for the dedication of the altar."

12 He who offered his offering the first day was Nahshon the son of Amminadab, of the tribe of Judah, 13 and his offering was:
one silver platter, the weight of which was one hundred and thirty shekels,[a]
one silver bowl of seventy shekels, according to the shekel of the sanctuary, both of them full of fine flour mixed with oil for a meal offering;
14 one golden ladle of ten shekels, full of incense;
15 one young bull,
one ram,
one male lamb a year old, for a burnt offering;
16 one male goat for a sin offering;
17 and for the sacrifice of peace offerings, two head of cattle, five rams, five male goats, and five male lambs a year old. This was the offering of Nahshon the son of Amminadab.

18 On the second day Nethanel the son of Zuar, prince of Issachar, gave his offering. 19 He offered for his offering:
one silver platter, the weight of which was one hundred and thirty shekels,
one silver bowl of seventy shekels, according to the shekel of the sanctuary, both of them full of fine flour mixed with oil for a meal offering;
20 one golden ladle of ten shekels, full of incense;
21 one young bull,
one ram,
one male lamb a year old, for a burnt offering;
22 one male goat for a sin offering;
23 and for the sacrifice of peace offerings, two head of cattle, five rams, five male goats, five male lambs a year old. This was the offering of Nethanel the son of Zuar.

24 On the third day Eliab the son of Helon, prince of the children of Zebulun, 25 gave his offering:
one silver platter, the weight of which was a hundred and thirty shekels,
one silver bowl of seventy shekels, according to the shekel of the sanctuary, both of them full of fine flour mixed with oil for a meal offering;
26 one golden ladle of ten shekels, full of incense;
27 one young bull,
one ram,
one male lamb a year old, for a burnt offering;

28 one male goat for a sin offering;
29 and for the sacrifice of peace offerings, two head of cattle, five rams, five male goats, and five male lambs a year old. This was the offering of Eliab the son of Helon.

30 On the fourth day Elizur the son of Shedeur, prince of the children of Reuben, 31 gave his offering:
one silver platter, the weight of which was one hundred and thirty shekels,
one silver bowl of seventy shekels, according to the shekel of the sanctuary, both of them full of fine flour mixed with oil for a meal offering;
32 one golden ladle of ten shekels, full of incense;
33 one young bull,
one ram,
one male lamb a year old, for a burnt offering;
34 one male goat for a sin offering;
35 and for the sacrifice of peace offerings, two head of cattle, five rams, five male goats, and five male lambs a year old. This was the offering of Elizur the son of Shedeur.

36 On the fifth day Shelumiel the son of Zurishaddai, prince of the children of Simeon, 37 gave his offering:
one silver platter, the weight of which was one hundred and thirty shekels,
one silver bowl of seventy shekels, according to the shekel of the sanctuary, both of them full of fine flour mixed with oil for a meal offering;
38 one golden ladle of ten shekels, full of incense;
39 one young bull,
one ram,
one male lamb a year old, for a burnt offering;
40 one male goat for a sin offering;
41 and for the sacrifice of peace offerings, two head of cattle, five rams, five male goats, and five male lambs a year old: this was the offering of Shelumiel the son of Zurishaddai.

42 On the sixth day, Eliasaph the son of Deuel, prince of the children of Gad, 43 gave his offering:
one silver platter, the weight of which was one hundred and thirty shekels,
one silver bowl of seventy shekels, according to the shekel of the sanctuary, both of them full of fine flour mixed with oil for a meal offering;
44 one golden ladle of ten shekels, full of incense;
45 one young bull,
one ram,
one male lamb a year old, for a burnt offering;
46 one male goat for a sin offering;
47 and for the sacrifice of peace offerings, two head of cattle, five rams, five male goats, and five male lambs a year old. This was the offering of Eliasaph the son of Deuel.

48 On the seventh day Elishama the son of Ammihud, prince of the children of Ephraim, 49 gave his offering:
one silver platter, the weight of which was one hundred and thirty shekels,
one silver bowl of seventy shekels, according to the shekel of the sanctuary, both of them full of fine flour mixed with oil for a meal offering;
50 one golden ladle of ten shekels, full of incense;
51 one young bull,
one ram,
one male lamb a year old, for a burnt offering;
52 one male goat for a sin offering;
53 and for the sacrifice of peace offerings, two head of cattle, five rams, five male goats, and five male lambs a year old. This was the offering of Elishama the son of Ammihud.

54 On the eighth day Gamaliel the son of Pedahzur, prince of the children of Manasseh, 55 gave his offering:
one silver platter, the weight of which was one hundred and thirty shekels,
one silver bowl of seventy shekels, according to the shekel of the sanctuary, both of them full of fine flour mixed with oil for a meal offering;
56 one golden ladle of ten shekels, full of incense;
57 one young bull,
one ram,
one male lamb a year old, for a burnt offering;
58 one male goat for a sin offering;
59 and for the sacrifice of peace offerings, two head of cattle, five rams, five male goats, and five male lambs a year old. This was the offering of Gamaliel the son of Pedahzur.

60 On the ninth day Abidan the son of Gideoni, prince of the children of Benjamin, 61 gave his offering:
one silver platter, the weight of which was one hundred and thirty shekels,
one silver bowl of seventy shekels, according to the shekel of the sanctuary, both of them full of fine flour mixed with oil for a meal offering;
62 one golden ladle of ten shekels, full of incense;
63 one young bull,
one ram,
one male lamb a year old, for a burnt offering;
64 one male goat for a sin offering;

---

65 and for the sacrifice of peace offerings, two head of cattle, five rams, five male goats, and five male lambs a year old. This was the offering of Abidan the son of Gideoni.

66 On the tenth day Ahiezer the son of Ammishaddai, prince of the children of Dan, 67 gave his offering:

one silver platter, the weight of which was one hundred and thirty shekels,

one silver bowl of seventy shekels, according to the shekel of the sanctuary, both of them full of fine flour mixed with oil for a meal offering;

68 one golden ladle of ten shekels, full of incense;

69 one young bull,

one ram,

one male lamb a year old, for a burnt offering;

70 one male goat for a sin offering;

71 and for the sacrifice of peace offerings, two head of cattle, five rams, five male goats, and five male lambs a year old. This was the offering of Ahiezer the son of Ammishaddai.

72 On the eleventh day Pagiel the son of Ochran, prince of the children of Asher, 73 gave his offering:

one silver platter, the weight of which was one hundred and thirty shekels,

one silver bowl of seventy shekels, according to the shekel of the sanctuary, both of them full of fine flour mixed with oil for a meal offering;

74 one golden ladle of ten shekels, full of incense;

75 one young bull,

one ram,

one male lamb a year old, for a burnt offering;

76 one male goat for a sin offering;

77 and for the sacrifice of peace offerings, two head of cattle, five rams, five male goats, and five male lambs a year old. This was the offering of Pagiel the son of Ochran.

78 On the twelfth day Ahira the son of Enan, prince of the children of Naphtali, 79 gave his offering:

one silver platter, the weight of which was one hundred and thirty shekels,

one silver bowl of seventy shekels, according to the shekel of the sanctuary, both of them full of fine flour mixed with oil for a meal offering;

80 one golden ladle of ten shekels, full of incense;

81 one young bull,

one ram,

one male lamb a year old, for a burnt offering;

82 one male goat for a sin offering;

83 and for the sacrifice of peace offerings, two head of cattle, five rams, five male goats, and five male lambs a year old. This was the offering of Ahira the son of Enan.

84 This was the dedication offering of the altar, on the day when it was anointed, by the princes of Israel: twelve silver platters, twelve silver bowls, twelve golden ladles; 85 each silver platter weighing one hundred and thirty shekels, and each bowl seventy; all the silver of the vessels two thousand and four hundred shekels, according to the shekel of the sanctuary; 86 the twelve golden ladles, full of incense, weighing ten shekels apiece, according to the shekel of the sanctuary; all the gold of the ladles weighed one hundred and twenty shekels; 87 all the cattle for the burnt offering twelve bulls, the rams twelve, the male lambs a year old twelve, and their meal offering; and twelve male goats for a sin offering; 88 and all the cattle for the sacrifice of peace offerings: twenty-four bulls, sixty rams, sixty male goats, and sixty male lambs a year old. This was the dedication offering of the altar, after it was anointed.

89 When Moses went into the Tent of Meeting to speak with the LORD, he heard his voice speaking to him from above the mercy seat that was on the ark of the Testimony, from between the two cherubim; and he spoke to him.

8

1 The LORD spoke to Moses, saying, 2 "Speak to Aaron, and tell him, 'When you light the lamps, the seven lamps shall give light in front of the lamp stand.'"

3 Aaron did so. He lit its lamps to light the area in front of the lamp stand, as the LORD commanded Moses. 4 This was the workmanship of the lamp stand, beaten work of gold. From its base to its flowers, it was beaten work. He made the lamp stand according to the pattern which the LORD had shown Moses.

5 The LORD spoke to Moses, saying, 6 "Take the Levites from amongst the children of Israel, and cleanse them. 7 You shall do this to them to cleanse them: sprinkle the water of cleansing on them, let them shave their whole bodies with a razor, let them wash their clothes, and cleanse themselves. 8 Then let them take a young bull and its meal offering, fine flour mixed with oil; and another young bull you shall take for a sin offering. 9 You shall present the Levites before the Tent of Meeting. You shall assemble the whole congregation of the children of Israel. 10 You shall present the Levites before the LORD. The children of Israel shall lay their hands on the Levites, 11 and Aaron shall offer the Levites before the LORD for a wave offering on the behalf of the children of Israel, that it may be theirs to do the service of the LORD.

12 "The Levites shall lay their hands on the heads of the bulls, and you shall offer the one for a sin offering and the other for a burnt offering to the LORD, to make atonement for the Levites. 13 You shall set the Levites before Aaron and before his sons, and offer them as a wave offering to the LORD. 14 Thus you shall separate the Levites from amongst the children of Israel, and the Levites shall be mine.

15 "After that, the Levites shall go in to do the service of the Tent of Meeting. You shall cleanse them, and offer them as a wave offering. 16 For they are wholly given to me from amongst the children of Israel; instead of all who open the womb, even the firstborn of all the children of Israel, I have taken them to me. 17 For all the firstborn amongst the children of Israel are mine, both man and animal. On the day that I struck all the firstborn in the land of Egypt, I sanctified them for myself. 18 I have taken the Levites instead of all the firstborn amongst the children of Israel. 19 I have given the Levites as a gift to Aaron and to his sons from amongst the children of Israel, to do the service of the children of Israel in the Tent of Meeting, and to make atonement for the children of Israel, so that there will be no plague amongst the children of Israel when the children of Israel come near to the sanctuary."

20 Moses, and Aaron, and all the congregation of the children of Israel did so to the Levites. According to all that the LORD commanded Moses concerning the Levites, so the children of Israel did to them. 21 The Levites purified themselves from sin, and they washed their clothes; and Aaron offered them for a wave offering before the LORD and Aaron made atonement for them to cleanse them. 22 After that, the Levites went in to do their service in the Tent of Meeting before Aaron and before his sons: as the LORD had commanded Moses concerning the Levites, so they did to them.

23 The LORD spoke to Moses, saying, 24 "This is what is assigned to the Levites: from twenty-five years old and upward they shall go in to wait on the service in the work of the Tent of Meeting; 25 and from the age of fifty years they shall retire from doing the work, and shall serve no more, 26 but shall assist their brothers in the Tent of Meeting, to perform the duty, and shall perform no service. This is how you shall have the Levites do their duties."

9

1 The LORD spoke to Moses in the wilderness of Sinai, in the first month of the second year after they had come out of the land of Egypt, saying, 2 "Let the children of Israel keep the Passover in its appointed season. 3 On the fourteenth day of this month, at evening, you shall keep it in its appointed season. You shall keep it according to all its statutes and according to all its ordinances."

4 Moses told the children of Israel that they should keep the Passover. 5 They kept the Passover in the first month, on the fourteenth day of the month at evening, in the wilderness of Sinai. According to all that the LORD commanded Moses, so the children of Israel did. 6 There were certain men who were unclean because of the dead body of a man, so that they could not keep the Passover on that day, and they came before Moses and Aaron on that day. 7 Those men said to him, "We are unclean because of the dead body of a man. Why are we kept back, that we may not offer the offering of the LORD in its appointed season amongst the children of Israel?"

8 Moses answered them, "Wait, that I may hear what the LORD will command concerning you."

9 The LORD spoke to Moses, saying, 10 "Say to the children of Israel, 'If any man of you or of your generations is unclean by reason of a dead body, or is on a journey far away, he shall still keep the Passover to the LORD. 11 In the second month, on the fourteenth day at evening they shall keep it; they shall eat it with unleavened bread and bitter herbs. 12 They shall leave none of it until the morning, nor break a bone of it. According to all the statute of the Passover they shall keep it. 13 But the man who is clean, and is not on a journey, and fails to keep the Passover, that soul shall be cut off from his people. Because he didn't offer the offering of the LORD in its appointed season, that man shall bear his sin.

14 "'If a foreigner lives amongst you and desires to keep the Passover to the LORD, then he shall do so according to the statute of the Passover, and according to its ordinance. You shall have one statute, both for the foreigner and for him who is born in the land.'"

15 On the day that the tabernacle was raised up, the cloud covered the tabernacle, even the Tent of the Testimony. At evening it was over the tabernacle, as it were the appearance of fire, until morning. 16 So it was continually. The cloud covered it, and the appearance of fire by night. 17 Whenever the cloud was taken up from over the Tent, then after that the children of Israel travelled; and in the place where the cloud remained, there the children of Israel encamped. 18 At the commandment of the LORD, the children of Israel travelled, and at the commandment of the LORD they encamped. As long as the cloud remained on the tabernacle they remained encamped. 19 When the cloud stayed on the tabernacle many days, then the children of Israel kept the LORD's command, and didn't travel. 20 Sometimes the cloud was a few days on the tabernacle; then according to the commandment of the LORD they remained encamped, and according to the commandment of the LORD they travelled. 21 Sometimes the cloud was from evening until morning; and when the cloud was taken up in the morning, they travelled; or by day and by night, when the cloud was taken up, they travelled. 22 Whether it was two days, or a month, or a year that the cloud stayed on the tabernacle, remaining on it, the children of Israel remained encamped, and didn't travel; but when it was taken up, they travelled. 23 At the commandment of the LORD they encamped, and at the commandment of the LORD they travelled. They kept the LORD's command, at the commandment of the LORD by Moses.

10

1 The LORD spoke to Moses, saying, 2 "Make two trumpets of silver. You shall make them of beaten work. You shall use them for the calling of the congregation and for the journeying of the camps. 3 When they blow them, all the congregation shall gather themselves to you at the door of the

Tent of Meeting. 4 If they blow just one, then the princes, the heads of the thousands of Israel, shall gather themselves to you. 5 When you blow an alarm, the camps that lie on the east side shall go forward. 6 When you blow an alarm the second time, the camps that lie on the south side shall go forward. They shall blow an alarm for their journeys. 7 But when the assembly is to be gathered together, you shall blow, but you shall not sound an alarm.

8 "The sons of Aaron, the priests, shall blow the trumpets. This shall be to you for a statute forever throughout your generations. 9 When you go to war in your land against the adversary who oppresses you, then you shall sound an alarm with the trumpets. Then you will be remembered before the LORD your God, and you will be saved from your enemies.

10 "Also in the day of your gladness, and in your set feasts, and in the beginnings of your months, you shall blow the trumpets over your burnt offerings, and over the sacrifices of your peace offerings; and they shall be to you for a memorial before your God. I am the LORD your God."

11 In the second year, in the second month, on the twentieth day of the month, the cloud was taken up from over the tabernacle of the covenant. 12 The children of Israel went forward on their journeys out of the wilderness of Sinai; and the cloud stayed in the wilderness of Paran. 13 They first went forward according to the commandment of the LORD by Moses.

14 First, the standard of the camp of the children of Judah went forward according to their armies. Nahshon the son of Amminadab was over his army. 15 Nethanel the son of Zuar was over the army of the tribe of the children of Issachar. 16 Eliab the son of Helon was over the army of the tribe of the children of Zebulun. 17 The tabernacle was taken down; and the sons of Gershon and the sons of Merari, who bore the tabernacle, went forward. 18 The standard of the camp of Reuben went forward according to their armies. Elizur the son of Shedeur was over his army. 19 Shelumiel the son of Zurishaddai was over the army of the tribe of the children of Simeon. 20 Eliasaph the son of Deuel was over the army of the tribe of the children of Gad.

21 The Kohathites set forward, bearing the sanctuary. The others set up the tabernacle before they arrived.

22 The standard of the camp of the children of Ephraim set forward according to their armies. Elishama the son of Ammihud was over his army. 23 Gamaliel the son of Pedahzur was over the army of the tribe of the children of Manasseh. 24 Abidan the son of Gideoni was over the army of the tribe of the children of Benjamin.

25 The standard of the camp of the children of Dan, which was the rear guard of all the camps, set forward according to their armies. Ahiezer the son of Ammishaddai was over his army. 26 Pagiel the son of Ochran was over the army of the tribe of the children of Asher. 27 Ahira the son of Enan was over the army of the tribe of the children of Naphtali. 28 Thus were the travels of the children of Israel according to their armies; and they went forward.

29 Moses said to Hobab, the son of Reuel the Midianite, Moses' father-in-law, "We are journeying to the place of which the LORD said, 'I will give it to you.' Come with us, and we will treat you well; for the LORD has spoken good concerning Israel."

30 He said to him, "I will not go; but I will depart to my own land, and to my relatives."

31 Moses said, "Don't leave us, please; because you know how we are to encamp in the wilderness, and you can be our eyes. 32 It shall be, if you go with us—yes, it shall be—that whatever good the LORD does to us, we will do the same to you."

33 They set forward from the Mount of the LORD three days' journey. The ark of the LORD's covenant went before them three days' journey, to seek out a resting place for them. 34 The cloud of the LORD was over them by day, when they set forward from the camp. 35 When the ark went forward, Moses said, "Rise up, LORD, and let your enemies be scattered! Let those who hate you flee before you!" 36 When it rested, he said, "Return, LORD, to the ten thousands of the thousands of Israel."

11

1 The people were complaining in the ears of the LORD. When the LORD heard it, his anger burnt; and the LORD's fire burnt amongst them, and consumed some of the outskirts of the camp. 2 The people cried to Moses; and Moses prayed to the LORD, and the fire abated. 3 The name of that place was called Taberah,ᵃ because the LORD's fire burnt amongst them.

4 The mixed multitude that was amongst them lusted exceedingly; and the children of Israel also wept again, and said, "Who will give us meat to eat? 5 We remember the fish, which we ate in Egypt for nothing; the cucumbers, and the melons, and the leeks, and the onions, and the garlic; 6 but now we have lost our appetite. There is nothing at all except this manna to look at." 7 The manna was like coriander seed, and it looked like bdellium.ᵇ 8 The people went around, gathered it, and ground it in mills, or beat it in mortars, and boiled it in pots, and made cakes of it. Its taste was like the taste of fresh oil. 9 When the dew fell on the camp in the night, the manna fell on it.

10 Moses heard the people weeping throughout their families, every man at the door of his tent; and the LORD's anger burnt greatly; and Moses was displeased. 11 Moses said to the LORD, "Why have you treated your servant so badly? Why haven't I found favour in your sight, that you lay the burden of all this people on me? 12 Have I conceived all this people? Have I brought them out, that you should tell me, 'Carry them in your bosom, as a nurse carries a nursing infant, to the land which you swore to their fathers'? 13 Where could I get meat to give all these people? For they weep before me, saying, 'Give us meat, that we may eat.' 14 I am not able to bear all this people alone, because it is too heavy for me. 15 If you treat me this way, please kill me right now, if I have found favour in your sight; and don't let me see my wretchedness."

16 The LORD said to Moses, "Gather to me seventy men of the elders of Israel, whom you know to be the elders of the people and officers over them; and bring them to the Tent of Meeting, that they may stand there with you. 17 I will come down and talk with you there. I will take of the Spirit which is on you, and will put it on them; and they shall bear the burden of the people with you, that you don't bear it yourself alone.

18 "Say to the people, 'Sanctify yourselves in preparation for tomorrow, and you will eat meat; for you have wept in the ears of the LORD, saying, "Who will give us meat to eat? For it was well with us in Egypt." Therefore the LORD will give you meat, and you will eat. 19 You will not eat just one day, or two days, or five days, or ten days, or twenty days, 20 but a whole month, until it comes out at your nostrils, and it is loathsome to you; because you have rejected the LORD who is amongst you, and have wept before him, saying, "Why did we come out of Egypt?"'"

21 Moses said, "The people, amongst whom I am, are six hundred thousand men on foot; and you have said, 'I will give them meat, that they may eat a whole month.' 22 Shall flocks and herds be slaughtered for them, to be sufficient for them? Shall all the fish of the sea be gathered together for them, to be sufficient for them?"

23 The LORD said to Moses, "Has the LORD's hand grown short? Now you will see whether my word will happen to you or not."

24 Moses went out, and told the people the LORD's words; and he gathered seventy men of the elders of the people, and set them around the Tent. 25 The LORD came down in the cloud, and spoke to him, and took of the Spirit that was on him, and put it on the seventy elders. When the Spirit rested on them, they prophesied, but they did so no more. 26 But two men remained in the camp. The name of one was Eldad, and the name of the other Medad; and the Spirit rested on them. They were of those who were written, but had not gone out to the Tent; and they prophesied in the camp. 27 A young man ran, and told Moses, and said, "Eldad and Medad are prophesying in the camp!"

28 Joshua the son of Nun, the servant of Moses, one of his chosen men, answered, "My lord Moses, forbid them!"

29 Moses said to him, "Are you jealous for my sake? I wish that all the LORD's people were prophets, that the LORD would put his Spirit on them!"

30 Moses went into the camp, he and the elders of Israel. 31 A wind from the LORD went out and brought quails from the sea, and let them fall by the camp, about a day's journey on this side, and a day's journey on the other side, around the camp, and about two cubitsᶜ above the surface of the earth. 32 The people rose up all that day, and all of that night, and all the next day, and gathered the quails. He who gathered least gathered ten homers;ᵈ and they spread them all out for themselves around the camp. 33 While the meat was still between their teeth, before it was chewed, the LORD's anger burnt against the people, and the LORD struck the people with a very great plague. 34 The name of that place was called Kibroth Hattaavah,ᵉ because there they buried the people who lusted.

35 From Kibroth Hattaavah the people travelled to Hazeroth; and they stayed at Hazeroth.

12

1 Miriam and Aaron spoke against Moses because of the Cushite woman whom he had married; for he had married a Cushite woman. 2 They said, "Has the LORD indeed spoken only with Moses? Hasn't he spoken also with us?" And the LORD heard it.

3 Now the man Moses was very humble, more than all the men who were on the surface of the earth. 4 The LORD spoke suddenly to Moses, to Aaron, and to Miriam, "You three come out to the Tent of Meeting!"

The three of them came out. 5 The LORD came down in a pillar of cloud, and stood at the door of the Tent, and called Aaron and Miriam; and they both came forward. 6 He said, "Now hear my words. If there is a prophet amongst you, I, the LORD, will make myself known to him in a vision. I will speak with him in a dream. 7 My servant Moses is not so. He is faithful in all my house. 8 With him, I will speak mouth to mouth, even plainly, and not in riddles; and he shall see the LORD's form. Why then were you not afraid to speak against my servant, against Moses?" 9 The LORD's anger burnt against them; and he departed.

10 The cloud departed from over the Tent; and behold, Miriam was leprous, as white as snow. Aaron looked at Miriam, and behold, she was leprous.

11 Aaron said to Moses, "Oh, my lord, please don't count this sin against us, in which we have done foolishly, and in which we have sinned. 12 Let her not, I pray, be as one dead, of whom the flesh is half consumed when he comes out of his mother's womb."

13 Moses cried to the LORD, saying, "Heal her, God, I beg you!"

ᵃ *11:3* Taberah means "burning"
ᵇ *11:7* Bdellium is a resin extracted from certain African trees.
ᶜ *11:31* A cubit is the length from the tip of the middle finger to the elbow on a man's arm, or about 18 inches or 46 centimetres.

ᵈ *11:32* 1 homer is about 220 litres or 6 bushels
ᵉ *11:34* Kibroth Hattaavah means "graves of lust"

₁₄ The LORD said to Moses, "If her father had but spit in her face, shouldn't she be ashamed seven days? Let her be shut up outside of the camp seven days, and after that she shall be brought in again."

₁₅ Miriam was shut up outside of the camp seven days, and the people didn't travel until Miriam was brought in again. ₁₆ Afterward the people travelled from Hazeroth, and encamped in the wilderness of Paran.

13

₁ The LORD spoke to Moses, saying, ₂ "Send men, that they may spy out the land of Canaan, which I give to the children of Israel. Of every tribe of their fathers, you shall send a man, every one a prince amongst them."

₃ Moses sent them from the wilderness of Paran according to the commandment of the LORD. All of them were men who were heads of the children of Israel. ₄ These were their names:

Of the tribe of Reuben, Shammua the son of Zaccur.

₅ Of the tribe of Simeon, Shaphat the son of Hori.

₆ Of the tribe of Judah, Caleb the son of Jephunneh.

₇ Of the tribe of Issachar, Igal the son of Joseph.

₈ Of the tribe of Ephraim, Hoshea the son of Nun.

₉ Of the tribe of Benjamin, Palti the son of Raphu.

₁₀ Of the tribe of Zebulun, Gaddiel the son of Sodi.

₁₁ Of the tribe of Joseph, of the tribe of Manasseh, Gaddi the son of Susi.

₁₂ Of the tribe of Dan, Ammiel the son of Gemalli.

₁₃ Of the tribe of Asher, Sethur the son of Michael.

₁₄ Of the tribe of Naphtali, Nahbi the son of Vophsi.

₁₅ Of the tribe of Gad, Geuel the son of Machi.

₁₆ These are the names of the men who Moses sent to spy out the land. Moses called Hoshea the son of Nun Joshua. ₁₇ Moses sent them to spy out the land of Canaan, and said to them, "Go up this way by the South, and go up into the hill country. ₁₈ See the land, what it is; and the people who dwell therein, whether they are strong or weak, whether they are few or many; ₁₉ and what the land is that they dwell in, whether it is good or bad; and what cities they are that they dwell in, whether in camps, or in strongholds; ₂₀ and what the land is, whether it is fertile or poor, whether there is wood therein, or not. Be courageous, and bring some of the fruit of the land." Now the time was the time of the first-ripe grapes.

₂₁ So they went up, and spied out the land from the wilderness of Zin to Rehob, to the entrance of Hamath. ₂₂ They went up by the South, and came to Hebron; and Ahiman, Sheshai, and Talmai, the children of Anak, were there. (Now Hebron was built seven years before Zoan in Egypt.) ₂₃ They came to the valley of Eshcol, and cut down from there a branch with one cluster of grapes, and they bore it on a staff between two. They also brought some of the pomegranates and figs. ₂₄ That place was called the valley of Eshcol, because of the cluster which the children of Israel cut down from there. ₂₅ They returned from spying out the land at the end of forty days. ₂₆ They went and came to Moses, to Aaron, and to all the congregation of the children of Israel, to the wilderness of Paran, to Kadesh; and brought back word to them and to all the congregation. They showed them the fruit of the land. ₂₇ They told him, and said, "We came to the land where you sent us. Surely it flows with milk and honey, and this is its fruit. ₂₈ However, the people who dwell in the land are strong, and the cities are fortified and very large. Moreover, we saw the children of Anak there. ₂₉ Amalek dwells in the land of the South. The Hittite, the Jebusite, and the Amorite dwell in the hill country. The Canaanite dwells by the sea, and along the side of the Jordan."

₃₀ Caleb stilled the people before Moses, and said, "Let's go up at once, and possess it; for we are well able to overcome it!"

₃₁ But the men who went up with him said, "We aren't able to go up against the people; for they are stronger than we." ₃₂ They brought up an evil report of the land which they had spied out to the children of Israel, saying, "The land, through which we have gone to spy it out, is a land that eats up its inhabitants; and all the people who we saw in it are men of great stature. ₃₃ There we saw the Nephilim,ᵃ the sons of Anak, who come from the Nephilim.ᵇ We were in our own sight as grasshoppers, and so we were in their sight."

14

₁ All the congregation lifted up their voice, and cried; and the people wept that night. ₂ All the children of Israel murmured against Moses and against Aaron. The whole congregation said to them, "We wish that we had died in the land of Egypt, or that we had died in this wilderness! ₃ Why does the LORD bring us to this land, to fall by the sword? Our wives and our little ones will be captured or killed! Wouldn't it be better for us to return into Egypt?" ₄ They said to one another, "Let's choose a leader, and let's return into Egypt."

₅ Then Moses and Aaron fell on their faces before all the assembly of the congregation of the children of Israel.

₆ Joshua the son of Nun and Caleb the son of Jephunneh, who were of those who spied out the land, tore their clothes. ₇ They spoke to all the congregation of the children of Israel, saying, "The land, which we passed through to spy it out, is an exceedingly good land. ₈ If the LORD delights in us, then he will bring us into this land, and give it to us: a land which flows with milk and honey. ₉ Only don't rebel against the LORD, neither fear the people of the land; for they are bread for us. Their defence is removed from over them, and the LORD is with us. Don't fear them."

₁₀ But all the congregation threatened to stone them with stones.

The LORD's glory appeared in the Tent of Meeting to all the children of Israel. ₁₁ The LORD said to Moses, "How long will this people despise me? How long will they not believe in me, for all the signs which I have worked amongst them? ₁₂ I will strike them with the pestilence, and disinherit them, and will make of you a nation greater and mightier than they."

₁₃ Moses said to the LORD, "Then the Egyptians will hear it; for you brought up this people in your might from amongst them. ₁₄ They will tell it to the inhabitants of this land. They have heard that you LORD are amongst this people; for you LORD are seen face to face, and your cloud stands over them, and you go before them, in a pillar of cloud by day, and in a pillar of fire by night. ₁₅ Now if you killed this people as one man, then the nations which have heard the fame of you will speak, saying, ₁₆ 'Because the LORD was not able to bring this people into the land which he swore to them, therefore he has slain them in the wilderness.' ₁₇ Now please let the power of the Lordᶜ be great, according as you have spoken, saying, ₁₈ 'The LORD is slow to anger, and abundant in loving kindness, forgiving iniquity and disobedience; and he will by no means clear the guilty, visiting the iniquity of the fathers on the children, on the third and on the fourth generation.' ₁₉ Please pardon the iniquity of this people according to the greatness of your loving kindness, and just as you have forgiven this people, from Egypt even until now."

₂₀ The LORD said, "I have pardoned according to your word; ₂₁ but in very deed—as I live, and as all the earth shall be filled with the LORD's glory— ₂₂ because all those men who have seen my glory and my signs, which I worked in Egypt and in the wilderness, yet have tempted me these ten times, and have not listened to my voice; ₂₃ surely they shall not see the land which I swore to their fathers, neither shall any of those who despised me see it. ₂₄ But my servant Caleb, because he had another spirit with him, and has followed me fully, him I will bring into the land into which he went. His offspring shall possess it. ₂₅ Since the Amalekite and the Canaanite dwell in the valley, tomorrow turn and go into the wilderness by the way to the Red Sea. ₂₆ The LORD spoke to Moses and to Aaron, saying, ₂₇ "How long shall I bear with this evil congregation that complain against me? I have heard the complaints of the children of Israel, which they complain against me. ₂₈ Tell them, 'As I live, says the LORD, surely as you have spoken in my ears, so I will do to you. ₂₉ Your dead bodies shall fall in this wilderness; and all who were counted of you, according to your whole number, from twenty years old and upward, who have complained against me, ₃₀ surely you shall not come into the land concerning which I swore that I would make you dwell therein, except Caleb the son of Jephunneh, and Joshua the son of Nun. ₃₁ But I will bring in your little ones that you said should be captured or killed, and they shall know the land which you have rejected. ₃₂ But as for you, your dead bodies shall fall in this wilderness. ₃₃ Your children shall be wanderers in the wilderness forty years, and shall bear your prostitution, until your dead bodies are consumed in the wilderness. ₃₄ After the number of the days in which you spied out the land, even forty days, for every day a year, you will bear your iniquities, even forty years, and you will know my alienation.' ₃₅ I, the LORD, have spoken. I will surely do this to all this evil congregation who are gathered together against me. In this wilderness they shall be consumed, and there they shall die."

₃₆ The men whom Moses sent to spy out the land, who returned and made all the congregation to murmur against him by bringing up an evil report against the land, ₃₇ even those men who brought up an evil report of the land, died by the plague before the LORD. ₃₈ But Joshua the son of Nun and Caleb the son of Jephunneh remained alive of those men who went to spy out the land.

₃₉ Moses told these words to all the children of Israel, and the people mourned greatly. ₄₀ They rose up early in the morning and went up to the top of the mountain, saying, "Behold, we are here, and will go up to the place which the LORD has promised; for we have sinned."

₄₁ Moses said, "Why now do you disobey the commandment of the LORD, since it shall not prosper? ₄₂ Don't go up, for the LORD isn't amongst you; that way you won't be struck down before your enemies. ₄₃ For there the Amalekite and the Canaanite are before you, and you will fall by the sword because you turned back from following the LORD; therefore the LORD will not be with you."

₄₄ But they presumed to go up to the top of the mountain. Nevertheless, the ark of the LORD's covenant and Moses didn't depart out of the camp. ₄₅ Then the Amalekites came down, and the Canaanites who lived in that mountain, and struck them and beat them down even to Hormah.

15

₁ The LORD spoke to Moses, saying, ₂ "Speak to the children of Israel, and tell them, 'When you have come into the land of your habitations, which I give to you, ₃ and will make an offering by fire to the LORD—a burnt offering, or a sacrifice, to accomplish a vow, or as a free will offering, or in your set feasts, to make a pleasant aroma to the LORD, of the herd, or of the flock— ₄ then he who offers his offering shall offer to the LORD a meal offering of one tenth of an ephahᵈ of fine flour mixed with one fourth of a hinᵉ of oil. ₅ You shall prepare wine for the drink offering, one fourth of a hin, with the burnt offering or for the sacrifice, for each lamb.

₆ "'For a ram, you shall prepare for a meal offering two tenths of an ephahᶠ of fine flour mixed with the third part of a hin of oil; ₇ and for the

---

ᵃ *13:33* or, giants

ᵇ *13:33* or, giants

ᶜ *14:17* The word translated "Lord" is "Adonai."

ᵈ *15:4* 1 ephah is about 22 litres or about 2/3 of a bushel

ᵉ *15:4* A hin is about 6.5 litres or 1.7 gallons.

ᶠ *15:6* 1 ephah is about 22 litres or about 2/3 of a bushel drink offering you shall offer the third part of a hin of wine, of a pleasant aroma to the LORD. ₈ When you prepare a bull for a burnt offering or for a sacrifice, to accomplish a vow, or for peace offerings to the LORD, ₉ then he shall offer with the bull a meal offering of three tenths of an ephah[a] of fine flour mixed with half a hin of oil; ₁₀ and you shall offer for the drink offering half a hin of wine, for an offering made by fire, of a pleasant aroma to the LORD. ₁₁ Thus it shall be done for each bull, for each ram, for each of the male lambs, or of the young goats. ₁₂ According to the number that you shall prepare, so you shall do to everyone according to their number.

₁₃ "'All who are native-born shall do these things in this way, in offering an offering made by fire, of a pleasant aroma to the LORD. ₁₄ If a stranger lives as a foreigner with you, or whoever may be amongst you throughout your generations, and will offer an offering made by fire, of a pleasant aroma to the LORD, as you do, so he shall do. ₁₅ For the assembly, there shall be one statute for you and for the stranger who lives as a foreigner, a statute forever throughout your generations. As you are, so the foreigner shall be before the LORD. ₁₆ One law and one ordinance shall be for you and for the stranger who lives as a foreigner with you.'"

₁₇ The LORD spoke to Moses, saying, ₁₈ "Speak to the children of Israel, and tell them, 'When you come into the land where I bring you, ₁₉ then it shall be that when you eat of the bread of the land, you shall offer up a wave offering to the LORD. ₂₀ Of the first of your dough you shall offer up a cake for a wave offering. As the wave offering of the threshing floor, so you shall heave it. ₂₁ Of the first of your dough, you shall give to the LORD a wave offering throughout your generations.

₂₂ "When you err, and don't observe all these commandments which the LORD has spoken to Moses— ₂₃ even all that the LORD has commanded you by Moses, from the day that the LORD gave commandment and onward throughout your generations— ₂₄ then it shall be, if it was done unwittingly, without the knowledge of the congregation, that all the congregation shall offer one young bull for a burnt offering, for a pleasant aroma to the LORD, with its meal offering and its drink offering, according to the ordinance, and one male goat for a sin offering. ₂₅ The priest shall make atonement for all the congregation of the children of Israel, and they shall be forgiven; for it was an error, and they have brought their offering, an offering made by fire to the LORD, and their sin offering before the LORD, for their error. ₂₆ All the congregation of the children of Israel shall be forgiven, as well as the stranger who lives as a foreigner amongst them; for with regard to all the people, it was done unwittingly.

₂₇ "'If a person sins unwittingly, then he shall offer a female goat a year old for a sin offering. ₂₈ The priest shall make atonement for the soul who errs when he sins unwittingly before the LORD. He shall make atonement for him; and he shall be forgiven. ₂₉ You shall have one law for him who does anything unwittingly, for him who is native-born amongst the children of Israel, and for the stranger who lives as a foreigner amongst them.

₃₀ "'But the soul who does anything with a high hand, whether he is native-born or a foreigner, blasphemes the LORD. That soul shall be cut off from amongst his people. ₃₁ Because he has despised the LORD's word, and has broken his commandment, that soul shall be utterly cut off. His iniquity shall be on him."

₃₂ While the children of Israel were in the wilderness, they found a man gathering sticks on the Sabbath day. ₃₃ Those who found him gathering sticks brought him to Moses and Aaron, and to all the congregation. ₃₄ They put him in custody, because it had not been declared what should be done to him.

₃₅ The LORD said to Moses, "The man shall surely be put to death. All the congregation shall stone him with stones outside of the camp." ₃₆ All the congregation brought him outside of the camp, and stoned him to death with stones, as the LORD commanded Moses.

₃₇ The LORD spoke to Moses, saying, ₃₈ "Speak to the children of Israel, and tell them that they should make themselves fringes[b] on the borders of their garments throughout their generations, and that they put on the fringe[c] of each border a cord of blue. ₃₉ It shall be to you for a fringe,[d] that you may see it, and remember all the LORD's commandments, and do them; and that you don't follow your own heart and your own eyes, after which you used to play the prostitute; ₄₀ so that you may remember and do all my commandments, and be holy to your God. ₄₁ I am the LORD your God, who brought you out of the land of Egypt, to be your God: I am the LORD your God."

16

₁ Now Korah, the son of Izhar, the son of Kohath, the son of Levi, with Dathan and Abiram, the sons of Eliab, and On, the son of Peleth, sons of Reuben, took some men. ₂ They rose up before Moses, with some of the children of Israel, two hundred and fifty princes of the congregation, called to the assembly, men of renown. ₃ They assembled themselves together against Moses and against Aaron, and said to them, "You take too much on yourself, since all the congregation are holy, everyone of them, and the LORD is amongst them! Why do you lift yourselves up above the LORD's assembly?"

₄ When Moses heard it, he fell on his face. ₅ He said to Korah and to all his company, "In the morning, the LORD will show who are his, and who is holy, and will cause him to come near to him. Even him whom he shall choose, he will cause to come near to him. ₆ Do this: have Korah and all his company take censers, ₇ put fire in them, and put incense on them before

the LORD tomorrow. It shall be that the man whom the LORD chooses, he shall be holy. You have gone too far, you sons of Levi!"

₈ Moses said to Korah, "Hear now, you sons of Levi! ₉ Is it a small thing to you that the God of Israel has separated you from the congregation of Israel, to bring you near to himself, to do the service of the LORD's tabernacle, and to stand before the congregation to minister to them; ₁₀ and that he has brought you near, and all your brothers the sons of Levi with you? Do you seek the priesthood also? ₁₁ Therefore you and all your company have gathered together against the LORD! What is Aaron that you complain against him?"

₁₂ Moses sent to call Dathan and Abiram, the sons of Eliab; and they said, "We won't come up! ₁₃ Is it a small thing that you have brought us up out of a land flowing with milk and honey, to kill us in the wilderness, but you must also make yourself a prince over us? ₁₄ Moreover you haven't brought us into a land flowing with milk and honey, nor given us inheritance of fields and vineyards. Will you put out the eyes of these men? We won't come up."

₁₅ Moses was very angry, and said to the LORD, "Don't respect their offering. I have not taken one donkey from them, neither have I hurt one of them."

₁₆ Moses said to Korah, "You and all your company go before the LORD, you, and they, and Aaron, tomorrow. ₁₇ Each man take his censer and put incense on it, and each man bring before the LORD his censer, two hundred and fifty censers; you also, and Aaron, each with his censer."

₁₈ They each took his censer, and put fire in it, and laid incense on it, and stood at the door of the Tent of Meeting with Moses and Aaron. ₁₉ Korah assembled all the congregation opposite them to the door of the Tent of Meeting.

The LORD's glory appeared to all the congregation. ₂₀ The LORD spoke to Moses and to Aaron, saying, ₂₁ "Separate yourselves from amongst this congregation, that I may consume them in a moment!"

₂₂ They fell on their faces, and said, "God, the God of the spirits of all flesh, shall one man sin, and will you be angry with all the congregation?"

₂₃ The LORD spoke to Moses, saying, ₂₄ "Speak to the congregation, saying, 'Get away from around the tent of Korah, Dathan, and Abiram!'"

₂₅ Moses rose up and went to Dathan and Abiram; and the elders of Israel followed him. ₂₆ He spoke to the congregation, saying, "Depart, please, from the tents of these wicked men, and touch nothing of theirs, lest you be consumed in all their sins!"

₂₇ So they went away from the tent of Korah, Dathan, and Abiram, on every side. Dathan and Abiram came out, and stood at the door of their tents with their wives, their sons, and their little ones.

₂₈ Moses said, "Hereby you shall know that the LORD has sent me to do all these works; for they are not from my own mind. ₂₉ If these men die the common death of all men, or if they experience what all men experience, then the LORD hasn't sent me. ₃₀ But if the LORD makes a new thing, and the ground opens its mouth, and swallows them up with all that belong to them, and they go down alive into Sheol,[e] then you shall understand that these men have despised the LORD."

₃₁ As he finished speaking all these words, the ground that was under them split apart. ₃₂ The earth opened its mouth and swallowed them up with their households, all of Korah's men, and all their goods. ₃₃ So they, and all that belonged to them went down alive into Sheol.[f] The earth closed on them, and they perished from amongst the assembly. ₃₄ All Israel that were around them fled at their cry; for they said, "Lest the earth swallow us up!" ₃₅ Fire came out from the LORD, and devoured the two hundred and fifty men who offered the incense.

₃₆ The LORD spoke to Moses, saying, ₃₇ "Speak to Eleazar the son of Aaron the priest, that he take up the censers out of the burning, and scatter the fire away from the camp; for they are holy, ₃₈ even the censers of those who sinned against their own lives. Let them be beaten into plates for a covering of the altar, for they offered them before the LORD. Therefore they are holy. They shall be a sign to the children of Israel."

₃₉ Eleazar the priest took the bronze censers which those who were burnt had offered; and they beat them out for a covering of the altar, ₄₀ to be a memorial to the children of Israel, to the end that no stranger who isn't of the offspring of Aaron, would come near to burn incense before the LORD, that he not be as Korah and as his company; as the LORD spoke to him by Moses.

₄₁ But on the next day all the congregation of the children of Israel complained against Moses and against Aaron, saying, "You have killed the LORD's people!"

₄₂ When the congregation was assembled against Moses and against Aaron, they looked towards the Tent of Meeting. Behold, the cloud covered it, and the LORD's glory appeared. ₄₃ Moses and Aaron came to the front of the Tent of Meeting. ₄₄ The LORD spoke to Moses, saying, ₄₅ "Get away from amongst this congregation, that I may consume them in a moment!" They fell on their faces.

₄₆ Moses said to Aaron, "Take your censer, put fire from the altar in it, lay incense on it, carry it quickly to the congregation, and make atonement for them; for wrath has gone out from the LORD! The plague has begun."

₄₇ Aaron did as Moses said, and ran into the middle of the assembly. The plague had already begun amongst the people. He put on the incense, and made atonement for the people. ₄₈ He stood between the dead and the living; and the plague was stayed. ₄₉ Now those who died by the plague

---

a *15:9* 1 ephah is about 22 litres or about 2/3 of a bushel
b *15:38* or, tassels (Hebrew צִיצִת)
c *15:38* or, tassel
d *15:39* or, tassel
e *16:30* Sheol is the place of the dead.
f *16:33* Sheol is the place of the dead.

were fourteen thousand and seven hundred, in addition to those who died about the matter of Korah. 50 Aaron returned to Moses to the door of the Tent of Meeting, and the plague was stopped.

17

1 The LORD spoke to Moses, saying, 2 "Speak to the children of Israel, and take rods from them, one for each fathers' house, of all their princes according to their fathers' houses, twelve rods. Write each man's name on his rod. 3 You shall write Aaron's name on Levi's rod. There shall be one rod for each head of their fathers' houses. 4 You shall lay them up in the Tent of Meeting before the covenant, where I meet with you. 5 It shall happen that the rod of the man whom I shall choose shall bud. I will make the murmurings of the children of Israel, which they murmur against you, cease from me."

6 Moses spoke to the children of Israel; and all their princes gave him rods, for each prince one, according to their fathers' houses, a total of twelve rods. Aaron's rod was amongst their rods. 7 Moses laid up the rods before the LORD in the Tent of the Testimony.

8 On the next day, Moses went into the Tent of the Testimony; and behold, Aaron's rod for the house of Levi had sprouted, budded, produced blossoms, and bore ripe almonds. 9 Moses brought out all the rods from before the LORD to all the children of Israel. They looked, and each man took his rod.

10 The LORD said to Moses, "Put back the rod of Aaron before the covenant, to be kept for a token against the children of rebellion; that you may make an end of their complaining against me, that they not die." 11 Moses did so. As the LORD commanded him, so he did.

12 The children of Israel spoke to Moses, saying, "Behold, we perish! We are undone! We are all undone! 13 Everyone who keeps approaching the LORD's tabernacle, dies! Will we all perish?"

18

1 The LORD said to Aaron, "You and your sons and your fathers' house with you shall bear the iniquity of the sanctuary; and you and your sons with you shall bear the iniquity of your priesthood. 2 Bring your brothers also, the tribe of Levi, the tribe of your father, near with you, that they may be joined to you, and minister to you; but you and your sons with you shall be before the Tent of the Testimony. 3 They shall keep your commands and the duty of the whole Tent; only they shall not come near to the vessels of the sanctuary and to the altar, that they not die, neither they nor you. 4 They shall be joined to you and keep the responsibility of the Tent of Meeting, for all the service of the Tent. A stranger shall not come near to you.

5 "You shall perform the duty of the sanctuary and the duty of the altar, that there be no more wrath on the children of Israel. 6 Behold, I myself have taken your brothers the Levites from amongst the children of Israel. They are a gift to you, dedicated to the LORD, to do the service of the Tent of Meeting. 7 You and your sons with you shall keep your priesthood for everything of the altar, and for that within the veil. You shall serve. I give you the service of the priesthood as a gift. The stranger who comes near shall be put to death."

8 The LORD spoke to Aaron, "Behold, I myself have given you the command of my wave offerings, even all the holy things of the children of Israel. I have given them to you by reason of the anointing, and to your sons, as a portion forever. 9 This shall be yours of the most holy things from the fire: every offering of theirs, even every meal offering of theirs, and every sin offering of theirs, and every trespass offering of theirs, which they shall render to me, shall be most holy for you and for your sons. 10 You shall eat of it like the most holy things. Every male shall eat of it. It shall be holy to you.

11 "This is yours, too: the wave offering of their gift, even all the wave offerings of the children of Israel. I have given them to you, and to your sons and to your daughters with you, as a portion forever. Everyone who is clean in your house shall eat of it.

12 "I have given to you all the best of the oil, all the best of the vintage, and of the grain, the first fruits of them which they give to the LORD. 13 The first-ripe fruits of all that is in their land, which they bring to the LORD, shall be yours. Everyone who is clean in your house shall eat of it.

14 "Everything devoted in Israel shall be yours. 15 Everything that opens the womb, of all flesh which they offer to the LORD, both of man and animal, shall be yours. Nevertheless, you shall surely redeem the firstborn of man, and you shall redeem the firstborn of unclean animals. 16 You shall redeem those who are to be redeemed of them from a month old, according to your estimation, for five shekels of money, according to the shekel[a] of the sanctuary, which weighs twenty gerahs.[b]

17 "But you shall not redeem the firstborn of a cow, or the firstborn of a sheep, or the firstborn of a goat. They are holy. You shall sprinkle their blood on the altar, and shall burn their fat for an offering made by fire, for a pleasant aroma to the LORD. 18 Their meat shall be yours, as the wave offering breast and as the right thigh, it shall be yours. 19 All the wave offerings of the holy things which the children of Israel offer to the LORD, I have given you and your sons and your daughters with you, as a portion forever. It is a covenant of salt forever before the LORD to you and to your offspring with you."

20 The LORD said to Aaron, "You shall have no inheritance in their land, neither shall you have any portion amongst them. I am your portion and your inheritance amongst the children of Israel.

21 "To the children of Levi, behold, I have given all the tithe in Israel for an inheritance, in return for their service which they serve, even the service of the Tent of Meeting. 22 Henceforth the children of Israel shall not come near the Tent of Meeting, lest they bear sin, and die. 23 But the Levites shall do the service of the Tent of Meeting, and they shall bear their iniquity. It shall be a statute forever throughout your generations. Amongst the children of Israel, they shall have no inheritance. 24 For the tithe of the children of Israel, which they offer as a wave offering to the LORD, I have given to the Levites for an inheritance. Therefore I have said to them, 'Amongst the children of Israel they shall have no inheritance.'"

25 The LORD spoke to Moses, saying, 26 "Moreover you shall speak to the Levites, and tell them, 'When you take of the children of Israel the tithe which I have given you from them for your inheritance, then you shall offer up a wave offering of it for the LORD, a tithe of the tithe. 27 Your wave offering shall be credited to you, as though it were the grain of the threshing floor, and as the fullness of the wine press. 28 Thus you also shall offer a wave offering to the LORD of all your tithes, which you receive of the children of Israel; and of it you shall give the LORD's wave offering to Aaron the priest. 29 Out of all your gifts, you shall offer every wave offering to the LORD, of all its best parts, even the holy part of it.'

30 "Therefore you shall tell them, 'When you heave its best from it, then it shall be credited to the Levites as the increase of the threshing floor, and as the increase of the wine press. 31 You may eat it anywhere, you and your households, for it is your reward in return for your service in the Tent of Meeting. 32 You shall bear no sin by reason of it, when you have heaved from it its best. You shall not profane the holy things of the children of Israel, that you not die.'"

19

1 The LORD spoke to Moses and to Aaron, saying, 2 "This is the statute of the law which the LORD has commanded. Tell the children of Israel to bring you a red heifer without spot, in which is no defect, and which was never yoked. 3 You shall give her to Eleazar the priest, and he shall bring her outside of the camp, and one shall kill her before his face. 4 Eleazar the priest shall take some of her blood with his finger, and sprinkle her blood towards the front of the Tent of Meeting seven times. 5 One shall burn the heifer in his sight; her skin, and her meat, and her blood, with her dung, shall he burn. 6 The priest shall take cedar wood, hyssop, and scarlet, and cast it into the middle of the burning of the heifer. 7 Then the priest shall wash his clothes, and he shall bathe his flesh in water, and afterward he shall come into the camp, and the priest shall be unclean until the evening. 8 He who burns her shall wash his clothes in water, and bathe his flesh in water, and shall be unclean until the evening.

9 "A man who is clean shall gather up the ashes of the heifer, and lay them up outside of the camp in a clean place; and it shall be kept for the congregation of the children of Israel for use in water for cleansing impurity. It is a sin offering. 10 He who gathers the ashes of the heifer shall wash his clothes, and be unclean until the evening. It shall be to the children of Israel, and to the stranger who lives as a foreigner amongst them, for a statute forever.

11 "He who touches the dead body of any man shall be unclean seven days. 12 He shall purify himself with water on the third day, and on the seventh day he shall be clean; but if he doesn't purify himself the third day, then the seventh day he shall not be clean. 13 Whoever touches a dead person, the body of a man who has died, and doesn't purify himself, defiles the LORD's tabernacle; and that soul shall be cut off from Israel; because the water for impurity was not sprinkled on him, he shall be unclean. His uncleanness is yet on him.

14 "This is the law when a man dies in a tent: everyone who comes into the tent, and everyone who is in the tent, shall be unclean seven days. 15 Every open vessel, which has no covering bound on it, is unclean.

16 "Whoever in the open field touches one who is slain with a sword, or a dead body, or a bone of a man, or a grave, shall be unclean seven days. 17 "For the unclean, they shall take of the ashes of the burning of the sin offering; and running water shall be poured on them in a vessel. 18 A clean person shall take hyssop, dip it in the water, and sprinkle it on the tent, on all the vessels, on the persons who were there, and on him who touched the bone, or the slain, or the dead, or the grave. 19 The clean person shall sprinkle on the unclean on the third day, and on the seventh day. On the seventh day, he shall purify him. He shall wash his clothes and bathe himself in water, and shall be clean at evening. 20 But the man who shall be unclean, and shall not purify himself, that soul shall be cut off from amongst the assembly, because he has defiled the sanctuary of the LORD. The water for impurity has not been sprinkled on him. He is unclean. 21 It shall be a perpetual statute to them. He who sprinkles the water for impurity shall wash his clothes, and he who touches the water for impurity shall be unclean until evening.

22 "Whatever the unclean person touches shall be unclean; and the soul that touches it shall be unclean until evening."

20

1 The children of Israel, even the whole congregation, came into the wilderness of Zin in the first month. The people stayed in Kadesh. Miriam died there, and was buried there. 2 There was no water for the congregation; and they assembled themselves together against Moses and against Aaron. 3 The people quarrelled with Moses, and spoke, saying, "We wish that we had died when our brothers died before the LORD! 4 Why have you brought the LORD's assembly into this wilderness, that we should die

---

a 18:16 A shekel is about 10 grams or about 0.35 ounces.

b 18:16 A gerah is about 0.5 grams or about 7.7 grains.

there, we and our animals? 5 Why have you made us to come up out of Egypt, to bring us in to this evil place? It is no place of seed, or of figs, or of vines, or of pomegranates; neither is there any water to drink."

6 Moses and Aaron went from the presence of the assembly to the door of the Tent of Meeting, and fell on their faces. The LORD's glory appeared to them. 7 The LORD spoke to Moses, saying, 8 "Take the rod, and assemble the congregation, you, and Aaron your brother, and speak to the rock before their eyes, that it pour out its water. You shall bring water to them out of the rock; so you shall give the congregation and their livestock drink."

9 Moses took the rod from before the LORD, as he commanded him. 10 Moses and Aaron gathered the assembly together before the rock, and he said to them, "Hear now, you rebels! Shall we bring water out of this rock for you?" 11 Moses lifted up his hand, and struck the rock with his rod twice, and water came out abundantly. The congregation and their livestock drank.

12 The LORD said to Moses and Aaron, "Because you didn't believe in me, to sanctify me in the eyes of the children of Israel, therefore you shall not bring this assembly into the land which I have given them."

13 These are the waters of Meribah;[a] because the children of Israel strove with the LORD, and he was sanctified in them.

14 Moses sent messengers from Kadesh to the king of Edom, saying:

"Your brother Israel says: You know all the travail that has happened to us; 15 how our fathers went down into Egypt, and we lived in Egypt a long time. The Egyptians mistreated us and our fathers. 16 When we cried to the LORD, he heard our voice, sent an angel, and brought us out of Egypt. Behold, we are in Kadesh, a city in the edge of your border.

17 "Please let us pass through your land. We will not pass through field or through vineyard, neither will we drink from the water of the wells. We will go along the king's highway. We will not turn away to the right hand nor to the left, until we have passed your border."

18 Edom said to him, "You shall not pass through me, lest I come out with the sword against you."

19 The children of Israel said to him, "We will go up by the highway; and if we drink your water, I and my livestock, then I will give its price. Only let me, without doing anything else, pass through on my feet."

20 He said, "You shall not pass through." Edom came out against him with many people, and with a strong hand. 21 Thus Edom refused to give Israel passage through his border, so Israel turned away from him.

22 They travelled from Kadesh, and the children of Israel, even the whole congregation, came to Mount Hor. 23 The LORD spoke to Moses and Aaron in Mount Hor, by the border of the land of Edom, saying, 24 "Aaron shall be gathered to his people; for he shall not enter into the land which I have given to the children of Israel, because you rebelled against my word at the waters of Meribah. 25 Take Aaron and Eleazar his son, and bring them up to Mount Hor; 26 and strip Aaron of his garments, and put them on Eleazar his son. Aaron shall be gathered, and shall die there."

27 Moses did as the LORD commanded. They went up onto Mount Hor in the sight of all the congregation. 28 Moses stripped Aaron of his garments, and put them on Eleazar his son. Aaron died there on the top of the mountain, and Moses and Eleazar came down from the mountain. 29 When all the congregation saw that Aaron was dead, they wept for Aaron thirty days, even all the house of Israel.

21

1 The Canaanite, the king of Arad, who lived in the South, heard that Israel came by the way of Atharim. He fought against Israel, and took some of them captive. 2 Israel vowed a vow to the LORD, and said, "If you will indeed deliver this people into my hand, then I will utterly destroy their cities." 3 The LORD listened to the voice of Israel, and delivered up the Canaanites; and they utterly destroyed them and their cities. The name of the place was called Hormah.[b]

4 They travelled from Mount Hor by the way to the Red Sea, to go around the land of Edom. The soul of the people was very discouraged because of the journey. 5 The people spoke against God and against Moses: "Why have you brought us up out of Egypt to die in the wilderness? For there is no bread, there is no water, and our soul loathes this disgusting food!"

6 The LORD sent venomous snakes amongst the people, and they bit the people. Many people of Israel died. 7 The people came to Moses, and said, "We have sinned, because we have spoken against the LORD and against you. Pray to the LORD, that he take away the serpents from us." Moses prayed for the people.

8 The LORD said to Moses, "Make a venomous snake, and set it on a pole. It shall happen that everyone who is bitten, when he sees it, shall live." 9 Moses made a serpent of bronze, and set it on the pole. If a serpent had bitten any man, when he looked at the serpent of bronze, he lived.

10 The children of Israel travelled, and encamped in Oboth. 11 They travelled from Oboth, and encamped at Iyeabarim, in the wilderness which is before Moab, towards the sunrise. 12 From there they travelled, and encamped in the valley of Zered. 13 From there they travelled, and encamped on the other side of the Arnon, which is in the wilderness that comes out of the border of the Amorites; for the Arnon is the border of Moab, between Moab and the Amorites. 14 Therefore it is said in *The Book of the Wars of the LORD*, "Vaheb in Suphah, the valleys of the Arnon, 15 the slope of the valleys that incline towards the dwelling of Ar, leans on the border of Moab."

16 From there they travelled to Beer; that is the well of which the LORD said to Moses, "Gather the people together, and I will give them water."

17 Then Israel sang this song:

"Spring up, well! Sing to it,
18 the well, which the princes dug,
which the nobles of the people dug,
with the sceptre, and with their poles."

From the wilderness they travelled to Mattanah; 19 and from Mattanah to Nahaliel; and from Nahaliel to Bamoth; 20 and from Bamoth to the valley that is in the field of Moab, to the top of Pisgah, which looks down on the desert. 21 Israel sent messengers to Sihon king of the Amorites, saying, 22 "Let me pass through your land. We will not turn away into field or vineyard. We will not drink of the water of the wells. We will go by the king's highway, until we have passed your border."

23 Sihon would not allow Israel to pass through his border, but Sihon gathered all his people together, and went out against Israel into the wilderness, and came to Jahaz. He fought against Israel. 24 Israel struck him with the edge of the sword, and possessed his land from the Arnon to the Jabbok, even to the children of Ammon; for the border of the children of Ammon was fortified. 25 Israel took all these cities. Israel lived in all the cities of the Amorites, in Heshbon, and in all its villages. 26 For Heshbon was the city of Sihon the king of the Amorites, who had fought against the former king of Moab, and taken all his land out of his hand, even to the Arnon. 27 Therefore those who speak in proverbs say,

"Come to Heshbon.
Let the city of Sihon be built and established;
28 for a fire has gone out of Heshbon,
a flame from the city of Sihon.
It has devoured Ar of Moab,
The lords of the high places of the Arnon.
29 Woe to you, Moab!
You are undone, people of Chemosh!
He has given his sons as fugitives,
and his daughters into captivity,
to Sihon king of the Amorites.
30 We have shot at them.
Heshbon has perished even to Dibon.
We have laid waste even to Nophah,
Which reaches to Medeba."

31 Thus Israel lived in the land of the Amorites. 32 Moses sent to spy out Jazer. They took its villages, and drove out the Amorites who were there. 33 They turned and went up by the way of Bashan. Og the king of Bashan went out against them, he and all his people, to battle at Edrei.

34 The LORD said to Moses, "Don't fear him, for I have delivered him into your hand, with all his people, and his land. You shall do to him as you did to Sihon king of the Amorites, who lived at Heshbon."

35 So they struck him, with his sons and all his people, until there were no survivors; and they possessed his land.

22

1 The children of Israel travelled, and encamped in the plains of Moab beyond the Jordan at Jericho. 2 Balak the son of Zippor saw all that Israel had done to the Amorites. 3 Moab was very afraid of the people, because they were many. Moab was distressed because of the children of Israel. 4 Moab said to the elders of Midian, "Now this multitude will lick up all that is around us, as the ox licks up the grass of the field."

Balak the son of Zippor was king of Moab at that time. 5 He sent messengers to Balaam the son of Beor, to Pethor, which is by the River, to the land of the children of his people, to call him, saying, "Behold, there is a people who came out of Egypt. Behold, they cover the surface of the earth, and they are staying opposite me. 6 Please come now therefore, and curse this people for me; for they are too mighty for me. Perhaps I shall prevail, that we may strike them, and that I may drive them out of the land; for I know that he whom you bless is blessed, and he whom you curse is cursed."

7 The elders of Moab and the elders of Midian departed with the rewards of divination in their hand. They came to Balaam, and spoke to him the words of Balak.

8 He said to them, "Lodge here this night, and I will bring you word again, as the LORD shall speak to me." The princes of Moab stayed with Balaam.

9 God came to Balaam, and said, "Who are these men with you?"

10 Balaam said to God, "Balak the son of Zippor, king of Moab, has said to me, 11 'Behold, the people that has come out of Egypt covers the surface of the earth. Now, come curse them for me. Perhaps I shall be able to fight against them, and shall drive them out.'"

12 God said to Balaam, "You shall not go with them. You shall not curse the people, for they are blessed."

13 Balaam rose up in the morning, and said to the princes of Balak, "Go to your land; for the LORD refuses to permit me to go with you."

14 The princes of Moab rose up, and they went to Balak, and said, "Balaam refuses to come with us."

15 Balak again sent princes, more, and more honourable than they. 16 They came to Balaam, and said to him, "Balak the son of Zippor says, 'Please let nothing hinder you from coming to me, 17 for I will promote you to very great honour, and whatever you say to me I will do. Please come therefore, and curse this people for me.'"

---

[a] 20:13 "Meribah" means "quarrelling".

[b] 21:3 "Hormah" means "destruction".

18 Balaam answered the servants of Balak, "If Balak would give me his house full of silver and gold, I can't go beyond the word of the LORD my God, to do less or more. 19 Now therefore please stay here tonight as well, that I may know what else the LORD will speak to me."

20 God came to Balaam at night, and said to him, "If the men have come to call you, rise up, go with them; but only the word which I speak to you, that you shall do."

21 Balaam rose up in the morning, and saddled his donkey, and went with the princes of Moab. 22 God's anger burnt because he went; and the LORD's angel placed himself in the way as an adversary against him. Now he was riding on his donkey, and his two servants were with him. 23 The donkey saw the LORD's angel standing in the way, with his sword drawn in his hand; and the donkey turned out of the path, and went into the field. Balaam struck the donkey, to turn her into the path. 24 Then the LORD's angel stood in a narrow path between the vineyards, a wall being on this side, and a wall on that side. 25 The donkey saw the LORD's angel, and she thrust herself to the wall, and crushed Balaam's foot against the wall. He struck her again.

26 The LORD's angel went further, and stood in a narrow place, where there was no way to turn either to the right hand or to the left. 27 The donkey saw the LORD's angel, and she lay down under Balaam. Balaam's anger burnt, and he struck the donkey with his staff.

28 The LORD opened the mouth of the donkey, and she said to Balaam, "What have I done to you, that you have struck me these three times?"

29 Balaam said to the donkey, "Because you have mocked me, I wish there were a sword in my hand, for now I would have killed you."

30 The donkey said to Balaam, "Am I not your donkey, on which you have ridden all your life long until today? Was I ever in the habit of doing so to you?"

He said, "No."

31 Then the LORD opened the eyes of Balaam, and he saw the LORD's angel standing in the way, with his sword drawn in his hand; and he bowed his head, and fell on his face. 32 The LORD's angel said to him, "Why have you struck your donkey these three times? Behold, I have come out as an adversary, because your way is perverse before me. 33 The donkey saw me, and turned away before me these three times. Unless she had turned away from me, surely now I would have killed you, and saved her alive."

34 Balaam said to the LORD's angel, "I have sinned; for I didn't know that you stood in the way against me. Now therefore, if it displeases you, I will go back again."

35 The LORD's angel said to Balaam, "Go with the men; but you shall only speak the word that I shall speak to you."

So Balaam went with the princes of Balak. 36 When Balak heard that Balaam had come, he went out to meet him to the City of Moab, which is on the border of the Arnon, which is in the utmost part of the border. 37 Balak said to Balaam, "Didn't I earnestly send for you to summon you? Why didn't you come to me? Am I not able indeed to promote you to honour?"

38 Balaam said to Balak, "Behold, I have come to you. Have I now any power at all to speak anything? I will speak the word that God puts in my mouth."

39 Balaam went with Balak, and they came to Kiriath Huzoth. 40 Balak sacrificed cattle and sheep, and sent to Balaam, and to the princes who were with him. 41 In the morning, Balak took Balaam, and brought him up into the high places of Baal; and he saw from there part of the people.

23

1 Balaam said to Balak, "Build here seven altars for me, and prepare here seven bulls and seven rams for me."

2 Balak did as Balaam had spoken; and Balak and Balaam offered on every altar a bull and a ram. 3 Balaam said to Balak, "Stand by your burnt offering, and I will go. Perhaps the LORD will come to meet me. Whatever he shows me I will tell you."

He went to a bare height. 4 God met Balaam, and he said to him, "I have prepared the seven altars, and I have offered up a bull and a ram on every altar."

5 The LORD put a word in Balaam's mouth, and said, "Return to Balak, and thus you shall speak."

6 He returned to him, and behold, he was standing by his burnt offering, he, and all the princes of Moab. 7 He took up his parable, and said,
"From Aram has Balak brought me,
    the king of Moab from the mountains of the East.
Come, curse Jacob for me.
    Come, defy Israel.
8 How shall I curse whom God has not cursed?
    How shall I defy whom the LORD has not defied?
9 For from the top of the rocks I see him.
    From the hills I see him.
Behold, it is a people that dwells alone,
    and shall not be listed amongst the nations.
10 Who can count the dust of Jacob,
    or count the fourth part of Israel?
Let me die the death of the righteous!
    Let my last end be like his!"

11 Balak said to Balaam, "What have you done to me? I took you to curse my enemies, and behold, you have blessed them altogether."

12 He answered and said, "Must I not take heed to speak that which the LORD puts in my mouth?"

13 Balak said to him, "Please come with me to another place, where you may see them. You shall see just part of them, and shall not see them all. Curse them from there for me."

14 He took him into the field of Zophim, to the top of Pisgah, and built seven altars, and offered up a bull and a ram on every altar. 15 He said to Balak, "Stand here by your burnt offering, while I meet God over there."

16 The LORD met Balaam, and put a word in his mouth, and said, "Return to Balak, and say this."

17 He came to him, and behold, he was standing by his burnt offering, and the princes of Moab with him. Balak said to him, "What has the LORD spoken?"

18 He took up his parable, and said,
"Rise up, Balak, and hear!
    Listen to me, you son of Zippor.
19 God is not a man, that he should lie,
    nor a son of man, that he should repent.
Has he said, and he won't do it?
    Or has he spoken, and he won't make it good?
20 Behold, I have received a command to bless.
    He has blessed, and I can't reverse it.
21 He has not seen iniquity in Jacob.
    Neither has he seen perverseness in Israel.
The LORD his God is with him.
    The shout of a king is amongst them.
22 God brings them out of Egypt.
    He has as it were the strength of the wild ox.
23 Surely there is no enchantment with Jacob;
    neither is there any divination with Israel.
Now it shall be said of Jacob and of Israel,
    'What has God done!'
24 Behold, a people rises up as a lioness.
    As a lion he lifts himself up.
He shall not lie down until he eats of the prey,
    and drinks the blood of the slain."

25 Balak said to Balaam, "Neither curse them at all, nor bless them at all."

26 But Balaam answered Balak, "Didn't I tell you, saying, 'All that the LORD speaks, that I must do'?"

27 Balak said to Balaam, "Come now, I will take you to another place; perhaps it will please God that you may curse them for me from there."

28 Balak took Balaam to the top of Peor, that looks down on the desert. 29 Balaam said to Balak, "Build seven altars for me here, and prepare seven bulls and seven rams for me here."

30 Balak did as Balaam had said, and offered up a bull and a ram on every altar.

24

1 When Balaam saw that it pleased the LORD to bless Israel, he didn't go, as at the other times, to use divination, but he set his face towards the wilderness. 2 Balaam lifted up his eyes, and he saw Israel dwelling according to their tribes; and the Spirit of God came on him. 3 He took up his parable, and said,
"Balaam the son of Beor says,
    the man whose eyes are open says;
4 he says, who hears the words of God,
    who sees the vision of the Almighty,
    falling down, and having his eyes open:
5 How goodly are your tents, Jacob,
    and your dwellings, Israel!
6 As valleys they are spread out,
    as gardens by the riverside,
    as aloes which the LORD has planted,
    as cedar trees beside the waters.
7 Water shall flow from his buckets.
    His seed shall be in many waters.
His king shall be higher than Agag.
    His kingdom shall be exalted.
8 God brings him out of Egypt.
    He has as it were the strength of the wild ox.
He shall consume the nations his adversaries,
    shall break their bones in pieces,
    and pierce them with his arrows.
9 He couched, he lay down as a lion,
    as a lioness;
    who shall rouse him up?
Everyone who blesses you is blessed.
    Everyone who curses you is cursed."

10 Balak's anger burnt against Balaam, and he struck his hands together. Balak said to Balaam, "I called you to curse my enemies, and, behold, you have altogether blessed them these three times. 11 Therefore, flee to your place, now! I thought to promote you to great honour; but, behold, the LORD has kept you back from honour."

12 Balaam said to Balak, "Didn't I also tell your messengers whom you sent to me, saying, 13 'If Balak would give me his house full of silver and gold, I can't go beyond the LORD's word, to do either good or bad from my own mind. I will say what the LORD says'? 14 Now, behold, I go to my people. Come, I will inform you what this people shall do to your people in the latter days."

15 He took up his parable, and said,
"Balaam the son of Beor says,

the man whose eyes are open says;

 16 he says, who hears the words of God,
 knows the knowledge of the Most High,
 and who sees the vision of the Almighty,
 falling down, and having his eyes open:
 17 I see him, but not now.
 I see him, but not near.
 A star will come out of Jacob.
 A sceptre will rise out of Israel,
 and shall strike through the corners of Moab,
 and crush all the sons of Sheth.
 18 Edom shall be a possession.
 Seir, his enemy, also shall be a possession,
 while Israel does valiantly.
 19 Out of Jacob shall one have dominion,
 and shall destroy the remnant from the city."
 20 He looked at Amalek, and took up his parable, and said,
 "Amalek was the first of the nations,
 but his latter end shall come to destruction."
 21 He looked at the Kenite, and took up his parable, and said,
 "Your dwelling place is strong.
 Your nest is set in the rock.
 22 Nevertheless Kain shall be wasted,
 until Asshur carries you away captive."
 23 He took up his parable, and said,
 "Alas, who shall live when God does this?
 24 But ships shall come from the coast of Kittim.
 They shall afflict Asshur, and shall afflict Eber.
 He also shall come to destruction."
 25 Balaam rose up, and went and returned to his place; and Balak also went his way.

25

 1 Israel stayed in Shittim; and the people began to play the prostitute with the daughters of Moab; 2 for they called the people to the sacrifices of their gods. The people ate and bowed down to their gods. 3 Israel joined himself to Baal Peor, and the LORD's anger burnt against Israel. 4 The LORD said to Moses, "Take all the chiefs of the people, and hang them up to the LORD before the sun, that the fierce anger of the LORD may turn away from Israel."

 5 Moses said to the judges of Israel, "Everyone kill his men who have joined themselves to Baal Peor."

 6 Behold, one of the children of Israel came and brought to his brothers a Midianite woman in the sight of Moses, and in the sight of all the congregation of the children of Israel, while they were weeping at the door of the Tent of Meeting. 7 When Phinehas, the son of Eleazar, the son of Aaron the priest, saw it, he rose up from the middle of the congregation, and took a spear in his hand. 8 He went after the man of Israel into the pavilion, and thrust both of them through, the man of Israel, and the woman through her body. So the plague was stopped amongst the children of Israel. 9 Those who died by the plague were twenty-four thousand.

 10 The LORD spoke to Moses, saying, 11 "Phinehas, the son of Eleazar, the son of Aaron the priest, has turned my wrath away from the children of Israel, in that he was jealous with my jealousy amongst them, so that I didn't consume the children of Israel in my jealousy. 12 Therefore say, 'Behold, I give to him my covenant of peace. 13 It shall be to him, and to his offspring after him, the covenant of an everlasting priesthood, because he was jealous for his God, and made atonement for the children of Israel.'"

 14 Now the name of the man of Israel that was slain, who was slain with the Midianite woman, was Zimri, the son of Salu, a prince of a fathers' house amongst the Simeonites. 15 The name of the Midianite woman who was slain was Cozbi, the daughter of Zur. He was head of the people of a fathers' house in Midian.

 16 The LORD spoke to Moses, saying, 17 "Harass the Midianites, and strike them; 18 for they harassed you with their wiles, wherein they have deceived you in the matter of Peor, and in the incident regarding Cozbi, the daughter of the prince of Midian, their sister, who was slain on the day of the plague in the matter of Peor."

26

 1 After the plague, the LORD spoke to Moses and to Eleazar the son of Aaron the priest, saying, 2 "Take a census of all the congregation of the children of Israel, from twenty years old and upward, by their fathers' houses, all who are able to go out to war in Israel." 3 Moses and Eleazar the priest spoke with them in the plains of Moab by the Jordan at Jericho, saying, 4 "Take a census, from twenty years old and upward, as the LORD commanded Moses and the children of Israel."

 These are those who came out of the land of Egypt. 5 Reuben, the firstborn of Israel; the sons of Reuben: of Hanoch, the family of the Hanochites; of Pallu, the family of the Palluites; 6 of Hezron, the family of the Hezronites; of Carmi, the family of the Carmites. 7 These are the families of the Reubenites; and those who were counted of them were forty-three thousand and seven hundred and thirty. 8 The son of Pallu: Eliab. 9 The sons of Eliab: Nemuel, Dathan, and Abiram. These are that Dathan and Abiram who were called by the congregation, who rebelled against Moses and against Aaron in the company of Korah when they rebelled against the LORD; 10 and the earth opened its mouth, and swallowed them up together with Korah when that company died; at the time the fire devoured two hundred and fifty men, and they became a sign. 11 Notwithstanding, the sons of Korah didn't die. 12 The sons of Simeon after their families: of

Nemuel, the family of the Nemuelites; of Jamin, the family of the Jaminites; of Jachin, the family of the Jachinites; 13 of Zerah, the family of the Zerahites; of Shaul, the family of the Shaulites. 14 These are the families of the Simeonites, twenty-two thousand and two hundred. 15 The sons of Gad after their families: of Zephon, the family of the Zephonites; of Haggi, the family of the Haggites; of Shuni, the family of the Shunites; 16 of Ozni, the family of the Oznites; of Eri, the family of the Erites; 17 of Arod, the family of the Arodites; of Areli, the family of the Arelites. 18 These are the families of the sons of Gad according to those who were counted of them, forty thousand and five hundred. 19 The sons of Judah: Er and Onan. Er and Onan died in the land of Canaan. 20 The sons of Judah after their families were: of Shelah, the family of the Shelanites; of Perez, the family of the Perezites; of Zerah, the family of the Zerahites. 21 The sons of Perez were: of Hezron, the family of the Hezronites; of Hamul, the family of the Hamulites. 22 These are the families of Judah according to those who were counted of them, seventy-six thousand and five hundred. 23 The sons of Issachar after their families: of Tola, the family of the Tolaites; of Puvah, the family of the Punites; 24 of Jashub, the family of the Jashubites; of Shimron, the family of the Shimronites. 25 These are the families of Issachar according to those who were counted of them, sixty-four thousand and three hundred. 26 The sons of Zebulun after their families: of Sered, the family of the Seredites; of Elon, the family of the Elonites; of Jahleel, the family of the Jahleelites. 27 These are the families of the Zebulunites according to those who were counted of them, sixty thousand and five hundred. 28 The sons of Joseph after their families: Manasseh and Ephraim. 29 The sons of Manasseh: of Machir, the family of the Machirites; and Machir became the father of Gilead; of Gilead, the family of the Gileadites. 30 These are the sons of Gilead: of Iezer, the family of the Iezerites; of Helek, the family of the Helekites; 31 and Asriel, the family of the Asrielites; and Shechem, the family of the Shechemites; 32 and Shemida, the family of the Shemidaites; and Hepher, the family of the Hepherites. 33 Zelophehad the son of Hepher had no sons, but daughters: and the names of the daughters of Zelophehad were Mahlah, Noah, Hoglah, Milcah, and Tirzah. 34 These are the families of Manasseh. Those who were counted of them were fifty-two thousand and seven hundred. 35 These are the sons of Ephraim after their families: of Shuthelah, the family of the Shuthelahites; of Becher, the family of the Becherites; of Tahan, the family of the Tahanites. 36 These are the sons of Shuthelah: of Eran, the family of the Eranites. 37 These are the families of the sons of Ephraim according to those who were counted of them, thirty-two thousand and five hundred. These are the sons of Joseph after their families. 38 The sons of Benjamin after their families: of Bela, the family of the Belaites; of Ashbel, the family of the Ashbelites; of Ahiram, the family of the Ahiramites; 39 of Shephupham, the family of the Shuphamites; of Hupham, the family of the Huphamites. 40 The sons of Bela were Ard and Naaman: the family of the Ardites; and of Naaman, the family of the Naamites. 41 These are the sons of Benjamin after their families; and those who were counted of them were forty-five thousand and six hundred. 42 These are the sons of Dan after their families: of Shuham, the family of the Shuhamites. These are the families of Dan after their families. 43 All the families of the Shuhamites, according to those who were counted of them, were sixty-four thousand and four hundred. 44 The sons of Asher after their families: of Imnah, the family of the Imnites; of Ishvi, the family of the Ishvites; of Beriah, the family of the Berites. 45 Of the sons of Beriah: of Heber, the family of the Heberites; of Malchiel, the family of the Malchielites. 46 The name of the daughter of Asher was Serah. 47 These are the families of the sons of Asher according to those who were counted of them, fifty-three thousand and four hundred. 48 The sons of Naphtali after their families: of Jahzeel, the family of the Jahzeelites; of Guni, the family of the Gunites; 49 of Jezer, the family of the Jezerites; of Shillem, the family of the Shillemites. 50 These are the families of Naphtali according to their families; and those who were counted of them were forty-five thousand and four hundred. 51 These are those who were counted of the children of Israel, six hundred and one thousand and seven hundred and thirty.

 52 The LORD spoke to Moses, saying, 53 "To these the land shall be divided for an inheritance according to the number of names. 54 To the more you shall give the more inheritance, and to the fewer you shall give the less inheritance. To everyone according to those who were counted of him shall his inheritance be given. 55 Notwithstanding, the land shall be divided by lot. According to the names of the tribes of their fathers they shall inherit. 56 According to the lot shall their inheritance be divided between the more and the fewer."

 57 These are those who were counted of the Levites after their families: of Gershon, the family of the Gershonites; of Kohath, the family of the Kohathites; of Merari, the family of the Merarites. 58 These are the families of Levi: the family of the Libnites, the family of the Hebronites, the family of the Mahlites, the family of the Mushites, and the family of the Korahites. Kohath became the father of Amram. 59 The name of Amram's wife was Jochebed, the daughter of Levi, who was born to Levi in Egypt. She bore to Amram Aaron and Moses, and Miriam their sister. 60 To Aaron were born Nadab and Abihu, Eleazar and Ithamar. 61 Nadab and Abihu died when they offered strange fire before the LORD. 62 Those who were counted of them were twenty-three thousand, every male from a month old and upward; for they were not counted amongst the children of Israel, because there was no inheritance given them amongst the children of Israel. 63 These are those who were counted by Moses and Eleazar the priest, who counted the children of Israel in the plains of Moab by the Jordan at Jericho. 64 But amongst these there was not a man of them who were counted by Moses and Aaron the priest, who counted the children of Israel in the wilderness of Sinai. 65 For the LORD had said of them, "They

shall surely die in the wilderness." There was not a man left of them, except Caleb the son of Jephunneh, and Joshua the son of Nun.

27

1 Then the daughters of Zelophehad, the son of Hepher, the son of Gilead, the son of Machir, the son of Manasseh, of the families of Manasseh the son of Joseph came near. These are the names of his daughters: Mahlah, Noah, Hoglah, Milcah, and Tirzah. 2 They stood before Moses, before Eleazar the priest, and before the princes and all the congregation, at the door of the Tent of Meeting, saying, 3 "Our father died in the wilderness. He was not amongst the company of those who gathered themselves together against the LORD in the company of Korah, but he died in his own sin. He had no sons. 4 Why should the name of our father be taken away from amongst his family, because he had no son? Give to us a possession amongst the brothers of our father."

5 Moses brought their cause before the LORD. 6 The LORD spoke to Moses, saying, 7 "The daughters of Zelophehad speak right. You shall surely give them a possession of an inheritance amongst their father's brothers. You shall cause the inheritance of their father to pass to them. 8 You shall speak to the children of Israel, saying, 'If a man dies, and has no son, then you shall cause his inheritance to pass to his daughter. 9 If he has no daughter, then you shall give his inheritance to his brothers. 10 If he has no brothers, then you shall give his inheritance to his father's brothers. 11 If his father has no brothers, then you shall give his inheritance to his kinsman who is next to him of his family, and he shall possess it. This shall be a statute and ordinance for the children of Israel, as the LORD commanded Moses.'"

12 The LORD said to Moses, "Go up into this mountain of Abarim, and see the land which I have given to the children of Israel. 13 When you have seen it, you also shall be gathered to your people, as Aaron your brother was gathered; 14 because in the strife of the congregation, you rebelled against my word in the wilderness of Zin, to honour me as holy at the waters before their eyes." (These are the waters of Meribah of Kadesh in the wilderness of Zin.)

15 Moses spoke to the LORD, saying, 16 "Let the LORD, the God of the spirits of all flesh, appoint a man over the congregation, 17 who may go out before them, and who may come in before them, and who may lead them out, and who may bring them in, that the congregation of the LORD may not be as sheep which have no shepherd."

18 The LORD said to Moses, "Take Joshua the son of Nun, a man in whom is the Spirit, and lay your hand on him. 19 Set him before Eleazar the priest, and before all the congregation; and commission him in their sight. 20 You shall give authority to him, that all the congregation of the children of Israel may obey. 21 He shall stand before Eleazar the priest, who shall enquire for him by the judgement of the Urim before the LORD. At his word they shall go out, and at his word they shall come in, both he and all the children of Israel with him, even all the congregation."

22 Moses did as the LORD commanded him. He took Joshua, and set him before Eleazar the priest and before all the congregation. 23 He laid his hands on him and commissioned him, as the LORD spoke by Moses.

28

1 The LORD spoke to Moses, saying, 2 "Command the children of Israel, and tell them, 'See that you present my offering, my food for my offerings made by fire, as a pleasant aroma to me, in their due season.' 3 You shall tell them, 'This is the offering made by fire which you shall offer to the LORD: male lambs a year old without defect, two day by day, for a continual burnt offering. 4 You shall offer the one lamb in the morning, and you shall offer the other lamb at evening, 5 with one tenth of an ephah[a] of fine flour for a meal offering, mixed with the fourth part of a hin[b] of beaten oil. 6 It is a continual burnt offering which was ordained in Mount Sinai for a pleasant aroma, an offering made by fire to the LORD. 7 Its drink offering shall be the fourth part of a hin[c] for each lamb. You shall pour out a drink offering of strong drink to the LORD in the holy place. 8 The other lamb you shall offer at evening. As the meal offering of the morning, and as its drink offering, you shall offer it, an offering made by fire, for a pleasant aroma to the LORD.

9 "'On the Sabbath day, you shall offer two male lambs a year old without defect, and two tenths of an ephah[d] of fine flour for a meal offering mixed with oil, and its drink offering: 10 this is the burnt offering of every Sabbath, in addition to the continual burnt offering and its drink offering.

11 "'In the beginnings of your months, you shall offer a burnt offering to the LORD: two young bulls, one ram, seven male lambs a year old without defect, 12 and three tenths of an ephah[e] of fine flour for a meal offering mixed with oil, for each bull; and two tenth parts of fine flour for a meal offering mixed with oil, for the one ram; 13 and one tenth part of fine flour mixed with oil for a meal offering to every lamb, as a burnt offering of a pleasant aroma, an offering made by fire to the LORD. 14 Their drink offerings shall be half a hin of wine for a bull, the third part of a hin for the ram, and the fourth part of a hin for a lamb. This is the burnt offering of every month throughout the months of the year. 15 Also, one male goat for a sin offering to the LORD shall be offered in addition to the continual burnt offering and its drink offering.

16 "'In the first month, on the fourteenth day of the month, is the LORD's Passover. 17 On the fifteenth day of this month shall be a feast. Unleavened bread shall be eaten for seven days. 18 In the first day shall be

a holy convocation. You shall do no regular work, 19 but you shall offer an offering made by fire, a burnt offering to the LORD: two young bulls, one ram, and seven male lambs a year old. They shall be without defect, 20 with their meal offering, fine flour mixed with oil. You shall offer three tenths for a bull, and two tenths for the ram. 21 You shall offer one tenth for every lamb of the seven lambs; 22 and one male goat for a sin offering, to make atonement for you. 23 You shall offer these in addition to the burnt offering of the morning, which is for a continual burnt offering. 24 In this way you shall offer daily, for seven days, the food of the offering made by fire, of a pleasant aroma to the LORD. It shall be offered in addition to the continual burnt offering and its drink offering. 25 On the seventh day you shall have a holy convocation. You shall do no regular work.

26 "'Also in the day of the first fruits, when you offer a new meal offering to the LORD in your feast of weeks, you shall have a holy convocation. You shall do no regular work; 27 but you shall offer a burnt offering for a pleasant aroma to the LORD: two young bulls, one ram, seven male lambs a year old; 28 and their meal offering, fine flour mixed with oil, three tenths for each bull, two tenths for the one ram, 29 one tenth for every lamb of the seven lambs; 30 and one male goat, to make atonement for you. 31 Besides the continual burnt offering and its meal offering, you shall offer them and their drink offerings. See that they are without defect.

29

1 "'In the seventh month, on the first day of the month, you shall have a holy convocation; you shall do no regular work. It is a day of blowing of trumpets to you. 2 You shall offer a burnt offering for a pleasant aroma to the LORD: one young bull, one ram, seven male lambs a year old without defect; 3 and their meal offering, fine flour mixed with oil: three tenths for the bull, two tenths for the ram, 4 and one tenth for every lamb of the seven lambs; 5 and one male goat for a sin offering, to make atonement for you; 6 in addition to the burnt offering of the new moon with its meal offering, and the continual burnt offering with its meal offering, and their drink offerings, according to their ordinance, for a pleasant aroma, an offering made by fire to the LORD.

7 "'On the tenth day of this seventh month you shall have a holy convocation. You shall afflict your souls. You shall do no kind of work; 8 but you shall offer a burnt offering to the LORD for a pleasant aroma: one young bull, one ram, seven male lambs a year old, all without defect; 9 and their meal offering, fine flour mixed with oil: three tenths for the bull, two tenths for the one ram, 10 one tenth for every lamb of the seven lambs; 11 one male goat for a sin offering, in addition to the sin offering of atonement, and the continual burnt offering, and its meal offering, and their drink offerings.

12 "'On the fifteenth day of the seventh month you shall have a holy convocation. You shall do no regular work. You shall keep a feast to the LORD seven days. 13 You shall offer a burnt offering, an offering made by fire, of a pleasant aroma to the LORD: thirteen young bulls, two rams, fourteen male lambs a year old, all without defect; 14 and their meal offering, fine flour mixed with oil: three tenths for every bull of the thirteen bulls, two tenths for each ram of the two rams, 15 and one tenth for every lamb of the fourteen lambs; 16 and one male goat for a sin offering, in addition to the continual burnt offering, its meal offering, and its drink offering.

17 "'On the second day you shall offer twelve young bulls, two rams, and fourteen male lambs a year old without defect; 18 and their meal offering and their drink offerings for the bulls, for the rams, and for the lambs, according to their number, after the ordinance; 19 and one male goat for a sin offering, in addition to the continual burnt offering, with its meal offering and their drink offerings.

20 "'On the third day: eleven bulls, two rams, fourteen male lambs a year old without defect; 21 and their meal offering and their drink offerings for the bulls, for the rams, and for the lambs, according to their number, after the ordinance; 22 and one male goat for a sin offering, in addition to the continual burnt offering, and its meal offering, and its drink offering.

23 "'On the fourth day ten bulls, two rams, fourteen male lambs a year old without defect; 24 their meal offering and their drink offerings for the bulls, for the rams, and for the lambs, according to their number, after the ordinance; 25 and one male goat for a sin offering; in addition to the continual burnt offering, its meal offering, and its drink offering.

26 "'On the fifth day: nine bulls, two rams, fourteen male lambs a year old without defect; 27 and their meal offering and their drink offerings for the bulls, for the rams, and for the lambs, according to their number, after the ordinance, 28 and one male goat for a sin offering, in addition to the continual burnt offering, and its meal offering, and its drink offering.

29 "'On the sixth day: eight bulls, two rams, fourteen male lambs a year old without defect; 30 and their meal offering and their drink offerings for the bulls, for the rams, and for the lambs, according to their number, after the ordinance, 31 and one male goat for a sin offering; in addition to the continual burnt offering, its meal offering, and the drink offerings of it.

32 "'On the seventh day: seven bulls, two rams, fourteen male lambs a year old without defect; 33 and their meal offering and their drink offerings for the bulls, for the rams, and for the lambs, according to their number, after the ordinance, 34 and one male goat for a sin offering; in addition to the continual burnt offering, its meal offering, and its drink offering.

---

a *28:5* 1 ephah is about 22 litres or about 2/3 of a bushel
b *28:5* A hin is about 6.5 litres or 1.7 gallons.
c *28:7* One hin is about 6.5 litres, so 1/4 hin is about 1.6 litres or 1.7 quarts.

d *28:9* 1 ephah is about 22 litres or about 2/3 of a bushel
e *28:12* 1 ephah is about 22 litres or about 2/3 of a bushel

35 "'On the eighth day you shall have a solemn assembly. You shall do no regular work; 36 but you shall offer a burnt offering, an offering made by fire, a pleasant aroma to the LORD: one bull, one ram, seven male lambs a year old without defect; 37 their meal offering and their drink offerings for the bull, for the ram, and for the lambs, shall be according to their number, after the ordinance, 38 and one male goat for a sin offering, in addition to the continual burnt offering, with its meal offering, and its drink offering.

39 "'You shall offer these to the LORD in your set feasts—in addition to your vows and your free will offerings—for your burnt offerings, your meal offerings, your drink offerings, and your peace offerings.'"

40 Moses told the children of Israel according to all that the LORD commanded Moses.

30

1 Moses spoke to the heads of the tribes of the children of Israel, saying, "This is the thing which the LORD has commanded. 2 When a man vows a vow to the LORD, or swears an oath to bind his soul with a bond, he shall not break his word. He shall do according to all that proceeds out of his mouth.

3 "Also, when a woman vows a vow to the LORD and binds herself by a pledge, being in her father's house, in her youth, 4 and her father hears her vow and her pledge with which she has bound her soul, and her father says nothing to her, then all her vows shall stand, and every pledge with which she has bound her soul shall stand. 5 But if her father forbids her in the day that he hears, none of her vows or of her pledges with which she has bound her soul, shall stand. The LORD will forgive her, because her father has forbidden her.

6 "If she has a husband, while her vows are on her, or the rash utterance of her lips with which she has bound her soul, 7 and her husband hears it, and says nothing to her in the day that he hears it; then her vows shall stand, and her pledges with which she has bound her soul shall stand. 8 But if her husband forbids her in the day that he hears it, then he makes void her vow which is on her and the rash utterance of her lips, with which she has bound her soul. The LORD will forgive her.

9 "But the vow of a widow, or of her who is divorced, everything with which she has bound her soul shall stand against her.

10 "If she vowed in her husband's house or bound her soul by a bond with an oath, 11 and her husband heard it, and held his peace at her and didn't disallow her, then all her vows shall stand, and every pledge with which she bound her soul shall stand. 12 But if her husband made them null and void in the day that he heard them, then whatever proceeded out of her lips concerning her vows, or concerning the bond of her soul, shall not stand. Her husband has made them void. The LORD will forgive her. 13 Every vow, and every binding oath to afflict the soul, her husband may establish it, or her husband may make it void. 14 But if her husband says nothing to her from day to day, then he establishes all her vows or all her pledges which are on her. He has established them, because he said nothing to her in the day that he heard them. 15 But if he makes them null and void after he has heard them, then he shall bear her iniquity."

16 These are the statutes which the LORD commanded Moses, between a man and his wife, between a father and his daughter, being in her youth, in her father's house.

31

1 The LORD spoke to Moses, saying, 2 "Avenge the children of Israel on the Midianites. Afterward you shall be gathered to your people."

3 Moses spoke to the people, saying, "Arm men from amongst you for war, that they may go against Midian, to execute the LORD's vengeance on Midian. 4 You shall send one thousand out of every tribe, throughout all the tribes of Israel, to the war." 5 So there were delivered, out of the thousands of Israel, a thousand from every tribe, twelve thousand armed for war. 6 Moses sent them, one thousand of every tribe, to the war with Phinehas the son of Eleazar the priest, to the war, with the vessels of the sanctuary and the trumpets for the alarm in his hand. 7 They fought against Midian, as the LORD commanded Moses. They killed every male. 8 They killed the kings of Midian with the rest of their slain: Evi, Rekem, Zur, Hur, and Reba, the five kings of Midian. They also killed Balaam the son of Beor with the sword. 9 The children of Israel took the women of Midian captive with their little ones; and all their livestock, all their flocks, and all their goods, they took as plunder. 10 All their cities in the places in which they lived, and all their encampments, they burnt with fire. 11 They took all the captives, and all the plunder, both of man and of animal. 12 They brought the captives with the prey and the plunder, to Moses, and to Eleazar the priest, and to the congregation of the children of Israel, to the camp at the plains of Moab, which are by the Jordan at Jericho. 13 Moses and Eleazar the priest, with all the princes of the congregation, went out to meet them outside of the camp. 14 Moses was angry with the officers of the army, the captains of thousands and the captains of hundreds, who came from the service of the war. 15 Moses said to them, "Have you saved all the women alive? 16 Behold, these caused the children of Israel, through the counsel of Balaam, to commit trespass against the LORD in the matter of Peor, and so the plague was amongst the congregation of the LORD. 17 Now therefore kill every male amongst the little ones, and kill every woman who has known man by lying with him. 18 But all the girls, who have not known man by lying with him, keep alive for yourselves.

19 "Encamp outside of the camp for seven days. Whoever has killed any person, and whoever has touched any slain, purify yourselves on the third day and on the seventh day, you and your captives. 20 You shall purify every garment, and all that is made of skin, and all work of goats' hair, and all things made of wood."

21 Eleazar the priest said to the men of war who went to the battle, "This is the statute of the law which the LORD has commanded Moses. 22 However the gold, and the silver, the bronze, the iron, the tin, and the lead, 23 everything that may withstand the fire, you shall make to go through the fire, and it shall be clean; nevertheless it shall be purified with the water for impurity. All that doesn't withstand the fire you shall make to go through the water. 24 You shall wash your clothes on the seventh day, and you shall be clean. Afterward you shall come into the camp."

25 The LORD spoke to Moses, saying, 26 "Count the plunder that was taken, both of man and of animal, you, and Eleazar the priest, and the heads of the fathers' households of the congregation; 27 and divide the plunder into two parts: between the men skilled in war, who went out to battle, and all the congregation. 28 Levy a tribute to the LORD of the men of war who went out to battle: one soul of five hundred; of the persons, of the cattle, of the donkeys, and of the flocks. 29 Take it from their half, and give it to Eleazar the priest, for the LORD's wave offering. 30 Of the children of Israel's half, you shall take one drawn out of every fifty, of the persons, of the cattle, of the donkeys, and of the flocks, of all the livestock, and give them to the Levites, who perform the duty of the LORD's tabernacle."

31 Moses and Eleazar the priest did as the LORD commanded Moses.

32 Now the plunder, over and above the booty which the men of war took, was six hundred and seventy-five thousand sheep, 33 seventy-two thousand head of cattle, 34 sixty-one thousand donkeys, 35 and thirty-two thousand persons in all, of the women who had not known man by lying with him. 36 The half, which was the portion of those who went out to war, was in number three hundred and thirty-seven thousand and five hundred sheep; 37 and the LORD's tribute of the sheep was six hundred and seventy-five. 38 The cattle were thirty-six thousand, of which the LORD's tribute was seventy-two. 39 The donkeys were thirty thousand and five hundred, of which the LORD's tribute was sixty-one. 40 The persons were sixteen thousand, of whom the LORD's tribute was thirty-two persons. 41 Moses gave the tribute, which was the LORD's wave offering, to Eleazar the priest, as the LORD commanded Moses. 42 Of the children of Israel's half, which Moses divided off from the men who fought 43 (now the congregation's half was three hundred and thirty-seven thousand and five hundred sheep, 44 thirty-six thousand head of cattle, 45 thirty thousand and five hundred donkeys, 46 and sixteen thousand persons), 47 even of the children of Israel's half, Moses took one drawn out of every fifty, both of man and of animal, and gave them to the Levites, who performed the duty of the LORD's tabernacle, as the LORD commanded Moses.

48 The officers who were over the thousands of the army, the captains of thousands, and the captains of hundreds, came near to Moses. 49 They said to Moses, "Your servants have taken the sum of the men of war who are under our command, and there lacks not one man of us. 50 We have brought the LORD's offering, what every man found: gold ornaments, armlets, bracelets, signet rings, earrings, and necklaces, to make atonement for our souls before the LORD."

51 Moses and Eleazar the priest took their gold, even all worked jewels. 52 All the gold of the wave offering that they offered up to the LORD, of the captains of thousands, and of the captains of hundreds, was sixteen thousand and seven hundred and fifty shekels.[a] 53 The men of war had taken booty, every man for himself. 54 Moses and Eleazar the priest took the gold of the captains of thousands and of hundreds, and brought it into the Tent of Meeting for a memorial for the children of Israel before the LORD.

32

1 Now the children of Reuben and the children of Gad had a very great multitude of livestock. They saw the land of Jazer, and the land of Gilead. Behold, the place was a place for livestock. 2 Then the children of Gad and the children of Reuben came and spoke to Moses, and to Eleazar the priest, and to the princes of the congregation, saying, 3 "Ataroth, Dibon, Jazer, Nimrah, Heshbon, Elealeh, Sebam, Nebo, and Beon, 4 the land which The LORD struck before the congregation of Israel, is a land for livestock; and your servants have livestock." 5 They said, "If we have found favour in your sight, let this land be given to your servants for a possession. Don't bring us over the Jordan."

6 Moses said to the children of Gad, and to the children of Reuben, "Shall your brothers go to war while you sit here? 7 Why do you discourage the heart of the children of Israel from going over into the land which the LORD has given them? 8 Your fathers did so when I sent them from Kadesh Barnea to see the land. 9 For when they went up to the valley of Eshcol, and saw the land, they discouraged the heart of the children of Israel, that they should not go into the land which the LORD had given them. 10 The LORD's anger burnt in that day, and he swore, saying, 11 'Surely none of the men who came up out of Egypt, from twenty years old and upward, shall see the land which I swore to Abraham, to Isaac, and to Jacob; because they have not wholly followed me, 12 except Caleb the son of Jephunneh the Kenizzite, and Joshua the son of Nun, because they have followed the LORD completely.' 13 The LORD's anger burnt against Israel, and he made them wander back and forth in the wilderness forty years, until all the generation who had done evil in the LORD's sight was consumed.

---

[a] *31:52* A shekel is about 10 grams or about 0.35 ounces, so 16,750 shekels is about 167.5 kilograms or about 368.5 pounds.

14 "Behold, you have risen up in your fathers' place, an increase of sinful men, to increase the fierce anger of the LORD towards Israel. 15 For if you turn away from after him, he will yet again leave them in the wilderness; and you will destroy all these people."

16 They came near to him, and said, "We will build sheepfolds here for our livestock, and cities for our little ones; 17 but we ourselves will be ready armed to go before the children of Israel, until we have brought them to their place. Our little ones shall dwell in the fortified cities because of the inhabitants of the land. 18 We will not return to our houses until the children of Israel have all received their inheritance. 19 For we will not inherit with them on the other side of the Jordan and beyond, because our inheritance has come to us on this side of the Jordan eastward."

20 Moses said to them: "If you will do this thing, if you will arm yourselves to go before the LORD to the war, 21 and every one of your armed men will pass over the Jordan before the LORD until he has driven out his enemies from before him, 22 and the land is subdued before the LORD; then afterward you shall return, and be clear of obligation to the LORD and to Israel. Then this land shall be your possession before the LORD.

23 "But if you will not do so, behold, you have sinned against the LORD; and be sure your sin will find you out. 24 Build cities for your little ones, and folds for your sheep; and do that which has proceeded out of your mouth."

25 The children of Gad and the children of Reuben spoke to Moses, saying, "Your servants will do as my lord commands. 26 Our little ones, our wives, our flocks, and all our livestock shall be there in the cities of Gilead; 27 but your servants will pass over, every man who is armed for war, before the LORD to battle, as my lord says."

28 So Moses commanded concerning them to Eleazar the priest, and to Joshua the son of Nun, and to the heads of the fathers' households of the tribes of the children of Israel. 29 Moses said to them, "If the children of Gad and the children of Reuben will pass with you over the Jordan, every man who is armed to battle before the LORD, and the land is subdued before you, then you shall give them the land of Gilead for a possession; 30 but if they will not pass over with you armed, they shall have possessions amongst you in the land of Canaan."

31 The children of Gad and the children of Reuben answered, saying, "As the LORD has said to your servants, so will we do. 32 We will pass over armed before the LORD into the land of Canaan, and the possession of our inheritance shall remain with us beyond the Jordan."

33 Moses gave to them, even to the children of Gad, and to the children of Reuben, and to the half-tribe of Manasseh the son of Joseph, the kingdom of Sihon king of the Amorites, and the kingdom of Og king of Bashan; the land, according to its cities and borders, even the cities of the surrounding land. 34 The children of Gad built Dibon, Ataroth, Aroer, 35 Atroth-shophan, Jazer, Jogbehah, 36 Beth Nimrah, and Beth Haran: fortified cities and folds for sheep. 37 The children of Reuben built Heshbon, Elealeh, Kiriathaim, 38 Nebo, and Baal Meon, (their names being changed), and Sibmah. They gave other names to the cities which they built. 39 The children of Machir the son of Manasseh went to Gilead, took it, and dispossessed the Amorites who were therein. 40 Moses gave Gilead to Machir the son of Manasseh; and he lived therein. 41 Jair the son of Manasseh went and took its villages, and called them Havvoth Jair. 42 Nobah went and took Kenath and its villages, and called it Nobah, after his own name.

33

1 These are the journeys of the children of Israel, when they went out of the land of Egypt by their armies under the hand of Moses and Aaron. 2 Moses wrote the starting points of their journeys by the commandment of the LORD. These are their journeys according to their starting points. 3 They travelled from Rameses in the first month, on the fifteenth day of the first month; on the next day after the Passover, the children of Israel went out with a high hand in the sight of all the Egyptians, 4 while the Egyptians were burying all their firstborn, whom the LORD had struck amongst them. The LORD also executed judgements on their gods. 5 The children of Israel travelled from Rameses, and encamped in Succoth. 6 They travelled from Succoth, and encamped in Etham, which is in the edge of the wilderness. 7 They travelled from Etham, and turned back to Pihahiroth, which is before Baal Zephon, and they encamped before Migdol. 8 They travelled from before Hahiroth, and crossed through the middle of the sea into the wilderness. They went three days' journey in the wilderness of Etham, and encamped in Marah. 9 They travelled from Marah, and came to Elim. In Elim, there were twelve springs of water and seventy palm trees, and they encamped there. 10 They travelled from Elim, and encamped by the Red Sea. 11 They travelled from the Red Sea, and encamped in the wilderness of Sin. 12 They travelled from the wilderness of Sin, and encamped in Dophkah. 13 They travelled from Dophkah, and encamped in Alush. 14 They travelled from Alush, and encamped in Rephidim, where there was no water for the people to drink. 15 They travelled from Rephidim, and encamped in the wilderness of Sinai. 16 They travelled from the wilderness of Sinai, and encamped in Kibroth Hattaavah. 17 They travelled from Kibroth Hattaavah, and encamped in Hazeroth. 18 They travelled from Hazeroth, and encamped in Rithmah. 19 They travelled from Rithmah, and encamped in Rimmon Perez. 20 They travelled from Rimmon Perez, and encamped in Libnah. 21 They travelled from Libnah, and encamped in Rissah. 22 They travelled from Rissah, and encamped in Kehelathah. 23 They travelled from Kehelathah, and encamped in Mount Shepher. 24 They travelled from Mount Shepher, and encamped in Haradah. 25 They travelled from Haradah, and encamped in Makheloth. 26 They travelled from Makheloth, and encamped in Tahath. 27 They travelled from Tahath, and encamped in Terah. 28 They travelled from Terah, and encamped in Mithkah. 29 They travelled from Mithkah, and encamped in Hashmonah. 30 They travelled from Hashmonah, and encamped in Moseroth. 31 They travelled from Moseroth, and encamped in Bene Jaakan. 32 They travelled from Bene Jaakan, and encamped in Hor Haggidgad. 33 They travelled from Hor Haggidgad, and encamped in Jotbathah. 34 They travelled from Jotbathah, and encamped in Abronah. 35 They travelled from Abronah, and encamped in Ezion Geber. 36 They travelled from Ezion Geber, and encamped at Kadesh in the wilderness of Zin. 37 They travelled from Kadesh, and encamped in Mount Hor, in the edge of the land of Edom. 38 Aaron the priest went up into Mount Hor at the commandment of the LORD and died there, in the fortieth year after the children of Israel had come out of the land of Egypt, in the fifth month, on the first day of the month. 39 Aaron was one hundred and twenty-three years old when he died in Mount Hor. 40 The Canaanite king of Arad, who lived in the South in the land of Canaan, heard of the coming of the children of Israel. 41 They travelled from Mount Hor, and encamped in Zalmonah. 42 They travelled from Zalmonah, and encamped in Punon. 43 They travelled from Punon, and encamped in Oboth. 44 They travelled from Oboth, and encamped in Iye Abarim, in the border of Moab. 45 They travelled from Iyim, and encamped in Dibon Gad. 46 They travelled from Dibon Gad, and encamped in Almon Diblathaim. 47 They travelled from Almon Diblathaim, and encamped in the mountains of Abarim, before Nebo. 48 They travelled from the mountains of Abarim, and encamped in the plains of Moab by the Jordan at Jericho. 49 They encamped by the Jordan, from Beth Jeshimoth even to Abel Shittim in the plains of Moab. 50 The LORD spoke to Moses in the plains of Moab by the Jordan at Jericho, saying, 51 Speak to the children of Israel, and tell them, "When you pass over the Jordan into the land of Canaan, 52 then you shall drive out all the inhabitants of the land from before you, destroy all their stone idols, destroy all their molten images, and demolish all their high places. 53 You shall take possession of the land, and dwell therein; for I have given the land to you to possess it. 54 You shall inherit the land by lot according to your families; to the larger groups you shall give a larger inheritance, and to the smaller you shall give a smaller inheritance. Wherever the lot falls to any man, that shall be his. You shall inherit according to the tribes of your fathers.

55 "But if you do not drive out the inhabitants of the land from before you, then those you let remain of them will be like pricks in your eyes and thorns in your sides. They will harass you in the land in which you dwell. 56 It shall happen that as I thought to do to them, so I will do to you."

34

1 The LORD spoke to Moses, saying, 2 "Command the children of Israel, and tell them, 'When you come into the land of Canaan (this is the land that shall fall to you for an inheritance, even the land of Canaan according to its borders), 3 then your south quarter shall be from the wilderness of Zin along by the side of Edom, and your south border shall be from the end of the Salt Sea eastward. 4 Your border shall turn about southward of the ascent of Akrabbim, and pass along to Zin; and it shall pass southward of Kadesh Barnea; and it shall go from there to Hazar Addar, and pass along to Azmon. 5 The border shall turn about from Azmon to the brook of Egypt, and it shall end at the sea.

6 "'For the western border, you shall have the great sea and its border. This shall be your west border.

7 "'This shall be your north border: from the great sea you shall mark out for yourselves Mount Hor. 8 From Mount Hor you shall mark out to the entrance of Hamath; and the border shall pass by Zedad. 9 Then the border shall go to Ziphron, and it shall end at Hazar Enan. This shall be your north border.

10 "'You shall mark out your east border from Hazar Enan to Shepham. 11 The border shall go down from Shepham to Riblah, on the east side of Ain. The border shall go down, and shall reach to the side of the sea of Chinnereth eastward. 12 The border shall go down to the Jordan, and end at the Salt Sea. This shall be your land according to its borders around it.'"

13 Moses commanded the children of Israel, saying, "This is the land which you shall inherit by lot, which the LORD has commanded to give to the nine tribes, and to the half-tribe; 14 for the tribe of the children of Reuben according to their fathers' houses, the tribe of the children of Gad according to their fathers' houses, and the half-tribe of Manasseh have received their inheritance. 15 The two tribes and the half-tribe have received their inheritance beyond the Jordan at Jericho eastward, towards the sunrise."

16 The LORD spoke to Moses, saying, 17 "These are the names of the men who shall divide the land to you for inheritance: Eleazar the priest, and Joshua the son of Nun. 18 You shall take one prince of every tribe, to divide the land for inheritance. 19 These are the names of the men: Of the tribe of Judah, Caleb the son of Jephunneh. 20 Of the tribe of the children of Simeon, Shemuel the son of Ammihud. 21 Of the tribe of Benjamin, Elidad the son of Chislon. 22 Of the tribe of the children of Dan a prince, Bukki the son of Jogli. 23 Of the children of Joseph: of the tribe of the children of Manasseh a prince, Hanniel the son of Ephod. 24 Of the tribe of the children of Ephraim a prince, Kemuel the son of Shiphtan. 25 Of the tribe of the children of Zebulun a prince, Elizaphan the son of Parnach. 26 Of the tribe of the children of Issachar a prince, Paltiel the son of Azzan. 27 Of the tribe of the children of Asher a prince, Ahihud the son of Shelomi. 28 Of the tribe of the children of Naphtali a prince, Pedahel the son of Ammihud." 29 These are they whom the LORD commanded to divide the inheritance to the children of Israel in the land of Canaan.

35

1 The LORD spoke to Moses in the plains of Moab by the Jordan at Jericho, saying, 2 "Command the children of Israel to give to the Levites cities to dwell in out of their inheritance. You shall give pasture lands for the cities around them to the Levites. 3 They shall have the cities to dwell in. Their pasture lands shall be for their livestock, and for their possessions, and for all their animals.

4 "The pasture lands of the cities, which you shall give to the Levites, shall be from the wall of the city and outward one thousand cubits[a] around it. 5 You shall measure outside of the city for the east side two thousand cubits, and for the south side two thousand cubits, and for the west side two thousand cubits, and for the north side two thousand cubits, the city being in the middle. This shall be the pasture lands of their cities.

6 "The cities which you shall give to the Levites, they shall be the six cities of refuge, which you shall give for the man slayer to flee to. Besides them you shall give forty-two cities. 7 All the cities which you shall give to the Levites shall be forty-eight cities together with their pasture lands. 8 Concerning the cities which you shall give of the possession of the children of Israel, from the many you shall take many, and from the few you shall take few. Everyone according to his inheritance which he inherits shall give some of his cities to the Levites." 9 The LORD spoke to Moses, saying, 10 "Speak to the children of Israel, and tell them, 'When you pass over the Jordan into the land of Canaan, 11 then you shall appoint for yourselves cities to be cities of refuge for you, that the man slayer who kills any person unwittingly may flee there. 12 The cities shall be for your refuge from the avenger, that the man slayer not die until he stands before the congregation for judgement. 13 The cities which you shall give shall be for you six cities of refuge. 14 You shall give three cities beyond the Jordan, and you shall give three cities in the land of Canaan. They shall be cities of refuge. 15 These six cities shall be refuge for the children of Israel, for the stranger, and for the foreigner living amongst them, that everyone who kills any person unwittingly may flee there.

16 "'But if he struck him with an instrument of iron, so that he died, he is a murderer. The murderer shall surely be put to death. 17 If he struck him with a stone in the hand, by which a man may die, and he died, he is a murderer. The murderer shall surely be put to death. 18 Or if he struck him with a weapon of wood in the hand, by which a man may die, and he died, he is a murderer. The murderer shall surely be put to death. 19 The avenger of blood shall himself put the murderer to death. When he meets him, he shall put him to death. 20 If he shoved him out of hatred, or hurled something at him while lying in wait, so that he died, 21 or in hostility struck him with his hand, so that he died, he who struck him shall surely be put to death. He is a murderer. The avenger of blood shall put the murderer to death when he meets him.

22 "'But if he shoved him suddenly without hostility, or hurled on him anything without lying in wait, 23 or with any stone, by which a man may die, not seeing him, and cast it on him so that he died, and he was not his enemy and not seeking his harm, 24 then the congregation shall judge between the striker and the avenger of blood according to these ordinances. 25 The congregation shall deliver the man slayer out of the hand of the avenger of blood, and the congregation shall restore him to his city of refuge, where he had fled. He shall dwell therein until the death of the high priest, who was anointed with the holy oil.

26 "'But if the man slayer shall at any time go beyond the border of his city of refuge where he flees, 27 and the avenger of blood finds him outside of the border of his city of refuge, and the avenger of blood kills the man slayer, he shall not be guilty of blood, 28 because he should have remained in his city of refuge until the death of the high priest. But after the death of the high priest, the man slayer shall return into the land of his possession.

29 "'These things shall be for a statute and ordinance to you throughout your generations in all your dwellings.

30 "'Whoever kills any person, the murderer shall be slain based on the testimony of witnesses; but one witness shall not testify alone against any person so that he dies.

31 "'Moreover you shall take no ransom for the life of a murderer who is guilty of death. He shall surely be put to death.

32 "'You shall take no ransom for him who has fled to his city of refuge, that he may come again to dwell in the land before the death of the priest.

33 "'So you shall not pollute the land where you live; for blood pollutes the land. No atonement can be made for the land for the blood that is shed in it, but by the blood of him who shed it. 34 You shall not defile the land which you inhabit, where I dwell; for I, the LORD, dwell amongst the children of Israel.'"

36

1 The heads of the fathers' households of the family of the children of Gilead, the son of Machir, the son of Manasseh, of the families of the sons of Joseph, came near and spoke before Moses and before the princes, the heads of the fathers' households of the children of Israel. 2 They said, "The LORD commanded my lord to give the land for inheritance by lot to the children of Israel. My lord was commanded by the LORD to give the inheritance of Zelophehad our brother to his daughters. 3 If they are married to any of the sons of the other tribes of the children of Israel, then their inheritance will be taken away from the inheritance of our fathers, and will be added to the inheritance of the tribe to which they shall belong. So it will be taken away from the lot of our inheritance. 4 When the jubilee of the children of Israel comes, then their inheritance will be added to the inheritance of the tribe to which they shall belong. So their inheritance will be taken away from the inheritance of the tribe of our fathers."

5 Moses commanded the children of Israel according to the LORD's word, saying, "The tribe of the sons of Joseph speak what is right. 6 This is the thing which the LORD commands concerning the daughters of Zelophehad, saying, 'Let them be married to whom they think best, only they shall marry into the family of the tribe of their father. 7 So shall no inheritance of the children of Israel move from tribe to tribe; for the children of Israel shall all keep the inheritance of the tribe of his fathers. 8 Every daughter who possesses an inheritance in any tribe of the children of Israel shall be wife to one of the family of the tribe of her father, that the children of Israel may each possess the inheritance of his fathers. 9 So shall no inheritance move from one tribe to another tribe; for the tribes of the children of Israel shall each keep his own inheritance.'"

10 The daughters of Zelophehad did as the LORD commanded Moses: 11 for Mahlah, Tirzah, Hoglah, Milcah, and Noah, the daughters of Zelophehad, were married to their father's brothers' sons. 12 They were married into the families of the sons of Manasseh the son of Joseph. Their inheritance remained in the tribe of the family of their father.

13 These are the commandments and the ordinances which the LORD commanded by Moses to the children of Israel in the plains of Moab by the Jordan at Jericho.

---

a *35:4* A cubit is the length from the tip of the middle finger to the elbow on a man's arm, or about 18 inches or 46 centimetres.

The Fifth Book of Moses, Commonly Called Deuteronomy

1

1 These are the words which Moses spoke to all Israel beyond the Jordan in the wilderness, in the Arabah opposite Suf, between Paran, Tophel, Laban, Hazeroth, and Dizahab. 2 It is eleven days' journey from Horeb by the way of Mount Seir to Kadesh Barnea. 3 In the fortieth year, in the eleventh month, on the first day of the month, Moses spoke to the children of Israel according to all that the LORD[a] had given him in commandment to them, 4 after he had struck Sihon the king of the Amorites who lived in Heshbon, and Og the king of Bashan who lived in Ashtaroth, at Edrei. 5 Beyond the Jordan, in the land of Moab, Moses began to declare this law, saying, 6 "The LORD our God[b] spoke to us in Horeb, saying, 'You have lived long enough at this mountain. 7 Turn, and take your journey, and go to the hill country of the Amorites and to all the places near there: in the Arabah, in the hill country, in the lowland, in the South, by the seashore, in the land of the Canaanites, and in Lebanon as far as the great river, the river Euphrates. 8 Behold,[c] I have set the land before you. Go in and possess the land which the LORD swore to your fathers—to Abraham, to Isaac, and to Jacob—to give to them and to their offspring[d] after them.'"

9 I spoke to you at that time, saying, "I am not able to bear you myself alone. 10 The LORD your God has multiplied you, and behold, you are today as the stars of the sky for multitude. 11 May the LORD, the God of your fathers, make you a thousand times as many as you are and bless you, as he has promised you! 12 How can I myself alone bear your problems, your burdens, and your strife? 13 Take wise men of understanding who are respected amongst your tribes, and I will make them heads over you."

14 You answered me, and said, "The thing which you have spoken is good to do." 15 So I took the heads of your tribes, wise and respected men, and made them heads over you, captains of thousands, captains of hundreds, captains of fifties, captains of tens, and officers, according to your tribes. 16 I commanded your judges at that time, saying, "Hear cases between your brothers and judge righteously between a man and his brother, and the foreigner who is living with him. 17 You shall not show partiality in judgement; you shall hear the small and the great alike. You shall not be afraid of the face of man, for the judgement is God's. The case that is too hard for you, you shall bring to me, and I will hear it." 18 I commanded you at that time all the things which you should do. 19 We travelled from Horeb and went through all that great and terrible wilderness which you saw, by the way to the hill country of the Amorites, as the LORD our God commanded us; and we came to Kadesh Barnea. 20 I said to you, "You have come to the hill country of the Amorites, which the LORD our God gives to us. 21 Behold, the LORD your God has set the land before you. Go up, take possession, as the LORD the God of your fathers has spoken to you. Don't be afraid, neither be dismayed."

22 You came near to me, everyone of you, and said, "Let's send men before us, that they may search the land for us, and bring back to us word of the way by which we must go up, and the cities to which we shall come." 23 The thing pleased me well. I took twelve of your men, one man for every tribe. 24 They turned and went up into the hill country, and came to the valley of Eshcol, and spied it out. 25 They took some of the fruit of the land in their hands and brought it down to us, and brought us word again, and said, "It is a good land which the LORD our God gives to us." 26 Yet you wouldn't go up, but rebelled against the commandment of the LORD your God. 27 You murmured in your tents, and said, "Because the LORD hated us, he has brought us out of the land of Egypt, to deliver us into the hand of the Amorites to destroy us. 28 Where are we going up? Our brothers have made our heart melt, saying, 'The people are greater and taller than we. The cities are great and fortified up to the sky. Moreover we have seen the sons of the Anakim there!'"

29 Then I said to you, "Don't be terrified. Don't be afraid of them. 30 The LORD your God, who goes before you, he will fight for you, according to all that he did for you in Egypt before your eyes, 31 and in the wilderness where you have seen how that the LORD your God carried you, as a man carries his son, in all the way that you went, until you came to this place."

32 Yet in this thing you didn't believe the LORD your God, 33 who went before you on the way, to seek out a place for you to pitch your tents in: in fire by night, to show you by what way you should go, and in the cloud by day. 34 The LORD heard the voice of your words and was angry, and swore, saying, 35 "Surely not one of these men of this evil generation shall see the good land which I swore to give to your fathers, 36 except Caleb the son of Jephunneh. He shall see it. I will give the land that he has trodden on to him and to his children, because he has wholly followed the LORD."

37 Also the LORD was angry with me for your sakes, saying, "You also shall not go in there. 38 Joshua the son of Nun, who stands before you, shall go in there. Encourage him, for he shall cause Israel to inherit it. 39 Moreover your little ones, whom you said would be captured or killed, your children, who today have no knowledge of good or evil, shall go in there. I will give it to them, and they shall possess it. 40 But as for you, turn, and take your journey into the wilderness by the way to the Red Sea."

41 Then you answered and said to me, "We have sinned against the LORD. We will go up and fight, according to all that the LORD our God commanded us." Every man of you put on his weapons of war, and presumed to go up into the hill country.

42 The LORD said to me, "Tell them, 'Don't go up and don't fight; for I am not amongst you, lest you be struck before your enemies.'"

43 So I spoke to you, and you didn't listen; but you rebelled against the commandment of the LORD, and were presumptuous, and went up into the hill country. 44 The Amorites, who lived in that hill country, came out against you and chased you as bees do, and beat you down in Seir, even to Hormah. 45 You returned and wept before the LORD, but the LORD didn't listen to your voice, nor turn his ear to you. 46 So you stayed in Kadesh many days, according to the days that you remained.

2

1 Then we turned, and took our journey into the wilderness by the way to the Red Sea, as the LORD spoke to me; and we encircled Mount Seir many days.

2 The LORD spoke to me, saying, 3 "You have encircled this mountain long enough. Turn northward. 4 Command the people, saying, 'You are to pass through the border of your brothers, the children of Esau, who dwell in Seir; and they will be afraid of you. Therefore be careful. 5 Don't contend with them; for I will not give you any of their land, no, not so much as for the sole of the foot to tread on, because I have given Mount Seir to Esau for a possession. 6 You shall purchase food from them for money, that you may eat. You shall also buy water from them for money, that you may drink.'"

7 For the LORD your God has blessed you in all the work of your hands. He has known your walking through this great wilderness. These forty years, the LORD your God has been with you. You have lacked nothing.

8 So we passed by from our brothers, the children of Esau, who dwell in Seir, from the way of the Arabah from Elath and from Ezion Geber. We turned and passed by the way of the wilderness of Moab.

9 The LORD said to me, "Don't bother Moab, neither contend with them in battle; for I will not give you any of his land for a possession, because I have given Ar to the children of Lot for a possession."

10 (The Emim lived there before, a great and numerous people, and tall as the Anakim. 11 These also are considered to be Rephaim, as the Anakim; but the Moabites call them Emim. 12 The Horites also lived in Seir in the past, but the children of Esau succeeded them. They destroyed them from before them, and lived in their place, as Israel did to the land of his possession, which the LORD gave to them.)

13 "Now rise up and cross over the brook Zered." We went over the brook Zered.

14 The days in which we came from Kadesh Barnea until we had come over the brook Zered were thirty-eight years, until all the generation of the men of war were consumed from the middle of the camp, as the LORD swore to them. 15 Moreover the LORD's hand was against them, to destroy them from the middle of the camp, until they were consumed. 16 So, when all the men of war were consumed and dead from amongst the people, 17 the LORD spoke to me, saying, 18 "You are to pass over Ar, the border of Moab, today. 19 When you come near the border of the children of Ammon, don't bother them, nor contend with them; for I will not give you any of the land of the children of Ammon for a possession, because I have given it to the children of Lot for a possession."

20 (That also is considered a land of Rephaim. Rephaim lived there in the past, but the Ammonites call them Zamzummim, 21 a great people, many, and tall, as the Anakim; but the LORD destroyed them from before Israel, and they succeeded them, and lived in their place, 22 as he did for the children of Esau who dwell in Seir, when he destroyed the Horites from before them; and they succeeded them, and lived in their place even to this day. 23 Then the Avvim, who lived in villages as far as Gaza: the Caphtorim, who came out of Caphtor, destroyed them and lived in their place.)

24 "Rise up, take your journey, and pass over the valley of the Arnon. Behold, I have given into your hand Sihon the Amorite, king of Heshbon, and his land; begin to possess it, and contend with him in battle. 25 Today I will begin to put the dread of you and the fear of you on the peoples who are under the whole sky, who shall hear the report of you, and shall tremble and be in anguish because of you."

26 I sent messengers out of the wilderness of Kedemoth to Sihon king of Heshbon with words of peace, saying, 27 "Let me pass through your land. I will go along by the highway. I will turn neither to the right hand nor to the left. 28 You shall sell me food for money, that I may eat; and give me water for money, that I may drink. Just let me pass through on my feet, 29 as the children of Esau who dwell in Seir, and the Moabites who dwell in Ar, did to me, until I pass over the Jordan into the land which the LORD our God gives us." 30 But Sihon king of Heshbon would not let us pass by him, for the LORD your God hardened his spirit and made his heart obstinate, that he might deliver him into your hand, as it is today.

31 The LORD said to me, "Behold, I have begun to deliver up Sihon and his land before you. Begin to possess, that you may inherit his land." 32 Then Sihon came out against us, he and all his people, to battle at Jahaz. 33 The LORD our God delivered him up before us; and we struck him, his sons, and all his people. 34 We took all his cities at that time, and utterly

---

[a] *1:3* When rendered in ALL CAPITAL LETTERS, "LORD" or "GOD" is the translation of God's Proper Name.
[b] *1:6* The Hebrew word rendered "God" is "אֱלֹהִים" (Elohim).
[c] *1:8* "Behold", from "הִנֵּה", means look at, take notice, observe, see, or gaze at. It is often used as an interjection.
[d] *1:8* or, seed

destroyed every inhabited city, with the women and the little ones. We left no one remaining. ₃₅ Only the livestock we took for plunder for ourselves, with the plunder of the cities which we had taken. ₃₆ From Aroer, which is on the edge of the valley of the Arnon, and the city that is in the valley, even to Gilead, there was not a city too high for us. The LORD our God delivered up all before us. ₃₇ Only to the land of the children of Ammon you didn't come near: all the banks of the river Jabbok, and the cities of the hill country, and wherever the LORD our God forbade us.

3

₁ Then we turned, and went up the way to Bashan. Og the king of Bashan came out against us, he and all his people, to battle at Edrei. ₂ The LORD said to me, "Don't fear him; for I have delivered him, with all his people and his land, into your hand. You shall do to him as you did to Sihon king of the Amorites, who lived at Heshbon."

₃ So the LORD our God also delivered into our hand Og, the king of Bashan, and all his people. We struck him until no one was left to him remaining. ₄ We took all his cities at that time. There was not a city which we didn't take from them: sixty cities, all the region of Argob, the kingdom of Og in Bashan. ₅ All these were cities fortified with high walls, gates, and bars, in addition to a great many villages without walls. ₆ We utterly destroyed them, as we did to Sihon king of Heshbon, utterly destroying every inhabited city, with the women and the little ones. ₇ But all the livestock, and the plunder of the cities, we took for plunder for ourselves. ₈ We took the land at that time out of the hand of the two kings of the Amorites who were beyond the Jordan, from the valley of the Arnon to Mount Hermon. ₉ (The Sidonians call Hermon Sirion, and the Amorites call it Senir.) ₁₀ We took all the cities of the plain, and all Gilead, and all Bashan, to Salecah and Edrei, cities of the kingdom of Og in Bashan. ₁₁ (For only Og king of Bashan remained of the remnant of the Rephaim. Behold, his bedstead was a bedstead of iron. Isn't it in Rabbah of the children of Ammon? Nine cubitsª was its length, and four cubits its width, after the cubit of a man.) ₁₂ This land we took in possession at that time: from Aroer, which is by the valley of the Arnon, and half the hill country of Gilead with its cities, I gave to the Reubenites and to the Gadites; ₁₃ and the rest of Gilead, and all Bashan, the kingdom of Og, I gave to the half-tribe of Manasseh—all the region of Argob, even all Bashan. (The same is called the land of Rephaim. ₁₄ Jair the son of Manasseh took all the region of Argob, to the border of the Geshurites and the Maacathites, and called them, even Bashan, after his own name, Havvoth Jair, to this day.) ₁₅ I gave Gilead to Machir. ₁₆ To the Reubenites and to the Gadites I gave from Gilead even to the valley of the Arnon, the middle of the valley, and its border, even to the river Jabbok, which is the border of the children of Ammon; ₁₇ the Arabah also, and the Jordan and its border, from Chinnereth even to the sea of the Arabah, the Salt Sea, under the slopes of Pisgah eastward.

₁₈ I commanded you at that time, saying, "The LORD your God has given you this land to possess it. All of you men of valour shall pass over armed before your brothers, the children of Israel. ₁₉ But your wives, and your little ones, and your livestock, (I know that you have much livestock), shall live in your cities which I have given you, ₂₀ until the LORD gives rest to your brothers, as to you, and they also possess the land which the LORD your God gives them beyond the Jordan. Then you shall each return to his own possession, which I have given you."

₂₁ I commanded Joshua at that time, saying, "Your eyes have seen all that the LORD your God has done to these two kings. So shall the LORD do to all the kingdoms where you go over. ₂₂ You shall not fear them; for the LORD your God himself fights for you."

₂₃ I begged GOD at that time, saying, ₂₄ "Lordᵇ GOD, you have begun to show your servant your greatness, and your strong hand. For what god is there in heaven or in earth that can do works like yours, and mighty acts like yours? ₂₅ Please let me go over and see the good land that is beyond the Jordan, that fine mountain, and Lebanon."

₂₆ But the LORD was angry with me because of you, and didn't listen to me. The LORD said to me, "That is enough! Speak no more to me of this matter. ₂₇ Go up to the top of Pisgah, and lift up your eyes westward, and northward, and southward, and eastward, and see with your eyes; for you shall not go over this Jordan. ₂₈ But commission Joshua, and encourage him, and strengthen him; for he shall go over before this people, and he shall cause them to inherit the land which you shall see." ₂₉ So we stayed in the valley near Beth Peor.

4

₁ Now, Israel, listen to the statutes and to the ordinances which I teach you, to do them, that you may live and go in and possess the land which the LORD, the God of your fathers, gives you. ₂ You shall not add to the word which I command you, neither shall you take away from it, that you may keep the commandments of the LORD your God which I command you. ₃ Your eyes have seen what the LORD did because of Baal Peor; for the LORD your God has destroyed all the men who followed Baal Peor from amongst you. ₄ But you who were faithful to the LORD your God are all alive today. ₅ Behold, I have taught you statutes and ordinances, even as the LORD my God commanded me, that you should do so in the middle of the land where you go in to possess it. ₆ Keep therefore and do them; for this is your wisdom and your understanding in the sight of the peoples who shall hear all these statutes and say, "Surely this great nation is a wise and understanding people." ₇ For what great nation is there that has a god so near to them as the LORD our God is whenever we call on him? ₈ What

great nation is there that has statutes and ordinances so righteous as all this law which I set before you today?

₉ Only be careful, and keep your soul diligently, lest you forget the things which your eyes saw, and lest they depart from your heart all the days of your life; but make them known to your children and your children's children— ₁₀ the day that you stood before the LORD your God in Horeb, when the LORD said to me, "Assemble the people to me, and I will make them hear my words, that they may learn to fear me all the days that they live on the earth, and that they may teach their children." ₁₁ You came near and stood under the mountain. The mountain burnt with fire to the heart of the sky, with darkness, cloud, and thick darkness. ₁₂ The LORD spoke to you out of the middle of the fire: you heard the voice of words, but you saw no form; you only heard a voice. ₁₃ He declared to you his covenant, which he commanded you to perform, even the ten commandments. He wrote them on two stone tablets. ₁₄ The LORD commanded me at that time to teach you statutes and ordinances, that you might do them in the land where you go over to possess it. ₁₅ Be very careful, for you saw no kind of form on the day that the LORD spoke to you in Horeb out of the middle of the fire, ₁₆ lest you corrupt yourselves, and make yourself a carved image in the form of any figure, the likeness of male or female, ₁₇ the likeness of any animal that is on the earth, the likeness of any winged bird that flies in the sky, ₁₈ the likeness of anything that creeps on the ground, the likeness of any fish that is in the water under the earth; ₁₉ and lest you lift up your eyes to the sky, and when you see the sun and the moon and the stars, even all the army of the sky, you are drawn away and worship them, and serve them, which the LORD your God has allotted to all the peoples under the whole sky. ₂₀ But the LORD has taken you, and brought you out of the iron furnace, out of Egypt, to be to him a people of inheritance, as it is today.

₂₁ Furthermore the LORD was angry with me for your sakes, and swore that I should not go over the Jordan, and that I should not go in to that good land which the LORD your God gives you for an inheritance; ₂₂ but I must die in this land. I must not go over the Jordan, but you shall go over and possess that good land. ₂₃ Be careful, lest you forget the covenant of the LORD your God, which he made with you, and make yourselves a carved image in the form of anything which the LORD your God has forbidden you. ₂₄ For the LORD your God is a devouring fire, a jealous God. ₂₅ When you father children and children's children, and you have been long in the land, and then corrupt yourselves, and make a carved image in the form of anything, and do that which is evil in the LORD your God's sight to provoke him to anger, ₂₆ I call heaven and earth to witness against you today, that you will soon utterly perish from off the land which you go over the Jordan to possess it. You will not prolong your days on it, but will utterly be destroyed. ₂₇ The LORD will scatter you amongst the peoples, and you will be left few in number amongst the nations where the LORD will lead you away. ₂₈ There you will serve gods, the work of men's hands, wood and stone, which neither see, nor hear, nor eat, nor smell. ₂₉ But from there you shall seek the LORD your God, and you will find him when you search after him with all your heart and with all your soul. ₃₀ When you are in oppression, and all these things have come on you, in the latter days you shall return to the LORD your God and listen to his voice. ₃₁ For the LORD your God is a merciful God. He will not fail you nor destroy you, nor forget the covenant of your fathers which he swore to them. ₃₂ For ask now of the days that are past, which were before you, since the day that God created man on the earth, and from the one end of the sky to the other, whether there has been anything as great as this thing is, or has been heard like it? ₃₃ Did a people ever hear the voice of God speaking out of the middle of the fire, as you have heard, and live? ₃₄ Or has God tried to go and take a nation for himself from amongst another nation, by trials, by signs, by wonders, by war, by a mighty hand, by an outstretched arm, and by great terrors, according to all that the LORD your God did for you in Egypt before your eyes? ₃₅ It was shown to you so that you might know that the LORD is God. There is no one else besides him. ₃₆ Out of heaven he made you to hear his voice, that he might instruct you. On earth he made you to see his great fire; and you heard his words out of the middle of the fire. ₃₇ Because he loved your fathers, therefore he chose their offspring after them, and brought you out with his presence, with his great power, out of Egypt; ₃₈ to drive out nations from before you greater and mightier than you, to bring you in, to give you their land for an inheritance, as it is today. ₃₉ Know therefore today, and take it to heart, that the LORD himself is God in heaven above and on the earth beneath. There is no one else. ₄₀ You shall keep his statutes and his commandments which I command you today, that it may go well with you and with your children after you, and that you may prolong your days in the land which the LORD your God gives you for all time.

₄₁ Then Moses set apart three cities beyond the Jordan towards the sunrise, ₄₂ that the man slayer might flee there, who kills his neighbour unintentionally and didn't hate him in time past, and that fleeing to one of these cities he might live: ₄₃ Bezer in the wilderness, in the plain country, for the Reubenites; and Ramoth in Gilead for the Gadites; and Golan in Bashan for the Manassites.

₄₄ This is the law which Moses set before the children of Israel. ₄₅ These are the testimonies, and the statutes, and the ordinances which Moses spoke to the children of Israel when they came out of Egypt, ₄₆ beyond the Jordan, in the valley opposite Beth Peor, in the land of Sihon king of the Amorites, who lived at Heshbon, whom Moses and the children of Israel struck when they came out of Egypt. ₄₇ They took possession of his land and the land of Og king of Bashan, the two kings of the Amorites,

---

ª *3:11* A cubit is the length from the tip of the middle finger to the elbow on a man's arm, or about 18 inches or 46 centimetres.

ᵇ *3:24* The word translated "Lord" is "Adonai."

who were beyond the Jordan towards the sunrise; 48 from Aroer, which is on the edge of the valley of the Arnon, even to Mount Zion (also called Hermon), 49 and all the Arabah beyond the Jordan eastward, even to the sea of the Arabah, under the slopes of Pisgah.

5

1 Moses called to all Israel, and said to them, "Hear, Israel, the statutes and the ordinances which I speak in your ears today, that you may learn them, and observe to do them." 2 The LORD our God made a covenant with us in Horeb. 3 The LORD didn't make this covenant with our fathers, but with us, even us, who are all of us here alive today. 4 The LORD spoke with you face to face on the mountain out of the middle of the fire, 5 (I stood between the LORD and you at that time, to show you the LORD's word; for you were afraid because of the fire, and didn't go up onto the mountain) saying,

6 "I am the LORD your God, who brought you out of the land of Egypt, out of the house of bondage.

7 "You shall have no other gods before me.

8 "You shall not make a carved image for yourself—any likeness of what is in heaven above, or what is in the earth beneath, or that is in the water under the earth. 9 You shall not bow yourself down to them, nor serve them, for I, the LORD your God, am a jealous God, visiting the iniquity of the fathers on the children and on the third and on the fourth generation of those who hate me 10 and showing loving kindness to thousands of those who love me and keep my commandments.

11 "You shall not misuse the name of the LORD your God;[a] for the LORD will not hold him guiltless who misuses his name.

12 "Observe the Sabbath day, to keep it holy, as the LORD your God commanded you. 13 You shall labour six days, and do all your work; 14 but the seventh day is a Sabbath to the LORD your God, in which you shall not do any work— neither you, nor your son, nor your daughter, nor your male servant, nor your female servant, nor your ox, nor your donkey, nor any of your livestock, nor your stranger who is within your gates; that your male servant and your female servant may rest as well as you. 15 You shall remember that you were a servant in the land of Egypt, and the LORD your God brought you out of there by a mighty hand and by an outstretched arm. Therefore the LORD your God commanded you to keep the Sabbath day.

16 "Honour your father and your mother, as the LORD your God commanded you, that your days may be long and that it may go well with you in the land which the LORD your God gives you.

17 "You shall not murder.

18 "You shall not commit adultery.

19 "You shall not steal.

20 "You shall not give false testimony against your neighbour.

21 "You shall not covet your neighbour's wife. Neither shall you desire your neighbour's house, his field, or his male servant, or his female servant, his ox, or his donkey, or anything that is your neighbour's."

22 The LORD spoke these words to all your assembly on the mountain out of the middle of the fire, of the cloud, and of the thick darkness, with a great voice. He added no more. He wrote them on two stone tablets, and gave them to me. 23 When you heard the voice out of the middle of the darkness, while the mountain was burning with fire, you came near to me, even all the heads of your tribes, and your elders; 24 and you said, "Behold, the LORD our God has shown us his glory and his greatness, and we have heard his voice out of the middle of the fire. We have seen today that God does speak with man, and he lives. 25 Now therefore, why should we die? For this great fire will consume us. If we hear the LORD our God's voice any more, then we shall die. 26 For who is there of all flesh who has heard the voice of the living God speaking out of the middle of the fire, as we have, and lived? 27 Go near, and hear all that the LORD our God shall say, and tell us all that the LORD our God tells you; and we will hear it, and do it."

28 The LORD heard the voice of your words when you spoke to me; and the LORD said to me, "I have heard the voice of the words of this people which they have spoken to you. They have well said all that they have spoken. 29 Oh that there were such a heart in them that they would fear me and keep all my commandments always, that it might be well with them and with their children forever!

30 "Go tell them, 'Return to your tents.' 31 But as for you, stand here by me, and I will tell you all the commandments, and the statutes, and the ordinances, which you shall teach them, that they may do them in the land which I give them to possess."

32 You shall observe to do therefore as the LORD your God has commanded you. You shall not turn away to the right hand or to the left. 33 You shall walk in all the way which the LORD your God has commanded you, that you may live and that it may be well with you, and that you may prolong your days in the land which you shall possess.

6

1 Now these are the commandments, the statutes, and the ordinances, which the LORD your God commanded to teach you, that you might do them in the land that you go over to possess; 2 that you might fear the LORD your God, to keep all his statutes and his commandments, which I command you—you, your son, and your son's son, all the days of your life; and that your days may be prolonged. 3 Hear therefore, Israel, and observe to do it, that it may be well with you, and that you may increase mightily, as the LORD, the God of your fathers, has promised to you, in a land flowing with milk and honey.

4 Hear, Israel: the LORD is our God. The LORD is one. 5 You shall love the LORD your God with all your heart, with all your soul, and with all your might. 6 These words, which I command you today, shall be on your heart; 7 and you shall teach them diligently to your children, and shall talk of them when you sit in your house, and when you walk by the way, and when you lie down, and when you rise up. 8 You shall bind them for a sign on your hand, and they shall be for frontlets between your eyes. 9 You shall write them on the door posts of your house and on your gates.

10 It shall be, when the LORD your God brings you into the land which he swore to your fathers, to Abraham, to Isaac, and to Jacob, to give you, great and goodly cities which you didn't build, 11 and houses full of all good things which you didn't fill, and cisterns dug out which you didn't dig, vineyards and olive trees which you didn't plant, and you shall eat and be full; 12 then beware lest you forget the LORD, who brought you out of the land of Egypt, out of the house of bondage. 13 You shall fear the LORD your God; and you shall serve him, and shall swear by his name. 14 You shall not go after other gods, of the gods of the peoples who are around you, 15 for the LORD your God amongst you is a jealous God, lest the anger of the LORD your God be kindled against you, and he destroy you from off the face of the earth. 16 You shall not tempt the LORD your God, as you tempted him in Massah. 17 You shall diligently keep the commandments of the LORD your God, and his testimonies, and his statutes, which he has commanded you. 18 You shall do that which is right and good in the LORD's sight, that it may be well with you and that you may go in and possess the good land which the LORD swore to your fathers, 19 to thrust out all your enemies from before you, as the LORD has spoken.

20 When your son asks you in time to come, saying, "What do the testimonies, the statutes, and the ordinances, which the LORD our God has commanded you mean?" 21 then you shall tell your son, "We were Pharaoh's slaves in Egypt. The LORD brought us out of Egypt with a mighty hand; 22 and the LORD showed great and awesome signs and wonders on Egypt, on Pharaoh, and on all his house, before our eyes; 23 and he brought us out from there, that he might bring us in, to give us the land which he swore to our fathers. 24 The LORD commanded us to do all these statutes, to fear the LORD our God, for our good always, that he might preserve us alive, as we are today. 25 It shall be righteousness to us, if we observe to do all these commandments before the LORD our God, as he has commanded us."

7

1 When the LORD your God brings you into the land where you go to possess it, and casts out many nations before you—the Hittite, the Girgashite, the Amorite, the Canaanite, the Perizzite, the Hivite, and the Jebusite—seven nations greater and mightier than you; 2 and when the LORD your God delivers them up before you, and you strike them, then you shall utterly destroy them. You shall make no covenant with them, nor show mercy to them. 3 You shall not make marriages with them. You shall not give your daughter to his son, nor shall you take his daughter for your son. 4 For that would turn away your sons from following me, that they may serve other gods. So the LORD's anger would be kindled against you, and he would destroy you quickly. 5 But you shall deal with them like this: you shall break down their altars, dash their pillars in pieces, cut down their Asherah poles, and burn their engraved images with fire. 6 For you are a holy people to the LORD your God. The LORD your God has chosen you to be a people for his own possession, above all peoples who are on the face of the earth. 7 The LORD didn't set his love on you nor choose you, because you were more in number than any people; for you were the fewest of all peoples; 8 but because the LORD loves you, and because he desires to keep the oath which he swore to your fathers, the LORD has brought you out with a mighty hand and redeemed you out of the house of bondage, from the hand of Pharaoh king of Egypt. 9 Know therefore that the LORD your God himself is God, the faithful God, who keeps covenant and loving kindness to a thousand generations with those who love him and keep his commandments, 10 and repays those who hate him to their face, to destroy them. He will not be slack to him who hates him. He will repay him to his face. 11 You shall therefore keep the commandments, the statutes, and the ordinances which I command you today, to do them. 12 It shall happen, because you listen to these ordinances and keep and do them, that the LORD your God will keep with you the covenant and the loving kindness which he swore to your fathers. 13 He will love you, bless you, and multiply you. He will also bless the fruit of your body and the fruit of your ground, your grain and your new wine and your oil, the increase of your livestock and the young of your flock, in the land which he swore to your fathers to give you. 14 You will be blessed above all peoples. There won't be male or female barren amongst you, or amongst your livestock. 15 The LORD will take away from you all sickness; and he will put none of the evil diseases of Egypt, which you know, on you, but will lay them on all those who hate you. 16 You shall consume all the peoples whom the LORD your God shall deliver to you. Your eye shall not pity them. You shall not serve their gods; for that would be a snare to you. 17 If you shall say in your heart, "These nations are more than I; how can I dispossess them?" 18 you shall not be afraid of them. You shall remember well what the LORD your God did to Pharaoh and to all Egypt: 19 the great trials which your eyes saw, the signs, the wonders, the mighty hand, and the outstretched arm, by which the LORD your God brought you out. So shall the LORD your God do to all the peoples of whom you are afraid. 20 Moreover the LORD your God will send the hornet amongst them, until those who are left, and hide themselves,

---

[a] 5:11 or, You shall not take the name of the LORD your God in vain;

perish from before you. 21 You shall not be scared of them; for the LORD your God is amongst you, a great and awesome God. 22 The LORD your God will cast out those nations before you little by little. You may not consume them at once, lest the animals of the field increase on you. 23 But the LORD your God will deliver them up before you, and will confuse them with a great confusion, until they are destroyed. 24 He will deliver their kings into your hand, and you shall make their name perish from under the sky. No one will be able to stand before you until you have destroyed them. 25 You shall burn the engraved images of their gods with fire. You shall not covet the silver or the gold that is on them, nor take it for yourself, lest you be snared in it; for it is an abomination to the LORD your God. 26 You shall not bring an abomination into your house and become a devoted thing like it. You shall utterly detest it. You shall utterly abhor it; for it is a devoted thing.

8

1 You shall observe to do all the commandments which I command you today, that you may live, and multiply, and go in and possess the land which the LORD swore to your fathers. 2 You shall remember all the way which the LORD your God has led you these forty years in the wilderness, that he might humble you, to test you, to know what was in your heart, whether you would keep his commandments or not. 3 He humbled you, allowed you to be hungry, and fed you with manna, which you didn't know, neither did your fathers know, that he might teach you that man does not live by bread only, but man lives by every word that proceeds out of the LORD's mouth. 4 Your clothing didn't grow old on you, neither did your foot swell, these forty years. 5 You shall consider in your heart that as a man disciplines his son, so the LORD your God disciplines you. 6 You shall keep the commandments of the LORD your God, to walk in his ways, and to fear him. 7 For the LORD your God brings you into a good land, a land of brooks of water, of springs, and underground water flowing into valleys and hills; 8 a land of wheat, barley, vines, fig trees, and pomegranates; a land of olive trees and honey; 9 a land in which you shall eat bread without scarcity, you shall not lack anything in it; a land whose stones are iron, and out of whose hills you may dig copper. 10 You shall eat and be full, and you shall bless the LORD your God for the good land which he has given you.

11 Beware lest you forget the LORD your God, in not keeping his commandments, his ordinances, and his statutes, which I command you today; 12 lest, when you have eaten and are full, and have built fine houses and lived in them; 13 and when your herds and your flocks multiply, and your silver and your gold is multiplied, and all that you have is multiplied; 14 then your heart might be lifted up, and you forget the LORD your God, who brought you out of the land of Egypt, out of the house of bondage; 15 who led you through the great and terrible wilderness, with venomous snakes and scorpions, and thirsty ground where there was no water; who poured water for you out of the rock of flint; 16 who fed you in the wilderness with manna, which your fathers didn't know, that he might humble you, and that he might prove you, to do you good at your latter end; 17 and lest you say in your heart, "My power and the might of my hand has gotten me this wealth." 18 But you shall remember the LORD your God, for it is he who gives you power to get wealth, that he may establish his covenant which he swore to your fathers, as it is today.

19 It shall be, if you shall forget the LORD your God, and walk after other gods, and serve them and worship them, I testify against you today that you shall surely perish. 20 As the nations that the LORD makes to perish before you, so you shall perish, because you wouldn't listen to the LORD your God's voice.

9

1 Hear, Israel! You are to pass over the Jordan today, to go in to dispossess nations greater and mightier than yourself, cities great and fortified up to the sky, 2 a people great and tall, the sons of the Anakim, whom you know, and of whom you have heard say, "Who can stand before the sons of Anak?" 3 Know therefore today that the LORD your God is he who goes over before you as a devouring fire. He will destroy them and he will bring them down before you. So you shall drive them out and make them perish quickly, as the LORD has spoken to you.

4 Don't say in your heart, after the LORD your God has thrust them out from before you, "For my righteousness the LORD has brought me in to possess this land;" because the LORD drives them out before you because of the wickedness of these nations. 5 Not for your righteousness or for the uprightness of your heart do you go in to possess their land; but for the wickedness of these nations the LORD your God does drive them out from before you, and that he may establish the word which the LORD swore to your fathers, to Abraham, to Isaac, and to Jacob. 6 Know therefore that the LORD your God doesn't give you this good land to possess for your righteousness, for you are a stiff-necked people. 7 Remember, and don't forget, how you provoked the LORD your God to wrath in the wilderness. From the day that you left the land of Egypt until you came to this place, you have been rebellious against the LORD. 8 Also in Horeb you provoked the LORD to wrath, and the LORD was angry with you to destroy you. 9 When I had gone up onto the mountain to receive the stone tablets, even the tablets of the covenant which the LORD made with you, then I stayed on the mountain forty days and forty nights. I neither ate bread nor drank water. 10 The LORD delivered to me the two stone tablets written with God's finger. On them were all the words which the LORD spoke with you on the mountain out of the middle of the fire in the day of the assembly.

11 It came to pass at the end of forty days and forty nights that the LORD gave me the two stone tablets, even the tablets of the covenant. 12 The LORD said to me, "Arise, get down quickly from here; for your people

whom you have brought out of Egypt have corrupted themselves. They have quickly turned away from the way which I commanded them. They have made a molten image for themselves!"

13 Furthermore the LORD spoke to me, saying, "I have seen these people, and behold, they are a stiff-necked people. 14 Leave me alone, that I may destroy them, and blot out their name from under the sky; and I will make of you a nation mightier and greater than they."

15 So I turned and came down from the mountain, and the mountain was burning with fire. The two tablets of the covenant were in my two hands. 16 I looked, and behold, you had sinned against the LORD your God. You had made yourselves a moulded calf. You had quickly turned away from the way which the LORD had commanded you. 17 I took hold of the two tablets, and threw them out of my two hands, and broke them before your eyes. 18 I fell down before the LORD, as at the first, forty days and forty nights. I neither ate bread nor drank water, because of all your sin which you sinned, in doing that which was evil in the LORD's sight, to provoke him to anger. 19 For I was afraid of the anger and hot displeasure with which the LORD was angry against you to destroy you. But the LORD listened to me that time also. 20 The LORD was angry enough with Aaron to destroy him. I prayed for Aaron also at the same time. 21 I took your sin, the calf which you had made, and burnt it with fire, and crushed it, grinding it very small, until it was as fine as dust. I threw its dust into the brook that descended out of the mountain. 22 At Taberah, at Massah, and at Kibroth Hattaavah you provoked the LORD to wrath. 23 When the LORD sent you from Kadesh Barnea, saying, "Go up and possess the land which I have given you," you rebelled against the commandment of the LORD your God, and you didn't believe him or listen to his voice. 24 You have been rebellious against the LORD from the day that I knew you. 25 So I fell down before the LORD the forty days and forty nights that I fell down, because the LORD had said he would destroy you. 26 I prayed to the LORD, and said, "Lord GOD, don't destroy your people and your inheritance that you have redeemed through your greatness, that you have brought out of Egypt with a mighty hand. 27 Remember your servants, Abraham, Isaac, and Jacob. Don't look at the stubbornness of this people, nor at their wickedness, nor at their sin, 28 lest the land you brought us out from say, 'Because the LORD was not able to bring them into the land which he promised to them, and because he hated them, he has brought them out to kill them in the wilderness.' 29 Yet they are your people and your inheritance, which you brought out by your great power and by your outstretched arm."

10

1 At that time the LORD said to me, "Cut two stone tablets like the first, and come up to me onto the mountain, and make an ark of wood. 2 I will write on the tablets the words that were on the first tablets which you broke, and you shall put them in the ark." 3 So I made an ark of acacia wood, and cut two stone tablets like the first, and went up onto the mountain, having the two tablets in my hand. 4 He wrote on the tablets, according to the first writing, the ten commandments, which the LORD spoke to you on the mountain out of the middle of the fire in the day of the assembly; and the LORD gave them to me. 5 I turned and came down from the mountain, and put the tablets in the ark which I had made; and there they are as the LORD commanded me.

6 (The children of Israel travelled from Beeroth Bene Jaakan to Moserah. There Aaron died, and there he was buried; and Eleazar his son ministered in the priest's office in his place. 7 From there they travelled to Gudgodah; and from Gudgodah to Jotbathah, a land of brooks of water. 8 At that time the LORD set apart the tribe of Levi to bear the ark of the LORD's covenant, to stand before the LORD to minister to him, and to bless in his name, to this day. 9 Therefore Levi has no portion nor inheritance with his brothers; the LORD is his inheritance, according as the LORD your God spoke to him.)

10 I stayed on the mountain, as at the first time, forty days and forty nights; and the LORD listened to me that time also. The LORD would not destroy you. 11 The LORD said to me, "Arise, take your journey before the people; and they shall go in and possess the land which I swore to their fathers to give to them."

12 Now, Israel, what does the LORD your God require of you, but to fear the LORD your God, to walk in all his ways, to love him, and to serve the LORD your God with all your heart and with all your soul, 13 to keep the LORD's commandments and statutes, which I command you today for your good? 14 Behold, to the LORD your God belongs heaven, the heaven of heavens, and the earth, with all that is therein. 15 Only the LORD had a delight in your fathers to love them, and he chose their offspring after them, even you above all peoples, as it is today. 16 Circumcise therefore the foreskin of your heart, and be no more stiff-necked. 17 For the LORD your God, he is God of gods and Lord of lords, the great God, the mighty, and the awesome, who doesn't respect persons or take bribes. 18 He executes justice for the fatherless and widow and loves the foreigner in giving him food and clothing. 19 Therefore love the foreigner, for you were foreigners in the land of Egypt. 20 You shall fear the LORD your God. You shall serve him. You shall cling to him, and you shall swear by his name. 21 He is your praise, and he is your God, who has done for you these great and awesome things which your eyes have seen. 22 Your fathers went down into Egypt with seventy persons; and now the LORD your God has made you as the stars of the sky for multitude.

11

1 Therefore you shall love the LORD your God, and keep his instructions, his statutes, his ordinances, and his commandments, always. 2 Know this day—for I don't speak with your children who have not known,

and who have not seen the chastisement of the LORD your God, his greatness, his mighty hand, his outstretched arm, ₃ his signs, and his works, which he did in the middle of Egypt to Pharaoh the king of Egypt, and to all his land; ₄ and what he did to the army of Egypt, to their horses, and to their chariots; how he made the water of the Red Sea to overflow them as they pursued you, and how the LORD has destroyed them to this day; ₅ and what he did to you in the wilderness until you came to this place; ₆ and what he did to Dathan and Abiram, the sons of Eliab, the son of Reuben—how the earth opened its mouth and swallowed them up, with their households, their tents, and every living thing that followed them, in the middle of all Israel; ₇ but your eyes have seen all of the LORD's great work which he did.

₈ Therefore you shall keep the entire commandment which I command you today, that you may be strong, and go in and possess the land that you go over to possess; ₉ and that you may prolong your days in the land which the LORD swore to your fathers to give to them and to their offspring, a land flowing with milk and honey. ₁₀ For the land, where you go in to possess isn't like the land of Egypt that you came out of, where you sowed your seed and watered it with your foot, as a garden of herbs; ₁₁ but the land that you go over to possess is a land of hills and valleys which drinks water from the rain of the sky, ₁₂ a land which the LORD your God cares for. The LORD your God's eyes are always on it, from the beginning of the year even to the end of the year. ₁₃ It shall happen, if you shall listen diligently to my commandments which I command you today, to love the LORD your God, and to serve him with all your heart and with all your soul, ₁₄ that I will give the rain for your land in its season, the early rain and the latter rain, that you may gather in your grain, your new wine, and your oil. ₁₅ I will give grass in your fields for your livestock, and you shall eat and be full. ₁₆ Be careful, lest your heart be deceived, and you turn away to serve other gods and worship them; ₁₇ and the LORD's anger be kindled against you, and he shut up the sky so that there is no rain, and the land doesn't yield its fruit; and you perish quickly from off the good land which the LORD gives you. ₁₈ Therefore you shall lay up these words of mine in your heart and in your soul. You shall bind them for a sign on your hand, and they shall be for frontlets between your eyes. ₁₉ You shall teach them to your children, talking of them when you sit in your house, when you walk by the way, when you lie down, and when you rise up. ₂₀ You shall write them on the door posts of your house and on your gates; ₂₁ that your days and your children's days may be multiplied in the land which the LORD swore to your fathers to give them, as the days of the heavens above the earth. ₂₂ For if you shall diligently keep all these commandments which I command you—to do them, to love the LORD your God, to walk in all his ways, and to cling to him— ₂₃ then the LORD will drive out all these nations from before you, and you shall dispossess nations greater and mightier than yourselves. ₂₄ Every place on which the sole of your foot treads shall be yours: from the wilderness and Lebanon, from the river, the river Euphrates, even to the western sea shall be your border. ₂₅ No man will be able to stand before you. The LORD your God will lay the fear of you and the dread of you on all the land that you tread on, as he has spoken to you. ₂₆ Behold, I set before you today a blessing and a curse: ₂₇ the blessing, if you listen to the commandments of the LORD your God, which I command you today; ₂₈ and the curse, if you do not listen to the commandments of the LORD your God, but turn away out of the way which I command you today, to go after other gods which you have not known. ₂₉ It shall happen, when the LORD your God brings you into the land that you go to possess, that you shall set the blessing on Mount Gerizim, and the curse on Mount Ebal. ₃₀ Aren't they beyond the Jordan, behind the way of the going down of the sun, in the land of the Canaanites who dwell in the Arabah near Gilgal, beside the oaks of Moreh? ₃₁ For you are to pass over the Jordan to go in to possess the land which the LORD your God gives you, and you shall possess it and dwell in it. ₃₂ You shall observe to do all the statutes and the ordinances which I set before you today.

12

₁ These are the statutes and the ordinances which you shall observe to do in the land which the LORD, the God of your fathers, has given you to possess all the days that you live on the earth. ₂ You shall surely destroy all the places in which the nations that you shall dispossess served their gods: on the high mountains, and on the hills, and under every green tree. ₃ You shall break down their altars, dash their pillars in pieces, and burn their Asherah poles with fire. You shall cut down the engraved images of their gods. You shall destroy their name out of that place. ₄ You shall not do so to the LORD your God. ₅ But to the place which the LORD your God shall choose out of all your tribes, to put his name there, you shall seek his habitation, and you shall come there. ₆ You shall bring your burnt offerings, your sacrifices, your tithes, the wave offering of your hand, your vows, your free will offerings, and the firstborn of your herd and of your flock there. ₇ There you shall eat before the LORD your God, and you shall rejoice in all that you put your hand to, you and your households, in which the LORD your God has blessed you. ₈ You shall not do all the things that we do here today, every man whatever is right in his own eyes; ₉ for you haven't yet come to the rest and to the inheritance which the LORD your God gives you. ₁₀ But when you go over the Jordan and dwell in the land which the LORD your God causes you to inherit, and he gives you rest from all your enemies around you, so that you dwell in safety, ₁₁ then it shall happen that to the place which the LORD your God shall choose, to cause his name to dwell there, there you shall bring all that I command you: your burnt offerings, your sacrifices, your tithes, the wave offering of your hand, and all your choice vows which you vow to the LORD. ₁₂ You shall rejoice before the LORD your God—you, and your sons, your daughters, your male

servants, your female servants, and the Levite who is within your gates, because he has no portion nor inheritance with you. ₁₃ Be careful that you don't offer your burnt offerings in every place that you see; ₁₄ but in the place which the LORD chooses in one of your tribes, there you shall offer your burnt offerings, and there you shall do all that I command you.

₁₅ Yet you may kill and eat meat within all your gates, after all the desire of your soul, according to the LORD your God's blessing which he has given you. The unclean and the clean may eat of it, as of the gazelle and the deer. ₁₆ Only you shall not eat the blood. You shall pour it out on the earth like water. ₁₇ You may not eat within your gates the tithe of your grain, or of your new wine, or of your oil, or the firstborn of your herd or of your flock, nor any of your vows which you vow, nor your free will offerings, nor the wave offering of your hand; ₁₈ but you shall eat them before the LORD your God in the place which the LORD your God shall choose: you, your son, your daughter, your male servant, your female servant, and the Levite who is within your gates. You shall rejoice before the LORD your God in all that you put your hand to. ₁₉ Be careful that you don't forsake the Levite as long as you live in your land.

₂₀ When the LORD your God enlarges your border, as he has promised you, and you say, "I want to eat meat," because your soul desires to eat meat, you may eat meat, after all the desire of your soul. ₂₁ If the place which the LORD your God shall choose to put his name is too far from you, then you shall kill of your herd and of your flock, which the LORD has given you, as I have commanded you; and you may eat within your gates, after all the desire of your soul. ₂₂ Even as the gazelle and as the deer is eaten, so you shall eat of it. The unclean and the clean may eat of it alike. ₂₃ Only be sure that you don't eat the blood; for the blood is the life. You shall not eat the life with the meat. ₂₄ You shall not eat it. You shall pour it out on the earth like water. ₂₅ You shall not eat it, that it may go well with you and with your children after you, when you do that which is right in the LORD's eyes. ₂₆ Only your holy things which you have, and your vows, you shall take and go to the place which the LORD shall choose. ₂₇ You shall offer your burnt offerings, the meat and the blood, on the LORD your God's altar. The blood of your sacrifices shall be poured out on the LORD your God's altar, and you shall eat the meat. ₂₈ Observe and hear all these words which I command you, that it may go well with you and with your children after you forever, when you do that which is good and right in the LORD your God's eyes.

₂₉ When the LORD your God cuts off the nations from before you where you go in to dispossess them, and you dispossess them and dwell in their land, ₃₀ be careful that you are not ensnared to follow them after they are destroyed from before you, and that you not enquire after their gods, saying, "How do these nations serve their gods? I will do likewise." ₃₁ You shall not do so to the LORD your God; for every abomination to the LORD, which he hates, they have done to their gods; for they even burn their sons and their daughters in the fire to their gods. ₃₂ Whatever thing I command you, that you shall observe to do. You shall not add to it, nor take away from it.

13

₁ If a prophet or a dreamer of dreams arises amongst you, and he gives you a sign or a wonder, ₂ and the sign or the wonder comes to pass, of which he spoke to you, saying, "Let's go after other gods" (which you have not known) "and let's serve them," ₃ you shall not listen to the words of that prophet, or to that dreamer of dreams; for the LORD your God is testing you, to know whether you love the LORD your God with all your heart and with all your soul. ₄ You shall walk after the LORD your God, fear him, keep his commandments, and obey his voice. You shall serve him, and cling to him. ₅ That prophet, or that dreamer of dreams, shall be put to death, because he has spoken rebellion against the LORD your God, who brought you out of the land of Egypt and redeemed you out of the house of bondage, to draw you aside out of the way which the LORD your God commanded you to walk in. So you shall remove the evil from amongst you.

₆ If your brother, the son of your mother, or your son, or your daughter, or the wife of your bosom, or your friend who is as your own soul, entices you secretly, saying, "Let's go and serve other gods"—which you have not known, you, nor your fathers; ₇ of the gods of the peoples who are around you, near to you, or far off from you, from the one end of the earth even to the other end of the earth— ₈ you shall not consent to him nor listen to him; neither shall your eye pity him, neither shall you spare, neither shall you conceal him; ₉ but you shall surely kill him. Your hand shall be first on him to put him to death, and afterwards the hands of all the people. ₁₀ You shall stone him to death with stones, because he has sought to draw you away from the LORD your God, who brought you out of the land of Egypt, out of the house of bondage. ₁₁ All Israel shall hear, and fear, and shall not do any more wickedness like this amongst you.

₁₂ If you hear about one of your cities, which the LORD your God gives you to dwell there, that ₁₃ certain wicked fellows have gone out from amongst you and have drawn away the inhabitants of their city, saying, "Let's go and serve other gods," which you have not known, ₁₄ then you shall enquire, investigate, and ask diligently. Behold, if it is true, and the thing certain, that such abomination was done amongst you, ₁₅ you shall surely strike the inhabitants of that city with the edge of the sword, destroying it utterly, with all that is therein and its livestock, with the edge of the sword. ₁₆ You shall gather all its plunder into the middle of its street, and shall burn with fire the city, with all of its plunder, to the LORD your God. It shall be a heap forever. It shall not be built again. ₁₇ Nothing of the devoted thing shall cling to your hand, that the LORD may turn from the fierceness of his anger and show you mercy, and have compassion on you and multiply you, as he has sworn to your fathers, ₁₈ when you listen to the

LORD your God's voice, to keep all his commandments which I command you today, to do that which is right in the LORD your God's eyes.

14

1 You are the children of the LORD your God. You shall not cut yourselves, nor make any baldness between your eyes for the dead. 2 For you are a holy people to the LORD your God, and the LORD has chosen you to be a people for his own possession, above all peoples who are on the face of the earth.

3 You shall not eat any abominable thing. 4 These are the animals which you may eat: the ox, the sheep, the goat, 5 the deer, the gazelle, the roebuck, the wild goat, the ibex, the antelope, and the chamois. 6 Every animal that parts the hoof, and has the hoof split in two and chews the cud, amongst the animals, you may eat. 7 Nevertheless these you shall not eat of them that chew the cud, or of those who have the hoof split: the camel, the hare, and the rabbit. Because they chew the cud but don't part the hoof, they are unclean to you. 8 The pig, because it has a split hoof but doesn't chew the cud, is unclean to you. You shall not eat their meat. You shall not touch their carcasses. 9 These you may eat of all that are in the waters: you may eat whatever has fins and scales. 10 You shall not eat whatever doesn't have fins and scales. It is unclean to you. 11 Of all clean birds you may eat. 12 But these are they of which you shall not eat: the eagle, the vulture, the osprey, 13 the red kite, the falcon, the kite of any kind, 14 every raven of any kind, 15 the ostrich, the owl, the seagull, the hawk of any kind, 16 the little owl, the great owl, the horned owl, 17 the pelican, the vulture, the cormorant, 18 the stork, the heron after its kind, the hoopoe, and the bat. 19 All winged creeping things are unclean to you. They shall not be eaten. 20 Of all clean birds you may eat.

21 You shall not eat of anything that dies of itself. You may give it to the foreigner living amongst you who is within your gates, that he may eat it; or you may sell it to a foreigner; for you are a holy people to the LORD your God.

You shall not boil a young goat in its mother's milk.

22 You shall surely tithe all the increase of your seed, that which comes out of the field year by year. 23 You shall eat before the LORD your God, in the place which he chooses to cause his name to dwell, the tithe of your grain, of your new wine, and of your oil, and the firstborn of your herd and of your flock; that you may learn to fear the LORD your God always. 24 If the way is too long for you, so that you are not able to carry it because the place which the LORD your God shall choose to set his name there is too far from you, when the LORD your God blesses you, 25 then you shall turn it into money, bind up the money in your hand, and shall go to the place which the LORD your God shall choose. 26 You shall trade the money for whatever your soul desires: for cattle, or for sheep, or for wine, or for strong drink, or for whatever your soul asks of you. You shall eat there before the LORD your God, and you shall rejoice, you and your household. 27 You shall not forsake the Levite who is within your gates, for he has no portion nor inheritance with you. 28 At the end of every three years you shall bring all the tithe of your increase in the same year, and shall store it within your gates. 29 The Levite, because he has no portion nor inheritance with you, as well as the foreigner living amongst you, the fatherless, and the widow who are within your gates shall come, and shall eat and be satisfied; that the LORD your God may bless you in all the work of your hand which you do.

15

1 At the end of every seven years, you shall cancel debts. 2 This is the way it shall be done: every creditor shall release that which he has lent to his neighbour. He shall not require payment from his neighbour and his brother, because the LORD's release has been proclaimed. 3 Of a foreigner you may require it; but whatever of yours is with your brother, your hand shall release. 4 However there will be no poor with you (for the LORD will surely bless you in the land which the LORD your God gives you for an inheritance to possess) 5 if only you diligently listen to the LORD your God's voice, to observe to do all this commandment which I command you today. 6 For the LORD your God will bless you, as he promised you. You will lend to many nations, but you will not borrow. You will rule over many nations, but they will not rule over you. 7 If a poor man, one of your brothers, is with you within any of your gates in your land which the LORD your God gives you, you shall not harden your heart, nor shut your hand from your poor brother; 8 but you shall surely open your hand to him, and shall surely lend him sufficient for his need, which he lacks. 9 Beware that there not be a wicked thought in your heart, saying, "The seventh year, the year of release, is at hand," and your eye be evil against your poor brother and you give him nothing; and he cry to the LORD against you, and it be sin to you. 10 You shall surely give, and your heart shall not be grieved when you give to him, because it is for this thing the LORD your God will bless you in all your work and in all that you put your hand to. 11 For the poor will never cease out of the land. Therefore I command you to surely open your hand to your brother, to your needy, and to your poor, in your land. 12 If your brother, a Hebrew man, or a Hebrew woman, is sold to you and serves you six years, then in the seventh year you shall let him go free from you. 13 When you let him go free from you, you shall not let him go empty. 14 You shall furnish him liberally out of your flock, out of your threshing floor, and out of your wine press. As the LORD your God has blessed you, you shall give to him. 15 You shall remember that you were a slave in the land of Egypt, and the LORD your God redeemed you. Therefore I command you this thing today. 16 It shall be, if he tells you, "I will not go out from you," because he loves you and your house, because he is well with you, 17 then you shall take an awl, and thrust it through his ear to the door, and he shall

be your servant forever. Also to your female servant you shall do likewise. 18 It shall not seem hard to you when you let him go free from you, for he has been double the value of a hired hand as he served you six years. The LORD your God will bless you in all that you do. 19 You shall dedicate all the firstborn males that are born of your herd and of your flock to the LORD your God. You shall do no work with the firstborn of your herd, nor shear the firstborn of your flock. 20 You shall eat it before the LORD your God year by year in the place which the LORD shall choose, you and your household. 21 If it has any defect—is lame or blind, or has any defect whatever, you shall not sacrifice it to the LORD your God. 22 You shall eat it within your gates. The unclean and the clean shall eat it alike, as the gazelle and as the deer. 23 Only you shall not eat its blood. You shall pour it out on the ground like water.

16

1 Observe the month of Abib, and keep the Passover to the LORD your God; for in the month of Abib the LORD your God brought you out of Egypt by night. 2 You shall sacrifice the Passover to the LORD your God, of the flock and the herd, in the place which the LORD shall choose to cause his name to dwell there. 3 You shall eat no leavened bread with it. You shall eat unleavened bread with it seven days, even the bread of affliction (for you came out of the land of Egypt in haste) that you may remember the day when you came out of the land of Egypt all the days of your life. 4 No yeast shall be seen with you in all your borders seven days; neither shall any of the meat, which you sacrifice the first day at evening, remain all night until the morning. 5 You may not sacrifice the Passover within any of your gates which the LORD your God gives you; 6 but at the place which the LORD your God shall choose to cause his name to dwell in, there you shall sacrifice the Passover at evening, at the going down of the sun, at the season that you came out of Egypt. 7 You shall roast and eat it in the place which the LORD your God chooses. In the morning you shall return to your tents. 8 Six days you shall eat unleavened bread. On the seventh day shall be a solemn assembly to the LORD your God. You shall do no work.

9 You shall count for yourselves seven weeks. From the time you begin to put the sickle to the standing grain you shall begin to count seven weeks. 10 You shall keep the feast of weeks to the LORD your God with a tribute of a free will offering of your hand, which you shall give according to how the LORD your God blesses you. 11 You shall rejoice before the LORD your God: you, your son, your daughter, your male servant, your female servant, the Levite who is within your gates, the foreigner, the fatherless, and the widow who are amongst you, in the place which the LORD your God shall choose to cause his name to dwell there. 12 You shall remember that you were a slave in Egypt. You shall observe and do these statutes.

13 You shall keep the feast of booths seven days, after you have gathered in from your threshing floor and from your wine press. 14 You shall rejoice in your feast, you, your son, your daughter, your male servant, your female servant, the Levite, the foreigner, the fatherless, and the widow who are within your gates. 15 You shall keep a feast to the LORD your God seven days in the place which the LORD chooses, because the LORD your God will bless you in all your increase and in all the work of your hands, and you shall be altogether joyful. 16 Three times in a year all of your males shall appear before the LORD your God in the place which he chooses: in the feast of unleavened bread, in the feast of weeks, and in the feast of booths. They shall not appear before the LORD empty. 17 Every man shall give as he is able, according to the LORD your God's blessing which he has given you. 18 You shall make judges and officers in all your gates, which the LORD your God gives you, according to your tribes; and they shall judge the people with righteous judgement. 19 You shall not pervert justice. You shall not show partiality. You shall not take a bribe, for a bribe blinds the eyes of the wise and perverts the words of the righteous. 20 You shall follow that which is altogether just, that you may live and inherit the land which the LORD your God gives you. 21 You shall not plant for yourselves an Asherah of any kind of tree beside the LORD your God's altar, which you shall make for yourselves. 22 Neither shall you set yourself up a sacred stone which the LORD your God hates.

17

1 You shall not sacrifice to the LORD your God an ox or a sheep in which is a defect or anything evil; for that is an abomination to the LORD your God.

2 If there is found amongst you, within any of your gates which the LORD your God gives you, a man or woman who does that which is evil in the LORD your God's sight in transgressing his covenant, 3 and has gone and served other gods and worshipped them, or the sun, or the moon, or any of the stars of the sky, which I have not commanded, 4 and you are told, and you have heard of it, then you shall enquire diligently. Behold, if it is true, and the thing certain, that such abomination is done in Israel, 5 then you shall bring out that man or that woman who has done this evil thing to your gates, even that same man or woman; and you shall stone them to death with stones. 6 At the mouth of two witnesses, or three witnesses, he who is to die shall be put to death. At the mouth of one witness he shall not be put to death. 7 The hands of the witnesses shall be first on him to put him to death, and afterward the hands of all the people. So you shall remove the evil from amongst you.

8 If there arises a matter too hard for you in judgement, between blood and blood, between plea and plea, and between stroke and stroke, being matters of controversy within your gates, then you shall arise, and go up to the place which the LORD your God chooses. 9 You shall come to the priests who are Levites and to the judge who shall be in those days. You shall enquire, and they shall give you the verdict. 10 You shall do according

to the decisions of the verdict which they shall give you from that place which the LORD chooses. You shall observe to do according to all that they shall teach you. ₁₁ According to the decisions of the law which they shall teach you, and according to the judgement which they shall tell you, you shall do. You shall not turn away from the sentence which they announce to you, to the right hand, nor to the left. ₁₂ The man who does presumptuously in not listening to the priest who stands to minister there before the LORD your God, or to the judge, even that man shall die. You shall put away the evil from Israel. ₁₃ All the people shall hear and fear, and do no more presumptuously.

₁₄ When you have come to the land which the LORD your God gives you, and possess it and dwell in it, and say, "I will set a king over me, like all the nations that are around me," ₁₅ you shall surely set him whom the LORD your God chooses as king over yourselves. You shall set as king over you one from amongst your brothers. You may not put a foreigner over you, who is not your brother. ₁₆ Only he shall not multiply horses to himself, nor cause the people to return to Egypt, to the end that he may multiply horses; because the LORD has said to you, "You shall not go back that way again." ₁₇ He shall not multiply wives to himself, that his heart not turn away. He shall not greatly multiply to himself silver and gold.

₁₈ It shall be, when he sits on the throne of his kingdom, that he shall write himself a copy of this law in a book, out of that which is before the Levitical priests. ₁₉ It shall be with him, and he shall read from it all the days of his life, that he may learn to fear the LORD his God, to keep all the words of this law and these statutes, to do them; ₂₀ that his heart not be lifted up above his brothers, and that he not turn away from the commandment to the right hand, or to the left, to the end that he may prolong his days in his kingdom, he and his children, in the middle of Israel.

18

₁ The priests and the Levites—all the tribe of Levi—shall have no portion nor inheritance with Israel. They shall eat the offerings of the LORD made by fire and his portion. ₂ They shall have no inheritance amongst their brothers. The LORD is their inheritance, as he has spoken to them. ₃ This shall be the priests' due from the people, from those who offer a sacrifice, whether it be ox or sheep, that they shall give to the priest: the shoulder, the two cheeks, and the inner parts. ₄ You shall give him the first fruits of your grain, of your new wine, and of your oil, and the first of the fleece of your sheep. ₅ For the LORD your God has chosen him out of all your tribes to stand to minister in the LORD's name, him and his sons forever.

₆ If a Levite comes from any of your gates out of all Israel where he lives, and comes with all the desire of his soul to the place which the LORD shall choose, ₇ then he shall minister in the name of the LORD his God, as all his brothers the Levites do, who stand there before the LORD. ₈ They shall have like portions to eat, in addition to that which comes from the sale of his family possessions.

₉ When you have come into the land which the LORD your God gives you, you shall not learn to imitate the abominations of those nations. ₁₀ There shall not be found with you anyone who makes his son or his daughter to pass through the fire, one who uses divination, one who tells fortunes, or an enchanter, or a sorcerer, ₁₁ or a charmer, or someone who consults with a familiar spirit, or a wizard, or a necromancer. ₁₂ For whoever does these things is an abomination to the LORD. Because of these abominations, the LORD your God drives them out from before you. ₁₃ You shall be blameless with the LORD your God. ₁₄ For these nations that you shall dispossess listen to those who practise sorcery and to diviners; but as for you, the LORD your God has not allowed you so to do. ₁₅ The LORD your God will raise up to you a prophet from amongst you, of your brothers, like me. You shall listen to him. ₁₆ This is according to all that you desired of the LORD your God in Horeb in the day of the assembly, saying, "Let me not hear again the LORD my God's voice, neither let me see this great fire any more, that I not die."

₁₇ The LORD said to me, "They have well said that which they have spoken. ₁₈ I will raise them up a prophet from amongst their brothers, like you. I will put my words in his mouth, and he shall speak to them all that I shall command him. ₁₉ It shall happen, that whoever will not listen to my words which he shall speak in my name, I will require it of him. ₂₀ But the prophet who speaks a word presumptuously in my name, which I have not commanded him to speak, or who speaks in the name of other gods, that same prophet shall die."

₂₁ You may say in your heart, "How shall we know the word which the LORD has not spoken?" ₂₂ When a prophet speaks in the LORD's name, if the thing doesn't follow, nor happen, that is the thing which the LORD has not spoken. The prophet has spoken it presumptuously. You shall not be afraid of him.

19

₁ When the LORD your God cuts off the nations whose land the LORD your God gives you, and you succeed them and dwell in their cities and in their houses, ₂ you shall set apart three cities for yourselves in the middle of your land, which the LORD your God gives you to possess. ₃ You shall prepare the way, and divide the borders of your land which the LORD your God causes you to inherit into three parts, that every man slayer may flee there. ₄ This is the case of the man slayer who shall flee there and live: Whoever kills his neighbour unintentionally, and didn't hate him in time past— ₅ as when a man goes into the forest with his neighbour to chop wood and his hand swings the axe to cut down the tree, and the head slips from the handle and hits his neighbour so that he dies—he shall flee to one of these cities and live. ₆ Otherwise, the avenger of blood might pursue the

man slayer while hot anger is in his heart and overtake him, because the way is long, and strike him mortally, even though he was not worthy of death, because he didn't hate him in time past. ₇ Therefore I command you to set apart three cities for yourselves. ₈ If the LORD your God enlarges your border, as he has sworn to your fathers, and gives you all the land which he promised to give to your fathers; ₉ and if you keep all this commandment to do it, which I command you today, to love the LORD your God, and to walk ever in his ways, then you shall add three cities more for yourselves, in addition to these three. ₁₀ This is so that innocent blood will not be shed in the middle of your land which the LORD your God gives you for an inheritance, leaving blood guilt on you. ₁₁ But if any man hates his neighbour, lies in wait for him, rises up against him, strikes him mortally so that he dies, and he flees into one of these cities; ₁₂ then the elders of his city shall send and bring him there, and deliver him into the hand of the avenger of blood, that he may die. ₁₃ Your eye shall not pity him, but you shall purge the innocent blood from Israel that it may go well with you.

₁₄ You shall not remove your neighbour's landmark, which they of old time have set, in your inheritance which you shall inherit, in the land that the LORD your God gives you to possess.

₁₅ One witness shall not rise up against a man for any iniquity, or for any sin that he sins. At the mouth of two witnesses, or at the mouth of three witnesses, shall a matter be established. ₁₆ If an unrighteous witness rises up against any man to testify against him of wrongdoing, ₁₇ then both the men, between whom the controversy is, shall stand before the LORD, before the priests and the judges who shall be in those days; ₁₈ and the judges shall make diligent inquisition; and behold, if the witness is a false witness, and has testified falsely against his brother, ₁₉ then you shall do to him as he had thought to do to his brother. So you shall remove the evil from amongst you. ₂₀ Those who remain shall hear, and fear, and will never again commit any such evil amongst you. ₂₁ Your eyes shall not pity: life for life, eye for eye, tooth for tooth, hand for hand, foot for foot.

20

₁ When you go out to battle against your enemies, and see horses, chariots, and a people more numerous than you, you shall not be afraid of them; for the LORD your God, who brought you up out of the land of Egypt, is with you. ₂ It shall be, when you draw near to the battle, that the priest shall approach and speak to the people, ₃ and shall tell them, "Hear, Israel, you draw near today to battle against your enemies. Don't let your heart faint! Don't be afraid, nor tremble, neither be scared of them; ₄ for the LORD your God is he who goes with you, to fight for you against your enemies, to save you."

₅ The officers shall speak to the people, saying, "What man is there who has built a new house, and has not dedicated it? Let him go and return to his house, lest he die in the battle, and another man dedicate it. ₆ What man is there who has planted a vineyard, and has not used its fruit? Let him go and return to his house, lest he die in the battle, and another man use its fruit. ₇ What man is there who has pledged to be married to a wife, and has not taken her? Let him go and return to his house, lest he die in the battle, and another man take her." ₈ The officers shall speak further to the people, and they shall say, "What man is there who is fearful and faint-hearted? Let him go and return to his house, lest his brother's heart melt as his heart." ₉ It shall be, when the officers have finished speaking to the people, that they shall appoint captains of armies at the head of the people.

₁₀ When you draw near to a city to fight against it, then proclaim peace to it. ₁₁ It shall be, if it gives you answer of peace and opens to you, then it shall be that all the people who are found therein shall become forced labourers to you, and shall serve you. ₁₂ If it will make no peace with you, but will make war against you, then you shall besiege it. ₁₃ When the LORD your God delivers it into your hand, you shall strike every male of it with the edge of the sword; ₁₄ but the women, the little ones, the livestock, and all that is in the city, even all its plunder, you shall take for plunder for yourself. You may use the plunder of your enemies, which the LORD your God has given you. ₁₅ Thus you shall do to all the cities which are very far off from you, which are not of the cities of these nations. ₁₆ But of the cities of these peoples that the LORD your God gives you for an inheritance, you shall save alive nothing that breathes; ₁₇ but you shall utterly destroy them: the Hittite, the Amorite, the Canaanite, the Perizzite, the Hivite, and the Jebusite, as the LORD your God has commanded you; ₁₈ that they not teach you to follow all their abominations, which they have done for their gods; so would you sin against the LORD your God. ₁₉ When you shall besiege a city a long time, in making war against it to take it, you shall not destroy its trees by wielding an axe against them; for you may eat of them. You shall not cut them down, for is the tree of the field man, that it should be besieged by you? ₂₀ Only the trees that you know are not trees for food, you shall destroy and cut them down. You shall build bulwarks against the city that makes war with you, until it falls.

21

₁ If someone is found slain in the land which the LORD your God gives you to possess, lying in the field, and it isn't known who has struck him, ₂ then your elders and your judges shall come out, and they shall measure to the cities which are around him who is slain. ₃ It shall be that the elders of the city which is nearest to the slain man shall take a heifer of the herd, which hasn't been worked with and which has not drawn in the yoke. ₄ The elders of that city shall bring the heifer down to a valley with running water, which is neither ploughed nor sown, and shall break the heifer's neck there in the valley. ₅ The priests the sons of Levi shall come near, for them the LORD your God has chosen to minister to him, and to bless in the LORD's name; and according to their word shall every controversy and every assault be decided. 6 All the elders of that city which is nearest to the slain man shall wash their hands over the heifer whose neck was broken in the valley. 7 They shall answer and say, "Our hands have not shed this blood, neither have our eyes seen it. 8 Forgive, LORD, your people Israel, whom you have redeemed, and don't allow innocent blood amongst your people Israel." The blood shall be forgiven them. 9 So you shall put away the innocent blood from amongst you, when you shall do that which is right in the LORD's eyes.

10 When you go out to battle against your enemies, and the LORD your God delivers them into your hands and you carry them away captive, 11 and see amongst the captives a beautiful woman, and you are attracted to her, and desire to take her as your wife, 12 then you shall bring her home to your house. She shall shave her head and trim her nails. 13 She shall take off the clothing of her captivity, and shall remain in your house, and bewail her father and her mother a full month. After that you shall go in to her and be her husband, and she shall be your wife. 14 It shall be, if you have no delight in her, then you shall let her go where she desires; but you shall not sell her at all for money. You shall not deal with her as a slave, because you have humbled her.

15 If a man has two wives, the one beloved and the other hated, and they have borne him children, both the beloved and the hated, and if the firstborn son is hers who was hated, 16 then it shall be, in the day that he causes his sons to inherit that which he has, that he may not give the son of the beloved the rights of the firstborn before the son of the hated, who is the firstborn; 17 but he shall acknowledge the firstborn, the son of the hated, by giving him a double portion of all that he has; for he is the beginning of his strength. The right of the firstborn is his.

18 If a man has a stubborn and rebellious son who will not obey the voice of his father or the voice of his mother, and though they chasten him, will not listen to them, 19 then his father and his mother shall take hold of him and bring him out to the elders of his city and to the gate of his place. 20 They shall tell the elders of his city, "This our son is stubborn and rebellious. He will not obey our voice. He is a glutton and a drunkard." 21 All the men of his city shall stone him to death with stones. So you shall remove the evil from amongst you. All Israel shall hear, and fear.

22 If a man has committed a sin worthy of death, and he is put to death, and you hang him on a tree, 23 his body shall not remain all night on the tree, but you shall surely bury him the same day; for he who is hanged is accursed of God. Don't defile your land which the LORD your God gives you for an inheritance.

22

1 You shall not see your brother's ox or his sheep go astray and hide yourself from them. You shall surely bring them again to your brother. 2 If your brother isn't near to you, or if you don't know him, then you shall bring it home to your house, and it shall be with you until your brother comes looking for it, and you shall restore it to him. 3 So you shall do with his donkey. So you shall do with his garment. So you shall do with every lost thing of your brother's, which he has lost and you have found. You may not hide yourself. 4 You shall not see your brother's donkey or his ox fallen down by the way, and hide yourself from them. You shall surely help him to lift them up again.

5 A woman shall not wear men's clothing, neither shall a man put on women's clothing; for whoever does these things is an abomination to the LORD your God.

6 If you come across a bird's nest on the way, in any tree or on the ground, with young ones or eggs, and the hen sitting on the young, or on the eggs, you shall not take the hen with the young. 7 You shall surely let the hen go, but the young you may take for yourself, that it may be well with you, and that you may prolong your days.

8 When you build a new house, then you shall make a railing around your roof, so that you don't bring blood on your house if anyone falls from there.

9 You shall not sow your vineyard with two kinds of seed, lest all the fruit be defiled, the seed which you have sown, and the increase of the vineyard. 10 You shall not plough with an ox and a donkey together. 11 You shall not wear clothes of wool and linen woven together.

12 You shall make yourselves fringes[a] on the four corners of your cloak with which you cover yourself.

13 If any man takes a wife, and goes in to her, hates her, 14 accuses her of shameful things, gives her a bad name, and says, "I took this woman, and when I came near to her, I didn't find in her the tokens of virginity;" 15 then the young lady's father and mother shall take and bring the tokens of the young lady's virginity to the elders of the city in the gate. 16 The young lady's father shall tell the elders, "I gave my daughter to this man as his wife, and he hates her. 17 Behold, he has accused her of shameful things, saying, 'I didn't find in your daughter the tokens of virginity;' and yet these are the tokens of my daughter's virginity." They shall spread the cloth before the elders of the city. 18 The elders of that city shall take the man and chastise him. 19 They shall fine him one hundred shekels of silver,[b] and give them to the father of the young lady, because he has given a bad name to a virgin of Israel. She shall be his wife. He may not put her away all his days.

20 But if this thing is true, that the tokens of virginity were not found in the young lady, 21 then they shall bring out the young lady to the door of her father's house, and the men of her city shall stone her to death with stones, because she has done folly in Israel, to play the prostitute in her father's house. So you shall remove the evil from amongst you.

22 If a man is found lying with a woman married to a husband, then they shall both die, the man who lay with the woman and the woman. So you shall remove the evil from Israel. 23 If there is a young lady who is a virgin pledged to be married to a husband, and a man finds her in the city, and lies with her, 24 then you shall bring them both out to the gate of that city, and you shall stone them to death with stones; the lady, because she didn't cry, being in the city; and the man, because he has humbled his neighbour's wife. So you shall remove the evil from amongst you. 25 But if the man finds the lady who is pledged to be married in the field, and the man forces her and lies with her, then only the man who lay with her shall die; 26 but to the lady you shall do nothing. There is in the lady no sin worthy of death; for as when a man rises against his neighbour and kills him, even so is this matter; 27 for he found her in the field, the pledged to be married lady cried, and there was no one to save her. 28 If a man finds a lady who is a virgin, who is not pledged to be married, grabs her and lies with her, and they are found, 29 then the man who lay with her shall give to the lady's father fifty shekels[c] of silver. She shall be his wife, because he has humbled her. He may not put her away all his days. 30 A man shall not take his father's wife, and shall not uncover his father's skirt.

23

1 He who is emasculated by crushing or cutting shall not enter into the LORD's assembly. 2 A person born of a forbidden union shall not enter into the LORD's assembly; even to the tenth generation shall no one of his enter into the LORD's assembly. 3 An Ammonite or a Moabite shall not enter into the LORD's assembly; even to the tenth generation shall no one belonging to them enter into the LORD's assembly forever, 4 because they didn't meet you with bread and with water on the way when you came out of Egypt, and because they hired against you Balaam the son of Beor from Pethor of Mesopotamia, to curse you. 5 Nevertheless the LORD your God wouldn't listen to Balaam, but the LORD your God turned the curse into a blessing to you, because the LORD your God loved you. 6 You shall not seek their peace nor their prosperity all your days forever. 7 You shall not abhor an Edomite, for he is your brother. You shall not abhor an Egyptian, because you lived as a foreigner in his land. 8 The children of the third generation who are born to them may enter into the LORD's assembly.

9 When you go out and camp against your enemies, then you shall keep yourselves from every evil thing. 10 If there is amongst you any man who is not clean by reason of that which happens to him by night, then shall he go outside of the camp. He shall not come within the camp; 11 but it shall be, when evening comes, he shall bathe himself in water. When the sun is down, he shall come within the camp. 12 You shall have a place also outside of the camp where you go relieve yourself. 13 You shall have a trowel amongst your weapons. It shall be, when you relieve yourself, you shall dig with it, and shall turn back and cover your excrement; 14 for the LORD your God walks in the middle of your camp, to deliver you, and to give up your enemies before you. Therefore your camp shall be holy, that he may not see an unclean thing in you, and turn away from you.

15 You shall not deliver to his master a servant who has escaped from his master to you. 16 He shall dwell with you, amongst you, in the place which he shall choose within one of your gates, where it pleases him best. You shall not oppress him.

17 There shall be no prostitute of the daughters of Israel, neither shall there be a sodomite of the sons of Israel. 18 You shall not bring the hire of a prostitute, or the wages of a male prostitute,[d] into the house of the LORD your God for any vow; for both of these are an abomination to the LORD your God.

19 You shall not lend on interest to your brother: interest of money, interest of food, interest of anything that is lent on interest. 20 You may charge a foreigner interest; but you shall not charge your brother interest, that the LORD your God may bless you in all that you put your hand to, in the land where you go in to possess it.

21 When you vow a vow to the LORD your God, you shall not be slack to pay it, for the LORD your God will surely require it of you; and it would be sin in you. 22 But if you refrain from making a vow, it shall be no sin in you. 23 You shall observe and do that which has gone out of your lips. Whatever you have vowed to the LORD your God as a free will offering, which you have promised with your mouth, you must do. 24 When you come into your neighbour's vineyard, then you may eat your fill of grapes at your own pleasure; but you shall not put any in your container. 25 When you come into your neighbour's standing grain, then you may pluck the ears with your hand; but you shall not use a sickle on your neighbour's standing grain.

24

1 When a man takes a wife and marries her, then it shall be, if she finds no favour in his eyes because he has found some unseemly thing in her, that he shall write her a certificate of divorce, put it in her hand, and send her out of his house. 2 When she has departed out of his house, she may go and be another man's wife. 3 If the latter husband hates her, and writes her a certificate of divorce, puts it in her hand, and sends her out of his house; or if the latter husband dies, who took her to be his wife; 4 her former husband, who sent her away, may not take her again to be his wife

---

a 22:12 or, tassels
b 22:19 A shekel is about 10 grams or about 0.35 ounces, so 100 shekels is about a kilogram or 2.2 pounds.
c 22:29 A shekel is about 10 grams or about 0.35 ounces.
d 23:18 literally, dog

after she is defiled; for that would be an abomination to the LORD. You shall not cause the land to sin, which the LORD your God gives you for an inheritance. ₅ When a man takes a new wife, he shall not go out in the army, neither shall he be assigned any business. He shall be free at home one year, and shall cheer his wife whom he has taken.

₆ No man shall take the mill or the upper millstone as a pledge, for he takes a life in pledge.

₇ If a man is found stealing any of his brothers of the children of Israel, and he deals with him as a slave, or sells him, then that thief shall die. So you shall remove the evil from amongst you.

₈ Be careful in the plague of leprosy, that you observe diligently and do according to all that the Levitical priests teach you. As I commanded them, so you shall observe to do. ₉ Remember what the LORD your God did to Miriam, by the way as you came out of Egypt.

₁₀ When you lend your neighbour any kind of loan, you shall not go into his house to get his pledge. ₁₁ You shall stand outside, and the man to whom you lend shall bring the pledge outside to you. ₁₂ If he is a poor man, you shall not sleep with his pledge. ₁₃ You shall surely restore to him the pledge when the sun goes down, that he may sleep in his garment and bless you. It shall be righteousness to you before the LORD your God.

₁₄ You shall not oppress a hired servant who is poor and needy, whether he is one of your brothers or one of the foreigners who are in your land within your gates. ₁₅ In his day you shall give him his wages, neither shall the sun go down on it, for he is poor and sets his heart on it, lest he cry against you to the LORD, and it be sin to you.

₁₆ The fathers shall not be put to death for the children, neither shall the children be put to death for the fathers. Every man shall be put to death for his own sin.

₁₇ You shall not deprive the foreigner or the fatherless of justice, nor take a widow's clothing in pledge; ₁₈ but you shall remember that you were a slave in Egypt, and the LORD your God redeemed you there. Therefore I command you to do this thing.

₁₉ When you reap your harvest in your field, and have forgotten a sheaf in the field, you shall not go again to get it. It shall be for the foreigner, for the fatherless, and for the widow, that the LORD your God may bless you in all the work of your hands. ₂₀ When you beat your olive tree, you shall not go over the boughs again. It shall be for the foreigner, for the fatherless, and for the widow.

₂₁ When you harvest your vineyard, you shall not glean it after yourselves. It shall be for the foreigner, for the fatherless, and for the widow. ₂₂ You shall remember that you were a slave in the land of Egypt. Therefore I command you to do this thing.

25

₁ If there is a controversy between men, and they come to judgement and the judges judge them, then they shall justify the righteous and condemn the wicked. ₂ It shall be, if the wicked man is worthy to be beaten, that the judge shall cause him to lie down and to be beaten before his face, according to his wickedness, by number. ₃ He may sentence him to no more than forty stripes. He shall not give more, lest if he should give more and beat him more than that many stripes, then your brother will be degraded in your sight.

₄ You shall not muzzle the ox when he treads out the grain.

₅ If brothers dwell together, and one of them dies and has no son, the wife of the dead shall not be married outside to a stranger. Her husband's brother shall go in to her, and take her as his wife, and perform the duty of a husband's brother to her. ₆ It shall be that the firstborn whom she bears shall succeed in the name of his brother who is dead, that his name not be blotted out of Israel.

₇ If the man doesn't want to take his brother's wife, then his brother's wife shall go up to the gate to the elders, and say, "My husband's brother refuses to raise up to his brother a name in Israel. He will not perform the duty of a husband's brother to me." ₈ Then the elders of his city shall call him, and speak to him. If he stands and says, "I don't want to take her," ₉ then his brother's wife shall come to him in the presence of the elders, and loose his sandal from off his foot, and spit in his face. She shall answer and say, "So shall it be done to the man who does not build up his brother's house." ₁₀ His name shall be called in Israel, "The house of him who had his sandal removed."

₁₁ When men strive against each other, and the wife of one draws near to deliver her husband out of the hand of him who strikes him, and puts out her hand, and grabs him by his private parts, ₁₂ then you shall cut off her hand. Your eye shall have no pity.

₁₃ You shall not have in your bag diverse weights, one heavy and one light. ₁₄ You shall not have in your house diverse measures, one large and one small. ₁₅ You shall have a perfect and just weight. You shall have a perfect and just measure, that your days may be long in the land which the LORD your God gives you. ₁₆ For all who do such things, all who do unrighteously, are an abomination to the LORD your God.

₁₇ Remember what Amalek did to you by the way as you came out of Egypt, ₁₈ how he met you by the way, and struck the rearmost of you, all who were feeble behind you, when you were faint and weary; and he didn't fear God. ₁₉ Therefore it shall be, when the LORD your God has given you rest from all your enemies all around, in the land which the LORD your God gives you for an inheritance to possess it, that you shall blot out the memory of Amalek from under the sky. You shall not forget.

26

₁ It shall be, when you have come in to the land which the LORD your God gives you for an inheritance, possess it, and dwell in it, ₂ that you shall take some of the first of all the fruit of the ground, which you shall bring in from your land that the LORD your God gives you. You shall put it in a basket, and shall go to the place which the LORD your God shall choose to cause his name to dwell there. ₃ You shall come to the priest who shall be in those days, and tell him, "I profess today to the LORD your God, that I have come to the land which the LORD swore to our fathers to give us." ₄ The priest shall take the basket out of your hand, and set it down before the LORD your God's altar. ₅ You shall answer and say before the LORD your God, "My fatherᵃ was a Syrian ready to perish. He went down into Egypt, and lived there, few in number. There he became a great, mighty, and populous nation. ₆ The Egyptians mistreated us, afflicted us, and imposed hard labour on us. ₇ Then we cried to the LORD, the God of our fathers. The LORD heard our voice, and saw our affliction, our toil, and our oppression. ₈ The LORD brought us out of Egypt with a mighty hand, with an outstretched arm, with great terror, with signs, and with wonders; ₉ and he has brought us into this place, and has given us this land, a land flowing with milk and honey. ₁₀ Now, behold, I have brought the first of the fruit of the ground, which you, the LORD, have given me." You shall set it down before the LORD your God, and worship before the LORD your God. ₁₁ You shall rejoice in all the good which the LORD your God has given to you, and to your house, you, and the Levite, and the foreigner who is amongst you.

₁₂ When you have finished tithing all the tithe of your increase in the third year, which is the year of tithing, then you shall give it to the Levite, to the foreigner, to the fatherless, and to the widow, that they may eat within your gates and be filled. ₁₃ You shall say before the LORD your God, "I have put away the holy things out of my house, and also have given them to the Levite, to the foreigner, to the fatherless, and to the widow, according to all your commandment which you have commanded me. I have not transgressed any of your commandments, neither have I forgotten them. ₁₄ I have not eaten of it in my mourning, neither have I removed any of it while I was unclean, nor given of it for the dead. I have listened to the LORD my God's voice. I have done according to all that you have commanded me. ₁₅ Look down from your holy habitation, from heaven, and bless your people Israel, and the ground which you have given us, as you swore to our fathers, a land flowing with milk and honey."

₁₆ Today the LORD your God commands you to do these statutes and ordinances. You shall therefore keep and do them with all your heart and with all your soul. ₁₇ You have declared today that the LORD is your God, and that you would walk in his ways, keep his statutes, his commandments, and his ordinances, and listen to his voice. ₁₈ The LORD has declared today that you are a people for his own possession, as he has promised you, and that you should keep all his commandments. ₁₉ He will make you high above all nations that he has made, in praise, in name, and in honour, and that you may be a holy people to the LORD your God, as he has spoken.

27

₁ Moses and the elders of Israel commanded the people, saying, "Keep all the commandment which I command you today. ₂ It shall be on the day when you shall pass over the Jordan to the land which the LORD your God gives you, that you shall set yourself up great stones, and coat them with plaster. ₃ You shall write on them all the words of this law, when you have passed over, that you may go in to the land which the LORD your God gives you, a land flowing with milk and honey, as the LORD, the God of your fathers, has promised you. ₄ It shall be, when you have crossed over the Jordan, that you shall set up these stones, which I command you today, on Mount Ebal, and you shall coat them with plaster. ₅ There you shall build an altar to the LORD your God, an altar of stones. You shall not use any iron tool on them. ₆ You shall build the LORD your God's altar of uncut stones. You shall offer burnt offerings on it to the LORD your God. ₇ You shall sacrifice peace offerings, and shall eat there. You shall rejoice before the LORD your God. ₈ You shall write on the stones all the words of this law very plainly."

₉ Moses and the Levitical priests spoke to all Israel, saying, "Be silent and listen, Israel! Today you have become the people of the LORD your God. ₁₀ You shall therefore obey the LORD your God's voice, and do his commandments and his statutes, which I command you today."

₁₁ Moses commanded the people the same day, saying, ₁₂ "These shall stand on Mount Gerizim to bless the people, when you have crossed over the Jordan: Simeon, Levi, Judah, Issachar, Joseph, and Benjamin. ₁₃ These shall stand on Mount Ebal for the curse: Reuben, Gad, Asher, Zebulun, Dan, and Naphtali. ₁₄ With a loud voice, the Levites shall say to all the men of Israel, ₁₅ 'Cursed is the man who makes an engraved or molten image, an abomination to the LORD, the work of the hands of the craftsman, and sets it up in secret.'

All the people shall answer and say, 'Amen.'

₁₆ 'Cursed is he who dishonours his father or his mother.'

All the people shall say, 'Amen.'

₁₇ 'Cursed is he who removes his neighbour's landmark.'

All the people shall say, 'Amen.'

₁₈ 'Cursed is he who leads the blind astray on the road.'

All the people shall say, 'Amen.'

₁₉ 'Cursed is he who withholds justice from the foreigner, fatherless, and widow.'

All the people shall say, 'Amen.'

ᵃ *26:5 or, forefather*

20 'Cursed is he who lies with[a] his father's wife, because he dishonours his father's bed.'

All the people shall say, 'Amen.'

21 'Cursed is he who lies with any kind of animal.'

All the people shall say, 'Amen.'

22 'Cursed is he who lies with his sister, his father's daughter or his mother's daughter.'

All the people shall say, 'Amen.'

23 'Cursed is he who lies with his mother-in-law.'

All the people shall say, 'Amen.'

24 'Cursed is he who secretly kills his neighbour.'

All the people shall say, 'Amen.'

25 'Cursed is he who takes a bribe to kill an innocent person.'

All the people shall say, 'Amen.'

26 'Cursed is he who doesn't uphold the words of this law by doing them.'

All the people shall say, 'Amen.'"

28

1 It shall happen, if you shall listen diligently to the LORD your God's voice, to observe to do all his commandments which I command you today, that the LORD your God will set you high above all the nations of the earth. 2 All these blessings will come upon you, and overtake you, if you listen to the LORD your God's voice. 3 You shall be blessed in the city, and you shall be blessed in the field. 4 You shall be blessed in the fruit of your body, the fruit of your ground, the fruit of your animals, the increase of your livestock, and the young of your flock. 5 Your basket and your kneading trough shall be blessed. 6 You shall be blessed when you come in, and you shall be blessed when you go out. 7 The LORD will cause your enemies who rise up against you to be struck before you. They will come out against you one way, and will flee before you seven ways. 8 The LORD will command the blessing on you in your barns, and in all that you put your hand to. He will bless you in the land which the LORD your God gives you. 9 The LORD will establish you for a holy people to himself, as he has sworn to you, if you shall keep the commandments of the LORD your God, and walk in his ways. 10 All the peoples of the earth shall see that you are called by the LORD's name, and they will be afraid of you. 11 The LORD will grant you abundant prosperity in the fruit of your body, in the fruit of your livestock, and in the fruit of your ground, in the land which the LORD swore to your fathers to give you. 12 The LORD will open to you his good treasure in the sky, to give the rain of your land in its season, and to bless all the work of your hand. You will lend to many nations, and you will not borrow. 13 The LORD will make you the head, and not the tail. You will be above only, and you will not be beneath, if you listen to the commandments of the LORD your God which I command you today, to observe and to do, 14 and shall not turn away from any of the words which I command you today, to the right hand or to the left, to go after other gods to serve them.

15 But it shall come to pass, if you will not listen to the LORD your God's voice, to observe to do all his commandments and his statutes which I command you today, that all these curses will come on you and overtake you. 16 You will be cursed in the city, and you will be cursed in the field. 17 Your basket and your kneading trough will be cursed. 18 The fruit of your body, the fruit of your ground, the increase of your livestock, and the young of your flock will be cursed. 19 You will be cursed when you come in, and you will be cursed when you go out. 20 The LORD will send on you cursing, confusion, and rebuke in all that you put your hand to do, until you are destroyed and until you perish quickly, because of the evil of your doings, by which you have forsaken me. 21 The LORD will make the pestilence cling to you, until he has consumed you from off the land where you go in to possess it. 22 The LORD will strike you with consumption, with fever, with inflammation, with fiery heat, with the sword, with blight, and with mildew. They will pursue you until you perish. 23 Your sky that is over your head will be bronze, and the earth that is under you will be iron. 24 The LORD will make the rain of your land powder and dust. It will come down on you from the sky, until you are destroyed. 25 The LORD will cause you to be struck before your enemies. You will go out one way against them, and will flee seven ways before them. You will be tossed back and forth amongst all the kingdoms of the earth. 26 Your dead bodies will be food to all birds of the sky, and to the animals of the earth; and there will be no one to frighten them away. 27 The LORD will strike you with the boils of Egypt, with the tumours, with the scurvy, and with the itch, of which you can not be healed. 28 The LORD will strike you with madness, with blindness, and with astonishment of heart. 29 You will grope at noonday, as the blind gropes in darkness, and you shall not prosper in your ways. You will only be oppressed and robbed always, and there will be no one to save you. 30 You will betroth a wife, and another man shall lie with her. You will build a house, and you won't dwell in it. You will plant a vineyard, and not use its fruit. 31 Your ox will be slain before your eyes, and you will not eat any of it. Your donkey will be violently taken away from before your face, and will not be restored to you. Your sheep will be given to your enemies, and you will have no one to save you. 32 Your sons and your daughters will be given to another people. Your eyes will look and fail with longing for them all day long. There will be no power in your hand. 33 A nation which you don't know will eat the fruit of your ground and all of your work. You will only be oppressed and crushed always, 34 so that the sights that you see with your eyes will drive you mad. 35 The LORD will strike you in the knees and in the legs with a sore boil, of which you cannot be healed, from the sole of your

foot to the crown of your head. 36 The LORD will bring you, and your king whom you will set over yourselves, to a nation that you have not known, you nor your fathers. There you will serve other gods of wood and stone. 37 You will become an astonishment, a proverb, and a byword amongst all the peoples where the LORD will lead you away. 38 You will carry much seed out into the field, and will gather little in, for the locust will consume it. 39 You will plant vineyards and dress them, but you will neither drink of the wine, nor harvest, because worms will eat them. 40 You will have olive trees throughout all your borders, but you won't anoint yourself with the oil, for your olives will drop off. 41 You will father sons and daughters, but they will not be yours, for they will go into captivity. 42 Locusts will consume all of your trees and the fruit of your ground. 43 The foreigner who is amongst you will mount up above you higher and higher, and you will come down lower and lower. 44 He will lend to you, and you won't lend to him. He will be the head, and you will be the tail.

45 All these curses will come on you, and will pursue you and overtake you, until you are destroyed, because you didn't listen to the LORD your God's voice, to keep his commandments and his statutes which he commanded you. 46 They will be for a sign and for a wonder to you and to your offspring forever. 47 Because you didn't serve the LORD your God with joyfulness and with gladness of heart, by reason of the abundance of all things; 48 therefore you will serve your enemies whom the LORD sends against you, in hunger, in thirst, in nakedness, and in lack of all things. He will put an iron yoke on your neck until he has destroyed you. 49 The LORD will bring a nation against you from far away, from the end of the earth, as the eagle flies: a nation whose language you will not understand, 50 a nation of fierce facial expressions, that doesn't respect the elderly, nor show favour to the young. 51 They will eat the fruit of your livestock and the fruit of your ground, until you are destroyed. They also won't leave you grain, new wine, oil, the increase of your livestock, or the young of your flock, until they have caused you to perish. 52 They will besiege you in all your gates until your high and fortified walls in which you trusted come down throughout all your land. They will besiege you in all your gates throughout all your land which the LORD your God has given you. 53 You will eat the fruit of your own body, the flesh of your sons and of your daughters, whom the LORD your God has given you, in the siege and in the distress with which your enemies will distress you. 54 The man who is tender amongst you, and very delicate, his eye will be evil towards his brother, towards the wife whom he loves, and towards the remnant of his children whom he has remaining, 55 so that he will not give to any of them of the flesh of his children whom he will eat, because he has nothing left to him, in the siege and in the distress with which your enemy will distress you in all your gates. 56 The tender and delicate woman amongst you, who would not venture to set the sole of her foot on the ground for delicateness and tenderness, her eye will be evil towards the husband that she loves, towards her son, towards her daughter, 57 towards her young one who comes out from between her feet, and towards her children whom she bears; for she will eat them secretly for lack of all things in the siege and in the distress with which your enemy will distress you in your gates. 58 If you will not observe to do all the words of this law that are written in this book, that you may fear this glorious and fearful name, THE LORD your God, 59 then the LORD will make your plagues and the plagues of your offspring fearful, even great plagues, and of long duration, and severe sicknesses, and of long duration. 60 He will bring on you again all the diseases of Egypt, which you were afraid of; and they will cling to you. 61 Also every sickness and every plague which is not written in the book of this law, the LORD will bring them on you until you are destroyed. 62 You will be left few in number, even though you were as the stars of the sky for multitude, because you didn't listen to the LORD your God's voice. 63 It will happen that as the LORD rejoiced over you to do you good, and to multiply you, so the LORD will rejoice over you to cause you to perish and to destroy you. You will be plucked from the land that you are going in to possess. 64 The LORD will scatter you amongst all peoples, from one end of the earth to the other end of the earth. There you will serve other gods which you have not known, you nor your fathers, even wood and stone. 65 Amongst these nations you will find no ease, and there will be no rest for the sole of your foot; but the LORD will give you there a trembling heart, failing of eyes, and pining of soul. 66 Your life will hang in doubt before you. You will be afraid night and day, and will have no assurance of your life. 67 In the morning you will say, "I wish it were evening!" and at evening you will say, "I wish it were morning!" for the fear of your heart which you will fear, and for the sights which your eyes will see. 68 The LORD will bring you into Egypt again with ships, by the way of which I told to you that you would never see it again. There you will offer yourselves to your enemies for male and female slaves, and nobody will buy you.

29

1 These are the words of the covenant which the LORD commanded Moses to make with the children of Israel in the land of Moab, in addition to the covenant which he made with them in Horeb. 2 Moses called to all Israel, and said to them:

Your eyes have seen all that the LORD did in the land of Egypt to Pharaoh, and to all his servants, and to all his land; 3 the great trials which your eyes saw, the signs, and those great wonders. 4 But the LORD has not given you a heart to know, eyes to see, and ears to hear, to this day. 5 I have led you forty years in the wilderness. Your clothes have not grown old on you, and your sandals have not grown old on your feet. 6 You have not

---

a 27:20 i.e., has sexual relations with

eaten bread, neither have you drunk wine or strong drink, that you may know that I am the LORD your God. 7 When you came to this place, Sihon the king of Heshbon and Og the king of Bashan came out against us to battle, and we struck them. 8 We took their land, and gave it for an inheritance to the Reubenites, and to the Gadites, and to the half-tribe of the Manassites. 9 Therefore keep the words of this covenant and do them, that you may prosper in all that you do. 10 All of you stand today in the presence of the LORD your God: your heads, your tribes, your elders, and your officers, even all the men of Israel, 11 your little ones, your wives, and the foreigners who are in the middle of your camps, from the one who cuts your wood to the one who draws your water, 12 that you may enter into the covenant of the LORD your God, and into his oath, which the LORD your God makes with you today, 13 that he may establish you today as his people, and that he may be your God, as he spoke to you and as he swore to your fathers, to Abraham, to Isaac, and to Jacob. 14 Neither do I make this covenant and this oath with you only, 15 but with those who stand here with us today before the LORD our God, and also with those who are not here with us today 16 (for you know how we lived in the land of Egypt, and how we came through the middle of the nations through which you passed; 17 and you have seen their abominations and their idols of wood, stone, silver, and gold, which were amongst them); 18 lest there should be amongst you man, woman, family, or tribe whose heart turns away today from the LORD our God, to go to serve the gods of those nations; lest there should be amongst you a root that produces bitter poison; 19 and it happen, when he hears the words of this curse, that he bless himself in his heart, saying, "I shall have peace, though I walk in the stubbornness of my heart," to destroy the moist with the dry. 20 The LORD will not pardon him, but then the LORD's anger and his jealousy will smoke against that man, and all the curse that is written in this book will fall on him, and the LORD will blot out his name from under the sky. 21 The LORD will set him apart for evil out of all the tribes of Israel, according to all the curses of the covenant written in this book of the law.

22 The generation to come—your children who will rise up after you, and the foreigner who will come from a far land—will say, when they see the plagues of that land, and the sicknesses with which the LORD has made it sick, 23 that all of its land is sulphur, salt, and burning, that it is not sown, doesn't produce, nor does any grass grow in it, like the overthrow of Sodom, Gomorrah, Admah, and Zeboiim, which the LORD overthrew in his anger, and in his wrath. 24 Even all the nations will say, "Why has the LORD done this to this land? What does the heat of this great anger mean?"

25 Then men will say, "Because they abandoned the covenant of the LORD, the God of their fathers, which he made with them when he brought them out of the land of Egypt, 26 and went and served other gods and worshipped them, gods that they didn't know and that he had not given to them. 27 Therefore the LORD's anger burnt against this land, to bring on it all the curses that are written in this book. 28 The LORD rooted them out of their land in anger, in wrath, and in great indignation, and thrust them into another land, as it is today."

29 The secret things belong to the LORD our God; but the things that are revealed belong to us and to our children forever, that we may do all the words of this law.

30

1 It shall happen, when all these things have come on you, the blessing and the curse, which I have set before you, and you shall call them to mind amongst all the nations where the LORD your God has driven you, 2 and return to the LORD your God and obey his voice according to all that I command you today, you and your children, with all your heart and with all your soul, 3 that then the LORD your God will release you from captivity, have compassion on you, and will return and gather you from all the peoples where the LORD your God has scattered you. 4 If your outcasts are in the uttermost parts of the heavens, from there the LORD your God will gather you, and from there he will bring you back. 5 The LORD your God will bring you into the land which your fathers possessed, and you will possess it. He will do you good, and increase your numbers more than your fathers. 6 The LORD your God will circumcise your heart, and the heart of your offspring, to love the LORD your God with all your heart and with all your soul, that you may live. 7 The LORD your God will put all these curses on your enemies and on those who hate you, who persecuted you. 8 You shall return and obey the LORD's voice, and do all his commandments which I command you today. 9 The LORD your God will make you prosperous in all the work of your hand, in the fruit of your body, in the fruit of your livestock, and in the fruit of your ground, for good; for the LORD will again rejoice over you for good, as he rejoiced over your fathers, 10 if you will obey the LORD your God's voice, to keep his commandments and his statutes which are written in this book of the law, if you turn to the LORD your God with all your heart and with all your soul.

11 For this commandment which I command you today is not too hard for you or too distant. 12 It is not in heaven, that you should say, "Who will go up for us to heaven, bring it to us, and proclaim it to us, that we may do it?" 13 Neither is it beyond the sea, that you should say, "Who will go over the sea for us, bring it to us, and proclaim it to us, that we may do it?" 14 But the word is very near to you, in your mouth and in your heart, that you may do it. 15 Behold, I have set before you today life and prosperity, and death and evil. 16 For I command you today to love the LORD your God, to walk in his ways and to keep his commandments, his statutes, and his ordinances, that you may live and multiply, and that the LORD your God may bless you in the land where you go in to possess it. 17 But if your heart turns away, and you will not hear, but are drawn away and worship other gods, and serve them, 18 I declare to you today that you will surely perish.

You will not prolong your days in the land where you pass over the Jordan to go in to possess it. 19 I call heaven and earth to witness against you today that I have set before you life and death, the blessing and the curse. Therefore choose life, that you may live, you and your descendants, 20 to love the LORD your God, to obey his voice, and to cling to him; for he is your life, and the length of your days, that you may dwell in the land which the LORD swore to your fathers, to Abraham, to Isaac, and to Jacob, to give them.

31

1 Moses went and spoke these words to all Israel. 2 He said to them, "I am one hundred and twenty years old today. I can no more go out and come in. The LORD has said to me, 'You shall not go over this Jordan.' 3 The LORD your God himself will go over before you. He will destroy these nations from before you, and you shall dispossess them. Joshua will go over before you, as the LORD has spoken. 4 The LORD will do to them as he did to Sihon and to Og, the kings of the Amorites, and to their land, when he destroyed them. 5 The LORD will deliver them up before you, and you shall do to them according to all the commandment which I have commanded you. 6 Be strong and courageous. Don't be afraid or scared of them, for the LORD your God himself is who goes with you. He will not fail you nor forsake you."

7 Moses called to Joshua, and said to him in the sight of all Israel, "Be strong and courageous, for you shall go with this people into the land which the LORD has sworn to their fathers to give them; and you shall cause them to inherit it. 8 The LORD himself is who goes before you. He will be with you. He will not fail you nor forsake you. Don't be afraid. Don't be discouraged."

9 Moses wrote this law and delivered it to the priests the sons of Levi, who bore the ark of the LORD's covenant, and to all the elders of Israel. 10 Moses commanded them, saying, "At the end of every seven years, in the set time of the year of release, in the feast of booths, 11 when all Israel has come to appear before the LORD your God in the place which he will choose, you shall read this law before all Israel in their hearing. 12 Assemble the people, the men and the women and the little ones, and the foreigners who are within your gates, that they may hear, learn, fear the LORD your God, and observe to do all the words of this law, 13 and that their children, who have not known, may hear and learn to fear the LORD your God, as long as you live in the land where you go over the Jordan to possess it."

14 The LORD said to Moses, "Behold, your days approach that you must die. Call Joshua, and present yourselves in the Tent of Meeting, that I may commission him."

Moses and Joshua went, and presented themselves in the Tent of Meeting.

15 The LORD appeared in the Tent in a pillar of cloud, and the pillar of cloud stood over the Tent's door. 16 The LORD said to Moses, "Behold, you shall sleep with your fathers. This people will rise up and play the prostitute after the strange gods of the land where they go to be amongst them, and will forsake me and break my covenant which I have made with them. 17 Then my anger shall be kindled against them in that day, and I will forsake them, and I will hide my face from them, and they shall be devoured, and many evils and troubles shall come on them; so that they will say in that day, 'Haven't these evils come on us because our God is not amongst us?' 18 I will surely hide my face in that day for all the evil which they have done, in that they have turned to other gods.

19 "Now therefore write this song for yourselves, and teach it to the children of Israel. Put it in their mouths, that this song may be a witness for me against the children of Israel. 20 For when I have brought them into the land which I swore to their fathers, flowing with milk and honey, and they have eaten and filled themselves, and grown fat, then they will turn to other gods, and serve them, and despise me, and break my covenant. 21 It will happen, when many evils and troubles have come on them, that this song will testify before them as a witness; for it will not be forgotten out of the mouths of their descendants; for I know their ways and what they are doing today, before I have brought them into the land which I promised them."

22 So Moses wrote this song the same day, and taught it to the children of Israel.

23 He commissioned Joshua the son of Nun, and said, "Be strong and courageous; for you shall bring the children of Israel into the land which I swore to them. I will be with you."

24 When Moses had finished writing the words of this law in a book, until they were finished, 25 Moses commanded the Levites, who bore the ark of the LORD's covenant, saying, 26 "Take this book of the law, and put it by the side of the ark of the LORD your God's covenant, that it may be there for a witness against you. 27 For I know your rebellion and your stiff neck. Behold, while I am yet alive with you today, you have been rebellious against the LORD. How much more after my death? 28 Assemble to me all the elders of your tribes and your officers, that I may speak these words in their ears, and call heaven and earth to witness against them. 29 For I know that after my death you will utterly corrupt yourselves, and turn away from the way which I have commanded you; and evil will happen to you in the latter days, because you will do that which is evil in the LORD's sight, to provoke him to anger through the work of your hands."

30 Moses spoke in the ears of all the assembly of Israel the words of this song, until they were finished.

32

1 Give ear, you heavens, and I will speak.
Let the earth hear the words of my mouth.

2 My doctrine will drop as the rain.
  My speech will condense as the dew,
    as the misty rain on the tender grass,
    as the showers on the herb.
3 For I will proclaim the LORD's name.
  Ascribe greatness to our God!
4 The Rock: his work is perfect,
  for all his ways are just.
  A God of faithfulness who does no wrong,
  just and right is he.
5 They have dealt corruptly with him.
  They are not his children, because of their defect.
  They are a perverse and crooked generation.
6 Is this the way you repay the LORD,
  foolish and unwise people?
Isn't he your father who has bought you?
  He has made you and established you.
7 Remember the days of old.
  Consider the years of many generations.
Ask your father, and he will show you;
  your elders, and they will tell you.
8 When the Most High gave to the nations their inheritance,
  when he separated the children of men,
he set the bounds of the peoples
  according to the number of the children of Israel.
9 For the LORD's portion is his people.
  Jacob is the lot of his inheritance.
10 He found him in a desert land,
  in the waste howling wilderness.
He surrounded him.
  He cared for him.
  He kept him as the apple of his eye.
11 As an eagle that stirs up her nest,
  that flutters over her young,
he spread abroad his wings,
  he took them,
  he bore them on his feathers.
12 The LORD alone led him.
  There was no foreign god with him.
13 He made him ride on the high places of the earth.
  He ate the increase of the field.
He caused him to suck honey out of the rock,
  oil out of the flinty rock;
14 butter from the herd, and milk from the flock,
  with fat of lambs,
  rams of the breed of Bashan, and goats,
  with the finest of the wheat.
  From the blood of the grape, you drank wine.
15 But Jeshurun grew fat, and kicked.
  You have grown fat.
  You have grown thick.
  You have become sleek.
Then he abandoned God who made him,
  and rejected the Rock of his salvation.
16 They moved him to jealousy with strange gods.
  They provoked him to anger with abominations.
17 They sacrificed to demons, not God,
  to gods that they didn't know,
  to new gods that came up recently,
  which your fathers didn't dread.
18 Of the Rock who became your father, you are unmindful,
  and have forgotten God who gave you birth.
19 The LORD saw and abhorred,
  because of the provocation of his sons and his daughters.
20 He said, "I will hide my face from them.
  I will see what their end will be;
for they are a very perverse generation,
  children in whom is no faithfulness.
21 They have moved me to jealousy with that which is not God.
  They have provoked me to anger with their vanities.
I will move them to jealousy with those who are not a people.
  I will provoke them to anger with a foolish nation.
22 For a fire is kindled in my anger,
  that burns to the lowest Sheol,ᵃ
  devours the earth with its increase,
  and sets the foundations of the mountains on fire.

23 "I will heap evils on them.
  I will spend my arrows on them.
24 They shall be wasted with hunger,
  and devoured with burning heat
  and bitter destruction.
I will send the teeth of animals on them,
  with the venom of vipers that glide in the dust.
25 Outside the sword will bereave,

and in the rooms,
  terror on both young man and virgin,
  the nursing infant with the grey-haired man.
26 I said that I would scatter them afar.
  I would make their memory to cease from amongst men;
27 were it not that I feared the provocation of the enemy,
  lest their adversaries should judge wrongly,
  lest they should say, 'Our hand is exalted;
  the LORD has not done all this.'"

28 For they are a nation void of counsel.
  There is no understanding in them.
29 Oh that they were wise, that they understood this,
  that they would consider their latter end!
30 How could one chase a thousand,
  and two put ten thousand to flight,
unless their Rock had sold them,
  and the LORD had delivered them up?
31 For their rock is not as our Rock,
  even our enemies themselves concede.
32 For their vine is of the vine of Sodom,
  of the fields of Gomorrah.
Their grapes are poison grapes.
  Their clusters are bitter.
33 Their wine is the poison of serpents,
  the cruel venom of asps.

34 "Isn't this laid up in store with me,
  sealed up amongst my treasures?
35 Vengeance is mine, and recompense,
  at the time when their foot slides,
for the day of their calamity is at hand.
  Their doom rushes at them."

36 For the LORD will judge his people,
  and have compassion on his servants,
when he sees that their power is gone,
  that there is no one remaining, shut up or left at large.
37 He will say, "Where are their gods,
  the rock in which they took refuge,
38 which ate the fat of their sacrifices,
  and drank the wine of their drink offering?
Let them rise up and help you!
  Let them be your protection.

39 "See now that I myself am he.
  There is no god with me.
I kill and I make alive.
  I wound and I heal.
  There is no one who can deliver out of my hand.
40 For I lift up my hand to heaven and declare,
  as I live forever,
41 if I sharpen my glittering sword,
  my hand grasps it in judgement;
I will take vengeance on my adversaries,
  and will repay those who hate me.
42 I will make my arrows drunk with blood.
  My sword shall devour flesh with the blood of the slain and the
    captives,
  from the head of the leaders of the enemy."

43 Rejoice, you nations, with his people,
  for he will avenge the blood of his servants.
  He will take vengeance on his adversaries,
  and will make atonement for his land and for his people.ᵇ
44 Moses came and spoke all the words of this song in the ears of the people, he and Joshua the son of Nun. 45 Moses finished reciting all these words to all Israel. 46 He said to them, "Set your heart to all the words which I testify to you today, which you shall command your children to observe to do, all the words of this law. 47 For it is no vain thing for you, because it is your life, and through this thing you shall prolong your days in the land, where you go over the Jordan to possess it."

48 The LORD spoke to Moses that same day, saying, 49 "Go up into this mountain of Abarim, to Mount Nebo, which is in the land of Moab, that is across from Jericho; and see the land of Canaan, which I give to the children of Israel for a possession. 50 Die on the mountain where you go up, and be gathered to your people, as Aaron your brother died on Mount Hor, and was gathered to his people; 51 because you trespassed against me amongst the children of Israel at the waters of Meribah of Kadesh, in the wilderness of Zin; because you didn't uphold my holiness amongst the children of Israel. 52 For you shall see the land from a distance; but you shall not go there into the land which I give the children of Israel."

ᵃ *32:22* Sheol is the place of the dead.
ᵇ *32:43* For this verse, LXX reads: Rejoice, you heavens, with him, and let all the angels of God worship him; rejoice you Gentiles, with his people, and let all the sons of God strengthen themselves in him; for he will avenge the blood of his sons, and he will render vengeance, and recompense justice to his enemies, and will reward them that hate him; and the Lord shall purge the land of his people.

33

1 This is the blessing with which Moses the man of God blessed the children of Israel before his death. 2 He said,

"The LORD came from Sinai,
  and rose from Seir to them.
He shone from Mount Paran.
  He came from the ten thousands of holy ones.
  At his right hand was a fiery law for them.ᵃ
3 Yes, he loves the people.
  All his saints are in your hand.
  They sat down at your feet.
  Each receives your words.
4 Moses commanded us a law,
  an inheritance for the assembly of Jacob.
5 He was king in Jeshurun,
  when the heads of the people were gathered,
  all the tribes of Israel together.

6 "Let Reuben live, and not die;
  Nor let his men be few."
7 This is for Judah. He said,
"Hear, LORD, the voice of Judah.
  Bring him in to his people.
With his hands he contended for himself.
  You shall be a help against his adversaries."
8 About Levi he said,
"Your Thummim and your Urim are with your godly one,
  whom you proved at Massah,
  with whom you contended at the waters of Meribah.
9 He said of his father, and of his mother, 'I have not seen him.'
  He didn't acknowledge his brothers,
  nor did he know his own children;
for they have observed your word,
  and keep your covenant.
10 They shall teach Jacob your ordinances,
  and Israel your law.
They shall put incense before you,
  and whole burnt offering on your altar.
11 LORD, bless his skills.
  Accept the work of his hands.
Strike through the hips of those who rise up against him,
  of those who hate him, that they not rise again."
12 About Benjamin he said,
"The beloved of the LORD will dwell in safety by him.
  He covers him all day long.
  He dwells between his shoulders."
13 About Joseph he said,
"His land is blessed by the LORD,
  for the precious things of the heavens, for the dew,
  for the deep that couches beneath,
14 for the precious things of the fruits of the sun,
  for the precious things that the moon can yield,
15 for the best things of the ancient mountains,
  for the precious things of the everlasting hills,
16 for the precious things of the earth and its fullness,
  the good will of him who lived in the bush.ᵇ
Let this come on the head of Joseph,
  on the crown of the head of him who was separated from his brothers.
17 Majesty belongs to the firstborn of his herd.
  His horns are the horns of the wild ox.
  With them he will push all the peoples to the ends of the earth.
They are the ten thousands of Ephraim.
  They are the thousands of Manasseh."
18 About Zebulun he said,
"Rejoice, Zebulun, in your going out;
  and Issachar, in your tents.
19 They will call the peoples to the mountain.
  There they will offer sacrifices of righteousness,
for they will draw out the abundance of the seas,
  the hidden treasures of the sand."
20 About Gad he said,
"He who enlarges Gad is blessed.
  He dwells as a lioness,
  and tears the arm and the crown of the head.
21 He provided the first part for himself,
  for the lawgiver's portion was reserved for him.
He came with the heads of the people.
  He executed the righteousness of the LORD,
  His ordinances with Israel."
22 About Dan he said,
"Dan is a lion's cub
  that leaps out of Bashan."
23 About Naphtali he said,
"Naphtali, satisfied with favour,
  full of the LORD's blessing,

Possess the west and the south."
24 About Asher he said,
"Asher is blessed with children.
  Let him be acceptable to his brothers.
  Let him dip his foot in oil.
25 Your bars will be iron and bronze.
  As your days, so your strength will be.

26 "There is no one like God, Jeshurun,
  who rides on the heavens for your help,
  in his excellency on the skies.
27 The eternal God is your dwelling place.
  Underneath are the everlasting arms.
He thrust out the enemy from before you,
  and said, 'Destroy!'
28 Israel dwells in safety,
  the fountain of Jacob alone,
In a land of grain and new wine.
  Yes, his heavens drop down dew.
29 You are happy, Israel!
  Who is like you, a people saved by the LORD,
  the shield of your help,
  the sword of your excellency?
Your enemies will submit themselves to you.
  You will tread on their high places."

34

1 Moses went up from the plains of Moab to Mount Nebo, to the top of Pisgah, that is opposite Jericho. The LORD showed him all the land of Gilead to Dan, 2 and all Naphtali, and the land of Ephraim and Manasseh, and all the land of Judah, to the Western Sea, 3 and the south,ᶜ and the Plain of the valley of Jericho the city of palm trees, to Zoar. 4 The LORD said to him, "This is the land which I swore to Abraham, to Isaac, and to Jacob, saying, 'I will give it to your offspring.' I have caused you to see it with your eyes, but you shall not go over there."

5 So Moses the servant of the LORD died there in the land of Moab, according to the LORD's word. 6 He buried him in the valley in the land of Moab opposite Beth Peor, but no man knows where his tomb is to this day. 7 Moses was one hundred and twenty years old when he died. His eye was not dim, nor his strength gone. 8 The children of Israel wept for Moses in the plains of Moab thirty days, until the days of weeping in the mourning for Moses were ended. 9 Joshua the son of Nun was full of the spirit of wisdom, for Moses had laid his hands on him. The children of Israel listened to him, and did as the LORD commanded Moses. 10 Since then, there has not arisen a prophet in Israel like Moses, whom the LORD knew face to face, 11 in all the signs and the wonders which the LORD sent him to do in the land of Egypt, to Pharaoh, and to all his servants, and to all his land, 12 and in all the mighty hand, and in all the awesome deeds, which Moses did in the sight of all Israel.

ᵃ *33:2* another manuscript reads "He came with myriads of holy ones from the south, from his mountain slopes."

ᵇ *33:16* i.e., the burning bush of Exodus 3:3-4.

ᶜ *34:3* or, Negev

The Book of Joshua

1

1 Now after the death of Moses the servant of the LORD,[a] the LORD spoke to Joshua the son of Nun, Moses' servant, saying, 2 "Moses my servant is dead. Now therefore arise, go across this Jordan, you and all these people, to the land which I am giving to them, even to the children of Israel. 3 I have given you every place that the sole of your foot will tread on, as I told Moses. 4 From the wilderness and this Lebanon even to the great river, the river Euphrates, all the land of the Hittites, and to the great sea towards the going down of the sun, shall be your border. 5 No man will be able to stand before you all the days of your life. As I was with Moses, so I will be with you. I will not fail you nor forsake you.

6 "Be strong and courageous; for you shall cause this people to inherit the land which I swore to their fathers to give them. 7 Only be strong and very courageous. Be careful to observe to do according to all the law which Moses my servant commanded you. Don't turn from it to the right hand or to the left, that you may have good success wherever you go. 8 This book of the law shall not depart from your mouth, but you shall meditate on it day and night, that you may observe to do according to all that is written in it; for then you shall make your way prosperous, and then you shall have good success. 9 Haven't I commanded you? Be strong and courageous. Don't be afraid. Don't be dismayed, for the LORD your God[b] is with you wherever you go."

10 Then Joshua commanded the officers of the people, saying, 11 "Pass through the middle of the camp, and command the people, saying, 'Prepare food; for within three days you are to pass over this Jordan, to go in to possess the land which the LORD your God gives you to possess.'"

12 Joshua spoke to the Reubenites, and to the Gadites, and to the half-tribe of Manasseh, saying, 13 "Remember the word which Moses the servant of the LORD commanded you, saying, 'The LORD your God gives you rest, and will give you this land. 14 Your wives, your little ones, and your livestock shall live in the land which Moses gave you beyond the Jordan; but you shall pass over before your brothers armed, all the mighty men of valour, and shall help them 15 until the LORD has given your brothers rest, as he has given you, and they have also possessed the land which the LORD your God gives them. Then you shall return to the land of your possession and possess it, which Moses the servant of the LORD gave you beyond the Jordan towards the sunrise.'"

16 They answered Joshua, saying, "All that you have commanded us we will do, and wherever you send us we will go. 17 Just as we listened to Moses in all things, so will we listen to you. Only may the LORD your God be with you, as he was with Moses. 18 Whoever rebels against your commandment, and doesn't listen to your words in all that you command him shall himself be put to death. Only be strong and courageous."

2

1 Joshua the son of Nun secretly sent two men out of Shittim as spies, saying, "Go, view the land, including Jericho." They went and came into the house of a prostitute whose name was Rahab, and slept there.

2 The king of Jericho was told, "Behold,[c] men of the children of Israel came in here tonight to spy out the land."

3 Jericho's king sent to Rahab, saying, "Bring out the men who have come to you, who have entered into your house; for they have come to spy out all the land."

4 The woman took the two men and hid them. Then she said, "Yes, the men came to me, but I didn't know where they came from. 5 About the time of the shutting of the gate, when it was dark, the men went out. Where the men went, I don't know. Pursue them quickly. You may catch up with them." 6 But she had brought them up to the roof, and hidden them under the stalks of flax which she had laid in order on the roof. 7 The men pursued them along the way to the fords of the Jordan River. As soon as those who pursued them had gone out, they shut the gate. 8 Before they had lain down, she came up to them on the roof. 9 She said to the men, "I know that the LORD has given you the land, and that the fear of you has fallen upon us, and that all the inhabitants of the land melt away before you. 10 For we have heard how the LORD dried up the water of the Red Sea before you, when you came out of Egypt; and what you did to the two kings of the Amorites, who were beyond the Jordan, to Sihon and to Og, whom you utterly destroyed. 11 As soon as we had heard it, our hearts melted, and there wasn't any more spirit in any man, because of you: for the LORD your God, he is God in heaven above, and on earth beneath. 12 Now therefore, please swear to me by the LORD, since I have dealt kindly with you, that you also will deal kindly with my father's house, and give me a true sign; 13 and that you will save alive my father, my mother, my brothers, and my sisters, and all that they have, and will deliver our lives from death."

14 The men said to her, "Our life for yours, if you don't talk about this business of ours; and it shall be, when the LORD gives us the land, that we will deal kindly and truly with you."

15 Then she let them down by a cord through the window; for her house was on the side of the wall, and she lived on the wall. 16 She said to them, "Go to the mountain, lest the pursuers find you. Hide yourselves there three days, until the pursuers have returned. Afterward, you may go your way."

17 The men said to her, "We will be guiltless of this your oath which you've made us to swear. 18 Behold, when we come into the land, tie this line of scarlet thread in the window which you used to let us down. Gather to yourself into the house your father, your mother, your brothers, and all your father's household. 19 It shall be that whoever goes out of the doors of your house into the street, his blood will be on his head, and we will be guiltless. Whoever is with you in the house, his blood shall be on our head, if any hand is on him. 20 But if you talk about this business of ours, then we shall be guiltless of your oath which you've made us to swear."

21 She said, "Let it be as you have said." She sent them away, and they departed. Then she tied the scarlet line in the window.

22 They went and came to the mountain, and stayed there three days, until the pursuers had returned. The pursuers sought them all along the way, but didn't find them. 23 Then the two men returned, descended from the mountain, crossed the river, and came to Joshua the son of Nun. They told him all that had happened to them. 24 They said to Joshua, "Truly the LORD has delivered all the land into our hands. Moreover, all the inhabitants of the land melt away before us."

3

1 Joshua got up early in the morning; and they moved from Shittim and came to the Jordan, he and all the children of Israel. They camped there before they crossed over. 2 After three days, the officers went through the middle of the camp; 3 and they commanded the people, saying, "When you see the ark of the LORD your God's covenant, and the Levitical priests bearing it, then leave your place, and follow it. 4 Yet there shall be a space between you and it of about two thousand cubits[d] by measure—don't come closer to it—that you may know the way by which you must go; for you have not passed this way before."

5 Joshua said to the people, "Sanctify yourselves; for tomorrow the LORD will do wonders amongst you."

6 Joshua spoke to the priests, saying, "Take up the ark of the covenant, and cross over before the people." They took up the ark of the covenant, and went before the people.

7 The LORD said to Joshua, "Today I will begin to magnify you in the sight of all Israel, that they may know that as I was with Moses, so I will be with you. 8 You shall command the priests who bear the ark of the covenant, saying, 'When you come to the brink of the waters of the Jordan, you shall stand still in the Jordan.'"

9 Joshua said to the children of Israel, "Come here, and hear the words of the LORD your God." 10 Joshua said, "By this you shall know that the living God is amongst you, and that he will without fail drive the Canaanite, the Hittite, the Hivite, the Perizzite, the Girgashite, the Amorite, and the Jebusite out from before you. 11 Behold, the ark of the covenant of the Lord[e] of all the earth passes over before you into the Jordan. 12 Now therefore take twelve men out of the tribes of Israel, for every tribe a man. 13 It shall be that when the soles of the feet of the priests who bear the ark of the LORD, the Lord of all the earth, rest in the waters of the Jordan, that the waters of the Jordan will be cut off. The waters that come down from above shall stand in one heap."

14 When the people moved from their tents to pass over the Jordan, the priests who bore the ark of the covenant being before the people, 15 and when those who bore the ark had come to the Jordan, and the feet of the priests who bore the ark had dipped in the edge of the water (for the Jordan overflows all its banks all the time of harvest), 16 the waters which came down from above stood, and rose up in one heap a great way off, at Adam, the city that is beside Zarethan; and those that went down towards the sea of the Arabah, even the Salt Sea, were wholly cut off. Then the people passed over near Jericho. 17 The priests who bore the ark of the LORD's covenant stood firm on dry ground in the middle of the Jordan; and all Israel crossed over on dry ground, until all the nation had passed completely over the Jordan.

4

1 When all the nation had completely crossed over the Jordan, the LORD spoke to Joshua, saying, 2 "Take twelve men out of the people, a man out of every tribe, 3 and command them, saying, 'Take from out of the middle of the Jordan, out of the place where the priests' feet stood firm, twelve stones, carry them over with you, and lay them down in the place where you'll camp tonight.'"

4 Then Joshua called the twelve men whom he had prepared of the children of Israel, a man out of every tribe. 5 Joshua said to them, "Cross before the ark of the LORD your God into the middle of the Jordan, and each of you pick up a stone and put it on your shoulder, according to the number of the tribes of the children of Israel; 6 that this may be a sign amongst you, that when your children ask in the future, saying, 'What do you mean by these stones?' 7 then you shall tell them, 'Because the waters of the Jordan were cut off before the ark of the LORD's covenant. When it crossed over the Jordan, the waters of the Jordan were cut off. These stones shall be for a memorial to the children of Israel forever.'"

---

a 1:1 When rendered in ALL CAPITAL LETTERS, "LORD" or "GOD" is the translation of God's Proper Name.

b 1:9 The Hebrew word rendered "God" is "אֱלֹהִים" (Elohim).

c 2:2 "Behold", from "הִנֵּה", means look at, take notice, observe, see, or gaze at. It is often used as an interjection.

d 3:4 A cubit is the length from the tip of the middle finger to the elbow on a man's arm, or about 18 inches or 46 centimetres, so 2,000 cubits is about 920 metres.

e 3:11 The word translated "Lord" is "Adonai."

8 The children of Israel did as Joshua commanded, and took up twelve stones out of the middle of the Jordan, as the LORD spoke to Joshua, according to the number of the tribes of the children of Israel. They carried them over with them to the place where they camped, and laid them down there. 9 Joshua set up twelve stones in the middle of the Jordan, in the place where the feet of the priests who bore the ark of the covenant stood; and they are there to this day. 10 For the priests who bore the ark stood in the middle of the Jordan until everything was finished that the LORD commanded Joshua to speak to the people, according to all that Moses commanded Joshua; and the people hurried and passed over. 11 When all the people had completely crossed over, the LORD's ark crossed over with the priests in the presence of the people.

12 The children of Reuben, and the children of Gad, and the half-tribe of Manasseh crossed over armed before the children of Israel, as Moses spoke to them. 13 About forty thousand men, ready and armed for war, passed over before the LORD to battle, to the plains of Jericho. 14 On that day, the LORD magnified Joshua in the sight of all Israel; and they feared him, as they feared Moses, all the days of his life.

15 The LORD spoke to Joshua, saying, 16 "Command the priests who bear the ark of the covenant, that they come up out of the Jordan."

17 Joshua therefore commanded the priests, saying, "Come up out of the Jordan!" 18 When the priests who bore the ark of the LORD's covenant had come up out of the middle of the Jordan, and the soles of the priests' feet had been lifted up to the dry ground, the waters of the Jordan returned to their place, and went over all its banks, as before. 19 The people came up out of the Jordan on the tenth day of the first month, and encamped in Gilgal, on the east border of Jericho.

20 Joshua set up those twelve stones, which they took out of the Jordan, in Gilgal. 21 He spoke to the children of Israel, saying, "When your children ask their fathers in time to come, saying, 'What do these stones mean?' 22 Then you shall let your children know, saying, 'Israel came over this Jordan on dry land. 23 For the LORD your God dried up the waters of the Jordan from before you until you had crossed over, as the LORD your God did to the Red Sea, which he dried up from before us, until we had crossed over, 24 that all the peoples of the earth may know that the LORD's hand is mighty, and that you may fear the LORD your God forever.'"

5

1 When all the kings of the Amorites, who were beyond the Jordan westward, and all the kings of the Canaanites, who were by the sea, heard how the LORD had dried up the waters of the Jordan from before the children of Israel until we had crossed over, their heart melted, and there was no more spirit in them, because of the children of Israel. 2 At that time, the LORD said to Joshua, "Make flint knives, and circumcise again the sons of Israel the second time." 3 Joshua made himself flint knives, and circumcised the sons of Israel at the hill of the foreskins. 4 This is the reason Joshua circumcised them: all the people who came out of Egypt, who were males, even all the men of war, died in the wilderness along the way, after they came out of Egypt. 5 For all the people who came out were circumcised; but all the people who were born in the wilderness along the way as they came out of Egypt had not been circumcised. 6 For the children of Israel walked forty years in the wilderness until all the nation, even the men of war who came out of Egypt, were consumed, because they didn't listen to the LORD's voice. The LORD swore to them that he wouldn't let them see the land which the LORD swore to their fathers that he would give us, a land flowing with milk and honey. 7 Their children, whom he raised up in their place, were circumcised by Joshua, for they were uncircumcised, because they had not circumcised them on the way. 8 When they were done circumcising the whole nation, they stayed in their places in the camp until they were healed.

9 The LORD said to Joshua, "Today I have rolled away the reproach of Egypt from you." Therefore the name of that place was called Gilgal[a] to this day. 10 The children of Israel encamped in Gilgal. They kept the Passover on the fourteenth day of the month at evening in the plains of Jericho. 11 They ate unleavened cakes and parched grain of the produce of the land on the next day after the Passover, in the same day. 12 The manna ceased on the next day, after they had eaten of the produce of the land. The children of Israel didn't have manna any more, but they ate of the fruit of the land of Canaan that year.

13 When Joshua was by Jericho, he lifted up his eyes and looked, and behold, a man stood in front of him with his sword drawn in his hand. Joshua went to him and said to him, "Are you for us, or for our enemies?"

14 He said, "No; but I have come now as commander of the LORD's army."

Joshua fell on his face to the earth, and worshipped, and asked him, "What does my lord say to his servant?"

15 The prince of the LORD's army said to Joshua, "Take off your sandals, for the place on which you stand is holy." Joshua did so.

6

1 Now Jericho was tightly shut up because of the children of Israel. No one went out, and no one came in. 2 The LORD said to Joshua, "Behold, I have given Jericho into your hand, with its king and the mighty men of valour. 3 All of your men of war shall march around the city, going around the city once. You shall do this six days. 4 Seven priests shall bear seven trumpets of rams' horns before the ark. On the seventh day, you shall march around the city seven times, and the priests shall blow the trumpets. 5 It shall be that when they make a long blast with the ram's horn, and when you hear the sound of the trumpet, all the people shall shout with a great shout; then the city wall will fall down flat, and the people shall go up, every man straight in front of him."

6 Joshua the son of Nun called the priests, and said to them, "Take up the ark of the covenant, and let seven priests bear seven trumpets of rams' horns before the LORD's ark."

7 They said to the people, "Advance! March around the city, and let the armed men pass on before the LORD's ark."

8 It was so, that when Joshua had spoken to the people, the seven priests bearing the seven trumpets of rams' horns before the LORD advanced and blew the trumpets, and the ark of the LORD's covenant followed them. 9 The armed men went before the priests who blew the trumpets, and the ark went after them. The trumpets sounded as they went.

10 Joshua commanded the people, saying, "You shall not shout nor let your voice be heard, neither shall any word proceed out of your mouth until the day I tell you to shout. Then you shall shout." 11 So he caused the LORD's ark to go around the city, circling it once. Then they came into the camp, and stayed in the camp. 12 Joshua rose early in the morning, and the priests took up the LORD's ark. 13 The seven priests bearing the seven trumpets of rams' horns in front of the LORD's ark went on continually, and blew the trumpets. The armed men went in front of them. The rear guard came after the LORD's ark. The trumpets sounded as they went. 14 The second day they marched around the city once, and returned into the camp. They did this six days.

15 On the seventh day, they rose early at the dawning of the day, and marched around the city in the same way seven times. On this day only they marched around the city seven times. 16 At the seventh time, when the priests blew the trumpets, Joshua said to the people, "Shout, for the LORD has given you the city! 17 The city shall be devoted, even it and all that is in it, to the LORD. Only Rahab the prostitute shall live, she and all who are with her in the house, because she hid the messengers that we sent. 18 But as for you, only keep yourselves from what is devoted to destruction, lest when you have devoted it, you take of the devoted thing; so you would make the camp of Israel accursed and trouble it. 19 But all the silver, gold, and vessels of bronze and iron are holy to the LORD. They shall come into the LORD's treasury."

20 So the people shouted and the priests blew the trumpets. When the people heard the sound of the trumpet, the people shouted with a great shout, and the wall fell down flat, so that the people went up into the city, every man straight in front of him, and they took the city. 21 They utterly destroyed all that was in the city, both man and woman, both young and old, and ox, sheep, and donkey, with the edge of the sword. 22 Joshua said to the two men who had spied out the land, "Go into the prostitute's house, and bring the woman and all that she has out from there, as you swore to her." 23 The young men who were spies went in, and brought out Rahab with her father, her mother, her brothers, and all that she had. They also brought out all of her relatives, and they set them outside of the camp of Israel. 24 They burnt the city with fire, and all that was in it. Only they put the silver, the gold, and the vessels of bronze and of iron into the treasury of the LORD's house. 25 But Rahab the prostitute, her father's household, and all that she had, Joshua saved alive. She lives in the middle of Israel to this day, because she hid the messengers whom Joshua sent to spy out Jericho.

26 Joshua commanded them with an oath at that time, saying, "Cursed is the man before the LORD who rises up and builds this city Jericho. With the loss of his firstborn he will lay its foundation, and with the loss of his youngest son he will set up its gates." 27 So the LORD was with Joshua; and his fame was in all the land.

7

1 But the children of Israel committed a trespass in the devoted things; for Achan, the son of Carmi, the son of Zabdi, the son of Zerah, of the tribe of Judah, took some of the devoted things. Therefore the LORD's anger burnt against the children of Israel. 2 Joshua sent men from Jericho to Ai, which is beside Beth Aven, on the east side of Bethel, and spoke to them, saying, "Go up and spy out the land."

The men went up and spied out Ai. 3 They returned to Joshua, and said to him, "Don't let all the people go up, but let about two or three thousand men go up and strike Ai. Don't make all the people to toil there, for there are only a few of them." 4 So about three thousand men of the people went up there, and they fled before the men of Ai. 5 The men of Ai struck about thirty-six men of them. They chased them from before the gate even to Shebarim, and struck them at the descent. The hearts of the people melted, and became like water. 6 Joshua tore his clothes, and fell to the earth on his face before the LORD's ark until the evening, he and the elders of Israel; and they put dust on their heads. 7 Joshua said, "Alas, Lord GOD, why have you brought this people over the Jordan at all, to deliver us into the hand of the Amorites, to cause us to perish? I wish that we had been content and lived beyond the Jordan! 8 Oh, Lord, what shall I say, after Israel has turned their backs before their enemies? 9 For the Canaanites and all the inhabitants of the land will hear of it, and will surround us, and cut off our name from the earth. What will you do for your great name?"

10 The LORD said to Joshua, "Get up! Why have you fallen on your face like that? 11 Israel has sinned. Yes, they have even transgressed my covenant which I commanded them. Yes, they have even taken some of the devoted things, and have also stolen, and also deceived. They have even put it amongst their own stuff. 12 Therefore the children of Israel can't stand

a 5:9 "Gilgal" sounds like the Hebrew for "roll."

before their enemies. They turn their backs before their enemies, because they have become devoted for destruction. I will not be with you any more, unless you destroy the devoted things from amongst you. 13 Get up! Sanctify the people, and say, 'Sanctify yourselves for tomorrow, for the LORD, the God of Israel, says, "There is a devoted thing amongst you, Israel. You cannot stand before your enemies until you take away the devoted thing from amongst you." 14 In the morning therefore you shall be brought near by your tribes. It shall be that the tribe which the LORD selects shall come near by families. The family which the LORD selects shall come near by households. The household which the LORD selects shall come near man by man. 15 It shall be, that he who is taken with the devoted thing shall be burnt with fire, he and all that he has, because he has transgressed the LORD's covenant, and because he has done a disgraceful thing in Israel.'"

16 So Joshua rose up early in the morning and brought Israel near by their tribes. The tribe of Judah was selected. 17 He brought near the family of Judah, and he selected the family of the Zerahites. He brought near the family of the Zerahites man by man, and Zabdi was selected. 18 He brought near his household man by man, and Achan, the son of Carmi, the son of Zabdi, the son of Zerah, of the tribe of Judah, was selected. 19 Joshua said to Achan, "My son, please give glory to the LORD, the God of Israel, and make confession to him. Tell me now what you have done! Don't hide it from me!"

20 Achan answered Joshua, and said, "I have truly sinned against the LORD, the God of Israel, and this is what I have done. 21 When I saw amongst the plunder a beautiful Babylonian robe, two hundred shekels[a] of silver, and a wedge of gold weighing fifty shekels, then I coveted them and took them. Behold, they are hidden in the ground in the middle of my tent, with the silver under it."

22 So Joshua sent messengers, and they ran to the tent. Behold, it was hidden in his tent, with the silver under it. 23 They took them from the middle of the tent, and brought them to Joshua and to all the children of Israel. They laid them down before the LORD. 24 Joshua, and all Israel with him, took Achan the son of Zerah, the silver, the robe, the wedge of gold, his sons, his daughters, his cattle, his donkeys, his sheep, his tent, and all that he had; and they brought them up to the valley of Achor. 25 Joshua said, "Why have you troubled us? The LORD will trouble you today." All Israel stoned him with stones, and they burnt them with fire and stoned them with stones. 26 They raised over him a great heap of stones that remains to this day. The LORD turned from the fierceness of his anger. Therefore the name of that place was called "The valley of Achor" to this day.

8

1 The LORD said to Joshua, "Don't be afraid, and don't be dismayed. Take all the warriors with you, and arise, go up to Ai. Behold, I have given into your hand the king of Ai, with his people, his city, and his land. 2 You shall do to Ai and her king as you did to Jericho and her king, except you shall take its goods and its livestock for yourselves. Set an ambush for the city behind it."

3 So Joshua arose, with all the warriors, to go up to Ai. Joshua chose thirty thousand men, the mighty men of valour, and sent them out by night. 4 He commanded them, saying, "Behold, you shall lie in ambush against the city, behind the city. Don't go very far from the city, but all of you be ready. 5 I and all the people who are with me will approach the city. It shall happen, when they come out against us, as at the first, that we will flee before them. 6 They will come out after us until we have drawn them away from the city; for they will say, 'They flee before us, like the first time.' So we will flee before them, 7 and you shall rise up from the ambush, and take possession of the city; for the LORD your God will deliver it into your hand. 8 It shall be, when you have seized the city, that you shall set the city on fire. You shall do this according to the LORD's word. Behold, I have commanded you."

9 Joshua sent them out; and they went to set up the ambush, and stayed between Bethel and Ai on the west side of Ai; but Joshua stayed amongst the people that night. 10 Joshua rose up early in the morning, mustered the people, and went up, he and the elders of Israel, before the people to Ai. 11 All the people, even the men of war who were with him, went up and came near, and came before the city and encamped on the north side of Ai. Now there was a valley between him and Ai. 12 He took about five thousand men, and set them in ambush between Bethel and Ai, on the west side of the city. 13 So they set the people, even all the army who was on the north of the city, and their ambush on the west of the city; and Joshua went that night into the middle of the valley. 14 When the king of Ai saw it, they hurried and rose up early, and the men of the city went out against Israel to battle, he and all his people, at the time appointed, before the Arabah; but he didn't know that there was an ambush against him behind the city. 15 Joshua and all Israel made as if they were beaten before them, and fled by the way of the wilderness. 16 All the people who were in the city were called together to pursue after them. They pursued Joshua, and were drawn away from the city. 17 There was not a man left in Ai or Bethel who didn't go out after Israel. They left the city open, and pursued Israel.

18 The LORD said to Joshua, "Stretch out the javelin that is in your hand towards Ai, for I will give it into your hand."

Joshua stretched out the javelin that was in his hand towards the city. 19 The ambush arose quickly out of their place, and they ran as soon as he had stretched out his hand and entered into the city and took it. They

hurried and set the city on fire. 20 When the men of Ai looked behind them, they saw, and behold, the smoke of the city ascended up to heaven, and they had no power to flee this way or that way. The people who fled to the wilderness turned back on the pursuers. 21 When Joshua and all Israel saw that the ambush had taken the city, and that the smoke of the city ascended, then they turned back and killed the men of Ai. 22 The others came out of the city against them, so they were in the middle of Israel, some on this side, and some on that side. They struck them, so that they let none of them remain or escape. 23 They captured the king of Ai alive, and brought him to Joshua.

24 When Israel had finished killing all the inhabitants of Ai in the field, in the wilderness in which they pursued them, and they had all fallen by the edge of the sword until they were consumed, all Israel returned to Ai and struck it with the edge of the sword. 25 All that fell that day, both of men and women, were twelve thousand, even all the people of Ai. 26 For Joshua didn't draw back his hand, with which he stretched out the javelin, until he had utterly destroyed all the inhabitants of Ai. 27 Israel took for themselves only the livestock and the goods of that city, according to the LORD's word which he commanded Joshua. 28 So Joshua burnt Ai and made it a heap forever, even a desolation, to this day. 29 He hanged the king of Ai on a tree until the evening. At sundown, Joshua commanded, and they took his body down from the tree and threw it at the entrance of the gate of the city, and raised a great heap of stones on it that remains to this day.

30 Then Joshua built an altar to the LORD, the God of Israel, on Mount Ebal, 31 as Moses the servant of the LORD commanded the children of Israel, as it is written in the book of the law of Moses: an altar of uncut stones, on which no one had lifted up any iron. They offered burnt offerings on it to the LORD and sacrificed peace offerings. 32 He wrote there on the stones a copy of Moses' law, which he wrote in the presence of the children of Israel. 33 All Israel, with their elders, officers, and judges, stood on both sides of the ark before the Levitical priests, who carried the ark of the LORD's covenant, the foreigner as well as the native; half of them in front of Mount Gerizim, and half of them in front of Mount Ebal, as Moses the servant of the LORD had commanded at the first, that they should bless the people of Israel. 34 Afterward he read all the words of the law, the blessing and the curse, according to all that is written in the book of the law. 35 There was not a word of all that Moses commanded which Joshua didn't read before all the assembly of Israel, with the women, the little ones, and the foreigners who were amongst them.

9

1 When all the kings who were beyond the Jordan, in the hill country, and in the lowland, and on all the shore of the great sea in front of Lebanon, the Hittite, the Amorite, the Canaanite, the Perizzite, the Hivite, and the Jebusite, heard of it 2 they gathered themselves together to fight with Joshua and with Israel, with one accord. 3 But when the inhabitants of Gibeon heard what Joshua had done to Jericho and to Ai, 4 they also resorted to a ruse, and went and made as if they had been ambassadors, and took old sacks on their donkeys, and old, torn-up and bound up wine skins, 5 and old and patched sandals on their feet, and wore old garments. All the bread of their food supply was dry and mouldy. 6 They went to Joshua at the camp at Gilgal, and said to him and to the men of Israel, "We have come from a far country. Now therefore make a covenant with us."

7 The men of Israel said to the Hivites, "What if you live amongst us? How could we make a covenant with you?"

8 They said to Joshua, "We are your servants."

Joshua said to them, "Who are you? Where do you come from?"

9 They said to him, "Your servants have come from a very far country because of the name of the LORD your God; for we have heard of his fame, all that he did in Egypt, 10 and all that he did to the two kings of the Amorites who were beyond the Jordan, to Sihon king of Heshbon and to Og king of Bashan, who was at Ashtaroth. 11 Our elders and all the inhabitants of our country spoke to us, saying, 'Take supplies in your hand for the journey, and go to meet them. Tell them, "We are your servants. Now make a covenant with us."' 12 This our bread we took hot for our supplies out of our houses on the day we went out to go to you; but now, behold, it is dry, and has become mouldy. 13 These wine skins, which we filled, were new; and behold, they are torn. These our garments and our sandals have become old because of the very long journey."

14 The men sampled their provisions, and didn't ask counsel from the LORD's mouth. 15 Joshua made peace with them, and made a covenant with them, to let them live. The princes of the congregation swore to them. 16 At the end of three days after they had made a covenant with them, they heard that they were their neighbours, and that they lived amongst them. 17 The children of Israel travelled and came to their cities on the third day. Now their cities were Gibeon, Chephirah, Beeroth, and Kiriath Jearim. 18 The children of Israel didn't strike them, because the princes of the congregation had sworn to them by the LORD, the God of Israel. All the congregation murmured against the princes. 19 But all the princes said to all the congregation, "We have sworn to them by the LORD, the God of Israel. Now therefore we may not touch them. 20 We will do this to them, and let them live; lest wrath be on us, because of the oath which we swore to them." 21 The princes said to them, "Let them live." So they became wood cutters and drawers of water for all the congregation, as the princes had spoken to them.

22 Joshua called for them, and he spoke to them, saying, "Why have you deceived us, saying, 'We are very far from you,' when you live amongst

---

a *7:21* A shekel is about 10 grams or about 0.35 ounces.

us? 23 Now therefore you are cursed, and some of you will never fail to be slaves, both wood cutters and drawers of water for the house of my God."

24 They answered Joshua, and said, "Because your servants were certainly told how the LORD your God commanded his servant Moses to give you all the land, and to destroy all the inhabitants of the land from before you. Therefore we were very afraid for our lives because of you, and have done this thing. 25 Now, behold, we are in your hand. Do to us as it seems good and right to you to do."

26 He did so to them, and delivered them out of the hand of the children of Israel, so that they didn't kill them. 27 That day Joshua made them wood cutters and drawers of water for the congregation and for the LORD's altar to this day, in the place which he should choose.

10

1 Now when Adoni-Zedek king of Jerusalem heard how Joshua had taken Ai, and had utterly destroyed it; as he had done to Jericho and her king, so he had done to Ai and her king; and how the inhabitants of Gibeon had made peace with Israel, and were amongst them, 2 they were very afraid, because Gibeon was a great city, as one of the royal cities, and because it was greater than Ai, and all its men were mighty. 3 Therefore Adoni-Zedek king of Jerusalem sent to Hoham king of Hebron, Piram king of Jarmuth, Japhia king of Lachish, and Debir king of Eglon, saying, 4 "Come up to me and help me. Let's strike Gibeon; for they have made peace with Joshua and with the children of Israel." 5 Therefore the five kings of the Amorites, the king of Jerusalem, the king of Hebron, the king of Jarmuth, the king of Lachish, and the king of Eglon, gathered themselves together and went up, they and all their armies, and encamped against Gibeon, and made war against it. 6 The men of Gibeon sent to Joshua at the camp at Gilgal, saying, "Don't abandon your servants! Come up to us quickly and save us! Help us; for all the kings of the Amorites that dwell in the hill country have gathered together against us."

7 So Joshua went up from Gilgal, he and the whole army with him, including all the mighty men of valour. 8 The LORD said to Joshua, "Don't fear them, for I have delivered them into your hands. Not a man of them will stand before you."

9 Joshua therefore came to them suddenly. He marched from Gilgal all night. 10 The LORD confused them before Israel. He killed them with a great slaughter at Gibeon, and chased them by the way of the ascent of Beth Horon, and struck them to Azekah and to Makkedah. 11 As they fled from before Israel, while they were at the descent of Beth Horon, the LORD hurled down great stones from the sky on them to Azekah, and they died. There were more who died from the hailstones than those whom the children of Israel killed with the sword.

12 Then Joshua spoke to the LORD in the day when the LORD delivered up the Amorites before the children of Israel. He said in the sight of Israel, "Sun, stand still on Gibeon! You, moon, stop in the valley of Aijalon!"

13 The sun stood still, and the moon stayed, until the nation had avenged themselves on their enemies. Isn't this written in the book of Jashar? The sun stayed in the middle of the sky, and didn't hurry to go down about a whole day. 14 There was no day like that before it or after it, that the LORD listened to the voice of a man; for the LORD fought for Israel.

15 Joshua returned, and all Israel with him, to the camp to Gilgal. 16 These five kings fled, and hid themselves in the cave at Makkedah. 17 Joshua was told, saying, "The five kings have been found, hidden in the cave at Makkedah."

18 Joshua said, "Roll large stones to cover the cave's entrance, and set men by it to guard them; 19 but don't stay there. Pursue your enemies, and attack them from the rear. Don't allow them to enter into their cities; for the LORD your God has delivered them into your hand."

20 When Joshua and the children of Israel had finished killing them with a very great slaughter until they were consumed, and the remnant which remained of them had entered into the fortified cities, 21 all the people returned to the camp to Joshua at Makkedah in peace. None moved his tongue against any of the children of Israel. 22 Then Joshua said, "Open the cave entrance, and bring those five kings out of the cave to me."

23 They did so, and brought those five kings out of the cave to him: the king of Jerusalem, the king of Hebron, the king of Jarmuth, the king of Lachish, and the king of Eglon. 24 When they brought those kings out to Joshua, Joshua called for all the men of Israel, and said to the chiefs of the men of war who went with him, "Come near. Put your feet on the necks of these kings."

They came near, and put their feet on their necks.

25 Joshua said to them, "Don't be afraid, nor be dismayed. Be strong and courageous, for the LORD will do this to all your enemies against whom you fight."

26 Afterward Joshua struck them, put them to death, and hanged them on five trees. They were hanging on the trees until the evening. 27 At the time of the going down of the sun, Joshua commanded, and they took them down off the trees, and threw them into the cave in which they had hidden themselves, and laid great stones on the mouth of the cave, which remain to this very day.

28 Joshua took Makkedah on that day, and struck it with the edge of the sword, with its king. He utterly destroyed it and all the souls who were in it. He left no one remaining. He did to the king of Makkedah as he had done to the king of Jericho.

29 Joshua passed from Makkedah, and all Israel with him, to Libnah, and fought against Libnah. 30 The LORD delivered it also, with its king, into the hand of Israel. He struck it with the edge of the sword, and all the souls who were in it. He left no one remaining in it. He did to its king as he had done to the king of Jericho.

31 Joshua passed from Libnah, and all Israel with him, to Lachish, and encamped against it, and fought against it. 32 The LORD delivered Lachish into the hand of Israel. He took it on the second day, and struck it with the edge of the sword, with all the souls who were in it, according to all that he had done to Libnah. 33 Then Horam king of Gezer came up to help Lachish; and Joshua struck him and his people, until he had left him no one remaining.

34 Joshua passed from Lachish, and all Israel with him, to Eglon; and they encamped against it and fought against it. 35 They took it on that day, and struck it with the edge of the sword. He utterly destroyed all the souls who were in it that day, according to all that he had done to Lachish.

36 Joshua went up from Eglon, and all Israel with him, to Hebron; and they fought against it. 37 They took it, and struck it with the edge of the sword, with its king and all its cities, and all the souls who were in it. He left no one remaining, according to all that he had done to Eglon; but he utterly destroyed it, and all the souls who were in it.

38 Joshua returned, and all Israel with him, to Debir, and fought against it. 39 He took it, with its king and all its cities. They struck them with the edge of the sword, and utterly destroyed all the souls who were in it. He left no one remaining. As he had done to Hebron, so he did to Debir, and to its king; as he had done also to Libnah, and to its king. 40 So Joshua struck all the land, the hill country, the South, the lowland, the slopes, and all their kings. He left no one remaining, but he utterly destroyed all that breathed, as the LORD, the God of Israel, commanded. 41 Joshua struck them from Kadesh Barnea even to Gaza, and all the country of Goshen, even to Gibeon. 42 Joshua took all these kings and their land at one time because the LORD, the God of Israel, fought for Israel. 43 Joshua returned, and all Israel with him, to the camp to Gilgal.

11

1 When Jabin king of Hazor heard of it, he sent to Jobab king of Madon, to the king of Shimron, to the king of Achshaph, 2 and to the kings who were on the north, in the hill country, in the Arabah south of Chinneroth, in the lowland, and in the heights of Dor on the west, 3 to the Canaanite on the east and on the west, the Amorite, the Hittite, the Perizzite, the Jebusite in the hill country, and the Hivite under Hermon in the land of Mizpah. 4 They went out, they and all their armies with them, many people, even as the sand that is on the seashore in multitude, with very many horses and chariots. 5 All these kings met together; and they came and encamped together at the waters of Merom, to fight with Israel.

6 The LORD said to Joshua, "Don't be afraid because of them; for tomorrow at this time, I will deliver them up all slain before Israel. You shall hamstring their horses and burn their chariots with fire."

7 So Joshua came suddenly, with all the warriors, against them by the waters of Merom, and attacked them. 8 The LORD delivered them into the hand of Israel, and they struck them, and chased them to great Sidon, and to Misrephoth Maim, and to the valley of Mizpah eastward. They struck them until they left them no one remaining. 9 Joshua did to them as the LORD told him. He hamstrung their horses and burnt their chariots with fire.

10 Joshua turned back at that time, and took Hazor, and struck its king with the sword; for Hazor used to be the head of all those kingdoms. 11 They struck all the souls who were in it with the edge of the sword, utterly destroying them. There was no one left who breathed. He burnt Hazor with fire. 12 Joshua captured all the cities of those kings, with their kings, and he struck them with the edge of the sword, and utterly destroyed them, as Moses the servant of the LORD commanded. 13 But as for the cities that stood on their mounds, Israel burnt none of them, except Hazor only. Joshua burnt that. 14 The children of Israel took all the plunder of these cities, with the livestock, as plunder for themselves; but every man they struck with the edge of the sword, until they had destroyed them. They didn't leave any who breathed.

15 As the LORD commanded Moses his servant, so Moses commanded Joshua. Joshua did so. He left nothing undone of all that the LORD commanded Moses. 16 So Joshua captured all that land, the hill country, all the South, all the land of Goshen, the lowland, the Arabah, the hill country of Israel, and the lowland of the same, 17 from Mount Halak, that goes up to Seir, even to Baal Gad in the valley of Lebanon under Mount Hermon. He took all their kings, struck them, and put them to death. 18 Joshua made war a long time with all those kings. 19 There was not a city that made peace with the children of Israel, except the Hivites, the inhabitants of Gibeon. They took all in battle. 20 For it was of the LORD to harden their hearts, to come against Israel in battle, that he might utterly destroy them, that they might have no favour, but that he might destroy them, as the LORD commanded Moses. 21 Joshua came at that time, and cut off the Anakim from the hill country, from Hebron, from Debir, from Anab, and from all the hill country of Judah, and from all the hill country of Israel. Joshua utterly destroyed them with their cities. 22 There were none of the Anakim left in the land of the children of Israel. Only in Gaza, in Gath, and in Ashdod, did some remain. 23 So Joshua took the whole land, according to all that the LORD spoke to Moses; and Joshua gave it for an inheritance to Israel according to their divisions by their tribes. Then the land had rest from war.

12

1 Now these are the kings of the land, whom the children of Israel struck, and possessed their land beyond the Jordan towards the sunrise, from the valley of the Arnon to Mount Hermon, and all the Arabah eastward: 2 Sihon king of the Amorites, who lived in Heshbon, and ruled from Aroer,

which is on the edge of the valley of the Arnon, and the middle of the valley, and half Gilead, even to the river Jabbok, the border of the children of Ammon; 3 and the Arabah to the sea of Chinneroth, eastward, and to the sea of the Arabah, even the Salt Sea, eastward, the way to Beth Jeshimoth; and on the south, under the slopes of Pisgah: 4 and the border of Og king of Bashan, of the remnant of the Rephaim, who lived at Ashtaroth and at Edrei, 5 and ruled in Mount Hermon, and in Salecah, and in all Bashan, to the border of the Geshurites and the Maacathites, and half Gilead, the border of Sihon king of Heshbon. 6 Moses the servant of the LORD and the children of Israel struck them. Moses the servant of the LORD gave it for a possession to the Reubenites, and the Gadites, and the half-tribe of Manasseh.

7 These are the kings of the land whom Joshua and the children of Israel struck beyond the Jordan westward, from Baal Gad in the valley of Lebanon even to Mount Halak, that goes up to Seir. Joshua gave it to the tribes of Israel for a possession according to their divisions; 8 in the hill country, and in the lowland, and in the Arabah, and in the slopes, and in the wilderness, and in the South; the Hittite, the Amorite, and the Canaanite, the Perizzite, the Hivite, and the Jebusite:

9 the king of Jericho, one;
the king of Ai, which is beside Bethel, one;
10 the king of Jerusalem, one;
the king of Hebron, one;
11 the king of Jarmuth, one;
the king of Lachish, one;
12 the king of Eglon, one;
the king of Gezer, one;
13 the king of Debir, one;
the king of Geder, one;
14 the king of Hormah, one;
the king of Arad, one;
15 the king of Libnah, one;
the king of Adullam, one;
16 the king of Makkedah, one;
the king of Bethel, one;
17 the king of Tappuah, one;
the king of Hepher, one;
18 the king of Aphek, one;
the king of Lassharon, one;
19 the king of Madon, one;
the king of Hazor, one;
20 the king of Shimron Meron, one;
the king of Achshaph, one;
21 the king of Taanach, one;
the king of Megiddo, one;
22 the king of Kedesh, one;
the king of Jokneam in Carmel, one;
23 the king of Dor in the height of Dor, one;
the king of Goiim in Gilgal, one;
24 the king of Tirzah, one:
all the kings thirty-one.

13

1 Now Joshua was old and well advanced in years. The LORD said to him, "You are old and advanced in years, and there remains yet very much land to be possessed.

2 "This is the land that still remains: all the regions of the Philistines, and all the Geshurites; 3 from the Shihor, which is before Egypt, even to the border of Ekron northward, which is counted as Canaanite; the five lords of the Philistines; the Gazites, and the Ashdodites, the Ashkelonites, the Gittites, and the Ekronites; also the Avvim, 4 on the south; all the land of the Canaanites, and Mearah that belongs to the Sidonians, to Aphek, to the border of the Amorites; 5 and the land of the Gebalites, and all Lebanon, towards the sunrise, from Baal Gad under Mount Hermon to the entrance of Hamath; 6 all the inhabitants of the hill country from Lebanon to Misrephoth Maim, even all the Sidonians. I will drive them out from before the children of Israel. Just allocate it to Israel for an inheritance, as I have commanded you. 7 Now therefore divide this land for an inheritance to the nine tribes and the half-tribe of Manasseh." 8 With him the Reubenites and the Gadites received their inheritance, which Moses gave them, beyond the Jordan eastward, even as Moses the servant of the LORD gave them: 9 from Aroer, that is on the edge of the valley of the Arnon, and the city that is in the middle of the valley, and all the plain of Medeba to Dibon; 10 and all the cities of Sihon king of the Amorites, who reigned in Heshbon, to the border of the children of Ammon; 11 and Gilead, and the border of the Geshurites and Maacathites, and all Mount Hermon, and all Bashan to Salecah; 12 all the kingdom of Og in Bashan, who reigned in Ashtaroth and in Edrei (who was left of the remnant of the Rephaim); for Moses attacked these, and drove them out. 13 Nevertheless the children of Israel didn't drive out the Geshurites, nor the Maacathites: but Geshur and Maacath live within Israel to this day. 14 Only he gave no inheritance to the tribe of Levi. The offerings of the LORD, the God of Israel, made by fire are his inheritance, as he spoke to him. 15 Moses gave to the tribe of the children of Reuben according to their families. 16 Their border was from Aroer, that is on the edge of the valley of the Arnon, and the city that is in the middle of the valley, and all the plain by Medeba; 17 Heshbon, and all its cities that are in the plain; Dibon, Bamoth Baal, Beth Baal Meon, 18 Jahaz, Kedemoth, Mephaath, 19 Kiriathaim, Sibmah, Zereth Shahar in the mount of the valley, 20 Beth Peor, the slopes of Pisgah, Beth Jeshimoth, 21 all the cities of the plain, and all the kingdom of Sihon king of the Amorites, who reigned in

Heshbon, whom Moses struck with the chiefs of Midian, Evi, Rekem, Zur, Hur, and Reba, the princes of Sihon, who lived in the land. 22 The children of Israel also killed Balaam the son of Beor, the soothsayer, with the sword, amongst the rest of their slain.

23 The border of the children of Reuben was the bank of the Jordan. This was the inheritance of the children of Reuben according to their families, the cities and its villages.

24 Moses gave to the tribe of Gad, to the children of Gad, according to their families. 25 Their border was Jazer, and all the cities of Gilead, and half the land of the children of Ammon, to Aroer that is near Rabbah; 26 and from Heshbon to Ramath Mizpeh, and Betonim; and from Mahanaim to the border of Debir; 27 and in the valley, Beth Haram, Beth Nimrah, Succoth, and Zaphon, the rest of the kingdom of Sihon king of Heshbon, the Jordan's bank, to the uttermost part of the sea of Chinnereth beyond the Jordan eastward. 28 This is the inheritance of the children of Gad according to their families, the cities and its villages.

29 Moses gave an inheritance to the half-tribe of Manasseh. It was for the half-tribe of the children of Manasseh according to their families. 30 Their border was from Mahanaim, all Bashan, all the kingdom of Og king of Bashan, and all the villages of Jair, which are in Bashan, sixty cities. 31 Half Gilead, Ashtaroth, and Edrei, the cities of the kingdom of Og in Bashan, were for the children of Machir the son of Manasseh, even for the half of the children of Machir according to their families.

32 These are the inheritances which Moses distributed in the plains of Moab, beyond the Jordan at Jericho, eastward. 33 But Moses gave no inheritance to the tribe of Levi. The LORD, the God of Israel, is their inheritance, as he spoke to them.

14

1 These are the inheritances which the children of Israel took in the land of Canaan, which Eleazar the priest, Joshua the son of Nun, and the heads of the fathers' houses of the tribes of the children of Israel, distributed to them, 2 by the lot of their inheritance, as the LORD commanded by Moses, for the nine tribes, and for the half-tribe. 3 For Moses had given the inheritance of the two tribes and the half-tribe beyond the Jordan; but to the Levites he gave no inheritance amongst them. 4 For the children of Joseph were two tribes, Manasseh and Ephraim. They gave no portion to the Levites in the land, except cities to dwell in, with their pasture lands for their livestock and for their property. 5 The children of Israel did as the LORD commanded Moses, and they divided the land.

6 Then the children of Judah came near to Joshua in Gilgal. Caleb the son of Jephunneh the Kenizzite said to him, "You know the thing that the LORD spoke to Moses the man of God concerning me and concerning you in Kadesh Barnea. 7 I was forty years old when Moses the servant of the LORD sent me from Kadesh Barnea to spy out the land. I brought him word again as it was in my heart. 8 Nevertheless, my brothers who went up with me made the heart of the people melt; but I wholly followed the LORD my God. 9 Moses swore on that day, saying, 'Surely the land where you walked shall be an inheritance to you and to your children forever, because you have wholly followed the LORD my God.'

10 "Now, behold, the LORD has kept me alive, as he spoke, these forty-five years, from the time that the LORD spoke this word to Moses, while Israel walked in the wilderness. Now, behold, I am eighty-five years old, today. 11 As yet I am as strong today as I was in the day that Moses sent me. As my strength was then, even so is my strength now for war, to go out and to come in. 12 Now therefore give me this hill country, of which the LORD spoke in that day; for you heard in that day how the Anakim were there, and great and fortified cities. It may be that the LORD will be with me, and I shall drive them out, as the LORD said."

13 Joshua blessed him; and he gave Hebron to Caleb the son of Jephunneh for an inheritance. 14 Therefore Hebron became the inheritance of Caleb the son of Jephunneh the Kenizzite to this day, because he followed the LORD, the God of Israel wholeheartedly. 15 Now the name of Hebron before was Kiriath Arba, after the greatest man amongst the Anakim. Then the land had rest from war.

15

1 The lot for the tribe of the children of Judah according to their families was to the border of Edom, even to the wilderness of Zin southward, at the uttermost part of the south. 2 Their south border was from the uttermost part of the Salt Sea, from the bay that looks southward; 3 and it went out southward of the ascent of Akrabbim, and passed along to Zin, and went up by the south of Kadesh Barnea, and passed along by Hezron, went up to Addar, and turned towards Karka; 4 and it passed along to Azmon, went out at the brook of Egypt; and the border ended at the sea. This shall be your south border. 5 The east border was the Salt Sea, even to the end of the Jordan. The border of the north quarter was from the bay of the sea at the end of the Jordan. 6 The border went up to Beth Hoglah, and passed along by the north of Beth Arabah; and the border went up to the stone of Bohan the son of Reuben. 7 The border went up to Debir from the valley of Achor, and so northward, looking towards Gilgal, that faces the ascent of Adummim, which is on the south side of the river. The border passed along to the waters of En Shemesh, and ended at En Rogel. 8 The border went up by the valley of the son of Hinnom to the side of the Jebusite (also called Jerusalem) southward; and the border went up to the top of the mountain that lies before the valley of Hinnom westward, which is at the farthest part of the valley of Rephaim northward. 9 The border extended from the top of the mountain to the spring of the waters of Nephtoah, and went out to the cities of Mount Ephron; and the border extended to Baalah (also called Kiriath Jearim); 10 and the border turned

about from Baalah westward to Mount Seir, and passed along to the side of Mount Jearim (also called Chesalon) on the north, and went down to Beth Shemesh, and passed along by Timnah; 11 and the border went out to the side of Ekron northward; and the border extended to Shikkeron, and passed along to Mount Baalah, and went out at Jabneel; and the goings out of the border were at the sea. 12 The west border was to the shore of the great sea. This is the border of the children of Judah according to their families.

13 He gave to Caleb the son of Jephunneh a portion amongst the children of Judah, according to the commandment of the LORD to Joshua, even Kiriath Arba, named after the father of Anak (also called Hebron). 14 Caleb drove out the three sons of Anak: Sheshai, and Ahiman, and Talmai, the children of Anak. 15 He went up against the inhabitants of Debir: now the name of Debir before was Kiriath Sepher. 16 Caleb said, "He who strikes Kiriath Sepher, and takes it, to him I will give Achsah my daughter as wife." 17 Othniel the son of Kenaz, the brother of Caleb, took it: and he gave him Achsah his daughter as wife. 18 When she came, she had him ask her father for a field. She got off her donkey, and Caleb said, "What do you want?"

19 She said, "Give me a blessing. Because you have set me in the land of the South, give me also springs of water."

So he gave her the upper springs and the lower springs.

20 This is the inheritance of the tribe of the children of Judah according to their families. 21 The farthest cities of the tribe of the children of Judah towards the border of Edom in the South were Kabzeel, Eder, Jagur, 22 Kinah, Dimonah, Adadah, 23 Kedesh, Hazor, Ithnan, 24 Ziph, Telem, Bealoth, 25 Hazor Hadattah, Kerioth Hezron (also called Hazor), 26 Amam, Shema, Moladah, 27 Hazar Gaddah, Heshmon, Beth Pelet, 28 Hazar Shual, Beersheba, Biziothiah, 29 Baalah, Iim, Ezem, 30 Eltolad, Chesil, Hormah, 31 Ziklag, Madmannah, Sansannah, 32 Lebaoth, Shilhim, Ain, and Rimmon. All the cities are twenty-nine, with their villages.

33 In the lowland, Eshtaol, Zorah, Ashnah, 34 Zanoah, En Gannim, Tappuah, Enam, 35 Jarmuth, Adullam, Socoh, Azekah, 36 Shaaraim, Adithaim and Gederah (or Gederothaim); fourteen cities with their villages.

37 Zenan, Hadashah, Migdal Gad, 38 Dilean, Mizpah, Joktheel, 39 Lachish, Bozkath, Eglon, 40 Cabbon, Lahmam, Chitlish, 41 Gederoth, Beth Dagon, Naamah, and Makkedah; sixteen cities with their villages.

42 Libnah, Ether, Ashan, 43 Iphtah, Ashnah, Nezib, 44 Keilah, Achzib, and Mareshah; nine cities with their villages.

45 Ekron, with its towns and its villages; 46 from Ekron even to the sea, all that were by the side of Ashdod, with their villages. 47 Ashdod, its towns and its villages; Gaza, its towns and its villages; to the brook of Egypt, and the great sea with its coastline.

48 In the hill country, Shamir, Jattir, Socoh, 49 Dannah, Kiriath Sannah (which is Debir), 50 Anab, Eshtemoh, Anim, 51 Goshen, Holon, and Giloh; eleven cities with their villages.

52 Arab, Dumah, Eshan, 53 Janim, Beth Tappuah, Aphekah, 54 Humtah, Kiriath Arba (also called Hebron), and Zior; nine cities with their villages.

55 Maon, Carmel, Ziph, Jutah, 56 Jezreel, Jokdeam, Zanoah, 57 Kain, Gibeah, and Timnah; ten cities with their villages.

58 Halhul, Beth Zur, Gedor, 59 Maarath, Beth Anoth, and Eltekon; six cities with their villages. 60 Kiriath Baal (also called Kiriath Jearim), and Rabbah; two cities with their villages.

61 In the wilderness, Beth Arabah, Middin, Secacah, 62 Nibshan, the City of Salt, and En Gedi; six cities with their villages.

63 As for the Jebusites, the inhabitants of Jerusalem, the children of Judah couldn't drive them out; but the Jebusites live with the children of Judah at Jerusalem to this day.

16

1 The lot came out for the children of Joseph from the Jordan at Jericho, at the waters of Jericho on the east, even the wilderness, going up from Jericho through the hill country to Bethel. 2 It went out from Bethel to Luz, and passed along to the border of the Archites to Ataroth; 3 and it went down westward to the border of the Japhletites, to the border of Beth Horon the lower, and on to Gezer; and ended at the sea.

4 The children of Joseph, Manasseh and Ephraim, took their inheritance. 5 This was the border of the children of Ephraim according to their families. The border of their inheritance eastward was Ataroth Addar, to Beth Horon the upper. 6 The border went out westward at Michmethath on the north. The border turned about eastward to Taanath Shiloh, and passed along it on the east of Janoah. 7 It went down from Janoah to Ataroth, to Naarah, reached to Jericho, and went out at the Jordan. 8 From Tappuah the border went along westward to the brook of Kanah; and ended at the sea. This is the inheritance of the tribe of the children of Ephraim according to their families; 9 together with the cities which were set apart for the children of Ephraim in the middle of the inheritance of the children of Manasseh, all the cities with their villages. 10 They didn't drive out the Canaanites who lived in Gezer; but the Canaanites dwell in the territory of Ephraim to this day, and have become servants to do forced labour.

17

1 This was the lot for the tribe of Manasseh, for he was the firstborn of Joseph. As for Machir the firstborn of Manasseh, the father of Gilead, because he was a man of war, therefore he had Gilead and Bashan. 2 So this was for the rest of the children of Manasseh according to their families: for the children of Abiezer, for the children of Helek, for the children of Asriel, for the children of Shechem, for the children of Hepher, and for the children of Shemida. These were the male children of Manasseh the son of Joseph according to their families. 3 But Zelophehad, the son of Hepher, the son of Gilead, the son of Machir, the son of Manasseh, had no sons, but

daughters. These are the names of his daughters: Mahlah, Noah, Hoglah, Milcah, and Tirzah. 4 They came to Eleazar the priest, and to Joshua the son of Nun, and to the princes, saying, "The LORD commanded Moses to give us an inheritance amongst our brothers." Therefore according to the commandment of the LORD he gave them an inheritance amongst the brothers of their father. 5 Ten parts fell to Manasseh, in addition to the land of Gilead and Bashan, which is beyond the Jordan; 6 because the daughters of Manasseh had an inheritance amongst his sons. The land of Gilead belonged to the rest of the sons of Manasseh. 7 The border of Manasseh was from Asher to Michmethath, which is before Shechem. The border went along to the right hand, to the inhabitants of En Tappuah. 8 The land of Tappuah belonged to Manasseh; but Tappuah on the border of Manasseh belonged to the children of Ephraim. 9 The border went down to the brook of Kanah, southward of the brook. These cities belonged to Ephraim amongst the cities of Manasseh. The border of Manasseh was on the north side of the brook, and ended at the sea. 10 Southward it was Ephraim's, and northward it was Manasseh's, and the sea was his border. They reached to Asher on the north, and to Issachar on the east. 11 Manasseh had three heights in Issachar, in Asher Beth Shean and its towns, and Ibleam and its towns, and the inhabitants of Dor and its towns, and the inhabitants of Endor and its towns, and the inhabitants of Taanach and its towns, and the inhabitants of Megiddo and its towns. 12 Yet the children of Manasseh couldn't drive out the inhabitants of those cities; but the Canaanites would dwell in that land.

13 When the children of Israel had grown strong, they put the Canaanites to forced labour, and didn't utterly drive them out. 14 The children of Joseph spoke to Joshua, saying, "Why have you given me just one lot and one part for an inheritance, since we are a numerous people, because the LORD has blessed us so far?"

15 Joshua said to them, "If you are a numerous people, go up to the forest, and clear land for yourself there in the land of the Perizzites and of the Rephaim, since the hill country of Ephraim is too narrow for you."

16 The children of Joseph said, "The hill country is not enough for us. All the Canaanites who dwell in the land of the valley have chariots of iron, both those who are in Beth Shean and its towns, and those who are in the valley of Jezreel."

17 Joshua spoke to the house of Joseph, that is, to Ephraim and to Manasseh, saying, "You are a numerous people, and have great power. You shall not have one lot only; 18 but the hill country shall be yours. Although it is a forest, you shall cut it down, and it's farthest extent shall be yours; for you shall drive out the Canaanites, though they have chariots of iron, and though they are strong."

18

1 The whole congregation of the children of Israel assembled themselves together at Shiloh, and set up the Tent of Meeting there. The land was subdued before them. 2 Seven tribes remained amongst the children of Israel, which had not yet divided their inheritance. 3 Joshua said to the children of Israel, "How long will you neglect to go in to possess the land, which the LORD, the God of your fathers, has given you? 4 Appoint for yourselves three men from each tribe. I will send them, and they shall arise, walk through the land, and describe it according to their inheritance; then they shall come to me. 5 They shall divide it into seven portions. Judah shall live in his borders on the south, and the house of Joseph shall live in their borders on the north. 6 You shall survey the land into seven parts, and bring the description here to me; and I will cast lots for you here before the LORD our God. 7 However, the Levites have no portion amongst you; for the priesthood of the LORD is their inheritance. Gad, Reuben, and the half-tribe of Manasseh have received their inheritance east of the Jordan, which Moses the servant of the LORD gave them."

8 The men arose and went. Joshua commanded those who went to survey the land, saying, "Go walk through the land, survey it, and come again to me. I will cast lots for you here before the LORD in Shiloh."

9 The men went and passed through the land, and surveyed it by cities into seven portions in a book. They came to Joshua to the camp at Shiloh. 10 Joshua cast lots for them in Shiloh before the LORD. There Joshua divided the land to the children of Israel according to their divisions.

11 The lot of the tribe of the children of Benjamin came up according to their families. The border of their lot went out between the children of Judah and the children of Joseph. 12 Their border on the north quarter was from the Jordan. The border went up to the side of Jericho on the north, and went up through the hill country westward. It ended at the wilderness of Beth Aven. 13 The border passed along from there to Luz, to the side of Luz (also called Bethel), southward. The border went down to Ataroth Addar, by the mountain that lies on the south of Beth Horon the lower. 14 The border extended, and turned around on the west quarter southward, from the mountain that lies before Beth Horon southward; and ended at Kiriath Baal (also called Kiriath Jearim), a city of the children of Judah. This was the west quarter. 15 The south quarter was from the farthest part of Kiriath Jearim. The border went out westward, and went out to the spring of the waters of Nephtoah. 16 The border went down to the farthest part of the mountain that lies before the valley of the son of Hinnom, which is in the valley of Rephaim northward. It went down to the valley of Hinnom, to the side of the Jebusite southward, and went down to En Rogel. 17 It extended northward, went out at En Shemesh, and went out to Geliloth, which is opposite the ascent of Adummim. It went down to the stone of Bohan the son of Reuben. 18 It passed along to the side opposite the Arabah northward, and went down to the Arabah. 19 The border passed along to the side of Beth Hoglah northward; and the border ended at the north bay of the

Salt Sea, at the south end of the Jordan. This was the south border. 20 The Jordan was its border on the east quarter. This was the inheritance of the children of Benjamin, by the borders around it, according to their families. 21 Now the cities of the tribe of the children of Benjamin according to their families were Jericho, Beth Hoglah, Emek Keziz, 22 Beth Arabah, Zemaraim, Bethel, 23 Avvim, Parah, Ophrah, 24 Chephar Ammoni, Ophni, and Geba; twelve cities with their villages. 25 Gibeon, Ramah, Beeroth, 26 Mizpeh, Chephirah, Mozah, 27 Rekem, Irpeel, Taralah, 28 Zelah, Eleph, the Jebusite (also called Jerusalem), Gibeath, and Kiriath; fourteen cities with their villages. This is the inheritance of the children of Benjamin according to their families.

19

1 The second lot came out for Simeon, even for the tribe of the children of Simeon according to their families. Their inheritance was in the middle of the inheritance of the children of Judah. 2 They had for their inheritance Beersheba (or Sheba), Moladah, 3 Hazar Shual, Balah, Ezem, 4 Eltolad, Bethul, Hormah, 5 Ziklag, Beth Marcaboth, Hazar Susah, 6 Beth Lebaoth, and Sharuhen; thirteen cities with their villages; 7 Ain, Rimmon, Ether, and Ashan; four cities with their villages; 8 and all the villages that were around these cities to Baalath Beer, Ramah of the South. This is the inheritance of the tribe of the children of Simeon according to their families. 9 Out of the part of the children of Judah was the inheritance of the children of Simeon; for the portion of the children of Judah was too much for them. Therefore the children of Simeon had inheritance in the middle of their inheritance.

10 The third lot came up for the children of Zebulun according to their families. The border of their inheritance was to Sarid. 11 Their border went up westward, even to Maralah, and reached to Dabbesheth. It reached to the brook that is before Jokneam. 12 It turned from Sarid eastward towards the sunrise to the border of Chisloth Tabor. It went out to Daberath, and went up to Japhia. 13 From there it passed along eastward to Gath Hepher, to Ethkazin; and it went out at Rimmon which stretches to Neah. 14 The border turned around it on the north to Hannathon; and it ended at the valley of Iphtah El; 15 Kattath, Nahalal, Shimron, Idalah, and Bethlehem: twelve cities with their villages. 16 This is the inheritance of the children of Zebulun according to their families, these cities with their villages.

17 The fourth lot came out for Issachar, even for the children of Issachar according to their families. 18 Their border was to Jezreel, Chesulloth, Shunem, 19 Hapharaim, Shion, Anaharath, 20 Rabbith, Kishion, Ebez, 21 Remeth, Engannim, En Haddah, and Beth Pazzez. 22 The border reached to Tabor, Shahazumah, and Beth Shemesh. Their border ended at the Jordan: sixteen cities with their villages. 23 This is the inheritance of the tribe of the children of Issachar according to their families, the cities with their villages.

24 The fifth lot came out for the tribe of the children of Asher according to their families. 25 Their border was Helkath, Hali, Beten, Achshaph, 26 Allammelech, Amad, Mishal. It reached to Carmel westward, and to Shihorlibnath. 27 It turned towards the sunrise to Beth Dagon, and reached to Zebulun, and to the valley of Iphtah El northward to Beth Emek and Neiel. It went out to Cabul on the left hand, 28 and Ebron, Rehob, Hammon, and Kanah, even to great Sidon. 29 The border turned to Ramah, to the fortified city of Tyre; and the border turned to Hosah. It ended at the sea by the region of Achzib; 30 Ummah also, and Aphek, and Rehob: twenty-two cities with their villages. 31 This is the inheritance of the tribe of the children of Asher according to their families, these cities with their villages.

32 The sixth lot came out for the children of Naphtali, even for the children of Naphtali according to their families. 33 Their border was from Heleph, from the oak in Zaanannim, Adami-nekeb, and Jabneel, to Lakkum. It ended at the Jordan. 34 The border turned westward to Aznoth Tabor, and went out from there to Hukkok. It reached to Zebulun on the south, and reached to Asher on the west, and to Judah at the Jordan towards the sunrise. 35 The fortified cities were Ziddim, Zer, Hammath, Rakkath, Chinnereth, 36 Adamah, Ramah, Hazor, 37 Kedesh, Edrei, En Hazor, 38 Iron, Migdal El, Horem, Beth Anath, and Beth Shemesh; nineteen cities with their villages. 39 This is the inheritance of the tribe of the children of Naphtali according to their families, the cities with their villages.

40 The seventh lot came out for the tribe of the children of Dan according to their families. 41 The border of their inheritance was Zorah, Eshtaol, Irshemesh, 42 Shaalabbin, Aijalon, Ithlah, 43 Elon, Timnah, Ekron, 44 Eltekeh, Gibbethon, Baalath, 45 Jehud, Bene Berak, Gath Rimmon, 46 Me Jarkon, and Rakkon, with the border opposite Joppa. 47 The border of the children of Dan went out beyond them; for the children of Dan went up and fought against Leshem, and took it, and struck it with the edge of the sword, and possessed it, and lived therein, and called Leshem, Dan, after the name of Dan their forefather. 48 This is the inheritance of the tribe of the children of Dan according to their families, these cities with their villages.

49 So they finished distributing the land for inheritance by its borders. The children of Israel gave an inheritance to Joshua the son of Nun amongst them. 50 According to the LORD's commandment, they gave him the city which he asked, even Timnathserah in the hill country of Ephraim; and he built the city, and lived there. 51 These are the inheritances, which Eleazar the priest, Joshua the son of Nun, and the heads of the fathers' houses of the tribes of the children of Israel, distributed for inheritance by lot in Shiloh before the LORD, at the door of the Tent of Meeting. So they finished dividing the land.

20

1 The LORD spoke to Joshua, saying, 2 "Speak to the children of Israel, saying, 'Assign the cities of refuge, of which I spoke to you by Moses, 3 that the man slayer who kills any person accidentally or unintentionally may flee there. They shall be to you for a refuge from the avenger of blood. 4 He shall flee to one of those cities, and shall stand at the entrance of the gate of the city, and declare his case in the ears of the elders of that city. They shall take him into the city with them, and give him a place, that he may live amongst them. 5 If the avenger of blood pursues him, then they shall not deliver up the man slayer into his hand; because he struck his neighbour unintentionally, and didn't hate him before. 6 He shall dwell in that city until he stands before the congregation for judgement, until the death of the high priest that shall be in those days. Then the man slayer shall return, and come to his own city, and to his own house, to the city he fled from.'"

7 They set apart Kedesh in Galilee in the hill country of Naphtali, Shechem in the hill country of Ephraim, and Kiriath Arba (also called Hebron) in the hill country of Judah. 8 Beyond the Jordan at Jericho eastward, they assigned Bezer in the wilderness in the plain out of the tribe of Reuben, Ramoth in Gilead out of the tribe of Gad, and Golan in Bashan out of the tribe of Manasseh. 9 These were the appointed cities for all the children of Israel, and for the alien who lives amongst them, that whoever kills any person unintentionally might flee there, and not die by the hand of the avenger of blood, until he stands trial before the congregation.

21

1 Then the heads of fathers' houses of the Levites came near to Eleazar the priest, and to Joshua the son of Nun, and to the heads of fathers' houses of the tribes of the children of Israel. 2 They spoke to them at Shiloh in the land of Canaan, saying, "The LORD commanded through Moses to give us cities to dwell in, with their pasture lands for our livestock."

3 The children of Israel gave to the Levites out of their inheritance, according to the commandment of the LORD, these cities with their pasture lands. 4 The lot came out for the families of the Kohathites. The children of Aaron the priest, who were of the Levites, had thirteen cities by lot out of the tribe of Judah, out of the tribe of the Simeonites, and out of the tribe of Benjamin. 5 The rest of the children of Kohath had ten cities by lot out of the families of the tribe of Ephraim, out of the tribe of Dan, and out of the half-tribe of Manasseh. 6 The children of Gershon had thirteen cities by lot out of the families of the tribe of Issachar, out of the tribe of Asher, out of the tribe of Naphtali, and out of the half-tribe of Manasseh in Bashan. 7 The children of Merari according to their families had twelve cities out of the tribe of Reuben, out of the tribe of Gad, and out of the tribe of Zebulun. 8 The children of Israel gave these cities with their pasture lands by lot to the Levites, as the LORD commanded by Moses. 9 They gave out of the tribe of the children of Judah, and out of the tribe of the children of Simeon, these cities which are mentioned by name: 10 and they were for the children of Aaron, of the families of the Kohathites, who were of the children of Levi; for theirs was the first lot. 11 They gave them Kiriath Arba, named after the father of Anak (also called Hebron), in the hill country of Judah, with its pasture lands around it. 12 But they gave the fields of the city and its villages to Caleb the son of Jephunneh for his possession. 13 To the children of Aaron the priest they gave Hebron with its pasture lands, the city of refuge for the man slayer, Libnah with its pasture lands, 14 Jattir with its pasture lands, Eshtemoa with its pasture lands, 15 Holon with its pasture lands, Debir with its pasture lands, 16 Ain with its pasture lands, Juttah with its pasture lands, and Beth Shemesh with its pasture lands: nine cities out of those two tribes. 17 Out of the tribe of Benjamin, Gibeon with its pasture lands, Geba with its pasture lands, 18 Anathoth with its pasture lands, and Almon with its pasture lands: four cities. 19 All the cities of the children of Aaron, the priests, were thirteen cities with their pasture lands.

20 The families of the children of Kohath, the Levites, even the rest of the children of Kohath, had the cities of their lot out of the tribe of Ephraim. 21 They gave them Shechem with its pasture lands in the hill country of Ephraim, the city of refuge for the man slayer, and Gezer with its pasture lands, 22 Kibzaim with its pasture lands, and Beth Horon with its pasture lands: four cities. 23 Out of the tribe of Dan, Elteke with its pasture lands, Gibbethon with its pasture lands, 24 Aijalon with its pasture lands, Gath Rimmon with its pasture lands: four cities. 25 Out of the half-tribe of Manasseh, Taanach with its pasture lands, and Gath Rimmon with its pasture lands: two cities. 26 All the cities of the families of the rest of the children of Kohath were ten with their pasture lands.

27 They gave to the children of Gershon, of the families of the Levites, out of the half-tribe of Manasseh Golan in Bashan with its pasture lands, the city of refuge for the man slayer, and Be Eshterah with its pasture lands: two cities. 28 Out of the tribe of Issachar, Kishion with its pasture lands, Daberath with its pasture lands, 29 Jarmuth with its pasture lands, En Gannim with its pasture lands: four cities. 30 Out of the tribe of Asher, Mishal with its pasture lands, Abdon with its pasture lands, 31 Helkath with its pasture lands, and Rehob with its pasture lands: four cities. 32 Out of the tribe of Naphtali, Kedesh in Galilee with its pasture lands, the city of refuge for the man slayer, Hammothdor with its pasture lands, and Kartan with its pasture lands: three cities. 33 All the cities of the Gershonites according to their families were thirteen cities with their pasture lands.

34 To the families of the children of Merari, the rest of the Levites, out of the tribe of Zebulun, Jokneam with its pasture lands, Kartah with its pasture lands, 35 Dimnah with its pasture lands, and Nahalal with its pasture lands: four cities. 36 Out of the tribe of Reuben, Bezer with its

pasture lands, Jahaz with its pasture lands, 37 Kedemoth with its pasture lands, and Mephaath with its pasture lands: four cities. 38 Out of the tribe of Gad, Ramoth in Gilead with its pasture lands, the city of refuge for the man slayer, and Mahanaim with its pasture lands, 39 Heshbon with its pasture lands, Jazer with its pasture lands: four cities in all. 40 All these were the cities of the children of Merari according to their families, even the rest of the families of the Levites. Their lot was twelve cities.

41 All the cities of the Levites amongst the possessions of the children of Israel were forty-eight cities with their pasture lands. 42 Each of these cities included their pasture lands around them. It was this way with all these cities.

43 So the LORD gave to Israel all the land which he swore to give to their fathers. They possessed it, and lived in it. 44 The LORD gave them rest all around, according to all that he swore to their fathers. Not a man of all their enemies stood before them. The LORD delivered all their enemies into their hand. 45 Nothing failed of any good thing which the LORD had spoken to the house of Israel. All came to pass.

22

1 Then Joshua called the Reubenites, the Gadites, and the half-tribe of Manasseh, 2 and said to them, "You have kept all that Moses the servant of the LORD commanded you, and have listened to my voice in all that I commanded you. 3 You have not left your brothers these many days to this day, but have performed the duty of the commandment of the LORD your God. 4 Now the LORD your God has given rest to your brothers, as he spoke to them. Therefore now return and go to your tents, to the land of your possession, which Moses the servant of the LORD gave you beyond the Jordan. 5 Only take diligent heed to do the commandment and the law which Moses the servant of the LORD commanded you, to love the LORD your God, to walk in all his ways, to keep his commandments, to hold fast to him, and to serve him with all your heart and with all your soul."

6 So Joshua blessed them, and sent them away; and they went to their tents. 7 Now to the one half-tribe of Manasseh Moses had given inheritance in Bashan; but Joshua gave to the other half amongst their brothers beyond the Jordan westward. Moreover when Joshua sent them away to their tents, he blessed them, 8 and spoke to them, saying, "Return with much wealth to your tents, with very much livestock, with silver, with gold, with bronze, with iron, and with very much clothing. Divide the plunder of your enemies with your brothers."

9 The children of Reuben and the children of Gad and the half-tribe of Manasseh returned, and departed from the children of Israel out of Shiloh, which is in the land of Canaan, to go to the land of Gilead, to the land of their possession, which they owned, according to the commandment of the LORD by Moses. 10 When they came to the region near the Jordan, that is in the land of Canaan, the children of Reuben and the children of Gad and the half-tribe of Manasseh built an altar there by the Jordan, a great altar to look at. 11 The children of Israel heard this, "Behold, the children of Reuben and the children of Gad and the half-tribe of Manasseh have built an altar along the border of the land of Canaan, in the region around the Jordan, on the side that belongs to the children of Israel." 12 When the children of Israel heard of it, the whole congregation of the children of Israel gathered themselves together at Shiloh, to go up against them to war. 13 The children of Israel sent to the children of Reuben, and to the children of Gad, and to the half-tribe of Manasseh, into the land of Gilead, Phinehas the son of Eleazar the priest. 14 With him were ten princes, one prince of a fathers' house for each of the tribes of Israel; and they were each head of their fathers' houses amongst the thousands of Israel. 15 They came to the children of Reuben, and to the children of Gad, and to the half-tribe of Manasseh, to the land of Gilead, and they spoke with them, saying, 16 "The whole congregation of the LORD says, 'What trespass is this that you have committed against the God of Israel, to turn away today from following the LORD, in that you have built yourselves an altar, to rebel today against the LORD? 17 Is the iniquity of Peor too little for us, from which we have not cleansed ourselves to this day, although there came a plague on the congregation of the LORD, 18 that you must turn away today from following the LORD? It will be, since you rebel today against the LORD, that tomorrow he will be angry with the whole congregation of Israel. 19 However, if the land of your possession is unclean, then pass over to the land of the possession of the LORD, in which the LORD's tabernacle dwells, and take possession amongst us; but don't rebel against the LORD, nor rebel against us, in building an altar other than the LORD our God's altar. 20 Didn't Achan the son of Zerah commit a trespass in the devoted thing, and wrath fell on all the congregation of Israel? That man didn't perish alone in his iniquity.'"

21 Then the children of Reuben and the children of Gad and the half-tribe of Manasseh answered, and spoke to the heads of the thousands of Israel, 22 "The Mighty One, God, the LORD, the Mighty One, God, the LORD, he knows; and Israel shall know: if it was in rebellion, or if in trespass against the LORD (don't save us today), 23 that we have built us an altar to turn away from following the LORD; or if to offer burnt offering or meal offering, or if to offer sacrifices of peace offerings, let the LORD himself require it.

24 "If we have not out of concern done this, and for a reason, saying, 'In time to come your children might speak to our children, saying, "What have you to do with the LORD, the God of Israel? 25 For the LORD has made the Jordan a border between us and you, you children of Reuben and

children of Gad. You have no portion in the LORD.'" So your children might make our children cease from fearing the LORD.

26 "Therefore we said, 'Let's now prepare to build ourselves an altar, not for burnt offering, nor for sacrifice; 27 but it will be a witness between us and you, and between our generations after us, that we may perform the service of the LORD before him with our burnt offerings, with our sacrifices, and with our peace offerings;' that your children may not tell our children in time to come, 'You have no portion in the LORD.'

28 "Therefore we said, 'It shall be, when they tell us or our generations this in time to come, that we shall say, "Behold the pattern of the LORD's altar, which our fathers made, not for burnt offering, nor for sacrifice; but it is a witness between us and you."'

29 "Far be it from us that we should rebel against the LORD, and turn away today from following the LORD, to build an altar for burnt offering, for meal offering, or for sacrifice, besides the LORD our God's altar that is before his tabernacle!"

30 When Phinehas the priest, and the princes of the congregation, even the heads of the thousands of Israel that were with him, heard the words that the children of Reuben and the children of Gad and the children of Manasseh spoke, it pleased them well. 31 Phinehas the son of Eleazar the priest said to the children of Reuben, to the children of Gad, and to the children of Manasseh, "Today we know that the LORD is amongst us, because you have not committed this trespass against the LORD. Now you have delivered the children of Israel out of the LORD's hand." 32 Phinehas the son of Eleazar the priest, and the princes, returned from the children of Reuben, and from the children of Gad, out of the land of Gilead, to the land of Canaan, to the children of Israel, and brought them word again. 33 The thing pleased the children of Israel; and the children of Israel blessed God, and spoke no more of going up against them to war, to destroy the land in which the children of Reuben and the children of Gad lived. 34 The children of Reuben and the children of Gad named the altar "A Witness Between Us that the LORD is God."

23

1 After many days, when the LORD had given rest to Israel from their enemies all around, and Joshua was old and well advanced in years, 2 Joshua called for all Israel, for their elders and for their heads, and for their judges and for their officers, and said to them, "I am old and well advanced in years. 3 You have seen all that the LORD your God has done to all these nations because of you; for it is the LORD your God who has fought for you. 4 Behold, I have allotted to you these nations that remain, to be an inheritance for your tribes, from the Jordan, with all the nations that I have cut off, even to the great sea towards the going down of the sun. 5 The LORD your God will thrust them out from before you, and drive them from out of your sight. You shall possess their land, as the LORD your God spoke to you.

6 "Therefore be very courageous to keep and to do all that is written in the book of the law of Moses, that you not turn away from it to the right hand or to the left; 7 that you not come amongst these nations, these that remain amongst you; neither make mention of the name of their gods, nor cause to swear by them, neither serve them, nor bow down yourselves to them; 8 but hold fast to the LORD your God, as you have done to this day.

9 "For the LORD has driven great and strong nations out from before you. But as for you, no man has stood before you to this day. 10 One man of you shall chase a thousand; for it is the LORD your God who fights for you, as he spoke to you. 11 Take good heed therefore to yourselves, that you love the LORD your God.

12 "But if you do at all go back, and hold fast to the remnant of these nations, even these who remain amongst you, and make marriages with them, and go in to them, and they to you; 13 know for a certainty that the LORD your God will no longer drive these nations from out of your sight; but they shall be a snare and a trap to you, a scourge in your sides, and thorns in your eyes, until you perish from off this good land which the LORD your God has given you.

14 "Behold, today I am going the way of all the earth. You know in all your hearts and in all your souls that not one thing has failed of all the good things which the LORD your God spoke concerning you. All have happened to you. Not one thing has failed of it. 15 It shall happen that as all the good things have come on you of which the LORD your God spoke to you, so the LORD will bring on you all the evil things, until he has destroyed you from off this good land which the LORD your God has given you, 16 when you disobey the covenant of the LORD your God, which he commanded you, and go and serve other gods, and bow down yourselves to them. Then the LORD's anger will be kindled against you, and you will perish quickly from off the good land which he has given to you."

24

1 Joshua gathered all the tribes of Israel to Shechem, and called for the elders of Israel, for their heads, for their judges, and for their officers; and they presented themselves before God. 2 Joshua said to all the people, "The LORD, the God of Israel, says, 'Your fathers lived of old time beyond the River, even Terah, the father of Abraham, and the father of Nahor. They served other gods. 3 I took your father Abraham from beyond the River, and led him throughout all the land of Canaan, and multiplied his offspring,[a] and gave him Isaac. 4 I gave to Isaac Jacob and Esau: and I gave to Esau Mount Seir, to possess it. Jacob and his children went down into Egypt.

5 "'I sent Moses and Aaron, and I plagued Egypt, according to that which I did amongst them: and afterward I brought you out. 6 I brought

---

a 24:3 or, seed

your fathers out of Egypt: and you came to the sea. The Egyptians pursued your fathers with chariots and with horsemen to the Red Sea. ⁷ When they cried out to the LORD, he put darkness between you and the Egyptians, and brought the sea on them, and covered them; and your eyes saw what I did in Egypt. You lived in the wilderness many days.

⁸ "'I brought you into the land of the Amorites, that lived beyond the Jordan. They fought with you, and I gave them into your hand. You possessed their land, and I destroyed them from before you. ⁹ Then Balak the son of Zippor, king of Moab, arose and fought against Israel. He sent and called Balaam the son of Beor to curse you, ¹⁰ but I would not listen to Balaam; therefore he blessed you still. So I delivered you out of his hand.

¹¹ "'You went over the Jordan, and came to Jericho. The men of Jericho fought against you, the Amorite, the Perizzite, the Canaanite, the Hittite, the Girgashite, the Hivite, and the Jebusite; and I delivered them into your hand. ¹² I sent the hornet before you, which drove them out from before you, even the two kings of the Amorites; not with your sword, nor with your bow. ¹³ I gave you a land on which you had not laboured, and cities which you didn't build, and you live in them. You eat of vineyards and olive groves which you didn't plant.'

¹⁴ "Now therefore fear the LORD, and serve him in sincerity and in truth. Put away the gods which your fathers served beyond the River, in Egypt; and serve the LORD. ¹⁵ If it seems evil to you to serve the LORD, choose today whom you will serve; whether the gods which your fathers served that were beyond the River, or the gods of the Amorites, in whose land you dwell; but as for me and my house, we will serve the LORD."

¹⁶ The people answered, "Far be it from us that we should forsake the LORD, to serve other gods; ¹⁷ for it is the LORD our God who brought us and our fathers up out of the land of Egypt, from the house of bondage, and who did those great signs in our sight, and preserved us in all the way in which we went, and amongst all the peoples through the middle of whom we passed. ¹⁸ The LORD drove out from before us all the peoples, even the Amorites who lived in the land. Therefore we also will serve the LORD; for he is our God."

¹⁹ Joshua said to the people, "You can't serve the LORD, for he is a holy God. He is a jealous God. He will not forgive your disobedience nor your sins. ²⁰ If you forsake the LORD, and serve foreign gods, then he will turn and do you evil, and consume you, after he has done you good."

²¹ The people said to Joshua, "No, but we will serve the LORD." ²² Joshua said to the people, "You are witnesses against yourselves that you have chosen the LORD yourselves, to serve him."

They said, "We are witnesses."

²³ "Now therefore put away the foreign gods which are amongst you, and incline your heart to the LORD, the God of Israel."

²⁴ The people said to Joshua, "We will serve the LORD our God, and we will listen to his voice."

²⁵ So Joshua made a covenant with the people that day, and made for them a statute and an ordinance in Shechem. ²⁶ Joshua wrote these words in the book of the law of God; and he took a great stone, and set it up there under the oak that was by the sanctuary of the LORD. ²⁷ Joshua said to all the people, "Behold, this stone shall be a witness against us, for it has heard all the LORD's words which he spoke to us. It shall be therefore a witness against you, lest you deny your God." ²⁸ So Joshua sent the people away, each to his own inheritance.

²⁹ After these things, Joshua the son of Nun, the servant of the LORD, died, being one hundred and ten years old. ³⁰ They buried him in the border of his inheritance in Timnathserah, which is in the hill country of Ephraim, on the north of the mountain of Gaash. ³¹ Israel served the LORD all the days of Joshua, and all the days of the elders who outlived Joshua, and had known all the work of the LORD, that he had worked for Israel. ³² They buried the bones of Joseph, which the children of Israel brought up out of Egypt, in Shechem, in the parcel of ground which Jacob bought from the sons of Hamor the father of Shechem for a hundred pieces of silver.ᵃ They became the inheritance of the children of Joseph. ³³ Eleazar the son of Aaron died. They buried him in the hill of Phinehas his son, which was given him in the hill country of Ephraim.

ᵃ *24:32* Hebrew: kesitahs. A kesitah was a kind of silver coin.

The Book of Judges

1

1 After the death of Joshua, the children of Israel asked of the LORD,[a] saying, "Who should go up for us first against the Canaanites, to fight against them?"

2 The LORD said, "Judah shall go up. Behold,[b] I have delivered the land into his hand."

3 Judah said to Simeon his brother, "Come up with me into my lot, that we may fight against the Canaanites; and I likewise will go with you into your lot." So Simeon went with him. 4 Judah went up, and the LORD delivered the Canaanites and the Perizzites into their hand. They struck ten thousand men in Bezek. 5 They found Adoni-Bezek in Bezek, and they fought against him. They struck the Canaanites and the Perizzites. 6 But Adoni-Bezek fled. They pursued him, caught him, and cut off his thumbs and his big toes. 7 Adoni-Bezek said, "Seventy kings, having their thumbs and their big toes cut off, scavenged under my table. As I have done, so God[c] has done to me." They brought him to Jerusalem, and he died there. 8 The children of Judah fought against Jerusalem, took it, struck it with the edge of the sword, and set the city on fire.

9 After that, the children of Judah went down to fight against the Canaanites who lived in the hill country, and in the South, and in the lowland. 10 Judah went against the Canaanites who lived in Hebron. (The name of Hebron before that was Kiriath Arba.) They struck Sheshai, Ahiman, and Talmai.

11 From there he went against the inhabitants of Debir. (The name of Debir before that was Kiriath Sepher.) 12 Caleb said, "I will give Achsah my daughter as wife to the man who strikes Kiriath Sepher, and takes it." 13 Othniel the son of Kenaz, Caleb's younger brother, took it, so he gave him Achsah his daughter as his wife.

14 When she came, she got him to ask her father for a field. She got off her donkey; and Caleb said to her, "What would you like?"

15 She said to him, "Give me a blessing; because you have set me in the land of the South, give me also springs of water." Then Caleb gave her the upper springs and the lower springs. 16 The children of the Kenite, Moses' brother-in-law, went up out of the city of palm trees with the children of Judah into the wilderness of Judah, which is in the south of Arad; and they went and lived with the people. 17 Judah went with Simeon his brother, and they struck the Canaanites who inhabited Zephath, and utterly destroyed it. The name of the city was called Hormah. 18 Also Judah took Gaza with its border, and Ashkelon with its border, and Ekron with its border. 19 The LORD was with Judah, and drove out the inhabitants of the hill country; for he could not drive out the inhabitants of the valley, because they had chariots of iron. 20 They gave Hebron to Caleb, as Moses had said, and he drove the three sons of Anak out of there. 21 The children of Benjamin didn't drive out the Jebusites who inhabited Jerusalem, but the Jebusites dwell with the children of Benjamin in Jerusalem to this day.

22 The house of Joseph also went up against Bethel, and the LORD was with them. 23 The house of Joseph sent to spy out Bethel. (The name of the city before that was Luz.) 24 The watchers saw a man come out of the city, and they said to him, "Please show us the entrance into the city, and we will deal kindly with you." 25 He showed them the entrance into the city, and they struck the city with the edge of the sword; but they let the man and all his family go. 26 The man went into the land of the Hittites, built a city, and called its name Luz, which is its name to this day.

27 Manasseh didn't drive out the inhabitants of Beth Shean and its towns, nor Taanach and its towns, nor the inhabitants of Dor and its towns, nor the inhabitants of Ibleam and its towns, nor the inhabitants of Megiddo and its towns; but the Canaanites would dwell in that land. 28 When Israel had grown strong, they put the Canaanites to forced labour, and didn't utterly drive them out. 29 Ephraim didn't drive out the Canaanites who lived in Gezer, but the Canaanites lived in Gezer amongst them. 30 Zebulun didn't drive out the inhabitants of Kitron, nor the inhabitants of Nahalol; but the Canaanites lived amongst them, and became subject to forced labour. 31 Asher didn't drive out the inhabitants of Acco, nor the inhabitants of Sidon, nor of Ahlab, nor of Achzib, nor of Helbah, nor of Aphik, nor of Rehob; 32 but the Asherites lived amongst the Canaanites, the inhabitants of the land, for they didn't drive them out. 33 Naphtali didn't drive out the inhabitants of Beth Shemesh, nor the inhabitants of Beth Anath; but he lived amongst the Canaanites, the inhabitants of the land. Nevertheless the inhabitants of Beth Shemesh and of Beth Anath became subject to forced labour. 34 The Amorites forced the children of Dan into the hill country, for they would not allow them to come down to the valley; 35 but the Amorites would dwell in Mount Heres, in Aijalon, and in Shaalbim. Yet the hand of the house of Joseph prevailed, so that they became subject to forced labour. 36 The border of the Amorites was from the ascent of Akrabbim, from the rock, and upward.

2

1 The LORD's angel came up from Gilgal to Bochim. He said, "I brought you out of Egypt, and have brought you to the land which I swore to give your fathers. I said, 'I will never break my covenant with you. 2 You shall make no covenant with the inhabitants of this land. You shall break down their altars.' But you have not listened to my voice. Why have you done this? 3 Therefore I also said, 'I will not drive them out from before you; but they shall be in your sides, and their gods will be a snare to you.'"

4 When the LORD's angel spoke these words to all the children of Israel, the people lifted up their voice and wept. 5 They called the name of that place Bochim,[d] and they sacrificed there to the LORD. 6 Now when Joshua had sent the people away, the children of Israel each went to his inheritance to possess the land. 7 The people served the LORD all the days of Joshua, and all the days of the elders who outlived Joshua, who had seen all the great work of the LORD that he had worked for Israel. 8 Joshua the son of Nun, the servant of the LORD, died, being one hundred and ten years old. 9 They buried him in the border of his inheritance in Timnath Heres, in the hill country of Ephraim, on the north of the mountain of Gaash. 10 After all that generation were gathered to their fathers, another generation arose after them who didn't know the LORD, nor the work which he had done for Israel. 11 The children of Israel did that which was evil in the LORD's sight, and served the Baals. 12 They abandoned the LORD, the God of their fathers, who brought them out of the land of Egypt, and followed other gods, of the gods of the peoples who were around them, and bowed themselves down to them; and they provoked the LORD to anger. 13 They abandoned the LORD, and served Baal and the Ashtaroth. 14 The LORD's anger burnt against Israel, and he delivered them into the hands of raiders who plundered them. He sold them into the hands of their enemies all around, so that they could no longer stand before their enemies. 15 Wherever they went out, the LORD's hand was against them for evil, as the LORD had spoken, and as the LORD had sworn to them; and they were very distressed. 16 The LORD raised up judges, who saved them out of the hand of those who plundered them. 17 Yet they didn't listen to their judges; for they prostituted themselves to other gods, and bowed themselves down to them. They quickly turned away from the way in which their fathers walked, obeying the LORD's commandments. They didn't do so. 18 When the LORD raised up judges for them, then the LORD was with the judge, and saved them out of the hand of their enemies all the days of the judge; for it grieved the LORD because of their groaning by reason of those who oppressed them and troubled them. 19 But when the judge was dead, they turned back, and dealt more corruptly than their fathers in following other gods to serve them and to bow down to them. They didn't cease what they were doing, or give up their stubborn ways. 20 The LORD's anger burnt against Israel; and he said, "Because this nation transgressed my covenant which I commanded their fathers, and has not listened to my voice, 21 I also will no longer drive out any of the nations that Joshua left when he died from before them; 22 that by them I may test Israel, to see if they will keep the LORD's way to walk therein, as their fathers kept it, or not." 23 So the LORD left those nations, without driving them out hastily. He didn't deliver them into Joshua's hand.

3

1 Now these are the nations which the LORD left, to test Israel by them, even as many as had not known all the wars of Canaan; 2 only that the generations of the children of Israel might know, to teach them war, at least those who knew nothing of it before: 3 the five lords of the Philistines, all the Canaanites, the Sidonians, and the Hivites who lived on Mount Lebanon, from Mount Baal Hermon to the entrance of Hamath. 4 They were left to test Israel by them, to know whether they would listen to the LORD's commandments, which he commanded their fathers by Moses. 5 The children of Israel lived amongst the Canaanites, the Hittites, the Amorites, the Perizzites, the Hivites, and the Jebusites. 6 They took their daughters to be their wives, and gave their own daughters to their sons and served their gods. 7 The children of Israel did that which was evil in the LORD's sight, and forgot the LORD their God, and served the Baals and the Asheroth. 8 Therefore the LORD's anger burnt against Israel, and he sold them into the hand of Cushan Rishathaim king of Mesopotamia; and the children of Israel served Cushan Rishathaim eight years. 9 When the children of Israel cried to the LORD, the LORD raised up a saviour to the children of Israel, who saved them, even Othniel the son of Kenaz, Caleb's younger brother. 10 The LORD's Spirit came on him, and he judged Israel; and he went out to war, and the LORD delivered Cushan Rishathaim king of Mesopotamia into his hand. His hand prevailed against Cushan Rishathaim. 11 The land had rest forty years, then Othniel the son of Kenaz died.

12 The children of Israel again did that which was evil in the LORD's sight, and the LORD strengthened Eglon the king of Moab against Israel, because they had done that which was evil in the LORD's sight. 13 He gathered the children of Ammon and Amalek to himself; and he went and struck Israel, and they possessed the city of palm trees. 14 The children of Israel served Eglon the king of Moab eighteen years. 15 But when the children of Israel cried to the LORD, the LORD raised up a saviour for them: Ehud the son of Gera, the Benjamite, a left-handed man. The children of Israel sent tribute by him to Eglon the king of Moab. 16 Ehud made himself a sword which had two edges, a cubit[e] in length; and he wore it under his clothing on his right thigh. 17 He offered the tribute to Eglon king of Moab. Now Eglon was a very fat man. 18 When Ehud had finished offering the tribute, he sent away the people who carried the tribute. 19 But he himself

---

turned back from the stone idols that were by Gilgal, and said, "I have a secret message for you, O king."

The king said, "Keep silence!" All who stood by him left him.

20 Ehud came to him; and he was sitting by himself alone in the cool upper room. Ehud said, "I have a message from God to you." He arose out of his seat. 21 Ehud put out his left hand, and took the sword from his right thigh, and thrust it into his body. 22 The handle also went in after the blade; and the fat closed on the blade, for he didn't draw the sword out of his body; and it came out behind. 23 Then Ehud went out onto the porch, and shut the doors of the upper room on him, and locked them.

24 After he had gone, his servants came and saw that the doors of the upper room were locked. They said, "Surely he is covering his feet[a] in the upper room." 25 They waited until they were ashamed; and behold, he didn't open the doors of the upper room. Therefore they took the key and opened them, and behold, their lord had fallen down dead on the floor.

26 Ehud escaped while they waited, passed beyond the stone idols, and escaped to Seirah. 27 When he had come, he blew a trumpet in the hill country of Ephraim; and the children of Israel went down with him from the hill country, and he led them.

28 He said to them, "Follow me; for the LORD has delivered your enemies the Moabites into your hand." They followed him, and took the fords of the Jordan against the Moabites, and didn't allow any man to pass over. 29 They struck at that time about ten thousand men of Moab, every strong man and every man of valour. No man escaped. 30 So Moab was subdued that day under the hand of Israel. Then the land had rest eighty years.

31 After him was Shamgar the son of Anath, who struck six hundred men of the Philistines with an ox goad. He also saved Israel.

4

1 The children of Israel again did that which was evil in the LORD's sight, when Ehud was dead. 2 The LORD sold them into the hand of Jabin king of Canaan, who reigned in Hazor; the captain of whose army was Sisera, who lived in Harosheth of the Gentiles. 3 The children of Israel cried to the LORD, for he had nine hundred chariots of iron; and he mightily oppressed the children of Israel for twenty years. 4 Now Deborah, a prophetess, the wife of Lappidoth, judged Israel at that time. 5 She lived under Deborah's palm tree between Ramah and Bethel in the hill country of Ephraim; and the children of Israel came up to her for judgement. 6 She sent and called Barak the son of Abinoam out of Kedesh Naphtali, and said to him, "Hasn't the LORD, the God of Israel, commanded, 'Go and lead the way to Mount Tabor, and take with you ten thousand men of the children of Naphtali and of the children of Zebulun? 7 I will draw to you, to the river Kishon, Sisera, the captain of Jabin's army, with his chariots and his multitude; and I will deliver him into your hand.'"

8 Barak said to her, "If you will go with me, then I will go; but if you will not go with me, I will not go."

9 She said, "I will surely go with you. Nevertheless, the journey that you take won't be for your honour; for the LORD will sell Sisera into a woman's hand." Deborah arose, and went with Barak to Kedesh.

10 Barak called Zebulun and Naphtali together to Kedesh. Ten thousand men followed him; and Deborah went up with him. 11 Now Heber the Kenite had separated himself from the Kenites, even from the children of Hobab, Moses' brother-in-law, and had pitched his tent as far as the oak in Zaanannim, which is by Kedesh. 12 They told Sisera that Barak the son of Abinoam had gone up to Mount Tabor. 13 Sisera gathered together all his chariots, even nine hundred chariots of iron, and all the people who were with him, from Harosheth of the Gentiles, to the river Kishon.

14 Deborah said to Barak, "Go; for this is the day in which the LORD has delivered Sisera into your hand. Hasn't the LORD gone out before you?" So Barak went down from Mount Tabor, and ten thousand men after him. 15 The LORD confused Sisera, all his chariots, and all his army, with the edge of the sword before Barak. Sisera abandoned his chariot and fled away on his feet. 16 But Barak pursued the chariots and the army to Harosheth of the Gentiles; and all the army of Sisera fell by the edge of the sword. There was not a man left.

17 However Sisera fled away on his feet to the tent of Jael the wife of Heber the Kenite; for there was peace between Jabin the king of Hazor and the house of Heber the Kenite. 18 Jael went out to meet Sisera, and said to him, "Turn in, my lord, turn in to me; don't be afraid." He came in to her into the tent, and she covered him with a rug.

19 He said to her, "Please give me a little water to drink; for I am thirsty."

She opened a container of milk, and gave him a drink, and covered him.

20 He said to her, "Stand in the door of the tent, and if any man comes and enquires of you, and says, 'Is there any man here?' you shall say, 'No.'"

21 Then Jael, Heber's wife, took a tent peg, and took a hammer in her hand, and went softly to him, and struck the pin into his temples, and it pierced through into the ground, for he was in a deep sleep; so he fainted and died. 22 Behold, as Barak pursued Sisera, Jael came out to meet him, and said to him, "Come, and I will show you the man whom you seek." He came to her; and behold, Sisera lay dead, and the tent peg was in his temples. 23 So God subdued Jabin the king of Canaan before the children of Israel on that day. 24 The hand of the children of Israel prevailed more and more against Jabin the king of Canaan, until they had destroyed Jabin king of Canaan.

5

1 Then Deborah and Barak the son of Abinoam sang on that day, saying,

2 "Because the leaders took the lead in Israel,
because the people offered themselves willingly,
be blessed, LORD!

3 "Hear, you kings!
Give ear, you princes!
I, even I, will sing to the LORD.
I will sing praise to the LORD, the God of Israel.

4 "LORD, when you went out of Seir,
when you marched out of the field of Edom,
the earth trembled, the sky also dropped.
Yes, the clouds dropped water.
5 The mountains quaked at the LORD's presence,
even Sinai at the presence of the LORD, the God of Israel.

6 "In the days of Shamgar the son of Anath,
in the days of Jael, the highways were unoccupied.
The travellers walked through byways.
7 The rulers ceased in Israel.
They ceased until I, Deborah, arose;
Until I arose a mother in Israel.
8 They chose new gods.
Then war was in the gates.
Was there a shield or spear seen amongst forty thousand in Israel?
9 My heart is towards the governors of Israel,
who offered themselves willingly amongst the people.
Bless the LORD!

10 "Speak, you who ride on white donkeys,
you who sit on rich carpets,
and you who walk by the way.
11 Far from the noise of archers, in the places of drawing water,
there they will rehearse the LORD's righteous acts,
the righteous acts of his rule in Israel.

"Then the LORD's people went down to the gates.
12 'Awake, awake, Deborah!
Awake, awake, utter a song!
Arise, Barak, and lead away your captives, you son of Abinoam.'

13 "Then a remnant of the nobles and the people came down.
The LORD came down for me against the mighty.
14 Those whose root is in Amalek came out of Ephraim,
after you, Benjamin, amongst your peoples.
Governors come down out of Machir.
Those who handle the marshal's staff came out of Zebulun.
15 The princes of Issachar were with Deborah.
As was Issachar, so was Barak.
They rushed into the valley at his feet.
By the watercourses of Reuben,
there were great resolves of heart.
16 Why did you sit amongst the sheepfolds?
To hear the whistling for the flocks?
At the watercourses of Reuben,
there were great searchings of heart.
17 Gilead lived beyond the Jordan.
Why did Dan remain in ships?
Asher sat still at the haven of the sea,
and lived by his creeks.
18 Zebulun was a people that jeopardised their lives to the death;
Naphtali also, on the high places of the field.

19 "The kings came and fought,
then the kings of Canaan fought at Taanach by the waters of Megiddo.
They took no plunder of silver.
20 From the sky the stars fought.
From their courses, they fought against Sisera.
21 The river Kishon swept them away,
that ancient river, the river Kishon.
My soul, march on with strength.
22 Then the horse hoofs stamped because of the prancing,
the prancing of their strong ones.
23 'Curse Meroz,' said the LORD's angel.
'Curse bitterly its inhabitants,
because they didn't come to help the LORD,
to help the LORD against the mighty.'

24 "Jael shall be blessed above women,
the wife of Heber the Kenite;
blessed shall she be above women in the tent.
25 He asked for water.
She gave him milk.

She brought him butter in a lordly dish.
26 She put her hand to the tent peg,
  and her right hand to the workmen's hammer.
With the hammer she struck Sisera.
  She struck through his head.
  Yes, she pierced and struck through his temples.
27 At her feet he bowed, he fell, he lay.
  At her feet he bowed, he fell.
  Where he bowed, there he fell down dead.

28 "Through the window she looked out, and cried:
  Sisera's mother looked through the lattice.
'Why is his chariot so long in coming?
  Why do the wheels of his chariots wait?'
29 Her wise ladies answered her,
  Yes, she returned answer to herself,
30 'Have they not found, have they not divided the plunder?
  A lady, two ladies to every man;
to Sisera a plunder of dyed garments,
  a plunder of dyed garments embroidered,
  of dyed garments embroidered on both sides, on the necks of the
    plunder?'

31 "So let all your enemies perish, LORD,
  but let those who love him be as the sun when it rises in its strength."

Then the land had rest forty years.

6

1 The children of Israel did that which was evil in the LORD's sight, so the LORD delivered them into the hand of Midian seven years. 2 The hand of Midian prevailed against Israel; and because of Midian the children of Israel made themselves the dens which are in the mountains, the caves, and the strongholds. 3 So it was, when Israel had sown, that the Midianites, the Amalekites, and the children of the east came up against them. 4 They encamped against them, and destroyed the increase of the earth, until you come to Gaza. They left no sustenance in Israel, and no sheep, ox, or donkey. 5 For they came up with their livestock and their tents. They came in as locusts for multitude. Both they and their camels were without number; and they came into the land to destroy it. 6 Israel was brought very low because of Midian; and the children of Israel cried to the LORD.

7 When the children of Israel cried to the LORD because of Midian, 8 The LORD sent a prophet to the children of Israel; and he said to them, "The LORD, the God of Israel, says, 'I brought you up from Egypt, and brought you out of the house of bondage. 9 I delivered you out of the hand of the Egyptians and out of the hand of all who oppressed you, and drove them out from before you, and gave you their land. 10 I said to you, "I am the LORD your God. You shall not fear the gods of the Amorites, in whose land you dwell." But you have not listened to my voice.'"

11 The LORD's angel came and sat under the oak which was in Ophrah, that belonged to Joash the Abiezrite. His son Gideon was beating out wheat in the wine press, to hide it from the Midianites. 12 The LORD's angel appeared to him, and said to him, "The LORD is with you, you mighty man of valour!"

13 Gideon said to him, "Oh, my lord, if the LORD is with us, why then has all this happened to us? Where are all his wondrous works which our fathers told us of, saying, 'Didn't the LORD bring us up from Egypt?' But now the LORD has cast us off, and delivered us into the hand of Midian."

14 The LORD looked at him, and said, "Go in this your might, and save Israel from the hand of Midian. Haven't I sent you?"

15 He said to him, "O Lord,[a] how shall I save Israel? Behold, my family is the poorest in Manasseh, and I am the least in my father's house."

16 The LORD said to him, "Surely I will be with you, and you shall strike the Midianites as one man."

17 He said to him, "If now I have found favour in your sight, then show me a sign that it is you who talk with me. 18 Please don't go away until I come to you, and bring out my present, and lay it before you."

He said, "I will wait until you come back."

19 Gideon went in and prepared a young goat and unleavened cakes of an ephah[b] of meal. He put the meat in a basket and he put the broth in a pot, and brought it out to him under the oak, and presented it.

20 The angel of God said to him, "Take the meat and the unleavened cakes, and lay them on this rock, and pour out the broth."

He did so. 21 Then the LORD's angel stretched out the end of the staff that was in his hand, and touched the meat and the unleavened cakes; and fire went up out of the rock and consumed the meat and the unleavened cakes. Then the LORD's angel departed out of his sight.

22 Gideon saw that he was the LORD's angel; and Gideon said, "Alas, Lord GOD! Because I have seen the LORD's angel face to face!"

23 The LORD said to him, "Peace be to you! Don't be afraid. You shall not die."

24 Then Gideon built an altar there to the LORD, and called it "The LORD is Peace."[c] To this day it is still in Ophrah of the Abiezrites.

25 That same night, the LORD said to him, "Take your father's bull, even the second bull seven years old, and throw down the altar of Baal that your father has, and cut down the Asherah that is by it. 26 Then build an altar to the LORD your God on the top of this stronghold, in an orderly way, and take the second bull, and offer a burnt offering with the wood of the Asherah which you shall cut down."

27 Then Gideon took ten men of his servants, and did as the LORD had spoken to him. Because he feared his father's household and the men of the city, he could not do it by day, but he did it by night.

28 When the men of the city arose early in the morning, behold, the altar of Baal was broken down, and the Asherah was cut down that was by it, and the second bull was offered on the altar that was built. 29 They said to one another, "Who has done this thing?"

When they enquired and asked, they said, "Gideon the son of Joash has done this thing."

30 Then the men of the city said to Joash, "Bring out your son, that he may die, because he has broken down the altar of Baal, and because he has cut down the Asherah that was by it." 31 Joash said to all who stood against him, "Will you contend for Baal? Or will you save him? He who will contend for him, let him be put to death by morning! If he is a god, let him contend for himself, because someone has broken down his altar!" 32 Therefore on that day he named him Jerub-Baal,[d] saying, "Let Baal contend against him, because he has broken down his altar."

33 Then all the Midianites and the Amalekites and the children of the east assembled themselves together; and they passed over, and encamped in the valley of Jezreel. 34 But the LORD's Spirit came on Gideon, and he blew a trumpet; and Abiezer was gathered together to follow him. 35 He sent messengers throughout all Manasseh, and they also were gathered together to follow him. He sent messengers to Asher, to Zebulun, and to Naphtali; and they came up to meet them.

36 Gideon said to God, "If you will save Israel by my hand, as you have spoken, 37 behold, I will put a fleece of wool on the threshing floor. If there is dew on the fleece only, and it is dry on all the ground, then I'll know that you will save Israel by my hand, as you have spoken."

38 It was so; for he rose up early on the next day, and pressed the fleece together, and wrung the dew out of the fleece, a bowl full of water.

39 Gideon said to God, "Don't let your anger be kindled against me, and I will speak but this once. Please let me make a trial just this once with the fleece. Let it now be dry only on the fleece, and on all the ground let there be dew."

40 God did so that night; for it was dry on the fleece only, and there was dew on all the ground.

7

1 Then Jerubbaal, who is Gideon, and all the people who were with him, rose up early and encamped beside the spring of Harod. Midian's camp was on the north side of them, by the hill of Moreh, in the valley. 2 The LORD said to Gideon, "The people who are with you are too many for me to give the Midianites into their hand, lest Israel brag against me, saying, 'My own hand has saved me.' 3 Now therefore proclaim in the ears of the people, saying, 'Whoever is fearful and trembling, let him return and depart from Mount Gilead.'" So twenty-two thousand of the people returned, and ten thousand remained.

4 The LORD said to Gideon, "There are still too many people. Bring them down to the water, and I will test them for you there. It shall be, that those whom I tell you, 'This shall go with you,' shall go with you; and whoever I tell you, 'This shall not go with you,' shall not go." 5 So he brought down the people to the water; and the LORD said to Gideon, "Everyone who laps of the water with his tongue, like a dog laps, you shall set him by himself; likewise everyone who bows down on his knees to drink." 6 The number of those who lapped, putting their hand to their mouth, was three hundred men; but all the rest of the people bowed down on their knees to drink water. 7 The LORD said to Gideon, "I will save you by the three hundred men who lapped, and deliver the Midianites into your hand. Let all the other people go, each to his own place."

8 So the people took food in their hand, and their trumpets; and he sent all the rest of the men of Israel to their own tents, but retained the three hundred men; and the camp of Midian was beneath him in the valley. 9 That same night, the LORD said to him, "Arise, go down into the camp, for I have delivered it into your hand. 10 But if you are afraid to go down, go with Purah your servant down to the camp. 11 You will hear what they say; and afterward your hands will be strengthened to go down into the camp." Then went he down with Purah his servant to the outermost part of the armed men who were in the camp.

12 The Midianites and the Amalekites and all the children of the east lay along in the valley like locusts for multitude; and their camels were without number, as the sand which is on the seashore for multitude.

13 When Gideon had come, behold, there was a man telling a dream to his fellow. He said, "Behold, I dreamt a dream; and behold, a cake of barley bread tumbled into the camp of Midian, came to the tent, and struck it so that it fell, and turned it upside down, so that the tent lay flat."

14 His fellow answered, "This is nothing other than the sword of Gideon the son of Joash, a man of Israel. God has delivered Midian into his hand, with all the army."

15 It was so, when Gideon heard the telling of the dream and its interpretation, that he worshipped. Then he returned into the camp of Israel and said, "Arise, for the LORD has delivered the army of Midian into your hand!"

---

16 He divided the three hundred men into three companies, and he put into the hands of all of them trumpets and empty pitchers, with torches within the pitchers.

17 He said to them, "Watch me, and do likewise. Behold, when I come to the outermost part of the camp, it shall be that, as I do, so you shall do. 18 When I blow the trumpet, I and all who are with me, then blow the trumpets also on every side of all the camp, and shout, 'For the LORD and for Gideon!'"

19 So Gideon and the hundred men who were with him came to the outermost part of the camp in the beginning of the middle watch, when they had but newly set the watch. Then they blew the trumpets and broke in pieces the pitchers that were in their hands. 20 The three companies blew the trumpets, broke the pitchers, and held the torches in their left hands and the trumpets in their right hands with which to blow; and they shouted, "The sword of the LORD and of Gideon!" 21 They each stood in his place around the camp, and all the army ran; and they shouted, and put them to flight. 22 They blew the three hundred trumpets, and the LORD set every man's sword against his fellow and against all the army; and the army fled as far as Beth Shittah towards Zererah, as far as the border of Abel Meholah, by Tabbath. 23 The men of Israel were gathered together out of Naphtali, out of Asher, and out of all Manasseh, and pursued Midian. 24 Gideon sent messengers throughout all the hill country of Ephraim, saying, "Come down against Midian and take the waters before them as far as Beth Barah, even the Jordan!" So all the men of Ephraim were gathered together and took the waters as far as Beth Barah, even the Jordan. 25 They took the two princes of Midian, Oreb and Zeeb. They killed Oreb at Oreb's rock, and Zeeb they killed at Zeeb's wine press, as they pursued Midian. Then they brought the heads of Oreb and Zeeb to Gideon beyond the Jordan.

8

1 The men of Ephraim said to him, "Why have you treated us this way, that you didn't call us when you went to fight with Midian?" They rebuked him sharply. 2 He said to them, "What have I now done in comparison with you? Isn't the gleaning of the grapes of Ephraim better than the vintage of Abiezer? 3 God has delivered into your hand the princes of Midian, Oreb and Zeeb! What was I able to do in comparison with you?" Then their anger was abated towards him when he had said that.

4 Gideon came to the Jordan and passed over, he and the three hundred men who were with him, faint, yet pursuing. 5 He said to the men of Succoth, "Please give loaves of bread to the people who follow me; for they are faint, and I am pursuing after Zebah and Zalmunna, the kings of Midian."

6 The princes of Succoth said, "Are the hands of Zebah and Zalmunna now in your hand, that we should give bread to your army?"

7 Gideon said, "Therefore when the LORD has delivered Zebah and Zalmunna into my hand, then I will tear your flesh with the thorns of the wilderness and with briers."

8 He went up there to Penuel, and spoke to them in the same way; and the men of Penuel answered him as the men of Succoth had answered. 9 He spoke also to the men of Penuel, saying, "When I come again in peace, I will break down this tower."

10 Now Zebah and Zalmunna were in Karkor, and their armies with them, about fifteen thousand men, all who were left of all the army of the children of the east; for there fell one hundred and twenty thousand men who drew sword. 11 Gideon went up by the way of those who lived in tents on the east of Nobah and Jogbehah, and struck the army; for the army felt secure. 12 Zebah and Zalmunna fled and he pursued them. He took the two kings of Midian, Zebah and Zalmunna, and confused all the army. 13 Gideon the son of Joash returned from the battle from the ascent of Heres. 14 He caught a young man of the men of Succoth, and enquired of him; and he described for him the princes of Succoth, and its elders, seventy-seven men. 15 He came to the men of Succoth, and said, "See Zebah and Zalmunna, concerning whom you taunted me, saying, 'Are the hands of Zebah and Zalmunna now in your hand, that we should give bread to your men who are weary?'" 16 He took the elders of the city, and thorns of the wilderness and briers, and with them he taught the men of Succoth. 17 He broke down the tower of Penuel, and killed the men of the city.

18 Then he said to Zebah and Zalmunna, "What kind of men were they whom you killed at Tabor?"

They answered, "They were like you. They all resembled the children of a king."

19 He said, "They were my brothers, the sons of my mother. As the LORD lives, if you had saved them alive, I would not kill you." 20 He said to Jether his firstborn, "Get up and kill them!" But the youth didn't draw his sword; for he was afraid, because he was yet a youth.

21 Then Zebah and Zalmunna said, "You rise and fall on us; for as the man is, so is his strength." Gideon arose, and killed Zebah and Zalmunna, and took the crescents that were on their camels' necks.

22 Then the men of Israel said to Gideon, "Rule over us, both you, your son, and your son's son also; for you have saved us out of the hand of Midian."

23 Gideon said to them, "I will not rule over you, neither shall my son rule over you. The LORD shall rule over you. 24 Gideon said to them, "I do have a request: that you would each give me the earrings of his plunder." (For they had golden earrings, because they were Ishmaelites.)

25 They answered, "We will willingly give them." They spread a garment, and every man threw the earrings of his plunder into it. 26 The weight of the golden earrings that he requested was one thousand and seven hundred shekels[a] of gold, in addition to the crescents, and the pendants, and the purple clothing that was on the kings of Midian, and in addition to the chains that were about their camels' necks. 27 Gideon made an ephod out of it, and put it in Ophrah, his city. Then all Israel played the prostitute with it there; and it became a snare to Gideon and to his house. 28 So Midian was subdued before the children of Israel, and they lifted up their heads no more. The land had rest forty years in the days of Gideon.

29 Jerubbaal the son of Joash went and lived in his own house. 30 Gideon had seventy sons conceived from his body, for he had many wives. 31 His concubine who was in Shechem also bore him a son, and he named him Abimelech. 32 Gideon the son of Joash died in a good old age, and was buried in the tomb of Joash his father, in Ophrah of the Abiezrites.

33 As soon as Gideon was dead, the children of Israel turned again and played the prostitute following the Baals, and made Baal Berith their god. 34 The children of Israel didn't remember the LORD their God, who had delivered them out of the hand of all their enemies on every side; 35 neither did they show kindness to the house of Jerubbaal, that is, Gideon, according to all the goodness which he had shown to Israel.

9

1 Abimelech the son of Jerubbaal went to Shechem to his mother's brothers, and spoke with them and with all the family of the house of his mother's father, saying, 2 "Please speak in the ears of all the men of Shechem, 'Is it better for you that all the sons of Jerubbaal, who are seventy persons, rule over you, or that one rule over you?' Remember also that I am your bone and your flesh."

3 His mother's brothers spoke of him in the ears of all the men of Shechem all these words. Their hearts inclined to follow Abimelech; for they said, "He is our brother." 4 They gave him seventy pieces of silver out of the house of Baal Berith, with which Abimelech hired vain and reckless fellows who followed him. 5 He went to his father's house at Ophrah, and killed his brothers the sons of Jerubbaal, being seventy persons, on one stone; but Jotham the youngest son of Jerubbaal was left, for he hid himself. 6 All the men of Shechem assembled themselves together with all the house of Millo, and went and made Abimelech king by the oak of the pillar that was in Shechem. 7 When they told it to Jotham, he went and stood on the top of Mount Gerizim and lifted up his voice, cried out, and said to them, "Listen to me, you men of Shechem, that God may listen to you. 8 The trees set out to anoint a king over themselves. They said to the olive tree, 'Reign over us.'

9 "But the olive tree said to them, 'Should I stop producing my oil, with which they honour God and man by me, and go to wave back and forth over the trees?'

10 "The trees said to the fig tree, 'Come and reign over us.'

11 "But the fig tree said to them, 'Should I leave my sweetness, and my good fruit, and go to wave back and forth over the trees?'

12 "The trees said to the vine, 'Come and reign over us.'

13 "The vine said to them, 'Should I leave my new wine, which cheers God and man, and go to wave back and forth over the trees?'

14 "Then all the trees said to the bramble, 'Come and reign over us.'

15 "The bramble said to the trees, 'If in truth you anoint me king over you, then come and take refuge in my shade; and if not, let fire come out of the bramble, and devour the cedars of Lebanon.'

16 "Now therefore, if you have dealt truly and righteously, in that you have made Abimelech king, and if you have dealt well with Jerubbaal and his house, and have done to him according to the deserving of his hands 17 (for my father fought for you, risked his life, and delivered you out of the hand of Midian; 18 and you have risen up against my father's house today and have slain his sons, seventy persons, on one stone, and have made Abimelech, the son of his female servant, king over the men of Shechem, because he is your brother); 19 if you then have dealt truly and righteously with Jerubbaal and with his house today, then rejoice in Abimelech, and let him also rejoice in you; 20 but if not, let fire come out from Abimelech and devour the men of Shechem and the house of Millo; and let fire come out from the men of Shechem and from the house of Millo and devour Abimelech."

21 Jotham ran away and fled, and went to Beer[b] and lived there, for fear of Abimelech his brother.

22 Abimelech was prince over Israel three years. 23 Then God sent an evil spirit between Abimelech and the men of Shechem; and the men of Shechem dealt treacherously with Abimelech, 24 that the violence done to the seventy sons of Jerubbaal might come, and that their blood might be laid on Abimelech their brother who killed them, and on the men of Shechem who strengthened his hands to kill his brothers. 25 The men of Shechem set an ambush for him on the tops of the mountains, and they robbed all who came along that way by them; and Abimelech was told about it.

26 Gaal the son of Ebed came with his brothers and went over to Shechem; and the men of Shechem put their trust in him. 27 They went out into the field, harvested their vineyards, trod the grapes, celebrated, and went into the house of their god and ate and drank, and cursed Abimelech. 28 Gaal the son of Ebed said, "Who is Abimelech, and who is Shechem, that we should serve him? Isn't he the son of Jerubbaal? Isn't Zebul his officer?

---

a 8:26 A shekel is about 10 grams or about 0.32 Troy ounces, so 1700 shekels is about 17 kilograms or 37.4 pounds.

b 9:21 "Beer" is Hebrew for "well", i.e., a village named for its well.

Serve the men of Hamor the father of Shechem, but why should we serve him? 29 I wish that this people were under my hand! Then I would remove Abimelech." He said to Abimelech, "Increase your army and come out!"

30 When Zebul the ruler of the city heard the words of Gaal the son of Ebed, his anger burnt. 31 He sent messengers to Abimelech craftily, saying, "Behold, Gaal the son of Ebed and his brothers have come to Shechem; and behold, they incite the city against you. 32 Now therefore, go up by night, you and the people who are with you, and lie in wait in the field. 33 It shall be that in the morning, as soon as the sun is up, you shall rise early and rush on the city. Behold, when he and the people who are with him come out against you, then may you do to them as you shall find occasion."

34 Abimelech rose up, and all the people who were with him, by night, and they laid wait against Shechem in four companies. 35 Gaal the son of Ebed went out, and stood in the entrance of the gate of the city. Abimelech rose up, and the people who were with him, from the ambush.

36 When Gaal saw the people, he said to Zebul, "Behold, people are coming down from the tops of the mountains."

Zebul said to him, "You see the shadows of the mountains as if they were men."

37 Gaal spoke again and said, "Behold, people are coming down by the middle of the land, and one company comes by the way of the oak of Meonenim."

38 Then Zebul said to him, "Now where is your mouth, that you said, 'Who is Abimelech, that we should serve him?' Isn't this the people that you have despised? Please go out now and fight with them."

39 Gaal went out before the men of Shechem, and fought with Abimelech. 40 Abimelech chased him, and he fled before him, and many fell wounded, even to the entrance of the gate. 41 Abimelech lived at Arumah; and Zebul drove out Gaal and his brothers, that they should not dwell in Shechem. 42 On the next day, the people went out into the field; and they told Abimelech. 43 He took the people and divided them into three companies, and laid wait in the field; and he looked, and behold, the people came out of the city. So, he rose up against them and struck them. 44 Abimelech and the companies that were with him rushed forward and stood in the entrance of the gate of the city; and the two companies rushed on all who were in the field and struck them. 45 Abimelech fought against the city all that day; and he took the city and killed the people in it. He beat down the city and sowed it with salt.

46 When all the men of the tower of Shechem heard of it, they entered into the stronghold of the house of Elberith. 47 Abimelech was told that all the men of the tower of Shechem were gathered together. 48 Abimelech went up to Mount Zalmon, he and all the people who were with him; and Abimelech took an axe in his hand, and cut down a bough from the trees, and took it up, and laid it on his shoulder. Then he said to the people who were with him, "What you have seen me do, make haste, and do as I have done!" 49 All the people likewise each cut down his bough, followed Abimelech, and put them at the base of the stronghold, and set the stronghold on fire over them, so that all the people of the tower of Shechem died also, about a thousand men and women. 50 Then Abimelech went to Thebez and encamped against Thebez, and took it. 51 But there was a strong tower within the city, and all the men and women of the city fled there, and shut themselves in, and went up to the roof of the tower. 52 Abimelech came to the tower and fought against it, and came near to the door of the tower to burn it with fire. 53 A certain woman cast an upper millstone on Abimelech's head, and broke his skull.

54 Then he called hastily to the young man, his armour bearer, and said to him, "Draw your sword and kill me, that men not say of me, 'A woman killed him.'" His young man thrust him through, and he died.

55 When the men of Israel saw that Abimelech was dead, they each departed to his place. 56 Thus God repaid the wickedness of Abimelech, which he did to his father in killing his seventy brothers; 57 and God repaid all the wickedness of the men of Shechem on their heads; and the curse of Jotham the son of Jerubbaal came on them.

10

1 After Abimelech, Tola the son of Puah, the son of Dodo, a man of Issachar, arose to save Israel. He lived in Shamir in the hill country of Ephraim. 2 He judged Israel twenty-three years, and died, and was buried in Shamir.

3 After him Jair, the Gileadite, arose. He judged Israel twenty-two years. 4 He had thirty sons who rode on thirty donkey colts. They had thirty cities, which are called Havvoth Jair to this day, which are in the land of Gilead. 5 Jair died, and was buried in Kamon.

6 The children of Israel again did that which was evil in the LORD's sight, and served the Baals, the Ashtaroth, the gods of Syria, the gods of Sidon, the gods of Moab, the gods of the children of Ammon, and the gods of the Philistines. They abandoned the LORD, and didn't serve him. 7 The LORD's anger burnt against Israel, and he sold them into the hand of the Philistines and into the hand of the children of Ammon. 8 They troubled and oppressed the children of Israel that year. For eighteen years they oppressed all the children of Israel that were beyond the Jordan in the land of the Amorites, which is in Gilead. 9 The children of Ammon passed over the Jordan to fight also against Judah, and against Benjamin, and against the house of Ephraim, so that Israel was very distressed. 10 The children of Israel cried to the LORD, saying, "We have sinned against you, even because we have forsaken our God, and have served the Baals."

11 The LORD said to the children of Israel, "Didn't I save you from the Egyptians, and from the Amorites, from the children of Ammon, and from the Philistines? 12 The Sidonians also, and the Amalekites, and the

Maonites, oppressed you; and you cried to me, and I saved you out of their hand. 13 Yet you have forsaken me and served other gods. Therefore I will save you no more. 14 Go and cry to the gods which you have chosen. Let them save you in the time of your distress!"

15 The children of Israel said to the LORD, "We have sinned! Do to us whatever seems good to you; only deliver us, please, today." 16 They put away the foreign gods from amongst them and served the LORD; and his soul was grieved for the misery of Israel.

17 Then the children of Ammon were gathered together and encamped in Gilead. The children of Israel assembled themselves together and encamped in Mizpah. 18 The people, the princes of Gilead, said to one another, "Who is the man who will begin to fight against the children of Ammon? He shall be head over all the inhabitants of Gilead."

11

1 Now Jephthah the Gileadite was a mighty man of valour. He was the son of a prostitute. Gilead became the father of Jephthah. 2 Gilead's wife bore him sons. When his wife's sons grew up, they drove Jephthah out and said to him, "You will not inherit in our father's house, for you are the son of another woman." 3 Then Jephthah fled from his brothers and lived in the land of Tob. Outlaws joined up with Jephthah, and they went out with him.

4 After a while, the children of Ammon made war against Israel. 5 When the children of Ammon made war against Israel, the elders of Gilead went to get Jephthah out of the land of Tob. 6 They said to Jephthah, "Come and be our chief, that we may fight with the children of Ammon."

7 Jephthah said to the elders of Gilead, "Didn't you hate me, and drive me out of my father's house? Why have you come to me now when you are in distress?"

8 The elders of Gilead said to Jephthah, "Therefore we have turned again to you now, that you may go with us and fight with the children of Ammon. You will be our head over all the inhabitants of Gilead."

9 Jephthah said to the elders of Gilead, "If you bring me home again to fight with the children of Ammon, and the LORD delivers them before me, will I be your head?"

10 The elders of Gilead said to Jephthah, "The LORD will be witness between us. Surely we will do what you say."

11 Then Jephthah went with the elders of Gilead, and the people made him head and chief over them. Jephthah spoke all his words before the LORD in Mizpah.

12 Jephthah sent messengers to the king of the children of Ammon, saying, "What do you have to do with me, that you have come to me to fight against my land?"

13 The king of the children of Ammon answered the messengers of Jephthah, "Because Israel took away my land when he came up out of Egypt, from the Arnon even to the Jabbok, and to the Jordan. Now therefore restore that territory again peaceably."

14 Jephthah sent messengers again to the king of the children of Ammon; 15 and he said to him, "Jephthah says: Israel didn't take away the land of Moab, nor the land of the children of Ammon; 16 but when they came up from Egypt, and Israel went through the wilderness to the Red Sea, and came to Kadesh, 17 then Israel sent messengers to the king of Edom, saying, 'Please let me pass through your land;' but the king of Edom didn't listen. In the same way, he sent to the king of Moab, but he refused; so Israel stayed in Kadesh. 18 Then they went through the wilderness, and went around the land of Edom, and the land of Moab, and came by the east side of the land of Moab, and they encamped on the other side of the Arnon; but they didn't come within the border of Moab, for the Arnon was the border of Moab. 19 Israel sent messengers to Sihon king of the Amorites, the king of Heshbon; and Israel said to him, 'Please let us pass through your land to my place.' 20 But Sihon didn't trust Israel to pass through his border; but Sihon gathered all his people together, and encamped in Jahaz, and fought against Israel. 21 The LORD, the God of Israel, delivered Sihon and all his people into the hand of Israel, and they struck them. So Israel possessed all the land of the Amorites, the inhabitants of that country. 22 They possessed all the border of the Amorites, from the Arnon even to the Jabbok, and from the wilderness even to the Jordan. 23 So now the LORD, the God of Israel, has dispossessed the Amorites from before his people Israel, and should you possess them? 24 Won't you possess that which Chemosh your god gives you to possess? So whoever the LORD our God has dispossessed from before us, them will we possess. 25 Now are you anything better than Balak the son of Zippor, king of Moab? Did he ever strive against Israel, or did he ever fight against them? 26 Israel lived in Heshbon and its towns, and in Aroer and its towns, and in all the cities that are along the side of the Arnon for three hundred years! Why didn't you recover them within that time? 27 Therefore I have not sinned against you, but you do me wrong to war against me. May The LORD the Judge be judge today between the children of Israel and the children of Ammon."

28 However, the king of the children of Ammon didn't listen to the words of Jephthah which he sent him. 29 Then the LORD's Spirit came on Jephthah, and he passed over Gilead and Manasseh, and passed over Mizpah of Gilead, and from Mizpah of Gilead he passed over to the children of Ammon.

30 Jephthah vowed a vow to the LORD, and said, "If you will indeed deliver the children of Ammon into my hand, 31 then it shall be, that whatever comes out of the doors of my house to meet me when I return in peace from the children of Ammon, it shall be the LORD's, and I will offer it up for a burnt offering. 32 So Jephthah passed over to the children of Ammon to fight against them; and the LORD delivered them into his hand. 33 He struck them from

Aroer until you come to Minnith, even twenty cities, and to Abelcheramim, with a very great slaughter. So the children of Ammon were subdued before the children of Israel.

34 Jephthah came to Mizpah to his house; and behold, his daughter came out to meet him with tambourines and with dances. She was his only child. Besides her he had neither son nor daughter. 35 When he saw her, he tore his clothes, and said, "Alas, my daughter! You have brought me very low, and you are one of those who trouble me; for I have opened my mouth to the LORD, and I can't go back."

36 She said to him, "My father, you have opened your mouth to the LORD; do to me according to that which has proceeded out of your mouth, because the LORD has taken vengeance for you on your enemies, even on the children of Ammon." 37 Then she said to her father, "Let this thing be done for me. Leave me alone two months, that I may depart and go down on the mountains, and bewail my virginity, I and my companions."

38 He said, "Go." He sent her away for two months; and she departed, she and her companions, and mourned her virginity on the mountains. 39 At the end of two months, she returned to her father, who did with her according to his vow which he had vowed. She was a virgin. It became a custom in Israel 40 that the daughters of Israel went yearly to celebrate the daughter of Jephthah the Gileadite four days in a year.

12

1 The men of Ephraim were gathered together, and passed northward; and they said to Jephthah, "Why did you pass over to fight against the children of Ammon, and didn't call us to go with you? We will burn your house around you with fire!"

2 Jephthah said to them, "I and my people were at great strife with the children of Ammon; and when I called you, you didn't save me out of their hand. 3 When I saw that you didn't save me, I put my life in my hand, and passed over against the children of Ammon, and the LORD delivered them into my hand. Why then have you come up to me today, to fight against me?"

4 Then Jephthah gathered together all the men of Gilead, and fought with Ephraim. The men of Gilead struck Ephraim, because they said, "You are fugitives of Ephraim, you Gileadites, in the middle of Ephraim, and in the middle of Manasseh." 5 The Gileadites took the fords of the Jordan against the Ephraimites. Whenever a fugitive of Ephraim said, "Let me go over," the men of Gilead said to him, "Are you an Ephraimite?" If he said, "No;" 6 then they said to him, "Now say 'Shibboleth;'" and he said "Sibboleth;" for he couldn't manage to pronounce it correctly, then they seized him and killed him at the fords of the Jordan. At that time, forty-two thousand of Ephraim fell.

7 Jephthah judged Israel six years. Then Jephthah the Gileadite died, and was buried in the cities of Gilead.

8 After him Ibzan of Bethlehem judged Israel. 9 He had thirty sons. He sent his thirty daughters outside his clan, and he brought in thirty daughters from outside his clan for his sons. He judged Israel seven years. 10 Ibzan died, and was buried at Bethlehem.

11 After him, Elon the Zebulunite judged Israel; and he judged Israel ten years. 12 Elon the Zebulunite died, and was buried in Aijalon in the land of Zebulun.

13 After him, Abdon the son of Hillel the Pirathonite judged Israel. 14 He had forty sons and thirty sons' sons who rode on seventy donkey colts. He judged Israel eight years. 15 Abdon the son of Hillel the Pirathonite died, and was buried in Pirathon in the land of Ephraim, in the hill country of the Amalekites.

13

1 The children of Israel again did that which was evil in the LORD's sight; and the LORD delivered them into the hand of the Philistines forty years.

2 There was a certain man of Zorah, of the family of the Danites, whose name was Manoah; and his wife was barren, and childless. 3 The LORD's angel appeared to the woman, and said to her, "See now, you are barren and childless; but you shall conceive and bear a son. 4 Now therefore please beware and drink no wine nor strong drink, and don't eat any unclean thing; 5 for, behold, you shall conceive and give birth to a son. No razor shall come on his head, for the child shall be a Nazirite to God from the womb. He shall begin to save Israel out of the hand of the Philistines."

6 Then the woman came and told her husband, saying, "A man of God came to me, and his face was like the face of the angel of God, very awesome. I didn't ask him where he was from, neither did he tell me his name; 7 but he said to me, 'Behold, you shall conceive and bear a son; and now drink no wine nor strong drink. Don't eat any unclean thing, for the child shall be a Nazirite to God from the womb to the day of his death.'"

8 Then Manoah entreated the LORD, and said, "Oh, Lord, please let the man of God whom you sent come again to us, and teach us what we should do to the child who shall be born."

9 God listened to the voice of Manoah, and the angel of God came again to the woman as she sat in the field; but Manoah, her husband, wasn't with her. 10 The woman hurried and ran, and told her husband, saying to him, "Behold, the man who came to me that day has appeared to me."

11 Manoah arose and followed his wife, and came to the man, and said to him, "Are you the man who spoke to my wife?"

He said, "I am."

12 Manoah said, "Now let your words happen. What shall the child's way of life and mission be?"

13 The LORD's angel said to Manoah, "Of all that I said to the woman let her beware. 14 She may not eat of anything that comes of the vine, neither let her drink wine or strong drink, nor eat any unclean thing. Let her observe all that I commanded her."

15 Manoah said to the LORD's angel, "Please stay with us, that we may make a young goat ready for you."

16 The LORD's angel said to Manoah, "Though you detain me, I won't eat your bread. If you will prepare a burnt offering, you must offer it to the LORD." For Manoah didn't know that he was the LORD's angel.

17 Manoah said to the LORD's angel, "What is your name, that when your words happen, we may honour you?"

18 The LORD's angel said to him, "Why do you ask about my name, since it is incomprehensible[a]?"

19 So Manoah took the young goat with the meal offering, and offered it on the rock to the LORD. Then the angel did an amazing thing as Manoah and his wife watched. 20 For when the flame went up towards the sky from off the altar, the LORD's angel ascended in the flame of the altar. Manoah and his wife watched; and they fell on their faces to the ground. 21 But the LORD's angel didn't appear to Manoah or to his wife any more. Then Manoah knew that he was the LORD's angel. 22 Manoah said to his wife, "We shall surely die, because we have seen God."

23 But his wife said to him, "If the LORD were pleased to kill us, he wouldn't have received a burnt offering and a meal offering at our hand, and he wouldn't have shown us all these things, nor would he have told us such things as these at this time." 24 The woman bore a son and named him Samson. The child grew, and the LORD blessed him. 25 The LORD's Spirit began to move him in Mahaneh Dan, between Zorah and Eshtaol.

14

1 Samson went down to Timnah, and saw a woman in Timnah of the daughters of the Philistines. 2 He came up, and told his father and his mother, saying, "I have seen a woman in Timnah of the daughters of the Philistines. Now therefore get her for me as my wife."

3 Then his father and his mother said to him, "Isn't there a woman amongst your brothers' daughters, or amongst all my people, that you go to take a wife of the uncircumcised Philistines?"

Samson said to his father, "Get her for me, for she pleases me well."

4 But his father and his mother didn't know that it was of the LORD; for he sought an occasion against the Philistines. Now at that time the Philistines ruled over Israel.

5 Then Samson went down to Timnah with his father and his mother, and came to the vineyards of Timnah; and behold, a young lion roared at him. 6 The LORD's Spirit came mightily on him, and he tore him as he would have torn a young goat with his bare hands, but he didn't tell his father or his mother what he had done. 7 He went down and talked with the woman, and she pleased Samson well. 8 After a while he returned to take her, and he went over to see the carcass of the lion; and behold, there was a swarm of bees in the body of the lion, and honey. 9 He took it into his hands, and went on, eating as he went. He came to his father and mother and gave to them, and they ate, but he didn't tell them that he had taken the honey out of the lion's body. 10 His father went down to the woman; and Samson made a feast there, for the young men used to do so. 11 When they saw him, they brought thirty companions to be with him.

12 Samson said to them, "Let me tell you a riddle now. If you can tell me the answer within the seven days of the feast, and find it out, then I will give you thirty linen garments and thirty changes of clothing; 13 but if you can't tell me the answer, then you shall give me thirty linen garments and thirty changes of clothing."

They said to him, "Tell us your riddle, that we may hear it."

14 He said to them,

"Out of the eater came out food.
    Out of the strong came out sweetness."

They couldn't in three days declare the riddle. 15 On the seventh day, they said to Samson's wife, "Entice your husband, that he may declare to us the riddle, lest we burn you and your father's house with fire. Have you called us to impoverish us? Isn't that so?"

16 Samson's wife wept before him, and said, "You just hate me, and don't love me. You've told a riddle to the children of my people, and haven't told it to me."

He said to her, "Behold, I haven't told my father or my mother, so why should I tell you?"

17 She wept before him the seven days, while their feast lasted; and on the seventh day, he told her, because she pressed him severely; and she told the riddle to the children of her people. 18 The men of the city said to him on the seventh day before the sun went down, "What is sweeter than honey? What is stronger than a lion?"

He said to them,

"If you hadn't ploughed with my heifer,
    you wouldn't have found out my riddle."

19 The LORD's Spirit came mightily on him, and he went down to Ashkelon and struck thirty men of them. He took their plunder, then gave the changes of clothing to those who declared the riddle. His anger burnt, and he went up to his father's house. 20 But Samson's wife was given to his companion, who had been his friend.

---

a 13:18 or, wonderful

15

1 But after a while, in the time of wheat harvest, Samson visited his wife with a young goat. He said, "I will go in to my wife's room."

But her father wouldn't allow him to go in. 2 Her father said, "I most certainly thought that you utterly hated her; therefore I gave her to your companion. Isn't her younger sister more beautiful than she? Please, take her instead."

3 Samson said to them, "This time I will be blameless in the case of the Philistines when I harm them." 4 Samson went and caught three hundred foxes, and took torches, and turned tail to tail, and put a torch in the middle between every two tails. 5 When he had set the torches on fire, he let them go into the standing grain of the Philistines, and burnt up both the shocks and the standing grain, and also the olive groves.

6 Then the Philistines said, "Who has done this?"

They said, "Samson, the son-in-law of the Timnite, because he has taken his wife and given her to his companion." The Philistines came up, and burnt her and her father with fire.

7 Samson said to them, "If you behave like this, surely I will take revenge on you, and after that I will cease." 8 He struck them hip and thigh with a great slaughter; and he went down and lived in the cave in Etam's rock. 9 Then the Philistines went up, encamped in Judah, and spread themselves in Lehi.

10 The men of Judah said, "Why have you come up against us?"

They said, "We have come up to bind Samson, to do to him as he has done to us."

11 Then three thousand men of Judah went down to the cave in Etam's rock, and said to Samson, "Don't you know that the Philistines are rulers over us? What then is this that you have done to us?"

He said to them, "As they did to me, so I have done to them."

12 They said to him, "We have come down to bind you, that we may deliver you into the hand of the Philistines."

Samson said to them, "Swear to me that you will not attack me yourselves."

13 They spoke to him, saying, "No, but we will bind you securely and deliver you into their hands; but surely we will not kill you." They bound him with two new ropes, and brought him up from the rock.

14 When he came to Lehi, the Philistines shouted as they met him. Then the LORD's Spirit came mightily on him, and the ropes that were on his arms became as flax that was burnt with fire; and his bands dropped from off his hands. 15 He found a fresh jawbone of a donkey, put out his hand, took it, and struck a thousand men with it. 16 Samson said, "With the jawbone of a donkey, heaps on heaps; with the jawbone of a donkey I have struck a thousand men." 17 When he had finished speaking, he threw the jawbone out of his hand; and that place was called Ramath Lehi.[a]

18 He was very thirsty, and called on the LORD and said, "You have given this great deliverance by the hand of your servant; and now shall I die of thirst, and fall into the hand of the uncircumcised?"

19 But God split the hollow place that is in Lehi, and water came out of it. When he had drunk, his spirit came again, and he revived. Therefore its name was called En Hakkore, which is in Lehi, to this day. 20 He judged Israel twenty years in the days of the Philistines.

16

1 Samson went to Gaza, and saw there a prostitute, and went in to her. 2 The Gazites were told, "Samson is here!" They surrounded him and laid wait for him all night in the gate of the city, and were quiet all the night, saying, "Wait until morning light; then we will kill him." 3 Samson lay until midnight, then arose at midnight and took hold of the doors of the gate of the city, with the two posts, and plucked them up, bar and all, and put them on his shoulders and carried them up to the top of the mountain that is before Hebron.

4 It came to pass afterward that he loved a woman in the valley of Sorek, whose name was Delilah. 5 The lords of the Philistines came up to her and said to her, "Entice him, and see in which his great strength lies, and by what means we may prevail against him, that we may bind him to afflict him; and we will each give you eleven hundred pieces of silver."

6 Delilah said to Samson, "Please tell me where your great strength lies, and what you might be bound to afflict you."

7 Samson said to her, "If they bind me with seven green cords that were never dried, then shall I become weak, and be as another man."

8 Then the lords of the Philistines brought up to her seven green cords which had not been dried, and she bound him with them. 9 Now she had an ambush waiting in the inner room. She said to him, "The Philistines are on you, Samson!" He broke the cords as a flax thread is broken when it touches the fire. So his strength was not known.

10 Delilah said to Samson, "Behold, you have mocked me, and told me lies. Now please tell me how you might be bound."

11 He said to her, "If they only bind me with new ropes with which no work has been done, then shall I become weak, and be as another man."

12 So Delilah took new ropes and bound him with them, then said to him, "The Philistines are on you, Samson!" The ambush was waiting in the inner room. He broke them off his arms like a thread.

13 Delilah said to Samson, "Until now, you have mocked me and told me lies. Tell me with what you might be bound."

He said to her, "If you weave the seven locks of my head with the fabric on the loom."

14 She fastened it with the pin, and said to him, "The Philistines are on you, Samson!" He awakened out of his sleep, and plucked away the pin of the beam and the fabric.

15 She said to him, "How can you say, 'I love you,' when your heart is not with me? You have mocked me these three times, and have not told me where your great strength lies."

16 When she pressed him daily with her words and urged him, his soul was troubled to death. 17 He told her all his heart and said to her, "No razor has ever come on my head; for I have been a Nazirite to God from my mother's womb. If I am shaved, then my strength will go from me and I will become weak, and be like any other man."

18 When Delilah saw that he had told her all his heart, she sent and called for the lords of the Philistines, saying, "Come up this once, for he has told me all his heart." Then the lords of the Philistines came up to her and brought the money in their hand. 19 She made him sleep on her knees; and she called for a man and shaved off the seven locks of his head; and she began to afflict him, and his strength went from him. 20 She said, "The Philistines are upon you, Samson!"

He awoke out of his sleep, and said, "I will go out as at other times, and shake myself free." But he didn't know that the LORD had departed from him. 21 The Philistines laid hold on him and put out his eyes; and they brought him down to Gaza and bound him with fetters of bronze; and he ground at the mill in the prison. 22 However, the hair of his head began to grow again after he was shaved.

23 The lords of the Philistines gathered together to offer a great sacrifice to Dagon their god, and to rejoice; for they said, "Our god has delivered Samson our enemy into our hand." 24 When the people saw him, they praised their god; for they said, "Our god has delivered our enemy and the destroyer of our country, who has slain many of us, into our hand."

25 When their hearts were merry, they said, "Call for Samson, that he may entertain us." They called for Samson out of the prison; and he performed before them. They set him between the pillars; 26 and Samson said to the boy who held him by the hand, "Allow me to feel the pillars on which the house rests, that I may lean on them." 27 Now the house was full of men and women; and all the lords of the Philistines were there; and there were on the roof about three thousand men and women, who saw while Samson performed. 28 Samson called to the LORD, and said, "Lord GOD, remember me, please, and strengthen me, please, only this once, God, that I may be at once avenged of the Philistines for my two eyes." 29 Samson took hold of the two middle pillars on which the house rested and leaned on them, the one with his right hand and the other with his left. 30 Samson said, "Let me die with the Philistines!" He bowed himself with all his might; and the house fell on the lords, and on all the people who were in it. So the dead that he killed at his death were more than those who he killed in his life.

31 Then his brothers and all the house of his father came down and took him, and brought him up and buried him between Zorah and Eshtaol in the burial site of Manoah his father. He judged Israel twenty years.

17

1 There was a man of the hill country of Ephraim, whose name was Micah. 2 He said to his mother, "The eleven hundred pieces of silver that were taken from you, about which you uttered a curse, and also spoke it in my ears—behold, the silver is with me. I took it."

His mother said, "May the LORD bless my son!"

3 He restored the eleven hundred pieces of silver to his mother, then his mother said, "I most certainly dedicate the silver to the LORD from my hand for my son, to make a carved image and a molten image. Now therefore I will restore it to you."

4 When he restored the money to his mother, his mother took two hundred pieces of silver, and gave them to a silversmith, who made a carved image and a molten image out of it. It was in the house of Micah.

5 The man Micah had a house of gods, and he made an ephod, and teraphim,[b] and consecrated one of his sons, who became his priest. 6 In those days there was no king in Israel. Everyone did that which was right in his own eyes. 7 There was a young man out of Bethlehem Judah, of the family of Judah, who was a Levite; and he lived there. 8 The man departed out of the city, out of Bethlehem Judah, to live where he could find a place, and he came to the hill country of Ephraim, to the house of Micah, as he travelled. 9 Micah said to him, "Where did you come from?"

He said to him, "I am a Levite of Bethlehem Judah, and I am looking for a place to live."

10 Micah said to him, "Dwell with me, and be to me a father and a priest, and I will give you ten pieces of silver per year, a suit of clothing, and your food." So the Levite went in. 11 The Levite was content to dwell with the man; and the young man was to him as one of his sons. 12 Micah consecrated the Levite, and the young man became his priest, and was in the house of Micah. 13 Then Micah said, "Now I know that the LORD will do good to me, since I have a Levite as my priest."

18

1 In those days there was no king in Israel. In those days the tribe of the Danites sought an inheritance to dwell in; for to that day, their inheritance had not fallen to them amongst the tribes of Israel. 2 The children of Dan sent five men of their family from their whole number, men of valour, from Zorah and from Eshtaol, to spy out the land and to search it. They said to them, "Go, explore the land!"

---

a 15:17 "Ramath" means "hill" and "Lehi" means "jawbone".

b 17:5 teraphim were household idols that may have been associated with inheritance rights to the household property.

They came to the hill country of Ephraim, to the house of Micah, and lodged there. 3 When they were by the house of Micah, they knew the voice of the young man the Levite; so they went over there and said to him, "Who brought you here? What do you do in this place? What do you have here?"

4 He said to them, "Thus and thus has Micah dealt with me, and he has hired me, and I have become his priest."

5 They said to him, "Please ask counsel of God, that we may know whether our way which we go shall be prosperous."

6 The priest said to them, "Go in peace. Your way in which you go is before the LORD."

7 Then the five men departed and came to Laish and saw the people who were there, how they lived in safety, in the way of the Sidonians, quiet and secure; for there was no one in the land possessing authority, that might put them to shame in anything, and they were far from the Sidonians, and had no dealings with anyone else. 8 They came to their brothers at Zorah and Eshtaol; and their brothers asked them, "What do you say?"

9 They said, "Arise, and let's go up against them; for we have seen the land, and behold, it is very good. Do you stand still? Don't be slothful to go and to enter in to possess the land. 10 When you go, you will come to an unsuspecting people, and the land is large; for God has given it into your hand, a place where there is no lack of anything that is in the earth."

11 The family of the Danites set out from Zorah and Eshtaol with six hundred men armed with weapons of war. 12 They went up and encamped in Kiriath Jearim in Judah. Therefore they call that place Mahaneh Dan to this day. Behold, it is behind Kiriath Jearim. 13 They passed from there to the hill country of Ephraim, and came to the house of Micah.

14 Then the five men who went to spy out the country of Laish answered and said to their brothers, "Do you know that there is in these houses an ephod, and teraphim,[a] and a carved image, and a molten image? Now therefore consider what you have to do." 15 They went over there and came to the house of the young Levite man, even to the house of Micah, and asked him how he was doing. 16 The six hundred men armed with their weapons of war, who were of the children of Dan, stood by the entrance of the gate. 17 The five men who went to spy out the land went up, and came in there, and took the engraved image, the ephod, the teraphim, and the molten image; and the priest stood by the entrance of the gate with the six hundred men armed with weapons of war.

18 When these went into Micah's house, and took the engraved image, the ephod, the teraphim, and the molten image, the priest said to them, "What are you doing?"

19 They said to him, "Hold your peace, put your hand on your mouth, and go with us. Be a father and a priest to us. Is it better for you to be priest to the house of one man, or to be priest to a tribe and a family in Israel?"

20 The priest's heart was glad, and he took the ephod, the teraphim, and the engraved image, and went with the people. 21 So they turned and departed, and put the little ones, the livestock, and the goods before them. 22 When they were a good way from the house of Micah, the men who were in the houses near Micah's house gathered together and overtook the children of Dan. 23 As they called to the children of Dan, they turned their faces, and said to Micah, "What ails you, that you come with such a company?"

24 He said, "You have taken away my gods which I made, and the priest, and have gone away! What more do I have? How can you ask me, 'What ails you?'"

25 The children of Dan said to him, "Don't let your voice be heard amongst us, lest angry fellows fall on you, and you lose your life, with the lives of your household."

26 The children of Dan went their way; and when Micah saw that they were too strong for him, he turned and went back to his house. 27 They took that which Micah had made, and the priest whom he had, and came to Laish, to a people quiet and unsuspecting, and struck them with the edge of the sword; then they burnt the city with fire. 28 There was no deliverer, because it was far from Sidon, and they had no dealings with anyone else; and it was in the valley that lies by Beth Rehob. They built the city and lived in it. 29 They called the name of the city Dan, after the name of Dan their father, who was born to Israel; however the name of the city used to be Laish. 30 The children of Dan set up for themselves the engraved image; and Jonathan, the son of Gershom, the son of Moses, and his sons were priests to the tribe of the Danites until the day of the captivity of the land. 31 So they set up for themselves Micah's engraved image which he made, and it remained all the time that God's house was in Shiloh.

19

1 In those days, when there was no king in Israel, there was a certain Levite living on the farther side of the hill country of Ephraim, who took for himself a concubine out of Bethlehem Judah. 2 His concubine played the prostitute against him, and went away from him to her father's house to Bethlehem Judah, and was there for four months. 3 Her husband arose and went after her to speak kindly to her, to bring her again, having his servant with him and a couple of donkeys. She brought him into her father's house; and when the father of the young lady saw him, he rejoiced to meet him. 4 His father-in-law, the young lady's father, kept him there; and he stayed with him three days. So they ate and drank, and stayed there.

5 On the fourth day, they got up early in the morning, and he rose up to depart. The young lady's father said to his son-in-law, "Strengthen your heart with a morsel of bread, and afterward you shall go your way." 6 So

they sat down, ate, and drank, both of them together. Then the young lady's father said to the man, "Please be pleased to stay all night, and let your heart be merry." 7 The man rose up to depart; but his father-in-law urged him, and he stayed there again. 8 He arose early in the morning on the fifth day to depart; and the young lady's father said, "Please strengthen your heart and stay until the day declines;" and they both ate.

9 When the man rose up to depart, he, and his concubine, and his servant, his father-in-law, the young lady's father, said to him, "Behold, now the day draws towards evening, please stay all night. Behold, the day is ending. Stay here, that your heart may be merry; and tomorrow go on your way early, that you may go home." 10 But the man wouldn't stay that night, but he rose up and went near Jebus (also called Jerusalem). With him were a couple of saddled donkeys. His concubine also was with him.

11 When they were by Jebus, the day was far spent; and the servant said to his master, "Please come and let's enter into this city of the Jebusites, and stay in it."

12 His master said to him, "We won't enter into the city of a foreigner that is not of the children of Israel; but we will pass over to Gibeah." 13 He said to his servant, "Come and let's draw near to one of these places; and we will lodge in Gibeah, or in Ramah." 14 So they passed on and went their way; and the sun went down on them near Gibeah, which belongs to Benjamin. 15 They went over there, to go in to stay in Gibeah. He went in, and sat down in the street of the city; for there was no one who took them into his house to stay.

16 Behold, an old man came from his work out of the field at evening. Now the man was from the hill country of Ephraim, and he lived in Gibeah; but the men of the place were Benjamites. 17 He lifted up his eyes, and saw the wayfaring man in the street of the city; and the old man said, "Where are you going? Where did you come from?"

18 He said to him, "We are passing from Bethlehem Judah to the farther side of the hill country of Ephraim. I am from there, and I went to Bethlehem Judah. I am going to the LORD's house; and there is no one who has taken me into his house. 19 Yet there is both straw and feed for our donkeys; and there is bread and wine also for me, and for your servant, and for the young man who is with your servants. There is no lack of anything."

20 The old man said, "Peace be to you! Just let me supply all your needs, but don't sleep in the street." 21 So he brought him into his house, and gave the donkeys fodder. Then they washed their feet, and ate and drank. 22 As they were making their hearts merry, behold, the men of the city, certain wicked fellows, surrounded the house, beating at the door; and they spoke to the master of the house, the old man, saying, "Bring out the man who came into your house, that we can have sex with him!"

23 The man, the master of the house, went out to them, and said to them, "No, my brothers, please don't act so wickedly; since this man has come into my house, don't do this folly. 24 Behold, here is my virgin daughter and his concubine. I will bring them out now. Humble them, and do with them what seems good to you; but to this man don't do any such folly."

25 But the men wouldn't listen to him; so the man grabbed his concubine, and brought her out to them; and they had sex with her, and abused her all night until the morning. When the day began to dawn, they let her go. 26 Then the woman came in the dawning of the day, and fell down at the door of the man's house where her lord was, until it was light. 27 Her lord rose up in the morning and opened the doors of the house, and went out to go his way; and behold, the woman his concubine had fallen down at the door of the house, with her hands on the threshold.

28 He said to her, "Get up, and let's get going!" but no one answered. Then he took her up on the donkey; and the man rose up, and went to his place.

29 When he had come into his house, he took a knife and cut up his concubine, and divided her, limb by limb, into twelve pieces, and sent her throughout all the borders of Israel. 30 It was so, that all who saw it said, "Such a deed has not been done or seen from the day that the children of Israel came up out of the land of Egypt to this day! Consider it, take counsel, and speak."

20

1 Then all the children of Israel went out, and the congregation was assembled as one man, from Dan even to Beersheba, with the land of Gilead, to the LORD at Mizpah. 2 The chiefs of all the people, even of all the tribes of Israel, presented themselves in the assembly of the people of God, four hundred thousand footmen who drew sword. 3 (Now the children of Benjamin heard that the children of Israel had gone up to Mizpah.) The children of Israel said, "Tell us, how did this wickedness happen?"

4 The Levite, the husband of the woman who was murdered, answered, "I came into Gibeah that belongs to Benjamin, I and my concubine, to spend the night. 5 The men of Gibeah rose against me, and surrounded the house by night. They intended to kill me and they raped my concubine, and she is dead. 6 I took my concubine and cut her in pieces, and sent her throughout all the country of the inheritance of Israel; for they have committed lewdness and folly in Israel. 7 Behold, you children of Israel, all of you, give here your advice and counsel."

8 All the people arose as one man, saying, "None of us will go to his tent, neither will any of us turn to his house. 9 But now this is the thing which we will do to Gibeah: we will go up against it by lot; 10 and we will take ten men of one hundred throughout all the tribes of Israel, and one

hundred of one thousand, and a thousand out of ten thousand to get food for the people, that they may do, when they come to Gibeah of Benjamin, according to all the folly that the men of Gibeah have done in Israel." 11 So all the men of Israel were gathered against the city, knit together as one man.

12 The tribes of Israel sent men through all the tribe of Benjamin, saying, "What wickedness is this that has happened amongst you? 13 Now therefore deliver up the men, the wicked fellows who are in Gibeah, that we may put them to death and put away evil from Israel."

But Benjamin would not listen to the voice of their brothers, the children of Israel. 14 The children of Benjamin gathered themselves together out of the cities to Gibeah, to go out to battle against the children of Israel. 15 The children of Benjamin were counted on that day out of the cities twenty-six thousand men who drew the sword, in addition to the inhabitants of Gibeah, who were counted seven hundred chosen men. 16 Amongst all these soldiers there were seven hundred chosen men who were left-handed. Every one of them could sling a stone at a hair and not miss. 17 The men of Israel, besides Benjamin, were counted four hundred thousand men who drew sword. All these were men of war.

18 The children of Israel arose, went up to Bethel, and asked counsel of God. They asked, "Who shall go up for us first to battle against the children of Benjamin?"

The LORD said, "Judah first."

19 The children of Israel rose up in the morning and encamped against Gibeah. 20 The men of Israel went out to battle against Benjamin; and the men of Israel set the battle in array against them at Gibeah. 21 The children of Benjamin came out of Gibeah, and on that day destroyed twenty-two thousand of the Israelite men down to the ground. 22 The people, the men of Israel, encouraged themselves, and set the battle again in array in the place where they set themselves in array the first day. 23 The children of Israel went up and wept before the LORD until evening; and they asked of the LORD, saying, "Shall I again draw near to battle against the children of Benjamin my brother?"

The LORD said, "Go up against him."

24 The children of Israel came near against the children of Benjamin the second day. 25 Benjamin went out against them out of Gibeah the second day, and destroyed down to the ground of the children of Israel again eighteen thousand men. All these drew the sword.

26 Then all the children of Israel and all the people went up, and came to Bethel, and wept, and sat there before the LORD, and fasted that day until evening; then they offered burnt offerings and peace offerings before the LORD. 27 The children of Israel asked the LORD (for the ark of the covenant of God was there in those days, 28 and Phinehas, the son of Eleazar, the son of Aaron, stood before it in those days), saying, "Shall I yet again go out to battle against the children of Benjamin my brother, or shall I cease?"

The LORD said, "Go up; for tomorrow I will deliver him into your hand."

29 Israel set ambushes all around Gibeah. 30 The children of Israel went up against the children of Benjamin on the third day, and set themselves in array against Gibeah, as at other times. 31 The children of Benjamin went out against the people, and were drawn away from the city; and they began to strike and kill of the people as at other times, in the highways, of which one goes up to Bethel and the other to Gibeah, in the field, about thirty men of Israel.

32 The children of Benjamin said, "They are struck down before us, as at the first." But the children of Israel said, "Let's flee, and draw them away from the city to the highways."

33 All the men of Israel rose up out of their place and set themselves in array at Baal Tamar. Then the ambushers of Israel broke out of their place, even out of Maareh Geba. 34 Ten thousand chosen men out of all Israel came over against Gibeah, and the battle was severe; but they didn't know that disaster was close to them. 35 The LORD struck Benjamin before Israel; and the children of Israel destroyed of Benjamin that day twenty-five thousand and one hundred men. All these drew the sword. 36 So the children of Benjamin saw that they were struck, for the men of Israel yielded to Benjamin because they trusted the ambushers whom they had set against Gibeah. 37 The ambushers hurried, and rushed on Gibeah; then the ambushers spread out, and struck all the city with the edge of the sword. 38 Now the appointed sign between the men of Israel and the ambushers was that they should make a great cloud of smoke rise up out of the city. 39 The men of Israel turned in the battle, and Benjamin began to strike and kill of the men of Israel about thirty persons; for they said, "Surely they are struck down before us, as in the first battle." 40 But when the cloud began to arise up out of the city in a pillar of smoke, the Benjamites looked behind them; and behold, the whole city went up in smoke to the sky. 41 The men of Israel turned, and the men of Benjamin were dismayed; for they saw that disaster had come on them. 42 Therefore they turned their backs before the men of Israel to the way of the wilderness, but the battle followed hard after them; and those who came out of the cities destroyed them in the middle of it. 43 They surrounded the Benjamites, chased them, and trod them down at their resting place, as far as near Gibeah towards the sunrise. 44 Eighteen thousand men of Benjamin fell; all these were men of valour. 45 They turned and fled towards the wilderness to the rock of Rimmon. They gleaned five thousand men of them in the highways, and followed hard after them to Gidom, and struck two thousand men of them. 46 So that all who fell that day of Benjamin were twenty-five thousand men who drew the sword. All these were men of valour. 47 But six hundred men turned and fled towards the wilderness to

the rock of Rimmon, and stayed in the rock of Rimmon four months. 48 The men of Israel turned again on the children of Benjamin, and struck them with the edge of the sword—including the entire city, the livestock, and all that they found. Moreover they set all the cities which they found on fire.

21

1 Now the men of Israel had sworn in Mizpah, saying, "None of us will give his daughter to Benjamin as a wife." 2 The people came to Bethel and sat there until evening before God, and lifted up their voices, and wept severely. 3 They said, "The LORD, the God of Israel, why has this happened in Israel, that there should be one tribe lacking in Israel today?"

4 On the next day, the people rose early and built an altar there, and offered burnt offerings and peace offerings. 5 The children of Israel said, "Who is there amongst all the tribes of Israel who didn't come up in the assembly to the LORD?" For they had made a great oath concerning him who didn't come up to the LORD to Mizpah, saying, "He shall surely be put to death." 6 The children of Israel grieved for Benjamin their brother, and said, "There is one tribe cut off from Israel today. 7 How shall we provide wives for those who remain, since we have sworn by the LORD that we will not give them of our daughters to wives?" 8 They said, "What one is there of the tribes of Israel who didn't come up to the LORD to Mizpah?" Behold, no one came from Jabesh Gilead to the camp to the assembly. 9 For when the people were counted, behold, there were none of the inhabitants of Jabesh Gilead there. 10 The congregation sent twelve thousand of the most valiant men there, and commanded them, saying, "Go and strike the inhabitants of Jabesh Gilead with the edge of the sword, with the women and the little ones. 11 This is the thing that you shall do: you shall utterly destroy every male, and every woman who has lain with a man." 12 They found amongst the inhabitants of Jabesh Gilead four hundred young virgins who had not known man by lying with him; and they brought them to the camp to Shiloh, which is in the land of Canaan.

13 The whole congregation sent and spoke to the children of Benjamin who were in the rock of Rimmon, and proclaimed peace to them. 14 Benjamin returned at that time; and they gave them the women whom they had saved alive of the women of Jabesh Gilead. There still weren't enough for them. 15 The people grieved for Benjamin, because the LORD had made a breach in the tribes of Israel. 16 Then the elders of the congregation said, "How shall we provide wives for those who remain, since the women are destroyed out of Benjamin?" 17 They said, "There must be an inheritance for those who are escaped of Benjamin, that a tribe not be blotted out from Israel. 18 However, we may not give them wives of our daughters, for the children of Israel had sworn, saying, 'Cursed is he who gives a wife to Benjamin.'" 19 They said, "Behold, there is a feast of the LORD from year to year in Shiloh, which is on the north of Bethel, on the east side of the highway that goes up from Bethel to Shechem, and on the south of Lebonah." 20 They commanded the children of Benjamin, saying, "Go and lie in wait in the vineyards, 21 and see, and behold, if the daughters of Shiloh come out to dance in the dances, then come out of the vineyards, and each man catch his wife of the daughters of Shiloh, and go to the land of Benjamin. 22 It shall be, when their fathers or their brothers come to complain to us, that we will say to them, 'Grant them graciously to us, because we didn't take for each man his wife in battle, neither did you give them to them; otherwise you would now be guilty.'"

23 The children of Benjamin did so, and took wives for themselves according to their number, of those who danced, whom they carried off. They went and returned to their inheritance, built the cities, and lived in them. 24 The children of Israel departed from there at that time, every man to his tribe and to his family, and they each went out from there to his own inheritance. 25 In those days there was no king in Israel. Everyone did that which was right in his own eyes.

The Book of Ruth

1

1 In the days when the judges judged, there was a famine in the land. A certain man of Bethlehem Judah went to live in the country of Moab with his wife and his two sons. 2 The name of the man was Elimelech, and the name of his wife Naomi. The names of his two sons were Mahlon and Chilion, Ephrathites of Bethlehem Judah. They came into the country of Moab and lived there. 3 Elimelech, Naomi's husband, died; and she was left with her two sons. 4 They took for themselves wives of the women of Moab. The name of the one was Orpah, and the name of the other was Ruth. They lived there about ten years. 5 Mahlon and Chilion both died, and the woman was bereaved of her two children and of her husband. 6 Then she arose with her daughters-in-law, that she might return from the country of Moab; for she had heard in the country of Moab how the LORD[a] had visited his people in giving them bread. 7 She went out of the place where she was, and her two daughters-in-law with her. They went on the way to return to the land of Judah. 8 Naomi said to her two daughters-in-law, "Go, return each of you to her mother's house. May the LORD deal kindly with you, as you have dealt with the dead and with me. 9 May The LORD grant you that you may find rest, each of you in the house of her husband."

Then she kissed them, and they lifted up their voices, and wept. 10 They said to her, "No, but we will return with you to your people."

11 Naomi said, "Go back, my daughters. Why do you want to go with me? Do I still have sons in my womb, that they may be your husbands? 12 Go back, my daughters, go your way; for I am too old to have a husband. If I should say, 'I have hope,' if I should even have a husband tonight, and should also bear sons, 13 would you then wait until they were grown? Would you then refrain from having husbands? No, my daughters, for it grieves me seriously for your sakes, for the LORD's hand has gone out against me."

14 They lifted up their voices and wept again; then Orpah kissed her mother-in-law, but Ruth stayed with her. 15 She said, "Behold,[b] your sister-in-law has gone back to her people and to her god. Follow your sister-in-law."

16 Ruth said, "Don't urge me to leave you, and to return from following you, for where you go, I will go; and where you stay, I will stay. Your people will be my people, and your God[c] my God. 17 Where you die, I will die, and there I will be buried. May The LORD do so to me, and more also, if anything but death parts you and me."

18 When Naomi saw that she was determined to go with her, she stopped urging her.

19 So they both went until they came to Bethlehem. When they come to Bethlehem, all the city was excited about them, and they asked, "Is this Naomi?"

20 She said to them, "Don't call me Naomi.[d] Call me Mara,[e] for the Almighty has dealt very bitterly with me. 21 I went out full, and the LORD has brought me home again empty. Why do you call me Naomi, since the LORD has testified against me, and the Almighty has afflicted me?" 22 So Naomi returned, and Ruth the Moabitess, her daughter-in-law, with her, who returned out of the country of Moab. They came to Bethlehem in the beginning of barley harvest.

2

1 Naomi had a relative of her husband's, a mighty man of wealth, of the family of Elimelech, and his name was Boaz. 2 Ruth the Moabitess said to Naomi, "Let me now go to the field, and glean amongst the ears of grain after him in whose sight I find favour."

She said to her, "Go, my daughter." 3 She went, and came and gleaned in the field after the reapers; and she happened to come to the portion of the field belonging to Boaz, who was of the family of Elimelech.

4 Behold, Boaz came from Bethlehem, and said to the reapers, "May The LORD be with you."

They answered him, "May The LORD bless you."

5 Then Boaz said to his servant who was set over the reapers, "Whose young lady is this?"

6 The servant who was set over the reapers answered, "It is the Moabite lady who came back with Naomi out of the country of Moab. 7 She said, 'Please let me glean and gather after the reapers amongst the sheaves.' So she came, and has continued even from the morning until now, except that she rested a little in the house."

8 Then Boaz said to Ruth, "Listen, my daughter. Don't go to glean in another field, and don't go from here, but stay here close to my maidens. 9 Let your eyes be on the field that they reap, and go after them. Haven't I commanded the young men not to touch you? When you are thirsty, go to the vessels, and drink from that which the young men have drawn."

10 Then she fell on her face and bowed herself to the ground, and said to him, "Why have I found favour in your sight, that you should take knowledge of me, since I am a foreigner?"

11 Boaz answered her, "I have been told all about what you have done for your mother-in-law since the death of your husband, and how you have left your father, your mother, and the land of your birth, and have come to a people that you didn't know before. 12 May the LORD repay your work, and a full reward be given to you from the LORD, the God of Israel, under whose wings you have come to take refuge."

13 Then she said, "Let me find favour in your sight, my lord, because you have comforted me, and because you have spoken kindly to your servant, though I am not as one of your servants."

14 At meal time Boaz said to her, "Come here, and eat some bread, and dip your morsel in the vinegar."

She sat beside the reapers, and they passed her parched grain. She ate, was satisfied, and left some of it. 15 When she had risen up to glean, Boaz commanded his young men, saying, "Let her glean even amongst the sheaves, and don't reproach her. 16 Also pull out some for her from the bundles, and leave it. Let her glean, and don't rebuke her."

17 So she gleaned in the field until evening; and she beat out that which she had gleaned, and it was about an ephah[f] of barley. 18 She took it up, and went into the city. Then her mother-in-law saw what she had gleaned; and she brought out and gave to her that which she had left after she had enough.

19 Her mother-in-law said to her, "Where have you gleaned today? Where have you worked? Blessed be he who noticed you."

She told her mother-in-law with whom she had worked, "The man's name with whom I worked today is Boaz." 20 Naomi said to her daughter-in-law, "May he be blessed by the LORD, who has not abandoned his kindness to the living and to the dead." Naomi said to her, "The man is a close relative to us, one of our near kinsmen."

21 Ruth the Moabitess said, "Yes, he said to me, 'You shall stay close to my young men until they have finished all my harvest.'"

22 Naomi said to Ruth her daughter-in-law, "It is good, my daughter, that you go out with his maidens, and that they not meet you in any other field." 23 So she stayed close to the maidens of Boaz, to glean to the end of barley harvest and of wheat harvest; and she lived with her mother-in-law.

3

1 Naomi her mother-in-law said to her, "My daughter, shall I not seek rest for you, that it may be well with you? 2 Now isn't Boaz our kinsman, with whose maidens you were? Behold, he will be winnowing barley tonight on the threshing floor. 3 Therefore wash yourself, anoint yourself, get dressed, and go down to the threshing floor; but don't make yourself known to the man until he has finished eating and drinking. 4 It shall be, when he lies down, that you shall note the place where he is lying. Then you shall go in, uncover his feet, and lie down. Then he will tell you what to do."

5 She said to her, "All that you say, I will do." 6 She went down to the threshing floor, and did everything that her mother-in-law told her. 7 When Boaz had eaten and drunk, and his heart was merry, he went to lie down at the end of the heap of grain. She came softly, uncovered his feet, and lay down. 8 At midnight, the man was startled and turned himself; and behold, a woman lay at his feet. 9 He said, "Who are you?"

She answered, "I am Ruth your servant. Therefore spread the corner of your garment over your servant; for you are a near kinsman."

10 He said, "You are blessed by the LORD, my daughter. You have shown more kindness in the latter end than at the beginning, because you didn't follow young men, whether poor or rich. 11 Now, my daughter, don't be afraid. I will do to you all that you say; for all the city of my people knows that you are a worthy woman. 12 Now it is true that I am a near kinsman. However, there is a kinsman nearer than I. 13 Stay this night, and in the morning, if he will perform for you the part of a kinsman, good. Let him do the kinsman's duty. But if he will not do the duty of a kinsman for you, then I will do the duty of a kinsman for you, as the LORD lives. Lie down until the morning."

14 She lay at his feet until the morning, then she rose up before one could discern another. For he said, "Let it not be known that the woman came to the threshing floor." 15 He said, "Bring the mantle that is on you, and hold it." She held it; and he measured six measures of barley, and laid it on her; then he went into the city.

16 When she came to her mother-in-law, she said, "How did it go, my daughter?"

She told her all that the man had done for her. 17 She said, "He gave me these six measures of barley; for he said, 'Don't go empty to your mother-in-law.'"

18 Then she said, "Wait, my daughter, until you know what will happen; for the man will not rest until he has settled this today."

4

1 Now Boaz went up to the gate and sat down there. Behold, the near kinsman of whom Boaz spoke came by. Boaz said to him, "Come over here, friend, and sit down!" He came over, and sat down. 2 Boaz took ten men of the elders of the city, and said, "Sit down here," and they sat down. 3 He said to the near kinsman, "Naomi, who has come back out of the country of Moab, is selling the parcel of land, which was our brother Elimelech's. 4 I thought I should tell you, saying, 'Buy it before those who sit here, and before the elders of my people.' If you will redeem it, redeem it; but if you will not redeem it, then tell me, that I may know. For there is no one to redeem it besides you; and I am after you."

He said, "I will redeem it."

---

a *1:6* When rendered in ALL CAPITAL LETTERS, "LORD" or "GOD" is the translation of God's Proper Name.
b *1:15* "Behold", from "הִנֵּה", means look at, take notice, observe, see, or gaze at. It is often used as an interjection.

c *1:16* The Hebrew word rendered "God" is "אֱלֹהִים" (Elohim).
d *1:20* "Naomi" means "pleasant".
e *1:20* "Mara" means "bitter".
f *2:17* 1 ephah is about 22 litres or about 2/3 of a bushel

5 Then Boaz said, "On the day you buy the field from the hand of Naomi, you must buy it also from Ruth the Moabitess, the wife of the dead, to raise up the name of the dead on his inheritance."

6 The near kinsman said, "I can't redeem it for myself, lest I endanger my own inheritance. Take my right of redemption for yourself; for I can't redeem it."

7 Now this was the custom in former time in Israel concerning redeeming and concerning exchanging, to confirm all things: a man took off his sandal, and gave it to his neighbour; and this was the way of formalizing transactions in Israel. 8 So the near kinsman said to Boaz, "Buy it for yourself," then he took off his sandal.

9 Boaz said to the elders and to all the people, "You are witnesses today, that I have bought all that was Elimelech's, and all that was Chilion's and Mahlon's, from the hand of Naomi. 10 Moreover, Ruth the Moabitess, the wife of Mahlon, I have purchased to be my wife, to raise up the name of the dead on his inheritance, that the name of the dead may not be cut off from amongst his brothers and from the gate of his place. You are witnesses today."

11 All the people who were in the gate, and the elders, said, "We are witnesses. May the LORD make the woman who has come into your house like Rachel and like Leah, which both built the house of Israel; and treat you worthily in Ephrathah, and be famous in Bethlehem. 12 Let your house be like the house of Perez, whom Tamar bore to Judah, of the offspring[a] which the LORD will give you by this young woman."

13 So Boaz took Ruth and she became his wife; and he went in to her, and the LORD enabled her to conceive, and she bore a son. 14 The women said to Naomi, "Blessed be the LORD, who has not left you today without a near kinsman. Let his name be famous in Israel. 15 He shall be to you a restorer of life and sustain you in your old age; for your daughter-in-law, who loves you, who is better to you than seven sons, has given birth to him." 16 Naomi took the child, laid him in her bosom, and became nurse to him. 17 The women, her neighbours, gave him a name, saying, "A son is born to Naomi". They named him Obed. He is the father of Jesse, the father of David.

18 Now this is the history of the generations of Perez: Perez became the father of Hezron, 19 and Hezron became the father of Ram, and Ram became the father of Amminadab, 20 and Amminadab became the father of Nahshon, and Nahshon became the father of Salmon, 21 and Salmon became the father of Boaz, and Boaz became the father of Obed, 22 and Obed became the father of Jesse, and Jesse became the father of David.

---

[a] *4:12* or, seed

The First Book of Samuel

1

1 Now there was a certain man of Ramathaim Zophim, of the hill country of Ephraim, and his name was Elkanah, the son of Jeroham, the son of Elihu, the son of Tohu, the son of Zuph, an Ephraimite. 2 He had two wives. The name of one was Hannah, and the name of the other Peninnah. Peninnah had children, but Hannah had no children. 3 This man went up out of his city from year to year to worship and to sacrifice to the LORD[a] of Armies in Shiloh. The two sons of Eli, Hophni and Phinehas, priests to the LORD, were there. 4 When the day came that Elkanah sacrificed, he gave portions to Peninnah his wife and to all her sons and her daughters; 5 but he gave a double portion to Hannah, for he loved Hannah, but the LORD had shut up her womb. 6 Her rival provoked her severely, to irritate her, because the LORD had shut up her womb. 7 So year by year, when she went up to the LORD's house, her rival provoked her. Therefore she wept, and didn't eat. 8 Elkanah her husband said to her, "Hannah, why do you weep? Why don't you eat? Why is your heart grieved? Am I not better to you than ten sons?"

9 So Hannah rose up after they had finished eating and drinking in Shiloh. Now Eli the priest was sitting on his seat by the doorpost of the LORD's temple. 10 She was in bitterness of soul, and prayed to the LORD, weeping bitterly. 11 She vowed a vow, and said, "LORD of Armies, if you will indeed look at the affliction of your servant and remember me, and not forget your servant, but will give to your servant a boy, then I will give him to the LORD all the days of his life, and no razor shall come on his head."

12 As she continued praying before the LORD, Eli saw her mouth. 13 Now Hannah spoke in her heart. Only her lips moved, but her voice was not heard. Therefore Eli thought she was drunk. 14 Eli said to her, "How long will you be drunk? Get rid of your wine!"

15 Hannah answered, "No, my lord, I am a woman of a sorrowful spirit. I have not been drinking wine or strong drink, but I poured out my soul before the LORD. 16 Don't consider your servant a wicked woman; for I have been speaking out of the abundance of my complaint and my provocation."

17 Then Eli answered, "Go in peace; and may the God[b] of Israel grant your petition that you have asked of him."

18 She said, "Let your servant find favour in your sight." So the woman went her way and ate; and her facial expression wasn't sad any more.

19 They rose up in the morning early and worshipped the LORD, then returned and came to their house to Ramah. Then Elkanah knew Hannah his wife; and the LORD remembered her.

20 When the time had come, Hannah conceived, and bore a son; and she named him Samuel,[c] saying, "Because I have asked him of the LORD."

21 The man Elkanah, and all his house, went up to offer to the LORD the yearly sacrifice and his vow. 22 But Hannah didn't go up, for she said to her husband, "Not until the child is weaned; then I will bring him, that he may appear before the LORD, and stay there forever."

23 Elkanah her husband said to her, "Do what seems good to you. Wait until you have weaned him; only may the LORD establish his word."

So the woman waited and nursed her son until she weaned him. 24 When she had weaned him, she took him up with her, with three bulls, and one ephah[d] of meal, and a container of wine, and brought him to the LORD's house in Shiloh. The child was young. 25 They killed the bull, and brought the child to Eli. 26 She said, "Oh, my lord, as your soul lives, my lord, I am the woman who stood by you here, praying to the LORD. 27 I prayed for this child, and the LORD has given me my petition which I asked of him. 28 Therefore I have also given him to the LORD. As long as he lives he is given to the LORD." He worshipped the LORD there.

2

1 Hannah prayed, and said,
"My heart exults in the LORD!
    My horn is exalted in the LORD.
My mouth is enlarged over my enemies,
    because I rejoice in your salvation.
2 There is no one as holy as the LORD,
    for there is no one besides you,
    nor is there any rock like our God.

3 "Don't keep talking so exceedingly proudly.
    Don't let arrogance come out of your mouth,
    for the LORD is a God of knowledge.
    By him actions are weighed.

4 "The bows of the mighty men are broken.
    Those who stumbled are armed with strength.
5 Those who were full have hired themselves out for bread.
    Those who were hungry are satisfied.
Yes, the barren has borne seven.
    She who has many children languishes.

6 "The LORD kills and makes alive.
    He brings down to Sheol[e] and brings up.
7 The LORD makes poor and makes rich.
    He brings low, he also lifts up.
8 He raises up the poor out of the dust.
    He lifts up the needy from the dunghill
    to make them sit with princes
    and inherit the throne of glory.
For the pillars of the earth are the LORD's.
    He has set the world on them.
9 He will keep the feet of his holy ones,
    but the wicked will be put to silence in darkness;
    for no man will prevail by strength.
10 Those who strive with the LORD shall be broken to pieces.
    He will thunder against them in the sky.

"The LORD will judge the ends of the earth.
    He will give strength to his king,
    and exalt the horn of his anointed."

11 Elkanah went to Ramah to his house. The child served the LORD before Eli the priest.

12 Now the sons of Eli were wicked men. They didn't know the LORD. 13 The custom of the priests with the people was that when anyone offered a sacrifice, the priest's servant came while the meat was boiling, with a fork of three teeth in his hand; 14 and he stabbed it into the pan, or kettle, or cauldron, or pot. The priest took all that the fork brought up for himself. They did this to all the Israelites who came there to Shiloh. 15 Yes, before they burnt the fat, the priest's servant came, and said to the man who sacrificed, "Give meat to roast for the priest; for he will not accept boiled meat from you, but raw."

16 If the man said to him, "Let the fat be burnt first, and then take as much as your soul desires;" then he would say, "No, but you shall give it to me now; and if not, I will take it by force." 17 The sin of the young men was very great before the LORD; for the men despised the LORD's offering. 18 But Samuel ministered before the LORD, being a child, clothed with a linen ephod. 19 Moreover his mother made him a little robe, and brought it to him from year to year when she came up with her husband to offer the yearly sacrifice. 20 Eli blessed Elkanah and his wife, and said, "May The LORD give you offspring[f] from this woman for the petition which was asked of the LORD." Then they went to their own home. 21 The LORD visited Hannah, and she conceived and bore three sons and two daughters. The child Samuel grew before the LORD.

22 Now Eli was very old; and he heard all that his sons did to all Israel, and how that they slept with the women who served at the door of the Tent of Meeting. 23 He said to them, "Why do you do such things? For I hear of your evil dealings from all these people. 24 No, my sons; for it is not a good report that I hear! You make the LORD's people disobey. 25 If one man sins against another, God will judge him; but if a man sins against the LORD, who will intercede for him?" Notwithstanding, they didn't listen to the voice of their father, because the LORD intended to kill them.

26 The child Samuel grew on, and increased in favour both with the LORD and also with men.

27 A man of God came to Eli and said to him, "The LORD says, 'Did I reveal myself to the house of your father when they were in Egypt in bondage to Pharaoh's house? 28 Didn't I choose him out of all the tribes of Israel to be my priest, to go up to my altar, to burn incense, to wear an ephod before me? Didn't I give to the house of your father all the offerings of the children of Israel made by fire? 29 Why do you kick at my sacrifice and at my offering, which I have commanded in my habitation, and honour your sons above me, to make yourselves fat with the best of all the offerings of Israel my people?' 30 "Therefore the LORD, the God of Israel, says, 'I said indeed that your house and the house of your father should walk before me forever.' But now the LORD says, 'Far be it from me; for those who honour me I will honour, and those who despise me will be cursed. 31 Behold,[g] the days come that I will cut off your arm and the arm of your father's house, that there will not be an old man in your house. 32 You will see the affliction of my habitation, in all the wealth which I will give Israel. There shall not be an old man in your house forever. 33 The man of yours whom I don't cut off from my altar will consume your eyes[h] and grieve your heart. All the increase of your house will die in the flower of their age. 34 This will be the sign to you that will come on your two sons, on Hophni and Phinehas: in one day they will both die. 35 I will raise up a faithful priest for myself who will do according to that which is in my heart and in my mind. I will build him a sure house. He will walk before my anointed forever. 36 It will happen that everyone who is left in your house will come and bow down to him for a piece of silver and a loaf of bread, and will say, "Please put me into one of the priests' offices, that I may eat a morsel of bread."'"

3

1 The child Samuel ministered to the LORD before Eli. The LORD's word was rare in those days. There were not many visions, then. 2 At that time, when Eli was laid down in his place (now his eyes had begun to grow

---

a 1:3 When rendered in ALL CAPITAL LETTERS, "LORD" or "GOD" is the translation of God's Proper Name.
b 1:17 The Hebrew word rendered "God" is "אֱלֹהִים" (Elohim).
c 1:20 Samuel sounds like the Hebrew for "heard by God."
d 1:24 1 ephah is about 22 litres or about 2/3 of a bushel

e 2:6 Sheol is the place of the dead.
f 2:20 or, seed
g 2:31 "Behold", from "הִנֵּה", means look at, take notice, observe, see, or gaze at. It is often used as an interjection.
h 2:33 or, blind your eyes with tears

dim, so that he could not see), 3 and God's lamp hadn't yet gone out, and Samuel had laid down in the LORD's temple where God's ark was, 4 The LORD called Samuel. He said, "Here I am."

5 He ran to Eli and said, "Here I am; for you called me."

He said, "I didn't call. Lie down again."

He went and lay down. 6 The LORD called yet again, "Samuel!"

Samuel arose and went to Eli and said, "Here I am; for you called me."

He answered, "I didn't call, my son. Lie down again." 7 Now Samuel didn't yet know the LORD, neither was the LORD's word yet revealed to him. 8 The LORD called Samuel again the third time. He arose and went to Eli and said, "Here I am; for you called me."

Eli perceived that the LORD had called the child. 9 Therefore Eli said to Samuel, "Go, lie down. It shall be, if he calls you, that you shall say, 'Speak, LORD; for your servant hears.'" So Samuel went and lay down in his place. 10 The LORD came, and stood, and called as at other times, "Samuel! Samuel!"

Then Samuel said, "Speak; for your servant hears."

11 The LORD said to Samuel, "Behold, I will do a thing in Israel at which both the ears of everyone who hears it will tingle. 12 In that day I will perform against Eli all that I have spoken concerning his house, from the beginning even to the end. 13 For I have told him that I will judge his house forever for the iniquity which he knew, because his sons brought a curse on themselves, and he didn't restrain them. 14 Therefore I have sworn to the house of Eli that the iniquity of Eli's house shall not be removed with sacrifice or offering forever."

15 Samuel lay until the morning, and opened the doors of the LORD's house. Samuel was afraid to show Eli the vision. 16 Then Eli called Samuel and said, "Samuel, my son!"

He said, "Here I am."

17 He said, "What is the thing that he has spoken to you? Please don't hide it from me. God do so to you, and more also, if you hide anything from me of all the things that he spoke to you."

18 Samuel told him every bit, and hid nothing from him.

He said, "It is the LORD. Let him do what seems good to him."

19 Samuel grew, and the LORD was with him and let none of his words fall to the ground. 20 All Israel from Dan even to Beersheba knew that Samuel was established to be a prophet of the LORD. 21 The LORD appeared again in Shiloh; for the LORD revealed himself to Samuel in Shiloh by the LORD's word.

4

1 The word of Samuel came to all Israel.

Now Israel went out against the Philistines to battle, and encamped beside Ebenezer; and the Philistines encamped in Aphek. 2 The Philistines put themselves in array against Israel. When they joined battle, Israel was defeated by the Philistines, who killed about four thousand men of the army in the field. 3 When the people had come into the camp, the elders of Israel said, "Why has the LORD defeated us today before the Philistines? Let's get the ark of the LORD's covenant out of Shiloh and bring it to us, that it may come amongst us and save us out of the hand of our enemies."

4 So the people sent to Shiloh, and they brought from there the ark of the covenant of the LORD of Armies, who sits above the cherubim; and the two sons of Eli, Hophni and Phinehas, were there with the ark of the covenant of God. 5 When the ark of the LORD's covenant came into the camp, all Israel shouted with a great shout, so that the earth resounded. 6 When the Philistines heard the noise of the shout, they said, "What does the noise of this great shout in the camp of the Hebrews mean?" They understood that the LORD's ark had come into the camp. 7 The Philistines were afraid, for they said, "God has come into the camp." They said, "Woe to us! For there has not been such a thing before. 8 Woe to us! Who shall deliver us out of the hand of these mighty gods? These are the gods that struck the Egyptians with all kinds of plagues in the wilderness. 9 Be strong and behave like men, O you Philistines, that you not be servants to the Hebrews, as they have been to you. Strengthen yourselves like men, and fight!" 10 The Philistines fought, and Israel was defeated, and each man fled to his tent. There was a very great slaughter; for thirty thousand footmen of Israel fell. 11 God's ark was taken; and the two sons of Eli, Hophni and Phinehas, were slain.

12 A man of Benjamin ran out of the army and came to Shiloh the same day, with his clothes torn and with dirt on his head. 13 When he came, behold, Eli was sitting on his seat by the road watching, for his heart trembled for God's ark. When the man came into the city and told about it, all the city cried out. 14 When Eli heard the noise of the crying, he said, "What does the noise of this tumult mean?"

The man hurried, and came and told Eli. 15 Now Eli was ninety-eight years old. His eyes were set, so that he could not see. 16 The man said to Eli, "I am he who came out of the army, and I fled today out of the army."

He said, "How did the matter go, my son?"

17 He who brought the news answered, "Israel has fled before the Philistines, and there has been also a great slaughter amongst the people. Your two sons also, Hophni and Phinehas, are dead, and God's ark has been captured."

18 When he made mention of God's ark, Eli fell from off his seat backward by the side of the gate; and his neck broke, and he died, for he was an old man and heavy. He had judged Israel forty years.

19 His daughter-in-law, Phinehas' wife, was with child, near to giving birth. When she heard the news that God's ark was taken and that her father-in-law and her husband were dead, she bowed herself and gave birth; for her pains came on her. 20 About the time of her death the women who stood by her said to her, "Don't be afraid, for you have given birth to a son." But she didn't answer, neither did she regard it. 21 She named the child Ichabod,[a] saying, "The glory has departed from Israel!" because God's ark was taken, and because of her father-in-law and her husband. 22 She said, "The glory has departed from Israel; for God's ark has been taken."

5

1 Now the Philistines had taken God's ark, and they brought it from Ebenezer to Ashdod. 2 The Philistines took God's ark, and brought it into the house of Dagon and set it by Dagon. 3 When the people of Ashdod arose early on the next day, behold, Dagon had fallen on his face to the ground before the LORD's ark. They took Dagon and set him in his place again. 4 When they arose early on the following morning, behold, Dagon had fallen on his face to the ground before the LORD's ark; and the head of Dagon and both the palms of his hands were cut off on the threshold. Only Dagon's torso was intact. 5 Therefore neither the priests of Dagon nor any who come into Dagon's house step on the threshold of Dagon in Ashdod to this day. 6 But the LORD's hand was heavy on the people of Ashdod, and he destroyed them and struck them with tumours, even Ashdod and its borders.

7 When the men of Ashdod saw that it was so, they said, "The ark of the God of Israel shall not stay with us, for his hand is severe on us and on Dagon our god." 8 They sent therefore and gathered together all the lords of the Philistines, and said, "What shall we do with the ark of the God of Israel?"

They answered, "Let the ark of the God of Israel be carried over to Gath." They carried the ark of the God of Israel there. 9 It was so, that after they had carried it there, the LORD's hand was against the city with a very great confusion; and he struck the men of the city, both small and great, so that tumours broke out on them. 10 So they sent God's ark to Ekron.

As God's ark came to Ekron, the Ekronites cried out, saying, "They have brought the ark of the God of Israel here to us, to kill us and our people." 11 They sent therefore and gathered together all the lords of the Philistines, and they said, "Send the ark of the God of Israel away, and let it go again to its own place, that it not kill us and our people." For there was a deadly panic throughout all the city. The hand of God was very heavy there. 12 The men who didn't die were struck with the tumours; and the cry of the city went up to heaven.

6

1 The LORD's ark was in the country of the Philistines seven months. 2 The Philistines called for the priests and the diviners, saying, "What shall we do with the LORD's ark? Show us how we should send it to its place."

3 They said, "If you send away the ark of the God of Israel, don't send it empty; but by all means return a trespass offering to him. Then you will be healed, and it will be known to you why his hand is not removed from you."

4 Then they said, "What should the trespass offering be which we shall return to him?"

They said, "Five golden tumours and five golden mice, for the number of the lords of the Philistines; for one plague was on you all, and on your lords. 5 Therefore you shall make images of your tumours and images of your mice that mar the land; and you shall give glory to the God of Israel. Perhaps he will release his hand from you, from your gods, and from your land. 6 Why then do you harden your hearts as the Egyptians and Pharaoh hardened their hearts? When he had worked wonderfully amongst them, didn't they let the people go, and they departed?

7 "Now therefore take and prepare yourselves a new cart and two milk cows on which there has come no yoke; and tie the cows to the cart, and bring their calves home from them; 8 and take the LORD's ark and lay it on the cart. Put the jewels of gold, which you return him for a trespass offering, in a box by its side; and send it away, that it may go. 9 Behold, if it goes up by the way of its own border to Beth Shemesh, then he has done us this great evil; but if not, then we shall know that it is not his hand that struck us. It was a chance that happened to us."

10 The men did so, and took two milk cows and tied them to the cart, and shut up their calves at home. 11 They put the LORD's ark on the cart, and the box with the golden mice and the images of their tumours. 12 The cows took the straight way by the way to Beth Shemesh. They went along the highway, lowing as they went, and didn't turn away to the right hand or to the left; and the lords of the Philistines went after them to the border of Beth Shemesh. 13 The people of Beth Shemesh were reaping their wheat harvest in the valley; and they lifted up their eyes and saw the ark, and rejoiced to see it. 14 The cart came into the field of Joshua of Beth Shemesh, and stood there, where there was a great stone. Then they split the wood of the cart and offered up the cows for a burnt offering to the LORD. 15 The Levites took down the LORD's ark and the box that was with it, in which the jewels of gold were, and put them on the great stone; and the men of Beth Shemesh offered burnt offerings and sacrificed sacrifices the same day to the LORD. 16 When the five lords of the Philistines had seen it, they returned to Ekron the same day. 17 These are the golden tumours which the Philistines returned for a trespass offering to the LORD: for Ashdod one, for Gaza one, for Ashkelon one, for Gath one, for Ekron one; 18 and the golden mice, according to the number of all the cities of the Philistines belonging to the five lords, both of fortified cities and of country villages, even to the great stone on which they set down the LORD's ark.

That stone remains to this day in the field of Joshua of Beth Shemesh. ₁₉ He struck of the men of Beth Shemesh, because they had looked into the LORD's ark, he struck fifty thousand and seventy of the men. Then the people mourned, because the LORD had struck the people with a great slaughter. ₂₀ The men of Beth Shemesh said, "Who is able to stand before the LORD, this holy God? To whom shall he go up from us?"

₂₁ They sent messengers to the inhabitants of Kiriath Jearim, saying, "The Philistines have brought back the LORD's ark. Come down and bring it up to yourselves."

7

₁ The men of Kiriath Jearim came and took the LORD's ark, and brought it into Abinadab's house on the hill, and consecrated Eleazar his son to keep the LORD's ark. ₂ From the day that the ark stayed in Kiriath Jearim, the time was long—for it was twenty years; and all the house of Israel lamented after the LORD. ₃ Samuel spoke to all the house of Israel, saying, "If you are returning to the LORD with all your heart, then put away the foreign gods and the Ashtaroth from amongst you, and direct your hearts to the LORD, and serve him only; and he will deliver you out of the hand of the Philistines." ₄ Then the children of Israel removed the Baals and the Ashtaroth, and served the LORD only. ₅ Samuel said, "Gather all Israel to Mizpah, and I will pray to the LORD for you." ₆ They gathered together to Mizpah, and drew water, and poured it out before the LORD, and fasted on that day, and said there, "We have sinned against the LORD." Samuel judged the children of Israel in Mizpah.

₇ When the Philistines heard that the children of Israel were gathered together at Mizpah, the lords of the Philistines went up against Israel. When the children of Israel heard it, they were afraid of the Philistines. ₈ The children of Israel said to Samuel, "Don't stop crying to the LORD our God for us, that he will save us out of the hand of the Philistines." ₉ Samuel took a suckling lamb, and offered it for a whole burnt offering to the LORD. Samuel cried to the LORD for Israel, and the LORD answered him. ₁₀ As Samuel was offering up the burnt offering, the Philistines came near to battle against Israel; but the LORD thundered with a great thunder on that day on the Philistines and confused them; and they were struck down before Israel. ₁₁ The men of Israel went out of Mizpah and pursued the Philistines, and struck them until they came under Beth Kar.

₁₂ Then Samuel took a stone and set it between Mizpah and Shen, and called its name Ebenezer,ª saying, "The LORD helped us until now." ₁₃ So the Philistines were subdued, and they stopped coming within the border of Israel. The LORD's hand was against the Philistines all the days of Samuel. ₁₄ The cities which the Philistines had taken from Israel were restored to Israel, from Ekron even to Gath; and Israel recovered its border out of the hand of the Philistines. There was peace between Israel and the Amorites.

₁₅ Samuel judged Israel all the days of his life. ₁₆ He went from year to year in a circuit to Bethel, Gilgal, and Mizpah; and he judged Israel in all those places. ₁₇ His return was to Ramah, for his house was there, and he judged Israel there; and he built an altar to the LORD there.

8

₁ When Samuel was old, he made his sons judges over Israel. ₂ Now the name of his firstborn was Joel, and the name of his second, Abijah. They were judges in Beersheba. ₃ His sons didn't walk in his ways, but turned away after dishonest gain, took bribes, and perverted justice.

₄ Then all the elders of Israel gathered themselves together and came to Samuel to Ramah. ₅ They said to him, "Behold, you are old, and your sons don't walk in your ways. Now make us a king to judge us like all the nations." ₆ But the thing displeased Samuel when they said, "Give us a king to judge us."

Samuel prayed to the LORD. ₇ The LORD said to Samuel, "Listen to the voice of the people in all that they tell you; for they have not rejected you, but they have rejected me as the king over them. ₈ According to all the works which they have done since the day that I brought them up out of Egypt even to this day, in that they have forsaken me and served other gods, so they also do to you. ₉ Now therefore, listen to their voice. However, you shall protest solemnly to them, and shall show them the way of the king who will reign over them."

₁₀ Samuel told all the LORD's words to the people who asked him for a king. ₁₁ He said, "This will be the way of the king who shall reign over you: he will take your sons and appoint them as his servants, for his chariots and to be his horsemen; and they will run before his chariots. ₁₂ He will appoint them to him for captains of thousands and captains of fifties; and he will assign some to plough his ground and to reap his harvest; and to make his instruments of war and the instruments of his chariots. ₁₃ He will take your daughters to be perfumers, to be cooks, and to be bakers. ₁₄ He will take your fields, your vineyards, and your olive groves, even your best, and give them to his servants. ₁₅ He will take one tenth of your seed and of your vineyards, and give it to his officers and to his servants. ₁₆ He will take your male servants, your female servants, your best young men, and your donkeys, and assign them to his own work. ₁₇ He will take one tenth of your flocks; and you will be his servants. ₁₈ You will cry out in that day because of your king whom you will have chosen for yourselves; and the LORD will not answer you in that day."

₁₉ But the people refused to listen to the voice of Samuel; and they said, "No, but we will have a king over us, ₂₀ that we also may be like all the nations; and that our king may judge us, and go out before us, and fight our battles."

₂₁ Samuel heard all the words of the people, and he rehearsed them in the ears of the LORD. ₂₂ The LORD said to Samuel, "Listen to their voice, and make them a king."

Samuel said to the men of Israel, "Everyone go to your own city."

9

₁ Now there was a man of Benjamin, whose name was Kish the son of Abiel, the son of Zeror, the son of Becorath, the son of Aphiah, the son of a Benjamite, a mighty man of valour. ₂ He had a son whose name was Saul, an impressive young man; and there was not amongst the children of Israel a more handsome person than he. From his shoulders and upward he was taller than any of the people.

₃ The donkeys of Kish, Saul's father, were lost. Kish said to Saul his son, "Now take one of the servants with you, and arise, go look for the donkeys." ₄ He passed through the hill country of Ephraim, and passed through the land of Shalishah, but they didn't find them. Then they passed through the land of Shaalim, and they weren't there. Then he passed through the land of the Benjamites, but they didn't find them.

₅ When they had come to the land of Zuph, Saul said to his servant who was with him, "Come! Let's return, lest my father stop caring about the donkeys and be anxious for us."

₆ The servant said to him, "Behold now, there is a man of God in this city, and he is a man who is held in honour. All that he says surely happens. Now let's go there. Perhaps he can tell us which way to go."

₇ Then Saul said to his servant, "But behold, if we go, what should we bring the man? For the bread is spent in our sacks, and there is not a present to bring to the man of God. What do we have?"

₈ The servant answered Saul again and said, "Behold, I have in my hand the fourth part of a shekelᵇ of silver. I will give that to the man of God, to tell us our way." ₉ (In earlier times in Israel, when a man went to enquire of God, he said, "Come! Let's go to the seer;" for he who is now called a prophet was before called a seer.)

₁₀ Then Saul said to his servant, "Well said. Come! Let's go." So they went to the city where the man of God was. ₁₁ As they went up the ascent to the city, they found young maidens going out to draw water, and said to them, "Is the seer here?"

₁₂ They answered them and said, "He is. Behold, he is before you. Hurry now, for he has come today into the city; for the people have a sacrifice today in the high place. ₁₃ As soon as you have come into the city, you will immediately find him before he goes up to the high place to eat; for the people will not eat until he comes, because he blesses the sacrifice. Afterwards those who are invited eat. Now therefore go up; for at this time you will find him."

₁₄ They went up to the city. As they came within the city, behold, Samuel came out towards them to go up to the high place.

₁₅ Now the LORD had revealed to Samuel a day before Saul came, saying, ₁₆ "Tomorrow about this time I will send you a man out of the land of Benjamin, and you shall anoint him to be prince over my people Israel. He will save my people out of the hand of the Philistines; for I have looked upon my people, because their cry has come to me."

₁₇ When Samuel saw Saul, the LORD said to him, "Behold, the man of whom I spoke to you! He will have authority over my people."

₁₈ Then Saul approached Samuel in the gateway, and said, "Please tell me where the seer's house is."

₁₉ Samuel answered Saul and said, "I am the seer. Go up before me to the high place, for you are to eat with me today. In the morning I will let you go and will tell you all that is in your heart. ₂₀ As for your donkeys who were lost three days ago, don't set your mind on them, for they have been found. For whom does all Israel desire? Is it not you and all your father's house?"

₂₁ Saul answered, "Am I not a Benjamite, of the smallest of the tribes of Israel? And my family the least of all the families of the tribe of Benjamin? Why then do you speak to me like this?"

₂₂ Samuel took Saul and his servant and brought them into the guest room, and made them sit in the best place amongst those who were invited, who were about thirty persons. ₂₃ Samuel said to the cook, "Bring the portion which I gave you, of which I said to you, 'Set it aside.'" ₂₄ The cook took up the thigh, and that which was on it, and set it before Saul. Samuel said, "Behold, that which has been reserved! Set it before yourself and eat; because it has been kept for you for the appointed time, for I said, 'I have invited the people.'" So Saul ate with Samuel that day.

₂₅ When they had come down from the high place into the city, he talked with Saul on the housetop. ₂₆ They arose early; and about daybreak, Samuel called to Saul on the housetop, saying, "Get up, that I may send you away." Saul arose, and they both went outside, he and Samuel, together. ₂₇ As they were going down at the end of the city, Samuel said to Saul, "Tell the servant to go on ahead of us." He went ahead, then Samuel said, "But stand still first, that I may cause you to hear God's message."

10

₁ Then Samuel took the vial of oil and poured it on his head, then kissed him and said, "Hasn't the LORD anointed you to be prince over his inheritance? ₂ When you have departed from me today, then you will find two men by Rachel's tomb, on the border of Benjamin at Zelzah. They will tell you, 'The donkeys which you went to look for have been found; and behold, your father has stopped caring about the donkeys and is anxious for you, saying, "What shall I do for my son?"'

ª *7:12* "Ebenezer" means "stone of help".

ᵇ *9:8* A shekel is about 10 grams or about 0.35 ounces, so 1/4 shekel would be a small coin of about 2.5 grams.

3 "Then you will go on forward from there, and you will come to the oak of Tabor. Three men will meet you there going up to God to Bethel: one carrying three young goats, and another carrying three loaves of bread, and another carrying a container of wine. 4 They will greet you and give you two loaves of bread, which you shall receive from their hand.

5 "After that you will come to the hill of God, where the garrison of the Philistines is; and it will happen, when you have come there to the city, that you will meet a band of prophets coming down from the high place with a lute, a tambourine, a pipe, and a harp before them; and they will be prophesying. 6 Then the LORD's Spirit will come mightily on you, then you will prophesy with them and will be turned into another man. 7 Let it be, when these signs have come to you, that you do what is appropriate for the occasion; for God is with you.

8 "Go down ahead of me to Gilgal; and behold, I will come down to you to offer burnt offerings and to sacrifice sacrifices of peace offerings. Wait seven days, until I come to you and show you what you are to do." 9 It was so, that when he had turned his back to go from Samuel, God gave him another heart; and all those signs happened that day. 10 When they came there to the hill, behold, a band of prophets met him; and the Spirit of God came mightily on him, and he prophesied amongst them. 11 When all who knew him before saw that, behold, he prophesied with the prophets, then the people said to one another, "What is this that has come to the son of Kish? Is Saul also amongst the prophets?"

12 One from the same place answered, "Who is their father?" Therefore it became a proverb, "Is Saul also amongst the prophets?" 13 When he had finished prophesying, he came to the high place.

14 Saul's uncle said to him and to his servant, "Where did you go?"

He said, "To seek the donkeys. When we saw that they were not found, we came to Samuel."

15 Saul's uncle said, "Please tell me what Samuel said to you."

16 Saul said to his uncle, "He told us plainly that the donkeys were found." But concerning the matter of the kingdom, of which Samuel spoke, he didn't tell him.

17 Samuel called the people together to the LORD to Mizpah; 18 and he said to the children of Israel, "The LORD, the God of Israel, says 'I brought Israel up out of Egypt and I delivered you out of the hand of the Egyptians, and out of the hand of all the kingdoms that oppressed you.' 19 But you have today rejected your God, who himself saves you out of all your calamities and your distresses; and you have said to him, 'No! Set a king over us!' Now therefore present yourselves before the LORD by your tribes and by your thousands."

20 So Samuel brought all the tribes of Israel near, and the tribe of Benjamin was chosen. 21 He brought the tribe of Benjamin near by their families and the family of the Matrites was chosen. Then Saul the son of Kish was chosen; but when they looked for him, he could not be found. 22 Therefore they asked of the LORD further, "Is there yet a man to come here?"

The LORD answered, "Behold, he has hidden himself amongst the baggage."

23 They ran and got him there. When he stood amongst the people, he was higher than any of the people from his shoulders and upward. 24 Samuel said to all the people, "Do you see him whom the LORD has chosen, that there is no one like him amongst all the people?"

All the people shouted and said, "Long live the king!"

25 Then Samuel told the people the regulations of the kingdom, and wrote it in a book and laid it up before the LORD. Samuel sent all the people away, every man to his house. 26 Saul also went to his house in Gibeah; and the army went with him, whose hearts God had touched. 27 But certain worthless fellows said, "How could this man save us?" They despised him, and brought him no tribute. But he held his peace.

11

1 Then Nahash the Ammonite came up and encamped against Jabesh Gilead; and all the men of Jabesh said to Nahash, "Make a covenant with us, and we will serve you."

2 Nahash the Ammonite said to them, "On this condition I will make it with you, that all your right eyes be gouged out. I will make this dishonour all Israel."

3 The elders of Jabesh said to him, "Give us seven days, that we may send messengers to all the borders of Israel; and then, if there is no one to save us, we will come out to you." 4 Then the messengers came to Gibeah of Saul, and spoke these words in the ears of the people, then all the people lifted up their voice and wept.

5 Behold, Saul came following the oxen out of the field; and Saul said, "What ails the people that they weep?" They told him the words of the men of Jabesh. 6 God's Spirit came mightily on Saul when he heard those words, and his anger burnt hot. 7 He took a yoke of oxen and cut them in pieces, then sent them throughout all the borders of Israel by the hand of messengers, saying, "Whoever doesn't come out after Saul and after Samuel, so shall it be done to his oxen." The dread of the LORD fell on the people, and they came out as one man. 8 He counted them in Bezek; and the children of Israel were three hundred thousand, and the men of Judah thirty thousand. 9 They said to the messengers who came, "Tell the men of Jabesh Gilead, 'Tomorrow, by the time the sun is hot, you will be rescued.'" The messengers came and told the men of Jabesh; and they were glad. 10 Therefore the men of Jabesh said, "Tomorrow we will come out to you, and

you shall do with us all that seems good to you." 11 On the next day, Saul put the people in three companies; and they came into the middle of the camp in the morning watch, and struck the Ammonites until the heat of the day. Those who remained were scattered, so that no two of them were left together.

12 The people said to Samuel, "Who is he who said, 'Shall Saul reign over us?' Bring those men, that we may put them to death!"

13 Saul said, "No man shall be put to death today; for today the LORD has rescued Israel."

14 Then Samuel said to the people, "Come! Let's go to Gilgal, and renew the kingdom there." 15 All the people went to Gilgal; and there they made Saul king before the LORD in Gilgal. There they offered sacrifices of peace offerings before the LORD; and there Saul and all the men of Israel rejoiced greatly.

12

1 Samuel said to all Israel, "Behold, I have listened to your voice in all that you said to me, and have made a king over you. 2 Now, behold, the king walks before you. I am old and grey-headed. Behold, my sons are with you. I have walked before you from my youth to this day. 3 Here I am. Witness against me before the LORD and before his anointed. Whose ox have I taken? Whose donkey have I taken? Whom have I defrauded? Whom have I oppressed? Of whose hand have I taken a bribe to make me blind my eyes? I will restore it to you."

4 They said, "You have not defrauded us, nor oppressed us, neither have you taken anything from anyone's hand."

5 He said to them, "The LORD is witness against you, and his anointed is witness today, that you have not found anything in my hand."

They said, "He is witness." 6 Samuel said to the people, "It is the LORD who appointed Moses and Aaron, and that brought your fathers up out of the land of Egypt. 7 Now therefore stand still, that I may plead with you before the LORD concerning all the righteous acts of the LORD, which he did to you and to your fathers.

8 "When Jacob had come into Egypt, and your fathers cried to the LORD, then the LORD sent Moses and Aaron, who brought your fathers out of Egypt, and made them to dwell in this place. 9 But they forgot the LORD their God; and he sold them into the hand of Sisera, captain of the army of Hazor, and into the hand of the Philistines, and into the hand of the king of Moab; and they fought against them. 10 They cried to the LORD, and said, 'We have sinned, because we have forsaken the LORD and have served the Baals and the Ashtaroth; but now deliver us out of the hand of our enemies, and we will serve you.' 11 The LORD sent Jerubbaal, Bedan, Jephthah, and Samuel, and delivered you out of the hand of your enemies on every side; and you lived in safety.

12 "When you saw that Nahash the king of the children of Ammon came against you, you said to me, 'No, but a king shall reign over us,' when the LORD your God was your king. 13 Now therefore see the king whom you have chosen and whom you have asked for. Behold, the LORD has set a king over you. 14 If you will fear the LORD, and serve him, and listen to his voice, and not rebel against the commandment of the LORD, then both you and also the king who reigns over you are followers of the LORD your God. 15 But if you will not listen to the LORD's voice, but rebel against the commandment of the LORD, then the LORD's hand will be against you, as it was against your fathers.

16 "Now therefore stand still and see this great thing, which the LORD will do before your eyes. 17 Isn't it wheat harvest today? I will call to the LORD, that he may send thunder and rain; and you will know and see that your wickedness is great, which you have done in the LORD's sight, in asking for a king."

18 So Samuel called to the LORD, and the LORD sent thunder and rain that day. Then all the people greatly feared the LORD and Samuel.

19 All the people said to Samuel, "Pray for your servants to the LORD your God, that we not die; for we have added to all our sins this evil, to ask for a king."

20 Samuel said to the people, "Don't be afraid. You have indeed done all this evil; yet don't turn away from following the LORD, but serve the LORD with all your heart. 21 Don't turn away to go after vain things which can't profit or deliver, for they are vain. 22 For the LORD will not forsake his people for his great name's sake, because it has pleased the LORD to make you a people for himself. 23 Moreover, as for me, far be it from me that I should sin against the LORD in ceasing to pray for you; but I will instruct you in the good and the right way. 24 Only fear the LORD, and serve him in truth with all your heart; for consider what great things he has done for you. 25 But if you keep doing evil, you will be consumed, both you and your king."

13

1 Saul was thirty years old when he became king, and he reigned over Israel forty-two years.[a]

2 Saul chose for himself three thousand men of Israel, of which two thousand were with Saul in Michmash and in the Mount of Bethel, and one thousand were with Jonathan in Gibeah of Benjamin. He sent the rest of the people to their own tents. 3 Jonathan struck the garrison of the Philistines that was in Geba, and the Philistines heard of it. Saul blew the trumpet throughout all the land, saying, "Let the Hebrews hear!" 4 All Israel heard that Saul had struck the garrison of the Philistines, and also that Israel was considered an abomination to the Philistines. The people were gathered

---

a 13:1 The traditional Hebrew text omits "thirty" and "forty-". The blanks are filled in here from a few manuscripts of the Septuagint.

together after Saul to Gilgal. 5 The Philistines assembled themselves together to fight with Israel: thirty thousand chariots, six thousand horsemen, and people as the sand which is on the seashore in multitude. They came up and encamped in Michmash, eastward of Beth Aven. 6 When the men of Israel saw that they were in trouble (for the people were distressed), then the people hid themselves in caves, in thickets, in rocks, in tombs, and in pits. 7 Now some of the Hebrews had gone over the Jordan to the land of Gad and Gilead; but as for Saul, he was yet in Gilgal, and all the people followed him trembling. 8 He stayed seven days, according to the time set by Samuel; but Samuel didn't come to Gilgal, and the people were scattering from him. 9 Saul said, "Bring the burnt offering to me here, and the peace offerings." He offered the burnt offering.

10 It came to pass that as soon as he had finished offering the burnt offering, behold, Samuel came; and Saul went out to meet him, that he might greet him. 11 Samuel said, "What have you done?"

Saul said, "Because I saw that the people were scattered from me, and that you didn't come within the days appointed, and that the Philistines assembled themselves together at Michmash, 12 therefore I said, 'Now the Philistines will come down on me to Gilgal, and I haven't entreated the favour of the LORD.' I forced myself therefore, and offered the burnt offering."

13 Samuel said to Saul, "You have done foolishly. You have not kept the commandment of the LORD your God, which he commanded you; for now the LORD would have established your kingdom on Israel forever. 14 But now your kingdom will not continue. The LORD has sought for himself a man after his own heart, and the LORD has appointed him to be prince over his people, because you have not kept that which the LORD commanded you."

15 Samuel arose, and went from Gilgal to Gibeah of Benjamin. Saul counted the people who were present with him, about six hundred men. 16 Saul, and Jonathan his son, and the people who were present with them, stayed in Geba of Benjamin; but the Philistines encamped in Michmash. 17 The raiders came out of the camp of the Philistines in three companies: one company turned to the way that leads to Ophrah, to the land of Shual; 18 another company turned the way to Beth Horon; and another company turned the way of the border that looks down on the valley of Zeboim towards the wilderness. 19 Now there was no blacksmith found throughout all the land of Israel, for the Philistines said, "Lest the Hebrews make themselves swords or spears"; 20 but all the Israelites went down to the Philistines, each man to sharpen his own ploughshare, mattock, axe, and sickle. 21 The price was one payim[a] each to sharpen mattocks, ploughshares, pitchforks, axes, and goads. 22 So it came to pass in the day of battle that neither sword nor spear was found in the hand of any of the people who were with Saul and Jonathan; but Saul and Jonathan his son had them.

23 The garrison of the Philistines went out to the pass of Michmash.

14

1 Now it happened on a day that Jonathan the son of Saul said to the young man who bore his armour, "Come! Let's go over to the Philistines' garrison that is on the other side." But he didn't tell his father. 2 Saul stayed in the uttermost part of Gibeah under the pomegranate tree which is in Migron; and the people who were with him were about six hundred men, 3 including Ahijah the son of Ahitub, Ichabod's brother, the son of Phinehas, the son of Eli the priest of the LORD in Shiloh, wearing an ephod. The people didn't know that Jonathan was gone.

4 Between the passes, by which Jonathan sought to go over to the Philistines' garrison, there was a rocky crag on the one side and a rocky crag on the other side; and the name of the one was Bozez, and the name of the other Seneh. 5 The one crag rose up on the north in front of Michmash, and the other on the south in front of Geba. 6 Jonathan said to the young man who bore his armour, "Come! Let's go over to the garrison of these uncircumcised. It may be that the LORD will work for us, for there is no restraint on the LORD to save by many or by few."

7 His armour bearer said to him, "Do all that is in your heart. Go, and behold, I am with you according to your heart."

8 Then Jonathan said, "Behold, we will pass over to the men, and we will reveal ourselves to them. 9 If they say this to us, 'Wait until we come to you!' then we will stand still in our place and will not go up to them. 10 But if they say this, 'Come up to us!' then we will go up, for the LORD has delivered them into our hand. This shall be the sign to us."

11 Both of them revealed themselves to the garrison of the Philistines; and the Philistines said, "Behold, the Hebrews are coming out of the holes where they had hidden themselves!" 12 The men of the garrison answered Jonathan and his armour bearer, and said, "Come up to us, and we will show you something!"

Jonathan said to his armour bearer, "Come up after me, for the LORD has delivered them into the hand of Israel." 13 Jonathan climbed up on his hands and on his feet, and his armour bearer after him, and they fell before Jonathan; and his armour bearer killed them after him. 14 That first slaughter, which Jonathan and his armour bearer made, was about twenty men, within as it were half a furrow's length in an acre of land.

15 There was a trembling in the camp, in the field, and amongst all the people; the garrison and the raiders also trembled; and the earth quaked, so there was an exceedingly great trembling. 16 The watchmen of Saul in Gibeah of Benjamin looked; and behold, the multitude melted away and scattered. 17 Then Saul said to the people who were with him, "Count now,

and see who is missing from us." When they had counted, behold, Jonathan and his armour bearer were not there.

18 Saul said to Ahijah, "Bring God's ark here." For God's ark was with the children of Israel at that time. 19 While Saul talked to the priest, the tumult that was in the camp of the Philistines went on and increased; and Saul said to the priest, "Withdraw your hand!"

20 Saul and all the people who were with him were gathered together, and came to the battle; and behold, they were all striking each other with their swords in very great confusion. 21 Now the Hebrews who were with the Philistines before and who went up with them into the camp from all around, even they also turned to be with the Israelites who were with Saul and Jonathan. 22 Likewise all the men of Israel who had hidden themselves in the hill country of Ephraim, when they heard that the Philistines fled, even they also followed hard after them in the battle. 23 So the LORD saved Israel that day; and the battle passed over by Beth Aven.

24 The men of Israel were distressed that day; for Saul had adjured the people, saying, "Cursed is the man who eats any food until it is evening, and I am avenged of my enemies." So none of the people tasted food.

25 All the people came into the forest; and there was honey on the ground. 26 When the people had come to the forest, behold, honey was dripping, but no one put his hand to his mouth, for the people feared the oath. 27 But Jonathan didn't hear when his father commanded the people with the oath. Therefore he put out the end of the rod that was in his hand and dipped it in the honeycomb, and put his hand to his mouth; and his eyes brightened. 28 Then one of the people answered, and said, "Your father directly commanded the people with an oath, saying, 'Cursed is the man who eats food today.'" So the people were faint.

29 Then Jonathan said, "My father has troubled the land. Please look how my eyes have brightened because I tasted a little of this honey. 30 How much more, if perhaps the people had eaten freely today of the plunder of their enemies which they found? For now there has been no great slaughter amongst the Philistines." 31 They struck the Philistines that day from Michmash to Aijalon. The people were very faint; 32 and the people pounced on the plunder, and took sheep, cattle, and calves, and killed them on the ground; and the people ate them with the blood. 33 Then they told Saul, saying, "Behold, the people are sinning against the LORD, in that they eat meat with the blood."

He said, "You have dealt treacherously. Roll a large stone to me today!" 34 Saul said, "Disperse yourselves amongst the people, and tell them, 'Every man bring me here his ox, and every man his sheep, and kill them here, and eat; and don't sin against the LORD in eating meat with the blood.'" All the people brought every man his ox with him that night, and killed them there.

35 Saul built an altar to the LORD. This was the first altar that he built to the LORD. 36 Saul said, "Let's go down after the Philistines by night, and take plunder amongst them until the morning light. Let's not leave a man of them."

They said, "Do whatever seems good to you."

Then the priest said, "Let's draw near here to God."

37 Saul asked counsel of God: "Shall I go down after the Philistines? Will you deliver them into the hand of Israel?" But he didn't answer him that day. 38 Saul said, "Draw near here, all you chiefs of the people, and know and see in whom this sin has been today. 39 For as the LORD lives, who saves Israel, though it is in Jonathan my son, he shall surely die." But there was not a man amongst all the people who answered him. 40 Then he said to all Israel, "You be on one side, and I and Jonathan my son will be on the other side."

The people said to Saul, "Do what seems good to you."

41 Therefore Saul said to the LORD, the God of Israel, "Show the right."

Jonathan and Saul were chosen, but the people escaped. 42 Saul said, "Cast lots between me and Jonathan my son."

Jonathan was selected.

43 Then Saul said to Jonathan, "Tell me what you have done!"

Jonathan told him, and said, "I certainly did taste a little honey with the end of the rod that was in my hand; and behold, I must die."

44 Saul said, "God do so and more also; for you shall surely die, Jonathan."

45 The people said to Saul, "Shall Jonathan die, who has worked this great salvation in Israel? Far from it! As the LORD lives, there shall not one hair of his head fall to the ground, for he has worked with God today!" So the people rescued Jonathan, so he didn't die. 46 Then Saul went up from following the Philistines; and the Philistines went to their own place.

47 Now when Saul had taken the kingdom over Israel, he fought against all his enemies on every side: against Moab, and against the children of Ammon, and against Edom, and against the kings of Zobah, and against the Philistines. Wherever he turned himself, he defeated them. 48 He did valiantly and struck the Amalekites, and delivered Israel out of the hands of those who plundered them. 49 Now the sons of Saul were Jonathan, Ishvi, and Malchishua; and the names of his two daughters were these: the name of the firstborn Merab, and the name of the younger Michal. 50 The name of Saul's wife was Ahinoam the daughter of Ahimaaz. The name of the captain of his army was Abner the son of Ner, Saul's uncle. 51 Kish was the father of Saul, and Ner the father of Abner was the son of Abiel.

---

a *13:21* A payim (or pim) was 2/3 shekel of silver, or 0.26 ounces, or 7.6 grams

52 There was severe war against the Philistines all the days of Saul; and when Saul saw any mighty man or any valiant man, he took him into his service.

15

1 Samuel said to Saul, "The LORD sent me to anoint you to be king over his people, over Israel. Now therefore listen to the voice of the LORD's words. 2 The LORD of Armies says, 'I remember what Amalek did to Israel, how he set himself against him on the way when he came up out of Egypt. 3 Now go and strike Amalek, and utterly destroy all that they have, and don't spare them; but kill both man and woman, infant and nursing baby, ox and sheep, camel and donkey.'"

4 Saul summoned the people, and counted them in Telaim, two hundred thousand footmen and ten thousand men of Judah. 5 Saul came to the city of Amalek, and set an ambush in the valley. 6 Saul said to the Kenites, "Go, depart, go down from amongst the Amalekites, lest I destroy you with them; for you showed kindness to all the children of Israel when they came up out of Egypt." So the Kenites departed from amongst the Amalekites.

7 Saul struck the Amalekites, from Havilah as you go to Shur, which is before Egypt. 8 He took Agag the king of the Amalekites alive, and utterly destroyed all the people with the edge of the sword. 9 But Saul and the people spared Agag and the best of the sheep, of the cattle, of the fat calves, of the lambs, and all that was good, and were not willing to utterly destroy them; but everything that was vile and refuse, that they destroyed utterly.

10 Then the LORD's word came to Samuel, saying, 11 "It grieves me that I have set up Saul to be king, for he has turned back from following me, and has not performed my commandments." Samuel was angry; and he cried to the LORD all night.

12 Samuel rose early to meet Saul in the morning; and Samuel was told, saying, "Saul came to Carmel, and behold, he set up a monument for himself, turned, passed on, and went down to Gilgal."

13 Samuel came to Saul; and Saul said to him, "You are blessed by the LORD! I have performed the commandment of the LORD."

14 Samuel said, "Then what does this bleating of the sheep in my ears and the lowing of the cattle which I hear mean?"

15 Saul said, "They have brought them from the Amalekites; for the people spared the best of the sheep and of the cattle, to sacrifice to the LORD your God. We have utterly destroyed the rest."

16 Then Samuel said to Saul, "Stay, and I will tell you what the LORD said to me last night."

He said to him, "Say on."

17 Samuel said, "Though you were little in your own sight, weren't you made the head of the tribes of Israel? The LORD anointed you king over Israel; 18 and the LORD sent you on a journey, and said, 'Go, and utterly destroy the sinners the Amalekites, and fight against them until they are consumed.' 19 Why then didn't you obey the LORD's voice, but took the plunder, and did that which was evil in the LORD's sight?"

20 Saul said to Samuel, "But I have obeyed the LORD's voice, and have gone the way which the LORD sent me, and have brought Agag the king of Amalek, and have utterly destroyed the Amalekites. 21 But the people took of the plunder, sheep and cattle, the best of the devoted things, to sacrifice to the LORD your God in Gilgal."

22 Samuel said, "Has the LORD as great delight in burnt offerings and sacrifices, as in obeying the LORD's voice? Behold, to obey is better than sacrifice, and to listen than the fat of rams. 23 For rebellion is as the sin of witchcraft, and stubbornness is as idolatry and teraphim.[a] Because you have rejected the LORD's word, he has also rejected you from being king."

24 Saul said to Samuel, "I have sinned; for I have transgressed the commandment of the LORD and your words, because I feared the people and obeyed their voice. 25 Now therefore, please pardon my sin, and turn again with me, that I may worship the LORD."

26 Samuel said to Saul, "I will not return with you; for you have rejected the LORD's word, and the LORD has rejected you from being king over Israel." 27 As Samuel turned around to go away, Saul grabbed the skirt of his robe, and it tore. 28 Samuel said to him, "The LORD has torn the kingdom of Israel from you today, and has given it to a neighbour of yours who is better than you. 29 Also the Strength of Israel will not lie nor repent; for he is not a man, that he should repent."

30 Then he said, "I have sinned; yet please honour me now before the elders of my people and before Israel, and come back with me, that I may worship the LORD your God."

31 So Samuel went back with Saul; and Saul worshipped the LORD. 32 Then Samuel said, "Bring Agag the king of the Amalekites here to me!"

Agag came to him cheerfully. Agag said, "Surely the bitterness of death is past."

33 Samuel said, "As your sword has made women childless, so your mother will be childless amongst women!" Then Samuel cut Agag in pieces before the LORD in Gilgal.

34 Then Samuel went to Ramah; and Saul went up to his house to Gibeah of Saul. 35 Samuel came no more to see Saul until the day of his death, but Samuel mourned for Saul. The LORD grieved that he had made Saul king over Israel.

16

1 The LORD said to Samuel, "How long will you mourn for Saul, since I have rejected him from being king over Israel? Fill your horn with oil, and go. I will send you to Jesse the Bethlehemite, for I have provided a king for myself amongst his sons."

2 Samuel said, "How can I go? If Saul hears it, he will kill me."

The LORD said, "Take a heifer with you, and say, 'I have come to sacrifice to the LORD.' 3 Call Jesse to the sacrifice, and I will show you what you shall do. You shall anoint to me him whom I name to you."

4 Samuel did that which the LORD spoke, and came to Bethlehem. The elders of the city came to meet him trembling, and said, "Do you come peaceably?"

5 He said, "Peaceably; I have come to sacrifice to the LORD. Sanctify yourselves, and come with me to the sacrifice." He sanctified Jesse and his sons, and called them to the sacrifice. 6 When they had come, he looked at Eliab, and said, "Surely the LORD's anointed is before him."

7 But the LORD said to Samuel, "Don't look on his face, or on the height of his stature, because I have rejected him; for I don't see as man sees. For man looks at the outward appearance, but the LORD looks at the heart."

8 Then Jesse called Abinadab, and made him pass before Samuel. He said, "The LORD has not chosen this one, either." 9 Then Jesse made Shammah to pass by. He said, "The LORD has not chosen this one, either." 10 Jesse made seven of his sons to pass before Samuel. Samuel said to Jesse, "The LORD has not chosen these." 11 Samuel said to Jesse, "Are all your children here?"

He said, "There remains yet the youngest. Behold, he is keeping the sheep."

Samuel said to Jesse, "Send and get him, for we will not sit down until he comes here."

12 He sent, and brought him in. Now he was ruddy, with a handsome face and good appearance. The LORD said, "Arise! Anoint him, for this is he."

13 Then Samuel took the horn of oil and anointed him in the middle of his brothers. Then the LORD's Spirit came mightily on David from that day forward. So Samuel rose up and went to Ramah. 14 Now the LORD's Spirit departed from Saul, and an evil spirit from the LORD troubled him. 15 Saul's servants said to him, "See now, an evil spirit from God troubles you. 16 Let our lord now command your servants who are in front of you to seek out a man who is a skilful player on the harp. Then when the evil spirit from God is on you, he will play with his hand, and you will be well."

17 Saul said to his servants, "Provide me now a man who can play well, and bring him to me."

18 Then one of the young men answered and said, "Behold, I have seen a son of Jesse the Bethlehemite who is skilful in playing, a mighty man of valour, a man of war, prudent in speech, and a handsome person; and the LORD is with him."

19 Therefore Saul sent messengers to Jesse, and said, "Send me David your son, who is with the sheep."

20 Jesse took a donkey loaded with bread, a container of wine, and a young goat, and sent them by David his son to Saul. 21 David came to Saul and stood before him. He loved him greatly; and he became his armour bearer. 22 Saul sent to Jesse, saying, "Please let David stand before me, for he has found favour in my sight." 23 When the spirit from God was on Saul, David took the harp and played with his hand; so Saul was refreshed and was well, and the evil spirit departed from him.

17

1 Now the Philistines gathered together their armies to battle; and they were gathered together at Socoh, which belongs to Judah, and encamped between Socoh and Azekah in Ephesdammim. 2 Saul and the men of Israel were gathered together, and encamped in the valley of Elah, and set the battle in array against the Philistines. 3 The Philistines stood on the mountain on the one side, and Israel stood on the mountain on the other side: and there was a valley between them. 4 A champion out of the camp of the Philistines named Goliath of Gath, whose height was six cubits and a span[b] went out. 5 He had a helmet of bronze on his head, and he wore a coat of mail; and the weight of the coat was five thousand shekels[c] of bronze. 6 He had bronze shin armour on his legs and a bronze javelin between his shoulders. 7 The staff of his spear was like a weaver's beam; and his spear's head weighed six hundred shekels of iron.[d] His shield bearer went before him. 8 He stood and cried to the armies of Israel, and said to them, "Why have you come out to set your battle in array? Am I not a Philistine, and you servants to Saul? Choose a man for yourselves, and let him come down to me. 9 If he is able to fight with me and kill me, then will we be your servants; but if I prevail against him and kill him, then you will be our servants and serve us." 10 The Philistine said, "I defy the armies of Israel today! Give me a man, that we may fight together!"

11 When Saul and all Israel heard those words of the Philistine, they were dismayed and greatly afraid. 12 Now David was the son of that

---

a 15:23 teraphim were household idols that may have been associated with inheritance rights to the household property.

b 17:4 A cubit is the length from the tip of the middle finger to the elbow on a man's arm, or about 18 inches or 46 centimetres. A span is the length from the tip of a man's thumb to the tip of his little finger when his hand is stretched out

(about half a cubit, or 9 inches, or 22.8 cm.) Therefore, Goliath was about 9 feet and 9 inches or 2.97 metres tall.

c 17:5 A shekel is about 10 grams or about 0.35 ounces, so 5000 shekels is about 50 kilograms or 110 pounds.

d 17:7 A shekel is about 10 grams or about 0.35 ounces, so 600 shekels is about 6 kilograms or about 13 pounds.

Ephrathite of Bethlehem Judah, whose name was Jesse; and he had eight sons. The man was an elderly old man in the days of Saul. 13 The three oldest sons of Jesse had gone after Saul to the battle; and the names of his three sons who went to the battle were Eliab the firstborn, and next to him Abinadab, and the third Shammah. 14 David was the youngest; and the three oldest followed Saul. 15 Now David went back and forth from Saul to feed his father's sheep at Bethlehem.

16 The Philistine came near morning and evening, and presented himself forty days.

17 Jesse said to David his son, "Now take for your brothers an ephah[a] of this parched grain and these ten loaves, and carry them quickly to the camp to your brothers; 18 and bring these ten cheeses to the captain of their thousand; and see how your brothers are doing, and bring back news." 19 Now Saul, and they, and all the men of Israel were in the valley of Elah, fighting with the Philistines.

20 David rose up early in the morning and left the sheep with a keeper, and took the provisions and went, as Jesse had commanded him. He came to the place of the wagons as the army which was going out to the fight shouted for the battle. 21 Israel and the Philistines put the battle in array, army against army. 22 David left his baggage in the hand of the keeper of the baggage and ran to the army, and came and greeted his brothers. 23 As he talked with them, behold, the champion, the Philistine of Gath, Goliath by name, came up out of the ranks of the Philistines, and said the same words; and David heard them. 24 All the men of Israel, when they saw the man, fled from him and were terrified. 25 The men of Israel said, "Have you seen this man who has come up? He has surely come up to defy Israel. The king will give great riches to the man who kills him, and will give him his daughter, and will make his father's house tax-free in Israel."

26 David spoke to the men who stood by him, saying, "What shall be done to the man who kills this Philistine and takes away the reproach from Israel? For who is this uncircumcised Philistine, that he should defy the armies of the living God?"

27 The people answered him in this way, saying, "So shall it be done to the man who kills him."

28 Eliab his oldest brother heard when he spoke to the men; and Eliab's anger burnt against David, and he said, "Why have you come down? With whom have you left those few sheep in the wilderness? I know your pride and the evil of your heart; for you have come down that you might see the battle."

29 David said, "What have I now done? Is there not a cause?" 30 He turned away from him towards another, and spoke like that again; and the people answered him again the same way. 31 When the words were heard which David spoke, they rehearsed them before Saul; and he sent for him. 32 David said to Saul, "Let no man's heart fail because of him. Your servant will go and fight with this Philistine."

33 Saul said to David, "You are not able to go against this Philistine to fight with him; for you are but a youth, and he a man of war from his youth."

34 David said to Saul, "Your servant was keeping his father's sheep; and when a lion or a bear came and took a lamb out of the flock, 35 I went out after him, struck him, and rescued it out of his mouth. When he arose against me, I caught him by his beard, struck him, and killed him. 36 Your servant struck both the lion and the bear. This uncircumcised Philistine shall be as one of them, since he has defied the armies of the living God." 37 David said, "The LORD, who delivered me out of the paw of the lion and out of the paw of the bear, will deliver me out of the hand of this Philistine."

Saul said to David, "Go! The LORD will be with you."

38 Saul dressed David with his clothing. He put a helmet of bronze on his head, and he clad him with a coat of mail. 39 David strapped his sword on his clothing and he tried to move, for he had not tested it. David said to Saul, "I can't go with these, for I have not tested them." Then David took them off.

40 He took his staff in his hand, and chose for himself five smooth stones out of the brook, and put them in the pouch of his shepherd's bag which he had. His sling was in his hand; and he came near to the Philistine. 41 The Philistine walked and came near to David; and the man who bore the shield went before him. 42 When the Philistine looked around and saw David, he disdained him; for he was but a youth, and ruddy, and had a good looking face. 43 The Philistine said to David, "Am I a dog, that you come to me with sticks?" The Philistine cursed David by his gods. 44 The Philistine said to David, "Come to me, and I will give your flesh to the birds of the sky and to the animals of the field."

45 Then David said to the Philistine, "You come to me with a sword, with a spear, and with a javelin; but I come to you in the name of the LORD of Armies, the God of the armies of Israel, whom you have defied. 46 Today, the LORD will deliver you into my hand. I will strike you and take your head from off you. I will give the dead bodies of the army of the Philistines today to the birds of the sky and to the wild animals of the earth, that all the earth may know that there is a God in Israel, 47 and that all this assembly may know that the LORD doesn't save with sword and spear; for the battle is the LORD's, and he will give you into our hand."

48 When the Philistine arose, and walked and came near to meet David, David hurried and ran towards the army to meet the Philistine. 49 David put his hand in his bag, took a stone and slung it, and struck the Philistine in his forehead. The stone sank into his forehead, and he fell on his face to the earth. 50 So David prevailed over the Philistine with a sling and with a stone, and struck the Philistine and killed him; but there was no

sword in David's hand. 51 Then David ran, stood over the Philistine, took his sword, drew it out of its sheath, killed him, and cut off his head with it.

When the Philistines saw that their champion was dead, they fled. 52 The men of Israel and of Judah arose and shouted, and pursued the Philistines as far as Gai and to the gates of Ekron. The wounded of the Philistines fell down by the way to Shaaraim, even to Gath and to Ekron. 53 The children of Israel returned from chasing after the Philistines, and they plundered their camp. 54 David took the head of the Philistine and brought it to Jerusalem, but he put his armour in his tent. 55 When Saul saw David go out against the Philistine, he said to Abner, the captain of the army, "Abner, whose son is this youth?"

Abner said, "As your soul lives, O king, I can't tell."

56 The king said, "Enquire whose son the young man is!"

57 As David returned from the slaughter of the Philistine, Abner took him and brought him before Saul with the head of the Philistine in his hand. 58 Saul said to him, "Whose son are you, you young man?"

David answered, "I am the son of your servant Jesse the Bethlehemite."

18

1 When he had finished speaking to Saul, the soul of Jonathan was knit with the soul of David, and Jonathan loved him as his own soul. 2 Saul took him that day, and wouldn't let him go home to his father's house any more. 3 Then Jonathan and David made a covenant, because he loved him as his own soul. 4 Jonathan stripped himself of the robe that was on him and gave it to David with his clothing, even including his sword, his bow, and his sash.

5 David went out wherever Saul sent him, and behaved himself wisely; and Saul set him over the men of war. It was good in the sight of all the people, and also in the sight of Saul's servants.

6 As they came, when David returned from the slaughter of the Philistine, the women came out of all the cities of Israel, singing and dancing, to meet King Saul with tambourines, with joy, and with instruments of music. 7 The women sang to one another as they played, and said,
"Saul has slain his thousands,
    and David his ten thousands."

8 Saul was very angry, and this saying displeased him. He said, "They have credited David with ten thousands, and they have only credited me with thousands. What can he have more but the kingdom?" 9 Saul watched David from that day and forward. 10 On the next day, an evil spirit from God came mightily on Saul, and he prophesied in the middle of the house. David played with his hand, as he did day by day. Saul had his spear in his hand; 11 and Saul threw the spear, for he said, "I will pin David to the wall!" David escaped from his presence twice. 12 Saul was afraid of David, because the LORD was with him, and had departed from Saul. 13 Therefore Saul removed him from his presence, and made him his captain over a thousand; and he went out and came in before the people.

14 David behaved himself wisely in all his ways; and the LORD was with him. 15 When Saul saw that he behaved himself very wisely, he stood in awe of him. 16 But all Israel and Judah loved David; for he went out and came in before them. 17 Saul said to David, "Behold, my elder daughter Merab. I will give her to you as wife. Only be valiant for me, and fight the LORD's battles." For Saul said, "Don't let my hand be on him, but let the hand of the Philistines be on him."

18 David said to Saul, "Who am I, and what is my life, or my father's family in Israel, that I should be son-in-law to the king?"

19 But at the time when Merab, Saul's daughter, should have been given to David, she was given to Adriel the Meholathite as wife.

20 Michal, Saul's daughter, loved David; and they told Saul, and the thing pleased him. 21 Saul said, I will give her to him, that she may be a snare to him and that the hand of the Philistines may be against him. Therefore Saul said to David a second time, "You shall today be my son-in-law."

22 Saul commanded his servants, "Talk with David secretly, and say, 'Behold, the king has delight in you, and all his servants love you. Now therefore be the king's son-in-law.'"

23 Saul's servants spoke those words in the ears of David. David said, "Does it seem to you a light thing to be the king's son-in-law, since I am a poor man and little known?"

24 The servants of Saul told him, saying, "David spoke like this."

25 Saul said, "Tell David, 'The king desires no dowry except one hundred foreskins of the Philistines, to be avenged of the king's enemies.'" Now Saul thought he would make David fall by the hand of the Philistines. 26 When his servants told David these words, it pleased David well to be the king's son-in-law. Before the deadline, 27 David arose and went, he and his men, and killed two hundred men of the Philistines. Then David brought their foreskins, and they gave them in full number to the king, that he might be the king's son-in-law. Then Saul gave him Michal his daughter as wife. 28 Saul saw and knew that the LORD was with David; and Michal, Saul's daughter, loved him. 29 Saul was even more afraid of David; and Saul was David's enemy continually.

30 Then the princes of the Philistines went out; and as often as they went out, David behaved himself more wisely than all the servants of Saul, so that his name was highly esteemed.

---

[a] *17:17* 1 ephah is about 22 litres or about 2/3 of a bushel

19

1 Saul spoke to Jonathan his son and to all his servants, that they should kill David. But Jonathan, Saul's son, greatly delighted in David. 2 Jonathan told David, saying, "Saul my father seeks to kill you. Now therefore, please take care of yourself in the morning, live in a secret place, and hide yourself. 3 I will go out and stand beside my father in the field where you are, and I will talk with my father about you; and if I see anything, I will tell you."

4 Jonathan spoke good of David to Saul his father, and said to him, "Don't let the king sin against his servant, against David; because he has not sinned against you, and because his works have been very good towards you; 5 for he put his life in his hand and struck the Philistine, and the LORD worked a great victory for all Israel. You saw it and rejoiced. Why then will you sin against innocent blood, to kill David without a cause?"

6 Saul listened to the voice of Jonathan; and Saul swore, "As the LORD lives, he shall not be put to death."

7 Jonathan called David, and Jonathan showed him all those things. Then Jonathan brought David to Saul, and he was in his presence as before.

8 There was war again. David went out and fought with the Philistines, and killed them with a great slaughter; and they fled before him.

9 An evil spirit from the LORD was on Saul as he sat in his house with his spear in his hand; and David was playing music with his hand. 10 Saul sought to pin David to the wall with the spear, but he slipped away out of Saul's presence; and he stuck the spear into the wall. David fled and escaped that night. 11 Saul sent messengers to David's house to watch him and to kill him in the morning. Michal, David's wife, told him, saying, "If you don't save your life tonight, tomorrow you will be killed." 12 So Michal let David down through the window. He went away, fled, and escaped. 13 Michal took the teraphim[a] and laid it in the bed, and put a pillow of goats' hair at its head and covered it with clothes. 14 When Saul sent messengers to take David, she said, "He is sick."

15 Saul sent the messengers to see David, saying, "Bring him up to me in the bed, that I may kill him." 16 When the messengers came in, behold, the teraphim was in the bed, with the pillow of goats' hair at its head.

17 Saul said to Michal, "Why have you deceived me like this and let my enemy go, so that he has escaped?"

Michal answered Saul, "He said to me, 'Let me go! Why should I kill you?'"

18 Now David fled and escaped, and came to Samuel at Ramah, and told him all that Saul had done to him. He and Samuel went and lived in Naioth. 19 Saul was told, saying, "Behold, David is at Naioth in Ramah." 20 Saul sent messengers to seize David; and when they saw the company of the prophets prophesying, and Samuel standing as head over them, God's Spirit came on Saul's messengers, and they also prophesied. 21 When Saul was told, he sent other messengers, and they also prophesied. Saul sent messengers again the third time, and they also prophesied. 22 Then he also went to Ramah, and came to the great well that is in Secu: and he asked, "Where are Samuel and David?"

One said, "Behold, they are at Naioth in Ramah."

23 He went there to Naioth in Ramah. Then God's Spirit came on him also, and he went on, and prophesied, until he came to Naioth in Ramah. 24 He also stripped off his clothes. He also prophesied before Samuel and lay down naked all that day and all that night. Therefore they say, "Is Saul also amongst the prophets?"

20

1 David fled from Naioth in Ramah, and came and said to Jonathan, "What have I done? What is my iniquity? What is my sin before your father, that he seeks my life?"

2 He said to him, "Far from it; you will not die. Behold, my father does nothing either great or small, but that he discloses it to me. Why would my father hide this thing from me? It is not so."

3 David swore moreover, and said, "Your father knows well that I have found favour in your eyes; and he says, 'Don't let Jonathan know this, lest he be grieved;' but truly as the LORD lives, and as your soul lives, there is but a step between me and death."

4 Then Jonathan said to David, "Whatever your soul desires, I will even do it for you."

5 David said to Jonathan, "Behold, tomorrow is the new moon, and I should not fail to dine with the king; but let me go, that I may hide myself in the field to the third day at evening. 6 If your father misses me at all, then say, 'David earnestly asked leave of me that he might run to Bethlehem, his city; for it is the yearly sacrifice there for all the family.' 7 If he says, 'It is well,' your servant shall have peace; but if he is angry, then know that evil is determined by him. 8 Therefore deal kindly with your servant, for you have brought your servant into a covenant of the LORD with you; but if there is iniquity in me, kill me yourself, for why should you bring me to your father?"

9 Jonathan said, "Far be it from you; for if I should at all know that evil were determined by my father to come on you, then wouldn't I tell you that?"

10 Then David said to Jonathan, "Who will tell me if your father answers you roughly?"

11 Jonathan said to David, "Come! Let's go out into the field." They both went out into the field. 12 Jonathan said to David, "By the LORD, the God of Israel, when I have sounded out my father about this time tomorrow, or the third day, behold, if there is good towards David, won't I then send to you and disclose it to you? 13 The LORD do so to Jonathan and more also, should it please my father to do you evil, if I don't disclose it to you and send you away, that you may go in peace. May the LORD be with you as he has been with my father. 14 You shall not only show me the loving kindness of the LORD while I still live, that I not die; 15 but you shall also not cut off your kindness from my house forever, no, not when the LORD has cut off every one of the enemies of David from the surface of the earth." 16 So Jonathan made a covenant with David's house, saying, "The LORD will require it at the hand of David's enemies."

17 Jonathan caused David to swear again, for the love that he had to him; for he loved him as he loved his own soul. 18 Then Jonathan said to him, "Tomorrow is the new moon, and you will be missed, because your seat will be empty. 19 When you have stayed three days, go down quickly and come to the place where you hid yourself when this started, and remain by the stone Ezel. 20 I will shoot three arrows on its side, as though I shot at a mark. 21 Behold, I will send the boy, saying, 'Go, find the arrows!' If I tell the boy, 'Behold, the arrows are on this side of you. Take them;' then come, for there is peace to you and no danger, as the LORD lives. 22 But if I say this to the boy, 'Behold, the arrows are beyond you,' then go your way, for the LORD has sent you away. 23 Concerning the matter which you and I have spoken of, behold, the LORD is between you and me forever."

24 So David hid himself in the field. When the new moon had come, the king sat himself down to eat food. 25 The king sat on his seat, as at other times, even on the seat by the wall; and Jonathan stood up, and Abner sat by Saul's side, but David's place was empty. 26 Nevertheless Saul didn't say anything that day, for he thought, "Something has happened to him. He is not clean. Surely he is not clean."

27 On the next day after the new moon, the second day, David's place was empty. Saul said to Jonathan his son, "Why didn't the son of Jesse come to eat, either yesterday, or today?"

28 Jonathan answered Saul, "David earnestly asked permission of me to go to Bethlehem. 29 He said, 'Please let me go, for our family has a sacrifice in the city. My brother has commanded me to be there. Now, if I have found favour in your eyes, please let me go away and see my brothers.' Therefore he has not come to the king's table."

30 Then Saul's anger burnt against Jonathan, and he said to him, "You son of a perverse rebellious woman, don't I know that you have chosen the son of Jesse to your own shame, and to the shame of your mother's nakedness? 31 For as long as the son of Jesse lives on the earth, you will not be established, nor will your kingdom. Therefore now send and bring him to me, for he shall surely die!"

32 Jonathan answered Saul his father, and said to him, "Why should he be put to death? What has he done?"

33 Saul cast his spear at him to strike him. By this Jonathan knew that his father was determined to put David to death. 34 So Jonathan arose from the table in fierce anger, and ate no food the second day of the month; for he was grieved for David, because his father had treated him shamefully.

35 In the morning, Jonathan went out into the field at the time appointed with David, and a little boy with him. 36 He said to his boy, "Run, find now the arrows which I shoot." As the boy ran, he shot an arrow beyond him. 37 When the boy had come to the place of the arrow which Jonathan had shot, Jonathan cried after the boy, and said, "Isn't the arrow beyond you?" 38 Jonathan cried after the boy, "Go fast! Hurry! Don't delay!" Jonathan's boy gathered up the arrows, and came to his master. 39 But the boy didn't know anything. Only Jonathan and David knew the matter. 40 Jonathan gave his weapons to his boy, and said to him, "Go, carry them to the city."

41 As soon as the boy was gone, David arose out of the south, and fell on his face to the ground, and bowed himself three times. They kissed one another and wept with one another, and David wept the most. 42 Jonathan said to David, "Go in peace, because we have both sworn in the LORD's name, saying, 'The LORD is between me and you, and between my offspring and your offspring, forever.'" He arose and departed; and Jonathan went into the city.

21

1 Then David came to Nob to Ahimelech the priest. Ahimelech came to meet David trembling, and said to him, "Why are you alone, and no man with you?" 2 David said to Ahimelech the priest, "The king has commanded me to do something, and has said to me, 'Let no one know anything about the business about which I send you, and what I have commanded you. I have sent the young men to a certain place.' 3 Now therefore what is under your hand? Please give me five loaves of bread in my hand, or whatever is available."

4 The priest answered David, and said, "I have no common bread, but there is holy bread; if only the young men have kept themselves from women."

5 David answered the priest, and said to him, "Truly, women have been kept from us as usual these three days. When I came out, the vessels of the young men were holy, though it was only a common journey. How much more then today shall their vessels be holy?" 6 So the priest gave him holy bread; for there was no bread there but the show bread that was taken from before the LORD, to be replaced with hot bread in the day when it was taken away.

---

a *19:13* teraphim were household idols that may have been associated with inheritance rights to the household property.

7 Now a certain man of the servants of Saul was there that day, detained before the LORD; and his name was Doeg the Edomite, the best of the herdsmen who belonged to Saul.

8 David said to Ahimelech, "Isn't there here under your hand spear or sword? For I haven't brought my sword or my weapons with me, because the king's business required haste."

9 The priest said, "Behold, the sword of Goliath the Philistine, whom you killed in the valley of Elah, is here wrapped in a cloth behind the ephod. If you would like to take that, take it, for there is no other except that here."

David said, "There is none like that. Give it to me."

10 David arose and fled that day for fear of Saul, and went to Achish the king of Gath. 11 The servants of Achish said to him, "Isn't this David the king of the land? Didn't they sing to one another about him in dances, saying,

'Saul has slain his thousands,
    and David his ten thousands'?"

12 David laid up these words in his heart, and was very afraid of Achish the king of Gath. 13 He changed his behaviour before them and pretended to be insane in their hands, and scribbled on the doors of the gate, and let his spittle fall down on his beard. 14 Then Achish said to his servants, "Look, you see the man is insane. Why then have you brought him to me? 15 Do I lack madmen, that you have brought this fellow to play the madman in my presence? Should this fellow come into my house?"

22

1 David therefore departed from there and escaped to Adullam's cave. When his brothers and all his father's house heard it, they went down there to him. 2 Everyone who was in distress, everyone who was in debt, and everyone who was discontented gathered themselves to him; and he became captain over them. There were with him about four hundred men. 3 David went from there to Mizpeh of Moab; and he said to the king of Moab, "Please let my father and my mother come out to you, until I know what God will do for me." 4 He brought them before the king of Moab; and they lived with him all the time that David was in the stronghold. 5 The prophet Gad said to David, "Don't stay in the stronghold. Depart, and go into the land of Judah."

Then David departed, and came into the forest of Hereth.

6 Saul heard that David was discovered, with the men who were with him. Now Saul was sitting in Gibeah, under the tamarisk tree in Ramah, with his spear in his hand, and all his servants were standing around him. 7 Saul said to his servants who stood around him, "Hear now, you Benjamites! Will the son of Jesse give everyone of you fields and vineyards? Will he make you all captains of thousands and captains of hundreds? 8 Is that why all of you have conspired against me, and there is no one who discloses to me when my son makes a treaty with the son of Jesse, and there is none of you who is sorry for me, or discloses to me that my son has stirred up my servant against me, to lie in wait, as it is today?"

9 Then Doeg the Edomite, who stood by the servants of Saul, answered and said, "I saw the son of Jesse coming to Nob, to Ahimelech the son of Ahitub. 10 He enquired of the LORD for him, gave him food, and gave him the sword of Goliath the Philistine."

11 Then the king sent to call Ahimelech the priest, the son of Ahitub, and all his father's house, the priests who were in Nob; and they all came to the king. 12 Saul said, "Hear now, you son of Ahitub."

He answered, "Here I am, my lord."

13 Saul said to him, "Why have you conspired against me, you and the son of Jesse, in that you have given him bread, and a sword, and have enquired of God for him, that he should rise against me, to lie in wait, as it is today?"

14 Then Ahimelech answered the king, and said, "Who amongst all your servants is so faithful as David, who is the king's son-in-law, captain of your body guard, and honoured in your house? 15 Have I today begun to enquire of God for him? Be it far from me! Don't let the king impute anything to his servant, nor to all the house of my father; for your servant knew nothing of all this, less or more."

16 The king said, "You shall surely die, Ahimelech, you and all your father's house." 17 The king said to the guard who stood about him, "Turn and kill the priests of the LORD, because their hand also is with David, and because they knew that he fled and didn't disclose it to me." But the servants of the king wouldn't put out their hand to fall on the priests of the LORD.

18 The king said to Doeg, "Turn and attack the priests!"

Doeg the Edomite turned, and he attacked the priests, and he killed on that day eighty-five people who wore a linen ephod. 19 He struck Nob, the city of the priests, with the edge of the sword—both men and women, children and nursing babies, and cattle, donkeys, and sheep, with the edge of the sword. 20 One of the sons of Ahimelech the son of Ahitub, named Abiathar, escaped and fled after David. 21 Abiathar told David that Saul had slain the LORD's priests.

22 David said to Abiathar, "I knew on that day, when Doeg the Edomite was there, that he would surely tell Saul. I am responsible for the death of all the persons of your father's house. 23 Stay with me. Don't be afraid, for he who seeks my life seeks your life. You will be safe with me."

23

1 David was told, "Behold, the Philistines are fighting against Keilah, and are robbing the threshing floors."

2 Therefore David enquired of the LORD, saying, "Shall I go and strike these Philistines?"

The LORD said to David, "Go strike the Philistines, and save Keilah."

3 David's men said to him, "Behold, we are afraid here in Judah. How much more then if we go to Keilah against the armies of the Philistines?"

4 Then David enquired of the LORD yet again. The LORD answered him, and said, "Arise, go down to Keilah; for I will deliver the Philistines into your hand."

5 David and his men went to Keilah and fought with the Philistines, and brought away their livestock, and killed them with a great slaughter. So David saved the inhabitants of Keilah.

6 When Abiathar the son of Ahimelech fled to David to Keilah, he came down with an ephod in his hand.

7 Saul was told that David had come to Keilah. Saul said, "God has delivered him into my hand, for he is shut in by entering into a town that has gates and bars." 8 Saul summoned all the people to war, to go down to Keilah to besiege David and his men. 9 David knew that Saul was devising mischief against him. He said to Abiathar the priest, "Bring the ephod here." 10 Then David said, "O LORD, the God of Israel, your servant has surely heard that Saul seeks to come to Keilah to destroy the city for my sake. 11 Will the men of Keilah deliver me up into his hand? Will Saul come down, as your servant has heard? LORD, the God of Israel, I beg you, tell your servant."

The LORD said, "He will come down."

12 Then David said, "Will the men of Keilah deliver me and my men into the hand of Saul?"

The LORD said, "They will deliver you up."

13 Then David and his men, who were about six hundred, arose and departed out of Keilah and went wherever they could go. Saul was told that David had escaped from Keilah; and he gave up going there. 14 David stayed in the wilderness in the strongholds, and remained in the hill country in the wilderness of Ziph. Saul sought him every day, but God didn't deliver him into his hand. 15 David saw that Saul had come out to seek his life. David was in the wilderness of Ziph in the woods.

16 Jonathan, Saul's son, arose and went to David into the woods, and strengthened his hand in God. 17 He said to him, "Don't be afraid, for the hand of Saul my father won't find you; and you will be king over Israel, and I will be next to you; and Saul my father knows that also." 18 They both made a covenant before the LORD. Then David stayed in the woods and Jonathan went to his house.

19 Then the Ziphites came up to Saul to Gibeah, saying, "Doesn't David hide himself with us in the strongholds in the woods, in the hill of Hachilah, which is on the south of the desert? 20 Now therefore, O king, come down. According to all the desire of your soul to come down; and our part will be to deliver him up into the king's hand."

21 Saul said, "You are blessed by the LORD, for you have had compassion on me. 22 Please go make yet more sure, and know and see his place where his haunt is, and who has seen him there; for I have been told that he is very cunning. 23 See therefore, and take knowledge of all the lurking places where he hides himself; and come again to me with certainty, and I will go with you. It shall happen, if he is in the land, that I will search him out amongst all the thousands of Judah."

24 They arose, and went to Ziph before Saul; but David and his men were in the wilderness of Maon, in the Arabah on the south of the desert. 25 Saul and his men went to seek him. When David was told, he went down to the rock, and stayed in the wilderness of Maon. When Saul heard that, he pursued David in the wilderness of Maon. 26 Saul went on this side of the mountain, and David and his men on that side of the mountain; and David hurried to get away for fear of Saul, for Saul and his men surrounded David and his men to take them. 27 But a messenger came to Saul, saying, "Hurry and come, for the Philistines have made a raid on the land!" 28 So Saul returned from pursuing David, and went against the Philistines. Therefore they called that place Sela Hammahlekoth.ᵃ

29 David went up from there and lived in the strongholds of En Gedi.

24

1 When Saul had returned from following the Philistines, he was told, "Behold, David is in the wilderness of En Gedi." 2 Then Saul took three thousand chosen men out of all Israel, and went to seek David and his men on the rocks of the wild goats. 3 He came to the sheep pens by the way, where there was a cave; and Saul went in to relieve himself. Now David and his men were staying in the innermost parts of the cave. 4 David's men said to him, "Behold, the day of which the LORD said to you, 'Behold, I will deliver your enemy into your hand, and you shall do to him as it shall seem good to you.'" Then David arose and cut off the skirt of Saul's robe secretly. 5 Afterward, David's heart struck him because he had cut off Saul's skirt. 6 He said to his men, "The LORD forbid that I should do this thing to my lord, the LORD's anointed, to stretch out my hand against him, since he is the LORD's anointed." 7 So David checked his men with these words, and didn't allow them to rise against Saul. Saul rose up out of the cave, and went on his way. 8 David also arose afterward, and went out of the cave and cried after Saul, saying, "My lord the king!"

When Saul looked behind him, David bowed with his face to the earth, and showed respect. 9 David said to Saul, "Why do you listen to men's words, saying, 'Behold, David seeks to harm you'? 10 Behold, today your eyes have seen how the LORD had delivered you today into my hand in the cave. Some urged me to kill you, but I spared you. I said, 'I will not stretch

---

ᵃ 23:28 "Sela Hammahlekoth" means "rock of parting".

out my hand against my lord, for he is the LORD's anointed.' 11 Moreover, my father, behold, yes, see the skirt of your robe in my hand; for in that I cut off the skirt of your robe and didn't kill you, know and see that there is neither evil nor disobedience in my hand. I have not sinned against you, though you hunt for my life to take it. 12 May the LORD judge between me and you, and may the LORD avenge me of you; but my hand will not be on you. 13 As the proverb of the ancients says, 'Out of the wicked comes wickedness;' but my hand will not be on you. 14 Against whom has the king of Israel come out? Whom do you pursue? A dead dog? A flea? 15 May the LORD therefore be judge, and give sentence between me and you, and see, and plead my cause, and deliver me out of your hand."

16 It came to pass, when David had finished speaking these words to Saul, that Saul said, "Is that your voice, my son David?" Saul lifted up his voice and wept. 17 He said to David, "You are more righteous than I; for you have done good to me, whereas I have done evil to you. 18 You have declared today how you have dealt well with me, because when the LORD had delivered me up into your hand, you didn't kill me. 19 For if a man finds his enemy, will he let him go away unharmed? Therefore may the LORD reward you good for that which you have done to me today. 20 Now, behold, I know that you will surely be king, and that the kingdom of Israel will be established in your hand. 21 Swear now therefore to me by the LORD that you will not cut off my offspring after me, and that you will not destroy my name out of my father's house."

22 David swore to Saul. Saul went home, but David and his men went up to the stronghold.

25

1 Samuel died; and all Israel gathered themselves together and mourned for him, and buried him at his house at Ramah.

Then David arose and went down to the wilderness of Paran. 2 There was a man in Maon whose possessions were in Carmel; and the man was very great. He had three thousand sheep and a thousand goats; and he was shearing his sheep in Carmel. 3 Now the name of the man was Nabal; and the name of his wife Abigail. This woman was intelligent and had a beautiful face; but the man was surly and evil in his doings. He was of the house of Caleb. 4 David heard in the wilderness that Nabal was shearing his sheep. 5 David sent ten young men; and David said to the young men, "Go up to Carmel, and go to Nabal, and greet him in my name. 6 Tell him, 'Long life to you! Peace be to you! Peace be to your house! Peace be to all that you have! 7 Now I have heard that you have shearers. Your shepherds have now been with us, and we didn't harm them. Nothing was missing from them all the time they were in Carmel. 8 Ask your young men, and they will tell you. Therefore let the young men find favour in your eyes, for we come on a good day. Please give whatever comes to your hand to your servants and to your son David.'"

9 When David's young men came, they spoke to Nabal all those words in the name of David, and waited.

10 Nabal answered David's servants and said, "Who is David? Who is the son of Jesse? There are many servants who break away from their masters these days. 11 Shall I then take my bread, my water, and my meat that I have killed for my shearers, and give it to men who I don't know where they come from?"

12 So David's young men turned on their way and went back, and came and told him all these words.

13 David said to his men, "Every man put on his sword!"

Every man put on his sword. David also put on his sword. About four hundred men followed David, and two hundred stayed by the baggage.

14 But one of the young men told Abigail, Nabal's wife, saying, "Behold, David sent messengers out of the wilderness to greet our master; and he insulted them. 15 But the men were very good to us, and we were not harmed, and we didn't miss anything as long as we went with them, when we were in the fields. 16 They were a wall to us both by night and by day, all the while we were with them keeping the sheep. 17 Now therefore know and consider what you will do; for evil is determined against our master and against all his house, for he is such a worthless fellow that one can't speak to him."

18 Then Abigail hurried and took two hundred loaves of bread, two containers of wine, five sheep ready dressed, five seahs[a] of parched grain, one hundred clusters of raisins, and two hundred cakes of figs, and laid them on donkeys. 19 She said to her young men, "Go on before me. Behold, I am coming after you." But she didn't tell her husband, Nabal. 20 As she rode on her donkey, and came down hidden by the mountain, behold, David and his men came down towards her, and she met them.

21 Now David had said, "Surely in vain I have kept all that this fellow has in the wilderness, so that nothing was missed of all that pertained to him. He has returned me evil for good. 22 God do so to the enemies of David, and more also, if I leave of all that belongs to him by the morning light so much as one who urinates on a wall."[b]

23 When Abigail saw David, she hurried and got off her donkey, and fell before David on her face and bowed herself to the ground. 24 She fell at his feet and said, "On me, my lord, on me be the blame! Please let your servant speak in your ears. Hear the words of your servant. 25 Please don't let my lord pay attention to this worthless fellow, Nabal, for as his name is, so is he. Nabal[c] is his name, and folly is with him; but I, your servant, didn't see my lord's young men whom you sent. 26 Now therefore, my lord, as the LORD lives and as your soul lives, since the LORD has withheld you from

blood guiltiness and from avenging yourself with your own hand, now therefore let your enemies and those who seek evil to my lord be as Nabal. 27 Now this present which your servant has brought to my lord, let it be given to the young men who follow my lord. 28 Please forgive the trespass of your servant. For the LORD will certainly make my lord a sure house, because my lord fights the LORD's battles. Evil will not be found in you all your days. 29 Though men may rise up to pursue you and to seek your soul, yet the soul of my lord will be bound in the bundle of life with the LORD your God. He will sling out the souls of your enemies as from a sling's pocket. 30 It will come to pass, when the LORD has done to my lord according to all the good that he has spoken concerning you, and has appointed you prince over Israel, 31 that this shall be no grief to you, nor offence of heart to my lord, either that you have shed blood without cause, or that my lord has avenged himself. When the LORD has dealt well with my lord, then remember your servant."

32 David said to Abigail, "Blessed is the LORD, the God of Israel, who sent you today to meet me! 33 Blessed is your discretion, and blessed are you, who have kept me today from blood guiltiness, and from avenging myself with my own hand. 34 For indeed, as the LORD the God of Israel lives, who has withheld me from harming you, unless you had hurried and come to meet me, surely there wouldn't have been left to Nabal by the morning light so much as one who urinates on a wall."[d]

35 So David received from her hand that which she had brought him. Then he said to her, "Go up in peace to your house. Behold, I have listened to your voice and have granted your request."

36 Abigail came to Nabal; and behold, he held a feast in his house like the feast of a king. Nabal's heart was merry within him, for he was very drunk. Therefore she told him nothing until the morning light. 37 In the morning, when the wine had gone out of Nabal, his wife told him these things; and his heart died within him, and he became as a stone. 38 About ten days later, the LORD struck Nabal, so that he died. 39 When David heard that Nabal was dead, he said, "Blessed is the LORD, who has pleaded the cause of my reproach from the hand of Nabal, and has kept back his servant from evil. The LORD has returned the evildoing of Nabal on his own head."

David sent and spoke concerning Abigail, to take her to himself as wife. 40 When David's servants had come to Abigail to Carmel, they spoke to her, saying, "David has sent us to you, to take you to him as wife."

41 She arose and bowed herself with her face to the earth, and said, "Behold, your servant is a servant to wash the feet of the servants of my lord." 42 Abigail hurriedly arose and rode on a donkey with her five maids who followed her; and she went after the messengers of David, and became his wife. 43 David also took Ahinoam of Jezreel; and they both became his wives.

44 Now Saul had given Michal his daughter, David's wife, to Palti the son of Laish, who was of Gallim.

26

1 The Ziphites came to Saul to Gibeah, saying, "Doesn't David hide himself in the hill of Hachilah, which is before the desert?" 2 Then Saul arose and went down to the wilderness of Ziph, having three thousand chosen men of Israel with him, to seek David in the wilderness of Ziph. 3 Saul encamped in the hill of Hachilah, which is before the desert, by the way. But David stayed in the wilderness, and he saw that Saul came after him into the wilderness. 4 David therefore sent out spies, and understood that Saul had certainly come. 5 Then David arose and came to the place where Saul had encamped; and David saw the place where Saul lay, with Abner the son of Ner, the captain of his army. Saul lay within the place of the wagons, and the people were encamped around him.

6 Then David answered and said to Ahimelech the Hittite, and to Abishai the son of Zeruiah, brother of Joab, saying, "Who will go down with me to Saul to the camp?"

Abishai said, "I will go down with you." 7 So David and Abishai came to the people by night; and, behold, Saul lay sleeping within the place of the wagons, with his spear stuck in the ground at his head; and Abner and the people lay around him. 8 Then Abishai said to David, "God has delivered up your enemy into your hand today. Now therefore please let me strike him with the spear to the earth at one stroke, and I will not strike him the second time."

9 David said to Abishai, "Don't destroy him, for who can stretch out his hand against the LORD's anointed, and be guiltless?" 10 David said, "As the LORD lives, the LORD will strike him; or his day shall come to die, or he shall go down into battle and perish. 11 The LORD forbid that I should stretch out my hand against the LORD's anointed; but now please take the spear that is at his head and the jar of water, and let's go."

12 So David took the spear and the jar of water from Saul's head, and they went away. No man saw it, or knew it, nor did any awake; for they were all asleep, because a deep sleep from the LORD had fallen on them. 13 Then David went over to the other side, and stood on the top of the mountain far away, a great space being between them; 14 and David cried to the people, and to Abner the son of Ner, saying, "Don't you answer, Abner?"

Then Abner answered, "Who are you who calls to the king?"

15 David said to Abner, "Aren't you a man? Who is like you in Israel? Why then have you not kept watch over your lord the king? For one of the people came in to destroy your lord the king. 16 This thing isn't good that you have done. As the LORD lives, you are worthy to die, because you have

---

a 25:18 1 seah is about 7 litres or 1.9 gallons or 0.8 pecks
b 25:22 or, male.

c 25:25 "Nabal" means "foolish".
d 25:34 or, one male.

not kept watch over your lord, the LORD's anointed. Now see where the king's spear is, and the jar of water that was at his head."

17 Saul recognised David's voice, and said, "Is this your voice, my son David?"

David said, "It is my voice, my lord, O king." 18 He said, "Why does my lord pursue his servant? For what have I done? What evil is in my hand? 19 Now therefore, please let my lord the king hear the words of his servant. If it is so that the LORD has stirred you up against me, let him accept an offering. But if it is the children of men, they are cursed before the LORD; for they have driven me out today that I shouldn't cling to the LORD's inheritance, saying, 'Go, serve other gods!' 20 Now therefore, don't let my blood fall to the earth away from the presence of the LORD; for the king of Israel has come out to seek a flea, as when one hunts a partridge in the mountains."

21 Then Saul said, "I have sinned. Return, my son David; for I will no more do you harm, because my life was precious in your eyes today. Behold, I have played the fool, and have erred exceedingly."

22 David answered, "Behold the spear, O king! Let one of the young men come over and get it. 23 The LORD will render to every man his righteousness and his faithfulness; because the LORD delivered you into my hand today, and I wouldn't stretch out my hand against the LORD's anointed. 24 Behold, as your life was respected today in my eyes, so let my life be respected in the LORD's eyes, and let him deliver me out of all oppression."

25 Then Saul said to David, "You are blessed, my son David. You will both do mightily, and will surely prevail."

So David went his way, and Saul returned to his place.

27

1 David said in his heart, "I will now perish one day by the hand of Saul. There is nothing better for me than that I should escape into the land of the Philistines; and Saul will despair of me, to seek me any more in all the borders of Israel. So I will escape out of his hand." 2 David arose and passed over, he and the six hundred men who were with him, to Achish the son of Maoch, king of Gath. 3 David lived with Achish at Gath, he and his men, every man with his household, even David with his two wives, Ahinoam the Jezreelitess and Abigail the Carmelitess, Nabal's wife. 4 Saul was told that David had fled to Gath, so he stopped looking for him.

5 David said to Achish, "If now I have found favour in your eyes, let them give me a place in one of the cities in the country, that I may dwell there. For why should your servant dwell in the royal city with you?" 6 Then Achish gave him Ziklag that day: therefore Ziklag belongs to the kings of Judah to this day. 7 The number of the days that David lived in the country of the Philistines was a full year and four months.

8 David and his men went up and raided the Geshurites, the Girzites, and the Amalekites; for those were the inhabitants of the land who were of old, on the way to Shur, even to the land of Egypt. 9 David struck the land, and saved no man or woman alive, and took away the sheep, the cattle, the donkeys, the camels, and the clothing. Then he returned, and came to Achish.

10 Achish said, "Against whom have you made a raid today?"

David said, "Against the South of Judah, against the South of the Jerahmeelites, and against the South of the Kenites." 11 David saved neither man nor woman alive to bring them to Gath, saying, "Lest they should tell about us, saying, 'David did this, and this has been his way all the time he has lived in the country of the Philistines.'"

12 Achish believed David, saying, "He has made his people Israel utterly to abhor him. Therefore he will be my servant forever."

28

1 In those days, the Philistines gathered their armies together for warfare, to fight with Israel. Achish said to David, "Know assuredly that you will go out with me in the army, you and your men."

2 David said to Achish, "Therefore you will know what your servant can do."

Achish said to David, "Therefore I will make you my bodyguard forever."

3 Now Samuel was dead, and all Israel had mourned for him and buried him in Ramah, even in his own city. Saul had sent away those who had familiar spirits and the wizards out of the land.

4 The Philistines gathered themselves together, and came and encamped in Shunem; and Saul gathered all Israel together, and they encamped in Gilboa. 5 When Saul saw the army of the Philistines, he was afraid, and his heart trembled greatly. 6 When Saul enquired of the LORD, the LORD didn't answer him by dreams, by Urim, or by prophets. 7 Then Saul said to his servants, "Seek for me a woman who has a familiar spirit, that I may go to her and enquire of her."

His servants said to him, "Behold, there is a woman who has a familiar spirit at Endor."

8 Saul disguised himself and put on other clothing, and went, he and two men with him, and they came to the woman by night. Then he said, "Please consult for me by the familiar spirit, and bring me up whomever I shall name to you."

9 The woman said to him, "Behold, you know what Saul has done, how he has cut off those who have familiar spirits and the wizards out of the land. Why then do you lay a snare for my life, to cause me to die?"

10 Saul swore to her by the LORD, saying, "As the LORD lives, no punishment will happen to you for this thing."

11 Then the woman said, "Whom shall I bring up to you?"

He said, "Bring Samuel up for me."

12 When the woman saw Samuel, she cried with a loud voice; and the woman spoke to Saul, saying, "Why have you deceived me? For you are Saul!"

13 The king said to her, "Don't be afraid! What do you see?"

The woman said to Saul, "I see a god coming up out of the earth."

14 He said to her, "What does he look like?"

She said, "An old man comes up. He is covered with a robe." Saul perceived that it was Samuel, and he bowed with his face to the ground, and showed respect.

15 Samuel said to Saul, "Why have you disturbed me, to bring me up?"

Saul answered, "I am very distressed; for the Philistines make war against me, and God has departed from me, and answers me no more, by prophets, or by dreams. Therefore I have called you, that you may make known to me what I shall do."

16 Samuel said, "Why then do you ask me, since the LORD has departed from you and has become your adversary? 17 The LORD has done to you as he spoke by me. The LORD has torn the kingdom out of your hand and given it to your neighbour, even to David. 18 Because you didn't obey the LORD's voice, and didn't execute his fierce wrath on Amalek, therefore the LORD has done this thing to you today. 19 Moreover the LORD will deliver Israel also with you into the hand of the Philistines; and tomorrow you and your sons will be with me. The LORD will deliver the army of Israel also into the hand of the Philistines."

20 Then Saul fell immediately his full length on the earth, and was terrified, because of Samuel's words. There was no strength in him, for he had eaten no bread all day long or all night long.

21 The woman came to Saul and saw that he was very troubled, and said to him, "Behold, your servant has listened to your voice, and I have put my life in my hand, and have listened to your words which you spoke to me. 22 Now therefore, please listen also to the voice of your servant, and let me set a morsel of bread before you. Eat, that you may have strength when you go on your way."

23 But he refused, and said, "I will not eat." But his servants, together with the woman, constrained him; and he listened to their voice. So he arose from the earth and sat on the bed. 24 The woman had a fattened calf in the house. She hurried and killed it; and she took flour and kneaded it, and baked unleavened bread of it. 25 She brought it before Saul and before his servants, and they ate. Then they rose up and went away that night.

29

1 Now the Philistines gathered together all their armies to Aphek; and the Israelites encamped by the spring which is in Jezreel. 2 The lords of the Philistines passed on by hundreds and by thousands; and David and his men passed on in the rear with Achish.

3 Then the princes of the Philistines said, "What about these Hebrews?"

Achish said to the princes of the Philistines, "Isn't this David, the servant of Saul the king of Israel, who has been with me these days, or rather these years? I have found no fault in him since he fell away until today."

4 But the princes of the Philistines were angry with him; and the princes of the Philistines said to him, "Make the man return, that he may go back to his place where you have appointed him, and let him not go down with us to battle, lest in the battle he become an adversary to us. For with what should this fellow reconcile himself to his lord? Should it not be with the heads of these men? 5 Isn't this David, of whom people sang to one another in dances, saying,

'Saul has slain his thousands,
    and David his ten thousands'?"

6 Then Achish called David and said to him, "As the LORD lives, you have been upright, and your going out and your coming in with me in the army is good in my sight; for I have not found evil in you since the day of your coming to me to this day. Nevertheless, the lords don't favour you. 7 Therefore now return, and go in peace, that you not displease the lords of the Philistines."

8 David said to Achish, "But what have I done? What have you found in your servant so long as I have been before you to this day, that I may not go and fight against the enemies of my lord the king?"

9 Achish answered David, "I know that you are good in my sight, as an angel of God. Notwithstanding, the princes of the Philistines have said, 'He shall not go up with us to the battle.' 10 Therefore now rise up early in the morning with the servants of your lord who have come with you; and as soon as you are up early in the morning and have light, depart."

11 So David rose up early, he and his men, to depart in the morning, to return into the land of the Philistines; and the Philistines went up to Jezreel.

30

1 When David and his men had come to Ziklag on the third day, the Amalekites had made a raid on the South and on Ziklag, and had struck Ziklag and burnt it with fire, 2 and had taken captive the women and all who were in it, both small and great. They didn't kill any, but carried them off and went their way. 3 When David and his men came to the city, behold, it was burnt with fire; and their wives, their sons, and their daughters were taken captive. 4 Then David and the people who were with him lifted up their voice and wept until they had no more power to weep. 5 David's two wives were taken captive, Ahinoam the Jezreelitess, and Abigail the wife of Nabal the Carmelite. 6 David was greatly distressed, for the people spoke of stoning him, because the souls of all the people were grieved, every man for his sons and for his daughters; but David strengthened himself in the

LORD his God. 7 David said to Abiathar the priest, the son of Ahimelech, "Please bring the ephod here to me."

Abiathar brought the ephod to David. 8 David enquired of the LORD, saying, "If I pursue after this troop, will I overtake them?"

He answered him, "Pursue, for you will surely overtake them, and will without fail recover all."

9 So David went, he and the six hundred men who were with him, and came to the brook Besor, where those who were left behind stayed. 10 But David pursued, he and four hundred men; for two hundred stayed behind, who were so faint that they couldn't go over the brook Besor. 11 They found an Egyptian in the field, and brought him to David, and gave him bread, and he ate; and they gave him water to drink. 12 They gave him a piece of a cake of figs and two clusters of raisins. When he had eaten, his spirit came again to him; for he had eaten no bread, and drank no water for three days and three nights. 13 David asked him, "To whom do you belong? Where are you from?"

He said, "I am a young man of Egypt, servant to an Amalekite; and my master left me, because three days ago I got sick. 14 We made a raid on the South of the Cherethites, and on that which belongs to Judah, and on the South of Caleb; and we burnt Ziklag with fire."

15 David said to him, "Will you bring me down to this troop?"

He said, "Swear to me by God that you will not kill me and not deliver me up into the hands of my master, and I will bring you down to this troop."

16 When he had brought him down, behold, they were spread around over all the ground, eating, drinking, and dancing, because of all the great plunder that they had taken out of the land of the Philistines, and out of the land of Judah. 17 David struck them from the twilight even to the evening of the next day. Not a man of them escaped from there, except four hundred young men who rode on camels and fled. 18 David recovered all that the Amalekites had taken, and David rescued his two wives. 19 There was nothing lacking to them, neither small nor great, neither sons nor daughters, neither plunder, nor anything that they had taken. David brought them all back. 20 David took all the flocks and the herds, which they drove before those other livestock, and said, "This is David's plunder."

21 David came to the two hundred men, who were so faint that they could not follow David, whom also they had made to stay at the brook Besor; and they went out to meet David, and to meet the people who were with him. When David came near to the people, he greeted them. 22 Then all the wicked men and worthless fellows of those who went with David answered and said, "Because they didn't go with us, we will not give them anything of the plunder that we have recovered, except to every man his wife and his children, that he may lead them away and depart."

23 Then David said, "Do not do so, my brothers, with that which the LORD has given to us, who has preserved us, and delivered the troop that came against us into our hand. 24 Who will listen to you in this matter? For as his share is who goes down to the battle, so shall his share be who stays with the baggage. They shall share alike." 25 It was so from that day forward that he made it a statute and an ordinance for Israel to this day.

26 When David came to Ziklag, he sent some of the plunder to the elders of Judah, even to his friends, saying, "Behold, a present for you from the plunder of the LORD's enemies." 27 He sent it to those who were in Bethel, to those who were in Ramoth of the South, to those who were in Jattir, 28 to those who were in Aroer, to those who were in Siphmoth, to those who were in Eshtemoa, 29 to those who were in Racal, to those who were in the cities of the Jerahmeelites, to those who were in the cities of the Kenites, 30 to those who were in Hormah, to those who were in Borashan, to those who were in Athach, 31 to those who were in Hebron, and to all the places where David himself and his men used to stay.

31

1 Now the Philistines fought against Israel; and the men of Israel fled from before the Philistines, and fell down slain on Mount Gilboa. 2 The Philistines overtook Saul and his sons; and the Philistines killed Jonathan, Abinadab, and Malchishua, the sons of Saul. 3 The battle went hard against Saul, and the archers overtook him; and he was greatly distressed by reason of the archers. 4 Then Saul said to his armour bearer, "Draw your sword, and thrust me through with it, lest these uncircumcised come and thrust me through and abuse me!" But his armour bearer would not, for he was terrified. Therefore Saul took his sword and fell on it. 5 When his armour bearer saw that Saul was dead, he likewise fell on his sword, and died with him. 6 So Saul died with his three sons, his armour bearer, and all his men that same day together.

7 When the men of Israel who were on the other side of the valley, and those who were beyond the Jordan, saw that the men of Israel fled and that Saul and his sons were dead, they abandoned the cities and fled; and the Philistines came and lived in them. 8 On the next day, when the Philistines came to strip the slain, they found Saul and his three sons fallen on Mount Gilboa. 9 They cut off his head, stripped off his armour, and sent into the land of the Philistines all around, to carry the news to the house of their idols and to the people. 10 They put his armour in the house of the Ashtaroth, and they fastened his body to the wall of Beth Shan. 11 When the inhabitants of Jabesh Gilead heard what the Philistines had done to Saul, 12 all the valiant men arose, went all night, and took the body of Saul and the bodies of his sons from the wall of Beth Shan; and they came to Jabesh and burnt them there. 13 They took their bones and buried them under the tamarisk[a] tree in Jabesh, and fasted seven days.

---

a *31:13* or, salt cedar

The Second Book of Samuel

1

1 After the death of Saul, when David had returned from the slaughter of the Amalekites, and David had stayed two days in Ziklag, 2 on the third day, behold,[a] a man came out of the camp from Saul, with his clothes torn and earth on his head. When he came to David, he fell to the earth and showed respect.

3 David said to him, "Where do you come from?"

He said to him, "I have escaped out of the camp of Israel."

4 David said to him, "How did it go? Please tell me."

He answered, "The people have fled from the battle, and many of the people also have fallen and are dead. Saul and Jonathan his son are dead also."

5 David said to the young man who told him, "How do you know that Saul and Jonathan his son are dead?"

6 The young man who told him said, "As I happened by chance on Mount Gilboa, behold, Saul was leaning on his spear; and behold, the chariots and the horsemen followed close behind him. 7 When he looked behind him, he saw me and called to me. I answered, 'Here I am.' 8 He said to me, 'Who are you?' I answered him, 'I am an Amalekite.' 9 He said to me, 'Please stand beside me, and kill me, for anguish has taken hold of me because my life lingers in me.' 10 So I stood beside him and killed him, because I was sure that he could not live after he had fallen. I took the crown that was on his head and the bracelet that was on his arm, and have brought them here to my lord."

11 Then David took hold on his clothes and tore them; and all the men who were with him did likewise. 12 They mourned, wept, and fasted until evening for Saul and for Jonathan his son, and for the people of the LORD,[b] and for the house of Israel, because they had fallen by the sword.

13 David said to the young man who told him, "Where are you from?"

He answered, "I am the son of a foreigner, an Amalekite."

14 David said to him, "Why were you not afraid to stretch out your hand to destroy the LORD's anointed?" 15 David called one of the young men and said, "Go near, and cut him down!" He struck him so that he died. 16 David said to him, "Your blood be on your head, for your mouth has testified against you, saying, 'I have slain the LORD's anointed.'"

17 David lamented with this lamentation over Saul and over Jonathan his son 18 (and he commanded them to teach the children of Judah the song of the bow; behold, it is written in the book of Jashar):

19 "Your glory, Israel, was slain on your high places!
How the mighty have fallen!
20 Don't tell it in Gath.
Don't publish it in the streets of Ashkelon,
lest the daughters of the Philistines rejoice,
lest the daughters of the uncircumcised triumph.
21 You mountains of Gilboa,
let there be no dew or rain on you, and no fields of offerings;
for there the shield of the mighty was defiled and cast away,
the shield of Saul was not anointed with oil.
22 From the blood of the slain,
from the fat of the mighty,
Jonathan's bow didn't turn back.
Saul's sword didn't return empty.
23 Saul and Jonathan were lovely and pleasant in their lives.
In their death, they were not divided.
They were swifter than eagles.
They were stronger than lions.
24 You daughters of Israel, weep over Saul,
who clothed you delicately in scarlet,
who put ornaments of gold on your clothing.
25 How the mighty have fallen in the middle of the battle!
Jonathan was slain on your high places.
26 I am distressed for you, my brother Jonathan.
You have been very pleasant to me.
Your love to me was wonderful,
surpassing the love of women.
27 How the mighty have fallen,
and the weapons of war have perished!"

2

1 After this, David enquired of the LORD, saying, "Shall I go up into any of the cities of Judah?"

The LORD said to him, "Go up."

David said, "Where shall I go up?"

He said, "To Hebron."

2 So David went up there with his two wives, Ahinoam the Jezreelitess, and Abigail the wife of Nabal the Carmelite. 3 David brought up his men who were with him, every man with his household. They lived in the cities of Hebron. 4 The men of Judah came, and there they anointed David king over the house of Judah. They told David, "The men of Jabesh Gilead were those who buried Saul." 5 David sent messengers to the men of Jabesh Gilead, and said to them, "Blessed are you by the LORD, that you have shown this kindness to your lord, even to Saul, and have buried him. 6 Now may the LORD show loving kindness and truth to you. I also will reward you for this kindness, because you have done this thing. 7 Now therefore let your hands be strong, and be valiant; for Saul your lord is dead, and also the house of Judah have anointed me king over them."

8 Now Abner the son of Ner, captain of Saul's army, had taken Ishbosheth the son of Saul and brought him over to Mahanaim. 9 He made him king over Gilead, over the Ashurites, over Jezreel, over Ephraim, over Benjamin, and over all Israel. 10 Ishbosheth, Saul's son, was forty years old when he began to reign over Israel, and he reigned two years. But the house of Judah followed David. 11 The time that David was king in Hebron over the house of Judah was seven years and six months.

12 Abner the son of Ner, and the servants of Ishbosheth the son of Saul, went out from Mahanaim to Gibeon. 13 Joab the son of Zeruiah and David's servants went out, and met them by the pool of Gibeon; and they sat down, the one on the one side of the pool and the other on the other side of the pool. 14 Abner said to Joab, "Please let the young men arise and compete before us!"

Joab said, "Let them arise!" 15 Then they arose and went over by number: twelve for Benjamin and for Ishbosheth the son of Saul, and twelve of David's servants. 16 They each caught his opponent by the head and thrust his sword in his fellow's side; so they fell down together. Therefore that place in Gibeon was called Helkath Hazzurim.[c] 17 The battle was very severe that day; and Abner was beaten, and the men of Israel, before David's servants. 18 The three sons of Zeruiah were there: Joab, Abishai, and Asahel. Asahel was as light of foot as a wild gazelle. 19 Asahel pursued Abner. He didn't turn to the right hand or to the left from following Abner.

20 Then Abner looked behind him and said, "Is that you, Asahel?"

He answered, "It is."

21 Abner said to him, "Turn away to your right hand or to your left, and grab one of the young men, and take his armour." But Asahel would not turn away from following him. 22 Abner said again to Asahel, "Turn away from following me. Why should I strike you to the ground? How then could I look Joab your brother in the face?" 23 However, he refused to turn away. Therefore Abner with the back end of the spear struck him in the body, so that the spear came out behind him; and he fell down there and died in the same place. As many as came to the place where Asahel fell down and died stood still.

24 But Joab and Abishai pursued Abner. The sun went down when they had come to the hill of Ammah, that lies before Giah by the way of the wilderness of Gibeon. 25 The children of Benjamin gathered themselves together after Abner and became one band, and stood on the top of a hill. 26 Then Abner called to Joab, and said, "Shall the sword devour forever? Don't you know that it will be bitterness in the latter end? How long will it be then, before you ask the people to return from following their brothers?"

27 Joab said, "As God[d] lives, if you had not spoken, surely then in the morning the people would have gone away, and not each followed his brother." 28 So Joab blew the trumpet; and all the people stood still and pursued Israel no more, and they fought no more. 29 Abner and his men went all that night through the Arabah; and they passed over the Jordan, and went through all Bithron, and came to Mahanaim.

30 Joab returned from following Abner; and when he had gathered all the people together, nineteen men of David's and Asahel were missing. 31 But David's servants had struck Benjamin Abner's men so that three hundred and sixty men died. 32 They took up Asahel and buried him in the tomb of his father, which was in Bethlehem. Joab and his men went all night, and the day broke on them at Hebron.

3

1 Now there was long war between Saul's house and David's house. David grew stronger and stronger, but Saul's house grew weaker and weaker. 2 Sons were born to David in Hebron. His firstborn was Amnon, of Ahinoam the Jezreelitess; 3 and his second, Chileab, of Abigail the wife of Nabal the Carmelite; and the third, Absalom the son of Maacah the daughter of Talmai king of Geshur; 4 and the fourth, Adonijah the son of Haggith; and the fifth, Shephatiah the son of Abital; 5 and the sixth, Ithream, of Eglah, David's wife. These were born to David in Hebron.

6 While there was war between Saul's house and David's house, Abner made himself strong in Saul's house. 7 Now Saul had a concubine, whose name was Rizpah, the daughter of Aiah; and Ishbosheth said to Abner, "Why have you gone in to my father's concubine?"

8 Then Abner was very angry about Ishbosheth's words, and said, "Am I a dog's head that belongs to Judah? Today I show kindness to your father Saul's house, to his brothers, and to his friends, and have not delivered you into the hand of David; and yet you charge me today with a fault concerning this woman! 9 God do so to Abner, and more also, if, as the LORD has sworn to David, I don't do even so to him: 10 to transfer the kingdom from Saul's house, and to set up David's throne over Israel and over Judah, from Dan even to Beersheba."

11 He could not answer Abner another word, because he was afraid of him.

---

a 1:2 "Behold", from "הִנֵּה", means look at, take notice, observe, see, or gaze at. It is often used as an interjection.
b 1:12 When rendered in ALL CAPITAL LETTERS, "LORD" or "GOD" is the translation of God's Proper Name.
c 2:16 "Helkath Hazzurim" means "field of daggers".
d 2:27 The Hebrew word rendered "God" is "אֱלֹהִים" (Elohim).

12 Abner sent messengers to David on his behalf, saying, "Whose is the land?" and saying, "Make your alliance with me, and behold, my hand will be with you to bring all Israel around to you."

13 David said, "Good. I will make a treaty with you, but one thing I require of you. That is, you will not see my face unless you first bring Michal, Saul's daughter, when you come to see my face." 14 David sent messengers to Ishbosheth, Saul's son, saying, "Deliver me my wife Michal, whom I was given to marry for one hundred foreskins of the Philistines."

15 Ishbosheth sent and took her from her husband, Paltiel the son of Laish. 16 Her husband went with her, weeping as he went, and followed her to Bahurim. Then Abner said to him, "Go! Return!" and he returned.

17 Abner had communication with the elders of Israel, saying, "In times past, you sought for David to be king over you. 18 Now then do it! For the LORD has spoken of David, saying, 'By the hand of my servant David, I will save my people Israel out of the hand of the Philistines, and out of the hand of all their enemies.'"

19 Abner also spoke in the ears of Benjamin; and Abner went also to speak in the ears of David in Hebron all that seemed good to Israel and to the whole house of Benjamin. 20 So Abner came to David to Hebron, and twenty men with him. David made Abner and the men who were with him a feast. 21 Abner said to David, "I will arise and go, and will gather all Israel to my lord the king, that they may make a covenant with you, and that you may reign over all that your soul desires." David sent Abner away; and he went in peace.

22 Behold, David's servants and Joab came from a raid and brought in a great plunder with them; but Abner was not with David in Hebron, for he had sent him away, and he had gone in peace. 23 When Joab and all the army who was with him had come, they told Joab, "Abner the son of Ner came to the king, and he has sent him away, and he has gone in peace."

24 Then Joab came to the king and said, "What have you done? Behold, Abner came to you. Why is it that you have sent him away, and he is already gone? 25 You know Abner the son of Ner. He came to deceive you, and to know your going out and your coming in, and to know all that you do."

26 When Joab had come out from David, he sent messengers after Abner, and they brought him back from the well of Sirah; but David didn't know it. 27 When Abner had returned to Hebron, Joab took him aside into the middle of the gate to speak with him quietly, and struck him there in the body, so that he died for the blood of Asahel his brother. 28 Afterward, when David heard it, he said, "I and my kingdom are guiltless before the LORD forever of the blood of Abner the son of Ner. 29 Let it fall on the head of Joab and on all his father's house. Let there not fail from the house of Joab one who has a discharge, or who is a leper, or who leans on a staff, or who falls by the sword, or who lacks bread." 30 So Joab and Abishai his brother killed Abner, because he had killed their brother Asahel at Gibeon in the battle.

31 David said to Joab and to all the people who were with him, "Tear your clothes, and clothe yourselves with sackcloth, and mourn in front of Abner." King David followed the bier. 32 They buried Abner in Hebron; and the king lifted up his voice and wept at Abner's grave; and all the people wept. 33 The king lamented for Abner, and said, "Should Abner die as a fool dies? 34 Your hands weren't bound, and your feet weren't put into fetters. As a man falls before the children of iniquity, so you fell."

All the people wept again over him. 35 All the people came to urge David to eat bread while it was yet day; but David swore, saying, "God do so to me, and more also, if I taste bread or anything else, until the sun goes down."

36 All the people took notice of it, and it pleased them, as whatever the king did pleased all the people. 37 So all the people and all Israel understood that day that it was not of the king to kill Abner the son of Ner. 38 The king said to his servants, "Don't you know that a prince and a great man has fallen today in Israel? 39 I am weak today, though anointed king. These men, the sons of Zeruiah are too hard for me. May the LORD reward the evildoer according to his wickedness."

4

1 When Saul's son heard that Abner was dead in Hebron, his hands became feeble, and all the Israelites were troubled. 2 Saul's son had two men who were captains of raiding bands. The name of one was Baanah and the name of the other Rechab, the sons of Rimmon the Beerothite, of the children of Benjamin (for Beeroth also is considered a part of Benjamin; 3 and the Beerothites fled to Gittaim, and have lived as foreigners there until today).

4 Now Jonathan, Saul's son, had a son who was lame in his feet. He was five years old when the news came about Saul and Jonathan out of Jezreel; and his nurse picked him up and fled. As she hurried to flee, he fell and became lame. His name was Mephibosheth.

5 The sons of Rimmon the Beerothite, Rechab and Baanah, went out and came at about the heat of the day to the house of Ishbosheth as he took his rest at noon. 6 They came there into the middle of the house as though they would have fetched wheat, and they struck him in the body; and Rechab and Baanah his brother escaped. 7 Now when they came into the house as he lay on his bed in his bedroom, they struck him, killed him, beheaded him, and took his head, and went by the way of the Arabah all night. 8 They brought the head of Ishbosheth to David to Hebron, and said to the king, "Behold, the head of Ishbosheth, the son of Saul, your enemy, who sought your life! The LORD has avenged my lord the king today of Saul and of his offspring.ᵃ"

9 David answered Rechab and Baanah his brother, the sons of Rimmon the Beerothite, and said to them, "As the LORD lives, who has redeemed my soul out of all adversity, 10 when someone told me, 'Behold, Saul is dead,' thinking that he brought good news, I seized him and killed him in Ziklag, which was the reward I gave him for his news. 11 How much more, when wicked men have slain a righteous person in his own house on his bed, should I not now require his blood from your hand, and rid the earth of you?" 12 David commanded his young men, and they killed them, cut off their hands and their feet, and hanged them up beside the pool in Hebron. But they took the head of Ishbosheth and buried it in Abner's grave in Hebron.

5

1 Then all the tribes of Israel came to David at Hebron and spoke, saying, "Behold, we are your bone and your flesh. 2 In times past, when Saul was king over us, it was you who led Israel out and in. The LORD said to you, 'You will be shepherd of my people Israel, and you will be prince over Israel.'" 3 So all the elders of Israel came to the king to Hebron, and King David made a covenant with them in Hebron before the LORD; and they anointed David king over Israel.

4 David was thirty years old when he began to reign, and he reigned forty years. 5 In Hebron he reigned over Judah seven years and six months, and in Jerusalem he reigned thirty-three years over all Israel and Judah.

6 The king and his men went to Jerusalem against the Jebusites, the inhabitants of the land, who spoke to David, saying, "The blind and the lame will keep you out of here," thinking, "David can't come in here." 7 Nevertheless David took the stronghold of Zion. This is David's city. 8 David said on that day, "Whoever strikes the Jebusites, let him go up to the watercourse and strike those lame and blind, who are hated by David's soul." Therefore they say, "The blind and the lame can't come into the house."

9 David lived in the stronghold, and called it David's city. David built around from Millo and inward. 10 David grew greater and greater, for the LORD, the God of Armies, was with him. 11 Hiram king of Tyre sent messengers to David, with cedar trees, carpenters, and masons; and they built David a house. 12 David perceived that the LORD had established him king over Israel, and that he had exalted his kingdom for his people Israel's sake.

13 David took more concubines and wives for himself out of Jerusalem, after he had come from Hebron; and more sons and daughters were born to David. 14 These are the names of those who were born to him in Jerusalem: Shammua, Shobab, Nathan, Solomon, 15 Ibhar, Elishua, Nepheg, Japhia, 16 Elishama, Eliada, and Eliphelet.

17 When the Philistines heard that they had anointed David king over Israel, all the Philistines went up to seek David, but David heard about it and went down to the stronghold. 18 Now the Philistines had come and spread themselves in the valley of Rephaim. 19 David enquired of the LORD, saying, "Shall I go up against the Philistines? Will you deliver them into my hand?"

The LORD said to David, "Go up; for I will certainly deliver the Philistines into your hand."

20 David came to Baal Perazim, and David struck them there. Then he said, "The LORD has broken my enemies before me, like the breach of waters." Therefore he called the name of that place Baal Perazim.ᵇ 21 They left their images there, and David and his men took them away.

22 The Philistines came up yet again and spread themselves in the valley of Rephaim. 23 When David enquired of the LORD, he said, "You shall not go up. Circle around behind them, and attack them in front of the mulberry trees. 24 When you hear the sound of marching in the tops of the mulberry trees, then stir yourself up; for then the LORD has gone out before you to strike the army of the Philistines."

25 David did so, as the LORD commanded him, and struck the Philistines all the way from Geba to Gezer.

6

1 David again gathered together all the chosen men of Israel, thirty thousand. 2 David arose and went with all the people who were with him from Baale Judah, to bring up from there God's ark, which is called by the Name, even the name of the LORD of Armies who sits above the cherubim. 3 They set God's ark on a new cart, and brought it out of Abinadab's house that was on the hill; and Uzzah and Ahio, the sons of Abinadab, drove the new cart. 4 They brought it out of Abinadab's house which was in the hill, with God's ark; and Ahio went before the ark. 5 David and all the house of Israel played before the LORD with all kinds of instruments made of cypress wood, with harps, with stringed instruments, with tambourines, with castanets, and with cymbals.

6 When they came to the threshing floor of Nacon, Uzzah reached for God's ark and took hold of it, for the cattle stumbled. 7 The LORD's anger burnt against Uzzah, and God struck him there for his error; and he died there by God's ark. 8 David was displeased because the LORD had broken out against Uzzah; and he called that place Perez Uzzahᶜ to this day. 9 David was afraid of the LORD that day; and he said, "How could the LORD's ark come to me?" 10 So David would not move the LORD's ark to be with him in David's city; but David carried it aside into Obed-Edom the Gittite's house. 11 The LORD's ark remained in Obed-Edom the Gittite's house three

---

ᵃ 4:8 or, seed
ᵇ 5:20 "Baal Perazim" means "Lord who breaks out".

ᶜ 6:8 "Perez Uzzah" means "outbreak against Uzzah".

months; and the LORD blessed Obed-Edom and all his house. 12 King David was told, "The LORD has blessed the house of Obed-Edom, and all that belongs to him, because of God's ark."

So David went and brought up God's ark from the house of Obed-Edom into David's city with joy. 13 When those who bore the LORD's ark had gone six paces, he sacrificed an ox and a fattened calf. 14 David danced before the LORD with all his might; and David was clothed in a linen ephod. 15 So David and all the house of Israel brought up the LORD's ark with shouting and with the sound of the trumpet.

16 As the LORD's ark came into David's city, Michal the daughter of Saul looked out through the window and saw King David leaping and dancing before the LORD; and she despised him in her heart. 17 They brought in the LORD's ark, and set it in its place in the middle of the tent that David had pitched for it; and David offered burnt offerings and peace offerings before the LORD. 18 When David had finished offering the burnt offering and the peace offerings, he blessed the people in the name of the LORD of Armies. 19 He gave to all the people, even amongst the whole multitude of Israel, both to men and women, to everyone a portion of bread, dates, and raisins. So all the people departed, each to his own house.

20 Then David returned to bless his household. Michal the daughter of Saul came out to meet David, and said, "How glorious the king of Israel was today, who uncovered himself today in the eyes of his servants' maids, as one of the vain fellows shamelessly uncovers himself!"

21 David said to Michal, "It was before the LORD, who chose me above your father, and above all his house, to appoint me prince over the people of the LORD, over Israel. Therefore I will celebrate before the LORD. 22 I will be yet more undignified than this, and will be worthless in my own sight. But the maids of whom you have spoken will honour me."

23 Michal the daughter of Saul had no child to the day of her death.

7

1 When the king lived in his house, and the LORD had given him rest from all his enemies all around, 2 the king said to Nathan the prophet, "See now, I dwell in a house of cedar, but God's ark dwells within curtains."

3 Nathan said to the king, "Go, do all that is in your heart, for the LORD is with you."

4 That same night, the LORD's word came to Nathan, saying, 5 "Go and tell my servant David, 'The LORD says, "Should you build me a house for me to dwell in? 6 For I have not lived in a house since the day that I brought the children of Israel up out of Egypt, even to this day, but have moved around in a tent and in a tabernacle. 7 In all places in which I have walked with all the children of Israel, did I say a word to anyone from the tribes of Israel whom I commanded to be shepherd of my people Israel, saying, 'Why have you not built me a house of cedar?'"' 8 Now therefore tell my servant David this: 'The LORD of Armies says, "I took you from the sheep pen, from following the sheep, to be prince over my people, over Israel. 9 I have been with you wherever you went, and have cut off all your enemies from before you. I will make you a great name, like the name of the great ones who are in the earth. 10 I will appoint a place for my people Israel, and will plant them, that they may dwell in their own place and be moved no more. The children of wickedness will not afflict them any more, as at the first, 11 and as from the day that I commanded judges to be over my people Israel. I will cause you to rest from all your enemies. Moreover the LORD tells you that the LORD will make you a house. 12 When your days are fulfilled and you sleep with your fathers, I will set up your offspring after you, who will proceed out of your body, and I will establish his kingdom. 13 He will build a house for my name, and I will establish the throne of his kingdom forever. 14 I will be his father, and he will be my son. If he commits iniquity, I will chasten him with the rod of men and with the stripes of the children of men; 15 but my loving kindness will not depart from him, as I took it from Saul, whom I put away before you. 16 Your house and your kingdom will be made sure forever before you. Your throne will be established forever."'" 17 Nathan spoke to David all these words, and according to all this vision.

18 Then David the king went in and sat before the LORD; and he said, "Who am I, Lord[a] GOD, and what is my house, that you have brought me this far? 19 This was yet a small thing in your eyes, Lord GOD, but you have spoken also of your servant's house for a great while to come; and this amongst men, Lord GOD! 20 What more can David say to you? For you know your servant, Lord GOD. 21 For your word's sake, and according to your own heart, you have worked all this greatness, to make your servant know it. 22 Therefore you are great, LORD God. For there is no one like you, neither is there any God besides you, according to all that we have heard with our ears. 23 What one nation in the earth is like your people, even like Israel, whom God went to redeem to himself for a people, and to make himself a name, and to do great things for you, and awesome things for your land, before your people, whom you redeemed to yourself out of Egypt, from the nations and their gods? 24 You established for yourself your people Israel to be your people forever; and you, LORD, became their God.

25 "Now, LORD God, the word that you have spoken concerning your servant, and concerning his house, confirm it forever, and do as you have spoken. 26 Let your name be magnified forever, saying, 'The LORD of Armies is God over Israel; and the house of your servant David will be established before you.' 27 For you, LORD of Armies, the God of Israel, have revealed to your servant, saying, 'I will build you a house.' Therefore your servant has found in his heart to pray this prayer to you.

28 "Now, O Lord GOD, you are God, and your words are truth, and you have promised this good thing to your servant. 29 Now therefore, let it please you to bless the house of your servant, that it may continue forever before you; for you, Lord GOD, have spoken it. Let the house of your servant be blessed forever with your blessing."

8

1 After this, David struck the Philistines and subdued them; and David took the bridle of the mother city out of the hand of the Philistines. 2 He defeated Moab, and measured them with the line, making them to lie down on the ground; and he measured two lines to put to death, and one full line to keep alive. The Moabites became servants to David, and brought tribute.

3 David also struck Hadadezer the son of Rehob, king of Zobah, as he went to recover his dominion at the River. 4 David took from him one thousand and seven hundred horsemen and twenty thousand footmen. David hamstrung the chariot horses, but reserved enough of them for one hundred chariots. 5 When the Syrians of Damascus came to help Hadadezer king of Zobah, David struck twenty two thousand men of the Syrians. 6 Then David put garrisons in Syria of Damascus; and the Syrians became servants to David, and brought tribute. The LORD gave victory to David wherever he went. 7 David took the shields of gold that were on the servants of Hadadezer, and brought them to Jerusalem. 8 From Betah and from Berothai, cities of Hadadezer, King David took a great quantity of bronze.

9 When Toi king of Hamath heard that David had struck all the army of Hadadezer, 10 then Toi sent Joram his son to King David to greet him and to bless him, because he had fought against Hadadezer and struck him; for Hadadezer had wars with Toi. Joram brought with him vessels of silver, vessels of gold, and vessels of bronze. 11 King David also dedicated these to the LORD, with the silver and gold that he dedicated of all the nations which he subdued— 12 of Syria, of Moab, of the children of Ammon, of the Philistines, of Amalek, and of the plunder of Hadadezer, son of Rehob, king of Zobah.

13 David earned a reputation when he returned from striking down eighteen thousand men of the Syrians in the Valley of Salt. 14 He put garrisons in Edom. Throughout all Edom, he put garrisons, and all the Edomites became servants to David. The LORD gave victory to David wherever he went.

15 David reigned over all Israel; and David executed justice and righteousness for all his people. 16 Joab the son of Zeruiah was over the army, Jehoshaphat the son of Ahilud was recorder, 17 Zadok the son of Ahitub and Ahimelech the son of Abiathar were priests, Seraiah was scribe, 18 Benaiah the son of Jehoiada was over the Cherethites and the Pelethites; and David's sons were chief ministers.

9

1 David said, "Is there yet any who is left of Saul's house, that I may show him kindness for Jonathan's sake?" 2 There was of Saul's house a servant whose name was Ziba, and they called him to David; and the king said to him, "Are you Ziba?"

He said, "I am your servant."

3 The king said, "Is there not yet any of Saul's house, that I may show the kindness of God to him?"

Ziba said to the king, "Jonathan still has a son, who is lame in his feet."

4 The king said to him, "Where is he?"

Ziba said to the king, "Behold, he is in the house of Machir the son of Ammiel, in Lo Debar."

5 Then King David sent and brought him out of the house of Machir the son of Ammiel, from Lo Debar. 6 Mephibosheth, the son of Jonathan, the son of Saul, came to David, fell on his face, and showed respect. David said, "Mephibosheth?"

He answered, "Behold, your servant!"

7 David said to him, "Don't be afraid, for I will surely show you kindness for Jonathan your father's sake, and will restore to you all the land of Saul your father. You will eat bread at my table continually."

8 He bowed down, and said, "What is your servant, that you should look at such a dead dog as I am?"

9 Then the king called to Ziba, Saul's servant, and said to him, "All that belonged to Saul and to all his house I have given to your master's son. 10 Till the land for him—you, your sons, and your servants. Bring in the harvest, that your master's son may have bread to eat; but Mephibosheth your master's son will always eat bread at my table."

Now Ziba had fifteen sons and twenty servants. 11 Then Ziba said to the king, "According to all that my lord the king commands his servant, so your servant will do." So Mephibosheth ate at the king's table like one of the king's sons. 12 Mephibosheth had a young son, whose name was Mica. All who lived in Ziba's house were servants to Mephibosheth. 13 So Mephibosheth lived in Jerusalem, for he ate continually at the king's table. He was lame in both his feet.

10

1 After this, the king of the children of Ammon died, and Hanun his son reigned in his place. 2 David said, "I will show kindness to Hanun the son of Nahash, as his father showed kindness to me." So David sent by his servants to comfort him concerning his father. David's servants came into the land of the children of Ammon.

---

a *7:18* The word translated "Lord" is "Adonai."

3 But the princes of the children of Ammon said to Hanun their lord, "Do you think that David honours your father, in that he has sent comforters to you? Hasn't David sent his servants to you to search the city, to spy it out, and to overthrow it?"

4 So Hanun took David's servants, shaved off one half of their beards, and cut off their garments in the middle, even to their buttocks, and sent them away. 5 When they told David this, he sent to meet them, for the men were greatly ashamed. The king said, "Wait at Jericho until your beards have grown, and then return."

6 When the children of Ammon saw that they had become odious to David, the children of Ammon sent and hired the Syrians of Beth Rehob and the Syrians of Zobah, twenty thousand footmen, and the king of Maacah with one thousand men, and the men of Tob twelve thousand men. 7 When David heard of it, he sent Joab and all the army of the mighty men. 8 The children of Ammon came out, and put the battle in array at the entrance of the gate. The Syrians of Zobah and of Rehob and the men of Tob and Maacah were by themselves in the field. 9 Now when Joab saw that the battle was set against him before and behind, he chose of all the choice men of Israel and put them in array against the Syrians. 10 The rest of the people he committed into the hand of Abishai his brother; and he put them in array against the children of Ammon. 11 He said, "If the Syrians are too strong for me, then you shall help me; but if the children of Ammon are too strong for you, then I will come and help you. 12 Be courageous, and let's be strong for our people and for the cities of our God; and may the LORD do what seems good to him." 13 So Joab and the people who were with him came near to the battle against the Syrians, and they fled before him. 14 When the children of Ammon saw that the Syrians had fled, they likewise fled before Abishai, and entered into the city. Then Joab returned from the children of Ammon and came to Jerusalem.

15 When the Syrians saw that they were defeated by Israel, they gathered themselves together. 16 Hadadezer sent and brought out the Syrians who were beyond the River; and they came to Helam, with Shobach the captain of the army of Hadadezer at their head. 17 David was told that; and he gathered all Israel together, passed over the Jordan, and came to Helam. The Syrians set themselves in array against David and fought with him. 18 The Syrians fled before Israel; and David killed seven hundred charioteers of the Syrians and forty thousand horsemen, and struck Shobach the captain of their army, so that he died there. 19 When all the kings who were servants to Hadadezer saw that they were defeated before Israel, they made peace with Israel and served them. So the Syrians were afraid to help the children of Ammon any more.

11

1 At the return of the year, at the time when kings go out, David sent Joab and his servants with him, and all Israel; and they destroyed the children of Ammon and besieged Rabbah. But David stayed at Jerusalem. 2 At evening, David arose from his bed and walked on the roof of the king's house. From the roof, he saw a woman bathing, and the woman was very beautiful to look at. 3 David sent and enquired after the woman. One said, "Isn't this Bathsheba, the daughter of Eliam, Uriah the Hittite's wife?"

4 David sent messengers, and took her; and she came in to him, and he lay with her (for she was purified from her uncleanness); and she returned to her house. 5 The woman conceived; and she sent and told David, and said, "I am with child."

6 David sent to Joab, "Send me Uriah the Hittite." Joab sent Uriah to David. 7 When Uriah had come to him, David asked him how Joab did, and how the people fared, and how the war prospered. 8 David said to Uriah, "Go down to your house and wash your feet." Uriah departed out of the king's house, and a gift from the king was sent after him. 9 But Uriah slept at the door of the king's house with all the servants of his lord, and didn't go down to his house. 10 When they had told David, saying, "Uriah didn't go down to his house," David said to Uriah, "Haven't you come from a journey? Why didn't you go down to your house?"

11 Uriah said to David, "The ark, Israel, and Judah, are staying in tents; and my lord Joab and the servants of my lord are encamped in the open field. Shall I then go into my house to eat and to drink, and to lie with my wife? As you live, and as your soul lives, I will not do this thing!"

12 David said to Uriah, "Stay here today also, and tomorrow I will let you depart." So Uriah stayed in Jerusalem that day and the next day. 13 When David had called him, he ate and drank before him; and he made him drunk. At evening, he went out to lie on his bed with the servants of his lord, but didn't go down to his house. 14 In the morning, David wrote a letter to Joab and sent it by the hand of Uriah. 15 He wrote in the letter, saying, "Send Uriah to the forefront of the hottest battle, and retreat from him, that he may be struck and die."

16 When Joab kept watch on the city, he assigned Uriah to the place where he knew that valiant men were. 17 The men of the city went out and fought with Joab. Some of the people fell, even of David's servants; and Uriah the Hittite died also. 18 Then Joab sent and told David all the things concerning the war; 19 and he commanded the messenger, saying, "When you have finished telling all the things concerning the war to the king, 20 it shall be that, if the king's wrath arise, and he asks you, 'Why did you go so near to the city to fight? Didn't you know that they would shoot from the wall? 21 Who struck Abimelech the son of Jerubbesheth? Didn't a woman cast an upper millstone on him from the wall, so that he died at Thebez? Why did you go so near the wall?' then you shall say, 'Your servant Uriah the Hittite is also dead.'"

22 So the messenger went, and came and showed David all that Joab had sent him for. 23 The messenger said to David, "The men prevailed against us, and came out to us into the field; and we were on them even to the entrance of the gate. 24 The shooters shot at your servants from off the wall; and some of the king's servants are dead, and your servant Uriah the Hittite is also dead."

25 Then David said to the messenger, "Tell Joab, 'Don't let this thing displease you, for the sword devours one as well as another. Make your battle stronger against the city, and overthrow it.' Encourage him."

26 When Uriah's wife heard that Uriah her husband was dead, she mourned for her husband. 27 When the mourning was past, David sent and took her home to his house, and she became his wife and bore him a son. But the thing that David had done displeased the LORD.

12

1 The LORD sent Nathan to David. He came to him, and said to him, "There were two men in one city: the one rich, and the other poor. 2 The rich man had very many flocks and herds, 3 but the poor man had nothing, except one little ewe lamb, which he had bought and raised. It grew up together with him and with his children. It ate of his own food, drank of his own cup, and lay in his bosom, and was like a daughter to him. 4 A traveller came to the rich man, and he didn't want to take of his own flock and of his own herd to prepare for the wayfaring man who had come to him, but took the poor man's lamb and prepared it for the man who had come to him."

5 David's anger burnt hot against the man, and he said to Nathan, "As the LORD lives, the man who has done this deserves to die! 6 He must restore the lamb fourfold, because he did this thing and because he had no pity!"

7 Nathan said to David, "You are the man! This is what the LORD, the God of Israel, says: 'I anointed you king over Israel, and I delivered you out of the hand of Saul. 8 I gave you your master's house and your master's wives into your bosom, and gave you the house of Israel and of Judah; and if that would have been too little, I would have added to you many more such things. 9 Why have you despised the LORD's word, to do that which is evil in his sight? You have struck Uriah the Hittite with the sword, have taken his wife to be your wife, and have slain him with the sword of the children of Ammon. 10 Now therefore the sword will never depart from your house, because you have despised me and have taken Uriah the Hittite's wife to be your wife.'

11 "This is what the LORD says: 'Behold, I will raise up evil against you out of your own house; and I will take your wives before your eyes and give them to your neighbour, and he will lie with your wives in the sight of this sun. 12 For you did this secretly, but I will do this thing before all Israel, and before the sun.'"

13 David said to Nathan, "I have sinned against the LORD."

Nathan said to David, "The LORD also has put away your sin. You will not die. 14 However, because by this deed you have given great occasion to the LORD's enemies to blaspheme, the child also who is born to you will surely die." 15 Then Nathan departed to his house.

The LORD struck the child that Uriah's wife bore to David, and he was very sick. 16 David therefore begged God for the child; and David fasted, and went in and lay all night on the ground. 17 The elders of his house arose beside him, to raise him up from the earth; but he would not, and he didn't eat bread with them. 18 On the seventh day, the child died. David's servants were afraid to tell him that the child was dead, for they said, "Behold, while the child was yet alive, we spoke to him and he didn't listen to our voice. How will he then harm himself if we tell him that the child is dead?"

19 But when David saw that his servants were whispering together, David perceived that the child was dead; and David said to his servants, "Is the child dead?"

They said, "He is dead."

20 Then David arose from the earth, and washed and anointed himself, and changed his clothing; and he came into the LORD's house, and worshipped. Then he came to his own house; and when he requested, they set bread before him and he ate. 21 Then his servants said to him, "What is this that you have done? You fasted and wept for the child while he was alive, but when the child was dead, you rose up and ate bread."

22 He said, "While the child was yet alive, I fasted and wept; for I said, 'Who knows whether the LORD will not be gracious to me, that the child may live?' 23 But now he is dead. Why should I fast? Can I bring him back again? I will go to him, but he will not return to me."

24 David comforted Bathsheba his wife, and went in to her, and lay with her. She bore a son, and he called his name Solomon. The LORD loved him; 25 and he sent by the hand of Nathan the prophet, and he named him Jedidiah,[a] for the LORD's sake.

26 Now Joab fought against Rabbah of the children of Ammon, and took the royal city. 27 Joab sent messengers to David, and said, "I have fought against Rabbah. Yes, I have taken the city of waters. 28 Now therefore gather the rest of the people together, and encamp against the city and take it; lest I take the city, and it be called by my name."

29 David gathered all the people together and went to Rabbah, and fought against it and took it. 30 He took the crown of their king from off his head; and its weight was a talent[b] of gold, and in it were precious stones; and it was set on David's head. He brought a great quantity of plunder out of the city. 31 He brought out the people who were in it, and put them to work under saws, under iron picks, under axes of iron, and made them go

---

a 12:25 "Jedidiah" means "loved by the LORD".

b 12:30 A talent is about 30 kilograms or 66 pounds or 965 Troy ounces to the brick kiln; and he did so to all the cities of the children of Ammon. Then David and all the people returned to Jerusalem.

13

₁ After this, Absalom the son of David had a beautiful sister, whose name was Tamar; and Amnon the son of David loved her. ₂ Amnon was so troubled that he became sick because of his sister Tamar, for she was a virgin, and it seemed hard to Amnon to do anything to her. ₃ But Amnon had a friend whose name was Jonadab the son of Shimeah, David's brother; and Jonadab was a very subtle man. ₄ He said to him, "Why, son of the king, are you so sad from day to day? Won't you tell me?"

Amnon said to him, "I love Tamar, my brother Absalom's sister."

₅ Jonadab said to him, "Lay down on your bed and pretend to be sick. When your father comes to see you, tell him, 'Please let my sister Tamar come and give me bread to eat, and prepare the food in my sight, that I may see it and eat it from her hand.'"

₆ So Amnon lay down and faked being sick. When the king came to see him, Amnon said to the king, "Please let my sister Tamar come and make me a couple of cakes in my sight, that I may eat from her hand."

₇ Then David sent home to Tamar, saying, "Go now to your brother Amnon's house, and prepare food for him." ₈ So Tamar went to her brother Amnon's house; and he was lying down. She took dough, kneaded it, made cakes in his sight, and baked the cakes. ₉ She took the pan and poured them out before him, but he refused to eat. Amnon said, "Have all men leave me." Then every man went out from him. ₁₀ Amnon said to Tamar, "Bring the food into the room, that I may eat from your hand." Tamar took the cakes which she had made, and brought them into the room to Amnon her brother. ₁₁ When she had brought them near to him to eat, he took hold of her and said to her, "Come, lie with me, my sister!"

₁₂ She answered him, "No, my brother, do not force me! For no such thing ought to be done in Israel. Don't you do this folly! ₁₃ As for me, where would I carry my shame? And as for you, you will be as one of the fools in Israel. Now therefore, please speak to the king; for he will not withhold me from you."

₁₄ However, he would not listen to her voice; but being stronger than she, he forced her and lay with her. ₁₅ Then Amnon hated her with exceedingly great hatred; for the hatred with which he hated her was greater than the love with which he had loved her. Amnon said to her, "Arise, be gone!"

₁₆ She said to him, "Not so, because this great wrong in sending me away is worse than the other that you did to me!"

But he would not listen to her. ₁₇ Then he called his servant who ministered to him, and said, "Now put this woman out from me, and bolt the door after her."

₁₈ She had a garment of various colours on her, for the king's daughters who were virgins dressed in such robes. Then his servant brought her out and bolted the door after her. ₁₉ Tamar put ashes on her head, and tore her garment of various colours that was on her; and she laid her hand on her head and went her way, crying aloud as she went.

₂₀ Absalom her brother said to her, "Has Amnon your brother been with you? But now hold your peace, my sister. He is your brother. Don't take this thing to heart."

So Tamar remained desolate in her brother Absalom's house. ₂₁ But when King David heard of all these things, he was very angry. ₂₂ Absalom spoke to Amnon neither good nor bad; for Absalom hated Amnon, because he had forced his sister Tamar.

₂₃ After two full years, Absalom had sheep shearers in Baal Hazor, which is beside Ephraim; and Absalom invited all the king's sons. ₂₄ Absalom came to the king and said, "See now, your servant has sheep shearers. Please let the king and his servants go with your servant."

₂₅ The king said to Absalom, "No, my son, let's not all go, lest we be burdensome to you." He pressed him; however he would not go, but blessed him.

₂₆ Then Absalom said, "If not, please let my brother Amnon go with us."

The king said to him, "Why should he go with you?"

₂₇ But Absalom pressed him, and he let Amnon and all the king's sons go with him. ₂₈ Absalom commanded his servants, saying, "Mark now, when Amnon's heart is merry with wine; and when I tell you, 'Strike Amnon,' then kill him. Don't be afraid. Haven't I commanded you? Be courageous, and be valiant!"

₂₉ The servants of Absalom did to Amnon as Absalom had commanded. Then all the king's sons arose, and every man got up on his mule and fled.

₃₀ While they were on the way, the news came to David, saying, "Absalom has slain all the king's sons, and there is not one of them left!"

₃₁ Then the king arose, and tore his garments, and lay on the earth; and all his servants stood by with their clothes torn. ₃₂ Jonadab the son of Shimeah, David's brother, answered, "Don't let my lord suppose that they have killed all the young men, the king's sons, for Amnon only is dead; for by the appointment of Absalom this has been determined from the day that he forced his sister Tamar. ₃₃ Now therefore don't let my lord the king take the thing to his heart, to think that all the king's sons are dead; for only Amnon is dead." ₃₄ But Absalom fled. The young man who kept the watch lifted up his eyes and looked, and behold, many people were coming by way of the hillside behind him. ₃₅ Jonadab said to the king, "Behold, the

king's sons are coming! It is as your servant said." ₃₆ As soon as he had finished speaking, behold, the king's sons came, and lifted up their voices and wept. The king also and all his servants wept bitterly.

₃₇ But Absalom fled and went to Talmai the son of Ammihur, king of Geshur. David mourned for his son every day. ₃₈ So Absalom fled and went to Geshur, and was there three years. ₃₉ King David longed to go out to Absalom, for he was comforted concerning Amnon, since he was dead.

14

₁ Now Joab the son of Zeruiah perceived that the king's heart was towards Absalom. ₂ Joab sent to Tekoa and brought a wise woman from there, and said to her, "Please act like a mourner, and put on mourning clothing, please, and don't anoint yourself with oil; but be as a woman who has mourned a long time for the dead. ₃ Go in to the king and speak like this to him." So Joab put the words in her mouth.

₄ When the woman of Tekoa spoke to the king, she fell on her face to the ground, showed respect, and said, "Help, O king!"

₅ The king said to her, "What ails you?"

She answered, "Truly I am a widow, and my husband is dead. ₆ Your servant had two sons; and they both fought together in the field, and there was no one to part them, but the one struck the other and killed him. ₇ Behold, the whole family has risen against your servant, and they say, 'Deliver him who struck his brother, that we may kill him for the life of his brother whom he killed, and so destroy the heir also.' Thus they would quench my coal which is left, and would leave to my husband neither name nor remainder on the surface of the earth."

₈ The king said to the woman, "Go to your house, and I will give a command concerning you."

₉ The woman of Tekoa said to the king, "My lord, O king, may the iniquity be on me, and on my father's house; and may the king and his throne be guiltless."

₁₀ The king said, "Whoever says anything to you, bring him to me, and he will not bother you any more."

₁₁ Then she said, "Please let the king remember the LORD your God, that the avenger of blood destroy not any more, lest they destroy my son."

He said, "As the LORD lives, not one hair of your son shall fall to the earth."

₁₂ Then the woman said, "Please let your servant speak a word to my lord the king."

He said, "Say on."

₁₃ The woman said, "Why then have you devised such a thing against the people of God? For in speaking this word the king is as one who is guilty, in that the king does not bring home again his banished one. ₁₄ For we must die, and are like water spilled on the ground, which can't be gathered up again; neither does God take away life, but devises means, that he who is banished not be an outcast from him. ₁₅ Now therefore, seeing that I have come to speak this word to my lord the king, it is because the people have made me afraid. Your servant said, 'I will now speak to the king; it may be that the king will perform the request of his servant.' ₁₆ For the king will hear, to deliver his servant out of the hand of the man who would destroy me and my son together out of the inheritance of God. ₁₇ Then your servant said, 'Please let the word of my lord the king bring rest; for as an angel of God, so is my lord the king to discern good and bad. May the LORD, your God, be with you.'"

₁₈ Then the king answered the woman, "Please don't hide anything from me that I ask you."

The woman said, "Let my lord the king now speak."

₁₉ The king said, "Is the hand of Joab with you in all this?"

The woman answered, "As your soul lives, my lord the king, no one can turn to the right hand or to the left from anything that my lord the king has spoken; for your servant Joab urged me, and he put all these words in the mouth of your servant. ₂₀ Your servant Joab has done this thing to change the face of the matter. My lord is wise, according to the wisdom of an angel of God, to know all things that are in the earth."

₂₁ The king said to Joab, "Behold now, I have granted this thing. Go therefore, and bring the young man Absalom back."

₂₂ Joab fell to the ground on his face, showed respect, and blessed the king. Joab said, "Today your servant knows that I have found favour in your sight, my lord, O king, in that the king has performed the request of his servant."

₂₃ So Joab arose and went to Geshur, and brought Absalom to Jerusalem. ₂₄ The king said, "Let him return to his own house, but let him not see my face." So Absalom returned to his own house, and didn't see the king's face. ₂₅ Now in all Israel there was no one to be so much praised as Absalom for his beauty. From the sole of his foot even to the crown of his head there was no defect in him. ₂₆ When he cut the hair of his head (now it was at every year's end that he cut it; because it was heavy on him, therefore he cut it), he weighed the hair of his head at two hundred shekels,[a] after the king's weight. ₂₇ Three sons were born to Absalom, and one daughter, whose name was Tamar. She was a woman with a beautiful face. ₂₈ Absalom lived two full years in Jerusalem, and he didn't see the king's face. ₂₉ Then Absalom sent for Joab, to send him to the king, but he would not come to him. Then he sent again a second time, but he would not come. ₃₀ Therefore he said to his servants, "Behold, Joab's field is near mine, and he has barley there. Go and set it on fire." So Absalom's servants set the field on fire.

---

[a] *14:26* A shekel is about 10 grams or about 0.35 ounces, so 200 shekels is about 2 kilograms or about 4.4 pounds.

31 Then Joab arose and came to Absalom to his house, and said to him, "Why have your servants set my field on fire?"

32 Absalom answered Joab, "Behold, I sent to you, saying, 'Come here, that I may send you to the king, to say, "Why have I come from Geshur? It would be better for me to be there still. Now therefore, let me see the king's face; and if there is iniquity in me, let him kill me."'"

33 So Joab came to the king and told him; and when he had called for Absalom, he came to the king and bowed himself on his face to the ground before the king; and the king kissed Absalom.

15

1 After this, Absalom prepared a chariot and horses for himself, and fifty men to run before him. 2 Absalom rose up early, and stood beside the way of the gate. When any man had a suit which should come to the king for judgement, then Absalom called to him, and said, "What city are you from?"

He said, "Your servant is of one of the tribes of Israel."

3 Absalom said to him, "Behold, your matters are good and right; but there is no man deputized by the king to hear you." 4 Absalom said moreover, "Oh that I were made judge in the land, that every man who has any suit or cause might come to me, and I would do him justice!" 5 It was so, that when any man came near to bow down to him, he stretched out his hand, took hold of him, and kissed him. 6 Absalom did this sort of thing to all Israel who came to the king for judgement. So Absalom stole the hearts of the men of Israel.

7 At the end of forty years, Absalom said to the king, "Please let me go and pay my vow, which I have vowed to the LORD, in Hebron. 8 For your servant vowed a vow while I stayed at Geshur in Syria, saying, 'If the LORD shall indeed bring me again to Jerusalem, then I will serve the LORD.'"

9 The king said to him, "Go in peace."

So he arose and went to Hebron. 10 But Absalom sent spies throughout all the tribes of Israel, saying, "As soon as you hear the sound of the trumpet, then you shall say, 'Absalom is king in Hebron!'"

11 Two hundred men went with Absalom out of Jerusalem, who were invited, and went in their simplicity; and they didn't know anything. 12 Absalom sent for Ahithophel the Gilonite, David's counsellor, from his city, even from Giloh, while he was offering the sacrifices. The conspiracy was strong, for the people increased continually with Absalom. 13 A messenger came to David, saying, "The hearts of the men of Israel are after Absalom."

14 David said to all his servants who were with him at Jerusalem, "Arise! Let's flee, or else none of us will escape from Absalom. Hurry to depart, lest he overtake us quickly and bring down evil on us, and strike the city with the edge of the sword."

15 The king's servants said to the king, "Behold, your servants are ready to do whatever my lord the king chooses."

16 The king went out, and all his household after him. The king left ten women, who were concubines, to keep the house. 17 The king went out, and all the people after him; and they stayed in Beth Merhak. 18 All his servants passed on beside him; and all the Cherethites, and all the Pelethites, and all the Gittites, six hundred men who came after him from Gath, passed on before the king.

19 Then the king said to Ittai the Gittite, "Why do you also go with us? Return, and stay with the king; for you are a foreigner and also an exile. Return to your own place. 20 Whereas you came but yesterday, should I today make you go up and down with us, since I go where I may? Return, and take back your brothers. Mercy and truth be with you."

21 Ittai answered the king and said, "As the LORD lives, and as my lord the king lives, surely in what place my lord the king is, whether for death or for life, your servant will be there also."

22 David said to Ittai, "Go and pass over." Ittai the Gittite passed over, and all his men, and all the little ones who were with him. 23 All the country wept with a loud voice, and all the people passed over. The king also himself passed over the brook Kidron, and all the people passed over towards the way of the wilderness. 24 Behold, Zadok also came, and all the Levites with him, bearing the ark of the covenant of God; and they set down God's ark; and Abiathar went up until all the people finished passing out of the city. 25 The king said to Zadok, "Carry God's ark back into the city. If I find favour in the LORD's eyes, he will bring me again, and show me both it and his habitation; 26 but if he says, 'I have no delight in you,' behold, here I am. Let him do to me as seems good to him." 27 The king said also to Zadok the priest, "Aren't you a seer? Return into the city in peace, and your two sons with you, Ahimaaz your son and Jonathan the son of Abiathar. 28 Behold, I will stay at the fords of the wilderness until word comes from you to inform me." 29 Zadok therefore and Abiathar carried God's ark to Jerusalem again; and they stayed there. 30 David went up by the ascent of the Mount of Olives, and wept as he went up; and he had his head covered and went barefoot. All the people who were with him each covered his head, and they went up, weeping as they went up.

31 Someone told David, saying, "Ahithophel is amongst the conspirators with Absalom."

David said, "LORD, please turn the counsel of Ahithophel into foolishness."

32 When David had come to the top, where God was worshipped, behold, Hushai the Archite came to meet him with his tunic torn and earth on his head. 33 David said to him, "If you pass on with me, then you will be a burden to me; 34 but if you return to the city, and tell Absalom, 'I will be your servant, O king. As I have been your father's servant in time past, so I will now be your servant; then will you defeat for me the counsel of Ahithophel.' 35 Don't you have Zadok and Abiathar the priests there with

you? Therefore whatever you hear out of the king's house, tell it to Zadok and Abiathar the priests. 36 Behold, they have there with them their two sons, Ahimaaz, Zadok's son, and Jonathan, Abiathar's son. Send to me everything that you shall hear by them."

37 So Hushai, David's friend, came into the city; and Absalom came into Jerusalem.

16

1 When David was a little past the top, behold, Ziba the servant of Mephibosheth met him with a couple of donkeys saddled, and on them two hundred loaves of bread, and one hundred clusters of raisins, and one hundred summer fruits, and a container of wine. 2 The king said to Ziba, "What do you mean by these?"

Ziba said, "The donkeys are for the king's household to ride on; and the bread and summer fruit for the young men to eat; and the wine, that those who are faint in the wilderness may drink."

3 The king said, "Where is your master's son?"

Ziba said to the king, "Behold, he is staying in Jerusalem; for he said, 'Today the house of Israel will restore me the kingdom of my father.'"

4 Then the king said to Ziba, "Behold, all that belongs to Mephibosheth is yours."

Ziba said, "I bow down. Let me find favour in your sight, my lord, O king."

5 When King David came to Bahurim, behold, a man of the family of Saul's house came out, whose name was Shimei, the son of Gera. He came out and cursed as he came. 6 He cast stones at David and at all the servants of King David, and all the people and all the mighty men were on his right hand and on his left. 7 Shimei said when he cursed, "Be gone, be gone, you man of blood, and wicked fellow! 8 The LORD has returned on you all the blood of Saul's house, in whose place you have reigned! The LORD has delivered the kingdom into the hand of Absalom your son! Behold, you are caught by your own mischief, because you are a man of blood!"

9 Then Abishai the son of Zeruiah said to the king, "Why should this dead dog curse my lord the king? Please let me go over and take off his head." 10 The king said, "What have I to do with you, you sons of Zeruiah? Because he curses, and because the LORD has said to him, 'Curse David,' who then shall say, 'Why have you done so?'"

11 David said to Abishai and to all his servants, "Behold, my son, who came out of my bowels, seeks my life. How much more this Benjamite, now? Leave him alone, and let him curse; for the LORD has invited him. 12 It may be that the LORD will look on the wrong done to me, and that the LORD will repay me good for the cursing of me today." 13 So David and his men went by the way; and Shimei went along on the hillside opposite him and cursed as he went, threw stones at him, and threw dust. 14 The king and all the people who were with him arrived weary; and he refreshed himself there.

15 Absalom and all the people, the men of Israel, came to Jerusalem, and Ahithophel with him. 16 When Hushai the Archite, David's friend, had come to Absalom, Hushai said to Absalom, "Long live the king! Long live the king!"

17 Absalom said to Hushai, "Is this your kindness to your friend? Why didn't you go with your friend?"

18 Hushai said to Absalom, "No; but whomever the LORD and this people and all the men of Israel have chosen, I will be his, and I will stay with him. 19 Again, whom should I serve? Shouldn't I serve in the presence of his son? As I have served in your father's presence, so I will be in your presence."

20 Then Absalom said to Ahithophel, "Give your counsel what we shall do."

21 Ahithophel said to Absalom, "Go in to your father's concubines that he has left to keep the house. Then all Israel will hear that you are abhorred by your father. Then the hands of all who are with you will be strong."

22 So they spread a tent for Absalom on the top of the house, and Absalom went in to his father's concubines in the sight of all Israel.

23 The counsel of Ahithophel, which he gave in those days, was as if a man enquired at the inner sanctuary of God. All the counsel of Ahithophel was like this both with David and with Absalom.

17

1 Moreover Ahithophel said to Absalom, "Let me now choose twelve thousand men, and I will arise and pursue after David tonight. 2 I will come on him while he is weary and exhausted, and will make him afraid. All the people who are with him will flee. I will strike the king only, 3 and I will bring back all the people to you. The man whom you seek is as if all returned. All the people shall be in peace."

4 The saying pleased Absalom well, and all the elders of Israel. 5 Then Absalom said, "Now call Hushai the Archite also, and let's hear likewise what he says."

6 When Hushai had come to Absalom, Absalom spoke to him, saying, "Ahithophel has spoken like this. Shall we do what he says? If not, speak up."

7 Hushai said to Absalom, "The counsel that Ahithophel has given this time is not good." 8 Hushai said moreover, "You know your father and his men, that they are mighty men, and they are fierce in their minds, like a bear robbed of her cubs in the field. Your father is a man of war, and will not lodge with the people. 9 Behold, he is now hidden in some pit, or in some other place. It will happen, when some of them have fallen at the first, that whoever hears it will say, 'There is a slaughter amongst the people who follow Absalom!' 10 Even he who is valiant, whose heart is as the heart of a

lion, will utterly melt; for all Israel knows that your father is a mighty man, and those who are with him are valiant men. 11 But I counsel that all Israel be gathered together to you, from Dan even to Beersheba, as the sand that is by the sea for multitude; and that you go to battle in your own person. 12 So we will come on him in some place where he will be found, and we will light on him as the dew falls on the ground, then we will not leave so much as one of him and of all the men who are with him. 13 Moreover, if he has gone into a city, then all Israel will bring ropes to that city, and we will draw it into the river, until there isn't one small stone found there."

14 Absalom and all the men of Israel said, "The counsel of Hushai the Archite is better than the counsel of Ahithophel." For the LORD had ordained to defeat the good counsel of Ahithophel, to the intent that the LORD might bring evil on Absalom.

15 Then Hushai said to Zadok and to Abiathar the priests, "Ahithophel counselled Absalom and the elders of Israel that way; and I have counselled this way. 16 Now therefore send quickly, and tell David, saying, 'Don't lodge tonight at the fords of the wilderness, but by all means pass over, lest the king be swallowed up, and all the people who are with him.'"

17 Now Jonathan and Ahimaaz were staying by En Rogel; and a female servant used to go and report to them, and they went and told King David; for they couldn't risk being seen coming into the city. 18 But a boy saw them, and told Absalom. Then they both went away quickly and came to the house of a man in Bahurim, who had a well in his court; and they went down there. 19 The woman took and spread the covering over the well's mouth, and spread out crushed grain on it; and nothing was known. 20 Absalom's servants came to the woman to the house; and they said, "Where are Ahimaaz and Jonathan?"

The woman said to them, "They have gone over the brook of water."

When they had sought and could not find them, they returned to Jerusalem. 21 After they had departed, they came up out of the well and went and told King David; and they said to David, "Arise and pass quickly over the water; for thus has Ahithophel counselled against you." 22 Then David arose, and all the people who were with him, and they passed over the Jordan. By the morning light there lacked not one of them who had not gone over the Jordan.

23 When Ahithophel saw that his counsel was not followed, he saddled his donkey, arose, and went home to his city, set his house in order, and hanged himself; and he died, and was buried in the tomb of his father.

24 Then David came to Mahanaim. Absalom passed over the Jordan, he and all the men of Israel with him. 25 Absalom set Amasa over the army instead of Joab. Now Amasa was the son of a man whose name was Ithra the Israelite, who went in to Abigail the daughter of Nahash, sister to Zeruiah, Joab's mother. 26 Israel and Absalom encamped in the land of Gilead.

27 When David had come to Mahanaim, Shobi the son of Nahash of Rabbah of the children of Ammon, and Machir the son of Ammiel of Lodebar, and Barzillai the Gileadite of Rogelim, 28 brought beds, basins, earthen vessels, wheat, barley, meal, parched grain, beans, lentils, roasted grain, 29 honey, butter, sheep, and cheese of the herd, for David and for the people who were with him to eat; for they said, "The people are hungry, weary, and thirsty in the wilderness."

18

1 David counted the people who were with him, and set captains of thousands and captains of hundreds over them. 2 David sent the people out, a third part under the hand of Joab, and a third part under the hand of Abishai the son of Zeruiah, Joab's brother, and a third part under the hand of Ittai the Gittite. The king said to the people, "I will also surely go out with you myself."

3 But the people said, "You shall not go out, for if we flee away, they will not care for us, neither if half of us die, will they care for us. But you are worth ten thousand of us. Therefore now it is better that you are ready to help us out of the city."

4 The king said to them, "I will do what seems best to you."

The king stood beside the gate, and all the people went out by hundreds and by thousands. 5 The king commanded Joab and Abishai and Ittai, saying, "Deal gently for my sake with the young man Absalom." All the people heard when the king commanded all the captains concerning Absalom.

6 So the people went out into the field against Israel; and the battle was in the forest of Ephraim. 7 The people of Israel were struck there before David's servants, and there was a great slaughter there that day of twenty thousand men. 8 For the battle was there spread over the surface of all the country, and the forest devoured more people that day than the sword devoured.

9 Absalom happened to meet David's servants. Absalom was riding on his mule, and the mule went under the thick boughs of a great oak; and his head caught hold of the oak, and he was hanging between the sky and earth; and the mule that was under him went on. 10 A certain man saw it, and told Joab, and said, "Behold, I saw Absalom hanging in an oak."

11 Joab said to the man who told him, "Behold, you saw it, and why didn't you strike him there to the ground? I would have given you ten pieces of silver and a sash."

12 The man said to Joab, "Though I should receive a thousand pieces of silver in my hand, I still wouldn't stretch out my hand against the king's son; for in our hearing the king commanded you and Abishai and Ittai, saying, 'Beware that no one touch the young man Absalom.' 13 Otherwise, if I had dealt falsely against his life (and there is no matter hidden from the king), then you yourself would have set yourself against me."

14 Then Joab said, "I'm not going to wait like this with you." He took three darts in his hand and thrust them through Absalom's heart while he was still alive in the middle of the oak. 15 Ten young men who bore Joab's armour surrounded and struck Absalom, and killed him. 16 Joab blew the trumpet, and the people returned from pursuing after Israel; for Joab held the people back. 17 They took Absalom and cast him into a great pit in the forest, and raised over him a very great heap of stones. Then all Israel fled, each to his own tent.

18 Now Absalom in his lifetime had taken and reared up for himself the pillar which is in the king's valley, for he said, "I have no son to keep my name in memory." He called the pillar after his own name. It is called Absalom's monument, to this day.

19 Then Ahimaaz the son of Zadok said, "Let me now run and carry the king news, how the LORD has avenged him of his enemies."

20 Joab said to him, "You must not be the bearer of news today, but you must carry news another day. But today you must carry no news, because the king's son is dead."

21 Then Joab said to the Cushite, "Go, tell the king what you have seen!" The Cushite bowed himself to Joab, and ran.

22 Then Ahimaaz the son of Zadok said yet again to Joab, "But come what may, please let me also run after the Cushite."

Joab said, "Why do you want to run, my son, since you will have no reward for the news?"

23 "But come what may," he said, "I will run."

He said to him, "Run!" Then Ahimaaz ran by the way of the Plain, and outran the Cushite.

24 Now David was sitting between the two gates; and the watchman went up to the roof of the gate to the wall, and lifted up his eyes and looked, and, behold, a man running alone. The watchman shouted and told the king. The king said, "If he is alone, there is news in his mouth." He came closer and closer.

26 The watchman saw another man running; and the watchman called to the gatekeeper and said, "Behold, a man running alone!"

The king said, "He also brings news."

27 The watchman said, "I think the running of the first one is like the running of Ahimaaz the son of Zadok."

The king said, "He is a good man, and comes with good news."

28 Ahimaaz called, and said to the king, "All is well." He bowed himself before the king with his face to the earth, and said, "Blessed is the LORD your God, who has delivered up the men who lifted up their hand against my lord the king!"

29 The king said, "Is it well with the young man Absalom?"

Ahimaaz answered, "When Joab sent the king's servant, even me your servant, I saw a great tumult, but I don't know what it was."

30 The king said, "Come and stand here." He came and stood still.

31 Behold, the Cushite came. The Cushite said, "Good news for my lord the king, for the LORD has avenged you today of all those who rose up against you."

32 The king said to the Cushite, "Is it well with the young man Absalom?"

The Cushite answered, "May the enemies of my lord the king, and all who rise up against you to do you harm, be as that young man is."

33 The king was much moved, and went up to the room over the gate and wept. As he went, he said, "My son Absalom! My son, my son Absalom! I wish I had died instead of you, Absalom, my son, my son!"

19

1 Joab was told, "Behold, the king weeps and mourns for Absalom." 2 The victory that day was turned into mourning amongst all the people, for the people heard it said that day, "The king grieves for his son."

3 The people sneaked into the city that day, as people who are ashamed steal away when they flee in battle. 4 The king covered his face, and the king cried with a loud voice, "My son Absalom, Absalom, my son, my son!"

5 Joab came into the house to the king, and said, "Today you have shamed the faces of all your servants who today have saved your life, and the lives of your sons and of your daughters, and the lives of your wives, and the lives of your concubines; 6 in that you love those who hate you and hate those who love you. For you have declared today that princes and servants are nothing to you. For today I perceive that if Absalom had lived and we had all died today, then it would have pleased you well. 7 Now therefore arise, go out and speak to comfort your servants; for I swear by the LORD, if you don't go out, not a man will stay with you this night. That would be worse to you than all the evil that has happened to you from your youth until now."

8 Then the king arose and sat in the gate. The people were all told, "Behold, the king is sitting in the gate." All the people came before the king. Now Israel had fled every man to his tent. 9 All the people were at strife throughout all the tribes of Israel, saying, "The king delivered us out of the hand of our enemies, and he saved us out of the hand of the Philistines; and now he has fled out of the land from Absalom. 10 Absalom, whom we anointed over us, is dead in battle. Now therefore why don't you speak a word of bringing the king back?"

11 King David sent to Zadok and to Abiathar the priests, saying, "Speak to the elders of Judah, saying, 'Why are you the last to bring the king back to his house, since the speech of all Israel has come to the king, to return him to his house? 12 You are my brothers. You are my bone and my flesh. Why then are you the last to bring back the king?' 13 Say to Amasa, 'Aren't you my bone and my flesh? God do so to me, and more also, if you aren't captain of the army before me continually instead of

Joab.'" 14 He bowed the heart of all the men of Judah, even as one man, so that they sent to the king, saying, "Return, you and all your servants."

15 So the king returned, and came to the Jordan. Judah came to Gilgal, to go to meet the king, to bring the king over the Jordan. 16 Shimei the son of Gera, the Benjamite, who was of Bahurim, hurried and came down with the men of Judah to meet King David. 17 There were a thousand men of Benjamin with him, and Ziba the servant of Saul's house, and his fifteen sons and his twenty servants with him; and they went through the Jordan in the presence of the king. 18 A ferry boat went to bring over the king's household, and to do what he thought good.

Shimei the son of Gera fell down before the king when he had come over the Jordan. 19 He said to the king, "Don't let my lord impute iniquity to me, or remember that which your servant did perversely the day that my lord the king went out of Jerusalem, that the king should take it to his heart. 20 For your servant knows that I have sinned. Therefore behold, I have come today as the first of all the house of Joseph to go down to meet my lord the king."

21 But Abishai the son of Zeruiah answered, "Shouldn't Shimei be put to death for this, because he cursed the LORD's anointed?"

22 David said, "What have I to do with you, you sons of Zeruiah, that you should be adversaries to me today? Shall any man be put to death today in Israel? For don't I know that I am king over Israel today?" 23 The king said to Shimei, "You will not die." The king swore to him.

24 Mephibosheth the son of Saul came down to meet the king; and he had neither groomed his feet, nor trimmed his beard, nor washed his clothes, from the day the king departed until the day he came home in peace. 25 When he had come to Jerusalem to meet the king, the king said to him, "Why didn't you go with me, Mephibosheth?"

26 He answered, "My lord, O king, my servant deceived me. For your servant said, 'I will saddle a donkey for myself, that I may ride on it and go with the king,' because your servant is lame. 27 He has slandered your servant to my lord the king, but my lord the king is as an angel of God. Therefore do what is good in your eyes. 28 For all my father's house were but dead men before my lord the king; yet you set your servant amongst those who ate at your own table. What right therefore have I yet that I should appeal any more to the king?"

29 The king said to him, "Why do you speak any more of your matters? I say, you and Ziba divide the land."

30 Mephibosheth said to the king, "Yes, let him take all, because my lord the king has come in peace to his own house."

31 Barzillai the Gileadite came down from Rogelim; and he went over the Jordan with the king to conduct him over the Jordan. 32 Now Barzillai was a very aged man, even eighty years old. He had provided the king with sustenance while he stayed at Mahanaim, for he was a very great man. 33 The king said to Barzillai, "Come over with me, and I will sustain you with me in Jerusalem."

34 Barzillai said to the king, "How many are the days of the years of my life, that I should go up with the king to Jerusalem? 35 I am eighty years old, today. Can I discern between good and bad? Can your servant taste what I eat or what I drink? Can I hear the voice of singing men and singing women any more? Why then should your servant be a burden to my lord the king? 36 Your servant will just go over the Jordan with the king. Why should the king repay me with such a reward? 37 Please let your servant turn back again, that I may die in my own city, by the grave of my father and my mother. But behold, your servant Chimham; let him go over with my lord the king; and do to him what shall seem good to you."

38 The king answered, "Chimham shall go over with me, and I will do to him that which shall seem good to you. Whatever you request of me, that I will do for you."

39 All the people went over the Jordan, and the king went over. Then the king kissed Barzillai and blessed him; and he returned to his own place. 40 So the king went over to Gilgal, and Chimham went over with him. All the people of Judah brought the king over, and also half the people of Israel. 41 Behold, all the men of Israel came to the king, and said to the king, "Why have our brothers the men of Judah stolen you away, and brought the king and his household, over the Jordan, and all David's men with him?"

42 All the men of Judah answered the men of Israel, "Because the king is a close relative to us. Why then are you angry about this matter? Have we eaten at all at the king's cost? Or has he given us any gift?"

43 The men of Israel answered the men of Judah, and said, "We have ten parts in the king, and we have also more claim to David than you. Why then did you despise us, that our advice should not be first had in bringing back our king?" The words of the men of Judah were fiercer than the words of the men of Israel.

20

1 There happened to be there a wicked fellow, whose name was Sheba the son of Bichri, a Benjamite; and he blew the trumpet, and said, "We have no portion in David, neither have we inheritance in the son of Jesse. Every man to his tents, Israel!"

2 So all the men of Israel went up from following David, and followed Sheba the son of Bichri; but the men of Judah joined with their king, from the Jordan even to Jerusalem.

3 David came to his house at Jerusalem; and the king took the ten women his concubines, whom he had left to keep the house, and put them in custody and provided them with sustenance, but didn't go in to them. So they were shut up to the day of their death, living in widowhood.

4 Then the king said to Amasa, "Call me the men of Judah together within three days, and be here present."

5 So Amasa went to call the men of Judah together, but he stayed longer than the set time which had been appointed to him. 6 David said to Abishai, "Now Sheba the son of Bichri will do us more harm than Absalom did. Take your lord's servants and pursue after him, lest he get himself fortified cities, and escape out of our sight."

7 Joab's men went out after him with the Cherethites, the Pelethites, and all the mighty men; and they went out of Jerusalem to pursue Sheba the son of Bichri. 8 When they were at the great stone which is in Gibeon, Amasa came to meet them. Joab was clothed in his apparel of war that he had put on, and on it was a sash with a sword fastened on his waist in its sheath; and as he went along it fell out. 9 Joab said to Amasa, "Is it well with you, my brother?" Joab took Amasa by the beard with his right hand to kiss him. 10 But Amasa took no heed to the sword that was in Joab's hand. So he struck him with it in the body and shed out his bowels to the ground, and didn't strike him again; and he died. Joab and Abishai his brother pursued Sheba the son of Bichri. 11 One of Joab's young men stood by him, and said, "He who favours Joab, and he who is for David, let him follow Joab!"

12 Amasa lay wallowing in his blood in the middle of the highway. When the man saw that all the people stood still, he carried Amasa out of the highway into the field, and cast a garment over him when he saw that everyone who came by him stood still. 13 When he was removed out of the highway, all the people went on after Joab to pursue Sheba the son of Bichri. 14 He went through all the tribes of Israel to Abel, to Beth Maacah, and all the Berites. They were gathered together, and went also after him. 15 They came and besieged him in Abel of Beth Maacah, and they cast up a mound against the city, and it stood against the rampart; and all the people who were with Joab battered the wall to throw it down.

16 Then a wise woman cried out of the city, "Hear, hear! Please say to Joab, 'Come near here, that I may speak with you.'" 17 He came near to her; and the woman said, "Are you Joab?"

He answered, "I am."

Then she said to him, "Hear the words of your servant."

He answered, "I'm listening."

18 Then she spoke, saying, "They used to say in old times, 'They shall surely ask counsel at Abel,' and so they settled a matter. 19 I am amongst those who are peaceable and faithful in Israel. You seek to destroy a city and a mother in Israel. Why will you swallow up the LORD's inheritance?"

20 Joab answered, "Far be it, far be it from me, that I should swallow up or destroy. 21 The matter is not so. But a man of the hill country of Ephraim, Sheba the son of Bichri by name, has lifted up his hand against the king, even against David. Just deliver him, and I will depart from the city."

The woman said to Joab, "Behold, his head will be thrown to you over the wall."

22 Then the woman went to all the people in her wisdom. They cut off the head of Sheba the son of Bichri, and threw it out to Joab. He blew the trumpet, and they were dispersed from the city, every man to his tent. Then Joab returned to Jerusalem to the king.

23 Now Joab was over all the army of Israel, Benaiah the son of Jehoiada was over the Cherethites and over the Pelethites, 24 Adoram was over the men subject to forced labour, Jehoshaphat the son of Ahilud was the recorder, 25 Sheva was scribe, Zadok and Abiathar were priests, 26 and Ira the Jairite was chief minister to David.

21

1 There was a famine in the days of David for three years, year after year; and David sought the face of the LORD. The LORD said, "It is for Saul, and for his bloody house, because he put the Gibeonites to death."

2 The king called the Gibeonites and said to them (now the Gibeonites were not of the children of Israel, but of the remnant of the Amorites, and the children of Israel had sworn to them; and Saul sought to kill them in his zeal for the children of Israel and Judah); 3 and David said to the Gibeonites, "What should I do for you? And with what should I make atonement, that you may bless the LORD's inheritance?"

4 The Gibeonites said to him, "It is no matter of silver or gold between us and Saul or his house; neither is it for us to put any man to death in Israel."

He said, "I will do for you whatever you say."

5 They said to the king, "The man who consumed us and who plotted against us, that we should be destroyed from remaining in any of the borders of Israel, 6 let seven men of his sons be delivered to us, and we will hang them up to the LORD in Gibeah of Saul, the chosen of the LORD."

The king said, "I will give them."

7 But the king spared Mephibosheth the son of Jonathan the son of Saul, because of the LORD's oath that was between them, between David and Jonathan the son of Saul. 8 But the king took the two sons of Rizpah the daughter of Aiah, whom she bore to Saul, Armoni and Mephibosheth; and the five sons of Merab the daughter of Saul, whom she bore to Adriel the son of Barzillai the Meholathite. 9 He delivered them into the hands of the Gibeonites; and they hanged them on the mountain before the LORD, and all seven of them fell together. They were put to death in the days of harvest, in the first days, at the beginning of barley harvest.

10 Rizpah the daughter of Aiah took sackcloth and spread it for herself on the rock, from the beginning of harvest until water poured on them from the sky. She allowed neither the birds of the sky to rest on them by day, nor the animals of the field by night. 11 David was told what Rizpah the daughter of Aiah, the concubine of Saul, had done. 12 So David went and took the bones of Saul and the bones of Jonathan his son from the men of Jabesh Gilead, who had stolen them from the street of Beth Shan, where

the Philistines had hanged them in the day that the Philistines killed Saul in Gilboa; 13 and he brought up from there the bones of Saul and the bones of Jonathan his son. They also gathered the bones of those who were hanged. 14 They buried the bones of Saul and Jonathan his son in the country of Benjamin in Zela, in the tomb of Kish his father; and they performed all that the king commanded. After that, God answered prayer for the land.

15 The Philistines had war again with Israel; and David went down, and his servants with him, and fought against the Philistines. David grew faint; 16 and Ishbibenob, who was of the sons of the giant, the weight of whose spear was three hundred shekels of bronze in weight, he being armed with a new sword, thought he would kill David. 17 But Abishai the son of Zeruiah helped him, and struck the Philistine and killed him. Then the men of David swore to him, saying, "Don't go out with us to battle any more, so that you don't quench the lamp of Israel."

18 After this, there was again war with the Philistines at Gob. Then Sibbecai the Hushathite killed Saph, who was of the sons of the giant. 19 There was again war with the Philistines at Gob, and Elhanan the son of Jaare-Oregim the Bethlehemite killed Goliath the Gittite's brother, the staff of whose spear was like a weaver's beam. 20 There was again war at Gath, where there was a man of great stature, who had six fingers on every hand and six toes on every foot, twenty-four in number, and he also was born to the giant. 21 When he defied Israel, Jonathan the son of Shimei, David's brother, killed him. 22 These four were born to the giant in Gath; and they fell by the hand of David and by the hand of his servants.

22

1 David spoke to the LORD the words of this song in the day that the LORD delivered him out of the hand of all his enemies, and out of the hand of Saul, 2 and he said:
"The LORD is my rock,
 my fortress,
 and my deliverer, even mine;
3 God is my rock in whom I take refuge;
 my shield, and the horn of my salvation,
 my high tower, and my refuge.
 My saviour, you save me from violence.
4 I call on the LORD, who is worthy to be praised;
 So shall I be saved from my enemies.

5 For the waves of death surrounded me.
 The floods of ungodliness made me afraid.
6 The cords of Sheol[a] were around me.
 The snares of death caught me.
7 In my distress, I called on the LORD.
 Yes, I called to my God.
He heard my voice out of his temple.
 My cry came into his ears.
8 Then the earth shook and trembled.
 The foundations of heaven quaked and were shaken,
 because he was angry.
9 Smoke went up out of his nostrils.
 Consuming fire came out of his mouth.
 Coals were kindled by it.
10 He bowed the heavens also, and came down.
 Thick darkness was under his feet.
11 He rode on a cherub, and flew.
 Yes, he was seen on the wings of the wind.
12 He made darkness a shelter around himself,
 gathering of waters, and thick clouds of the skies.
13 At the brightness before him,
 coals of fire were kindled.
14 The LORD thundered from heaven.
 The Most High uttered his voice.
15 He sent out arrows and scattered them,
 lightning and confused them.
16 Then the channels of the sea appeared.
 The foundations of the world were laid bare by the LORD's rebuke,
 at the blast of the breath of his nostrils.

17 He sent from on high and he took me.
 He drew me out of many waters.
18 He delivered me from my strong enemy,
 from those who hated me, for they were too mighty for me.
19 They came on me in the day of my calamity,
 but the LORD was my support.
20 He also brought me out into a large place.
 He delivered me, because he delighted in me.
21 The LORD rewarded me according to my righteousness.
 He rewarded me according to the cleanness of my hands.
22 For I have kept the LORD's ways,
 and have not wickedly departed from my God.
23 For all his ordinances were before me.
 As for his statutes, I didn't depart from them.
24 I was also perfect towards him.
 I kept myself from my iniquity.
25 Therefore the LORD has rewarded me according to my righteousness,

According to my cleanness in his eyesight.

26 With the merciful you will show yourself merciful.
 With the perfect man you will show yourself perfect.
27 With the pure you will show yourself pure.
 With the crooked you will show yourself shrewd.
28 You will save the afflicted people,
 but your eyes are on the arrogant, that you may bring them down.
29 For you are my lamp, LORD.
 The LORD will light up my darkness.
30 For by you, I run against a troop.
 By my God, I leap over a wall.
31 As for God, his way is perfect.
 The LORD's word is tested.
 He is a shield to all those who take refuge in him.

32 For who is God, besides the LORD?
 Who is a rock, besides our God?
33 God is my strong fortress.
 He makes my way perfect.
34 He makes his feet like hinds' feet,
 and sets me on my high places.
35 He teaches my hands to war,
 so that my arms bend a bow of bronze.
36 You have also given me the shield of your salvation.
 Your gentleness has made me great.
37 You have enlarged my steps under me.
 My feet have not slipped.
38 I have pursued my enemies and destroyed them.
 I didn't turn again until they were consumed.
39 I have consumed them,
 and struck them through,
 so that they can't arise.
 Yes, they have fallen under my feet.
40 For you have armed me with strength for the battle.
 You have subdued under me those who rose up against me.
41 You have also made my enemies turn their backs to me,
 that I might cut off those who hate me.
42 They looked, but there was no one to save;
 even to the LORD, but he didn't answer them.
43 Then I beat them as small as the dust of the earth.
 I crushed them as the mire of the streets, and spread them abroad.

44 You also have delivered me from the strivings of my people.
 You have kept me to be the head of the nations.
 A people whom I have not known will serve me.
45 The foreigners will submit themselves to me.
 As soon as they hear of me, they will obey me.
46 The foreigners will fade away,
 and will come trembling out of their close places.

47 The LORD lives!
 Blessed be my rock!
Exalted be God, the rock of my salvation,
 48 even the God who executes vengeance for me,
 who brings down peoples under me,
 49 who brings me away from my enemies.
Yes, you lift me up above those who rise up against me.
 You deliver me from the violent man.
50 Therefore I will give thanks to you, LORD, amongst the nations,
 and will sing praises to your name.
51 He gives great deliverance to his king,
 and shows loving kindness to his anointed,
 to David and to his offspring, forever more."

23

1 Now these are the last words of David.
David the son of Jesse says,
 the man who was raised on high says,
 the anointed of the God of Jacob,
 the sweet psalmist of Israel:
2 "The LORD's Spirit spoke by me.
 His word was on my tongue.
3 The God of Israel said,
 the Rock of Israel spoke to me,
 'One who rules over men righteously,
 who rules in the fear of God,
4 shall be as the light of the morning when the sun rises,
 a morning without clouds,
 when the tender grass springs out of the earth,
 through clear shining after rain.'

5 Isn't my house so with God?
 Yet he has made with me an everlasting covenant,
 ordered in all things, and sure,
 for it is all my salvation and all my desire.
 Won't he make it grow?

---

a *22:6 Sheol is the place of the dead.*

6 But all the ungodly will be as thorns to be thrust away,
  because they can't be taken with the hand.
7 The man who touches them must be armed with iron and the staff of a
  spear.
They will be utterly burnt with fire in their place."

8 These are the names of the mighty men whom David had: Josheb Basshebeth a Tahchemonite, chief of the captains; he was called Adino the Eznite, who killed eight hundred at one time. 9 After him was Eleazar the son of Dodai the son of an Ahohite, one of the three mighty men with David when they defied the Philistines who were there gathered together to battle, and the men of Israel had gone away. 10 He arose and struck the Philistines until his hand was weary, and his hand froze to the sword; and the LORD worked a great victory that day; and the people returned after him only to take plunder. 11 After him was Shammah the son of Agee a Hararite. The Philistines had gathered together into a troop where there was a plot of ground full of lentils; and the people fled from the Philistines. 12 But he stood in the middle of the plot and defended it, and killed the Philistines; and the LORD worked a great victory.

13 Three of the thirty chief men went down, and came to David in the harvest time to the cave of Adullam; and the troop of the Philistines was encamped in the valley of Rephaim. 14 David was then in the stronghold; and the garrison of the Philistines was then in Bethlehem. 15 David said longingly, "Oh that someone would give me water to drink from the well of Bethlehem, which is by the gate!"

16 The three mighty men broke through the army of the Philistines, and drew water out of the well of Bethlehem that was by the gate and took it and brought it to David; but he would not drink of it, but poured it out to the LORD. 17 He said, "Be it far from me, LORD, that I should do this! Isn't this the blood of the men who risked their lives to go?" Therefore he would not drink it. The three mighty men did these things.

18 Abishai, the brother of Joab, the son of Zeruiah, was chief of the three. He lifted up his spear against three hundred and killed them, and had a name amongst the three. 19 Wasn't he the most honourable of the three? Therefore he was made their captain. However he wasn't included as one of the three.

20 Benaiah the son of Jehoiada, the son of a valiant man of Kabzeel, who had done mighty deeds, killed the two sons of Ariel of Moab. He also went down and killed a lion in the middle of a pit in a time of snow. 21 He killed a huge Egyptian, and the Egyptian had a spear in his hand; but he went down to him with a staff and plucked the spear out of the Egyptian's hand, and killed him with his own spear. 22 Benaiah the son of Jehoiada did these things, and had a name amongst the three mighty men. 23 He was more honourable than the thirty, but he didn't attain to the three. David set him over his guard.

24 Asahel the brother of Joab was one of the thirty: Elhanan the son of Dodo of Bethlehem, 25 Shammah the Harodite, Elika the Harodite, 26 Helez the Paltite, Ira the son of Ikkesh the Tekoite, 27 Abiezer the Anathothite, Mebunnai the Hushathite, 28 Zalmon the Ahohite, Maharai the Netophathite, 29 Heleb the son of Baanah the Netophathite, Ittai the son of Ribai of Gibeah of the children of Benjamin, 30 Benaiah a Pirathonite, Hiddai of the brooks of Gaash. 31 Abialbon the Arbathite, Azmaveth the Barhumite, 32 Eliahba the Shaalbonite, the sons of Jashen, Jonathan, 33 Shammah the Hararite, Ahiam the son of Sharar the Ararite, 34 Eliphelet the son of Ahasbai, the son of the Maacathite, Eliam the son of Ahithophel the Gilonite, 35 Hezro the Carmelite, Paarai the Arbite, 36 Igal the son of Nathan of Zobah, Bani the Gadite, 37 Zelek the Ammonite, Naharai the Beerothite, armour bearers to Joab the son of Zeruiah, 38 Ira the Ithrite, Gareb the Ithrite, 39 and Uriah the Hittite: thirty-seven in all.

24

1 Again the LORD's anger burnt against Israel, and he moved David against them, saying, "Go, count Israel and Judah." 2 The king said to Joab the captain of the army, who was with him, "Now go back and forth through all the tribes of Israel, from Dan even to Beersheba, and count the people, that I may know the sum of the people."

3 Joab said to the king, "Now may the LORD your God add to the people, however many they may be, one hundred times; and may the eyes of my lord the king see it. But why does my lord the king delight in this thing?"

4 Notwithstanding, the king's word prevailed against Joab and against the captains of the army. Joab and the captains of the army went out from the presence of the king to count the people of Israel. 5 They passed over the Jordan and encamped in Aroer, on the right side of the city that is in the middle of the valley of Gad, and to Jazer; 6 then they came to Gilead and to the land of Tahtim Hodshi; and they came to Dan Jaan and around to Sidon, 7 and came to the stronghold of Tyre, and to all the cities of the Hivites and of the Canaanites; and they went out to the south of Judah, at Beersheba.

8 So when they had gone back and forth through all the land, they came to Jerusalem at the end of nine months and twenty days. 9 Joab gave up the sum of the counting of the people to the king; and there were in Israel eight hundred thousand valiant men who drew the sword, and the men of Judah were five hundred thousand men.

10 David's heart struck him after he had counted the people. David said to the LORD, "I have sinned greatly in that which I have done. But now, the LORD, put away, I beg you, the iniquity of your servant; for I have done very foolishly."

11 When David rose up in the morning, the LORD's word came to the prophet Gad, David's seer, saying, 12 "Go and speak to David, 'The LORD says, "I offer you three things. Choose one of them, that I may do it to you."'"

13 So Gad came to David, and told him, saying, "Shall seven years of famine come to you in your land? Or will you flee three months before your foes while they pursue you? Or shall there be three days' pestilence in your land? Now answer, and consider what answer I shall return to him who sent me."

14 David said to Gad, "I am in distress. Let us fall now into the LORD's hand, for his mercies are great. Let me not fall into man's hand."

15 So the LORD sent a pestilence on Israel from the morning even to the appointed time; and seventy thousand men died of the people from Dan even to Beersheba. 16 When the angel stretched out his hand towards Jerusalem to destroy it, the LORD relented of the disaster, and said to the angel who destroyed the people, "It is enough. Now withdraw your hand." The LORD's angel was by the threshing floor of Araunah the Jebusite.

17 David spoke to the LORD when he saw the angel who struck the people, and said, "Behold, I have sinned, and I have done perversely; but these sheep, what have they done? Please let your hand be against me, and against my father's house."

18 Gad came that day to David and said to him, "Go up, build an altar to the LORD on the threshing floor of Araunah the Jebusite."

19 David went up according to the saying of Gad, as the LORD commanded. 20 Araunah looked out, and saw the king and his servants coming on towards him. Then Araunah went out and bowed himself before the king with his face to the ground. 21 Araunah said, "Why has my lord the king come to his servant?"

David said, "To buy your threshing floor, to build an altar to the LORD, that the plague may be stopped from afflicting the people."

22 Araunah said to David, "Let my lord the king take and offer up what seems good to him. Behold, the cattle for the burnt offering, and the threshing sledges and the yokes of the oxen for the wood. 23 All this, O king, does Araunah give to the king." Araunah said to the king, "May the LORD your God accept you."

24 The king said to Araunah, "No, but I will most certainly buy it from you for a price. I will not offer burnt offerings to the LORD my God which cost me nothing." So David bought the threshing floor and the oxen for fifty shekels[a] of silver. 25 David built an altar to the LORD there, and offered burnt offerings and peace offerings. So the LORD was entreated for the land, and the plague was removed from Israel.

---

a *24:24* A shekel is about 10 grams or about 0.35 ounces, so 50 shekels is about 0.5 kilograms or 1.1 pounds.

The First Book of Kings

1

1 Now King David was old and advanced in years; and they covered him with clothes, but he couldn't keep warm. 2 Therefore his servants said to him, "Let a young virgin be sought for my lord the king. Let her stand before the king, and cherish him; and let her lie in your bosom, that my lord the king may keep warm." 3 So they sought for a beautiful young lady throughout all the borders of Israel, and found Abishag the Shunammite, and brought her to the king. 4 The young lady was very beautiful; and she cherished the king, and served him; but the king didn't know her intimately.

5 Then Adonijah the son of Haggith exalted himself, saying, "I will be king." Then he prepared him chariots and horsemen, and fifty men to run before him. 6 His father had not displeased him at any time in saying, "Why have you done so?" and he was also a very handsome man; and he was born after Absalom. 7 He conferred with Joab the son of Zeruiah and with Abiathar the priest; and they followed Adonijah and helped him. 8 But Zadok the priest, Benaiah the son of Jehoiada, Nathan the prophet, Shimei, Rei, and the mighty men who belonged to David, were not with Adonijah.

9 Adonijah killed sheep, cattle, and fatlings by the stone of Zoheleth, which is beside En Rogel; and he called all his brothers, the king's sons, and all the men of Judah, the king's servants; 10 but he didn't call Nathan the prophet, and Benaiah, and the mighty men, and Solomon his brother.

11 Then Nathan spoke to Bathsheba the mother of Solomon, saying, "Haven't you heard that Adonijah the son of Haggith reigns, and David our lord doesn't know it? 12 Now therefore come, please let me give you counsel, that you may save your own life and your son Solomon's life. 13 Go in to King David, and tell him, 'Didn't you, my lord the king, swear to your servant, saying, "Assuredly Solomon your son shall reign after me, and he shall sit on my throne"? Why then does Adonijah reign?' 14 Behold,[a] while you are still talking there with the king, I will also come in after you and confirm your words."

15 Bathsheba went in to the king in his room. The king was very old; and Abishag the Shunammite was serving the king. 16 Bathsheba bowed and showed respect to the king. The king said, "What would you like?"

17 She said to him, "My lord, you swore by the LORD[b] your God[c] to your servant, 'Assuredly Solomon your son shall reign after me, and he shall sit on my throne.' 18 Now, behold, Adonijah reigns; and you, my lord the king, don't know it. 19 He has slain cattle and fatlings and sheep in abundance, and has called all the sons of the king, Abiathar the priest, and Joab the captain of the army; but he hasn't called Solomon your servant. 20 You, my lord the king, the eyes of all Israel are on you, that you should tell them who will sit on the throne of my lord the king after him. 21 Otherwise it will happen, when my lord the king sleeps with his fathers, that I and my son Solomon will be considered criminals."

22 Behold, while she was still talking with the king, Nathan the prophet came in. 23 They told the king, saying, "Behold, Nathan the prophet!"

When he had come in before the king, he bowed himself before the king with his face to the ground. 24 Nathan said, "My lord, King, have you said, 'Adonijah shall reign after me, and he shall sit on my throne'? 25 For he has gone down today, and has slain cattle, fatlings, and sheep in abundance, and has called all the king's sons, the captains of the army, and Abiathar the priest. Behold, they are eating and drinking before him, and saying, 'Long live King Adonijah!' 26 But he hasn't called me, even me your servant, Zadok the priest, and Benaiah the son of Jehoiada, and your servant Solomon. 27 Was this thing done by my lord the king, and you haven't shown to your servants who should sit on the throne of my lord the king after him?"

28 Then King David answered, "Call Bathsheba in to me." She came into the king's presence and stood before the king. 29 The king vowed and said, "As the LORD lives, who has redeemed my soul out of all adversity, 30 most certainly as I swore to you by the LORD, the God of Israel, saying, 'Assuredly Solomon your son shall reign after me, and he shall sit on my throne in my place;' I will most certainly do this today."

31 Then Bathsheba bowed with her face to the earth and showed respect to the king, and said, "Let my lord King David live forever!"

32 King David said, "Call to me Zadok the priest, Nathan the prophet, and Benaiah the son of Jehoiada." They came before the king. 33 The king said to them, "Take with you the servants of your lord, and cause Solomon my son to ride on my own mule, and bring him down to Gihon. 34 Let Zadok the priest and Nathan the prophet anoint him there king over Israel. Blow the trumpet, and say, 'Long live King Solomon!' 35 Then come up after him, and he shall come and sit on my throne; for he shall be king in my place. I have appointed him to be prince over Israel and over Judah."

36 Benaiah the son of Jehoiada answered the king, and said, "Amen. May the LORD, the God of my lord the king, say so. 37 As the LORD has been with my lord the king, even so may he be with Solomon, and make his throne greater than the throne of my lord King David."

38 So Zadok the priest, Nathan the prophet, Benaiah the son of Jehoiada, and the Cherethites and the Pelethites went down and had Solomon ride on King David's mule, and brought him to Gihon. 39 Zadok the priest took the horn of oil from the Tent, and anointed Solomon. They blew the trumpet; and all the people said, "Long live King Solomon!"

40 All the people came up after him, and the people piped with pipes, and rejoiced with great joy, so that the earth shook with their sound. 41 Adonijah and all the guests who were with him heard it as they had finished eating. When Joab heard the sound of the trumpet, he said, "Why is this noise of the city being in an uproar?"

42 While he yet spoke, behold, Jonathan the son of Abiathar the priest came; and Adonijah said, "Come in; for you are a worthy man, and bring good news."

43 Jonathan answered Adonijah, "Most certainly our lord King David has made Solomon king. 44 The king has sent with him Zadok the priest, Nathan the prophet, Benaiah the son of Jehoiada, and the Cherethites and the Pelethites; and they have caused him to ride on the king's mule. 45 Zadok the priest and Nathan the prophet have anointed him king in Gihon. They have come up from there rejoicing, so that the city rang again. This is the noise that you have heard. 46 Also, Solomon sits on the throne of the kingdom. 47 Moreover the king's servants came to bless our lord King David, saying, 'May your God make the name of Solomon better than your name, and make his throne greater than your throne;' and the king bowed himself on the bed. 48 Also thus said the king, 'Blessed be the LORD, the God of Israel, who has given one to sit on my throne today, my eyes even seeing it.'"

49 All the guests of Adonijah were afraid, and rose up, and each man went his way. 50 Adonijah was afraid because of Solomon; and he arose, and went, and hung onto the horns of the altar. 51 Solomon was told, "Behold, Adonijah fears King Solomon; for, behold, he is hanging onto the horns of the altar, saying, 'Let King Solomon swear to me first that he will not kill his servant with the sword.'"

52 Solomon said, "If he shows himself a worthy man, not a hair of his shall fall to the earth; but if wickedness is found in him, he shall die."

53 So King Solomon sent, and they brought him down from the altar. He came and bowed down to King Solomon; and Solomon said to him, "Go to your house."

2

1 Now the days of David came near that he should die; and he commanded Solomon his son, saying, 2 "I am going the way of all the earth. You be strong therefore, and show yourself a man; 3 and keep the instruction of the LORD your God, to walk in his ways, to keep his statutes, his commandments, his ordinances, and his testimonies, according to that which is written in the law of Moses, that you may prosper in all that you do and wherever you turn yourself. 4 Then the LORD may establish his word which he spoke concerning me, saying, 'If your children are careful of their way, to walk before me in truth with all their heart and with all their soul, there shall not fail you,' he said, 'a man on the throne of Israel.'

5 "Moreover you know also what Joab the son of Zeruiah did to me, even what he did to the two captains of the armies of Israel, to Abner the son of Ner and to Amasa the son of Jether, whom he killed, and shed the blood of war in peace, and put the blood of war on his sash that was around his waist and in his sandals that were on his feet. 6 Do therefore according to your wisdom, and don't let his grey head go down to Sheol[d] in peace. 7 But show kindness to the sons of Barzillai the Gileadite, and let them be amongst those who eat at your table; for so they came to me when I fled from Absalom your brother.

8 "Behold, there is with you Shimei the son of Gera, the Benjamite of Bahurim, who cursed me with a grievous curse in the day when I went to Mahanaim; but he came down to meet me at the Jordan, and I swore to him by the LORD, saying, 'I will not put you to death with the sword.' 9 Now therefore don't hold him guiltless, for you are a wise man; and you will know what you ought to do to him, and you shall bring his grey head down to Sheol[e] with blood."

10 David slept with his fathers, and was buried in David's city. 11 The days that David reigned over Israel were forty years; he reigned seven years in Hebron, and he reigned thirty-three years in Jerusalem. 12 Solomon sat on David his father's throne; and his kingdom was firmly established.

13 Then Adonijah the son of Haggith came to Bathsheba the mother of Solomon. She said, "Do you come peaceably?"

He said, "Peaceably. 14 He said moreover, I have something to tell you."

She said, "Say on."

15 He said, "You know that the kingdom was mine, and that all Israel set their faces on me, that I should reign. However, the kingdom is turned around, and has become my brother's; for it was his from the LORD. 16 Now I ask one petition of you. Don't deny me."

She said to him, "Say on."

17 He said, "Please speak to Solomon the king (for he will not tell you 'no'), that he give me Abishag the Shunammite as wife."

18 Bathsheba said, "All right. I will speak for you to the king."

19 Bathsheba therefore went to King Solomon, to speak to him for Adonijah. The king rose up to meet her and bowed himself to her, and sat down on his throne and caused a throne to be set for the king's mother; and she sat on his right hand. 20 Then she said, "I ask one small petition of you; don't deny me."

---

a *1:14* "Behold", from "הִנֵּה", means look at, take notice, observe, see, or gaze at. It is often used as an interjection.

b *1:17* When rendered in ALL CAPITAL LETTERS, "LORD" or "GOD" is the translation of God's Proper Name.

c *1:17* The Hebrew word rendered "God" is "אֱלֹהִים" (Elohim).

d *2:6* Sheol is the place of the dead.

e *2:9* Sheol is the place of the dead.

The king said to her, "Ask on, my mother, for I will not deny you."

21 She said, "Let Abishag the Shunammite be given to Adonijah your brother as wife."

22 King Solomon answered his mother, "Why do you ask Abishag the Shunammite for Adonijah? Ask for him the kingdom also, for he is my elder brother; even for him, and for Abiathar the priest, and for Joab the son of Zeruiah." 23 Then King Solomon swore by the LORD, saying, "God do so to me, and more also, if Adonijah has not spoken this word against his own life. 24 Now therefore as the LORD lives, who has established me and set me on my father David's throne, and who has made me a house as he promised, surely Adonijah shall be put to death today."

25 King Solomon sent Benaiah the son of Jehoiada; and he fell on him, so that he died. 26 To Abiathar the priest the king said, "Go to Anathoth, to your own fields, for you are worthy of death. But I will not at this time put you to death, because you bore the Lord[a] GOD's ark before David my father, and because you were afflicted in all in which my father was afflicted." 27 So Solomon thrust Abiathar out from being priest to the LORD, that he might fulfil the LORD's word which he spoke concerning the house of Eli in Shiloh.

28 This news came to Joab; for Joab had followed Adonijah, although he didn't follow Absalom. Joab fled to the LORD's Tent, and held onto the horns of the altar. 29 King Solomon was told, "Joab has fled to the LORD's Tent; and behold, he is by the altar." Then Solomon sent Benaiah the son of Jehoiada, saying, "Go, fall on him."

30 Benaiah came to the LORD's Tent, and said to him, "The king says, 'Come out!'"

He said, "No; but I will die here."

Benaiah brought the king word again, saying, "This is what Joab said, and this is how he answered me."

31 The king said to him, "Do as he has said, and fall on him, and bury him, that you may take away the blood, which Joab shed without cause, from me and from my father's house. 32 The LORD will return his blood on his own head, because he fell on two men more righteous and better than he, and killed them with the sword, and my father David didn't know it: Abner the son of Ner, captain of the army of Israel, and Amasa the son of Jether, captain of the army of Judah. 33 So their blood will return on the head of Joab and on the head of his offspring[b] forever. But for David, for his offspring, for his house, and for his throne, there will be peace forever from the LORD."

34 Then Benaiah the son of Jehoiada went up and fell on him, and killed him; and he was buried in his own house in the wilderness. 35 The king put Benaiah the son of Jehoiada in his place over the army; and the king put Zadok the priest in the place of Abiathar.

36 The king sent and called for Shimei, and said to him, "Build yourself a house in Jerusalem, and live there, and don't go anywhere else. 37 For on the day you go out and pass over the brook Kidron, know for certain that you will surely die. Your blood will be on your own head."

38 Shimei said to the king, "What you say is good. As my lord the king has said, so will your servant do." Shimei lived in Jerusalem many days.

39 At the end of three years, two of Shimei's slaves ran away to Achish, son of Maacah, king of Gath. They told Shimei, saying, "Behold, your slaves are in Gath."

40 Shimei arose, saddled his donkey, and went to Gath to Achish to seek his slaves; and Shimei went and brought his slaves from Gath. 41 Solomon was told that Shimei had gone from Jerusalem to Gath, and had come again.

42 The king sent and called for Shimei, and said to him, "Didn't I adjure you by the LORD and warn you, saying, 'Know for certain that on the day you go out and walk anywhere else, you shall surely die'? You said to me, 'The saying that I have heard is good.' 43 Why then have you not kept the oath of the LORD and the commandment that I have instructed you with?" 44 The king said moreover to Shimei, "You know in your heart all the wickedness that you did to David my father. Therefore the LORD will return your wickedness on your own head. 45 But King Solomon will be blessed, and David's throne will be established before the LORD forever." 46 So the king commanded Benaiah the son of Jehoiada; and he went out, and fell on him, so that he died. The kingdom was established in the hand of Solomon.

3

1 Solomon made a marriage alliance with Pharaoh king of Egypt. He took Pharaoh's daughter and brought her into David's city until he had finished building his own house, the LORD's house, and the wall around Jerusalem. 2 However, the people sacrificed in the high places, because there was not yet a house built for the LORD's name. 3 Solomon loved the LORD, walking in the statutes of David his father, except that he sacrificed and burnt incense in the high places. 4 The king went to Gibeon to sacrifice there, for that was the great high place. Solomon offered a thousand burnt offerings on that altar. 5 In Gibeon, the LORD appeared to Solomon in a dream by night; and God said, "Ask for what I should give you."

6 Solomon said, "You have shown to your servant David my father great loving kindness, because he walked before you in truth, in righteousness, and in uprightness of heart with you. You have kept for him this great loving kindness, that you have given him a son to sit on his throne, as it is today. 7 Now, LORD my God, you have made your servant king instead of David my father. I am just a little child. I don't know how to go out or come in. 8 Your servant is amongst your people which you have chosen, a great people, that can't be numbered or counted for multitude. 9 Give your servant therefore an understanding heart to judge your people, that I may discern between good and evil; for who is able to judge this great people of yours?"

10 This request pleased the Lord, that Solomon had asked this thing. 11 God said to him, "Because you have asked this thing, and have not asked for yourself long life, nor have you asked for riches for yourself, nor have you asked for the life of your enemies, but have asked for yourself understanding to discern justice, 12 behold, I have done according to your word. Behold, I have given you a wise and understanding heart, so that there has been no one like you before you, and after you none will arise like you. 13 I have also given you that which you have not asked, both riches and honour, so that there will not be any amongst the kings like you for all your days. 14 If you will walk in my ways, to keep my statutes and my commandments, as your father David walked, then I will lengthen your days."

15 Solomon awoke; and behold, it was a dream. Then he came to Jerusalem and stood before the ark of the LORD's covenant, and offered up burnt offerings, offered peace offerings, and made a feast for all his servants.

16 Then two women who were prostitutes came to the king, and stood before him. 17 The one woman said, "Oh, my lord, I and this woman dwell in one house. I delivered a child with her in the house. 18 The third day after I delivered, this woman delivered also. We were together. There was no stranger with us in the house, just us two in the house. 19 This woman's child died in the night, because she lay on it. 20 She arose at midnight, and took my son from beside me while your servant slept, and laid it in her bosom, and laid her dead child in my bosom. 21 When I rose in the morning to nurse my child, behold, he was dead; but when I had looked at him in the morning, behold, it was not my son whom I bore."

22 The other woman said, "No! But the living one is my son, and the dead one is your son."

The first one said, "No! But the dead one is your son, and the living one is my son." They argued like this before the king.

23 Then the king said, "One says, 'This is my son who lives, and your son is the dead;' and the other says, 'No! But your son is the dead one, and my son is the living one.'"

24 The king said, "Get me a sword." So they brought a sword before the king.

25 The king said, "Divide the living child in two, and give half to the one, and half to the other."

26 Then the woman whose the living child was spoke to the king, for her heart yearned over her son, and she said, "Oh, my lord, give her the living child, and in no way kill him!"

But the other said, "He shall be neither mine nor yours. Divide him."

27 Then the king answered, "Give the first woman the living child, and definitely do not kill him. She is his mother."

28 All Israel heard of the judgement which the king had judged; and they feared the king, for they saw that the wisdom of God was in him to do justice.

4

1 King Solomon was king over all Israel. 2 These were the princes whom he had: Azariah the son of Zadok, the priest; 3 Elihoreph and Ahijah, the sons of Shisha, scribes; Jehoshaphat the son of Ahilud, the recorder; 4 Benaiah the son of Jehoiada was over the army; Zadok and Abiathar were priests; 5 Azariah the son of Nathan was over the officers; Zabud the son of Nathan was chief minister, the king's friend; 6 Ahishar was over the household; and Adoniram the son of Abda was over the men subject to forced labour.

7 Solomon had twelve officers over all Israel, who provided food for the king and his household. Each man had to make provision for a month in the year. 8 These are their names: Ben Hur, in the hill country of Ephraim; 9 Ben Deker, in Makaz, in Shaalbim, Beth Shemesh, and Elon Beth Hanan; 10 Ben Hesed, in Arubboth (Socoh and all the land of Hepher belonged to him); 11 Ben Abinadab, in all the height of Dor (he had Taphath, Solomon's daughter, as wife); 12 Baana the son of Ahilud, in Taanach and Megiddo, and all Beth Shean which is beside Zarethan, beneath Jezreel, from Beth Shean to Abel Meholah, as far as beyond Jokmeam; 13 Ben Geber, in Ramoth Gilead (the towns of Jair the son of Manasseh, which are in Gilead, belonged to him; and the region of Argob, which is in Bashan, sixty great cities with walls and bronze bars, belonged to him); 14 Ahinadab the son of Iddo, in Mahanaim; 15 Ahimaaz, in Naphtali (he also took Basemath the daughter of Solomon as wife); 16 Baana the son of Hushai, in Asher and Bealoth; 17 Jehoshaphat the son of Paruah, in Issachar; 18 Shimei the son of Ela, in Benjamin; 19 Geber the son of Uri, in the land of Gilead, the country of Sihon king of the Amorites and of Og king of Bashan; and he was the only officer who was in the land.

20 Judah and Israel were numerous as the sand which is by the sea in multitude, eating and drinking and making merry. 21 Solomon ruled over all the kingdoms from the River to the land of the Philistines, and to the border of Egypt. They brought tribute and served Solomon all the days of his life. 22 Solomon's provision for one day was thirty cors[c] of fine flour, sixty measures of meal, 23 ten head of fat cattle, twenty head of cattle out of the pastures, and one hundred sheep, in addition to deer, gazelles, roebucks, and fattened fowl. 24 For he had dominion over all on this side the River,

---

a 2:26 The word translated "Lord" is "Adonai."

b 2:33 or, seed

c 4:22 1 cor is the same as a homer, or about 55.9 U. S. gallons (liquid) or 211 litres or 6 bushels from Tiphsah even to Gaza, over all the kings on this side the River; and he had peace on all sides around him. 25 Judah and Israel lived safely, every man under his vine and under his fig tree, from Dan even to Beersheba, all the days of Solomon. 26 Solomon had forty thousand stalls of horses for his chariots, and twelve thousand horsemen. 27 Those officers provided food for King Solomon, and for all who came to King Solomon's table, every man in his month. They let nothing be lacking. 28 They also brought barley and straw for the horses and swift steeds to the place where the officers were, each man according to his duty. 29 God gave Solomon abundant wisdom, understanding, and breadth of mind like the sand that is on the seashore. 30 Solomon's wisdom excelled the wisdom of all the children of the east and all the wisdom of Egypt. 31 For he was wiser than all men—wiser than Ethan the Ezrahite, Heman, Calcol, and Darda, the sons of Mahol; and his fame was in all the nations all around. 32 He spoke three thousand proverbs, and his songs numbered one thousand and five. 33 He spoke of trees, from the cedar that is in Lebanon even to the hyssop that grows out of the wall; he also spoke of animals, of birds, of creeping things, and of fish. 34 People of all nations came to hear the wisdom of Solomon, sent by all kings of the earth who had heard of his wisdom.

5

1 Hiram king of Tyre sent his servants to Solomon, for he had heard that they had anointed him king in the place of his father, and Hiram had always loved David. 2 Solomon sent to Hiram, saying, 3 "You know that David my father could not build a house for the name of the LORD his God because of the wars which were around him on every side, until the LORD put his enemies under the soles of his feet. 4 But now the LORD my God has given me rest on every side. There is no enemy and no evil occurrence. 5 Behold, I intend to build a house for the name of the LORD my God, as the LORD spoke to David my father, saying, 'Your son, whom I will set on your throne in your place shall build the house for my name.' 6 Now therefore command that cedar trees be cut for me out of Lebanon. My servants will be with your servants; and I will give you wages for your servants according to all that you say. For you know that there is nobody amongst us who knows how to cut timber like the Sidonians."

7 When Hiram heard the words of Solomon, he rejoiced greatly, and said, "Blessed is the LORD today, who has given to David a wise son to rule over this great people." 8 Hiram sent to Solomon, saying, "I have heard the message which you have sent to me. I will do all your desire concerning timber of cedar, and concerning cypress timber. 9 My servants will bring them down from Lebanon to the sea. I will make them into rafts to go by sea to the place that you specify to me, and will cause them to be broken up there, and you will receive them. You will accomplish my desire, in giving food for my household."

10 So Hiram gave Solomon cedar timber and cypress timber according to all his desire. 11 Solomon gave Hiram twenty thousand cors[a] of wheat for food to his household, and twenty cors[b] of pure oil. Solomon gave this to Hiram year by year. 12 The LORD gave Solomon wisdom, as he promised him. There was peace between Hiram and Solomon, and the two of them made a treaty together.

13 King Solomon raised a levy out of all Israel; and the levy was thirty thousand men. 14 He sent them to Lebanon, ten thousand a month by courses: for a month they were in Lebanon, and two months at home; and Adoniram was over the men subject to forced labour. 15 Solomon had seventy thousand who bore burdens, and eighty thousand who were stone cutters in the mountains, 16 besides Solomon's chief officers who were over the work: three thousand and three hundred who ruled over the people who laboured in the work. 17 The king commanded, and they cut out large stones, costly stones, to lay the foundation of the house with worked stone. 18 Solomon's builders and Hiram's builders and the Gebalites cut them, and prepared the timber and the stones to build the house.

6

1 In the four hundred and eightieth year after the children of Israel had come out of the land of Egypt, in the fourth year of Solomon's reign over Israel, in the month Ziv, which is the second month, he began to build the LORD's house. 2 The house which King Solomon built for the LORD had a length of sixty cubits,[c] and its width twenty, and its height thirty cubits. 3 The porch in front of the temple of the house had a length of twenty cubits, which was along the width of the house. Ten cubits was its width in front of the house. 4 He made windows of fixed lattice work for the house. 5 Against the wall of the house, he built floors all around, against the walls of the house all around, both of the temple and of the inner sanctuary; and he made side rooms all around. 6 The lowest floor was five cubits wide, and the middle was six cubits wide, and the third was seven cubits wide; for on the outside he made offsets in the wall of the house all around, that the beams should not be inserted into the walls of the house. 7 The house, when it was under construction, was built of stone prepared at the quarry; and no hammer or axe or any tool of iron was heard in the house while it was under construction. 8 The door for the middle side rooms was in the right side of the house. They went up by winding stairs into the middle floor, and out of the middle into the third. 9 So he built the house and finished it; and he covered the house with beams and planks of cedar. 10 He

built the floors all along the house, each five cubits high; and they rested on the house with timbers of cedar.

11 The LORD's word came to Solomon, saying, 12 "Concerning this house which you are building, if you will walk in my statutes, and execute my ordinances, and keep all my commandments to walk in them, then I will establish my word with you, which I spoke to David your father. 13 I will dwell amongst the children of Israel, and will not forsake my people Israel."

14 So Solomon built the house and finished it. 15 He built the walls of the house within with boards of cedar; from the floor of the house to the walls of the ceiling, he covered them on the inside with wood. He covered the floor of the house with cypress boards. 16 He built twenty cubits of the back part of the house with boards of cedar from the floor to the ceiling. He built this within, for an inner sanctuary, even for the most holy place. 17 In front of the temple sanctuary was forty cubits long. 18 There was cedar on the house within, carved with buds and open flowers. All was cedar. No stone was visible. 19 He prepared an inner sanctuary in the middle of the house within, to set the ark of the LORD's covenant there. 20 Within the inner sanctuary was twenty cubits in length, and twenty cubits in width, and twenty cubits in its height. He overlaid it with pure gold. He covered the altar with cedar. 21 So Solomon overlaid the house within with pure gold. He drew chains of gold across before the inner sanctuary, and he overlaid it with gold. 22 He overlaid the whole house with gold, until all the house was finished. He also overlaid the whole altar that belonged to the inner sanctuary with gold.

23 In the inner sanctuary he made two cherubim[d] of olive wood, each ten cubits high. 24 Five cubits was the length of one wing of the cherub, and five cubits was the length of the other wing of the cherub. From the tip of one wing to the tip of the other was ten cubits. 25 The other cherub was ten cubits. Both the cherubim were of one measure and one form. 26 One cherub was ten cubits high, and so was the other cherub. 27 He set the cherubim within the inner house. The wings of the cherubim were stretched out, so that the wing of the one touched the one wall and the wing of the other cherub touched the other wall; and their wings touched one another in the middle of the house. 28 He overlaid the cherubim with gold.

29 He carved all the walls of the house around with carved figures of cherubim, palm trees, and open flowers, inside and outside. 30 He overlaid the floor of the house with gold, inside and outside. 31 For the entrance of the inner sanctuary, he made doors of olive wood. The lintel and door posts were a fifth part of the wall. 32 So he made two doors of olive wood; and he carved on them carvings of cherubim, palm trees, and open flowers, and overlaid them with gold. He spread the gold on the cherubim and on the palm trees. 33 He also made the entrance of the temple door posts of olive wood, out of a fourth part of the wall, 34 and two doors of cypress wood. The two leaves of the one door were folding, and the two leaves of the other door were folding. 35 He carved cherubim, palm trees, and open flowers; and he overlaid them with gold fitted on the engraved work. 36 He built the inner court with three courses of cut stone and a course of cedar beams.

37 The foundation of the LORD's house was laid in the fourth year, in the month Ziv. 38 In the eleventh year, in the month Bul, which is the eighth month, the house was finished throughout all its parts and according to all its specifications. So he spent seven years building it.

7

1 Solomon was building his own house thirteen years, and he finished all his house. 2 For he built the House of the Forest of Lebanon. Its length was one hundred cubits,[e] its width fifty cubits, and its height thirty cubits, on four rows of cedar pillars, with cedar beams on the pillars. 3 It was covered with cedar above over the forty-five beams that were on the pillars, fifteen in a row. 4 There were beams in three rows, and window was facing window in three ranks. 5 All the doors and posts were made square with beams; and window was facing window in three ranks. 6 He made the hall of pillars. Its length was fifty cubits and its width thirty cubits, with a porch before them, and pillars and a threshold before them. 7 He made the porch of the throne where he was to judge, even the porch of judgement; and it was covered with cedar from floor to floor. 8 His house where he was to dwell, the other court within the porch, was of the same construction. He made also a house for Pharaoh's daughter (whom Solomon had taken as wife), like this porch. 9 All these were of costly stones, even of stone cut according to measure, sawed with saws, inside and outside, even from the foundation to the coping, and so on the outside to the great court. 10 The foundation was of costly stones, even great stones, stones of ten cubits and stones of eight cubits. 11 Above were costly stones, even cut stone, according to measure, and cedar wood. 12 The great court around had three courses of cut stone with a course of cedar beams, like the inner court of the LORD's house and the porch of the house.

13 King Solomon sent and brought Hiram out of Tyre. 14 He was the son of a widow of the tribe of Naphtali, and his father was a man of Tyre, a worker in bronze; and he was filled with wisdom and understanding and skill to work all works in bronze. He came to King Solomon and performed all his work. 15 For he fashioned the two pillars of bronze, eighteen cubits high apiece; and a line of twelve cubits encircled either of them. 16 He made two capitals of molten bronze to set on the tops of the pillars. The height of the one capital was five cubits, and the height of the other capital was five

---

a 5:11 20,000 cors would be about 120,000 bushels or about 4.2 megalitres of wheat, which would weigh about 3,270 metric tonnes.
b 5:11 20 cors is about 1,100 gallons or about 4220 litres.
c 6:2 A cubit is the length from the tip of the middle finger to the elbow on a man's arm, or about 18 inches or 46 centimetres.

d 6:23 "Cherubim" is plural of "cherub", an angelic being.
e 7:2 A cubit is the length from the tip of the middle finger to the elbow on a man's arm, or about 18 inches or 46 centimetres.

cubits. 17 There were nets of checker work and wreaths of chain work for the capitals which were on the top of the pillars: seven for the one capital, and seven for the other capital. 18 So he made the pillars; and there were two rows of pomegranates around the one network, to cover the capitals that were on the top of the pillars; and he did so for the other capital. 19 The capitals that were on the top of the pillars in the porch were of lily work, four cubits. 20 There were capitals above also on the two pillars, close by the belly which was beside the network. There were two hundred pomegranates in rows around the other capital. 21 He set up the pillars at the porch of the temple. He set up the right pillar and called its name Jachin; and he set up the left pillar and called its name Boaz. 22 On the tops of the pillars was lily work. So the work of the pillars was finished.

23 He made the molten sea ten cubits from brim to brim, round in shape. Its height was five cubits; and a line of thirty cubits encircled it. 24 Under its brim around there were buds which encircled it for ten cubits, encircling the sea. The buds were in two rows, cast when it was cast. 25 It stood on twelve oxen, three looking towards the north, and three looking towards the west, and three looking towards the south, and three looking towards the east; and the sea was set on them above, and all their hindquarters were inward. 26 It was a hand width thick. Its brim was worked like the brim of a cup, like the flower of a lily. It held two thousand baths.

27 He made the ten bases of bronze. The length of one base was four cubits, four cubits its width, and three cubits its height. 28 The work of the bases was like this: they had panels; and there were panels between the ledges; 29 and on the panels that were between the ledges were lions, oxen, and cherubim; and on the ledges there was a pedestal above; and beneath the lions and oxen were wreaths of hanging work. 30 Every base had four bronze wheels and axles of bronze; and its four feet had supports. The supports were cast beneath the basin, with wreaths at the side of each. 31 Its opening within the capital and above was a cubit. Its opening was round like the work of a pedestal, a cubit and a half; and also on its opening were engravings, and their panels were square, not round. 32 The four wheels were underneath the panels; and the axles of the wheels were in the base. The height of a wheel was a cubit and half a cubit. 33 The work of the wheels was like the work of a chariot wheel. Their axles, their rims, their spokes, and their hubs were all of cast metal. 34 There were four supports at the four corners of each base. Its supports were of the base itself. 35 In the top of the base there was a round half a cubit high; and on the top of the base its supports and its panels were the same. 36 On the plates of its supports and on its panels, he engraved cherubim, lions, and palm trees, each in its space, with wreaths all around. 37 He made the ten bases in this way: all of them had one casting, one measure, and one form. 38 He made ten basins of bronze. One basin contained forty baths.ᵃ Every basin measured four cubits. One basin was on every one of the ten bases. 39 He set the bases, five on the right side of the house and five on the left side of the house. He set the sea on the right side of the house eastward and towards the south.

40 Hiram made the pots, the shovels, and the basins. So Hiram finished doing all the work that he worked for King Solomon in the LORD's house: 41 the two pillars; the two bowls of the capitals that were on the top of the pillars; the two networks to cover the two bowls of the capitals that were on the top of the pillars; 42 the four hundred pomegranates for the two networks; two rows of pomegranates for each network, to cover the two bowls of the capitals that were on the pillars; 43 the ten bases; the ten basins on the bases; 44 the one sea; the twelve oxen under the sea; 45 the pots; the shovels; and the basins. All of these vessels, which Hiram made for King Solomon in the LORD's house, were of burnished bronze. 46 The king cast them in the plain of the Jordan, in the clay ground between Succoth and Zarethan. 47 Solomon left all the vessels unweighed, because there were so many of them. The weight of the bronze could not be determined.

48 Solomon made all the vessels that were in the LORD's house: the golden altar and the table that the show bread was on, of gold; 49 and the lamp stands, five on the right side and five on the left, in front of the inner sanctuary, of pure gold; and the flowers, the lamps, and the tongs, of gold; 50 the cups, the snuffers, the basins, the spoons, and the fire pans, of pure gold; and the hinges, both for the doors of the inner house, the most holy place, and for the doors of the house, of the temple, of gold.

51 Thus all the work that King Solomon did in the LORD's house was finished. Solomon brought in the things which David his father had dedicated—the silver, the gold, and the vessels—and put them in the treasuries of the LORD's house.

8

1 Then Solomon assembled the elders of Israel with all the heads of the tribes, the princes of the fathers' households of the children of Israel, to King Solomon in Jerusalem, to bring up the ark of the LORD's covenant out of David's city, which is Zion. 2 All the men of Israel assembled themselves to King Solomon at the feast in the month Ethanim, which is the seventh month. 3 All the elders of Israel came, and the priests picked up the ark. 4 They brought up the LORD's ark, the Tent of Meeting, and all the holy vessels that were in the Tent. The priests and the Levites brought these up. 5 King Solomon and all the congregation of Israel, who were assembled to him, were with him before the ark, sacrificing sheep and cattle that could not be counted or numbered for multitude. 6 The priests brought in the ark of the LORD's covenant to its place, into the inner sanctuary of the house,

to the most holy place, even under the cherubim's wings. 7 For the cherubim spread their wings out over the place of the ark, and the cherubim covered the ark and its poles above. 8 The poles were so long that the ends of the poles were seen from the holy place before the inner sanctuary, but they were not seen outside. They are there to this day. 9 There was nothing in the ark except the two stone tablets which Moses put there at Horeb, when the LORD made a covenant with the children of Israel, when they came out of the land of Egypt. 10 It came to pass, when the priests had come out of the holy place, that the cloud filled the LORD's house, 11 so that the priests could not stand to minister by reason of the cloud; for the LORD's glory filled the LORD's house.

12 Then Solomon said, "The LORD has said that he would dwell in the thick darkness. 13 I have surely built you a house of habitation, a place for you to dwell in forever."

14 The king turned his face around and blessed all the assembly of Israel; and all the assembly of Israel stood. 15 He said, "Blessed is the LORD, the God of Israel, who spoke with his mouth to David your father, and has with his hand fulfilled it, saying, 16 'Since the day that I brought my people Israel out of Egypt, I chose no city out of all the tribes of Israel to build a house, that my name might be there; but I chose David to be over my people Israel.'

17 "Now it was in the heart of David my father to build a house for the name of the LORD, the God of Israel. 18 But the LORD said to David my father, 'Whereas it was in your heart to build a house for my name, you did well that it was in your heart. 19 Nevertheless, you shall not build the house; but your son who shall come out of your body, he shall build the house for my name.' 20 The LORD has established his word that he spoke; for I have risen up in the place of David my father, and I sit on the throne of Israel, as the LORD promised, and have built the house for the name of the LORD, the God of Israel. 21 There I have set a place for the ark, in which is the LORD's covenant, which he made with our fathers when he brought them out of the land of Egypt."

22 Solomon stood before the LORD's altar in the presence of all the assembly of Israel, and spread out his hands towards heaven; 23 and he said, "LORD, the God of Israel, there is no God like you, in heaven above, or on earth beneath; who keeps covenant and loving kindness with your servants who walk before you with all their heart; 24 who has kept with your servant David my father that which you promised him. Yes, you spoke with your mouth, and have fulfilled it with your hand, as it is today. 25 Now therefore, may LORD, the God of Israel, keep with your servant David my father that which you have promised him, saying, 'There shall not fail from you a man in my sight to sit on the throne of Israel, if only your children take heed to their way, to walk before me as you have walked before me.'

26 "Now therefore, God of Israel, please let your word be verified, which you spoke to your servant David my father. 27 But will God in very deed dwell on the earth? Behold, heaven and the heaven of heavens can't contain you; how much less this house that I have built! 28 Yet have respect for the prayer of your servant and for his supplication, LORD my God, to listen to the cry and to the prayer which your servant prays before you today; 29 that your eyes may be open towards this house night and day, even towards the place of which you have said, 'My name shall be there;' to listen to the prayer which your servant prays towards this place. 30 Listen to the supplication of your servant, and of your people Israel, when they pray towards this place. Yes, hear in heaven, your dwelling place; and when you hear, forgive.

31 "If a man sins against his neighbour, and an oath is laid on him to cause him to swear, and he comes and swears before your altar in this house, 32 then hear in heaven, and act, and judge your servants, condemning the wicked, to bring his way on his own head, and justifying the righteous, to give him according to his righteousness.

33 "When your people Israel are struck down before the enemy because they have sinned against you, if they turn again to you and confess your name, and pray and make supplication to you in this house, 34 then hear in heaven, and forgive the sin of your people Israel, and bring them again to the land which you gave to their fathers.

35 "When the sky is shut up and there is no rain because they have sinned against you, if they pray towards this place and confess your name, and turn from their sin when you afflict them, 36 then hear in heaven, and forgive the sin of your servants, and of your people Israel, when you teach them the good way in which they should walk; and send rain on your land which you have given to your people for an inheritance.

37 "If there is famine in the land, if there is pestilence, if there is blight, mildew, locust or caterpillar; if their enemy besieges them in the land of their cities, whatever plague, whatever sickness there is, 38 whatever prayer and supplication is made by any man, or by all your people Israel, who shall each know the plague of his own heart, and spread out his hands towards this house, 39 then hear in heaven, your dwelling place, and forgive, and act, and give to every man according to all his ways, whose heart you know (for you, even you only, know the hearts of all the children of men); 40 that they may fear you all the days that they live in the land which you gave to our fathers.

41 "Moreover, concerning the foreigner, who is not of your people Israel, when he comes out of a far country for your name's sake 42 (for they shall hear of your great name and of your mighty hand and of your outstretched arm), when he comes and prays towards this house, 43 hear in heaven, your dwelling place, and do according to all that the foreigner calls

---

ᵃ 7:38 1 bath is one tenth of a cor, or about 5.6 U. S. gallons or 21 litres, so 40 baths was about 224 gallons or 840 litres.

to you for; that all the peoples of the earth may know your name, to fear you, as do your people Israel, and that they may know that this house which I have built is called by your name.

44 "If your people go out to battle against their enemy, by whatever way you shall send them, and they pray to the LORD towards the city which you have chosen, and towards the house which I have built for your name, 45 then hear in heaven their prayer and their supplication, and maintain their cause. 46 If they sin against you (for there is no man who doesn't sin), and you are angry with them and deliver them to the enemy, so that they carry them away captive to the land of the enemy, far off or near; 47 yet if they repent in the land where they are carried captive, and turn again, and make supplication to you in the land of those who carried them captive, saying, 'We have sinned and have done perversely; we have dealt wickedly,' 48 if they return to you with all their heart and with all their soul in the land of their enemies who carried them captive, and pray to you towards their land which you gave to their fathers, the city which you have chosen and the house which I have built for your name, 49 then hear their prayer and their supplication in heaven, your dwelling place, and maintain their cause; 50 and forgive your people who have sinned against you, and all their transgressions in which they have transgressed against you; and give them compassion before those who carried them captive, that they may have compassion on them 51 (for they are your people and your inheritance, which you brought out of Egypt, from the middle of the iron furnace); 52 that your eyes may be open to the supplication of your servant and to the supplication of your people Israel, to listen to them whenever they cry to you. 53 For you separated them from amongst all the peoples of the earth to be your inheritance, as you spoke by Moses your servant, when you brought our fathers out of Egypt, Lord GOD."

54 It was so, that when Solomon had finished praying all this prayer and supplication to the LORD, he arose from before the LORD's altar, from kneeling on his knees with his hands spread out towards heaven. 55 He stood and blessed all the assembly of Israel with a loud voice, saying, 56 "Blessed be the LORD, who has given rest to his people Israel, according to all that he promised. There has not failed one word of all his good promise, which he promised by Moses his servant. 57 May the LORD our God be with us as he was with our fathers. Let him not leave us or forsake us, 58 that he may incline our hearts to him, to walk in all his ways, and to keep his commandments, his statutes, and his ordinances, which he commanded our fathers. 59 Let these my words, with which I have made supplication before the LORD, be near to the LORD our God day and night, that he may maintain the cause of his servant and the cause of his people Israel, as every day requires; 60 that all the peoples of the earth may know that the LORD himself is God. There is no one else.

61 "Let your heart therefore be perfect with the LORD our God, to walk in his statutes, and to keep his commandments, as it is today."

62 The king, and all Israel with him, offered sacrifice before the LORD. 63 Solomon offered for the sacrifice of peace offerings, which he offered to the LORD, twenty two thousand head of cattle and one hundred and twenty thousand sheep. So the king and all the children of Israel dedicated the LORD's house. 64 The same day the king made the middle of the court holy that was before the LORD's house; for there he offered the burnt offering, the meal offering, and the fat of the peace offerings, because the bronze altar that was before the LORD was too little to receive the burnt offering, the meal offering, and the fat of the peace offerings.

65 So Solomon held the feast at that time, and all Israel with him, a great assembly, from the entrance of Hamath to the brook of Egypt, before the LORD our God, seven days and seven more days, even fourteen days. 66 On the eighth day he sent the people away; and they blessed the king, and went to their tents joyful and glad in their hearts for all the goodness that the LORD had shown to David his servant, and to Israel his people.

9

1 When Solomon had finished the building of the LORD's house, the king's house, and all Solomon's desire which he was pleased to do, 2 The LORD appeared to Solomon the second time, as he had appeared to him at Gibeon. 3 The LORD said to him, "I have heard your prayer and your supplication that you have made before me. I have made this house holy, which you have built, to put my name there forever; and my eyes and my heart shall be there perpetually. 4 As for you, if you will walk before me as David your father walked, in integrity of heart and in uprightness, to do according to all that I have commanded you, and will keep my statutes and my ordinances, 5 then I will establish the throne of your kingdom over Israel forever, as I promised to David your father, saying, 'There shall not fail from you a man on the throne of Israel.' 6 But if you turn away from following me, you or your children, and not keep my commandments and my statutes which I have set before you, but go and serve other gods and worship them, 7 then I will cut off Israel out of the land which I have given them; and I will cast this house, which I have made holy for my name, out of my sight; and Israel will be a proverb and a byword amongst all peoples. 8 Though this house is so high, yet everyone who passes by it will be astonished and hiss; and they will say, 'Why has the LORD done this to this land and to this house?' 9 and they will answer, 'Because they abandoned the LORD their God, who brought their fathers out of the land of Egypt, and embraced other gods, and worshipped them, and served them. Therefore the LORD has brought all this evil on them.'"

10 At the end of twenty years, in which Solomon had built the two houses, the LORD's house and the king's house, 11 (now Hiram the king of Tyre had furnished Solomon with cedar trees and cypress trees, and with gold, according to all his desire), King Solomon gave Hiram twenty cities in the land of Galilee. 12 Hiram came out of Tyre to see the cities which Solomon had given him; and they didn't please him. 13 He said, "What cities are these which you have given me, my brother?" He called them the land of Cabul[a] to this day. 14 Hiram sent to the king one hundred and twenty talents[b] of gold.

15 This is the reason of the forced labour which King Solomon conscripted: to build the LORD's house, his own house, Millo, Jerusalem's wall, Hazor, Megiddo, and Gezer. 16 Pharaoh king of Egypt had gone up, taken Gezer, burnt it with fire, killed the Canaanites who lived in the city, and given it for a wedding gift to his daughter, Solomon's wife. 17 Solomon built in the land Gezer, Beth Horon the lower, 18 Baalath, Tamar in the wilderness, 19 all the storage cities that Solomon had, the cities for his chariots, the cities for his horsemen, and that which Solomon desired to build for his pleasure in Jerusalem, and in Lebanon, and in all the land of his dominion. 20 As for all the people who were left of the Amorites, the Hittites, the Perizzites, the Hivites, and the Jebusites, who were not of the children of Israel— 21 their children who were left after them in the land, whom the children of Israel were not able utterly to destroy—of them Solomon raised a levy of bondservants to this day. 22 But of the children of Israel Solomon made no bondservants; but they were the men of war, his servants, his princes, his captains, and rulers of his chariots and of his horsemen. 23 These were the five hundred and fifty chief officers who were over Solomon's work, who ruled over the people who laboured in the work.

24 But Pharaoh's daughter came up out of David's city to her house which Solomon had built for her. Then he built Millo.

25 Solomon offered burnt offerings and peace offerings on the altar which he built to the LORD three times per year, burning incense with them on the altar that was before the LORD. So he finished the house.

26 King Solomon made a fleet of ships in Ezion Geber, which is beside Eloth, on the shore of the Red Sea, in the land of Edom. 27 Hiram sent in the fleet his servants, sailors who had knowledge of the sea, with the servants of Solomon. 28 They came to Ophir, and fetched from there gold, four hundred and twenty talents,[c] and brought it to King Solomon.

10

1 When the queen of Sheba heard of the fame of Solomon concerning the LORD's name, she came to test him with hard questions. 2 She came to Jerusalem with a very great caravan, with camels that bore spices, very much gold, and precious stones; and when she had come to Solomon, she talked with him about all that was in her heart. 3 Solomon answered all her questions. There wasn't anything hidden from the king which he didn't tell her. 4 When the queen of Sheba had seen all the wisdom of Solomon, the house that he had built, 5 the food of his table, the sitting of his servants, the attendance of his officials, their clothing, his cup bearers, and his ascent by which he went up to the LORD's house, there was no more spirit in her. 6 She said to the king, "It was a true report that I heard in my own land of your acts and of your wisdom. 7 However, I didn't believe the words until I came and my eyes had seen it. Behold, not even half was told me! Your wisdom and prosperity exceed the fame which I heard. 8 Happy are your men, happy are these your servants who stand continually before you, who hear your wisdom. 9 Blessed is the LORD your God, who delighted in you, to set you on the throne of Israel. Because the LORD loved Israel forever, therefore he made you king, to do justice and righteousness." 10 She gave the king one hundred and twenty talents of gold, and a very great quantity of spices, and precious stones. Never again was there such an abundance of spices as these which the queen of Sheba gave to King Solomon.

11 The fleet of Hiram that brought gold from Ophir also brought in from Ophir great quantities of almug trees[d] and precious stones. 12 The king made of the almug trees pillars for the LORD's house and for the king's house, harps also and stringed instruments for the singers; no such almug trees came or were seen to this day.

13 King Solomon gave to the queen of Sheba all her desire, whatever she asked, in addition to that which Solomon gave her of his royal bounty. So she turned and went to her own land, she and her servants.

14 Now the weight of gold that came to Solomon in one year was six hundred and sixty-six talents[e] of gold, 15 in addition to that which the traders brought, and the traffic of the merchants, and of all the kings of the mixed people, and of the governors of the country. 16 King Solomon made two hundred bucklers of beaten gold; six hundred shekels[f] of gold went to one buckler. 17 He made three hundred shields of beaten gold; three minas[g] of gold went to one shield; and the king put them in the House of the Forest of Lebanon. 18 Moreover the king made a great throne of ivory, and overlaid

---

a 9:13 "Cabul" sounds like Hebrew for "good-for-nothing".

b 9:14 A talent is about 30 kilograms or 66 pounds or 965 Troy ounces, so 120 talents is about 3.6 metric tonnes

c 9:28 A talent is about 30 kilograms or 66 pounds or 965 Troy ounces, so 420 talents is about 12.6 metric tonnes

d 10:11 possibly an Indian sandalwood, with nice grain and a pleasant scent, and good for woodworking

e 10:14 A talent is about 30 kilograms or 66 pounds or 965 Troy ounces, so 666 talents is about 20 metric tonnes

f 10:16 A shekel is about 10 grams or about 0.32 Troy ounces, so 600 shekels is about 6 kilograms or 13.2 pounds or 192 Troy ounces.

g 10:17 A mina is about 600 grams or 1.3 U. S. pounds.

it with the finest gold. ₁₉ There were six steps to the throne, and the top of the throne was round behind; and there were armrests on either side by the place of the seat, and two lions standing beside the armrests. ₂₀ Twelve lions stood there on the one side and on the other on the six steps. Nothing like it was made in any kingdom. ₂₁ All King Solomon's drinking vessels were of gold, and all the vessels of the House of the Forest of Lebanon were of pure gold. None were of silver, because it was considered of little value in the days of Solomon. ₂₂ For the king had a fleet of ships of Tarshish at sea with Hiram's fleet. Once every three years the fleet of Tarshish came bringing gold, silver, ivory, apes, and peacocks.

₂₃ So King Solomon exceeded all the kings of the earth in riches and in wisdom. ₂₄ All the earth sought the presence of Solomon to hear his wisdom which God had put in his heart. ₂₅ Year after year, every man brought his tribute, vessels of silver, vessels of gold, clothing, armour, spices, horses, and mules.

₂₆ Solomon gathered together chariots and horsemen. He had one thousand and four hundred chariots and twelve thousand horsemen. He kept them in the chariot cities and with the king at Jerusalem. ₂₇ The king made silver as common as stones in Jerusalem, and cedars as common as the sycamore trees that are in the lowland. ₂₈ The horses which Solomon had were brought out of Egypt. The king's merchants received them in droves, each drove at a price. ₂₉ A chariot was imported from Egypt for six hundred shekels[a] of silver, and a horse for one hundred and fifty shekels; and so they exported them to all the kings of the Hittites and to the kings of Syria.

11

₁ Now King Solomon loved many foreign women, together with the daughter of Pharaoh: women of the Moabites, Ammonites, Edomites, Sidonians, and Hittites, ₂ of the nations concerning which the LORD said to the children of Israel, "You shall not go amongst them, neither shall they come amongst you, for surely they will turn away your heart after their gods." Solomon joined to these in love. ₃ He had seven hundred wives, princesses, and three hundred concubines. His wives turned his heart away. ₄ When Solomon was old, his wives turned away his heart after other gods; and his heart was not perfect with the LORD his God, as the heart of David his father was. ₅ For Solomon went after Ashtoreth the goddess of the Sidonians, and after Milcom the abomination of the Ammonites. ₆ Solomon did that which was evil in the LORD's sight, and didn't go fully after the LORD, as David his father did. ₇ Then Solomon built a high place for Chemosh the abomination of Moab, on the mountain that is before Jerusalem, and for Molech the abomination of the children of Ammon. ₈ So he did for all his foreign wives, who burnt incense and sacrificed to their gods. ₉ The LORD was angry with Solomon, because his heart was turned away from the LORD, the God of Israel, who had appeared to him twice, ₁₀ and had commanded him concerning this thing, that he should not go after other gods; but he didn't keep that which the LORD commanded. ₁₁ Therefore the LORD said to Solomon, "Because this is done by you, and you have not kept my covenant and my statutes, which I have commanded you, I will surely tear the kingdom from you, and will give it to your servant. ₁₂ Nevertheless, I will not do it in your days, for David your father's sake; but I will tear it out of your son's hand. ₁₃ However, I will not tear away all the kingdom; but I will give one tribe to your son, for David my servant's sake, and for Jerusalem's sake which I have chosen."

₁₄ The LORD raised up an adversary to Solomon: Hadad the Edomite. He was one of the king's offspring in Edom. ₁₅ For when David was in Edom, and Joab the captain of the army had gone up to bury the slain, and had struck every male in Edom ₁₆ (for Joab and all Israel remained there six months, until he had cut off every male in Edom), ₁₇ Hadad fled, he and certain Edomites of his father's servants with him, to go into Egypt, when Hadad was still a little child. ₁₈ They arose out of Midian and came to Paran; and they took men with them out of Paran, and they came to Egypt, to Pharaoh king of Egypt, who gave him a house, and appointed him food, and gave him land. ₁₉ Hadad found great favour in the sight of Pharaoh, so that he gave him as wife the sister of his own wife, the sister of Tahpenes the queen. ₂₀ The sister of Tahpenes bore him Genubath his son, whom Tahpenes weaned in Pharaoh's house; and Genubath was in Pharaoh's house amongst the sons of Pharaoh. ₂₁ When Hadad heard in Egypt that David slept with his fathers, and that Joab the captain of the army was dead, Hadad said to Pharaoh, "Let me depart, that I may go to my own country."

₂₂ Then Pharaoh said to him, "But what have you lacked with me, that behold, you seek to go to your own country?"

He answered, "Nothing, however only let me depart."

₂₃ God raised up an adversary to him, Rezon the son of Eliada, who had fled from his lord, Hadadezer king of Zobah. ₂₄ He gathered men to himself, and became captain over a troop, when David killed them of Zobah. They went to Damascus and lived there, and reigned in Damascus. ₂₅ He was an adversary to Israel all the days of Solomon, in addition to the mischief of Hadad. He abhorred Israel, and reigned over Syria.

₂₆ Jeroboam the son of Nebat, an Ephraimite of Zeredah, a servant of Solomon, whose mother's name was Zeruah, a widow, also lifted up his hand against the king. ₂₇ This was the reason why he lifted up his hand against the king: Solomon built Millo, and repaired the breach of his father David's city. ₂₈ The man Jeroboam was a mighty man of valour; and Solomon saw the young man that he was industrious, and he put him in charge of all the labour of the house of Joseph. ₂₉ At that time, when

Jeroboam went out of Jerusalem, the prophet Ahijah the Shilonite found him on the way. Now Ahijah had clad himself with a new garment; and the two of them were alone in the field. ₃₀ Ahijah took the new garment that was on him, and tore it in twelve pieces. ₃₁ He said to Jeroboam, "Take ten pieces; for the LORD, the God of Israel, says, 'Behold, I will tear the kingdom out of the hand of Solomon and will give ten tribes to you ₃₂ (but he shall have one tribe, for my servant David's sake and for Jerusalem's sake, the city which I have chosen out of all the tribes of Israel), ₃₃ because they have forsaken me, and have worshipped Ashtoreth the goddess of the Sidonians, Chemosh the god of Moab, and Milcom the god of the children of Ammon. They have not walked in my ways, to do that which is right in my eyes, and to keep my statutes and my ordinances, as David his father did.

₃₄ "'However, I will not take the whole kingdom out of his hand, but I will make him prince all the days of his life for David my servant's sake whom I chose, who kept my commandments and my statutes, ₃₅ but I will take the kingdom out of his son's hand and will give it to you, even ten tribes. ₃₆ I will give one tribe to his son, that David my servant may have a lamp always before me in Jerusalem, the city which I have chosen for myself to put my name there. ₃₇ I will take you, and you shall reign according to all that your soul desires, and shall be king over Israel. ₃₈ It shall be, if you will listen to all that I command you, and will walk in my ways, and do that which is right in my eyes, to keep my statutes and my commandments, as David my servant did, that I will be with you, and will build you a sure house, as I built for David, and will give Israel to you. ₃₉ I will afflict the offspring of David for this, but not forever.'"

₄₀ Therefore Solomon sought to kill Jeroboam, but Jeroboam arose and fled into Egypt, to Shishak king of Egypt, and was in Egypt until the death of Solomon.

₄₁ Now the rest of the acts of Solomon, and all that he did, and his wisdom, aren't they written in the book of the acts of Solomon? ₄₂ The time that Solomon reigned in Jerusalem over all Israel was forty years. ₄₃ Solomon slept with his fathers, and was buried in his father David's city; and Rehoboam his son reigned in his place.

12

₁ Rehoboam went to Shechem, for all Israel had come to Shechem to make him king. ₂ When Jeroboam the son of Nebat heard of it (for he was yet in Egypt, where he had fled from the presence of King Solomon, and Jeroboam lived in Egypt; ₃ and they sent and called him), Jeroboam and all the assembly of Israel came, and spoke to Rehoboam, saying, ₄ "Your father made our yoke difficult. Now therefore make the hard service of your father, and his heavy yoke which he put on us, lighter, and we will serve you."

₅ He said to them, "Depart for three days, then come back to me." So the people departed.

₆ King Rehoboam took counsel with the old men who had stood before Solomon his father while he yet lived, saying, "What counsel do you give me to answer these people?"

₇ They replied, "If you will be a servant to this people today, and will serve them, and answer them with good words, then they will be your servants forever."

₈ But he abandoned the counsel of the old men which they had given him, and took counsel with the young men who had grown up with him, who stood before him. ₉ He said to them, "What counsel do you give, that we may answer these people who have spoken to me, saying, 'Make the yoke that your father put on us lighter'?"

₁₀ The young men who had grown up with him said to him, "Tell these people who spoke to you, saying, 'Your father made our yoke heavy, but make it lighter to us'— tell them, 'My little finger is thicker than my father's waist. ₁₁ Now my father burdened you with a heavy yoke, but I will add to your yoke. My father chastised you with whips, but I will chastise you with scorpions.'"

₁₂ So Jeroboam and all the people came to Rehoboam the third day, as the king asked, saying, "Come to me again the third day." ₁₃ The king answered the people roughly, and abandoned the counsel of the old men which they had given him, ₁₄ and spoke to them according to the counsel of the young men, saying, "My father made your yoke heavy, but I will add to your yoke. My father chastised you with whips, but I will chastise you with scorpions."

₁₅ So the king didn't listen to the people; for it was a thing brought about from the LORD, that he might establish his word, which the LORD spoke by Ahijah the Shilonite to Jeroboam the son of Nebat. ₁₆ When all Israel saw that the king didn't listen to them, the people answered the king, saying, "What portion have we in David? We don't have an inheritance in the son of Jesse. To your tents, Israel! Now see to your own house, David." So Israel departed to their tents.

₁₇ But as for the children of Israel who lived in the cities of Judah, Rehoboam reigned over them. ₁₈ Then King Rehoboam sent Adoram, who was over the men subject to forced labour; and all Israel stoned him to death with stones. King Rehoboam hurried to get himself up to his chariot, to flee to Jerusalem. ₁₉ So Israel rebelled against David's house to this day.

₂₀ When all Israel heard that Jeroboam had returned, they sent and called him to the congregation, and made him king over all Israel. There was no one who followed David's house, except for the tribe of Judah only.

₂₁ When Rehoboam had come to Jerusalem, he assembled all the house of Judah and the tribe of Benjamin, a hundred and eighty thousand

---

a *10:29* A shekel is about 10 grams or about 0.35 ounces.

chosen men who were warriors, to fight against the house of Israel, to bring the kingdom again to Rehoboam the son of Solomon. 22 But the word of God came to Shemaiah the man of God, saying, 23 "Speak to Rehoboam the son of Solomon, king of Judah, and to all the house of Judah and Benjamin, and to the rest of the people, saying, 24 'The LORD says, "You shall not go up or fight against your brothers, the children of Israel. Everyone return to his house; for this thing is from me."'" So they listened to the LORD's word, and returned and went their way, according to the LORD's word.

25 Then Jeroboam built Shechem in the hill country of Ephraim, and lived in it; and he went out from there and built Penuel. 26 Jeroboam said in his heart, "Now the kingdom will return to David's house. 27 If this people goes up to offer sacrifices in the LORD's house at Jerusalem, then the heart of this people will turn again to their lord, even to Rehoboam king of Judah; and they will kill me, and return to Rehoboam king of Judah." 28 So the king took counsel, and made two calves of gold; and he said to them, "It is too much for you to go up to Jerusalem. Look and behold your gods, Israel, which brought you up out of the land of Egypt!" 29 He set the one in Bethel, and the other he put in Dan. 30 This thing became a sin, for the people went even as far as Dan to worship before the one there. 31 He made houses of high places, and made priests from amongst all the people, who were not of the sons of Levi. 32 Jeroboam ordained a feast in the eighth month, on the fifteenth day of the month, like the feast that is in Judah, and he went up to the altar. He did so in Bethel, sacrificing to the calves that he had made, and he placed in Bethel the priests of the high places that he had made. 33 He went up to the altar which he had made in Bethel on the fifteenth day in the eighth month, even in the month which he had devised of his own heart; and he ordained a feast for the children of Israel, and went up to the altar to burn incense.

13

1 Behold, a man of God came out of Judah by the LORD's word to Bethel; and Jeroboam was standing by the altar to burn incense. 2 He cried against the altar by the LORD's word, and said, "Altar! Altar! the LORD says: 'Behold, a son will be born to David's house, Josiah by name. On you he will sacrifice the priests of the high places who burn incense on you, and they will burn men's bones on you.'" 3 He gave a sign the same day, saying, "This is the sign which the LORD has spoken: Behold, the altar will be split apart, and the ashes that are on it will be poured out."

4 When the king heard the saying of the man of God, which he cried against the altar in Bethel, Jeroboam put out his hand from the altar, saying, "Seize him!" His hand, which he put out against him, dried up, so that he could not draw it back again to himself. 5 The altar was also split apart, and the ashes poured out from the altar, according to the sign which the man of God had given by the LORD's word. 6 The king answered the man of God, "Now intercede for the favour of the LORD your God, and pray for me, that my hand may be restored me again."

The man of God interceded with the LORD, and the king's hand was restored to him again, and became as it was before.

7 The king said to the man of God, "Come home with me and refresh yourself, and I will give you a reward."

8 The man of God said to the king, "Even if you gave me half of your house, I would not go in with you, neither would I eat bread nor drink water in this place; 9 for so was it commanded me by the LORD's word, saying, 'You shall eat no bread, drink no water, and don't return by the way that you came.'" 10 So he went another way, and didn't return by the way that he came to Bethel.

11 Now an old prophet lived in Bethel, and one of his sons came and told him all the works that the man of God had done that day in Bethel. They also told their father the words which he had spoken to the king.

12 Their father said to them, "Which way did he go?" Now his sons had seen which way the man of God went, who came from Judah. 13 He said to his sons, "Saddle the donkey for me." So they saddled the donkey for him; and he rode on it. 14 He went after the man of God, and found him sitting under an oak. He said to him, "Are you the man of God who came from Judah?"

He said, "I am."

15 Then he said to him, "Come home with me and eat bread."

16 He said, "I may not return with you, nor go in with you. I will not eat bread or drink water with you in this place. 17 For it was said to me by the LORD's word, 'You shall eat no bread or drink water there, and don't turn again to go by the way that you came.'"

18 He said to him, "I also am a prophet as you are; and an angel spoke to me by the LORD's word, saying, 'Bring him back with you into your house, that he may eat bread and drink water.'" He lied to him.

19 So he went back with him, ate bread in his house, and drank water. 20 As they sat at the table, the LORD's word came to the prophet who brought him back; 21 and he cried out to the man of God who came from Judah, saying, "The LORD says, 'Because you have been disobedient to the LORD's word, and have not kept the commandment which the LORD your God commanded you, 22 but came back, and have eaten bread and drank water in the place of which he said to you, "Eat no bread, and drink no water," your body will not come to the tomb of your fathers.'"

23 After he had eaten bread and after he drank, he saddled the donkey for the prophet whom he had brought back. 24 When he had gone, a lion met him by the way and killed him. His body was thrown on the path, and the donkey stood by it. The lion also stood by the body. 25 Behold, men passed by and saw the body thrown on the path, and the lion standing by

the body; and they came and told it in the city where the old prophet lived.

26 When the prophet who brought him back from the way heard of it, he said, "It is the man of God who was disobedient to the LORD's word. Therefore the LORD has delivered him to the lion, which has mauled him and slain him, according to the LORD's word which he spoke to him." 27 He said to his sons, saying, "Saddle the donkey for me," and they saddled it. 28 He went and found his body thrown on the path, and the donkey and the lion standing by the body. The lion had not eaten the body nor mauled the donkey. 29 The prophet took up the body of the man of God, and laid it on the donkey, and brought it back. He came to the city of the old prophet to mourn, and to bury him. 30 He laid his body in his own grave; and they mourned over him, saying, "Alas, my brother!"

31 After he had buried him, he spoke to his sons, saying, "When I am dead, bury me in the tomb in which the man of God is buried. Lay my bones beside his bones. 32 For the saying which he cried by the LORD's word against the altar in Bethel, and against all the houses of the high places which are in the cities of Samaria, will surely happen."

33 After this thing, Jeroboam didn't turn from his evil way, but again made priests of the high places from amongst all the people. Whoever wanted to, he consecrated him, that there might be priests of the high places. 34 This thing became sin to the house of Jeroboam, even to cut it off and to destroy it from off the surface of the earth.

14

1 At that time Abijah the son of Jeroboam became sick. 2 Jeroboam said to his wife, "Please get up and disguise yourself, so that you won't be recognised as Jeroboam's wife. Go to Shiloh. Behold, Ahijah the prophet is there, who said that I would be king over this people. 3 Take with you ten loaves of bread, some cakes, and a jar of honey, and go to him. He will tell you what will become of the child."

4 Jeroboam's wife did so, and arose and went to Shiloh, and came to Ahijah's house. Now Ahijah could not see, for his eyes were set by reason of his age. 5 The LORD said to Ahijah, "Behold, Jeroboam's wife is coming to enquire of you concerning her son, for he is sick. Tell her such and such; for it will be, when she comes in, that she will pretend to be another woman."

6 So when Ahijah heard the sound of her feet as she came in at the door, he said, "Come in, Jeroboam's wife! Why do you pretend to be another? For I am sent to you with heavy news. 7 Go, tell Jeroboam, 'The LORD, the God of Israel, says: "Because I exalted you from amongst the people, and made you prince over my people Israel, 8 and tore the kingdom away from David's house, and gave it you; and yet you have not been as my servant David, who kept my commandments, and who followed me with all his heart, to do that only which was right in my eyes, 9 but have done evil above all who were before you, and have gone and made for yourself other gods, molten images, to provoke me to anger, and have cast me behind your back, 10 therefore, behold, I will bring evil on the house of Jeroboam, and will cut off from Jeroboam everyone who urinates on a wall,[a] he who is shut up and he who is left at large in Israel, and will utterly sweep away the house of Jeroboam, as a man sweeps away dung until it is all gone. 11 The dogs will eat he who belongs to Jeroboam who dies in the city; and the birds of the sky will eat he who dies in the field, for the LORD has spoken it.'" 12 Arise therefore, and go to your house. When your feet enter into the city, the child will die. 13 All Israel will mourn for him and bury him; for he only of Jeroboam will come to the grave, because in him there is found some good thing towards the LORD, the God of Israel, in the house of Jeroboam. 14 Moreover the LORD will raise up a king for himself over Israel who will cut off the house of Jeroboam. This is the day! What? Even now. 15 For the LORD will strike Israel, as a reed is shaken in the water; and he will root up Israel out of this good land which he gave to their fathers, and will scatter them beyond the River,[b] because they have made their Asherah poles, provoking the LORD to anger. 16 He will give Israel up because of the sins of Jeroboam, which he has sinned, and with which he has made Israel to sin."

17 Jeroboam's wife arose and departed, and came to Tirzah. As she came to the threshold of the house, the child died. 18 All Israel buried him and mourned for him, according to the LORD's word, which he spoke by his servant Ahijah the prophet.

19 The rest of the acts of Jeroboam, how he fought and how he reigned, behold, they are written in the book of the chronicles of the kings of Israel. 20 The days which Jeroboam reigned were twenty two years; then he slept with his fathers, and Nadab his son reigned in his place.

21 Rehoboam the son of Solomon reigned in Judah. Rehoboam was forty-one years old when he began to reign, and he reigned seventeen years in Jerusalem, the city which the LORD had chosen out of all the tribes of Israel, to put his name there. His mother's name was Naamah the Ammonitess. 22 Judah did that which was evil in the LORD's sight, and they provoked him to jealousy with their sins which they committed, above all that their fathers had done. 23 For they also built for themselves high places, sacred pillars, and Asherah poles on every high hill and under every green tree. 24 There were also sodomites in the land. They did according to all the abominations of the nations which the LORD drove out before the children of Israel.

25 In the fifth year of King Rehoboam, Shishak king of Egypt came up against Jerusalem; 26 and he took away the treasures of the LORD's house and the treasures of the king's house. He even took away all of it, including all the gold shields which Solomon had made. 27 King Rehoboam made

---

a *14:10* or, male

b *14:15* That is, the Euphrates.

shields of bronze in their place, and committed them to the hands of the captains of the guard, who kept the door of the king's house. 28 It was so, that as often as the king went into the LORD's house, the guard bore them, and brought them back into the guard room.

29 Now the rest of the acts of Rehoboam, and all that he did, aren't they written in the book of the chronicles of the kings of Judah? 30 There was war between Rehoboam and Jeroboam continually. 31 Rehoboam slept with his fathers, and was buried with his fathers in David's city. His mother's name was Naamah the Ammonitess. Abijam his son reigned in his place.

15

1 Now in the eighteenth year of King Jeroboam the son of Nebat, Abijam began to reign over Judah. 2 He reigned three years in Jerusalem. His mother's name was Maacah the daughter of Abishalom. 3 He walked in all the sins of his father, which he had done before him; and his heart was not perfect with the LORD his God, as the heart of David his father. 4 Nevertheless for David's sake, the LORD his God gave him a lamp in Jerusalem, to set up his son after him and to establish Jerusalem; 5 because David did that which was right in the LORD's eyes, and didn't turn away from anything that he commanded him all the days of his life, except only in the matter of Uriah the Hittite. 6 Now there was war between Rehoboam and Jeroboam all the days of his life. 7 The rest of the acts of Abijam, and all that he did, aren't they written in the book of the chronicles of the kings of Judah? There was war between Abijam and Jeroboam. 8 Abijam slept with his fathers, and they buried him in David's city; and Asa his son reigned in his place.

9 In the twentieth year of Jeroboam king of Israel, Asa began to reign over Judah. 10 He reigned forty-one years in Jerusalem. His mother's name was Maacah the daughter of Abishalom. 11 Asa did that which was right in the LORD's eyes, as David his father did. 12 He put away the sodomites out of the land, and removed all the idols that his fathers had made. 13 He also removed Maacah his mother from being queen, because she had made an abominable image for an Asherah. Asa cut down her image and burnt it at the brook Kidron. 14 But the high places were not taken away. Nevertheless the heart of Asa was perfect with the LORD all his days. 15 He brought into the LORD's house the things that his father had dedicated, and the things that he himself had dedicated: silver, gold, and utensils.

16 There was war between Asa and Baasha king of Israel all their days. 17 Baasha king of Israel went up against Judah, and built Ramah, that he might not allow anyone to go out or come in to Asa king of Judah. 18 Then Asa took all the silver and the gold that was left in the treasures of the LORD's house, and the treasures of the king's house, and delivered it into the hand of his servants. Then King Asa sent them to Ben Hadad, the son of Tabrimmon, the son of Hezion, king of Syria, who lived at Damascus, saying, 19 "Let there be a treaty between me and you, like that between my father and your father. Behold, I have sent to you a present of silver and gold. Go, break your treaty with Baasha king of Israel, that he may depart from me." 20 Ben Hadad listened to King Asa, and sent the captains of his armies against the cities of Israel, and struck Ijon, and Dan, and Abel Beth Maacah, and all Chinneroth, with all the land of Naphtali. 21 When Baasha heard of it, he stopped building Ramah, and lived in Tirzah. 22 Then King Asa made a proclamation to all Judah. No one was exempted. They carried away the stones of Ramah, and its timber, with which Baasha had built; and King Asa used it to build Geba of Benjamin, and Mizpah. 23 Now the rest of all the acts of Asa, and all his might, and all that he did, and the cities which he built, aren't they written in the book of the chronicles of the kings of Judah? But in the time of his old age he was diseased in his feet. 24 Asa slept with his fathers, and was buried with his fathers in his father David's city; and Jehoshaphat his son reigned in his place.

25 Nadab the son of Jeroboam began to reign over Israel in the second year of Asa king of Judah; and he reigned over Israel two years. 26 He did that which was evil in the LORD's sight, and walked in the way of his father, and in his sin with which he made Israel to sin. 27 Baasha the son of Ahijah, of the house of Issachar, conspired against him; and Baasha struck him at Gibbethon, which belonged to the Philistines; for Nadab and all Israel were besieging Gibbethon. 28 Even in the third year of Asa king of Judah, Baasha killed him and reigned in his place. 29 As soon as he was king, he struck all the house of Jeroboam. He didn't leave to Jeroboam any who breathed, until he had destroyed him, according to the saying of the LORD, which he spoke by his servant Ahijah the Shilonite; 30 for the sins of Jeroboam which he sinned, and with which he made Israel to sin, because of his provocation with which he provoked the LORD, the God of Israel, to anger.

31 Now the rest of the acts of Nadab, and all that he did, aren't they written in the book of the chronicles of the kings of Israel? 32 There was war between Asa and Baasha king of Israel all their days.

33 In the third year of Asa king of Judah, Baasha the son of Ahijah began to reign over all Israel in Tirzah for twenty-four years. 34 He did that which was evil in the LORD's sight, and walked in the way of Jeroboam, and in his sin with which he made Israel to sin.

16

1 The LORD's word came to Jehu the son of Hanani against Baasha, saying, 2 "Because I exalted you out of the dust and made you prince over my people Israel, and you have walked in the way of Jeroboam and have made my people Israel to sin, to provoke me to anger with their sins, 3 behold, I will utterly sweep away Baasha and his house; and I will make your house like the house of Jeroboam the son of Nebat. 4 The dogs will eat Baasha's descendants who die in the city; and he who dies of his in the field, the birds of the sky will eat."

5 Now the rest of the acts of Baasha, and what he did, and his might, aren't they written in the book of the chronicles of the kings of Israel? 6 Baasha slept with his fathers, and was buried in Tirzah; and Elah his son reigned in his place.

7 Moreover the LORD's word came by the prophet Jehu the son of Hanani against Baasha and against his house, both because of all the evil that he did in the LORD's sight, to provoke him to anger with the work of his hands, in being like the house of Jeroboam, and because he struck him.

8 In the twenty-sixth year of Asa king of Judah, Elah the son of Baasha began to reign over Israel in Tirzah for two years. 9 His servant Zimri, captain of half his chariots, conspired against him. Now he was in Tirzah, drinking himself drunk in the house of Arza, who was over the household in Tirzah; 10 and Zimri went in and struck him and killed him in the twenty-seventh year of Asa king of Judah, and reigned in his place.

11 When he began to reign, as soon as he sat on his throne, he attacked all the house of Baasha. He didn't leave him a single one who urinates on a wall[a] amongst his relatives or his friends. 12 Thus Zimri destroyed all the house of Baasha, according to the LORD's word which he spoke against Baasha by Jehu the prophet, 13 for all the sins of Baasha, and the sins of Elah his son, which they sinned and with which they made Israel to sin, to provoke the LORD, the God of Israel, to anger with their vanities. 14 Now the rest of the acts of Elah, and all that he did, aren't they written in the book of the chronicles of the kings of Israel?

15 In the twenty-seventh year of Asa king of Judah, Zimri reigned seven days in Tirzah. Now the people were encamped against Gibbethon, which belonged to the Philistines. 16 The people who were encamped heard that Zimri had conspired, and had also killed the king. Therefore all Israel made Omri, the captain of the army, king over Israel that day in the camp. 17 Omri went up from Gibbethon, and all Israel with him, and they besieged Tirzah. 18 When Zimri saw that the city was taken, he went into the fortified part of the king's house and burnt the king's house over him with fire, and died, 19 for his sins which he sinned in doing that which was evil in the LORD's sight, in walking in the way of Jeroboam, and in his sin which he did to make Israel to sin. 20 Now the rest of the acts of Zimri, and his treason that he committed, aren't they written in the book of the chronicles of the kings of Israel?

21 Then the people of Israel were divided into two parts: half of the people followed Tibni the son of Ginath, to make him king, and half followed Omri. 22 But the people who followed Omri prevailed against the people who followed Tibni the son of Ginath; so Tibni died, and Omri reigned. 23 In the thirty-first year of Asa king of Judah, Omri began to reign over Israel for twelve years. He reigned six years in Tirzah. 24 He bought the hill Samaria of Shemer for two talents[b] of silver; and he built on the hill, and called the name of the city which he built, Samaria, after the name of Shemer, the owner of the hill. 25 Omri did that which was evil in the LORD's sight, and dealt wickedly above all who were before him. 26 For he walked in all the way of Jeroboam the son of Nebat, and in his sins with which he made Israel to sin, to provoke the LORD, the God of Israel, to anger with their vanities. 27 Now the rest of the acts of Omri which he did, and his might that he showed, aren't they written in the book of the chronicles of the kings of Israel? 28 So Omri slept with his fathers, and was buried in Samaria; and Ahab his son reigned in his place.

29 In the thirty-eighth year of Asa king of Judah, Ahab the son of Omri began to reign over Israel. Ahab the son of Omri reigned over Israel in Samaria twenty-two years. 30 Ahab the son of Omri did that which was evil in the LORD's sight above all that were before him. 31 As if it had been a light thing for him to walk in the sins of Jeroboam the son of Nebat, he took as wife Jezebel the daughter of Ethbaal king of the Sidonians, and went and served Baal and worshipped him. 32 He raised up an altar for Baal in the house of Baal, which he had built in Samaria. 33 Ahab made the Asherah; and Ahab did more yet to provoke the LORD, the God of Israel, to anger than all the kings of Israel who were before him. 34 In his days Hiel the Bethelite built Jericho. He laid its foundation with the loss of Abiram his firstborn, and set up its gates with the loss of his youngest son Segub, according to the LORD's word, which he spoke by Joshua the son of Nun.

17

1 Elijah the Tishbite, who was one of the settlers of Gilead, said to Ahab, "As the LORD, the God of Israel, lives, before whom I stand, there shall not be dew nor rain these years, but according to my word."

2 Then the LORD's word came to him, saying, 3 "Go away from here, turn eastward, and hide yourself by the brook Cherith, that is before the Jordan. 4 You shall drink from the brook. I have commanded the ravens to feed you there." 5 So he went and did according to the LORD's word, for he went and lived by the brook Cherith that is before the Jordan. 6 The ravens brought him bread and meat in the morning, and bread and meat in the evening; and he drank from the brook. 7 After a while, the brook dried up, because there was no rain in the land.

8 The LORD's word came to him, saying, 9 "Arise, go to Zarephath, which belongs to Sidon, and stay there. Behold, I have commanded a widow there to sustain you."

10 So he arose and went to Zarephath; and when he came to the gate of the city, behold, a widow was there gathering sticks. He called to her and said, "Please get me a little water in a jar, that I may drink."

---

a 16:11 or, male

b 16:24 A talent is about 30 kilograms or 66 pounds.

11 As she was going to get it, he called to her and said, "Please bring me a morsel of bread in your hand."

12 She said, "As the LORD your God lives, I don't have anything baked, but only a handful of meal in a jar and a little oil in a jar. Behold, I am gathering two sticks, that I may go in and bake it for me and my son, that we may eat it, and die."

13 Elijah said to her, "Don't be afraid. Go and do as you have said; but make me a little cake from it first, and bring it out to me, and afterward make some for you and for your son. 14 For the LORD, the God of Israel, says, 'The jar of meal will not run out, and the jar of oil will not fail, until the day that the LORD sends rain on the earth.'"

15 She went and did according to the saying of Elijah; and she, he, and her household ate many days. 16 The jar of meal didn't run out and the jar of oil didn't fail, according to the LORD's word, which he spoke by Elijah.

17 After these things, the son of the woman, the mistress of the house, became sick; and his sickness was so severe that there was no breath left in him. 18 She said to Elijah, "What have I to do with you, you man of God? You have come to me to bring my sin to memory, and to kill my son!"

19 He said to her, "Give me your son." He took him out of her bosom, and carried him up into the room where he stayed, and laid him on his own bed. 20 He cried to the LORD and said, "LORD my God, have you also brought evil on the widow with whom I am staying, by killing her son?"

21 He stretched himself on the child three times, and cried to the LORD and said, "LORD my God, please let this child's soul come into him again."

22 The LORD listened to the voice of Elijah; and the soul of the child came into him again, and he revived. 23 Elijah took the child and brought him down out of the room into the house, and delivered him to his mother; and Elijah said, "Behold, your son lives."

24 The woman said to Elijah, "Now I know that you are a man of God, and that the LORD's word in your mouth is truth."

18

1 After many days, the LORD's word came to Elijah, in the third year, saying, "Go, show yourself to Ahab; and I will send rain on the earth."

2 Elijah went to show himself to Ahab. The famine was severe in Samaria. 3 Ahab called Obadiah, who was over the household. (Now Obadiah feared the LORD greatly; 4 for when Jezebel cut off the LORD's prophets, Obadiah took one hundred prophets, and hid them fifty to a cave, and fed them with bread and water.) 5 Ahab said to Obadiah, "Go through the land, to all the springs of water, and to all the brooks. Perhaps we may find grass and save the horses and mules alive, that we not lose all the animals."

6 So they divided the land between them to pass throughout it. Ahab went one way by himself, and Obadiah went another way by himself. 7 As Obadiah was on the way, behold, Elijah met him. He recognised him, and fell on his face, and said, "Is it you, my lord Elijah?"

8 He answered him, "It is I. Go, tell your lord, 'Behold, Elijah is here!'"

9 He said, "How have I sinned, that you would deliver your servant into the hand of Ahab, to kill me? 10 As the LORD your God lives, there is no nation or kingdom where my lord has not sent to seek you. When they said, 'He is not here,' he took an oath of the kingdom and nation that they didn't find you. 11 Now you say, 'Go, tell your lord, "Behold, Elijah is here."' 12 It will happen, as soon as I leave you, that the LORD's Spirit will carry you I don't know where; and so when I come and tell Ahab, and he can't find you, he will kill me. But I, your servant, have feared the LORD from my youth. 13 Wasn't it told my lord what I did when Jezebel killed the LORD's prophets, how I hid one hundred men of the LORD's prophets with fifty to a cave, and fed them with bread and water? 14 Now you say, 'Go, tell your lord, "Behold, Elijah is here".' He will kill me."

15 Elijah said, "As the LORD of Armies lives, before whom I stand, I will surely show myself to him today." 16 So Obadiah went to meet Ahab, and told him; and Ahab went to meet Elijah.

17 When Ahab saw Elijah, Ahab said to him, "Is that you, you troubler of Israel?"

18 He answered, "I have not troubled Israel, but you and your father's house, in that you have forsaken the LORD's commandments and you have followed the Baals. 19 Now therefore send, and gather to me all Israel to Mount Carmel, and four hundred and fifty of the prophets of Baal, and four hundred of the prophets of the Asherah, who eat at Jezebel's table."

20 So Ahab sent to all the children of Israel, and gathered the prophets together to Mount Carmel. 21 Elijah came near to all the people, and said, "How long will you waver between the two sides? If the LORD is God, follow him; but if Baal, then follow him."

The people didn't say a word.

22 Then Elijah said to the people, "I, even I only, am left as a prophet of the LORD; but Baal's prophets are four hundred and fifty men. 23 Let them therefore give us two bulls; and let them choose one bull for themselves, and cut it in pieces, and lay it on the wood, and put no fire under; and I will dress the other bull, and lay it on the wood, and put no fire under it. 24 You call on the name of your god, and I will call on the LORD's name. The God who answers by fire, let him be God."

All the people answered, "What you say is good."

25 Elijah said to the prophets of Baal, "Choose one bull for yourselves, and dress it first, for you are many; and call on the name of your god, but put no fire under it."

26 They took the bull which was given them, and they dressed it, and called on the name of Baal from morning even until noon, saying, "Baal,

hear us!" But there was no voice, and nobody answered. They leapt about the altar which was made.

27 At noon, Elijah mocked them, and said, "Cry aloud, for he is a god. Either he is deep in thought, or he has gone somewhere, or he is on a journey, or perhaps he sleeps and must be awakened."

28 They cried aloud, and cut themselves in their way with knives and lances until the blood gushed out on them. 29 When midday was past, they prophesied until the time of the evening offering; but there was no voice, no answer, and nobody paid attention.

30 Elijah said to all the people, "Come near to me!"; and all the people came near to him. He repaired the LORD's altar that had been thrown down. 31 Elijah took twelve stones, according to the number of the tribes of the sons of Jacob, to whom the LORD's word came, saying, "Israel shall be your name." 32 With the stones he built an altar in the LORD's name. He made a trench around the altar large enough to contain two seahs^a of seed. 33 He put the wood in order, and cut the bull in pieces and laid it on the wood. He said, "Fill four jars with water, and pour it on the burnt offering and on the wood." 34 He said, "Do it a second time;" and they did it the second time. He said, "Do it a third time;" and they did it the third time. 35 The water ran around the altar; and he also filled the trench with water.

36 At the time of the evening offering, Elijah the prophet came near and said, "LORD, the God of Abraham, of Isaac, and of Israel, let it be known today that you are God in Israel and that I am your servant, and that I have done all these things at your word. 37 Hear me, LORD, hear me, that this people may know that you, LORD, are God, and that you have turned their heart back again."

38 Then the LORD's fire fell and consumed the burnt offering, the wood, the stones, and the dust; and it licked up the water that was in the trench. 39 When all the people saw it, they fell on their faces. They said, "The LORD, he is God! The LORD, he is God!"

40 Elijah said to them, "Seize the prophets of Baal! Don't let one of them escape!"

They seized them; and Elijah brought them down to the brook Kishon, and killed them there.

41 Elijah said to Ahab, "Get up, eat and drink; for there is the sound of abundance of rain."

42 So Ahab went up to eat and to drink. Elijah went up to the top of Carmel; and he bowed himself down on the earth, and put his face between his knees. 43 He said to his servant, "Go up now and look towards the sea."

He went up and looked, then said, "There is nothing."

He said, "Go again" seven times.

44 On the seventh time, he said, "Behold, a small cloud, like a man's hand, is rising out of the sea."

He said, "Go up, tell Ahab, 'Get ready and go down, so that the rain doesn't stop you.'"

45 In a little while, the sky grew black with clouds and wind, and there was a great rain. Ahab rode, and went to Jezreel. 46 The LORD's hand was on Elijah; and he tucked his cloak into his belt and ran before Ahab to the entrance of Jezreel.

19

1 Ahab told Jezebel all that Elijah had done, and how he had killed all the prophets with the sword. 2 Then Jezebel sent a messenger to Elijah, saying, "So let the gods do to me, and more also, if I don't make your life as the life of one of them by tomorrow about this time!"

3 When he saw that, he arose and ran for his life, and came to Beersheba, which belongs to Judah, and left his servant there. 4 But he himself went a day's journey into the wilderness, and came and sat down under a juniper tree. Then he requested for himself that he might die, and said, "It is enough. Now, O LORD, take away my life; for I am not better than my fathers."

5 He lay down and slept under a juniper tree; and behold, an angel touched him, and said to him, "Arise and eat!"

6 He looked, and behold, there was at his head a cake baked on the coals, and a jar of water. He ate and drank, and lay down again. 7 The LORD's angel came again the second time, and touched him, and said, "Arise and eat, because the journey is too great for you."

8 He arose, and ate and drank, and went in the strength of that food forty days and forty nights to Horeb, God's Mountain. 9 He came to a cave there, and camped there; and behold, the LORD's word came to him, and he said to him, "What are you doing here, Elijah?"

10 He said, "I have been very jealous for the LORD, the God of Armies; for the children of Israel have forsaken your covenant, thrown down your altars, and killed your prophets with the sword. I, even I only, am left; and they seek my life, to take it away."

11 He said, "Go out and stand on the mountain before the LORD."

Behold, the LORD passed by, and a great and strong wind tore the mountains and broke in pieces the rocks before the LORD; but the LORD was not in the wind. After the wind there was an earthquake; but the LORD was not in the earthquake. 12 After the earthquake a fire passed; but the LORD was not in the fire. After the fire, there was a still small voice. 13 When Elijah heard it, he wrapped his face in his mantle, went out, and stood in the entrance of the cave. Behold, a voice came to him, and said, "What are you doing here, Elijah?"

14 He said, "I have been very jealous for the LORD, the God of Armies; for the children of Israel have forsaken your covenant, thrown down your

---

^a *18:32* 1 seah is about 7 litres or 1.9 gallons or 0.8 pecks

altars, and killed your prophets with the sword. I, even I only, am left; and they seek my life, to take it away."

₁₅ The LORD said to him, "Go, return on your way to the wilderness of Damascus. When you arrive, anoint Hazael to be king over Syria. ₁₆ Anoint Jehu the son of Nimshi to be king over Israel; and anoint Elisha the son of Shaphat of Abel Meholah to be prophet in your place. ₁₇ He who escapes from the sword of Hazael, Jehu will kill; and he who escapes from the sword of Jehu, Elisha will kill. ₁₈ Yet I reserved seven thousand in Israel, all the knees of which have not bowed to Baal, and every mouth which has not kissed him."

₁₉ So he departed from there and found Elisha the son of Shaphat, who was ploughing with twelve yoke of oxen before him, and he with the twelfth. Elijah went over to him and put his mantle on him. ₂₀ Elisha left the oxen and ran after Elijah, and said, "Let me please kiss my father and my mother, and then I will follow you."

He said to him, "Go back again; for what have I done to you?"

₂₁ He returned from following him, and took the yoke of oxen, killed them, and boiled their meat with the oxen's equipment, and gave to the people; and they ate. Then he arose, and went after Elijah, and served him.

20

₁ Ben Hadad the king of Syria gathered all his army together; and there were thirty-two kings with him, with horses and chariots. He went up and besieged Samaria, and fought against it. ₂ He sent messengers into the city to Ahab king of Israel and said to him, "Ben Hadad says, ₃ 'Your silver and your gold are mine. Your wives also and your children, even the best, are mine.'"

₄ The king of Israel answered, "It is according to your saying, my lord, O king. I am yours, and all that I have."

₅ The messengers came again and said, "Ben Hadad says, 'I sent indeed to you, saying, "You shall deliver me your silver, your gold, your wives, and your children; ₆ but I will send my servants to you tomorrow about this time, and they will search your house and the houses of your servants. Whatever is pleasant in your eyes, they will put it in their hand, and take it away."'"

₇ Then the king of Israel called all the elders of the land, and said, "Please notice how this man seeks mischief; for he sent to me for my wives, and for my children, and for my silver, and for my gold; and I didn't deny him."

₈ All the elders and all the people said to him, "Don't listen, and don't consent."

₉ Therefore he said to the messengers of Ben Hadad, "Tell my lord the king, 'All that you sent for to your servant at the first I will do, but this thing I cannot do.'"

The messengers departed and brought him back the message. ₁₀ Ben Hadad sent to him, and said, "The gods do so to me, and more also, if the dust of Samaria will be enough for handfuls for all the people who follow me."

₁₁ The king of Israel answered, "Tell him, 'Don't let him who puts on his armour brag like he who takes it off.'"

₁₂ When Ben Hadad heard this message as he was drinking, he and the kings in the pavilions, he said to his servants, "Prepare to attack!" So they prepared to attack the city.

₁₃ Behold, a prophet came near to Ahab king of Israel, and said, "The LORD says, 'Have you seen all this great multitude? Behold, I will deliver it into your hand today. Then you will know that I am the LORD.'"

₁₄ Ahab said, "By whom?"

He said, "The LORD says, 'By the young men of the princes of the provinces.'"

Then he said, "Who shall begin the battle?"

He answered, "You."

₁₅ Then he mustered the young men of the princes of the provinces, and they were two hundred and thirty-two. After them, he mustered all the people, even all the children of Israel, being seven thousand. ₁₆ They went out at noon. But Ben Hadad was drinking himself drunk in the pavilions, he and the kings, the thirty-two kings who helped him. ₁₇ The young men of the princes of the provinces went out first; and Ben Hadad sent out, and they told him, saying, "Men are coming out from Samaria."

₁₈ He said, "If they have come out for peace, take them alive; or if they have come out for war, take them alive."

₁₉ So these went out of the city, the young men of the princes of the provinces, and the army which followed them. ₂₀ They each killed his man. The Syrians fled, and Israel pursued them. Ben Hadad the king of Syria escaped on a horse with horsemen. ₂₁ The king of Israel went out and struck the horses and chariots, and killed the Syrians with a great slaughter. ₂₂ The prophet came near to the king of Israel and said to him, "Go, strengthen yourself, and plan what you must do, for at the return of the year, the king of Syria will come up against you."

₂₃ The servants of the king of Syria said to him, "Their god is a god of the hills; therefore they were stronger than we. But let's fight against them in the plain, and surely we will be stronger than they. ₂₄ Do this thing: take the kings away, every man out of his place, and put captains in their place. ₂₅ Muster an army like the army that you have lost, horse for horse and chariot for chariot. We will fight against them in the plain, and surely we will be stronger than they are."

He listened to their voice and did so. ₂₆ At the return of the year, Ben Hadad mustered the Syrians and went up to Aphek to fight against Israel. ₂₇ The children of Israel were mustered and given provisions, and went against them. The children of Israel encamped before them like two little flocks of young goats, but the Syrians filled the country. ₂₈ A man of God came near and spoke to the king of Israel, and said, "The LORD says, 'Because the Syrians have said, "The LORD is a god of the hills, but he is not a god of the valleys," therefore I will deliver all this great multitude into your hand, and you shall know that I am the LORD.'"

₂₉ They encamped opposite each other for seven days. Then on the seventh day the battle was joined; and the children of Israel killed one hundred thousand footmen of the Syrians in one day. ₃₀ But the rest fled to Aphek, into the city; and the wall fell on twenty-seven thousand men who were left. Ben Hadad fled and came into the city, into an inner room. ₃₁ His servants said to him, "See now, we have heard that the kings of the house of Israel are merciful kings. Please let us put sackcloth on our bodies and ropes on our heads, and go out to the king of Israel. Maybe he will save your life."

₃₂ So they put sackcloth on their bodies and ropes on their heads, and came to the king of Israel, and said, "Your servant Ben Hadad says, 'Please let me live.'"

He said, "Is he still alive? He is my brother."

₃₃ Now the men observed diligently and hurried to take this phrase; and they said, "Your brother Ben Hadad."

Then he said, "Go, bring him."

Then Ben Hadad came out to him; and he caused him to come up into the chariot. ₃₄ Ben Hadad said to him, "The cities which my father took from your father I will restore. You shall make streets for yourself in Damascus, as my father made in Samaria."

"I", said Ahab, "will let you go with this covenant." So he made a covenant with him and let him go.

₃₅ A certain man of the sons of the prophets said to his fellow by the LORD's word, "Please strike me!"

The man refused to strike him. ₃₆ Then he said to him, "Because you have not obeyed the LORD's voice, behold, as soon as you have departed from me, a lion will kill you." As soon as he had departed from him, a lion found him and killed him.

₃₇ Then he found another man, and said, "Please strike me."

The man struck him and wounded him. ₃₈ So the prophet departed and waited for the king by the way, and disguised himself with his headband over his eyes. ₃₉ As the king passed by, he cried to the king, and he said, "Your servant went out into the middle of the battle; and behold, a man came over and brought a man to me, and said, 'Guard this man! If by any means he is missing, then your life shall be for his life, or else you shall pay a talent[a] of silver.' ₄₀ As your servant was busy here and there, he was gone."

The king of Israel said to him, "So shall your judgement be. You yourself have decided it."

₄₁ He hurried, and took the headband away from his eyes; and the king of Israel recognised that he was one of the prophets. ₄₂ He said to him, "The LORD says, 'Because you have let go out of your hand the man whom I had devoted to destruction, therefore your life will take the place of his life, and your people take the place of his people.'"

₄₃ The king of Israel went to his house sullen and angry, and came to Samaria.

21

₁ After these things, Naboth the Jezreelite had a vineyard which was in Jezreel, next to the palace of Ahab king of Samaria. ₂ Ahab spoke to Naboth, saying, "Give me your vineyard, that I may have it for a garden of herbs, because it is near my house; and I will give you for it a better vineyard than it. Or, if it seems good to you, I will give you its worth in money."

₃ Naboth said to Ahab, "May the LORD forbid me, that I should give the inheritance of my fathers to you!"

₄ Ahab came into his house sullen and angry because of the word which Naboth the Jezreelite had spoken to him, for he had said, "I will not give you the inheritance of my fathers." He laid himself down on his bed, and turned away his face, and would eat no bread. ₅ But Jezebel his wife came to him, and said to him, "Why is your spirit so sad that you eat no bread?"

₆ He said to her, "Because I spoke to Naboth the Jezreelite, and said to him, 'Give me your vineyard for money; or else, if it pleases you, I will give you another vineyard for it.' He answered, 'I will not give you my vineyard.'"

₇ Jezebel his wife said to him, "Do you now govern the kingdom of Israel? Arise, and eat bread, and let your heart be merry. I will give you the vineyard of Naboth the Jezreelite." ₈ So she wrote letters in Ahab's name and sealed them with his seal, and sent the letters to the elders and to the nobles who were in his city, who lived with Naboth. ₉ She wrote in the letters, saying, "Proclaim a fast, and set Naboth on high amongst the people. ₁₀ Set two men, wicked fellows, before him, and let them testify against him, saying, 'You cursed God and the king!' Then carry him out, and stone him to death."

₁₁ The men of his city, even the elders and the nobles who lived in his city, did as Jezebel had instructed them in the letters which she had written and sent to them. ₁₂ They proclaimed a fast, and set Naboth on high amongst the people. ₁₃ The two men, the wicked fellows, came in and sat before him. The wicked fellows testified against him, even against Naboth,

---

ᵃ *20:39* A talent is about 30 kilograms or 66 pounds

in the presence of the people, saying, "Naboth cursed God and the king!" Then they carried him out of the city and stoned him to death with stones. ₁₄ Then they sent to Jezebel, saying, "Naboth has been stoned and is dead."

₁₅ When Jezebel heard that Naboth had been stoned and was dead, Jezebel said to Ahab, "Arise, take possession of the vineyard of Naboth the Jezreelite, which he refused to give you for money; for Naboth is not alive, but dead."

₁₆ When Ahab heard that Naboth was dead, Ahab rose up to go down to the vineyard of Naboth the Jezreelite, to take possession of it.

₁₇ The LORD's word came to Elijah the Tishbite, saying, ₁₈ "Arise, go down to meet Ahab king of Israel, who dwells in Samaria. Behold, he is in the vineyard of Naboth, where he has gone down to take possession of it. ₁₉ You shall speak to him, saying, 'The LORD says, "Have you killed and also taken possession?"' You shall speak to him, saying, 'The LORD says, "In the place where dogs licked the blood of Naboth, dogs will lick your blood, even yours."'"

₂₀ Ahab said to Elijah, "Have you found me, my enemy?"

He answered, "I have found you, because you have sold yourself to do that which is evil in the LORD's sight. ₂₁ Behold, I will bring evil on you, and will utterly sweep you away and will cut off from Ahab everyone who urinates against a wall,ª and him who is shut up and him who is left at large in Israel. ₂₂ I will make your house like the house of Jeroboam the son of Nebat, and like the house of Baasha the son of Ahijah, for the provocation with which you have provoked me to anger, and have made Israel to sin." ₂₃ The LORD also spoke of Jezebel, saying, "The dogs will eat Jezebel by the rampart of Jezreel. ₂₄ The dogs will eat he who dies of Ahab in the city; and the birds of the sky will eat he who dies in the field."

₂₅ But there was no one like Ahab, who sold himself to do that which was evil in the LORD's sight, whom Jezebel his wife stirred up. ₂₆ He did very abominably in following idols, according to all that the Amorites did, whom the LORD cast out before the children of Israel.

₂₇ When Ahab heard those words, he tore his clothes, put sackcloth on his body, fasted, lay in sackcloth, and went about despondently.

₂₈ The LORD's word came to Elijah the Tishbite, saying, ₂₉ " See how Ahab humbles himself before me? Because he humbles himself before me, I will not bring the evil in his days; but I will bring the evil on his house in his son's day."

22

₁ They continued three years without war between Syria and Israel. ₂ In the third year, Jehoshaphat the king of Judah came down to the king of Israel. ₃ The king of Israel said to his servants, "You know that Ramoth Gilead is ours, and we do nothing, and don't take it out of the hand of the king of Syria?" ₄ He said to Jehoshaphat, "Will you go with me to battle to Ramoth Gilead?"

Jehoshaphat said to the king of Israel, "I am as you are, my people as your people, my horses as your horses." ₅ Jehoshaphat said to the king of Israel, "Please enquire first for the LORD's word."

₆ Then the king of Israel gathered the prophets together, about four hundred men, and said to them, "Should I go against Ramoth Gilead to battle, or should I refrain?"

They said, "Go up; for the Lord will deliver it into the hand of the king."

₇ But Jehoshaphat said, "Isn't there here a prophet of the LORD, that we may enquire of him?"

₈ The king of Israel said to Jehoshaphat, "There is yet one man by whom we may enquire of the LORD, Micaiah the son of Imlah; but I hate him, for he does not prophesy good concerning me, but evil."

Jehoshaphat said, "Don't let the king say so."

₉ Then the king of Israel called an officer, and said, "Quickly get Micaiah the son of Imlah."

₁₀ Now the king of Israel and Jehoshaphat the king of Judah were sitting each on his throne, arrayed in their robes, in an open place at the entrance of the gate of Samaria; and all the prophets were prophesying before them. ₁₁ Zedekiah the son of Chenaanah made himself horns of iron, and said, "The LORD says, 'With these you will push the Syrians, until they are consumed.'" ₁₂ All the prophets prophesied so, saying, "Go up to Ramoth Gilead and prosper; for the LORD will deliver it into the hand of the king."

₁₃ The messenger who went to call Micaiah spoke to him, saying, "See now, the prophets declare good to the king with one mouth. Please let your word be like the word of one of them, and speak good."

₁₄ Micaiah said, "As the LORD lives, what the LORD says to me, that I will speak."

₁₅ When he had come to the king, the king said to him, "Micaiah, shall we go to Ramoth Gilead to battle, or shall we forbear?"

He answered him, "Go up and prosper; and the LORD will deliver it into the hand of the king."

₁₆ The king said to him, "How many times do I have to adjure you that you speak to me nothing but the truth in the LORD's name?"

₁₇ He said, "I saw all Israel scattered on the mountains, as sheep that have no shepherd. The LORD said, 'These have no master. Let them each return to his house in peace.'"

₁₈ The king of Israel said to Jehoshaphat, "Didn't I tell you that he would not prophesy good concerning me, but evil?"

₁₉ Micaiah said, "Therefore hear the LORD's word. I saw the LORD sitting on his throne, and all the army of heaven standing by him on his right hand and on his left. ₂₀ The LORD said, 'Who will entice Ahab, that he may go up and fall at Ramoth Gilead?' One said one thing, and another said another.

₂₁ A spirit came out and stood before the LORD, and said, 'I will entice him.'

₂₂ The LORD said to him, 'How?'

He said, 'I will go out and will be a lying spirit in the mouth of all his prophets.'

He said, 'You will entice him, and will also prevail. Go out and do so.' ₂₃ Now therefore, behold, the LORD has put a lying spirit in the mouth of all these your prophets; and the LORD has spoken evil concerning you."

₂₄ Then Zedekiah the son of Chenaanah came near and struck Micaiah on the cheek, and said, "Which way did the LORD's Spirit go from me to speak to you?"

₂₅ Micaiah said, "Behold, you will see on that day when you go into an inner room to hide yourself."

₂₆ The king of Israel said, "Take Micaiah, and carry him back to Amon the governor of the city and to Joash the king's son. ₂₇ Say, 'The king says, "Put this fellow in the prison, and feed him with bread of affliction and with water of affliction, until I come in peace."'"

₂₈ Micaiah said, "If you return at all in peace, the LORD has not spoken by me." He said, "Listen, all you people!"

₂₉ So the king of Israel and Jehoshaphat the king of Judah went up to Ramoth Gilead. ₃₀ The king of Israel said to Jehoshaphat, "I will disguise myself and go into the battle, but you put on your robes." The king of Israel disguised himself and went into the battle.

₃₁ Now the king of Syria had commanded the thirty-two captains of his chariots, saying, "Don't fight with small nor great, except only with the king of Israel."

₃₂ When the captains of the chariots saw Jehoshaphat, they said, "Surely that is the king of Israel!" and they came over to fight against him. Jehoshaphat cried out. ₃₃ When the captains of the chariots saw that it was not the king of Israel, they turned back from pursuing him. ₃₄ A certain man drew his bow at random, and struck the king of Israel between the joints of the armour. Therefore he said to the driver of his chariot, "Turn around, and carry me out of the battle, for I am severely wounded." ₃₅ The battle increased that day. The king was propped up in his chariot facing the Syrians, and died at evening. The blood ran out of the wound into the bottom of the chariot. ₃₆ A cry went throughout the army about the going down of the sun, saying, "Every man to his city, and every man to his country!"

₃₇ So the king died, and was brought to Samaria; and they buried the king in Samaria. ₃₈ They washed the chariot by the pool of Samaria; and the dogs licked up his blood where the prostitutes washed themselves, according to the LORD's word which he spoke.

₃₉ Now the rest of the acts of Ahab, and all that he did, and the ivory house which he built, and all the cities that he built, aren't they written in the book of the chronicles of the kings of Israel? ₄₀ So Ahab slept with his fathers; and Ahaziah his son reigned in his place.

₄₁ Jehoshaphat the son of Asa began to reign over Judah in the fourth year of Ahab king of Israel. ₄₂ Jehoshaphat was thirty-five years old when he began to reign; and he reigned twenty-five years in Jerusalem. His mother's name was Azubah the daughter of Shilhi. ₄₃ He walked in all the way of Asa his father. He didn't turn away from it, doing that which was right in the LORD's eyes. However, the high places were not taken away. The people still sacrificed and burnt incense on the high places. ₄₄ Jehoshaphat made peace with the king of Israel.

₄₅ Now the rest of the acts of Jehoshaphat, and his might that he showed, and how he fought, aren't they written in the book of the chronicles of the kings of Judah? ₄₆ The remnant of the sodomites, that remained in the days of his father Asa, he put away out of the land. ₄₇ There was no king in Edom. A deputy ruled. ₄₈ Jehoshaphat made ships of Tarshish to go to Ophir for gold, but they didn't go, for the ships wrecked at Ezion Geber. ₄₉ Then Ahaziah the son of Ahab said to Jehoshaphat, "Let my servants go with your servants in the ships." But Jehoshaphat would not. ₅₀ Jehoshaphat slept with his fathers, and was buried with his fathers in his father David's city. Jehoram his son reigned in his place.

₅₁ Ahaziah the son of Ahab began to reign over Israel in Samaria in the seventeenth year of Jehoshaphat king of Judah, and he reigned two years over Israel. ₅₂ He did that which was evil in the LORD's sight, and walked in the way of his father, and in the way of his mother, and in the way of Jeroboam the son of Nebat, in which he made Israel to sin. ₅₃ He served Baal and worshipped him, and provoked the LORD, the God of Israel, to anger in all the ways that his father had done so.

ª 21:21 or, male

The Second Book of Kings

1

1 Moab rebelled against Israel after the death of Ahab.

2 Ahaziah fell down through the lattice in his upper room that was in Samaria, and was sick. So he sent messengers, and said to them, "Go, enquire of Baal Zebub, the god of Ekron, whether I will recover of this sickness."

3 But the LORD's[a] angel said to Elijah the Tishbite, "Arise, go up to meet the messengers of the king of Samaria, and tell them, 'Is it because there is no God[b] in Israel that you go to enquire of Baal Zebub, the god of Ekron? 4 Now therefore the LORD says, "You will not come down from the bed where you have gone up, but you will surely die."'" Then Elijah departed.

5 The messengers returned to him, and he said to them, "Why is it that you have returned?"

6 They said to him, "A man came up to meet us, and said to us, 'Go, return to the king who sent you, and tell him, "The LORD says, 'Is it because there is no God in Israel that you send to enquire of Baal Zebub, the god of Ekron? Therefore you will not come down from the bed where you have gone up, but you will surely die.'"'"

7 He said to them, "What kind of man was he who came up to meet you and told you these words?"

8 They answered him, "He was a hairy man, and wearing a leather belt around his waist."

He said, "It's Elijah the Tishbite."

9 Then the king sent a captain of fifty with his fifty to him. He went up to him; and behold,[c] he was sitting on the top of the hill. He said to him, "Man of God, the king has said, 'Come down!'"

10 Elijah answered to the captain of fifty, "If I am a man of God, then let fire come down from the sky and consume you and your fifty!" Then fire came down from the sky, and consumed him and his fifty.

11 Again he sent to him another captain of fifty with his fifty. He answered him, "Man of God, the king has said, 'Come down quickly!'"

12 Elijah answered them, "If I am a man of God, then let fire come down from the sky and consume you and your fifty!" Then God's fire came down from the sky, and consumed him and his fifty.

13 Again he sent the captain of a third fifty with his fifty. The third captain of fifty went up, and came and fell on his knees before Elijah, and begged him, and said to him, "Man of God, please let my life and the life of these fifty of your servants be precious in your sight. 14 Behold, fire came down from the sky and consumed the last two captains of fifty with their fifties. But now let my life be precious in your sight."

15 The LORD's angel said to Elijah, "Go down with him. Don't be afraid of him."

Then he arose and went down with him to the king. 16 He said to him, "The LORD says, 'Because you have sent messengers to enquire of Baal Zebub, the god of Ekron, is it because there is no God in Israel to enquire of his word? Therefore you will not come down from the bed where you have gone up, but you will surely die.'"

17 So he died according to the LORD's word which Elijah had spoken. Jehoram began to reign in his place in the second year of Jehoram the son of Jehoshaphat king of Judah, because he had no son. 18 Now the rest of the acts of Ahaziah which he did, aren't they written in the book of the chronicles of the kings of Israel?

2

1 When the LORD was about to take Elijah up by a whirlwind into heaven, Elijah went with Elisha from Gilgal. 2 Elijah said to Elisha, "Please wait here, for the LORD has sent me as far as Bethel."

Elisha said, "As the LORD lives, and as your soul lives, I will not leave you." So they went down to Bethel.

3 The sons of the prophets who were at Bethel came out to Elisha, and said to him, "Do you know that the LORD will take away your master from over you today?"

He said, "Yes, I know it. Hold your peace."

4 Elijah said to him, "Elisha, please wait here, for the LORD has sent me to Jericho."

He said, "As the LORD lives, and as your soul lives, I will not leave you." So they came to Jericho.

5 The sons of the prophets who were at Jericho came near to Elisha, and said to him, "Do you know that the LORD will take away your master from over you today?"

He answered, "Yes, I know it. Hold your peace."

6 Elijah said to him, "Please wait here, for the LORD has sent me to the Jordan."

He said, "As the LORD lives, and as your soul lives, I will not leave you." Then they both went on. 7 Fifty men of the sons of the prophets went and stood opposite them at a distance; and they both stood by the Jordan. 8 Elijah took his mantle, and rolled it up, and struck the waters; and they were divided here and there, so that they both went over on dry ground. 9 When they had gone over, Elijah said to Elisha, "Ask what I shall do for you, before I am taken from you."

Elisha said, "Please let a double portion of your spirit be on me."

10 He said, "You have asked a hard thing. If you see me when I am taken from you, it will be so for you; but if not, it will not be so."

11 As they continued on and talked, behold, a chariot of fire and horses of fire separated them; and Elijah went up by a whirlwind into heaven. 12 Elisha saw it, and he cried, "My father, my father, the chariots of Israel and its horsemen!"

He saw him no more. Then he took hold of his own clothes and tore them in two pieces. 13 He also took up Elijah's mantle that fell from him, and went back and stood by the bank of the Jordan. 14 He took Elijah's mantle that fell from him, and struck the waters, and said, "Where is the LORD, the God of Elijah?" When he also had struck the waters, they were divided apart, and Elisha went over.

15 When the sons of the prophets who were at Jericho facing him saw him, they said, "The spirit of Elijah rests on Elisha." They came to meet him, and bowed themselves to the ground before him. 16 They said to him, "See now, there are with your servants fifty strong men. Please let them go and seek your master. Perhaps the LORD's Spirit has taken him up, and put him on some mountain or into some valley."

He said, "Don't send them."

17 When they urged him until he was ashamed, he said, "Send them."

Therefore they sent fifty men; and they searched for three days, but didn't find him. 18 They came back to him while he stayed at Jericho; and he said to them, "Didn't I tell you, 'Don't go'?"

19 The men of the city said to Elisha, "Behold, please, the situation of this city is pleasant, as my lord sees; but the water is bad, and the land is barren."

20 He said, "Bring me a new jar, and put salt in it." Then they brought it to him. 21 He went out to the spring of the waters, and threw salt into it, and said, "The LORD says, 'I have healed these waters. There shall not be from there any more death or barren wasteland.'" 22 So the waters were healed to this day, according to Elisha's word which he spoke.

23 He went up from there to Bethel. As he was going up by the way, some youths came out of the city and mocked him, and said to him, "Go up, you baldy! Go up, you baldy!" 24 He looked behind him and saw them, and cursed them in the LORD's name. Then two female bears came out of the woods and mauled forty-two of those youths. 25 He went from there to Mount Carmel, and from there he returned to Samaria.

3

1 Now Jehoram the son of Ahab began to reign over Israel in Samaria in the eighteenth year of Jehoshaphat king of Judah, and reigned twelve years. 2 He did that which was evil in the LORD's sight, but not like his father and like his mother, for he put away the pillar of Baal that his father had made. 3 Nevertheless he held to the sins of Jeroboam the son of Nebat, with which he made Israel to sin. He didn't depart from them.

4 Now Mesha king of Moab was a sheep breeder; and he supplied the king of Israel with one hundred thousand lambs and the wool of one hundred thousand rams. 5 But when Ahab was dead, the king of Moab rebelled against the king of Israel. 6 King Jehoram went out of Samaria at that time, and mustered all Israel. 7 He went and sent to Jehoshaphat the king of Judah, saying, "The king of Moab has rebelled against me. Will you go with me against Moab to battle?"

He said, "I will go up. I am as you are, my people as your people, my horses as your horses." 8 Then he said, "Which way shall we go up?"

Jehoram answered, "The way of the wilderness of Edom."

9 So the king of Israel went with the king of Judah and the king of Edom, and they marched for seven days along a circuitous route. There was no water for the army or for the animals that followed them. 10 The king of Israel said, "Alas! For the LORD has called these three kings together to deliver them into the hand of Moab."

11 But Jehoshaphat said, "Isn't there a prophet of the LORD here, that we may enquire of the LORD by him?"

One of the king of Israel's servants answered, "Elisha the son of Shaphat, who poured water on the hands of Elijah, is here."

12 Jehoshaphat said, "The LORD's word is with him." So the king of Israel and Jehoshaphat and the king of Edom went down to him.

13 Elisha said to the king of Israel, "What have I to do with you? Go to the prophets of your father, and to the prophets of your mother."

The king of Israel said to him, "No, for the LORD has called these three kings together to deliver them into the hand of Moab."

14 Elisha said, "As the LORD of Armies lives, before whom I stand, surely, were it not that I respect the presence of Jehoshaphat the king of Judah, I would not look towards you, nor see you. 15 But now bring me a musician." When the musician played, the LORD's hand came on him. 16 He said, "The LORD says, 'Make this valley full of trenches.' 17 For the LORD says, 'You will not see wind, neither will you see rain, yet that valley will be filled with water, and you will drink, both you and your livestock and your other animals. 18 This is an easy thing in the LORD's sight. He will also deliver the Moabites into your hand. 19 You shall strike every fortified city and every choice city, and shall fell every good tree, and stop all springs of water, and mar every good piece of land with stones.'"

20 In the morning, about the time of offering the sacrifice, behold, water came by the way of Edom, and the country was filled with water.

a 1:3 When rendered in ALL CAPITAL LETTERS, "LORD" or "GOD" is the translation of God's Proper Name.
b 1:3 The Hebrew word rendered "God" is "אֱלֹהִים" (Elohim).

c 1:9 "Behold", from "הִנֵּה", means look at, take notice, observe, see, or gaze at. It is often used as an interjection.

21 Now when all the Moabites heard that the kings had come up to fight against them, they gathered themselves together, all who were able to put on armour, young and old, and stood on the border. 22 They rose up early in the morning, and the sun shone on the water, and the Moabites saw the water opposite them as red as blood. 23 They said, "This is blood. The kings are surely destroyed, and they have struck each other. Now therefore, Moab, to the plunder!"

24 When they came to the camp of Israel, the Israelites rose up and struck the Moabites, so that they fled before them; and they went forward into the land attacking the Moabites. 25 They beat down the cities; and on every good piece of land each man cast his stone, and filled it. They also stopped all the springs of water and cut down all the good trees, until in Kir Hareseth all they left was its stones; however the men armed with slings went around it and attacked it. 26 When the king of Moab saw that the battle was too severe for him, he took with him seven hundred men who drew a sword, to break through to the king of Edom; but they could not. 27 Then he took his oldest son who would have reigned in his place, and offered him for a burnt offering on the wall. There was great wrath against Israel; and they departed from him, and returned to their own land.

4

1 Now a certain woman of the wives of the sons of the prophets cried out to Elisha, saying, "Your servant my husband is dead. You know that your servant feared the LORD. Now the creditor has come to take for himself my two children to be slaves."

2 Elisha said to her, "What should I do for you? Tell me, what do you have in the house?"

She said, "Your servant has nothing in the house, except a pot of oil."

3 Then he said, "Go, borrow empty containers from all your neighbours. Don't borrow just a few containers. 4 Go in and shut the door on you and on your sons, and pour oil into all those containers; and set aside those which are full."

5 So she went from him, and shut the door on herself and on her sons. They brought the containers to her, and she poured oil. 6 When the containers were full, she said to her son, "Bring me another container."

He said to her, "There isn't another container." Then the oil stopped flowing.

7 Then she came and told the man of God. He said, "Go, sell the oil, and pay your debt; and you and your sons live on the rest."

8 One day Elisha went to Shunem, where there was a prominent woman; and she persuaded him to eat bread. So it was, that as often as he passed by, he turned in there to eat bread. 9 She said to her husband, "See now, I perceive that this is a holy man of God who passes by us continually. 10 Please, let's make a little room on the roof. Let's set a bed, a table, a chair, and a lamp stand for him there. When he comes to us, he can stay there."

11 One day he came there, and he went to the room and lay there. 12 He said to Gehazi his servant, "Call this Shunammite." When he had called her, she stood before him. 13 He said to him, "Say now to her, 'Behold, you have cared for us with all this care. What is to be done for you? Would you like to be spoken for to the king, or to the captain of the army?'"

She answered, "I dwell amongst my own people."

14 He said, "What then is to be done for her?"

Gehazi answered, "Most certainly she has no son, and her husband is old."

15 He said, "Call her." When he had called her, she stood in the door. 16 He said, "At this season next year, you will embrace a son."

She said, "No, my lord, you man of God, do not lie to your servant."

17 The woman conceived, and bore a son at that season when the time came around, as Elisha had said to her. 18 When the child was grown, one day he went out to his father to the reapers. 19 He said to his father, "My head! My head!"

He said to his servant, "Carry him to his mother."

20 When he had taken him and brought him to his mother, he sat on her knees until noon, and then died. 21 She went up and laid him on the man of God's bed, and shut the door on him, and went out. 22 She called to her husband and said, "Please send me one of the servants, and one of the donkeys, that I may run to the man of God and come again."

23 He said, "Why would you want to go to him today? It is not a new moon or a Sabbath."

She said, "It's all right."

24 Then she saddled a donkey, and said to her servant, "Drive, and go forward! Don't slow down for me, unless I ask you to."

25 So she went, and came to the man of God to Mount Carmel. When the man of God saw her afar off, he said to Gehazi his servant, "Behold, there is the Shunammite. 26 Please run now to meet her, and ask her, 'Is it well with you? Is it well with your husband? Is it well with your child?'"

She answered, "It is well."

27 When she came to the man of God to the hill, she caught hold of his feet. Gehazi came near to thrust her away; but the man of God said, "Leave her alone, for her soul is troubled within her; and the LORD has hidden it from me, and has not told me."

28 Then she said, "Did I ask you for a son, my lord? Didn't I say, 'Do not deceive me'?"

29 Then he said to Gehazi, "Tuck your cloak into your belt, take my staff in your hand, and go your way. If you meet any man, don't greet him; and if anyone greets you, don't answer him again. Then lay my staff on the child's face."

30 The child's mother said, "As the LORD lives, and as your soul lives, I will not leave you."

So he arose, and followed her.

31 Gehazi went ahead of them, and laid the staff on the child's face; but there was no voice and no hearing. Therefore he returned to meet him, and told him, "The child has not awakened."

32 When Elisha had come into the house, behold, the child was dead, and lying on his bed. 33 He went in therefore, and shut the door on them both, and prayed to the LORD. 34 He went up and lay on the child, and put his mouth on his mouth, and his eyes on his eyes, and his hands on his hands; and he stretched himself on him; and the child's flesh grew warm. 35 Then he returned, and walked in the house once back and forth, then went up and stretched himself out on him. Then the child sneezed seven times, and the child opened his eyes. 36 He called Gehazi, and said, "Call this Shunammite!" So he called her.

When she had come in to him, he said, "Take up your son."

37 Then she went in, fell at his feet, and bowed herself to the ground; then she picked up her son, and went out.

38 Elisha came again to Gilgal. There was a famine in the land; and the sons of the prophets were sitting before him; and he said to his servant, "Get the large pot, and boil stew for the sons of the prophets."

39 One went out into the field to gather herbs, and found a wild vine, and gathered a lap full of wild gourds from it, and came and cut them up into the pot of stew; for they didn't recognise them. 40 So they poured out for the men to eat. As they were eating some of the stew, they cried out and said, "Man of God, there is death in the pot!" And they could not eat it.

41 But he said, "Then bring meal." He threw it into the pot; and he said, "Serve it to the people, that they may eat." And there was nothing harmful in the pot.

42 A man from Baal Shalishah came, and brought the man of God some bread of the first fruits: twenty loaves of barley and fresh ears of grain in his sack. Elisha said, "Give to the people, that they may eat."

43 His servant said, "What, should I set this before a hundred men?"

But he said, "Give it to the people, that they may eat; for the LORD says, 'They will eat, and will have some left over.'"

44 So he set it before them and they ate and had some left over, according to the LORD's word.

5

1 Now Naaman, captain of the army of the king of Syria, was a great man with his master, and honourable, because by him the LORD had given victory to Syria; he was also a mighty man of valour, but he was a leper. 2 The Syrians had gone out in bands, and had brought away captive out of the land of Israel a little girl, and she waited on Naaman's wife. 3 She said to her mistress, "I wish that my lord were with the prophet who is in Samaria! Then he would heal him of his leprosy."

4 Someone went in and told his lord, saying, "The girl who is from the land of Israel said this."

5 The king of Syria said, "Go now, and I will send a letter to the king of Israel."

He departed, and took with him ten talents[a] of silver, six thousand pieces of gold, and ten changes of clothing. 6 He brought the letter to the king of Israel, saying, "Now when this letter has come to you, behold, I have sent Naaman my servant to you, that you may heal him of his leprosy."

7 When the king of Israel had read the letter, he tore his clothes and said, "Am I God, to kill and to make alive, that this man sends to me to heal a man of his leprosy? But please consider and see how he seeks a quarrel against me."

8 It was so, when Elisha the man of God heard that the king of Israel had torn his clothes, that he sent to the king, saying, "Why have you torn your clothes? Let him come now to me, and he shall know that there is a prophet in Israel."

9 So Naaman came with his horses and with his chariots, and stood at the door of the house of Elisha. 10 Elisha sent a messenger to him, saying, "Go and wash in the Jordan seven times, and your flesh shall come again to you, and you shall be clean."

11 But Naaman was angry, and went away and said, "Behold, I thought, 'He will surely come out to me, and stand, and call on the name of the LORD his God, and wave his hand over the place, and heal the leper.' 12 Aren't Abanah and Pharpar, the rivers of Damascus, better than all the waters of Israel? Couldn't I wash in them and be clean?" So he turned and went away in a rage.

13 His servants came near and spoke to him, and said, "My father, if the prophet had asked you do some great thing, wouldn't you have done it? How much rather then, when he says to you, 'Wash, and be clean'?"

14 Then went he down and dipped himself seven times in the Jordan, according to the saying of the man of God; and his flesh was restored like the flesh of a little child, and he was clean. 15 He returned to the man of God, he and all his company, and came, and stood before him; and he said, "See now, I know that there is no God in all the earth, but in Israel. Now therefore, please take a gift from your servant."

16 But he said, "As the LORD lives, before whom I stand, I will receive none."

He urged him to take it; but he refused. 17 Naaman said, "If not, then, please let two mules' load of earth be given to your servant; for your

---

a *5:5* A talent is about 30 kilograms or 66 pounds

servant will from now on offer neither burnt offering nor sacrifice to other gods, but to the LORD. 18 In this thing may the LORD pardon your servant: when my master goes into the house of Rimmon to worship there, and he leans on my hand, and I bow myself in the house of Rimmon. When I bow myself in the house of Rimmon, may the LORD pardon your servant in this thing."

19 He said to him, "Go in peace."

So he departed from him a little way. 20 But Gehazi the servant of Elisha the man of God, said, "Behold, my master has spared this Naaman the Syrian, in not receiving at his hands that which he brought. As the LORD lives, I will run after him, and take something from him."

21 So Gehazi followed after Naaman. When Naaman saw one running after him, he came down from the chariot to meet him, and said, "Is all well?"

22 He said, "All is well. My master has sent me, saying, 'Behold, even now two young men of the sons of the prophets have come to me from the hill country of Ephraim. Please give them a talent[a] of silver and two changes of clothing.'"

23 Naaman said, "Be pleased to take two talents." He urged him, and bound two talents of silver in two bags, with two changes of clothing, and laid them on two of his servants; and they carried them before him. 24 When he came to the hill, he took them from their hand, and stored them in the house. Then he let the men go, and they departed. 25 But he went in, and stood before his master. Elisha said to him, "Where did you come from, Gehazi?"

He said, "Your servant went nowhere."

26 He said to him, "Didn't my heart go with you when the man turned from his chariot to meet you? Is it a time to receive money, and to receive garments, and olive groves and vineyards, and sheep and cattle, and male servants and female servants? 27 Therefore the leprosy of Naaman will cling to you and to your offspring[b] forever."

He went out from his presence a leper, as white as snow.

6

1 The sons of the prophets said to Elisha, "See now, the place where we live and meet with you is too small for us. 2 Please let us go to the Jordan, and each man take a beam from there, and let's make us a place there, where we may live."

He answered, "Go!"

3 One said, "Please be pleased to go with your servants."

He answered, "I will go." 4 So he went with them. When they came to the Jordan, they cut down wood. 5 But as one was cutting down a tree, the axe head fell into the water. Then he cried out and said, "Alas, my master! For it was borrowed."

6 The man of God asked, "Where did it fall?" He showed him the place. He cut down a stick, threw it in there, and made the iron float. 7 He said, "Take it." So he put out his hand and took it.

8 Now the king of Syria was at war against Israel; and he took counsel with his servants, saying, "My camp will be in such and such a place."

9 The man of God sent to the king of Israel, saying, "Beware that you not pass this place, for the Syrians are coming down there." 10 The king of Israel sent to the place which the man of God told him and warned him of; and he saved himself there, not once or twice. 11 The king of Syria's heart was very troubled about this. He called his servants, and said to them, "Won't you show me which of us is for the king of Israel?"

12 One of his servants said, "No, my lord, O king; but Elisha, the prophet who is in Israel, tells the king of Israel the words that you speak in your bedroom."

13 He said, "Go and see where he is, that I may send and get him."

He was told, "Behold, he is in Dothan."

14 Therefore he sent horses, chariots, and a great army there. They came by night, and surrounded the city. 15 When the servant of the man of God had risen early and gone out, behold, an army with horses and chariots was around the city. His servant said to him, "Alas, my master! What shall we do?"

16 He answered, "Don't be afraid, for those who are with us are more than those who are with them." 17 Elisha prayed, and said, "LORD, please open his eyes, that he may see." the LORD opened the young man's eyes, and he saw; and behold, the mountain was full of horses and chariots of fire around Elisha. 18 When they came down to him, Elisha prayed to the LORD, and said, "Please strike this people with blindness."

He struck them with blindness according to Elisha's word.

19 Elisha said to them, "This is not the way, neither is this the city. Follow me, and I will bring you to the man whom you seek." He led them to Samaria. 20 When they had come into Samaria, Elisha said, "LORD, open these men's eyes, that they may see."

The LORD opened their eyes, and they saw; and behold, they were in the middle of Samaria.

21 The king of Israel said to Elisha, when he saw them, "My father, shall I strike them? Shall I strike them?"

22 He answered, "You shall not strike them. Would you strike those whom you have taken captive with your sword and with your bow? Set

bread and water before them, that they may eat and drink, then go to their master."

23 He prepared a great feast for them. After they ate and drank, he sent them away and they went to their master. So the bands of Syria stopped raiding the land of Israel.

24 After this, Benhadad king of Syria gathered all his army, and went up and besieged Samaria. 25 There was a great famine in Samaria. Behold, they besieged it until a donkey's head was sold for eighty pieces of silver, and the fourth part of a kab[c] of dove's dung for five pieces of silver. 26 As the king of Israel was passing by on the wall, a woman cried to him, saying, "Help, my lord, O king!"

27 He said, "If the LORD doesn't help you, where could I get help for you? From the threshing floor, or from the wine press?" 28 Then the king asked her, "What is your problem?"

She answered, "This woman said to me, 'Give your son, that we may eat him today, and we will eat my son tomorrow.' 29 So we boiled my son and ate him; and I said to her on the next day, 'Give up your son, that we may eat him;' and she has hidden her son."

30 When the king heard the words of the woman, he tore his clothes. Now he was passing by on the wall, and the people looked, and behold, he had sackcloth underneath on his body. 31 Then he said, "God do so to me, and more also, if the head of Elisha the son of Shaphat stays on him today."

32 But Elisha was sitting in his house, and the elders were sitting with him. Then the king sent a man from before him; but before the messenger came to him, he said to the elders, "Do you see how this son of a murderer has sent to take away my head? Behold, when the messenger comes, shut the door, and hold the door shut against him. Isn't the sound of his master's feet behind him?"

33 While he was still talking with them, behold, the messenger came down to him. Then he said, "Behold, this evil is from the LORD. Why should I wait for the LORD any longer?"

7

1 Elisha said, "Hear the LORD's word. The LORD says, 'Tomorrow about this time a seah[d] of fine flour will be sold for a shekel,[e] and two seahs of barley for a shekel, in the gate of Samaria.'"

2 Then the captain on whose hand the king leaned answered the man of God, and said, "Behold, if the LORD made windows in heaven, could this thing be?"

He said, "Behold, you will see it with your eyes, but will not eat of it."

3 Now there were four leprous men at the entrance of the gate. They said to one another, "Why do we sit here until we die? 4 If we say, 'We will enter into the city,' then the famine is in the city, and we will die there. If we sit still here, we also die. Now therefore come, and let's surrender to the army of the Syrians. If they save us alive, we will live; and if they kill us, we will only die."

5 They rose up in the twilight to go to the camp of the Syrians. When they had come to the outermost part of the camp of the Syrians, behold, no man was there. 6 For the Lord[f] had made the army of the Syrians to hear the sound of chariots and the sound of horses, even the noise of a great army; and they said to one another, "Behold, the king of Israel has hired against us the kings of the Hittites and the kings of the Egyptians to attack us." 7 Therefore they arose and fled in the twilight, and left their tents, their horses, and their donkeys, even the camp as it was, and fled for their life. 8 When these lepers came to the outermost part of the camp, they went into one tent, and ate and drank, then carried away silver, gold, and clothing and went and hid it. Then they came back, and entered into another tent and carried things from there also, and went and hid them. 9 Then they said to one another, "We aren't doing right. Today is a day of good news, and we keep silent. If we wait until the morning light, punishment will overtake us. Now therefore come, let's go and tell the king's household."

10 So they came and called to the city gatekeepers; and they told them, "We came to the camp of the Syrians, and, behold, there was no man there, not even a man's voice, but the horses tied, and the donkeys tied, and the tents as they were."

11 Then the gatekeepers called out and told it to the king's household within.

12 The king arose in the night, and said to his servants, "I will now show you what the Syrians have done to us. They know that we are hungry. Therefore they have gone out of the camp to hide themselves in the field, saying, 'When they come out of the city, we shall take them alive, and get into the city.'"

13 One of his servants answered, "Please let some people take five of the horses that remain, which are left in the city. Behold, they are like all the multitude of Israel who are left in it. Behold, they are like all the multitude of Israel who are consumed. Let's send and see."

14 Therefore they took two chariots with horses; and the king sent them out to the Syrian army, saying, "Go and see." 15 They went after them to the Jordan; and behold, all the path was full of garments and equipment which the Syrians had cast away in their haste. The messengers returned and told the king. 16 The people went out and plundered the camp of the Syrians. So a seah[g] of fine flour was sold for a

---

a *5:22* A talent is about 30 kilograms or 66 pounds

b *5:27* or, seed

c *6:25* A kab was about 2 litres, so a fourth of a kab would be about 500 milliliters or about a pint

d *7:1* 1 seah is about 7 litres or 1.9 gallons or 0.8 pecks

e *7:1* A shekel is about 10 grams or about 0.35 ounces. In this context, it was probably a silver coin weighing that much.

f *7:6* The word translated "Lord" is "Adonai."

g *7:16* 1 seah is about 7 litres or 1.9 gallons or 0.8 pecks shekel, and two measures of barley for a shekel,[a] according to the LORD's word. 17 The king had appointed the captain on whose hand he leaned to be in charge of the gate; and the people trampled over him in the gate, and he died as the man of God had said, who spoke when the king came down to him. 18 It happened as the man of God had spoken to the king, saying, "Two seahs[b] of barley for a shekel,[c] and a seah of fine flour for a shekel, shall be tomorrow about this time in the gate of Samaria;" 19 and that captain answered the man of God, and said, "Now, behold, if the LORD made windows in heaven, might such a thing be?" and he said, "Behold, you will see it with your eyes, but will not eat of it." 20 It happened like that to him, for the people trampled over him in the gate, and he died.

8

1 Now Elisha had spoken to the woman whose son he had restored to life, saying, "Arise, and go, you and your household, and stay for a while wherever you can; for the LORD has called for a famine. It will also come on the land for seven years."

2 The woman arose, and did according to the man of God's word. She went with her household, and lived in the land of the Philistines for seven years. 3 At the end of seven years, the woman returned from the land of the Philistines. Then she went out to beg the king for her house and for her land. 4 Now the king was talking with Gehazi the servant of the man of God, saying, "Please tell me all the great things that Elisha has done." 5 As he was telling the king how he had restored to life him who was dead, behold, the woman whose son he had restored to life begged the king for her house and for her land. Gehazi said, "My lord, O king, this is the woman, and this is her son, whom Elisha restored to life."

6 When the king asked the woman, she told him. So the king appointed to her a certain officer, saying, "Restore all that was hers, and all the fruits of the field since the day that she left the land, even until now."

7 Elisha came to Damascus; and Benhadad the king of Syria was sick. He was told, "The man of God has come here."

8 The king said to Hazael, "Take a present in your hand, and go meet the man of God, and enquire of the LORD by him, saying, 'Will I recover from this sickness?'"

9 So Hazael went to meet him and took a present with him, even of every good thing of Damascus, forty camels' burden, and came and stood before him and said, "Your son Benhadad king of Syria has sent me to you, saying, 'Will I recover from this sickness?'"

10 Elisha said to him, "Go, tell him, 'You will surely recover;' however the LORD has shown me that he will surely die." 11 He settled his gaze steadfastly on him, until he was ashamed. Then the man of God wept.

12 Hazael said, "Why do you weep, my lord?"

He answered, "Because I know the evil that you will do to the children of Israel. You will set their strongholds on fire, and you will kill their young men with the sword, and will dash their little ones in pieces, and rip up their pregnant women."

13 Hazael said, "But what is your servant, who is but a dog, that he could do this great thing?"

Elisha answered, "The LORD has shown me that you will be king over Syria."

14 Then he departed from Elisha, and came to his master, who said to him, "What did Elisha say to you?"

He answered, "He told me that you would surely recover."

15 On the next day, he took a thick cloth, dipped it in water, and spread it on the king's face, so that he died. Then Hazael reigned in his place.

16 In the fifth year of Joram the son of Ahab king of Israel, Jehoshaphat being king of Judah then, Jehoram the son of Jehoshaphat king of Judah began to reign. 17 He was thirty-two years old when he began to reign. He reigned eight years in Jerusalem. 18 He walked in the way of the kings of Israel, as did Ahab's house, for he married Ahab's daughter. He did that which was evil in the LORD's sight. 19 However, the LORD would not destroy Judah, for David his servant's sake, as he promised to give to him a lamp for his children always.

20 In his days Edom revolted from under the hand of Judah, and made a king over themselves. 21 Then Joram crossed over to Zair, and all his chariots with him; and he rose up by night and struck the Edomites who surrounded him with the captains of the chariots; and the people fled to their tents. 22 So Edom revolted from under the hand of Judah to this day. Then Libnah revolted at the same time. 23 The rest of the acts of Joram, and all that he did, aren't they written in the book of the chronicles of the kings of Judah? 24 Joram slept with his fathers, and was buried with his fathers in David's city; and Ahaziah his son reigned in his place.

25 In the twelfth year of Joram the son of Ahab king of Israel, Ahaziah the son of Jehoram king of Judah began to reign. 26 Ahaziah was twenty-two years old when he began to reign; and he reigned one year in Jerusalem. His mother's name was Athaliah the daughter of Omri king of Israel. 27 He walked in the way of Ahab's house and did that which was evil in the LORD's sight, as did Ahab's house, for he was the son-in-law of Ahab's house.

28 He went with Joram the son of Ahab to war against Hazael king of Syria at Ramoth Gilead, and the Syrians wounded Joram. 29 King Joram returned to be healed in Jezreel from the wounds which the Syrians had given him at Ramah, when he fought against Hazael king of Syria. Ahaziah

the son of Jehoram, king of Judah, went down to see Joram the son of Ahab in Jezreel, because he was sick.

9

1 Elisha the prophet called one of the sons of the prophets, and said to him, "Put your belt on your waist, take this vial of oil in your hand, and go to Ramoth Gilead. 2 When you come there, find Jehu the son of Jehoshaphat the son of Nimshi, and go in and make him rise up from amongst his brothers, and take him to an inner room. 3 Then take the vial of oil, and pour it on his head, and say, 'The LORD says, "I have anointed you king over Israel."' Then open the door, flee, and don't wait."

4 So the young man, the young prophet, went to Ramoth Gilead. 5 When he came, behold, the captains of the army were sitting. Then he said, "I have a message for you, captain."

Jehu said, "To which one of us?"

He said, "To you, O captain." 6 He arose, and went into the house. Then he poured the oil on his head, and said to him, "The LORD, the God of Israel, says, 'I have anointed you king over the people of the LORD, even over Israel. 7 You must strike your master Ahab's house, that I may avenge the blood of my servants the prophets, and the blood of all the servants of the LORD, at the hand of Jezebel. 8 For the whole house of Ahab will perish. I will cut off from Ahab everyone who urinates against a wall,[d] both him who is shut up and him who is left at large in Israel. 9 I will make Ahab's house like the house of Jeroboam the son of Nebat, and like the house of Baasha the son of Ahijah. 10 The dogs will eat Jezebel on the plot of ground of Jezreel, and there shall be no one to bury her.'" Then he opened the door and fled.

11 When Jehu came out to the servants of his lord and one said to him, "Is all well? Why did this madman come to you?"

He said to them, "You know the man and how he talks."

12 They said, "That is a lie. Tell us now."

He said, "He said to me, 'The LORD says, I have anointed you king over Israel.'"

13 Then they hurried, and each man took his cloak, and put it under him on the top of the stairs, and blew the trumpet, saying, "Jehu is king."

14 So Jehu the son of Jehoshaphat the son of Nimshi conspired against Joram. (Now Joram was defending Ramoth Gilead, he and all Israel, because of Hazael king of Syria; 15 but King Joram had returned to be healed in Jezreel of the wounds which the Syrians had given him when he fought with Hazael king of Syria.) Jehu said, "If this is your thinking, then let no one escape and go out of the city to go to tell it in Jezreel." 16 So Jehu rode in a chariot and went to Jezreel, for Joram lay there. Ahaziah king of Judah had come down to see Joram. 17 Now the watchman was standing on the tower in Jezreel, and he spied the company of Jehu as he came, and said, "I see a company."

Joram said, "Take a horseman, and send to meet them, and let him say, 'Is it peace?'"

18 So one went on horseback to meet him, and said, "the king says, 'Is it peace?'"

Jehu said, "What do you have to do with peace? Fall in behind me!"

The watchman said, "The messenger came to them, but he isn't coming back."

19 Then he sent out a second on horseback, who came to them and said, "The king says, 'Is it peace?'"

Jehu answered, "What do you have to do with peace? Fall in behind me!"

20 The watchman said, "He came to them, and isn't coming back. The driving is like the driving of Jehu the son of Nimshi, for he drives furiously."

21 Joram said, "Get ready!"

They got his chariot ready. Then Joram king of Israel and Ahaziah king of Judah went out, each in his chariot; and they went out to meet Jehu, and found him on Naboth the Jezreelite's land. 22 When Joram saw Jehu, he said, "Is it peace, Jehu?"

He answered, "What peace, so long as the prostitution of your mother Jezebel and her witchcraft abound?"

23 Joram turned his hands and fled, and said to Ahaziah, "This is treason, Ahaziah!"

24 Jehu drew his bow with his full strength, and struck Joram between his arms; and the arrow went out at his heart, and he sunk down in his chariot. 25 Then Jehu said to Bidkar his captain, "Pick him up, and throw him in the plot of the field of Naboth the Jezreelite; for remember how, when you and I rode together after Ahab his father, the LORD laid this burden on him: 26 'Surely I have seen yesterday the blood of Naboth, and the blood of his sons,' says the LORD; 'and I will repay you in this plot of ground,' says the LORD. Now therefore take and cast him onto the plot of ground, according to the LORD's word."

27 But when Ahaziah the king of Judah saw this, he fled by the way of the garden house. Jehu followed after him, and said, "Strike him also in the chariot!" They struck him at the ascent of Gur, which is by Ibleam. He fled to Megiddo, and died there. 28 His servants carried him in a chariot to Jerusalem, and buried him in his tomb with his fathers in David's city. 29 In the eleventh year of Joram the son of Ahab, Ahaziah began to reign over Judah.

30 When Jehu had come to Jezreel, Jezebel heard of it; and she painted her eyes, and adorned her head, and looked out at the window. 31

---

a *7:16* A shekel is about 10 grams or about 0.35 ounces. In this context, it was probably a silver coin weighing that much.

b *7:18* 1 seah is about 7 litres or 1.9 gallons or 0.8 pecks

c *7:18* A shekel is about 10 grams or about 0.35 ounces. In this context, it was probably a silver coin weighing that much.

d *9:8* or, male

As Jehu entered in at the gate, she said, "Do you come in peace, Zimri, you murderer of your master?"

32 He lifted up his face to the window, and said, "Who is on my side? Who?"

Two or three eunuchs looked out at him.

33 He said, "Throw her down!"

So they threw her down; and some of her blood was sprinkled on the wall, and on the horses. Then he trampled her under foot. 34 When he had come in, he ate and drank. Then he said, "See now to this cursed woman, and bury her; for she is a king's daughter."

35 They went to bury her, but they found no more of her than the skull, the feet, and the palms of her hands. 36 Therefore they came back, and told him.

He said, "This is the LORD's word, which he spoke by his servant Elijah the Tishbite, saying, 'The dogs will eat the flesh of Jezebel on the plot of Jezreel, 37 and the body of Jezebel will be as dung on the surface of the field on Jezreel's land, so that they won't say, "This is Jezebel."'"

10

1 Now Ahab had seventy sons in Samaria. Jehu wrote letters and sent them to Samaria, to the rulers of Jezreel, even the elders, and to those who brought up Ahab's sons, saying, 2 "Now as soon as this letter comes to you, since your master's sons are with you, and you have chariots and horses, a fortified city also, and armour, 3 select the best and fittest of your master's sons, set him on his father's throne, and fight for your master's house."

4 But they were exceedingly afraid, and said, "Behold, the two kings didn't stand before him! How then shall we stand?" 5 He who was over the household, and he who was over the city, the elders also, and those who raised the children, sent to Jehu, saying, "We are your servants, and will do all that you ask us. We will not make any man king. You do that which is good in your eyes."

6 Then he wrote a letter the second time to them, saying, "If you are on my side, and if you will listen to my voice, take the heads of the men who are your master's sons, and come to me to Jezreel by tomorrow this time."

Now the king's sons, being seventy persons, were with the great men of the city, who brought them up. 7 When the letter came to them, they took the king's sons and killed them, even seventy people, and put their heads in baskets, and sent them to him to Jezreel. 8 A messenger came and told him, "They have brought the heads of the king's sons."

He said, "Lay them in two heaps at the entrance of the gate until the morning." 9 In the morning, he went out and stood, and said to all the people, "You are righteous. Behold, I conspired against my master and killed him, but who killed all these? 10 Know now that nothing will fall to the earth of the LORD's word, which the LORD spoke concerning Ahab's house. For the LORD has done that which he spoke by his servant Elijah."

11 So Jehu struck all that remained of Ahab's house in Jezreel, with all his great men, his familiar friends, and his priests, until he left him no one remaining.

12 He arose and departed, and went to Samaria. As he was at the shearing house of the shepherds on the way, 13 Jehu met with the brothers of Ahaziah king of Judah, and said, "Who are you?"

They answered, "We are the brothers of Ahaziah. We are going down to greet the children of the king and the children of the queen."

14 He said, "Take them alive!"

They took them alive, and killed them at the pit of the shearing house, even forty-two men. He didn't leave any of them.

15 When he had departed from there, he met Jehonadab the son of Rechab coming to meet him. He greeted him, and said to him, "Is your heart right, as my heart is with your heart?"

Jehonadab answered, "It is."

"If it is, give me your hand." He gave him his hand; and he took him up to him into the chariot. 16 He said, "Come with me, and see my zeal for the LORD." So they made him ride in his chariot. 17 When he came to Samaria, he struck all who remained to Ahab in Samaria, until he had destroyed them, according to the LORD's word which he spoke to Elijah.

18 Jehu gathered all the people together, and said to them, "Ahab served Baal a little, but Jehu will serve him much. 19 Now therefore call to me all the prophets of Baal, all of his worshippers, and all of his priests. Let no one be absent, for I have a great sacrifice to Baal. Whoever is absent, he shall not live." But Jehu did deceptively, intending to destroy the worshippers of Baal.

20 Jehu said, "Sanctify a solemn assembly for Baal!"

So they proclaimed it. 21 Jehu sent through all Israel; and all the worshippers of Baal came, so that there was not a man left that didn't come. They came into the house of Baal; and the house of Baal was filled from one end to another. 22 He said to him who kept the wardrobe, "Bring out robes for all the worshippers of Baal!"

So he brought robes out to them. 23 Jehu went with Jehonadab the son of Rechab into the house of Baal. Then he said to the worshippers of Baal, "Search, and see that none of the servants of the LORD are here with you, but only the worshippers of Baal."

24 So they went in to offer sacrifices and burnt offerings. Now Jehu had appointed for himself eighty men outside, and said, "If any of the men whom I bring into your hands escape, he who lets him go, his life shall be for the life of him."

25 As soon as he had finished offering the burnt offering, Jehu said to the guard and to the captains, "Go in and kill them! Let no one escape." So they struck them with the edge of the sword. The guard and the captains

threw the bodies out, and went to the inner shrine of the house of Baal. 26 They brought out the pillars that were in the house of Baal and burnt them. 27 They broke down the pillar of Baal, and broke down the house of Baal, and made it a latrine, to this day. 28 Thus Jehu destroyed Baal out of Israel.

29 However, Jehu didn't depart from the sins of Jeroboam the son of Nebat, with which he made Israel to sin—the golden calves that were in Bethel and that were in Dan. 30 The LORD said to Jehu, "Because you have done well in executing that which is right in my eyes, and have done to Ahab's house according to all that was in my heart, your descendants shall sit on the throne of Israel to the fourth generation."

31 But Jehu took no heed to walk in the law of the LORD, the God of Israel, with all his heart. He didn't depart from the sins of Jeroboam, with which he made Israel to sin.

32 In those days the LORD began to cut away parts of Israel; and Hazael struck them in all the borders of Israel 33 from the Jordan eastward, all the land of Gilead, the Gadites, and the Reubenites, and the Manassites, from Aroer, which is by the valley of the Arnon, even Gilead and Bashan. 34 Now the rest of the acts of Jehu, and all that he did, and all his might, aren't they written in the book of the chronicles of the kings of Israel? 35 Jehu slept with his fathers; and they buried him in Samaria. Jehoahaz his son reigned in his place. 36 The time that Jehu reigned over Israel in Samaria was twenty-eight years.

11

1 Now when Athaliah the mother of Ahaziah saw that her son was dead, she arose and destroyed all the royal offspring. 2 But Jehosheba, the daughter of King Joram, sister of Ahaziah, took Joash the son of Ahaziah, and stole him away from amongst the king's sons who were slain, even him and his nurse, and put them in the bedroom; and they hid him from Athaliah, so that he was not slain. 3 He was with her hidden in the LORD's house six years while Athaliah reigned over the land.

4 In the seventh year Jehoiada sent and fetched the captains over hundreds of the Carites and of the guard, and brought them to him into the LORD's house; and he made a covenant with them, and made a covenant with them in the LORD's house, and showed them the king's son. 5 He commanded them, saying, "This is what you must do: a third of you, who come in on the Sabbath, shall be keepers of the watch of the king's house; 6 a third of you shall be at the gate Sur; and a third of you at the gate behind the guard. So you shall keep the watch of the house, and be a barrier. 7 The two companies of you, even all who go out on the Sabbath, shall keep the watch of the LORD's house around the king. 8 You shall surround the king, every man with his weapons in his hand; and he who comes within the ranks, let him be slain. Be with the king when he goes out, and when he comes in."

9 The captains over hundreds did according to all that Jehoiada the priest commanded; and they each took his men, those who were to come in on the Sabbath with those who were to go out on the Sabbath, and came to Jehoiada the priest. 10 The priest delivered to the captains over hundreds the spears and shields that had been King David's, which were in the LORD's house. 11 The guard stood, every man with his weapons in his hand, from the right side of the house to the left side of the house, along by the altar and the house, around the king. 12 Then he brought out the king's son, and put the crown on him, and gave him the covenant; and they made him king and anointed him; and they clapped their hands, and said, "Long live the king!"

13 When Athaliah heard the noise of the guard and of the people, she came to the people into the LORD's house; 14 and she looked, and behold, the king stood by the pillar, as the tradition was, with the captains and the trumpets by the king; and all the people of the land rejoiced, and blew trumpets. Then Athaliah tore her clothes and cried, "Treason! Treason!"

15 Jehoiada the priest commanded the captains of hundreds who were set over the army, and said to them, "Bring her out between the ranks. Kill anyone who follows her with the sword." For the priest said, "Don't let her be slain in the LORD's house." 16 So they seized her; and she went by the way of the horses' entry to the king's house, and she was slain there.

17 Jehoiada made a covenant between the LORD and the king and the people, that they should be the LORD's people; also between the king and the people. 18 All the people of the land went to the house of Baal, and broke it down. They broke his altars and his images in pieces thoroughly, and killed Mattan the priest of Baal before the altars. The priest appointed officers over the LORD's house. 19 He took the captains over hundreds, and the Carites, and the guard, and all the people of the land; and they brought down the king from the LORD's house, and came by the way of the gate of the guard to the king's house. He sat on the throne of the kings. 20 So all the people of the land rejoiced, and the city was quiet. They had slain Athaliah with the sword at the king's house.

21 Jehoash was seven years old when he began to reign.

12

1 Jehoash began to reign in the seventh year of Jehu, and he reigned forty years in Jerusalem. His mother's name was Zibiah of Beersheba. 2 Jehoash did that which was right in the LORD's eyes all his days in which Jehoiada the priest instructed him. 3 However, the high places were not taken away. The people still sacrificed and burnt incense in the high places.

4 Jehoash said to the priests, "All the money of the holy things that is brought into the LORD's house, in current money, the money of the people

for whom each man is evaluated,ᵃ and all the money that it comes into any man's heart to bring into the LORD's house, ₅ let the priests take it to them, each man from his donor; and they shall repair the damage to the house, wherever any damage is found."

₆ But it was so, that in the twenty-third year of King Jehoash the priests had not repaired the damage to the house. ₇ Then King Jehoash called for Jehoiada the priest, and for the other priests, and said to them, "Why aren't you repairing the damage to the house? Now therefore take no more money from your treasurers, but deliver it for repair of the damage to the house."

₈ The priests consented that they should take no more money from the people, and not repair the damage to the house. ₉ But Jehoiada the priest took a chest and bored a hole in its lid, and set it beside the altar, on the right side as one comes into the LORD's house; and the priests who kept the threshold put all the money that was brought into the LORD's house into it. ₁₀ When they saw that there was much money in the chest, the king's scribe and the high priest came up, and they put it in bags and counted the money that was found in the LORD's house. ₁₁ They gave the money that was weighed out into the hands of those who did the work, who had the oversight of the LORD's house; and they paid it out to the carpenters and the builders who worked on the LORD's house, ₁₂ and to the masons and the stone cutters, and for buying timber and cut stone to repair the damage to the LORD's house, and for all that was laid out for the house to repair it. ₁₃ But there were not made for the LORD's house cups of silver, snuffers, basins, trumpets, any vessels of gold or vessels of silver, of the money that was brought into the LORD's house; ₁₄ for they gave that to those who did the work, and repaired the LORD's house with it. ₁₅ Moreover they didn't demand an accounting from the men into whose hand they delivered the money to give to those who did the work; for they dealt faithfully. ₁₆ The money for the trespass offerings and the money for the sin offerings was not brought into the LORD's house. It was the priests'.

₁₇ Then Hazael king of Syria went up and fought against Gath, and took it; and Hazael set his face to go up to Jerusalem. ₁₈ Jehoash king of Judah took all the holy things that Jehoshaphat and Jehoram and Ahaziah, his fathers, kings of Judah, had dedicated, and his own holy things, and all the gold that was found in the treasures of the LORD's house, and of the king's house, and sent it to Hazael king of Syria; and he went away from Jerusalem.

₁₉ Now the rest of the acts of Joash, and all that he did, aren't they written in the book of the chronicles of the kings of Judah? ₂₀ His servants arose and made a conspiracy, and struck Joash at the house of Millo, on the way that goes down to Silla. ₂₁ For Jozacar the son of Shimeath, and Jehozabad the son of Shomer, his servants, struck him, and he died; and they buried him with his fathers in David's city; and Amaziah his son reigned in his place.

13

₁ In the twenty-third year of Joash the son of Ahaziah, king of Judah, Jehoahaz the son of Jehu began to reign over Israel in Samaria for seventeen years. ₂ He did that which was evil in the LORD's sight, and followed the sins of Jeroboam the son of Nebat, with which he made Israel to sin. He didn't depart from it. ₃ The LORD's anger burnt against Israel, and he delivered them into the hand of Hazael king of Syria, and into the hand of Benhadad the son of Hazael, continually. ₄ Jehoahaz begged the LORD, and the LORD listened to him; for he saw the oppression of Israel, how the king of Syria oppressed them. ₅ (The LORD gave Israel a saviour, so that they went out from under the hand of the Syrians; and the children of Israel lived in their tents as before. ₆ Nevertheless they didn't depart from the sins of the house of Jeroboam, with which he made Israel to sin, but walked in them; and the Asherah also remained in Samaria.) ₇ For he didn't leave to Jehoahaz of the people any more than fifty horsemen, and ten chariots, and ten thousand footmen; for the king of Syria destroyed them and made them like the dust in threshing. ₈ Now the rest of the acts of Jehoahaz, and all that he did, and his might, aren't they written in the book of the chronicles of the kings of Israel? ₉ Jehoahaz slept with his fathers; and they buried him in Samaria; and Joash his son reigned in his place.

₁₀ In the thirty-seventh year of Joash king of Judah, Jehoash the son of Jehoahaz began to reign over Israel in Samaria for sixteen years. ₁₁ He did that which was evil in the LORD's sight. He didn't depart from all the sins of Jeroboam the son of Nebat, with which he made Israel to sin; but he walked in them. ₁₂ Now the rest of the acts of Joash, and all that he did, and his might with which he fought against Amaziah king of Judah, aren't they written in the book of the chronicles of the kings of Israel? ₁₃ Joash slept with his fathers; and Jeroboam sat on his throne. Joash was buried in Samaria with the kings of Israel.

₁₄ Now Elisha became sick with the illness of which he died; and Joash the king of Israel came down to him, and wept over him, and said, "My father, my father, the chariots of Israel and its horsemen!"

₁₅ Elisha said to him, "Take bow and arrows;" and he took bow and arrows for himself. ₁₆ He said to the king of Israel, "Put your hand on the bow;" and he put his hand on it. Elisha laid his hands on the king's hands. ₁₇ He said, "Open the window eastward;" and he opened it. Then Elisha said, "Shoot!" and he shot. He said, "The LORD's arrow of victory, even the arrow of victory over Syria; for you will strike the Syrians in Aphek until you have consumed them."

₁₈ He said, "Take the arrows;" and he took them. He said to the king of Israel, "Strike the ground;" and he struck three times, and stopped. ₁₉ The man of God was angry with him, and said, "You should have struck five or six times. Then you would have struck Syria until you had consumed it, but now you will strike Syria just three times."

₂₀ Elisha died, and they buried him.

Now the bands of the Moabites invaded the land at the coming in of the year. ₂₁ As they were burying a man, behold, they saw a band of raiders; and they threw the man into Elisha's tomb. As soon as the man touched Elisha's bones, he revived, and stood up on his feet.

₂₂ Hazael king of Syria oppressed Israel all the days of Jehoahaz. ₂₃ But the LORD was gracious to them, and had compassion on them, and favoured them because of his covenant with Abraham, Isaac, and Jacob, and would not destroy them and he didn't cast them from his presence as yet.

₂₄ Hazael king of Syria died; and Benhadad his son reigned in his place. ₂₅ Jehoash the son of Jehoahaz took again out of the hand of Benhadad the son of Hazael the cities which he had taken out of the hand of Jehoahaz his father by war. Joash struck him three times, and recovered the cities of Israel.

14

₁ In the second year of Joash, son of Joahaz, king of Israel, Amaziah the son of Joash king of Judah began to reign. ₂ He was twenty-five years old when he began to reign; and he reigned twenty-nine years in Jerusalem. His mother's name was Jehoaddin of Jerusalem. ₃ He did that which was right in the LORD's eyes, yet not like David his father. He did according to all that Joash his father had done. ₄ However the high places were not taken away. The people still sacrificed and burnt incense in the high places. ₅ As soon as the kingdom was established in his hand, he killed his servants who had slain the king his father, ₆ but the children of the murderers he didn't put to death, according to that which is written in the book of the law of Moses, as the LORD commanded, saying, "The fathers shall not be put to death for the children, nor the children be put to death for the fathers; but every man shall die for his own sin."

₇ He killed ten thousand Edomites in the Valley of Salt, and took Sela by war, and called its name Joktheel, to this day. ₈ Then Amaziah sent messengers to Jehoash, the son of Jehoahaz son of Jehu, king of Israel, saying, "Come, let's look one another in the face."

₉ Jehoash the king of Israel sent to Amaziah king of Judah, saying, "The thistle that was in Lebanon sent to the cedar that was in Lebanon, saying, 'Give your daughter to my son as wife.' Then a wild animal that was in Lebanon passed by, and trampled down the thistle. ₁₀ You have indeed struck Edom, and your heart has lifted you up. Enjoy the glory of it, and stay at home; for why should you meddle to your harm, that you fall, even you, and Judah with you?"

₁₁ But Amaziah would not listen. So Jehoash king of Israel went up; and he and Amaziah king of Judah looked one another in the face at Beth Shemesh, which belongs to Judah. ₁₂ Judah was defeated by Israel; and each man fled to his tent. ₁₃ Jehoash king of Israel took Amaziah king of Judah, the son of Jehoash the son of Ahaziah, at Beth Shemesh and came to Jerusalem, then broke down the wall of Jerusalem from the gate of Ephraim to the corner gate, four hundred cubits.ᵃ ₁₄ He took all the gold and silver and all the vessels that were found in the LORD's house and in the treasures of the king's house, the hostages also, and returned to Samaria.

₁₅ Now the rest of the acts of Jehoash which he did, and his might, and how he fought with Amaziah king of Judah, aren't they written in the book of the chronicles of the kings of Israel? ₁₆ Jehoash slept with his fathers, and was buried in Samaria with the kings of Israel; and Jeroboam his son reigned in his place.

₁₇ Amaziah the son of Joash king of Judah lived after the death of Jehoash son of Jehoahaz, king of Israel, fifteen years. ₁₈ Now the rest of the acts of Amaziah, aren't they written in the book of the chronicles of the kings of Judah? ₁₉ They made a conspiracy against him in Jerusalem, and he fled to Lachish; but they sent after him to Lachish and killed him there. ₂₀ They brought him on horses, and he was buried at Jerusalem with his fathers in David's city.

₂₁ All the people of Judah took Azariah, who was sixteen years old, and made him king in the place of his father Amaziah. ₂₂ He built Elath and restored it to Judah. After that the king slept with his fathers.

₂₃ In the fifteenth year of Amaziah the son of Joash king of Judah, Jeroboam the son of Joash king of Israel began to reign in Samaria for forty-one years. ₂₄ He did that which was evil in the LORD's sight. He didn't depart from all the sins of Jeroboam the son of Nebat, with which he made Israel to sin. ₂₅ He restored the border of Israel from the entrance of Hamath to the sea of the Arabah, according to the LORD, the God of Israel's word, which he spoke by his servant Jonah the son of Amittai, the prophet, who was from Gath Hepher. ₂₆ For the LORD saw the affliction of Israel, that it was very bitter for all, slave and free; and there was no helper for Israel. ₂₇ The LORD didn't say that he would blot out the name of Israel from under the sky; but he saved them by the hand of Jeroboam the son of Joash. ₂₈ Now the rest of the acts of Jeroboam, and all that he did, and his might, how he fought, and how he recovered Damascus, and Hamath, which had belonged to Judah, for Israel, aren't they written in the book of the chronicles of the kings of Israel? ₂₉ Jeroboam slept with his fathers, even with the kings of Israel; and Zechariah his son reigned in his place.

** 12:4 Exodus 30:12

ᵃ *14:13* A cubit is the length from the tip of the middle finger to the elbow on a man's arm, or about 18 inches or 46 centimetres.

15

1 In the twenty-seventh year of Jeroboam king of Israel, Azariah son of Amaziah king of Judah began to reign. 2 He was sixteen years old when he began to reign, and he reigned fifty-two years in Jerusalem. His mother's name was Jecoliah of Jerusalem. 3 He did that which was right in the LORD's eyes, according to all that his father Amaziah had done. 4 However, the high places were not taken away. The people still sacrificed and burnt incense in the high places. 5 The LORD struck the king, so that he was a leper to the day of his death, and lived in a separate house. Jotham, the king's son, was over the household, judging the people of the land. 6 Now the rest of the acts of Azariah, and all that he did, aren't they written in the book of the chronicles of the kings of Judah? 7 Azariah slept with his fathers; and they buried him with his fathers in David's city; and Jotham his son reigned in his place.

8 In the thirty-eighth year of Azariah king of Judah, Zechariah the son of Jeroboam reigned over Israel in Samaria six months. 9 He did that which was evil in the LORD's sight, as his fathers had done. He didn't depart from the sins of Jeroboam the son of Nebat, with which he made Israel to sin. 10 Shallum the son of Jabesh conspired against him, and struck him before the people and killed him, and reigned in his place. 11 Now the rest of the acts of Zechariah, behold, they are written in the book of the chronicles of the kings of Israel. 12 This was the LORD's word which he spoke to Jehu, saying, "Your sons to the fourth generation shall sit on the throne of Israel." So it came to pass.

13 Shallum the son of Jabesh began to reign in the thirty-ninth year of Uzziah king of Judah, and he reigned for a month in Samaria. 14 Menahem the son of Gadi went up from Tirzah, came to Samaria, struck Shallum the son of Jabesh in Samaria, killed him, and reigned in his place. 15 Now the rest of the acts of Shallum, and his conspiracy which he made, behold, they are written in the book of the chronicles of the kings of Israel.

16 Then Menahem attacked Tiphsah and all who were in it and its border areas, from Tirzah. He attacked it because they didn't open their gates to him, and he ripped up all their women who were with child.

17 In the thirty ninth year of Azariah king of Judah, Menahem the son of Gadi began to reign over Israel for ten years in Samaria. 18 He did that which was evil in the LORD's sight. He didn't depart all his days from the sins of Jeroboam the son of Nebat, with which he made Israel to sin. 19 Pul the king of Assyria came against the land, and Menahem gave Pul one thousand talents[a] of silver, that his hand might be with him to confirm the kingdom in his hand. 20 Menahem exacted the money from Israel, even from all the mighty men of wealth, from each man fifty shekels[b] of silver, to give to the king of Assyria. So the king of Assyria turned back, and didn't stay there in the land. 21 Now the rest of the acts of Menahem, and all that he did, aren't they written in the book of the chronicles of the kings of Israel? 22 Menahem slept with his fathers, and Pekahiah his son reigned in his place.

23 In the fiftieth year of Azariah king of Judah, Pekahiah the son of Menahem began to reign over Israel in Samaria for two years. 24 He did that which was evil in the LORD's sight. He didn't depart from the sins of Jeroboam the son of Nebat, with which he made Israel to sin. 25 Pekah the son of Remaliah, his captain, conspired against him and attacked him in Samaria, in the fortress of the king's house, with Argob and Arieh; and with him were fifty men of the Gileadites. He killed him, and reigned in his place. 26 Now the rest of the acts of Pekahiah, and all that he did, behold, they are written in the book of the chronicles of the kings of Israel.

27 In the fifty-second year of Azariah king of Judah, Pekah the son of Remaliah began to reign over Israel in Samaria for twenty years. 28 He did that which was evil in the LORD's sight. He didn't depart from the sins of Jeroboam the son of Nebat, with which he made Israel to sin. 29 In the days of Pekah king of Israel, Tiglath Pileser king of Assyria came and took Ijon, Abel Beth Maacah, Janoah, Kedesh, Hazor, Gilead, and Galilee, all the land of Naphtali; and he carried them captive to Assyria. 30 Hoshea the son of Elah made a conspiracy against Pekah the son of Remaliah, attacked him, killed him, and reigned in his place, in the twentieth year of Jotham the son of Uzziah. 31 Now the rest of the acts of Pekah, and all that he did, behold, they are written in the book of the chronicles of the kings of Israel.

32 In the second year of Pekah the son of Remaliah king of Israel, Jotham the son of Uzziah king of Judah began to reign. 33 He was twenty-five years old when he began to reign, and he reigned sixteen years in Jerusalem. His mother's name was Jerusha the daughter of Zadok. 34 He did that which was right in the LORD's eyes. He did according to all that his father Uzziah had done. 35 However the high places were not taken away. The people still sacrificed and burnt incense in the high places. He built the upper gate of the LORD's house. 36 Now the rest of the acts of Jotham, and all that he did, aren't they written in the book of the chronicles of the kings of Judah? 37 In those days, the LORD began to send Rezin the king of Syria and Pekah the son of Remaliah against Judah. 38 Jotham slept with his fathers, and was buried with his fathers in his father David's city; and Ahaz his son reigned in his place.

16

1 In the seventeenth year of Pekah the son of Remaliah, Ahaz the son of Jotham king of Judah began to reign. 2 Ahaz was twenty years old when he began to reign, and he reigned sixteen years in Jerusalem. He didn't do that which was right in the LORD his God's eyes, like David his father. 3 But he walked in the way of the kings of Israel, and even made his son to pass through the fire, according to the abominations of the nations whom the LORD cast out from before the children of Israel. 4 He sacrificed and burnt incense in the high places, on the hills, and under every green tree.

5 Then Rezin king of Syria and Pekah son of Remaliah king of Israel came up to Jerusalem to wage war. They besieged Ahaz, but could not overcome him. 6 At that time Rezin king of Syria recovered Elath to Syria, and drove the Jews from Elath; and the Syrians came to Elath, and lived there to this day. 7 So Ahaz sent messengers to Tiglath Pileser king of Assyria, saying, "I am your servant and your son. Come up and save me out of the hand of the king of Syria and out of the hand of the king of Israel, who rise up against me." 8 Ahaz took the silver and gold that was found in the LORD's house, and in the treasures of the king's house, and sent it for a present to the king of Assyria. 9 The king of Assyria listened to him; and the king of Assyria went up against Damascus and took it, and carried its people captive to Kir, and killed Rezin.

10 King Ahaz went to Damascus to meet Tiglath Pileser king of Assyria, and saw the altar that was at Damascus; and King Ahaz sent to Urijah the priest a drawing of the altar and plans to build it. 11 Urijah the priest built an altar. According to all that King Ahaz had sent from Damascus, so Urijah the priest made it for the coming of King Ahaz from Damascus. 12 When the king had come from Damascus, the king saw the altar; and the king came near to the altar, and offered on it. 13 He burnt his burnt offering and his meal offering, poured his drink offering, and sprinkled the blood of his peace offerings on the altar. 14 The bronze altar, which was before the LORD, he brought from the front of the house, from between his altar and the LORD's house, and put it on the north side of his altar. 15 King Ahaz commanded Urijah the priest, saying, "On the great altar burn the morning burnt offering, the evening meal offering, the king's burnt offering and his meal offering, with the burnt offering of all the people of the land, their meal offering, and their drink offerings; and sprinkle on it all the blood of the burnt offering, and all the blood of the sacrifice; but the bronze altar will be for me to enquire by." 16 Urijah the priest did so, according to all that King Ahaz commanded.

17 King Ahaz cut off the panels of the bases, and removed the basin from off them, and took down the sea from off the bronze oxen that were under it, and put it on a pavement of stone. 18 He removed the covered way for the Sabbath that they had built in the house, and the king's outer entrance to the LORD's house, because of the king of Assyria. 19 Now the rest of the acts of Ahaz which he did, aren't they written in the book of the chronicles of the kings of Judah? 20 Ahaz slept with his fathers, and was buried with his fathers in David's city; and Hezekiah his son reigned in his place.

17

1 In the twelfth year of Ahaz king of Judah, Hoshea the son of Elah began to reign in Samaria over Israel for nine years. 2 He did that which was evil in the LORD's sight, yet not as the kings of Israel who were before him. 3 Shalmaneser king of Assyria came up against him; and Hoshea became his servant, and brought him tribute. 4 The king of Assyria discovered a conspiracy in Hoshea; for he had sent messengers to So king of Egypt, and offered no tribute to the king of Assyria, as he had done year by year. Therefore the king of Assyria seized him, and bound him in prison. 5 Then the king of Assyria came up throughout all the land, went up to Samaria, and besieged it three years. 6 In the ninth year of Hoshea the king of Assyria took Samaria and carried Israel away to Assyria, and placed them in Halah, and on the Habor, the river of Gozan, and in the cities of the Medes.

7 It was so because the children of Israel had sinned against the LORD their God, who brought them up out of the land of Egypt from under the hand of Pharaoh king of Egypt, and had feared other gods, 8 and walked in the statutes of the nations whom the LORD cast out from before the children of Israel, and of the kings of Israel, which they made. 9 The children of Israel secretly did things that were not right against the LORD their God; and they built high places for themselves in all their cities, from the tower of the watchmen to the fortified city; 10 and they set up for themselves pillars and Asherah poles on every high hill and under every green tree; 11 and there they burnt incense in all the high places, as the nations whom the LORD carried away before them did; and they did wicked things to provoke the LORD to anger; 12 and they served idols, of which the LORD had said to them, "You shall not do this thing." 13 Yet the LORD testified to Israel and to Judah, by every prophet and every seer, saying, "Turn from your evil ways, and keep my commandments and my statutes, according to all the law which I commanded your fathers, and which I sent to you by my servants the prophets." 14 Notwithstanding, they would not listen, but hardened their neck like the neck of their fathers who didn't believe in the LORD their God. 15 They rejected his statutes and his covenant that he made with their fathers, and his testimonies which he testified to them; and they followed vanity, and became vain, and followed the nations that were around them, concerning whom the LORD had commanded them that they should not do like them. 16 They abandoned all the commandments of the LORD their God, and made molten images for themselves, even two calves, and made an Asherah, and worshipped all the army of the sky, and served Baal. 17 They caused their sons and their daughters to pass through the fire, used divination and enchantments, and sold themselves to do that which was evil in the LORD's sight, to provoke him to anger. 18 Therefore the LORD was very angry with Israel, and

---

a 15:19 A talent is about 30 kilograms or 66 pounds, so 1000 talents is about 30 metric tonnes

b 15:20 A shekel is about 10 grams or about 0.35 ounces, so 50 shekels was about 0.5 kilograms or 1.1 pounds.

removed them out of his sight. There was none left but the tribe of Judah only.

19 Also Judah didn't keep the commandments of the LORD their God, but walked in the statutes of Israel which they made. 20 The LORD rejected all the offspring of Israel, afflicted them, and delivered them into the hands of raiders, until he had cast them out of his sight. 21 For he tore Israel from David's house; and they made Jeroboam the son of Nebat king; and Jeroboam drove Israel from following the LORD, and made them sin a great sin. 22 The children of Israel walked in all the sins of Jeroboam which he did; they didn't depart from them 23 until the LORD removed Israel out of his sight, as he said by all his servants the prophets. So Israel was carried away out of their own land to Assyria to this day.

24 The king of Assyria brought people from Babylon, from Cuthah, from Avva, and from Hamath and Sepharvaim, and placed them in the cities of Samaria instead of the children of Israel; and they possessed Samaria and lived in its cities. 25 So it was, at the beginning of their dwelling there, that they didn't fear the LORD. Therefore the LORD sent lions amongst them, which killed some of them. 26 Therefore they spoke to the king of Assyria, saying, "The nations which you have carried away and placed in the cities of Samaria don't know the law of the god of the land. Therefore he has sent lions amongst them; and behold, they kill them, because they don't know the law of the god of the land."

27 Then the king of Assyria commanded, saying, "Carry there one of the priests whom you brought from there; and let him[a] go and dwell there, and let him teach them the law of the god of the land."

28 So one of the priests whom they had carried away from Samaria came and lived in Bethel, and taught them how they should fear the LORD.

29 However every nation made gods of their own, and put them in the houses of the high places which the Samaritans had made, every nation in their cities in which they lived. 30 The men of Babylon made Succoth Benoth, and the men of Cuth made Nergal, and the men of Hamath made Ashima, 31 and the Avvites made Nibhaz and Tartak; and the Sepharvites burnt their children in the fire to Adrammelech and Anammelech, the gods of Sepharvaim. 32 So they feared the LORD, and also made from amongst themselves priests of the high places for themselves, who sacrificed for them in the houses of the high places. 33 They feared the LORD, and also served their own gods, after the ways of the nations from amongst whom they had been carried away. 34 To this day they do what they did before. They don't fear the LORD, and they do not follow the statutes, or the ordinances, or the law, or the commandment which the LORD commanded the children of Jacob, whom he named Israel; 35 with whom the LORD had made a covenant and commanded them, saying, "You shall not fear other gods, nor bow yourselves to them, nor serve them, nor sacrifice to them; 36 but you shall fear the LORD, who brought you up out of the land of Egypt with great power and with an outstretched arm, and you shall bow yourselves to him, and you shall sacrifice to him. 37 The statutes and the ordinances, and the law and the commandment which he wrote for you, you shall observe to do forever more. You shall not fear other gods. 38 You shall not forget the covenant that I have made with you. You shall not fear other gods. 39 But you shall fear the LORD your God, and he will deliver you out of the hand of all your enemies."

40 However they didn't listen, but they did what they did before. 41 So these nations feared the LORD, and also served their engraved images. Their children did likewise, and so did their children's children. They do as their fathers did to this day.

18

1 Now in the third year of Hoshea son of Elah king of Israel, Hezekiah the son of Ahaz king of Judah began to reign. 2 He was twenty-five years old when he began to reign, and he reigned twenty-nine years in Jerusalem. His mother's name was Abi the daughter of Zechariah. 3 He did that which was right in the LORD's eyes, according to all that David his father had done. 4 He removed the high places, broke the pillars, and cut down the Asherah. He also broke in pieces the bronze serpent that Moses had made, because in those days the children of Israel burnt incense to it; and he called it Nehushtan. 5 He trusted in the LORD, the God of Israel, so that after him was no one like him amongst all the kings of Judah, nor amongst them that were before him. 6 For he joined with the LORD. He didn't depart from following him, but kept his commandments, which the LORD commanded Moses. 7 The LORD was with him. Wherever he went, he prospered. He rebelled against the king of Assyria, and didn't serve him. 8 He struck the Philistines to Gaza and its borders, from the tower of the watchmen to the fortified city.

9 In the fourth year of King Hezekiah, which was the seventh year of Hoshea son of Elah king of Israel, Shalmaneser king of Assyria came up against Samaria and besieged it. 10 At the end of three years they took it. In the sixth year of Hezekiah, which was the ninth year of Hoshea king of Israel, Samaria was taken. 11 The king of Assyria carried Israel away to Assyria, and put them in Halah, and on the Habor, the river of Gozan, and in the cities of the Medes, 12 because they didn't obey the LORD their God's voice, but transgressed his covenant, even all that Moses the servant of the LORD commanded, and would not hear it or do it.

13 Now in the fourteenth year of King Hezekiah, Sennacherib king of Assyria came up against all the fortified cities of Judah and took them. 14 Hezekiah king of Judah sent to the king of Assyria at Lachish, saying, "I have offended you. Withdraw from me. That which you put on me, I will bear." The king of Assyria appointed to Hezekiah king of Judah three

hundred talents of silver and thirty talents[b] of gold. 15 Hezekiah gave him all the silver that was found in the LORD's house and in the treasures of the king's house. 16 At that time, Hezekiah cut off the gold from the doors of the LORD's temple, and from the pillars which Hezekiah king of Judah had overlaid, and gave it to the king of Assyria.

17 The king of Assyria sent Tartan, Rabsaris, and Rabshakeh from Lachish to King Hezekiah with a great army to Jerusalem. They went up and came to Jerusalem. When they had come up, they came and stood by the conduit of the upper pool, which is in the highway of the fuller's field. 18 When they had called to the king, Eliakim the son of Hilkiah, who was over the household, and Shebnah the scribe, and Joah the son of Asaph the recorder came out to them. 19 Rabshakeh said to them, "Say now to Hezekiah, 'The great king, the king of Assyria, says, "What confidence is this in which you trust? 20 You say (but they are but vain words), 'There is counsel and strength for war.' Now on whom do you trust, that you have rebelled against me? 21 Now, behold, you trust in the staff of this bruised reed, even in Egypt. If a man leans on it, it will go into his hand and pierce it. So is Pharaoh king of Egypt to all who trust on him. 22 But if you tell me, 'We trust in the LORD our God,' isn't that he whose high places and whose altars Hezekiah has taken away, and has said to Judah and to Jerusalem, 'You shall worship before this altar in Jerusalem'? 23 Now therefore, please give pledges to my master the king of Assyria, and I will give you two thousand horses if you are able on your part to set riders on them. 24 How then can you turn away the face of one captain of the least of my master's servants, and put your trust on Egypt for chariots and for horsemen? 25 Have I now come up without the LORD against this place to destroy it? the LORD said to me, 'Go up against this land, and destroy it.'"'"

26 Then Eliakim the son of Hilkiah, Shebnah, and Joah, said to Rabshakeh, "Please speak to your servants in the Syrian language, for we understand it. Don't speak with us in the Jews' language, in the hearing of the people who are on the wall."

27 But Rabshakeh said to them, "Has my master sent me to your master and to you, to speak these words? Hasn't he sent me to the men who sit on the wall, to eat their own dung, and to drink their own urine with you?"

28 Then Rabshakeh stood and cried with a loud voice in the Jews' language, and spoke, saying, "Hear the word of the great king, the king of Assyria. 29 The king says, 'Don't let Hezekiah deceive you, for he will not be able to deliver you out of his hand. 30 Don't let Hezekiah make you trust in the LORD, saying, "The LORD will surely deliver us, and this city shall not be given into the hand of the king of Assyria." 31 Don't listen to Hezekiah.' For the king of Assyria says, 'Make your peace with me, and come out to me; and everyone of you eat from his own vine, and everyone from his own fig tree, and everyone drink water from his own cistern; 32 until I come and take you away to a land like your own land, a land of grain and new wine, a land of bread and vineyards, a land of olive trees and of honey, that you may live and not die. Don't listen to Hezekiah when he persuades you, saying, "The LORD will deliver us." 33 Has any of the gods of the nations ever delivered his land out of the hand of the king of Assyria? 34 Where are the gods of Hamath and of Arpad? Where are the gods of Sepharvaim, of Hena, and Ivvah? Have they delivered Samaria out of my hand? 35 Who are they amongst all the gods of the countries, that have delivered their country out of my hand, that the LORD should deliver Jerusalem out of my hand?'"

36 But the people stayed quiet, and answered him not a word; for the king's commandment was, "Don't answer him." 37 Then Eliakim the son of Hilkiah, who was over the household, came with Shebna the scribe and Joah the son of Asaph the recorder to Hezekiah with their clothes torn, and told him Rabshakeh's words.

19

1 When King Hezekiah heard it, he tore his clothes, covered himself with sackcloth, and went into the LORD's house. 2 He sent Eliakim, who was over the household, Shebna the scribe, and the elders of the priests, covered with sackcloth, to Isaiah the prophet the son of Amoz. 3 They said to him, "Hezekiah says, 'Today is a day of trouble, of rebuke, and of rejection; for the children have come to the point of birth, and there is no strength to deliver them. 4 It may be the LORD your God will hear all the words of Rabshakeh, whom the king of Assyria his master has sent to defy the living God, and will rebuke the words which the LORD your God has heard. Therefore lift up your prayer for the remnant that is left.'"

5 So the servants of King Hezekiah came to Isaiah. 6 Isaiah said to them, "Tell your master this: 'The LORD says, "Don't be afraid of the words that you have heard, with which the servants of the king of Assyria have blasphemed me. 7 Behold, I will put a spirit in him, and he will hear news, and will return to his own land. I will cause him to fall by the sword in his own land."'"

8 So Rabshakeh returned and found the king of Assyria warring against Libnah; for he had heard that he had departed from Lachish. 9 When he heard it said of Tirhakah king of Ethiopia, "Behold, he has come out to fight against you," he sent messengers again to Hezekiah, saying, 10 "Tell Hezekiah king of Judah this: 'Don't let your God in whom you trust deceive you, saying, Jerusalem will not be given into the hand of the king of Assyria. 11 Behold, you have heard what the kings of Assyria have done to all lands, by destroying them utterly. Will you be delivered? 12 Have the gods of the nations delivered them, which my fathers have destroyed—Gozan, Haran, Rezeph, and the children of Eden who were in Telassar?

---

13 Where is the king of Hamath, the king of Arpad, and the king of the city of Sepharvaim, of Hena, and Ivvah?"'

14 Hezekiah received the letter from the hand of the messengers and read it. Then Hezekiah went up to the LORD's house, and spread it before the LORD. 15 Hezekiah prayed before the LORD, and said, "LORD, the God of Israel, who are enthroned above the cherubim, you are the God, even you alone, of all the kingdoms of the earth. You have made heaven and earth. 16 Incline your ear, LORD, and hear. Open your eyes, LORD, and see. Hear the words of Sennacherib, which he has sent to defy the living God. 17 Truly, LORD, the kings of Assyria have laid waste the nations and their lands, 18 and have cast their gods into the fire; for they were no gods, but the work of men's hands, wood and stone. Therefore they have destroyed them. 19 Now therefore, LORD our God, save us, I beg you, out of his hand, that all the kingdoms of the earth may know that you, LORD, are God alone."

20 Then Isaiah the son of Amoz sent to Hezekiah, saying, "The LORD, the God of Israel, says 'You have prayed to me against Sennacherib king of Assyria, and I have heard you. 21 This is the word that the LORD has spoken concerning him: 'The virgin daughter of Zion has despised you and ridiculed you. The daughter of Jerusalem has shaken her head at you. 22 Whom have you defied and blasphemed? Against whom have you exalted your voice and lifted up your eyes on high? Against the Holy One of Israel! 23 By your messengers, you have defied the Lord, and have said, "With the multitude of my chariots, I have come up to the height of the mountains, to the innermost parts of Lebanon, and I will cut down its tall cedars and its choice cypress trees; and I will enter into his farthest lodging place, the forest of his fruitful field. 24 I have dug and drunk strange waters, and I will dry up all the rivers of Egypt with the sole of my feet." 25 Haven't you heard how I have done it long ago, and formed it of ancient times? Now I have brought it to pass, that it should be yours to lay waste fortified cities into ruinous heaps. 26 Therefore their inhabitants had little power. They were dismayed and confounded. They were like the grass of the field and like the green herb, like the grass on the housetops and like grain blasted before it has grown up. 27 But I know your sitting down, your going out, your coming in, and your raging against me. 28 Because of your raging against me, and because your arrogance has come up into my ears, therefore I will put my hook in your nose, and my bridle in your lips, and I will turn you back by the way by which you came.'

29 "This will be the sign to you: This year, you will eat that which grows of itself, and in the second year that which springs from that; and in the third year sow and reap, and plant vineyards and eat their fruit. 30 The remnant that has escaped of the house of Judah will again take root downward, and bear fruit upward. 31 For out of Jerusalem a remnant will go out, and out of Mount Zion those who shall escape. The LORD's zeal will perform this.

32 "Therefore the LORD says concerning the king of Assyria, 'He will not come to this city, nor shoot an arrow there. He will not come before it with shield, nor cast up a mound against it. 33 He will return the same way that he came, and he will not come to this city,' says the LORD. 34 'For I will defend this city to save it, for my own sake and for my servant David's sake.'"

35 That night, the LORD's angel went out and struck one hundred and eighty-five thousand in the camp of the Assyrians. When men arose early in the morning, behold, these were all dead bodies. 36 So Sennacherib king of Assyria departed, went home, and lived at Nineveh. 37 As he was worshipping in the house of Nisroch his god, Adrammelech and Sharezer struck him with the sword; and they escaped into the land of Ararat. Esar Haddon his son reigned in his place.

20

1 In those days Hezekiah was sick and dying. Isaiah the prophet the son of Amoz came to him, and said to him, "The LORD says, 'Set your house in order; for you will die, and not live.'"

2 Then he turned his face to the wall, and prayed to the LORD, saying, 3 "Remember now, LORD, I beg you, how I have walked before you in truth and with a perfect heart, and have done that which is good in your sight." And Hezekiah wept bitterly.

4 Before Isaiah had gone out into the middle part of the city, the LORD's word came to him, saying, 5 "Turn back, and tell Hezekiah the prince of my people, 'The LORD, the God of David your father, says, "I have heard your prayer. I have seen your tears. Behold, I will heal you. On the third day, you will go up to the LORD's house. 6 I will add to your days fifteen years. I will deliver you and this city out of the hand of the king of Assyria. I will defend this city for my own sake, and for my servant David's sake."'"

7 Isaiah said, "Take a cake of figs."

They took and laid it on the boil, and he recovered.

8 Hezekiah said to Isaiah, "What will be the sign that the LORD will heal me, and that I will go up to the LORD's house the third day?"

9 Isaiah said, "This will be the sign to you from the LORD, that the LORD will do the thing that he has spoken: should the shadow go forward ten steps, or go back ten steps?"

10 Hezekiah answered, "It is a light thing for the shadow to go forward ten steps. No, but let the shadow return backward ten steps."

11 Isaiah the prophet cried to the LORD; and he brought the shadow ten steps backward, by which it had gone down on the sundial of Ahaz.

12 At that time Berodach Baladan the son of Baladan, king of Babylon, sent letters and a present to Hezekiah, for he had heard that Hezekiah had been sick. 13 Hezekiah listened to them, and showed them all the storehouse of his precious things—the silver, the gold, the spices, and the precious oil, and the house of his armour, and all that was found in his

treasures. There was nothing in his house, or in all his dominion, that Hezekiah didn't show them.

14 Then Isaiah the prophet came to King Hezekiah, and said to him, "What did these men say? From where did they come to you?"

Hezekiah said, "They have come from a far country, even from Babylon."

15 He said, "What have they seen in your house?"

Hezekiah answered, "They have seen all that is in my house. There is nothing amongst my treasures that I have not shown them."

16 Isaiah said to Hezekiah, "Hear the LORD's word. 17 'Behold, the days come that all that is in your house, and that which your fathers have laid up in store to this day, will be carried to Babylon. Nothing will be left,' says the LORD. 18 'They will take away some of your sons who will issue from you, whom you will father; and they will be eunuchs in the palace of the king of Babylon.'"

19 Then Hezekiah said to Isaiah, "The LORD's word which you have spoken is good." He said moreover, "Isn't it so, if peace and truth will be in my days?"

20 Now the rest of the acts of Hezekiah, and all his might, and how he made the pool, and the conduit, and brought water into the city, aren't they written in the book of the chronicles of the kings of Judah? 21 Hezekiah slept with his fathers, and Manasseh his son reigned in his place.

21

1 Manasseh was twelve years old when he began to reign, and he reigned fifty-five years in Jerusalem. His mother's name was Hephzibah. 2 He did that which was evil in the LORD's sight, after the abominations of the nations whom the LORD cast out before the children of Israel. 3 For he built again the high places which Hezekiah his father had destroyed; and he raised up altars for Baal, and made an Asherah, as Ahab king of Israel did, and worshipped all the army of the sky, and served them. 4 He built altars in the LORD's house, of which the LORD said, "I will put my name in Jerusalem." 5 He built altars for all the army of the sky in the two courts of the LORD's house. 6 He made his son to pass through the fire, practised sorcery, used enchantments, and dealt with those who had familiar spirits and with wizards. He did much evil in the LORD's sight, to provoke him to anger. 7 He set the engraved image of Asherah that he had made in the house of which the LORD said to David and to Solomon his son, "In this house, and in Jerusalem, which I have chosen out of all the tribes of Israel, I will put my name forever; 8 I will not cause the feet of Israel to wander any more out of the land which I gave their fathers, if only they will observe to do according to all that I have commanded them, and according to all the law that my servant Moses commanded them." 9 But they didn't listen, and Manasseh seduced them to do that which is evil more than the nations did whom the LORD destroyed before the children of Israel.

10 The LORD spoke by his servants the prophets, saying, 11 "Because Manasseh king of Judah has done these abominations, and has done wickedly above all that the Amorites did, who were before him, and has also made Judah to sin with his idols; 12 therefore the LORD the God of Israel says, 'Behold, I will bring such evil on Jerusalem and Judah that whoever hears of it, both his ears will tingle. 13 I will stretch over Jerusalem the line of Samaria, and the plumb line of Ahab's house; and I will wipe Jerusalem as a man wipes a dish, wiping it and turning it upside down. 14 I will cast off the remnant of my inheritance and deliver them into the hands of their enemies. They will become a prey and a plunder to all their enemies, 15 because they have done that which is evil in my sight, and have provoked me to anger since the day their fathers came out of Egypt, even to this day.'"

16 Moreover Manasseh shed innocent blood very much, until he had filled Jerusalem from one end to another; in addition to his sin with which he made Judah to sin, in doing that which was evil in the LORD's sight.

17 Now the rest of the acts of Manasseh, and all that he did, and his sin that he sinned, aren't they written in the book of the chronicles of the kings of Judah? 18 Manasseh slept with his fathers, and was buried in the garden of his own house, in the garden of Uzza; and Amon his son reigned in his place.

19 Amon was twenty-two years old when he began to reign; and he reigned two years in Jerusalem. His mother's name was Meshullemeth the daughter of Haruz of Jotbah. 20 He did that which was evil in the LORD's sight, as Manasseh his father did. 21 He walked in all the ways that his father walked in, and served the idols that his father served, and worshipped them; 22 and he abandoned the LORD, the God of his fathers, and didn't walk in the way of the LORD. 23 The servants of Amon conspired against him, and put the king to death in his own house. 24 But the people of the land killed all those who had conspired against King Amon; and the people of the land made Josiah his son king in his place. 25 Now the rest of the acts of Amon which he did, aren't they written in the book of the chronicles of the kings of Judah? 26 He was buried in his tomb in the garden of Uzza, and Josiah his son reigned in his place.

22

1 Josiah was eight years old when he began to reign, and he reigned thirty-one years in Jerusalem. His mother's name was Jedidah the daughter of Adaiah of Bozkath. 2 He did that which was right in the LORD's eyes, and walked in all the ways of David his father, and didn't turn away to the right hand or to the left.

3 In the eighteenth year of King Josiah, the king sent Shaphan, the son of Azaliah the son of Meshullam, the scribe, to the LORD's house, saying, 4 "Go up to Hilkiah the high priest, that he may count the money which is brought into the LORD's house, which the keepers of the threshold

have gathered of the people. 5 Let them deliver it into the hand of the workers who have the oversight of the LORD's house; and let them give it to the workers who are in the LORD's house, to repair the damage to the house, 6 to the carpenters, and to the builders, and to the masons, and for buying timber and cut stone to repair the house. 7 However, no accounting shall be asked of them for the money delivered into their hand, for they deal faithfully."

8 Hilkiah the high priest said to Shaphan the scribe, "I have found the book of the law in the LORD's house." Hilkiah delivered the book to Shaphan, and he read it. 9 Shaphan the scribe came to the king, and brought the king word again, and said, "Your servants have emptied out the money that was found in the house, and have delivered it into the hands of the workmen who have the oversight of the LORD's house." 10 Shaphan the scribe told the king, saying, "Hilkiah the priest has delivered a book to me." Then Shaphan read it before the king.

11 When the king had heard the words of the book of the law, he tore his clothes. 12 The king commanded Hilkiah the priest, Ahikam the son of Shaphan, Achbor the son of Micaiah, Shaphan the scribe, and Asaiah the king's servant, saying, 13 "Go enquire of the LORD for me, and for the people, and for all Judah, concerning the words of this book that is found; for great is the LORD's wrath that is kindled against us, because our fathers have not listened to the words of this book, to do according to all that which is written concerning us."

14 So Hilkiah the priest, Ahikam, Achbor, Shaphan, and Asaiah went to Huldah the prophetess, the wife of Shallum the son of Tikvah, the son of Harhas, keeper of the wardrobe (now she lived in Jerusalem in the second quarter); and they talked with her. 15 She said to them, "The LORD the God of Israel says, 'Tell the man who sent you to me, 16 "The LORD says, 'Behold, I will bring evil on this place and on its inhabitants, even all the words of the book which the king of Judah has read. 17 Because they have forsaken me and have burnt incense to other gods, that they might provoke me to anger with all the work of their hands, therefore my wrath shall be kindled against this place, and it will not be quenched.'" 18 But to the king of Judah, who sent you to enquire of The LORD, tell him, "the LORD the God of Israel says, 'Concerning the words which you have heard, 19 because your heart was tender, and you humbled yourself before the LORD when you heard what I spoke against this place and against its inhabitants, that they should become a desolation and a curse, and have torn your clothes and wept before me, I also have heard you,' says the LORD. 20 'Therefore behold, I will gather you to your fathers, and you will be gathered to your grave in peace. Your eyes will not see all the evil which I will bring on this place.'"'" So they brought this message back to the king.

23

1 The king sent, and they gathered to him all the elders of Judah and of Jerusalem. 2 The king went up to the LORD's house, and all the men of Judah and all the inhabitants of Jerusalem with him—with the priests, the prophets, and all the people, both small and great; and he read in their hearing all the words of the book of the covenant which was found in the LORD's house. 3 The king stood by the pillar and made a covenant before the LORD to walk after the LORD and to keep his commandments, his testimonies, and his statutes with all his heart and all his soul, to confirm the words of this covenant that were written in this book; and all the people agreed to the covenant.

4 The king commanded Hilkiah the high priest, and the priests of the second order, and the keepers of the threshold, to bring out of the LORD's temple all the vessels that were made for Baal, for the Asherah, and for all the army of the sky; and he burnt them outside of Jerusalem in the fields of the Kidron, and carried their ashes to Bethel. 5 He got rid of the idolatrous priests whom the kings of Judah had ordained to burn incense in the high places in the cities of Judah and in the places around Jerusalem; those also who burnt incense to Baal, to the sun, to the moon, to the planets, and to all the army of the sky. 6 He brought out the Asherah from the LORD's house, outside of Jerusalem, to the brook Kidron, and burnt it at the brook Kidron, and beat it to dust, and cast its dust on the graves of the common people. 7 He broke down the houses of the male shrine prostitutes that were in the LORD's house, where the women wove hangings for the Asherah. 8 He brought all the priests out of the cities of Judah, and defiled the high places where the priests had burnt incense, from Geba to Beersheba; and he broke down the high places of the gates that were at the entrance of the gate of Joshua the governor of the city, which were on a man's left hand at the gate of the city. 9 Nevertheless the priests of the high places didn't come up to the LORD's altar in Jerusalem, but they ate unleavened bread amongst their brothers. 10 He defiled Topheth, which is in the valley of the children of Hinnom, that no man might make his son or his daughter to pass through the fire to Molech. 11 He took away the horses that the kings of Judah had dedicated to the sun, at the entrance of the LORD's house, by the room of Nathan Melech the officer who was in the court; and he burnt the chariots of the sun with fire. 12 The king broke down the altars that were on the roof of the upper room of Ahaz, which the kings of Judah had made, and the altars which Manasseh had made in the two courts of the LORD's house, and beat them down from there, and cast their dust into the brook Kidron. 13 The king defiled the high places that were before Jerusalem, which were on the right hand of the mountain of corruption, which Solomon the king of Israel had built for Ashtoreth the abomination of the Sidonians, and for Chemosh the abomination of Moab, and for Milcom the abomination of the children of Ammon. 14 He broke in

pieces the pillars, cut down the Asherah poles, and filled their places with men's bones.

15 Moreover the altar that was at Bethel and the high place which Jeroboam the son of Nebat, who made Israel to sin, had made, even that altar and the high place he broke down; and he burnt the high place and beat it to dust, and burnt the Asherah. 16 As Josiah turned himself, he spied the tombs that were there in the mountain; and he sent, and took the bones out of the tombs, and burnt them on the altar, and defiled it, according to the LORD's word which the man of God proclaimed, who proclaimed these things. 17 Then he said, "What monument is that which I see?"

The men of the city told him, "It is the tomb of the man of God who came from Judah and proclaimed these things that you have done against the altar of Bethel."

18 He said, "Let him be! Let no one move his bones." So they let his bones alone, with the bones of the prophet who came out of Samaria. 19 All the houses also of the high places that were in the cities of Samaria, which the kings of Israel had made to provoke the LORD to anger, Josiah took away, and did to them according to all the acts that he had done in Bethel. 20 He killed all the priests of the high places that were there, on the altars, and burnt men's bones on them; and he returned to Jerusalem.

21 The king commanded all the people, saying, "Keep the Passover to the LORD your God, as it is written in this book of the covenant." 22 Surely there was not kept such a Passover from the days of the judges who judged Israel, nor in all the days of the kings of Israel, nor of the kings of Judah; 23 but in the eighteenth year of King Josiah, this Passover was kept to the LORD in Jerusalem.

24 Moreover, Josiah removed those who had familiar spirits, the wizards, and the teraphim,[a] and the idols, and all the abominations that were seen in the land of Judah and in Jerusalem, that he might confirm the words of the law which were written in the book that Hilkiah the priest found in the LORD's house. 25 There was no king like him before him, who turned to the LORD with all his heart, and with all his soul, and with all his might, according to all the law of Moses; and there was none like him who arose after him. 26 Notwithstanding, the LORD didn't turn from the fierceness of his great wrath, with which his anger burnt against Judah, because of all the provocation with which Manasseh had provoked him. 27 The LORD said, "I will also remove Judah out of my sight, as I have removed Israel; and I will cast off this city which I have chosen, even Jerusalem, and the house of which I said, 'My name shall be there.'"

28 Now the rest of the acts of Josiah, and all that he did, aren't they written in the book of the chronicles of the kings of Judah? 29 In his days Pharaoh Necoh king of Egypt went up against the king of Assyria to the river Euphrates; and King Josiah went against him, but Pharaoh Necoh killed him at Megiddo when he saw him. 30 His servants carried him dead in a chariot from Megiddo, brought him to Jerusalem, and buried him in his own tomb. The people of the land took Jehoahaz the son of Josiah, and anointed him, and made him king in his father's place.

31 Jehoahaz was twenty-three years old when he began to reign; and he reigned three months in Jerusalem. His mother's name was Hamutal the daughter of Jeremiah of Libnah. 32 He did that which was evil in the LORD's sight, according to all that his fathers had done. 33 Pharaoh Necoh put him in bonds at Riblah in the land of Hamath, that he might not reign in Jerusalem; and put the land to a tribute of one hundred talents of silver and a talent[b] of gold. 34 Pharaoh Necoh made Eliakim the son of Josiah king in the place of Josiah his father, and changed his name to Jehoiakim; but he took Jehoahaz away, and he came to Egypt and died there. 35 Jehoiakim gave the silver and the gold to Pharaoh; but he taxed the land to give the money according to the commandment of Pharaoh. He exacted the silver and the gold of the people of the land, from everyone according to his assessment, to give it to Pharaoh Necoh. 36 Jehoiakim was twenty-five years old when he began to reign, and he reigned eleven years in Jerusalem. His mother's name was Zebidah the daughter of Pedaiah of Rumah. 37 He did that which was evil in the LORD's sight, according to all that his fathers had done.

24

1 In his days Nebuchadnezzar king of Babylon came up, and Jehoiakim became his servant three years. Then he turned and rebelled against him. 2 The LORD sent against him bands of the Chaldeans, bands of the Syrians, bands of the Moabites, and bands of the children of Ammon, and sent them against Judah to destroy it, according to the LORD's word which he spoke by his servants the prophets. 3 Surely at the commandment of the LORD this came on Judah, to remove them out of his sight for the sins of Manasseh, according to all that he did, 4 and also for the innocent blood that he shed; for he filled Jerusalem with innocent blood, and the LORD would not pardon. 5 Now the rest of the acts of Jehoiakim, and all that he did, aren't they written in the book of the chronicles of the kings of Judah? 6 So Jehoiakim slept with his fathers, and Jehoiachin his son reigned in his place.

7 The king of Egypt didn't come out of his land any more; for the king of Babylon had taken, from the brook of Egypt to the river Euphrates, all that belonged to the king of Egypt.

8 Jehoiachin was eighteen years old when he began to reign, and he reigned in Jerusalem three months. His mother's name was Nehushta the daughter of Elnathan of Jerusalem. 9 He did that which was evil in the LORD's sight, according to all that his father had done. 10 At that time the servants of Nebuchadnezzar king of Babylon came up to Jerusalem, and

---

a 23:24 teraphim were household idols.

b 23:33 A talent is about 30 kilograms or 66 pounds or 965 Troy ounces the city was besieged. 11 Nebuchadnezzar king of Babylon came to the city while his servants were besieging it, 12 and Jehoiachin the king of Judah went out to the king of Babylon—he, his mother, his servants, his princes, and his officers; and the king of Babylon captured him in the eighth year of his reign. 13 He carried out from there all the treasures of the LORD's house and the treasures of the king's house, and cut in pieces all the vessels of gold which Solomon king of Israel had made in the LORD's temple, as the LORD had said. 14 He carried away all Jerusalem, and all the princes, and all the mighty men of valour, even ten thousand captives, and all the craftsmen and the smiths. No one remained except the poorest people of the land. 15 He carried away Jehoiachin to Babylon, with the king's mother, the king's wives, his officers, and the chief men of the land. He carried them into captivity from Jerusalem to Babylon. 16 All the men of might, even seven thousand, and the craftsmen and the smiths one thousand, all of them strong and fit for war, even them the king of Babylon brought captive to Babylon. 17 The king of Babylon made Mattaniah, Jehoiachin's father's brother, king in his place, and changed his name to Zedekiah.

18 Zedekiah was twenty-one years old when he began to reign, and he reigned eleven years in Jerusalem. His mother's name was Hamutal the daughter of Jeremiah of Libnah. 19 He did that which was evil in the LORD's sight, according to all that Jehoiakim had done. 20 For through the anger of the LORD, this happened in Jerusalem and Judah, until he had cast them out from his presence.

Then Zedekiah rebelled against the king of Babylon.

25

1 In the ninth year of his reign, in the tenth month, in the tenth day of the month, Nebuchadnezzar king of Babylon came, he and all his army, against Jerusalem, and encamped against it; and they built forts against it around it. 2 So the city was besieged until the eleventh year of King Zedekiah. 3 On the ninth day of the fourth month, the famine was severe in the city, so that there was no bread for the people of the land. 4 Then a breach was made in the city, and all the men of war fled by night by the way of the gate between the two walls, which was by the king's garden (now the Chaldeans were against the city around it); and the king went by the way of the Arabah. 5 But the Chaldean army pursued the king, and overtook him in the plains of Jericho; and all his army was scattered from him. 6 Then they captured the king and carried him up to the king of Babylon to Riblah; and they passed judgement on him. 7 They killed Zedekiah's sons before his eyes, then put out Zedekiah's eyes, bound him in fetters, and carried him to Babylon.

8 Now in the fifth month, on the seventh day of the month, which was the nineteenth year of King Nebuchadnezzar king of Babylon, Nebuzaradan the captain of the guard, a servant of the king of Babylon, came to Jerusalem. 9 He burnt the LORD's house, the king's house, and all the houses of Jerusalem. He burnt every great house with fire. 10 All the army of the Chaldeans, who were with the captain of the guard, broke down the walls around Jerusalem. 11 Nebuzaradan the captain of the guard carried away captive the rest of the people who were left in the city and those who had deserted to the king of Babylon—all the rest of the multitude. 12 But the captain of the guard left some of the poorest of the land to work the vineyards and fields.

13 The Chaldeans broke up the pillars of bronze that were in the LORD's house and the bases and the bronze sea that were in the LORD's house, and carried the bronze pieces to Babylon. 14 They took away the pots, the shovels, the snuffers, the spoons, and all the vessels of bronze with which they ministered. 15 The captain of the guard took away the fire pans, the basins, that which was of gold, for gold, and that which was of silver, for silver. 16 The two pillars, the one sea, and the bases, which Solomon had made for the LORD's house, the bronze of all these vessels was not weighed. 17 The height of the one pillar was eighteen cubits,[a] and a capital of bronze was on it. The height of the capital was three cubits, with network and pomegranates on the capital around it, all of bronze; and the second pillar with its network was like these.

18 The captain of the guard took Seraiah the chief priest, Zephaniah the second priest, and the three keepers of the threshold; 19 and out of the city he took an officer who was set over the men of war; and five men of those who saw the king's face, who were found in the city; and the scribe, the captain of the army, who mustered the people of the land, and sixty men of the people of the land who were found in the city. 20 Nebuzaradan the captain of the guard took them, and brought them to the king of Babylon to Riblah. 21 The king of Babylon attacked them and put them to death at Riblah in the land of Hamath. So Judah was carried away captive out of his land.

22 As for the people who were left in the land of Judah whom Nebuchadnezzar king of Babylon had left, even over them he made Gedaliah the son of Ahikam, the son of Shaphan, governor. 23 Now when all the captains of the forces, they and their men, heard that the king of Babylon had made Gedaliah governor, they came to Gedaliah to Mizpah, even Ishmael the son of Nethaniah, Johanan the son of Kareah, Seraiah the son of Tanhumeth the Netophathite, and Jaazaniah the son of the Maacathite, they and their men. 24 Gedaliah swore to them and to their men, and said to them, "Don't be afraid because of the servants of the Chaldeans. Dwell in the land and serve the king of Babylon, and it will be well with you."

25 But in the seventh month, Ishmael the son of Nethaniah, the son of Elishama, of the royal offspring came, and ten men with him, and struck Gedaliah so that he died, with the Jews and the Chaldeans that were with him at Mizpah. 26 All the people, both small and great, and the captains of the forces arose and came to Egypt; for they were afraid of the Chaldeans. 27 In the thirty-seventh year of the captivity of Jehoiachin king of Judah, in the twelfth month, on the twenty-seventh day of the month, Evilmerodach king of Babylon, in the year that he began to reign, released Jehoiachin king of Judah out of prison, 28 and he spoke kindly to him and set his throne above the throne of the kings who were with him in Babylon, 29 and changed his prison garments. Jehoiachin ate bread before him continually all the days of his life; 30 and for his allowance, there was a continual allowance given him from the king, every day a portion, all the days of his life.

---

a *25:17* A cubit is the length from the tip of the middle finger to the elbow on a man's arm, or about 18 inches or 46 centimetres.

The First Book of Chronicles

1

1 Adam, Seth, Enosh, 2 Kenan, Mahalalel, Jared, 3 Enoch, Methuselah, Lamech, 4 Noah, Shem, Ham, and Japheth.

5 The sons of Japheth: Gomer, Magog, Madai, Javan, Tubal, Meshech, and Tiras. 6 The sons of Gomer: Ashkenaz, Diphath, and Togarmah. 7 The sons of Javan: Elishah, Tarshish, Kittim, and Rodanim.

8 The sons of Ham: Cush, Mizraim, Put, and Canaan. 9 The sons of Cush: Seba, Havilah, Sabta, Raamah, Sabteca. The sons of Raamah: Sheba and Dedan. 10 Cush became the father of Nimrod. He began to be a mighty one in the earth. 11 Mizraim became the father of Ludim, Anamim, Lehabim, Naphtuhim, 12 Pathrusim, Casluhim (where the Philistines came from), and Caphtorim. 13 Canaan became the father of Sidon his firstborn, Heth, 14 the Jebusite, the Amorite, the Girgashite, 15 the Hivite, the Arkite, the Sinite, 16 the Arvadite, the Zemarite, and the Hamathite.

17 The sons of Shem: Elam, Asshur, Arpachshad, Lud, Aram, Uz, Hul, Gether, and Meshech. 18 Arpachshad became the father of Shelah, and Shelah became the father of Eber. 19 To Eber were born two sons: the name of the one was Peleg, for in his days the earth was divided; and his brother's name was Joktan. 20 Joktan became the father of Almodad, Sheleph, Hazarmaveth, Jerah, 21 Hadoram, Uzal, Diklah, 22 Ebal, Abimael, Sheba, 23 Ophir, Havilah, and Jobab. All these were the sons of Joktan. 24 Shem, Arpachshad, Shelah, 25 Eber, Peleg, Reu, 26 Serug, Nahor, Terah, 27 Abram (also called Abraham).

28 The sons of Abraham: Isaac and Ishmael. 29 These are their generations: the firstborn of Ishmael, Nebaioth; then Kedar, Adbeel, Mibsam, 30 Mishma, Dumah, Massa, Hadad, Tema, 31 Jetur, Naphish, and Kedemah. These are the sons of Ishmael.

32 The sons of Keturah, Abraham's concubine: she bore Zimran, Jokshan, Medan, Midian, Ishbak, and Shuah. The sons of Jokshan: Sheba and Dedan. 33 The sons of Midian: Ephah, Epher, Hanoch, Abida, and Eldaah. All these were the sons of Keturah.

34 Abraham became the father of Isaac. The sons of Isaac: Esau and Israel. 35 The sons of Esau: Eliphaz, Reuel, Jeush, Jalam, and Korah. 36 The sons of Eliphaz: Teman, Omar, Zephi, Gatam, Kenaz, Timna, and Amalek. 37 The sons of Reuel: Nahath, Zerah, Shammah, and Mizzah.

38 The sons of Seir: Lotan, Shobal, Zibeon, Anah, Dishon, Ezer, and Dishan. 39 The sons of Lotan: Hori and Homam; and Timna was Lotan's sister. 40 The sons of Shobal: Alian, Manahath, Ebal, Shephi, and Onam. The sons of Zibeon: Aiah and Anah. 41 The son of Anah: Dishon. The sons of Dishon: Hamran, Eshban, Ithran, and Cheran. 42 The sons of Ezer: Bilhan, Zaavan, and Jaakan. The sons of Dishan: Uz and Aran.

43 Now these are the kings who reigned in the land of Edom, before any king reigned over the children of Israel: Bela the son of Beor; and the name of his city was Dinhabah. 44 Bela died, and Jobab the son of Zerah of Bozrah reigned in his place. 45 Jobab died, and Husham of the land of the Temanites reigned in his place. 46 Husham died, and Hadad the son of Bedad, who struck Midian in the field of Moab, reigned in his place; and the name of his city was Avith. 47 Hadad died, and Samlah of Masrekah reigned in his place. 48 Samlah died, and Shaul of Rehoboth by the River reigned in his place. 49 Shaul died, and Baal Hanan the son of Achbor reigned in his place. 50 Baal Hanan died, and Hadad reigned in his place; and the name of his city was Pai. His wife's name was Mehetabel, the daughter of Matred, the daughter of Mezahab. 51 Then Hadad died. The chiefs of Edom were: chief Timna, chief Aliah, chief Jetheth, 52 chief Oholibamah, chief Elah, chief Pinon, 53 chief Kenaz, chief Teman, chief Mibzar, 54 chief Magdiel, and chief Iram. These are the chiefs of Edom.

2

1 These are the sons of Israel: Reuben, Simeon, Levi, Judah, Issachar, Zebulun, 2 Dan, Joseph, Benjamin, Naphtali, Gad, and Asher.

3 The sons of Judah: Er, Onan, and Shelah, which three were born to him of Shua's daughter the Canaanitess. Er, Judah's firstborn, was wicked in the LORD's[a] sight; and he killed him. 4 Tamar his daughter-in-law bore him Perez and Zerah. All the sons of Judah were five.

5 The sons of Perez: Hezron and Hamul. 6 The sons of Zerah: Zimri, Ethan, Heman, Calcol, and Dara—five of them in all. 7 The son of Carmi: Achar, the troubler of Israel, who committed a trespass in the devoted thing. 8 The son of Ethan: Azariah.

9 The sons also of Hezron, who were born to him: Jerahmeel, Ram, and Chelubai. 10 Ram became the father of Amminadab, and Amminadab became the father of Nahshon, prince of the children of Judah; 11 and Nahshon became the father of Salma, and Salma became the father of Boaz, 12 and Boaz became the father of Obed, and Obed became the father of Jesse; 13 and Jesse became the father of his firstborn Eliab, Abinadab the second, Shimea the third, 14 Nethanel the fourth, Raddai the fifth, 15 Ozem the sixth, and David the seventh; 16 and their sisters were Zeruiah and Abigail. The sons of Zeruiah: Abishai, Joab, and Asahel, three. 17 Abigail bore Amasa; and the father of Amasa was Jether the Ishmaelite.

18 Caleb the son of Hezron became the father of children by Azubah his wife, and by Jerioth; and these were her sons: Jesher, Shobab, and Ardon. 19 Azubah died, and Caleb married Ephrath, who bore him Hur. 20 Hur became the father of Uri, and Uri became the father of Bezalel.

21 Afterward Hezron went in to the daughter of Machir the father of Gilead, whom he took as wife when he was sixty years old; and she bore him Segub. 22 Segub became the father of Jair, who had twenty-three cities in the land of Gilead. 23 Geshur and Aram took the towns of Jair from them, with Kenath, and its villages, even sixty cities. All these were the sons of Machir the father of Gilead. 24 After Hezron died in Caleb Ephrathah, Abijah, Hezron's wife, bore him Ashhur the father of Tekoa.

25 The sons of Jerahmeel the firstborn of Hezron were Ram the firstborn, Bunah, Oren, Ozem, and Ahijah. 26 Jerahmeel had another wife, whose name was Atarah. She was the mother of Onam. 27 The sons of Ram the firstborn of Jerahmeel were Maaz, Jamin, and Eker. 28 The sons of Onam were Shammai and Jada. The sons of Shammai: Nadab and Abishur. 29 The name of the wife of Abishur was Abihail; and she bore him Ahban and Molid. 30 The sons of Nadab: Seled and Appaim; but Seled died without children. 31 The son of Appaim: Ishi. The son of Ishi: Sheshan. The son of Sheshan: Ahlai. 32 The sons of Jada the brother of Shammai: Jether and Jonathan; and Jether died without children. 33 The sons of Jonathan: Peleth and Zaza. These were the sons of Jerahmeel. 34 Now Sheshan had no sons, but only daughters. Sheshan had a servant, an Egyptian, whose name was Jarha. 35 Sheshan gave his daughter to Jarha his servant as wife; and she bore him Attai. 36 Attai became the father of Nathan, and Nathan became the father of Zabad, 37 and Zabad became the father of Ephlal, and Ephlal became the father of Obed, 38 and Obed became the father of Jehu, and Jehu became the father of Azariah, 39 and Azariah became the father of Helez, and Helez became the father of Eleasah, 40 and Eleasah became the father of Sismai, and Sismai became the father of Shallum, 41 and Shallum became the father of Jekamiah, and Jekamiah became the father of Elishama.

42 The sons of Caleb the brother of Jerahmeel were Mesha his firstborn, who was the father of Ziph, and the sons of Mareshah the father of Hebron. 43 The sons of Hebron: Korah, Tappuah, Rekem, and Shema. 44 Shema became the father of Raham, the father of Jorkeam; and Rekem became the father of Shammai. 45 The son of Shammai was Maon; and Maon was the father of Beth Zur. 46 Ephah, Caleb's concubine, bore Haran, Moza, and Gazez; and Haran became the father of Gazez. 47 The sons of Jahdai: Regem, Jotham, Geshan, Pelet, Ephah, and Shaaph. 48 Maacah, Caleb's concubine, bore Sheber and Tirhanah. 49 She bore also Shaaph the father of Madmannah, Sheva the father of Machbena and the father of Gibea; and the daughter of Caleb was Achsah.

50 These were the sons of Caleb, the son of Hur, the firstborn of Ephrathah: Shobal the father of Kiriath Jearim, 51 Salma the father of Bethlehem, and Hareph the father of Beth Gader. 52 Shobal the father of Kiriath Jearim had sons: Haroeh, half of the Menuhoth. 53 The families of Kiriath Jearim: the Ithrites, the Puthites, the Shumathites, and the Mishraites; from them came the Zorathites and the Eshtaolites. 54 The sons of Salma: Bethlehem, the Netophathites, Atroth Beth Joab, and half of the Manahathites, the Zorites. 55 The families of scribes who lived at Jabez: the Tirathites, the Shimeathites, and the Sucathites. These are the Kenites who came from Hammath, the father of the house of Rechab.

3

1 Now these were the sons of David, who were born to him in Hebron: the firstborn, Amnon, of Ahinoam the Jezreelitess; the second, Daniel, of Abigail the Carmelitess; 2 the third, Absalom the son of Maacah the daughter of Talmai king of Geshur; the fourth, Adonijah the son of Haggith; 3 the fifth, Shephatiah of Abital; the sixth, Ithream by Eglah his wife: 4 six were born to him in Hebron; and he reigned there seven years and six months. He reigned thirty-three years in Jerusalem; 5 and these were born to him in Jerusalem: Shimea, Shobab, Nathan, and Solomon, four, by Bathshua the daughter of Ammiel; 6 and Ibhar, Elishama, Eliphelet, 7 Nogah, Nepheg, Japhia, 8 Elishama, Eliada, and Eliphelet, nine. 9 All these were the sons of David, in addition to the sons of the concubines; and Tamar was their sister.

10 Solomon's son was Rehoboam, Abijah his son, Asa his son, Jehoshaphat his son, 11 Joram his son, Ahaziah his son, Joash his son, 12 Amaziah his son, Azariah his son, Jotham his son, 13 Ahaz his son, Hezekiah his son, Manasseh his son, 14 Amon his son, and Josiah his son. 15 The sons of Josiah: the firstborn Johanan, the second Jehoiakim, the third Zedekiah, and the fourth Shallum. 16 The sons of Jehoiakim: Jeconiah his son, and Zedekiah his son. 17 The sons of Jeconiah, the captive: Shealtiel his son, 18 Malchiram, Pedaiah, Shenazzar, Jekamiah, Hoshama, and Nedabiah. 19 The sons of Pedaiah: Zerubbabel and Shimei. The sons of Zerubbabel: Meshullam and Hananiah; and Shelomith was their sister; 20 and Hashubah, Ohel, Berechiah, Hasadiah, and Jushab Hesed, five. 21 The sons of Hananiah: Pelatiah and Jeshaiah; the sons of Rephaiah, the sons of Arnan, the sons of Obadiah, the sons of Shecaniah. 22 The son of Shecaniah: Shemaiah. The sons of Shemaiah: Hattush, Igal, Bariah, Neariah, and Shaphat, six. 23 The sons of Neariah: Elioenai, Hizkiah, and Azrikam, three. 24 The sons of Elioenai: Hodaviah, Eliashib, Pelaiah, Akkub, Johanan, Delaiah, and Anani, seven.

4

1 The sons of Judah: Perez, Hezron, Carmi, Hur, and Shobal. 2 Reaiah the son of Shobal became the father of Jahath; and Jahath became the father of Ahumai and Lahad. These are the families of the Zorathites. 3 These were the sons of the father of Etam: Jezreel, Ishma, and Idbash. The name of their sister was Hazzelelponi. 4 Penuel was the father of Gedor and

---

a 2:3 When rendered in ALL CAPITAL LETTERS, "LORD" or "GOD" is the translation of God's Proper Name.

Ezer the father of Hushah. These are the sons of Hur, the firstborn of Ephrathah, the father of Bethlehem. 5 Ashhur the father of Tekoa had two wives, Helah and Naarah. 6 Naarah bore him Ahuzzam, Hepher, Temeni, and Haahashtari. These were the sons of Naarah. 7 The sons of Helah were Zereth, Izhar, and Ethnan. 8 Hakkoz became the father of Anub, Zobebah, and the families of Aharhel the son of Harum.

9 Jabez was more honourable than his brothers. His mother named him Jabez,[a] saying, "Because I bore him with sorrow."

10 Jabez called on the God[b] of Israel, saying, "Oh that you would bless me indeed, and enlarge my border! May your hand be with me, and may you keep me from evil, that I may not cause pain!"

God granted him that which he requested.

11 Chelub the brother of Shuhah became the father of Mehir, who was the father of Eshton. 12 Eshton became the father of Beth Rapha, Paseah, and Tehinnah the father of Ir Nahash. These are the men of Recah. 13 The sons of Kenaz: Othniel and Seraiah. The sons of Othniel: Hathath.[c] 14 Meonothai became the father of Ophrah: and Seraiah became the father of Joab the father of Ge Harashim, for they were craftsmen. 15 The sons of Caleb the son of Jephunneh: Iru, Elah, and Naam. The son of Elah: Kenaz. 16 The sons of Jehallelel: Ziph, Ziphah, Tiria, and Asarel. 17 The sons of Ezrah: Jether, Mered, Epher, and Jalon; and Mered's wife bore Miriam, Shammai, and Ishbah the father of Eshtemoa. 18 His wife the Jewess bore Jered the father of Gedor, Heber the father of Soco, and Jekuthiel the father of Zanoah. These are the sons of Bithiah the daughter of Pharaoh, whom Mered took. 19 The sons of the wife of Hodiah, the sister of Naham, were the fathers of Keilah the Garmite and Eshtemoa the Maacathite. 20 The sons of Shimon: Amnon, Rinnah, Ben Hanan, and Tilon. The sons of Ishi: Zoheth, and Ben Zoheth. 21 The sons of Shelah the son of Judah: Er the father of Lecah, Laadah the father of Mareshah, and the families of the house of those who worked fine linen, of the house of Ashbea; 22 and Jokim, and the men of Cozeba, and Joash, and Saraph, who had dominion in Moab, and Jashubilehem. These records are ancient. 23 These were the potters, and the inhabitants of Netaim and Gederah; they lived there with the king for his work.

24 The sons of Simeon: Nemuel, Jamin, Jarib, Zerah, Shaul; 25 Shallum his son, Mibsam his son, and Mishma his son. 26 The sons of Mishma: Hammuel his son, Zaccur his son, Shimei his son. 27 Shimei had sixteen sons and six daughters; but his brothers didn't have many children, and all their family didn't multiply like the children of Judah. 28 They lived at Beersheba, Moladah, Hazarshual, 29 at Bilhah, at Ezem, at Tolad, 30 at Bethuel, at Hormah, at Ziklag, 31 at Beth Marcaboth, Hazar Susim, at Beth Biri, and at Shaaraim. These were their cities until David's reign. 32 Their villages were Etam, Ain, Rimmon, Tochen, and Ashan, five cities; 33 and all their villages that were around the same cities, as far as Baal. These were their settlements, and they kept their genealogy. 34 Meshobab, Jamlech, Joshah the son of Amaziah, 35 Joel, Jehu the son of Joshibiah, the son of Seraiah, the son of Asiel, 36 Elioenai, Jaakobah, Jeshohaiah, Asaiah, Adiel, Jesimiel, Benaiah, 37 and Ziza the son of Shiphi, the son of Allon, the son of Jedaiah, the son of Shimri, the son of Shemaiah— 38 these mentioned by name were princes in their families. Their fathers' houses increased greatly.

39 They went to the entrance of Gedor, even to the east side of the valley, to seek pasture for their flocks. 40 They found rich, good pasture, and the land was wide, and quiet, and peaceful, for those who lived there before were descended from Ham. 41 These written by name came in the days of Hezekiah king of Judah, and struck their tents and the Meunim who were found there; and they destroyed them utterly to this day, and lived in their place, because there was pasture there for their flocks. 42 Some of them, even of the sons of Simeon, five hundred men, went to Mount Seir, having for their captains Pelatiah, Neariah, Rephaiah, and Uzziel, the sons of Ishi. 43 They struck the remnant of the Amalekites who escaped, and have lived there to this day.

5

1 The sons of Reuben the firstborn of Israel (for he was the firstborn, but because he defiled his father's couch, his birthright was given to the sons of Joseph the son of Israel; and the genealogy is not to be listed according to the birthright. 2 For Judah prevailed above his brothers, and from him came the prince; but the birthright was Joseph's)— 3 the sons of Reuben the firstborn of Israel: Hanoch, Pallu, Hezron, and Carmi. 4 The sons of Joel: Shemaiah his son, Gog his son, Shimei his son, 5 Micah his son, Reaiah his son, Baal his son, 6 and Beerah his son, whom Tilgath Pilneser king of Assyria carried away captive. He was prince of the Reubenites. 7 His brothers by their families, when the genealogy of their generations was listed: the chief, Jeiel, and Zechariah, 8 and Bela the son of Azaz, the son of Shema, the son of Joel, who lived in Aroer, even to Nebo and Baal Meon; 9 and he lived eastward even to the entrance of the wilderness from the river Euphrates, because their livestock were multiplied in the land of Gilead.

10 In the days of Saul, they made war with the Hagrites, who fell by their hand; and they lived in their tents throughout all the land east of Gilead.

11 The sons of Gad lived beside them in the land of Bashan to Salecah: 12 Joel the chief, Shapham the second, Janai, and Shaphat in Bashan. 13 Their brothers of their fathers' houses: Michael, Meshullam, Sheba, Jorai, Jacan, Zia, and Eber, seven. 14 These were the sons of Abihail, the son of Huri, the son of Jaroah, the son of Gilead, the son of Michael, the son of

Jeshishai, the son of Jahdo, the son of Buz; 15 Ahi the son of Abdiel, the son of Guni, chief of their fathers' houses. 16 They lived in Gilead in Bashan and in its towns, and in all the pasture lands of Sharon as far as their borders. 17 All these were listed by genealogies in the days of Jotham king of Judah, and in the days of Jeroboam king of Israel.

18 The sons of Reuben, the Gadites, and the half-tribe of Manasseh, of valiant men, men able to bear buckler and sword, able to shoot with bow, and skilful in war, were forty-four thousand and seven hundred and sixty that were able to go out to war. 19 They made war with the Hagrites, with Jetur, and Naphish, and Nodab. 20 They were helped against them, and the Hagrites were delivered into their hand, and all who were with them; for they cried to God in the battle, and he answered them because they put their trust in him. 21 They took away their livestock: of their camels fifty thousand, and of sheep two hundred and fifty thousand, and of donkeys two thousand, and of men one hundred thousand. 22 For many fell slain, because the war was of God. They lived in their place until the captivity.

23 The children of the half-tribe of Manasseh lived in the land. They increased from Bashan to Baal Hermon, Senir, and Mount Hermon. 24 These were the heads of their fathers' houses: Epher, Ishi, Eliel, Azriel, Jeremiah, Hodaviah, and Jahdiel—mighty men of valour, famous men, heads of their fathers' houses. 25 They trespassed against the God of their fathers, and played the prostitute after the gods of the peoples of the land whom God destroyed before them. 26 So the God of Israel stirred up the spirit of Pul king of Assyria, and the spirit of Tilgath Pilneser king of Assyria, and he carried away the Reubenites, the Gadites, and the half-tribe of Manasseh, and brought them to Halah, Habor, Hara, and to the river of Gozan, to this day.

6

1 The sons of Levi: Gershon, Kohath, and Merari. 2 The sons of Kohath: Amram, Izhar, Hebron, and Uzziel. 3 The children of Amram: Aaron, Moses, and Miriam. The sons of Aaron: Nadab, Abihu, Eleazar, and Ithamar. 4 Eleazar became the father of Phinehas, Phinehas became the father of Abishua, 5 Abishua became the father of Bukki. Bukki became the father of Uzzi. 6 Uzzi became the father of Zerahiah. Zerahiah became the father of Meraioth. 7 Meraioth became the father of Amariah. Amariah became the father of Ahitub. 8 Ahitub became the father of Zadok. Zadok became the father of Ahimaaz. 9 Ahimaaz became the father of Azariah. Azariah became the father of Johanan. 10 Johanan became the father of Azariah, who executed the priest's office in the house that Solomon built in Jerusalem. 11 Azariah became the father of Amariah. Amariah became the father of Ahitub. 12 Ahitub became the father of Zadok. Zadok became the father of Shallum. 13 Shallum became the father of Hilkiah. Hilkiah became the father of Azariah. 14 Azariah became the father of Seraiah. Seraiah became the father of Jehozadak. 15 Jehozadak went into captivity when the LORD carried Judah and Jerusalem away by the hand of Nebuchadnezzar.

16 The sons of Levi: Gershon, Kohath, and Merari. 17 These are the names of the sons of Gershom: Libni and Shimei. 18 The sons of Kohath were Amram, Izhar, Hebron, and Uzziel. 19 The sons of Merari: Mahli and Mushi. These are the families of the Levites according to their fathers' households. 20 Of Gershom: Libni his son, Jahath his son, Zimmah his son, 21 Joah his son, Iddo his son, Zerah his son, and Jeatherai his son. 22 The sons of Kohath: Amminadab his son, Korah his son, Assir his son, 23 Elkanah his son, Ebiasaph his son, Assir his son, 24 Tahath his son, Uriel his son, Uzziah his son, and Shaul his son. 25 The sons of Elkanah: Amasai and Ahimoth. 26 As for Elkanah: Zophai his son, Nahath his son, 27 Eliab his son, Jeroham his son, and Elkanah his son. 28 The sons of Samuel: the firstborn, Joel, and the second, Abijah. 29 The sons of Merari: Mahli, Libni his son, Shimei his son, Uzzah his son, 30 Shimea his son, Haggiah his son, Asaiah his son.

31 These are they whom David set over the service of song in the LORD's house after the ark came to rest there. 32 They ministered with song before the tabernacle of the Tent of Meeting until Solomon had built the LORD's house in Jerusalem. They performed the duties of their office according to their order. 33 These are those who served, and their sons. Of the sons of the Kohathites: Heman the singer, the son of Joel, the son of Samuel, 34 the son of Elkanah, the son of Jeroham, the son of Eliel, the son of Toah, 35 the son of Zuph, the son of Elkanah, the son of Mahath, the son of Amasai, 36 the son of Elkanah, the son of Joel, the son of Azariah, the son of Zephaniah, 37 the son of Tahath, the son of Assir, the son of Ebiasaph, the son of Korah, 38 the son of Izhar, the son of Kohath, the son of Levi, the son of Israel. 39 His brother Asaph, who stood on his right hand, even Asaph the son of Berechiah, the son of Shimea, 40 the son of Michael, the son of Baaseiah, the son of Malchijah, 41 the son of Ethni, the son of Zerah, the son of Adaiah, 42 the son of Ethan, the son of Zimmah, the son of Shimei, 43 the son of Jahath, the son of Gershom, the son of Levi. 44 On the left hand their brothers the sons of Merari: Ethan the son of Kishi, the son of Abdi, the son of Malluch, 45 the son of Hashabiah, the son of Amaziah, the son of Hilkiah, 46 the son of Amzi, the son of Bani, the son of Shemer, 47 the son of Mahli, the son of Mushi, the son of Merari, the son of Levi. 48 Their brothers the Levites were appointed for all the service of the tabernacle of God's house. 49 But Aaron and his sons offered on the altar of burnt offering, and on the altar of incense, for all the work of the most holy place, and to make atonement for Israel, according to all that Moses the servant of God had commanded.

---

a 4:9 "Jabez" sounds similar to the Hebrew word for "pain".
b 4:10 The Hebrew word rendered "God" is "אֱלֹהִים" (Elohim).
c 4:13 Greek and Vulgate add "and Meonothai"

50 These are the sons of Aaron: Eleazar his son, Phinehas his son, Abishua his son, 51 Bukki his son, Uzzi his son, Zerahiah his son, 52 Meraioth his son, Amariah his son, Ahitub his son, 53 Zadok his son, and Ahimaaz his son. 54 Now these are their dwelling places according to their encampments in their borders: to the sons of Aaron, of the families of the Kohathites (for theirs was the first lot), 55 to them they gave Hebron in the land of Judah, and its pasture lands around it; 56 but the fields of the city and its villages, they gave to Caleb the son of Jephunneh. 57 To the sons of Aaron they gave the cities of refuge, Hebron, Libnah also with its pasture lands, Jattir, Eshtemoa with its pasture lands, 58 Hilen with its pasture lands, Debir with its pasture lands, 59 Ashan with its pasture lands, and Beth Shemesh with its pasture lands; 60 and out of the tribe of Benjamin, Geba with its pasture lands, Allemeth with its pasture lands, and Anathoth with its pasture lands. All their cities throughout their families were thirteen cities.

61 To the rest of the sons of Kohath were given by lot, out of the family of the tribe, out of the half-tribe, the half of Manasseh, ten cities. 62 To the sons of Gershom, according to their families, out of the tribe of Issachar, and out of the tribe of Asher, and out of the tribe of Naphtali, and out of the tribe of Manasseh in Bashan, thirteen cities. 63 To the sons of Merari were given by lot, according to their families, out of the tribe of Reuben, and out of the tribe of Gad, and out of the tribe of Zebulun, twelve cities. 64 The children of Israel gave to the Levites the cities with their pasture lands. 65 They gave by lot out of the tribe of the children of Judah, and out of the tribe of the children of Simeon, and out of the tribe of the children of Benjamin, these cities which are mentioned by name.

66 Some of the families of the sons of Kohath had cities of their borders out of the tribe of Ephraim. 67 They gave to them the cities of refuge, Shechem in the hill country of Ephraim with its pasture lands and Gezer with its pasture lands, 68 Jokmeam with its pasture lands, Beth Horon with its pasture lands, 69 Aijalon with its pasture lands, Gath Rimmon with its pasture lands; 70 and out of the half-tribe of Manasseh, Aner with its pasture lands, and Bileam with its pasture lands, for the rest of the family of the sons of Kohath.

71 To the sons of Gershom were given, out of the family of the half-tribe of Manasseh, Golan in Bashan with its pasture lands, and Ashtaroth with its pasture lands; 72 and out of the tribe of Issachar, Kedesh with its pasture lands, Daberath with its pasture lands, 73 Ramoth with its pasture lands, and Anem with its pasture lands; 74 and out of the tribe of Asher, Mashal with its pasture lands, Abdon with its pasture lands, 75 Hukok with its pasture lands, and Rehob with its pasture lands; 76 and out of the tribe of Naphtali, Kedesh in Galilee with its pasture lands, Hammon with its pasture lands, and Kiriathaim with its pasture lands.

77 To the rest of the Levites, the sons of Merari, were given, out of the tribe of Zebulun, Rimmono with its pasture lands, and Tabor with its pasture lands; 78 and beyond the Jordan at Jericho, on the east side of the Jordan, were given them out of the tribe of Reuben: Bezer in the wilderness with its pasture lands, Jahzah with its pasture lands, 79 Kedemoth with its pasture lands, and Mephaath with its pasture lands; 80 and out of the tribe of Gad, Ramoth in Gilead with its pasture lands, Mahanaim with its pasture lands, 81 Heshbon with its pasture lands, and Jazer with its pasture lands.

7

1 Of the sons of Issachar: Tola, Puah, Jashub, and Shimron, four. 2 The sons of Tola: Uzzi, Rephaiah, Jeriel, Jahmai, Ibsam, and Shemuel, heads of their fathers' houses, of Tola; mighty men of valour in their generations. Their number in the days of David was twenty-two thousand and six hundred. 3 The son of Uzzi: Izrahiah. The sons of Izrahiah: Michael, Obadiah, Joel, and Isshiah, five; all of them chief men. 4 With them, by their generations, after their fathers' houses, were bands of the army for war, thirty-six thousand; for they had many wives and sons. 5 Their brothers amongst all the families of Issachar, mighty men of valour, listed in all by genealogy, were eighty-seven thousand.

6 The sons of Benjamin: Bela, Becher, and Jediael, three. 7 The sons of Bela: Ezbon, Uzzi, Uzziel, Jerimoth, and Iri, five; heads of fathers' houses, mighty men of valour; and they were listed by genealogy twenty-two thousand and thirty-four. 8 The sons of Becher: Zemirah, Joash, Eliezer, Elioenai, Omri, Jeremoth, Abijah, Anathoth, and Alemeth. All these were the sons of Becher. 9 They were listed by genealogy, after their generations, heads of their fathers' houses, mighty men of valour, twenty thousand and two hundred. 10 The son of Jediael: Bilhan. The sons of Bilhan: Jeush, Benjamin, Ehud, Chenaanah, Zethan, Tarshish, and Ahishahar. 11 All these were sons of Jediael, according to the heads of their fathers' households, mighty men of valour, seventeen thousand and two hundred, who were able to go out in the army for war. 12 So were Shuppim, Huppim, the sons of Ir, Hushim, and the sons of Aher.

13 The sons of Naphtali: Jahziel, Guni, Jezer, Shallum, and the sons of Bilhah.

14 The sons of Manasseh: Asriel, whom his concubine the Aramitess bore. She bore Machir the father of Gilead. 15 Machir took a wife of Huppim and Shuppim, whose sister's name was Maacah. The name of the second was Zelophehad; and Zelophehad had daughters. 16 Maacah the wife of Machir bore a son, and she named him Peresh. The name of his brother was Sheresh; and his sons were Ulam and Rakem. 17 The sons of Ulam: Bedan. These were the sons of Gilead the son of Machir, the son of Manasseh. 18 His sister Hammolecheth bore Ishhod, Abiezer, and Mahlah. 19 The sons of Shemida were Ahian, Shechem, Likhi, and Aniam.

20 The sons of Ephraim: Shuthelah, Bered his son, Tahath his son, Eleadah his son, Tahath his son, 21 Zabad his son, Shuthelah his son, Ezer, and Elead, whom the men of Gath who were born in the land killed, because they came down to take away their livestock. 22 Ephraim their father mourned many days, and his brothers came to comfort him. 23 He went in to his wife, and she conceived and bore a son, and he named him Beriah,[a] because there was trouble with his house. 24 His daughter was Sheerah, who built Beth Horon the lower and the upper, and Uzzen Sheerah. 25 Rephah was his son, Resheph his son, Telah his son, Tahan his son, 26 Ladan his son, Ammihud his son, Elishama his son, 27 Nun his son, and Joshua his son. 28 Their possessions and settlements were Bethel and its towns, and eastward Naaran, and westward Gezer with its towns; Shechem also and its towns, to Azzah and its towns; 29 and by the borders of the children of Manasseh, Beth Shean and its towns, Taanach and its towns, Megiddo and its towns, and Dor and its towns. The children of Joseph the son of Israel lived in these.

30 The sons of Asher: Imnah, Ishvah, Ishvi, and Beriah. Serah was their sister. 31 The sons of Beriah: Heber and Malchiel, who was the father of Birzaith. 32 Heber became the father of Japhlet, Shomer, Hotham, and Shua their sister. 33 The sons of Japhlet: Pasach, Bimhal, and Ashvath. These are the children of Japhlet. 34 The sons of Shemer: Ahi, Rohgah, Jehubbah, and Aram. 35 The sons of Helem his brother: Zophah, Imna, Shelesh, and Amal. 36 The sons of Zophah: Suah, Harnepher, Shual, Beri, Imrah, 37 Bezer, Hod, Shamma, Shilshah, Ithran, and Beera. 38 The sons of Jether: Jephunneh, Pispa, and Ara. 39 The sons of Ulla: Arah, Hanniel, and Rizia. 40 All these were the children of Asher, heads of the fathers' houses, choice and mighty men of valour, chief of the princes. The number of them listed by genealogy for service in war was twenty-six thousand men.

8

1 Benjamin became the father of Bela his firstborn, Ashbel the second, Aharah the third, 2 Nohah the fourth, and Rapha the fifth. 3 Bela had sons: Addar, Gera, Abihud, 4 Abishua, Naaman, Ahoah, 5 Gera, Shephuphan, and Huram. 6 These are the sons of Ehud. These are the heads of fathers' households of the inhabitants of Geba, who were carried captive to Manahath: 7 Naaman, Ahijah, and Gera, who carried them captive; and he became the father of Uzza and Ahihud.

8 Shaharaim became the father of children in the field of Moab, after he had sent them away. Hushim and Baara were his wives. 9 By Hodesh his wife, he became the father of Jobab, Zibia, Mesha, Malcam, 10 Jeuz, Shachia, and Mirmah. These were his sons, heads of fathers' households. 11 By Hushim, he became the father of Abitub and Elpaal. 12 The sons of Elpaal: Eber, Misham, and Shemed, who built Ono and Lod, with its towns; 13 and Beriah and Shema, who were heads of fathers' households of the inhabitants of Aijalon, who put to flight the inhabitants of Gath; 14 and Ahio, Shashak, Jeremoth, 15 Zebadiah, Arad, Eder, 16 Michael, Ishpah, Joha, the sons of Beriah, 17 Zebadiah, Meshullam, Hizki, Heber, 18 Ishmerai, Izliah, Jobab, the sons of Elpaal, 19 Jakim, Zichri, Zabdi, 20 Elienai, Zillethai, Eliel, 21 Adaiah, Beraiah, Shimrath, the sons of Shimei, 22 Ishpan, Eber, Eliel, 23 Abdon, Zichri, Hanan, 24 Hananiah, Elam, Anthothijah, 25 Iphdeiah, Penuel, the sons of Shashak, 26 Shamsherai, Sheariah, Athaliah, 27 Jaareshiah, Elijah, Zichri, and the sons of Jeroham. 28 These were heads of fathers' households throughout their generations, chief men. These lived in Jerusalem.

29 The father of Gibeon, whose wife's name was Maacah, lived in Gibeon 30 with his firstborn son Abdon, Zur, Kish, Baal, Nadab, 31 Gedor, Ahio, Zecher, 32 and Mikloth, who became the father of Shimeah. They also lived with their families in Jerusalem, near their relatives. 33 Ner became the father of Kish. Kish became the father of Saul. Saul became the father of Jonathan, Malchishua, Abinadab, and Eshbaal. 34 The son of Jonathan was Merib-baal. Merib-baal became the father of Micah. 35 The sons of Micah: Pithon, Melech, Tarea, and Ahaz. 36 Ahaz became the father of Jehoaddah. Jehoaddah became the father of Alemeth, Azmaveth, and Zimri. Zimri became the father of Moza. 37 Moza became the father of Binea. Raphah was his son, Eleasah his son, and Azel his son. 38 Azel had six sons, whose names are these: Azrikam, Bocheru, Ishmael, Sheariah, Obadiah, and Hanan. All these were the sons of Azel. 39 The sons of Eshek his brother: Ulam his firstborn, Jeush the second, and Eliphelet the third. 40 The sons of Ulam were mighty men of valour, archers, and had many sons, and grandsons, one hundred and fifty. All these were of the sons of Benjamin.

9

1 So all Israel were listed by genealogies; and behold,[b] they are written in the book of the kings of Israel. Judah was carried away captive to Babylon for their disobedience. 2 Now the first inhabitants who lived in their possessions in their cities were Israel, the priests, the Levites, and the temple servants. 3 In Jerusalem, there lived of the children of Judah, of the children of Benjamin, and of the children of Ephraim and Manasseh: 4 Uthai the son of Ammihud, the son of Omri, the son of Imri, the son of Bani, of the children of Perez the son of Judah. 5 Of the Shilonites: Asaiah the firstborn and his sons. 6 Of the sons of Zerah: Jeuel and their brothers, six hundred and ninety. 7 Of the sons of Benjamin: Sallu the son of Meshullam, the son of Hodaviah, the son of Hassenuah; 8 Ibneiah the son of Jeroham, and Elah the son of Uzzi, the son of Michri; and Meshullam the son of Shephatiah, the son of Reuel, the son of Ibnijah; 9 and their brothers, according to their generations, nine hundred and fifty-six. All these men were heads of fathers' households by their fathers' houses.

---

a 7:23 "Beriah" is similar to the Hebrew word for "misfortune".

b 9:1 "Behold", from "הִנֵּה", means look at, take notice, observe, see, or gaze at. It is often used as an interjection.

10 Of the priests: Jedaiah, Jehoiarib, Jachin, 11 and Azariah the son of Hilkiah, the son of Meshullam, the son of Zadok, the son of Meraioth, the son of Ahitub, the ruler of God's house; 12 and Adaiah the son of Jeroham, the son of Pashhur, the son of Malchijah; and Maasai the son of Adiel, the son of Jahzerah, the son of Meshullam, the son of Meshillemith, the son of Immer; 13 and their brothers, heads of their fathers' houses, one thousand and seven hundred and sixty; they were very able men for the work of the service of God's house.

14 Of the Levites: Shemaiah the son of Hasshub, the son of Azrikam, the son of Hashabiah, of the sons of Merari; 15 and Bakbakkar, Heresh, Galal, and Mattaniah the son of Mica, the son of Zichri, the son of Asaph, 16 and Obadiah the son of Shemaiah, the son of Galal, the son of Jeduthun; and Berechiah the son of Asa, the son of Elkanah, who lived in the villages of the Netophathites.

17 The gatekeepers: Shallum, Akkub, Talmon, Ahiman, and their brothers (Shallum was the chief), 18 who previously served in the king's gate eastward. They were the gatekeepers for the camp of the children of Levi. 19 Shallum was the son of Kore, the son of Ebiasaph, the son of Korah, and his brothers, of his father's house, the Korahites, were over the work of the service, keepers of the thresholds of the tent. Their fathers had been over the LORD's camp, keepers of the entry. 20 Phinehas the son of Eleazar was ruler over them in time past, and the LORD was with him. 21 Zechariah the son of Meshelemiah was gatekeeper of the door of the Tent of Meeting. 22 All these who were chosen to be gatekeepers in the thresholds were two hundred and twelve. These were listed by genealogy in their villages, whom David and Samuel the seer ordained in their office of trust. 23 So they and their children had the oversight of the gates of the LORD's house, even the house of the tent, as guards. 24 On the four sides were the gatekeepers, towards the east, west, north, and south. 25 Their brothers, in their villages, were to come in every seven days from time to time to be with them, 26 for the four chief gatekeepers, who were Levites, were in an office of trust, and were over the rooms and over the treasuries in God's house. 27 They stayed around God's house, because that was their duty; and it was their duty to open it morning by morning.

28 Certain of them were in charge of the vessels of service, for these were brought in by count, and these were taken out by count. 29 Some of them also were appointed over the furniture, and over all the vessels of the sanctuary, over the fine flour, the wine, the oil, the frankincense, and the spices.

30 Some of the sons of the priests prepared the mixing of the spices. 31 Mattithiah, one of the Levites, who was the firstborn of Shallum the Korahite, had the office of trust over the things that were baked in pans. 32 Some of their brothers, of the sons of the Kohathites, were over the show bread, to prepare it every Sabbath.

33 These are the singers, heads of fathers' households of the Levites, who lived in the rooms and were free from other service, for they were employed in their work day and night. 34 These were heads of fathers' households of the Levites, throughout their generations, chief men. They lived at Jerusalem.

35 Jeiel the father of Gibeon, whose wife's name was Maacah, lived in Gibeon. 36 His firstborn son was Abdon, then Zur, Kish, Baal, Ner, Nadab, 37 Gedor, Ahio, Zechariah, and Mikloth. 38 Mikloth became the father of Shimeam. They also lived with their relatives in Jerusalem, near their relatives. 39 Ner became the father of Kish. Kish became the father of Saul. Saul became the father of Jonathan, Malchishua, Abinadab, and Eshbaal. 40 The son of Jonathan was Merib-baal. Merib-baal became the father of Micah. 41 The sons of Micah: Pithon, Melech, Tahrea, and Ahaz. 42 Ahaz became the father of Jarah. Jarah became the father of Alemeth, Azmaveth, and Zimri. Zimri became the father of Moza. 43 Moza became the father of Binea, Rephaiah his son, Eleasah his son, and Azel his son. 44 Azel had six sons, whose names are Azrikam, Bocheru, Ishmael, Sheariah, Obadiah, and Hanan. These were the sons of Azel.

10

1 Now the Philistines fought against Israel; and the men of Israel fled from before the Philistines, and fell down slain on Mount Gilboa. 2 The Philistines followed hard after Saul and after his sons; and the Philistines killed Jonathan, Abinadab, and Malchishua, the sons of Saul. 3 The battle went hard against Saul, and the archers overtook him; and he was distressed by reason of the archers. 4 Then Saul said to his armour bearer, "Draw your sword, and thrust me through with it, lest these uncircumcised come and abuse me."

But his armour bearer would not, for he was terrified. Therefore Saul took his sword and fell on it. 5 When his armour bearer saw that Saul was dead, he likewise fell on his sword and died. 6 So Saul died with his three sons; and all his house died together. 7 When all the men of Israel who were in the valley saw that they fled, and that Saul and his sons were dead, they abandoned their cities, and fled; and the Philistines came and lived in them.

8 On the next day, when the Philistines came to strip the slain, they found Saul and his sons fallen on Mount Gilboa. 9 They stripped him and took his head and his armour, then sent into the land of the Philistines all around to carry the news to their idols and to the people. 10 They put his armour in the house of their gods, and fastened his head in the house of Dagon. 11 When all Jabesh Gilead heard all that the Philistines had done to

Saul, 12 all the valiant men arose and took away the body of Saul and the bodies of his sons, and brought them to Jabesh, and buried their bones under the oak in Jabesh, and fasted seven days.

13 So Saul died for his trespass which he committed against the LORD, because of the LORD's word, which he didn't keep, and also because he asked counsel of one who had a familiar spirit, to enquire, 14 and didn't enquire of the LORD. Therefore he killed him, and turned the kingdom over to David the son of Jesse.

11

1 Then all Israel gathered themselves to David to Hebron, saying, "Behold, we are your bone and your flesh. 2 In times past, even when Saul was king, it was you who led out and brought in Israel. The LORD your God said to you, 'You shall be shepherd of my people Israel, and you shall be prince over my people Israel.'"

3 So all the elders of Israel came to the king to Hebron; and David made a covenant with them in Hebron before the LORD. They anointed David king over Israel, according to the LORD's word by Samuel.

4 David and all Israel went to Jerusalem (also called Jebus); and the Jebusites, the inhabitants of the land, were there. 5 The inhabitants of Jebus said to David, "You will not come in here!" Nevertheless David took the stronghold of Zion. The same is David's city. 6 David had said, "Whoever strikes the Jebusites first shall be chief and captain." Joab the son of Zeruiah went up first, and was made chief. 7 David lived in the stronghold; therefore they called it David's city. 8 He built the city all around, from Millo even around; and Joab repaired the rest of the city. 9 David grew greater and greater, for the LORD of Armies was with him.

10 Now these are the chief of the mighty men whom David had, who showed themselves strong with him in his kingdom, together with all Israel, to make him king, according to the LORD's word concerning Israel.

11 This is the number of the mighty men whom David had: Jashobeam, the son of a Hachmonite, the chief of the thirty; he lifted up his spear against three hundred and killed them at one time. 12 After him was Eleazar the son of Dodo, the Ahohite, who was one of the three mighty men. 13 He was with David at Pasdammim, and there the Philistines were gathered together to battle, where there was a plot of ground full of barley; and the people fled from before the Philistines. 14 They stood in the middle of the plot, defended it, and killed the Philistines; and the LORD saved them by a great victory.

15 Three of the thirty chief men went down to the rock to David, into the cave of Adullam; and the army of the Philistines were encamped in the valley of Rephaim. 16 David was then in the stronghold, and the garrison of the Philistines was in Bethlehem at that time. 17 David longed, and said, "Oh, that someone would give me water to drink from the well of Bethlehem, which is by the gate!"

18 The three broke through the army of the Philistines, and drew water out of the well of Bethlehem that was by the gate, took it, and brought it to David; but David would not drink any of it, but poured it out to the LORD, 19 and said, "My God forbid me, that I should do this! Shall I drink the blood of these men who have put their lives in jeopardy?" For they risked their lives to bring it. Therefore he would not drink it. The three mighty men did these things.

20 Abishai, the brother of Joab, was chief of the three; for he lifted up his spear against three hundred and killed them, and had a name amongst the three. 21 Of the three, he was more honourable than the two, and was made their captain; however he wasn't included in the three.

22 Benaiah the son of Jehoiada, the son of a valiant man of Kabzeel, who had done mighty deeds, killed the two sons of Ariel of Moab. He also went down and killed a lion in the middle of a pit on a snowy day. 23 He killed an Egyptian, a man of great stature, five cubits[a] high. In the Egyptian's hand was a spear like a weaver's beam; and he went down to him with a staff, plucked the spear out of the Egyptian's hand, and killed him with his own spear. 24 Benaiah the son of Jehoiada did these things and had a name amongst the three mighty men. 25 Behold, he was more honourable than the thirty, but he didn't attain to the three; and David set him over his guard.

26 The mighty men of the armies also include Asahel the brother of Joab, Elhanan the son of Dodo of Bethlehem, 27 Shammoth the Harorite, Helez the Pelonite, 28 Ira the son of Ikkesh the Tekoite, Abiezer the Anathothite, 29 Sibbecai the Hushathite, Ilai the Ahohite, 30 Maharai the Netophathite, Heled the son of Baanah the Netophathite, 31 Ithai the son of Ribai of Gibeah of the children of Benjamin, Benaiah the Pirathonite, 32 Hurai of the brooks of Gaash, Abiel the Arbathite, 33 Azmaveth the Baharumite, Eliahba the Shaalbonite, 34 the sons of Hashem the Gizonite, Jonathan the son of Shagee the Hararite, 35 Ahiam the son of Sacar the Hararite, Eliphal the son of Ur, 36 Hepher the Mecherathite, Ahijah the Pelonite, 37 Hezro the Carmelite, Naarai the son of Ezbai, 38 Joel the brother of Nathan, Mibhar the son of Hagri, 39 Zelek the Ammonite, Naharai the Berothite (the armour bearer of Joab the son of Zeruiah), 40 Ira the Ithrite, Gareb the Ithrite, 41 Uriah the Hittite, Zabad the son of Ahlai, 42 Adina the son of Shiza the Reubenite (a chief of the Reubenites), and thirty with him, 43 Hanan the son of Maacah, Joshaphat the Mithnite, 44 Uzzia the Ashterathite, Shama and Jeiel the sons of Hotham the Aroerite, 45 Jediael the son of Shimri, and Joha his brother, the Tizite, 46 Eliel the Mahavite, and Jeribai, and Joshaviah, the sons of Elnaam, and Ithmah the Moabite, 47 Eliel, Obed, and Jaasiel the Mezobaite.

---

a *11:23* A cubit is the length from the tip of the middle finger to the elbow on a man's arm, or about 18 inches or 46 centimetres. Therefore this Egyptian was about 7 feet and 6 inches or 2.28 metres tall.

12

1 Now these are those who came to David to Ziklag while he was a fugitive from Saul the son of Kish. They were amongst the mighty men, his helpers in war. 2 They were armed with bows, and could use both the right hand and the left in slinging stones and in shooting arrows from the bow. They were of Saul's relatives of the tribe of Benjamin. 3 The chief was Ahiezer, then Joash, the sons of Shemaah the Gibeathite; Jeziel and Pelet, the sons of Azmaveth; Beracah; Jehu the Anathothite; 4 Ishmaiah the Gibeonite, a mighty man amongst the thirty and a leader of the thirty; Jeremiah; Jahaziel; Johanan; Jozabad the Gederathite; 5 Eluzai; Jerimoth; Bealiah; Shemariah; Shephatiah the Haruphite; 6 Elkanah, Isshiah, Azarel, Joezer, and Jashobeam, the Korahites; 7 and Joelah and Zebadiah, the sons of Jeroham of Gedor.

8 Some Gadites joined David in the stronghold in the wilderness, mighty men of valour, men trained for war, who could handle shield and spear; whose faces were like the faces of lions, and they were as swift as the gazelles on the mountains: 9 Ezer the chief, Obadiah the second, Eliab the third, 10 Mishmannah the fourth, Jeremiah the fifth, 11 Attai the sixth, Eliel the seventh, 12 Johanan the eighth, Elzabad the ninth, 13 Jeremiah the tenth, and Machbannai the eleventh. 14 These of the sons of Gad were captains of the army. He who was least was equal to one hundred, and the greatest to one thousand. 15 These are those who went over the Jordan in the first month, when it had overflowed all its banks; and they put to flight all who lived in the valleys, both towards the east and towards the west.

16 Some of the children of Benjamin and Judah came to the stronghold to David. 17 David went out to meet them, and answered them, "If you have come peaceably to me to help me, my heart will be united with you; but if you have come to betray me to my adversaries, since there is no wrong in my hands, may the God of our fathers see this and rebuke it." 18 Then the Spirit came on Amasai, who was chief of the thirty, and he said, "We are yours, David, and on your side, you son of Jesse. Peace, peace be to you, and peace be to your helpers; for your God helps you." Then David received them and made them captains of the band.

19 Some of Manasseh also joined David when he came with the Philistines against Saul to battle, but they didn't help them, for the lords of the Philistines sent him away after consultation, saying, "He will desert to his master Saul to the jeopardy of our heads."

20 As he went to Ziklag, some from Manasseh joined him: Adnah, Jozabad, Jediael, Michael, Jozabad, Elihu, and Zillethai, captains of thousands who were of Manasseh. 21 They helped David against the band of raiders, for they were all mighty men of valour and were captains in the army. 22 For from day to day men came to David to help him, until there was a great army, like God's army.

23 These are the numbers of the heads of those who were armed for war, who came to David to Hebron to turn the kingdom of Saul to him, according to the LORD's word. 24 The children of Judah who bore shield and spear were six thousand and eight hundred, armed for war. 25 Of the children of Simeon, mighty men of valour for the war: seven thousand and one hundred. 26 Of the children of Levi: four thousand and six hundred. 27 Jehoiada was the leader of the household of Aaron; and with him were three thousand and seven hundred, 28 and Zadok, a young man mighty of valour, and of his father's house twenty-two captains. 29 Of the children of Benjamin, Saul's relatives: three thousand, for until then, the greatest part of them had kept their allegiance to Saul's house. 30 Of the children of Ephraim: twenty thousand and eight hundred, mighty men of valour, famous men in their fathers' houses. 31 Of the half-tribe of Manasseh: eighteen thousand, who were mentioned by name, to come and make David king. 32 Of the children of Issachar, men who had understanding of the times, to know what Israel ought to do, their heads were two hundred; and all their brothers were at their command. 33 Of Zebulun, such as were able to go out in the army, who could set the battle in array with all kinds of instruments of war: fifty thousand who could command and were not of double heart. 34 Of Naphtali: one thousand captains, and with them with shield and spear thirty-seven thousand. 35 Of the Danites who could set the battle in array: twenty-eight thousand and six hundred. 36 Of Asher, such as were able to go out in the army, who could set the battle in array: forty thousand. 37 On the other side of the Jordan, of the Reubenites, the Gadites, and of the half-tribe of Manasseh, with all kinds of instruments of war for the battle: one hundred and twenty thousand.

38 All these were men of war who could order the battle array, and came with a perfect heart to Hebron to make David king over all Israel; and all the rest also of Israel were of one heart to make David king. 39 They were there with David three days, eating and drinking; for their brothers had supplied provisions for them. 40 Moreover those who were near to them, as far as Issachar, Zebulun, and Naphtali, brought bread on donkeys, on camels, on mules, and on oxen: supplies of flour, cakes of figs, clusters of raisins, wine, oil, cattle, and sheep in abundance; for there was joy in Israel.

13

1 David consulted with the captains of thousands and of hundreds, even with every leader. 2 David said to all the assembly of Israel, "If it seems good to you, and if it is of the LORD our God, let's send word everywhere to our brothers who are left in all the land of Israel, with whom the priests and Levites are in their cities that have pasture lands, that they may gather themselves to us. 3 Also, let's bring the ark of our God back to us again, for we didn't seek it in the days of Saul."

4 All the assembly said that they would do so, for the thing was right in the eyes of all the people. 5 So David assembled all Israel together, from the Shihor River of Egypt even to the entrance of Hamath, to bring God's ark from Kiriath Jearim.

6 David went up with all Israel to Baalah, that is, to Kiriath Jearim, which belonged to Judah, to bring up from there God the LORD's ark that sits above the cherubim, that is called by the Name. 7 They carried God's ark on a new cart, and brought it out of Abinadab's house; and Uzza and Ahio drove the cart. 8 David and all Israel played before God with all their might, even with songs, with harps, with stringed instruments, with tambourines, with cymbals, and with trumpets.

9 When they came to Chidon's threshing floor, Uzza put out his hand to hold the ark, for the oxen stumbled. 10 The LORD's anger burnt against Uzza, and he struck him because he put his hand on the ark; and he died there before God. 11 David was displeased, because the LORD had broken out against Uzza. He called that place Perez Uzza, to this day. 12 David was afraid of God that day, saying, "How can I bring God's ark home to me?" 13 So David didn't move the ark with him into David's city, but carried it aside into Obed-Edom the Gittite's house. 14 God's ark remained with the family of Obed-Edom in his house three months; and the LORD blessed Obed-Edom's house and all that he had.

14

1 Hiram king of Tyre sent messengers to David with cedar trees, masons, and carpenters, to build him a house. 2 David perceived that the LORD had established him king over Israel, for his kingdom was highly exalted, for his people Israel's sake.

3 David took more wives in Jerusalem, and David became the father of more sons and daughters. 4 These are the names of the children whom he had in Jerusalem: Shammua, Shobab, Nathan, Solomon, 5 Ibhar, Elishua, Elpelet, 6 Nogah, Nepheg, Japhia, 7 Elishama, Beeliada, and Eliphelet.

8 When the Philistines heard that David was anointed king over all Israel, all the Philistines went up to seek David; and David heard of it, and went out against them. 9 Now the Philistines had come and made a raid in the valley of Rephaim. 10 David enquired of God, saying, "Shall I go up against the Philistines? Will you deliver them into my hand?"

The LORD said to him, "Go up; for I will deliver them into your hand."

11 So they came up to Baal Perazim, and David defeated them there. David said, God has broken my enemies by my hand, like waters breaking out. Therefore they called the name of that place Baal Perazim.ª 12 They left their gods there; and David gave a command, and they were burnt with fire.

13 The Philistines made another raid in the valley. 14 David enquired again of God; and God said to him, "You shall not go up after them. Turn away from them, and come on them opposite the mulberry trees. 15 When you hear the sound of marching in the tops of the mulberry trees, then go out to battle; for God has gone out before you to strike the army of the Philistines."

16 David did as God commanded him; and they attacked the army of the Philistines from Gibeon even to Gezer. 17 The fame of David went out into all lands; and the LORD brought the fear of him on all nations.

15

1 David made himself houses in David's city; and he prepared a place for God's ark, and pitched a tent for it. 2 Then David said, "No one ought to carry God's ark but the Levites. For the LORD has chosen them to carry God's ark, and to minister to him forever."

3 David assembled all Israel at Jerusalem, to bring up the LORD's ark to its place, which he had prepared for it. 4 David gathered together the sons of Aaron and the Levites: 5 of the sons of Kohath, Uriel the chief, and his brothers one hundred and twenty; 6 of the sons of Merari, Asaiah the chief, and his brothers two hundred and twenty; 7 of the sons of Gershom, Joel the chief, and his brothers one hundred and thirty; 8 of the sons of Elizaphan, Shemaiah the chief, and his brothers two hundred; 9 of the sons of Hebron, Eliel the chief, and his brothers eighty; 10 of the sons of Uzziel, Amminadab the chief, and his brothers one hundred and twelve.

11 David called for Zadok and Abiathar the priests, and for the Levites: for Uriel, Asaiah, Joel, Shemaiah, Eliel, and Amminadab, 12 and said to them, "You are the heads of the fathers' households of the Levites. Sanctify yourselves, both you and your brothers, that you may bring the ark of the LORD, the God of Israel, up to the place that I have prepared for it. 13 For because you didn't carry it at first, the LORD our God broke out in anger against us, because we didn't seek him according to the ordinance."

14 So the priests and the Levites sanctified themselves to bring up the ark of the LORD, the God of Israel. 15 The children of the Levites bore God's ark on their shoulders with its poles, as Moses commanded according to the LORD's word.

16 David spoke to the chief of the Levites to appoint their brothers as singers with instruments of music, stringed instruments, harps, and cymbals, sounding aloud and lifting up their voices with joy. 17 So the Levites appointed Heman the son of Joel; and of his brothers, Asaph the son of Berechiah; and of the sons of Merari their brothers, Ethan the son of Kushaiah; 18 and with them their brothers of the second rank: Zechariah, Ben, Jaaziel, Shemiramoth, Jehiel, Unni, Eliab, Benaiah, Maaseiah, Mattithiah, Eliphelehu, Mikneiah, Obed-Edom, and Jeiel, the doorkeepers. 19 So the singers, Heman, Asaph, and Ethan, were given cymbals of bronze to sound aloud; 20 and Zechariah, Aziel, Shemiramoth, Jehiel, Unni, Eliab, Maaseiah, and Benaiah, with stringed instruments set to Alamoth; 21 and Mattithiah, Eliphelehu, Mikneiah, Obed-Edom, Jeiel, and Azaziah, with harps

---

a 14:11 "Baal Perazim" means "The Lord who breaks out".

tuned to the eight-stringed lyre, to lead. 22 Chenaniah, chief of the Levites, was over the singing. He taught the singers, because he was skilful. 23 Berechiah and Elkanah were doorkeepers for the ark. 24 Shebaniah, Joshaphat, Nethanel, Amasai, Zechariah, Benaiah, and Eliezer, the priests, blew the trumpets before God's ark; and Obed-Edom and Jehiah were doorkeepers for the ark.

25 So David, the elders of Israel, and the captains over thousands went to bring the ark of the LORD's covenant up out of the house of Obed-Edom with joy. 26 When God helped the Levites who bore the ark of the LORD's covenant, they sacrificed seven bulls and seven rams. 27 David was clothed with a robe of fine linen, as were all the Levites who bore the ark, the singers, and Chenaniah the choir master with the singers; and David had an ephod of linen on him. 28 Thus all Israel brought the ark of the LORD's covenant up with shouting, with sound of the cornet, with trumpets, and with cymbals, sounding aloud with stringed instruments and harps. 29 As the ark of the LORD's covenant came to David's city, Michal the daughter of Saul looked out at the window, and saw king David dancing and playing; and she despised him in her heart.

16

1 They brought in God's ark, and set it in the middle of the tent that David had pitched for it; and they offered burnt offerings and peace offerings before God. 2 When David had finished offering the burnt offering and the peace offerings, he blessed the people in the LORD's name. 3 He gave to everyone of Israel, both man and woman, to everyone a loaf of bread, a portion of meat, and a cake of raisins.

4 He appointed some of the Levites to minister before the LORD's ark, and to commemorate, to thank, and to praise the LORD, the God of Israel: 5 Asaph the chief, and second to him Zechariah, then Jeiel, Shemiramoth, Jehiel, Mattithiah, Eliab, Benaiah, Obed-Edom, and Jeiel, with stringed instruments and with harps; and Asaph with cymbals, sounding aloud; 6 with Benaiah and Jahaziel the priests with trumpets continually, before the ark of the covenant of God.

7 Then on that day David first ordained giving of thanks to the LORD by the hand of Asaph and his brothers.

8 Oh give thanks to the LORD.
Call on his name.
Make what he has done known amongst the peoples.
9 Sing to him.
Sing praises to him.
Tell of all his marvellous works.
10 Glory in his holy name.
Let the heart of those who seek the LORD rejoice.
11 Seek the LORD and his strength.
Seek his face forever more.
12 Remember his marvellous works that he has done,
his wonders, and the judgements of his mouth,
13 you offspring[a] of Israel his servant,
you children of Jacob, his chosen ones.

14 He is the LORD our God.
His judgements are in all the earth.
15 Remember his covenant forever,
the word which he commanded to a thousand generations,
16 the covenant which he made with Abraham,
his oath to Isaac.
17 He confirmed it to Jacob for a statute,
and to Israel for an everlasting covenant,
18 saying, "I will give you the land of Canaan,
The lot of your inheritance,"
19 when you were but a few men in number,
yes, very few, and foreigners in it.
20 They went about from nation to nation,
from one kingdom to another people.
21 He allowed no man to do them wrong.
Yes, he reproved kings for their sakes,
22 "Don't touch my anointed ones!
Do my prophets no harm!"

23 Sing to the LORD, all the earth!
Display his salvation from day to day.
24 Declare his glory amongst the nations,
and his marvellous works amongst all the peoples.
25 For great is the LORD, and greatly to be praised.
He also is to be feared above all gods.
26 For all the gods of the peoples are idols,
but the LORD made the heavens.
27 Honour and majesty are before him.
Strength and gladness are in his place.
28 Ascribe to the LORD, you families of the peoples,
ascribe to the LORD glory and strength!
29 Ascribe to the LORD the glory due to his name.
Bring an offering, and come before him.
Worship the LORD in holy array.
30 Tremble before him, all the earth.
The world also is established that it can't be moved.

31 Let the heavens be glad,
and let the earth rejoice!
Let them say amongst the nations, "The LORD reigns!"
32 Let the sea roar, and its fullness!
Let the field exult, and all that is in it!
33 Then the trees of the forest will sing for joy before the LORD,
for he comes to judge the earth.
34 Oh give thanks to the LORD, for he is good,
for his loving kindness endures forever.
35 Say, "Save us, God of our salvation!
Gather us together and deliver us from the nations,
to give thanks to your holy name,
to triumph in your praise."
36 Blessed be the LORD, the God of Israel,
from everlasting even to everlasting.
All the people said, "Amen," and praised the LORD.

37 So he left Asaph and his brothers there before the ark of the LORD's covenant, to minister before the ark continually, as every day's work required; 38 and Obed-Edom with their sixty-eight relatives; Obed-Edom also the son of Jeduthun and Hosah to be doorkeepers; 39 and Zadok the priest and his brothers the priests, before the LORD's tabernacle in the high place that was at Gibeon, 40 to offer burnt offerings to the LORD on the altar of burnt offering continually morning and evening, even according to all that is written in the LORD's law, which he commanded to Israel; 41 and with them Heman and Jeduthun and the rest who were chosen, who were mentioned by name, to give thanks to the LORD, because his loving kindness endures forever; 42 and with them Heman and Jeduthun with trumpets and cymbals for those that should sound aloud, and with instruments for the songs of God, and the sons of Jeduthun to be at the gate. 43 All the people departed, each man to his house; and David returned to bless his house.

17

1 When David was living in his house, David said to Nathan the prophet, "Behold, I live in a cedar house, but the ark of the LORD's covenant is in a tent."

2 Nathan said to David, "Do all that is in your heart; for God is with you."

3 That same night, the word of God came to Nathan, saying, 4 "Go and tell David my servant, 'The LORD says, "You shall not build me a house to dwell in; 5 for I have not lived in a house since the day that I brought up Israel to this day, but have gone from tent to tent, and from one tent to another. 6 In all places in which I have walked with all Israel, did I speak a word with any of the judges of Israel, whom I commanded to be shepherd of my people, saying, 'Why have you not built me a house of cedar?'"'

7 "Now therefore, you shall tell my servant David, 'The LORD of Armies says, "I took you from the sheep pen, from following the sheep, to be prince over my people Israel. 8 I have been with you wherever you have gone, and have cut off all your enemies from before you. I will make you a name like the name of the great ones who are in the earth. 9 I will appoint a place for my people Israel, and will plant them, that they may dwell in their own place, and be moved no more. The children of wickedness will not waste them any more, as at the first, 10 and from the day that I commanded judges to be over my people Israel. I will subdue all your enemies. Moreover I tell you that the LORD will build you a house. 11 It will happen, when your days are fulfilled that you must go to be with your fathers, that I will set up your offspring after you, who will be of your sons; and I will establish his kingdom. 12 He will build me a house, and I will establish his throne forever. 13 I will be his father, and he will be my son. I will not take my loving kindness away from him, as I took it from him who was before you; 14 but I will settle him in my house and in my kingdom forever. His throne will be established forever."'" 15 According to all these words, and according to all this vision, so Nathan spoke to David.

16 Then David the king went in and sat before the LORD; and he said, "Who am I, LORD God, and what is my house, that you have brought me this far? 17 This was a small thing in your eyes, O God, but you have spoken of your servant's house for a great while to come, and have respected me according to the standard of a man of high degree, LORD God. 18 What can David say yet more to you concerning the honour which is done to your servant? For you know your servant. 19 LORD, for your servant's sake, and according to your own heart, you have done all this greatness, to make known all these great things. 20 LORD, there is no one like you, neither is there any God besides you, according to all that we have heard with our ears. 21 What one nation in the earth is like your people Israel, whom God went to redeem to himself for a people, to make you a name by great and awesome things, in driving out nations from before your people whom you redeemed out of Egypt? 22 For you made your people Israel your own people forever; and you, LORD, became their God. 23 Now, LORD, let the word that you have spoken concerning your servant, and concerning his house, be established forever, and do as you have spoken. 24 Let your name be established and magnified forever, saying, 'The LORD of Armies is the God of Israel, even a God to Israel. The house of David your servant is established before you.' 25 For you, my God, have revealed to your servant that you will build him a house. Therefore your servant has found courage to pray before you. 26 Now, LORD, you are God, and have promised this good thing to your servant. 27 Now it has pleased you to

---

a 16:13 or, seed

bless the house of your servant, that it may continue forever before you; for you, LORD, have blessed, and it is blessed forever."

18

1 After this, David defeated the Philistines and subdued them, and took Gath and its towns out of the hand of the Philistines. 2 He defeated Moab; and the Moabites became servants to David and brought tribute. 3 David defeated Hadadezer king of Zobah, towards Hamath, as he went to establish his dominion by the river Euphrates. 4 David took from him one thousand chariots, seven thousand horsemen, and twenty thousand footmen; and David hamstrung all the chariot horses, but reserved of them enough for one hundred chariots. 5 When the Syrians of Damascus came to help Hadadezer king of Zobah, David struck twenty-two thousand men of the Syrians. 6 Then David put garrisons in Syria of Damascus; and the Syrians became servants to David and brought tribute. The LORD gave victory to David wherever he went. 7 David took the shields of gold that were on the servants of Hadadezer, and brought them to Jerusalem. 8 From Tibhath and from Cun, cities of Hadadezer, David took very much bronze, with which Solomon made the bronze sea, the pillars, and the vessels of bronze.

9 When Tou king of Hamath heard that David had struck all the army of Hadadezer king of Zobah, 10 he sent Hadoram his son to King David to greet him and to bless him, because he had fought against Hadadezer and struck him (for Hadadezer had wars with Tou); and he had with him all kinds of vessels of gold and silver and bronze. 11 King David also dedicated these to the LORD, with the silver and the gold that he carried away from all the nations: from Edom, from Moab, from the children of Ammon, from the Philistines, and from Amalek.

12 Moreover Abishai the son of Zeruiah struck eighteen thousand of the Edomites in the Valley of Salt. 13 He put garrisons in Edom; and all the Edomites became servants to David. The LORD gave victory to David wherever he went.

14 David reigned over all Israel; and he executed justice and righteousness for all his people. 15 Joab the son of Zeruiah was over the army; Jehoshaphat the son of Ahilud was recorder; 16 Zadok the son of Ahitub and Abimelech the son of Abiathar were priests; Shavsha was scribe; 17 and Benaiah the son of Jehoiada was over the Cherethites and the Pelethites; and the sons of David were chief officials serving the king.

19

1 After this, Nahash the king of the children of Ammon died, and his son reigned in his place. 2 David said, "I will show kindness to Hanun the son of Nahash, because his father showed kindness to me."

So David sent messengers to comfort him concerning his father. David's servants came into the land of the children of Ammon to Hanun to comfort him. 3 But the princes of the children of Ammon said to Hanun, "Do you think that David honours your father, in that he has sent comforters to you? Haven't his servants come to you to search, to overthrow, and to spy out the land?" 4 So Hanun took David's servants, shaved them, and cut off their garments in the middle at their buttocks, and sent them away. 5 Then some people went and told David how the men were treated. He sent to meet them; for the men were greatly humiliated. The king said, "Stay at Jericho until your beards have grown, and then return."

6 When the children of Ammon saw that they had made themselves odious to David, Hanun and the children of Ammon sent one thousand talents[a] of silver to hire chariots and horsemen out of Mesopotamia, out of Aram-maacah, and out of Zobah. 7 So they hired for themselves thirty-two thousand chariots, and the king of Maacah with his people, who came and encamped near Medeba. The children of Ammon gathered themselves together from their cities, and came to battle. 8 When David heard of it, he sent Joab with all the army of the mighty men. 9 The children of Ammon came out, and put the battle in array at the gate of the city; and the kings who had come were by themselves in the field.

10 Now when Joab saw that the battle was set against him before and behind, he chose some of all the choice men of Israel, and put them in array against the Syrians. 11 The rest of the people he committed into the hand of Abishai his brother; and they put themselves in array against the children of Ammon. 12 He said, "If the Syrians are too strong for me, then you are to help me; but if the children of Ammon are too strong for you, then I will help you. 13 Be courageous, and let's be strong for our people and for the cities of our God. May the LORD do that which seems good to him."

14 So Joab and the people who were with him came near to the front of the Syrians to the battle; and they fled before him. 15 When the children of Ammon saw that the Syrians had fled, they likewise fled before Abishai his brother, and entered into the city. Then Joab came to Jerusalem.

16 When the Syrians saw that they were defeated by Israel, they sent messengers and called out the Syrians who were beyond the River,[b] with Shophach the captain of the army of Hadadezer leading them. 17 David was told that, so he gathered all Israel together, passed over the Jordan, came to them, and set the battle in array against them. So when David had put the battle in array against the Syrians, they fought with him. 18 The Syrians fled before Israel; and David killed of the Syrian men seven thousand charioteers and forty thousand footmen, and also killed Shophach the captain of the army. 19 When the servants of Hadadezer saw that they were defeated by Israel, they made peace with David and served him. The Syrians would not help the children of Ammon any more.

20

1 At the time of the return of the year, at the time when kings go out, Joab led out the army and wasted the country of the children of Ammon, and came and besieged Rabbah. But David stayed at Jerusalem. Joab struck Rabbah, and overthrew it. 2 David took the crown of their king from off his head, and found it to weigh a talent of gold,[c] and there were precious stones in it. It was set on David's head, and he brought very much plunder out of the city. 3 He brought out the people who were in it, and had them cut with saws, with iron picks, and with axes. David did so to all the cities of the children of Ammon. Then David and all the people returned to Jerusalem.

4 After this, war arose at Gezer with the Philistines. Then Sibbecai the Hushathite killed Sippai, of the sons of the giant; and they were subdued. 5 Again there was war with the Philistines; and Elhanan the son of Jair killed Lahmi the brother of Goliath the Gittite, the staff of whose spear was like a weaver's beam. 6 There was again war at Gath, where there was a man of great stature, who had twenty-four fingers and toes, six on each hand and six on each foot; and he also was born to the giant. 7 When he defied Israel, Jonathan the son of Shimea, David's brother, killed him. 8 These were born to the giant in Gath; and they fell by the hand of David and by the hand of his servants.

21

1 Satan stood up against Israel, and moved David to take a census of Israel. 2 David said to Joab and to the princes of the people, "Go, count Israel from Beersheba even to Dan; and bring me word, that I may know how many there are."

3 Joab said, "May the LORD make his people a hundred times as many as they are. But, my lord the king, aren't they all my lord's servants? Why does my lord require this thing? Why will he be a cause of guilt to Israel?"

4 Nevertheless the king's word prevailed against Joab. Therefore Joab departed and went throughout all Israel, then came to Jerusalem. 5 Joab gave the sum of the census of the people to David. All those of Israel were one million one hundred thousand men who drew a sword; and in Judah were four hundred and seventy thousand men who drew a sword. 6 But he didn't count Levi and Benjamin amongst them, for the king's word was abominable to Joab.

7 God was displeased with this thing; therefore he struck Israel. 8 David said to God, "I have sinned greatly, in that I have done this thing. But now put away, I beg you, the iniquity of your servant, for I have done very foolishly."

9 The LORD spoke to Gad, David's seer, saying, 10 "Go and speak to David, saying, 'The LORD says, "I offer you three things. Choose one of them, that I may do it to you."'"

11 So Gad came to David and said to him, "The LORD says, 'Take your choice: 12 either three years of famine; or three months to be consumed before your foes, while the sword of your enemies overtakes you; or else three days of the sword of the LORD, even pestilence in the land, and the LORD's angel destroying throughout all the borders of Israel. Now therefore consider what answer I shall return to him who sent me.'"

13 David said to Gad, "I am in distress. Let me fall, I pray, into the LORD's hand, for his mercies are very great. Don't let me fall into man's hand."

14 So the LORD sent a pestilence on Israel, and seventy thousand men of Israel fell. 15 God sent an angel to Jerusalem to destroy it. As he was about to destroy, the LORD saw, and he relented of the disaster, and said to the destroying angel, "It is enough. Now withdraw your hand." the LORD's angel was standing by the threshing floor of Ornan the Jebusite. 16 David lifted up his eyes, and saw the LORD's angel standing between earth and the sky, having a drawn sword in his hand stretched out over Jerusalem.

Then David and the elders, clothed in sackcloth, fell on their faces. 17 David said to God, "Isn't it I who commanded the people to be counted? It is even I who have sinned and done very wickedly; but these sheep, what have they done? Please let your hand, O LORD my God, be against me and against my father's house; but not against your people, that they should be plagued."

18 Then the LORD's angel commanded Gad to tell David that David should go up and raise an altar to the LORD on the threshing floor of Ornan the Jebusite. 19 David went up at the saying of Gad, which he spoke in the LORD's name.

20 Ornan turned back and saw the angel; and his four sons who were with him hid themselves. Now Ornan was threshing wheat. 21 As David came to Ornan, Ornan looked and saw David, and went out of the threshing floor, and bowed himself to David with his face to the ground.

22 Then David said to Ornan, "Sell me the place of this threshing floor, that I may build an altar to the LORD on it. You shall sell it to me for the full price, that the plague may be stopped from afflicting the people."

23 Ornan said to David, "Take it for yourself, and let my lord the king do that which is good in his eyes. Behold, I give the oxen for burnt offerings, and the threshing instruments for wood, and the wheat for the meal offering. I give it all."

24 King David said to Ornan, "No, but I will most certainly buy it for the full price. For I will not take that which is yours for the LORD, nor offer a burnt offering that costs me nothing."

---

a 19:6 A talent is about 30 kilograms or 66 pounds, so 1000 talents is about 30 metric tonnes

b 19:16 or, the Euphrates River

c 20:2 A talent is about 30 kilograms or 66 pounds or 965 Troy ounces

25 So David gave to Ornan six hundred shekels[a] of gold by weight for the place. 26 David built an altar to the LORD there, and offered burnt offerings and peace offerings, and called on the LORD; and he answered him from the sky by fire on the altar of burnt offering. 27 Then The LORD commanded the angel, and he put his sword back into its sheath. 28 At that time, when David saw that the LORD had answered him in the threshing floor of Ornan the Jebusite, then he sacrificed there. 29 For the LORD's tabernacle, which Moses made in the wilderness, and the altar of burnt offering, were at that time in the high place at Gibeon. 30 But David couldn't go before it to enquire of God, for he was afraid because of the sword of the LORD's angel.

22

1 Then David said, "This is the house of the LORD God, and this is the altar of burnt offering for Israel."

2 David gave orders to gather together the foreigners who were in the land of Israel; and he set masons to cut dressed stones to build God's house. 3 David prepared iron in abundance for the nails for the doors of the gates and for the couplings, and bronze in abundance without weight, 4 and cedar trees without number, for the Sidonians and the people of Tyre brought cedar trees in abundance to David. 5 David said, "Solomon my son is young and tender, and the house that is to be built for the LORD must be exceedingly magnificent, of fame and of glory throughout all countries. I will therefore make preparation for it." So David prepared abundantly before his death. 6 Then he called for Solomon his son, and commanded him to build a house for the LORD, the God of Israel. 7 David said to Solomon his son, "As for me, it was in my heart to build a house to the name of the LORD my God. 8 But the LORD's word came to me, saying, 'You have shed blood abundantly and have made great wars. You shall not build a house to my name, because you have shed much blood on the earth in my sight. 9 Behold, a son shall be born to you, who shall be a man of peace. I will give him rest from all his enemies all around; for his name shall be Solomon, and I will give peace and quietness to Israel in his days. 10 He shall build a house for my name; and he will be my son, and I will be his father; and I will establish the throne of his kingdom over Israel forever.' 11 Now, my son, may the LORD be with you and prosper you, and build the house of the LORD your God, as he has spoken concerning you. 12 May the LORD give you discretion and understanding, and put you in charge of Israel, so that you may keep the law of the LORD your God. 13 Then you will prosper, if you observe to do the statutes and the ordinances which the LORD gave Moses concerning Israel. Be strong and courageous. Don't be afraid and don't be dismayed. 14 Now, behold, in my affliction I have prepared for the LORD's house one hundred thousand talents[b] of gold, one million talents[c] of silver, and bronze and iron without weight; for it is in abundance. I have also prepared timber and stone; and you may add to them. 15 There are also workmen with you in abundance—cutters and workers of stone and timber, and all kinds of men who are skilful in every kind of work; 16 of the gold, the silver, the bronze, and the iron, there is no number. Arise and be doing, and may the LORD be with you."

17 David also commanded all the princes of Israel to help Solomon his son, saying, 18 "Isn't the LORD your God with you? Hasn't he given you rest on every side? For he has delivered the inhabitants of the land into my hand; and the land is subdued before the LORD and before his people. 19 Now set your heart and your soul to follow the LORD your God. Arise therefore, and build the sanctuary of the LORD God, to bring the ark of the LORD's covenant and the holy vessels of God into the house that is to be built for the LORD's name."

23

1 Now David was old and full of days; and he made Solomon his son king over Israel. 2 He gathered together all the princes of Israel, with the priests and the Levites. 3 The Levites were counted from thirty years old and upward; and their number by their polls, man by man, was thirty-eight thousand. 4 David said, "Of these, twenty-four thousand were to oversee the work of the LORD's house, six thousand were officers and judges, 5 four thousand were doorkeepers, and four thousand praised the LORD with the instruments which I made for giving praise."

6 David divided them into divisions according to the sons of Levi: Gershon, Kohath, and Merari.

7 Of the Gershonites: Ladan and Shimei. 8 The sons of Ladan: Jehiel the chief, Zetham, and Joel, three. 9 The sons of Shimei: Shelomoth, Haziel, and Haran, three. These were the heads of the fathers' households of Ladan. 10 The sons of Shimei: Jahath, Zina, Jeush, and Beriah. These four were the sons of Shimei. 11 Jahath was the chief, and Zizah the second; but Jeush and Beriah didn't have many sons; therefore they became a fathers' house in one reckoning.

12 The sons of Kohath: Amram, Izhar, Hebron, and Uzziel, four. 13 The sons of Amram: Aaron and Moses; and Aaron was separated that he should sanctify the most holy things, he and his sons forever, to burn incense before the LORD, to minister to him, and to bless in his name forever. 14 But as for Moses the man of God, his sons were named amongst the tribe of Levi. 15 The sons of Moses: Gershom and Eliezer. 16 The sons of Gershom: Shebuel the chief. 17 The son of Eliezer was Rehabiah the chief; and Eliezer had no other sons, but the sons of Rehabiah were very many. 18 The son of Izhar: Shelomith the chief. 19 The sons of Hebron: Jeriah the chief, Amariah

the second, Jahaziel the third, and Jekameam the fourth. 20 The sons of Uzziel: Micah the chief, and Isshiah the second.

21 The sons of Merari: Mahli and Mushi. The sons of Mahli: Eleazar and Kish. 22 Eleazar died, and had no sons, but daughters only; and their relatives, the sons of Kish, took them as wives. 23 The sons of Mushi: Mahli, Eder, and Jeremoth, three.

24 These were the sons of Levi after their fathers' houses, even the heads of the fathers' houses of those who were counted individually, in the number of names by their polls, who did the work for the service of the LORD's house, from twenty years old and upward. 25 For David said, "The LORD, the God of Israel, has given rest to his people; and he dwells in Jerusalem forever. 26 Also the Levites will no longer need to carry the tabernacle and all its vessels for its service." 27 For by the last words of David the sons of Levi were counted, from twenty years old and upward. 28 For their duty was to wait on the sons of Aaron for the service of the LORD's house—in the courts, in the rooms, and in the purifying of all holy things, even the work of the service of God's house; 29 for the show bread also, and for the fine flour for a meal offering, whether of unleavened wafers, or of that which is baked in the pan, or of that which is soaked, and for all measurements of quantity and size; 30 and to stand every morning to thank and praise the LORD, and likewise in the evening; 31 and to offer all burnt offerings to the LORD on the Sabbaths, on the new moons, and on the set feasts, in number according to the ordinance concerning them, continually before the LORD; 32 and that they should keep the duty of the Tent of Meeting, the duty of the holy place, and the duty of the sons of Aaron their brothers for the service of the LORD's house.

24

1 These were the divisions of the sons of Aaron. The sons of Aaron: Nadab, Abihu, Eleazar, and Ithamar. 2 But Nadab and Abihu died before their father, and had no children; therefore Eleazar and Ithamar served as priests. 3 David, with Zadok of the sons of Eleazar and Ahimelech of the sons of Ithamar, divided them according to their ordering in their service. 4 There were more chief men found of the sons of Eleazar than of the sons of Ithamar; and they were divided like this: of the sons of Eleazar there were sixteen, heads of fathers' houses; and of the sons of Ithamar, according to their fathers' houses, eight. 5 Thus they were divided impartially by drawing lots; for there were princes of the sanctuary and princes of God, both of the sons of Eleazar, and of the sons of Ithamar. 6 Shemaiah the son of Nethanel the scribe, who was of the Levites, wrote them in the presence of the king, the princes, Zadok the priest, Ahimelech the son of Abiathar, and the heads of the fathers' households of the priests and of the Levites; one fathers' house being taken for Eleazar, and one taken for Ithamar.

7 Now the first lot came out to Jehoiarib, the second to Jedaiah, 8 the third to Harim, the fourth to Seorim, 9 the fifth to Malchijah, the sixth to Mijamin, 10 the seventh to Hakkoz, the eighth to Abijah, 11 the ninth to Jeshua, the tenth to Shecaniah, 12 the eleventh to Eliashib, the twelfth to Jakim, 13 the thirteenth to Huppah, the fourteenth to Jeshebeab, 14 the fifteenth to Bilgah, the sixteenth to Immer, 15 the seventeenth to Hezir, the eighteenth to Happizzez, 16 the nineteenth to Pethahiah, the twentieth to Jehezkel, 17 the twenty-first to Jachin, the twenty-second to Gamul, 18 the twenty-third to Delaiah, and the twenty-fourth to Maaziah. 19 This was their ordering in their service, to come into the LORD's house according to the ordinance given to them by Aaron their father, as the LORD, the God of Israel, had commanded him.

20 Of the rest of the sons of Levi: of the sons of Amram, Shubael; of the sons of Shubael, Jehdeiah. 21 Of Rehabiah: of the sons of Rehabiah, Isshiah the chief. 22 Of the Izharites, Shelomoth; of the sons of Shelomoth, Jahath. 23 The sons of Hebron: Jeriah, Amariah the second, Jahaziel the third, and Jekameam the fourth. 24 The sons of Uzziel: Micah; of the sons of Micah, Shamir. 25 The brother of Micah: Isshiah; of the sons of Isshiah, Zechariah. 26 The sons of Merari: Mahli and Mushi. The son of Jaaziah: Beno. 27 The sons of Merari by Jaaziah: Beno, Shoham, Zaccur, and Ibri. 28 Of Mahli: Eleazar, who had no sons. 29 Of Kish, the son of Kish: Jerahmeel. 30 The sons of Mushi: Mahli, Eder, and Jerimoth. These were the sons of the Levites after their fathers' houses. 31 These likewise cast lots even as their brothers the sons of Aaron in the presence of David the king, Zadok, Ahimelech, and the heads of the fathers' households of the priests and of the Levites, the fathers' households of the chief even as those of his younger brother.

25

1 Moreover, David and the captains of the army set apart for the service certain of the sons of Asaph, of Heman, and of Jeduthun, who were to prophesy with harps, with stringed instruments, and with cymbals. The number of those who did the work according to their service was: 2 of the sons of Asaph: Zaccur, Joseph, Nethaniah, and Asharelah. The sons of Asaph were under the hand of Asaph, who prophesied at the order of the king. 3 Of Jeduthun, the sons of Jeduthun: Gedaliah, Zeri, Jeshaiah, Shimei, Hashabiah, and Mattithiah, six, under the hands of their father Jeduthun, who prophesied in giving thanks and praising the LORD with the harp. 4 Of Heman, the sons of Heman: Bukkiah, Mattaniah, Uzziel, Shebuel, Jerimoth, Hananiah, Hanani, Eliathah, Giddalti, Romamti-Ezer, Joshbekashah, Mallothi, Hothir, and Mahazioth. 5 All these were the sons of Heman the king's seer in the words of God, to lift up the horn. God gave to Heman fourteen sons and three daughters. 6 All these were under the

---

a 21:25 A shekel is about 10 grams or about 0.32 Troy ounces, so 600 shekels was about 6 kilograms or about 192 Troy ounces.

b 22:14 A talent is about 30 kilograms or 66 pounds or 965 Troy ounces, so 100,000 talents is about 3 metric tonnes

c 22:14 about 30,000 metric tonnes

hands of their father for song in the LORD's house, with cymbals, stringed instruments, and harps, for the service of God's house: Asaph, Jeduthun, and Heman being under the order of the king. 7 The number of them, with their brothers who were instructed in singing to the LORD, even all who were skilful, was two hundred and eighty-eight. 8 They cast lots for their offices, all alike, the small as well as the great, the teacher as well as the student.

9 Now the first lot came out for Asaph to Joseph; the second to Gedaliah, he and his brothers and sons were twelve; 10 the third to Zaccur, his sons and his brothers, twelve; 11 the fourth to Izri, his sons and his brothers, twelve; 12 the fifth to Nethaniah, his sons and his brothers, twelve; 13 the sixth to Bukkiah, his sons and his brothers, twelve; 14 the seventh to Jesharelah, his sons and his brothers, twelve; 15 the eighth to Jeshaiah, his sons and his brothers, twelve; 16 the ninth to Mattaniah, his sons and his brothers, twelve; 17 the tenth to Shimei, his sons and his brothers, twelve; 18 the eleventh to Azarel, his sons and his brothers, twelve; 19 the twelfth to Hashabiah, his sons and his brothers, twelve; 20 for the thirteenth, Shubael, his sons and his brothers, twelve; 21 for the fourteenth, Mattithiah, his sons and his brothers, twelve; 22 for the fifteenth to Jeremoth, his sons and his brothers, twelve; 23 for the sixteenth to Hananiah, his sons and his brothers, twelve; 24 for the seventeenth to Joshbekashah, his sons and his brothers, twelve; 25 for the eighteenth to Hanani, his sons and his brothers, twelve; 26 for the nineteenth to Mallothi, his sons and his brothers, twelve; 27 for the twentieth to Eliathah, his sons and his brothers, twelve; 28 for the twenty-first to Hothir, his sons and his brothers, twelve; 29 for the twenty-second to Giddalti, his sons and his brothers, twelve; 30 for the twenty-third to Mahazioth, his sons and his brothers, twelve; 31 for the twenty-fourth to Romamti-Ezer, his sons and his brothers, twelve.

26

1 For the divisions of the doorkeepers: of the Korahites, Meshelemiah the son of Kore, of the sons of Asaph. 2 Meshelemiah had sons: Zechariah the firstborn, Jediael the second, Zebadiah the third, Jathniel the fourth, 3 Elam the fifth, Jehohanan the sixth, and Eliehoenai the seventh. 4 Obed-Edom had sons: Shemaiah the firstborn, Jehozabad the second, Joah the third, Sacar the fourth, Nethanel the fifth, 5 Ammiel the sixth, Issachar the seventh, and Peullethai the eighth; for God blessed him. 6 Sons were also born to Shemaiah his son, who ruled over the house of their father; for they were mighty men of valour. 7 The sons of Shemaiah: Othni, Rephael, Obed, and Elzabad, whose relatives were valiant men, Elihu, and Semachiah. 8 All these were of the sons of Obed-Edom with their sons and their brothers, able men in strength for the service: sixty-two of Obed-Edom. 9 Meshelemiah had sons and brothers, eighteen valiant men. 10 Also Hosah, of the children of Merari, had sons: Shimri the chief (for though he was not the firstborn, yet his father made him chief), 11 Hilkiah the second, Tebaliah the third, and Zechariah the fourth. All the sons and brothers of Hosah were thirteen.

12 Of these were the divisions of the doorkeepers, even of the chief men, having offices like their brothers, to minister in the LORD's house. 13 They cast lots, the small as well as the great, according to their fathers' houses, for every gate. 14 The lot eastward fell to Shelemiah. Then for Zechariah his son, a wise counsellor, they cast lots; and his lot came out northward. 15 To Obed-Edom southward; and to his sons the storehouse. 16 To Shuppim and Hosah westward, by the gate of Shallecheth, at the causeway that goes up, watchman opposite watchman. 17 Eastward were six Levites, northward four a day, southward four a day, and for the storehouse two and two. 18 For Parbar westward, four at the causeway, and two at Parbar. 19 These were the divisions of the doorkeepers; of the sons of the Korahites, and of the sons of Merari.

20 Of the Levites, Ahijah was over the treasures of God's house and over the treasures of the dedicated things. 21 The sons of Ladan, the sons of the Gershonites belonging to Ladan, the heads of the fathers' households belonging to Ladan the Gershonite: Jehieli. 22 The sons of Jehieli: Zetham, and Joel his brother, over the treasures of the LORD's house. 23 Of the Amramites, of the Izharites, of the Hebronites, of the Uzzielites: 24 Shebuel the son of Gershom, the son of Moses, was ruler over the treasures. 25 His brothers: of Eliezer, Rehabiah his son, and Jeshaiah his son, and Joram his son, and Zichri his son, and Shelomoth his son. 26 This Shelomoth and his brothers were over all the treasuries of the dedicated things, which David the king, and the heads of the fathers' households, the captains over thousands and hundreds, and the captains of the army, had dedicated. 27 They dedicated some of the plunder won in battles to repair the LORD's house. 28 All that Samuel the seer, Saul the son of Kish, Abner the son of Ner, and Joab the son of Zeruiah had dedicated, whoever had dedicated anything, it was under the hand of Shelomoth and of his brothers.

29 Of the Izharites, Chenaniah and his sons were appointed to the outward business over Israel, for officers and judges. 30 Of the Hebronites, Hashabiah and his brothers, one thousand and seven hundred men of valour, had the oversight of Israel beyond the Jordan westward, for all the business of the LORD and for the service of the king. 31 Of the Hebronites, Jerijah was the chief of the Hebronites, according to their generations by fathers' households. They were sought for in the fortieth year of the reign of David, and mighty men of valour were found amongst them at Jazer of Gilead. 32 His relatives, men of valour, were two thousand and seven hundred, heads of fathers' households, whom King David made overseers over the Reubenites, the Gadites, and the half-tribe of the Manassites, for every matter pertaining to God and for the affairs of the king.

27

1 Now the children of Israel after their number, the heads of fathers' households and the captains of thousands and of hundreds, and their officers who served the king in any matter of the divisions which came in and went out month by month throughout all the months of the year—of every division were twenty-four thousand. 2 Over the first division for the first month was Jashobeam the son of Zabdiel. In his division were twenty-four thousand. 3 He was of the children of Perez, the chief of all the captains of the army for the first month. 4 Over the division of the second month was Dodai the Ahohite and his division, and Mikloth the ruler; and in his division were twenty-four thousand. 5 The third captain of the army for the third month was Benaiah, the son of Jehoiada the chief priest. In his division were twenty-four thousand. 6 This is that Benaiah who was the mighty man of the thirty and over the thirty. Of his division was Ammizabad his son. 7 The fourth captain for the fourth month was Asahel the brother of Joab, and Zebadiah his son after him. In his division were twenty-four thousand. 8 The fifth captain for the fifth month was Shamhuth the Izrahite. In his division were twenty-four thousand. 9 The sixth captain for the sixth month was Ira the son of Ikkesh the Tekoite. In his division were twenty-four thousand. 10 The seventh captain for the seventh month was Helez the Pelonite, of the children of Ephraim. In his division were twenty-four thousand. 11 The eighth captain for the eighth month was Sibbecai the Hushathite, of the Zerahites. In his division were twenty-four thousand. 12 The ninth captain for the ninth month was Abiezer the Anathothite, of the Benjamites. In his division were twenty-four thousand. 13 The tenth captain for the tenth month was Maharai the Netophathite, of the Zerahites. In his division were twenty-four thousand. 14 The eleventh captain for the eleventh month was Benaiah the Pirathonite, of the children of Ephraim. In his division were twenty-four thousand. 15 The twelfth captain for the twelfth month was Heldai the Netophathite, of Othniel. In his division were twenty-four thousand.

16 Furthermore over the tribes of Israel: of the Reubenites, Eliezer the son of Zichri was the ruler; of the Simeonites, Shephatiah the son of Maacah; 17 of Levi, Hashabiah the son of Kemuel; of Aaron, Zadok; 18 of Judah, Elihu, one of the brothers of David; of Issachar, Omri the son of Michael; 19 of Zebulun, Ishmaiah the son of Obadiah; of Naphtali, Jeremoth the son of Azriel; 20 of the children of Ephraim, Hoshea the son of Azaziah; of the half-tribe of Manasseh, Joel the son of Pedaiah; 21 of the half-tribe of Manasseh in Gilead, Iddo the son of Zechariah; of Benjamin, Jaasiel the son of Abner; 22 of Dan, Azarel the son of Jeroham. These were the captains of the tribes of Israel. 23 But David didn't take the number of them from twenty years old and under, because the LORD had said he would increase Israel like the stars of the sky. 24 Joab the son of Zeruiah began to take a census, but didn't finish; and wrath came on Israel for this. The number wasn't put into the account in the chronicles of King David.

25 Over the king's treasures was Azmaveth the son of Adiel. Over the treasures in the fields, in the cities, in the villages, and in the towers was Jonathan the son of Uzziah; 26 Over those who did the work of the field for tillage of the ground was Ezri the son of Chelub. 27 Over the vineyards was Shimei the Ramathite. Over the increase of the vineyards for the wine cellars was Zabdi the Shiphmite. 28 Over the olive trees and the sycamore trees that were in the lowland was Baal Hanan the Gederite. Over the cellars of oil was Joash. 29 Over the herds that fed in Sharon was Shitrai the Sharonite. Over the herds that were in the valleys was Shaphat the son of Adlai. 30 Over the camels was Obil the Ishmaelite. Over the donkeys was Jehdeiah the Meronothite. Over the flocks was Jaziz the Hagrite. 31 All these were the rulers of the property which was King David's.

32 Also Jonathan, David's uncle, was a counsellor, a man of understanding, and a scribe. Jehiel the son of Hachmoni was with the king's sons. 33 Ahithophel was the king's counsellor. Hushai the Archite was the king's friend. 34 After Ahithophel was Jehoiada the son of Benaiah, and Abiathar. Joab was the captain of the king's army.

28

1 David assembled all the princes of Israel, the princes of the tribes, the captains of the companies who served the king by division, the captains of thousands, the captains of hundreds, and the rulers over all the substance and possessions of the king and of his sons, with the officers and the mighty men, even all the mighty men of valour, to Jerusalem. 2 Then David the king stood up on his feet and said, "Hear me, my brothers and my people! As for me, it was in my heart to build a house of rest for the ark of the LORD's covenant, and for the footstool of our God; and I had prepared for the building. 3 But God said to me, 'You shall not build a house for my name, because you are a man of war and have shed blood.' 4 However the LORD, the God of Israel, chose me out of all the house of my father to be king over Israel forever. For he has chosen Judah to be prince; and in the house of Judah, the house of my father; and amongst the sons of my father he took pleasure in me to make me king over all Israel. 5 Of all my sons (for the LORD has given me many sons), he has chosen Solomon my son to sit on the throne of the LORD's kingdom over Israel. 6 He said to me, 'Solomon, your son, shall build my house and my courts; for I have chosen him to be my son, and I will be his father. 7 I will establish his kingdom forever if he continues to do my commandments and my ordinances, as it is today.'

8 Now therefore, in the sight of all Israel, the LORD's assembly, and in the audience of our God, observe and seek out all the commandments of the LORD your God, that you may possess this good land, and leave it for an inheritance to your children after you forever.

9 You, Solomon my son, know the God of your father, and serve him with a perfect heart and with a willing mind; for the LORD searches all hearts, and understands all the imaginations of the thoughts. If you seek him, he will be found by you; but if you forsake him, he will cast you off forever. 10 Take heed now, for the LORD has chosen you to build a house for the sanctuary. Be strong, and do it."

11 Then David gave to Solomon his son the plans for the porch of the temple, for its houses, for its treasuries, for its upper rooms, for its inner rooms, for the place of the mercy seat; 12 and the plans of all that he had by the Spirit, for the courts of the LORD's house, for all the surrounding rooms, for the treasuries of God's house, and for the treasuries of the dedicated things; 13 also for the divisions of the priests and the Levites, for all the work of the service of the LORD's house, and for all the vessels of service in the LORD's house— 14 of gold by weight for the gold for all vessels of every kind of service, for all the vessels of silver by weight, for all vessels of every kind of service; 15 by weight also for the lamp stands of gold, and for its lamps, of gold, by weight for every lamp stand and for its lamps; and for the lamp stands of silver, by weight for every lamp stand and for its lamps, according to the use of every lamp stand; 16 and the gold by weight for the tables of show bread, for every table; and silver for the tables of silver; 17 and the forks, the basins, and the cups, of pure gold; and for the golden bowls by weight for every bowl; and for the silver bowls by weight for every bowl; 18 and for the altar of incense, refined gold by weight; and gold for the plans for the chariot, and the cherubim that spread out and cover the ark of the LORD's covenant. 19 "All this", David said, "I have been made to understand in writing from the LORD's hand, even all the works of this pattern."

20 David said to Solomon his son, "Be strong and courageous, and do it. Don't be afraid, nor be dismayed, for the LORD God, even my God, is with you. He will not fail you nor forsake you, until all the work for the service of the LORD's house is finished. 21 Behold, there are the divisions of the priests and the Levites for all the service of God's house. Every willing man who has skill for any kind of service shall be with you in all kinds of work. Also the captains and all the people will be entirely at your command."

29

1 David the king said to all the assembly, "Solomon my son, whom alone God has chosen, is yet young and tender, and the work is great; for the palace is not for man, but for the LORD God. 2 Now I have prepared with all my might for the house of my God the gold for the things of gold, the silver for the things of silver, the bronze for the things of bronze, iron for the things of iron, and wood for the things of wood, also onyx stones, stones to be set, stones for inlaid work of various colours, all kinds of precious stones, and marble stones in abundance. 3 In addition, because I have set my affection on the house of my God, since I have a treasure of my own of gold and silver, I give it to the house of my God, over and above all that I have prepared for the holy house: 4 even three thousand talents of gold,[a] of the gold of Ophir, and seven thousand talents[b] of refined silver, with which to overlay the walls of the houses; 5 of gold for the things of gold, and of silver for the things of silver, and for all kinds of work to be made by the hands of artisans. Who then offers willingly to consecrate himself today to the LORD?"

6 Then the princes of the fathers' households, and the princes of the tribes of Israel, and the captains of thousands and of hundreds, with the rulers over the king's work, offered willingly; 7 and they gave for the service of God's house of gold five thousand talents[c] and ten thousand darics,[d] of silver ten thousand talents, of bronze eighteen thousand talents, and of iron one hundred thousand talents. 8 People with whom precious stones were found gave them to the treasure of the LORD's house, under the hand of Jehiel the Gershonite. 9 Then the people rejoiced, because they offered willingly, because with a perfect heart they offered willingly to the LORD; and David the king also rejoiced with great joy.

10 Therefore David blessed the LORD before all the assembly; and David said, "You are blessed, LORD, the God of Israel our father, forever and ever. 11 Yours, LORD, is the greatness, the power, the glory, the victory, and the majesty! For all that is in the heavens and in the earth is yours. Yours is the kingdom, LORD, and you are exalted as head above all. 12 Both riches and honour come from you, and you rule over all! In your hand is power and might! It is in your hand to make great, and to give strength to all! 13 Now therefore, our God, we thank you and praise your glorious name. 14 But who am I, and what is my people, that we should be able to offer so willingly as this? For all things come from you, and we have given you of your own. 15 For we are strangers before you and foreigners, as all our fathers were. Our days on the earth are as a shadow, and there is no remaining. 16 LORD our God, all this store that we have prepared to build you a house for your holy name comes from your hand, and is all your own. 17 I know also, my God, that you try the heart and have pleasure in uprightness. As for me, in the uprightness of my heart I have willingly offered all these things. Now I have seen with joy your people, who are present here, offer willingly to you. 18 LORD, the God of Abraham, of Isaac, and of Israel, our fathers, keep this desire forever in the thoughts of the heart of your people, and prepare their heart for you; 19 and give to Solomon my son a perfect heart, to keep your commandments, your

testimonies, and your statutes, and to do all these things, and to build the palace, for which I have made provision."

20 Then David said to all the assembly, "Now bless the LORD your God!"

All the assembly blessed the LORD, the God of their fathers, and bowed down their heads and prostrated themselves before the LORD and the king. 21 They sacrificed sacrifices to the LORD and offered burnt offerings to the LORD on the next day after that day, even one thousand bulls, one thousand rams, and one thousand lambs, with their drink offerings and sacrifices in abundance for all Israel, 22 and ate and drank before the LORD on that day with great gladness. They made Solomon the son of David king the second time, and anointed him before the LORD to be prince, and Zadok to be priest.

23 Then Solomon sat on the throne of the LORD as king instead of David his father, and prospered; and all Israel obeyed him. 24 All the princes, the mighty men, and also all of the sons of King David submitted themselves to Solomon the king. 25 The LORD magnified Solomon exceedingly in the sight of all Israel, and gave to him such royal majesty as had not been on any king before him in Israel.

26 Now David the son of Jesse reigned over all Israel. 27 The time that he reigned over Israel was forty years; he reigned seven years in Hebron, and he reigned thirty-three years in Jerusalem. 28 He died at a good old age, full of days, riches, and honour; and Solomon his son reigned in his place. 29 Now the acts of David the king, first and last, behold, they are written in the history of Samuel the seer, and in the history of Nathan the prophet, and in the history of Gad the seer, 30 with all his reign and his might, and the events that involved him, Israel, and all the kingdoms of the lands.

---

a 29:4 A talent is about 30 kilograms or 66 pounds or 965 Troy ounces, so 3000 talents is about 90 metric tonnes
b 29:4 about 210 metric tonnes

c 29:7 A talent is about 30 kilograms or 66 pounds or 965 Troy ounces, so 5000 talents is about 150 metric tonnes
d 29:7 a daric was a gold coin issued by a Persian king, weighing about 8.4 grams or about 0.27 troy ounces each.

The Second Book of Chronicles

1

1 Solomon the son of David was firmly established in his kingdom, and the LORD[a] his God[b] was with him, and made him exceedingly great.

2 Solomon spoke to all Israel, to the captains of thousands and of hundreds, to the judges, and to every prince in all Israel, the heads of the fathers' households. 3 Then Solomon, and all the assembly with him, went to the high place that was at Gibeon; for God's Tent of Meeting was there, which the LORD's servant Moses had made in the wilderness. 4 But David had brought God's ark up from Kiriath Jearim to the place that David had prepared for it; for he had pitched a tent for it at Jerusalem. 5 Moreover the bronze altar that Bezalel the son of Uri, the son of Hur, had made was there before the LORD's tabernacle; and Solomon and the assembly were seeking counsel there. 6 Solomon went up there to the bronze altar before the LORD, which was at the Tent of Meeting, and offered one thousand burnt offerings on it.

7 That night, God appeared to Solomon and said to him, "Ask for what you want me to give you."

8 Solomon said to God, "You have shown great loving kindness to David my father, and have made me king in his place. 9 Now, LORD God, let your promise to David my father be established; for you have made me king over a people like the dust of the earth in multitude. 10 Now give me wisdom and knowledge, that I may go out and come in before this people; for who can judge this great people of yours?"

11 God said to Solomon, "Because this was in your heart, and you have not asked riches, wealth, honour, or the life of those who hate you, nor yet have you asked for long life; but have asked for wisdom and knowledge for yourself, that you may judge my people, over whom I have made you king, 12 therefore wisdom and knowledge is granted to you. I will give you riches, wealth, and honour, such as none of the kings have had who have been before you, and none after you will have."

13 So Solomon came from the high place that was at Gibeon, from before the Tent of Meeting, to Jerusalem; and he reigned over Israel.

14 Solomon gathered chariots and horsemen. He had one thousand and four hundred chariots and twelve thousand horsemen that he placed in the chariot cities, and with the king at Jerusalem. 15 The king made silver and gold to be as common as stones in Jerusalem, and he made cedars to be as common as the sycamore trees that are in the lowland. 16 The horses which Solomon had were brought out of Egypt and from Kue. The king's merchants purchased them from Kue. 17 They imported from Egypt then exported a chariot for six hundred pieces of silver and a horse for one hundred and fifty.[c] They also exported them to the Hittite kings and the Syrian[d] kings.

2

1 Now Solomon decided to build a house for the LORD's name, and a house for his kingdom. 2 Solomon counted out seventy thousand men to bear burdens, eighty thousand men who were stone cutters in the mountains, and three thousand and six hundred to oversee them.

3 Solomon sent to Huram the king of Tyre, saying, "As you dealt with David my father, and sent him cedars to build him a house in which to dwell, so deal with me. 4 Behold,[e] I am about to build a house for the name of the LORD my God, to dedicate it to him, to burn before him incense of sweet spices, for the continual show bread, and for the burnt offerings morning and evening, on the Sabbaths, on the new moons, and on the set feasts of the LORD our God. This is an ordinance forever to Israel.

5 "The house which I am building will be great, for our God is greater than all gods. 6 But who is able to build him a house, since heaven and the heaven of heavens can't contain him? Who am I then, that I should build him a house, except just to burn incense before him?

7 "Now therefore send me a man skilful to work in gold, in silver, in bronze, in iron, and in purple, crimson, and blue, and who knows how to engrave engravings, to be with the skilful men who are with me in Judah and in Jerusalem, whom David my father provided.

8 "Send me also cedar trees, cypress trees, and algum trees out of Lebanon, for I know that your servants know how to cut timber in Lebanon. Behold, my servants will be with your servants, 9 even to prepare me timber in abundance; for the house which I am about to build will be great and wonderful. 10 Behold, I will give to your servants, the cutters who cut timber, twenty thousand cors[f] of beaten wheat, twenty thousand baths[g] of barley, twenty thousand baths of wine, and twenty thousand baths of oil."

11 Then Huram the king of Tyre answered in writing, which he sent to Solomon, "Because the LORD loves his people, he has made you king over them." 12 Huram continued, "Blessed be the LORD, the God of Israel, who made heaven and earth, who has given to David the king a wise son, endowed with discretion and understanding, who would build a house for the LORD and a house for his kingdom.

13 Now I have sent a skilful man, endowed with understanding, Huram-abi,[h] 14 the son of a woman of the daughters of Dan; and his father was a man of Tyre. He is skilful to work in gold, in silver, in bronze, in iron, in stone, in timber, in purple, in blue, in fine linen, and in crimson, also to engrave any kind of engraving and to devise any device, that there may be a place prepared to him with your skilful men, and with the skilful men of my lord David your father.

15 "Now therefore, the wheat, the barley, the oil, and the wine which my lord has spoken of, let him send to his servants; 16 and we will cut wood out of Lebanon, as much as you need. We will bring it to you in rafts by sea to Joppa; then you shall carry it up to Jerusalem."

17 Solomon counted all the foreigners who were in the land of Israel, after the census with which David his father had counted them; and they found one hundred and fifty-three thousand and six hundred. 18 He set seventy thousand of them to bear burdens, eighty thousand who were stone cutters in the mountains, and three thousand and six hundred overseers to assign the people their work.

3

1 Then Solomon began to build the LORD's house at Jerusalem on Mount Moriah, where the LORD appeared to David his father, which he prepared in the place that David had appointed, on the threshing floor of Ornan the Jebusite. 2 He began to build in the second day of the second month, in the fourth year of his reign. 3 Now these are the foundations which Solomon laid for the building of God's house: the length by cubits[i] after the first measure was sixty cubits, and the width twenty cubits. 4 The porch that was in front, its length, across the width of the house, was twenty cubits, and the height one hundred and twenty; and he overlaid it within with pure gold. 5 He made the larger room with a ceiling of cypress wood, which he overlaid with fine gold, and ornamented it with palm trees and chains. 6 He decorated the house with precious stones for beauty. The gold was gold from Parvaim. 7 He also overlaid the house, the beams, the thresholds, its walls, and its doors with gold, and engraved cherubim on the walls.

8 He made the most holy place. Its length, according to the width of the house, was twenty cubits, and its width twenty cubits; and he overlaid it with fine gold, amounting to six hundred talents.[j] 9 The weight of the nails was fifty shekels[k] of gold. He overlaid the upper rooms with gold.

10 In the most holy place he made two cherubim by carving, and they overlaid them with gold. 11 The wings of the cherubim were twenty cubits long: the wing of the one was five cubits, reaching to the wall of the house; and the other wing was five cubits, reaching to the wing of the other cherub. 12 The wing of the other cherub was five cubits, reaching to the wall of the house; and the other wing was five cubits, joining to the wing of the other cherub. 13 The wings of these cherubim spread themselves out twenty cubits. They stood on their feet, and their faces were towards the house. 14 He made the veil of blue, purple, crimson, and fine linen, and ornamented it with cherubim.

15 Also he made before the house two pillars thirty-five cubits high, and the capital that was on the top of each of them was five cubits. 16 He made chains in the inner sanctuary, and put them on the tops of the pillars; and he made one hundred pomegranates, and put them on the chains. 17 He set up the pillars before the temple, one on the right hand and the other on the left; and called the name of that on the right hand Jachin, and the name of that on the left Boaz.

4

1 Then he made an altar of bronze, twenty cubits[l] long, twenty cubits wide, and ten cubits high. 2 Also he made the molten sea[m] of ten cubits from brim to brim. It was round, five cubits high, and thirty cubits in circumference. 3 Under it was the likeness of oxen, which encircled it, for ten cubits, encircling the sea. The oxen were in two rows, cast when it was cast. 4 It stood on twelve oxen, three looking towards the north, three looking towards the west, three looking towards the south, and three looking towards the east; and the sea was set on them above, and all their hindquarters were inward. 5 It was a handbreadth thick. Its brim was made like the brim of a cup, like the flower of a lily. It received and held three thousand baths.[n] 6 He also made ten basins, and put five on the right hand and five on the left, to wash in them. The things that belonged to the burnt offering were washed in them, but the sea was for the priests to wash in.

---

a 1:1 When rendered in ALL CAPITAL LETTERS, "LORD" or "GOD" is the translation of God's Proper Name.

b 1:1 The Hebrew word rendered "God" is "אֱלֹהִים" (Elohim).

c 1:17 The pieces of silver were probably shekels, so 600 pieces would be about 13.2 pounds or 6 kilograms of silver, and 150 would be about 3.3 pounds or 1.5 kilograms of silver.

d 1:17 or, Aramean

e 2:4 "Behold", from "הִנֵּה", means look at, take notice, observe, see, or gaze at. It is often used as an interjection.

f 2:10 1 cor is the same as a homer, or about 55.9 U. S. gallons (liquid) or 211 litres or 6 bushels, so 20,000 cors of wheat would weigh about 545 metric tonnes

g 2:10 1 bath is one tenth of a cor, or about 5.6 U. S. gallons or 21 litres or 2.4 pecks. 20,000 baths of barley would weigh about 262 metric tonnes.

h 2:13 or, Huram, my father

i 3:3 A cubit is the length from the tip of the middle finger to the elbow on a man's arm, or about 18 inches or 46 centimetres.

j 3:8 A talent is about 30 kilograms or 66 pounds or 965 Troy ounces, so 600 talents is about 18 metric tonnes

k 3:9 A shekel is about 10 grams or about 0.32 Troy ounces, so 50 shekels was about 0.5 kilograms or about 16 Troy ounces.

l 4:1 A cubit is the length from the tip of the middle finger to the elbow on a man's arm, or about 18 inches or 46 centimetres.

m 4:2 or, pool, or, reservoir

n 4:5 A bath is about 5.6 U. S. gallons or 21.1 litres, so 3,000 baths is about 16,800 gallons or 63.3 kilolitres.

7 He made the ten lamp stands of gold according to the ordinance concerning them; and he set them in the temple, five on the right hand and five on the left. 8 He made also ten tables, and placed them in the temple, five on the right side and five on the left. He made one hundred basins of gold. 9 Furthermore he made the court of the priests, the great court, and doors for the court, and overlaid their doors with bronze. 10 He set the sea on the right side of the house eastward, towards the south.

11 Huram made the pots, the shovels, and the basins.

So Huram finished doing the work that he did for King Solomon in God's house: 12 the two pillars, the bowls, the two capitals which were on the top of the pillars, the two networks to cover the two bowls of the capitals that were on the top of the pillars, 13 and the four hundred pomegranates for the two networks—two rows of pomegranates for each network, to cover the two bowls of the capitals that were on the pillars. 14 He also made the bases, and he made the basins on the bases— 15 one sea, and the twelve oxen under it. 16 Huram-abi[a] also made the pots, the shovels, the forks, and all its vessels for the LORD's house, of bright bronze. 17 The king cast them in the plain of the Jordan, in the clay ground between Succoth and Zeredah. 18 Thus Solomon made all these vessels in great abundance, so that the weight of the bronze could not be determined.

19 Solomon made all the vessels that were in God's house: the golden altar, the tables with the show bread on them, 20 and the lamp stands with their lamps to burn according to the ordinance before the inner sanctuary, of pure gold; 21 and the flowers, the lamps, and the tongs of gold that was purest gold; 22 and the snuffers, the basins, the spoons, and the fire pans of pure gold. As for the entry of the house, its inner doors for the most holy place and the doors of the main hall of the temple were of gold.

5

1 Thus all the work that Solomon did for the LORD's house was finished. Solomon brought in the things that David his father had dedicated, even the silver, the gold, and all the vessels, and put them in the treasuries of God's house.

2 Then Solomon assembled the elders of Israel and all the heads of the tribes, the princes of the fathers' households of the children of Israel, to Jerusalem, to bring up the ark of the LORD's covenant out of David's city, which is Zion. 3 So all the men of Israel assembled themselves to the king at the feast, which was in the seventh month. 4 All the elders of Israel came. The Levites took up the ark. 5 They brought up the ark, the Tent of Meeting, and all the holy vessels that were in the Tent. The Levitical priests brought these up. 6 King Solomon and all the congregation of Israel who were assembled to him were before the ark, sacrificing sheep and cattle that could not be counted or numbered for multitude. 7 The priests brought in the ark of the LORD's covenant to its place, into the inner sanctuary of the house, to the most holy place, even under the wings of the cherubim. 8 For the cherubim spread out their wings over the place of the ark, and the cherubim covered the ark and its poles above. 9 The poles were so long that the ends of the poles were seen from the ark in front of the inner sanctuary, but they were not seen outside; and it is there to this day. 10 There was nothing in the ark except the two tablets which Moses put there at Horeb, when the LORD made a covenant with the children of Israel, when they came out of Egypt.

11 When the priests had come out of the holy place (for all the priests who were present had sanctified themselves, and didn't keep their divisions; 12 also the Levites who were the singers, all of them, even Asaph, Heman, Jeduthun, and their sons and their brothers, arrayed in fine linen, with cymbals and stringed instruments and harps, stood at the east end of the altar, and with them one hundred and twenty priests sounding with trumpets); 13 when the trumpeters and singers were as one, to make one sound to be heard in praising and thanking the LORD; and when they lifted up their voice with the trumpets and cymbals and instruments of music, and praised the LORD, saying,
"For he is good,
    for his loving kindness endures forever!"
then the house was filled with a cloud, even the LORD's house, 14 so that the priests could not stand to minister by reason of the cloud; for the LORD's glory filled God's house.

6

1 Then Solomon said, "The LORD has said that he would dwell in the thick darkness. 2 But I have built you a house and home, a place for you to dwell in forever."

3 The king turned his face, and blessed all the assembly of Israel; and all the assembly of Israel stood.

4 He said, "Blessed be the LORD, the God of Israel, who spoke with his mouth to David my father, and has with his hands fulfilled it, saying, 5 'Since the day that I brought my people out of the land of Egypt, I chose no city out of all the tribes of Israel to build a house in, that my name might be there, and I chose no man to be prince over my people Israel; 6 but now I have chosen Jerusalem, that my name might be there; and I have chosen David to be over my people Israel.' 7 Now it was in the heart of David my father to build a house for the name of the LORD, the God of Israel. 8 But the LORD said to David my father, 'Whereas it was in your heart to build a house for my name, you did well that it was in your heart; 9 nevertheless you shall not build the house, but your son who will come out of your body, he shall build the house for my name.'

10 "The LORD has performed his word that he spoke; for I have risen up in the place of David my father, and sit on the throne of Israel, as the LORD promised, and have built the house for the name of the LORD, the God of Israel. 11 There I have set the ark, in which is the LORD's covenant, which he made with the children of Israel."

12 He stood before the LORD's altar in the presence of all the assembly of Israel, and spread out his hands 13 (for Solomon had made a bronze platform, five cubits[b] long, five cubits wide, and three cubits high, and had set it in the middle of the court; and he stood on it, and knelt down on his knees before all the assembly of Israel, and spread out his hands towards heaven). 14 Then he said, "LORD, the God of Israel, there is no God like you in heaven or on earth—you who keep covenant and loving kindness with your servants who walk before you with all their heart; 15 who have kept with your servant David my father that which you promised him. Yes, you spoke with your mouth, and have fulfilled it with your hand, as it is today.

16 "Now therefore, LORD, the God of Israel, keep with your servant David my father that which you have promised him, saying, 'There shall not fail you a man in my sight to sit on the throne of Israel, if only your children take heed to their way, to walk in my law as you have walked before me.' 17 Now therefore, LORD, the God of Israel, let your word be verified, which you spoke to your servant David.

18 "But will God indeed dwell with men on the earth? Behold, heaven and the heaven of heavens can't contain you; how much less this house which I have built! 19 Yet have respect for the prayer of your servant and to his supplication, LORD my God, to listen to the cry and to the prayer which your servant prays before you; 20 that your eyes may be open towards this house day and night, even towards the place where you have said that you would put your name, to listen to the prayer which your servant will pray towards this place. 21 Listen to the petitions of your servant and of your people Israel, when they pray towards this place. Yes, hear from your dwelling place, even from heaven; and when you hear, forgive.

22 "If a man sins against his neighbour, and an oath is laid on him to cause him to swear, and he comes and swears before your altar in this house, 23 then hear from heaven, act, and judge your servants, bringing retribution to the wicked, to bring his way on his own head; and justifying the righteous, to give him according to his righteousness.

24 "If your people Israel are struck down before the enemy because they have sinned against you, and they turn again and confess your name, and pray and make supplication before you in this house, 25 then hear from heaven, and forgive the sin of your people Israel, and bring them again to the land which you gave to them and to their fathers.

26 "When the sky is shut up and there is no rain because they have sinned against you, if they pray towards this place and confess your name, and turn from their sin when you afflict them, 27 then hear in heaven, and forgive the sin of your servants, your people Israel, when you teach them the good way in which they should walk, and send rain on your land, which you have given to your people for an inheritance.

28 "If there is famine in the land, if there is pestilence, if there is blight or mildew, locust or caterpillar; if their enemies besiege them in the land of their cities; whatever plague or whatever sickness there is— 29 whatever prayer and supplication is made by any man, or by all your people Israel, who will each know his own plague and his own sorrow, and shall spread out his hands towards this house, 30 then hear from heaven your dwelling place and forgive, and render to every man according to all his ways, whose heart you know (for you, even you only, know the hearts of the children of men), 31 that they may fear you, to walk in your ways as long as they live in the land which you gave to our fathers.

32 "Moreover, concerning the foreigner, who is not of your people Israel, when he comes from a far country for your great name's sake and your mighty hand and your outstretched arm, when they come and pray towards this house, 33 then hear from heaven, even from your dwelling place, and do according to all that the foreigner calls to you for; that all the peoples of the earth may know your name and fear you, as do your people Israel, and that they may know that this house which I have built is called by your name.

34 "If your people go out to battle against their enemies, by whatever way you send them, and they pray to you towards this city which you have chosen, and the house which I have built for your name; 35 then hear from heaven their prayer and their supplication, and maintain their cause.

36 "If they sin against you (for there is no man who doesn't sin), and you are angry with them and deliver them to the enemy, so that they carry them away captive to a land far off or near; 37 yet if they come to their senses in the land where they are carried captive, and turn again, and make supplication to you in the land of their captivity, saying, 'We have sinned, we have done perversely, and have dealt wickedly;' 38 if they return to you with all their heart and with all their soul in the land of their captivity, where they have been taken captive, and pray towards their land which you gave to their fathers, and the city which you have chosen, and towards the house which I have built for your name; 39 then hear from heaven, even from your dwelling place, their prayer and their petitions, and maintain their cause, and forgive your people who have sinned against you.

40 "Now, my God, let, I beg you, your eyes be open, and let your ears be attentive to the prayer that is made in this place.

---

a 4:16 "abi" means "his father"

b 6:13 A cubit is the length from the tip of the middle finger to the elbow on a man's arm, or about 18 inches or 46 centimetres.

41 "Now therefore arise, LORD God, into your resting place, you, and the ark of your strength. Let your priests, LORD God, be clothed with salvation, and let your saints rejoice in goodness.

42 "LORD God, don't turn away the face of your anointed. Remember your loving kindnesses to David your servant."

7

1 Now when Solomon had finished praying, fire came down from heaven and consumed the burnt offering and the sacrifices; and the LORD's glory filled the house. 2 The priests could not enter into the LORD's house, because the LORD's glory filled the LORD's house. 3 All the children of Israel looked on, when the fire came down, and the LORD's glory was on the house. They bowed themselves with their faces to the ground on the pavement, worshipped, and gave thanks to the LORD, saying, "For he is good,

for his loving kindness endures forever!"

4 Then the king and all the people offered sacrifices before the LORD. 5 King Solomon offered a sacrifice of twenty-two thousand head of cattle and a hundred and twenty thousand sheep. So the king and all the people dedicated God's house. 6 The priests stood, according to their positions; the Levites also with instruments of music of the LORD, which David the king had made to give thanks to the LORD, when David praised by their ministry, saying "For his loving kindness endures forever." The priests sounded trumpets before them; and all Israel stood.

7 Moreover Solomon made the middle of the court that was before the LORD's house holy; for there he offered the burnt offerings and the fat of the peace offerings, because the bronze altar which Solomon had made was not able to receive the burnt offering, the meal offering, and the fat.

8 So Solomon held the feast at that time for seven days, and all Israel with him, a very great assembly, from the entrance of Hamath to the brook of Egypt.

9 On the eighth day, they held a solemn assembly; for they kept the dedication of the altar seven days, and the feast seven days. 10 On the twenty-third day of the seventh month, he sent the people away to their tents, joyful and glad of heart for the goodness that the LORD had shown to David, to Solomon, and to Israel his people.

11 Thus Solomon finished the LORD's house and the king's house; and he successfully completed all that came into Solomon's heart to make in the LORD's house and in his own house.

12 Then the LORD appeared to Solomon by night, and said to him, "I have heard your prayer, and have chosen this place for myself for a house of sacrifice.

13 "If I shut up the sky so that there is no rain, or if I command the locust to devour the land, or if I send pestilence amongst my people, 14 if my people who are called by my name will humble themselves, pray, seek my face, and turn from their wicked ways, then I will hear from heaven, will forgive their sin, and will heal their land. 15 Now my eyes will be open and my ears attentive to prayer that is made in this place. 16 For now I have chosen and made this house holy, that my name may be there forever; and my eyes and my heart will be there perpetually.

17 "As for you, if you will walk before me as David your father walked, and do according to all that I have commanded you, and will keep my statutes and my ordinances, 18 then I will establish the throne of your kingdom, according as I covenanted with David your father, saying, 'There shall not fail you a man to be ruler in Israel.'

19 But if you turn away and forsake my statutes and my commandments which I have set before you, and go and serve other gods and worship them, 20 then I will pluck them up by the roots out of my land which I have given them; and this house, which I have made holy for my name, I will cast out of my sight, and I will make it a proverb and a byword amongst all peoples. 21 This house, which is so high, everyone who passes by it will be astonished and say, 'Why has the LORD done this to this land and to this house?' 22 They shall answer, 'Because they abandoned the LORD, the God of their fathers, who brought them out of the land of Egypt, and took other gods, worshipped them, and served them. Therefore he has brought all this evil on them.'"

8

1 At the end of twenty years, in which Solomon had built the LORD's house and his own house, 2 Solomon built the cities which Huram had given to Solomon, and caused the children of Israel to dwell there.

3 Solomon went to Hamath Zobah, and prevailed against it. 4 He built Tadmor in the wilderness, and all the storage cities, which he built in Hamath. 5 Also he built Beth Horon the upper and Beth Horon the lower, fortified cities with walls, gates, and bars; 6 and Baalath, and all the storage cities that Solomon had, and all the cities for his chariots, the cities for his horsemen, and all that Solomon desired to build for his pleasure in Jerusalem, in Lebanon, and in all the land of his dominion.

7 As for all the people who were left of the Hittites, the Amorites, the Perizzites, the Hivites, and the Jebusites, who were not of Israel— 8 of their children who were left after them in the land, whom the children of Israel

didn't consume—of them Solomon conscripted forced labour to this day. 9 But of the children of Israel, Solomon made no servants for his work, but they were men of war, chief of his captains, and rulers of his chariots and of his horsemen. 10 These were the chief officers of King Solomon, even two-hundred and fifty, who ruled over the people.

11 Solomon brought up Pharaoh's daughter out of David's city to the house that he had built for her; for he said, "My wife shall not dwell in the house of David king of Israel, because the places where the LORD's ark has come are holy."

12 Then Solomon offered burnt offerings to the LORD on the LORD's altar which he had built before the porch, 13 even as the duty of every day required, offering according to the commandment of Moses on the Sabbaths, on the new moons, and on the set feasts, three times per year, during the feast of unleavened bread, during the feast of weeks, and during the feast of booths.ᵃ

14 He appointed, according to the ordinance of David his father, the divisions of the priests to their service, and the Levites to their offices, to praise and to minister before the priests, as the duty of every day required, the doorkeepers also by their divisions at every gate, for David the man of God had so commanded. 15 They didn't depart from the commandment of the king to the priests and Levites concerning any matter or concerning the treasures.

16 Now all the work of Solomon was accomplished from the day of the foundation of the LORD's house until it was finished. So the LORD's house was completed.

17 Then Solomon went to Ezion Geber and to Eloth, on the seashore in the land of Edom. 18 Huram sent him ships and servants who had knowledge of the sea by the hands of his servants; and they came with the servants of Solomon to Ophir, and brought from there four hundred and fifty talentsᵇ of gold, and brought them to King Solomon.

9

1 When the queen of Sheba heard of the fame of Solomon, she came to test Solomon with hard questions at Jerusalem, with a very great caravan, including camels that bore spices, gold in abundance, and precious stones. When she had come to Solomon, she talked with him about all that was in her heart. 2 Solomon answered all her questions. There wasn't anything hidden from Solomon which he didn't tell her. 3 When the queen of Sheba had seen the wisdom of Solomon, the house that he had built, 4 the food of his table, the seating of his servants, the attendance of his ministers, their clothing, his cup bearers and their clothing, and his ascent by which he went up to the LORD's house, there was no more spirit in her.ᶜ

5 She said to the king, "It was a true report that I heard in my own land of your acts and of your wisdom. 6 However I didn't believe their words until I came, and my eyes had seen it; and behold half of the greatness of your wisdom wasn't told me. You exceed the fame that I heard! 7 Happy are your men, and happy are these your servants, who stand continually before you and hear your wisdom. 8 Blessed be the LORD your God, who delighted in you and set you on his throne to be king for the LORD your God, because your God loved Israel, to establish them forever. Therefore he made you king over them, to do justice and righteousness."

9 She gave the king one hundred and twenty talentsᵈ of gold, spices in great abundance, and precious stones. There was never before such spice as the queen of Sheba gave to King Solomon.

10 The servants of Huram and the servants of Solomon, who brought gold from Ophir, also brought algum treesᵉ and precious stones. 11 The king used algum tree wood to make terraces for the LORD's house and for the king's house, and harps and stringed instruments for the singers. There were none like these seen before in the land of Judah. 12 King Solomon gave to the queen of Sheba all her desire, whatever she asked, more than that which she had brought to the king. So she turned and went to her own land, she and her servants.

13 Now the weight of gold that came to Solomon in one year was six hundred and sixty-six talentsᶠ of gold, 14 in addition to that which the traders and merchants brought. All the kings of Arabia and the governors of the country brought gold and silver to Solomon. 15 King Solomon made two hundred large shields of beaten gold. Six hundred shekelsᵍ of beaten gold went to one large shield. 16 He made three hundred shields of beaten gold. Three hundred shekelsʰ of gold went to one shield. The king put them in the House of the Forest of Lebanon. 17 Moreover the king made a great throne of ivory, and overlaid it with pure gold. 18 There were six steps to the throne, with a footstool of gold, which were fastened to the throne, and armrests on either side by the place of the seat, and two lions standing beside the armrests. 19 Twelve lions stood there on the one side and on the other on the six steps. There was nothing like it made in any other kingdom. 20 All King Solomon's drinking vessels were of gold, and all the vessels of the House of the Forest of Lebanon were of pure gold. Silver was not considered valuable in the days of Solomon. 21 For the king had ships that

---

ᵃ 8:13 or, feast of tents (Sukkot)

ᵇ 8:18 A talent is about 30 kilograms or 66 pounds or 965 Troy ounces, so 450 talents is about 13.5 metric tonnes

ᶜ 9:4 or, she was breathless.

ᵈ 9:9 A talent is about 30 kilograms or 66 pounds or 965 Troy ounces, so 120 talents is about 3.6 metric tonnes

ᵉ 9:10 possibly Indian sandalwood, which has nice grain and a pleasant scent and is good for woodworking

ᶠ 9:13 A talent is about 30 kilograms or 66 pounds or 965 Troy ounces, so 666 talents is about 20 metric tonnes

ᵍ 9:15 A shekel is about 10 grams or about 0.32 Troy ounces, so 600 shekels was about 6 kilograms or about 192 Troy ounces.

ʰ 9:16 A shekel is about 10 grams or about 0.32 Troy ounces, so 300 shekels was about 3 kilograms or about 96 Troy ounces.

went to Tarshish with Huram's servants. Once every three years, the ships of Tarshish came bringing gold, silver, ivory, apes, and peacocks.

22 So King Solomon exceeded all the kings of the earth in riches and wisdom. 23 All the kings of the earth sought the presence of Solomon to hear his wisdom, which God had put in his heart. 24 They each brought tribute: vessels of silver, vessels of gold, clothing, armour, spices, horses, and mules every year. 25 Solomon had four thousand stalls for horses and chariots, and twelve thousand horsemen that he stationed in the chariot cities and with the king at Jerusalem. 26 He ruled over all the kings from the River even to the land of the Philistines, and to the border of Egypt. 27 The king made silver as common in Jerusalem as stones, and he made cedars to be as abundant as the sycamore trees that are in the lowland. 28 They brought horses for Solomon out of Egypt and out of all lands.

29 Now the rest of the acts of Solomon, first and last, aren't they written in the history of Nathan the prophet, and in the prophecy of Ahijah the Shilonite, and in the visions of Iddo the seer concerning Jeroboam the son of Nebat? 30 Solomon reigned in Jerusalem over all Israel forty years. 31 Solomon slept with his fathers, and he was buried in his father David's city; and Rehoboam his son reigned in his place.

10

1 Rehoboam went to Shechem, for all Israel had come to Shechem to make him king. 2 When Jeroboam the son of Nebat heard of it (for he was in Egypt, where he had fled from the presence of King Solomon), Jeroboam returned out of Egypt. 3 They sent and called him; and Jeroboam and all Israel came, and they spoke to Rehoboam, saying, 4 "Your father made our yoke grievous. Now therefore make the grievous service of your father and his heavy yoke which he put on us, lighter, and we will serve you."

5 He said to them, "Come again to me after three days."

So the people departed.

6 King Rehoboam took counsel with the old men, who had stood before Solomon his father while he yet lived, saying, "What counsel do you give me about how to answer these people?"

7 They spoke to him, saying, "If you are kind to these people, please them, and speak good words to them, then they will be your servants forever."

8 But he abandoned the counsel of the old men which they had given him, and took counsel with the young men who had grown up with him, who stood before him. 9 He said to them, "What counsel do you give, that we may give an answer to these people, who have spoken to me, saying, 'Make the yoke that your father put on us lighter'?"

10 The young men who had grown up with him spoke to him, saying, "Thus you shall tell the people who spoke to you, saying, 'Your father made our yoke heavy, but make it lighter on us;' thus you shall say to them, 'My little finger is thicker than my father's waist. 11 Now whereas my father burdened you with a heavy yoke, I will add to your yoke. My father chastised you with whips, but I will chastise you with scorpions.'"

12 So Jeroboam and all the people came to Rehoboam the third day, as the king asked, saying, "Come to me again the third day." 13 The king answered them roughly; and King Rehoboam abandoned the counsel of the old men, 14 and spoke to them after the counsel of the young men, saying, "My father made your yoke heavy, but I will add to it. My father chastised you with whips, but I will chastise you with scorpions."

15 So the king didn't listen to the people; for it was brought about by God, that the LORD might establish his word, which he spoke by Ahijah the Shilonite to Jeroboam the son of Nebat.

16 When all Israel saw that the king didn't listen to them, the people answered the king, saying, "What portion do we have in David? We don't have an inheritance in the son of Jesse! Every man to your tents, Israel! Now see to your own house, David." So all Israel departed to their tents.

17 But as for the children of Israel who lived in the cities of Judah, Rehoboam reigned over them. 18 Then King Rehoboam sent Hadoram, who was over the men subject to forced labour; and the children of Israel stoned him to death with stones. King Rehoboam hurried to get himself up to his chariot, to flee to Jerusalem. 19 So Israel rebelled against David's house to this day.

11

1 When Rehoboam had come to Jerusalem, he assembled the house of Judah and Benjamin, one hundred and eighty thousand chosen men who were warriors, to fight against Israel, to bring the kingdom again to Rehoboam. 2 But the LORD's word came to Shemaiah the man of God, saying, 3 "Speak to Rehoboam the son of Solomon, king of Judah, and to all Israel in Judah and Benjamin, saying, 4 'The LORD says, "You shall not go up, nor fight against your brothers! Every man return to his house; for this thing is of me."'" So they listened to the LORD's words, and returned from going against Jeroboam.

5 Rehoboam lived in Jerusalem, and built cities for defence in Judah. 6 He built Bethlehem, Etam, Tekoa, 7 Beth Zur, Soco, Adullam, 8 Gath, Mareshah, Ziph, 9 Adoraim, Lachish, Azekah, 10 Zorah, Aijalon, and Hebron, which are fortified cities in Judah and in Benjamin. 11 He fortified the strongholds and put captains in them with stores of food, oil and wine. 12 He put shields and spears in every city, and made them exceedingly strong. Judah and Benjamin belonged to him.

13 The priests and the Levites who were in all Israel stood with him out of all their territory. 14 For the Levites left their pasture lands and their possessions, and came to Judah and Jerusalem; for Jeroboam and his sons cast them off, that they should not execute the priest's office to the LORD. 15 He himself appointed priests for the high places, for the male goat and calf idols which he had made. 16 After them, out of all the tribes of

Israel, those who set their hearts to seek the LORD, the God of Israel, came to Jerusalem to sacrifice to the LORD, the God of their fathers. 17 So they strengthened the kingdom of Judah and made Rehoboam the son of Solomon strong for three years, for they walked three years in the way of David and Solomon.

18 Rehoboam took a wife for himself, Mahalath the daughter of Jerimoth the son of David and of Abihail the daughter of Eliab the son of Jesse. 19 She bore him sons: Jeush, Shemariah, and Zaham. 20 After her, he took Maacah the granddaughter of Absalom; and she bore him Abijah, Attai, Ziza, and Shelomith. 21 Rehoboam loved Maacah the granddaughter of Absalom above all his wives and his concubines; for he took eighteen wives and sixty concubines, and became the father of twenty-eight sons and sixty daughters. 22 Rehoboam appointed Abijah the son of Maacah to be chief, the prince amongst his brothers, for he intended to make him king. 23 He dealt wisely, and dispersed some of his sons throughout all the lands of Judah and Benjamin, to every fortified city. He gave them food in abundance; and he sought many wives for them.

12

1 When the kingdom of Rehoboam was established and he was strong, he abandoned the LORD's law, and all Israel with him. 2 In the fifth year of King Rehoboam, Shishak king of Egypt came up against Jerusalem, because they had trespassed against the LORD, 3 with twelve hundred chariots and sixty thousand horsemen. The people were without number who came with him out of Egypt: the Lubim, the Sukkiim, and the Ethiopians. 4 He took the fortified cities which belonged to Judah, and came to Jerusalem. 5 Now Shemaiah the prophet came to Rehoboam and to the princes of Judah, who were gathered together to Jerusalem because of Shishak, and said to them, "The LORD says, 'You have forsaken me, therefore I have also left you in the hand of Shishak.'"

6 Then the princes of Israel and the king humbled themselves; and they said, "The LORD is righteous."

7 When the LORD saw that they humbled themselves, the LORD's word came to Shemaiah, saying, "They have humbled themselves. I will not destroy them, but I will grant them some deliverance, and my wrath won't be poured out on Jerusalem by the hand of Shishak. 8 Nevertheless they will be his servants, that they may know my service, and the service of the kingdoms of the countries."

9 So Shishak king of Egypt came up against Jerusalem and took away the treasures of the LORD's house and the treasures of the king's house. He took it all away. He also took away the shields of gold which Solomon had made. 10 King Rehoboam made shields of bronze in their place, and committed them to the hands of the captains of the guard, who kept the door of the king's house. 11 As often as the king entered into the LORD's house, the guard came and bore them, then brought them back into the guard room. 12 When he humbled himself, the LORD's wrath turned from him, so as not to destroy him altogether. Moreover, there were good things found in Judah.

13 So King Rehoboam strengthened himself in Jerusalem and reigned; for Rehoboam was forty-one years old when he began to reign, and he reigned seventeen years in Jerusalem, the city which the LORD had chosen out of all the tribes of Israel to put his name there. His mother's name was Naamah the Ammonitess. 14 He did that which was evil, because he didn't set his heart to seek the LORD.

15 Now the acts of Rehoboam, first and last, aren't they written in the histories of Shemaiah the prophet and of Iddo the seer, in the genealogies? There were wars between Rehoboam and Jeroboam continually. 16 Rehoboam slept with his fathers, and was buried in David's city; and Abijah his son reigned in his place.

13

1 In the eighteenth year of King Jeroboam, Abijah began to reign over Judah. 2 He reigned three years in Jerusalem. His mother's name was Micaiah the daughter of Uriel of Gibeah. There was war between Abijah and Jeroboam. 3 Abijah joined battle with an army of valiant men of war, even four hundred thousand chosen men; and Jeroboam set the battle in array against him with eight hundred thousand chosen men, who were mighty men of valour. 4 Abijah stood up on Mount Zemaraim, which is in the hill country of Ephraim, and said, "Hear me, Jeroboam and all Israel: 5 Ought you not to know that the LORD, the God of Israel, gave the kingdom over Israel to David forever, even to him and to his sons by a covenant of salt? 6 Yet Jeroboam the son of Nebat, the servant of Solomon the son of David, rose up, and rebelled against his lord. 7 Worthless men were gathered to him, wicked fellows who strengthened themselves against Rehoboam the son of Solomon, when Rehoboam was young and tender hearted, and could not withstand them.

8 "Now you intend to withstand the kingdom of the LORD in the hand of the sons of David. You are a great multitude, and the golden calves which Jeroboam made you for gods are with you. 9 Haven't you driven out the priests of the LORD, the sons of Aaron, and the Levites, and made priests for yourselves according to the ways of the peoples of other lands? Whoever comes to consecrate himself with a young bull and seven rams may be a priest of those who are no gods.

10 "But as for us, the LORD is our God, and we have not forsaken him. We have priests serving the LORD, the sons of Aaron, and the Levites in their work. 11 They burn to the LORD every morning and every evening burnt offerings and sweet incense. They also set the show bread in order on the pure table, and care for the gold lamp stand with its lamps, to burn every evening; for we keep the instruction of the LORD our God, but you have forsaken him. 12 Behold, God is with us at our head, and his priests

with the trumpets of alarm to sound an alarm against you. Children of Israel, don't fight against the LORD, the God of your fathers; for you will not prosper."

13 But Jeroboam caused an ambush to come about behind them; so they were before Judah, and the ambush was behind them. 14 When Judah looked back, behold, the battle was before and behind them; and they cried to the LORD, and the priests sounded with the trumpets. 15 Then the men of Judah gave a shout. As the men of Judah shouted, God struck Jeroboam and all Israel before Abijah and Judah. 16 The children of Israel fled before Judah, and God delivered them into their hand. 17 Abijah and his people killed them with a great slaughter, so five hundred thousand chosen men of Israel fell down slain. 18 Thus the children of Israel were brought under at that time, and the children of Judah prevailed, because they relied on the LORD, the God of their fathers. 19 Abijah pursued Jeroboam, and took cities from him: Bethel with its villages, Jeshanah with its villages, and Ephron with its villages.

20 Jeroboam didn't recover strength again in the days of Abijah. The LORD struck him, and he died. 21 But Abijah grew mighty and took for himself fourteen wives, and became the father of twenty-two sons and sixteen daughters. 22 The rest of the acts of Abijah, his ways, and his sayings are written in the commentary of the prophet Iddo.

14

1 So Abijah slept with his fathers, and they buried him in David's city; and Asa his son reigned in his place. In his days, the land was quiet ten years. 2 Asa did that which was good and right in the LORD his God's eyes, 3 for he took away the foreign altars and the high places, broke down the pillars, cut down the Asherah poles, 4 and commanded Judah to seek the LORD, the God of their fathers, and to obey his law and command. 5 Also he took away out of all the cities of Judah the high places and the sun images; and the kingdom was quiet before him. 6 He built fortified cities in Judah; for the land was quiet, and he had no war in those years, because the LORD had given him rest. 7 For he said to Judah, "Let's build these cities and make walls around them, with towers, gates, and bars. The land is yet before us, because we have sought the LORD our God. We have sought him, and he has given us rest on every side." So they built and prospered.

8 Asa had an army of three hundred thousand out of Judah who bore bucklers and spears, and two hundred and eighty thousand out of Benjamin who bore shields and drew bows. All these were mighty men of valour.

9 Zerah the Ethiopian came out against them with an army of a million troops and three hundred chariots, and he came to Mareshah. 10 Then Asa went out to meet him, and they set the battle in array in the valley of Zephathah at Mareshah. 11 Asa cried to the LORD his God, and said, "LORD, there is no one besides you to help, between the mighty and him who has no strength. Help us, LORD our God; for we rely on you, and in your name are we come against this multitude. LORD, you are our God. Don't let man prevail against you."

12 So the LORD struck the Ethiopians before Asa and before Judah; and the Ethiopians fled. 13 Asa and the people who were with him pursued them to Gerar. So many of the Ethiopians fell that they could not recover themselves, for they were destroyed before the LORD and before his army. Judah's army carried away very much booty. 14 They struck all the cities around Gerar, for the fear of the LORD came on them. They plundered all the cities, for there was much plunder in them. 15 They also struck the tents of those who had livestock, and carried away sheep and camels in abundance, then returned to Jerusalem.

15

1 The Spirit of God came on Azariah the son of Oded. 2 He went out to meet Asa, and said to him, "Hear me, Asa, and all Judah and Benjamin! The LORD is with you while you are with him; and if you seek him, he will be found by you; but if you forsake him, he will forsake you. 3 Now for a long time Israel was without the true God, without a teaching priest, and without law. 4 But when in their distress they turned to the LORD, the God of Israel, and sought him, he was found by them. 5 In those times there was no peace to him who went out, nor to him who came in; but great troubles were on all the inhabitants of the lands. 6 They were broken in pieces, nation against nation, and city against city; for God troubled them with all adversity. 7 But you be strong! Don't let your hands be slack, for your work will be rewarded."

8 When Asa heard these words and the prophecy of Oded the prophet, he took courage, and put away the abominations out of all the land of Judah and Benjamin, and out of the cities which he had taken from the hill country of Ephraim; and he renewed the LORD's altar that was before the LORD's porch. 9 He gathered all Judah and Benjamin, and those who lived with them out of Ephraim, Manasseh, and Simeon; for they came to him out of Israel in abundance when they saw that the LORD his God was with him. 10 So they gathered themselves together at Jerusalem in the third month, in the fifteenth year of Asa's reign. 11 They sacrificed to the LORD in that day, of the plunder which they had brought, seven hundred head of cattle and seven thousand sheep. 12 They entered into the covenant to seek the LORD, the God of their fathers, with all their heart and with all their soul; 13 and that whoever would not seek the LORD, the God of Israel, should be put to death, whether small or great, whether man or woman. 14 They swore to the LORD with a loud voice, with shouting, with trumpets, and with cornets. 15 All Judah rejoiced at the oath, for they had sworn with all their heart and sought him with their whole desire; and he was found by them. Then the LORD gave them rest all around.

16 Also Maacah, the mother of Asa the king, he removed from being queen mother, because she had made an abominable image for an Asherah; so Asa cut down her image, ground it into dust, and burnt it at the brook Kidron. 17 But the high places were not taken away out of Israel; nevertheless the heart of Asa was perfect all his days. 18 He brought the things that his father had dedicated and that he himself had dedicated, silver, gold, and vessels into God's house. 19 There was no more war to the thirty-fifth year of Asa's reign.

16

1 In the thirty-sixth year of Asa's reign, Baasha king of Israel went up against Judah, and built Ramah, that he might not allow anyone to go out or come in to Asa king of Judah. 2 Then Asa brought out silver and gold out of the treasures of the LORD's house and of the king's house, and sent to Ben Hadad king of Syria, who lived at Damascus, saying, 3 "Let there be a treaty between me and you, as there was between my father and your father. Behold, I have sent you silver and gold. Go, break your treaty with Baasha king of Israel, that he may depart from me."

4 Ben Hadad listened to King Asa, and sent the captains of his armies against the cities of Israel; and they struck Ijon, Dan, Abel Maim, and all the storage cities of Naphtali. 5 When Baasha heard of it, he stopped building Ramah, and let his work cease. 6 Then Asa the king took all Judah, and they carried away the stones and timber of Ramah, with which Baasha had built; and he built Geba and Mizpah with them.

7 At that time Hanani the seer came to Asa king of Judah, and said to him, "Because you have relied on the king of Syria, and have not relied on the LORD your God, therefore the army of the king of Syria has escaped out of your hand. 8 Weren't the Ethiopians and the Lubim a huge army, with chariots and exceedingly many horsemen? Yet, because you relied on the LORD, he delivered them into your hand. 9 For the LORD's eyes run back and forth throughout the whole earth, to show himself strong in the behalf of them whose heart is perfect towards him. You have done foolishly in this; for from now on you will have wars."

10 Then Asa was angry with the seer, and put him in the prison; for he was in a rage with him because of this thing. Asa oppressed some of the people at the same time.

11 Behold, the acts of Asa, first and last, behold, they are written in the book of the kings of Judah and Israel. 12 In the thirty-ninth year of his reign, Asa was diseased in his feet. His disease was exceedingly great; yet in his disease he didn't seek the LORD, but just the physicians. 13 Asa slept with his fathers, and died in the forty-first year of his reign. 14 They buried him in his own tomb, which he had dug out for himself in David's city, and laid him in the bed which was filled with sweet odours and various kinds of spices prepared by the perfumers' art; and they made a very great fire for him.

17

1 Jehoshaphat his son reigned in his place, and strengthened himself against Israel. 2 He placed forces in all the fortified cities of Judah, and set garrisons in the land of Judah and in the cities of Ephraim, which Asa his father had taken. 3 The LORD was with Jehoshaphat, because he walked in the first ways of his father David, and didn't seek the Baals, 4 but sought the God of his father, and walked in his commandments, and not in the ways of Israel. 5 Therefore the LORD established the kingdom in his hand. All Judah brought tribute to Jehoshaphat, and he had riches and honour in abundance. 6 His heart was lifted up in the ways of the LORD. Furthermore, he took away the high places and the Asherah poles out of Judah.

7 Also in the third year of his reign he sent his princes, even Ben Hail, Obadiah, Zechariah, Nethanel, and Micaiah, to teach in the cities of Judah; 8 and with them Levites, even Shemaiah, Nethaniah, Zebadiah, Asahel, Shemiramoth, Jehonathan, Adonijah, Tobijah, and Tobadonijah, the Levites; and with them Elishama and Jehoram, the priests. 9 They taught in Judah, having the book of the LORD's law with them. They went about throughout all the cities of Judah and taught amongst the people.

10 The fear of the LORD fell on all the kingdoms of the lands that were around Judah, so that they made no war against Jehoshaphat. 11 Some of the Philistines brought Jehoshaphat presents and silver for tribute. The Arabians also brought him flocks: seven thousand and seven hundred rams and seven thousand and seven hundred male goats. 12 Jehoshaphat grew great exceedingly; and he built fortresses and store cities in Judah. 13 He had many works in the cities of Judah; and men of war, mighty men of valour, in Jerusalem. 14 This was the numbering of them according to their fathers' houses: From Judah, the captains of thousands: Adnah the captain, and with him three hundred thousand mighty men of valour; 15 and next to him Jehohanan the captain, and with him two hundred and eighty thousand; 16 and next to him Amasiah the son of Zichri, who willingly offered himself to the LORD, and with him two hundred thousand mighty men of valour. 17 From Benjamin: Eliada, a mighty man of valour, and with him two hundred thousand armed with bow and shield; 18 and next to him Jehozabad, and with him one hundred and eighty thousand ready and prepared for war. 19 These were those who waited on the king, in addition to those whom the king put in the fortified cities throughout all Judah.

18

1 Now Jehoshaphat had riches and honour in abundance; and he allied himself with Ahab. 2 After some years, he went down to Ahab to Samaria. Ahab killed sheep and cattle for him in abundance, and for the people who were with him, and moved him to go up with him to Ramoth Gilead. 3 Ahab king of Israel said to Jehoshaphat king of Judah, "Will you go with me to Ramoth Gilead?"

He answered him, "I am as you are, and my people as your people. We will be with you in the war." 4 Jehoshaphat said to the king of Israel, "Please enquire first for the LORD's word."

5 Then the king of Israel gathered the prophets together, four hundred men, and said to them, "Shall we go to Ramoth Gilead to battle, or shall I forbear?"

They said, "Go up, for God will deliver it into the hand of the king."

6 But Jehoshaphat said, "Isn't there here a prophet of the LORD besides, that we may enquire of him?"

7 The king of Israel said to Jehoshaphat, "There is yet one man by whom we may enquire of the LORD; but I hate him, for he never prophesies good concerning me, but always evil. He is Micaiah the son of Imla."

Jehoshaphat said, "Don't let the king say so."

8 Then the king of Israel called an officer, and said, "Get Micaiah the son of Imla quickly."

9 Now the king of Israel and Jehoshaphat the king of Judah each sat on his throne, arrayed in their robes, and they were sitting in an open place at the entrance of the gate of Samaria; and all the prophets were prophesying before them. 10 Zedekiah the son of Chenaanah made himself horns of iron and said, "The LORD says, 'With these you shall push the Syrians, until they are consumed.'"

11 All the prophets prophesied so, saying, "Go up to Ramoth Gilead, and prosper; for the LORD will deliver it into the hand of the king."

12 The messenger who went to call Micaiah spoke to him, saying, "Behold, the words of the prophets declare good to the king with one mouth. Let your word therefore, please be like one of theirs, and speak good."

13 Micaiah said, "As the LORD lives, I will say what my God says."

14 When he had come to the king, the king said to him, "Micaiah, shall we go to Ramoth Gilead to battle, or shall I forbear?"

He said, "Go up, and prosper. They shall be delivered into your hand."

15 The king said to him, "How many times shall I adjure you that you speak to me nothing but the truth in the LORD's name?"

16 He said, "I saw all Israel scattered on the mountains, as sheep that have no shepherd. The LORD said, 'These have no master. Let them each return to his house in peace.'"

17 The king of Israel said to Jehoshaphat, "Didn't I tell you that he would not prophesy good concerning me, but evil?"

18 Micaiah said, "Therefore hear the LORD's word: I saw the LORD sitting on his throne, and all the army of heaven standing on his right hand and on his left. 19 The LORD said, 'Who will entice Ahab king of Israel, that he may go up and fall at Ramoth Gilead?' One spoke saying in this way, and another saying in that way. 20 A spirit came out, stood before the LORD, and said, 'I will entice him.'

"The LORD said to him, 'How?'

21 "He said, 'I will go, and will be a lying spirit in the mouth of all his prophets.'

"He said, 'You will entice him, and will prevail also. Go and do so.'

22 "Now therefore, behold, the LORD has put a lying spirit in the mouth of these your prophets; and the LORD has spoken evil concerning you."

23 Then Zedekiah the son of Chenaanah came near, and struck Micaiah on the cheek, and said, "Which way did the LORD's Spirit go from me to speak to you?"

24 Micaiah said, "Behold, you shall see on that day, when you go into an inner room to hide yourself."

25 The king of Israel said, "Take Micaiah, and carry him back to Amon the governor of the city, and to Joash the king's son; 26 and say, 'The king says, "Put this fellow in the prison, and feed him with bread of affliction and with water of affliction, until I return in peace."'"

27 Micaiah said, "If you return at all in peace, the LORD has not spoken by me." He said, "Listen, you people, all of you!"

28 So the king of Israel and Jehoshaphat the king of Judah went up to Ramoth Gilead. 29 The king of Israel said to Jehoshaphat, "I will disguise myself, and go into the battle; but you put on your robes." So the king of Israel disguised himself; and they went into the battle. 30 Now the king of Syria had commanded the captains of his chariots, saying, "Don't fight with small nor great, except only with the king of Israel."

31 When the captains of the chariots saw Jehoshaphat, they said, "It is the king of Israel!" Therefore they turned around to fight against him. But Jehoshaphat cried out, and the LORD helped him; and God moved them to depart from him. 32 When the captains of the chariots saw that it was not the king of Israel, they turned back from pursuing him. 33 A certain man drew his bow at random, and struck the king of Israel between the joints of the armour. Therefore he said to the driver of the chariot, "Turn around and carry me out of the battle, for I am severely wounded." 34 The battle increased that day. However, the king of Israel propped himself up in his chariot against the Syrians until the evening; and at about sunset, he died.

19

1 Jehoshaphat the king of Judah returned to his house in peace to Jerusalem. 2 Jehu the son of Hanani the seer went out to meet him, and said to King Jehoshaphat, "Should you help the wicked, and love those who hate the LORD? Because of this, wrath is on you from before the LORD. 3 Nevertheless there are good things found in you, in that you have put away the Asheroth out of the land, and have set your heart to seek God."

4 Jehoshaphat lived at Jerusalem; and he went out again amongst the people from Beersheba to the hill country of Ephraim, and brought them back to the LORD, the God of their fathers. 5 He set judges in the land throughout all the fortified cities of Judah, city by city, 6 and said to the judges, "Consider what you do, for you don't judge for man, but for the LORD; and he is with you in the judgement. 7 Now therefore let the fear of the LORD be on you. Take heed and do it; for there is no iniquity with the LORD our God, nor respect of persons, nor taking of bribes."

8 Moreover in Jerusalem Jehoshaphat appointed certain Levites, priests, and heads of the fathers' households of Israel to give judgement for the LORD and for controversies. They returned to Jerusalem. 9 He commanded them, saying, "You shall do this in the fear of the LORD, faithfully, and with a perfect heart. 10 Whenever any controversy comes to you from your brothers who dwell in their cities, between blood and blood, between law and commandment, statutes and ordinances, you must warn them, that they not be guilty towards the LORD, and so wrath come on you and on your brothers. Do this, and you will not be guilty. 11 Behold, Amariah the chief priest is over you in all matters of the LORD; and Zebadiah the son of Ishmael, the ruler of the house of Judah, in all the king's matters. Also the Levites shall be officers before you. Deal courageously, and may the LORD be with the good."

20

1 After this, the children of Moab, the children of Ammon, and with them some of the Ammonites, came against Jehoshaphat to battle. 2 Then some came who told Jehoshaphat, saying, "A great multitude is coming against you from beyond the sea from Syria. Behold, they are in Hazazon Tamar" (that is, En Gedi). 3 Jehoshaphat was alarmed, and set himself to seek the LORD. He proclaimed a fast throughout all Judah. 4 Judah gathered themselves together to seek help from the LORD. They came out of all the cities of Judah to seek the LORD.

5 Jehoshaphat stood in the assembly of Judah and Jerusalem, in the LORD's house, before the new court; 6 and he said, "LORD, the God of our fathers, aren't you God in heaven? Aren't you ruler over all the kingdoms of the nations? Power and might are in your hand, so that no one is able to withstand you. 7 Didn't you, our God, drive out the inhabitants of this land before your people Israel, and give it to the offspring[a] of Abraham your friend forever? 8 They lived in it, and have built you a sanctuary in it for your name, saying, 9 'If evil comes on us—the sword, judgement, pestilence, or famine—we will stand before this house, and before you (for your name is in this house), and cry to you in our affliction, and you will hear and save.' 10 Now, behold, the children of Ammon and Moab and Mount Seir, whom you would not let Israel invade when they came out of the land of Egypt, but they turned away from them, and didn't destroy them; 11 behold, how they reward us, to come to cast us out of your possession, which you have given us to inherit. 12 Our God, will you not judge them? For we have no might against this great company that comes against us. We don't know what to do, but our eyes are on you."

13 All Judah stood before the LORD, with their little ones, their wives, and their children.

14 Then the LORD's Spirit came on Jahaziel the son of Zechariah, the son of Benaiah, the son of Jeiel, the son of Mattaniah, the Levite, of the sons of Asaph, in the middle of the assembly; 15 and he said, "Listen, all Judah, and you inhabitants of Jerusalem, and you, King Jehoshaphat. The LORD says to you, 'Don't be afraid, and don't be dismayed because of this great multitude; for the battle is not yours, but God's. 16 Tomorrow, go down against them. Behold, they are coming up by the ascent of Ziz. You will find them at the end of the valley, before the wilderness of Jeruel. 17 You will not need to fight this battle. Set yourselves, stand still, and see the salvation of the LORD with you, O Judah and Jerusalem. Don't be afraid, nor be dismayed. Go out against them tomorrow, for the LORD is with you.'"

18 Jehoshaphat bowed his head with his face to the ground; and all Judah and the inhabitants of Jerusalem fell down before the LORD, worshipping the LORD. 19 The Levites, of the children of the Kohathites and of the children of the Korahites, stood up to praise the LORD, the God of Israel, with an exceedingly loud voice.

20 They rose early in the morning and went out into the wilderness of Tekoa. As they went out, Jehoshaphat stood and said, "Listen to me, Judah and you inhabitants of Jerusalem! Believe in the LORD your God, so you will be established! Believe his prophets, so you will prosper."

21 When he had taken counsel with the people, he appointed those who were to sing to the LORD and give praise in holy array as they go out before the army, and say, "Give thanks to the LORD, for his loving kindness endures forever." 22 When they began to sing and to praise, the LORD set ambushers against the children of Ammon, Moab, and Mount Seir, who had come against Judah; and they were struck. 23 For the children of Ammon and Moab stood up against the inhabitants of Mount Seir to utterly kill and destroy them. When they had finished the inhabitants of Seir, everyone helped to destroy each other.

24 When Judah came to the place overlooking the wilderness, they looked at the multitude; and behold, they were dead bodies fallen to the earth, and there were none who escaped. 25 When Jehoshaphat and his people came to take their plunder, they found amongst them in abundance both riches and dead bodies with precious jewels, which they stripped off for themselves, more than they could carry away. They took plunder for three days, it was so much. 26 On the fourth day, they assembled

---

a 20:7 or, seed

themselves in Beracah[a] Valley, for there they blessed the LORD. Therefore the name of that place was called "Beracah Valley" to this day. 27 Then they returned, every man of Judah and Jerusalem, with Jehoshaphat in front of them, to go again to Jerusalem with joy; for the LORD had made them to rejoice over their enemies. 28 They came to Jerusalem with stringed instruments, harps, and trumpets to the LORD's house. 29 The fear of God was on all the kingdoms of the countries when they heard that the LORD fought against the enemies of Israel. 30 So the realm of Jehoshaphat was quiet, for his God gave him rest all around.

31 So Jehoshaphat reigned over Judah. He was thirty-five years old when he began to reign. He reigned twenty-five years in Jerusalem. His mother's name was Azubah the daughter of Shilhi. 32 He walked in the way of Asa his father, and didn't turn away from it, doing that which was right in the LORD's eyes. 33 However the high places were not taken away, and the people had still not set their hearts on the God of their fathers.

34 Now the rest of the acts of Jehoshaphat, first and last, behold, they are written in the history of Jehu the son of Hanani, which is included in the book of the kings of Israel.

35 After this, Jehoshaphat king of Judah joined himself with Ahaziah king of Israel. The same did very wickedly. 36 He joined himself with him to make ships to go to Tarshish. They made the ships in Ezion Geber. 37 Then Eliezer the son of Dodavahu of Mareshah prophesied against Jehoshaphat, saying, "Because you have joined yourself with Ahaziah, the LORD has destroyed your works." The ships were wrecked, so that they were not able to go to Tarshish.

21

1 Jehoshaphat slept with his fathers, and was buried with his fathers in David's city; and Jehoram his son reigned in his place. 2 He had brothers, the sons of Jehoshaphat: Azariah, Jehiel, Zechariah, Azariah, Michael, and Shephatiah. All these were the sons of Jehoshaphat king of Israel. 3 Their father gave them great gifts of silver, of gold, and of precious things, with fortified cities in Judah; but he gave the kingdom to Jehoram, because he was the firstborn. 4 Now when Jehoram had risen up over the kingdom of his father, and had strengthened himself, he killed all his brothers with the sword, and also some of the princes of Israel. 5 Jehoram was thirty-two years old when he began to reign, and he reigned eight years in Jerusalem. 6 He walked in the way of the kings of Israel, as did Ahab's house, for he had Ahab's daughter as his wife. He did that which was evil in the LORD's sight. 7 However the LORD would not destroy David's house, because of the covenant that he had made with David, and as he promised to give a lamp to him and to his children always.

8 In his days Edom revolted from under the hand of Judah, and made a king over themselves. 9 Then Jehoram went there with his captains and all his chariots with him. He rose up by night and struck the Edomites who surrounded him, along with the captains of the chariots. 10 So Edom has been in revolt from under the hand of Judah to this day. Then Libnah revolted at the same time from under his hand, because he had forsaken the LORD, the God of his fathers.

11 Moreover he made high places in the mountains of Judah, and made the inhabitants of Jerusalem play the prostitute, and led Judah astray. 12 A letter came to him from Elijah the prophet, saying, "the LORD, the God of David your father, says, 'Because you have not walked in the ways of Jehoshaphat your father, nor in the ways of Asa king of Judah, 13 but have walked in the way of the kings of Israel, and have made Judah and the inhabitants of Jerusalem to play the prostitute like Ahab's house did, and also have slain your brothers of your father's house, who were better than yourself, 14 behold, the LORD will strike your people with a great plague, including your children, your wives, and all your possessions; 15 and you will have great sickness with a disease of your bowels, until your bowels fall out by reason of the sickness, day by day.'"

16 The LORD stirred up against Jehoram the spirit of the Philistines and of the Arabians who are beside the Ethiopians; 17 and they came up against Judah, broke into it, and carried away all the possessions that were found in the king's house, including his sons and his wives, so that there was no son left to him except Jehoahaz, the youngest of his sons.

18 After all this the LORD struck him in his bowels with an incurable disease. 19 In process of time, at the end of two years, his bowels fell out by reason of his sickness, and he died of severe diseases. His people made no burning for him, like the burning of his fathers. 20 He was thirty-two years old when he began to reign, and he reigned in Jerusalem eight years. He departed with no one's regret. They buried him in David's city, but not in the tombs of the kings.

22

1 The inhabitants of Jerusalem made Ahaziah his youngest son king in his place, because the band of men who came with the Arabians to the camp had slain all the oldest. So Ahaziah the son of Jehoram king of Judah reigned. 2 Ahaziah was forty-two years old when he began to reign, and he reigned one year in Jerusalem. His mother's name was Athaliah the daughter of Omri. 3 He also walked in the ways of Ahab's house, because his mother was his counsellor in acting wickedly. 4 He did that which was evil in the LORD's sight, as did Ahab's house, for they were his counsellors after the death of his father, to his destruction. 5 He also followed their counsel, and went with Jehoram the son of Ahab king of Israel to war against Hazael king of Syria at Ramoth Gilead; and the Syrians wounded Joram. 6 He returned to be healed in Jezreel of the wounds which they had given him at Ramah, when he fought against Hazael king of Syria. Azariah

the son of Jehoram, king of Judah, went down to see Jehoram the son of Ahab in Jezreel, because he was sick.

7 Now the destruction of Ahaziah was of God, in that he went to Joram; for when he had come, he went out with Jehoram against Jehu the son of Nimshi, whom the LORD had anointed to cut off Ahab's house. 8 When Jehu was executing judgement on Ahab's house, he found the princes of Judah and the sons of the brothers of Ahaziah serving Ahaziah, and killed them. 9 He sought Ahaziah, and they caught him (now he was hiding in Samaria), and they brought him to Jehu and killed him; and they buried him, for they said, "He is the son of Jehoshaphat, who sought the LORD with all his heart." The house of Ahaziah had no power to hold the kingdom.

10 Now when Athaliah the mother of Ahaziah saw that her son was dead, she arose and destroyed all the royal offspring of the house of Judah. 11 But Jehoshabeath, the king's daughter, took Joash the son of Ahaziah, and stealthily rescued him from amongst the king's sons who were slain, and put him and his nurse in the bedroom. So Jehoshabeath, the daughter of King Jehoram, the wife of Jehoiada the priest (for she was the sister of Ahaziah), hid him from Athaliah, so that she didn't kill him. 12 He was with them hidden in God's house six years while Athaliah reigned over the land.

23

1 In the seventh year, Jehoiada strengthened himself, and took the captains of hundreds—Azariah the son of Jeroham, Ishmael the son of Jehohanan, Azariah the son of Obed, Maaseiah the son of Adaiah, and Elishaphat the son of Zichri—into a covenant with him. 2 They went around in Judah and gathered the Levites out of all the cities of Judah, and the heads of fathers' households of Israel, and they came to Jerusalem. 3 All the assembly made a covenant with the king in God's house. Jehoiada[b] said to them, "Behold, the king's son must reign, as the LORD has spoken concerning the sons of David. 4 This is the thing that you must do: a third part of you, who come in on the Sabbath, of the priests and of the Levites, shall be gatekeepers of the thresholds. 5 A third part shall be at the king's house; and a third part at the gate of the foundation. All the people will be in the courts of the LORD's house. 6 But let no one come into the LORD's house except the priests and those who minister of the Levites. They shall come in, for they are holy, but all the people shall follow the LORD's instructions. 7 The Levites shall surround the king, every man with his weapons in his hand. Whoever comes into the house, let him be slain. Be with the king when he comes in and when he goes out."

8 So the Levites and all Judah did according to all that Jehoiada the priest commanded. They each took his men, those who were to come in on the Sabbath, with those who were to go out on the Sabbath, for Jehoiada the priest didn't dismiss the shift. 9 Jehoiada the priest delivered to the captains of hundreds the spears, bucklers, and shields that had been king David's, which were in God's house. 10 He set all the people, every man with his weapon in his hand, from the right side of the house to the left side of the house, near the altar and the house, around the king. 11 Then they brought out the king's son, put the crown on him, gave him the covenant, and made him king. Jehoiada and his sons anointed him, and they said, "Long live the king!"

12 When Athaliah heard the noise of the people running and praising the king, she came to the people into the LORD's house. 13 Then she looked, and behold, the king stood by his pillar at the entrance, with the captains and the trumpeters by the king. All the people of the land rejoiced and blew trumpets. The singers also played musical instruments, and led the singing of praise. Then Athaliah tore her clothes, and said, "Treason! treason!"

14 Jehoiada the priest brought out the captains of hundreds who were set over the army, and said to them, "Bring her out between the ranks; and whoever follows her, let him be slain with the sword." For the priest said, "Don't kill her in the LORD's house." 15 So they made way for her. She went to the entrance of the horse gate to the king's house; and they killed her there.

16 Jehoiada made a covenant between himself, all the people, and the king, that they should be the LORD's people. 17 All the people went to the house of Baal, broke it down, broke his altars and his images in pieces, and killed Mattan the priest of Baal before the altars. 18 Jehoiada appointed the officers of the LORD's house under the hand of the Levitical priests, whom David had distributed in the LORD's house, to offer the burnt offerings of the LORD, as it is written in the law of Moses, with rejoicing and with singing, as David had ordered. 19 He set the gatekeepers at the gates of the LORD's house, that no one who was unclean in anything should enter in. 20 He took the captains of hundreds, the nobles, the governors of the people, and all the people of the land, and brought the king down from the LORD's house. They came through the upper gate to the king's house, and set the king on the throne of the kingdom. 21 So all the people of the land rejoiced, and the city was quiet. They had slain Athaliah with the sword.

24

1 Joash was seven years old when he began to reign, and he reigned forty years in Jerusalem. His mother's name was Zibiah, of Beersheba. 2 Joash did that which was right in the LORD's eyes all the days of Jehoiada the priest. 3 Jehoiada took for him two wives, and he became the father of sons and daughters.

4 After this, Joash intended to restore the LORD's house. 5 He gathered together the priests and the Levites, and said to them, "Go out to the cities of Judah, and gather money to repair the house of your God from

---

[a] 20:26 "Beracah" means "blessing". | [b] 23:3 Hebrew He

all Israel from year to year. See that you expedite this matter." However the Levites didn't do it right away. 6 The king called for Jehoiada the chief, and said to him, "Why haven't you required of the Levites to bring in the tax of Moses the servant of the LORD, and of the assembly of Israel, out of Judah and out of Jerusalem, for the Tent of the Testimony?" 7 For the sons of Athaliah, that wicked woman, had broken up God's house; and they also gave all the dedicated things of the LORD's house to the Baals.

8 So the king commanded, and they made a chest, and set it outside at the gate of the LORD's house. 9 They made a proclamation through Judah and Jerusalem, to bring in for the LORD the tax that Moses the servant of God laid on Israel in the wilderness. 10 All the princes and all the people rejoiced, and brought in, and cast into the chest, until they had filled it. 11 Whenever the chest was brought to the king's officers by the hand of the Levites, and when they saw that there was much money, the king's scribe and the chief priest's officer came and emptied the chest, and took it, and carried it to its place again. Thus they did day by day, and gathered money in abundance. 12 The king and Jehoiada gave it to those who did the work of the service of the LORD's house. They hired masons and carpenters to restore the LORD's house, and also those who worked iron and bronze to repair the LORD's house. 13 So the workmen worked, and the work of repairing went forward in their hands. They set up God's house as it was designed, and strengthened it. 14 When they had finished, they brought the rest of the money before the king and Jehoiada, from which were made vessels for the LORD's house, even vessels with which to minister and to offer, including spoons and vessels of gold and silver. They offered burnt offerings in the LORD's house continually all the days of Jehoiada.

15 But Jehoiada grew old and was full of days, and he died. He was one hundred and thirty years old when he died. 16 They buried him in David's city amongst the kings, because he had done good in Israel, and towards God and his house.

17 Now after the death of Jehoiada, the princes of Judah came and bowed down to the king. Then the king listened to them. 18 They abandoned the house of the LORD, the God of their fathers, and served the Asherah poles and the idols, so wrath came on Judah and Jerusalem for this their guiltiness. 19 Yet he sent prophets to them to bring them again to the LORD, and they testified against them; but they would not listen.

20 The Spirit of God came on Zechariah the son of Jehoiada the priest; and he stood above the people, and said to them, "God says, 'Why do you disobey the LORD's commandments, so that you can't prosper? Because you have forsaken the LORD, he has also forsaken you.'"

21 They conspired against him, and stoned him with stones at the commandment of the king in the court of the LORD's house. 22 Thus Joash the king didn't remember the kindness which Jehoiada his father had done to him, but killed his son. When he died, he said, "May the LORD look at it, and repay it."

23 At the end of the year, the army of the Syrians came up against him. They came to Judah and Jerusalem, and destroyed all the princes of the people from amongst the people, and sent all their plunder to the king of Damascus. 24 For the army of the Syrians came with a small company of men; and the LORD delivered a very great army into their hand, because they had forsaken the LORD, the God of their fathers. So they executed judgement on Joash.

25 When they had departed from him (for they left him seriously wounded), his own servants conspired against him for the blood of the sons of Jehoiada the priest, and killed him on his bed, and he died. They buried him in David's city, but they didn't bury him in the tombs of the kings. 26 These are those who conspired against him: Zabad the son of Shimeath the Ammonitess and Jehozabad the son of Shimrith the Moabitess. 27 Now concerning his sons, the greatness of the burdens laid on him, and the rebuilding of God's house, behold, they are written in the commentary of the book of the kings. Amaziah his son reigned in his place.

25

1 Amaziah was twenty-five years old when he began to reign, and he reigned twenty-nine years in Jerusalem. His mother's name was Jehoaddan, of Jerusalem. 2 He did that which was right in the LORD's eyes, but not with a perfect heart. 3 Now when the kingdom was established to him, he killed his servants who had killed his father the king. 4 But he didn't put their children to death, but did according to that which is written in the law in the book of Moses, as the LORD commanded, saying, "The fathers shall not die for the children, neither shall the children die for the fathers; but every man shall die for his own sin."

5 Moreover Amaziah gathered Judah together and ordered them according to their fathers' houses, under captains of thousands and captains of hundreds, even all Judah and Benjamin. He counted them from twenty years old and upward, and found that there were three hundred thousand chosen men, able to go out to war, who could handle spear and shield. 6 He also hired one hundred thousand mighty men of valour out of Israel for one hundred talents[a] of silver. 7 A man of God came to him, saying, "O king, don't let the army of Israel go with you, for the LORD is not with Israel, with all the children of Ephraim. 8 But if you will go, take action, and be strong for the battle. God will overthrow you before the enemy; for God has power to help, and to overthrow."

9 Amaziah said to the man of God, "But what shall we do for the hundred talents[b] which I have given to the army of Israel?"

The man of God answered, "The LORD is able to give you much more than this."

10 Then Amaziah separated them, the army that had come to him out of Ephraim, to go home again. Therefore their anger was greatly kindled against Judah, and they returned home in fierce anger.

11 Amaziah took courage, and led his people out and went to the Valley of Salt, and struck ten thousand of the children of Seir. 12 The children of Judah carried away ten thousand alive, and brought them to the top of the rock, and threw them down from the top of the rock, so that they all were broken in pieces. 13 But the men of the army whom Amaziah sent back, that they should not go with him to battle, fell on the cities of Judah from Samaria even to Beth Horon, and struck of them three thousand, and took much plunder.

14 Now after Amaziah had come from the slaughter of the Edomites, he brought the gods of the children of Seir, and set them up to be his gods, and bowed down himself before them and burnt incense to them. 15 Therefore the LORD's anger burnt against Amaziah, and he sent to him a prophet who said to him, "Why have you sought after the gods of the people, which have not delivered their own people out of your hand?"

16 As he talked with him, the king said to him, "Have we made you one of the king's counsellors? Stop! Why should you be struck down?"

Then the prophet stopped, and said, "I know that God has determined to destroy you, because you have done this and have not listened to my counsel."

17 Then Amaziah king of Judah consulted his advisers, and sent to Joash, the son of Jehoahaz, the son of Jehu, king of Israel, saying, "Come! Let's look one another in the face."

18 Joash king of Israel sent to Amaziah king of Judah, saying, "The thistle that was in Lebanon sent to the cedar that was in Lebanon, saying, 'Give your daughter to my son as his wife. Then a wild animal that was in Lebanon passed by and trampled down the thistle. 19 You say to yourself that you have struck Edom; and your heart lifts you up to boast. Now stay at home. Why should you meddle with trouble, that you should fall, even you and Judah with you?'"

20 But Amaziah would not listen; for it was of God, that he might deliver them into the hand of their enemies, because they had sought after the gods of Edom. 21 So Joash king of Israel went up, and he and Amaziah king of Judah looked one another in the face at Beth Shemesh, which belongs to Judah. 22 Judah was defeated by Israel; so every man fled to his tent.

23 Joash king of Israel took Amaziah king of Judah, the son of Joash the son of Jehoahaz, at Beth Shemesh and brought him to Jerusalem, and broke down the wall of Jerusalem from the gate of Ephraim to the corner gate, four hundred cubits.[c] 24 He took all the gold and silver, and all the vessels that were found in God's house with Obed-Edom, and the treasures of the king's house, and the hostages, and returned to Samaria.

25 Amaziah the son of Joash, king of Judah, lived for fifteen years after the death of Joash, son of Jehoahaz, king of Israel. 26 Now the rest of the acts of Amaziah, first and last, behold, aren't they written in the book of the kings of Judah and Israel? 27 Now from the time that Amaziah turned away from following the LORD, they made a conspiracy against him in Jerusalem. He fled to Lachish, but they sent after him to Lachish and killed him there. 28 They brought him on horses and buried him with his fathers in the City of Judah.

26

1 All the people of Judah took Uzziah, who was sixteen years old, and made him king in the place of his father Amaziah. 2 He built Eloth and restored it to Judah. After that the king slept with his fathers. 3 Uzziah was sixteen years old when he began to reign; and he reigned fifty-two years in Jerusalem. His mother's name was Jechiliah, of Jerusalem. 4 He did that which was right in the LORD's eyes, according to all that his father Amaziah had done. 5 He set himself to seek God in the days of Zechariah, who had understanding in the vision of God; and as long as he sought the LORD, God made him prosper.

6 He went out and fought against the Philistines, and broke down the wall of Gath, the wall of Jabneh, and the wall of Ashdod; and he built cities in the country of Ashdod, and amongst the Philistines. 7 God helped him against the Philistines, and against the Arabians who lived in Gur Baal, and the Meunim. 8 The Ammonites gave tribute to Uzziah. His name spread abroad even to the entrance of Egypt, for he grew exceedingly strong. 9 Moreover Uzziah built towers in Jerusalem at the corner gate, at the valley gate, and at the turning of the wall, and fortified them. 10 He built towers in the wilderness, and dug out many cisterns, for he had much livestock, both in the lowlands and in the plains. He had farmers and vineyard keepers in the mountains and in the fruitful fields, for he loved farming. 11 Moreover Uzziah had an army of fighting men who went out to war by bands, according to the number of their reckoning made by Jeiel the scribe and Maaseiah the officer, under the hand of Hananiah, one of the king's captains. 12 The whole number of the heads of fathers' households, even the mighty men of valour, was two thousand and six hundred. 13 Under their hand was an army, three hundred and seven thousand and five hundred, who made war with mighty power, to help the king against the

---

a *25:6* A talent is about 30 kilograms or 66 pounds
b *25:9* A talent is about 30 kilograms or 66 pounds

c *25:23* A cubit is the length from the tip of the middle finger to the elbow on a man's arm, or about 18 inches or 46 centimetres, so 400 cubits is about 200 yards or 184 metres.

enemy. 14 Uzziah prepared for them, even for all the army, shields, spears, helmets, coats of mail, bows, and stones for slinging. 15 In Jerusalem, he made devices, invented by skilful men, to be on the towers and on the battlements, with which to shoot arrows and great stones. His name spread far abroad, because he was marvellously helped until he was strong.

16 But when he was strong, his heart was lifted up, so that he did corruptly and he trespassed against the LORD his God, for he went into the LORD's temple to burn incense on the altar of incense. 17 Azariah the priest went in after him, and with him eighty priests of the LORD, who were valiant men. 18 They resisted Uzziah the king, and said to him, "It isn't for you, Uzziah, to burn incense to the LORD, but for the priests the sons of Aaron, who are consecrated to burn incense. Go out of the sanctuary, for you have trespassed. It will not be for your honour from the LORD God."

19 Then Uzziah was angry. He had a censer in his hand to burn incense, and while he was angry with the priests, the leprosy broke out on his forehead before the priests in the LORD's house, beside the altar of incense. 20 Azariah the chief priest and all the priests looked at him, and behold, he was leprous in his forehead; and they thrust him out quickly from there. Indeed, he himself also hurried to go out, because the LORD had struck him. 21 Uzziah the king was a leper to the day of his death, and lived in a separate house, being a leper; for he was cut off from the LORD's house. Jotham his son was over the king's house, judging the people of the land.

22 Now the rest of the acts of Uzziah, first and last, Isaiah the prophet, the son of Amoz, wrote. 23 So Uzziah slept with his fathers; and they buried him with his fathers in the field of burial which belonged to the kings, for they said, "He is a leper." Jotham his son reigned in his place.

27

1 Jotham was twenty-five years old when he began to reign, and he reigned sixteen years in Jerusalem. His mother's name was Jerushah the daughter of Zadok. 2 He did that which was right in the LORD's eyes, according to all that his father Uzziah had done. However he didn't enter into the LORD's temple. The people still acted corruptly. 3 He built the upper gate of the LORD's house, and he built much on the wall of Ophel. 4 Moreover he built cities in the hill country of Judah, and in the forests he built fortresses and towers. 5 He also fought with the king of the children of Ammon, and prevailed against them. The children of Ammon gave him the same year one hundred talents[a] of silver, ten thousand cors[b] of wheat, and ten thousand cors of barley.[c] The children of Ammon also gave that much to him in the second year, and in the third. 6 So Jotham became mighty, because he ordered his ways before the LORD his God. 7 Now the rest of the acts of Jotham, and all his wars and his ways, behold, they are written in the book of the kings of Israel and Judah. 8 He was twenty-five years old when he began to reign, and reigned sixteen years in Jerusalem. 9 Jotham slept with his fathers, and they buried him in David's city; and Ahaz his son reigned in his place.

28

1 Ahaz was twenty years old when he began to reign, and he reigned sixteen years in Jerusalem. He didn't do that which was right in the LORD's eyes, like David his father, 2 but he walked in the ways of the kings of Israel, and also made molten images for the Baals. 3 Moreover he burnt incense in the valley of the son of Hinnom, and burnt his children in the fire, according to the abominations of the nations whom the LORD cast out before the children of Israel. 4 He sacrificed and burnt incense in the high places, and on the hills, and under every green tree.

5 Therefore the LORD his God delivered him into the hand of the king of Syria. They struck him, and carried away from him a great multitude of captives, and brought them to Damascus. He was also delivered into the hand of the king of Israel, who struck him with a great slaughter. 6 For Pekah the son of Remaliah killed in Judah one hundred and twenty thousand in one day, all of them valiant men, because they had forsaken the LORD, the God of their fathers. 7 Zichri, a mighty man of Ephraim, killed Maaseiah the king's son, Azrikam the ruler of the house, and Elkanah who was next to the king. 8 The children of Israel carried away captive of their brothers two hundred thousand women, sons, and daughters, and also took away much plunder from them, and brought the plunder to Samaria. 9 But a prophet of the LORD was there, whose name was Oded; and he went out to meet the army that came to Samaria, and said to them, "Behold, because the LORD, the God of your fathers, was angry with Judah, he has delivered them into your hand, and you have slain them in a rage which has reached up to heaven. 10 Now you intend to degrade the children of Judah and Jerusalem as male and female slaves for yourselves. Aren't there even with you trespasses of your own against the LORD your God? 11 Now hear me therefore, and send back the captives that you have taken captive from your brothers, for the fierce wrath of the LORD is on you." 12 Then some of the heads of the children of Ephraim, Azariah the son of Johanan, Berechiah the son of Meshillemoth, Jehizkiah the son of Shallum, and Amasa the son of Hadlai, stood up against those who came from the war, 13 and said to them, "You must not bring in the captives here, for you intend that which will bring on us a trespass against the LORD, to add to our sins and to our guilt; for our guilt is great, and there is fierce wrath against Israel."

14 So the armed men left the captives and the plunder before the princes and all the assembly. 15 The men who have been mentioned by name rose up and took the captives, and with the plunder clothed all who were naked amongst them, dressed them, gave them sandals, gave them something to eat and to drink, anointed them, carried all the feeble of them on donkeys, and brought them to Jericho, the city of palm trees, to their brothers. Then they returned to Samaria.

16 At that time King Ahaz sent to the kings of Assyria to help him. 17 For again the Edomites had come and struck Judah, and carried away captives. 18 The Philistines also had invaded the cities of the lowland and of the South of Judah, and had taken Beth Shemesh, Aijalon, Gederoth, Soco with its villages, Timnah with its villages, and also Gimzo and its villages; and they lived there. 19 For the LORD brought Judah low because of Ahaz king of Israel, because he acted without restraint in Judah and trespassed severely against the LORD. 20 Tilgath-pilneser king of Assyria came to him and gave him trouble, but didn't strengthen him. 21 For Ahaz took away a portion out of the LORD's house, and out of the house of the king and of the princes, and gave it to the king of Assyria; but it didn't help him.

22 In the time of his distress, he trespassed yet more against the LORD, this same King Ahaz. 23 For he sacrificed to the gods of Damascus which had defeated him. He said, "Because the gods of the kings of Syria helped them, I will sacrifice to them, that they may help me." But they were the ruin of him and of all Israel. 24 Ahaz gathered together the vessels of God's house, cut the vessels of God's house in pieces, and shut up the doors of the LORD's house; and he made himself altars in every corner of Jerusalem. 25 In every city of Judah he made high places to burn incense to other gods, and provoked the LORD, the God of his fathers, to anger.

26 Now the rest of his acts, and all his ways, first and last, behold, they are written in the book of the kings of Judah and Israel. 27 Ahaz slept with his fathers, and they buried him in the city, even in Jerusalem, because they didn't bring him into the tombs of the kings of Israel; and Hezekiah his son reigned in his place.

29

1 Hezekiah began to reign when he was twenty-five years old, and he reigned twenty-nine years in Jerusalem. His mother's name was Abijah, the daughter of Zechariah. 2 He did that which was right in the LORD's eyes, according to all that David his father had done. 3 In the first year of his reign, in the first month, he opened the doors of the LORD's house and repaired them. 4 He brought in the priests and the Levites and gathered them together into the wide place on the east, 5 and said to them, "Listen to me, you Levites! Now sanctify yourselves, and sanctify the house of the LORD, the God of your fathers, and carry the filthiness out of the holy place. 6 For our fathers were unfaithful, and have done that which was evil in the LORD our God's sight, and have forsaken him, and have turned away their faces from the habitation of the LORD, and turned their backs. 7 Also they have shut up the doors of the porch, and put out the lamps, and have not burnt incense nor offered burnt offerings in the holy place to the God of Israel. 8 Therefore the LORD's wrath was on Judah and Jerusalem, and he has delivered them to be tossed back and forth, to be an astonishment and a hissing, as you see with your eyes. 9 For behold, our fathers have fallen by the sword, and our sons and our daughters and our wives are in captivity for this. 10 Now it is in my heart to make a covenant with the LORD, the God of Israel, that his fierce anger may turn away from us. 11 My sons, don't be negligent now; for the LORD has chosen you to stand before him, to minister to him, and that you should be his ministers and burn incense."

12 Then the Levites arose: Mahath, the son of Amasai, and Joel the son of Azariah, of the sons of the Kohathites; and of the sons of Merari, Kish the son of Abdi, and Azariah the son of Jehallelel; and of the Gershonites, Joah the son of Zimmah, and Eden the son of Joah; 13 and of the sons of Elizaphan, Shimri and Jeuel; and of the sons of Asaph, Zechariah and Mattaniah; 14 and of the sons of Heman, Jehuel and Shimei; and of the sons of Jeduthun, Shemaiah and Uzziel. 15 They gathered their brothers, sanctified themselves, and went in, according to the commandment of the king by the LORD's words, to cleanse the LORD's house. 16 The priests went into the inner part of the LORD's house to cleanse it, and brought out all the uncleanness that they found in the LORD's temple into the court of the LORD's house. The Levites took it from there to carry it out to the brook Kidron. 17 Now they began on the first day of the first month to sanctify, and on the eighth day of the month they came to the LORD's porch. They sanctified the LORD's house in eight days, and on the sixteenth day of the first month they finished. 18 Then they went in to Hezekiah the king within the palace and said, "We have cleansed all the LORD's house, including the altar of burnt offering with all its vessels, and the table of show bread with all its vessels. 19 Moreover, we have prepared and sanctified all the vessels which King Ahaz threw away in his reign when he was unfaithful. Behold, they are before the LORD's altar."

20 Then Hezekiah the king arose early, gathered the princes of the city, and went up to the LORD's house. 21 They brought seven bulls, seven rams, seven lambs, and seven male goats, for a sin offering for the kingdom, for the sanctuary, and for Judah. He commanded the priests the sons of Aaron to offer them on the LORD's altar. 22 So they killed the bulls, and the priests received the blood and sprinkled it on the altar. They killed the rams and sprinkled the blood on the altar. They also killed the lambs and sprinkled the blood on the altar. 23 They brought near the male goats for the sin offering before the king and the assembly; and they laid their

---

[a] *27:5* A talent is about 30 kilograms or 66 pounds
[b] *27:5* 1 cor is the same as a homer, or about 55.9 U. S. gallons (liquid) or 211 litres or 6 bushels. 10,000 cors of wheat would weigh about 1,640 metric tonnes.
[c] *27:5* 10,000 cors of barley would weigh about 1,310 metric tonnes.

hands on them. 24 Then the priests killed them, and they made a sin offering with their blood on the altar, to make atonement for all Israel; for the king commanded that the burnt offering and the sin offering should be made for all Israel.

25 He set the Levites in the LORD's house with cymbals, with stringed instruments, and with harps, according to the commandment of David, of Gad the king's seer, and Nathan the prophet; for the commandment was from the LORD by his prophets. 26 The Levites stood with David's instruments, and the priests with the trumpets. 27 Hezekiah commanded them to offer the burnt offering on the altar. When the burnt offering began, the LORD's song also began, along with the trumpets and instruments of David king of Israel. 28 All the assembly worshipped, the singers sang, and the trumpeters sounded. All this continued until the burnt offering was finished.

29 When they had finished offering, the king and all who were present with him bowed themselves and worshipped. 30 Moreover Hezekiah the king and the princes commanded the Levites to sing praises to the LORD with the words of David, and of Asaph the seer. They sang praises with gladness, and they bowed their heads and worshipped.

31 Then Hezekiah answered, "Now you have consecrated yourselves to the LORD. Come near and bring sacrifices and thank offerings into the LORD's house." The assembly brought in sacrifices and thank offerings, and as many as were of a willing heart brought burnt offerings. 32 The number of the burnt offerings which the assembly brought was seventy bulls, one hundred rams, and two hundred lambs. All these were for a burnt offering to the LORD. 33 The consecrated things were six hundred head of cattle and three thousand sheep. 34 But the priests were too few, so that they could not skin all the burnt offerings. Therefore their brothers the Levites helped them until the work was ended, and until the priests had sanctified themselves, for the Levites were more upright in heart to sanctify themselves than the priests. 35 Also the burnt offerings were in abundance, with the fat of the peace offerings and with the drink offerings for every burnt offering. So the service of the LORD's house was set in order. 36 Hezekiah and all the people rejoiced because of that which God had prepared for the people; for the thing was done suddenly.

30

1 Hezekiah sent to all Israel and Judah, and wrote letters also to Ephraim and Manasseh, that they should come to the LORD's house at Jerusalem, to keep the Passover to the LORD, the God of Israel. 2 For the king had taken counsel with his princes and all the assembly in Jerusalem to keep the Passover in the second month. 3 For they could not keep it at that time, because the priests had not sanctified themselves in sufficient number, and the people had not gathered themselves together to Jerusalem. 4 The thing was right in the eyes of the king and of all the assembly. 5 So they established a decree to make proclamation throughout all Israel, from Beersheba even to Dan, that they should come to keep the Passover to the LORD, the God of Israel, at Jerusalem, for they had not kept it in great numbers in the way it is written.

6 So the couriers went with the letters from the king and his princes throughout all Israel and Judah, according to the commandment of the king, saying, "You children of Israel, turn again to the LORD, the God of Abraham, Isaac, and Israel, that he may return to the remnant of you that have escaped out of the hand of the kings of Assyria. 7 Don't be like your fathers and like your brothers, who trespassed against the LORD, the God of their fathers, so that he gave them up to desolation, as you see. 8 Now don't be stiff-necked, as your fathers were, but yield yourselves to the LORD, and enter into his sanctuary, which he has sanctified forever, and serve the LORD your God, that his fierce anger may turn away from you. 9 For if you turn again to the LORD, your brothers and your children will find compassion with those who led them captive, and will come again into this land, because the LORD your God is gracious and merciful, and will not turn away his face from you if you return to him."

10 So the couriers passed from city to city through the country of Ephraim and Manasseh, even to Zebulun, but people ridiculed them and mocked them. 11 Nevertheless some men of Asher, Manasseh, and Zebulun humbled themselves and came to Jerusalem. 12 Also the hand of God came on Judah to give them one heart, to do the commandment of the king and of the princes by the LORD's word.

13 Many people assembled at Jerusalem to keep the feast of unleavened bread in the second month, a very great assembly. 14 They arose and took away the altars that were in Jerusalem, and they took away all the altars for incense and threw them into the brook Kidron. 15 Then they killed the Passover on the fourteenth day of the second month. The priests and the Levites were ashamed, and sanctified themselves, and brought burnt offerings into the LORD's house. 16 They stood in their place after their order, according to the law of Moses the man of God. The priests sprinkled the blood which they received of the hand of the Levites. 17 For there were many in the assembly who had not sanctified themselves; therefore the Levites were in charge of killing the Passovers for everyone who was not clean, to sanctify them to the LORD. 18 For a multitude of the people, even many of Ephraim, Manasseh, Issachar, and Zebulun, had not cleansed themselves, yet they ate the Passover other than the way it is written. For Hezekiah had prayed for them, saying, "May the good LORD pardon everyone 19 who sets his heart to seek God, the LORD, the God of his fathers, even if they aren't clean according to the purification of the sanctuary."

20 The LORD listened to Hezekiah, and healed the people. 21 The children of Israel who were present at Jerusalem kept the feast of unleavened bread seven days with great gladness. The Levites and the

priests praised the LORD day by day, singing with loud instruments to the LORD. 22 Hezekiah spoke encouragingly to all the Levites who had good understanding in the service of the LORD. So they ate throughout the feast for the seven days, offering sacrifices of peace offerings and making confession to the LORD, the God of their fathers.

23 The whole assembly took counsel to keep another seven days, and they kept another seven days with gladness. 24 For Hezekiah king of Judah gave to the assembly for offerings one thousand bulls and seven thousand sheep; and the princes gave to the assembly a thousand bulls and ten thousand sheep; and a great number of priests sanctified themselves. 25 All the assembly of Judah, with the priests and the Levites, and all the assembly who came out of Israel, and the foreigners who came out of the land of Israel and who lived in Judah, rejoiced. 26 So there was great joy in Jerusalem; for since the time of Solomon the son of David king of Israel there was nothing like this in Jerusalem. 27 Then the Levitical priests arose and blessed the people. Their voice was heard, and their prayer came up to his holy habitation, even to heaven.

31

1 Now when all this was finished, all Israel who were present went out to the cities of Judah and broke the pillars in pieces, cut down the Asherah poles, and broke down the high places and the altars out of all Judah and Benjamin, also in Ephraim and Manasseh, until they had destroyed them all. Then all the children of Israel returned, every man to his possession, into their own cities.

2 Hezekiah appointed the divisions of the priests and the Levites after their divisions, every man according to his service, both the priests and the Levites, for burnt offerings and for peace offerings, to minister, to give thanks, and to praise in the gates of the LORD's camp. 3 He also appointed the king's portion of his possessions for the burnt offerings: for the morning and evening burnt offerings, and the burnt offerings for the Sabbaths, for the new moons, and for the set feasts, as it is written in the LORD's law. 4 Moreover he commanded the people who lived in Jerusalem to give the portion of the priests and the Levites, that they might give themselves to the LORD's law. 5 As soon as the commandment went out, the children of Israel gave in abundance the first fruits of grain, new wine, oil, honey, and of all the increase of the field; and they brought in the tithe of all things abundantly. 6 The children of Israel and Judah, who lived in the cities of Judah, also brought in the tithe of cattle and sheep, and the tithe of dedicated things which were consecrated to the LORD their God, and laid them in heaps.

7 In the third month, they began to lay the foundation of the heaps, and finished them in the seventh month. 8 When Hezekiah and the princes came and saw the heaps, they blessed the LORD and his people Israel. 9 Then Hezekiah questioned the priests and the Levites about the heaps. 10 Azariah the chief priest, of the house of Zadok, answered him and said, "Since people began to bring the offerings into the LORD's house, we have eaten and had enough, and have plenty left over, for the LORD has blessed his people; and that which is left is this great store."

11 Then Hezekiah commanded them to prepare rooms in the LORD's house, and they prepared them. 12 They brought in the offerings, the tithes, and the dedicated things faithfully. Conaniah the Levite was ruler over them, and Shimei his brother was second. 13 Jehiel, Azaziah, Nahath, Asahel, Jerimoth, Jozabad, Eliel, Ismachiah, Mahath, and Benaiah were overseers under the hand of Conaniah and Shimei his brother, by the appointment of Hezekiah the king and Azariah the ruler of God's house. 14 Kore the son of Imnah the Levite, the gatekeeper at the east gate, was over the free will offerings of God, to distribute the LORD's offerings and the most holy things. 15 Under him were Eden, Miniamin, Jeshua, Shemaiah, Amariah, and Shecaniah, in the cities of the priests, in their office of trust, to give to their brothers by divisions, to the great as well as to the small; 16 in addition to those who were listed by genealogy of males, from three years old and upward, even everyone who entered into the LORD's house, as the duty of every day required, for their service in their offices according to their divisions; 17 and those who were listed by genealogy of the priests by their fathers' houses, and the Levites from twenty years old and upward, in their offices by their divisions; 18 and those who were listed by genealogy of all their little ones, their wives, their sons, and their daughters, through all the congregation; for in their office of trust they sanctified themselves in holiness. 19 Also for the sons of Aaron the priests, who were in the fields of the pasture lands of their cities, in every city, there were men who were mentioned by name to give portions to all the males amongst the priests and to all who were listed by genealogy amongst the Levites.

20 Hezekiah did so throughout all Judah; and he did that which was good, right, and faithful before the LORD his God. 21 In every work that he began in the service of God's house, in the law, and in the commandments, to seek his God, he did it with all his heart and prospered.

32

1 After these things and this faithfulness, Sennacherib king of Assyria came, entered into Judah, encamped against the fortified cities, and intended to win them for himself. 2 When Hezekiah saw that Sennacherib had come, and that he was planning to fight against Jerusalem, 3 he took counsel with his princes and his mighty men to stop the waters of the springs which were outside of the city, and they helped him. 4 Then many people gathered together and they stopped all the springs and the brook that flowed through the middle of the land, saying, "Why should the kings of Assyria come, and find abundant water?"

5 He took courage, built up all the wall that was broken down, and raised it up to the towers, with the other wall outside, and strengthened Millo in David's city, and made weapons and shields in abundance. 6 He set captains of war over the people, gathered them together to him in the wide place at the gate of the city, and spoke encouragingly to them, saying, 7 "Be strong and courageous. Don't be afraid or dismayed because of the king of Assyria, nor for all the multitude who is with him; for there is a greater one with us than with him. 8 An arm of flesh is with him, but the LORD our God is with us to help us and to fight our battles." The people rested themselves on the words of Hezekiah king of Judah.

9 After this, Sennacherib king of Assyria sent his servants to Jerusalem, (now he was attacking Lachish, and all his forces were with him), to Hezekiah king of Judah, and to all Judah who were at Jerusalem, saying, 10 Sennacherib king of Assyria says, "In whom do you trust, that you remain under siege in Jerusalem? 11 Doesn't Hezekiah persuade you to give you over to die by famine and by thirst, saying, 'The LORD our God will deliver us out of the hand of the king of Assyria'? 12 Hasn't the same Hezekiah taken away his high places and his altars, and commanded Judah and Jerusalem, saying, 'You shall worship before one altar, and you shall burn incense on it'? 13 Don't you know what I and my fathers have done to all the peoples of the lands? Were the gods of the nations of those lands in any way able to deliver their land out of my hand? 14 Who was there amongst all the gods of those nations which my fathers utterly destroyed that could deliver his people out of my hand, that your God should be able to deliver you out of my hand? 15 Now therefore don't let Hezekiah deceive you nor persuade you in this way. Don't believe him, for no god of any nation or kingdom was able to deliver his people out of my hand, and out of the hand of my fathers. How much less will your God deliver you out of my hand?"

16 His servants spoke yet more against the LORD God and against his servant Hezekiah. 17 He also wrote letters insulting the LORD, the God of Israel, and speaking against him, saying, "As the gods of the nations of the lands, which have not delivered their people out of my hand, so shall the God of Hezekiah not deliver his people out of my hand." 18 They called out with a loud voice in the Jews' language to the people of Jerusalem who were on the wall, to frighten them and to trouble them, that they might take the city. 19 They spoke of the God of Jerusalem as of the gods of the peoples of the earth, which are the work of men's hands.

20 Hezekiah the king and Isaiah the prophet, the son of Amoz, prayed because of this, and cried to heaven.

21 The LORD sent an angel, who cut off all the mighty men of valour, the leaders, and captains in the camp of the king of Assyria. So he returned with shame of face to his own land. When he had come into the house of his god, those who came out of his own body[a] killed him there with the sword. 22 Thus the LORD saved Hezekiah and the inhabitants of Jerusalem from the hand of Sennacherib the king of Assyria and from the hand of all others, and guided them on every side. 23 Many brought gifts to the LORD to Jerusalem, and precious things to Hezekiah king of Judah, so that he was exalted in the sight of all nations from then on.

24 In those days Hezekiah was terminally ill, and he prayed to the LORD; and he spoke to him, and gave him a sign. 25 But Hezekiah didn't reciprocate appropriate to the benefit done for him, because his heart was lifted up. Therefore there was wrath on him, Judah, and Jerusalem. 26 However, Hezekiah humbled himself for the pride of his heart, both he and the inhabitants of Jerusalem, so that the LORD's wrath didn't come on them in the days of Hezekiah.

27 Hezekiah had exceedingly great riches and honour. He provided himself with treasuries for silver, for gold, for precious stones, for spices, for shields, and for all kinds of valuable vessels; 28 also storehouses for the increase of grain, new wine, and oil; and stalls for all kinds of animals, and flocks in folds. 29 Moreover he provided for himself cities, and possessions of flocks and herds in abundance; for God had given him abundant possessions. 30 This same Hezekiah also stopped the upper spring of the waters of Gihon, and brought them straight down on the west side of David's city. Hezekiah prospered in all his works.

31 However, concerning the ambassadors of the princes of Babylon, who sent to him to enquire of the wonder that was done in the land, God left him to test him, that he might know all that was in his heart.

32 Now the rest of the acts of Hezekiah and his good deeds, behold, they are written in the vision of Isaiah the prophet, the son of Amoz, in the book of the kings of Judah and Israel. 33 Hezekiah slept with his fathers, and they buried him in the ascent to the tombs of the sons of David. All Judah and the inhabitants of Jerusalem honoured him at his death. Manasseh his son reigned in his place.

33

1 Manasseh was twelve years old when he began to reign, and he reigned fifty-five years in Jerusalem. 2 He did that which was evil in the LORD's sight, after the abominations of the nations whom the LORD cast out before the children of Israel. 3 For he built again the high places which Hezekiah his father had broken down; and he raised up altars for the Baals, made Asheroth, and worshipped all the army of the sky, and served them. 4 He built altars in the LORD's house, of which the LORD said, "My name shall be in Jerusalem forever." 5 He built altars for all the army of the sky in the two courts of the LORD's house. 6 He also made his children to pass through the fire in the valley of the son of Hinnom. He practised sorcery, divination, and witchcraft, and dealt with those who had familiar spirits and

with wizards. He did much evil in the LORD's sight, to provoke him to anger. 7 He set the engraved image of the idol, which he had made, in God's house, of which God said to David and to Solomon his son, "In this house, and in Jerusalem, which I have chosen out of all the tribes of Israel, I will put my name forever. 8 I will not any more remove the foot of Israel from off the land which I have appointed for your fathers, if only they will observe to do all that I have commanded them, even all the law, the statutes, and the ordinances given by Moses." 9 Manasseh seduced Judah and the inhabitants of Jerusalem, so that they did more evil than did the nations whom the LORD destroyed before the children of Israel.

10 The LORD spoke to Manasseh and to his people, but they didn't listen. 11 Therefore the LORD brought on them the captains of the army of the king of Assyria, who took Manasseh in chains, bound him with fetters, and carried him to Babylon.

12 When he was in distress, he begged the LORD his God, and humbled himself greatly before the God of his fathers. 13 He prayed to him; and he was entreated by him, and heard his supplication, and brought him again to Jerusalem into his kingdom. Then Manasseh knew that the LORD was God.

14 Now after this, he built an outer wall to David's city on the west side of Gihon, in the valley, even to the entrance at the fish gate. He encircled Ophel with it, and raised it up to a very great height; and he put valiant captains in all the fortified cities of Judah. 15 He took away the foreign gods and the idol out of the LORD's house, and all the altars that he had built in the mountain of the LORD's house and in Jerusalem, and cast them out of the city. 16 He built up the LORD's altar, and offered sacrifices of peace offerings and of thanksgiving on it, and commanded Judah to serve the LORD, the God of Israel. 17 Nevertheless the people still sacrificed in the high places, but only to the LORD their God.

18 Now the rest of the acts of Manasseh, and his prayer to his God, and the words of the seers who spoke to him in the name of the LORD, the God of Israel, behold, they are written amongst the acts of the kings of Israel. 19 His prayer also, and how God listened to his request, and all his sin and his trespass, and the places in which he built high places and set up the Asherah poles and the engraved images before he humbled himself: behold, they are written in the history of Hozai.[b] 20 So Manasseh slept with his fathers, and they buried him in his own house; and Amon his son reigned in his place.

21 Amon was twenty-two years old when he began to reign; and he reigned two years in Jerusalem. 22 He did that which was evil in the LORD's sight, as did Manasseh his father; and Amon sacrificed to all the engraved images which Manasseh his father had made, and served them. 23 He didn't humble himself before the LORD, as Manasseh his father had humbled himself; but this same Amon trespassed more and more. 24 His servants conspired against him, and put him to death in his own house. 25 But the people of the land killed all those who had conspired against King Amon; and the people of the land made Josiah his son king in his place.

34

1 Josiah was eight years old when he began to reign, and he reigned thirty-one years in Jerusalem. 2 He did that which was right in the LORD's eyes, and walked in the ways of David his father, and didn't turn away to the right hand or to the left. 3 For in the eighth year of his reign, while he was yet young, he began to seek after the God of David his father; and in the twelfth year he began to purge Judah and Jerusalem from the high places, the Asherah poles, the engraved images, and the molten images. 4 They broke down the altars of the Baals in his presence; and he cut down the incense altars that were on high above them. He broke the Asherah poles, the engraved images, and the molten images in pieces, made dust of them, and scattered it on the graves of those who had sacrificed to them. 5 He burnt the bones of the priests on their altars, and purged Judah and Jerusalem. 6 He did this in the cities of Manasseh, Ephraim, and Simeon, even to Naphtali, around in their ruins. 7 He broke down the altars, beat the Asherah poles and the engraved images into powder, and cut down all the incense altars throughout all the land of Israel, then returned to Jerusalem.

8 Now in the eighteenth year of his reign, when he had purged the land and the house, he sent Shaphan the son of Azaliah, Maaseiah the governor of the city, and Joah the son of Joahaz the recorder to repair the house of the LORD his God. 9 They came to Hilkiah the high priest and delivered the money that was brought into God's house, which the Levites, the keepers of the threshold, had gathered from the hands of Manasseh, Ephraim, of all the remnant of Israel, of all Judah and Benjamin, and of the inhabitants of Jerusalem. 10 They delivered it into the hands of the workmen who had the oversight of the LORD's house; and the workmen who laboured in the LORD's house gave it to mend and repair the house. 11 They gave it to the carpenters and to the builders to buy cut stone and timber for couplings, and to make beams for the houses which the kings of Judah had destroyed. 12 The men did the work faithfully. Their overseers were Jahath and Obadiah the Levites, of the sons of Merari; and Zechariah and Meshullam, of the sons of the Kohathites, to give direction; and others of the Levites, who were all skilful with musical instruments. 13 Also they were over the bearers of burdens, and directed all who did the work in every kind of service. Of the Levites, there were scribes, officials, and gatekeepers.

14 When they brought out the money that was brought into the LORD's house, Hilkiah the priest found the book of the LORD's law given by Moses.

---

a 32:21 i.e., his own sons

b 33:19 or, the seers

15 Hilkiah answered Shaphan the scribe, "I have found the book of the law in the LORD's house." So Hilkiah delivered the book to Shaphan.

16 Shaphan carried the book to the king, and moreover brought back word to the king, saying, "All that was committed to your servants, they are doing. 17 They have emptied out the money that was found in the LORD's house, and have delivered it into the hand of the overseers and into the hand of the workmen." 18 Shaphan the scribe told the king, saying, "Hilkiah the priest has delivered me a book." Shaphan read from it to the king.

19 When the king had heard the words of the law, he tore his clothes. 20 The king commanded Hilkiah, Ahikam the son of Shaphan, Abdon the son of Micah, Shaphan the scribe, and Asaiah the king's servant, saying, 21 "Go enquire of the LORD for me, and for those who are left in Israel and in Judah, concerning the words of the book that is found; for great is the LORD's wrath that is poured out on us, because our fathers have not kept the LORD's word, to do according to all that is written in this book."

22 So Hilkiah and those whom the king had commanded went to Huldah the prophetess, the wife of Shallum the son of Tokhath, the son of Hasrah, keeper of the wardrobe (now she lived in Jerusalem in the second quarter), and they spoke to her to that effect.

23 She said to them, "The LORD, the God of Israel says: 'Tell the man who sent you to me, 24 The LORD says, 'Behold, I will bring evil on this place and on its inhabitants, even all the curses that are written in the book which they have read before the king of Judah. 25 Because they have forsaken me, and have burnt incense to other gods, that they might provoke me to anger with all the works of their hands, therefore my wrath is poured out on this place, and it will not be quenched.'"' 26 But to the king of Judah, who sent you to enquire of the LORD, you shall tell him this, 'The LORD, the God of Israel says: "About the words which you have heard, 27 because your heart was tender, and you humbled yourself before God when you heard his words against this place and against its inhabitants, and have humbled yourself before me, and have torn your clothes and wept before me, I also have heard you," says the LORD. 28 "Behold, I will gather you to your fathers, and you will be gathered to your grave in peace. Your eyes won't see all the evil that I will bring on this place and on its inhabitants."'"

They brought back this message to the king.

29 Then the king sent and gathered together all the elders of Judah and Jerusalem. 30 The king went up to the LORD's house with all the men of Judah and the inhabitants of Jerusalem—the priests, the Levites, and all the people, both great and small—and he read in their hearing all the words of the book of the covenant that was found in the LORD's house. 31 The king stood in his place and made a covenant before the LORD, to walk after the LORD, and to keep his commandments, his testimonies, and his statutes with all his heart and with all his soul, to perform the words of the covenant that were written in this book. 32 He caused all who were found in Jerusalem and Benjamin to stand. The inhabitants of Jerusalem did according to the covenant of God, the God of their fathers. 33 Josiah took away all the abominations out of all the countries that belonged to the children of Israel, and made all who were found in Israel to serve, even to serve the LORD their God. All his days they didn't depart from following the LORD, the God of their fathers.

35

1 Josiah kept a Passover to the LORD in Jerusalem. They killed the Passover on the fourteenth day of the first month. 2 He set the priests in their offices and encouraged them in the service of the LORD's house. 3 He said to the Levites who taught all Israel, who were holy to the LORD, "Put the holy ark in the house which Solomon the son of David king of Israel built. It will no longer be a burden on your shoulders. Now serve the LORD your God and his people Israel. 4 Prepare yourselves after your fathers' houses by your divisions, according to the writing of David king of Israel, and according to the writing of Solomon his son. 5 Stand in the holy place according to the divisions of the fathers' houses of your brothers the children of the people, and let there be for each a portion of a fathers' house of the Levites. 6 Kill the Passover lamb, sanctify yourselves, and prepare for your brothers, to do according to the LORD's word by Moses."

7 Josiah gave to the children of the people, of the flock, lambs and young goats, all of them for the Passover offerings, to all who were present, to the number of thirty thousand, and three thousand bulls. These were of the king's substance. 8 His princes gave a free will offering to the people, to the priests, and to the Levites. Hilkiah, Zechariah, and Jehiel, the rulers of God's house, gave to the priests for the Passover offerings two thousand and six hundred small livestock, and three hundred head of cattle. 9 Conaniah also, and Shemaiah and Nethanel, his brothers, and Hashabiah, Jeiel, and Jozabad, the chiefs of the Levites, gave to the Levites for the Passover offerings five thousand small livestock and five hundred head of cattle.

10 So the service was prepared, and the priests stood in their place, and the Levites by their divisions, according to the king's commandment. 11 They killed the Passover lambs, and the priests sprinkled the blood which they received from their hands, and the Levites skinned them. 12 They removed the burnt offerings, that they might give them according to the divisions of the fathers' houses of the children of the people, to offer to the LORD, as it is written in the book of Moses. They did the same with the cattle. 13 They roasted the Passover with fire according to the ordinance. They boiled the holy offerings in pots, in cauldrons, and in pans, and carried them quickly to all the children of the people. 14 Afterward they prepared for themselves and for the priests, because the priests the sons of Aaron were busy with offering the burnt offerings and the fat until night. Therefore the Levites prepared for themselves and for the priests the sons of Aaron. 15 The singers, the sons of Asaph, were in their place, according to the commandment of David, Asaph, Heman, and Jeduthun the king's seer; and the gatekeepers were at every gate. They didn't need to depart from their service, because their brothers the Levites prepared for them.

16 So all the service of the LORD was prepared the same day, to keep the Passover, and to offer burnt offerings on the LORD's altar, according to the commandment of King Josiah. 17 The children of Israel who were present kept the Passover at that time, and the feast of unleavened bread seven days. 18 There was no Passover like that kept in Israel from the days of Samuel the prophet, nor did any of the kings of Israel keep such a Passover as Josiah kept—with the priests, the Levites, and all Judah and Israel who were present, and the inhabitants of Jerusalem. 19 This Passover was kept in the eighteenth year of the reign of Josiah.

20 After all this, when Josiah had prepared the temple, Neco king of Egypt went up to fight against Carchemish by the Euphrates, and Josiah went out against him. 21 But he sent ambassadors to him, saying, "What have I to do with you, you king of Judah? I come not against you today, but against the house with which I have war. God has commanded me to make haste. Beware that it is God who is with me, that he not destroy you."

22 Nevertheless Josiah would not turn his face from him, but disguised himself, that he might fight with him, and didn't listen to the words of Neco from the mouth of God, and came to fight in the valley of Megiddo. 23 The archers shot at King Josiah; and the king said to his servants, "Take me away, because I am seriously wounded!"

24 So his servants took him out of the chariot, and put him in the second chariot that he had, and brought him to Jerusalem; and he died, and was buried in the tombs of his fathers. All Judah and Jerusalem mourned for Josiah. 25 Jeremiah lamented for Josiah, and all the singing men and singing women spoke of Josiah in their lamentations to this day; and they made them an ordinance in Israel. Behold, they are written in the lamentations. 26 Now the rest of the acts of Josiah and his good deeds, according to that which is written in the LORD's law, 27 and his acts, first and last, behold, they are written in the book of the kings of Israel and Judah.

36

1 Then the people of the land took Jehoahaz the son of Josiah, and made him king in his father's place in Jerusalem. 2 Joahaz was twenty-three years old when he began to reign; and he reigned three months in Jerusalem. 3 The king of Egypt removed him from office at Jerusalem, and fined the land one hundred talents of silver and a talent[a] of gold. 4 The king of Egypt made Eliakim his brother king over Judah and Jerusalem, and changed his name to Jehoiakim. Neco took Joahaz his brother, and carried him to Egypt.

5 Jehoiakim was twenty-five years old when he began to reign, and he reigned eleven years in Jerusalem. He did that which was evil in the LORD his God's sight. 6 Nebuchadnezzar king of Babylon came up against him, and bound him in fetters to carry him to Babylon. 7 Nebuchadnezzar also carried some of the vessels of the LORD's house to Babylon, and put them in his temple at Babylon. 8 Now the rest of the acts of Jehoiakim, and his abominations which he did, and that which was found in him, behold, they are written in the book of the kings of Israel and Judah; and Jehoiachin his son reigned in his place.

9 Jehoiachin was eight years old when he began to reign, and he reigned three months and ten days in Jerusalem. He did that which was evil in the LORD's sight. 10 At the return of the year, King Nebuchadnezzar sent and brought him to Babylon, with the valuable vessels of the LORD's house, and made Zedekiah his brother king over Judah and Jerusalem.

11 Zedekiah was twenty-one years old when he began to reign, and he reigned eleven years in Jerusalem. 12 He did that which was evil in the LORD his God's sight. He didn't humble himself before Jeremiah the prophet speaking from the LORD's mouth. 13 He also rebelled against King Nebuchadnezzar, who had made him swear by God; but he stiffened his neck, and hardened his heart against turning to the LORD, the God of Israel. 14 Moreover all the chiefs of the priests and the people trespassed very greatly after all the abominations of the nations; and they polluted the LORD's house which he had made holy in Jerusalem.

15 The LORD, the God of their fathers, sent to them by his messengers, rising up early and sending, because he had compassion on his people and on his dwelling place; 16 but they mocked the messengers of God, despised his words, and scoffed at his prophets, until the LORD's wrath arose against his people, until there was no remedy.

17 Therefore he brought on them the king of the Chaldeans, who killed their young men with the sword in the house of their sanctuary, and had no compassion on young man or virgin, old man or infirm. He gave them all into his hand. 18 All the vessels of God's house, great and small, and the treasures of the LORD's house, and the treasures of the king and of his princes, all these he brought to Babylon. 19 They burnt God's house, broke down the wall of Jerusalem, burnt all its palaces with fire, and destroyed all of its valuable vessels. 20 He carried those who had escaped from the sword away to Babylon, and they were servants to him and his sons until the reign of the kingdom of Persia, 21 to fulfil the LORD's word by Jeremiah's mouth, until the land had enjoyed its Sabbaths. As long as it lay desolate, it kept Sabbath, to fulfil seventy years.

---

a *36:3* A talent is about 30 kilograms or 66 pounds or 965 Troy ounces

22 Now in the first year of Cyrus king of Persia, that the LORD's word by the mouth of Jeremiah might be accomplished, the LORD stirred up the spirit of Cyrus king of Persia, so that he made a proclamation throughout all his kingdom, and put it also in writing, saying, 23 " Cyrus king of Persia says, 'The LORD, the God of heaven, has given all the kingdoms of the earth to me; and he has commanded me to build him a house in Jerusalem, which is in Judah. Whoever there is amongst you of all his people, the LORD his God be with him, and let him go up.'"

The Book of Ezra

1

1 Now in the first year of Cyrus king of Persia, that the LORD's[a] word by Jeremiah's mouth might be accomplished, the LORD stirred up the spirit of Cyrus king of Persia, so that he made a proclamation throughout all his kingdom, and put it also in writing, saying,

2 "Cyrus king of Persia says, 'The LORD, the God[b] of heaven, has given me all the kingdoms of the earth; and he has commanded me to build him a house in Jerusalem, which is in Judah. 3 Whoever there is amongst you of all his people, may his God be with him, and let him go up to Jerusalem, which is in Judah, and build the house of the LORD, the God of Israel (he is God), which is in Jerusalem. 4 Whoever is left, in any place where he lives, let the men of his place help him with silver, with gold, with goods, and with animals, in addition to the free will offering for God's house which is in Jerusalem.'"

5 Then the heads of fathers' households of Judah and Benjamin, the priests and the Levites, all whose spirit God had stirred to go up, rose up to build the LORD's house which is in Jerusalem. 6 All those who were around them strengthened their hands with vessels of silver, with gold, with goods, with animals, and with precious things, in addition to all that was willingly offered. 7 Also Cyrus the king brought out the vessels of the LORD's house, which Nebuchadnezzar had brought out of Jerusalem, and had put in the house of his gods; 8 even those, Cyrus king of Persia brought out by the hand of Mithredath the treasurer, and counted them out to Sheshbazzar the prince of Judah. 9 This is the number of them: thirty platters of gold, one thousand platters of silver, twenty-nine knives, 10 thirty bowls of gold, four hundred and ten silver bowls of a second kind, and one thousand other vessels. 11 All the vessels of gold and of silver were five thousand and four hundred. Sheshbazzar brought all these up when the captives were brought up from Babylon to Jerusalem.

2

1 Now these are the children of the province who went up out of the captivity of those who had been carried away, whom Nebuchadnezzar the king of Babylon had carried away to Babylon, and who returned to Jerusalem and Judah, everyone to his city; 2 who came with Zerubbabel, Jeshua, Nehemiah, Seraiah, Reelaiah, Mordecai, Bilshan, Mispar, Bigvai, Rehum, and Baanah.

The number of the men of the people of Israel: 3 The children of Parosh, two thousand and one hundred and seventy-two. 4 The children of Shephatiah, three hundred and seventy-two. 5 The children of Arah, seven hundred and seventy-five. 6 The children of Pahathmoab, of the children of Jeshua and Joab, two thousand and eight hundred and twelve. 7 The children of Elam, one thousand and two hundred and fifty-four. 8 The children of Zattu, nine hundred and forty-five. 9 The children of Zaccai, seven hundred and sixty. 10 The children of Bani, six hundred and forty-two. 11 The children of Bebai, six hundred and twenty-three. 12 The children of Azgad, one thousand and two hundred and twenty-two. 13 The children of Adonikam, six hundred and sixty-six. 14 The children of Bigvai, two thousand and fifty-six. 15 The children of Adin, four hundred and fifty-four. 16 The children of Ater, of Hezekiah, ninety-eight. 17 The children of Bezai, three hundred and twenty-three. 18 The children of Jorah, one hundred and twelve. 19 The children of Hashum, two hundred and twenty-three. 20 The children of Gibbar, ninety-five. 21 The children of Bethlehem, one hundred and twenty-three. 22 The men of Netophah, fifty-six. 23 The men of Anathoth, one hundred and twenty-eight. 24 The children of Azmaveth, forty-two. 25 The children of Kiriath Arim, Chephirah, and Beeroth, seven hundred and forty-three. 26 The children of Ramah and Geba, six hundred and twenty-one. 27 The men of Michmas, one hundred and twenty-two. 28 The men of Bethel and Ai, two hundred and twenty-three. 29 The children of Nebo, fifty-two. 30 The children of Magbish, one hundred and fifty-six. 31 The children of the other Elam, one thousand and two hundred and fifty-four. 32 The children of Harim, three hundred and twenty. 33 The children of Lod, Hadid, and Ono, seven hundred and twenty-five. 34 The children of Jericho, three hundred and forty-five. 35 The children of Senaah, three thousand and six hundred and thirty.

36 The priests: the children of Jedaiah, of the house of Jeshua, nine hundred and seventy-three. 37 The children of Immer, one thousand and fifty-two. 38 The children of Pashhur, one thousand and two hundred and forty-seven. 39 The children of Harim, one thousand and seventeen.

40 The Levites: the children of Jeshua and Kadmiel, of the children of Hodaviah, seventy-four. 41 The singers: the children of Asaph, one hundred and twenty-eight. 42 The children of the gatekeepers: the children of Shallum, the children of Ater, the children of Talmon, the children of Akkub, the children of Hatita, the children of Shobai, in all one hundred and thirty-nine.

43 The temple servants: the children of Ziha, the children of Hasupha, the children of Tabbaoth, 44 the children of Keros, the children of Siaha, the children of Padon, 45 the children of Lebanah, the children of Hagabah, the children of Akkub, 46 the children of Hagab, the children of Shamlai, the children of Hanan, 47 the children of Giddel, the children of Gahar, the children of Reaiah, 48 the children of Rezin, the children of Nekoda, the children of Gazzam, 49 the children of Uzza, the children of Paseah, the children of Besai, 50 the children of Asnah, the children of Meunim, the children of Nephisim, 51 the children of Bakbuk, the children of Hakupha, the children of Harhur, 52 the children of Bazluth, the children of Mehida, the children of Harsha, 53 the children of Barkos, the children of Sisera, the children of Temah, 54 the children of Neziah, the children of Hatipha.

55 The children of Solomon's servants: the children of Sotai, the children of Hassophereth, the children of Peruda, 56 the children of Jaalah, the children of Darkon, the children of Giddel, 57 the children of Shephatiah, the children of Hattil, the children of Pochereth Hazzebaim, the children of Ami. 58 All the temple servants, and the children of Solomon's servants, were three hundred and ninety-two.

59 These were those who went up from Tel Melah, Tel Harsha, Cherub, Addan, and Immer; but they could not show their fathers' houses and their offspring,[c] whether they were of Israel: 60 the children of Delaiah, the children of Tobiah, the children of Nekoda, six hundred and fifty-two. 61 Of the children of the priests: the children of Habaiah, the children of Hakkoz, and the children of Barzillai, who took a wife of the daughters of Barzillai the Gileadite, and was called after their name. 62 These sought their place amongst those who were registered by genealogy, but they were not found; therefore they were deemed disqualified and removed from the priesthood. 63 The governor told them that they should not eat of the most holy things until a priest stood up to serve with Urim and with Thummim.

64 The whole assembly together was forty-two thousand and three hundred and sixty, 65 in addition to their male servants and their female servants, of whom there were seven thousand and three hundred and thirty-seven; and they had two hundred singing men and singing women. 66 Their horses were seven hundred and thirty-six; their mules, two hundred and forty-five; 67 their camels, four hundred and thirty-five; their donkeys, six thousand and seven hundred and twenty.

68 Some of the heads of fathers' households, when they came to the LORD's house which is in Jerusalem, offered willingly for God's house to set it up in its place. 69 They gave according to their ability into the treasury of the work sixty-one thousand darics of gold,[d] five thousand minas[e] of silver, and one hundred priests' garments.

70 So the priests and the Levites, with some of the people, the singers, the gatekeepers, and the temple servants, lived in their cities, and all Israel in their cities.

3

1 When the seventh month had come, and the children of Israel were in the cities, the people gathered themselves together as one man to Jerusalem. 2 Then Jeshua the son of Jozadak stood up with his brothers the priests and Zerubbabel the son of Shealtiel and his relatives, and built the altar of the God of Israel, to offer burnt offerings on it, as it is written in the law of Moses the man of God. 3 In spite of their fear because of the peoples of the surrounding lands, they set the altar on its base; and they offered burnt offerings on it to the LORD, even burnt offerings morning and evening. 4 They kept the feast of booths, as it is written, and offered the daily burnt offerings by number, according to the ordinance, as the duty of every day required; 5 and afterward the continual burnt offering, the offerings of the new moons, of all the set feasts of the LORD that were consecrated, and of everyone who willingly offered a free will offering to the LORD. 6 From the first day of the seventh month, they began to offer burnt offerings to the LORD; but the foundation of the LORD's temple was not yet laid. 7 They also gave money to the masons and to the carpenters. They also gave food, drink, and oil to the people of Sidon and Tyre to bring cedar trees from Lebanon to the sea, to Joppa, according to the grant that they had from Cyrus King of Persia.

8 Now in the second year of their coming to God's house at Jerusalem, in the second month, Zerubbabel the son of Shealtiel, Jeshua the son of Jozadak, and the rest of their brothers the priests and the Levites, and all those who had come out of the captivity to Jerusalem, began the work and appointed the Levites, from twenty years old and upward, to have the oversight of the work of the LORD's house. 9 Then Jeshua stood with his sons and his brothers, Kadmiel and his sons, the sons of Judah, together to have the oversight of the workmen in God's house: the sons of Henadad, with their sons and their brothers the Levites.

10 When the builders laid the foundation of the LORD's temple, they set the priests in their vestments with trumpets, with the Levites the sons of Asaph with cymbals, to praise the LORD, according to the directions of David king of Israel. 11 They sang to one another in praising and giving thanks to the LORD, "For he is good, for his loving kindness endures forever towards Israel." All the people shouted with a great shout, when they praised the LORD, because the foundation of the LORD's house had been laid.

12 But many of the priests and Levites and heads of fathers' households, the old men who had seen the first house, when the foundation of this house was laid before their eyes, wept with a loud voice. Many also shouted aloud for joy, 13 so that the people could not discern the noise of the shout of joy from the noise of the weeping of the people; for the people shouted with a loud shout, and the noise was heard far away.

---

a 1:1 When rendered in ALL CAPITAL LETTERS, "LORD" or "GOD" is the translation of God's Proper Name.

b 1:2 The Hebrew word rendered "God" is "אֱלֹהִים" (Elohim).

c 2:59 or, seed

d 2:69 a daric was a gold coin issued by a Persian king, weighing about 8.4 grams or about 0.27 troy ounces each.

e 2:69 A mina is about 600 grams or 1.3 U. S. pounds, so 5,000 minas is about 3 metric tonnes.

4

1 Now when the adversaries of Judah and Benjamin heard that the children of the captivity were building a temple to the LORD, the God of Israel, 2 they came near to Zerubbabel, and to the heads of fathers' households, and said to them, "Let us build with you, for we seek your God as you do; and we have been sacrificing to him since the days of Esar Haddon king of Assyria, who brought us up here."

3 But Zerubbabel, Jeshua, and the rest of the heads of fathers' households of Israel said to them, "You have nothing to do with us in building a house to our God; but we ourselves together will build to the LORD, the God of Israel, as King Cyrus the king of Persia has commanded us."

4 Then the people of the land weakened the hands of the people of Judah, and troubled them in building. 5 They hired counsellors against them to frustrate their purpose all the days of Cyrus king of Persia, even until the reign of Darius king of Persia. 6 In the reign of Ahasuerus, in the beginning of his reign, they wrote an accusation against the inhabitants of Judah and Jerusalem.

7 In the days of Artaxerxes, Bishlam, Mithredath, Tabeel, and the rest of his companions wrote to Artaxerxes king of Persia; and the writing of the letter was written in Syrian and delivered in the Syrian language. 8 Rehum the chancellor and Shimshai the scribe wrote a letter against Jerusalem to Artaxerxes the king as follows. 9 Then Rehum the chancellor, Shimshai the scribe, and the rest of their companions, the Dinaites, and the Apharsathchites, the Tarpelites, the Apharsites, the Archevites, the Babylonians, the Shushanchites, the Dehaites, the Elamites, 10 and the rest of the nations whom the great and noble Osnappar brought over and settled in the city of Samaria, and in the rest of the country beyond the River, and so forth, wrote.

11 This is the copy of the letter that they sent:

To King Artaxerxes, from your servants, the people beyond the River.

12 Be it known to the king that the Jews who came up from you have come to us to Jerusalem. They are building the rebellious and bad city, and have finished the walls and repaired the foundations. 13 Be it known now to the king that if this city is built and the walls finished, they will not pay tribute, custom, or toll, and in the end it will be hurtful to the kings. 14 Now because we eat the salt of the palace and it is not appropriate for us to see the king's dishonour, therefore we have sent and informed the king, 15 that search may be made in the book of the records of your fathers. You will see in the book of the records, and know that this city is a rebellious city, and hurtful to kings and provinces, and that they have started rebellions within it in the past. That is why this city was destroyed. 16 We inform the king that if this city is built and the walls finished, then you will have no possession beyond the River.

17 Then the king sent an answer to Rehum the chancellor, and to Shimshai the scribe, and to the rest of their companions who live in Samaria, and in the rest of the country beyond the River:

Peace.

18 The letter which you sent to us has been plainly read before me. 19 I decreed, and search has been made, and it was found that this city has made insurrection against kings in the past, and that rebellion and revolts have been made in it. 20 There have also been mighty kings over Jerusalem who have ruled over all the country beyond the River; and tribute, custom, and toll was paid to them. 21 Make a decree now to cause these men to cease, and that this city not be built until a decree is made by me. 22 Be careful that you not be slack doing so. Why should damage grow to the hurt of the kings?

23 Then when the copy of King Artaxerxes' letter was read before Rehum, Shimshai the scribe, and their companions, they went in haste to Jerusalem to the Jews, and made them to cease by force of arms. 24 Then work stopped on God's house which is at Jerusalem. It stopped until the second year of the reign of Darius king of Persia.

5

1 Now the prophets, Haggai the prophet and Zechariah the son of Iddo, prophesied to the Jews who were in Judah and Jerusalem. They prophesied to them in the name of the God of Israel. 2 Then Zerubbabel the son of Shealtiel, and Jeshua the son of Jozadak rose up and began to build God's house which is at Jerusalem; and with them were the prophets of God, helping them.

3 At the same time Tattenai, the governor beyond the River, came to them, with Shetharbozenai and their companions, and asked them, "Who gave you a decree to build this house and to finish this wall?" 4 They also asked for the names of the men who were making this building. 5 But the eye of their God was on the elders of the Jews, and they didn't make them cease until the matter should come to Darius, and an answer should be returned by letter concerning it.

6 The copy of the letter that Tattenai, the governor beyond the River, and Shetharbozenai, and his companions the Apharsachites who were beyond the River, sent to Darius the king follows. 7 They sent a letter to him, in which was written:

To Darius the king, all peace.

8 Be it known to the king that we went into the province of Judah, to the house of the great God, which is being built with great stones and timber is laid in the walls. This work goes on with diligence and prospers in their hands. 9 Then we asked those elders, and said to them thus, "Who gave you a decree to build this house, and to finish this wall?" 10 We asked them their names also, to inform you that we might write the names of the men who were at their head. 11 Thus they returned us answer, saying, "We are the servants of the God of heaven and earth and are building the house that was built these many years ago, which a great king of Israel built and finished. 12 But after our fathers had provoked the God of heaven to wrath, he gave them into the hand of Nebuchadnezzar king of Babylon, the Chaldean, who destroyed this house and carried the people away into Babylon. 13 But in the first year of Cyrus king of Babylon, Cyrus the king made a decree to build this house of God. 14 The gold and silver vessels of God's house, which Nebuchadnezzar took out of the temple that was in Jerusalem and brought into the temple of Babylon, those Cyrus the king also took out of the temple of Babylon, and they were delivered to one whose name was Sheshbazzar, whom he had made governor. 15 He said to him, 'Take these vessels, go, put them in the temple that is in Jerusalem, and let God's house be built in its place.' 16 Then the same Sheshbazzar came and laid the foundations of God's house which is in Jerusalem. Since that time even until now it has been being built, and yet it is not completed.

17 Now therefore, if it seems good to the king, let a search be made in the king's treasure house, which is there at Babylon, whether it is so that a decree was made by Cyrus the king to build this house of God at Jerusalem; and let the king send his pleasure to us concerning this matter."

6

1 Then Darius the king made a decree, and the house of the archives, where the treasures were laid up in Babylon, was searched. 2 A scroll was found at Achmetha, in the palace that is in the province of Media, and in it this was written for a record:

3 In the first year of Cyrus the king, Cyrus the king made a decree: Concerning God's house at Jerusalem, let the house be built, the place where they offer sacrifices, and let its foundations be strongly laid, with its height sixty cubits[a] and its width sixty cubits; 4 with three courses of great stones and a course of new timber. Let the expenses be given out of the king's house. 5 Also let the gold and silver vessels of God's house, which Nebuchadnezzar took out of the temple which is at Jerusalem and brought to Babylon, be restored and brought again to the temple which is at Jerusalem, everything to its place. You shall put them in God's house.

6 Now therefore, Tattenai, governor beyond the River, Shetharbozenai, and your companions the Apharsachites, who are beyond the River, you must stay far from there. 7 Leave the work of this house of God alone; let the governor of the Jews and the elders of the Jews build this house of God in its place. 8 Moreover I make a decree regarding what you shall do for these elders of the Jews for the building of this house of God: that of the king's goods, even of the tribute beyond the River, expenses must be given with all diligence to these men, that they not be hindered. 9 That which they have need of, including young bulls, rams, and lambs, for burnt offerings to the God of heaven; also wheat, salt, wine, and oil, according to the word of the priests who are at Jerusalem, let it be given them day by day without fail, 10 that they may offer sacrifices of pleasant aroma to the God of heaven, and pray for the life of the king and of his sons. 11 I have also made a decree that whoever alters this message, let a beam be pulled out from his house, and let him be lifted up and fastened on it; and let his house be made a dunghill for this. 12 May the God who has caused his name to dwell there overthrow all kings and peoples who stretch out their hand to alter this, to destroy this house of God which is at Jerusalem. I Darius have made a decree. Let it be done with all diligence.

13 Then Tattenai, the governor beyond the River, Shetharbozenai, and their companions did accordingly with all diligence, because Darius the king had sent a decree. 14 The elders of the Jews built and prospered, through the prophesying of Haggai the prophet and Zechariah the son of Iddo. They built and finished it, according to the commandment of the God of Israel, and according to the decree of Cyrus, Darius, and Artaxerxes king of

---

a 6:3 A cubit is the length from the tip of the middle finger to the elbow on a man's arm, or about 18 inches or 46 centimetres.

Persia. 15 This house was finished on the third day of the month Adar, which was in the sixth year of the reign of Darius the king.

16 The children of Israel, the priests, the Levites, and the rest of the children of the captivity, kept the dedication of this house of God with joy. 17 They offered at the dedication of this house of God one hundred bulls, two hundred rams, four hundred lambs; and for a sin offering for all Israel, twelve male goats, according to the number of the tribes of Israel. 18 They set the priests in their divisions and the Levites in their courses, for the service of God which is at Jerusalem, as it is written in the book of Moses.

19 The children of the captivity kept the Passover on the fourteenth day of the first month. 20 Because the priests and the Levites had purified themselves together, all of them were pure. They killed the Passover for all the children of the captivity, for their brothers the priests, and for themselves. 21 The children of Israel who had returned out of the captivity, and all who had separated themselves to them from the filthiness of the nations of the land to seek the LORD, the God of Israel, ate, 22 and kept the feast of unleavened bread seven days with joy; because the LORD had made them joyful, and had turned the heart of the king of Assyria to them, to strengthen their hands in the work of God, the God of Israel's house.

7

1 Now after these things, in the reign of Artaxerxes king of Persia, Ezra the son of Seraiah, the son of Azariah, the son of Hilkiah, 2 the son of Shallum, the son of Zadok, the son of Ahitub, 3 the son of Amariah, the son of Azariah, the son of Meraioth, 4 the son of Zerahiah, the son of Uzzi, the son of Bukki, 5 the son of Abishua, the son of Phinehas, the son of Eleazar, the son of Aaron the chief priest— 6 this Ezra went up from Babylon. He was a skilled scribe in the law of Moses, which the LORD, the God of Israel, had given; and the king granted him all his request, according to the LORD his God's hand on him. 7 Some of the children of Israel, including some of the priests, the Levites, the singers, the gatekeepers, and the temple servants went up to Jerusalem in the seventh year of Artaxerxes the king. 8 He came to Jerusalem in the fifth month, which was in the seventh year of the king. 9 For on the first day of the first month he began to go up from Babylon; and on the first day of the fifth month he came to Jerusalem, according to the good hand of his God on him. 10 For Ezra had set his heart to seek the LORD's law, and to do it, and to teach statutes and ordinances in Israel.

11 Now this is the copy of the letter that King Artaxerxes gave to Ezra the priest, the scribe, even the scribe of the words of the LORD's commandments, and of his statutes to Israel:

12 Artaxerxes, king of kings,
To Ezra the priest, the scribe of the law of the perfect God of heaven.

Now 13 I make a decree that all those of the people of Israel and their priests and the Levites in my realm, who intend of their own free will to go to Jerusalem, go with you. 14 Because you are sent by the king and his seven counsellors to enquire concerning Judah and Jerusalem, according to the law of your God which is in your hand, 15 and to carry the silver and gold, which the king and his counsellors have freely offered to the God of Israel, whose habitation is in Jerusalem, 16 and all the silver and gold that you will find in all the province of Babylon, with the free will offering of the people and of the priests, offering willingly for the house of their God which is in Jerusalem. 17 Therefore you shall with all diligence buy with this money bulls, rams, and lambs with their meal offerings and their drink offerings, and shall offer them on the altar of the house of your God which is in Jerusalem. 18 Whatever seems good to you and to your brothers to do with the rest of the silver and the gold, do that according to the will of your God. 19 The vessels that are given to you for the service of the house of your God, deliver before the God of Jerusalem. 20 Whatever more will be needed for the house of your God, which you may have occasion to give, give it out of the king's treasure house.

21 I, even I, Artaxerxes the king, make a decree to all the treasurers who are beyond the River, that whatever Ezra the priest, the scribe of the law of the God of heaven, requires of you, it shall be done with all diligence, 22 up to one hundred talents[a] of silver, and to one hundred cors[b] of wheat, and to one hundred baths[c] of wine, and to one hundred baths of oil, and salt without prescribing how much. 23 Whatever is commanded by the God of heaven, let it be done exactly for the house of the God of heaven; for why should there be wrath against the realm of the king and his sons?

24 Also we inform you that it shall not be lawful to impose tribute, custom, or toll on any of the priests, Levites, singers, gatekeepers, temple servants, or labourers of this house of God.

25 You, Ezra, according to the wisdom of your God that is in your hand, appoint magistrates and judges who may judge all the people who are beyond the River, who all know the laws of your God; and teach him who doesn't know them. 26 Whoever will not

do the law of your God and the law of the king, let judgement be executed on him with all diligence, whether it is to death, or to banishment, or to confiscation of goods, or to imprisonment.

27 Blessed be the LORD, the God of our fathers, who has put such a thing as this in the king's heart, to beautify the LORD's house which is in Jerusalem; 28 and has extended loving kindness to me before the king and his counsellors, and before all the king's mighty princes. I was strengthened according to the LORD my God's hand on me, and I gathered together chief men out of Israel to go up with me.

8

1 Now these are the heads of their fathers' households, and this is the genealogy of those who went up with me from Babylon, in the reign of Artaxerxes the king:
2 Of the sons of Phinehas, Gershom.
Of the sons of Ithamar, Daniel.
Of the sons of David, Hattush.
3 Of the sons of Shecaniah, of the sons of Parosh, Zechariah; and with him were listed by genealogy of the males one hundred and fifty.
4 Of the sons of Pahathmoab, Eliehoenai the son of Zerahiah; and with him two hundred males.
5 Of the sons of Shecaniah, the son of Jahaziel; and with him three hundred males.
6 Of the sons of Adin, Ebed the son of Jonathan; and with him fifty males.
7 Of the sons of Elam, Jeshaiah the son of Athaliah; and with him seventy males.
8 Of the sons of Shephatiah, Zebadiah the son of Michael; and with him eighty males.
9 Of the sons of Joab, Obadiah the son of Jehiel; and with him two hundred and eighteen males.
10 Of the sons of Shelomith, the son of Josiphiah; and with him one hundred and sixty males.
11 Of the sons of Bebai, Zechariah the son of Bebai; and with him twenty-eight males.
12 Of the sons of Azgad, Johanan the son of Hakkatan; and with him one hundred and ten males.
13 Of the sons of Adonikam, who were the last, their names are: Eliphelet, Jeuel, and Shemaiah; and with them sixty males.
14 Of the sons of Bigvai, Uthai and Zabbud; and with them seventy males.

15 I gathered them together to the river that runs to Ahava; and there we encamped three days. Then I looked around at the people and the priests, and found there were none of the sons of Levi. 16 Then I sent for Eliezer, for Ariel, for Shemaiah, for Elnathan, for Jarib, for Elnathan, for Nathan, for Zechariah, and for Meshullam, chief men; also for Joiarib and for Elnathan, who were teachers. 17 I sent them out to Iddo the chief at the place Casiphia; and I told them what they should tell Iddo and his brothers the temple servants at the place Casiphia, that they should bring to us ministers for the house of our God. 18 According to the good hand of our God on us they brought us a man of discretion, of the sons of Mahli, the son of Levi, the son of Israel, namely Sherebiah, with his sons and his brothers, eighteen; 19 and Hashabiah, and with him Jeshaiah of the sons of Merari, his brothers and their sons, twenty; 20 and of the temple servants, whom David and the princes had given for the service of the Levites, two hundred and twenty temple servants. All of them were mentioned by name.

21 Then I proclaimed a fast there at the river Ahava, that we might humble ourselves before our God, to seek from him a straight way for us, for our little ones, and for all our possessions. 22 For I was ashamed to ask of the king a band of soldiers and horsemen to help us against the enemy on the way, because we had spoken to the king, saying, "The hand of our God is on all those who seek him, for good; but his power and his wrath is against all those who forsake him." 23 So we fasted and begged our God for this, and he granted our request.

24 Then I set apart twelve of the chiefs of the priests, even Sherebiah, Hashabiah, and ten of their brothers with them, 25 and weighed to them the silver, the gold, and the vessels, even the offering for the house of our God, which the king, his counsellors, his princes, and all Israel there present, had offered. 26 I weighed into their hand six hundred and fifty talents of silver,[d] one hundred talents of silver vessels, one hundred talents of gold, 27 twenty bowls of gold weighing one thousand darics,[e] and two vessels of fine bright bronze, precious as gold. 28 I said to them, "You are holy to the LORD, and the vessels are holy. The silver and the gold are a free will offering to the LORD, the God of your fathers. 29 Watch and keep them until you weigh them before the chiefs of the priests, the Levites, and the princes of the fathers' households of Israel at Jerusalem, in the rooms of the LORD's house."

30 So the priests and the Levites received the weight of the silver, the gold, and the vessels, to bring them to Jerusalem to the house of our God.

31 Then we departed from the river Ahava on the twelfth day of the first month, to go to Jerusalem. The hand of our God was on us, and he delivered us from the hand of the enemy and the bandits by the way. 32 We came to Jerusalem, and stayed there three days. 33 On the fourth day the silver and the gold and the vessels were weighed in the house of our God

---

a *7:22* A talent is about 30 kilograms or 66 pounds or 965 Troy ounces
b *7:22* 1 cor is the same as a homer, or about 55.9 U. S. gallons (liquid) or 211 litres or 6 bushels.
c *7:22* 1 bath is one tenth of a cor, or about 5.6 U. S. gallons or 21 litres or 2.4 pecks. 100 baths would be about 2,100 litres.

d *8:26* A talent is about 30 kilograms or 66 pounds or 965 Troy ounces
e *8:27* a daric was a gold coin issued by a Persian king, weighing about 8.4 grams or about 0.27 troy ounces each.

into the hand of Meremoth the son of Uriah the priest; and with him was Eleazar the son of Phinehas; and with them were Jozabad the son of Jeshua, and Noadiah the son of Binnui, the Levites. 34 Everything was counted and weighed; and all the weight was written at that time.

35 The children of the captivity, who had come out of exile, offered burnt offerings to the God of Israel: twelve bulls for all Israel, ninety-six rams, seventy-seven lambs, and twelve male goats for a sin offering. All this was a burnt offering to the LORD. 36 They delivered the king's commissions to the king's local governors and to the governors beyond the River. So they supported the people and God's house.

9

1 Now when these things were done, the princes came near to me, saying, "The people of Israel, the priests, and the Levites have not separated themselves from the peoples of the lands, following their abominations, even those of the Canaanites, the Hittites, the Perizzites, the Jebusites, the Ammonites, the Moabites, the Egyptians, and the Amorites. 2 For they have taken of their daughters for themselves and for their sons, so that the holy offspring have mixed themselves with the peoples of the lands. Yes, the hand of the princes and rulers has been chief in this trespass."

3 When I heard this thing, I tore my garment and my robe, and pulled the hair out of my head and of my beard, and sat down confounded. 4 Then everyone who trembled at the words of the God of Israel were assembled to me because of the trespass of the exiles; and I sat confounded until the evening offering.

5 At the evening offering I rose up from my humiliation, even with my garment and my robe torn; and I fell on my knees, and spread out my hands to the LORD my God; 6 and I said, "My God, I am ashamed and blush to lift up my face to you, my God, for our iniquities have increased over our head, and our guiltiness has grown up to the heavens. 7 Since the days of our fathers we have been exceedingly guilty to this day; and for our iniquities we, our kings, and our priests have been delivered into the hand of the kings of the lands, to the sword, to captivity, to plunder, and to confusion of face, as it is this day. 8 Now for a little moment grace has been shown from the LORD our God, to leave us a remnant to escape, and to give us a stake in his holy place, that our God may lighten our eyes, and revive us a little in our bondage. 9 For we are bondservants; yet our God has not forsaken us in our bondage, but has extended loving kindness to us in the sight of the kings of Persia, to revive us, to set up the house of our God, and to repair its ruins, and to give us a wall in Judah and in Jerusalem.

10 "Now, our God, what shall we say after this? For we have forsaken your commandments, 11 which you have commanded by your servants the prophets, saying, 'The land to which you go to possess is an unclean land through the uncleanness of the peoples of the lands, through their abominations, which have filled it from one end to another with their filthiness. 12 Now therefore don't give your daughters to their sons. Don't take their daughters to your sons, nor seek their peace or their prosperity forever, that you may be strong and eat the good of the land, and leave it for an inheritance to your children forever.'

13 "After all that has come on us for our evil deeds and for our great guilt, since you, our God, have punished us less than our iniquities deserve, and have given us such a remnant, 14 shall we again break your commandments, and join ourselves with the peoples that do these abominations? Wouldn't you be angry with us until you had consumed us, so that there would be no remnant, nor any to escape? 15 LORD, the God of Israel, you are righteous; for we are left a remnant that has escaped, as it is today. Behold,[a] we are before you in our guiltiness; for no one can stand before you because of this."

10

1 Now while Ezra prayed and made confession, weeping and casting himself down before God's house, there was gathered together to him out of Israel a very great assembly of men and women and children; for the people wept very bitterly. 2 Shecaniah the son of Jehiel, one of the sons of Elam, answered Ezra, "We have trespassed against our God, and have married foreign women of the peoples of the land. Yet now there is hope for Israel concerning this thing. 3 Now therefore let's make a covenant with our God to put away all the wives and those who are born of them, according to the counsel of my lord and of those who tremble at the commandment of our God. Let it be done according to the law. 4 Arise, for the matter belongs to you and we are with you. Be courageous, and do it."

5 Then Ezra arose, and made the chiefs of the priests, the Levites, and all Israel to swear that they would do according to this word. So they swore. 6 Then Ezra rose up from before God's house, and went into the room of Jehohanan the son of Eliashib. When he came there, he didn't eat bread or drink water, for he mourned because of the trespass of the exiles. 7 They made a proclamation throughout Judah and Jerusalem to all the children of the captivity, that they should gather themselves together to Jerusalem; 8 and that whoever didn't come within three days, according to the counsel of the princes and the elders, all his possessions should be forfeited, and he himself separated from the assembly of the captivity.

9 Then all the men of Judah and Benjamin gathered themselves together to Jerusalem within the three days. It was the ninth month, on the twentieth day of the month; and all the people sat in the wide place in front of God's house, trembling because of this matter, and because of the great rain.

10 Ezra the priest stood up and said to them, "You have trespassed, and have married foreign women, increasing the guilt of Israel. 11 Now therefore make confession to the LORD, the God of your fathers and do his pleasure. Separate yourselves from the peoples of the land and from the foreign women."

12 Then all the assembly answered with a loud voice, "We must do as you have said concerning us. 13 But the people are many, and it is a time of much rain, and we are not able to stand outside. This is not a work of one day or two, for we have greatly transgressed in this matter. 14 Now let our princes be appointed for all the assembly, and let all those who are in our cities who have married foreign women come at appointed times, and with them the elders of every city and its judges, until the fierce wrath of our God is turned from us, until this matter is resolved."

15 Only Jonathan the son of Asahel and Jahzeiah the son of Tikvah stood up against this; and Meshullam and Shabbethai the Levite helped them.

16 The children of the captivity did so. Ezra the priest, with certain heads of fathers' households, after their fathers' houses, and all of them by their names, were set apart; and they sat down in the first day of the tenth month to examine the matter. 17 They finished with all the men who had married foreign women by the first day of the first month.

18 Amongst the sons of the priests there were found who had married foreign women:

of the sons of Jeshua, the son of Jozadak, and his brothers: Maaseiah, Eliezer, Jarib, and Gedaliah. 19 They gave their hand that they would put away their wives; and being guilty, they offered a ram of the flock for their guilt.

20 Of the sons of Immer: Hanani and Zebadiah.
21 Of the sons of Harim: Maaseiah, Elijah, Shemaiah, Jehiel, and Uzziah.
22 Of the sons of Pashhur: Elioenai, Maaseiah, Ishmael, Nethanel, Jozabad, and Elasah.
23 Of the Levites: Jozabad, Shimei, Kelaiah (also called Kelita), Pethahiah, Judah, and Eliezer.
24 Of the singers: Eliashib.
Of the gatekeepers: Shallum, Telem, and Uri.
25 Of Israel: Of the sons of Parosh: Ramiah, Izziah, Malchijah, Mijamin, Eleazar, Malchijah, and Benaiah.
26 Of the sons of Elam: Mattaniah, Zechariah, Jehiel, Abdi, Jeremoth, and Elijah.
27 Of the sons of Zattu: Elioenai, Eliashib, Mattaniah, Jeremoth, Zabad, and Aziza.
28 Of the sons of Bebai: Jehohanan, Hananiah, Zabbai, and Athlai.
29 Of the sons of Bani: Meshullam, Malluch, Adaiah, Jashub, Sheal, and Jeremoth.
30 Of the sons of Pahathmoab: Adna, Chelal, Benaiah, Maaseiah, Mattaniah, Bezalel, Binnui, and Manasseh.
31 Of the sons of Harim: Eliezer, Isshijah, Malchijah, Shemaiah, Shimeon, 32 Benjamin, Malluch, and Shemariah.
33 Of the sons of Hashum: Mattenai, Mattattah, Zabad, Eliphelet, Jeremai, Manasseh, and Shimei.
34 Of the sons of Bani: Maadai, Amram, Uel, 35 Benaiah, Bedeiah, Cheluhi, 36 Vaniah, Meremoth, Eliashib, 37 Mattaniah, Mattenai, Jaasu, 38 Bani, Binnui, Shimei, 39 Shelemiah, Nathan, Adaiah, 40 Machnadebai, Shashai, Sharai, 41 Azarel, Shelemiah, Shemariah, 42 Shallum, Amariah, and Joseph.
43 Of the sons of Nebo: Jeiel, Mattithiah, Zabad, Zebina, Iddo, Joel, and Benaiah.

44 All these had taken foreign wives. Some of them had wives by whom they had children.

---

a *9:15* "Behold", from "הִנֵּה", means look at, take notice, observe, see, or gaze at. It is often used as an interjection.

The Book of Nehemiah

1

1 The words of Nehemiah the son of Hacaliah.

Now in the month Chislev, in the twentieth year, as I was in Susa the palace, 2 Hanani, one of my brothers, came, he and certain men out of Judah; and I asked them about the Jews who had escaped, who were left of the captivity, and concerning Jerusalem. 3 They said to me, "The remnant who are left of the captivity there in the province are in great affliction and reproach. The wall of Jerusalem is also broken down, and its gates are burnt with fire."

4 When I heard these words, I sat down and wept, and mourned several days; and I fasted and prayed before the God[a] of heaven, 5 and said, "I beg you, LORD,[b] the God of heaven, the great and awesome God who keeps covenant and loving kindness with those who love him and keep his commandments, 6 let your ear now be attentive and your eyes open, that you may listen to the prayer of your servant which I pray before you at this time, day and night, for the children of Israel your servants, while I confess the sins of the children of Israel which we have sinned against you. Yes, I and my father's house have sinned. 7 We have dealt very corruptly against you, and have not kept the commandments, nor the statutes, nor the ordinances, which you commanded your servant Moses.

8 "Remember, I beg you, the word that you commanded your servant Moses, saying, 'If you trespass, I will scatter you amongst the peoples; 9 but if you return to me, and keep my commandments and do them, though your outcasts were in the uttermost part of the heavens, yet I will gather them from there, and will bring them to the place that I have chosen, to cause my name to dwell there.'

10 "Now these are your servants and your people, whom you have redeemed by your great power and by your strong hand. 11 Lord,[c] I beg you, let your ear be attentive now to the prayer of your servant, and to the prayer of your servants who delight to fear your name; and please prosper your servant today, and grant him mercy in the sight of this man."

Now I was cup bearer to the king.

2

1 In the month Nisan, in the twentieth year of Artaxerxes the king, when wine was before him, I picked up the wine, and gave it to the king. Now I had not been sad before in his presence. 2 The king said to me, "Why is your face sad, since you are not sick? This is nothing else but sorrow of heart."

Then I was very much afraid. 3 I said to the king, "Let the king live forever! Why shouldn't my face be sad, when the city, the place of my fathers' tombs, lies waste, and its gates have been consumed with fire?"

4 Then the king said to me, "What is your request?"

So I prayed to the God of heaven. 5 I said to the king, "If it pleases the king, and if your servant has found favour in your sight, I ask that you would send me to Judah, to the city of my fathers' tombs, that I may build it."

6 The king said to me (the queen was also sitting by him), "How long will your journey be? When will you return?"

So it pleased the king to send me, and I set a time for him. 7 Moreover I said to the king, "If it pleases the king, let letters be given me to the governors beyond the River, that they may let me pass through until I come to Judah; 8 and a letter to Asaph the keeper of the king's forest, that he may give me timber to make beams for the gates of the citadel by the temple, for the wall of the city, and for the house that I will occupy."

The king granted my requests, because of the good hand of my God on me. 9 Then I came to the governors beyond the River, and gave them the king's letters. Now the king had sent captains of the army and horsemen with me. 10 When Sanballat the Horonite and Tobiah the Ammonite servant heard of it, it grieved them exceedingly, because a man had come to seek the welfare of the children of Israel.

11 So I came to Jerusalem, and was there three days. 12 I arose in the night, I and a few men with me. I didn't tell anyone what my God put into my heart to do for Jerusalem. There wasn't any animal with me except the animal that I rode on. 13 I went out by night by the valley gate towards the jackal's well, then to the dung gate; and I inspected the walls of Jerusalem, which were broken down, and its gates were consumed with fire. 14 Then I went on to the spring gate and to the king's pool, but there was no place for the animal that was under me to pass. 15 Then I went up in the night by the brook and inspected the wall; and I turned back, and entered by the valley gate, and so returned. 16 The rulers didn't know where I went, or what I did. I had not as yet told it to the Jews, nor to the priests, nor to the nobles, nor to the rulers, nor to the rest who did the work.

17 Then I said to them, "You see the bad situation that we are in, how Jerusalem lies waste, and its gates are burnt with fire. Come, let's build up the wall of Jerusalem, that we won't be disgraced." 18 I told them about the hand of my God which was good on me, and also about the king's words that he had spoken to me.

They said, "Let's rise up and build." So they strengthened their hands for the good work.

19 But when Sanballat the Horonite, Tobiah the Ammonite servant, and Geshem the Arabian, heard it, they ridiculed us and despised us, and said, "What is this thing that you are doing? Will you rebel against the king?"

20 Then I answered them, and said to them, "The God of heaven will prosper us. Therefore we, his servants, will arise and build; but you have no portion, nor right, nor memorial in Jerusalem."

3

1 Then Eliashib the high priest rose up with his brothers the priests, and they built the sheep gate. They sanctified it, and set up its doors. They sanctified it even to the tower of Hammeah, to the tower of Hananel. 2 Next to him the men of Jericho built. Next to them Zaccur the son of Imri built.

3 The sons of Hassenaah built the fish gate. They laid its beams, and set up its doors, its bolts, and its bars. 4 Next to them, Meremoth the son of Uriah, the son of Hakkoz made repairs. Next to them, Meshullam the son of Berechiah, the son of Meshezabel made repairs. Next to them, Zadok the son of Baana made repairs. 5 Next to them, the Tekoites made repairs; but their nobles didn't put their necks to the Lord's work.

6 Joiada the son of Paseah and Meshullam the son of Besodeiah repaired the old gate. They laid its beams and set up its doors, its bolts, and its bars. 7 Next to them, Melatiah the Gibeonite and Jadon the Meronothite, the men of Gibeon and of Mizpah, repaired the residence of the governor beyond the River. 8 Next to him, Uzziel the son of Harhaiah, goldsmiths, made repairs. Next to him, Hananiah, one of the perfumers, made repairs, and they fortified Jerusalem even to the wide wall. 9 Next to them, Rephaiah the son of Hur, the ruler of half the district of Jerusalem, made repairs. 10 Next to them, Jedaiah the son of Harumaph made repairs across from his house. Next to him, Hattush the son of Hashabneiah made repairs. 11 Malchijah the son of Harim and Hasshub the son of Pahathmoab repaired another portion and the tower of the furnaces. 12 Next to him, Shallum the son of Hallohesh, the ruler of half the district of Jerusalem, he and his daughters made repairs.

13 Hanun and the inhabitants of Zanoah repaired the valley gate. They built it, and set up its doors, its bolts, and its bars, and one thousand cubits[d] of the wall to the dung gate.

14 Malchijah the son of Rechab, the ruler of the district of Beth Haccherem, repaired the dung gate. He built it, and set up its doors, its bolts, and its bars.

15 Shallun the son of Colhozeh, the ruler of the district of Mizpah, repaired the spring gate. He built it, covered it, and set up its doors, its bolts, and its bars; and he repaired the wall of the pool of Shelah by the king's garden, even to the stairs that go down from David's city. 16 After him, Nehemiah the son of Azbuk, the ruler of half the district of Beth Zur, made repairs to the place opposite the tombs of David, and to the pool that was made, and to the house of the mighty men. 17 After him, the Levites—Rehum the son of Bani made repairs. Next to him, Hashabiah, the ruler of half the district of Keilah, made repairs for his district. 18 After him, their brothers, Bavvai the son of Henadad, the ruler of half the district of Keilah made repairs. 19 Next to him, Ezer the son of Jeshua, the ruler of Mizpah, repaired another portion across from the ascent to the armoury at the turning of the wall. 20 After him, Baruch the son of Zabbai earnestly repaired another portion, from the turning of the wall to the door of the house of Eliashib the high priest. 21 After him, Meremoth the son of Uriah the son of Hakkoz repaired another portion, from the door of the house of Eliashib even to the end of the house of Eliashib. 22 After him, the priests, the men of the surrounding area made repairs. 23 After them, Benjamin and Hasshub made repairs across from their house. After them, Azariah the son of Maaseiah the son of Ananiah made repairs beside his own house. 24 After him, Binnui the son of Henadad repaired another portion, from the house of Azariah to the turning of the wall, and to the corner. 25 Palal the son of Uzai made repairs opposite the turning of the wall, and the tower that stands out from the upper house of the king, which is by the court of the guard. After him Pedaiah the son of Parosh made repairs. 26 (Now the temple servants lived in Ophel, to the place opposite the water gate towards the east, and the tower that stands out.) 27 After him the Tekoites repaired another portion, opposite the great tower that stands out, and to the wall of Ophel.

28 Above the horse gate, the priests made repairs, everyone across from his own house. 29 After them, Zadok the son of Immer made repairs across from his own house. After him, Shemaiah the son of Shecaniah, the keeper of the east gate, made repairs. 30 After him, Hananiah the son of Shelemiah, and Hanun, the sixth son of Zalaph, repaired another portion. After him, Meshullam the son of Berechiah made repairs across from his room. 31 After him, Malchijah, one of the goldsmiths to the house of the temple servants, and of the merchants, made repairs opposite the gate of Hammiphkad and to the ascent of the corner. 32 Between the ascent of the corner and the sheep gate, the goldsmiths and the merchants made repairs.

4

1 But when Sanballat heard that we were building the wall, he was angry, and was very indignant, and mocked the Jews. 2 He spoke before his brothers and the army of Samaria, and said, "What are these feeble Jews doing? Will they fortify themselves? Will they sacrifice? Will they finish in a day? Will they revive the stones out of the heaps of rubbish, since they are burnt?"

3 Now Tobiah the Ammonite was by him, and he said, "What they are building, if a fox climbed up it, he would break down their stone wall."

---

a 1:4 The Hebrew word rendered "God" is "אֱלֹהִים" (Elohim).
b 1:5 When rendered in ALL CAPITAL LETTERS, "LORD" or "GOD" is the translation of God's Proper Name.

c 1:11 The word translated "Lord" is "Adonai."
d 3:13 A cubit is the length from the tip of the middle finger to the elbow on a man's arm, or about 18 inches or 46 centimetres.

Page | 169

4 "Hear, our God, for we are despised. Turn back their reproach on their own head. Give them up for a plunder in a land of captivity. 5 Don't cover their iniquity. Don't let their sin be blotted out from before you; for they have insulted the builders."

6 So we built the wall; and all the wall was joined together to half its height, for the people had a mind to work.

7 But when Sanballat, Tobiah, the Arabians, the Ammonites, and the Ashdodites heard that the repairing of the walls of Jerusalem went forward, and that the breaches began to be filled, they were very angry; 8 and they all conspired together to come and fight against Jerusalem, and to cause confusion amongst us. 9 But we made our prayer to our God, and set a watch against them day and night because of them.

10 Judah said, "The strength of the bearers of burdens is fading and there is much rubble, so that we are not able to build the wall." 11 Our adversaries said, "They will not know or see, until we come in amongst them and kill them, and cause the work to cease."

12 When the Jews who lived by them came, they said to us ten times from all places, "Wherever you turn, they will attack us."

13 Therefore I set guards in the lowest parts of the space behind the wall, in the open places. I set the people by family groups with their swords, their spears, and their bows. 14 I looked, and rose up, and said to the nobles, to the rulers, and to the rest of the people, "Don't be afraid of them! Remember the Lord, who is great and awesome, and fight for your brothers, your sons, your daughters, your wives, and your houses."

15 When our enemies heard that it was known to us, and God had brought their counsel to nothing, all of us returned to the wall, everyone to his work. 16 From that time forth, half of my servants did the work, and half of them held the spears, the shields, the bows, and the coats of mail; and the rulers were behind all the house of Judah. 17 Those who built the wall, and those who bore burdens loaded themselves; everyone with one of his hands did the work, and with the other held his weapon. 18 Amongst the builders, everyone wore his sword at his side, and so built. He who sounded the trumpet was by me. 19 I said to the nobles, and to the rulers and to the rest of the people, "The work is great and widely spread out, and we are separated on the wall, far from one another. 20 Wherever you hear the sound of the trumpet, rally there to us. Our God will fight for us."

21 So we did the work. Half of the people held the spears from the rising of the morning until the stars appeared. 22 Likewise at the same time I said to the people, "Let everyone with his servant lodge within Jerusalem, that in the night they may be a guard to us, and may labour in the day." 23 So neither I, nor my brothers, nor my servants, nor the men of the guard who followed me took off our clothes. Everyone took his weapon to the water.

5

1 Then there arose a great cry of the people and of their wives against their brothers the Jews. 2 For there were some who said, "We, our sons and our daughters, are many. Let us get grain, that we may eat and live." 3 There were also some who said, "We are mortgaging our fields, our vineyards, and our houses. Let us get grain, because of the famine." 4 There were also some who said, "We have borrowed money for the king's tribute using our fields and our vineyards as collateral. 5 Yet now our flesh is as the flesh of our brothers, our children as their children. Behold,[a] we bring our sons and our daughters into bondage to be servants, and some of our daughters have been brought into bondage. It is also not in our power to help it, because other men have our fields and our vineyards."

6 I was very angry when I heard their cry and these words. 7 Then I consulted with myself, and contended with the nobles and the rulers, and said to them, "You exact usury, everyone of his brother." I held a great assembly against them. 8 I said to them, "We, after our ability, have redeemed our brothers the Jews that were sold to the nations; and would you even sell your brothers, and should they be sold to us?" Then they held their peace, and found not a word to say. 9 Also I said, "The thing that you do is not good. Shouldn't you walk in the fear of our God because of the reproach of the nations, our enemies? 10 I likewise, my brothers and my servants, lend them money and grain. Please let us stop this usury. 11 Please restore to them, even today, their fields, their vineyards, their olive groves, and their houses, also the hundredth part of the money, and of the grain, the new wine, and the oil, that you are charging them."

12 Then they said, "We will restore them, and will require nothing of them. We will do so, even as you say."

Then I called the priests, and took an oath of them, that they would do according to this promise. 13 Also I shook out my lap, and said, "So may God shake out every man from his house, and from his labour, that doesn't perform this promise; even may he be shaken out and emptied like this."

All the assembly said, "Amen," and praised the LORD. The people did according to this promise.

14 Moreover from the time that I was appointed to be their governor in the land of Judah, from the twentieth year even to the thirty-second year of Artaxerxes the king, that is, twelve years, I and my brothers have not eaten the bread of the governor. 15 But the former governors who were before me were supported by the people, and took bread and wine from them, plus forty shekels[b] of silver; yes, even their servants ruled over the people, but I didn't do so, because of the fear of God. 16 Yes, I also continued in the work of this wall. We didn't buy any land. All my servants were gathered there to the work. 17 Moreover there were at my table, of the Jews and the rulers, one

hundred and fifty men, in addition to those who came to us from amongst the nations that were around us. 18 Now that which was prepared for one day was one ox and six choice sheep. Also fowls were prepared for me, and once in ten days a store of all sorts of wine. Yet for all this, I didn't demand the governor's pay, because the bondage was heavy on this people. 19 Remember me, my God, for all the good that I have done for this people.

6

1 Now when it was reported to Sanballat, Tobiah, Geshem the Arabian, and to the rest of our enemies that I had built the wall, and that there was no breach left in it (though even to that time I had not set up the doors in the gates), 2 Sanballat and Geshem sent to me, saying, "Come! Let's meet together in the villages in the plain of Ono." But they intended to harm me.

3 I sent messengers to them, saying, "I am doing a great work, so that I can't come down. Why should the work cease while I leave it and come down to you?"

4 They sent to me four times like this; and I answered them the same way. 5 Then Sanballat sent his servant to me the same way the fifth time with an open letter in his hand, 6 in which was written, "It is reported amongst the nations, and let's says it, that you and the Jews intend to rebel. Because of that, you are building the wall. You would be their king, according to these words. 7 You have also appointed prophets to proclaim of you at Jerusalem, saying, 'There is a king in Judah!' Now it will be reported to the king according to these words. Come now therefore, and let's take counsel together."

8 Then I sent to him, saying, "There are no such things done as you say, but you imagine them out of your own heart." 9 For they all would have made us afraid, saying, "Their hands will be weakened from the work, that it not be done." But now, strengthen my hands.

10 I went to the house of Shemaiah the son of Delaiah the son of Mehetabel, who was shut in at his home; and he said, "Let us meet together in God's house, within the temple, and let's shut the doors of the temple; for they will come to kill you. Yes, in the night they will come to kill you."

11 I said, "Should a man like me flee? Who is there that, being such as I, would go into the temple to save his life? I will not go in." 12 I discerned, and behold, God had not sent him, but he pronounced this prophecy against me. Tobiah and Sanballat had hired him. 13 He was hired so that I would be afraid, do so, and sin, and that they might have material for an evil report, that they might reproach me. 14 "Remember, my God, Tobiah and Sanballat according to these their works, and also the prophetess Noadiah and the rest of the prophets that would have put me in fear."

15 So the wall was finished in the twenty-fifth day of Elul, in fifty-two days. 16 When all our enemies heard of it, all the nations that were around us were afraid, and they lost their confidence; for they perceived that this work was done by our God. 17 Moreover in those days the nobles of Judah sent many letters to Tobiah, and Tobiah's letters came to them. 18 For there were many in Judah sworn to him because he was the son-in-law of Shecaniah the son of Arah; and his son Jehohanan had taken the daughter of Meshullam the son of Berechiah as wife. 19 Also they spoke of his good deeds before me, and reported my words to him. Tobiah sent letters to put me in fear.

7

1 Now when the wall was built and I had set up the doors, and the gatekeepers and the singers and the Levites were appointed, 2 I put my brother Hanani, and Hananiah the governor of the fortress, in charge of Jerusalem; for he was a faithful man and feared God above many. 3 I said to them, "Don't let the gates of Jerusalem be opened until the sun is hot; and while they stand guard, let them shut the doors, and you bar them; and appoint watches of the inhabitants of Jerusalem, everyone in his watch, with everyone near his house."

4 Now the city was wide and large; but the people were few therein, and the houses were not built.

5 My God put into my heart to gather together the nobles, and the rulers, and the people, that they might be listed by genealogy. I found the book of the genealogy of those who came up at the first, and I found this written in it:

6 These are the children of the province who went up out of the captivity of those who had been carried away, whom Nebuchadnezzar the king of Babylon had carried away, and who returned to Jerusalem and to Judah, everyone to his city, 7 who came with Zerubbabel, Jeshua, Nehemiah, Azariah, Raamiah, Nahamani, Mordecai, Bilshan, Mispereth, Bigvai, Nehum, and Baanah.

The number of the men of the people of Israel:

8 The children of Parosh: two thousand and one hundred and seventy-two.

9 The children of Shephatiah: three hundred and seventy-two.

10 The children of Arah: six hundred and fifty-two.

11 The children of Pahathmoab, of the children of Jeshua and Joab: two thousand and eight hundred and eighteen.

12 The children of Elam: one thousand and two hundred and fifty-four.

13 The children of Zattu: eight hundred and forty-five.

14 The children of Zaccai: seven hundred and sixty.

15 The children of Binnui: six hundred and forty-eight.

16 The children of Bebai: six hundred and twenty-eight.

17 The children of Azgad: two thousand and three hundred and twenty-two.

18 The children of Adonikam: six hundred and sixty-seven.

19 The children of Bigvai: two thousand and sixty-seven.

---

a 5:5 "Behold", from "הִנֵּה", means look at, take notice, observe, see, or gaze at. It is often used as an interjection.

b 5:15 A shekel is about 10 grams or about 0.35 ounces.

20 The children of Adin: six hundred and fifty-five.
21 The children of Ater: of Hezekiah, ninety-eight.
22 The children of Hashum: three hundred and twenty-eight.
23 The children of Bezai: three hundred and twenty-four.
24 The children of Hariph: one hundred and twelve.
25 The children of Gibeon: ninety-five.
26 The men of Bethlehem and Netophah: one hundred and eighty-eight.
27 The men of Anathoth: one hundred and twenty-eight.
28 The men of Beth Azmaveth: forty-two.
29 The men of Kiriath Jearim, Chephirah, and Beeroth: seven hundred and forty-three.
30 The men of Ramah and Geba: six hundred and twenty-one.
31 The men of Michmas: one hundred and twenty-two.
32 The men of Bethel and Ai: one hundred and twenty-three.
33 The men of the other Nebo: fifty-two.
34 The children of the other Elam: one thousand and two hundred and fifty-four.
35 The children of Harim: three hundred and twenty.
36 The children of Jericho: three hundred and forty-five.
37 The children of Lod, Hadid, and Ono: seven hundred and twenty-one.
38 The children of Senaah: three thousand and nine hundred and thirty.

39 The priests: The children of Jedaiah, of the house of Jeshua: nine hundred and seventy-three.
40 The children of Immer: one thousand and fifty-two.
41 The children of Pashhur: one thousand and two hundred and forty-seven.
42 The children of Harim: one thousand and seventeen.

43 The Levites: the children of Jeshua, of Kadmiel, of the children of Hodevah: seventy-four.
44 The singers: the children of Asaph: one hundred and forty-eight.
45 The gatekeepers: the children of Shallum, the children of Ater, the children of Talmon, the children of Akkub, the children of Hatita, the children of Shobai: one hundred and thirty-eight.
46 The temple servants: the children of Ziha, the children of Hasupha, the children of Tabbaoth, 47 the children of Keros, the children of Sia, the children of Padon, 48 the children of Lebana, the children of Hagaba, the children of Salmai, 49 the children of Hanan, the children of Giddel, the children of Gahar, 50 the children of Reaiah, the children of Rezin, the children of Nekoda, 51 the children of Gazzam, the children of Uzza, the children of Paseah, 52 the children of Besai, the children of Meunim, the children of Nephushesim, 53 the children of Bakbuk, the children of Hakupha, the children of Harhur, 54 the children of Bazlith, the children of Mehida, the children of Harsha, 55 the children of Barkos, the children of Sisera, the children of Temah, 56 the children of Neziah, and the children of Hatipha.
57 The children of Solomon's servants: the children of Sotai, the children of Sophereth, the children of Perida, 58 the children of Jaala, the children of Darkon, the children of Giddel, 59 the children of Shephatiah, the children of Hattil, the children of Pochereth Hazzebaim, and the children of Amon. 60 All the temple servants and the children of Solomon's servants were three hundred and ninety-two.
61 These were those who went up from Tel Melah, Tel Harsha, Cherub, Addon, and Immer; but they could not show their fathers' houses, nor their offspring,[a] whether they were of Israel:
62 The children of Delaiah, the children of Tobiah, the children of Nekoda: six hundred and forty-two.
63 Of the priests: the children of Hobaiah, the children of Hakkoz, the children of Barzillai, who took a wife of the daughters of Barzillai the Gileadite, and was called after their name.
64 These searched for their genealogical records, but couldn't find them. Therefore they were deemed disqualified and removed from the priesthood. 65 The governor told them not to eat of the most holy things until a priest stood up to minister with Urim and Thummim.
66 The whole assembly together was forty-two thousand and three hundred and sixty, 67 in addition to their male servants and their female servants, of whom there were seven thousand and three hundred and thirty-seven. They had two hundred and forty-five singing men and singing women. 68 Their horses were seven hundred and thirty-six; their mules, two hundred and forty-five; 69 their camels, four hundred and thirty-five; their donkeys, six thousand and seven hundred and twenty.
70 Some from amongst the heads of fathers' households gave to the work. The governor gave to the treasury one thousand darics of gold,[b] fifty basins, and five hundred and thirty priests' garments. 71 Some of the heads of fathers' households gave into the treasury of the work twenty thousand darics of gold, and two thousand and two hundred minas[c] of silver. 72 That which the rest of the people gave was twenty thousand darics of gold, plus two thousand minas of silver, and sixty-seven priests' garments.
73 So the priests, the Levites, the gatekeepers, the singers, some of the people, the temple servants, and all Israel lived in their cities.

When the seventh month had come, the children of Israel were in their cities.

8

1 All the people gathered themselves together as one man into the wide place that was in front of the water gate; and they spoke to Ezra the scribe to bring the book of the law of Moses, which the LORD had commanded to Israel. 2 Ezra the priest brought the law before the assembly, both men and women, and all who could hear with understanding, on the first day of the seventh month. 3 He read from it before the wide place that was in front of the water gate from early morning until midday, in the presence of the men and the women, and of those who could understand. The ears of all the people were attentive to the book of the law. 4 Ezra the scribe stood on a pulpit of wood, which they had made for the purpose; and beside him stood Mattithiah, Shema, Anaiah, Uriah, Hilkiah, and Maaseiah, on his right hand; and on his left hand, Pedaiah, Mishael, Malchijah, Hashum, Hashbaddanah, Zechariah, and Meshullam. 5 Ezra opened the book in the sight of all the people (for he was above all the people), and when he opened it, all the people stood up. 6 Then Ezra blessed the LORD, the great God.

All the people answered, "Amen, Amen," with the lifting up of their hands. They bowed their heads, and worshipped the LORD with their faces to the ground. 7 Also Jeshua, Bani, Sherebiah, Jamin, Akkub, Shabbethai, Hodiah, Maaseiah, Kelita, Azariah, Jozabad, Hanan, Pelaiah, and the Levites, caused the people to understand the law; and the people stayed in their place. 8 They read in the book, in the law of God, distinctly; and they gave the sense, so that they understood the reading.

9 Nehemiah, who was the governor, Ezra the priest and scribe, and the Levites who taught the people said to all the people, "Today is holy to the LORD your God. Don't mourn, nor weep." For all the people wept when they heard the words of the law. 10 Then he said to them, "Go your way. Eat the fat, drink the sweet, and send portions to him for whom nothing is prepared, for today is holy to our Lord. Don't be grieved, for the joy of the LORD is your strength."

11 So the Levites calmed all the people, saying, "Hold your peace, for the day is holy. Don't be grieved."

12 All the people went their way to eat, to drink, to send portions, and to celebrate, because they had understood the words that were declared to them.

13 On the second day, the heads of fathers' households of all the people, the priests, and the Levites were gathered together to Ezra the scribe, to study the words of the law. 14 They found written in the law how the LORD had commanded by Moses that the children of Israel should dwell in booths in the feast of the seventh month; 15 and that they should publish and proclaim in all their cities and in Jerusalem, saying, "Go out to the mountain, and get olive branches, branches of wild olive, myrtle branches, palm branches, and branches of thick trees, to make temporary shelters,[d] as it is written."

16 So the people went out and brought them, and made themselves temporary shelters,[e] everyone on the roof of his house, in their courts, in the courts of God's house, in the wide place of the water gate, and in the wide place of Ephraim's gate. 17 All the assembly of those who had come back out of the captivity made temporary shelters[f] and lived in the temporary shelters, for since the days of Joshua the son of Nun to that day the children of Israel had not done so. There was very great gladness. 18 Also day by day, from the first day to the last day, he read in the book of the law of God. They kept the feast seven days; and on the eighth day was a solemn assembly, according to the ordinance.

9

1 Now in the twenty-fourth day of this month the children of Israel were assembled with fasting, with sackcloth, and dirt on them. 2 The offspring of Israel separated themselves from all foreigners and stood and confessed their sins and the iniquities of their fathers. 3 They stood up in their place, and read in the book of the law of the LORD their God a fourth part of the day; and a fourth part they confessed and worshipped the LORD their God. 4 Then Jeshua, Bani, Kadmiel, Shebaniah, Bunni, Sherebiah, Bani, and Chenani of the Levites stood up on the stairs, and cried with a loud voice to the LORD their God.

5 Then the Levites, Jeshua, and Kadmiel, Bani, Hashabneiah, Sherebiah, Hodiah, Shebaniah, and Pethahiah, said, "Stand up and bless the LORD your God from everlasting to everlasting! Blessed be your glorious name, which is exalted above all blessing and praise! 6 You are the LORD, even you alone. You have made heaven, the heaven of heavens, with all their army, the earth and all things that are on it, the seas and all that is in them, and you preserve them all. The army of heaven worships you. 7 You are the LORD, the God who chose Abram, brought him out of Ur of the Chaldees, gave him the name of Abraham, 8 found his heart faithful before you, and made a covenant with him to give the land of the Canaanite, the Hittite, the Amorite, the Perizzite, the Jebusite, and the Girgashite, to give it to his offspring, and have performed your words, for you are righteous.

9 "You saw the affliction of our fathers in Egypt, and heard their cry by the Red Sea, 10 and showed signs and wonders against Pharaoh, against all his servants, and against all the people of his land, for you knew that they dealt proudly against them, and made a name for yourself, as it is today. 11 You divided the sea before them, so that they went through the middle of

---

[a] 7:61 or, seed
[b] 7:70 a daric was a gold coin issued by a Persian king, weighing about 8.4 grams or about 0.27 troy ounces each.
[c] 7:71 A mina is about 600 grams or 1.3 U. S. pounds, so 2,200 minas is about 1.3 metric tonnes.

[d] 8:15 or, booths
[e] 8:16 or, booths
[f] 8:17 or, booths

the sea on the dry land; and you cast their pursuers into the depths, as a stone into the mighty waters. 12 Moreover, in a pillar of cloud you led them by day; and in a pillar of fire by night, to give them light in the way in which they should go.

13 "You also came down on Mount Sinai, and spoke with them from heaven, and gave them right ordinances and true laws, good statutes and commandments, 14 and made known to them your holy Sabbath, and commanded them commandments, statutes, and a law, by Moses your servant, 15 and gave them bread from the sky for their hunger, and brought water out of the rock for them for their thirst, and commanded them that they should go in to possess the land which you had sworn to give them.

16 "But they and our fathers behaved proudly, hardened their neck, didn't listen to your commandments, 17 and refused to obey. They weren't mindful of your wonders that you did amongst them, but hardened their neck, and in their rebellion appointed a captain to return to their bondage. But you are a God ready to pardon, gracious and merciful, slow to anger, and abundant in loving kindness, and didn't forsake them. 18 Yes, when they had made themselves a moulded calf, and said, 'This is your God who brought you up out of Egypt,' and had committed awful blasphemies, 19 yet you in your manifold mercies didn't forsake them in the wilderness. The pillar of cloud didn't depart from over them by day, to lead them in the way; neither did the pillar of fire by night, to show them light, and the way in which they should go. 20 You gave also your good Spirit to instruct them, and didn't withhold your manna from their mouth, and gave them water for their thirst.

21 "Yes, forty years you sustained them in the wilderness. They lacked nothing. Their clothes didn't grow old, and their feet didn't swell. 22 Moreover you gave them kingdoms and peoples, which you allotted according to their portions. So they possessed the land of Sihon, even the land of the king of Heshbon, and the land of Og king of Bashan. 23 You also multiplied their children as the stars of the sky, and brought them into the land concerning which you said to their fathers that they should go in to possess it.

24 "So the children went in and possessed the land; and you subdued before them the inhabitants of the land, the Canaanites, and gave them into their hands, with their kings and the peoples of the land, that they might do with them as they pleased. 25 They took fortified cities and a rich land, and possessed houses full of all good things, cisterns dug out, vineyards, olive groves, and fruit trees in abundance. So they ate, were filled, became fat, and delighted themselves in your great goodness.

26 "Nevertheless they were disobedient and rebelled against you, cast your law behind their back, killed your prophets that testified against them to turn them again to you, and they committed awful blasphemies. 27 Therefore you delivered them into the hand of their adversaries, who distressed them. In the time of their trouble, when they cried to you, you heard from heaven; and according to your manifold mercies you gave them saviours who saved them out of the hands of their adversaries. 28 But after they had rest, they did evil again before you; therefore you left them in the hands of their enemies, so that they had the dominion over them; yet when they returned and cried to you, you heard from heaven; and many times you delivered them according to your mercies, 29 and testified against them, that you might bring them again to your law. Yet they were arrogant, and didn't listen to your commandments, but sinned against your ordinances (which if a man does, he shall live in them), turned their backs, stiffened their neck, and would not hear. 30 Yet many years you put up with them, and testified against them by your Spirit through your prophets. Yet they would not listen. Therefore you gave them into the hand of the peoples of the lands.

31 "Nevertheless in your manifold mercies you didn't make a full end of them, nor forsake them; for you are a gracious and merciful God.

32 Now therefore, our God, the great, the mighty, and the awesome God, who keeps covenant and loving kindness, don't let all the travail seem little before you that has come on us, on our kings, on our princes, on our priests, on our prophets, on our fathers, and on all your people, since the time of the kings of Assyria to this day. 33 However you are just in all that has come on us; for you have dealt truly, but we have done wickedly. 34 Also our kings, our princes, our priests, and our fathers have not kept your law, nor listened to your commandments and your testimonies with which you testified against them. 35 For they have not served you in their kingdom, and in your great goodness that you gave them, and in the large and rich land which you gave before them. They didn't turn from their wicked works.

36 "Behold, we are servants today, and as for the land that you gave to our fathers to eat its fruit and its good, behold, we are servants in it. 37 It yields much increase to the kings whom you have set over us because of our sins. Also they have power over our bodies and over our livestock, at their pleasure, and we are in great distress. 38 Yet for all this, we make a sure covenant, and write it; and our princes, our Levites, and our priests, seal it."

10

1 Now those who sealed were: Nehemiah the governor, the son of Hacaliah, and Zedekiah, 2 Seraiah, Azariah, Jeremiah, 3 Pashhur, Amariah, Malchijah, 4 Hattush, Shebaniah, Malluch, 5 Harim, Meremoth, Obadiah, 6 Daniel, Ginnethon, Baruch, 7 Meshullam, Abijah, Mijamin, 8 Maaziah, Bilgai, and Shemaiah. These were the priests. 9 The Levites: Jeshua the son of Azaniah, Binnui of the sons of Henadad, Kadmiel; 10 and their brothers,

Shebaniah, Hodiah, Kelita, Pelaiah, Hanan, 11 Mica, Rehob, Hashabiah, 12 Zaccur, Sherebiah, Shebaniah, 13 Hodiah, Bani, and Beninu. 14 The chiefs of the people: Parosh, Pahathmoab, Elam, Zattu, Bani, 15 Bunni, Azgad, Bebai, 16 Adonijah, Bigvai, Adin, 17 Ater, Hezekiah, Azzur, 18 Hodiah, Hashum, Bezai, 19 Hariph, Anathoth, Nobai, 20 Magpiash, Meshullam, Hezir, 21 Meshezabel, Zadok, Jaddua, 22 Pelatiah, Hanan, Anaiah, 23 Hoshea, Hananiah, Hasshub, 24 Hallohesh, Pilha, Shobek, 25 Rehum, Hashabnah, Maaseiah, 26 Ahiah, Hanan, Anan, 27 Malluch, Harim, and Baanah.

28 The rest of the people, the priests, the Levites, the gatekeepers, the singers, the temple servants, and all those who had separated themselves from the peoples of the lands to the law of God, their wives, their sons, and their daughters—everyone who had knowledge and understanding— 29 joined with their brothers, their nobles, and entered into a curse and into an oath, to walk in God's law, which was given by Moses the servant of God, and to observe and do all the commandments of the LORD our Lord, and his ordinances and his statutes; 30 and that we would not give our daughters to the peoples of the land, nor take their daughters for our sons; 31 and if the peoples of the land bring wares or any grain on the Sabbath day to sell, that we would not buy from them on the Sabbath, or on a holy day; and that we would forego the seventh year crops and the exaction of every debt.

32 Also we made ordinances for ourselves, to charge ourselves yearly with the third part of a shekel[a] for the service of the house of our God: 33 for the show bread, for the continual meal offering, for the continual burnt offering, for the Sabbaths, for the new moons, for the set feasts, for the holy things, for the sin offerings to make atonement for Israel, and for all the work of the house of our God. 34 We, the priests, the Levites, and the people, cast lots for the wood offering, to bring it into the house of our God, according to our fathers' houses, at times appointed year by year, to burn on the LORD our God's altar, as it is written in the law; 35 and to bring the first fruits of our ground and the first fruits of all fruit of all kinds of trees, year by year, to the LORD's house; 36 also the firstborn of our sons and of our livestock, as it is written in the law, and the firstborn of our herds and of our flocks, to bring to the house of our God, to the priests who minister in the house of our God; 37 and that we should bring the first fruits of our dough, our wave offerings, the fruit of all kinds of trees, and the new wine and the oil, to the priests, to the rooms of the house of our God; and the tithes of our ground to the Levites; for they, the Levites, take the tithes in all our farming villages. 38 The priest, the descendent of Aaron, shall be with the Levites when the Levites take tithes. The Levites shall bring up the tithe of the tithes to the house of our God, to the rooms, into the treasure house. 39 For the children of Israel and the children of Levi shall bring the wave offering of the grain, of the new wine, and of the oil, to the rooms where the vessels of the sanctuary are, and the priests who minister, with the gatekeepers and the singers. We will not forsake the house of our God.

11

1 The princes of the people lived in Jerusalem. The rest of the people also cast lots to bring one of ten to dwell in Jerusalem, the holy city, and nine parts in the other cities. 2 The people blessed all the men who willingly offered themselves to dwell in Jerusalem.

3 Now these are the chiefs of the province who lived in Jerusalem; but in the cities of Judah, everyone lived in his possession in their cities— Israel, the priests, the Levites, the temple servants, and the children of Solomon's servants. 4 Some of the children of Judah and of the children of Benjamin lived in Jerusalem. Of the children of Judah: Athaiah the son of Uzziah, the son of Zechariah, the son of Amariah, the son of Shephatiah, the son of Mahalalel, of the children of Perez; 5 and Maaseiah the son of Baruch, the son of Colhozeh, the son of Hazaiah, the son of Adaiah, the son of Joiarib, the son of Zechariah, the son of the Shilonite. 6 All the sons of Perez who lived in Jerusalem were four hundred and sixty-eight valiant men.

7 These are the sons of Benjamin: Sallu the son of Meshullam, the son of Joed, the son of Pedaiah, the son of Kolaiah, the son of Maaseiah, the son of Ithiel, the son of Jeshaiah. 8 After him Gabbai and Sallai, nine hundred and twenty-eight. 9 Joel the son of Zichri was their overseer; and Judah the son of Hassenuah was second over the city.

10 Of the priests: Jedaiah the son of Joiarib, Jachin, 11 Seraiah the son of Hilkiah, the son of Meshullam, the son of Zadok, the son of Meraioth, the son of Ahitub, the ruler of God's house, 12 and their brothers who did the work of the house, eight hundred and twenty-two; and Adaiah the son of Jeroham, the son of Pelaliah, the son of Amzi, the son of Zechariah, the son of Pashhur, the son of Malchijah, 13 and his brothers, chiefs of fathers' households, two hundred and forty-two; and Amashsai the son of Azarel, the son of Ahzai, the son of Meshillemoth, the son of Immer, 14 and their brothers, mighty men of valour, one hundred and twenty-eight; and their overseer was Zabdiel, the son of Haggedolim.

15 Of the Levites: Shemaiah the son of Hasshub, the son of Azrikam, the son of Hashabiah, the son of Bunni; 16 and Shabbethai and Jozabad, of the chiefs of the Levites, who had the oversight of the outward business of God's house; 17 and Mattaniah the son of Mica, the son of Zabdi, the son of Asaph, who was the chief to begin the thanksgiving in prayer, and Bakbukiah, the second amongst his brothers; and Abda the son of Shammua, the son of Galal, the son of Jeduthun. 18 All the Levites in the holy city were two hundred and eighty-four.

19 Moreover the gatekeepers, Akkub, Talmon, and their brothers, who kept watch at the gates, were one hundred and seventy-two. 20 The residue

---

a 10:32 A shekel is about 10 grams or about 0.35 ounces.

of Israel, of the priests, and the Levites were in all the cities of Judah, everyone in his inheritance. 21 But the temple servants lived in Ophel; and Ziha and Gishpa were over the temple servants.

22 The overseer also of the Levites at Jerusalem was Uzzi the son of Bani, the son of Hashabiah, the son of Mattaniah, the son of Mica, of the sons of Asaph, the singers responsible for the service of God's house. 23 For there was a commandment from the king concerning them, and a settled provision for the singers, as every day required. 24 Pethahiah the son of Meshezabel, of the children of Zerah the son of Judah, was at the king's hand in all matters concerning the people.

25 As for the villages with their fields, some of the children of Judah lived in Kiriath Arba and its towns, in Dibon and its towns, in Jekabzeel and its villages, 26 in Jeshua, in Moladah, Beth Pelet, 27 in Hazar Shual, in Beersheba and its towns, 28 in Ziklag, in Meconah and in its towns, 29 in En Rimmon, in Zorah, in Jarmuth, 30 Zanoah, Adullam, and their villages, Lachish and its fields, and Azekah and its towns. So they encamped from Beersheba to the valley of Hinnom. 31 The children of Benjamin also lived from Geba onward, at Michmash and Aija, and at Bethel and its towns, 32 at Anathoth, Nob, Ananiah, 33 Hazor, Ramah, Gittaim, 34 Hadid, Zeboim, Neballat, 35 Lod, and Ono, the valley of craftsmen. 36 Of the Levites, certain divisions in Judah settled in Benjamin's territory.

12

1 Now these are the priests and the Levites who went up with Zerubbabel the son of Shealtiel, and Jeshua: Seraiah, Jeremiah, Ezra, 2 Amariah, Malluch, Hattush, 3 Shecaniah, Rehum, Meremoth, 4 Iddo, Ginnethoi, Abijah, 5 Mijamin, Maadiah, Bilgah, 6 Shemaiah, Joiarib, Jedaiah, 7 Sallu, Amok, Hilkiah, and Jedaiah. These were the chiefs of the priests and of their brothers in the days of Jeshua.

8 Moreover the Levites were Jeshua, Binnui, Kadmiel, Sherebiah, Judah, and Mattaniah, who was over the thanksgiving songs, he and his brothers. 9 Also Bakbukiah and Unno, their brothers, were close to them according to their offices. 10 Jeshua became the father of Joiakim, and Joiakim became the father of Eliashib, and Eliashib became the father of Joiada, 11 and Joiada became the father of Jonathan, and Jonathan became the father of Jaddua.

12 In the days of Joiakim were priests, heads of fathers' households: of Seraiah, Meraiah; of Jeremiah, Hananiah; 13 of Ezra, Meshullam; of Amariah, Jehohanan; 14 of Malluchi, Jonathan; of Shebaniah, Joseph; 15 of Harim, Adna; of Meraioth, Helkai; 16 of Iddo, Zechariah; of Ginnethon, Meshullam; 17 of Abijah, Zichri; of Miniamin, of Moadiah, Piltai; 18 of Bilgah, Shammua; of Shemaiah, Jehonathan; 19 of Joiarib, Mattenai; of Jedaiah, Uzzi; 20 of Sallai, Kallai; of Amok, Eber; 21 of Hilkiah, Hashabiah; of Jedaiah, Nethanel.

22 As for the Levites, in the days of Eliashib, Joiada, Johanan, and Jaddua, there were recorded the heads of fathers' households; also the priests, in the reign of Darius the Persian. 23 The sons of Levi, heads of fathers' households, were written in the book of the chronicles, even until the days of Johanan the son of Eliashib. 24 The chiefs of the Levites: Hashabiah, Sherebiah, and Jeshua the son of Kadmiel, with their brothers close to them, to praise and give thanks according to the commandment of David the man of God, section next to section. 25 Mattaniah, Bakbukiah, Obadiah, Meshullam, Talmon, and Akkub were gatekeepers keeping the watch at the storehouses of the gates. 26 These were in the days of Joiakim the son of Jeshua, the son of Jozadak, and in the days of Nehemiah the governor, and of Ezra the priest and scribe.

27 At the dedication of the wall of Jerusalem, they sought the Levites out of all their places, to bring them to Jerusalem to keep the dedication with gladness, both with giving thanks and with singing, with cymbals, stringed instruments, and with harps. 28 The sons of the singers gathered themselves together, both out of the plain around Jerusalem and from the villages of the Netophathites; 29 also from Beth Gilgal and out of the fields of Geba and Azmaveth, for the singers had built themselves villages around Jerusalem. 30 The priests and the Levites purified themselves; and they purified the people, the gates, and the wall.

31 Then I brought the princes of Judah up on the wall, and appointed two great companies who gave thanks and went in procession. One went on the right hand on the wall towards the dung gate; 32 and after them went Hoshaiah, with half of the princes of Judah, 33 and Azariah, Ezra, and Meshullam, 34 Judah, Benjamin, Shemaiah, Jeremiah, 35 and some of the priests' sons with trumpets: Zechariah the son of Jonathan, the son of Shemaiah, the son of Mattaniah, the son of Micaiah, the son of Zaccur, the son of Asaph; 36 and his brothers, Shemaiah, Azarel, Milalai, Gilalai, Maai, Nethanel, Judah, and Hanani, with the musical instruments of David the man of God; and Ezra the scribe was before them. 37 By the spring gate, and straight before them, they went up by the stairs of David's city, at the ascent of the wall, above David's house, even to the water gate eastward.

38 The other company of those who gave thanks went to meet them, and I after them, with the half of the people on the wall above the tower of the furnaces, even to the wide wall, 39 and above the gate of Ephraim, and by the old gate, and by the fish gate, the tower of Hananel, and the tower of Hammeah, even to the sheep gate; and they stood still in the gate of the guard. 40 So the two companies of those who gave thanks in God's house stood, and I and the half of the rulers with me; 41 and the priests, Eliakim, Maaseiah, Miniamin, Micaiah, Elioenai, Zechariah, and Hananiah, with trumpets; 42 and Maaseiah, Shemaiah, Eleazar, Uzzi, Jehohanan, Malchijah, Elam, and Ezer. The singers sang loud, with Jezrahiah their overseer. 43 They offered great sacrifices that day, and rejoiced, for God had made them rejoice with great joy; and the women and the children also rejoiced, so that the joy of Jerusalem was heard even far away.

44 On that day, men were appointed over the rooms for the treasures, for the wave offerings, for the first fruits, and for the tithes, to gather into them according to the fields of the cities the portions appointed by the law for the priests and Levites; for Judah rejoiced for the priests and for the Levites who served. 45 They performed the duty of their God and the duty of the purification, and so did the singers and the gatekeepers, according to the commandment of David and of Solomon his son. 46 For in the days of David and Asaph of old there was a chief of the singers, and songs of praise and thanksgiving to God. 47 All Israel in the days of Zerubbabel and in the days of Nehemiah gave the portions of the singers and the gatekeepers, as every day required; and they set apart that which was for the Levites; and the Levites set apart that which was for the sons of Aaron.

13

1 On that day they read in the book of Moses in the hearing of the people; and it was found written in it that an Ammonite and a Moabite should not enter into the assembly of God forever, 2 because they didn't meet the children of Israel with bread and with water, but hired Balaam against them to curse them; however, our God turned the curse into a blessing. 3 It came to pass, when they had heard the law, that they separated all the mixed multitude from Israel.

4 Now before this, Eliashib the priest, who was appointed over the rooms of the house of our God, being allied to Tobiah, 5 had prepared for him a great room, where before they laid the meal offerings, the frankincense, the vessels, and the tithes of the grain, the new wine, and the oil, which were given by commandment to the Levites, the singers, and the gatekeepers; and the wave offerings for the priests. 6 But in all this, I was not at Jerusalem; for in the thirty-second year of Artaxerxes king of Babylon I went to the king; and after some days I asked leave of the king, 7 and I came to Jerusalem, and understood the evil that Eliashib had done for Tobiah, in preparing him a room in the courts of God's house. 8 It grieved me severely. Therefore I threw all Tobiah's household stuff out of the room. 9 Then I commanded, and they cleansed the rooms. I brought into them the vessels of God's house, with the meal offerings and the frankincense again.

10 I perceived that the portions of the Levites had not been given them, so that the Levites and the singers, who did the work, had each fled to his field. 11 Then I contended with the rulers, and said, "Why is God's house forsaken?" I gathered them together, and set them in their place. 12 Then all Judah brought the tithe of the grain, the new wine, and the oil to the treasuries. 13 I made treasurers over the treasuries, Shelemiah the priest, and Zadok the scribe, and of the Levites, Pedaiah: and next to them was Hanan the son of Zaccur, the son of Mattaniah; for they were counted faithful, and their business was to distribute to their brothers.

14 Remember me, my God, concerning this, and don't wipe out my good deeds that I have done for the house of my God, and for its observances.

15 In those days I saw some men treading wine presses on the Sabbath in Judah, bringing in sheaves, and loading donkeys with wine, grapes, figs, and all kinds of burdens which they brought into Jerusalem on the Sabbath day; and I testified against them in the day in which they sold food. 16 Some men of Tyre also lived there, who brought in fish and all kinds of wares, and sold on the Sabbath to the children of Judah, and in Jerusalem. 17 Then I contended with the nobles of Judah, and said to them, "What evil thing is this that you do, and profane the Sabbath day? 18 Didn't your fathers do this, and didn't our God bring all this evil on us and on this city? Yet you bring more wrath on Israel by profaning the Sabbath."

19 It came to pass that when the gates of Jerusalem began to be dark before the Sabbath, I commanded that the doors should be shut, and commanded that they should not be opened until after the Sabbath. I set some of my servants over the gates, so that no burden should be brought in on the Sabbath day. 20 So the merchants and sellers of all kinds of wares camped outside of Jerusalem once or twice. 21 Then I testified against them, and said to them, "Why do you stay around the wall? If you do so again, I will lay hands on you." From that time on, they didn't come on the Sabbath. 22 I commanded the Levites that they should purify themselves, and that they should come and keep the gates, to sanctify the Sabbath day. Remember me for this also, my God, and spare me according to the greatness of your loving kindness.

23 In those days I also saw the Jews who had married women of Ashdod, of Ammon, and of Moab; 24 and their children spoke half in the speech of Ashdod, and could not speak in the Jews' language, but according to the language of each people. 25 I contended with them, cursed them, struck certain of them, plucked off their hair, and made them swear by God, "You shall not give your daughters to their sons, nor take their daughters for your sons, or for yourselves. 26 Didn't Solomon king of Israel sin by these things? Yet amongst many nations there was no king like him, and he was loved by his God, and God made him king over all Israel. Nevertheless foreign women caused even him to sin. 27 Shall we then listen to you to do all this great evil, to trespass against our God in marrying foreign women?"

28 One of the sons of Joiada, the son of Eliashib the high priest, was son-in-law to Sanballat the Horonite; therefore I chased him from me. 29 Remember them, my God, because they have defiled the priesthood and the covenant of the priesthood and of the Levites.

30 Thus I cleansed them from all foreigners and appointed duties for the priests and for the Levites, everyone in his work; 31 and for the wood offering, at appointed times, and for the first fruits. Remember me, my God, for good.

The Book of Esther

1

₁ Now in the days of Ahasuerus (this is Ahasuerus who reigned from India even to Ethiopia, over one hundred and twenty-seven provinces), ₂ in those days, when the King Ahasuerus sat on the throne of his kingdom, which was in Susa the palace, ₃ in the third year of his reign, he made a feast for all his princes and his servants; the army of Persia and Media, the nobles and princes of the provinces being before him. ₄ He displayed the riches of his glorious kingdom and the honour of his excellent majesty many days, even one hundred and eighty days.

₅ When these days were fulfilled, the king made a seven day feast for all the people who were present in Susa the palace, both great and small, in the court of the garden of the king's palace. ₆ There were hangings of white and blue material, fastened with cords of fine linen and purple to silver rings and marble pillars. The couches were of gold and silver, on a pavement of red, white, yellow, and black marble. ₇ They gave them drinks in golden vessels of various kinds, including royal wine in abundance, according to the bounty of the king. ₈ In accordance with the law, the drinking was not compulsory; for so the king had instructed all the officials of his house, that they should do according to every man's pleasure.

₉ Also Vashti the queen made a feast for the women in the royal house which belonged to King Ahasuerus.

₁₀ On the seventh day, when the heart of the king was merry with wine, he commanded Mehuman, Biztha, Harbona, Bigtha, and Abagtha, Zethar, and Carcass, the seven eunuchs who served in the presence of Ahasuerus the king, ₁₁ to bring Vashti the queen before the king wearing the royal crown, to show the people and the princes her beauty; for she was beautiful. ₁₂ But the queen Vashti refused to come at the king's commandment by the eunuchs. Therefore the king was very angry, and his anger burnt in him.

₁₃ Then the king said to the wise men, who knew the times (for it was the king's custom to consult those who knew law and judgement; ₁₄ and next to him were Carshena, Shethar, Admatha, Tarshish, Meres, Marsena, and Memucan, the seven princes of Persia and Media, who saw the king's face, and sat first in the kingdom), ₁₅ "What shall we do to Queen Vashti according to law, because she has not done the bidding of the King Ahasuerus by the eunuchs?"

₁₆ Memucan answered before the king and the princes, "Vashti the queen has not done wrong to just the king, but also to all the princes, and to all the people who are in all the provinces of the King Ahasuerus. ₁₇ For this deed of the queen will become known to all women, causing them to show contempt for their husbands when it is reported, 'King Ahasuerus commanded Vashti the queen to be brought in before him, but she didn't come.' ₁₈ Today, the princesses of Persia and Media who have heard of the queen's deed will tell all the king's princes. This will cause much contempt and wrath.

₁₉ "If it pleases the king, let a royal commandment go from him, and let it be written amongst the laws of the Persians and the Medes, so that it cannot be altered, that Vashti may never again come before King Ahasuerus; and let the king give her royal estate to another who is better than she. ₂₀ When the king's decree which he shall make is published throughout all his kingdom (for it is great), all the wives will give their husbands honour, both great and small."

₂₁ This advice pleased the king and the princes, and the king did according to the word of Memucan: ₂₂ for he sent letters into all the king's provinces, into every province according to its writing, and to every people in their language, that every man should rule his own house, speaking in the language of his own people.

2

₁ After these things, when the wrath of King Ahasuerus was pacified, he remembered Vashti, and what she had done, and what was decreed against her. ₂ Then the king's servants who served him said, "Let beautiful young virgins be sought for the king. ₃ Let the king appoint officers in all the provinces of his kingdom, that they may gather together all the beautiful young virgins to the citadel of Susa, to the women's house, to the custody of Hegai the king's eunuch, keeper of the women. Let cosmetics be given them; ₄ and let the maiden who pleases the king be queen instead of Vashti." The thing pleased the king, and he did so.

₅ There was a certain Jew in the citadel of Susa whose name was Mordecai, the son of Jair, the son of Shimei, the son of Kish, a Benjamite, ₆ who had been carried away from Jerusalem with the captives who had been carried away with Jeconiah king of Judah, whom Nebuchadnezzar the king of Babylon had carried away. ₇ He brought up Hadassah, that is, Esther, his uncle's daughter; for she had neither father nor mother. The maiden was fair and beautiful; and when her father and mother were dead, Mordecai took her for his own daughter.

₈ So, when the king's commandment and his decree was heard, and when many maidens were gathered together to the citadel of Susa, to the custody of Hegai, Esther was taken into the king's house, to the custody of Hegai, keeper of the women. ₉ The maiden pleased him, and she obtained kindness from him. He quickly gave her cosmetics and her portions of food, and the seven choice maidens who were to be given her out of the king's house. He moved her and her maidens to the best place in the women's house. ₁₀ Esther had not made known her people nor her relatives, because Mordecai had instructed her that she should not make it known. ₁₁ Mordecai walked every day in front of the court of the women's house, to find out how Esther was doing, and what would become of her.

₁₂ Each young woman's turn came to go in to King Ahasuerus after her purification for twelve months (for so were the days of their purification accomplished, six months with oil of myrrh, and six months with sweet fragrances and with preparations for beautifying women). ₁₃ The young woman then came to the king like this: whatever she desired was given her to go with her out of the women's house to the king's house. ₁₄ In the evening she went, and on the next day she returned into the second women's house, to the custody of Shaashgaz, the king's eunuch, who kept the concubines. She came in to the king no more, unless the king delighted in her, and she was called by name.

₁₅ Now when the turn of Esther, the daughter of Abihail the uncle of Mordecai, who had taken her for his daughter, came to go in to the king, she required nothing but what Hegai the king's eunuch, the keeper of the women, advised. Esther obtained favour in the sight of all those who looked at her.

₁₆ So Esther was taken to King Ahasuerus into his royal house in the tenth month, which is the month Tebeth, in the seventh year of his reign. ₁₇ The king loved Esther more than all the women, and she obtained favour and kindness in his sight more than all the virgins; so that he set the royal crown on her head, and made her queen instead of Vashti. ₁₈ Then the king made a great feast for all his princes and his servants, even Esther's feast; and he proclaimed a holiday in the provinces, and gave gifts according to the king's bounty.

₁₉ When the virgins were gathered together the second time, Mordecai was sitting in the king's gate. ₂₀ Esther had not yet made known her relatives nor her people, as Mordecai had commanded her; for Esther obeyed Mordecai, like she did when she was brought up by him. ₂₁ In those days, while Mordecai was sitting in the king's gate, two of the king's eunuchs, Bigthan and Teresh, who were doorkeepers, were angry, and sought to lay hands on the King Ahasuerus. ₂₂ This thing became known to Mordecai, who informed Esther the queen; and Esther informed the king in Mordecai's name. ₂₃ When this matter was investigated, and it was found to be so, they were both hanged on a gallows; and it was written in the book of the chronicles in the king's presence.

3

₁ After these things King Ahasuerus promoted Haman the son of Hammedatha the Agagite, and advanced him, and set his seat above all the princes who were with him. ₂ All the king's servants who were in the king's gate bowed down and paid homage to Haman, for the king had so commanded concerning him. But Mordecai didn't bow down or pay him homage. ₃ Then the king's servants who were in the king's gate said to Mordecai, "Why do you disobey the king's commandment?" ₄ Now it came to pass, when they spoke daily to him, and he didn't listen to them, that they told Haman, to see whether Mordecai's reason would stand; for he had told them that he was a Jew. ₅ When Haman saw that Mordecai didn't bow down nor pay him homage, Haman was full of wrath. ₆ But he scorned the thought of laying hands on Mordecai alone, for they had made known to him Mordecai's people. Therefore Haman sought to destroy all the Jews who were throughout the whole kingdom of Ahasuerus, even Mordecai's people.

₇ In the first month, which is the month Nisan, in the twelfth year of King Ahasuerus, they cast Pur, that is, the lot, before Haman from day to day, and from month to month, and chose the twelfth month, which is the month Adar. ₈ Haman said to King Ahasuerus, "There is a certain people scattered abroad and dispersed amongst the peoples in all the provinces of your kingdom, and their laws are different from other people's. They don't keep the king's laws. Therefore it is not for the king's profit to allow them to remain. ₉ If it pleases the king, let it be written that they be destroyed; and I will pay ten thousand talents[a] of silver into the hands of those who are in charge of the king's business, to bring it into the king's treasuries."

₁₀ The king took his ring from his hand, and gave it to Haman the son of Hammedatha the Agagite, the Jews' enemy. ₁₁ The king said to Haman, "The silver is given to you, the people also, to do with them as it seems good to you."

₁₂ Then the king's scribes were called in on the first month, on the thirteenth day of the month; and all that Haman commanded was written to the king's local governors, and to the governors who were over every province, and to the princes of every people, to every province according to its writing, and to every people in their language. It was written in the name of King Ahasuerus, and it was sealed with the king's ring. ₁₃ Letters were sent by couriers into all the king's provinces, to destroy, to kill, and to cause to perish, all Jews, both young and old, little children and women, in one day, even on the thirteenth day of the twelfth month, which is the month Adar, and to plunder their possessions. ₁₄ A copy of the letter, that the decree should be given out in every province, was published to all the peoples, that they should be ready against that day. ₁₅ The couriers went out in haste by the king's commandment, and the decree was given out in the citadel of Susa. The king and Haman sat down to drink; but the city of Susa was perplexed.

4

₁ Now when Mordecai found out all that was done, Mordecai tore his clothes and put on sackcloth with ashes, and went out into the middle of

---

^a *3:9* A talent is about 30 kilograms or 66 pounds or 965 Troy ounces

the city, and wailed loudly and bitterly. ₂ He came even before the king's gate, for no one is allowed inside the king's gate clothed with sackcloth. ₃ In every province, wherever the king's commandment and his decree came, there was great mourning amongst the Jews, and fasting, and weeping, and wailing; and many lay in sackcloth and ashes.

₄ Esther's maidens and her eunuchs came and told her this, and the queen was exceedingly grieved. She sent clothing to Mordecai, to replace his sackcloth, but he didn't receive it. ₅ Then Esther called for Hathach, one of the king's eunuchs, whom he had appointed to attend her, and commanded him to go to Mordecai, to find out what this was, and why it was. ₆ So Hathach went out to Mordecai, to the city square which was before the king's gate. ₇ Mordecai told him of all that had happened to him, and the exact sum of the money that Haman had promised to pay to the king's treasuries for the destruction of the Jews. ₈ He also gave him the copy of the writing of the decree that was given out in Susa to destroy them, to show it to Esther, and to declare it to her, and to urge her to go in to the king to make supplication to him, and to make request before him for her people.

₉ Hathach came and told Esther the words of Mordecai. ₁₀ Then Esther spoke to Hathach, and gave him a message to Mordecai: ₁₁ "All the king's servants and the people of the king's provinces know that whoever, whether man or woman, comes to the king into the inner court without being called, there is one law for him, that he be put to death, except those to whom the king might hold out the golden sceptre, that he may live. I have not been called to come in to the king these thirty days."

₁₂ They told Esther's words to Mordecai. ₁₃ Then Mordecai asked them to return this answer to Esther: "Don't think to yourself that you will escape in the king's house any more than all the Jews. ₁₄ For if you remain silent now, then relief and deliverance will come to the Jews from another place, but you and your father's house will perish. Who knows if you haven't come to the kingdom for such a time as this?"

₁₅ Then Esther asked them to answer Mordecai, ₁₆ "Go, gather together all the Jews who are present in Susa, and fast for me, and neither eat nor drink three days, night or day. I and my maidens will also fast the same way. Then I will go in to the king, which is against the law; and if I perish, I perish." ₁₇ So Mordecai went his way, and did according to all that Esther had commanded him.

5

₁ Now on the third day, Esther put on her royal clothing and stood in the inner court of the king's house, next to the king's house. The king sat on his royal throne in the royal house, next to the entrance of the house. ₂ When the king saw Esther the queen standing in the court, she obtained favour in his sight; and the king held out to Esther the golden sceptre that was in his hand. So Esther came near and touched the top of the sceptre. ₃ Then the king asked her, "What would you like, queen Esther? What is your request? It shall be given you even to the half of the kingdom."

₄ Esther said, "If it seems good to the king, let the king and Haman come today to the banquet that I have prepared for him."

₅ Then the king said, "Bring Haman quickly, so that it may be done as Esther has said." So the king and Haman came to the banquet that Esther had prepared.

₆ The king said to Esther at the banquet of wine, "What is your petition? It shall be granted you. What is your request? Even to the half of the kingdom it shall be performed."

₇ Then Esther answered and said, "My petition and my request is this. ₈ If I have found favour in the sight of the king, and if it pleases the king to grant my petition and to perform my request, let the king and Haman come to the banquet that I will prepare for them, and I will do tomorrow as the king has said."

₉ Then Haman went out that day joyful and glad of heart, but when Haman saw Mordecai in the king's gate, that he didn't stand up nor move for him, he was filled with wrath against Mordecai. ₁₀ Nevertheless Haman restrained himself, and went home. There, he sent and called for his friends and Zeresh his wife. ₁₁ Haman recounted to them the glory of his riches, the multitude of his children, all the things in which the king had promoted him, and how he had advanced him above the princes and servants of the king.

₁₂ Haman also said, "Yes, Esther the queen let no man come in with the king to the banquet that she had prepared but myself; and tomorrow I am also invited by her together with the king. ₁₃ Yet all this avails me nothing, so long as I see Mordecai the Jew sitting at the king's gate."

₁₄ Then Zeresh his wife and all his friends said to him, "Let a gallows be made fifty cubitsª high, and in the morning speak to the king about hanging Mordecai on it. Then go in merrily with the king to the banquet." This pleased Haman, so he had the gallows made.

6

₁ On that night, the king couldn't sleep. He commanded the book of records of the chronicles to be brought, and they were read to the king. ₂ It was found written that Mordecai had told of Bigthana and Teresh, two of the king's eunuchs, who were doorkeepers, who had tried to lay hands on the King Ahasuerus. ₃ The king said, "What honour and dignity has been given to Mordecai for this?"

Then the king's servants who attended him said, "Nothing has been done for him."

₄ The king said, "Who is in the court?" Now Haman had come into the outer court of the king's house, to speak to the king about hanging Mordecai on the gallows that he had prepared for him.

₅ The king's servants said to him, "Behold,ᵇ Haman stands in the court."

The king said, "Let him come in." ₆ So Haman came in. The king said to him, "What shall be done to the man whom the king delights to honour?"

Now Haman said in his heart, "Who would the king delight to honour more than myself?" ₇ Haman said to the king, "For the man whom the king delights to honour, ₈ let royal clothing be brought which the king uses to wear, and the horse that the king rides on, and on the head of which a royal crown is set. ₉ Let the clothing and the horse be delivered to the hand of one of the king's most noble princes, that they may array the man whom the king delights to honour with them, and have him ride on horseback through the city square, and proclaim before him, 'Thus it shall be done to the man whom the king delights to honour!'"

₁₀ Then the king said to Haman, "Hurry and take the clothing and the horse, as you have said, and do this for Mordecai the Jew, who sits at the king's gate. Let nothing fail of all that you have spoken."

₁₁ Then Haman took the clothing and the horse, and arrayed Mordecai, and had him ride through the city square, and proclaimed before him, "Thus it shall be done to the man whom the king delights to honour!"

₁₂ Mordecai came back to the king's gate, but Haman hurried to his house, mourning and having his head covered. ₁₃ Haman recounted to Zeresh his wife and all his friends everything that had happened to him. Then his wise men and Zeresh his wife said to him, "If Mordecai, before whom you have begun to fall, is of Jewish descent, you will not prevail against him, but you will surely fall before him." ₁₄ While they were yet talking with him, the king's eunuchs came, and hurried to bring Haman to the banquet that Esther had prepared.

7

₁ So the king and Haman came to banquet with Esther the queen. ₂ The king said again to Esther on the second day at the banquet of wine, "What is your petition, queen Esther? It shall be granted you. What is your request? Even to the half of the kingdom it shall be performed."

₃ Then Esther the queen answered, "If I have found favour in your sight, O king, and if it pleases the king, let my life be given me at my petition, and my people at my request. ₄ For we are sold, I and my people, to be destroyed, to be slain, and to perish. But if we had been sold for male and female slaves, I would have held my peace, although the adversary could not have compensated for the king's loss."

₅ Then King Ahasuerus said to Esther the queen, "Who is he, and where is he who dared presume in his heart to do so?"

₆ Esther said, "An adversary and an enemy, even this wicked Haman!"

Then Haman was afraid before the king and the queen. ₇ The king arose in his wrath from the banquet of wine and went into the palace garden. Haman stood up to make request for his life to Esther the queen, for he saw that there was evil determined against him by the king. ₈ Then the king returned out of the palace garden into the place of the banquet of wine; and Haman had fallen on the couch where Esther was. Then the king said, "Will he even assault the queen in front of me in the house?" As the word went out of the king's mouth, they covered Haman's face.

₉ Then Harbonah, one of the eunuchs who were with the king, said, "Behold, the gallows fifty cubitsᶜ high, which Haman has made for Mordecai, who spoke good for the king, is standing at Haman's house."

The king said, "Hang him on it!"

₁₀ So they hanged Haman on the gallows that he had prepared for Mordecai. Then the king's wrath was pacified.

8

₁ On that day, King Ahasuerus gave the house of Haman, the Jews' enemy, to Esther the queen. Mordecai came before the king; for Esther had told what he was to her. ₂ The king took off his ring, which he had taken from Haman, and gave it to Mordecai. Esther set Mordecai over the house of Haman.

₃ Esther spoke yet again before the king, and fell down at his feet and begged him with tears to put away the mischief of Haman the Agagite, and his plan that he had planned against the Jews. ₄ Then the king held out to Esther the golden sceptre. So Esther arose, and stood before the king. ₅ She said, "If it pleases the king, and if I have found favour in his sight, and the thing seems right to the king, and I am pleasing in his eyes, let it be written to reverse the letters devised by Haman, the son of Hammedatha the Agagite, which he wrote to destroy the Jews who are in all the king's provinces. ₆ For how can I endure to see the evil that would come to my people? How can I endure to see the destruction of my relatives?"

₇ Then King Ahasuerus said to Esther the queen and to Mordecai the Jew, "See, I have given Esther the house of Haman, and they have hanged him on the gallows because he laid his hand on the Jews. ₈ Write also to the Jews as it pleases you, in the king's name, and seal it with the king's ring; for the writing which is written in the king's name, and sealed with the king's ring, may not be reversed by any man."

₉ Then the king's scribes were called at that time, in the third month, which is the month Sivan, on the twenty-third day of the month; and it was written according to all that Mordecai commanded to the Jews, and to the

---

ª *5:14* A cubit is the length from the tip of the middle finger to the elbow on a man's arm, or about 18 inches or 46 centimetres.
ᵇ *6:5* "Behold", from "הִנֵּה", means look at, take notice, observe, see, or gaze at. It is often used as an interjection.

ᶜ *7:9* A cubit is the length from the tip of the middle finger to the elbow on a man's arm, or about 18 inches or 46 centimetres.

local governors, and the governors and princes of the provinces which are from India to Ethiopia, one hundred and twenty-seven provinces, to every province according to its writing, and to every people in their language, and to the Jews in their writing, and in their language. 10 He wrote in the name of King Ahasuerus, and sealed it with the king's ring, and sent letters by courier on horseback, riding on royal horses that were bred from swift steeds. 11 In those letters, the king granted the Jews who were in every city to gather themselves together and to defend their lives—to destroy, to kill, and to cause to perish all the power of the people and province that would assault them, their little ones and women, and to plunder their possessions, 12 on one day in all the provinces of King Ahasuerus, on the thirteenth day of the twelfth month, which is the month Adar. 13 A copy of the letter, that the decree should be given out in every province, was published to all the peoples, that the Jews should be ready for that day to avenge themselves on their enemies. 14 So the couriers who rode on royal horses went out, hastened and pressed on by the king's commandment. The decree was given out in the citadel of Susa.

15 Mordecai went out of the presence of the king in royal clothing of blue and white, and with a great crown of gold, and with a robe of fine linen and purple; and the city of Susa shouted and was glad. 16 The Jews had light, gladness, joy, and honour. 17 In every province and in every city, wherever the king's commandment and his decree came, the Jews had gladness, joy, a feast and a holiday. Many from amongst the peoples of the land became Jews, for the fear of the Jews had fallen on them.

9

1 Now in the twelfth month, which is the month Adar, on the thirteenth day of the month, when the king's commandment and his decree came near to be put in execution, on the day that the enemies of the Jews hoped to conquer them, (but it turned out that the opposite happened, that the Jews conquered those who hated them), 2 the Jews gathered themselves together in their cities throughout all the provinces of the King Ahasuerus, to lay hands on those who wanted to harm them. No one could withstand them, because the fear of them had fallen on all the people. 3 All the princes of the provinces, the local governors, the governors, and those who did the king's business helped the Jews, because the fear of Mordecai had fallen on them. 4 For Mordecai was great in the king's house, and his fame went out throughout all the provinces, for the man Mordecai grew greater and greater. 5 The Jews struck all their enemies with the stroke of the sword, and with slaughter and destruction, and did what they wanted to those who hated them. 6 In the citadel of Susa, the Jews killed and destroyed five hundred men. 7 They killed Parshandatha, Dalphon, Aspatha, 8 Poratha, Adalia, Aridatha, 9 Parmashta, Arisai, Aridai, and Vaizatha, 10 the ten sons of Haman the son of Hammedatha, the Jews' enemy, but they didn't lay their hand on the plunder.

11 On that day, the number of those who were slain in the citadel of Susa was brought before the king. 12 The king said to Esther the queen, "The Jews have slain and destroyed five hundred men in the citadel of Susa, including the ten sons of Haman; what then have they done in the rest of the king's provinces! Now what is your petition? It shall be granted you. What is your further request? It shall be done."

13 Then Esther said, "If it pleases the king, let it be granted to the Jews who are in Susa to do tomorrow also according to today's decree, and let Haman's ten sons be hanged on the gallows."

14 The king commanded this to be done. A decree was given out in Susa; and they hanged Haman's ten sons. 15 The Jews who were in Susa gathered themselves together on the fourteenth day also of the month Adar, and killed three hundred men in Susa; but they didn't lay their hand on the plunder.

16 The other Jews who were in the king's provinces gathered themselves together, defended their lives, had rest from their enemies, and killed seventy-five thousand of those who hated them; but they didn't lay their hand on the plunder. 17 This was done on the thirteenth day of the month Adar; and on the fourteenth day of that month they rested and made it a day of feasting and gladness.

18 But the Jews who were in Susa assembled together on the thirteenth and on the fourteenth days of the month; and on the fifteenth day of that month, they rested, and made it a day of feasting and gladness. 19 Therefore the Jews of the villages, who live in the unwalled towns, make the fourteenth day of the month Adar a day of gladness and feasting, a holiday, and a day of sending presents of food to one another.

20 Mordecai wrote these things, and sent letters to all the Jews who were in all the provinces of the King Ahasuerus, both near and far, 21 to enjoin them that they should keep the fourteenth and fifteenth days of the month Adar yearly, 22 as the days in which the Jews had rest from their enemies, and the month which was turned to them from sorrow to gladness, and from mourning into a holiday; that they should make them days of feasting and gladness, and of sending presents of food to one another, and gifts to the needy. 23 The Jews accepted the custom that they had begun, as Mordecai had written to them, 24 because Haman the son of Hammedatha, the Agagite, the enemy of all the Jews, had plotted against the Jews to destroy them, and had cast "Pur", that is the lot, to consume them and to destroy them; 25 but when this became known to the king, he commanded by letters that his wicked plan, which he had planned against the Jews, should return on his own head, and that he and his sons should be hanged on the gallows.

26 Therefore they called these days "Purim",[a] from the word "Pur." Therefore because of all the words of this letter, and of that which they had seen concerning this matter, and that which had come to them, 27 the Jews established and imposed on themselves, on their descendants, and on all those who joined themselves to them, so that it should not fail that they would keep these two days according to what was written and according to its appointed time every year; 28 and that these days should be remembered and kept throughout every generation, every family, every province, and every city; and that these days of Purim should not fail from amongst the Jews, nor their memory perish from their offspring.[b]

29 Then Esther the queen, the daughter of Abihail, and Mordecai the Jew wrote with all authority to confirm this second letter of Purim. 30 He sent letters to all the Jews in the hundred and twenty-seven provinces of the kingdom of Ahasuerus with words of peace and truth, 31 to confirm these days of Purim in their appointed times, as Mordecai the Jew and Esther the queen had decreed, and as they had imposed upon themselves and their descendants in the matter of the fastings and their mourning. 32 The commandment of Esther confirmed these matters of Purim; and it was written in the book.

10

1 King Ahasuerus laid a tribute on the land and on the islands of the sea. 2 Aren't all the acts of his power and of his might, and the full account of the greatness of Mordecai, to which the king advanced him, written in the book of the chronicles of the kings of Media and Persia? 3 For Mordecai the Jew was next to King Ahasuerus, and great amongst the Jews and accepted by the multitude of his brothers, seeking the good of his people and speaking peace to all his descendants.

---

a *9:26* Purim is the Hebrew plural for pur, which means lot. | b *9:28* or, seed

The Book of Job

1

1 There was a man in the land of Uz, whose name was Job. That man was blameless and upright, and one who feared God,[a] and turned away from evil. 2 There were born to him seven sons and three daughters. 3 His possessions also were seven thousand sheep, three thousand camels, five hundred yoke of oxen, five hundred female donkeys, and a very great household; so that this man was the greatest of all the children of the east. 4 His sons went and held a feast in the house of each one on his birthday; and they sent and called for their three sisters to eat and to drink with them. 5 It was so, when the days of their feasting had run their course, that Job sent and sanctified them, and rose up early in the morning, and offered burnt offerings according to the number of them all. For Job said, "It may be that my sons have sinned, and renounced God in their hearts." Job did so continually.

6 Now on the day when God's sons came to present themselves before the LORD,[b] Satan also came amongst them. 7 The LORD said to Satan, "Where have you come from?"

Then Satan answered the LORD, and said, "From going back and forth in the earth, and from walking up and down in it."

8 The LORD said to Satan, "Have you considered my servant, Job? For there is no one like him in the earth, a blameless and an upright man, one who fears God, and turns away from evil."

9 Then Satan answered the LORD, and said, "Does Job fear God for nothing? 10 Haven't you made a hedge around him, and around his house, and around all that he has, on every side? You have blessed the work of his hands, and his substance is increased in the land. 11 But stretch out your hand now, and touch all that he has, and he will renounce you to your face."

12 The LORD said to Satan, "Behold,[c] all that he has is in your power. Only on himself don't stretch out your hand."

So Satan went out from the presence of the LORD. 13 It fell on a day when his sons and his daughters were eating and drinking wine in their oldest brother's house, 14 that a messenger came to Job, and said, "The oxen were ploughing, and the donkeys feeding beside them, 15 and the Sabeans attacked, and took them away. Yes, they have killed the servants with the edge of the sword, and I alone have escaped to tell you."

16 While he was still speaking, another also came and said, "The fire of God has fallen from the sky, and has burnt up the sheep and the servants, and consumed them, and I alone have escaped to tell you."

17 While he was still speaking, another also came and said, "The Chaldeans made three bands, and swept down on the camels, and have taken them away, yes, and killed the servants with the edge of the sword; and I alone have escaped to tell you."

18 While he was still speaking, there came also another, and said, "Your sons and your daughters were eating and drinking wine in their oldest brother's house, 19 and behold, there came a great wind from the wilderness, and struck the four corners of the house, and it fell on the young men, and they are dead. I alone have escaped to tell you."

20 Then Job arose, and tore his robe, and shaved his head, and fell down on the ground, and worshipped. 21 He said, "Naked I came out of my mother's womb, and naked will I return there. The LORD gave, and the LORD has taken away. Blessed be the LORD's name." 22 In all this, Job didn't sin, nor charge God with wrongdoing.

2

1 Again, on the day when God's sons came to present themselves before the LORD, Satan came also amongst them to present himself before the LORD. 2 The LORD said to Satan, "Where have you come from?"

Satan answered the LORD, and said, "From going back and forth in the earth, and from walking up and down in it."

3 The LORD said to Satan, "Have you considered my servant Job? For there is no one like him in the earth, a blameless and an upright man, one who fears God, and turns away from evil. He still maintains his integrity, although you incited me against him, to ruin him without cause."

4 Satan answered the LORD, and said, "Skin for skin. Yes, all that a man has he will give for his life. 5 But stretch out your hand now, and touch his bone and his flesh, and he will renounce you to your face."

6 The LORD said to Satan, "Behold, he is in your hand. Only spare his life."

7 So Satan went out from the presence of the LORD, and struck Job with painful sores from the sole of his foot to his head. 8 He took for himself a potsherd to scrape himself with, and he sat amongst the ashes. 9 Then his wife said to him, "Do you still maintain your integrity? Renounce God, and die."

10 But he said to her, "You speak as one of the foolish women would speak. What? Shall we receive good at the hand of God, and shall we not receive evil?"

In all this Job didn't sin with his lips. 11 Now when Job's three friends heard of all this evil that had come on him, they each came from his own place: Eliphaz the Temanite, Bildad the Shuhite, and Zophar the Naamathite; and they made an appointment together to come to sympathise with him and to comfort him. 12 When they lifted up their eyes from a distance, and didn't recognise him, they raised their voices, and wept; and they each tore his robe, and sprinkled dust on their heads towards the sky. 13 So they sat down with him on the ground seven days and seven nights, and no one spoke a word to him, for they saw that his grief was very great.

3

1 After this Job opened his mouth, and cursed the day of his birth. 2 Job answered:

3 "Let the day perish in which I was born,
  the night which said, 'There is a boy conceived.'
4 Let that day be darkness.
  Don't let God from above seek for it,
  neither let the light shine on it.
5 Let darkness and the shadow of death claim it for their own.
  Let a cloud dwell on it.
  Let all that makes the day black terrify it.
6 As for that night, let thick darkness seize on it.
  Let it not rejoice amongst the days of the year.
  Let it not come into the number of the months.
7 Behold, let that night be barren.
  Let no joyful voice come therein.
8 Let them curse it who curse the day,
  who are ready to rouse up leviathan.
9 Let the stars of its twilight be dark.
  Let it look for light, but have none,
  neither let it see the eyelids of the morning,
10 because it didn't shut up the doors of my mother's womb,
  nor did it hide trouble from my eyes.

11 "Why didn't I die from the womb?
  Why didn't I give up the spirit when my mother bore me?
12 Why did the knees receive me?
  Or why the breast, that I should nurse?
13 For now I should have lain down and been quiet.
  I should have slept, then I would have been at rest,
14 with kings and counsellors of the earth,
  who built up waste places for themselves;
15 or with princes who had gold,
  who filled their houses with silver;
16 or as a hidden untimely birth I had not been,
  as infants who never saw light.
17 There the wicked cease from troubling.
  There the weary are at rest.
18 There the prisoners are at ease together.
  They don't hear the voice of the taskmaster.
19 The small and the great are there.
  The servant is free from his master.

20 "Why is light given to him who is in misery,
  life to the bitter in soul,
21 who long for death, but it doesn't come;
  and dig for it more than for hidden treasures,
22 who rejoice exceedingly,
  and are glad, when they can find the grave?
23 Why is light given to a man whose way is hidden,
  whom God has hedged in?
24 For my sighing comes before I eat.
  My groanings are poured out like water.
25 For the thing which I fear comes on me,
  that which I am afraid of comes to me.
26 I am not at ease, neither am I quiet, neither do I have rest;
  but trouble comes."

4

1 Then Eliphaz the Temanite answered,
2 "If someone ventures to talk with you, will you be grieved?
  But who can withhold himself from speaking?
3 Behold, you have instructed many,
  you have strengthened the weak hands.
4 Your words have supported him who was falling,
  you have made the feeble knees firm.
5 But now it has come to you, and you faint.
  It touches you, and you are troubled.
6 Isn't your piety your confidence?
  Isn't the integrity of your ways your hope?

7 "Remember, now, whoever perished, being innocent?
  Or where were the upright cut off?
8 According to what I have seen, those who plough iniquity
  and sow trouble, reap the same.
9 By the breath of God they perish.
  By the blast of his anger are they consumed.
10 The roaring of the lion,
  and the voice of the fierce lion,
  the teeth of the young lions, are broken.

---

a *1:1* The Hebrew word rendered "God" is "אֱלֹהִים" (Elohim).
b *1:6* When rendered in ALL CAPITAL LETTERS, "LORD" or "GOD" is the translation of God's Proper Name.
c *1:12* "Behold", from "הִנֵּה", means look at, take notice, observe, see, or gaze at. It is often used as an interjection.

11 The old lion perishes for lack of prey.
The cubs of the lioness are scattered abroad.

12 "Now a thing was secretly brought to me.
My ear received a whisper of it.
13 In thoughts from the visions of the night,
when deep sleep falls on men,
14 fear came on me, and trembling,
which made all my bones shake.
15 Then a spirit passed before my face.
The hair of my flesh stood up.
16 It stood still, but I couldn't discern its appearance.
A form was before my eyes.
Silence, then I heard a voice, saying,
17 'Shall mortal man be more just than God?
Shall a man be more pure than his Maker?
18 Behold, he puts no trust in his servants.
He charges his angels with error.
19 How much more those who dwell in houses of clay,
whose foundation is in the dust,
who are crushed before the moth!
20 Between morning and evening they are destroyed.
They perish forever without any regarding it.
21 Isn't their tent cord plucked up within them?
They die, and that without wisdom.'

5

1 "Call now; is there any who will answer you?
To which of the holy ones will you turn?
2 For resentment kills the foolish man,
and jealousy kills the simple.
3 I have seen the foolish taking root,
but suddenly I cursed his habitation.
4 His children are far from safety.
They are crushed in the gate.
Neither is there any to deliver them,
5 whose harvest the hungry eat up,
and take it even out of the thorns.
The snare gapes for their substance.
6 For affliction doesn't come out of the dust,
neither does trouble spring out of the ground;
7 but man is born to trouble,
as the sparks fly upward.

8 "But as for me, I would seek God.
I would commit my cause to God,
9 who does great things that can't be fathomed,
marvellous things without number;
10 who gives rain on the earth,
and sends waters on the fields;
11 so that he sets up on high those who are low,
those who mourn are exalted to safety.
12 He frustrates the plans of the crafty,
so that their hands can't perform their enterprise.
13 He takes the wise in their own craftiness;
the counsel of the cunning is carried headlong.
14 They meet with darkness in the day time,
and grope at noonday as in the night.
15 But he saves from the sword of their mouth,
even the needy from the hand of the mighty.
16 So the poor has hope,
and injustice shuts her mouth.

17 "Behold, happy is the man whom God corrects.
Therefore do not despise the chastening of the Almighty.
18 For he wounds and binds up.
He injures and his hands make whole.
19 He will deliver you in six troubles;
yes, in seven no evil will touch you.
20 In famine he will redeem you from death;
in war, from the power of the sword.
21 You will be hidden from the scourge of the tongue,
neither will you be afraid of destruction when it comes.
22 You will laugh at destruction and famine,
neither will you be afraid of the animals of the earth.
23 For you will be allied with the stones of the field.
The animals of the field will be at peace with you.
24 You will know that your tent is in peace.
You will visit your fold, and will miss nothing.
25 You will know also that your offspringª will be great,
your offspring as the grass of the earth.
26 You will come to your grave in a full age,
like a shock of grain comes in its season.
27 Behold, we have researched it. It is so.
Hear it, and know it for your good."

ª *5:25 or, seed*

6

1 Then Job answered,
2 "Oh that my anguish were weighed,
and all my calamity laid in the balances!
3 For now it would be heavier than the sand of the seas,
therefore my words have been rash.
4 For the arrows of the Almighty are within me.
My spirit drinks up their poison.
The terrors of God set themselves in array against me.
5 Does the wild donkey bray when he has grass?
Or does the ox low over his fodder?
6 Can that which has no flavour be eaten without salt?
Or is there any taste in the white of an egg?
7 My soul refuses to touch them.
They are as loathsome food to me.

8 "Oh that I might have my request,
that God would grant the thing that I long for,
9 even that it would please God to crush me;
that he would let loose his hand, and cut me off!
10 Let it still be my consolation,
yes, let me exult in pain that doesn't spare,
that I have not denied the words of the Holy One.
11 What is my strength, that I should wait?
What is my end, that I should be patient?
12 Is my strength the strength of stones?
Or is my flesh of bronze?
13 Isn't it that I have no help in me,
that wisdom is driven away from me?

14 "To him who is ready to faint, kindness should be shown from his friend;
even to him who forsakes the fear of the Almighty.
15 My brothers have dealt deceitfully as a brook,
as the channel of brooks that pass away;
16 which are black by reason of the ice,
in which the snow hides itself.
17 In the dry season, they vanish.
When it is hot, they are consumed out of their place.
18 The caravans that travel beside them turn away.
They go up into the waste, and perish.
19 The caravans of Tema looked.
The companies of Sheba waited for them.
20 They were distressed because they were confident.
They came there, and were confounded.
21 For now you are nothing.
You see a terror, and are afraid.
22 Did I ever say, 'Give to me'?
or, 'Offer a present for me from your substance'?
23 or, 'Deliver me from the adversary's hand'?
or, 'Redeem me from the hand of the oppressors'?

24 "Teach me, and I will hold my peace.
Cause me to understand my error.
25 How forcible are words of uprightness!
But your reproof, what does it reprove?
26 Do you intend to reprove words,
since the speeches of one who is desperate are as wind?
27 Yes, you would even cast lots for the fatherless,
and make merchandise of your friend.
28 Now therefore be pleased to look at me,
for surely I will not lie to your face.
29 Please return.
Let there be no injustice.
Yes, return again.
My cause is righteous.
30 Is there injustice on my tongue?
Can't my taste discern mischievous things?

7

1 "Isn't a man forced to labour on earth?
Aren't his days like the days of a hired hand?
2 As a servant who earnestly desires the shadow,
as a hireling who looks for his wages,
3 so I am made to possess months of misery,
wearisome nights are appointed to me.
4 When I lie down, I say,
'When will I arise, and the night be gone?'
I toss and turn until the dawning of the day.
5 My flesh is clothed with worms and clods of dust.
My skin closes up, and breaks out afresh.
6 My days are swifter than a weaver's shuttle,
and are spent without hope.
7 Oh remember that my life is a breath.
My eye will no more see good.
8 The eye of him who sees me will see me no more.
Your eyes will be on me, but I will not be.

9 As the cloud is consumed and vanishes away,
    so he who goes down to Sheol[a] will come up no more.
10 He will return no more to his house,
    neither will his place know him any more.

11 "Therefore I will not keep silent.
    I will speak in the anguish of my spirit.
    I will complain in the bitterness of my soul.
12 Am I a sea, or a sea monster,
    that you put a guard over me?
13 When I say, 'My bed will comfort me.
    My couch will ease my complaint,'
14 then you scare me with dreams
    and terrify me through visions,
15 so that my soul chooses strangling,
    death rather than my bones.
16 I loathe my life.
    I don't want to live forever.
    Leave me alone, for my days are but a breath.
17 What is man, that you should magnify him,
    that you should set your mind on him,
18 that you should visit him every morning,
    and test him every moment?
19 How long will you not look away from me,
    nor leave me alone until I swallow down my spittle?
20 If I have sinned, what do I do to you, you watcher of men?
    Why have you set me as a mark for you,
    so that I am a burden to myself?
21 Why do you not pardon my disobedience, and take away my iniquity?
    For now will I lie down in the dust.
    You will seek me diligently, but I will not be."

8

1 Then Bildad the Shuhite answered,
2 "How long will you speak these things?
    Shall the words of your mouth be a mighty wind?
3 Does God pervert justice?
    Or does the Almighty pervert righteousness?
4 If your children have sinned against him,
    he has delivered them into the hand of their disobedience.
5 If you want to seek God diligently,
    make your supplication to the Almighty.
6 If you were pure and upright,
    surely now he would awaken for you,
and make the habitation of your righteousness prosperous.
7 Though your beginning was small,
yet your latter end would greatly increase.

8 "Please enquire of past generations.
    Find out about the learning of their fathers.
9 (For we are but of yesterday, and know nothing,
    because our days on earth are a shadow.)
10 Shall they not teach you, tell you,
    and utter words out of their heart?

11 "Can the papyrus grow up without mire?
    Can the rushes grow without water?
12 While it is yet in its greenness, not cut down,
    it withers before any other reed.
13 So are the paths of all who forget God.
    The hope of the godless man will perish,
14 whose confidence will break apart,
    whose trust is a spider's web.
15 He will lean on his house, but it will not stand.
    He will cling to it, but it will not endure.
16 He is green before the sun.
    His shoots go out along his garden.
17 His roots are wrapped around the rock pile.
    He sees the place of stones.
18 If he is destroyed from his place,
    then it will deny him, saying, 'I have not seen you.'
19 Behold, this is the joy of his way.
    Out of the earth, others will spring.

20 "Behold, God will not cast away a blameless man,
    neither will he uphold the evildoers.
21 He will still fill your mouth with laughter,
    your lips with shouting.
22 Those who hate you will be clothed with shame.
    The tent of the wicked will be no more."

9

1 Then Job answered,
2 "Truly I know that it is so,
    but how can man be just with God?
3 If he is pleased to contend with him,
    he can't answer him one time in a thousand.
4 God is wise in heart, and mighty in strength.

Who has hardened himself against him and prospered?
5 He removes the mountains, and they don't know it,
    when he overturns them in his anger.
6 He shakes the earth out of its place.
    Its pillars tremble.
7 He commands the sun and it doesn't rise,
    and seals up the stars.
8 He alone stretches out the heavens,
    and treads on the waves of the sea.
9 He makes the Bear, Orion, and the Pleiades,
    and the rooms of the south.
10 He does great things past finding out;
    yes, marvellous things without number.
11 Behold, he goes by me, and I don't see him.
    He passes on also, but I don't perceive him.
12 Behold, he snatches away.
    Who can hinder him?
    Who will ask him, 'What are you doing?'

13 "God will not withdraw his anger.
    The helpers of Rahab stoop under him.
14 How much less will I answer him,
    and choose my words to argue with him?
15 Though I were righteous, yet I wouldn't answer him.
    I would make supplication to my judge.
16 If I had called, and he had answered me,
    yet I wouldn't believe that he listened to my voice.
17 For he breaks me with a storm,
    and multiplies my wounds without cause.
18 He will not allow me to catch my breath,
    but fills me with bitterness.
19 If it is a matter of strength, behold, he is mighty!
    If of justice, 'Who,' says he, 'will summon me?'
20 Though I am righteous, my own mouth will condemn me.
    Though I am blameless, it will prove me perverse.
21 I am blameless.
    I don't respect myself.
    I despise my life.

22 "It is all the same.
    Therefore I say he destroys the blameless and the wicked.
23 If the scourge kills suddenly,
    he will mock at the trial of the innocent.
24 The earth is given into the hand of the wicked.
    He covers the faces of its judges.
    If not he, then who is it?

25 "Now my days are swifter than a runner.
    They flee away. They see no good.
26 They have passed away as the swift ships,
    as the eagle that swoops on the prey.
27 If I say, 'I will forget my complaint,
    I will put off my sad face, and cheer up,'
28 I am afraid of all my sorrows.
    I know that you will not hold me innocent.
29 I will be condemned.
    Why then do I labour in vain?
30 If I wash myself with snow,
    and cleanse my hands with lye,
31 yet you will plunge me in the ditch.
    My own clothes will abhor me.
32 For he is not a man, as I am, that I should answer him,
    that we should come together in judgement.
33 There is no umpire between us,
    that might lay his hand on us both.
34 Let him take his rod away from me.
    Let his terror not make me afraid;
35 then I would speak, and not fear him,
    for I am not so in myself.

10

1 "My soul is weary of my life.
    I will give free course to my complaint.
    I will speak in the bitterness of my soul.
2 I will tell God, 'Do not condemn me.
    Show me why you contend with me.
3 Is it good to you that you should oppress,
    that you should despise the work of your hands,
    and smile on the counsel of the wicked?
4 Do you have eyes of flesh?
    Or do you see as man sees?
5 Are your days as the days of mortals,
    or your years as man's years,
6 that you enquire after my iniquity,
    and search after my sin?

_____

a *7:9* Sheol is the place of the dead.

7 Although you know that I am not wicked,
there is no one who can deliver out of your hand.

8 "'Your hands have framed me and fashioned me altogether,
yet you destroy me.
9 Remember, I beg you, that you have fashioned me as clay.
Will you bring me into dust again?
10 Haven't you poured me out like milk,
and curdled me like cheese?
11 You have clothed me with skin and flesh,
and knit me together with bones and sinews.
12 You have granted me life and loving kindness.
Your visitation has preserved my spirit.
13 Yet you hid these things in your heart.
I know that this is with you:
14 if I sin, then you mark me.
You will not acquit me from my iniquity.
15 If I am wicked, woe to me.
If I am righteous, I still will not lift up my head,
being filled with disgrace,
and conscious of my affliction.
16 If my head is held high, you hunt me like a lion.
Again you show yourself powerful to me.
17 You renew your witnesses against me,
and increase your indignation on me.
Changes and warfare are with me.

18 "'Why, then, have you brought me out of the womb?
I wish I had given up the spirit, and no eye had seen me.
19 I should have been as though I had not been.
I should have been carried from the womb to the grave.
20 Aren't my days few?
Stop!
Leave me alone, that I may find a little comfort,
21 before I go where I will not return from,
to the land of darkness and of the shadow of death;
22 the land dark as midnight,
of the shadow of death,
without any order,
where the light is as midnight.'"

11

1 Then Zophar, the Naamathite, answered,
2 "Shouldn't the multitude of words be answered?
Should a man full of talk be justified?
3 Should your boastings make men hold their peace?
When you mock, will no man make you ashamed?
4 For you say, 'My doctrine is pure.
I am clean in your eyes.'
5 But oh that God would speak,
and open his lips against you,
6 that he would show you the secrets of wisdom!
For true wisdom has two sides.
Know therefore that God exacts of you less than your iniquity
deserves.

7 "Can you fathom the mystery of God?
Or can you probe the limits of the Almighty?
8 They are high as heaven. What can you do?
They are deeper than Sheol.ᵃ What can you know?
9 Its measure is longer than the earth,
and broader than the sea.
10 If he passes by, or confines,
or convenes a court, then who can oppose him?
11 For he knows false men.
He sees iniquity also, even though he doesn't consider it.
12 An empty-headed man becomes wise
when a man is born as a wild donkey's colt.

13 "If you set your heart aright,
stretch out your hands towards him.
14 If iniquity is in your hand, put it far away.
Don't let unrighteousness dwell in your tents.
15 Surely then you will lift up your face without spot.
Yes, you will be steadfast, and will not fear,
16 for you will forget your misery.
You will remember it like waters that have passed away.
17 Life will be clearer than the noonday.
Though there is darkness, it will be as the morning.
18 You will be secure, because there is hope.
Yes, you will search, and will take your rest in safety.
19 Also you will lie down, and no one will make you afraid.
Yes, many will court your favour.
20 But the eyes of the wicked will fail.
They will have no way to flee.
Their hope will be the giving up of the spirit."

12

1 Then Job answered,
2 "No doubt, but you are the people,
and wisdom will die with you.
3 But I have understanding as well as you;
I am not inferior to you.
Yes, who doesn't know such things as these?
4 I am like one who is a joke to his neighbour,
I, who called on God, and he answered.
The just, the blameless man is a joke.
5 In the thought of him who is at ease there is contempt for misfortune.
It is ready for them whose foot slips.
6 The tents of robbers prosper.
Those who provoke God are secure,
who carry their god in their hands.

7 "But ask the animals now, and they will teach you;
the birds of the sky, and they will tell you.
8 Or speak to the earth, and it will teach you.
The fish of the sea will declare to you.
9 Who doesn't know that in all these,
the LORD's hand has done this,
10 in whose hand is the life of every living thing,
and the breath of all mankind?
11 Doesn't the ear try words,
even as the palate tastes its food?
12 With aged men is wisdom,
in length of days understanding.

13 "With God is wisdom and might.
He has counsel and understanding.
14 Behold, he breaks down, and it can't be built again.
He imprisons a man, and there can be no release.
15 Behold, he withholds the waters, and they dry up.
Again, he sends them out, and they overturn the earth.
16 With him is strength and wisdom.
The deceived and the deceiver are his.
17 He leads counsellors away stripped.
He makes judges fools.
18 He loosens the bond of kings.
He binds their waist with a belt.
19 He leads priests away stripped,
and overthrows the mighty.
20 He removes the speech of those who are trusted,
and takes away the understanding of the elders.
21 He pours contempt on princes,
and loosens the belt of the strong.
22 He uncovers deep things out of darkness,
and brings out to light the shadow of death.
23 He increases the nations, and he destroys them.
He enlarges the nations, and he leads them captive.
24 He takes away understanding from the chiefs of the people of the earth,
and causes them to wander in a wilderness where there is no way.
25 They grope in the dark without light.
He makes them stagger like a drunken man.

13

1 "Behold, my eye has seen all this.
My ear has heard and understood it.
2 What you know, I know also.
I am not inferior to you.

3 "Surely I would speak to the Almighty.
I desire to reason with God.
4 But you are forgers of lies.
You are all physicians of no value.
5 Oh that you would be completely silent!
Then you would be wise.
6 Hear now my reasoning.
Listen to the pleadings of my lips.
7 Will you speak unrighteously for God,
and talk deceitfully for him?
8 Will you show partiality to him?
Will you contend for God?
9 Is it good that he should search you out?
Or as one deceives a man, will you deceive him?
10 He will surely reprove you
if you secretly show partiality.
11 Won't his majesty make you afraid
and his dread fall on you?
12 Your memorable sayings are proverbs of ashes.
Your defences are defences of clay.

13 "Be silent!
Leave me alone, that I may speak,

ᵃ *11:8* Sheol is the place of the dead.

Let come on me what will.
14 Why should I take my flesh in my teeth,
and put my life in my hand?
15 Behold, he will kill me.
I have no hope.
Nevertheless, I will maintain my ways before him.
16 This also will be my salvation,
that a godless man will not come before him.
17 Listen carefully to my speech.
Let my declaration be in your ears.
18 See now, I have set my cause in order.
I know that I am righteous.
19 Who is he who will contend with me?
For then would I hold my peace and give up the spirit.

20 "Only don't do two things to me,
then I will not hide myself from your face:
21 withdraw your hand far from me,
and don't let your terror make me afraid.
22 Then call, and I will answer,
or let me speak, and you answer me.
23 How many are my iniquities and sins?
Make me know my disobedience and my sin.
24 Why do you hide your face,
and consider me your enemy?
25 Will you harass a driven leaf?
Will you pursue the dry stubble?
26 For you write bitter things against me,
and make me inherit the iniquities of my youth.
27 You also put my feet in the stocks,
and mark all my paths.
You set a bound to the soles of my feet,
28 though I am decaying like a rotten thing,
like a garment that is moth-eaten.

14

1 "Man, who is born of a woman,
is of few days, and full of trouble.
2 He grows up like a flower, and is cut down.
He also flees like a shadow, and doesn't continue.
3 Do you open your eyes on such a one,
and bring me into judgement with you?
4 Who can bring a clean thing out of an unclean?
Not one.
5 Seeing his days are determined,
the number of his months is with you,
and you have appointed his bounds that he can't pass.
6 Look away from him, that he may rest,
until he accomplishes, as a hireling, his day.

7 "For there is hope for a tree if it is cut down,
that it will sprout again,
that the tender branch of it will not cease.
8 Though its root grows old in the earth,
and its stock dies in the ground,
9 yet through the scent of water it will bud,
and sprout boughs like a plant.
10 But man dies, and is laid low.
Yes, man gives up the spirit, and where is he?
11 As the waters fail from the sea,
and the river wastes and dries up,
12 so man lies down and doesn't rise.
Until the heavens are no more, they will not awake,
nor be roused out of their sleep.

13 "Oh that you would hide me in Sheol,[a]
that you would keep me secret until your wrath is past,
that you would appoint me a set time and remember me!
14 If a man dies, will he live again?
I would wait all the days of my warfare,
until my release should come.
15 You would call, and I would answer you.
You would have a desire for the work of your hands.
16 But now you count my steps.
Don't you watch over my sin?
17 My disobedience is sealed up in a bag.
You fasten up my iniquity.

18 "But the mountain falling comes to nothing.
The rock is removed out of its place.
19 The waters wear the stones.
The torrents of it wash away the dust of the earth.
So you destroy the hope of man.
20 You forever prevail against him, and he departs.
You change his face, and send him away.

21 His sons come to honour, and he doesn't know it.
They are brought low, but he doesn't perceive it of them.
22 But his flesh on him has pain,
and his soul within him mourns."

15

1 Then Eliphaz the Temanite answered,
2 "Should a wise man answer with vain knowledge,
and fill himself with the east wind?
3 Should he reason with unprofitable talk,
or with speeches with which he can do no good?
4 Yes, you do away with fear,
and hinder devotion before God.
5 For your iniquity teaches your mouth,
and you choose the language of the crafty.
6 Your own mouth condemns you, and not I.
Yes, your own lips testify against you.

7 "Are you the first man who was born?
Or were you brought out before the hills?
8 Have you heard the secret counsel of God?
Do you limit wisdom to yourself?
9 What do you know that we don't know?
What do you understand which is not in us?
10 With us are both the grey-headed and the very aged men,
much older than your father.
11 Are the consolations of God too small for you,
even the word that is gentle towards you?
12 Why does your heart carry you away?
Why do your eyes flash,
13 that you turn your spirit against God,
and let such words go out of your mouth?
14 What is man, that he should be clean?
What is he who is born of a woman, that he should be righteous?
15 Behold, he puts no trust in his holy ones.
Yes, the heavens are not clean in his sight;
16 how much less one who is abominable and corrupt,
a man who drinks iniquity like water!

17 "I will show you, listen to me;
that which I have seen I will declare
18 (which wise men have told by their fathers,
and have not hidden it;
19 to whom alone the land was given,
and no stranger passed amongst them):
20 the wicked man writhes in pain all his days,
even the number of years that are laid up for the oppressor.
21 A sound of terrors is in his ears.
In prosperity the destroyer will come on him.
22 He doesn't believe that he will return out of darkness.
He is waited for by the sword.
23 He wanders abroad for bread, saying, 'Where is it?'
He knows that the day of darkness is ready at his hand.
24 Distress and anguish make him afraid.
They prevail against him, as a king ready to the battle.
25 Because he has stretched out his hand against God,
and behaves himself proudly against the Almighty,
26 he runs at him with a stiff neck,
with the thick shields of his bucklers,
27 because he has covered his face with his fatness,
and gathered fat on his thighs.
28 He has lived in desolate cities,
in houses which no one inhabited,
which were ready to become heaps.
29 He will not be rich, neither will his substance continue,
neither will their possessions be extended on the earth.
30 He will not depart out of darkness.
The flame will dry up his branches.
He will go away by the breath of God's mouth.
31 Let him not trust in emptiness, deceiving himself,
for emptiness will be his reward.
32 It will be accomplished before his time.
His branch will not be green.
33 He will shake off his unripe grape as the vine,
and will cast off his flower as the olive tree.
34 For the company of the godless will be barren,
and fire will consume the tents of bribery.
35 They conceive mischief and produce iniquity.
Their heart prepares deceit."

16

1 Then Job answered,
2 "I have heard many such things.
You are all miserable comforters!
3 Shall vain words have an end?
Or what provokes you that you answer?

---

a 14:13 Sheol is the place of the dead.

4 I also could speak as you do.
    If your soul were in my soul's place,
    I could join words together against you,
    and shake my head at you,
5 but I would strengthen you with my mouth.
    The solace of my lips would relieve you.

6 "Though I speak, my grief is not subsided.
    Though I forbear, what am I eased?
7 But now, God, you have surely worn me out.
    You have made all my company desolate.
8 You have shriveled me up. This is a witness against me.
    My leanness rises up against me.
    It testifies to my face.
9 He has torn me in his wrath and persecuted me.
    He has gnashed on me with his teeth.
    My adversary sharpens his eyes on me.
10 They have gaped on me with their mouth.
    They have struck me on the cheek reproachfully.
    They gather themselves together against me.
11 God delivers me to the ungodly,
    and casts me into the hands of the wicked.
12 I was at ease, and he broke me apart.
    Yes, he has taken me by the neck, and dashed me to pieces.
    He has also set me up for his target.
13 His archers surround me.
    He splits my kidneys apart, and does not spare.
    He pours out my bile on the ground.
14 He breaks me with breach on breach.
    He runs at me like a giant.
15 I have sewed sackcloth on my skin,
    and have thrust my horn in the dust.
16 My face is red with weeping.
    Deep darkness is on my eyelids,
17 although there is no violence in my hands,
    and my prayer is pure.

18 "Earth, don't cover my blood.
    Let my cry have no place to rest.
19 Even now, behold, my witness is in heaven.
    He who vouches for me is on high.
20 My friends scoff at me.
    My eyes pour out tears to God,
21 that he would maintain the right of a man with God,
    of a son of man with his neighbour!
22 For when a few years have come,
    I will go the way of no return.

17

1 "My spirit is consumed.
    My days are extinct
    and the grave is ready for me.
2 Surely there are mockers with me.
    My eye dwells on their provocation.

3 "Now give a pledge. Be collateral for me with yourself.
    Who is there who will strike hands with me?
4 For you have hidden their heart from understanding,
    therefore you will not exalt them.
5 He who denounces his friends for plunder,
    even the eyes of his children will fail.

6 "But he has made me a byword of the people.
    They spit in my face.
7 My eye also is dim by reason of sorrow.
    All my members are as a shadow.
8 Upright men will be astonished at this.
    The innocent will stir himself up against the godless.
9 Yet the righteous will hold to his way.
    He who has clean hands will grow stronger and stronger.
10 But as for you all, come back.
    I will not find a wise man amongst you.
11 My days are past.
    My plans are broken off,
    as are the thoughts of my heart.
12 They change the night into day,
    saying 'The light is near' in the presence of darkness.
13 If I look for Sheol[a] as my house,
    if I have spread my couch in the darkness,
14 if I have said to corruption, 'You are my father,'
    and to the worm, 'My mother,' and 'My sister,'
15 where then is my hope?
    As for my hope, who will see it?
16 Shall it go down with me to the gates of Sheol,[b]
    or descend together into the dust?"

18

1 Then Bildad the Shuhite answered,
2 "How long will you hunt for words?
    Consider, and afterwards we will speak.
3 Why are we counted as animals,
    which have become unclean in your sight?
4 You who tear yourself in your anger,
    will the earth be forsaken for you?
    Or will the rock be removed out of its place?

5 "Yes, the light of the wicked will be put out.
    The spark of his fire won't shine.
6 The light will be dark in his tent.
    His lamp above him will be put out.
7 The steps of his strength will be shortened.
    His own counsel will cast him down.
8 For he is cast into a net by his own feet,
    and he wanders into its mesh.
9 A snare will take him by the heel.
    A trap will catch him.
10 A noose is hidden for him in the ground,
    a trap for him on the path.
11 Terrors will make him afraid on every side,
    and will chase him at his heels.
12 His strength will be famished.
    Calamity will be ready at his side.
13 The members of his body will be devoured.
    The firstborn of death will devour his members.
14 He will be rooted out of the security of his tent.
    He will be brought to the king of terrors.
15 There will dwell in his tent that which is none of his.
    Sulphur will be scattered on his habitation.
16 His roots will be dried up beneath.
    His branch will be cut off above.
17 His memory will perish from the earth.
    He will have no name in the street.
18 He will be driven from light into darkness,
    and chased out of the world.
19 He will have neither son nor grandson amongst his people,
    nor any remaining where he lived.
20 Those who come after will be astonished at his day,
    as those who went before were frightened.
21 Surely such are the dwellings of the unrighteous.
    This is the place of him who doesn't know God."

19

1 Then Job answered,
2 "How long will you torment me,
    and crush me with words?
3 You have reproached me ten times.
    You aren't ashamed that you attack me.
4 If it is true that I have erred,
    my error remains with myself.
5 If indeed you will magnify yourselves against me,
    and plead against me my reproach,
6 know now that God has subverted me,
    and has surrounded me with his net.

7 "Behold, I cry out of wrong, but I am not heard.
    I cry for help, but there is no justice.
8 He has walled up my way so that I can't pass,
    and has set darkness in my paths.
9 He has stripped me of my glory,
    and taken the crown from my head.
10 He has broken me down on every side, and I am gone.
    He has plucked my hope up like a tree.
11 He has also kindled his wrath against me.
    He counts me amongst his adversaries.
12 His troops come on together,
    build a siege ramp against me,
    and encamp around my tent.

13 "He has put my brothers far from me.
    My acquaintances are wholly estranged from me.
14 My relatives have gone away.
    My familiar friends have forgotten me.
15 Those who dwell in my house and my maids consider me a stranger.
    I am an alien in their sight.
16 I call to my servant, and he gives me no answer.
    I beg him with my mouth.
17 My breath is offensive to my wife.
    I am loathsome to the children of my own mother.
18 Even young children despise me.
    If I arise, they speak against me.
19 All my familiar friends abhor me.
    They whom I loved have turned against me.
20 My bones stick to my skin and to my flesh.

---

a *17:13* Sheol is the place of the dead.

b *17:16* Sheol is the place of the dead.

I have escaped by the skin of my teeth.

21 "Have pity on me. Have pity on me, you my friends,
    for the hand of God has touched me.
22 Why do you persecute me as God,
    and are not satisfied with my flesh?

23 "Oh that my words were now written!
    Oh that they were inscribed in a book!
24 That with an iron pen and lead
    they were engraved in the rock forever!
25 But as for me, I know that my Redeemer lives.
    In the end, he will stand upon the earth.
26 After my skin is destroyed,
    then I will see God in my flesh,
27 whom I, even I, will see on my side.
    My eyes will see, and not as a stranger.

"My heart is consumed within me.
28 If you say, 'How we will persecute him!'
    because the root of the matter is found in me,
29 be afraid of the sword,
    for wrath brings the punishments of the sword,
    that you may know there is a judgement."

20

1 Then Zophar the Naamathite answered,
2 "Therefore my thoughts answer me,
    even by reason of my haste that is in me.
3 I have heard the reproof which puts me to shame.
    The spirit of my understanding answers me.
4 Don't you know this from old time,
    since man was placed on earth,
5 that the triumphing of the wicked is short,
    the joy of the godless but for a moment?
6 Though his height mount up to the heavens,
    and his head reach to the clouds,
7 yet he will perish forever like his own dung.
    Those who have seen him will say, 'Where is he?'
8 He will fly away as a dream, and will not be found.
    Yes, he will be chased away like a vision of the night.
9 The eye which saw him will see him no more,
    neither will his place see him any more.
10 His children will seek the favour of the poor.
    His hands will give back his wealth.
11 His bones are full of his youth,
    but youth will lie down with him in the dust.

12 "Though wickedness is sweet in his mouth,
    though he hide it under his tongue,
13 though he spare it, and will not let it go,
    but keep it still within his mouth,
14 yet his food in his bowels is turned.
    It is cobra venom within him.
15 He has swallowed down riches, and he will vomit them up again.
    God will cast them out of his belly.
16 He will suck cobra venom.
    The viper's tongue will kill him.
17 He will not look at the rivers,
    the flowing streams of honey and butter.
18 He will restore that for which he laboured, and will not swallow it down.
    He will not rejoice according to the substance that he has gotten.
19 For he has oppressed and forsaken the poor.
    He has violently taken away a house, and he will not build it up.

20 "Because he knew no quietness within him,
    he will not save anything of that in which he delights.
21 There was nothing left that he didn't devour,
    therefore his prosperity will not endure.
22 In the fullness of his sufficiency, distress will overtake him.
    The hand of everyone who is in misery will come on him.
23 When he is about to fill his belly, God will cast the fierceness of his wrath
        on him.
    It will rain on him while he is eating.
24 He will flee from the iron weapon.
    The bronze arrow will strike him through.
25 He draws it out, and it comes out of his body.
    Yes, the glittering point comes out of his liver.
    Terrors are on him.
26 All darkness is laid up for his treasures.
    An unfanned fire will devour him.
    It will consume that which is left in his tent.
27 The heavens will reveal his iniquity.
    The earth will rise up against him.
28 The increase of his house will depart.
    They will rush away in the day of his wrath.
29 This is the portion of a wicked man from God,

_____
a *21:13* Sheol is the place of the dead.

the heritage appointed to him by God."

21

1 Then Job answered,
2 "Listen diligently to my speech.
    Let this be your consolation.
3 Allow me, and I also will speak.
    After I have spoken, mock on.
4 As for me, is my complaint to man?
    Why shouldn't I be impatient?
5 Look at me, and be astonished.
    Lay your hand on your mouth.
6 When I remember, I am troubled.
    Horror takes hold of my flesh.

7 "Why do the wicked live,
    become old, yes, and grow mighty in power?
8 Their child is established with them in their sight,
    their offspring before their eyes.
9 Their houses are safe from fear,
    neither is the rod of God upon them.
10 Their bulls breed without fail.
    Their cows calve, and don't miscarry.
11 They send out their little ones like a flock.
    Their children dance.
12 They sing to the tambourine and harp,
    and rejoice at the sound of the pipe.
13 They spend their days in prosperity.
    In an instant they go down to Sheol.ᵃ
14 They tell God, 'Depart from us,
    for we don't want to know about your ways.
15 What is the Almighty, that we should serve him?
    What profit should we have, if we pray to him?'
16 Behold, their prosperity is not in their hand.
    The counsel of the wicked is far from me.

17 "How often is it that the lamp of the wicked is put out,
    that their calamity comes on them,
    that God distributes sorrows in his anger?
18 How often is it that they are as stubble before the wind,
    as chaff that the storm carries away?
19 You say, 'God lays up his iniquity for his children.'
    Let him recompense it to himself, that he may know it.
20 Let his own eyes see his destruction.
    Let him drink of the wrath of the Almighty.
21 For what does he care for his house after him,
    when the number of his months is cut off?

22 "Shall any teach God knowledge,
    since he judges those who are high?
23 One dies in his full strength,
    being wholly at ease and quiet.
24 His pails are full of milk.
    The marrow of his bones is moistened.
25 Another dies in bitterness of soul,
    and never tastes of good.
26 They lie down alike in the dust.
    The worm covers them.

27 "Behold, I know your thoughts,
    the plans with which you would wrong me.
28 For you say, 'Where is the house of the prince?
    Where is the tent in which the wicked lived?'
29 Haven't you asked wayfaring men?
    Don't you know their evidences,
30 that the evil man is reserved to the day of calamity,
    that they are led out to the day of wrath?
31 Who will declare his way to his face?
    Who will repay him what he has done?
32 Yet he will be borne to the grave.
    Men will keep watch over the tomb.
33 The clods of the valley will be sweet to him.
    All men will draw after him,
    as there were innumerable before him.
34 So how can you comfort me with nonsense,
    because in your answers there remains only falsehood?"

22

1 Then Eliphaz the Temanite answered,
2 "Can a man be profitable to God?
    Surely he who is wise is profitable to himself.
3 Is it any pleasure to the Almighty that you are righteous?
    Or does it benefit him that you make your ways perfect?
4 Is it for your piety that he reproves you,
    that he enters with you into judgement?
5 Isn't your wickedness great?
    Neither is there any end to your iniquities.
6 For you have taken pledges from your brother for nothing,

and stripped the naked of their clothing.
7 You haven't given water to the weary to drink,
and you have withheld bread from the hungry.
8 But as for the mighty man, he had the earth.
The honourable man, he lived in it.
9 You have sent widows away empty,
and the arms of the fatherless have been broken.
10 Therefore snares are around you.
Sudden fear troubles you,
11 or darkness, so that you can not see,
and floods of waters cover you.

12 "Isn't God in the heights of heaven?
See the height of the stars, how high they are!
13 You say, 'What does God know?
Can he judge through the thick darkness?
14 Thick clouds are a covering to him, so that he doesn't see.
He walks on the vault of the sky.'
15 Will you keep the old way,
which wicked men have trodden,
16 who were snatched away before their time,
whose foundation was poured out as a stream,
17 who said to God, 'Depart from us!'
and, 'What can the Almighty do for us?'
18 Yet he filled their houses with good things,
but the counsel of the wicked is far from me.
19 The righteous see it, and are glad.
The innocent ridicule them,
20 saying, 'Surely those who rose up against us are cut off.
The fire has consumed their remnant.'

21 "Acquaint yourself with him now, and be at peace.
By it, good will come to you.
22 Please receive instruction from his mouth,
and lay up his words in your heart.
23 If you return to the Almighty, you will be built up,
if you put away unrighteousness far from your tents.
24 Lay your treasure in the dust,
the gold of Ophir amongst the stones of the brooks.
25 The Almighty will be your treasure,
and precious silver to you.
26 For then you will delight yourself in the Almighty,
and will lift up your face to God.
27 You will make your prayer to him, and he will hear you.
You will pay your vows.
28 You will also decree a thing, and it will be established to you.
Light will shine on your ways.
29 When they cast down, you will say, 'be lifted up.'
He will save the humble person.
30 He will even deliver him who is not innocent.
Yes, he will be delivered through the cleanness of your hands."

23

1 Then Job answered,
2 "Even today my complaint is rebellious.
His hand is heavy in spite of my groaning.
3 Oh that I knew where I might find him!
That I might come even to his seat!
4 I would set my cause in order before him,
and fill my mouth with arguments.
5 I would know the words which he would answer me,
and understand what he would tell me.
6 Would he contend with me in the greatness of his power?
No, but he would listen to me.
7 There the upright might reason with him,
so I should be delivered forever from my judge.

8 "If I go east, he is not there.
If I go west, I can't find him.
9 He works to the north, but I can't see him.
He turns south, but I can't catch a glimpse of him.

10 But he knows the way that I take.
When he has tried me, I will come out like gold.
11 My foot has held fast to his steps.
I have kept his way, and not turned away.
12 I haven't gone back from the commandment of his lips.
I have treasured up the words of his mouth more than my necessary food.
13 But he stands alone, and who can oppose him?
What his soul desires, even that he does.
14 For he performs that which is appointed for me.
Many such things are with him.
15 Therefore I am terrified at his presence.
When I consider, I am afraid of him.
16 For God has made my heart faint.
The Almighty has terrified me.

17 Because I was not cut off before the darkness,
neither did he cover the thick darkness from my face.

24

1 "Why aren't times laid up by the Almighty?
Why don't those who know him see his days?
2 There are people who remove the landmarks.
They violently take away flocks, and feed them.
3 They drive away the donkey of the fatherless,
and they take the widow's ox for a pledge.
4 They turn the needy out of the way.
The poor of the earth all hide themselves.
5 Behold, as wild donkeys in the desert,
they go out to their work, seeking diligently for food.
The wilderness yields them bread for their children.
6 They cut their food in the field.
They glean the vineyard of the wicked.
7 They lie all night naked without clothing,
and have no covering in the cold.
8 They are wet with the showers of the mountains,
and embrace the rock for lack of a shelter.
9 There are those who pluck the fatherless from the breast,
and take a pledge of the poor,
10 so that they go around naked without clothing.
Being hungry, they carry the sheaves.
11 They make oil within the walls of these men.
They tread wine presses, and suffer thirst.
12 From out of the populous city, men groan.
The soul of the wounded cries out,
yet God doesn't regard the folly.

13 "These are of those who rebel against the light.
They don't know its ways,
nor stay in its paths.
14 The murderer rises with the light.
He kills the poor and needy.
In the night he is like a thief.
15 The eye also of the adulterer waits for the twilight,
saying, 'No eye will see me.'
He disguises his face.
16 In the dark they dig through houses.
They shut themselves up in the daytime.
They don't know the light.
17 For the morning is to all of them like thick darkness,
for they know the terrors of the thick darkness.

18 "They are foam on the surface of the waters.
Their portion is cursed in the earth.
They don't turn into the way of the vineyards.
19 Drought and heat consume the snow waters,
so does Sheol[a] those who have sinned.
20 The womb will forget him.
The worm will feed sweetly on him.
He will be no more remembered.
Unrighteousness will be broken as a tree.
21 He devours the barren who don't bear.
He shows no kindness to the widow.
22 Yet God preserves the mighty by his power.
He rises up who has no assurance of life.
23 God gives them security, and they rest in it.
His eyes are on their ways.
24 They are exalted; yet a little while, and they are gone.
Yes, they are brought low, they are taken out of the way as all others,
and are cut off as the tops of the ears of grain.
25 If it isn't so now, who will prove me a liar,
and make my speech worth nothing?"

25

1 Then Bildad the Shuhite answered,
2 "Dominion and fear are with him.
He makes peace in his high places.
3 Can his armies be counted?
On whom does his light not arise?
4 How then can man be just with God?
Or how can he who is born of a woman be clean?
5 Behold, even the moon has no brightness,
and the stars are not pure in his sight;
6 How much less man, who is a worm,
and the son of man, who is a worm!"

26

1 Then Job answered,
2 "How have you helped him who is without power!
How have you saved the arm that has no strength!
3 How have you counselled him who has no wisdom,

---

a *24:19* Sheol is the place of the dead.

and plentifully declared sound knowledge!
4 To whom have you uttered words?
    Whose spirit came out of you?

5 "The departed spirits tremble,
    those beneath the waters and all that live in them.
6 Sheol[a] is naked before God,
    and Abaddon[b] has no covering.
7 He stretches out the north over empty space,
    and hangs the earth on nothing.
8 He binds up the waters in his thick clouds,
    and the cloud is not burst under them.
9 He encloses the face of his throne,
    and spreads his cloud on it.
10 He has described a boundary on the surface of the waters,
    and to the confines of light and darkness.
11 The pillars of heaven tremble
    and are astonished at his rebuke.
12 He stirs up the sea with his power,
    and by his understanding he strikes through Rahab.
13 By his Spirit the heavens are garnished.
    His hand has pierced the swift serpent.
14 Behold, these are but the outskirts of his ways.
    How small a whisper do we hear of him!
    But the thunder of his power who can understand?"

27

1 Job again took up his parable, and said,
2 "As God lives, who has taken away my right,
    the Almighty, who has made my soul bitter
3 (for the length of my life is still in me,
    and the spirit of God is in my nostrils);
4 surely my lips will not speak unrighteousness,
    neither will my tongue utter deceit.
5 Far be it from me that I should justify you.
    Until I die I will not put away my integrity from me.
6 I hold fast to my righteousness, and will not let it go.
    My heart will not reproach me so long as I live.

7 "Let my enemy be as the wicked.
    Let him who rises up against me be as the unrighteous.

8 For what is the hope of the godless, when he is cut off,
    when God takes away his life?
9 Will God hear his cry when trouble comes on him?
10 Will he delight himself in the Almighty,
    and call on God at all times?
11 I will teach you about the hand of God.
    I will not conceal that which is with the Almighty.
12 Behold, all of you have seen it yourselves;
    why then have you become altogether vain?

13 "This is the portion of a wicked man with God,
    the heritage of oppressors, which they receive from the Almighty.
14 If his children are multiplied, it is for the sword.
    His offspring will not be satisfied with bread.
15 Those who remain of him will be buried in death.
    His widows will make no lamentation.
16 Though he heap up silver as the dust,
    and prepare clothing as the clay;
17 he may prepare it, but the just will put it on,
    and the innocent will divide the silver.
18 He builds his house as the moth,
    as a booth which the watchman makes.
19 He lies down rich, but he will not do so again.
    He opens his eyes, and he is not.
20 Terrors overtake him like waters.
    A storm steals him away in the night.
21 The east wind carries him away, and he departs.
    It sweeps him out of his place.
22 For it hurls at him, and does not spare,
    as he flees away from his hand.
23 Men will clap their hands at him,
    and will hiss him out of his place.

28

1 "Surely there is a mine for silver,
    and a place for gold which they refine.
2 Iron is taken out of the earth,
    and copper is smelted out of the ore.
3 Man sets an end to darkness,
    and searches out, to the furthest bound,
    the stones of obscurity and of thick darkness.
4 He breaks open a shaft away from where people live.
    They are forgotten by the foot.

They hang far from men, they swing back and forth.
5 As for the earth, out of it comes bread.
    Underneath it is turned up as it were by fire.
6 Sapphires come from its rocks.
    It has dust of gold.
7 That path no bird of prey knows,
    neither has the falcon's eye seen it.
8 The proud animals have not trodden it,
    nor has the fierce lion passed by there.
9 He puts his hand on the flinty rock,
    and he overturns the mountains by the roots.
10 He cuts out channels amongst the rocks.
    His eye sees every precious thing.
11 He binds the streams that they don't trickle.
    The thing that is hidden he brings out to light.

12 "But where will wisdom be found?
    Where is the place of understanding?
13 Man doesn't know its price,
    and it isn't found in the land of the living.
14 The deep says, 'It isn't in me.'
    The sea says, 'It isn't with me.'
15 It can't be gotten for gold,
    neither will silver be weighed for its price.
16 It can't be valued with the gold of Ophir,
    with the precious onyx, or the sapphire.[c]
17 Gold and glass can't equal it,
    neither will it be exchanged for jewels of fine gold.
18 No mention will be made of coral or of crystal.
    Yes, the price of wisdom is above rubies.
19 The topaz of Ethiopia will not equal it.
    It won't be valued with pure gold.
20 Where then does wisdom come from?
    Where is the place of understanding?
21 Seeing it is hidden from the eyes of all living,
    and kept close from the birds of the sky.
22 Destruction and Death say,
    'We have heard a rumour of it with our ears.'

23 "God understands its way,
    and he knows its place.
24 For he looks to the ends of the earth,
    and sees under the whole sky.
25 He establishes the force of the wind.
    Yes, he measures out the waters by measure.
26 When he made a decree for the rain,
    and a way for the lightning of the thunder,
27 then he saw it, and declared it.
    He established it, yes, and searched it out.
28 To man he said,
    'Behold, the fear of the Lord,[d] that is wisdom.
    To depart from evil is understanding.'"

29

1 Job again took up his parable, and said,
2 "Oh that I were as in the months of old,
    as in the days when God watched over me;
3 when his lamp shone on my head,
    and by his light I walked through darkness,
4 as I was in my prime,
    when the friendship of God was in my tent,
5 when the Almighty was yet with me,
    and my children were around me,
6 when my steps were washed with butter,
    and the rock poured out streams of oil for me,
7 when I went out to the city gate,
    when I prepared my seat in the street.
8 The young men saw me and hid themselves.
    The aged rose up and stood.
9 The princes refrained from talking,
    and laid their hand on their mouth.
10 The voice of the nobles was hushed,
    and their tongue stuck to the roof of their mouth.
11 For when the ear heard me, then it blessed me,
    and when the eye saw me, it commended me,
12 because I delivered the poor who cried,
    and the fatherless also, who had no one to help him,
13 the blessing of him who was ready to perish came on me,
    and I caused the widow's heart to sing for joy.
14 I put on righteousness, and it clothed me.
    My justice was as a robe and a diadem.
15 I was eyes to the blind,
    and feet to the lame.
16 I was a father to the needy.
    I researched the cause of him whom I didn't know.

---

a 26:6 Sheol is the place of the dead.
b 26:6 Abaddon means Destroyer.

c 28:16 or, lapis lazuli
d 28:28 The word translated "Lord" is "Adonai."

17 I broke the jaws of the unrighteous
  and plucked the prey out of his teeth.
18 Then I said, 'I will die in my own house,
  I will count my days as the sand.
19 My root is spread out to the waters.
  The dew lies all night on my branch.
20 My glory is fresh in me.
  My bow is renewed in my hand.'

21 "Men listened to me, waited,
  and kept silence for my counsel.
22 After my words they didn't speak again.
  My speech fell on them.
23 They waited for me as for the rain.
  Their mouths drank as with the spring rain.
24 I smiled on them when they had no confidence.
  They didn't reject the light of my face.
25 I chose out their way, and sat as chief.
  I lived as a king in the army,
  as one who comforts the mourners.

30

1 "But now those who are younger than I have me in derision,
  whose fathers I considered unworthy to put with my sheep dogs.
2 Of what use is the strength of their hands to me,
  men in whom ripe age has perished?
3 They are gaunt from lack and famine.
  They gnaw the dry ground, in the gloom of waste and desolation.
4 They pluck salt herbs by the bushes.
  The roots of the broom tree are their food.
5 They are driven out from amongst men.
  They cry after them as after a thief,
6 so that they live in frightful valleys,
  and in holes of the earth and of the rocks.
7 They bray amongst the bushes.
  They are gathered together under the nettles.
8 They are children of fools, yes, children of wicked men.
  They were flogged out of the land.

9 "Now I have become their song.
  Yes, I am a byword to them.
10 They abhor me, they stand aloof from me,
  and don't hesitate to spit in my face.
11 For he has untied his cord, and afflicted me;
  and they have thrown off restraint before me.
12 On my right hand rise the rabble.
  They thrust aside my feet.
  They cast their ways of destruction up against me.
13 They mar my path.
  They promote my destruction
  without anyone's help.
14 As through a wide breach they come.
  They roll themselves in amid the ruin.
15 Terrors have turned on me.
  They chase my honour as the wind.
  My welfare has passed away as a cloud.

16 "Now my soul is poured out within me.
  Days of affliction have taken hold of me.
17 In the night season my bones are pierced in me,
  and the pains that gnaw me take no rest.
18 My garment is disfigured by great force.
  It binds me about as the collar of my tunic.
19 He has cast me into the mire.
  I have become like dust and ashes.
20 I cry to you, and you do not answer me.
  I stand up, and you gaze at me.
21 You have turned to be cruel to me.
  With the might of your hand you persecute me.
22 You lift me up to the wind, and drive me with it.
  You dissolve me in the storm.
23 For I know that you will bring me to death,
  to the house appointed for all living.

24 "However doesn't one stretch out a hand in his fall?
  Or in his calamity therefore cry for help?
25 Didn't I weep for him who was in trouble?
  Wasn't my soul grieved for the needy?
26 When I looked for good, then evil came.
  When I waited for light, darkness came.
27 My heart is troubled, and doesn't rest.
  Days of affliction have come on me.
28 I go mourning without the sun.
  I stand up in the assembly, and cry for help.
29 I am a brother to jackals,
  and a companion to ostriches.
30 My skin grows black and peels from me.
  My bones are burnt with heat.

31 Therefore my harp has turned to mourning,
  and my pipe into the voice of those who weep.

31

1 "I made a covenant with my eyes;
  how then should I look lustfully at a young woman?
2 For what is the portion from God above,
  and the heritage from the Almighty on high?
3 Is it not calamity to the unrighteous,
  and disaster to the workers of iniquity?
4 Doesn't he see my ways,
  and count all my steps?

5 "If I have walked with falsehood,
  and my foot has hurried to deceit
6 (let me be weighed in an even balance,
  that God may know my integrity);
7 if my step has turned out of the way,
  if my heart walked after my eyes,
  if any defilement has stuck to my hands,
8 then let me sow, and let another eat.
  Yes, let the produce of my field be rooted out.

9 "If my heart has been enticed to a woman,
  and I have laid wait at my neighbour's door,
10 then let my wife grind for another,
  and let others sleep with her.
11 For that would be a heinous crime.
  Yes, it would be an iniquity to be punished by the judges,
12 for it is a fire that consumes to destruction,
  and would root out all my increase.
13 "If I have despised the cause of my male servant
  or of my female servant,
  when they contended with me,
14 what then will I do when God rises up?
  When he visits, what will I answer him?
15 Didn't he who made me in the womb make him?
  Didn't one fashion us in the womb?
16 "If I have withheld the poor from their desire,
  or have caused the eyes of the widow to fail,
17 or have eaten my morsel alone,
  and the fatherless has not eaten of it
18 (no, from my youth he grew up with me as with a father,
  I have guided her from my mother's womb);
19 if I have seen any perish for want of clothing,
  or that the needy had no covering;
20 if his heart hasn't blessed me,
  if he hasn't been warmed with my sheep's fleece;
21 if I have lifted up my hand against the fatherless,
  because I saw my help in the gate;
22 then let my shoulder fall from the shoulder blade,
  and my arm be broken from the bone.
23 For calamity from God is a terror to me.
  Because of his majesty, I can do nothing.
24 "If I have made gold my hope,
  and have said to the fine gold, 'You are my confidence;'
25 If I have rejoiced because my wealth was great,
  and because my hand had gotten much;
26 if I have seen the sun when it shined,
  or the moon moving in splendour,
27 and my heart has been secretly enticed,
  and my hand threw a kiss from my mouth;
28 this also would be an iniquity to be punished by the judges,
  for I would have denied the God who is above.
29 "If I have rejoiced at the destruction of him who hated me,
  or lifted up myself when evil found him
30 (I have certainly not allowed my mouth to sin
  by asking his life with a curse);
31 if the men of my tent have not said,
  'Who can find one who has not been filled with his meat?'
32 (the foreigner has not camped in the street,
  but I have opened my doors to the traveller);
33 if like Adam I have covered my transgressions,
  by hiding my iniquity in my heart,
34 because I feared the great multitude,
  and the contempt of families terrified me,
  so that I kept silence, and didn't go out of the door—
35 oh that I had one to hear me!
  Behold, here is my signature! Let the Almighty answer me!
  Let the accuser write my indictment!
36 Surely I would carry it on my shoulder,
  and I would bind it to me as a crown.
37 I would declare to him the number of my steps.
  I would go near to him like a prince.
38 If my land cries out against me,
  and its furrows weep together;
39 if I have eaten its fruits without money,
  or have caused its owners to lose their life,

40 let briers grow instead of wheat,
and stinkweed instead of barley."

The words of Job are ended.

32

1 So these three men ceased to answer Job, because he was righteous in his own eyes. 2 Then the wrath of Elihu the son of Barachel, the Buzite, of the family of Ram, was kindled against Job. His wrath was kindled because he justified himself rather than God. 3 Also his wrath was kindled against his three friends, because they had found no answer, and yet had condemned Job. 4 Now Elihu had waited to speak to Job, because they were older than he. 5 When Elihu saw that there was no answer in the mouth of these three men, his wrath was kindled.

6 Elihu the son of Barachel the Buzite answered,
"I am young, and you are very old.
    Therefore I held back, and didn't dare show you my opinion.
7 I said, 'Days should speak,
    and multitude of years should teach wisdom.'
8 But there is a spirit in man,
    and the Spirit[a] of the Almighty gives them understanding.
9 It is not the great who are wise,
    nor the aged who understand justice.
10 Therefore I said, 'Listen to me;
    I also will show my opinion.'

11 "Behold, I waited for your words,
    and I listened for your reasoning,
    while you searched out what to say.
12 Yes, I gave you my full attention,
    but there was no one who convinced Job,
    or who answered his words, amongst you.
13 Beware lest you say, 'We have found wisdom.
    God may refute him, not man;'
14 for he has not directed his words against me;
    neither will I answer him with your speeches.

15 "They are amazed. They answer no more.
    They don't have a word to say.
16 Shall I wait, because they don't speak,
    because they stand still, and answer no more?
17 I also will answer my part,
    and I also will show my opinion.
18 For I am full of words.
    The spirit within me constrains me.
19 Behold, my breast is as wine which has no vent;
    like new wineskins it is ready to burst.
20 I will speak, that I may be refreshed.
    I will open my lips and answer.
21 Please don't let me respect any man's person,
    neither will I give flattering titles to any man.
22 For I don't know how to give flattering titles,
    or else my Maker would soon take me away.

33

1 "However, Job, please hear my speech,
    and listen to all my words.
2 See now, I have opened my mouth.
    My tongue has spoken in my mouth.
3 My words will utter the uprightness of my heart.
    That which my lips know they will speak sincerely.
4 The Spirit of God has made me,
    and the breath of the Almighty gives me life.
5 If you can, answer me.
    Set your words in order before me, and stand up.
6 Behold, I am towards God even as you are.
    I am also formed out of the clay.
7 Behold, my terror will not make you afraid,
    neither will my pressure be heavy on you.

8 "Surely you have spoken in my hearing,
    I have heard the voice of your words, saying,
9 'I am clean, without disobedience.
    I am innocent, neither is there iniquity in me.
10 Behold, he finds occasions against me.
    He counts me for his enemy.
11 He puts my feet in the stocks.
    He marks all my paths.'

12 "Behold, I will answer you. In this you are not just,
    for God is greater than man.
13 Why do you strive against him,
    because he doesn't give account of any of his matters?
14 For God speaks once,
    yes twice, though man pays no attention.

a *32:8* or, breath

15 In a dream, in a vision of the night,
    when deep sleep falls on men,
    in slumbering on the bed,
16 then he opens the ears of men,
    and seals their instruction,
17 that he may withdraw man from his purpose,
    and hide pride from man.
18 He keeps back his soul from the pit,
    and his life from perishing by the sword.

19 "He is chastened also with pain on his bed,
    with continual strife in his bones,
20 so that his life abhors bread,
    and his soul dainty food.
21 His flesh is so consumed away that it can't be seen.
    His bones that were not seen stick out.
22 Yes, his soul draws near to the pit,
    and his life to the destroyers.

23 "If there is beside him an angel,
    an interpreter, one amongst a thousand,
    to show to man what is right for him,
24 then God is gracious to him, and says,
    'Deliver him from going down to the pit,
    I have found a ransom.'
25 His flesh will be fresher than a child's.
    He returns to the days of his youth.
26 He prays to God, and he is favourable to him,
    so that he sees his face with joy.
    He restores to man his righteousness.
27 He sings before men, and says,
    'I have sinned, and perverted that which was right,
    and it didn't profit me.
28 He has redeemed my soul from going into the pit.
    My life will see the light.'

29 "Behold, God does all these things,
    twice, yes three times, with a man,
30 to bring back his soul from the pit,
    that he may be enlightened with the light of the living.
31 Mark well, Job, and listen to me.
    Hold your peace, and I will speak.
32 If you have anything to say, answer me.
    Speak, for I desire to justify you.
33 If not, listen to me.
    Hold your peace, and I will teach you wisdom."

34

1 Moreover Elihu answered,
2 "Hear my words, you wise men.
    Give ear to me, you who have knowledge.
3 For the ear tries words,
    as the palate tastes food.
4 Let us choose for us that which is right.
    Let us know amongst ourselves what is good.
5 For Job has said, 'I am righteous,
    God has taken away my right.
6 Notwithstanding my right I am considered a liar.
    My wound is incurable, though I am without disobedience.'
7 What man is like Job,
    who drinks scorn like water,
8 who goes in company with the workers of iniquity,
    and walks with wicked men?
9 For he has said, 'It profits a man nothing
    that he should delight himself with God.'

10 "Therefore listen to me, you men of understanding:
    far be it from God, that he should do wickedness,
    from the Almighty, that he should commit iniquity.
11 For the work of a man he will render to him,
    and cause every man to find according to his ways.
12 Yes surely, God will not do wickedly,
    neither will the Almighty pervert justice.
13 Who put him in charge of the earth?
    Or who has appointed him over the whole world?
14 If he set his heart on himself,
    if he gathered to himself his spirit and his breath,
15 all flesh would perish together,
    and man would turn again to dust.

16 "If now you have understanding, hear this.
    Listen to the voice of my words.
17 Should even one who hates justice govern?
    Will you condemn him who is righteous and mighty,
18 who says to a king, 'Vile!'
    or to nobles, 'Wicked!'?

19 He doesn't respect the persons of princes,
    nor respect the rich more than the poor,
    for they all are the work of his hands.
20 In a moment they die, even at midnight.
    The people are shaken and pass away.
    The mighty are taken away without a hand.

21 "For his eyes are on the ways of a man.
    He sees all his goings.
22 There is no darkness, nor thick gloom,
    where the workers of iniquity may hide themselves.
23 For he doesn't need to consider a man further,
    that he should go before God in judgement.
24 He breaks mighty men in pieces in ways past finding out,
    and sets others in their place.
25 Therefore he takes knowledge of their works.
    He overturns them in the night, so that they are destroyed.
26 He strikes them as wicked men
    in the open sight of others;
27 because they turned away from following him,
    and wouldn't pay attention to any of his ways,
28 so that they caused the cry of the poor to come to him.
    He heard the cry of the afflicted.
29 When he gives quietness, who then can condemn?
    When he hides his face, who then can see him?
    He is over a nation or a man alike,
30 that the godless man may not reign,
    that there be no one to ensnare the people.

31 "For has any said to God,
    'I am guilty, but I will not offend any more.
32 Teach me that which I don't see.
    If I have done iniquity, I will do it no more'?
33 Shall his recompense be as you desire, that you refuse it?
    For you must choose, and not I.
    Therefore speak what you know.
34 Men of understanding will tell me,
    yes, every wise man who hears me:
35 'Job speaks without knowledge.
    His words are without wisdom.'
36 I wish that Job were tried to the end,
    because of his answering like wicked men.
37 For he adds rebellion to his sin.
    He claps his hands amongst us,
    and multiplies his words against God."

35

1 Moreover Elihu answered,
2 "Do you think this to be your right,
    or do you say, 'My righteousness is more than God's,'
3 that you ask, 'What advantage will it be to you?
    What profit will I have, more than if I had sinned?'
4 I will answer you,
    and your companions with you.
5 Look to the skies, and see.
    See the skies, which are higher than you.
6 If you have sinned, what effect do you have against him?
    If your transgressions are multiplied, what do you do to him?
7 If you are righteous, what do you give him?
    Or what does he receive from your hand?
8 Your wickedness may hurt a man as you are,
    and your righteousness may profit a son of man.

9 "By reason of the multitude of oppressions they cry out.
    They cry for help by reason of the arm of the mighty.
10 But no one says, 'Where is God my Maker,
    who gives songs in the night,
11 who teaches us more than the animals of the earth,
    and makes us wiser than the birds of the sky?'
12 There they cry, but no one answers,
    because of the pride of evil men.
13 Surely God will not hear an empty cry,
    neither will the Almighty regard it.
14 How much less when you say you don't see him.
    The cause is before him, and you wait for him!
15 But now, because he has not visited in his anger,
    neither does he greatly regard arrogance,
16 therefore Job opens his mouth with empty talk,
    and he multiplies words without knowledge."

36

1 Elihu also continued, and said,
2 "Bear with me a little, and I will show you;
    for I still have something to say on God's behalf.
3 I will get my knowledge from afar,
    and will ascribe righteousness to my Maker.
4 For truly my words are not false.
    One who is perfect in knowledge is with you.

5 "Behold, God is mighty, and doesn't despise anyone.
    He is mighty in strength of understanding.
6 He doesn't preserve the life of the wicked,
    but gives justice to the afflicted.
7 He doesn't withdraw his eyes from the righteous,
    but with kings on the throne,
    he sets them forever, and they are exalted.
8 If they are bound in fetters,
    and are taken in the cords of afflictions,
9 then he shows them their work,
    and their transgressions, that they have behaved themselves proudly.
10 He also opens their ears to instruction,
    and commands that they return from iniquity.
11 If they listen and serve him,
    they will spend their days in prosperity,
    and their years in pleasures.
12 But if they don't listen, they will perish by the sword;
    they will die without knowledge.

13 "But those who are godless in heart lay up anger.
    They don't cry for help when he binds them.
14 They die in youth.
    Their life perishes amongst the unclean.
15 He delivers the afflicted by their affliction,
    and opens their ear in oppression.
16 Yes, he would have allured you out of distress,
    into a wide place, where there is no restriction.
    That which is set on your table would be full of fatness.

17 "But you are full of the judgement of the wicked.
    Judgement and justice take hold of you.
18 Don't let riches entice you to wrath,
    neither let the great size of a bribe turn you aside.
19 Would your wealth sustain you in distress,
    or all the might of your strength?
20 Don't desire the night,
    when people are cut off in their place.
21 Take heed, don't regard iniquity;
    for you have chosen this rather than affliction.
22 Behold, God is exalted in his power.
    Who is a teacher like him?
23 Who has prescribed his way for him?
    Or who can say, 'You have committed unrighteousness'?

24 "Remember that you magnify his work,
    about which men have sung.
25 All men have looked on it.
    Man sees it afar off.
26 Behold, God is great, and we don't know him.
    The number of his years is unsearchable.
27 For he draws up the drops of water,
    which distill in rain from his vapour,
28 which the skies pour down
    and which drop on man abundantly.
29 Indeed, can anyone understand the spreading of the clouds
    and the thunderings of his pavilion?
30 Behold, he spreads his light around him.
    He covers the bottom of the sea.
31 For by these he judges the people.
    He gives food in abundance.
32 He covers his hands with the lightning,
    and commands it to strike the mark.
33 Its noise tells about him,
    and the livestock also, concerning the storm that comes up.

37

1 "Yes, at this my heart trembles,
    and is moved out of its place.
2 Hear, oh, hear the noise of his voice,
    the sound that goes out of his mouth.
3 He sends it out under the whole sky,
    and his lightning to the ends of the earth.
4 After it a voice roars.
    He thunders with the voice of his majesty.
    He doesn't hold back anything when his voice is heard.
5 God thunders marvellously with his voice.
    He does great things, which we can't comprehend.
6 For he says to the snow, 'Fall on the earth,'
    likewise to the shower of rain,
    and to the showers of his mighty rain.
7 He seals up the hand of every man,
    that all men whom he has made may know it.
8 Then the animals take cover,
    and remain in their dens.
9 Out of its room comes the storm,
    and cold out of the north.
10 By the breath of God, ice is given,
    and the width of the waters is frozen.

11 Yes, he loads the thick cloud with moisture.
  He spreads abroad the cloud of his lightning.
12 It is turned around by his guidance,
  that they may do whatever he commands them
  on the surface of the habitable world,
13 whether it is for correction, or for his land,
  or for loving kindness, that he causes it to come.

14 "Listen to this, Job.
  Stand still, and consider the wondrous works of God.
15 Do you know how God controls them,
  and causes the lightning of his cloud to shine?
16 Do you know the workings of the clouds,
  the wondrous works of him who is perfect in knowledge?
17 You whose clothing is warm
  when the earth is still by reason of the south wind?
18 Can you, with him, spread out the sky,
  which is strong as a cast metal mirror?
19 Teach us what we will tell him,
  for we can't make our case by reason of darkness.
20 Will it be told him that I would speak?
  Or should a man wish that he were swallowed up?

21 Now men don't see the light which is bright in the skies,
  but the wind passes, and clears them.
22 Out of the north comes golden splendour.
  With God is awesome majesty.
23 We can't reach the Almighty.
  He is exalted in power.
  In justice and great righteousness, he will not oppress.
24 Therefore men revere him.
  He doesn't regard any who are wise of heart."

38

1 Then the LORD answered Job out of the whirlwind,
2 "Who is this who darkens counsel
  by words without knowledge?
3 Brace yourself like a man,
  for I will question you, then you answer me!

4 "Where were you when I laid the foundations of the earth?
  Declare, if you have understanding.
5 Who determined its measures, if you know?
  Or who stretched the line on it?
6 What were its foundations fastened on?
  Or who laid its cornerstone,
7 when the morning stars sang together,
  and all the sons of God shouted for joy?

8 "Or who shut up the sea with doors,
  when it broke out of the womb,
9 when I made clouds its garment,
  and wrapped it in thick darkness,
10 marked out for it my bound,
  set bars and doors,
11 and said, 'You may come here, but no further.
  Your proud waves shall be stopped here'?

12 "Have you commanded the morning in your days,
  and caused the dawn to know its place,
13 that it might take hold of the ends of the earth,
  and shake the wicked out of it?
14 It is changed as clay under the seal,
  and presented as a garment.
15 From the wicked, their light is withheld.
  The high arm is broken.

16 "Have you entered into the springs of the sea?
  Or have you walked in the recesses of the deep?
17 Have the gates of death been revealed to you?
  Or have you seen the gates of the shadow of death?
18 Have you comprehended the earth in its width?
  Declare, if you know it all.

19 "What is the way to the dwelling of light?
  As for darkness, where is its place,
20 that you should take it to its bound,
  that you should discern the paths to its house?
21 Surely you know, for you were born then,
  and the number of your days is great!
22 Have you entered the storehouses of the snow,
  or have you seen the storehouses of the hail,
23 which I have reserved against the time of trouble,
  against the day of battle and war?
24 By what way is the lightning distributed,
  or the east wind scattered on the earth?

25 Who has cut a channel for the flood water,
  or the path for the thunderstorm,

26 to cause it to rain on a land where there is no man,
  on the wilderness, in which there is no man,
27 to satisfy the waste and desolate ground,
  to cause the tender grass to grow?
28 Does the rain have a father?
  Or who fathers the drops of dew?
29 Whose womb did the ice come out of?
  Who has given birth to the grey frost of the sky?
30 The waters become hard like stone,
  when the surface of the deep is frozen.

31 "Can you bind the cluster of the Pleiades,
  or loosen the cords of Orion?
32 Can you lead the constellations out in their season?
  Or can you guide the Bear with her cubs?
33 Do you know the laws of the heavens?
  Can you establish its dominion over the earth?

34 "Can you lift up your voice to the clouds,
  that abundance of waters may cover you?
35 Can you send out lightnings, that they may go?
  Do they report to you, 'Here we are'?
36 Who has put wisdom in the inward parts?
  Or who has given understanding to the mind?
37 Who can count the clouds by wisdom?
  Or who can pour out the containers of the sky,
38 when the dust runs into a mass,
  and the clods of earth stick together?

39 "Can you hunt the prey for the lioness,
  or satisfy the appetite of the young lions,
40 when they crouch in their dens,
  and lie in wait in the thicket?
41 Who provides for the raven his prey,
  when his young ones cry to God,
  and wander for lack of food?

39

1 "Do you know the time when the mountain goats give birth?
  Do you watch when the doe bears fawns?
2 Can you count the months that they fulfil?
  Or do you know the time when they give birth?
3 They bow themselves. They bear their young.
  They end their labour pains.
4 Their young ones become strong.
  They grow up in the open field.
  They go out, and don't return again.

5 "Who has set the wild donkey free?
  Or who has loosened the bonds of the swift donkey,
6 whose home I have made the wilderness,
  and the salt land his dwelling place?
7 He scorns the tumult of the city,
  neither does he hear the shouting of the driver.
8 The range of the mountains is his pasture.
  He searches after every green thing.

9 "Will the wild ox be content to serve you?
  Or will he stay by your feeding trough?
10 Can you hold the wild ox in the furrow with his harness?
  Or will he till the valleys after you?
11 Will you trust him, because his strength is great?
  Or will you leave to him your labour?
12 Will you confide in him, that he will bring home your seed,
  and gather the grain of your threshing floor?

13 "The wings of the ostrich wave proudly,
  but are they the feathers and plumage of love?
14 For she leaves her eggs on the earth,
  warms them in the dust,
15 and forgets that the foot may crush them,
  or that the wild animal may trample them.
16 She deals harshly with her young ones, as if they were not hers.
  Though her labour is in vain, she is without fear,
17 because God has deprived her of wisdom,
  neither has he imparted to her understanding.
18 When she lifts up herself on high,
  she scorns the horse and his rider.

19 "Have you given the horse might?
  Have you clothed his neck with a quivering mane?
20 Have you made him to leap as a locust?
  The glory of his snorting is awesome.
21 He paws in the valley, and rejoices in his strength.
  He goes out to meet the armed men.
22 He mocks at fear, and is not dismayed,
  neither does he turn back from the sword.
23 The quiver rattles against him,
  the flashing spear and the javelin.

24 He eats up the ground with fierceness and rage,
    neither does he stand still at the sound of the trumpet.
25 As often as the trumpet sounds he snorts, 'Aha!'
    He smells the battle afar off,
    the thunder of the captains, and the shouting.

26 "Is it by your wisdom that the hawk soars,
    and stretches her wings towards the south?
27 Is it at your command that the eagle mounts up,
    and makes his nest on high?
28 On the cliff he dwells and makes his home,
    on the point of the cliff and the stronghold.
29 From there he spies out the prey.
    His eyes see it afar off.
30 His young ones also suck up blood.
    Where the slain are, there he is."

40

1 Moreover the LORD answered Job,
2 "Shall he who argues contend with the Almighty?
    He who argues with God, let him answer it."

3 Then Job answered the LORD,
4 "Behold, I am of small account. What will I answer you?
    I lay my hand on my mouth.
5 I have spoken once, and I will not answer;
    Yes, twice, but I will proceed no further."

6 Then the LORD answered Job out of the whirlwind:
7 "Now brace yourself like a man.
    I will question you, and you will answer me.
8 Will you even annul my judgement?
    Will you condemn me, that you may be justified?
9 Or do you have an arm like God?
    Can you thunder with a voice like him?

10 "Now deck yourself with excellency and dignity.
    Array yourself with honour and majesty.
11 Pour out the fury of your anger.
    Look at everyone who is proud, and bring him low.
12 Look at everyone who is proud, and humble him.
    Crush the wicked in their place.
13 Hide them in the dust together.
    Bind their faces in the hidden place.
14 Then I will also admit to you
    that your own right hand can save you.

15 "See now behemoth, which I made as well as you.
    He eats grass as an ox.
16 Look now, his strength is in his thighs.
    His force is in the muscles of his belly.
17 He moves his tail like a cedar.
    The sinews of his thighs are knit together.
18 His bones are like tubes of bronze.
    His limbs are like bars of iron.

19 He is the chief of the ways of God.
    He who made him gives him his sword.
20 Surely the mountains produce food for him,
    where all the animals of the field play.
21 He lies under the lotus trees,
    in the covert of the reed, and the marsh.
22 The lotuses cover him with their shade.
    The willows of the brook surround him.
23 Behold, if a river overflows, he doesn't tremble.
    He is confident, though the Jordan swells even to his mouth.
24 Shall any take him when he is on the watch,
    or pierce through his nose with a snare?

41

1 "Can you draw out Leviathanᵃ with a fish hook,
    or press down his tongue with a cord?
2 Can you put a rope into his nose,
    or pierce his jaw through with a hook?
3 Will he make many petitions to you,
    or will he speak soft words to you?
4 Will he make a covenant with you,
    that you should take him for a servant forever?
5 Will you play with him as with a bird?
    Or will you bind him for your girls?
6 Will traders barter for him?
    Will they part him amongst the merchants?
7 Can you fill his skin with barbed irons,
    or his head with fish spears?
8 Lay your hand on him.

ᵃ *41:1 Leviathan is a name for a crocodile or similar creature.*

Remember the battle, and do so no more.
9 Behold, the hope of him is in vain.
    Won't one be cast down even at the sight of him?

10 None is so fierce that he dare stir him up.
    Who then is he who can stand before me?
11 Who has first given to me, that I should repay him?
    Everything under the heavens is mine.

12 "I will not keep silence concerning his limbs,
    nor his mighty strength, nor his goodly frame.
13 Who can strip off his outer garment?
    Who will come within his jaws?
14 Who can open the doors of his face?
    Around his teeth is terror.
15 Strong scales are his pride,
    shut up together with a close seal.
16 One is so near to another,
    that no air can come between them.
17 They are joined to one another.
    They stick together, so that they can't be pulled apart.
18 His sneezing flashes out light.
    His eyes are like the eyelids of the morning.
19 Out of his mouth go burning torches.
    Sparks of fire leap out.
20 Out of his nostrils a smoke goes,
    as of a boiling pot over a fire of reeds.
21 His breath kindles coals.
    A flame goes out of his mouth.
22 There is strength in his neck.
    Terror dances before him.
23 The flakes of his flesh are joined together.
    They are firm on him.
    They can't be moved.
24 His heart is as firm as a stone,
    yes, firm as the lower millstone.
25 When he raises himself up, the mighty are afraid.
    They retreat before his thrashing.
26 If one attacks him with the sword, it can't prevail;
    nor the spear, the dart, nor the pointed shaft.
27 He counts iron as straw,
    and bronze as rotten wood.
28 The arrow can't make him flee.
    Sling stones are like chaff to him.
29 Clubs are counted as stubble.
    He laughs at the rushing of the javelin.
30 His undersides are like sharp potsherds,
    leaving a trail in the mud like a threshing sledge.
31 He makes the deep to boil like a pot.
    He makes the sea like a pot of ointment.
32 He makes a path shine after him.
    One would think the deep had white hair.
33 On earth there is not his equal,
    that is made without fear.
34 He sees everything that is high.
    He is king over all the sons of pride."

42

1 Then Job answered the LORD:
2 "I know that you can do all things,
    and that no purpose of yours can be restrained.
3 You asked, 'Who is this who hides counsel without knowledge?'
    therefore I have uttered that which I didn't understand,
    things too wonderful for me, which I didn't know.
4 You said, 'Listen, now, and I will speak;
    I will question you, and you will answer me.'
5 I had heard of you by the hearing of the ear,
    but now my eye sees you.
6 Therefore I abhor myself,
    and repent in dust and ashes."

7 It was so, that after the LORD had spoken these words to Job, the LORD said to Eliphaz the Temanite, "My wrath is kindled against you, and against your two friends; for you have not spoken of me the thing that is right, as my servant Job has. 8 Now therefore, take to yourselves seven bulls and seven rams, and go to my servant Job, and offer up for yourselves a burnt offering; and my servant Job shall pray for you, for I will accept him, that I not deal with you according to your folly. For you have not spoken of me the thing that is right, as my servant Job has."

9 So Eliphaz the Temanite and Bildad the Shuhite and Zophar the Naamathite went and did what the LORD commanded them, and the LORD accepted Job.

10 The LORD restored Job's prosperity when he prayed for his friends. The LORD gave Job twice as much as he had before. 11 Then all his brothers, all his sisters, and all those who had been of his acquaintance

before, came to him and ate bread with him in his house. They comforted him, and consoled him concerning all the evil that the LORD had brought on him. Everyone also gave him a piece of money,[a] and everyone a ring of gold.

12 So the LORD blessed the latter end of Job more than his beginning. He had fourteen thousand sheep, six thousand camels, one thousand yoke of oxen, and a thousand female donkeys. 13 He had also seven sons and three daughters. 14 He called the name of the first, Jemimah; and the name of the second, Keziah; and the name of the third, Keren Happuch. 15 In all the land were no women found so beautiful as the daughters of Job. Their father gave them an inheritance amongst their brothers. 16 After this Job lived one hundred and forty years, and saw his sons, and his sons' sons, to four generations. 17 So Job died, being old and full of days.

---

[a] 42:11 literally, kesitah, a unit of money, probably silver

The Psalms

1

Book 1

1 Blessed is the man who doesn't walk in the counsel of the wicked,
  nor stand on the path of sinners,
  nor sit in the seat of scoffers;
2 but his delight is in the LORD's[a] law.
  On his law he meditates day and night.
3 He will be like a tree planted by the streams of water,
  that produces its fruit in its season,
  whose leaf also does not wither.
  Whatever he does shall prosper.
4 The wicked are not so,
  but are like the chaff which the wind drives away.
5 Therefore the wicked shall not stand in the judgement,
  nor sinners in the congregation of the righteous.
6 For the LORD knows the way of the righteous,
  but the way of the wicked shall perish.

2

1 Why do the nations rage,
  and the peoples plot a vain thing?
2 The kings of the earth take a stand,
  and the rulers take counsel together,
  against the LORD, and against his Anointed,[b] saying,
3 "Let's break their bonds apart,
  and cast their cords from us."
4 He who sits in the heavens will laugh.
  The Lord[c] will have them in derision.
5 Then he will speak to them in his anger,
  and terrify them in his wrath:
6 "Yet I have set my King on my holy hill of Zion."
7 I will tell of the decree:
The LORD said to me, "You are my son.
  Today I have become your father.
8 Ask of me, and I will give the nations for your inheritance,
  the uttermost parts of the earth for your possession.
9 You shall break them with a rod of iron.
  You shall dash them in pieces like a potter's vessel."
10 Now therefore be wise, you kings.
  Be instructed, you judges of the earth.
11 Serve the LORD with fear,
  and rejoice with trembling.
12 Give sincere homage to the Son,[d] lest he be angry, and you perish on the way,
  for his wrath will soon be kindled.
  Blessed are all those who take refuge in him.

3

A Psalm by David, when he fled from Absalom his son.

1 LORD, how my adversaries have increased!
  Many are those who rise up against me.
2 Many there are who say of my soul,
  "There is no help for him in God."[e] Selah.
3 But you, LORD, are a shield around me,
  my glory, and the one who lifts up my head.
4 I cry to the LORD with my voice,
  and he answers me out of his holy hill. Selah.
5 I laid myself down and slept.
  I awakened, for the LORD sustains me.
6 I will not be afraid of tens of thousands of people
  who have set themselves against me on every side.
7 Arise, LORD!
  Save me, my God!
For you have struck all of my enemies on the cheek bone.
  You have broken the teeth of the wicked.
8 Salvation belongs to the LORD.
  May your blessing be on your people. Selah.

4

For the Chief Musician; on stringed instruments. A Psalm by David.

1 Answer me when I call, God of my righteousness.
  Give me relief from my distress.
  Have mercy on me, and hear my prayer.
2 You sons of men, how long shall my glory be turned into dishonour?
  Will you love vanity and seek after falsehood? Selah.
3 But know that the LORD has set apart for himself him who is godly;
  The LORD will hear when I call to him.
4 Stand in awe, and don't sin.
  Search your own heart on your bed, and be still. Selah.
5 Offer the sacrifices of righteousness.
  Put your trust in the LORD.

6 Many say, "Who will show us any good?"
  LORD, let the light of your face shine on us.
7 You have put gladness in my heart,
  more than when their grain and their new wine are increased.
8 In peace I will both lay myself down and sleep,
  for you alone, LORD, make me live in safety.

5

For the Chief Musician, with the flutes. A Psalm by David.

1 Give ear to my words, LORD.
  Consider my meditation.
2 Listen to the voice of my cry, my King and my God,
  for I pray to you.
3 LORD, in the morning you will hear my voice.
  In the morning I will lay my requests before you, and will watch expectantly.
4 For you are not a God who has pleasure in wickedness.
  Evil can't live with you.
5 The arrogant will not stand in your sight.
  You hate all workers of iniquity.
6 You will destroy those who speak lies.
  The LORD abhors the bloodthirsty and deceitful man.
7 But as for me, in the abundance of your loving kindness I will come into your house.
  I will bow towards your holy temple in reverence of you.
8 Lead me, LORD, in your righteousness because of my enemies.
  Make your way straight before my face.
9 For there is no faithfulness in their mouth.
  Their heart is destruction.
  Their throat is an open tomb.
  They flatter with their tongue.
10 Hold them guilty, God.
  Let them fall by their own counsels.
Thrust them out in the multitude of their transgressions,
  for they have rebelled against you.
11 But let all those who take refuge in you rejoice.
  Let them always shout for joy, because you defend them.
Let them also who love your name be joyful in you.
12 For you will bless the righteous.
LORD, you will surround him with favour as with a shield.

6

For the Chief Musician; on stringed instruments, upon the eight-stringed lyre. A Psalm by David.

1 LORD, don't rebuke me in your anger,
  neither discipline me in your wrath.
2 Have mercy on me, LORD, for I am faint.
  LORD, heal me, for my bones are troubled.
3 My soul is also in great anguish.
  But you, LORD—how long?
4 Return, LORD. Deliver my soul,
  and save me for your loving kindness' sake.
5 For in death there is no memory of you.
  In Sheol,[f] who shall give you thanks?
6 I am weary with my groaning.
  Every night I flood my bed.
  I drench my couch with my tears.
7 My eye wastes away because of grief.
  It grows old because of all my adversaries.
8 Depart from me, all you workers of iniquity,
  for the LORD has heard the voice of my weeping.
9 The LORD has heard my supplication.
  The LORD accepts my prayer.
10 May all my enemies be ashamed and dismayed.
  They shall turn back, they shall be disgraced suddenly.

7

A meditation by David, which he sang to the LORD, concerning the words of Cush, the Benjamite.

1 LORD, my God, I take refuge in you.
  Save me from all those who pursue me, and deliver me,
2 lest they tear apart my soul like a lion,
  ripping it in pieces, while there is no one to deliver.
3 LORD, my God, if I have done this,
  if there is iniquity in my hands,
4 if I have rewarded evil to him who was at peace with me
  (yes, I have delivered him who without cause was my adversary),
5 let the enemy pursue my soul, and overtake it;
yes, let him tread my life down to the earth,
  and lay my glory in the dust. Selah.
6 Arise, LORD, in your anger.
  Lift up yourself against the rage of my adversaries.
Awake for me. You have commanded judgement.
7 Let the congregation of the peoples surround you.
  Rule over them on high.

---

a 1:2 When rendered in ALL CAPITAL LETTERS, "LORD" or "GOD" is the translation of God's Proper Name.
b 2:2 The word "Anointed" is the same as the word for "Messiah" or "Christ"
c 2:4 The word translated "Lord" is "Adonai."
d 2:12 or, Kiss the son
e 3:2 The Hebrew word rendered "God" is "אֱלֹהִים" (Elohim).
f 6:5 Sheol is the place of the dead.

8 The LORD administers judgement to the peoples.
   Judge me, LORD, according to my righteousness,
      and to my integrity that is in me.
9 Oh let the wickedness of the wicked come to an end,
      but establish the righteous;
      their minds and hearts are searched by the righteous God.
10 My shield is with God,
      who saves the upright in heart.
11 God is a righteous judge,
      yes, a God who has indignation every day.
12 If a man doesn't repent, he will sharpen his sword;
      he has bent and strung his bow.
13 He has also prepared for himself the instruments of death.
      He makes ready his flaming arrows.
14 Behold,[a] he travails with iniquity.
      Yes, he has conceived mischief,
      and brought out falsehood.
15 He has dug a hole,
      and has fallen into the pit which he made.
16 The trouble he causes shall return to his own head.
      His violence shall come down on the crown of his own head.
17 I will give thanks to the LORD according to his righteousness,
      and will sing praise to the name of the LORD Most High.

8

For the Chief Musician; on an instrument of Gath. A Psalm by David.
1 LORD, our Lord, how majestic is your name in all the earth!
      You have set your glory above the heavens!
2 From the lips of babes and infants you have established strength,
      because of your adversaries, that you might silence the enemy and
         the avenger.
3 When I consider your heavens, the work of your fingers,
      the moon and the stars, which you have ordained,
4 what is man, that you think of him?
      What is the son of man, that you care for him?
5 For you have made him a little lower than the angels,[b]
      and crowned him with glory and honour.
6 You make him ruler over the works of your hands.
      You have put all things under his feet:
7 All sheep and cattle,
      yes, and the animals of the field,
      8 the birds of the sky, the fish of the sea,
      and whatever passes through the paths of the seas.
9 LORD, our Lord,
      how majestic is your name in all the earth!

9

For the Chief Musician. Set to "The Death of the Son." A Psalm by David.
1 I will give thanks to the LORD with my whole heart.
      I will tell of all your marvellous works.
2 I will be glad and rejoice in you.
      I will sing praise to your name, O Most High.
3 When my enemies turn back,
      they stumble and perish in your presence.
4 For you have maintained my just cause.
      You sit on the throne judging righteously.
5 You have rebuked the nations.
      You have destroyed the wicked.
      You have blotted out their name forever and ever.
6 The enemy is overtaken by endless ruin.
      The very memory of the cities which you have overthrown has
         perished.
7 But the LORD reigns forever.
      He has prepared his throne for judgement.
8 He will judge the world in righteousness.
      He will administer judgement to the peoples in uprightness.
9 The LORD will also be a high tower for the oppressed;
      a high tower in times of trouble.
10 Those who know your name will put their trust in you,
      for you, LORD, have not forsaken those who seek you.
11 Sing praises to the LORD, who dwells in Zion,
      and declare amongst the people what he has done.
12 For he who avenges blood remembers them.
      He doesn't forget the cry of the afflicted.
13 Have mercy on me, LORD.
      See my affliction by those who hate me,
and lift me up from the gates of death,
      14 that I may show all of your praise.
      I will rejoice in your salvation in the gates of the daughter of Zion.
15 The nations have sunk down in the pit that they made.
      In the net which they hid, their own foot is taken.
16 The LORD has made himself known.
      He has executed judgement.
      The wicked is snared by the work of his own hands. Meditation. Selah.
17 The wicked shall be turned back to Sheol,[c]

even all the nations that forget God.
18 For the needy shall not always be forgotten,
      nor the hope of the poor perish forever.
19 Arise, LORD! Don't let man prevail.
      Let the nations be judged in your sight.
20 Put them in fear, LORD.
      Let the nations know that they are only men. Selah.

10

1 Why do you stand far off, LORD?
      Why do you hide yourself in times of trouble?
2 In arrogance, the wicked hunt down the weak.
      They are caught in the schemes that they devise.
3 For the wicked boasts of his heart's cravings.
      He blesses the greedy and condemns the LORD.
4 The wicked, in the pride of his face,
      has no room in his thoughts for God.
5 His ways are prosperous at all times.
      He is arrogant, and your laws are far from his sight.
As for all his adversaries, he sneers at them.
      6 He says in his heart, "I shall not be shaken.
      For generations I shall have no trouble."
7 His mouth is full of cursing, deceit, and oppression.
      Under his tongue is mischief and iniquity.
8 He lies in wait near the villages.
      From ambushes, he murders the innocent.
His eyes are secretly set against the helpless.
9 He lurks in secret as a lion in his ambush.
      He lies in wait to catch the helpless.
      He catches the helpless when he draws him in his net.
10 The helpless are crushed.
      They collapse.
      They fall under his strength.
11 He says in his heart, "God has forgotten.
      He hides his face.
      He will never see it."

12 Arise, LORD!
      God, lift up your hand!
      Don't forget the helpless.
13 Why does the wicked person condemn God,
      and say in his heart, "God won't call me into account"?
14 But you do see trouble and grief.
      You consider it to take it into your hand.
      You help the victim and the fatherless.
15 Break the arm of the wicked.
      As for the evil man, seek out his wickedness until you find none.
16 The LORD is King forever and ever!
      The nations will perish out of his land.
17 LORD, you have heard the desire of the humble.
      You will prepare their heart.
      You will cause your ear to hear,
      18 to judge the fatherless and the oppressed,
      that man who is of the earth may terrify no more.

11

For the Chief Musician. By David.
1 In the LORD, I take refuge.
      How can you say to my soul, "Flee as a bird to your mountain"?
2 For, behold, the wicked bend their bows.
      They set their arrows on the strings,
      that they may shoot in darkness at the upright in heart.
3 If the foundations are destroyed,
      what can the righteous do?
4 The LORD is in his holy temple.
      The LORD is on his throne in heaven.
His eyes observe.
      His eyes examine the children of men.
5 The LORD examines the righteous,
      but his soul hates the wicked and him who loves violence.
6 On the wicked he will rain blazing coals;
      fire, sulphur, and scorching wind shall be the portion of their cup.
7 For the LORD is righteous.
      He loves righteousness.
      The upright shall see his face.

12

For the Chief Musician; upon an eight-stringed lyre. A Psalm of David.
1 Help, LORD; for the godly man ceases.
      For the faithful fail from amongst the children of men.
2 Everyone lies to his neighbour.
      They speak with flattering lips, and with a double heart.
3 May the LORD cut off all flattering lips,
      and the tongue that boasts,
4 who have said, "With our tongue we will prevail.

---

[a] *7:14* "Behold", from "הִנֵּה", means look at, take notice, observe, see, or gaze at. It is often used as an interjection.

[b] *8:5* Hebrew: Elohim. The word Elohim, used here, usually means "God", but can also mean "gods", "princes", or "angels". The Septuagint reads "angels" here. See also the quote from the Septuagint in Hebrews 2:7.
[c] *9:17* Sheol is the place of the dead.

Our lips are our own.
Who is lord over us?"

5 "Because of the oppression of the weak and because of the groaning of
the needy,
I will now arise," says the LORD;
"I will set him in safety from those who malign him."

6 The LORD's words are flawless words,
as silver refined in a clay furnace, purified seven times.

7 You will keep them, LORD.
You will preserve them from this generation forever.

8 The wicked walk on every side,
when what is vile is exalted amongst the sons of men.

13

For the Chief Musician. A Psalm by David.

1 How long, LORD?
Will you forget me forever?
How long will you hide your face from me?

2 How long shall I take counsel in my soul,
having sorrow in my heart every day?
How long shall my enemy triumph over me?

3 Behold, and answer me, LORD, my God.
Give light to my eyes, lest I sleep in death;
4 lest my enemy say, "I have prevailed against him;"
lest my adversaries rejoice when I fall.

5 But I trust in your loving kindness.
My heart rejoices in your salvation.

6 I will sing to the LORD,
because he has been good to me.

14

For the Chief Musician. By David.

1 The fool has said in his heart, "There is no God."
They are corrupt.
They have done abominable deeds.
There is no one who does good.

2 The LORD looked down from heaven on the children of men,
to see if there were any who understood,
who sought after God.

3 They have all gone aside.
They have together become corrupt.
There is no one who does good, no, not one.

4 Have all the workers of iniquity no knowledge,
who eat up my people as they eat bread,
and don't call on the LORD?

5 There they were in great fear,
for God is in the generation of the righteous.

6 You frustrate the plan of the poor,
because the LORD is his refuge.

7 Oh that the salvation of Israel would come out of Zion!
When the LORD restores the fortunes of his people,
then Jacob shall rejoice, and Israel shall be glad.

15

A Psalm by David.

1 LORD, who shall dwell in your sanctuary?
Who shall live on your holy hill?

2 He who walks blamelessly and does what is right,
and speaks truth in his heart;

3 he who doesn't slander with his tongue,
nor does evil to his friend,
nor casts slurs against his fellow man;

4 in whose eyes a vile man is despised,
but who honours those who fear the LORD;
he who keeps an oath even when it hurts, and doesn't change;

5 he who doesn't lend out his money for usury,
nor take a bribe against the innocent.

He who does these things shall never be shaken.

16

A Poem by David.

1 Preserve me, God, for I take refuge in you.

2 My soul, you have said to the LORD, "You are my Lord.
Apart from you I have no good thing."

3 As for the saints who are in the earth,
they are the excellent ones in whom is all my delight.

4 Their sorrows shall be multiplied who give gifts to another god.
Their drink offerings of blood I will not offer,
nor take their names on my lips.

5 The LORD assigned my portion and my cup.
You made my lot secure.

6 The lines have fallen to me in pleasant places.
Yes, I have a good inheritance.

7 I will bless the LORD, who has given me counsel.
Yes, my heart instructs me in the night seasons.

---

a *16:10* Sheol is the place of the dead.

8 I have set the LORD always before me.
Because he is at my right hand, I shall not be moved.

9 Therefore my heart is glad, and my tongue rejoices.
My body shall also dwell in safety.

10 For you will not leave my soul in Sheol,[a]
neither will you allow your holy one to see corruption.

11 You will show me the path of life.
In your presence is fullness of joy.
In your right hand there are pleasures forever more.

17

A Prayer by David.

1 Hear, LORD, my righteous plea.
Give ear to my prayer that doesn't go out of deceitful lips.

2 Let my sentence come out of your presence.
Let your eyes look on equity.

3 You have proved my heart.
You have visited me in the night.
You have tried me, and found nothing.
I have resolved that my mouth shall not disobey.

4 As for the deeds of men, by the word of your lips,
I have kept myself from the ways of the violent.

5 My steps have held fast to your paths.
My feet have not slipped.

6 I have called on you, for you will answer me, God.
Turn your ear to me.
Hear my speech.

7 Show your marvellous loving kindness,
you who save those who take refuge by your right hand from their
enemies.

8 Keep me as the apple of your eye.
Hide me under the shadow of your wings,

9 from the wicked who oppress me,
my deadly enemies, who surround me.

10 They close up their callous hearts.
With their mouth they speak proudly.

11 They have now surrounded us in our steps.
They set their eyes to cast us down to the earth.

12 He is like a lion that is greedy of his prey,
as it were a young lion lurking in secret places.

13 Arise, LORD, confront him.
Cast him down.
Deliver my soul from the wicked by your sword,
14 from men by your hand, LORD,
from men of the world, whose portion is in this life.
You fill the belly of your cherished ones.
Your sons have plenty,
and they store up wealth for their children.

15 As for me, I shall see your face in righteousness.
I shall be satisfied, when I awake, with seeing your form.

18

For the Chief Musician. By David the servant of the LORD, who spoke to the
LORD the words of this song in the day that the LORD delivered him from
the hand of all his enemies, and from the hand of Saul. He said,

1 I love you, LORD, my strength.

2 The LORD is my rock, my fortress, and my deliverer;
my God, my rock, in whom I take refuge;
my shield, and the horn of my salvation, my high tower.

3 I call on the LORD, who is worthy to be praised;
and I am saved from my enemies.

4 The cords of death surrounded me.
The floods of ungodliness made me afraid.

5 The cords of Sheol[b] were around me.
The snares of death came on me.

6 In my distress I called on the LORD,
and cried to my God.
He heard my voice out of his temple.
My cry before him came into his ears.

7 Then the earth shook and trembled.
The foundations also of the mountains quaked and were shaken,
because he was angry.

8 Smoke went out of his nostrils.
Consuming fire came out of his mouth.
Coals were kindled by it.

9 He bowed the heavens also, and came down.
Thick darkness was under his feet.

10 He rode on a cherub, and flew.
Yes, he soared on the wings of the wind.

11 He made darkness his hiding place, his pavilion around him,
darkness of waters, thick clouds of the skies.

12 At the brightness before him his thick clouds passed,
hailstones and coals of fire.

13 The LORD also thundered in the sky.
The Most High uttered his voice:
hailstones and coals of fire.

14 He sent out his arrows, and scattered them.
He routed them with great lightning bolts.

---

b *18:5* Sheol is the place of the dead.

15 Then the channels of waters appeared.
The foundations of the world were laid bare at your rebuke, LORD,
at the blast of the breath of your nostrils.
16 He sent from on high.
He took me.
He drew me out of many waters.
17 He delivered me from my strong enemy,
from those who hated me; for they were too mighty for me.
18 They came on me in the day of my calamity,
but the LORD was my support.
19 He brought me out also into a large place.
He delivered me, because he delighted in me.
20 The LORD has rewarded me according to my righteousness.
According to the cleanness of my hands, he has recompensed me.
21 For I have kept the ways of the LORD,
and have not wickedly departed from my God.
22 For all his ordinances were before me.
I didn't put away his statutes from me.
23 I was also blameless with him.
I kept myself from my iniquity.
24 Therefore the LORD has rewarded me according to my righteousness,
according to the cleanness of my hands in his eyesight.
25 With the merciful you will show yourself merciful.
With the perfect man, you will show yourself perfect.
26 With the pure, you will show yourself pure.
With the crooked you will show yourself shrewd.
27 For you will save the afflicted people,
but the arrogant eyes you will bring down.
28 For you will light my lamp, LORD.
My God will light up my darkness.
29 For by you, I advance through a troop.
By my God, I leap over a wall.
30 As for God, his way is perfect.
The LORD's word is tried.
He is a shield to all those who take refuge in him.
31 For who is God, except the LORD?
Who is a rock, besides our God,
32 the God who arms me with strength, and makes my way perfect?
33 He makes my feet like deer's feet,
and sets me on my high places.
34 He teaches my hands to war,
so that my arms bend a bow of bronze.
35 You have also given me the shield of your salvation.
Your right hand sustains me.
Your gentleness has made me great.
36 You have enlarged my steps under me,
My feet have not slipped.
37 I will pursue my enemies, and overtake them.
I won't turn away until they are consumed.
38 I will strike them through, so that they will not be able to rise.
They shall fall under my feet.
39 For you have armed me with strength to the battle.
You have subdued under me those who rose up against me.
40 You have also made my enemies turn their backs to me,
that I might cut off those who hate me.
41 They cried, but there was no one to save;
even to the LORD, but he didn't answer them.
42 Then I beat them small as the dust before the wind.
I cast them out as the mire of the streets.
43 You have delivered me from the strivings of the people.
You have made me the head of the nations.
A people whom I have not known shall serve me.
44 As soon as they hear of me they shall obey me.
The foreigners shall submit themselves to me.
45 The foreigners shall fade away,
and shall come trembling out of their strongholds.
46 The LORD lives! Blessed be my rock.
Exalted be the God of my salvation,
47 even the God who executes vengeance for me,
and subdues peoples under me.
48 He rescues me from my enemies.
Yes, you lift me up above those who rise up against me.
You deliver me from the violent man.
49 Therefore I will give thanks to you, LORD, amongst the nations,
and will sing praises to your name.
50 He gives great deliverance to his king,
and shows loving kindness to his anointed,
to David and to his offspring,[a] forever more.

19

For the Chief Musician. A Psalm by David.
1 The heavens declare the glory of God.
The expanse shows his handiwork.
2 Day after day they pour out speech,
and night after night they display knowledge.
3 There is no speech nor language
where their voice is not heard.

4 Their voice has gone out through all the earth,
their words to the end of the world.
In them he has set a tent for the sun,
5 which is as a bridegroom coming out of his room,
like a strong man rejoicing to run his course.
6 His going out is from the end of the heavens,
his circuit to its ends.
There is nothing hidden from its heat.

7 The LORD's law is perfect, restoring the soul.
The LORD's covenant is sure, making wise the simple.
8 The LORD's precepts are right, rejoicing the heart.
The LORD's commandment is pure, enlightening the eyes.
9 The fear of the LORD is clean, enduring forever.
The LORD's ordinances are true, and righteous altogether.
10 They are more to be desired than gold, yes, than much fine gold,
sweeter also than honey and the extract of the honeycomb.
11 Moreover your servant is warned by them.
In keeping them there is great reward.
12 Who can discern his errors?
Forgive me from hidden errors.

13 Keep back your servant also from presumptuous sins.
Let them not have dominion over me.
Then I will be upright.
I will be blameless and innocent of great transgression.
14 Let the words of my mouth and the meditation of my heart
be acceptable in your sight,
LORD, my rock, and my redeemer.

20

For the Chief Musician. A Psalm by David.
1 May the LORD answer you in the day of trouble.
May the name of the God of Jacob set you up on high,
2 send you help from the sanctuary,
grant you support from Zion,
3 remember all your offerings,
and accept your burnt sacrifice. Selah.
4 May he grant you your heart's desire,
and fulfil all your counsel.
5 We will triumph in your salvation.
In the name of our God, we will set up our banners.
May the LORD grant all your requests.
6 Now I know that the LORD saves his anointed.
He will answer him from his holy heaven,
with the saving strength of his right hand.
7 Some trust in chariots, and some in horses,
but we trust in the name of the LORD our God.
8 They are bowed down and fallen,
but we rise up, and stand upright.
9 Save, LORD!
Let the King answer us when we call!

21

For the Chief Musician. A Psalm by David.
1 The king rejoices in your strength, LORD!
How greatly he rejoices in your salvation!
2 You have given him his heart's desire,
and have not withheld the request of his lips. Selah.
3 For you meet him with the blessings of goodness.
You set a crown of fine gold on his head.
4 He asked life of you and you gave it to him,
even length of days forever and ever.
5 His glory is great in your salvation.
You lay honour and majesty on him.
6 For you make him most blessed forever.
You make him glad with joy in your presence.
7 For the king trusts in the LORD.
Through the loving kindness of the Most High, he shall not be moved.
8 Your hand will find out all of your enemies.
Your right hand will find out those who hate you.
9 You will make them as a fiery furnace in the time of your anger.
The LORD will swallow them up in his wrath.
The fire shall devour them.
10 You will destroy their descendants from the earth,
their posterity from amongst the children of men.
11 For they intended evil against you.
They plotted evil against you which cannot succeed.
12 For you will make them turn their back,
when you aim drawn bows at their face.
13 Be exalted, LORD, in your strength,
so we will sing and praise your power.

22

For the Chief Musician; set to "The Doe of the Morning." A Psalm by David.
1 My God, my God, why have you forsaken me?
Why are you so far from helping me, and from the words of my
groaning?

---

a *18:50* or, seed

2 My God, I cry in the daytime, but you don't answer;
  in the night season, and am not silent.
3 But you are holy,
  you who inhabit the praises of Israel.
4 Our fathers trusted in you.
  They trusted, and you delivered them.
5 They cried to you, and were delivered.
  They trusted in you, and were not disappointed.
6 But I am a worm, and no man;
  a reproach of men, and despised by the people.
7 All those who see me mock me.
  They insult me with their lips. They shake their heads, saying,
  8 "He trusts in the LORD.
  Let him deliver him.
  Let him rescue him, since he delights in him."
9 But you brought me out of the womb.
  You made me trust while at my mother's breasts.
10 I was thrown on you from my mother's womb.
  You are my God since my mother bore me.
11 Don't be far from me, for trouble is near.
  For there is no one to help.
12 Many bulls have surrounded me.
  Strong bulls of Bashan have encircled me.
13 They open their mouths wide against me,
  lions tearing prey and roaring.
14 I am poured out like water.
  All my bones are out of joint.
My heart is like wax.
  It is melted within me.
15 My strength is dried up like a potsherd.
  My tongue sticks to the roof of my mouth.
You have brought me into the dust of death.
16 For dogs have surrounded me.
  A company of evildoers have enclosed me.
  They have pierced my hands and feet.[a]
17 I can count all of my bones.
They look and stare at me.
18 They divide my garments amongst them.
  They cast lots for my clothing.

19 But don't be far off, LORD.
  You are my help. Hurry to help me!
20 Deliver my soul from the sword,
  my precious life from the power of the dog.
21 Save me from the lion's mouth!
  Yes, you have rescued me from the horns of the wild oxen.

22 I will declare your name to my brothers.
  Amongst the assembly, I will praise you.
23 You who fear the LORD, praise him!
  All you descendants of Jacob, glorify him!
  Stand in awe of him, all you descendants of Israel!
24 For he has not despised nor abhorred the affliction of the afflicted,
  neither has he hidden his face from him;
  but when he cried to him, he heard.

25 My praise of you comes in the great assembly.
  I will pay my vows before those who fear him.
26 The humble shall eat and be satisfied.
  They shall praise the LORD who seek after him.
  Let your hearts live forever.
27 All the ends of the earth shall remember and turn to the LORD.
  All the relatives of the nations shall worship before you.
28 For the kingdom is the LORD's.
  He is the ruler over the nations.
29 All the rich ones of the earth shall eat and worship.
  All those who go down to the dust shall bow before him,
  even he who can't keep his soul alive.
30 Posterity shall serve him.
  Future generations shall be told about the Lord.
31 They shall come and shall declare his righteousness to a people that
      shall be born,
  for he has done it.

23

A Psalm by David.
1 The LORD is my shepherd;
  I shall lack nothing.
2 He makes me lie down in green pastures.
  He leads me beside still waters.
3 He restores my soul.
  He guides me in the paths of righteousness for his name's sake.
4 Even though I walk through the valley of the shadow of death,
  I will fear no evil, for you are with me.
Your rod and your staff,
  they comfort me.

5 You prepare a table before me
  in the presence of my enemies.
You anoint my head with oil.
  My cup runs over.
6 Surely goodness and loving kindness shall follow me all the days of my
      life,
  and I will dwell in the LORD's house forever.

24

A Psalm by David.
1 The earth is the LORD's, with its fullness;
  the world, and those who dwell in it.
2 For he has founded it on the seas,
  and established it on the floods.

3 Who may ascend to the LORD's hill?
  Who may stand in his holy place?
4 He who has clean hands and a pure heart;
  who has not lifted up his soul to falsehood,
  and has not sworn deceitfully.
5 He shall receive a blessing from the LORD,
  righteousness from the God of his salvation.
6 This is the generation of those who seek Him,
  who seek your face—even Jacob. Selah.

7 Lift up your heads, you gates!
  Be lifted up, you everlasting doors,
  and the King of glory will come in.
8 Who is the King of glory?
  The LORD strong and mighty,
  the LORD mighty in battle.
9 Lift up your heads, you gates;
  yes, lift them up, you everlasting doors,
  and the King of glory will come in.
10 Who is this King of glory?
  The LORD of Armies is the King of glory! Selah.

25

By David.
1 To you, LORD, I lift up my soul.
2 My God, I have trusted in you.
  Don't let me be shamed.
  Don't let my enemies triumph over me.
3 Yes, no one who waits for you will be shamed.
  They will be shamed who deal treacherously without cause.

4 Show me your ways, LORD.
  Teach me your paths.
5 Guide me in your truth, and teach me,
  for you are the God of my salvation.
  I wait for you all day long.
6 LORD, remember your tender mercies and your loving kindness,
  for they are from old times.
7 Don't remember the sins of my youth, nor my transgressions.
  Remember me according to your loving kindness,
  for your goodness' sake, LORD.
8 Good and upright is the LORD,
  therefore he will instruct sinners in the way.
9 He will guide the humble in justice.
  He will teach the humble his way.
10 All the paths of the LORD are loving kindness and truth
  to such as keep his covenant and his testimonies.
11 For your name's sake, LORD,
  pardon my iniquity, for it is great.
12 What man is he who fears the LORD?
  He shall instruct him in the way that he shall choose.
13 His soul will dwell at ease.
  His offspring will inherit the land.
14 The friendship of the LORD is with those who fear him.
  He will show them his covenant.

15 My eyes are ever on the LORD,
  for he will pluck my feet out of the net.
16 Turn to me, and have mercy on me,
  for I am desolate and afflicted.
17 The troubles of my heart are enlarged.
  Oh bring me out of my distresses.
18 Consider my affliction and my travail.
  Forgive all my sins.
19 Consider my enemies, for they are many.
  They hate me with cruel hatred.
20 Oh keep my soul, and deliver me.
  Let me not be disappointed, for I take refuge in you.
21 Let integrity and uprightness preserve me,
  for I wait for you.
22 God, redeem Israel
  out of all his troubles.

---

a *22:16* So Dead Sea Scrolls. Masoretic Text reads, "Like a lion, they pin my
hands and feet."

26

By David.

1 Judge me, LORD, for I have walked in my integrity.
     I have trusted also in the LORD without wavering.
2 Examine me, LORD, and prove me.
     Try my heart and my mind.
3 For your loving kindness is before my eyes.
     I have walked in your truth.
4 I have not sat with deceitful men,
     neither will I go in with hypocrites.
5 I hate the assembly of evildoers,
     and will not sit with the wicked.
6 I will wash my hands in innocence,
     so I will go about your altar, LORD,
         7 that I may make the voice of thanksgiving to be heard
     and tell of all your wondrous deeds.
8 LORD, I love the habitation of your house,
     the place where your glory dwells.
9 Don't gather my soul with sinners,
     nor my life with bloodthirsty men
         10 in whose hands is wickedness;
     their right hand is full of bribes.

11 But as for me, I will walk in my integrity.
     Redeem me, and be merciful to me.
12 My foot stands in an even place.
     In the congregations I will bless the LORD.

27

By David.

1 The LORD is my light and my salvation.
     Whom shall I fear?
The LORD is the strength of my life.
     Of whom shall I be afraid?
2 When evildoers came at me to eat up my flesh,
     even my adversaries and my foes, they stumbled and fell.
3 Though an army should encamp against me,
     my heart shall not fear.
Though war should rise against me,
     even then I will be confident.
4 One thing I have asked of the LORD, that I will seek after:
     that I may dwell in the LORD's house all the days of my life,
     to see the LORD's beauty,
     and to enquire in his temple.
5 For in the day of trouble, he will keep me secretly in his pavilion.
     In the secret place of his tabernacle, he will hide me.
     He will lift me up on a rock.
6 Now my head will be lifted up above my enemies around me.
I will offer sacrifices of joy in his tent.
     I will sing, yes, I will sing praises to the LORD.

7 Hear, LORD, when I cry with my voice.
     Have mercy also on me, and answer me.
8 When you said, "Seek my face,"
     my heart said to you, "I will seek your face, LORD."
9 Don't hide your face from me.
     Don't put your servant away in anger.
You have been my help.
     Don't abandon me,
     neither forsake me, God of my salvation.
10 When my father and my mother forsake me,
     then the LORD will take me up.
11 Teach me your way, LORD.
     Lead me in a straight path, because of my enemies.
12 Don't deliver me over to the desire of my adversaries,
     for false witnesses have risen up against me,
     such as breathe out cruelty.
13 I am still confident of this:
     I will see the goodness of the LORD in the land of the living.
14 Wait for the LORD.
     Be strong, and let your heart take courage.
Yes, wait for the LORD.

28

By David.

1 To you, LORD, I call.
     My rock, don't be deaf to me,
     lest, if you are silent to me,
     I would become like those who go down into the pit.
2 Hear the voice of my petitions, when I cry to you,
     when I lift up my hands towards your Most Holy Place.
3 Don't draw me away with the wicked,
     with the workers of iniquity who speak peace with their neighbours,
     but mischief is in their hearts.
4 Give them according to their work, and according to the wickedness of
         their doings.
     Give them according to the operation of their hands.

Bring back on them what they deserve.
5 Because they don't respect the works of the LORD,
     nor the operation of his hands,
     he will break them down and not build them up.

6 Blessed be the LORD,
     because he has heard the voice of my petitions.
7 The LORD is my strength and my shield.
     My heart has trusted in him, and I am helped.
Therefore my heart greatly rejoices.
     With my song I will thank him.
8 The LORD is their strength.
     He is a stronghold of salvation to his anointed.
9 Save your people,
     and bless your inheritance.
Be their shepherd also,
     and bear them up forever.

29

A Psalm by David.

1 Ascribe to the LORD, you sons of the mighty,
     ascribe to the LORD glory and strength.
2 Ascribe to the LORD the glory due to his name.
     Worship the LORD in holy array.

3 The LORD's voice is on the waters.
     The God of glory thunders, even the LORD on many waters.
4 The LORD's voice is powerful.
     The LORD's voice is full of majesty.
5 The LORD's voice breaks the cedars.
     Yes, the LORD breaks in pieces the cedars of Lebanon.
6 He makes them also to skip like a calf;
     Lebanon and Sirion like a young, wild ox.
7 The LORD's voice strikes with flashes of lightning.
         8 The LORD's voice shakes the wilderness.
     The LORD shakes the wilderness of Kadesh.
9 The LORD's voice makes the deer calve,
     and strips the forests bare.
     In his temple everything says, "Glory!"

10 The LORD sat enthroned at the Flood.
     Yes, the LORD sits as King forever.
11 The LORD will give strength to his people.
     The LORD will bless his people with peace.

30

A Psalm. A Song for the Dedication of the Temple. By David.

1 I will extol you, LORD, for you have raised me up,
     and have not made my foes to rejoice over me.
2 LORD my God, I cried to you,
     and you have healed me.
3 LORD, you have brought up my soul from Sheol.[a]
     You have kept me alive, that I should not go down to the pit.
4 Sing praise to the LORD, you saints of his.
     Give thanks to his holy name.
5 For his anger is but for a moment.
     His favour is for a lifetime.
Weeping may stay for the night,
     but joy comes in the morning.
6 As for me, I said in my prosperity,
     "I shall never be moved."
7 You, LORD, when you favoured me, made my mountain stand strong;
     but when you hid your face, I was troubled.
8 I cried to you, LORD.
     I made supplication to the Lord:
9 "What profit is there in my destruction, if I go down to the pit?
     Shall the dust praise you?
     Shall it declare your truth?
10 Hear, LORD, and have mercy on me.
     LORD, be my helper."
11 You have turned my mourning into dancing for me.
     You have removed my sackcloth, and clothed me with gladness,
         12 to the end that my heart may sing praise to you, and not be silent.
LORD my God, I will give thanks to you forever!

31

For the Chief Musician. A Psalm by David.

1 In you, LORD, I take refuge.
     Let me never be disappointed.
     Deliver me in your righteousness.
2 Bow down your ear to me.
     Deliver me speedily.
Be to me a strong rock,
     a house of defence to save me.
3 For you are my rock and my fortress,
     therefore for your name's sake lead me and guide me.
4 Pluck me out of the net that they have laid secretly for me,
     for you are my stronghold.

---

a *30:3* Sheol is the place of the dead.

5 Into your hand I commend my spirit.
    You redeem me, LORD, God of truth.
6 I hate those who regard lying vanities,
    but I trust in the LORD.
7 I will be glad and rejoice in your loving kindness,
    for you have seen my affliction.
    You have known my soul in adversities.
8 You have not shut me up into the hand of the enemy.
    You have set my feet in a large place.
9 Have mercy on me, LORD, for I am in distress.
    My eye, my soul, and my body waste away with grief.
10 For my life is spent with sorrow,
    my years with sighing.
My strength fails because of my iniquity.
    My bones are wasted away.
11 Because of all my adversaries I have become utterly contemptible to my
        neighbours,
    a horror to my acquaintances.
    Those who saw me on the street fled from me.
12 I am forgotten from their hearts like a dead man.
    I am like broken pottery.
13 For I have heard the slander of many, terror on every side,
    while they conspire together against me,
    they plot to take away my life.
14 But I trust in you, LORD.
    I said, "You are my God."
15 My times are in your hand.
    Deliver me from the hand of my enemies, and from those who
        persecute me.
16 Make your face to shine on your servant.
    Save me in your loving kindness.
17 Let me not be disappointed, LORD, for I have called on you.
    Let the wicked be disappointed.
    Let them be silent in Sheol.[a]
18 Let the lying lips be mute,
    which speak against the righteous insolently, with pride and
        contempt.
19 Oh how great is your goodness,
    which you have laid up for those who fear you,
    which you have worked for those who take refuge in you,
    before the sons of men!
20 In the shelter of your presence you will hide them from the plotting of
        man.
    You will keep them secretly in a dwelling away from the strife of
        tongues.
21 Praise be to the LORD,
    for he has shown me his marvellous loving kindness in a strong city.
22 As for me, I said in my haste, "I am cut off from before your eyes."
    Nevertheless you heard the voice of my petitions when I cried to you.
23 Oh love the LORD, all you his saints!
    The LORD preserves the faithful,
and fully recompenses him who behaves arrogantly.
24 Be strong, and let your heart take courage,
    all you who hope in the LORD.

32

By David. A contemplative psalm.
1 Blessed is he whose disobedience is forgiven,
    whose sin is covered.
2 Blessed is the man to whom the LORD doesn't impute iniquity,
    in whose spirit there is no deceit.
3 When I kept silence, my bones wasted away through my groaning all day
        long.
4 For day and night your hand was heavy on me.
    My strength was sapped in the heat of summer. Selah.
5 I acknowledged my sin to you.
    I didn't hide my iniquity.
I said, I will confess my transgressions to the LORD,
    and you forgave the iniquity of my sin. Selah.
6 For this, let everyone who is godly pray to you in a time when you may be
        found.
    Surely when the great waters overflow, they shall not reach to him.
7 You are my hiding place.
    You will preserve me from trouble.
    You will surround me with songs of deliverance. Selah.
8 I will instruct you and teach you in the way which you shall go.
    I will counsel you with my eye on you.
9 Don't be like the horse, or like the mule, which have no understanding,
    who are controlled by bit and bridle, or else they will not come near to
        you.
10 Many sorrows come to the wicked,
    but loving kindness shall surround him who trusts in the LORD.
11 Be glad in the LORD, and rejoice, you righteous!
    Shout for joy, all you who are upright in heart!

33

1 Rejoice in the LORD, you righteous!
    Praise is fitting for the upright.
2 Give thanks to the LORD with the lyre.
    Sing praises to him with the harp of ten strings.
3 Sing to him a new song.
    Play skilfully with a shout of joy!
4 For the LORD's word is right.
    All his work is done in faithfulness.
5 He loves righteousness and justice.
    The earth is full of the loving kindness of the LORD.
6 By the LORD's word, the heavens were made:
    all their army by the breath of his mouth.
7 He gathers the waters of the sea together as a heap.
    He lays up the deeps in storehouses.
8 Let all the earth fear the LORD.
    Let all the inhabitants of the world stand in awe of him.
9 For he spoke, and it was done.
    He commanded, and it stood firm.
10 The LORD brings the counsel of the nations to nothing.
    He makes the thoughts of the peoples to be of no effect.
11 The counsel of the LORD stands fast forever,
    the thoughts of his heart to all generations.
12 Blessed is the nation whose God is the LORD,
    the people whom he has chosen for his own inheritance.
13 The LORD looks from heaven.
    He sees all the sons of men.
14 From the place of his habitation he looks out on all the inhabitants of the
        earth,
    15 he who fashions all of their hearts;
    and he considers all of their works.
16 There is no king saved by the multitude of an army.
    A mighty man is not delivered by great strength.
17 A horse is a vain thing for safety,
    neither does he deliver any by his great power.
18 Behold, the LORD's eye is on those who fear him,
    on those who hope in his loving kindness,
    19 to deliver their soul from death,
    to keep them alive in famine.
20 Our soul has waited for the LORD.
    He is our help and our shield.
21 For our heart rejoices in him,
    because we have trusted in his holy name.
22 Let your loving kindness be on us, LORD,
    since we have hoped in you.

34

By David; when he pretended to be insane before Abimelech, who drove
him away, and he departed.
1 [b] I will bless the LORD at all times.
    His praise will always be in my mouth.
2 My soul shall boast in the LORD.
    The humble shall hear of it and be glad.
3 Oh magnify the LORD with me.
    Let's exalt his name together.
4 I sought the LORD, and he answered me,
    and delivered me from all my fears.
5 They looked to him, and were radiant.
    Their faces shall never be covered with shame.
6 This poor man cried, and the LORD heard him,
    and saved him out of all his troubles.
7 The LORD's angel encamps around those who fear him,
    and delivers them.
8 Oh taste and see that the LORD is good.
    Blessed is the man who takes refuge in him.
9 Oh fear the LORD, you his saints,
    for there is no lack with those who fear him.
10 The young lions do lack, and suffer hunger,
    but those who seek the LORD shall not lack any good thing.

11 Come, you children, listen to me.
    I will teach you the fear of the LORD.
12 Who is someone who desires life,
    and loves many days, that he may see good?
13 Keep your tongue from evil,
    and your lips from speaking lies.
14 Depart from evil, and do good.
    Seek peace, and pursue it.
15 The LORD's eyes are towards the righteous.
    His ears listen to their cry.
16 The LORD's face is against those who do evil,
    to cut off their memory from the earth.
17 The righteous cry, and the LORD hears,
    and delivers them out of all their troubles.
18 The LORD is near to those who have a broken heart,
    and saves those who have a crushed spirit.
19 Many are the afflictions of the righteous,
    but the LORD delivers him out of them all.

---

[a] *31:17* Sheol is the place of the dead.

[b] *34:1* Psalm 34 is an acrostic poem, with each verse starting with a letter of the
alphabet (ordered from Alef to Tav).

20 He protects all of his bones.
Not one of them is broken.
21 Evil shall kill the wicked.
Those who hate the righteous shall be condemned.
22 The LORD redeems the soul of his servants.
None of those who take refuge in him shall be condemned.

35

By David.
1 Contend, LORD, with those who contend with me.
Fight against those who fight against me.
2 Take hold of shield and buckler,
and stand up for my help.
3 Brandish the spear and block those who pursue me.
Tell my soul, "I am your salvation."
4 Let those who seek after my soul be disappointed and brought to
dishonour.
Let those who plot my ruin be turned back and confounded.
5 Let them be as chaff before the wind,
the LORD's angel driving them on.
6 Let their way be dark and slippery,
the LORD's angel pursuing them.
7 For without cause they have hidden their net in a pit for me.
Without cause they have dug a pit for my soul.
8 Let destruction come on him unawares.
Let his net that he has hidden catch himself.
Let him fall into that destruction.

9 My soul shall be joyful in the LORD.
It shall rejoice in his salvation.
10 All my bones shall say, "LORD, who is like you,
who delivers the poor from him who is too strong for him;
yes, the poor and the needy from him who robs him?"
11 Unrighteous witnesses rise up.
They ask me about things that I don't know about.
12 They reward me evil for good,
to the bereaving of my soul.

13 But as for me, when they were sick, my clothing was sackcloth.
I afflicted my soul with fasting.
My prayer returned into my own bosom.
14 I behaved myself as though it had been my friend or my brother.
I bowed down mourning, as one who mourns his mother.
15 But in my adversity, they rejoiced, and gathered themselves together.
The attackers gathered themselves together against me, and I didn't
know it.
They tore at me, and didn't cease.
16 Like the profane mockers in feasts,
they gnashed their teeth at me.
17 Lord, how long will you look on?
Rescue my soul from their destruction,
my precious life from the lions.
18 I will give you thanks in the great assembly.
I will praise you amongst many people.
19 Don't let those who are my enemies wrongfully rejoice over me;
neither let those who hate me without a cause wink their eyes.
20 For they don't speak peace,
but they devise deceitful words against those who are quiet in the
land.
21 Yes, they opened their mouth wide against me.
They said, "Aha! Aha! Our eye has seen it!"
22 You have seen it, LORD. Don't keep silent.
Lord, don't be far from me.
23 Wake up! Rise up to defend me, my God!
My Lord, contend for me!
24 Vindicate me, LORD my God, according to your righteousness.
Don't let them gloat over me.
25 Don't let them say in their heart, "Aha! That's the way we want it!"
Don't let them say, "We have swallowed him up!"
26 Let them be disappointed and confounded together who rejoice at my
calamity.
Let them be clothed with shame and dishonour who magnify
themselves against me.

27 Let those who favour my righteous cause shout for joy and be glad.
Yes, let them say continually, "May The LORD be magnified,
who has pleasure in the prosperity of his servant!"
28 My tongue shall talk about your righteousness and about your praise all
day long.

36

For the Chief Musician. By David, the servant of the LORD.
1 A revelation is within my heart about the disobedience of the wicked:
There is no fear of God before his eyes.
2 For he flatters himself in his own eyes,
too much to detect and hate his sin.
3 The words of his mouth are iniquity and deceit.
He has ceased to be wise and to do good.
4 He plots iniquity on his bed.
He sets himself in a way that is not good.

He doesn't abhor evil.
5 Your loving kindness, LORD, is in the heavens.
Your faithfulness reaches to the skies.
6 Your righteousness is like the mountains of God.
Your judgements are like a great deep.
LORD, you preserve man and animal.
7 How precious is your loving kindness, God!
The children of men take refuge under the shadow of your wings.
8 They shall be abundantly satisfied with the abundance of your house.
You will make them drink of the river of your pleasures.
9 For with you is the spring of life.
In your light we will see light.
10 Oh continue your loving kindness to those who know you,
your righteousness to the upright in heart.
11 Don't let the foot of pride come against me.
Don't let the hand of the wicked drive me away.
12 There the workers of iniquity are fallen.
They are thrust down, and shall not be able to rise.

37

By David.
1 Don't fret because of evildoers,
neither be envious against those who work unrighteousness.
2 For they shall soon be cut down like the grass,
and wither like the green herb.
3 Trust in the LORD, and do good.
Dwell in the land, and enjoy safe pasture.
4 Also delight yourself in the LORD,
and he will give you the desires of your heart.
5 Commit your way to the LORD.
Trust also in him, and he will do this:
6 he will make your righteousness shine out like light,
and your justice as the noon day sun.
7 Rest in the LORD, and wait patiently for him.
Don't fret because of him who prospers in his way,
because of the man who makes wicked plots happen.
8 Cease from anger, and forsake wrath.
Don't fret; it leads only to evildoing.
9 For evildoers shall be cut off,
but those who wait for the LORD shall inherit the land.
10 For yet a little while, and the wicked will be no more.
Yes, though you look for his place, he isn't there.
11 But the humble shall inherit the land,
and shall delight themselves in the abundance of peace.
12 The wicked plots against the just,
and gnashes at him with his teeth.
13 The Lord will laugh at him,
for he sees that his day is coming.
14 The wicked have drawn out the sword, and have bent their bow,
to cast down the poor and needy,
to kill those who are upright on the path.
15 Their sword shall enter into their own heart.
Their bows shall be broken.
16 Better is a little that the righteous has,
than the abundance of many wicked.
17 For the arms of the wicked shall be broken,
but the LORD upholds the righteous.
18 The LORD knows the days of the perfect.
Their inheritance shall be forever.
19 They shall not be disappointed in the time of evil.
In the days of famine they shall be satisfied.

20 But the wicked shall perish.
The enemies of the LORD shall be like the beauty of the fields.
They will vanish—
vanish like smoke.
21 The wicked borrow, and don't pay back,
but the righteous give generously.
22 For such as are blessed by him shall inherit the land.
Those who are cursed by him shall be cut off.
23 A man's steps are established by the LORD.
He delights in his way.
24 Though he stumble, he shall not fall,
for the LORD holds him up with his hand.
25 I have been young, and now am old,
yet I have not seen the righteous forsaken,
nor his children begging for bread.
26 All day long he deals graciously, and lends.
His offspring is blessed.
27 Depart from evil, and do good.
Live securely forever.
28 For the LORD loves justice,
and doesn't forsake his saints.
They are preserved forever,
but the children of the wicked shall be cut off.
29 The righteous shall inherit the land,
and live in it forever.

30 The mouth of the righteous talks of wisdom.

His tongue speaks justice.
31 The law of his God is in his heart.
None of his steps shall slide.
32 The wicked watch the righteous,
and seek to kill him.
33 The LORD will not leave him in his hand,
nor condemn him when he is judged.
34 Wait for the LORD, and keep his way,
and he will exalt you to inherit the land.
When the wicked are cut off, you shall see it.

35 I have seen the wicked in great power,
spreading himself like a green tree in its native soil.
36 But he passed away, and behold, he was not.
Yes, I sought him, but he could not be found.
37 Mark the perfect man, and see the upright,
for there is a future for the man of peace.
38 As for transgressors, they shall be destroyed together.
The future of the wicked shall be cut off.
39 But the salvation of the righteous is from the LORD.
He is their stronghold in the time of trouble.
40 The LORD helps them and rescues them.
He rescues them from the wicked and saves them,
because they have taken refuge in him.

38

A Psalm by David, for a memorial.
1 LORD, don't rebuke me in your wrath,
neither chasten me in your hot displeasure.
2 For your arrows have pierced me,
your hand presses hard on me.
3 There is no soundness in my flesh because of your indignation,
neither is there any health in my bones because of my sin.
4 For my iniquities have gone over my head.
As a heavy burden, they are too heavy for me.
5 My wounds are loathsome and corrupt
because of my foolishness.
6 I am in pain and bowed down greatly.
I go mourning all day long.
7 For my waist is filled with burning.
There is no soundness in my flesh.
8 I am faint and severely bruised.
I have groaned by reason of the anguish of my heart.
9 Lord, all my desire is before you.
My groaning is not hidden from you.
10 My heart throbs.
My strength fails me.
As for the light of my eyes, it has also left me.
11 My lovers and my friends stand aloof from my plague.
My kinsmen stand far away.
12 They also who seek after my life lay snares.
Those who seek my hurt speak mischievous things,
and meditate deceits all day long.
13 But I, as a deaf man, don't hear.
I am as a mute man who doesn't open his mouth.
14 Yes, I am as a man who doesn't hear,
in whose mouth are no reproofs.
15 For I hope in you, LORD.
You will answer, Lord my God.
16 For I said, "Don't let them gloat over me,
or exalt themselves over me when my foot slips."
17 For I am ready to fall.
My pain is continually before me.
18 For I will declare my iniquity.
I will be sorry for my sin.
19 But my enemies are vigorous and many.
Those who hate me without reason are numerous.
20 They who render evil for good are also adversaries to me,
because I follow what is good.
21 Don't forsake me, LORD.
My God, don't be far from me.
22 Hurry to help me,
Lord, my salvation.

39

For the Chief Musician. For Jeduthun. A Psalm by David.
1 I said, "I will watch my ways, so that I don't sin with my tongue.
I will keep my mouth with a bridle while the wicked is before me."
2 I was mute with silence.
I held my peace, even from good.
My sorrow was stirred.
3 My heart was hot within me.
While I meditated, the fire burnt.
I spoke with my tongue:
4 "LORD, show me my end,
what is the measure of my days.
Let me know how frail I am.
5 Behold, you have made my days hand widths.
My lifetime is as nothing before you.
Surely every man stands as a breath." Selah.

6 "Surely every man walks like a shadow.
Surely they busy themselves in vain.
He heaps up, and doesn't know who shall gather.
7 Now, Lord, what do I wait for?
My hope is in you.
8 Deliver me from all my transgressions.
Don't make me the reproach of the foolish.
9 I was mute.
I didn't open my mouth,
because you did it.
10 Remove your scourge away from me.
I am overcome by the blow of your hand.
11 When you rebuke and correct man for iniquity,
you consume his wealth like a moth.
Surely every man is but a breath." Selah.
12 "Hear my prayer, LORD, and give ear to my cry.
Don't be silent at my tears.
For I am a stranger with you,
a foreigner, as all my fathers were.
13 Oh spare me, that I may recover strength,
before I go away and exist no more."

40

For the Chief Musician. A Psalm by David.
1 I waited patiently for the LORD.
He turned to me, and heard my cry.
2 He brought me up also out of a horrible pit,
out of the miry clay.
He set my feet on a rock,
and gave me a firm place to stand.
3 He has put a new song in my mouth, even praise to our God.
Many shall see it, and fear, and shall trust in the LORD.
4 Blessed is the man who makes the LORD his trust,
and doesn't respect the proud, nor such as turn away to lies.
5 Many, LORD, my God, are the wonderful works which you have done,
and your thoughts which are towards us.
They can't be declared back to you.
If I would declare and speak of them, they are more than can be
counted.
6 Sacrifice and offering you didn't desire.
You have opened my ears.
You have not required burnt offering and sin offering.
7 Then I said, "Behold, I have come.
It is written about me in the book in the scroll.
8 I delight to do your will, my God.
Yes, your law is within my heart."
9 I have proclaimed glad news of righteousness in the great assembly.
Behold, I will not seal my lips, LORD, you know.
10 I have not hidden your righteousness within my heart.
I have declared your faithfulness and your salvation.
I have not concealed your loving kindness and your truth from the
great assembly.
11 Don't withhold your tender mercies from me, LORD.
Let your loving kindness and your truth continually preserve me.
12 For innumerable evils have surrounded me.
My iniquities have overtaken me, so that I am not able to look up.
They are more than the hairs of my head.
My heart has failed me.
13 Be pleased, LORD, to deliver me.
Hurry to help me, LORD.
14 Let them be disappointed and confounded together who seek after my
soul to destroy it.
Let them be turned backward and brought to dishonour who delight in
my hurt.
15 Let them be desolate by reason of their shame that tell me, "Aha! Aha!"
16 Let all those who seek you rejoice and be glad in you.
Let such as love your salvation say continually, "Let the LORD be
exalted!"
17 But I am poor and needy.
May the Lord think about me.
You are my help and my deliverer.
Don't delay, my God.

41

For the Chief Musician. A Psalm by David.
1 Blessed is he who considers the poor.
The LORD will deliver him in the day of evil.
2 The LORD will preserve him, and keep him alive.
He shall be blessed on the earth,
and he will not surrender him to the will of his enemies.
3 The LORD will sustain him on his sickbed,
and restore him from his bed of illness.
4 I said, "LORD, have mercy on me!
Heal me, for I have sinned against you."
5 My enemies speak evil against me:
"When will he die, and his name perish?"
6 If he comes to see me, he speaks falsehood.
His heart gathers iniquity to itself.
When he goes abroad, he tells it.
7 All who hate me whisper together against me.

They imagine the worst for me.
8 "An evil disease", they say, "has afflicted him.
Now that he lies he shall rise up no more."
9 Yes, my own familiar friend, in whom I trusted,
who ate bread with me,
has lifted up his heel against me.

10 But you, LORD, have mercy on me, and raise me up,
that I may repay them.
11 By this I know that you delight in me,
because my enemy doesn't triumph over me.
12 As for me, you uphold me in my integrity,
and set me in your presence forever.

13 Blessed be the LORD, the God of Israel,
from everlasting and to everlasting!
Amen and amen.

42
Book 2
For the Chief Musician. A contemplation by the sons of Korah.
1 As the deer pants for the water brooks,
so my soul pants after you, God.[a]
2 My soul thirsts for God, for the living God.
When shall I come and appear before God?
3 My tears have been my food day and night,
while they continually ask me, "Where is your God?"
4 These things I remember, and pour out my soul within me,
how I used to go with the crowd, and led them to God's house,
with the voice of joy and praise, a multitude keeping a holy day.
5 Why are you in despair, my soul?
Why are you disturbed within me?
Hope in God!
For I shall still praise him for the saving help of his presence.
6 My God, my soul is in despair within me.
Therefore I remember you from the land of the Jordan,
the heights of Hermon, from the hill Mizar.
7 Deep calls to deep at the noise of your waterfalls.
All your waves and your billows have swept over me.

8 GOD[b] will command his loving kindness in the daytime.
In the night his song shall be with me:
a prayer to the God of my life.
9 I will ask God, my rock, "Why have you forgotten me?
Why do I go mourning because of the oppression of the enemy?"
10 As with a sword in my bones, my adversaries reproach me,
while they continually ask me, "Where is your God?"
11 Why are you in despair, my soul?
Why are you disturbed within me?
Hope in God! For I shall still praise him,
the saving help of my countenance, and my God.

43
1 Vindicate me, God, and plead my cause against an ungodly nation.
Oh, deliver me from deceitful and wicked men.
2 For you are the God of my strength. Why have you rejected me?
Why do I go mourning because of the oppression of the enemy?
3 Oh, send out your light and your truth.
Let them lead me.
Let them bring me to your holy hill,
to your tents.
4 Then I will go to the altar of God,
to God, my exceeding joy.
I will praise you on the harp, God, my God.
5 Why are you in despair, my soul?
Why are you disturbed within me?
Hope in God!
For I shall still praise him:
my Saviour, my helper, and my God.

44
For the Chief Musician. By the sons of Korah. A contemplative psalm.
1 We have heard with our ears, God;
our fathers have told us what work you did in their days,
in the days of old.
2 You drove out the nations with your hand,
but you planted them.
You afflicted the peoples,
but you spread them abroad.
3 For they didn't get the land in possession by their own sword,
neither did their own arm save them;
but your right hand, your arm, and the light of your face,
because you were favourable to them.
4 God, you are my King.

Command victories for Jacob!
5 Through you, we will push down our adversaries.
Through your name, we will tread down those who rise up against us.
6 For I will not trust in my bow,
neither will my sword save me.
7 But you have saved us from our adversaries,
and have shamed those who hate us.
8 In God we have made our boast all day long.
We will give thanks to your name forever. Selah.

9 But now you rejected us, and brought us to dishonour,
and don't go out with our armies.
10 You make us turn back from the adversary.
Those who hate us take plunder for themselves.
11 You have made us like sheep for food,
and have scattered us amongst the nations.
12 You sell your people for nothing,
and have gained nothing from their sale.
13 You make us a reproach to our neighbours,
a scoffing and a derision to those who are around us.
14 You make us a byword amongst the nations,
a shaking of the head amongst the peoples.
15 All day long my dishonour is before me,
and shame covers my face,
16 at the taunt of one who reproaches and verbally abuses,
because of the enemy and the avenger.
17 All this has come on us,
yet we haven't forgotten you.
We haven't been false to your covenant.
18 Our heart has not turned back,
neither have our steps strayed from your path,
19 though you have crushed us in the haunt of jackals,
and covered us with the shadow of death.
20 If we have forgotten the name of our God,
or spread out our hands to a strange god,
21 won't God search this out?
For he knows the secrets of the heart.
22 Yes, for your sake we are killed all day long.
We are regarded as sheep for the slaughter.
23 Wake up!
Why do you sleep, Lord?[c]
Arise!
Don't reject us forever.
24 Why do you hide your face,
and forget our affliction and our oppression?
25 For our soul is bowed down to the dust.
Our body clings to the earth.
26 Rise up to help us.
Redeem us for your loving kindness' sake.

45
For the Chief Musician. Set to "The Lilies." A contemplation by the sons of Korah. A wedding song.
1 My heart overflows with a noble theme.
I recite my verses for the king.
My tongue is like the pen of a skilful writer.
2 You are the most excellent of the sons of men.
Grace has anointed your lips,
therefore God has blessed you forever.
3 Strap your sword on your thigh, O mighty one,
in your splendour and your majesty.
4 In your majesty ride on victoriously on behalf of truth, humility, and righteousness.
Let your right hand display awesome deeds.
5 Your arrows are sharp.
The nations fall under you, with arrows in the heart of the king's enemies.
6 Your throne, God, is forever and ever.
A sceptre of equity is the sceptre of your kingdom.
7 You have loved righteousness, and hated wickedness.
Therefore God, your God, has anointed you with the oil of gladness above your fellows.
8 All your garments smell like myrrh, aloes, and cassia.
Out of ivory palaces stringed instruments have made you glad.
9 Kings' daughters are amongst your honourable women.
At your right hand the queen stands in gold of Ophir.
10 Listen, daughter, consider, and turn your ear.
Forget your own people, and also your father's house.
11 So the king will desire your beauty,
honour him, for he is your lord.
12 The daughter of Tyre comes with a gift.
The rich amongst the people entreat your favour.
13 The princess inside is all glorious.
Her clothing is interwoven with gold.
14 She shall be led to the king in embroidered work.

---

a *42:1* The Hebrew word rendered "God" is "אֱלֹהִים" (Elohim).
b *42:8* When rendered in ALL CAPITAL LETTERS, "LORD" or "GOD" is the translation of God's Proper Name.

c *44:23* The word translated "Lord" is "Adonai."

The virgins, her companions who follow her, shall be brought to you.
15 With gladness and rejoicing they shall be led.
They shall enter into the king's palace.
16 Your sons will take the place of your fathers.
You shall make them princes in all the earth.
17 I will make your name to be remembered in all generations.
Therefore the peoples shall give you thanks forever and ever.

46

For the Chief Musician. By the sons of Korah. According to Alamoth.[a]
1 God is our refuge and strength,
a very present help in trouble.
2 Therefore we won't be afraid, though the earth changes,
though the mountains are shaken into the heart of the seas;
3 though its waters roar and are troubled,
though the mountains tremble with their swelling. Selah.

4 There is a river, the streams of which make the city of God glad,
the holy place of the tents of the Most High.
5 God is within her. She shall not be moved.
God will help her at dawn.
6 The nations raged. The kingdoms were moved.
He lifted his voice and the earth melted.
7 The LORD of Armies is with us.
The God of Jacob is our refuge. Selah.

8 Come, see the LORD's works,
what desolations he has made in the earth.
9 He makes wars cease to the end of the earth.
He breaks the bow, and shatters the spear.
He burns the chariots in the fire.
10 "Be still, and know that I am God.
I will be exalted amongst the nations.
I will be exalted in the earth."
11 The LORD of Armies is with us.
The God of Jacob is our refuge. Selah.

47

For the Chief Musician. A Psalm by the sons of Korah.
1 Oh clap your hands, all you nations.
Shout to God with the voice of triumph!
2 For the LORD Most High is awesome.
He is a great King over all the earth.
3 He subdues nations under us,
and peoples under our feet.
4 He chooses our inheritance for us,
the glory of Jacob whom he loved. Selah.
5 God has gone up with a shout,
the LORD with the sound of a trumpet.
6 Sing praises to God! Sing praises!
Sing praises to our King! Sing praises!
7 For God is the King of all the earth.
Sing praises with understanding.
8 God reigns over the nations.
God sits on his holy throne.
9 The princes of the peoples are gathered together,
the people of the God of Abraham.
For the shields of the earth belong to God.
He is greatly exalted!

48

A Song. A Psalm by the sons of Korah.
1 Great is the LORD, and greatly to be praised,
in the city of our God, in his holy mountain.
2 Beautiful in elevation, the joy of the whole earth,
is Mount Zion, on the north sides,
the city of the great King.
3 God has shown himself in her citadels as a refuge.
4 For, behold, the kings assembled themselves,
they passed by together.
5 They saw it, then they were amazed.
They were dismayed.
They hurried away.
6 Trembling took hold of them there,
pain, as of a woman in travail.
7 With the east wind, you break the ships of Tarshish.
8 As we have heard, so we have seen,
in the city of the LORD of Armies, in the city of our God.
God will establish it forever. Selah.
9 We have thought about your loving kindness, God,
in the middle of your temple.
10 As is your name, God,
so is your praise to the ends of the earth.
Your right hand is full of righteousness.
11 Let Mount Zion be glad!
Let the daughters of Judah rejoice because of your judgements.

12 Walk about Zion, and go around her.
Number its towers.
13 Notice her bulwarks.
Consider her palaces,
that you may tell it to the next generation.
14 For this God is our God forever and ever.
He will be our guide even to death.

49

For the Chief Musician. A Psalm by the sons of Korah.
1 Hear this, all you peoples.
Listen, all you inhabitants of the world,
2 both low and high,
rich and poor together.
3 My mouth will speak words of wisdom.
My heart will utter understanding.
4 I will incline my ear to a proverb.
I will solve my riddle on the harp.
5 Why should I fear in the days of evil,
when iniquity at my heels surrounds me?
6 Those who trust in their wealth,
and boast in the multitude of their riches—
7 none of them can by any means redeem his brother,
nor give God a ransom for him.
8 For the redemption of their life is costly,
no payment is ever enough,
9 that he should live on forever,
that he should not see corruption.
10 For he sees that wise men die;
likewise the fool and the senseless perish,
and leave their wealth to others.
11 Their inward thought is that their houses will endure forever,
and their dwelling places to all generations.
They name their lands after themselves.
12 But man, despite his riches, doesn't endure.
He is like the animals that perish.

13 This is the destiny of those who are foolish,
and of those who approve their sayings. Selah.
14 They are appointed as a flock for Sheol.[b]
Death shall be their shepherd.
The upright shall have dominion over them in the morning.
Their beauty shall decay in Sheol,[c]
far from their mansion.
15 But God will redeem my soul from the power of Sheol,[d]
for he will receive me. Selah.
16 Don't be afraid when a man is made rich,
when the glory of his house is increased;
17 for when he dies he will carry nothing away.
His glory won't descend after him.
18 Though while he lived he blessed his soul—
and men praise you when you do well for yourself—
19 he shall go to the generation of his fathers.
They shall never see the light.
20 A man who has riches without understanding,
is like the animals that perish.

50

A Psalm by Asaph.
1 The Mighty One, God, the LORD, speaks,
and calls the earth from sunrise to sunset.
2 Out of Zion, the perfection of beauty,
God shines out.
3 Our God comes, and does not keep silent.
A fire devours before him.
It is very stormy around him.
4 He calls to the heavens above,
to the earth, that he may judge his people:
5 "Gather my saints together to me,
those who have made a covenant with me by sacrifice."
6 The heavens shall declare his righteousness,
for God himself is judge. Selah.
7 "Hear, my people, and I will speak.
Israel, I will testify against you.
I am God, your God.
8 I don't rebuke you for your sacrifices.
Your burnt offerings are continually before me.
9 I have no need for a bull from your stall,
nor male goats from your pens.
10 For every animal of the forest is mine,
and the livestock on a thousand hills.
11 I know all the birds of the mountains.
The wild animals of the field are mine.
12 If I were hungry, I would not tell you,
for the world is mine, and all that is in it.
13 Will I eat the meat of bulls,
or drink the blood of goats?

---

a 46:0 Alamoth is a musical term.
b 49:14 Sheol is the place of the dead.
c 49:14 Sheol is the place of the dead.
d 49:15 Sheol is the place of the dead.

14 Offer to God the sacrifice of thanksgiving.
   Pay your vows to the Most High.
15 Call on me in the day of trouble.
   I will deliver you, and you will honour me."

16 But to the wicked God says,
   "What right do you have to declare my statutes,
   that you have taken my covenant on your lips,
   17 since you hate instruction,
   and throw my words behind you?
18 When you saw a thief, you consented with him,
   and have participated with adulterers.

19 "You give your mouth to evil.
   Your tongue frames deceit.
20 You sit and speak against your brother.
   You slander your own mother's son.
21 You have done these things, and I kept silent.
   You thought that I was just like you.
   I will rebuke you, and accuse you in front of your eyes.

22 "Now consider this, you who forget God,
   lest I tear you into pieces, and there be no one to deliver.
23 Whoever offers the sacrifice of thanksgiving glorifies me,
   and prepares his way so that I will show God's salvation to him."

51

For the Chief Musician. A Psalm by David, when Nathan the prophet came
to him, after he had gone in to Bathsheba.
1 Have mercy on me, God, according to your loving kindness.
   According to the multitude of your tender mercies, blot out my
      transgressions.
2 Wash me thoroughly from my iniquity.
   Cleanse me from my sin.
3 For I know my transgressions.
   My sin is constantly before me.
4 Against you, and you only, I have sinned,
   and done that which is evil in your sight,
so you may be proved right when you speak,
   and justified when you judge.
5 Behold, I was born in iniquity.
   My mother conceived me in sin.
6 Behold, you desire truth in the inward parts.
   You teach me wisdom in the inmost place.
7 Purify me with hyssop, and I will be clean.
   Wash me, and I will be whiter than snow.
8 Let me hear joy and gladness,
   that the bones which you have broken may rejoice.
9 Hide your face from my sins,
   and blot out all of my iniquities.
10 Create in me a clean heart, O God.
   Renew a right spirit within me.
11 Don't throw me from your presence,
   and don't take your Holy Spirit from me.
12 Restore to me the joy of your salvation.
   Uphold me with a willing spirit.
13 Then I will teach transgressors your ways.
   Sinners will be converted to you.
14 Deliver me from the guilt of bloodshed, O God, the God of my salvation.
   My tongue will sing aloud of your righteousness.
15 Lord, open my lips.
   My mouth will declare your praise.
16 For you don't delight in sacrifice, or else I would give it.
   You have no pleasure in burnt offering.
17 The sacrifices of God are a broken spirit.
   O God, you will not despise a broken and contrite heart.

18 Do well in your good pleasure to Zion.
   Build the walls of Jerusalem.
19 Then you will delight in the sacrifices of righteousness,
   in burnt offerings and in whole burnt offerings.
Then they will offer bulls on your altar.

52

For the Chief Musician. A contemplation by David, when Doeg the Edomite
came and told Saul, "David has come to Ahimelech's house."
1 Why do you boast of mischief, mighty man?
   God's loving kindness endures continually.
2 Your tongue plots destruction,
   like a sharp razor, working deceitfully.
3 You love evil more than good,
   lying rather than speaking the truth. Selah.
4 You love all devouring words,
   you deceitful tongue.
5 God will likewise destroy you forever.
   He will take you up, and pluck you out of your tent,
   and root you out of the land of the living. Selah.
6 The righteous also will see it, and fear,
   and laugh at him, saying,
7 "Behold, this is the man who didn't make God his strength,

but trusted in the abundance of his riches,
   and strengthened himself in his wickedness."
8 But as for me, I am like a green olive tree in God's house.
   I trust in God's loving kindness forever and ever.
9 I will give you thanks forever, because you have done it.
   I will hope in your name, for it is good,
   in the presence of your saints.

53

For the Chief Musician. To the tune of "Mahalath." A contemplation by
David.
1 The fool has said in his heart, "There is no God."
   They are corrupt, and have done abominable iniquity.
   There is no one who does good.
2 God looks down from heaven on the children of men,
   to see if there are any who understood,
   who seek after God.
3 Every one of them has gone back.
   They have become filthy together.
   There is no one who does good, no, not one.
4 Have the workers of iniquity no knowledge,
   who eat up my people as they eat bread,
   and don't call on God?
5 There they were in great fear, where no fear was,
   for God has scattered the bones of him who encamps against you.
You have put them to shame,
   because God has rejected them.
6 Oh that the salvation of Israel would come out of Zion!
   When God brings back his people from captivity,
   then Jacob shall rejoice,
   and Israel shall be glad.

54

For the Chief Musician. On stringed instruments. A contemplation by David,
when the Ziphites came and said to Saul, "Isn't David hiding himself
amongst us?"
1 Save me, God, by your name.
   Vindicate me in your might.
2 Hear my prayer, God.
   Listen to the words of my mouth.
3 For strangers have risen up against me.
   Violent men have sought after my soul.
   They haven't set God before them. Selah.
4 Behold, God is my helper.
   The Lord is the one who sustains my soul.
5 He will repay the evil to my enemies.
   Destroy them in your truth.
6 With a free will offering, I will sacrifice to you.
   I will give thanks to your name, LORD, for it is good.
7 For he has delivered me out of all trouble.
   My eye has seen triumph over my enemies.

55

For the Chief Musician. On stringed instruments. A contemplation by David.
1 Listen to my prayer, God.
   Don't hide yourself from my supplication.
2 Attend to me, and answer me.
   I am restless in my complaint,
   and moan 3 because of the voice of the enemy,
   because of the oppression of the wicked.
For they bring suffering on me.
   In anger they hold a grudge against me.
4 My heart is severely pained within me.
   The terrors of death have fallen on me.
5 Fearfulness and trembling have come on me.
   Horror has overwhelmed me.
6 I said, "Oh that I had wings like a dove!
   Then I would fly away, and be at rest.
7 Behold, then I would wander far off.
   I would lodge in the wilderness." Selah.
8 "I would hurry to a shelter from the stormy wind and storm."
9 Confuse them, Lord, and confound their language,
   for I have seen violence and strife in the city.
10 Day and night they prowl around on its walls.
   Malice and abuse are also within her.
11 Destructive forces are within her.
   Threats and lies don't depart from her streets.
12 For it was not an enemy who insulted me,
   then I could have endured it.
Neither was it he who hated me who raised himself up against me,
   then I would have hidden myself from him.
13 But it was you, a man like me,
   my companion, and my familiar friend.
14 We took sweet fellowship together.
   We walked in God's house with company.
15 Let death come suddenly on them.

Let them go down alive into Sheol.[a]
For wickedness is amongst them, in their dwelling.
16 As for me, I will call on God.
The LORD will save me.
17 Evening, morning, and at noon, I will cry out in distress.
He will hear my voice.
18 He has redeemed my soul in peace from the battle that was against me,
although there are many who oppose me.
19 God, who is enthroned forever,
will hear and answer them. Selah.

They never change
and don't fear God.
20 He raises his hands against his friends.
He has violated his covenant.
21 His mouth was smooth as butter,
but his heart was war.
His words were softer than oil,
yet they were drawn swords.

22 Cast your burden on the LORD and he will sustain you.
He will never allow the righteous to be moved.
23 But you, God, will bring them down into the pit of destruction.
Bloodthirsty and deceitful men shall not live out half their days,
but I will trust in you.

56

For the Chief Musician. To the tune of "Silent Dove in Distant Lands." A poem by David, when the Philistines seized him in Gath.
1 Be merciful to me, God, for man wants to swallow me up.
All day long, he attacks and oppresses me.
2 My enemies want to swallow me up all day long,
for they are many who fight proudly against me.
3 When I am afraid,
I will put my trust in you.
4 In God, I praise his word.
In God, I put my trust.
I will not be afraid.
What can flesh do to me?
5 All day long they twist my words.
All their thoughts are against me for evil.
6 They conspire and lurk,
watching my steps.
They are eager to take my life.
7 Shall they escape by iniquity?
In anger cast down the peoples, God.
8 You count my wanderings.
You put my tears into your container.
Aren't they in your book?
9 Then my enemies shall turn back in the day that I call.
I know this: that God is for me.
10 In God, I will praise his word.
In the LORD, I will praise his word.
11 I have put my trust in God.
I will not be afraid.
What can man do to me?
12 Your vows are on me, God.
I will give thank offerings to you.
13 For you have delivered my soul from death,
and prevented my feet from falling,
that I may walk before God in the light of the living.

57

For the Chief Musician. To the tune of "Do Not Destroy." A poem by David, when he fled from Saul, in the cave.
1 Be merciful to me, God, be merciful to me,
for my soul takes refuge in you.
Yes, in the shadow of your wings, I will take refuge,
until disaster has passed.
2 I cry out to God Most High,
to God who accomplishes my requests for me.
3 He will send from heaven, and save me,
he rebukes the one who is pursuing me. Selah.
God will send out his loving kindness and his truth.
4 My soul is amongst lions.
I lie amongst those who are set on fire,
even the sons of men, whose teeth are spears and arrows,
and their tongue a sharp sword.
5 Be exalted, God, above the heavens!
Let your glory be above all the earth!

6 They have prepared a net for my steps.
My soul is bowed down.
They dig a pit before me.
They fall into the middle of it themselves. Selah.
7 My heart is steadfast, God.
My heart is steadfast.
I will sing, yes, I will sing praises.

8 Wake up, my glory! Wake up, lute and harp!
I will wake up the dawn.
9 I will give thanks to you, Lord, amongst the peoples.
I will sing praises to you amongst the nations.
10 For your great loving kindness reaches to the heavens,
and your truth to the skies.
11 Be exalted, God, above the heavens.
Let your glory be over all the earth.

58

For the Chief Musician. To the tune of "Do Not Destroy." A poem by David.
1 Do you indeed speak righteousness, silent ones?
Do you judge blamelessly, you sons of men?
2 No, in your heart you plot injustice.
You measure out the violence of your hands in the earth.
3 The wicked go astray from the womb.
They are wayward as soon as they are born, speaking lies.
4 Their poison is like the poison of a snake,
like a deaf cobra that stops its ear,
5 which doesn't listen to the voice of charmers,
no matter how skilful the charmer may be.
6 Break their teeth, God, in their mouth.
Break out the great teeth of the young lions, LORD.
7 Let them vanish like water that flows away.
When they draw the bow, let their arrows be made blunt.
8 Let them be like a snail which melts and passes away,
like the stillborn child, who has not seen the sun.
9 Before your pots can feel the heat of the thorns,
he will sweep away the green and the burning alike.
10 The righteous shall rejoice when he sees the vengeance.
He shall wash his feet in the blood of the wicked,
11 so that men shall say, "Most certainly there is a reward for the righteous.
Most certainly there is a God who judges the earth."

59

For the Chief Musician. To the tune of "Do Not Destroy." A poem by David, when Saul sent, and they watched the house to kill him.
1 Deliver me from my enemies, my God.
Set me on high from those who rise up against me.
2 Deliver me from the workers of iniquity.
Save me from the bloodthirsty men.
3 For, behold, they lie in wait for my soul.
The mighty gather themselves together against me,
not for my disobedience, nor for my sin, LORD.
4 I have done no wrong, yet they are ready to attack me.
Rise up, behold, and help me!
5 You, LORD God of Armies, the God of Israel,
rouse yourself to punish the nations.
Show no mercy to the wicked traitors. Selah.
6 They return at evening, howling like dogs,
and prowl around the city.
7 Behold, they spew with their mouth.
Swords are in their lips,
"For", they say, "who hears us?"
8 But you, LORD, laugh at them.
You scoff at all the nations.
9 Oh, my Strength, I watch for you,
for God is my high tower.
10 My God will go before me with his loving kindness.
God will let me look at my enemies in triumph.
11 Don't kill them, or my people may forget.
Scatter them by your power, and bring them down, Lord our shield.
12 For the sin of their mouth, and the words of their lips,
let them be caught in their pride,
for the curses and lies which they utter.
13 Consume them in wrath.
Consume them, and they will be no more.
Let them know that God rules in Jacob,
to the ends of the earth. Selah.
14 At evening let them return.
Let them howl like a dog, and go around the city.
15 They shall wander up and down for food,
and wait all night if they aren't satisfied.

16 But I will sing of your strength.
Yes, I will sing aloud of your loving kindness in the morning.
For you have been my high tower,
a refuge in the day of my distress.
17 To you, my strength, I will sing praises.
For God is my high tower, the God of my mercy.

60

For the Chief Musician. To the tune of "The Lily of the Covenant." A teaching poem by David, when he fought with Aram Naharaim and with Aram Zobah, and Joab returned, and killed twelve thousand of Edom in the Valley of Salt.
1 God, you have rejected us.
You have broken us down.

---

[a] 55:15 Sheol is the place of the dead.

You have been angry.
    Restore us, again.
2 You have made the land tremble.
    You have torn it.
Mend its fractures,
    for it quakes.
3 You have shown your people hard things.
    You have made us drink the wine that makes us stagger.
4 You have given a banner to those who fear you,
    that it may be displayed because of the truth. Selah.

5 So that your beloved may be delivered,
    save with your right hand, and answer us.
6 God has spoken from his sanctuary:
    "I will triumph.
    I will divide Shechem,
    and measure out the valley of Succoth.
7 Gilead is mine, and Manasseh is mine.
    Ephraim also is the defence of my head.
    Judah is my sceptre.
8 Moab is my wash basin.
    I will throw my sandal on Edom.
    I shout in triumph over Philistia."

9 Who will bring me into the strong city?
    Who has led me to Edom?
10 Haven't you, God, rejected us?
    You don't go out with our armies, God.
11 Give us help against the adversary,
    for the help of man is vain.
12 Through God we will do valiantly,
    for it is he who will tread down our adversaries.

61

For the Chief Musician. For a stringed instrument. By David.
1 Hear my cry, God.
    Listen to my prayer.
2 From the end of the earth, I will call to you when my heart is
      overwhelmed.
    Lead me to the rock that is higher than I.
3 For you have been a refuge for me,
    a strong tower from the enemy.
4 I will dwell in your tent forever.
    I will take refuge in the shelter of your wings. Selah.
5 For you, God, have heard my vows.
    You have given me the heritage of those who fear your name.
6 You will prolong the king's life.
    His years will be for generations.
7 He shall be enthroned in God's presence forever.
    Appoint your loving kindness and truth, that they may preserve him.
8 So I will sing praise to your name forever,
    that I may fulfil my vows daily.

62

For the Chief Musician. To Jeduthun. A Psalm by David.
1 My soul rests in God alone.
    My salvation is from him.
2 He alone is my rock, my salvation, and my fortress.
    I will never be greatly shaken.
3 How long will you assault a man?
    Would all of you throw him down,
    like a leaning wall, like a tottering fence?
4 They fully intend to throw him down from his lofty place.
    They delight in lies.
    They bless with their mouth, but they curse inwardly. Selah.
5 My soul, wait in silence for God alone,
    for my expectation is from him.
6 He alone is my rock and my salvation, my fortress.
    I will not be shaken.
7 My salvation and my honour is with God.
    The rock of my strength, and my refuge, is in God.
8 Trust in him at all times, you people.
    Pour out your heart before him.
    God is a refuge for us. Selah.
9 Surely men of low degree are just a breath,
    and men of high degree are a lie.
In the balances they will go up.
    They are together lighter than a breath.
10 Don't trust in oppression.
    Don't become vain in robbery.
If riches increase,
    don't set your heart on them.
11 God has spoken once;
    twice I have heard this,
    that power belongs to God.
12 Also to you, Lord, belongs loving kindness,
    for you reward every man according to his work.

63

A Psalm by David, when he was in the desert of Judah.
1 God, you are my God.
    I will earnestly seek you.
My soul thirsts for you.
    My flesh longs for you,
    in a dry and weary land, where there is no water.
2 So I have seen you in the sanctuary,
    watching your power and your glory.
3 Because your loving kindness is better than life,
    my lips shall praise you.
4 So I will bless you while I live.
    I will lift up my hands in your name.
5 My soul shall be satisfied as with the richest food.
    My mouth shall praise you with joyful lips,
    6 when I remember you on my bed,
    and think about you in the night watches.
7 For you have been my help.
    I will rejoice in the shadow of your wings.
8 My soul stays close to you.
    Your right hand holds me up.
9 But those who seek my soul to destroy it
    shall go into the lower parts of the earth.
10 They shall be given over to the power of the sword.
    They shall be jackal food.
11 But the king shall rejoice in God.
    Everyone who swears by him will praise him,
    for the mouth of those who speak lies shall be silenced.

64

For the Chief Musician. A Psalm by David.
1 Hear my voice, God, in my complaint.
    Preserve my life from fear of the enemy.
2 Hide me from the conspiracy of the wicked,
    from the noisy crowd of the ones doing evil;
3 who sharpen their tongue like a sword,
    and aim their arrows, deadly words,
    4 to shoot innocent men from ambushes.
    They shoot at him suddenly and fearlessly.
5 They encourage themselves in evil plans.
    They talk about laying snares secretly.
    They say, "Who will see them?"
6 They plot injustice, saying, "We have made a perfect plan!"
    Surely man's mind and heart are cunning.
7 But God will shoot at them.
    They will be suddenly struck down with an arrow.
8 Their own tongues shall ruin them.
    All who see them will shake their heads.
9 All mankind shall be afraid.
    They shall declare the work of God,
    and shall wisely ponder what he has done.
10 The righteous shall be glad in the LORD,
    and shall take refuge in him.
    All the upright in heart shall praise him!

65

For the Chief Musician. A Psalm by David. A song.
1 Praise waits for you, God, in Zion.
    Vows shall be performed to you.
2 You who hear prayer,
    all men will come to you.
3 Sins overwhelmed me,
    but you atoned for our transgressions.
4 Blessed is the one whom you choose and cause to come near,
    that he may live in your courts.
    We will be filled with the goodness of your house,
    your holy temple.
5 By awesome deeds of righteousness, you answer us,
    God of our salvation.
You who are the hope of all the ends of the earth,
    of those who are far away on the sea.
6 By your power, you form the mountains,
    having armed yourself with strength.
7 You still the roaring of the seas,
    the roaring of their waves,
    and the turmoil of the nations.
8 They also who dwell in faraway places are afraid at your wonders.
    You call the morning's dawn and the evening with songs of joy.
9 You visit the earth, and water it.
    You greatly enrich it.
The river of God is full of water.
    You provide them grain, for so you have ordained it.
10 You drench its furrows.
    You level its ridges.
    You soften it with showers.
    You bless it with a crop.
11 You crown the year with your bounty.
    Your carts overflow with abundance.
12 The wilderness grasslands overflow.

The hills are clothed with gladness.
13 The pastures are covered with flocks.
The valleys also are clothed with grain.
They shout for joy!
They also sing.

66

For the Chief Musician. A song. A Psalm.
1 Make a joyful shout to God, all the earth!
2 Sing to the glory of his name!
Offer glory and praise!
3 Tell God, "How awesome are your deeds!
Through the greatness of your power, your enemies submit themselves to you.
4 All the earth will worship you,
and will sing to you;
they will sing to your name." Selah.
5 Come, and see God's deeds—
awesome work on behalf of the children of men.
6 He turned the sea into dry land.
They went through the river on foot.
There, we rejoiced in him.
7 He rules by his might forever.
His eyes watch the nations.
Don't let the rebellious rise up against him. Selah.
8 Praise our God, you peoples!
Make the sound of his praise heard,
9 who preserves our life amongst the living,
and doesn't allow our feet to be moved.
10 For you, God, have tested us.
You have refined us, as silver is refined.
11 You brought us into prison.
You laid a burden on our backs.
12 You allowed men to ride over our heads.
We went through fire and through water,
but you brought us to the place of abundance.
13 I will come into your temple with burnt offerings.
I will pay my vows to you, 14 which my lips promised,
and my mouth spoke, when I was in distress.
15 I will offer to you burnt offerings of fat animals,
with the offering of rams,
I will offer bulls with goats. Selah.
16 Come and hear, all you who fear God.
I will declare what he has done for my soul.
17 I cried to him with my mouth.
He was extolled with my tongue.
18 If I cherished sin in my heart,
the Lord wouldn't have listened.
19 But most certainly, God has listened.
He has heard the voice of my prayer.
20 Blessed be God, who has not turned away my prayer,
nor his loving kindness from me.

67

For the Chief Musician. With stringed instruments. A Psalm. A song.
1 May God be merciful to us, bless us,
and cause his face to shine on us. Selah.
2 That your way may be known on earth,
and your salvation amongst all nations,
3 let the peoples praise you, God.
Let all the peoples praise you.
4 Oh let the nations be glad and sing for joy,
for you will judge the peoples with equity,
and govern the nations on earth. Selah.
5 Let the peoples praise you, God.
Let all the peoples praise you.
6 The earth has yielded its increase.
God, even our own God, will bless us.
7 God will bless us.
All the ends of the earth shall fear him.

68

For the Chief Musician. A Psalm by David. A song.
1 Let God arise!
Let his enemies be scattered!
Let them who hate him also flee before him.
2 As smoke is driven away,
so drive them away.
As wax melts before the fire,
so let the wicked perish at the presence of God.
3 But let the righteous be glad.
Let them rejoice before God.
Yes, let them rejoice with gladness.
4 Sing to God! Sing praises to his name!
Extol him who rides on the clouds:
to the LORD, his name!
Rejoice before him!
5 A father of the fatherless, and a defender of the widows,
is God in his holy habitation.
6 God sets the lonely in families.

He brings out the prisoners with singing,
but the rebellious dwell in a sun-scorched land.

7 God, when you went out before your people,
when you marched through the wilderness... Selah.
8 The earth trembled.
The sky also poured down rain at the presence of the God of Sinai—
at the presence of God, the God of Israel.
9 You, God, sent a plentiful rain.
You confirmed your inheritance when it was weary.
10 Your congregation lived therein.
You, God, prepared your goodness for the poor.
11 The Lord announced the word.
The ones who proclaim it are a great company.
12 "Kings of armies flee! They flee!"
She who waits at home divides the plunder,
13 while you sleep amongst the camp fires,
the wings of a dove sheathed with silver,
her feathers with shining gold.
14 When the Almighty scattered kings in her,
it snowed on Zalmon.
15 The mountains of Bashan are majestic mountains.
The mountains of Bashan are rugged.
16 Why do you look in envy, you rugged mountains,
at the mountain where God chooses to reign?
Yes, the LORD will dwell there forever.
17 The chariots of God are tens of thousands and thousands of thousands.
The Lord is amongst them, from Sinai, into the sanctuary.
18 You have ascended on high.
You have led away captives.
You have received gifts amongst people,
yes, amongst the rebellious also, that the LORD God might dwell there.

19 Blessed be the Lord, who daily bears our burdens,
even the God who is our salvation. Selah.
20 God is to us a God of deliverance.
To the LORD, the Lord, belongs escape from death.
21 But God will strike through the head of his enemies,
the hairy scalp of such a one as still continues in his guiltiness.
22 The Lord said, "I will bring you again from Bashan,
I will bring you again from the depths of the sea,
23 that you may crush them, dipping your foot in blood,
that the tongues of your dogs may have their portion from your enemies."
24 They have seen your processions, God,
even the processions of my God, my King, into the sanctuary.
25 The singers went before, the minstrels followed after,
amongst the ladies playing with tambourines,
26 "Bless God in the congregations,
even the Lord in the assembly of Israel!"
27 There is little Benjamin, their ruler,
the princes of Judah, their council,
the princes of Zebulun, and the princes of Naphtali.

28 Your God has commanded your strength.
Strengthen, God, that which you have done for us.
29 Because of your temple at Jerusalem,
kings shall bring presents to you.
30 Rebuke the wild animal of the reeds,
the multitude of the bulls with the calves of the peoples.
Trample under foot the bars of silver.
Scatter the nations who delight in war.
31 Princes shall come out of Egypt.
Ethiopia shall hurry to stretch out her hands to God.
32 Sing to God, you kingdoms of the earth!
Sing praises to the Lord— Selah—
33 to him who rides on the heaven of heavens, which are of old;
behold, he utters his voice, a mighty voice.
34 Ascribe strength to God!
His excellency is over Israel,
his strength is in the skies.
35 You are awesome, God, in your sanctuaries.
The God of Israel gives strength and power to his people.
Praise be to God!

69

For the Chief Musician. To the tune of "Lilies." By David.
1 Save me, God,
for the waters have come up to my neck!
2 I sink in deep mire, where there is no foothold.
I have come into deep waters, where the floods overflow me.
3 I am weary with my crying.
My throat is dry.
My eyes fail looking for my God.
4 Those who hate me without a cause are more than the hairs of my head.
Those who want to cut me off, being my enemies wrongfully, are mighty.
I have to restore what I didn't take away.
5 God, you know my foolishness.

My sins aren't hidden from you.

6 Don't let those who wait for you be shamed through me, Lord GOD of Armies.

  Don't let those who seek you be brought to dishonour through me, God of Israel.

7 Because for your sake, I have borne reproach.

  Shame has covered my face.

8 I have become a stranger to my brothers,

  an alien to my mother's children.

9 For the zeal of your house consumes me.

  The reproaches of those who reproach you have fallen on me.

10 When I wept and I fasted,

  that was to my reproach.

11 When I made sackcloth my clothing,

  I became a byword to them.

12 Those who sit in the gate talk about me.

  I am the song of the drunkards.

13 But as for me, my prayer is to you, LORD, in an acceptable time.

  God, in the abundance of your loving kindness, answer me in the truth of your salvation.

14 Deliver me out of the mire, and don't let me sink.

  Let me be delivered from those who hate me, and out of the deep waters.

15 Don't let the flood waters overwhelm me,

  neither let the deep swallow me up.

  Don't let the pit shut its mouth on me.

16 Answer me, LORD, for your loving kindness is good.

  According to the multitude of your tender mercies, turn to me.

17 Don't hide your face from your servant,

  for I am in distress.

  Answer me speedily!

18 Draw near to my soul and redeem it.

  Ransom me because of my enemies.

19 You know my reproach, my shame, and my dishonour.

  My adversaries are all before you.

20 Reproach has broken my heart, and I am full of heaviness.

  I looked for some to take pity, but there was none;

  for comforters, but I found none.

21 They also gave me poison for my food.

  In my thirst, they gave me vinegar to drink.

22 Let their table before them become a snare.

  May it become a retribution and a trap.

23 Let their eyes be darkened, so that they can't see.

  Let their backs be continually bent.

24 Pour out your indignation on them.

  Let the fierceness of your anger overtake them.

25 Let their habitation be desolate.

  Let no one dwell in their tents.

26 For they persecute him whom you have wounded.

  They tell of the sorrow of those whom you have hurt.

27 Charge them with crime upon crime.

  Don't let them come into your righteousness.

28 Let them be blotted out of the book of life,

  and not be written with the righteous.

29 But I am in pain and distress.

  Let your salvation, God, protect me.

30 I will praise the name of God with a song,

  and will magnify him with thanksgiving.

31 It will please the LORD better than an ox,

  or a bull that has horns and hoofs.

32 The humble have seen it, and are glad.

  You who seek after God, let your heart live.

33 For the LORD hears the needy,

  and doesn't despise his captive people.

34 Let heaven and earth praise him;

  the seas, and everything that moves therein!

35 For God will save Zion, and build the cities of Judah.

  They shall settle there, and own it.

36 The children also of his servants shall inherit it.

  Those who love his name shall dwell therein.

70

For the Chief Musician. By David. A reminder.

1 Hurry, God, to deliver me.

  Come quickly to help me, LORD.

2 Let them be disappointed and confounded who seek my soul.

  Let those who desire my ruin be turned back in disgrace.

3 Let them be turned because of their shame

  who say, "Aha! Aha!"

4 Let all those who seek you rejoice and be glad in you.

  Let those who love your salvation continually say,

  "Let God be exalted!"

5 But I am poor and needy.

  Come to me quickly, God.

You are my help and my deliverer.

  LORD, don't delay.

71

1 In you, LORD, I take refuge.

Never let me be disappointed.

2 Deliver me in your righteousness, and rescue me.

  Turn your ear to me, and save me.

3 Be to me a rock of refuge to which I may always go.

  Give the command to save me,

  for you are my rock and my fortress.

4 Rescue me, my God, from the hand of the wicked,

  from the hand of the unrighteous and cruel man.

5 For you are my hope, Lord GOD,

  my confidence from my youth.

6 I have relied on you from the womb.

  You are he who took me out of my mother's womb.

  I will always praise you.

7 I am a marvel to many,

  but you are my strong refuge.

8 My mouth shall be filled with your praise,

  with your honour all day long.

9 Don't reject me in my old age.

  Don't forsake me when my strength fails.

10 For my enemies talk about me.

  Those who watch for my soul conspire together,

  11 saying, "God has forsaken him.

  Pursue and take him, for no one will rescue him."

12 God, don't be far from me.

  My God, hurry to help me.

13 Let my accusers be disappointed and consumed.

  Let them be covered with disgrace and scorn who want to harm me.

14 But I will always hope,

  and will add to all of your praise.

15 My mouth will tell about your righteousness,

  and of your salvation all day,

  though I don't know its full measure.

16 I will come with the mighty acts of the Lord GOD.

  I will make mention of your righteousness, even of yours alone.

17 God, you have taught me from my youth.

  Until now, I have declared your wondrous works.

18 Yes, even when I am old and grey-haired, God, don't forsake me,

  until I have declared your strength to the next generation,

  your might to everyone who is to come.

19 God, your righteousness also reaches to the heavens.

  You have done great things.

  God, who is like you?

20 You, who have shown us many and bitter troubles,

  you will let me live.

  You will bring us up again from the depths of the earth.

21 Increase my honour

  and comfort me again.

22 I will also praise you with the harp for your faithfulness, my God.

  I sing praises to you with the lyre, Holy One of Israel.

23 My lips shall shout for joy!

  My soul, which you have redeemed, sings praises to you!

24 My tongue will also talk about your righteousness all day long,

  for they are disappointed, and they are confounded,

  who want to harm me.

72

By Solomon.

1 God, give the king your justice;

  your righteousness to the royal son.

2 He will judge your people with righteousness,

  and your poor with justice.

3 The mountains shall bring prosperity to the people.

  The hills bring the fruit of righteousness.

4 He will judge the poor of the people.

  He will save the children of the needy,

  and will break the oppressor in pieces.

5 They shall fear you while the sun endures;

  and as long as the moon, throughout all generations.

6 He will come down like rain on the mown grass,

  as showers that water the earth.

7 In his days, the righteous shall flourish,

  and abundance of peace, until the moon is no more.

8 He shall have dominion also from sea to sea,

  from the River to the ends of the earth.

9 Those who dwell in the wilderness shall bow before him.

  His enemies shall lick the dust.

10 The kings of Tarshish and of the islands will bring tribute.

  The kings of Sheba and Seba shall offer gifts.

11 Yes, all kings shall fall down before him.

  All nations shall serve him.

12 For he will deliver the needy when he cries;

  the poor, who has no helper.

13 He will have pity on the poor and needy.

  He will save the souls of the needy.

14 He will redeem their soul from oppression and violence.

  Their blood will be precious in his sight.

15 He will live; and Sheba's gold will be given to him.

  Men will pray for him continually.

  They will bless him all day long.

16 Abundance of grain shall be throughout the land.

Its fruit sways like Lebanon.
    Let it flourish, thriving like the grass of the field.
17 His name endures forever.
    His name continues as long as the sun.
Men shall be blessed by him.
    All nations will call him blessed.

18 Praise be to the LORD God, the God of Israel,
    who alone does marvellous deeds.
19 Blessed be his glorious name forever!
    Let the whole earth be filled with his glory!
Amen and amen.

20 This ends the prayers by David, the son of Jesse.

73

Book 3

A Psalm by Asaph.

1 Surely God[a] is good to Israel,
    to those who are pure in heart.
2 But as for me, my feet were almost gone.
    My steps had nearly slipped.
3 For I was envious of the arrogant,
    when I saw the prosperity of the wicked.
4 For there are no struggles in their death,
    but their strength is firm.
5 They are free from burdens of men,
    neither are they plagued like other men.
6 Therefore pride is like a chain around their neck.
    Violence covers them like a garment.
7 Their eyes bulge with fat.
    Their minds pass the limits of conceit.
8 They scoff and speak with malice.
    In arrogance, they threaten oppression.
9 They have set their mouth in the heavens.
    Their tongue walks through the earth.
10 Therefore their people return to them,
    and they drink up waters of abundance.
11 They say, "How does God know?
    Is there knowledge in the Most High?"
12 Behold, these are the wicked.
    Being always at ease, they increase in riches.
13 Surely I have cleansed my heart in vain,
    and washed my hands in innocence,
14 For all day long I have been plagued,
    and punished every morning.
15 If I had said, "I will speak thus",
    behold, I would have betrayed the generation of your children.
16 When I tried to understand this,
    it was too painful for me—
17 until I entered God's sanctuary,
    and considered their latter end.
18 Surely you set them in slippery places.
    You throw them down to destruction.
19 How they are suddenly destroyed!
    They are completely swept away with terrors.
20 As a dream when one wakes up,
    so, Lord,[b] when you awake, you will despise their fantasies.
21 For my soul was grieved.
    I was embittered in my heart.
22 I was so senseless and ignorant.
    I was a brute beast before you.
23 Nevertheless, I am continually with you.
    You have held my right hand.
24 You will guide me with your counsel,
    and afterward receive me to glory.
25 Whom do I have in heaven?
    There is no one on earth whom I desire besides you.
26 My flesh and my heart fails,
    but God is the strength of my heart and my portion forever.
27 For, behold, those who are far from you shall perish.
    You have destroyed all those who are unfaithful to you.
28 But it is good for me to come close to God.
    I have made the Lord the LORD[c] my refuge,
    that I may tell of all your works.

74

A contemplation by Asaph.

1 God, why have you rejected us forever?
    Why does your anger smoulder against the sheep of your pasture?
2 Remember your congregation, which you purchased of old,
    which you have redeemed to be the tribe of your inheritance:
    Mount Zion, in which you have lived.
3 Lift up your feet to the perpetual ruins,
    all the evil that the enemy has done in the sanctuary.
4 Your adversaries have roared in the middle of your assembly.

    They have set up their standards as signs.
5 They behaved like men wielding axes,
    cutting through a thicket of trees.
6 Now they break all its carved work down with hatchet and hammers.
7 They have burnt your sanctuary to the ground.
    They have profaned the dwelling place of your Name.
8 They said in their heart, "We will crush them completely."
    They have burnt up all the places in the land where God was
        worshipped.
9 We see no miraculous signs.
    There is no longer any prophet,
    neither is there amongst us anyone who knows how long.
10 How long, God, shall the adversary reproach?
    Shall the enemy blaspheme your name forever?
11 Why do you draw back your hand, even your right hand?
    Take it from your chest and consume them!

12 Yet God is my King of old,
    working salvation throughout the earth.
13 You divided the sea by your strength.
    You broke the heads of the sea monsters in the waters.
14 You broke the heads of Leviathan in pieces.
    You gave him as food to people and desert creatures.
15 You opened up spring and stream.
    You dried up mighty rivers.
16 The day is yours, the night is also yours.
    You have prepared the light and the sun.
17 You have set all the boundaries of the earth.
    You have made summer and winter.

18 Remember this, that the enemy has mocked you, LORD.
    Foolish people have blasphemed your name.
19 Don't deliver the soul of your dove to wild beasts.
    Don't forget the life of your poor forever.
20 Honour your covenant,
    for haunts of violence fill the dark places of the earth.
21 Don't let the oppressed return ashamed.
    Let the poor and needy praise your name.
22 Arise, God! Plead your own cause.
    Remember how the foolish man mocks you all day.
23 Don't forget the voice of your adversaries.
    The tumult of those who rise up against you ascends continually.

75

For the Chief Musician. To the tune of "Do Not Destroy." A Psalm by Asaph. A song.

1 We give thanks to you, God.
    We give thanks, for your Name is near.
    Men tell about your wondrous works.

2 When I choose the appointed time,
    I will judge blamelessly.
3 The earth and all its inhabitants quake.
    I firmly hold its pillars. Selah.
4 I said to the arrogant, "Don't boast!"
    I said to the wicked, "Don't lift up the horn.
5 Don't lift up your horn on high.
    Don't speak with a stiff neck."
6 For neither from the east, nor from the west,
    nor yet from the south, comes exaltation.
7 But God is the judge.
    He puts down one, and lifts up another.
8 For in the LORD's hand there is a cup,
    full of foaming wine mixed with spices.
He pours it out.
    Indeed the wicked of the earth drink and drink it to its very dregs.

9 But I will declare this forever:
    I will sing praises to the God of Jacob.
10 I will cut off all the horns of the wicked,
    but the horns of the righteous shall be lifted up.

76

For the Chief Musician. On stringed instruments. A Psalm by Asaph. A song.

1 In Judah, God is known.
    His name is great in Israel.
2 His tabernacle is also in Salem.
    His dwelling place in Zion.
3 There he broke the flaming arrows of the bow,
    the shield, and the sword, and the weapons of war. Selah.
4 Glorious are you, and excellent,
    more than mountains of game.
5 Valiant men lie plundered,
    they have slept their last sleep.

---

a 73:1 The Hebrew word rendered "God" is "אֱלֹהִים" (Elohim).
b 73:20 The word translated "Lord" is "Adonai."

c 73:28 When rendered in ALL CAPITAL LETTERS, "LORD" or "GOD" is the translation of God's Proper Name.

None of the men of war can lift their hands.
6 At your rebuke, God of Jacob,
both chariot and horse are cast into a dead sleep.
7 You, even you, are to be feared.
Who can stand in your sight when you are angry?
8 You pronounced judgement from heaven.
The earth feared, and was silent,
9 when God arose to judgement,
to save all the afflicted ones of the earth. Selah.
10 Surely the wrath of man praises you.
The survivors of your wrath are restrained.
11 Make vows to the LORD your God, and fulfil them!
Let all of his neighbours bring presents to him who is to be feared.
12 He will cut off the spirit of princes.
He is feared by the kings of the earth.

77

For the Chief Musician. To Jeduthun. A Psalm by Asaph.
1 My cry goes to God!
Indeed, I cry to God for help,
and for him to listen to me.
2 In the day of my trouble I sought the Lord.
My hand was stretched out in the night, and didn't get tired.
My soul refused to be comforted.
3 I remember God, and I groan.
I complain, and my spirit is overwhelmed. Selah.

4 You hold my eyelids open.
I am so troubled that I can't speak.
5 I have considered the days of old,
the years of ancient times.
6 I remember my song in the night.
I consider in my own heart;
my spirit diligently enquires:
7 "Will the Lord reject us forever?
Will he be favourable no more?
8 Has his loving kindness vanished forever?
Does his promise fail for generations?
9 Has God forgotten to be gracious?
Has he, in anger, withheld his compassion?" Selah.
10 Then I thought, "I will appeal to this:
the years of the right hand of the Most High."
11 I will remember the LORD's deeds;
for I will remember your wonders of old.
12 I will also meditate on all your work,
and consider your doings.
13 Your way, God, is in the sanctuary.
What god is great like God?
14 You are the God who does wonders.
You have made your strength known amongst the peoples.
15 You have redeemed your people with your arm,
the sons of Jacob and Joseph. Selah.
16 The waters saw you, God.
The waters saw you, and they writhed.
The depths also convulsed.
17 The clouds poured out water.
The skies resounded with thunder.
Your arrows also flashed around.
18 The voice of your thunder was in the whirlwind.
The lightnings lit up the world.
The earth trembled and shook.
19 Your way was through the sea,
your paths through the great waters.
Your footsteps were not known.
20 You led your people like a flock,
by the hand of Moses and Aaron.

78

A contemplation by Asaph.
1 Hear my teaching, my people.
Turn your ears to the words of my mouth.
2 I will open my mouth in a parable.
I will utter dark sayings of old,
3 which we have heard and known,
and our fathers have told us.
4 We will not hide them from their children,
telling to the generation to come the praises of the LORD,
his strength, and his wondrous deeds that he has done.
5 For he established a covenant in Jacob,
and appointed a teaching in Israel,
which he commanded our fathers,
that they should make them known to their children;
6 that the generation to come might know, even the children who should be born;
who should arise and tell their children,
7 that they might set their hope in God,
and not forget God's deeds,
but keep his commandments,

8 and might not be as their fathers—
a stubborn and rebellious generation,
a generation that didn't make their hearts loyal,
whose spirit was not steadfast with God.
9 The children of Ephraim, being armed and carrying bows,
turned back in the day of battle.
10 They didn't keep God's covenant,
and refused to walk in his law.
11 They forgot his doings,
his wondrous deeds that he had shown them.
12 He did marvellous things in the sight of their fathers,
in the land of Egypt, in the field of Zoan.
13 He split the sea, and caused them to pass through.
He made the waters stand as a heap.
14 In the daytime he also led them with a cloud,
and all night with a light of fire.
15 He split rocks in the wilderness,
and gave them drink abundantly as out of the depths.
16 He brought streams also out of the rock,
and caused waters to run down like rivers.
17 Yet they still went on to sin against him,
to rebel against the Most High in the desert.
18 They tempted God in their heart
by asking food according to their desire.
19 Yes, they spoke against God.
They said, "Can God prepare a table in the wilderness?
20 Behold, he struck the rock, so that waters gushed out,
and streams overflowed.
Can he give bread also?
Will he provide meat for his people?"
21 Therefore the LORD heard, and was angry.
A fire was kindled against Jacob,
anger also went up against Israel,
22 because they didn't believe in God,
and didn't trust in his salvation.
23 Yet he commanded the skies above,
and opened the doors of heaven.
24 He rained down manna on them to eat,
and gave them food from the sky.
25 Man ate the bread of angels.
He sent them food to the full.
26 He caused the east wind to blow in the sky.
By his power he guided the south wind.
27 He also rained meat on them as the dust,
winged birds as the sand of the seas.
28 He let them fall in the middle of their camp,
around their habitations.
29 So they ate, and were well filled.
He gave them their own desire.
30 They didn't turn from their cravings.
Their food was yet in their mouths,
31 when the anger of God went up against them,
killed some of their strongest,
and struck down the young men of Israel.
32 For all this they still sinned,
and didn't believe in his wondrous works.
33 Therefore he consumed their days in vanity,
and their years in terror.
34 When he killed them, then they enquired after him.
They returned and sought God earnestly.
35 They remembered that God was their rock,
the Most High God, their redeemer.
36 But they flattered him with their mouth,
and lied to him with their tongue.
37 For their heart was not right with him,
neither were they faithful in his covenant.
38 But he, being merciful, forgave iniquity, and didn't destroy them.
Yes, many times he turned his anger away,
and didn't stir up all his wrath.
39 He remembered that they were but flesh,
a wind that passes away, and doesn't come again.
40 How often they rebelled against him in the wilderness,
and grieved him in the desert!
41 They turned again and tempted God,
and provoked the Holy One of Israel.
42 They didn't remember his hand,
nor the day when he redeemed them from the adversary;
43 how he set his signs in Egypt,
his wonders in the field of Zoan,
44 he turned their rivers into blood,
and their streams, so that they could not drink.
45 He sent amongst them swarms of flies, which devoured them;
and frogs, which destroyed them.
46 He also gave their increase to the caterpillar,
and their labour to the locust.
47 He destroyed their vines with hail,
their sycamore fig trees with frost.
48 He also gave over their livestock to the hail,
and their flocks to hot thunderbolts.

49 He threw on them the fierceness of his anger,
   wrath, indignation, and trouble,
   and a band of angels of evil.
50 He made a path for his anger.
   He didn't spare their soul from death,
   but gave their life over to the pestilence,
51 and struck all the firstborn in Egypt,
   the chief of their strength in the tents of Ham.
52 But he led out his own people like sheep,
   and guided them in the wilderness like a flock.
53 He led them safely, so that they weren't afraid,
   but the sea overwhelmed their enemies.
54 He brought them to the border of his sanctuary,
   to this mountain, which his right hand had taken.
55 He also drove out the nations before them,
   allotted them for an inheritance by line,
   and made the tribes of Israel to dwell in their tents.
56 Yet they tempted and rebelled against the Most High God,
   and didn't keep his testimonies,
57 but turned back, and dealt treacherously like their fathers.
   They were twisted like a deceitful bow.
58 For they provoked him to anger with their high places,
   and moved him to jealousy with their engraved images.
59 When God heard this, he was angry,
   and greatly abhorred Israel,
60 so that he abandoned the tent of Shiloh,
   the tent which he placed amongst men,
61 and delivered his strength into captivity,
   his glory into the adversary's hand.
62 He also gave his people over to the sword,
   and was angry with his inheritance.
63 Fire devoured their young men.
   Their virgins had no wedding song.
64 Their priests fell by the sword,
   and their widows couldn't weep.
65 Then the Lord awakened as one out of sleep,
   like a mighty man who shouts by reason of wine.
66 He struck his adversaries backward.
   He put them to a perpetual reproach.
67 Moreover he rejected the tent of Joseph,
   and didn't choose the tribe of Ephraim,
68 But chose the tribe of Judah,
   Mount Zion which he loved.
69 He built his sanctuary like the heights,
   like the earth which he has established forever.
70 He also chose David his servant,
   and took him from the sheepfolds;
71 from following the ewes that have their young,
   he brought him to be the shepherd of Jacob, his people,
   and Israel, his inheritance.
72 So he was their shepherd according to the integrity of his heart,
   and guided them by the skilfulness of his hands.

79

A Psalm by Asaph.
1 God, the nations have come into your inheritance.
   They have defiled your holy temple.
   They have laid Jerusalem in heaps.
2 They have given the dead bodies of your servants to be food for the birds
     of the sky,
   the flesh of your saints to the animals of the earth.
3 They have shed their blood like water around Jerusalem.
   There was no one to bury them.
4 We have become a reproach to our neighbours,
   a scoffing and derision to those who are around us.
5 How long, LORD?
   Will you be angry forever?
   Will your jealousy burn like fire?
6 Pour out your wrath on the nations that don't know you,
   on the kingdoms that don't call on your name,
7 for they have devoured Jacob,
   and destroyed his homeland.
8 Don't hold the iniquities of our forefathers against us.
   Let your tender mercies speedily meet us,
   for we are in desperate need.
9 Help us, God of our salvation, for the glory of your name.
   Deliver us, and forgive our sins, for your name's sake.
10 Why should the nations say, "Where is their God?"
   Let it be known amongst the nations, before our eyes,
   that vengeance for your servants' blood is being poured out.
11 Let the sighing of the prisoner come before you.
   According to the greatness of your power, preserve those who are
     sentenced to death.
12 Pay back to our neighbours seven times into their bosom
   their reproach with which they have reproached you, Lord.
13 So we, your people and sheep of your pasture,
   will give you thanks forever.
   We will praise you forever, to all generations.

80

For the Chief Musician. To the tune of "The Lilies of the Covenant." A Psalm
by Asaph.
1 Hear us, Shepherd of Israel,
   you who lead Joseph like a flock,
   you who sit above the cherubim, shine out.
2 Before Ephraim, Benjamin, and Manasseh, stir up your might!
   Come to save us!
3 Turn us again, God.
   Cause your face to shine,
   and we will be saved.

4 LORD God of Armies,
   how long will you be angry against the prayer of your people?
5 You have fed them with the bread of tears,
   and given them tears to drink in large measure.
6 You make us a source of contention to our neighbours.
   Our enemies laugh amongst themselves.
7 Turn us again, God of Armies.
   Cause your face to shine,
   and we will be saved.

8 You brought a vine out of Egypt.
   You drove out the nations, and planted it.
9 You cleared the ground for it.
   It took deep root, and filled the land.
10 The mountains were covered with its shadow.
   Its boughs were like God's cedars.
11 It sent out its branches to the sea,
   its shoots to the River.
12 Why have you broken down its walls,
   so that all those who pass by the way pluck it?
13 The boar out of the wood ravages it.
   The wild animals of the field feed on it.
14 Turn again, we beg you, God of Armies.
   Look down from heaven, and see, and visit this vine,
15 the stock which your right hand planted,
   the branch that you made strong for yourself.
16 It's burnt with fire.
   It's cut down.
   They perish at your rebuke.
17 Let your hand be on the man of your right hand,
   on the son of man whom you made strong for yourself.
18 So we will not turn away from you.
   Revive us, and we will call on your name.
19 Turn us again, LORD God of Armies.
   Cause your face to shine, and we will be saved.

81

For the Chief Musician. On an instrument of Gath. By Asaph.
1 Sing aloud to God, our strength!
   Make a joyful shout to the God of Jacob!
2 Raise a song, and bring here the tambourine,
   the pleasant lyre with the harp.
3 Blow the trumpet at the New Moon,
   at the full moon, on our feast day.
4 For it is a statute for Israel,
   an ordinance of the God of Jacob.
5 He appointed it in Joseph for a covenant,
   when he went out over the land of Egypt,
   I heard a language that I didn't know.
6 "I removed his shoulder from the burden.
   His hands were freed from the basket.
7 You called in trouble, and I delivered you.
   I answered you in the secret place of thunder.
   I tested you at the waters of Meribah." Selah.

8 "Hear, my people, and I will testify to you,
   Israel, if you would listen to me!
9 There shall be no strange god in you,
   neither shall you worship any foreign god.
10 I am the LORD, your God,
   who brought you up out of the land of Egypt.
   Open your mouth wide, and I will fill it.
11 But my people didn't listen to my voice.
   Israel desired none of me.
12 So I let them go after the stubbornness of their hearts,
   that they might walk in their own counsels.
13 Oh that my people would listen to me,
   that Israel would walk in my ways!
14 I would soon subdue their enemies,
   and turn my hand against their adversaries.
15 The haters of the LORD would cringe before him,
   and their punishment would last forever.
16 But he would have also fed them with the finest of the wheat.
   I will satisfy you with honey out of the rock."

82

A Psalm by Asaph.

1 God presides in the great assembly.
  He judges amongst the gods.
2 "How long will you judge unjustly,
  and show partiality to the wicked?" Selah.

3 "Defend the weak, the poor, and the fatherless.
  Maintain the rights of the poor and oppressed.
4 Rescue the weak and needy.
  Deliver them out of the hand of the wicked."
5 They don't know, neither do they understand.
  They walk back and forth in darkness.
  All the foundations of the earth are shaken.
6 I said, "You are gods,
  all of you are sons of the Most High.
7 Nevertheless you shall die like men,
  and fall like one of the rulers."
8 Arise, God, judge the earth,
  for you inherit all of the nations.

83

A song. A Psalm by Asaph.

1 God, don't keep silent.
  Don't keep silent,
  and don't be still, God.
2 For, behold, your enemies are stirred up.
  Those who hate you have lifted up their heads.
3 They conspire with cunning against your people.
  They plot against your cherished ones.
4 "Come," they say, "let's destroy them as a nation,
  that the name of Israel may be remembered no more."
5 For they have conspired together with one mind.
  They form an alliance against you.
6 The tents of Edom and the Ishmaelites;
  Moab, and the Hagrites;
7 Gebal, Ammon, and Amalek;
  Philistia with the inhabitants of Tyre;
8 Assyria also is joined with them.
  They have helped the children of Lot. Selah.
9 Do to them as you did to Midian,
  as to Sisera, as to Jabin, at the river Kishon;
10 who perished at Endor,
  who became as dung for the earth.
11 Make their nobles like Oreb and Zeeb,
  yes, all their princes like Zebah and Zalmunna,
  12 who said, "Let's take possession of God's pasture lands."
13 My God, make them like tumbleweed,
  like chaff before the wind.
14 As the fire that burns the forest,
  as the flame that sets the mountains on fire,
  15 so pursue them with your tempest,
  and terrify them with your storm.
16 Fill their faces with confusion,
  that they may seek your name, LORD.
17 Let them be disappointed and dismayed forever.
  Yes, let them be confounded and perish;
  18 that they may know that you alone, whose name is the LORD,
  are the Most High over all the earth.

84

For the Chief Musician. On an instrument of Gath. A Psalm by the sons of Korah.

1 How lovely are your dwellings,
  LORD of Armies!
2 My soul longs, and even faints for the courts of the LORD.
  My heart and my flesh cry out for the living God.
3 Yes, the sparrow has found a home,
  and the swallow a nest for herself, where she may have her young,
  near your altars, LORD of Armies, my King, and my God.
4 Blessed are those who dwell in your house.
  They are always praising you. Selah.
5 Blessed are those whose strength is in you,
  who have set their hearts on a pilgrimage.
6 Passing through the valley of Weeping, they make it a place of springs.
  Yes, the autumn rain covers it with blessings.
7 They go from strength to strength.
  Every one of them appears before God in Zion.
8 LORD, God of Armies, hear my prayer.
  Listen, God of Jacob. Selah.
9 Behold, God our shield,
  look at the face of your anointed.
10 For a day in your courts is better than a thousand.
  I would rather be a doorkeeper in the house of my God,
  than to dwell in the tents of wickedness.
11 For the LORD God is a sun and a shield.
  The LORD will give grace and glory.

He withholds no good thing from those who walk blamelessly.
12 LORD of Armies,
  blessed is the man who trusts in you.

85

For the Chief Musician. A Psalm by the sons of Korah.

1 LORD, you have been favourable to your land.
  You have restored the fortunes of Jacob.
2 You have forgiven the iniquity of your people.
  You have covered all their sin. Selah.
3 You have taken away all your wrath.
  You have turned from the fierceness of your anger.
4 Turn us, God of our salvation,
  and cause your indignation towards us to cease.
5 Will you be angry with us forever?
  Will you draw out your anger to all generations?
6 Won't you revive us again,
  that your people may rejoice in you?
7 Show us your loving kindness, LORD.
  Grant us your salvation.
8 I will hear what God, the LORD, will speak,
  for he will speak peace to his people, his saints;
  but let them not turn again to folly.
9 Surely his salvation is near those who fear him,
  that glory may dwell in our land.
10 Mercy and truth meet together.
  Righteousness and peace have kissed each other.
11 Truth springs out of the earth.
  Righteousness has looked down from heaven.
12 Yes, the LORD will give that which is good.
  Our land will yield its increase.
13 Righteousness goes before him,
  and prepares the way for his steps.

86

A Prayer by David.

1 Hear, LORD, and answer me,
  for I am poor and needy.
2 Preserve my soul, for I am godly.
  You, my God, save your servant who trusts in you.
3 Be merciful to me, Lord,
  for I call to you all day long.
4 Bring joy to the soul of your servant,
  for to you, Lord, do I lift up my soul.
5 For you, Lord, are good, and ready to forgive,
  abundant in loving kindness to all those who call on you.
6 Hear, LORD, my prayer.
  Listen to the voice of my petitions.
7 In the day of my trouble I will call on you,
  for you will answer me.
8 There is no one like you amongst the gods, Lord,
  nor any deeds like your deeds.
9 All nations you have made will come and worship before you, Lord.
  They shall glorify your name.
10 For you are great, and do wondrous things.
  You are God alone.
11 Teach me your way, LORD.
  I will walk in your truth.
  Make my heart undivided to fear your name.
12 I will praise you, Lord my God, with my whole heart.
  I will glorify your name forever more.
13 For your loving kindness is great towards me.
  You have delivered my soul from the lowest Sheol.[a]
14 God, the proud have risen up against me.
  A company of violent men have sought after my soul,
  and they don't hold regard for you before them.
15 But you, Lord, are a merciful and gracious God,
  slow to anger, and abundant in loving kindness and truth.
16 Turn to me, and have mercy on me!
  Give your strength to your servant.
  Save the son of your servant.
17 Show me a sign of your goodness,
  that those who hate me may see it, and be shamed,
  because you, LORD, have helped me, and comforted me.

87

A Psalm by the sons of Korah; a Song.

1 His foundation is in the holy mountains.
  2 The LORD loves the gates of Zion more than all the dwellings of Jacob.
3 Glorious things are spoken about you, city of God. Selah.
4 I will record Rahab[b] and Babylon amongst those who acknowledge me.
  Behold, Philistia, Tyre, and also Ethiopia:
  "This one was born there."
5 Yes, of Zion it will be said, "This one and that one was born in her;"
  the Most High himself will establish her.
6 The LORD will count, when he writes up the peoples,
  "This one was born there." Selah.

_____

a 86:13 Sheol is the place of the dead.

b 87:4 Rahab is a reference to Egypt.

7 Those who sing as well as those who dance say,
   "All my springs are in you."

88

A Song. A Psalm by the sons of Korah. For the Chief Musician. To the tune
of "The Suffering of Affliction." A contemplation by Heman, the Ezrahite.
1 LORD, the God of my salvation,
   I have cried day and night before you.
2 Let my prayer enter into your presence.
   Turn your ear to my cry.
3 For my soul is full of troubles.
   My life draws near to Sheol.[a]
4 I am counted amongst those who go down into the pit.
   I am like a man who has no help,
5 set apart amongst the dead,
   like the slain who lie in the grave,
   whom you remember no more.
   They are cut off from your hand.
6 You have laid me in the lowest pit,
   in the darkest depths.
7 Your wrath lies heavily on me.
   You have afflicted me with all your waves. Selah.
8 You have taken my friends from me.
   You have made me an abomination to them.
   I am confined, and I can't escape.
9 My eyes are dim from grief.
   I have called on you daily, LORD.
   I have spread out my hands to you.
10 Do you show wonders to the dead?
   Do the departed spirits rise up and praise you? Selah.
11 Is your loving kindness declared in the grave?
   Or your faithfulness in Destruction?
12 Are your wonders made known in the dark?
   Or your righteousness in the land of forgetfulness?
13 But to you, LORD, I have cried.
   In the morning, my prayer comes before you.
14 LORD, why do you reject my soul?
   Why do you hide your face from me?
15 I am afflicted and ready to die from my youth up.
   While I suffer your terrors, I am distracted.
16 Your fierce wrath has gone over me.
   Your terrors have cut me off.
17 They came around me like water all day long.
   They completely engulfed me.
18 You have put lover and friend far from me,
   and my friends into darkness.

89

A contemplation by Ethan, the Ezrahite.
1 I will sing of the loving kindness of the LORD forever.
   With my mouth, I will make known your faithfulness to all generations.
2 I indeed declare, "Love stands firm forever.
   You established the heavens.
   Your faithfulness is in them."

3 "I have made a covenant with my chosen one,
   I have sworn to David, my servant,
4 'I will establish your offspring forever,
   and build up your throne to all generations.'" Selah.
5 The heavens will praise your wonders, LORD,
   your faithfulness also in the assembly of the holy ones.
6 For who in the skies can be compared to the LORD?
   Who amongst the sons of the heavenly beings is like the LORD?
7 a very awesome God in the council of the holy ones,
   to be feared above all those who are around him?
8 LORD, God of Armies, who is a mighty one, like you?
   The LORD, your faithfulness is around you.
9 You rule the pride of the sea.
   When its waves rise up, you calm them.
10 You have broken Rahab in pieces, like one of the slain.
   You have scattered your enemies with your mighty arm.
11 The heavens are yours.
   The earth also is yours,
   the world and its fullness.
   You have founded them.
12 You have created the north and the south.
   Tabor and Hermon rejoice in your name.
13 You have a mighty arm.
   Your hand is strong, and your right hand is exalted.
14 Righteousness and justice are the foundation of your throne.
   Loving kindness and truth go before your face.
15 Blessed are the people who learn to acclaim you.
   They walk in the light of your presence, LORD.
16 In your name they rejoice all day.
   In your righteousness, they are exalted.
17 For you are the glory of their strength.
   In your favour, our horn will be exalted.

18 For our shield belongs to the LORD,
   our king to the Holy One of Israel.

19 Then you spoke in vision to your saints,
   and said, "I have given strength to the warrior.
   I have exalted a young man from the people.
20 I have found David, my servant.
   I have anointed him with my holy oil,
21 with whom my hand shall be established.
   My arm will also strengthen him.
22 No enemy will tax him.
   No wicked man will oppress him.
23 I will beat down his adversaries before him,
   and strike those who hate him.
24 But my faithfulness and my loving kindness will be with him.
   In my name, his horn will be exalted.
25 I will set his hand also on the sea,
   and his right hand on the rivers.
26 He will call to me, 'You are my Father,
   my God, and the rock of my salvation!'
27 I will also appoint him my firstborn,
   the highest of the kings of the earth.
28 I will keep my loving kindness for him forever more.
   My covenant will stand firm with him.
29 I will also make his offspring endure forever,
   and his throne as the days of heaven.
30 If his children forsake my law,
   and don't walk in my ordinances;
31 if they break my statutes,
   and don't keep my commandments;
32 then I will punish their sin with the rod,
   and their iniquity with stripes.
33 But I will not completely take my loving kindness from him,
   nor allow my faithfulness to fail.
34 I will not break my covenant,
   nor alter what my lips have uttered.
35 Once I have sworn by my holiness,
   I will not lie to David.
36 His offspring will endure forever,
   his throne like the sun before me.
37 It will be established forever like the moon,
   the faithful witness in the sky." Selah.

38 But you have rejected and spurned.
   You have been angry with your anointed.
39 You have renounced the covenant of your servant.
   You have defiled his crown in the dust.
40 You have broken down all his hedges.
   You have brought his strongholds to ruin.
41 All who pass by the way rob him.
   He has become a reproach to his neighbours.
42 You have exalted the right hand of his adversaries.
   You have made all of his enemies rejoice.
43 Yes, you turn back the edge of his sword,
   and haven't supported him in battle.
44 You have ended his splendour,
   and thrown his throne down to the ground.
45 You have shortened the days of his youth.
   You have covered him with shame. Selah.
46 How long, LORD?
   Will you hide yourself forever?
   Will your wrath burn like fire?
47 Remember how short my time is,
   for what vanity you have created all the children of men!
48 What man is he who shall live and not see death,
   who shall deliver his soul from the power of Sheol?[b] Selah.
49 Lord, where are your former loving kindnesses,
   which you swore to David in your faithfulness?
50 Remember, Lord, the reproach of your servants,
   how I bear in my heart the taunts of all the mighty peoples,
51 With which your enemies have mocked, LORD,
   with which they have mocked the footsteps of your anointed one.

52 Blessed be the LORD forever more.
Amen, and Amen.

90
Book 4

A Prayer by Moses, the man of God.[c]
1 Lord,[d] you have been our dwelling place for all generations.
   2 Before the mountains were born,
   before you had formed the earth and the world,
   even from everlasting to everlasting, you are God.
3 You turn man to destruction, saying,
   "Return, you children of men."
4 For a thousand years in your sight are just like yesterday when it is past,

_____

a 88:3 Sheol is the place of the dead.
b 89:48 Sheol is the place of the dead.

c 90:0 The Hebrew word rendered "God" is "אֱלֹהִים" (Elohim).
d 90:1 The word translated "Lord" is "Adonai."

like a watch in the night.
5 You sweep them away as they sleep.
In the morning they sprout like new grass.
6 In the morning it sprouts and springs up.
By evening, it is withered and dry.
7 For we are consumed in your anger.
We are troubled in your wrath.
8 You have set our iniquities before you,
our secret sins in the light of your presence.
9 For all our days have passed away in your wrath.
We bring our years to an end as a sigh.
10 The days of our years are seventy,
or even by reason of strength eighty years;
yet their pride is but labour and sorrow,
for it passes quickly, and we fly away.
11 Who knows the power of your anger,
your wrath according to the fear that is due to you?
12 So teach us to count our days,
that we may gain a heart of wisdom.
13 Relent, LORD![a]
How long?
Have compassion on your servants!
14 Satisfy us in the morning with your loving kindness,
that we may rejoice and be glad all our days.
15 Make us glad for as many days as you have afflicted us,
for as many years as we have seen evil.
16 Let your work appear to your servants,
your glory to their children.
17 Let the favour of the Lord our God be on us.
Establish the work of our hands for us.
Yes, establish the work of our hands.

91

1 He who dwells in the secret place of the Most High
will rest in the shadow of the Almighty.
2 I will say of the LORD, "He is my refuge and my fortress;
my God, in whom I trust."
3 For he will deliver you from the snare of the fowler,
and from the deadly pestilence.
4 He will cover you with his feathers.
Under his wings you will take refuge.
His faithfulness is your shield and rampart.
5 You shall not be afraid of the terror by night,
nor of the arrow that flies by day,
6 nor of the pestilence that walks in darkness,
nor of the destruction that wastes at noonday.
7 A thousand may fall at your side,
and ten thousand at your right hand;
but it will not come near you.
8 You will only look with your eyes,
and see the recompense of the wicked.
9 Because you have made the LORD your refuge,
and the Most High your dwelling place,
10 no evil shall happen to you,
neither shall any plague come near your dwelling.
11 For he will put his angels in charge of you,
to guard you in all your ways.
12 They will bear you up in their hands,
so that you won't dash your foot against a stone.
13 You will tread on the lion and cobra.
You will trample the young lion and the serpent underfoot.
14 "Because he has set his love on me, therefore I will deliver him.
I will set him on high, because he has known my name.
15 He will call on me, and I will answer him.
I will be with him in trouble.
I will deliver him, and honour him.
16 I will satisfy him with long life,
and show him my salvation."

92

A Psalm. A song for the Sabbath day.
1 It is a good thing to give thanks to the LORD,
to sing praises to your name, Most High,
2 to proclaim your loving kindness in the morning,
and your faithfulness every night,
3 with the ten-stringed lute, with the harp,
and with the melody of the lyre.
4 For you, LORD, have made me glad through your work.
I will triumph in the works of your hands.
5 How great are your works, LORD!
Your thoughts are very deep.
6 A senseless man doesn't know,
neither does a fool understand this:
7 though the wicked spring up as the grass,
and all the evildoers flourish,
they will be destroyed forever.
8 But you, LORD, are on high forever more.

9 For behold, your enemies, LORD,
for behold, your enemies shall perish.
All the evildoers will be scattered.
10 But you have exalted my horn like that of the wild ox.
I am anointed with fresh oil.
11 My eye has also seen my enemies.
My ears have heard of the wicked enemies who rise up against me.
12 The righteous shall flourish like the palm tree.
He will grow like a cedar in Lebanon.
13 They are planted in the LORD's house.
They will flourish in our God's courts.
14 They will still produce fruit in old age.
They will be full of sap and green,
15 to show that the LORD is upright.
He is my rock,
and there is no unrighteousness in him.

93

1 The LORD reigns!
He is clothed with majesty!
The LORD is armed with strength.
The world also is established.
It can't be moved.
2 Your throne is established from long ago.
You are from everlasting.
3 The floods have lifted up, LORD,
the floods have lifted up their voice.
The floods lift up their waves.
4 Above the voices of many waters,
the mighty breakers of the sea,
the LORD on high is mighty.
5 Your statutes stand firm.
Holiness adorns your house,
LORD, forever more.

94

1 LORD, you God to whom vengeance belongs,
you God to whom vengeance belongs, shine out.
2 Rise up, you judge of the earth.
Pay back the proud what they deserve.
3 LORD, how long will the wicked,
how long will the wicked triumph?
4 They pour out arrogant words.
All the evildoers boast.
5 They break your people in pieces, LORD,
and afflict your heritage.
6 They kill the widow and the alien,
and murder the fatherless.
7 They say, "The LORD will not see,
neither will Jacob's God consider."
8 Consider, you senseless amongst the people;
you fools, when will you be wise?
9 He who implanted the ear, won't he hear?
He who formed the eye, won't he see?
10 He who disciplines the nations, won't he punish?
He who teaches man knows.
11 The LORD knows the thoughts of man,
that they are futile.
12 Blessed is the man whom you discipline, LORD,
and teach out of your law,
13 that you may give him rest from the days of adversity,
until the pit is dug for the wicked.
14 For the LORD won't reject his people,
neither will he forsake his inheritance.
15 For judgement will return to righteousness.
All the upright in heart shall follow it.
16 Who will rise up for me against the wicked?
Who will stand up for me against the evildoers?
17 Unless the LORD had been my help,
my soul would have soon lived in silence.
18 When I said, "My foot is slipping!"
Your loving kindness, LORD, held me up.
19 In the multitude of my thoughts within me,
your comforts delight my soul.
20 Shall the throne of wickedness have fellowship with you,
which brings about mischief by statute?
21 They gather themselves together against the soul of the righteous,
and condemn the innocent blood.
22 But the LORD has been my high tower,
my God, the rock of my refuge.
23 He has brought on them their own iniquity,
and will cut them off in their own wickedness.
The LORD, our God, will cut them off.

95

1 Oh come, let's sing to the LORD.
Let's shout aloud to the rock of our salvation!

a *90:13* When rendered in ALL CAPITAL LETTERS, "LORD" or "GOD" is the
translation of God's Proper Name.

2 Let's come before his presence with thanksgiving.
 Let's extol him with songs!
3 For the LORD is a great God,
 a great King above all gods.
4 In his hand are the deep places of the earth.
 The heights of the mountains are also his.
5 The sea is his, and he made it.
 His hands formed the dry land.
6 Oh come, let's worship and bow down.
 Let's kneel before the LORD, our Maker,
7 for he is our God.
We are the people of his pasture,
 and the sheep in his care.
Today, oh that you would hear his voice!
 8 Don't harden your heart, as at Meribah,
 as in the day of Massah in the wilderness,
9 when your fathers tempted me,
 tested me, and saw my work.
10 Forty long years I was grieved with that generation,
 and said, "They are a people who err in their heart.
 They have not known my ways."
11 Therefore I swore in my wrath,
 "They won't enter into my rest."

96

1 Sing to the LORD a new song!
 Sing to the LORD, all the earth.
2 Sing to the LORD!
 Bless his name!
 Proclaim his salvation from day to day!
3 Declare his glory amongst the nations,
 his marvellous works amongst all the peoples.
4 For the LORD is great, and greatly to be praised!
 He is to be feared above all gods.
5 For all the gods of the peoples are idols,
 but the LORD made the heavens.
6 Honour and majesty are before him.
 Strength and beauty are in his sanctuary.
7 Ascribe to the LORD, you families of nations,
 ascribe to the LORD glory and strength.
8 Ascribe to the LORD the glory due to his name.
 Bring an offering, and come into his courts.
9 Worship the LORD in holy array.
 Tremble before him, all the earth.
10 Say amongst the nations, "The LORD reigns."
 The world is also established.
 It can't be moved.
 He will judge the peoples with equity.
11 Let the heavens be glad, and let the earth rejoice.
 Let the sea roar, and its fullness!
 12 Let the field and all that is in it exult!
 Then all the trees of the woods shall sing for joy
 13 before the LORD; for he comes,
 for he comes to judge the earth.
He will judge the world with righteousness,
 the peoples with his truth.

97

1 The LORD reigns!
 Let the earth rejoice!
 Let the multitude of islands be glad!
2 Clouds and darkness are around him.
 Righteousness and justice are the foundation of his throne.
3 A fire goes before him,
 and burns up his adversaries on every side.
4 His lightning lights up the world.
 The earth sees, and trembles.
5 The mountains melt like wax at the presence of the LORD,
 at the presence of the Lord of the whole earth.
6 The heavens declare his righteousness.
 All the peoples have seen his glory.
7 Let all them be shamed who serve engraved images,
 who boast in their idols.
 Worship him, all you gods!ª
8 Zion heard and was glad.
 The daughters of Judah rejoiced
 because of your judgements, LORD.
9 For you, LORD, are most high above all the earth.
 You are exalted far above all gods.
10 You who love the LORD, hate evil!
 He preserves the souls of his saints.
 He delivers them out of the hand of the wicked.
11 Light is sown for the righteous,
 and gladness for the upright in heart.
12 Be glad in the LORD, you righteous people!
 Give thanks to his holy Name.

ª 97:7 LXX reads "angels" instead of "gods".

98

A Psalm.
1 Sing to the LORD a new song,
 for he has done marvellous things!
 His right hand and his holy arm have worked salvation for him.
2 The LORD has made known his salvation.
 He has openly shown his righteousness in the sight of the nations.
3 He has remembered his loving kindness and his faithfulness towards the
 house of Israel.
 All the ends of the earth have seen the salvation of our God.
4 Make a joyful noise to the LORD, all the earth!
 Burst out and sing for joy, yes, sing praises!
5 Sing praises to the LORD with the harp,
 with the harp and the voice of melody.
6 With trumpets and sound of the ram's horn,
 make a joyful noise before the King, the LORD.
7 Let the sea roar with its fullness;
 the world, and those who dwell therein.
8 Let the rivers clap their hands.
 Let the mountains sing for joy together.
9 Let them sing before the LORD,
 for he comes to judge the earth.
He will judge the world with righteousness,
 and the peoples with equity.

99

1 The LORD reigns! Let the peoples tremble.
 He sits enthroned amongst the cherubim.
 Let the earth be moved.
2 The LORD is great in Zion.
 He is high above all the peoples.
3 Let them praise your great and awesome name.
 He is Holy!

4 The King's strength also loves justice.
 You establish equity.
 You execute justice and righteousness in Jacob.
5 Exalt the LORD our God.
 Worship at his footstool.
 He is Holy!

6 Moses and Aaron were amongst his priests,
 Samuel was amongst those who call on his name.
 They called on the LORD, and he answered them.
7 He spoke to them in the pillar of cloud.
 They kept his testimonies,
 the statute that he gave them.
8 You answered them, LORD our God.
 You are a God who forgave them,
 although you took vengeance for their doings.
9 Exalt the LORD, our God.
 Worship at his holy hill,
 for the LORD, our God, is holy!

100

A Psalm of thanksgiving.
1 Shout for joy to the LORD, all you lands!
 2 Serve the LORD with gladness.
 Come before his presence with singing.
3 Know that the LORD, he is God.
 It is he who has made us, and we are his.
 We are his people, and the sheep of his pasture.
4 Enter into his gates with thanksgiving,
 and into his courts with praise.
 Give thanks to him, and bless his name.
5 For the LORD is good.
 His loving kindness endures forever,
 his faithfulness to all generations.

101

A Psalm by David.
1 I will sing of loving kindness and justice.
 To you, LORD, I will sing praises.
2 I will be careful to live a blameless life.
 When will you come to me?
 I will walk within my house with a blameless heart.
3 I will set no vile thing before my eyes.
 I hate the deeds of faithless men.
 They will not cling to me.
4 A perverse heart will be far from me.
 I will have nothing to do with evil.
5 I will silence whoever secretly slanders his neighbour.
 I won't tolerate one who is arrogant and conceited.
6 My eyes will be on the faithful of the land,
 that they may dwell with me.
He who walks in a perfect way,
 he will serve me.
7 He who practices deceit won't dwell within my house.

He who speaks falsehood won't be established before my eyes.
8 Morning by morning, I will destroy all the wicked of the land,
to cut off all the workers of iniquity from the LORD's city.

102

A Prayer of the afflicted, when he is overwhelmed and pours out his complaint before the LORD.
1 Hear my prayer, LORD!
Let my cry come to you.
2 Don't hide your face from me in the day of my distress.
Turn your ear to me.
Answer me quickly in the day when I call.
3 For my days consume away like smoke.
My bones are burnt as a torch.
4 My heart is blighted like grass, and withered,
for I forget to eat my bread.
5 By reason of the voice of my groaning,
my bones stick to my skin.
6 I am like a pelican of the wilderness.
I have become as an owl of the waste places.
7 I watch, and have become like a sparrow that is alone on the housetop.
8 My enemies reproach me all day.
Those who are mad at me use my name as a curse.
9 For I have eaten ashes like bread,
and mixed my drink with tears,
10 because of your indignation and your wrath;
for you have taken me up and thrown me away.
11 My days are like a long shadow.
I have withered like grass.

12 But you, LORD, will remain forever;
your renown endures to all generations.
13 You will arise and have mercy on Zion,
for it is time to have pity on her.
Yes, the set time has come.
14 For your servants take pleasure in her stones,
and have pity on her dust.
15 So the nations will fear the LORD's name,
all the kings of the earth your glory.
16 For the LORD has built up Zion.
He has appeared in his glory.
17 He has responded to the prayer of the destitute,
and has not despised their prayer.
18 This will be written for the generation to come.
A people which will be created will praise the LORD,
19 for he has looked down from the height of his sanctuary.
From heaven, the LORD saw the earth,
20 to hear the groans of the prisoner,
to free those who are condemned to death,
21 that men may declare the LORD's name in Zion,
and his praise in Jerusalem,
22 when the peoples are gathered together,
the kingdoms, to serve the LORD.

23 He weakened my strength along the course.
He shortened my days.
24 I said, "My God, don't take me away in the middle of my days.
Your years are throughout all generations.
25 Of old, you laid the foundation of the earth.
The heavens are the work of your hands.
26 They will perish, but you will endure.
Yes, all of them will wear out like a garment.
You will change them like a cloak, and they will be changed.
27 But you are the same.
Your years will have no end.
28 The children of your servants will continue.
Their offspring will be established before you."

103

By David.
1 Praise the LORD, my soul!
All that is within me, praise his holy name!
2 Praise the LORD, my soul,
and don't forget all his benefits,
3 who forgives all your sins,
who heals all your diseases.
4 who redeems your life from destruction,
who crowns you with loving kindness and tender mercies,
5 who satisfies your desire with good things,
so that your youth is renewed like the eagle's.
6 The LORD executes righteous acts,
and justice for all who are oppressed.
7 He made known his ways to Moses,
his deeds to the children of Israel.
8 The LORD is merciful and gracious,
slow to anger, and abundant in loving kindness.
9 He will not always accuse;

neither will he stay angry forever.
10 He has not dealt with us according to our sins,
nor repaid us for our iniquities.
11 For as the heavens are high above the earth,
so great is his loving kindness towards those who fear him.
12 As far as the east is from the west,
so far has he removed our transgressions from us.
13 Like a father has compassion on his children,
so the LORD has compassion on those who fear him.
14 For he knows how we are made.
He remembers that we are dust.
15 As for man, his days are like grass.
As a flower of the field, so he flourishes.
16 For the wind passes over it, and it is gone.
Its place remembers it no more.
17 But the LORD's loving kindness is from everlasting to everlasting with those who fear him,
his righteousness to children's children,
18 to those who keep his covenant,
to those who remember to obey his precepts.
19 The LORD has established his throne in the heavens.
His kingdom rules over all.
20 Praise the LORD, you angels of his,
who are mighty in strength, who fulfil his word,
obeying the voice of his word.
21 Praise the LORD, all you armies of his,
you servants of his, who do his pleasure.
22 Praise the LORD, all you works of his,
in all places of his dominion.
Praise the LORD, my soul!

104

1 Bless the LORD, my soul.
The LORD, my God, you are very great.
You are clothed with honour and majesty.
2 He covers himself with light as with a garment.
He stretches out the heavens like a curtain.
3 He lays the beams of his rooms in the waters.
He makes the clouds his chariot.
He walks on the wings of the wind.
4 He makes his messengers[a] winds,
and his servants flames of fire.
5 He laid the foundations of the earth,
that it should not be moved forever.
6 You covered it with the deep as with a cloak.
The waters stood above the mountains.
7 At your rebuke they fled.
At the voice of your thunder they hurried away.
8 The mountains rose,
the valleys sank down,
to the place which you had assigned to them.
9 You have set a boundary that they may not pass over,
that they don't turn again to cover the earth.
10 He sends springs into the valleys.
They run amongst the mountains.
11 They give drink to every animal of the field.
The wild donkeys quench their thirst.
12 The birds of the sky nest by them.
They sing amongst the branches.
13 He waters the mountains from his rooms.
The earth is filled with the fruit of your works.
14 He causes the grass to grow for the livestock,
and plants for man to cultivate,
that he may produce food out of the earth:
15 wine that makes the heart of man glad,
oil to make his face to shine,
and bread that strengthens man's heart.
16 The LORD's trees are well watered,
the cedars of Lebanon, which he has planted,
17 where the birds make their nests.
The stork makes its home in the cypress trees.
18 The high mountains are for the wild goats.
The rocks are a refuge for the rock badgers.
19 He appointed the moon for seasons.
The sun knows when to set.
20 You make darkness, and it is night,
in which all the animals of the forest prowl.
21 The young lions roar after their prey,
and seek their food from God.
22 The sun rises, and they steal away,
and lie down in their dens.
23 Man goes out to his work,
to his labour until the evening.
24 LORD, how many are your works!
In wisdom, you have made them all.
The earth is full of your riches.
25 There is the sea, great and wide,

---

a *104:4 or, angels*

in which are innumerable living things,
both small and large animals.
26 There the ships go,
and leviathan, whom you formed to play there.
27 These all wait for you,
that you may give them their food in due season.
28 You give to them; they gather.
You open your hand; they are satisfied with good.
29 You hide your face; they are troubled.
You take away their breath; they die and return to the dust.
30 You send out your Spirit and they are created.
You renew the face of the ground.
31 Let the LORD's glory endure forever.
Let the LORD rejoice in his works.
32 He looks at the earth, and it trembles.
He touches the mountains, and they smoke.
33 I will sing to the LORD as long as I live.
I will sing praise to my God while I have any being.
34 Let my meditation be sweet to him.
I will rejoice in the LORD.
35 Let sinners be consumed out of the earth.
Let the wicked be no more.
Bless the LORD, my soul.
Praise the LORD!

105

1 Give thanks to the LORD! Call on his name!
Make his doings known amongst the peoples.
2 Sing to him, sing praises to him!
Tell of all his marvellous works.
3 Glory in his holy name.
Let the heart of those who seek the LORD rejoice.
4 Seek the LORD and his strength.
Seek his face forever more.
5 Remember his marvellous works that he has done:
his wonders, and the judgements of his mouth,
6 you offspring of Abraham, his servant,
you children of Jacob, his chosen ones.
7 He is the LORD, our God.
His judgements are in all the earth.
8 He has remembered his covenant forever,
the word which he commanded to a thousand generations,
9 the covenant which he made with Abraham,
his oath to Isaac,
10 and confirmed it to Jacob for a statute;
to Israel for an everlasting covenant,
11 saying, "To you I will give the land of Canaan,
the lot of your inheritance,"
12 when they were but a few men in number,
yes, very few, and foreigners in it.
13 They went about from nation to nation,
from one kingdom to another people.
14 He allowed no one to do them wrong.
Yes, he reproved kings for their sakes,
15 "Don't touch my anointed ones!
Do my prophets no harm!"
16 He called for a famine on the land.
He destroyed the food supplies.
17 He sent a man before them.
Joseph was sold for a slave.
18 They bruised his feet with shackles.
His neck was locked in irons,
19 until the time that his word happened,
and the LORD's word proved him true.
20 The king sent and freed him,
even the ruler of peoples, and let him go free.
21 He made him lord of his house,
and ruler of all of his possessions,
22 to discipline his princes at his pleasure,
and to teach his elders wisdom.
23 Israel also came into Egypt.
Jacob lived in the land of Ham.
24 He increased his people greatly,
and made them stronger than their adversaries.
25 He turned their heart to hate his people,
to conspire against his servants.
26 He sent Moses, his servant,
and Aaron, whom he had chosen.
27 They performed miracles amongst them,
and wonders in the land of Ham.
28 He sent darkness, and made it dark.
They didn't rebel against his words.
29 He turned their waters into blood,
and killed their fish.
30 Their land swarmed with frogs,
even in the rooms of their kings.
31 He spoke, and swarms of flies came,
and lice in all their borders.
32 He gave them hail for rain,
with lightning in their land.

33 He struck their vines and also their fig trees,
and shattered the trees of their country.
34 He spoke, and the locusts came
with the grasshoppers, without number.
35 They ate up every plant in their land,
and ate up the fruit of their ground.
36 He struck also all the firstborn in their land,
the first fruits of all their manhood.
37 He brought them out with silver and gold.
There was not one feeble person amongst his tribes.
38 Egypt was glad when they departed,
for the fear of them had fallen on them.
39 He spread a cloud for a covering,
fire to give light in the night.
40 They asked, and he brought quails,
and satisfied them with the bread of the sky.
41 He opened the rock, and waters gushed out.
They ran as a river in the dry places.
42 For he remembered his holy word,
and Abraham, his servant.
43 He brought his people out with joy,
his chosen with singing.
44 He gave them the lands of the nations.
They took the labour of the peoples in possession,
45 that they might keep his statutes,
and observe his laws.
Praise the LORD!

106

1 Praise the LORD!
Give thanks to the LORD, for he is good,
for his loving kindness endures forever.
2 Who can utter the mighty acts of the LORD,
or fully declare all his praise?
3 Blessed are those who keep justice.
Blessed is one who does what is right at all times.
4 Remember me, LORD, with the favour that you show to your people.
Visit me with your salvation,
5 that I may see the prosperity of your chosen,
that I may rejoice in the gladness of your nation,
that I may glory with your inheritance.

6 We have sinned with our fathers.
We have committed iniquity.
We have done wickedly.
7 Our fathers didn't understand your wonders in Egypt.
They didn't remember the multitude of your loving kindnesses,
but were rebellious at the sea, even at the Red Sea.
8 Nevertheless he saved them for his name's sake,
that he might make his mighty power known.
9 He rebuked the Red Sea also, and it was dried up;
so he led them through the depths, as through a desert.
10 He saved them from the hand of him who hated them,
and redeemed them from the hand of the enemy.
11 The waters covered their adversaries.
There was not one of them left.
12 Then they believed his words.
They sang his praise.

13 They soon forgot his works.
They didn't wait for his counsel,
14 but gave in to craving in the desert,
and tested God in the wasteland.
15 He gave them their request,
but sent leanness into their soul.
16 They envied Moses also in the camp,
and Aaron, the LORD's saint.
17 The earth opened and swallowed up Dathan,
and covered the company of Abiram.
18 A fire was kindled in their company.
The flame burnt up the wicked.
19 They made a calf in Horeb,
and worshipped a molten image.
20 Thus they exchanged their glory
for an image of a bull that eats grass.
21 They forgot God, their Saviour,
who had done great things in Egypt,
22 wondrous works in the land of Ham,
and awesome things by the Red Sea.
23 Therefore he said that he would destroy them,
had Moses, his chosen, not stood before him in the breach,
to turn away his wrath, so that he wouldn't destroy them.
24 Yes, they despised the pleasant land.
They didn't believe his word,
25 but murmured in their tents,
and didn't listen to the LORD's voice.
26 Therefore he swore to them
that he would overthrow them in the wilderness,
27 that he would overthrow their offspring amongst the nations,
and scatter them in the lands.

28 They joined themselves also to Baal Peor,
and ate the sacrifices of the dead.
29 Thus they provoked him to anger with their deeds.
The plague broke in on them.
30 Then Phinehas stood up and executed judgement,
so the plague was stopped.
31 That was credited to him for righteousness,
for all generations to come.
32 They angered him also at the waters of Meribah,
so that Moses was troubled for their sakes;
33 because they were rebellious against his spirit,
he spoke rashly with his lips.
34 They didn't destroy the peoples,
as the LORD commanded them,
35 but mixed themselves with the nations,
and learnt their works.
36 They served their idols,
which became a snare to them.
37 Yes, they sacrificed their sons and their daughters to demons.
38 They shed innocent blood,
even the blood of their sons and of their daughters,
whom they sacrificed to the idols of Canaan.
The land was polluted with blood.
39 Thus they were defiled with their works,
and prostituted themselves in their deeds.
40 Therefore the LORD burnt with anger against his people.
He abhorred his inheritance.
41 He gave them into the hand of the nations.
Those who hated them ruled over them.
42 Their enemies also oppressed them.
They were brought into subjection under their hand.
43 He rescued them many times,
but they were rebellious in their counsel,
and were brought low in their iniquity.
44 Nevertheless he regarded their distress,
when he heard their cry.
45 He remembered for them his covenant,
and repented according to the multitude of his loving kindnesses.
46 He made them also to be pitied
by all those who carried them captive.

47 Save us, LORD, our God,
gather us from amongst the nations,
to give thanks to your holy name,
to triumph in your praise!

48 Blessed be the LORD, the God of Israel,
from everlasting even to everlasting!
Let all the people say, "Amen."
Praise the LORD!

107

Book 5

1 Give thanks to the LORD,[a] for he is good,
for his loving kindness endures forever.
2 Let the redeemed by the LORD say so,
whom he has redeemed from the hand of the adversary,
3 and gathered out of the lands,
from the east and from the west,
from the north and from the south.

4 They wandered in the wilderness in a desert way.
They found no city to live in.
5 Hungry and thirsty,
their soul fainted in them.
6 Then they cried to the LORD in their trouble,
and he delivered them out of their distresses.
7 He led them also by a straight way,
that they might go to a city to live in.
8 Let them praise the LORD for his loving kindness,
for his wonderful deeds to the children of men!

9 For he satisfies the longing soul.
He fills the hungry soul with good.

10 Some sat in darkness and in the shadow of death,
being bound in affliction and iron,
11 because they rebelled against the words of God,[b]
and condemned the counsel of the Most High.
12 Therefore he brought down their heart with labour.
They fell down, and there was no one to help.
13 Then they cried to the LORD in their trouble,
and he saved them out of their distresses.
14 He brought them out of darkness and the shadow of death,
and broke away their chains.
15 Let them praise the LORD for his loving kindness,

for his wonderful deeds to the children of men!

16 For he has broken the gates of bronze,
and cut through bars of iron.

17 Fools are afflicted because of their disobedience,
and because of their iniquities.
18 Their soul abhors all kinds of food.
They draw near to the gates of death.
19 Then they cry to the LORD in their trouble,
and he saves them out of their distresses.
20 He sends his word, and heals them,
and delivers them from their graves.
21 Let them praise the LORD for his loving kindness,
for his wonderful deeds to the children of men!

22 Let them offer the sacrifices of thanksgiving,
and declare his deeds with singing.

23 Those who go down to the sea in ships,
who do business in great waters,
24 these see the LORD's deeds,
and his wonders in the deep.
25 For he commands, and raises the stormy wind,
which lifts up its waves.
26 They mount up to the sky; they go down again to the depths.
Their soul melts away because of trouble.
27 They reel back and forth, and stagger like a drunken man,
and are at their wits' end.
28 Then they cry to the LORD in their trouble,
and he brings them out of their distress.
29 He makes the storm a calm,
so that its waves are still.
30 Then they are glad because it is calm,
so he brings them to their desired haven.
31 Let them praise the LORD for his loving kindness,
for his wonderful deeds for the children of men!

32 Let them exalt him also in the assembly of the people,
and praise him in the seat of the elders.

33 He turns rivers into a desert,
water springs into a thirsty ground,
34 and a fruitful land into a salt waste,
for the wickedness of those who dwell in it.
35 He turns a desert into a pool of water,
and a dry land into water springs.
36 There he makes the hungry live,
that they may prepare a city to live in,
37 sow fields, plant vineyards,
and reap the fruits of increase.
38 He blesses them also, so that they are multiplied greatly.
He doesn't allow their livestock to decrease.
39 Again, they are diminished and bowed down
through oppression, trouble, and sorrow.
40 He pours contempt on princes,
and causes them to wander in a trackless waste.
41 Yet he lifts the needy out of their affliction,
and increases their families like a flock.
42 The upright will see it, and be glad.
All the wicked will shut their mouths.
43 Whoever is wise will pay attention to these things.
They will consider the loving kindnesses of the LORD.

108

A Song. A Psalm by David.

1 My heart is steadfast, God.
I will sing and I will make music with my soul.
2 Wake up, harp and lyre!
I will wake up the dawn.
3 I will give thanks to you, LORD, amongst the nations.
I will sing praises to you amongst the peoples.
4 For your loving kindness is great above the heavens.
Your faithfulness reaches to the skies.
5 Be exalted, God, above the heavens!
Let your glory be over all the earth.
6 That your beloved may be delivered,
save with your right hand, and answer us.
7 God has spoken from his sanctuary: "In triumph,
I will divide Shechem, and measure out the valley of Succoth.
8 Gilead is mine. Manasseh is mine.
Ephraim also is my helmet.
Judah is my sceptre.
9 Moab is my wash pot.
I will toss my sandal on Edom.
I will shout over Philistia."

---

a *107:1* When rendered in ALL CAPITAL LETTERS, "LORD" or "GOD" is the translation of God's Proper Name.

b *107:11* The Hebrew word rendered "God" is "אֱלֹהִים" (Elohim).

¹⁰ Who will bring me into the fortified city?
  Who will lead me to Edom?
¹¹ Haven't you rejected us, God?
  You don't go out, God, with our armies.
¹² Give us help against the enemy,
  for the help of man is vain.
¹³ Through God, we will do valiantly,
  for it is he who will tread down our enemies.

109

For the Chief Musician. A Psalm by David.
¹ God of my praise, don't remain silent,
    ² for they have opened the mouth of the wicked and the mouth of deceit against me.
  They have spoken to me with a lying tongue.
³ They have also surrounded me with words of hatred,
  and fought against me without a cause.
⁴ In return for my love, they are my adversaries;
  but I am in prayer.
⁵ They have rewarded me evil for good,
  and hatred for my love.
⁶ Set a wicked man over him.
  Let an adversary stand at his right hand.
⁷ When he is judged, let him come out guilty.
  Let his prayer be turned into sin.
⁸ Let his days be few.
  Let another take his office.
⁹ Let his children be fatherless,
  and his wife a widow.
¹⁰ Let his children be wandering beggars.
  Let them be sought from their ruins.
¹¹ Let the creditor seize all that he has.
  Let strangers plunder the fruit of his labour.
¹² Let there be no one to extend kindness to him,
  neither let there be anyone to have pity on his fatherless children.
¹³ Let his posterity be cut off.
  In the generation following let their name be blotted out.
¹⁴ Let the iniquity of his fathers be remembered by the LORD.
  Don't let the sin of his mother be blotted out.
¹⁵ Let them be before the LORD continually,
  that he may cut off their memory from the earth;
¹⁶ because he didn't remember to show kindness,
  but persecuted the poor and needy man,
  the broken in heart, to kill them.
¹⁷ Yes, he loved cursing, and it came to him.
  He didn't delight in blessing, and it was far from him.
¹⁸ He clothed himself also with cursing as with his garment.
  It came into his inward parts like water,
  like oil into his bones.
¹⁹ Let it be to him as the clothing with which he covers himself,
  for the belt that is always around him.
²⁰ This is the reward of my adversaries from the LORD,
  of those who speak evil against my soul.

²¹ But deal with me, GOD the Lord,^a for your name's sake,
  because your loving kindness is good, deliver me;
    ²² for I am poor and needy.
  My heart is wounded within me.
²³ I fade away like an evening shadow.
  I am shaken off like a locust.
²⁴ My knees are weak through fasting.
  My body is thin and lacks fat.
²⁵ I have also become a reproach to them.
  When they see me, they shake their head.
²⁶ Help me, LORD, my God.
  Save me according to your loving kindness;
²⁷ that they may know that this is your hand;
  that you, LORD, have done it.
²⁸ They may curse, but you bless.
  When they arise, they will be shamed,
  but your servant shall rejoice.
²⁹ Let my adversaries be clothed with dishonour.
  Let them cover themselves with their own shame as with a robe.
³⁰ I will give great thanks to the LORD with my mouth.
  Yes, I will praise him amongst the multitude.
³¹ For he will stand at the right hand of the needy,
  to save him from those who judge his soul.

110

A Psalm by David.
¹ The LORD says to my Lord, "Sit at my right hand,
  until I make your enemies your footstool for your feet."
² The LORD will send out the rod of your strength out of Zion.
  Rule amongst your enemies.
³ Your people offer themselves willingly in the day of your power, in holy array.

Out of the womb of the morning, you have the dew of your youth.
⁴ The LORD has sworn, and will not change his mind:
  "You are a priest forever in the order of Melchizedek."
⁵ The Lord is at your right hand.
  He will crush kings in the day of his wrath.
⁶ He will judge amongst the nations.
  He will heap up dead bodies.
  He will crush the ruler of the whole earth.
⁷ He will drink of the brook on the way;
  therefore he will lift up his head.

111

¹ Praise the LORD!^b
  I will give thanks to the LORD with my whole heart,
  in the council of the upright, and in the congregation.
² The LORD's works are great,
  pondered by all those who delight in them.
³ His work is honour and majesty.
  His righteousness endures forever.
⁴ He has caused his wonderful works to be remembered.
  The LORD is gracious and merciful.
⁵ He has given food to those who fear him.
  He always remembers his covenant.
⁶ He has shown his people the power of his works,
  in giving them the heritage of the nations.
⁷ The works of his hands are truth and justice.
  All his precepts are sure.
⁸ They are established forever and ever.
  They are done in truth and uprightness.
⁹ He has sent redemption to his people.
  He has ordained his covenant forever.
  His name is holy and awesome!
¹⁰ The fear of the LORD is the beginning of wisdom.
  All those who do his work have a good understanding.
His praise endures forever!

112

¹ Praise the LORD!^c
  Blessed is the man who fears the LORD,
  who delights greatly in his commandments.
² His offspring will be mighty in the land.
  The generation of the upright will be blessed.
³ Wealth and riches are in his house.
  His righteousness endures forever.
⁴ Light dawns in the darkness for the upright,
  gracious, merciful, and righteous.
⁵ It is well with the man who deals graciously and lends.
  He will maintain his cause in judgement.
⁶ For he will never be shaken.
  The righteous will be remembered forever.
⁷ He will not be afraid of evil news.
  His heart is steadfast, trusting in the LORD.
⁸ His heart is established.
  He will not be afraid in the end when he sees his adversaries.
⁹ He has dispersed, he has given to the poor.
  His righteousness endures forever.
  His horn will be exalted with honour.
¹⁰ The wicked will see it, and be grieved.
  He shall gnash with his teeth, and melt away.
  The desire of the wicked will perish.

113

¹ Praise the LORD!
  Praise, you servants of the LORD,
  praise the LORD's name.
² Blessed be the LORD's name,
  from this time forward and forever more.
³ From the rising of the sun to its going down,
  the LORD's name is to be praised.
⁴ The LORD is high above all nations,
  his glory above the heavens.
⁵ Who is like the LORD, our God,
  who has his seat on high,
    ⁶ who stoops down to see in heaven and in the earth?
⁷ He raises up the poor out of the dust,
  and lifts up the needy from the ash heap,
⁸ that he may set him with princes,
  even with the princes of his people.
⁹ He settles the barren woman in her home
  as a joyful mother of children.
Praise the LORD!

114

¹ When Israel went out of Egypt,
  the house of Jacob from a people of foreign language,
² Judah became his sanctuary,
  Israel his dominion.

---

^a *109:21* The word translated "Lord" is "Adonai."
^b *111:1* Psalm 111 is an acrostic poem, with each verse after the initial "Praise the LORD!" starting with a letter of the alphabet (ordered from Alef to Tav).

^c *112:1* Psalm 112 is an acrostic poem, with each verse after the initial "Praise the LORD!" starting with a letter of the alphabet (ordered from Alef to Tav).

3 The sea saw it, and fled.
　　The Jordan was driven back.
4 The mountains skipped like rams,
　　the little hills like lambs.
5 What was it, you sea, that you fled?
　　You Jordan, that you turned back?
6 You mountains, that you skipped like rams?
　　You little hills, like lambs?
7 Tremble, you earth, at the presence of the Lord,
　　at the presence of the God of Jacob,
8 who turned the rock into a pool of water,
　　the flint into a spring of waters.

115

1 Not to us, LORD, not to us,
　　but to your name give glory,
　　for your loving kindness, and for your truth's sake.
2 Why should the nations say,
　　"Where is their God, now?"
3 But our God is in the heavens.
　　He does whatever he pleases.
4 Their idols are silver and gold,
　　the work of men's hands.
5 They have mouths, but they don't speak.
　　They have eyes, but they don't see.
6 They have ears, but they don't hear.
　　They have noses, but they don't smell.
7 They have hands, but they don't feel.
　　They have feet, but they don't walk,
　　neither do they speak through their throat.
8 Those who make them will be like them;
　　yes, everyone who trusts in them.
9 Israel, trust in the LORD!
　　He is their help and their shield.
10 House of Aaron, trust in the LORD!
　　He is their help and their shield.
11 You who fear the LORD, trust in the LORD!
　　He is their help and their shield.
12 The LORD remembers us. He will bless us.
　　He will bless the house of Israel.
　　He will bless the house of Aaron.
13 He will bless those who fear the LORD,
　　both small and great.
14 May the LORD increase you more and more,
　　you and your children.
15 Blessed are you by the LORD,
　　who made heaven and earth.
16 The heavens are the LORD's heavens,
　　but he has given the earth to the children of men.
17 The dead don't praise the LORD,
　　nor any who go down into silence,
18 but we will bless the LORD,
　　from this time forward and forever more.
Praise the LORD!

116

1 I love the LORD, because he listens to my voice,
　　and my cries for mercy.
2 Because he has turned his ear to me,
　　therefore I will call on him as long as I live.
3 The cords of death surrounded me,
　　the pains of Sheol[a] got a hold of me.
　　I found trouble and sorrow.
4 Then I called on the LORD's name:
　　"LORD, I beg you, deliver my soul."
5 The LORD is gracious and righteous.
　　Yes, our God is merciful.
6 The LORD preserves the simple.
　　I was brought low, and he saved me.
7 Return to your rest, my soul,
　　for the LORD has dealt bountifully with you.
8 For you have delivered my soul from death,
　　my eyes from tears,
　　and my feet from falling.
9 I will walk before the LORD in the land of the living.
10 I believed, therefore I said,
　　"I was greatly afflicted."
11 I said in my haste,
　　"All people are liars."
12 What will I give to the LORD for all his benefits towards me?
　　13 I will take the cup of salvation, and call on the LORD's name.
14 I will pay my vows to the LORD,
　　yes, in the presence of all his people.
15 Precious in the LORD's sight is the death of his saints.
16 LORD, truly I am your servant.
　　I am your servant, the son of your servant girl.
　　You have freed me from my chains.
17 I will offer to you the sacrifice of thanksgiving,

and will call on the LORD's name.
18 I will pay my vows to the LORD,
　　yes, in the presence of all his people,
19 in the courts of the LORD's house,
　　in the middle of you, Jerusalem.
Praise the LORD!

117

1 Praise the LORD, all you nations!
　　Extol him, all you peoples!
2 For his loving kindness is great towards us.
　　The LORD's faithfulness endures forever.
Praise the LORD!

118

1 Give thanks to the LORD, for he is good,
　　for his loving kindness endures forever.
2 Let Israel now say
　　that his loving kindness endures forever.
3 Let the house of Aaron now say
　　that his loving kindness endures forever.
4 Now let those who fear the LORD say
　　that his loving kindness endures forever.
5 Out of my distress, I called on the LORD.
　　The LORD answered me with freedom.
6 The LORD is on my side. I will not be afraid.
　　What can man do to me?
7 The LORD is on my side amongst those who help me.
　　Therefore I will look in triumph at those who hate me.
8 It is better to take refuge in the LORD,
　　than to put confidence in man.
9 It is better to take refuge in the LORD,
　　than to put confidence in princes.
10 All the nations surrounded me,
　　but in the LORD's name I cut them off.
11 They surrounded me, yes, they surrounded me.
　　In the LORD's name I indeed cut them off.
12 They surrounded me like bees.
　　They are quenched like the burning thorns.
　　In the LORD's name I cut them off.
13 You pushed me back hard, to make me fall,
　　but the LORD helped me.
14 The LORD is my strength and song.
　　He has become my salvation.
15 The voice of rejoicing and salvation is in the tents of the righteous.
　　"The right hand of the LORD does valiantly.
16 The right hand of the LORD is exalted!
　　The right hand of the LORD does valiantly!"
17 I will not die, but live,
　　and declare the LORD's works.
18 The LORD has punished me severely,
　　but he has not given me over to death.
19 Open to me the gates of righteousness.
　　I will enter into them.
　　I will give thanks to the LORD.
20 This is the gate of the LORD;
　　the righteous will enter into it.
21 I will give thanks to you, for you have answered me,
　　and have become my salvation.
22 The stone which the builders rejected
　　has become the cornerstone.[b]
23 This is the LORD's doing.
　　It is marvellous in our eyes.
24 This is the day that the LORD has made.
　　We will rejoice and be glad in it!
25 Save us now, we beg you, LORD!
　　LORD, we beg you, send prosperity now.
26 Blessed is he who comes in the LORD's name!
　　We have blessed you out of the LORD's house.
27 The LORD is God, and he has given us light.
　　Bind the sacrifice with cords, even to the horns of the altar.
28 You are my God, and I will give thanks to you.
　　You are my God, I will exalt you.
29 Oh give thanks to the LORD, for he is good,
　　for his loving kindness endures forever.

119

ALEPH
1 Blessed are those whose ways are blameless,
　　who walk according to the LORD's law.
2 Blessed are those who keep his statutes,
　　who seek him with their whole heart.
3 Yes, they do nothing wrong.
　　They walk in his ways.
4 You have commanded your precepts,
　　that we should fully obey them.
5 Oh that my ways were steadfast
　　to obey your statutes!

---

a *116:3* Sheol is the place of the dead.

b *118:22* Literally, head of the corner

6 Then I wouldn't be disappointed,
    when I consider all of your commandments.
7 I will give thanks to you with uprightness of heart,
    when I learn your righteous judgements.
8 I will observe your statutes.
    Don't utterly forsake me.

BETH

9 How can a young man keep his way pure?
    By living according to your word.
10 With my whole heart I have sought you.
    Don't let me wander from your commandments.
11 I have hidden your word in my heart,
    that I might not sin against you.
12 Blessed are you, LORD.
    Teach me your statutes.
13 With my lips,
    I have declared all the ordinances of your mouth.
14 I have rejoiced in the way of your testimonies,
    as much as in all riches.
15 I will meditate on your precepts,
    and consider your ways.
16 I will delight myself in your statutes.
    I will not forget your word.

GIMEL

17 Do good to your servant.
    I will live and I will obey your word.
18 Open my eyes,
    that I may see wondrous things out of your law.
19 I am a stranger on the earth.
    Don't hide your commandments from me.
20 My soul is consumed with longing for your ordinances at all times.
21 You have rebuked the proud who are cursed,
    who wander from your commandments.
22 Take reproach and contempt away from me,
    for I have kept your statutes.
23 Though princes sit and slander me,
    your servant will meditate on your statutes.
24 Indeed your statutes are my delight,
    and my counsellors.

DALETH

25 My soul is laid low in the dust.
    Revive me according to your word!
26 I declared my ways, and you answered me.
    Teach me your statutes.
27 Let me understand the teaching of your precepts!
    Then I will meditate on your wondrous works.
28 My soul is weary with sorrow;
    strengthen me according to your word.
29 Keep me from the way of deceit.
    Grant me your law graciously!
30 I have chosen the way of truth.
    I have set your ordinances before me.
31 I cling to your statutes, LORD.
    Don't let me be disappointed.
32 I run in the path of your commandments,
    for you have set my heart free.

HE

33 Teach me, LORD, the way of your statutes.
    I will keep them to the end.
34 Give me understanding, and I will keep your law.
    Yes, I will obey it with my whole heart.
35 Direct me in the path of your commandments,
    for I delight in them.
36 Turn my heart towards your statutes,
    not towards selfish gain.
37 Turn my eyes away from looking at worthless things.
    Revive me in your ways.
38 Fulfil your promise to your servant,
    that you may be feared.
39 Take away my disgrace that I dread,
    for your ordinances are good.
40 Behold, I long for your precepts!
    Revive me in your righteousness.

VAV

41 Let your loving kindness also come to me, LORD,
    your salvation, according to your word.
42 So I will have an answer for him who reproaches me,
    for I trust in your word.
43 Don't snatch the word of truth out of my mouth,
    for I put my hope in your ordinances.
44 So I will obey your law continually,
    forever and ever.
45 I will walk in liberty,
    for I have sought your precepts.
46 I will also speak of your statutes before kings,
    and will not be disappointed.
47 I will delight myself in your commandments,
    because I love them.
48 I reach out my hands for your commandments, which I love.

    I will meditate on your statutes.

ZAYIN

49 Remember your word to your servant,
    because you gave me hope.
50 This is my comfort in my affliction,
    for your word has revived me.
51 The arrogant mock me excessively,
    but I don't swerve from your law.
52 I remember your ordinances of old, LORD,
    and have comforted myself.
53 Indignation has taken hold on me,
    because of the wicked who forsake your law.
54 Your statutes have been my songs
    in the house where I live.
55 I have remembered your name, LORD, in the night,
    and I obey your law.
56 This is my way,
    that I keep your precepts.

HETH

57 The LORD is my portion.
    I promised to obey your words.
58 I sought your favour with my whole heart.
    Be merciful to me according to your word.
59 I considered my ways,
    and turned my steps to your statutes.
60 I will hurry, and not delay,
    to obey your commandments.
61 The ropes of the wicked bind me,
    but I won't forget your law.
62 At midnight I will rise to give thanks to you,
    because of your righteous ordinances.
63 I am a friend of all those who fear you,
    of those who observe your precepts.
64 The earth is full of your loving kindness, LORD.
    Teach me your statutes.

TETH

65 You have treated your servant well,
    according to your word, LORD.
66 Teach me good judgement and knowledge,
    for I believe in your commandments.
67 Before I was afflicted, I went astray;
    but now I observe your word.
68 You are good, and do good.
    Teach me your statutes.
69 The proud have smeared a lie upon me.
    With my whole heart, I will keep your precepts.
70 Their heart is as callous as the fat,
    but I delight in your law.
71 It is good for me that I have been afflicted,
    that I may learn your statutes.
72 The law of your mouth is better to me than thousands of pieces of gold
        and silver.

YODH

73 Your hands have made me and formed me.
    Give me understanding, that I may learn your commandments.
74 Those who fear you will see me and be glad,
    because I have put my hope in your word.
75 LORD, I know that your judgements are righteous,
    that in faithfulness you have afflicted me.
76 Please let your loving kindness be for my comfort,
    according to your word to your servant.
77 Let your tender mercies come to me, that I may live;
    for your law is my delight.
78 Let the proud be disappointed, for they have overthrown me wrongfully.
    I will meditate on your precepts.
79 Let those who fear you turn to me.
    They will know your statutes.
80 Let my heart be blameless towards your decrees,
    that I may not be disappointed.

KAPF

81 My soul faints for your salvation.
    I hope in your word.
82 My eyes fail for your word.
    I say, "When will you comfort me?"
83 For I have become like a wineskin in the smoke.
    I don't forget your statutes.
84 How many are the days of your servant?
    When will you execute judgement on those who persecute me?
85 The proud have dug pits for me,
    contrary to your law.
86 All of your commandments are faithful.
    They persecute me wrongfully.
    Help me!
87 They had almost wiped me from the earth,
    but I didn't forsake your precepts.
88 Preserve my life according to your loving kindness,
    so I will obey the statutes of your mouth.

LAMEDH

89 LORD, your word is settled in heaven forever.

90 Your faithfulness is to all generations.
   You have established the earth, and it remains.
91 Your laws remain to this day,
   for all things serve you.
92 Unless your law had been my delight,
   I would have perished in my affliction.
93 I will never forget your precepts,
   for with them, you have revived me.
94 I am yours.
   Save me, for I have sought your precepts.
95 The wicked have waited for me, to destroy me.
   I will consider your statutes.
96 I have seen a limit to all perfection,
   but your commands are boundless.

MEM
97 How I love your law!
   It is my meditation all day.
98 Your commandments make me wiser than my enemies,
   for your commandments are always with me.
99 I have more understanding than all my teachers,
   for your testimonies are my meditation.
100 I understand more than the aged,
    because I have kept your precepts.
101 I have kept my feet from every evil way,
    that I might observe your word.
102 I have not turned away from your ordinances,
    for you have taught me.
103 How sweet are your promises to my taste,
    more than honey to my mouth!
104 Through your precepts, I get understanding;
    therefore I hate every false way.

NUN
105 Your word is a lamp to my feet,
    and a light for my path.
106 I have sworn, and have confirmed it,
    that I will obey your righteous ordinances.
107 I am afflicted very much.
    Revive me, LORD, according to your word.
108 Accept, I beg you, the willing offerings of my mouth.
    LORD, teach me your ordinances.
109 My soul is continually in my hand,
    yet I won't forget your law.
110 The wicked have laid a snare for me,
    yet I haven't gone astray from your precepts.
111 I have taken your testimonies as a heritage forever,
    for they are the joy of my heart.
112 I have set my heart to perform your statutes forever,
    even to the end.

SAMEKH
113 I hate double-minded men,
    but I love your law.
114 You are my hiding place and my shield.
    I hope in your word.
115 Depart from me, you evildoers,
    that I may keep the commandments of my God.
116 Uphold me according to your word, that I may live.
    Let me not be ashamed of my hope.
117 Hold me up, and I will be safe,
    and will have respect for your statutes continually.
118 You reject all those who stray from your statutes,
    for their deceit is in vain.
119 You put away all the wicked of the earth like dross.
    Therefore I love your testimonies.
120 My flesh trembles for fear of you.
    I am afraid of your judgements.

AYIN
121 I have done what is just and righteous.
    Don't leave me to my oppressors.
122 Ensure your servant's well-being.
    Don't let the proud oppress me.
123 My eyes fail looking for your salvation,
    for your righteous word.
124 Deal with your servant according to your loving kindness.
    Teach me your statutes.
125 I am your servant. Give me understanding,
    that I may know your testimonies.
126 It is time to act, LORD,
    for they break your law.
127 Therefore I love your commandments more than gold,
    yes, more than pure gold.
128 Therefore I consider all of your precepts to be right.
    I hate every false way.

PE
129 Your testimonies are wonderful,
    therefore my soul keeps them.
130 The entrance of your words gives light.
    It gives understanding to the simple.
131 I opened my mouth wide and panted,
    for I longed for your commandments.

132 Turn to me, and have mercy on me,
    as you always do to those who love your name.
133 Establish my footsteps in your word.
    Don't let any iniquity have dominion over me.
134 Redeem me from the oppression of man,
    so I will observe your precepts.
135 Make your face shine on your servant.
    Teach me your statutes.
136 Streams of tears run down my eyes,
    because they don't observe your law.

TZADHE
137 You are righteous, LORD.
    Your judgements are upright.
138 You have commanded your statutes in righteousness.
    They are fully trustworthy.
139 My zeal wears me out,
    because my enemies ignore your words.
140 Your promises have been thoroughly tested,
    and your servant loves them.
141 I am small and despised.
    I don't forget your precepts.
142 Your righteousness is an everlasting righteousness.
    Your law is truth.
143 Trouble and anguish have taken hold of me.
    Your commandments are my delight.
144 Your testimonies are righteous forever.
    Give me understanding, that I may live.

QOPH
145 I have called with my whole heart.
    Answer me, LORD!
    I will keep your statutes.
146 I have called to you. Save me!
    I will obey your statutes.
147 I rise before dawn and cry for help.
    I put my hope in your words.
148 My eyes stay open through the night watches,
    that I might meditate on your word.
149 Hear my voice according to your loving kindness.
    Revive me, LORD, according to your ordinances.
150 They draw near who follow after wickedness.
    They are far from your law.
151 You are near, LORD.
    All your commandments are truth.
152 Of old I have known from your testimonies,
    that you have founded them forever.

RESH
153 Consider my affliction, and deliver me,
    for I don't forget your law.
154 Plead my cause, and redeem me!
    Revive me according to your promise.
155 Salvation is far from the wicked,
    for they don't seek your statutes.
156 Great are your tender mercies, LORD.
    Revive me according to your ordinances.
157 Many are my persecutors and my adversaries.
    I haven't swerved from your testimonies.
158 I look at the faithless with loathing,
    because they don't observe your word.
159 Consider how I love your precepts.
    Revive me, LORD, according to your loving kindness.
160 All of your words are truth.
    Every one of your righteous ordinances endures forever.

SIN AND SHIN
161 Princes have persecuted me without a cause,
    but my heart stands in awe of your words.
162 I rejoice at your word,
    as one who finds great plunder.
163 I hate and abhor falsehood.
    I love your law.
164 Seven times a day, I praise you,
    because of your righteous ordinances.
165 Those who love your law have great peace.
    Nothing causes them to stumble.
166 I have hoped for your salvation, LORD.
    I have done your commandments.
167 My soul has observed your testimonies.
    I love them exceedingly.
168 I have obeyed your precepts and your testimonies,
    for all my ways are before you.

TAV
169 Let my cry come before you, LORD.
    Give me understanding according to your word.
170 Let my supplication come before you.
    Deliver me according to your word.
171 Let my lips utter praise,
    for you teach me your statutes.
172 Let my tongue sing of your word,
    for all your commandments are righteousness.
173 Let your hand be ready to help me,

for I have chosen your precepts.
174 I have longed for your salvation, LORD.
    Your law is my delight.
175 Let my soul live, that I may praise you.
    Let your ordinances help me.
176 I have gone astray like a lost sheep.
    Seek your servant, for I don't forget your commandments.

120

A Song of Ascents.
1 In my distress, I cried to the LORD.
    He answered me.
2 Deliver my soul, LORD, from lying lips,
    from a deceitful tongue.
3 What will be given to you, and what will be done more to you,
    you deceitful tongue?
4 Sharp arrows of the mighty,
    with coals of juniper.
5 Woe is me, that I live in Meshech,
    that I dwell amongst the tents of Kedar!
6 My soul has had her dwelling too long
    with him who hates peace.
7 I am for peace,
    but when I speak, they are for war.

121

A Song of Ascents.
1 I will lift up my eyes to the hills.
    Where does my help come from?
2 My help comes from the LORD,
    who made heaven and earth.

3 He will not allow your foot to be moved.
    He who keeps you will not slumber.
4 Behold, he who keeps Israel
    will neither slumber nor sleep.
5 The LORD is your keeper.
    The LORD is your shade on your right hand.
6 The sun will not harm you by day,
    nor the moon by night.
7 The LORD will keep you from all evil.
    He will keep your soul.
8 The LORD will keep your going out and your coming in,
    from this time forward, and forever more.

122

A Song of Ascents. By David.
1 I was glad when they said to me,
    "Let's go to the LORD's house!"
2 Our feet are standing within your gates, Jerusalem!
    3 Jerusalem is built as a city that is compact together,
4 where the tribes go up, even the LORD's tribes,
    according to an ordinance for Israel,
    to give thanks to the LORD's name.
5 For there are set thrones for judgement,
    the thrones of David's house.
6 Pray for the peace of Jerusalem.
    Those who love you will prosper.
7 Peace be within your walls,
    and prosperity within your palaces.
8 For my brothers' and companions' sakes,
    I will now say, "Peace be within you."
9 For the sake of the house of the LORD our God,
    I will seek your good.

123

A Song of Ascents.
1 I lift up my eyes to you,
    you who sit in the heavens.
2 Behold, as the eyes of servants look to the hand of their master,
    as the eyes of a maid to the hand of her mistress,
    so our eyes look to the LORD, our God,
    until he has mercy on us.
3 Have mercy on us, LORD, have mercy on us,
    for we have endured much contempt.
4 Our soul is exceedingly filled with the scoffing of those who are at ease,
    with the contempt of the proud.

124

A Song of Ascents. By David.
1 If it had not been the LORD who was on our side,
    let Israel now say,
2 if it had not been the LORD who was on our side,
    when men rose up against us,
3 then they would have swallowed us up alive,
    when their wrath was kindled against us,
4 then the waters would have overwhelmed us,
    the stream would have gone over our soul.
5 Then the proud waters would have gone over our soul.
6 Blessed be the LORD,
    who has not given us as a prey to their teeth.

7 Our soul has escaped like a bird out of the fowler's snare.
    The snare is broken, and we have escaped.
8 Our help is in the LORD's name,
    who made heaven and earth.

125

A Song of Ascents.
1 Those who trust in the LORD are as Mount Zion,
    which can't be moved, but remains forever.
2 As the mountains surround Jerusalem,
    so the LORD surrounds his people from this time forward and forever more.
3 For the sceptre of wickedness won't remain over the allotment of the righteous,
    so that the righteous won't use their hands to do evil.
4 Do good, LORD, to those who are good,
    to those who are upright in their hearts.
5 But as for those who turn away to their crooked ways,
    the LORD will lead them away with the workers of iniquity.
Peace be on Israel.

126

A Song of Ascents.
1 When the LORD brought back those who returned to Zion,
    we were like those who dream.
2 Then our mouth was filled with laughter,
    and our tongue with singing.
Then they said amongst the nations,
    "The LORD has done great things for them."
3 The LORD has done great things for us,
    and we are glad.
4 Restore our fortunes again, LORD,
    like the streams in the Negev.
5 Those who sow in tears will reap in joy.
6 He who goes out weeping, carrying seed for sowing,
    will certainly come again with joy, carrying his sheaves.

127

A Song of Ascents. By Solomon.
1 Unless the LORD builds the house,
    they who build it labour in vain.
Unless the LORD watches over the city,
    the watchman guards it in vain.
2 It is vain for you to rise up early,
    to stay up late,
    eating the bread of toil,
    for he gives sleep to his loved ones.
3 Behold, children are a heritage of the LORD.
    The fruit of the womb is his reward.
4 As arrows in the hand of a mighty man,
    so are the children of youth.
5 Happy is the man who has his quiver full of them.
    They won't be disappointed when they speak with their enemies in the gate.

128

A Song of Ascents.
1 Blessed is everyone who fears the LORD,
    who walks in his ways.
2 For you will eat the labour of your hands.
    You will be happy, and it will be well with you.
3 Your wife will be as a fruitful vine in the innermost parts of your house,
    your children like olive shoots around your table.
4 Behold, this is how the man who fears the LORD is blessed.
5 May the LORD bless you out of Zion,
    and may you see the good of Jerusalem all the days of your life.
6 Yes, may you see your children's children.
    Peace be upon Israel.

129

A Song of Ascents.
1 Many times they have afflicted me from my youth up.
    Let Israel now say:
2 many times they have afflicted me from my youth up,
    yet they have not prevailed against me.
3 The ploughers ploughed on my back.
    They made their furrows long.
4 The LORD is righteous.
    He has cut apart the cords of the wicked.
5 Let them be disappointed and turned backward,
    all those who hate Zion.
6 Let them be as the grass on the housetops,
    which withers before it grows up,
7 with which the reaper doesn't fill his hand,
    nor he who binds sheaves, his bosom.
8 Neither do those who go by say,
    "The blessing of the LORD be on you.
    We bless you in the LORD's name."

130

A Song of Ascents.
1 Out of the depths I have cried to you, LORD.

₂ Lord, hear my voice.
  Let your ears be attentive to the voice of my petitions.
₃ If you, LORD, kept a record of sins,
  Lord, who could stand?
₄ But there is forgiveness with you,
  therefore you are feared.
₅ I wait for the LORD.
  My soul waits.
  I hope in his word.
₆ My soul longs for the Lord more than watchmen long for the morning,
  more than watchmen for the morning.
₇ Israel, hope in the LORD,
  for there is loving kindness with the LORD.
  Abundant redemption is with him.
₈ He will redeem Israel from all their sins.

131

A Song of Ascents. By David.
₁ LORD, my heart isn't arrogant, nor my eyes lofty;
  nor do I concern myself with great matters,
  or things too wonderful for me.
₂ Surely I have stilled and quieted my soul,
  like a weaned child with his mother,
  like a weaned child is my soul within me.
₃ Israel, hope in the LORD,
  from this time forward and forever more.

132

A Song of Ascents.
₁ LORD, remember David and all his affliction,
₂ how he swore to the LORD,
  and vowed to the Mighty One of Jacob:
₃ "Surely I will not come into the structure of my house,
  nor go up into my bed;
₄ I will not give sleep to my eyes,
  or slumber to my eyelids,
₅ until I find out a place for the LORD,
  a dwelling for the Mighty One of Jacob."
₆ Behold, we heard of it in Ephrathah.
  We found it in the field of Jaar.
₇ "We will go into his dwelling place.
  We will worship at his footstool."
₈ Arise, LORD, into your resting place,
  you, and the ark of your strength.
₉ Let your priests be clothed with righteousness.
  Let your saints shout for joy!
₁₀ For your servant David's sake,
  don't turn away the face of your anointed one.
₁₁ The LORD has sworn to David in truth.
  He will not turn from it:
  "I will set the fruit of your body on your throne.
₁₂ If your children will keep my covenant,
  my testimony that I will teach them,
  their children also will sit on your throne forever more."
₁₃ For the LORD has chosen Zion.
  He has desired it for his habitation.
₁₄ "This is my resting place forever.
  I will live here, for I have desired it.
₁₅ I will abundantly bless her provision.
  I will satisfy her poor with bread.
₁₆ I will also clothe her priests with salvation.
  Her saints will shout aloud for joy.
₁₇ I will make the horn of David to bud there.
  I have ordained a lamp for my anointed.
₁₈ I will clothe his enemies with shame,
  but on himself, his crown will shine."

133

A Song of Ascents. By David.
₁ See how good and how pleasant it is
  for brothers to live together in unity!
₂ It is like the precious oil on the head,
  that ran down on the beard,
  even Aaron's beard,
  that came down on the edge of his robes,
₃ like the dew of Hermon,
  that comes down on the hills of Zion;
  for there the LORD gives the blessing,
  even life forever more.

134

A Song of Ascents.
₁ Look! Praise the LORD, all you servants of the LORD,
  who stand by night in the LORD's house!
₂ Lift up your hands in the sanctuary.
  Praise the LORD!
₃ May the LORD bless you from Zion,
  even he who made heaven and earth.

135

₁ Praise the LORD!
  Praise the LORD's name!
  Praise him, you servants of the LORD,
₂ you who stand in the LORD's house,
  in the courts of our God's house.
₃ Praise the LORD, for the LORD is good.
  Sing praises to his name, for that is pleasant.
₄ For the LORD has chosen Jacob for himself,
  Israel for his own possession.
₅ For I know that the LORD is great,
  that our Lord is above all gods.
₆ Whatever the LORD pleased, that he has done,
  in heaven and in earth, in the seas and in all deeps.
₇ He causes the clouds to rise from the ends of the earth.
  He makes lightnings with the rain.
  He brings the wind out of his treasuries.
₈ He struck the firstborn of Egypt,
  both of man and animal.
₉ He sent signs and wonders into the middle of you, Egypt,
  on Pharaoh, and on all his servants.
₁₀ He struck many nations,
  and killed mighty kings—
₁₁ Sihon king of the Amorites,
  Og king of Bashan,
  and all the kingdoms of Canaan—
₁₂ and gave their land for a heritage,
  a heritage to Israel, his people.
₁₃ Your name, LORD, endures forever;
  your renown, LORD, throughout all generations.
₁₄ For the LORD will judge his people
  and have compassion on his servants.

₁₅ The idols of the nations are silver and gold,
  the work of men's hands.
₁₆ They have mouths, but they can't speak.
  They have eyes, but they can't see.
₁₇ They have ears, but they can't hear,
  neither is there any breath in their mouths.
₁₈ Those who make them will be like them,
  yes, everyone who trusts in them.
₁₉ House of Israel, praise the LORD!
  House of Aaron, praise the LORD!
₂₀ House of Levi, praise the LORD!
  You who fear the LORD, praise the LORD!
₂₁ Blessed be the LORD from Zion,
  who dwells in Jerusalem.
Praise the LORD!

136

₁ Give thanks to the LORD, for he is good,
  for his loving kindness endures forever.
₂ Give thanks to the God of gods,
  for his loving kindness endures forever.
₃ Give thanks to the Lord of lords,
  for his loving kindness endures forever;
₄ to him who alone does great wonders,
  for his loving kindness endures forever;
₅ to him who by understanding made the heavens,
  for his loving kindness endures forever;
₆ to him who spread out the earth above the waters,
  for his loving kindness endures forever;
₇ to him who made the great lights,
  for his loving kindness endures forever;
₈ the sun to rule by day,
  for his loving kindness endures forever;
₉ the moon and stars to rule by night,
  for his loving kindness endures forever;
₁₀ to him who struck down the Egyptian firstborn,
  for his loving kindness endures forever;
₁₁ and brought out Israel from amongst them,
  for his loving kindness endures forever;
₁₂ with a strong hand, and with an outstretched arm,
  for his loving kindness endures forever;
₁₃ to him who divided the Red Sea apart,
  for his loving kindness endures forever;
₁₄ and made Israel to pass through the middle of it,
  for his loving kindness endures forever;
₁₅ but overthrew Pharaoh and his army in the Red Sea,
  for his loving kindness endures forever;
₁₆ to him who led his people through the wilderness,
  for his loving kindness endures forever;
₁₇ to him who struck great kings,
  for his loving kindness endures forever;
₁₈ and killed mighty kings,
  for his loving kindness endures forever;
₁₉ Sihon king of the Amorites,
  for his loving kindness endures forever;
₂₀ Og king of Bashan,
  for his loving kindness endures forever;
₂₁ and gave their land as an inheritance,
  for his loving kindness endures forever;

22 even a heritage to Israel his servant,
for his loving kindness endures forever;
23 who remembered us in our low estate,
for his loving kindness endures forever;
24 and has delivered us from our adversaries,
for his loving kindness endures forever;
25 who gives food to every creature,
for his loving kindness endures forever.
26 Oh give thanks to the God of heaven,
for his loving kindness endures forever.

137

1 By the rivers of Babylon, there we sat down.
Yes, we wept, when we remembered Zion.
2 On the willows in that land,
we hung up our harps.
3 For there, those who led us captive asked us for songs.
Those who tormented us demanded songs of joy:
"Sing us one of the songs of Zion!"
4 How can we sing the LORD's song in a foreign land?
5 If I forget you, Jerusalem,
let my right hand forget its skill.
6 Let my tongue stick to the roof of my mouth if I don't remember you,
if I don't prefer Jerusalem above my chief joy.
7 Remember, LORD, against the children of Edom in the day of Jerusalem,
who said, "Raze it!
Raze it even to its foundation!"
8 Daughter of Babylon, doomed to destruction,
he will be happy who repays you,
as you have done to us.
9 Happy shall he be,
who takes and dashes your little ones against the rock.

138

By David.
1 I will give you thanks with my whole heart.
Before the gods,[a] I will sing praises to you.
2 I will bow down towards your holy temple,
and give thanks to your Name for your loving kindness and for your truth;
for you have exalted your Name and your Word above all.
3 In the day that I called, you answered me.
You encouraged me with strength in my soul.
4 All the kings of the earth will give you thanks, LORD,
for they have heard the words of your mouth.
5 Yes, they will sing of the ways of the LORD,
for the LORD's glory is great!
6 For though the LORD is high, yet he looks after the lowly;
but he knows the proud from afar.
7 Though I walk in the middle of trouble, you will revive me.
You will stretch out your hand against the wrath of my enemies.
Your right hand will save me.
8 The LORD will fulfil that which concerns me.
Your loving kindness, LORD, endures forever.
Don't forsake the works of your own hands.

139

For the Chief Musician. A Psalm by David.
1 LORD, you have searched me,
and you know me.
2 You know my sitting down and my rising up.
You perceive my thoughts from afar.
3 You search out my path and my lying down,
and are acquainted with all my ways.
4 For there is not a word on my tongue,
but behold, LORD, you know it altogether.
5 You hem me in behind and before.
You laid your hand on me.
6 This knowledge is beyond me.
It's lofty.
I can't attain it.
7 Where could I go from your Spirit?
Or where could I flee from your presence?
8 If I ascend up into heaven, you are there.
If I make my bed in Sheol,[b] behold, you are there!
9 If I take the wings of the dawn,
and settle in the uttermost parts of the sea,
10 even there your hand will lead me,
and your right hand will hold me.
11 If I say, "Surely the darkness will overwhelm me.
The light around me will be night,"
12 even the darkness doesn't hide from you,
but the night shines as the day.
The darkness is like light to you.
13 For you formed my inmost being.
You knit me together in my mother's womb.
14 I will give thanks to you,

for I am fearfully and wonderfully made.
Your works are wonderful.
My soul knows that very well.
15 My frame wasn't hidden from you,
when I was made in secret,
woven together in the depths of the earth.
16 Your eyes saw my body.
In your book they were all written,
the days that were ordained for me,
when as yet there were none of them.
17 How precious to me are your thoughts, God!
How vast is their sum!
18 If I would count them, they are more in number than the sand.
When I wake up, I am still with you.
19 If only you, God, would kill the wicked.
Get away from me, you bloodthirsty men!
20 For they speak against you wickedly.
Your enemies take your name in vain.
21 LORD, don't I hate those who hate you?
Am I not grieved with those who rise up against you?
22 I hate them with perfect hatred.
They have become my enemies.
23 Search me, God, and know my heart.
Try me, and know my thoughts.
24 See if there is any wicked way in me,
and lead me in the everlasting way.

140

For the Chief Musician. A Psalm by David.
1 Deliver me, LORD, from evil men.
Preserve me from violent men:
2 those who devise mischief in their hearts.
They continually gather themselves together for war.
3 They have sharpened their tongues like a serpent.
Viper's poison is under their lips. Selah.
4 LORD, keep me from the hands of the wicked.
Preserve me from the violent men who have determined to trip my feet.
5 The proud have hidden a snare for me,
they have spread the cords of a net by the path.
They have set traps for me. Selah.
6 I said to the LORD, "You are my God."
Listen to the cry of my petitions, LORD.
7 LORD, the Lord, the strength of my salvation,
you have covered my head in the day of battle.
8 LORD, don't grant the desires of the wicked.
Don't let their evil plans succeed, or they will become proud. Selah.
9 As for the head of those who surround me,
let the mischief of their own lips cover them.
10 Let burning coals fall on them.
Let them be thrown into the fire,
into miry pits, from where they never rise.
11 An evil speaker won't be established in the earth.
Evil will hunt the violent man to overthrow him.
12 I know that the LORD will maintain the cause of the afflicted,
and justice for the needy.
13 Surely the righteous will give thanks to your name.
The upright will dwell in your presence.

141

A Psalm by David.
1 LORD, I have called on you.
Come to me quickly!
Listen to my voice when I call to you.
2 Let my prayer be set before you like incense;
the lifting up of my hands like the evening sacrifice.
3 Set a watch, LORD, before my mouth.
Keep the door of my lips.
4 Don't incline my heart to any evil thing,
to practise deeds of wickedness with men who work iniquity.
Don't let me eat of their delicacies.
5 Let the righteous strike me, it is kindness;
let him reprove me, it is like oil on the head;
don't let my head refuse it;
Yet my prayer is always against evil deeds.
6 Their judges are thrown down by the sides of the rock.
They will hear my words, for they are well spoken.
7 "As when one ploughs and breaks up the earth,
our bones are scattered at the mouth of Sheol."[c]
8 For my eyes are on you, LORD, the Lord.
I take refuge in you.
Don't leave my soul destitute.
9 Keep me from the snare which they have laid for me,
from the traps of the workers of iniquity.
10 Let the wicked fall together into their own nets
while I pass by.

---

a *138:1* The word elohim, used here, usually means "God" but can also mean "gods", "princes", or "angels".

b *139:8* Sheol is the place of the dead.
c *141:7* Sheol is the place of the dead.

142

A contemplation by David, when he was in the cave. A Prayer.

1 I cry with my voice to the LORD.
  With my voice, I ask the LORD for mercy.
2 I pour out my complaint before him.
  I tell him my troubles.
3 When my spirit was overwhelmed within me,
  you knew my route.
On the path in which I walk,
  they have hidden a snare for me.
4 Look on my right, and see;
  for there is no one who is concerned for me.
  Refuge has fled from me.
  No one cares for my soul.
5 I cried to you, LORD.
  I said, "You are my refuge,
  my portion in the land of the living."
6 Listen to my cry,
  for I am in desperate need.
Deliver me from my persecutors,
  for they are too strong for me.
7 Bring my soul out of prison,
  that I may give thanks to your name.
The righteous will surround me,
  for you will be good to me.

143

A Psalm by David.

1 Hear my prayer, LORD.
  Listen to my petitions.
  In your faithfulness and righteousness, relieve me.
2 Don't enter into judgement with your servant,
  for in your sight no man living is righteous.
3 For the enemy pursues my soul.
  He has struck my life down to the ground.
  He has made me live in dark places, as those who have been long
  dead.
4 Therefore my spirit is overwhelmed within me.
  My heart within me is desolate.
5 I remember the days of old.
  I meditate on all your doings.
  I contemplate the work of your hands.
6 I spread out my hands to you.
  My soul thirsts for you, like a parched land. Selah.
7 Hurry to answer me, LORD.
  My spirit fails.
Don't hide your face from me,
  so that I don't become like those who go down into the pit.
8 Cause me to hear your loving kindness in the morning,
  for I trust in you.
Cause me to know the way in which I should walk,
  for I lift up my soul to you.
9 Deliver me, LORD, from my enemies.
  I flee to you to hide me.
10 Teach me to do your will,
  for you are my God.
Your Spirit is good.
  Lead me in the land of uprightness.
11 Revive me, LORD, for your name's sake.
  In your righteousness, bring my soul out of trouble.
12 In your loving kindness, cut off my enemies,
  and destroy all those who afflict my soul,
  for I am your servant.

144

By David.

1 Blessed be the LORD, my rock,
  who trains my hands to war,
  and my fingers to battle—
2 my loving kindness, my fortress,
  my high tower, my deliverer,
  my shield, and he in whom I take refuge,
  who subdues my people under me.
3 LORD, what is man, that you care for him?
  Or the son of man, that you think of him?
4 Man is like a breath.
  His days are like a shadow that passes away.
5 Part your heavens, LORD, and come down.
  Touch the mountains, and they will smoke.
6 Throw out lightning, and scatter them.
  Send out your arrows, and rout them.
7 Stretch out your hand from above,
  rescue me, and deliver me out of great waters,
  out of the hands of foreigners,
  8 whose mouths speak deceit,
  whose right hand is a right hand of falsehood.

9 I will sing a new song to you, God.
  On a ten-stringed lyre, I will sing praises to you.
10 You are he who gives salvation to kings,
  who rescues David, his servant, from the deadly sword.
11 Rescue me, and deliver me out of the hands of foreigners,
  whose mouths speak deceit,
  whose right hand is a right hand of falsehood.

12 Then our sons will be like well-nurtured plants,
  our daughters like pillars carved to adorn a palace.
13 Our barns are full, filled with all kinds of provision.
  Our sheep produce thousands and ten thousands in our fields.
14 Our oxen will pull heavy loads.
  There is no breaking in, and no going away,
  and no outcry in our streets.
15 Happy are the people who are in such a situation.
  Happy are the people whose God is the LORD.

145

A praise psalm by David.[a]

1 I will exalt you, my God, the King.
  I will praise your name forever and ever.
2 Every day I will praise you.
  I will extol your name forever and ever.
3 Great is the LORD, and greatly to be praised!
  His greatness is unsearchable.
4 One generation will commend your works to another,
  and will declare your mighty acts.
5 I will meditate on the glorious majesty of your honour,
  on your wondrous works.
6 Men will speak of the might of your awesome acts.
  I will declare your greatness.
7 They will utter the memory of your great goodness,
  and will sing of your righteousness.
8 The LORD is gracious, merciful,
  slow to anger, and of great loving kindness.
9 The LORD is good to all.
  His tender mercies are over all his works.
10 All your works will give thanks to you, LORD.
  Your saints will extol you.
11 They will speak of the glory of your kingdom,
  and talk about your power,
12 to make known to the sons of men his mighty acts,
  the glory of the majesty of his kingdom.
13 Your kingdom is an everlasting kingdom.
  Your dominion endures throughout all generations.
The LORD is faithful in all his words,
  and loving in all his deeds.[b]
14 The LORD upholds all who fall,
  and raises up all those who are bowed down.
15 The eyes of all wait for you.
  You give them their food in due season.
16 You open your hand,
  and satisfy the desire of every living thing.
17 The LORD is righteous in all his ways,
  and gracious in all his works.
18 The LORD is near to all those who call on him,
  to all who call on him in truth.
19 He will fulfil the desire of those who fear him.
  He also will hear their cry, and will save them.
20 The LORD preserves all those who love him,
  but he will destroy all the wicked.
21 My mouth will speak the praise of the LORD.
  Let all flesh bless his holy name forever and ever.

146

1 Praise the LORD!
  Praise the LORD, my soul.
2 While I live, I will praise the LORD.
  I will sing praises to my God as long as I exist.
3 Don't put your trust in princes,
  in a son of man in whom there is no help.
4 His spirit departs, and he returns to the earth.
  In that very day, his thoughts perish.
5 Happy is he who has the God of Jacob for his help,
  whose hope is in the LORD, his God,
6 who made heaven and earth,
  the sea, and all that is in them;
  who keeps truth forever;
7 who executes justice for the oppressed;
  who gives food to the hungry.
The LORD frees the prisoners.
  8 The LORD opens the eyes of the blind.
  The LORD raises up those who are bowed down.
  The LORD loves the righteous.
9 The LORD preserves the foreigners.

---

a *145:0* This is an acrostic psalm, with every verse (including the second half of verse 13) starting with a consecutive letter of the Hebrew alphabet.

b *145:13* Some manuscripts omit these last two lines.

He upholds the fatherless and widow,
    but he turns the way of the wicked upside down.
10 The LORD will reign forever;
    your God, O Zion, to all generations.
Praise the LORD!

147

1 Praise the LORD,
    for it is good to sing praises to our God;
    for it is pleasant and fitting to praise him.
2 The LORD builds up Jerusalem.
    He gathers together the outcasts of Israel.
3 He heals the broken in heart,
    and binds up their wounds.
4 He counts the number of the stars.
    He calls them all by their names.
5 Great is our Lord, and mighty in power.
    His understanding is infinite.
6 The LORD upholds the humble.
    He brings the wicked down to the ground.
7 Sing to the LORD with thanksgiving.
    Sing praises on the harp to our God,
8 who covers the sky with clouds,
    who prepares rain for the earth,
    who makes grass grow on the mountains.
9 He provides food for the livestock,
    and for the young ravens when they call.
10 He doesn't delight in the strength of the horse.
    He takes no pleasure in the legs of a man.
11 The LORD takes pleasure in those who fear him,
    in those who hope in his loving kindness.
12 Praise the LORD, Jerusalem!
    Praise your God, Zion!
13 For he has strengthened the bars of your gates.
    He has blessed your children within you.
14 He makes peace in your borders.
    He fills you with the finest of the wheat.
15 He sends out his commandment to the earth.
    His word runs very swiftly.
16 He gives snow like wool,
    and scatters frost like ashes.
17 He hurls down his hail like pebbles.
    Who can stand before his cold?
18 He sends out his word, and melts them.
    He causes his wind to blow, and the waters flow.
19 He shows his word to Jacob,
    his statutes and his ordinances to Israel.
20 He has not done this for just any nation.
    They don't know his ordinances.
Praise the LORD!

148

1 Praise the LORD!
    Praise the LORD from the heavens!
    Praise him in the heights!
2 Praise him, all his angels!
    Praise him, all his army!
3 Praise him, sun and moon!
    Praise him, all you shining stars!
4 Praise him, you heavens of heavens,
    you waters that are above the heavens.
5 Let them praise the LORD's name,
    for he commanded, and they were created.
6 He has also established them forever and ever.
    He has made a decree which will not pass away.
7 Praise the LORD from the earth,
    you great sea creatures, and all depths,
8 lightning and hail, snow and clouds,
    stormy wind, fulfilling his word,
9 mountains and all hills,
    fruit trees and all cedars,
10 wild animals and all livestock,
    small creatures and flying birds,
11 kings of the earth and all peoples,
    princes and all judges of the earth,
12 both young men and maidens,
    old men and children.
13 Let them praise the LORD's name,
    for his name alone is exalted.
    His glory is above the earth and the heavens.
14 He has lifted up the horn of his people,
    the praise of all his saints,
    even of the children of Israel, a people near to him.
Praise the LORD!

149

1 Praise the LORD!
    Sing to the LORD a new song,
    his praise in the assembly of the saints.
2 Let Israel rejoice in him who made them.
    Let the children of Zion be joyful in their King.
3 Let them praise his name in the dance!
    Let them sing praises to him with tambourine and harp!
4 For the LORD takes pleasure in his people.
    He crowns the humble with salvation.
5 Let the saints rejoice in honour.
    Let them sing for joy on their beds.
6 May the high praises of God be in their mouths,
    and a two-edged sword in their hand,
7 to execute vengeance on the nations,
    and punishments on the peoples;
8 to bind their kings with chains,
    and their nobles with fetters of iron;
9 to execute on them the written judgement.
    All his saints have this honour.
Praise the LORD!

150

1 Praise the LORD!
    Praise God in his sanctuary!
    Praise him in his heavens for his acts of power!
2 Praise him for his mighty acts!
    Praise him according to his excellent greatness!
3 Praise him with the sounding of the trumpet!
    Praise him with harp and lyre!
4 Praise him with tambourine and dancing!
    Praise him with stringed instruments and flute!
5 Praise him with loud cymbals!
    Praise him with resounding cymbals!
6 Let everything that has breath praise the LORD!
    Praise the LORD!

The Proverbs

1

1 The proverbs of Solomon, the son of David, king of Israel:

2 to know wisdom and instruction;
  to discern the words of understanding;

3 to receive instruction in wise dealing,
  in righteousness, justice, and equity;

4 to give prudence to the simple,
  knowledge and discretion to the young man—

5 that the wise man may hear, and increase in learning;
  that the man of understanding may attain to sound counsel;

6 to understand a proverb and parables,
  the words and riddles of the wise.

7 The fear of the LORD[a] is the beginning of knowledge,
  but the foolish despise wisdom and instruction.

8 My son, listen to your father's instruction,
  and don't forsake your mother's teaching;

9 for they will be a garland to grace your head,
  and chains around your neck.

10 My son, if sinners entice you,
  don't consent.

11 If they say, "Come with us.
  Let's lie in wait for blood.
  Let's lurk secretly for the innocent without cause.

12 Let's swallow them up alive like Sheol,[b]
  and whole, like those who go down into the pit.

13 We'll find all valuable wealth.
  We'll fill our houses with plunder.

14 You shall cast your lot amongst us.
  We'll all have one purse"—

15 my son, don't walk on the path with them.
  Keep your foot from their path,

16 for their feet run to evil.
  They hurry to shed blood.

17 For the net is spread in vain in the sight of any bird;

18 but these lay in wait for their own blood.
  They lurk secretly for their own lives.

19 So are the ways of everyone who is greedy for gain.
  It takes away the life of its owners.

20 Wisdom calls aloud in the street.
  She utters her voice in the public squares.

21 She calls at the head of noisy places.
  At the entrance of the city gates, she utters her words:

22 "How long, you simple ones, will you love simplicity?
  How long will mockers delight themselves in mockery,
  and fools hate knowledge?

23 Turn at my reproof.
  Behold,[c] I will pour out my spirit on you.
  I will make known my words to you.

24 Because I have called, and you have refused;
  I have stretched out my hand, and no one has paid attention;

25 but you have ignored all my counsel,
  and wanted none of my reproof;

26 I also will laugh at your disaster.
  I will mock when calamity overtakes you,

27 when calamity overtakes you like a storm,
  when your disaster comes on like a whirlwind,
  when distress and anguish come on you.

28 Then they will call on me, but I will not answer.
  They will seek me diligently, but they will not find me,

29 because they hated knowledge,
  and didn't choose the fear of the LORD.

30 They wanted none of my counsel.
  They despised all my reproof.

31 Therefore they will eat of the fruit of their own way,
  and be filled with their own schemes.

32 For the backsliding of the simple will kill them.
  The careless ease of fools will destroy them.

33 But whoever listens to me will dwell securely,
  and will be at ease, without fear of harm."

2

1 My son, if you will receive my words,
  and store up my commandments within you,

2 so as to turn your ear to wisdom,
  and apply your heart to understanding;

3 yes, if you call out for discernment,
  and lift up your voice for understanding;

4 if you seek her as silver,
  and search for her as for hidden treasures;

5 then you will understand the fear of the LORD,
  and find the knowledge of God.[d]

6 For the LORD gives wisdom.
  Out of his mouth comes knowledge and understanding.

7 He lays up sound wisdom for the upright.
  He is a shield to those who walk in integrity,

8 that he may guard the paths of justice,
  and preserve the way of his saints.

9 Then you will understand righteousness and justice,
  equity and every good path.

10 For wisdom will enter into your heart.
  Knowledge will be pleasant to your soul.

11 Discretion will watch over you.
  Understanding will keep you,

12 to deliver you from the way of evil,
  from the men who speak perverse things,

13 who forsake the paths of uprightness,
  to walk in the ways of darkness,

14 who rejoice to do evil,
  and delight in the perverseness of evil,

15 who are crooked in their ways,
  and wayward in their paths,

16 to deliver you from the strange woman,
  even from the foreigner who flatters with her words,

17 who forsakes the friend of her youth,
  and forgets the covenant of her God;

18 for her house leads down to death,
  her paths to the departed spirits.

19 None who go to her return again,
  neither do they attain to the paths of life.

20 Therefore walk in the way of good men,
  and keep the paths of the righteous.

21 For the upright will dwell in the land.
  The perfect will remain in it.

22 But the wicked will be cut off from the land.
  The treacherous will be rooted out of it.

3

1 My son, don't forget my teaching,
  but let your heart keep my commandments,

2 for they will add to you length of days,
  years of life, and peace.

3 Don't let kindness and truth forsake you.
  Bind them around your neck.
  Write them on the tablet of your heart.

4 So you will find favour,
  and good understanding in the sight of God and man.

5 Trust in the LORD with all your heart,
  and don't lean on your own understanding.

6 In all your ways acknowledge him,
  and he will make your paths straight.

7 Don't be wise in your own eyes.
  Fear the LORD, and depart from evil.

8 It will be health to your body,
  and nourishment to your bones.

9 Honour the LORD with your substance,
  with the first fruits of all your increase;

10 so your barns will be filled with plenty,
  and your vats will overflow with new wine.

11 My son, don't despise the LORD's discipline,
  neither be weary of his correction;

12 for whom the LORD loves, he corrects,
  even as a father reproves the son in whom he delights.

13 Happy is the man who finds wisdom,
  the man who gets understanding.

14 For her good profit is better than getting silver,
  and her return is better than fine gold.

15 She is more precious than rubies.
  None of the things you can desire are to be compared to her.

16 Length of days is in her right hand.
  In her left hand are riches and honour.

17 Her ways are ways of pleasantness.
  All her paths are peace.

18 She is a tree of life to those who lay hold of her.
  Happy is everyone who retains her.

19 By wisdom the LORD founded the earth.
  By understanding, he established the heavens.

20 By his knowledge, the depths were broken up,
  and the skies drop down the dew.

21 My son, let them not depart from your eyes.
  Keep sound wisdom and discretion,

22 so they will be life to your soul,
  and grace for your neck.

23 Then you shall walk in your way securely.

---

a *1:7* When rendered in ALL CAPITAL LETTERS, "LORD" or "GOD" is the translation of God's Proper Name.

b *1:12* Sheol is the place of the dead.

c *1:23* "Behold," from "הִנֵּה", means look at, take notice, observe, see, or gaze at. It is often used as an interjection.

d *2:5* The Hebrew word rendered "God" is "אֱלֹהִים" (Elohim).

Your foot won't stumble.
24 When you lie down, you will not be afraid.
Yes, you will lie down, and your sleep will be sweet.
25 Don't be afraid of sudden fear,
neither of the desolation of the wicked, when it comes;
26 for the LORD will be your confidence,
and will keep your foot from being taken.

27 Don't withhold good from those to whom it is due,
when it is in the power of your hand to do it.
28 Don't say to your neighbour, "Go, and come again;
tomorrow I will give it to you,"
when you have it by you.
29 Don't devise evil against your neighbour,
since he dwells securely by you.
30 Don't strive with a man without cause,
if he has done you no harm.
31 Don't envy the man of violence.
Choose none of his ways.
32 For the perverse is an abomination to the LORD,
but his friendship is with the upright.
33 The LORD's curse is in the house of the wicked,
but he blesses the habitation of the righteous.
34 Surely he mocks the mockers,
but he gives grace to the humble.
35 The wise will inherit glory,
but shame will be the promotion of fools.

4

1 Listen, sons, to a father's instruction.
Pay attention and know understanding;
2 for I give you sound learning.
Don't forsake my law.
3 For I was a son to my father,
tender and an only child in the sight of my mother.
4 He taught me, and said to me:
"Let your heart retain my words.
Keep my commandments, and live.
5 Get wisdom.
Get understanding.
Don't forget, and don't deviate from the words of my mouth.
6 Don't forsake her, and she will preserve you.
Love her, and she will keep you.
7 Wisdom is supreme.
Get wisdom.
Yes, though it costs all your possessions, get understanding.
8 Esteem her, and she will exalt you.
She will bring you to honour when you embrace her.
9 She will give to your head a garland of grace.
She will deliver a crown of splendour to you."

10 Listen, my son, and receive my sayings.
The years of your life will be many.
11 I have taught you in the way of wisdom.
I have led you in straight paths.
12 When you go, your steps will not be hampered.
When you run, you will not stumble.
13 Take firm hold of instruction.
Don't let her go.
Keep her, for she is your life.
14 Don't enter into the path of the wicked.
Don't walk in the way of evil men.
15 Avoid it, and don't pass by it.
Turn from it, and pass on.
16 For they don't sleep unless they do evil.
Their sleep is taken away, unless they make someone fall.
17 For they eat the bread of wickedness
and drink the wine of violence.
18 But the path of the righteous is like the dawning light
that shines more and more until the perfect day.
19 The way of the wicked is like darkness.
They don't know what they stumble over.

20 My son, attend to my words.
Turn your ear to my sayings.
21 Let them not depart from your eyes.
Keep them in the centre of your heart.
22 For they are life to those who find them,
and health to their whole body.
23 Keep your heart with all diligence,
for out of it is the wellspring of life.
24 Put away from yourself a perverse mouth.
Put corrupt lips far from you.
25 Let your eyes look straight ahead.
Fix your gaze directly before you.
26 Make the path of your feet level.
Let all of your ways be established.

27 Don't turn to the right hand nor to the left.
Remove your foot from evil.

5

1 My son, pay attention to my wisdom.
Turn your ear to my understanding,
2 that you may maintain discretion,
that your lips may preserve knowledge.
3 For the lips of an adulteress drip honey.
Her mouth is smoother than oil,
4 but in the end she is as bitter as wormwood,
and as sharp as a two-edged sword.
5 Her feet go down to death.
Her steps lead straight to Sheol.[a]
6 She gives no thought to the way of life.
Her ways are crooked, and she doesn't know it.

7 Now therefore, my sons, listen to me.
Don't depart from the words of my mouth.
8 Remove your way far from her.
Don't come near the door of her house,
9 lest you give your honour to others,
and your years to the cruel one;
10 lest strangers feast on your wealth,
and your labours enrich another man's house.
11 You will groan at your latter end,
when your flesh and your body are consumed,
12 and say, "How I have hated instruction,
and my heart despised reproof.
13 I haven't obeyed the voice of my teachers,
nor turned my ear to those who instructed me!
14 I have come to the brink of utter ruin,
amongst the gathered assembly."

15 Drink water out of your own cistern,
running water out of your own well.
16 Should your springs overflow in the streets,
streams of water in the public squares?
17 Let them be for yourself alone,
not for strangers with you.
18 Let your spring be blessed.
Rejoice in the wife of your youth.
19 A loving doe and a graceful deer—
let her breasts satisfy you at all times.
Be captivated always with her love.
20 For why should you, my son, be captivated with an adulteress?
Why embrace the bosom of another?
21 For the ways of man are before the LORD's eyes.
He examines all his paths.
22 The evil deeds of the wicked ensnare him.
The cords of his sin hold him firmly.
23 He will die for lack of instruction.
In the greatness of his folly, he will go astray.

6

1 My son, if you have become collateral for your neighbour,
if you have struck your hands in pledge for a stranger,
2 you are trapped by the words of your mouth;
you are ensnared with the words of your mouth.
3 Do this now, my son, and deliver yourself,
since you have come into the hand of your neighbour.
Go, humble yourself.
Press your plea with your neighbour.
4 Give no sleep to your eyes,
nor slumber to your eyelids.
5 Free yourself, like a gazelle from the hand of the hunter,
like a bird from the snare of the fowler.

6 Go to the ant, you sluggard.
Consider her ways, and be wise;
7 which having no chief, overseer, or ruler,
8 provides her bread in the summer,
and gathers her food in the harvest.
9 How long will you sleep, sluggard?
When will you arise out of your sleep?
10 A little sleep, a little slumber,
a little folding of the hands to sleep—
11 so your poverty will come as a robber,
and your scarcity as an armed man.

12 A worthless person, a man of iniquity,
is he who walks with a perverse mouth,
13 who winks with his eyes, who signals with his feet,
who motions with his fingers,
14 in whose heart is perverseness,
who devises evil continually,
who always sows discord.
15 Therefore his calamity will come suddenly.

---

a 5:5 Sheol is the place of the dead.

He will be broken suddenly, and that without remedy.

16 There are six things which the LORD hates;
   yes, seven which are an abomination to him:
17 arrogant eyes, a lying tongue,
   hands that shed innocent blood,
18 a heart that devises wicked schemes,
   feet that are swift in running to mischief,
19 a false witness who utters lies,
   and he who sows discord amongst brothers.

20 My son, keep your father's commandment,
   and don't forsake your mother's teaching.
21 Bind them continually on your heart.
   Tie them around your neck.
22 When you walk, it will lead you.
   When you sleep, it will watch over you.
   When you awake, it will talk with you.
23 For the commandment is a lamp,
   and the law is light.
   Reproofs of instruction are the way of life,
24 to keep you from the immoral woman,
   from the flattery of the wayward wife's tongue.
25 Don't lust after her beauty in your heart,
   neither let her captivate you with her eyelids.
26 For a prostitute reduces you to a piece of bread.
   The adulteress hunts for your precious life.
27 Can a man scoop fire into his lap,
   and his clothes not be burnt?
28 Or can one walk on hot coals,
   and his feet not be scorched?
29 So is he who goes in to his neighbour's wife.
   Whoever touches her will not be unpunished.
30 Men don't despise a thief
   if he steals to satisfy himself when he is hungry,
31 but if he is found, he shall restore seven times.
   He shall give all the wealth of his house.
32 He who commits adultery with a woman is void of understanding.
   He who does it destroys his own soul.
33 He will get wounds and dishonour.
   His reproach will not be wiped away.
34 For jealousy arouses the fury of the husband.
   He won't spare in the day of vengeance.
35 He won't regard any ransom,
   neither will he rest content, though you give many gifts.

7

1 My son, keep my words.
   Lay up my commandments within you.
2 Keep my commandments and live!
   Guard my teaching as the apple of your eye.
3 Bind them on your fingers.
   Write them on the tablet of your heart.
4 Tell wisdom, "You are my sister."
   Call understanding your relative,
5 that they may keep you from the strange woman,
   from the foreigner who flatters with her words.
6 For at the window of my house,
   I looked out through my lattice.
7 I saw amongst the simple ones.
   I discerned amongst the youths a young man void of understanding,
8 passing through the street near her corner,
   he went the way to her house,
9 in the twilight, in the evening of the day,
   in the middle of the night and in the darkness.
10 Behold, there a woman met him with the attire of a prostitute,
   and with crafty intent.
11 She is loud and defiant.
   Her feet don't stay in her house.
12 Now she is in the streets, now in the squares,
   and lurking at every corner.
13 So she caught him, and kissed him.
   With an impudent face she said to him:
14 "Sacrifices of peace offerings are with me.
   Today I have paid my vows.
15 Therefore I came out to meet you,
   to diligently seek your face,
   and I have found you.
16 I have spread my couch with carpets of tapestry,
   with striped cloths of the yarn of Egypt.
17 I have perfumed my bed with myrrh, aloes, and cinnamon.
18 Come, let's take our fill of loving until the morning.
   Let's solace ourselves with loving.
19 For my husband isn't at home.
   He has gone on a long journey.
20 He has taken a bag of money with him.
   He will come home at the full moon."

21 With persuasive words, she led him astray.
   With the flattering of her lips, she seduced him.
22 He followed her immediately,
   as an ox goes to the slaughter,
   as a fool stepping into a noose.
23 Until an arrow strikes through his liver,
   as a bird hurries to the snare,
   and doesn't know that it will cost his life.

24 Now therefore, sons, listen to me.
   Pay attention to the words of my mouth.
25 Don't let your heart turn to her ways.
   Don't go astray in her paths,
26 for she has thrown down many wounded.
   Yes, all her slain are a mighty army.
27 Her house is the way to Sheol,ᵃ
   going down to the rooms of death.

8

1 Doesn't wisdom cry out?
   Doesn't understanding raise her voice?
2 On the top of high places by the way,
   where the paths meet, she stands.
3 Beside the gates, at the entry of the city,
   at the entry doors, she cries aloud:
4 "I call to you men!
   I send my voice to the sons of mankind.
5 You simple, understand prudence!
   You fools, be of an understanding heart!
6 Hear, for I will speak excellent things.
   The opening of my lips is for right things.
7 For my mouth speaks truth.
   Wickedness is an abomination to my lips.
8 All the words of my mouth are in righteousness.
   There is nothing crooked or perverse in them.
9 They are all plain to him who understands,
   right to those who find knowledge.
10 Receive my instruction rather than silver,
   knowledge rather than choice gold.
11 For wisdom is better than rubies.
   All the things that may be desired can't be compared to it.

12 "I, wisdom, have made prudence my dwelling.
   Find out knowledge and discretion.
13 The fear of the LORD is to hate evil.
   I hate pride, arrogance, the evil way, and the perverse mouth.
14 Counsel and sound knowledge are mine.
   I have understanding and power.
15 By me kings reign,
   and princes decree justice.
16 By me princes rule,
   nobles, and all the righteous rulers of the earth.
17 I love those who love me.
   Those who seek me diligently will find me.
18 With me are riches, honour,
   enduring wealth, and prosperity.
19 My fruit is better than gold, yes, than fine gold,
   my yield than choice silver.
20 I walk in the way of righteousness,
   in the middle of the paths of justice,
21 that I may give wealth to those who love me.
   I fill their treasuries.

22 "The LORD possessed me in the beginning of his work,
   before his deeds of old.
23 I was set up from everlasting, from the beginning,
   before the earth existed.
24 When there were no depths, I was born,
   when there were no springs abounding with water.
25 Before the mountains were settled in place,
   before the hills, I was born;
26 while as yet he had not made the earth, nor the fields,
   nor the beginning of the dust of the world.
27 When he established the heavens, I was there.
   When he set a circle on the surface of the deep,
28 when he established the clouds above,
   when the springs of the deep became strong,
29 when he gave to the sea its boundary,
   that the waters should not violate his commandment,
   when he marked out the foundations of the earth,
30 then I was the craftsman by his side.
   I was a delight day by day,
   always rejoicing before him,
31 rejoicing in his whole world.
   My delight was with the sons of men.

32 "Now therefore, my sons, listen to me,

ᵃ 7:27 Sheol is the place of the dead.

for blessed are those who keep my ways.
33 Hear instruction, and be wise.
　　Don't refuse it.
34 Blessed is the man who hears me,
　　watching daily at my gates,
　　waiting at my door posts.
35 For whoever finds me finds life,
　　and will obtain favour from the LORD.
36 But he who sins against me wrongs his own soul.
　　All those who hate me love death."

9

1 Wisdom has built her house.
　　She has carved out her seven pillars.
2 She has prepared her meat.
　　She has mixed her wine.
　　She has also set her table.
3 She has sent out her maidens.
　　She cries from the highest places of the city:
4 "Whoever is simple, let him turn in here!"
　　As for him who is void of understanding, she says to him,
5 "Come, eat some of my bread,
　　Drink some of the wine which I have mixed!
6 Leave your simple ways, and live.
　　Walk in the way of understanding."

7 One who corrects a mocker invites insult.
　　One who reproves a wicked man invites abuse.
8 Don't reprove a scoffer, lest he hate you.
　　Reprove a wise person, and he will love you.
9 Instruct a wise person, and he will be still wiser.
　　Teach a righteous person, and he will increase in learning.
10 The fear of the LORD is the beginning of wisdom.
　　The knowledge of the Holy One is understanding.
11 For by me your days will be multiplied.
　　The years of your life will be increased.
12 If you are wise, you are wise for yourself.
　　If you mock, you alone will bear it.

13 The foolish woman is loud,
　　undisciplined, and knows nothing.
14 She sits at the door of her house,
　　on a seat in the high places of the city,
15 to call to those who pass by,
　　who go straight on their ways,
16 "Whoever is simple, let him turn in here."
　　As for him who is void of understanding, she says to him,
17 "Stolen water is sweet.
　　Food eaten in secret is pleasant."
18 But he doesn't know that the departed spirits are there,
　　that her guests are in the depths of Sheol.ᵃ

10

1 The proverbs of Solomon.
A wise son makes a glad father;
　　but a foolish son brings grief to his mother.
2 Treasures of wickedness profit nothing,
　　but righteousness delivers from death.
3 The LORD will not allow the soul of the righteous to go hungry,
　　but he thrusts away the desire of the wicked.
4 He becomes poor who works with a lazy hand,
　　but the hand of the diligent brings wealth.
5 He who gathers in summer is a wise son,
　　but he who sleeps during the harvest is a son who causes shame.
6 Blessings are on the head of the righteous,
　　but violence covers the mouth of the wicked.
7 The memory of the righteous is blessed,
　　but the name of the wicked will rot.
8 The wise in heart accept commandments,
　　but a chattering fool will fall.
9 He who walks blamelessly walks surely,
　　but he who perverts his ways will be found out.
10 One who winks with the eye causes sorrow,
　　but a chattering fool will fall.
11 The mouth of the righteous is a spring of life,
　　but violence covers the mouth of the wicked.
12 Hatred stirs up strife,
　　but love covers all wrongs.
13 Wisdom is found on the lips of him who has discernment,
　　but a rod is for the back of him who is void of understanding.
14 Wise men lay up knowledge,
　　but the mouth of the foolish is near ruin.
15 The rich man's wealth is his strong city.
　　The destruction of the poor is their poverty.
16 The labour of the righteous leads to life.
　　The increase of the wicked leads to sin.
17 He is in the way of life who heeds correction,
　　but he who forsakes reproof leads others astray.

18 He who hides hatred has lying lips.
　　He who utters a slander is a fool.
19 In the multitude of words there is no lack of disobedience,
　　but he who restrains his lips does wisely.
20 The tongue of the righteous is like choice silver.
　　The heart of the wicked is of little worth.
21 The lips of the righteous feed many,
　　but the foolish die for lack of understanding.
22 The LORD's blessing brings wealth,
　　and he adds no trouble to it.
23 It is a fool's pleasure to do wickedness,
　　but wisdom is a man of understanding's pleasure.
24 What the wicked fear will overtake them,
　　but the desire of the righteous will be granted.
25 When the whirlwind passes, the wicked is no more;
　　but the righteous stand firm forever.
26 As vinegar to the teeth, and as smoke to the eyes,
　　so is the sluggard to those who send him.
27 The fear of the LORD prolongs days,
　　but the years of the wicked shall be shortened.
28 The prospect of the righteous is joy,
　　but the hope of the wicked will perish.
29 The way of the LORD is a stronghold to the upright,
　　but it is a destruction to the workers of iniquity.
30 The righteous will never be removed,
　　but the wicked will not dwell in the land.
31 The mouth of the righteous produces wisdom,
　　but the perverse tongue will be cut off.
32 The lips of the righteous know what is acceptable,
　　but the mouth of the wicked is perverse.

11

1 A false balance is an abomination to the LORD,
　　but accurate weights are his delight.
2 When pride comes, then comes shame,
　　but with humility comes wisdom.
3 The integrity of the upright shall guide them,
　　but the perverseness of the treacherous shall destroy them.
4 Riches don't profit in the day of wrath,
　　but righteousness delivers from death.
5 The righteousness of the blameless will direct his way,
　　but the wicked shall fall by his own wickedness.
6 The righteousness of the upright shall deliver them,
　　but the unfaithful will be trapped by evil desires.
7 When a wicked man dies, hope perishes,
　　and expectation of power comes to nothing.
8 A righteous person is delivered out of trouble,
　　and the wicked takes his place.
9 With his mouth the godless man destroys his neighbour,
　　but the righteous will be delivered through knowledge.
10 When it goes well with the righteous, the city rejoices.
　　When the wicked perish, there is shouting.
11 By the blessing of the upright, the city is exalted,
　　but it is overthrown by the mouth of the wicked.
12 One who despises his neighbour is void of wisdom,
　　but a man of understanding holds his peace.
13 One who brings gossip betrays a confidence,
　　but one who is of a trustworthy spirit is one who keeps a secret.
14 Where there is no wise guidance, the nation falls,
　　but in the multitude of counsellors there is victory.
15 He who is collateral for a stranger will suffer for it,
　　but he who refuses pledges of collateral is secure.
16 A gracious woman obtains honour,
　　but violent men obtain riches.
17 The merciful man does good to his own soul,
　　but he who is cruel troubles his own flesh.
18 Wicked people earn deceitful wages,
　　but one who sows righteousness reaps a sure reward.
19 He who is truly righteous gets life.
　　He who pursues evil gets death.
20 Those who are perverse in heart are an abomination to the LORD,
　　but those whose ways are blameless are his delight.
21 Most certainly, the evil man will not be unpunished,
　　but the offspringᵇ of the righteous will be delivered.
22 Like a gold ring in a pig's snout,
　　is a beautiful woman who lacks discretion.
23 The desire of the righteous is only good.
　　The expectation of the wicked is wrath.
24 There is one who scatters, and increases yet more.
　　There is one who withholds more than is appropriate, but gains poverty.
25 The liberal soul shall be made fat.
　　He who waters shall be watered also himself.
26 People curse someone who withholds grain,
　　but blessing will be on the head of him who sells it.
27 He who diligently seeks good seeks favour,
　　but he who searches after evil, it shall come to him.

ᵃ *9:18* Sheol is the place of the dead.

ᵇ *11:21* or, seed

28 He who trusts in his riches will fall,
　　but the righteous shall flourish as the green leaf.
29 He who troubles his own house shall inherit the wind.
　　The foolish shall be servant to the wise of heart.
30 The fruit of the righteous is a tree of life.
　　He who is wise wins souls.
31 Behold, the righteous shall be repaid in the earth,
　　how much more the wicked and the sinner!

12

1 Whoever loves correction loves knowledge,
　　but he who hates reproof is stupid.
2 A good man shall obtain favour from the LORD,
　　but he will condemn a man of wicked plans.
3 A man shall not be established by wickedness,
　　but the root of the righteous shall not be moved.
4 A worthy woman is the crown of her husband,
　　but a disgraceful wife is as rottenness in his bones.
5 The thoughts of the righteous are just,
　　but the advice of the wicked is deceitful.
6 The words of the wicked are about lying in wait for blood,
　　but the speech of the upright rescues them.
7 The wicked are overthrown, and are no more,
　　but the house of the righteous shall stand.
8 A man shall be commended according to his wisdom,
　　but he who has a warped mind shall be despised.
9 Better is he who is little known, and has a servant,
　　than he who honours himself and lacks bread.
10 A righteous man respects the life of his animal,
　　but the tender mercies of the wicked are cruel.
11 He who tills his land shall have plenty of bread,
　　but he who chases fantasies is void of understanding.
12 The wicked desires the plunder of evil men,
　　but the root of the righteous flourishes.
13 An evil man is trapped by sinfulness of lips,
　　but the righteous shall come out of trouble.
14 A man shall be satisfied with good by the fruit of his mouth.
　　The work of a man's hands shall be rewarded to him.
15 The way of a fool is right in his own eyes,
　　but he who is wise listens to counsel.
16 A fool shows his annoyance the same day,
　　but one who overlooks an insult is prudent.
17 He who is truthful testifies honestly,
　　but a false witness lies.
18 There is one who speaks rashly like the piercing of a sword,
　　but the tongue of the wise heals.
19 Truth's lips will be established forever,
　　but a lying tongue is only momentary.
20 Deceit is in the heart of those who plot evil,
　　but joy comes to the promoters of peace.
21 No mischief shall happen to the righteous,
　　but the wicked shall be filled with evil.
22 Lying lips are an abomination to the LORD,
　　but those who do the truth are his delight.
23 A prudent man keeps his knowledge,
　　but the hearts of fools proclaim foolishness.
24 The hands of the diligent ones shall rule,
　　but laziness ends in slave labour.
25 Anxiety in a man's heart weighs it down,
　　but a kind word makes it glad.
26 A righteous person is cautious in friendship,
　　but the way of the wicked leads them astray.
27 The slothful man doesn't roast his game,
　　but the possessions of diligent men are prized.
28 In the way of righteousness is life;
　　in its path there is no death.

13

1 A wise son listens to his father's instruction,
　　but a scoffer doesn't listen to rebuke.
2 By the fruit of his lips, a man enjoys good things,
　　but the unfaithful crave violence.
3 He who guards his mouth guards his soul.
　　One who opens wide his lips comes to ruin.
4 The soul of the sluggard desires, and has nothing,
　　but the desire of the diligent shall be fully satisfied.
5 A righteous man hates lies,
　　but a wicked man brings shame and disgrace.
6 Righteousness guards the way of integrity,
　　but wickedness overthrows the sinner.
7 There are some who pretend to be rich, yet have nothing.
　　There are some who pretend to be poor, yet have great wealth.
8 The ransom of a man's life is his riches,
　　but the poor hear no threats.
9 The light of the righteous shines brightly,
　　but the lamp of the wicked is snuffed out.
10 Pride only breeds quarrels,
　　but wisdom is with people who take advice.
11 Wealth gained dishonestly dwindles away,
　　but he who gathers by hand makes it grow.

12 Hope deferred makes the heart sick,
　　but when longing is fulfilled, it is a tree of life.
13 Whoever despises instruction will pay for it,
　　but he who respects a command will be rewarded.
14 The teaching of the wise is a spring of life,
　　to turn from the snares of death.
15 Good understanding wins favour,
　　but the way of the unfaithful is hard.
16 Every prudent man acts from knowledge,
　　but a fool exposes folly.
17 A wicked messenger falls into trouble,
　　but a trustworthy envoy gains healing.
18 Poverty and shame come to him who refuses discipline,
　　but he who heeds correction shall be honoured.
19 Longing fulfilled is sweet to the soul,
　　but fools detest turning from evil.
20 One who walks with wise men grows wise,
　　but a companion of fools suffers harm.
21 Misfortune pursues sinners,
　　but prosperity rewards the righteous.
22 A good man leaves an inheritance to his children's children,
　　but the wealth of the sinner is stored for the righteous.
23 An abundance of food is in poor people's fields,
　　but injustice sweeps it away.
24 One who spares the rod hates his son,
　　but one who loves him is careful to discipline him.
25 The righteous one eats to the satisfying of his soul,
　　but the belly of the wicked goes hungry.

14

1 Every wise woman builds her house,
　　but the foolish one tears it down with her own hands.
2 He who walks in his uprightness fears the LORD,
　　but he who is perverse in his ways despises him.
3 The fool's talk brings a rod to his back,
　　but the lips of the wise protect them.
4 Where no oxen are, the crib is clean,
　　but much increase is by the strength of the ox.
5 A truthful witness will not lie,
　　but a false witness pours out lies.
6 A scoffer seeks wisdom, and doesn't find it,
　　but knowledge comes easily to a discerning person.
7 Stay away from a foolish man,
　　for you won't find knowledge on his lips.
8 The wisdom of the prudent is to think about his way,
　　but the folly of fools is deceit.
9 Fools mock at making atonement for sins,
　　but amongst the upright there is good will.
10 The heart knows its own bitterness and joy;
　　he will not share these with a stranger.
11 The house of the wicked will be overthrown,
　　but the tent of the upright will flourish.
12 There is a way which seems right to a man,
　　but in the end it leads to death.
13 Even in laughter the heart may be sorrowful,
　　and mirth may end in heaviness.
14 The unfaithful will be repaid for his own ways;
　　likewise a good man will be rewarded for his ways.
15 A simple man believes everything,
　　but the prudent man carefully considers his ways.
16 A wise man fears and shuns evil,
　　but the fool is hot headed and reckless.
17 He who is quick to become angry will commit folly,
　　and a crafty man is hated.
18 The simple inherit folly,
　　but the prudent are crowned with knowledge.
19 The evil bow down before the good,
　　and the wicked at the gates of the righteous.
20 The poor person is shunned even by his own neighbour,
　　but the rich person has many friends.
21 He who despises his neighbour sins,
　　but he who has pity on the poor is blessed.
22 Don't they go astray who plot evil?
　　But love and faithfulness belong to those who plan good.
23 In all hard work there is profit,
　　but the talk of the lips leads only to poverty.
24 The crown of the wise is their riches,
　　but the folly of fools crowns them with folly.
25 A truthful witness saves souls,
　　but a false witness is deceitful.
26 In the fear of the LORD is a secure fortress,
　　and he will be a refuge for his children.
27 The fear of the LORD is a fountain of life,
　　turning people from the snares of death.
28 In the multitude of people is the king's glory,
　　but in the lack of people is the destruction of the prince.
29 He who is slow to anger has great understanding,
　　but he who has a quick temper displays folly.
30 The life of the body is a heart at peace,
　　but envy rots the bones.

31 He who oppresses the poor shows contempt for his Maker,
   but he who is kind to the needy honours him.
32 The wicked is brought down in his calamity,
   but in death, the righteous has a refuge.
33 Wisdom rests in the heart of one who has understanding,
   and is even made known in the inward part of fools.
34 Righteousness exalts a nation,
   but sin is a disgrace to any people.
35 The king's favour is towards a servant who deals wisely,
   but his wrath is towards one who causes shame.

15

1 A gentle answer turns away wrath,
   but a harsh word stirs up anger.
2 The tongue of the wise commends knowledge,
   but the mouths of fools gush out folly.
3 The LORD's eyes are everywhere,
   keeping watch on the evil and the good.
4 A gentle tongue is a tree of life,
   but deceit in it crushes the spirit.
5 A fool despises his father's correction,
   but he who heeds reproof shows prudence.
6 In the house of the righteous is much treasure,
   but the income of the wicked brings trouble.
7 The lips of the wise spread knowledge;
   not so with the heart of fools.
8 The sacrifice made by the wicked is an abomination to the LORD,
   but the prayer of the upright is his delight.
9 The way of the wicked is an abomination to the LORD,
   but he loves him who follows after righteousness.
10 There is stern discipline for one who forsakes the way.
   Whoever hates reproof shall die.
11 Sheolª and Abaddon are before the LORD—
   how much more then the hearts of the children of men!
12 A scoffer doesn't love to be reproved;
   he will not go to the wise.
13 A glad heart makes a cheerful face,
   but an aching heart breaks the spirit.
14 The heart of one who has understanding seeks knowledge,
   but the mouths of fools feed on folly.
15 All the days of the afflicted are wretched,
   but one who has a cheerful heart enjoys a continual feast.
16 Better is little, with the fear of the LORD,
   than great treasure with trouble.
17 Better is a dinner of herbs, where love is,
   than a fattened calf with hatred.
18 A wrathful man stirs up contention,
   but one who is slow to anger appeases strife.
19 The way of the sluggard is like a thorn patch,
   but the path of the upright is a highway.
20 A wise son makes a father glad,
   but a foolish man despises his mother.
21 Folly is joy to one who is void of wisdom,
   but a man of understanding keeps his way straight.
22 Where there is no counsel, plans fail;
   but in a multitude of counsellors they are established.
23 Joy comes to a man with the reply of his mouth.
   How good is a word at the right time!
24 The path of life leads upward for the wise,
   to keep him from going downward to Sheol.ᵇ
25 The LORD will uproot the house of the proud,
   but he will keep the widow's borders intact.
26 The LORD detests the thoughts of the wicked,
   but the thoughts of the pure are pleasing.
27 He who is greedy for gain troubles his own house,
   but he who hates bribes will live.
28 The heart of the righteous weighs answers,
   but the mouth of the wicked gushes out evil.
29 The LORD is far from the wicked,
   but he hears the prayer of the righteous.
30 The light of the eyes rejoices the heart.
   Good news gives health to the bones.
31 The ear that listens to reproof lives,
   and will be at home amongst the wise.
32 He who refuses correction despises his own soul,
   but he who listens to reproof gets understanding.
33 The fear of the LORD teaches wisdom.
   Before honour is humility.

16

1 The plans of the heart belong to man,
   but the answer of the tongue is from the LORD.
2 All the ways of a man are clean in his own eyes,
   but the LORD weighs the motives.
3 Commit your deeds to the LORD,
   and your plans shall succeed.
4 The LORD has made everything for its own end—
   yes, even the wicked for the day of evil.

5 Everyone who is proud in heart is an abomination to the LORD;
   they shall certainly not be unpunished.
6 By mercy and truth iniquity is atoned for.
   By the fear of the LORD men depart from evil.
7 When a man's ways please the LORD,
   he makes even his enemies to be at peace with him.
8 Better is a little with righteousness,
   than great revenues with injustice.
9 A man's heart plans his course,
   but the LORD directs his steps.
10 Inspired judgements are on the lips of the king.
   He shall not betray his mouth.
11 Honest balances and scales are the LORD's;
   all the weights in the bag are his work.
12 It is an abomination for kings to do wrong,
   for the throne is established by righteousness.
13 Righteous lips are the delight of kings.
   They value one who speaks the truth.
14 The king's wrath is a messenger of death,
   but a wise man will pacify it.
15 In the light of the king's face is life.
   His favour is like a cloud of the spring rain.
16 How much better it is to get wisdom than gold!
   Yes, to get understanding is to be chosen rather than silver.
17 The highway of the upright is to depart from evil.
   He who keeps his way preserves his soul.
18 Pride goes before destruction,
   and an arrogant spirit before a fall.
19 It is better to be of a lowly spirit with the poor,
   than to divide the plunder with the proud.
20 He who heeds the Word finds prosperity.
   Whoever trusts in the LORD is blessed.
21 The wise in heart shall be called prudent.
   Pleasantness of the lips promotes instruction.
22 Understanding is a fountain of life to one who has it,
   but the punishment of fools is their folly.
23 The heart of the wise instructs his mouth,
   and adds learning to his lips.
24 Pleasant words are a honeycomb,
   sweet to the soul, and health to the bones.
25 There is a way which seems right to a man,
   but in the end it leads to death.
26 The appetite of the labouring man labours for him,
   for his mouth urges him on.
27 A worthless man devises mischief.
   His speech is like a scorching fire.
28 A perverse man stirs up strife.
   A whisperer separates close friends.
29 A man of violence entices his neighbour,
   and leads him in a way that is not good.
30 One who winks his eyes to plot perversities,
   one who compresses his lips, is bent on evil.
31 Grey hair is a crown of glory.
   It is attained by a life of righteousness.
32 One who is slow to anger is better than the mighty;
   one who rules his spirit, than he who takes a city.
33 The lot is cast into the lap,
   but its every decision is from the LORD.

17

1 Better is a dry morsel with quietness,
   than a house full of feasting with strife.
2 A servant who deals wisely will rule over a son who causes shame,
   and shall have a part in the inheritance amongst the brothers.
3 The refining pot is for silver, and the furnace for gold,
   but the LORD tests the hearts.
4 An evildoer heeds wicked lips.
   A liar gives ear to a mischievous tongue.
5 Whoever mocks the poor reproaches his Maker.
   He who is glad at calamity shall not be unpunished.
6 Children's children are the crown of old men;
   the glory of children is their parents.
7 Excellent speech isn't fitting for a fool,
   much less do lying lips fit a prince.
8 A bribe is a precious stone in the eyes of him who gives it;
   wherever he turns, he prospers.
9 He who covers an offence promotes love;
   but he who repeats a matter separates best friends.
10 A rebuke enters deeper into one who has understanding
   than a hundred lashes into a fool.
11 An evil man seeks only rebellion;
   therefore a cruel messenger shall be sent against him.
12 Let a bear robbed of her cubs meet a man,
   rather than a fool in his folly.
13 Whoever rewards evil for good,
   evil shall not depart from his house.
14 The beginning of strife is like breaching a dam,

---

therefore stop contention before quarrelling breaks out.

15 He who justifies the wicked, and he who condemns the righteous,
   both of them alike are an abomination to the LORD.

16 Why is there money in the hand of a fool to buy wisdom,
   since he has no understanding?

17 A friend loves at all times;
   and a brother is born for adversity.

18 A man void of understanding strikes hands,
   and becomes collateral in the presence of his neighbour.

19 He who loves disobedience loves strife.
   One who builds a high gate seeks destruction.

20 One who has a perverse heart doesn't find prosperity,
   and one who has a deceitful tongue falls into trouble.

21 He who becomes the father of a fool grieves.
   The father of a fool has no joy.

22 A cheerful heart makes good medicine,
   but a crushed spirit dries up the bones.

23 A wicked man receives a bribe in secret,
   to pervert the ways of justice.

24 Wisdom is before the face of one who has understanding,
   but the eyes of a fool wander to the ends of the earth.

25 A foolish son brings grief to his father,
   and bitterness to her who bore him.

26 Also to punish the righteous is not good,
   nor to flog officials for their integrity.

27 He who spares his words has knowledge.
   He who is even tempered is a man of understanding.

28 Even a fool, when he keeps silent, is counted wise.
   When he shuts his lips, he is thought to be discerning.

18

1 A man who isolates himself pursues selfishness,
   and defies all sound judgement.

2 A fool has no delight in understanding,
   but only in revealing his own opinion.

3 When wickedness comes, contempt also comes,
   and with shame comes disgrace.

4 The words of a man's mouth are like deep waters.
   The fountain of wisdom is like a flowing brook.

5 To be partial to the faces of the wicked is not good,
   nor to deprive the innocent of justice.

6 A fool's lips come into strife,
   and his mouth invites beatings.

7 A fool's mouth is his destruction,
   and his lips are a snare to his soul.

8 The words of a gossip are like dainty morsels:
   they go down into a person's innermost parts.

9 One who is slack in his work
   is brother to him who is a master of destruction.

10 The LORD's name is a strong tower:
   the righteous run to him, and are safe.

11 The rich man's wealth is his strong city,
   like an unscalable wall in his own imagination.

12 Before destruction the heart of man is proud,
   but before honour is humility.

13 He who answers before he hears,
   that is folly and shame to him.

14 A man's spirit will sustain him in sickness,
   but a crushed spirit, who can bear?

15 The heart of the discerning gets knowledge.
   The ear of the wise seeks knowledge.

16 A man's gift makes room for him,
   and brings him before great men.

17 He who pleads his cause first seems right—
   until another comes and questions him.

18 The lot settles disputes,
   and keeps strong ones apart.

19 A brother offended is more difficult than a fortified city.
   Disputes are like the bars of a fortress.

20 A man's stomach is filled with the fruit of his mouth.
   With the harvest of his lips he is satisfied.

21 Death and life are in the power of the tongue;
   those who love it will eat its fruit.

22 Whoever finds a wife finds a good thing,
   and obtains favour of the LORD.

23 The poor plead for mercy,
   but the rich answer harshly.

24 A man of many companions may be ruined,
   but there is a friend who sticks closer than a brother.

19

1 Better is the poor who walks in his integrity
   than he who is perverse in his lips and is a fool.

2 It isn't good to have zeal without knowledge,
   nor being hasty with one's feet and missing the way.

3 The foolishness of man subverts his way;
   his heart rages against the LORD.

4 Wealth adds many friends,
   but the poor is separated from his friend.

5 A false witness shall not be unpunished.

He who pours out lies shall not go free.

6 Many will entreat the favour of a ruler,
   and everyone is a friend to a man who gives gifts.

7 All the relatives of the poor shun him;
   how much more do his friends avoid him!
   He pursues them with pleas, but they are gone.

8 He who gets wisdom loves his own soul.
   He who keeps understanding shall find good.

9 A false witness shall not be unpunished.
   He who utters lies shall perish.

10 Delicate living is not appropriate for a fool,
   much less for a servant to have rule over princes.

11 The discretion of a man makes him slow to anger.
   It is his glory to overlook an offence.

12 The king's wrath is like the roaring of a lion,
   but his favour is like dew on the grass.

13 A foolish son is the calamity of his father.
   A wife's quarrels are a continual dripping.

14 House and riches are an inheritance from fathers,
   but a prudent wife is from the LORD.

15 Slothfulness casts into a deep sleep.
   The idle soul shall suffer hunger.

16 He who keeps the commandment keeps his soul,
   but he who is contemptuous in his ways shall die.

17 He who has pity on the poor lends to the LORD;
   he will reward him.

18 Discipline your son, for there is hope;
   don't be a willing party to his death.

19 A hot-tempered man must pay the penalty,
   for if you rescue him, you must do it again.

20 Listen to counsel and receive instruction,
   that you may be wise in your latter end.

21 There are many plans in a man's heart,
   but the LORD's counsel will prevail.

22 That which makes a man to be desired is his kindness.
   A poor man is better than a liar.

23 The fear of the LORD leads to life, then contentment;
   he rests and will not be touched by trouble.

24 The sluggard buries his hand in the dish;
   he will not so much as bring it to his mouth again.

25 Flog a scoffer, and the simple will learn prudence;
   rebuke one who has understanding, and he will gain knowledge.

26 He who robs his father and drives away his mother
   is a son who causes shame and brings reproach.

27 If you stop listening to instruction, my son,
   you will stray from the words of knowledge.

28 A corrupt witness mocks justice,
   and the mouth of the wicked gulps down iniquity.

29 Penalties are prepared for scoffers,
   and beatings for the backs of fools.

20

1 Wine is a mocker and beer is a brawler.
   Whoever is led astray by them is not wise.

2 The terror of a king is like the roaring of a lion.
   He who provokes him to anger forfeits his own life.

3 It is an honour for a man to keep aloof from strife,
   but every fool will be quarrelling.

4 The sluggard will not plough by reason of the winter;
   therefore he shall beg in harvest, and have nothing.

5 Counsel in the heart of man is like deep water,
   but a man of understanding will draw it out.

6 Many men claim to be men of unfailing love,
   but who can find a faithful man?

7 A righteous man walks in integrity.
   Blessed are his children after him.

8 A king who sits on the throne of judgement
   scatters away all evil with his eyes.

9 Who can say, "I have made my heart pure.
   I am clean and without sin"?

10 Differing weights and differing measures,
   both of them alike are an abomination to the LORD.

11 Even a child makes himself known by his doings,
   whether his work is pure, and whether it is right.

12 The hearing ear, and the seeing eye,
   the LORD has made even both of them.

13 Don't love sleep, lest you come to poverty.
   Open your eyes, and you shall be satisfied with bread.

14 "It's no good, it's no good," says the buyer;
   but when he is gone his way, then he boasts.

15 There is gold and abundance of rubies,
   but the lips of knowledge are a rare jewel.

16 Take the garment of one who puts up collateral for a stranger;
   and hold him in pledge for a wayward woman.

17 Fraudulent food is sweet to a man,
   but afterwards his mouth is filled with gravel.

18 Plans are established by advice;
   by wise guidance you wage war!

19 He who goes about as a tale-bearer reveals secrets;

therefore don't keep company with him who opens wide his lips.

20 Whoever curses his father or his mother,
his lamp shall be put out in blackness of darkness.

21 An inheritance quickly gained at the beginning
won't be blessed in the end.

22 Don't say, "I will pay back evil."
Wait for the LORD, and he will save you.

23 The LORD detests differing weights,
and dishonest scales are not pleasing.

24 A man's steps are from the LORD;
how then can man understand his way?

25 It is a snare to a man to make a rash dedication,
then later to consider his vows.

26 A wise king winnows out the wicked,
and drives the threshing wheel over them.

27 The spirit of man is the LORD's lamp,
searching all his innermost parts.

28 Love and faithfulness keep the king safe.
His throne is sustained by love.

29 The glory of young men is their strength.
The splendour of old men is their grey hair.

30 Wounding blows cleanse away evil,
and beatings purge the innermost parts.

21

1 The king's heart is in the LORD's hand like the watercourses.
He turns it wherever he desires.

2 Every way of a man is right in his own eyes,
but the LORD weighs the hearts.

3 To do righteousness and justice
is more acceptable to the LORD than sacrifice.

4 A high look and a proud heart,
the lamp of the wicked, is sin.

5 The plans of the diligent surely lead to profit;
and everyone who is hasty surely rushes to poverty.

6 Getting treasures by a lying tongue
is a fleeting vapour for those who seek death.

7 The violence of the wicked will drive them away,
because they refuse to do what is right.

8 The way of the guilty is devious,
but the conduct of the innocent is upright.

9 It is better to dwell in the corner of the housetop
than to share a house with a contentious woman.

10 The soul of the wicked desires evil;
his neighbour finds no mercy in his eyes.

11 When the mocker is punished, the simple gains wisdom.
When the wise is instructed, he receives knowledge.

12 The Righteous One considers the house of the wicked,
and brings the wicked to ruin.

13 Whoever stops his ears at the cry of the poor,
he will also cry out, but shall not be heard.

14 A gift in secret pacifies anger,
and a bribe in the cloak, strong wrath.

15 It is joy to the righteous to do justice;
but it is a destruction to the workers of iniquity.

16 The man who wanders out of the way of understanding
shall rest in the assembly of the departed spirits.

17 He who loves pleasure will be a poor man.
He who loves wine and oil won't be rich.

18 The wicked is a ransom for the righteous,
the treacherous for the upright.

19 It is better to dwell in a desert land,
than with a contentious and fretful woman.

20 There is precious treasure and oil in the dwelling of the wise,
but a foolish man swallows it up.

21 He who follows after righteousness and kindness
finds life, righteousness, and honour.

22 A wise man scales the city of the mighty,
and brings down the strength of its confidence.

23 Whoever guards his mouth and his tongue
keeps his soul from troubles.

24 The proud and arrogant man—"Scoffer" is his name—
he works in the arrogance of pride.

25 The desire of the sluggard kills him,
for his hands refuse to labour.

26 There are those who covet greedily all day long;
but the righteous give and don't withhold.

27 The sacrifice of the wicked is an abomination—
how much more, when he brings it with a wicked mind!

28 A false witness will perish.
A man who listens speaks to eternity.

29 A wicked man hardens his face;
but as for the upright, he establishes his ways.

30 There is no wisdom nor understanding
nor counsel against the LORD.

31 The horse is prepared for the day of battle;
but victory is with the LORD.

22

1 A good name is more desirable than great riches,
and loving favour is better than silver and gold.

2 The rich and the poor have this in common:
The LORD is the maker of them all.

3 A prudent man sees danger and hides himself;
but the simple pass on, and suffer for it.

4 The result of humility and the fear of the LORD
is wealth, honour, and life.

5 Thorns and snares are in the path of the wicked;
whoever guards his soul stays far from them.

6 Train up a child in the way he should go,
and when he is old he will not depart from it.

7 The rich rule over the poor.
The borrower is servant to the lender.

8 He who sows wickedness reaps trouble,
and the rod of his fury will be destroyed.

9 He who has a generous eye will be blessed,
for he shares his food with the poor.

10 Drive out the mocker, and strife will go out;
yes, quarrels and insults will stop.

11 He who loves purity of heart and speaks gracefully
is the king's friend.

12 The LORD's eyes watch over knowledge,
but he frustrates the words of the unfaithful.

13 The sluggard says, "There is a lion outside!
I will be killed in the streets!"

14 The mouth of an adulteress is a deep pit.
He who is under the LORD's wrath will fall into it.

15 Folly is bound up in the heart of a child;
the rod of discipline drives it far from him.

16 Whoever oppresses the poor for his own increase and whoever gives to the rich,
both come to poverty.

17 Turn your ear, and listen to the words of the wise.
Apply your heart to my teaching.

18 For it is a pleasant thing if you keep them within you,
if all of them are ready on your lips.

19 I teach you today, even you,
so that your trust may be in the LORD.

20 Haven't I written to you thirty excellent things
of counsel and knowledge,

21 To teach you truth, reliable words,
to give sound answers to the ones who sent you?

22 Don't exploit the poor because he is poor;
and don't crush the needy in court;

23 for the LORD will plead their case,
and plunder the life of those who plunder them.

24 Don't befriend a hot-tempered man.
Don't associate with one who harbours anger,

25 lest you learn his ways
and ensnare your soul.

26 Don't you be one of those who strike hands,
of those who are collateral for debts.

27 If you don't have means to pay,
why should he take away your bed from under you?

28 Don't move the ancient boundary stone
which your fathers have set up.

29 Do you see a man skilled in his work?
He will serve kings.
He won't serve obscure men.

23

1 When you sit to eat with a ruler,
consider diligently what is before you;

2 put a knife to your throat
if you are a man given to appetite.

3 Don't be desirous of his dainties,
since they are deceitful food.

4 Don't weary yourself to be rich.
In your wisdom, show restraint.

5 Why do you set your eyes on that which is not?
For it certainly sprouts wings like an eagle and flies in the sky.

6 Don't eat the food of him who has a stingy eye,
and don't crave his delicacies,

7 for as he thinks about the cost, so he is.
"Eat and drink!" he says to you,
but his heart is not with you.

8 You will vomit up the morsel which you have eaten
and waste your pleasant words.

9 Don't speak in the ears of a fool,

for he will despise the wisdom of your words.

10 Don't move the ancient boundary stone.
    Don't encroach on the fields of the fatherless,
11 for their Defender is strong.
    He will plead their case against you.

12 Apply your heart to instruction,
    and your ears to the words of knowledge.
13 Don't withhold correction from a child.
    If you punish him with the rod, he will not die.
14 Punish him with the rod,
    and save his soul from Sheol.[a]

15 My son, if your heart is wise,
    then my heart will be glad, even mine.
16 Yes, my heart will rejoice
    when your lips speak what is right.
17 Don't let your heart envy sinners,
    but rather fear the LORD all day long.
18 Indeed surely there is a future hope,
    and your hope will not be cut off.
19 Listen, my son, and be wise,
    and keep your heart on the right path!
20 Don't be amongst ones drinking too much wine,
    or those who gorge themselves on meat;
21 for the drunkard and the glutton shall become poor;
    and drowsiness clothes them in rags.
22 Listen to your father who gave you life,
    and don't despise your mother when she is old.
23 Buy the truth, and don't sell it.
    Get wisdom, discipline, and understanding.
24 The father of the righteous has great joy.
    Whoever fathers a wise child delights in him.
25 Let your father and your mother be glad!
    Let her who bore you rejoice!
26 My son, give me your heart;
    and let your eyes keep in my ways.
27 For a prostitute is a deep pit;
    and a wayward wife is a narrow well.
28 Yes, she lies in wait like a robber,
    and increases the unfaithful amongst men.

29 Who has woe?
    Who has sorrow?
    Who has strife?
    Who has complaints?
    Who has needless bruises?
    Who has bloodshot eyes?
30 Those who stay long at the wine;
    those who go to seek out mixed wine.
31 Don't look at the wine when it is red,
    when it sparkles in the cup,
    when it goes down smoothly.
32 In the end, it bites like a snake,
    and poisons like a viper.
33 Your eyes will see strange things,
    and your mind will imagine confusing things.
34 Yes, you will be as he who lies down in the middle of the sea,
    or as he who lies on top of the rigging:
35 "They hit me, and I was not hurt!
    They beat me, and I don't feel it!
    When will I wake up? I can do it again.
    I will look for more."

24

1 Don't be envious of evil men,
    neither desire to be with them;
2 for their hearts plot violence
    and their lips talk about mischief.
3 Through wisdom a house is built;
    by understanding it is established;
4 by knowledge the rooms are filled
    with all rare and beautiful treasure.
5 A wise man has great power.
    A knowledgeable man increases strength,
6 for by wise guidance you wage your war,
    and victory is in many advisors.
7 Wisdom is too high for a fool.
    He doesn't open his mouth in the gate.
8 One who plots to do evil
    will be called a schemer.
9 The schemes of folly are sin.
    The mocker is detested by men.
10 If you falter in the time of trouble,
    your strength is small.

11 Rescue those who are being led away to death!
    Indeed, hold back those who are staggering to the slaughter!
12 If you say, "Behold, we didn't know this,"
    doesn't he who weighs the hearts consider it?
He who keeps your soul, doesn't he know it?
    Shall he not render to every man according to his work?
13 My son, eat honey, for it is good,
    the droppings of the honeycomb, which are sweet to your taste;
14 so you shall know wisdom to be to your soul.
    If you have found it, then there will be a reward:
    Your hope will not be cut off.
15 Don't lay in wait, wicked man, against the habitation of the righteous.
    Don't destroy his resting place;
16 for a righteous man falls seven times and rises up again,
    but the wicked are overthrown by calamity.
17 Don't rejoice when your enemy falls.
    Don't let your heart be glad when he is overthrown,
18 lest the LORD see it, and it displease him,
    and he turn away his wrath from him.
19 Don't fret yourself because of evildoers,
    neither be envious of the wicked;
20 for there will be no reward to the evil man.
    The lamp of the wicked will be snuffed out.
21 My son, fear the LORD and the king.
    Don't join those who are rebellious,
22 for their calamity will rise suddenly.
    Who knows what destruction may come from them both?

23 These also are sayings of the wise:

To show partiality in judgement is not good.
24 He who says to the wicked, "You are righteous,"
    peoples will curse him, and nations will abhor him—
25 but it will go well with those who convict the guilty,
    and a rich blessing will come on them.
26 An honest answer
    is like a kiss on the lips.
27 Prepare your work outside,
    and get your fields ready.
    Afterwards, build your house.
28 Don't be a witness against your neighbour without cause.
    Don't deceive with your lips.
29 Don't say, "I will do to him as he has done to me;
    I will repay the man according to his work."
30 I went by the field of the sluggard,
    by the vineyard of the man void of understanding.
31 Behold, it was all grown over with thorns.
    Its surface was covered with nettles,
    and its stone wall was broken down.
32 Then I saw, and considered well.
    I saw, and received instruction:
33 a little sleep, a little slumber,
    a little folding of the hands to sleep,
34 so your poverty will come as a robber
    and your want as an armed man.

25

1 These also are proverbs of Solomon, which the men of Hezekiah king of Judah copied out.
2 It is the glory of God to conceal a thing,
    but the glory of kings is to search out a matter.
3 As the heavens for height, and the earth for depth,
    so the hearts of kings are unsearchable.
4 Take away the dross from the silver,
    and material comes out for the refiner.
5 Take away the wicked from the king's presence,
    and his throne will be established in righteousness.
6 Don't exalt yourself in the presence of the king,
    or claim a place amongst great men;
7 for it is better that it be said to you, "Come up here,"
    than that you should be put lower in the presence of the prince,
    whom your eyes have seen.
8 Don't be hasty in bringing charges to court.
    What will you do in the end when your neighbour shames you?
9 Debate your case with your neighbour,
    and don't betray the confidence of another,
10 lest one who hears it put you to shame,
    and your bad reputation never depart.

11 A word fitly spoken
    is like apples of gold in settings of silver.
12 As an earring of gold, and an ornament of fine gold,
    so is a wise reprover to an obedient ear.
13 As the cold of snow in the time of harvest,
    so is a faithful messenger to those who send him;
    for he refreshes the soul of his masters.
14 As clouds and wind without rain,

---

[a] *23:14* Sheol is the place of the dead.

so is he who boasts of gifts deceptively.

15 By patience a ruler is persuaded.
  A soft tongue breaks the bone.
16 Have you found honey?
  Eat as much as is sufficient for you,
  lest you eat too much, and vomit it.
17 Let your foot be seldom in your neighbour's house,
  lest he be weary of you, and hate you.
18 A man who gives false testimony against his neighbour
  is like a club, a sword, or a sharp arrow.
19 Confidence in someone unfaithful in time of trouble
  is like a bad tooth or a lame foot.
20 As one who takes away a garment in cold weather,
  or vinegar on soda,
  so is one who sings songs to a heavy heart.
21 If your enemy is hungry, give him food to eat.
  If he is thirsty, give him water to drink;
22 for you will heap coals of fire on his head,
  and the LORD will reward you.
23 The north wind produces rain;
  so a backbiting tongue brings an angry face.
24 It is better to dwell in the corner of the housetop
  than to share a house with a contentious woman.
25 Like cold water to a thirsty soul,
  so is good news from a far country.
26 Like a muddied spring and a polluted well,
  so is a righteous man who gives way before the wicked.
27 It is not good to eat much honey,
  nor is it honourable to seek one's own honour.
28 Like a city that is broken down and without walls
  is a man whose spirit is without restraint.

26

1 Like snow in summer, and as rain in harvest,
  so honour is not fitting for a fool.
2 Like a fluttering sparrow,
  like a darting swallow,
  so the undeserved curse doesn't come to rest.
3 A whip is for the horse,
  a bridle for the donkey,
  and a rod for the back of fools!
4 Don't answer a fool according to his folly,
  lest you also be like him.
5 Answer a fool according to his folly,
  lest he be wise in his own eyes.
6 One who sends a message by the hand of a fool
  is cutting off feet and drinking violence.
7 Like the legs of the lame that hang loose,
  so is a parable in the mouth of fools.
8 As one who binds a stone in a sling,
  so is he who gives honour to a fool.
9 Like a thorn bush that goes into the hand of a drunkard,
  so is a parable in the mouth of fools.
10 As an archer who wounds all,
  so is he who hires a fool
  or he who hires those who pass by.
11 As a dog that returns to his vomit,
  so is a fool who repeats his folly.
12 Do you see a man wise in his own eyes?
  There is more hope for a fool than for him.
13 The sluggard says, "There is a lion in the road!
  A fierce lion roams the streets!"
14 As the door turns on its hinges,
  so does the sluggard on his bed.
15 The sluggard buries his hand in the dish.
  He is too lazy to bring it back to his mouth.
16 The sluggard is wiser in his own eyes
  than seven men who answer with discretion.
17 Like one who grabs a dog's ears
  is one who passes by and meddles in a quarrel not his own.
18 Like a madman who shoots torches, arrows, and death,
19 is the man who deceives his neighbour and says, "Am I not joking?"
20 For lack of wood a fire goes out.
  Without gossip, a quarrel dies down.
21 As coals are to hot embers,
  and wood to fire,
  so is a contentious man to kindling strife.
22 The words of a whisperer are as dainty morsels,
  they go down into the innermost parts.
23 Like silver dross on an earthen vessel
  are the lips of a fervent one with an evil heart.
24 A malicious man disguises himself with his lips,
  but he harbours evil in his heart.
25 When his speech is charming, don't believe him,
  for there are seven abominations in his heart.
26 His malice may be concealed by deception,

but his wickedness will be exposed in the assembly.
27 Whoever digs a pit shall fall into it.
  Whoever rolls a stone, it will come back on him.
28 A lying tongue hates those it hurts;
  and a flattering mouth works ruin.

27

1 Don't boast about tomorrow;
  for you don't know what a day may bring.
2 Let another man praise you,
  and not your own mouth;
  a stranger, and not your own lips.
3 A stone is heavy,
  and sand is a burden;
  but a fool's provocation is heavier than both.
4 Wrath is cruel,
  and anger is overwhelming;
  but who is able to stand before jealousy?
5 Better is open rebuke
  than hidden love.
6 The wounds of a friend are faithful,
  although the kisses of an enemy are profuse.
7 A full soul loathes a honeycomb;
  but to a hungry soul, every bitter thing is sweet.
8 As a bird that wanders from her nest,
  so is a man who wanders from his home.
9 Perfume and incense bring joy to the heart;
  so does earnest counsel from a man's friend.
10 Don't forsake your friend and your father's friend.
  Don't go to your brother's house in the day of your disaster.
  A neighbour who is near is better than a distant brother.
11 Be wise, my son,
  and bring joy to my heart,
  then I can answer my tormentor.
12 A prudent man sees danger and takes refuge;
  but the simple pass on, and suffer for it.
13 Take his garment when he puts up collateral for a stranger.
  Hold it for a wayward woman!
14 He who blesses his neighbour with a loud voice early in the morning,
  it will be taken as a curse by him.
15 A continual dropping on a rainy day
  and a contentious wife are alike:
16 restraining her is like restraining the wind,
  or like grasping oil in his right hand.

17 Iron sharpens iron;
  so a man sharpens his friend's countenance.
18 Whoever tends the fig tree shall eat its fruit.
  He who looks after his master shall be honoured.
19 Like water reflects a face,
  so a man's heart reflects the man.
20 Sheol[a] and Abaddon are never satisfied;
  and a man's eyes are never satisfied.
21 The crucible is for silver,
  and the furnace for gold;
  but man is refined by his praise.
22 Though you grind a fool in a mortar with a pestle along with grain,
  yet his foolishness will not be removed from him.

23 Know well the state of your flocks,
  and pay attention to your herds,
24 for riches are not forever,
  nor does the crown endure to all generations.
25 The hay is removed, and the new growth appears,
  the grasses of the hills are gathered in.
26 The lambs are for your clothing,
  and the goats are the price of a field.
27 There will be plenty of goats' milk for your food,
  for your family's food,
  and for the nourishment of your servant girls.

28

1 The wicked flee when no one pursues;
  but the righteous are as bold as a lion.
2 In rebellion, a land has many rulers,
  but order is maintained by a man of understanding and knowledge.
3 A needy man who oppresses the poor
  is like a driving rain which leaves no crops.
4 Those who forsake the law praise the wicked;
  but those who keep the law contend with them.
5 Evil men don't understand justice;
  but those who seek the LORD understand it fully.
6 Better is the poor who walks in his integrity
  than he who is perverse in his ways, and he is rich.
7 Whoever keeps the law is a wise son;
  but he who is a companion of gluttons shames his father.
8 He who increases his wealth by excessive interest
  gathers it for one who has pity on the poor.

---

9 He who turns away his ear from hearing the law,
   even his prayer is an abomination.
10 Whoever causes the upright to go astray in an evil way,
   he will fall into his own trap;
   but the blameless will inherit good.
11 The rich man is wise in his own eyes;
   but the poor who has understanding sees through him.
12 When the righteous triumph, there is great glory;
   but when the wicked rise, men hide themselves.
13 He who conceals his sins doesn't prosper,
   but whoever confesses and renounces them finds mercy.
14 Blessed is the man who always fears;
   but one who hardens his heart falls into trouble.
15 As a roaring lion or a charging bear,
   so is a wicked ruler over helpless people.
16 A tyrannical ruler lacks judgement.
   One who hates ill-gotten gain will have long days.
17 A man who is tormented by blood guilt will be a fugitive until death.
   No one will support him.
18 Whoever walks blamelessly is kept safe;
   but one with perverse ways will fall suddenly.
19 One who works his land will have an abundance of food;
   but one who chases fantasies will have his fill of poverty.
20 A faithful man is rich with blessings;
   but one who is eager to be rich will not go unpunished.
21 To show partiality is not good,
   yet a man will do wrong for a piece of bread.
22 A stingy man hurries after riches,
   and doesn't know that poverty waits for him.
23 One who rebukes a man will afterward find more favour
   than one who flatters with the tongue.
24 Whoever robs his father or his mother and says, "It's not wrong,"
   is a partner with a destroyer.
25 One who is greedy stirs up strife;
   but one who trusts in the LORD will prosper.
26 One who trusts in himself is a fool;
   but one who walks in wisdom is kept safe.
27 One who gives to the poor has no lack;
   but one who closes his eyes will have many curses.
28 When the wicked rise, men hide themselves;
   but when they perish, the righteous thrive.

29

1 He who is often rebuked and stiffens his neck
   will be destroyed suddenly, with no remedy.
2 When the righteous thrive, the people rejoice;
   but when the wicked rule, the people groan.
3 Whoever loves wisdom brings joy to his father;
   but a companion of prostitutes squanders his wealth.
4 The king by justice makes the land stable,
   but he who takes bribes tears it down.
5 A man who flatters his neighbour
   spreads a net for his feet.
6 An evil man is snared by his sin,
   but the righteous can sing and be glad.
7 The righteous care about justice for the poor.
   The wicked aren't concerned about knowledge.
8 Mockers stir up a city,
   but wise men turn away anger.
9 If a wise man goes to court with a foolish man,
   the fool rages or scoffs, and there is no peace.
10 The bloodthirsty hate a man of integrity;
   and they seek the life of the upright.
11 A fool vents all of his anger,
   but a wise man brings himself under control.
12 If a ruler listens to lies,
   all of his officials are wicked.
13 The poor man and the oppressor have this in common:
   The LORD gives sight to the eyes of both.
14 The king who fairly judges the poor,
   his throne shall be established forever.
15 The rod of correction gives wisdom,
   but a child left to himself causes shame to his mother.
16 When the wicked increase, sin increases;
   but the righteous will see their downfall.
17 Correct your son, and he will give you peace;
   yes, he will bring delight to your soul.
18 Where there is no revelation, the people cast off restraint;
   but one who keeps the law is blessed.
19 A servant can't be corrected by words.
   Though he understands, yet he will not respond.
20 Do you see a man who is hasty in his words?
   There is more hope for a fool than for him.
21 He who pampers his servant from youth
   will have him become a son in the end.
22 An angry man stirs up strife,
   and a wrathful man abounds in sin.

23 A man's pride brings him low,
   but one of lowly spirit gains honour.
24 Whoever is an accomplice of a thief is an enemy of his own soul.
   He takes an oath, but dares not testify.
25 The fear of man proves to be a snare,
   but whoever puts his trust in the LORD is kept safe.
26 Many seek the ruler's favour,
   but a man's justice comes from the LORD.
27 A dishonest man detests the righteous,
   and the upright in their ways detest the wicked.

30

1 The words of Agur the son of Jakeh, the revelation:
the man says to Ithiel,
   to Ithiel and Ucal:
2 "Surely I am the most ignorant man,
   and don't have a man's understanding.
3 I have not learnt wisdom,
   neither do I have the knowledge of the Holy One.
4 Who has ascended up into heaven, and descended?
   Who has gathered the wind in his fists?
   Who has bound the waters in his garment?
   Who has established all the ends of the earth?
   What is his name, and what is his son's name, if you know?

5 "Every word of God is flawless.
   He is a shield to those who take refuge in him.
6 Don't you add to his words,
   lest he reprove you, and you be found a liar.

7 "Two things I have asked of you.
   Don't deny me before I die.
8 Remove far from me falsehood and lies.
   Give me neither poverty nor riches.
   Feed me with the food that is needful for me,
9 lest I be full, deny you, and say, 'Who is the LORD?'
   or lest I be poor, and steal,
   and so dishonour the name of my God.

10 "Don't slander a servant to his master,
   lest he curse you, and you be held guilty.

11 There is a generation that curses their father,
   and doesn't bless their mother.
12 There is a generation that is pure in their own eyes,
   yet are not washed from their filthiness.
13 There is a generation, oh how lofty are their eyes!
   Their eyelids are lifted up.
14 There is a generation whose teeth are like swords,
   and their jaws like knives,
   to devour the poor from the earth, and the needy from amongst men.

15 "The leech has two daughters:
   'Give, give.'

"There are three things that are never satisfied;
   four that don't say, 'Enough!':
   16 Sheol,ᵃ
   the barren womb,
   the earth that is not satisfied with water,
   and the fire that doesn't say, 'Enough!'

17 "The eye that mocks at his father,
   and scorns obedience to his mother,
   the ravens of the valley shall pick it out,
   the young eagles shall eat it.

18 "There are three things which are too amazing for me,
   four which I don't understand:
   19 The way of an eagle in the air,
   the way of a serpent on a rock,
   the way of a ship in the middle of the sea,
   and the way of a man with a maiden.

20 "So is the way of an adulterous woman:
   She eats and wipes her mouth,
   and says, 'I have done nothing wrong.'

21 "For three things the earth trembles,
   and under four, it can't bear up:
   22 For a servant when he is king,
   a fool when he is filled with food,
   23 for an unloved woman when she is married,
   and a servant who is heir to her mistress.

24 "There are four things which are little on the earth,
   but they are exceedingly wise:

_____

ᵃ *30:16* Sheol is the place of the dead.

25 The ants are not a strong people,
  yet they provide their food in the summer.
26 The hyraxes are but a feeble folk,
  yet make they their houses in the rocks.
27 The locusts have no king,
  yet they advance in ranks.
28 You can catch a lizard with your hands,
  yet it is in kings' palaces.

29 "There are three things which are stately in their march,
  four which are stately in going:
  30 The lion, which is mightiest amongst animals,
  and doesn't turn away for any;
  31 the greyhound;
  the male goat;
  and the king against whom there is no rising up.

32 "If you have done foolishly in lifting up yourself,
  or if you have thought evil,
put your hand over your mouth.
  33 For as the churning of milk produces butter,
  and the wringing of the nose produces blood,
  so the forcing of wrath produces strife."

31

1 The words of King Lemuel—the revelation which his mother taught him:

2 "Oh, my son!
  Oh, son of my womb!
  Oh, son of my vows!
3 Don't give your strength to women,
  nor your ways to that which destroys kings.
4 It is not for kings, Lemuel,
  it is not for kings to drink wine,
  nor for princes to say, 'Where is strong drink?'
5 lest they drink, and forget the law,
  and pervert the justice due to anyone who is afflicted.
6 Give strong drink to him who is ready to perish,
  and wine to the bitter in soul.
7 Let him drink, and forget his poverty,
  and remember his misery no more.
8 Open your mouth for the mute,
  in the cause of all who are left desolate.
9 Open your mouth, judge righteously,
  and serve justice to the poor and needy."

10 ᵃWho can find a worthy woman?
  For her value is far above rubies.
11 The heart of her husband trusts in her.
  He shall have no lack of gain.
12 She does him good, and not harm,
  all the days of her life.
13 She seeks wool and flax,
  and works eagerly with her hands.
14 She is like the merchant ships.
  She brings her bread from afar.
15 She rises also while it is yet night,
  gives food to her household,
  and portions for her servant girls.
16 She considers a field, and buys it.
  With the fruit of her hands, she plants a vineyard.
17 She arms her waist with strength,
  and makes her arms strong.
18 She perceives that her merchandise is profitable.
  Her lamp doesn't go out by night.
19 She lays her hands to the distaff,
  and her hands hold the spindle.
20 She opens her arms to the poor;
  yes, she extends her hands to the needy.
21 She is not afraid of the snow for her household,
  for all her household are clothed with scarlet.
22 She makes for herself carpets of tapestry.
  Her clothing is fine linen and purple.
23 Her husband is respected in the gates,
  when he sits amongst the elders of the land.
24 She makes linen garments and sells them,
  and delivers sashes to the merchant.
25 Strength and dignity are her clothing.
  She laughs at the time to come.
26 She opens her mouth with wisdom.
  Kind instruction is on her tongue.
27 She looks well to the ways of her household,
  and doesn't eat the bread of idleness.
28 Her children rise up and call her blessed.
  Her husband also praises her:

29 "Many women do noble things,
  but you excel them all."
30 Charm is deceitful, and beauty is vain;
  but a woman who fears the LORD, she shall be praised.
31 Give her of the fruit of her hands!
  Let her works praise her in the gates!

ᵃ *31:10* Proverbs 31:10-31 form an acrostic, with each verse starting with each letter of the Hebrew alphabet, in order.

Ecclesiastes or The Preacher

1

1 The words of the Preacher, the son of David, king in Jerusalem: 2 "Vanity of vanities," says the Preacher; "Vanity of vanities, all is vanity." 3 What does man gain from all his labour in which he labours under the sun? 4 One generation goes, and another generation comes; but the earth remains forever. 5 The sun also rises, and the sun goes down, and hurries to its place where it rises. 6 The wind goes towards the south, and turns around to the north. It turns around continually as it goes, and the wind returns again to its courses. 7 All the rivers run into the sea, yet the sea is not full. To the place where the rivers flow, there they flow again. 8 All things are full of weariness beyond uttering. The eye is not satisfied with seeing, nor the ear filled with hearing. 9 That which has been is that which shall be, and that which has been done is that which shall be done; and there is no new thing under the sun. 10 Is there a thing of which it may be said, "Behold,[a] this is new"? It has been long ago, in the ages which were before us. 11 There is no memory of the former; neither shall there be any memory of the latter that are to come, amongst those that shall come after.

12 I, the Preacher, was king over Israel in Jerusalem. 13 I applied my heart to seek and to search out by wisdom concerning all that is done under the sky. It is a heavy burden that God[b] has given to the sons of men to be afflicted with. 14 I have seen all the works that are done under the sun; and behold, all is vanity and a chasing after wind. 15 That which is crooked can't be made straight; and that which is lacking can't be counted. 16 I said to myself, "Behold, I have obtained for myself great wisdom above all who were before me in Jerusalem. Yes, my heart has had great experience of wisdom and knowledge." 17 I applied my heart to know wisdom, and to know madness and folly. I perceived that this also was a chasing after wind. 18 For in much wisdom is much grief; and he who increases knowledge increases sorrow.

2

1 I said in my heart, "Come now, I will test you with mirth; therefore enjoy pleasure;" and behold, this also was vanity. 2 I said of laughter, "It is foolishness;" and of mirth, "What does it accomplish?"

3 I searched in my heart how to cheer my flesh with wine, my heart yet guiding me with wisdom, and how to lay hold of folly, until I might see what it was good for the sons of men that they should do under heaven all the days of their lives. 4 I made myself great works. I built myself houses. I planted myself vineyards. 5 I made myself gardens and parks, and I planted trees in them of all kinds of fruit. 6 I made myself pools of water, to water the forest where trees were grown. 7 I bought male servants and female servants, and had servants born in my house. I also had great possessions of herds and flocks, above all who were before me in Jerusalem. 8 I also gathered silver and gold for myself, and the treasure of kings and of the provinces. I got myself male and female singers, and the delights of the sons of men: musical instruments of all sorts. 9 So I was great, and increased more than all who were before me in Jerusalem. My wisdom also remained with me. 10 Whatever my eyes desired, I didn't keep from them. I didn't withhold my heart from any joy, for my heart rejoiced because of all my labour, and this was my portion from all my labour. 11 Then I looked at all the works that my hands had worked, and at the labour that I had laboured to do; and behold, all was vanity and a chasing after wind, and there was no profit under the sun.

12 I turned myself to consider wisdom, madness, and folly; for what can the king's successor do? Just that which has been done long ago. 13 Then I saw that wisdom excels folly, as far as light excels darkness. 14 The wise man's eyes are in his head, and the fool walks in darkness—and yet I perceived that one event happens to them all. 15 Then I said in my heart, "As it happens to the fool, so will it happen even to me; and why was I then more wise?" Then I said in my heart that this also is vanity. 16 For of the wise man, even as of the fool, there is no memory forever, since in the days to come all will have been long forgotten. Indeed, the wise man must die just like the fool!

17 So I hated life, because the work that is worked under the sun was grievous to me; for all is vanity and a chasing after wind. 18 I hated all my labour in which I laboured under the sun, because I must leave it to the man who comes after me. 19 Who knows whether he will be a wise man or a fool? Yet he will have rule over all of my labour in which I have laboured, and in which I have shown myself wise under the sun. This also is vanity.

20 Therefore I began to cause my heart to despair concerning all the labour in which I had laboured under the sun. 21 For there is a man whose labour is with wisdom, with knowledge, and with skilfulness; yet he shall leave it for his portion to a man who has not laboured for it. This also is vanity and a great evil. 22 For what does a man have of all his labour and of the striving of his heart, in which he labours under the sun? 23 For all his days are sorrows, and his travail is grief; yes, even in the night his heart takes no rest. This also is vanity. 24 There is nothing better for a man than that he should eat and drink, and make his soul enjoy good in his labour. This also I saw, that it is from the hand of God. 25 For who can eat, or who can have enjoyment, more than I? 26 For to the man who pleases him, God gives wisdom, knowledge, and joy; but to the sinner he gives travail, to gather and to heap up, that he may give to him who pleases God. This also is vanity and a chasing after wind.

3

1 For everything there is a season, and a time for every purpose under heaven:

2 a time to be born,
and a time to die;
a time to plant,
and a time to pluck up that which is planted;
3 a time to kill,
and a time to heal;
a time to break down,
and a time to build up;
4 a time to weep,
and a time to laugh;
a time to mourn,
and a time to dance;
5 a time to cast away stones,
and a time to gather stones together;
a time to embrace,
and a time to refrain from embracing;
6 a time to seek,
and a time to lose;
a time to keep,
and a time to cast away;
7 a time to tear,
and a time to sew;
a time to keep silence,
and a time to speak;
8 a time to love,
and a time to hate;
a time for war,
and a time for peace.

9 What profit has he who works in that in which he labours? 10 I have seen the burden which God has given to the sons of men to be afflicted with. 11 He has made everything beautiful in its time. He has also set eternity in their hearts, yet so that man can't find out the work that God has done from the beginning even to the end. 12 I know that there is nothing better for them than to rejoice, and to do good as long as they live. 13 Also that every man should eat and drink, and enjoy good in all his labour, is the gift of God. 14 I know that whatever God does, it shall be forever. Nothing can be added to it, nor anything taken from it; and God has done it, that men should fear before him. 15 That which is has been long ago, and that which is to be has been long ago. God seeks again that which is passed away.

16 Moreover I saw under the sun, in the place of justice, that wickedness was there; and in the place of righteousness, that wickedness was there. 17 I said in my heart, "God will judge the righteous and the wicked; for there is a time there for every purpose and for every work." 18 I said in my heart, "As for the sons of men, God tests them, so that they may see that they themselves are like animals. 19 For that which happens to the sons of men happens to animals. Even one thing happens to them. As the one dies, so the other dies. Yes, they have all one breath; and man has no advantage over the animals, for all is vanity. 20 All go to one place. All are from the dust, and all turn to dust again. 21 Who knows the spirit of man, whether it goes upward, and the spirit of the animal, whether it goes downward to the earth?"

22 Therefore I saw that there is nothing better than that a man should rejoice in his works, for that is his portion; for who can bring him to see what will be after him?

4

1 Then I returned and saw all the oppressions that are done under the sun: and behold, the tears of those who were oppressed, and they had no comforter; and on the side of their oppressors there was power; but they had no comforter. 2 Therefore I praised the dead who have been long dead more than the living who are yet alive. 3 Yes, better than them both is him who has not yet been, who has not seen the evil work that is done under the sun. 4 Then I saw all the labour and achievement that is the envy of a man's neighbour. This also is vanity and a striving after wind.

5 The fool folds his hands together and ruins himself. 6 Better is a handful, with quietness, than two handfuls with labour and chasing after wind.

7 Then I returned and saw vanity under the sun. 8 There is one who is alone, and he has neither son nor brother. There is no end to all of his labour, neither are his eyes satisfied with wealth. "For whom then do I labour and deprive my soul of enjoyment?" This also is vanity. Yes, it is a miserable business.

9 Two are better than one, because they have a good reward for their labour. 10 For if they fall, the one will lift up his fellow; but woe to him who is alone when he falls, and doesn't have another to lift him up. 11 Again, if two lie together, then they have warmth; but how can one keep warm alone? 12 If a man prevails against one who is alone, two shall withstand him; and a threefold cord is not quickly broken.

13 Better is a poor and wise youth than an old and foolish king who doesn't know how to receive admonition any more. 14 For out of prison he

---

[a] 1:10 "Behold", from "הִנֵּה", means look at, take notice, observe, see, or gaze at. It is often used as an interjection.

[b] 1:13 The Hebrew word rendered "God" is "אֱלֹהִים" (Elohim).

came out to be king; yes, even in his kingdom he was born poor. 15 I saw all the living who walk under the sun, that they were with the youth, the other, who succeeded him. 16 There was no end of all the people, even of all them over whom he was—yet those who come after shall not rejoice in him. Surely this also is vanity and a chasing after wind.

5

1 Guard your steps when you go to God's house; for to draw near to listen is better than to give the sacrifice of fools, for they don't know that they do evil. 2 Don't be rash with your mouth, and don't let your heart be hasty to utter anything before God; for God is in heaven, and you on earth. Therefore let your words be few. 3 For as a dream comes with a multitude of cares, so a fool's speech with a multitude of words. 4 When you vow a vow to God, don't defer to pay it; for he has no pleasure in fools. Pay that which you vow. 5 It is better that you should not vow, than that you should vow and not pay. 6 Don't allow your mouth to lead you into sin. Don't protest before the messenger that this was a mistake. Why should God be angry at your voice, and destroy the work of your hands? 7 For in the multitude of dreams there are vanities, as well as in many words; but you must fear God.

8 If you see the oppression of the poor, and the violent taking away of justice and righteousness in a district, don't marvel at the matter, for one official is eyed by a higher one, and there are officials over them. 9 Moreover the profit of the earth is for all. The king profits from the field.

10 He who loves silver shall not be satisfied with silver, nor he who loves abundance, with increase. This also is vanity. 11 When goods increase, those who eat them are increased; and what advantage is there to its owner, except to feast on them with his eyes?

12 The sleep of a labouring man is sweet, whether he eats little or much; but the abundance of the rich will not allow him to sleep.

13 There is a grievous evil which I have seen under the sun: wealth kept by its owner to his harm. 14 Those riches perish by misfortune, and if he has fathered a son, there is nothing in his hand. 15 As he came out of his mother's womb, naked shall he go again as he came, and shall take nothing for his labour, which he may carry away in his hand. 16 This also is a grievous evil, that in all points as he came, so shall he go. And what profit does he have who labours for the wind? 17 All his days he also eats in darkness, he is frustrated, and has sickness and wrath.

18 Behold, that which I have seen to be good and proper is for one to eat and to drink, and to enjoy good in all his labour, in which he labours under the sun, all the days of his life which God has given him; for this is his portion. 19 Every man also to whom God has given riches and wealth, and has given him power to eat of it, and to take his portion, and to rejoice in his labour—this is the gift of God. 20 For he shall not often reflect on the days of his life, because God occupies him with the joy of his heart.

6

1 There is an evil which I have seen under the sun, and it is heavy on men: 2 a man to whom God gives riches, wealth, and honour, so that he lacks nothing for his soul of all that he desires, yet God gives him no power to eat of it, but an alien eats it. This is vanity, and it is an evil disease.

3 If a man fathers a hundred children, and lives many years, so that the days of his years are many, but his soul is not filled with good, and moreover he has no burial, I say that a stillborn child is better than he; 4 for it comes in vanity, and departs in darkness, and its name is covered with darkness. 5 Moreover it has not seen the sun nor known it. This has rest rather than the other. 6 Yes, though he live a thousand years twice told, and yet fails to enjoy good, don't all go to one place? 7 All the labour of man is for his mouth, and yet the appetite is not filled. 8 For what advantage has the wise more than the fool? What has the poor man, that knows how to walk before the living? 9 Better is the sight of the eyes than the wandering of the desire. This also is vanity and a chasing after wind. 10 Whatever has been, its name was given long ago; and it is known what man is; neither can he contend with him who is mightier than he. 11 For there are many words that create vanity. What does that profit man? 12 For who knows what is good for man in life, all the days of his vain life which he spends like a shadow? For who can tell a man what will be after him under the sun?

7

1 A good name is better than fine perfume; and the day of death better than the day of one's birth. 2 It is better to go to the house of mourning than to go to the house of feasting; for that is the end of all men, and the living should take this to heart. 3 Sorrow is better than laughter; for by the sadness of the face the heart is made good. 4 The heart of the wise is in the house of mourning; but the heart of fools is in the house of mirth. 5 It is better to hear the rebuke of the wise than for a man to hear the song of fools. 6 For as the crackling of thorns under a pot, so is the laughter of the fool. This also is vanity. 7 Surely extortion makes the wise man foolish; and a bribe destroys the understanding. 8 Better is the end of a thing than its beginning.

The patient in spirit is better than the proud in spirit. 9 Don't be hasty in your spirit to be angry, for anger rests in the bosom of fools. 10 Don't say, "Why were the former days better than these?" For you do not ask wisely about this.

11 Wisdom is as good as an inheritance. Yes, it is more excellent for those who see the sun. 12 For wisdom is a defence, even as money is a defence; but the excellency of knowledge is that wisdom preserves the life of him who has it.

13 Consider the work of God, for who can make that straight which he has made crooked? 14 In the day of prosperity be joyful, and in the day of adversity consider; yes, God has made the one side by side with the other, to the end that man should not find out anything after him.

15 All this I have seen in my days of vanity: there is a righteous man who perishes in his righteousness, and there is a wicked man who lives long in his evildoing. 16 Don't be overly righteous, neither make yourself overly wise. Why should you destroy yourself? 17 Don't be too wicked, neither be foolish. Why should you die before your time? 18 It is good that you should take hold of this. Yes, also don't withdraw your hand from that; for he who fears God will come out of them all. 19 Wisdom is a strength to the wise man more than ten rulers who are in a city. 20 Surely there is not a righteous man on earth who does good and doesn't sin. 21 Also don't take heed to all words that are spoken, lest you hear your servant curse you; 22 for often your own heart knows that you yourself have likewise cursed others. 23 All this I have proved in wisdom. I said, "I will be wise;" but it was far from me. 24 That which is, is far off and exceedingly deep. Who can find it out? 25 I turned around, and my heart sought to know and to search out, and to seek wisdom and the scheme of things, and to know that wickedness is stupidity, and that foolishness is madness.

26 I find more bitter than death the woman whose heart is snares and traps, whose hands are chains. Whoever pleases God shall escape from her; but the sinner will be ensnared by her.

27 "Behold, I have found this," says the Preacher, "to one another, to find an explanation 28 which my soul still seeks, but I have not found. I have found one man amongst a thousand, but I have not found a woman amongst all those. 29 Behold, I have only found this: that God made mankind upright; but they search for many inventions."

8

1 Who is like the wise man? And who knows the interpretation of a thing? A man's wisdom makes his face shine, and the hardness of his face is changed.

2 I say, "Keep the king's command!" because of the oath to God. 3 Don't be hasty to go out of his presence. Don't persist in an evil thing, for he does whatever pleases him, 4 for the king's word is supreme. Who can say to him, "What are you doing?" 5 Whoever keeps the commandment shall not come to harm, and his wise heart will know the time and procedure. 6 For there is a time and procedure for every purpose, although the misery of man is heavy on him. 7 For he doesn't know that which will be; for who can tell him how it will be? 8 There is no man who has power over the spirit to contain the spirit; neither does he have power over the day of death. There is no discharge in war; neither shall wickedness deliver those who practise it.

9 All this I have seen, and applied my mind to every work that is done under the sun. There is a time in which one man has power over another to his hurt. 10 So I saw the wicked buried. Indeed they came also from holiness. They went and were forgotten in the city where they did this. This also is vanity. 11 Because sentence against an evil work is not executed speedily, therefore the heart of the sons of men is fully set in them to do evil. 12 Though a sinner commits crimes a hundred times, and lives long, yet surely I know that it will be better with those who fear God, who are reverent before him. 13 But it shall not be well with the wicked, neither shall he lengthen days like a shadow, because he doesn't fear God.

14 There is a vanity which is done on the earth, that there are righteous men to whom it happens according to the work of the wicked. Again, there are wicked men to whom it happens according to the work of the righteous. I said that this also is vanity. 15 Then I commended mirth, because a man has no better thing under the sun than to eat, to drink, and to be joyful: for that will accompany him in his labour all the days of his life which God has given him under the sun.

16 When I applied my heart to know wisdom, and to see the business that is done on the earth (even though eyes see no sleep day or night), 17 then I saw all the work of God, that man can't find out the work that is done under the sun, because however much a man labours to seek it out, yet he won't find it. Yes even though a wise man thinks he can comprehend it, he won't be able to find it.

9

1 For all this I laid to my heart, even to explore all this: that the righteous, and the wise, and their works, are in the hand of God; whether it is love or hatred, man doesn't know it; all is before them. 2 All things come alike to all. There is one event to the righteous and to the wicked; to the good, to the clean, to the unclean, to him who sacrifices, and to him who doesn't sacrifice. As is the good, so is the sinner; he who takes an oath, as he who fears an oath. 3 This is an evil in all that is done under the sun, that there is one event to all. Yes also, the heart of the sons of men is full of evil, and madness is in their heart while they live, and after that they go to the dead. 4 For to him who is joined with all the living there is hope; for a living dog is better than a dead lion. 5 For the living know that they will die, but the dead don't know anything, neither do they have any more a reward; for their memory is forgotten. 6 Also their love, their hatred, and their envy has perished long ago; neither do they any longer have a portion forever in anything that is done under the sun.

7 Go your way—eat your bread with joy, and drink your wine with a merry heart; for God has already accepted your works. 8 Let your garments be always white, and don't let your head lack oil. 9 Live joyfully with the wife whom you love all the days of your life of vanity, which he has given you under the sun, all your days of vanity, for that is your portion in life, and in your labour in which you labour under the sun. 10 Whatever your

hand finds to do, do it with your might; for there is no work, nor plan, nor knowledge, nor wisdom, in Sheol,[a] where you are going.

11 I returned and saw under the sun that the race is not to the swift, nor the battle to the strong, neither yet bread to the wise, nor yet riches to men of understanding, nor yet favour to men of skill; but time and chance happen to them all. 12 For man also doesn't know his time. As the fish that are taken in an evil net, and as the birds that are caught in the snare, even so are the sons of men snared in an evil time, when it falls suddenly on them.

13 I have also seen wisdom under the sun in this way, and it seemed great to me. 14 There was a little city, and few men within it; and a great king came against it, besieged it, and built great bulwarks against it. 15 Now a poor wise man was found in it, and he by his wisdom delivered the city; yet no man remembered that same poor man. 16 Then I said, "Wisdom is better than strength." Nevertheless the poor man's wisdom is despised, and his words are not heard. 17 The words of the wise heard in quiet are better than the cry of him who rules amongst fools. 18 Wisdom is better than weapons of war; but one sinner destroys much good.

10

1 Dead flies cause the oil of the perfumer to produce an evil odour;
    so does a little folly outweigh wisdom and honour.
2 A wise man's heart is at his right hand,
    but a fool's heart at his left. 3 Yes also when the fool walks by the way,
        his understanding fails him, and he says to everyone that he is
        a fool. 4 If the spirit of the ruler rises up against you, don't
        leave your place; for gentleness lays great offences to rest.

5 There is an evil which I have seen under the sun, the sort of error which proceeds from the ruler. 6 Folly is set in great dignity, and the rich sit in a low place. 7 I have seen servants on horses, and princes walking like servants on the earth. 8 He who digs a pit may fall into it; and whoever breaks through a wall may be bitten by a snake. 9 Whoever carves out stones may be injured by them. Whoever splits wood may be endangered by it. 10 If the axe is blunt, and one doesn't sharpen the edge, then he must use more strength; but skill brings success.

11 If the snake bites before it is charmed, then is there no profit for the charmer's tongue. 12 The words of a wise man's mouth are gracious; but a fool is swallowed by his own lips. 13 The beginning of the words of his mouth is foolishness; and the end of his talk is mischievous madness. 14 A fool also multiplies words.

Man doesn't know what will be; and that which will be after him, who can tell him? 15 The labour of fools wearies every one of them; for he doesn't know how to go to the city.

16 Woe to you, land, when your king is a child,
    and your princes eat in the morning!
17 Happy are you, land, when your king is the son of nobles,
    and your princes eat in due season,
    for strength, and not for drunkenness!
18 By slothfulness the roof sinks in;
    and through idleness of the hands the house leaks.
19 A feast is made for laughter,
    and wine makes the life glad;
    and money is the answer for all things.
20 Don't curse the king, no, not in your thoughts;
    and don't curse the rich in your bedroom,
    for a bird of the sky may carry your voice,
    and that which has wings may tell the matter.

11

1 Cast your bread on the waters;
    for you shall find it after many days.
2 Give a portion to seven, yes, even to eight;
    for you don't know what evil will be on the earth.
3 If the clouds are full of rain, they empty themselves on the earth;
    and if a tree falls towards the south, or towards the north,
    in the place where the tree falls, there shall it be.
4 He who observes the wind won't sow;
    and he who regards the clouds won't reap.
5 As you don't know what is the way of the wind,
    nor how the bones grow in the womb of her who is with child;
    even so you don't know the work of God who does all.
6 In the morning sow your seed,
    and in the evening don't withhold your hand;
    for you don't know which will prosper, whether this or that,
    or whether they both will be equally good.
7 Truly the light is sweet,
    and it is a pleasant thing for the eyes to see the sun.
8 Yes, if a man lives many years, let him rejoice in them all;
    but let him remember the days of darkness, for they shall be many.
    All that comes is vanity.
9 Rejoice, young man, in your youth,
    and let your heart cheer you in the days of your youth,
    and walk in the ways of your heart,
    and in the sight of your eyes;
    but know that for all these things God will bring you into judgement.
10 Therefore remove sorrow from your heart,
    and put away evil from your flesh;
    for youth and the dawn of life are vanity.

---

[a] 9:10 Sheol is the place of the dead.

12

1 Remember also your Creator in the days of your youth,
    before the evil days come, and the years draw near,
    when you will say, "I have no pleasure in them;"
2 Before the sun, the light, the moon, and the stars are darkened,
    and the clouds return after the rain;
3 in the day when the keepers of the house shall tremble,
    and the strong men shall bow themselves,
    and the grinders cease because they are few,
    and those who look out of the windows are darkened,
4 and the doors shall be shut in the street;
    when the sound of the grinding is low,
    and one shall rise up at the voice of a bird,
    and all the daughters of music shall be brought low;
5 yes, they shall be afraid of heights,
    and terrors will be on the way;
    and the almond tree shall blossom,
    and the grasshopper shall be a burden,
    and desire shall fail;
    because man goes to his everlasting home,
    and the mourners go about the streets;
6 before the silver cord is severed,
    or the golden bowl is broken,
    or the pitcher is broken at the spring,
    or the wheel broken at the cistern,
7 and the dust returns to the earth as it was,
    and the spirit returns to God who gave it.
8 "Vanity of vanities," says the Preacher.
    "All is vanity!"

9 Further, because the Preacher was wise, he still taught the people knowledge. Yes, he pondered, sought out, and set in order many proverbs. 10 The Preacher sought to find out acceptable words, and that which was written blamelessly, words of truth. 11 The words of the wise are like goads; and like nails well fastened are words from the masters of assemblies, which are given from one shepherd. 12 Furthermore, my son, be admonished: of making many books there is no end; and much study is a weariness of the flesh.

13 This is the end of the matter. All has been heard. Fear God and keep his commandments; for this is the whole duty of man. 14 For God will bring every work into judgement, with every hidden thing, whether it is good, or whether it is evil.

The Song of Solomon

1

1 The Song of songs, which is Solomon's.

Beloved

2 Let him kiss me with the kisses of his mouth;
    for your love is better than wine.
3 Your oils have a pleasing fragrance.
    Your name is oil poured out,
    therefore the virgins love you.
4 Take me away with you.
    Let's hurry.
    The king has brought me into his rooms.

Friends

We will be glad and rejoice in you.
    We will praise your love more than wine!

Beloved

They are right to love you.
5 I am dark, but lovely,
    you daughters of Jerusalem,
    like Kedar's tents,
    like Solomon's curtains.
6 Don't stare at me because I am dark,
    because the sun has scorched me.
My mother's sons were angry with me.
    They made me keeper of the vineyards.
    I haven't kept my own vineyard.
7 Tell me, you whom my soul loves,
    where you graze your flock,
    where you rest them at noon;
    for why should I be as one who is veiled
    beside the flocks of your companions?

Lover

8 If you don't know, most beautiful amongst women,
    follow the tracks of the sheep.
    Graze your young goats beside the shepherds' tents.

9 I have compared you, my love,
    to a steed in Pharaoh's chariots.
10 Your cheeks are beautiful with earrings,
    your neck with strings of jewels.

Friends

11 We will make you earrings of gold,
    with studs of silver.

Beloved

12 While the king sat at his table,
    my perfume spread its fragrance.
13 My beloved is to me a sachet of myrrh,
    that lies between my breasts.
14 My beloved is to me a cluster of henna blossoms
    from the vineyards of En Gedi.

Lover

15 Behold,[a] you are beautiful, my love.
    Behold, you are beautiful.
    Your eyes are like doves.

Beloved

16 Behold, you are beautiful, my beloved, yes, pleasant;
    and our couch is verdant.

Lover

17 The beams of our house are cedars.
    Our rafters are firs.

2

Beloved

1 I am a rose of Sharon,
    a lily of the valleys.

Lover

2 As a lily amongst thorns,

so is my love amongst the daughters.

Beloved

3 As the apple tree amongst the trees of the wood,
    so is my beloved amongst the sons.
I sat down under his shadow with great delight,
    his fruit was sweet to my taste.
4 He brought me to the banquet hall.
    His banner over me is love.
5 Strengthen me with raisins,
    refresh me with apples;
    for I am faint with love.
6 His left hand is under my head.
    His right hand embraces me.
7 I adjure you, daughters of Jerusalem,
    by the roes, or by the hinds of the field,
    that you not stir up, nor awaken love,
    until it so desires.

8 The voice of my beloved!
    Behold, he comes,
    leaping on the mountains,
    skipping on the hills.
9 My beloved is like a roe or a young deer.
    Behold, he stands behind our wall!
He looks in at the windows.
    He glances through the lattice.

10 My beloved spoke, and said to me,
    "Rise up, my love, my beautiful one, and come away.
11 For behold, the winter is past.
    The rain is over and gone.
12 The flowers appear on the earth.
    The time of the singing has come,
    and the voice of the turtledove is heard in our land.
13 The fig tree ripens her green figs.
    The vines are in blossom.
    They give out their fragrance.
Arise, my love, my beautiful one,
    and come away."

Lover

14 My dove in the clefts of the rock,
    in the hiding places of the mountainside,
    let me see your face.
    Let me hear your voice;
    for your voice is sweet and your face is lovely.
15 Catch for us the foxes,
    the little foxes that plunder the vineyards;
    for our vineyards are in blossom.

Beloved

16 My beloved is mine, and I am his.
    He browses amongst the lilies.
17 Until the day is cool, and the shadows flee away,
    turn, my beloved,
    and be like a roe or a young deer on the mountains of Bether.

3

1 By night on my bed,
    I sought him whom my soul loves.
    I sought him, but I didn't find him.
2 I will get up now, and go about the city;
    in the streets and in the squares I will seek him whom my soul loves.
    I sought him, but I didn't find him.
3 The watchmen who go about the city found me;
    "Have you seen him whom my soul loves?"
4 I had scarcely passed from them,
    when I found him whom my soul loves.
I held him, and would not let him go,
    until I had brought him into my mother's house,
    into the room of her who conceived me.

5 I adjure you, daughters of Jerusalem,
    by the roes, or by the hinds of the field,
    that you not stir up nor awaken love,
    until it so desires.

6 Who is this who comes up from the wilderness like pillars of smoke,
    perfumed with myrrh and frankincense,
    with all spices of the merchant?
7 Behold, it is Solomon's carriage!
    Sixty mighty men are around it,
    of the mighty men of Israel.
8 They all handle the sword, and are expert in war.

---

a *1:15* "Behold", from "הִנֵּה", means look at, take notice, observe, see, or gaze at. It is often used as an interjection.

Every man has his sword on his thigh,
because of fear in the night.

9 King Solomon made himself a carriage
of the wood of Lebanon.
10 He made its pillars of silver,
its bottom of gold, its seat of purple,
the middle of it being paved with love,
from the daughters of Jerusalem.
11 Go out, you daughters of Zion, and see King Solomon,
with the crown with which his mother has crowned him,
in the day of his weddings,
in the day of the gladness of his heart.

4

Lover

1 Behold, you are beautiful, my love.
Behold, you are beautiful.
Your eyes are like doves behind your veil.
Your hair is as a flock of goats,
that descend from Mount Gilead.
2 Your teeth are like a newly shorn flock,
which have come up from the washing,
where every one of them has twins.
None is bereaved amongst them.
3 Your lips are like scarlet thread.
Your mouth is lovely.
Your temples are like a piece of a pomegranate behind your veil.
4 Your neck is like David's tower built for an armoury,
on which a thousand shields hang,
all the shields of the mighty men.
5 Your two breasts are like two fawns
that are twins of a roe,
which feed amongst the lilies.

6 Until the day is cool, and the shadows flee away,
I will go to the mountain of myrrh,
to the hill of frankincense.

7 You are all beautiful, my love.
There is no spot in you.
8 Come with me from Lebanon, my bride,
with me from Lebanon.
Look from the top of Amana,
from the top of Senir and Hermon,
from the lions' dens,
from the mountains of the leopards.

9 You have ravished my heart, my sister, my bride.
You have ravished my heart with one of your eyes,
with one chain of your neck.
10 How beautiful is your love, my sister, my bride!
How much better is your love than wine,
the fragrance of your perfumes than all kinds of spices!
11 Your lips, my bride, drip like the honeycomb.
Honey and milk are under your tongue.
The smell of your garments is like the smell of Lebanon.
12 My sister, my bride, is a locked up garden;
a locked up spring,
a sealed fountain.
13 Your shoots are an orchard of pomegranates, with precious fruits,
henna with spikenard plants,
14 spikenard and saffron,
calamus and cinnamon, with every kind of incense tree;
myrrh and aloes, with all the best spices,
15 a fountain of gardens,
a well of living waters,
flowing streams from Lebanon.

Beloved

16 Awake, north wind, and come, you south!
Blow on my garden, that its spices may flow out.
Let my beloved come into his garden,
and taste his precious fruits.

5

Lover

1 I have come into my garden, my sister, my bride.
I have gathered my myrrh with my spice;
I have eaten my honeycomb with my honey;
I have drunk my wine with my milk.

Friends

Eat, friends!
Drink, yes, drink abundantly, beloved.

Beloved

2 I was asleep, but my heart was awake.
It is the voice of my beloved who knocks:
"Open to me, my sister, my love, my dove, my undefiled;
for my head is filled with dew,
and my hair with the dampness of the night."
3 I have taken off my robe. Indeed, must I put it on?
I have washed my feet. Indeed, must I soil them?
4 My beloved thrust his hand in through the latch opening.
My heart pounded for him.
5 I rose up to open for my beloved.
My hands dripped with myrrh,
my fingers with liquid myrrh,
on the handles of the lock.
6 I opened to my beloved;
but my beloved left, and had gone away.
My heart went out when he spoke.
I looked for him, but I didn't find him.
I called him, but he didn't answer.
7 The watchmen who go about the city found me.
They beat me.
They bruised me.
The keepers of the walls took my cloak away from me.

8 I adjure you, daughters of Jerusalem,
If you find my beloved,
that you tell him that I am faint with love.

Friends

9 How is your beloved better than another beloved,
you fairest amongst women?
How is your beloved better than another beloved,
that you do so adjure us?

Beloved

10 My beloved is white and ruddy.
The best amongst ten thousand.
11 His head is like the purest gold.
His hair is bushy, black as a raven.
12 His eyes are like doves beside the water brooks,
washed with milk, mounted like jewels.
13 His cheeks are like a bed of spices with towers of perfumes.
His lips are like lilies, dropping liquid myrrh.
14 His hands are like rings of gold set with beryl.
His body is like ivory work overlaid with sapphires.
15 His legs are like pillars of marble set on sockets of fine gold.
His appearance is like Lebanon, excellent as the cedars.
16 His mouth is sweetness;
yes, he is altogether lovely.
This is my beloved, and this is my friend,
daughters of Jerusalem.

6

Friends

1 Where has your beloved gone, you fairest amongst women?
Where has your beloved turned, that we may seek him with you?

Beloved

2 My beloved has gone down to his garden,
to the beds of spices,
to pasture his flock in the gardens, and to gather lilies.
3 I am my beloved's, and my beloved is mine.
He browses amongst the lilies.

Lover

4 You are beautiful, my love, as Tirzah,
lovely as Jerusalem,
awesome as an army with banners.
5 Turn away your eyes from me,
for they have overcome me.
Your hair is like a flock of goats,
that lie along the side of Gilead.
6 Your teeth are like a flock of ewes,
which have come up from the washing,
of which every one has twins;
not one is bereaved amongst them.
7 Your temples are like a piece of a pomegranate behind your veil.

8 There are sixty queens, eighty concubines,
and virgins without number.
9 My dove, my perfect one, is unique.
She is her mother's only daughter.
She is the favourite one of her who bore her.
The daughters saw her, and called her blessed.

The queens and the concubines saw her, and they praised her.

10 Who is she who looks out as the morning,
    beautiful as the moon,
    clear as the sun,
    and awesome as an army with banners?

11 I went down into the nut tree grove,
    to see the green plants of the valley,
    to see whether the vine budded,
    and the pomegranates were in flower.
12 Without realising it,
    my desire set me with my royal people's chariots.

Friends

13 Return, return, Shulammite!
    Return, return, that we may gaze at you.

Lover

Why do you desire to gaze at the Shulammite,
    as at the dance of Mahanaim?

7

1 How beautiful are your feet in sandals, prince's daughter!
    Your rounded thighs are like jewels,
    the work of the hands of a skilful workman.
2 Your body is like a round goblet,
    no mixed wine is wanting.
Your waist is like a heap of wheat,
    set about with lilies.
3 Your two breasts are like two fawns,
    that are twins of a roe.
4 Your neck is like an ivory tower.
    Your eyes are like the pools in Heshbon by the gate of Bathrabbim.
    Your nose is like the tower of Lebanon which looks towards
        Damascus.
5 Your head on you is like Carmel.
    The hair of your head like purple.
    The king is held captive in its tresses.
6 How beautiful and how pleasant you are,
    love, for delights!
7 This, your stature, is like a palm tree,
    your breasts like its fruit.
8 I said, "I will climb up into the palm tree.
    I will take hold of its fruit."
Let your breasts be like clusters of the vine,
    the smell of your breath like apples.
9 Your mouth is like the best wine,
    that goes down smoothly for my beloved,
    gliding through the lips of those who are asleep.

Beloved

10 I am my beloved's.
    His desire is towards me.
11 Come, my beloved! Let's go out into the field.
    Let's lodge in the villages.
12 Let's go early up to the vineyards.
    Let's see whether the vine has budded,
    its blossom is open,
    and the pomegranates are in flower.
    There I will give you my love.
13 The mandrakes produce fragrance.
    At our doors are all kinds of precious fruits, new and old,
    which I have stored up for you, my beloved.

8

1 Oh that you were like my brother,
    who nursed from the breasts of my mother!
If I found you outside, I would kiss you;
    yes, and no one would despise me.
2 I would lead you, bringing you into the house of my mother,
    who would instruct me.
I would have you drink spiced wine,
    of the juice of my pomegranate.
3 His left hand would be under my head.
    His right hand would embrace me.

4 I adjure you, daughters of Jerusalem,
    that you not stir up, nor awaken love,
    until it so desires.

Friends

5 Who is this who comes up from the wilderness,
    leaning on her beloved?

Beloved

Under the apple tree I awakened you.
    There your mother conceived you.
    There she was in labour and bore you.

6 Set me as a seal on your heart,
    as a seal on your arm;
    for love is strong as death.
    Jealousy is as cruel as Sheol.[a]
    Its flashes are flashes of fire,
    a very flame of the LORD.[b]
7 Many waters can't quench love,
    neither can floods drown it.
If a man would give all the wealth of his house for love,
    he would be utterly scorned.

Brothers

8 We have a little sister.
    She has no breasts.
What shall we do for our sister
    in the day when she is to be spoken for?

9 If she is a wall,
    we will build on her a turret of silver.
If she is a door,
    we will enclose her with boards of cedar.

Beloved

10 I am a wall, and my breasts like towers,
    then I was in his eyes like one who found peace.
11 Solomon had a vineyard at Baal Hamon.
    He leased out the vineyard to keepers.
    Each was to bring a thousand shekels[c] of silver for its fruit.
12 My own vineyard is before me.
    The thousand are for you, Solomon,
    two hundred for those who tend its fruit.

Lover

13 You who dwell in the gardens, with friends in attendance,
    let me hear your voice!

Beloved

14 Come away, my beloved!
    Be like a gazelle or a young stag on the mountains of spices!

---

[a] *8:6* Sheol is the place of the dead.
[b] *8:6* When rendered in ALL CAPITAL LETTERS, "LORD" or "GOD" is the translation of God's Proper Name

[c] *8:11* A shekel is about 10 grams or about 0.35 ounces, so 1000 shekels is about 10 kilograms or about 22 pounds.

The Book of the Prophet Isaiah

1

1 The vision of Isaiah the son of Amoz, which he saw concerning Judah and Jerusalem, in the days of Uzziah, Jotham, Ahaz, and Hezekiah, kings of Judah.

2 Hear, heavens,
and listen, earth; for the LORD[a] has spoken:
"I have nourished and brought up children
and they have rebelled against me.
3 The ox knows his owner,
and the donkey his master's crib;
but Israel doesn't know.
My people don't consider."
4 Ah sinful nation,
a people loaded with iniquity,
offspring[b] of evildoers,
children who deal corruptly!
They have forsaken the LORD.
They have despised the Holy One of Israel.
They are estranged and backward.
5 Why should you be beaten more,
that you revolt more and more?
The whole head is sick,
and the whole heart faint.
6 From the sole of the foot even to the head there is no soundness in it,
but wounds, welts, and open sores.
They haven't been closed, bandaged, or soothed with oil.
7 Your country is desolate.
Your cities are burnt with fire.
Strangers devour your land in your presence
and it is desolate,
as overthrown by strangers.
8 The daughter of Zion is left like a shelter in a vineyard,
like a hut in a field of melons,
like a besieged city.
9 Unless the LORD of Armies had left to us a very small remnant,
we would have been as Sodom.
We would have been like Gomorrah.

10 Hear the LORD's word, you rulers of Sodom!
Listen to the law of our God,[c] you people of Gomorrah!
11 "What are the multitude of your sacrifices to me?", says the LORD.
"I have had enough of the burnt offerings of rams
and the fat of fed animals.
I don't delight in the blood of bulls,
or of lambs,
or of male goats.
12 When you come to appear before me,
who has required this at your hand, to trample my courts?
13 Bring no more vain offerings.
Incense is an abomination to me.
New moons, Sabbaths, and convocations—
I can't stand evil assemblies.
14 My soul hates your New Moons and your appointed feasts.
They are a burden to me.
I am weary of bearing them.
15 When you spread out your hands, I will hide my eyes from you.
Yes, when you make many prayers, I will not hear.
Your hands are full of blood.
16 Wash yourselves. Make yourself clean.
Put away the evil of your doings from before my eyes.
Cease to do evil.
17 Learn to do well.
Seek justice.
Relieve the oppressed.
Defend the fatherless.
Plead for the widow."

18 "Come now, and let's reason together," says the LORD:
"Though your sins are as scarlet, they shall be as white as snow.
Though they are red like crimson, they shall be as wool.
19 If you are willing and obedient,
you will eat the good of the land;
20 but if you refuse and rebel, you will be devoured with the sword;
for the LORD's mouth has spoken it."

21 How the faithful city has become a prostitute!
She was full of justice.
Righteousness lodged in her,
but now there are murderers.
22 Your silver has become dross,
your wine mixed with water.
23 Your princes are rebellious and companions of thieves.
Everyone loves bribes and follows after rewards.
They don't defend the fatherless,
neither does the cause of the widow come to them.

24 Therefore the Lord,[d] GOD of Armies,
the Mighty One of Israel, says:
"Ah, I will get relief from my adversaries,
and avenge myself on my enemies.
25 I will turn my hand on you,
thoroughly purge away your dross,
and will take away all your tin.[e]
26 I will restore your judges as at the first,
and your counsellors as at the beginning.
Afterward you shall be called 'The city of righteousness,
a faithful town.'
27 Zion shall be redeemed with justice,
and her converts with righteousness.
28 But the destruction of transgressors and sinners shall be together,
and those who forsake the LORD shall be consumed.
29 For they shall be ashamed of the oaks which you have desired,
and you shall be confounded for the gardens that you have chosen.
30 For you shall be as an oak whose leaf fades,
and as a garden that has no water.
31 The strong will be like tinder,
and his work like a spark.
They will both burn together,
and no one will quench them."

2

1 This is what Isaiah the son of Amoz saw concerning Judah and Jerusalem.
2 It shall happen in the latter days, that the mountain of the LORD's house
shall be established on the top of the mountains,
and shall be raised above the hills;
and all nations shall flow to it.
3 Many peoples shall go and say,
"Come, let's go up to the mountain of the LORD,
to the house of the God of Jacob;
and he will teach us of his ways,
and we will walk in his paths."
For the law shall go out of Zion,
and the LORD's word from Jerusalem.
4 He will judge between the nations,
and will decide concerning many peoples.
They shall beat their swords into ploughshares,
and their spears into pruning hooks.
Nation shall not lift up sword against nation,
neither shall they learn war any more.

5 House of Jacob, come, and let's walk in the light of the LORD.
6 For you have forsaken your people, the house of Jacob,
because they are filled from the east,
with those who practise divination like the Philistines,
and they clasp hands with the children of foreigners.
7 Their land is full of silver and gold,
neither is there any end of their treasures.
Their land also is full of horses,
neither is there any end of their chariots.
8 Their land also is full of idols.
They worship the work of their own hands,
that which their own fingers have made.
9 Man is brought low,
and mankind is humbled;
therefore don't forgive them.
10 Enter into the rock,
and hide in the dust,
from before the terror of the LORD,
and from the glory of his majesty.
11 The lofty looks of man will be brought low,
the arrogance of men will be bowed down,
and the LORD alone will be exalted in that day.

12 For there will be a day of the LORD of Armies for all that is proud and arrogant,
and for all that is lifted up,
and it shall be brought low—
13 for all the cedars of Lebanon, that are high and lifted up,
for all the oaks of Bashan,
14 for all the high mountains,
for all the hills that are lifted up,
15 for every lofty tower,
for every fortified wall,

---

a *1:2* When rendered in ALL CAPITAL LETTERS, "LORD" or "GOD" is the translation of God's Proper Name.
b *1:4* or, seed
c *1:10* The Hebrew word rendered "God" is "אֱלֹהִים" (Elohim).

d *1:24* The word translated "Lord" is "Adonai."
e *1:25* tin is a metal that is separated from silver during the refining and purification process.

₁₆ for all the ships of Tarshish,
and for all pleasant imagery.
₁₇ The loftiness of man shall be bowed down,
and the arrogance of men shall be brought low;
and the LORD alone shall be exalted in that day.
₁₈ The idols shall utterly pass away.
₁₉ Men shall go into the caves of the rocks,
and into the holes of the earth,
from before the terror of the LORD,
and from the glory of his majesty,
when he arises to shake the earth mightily.
₂₀ In that day, men shall cast away their idols of silver
and their idols of gold,
which have been made for themselves to worship,
to the moles and to the bats,
₂₁ to go into the caverns of the rocks,
and into the clefts of the ragged rocks,
from before the terror of the LORD,
and from the glory of his majesty,
when he arises to shake the earth mightily.
₂₂ Stop trusting in man, whose breath is in his nostrils;
for of what account is he?

3

₁ For, behold,[a] the Lord, GOD of Armies, takes away from Jerusalem and from Judah supply and support,
the whole supply of bread,
and the whole supply of water;
₂ the mighty man,
the man of war,
the judge,
the prophet,
the diviner,
the elder,
₃ the captain of fifty,
the honourable man,
the counsellor,
the skilled craftsman,
and the clever enchanter.
₄ I will give boys to be their princes,
and children shall rule over them.
₅ The people will be oppressed,
everyone by another,
and everyone by his neighbour.
The child will behave himself proudly against the old man,
and the wicked against the honourable.
₆ Indeed a man shall take hold of his brother in the house of his father,
saying,
"You have clothing, you be our ruler,
and let this ruin be under your hand."
₇ In that day he will cry out, saying, "I will not be a healer;
for in my house is neither bread nor clothing.
You shall not make me ruler of the people."
₈ For Jerusalem is ruined, and Judah is fallen;
because their tongue and their doings are against the LORD,
to provoke the eyes of his glory.
₉ The look of their faces testify against them.
They parade their sin like Sodom.
They don't hide it.
Woe to their soul!
For they have brought disaster upon themselves.
₁₀ Tell the righteous that it will be well with them,
for they will eat the fruit of their deeds.
₁₁ Woe to the wicked!
Disaster is upon them,
for the deeds of their hands will be paid back to them.
₁₂ As for my people, children are their oppressors,
and women rule over them.
My people, those who lead you cause you to err,
and destroy the way of your paths.

₁₃ The LORD stands up to contend,
and stands to judge the peoples.
₁₄ The LORD will enter into judgement with the elders of his people
and their leaders:
"It is you who have eaten up the vineyard.
The plunder of the poor is in your houses.
₁₅ What do you mean that you crush my people,
and grind the face of the poor?" says the Lord, the LORD of Armies.

₁₆ Moreover the LORD said, "Because the daughters of Zion are arrogant,
and walk with outstretched necks and flirting eyes,
walking daintily as they go,

jingling ornaments on their feet;
₁₇ therefore the Lord brings sores on the crown of the head of the women of Zion,
and the LORD will make their scalps bald."
₁₈ In that day the Lord will take away the beauty of their anklets, the headbands, the crescent necklaces, ₁₉ the earrings, the bracelets, the veils, ₂₀ the headdresses, the ankle chains, the sashes, the perfume containers, the charms, ₂₁ the signet rings, the nose rings, ₂₂ the fine robes, the capes, the cloaks, the purses, ₂₃ the hand mirrors, the fine linen garments, the tiaras, and the shawls.
₂₄ It shall happen that instead of sweet spices, there shall be rottenness;
instead of a belt, a rope;
instead of well set hair, baldness;
instead of a robe, a wearing of sackcloth;
and branding instead of beauty.
₂₅ Your men shall fall by the sword,
and your mighty in the war.
₂₆ Her gates shall lament and mourn.
She shall be desolate and sit on the ground.

4

₁ Seven women shall take hold of one man in that day, saying, "We will eat our own bread, and wear our own clothing. Just let us be called by your name. Take away our reproach."
₂ In that day, the LORD's branch will be beautiful and glorious, and the fruit of the land will be the beauty and glory of the survivors of Israel. ₃ It will happen that he who is left in Zion and he who remains in Jerusalem shall be called holy, even everyone who is written amongst the living in Jerusalem, ₄ when the Lord shall have washed away the filth of the daughters of Zion, and shall have purged the blood of Jerusalem from within it, by the spirit of justice and by the spirit of burning. ₅ The LORD will create over the whole habitation of Mount Zion and over her assemblies, a cloud and smoke by day, and the shining of a flaming fire by night, for over all the glory will be a canopy. ₆ There will be a pavilion for a shade in the daytime from the heat, and for a refuge and for a shelter from storm and from rain.

5

₁ Let me sing for my well beloved a song of my beloved about his vineyard.
My beloved had a vineyard on a very fruitful hill.
₂ He dug it up,
gathered out its stones,
planted it with the choicest vine,
built a tower in the middle of it,
and also cut out a wine press in it.
He looked for it to yield grapes,
but it yielded wild grapes.

₃ "Now, inhabitants of Jerusalem and men of Judah,
please judge between me and my vineyard.
₄ What could have been done more to my vineyard, that I have not done in it?
Why, when I looked for it to yield grapes, did it yield wild grapes?
₅ Now I will tell you what I will do to my vineyard.
I will take away its hedge, and it will be eaten up.
I will break down its wall, and it will be trampled down.
₆ I will lay it a wasteland.
It won't be pruned or hoed,
but it will grow briers and thorns.
I will also command the clouds that they rain no rain on it."
₇ For the vineyard of the LORD of Armies is the house of Israel,
and the men of Judah his pleasant plant.
He looked for justice, but behold, oppression,
for righteousness, but behold, a cry of distress.

₈ Woe to those who join house to house,
who lay field to field, until there is no room,
and you are made to dwell alone in the middle of the land!
₉ In my ears, the LORD of Armies says: "Surely many houses will be desolate,
even great and beautiful, unoccupied.
₁₀ For ten acres[b] of vineyard shall yield one bath,[c]
and a homer[d] of seed shall yield an ephah."[e]
₁₁ Woe to those who rise up early in the morning, that they may follow strong drink,
who stay late into the night, until wine inflames them!
₁₂ The harp, lyre, tambourine, and flute, with wine, are at their feasts;
but they don't respect the work of the LORD,
neither have they considered the operation of his hands.

₁₃ Therefore my people go into captivity for lack of knowledge.
Their honourable men are famished,
and their multitudes are parched with thirst.
₁₄ Therefore Sheol[f] has enlarged its desire,

_a *3:1* "Behold", from "הִנֵּה", means look at, take notice, observe, see, or gaze at. It is often used as an interjection.
_b *5:10* literally, ten yokes, or the amount of land that ten yokes of oxen can plough in one day, which is about 10 acres or 4 hectares.
_c *5:10* 1 bath is about 22 litres or 5.8 U. S. gallons

_d *5:10* 1 homer is about 220 litres or 6 bushels
_e *5:10* 1 ephah is about 22 litres or 0.6 bushels or about 2 pecks—only one tenth of what was sown.
_f *5:14* Sheol is the place of the dead.

and opened its mouth without measure;
and their glory, their multitude, their pomp, and he who rejoices
amongst them, descend into it.
15 So man is brought low,
mankind is humbled,
and the eyes of the arrogant ones are humbled;
16 but the LORD of Armies is exalted in justice,
and God the Holy One is sanctified in righteousness.
17 Then the lambs will graze as in their pasture,
and strangers will eat the ruins of the rich.

18 Woe to those who draw iniquity with cords of falsehood,
and wickedness as with cart rope,
19 who say, "Let him make haste, let him hasten his work, that we may see it;
let the counsel of the Holy One of Israel draw near and come,
that we may know it!"
20 Woe to those who call evil good, and good evil;
who put darkness for light,
and light for darkness;
who put bitter for sweet,
and sweet for bitter!
21 Woe to those who are wise in their own eyes,
and prudent in their own sight!
22 Woe to those who are mighty to drink wine,
and champions at mixing strong drink;
23 who acquit the guilty for a bribe,
but deny justice for the innocent!

24 Therefore as the tongue of fire devours the stubble,
and as the dry grass sinks down in the flame,
so their root shall be as rottenness,
and their blossom shall go up as dust,
because they have rejected the law of the LORD of Armies,
and despised the word of the Holy One of Israel.
25 Therefore the LORD's anger burns against his people,
and he has stretched out his hand against them and has struck them.
The mountains tremble,
and their dead bodies are as refuse in the middle of the streets.
For all this, his anger is not turned away,
but his hand is still stretched out.

26 He will lift up a banner to the nations from far away,
and he will whistle for them from the end of the earth.
Behold, they will come speedily and swiftly.
27 No one shall be weary nor stumble amongst them;
no one shall slumber nor sleep,
neither shall the belt of their waist be untied,
nor the strap of their sandals be broken,
28 whose arrows are sharp,
and all their bows bent.
Their horses' hoofs will be like flint,
and their wheels like a whirlwind.
29 Their roaring will be like a lioness.
They will roar like young lions.
Yes, they shall roar,
and seize their prey and carry it off,
and there will be no one to deliver.
30 They will roar against them in that day like the roaring of the sea.
If one looks to the land, behold, darkness and distress.
The light is darkened in its clouds.

6

1 In the year that King Uzziah died, I saw the Lord sitting on a throne, high and lifted up; and his train filled the temple. 2 Above him stood the seraphim. Each one had six wings. With two he covered his face. With two he covered his feet. With two he flew. 3 One called to another, and said,
"Holy, holy, holy, is the LORD of Armies!
The whole earth is full of his glory!"
4 The foundations of the thresholds shook at the voice of him who called, and the house was filled with smoke. 5 Then I said, "Woe is me! For I am undone, because I am a man of unclean lips and I live amongst a people of unclean lips, for my eyes have seen the King, the LORD of Armies!"
6 Then one of the seraphim flew to me, having a live coal in his hand, which he had taken with the tongs from off the altar. 7 He touched my mouth with it, and said, "Behold, this has touched your lips; and your iniquity is taken away, and your sin forgiven."
8 I heard the Lord's voice, saying, "Whom shall I send, and who will go for us?"
Then I said, "Here I am. Send me!"
9 He said, "Go, and tell this people,
'You hear indeed,
but don't understand.
You see indeed,
but don't perceive.'

10 Make the heart of this people fat.
Make their ears heavy, and shut their eyes;
lest they see with their eyes,
hear with their ears,
understand with their heart,
and turn again, and be healed."
11 Then I said, "Lord, how long?"
He answered,
"Until cities are waste without inhabitant,
houses without man,
the land becomes utterly waste,
12 and the LORD has removed men far away,
and the forsaken places are many within the land.
13 If there is a tenth left in it,
that also will in turn be consumed,
as a terebinth, and as an oak whose stump remains when they are cut down,
so the holy seed is its stump."

7

1 In the days of Ahaz the son of Jotham, the son of Uzziah, king of Judah, Rezin the king of Syria and Pekah the son of Remaliah, king of Israel, went up to Jerusalem to war against it, but could not prevail against it. 2 David's house was told, "Syria is allied with Ephraim." His heart trembled, and the heart of his people, as the trees of the forest tremble with the wind.
3 Then the LORD said to Isaiah, "Go out now to meet Ahaz, you, and Shearjashub your son, at the end of the conduit of the upper pool, on the highway of the fuller's field. 4 Tell him, 'Be careful, and keep calm. Don't be afraid, neither let your heart be faint because of these two tails of smoking torches, for the fierce anger of Rezin and Syria, and of the son of Remaliah. 5 Because Syria, Ephraim, and the son of Remaliah, have plotted evil against you, saying, 6 "Let's go up against Judah, and tear it apart, and let's divide it amongst ourselves, and set up a king within it, even the son of Tabeel." 7 This is what the Lord GOD says: "It shall not stand, neither shall it happen." 8 For the head of Syria is Damascus, and the head of Damascus is Rezin. Within sixty-five years Ephraim shall be broken in pieces, so that it shall not be a people. 9 The head of Ephraim is Samaria, and the head of Samaria is Remaliah's son. If you will not believe, surely you shall not be established."'
10 The LORD spoke again to Ahaz, saying, 11 "Ask a sign of the LORD your God; ask it either in the depth, or in the height above."
12 But Ahaz said, "I won't ask. I won't tempt the LORD."
13 He said, "Listen now, house of David. Is it not enough for you to try the patience of men, that you will try the patience of my God also? 14 Therefore the Lord himself will give you a sign. Behold, the virgin will conceive, and bear a son, and shall call his name Immanuel.[a] 15 He shall eat butter and honey when he knows to refuse the evil and choose the good. 16 For before the child knows to refuse the evil and choose the good, the land whose two kings you abhor shall be forsaken. 17 The LORD will bring on you, on your people, and on your father's house days that have not come, from the day that Ephraim departed from Judah, even the king of Assyria.
18 It will happen in that day that the LORD will whistle for the fly that is in the uttermost part of the rivers of Egypt, and for the bee that is in the land of Assyria. 19 They shall come, and shall all rest in the desolate valleys, in the clefts of the rocks, on all thorn hedges, and on all pastures.
20 In that day the Lord will shave with a razor that is hired in the parts beyond the River, even with the king of Assyria, the head and the hair of the feet; and it shall also consume the beard.
21 It shall happen in that day that a man shall keep alive a young cow, and two sheep. 22 It shall happen, that because of the abundance of milk which they shall give he shall eat butter, for everyone will eat butter and honey that is left within the land.
23 It will happen in that day that every place where there were a thousand vines worth a thousand silver shekels,[b] will be for briers and thorns. 24 People will go there with arrows and with bow, because all the land will be briers and thorns. 25 All the hills that were cultivated with the hoe, you shall not come there for fear of briers and thorns; but it shall be for the sending out of oxen, and for sheep to tread on."

8

1 The LORD said to me, "Take a large tablet, and write on it with a man's pen, 'For Maher Shalal Hash Baz';[c] 2 and I will take for myself faithful witnesses to testify: Uriah the priest, and Zechariah the son of Jeberechiah."
3 I went to the prophetess, and she conceived, and bore a son. Then the LORD said to me, "Call his name 'Maher Shalal Hash Baz.' 4 For before the child knows how to say, 'My father' and 'My mother,' the riches of Damascus and the plunder of Samaria will be carried away by the king of Assyria."
5 The LORD spoke to me yet again, saying, 6 "Because this people has refused the waters of Shiloah that go softly, and rejoice in Rezin and Remaliah's son; 7 now therefore, behold, the Lord brings upon them the mighty flood waters of the River: the king of Assyria and all his glory. It will come up over all its channels, and go over all its banks. 8 It will sweep onward into Judah. It will overflow and pass through. It will reach even to

---

a 7:14 "Immanuel" means "God with us".
b 7:23 A shekel is about 10 grams or about 0.35 ounces, so 1000 shekels is about 10 kilograms or 22 pounds.

c 8:1 "Maher Shalal Hash Baz" means "quick to the plunder, swift to the prey".

the neck. The stretching out of its wings will fill the width of your land, O Immanuel.

9 Make an uproar, you peoples, and be broken in pieces! Listen, all you from far countries: dress for battle, and be shattered! Dress for battle, and be shattered! 10 Take counsel together, and it will be brought to nothing; speak the word, and it will not stand, for God is with us."

11 For the LORD spoke this to me with a strong hand, and instructed me not to walk in the way of this people, saying, 12 "Don't call a conspiracy all that this people call a conspiracy. Don't fear their threats or be terrorised. 13 The LORD of Armies is who you must respect as holy. He is the one you must fear. He is the one you must dread. 14 He will be a sanctuary, but for both houses of Israel, he will be a stumbling stone and a rock that makes them fall. For the people of Jerusalem, he will be a trap and a snare. 15 Many will stumble over it, fall, be broken, be snared, and be captured."

16 Wrap up the covenant. Seal the law amongst my disciples. 17 I will wait for the LORD, who hides his face from the house of Jacob, and I will look for him. 18 Behold, I and the children whom the LORD has given me are for signs and for wonders in Israel from the LORD of Armies, who dwells in Mount Zion.

19 When they tell you, "Consult with those who have familiar spirits and with the wizards, who chirp and who mutter," shouldn't a people consult with their God? Should they consult the dead on behalf of the living? 20 Turn to the law and to the covenant! If they don't speak according to this word, surely there is no morning for them. 21 They will pass through it, very distressed and hungry. It will happen that when they are hungry, they will worry, and curse their king and their God. They will turn their faces upward, 22 then look to the earth and see distress, darkness, and the gloom of anguish. They will be driven into thick darkness.

9

1 But there shall be no more gloom for her who was in anguish. In the former time, he brought into contempt the land of Zebulun and the land of Naphtali; but in the latter time he has made it glorious, by the way of the sea, beyond the Jordan, Galilee of the nations.

2 The people who walked in darkness have seen a great light.
The light has shined on those who lived in the land of the shadow of death.
3 You have multiplied the nation.
You have increased their joy.
They rejoice before you according to the joy in harvest, as men rejoice when they divide the plunder. 4 For the yoke of his burden, and the staff of his shoulder, the rod of his oppressor, you have broken as in the day of Midian. 5 For all the armour of the armed man in the noisy battle, and the garments rolled in blood, will be for burning, fuel for the fire. 6 For a child is born to us. A son is given to us; and the government will be on his shoulders. His name will be called Wonderful Counsellor, Mighty God, Everlasting Father, Prince of Peace. 7 Of the increase of his government and of peace there shall be no end, on David's throne, and on his kingdom, to establish it, and to uphold it with justice and with righteousness from that time on, even forever. The zeal of the LORD of Armies will perform this.

8 The Lord sent a word into Jacob,
and it falls on Israel.
9 All the people will know,
including Ephraim and the inhabitants of Samaria, who say in pride
and in arrogance of heart,
10 "The bricks have fallen,
but we will build with cut stone.
The sycamore fig trees have been cut down,
but we will put cedars in their place."
11 Therefore the LORD will set up on high against him the adversaries of Rezin,
and will stir up his enemies,
12 The Syrians in front,
and the Philistines behind;
and they will devour Israel with open mouth.
For all this, his anger is not turned away,
but his hand is stretched out still.

13 Yet the people have not turned to him who struck them,
neither have they sought the LORD of Armies.
14 Therefore the LORD will cut off from Israel head and tail,
palm branch and reed, in one day.
15 The elder and the honourable man is the head,
and the prophet who teaches lies is the tail.
16 For those who lead this people lead them astray;
and those who are led by them are destroyed.
17 Therefore the Lord will not rejoice over their young men,
neither will he have compassion on their fatherless and widows;
for everyone is profane and an evildoer,
and every mouth speaks folly.
For all this his anger is not turned away,
but his hand is stretched out still.

18 For wickedness burns like a fire.
It devours the briers and thorns;
yes, it kindles in the thickets of the forest,
and they roll upward in a column of smoke.
19 Through the LORD of Armies' wrath, the land is burnt up;
and the people are the fuel for the fire.

No one spares his brother.
20 One will devour on the right hand, and be hungry;
and he will eat on the left hand, and they will not be satisfied.
Everyone will eat the flesh of his own arm:
21 Manasseh eating Ephraim and Ephraim eating Manasseh, and they together will be against Judah.
For all this his anger is not turned away,
but his hand is stretched out still.

10

1 Woe to those who decree unrighteous decrees, and to the writers who write oppressive decrees 2 to deprive the needy of justice, and to rob the poor amongst my people of their rights, that widows may be their plunder, and that they may make the fatherless their prey! 3 What will you do in the day of visitation, and in the desolation which will come from afar? To whom will you flee for help? Where will you leave your wealth?
4 They will only bow down under the prisoners,
and will fall under the slain.
For all this his anger is not turned away,
but his hand is stretched out still.

5 Alas Assyrian, the rod of my anger, the staff in whose hand is my indignation! 6 I will send him against a profane nation, and against the people who anger me I will give him a command to take the plunder and to take the prey, and to tread them down like the mire of the streets. 7 However, he doesn't mean so, neither does his heart think so; but it is in his heart to destroy, and to cut off not a few nations. 8 For he says, "Aren't all of my princes kings? 9 Isn't Calno like Carchemish? Isn't Hamath like Arpad? Isn't Samaria like Damascus?" 10 As my hand has found the kingdoms of the idols, whose engraved images exceeded those of Jerusalem and of Samaria, 11 shall I not, as I have done to Samaria and her idols, so do to Jerusalem and her idols?

12 Therefore it will happen that when the Lord has performed his whole work on Mount Zion and on Jerusalem, I will punish the fruit of the wilful proud heart of the king of Assyria, and the insolence of his arrogant looks. 13 For he has said, "By the strength of my hand I have done it, and by my wisdom, for I have understanding. I have removed the boundaries of the peoples, and have robbed their treasures. Like a valiant man I have brought down their rulers. 14 My hand has found the riches of the peoples like a nest, and like one gathers eggs that are abandoned, I have gathered all the earth. There was no one who moved their wing, or that opened their mouth, or chirped."

15 Should an axe brag against him who chops with it? Should a saw exalt itself above him who saws with it? As if a rod should lift those who lift it up, or as if a staff should lift up someone who is not wood. 16 Therefore the Lord, the LORD of Armies, will send amongst his fat ones leanness; and under his glory a burning will be kindled like the burning of fire. 17 The light of Israel will be for a fire, and his Holy One for a flame; and it will burn and devour his thorns and his briers in one day. 18 He will consume the glory of his forest and of his fruitful field, both soul and body. It will be as when a standard bearer faints. 19 The remnant of the trees of his forest shall be few, so that a child could write their number.

20 It will come to pass in that day that the remnant of Israel, and those who have escaped from the house of Jacob will no more again lean on him who struck them, but shall lean on the LORD, the Holy One of Israel, in truth. 21 A remnant will return, even the remnant of Jacob, to the mighty God. 22 For though your people, Israel, are like the sand of the sea, only a remnant of them will return. A destruction is determined, overflowing with righteousness. 23 For the Lord, the LORD of Armies, will make a full end, and that determined, throughout all the earth.

24 Therefore the Lord, the LORD of Armies, says, "My people who dwell in Zion, don't be afraid of the Assyrian, though he strike you with the rod, and lift up his staff against you, as Egypt did. 25 For yet a very little while, and the indignation against you will be accomplished, and my anger will be directed to his destruction." 26 The LORD of Armies will stir up a scourge against him, as in the slaughter of Midian at the rock of Oreb. His rod will be over the sea, and he will lift it up like he did against Egypt. 27 It will happen in that day that his burden will depart from off your shoulder, and his yoke from off your neck, and the yoke shall be destroyed because of the anointing oil.

28 He has come to Aiath. He has passed through Migron. At Michmash he stores his baggage. 29 They have gone over the pass. They have taken up their lodging at Geba. Ramah trembles. Gibeah of Saul has fled. 30 Cry aloud with your voice, daughter of Gallim! Listen, Laishah! You poor Anathoth! 31 Madmenah is a fugitive. The inhabitants of Gebim flee for safety. 32 This very day he will halt at Nob. He shakes his hand at the mountain of the daughter of Zion, the hill of Jerusalem.

33 Behold, the Lord, the LORD of Armies, will lop the boughs with terror. The tall will be cut down, and the lofty will be brought low. 34 He will cut down the thickets of the forest with iron, and Lebanon will fall by the Mighty One.

11

1 A shoot will come out of the stock of Jesse,
and a branch out of his roots will bear fruit.
2 The LORD's Spirit will rest on him:
the spirit of wisdom and understanding,
the spirit of counsel and might,
the spirit of knowledge and of the fear of the LORD.
3 His delight will be in the fear of the LORD.

He will not judge by the sight of his eyes,
neither decide by the hearing of his ears;
₄ but he will judge the poor with righteousness,
and decide with equity for the humble of the earth.
He will strike the earth with the rod of his mouth;
and with the breath of his lips he will kill the wicked.
₅ Righteousness will be the belt around his waist,
and faithfulness the belt around his waist.

₆ The wolf will live with the lamb,
and the leopard will lie down with the young goat,
the calf, the young lion, and the fattened calf together;
and a little child will lead them.
₇ The cow and the bear will graze.
Their young ones will lie down together.
The lion will eat straw like the ox.
₈ The nursing child will play near a cobra's hole,
and the weaned child will put his hand on the viper's den.
₉ They will not hurt nor destroy in all my holy mountain;
for the earth will be full of the knowledge of the LORD,
as the waters cover the sea.

₁₀ It will happen in that day that the nations will seek the root of Jesse, who stands as a banner of the peoples; and his resting place will be glorious. ₁₁ It will happen in that day that the Lord will set his hand again the second time to recover the remnant that is left of his people from Assyria, from Egypt, from Pathros, from Cush, from Elam, from Shinar, from Hamath, and from the islands of the sea. ₁₂ He will set up a banner for the nations, and will assemble the outcasts of Israel, and gather together the dispersed of Judah from the four corners of the earth. ₁₃ The envy also of Ephraim will depart, and those who persecute Judah will be cut off. Ephraim won't envy Judah, and Judah won't persecute Ephraim. ₁₄ They will fly down on the shoulders of the Philistines on the west. Together they will plunder the children of the east. They will extend their power over Edom and Moab, and the children of Ammon will obey them. ₁₅ The LORD will utterly destroy the tongue of the Egyptian sea; and with his scorching wind he will wave his hand over the River, and will split it into seven streams, and cause men to march over in sandals. ₁₆ There will be a highway for the remnant that is left of his people from Assyria, like there was for Israel in the day that he came up out of the land of Egypt.

12

₁ In that day you will say, "I will give thanks to you, the LORD; for though you were angry with me, your anger has turned away and you comfort me. ₂ Behold, God is my salvation. I will trust, and will not be afraid; for the LORD, the LORD, is my strength and song; and he has become my salvation." ₃ Therefore with joy you will draw water out of the wells of salvation. ₄ In that day you will say, "Give thanks to the LORD! Call on his name! Declare his doings amongst the peoples! Proclaim that his name is exalted! ₅ Sing to the LORD, for he has done excellent things! Let this be known in all the earth! ₆ Cry aloud and shout, you inhabitant of Zion, for the Holy One of Israel is great amongst you!"

13

₁ The burden of Babylon, which Isaiah the son of Amoz saw.

₂ Set up a banner on the bare mountain! Lift up your voice to them! Wave your hand, that they may go into the gates of the nobles. ₃ I have commanded my consecrated ones; yes, I have called my mighty men for my anger, even my proudly exulting ones. ₄ The noise of a multitude is in the mountains, as of a great people; the noise of an uproar of the kingdoms of the nations gathered together! The LORD of Armies is mustering the army for the battle. ₅ They come from a far country, from the uttermost part of heaven, even the LORD, and the weapons of his indignation, to destroy the whole land.

₆ Wail, for the LORD's day is at hand! It will come as destruction from the Almighty. ₇ Therefore all hands will be feeble, and everyone's heart will melt. ₈ They will be dismayed. Pangs and sorrows will seize them. They will be in pain like a woman in labour. They will look in amazement one at another. Their faces will be faces of flame. ₉ Behold, the day of the LORD comes, cruel, with wrath and fierce anger; to make the land a desolation, and to destroy its sinners out of it. ₁₀ For the stars of the sky and its constellations will not give their light. The sun will be darkened in its going out, and the moon will not cause its light to shine. ₁₁ I will punish the world for their evil, and the wicked for their iniquity. I will cause the arrogance of the proud to cease, and will humble the arrogance of the terrible. ₁₂ I will make people more rare than fine gold, even a person than the pure gold of Ophir. ₁₃ Therefore I will make the heavens tremble, and the earth will be shaken out of its place in the LORD of Armies' wrath, and in the day of his fierce anger. ₁₄ It will happen that like a hunted gazelle and like sheep that no one gathers, they will each turn to their own people, and will each flee to their own land. ₁₅ Everyone who is found will be thrust through. Everyone who is captured will fall by the sword. ₁₆ Their infants also will be dashed in pieces before their eyes. Their houses will be ransacked, and their wives raped.

₁₇ Behold, I will stir up the Medes against them, who will not value silver, and as for gold, they will not delight in it. ₁₈ Their bows will dash the young men in pieces; and they shall have no pity on the fruit of the womb. Their eyes will not spare children. ₁₉ Babylon, the glory of kingdoms, the beauty of the Chaldeans' pride, will be like when God overthrew Sodom and Gomorrah. ₂₀ It will never be inhabited, neither will it be lived in from generation to generation. The Arabian will not pitch a tent there, neither will shepherds make their flocks lie down there. ₂₁ But wild animals of the desert will lie there, and their houses will be full of jackals. Ostriches will dwell there, and wild goats will frolic there. ₂₂ Hyenas will cry in their fortresses, and jackals in the pleasant palaces. Her time is near to come, and her days will not be prolonged.

14

₁ For the LORD will have compassion on Jacob, and will yet choose Israel, and set them in their own land. The foreigner will join himself with them, and they will unite with the house of Jacob. ₂ The peoples will take them, and bring them to their place. The house of Israel will possess them in the LORD's land for servants and for handmaids. They will take as captives those whose captives they were; and they shall rule over their oppressors.

₃ It will happen in the day that the LORD will give you rest from your sorrow, from your trouble, and from the hard service in which you were made to serve, ₄ that you will take up this parable against the king of Babylon, and say, "How the oppressor has ceased! The golden city has ceased!" ₅ The LORD has broken the staff of the wicked, the sceptre of the rulers, ₆ who struck the peoples in wrath with a continual stroke, who ruled the nations in anger, with a persecution that no one restrained. ₇ The whole earth is at rest, and is quiet. They break out in song. ₈ Yes, the cypress trees rejoice with you, with the cedars of Lebanon, saying, "Since you are humbled, no lumberjack has come up against us." ₉ Sheol[a] from beneath has moved for you to meet you at your coming. It stirs up the departed spirits for you, even all the rulers of the earth. It has raised up from their thrones all the kings of the nations. ₁₀ They all will answer and ask you, "Have you also become as weak as we are? Have you become like us?" ₁₁ Your pomp is brought down to Sheol,[b] with the sound of your stringed instruments. Maggots are spread out under you, and worms cover you.

₁₂ How you have fallen from heaven, shining one, son of the dawn! How you are cut down to the ground, who laid the nations low! ₁₃ You said in your heart, "I will ascend into heaven! I will exalt my throne above the stars of God! I will sit on the mountain of assembly, in the far north! ₁₄ I will ascend above the heights of the clouds! I will make myself like the Most High!" ₁₅ Yet you shall be brought down to Sheol,[c] to the depths of the pit.

₁₆ Those who see you will stare at you. They will ponder you, saying, "Is this the man who made the earth to tremble, who shook kingdoms, ₁₇ who made the world like a wilderness, and overthrew its cities, who didn't release his prisoners to their home?"

₁₈ All the kings of the nations sleep in glory, everyone in his own house. ₁₉ But you are cast away from your tomb like an abominable branch, clothed with the slain who are thrust through with the sword, who go down to the stones of the pit; like a dead body trodden under foot. ₂₀ You will not join them in burial, because you have destroyed your land. You have killed your people. The offspring of evildoers will not be named forever.

₂₁ Prepare for slaughter of his children because of the iniquity of their fathers, that they not rise up and possess the earth, and fill the surface of the world with cities. ₂₂ "I will rise up against them," says the LORD of Armies, "and cut off from Babylon name and remnant, and son and son's son," says the LORD. ₂₃ "I will also make it a possession for the porcupine, and pools of water. I will sweep it with the broom of destruction," says the LORD of Armies.

₂₄ The LORD of Armies has sworn, saying, "Surely, as I have thought, so shall it happen; and as I have purposed, so shall it stand: ₂₅ that I will break the Assyrian in my land, and tread him under foot on my mountains. Then his yoke will leave them, and his burden leave their shoulders. ₂₆ This is the plan that is determined for the whole earth. This is the hand that is stretched out over all the nations. ₂₇ For the LORD of Armies has planned, and who can stop it? His hand is stretched out, and who can turn it back?"

₂₈ This burden was in the year that King Ahaz died.

₂₉ Don't rejoice, O Philistia, all of you, because the rod that struck you is broken; for out of the serpent's root an adder will emerge, and his fruit will be a fiery flying serpent. ₃₀ The firstborn of the poor will eat, and the needy will lie down in safety; and I will kill your root with famine, and your remnant will be killed.

₃₁ Howl, gate! Cry, city! You are melted away, Philistia, all of you; for smoke comes out of the north, and there is no straggler in his ranks.

₃₂ What will they answer the messengers of the nation? That the LORD has founded Zion, and in her the afflicted of his people will take refuge.

15

₁ The burden of Moab.

For in a night, Ar of Moab is laid waste, and brought to nothing. For in a night Kir of Moab is laid waste, and brought to nothing. ₂ They have gone up to Bayith, and to Dibon, to the high places, to weep. Moab wails over Nebo and over Medeba. Baldness is on all of their heads. Every beard is cut off. ₃ In their streets, they clothe themselves in sackcloth. In their streets and on their housetops, everyone wails, weeping abundantly. ₄ Heshbon cries out with Elealeh. Their voice is heard even to Jahaz. Therefore the armed men of Moab cry aloud. Their souls tremble within them. ₅ My heart

---

a *14:9* Sheol is the place of the dead.
b *14:11* Sheol is the place of the dead.

c *14:15* Sheol is the place of the dead.

cries out for Moab! Her nobles flee to Zoar, to Eglath Shelishiyah; for they go up by the ascent of Luhith with weeping; for on the way to Horonaim, they raise up a cry of destruction. 6 For the waters of Nimrim will be desolate; for the grass has withered away, the tender grass fails, there is no green thing. 7 Therefore they will carry away the abundance they have gotten, and that which they have stored up, over the brook of the willows. 8 For the cry has gone around the borders of Moab, its wailing to Eglaim, and its wailing to Beer Elim. 9 For the waters of Dimon are full of blood; for I will bring yet more on Dimon, a lion on those of Moab who escape, and on the remnant of the land.

16

1 Send the lambs for the ruler of the land from Selah to the wilderness, to the mountain of the daughter of Zion. 2 For it will be that as wandering birds, as a scattered nest, so will the daughters of Moab be at the fords of the Arnon. 3 Give counsel! Execute justice! Make your shade like the night in the middle of the noonday! Hide the outcasts! Don't betray the fugitive! 4 Let my outcasts dwell with you! As for Moab, be a hiding place for him from the face of the destroyer. For the extortionist is brought to nothing. Destruction ceases. The oppressors are consumed out of the land. 5 A throne will be established in loving kindness. One will sit on it in truth, in the tent of David, judging, seeking justice, and swift to do righteousness.

6 We have heard of the pride of Moab, that he is very proud; even of his arrogance, his pride, and his wrath. His boastings are nothing. 7 Therefore Moab will wail for Moab. Everyone will wail. You will mourn for the raisin cakes of Kir Hareseth, utterly stricken. 8 For the fields of Heshbon languish with the vine of Sibmah. The lords of the nations have broken down its choice branches, which reached even to Jazer, which wandered into the wilderness. Its shoots were spread abroad. They passed over the sea. 9 Therefore I will weep with the weeping of Jazer for the vine of Sibmah. I will water you with my tears, Heshbon, and Elealeh: for on your summer fruits and on your harvest the battle shout has fallen. 10 Gladness is taken away, and joy out of the fruitful field; and in the vineyards there will be no singing, neither joyful noise. Nobody will tread out wine in the presses. I have made the shouting stop. 11 Therefore my heart sounds like a harp for Moab, and my inward parts for Kir Heres. 12 It will happen that when Moab presents himself, when he wearies himself on the high place, and comes to his sanctuary to pray, that he will not prevail.

13 This is the word that the LORD spoke concerning Moab in time past. 14 But now the LORD has spoken, saying, "Within three years, as a worker bound by contract would count them, the glory of Moab shall be brought into contempt, with all his great multitude; and the remnant will be very small and feeble."

17

1 The burden of Damascus.

"Behold, Damascus is taken away from being a city, and it will be a ruinous heap. 2 The cities of Aroer are forsaken. They will be for flocks, which shall lie down, and no one shall make them afraid. 3 The fortress shall cease from Ephraim, and the kingdom from Damascus, and the remnant of Syria. They will be as the glory of the children of Israel," says the LORD of Armies.

4 "It will happen in that day that the glory of Jacob will be made thin, and the fatness of his flesh will become lean. 5 It will be like when the harvester gathers the wheat, and his arm reaps the grain. Yes, it will be like when one gleans grain in the valley of Rephaim. 6 Yet gleanings will be left there, like the shaking of an olive tree, two or three olives in the top of the uppermost bough, four or five in the outermost branches of a fruitful tree," says the LORD, the God of Israel. 7 In that day, people will look to their Maker, and their eyes will have respect for the Holy One of Israel. 8 They will not look to the altars, the work of their hands; neither shall they respect that which their fingers have made, either the Asherah poles or the incense altars. 9 In that day, their strong cities will be like the forsaken places in the woods and on the mountain top, which were forsaken from before the children of Israel; and it will be a desolation. 10 For you have forgotten the God of your salvation, and have not remembered the rock of your strength. Therefore you plant pleasant plants, and set out foreign seedlings. 11 In the day of your planting, you hedge it in. In the morning, you make your seed blossom, but the harvest flees away in the day of grief and of desperate sorrow.

12 Ah, the uproar of many peoples who roar like the roaring of the seas; and the rushing of nations that rush like the rushing of mighty waters! 13 The nations will rush like the rushing of many waters, but he will rebuke them, and they will flee far off, and will be chased like the chaff of the mountains before the wind, and like the whirling dust before the storm. 14 At evening, behold, terror! Before the morning, they are no more. This is the portion of those who plunder us, and the lot of those who rob us.

18

1 Ah, the land of the rustling of wings, which is beyond the rivers of Ethiopia; 2 that sends ambassadors by the sea, even in vessels of papyrus on the waters, saying, "Go, you swift messengers, to a nation tall and smooth, to a people awesome from their beginning onward, a nation that measures out and treads down, whose land the rivers divide!" 3 All you inhabitants of the world, and you dwellers on the earth, when a banner is lifted up on the mountains, look! When the trumpet is blown, listen!

4 For the LORD said to me, "I will be still, and I will see in my dwelling place, like clear heat in sunshine, like a cloud of dew in the heat of harvest." 5 For before the harvest, when the blossom is over, and the flower

becomes a ripening grape, he will cut off the sprigs with pruning hooks, and he will cut down and take away the spreading branches. 6 They will be left together for the ravenous birds of the mountains, and for the animals of the earth. The ravenous birds will eat them in the summer, and all the animals of the earth will eat them in the winter. 7 In that time, a present will be brought to the LORD of Armies from a people tall and smooth, even from a people awesome from their beginning onward, a nation that measures out and treads down, whose land the rivers divide, to the place of the name of the LORD of Armies, Mount Zion.

19

1 The burden of Egypt.

"Behold, the LORD rides on a swift cloud, and comes to Egypt. The idols of Egypt will tremble at his presence; and the heart of Egypt will melt within it. 2 I will stir up the Egyptians against the Egyptians, and they will fight everyone against his brother, and everyone against his neighbour; city against city, and kingdom against kingdom. 3 The spirit of the Egyptians will fail within them. I will destroy their counsel. They will seek the idols, the charmers, those who have familiar spirits, and the wizards. 4 I will give over the Egyptians into the hand of a cruel lord. A fierce king will rule over them," says the Lord, the LORD of Armies.

5 The waters will fail from the sea, and the river will be wasted and become dry. 6 The rivers will become foul. The streams of Egypt will be diminished and dried up. The reeds and flags will wither away. 7 The meadows by the Nile, by the brink of the Nile, and all the sown fields of the Nile, will become dry, be driven away, and be no more. 8 The fishermen will lament, and all those who fish in the Nile will mourn, and those who spread nets on the waters will languish. 9 Moreover those who work in combed flax, and those who weave white cloth, will be confounded. 10 The pillars will be broken in pieces. All those who work for hire will be grieved in soul.

11 The princes of Zoan are utterly foolish. The counsel of the wisest counsellors of Pharaoh has become stupid. How do you say to Pharaoh, "I am the son of the wise, the son of ancient kings"? 12 Where then are your wise men? Let them tell you now; and let them know what the LORD of Armies has purposed concerning Egypt. 13 The princes of Zoan have become fools. The princes of Memphis are deceived. They have caused Egypt to go astray, those who are the cornerstone of her tribes. 14 The LORD has mixed a spirit of perverseness in the middle of her; and they have caused Egypt to go astray in all of its works, like a drunken man staggers in his vomit. 15 Neither shall there be any work for Egypt, which head or tail, palm branch or rush, may do. 16 In that day the Egyptians will be like women. They will tremble and fear because of the shaking of the LORD of Armies's hand, which he shakes over them. 17 The land of Judah will become a terror to Egypt. Everyone to whom mention is made of it will be afraid, because of the plans of the LORD of Armies, which he determines against it. 18 In that day, there will be five cities in the land of Egypt that speak the language of Canaan, and swear to the LORD of Armies. One will be called "The city of destruction."

19 In that day, there will be an altar to the LORD in the middle of the land of Egypt, and a pillar to the LORD at its border. 20 It will be for a sign and for a witness to the LORD of Armies in the land of Egypt; for they will cry to the LORD because of oppressors, and he will send them a saviour and a defender, and he will deliver them. 21 The LORD will be known to Egypt, and the Egyptians will know the LORD in that day. Yes, they will worship with sacrifice and offering, and will vow a vow to the LORD, and will perform it. 22 The LORD will strike Egypt, striking and healing. They will return to the LORD, and he will be entreated by them, and will heal them.

23 In that day there will be a highway out of Egypt to Assyria, and the Assyrian shall come into Egypt, and the Egyptian into Assyria; and the Egyptians will worship with the Assyrians.

24 In that day, Israel will be the third with Egypt and with Assyria, a blessing within the earth; 25 because the LORD of Armies has blessed them, saying, "Blessed be Egypt my people, Assyria the work of my hands, and Israel my inheritance."

20

1 In the year that Tartan came to Ashdod, when Sargon the king of Assyria sent him, and he fought against Ashdod and took it; 2 at that time the LORD spoke by Isaiah the son of Amoz, saying, "Go, and loosen the sackcloth from off your waist, and take your sandals from off your feet." He did so, walking naked and barefoot. 3 The LORD said, "As my servant Isaiah has walked naked and barefoot three years for a sign and a wonder concerning Egypt and concerning Ethiopia, 4 so the king of Assyria will lead away the captives of Egypt and the exiles of Ethiopia, young and old, naked and barefoot, and with buttocks uncovered, to the shame of Egypt. 5 They will be dismayed and confounded, because of Ethiopia their expectation, and of Egypt their glory. 6 The inhabitants of this coast land will say in that day, 'Behold, this is our expectation, where we fled for help to be delivered from the king of Assyria. And we, how will we escape?'"

21

1 The burden of the wilderness of the sea.

As whirlwinds in the South sweep through, it comes from the wilderness, from an awesome land. 2 A grievous vision is declared to me. The treacherous man deals treacherously, and the destroyer destroys. Go up, Elam; attack! I have stopped all of Media's sighing. 3 Therefore my thighs are filled with anguish. Pains have seized me, like the pains of a woman in labour. I am in so much pain that I can't hear. I am so dismayed that I can't see. 4 My heart flutters. Horror has frightened me. The twilight that I desired has been turned into trembling for me. 5 They prepare the table. They set the watch. They eat. They drink. Rise up, you princes, oil the shield! 6 For the Lord said to me, "Go, set a watchman. Let him declare what he sees. 7 When he sees a troop, horsemen in pairs, a troop of donkeys, a troop of camels, he shall listen diligently with great attentiveness." 8 He cried like a lion: "Lord, I stand continually on the watchtower in the daytime, and every night I stay at my post. 9 Behold, here comes a troop of men, horsemen in pairs." He answered, "Fallen, fallen is Babylon; and all the engraved images of her gods are broken to the ground.

10 You are my threshing, and the grain of my floor!" That which I have heard from the LORD of Armies, the God of Israel, I have declared to you.

11 The burden of Dumah.

One calls to me out of Seir, "Watchman, what of the night? Watchman, what of the night?" 12 The watchman said, "The morning comes, and also the night. If you will enquire, enquire. Come back again."

13 The burden on Arabia.

You will lodge in the thickets in Arabia, you caravans of Dedanites. 14 They brought water to him who was thirsty. The inhabitants of the land of Tema met the fugitives with their bread. 15 For they fled away from the swords, from the drawn sword, from the bent bow, and from the heat of battle. 16 For the Lord said to me, "Within a year, as a worker bound by contract would count it, all the glory of Kedar will fail, 17 and the residue of the number of the archers, the mighty men of the children of Kedar, will be few; for the LORD, the God of Israel, has spoken it."

22

1 The burden of the valley of vision.

What ails you now, that you have all gone up to the housetops? 2 You that are full of shouting, a tumultuous city, a joyous town, your slain are not slain with the sword, neither are they dead in battle. 3 All your rulers fled away together. They were bound by the archers. All who were found by you were bound together. They fled far away. 4 Therefore I said, "Look away from me. I will weep bitterly. Don't labour to comfort me for the destruction of the daughter of my people.

5 For it is a day of confusion, and of treading down, and of perplexity from the Lord, the LORD of Armies, in the valley of vision, a breaking down of the walls, and a crying to the mountains." 6 Elam carried his quiver, with chariots of men and horsemen; and Kir uncovered the shield. 7 Your choicest valleys were full of chariots, and the horsemen set themselves in array at the gate. 8 He took away the covering of Judah; and you looked in that day to the armour in the house of the forest. 9 You saw the breaches of David's city, that they were many; and you gathered together the waters of the lower pool. 10 You counted the houses of Jerusalem, and you broke down the houses to fortify the wall. 11 You also made a reservoir between the two walls for the water of the old pool. But you didn't look to him who had done this, neither did you have respect for him who planned it long ago.

12 In that day, the Lord, the LORD of Armies, called to weeping, to mourning, to baldness, and to dressing in sackcloth; 13 and behold, there is joy and gladness, killing cattle and killing sheep, eating meat and drinking wine: "Let's eat and drink, for tomorrow we will die." 14 The LORD of Armies revealed himself in my ears, "Surely this iniquity will not be forgiven you until you die," says the Lord, the LORD of Armies.

15 The Lord, the LORD of Armies says, "Go, get yourself to this treasurer, even to Shebna, who is over the house, and say, 16 'What are you doing here? Who has you here, that you have dug out a tomb here?' Cutting himself out a tomb on high, chiselling a habitation for himself in the rock!" 17 Behold, the LORD will overcome you and hurl you away violently. Yes, he will grasp you firmly. 18 He will surely wind you around and around, and throw you like a ball into a large country. There you will die, and there the chariots of your glory will be, you disgrace of your lord's house. 19 I will thrust you from your office. You will be pulled down from your station.

20 It will happen in that day that I will call my servant Eliakim the son of Hilkiah, 21 and I will clothe him with your robe, and strengthen him with your belt. I will commit your government into his hand; and he will be a father to the inhabitants of Jerusalem, and to the house of Judah. 22 I will lay the key of David's house on his shoulder. He will open, and no one will shut. He will shut, and no one will open. 23 I will fasten him like a nail in a sure place. He will be for a throne of glory to his father's house. 24 They will hang on him all the glory of his father's house, the offspring and the issue, every small vessel, from the cups even to all the pitchers. 25 "In that day," says the LORD of Armies, "the nail that was fastened in a sure place will give way. It will be cut down and fall. The burden that was on it will be cut off, for the LORD has spoken it."

23

1 The burden of Tyre.

Howl, you ships of Tarshish! For it is laid waste, so that there is no house, no entering in. From the land of Kittim it is revealed to them. 2 Be still, you inhabitants of the coast, you whom the merchants of Sidon that pass over the sea have replenished. 3 On great waters, the seed of the Shihor, the harvest of the Nile, was her revenue. She was the market of nations. 4 Be ashamed, Sidon; for the sea has spoken, the stronghold of the sea, saying, "I have not travailed, nor given birth, neither have I nourished young men, nor brought up virgins." 5 When the report comes to Egypt, they will be in anguish at the report of Tyre. 6 Pass over to Tarshish! Wail, you inhabitants of the coast! 7 Is this your joyous city, whose antiquity is of ancient days, whose feet carried her far away to travel?

8 Who has planned this against Tyre, the giver of crowns, whose merchants are princes, whose traders are the honourable of the earth? 9 The LORD of Armies has planned it, to stain the pride of all glory, to bring into contempt all the honourable of the earth. 10 Pass through your land like the Nile, daughter of Tarshish. There is no restraint any more. 11 He has stretched out his hand over the sea. He has shaken the kingdoms. The LORD has ordered the destruction of Canaan's strongholds. 12 He said, "You shall rejoice no more, you oppressed virgin daughter of Sidon. Arise, pass over to Kittim. Even there you will have no rest."

13 Behold, the land of the Chaldeans. This people didn't exist. The Assyrians founded it for those who dwell in the wilderness. They set up their towers. They overthrew its palaces. They made it a ruin. 14 Howl, you ships of Tarshish, for your stronghold is laid waste! 15 It will come to pass in that day that Tyre will be forgotten seventy years, according to the days of one king. After the end of seventy years it will be to Tyre like in the song of the prostitute. 16 Take a harp; go about the city, you prostitute that has been forgotten. Make sweet melody. Sing many songs, that you may be remembered. 17 It will happen after the end of seventy years that the LORD will visit Tyre. She will return to her wages, and will play the prostitute with all the kingdoms of the world on the surface of the earth. 18 Her merchandise and her wages will be holiness to the LORD. It will not be treasured nor laid up; for her merchandise will be for those who dwell before the LORD, to eat sufficiently, and for durable clothing.

24

1 Behold, the LORD makes the earth empty, makes it waste, turns it upside down, and scatters its inhabitants. 2 It will be as with the people, so with the priest; as with the servant, so with his master; as with the maid, so with her mistress; as with the buyer, so with the seller; as with the creditor, so with the debtor; as with the taker of interest, so with the giver of interest. 3 The earth will be utterly emptied and utterly laid waste; for the LORD has spoken this word. 4 The earth mourns and fades away. The world languishes and fades away. The lofty people of the earth languish. 5 The earth also is polluted under its inhabitants, because they have transgressed the laws, violated the statutes, and broken the everlasting covenant. 6 Therefore the curse has devoured the earth, and those who dwell therein are found guilty. Therefore the inhabitants of the earth are burnt, and few men are left. 7 The new wine mourns. The vine languishes. All the merry-hearted sigh. 8 The mirth of tambourines ceases. The sound of those who rejoice ends. The joy of the harp ceases. 9 They will not drink wine with a song. Strong drink will be bitter to those who drink it. 10 The confused city is broken down. Every house is shut up, that no man may come in. 11 There is a crying in the streets because of the wine. All joy is darkened. The mirth of the land is gone. 12 The city is left in desolation, and the gate is struck with destruction. 13 For it will be so within the earth amongst the peoples, as the shaking of an olive tree, as the gleanings when the vintage is done.

14 These shall lift up their voice. They will shout for the majesty of the LORD. They cry aloud from the sea. 15 Therefore glorify the LORD in the east, even the name of the LORD, the God of Israel, in the islands of the sea! 16 From the uttermost part of the earth have we heard songs. Glory to the righteous!

But I said, "I pine away! I pine away! woe is me!" The treacherous have dealt treacherously. Yes, the treacherous have dealt very treacherously. 17 Fear, the pit, and the snare are on you who inhabit the earth. 18 It will happen that he who flees from the noise of the fear will fall into the pit; and he who comes up out of the middle of the pit will be taken in the snare; for the windows on high are opened, and the foundations of the earth tremble. 19 The earth is utterly broken. The earth is torn apart. The earth is shaken violently. 20 The earth will stagger like a drunken man, and will sway back and forth like a hammock. Its disobedience will be heavy on it, and it will fall and not rise again.

21 It will happen in that day that the LORD will punish the army of the high ones on high, and the kings of the earth on the earth. 22 They will be gathered together, as prisoners are gathered in the pit, and will be shut up in the prison; and after many days they will be visited. 23 Then the moon will be confounded, and the sun ashamed; for the LORD of Armies will reign on Mount Zion and in Jerusalem; and glory will be before his elders.

25

1 The LORD, you are my God. I will exalt you! I will praise your name, for you have done wonderful things, things planned long ago, in complete faithfulness and truth. 2 For you have made a city into a heap, a fortified city into a ruin, a palace of strangers to be no city. It will never be built. 3 Therefore a strong people will glorify you. A city of awesome nations will fear you. 4 For you have been a stronghold to the poor, a stronghold to the needy in his distress, a refuge from the storm, a shade from the heat, when the blast of the dreaded ones is like a storm against the wall. 5 As the heat in a dry place you will bring down the noise of strangers; as the heat by the shade of a cloud, the song of the dreaded ones will be brought low.

6 In this mountain, the LORD of Armies will make all peoples a feast of choice meat,[a] a feast of choice wines, of choice meat full of marrow, of well refined choice wines. 7 He will destroy in this mountain the surface of the covering that covers all peoples, and the veil that is spread over all nations. 8 He has swallowed up death forever! The Lord GOD will wipe away tears from off all faces. He will take the reproach of his people away from off all the earth, for the LORD has spoken it.

9 It shall be said in that day, "Behold, this is our God! We have waited for him, and he will save us! This is the LORD! We have waited for him. We

---

a 25:6 literally, fat things

will be glad and rejoice in his salvation!" 10 For the LORD's hand will rest in this mountain.

Moab will be trodden down in his place, even like straw is trodden down in the water of the dunghill. 11 He will spread out his hands in the middle of it, like one who swims spreads out hands to swim, but his pride will be humbled together with the craft of his hands. 12 He has brought the high fortress of your walls down, laid low, and brought to the ground, even to the dust.

26

1 In that day, this song will be sung in the land of Judah:
"We have a strong city.
    God appoints salvation for walls and bulwarks.
2 Open the gates, that the righteous nation may enter:
    the one which keeps faith.
3 You will keep whoever's mind is steadfast in perfect peace,
    because he trusts in you.
4 Trust in the LORD forever;
    for in the LORD, the LORD, is an everlasting Rock.
5 For he has brought down those who dwell on high, the lofty city.
    He lays it low.
    He lays it low even to the ground.
    He brings it even to the dust.
6 The foot shall tread it down,
    even the feet of the poor
    and the steps of the needy."
7 The way of the just is uprightness.
    You who are upright make the path of the righteous level.

8 Yes, in the way of your judgements, LORD, we have waited for you.
    Your name and your renown are the desire of our soul.
9 With my soul I have desired you in the night.
    Yes, with my spirit within me I will seek you earnestly;
    for when your judgements are in the earth, the inhabitants of the world
        learn righteousness.
10 Let favour be shown to the wicked,
    yet he will not learn righteousness.
In the land of uprightness he will deal wrongfully,
    and will not see the LORD's majesty.

11 LORD, your hand is lifted up, yet they don't see;
    but they will see your zeal for the people and be disappointed.
    Yes, fire will consume your adversaries.
12 LORD, you will ordain peace for us,
    for you have also done all our work for us.
13 LORD our God, other lords besides you have had dominion over us,
    but we will only acknowledge your name.
14 The dead shall not live.
    The departed spirits shall not rise.
Therefore you have visited and destroyed them,
    and caused all memory of them to perish.
15 You have increased the nation, O LORD.
    You have increased the nation!
You are glorified!
    You have enlarged all the borders of the land.

16 LORD, in trouble they have visited you.
    They poured out a prayer when your chastening was on them.
17 Just as a woman with child, who draws near the time of her delivery,
    is in pain and cries out in her pangs,
    so we have been before you, LORD.
18 We have been with child.
    We have been in pain.
We gave birth, it seems, only to wind.
    We have not worked any deliverance in the earth;
    neither have the inhabitants of the world fallen.
19 Your dead shall live.
    Their dead bodies shall arise.
Awake and sing, you who dwell in the dust;
    for your dew is like the dew of herbs,
    and the earth will cast out the departed spirits.

20 Come, my people, enter into your rooms,
    and shut your doors behind you.
Hide yourself for a little moment,
    until the indignation is past.
21 For, behold, the LORD comes out of his place to punish the inhabitants
        of the earth for their iniquity.
    The earth also will disclose her blood, and will no longer cover her
        slain.

27

1 In that day, the LORD with his hard and great and strong sword will punish leviathan, the fleeing serpent, and leviathan, the twisted serpent; and he will kill the dragon that is in the sea.

2 In that day, sing to her, "A pleasant vineyard! 3 I, the LORD, am its keeper. I will water it every moment. Lest anyone damage it, I will keep it night and day. 4 Wrath is not in me, but if I should find briers and thorns, I

would do battle! I would march on them and I would burn them together. 5 Or else let him take hold of my strength, that he may make peace with me. Let him make peace with me."

6 In days to come, Jacob will take root. Israel will blossom and bud. They will fill the surface of the world with fruit. 7 Has he struck them as he struck those who struck them? Or are they killed like those who killed them were killed? 8 In measure, when you send them away, you contend with them. He has removed them with his rough blast in the day of the east wind. 9 Therefore by this the iniquity of Jacob will be forgiven, and this is all the fruit of taking away his sin: that he makes all the stones of the altar as chalk stones that are beaten in pieces, so that the Asherah poles and the incense altars shall rise no more. 10 For the fortified city is solitary, a habitation deserted and forsaken, like the wilderness. The calf will feed there, and there he will lie down, and consume its branches. 11 When its boughs are withered, they will be broken off. The women will come and set them on fire, for they are a people of no understanding. Therefore he who made them will not have compassion on them, and he who formed them will show them no favour.

12 It will happen in that day that the LORD will thresh from the flowing stream of the Euphrates to the brook of Egypt; and you will be gathered one by one, children of Israel.

13 It will happen in that day that a great trumpet will be blown; and those who were ready to perish in the land of Assyria, and those who were outcasts in the land of Egypt, shall come; and they will worship the LORD in the holy mountain at Jerusalem.

28

1 Woe to the crown of pride of the drunkards of Ephraim, and to the fading flower of his glorious beauty, which is on the head of the fertile valley of those who are overcome with wine! 2 Behold, the Lord has one who is mighty and strong. Like a storm of hail, a destroying storm, and like a storm of mighty waters overflowing, he will cast them down to the earth with his hand. 3 The crown of pride of the drunkards of Ephraim will be trodden under foot. 4 The fading flower of his glorious beauty, which is on the head of the fertile valley, shall be like the first-ripe fig before the summer, which someone picks and eats as soon as he sees it. 5 In that day, the LORD of Armies will become a crown of glory and a diadem of beauty to the residue of his people, 6 and a spirit of justice to him who sits in judgement, and strength to those who turn back the battle at the gate.

7 They also reel with wine, and stagger with strong drink. The priest and the prophet reel with strong drink. They are swallowed up by wine. They stagger with strong drink. They err in vision. They stumble in judgement. 8 For all tables are completely full of filthy vomit and filthiness.

9 Whom will he teach knowledge? To whom will he explain the message? Those who are weaned from the milk, and drawn from the breasts? 10 For it is precept on precept, precept on precept; line on line, line on line; here a little, there a little.

11 But he will speak to this nation with stammering lips and in another language, 12 to whom he said, "This is the resting place. Give rest to the weary," and "This is the refreshing;" yet they would not hear. 13 Therefore the LORD's word will be to them precept on precept, precept on precept; line on line, line on line; here a little, there a little; that they may go, fall backward, be broken, be snared, and be taken.

14 Therefore hear the LORD's word, you scoffers, that rule this people in Jerusalem: 15 "Because you have said, 'We have made a covenant with death, and we are in agreement with Sheol.[a] When the overflowing scourge passes through, it won't come to us; for we have made lies our refuge, and we have hidden ourselves under falsehood.'" 16 Therefore the Lord GOD says, "Behold, I lay in Zion for a foundation a stone, a tried stone, a precious cornerstone of a sure foundation. He who believes shall not act hastily. 17 I will make justice the measuring line, and righteousness the plumb line. The hail will sweep away the refuge of lies, and the waters will overflow the hiding place. 18 Your covenant with death shall be annulled, and your agreement with Sheol[b] shall not stand. When the overflowing scourge passes through, then you will be trampled down by it. 19 As often as it passes through, it will seize you; for morning by morning it will pass through, by day and by night; and it will be nothing but terror to understand the message." 20 For the bed is too short to stretch out on, and the blanket is too narrow to wrap oneself in. 21 For the LORD will rise up as on Mount Perazim. He will be angry as in the valley of Gibeon; that he may do his work, his unusual work, and bring to pass his act, his extraordinary act. 22 Now therefore don't be scoffers, lest your bonds be made strong; for I have heard a decree of destruction from the Lord, the LORD of Armies, on the whole earth.

23 Give ear, and hear my voice! Listen, and hear my speech! 24 Does he who ploughs to sow plough continually? Does he keep turning the soil and breaking the clods? 25 When he has levelled its surface, doesn't he plant the dill, and scatter the cumin seed, and put in the wheat in rows, the barley in the appointed place, and the spelt in its place? 26 For his God instructs him in right judgement and teaches him. 27 For the dill isn't threshed with a sharp instrument, neither is a cart wheel turned over the cumin; but the dill is beaten out with a stick, and the cumin with a rod. 28 Bread flour must be ground; so he will not always be threshing it. Although he drives the wheel of his threshing cart over it, his horses don't grind it. 29 This also comes out from the LORD of Armies, who is wonderful in counsel, and excellent in wisdom.

_____

29

1 Woe to Ariel! Ariel, the city where David encamped! Add year to year; let the feasts come around; 2 then I will distress Ariel, and there will be mourning and lamentation. She shall be to me as an altar hearth.[a] 3 I will encamp against you all around you, and will lay siege against you with posted troops. I will raise siege works against you. 4 You will be brought down, and will speak out of the ground. Your speech will mumble out of the dust. Your voice will be as of one who has a familiar spirit, out of the ground, and your speech will whisper out of the dust.

5 But the multitude of your foes will be like fine dust, and the multitude of the ruthless ones like chaff that blows away. Yes, it will be in an instant, suddenly. 6 She will be visited by the LORD of Armies with thunder, with earthquake, with great noise, with whirlwind and storm, and with the flame of a devouring fire. 7 The multitude of all the nations that fight against Ariel, even all who fight against her and her stronghold, and who distress her, will be like a dream, a vision of the night. 8 It will be like when a hungry man dreams, and behold, he eats; but he awakes, and his hunger isn't satisfied; or like when a thirsty man dreams, and behold, he drinks; but he awakes, and behold, he is faint, and he is still thirsty. The multitude of all the nations that fight against Mount Zion will be like that.

9 Pause and wonder! Blind yourselves and be blind! They are drunken, but not with wine; they stagger, but not with strong drink. 10 For the LORD has poured out on you a spirit of deep sleep, and has closed your eyes, the prophets; and he has covered your heads, the seers. 11 All vision has become to you like the words of a book that is sealed, which men deliver to one who is educated, saying, "Read this, please;" and he says, "I can't, for it is sealed;" 12 and the book is delivered to one who is not educated, saying, "Read this, please;" and he says, "I can't read."

13 The Lord said, "Because this people draws near with their mouth and honours me with their lips, but they have removed their heart far from me, and their fear of me is a commandment of men which has been taught; 14 therefore, behold, I will proceed to do a marvellous work amongst this people, even a marvellous work and a wonder; and the wisdom of their wise men will perish, and the understanding of their prudent men will be hidden."

15 Woe to those who deeply hide their counsel from the LORD, and whose deeds are in the dark, and who say, "Who sees us?" and "Who knows us?" 16 You turn things upside down! Should the potter be thought to be like clay, that the thing made should say about him who made it, "He didn't make me;" or the thing formed say of him who formed it, "He has no understanding"?

17 Isn't it yet a very little while, and Lebanon will be turned into a fruitful field, and the fruitful field will be regarded as a forest? 18 In that day, the deaf will hear the words of the book, and the eyes of the blind will see out of obscurity and out of darkness. 19 The humble also will increase their joy in the LORD, and the poor amongst men will rejoice in the Holy One of Israel. 20 For the ruthless is brought to nothing, and the scoffer ceases, and all those who are alert to do evil are cut off— 21 who cause a person to be indicted by a word, and lay a snare for one who reproves in the gate, and who deprive the innocent of justice with false testimony.

22 Therefore the LORD, who redeemed Abraham, says concerning the house of Jacob: "Jacob shall no longer be ashamed, neither shall his face grow pale. 23 But when he sees his children, the work of my hands, in the middle of him, they will sanctify my name. Yes, they will sanctify the Holy One of Jacob, and will stand in awe of the God of Israel. 24 They also who err in spirit will come to understanding, and those who grumble will receive instruction."

30

1 "Woe to the rebellious children", says the LORD, "who take counsel, but not from me; and who make an alliance, but not with my Spirit, that they may add sin to sin; 2 who set out to go down into Egypt without asking for my advice, to strengthen themselves in the strength of Pharaoh, and to take refuge in the shadow of Egypt! 3 Therefore the strength of Pharaoh will be your shame, and the refuge in the shadow of Egypt your confusion. 4 For their princes are at Zoan, and their ambassadors have come to Hanes. 5 They shall all be ashamed because of a people that can't profit them, that are not a help nor profit, but a shame, and also a reproach."

6 The burden of the animals of the South.

Through the land of trouble and anguish, of the lioness and the lion, the viper and fiery flying serpent, they carry their riches on the shoulders of young donkeys, and their treasures on the humps of camels, to an unprofitable people. 7 For Egypt helps in vain, and to no purpose; therefore I have called her Rahab who sits still. 8 Now go, write it before them on a tablet, and inscribe it in a book, that it may be for the time to come forever and ever. 9 For it is a rebellious people, lying children, children who will not hear the LORD's law; 10 who tell the seers, "Don't see!" and the prophets, "Don't prophesy to us right things. Tell us pleasant things. Prophesy deceits. 11 Get out of the way. Turn away from the path. Cause the Holy One of Israel to cease from before us." 12 Therefore the Holy One of Israel says, "Because you despise this word, and trust in oppression and perverseness, and rely on it, 13 therefore this iniquity shall be to you like a breach ready to fall, swelling out in a high wall, whose breaking comes suddenly in an instant. 14 He will break it as a potter's vessel is broken, breaking it in pieces without sparing, so that there won't be found amongst the broken pieces a piece good enough to take fire from the hearth, or to dip up water out of the cistern."

15 For thus said the Lord GOD, the Holy One of Israel, "You will be saved in returning and rest. Your strength will be in quietness and in confidence." You refused, 16 but you said, "No, for we will flee on horses;" therefore you will flee; and, "We will ride on the swift;" therefore those who pursue you will be swift. 17 One thousand will flee at the threat of one. At the threat of five, you will flee until you are left like a beacon on the top of a mountain, and like a banner on a hill.

18 Therefore the LORD will wait, that he may be gracious to you; and therefore he will be exalted, that he may have mercy on you, for the LORD is a God of justice. Blessed are all those who wait for him. 19 For the people will dwell in Zion at Jerusalem. You will weep no more. He will surely be gracious to you at the voice of your cry. When he hears you, he will answer you. 20 Though the Lord may give you the bread of adversity and the water of affliction, yet your teachers won't be hidden any more, but your eyes will see your teachers; 21 and when you turn to the right hand, and when you turn to the left, your ears will hear a voice behind you, saying, "This is the way. Walk in it." 22 You shall defile the overlaying of your engraved images of silver, and the plating of your molten images of gold. You shall cast them away as an unclean thing. You shall tell it, "Go away!"

23 He will give the rain for your seed, with which you will sow the ground; and bread of the increase of the ground will be rich and plentiful. In that day, your livestock will feed in large pastures. 24 The oxen likewise and the young donkeys that till the ground will eat savoury feed, which has been winnowed with the shovel and with the fork. 25 There will be brooks and streams of water on every lofty mountain and on every high hill in the day of the great slaughter, when the towers fall. 26 Moreover the light of the moon will be like the light of the sun, and the light of the sun will be seven times brighter, like the light of seven days, in the day that the LORD binds up the fracture of his people, and heals the wound they were struck with.

27 Behold, the LORD's name comes from far away, burning with his anger, and in thick rising smoke. His lips are full of indignation. His tongue is as a devouring fire. 28 His breath is as an overflowing stream that reaches even to the neck, to sift the nations with the sieve of destruction. A bridle that leads to ruin will be in the jaws of the peoples. 29 You will have a song, as in the night when a holy feast is kept, and gladness of heart, as when one goes with a flute to come to the LORD's mountain, to Israel's Rock. 30 The LORD will cause his glorious voice to be heard, and will show the descent of his arm, with the indignation of his anger and the flame of a devouring fire, with a blast, storm, and hailstones. 31 For through the LORD's voice the Assyrian will be dismayed. He will strike him with his rod. 32 Every stroke of the rod of punishment, which the LORD will lay on him, will be with the sound of tambourines and harps. He will fight with them in battles, brandishing weapons. 33 For his burning place has long been ready. Yes, it is prepared for the king. He has made its pyre deep and large with fire and much wood. The LORD's breath, like a stream of sulphur, kindles it.

31

1 Woe to those who go down to Egypt for help,
　and rely on horses,
　and trust in chariots because they are many,
　and in horsemen because they are very strong,
　but they don't look to the Holy One of Israel,
　and they don't seek the LORD!
2 Yet he also is wise, and will bring disaster,
　and will not call back his words, but will arise against the house of the
　　evildoers,
　and against the help of those who work iniquity.
3 Now the Egyptians are men, and not God;
　and their horses flesh, and not spirit.
When the LORD stretches out his hand, both he who helps shall stumble,
　and he who is helped shall fall,
　and they all shall be consumed together.

4 For the LORD says to me,
"As the lion and the young lion growling over his prey,
　if a multitude of shepherds is called together against him,
　will not be dismayed at their voice,
　nor abase himself for their noise,
　so the LORD of Armies will come down to fight on Mount Zion and on
　　its heights.
5 As birds hovering, so the LORD of Armies will protect Jerusalem.
　He will protect and deliver it.
　He will pass over and preserve it."
6 Return to him from whom you have deeply revolted, children of Israel. 7
　　For in that day everyone shall cast away his idols of silver and
　　　his idols of gold—sin which your own hands have made for
　　　you.
8 "The Assyrian will fall by the sword, not of man;
　and the sword, not of mankind, shall devour him.
He will flee from the sword,
　and his young men will become subject to forced labour.
9 His rock will pass away by reason of terror,
　and his princes will be afraid of the banner,"
says the LORD, whose fire is in Zion,
　and his furnace in Jerusalem.

---

[a] 29:2 or, Ariel

32

1 Behold, a king shall reign in righteousness,
    and princes shall rule in justice.
2 A man shall be as a hiding place from the wind,
    and a covert from the storm,
    as streams of water in a dry place,
    as the shade of a large rock in a weary land.
3 The eyes of those who see will not be dim,
    and the ears of those who hear will listen.
4 The heart of the rash will understand knowledge,
    and the tongue of the stammerers will be ready to speak plainly.
5 The fool will no longer be called noble,
    nor the scoundrel be highly respected.
6 For the fool will speak folly,
    and his heart will work iniquity,
    to practise profanity,
    and to utter error against the LORD,
    to make empty the soul of the hungry,
    and to cause the drink of the thirsty to fail.
7 The ways of the scoundrel are evil.
    He devises wicked plans to destroy the humble with lying words,
    even when the needy speaks right.
8 But the noble devises noble things,
    and he will continue in noble things.

9 Rise up, you women who are at ease! Hear my voice!
    You careless daughters, give ear to my speech!
10 For days beyond a year you will be troubled, you careless women;
    for the vintage will fail.
    The harvest won't come.
11 Tremble, you women who are at ease!
    Be troubled, you careless ones!
    Strip yourselves, make yourselves naked,
    and put sackcloth on your waist.
12 Beat your breasts for the pleasant fields,
    for the fruitful vine.
13 Thorns and briers will come up on my people's land;
    yes, on all the houses of joy in the joyous city.
14 For the palace will be forsaken.
    The populous city will be deserted.
    The hill and the watchtower will be for dens forever,
    a delight for wild donkeys,
    a pasture of flocks,
15 until the Spirit is poured on us from on high,
    and the wilderness becomes a fruitful field,
    and the fruitful field is considered a forest.

16 Then justice will dwell in the wilderness;
    and righteousness will remain in the fruitful field.
17 The work of righteousness will be peace,
    and the effect of righteousness, quietness and confidence forever.
18 My people will live in a peaceful habitation,
    in safe dwellings,
    and in quiet resting places,
19 though hail flattens the forest,
    and the city is levelled completely.
20 Blessed are you who sow beside all waters,
    who send out the feet of the ox and the donkey.

33

1 Woe to you who destroy, but you weren't destroyed,
    and who betray, but nobody betrayed you!
When you have finished destroying, you will be destroyed;
    and when you have finished betrayal, you will be betrayed.

2 LORD, be gracious to us. We have waited for you.
    Be our strength every morning,
    our salvation also in the time of trouble.
3 At the noise of the thunder, the peoples have fled.
    When you lift yourself up, the nations are scattered.
4 Your plunder will be gathered as the caterpillar gathers.
    Men will leap on it as locusts leap.
5 The LORD is exalted, for he dwells on high.
    He has filled Zion with justice and righteousness.
6 There will be stability in your times, abundance of salvation, wisdom, and
        knowledge.
    The fear of the LORD is your treasure.

7 Behold, their valiant ones cry outside;
    the ambassadors of peace weep bitterly.
8 The highways are desolate.
    The travelling man ceases.
    The covenant is broken.
    He has despised the cities.
    He doesn't respect man.
9 The land mourns and languishes.
    Lebanon is confounded and withers away.
    Sharon is like a desert, and Bashan and Carmel are stripped bare.
10 "Now I will arise," says the LORD.

"Now I will lift myself up.
    Now I will be exalted.
11 You will conceive chaff.
    You will give birth to stubble.
    Your breath is a fire that will devour you.
12 The peoples will be like the burning of lime,
    like thorns that are cut down and burnt in the fire.

13 Hear, you who are far off, what I have done;
    and, you who are near, acknowledge my might."
14 The sinners in Zion are afraid.
    Trembling has seized the godless ones.
Who amongst us can live with the devouring fire?
    Who amongst us can live with everlasting burning?
15 He who walks righteously
    and speaks blamelessly,
    he who despises the gain of oppressions,
    who gestures with his hands, refusing to take a bribe,
    who stops his ears from hearing of bloodshed,
    and shuts his eyes from looking at evil—
16 he will dwell on high.
    His place of defence will be the fortress of rocks.
    His bread will be supplied.
    His waters will be sure.

17 Your eyes will see the king in his beauty.
    They will see a distant land.
18 Your heart will meditate on the terror.
    Where is he who counted?
    Where is he who weighed?
    Where is he who counted the towers?
19 You will no longer see the fierce people,
    a people of a deep speech that you can't comprehend,
    with a strange language that you can't understand.
20 Look at Zion, the city of our appointed festivals.
    Your eyes will see Jerusalem, a quiet habitation,
    a tent that won't be removed.
Its stakes will never be plucked up,
    nor will any of its cords be broken.
21 But there the LORD will be with us in majesty,
    a place of wide rivers and streams,
    in which no galley with oars will go,
    neither will any gallant ship pass by there.
22 For the LORD is our judge.
    The LORD is our lawgiver.
    The LORD is our king.
    He will save us.

23 Your rigging is untied.
    They couldn't strengthen the foot of their mast.
    They couldn't spread the sail.
Then the prey of a great plunder was divided.
    The lame took the prey.

24 The inhabitant won't say, "I am sick."
    The people who dwell therein will be forgiven their iniquity.

34

1 Come near, you nations, to hear!
    Listen, you peoples.
    Let the earth and all it contains hear,
    the world, and everything that comes from it.
2 For the LORD is enraged against all the nations,
    and angry with all their armies.
He has utterly destroyed them.
    He has given them over for slaughter.
3 Their slain will also be cast out,
    and the stench of their dead bodies will come up.
    The mountains will melt in their blood.
4 All of the army of the sky will be dissolved.
    The sky will be rolled up like a scroll,
    and all its armies will fade away,
    as a leaf fades from off a vine or a fig tree.
5 For my sword has drunk its fill in the sky.
    Behold, it will come down on Edom,
    and on the people of my curse, for judgement.
6 The LORD's sword is filled with blood.
    It is covered with fat, with the blood of lambs and goats,
    with the fat of the kidneys of rams;
    for the LORD has a sacrifice in Bozrah,
    and a great slaughter in the land of Edom.
7 The wild oxen will come down with them,
    and the young bulls with the mighty bulls;
    and their land will be drunken with blood,
    and their dust made greasy with fat.

8 For the LORD has a day of vengeance,
    a year of recompense for the cause of Zion.
9 Its streams will be turned into pitch,
    its dust into sulphur,

and its land will become burning pitch.
10 It won't be quenched night or day.
    Its smoke will go up forever.
    From generation to generation, it will lie waste.
    No one will pass through it forever and ever.
11 But the pelican and the porcupine will possess it.
    The owl and the raven will dwell in it.
He will stretch the line of confusion over it,
    and the plumb line of emptiness.
12 They shall call its nobles to the kingdom, but none shall be there;
    and all its princes shall be nothing.
13 Thorns will come up in its palaces,
    nettles and thistles in its fortresses;
    and it will be a habitation of jackals,
    a court for ostriches.
14 The wild animals of the desert will meet with the wolves,
    and the wild goat will cry to his fellow.
Yes, the night creature[a] shall settle there,
    and shall find herself a place of rest.
15 The arrow snake will make her nest there,
    and lay, hatch, and gather under her shade.
    Yes, the kites will be gathered there, every one with her mate.

16 Search in the book of the LORD, and read:
    not one of these will be missing.
    None will lack her mate.
    For my mouth has commanded,
    and his Spirit has gathered them.
17 He has cast the lot for them,
    and his hand has divided it to them with a measuring line.
    They shall possess it forever.
    From generation to generation they will dwell in it.

35

1 The wilderness and the dry land will be glad.
    The desert will rejoice and blossom like a rose.
2 It will blossom abundantly,
    and rejoice even with joy and singing.
    Lebanon's glory will be given to it,
    the excellence of Carmel and Sharon.
    They will see the LORD's glory,
    the excellence of our God.

3 Strengthen the weak hands,
    and make the feeble knees firm.
4 Tell those who have a fearful heart, "Be strong!
    Don't be afraid!
Behold, your God will come with vengeance, God's retribution.
    He will come and save you.

5 Then the eyes of the blind will be opened,
    and the ears of the deaf will be unstopped.
6 Then the lame man will leap like a deer,
    and the tongue of the mute will sing;
    for waters will break out in the wilderness,
    and streams in the desert.
7 The burning sand will become a pool,
    and the thirsty ground springs of water.
    Grass with reeds and rushes will be in the habitation of jackals, where
    they lay.
8 A highway will be there, a road,
    and it will be called "The Holy Way".
The unclean shall not pass over it,
    but it will be for those who walk in the Way.
    Wicked fools shall not go there.
9 No lion will be there,
    nor will any ravenous animal go up on it.
    They will not be found there;
    but the redeemed will walk there.
10 Then the LORD's ransomed ones will return,
    and come with singing to Zion;
    and everlasting joy will be on their heads.
They will obtain gladness and joy,
    and sorrow and sighing will flee away."

36

1 Now in the fourteenth year of King Hezekiah, Sennacherib king of Assyria attacked all of the fortified cities of Judah and captured them. 2 The king of Assyria sent Rabshakeh from Lachish to Jerusalem to King Hezekiah with a large army. He stood by the aqueduct from the upper pool in the fuller's field highway. 3 Then Eliakim the son of Hilkiah, who was over the household, and Shebna the scribe, and Joah, the son of Asaph the recorder came out to him.

4 Rabshakeh said to them, "Now tell Hezekiah, 'The great king, the king of Assyria, says, "What confidence is this in which you trust? 5 I say that your counsel and strength for the war are only vain words. Now in whom do you trust, that you have rebelled against me? 6 Behold, you trust

in the staff of this bruised reed, even in Egypt, which if a man leans on it, it will go into his hand and pierce it. So is Pharaoh king of Egypt to all who trust in him. 7 But if you tell me, 'We trust in the LORD our God,' isn't that he whose high places and whose altars Hezekiah has taken away, and has said to Judah and to Jerusalem, 'You shall worship before this altar'?" 8 Now therefore, please make a pledge to my master the king of Assyria, and I will give you two thousand horses, if you are able on your part to set riders on them. 9 How then can you turn away the face of one captain of the least of my master's servants, and put your trust in Egypt for chariots and for horsemen? 10 Have I come up now without the LORD against this land to destroy it? the LORD said to me, "Go up against this land, and destroy it."'"

11 Then Eliakim, Shebna and Joah said to Rabshakeh, "Please speak to your servants in Aramaic, for we understand it. Don't speak to us in the Jews' language, in the hearing of the people who are on the wall."

12 But Rabshakeh said, "Has my master sent me only to your master and to you, to speak these words, and not to the men who sit on the wall, who will eat their own dung and drink their own urine with you?" 13 Then Rabshakeh stood, and called out with a loud voice in the Jews' language, and said, "Hear the words of the great king, the king of Assyria! 14 The king says, 'Don't let Hezekiah deceive you; for he will not be able to deliver you. 15 Don't let Hezekiah make you trust in the LORD, saying, "The LORD will surely deliver us. This city won't be given into the hand of the king of Assyria."' 16 Don't listen to Hezekiah, for the king of Assyria says, 'Make your peace with me, and come out to me; and each of you eat from his vine, and each one from his fig tree, and each one of you drink the waters of his own cistern; 17 until I come and take you away to a land like your own land, a land of grain and new wine, a land of bread and vineyards. 18 Beware lest Hezekiah persuade you, saying, "The LORD will deliver us." Have any of the gods of the nations delivered their lands from the hand of the king of Assyria? 19 Where are the gods of Hamath and Arpad? Where are the gods of Sepharvaim? Have they delivered Samaria from my hand? 20 Who are they amongst all the gods of these countries that have delivered their country out of my hand, that the LORD should deliver Jerusalem out of my hand?'"

21 But they remained silent, and said nothing in reply, for the king's commandment was, "Don't answer him."

22 Then Eliakim the son of Hilkiah, who was over the household, and Shebna the scribe, and Joah, the son of Asaph the recorder, came to Hezekiah with their clothes torn, and told him the words of Rabshakeh.

37

1 When King Hezekiah heard it, he tore his clothes, covered himself with sackcloth, and went into the LORD's house. 2 He sent Eliakim, who was over the household, and Shebna the scribe, and the elders of the priests, covered with sackcloth, to Isaiah the prophet, the son of Amoz. 3 They said to him, "Hezekiah says, 'Today is a day of trouble, and of rebuke, and of rejection; for the children have come to the birth, and there is no strength to give birth. 4 It may be the LORD your God will hear the words of Rabshakeh, whom the king of Assyria his master has sent to defy the living God, and will rebuke the words which the LORD your God has heard. Therefore lift up your prayer for the remnant that is left.'"

5 So the servants of King Hezekiah came to Isaiah.

6 Isaiah said to them, "Tell your master, 'The LORD says, "Don't be afraid of the words that you have heard, with which the servants of the king of Assyria have blasphemed me. 7 Behold, I will put a spirit in him and he will hear news, and will return to his own land. I will cause him to fall by the sword in his own land."'"

8 So Rabshakeh returned, and found the king of Assyria warring against Libnah, for he heard that he had departed from Lachish. 9 He heard news concerning Tirhakah king of Ethiopia, "He has come out to fight against you." When he heard it, he sent messengers to Hezekiah, saying, 10 "Thus you shall speak to Hezekiah king of Judah, saying, 'Don't let your God in whom you trust deceive you, saying, "Jerusalem won't be given into the hand of the king of Assyria." 11 Behold, you have heard what the kings of Assyria have done to all lands, by destroying them utterly. Shall you be delivered? 12 Have the gods of the nations delivered them, which my fathers have destroyed, Gozan, Haran, Rezeph, and the children of Eden who were in Telassar? 13 Where is the king of Hamath, and the king of Arpad, and the king of the city of Sepharvaim, of Hena, and Ivvah?'"

14 Hezekiah received the letter from the hand of the messengers and read it. Then Hezekiah went up to the LORD's house, and spread it before the LORD. 15 Hezekiah prayed to the LORD, saying, 16 "LORD of Armies, the God of Israel, who is enthroned amongst the cherubim, you are the God, even you alone, of all the kingdoms of the earth. You have made heaven and earth. 17 Turn your ear, LORD, and hear. Open your eyes, LORD, and behold. Hear all of the words of Sennacherib, who has sent to defy the living God. 18 Truly, LORD, the kings of Assyria have destroyed all the countries and their land, 19 and have cast their gods into the fire; for they were no gods, but the work of men's hands, wood and stone; therefore they have destroyed them. 20 Now therefore, LORD our God, save us from his hand, that all the kingdoms of the earth may know that you are the LORD, even you only."

21 Then Isaiah the son of Amoz sent to Hezekiah, saying, "The LORD, the God of Israel says, 'Because you have prayed to me against Sennacherib king of Assyria, 22 this is the word which the LORD has spoken concerning him: The virgin daughter of Zion has despised you and

---

a *34:14 literally, lilith, which could also be a night demon or night monster* ridiculed you. The daughter of Jerusalem has shaken her head at you. 23 Whom have you defied and blasphemed? Against whom have you exalted your voice and lifted up your eyes on high? Against the Holy One of Israel. 24 By your servants, you have defied the Lord, and have said, "With the multitude of my chariots I have come up to the height of the mountains, to the innermost parts of Lebanon. I will cut down its tall cedars and its choice cypress trees. I will enter into its farthest height, the forest of its fruitful field. 25 I have dug and drunk water, and with the sole of my feet I will dry up all the rivers of Egypt."

26 "'Have you not heard how I have done it long ago, and formed it in ancient times? Now I have brought it to pass, that it should be yours to destroy fortified cities, turning them into ruinous heaps. 27 Therefore their inhabitants had little power. They were dismayed and confounded. They were like the grass of the field, and like the green herb, like the grass on the housetops, and like a field before its crop has grown. 28 But I know your sitting down, your going out, your coming in, and your raging against me. 29 Because of your raging against me, and because your arrogance has come up into my ears, therefore I will put my hook in your nose and my bridle in your lips, and I will turn you back by the way by which you came.

30 "'This shall be the sign to you: You will eat this year that which grows of itself, and in the second year that which springs from it; and in the third year sow and reap and plant vineyards, and eat their fruit. 31 The remnant that is escaped of the house of Judah will again take root downward, and bear fruit upward. 32 For out of Jerusalem a remnant will go out, and survivors will escape from Mount Zion. The zeal of the LORD of Armies will perform this.'

33 "Therefore the LORD says concerning the king of Assyria, 'He will not come to this city, nor shoot an arrow there, neither will he come before it with shield, nor cast up a mound against it. 34 He will return the way that he came, and he won't come to this city,' says the LORD. 35 'For I will defend this city to save it, for my own sake, and for my servant David's sake.'"

36 Then the LORD's angel went out and struck one hundred and eighty-five thousand men in the camp of the Assyrians. When men arose early in the morning, behold, these were all dead bodies. 37 So Sennacherib king of Assyria departed, went away, returned to Nineveh, and stayed there. 38 As he was worshipping in the house of Nisroch his god, Adrammelech and Sharezer his sons struck him with the sword; and they escaped into the land of Ararat. Esar Haddon his son reigned in his place.

38

1 In those days Hezekiah was sick and near death. Isaiah the prophet, the son of Amoz, came to him, and said to him, "The LORD says, 'Set your house in order, for you will die, and not live.'"

2 Then Hezekiah turned his face to the wall and prayed to the LORD, 3 and said, "Remember now, the LORD, I beg you, how I have walked before you in truth and with a perfect heart, and have done that which is good in your sight." Then Hezekiah wept bitterly.

4 Then the LORD's word came to Isaiah, saying, 5 "Go, and tell Hezekiah, 'The LORD, the God of David your father, says, "I have heard your prayer. I have seen your tears. Behold, I will add fifteen years to your life. 6 I will deliver you and this city out of the hand of the king of Assyria, and I will defend this city. 7 This shall be the sign to you from the LORD, that the LORD will do this thing that he has spoken. 8 Behold, I will cause the shadow on the sundial, which has gone down on the sundial of Ahaz with the sun, to return backward ten steps."'" So the sun returned ten steps on the sundial on which it had gone down.

9 The writing of Hezekiah king of Judah, when he had been sick, and had recovered of his sickness:

10 I said, "In the middle of my life I go into the gates of Sheol.ᵃ
　I am deprived of the residue of my years."
11 I said, "I won't see the LORD,
　the LORD in the land of the living.
　I will see man no more with the inhabitants of the world.
12 My dwelling is removed,
　and is carried away from me like a shepherd's tent.
I have rolled up my life like a weaver.
　He will cut me off from the loom.
　From day even to night you will make an end of me.
13 I waited patiently until morning.
　He breaks all my bones like a lion.
　From day even to night you will make an end of me.
14 I chattered like a swallow or a crane.
　I moaned like a dove.
　My eyes weaken looking upward.
Lord, I am oppressed.
　Be my security."
15 What will I say?
　He has both spoken to me, and himself has done it.
　I will walk carefully all my years because of the anguish of my soul.
16 Lord, men live by these things;
　and my spirit finds life in all of them.
　You restore me, and cause me to live.
17 Behold, for peace I had great anguish,
　but you have in love for my soul delivered it from the pit of corruption;
　for you have cast all my sins behind your back.
18 For Sheolᵇ can't praise you.
　Death can't celebrate you.

Those who go down into the pit can't hope for your truth.
19 The living, the living, he shall praise you, as I do today.
　The father shall make known your truth to the children.
20 The LORD will save me.
　Therefore we will sing my songs with stringed instruments all the days of our life in the LORD's house.

21 Now Isaiah had said, "Let them take a cake of figs, and lay it for a poultice on the boil, and he shall recover." 22 Hezekiah also had said, "What is the sign that I will go up to the LORD's house?"

39

1 At that time, Merodach-baladan the son of Baladan, king of Babylon, sent letters and a present to Hezekiah, for he heard that he had been sick, and had recovered. 2 Hezekiah was pleased with them, and showed them the house of his precious things, the silver, the gold, the spices, and the precious oil, and all the house of his armour, and all that was found in his treasures. There was nothing in his house, nor in all his dominion, that Hezekiah didn't show them. 3 Then Isaiah the prophet came to King Hezekiah, and asked him, "What did these men say? From where did they come to you?"

Hezekiah said, "They have come from a country far from me, even from Babylon."

4 Then he asked, "What have they seen in your house?"

Hezekiah answered, "They have seen all that is in my house. There is nothing amongst my treasures that I have not shown them."

5 Then Isaiah said to Hezekiah, "Hear the word of the LORD of Armies: 6 'Behold, the days are coming when all that is in your house, and that which your fathers have stored up until today, will be carried to Babylon. Nothing will be left,' says the LORD. 7 'They will take away your sons who will issue from you, whom you shall father, and they will be eunuchs in the king of Babylon's palace.'"

8 Then Hezekiah said to Isaiah, "The LORD's word which you have spoken is good." He said moreover, "For there will be peace and truth in my days."

40

1 "Comfort, comfort my people," says your God. 2 "Speak comfortably to Jerusalem, and call out to her that her warfare is accomplished, that her iniquity is pardoned, that she has received of the LORD's hand double for all her sins."

3 The voice of one who calls out,
　"Prepare the way of the LORD in the wilderness!
　Make a level highway in the desert for our God.
4 Every valley shall be exalted,
　and every mountain and hill shall be made low.
　The uneven shall be made level,
　and the rough places a plain.
5 The LORD's glory shall be revealed,
　and all flesh shall see it together;
　for the mouth of the LORD has spoken it."

6 The voice of one saying, "Cry out!"
　One said, "What shall I cry?"
"All flesh is like grass,
　and all its glory is like the flower of the field.
7 The grass withers,
　the flower fades,
　because the LORD's breath blows on it.
　Surely the people are like grass.
8 The grass withers,
　the flower fades;
　but the word of our God stands forever."

9 You who tell good news to Zion, go up on a high mountain.
　You who tell good news to Jerusalem, lift up your voice with strength!
　Lift it up! Don't be afraid!
　Say to the cities of Judah, "Behold, your God!"
10 Behold, the Lord GOD will come as a mighty one,
　and his arm will rule for him.
　Behold, his reward is with him,
　and his recompense before him.
11 He will feed his flock like a shepherd.
　He will gather the lambs in his arm,
　and carry them in his bosom.
　He will gently lead those who have their young.

12 Who has measured the waters in the hollow of his hand,
　and marked off the sky with his span,
　and calculated the dust of the earth in a measuring basket,
　and weighed the mountains in scales,
　and the hills in a balance?
13 Who has directed the LORD's Spirit,
　or has taught him as his counsellor?
14 Who did he take counsel with,
　and who instructed him,
　and taught him in the path of justice,
　and taught him knowledge,
　and showed him the way of understanding?

ᵃ 38:10 Sheol is the place of the dead.

ᵇ 38:18 Sheol is the place of the dead.

15 Behold, the nations are like a drop in a bucket,
and are regarded as a speck of dust on a balance.
Behold, he lifts up the islands like a very little thing.
16 Lebanon is not sufficient to burn,
nor its animals sufficient for a burnt offering.
17 All the nations are like nothing before him.
They are regarded by him as less than nothing, and vanity.

18 To whom then will you liken God?
Or what likeness will you compare to him?
19 A workman has cast an image,
and the goldsmith overlays it with gold,
and casts silver chains for it.
20 He who is too impoverished for such an offering chooses a tree that will
not rot.
He seeks a skilful workman to set up a carved image for him that will
not be moved.

21 Haven't you known?
Haven't you heard?
Haven't you been told from the beginning?
Haven't you understood from the foundations of the earth?
22 It is he who sits above the circle of the earth,
and its inhabitants are like grasshoppers;
who stretches out the heavens like a curtain,
and spreads them out like a tent to dwell in,
23 who brings princes to nothing,
who makes the judges of the earth meaningless.
24 They are planted scarcely.
They are sown scarcely.
Their stock has scarcely taken root in the ground.
He merely blows on them, and they wither,
and the whirlwind takes them away as stubble.

25 "To whom then will you liken me?
Who is my equal?" says the Holy One.
26 Lift up your eyes on high,
and see who has created these,
who brings out their army by number.
He calls them all by name.
By the greatness of his might,
and because he is strong in power,
not one is lacking.

27 Why do you say, Jacob,
and speak, Israel,
"My way is hidden from the LORD,
and the justice due me is disregarded by my God"?
28 Haven't you known?
Haven't you heard?
The everlasting God, the LORD,
the Creator of the ends of the earth, doesn't faint.
He isn't weary.
His understanding is unsearchable.
29 He gives power to the weak.
He increases the strength of him who has no might.
30 Even the youths faint and get weary,
and the young men utterly fall;
31 but those who wait for the LORD will renew their strength.
They will mount up with wings like eagles.
They will run, and not be weary.
They will walk, and not faint.

41

1 "Keep silent before me, islands,
and let the peoples renew their strength.
Let them come near,
then let them speak.
Let's meet together for judgement.
2 Who has raised up one from the east?
Who called him to his feet in righteousness?
He hands over nations to him
and makes him rule over kings.
He gives them like the dust to his sword,
like the driven stubble to his bow.
3 He pursues them
and passes by safely,
even by a way that he had not gone with his feet.
4 Who has worked and done it,
calling the generations from the beginning?
I, the LORD, the first, and with the last, I am he."

5 The islands have seen, and fear.
The ends of the earth tremble.
They approach, and come.
6 Everyone helps his neighbour.
They say to their brothers, "Be strong!"
7 So the carpenter encourages the goldsmith.
He who smooths with the hammer encourages him who strikes the
anvil,

saying of the soldering, "It is good;"
and he fastens it with nails, that it might not totter.

8 "But you, Israel, my servant,
Jacob whom I have chosen,
the offspring of Abraham my friend,
9 you whom I have taken hold of from the ends of the earth,
and called from its corners,
and said to you, 'You are my servant. I have chosen you and have not
cast you away.'
10 Don't you be afraid, for I am with you.
Don't be dismayed, for I am your God.
I will strengthen you.
Yes, I will help you.
Yes, I will uphold you with the right hand of my righteousness.
11 Behold, all those who are incensed against you will be disappointed and
confounded.
Those who strive with you will be like nothing, and shall perish.
12 You will seek them, and won't find them,
even those who contend with you.
Those who war against you will be as nothing,
as a nonexistent thing.
13 For I, the LORD your God, will hold your right hand,
saying to you, 'Don't be afraid.
I will help you.'
14 Don't be afraid, you worm Jacob,
and you men of Israel.
I will help you," says the LORD.
"Your Redeemer is the Holy One of Israel.
15 Behold, I have made you into a new sharp threshing instrument with
teeth.
You will thresh the mountains,
and beat them small,
and will make the hills like chaff.
16 You will winnow them,
and the wind will carry them away,
and the whirlwind will scatter them.
You will rejoice in the LORD.
You will glory in the Holy One of Israel.

17 The poor and needy seek water, and there is none.
Their tongue fails for thirst.
I, the LORD, will answer them.
I, the God of Israel, will not forsake them.
18 I will open rivers on the bare heights,
and springs in the middle of the valleys.
I will make the wilderness a pool of water,
and the dry land springs of water.
19 I will put cedar, acacia, myrtle, and oil trees in the wilderness.
I will set cypress trees, pine, and box trees together in the desert;
20 that they may see, know, consider, and understand together,
that the LORD's hand has done this,
and the Holy One of Israel has created it.

21 Produce your cause," says the LORD.
"Bring out your strong reasons!" says the King of Jacob.
22 "Let them announce and declare to us what will happen!
Declare the former things, what they are,
that we may consider them, and know the latter end of them;
or show us things to come.
23 Declare the things that are to come hereafter,
that we may know that you are gods.
Yes, do good, or do evil,
that we may be dismayed,
and see it together.
24 Behold, you are nothing,
and your work is nothing.
He who chooses you is an abomination.

25 "I have raised up one from the north, and he has come,
from the rising of the sun, one who calls on my name,
and he shall come on rulers as on mortar,
and as the potter treads clay.
26 Who has declared it from the beginning, that we may know?
and before, that we may say, 'He is right'?
Surely, there is no one who declares.
Surely, there is no one who shows.
Surely, there is no one who hears your words.
27 I am the first to say to Zion, 'Behold, look at them;'
and I will give one who brings good news to Jerusalem.
28 When I look, there is no man,
even amongst them there is no counsellor who, when I ask, can
answer a word.
29 Behold, all of their deeds are vanity and nothing.
Their molten images are wind and confusion.

42

1 "Behold, my servant, whom I uphold,
my chosen, in whom my soul delights:
I have put my Spirit on him.

He will bring justice to the nations.
2 He will not shout,
    nor raise his voice,
    nor cause it to be heard in the street.
3 He won't break a bruised reed.
    He won't quench a dimly burning wick.
    He will faithfully bring justice.
4 He will not fail nor be discouraged,
    until he has set justice in the earth,
    and the islands wait for his law."

5 God the LORD,
    he who created the heavens and stretched them out,
    he who spread out the earth and that which comes out of it,
    he who gives breath to its people and spirit to those who walk in it,
        says:
6 "I, the LORD, have called you in righteousness.
    I will hold your hand.
    I will keep you,
    and make you a covenant for the people,
    as a light for the nations,
    7 to open the blind eyes,
    to bring the prisoners out of the dungeon,
    and those who sit in darkness out of the prison.

8 "I am the LORD.
    That is my name.
    I will not give my glory to another,
    nor my praise to engraved images.
9 Behold, the former things have happened
    and I declare new things.
    I tell you about them before they come up."

10 Sing to the LORD a new song,
    and his praise from the end of the earth,
    you who go down to the sea,
    and all that is therein,
    the islands and their inhabitants.
11 Let the wilderness and its cities raise their voices,
    with the villages that Kedar inhabits.
    Let the inhabitants of Sela sing.
    Let them shout from the top of the mountains!
12 Let them give glory to the LORD,
    and declare his praise in the islands.
13 The LORD will go out like a mighty man.
    He will stir up zeal like a man of war.
    He will raise a war cry.
    Yes, he will shout aloud.
    He will triumph over his enemies.

14 "I have been silent a long time.
    I have been quiet and restrained myself.
    Now I will cry out like a travailing woman. I will both gasp and pant.
15 I will destroy mountains and hills,
    and dry up all their herbs.
    I will make the rivers islands,
    and will dry up the pools.
16 I will bring the blind by a way that they don't know.
    I will lead them in paths that they don't know.
    I will make darkness light before them,
    and crooked places straight.
    I will do these things,
    and I will not forsake them.

17 "Those who trust in engraved images,
    who tell molten images,
    'You are our gods,'
    will be turned back.
    They will be utterly disappointed.

18 "Hear, you deaf,
    and look, you blind,
    that you may see.
19 Who is blind, but my servant?
    Or who is as deaf as my messenger whom I send?
Who is as blind as he who is at peace,
    and as blind as the LORD's servant?
20 You see many things, but don't observe.
    His ears are open, but he doesn't listen.
21 It pleased the LORD, for his righteousness' sake, to magnify the law
    and make it honourable.
22 But this is a robbed and plundered people.
    All of them are snared in holes,
    and they are hidden in prisons.
They have become captives, and no one delivers,
    and a plunder, and no one says, 'Restore them!'

23 Who is there amongst you who will give ear to this?
    Who will listen and hear for the time to come?

24 Who gave Jacob as plunder,
    and Israel to the robbers?
    Didn't the LORD, he against whom we have sinned?
    For they would not walk in his ways,
    and they disobeyed his law.
25 Therefore he poured the fierceness of his anger on him,
    and the strength of battle.
It set him on fire all around, but he didn't know.
    It burnt him, but he didn't take it to heart."

43

1 But now the LORD who created you, Jacob,
    and he who formed you, Israel, says:
"Don't be afraid, for I have redeemed you.
    I have called you by your name.
    You are mine.
2 When you pass through the waters, I will be with you,
    and through the rivers, they will not overflow you.
When you walk through the fire, you will not be burnt,
    and flame will not scorch you.
3 For I am the LORD your God,
    the Holy One of Israel,
    your Saviour.
I have given Egypt as your ransom,
    Ethiopia and Seba in your place.
4 Since you have been precious and honoured in my sight,
    and I have loved you,
    therefore I will give people in your place,
    and nations instead of your life.
5 Don't be afraid, for I am with you.
    I will bring your offspring from the east,
    and gather you from the west.
6 I will tell the north, 'Give them up!'
    and tell the south, 'Don't hold them back!
    Bring my sons from far away,
    and my daughters from the ends of the earth—
7 everyone who is called by my name,
    and whom I have created for my glory,
    whom I have formed,
    yes, whom I have made.'"

8 Bring out the blind people who have eyes,
    and the deaf who have ears.
9 Let all the nations be gathered together,
    and let the peoples be assembled.
Who amongst them can declare this,
    and show us former things?
Let them bring their witnesses, that they may be justified,
    or let them hear, and say, "That is true."

10 "You are my witnesses," says the LORD,
    "With my servant whom I have chosen;
    that you may know and believe me,
    and understand that I am he.
Before me there was no God formed,
    neither will there be after me.
11 I myself am the LORD.
    Besides me, there is no saviour.
12 I have declared, I have saved, and I have shown,
    and there was no strange god amongst you.
Therefore you are my witnesses",
    says the LORD, "and I am God.
13 Yes, since the day was, I am he.
    There is no one who can deliver out of my hand.
    I will work, and who can hinder it?"
14 The LORD, your Redeemer, the Holy One of Israel says: "For your
sake, I have sent to Babylon, and I will bring all of them down as fugitives,
even the Chaldeans, in the ships of their rejoicing. 15 I am the LORD, your
Holy One, the Creator of Israel, your King."
16 The LORD, who makes a way in the sea,
    and a path in the mighty waters,
17 who brings out the chariot and horse,
    the army and the mighty man
    (they lie down together, they shall not rise;
    they are extinct, they are quenched like a wick) says:
18 "Don't remember the former things,
    and don't consider the things of old.
19 Behold, I will do a new thing.
    It springs out now.
    Don't you know it?
I will even make a way in the wilderness,
    and rivers in the desert.
20 The animals of the field, the jackals and the ostriches, shall honour me,
    because I give water in the wilderness and rivers in the desert,
    to give drink to my people, my chosen,
    21 the people which I formed for myself,
    that they might declare my praise.

22 Yet you have not called on me, Jacob;
    but you have been weary of me, Israel.

23 You have not brought me any of your sheep for burnt offerings,
    neither have you honoured me with your sacrifices.
I have not burdened you with offerings,
    nor wearied you with frankincense.
24 You have bought me no sweet cane with money,
    nor have you filled me with the fat of your sacrifices,
but you have burdened me with your sins.
    You have wearied me with your iniquities.

25 I, even I, am he who blots out your transgressions for my own sake;
    and I will not remember your sins.
26 Put me in remembrance.
    Let us plead together.
Declare your case,
    that you may be justified.
27 Your first father sinned,
    and your teachers have transgressed against me.
28 Therefore I will profane the princes of the sanctuary;
    and I will make Jacob a curse,
    and Israel an insult."

44

1 Yet listen now, Jacob my servant,
    and Israel, whom I have chosen.
2 This is what the LORD who made you,
    and formed you from the womb,
    who will help you says:
"Don't be afraid, Jacob my servant;
    and you, Jeshurun, whom I have chosen.
3 For I will pour water on him who is thirsty,
    and streams on the dry ground.
I will pour my Spirit on your descendants,
    and my blessing on your offspring;
4 and they will spring up amongst the grass,
    as willows by the watercourses.
5 One will say, 'I am the LORD's.'
    Another will be called by the name of Jacob;
    and another will write with his hand 'to the LORD,'
    and honour the name of Israel."

6 This is what the LORD, the King of Israel,
    and his Redeemer, the LORD of Armies, says:
"I am the first, and I am the last;
    and besides me there is no God.
7 Who is like me?
    Who will call,
    and will declare it,
    and set it in order for me,
    since I established the ancient people?
Let them declare the things that are coming,
    and that will happen.
8 Don't fear,
    neither be afraid.
Haven't I declared it to you long ago,
    and shown it?
You are my witnesses.
    Is there a God besides me?
Indeed, there is not.
    I don't know any other Rock."

9 Everyone who makes a carved image is vain.
    The things that they delight in will not profit.
    Their own witnesses don't see, nor know, that they may be
        disappointed.
10 Who has fashioned a god,
    or moulds an image that is profitable for nothing?
11 Behold, all his fellows will be disappointed;
    and the workmen are mere men.
Let them all be gathered together.
    Let them stand up.
    They will fear.
    They will be put to shame together.

12 The blacksmith takes an axe,
    works in the coals,
    fashions it with hammers,
    and works it with his strong arm.
He is hungry,
    and his strength fails;
he drinks no water,
    and is faint.
13 The carpenter stretches out a line.
    He marks it out with a pencil.
    He shapes it with planes.
    He marks it out with compasses,
    and shapes it like the figure of a man,
    with the beauty of a man,
    to reside in a house.
14 He cuts down cedars for himself,
    and takes the cypress and the oak,

and strengthens for himself one amongst the trees of the forest.
He plants a cypress tree,
    and the rain nourishes it.
15 Then it will be for a man to burn;
    and he takes some of it and warms himself.
    Yes, he burns it and bakes bread.
Yes, he makes a god and worships it;
    he makes it a carved image, and falls down to it.
16 He burns part of it in the fire.
    With part of it, he eats meat.
    He roasts a roast and is satisfied.
Yes, he warms himself
    and says, "Aha! I am warm. I have seen the fire."
17 The rest of it he makes into a god,
    even his engraved image.
He bows down to it and worships,
    and prays to it, and says, "Deliver me, for you are my god!"

18 They don't know, neither do they consider,
    for he has shut their eyes, that they can't see,
    and their hearts, that they can't understand.
19 No one thinks,
    neither is there knowledge nor understanding to say,
    "I have burnt part of it in the fire.
    Yes, I have also baked bread on its coals.
    I have roasted meat and eaten it.
    Shall I make the rest of it into an abomination?
    Shall I bow down to a tree trunk?"
20 He feeds on ashes.
    A deceived heart has turned him aside;
    and he can't deliver his soul,
    nor say, "Isn't there a lie in my right hand?"

21 Remember these things, Jacob and Israel,
    for you are my servant.
    I have formed you.
    You are my servant.
    Israel, you will not be forgotten by me.
22 I have blotted out, as a thick cloud, your transgressions,
    and, as a cloud, your sins.
    Return to me, for I have redeemed you.

23 Sing, you heavens, for the LORD has done it!
    Shout, you lower parts of the earth!
    Break out into singing, you mountains, O forest, all of your trees,
    for the LORD has redeemed Jacob,
    and will glorify himself in Israel.

24 The LORD, your Redeemer,
    and he who formed you from the womb says:
"I am the LORD, who makes all things;
    who alone stretches out the heavens;
    who spreads out the earth by myself;
25 who frustrates the signs of the liars,
    and makes diviners mad;
who turns wise men backward,
    and makes their knowledge foolish;
26 who confirms the word of his servant,
    and performs the counsel of his messengers;
who says of Jerusalem, 'She will be inhabited;'
    and of the cities of Judah, 'They will be built,'
    and 'I will raise up its waste places;'
27 who says to the deep, 'Be dry,'
    and 'I will dry up your rivers,'
28 who says of Cyrus, 'He is my shepherd, and shall perform all my
        pleasure,'
    even saying of Jerusalem, 'She will be built;'
    and of the temple, 'Your foundation will be laid.'"

45

1 The LORD says to his anointed, to Cyrus, whose right hand I have
held to subdue nations before him and strip kings of their armour, to open
the doors before him, and the gates shall not be shut:
2 "I will go before you
    and make the rough places smooth.
I will break the doors of bronze in pieces
    and cut apart the bars of iron.
3 I will give you the treasures of darkness
    and hidden riches of secret places,
that you may know that it is I, the LORD, who calls you by your name,
    even the God of Israel.
4 For Jacob my servant's sake,
    and Israel my chosen,
I have called you by your name.
    I have given you a title,
    though you have not known me.
5 I am the LORD, and there is no one else.
    Besides me, there is no God.

I will strengthen[a] you,
>   though you have not known me,
6 that they may know from the rising of the sun,
>   and from the west,
that there is no one besides me.
>   I am the LORD, and there is no one else.
7 I form the light
>   and create darkness.
I make peace
>   and create calamity.
I am the LORD,
>   who does all these things.

8 Rain, you heavens, from above,
>   and let the skies pour down righteousness.
Let the earth open, that it may produce salvation,
>   and let it cause righteousness to spring up with it.
I, the LORD, have created it.

9 Woe to him who strives with his Maker—
>   a clay pot amongst the clay pots of the earth!
Shall the clay ask him who fashions it, 'What are you making?'
>   or your work, 'He has no hands'?
10 Woe to him who says to a father, 'What have you become the father of?'
>   or to a mother, 'What have you given birth to?'"

11 The LORD, the Holy One of Israel
>   and his Maker says:
"You ask me about the things that are to come, concerning my sons,
>   and you command me concerning the work of my hands!
12 I have made the earth, and created man on it.
>   I, even my hands, have stretched out the heavens.
>   I have commanded all their army.
13 I have raised him up in righteousness,
>   and I will make all his ways straight.
He shall build my city,
>   and he shall let my exiles go free,
>   not for price nor reward," says the LORD of Armies.

14 The LORD says: "The labour of Egypt,
>   and the merchandise of Ethiopia,
>   and the Sabeans, men of stature, will come over to you,
>   and they will be yours.
They will go after you.
>   They shall come over in chains.
>   They will bow down to you.
They will make supplication to you:
>   'Surely God is in you; and there is no one else.
>   There is no other god.
15 Most certainly you are a God who has hidden yourself,
>   God of Israel, the Saviour.'"
16 They will be disappointed,
>   yes, confounded, all of them.
>   Those who are makers of idols will go into confusion together.
17 Israel will be saved by the LORD with an everlasting salvation.
>   You will not be disappointed nor confounded to ages everlasting.

18 For the LORD who created the heavens,
>   the God who formed the earth and made it,
>   who established it and didn't create it a waste,
>   who formed it to be inhabited says:
"I am the LORD.
>   There is no other.
19 I have not spoken in secret,
>   in a place of the land of darkness.
I didn't say to the offspring of Jacob, 'Seek me in vain.'
>   I, the LORD, speak righteousness.
>   I declare things that are right.

20 "Assemble yourselves and come.
>   Draw near together, you who have escaped from the nations.
Those have no knowledge who carry the wood of their engraved image,
>   and pray to a god that can't save.
21 Declare and present it.
>   Yes, let them take counsel together.
Who has shown this from ancient time?
>   Who has declared it of old?
>   Haven't I, the LORD?
There is no other God besides me, a just God and a Saviour.
>   There is no one besides me.

22 "Look to me, and be saved, all the ends of the earth;
>   for I am God, and there is no other.
23 I have sworn by myself.
>   The word has gone out of my mouth in righteousness, and will not be revoked,
that to me every knee shall bow,

every tongue shall take an oath.
24 They will say of me,
>   'There is righteousness and strength only in the LORD.'"
Even to him will men come.
>   All those who raged against him will be disappointed.
25 All the offspring of Israel will be justified in the LORD,
>   and will rejoice!

46

1 Bel bows down.
>   Nebo stoops.
Their idols are carried by animals,
>   and on the livestock.
The things that you carried around are heavy loads,
>   a burden for the weary.
2 They stoop and they bow down together.
>   They could not deliver the burden,
>   but they have gone into captivity.

3 "Listen to me, house of Jacob,
>   and all the remnant of the house of Israel,
>   that have been carried from their birth,
>   that have been carried from the womb.
4 Even to old age I am he,
>   and even to grey hairs I will carry you.
I have made, and I will bear.
>   Yes, I will carry, and will deliver.

5 "To whom will you compare me, and consider my equal,
>   and compare me, as if we were the same?
6 Some pour out gold from the bag,
>   and weigh silver in the balance.
They hire a goldsmith,
>   and he makes it a god.
They fall down—
>   yes, they worship.
7 They bear it on their shoulder.
>   They carry it, and set it in its place, and it stands there.
>   It cannot move from its place.
Yes, one may cry to it, yet it can not answer.
>   It cannot save him out of his trouble.

8 "Remember this, and show yourselves men.
>   Bring it to mind again, you transgressors.
9 Remember the former things of old;
>   for I am God, and there is no other.
>   I am God, and there is none like me.
10 I declare the end from the beginning,
>   and from ancient times things that are not yet done.
I say: My counsel will stand,
>   and I will do all that I please.
11 I call a ravenous bird from the east,
>   the man of my counsel from a far country.
Yes, I have spoken.
>   I will also bring it to pass.
I have planned.
>   I will also do it.

12 Listen to me, you stubborn-hearted,
>   who are far from righteousness!
13 I bring my righteousness near.
>   It is not far off,
>   and my salvation will not wait.
I will grant salvation to Zion,
>   my glory to Israel.

47

1 "Come down and sit in the dust, virgin daughter of Babylon.
>   Sit on the ground without a throne, daughter of the Chaldeans.
>   For you will no longer be called tender and delicate.
2 Take the millstones and grind flour.
>   Remove your veil, lift up your skirt, uncover your legs,
>   and wade through the rivers.
3 Your nakedness will be uncovered.
>   Yes, your shame will be seen.
I will take vengeance,
>   and will spare no one."

4 Our Redeemer, the LORD of Armies is his name,
>   is the Holy One of Israel.

5 "Sit in silence, and go into darkness,
>   daughter of the Chaldeans.
For you shall no longer be called
>   the mistress of kingdoms.
6 I was angry with my people.
>   I profaned my inheritance

---

a 45:5 or, equip

and gave them into your hand.
You showed them no mercy.
    You laid a very heavy yoke on the aged.
7 You said, 'I will be a princess forever,'
    so that you didn't lay these things to your heart,
    nor did you remember the results.

8 "Now therefore hear this, you who are given to pleasures,
    who sit securely,
who say in your heart,
    'I am, and there is no one else besides me.
I won't sit as a widow,
    neither will I know the loss of children.'
9 But these two things will come to you in a moment in one day:
    the loss of children and widowhood.
They will come on you in their full measure,
    in the multitude of your sorceries,
    and the great abundance of your enchantments.
10 For you have trusted in your wickedness.
    You have said, 'No one sees me.'
Your wisdom and your knowledge has perverted you.
    You have said in your heart, 'I am, and there is no one else besides
        me.'
11 Therefore disaster will come on you.
    You won't know when it dawns.
Mischief will fall on you.
    You won't be able to put it away.
Desolation will come on you suddenly,
    which you don't understand.

12 "Stand now with your enchantments
    and with the multitude of your sorceries,
    in which you have laboured from your youth,
as if you might profit,
    as if you might prevail.
13 You are wearied in the multitude of your counsels.
    Now let the astrologers, the stargazers, and the monthly
        prognosticators stand up and save you from the things that
        will happen to you.
14 Behold, they are like stubble.
    The fire will burn them.
    They won't deliver themselves from the power of the flame.
It won't be a coal to warm at
    or a fire to sit by.
15 The things that you laboured in will be like this:
    those who have trafficked with you from your youth will each wander
        in his own way.
    There will be no one to save you.

48

1 "Hear this, house of Jacob,
    you who are called by the name of Israel,
    and have come out of the waters of Judah.
You swear by the LORD's name,
    and make mention of the God of Israel,
    but not in truth, nor in righteousness—
2 for they call themselves citizens of the holy city,
    and rely on the God of Israel;
    the LORD of Armies is his name.
3 I have declared the former things from of old.
    Yes, they went out of my mouth, and I revealed them.
    I did them suddenly, and they happened.
4 Because I knew that you are obstinate,
    and your neck is an iron sinew,
    and your brow bronze;
5 therefore I have declared it to you from of old;
    before it came to pass I showed it to you;
    lest you should say, 'My idol has done them.
    My engraved image and my molten image has commanded them.'
6 You have heard it.
    Now see all this.
    And you, won't you declare it?

"I have shown you new things from this time,
    even hidden things, which you have not known.
7 They are created now, and not from of old.
    Before today, you didn't hear them,
    lest you should say, 'Behold, I knew them.'
8 Yes, you didn't hear.
    Yes, you didn't know.
    Yes, from of old your ear was not opened,
for I knew that you dealt very treacherously,
    and were called a transgressor from the womb.
9 For my name's sake, I will defer my anger,
    and for my praise, I hold it back for you
    so that I don't cut you off.
10 Behold, I have refined you,
    but not as silver.
    I have chosen you in the furnace of affliction.

11 For my own sake,
    for my own sake, I will do it;
for how would my name be profaned?
    I will not give my glory to another.

12 "Listen to me, O Jacob,
    and Israel my called:
I am he.
    I am the first.
    I am also the last.
13 Yes, my hand has laid the foundation of the earth,
    and my right hand has spread out the heavens.
    when I call to them, they stand up together.

14 "Assemble yourselves, all of you, and hear!
    Who amongst them has declared these things?
He whom the LORD loves will do what he likes to Babylon,
    and his arm will be against the Chaldeans.
15 I, even I, have spoken.
    Yes, I have called him.
I have brought him
    and he shall make his way prosperous.
16 "Come near to me and hear this:

"From the beginning I have not spoken in secret;
    from the time that it happened, I was there."

Now the Lord GOD has sent me
    with his Spirit.

17 The LORD,
    your Redeemer,
    the Holy One of Israel, says:
"I am the LORD your God,
    who teaches you to profit,
    who leads you by the way that you should go.
18 Oh that you had listened to my commandments!
    Then your peace would have been like a river
    and your righteousness like the waves of the sea.
19 Your offspring also would have been as the sand
    and the descendants of your body like its grains.
    His name would not be cut off nor destroyed from before me."

20 Leave Babylon!
    Flee from the Chaldeans!
With the sound of joyful shouting announce this,
    tell it even to the end of the earth;
    say, "The LORD has redeemed his servant Jacob!"
21 They didn't thirst when he led them through the deserts.
    He caused the waters to flow out of the rock for them.
    He also split the rock and the waters gushed out.

22 "There is no peace", says the LORD, "for the wicked."

49

1 Listen, islands, to me.
    Listen, you peoples, from afar:
the LORD has called me from the womb;
    from the inside of my mother, he has mentioned my name.
2 He has made my mouth like a sharp sword.
    He has hidden me in the shadow of his hand.
He has made me a polished shaft.
    He has kept me close in his quiver.
3 He said to me, "You are my servant,
    Israel, in whom I will be glorified."
4 But I said, "I have laboured in vain.
    I have spent my strength in vain for nothing;
yet surely the justice due to me is with the LORD,
    and my reward with my God."

5 Now the LORD, he who formed me from the womb to be his servant,
    says to bring Jacob again to him,
    and to gather Israel to him,
    for I am honourable in the LORD's eyes,
    and my God has become my strength.
6 Indeed, he says, "It is too light a thing that you should be my servant to
        raise up the tribes of Jacob,
    and to restore the preserved of Israel.
I will also give you as a light to the nations,
    that you may be my salvation to the end of the earth."
7 The LORD, the Redeemer of Israel, and his Holy One,
    says to him whom man despises, to him whom the nation abhors, to a
        servant of rulers:
"Kings shall see and rise up,
    princes, and they shall worship,
    because of the LORD who is faithful, even the Holy One of Israel, who
        has chosen you."

8 The LORD says, "I have answered you in an acceptable time.
    I have helped you in a day of salvation.

I will preserve you and give you for a covenant of the people,
　　to raise up the land, to make them inherit the desolate heritage,
9 saying to those who are bound, 'Come out!';
　　to those who are in darkness, 'Show yourselves!'
"They shall feed along the paths,
　　and their pasture shall be on all treeless heights.
10 They shall not hunger nor thirst;
　　neither shall the heat nor sun strike them,
　　for he who has mercy on them will lead them.
He will guide them by springs of water.
11 I will make all my mountains a road,
　　and my highways shall be exalted.
12 Behold, these shall come from afar,
　　and behold, these from the north and from the west,
　　and these from the land of Sinim."
13 Sing, heavens, and be joyful, earth!
　　Break out into singing, mountains!
For the LORD has comforted his people,
　　and will have compassion on his afflicted.

14 But Zion said, "The LORD has forsaken me,
　　and the Lord has forgotten me."
15 "Can a woman forget her nursing child,
　　that she should not have compassion on the son of her womb?
Yes, these may forget,
　　yet I will not forget you!
16 Behold, I have engraved you on the palms of my hands.
　　Your walls are continually before me.
17 Your children hurry.
　　Your destroyers and those who devastated you will leave you.
18 Lift up your eyes all around, and see:
　　all these gather themselves together, and come to you.
As I live," says the LORD, "you shall surely clothe yourself with them all as
　　　　with an ornament,
　　and dress yourself with them, like a bride.
19 "For, as for your waste and your desolate places,
　　and your land that has been destroyed,
surely now that land will be too small for the inhabitants,
　　and those who swallowed you up will be far away.
20 The children of your bereavement will say in your ears,
　　'This place is too small for me.
　　Give me a place to live in.'
21 Then you will say in your heart, 'Who has conceived these for me, since I
　　　　have been bereaved of my children
　　and am alone, an exile, and wandering back and forth?
Who has brought these up?
　　Behold, I was left alone. Where were these?'"

22 The Lord GOD says, "Behold, I will lift up my hand to the nations,
　　and lift up my banner to the peoples.
They shall bring your sons in their bosom,
　　and your daughters shall be carried on their shoulders.
23 Kings shall be your foster fathers,
　　and their queens your nursing mothers.
They will bow down to you with their faces to the earth,
　　and lick the dust of your feet.
Then you will know that I am the LORD;
　　and those who wait for me won't be disappointed."

24 Shall the plunder be taken from the mighty,
　　or the lawful captives be delivered?
25 But the LORD says, "Even the captives of the mighty shall be taken
　　　　away,
　　and the plunder retrieved from the fierce,
for I will contend with him who contends with you
　　and I will save your children.
26 I will feed those who oppress you with their own flesh;
　　and they will be drunk on their own blood, as with sweet wine.
Then all flesh shall know that I, the LORD, am your Saviour
　　and your Redeemer, the Mighty One of Jacob."

50

1 The LORD says, "Where is the bill of your mother's divorce, with which I
　　　　have put her away?
　　Or to which of my creditors have I sold you?
Behold, you were sold for your iniquities,
　　and your mother was put away for your transgressions.
2 Why, when I came, was there no one?
　　When I called, why was there no one to answer?
Is my hand shortened at all, that it can't redeem?
　　Or have I no power to deliver?
Behold, at my rebuke I dry up the sea.
　　I make the rivers a wilderness.
　　Their fish stink because there is no water, and die of thirst.
3 I clothe the heavens with blackness.
　　I make sackcloth their covering."

4 The Lord GOD has given me the tongue of those who are taught,
　　that I may know how to sustain with words him who is weary.
He awakens morning by morning,

he awakens my ear to hear as those who are taught.
5 The Lord GOD has opened my ear.
　　I was not rebellious.
　　I have not turned back.
6 I gave my back to those who beat me,
　　and my cheeks to those who plucked off the hair.
　　I didn't hide my face from shame and spitting.
7 For the Lord GOD will help me.
　　Therefore I have not been confounded.
Therefore I have set my face like a flint,
　　and I know that I won't be disappointed.
8 He who justifies me is near.
　　Who will bring charges against me?
Let us stand up together.
　　Who is my adversary?
　　Let him come near to me.
9 Behold, the Lord GOD will help me!
　　Who is he who will condemn me?
Behold, they will all grow old like a garment.
　　The moths will eat them up.

10 Who amongst you fears the LORD
　　and obeys the voice of his servant?
He who walks in darkness
　　and has no light,
let him trust in the LORD's name,
　　and rely on his God.
11 Behold, all you who kindle a fire,
　　who adorn yourselves with torches around yourselves,
walk in the flame of your fire,
　　and amongst the torches that you have kindled.
You will have this from my hand:
　　you will lie down in sorrow.

51

1 "Listen to me, you who follow after righteousness,
　　you who seek the LORD.
Look to the rock you were cut from,
　　and to the quarry you were dug from.
2 Look to Abraham your father,
　　and to Sarah who bore you;
for when he was but one I called him,
　　I blessed him,
　　and made him many.
3 For the LORD has comforted Zion.
　　He has comforted all her waste places,
　　and has made her wilderness like Eden,
　　and her desert like the garden of the LORD.
Joy and gladness will be found in them,
　　thanksgiving, and the voice of melody.

4 "Listen to me, my people;
　　and hear me, my nation,
for a law will go out from me,
　　and I will establish my justice for a light to the peoples.
5 My righteousness is near.
　　My salvation has gone out,
　　and my arms will judge the peoples.
The islands will wait for me,
　　and they will trust my arm.
6 Lift up your eyes to the heavens,
　　and look at the earth beneath;
for the heavens will vanish away like smoke,
　　and the earth will wear out like a garment.
Its inhabitants will die in the same way,
　　but my salvation will be forever,
　　and my righteousness will not be abolished.

7 "Listen to me, you who know righteousness,
　　the people in whose heart is my law.
Don't fear the reproach of men,
　　and don't be dismayed at their insults.
8 For the moth will eat them up like a garment,
　　and the worm will eat them like wool;
but my righteousness will be forever,
　　and my salvation to all generations."

9 Awake, awake, put on strength, arm of the LORD!
　　Awake, as in the days of old,
　　the generations of ancient times.
Isn't it you who cut Rahab in pieces,
　　who pierced the monster?
10 Isn't it you who dried up the sea,
　　the waters of the great deep;
　　who made the depths of the sea a way for the redeemed to pass over?
11 Those ransomed by the LORD will return,
　　and come with singing to Zion.
　　Everlasting joy shall be on their heads.
They will obtain gladness and joy.
　　Sorrow and sighing shall flee away.

¹² "I, even I, am he who comforts you.
Who are you, that you are afraid of man who shall die,
and of the son of man who will be made as grass?
¹³ Have you forgotten the LORD your Maker,
who stretched out the heavens,
and laid the foundations of the earth?
Do you live in fear continually all day because of the fury of the oppressor,
when he prepares to destroy?
Where is the fury of the oppressor?
¹⁴ The captive exile will speedily be freed.
He will not die and go down into the pit.
His bread won't fail.
¹⁵ For I am the LORD your God, who stirs up the sea
so that its waves roar.
the LORD of Armies is his name.
¹⁶ I have put my words in your mouth
and have covered you in the shadow of my hand,
that I may plant the heavens,
and lay the foundations of the earth,
and tell Zion, 'You are my people.'"

¹⁷ Awake, awake!
Stand up, Jerusalem,
you who have drunk from the LORD's hand the cup of his wrath.
You have drunken the bowl of the cup of staggering,
and drained it.
¹⁸ There is no one to guide her amongst all the sons to whom she has given
birth;
and there is no one who takes her by the hand amongst all the sons
whom she has brought up.
¹⁹ These two things have happened to you—
who will grieve with you?—
desolation and destruction,
and famine and the sword.
How can I comfort you?
²⁰ Your sons have fainted.
They lie at the head of all the streets,
like an antelope in a net.
They are full of the LORD's wrath,
the rebuke of your God.

²¹ Therefore now hear this, you afflicted,
and drunken, but not with wine:
²² Your Lord GOD,
your God who pleads the cause of his people, says,
"Behold, I have taken out of your hand the cup of staggering,
even the bowl of the cup of my wrath.
You will not drink it any more.
²³ I will put it into the hand of those who afflict you,
who have said to your soul, 'Bow down, that we may walk over you;'
and you have laid your back as the ground,
like a street to those who walk over."

52

¹ Awake, awake! Put on your strength, Zion.
Put on your beautiful garments, Jerusalem, the holy city,
for from now on the uncircumcised and the unclean will no more come
into you.
² Shake yourself from the dust!
Arise, sit up, Jerusalem!
Release yourself from the bonds of your neck, captive daughter of
Zion!

³ For the LORD says, "You were sold for nothing;
and you will be redeemed without money."

⁴ For the Lord GOD says:
"My people went down at the first into Egypt to live there;
and the Assyrian has oppressed them without cause.

⁵ "Now therefore, what do I do here," says the LORD,
"seeing that my people are taken away for nothing?
Those who rule over them mock," says the LORD,
"and my name is blasphemed continually all day long.
⁶ Therefore my people shall know my name.
Therefore they shall know in that day that I am he who speaks.
Behold, it is I."

⁷ How beautiful on the mountains are the feet of him who brings good
news,
who publishes peace,
who brings good news,
who proclaims salvation,
who says to Zion, "Your God reigns!"
⁸ Your watchmen lift up their voice.

Together they sing;
for they shall see eye to eye when the LORD returns to Zion.
⁹ Break out into joy!
Sing together, you waste places of Jerusalem;
for the LORD has comforted his people.
He has redeemed Jerusalem.
¹⁰ The LORD has made his holy arm bare in the eyes of all the nations.
All the ends of the earth have seen the salvation of our God.

¹¹ Depart! Depart! Go out from there! Touch no unclean thing!
Go out from amongst her!
Cleanse yourselves, you who carry the LORD's vessels.
¹² For you shall not go out in haste,
neither shall you go by flight;
for the LORD will go before you,
and the God of Israel will be your rear guard.

¹³ Behold, my servant will deal wisely.
He will be exalted and lifted up,
and will be very high.
¹⁴ Just as many were astonished at you—
his appearance was marred more than any man, and his form more
than the sons of men—
¹⁵ so he will cleanse[a] many nations.
Kings will shut their mouths at him;
for they will see that which had not been told them,
and they will understand that which they had not heard.

53

¹ Who has believed our message?
To whom has the LORD's arm been revealed?
² For he grew up before him as a tender plant,
and as a root out of dry ground.
He has no good looks or majesty.
When we see him, there is no beauty that we should desire him.
³ He was despised
and rejected by men,
a man of suffering
and acquainted with disease.
He was despised as one from whom men hide their face;
and we didn't respect him.

⁴ Surely he has borne our sickness
and carried our suffering;
yet we considered him plagued,
struck by God, and afflicted.
⁵ But he was pierced for our transgressions.
He was crushed for our iniquities.
The punishment that brought our peace was on him;
and by his wounds we are healed.
⁶ All we like sheep have gone astray.
Everyone has turned to his own way;
and the LORD has laid on him the iniquity of us all.

⁷ He was oppressed,
yet when he was afflicted he didn't open his mouth.
As a lamb that is led to the slaughter,
and as a sheep that before its shearers is silent,
so he didn't open his mouth.
⁸ He was taken away by oppression and judgement.
As for his generation,
who considered that he was cut off out of the land of the living
and stricken for the disobedience of my people?
⁹ They made his grave with the wicked,
and with a rich man in his death,
although he had done no violence,
nor was any deceit in his mouth.

¹⁰ Yet it pleased the LORD to bruise him.
He has caused him to suffer.
When you make his soul an offering for sin,
he will see his offspring.
He will prolong his days
and the LORD's pleasure will prosper in his hand.
¹¹ After the suffering of his soul,
he will see the light[b] and be satisfied.
My righteous servant will justify many by the knowledge of himself;
and he will bear their iniquities.
¹² Therefore I will give him a portion with the great.
He will divide the plunder with the strong,
because he poured out his soul to death
and was counted with the transgressors;
yet he bore the sins of many
and made intercession for the transgressors.

54

¹ "Sing, barren, you who didn't give birth!

ᵃ *52:15 or, sprinkle*

ᵇ *53:11 So read the Dead Sea Scrolls and Septuagint. Masoretic Text omits*
"the light".

Break out into singing, and cry aloud, you who didn't travail with child!
For more are the children of the desolate than the children of the married wife," says the LORD.

2 "Enlarge the place of your tent,
and let them stretch out the curtains of your habitations;
don't spare; lengthen your cords, and strengthen your stakes.
3 For you will spread out on the right hand and on the left;
and your offspring will possess the nations
and settle in desolate cities.

4 "Don't be afraid, for you will not be ashamed.
Don't be confounded, for you will not be disappointed.
For you will forget the shame of your youth.
You will remember the reproach of your widowhood no more.
5 For your Maker is your husband; the LORD of Armies is his name.
The Holy One of Israel is your Redeemer.
He will be called the God of the whole earth.
6 For the LORD has called you as a wife forsaken and grieved in spirit,
even a wife of youth, when she is cast off," says your God.

7 "For a small moment I have forsaken you,
but I will gather you with great mercies.
8 In overflowing wrath I hid my face from you for a moment,
but with everlasting loving kindness I will have mercy on you," says the LORD your Redeemer.

9 "For this is like the waters of Noah to me;
for as I have sworn that the waters of Noah will no more go over the earth,
so I have sworn that I will not be angry with you, nor rebuke you.
10 For the mountains may depart,
and the hills be removed,
but my loving kindness will not depart from you,
and my covenant of peace will not be removed,"
says the LORD who has mercy on you.

11 "You afflicted, tossed with storms, and not comforted,
behold, I will set your stones in beautiful colours,
and lay your foundations with sapphires.
12 I will make your pinnacles of rubies,
your gates of sparkling jewels,
and all your walls of precious stones.
13 All your children will be taught by the LORD,
and your children's peace will be great.
14 You will be established in righteousness.
You will be far from oppression,
for you will not be afraid,
and far from terror,
for it shall not come near you.
15 Behold, they may gather together, but not by me.
Whoever gathers together against you will fall because of you.

16 "Behold, I have created the blacksmith who fans the coals into flame,
and forges a weapon for his work;
and I have created the destroyer to destroy.
17 No weapon that is formed against you will prevail;
and you will condemn every tongue that rises against you in judgement.
This is the heritage of the LORD's servants,
and their righteousness is of me," says the LORD.

55

1 "Hey! Come, everyone who thirsts, to the waters!
Come, he who has no money, buy, and eat!
Yes, come, buy wine and milk without money and without price.
2 Why do you spend money for that which is not bread,
and your labour for that which doesn't satisfy?
Listen diligently to me, and eat that which is good,
and let your soul delight itself in richness.
3 Turn your ear, and come to me.
Hear, and your soul will live.
I will make an everlasting covenant with you, even the sure mercies of David.
4 Behold, I have given him for a witness to the peoples,
a leader and commander to the peoples.
5 Behold, you shall call a nation that you don't know;
and a nation that didn't know you shall run to you,
because of the LORD your God,
and for the Holy One of Israel;
for he has glorified you."

6 Seek the LORD while he may be found.
Call on him while he is near.
7 Let the wicked forsake his way,
and the unrighteous man his thoughts.
Let him return to the LORD, and he will have mercy on him,
to our God, for he will freely pardon.

8 "For my thoughts are not your thoughts,

and your ways are not my ways," says the LORD.
9 "For as the heavens are higher than the earth,
so are my ways higher than your ways,
and my thoughts than your thoughts.
10 For as the rain comes down and the snow from the sky,
and doesn't return there, but waters the earth,
and makes it grow and bud,
and gives seed to the sower and bread to the eater;
11 so is my word that goes out of my mouth:
it will not return to me void,
but it will accomplish that which I please,
and it will prosper in the thing I sent it to do.
12 For you shall go out with joy,
and be led out with peace.
The mountains and the hills will break out before you into singing;
and all the trees of the fields will clap their hands.
13 Instead of the thorn the cypress tree will come up;
and instead of the brier the myrtle tree will come up.
It will make a name for the LORD,
for an everlasting sign that will not be cut off."

56

1 The LORD says:
"Maintain justice
and do what is right,
for my salvation is near
and my righteousness will soon be revealed.
2 Blessed is the man who does this,
and the son of man who holds it fast;
who keeps the Sabbath without profaning it
and keeps his hand from doing any evil."

3 Let no foreigner who has joined himself to the LORD speak, saying,
"The LORD will surely separate me from his people."
Do not let the eunuch say, "Behold, I am a dry tree."

4 For the LORD says, "To the eunuchs who keep my Sabbaths,
choose the things that please me,
and hold fast to my covenant,
5 I will give them in my house and within my walls a memorial and a name
better than of sons and of daughters.
I will give them an everlasting name that will not be cut off.

6 Also the foreigners who join themselves to the LORD
to serve him,
and to love the LORD's name,
to be his servants,
everyone who keeps the Sabbath from profaning it,
and holds fast my covenant,
7 I will bring these to my holy mountain,
and make them joyful in my house of prayer.
Their burnt offerings and their sacrifices will be accepted on my altar;
for my house will be called a house of prayer for all peoples."
8 The Lord GOD, who gathers the outcasts of Israel, says,
"I will yet gather others to him,
in addition to his own who are gathered."

9 All you animals of the field,
come to devour,
all you animals in the forest.
10 His watchmen are blind.
They are all without knowledge.
They are all mute dogs.
They can't bark—
dreaming, lying down, loving to slumber.
11 Yes, the dogs are greedy.
They can never have enough.
They are shepherds who can't understand.
They have all turned to their own way,
each one to his gain, from every quarter.
12 "Come," they say, "I will get wine,
and we will fill ourselves with strong drink;
and tomorrow will be as today,
great beyond measure."

57

1 The righteous perish,
and no one lays it to heart.
Merciful men are taken away,
and no one considers that the righteous is taken away from the evil.
2 He enters into peace.
They rest in their beds,
each one who walks in his uprightness.

3 "But draw near here, you sons of a sorceress,
you offspring of adulterers and prostitutes.
4 Whom do you mock?
Against whom do you make a wide mouth
and stick out your tongue?
Aren't you children of disobedience

and offspring of falsehood,
5 you who inflame yourselves amongst the oaks,
    under every green tree;
who kill the children in the valleys,
    under the clefts of the rocks?
6 Amongst the smooth stones of the valley is your portion.
    They, they are your lot.
You have even poured a drink offering to them.
    You have offered an offering.
    Shall I be appeased for these things?
7 On a high and lofty mountain you have set your bed.
    You also went up there to offer sacrifice.
8 You have set up your memorial behind the doors and the posts,
    for you have exposed yourself to someone besides me,
    and have gone up.
You have enlarged your bed
    and made you a covenant with them.
    You loved what you saw on their bed.
9 You went to the king with oil,
    increased your perfumes,
    sent your ambassadors far off,
    and degraded yourself even to Sheol.ᵃ
10 You were wearied with the length of your ways;
    yet you didn't say, 'It is in vain.'
You found a reviving of your strength;
    therefore you weren't faint.

11 "Whom have you dreaded and feared,
    so that you lie,
    and have not remembered me, nor laid it to your heart?
Haven't I held my peace for a long time,
    and you don't fear me?
12 I will declare your righteousness;
    and as for your works, they will not benefit you.
13 When you cry,
    let those whom you have gathered deliver you,
but the wind will take them.
    A breath will carry them all away,
but he who takes refuge in me will possess the land,
    and will inherit my holy mountain."

14 He will say, "Build up, build up, prepare the way!
    Remove the stumbling-block out of the way of my people."
15 For the high and lofty One who inhabits eternity,
    whose name is Holy, says:
"I dwell in the high and holy place, with him also who is of a contrite and
        humble spirit,
    to revive the spirit of the humble,
    and to revive the heart of the contrite.
16 For I will not contend forever, neither will I always be angry;
    for the spirit would faint before me,
    and the souls whom I have made.
17 I was angry because of the iniquity of his covetousness and struck him.
    I hid myself and was angry;
    and he went on backsliding in the way of his heart.
18 I have seen his ways, and will heal him.
    I will lead him also,
    and restore comforts to him and to his mourners.
19 I create the fruit of the lips:
    Peace, peace, to him who is far off and to him who is near,"
    says the LORD; "and I will heal them."
20 But the wicked are like the troubled sea;
    for it can't rest and its waters cast up mire and mud.
21 "There is no peace", says my God,
    "for the wicked."

58

1 "Cry aloud! Don't spare!
    Lift up your voice like a trumpet!
Declare to my people their disobedience,
    and to the house of Jacob their sins.
2 Yet they seek me daily,
    and delight to know my ways.
As a nation that did righteousness,
    and didn't forsake the ordinance of their God,
they ask of me righteous judgements.
    They delight to draw near to God.
3 'Why have we fasted,' they say, 'and you don't see?
    Why have we afflicted our soul, and you don't notice?'

"Behold, in the day of your fast you find pleasure,
    and oppress all your labourers.
4 Behold, you fast for strife and contention,
    and to strike with the fist of wickedness.
    You don't fast today so as to make your voice to be heard on high.
5 Is this the fast that I have chosen?
    A day for a man to humble his soul?

Is it to bow down his head like a reed,
    and to spread sackcloth and ashes under himself?
Will you call this a fast,
    and an acceptable day to the LORD?

6 "Isn't this the fast that I have chosen:
    to release the bonds of wickedness,
    to undo the straps of the yoke,
    to let the oppressed go free,
    and that you break every yoke?
7 Isn't it to distribute your bread to the hungry,
    and that you bring the poor who are cast out to your house?
When you see the naked,
    that you cover him;
    and that you not hide yourself from your own flesh?
8 Then your light will break out as the morning,
    and your healing will appear quickly;
then your righteousness shall go before you,
    and the LORD's glory will be your rear guard.
9 Then you will call, and the LORD will answer.
    You will cry for help, and he will say, 'Here I am.'

"If you take away from amongst you the yoke,
    finger pointing,
    and speaking wickedly;
10 and if you pour out your soul to the hungry,
    and satisfy the afflicted soul,
then your light will rise in darkness,
    and your obscurity will be as the noonday;
11 and the LORD will guide you continually,
    satisfy your soul in dry places,
    and make your bones strong.
You will be like a watered garden,
    and like a spring of water
    whose waters don't fail.
12 Those who will be of you will build the old waste places.
    You will raise up the foundations of many generations.
You will be called Repairer of the Breach,
    Restorer of Paths with Dwellings.

13 "If you turn away your foot from the Sabbath,
    from doing your pleasure on my holy day,
and call the Sabbath a delight,
    and the holy of the LORD honourable,
    and honour it,
    not doing your own ways,
    nor finding your own pleasure,
    nor speaking your own words,
14 then you will delight yourself in the LORD,
    and I will make you to ride on the high places of the earth,
    and I will feed you with the heritage of Jacob your father;"
    for the LORD's mouth has spoken it.

59

1 Behold, the LORD's hand is not shortened, that it can't save;
    nor his ear dull, that it can't hear.
2 But your iniquities have separated you and your God,
    and your sins have hidden his face from you,
    so that he will not hear.
3 For your hands are defiled with blood,
    and your fingers with iniquity.
Your lips have spoken lies.
    Your tongue mutters wickedness.
4 No one sues in righteousness,
    and no one pleads in truth.
They trust in vanity
    and speak lies.
They conceive mischief
    and give birth to iniquity.
5 They hatch adders' eggs
    and weave the spider's web.
He who eats of their eggs dies;
    and that which is crushed breaks out into a viper.
6 Their webs won't become garments.
    They won't cover themselves with their works.
Their works are works of iniquity,
    and acts of violence are in their hands.
7 Their feet run to evil,
    and they hurry to shed innocent blood.
Their thoughts are thoughts of iniquity.
    Desolation and destruction are in their paths.
8 They don't know the way of peace;
    and there is no justice in their ways.
They have made crooked paths for themselves;
    whoever goes in them doesn't know peace.

9 Therefore justice is far from us,

ᵃ 57:9 Sheol is the place of the dead.

and righteousness doesn't overtake us.
We look for light, but see darkness;
    for brightness, but we walk in obscurity.
10 We grope for the wall like the blind.
    Yes, we grope as those who have no eyes.
We stumble at noon as if it were twilight.
    Amongst those who are strong, we are like dead men.
11 We all roar like bears
    and moan sadly like doves.
We look for justice, but there is none,
    for salvation, but it is far off from us.

12 For our transgressions are multiplied before you,
    and our sins testify against us;
for our transgressions are with us,
    and as for our iniquities, we know them:
13 transgressing and denying the LORD,
    and turning away from following our God,
    speaking oppression and revolt,
    conceiving and uttering from the heart words of falsehood.
14 Justice is turned away backward,
    and righteousness stands far away;
for truth has fallen in the street,
    and uprightness can't enter.
15 Yes, truth is lacking;
    and he who departs from evil makes himself a prey.

The LORD saw it,
    and it displeased him that there was no justice.
16 He saw that there was no man,
    and wondered that there was no intercessor.
Therefore his own arm brought salvation to him;
    and his righteousness sustained him.
17 He put on righteousness as a breastplate,
    and a helmet of salvation on his head.
He put on garments of vengeance for clothing,
    and was clad with zeal as a mantle.
18 According to their deeds,
    he will repay as appropriate:
    wrath to his adversaries,
    recompense to his enemies.
He will repay the islands their due.
19 So they will fear the LORD's name from the west,
    and his glory from the rising of the sun;
for he will come as a rushing stream,
    which the LORD's breath drives.

20 "A Redeemer will come to Zion,
    and to those who turn from disobedience in Jacob," says the LORD.
    21 "As for me, this is my covenant with them," says the LORD. "My Spirit who is on you, and my words which I have put in your mouth shall not depart out of your mouth, nor out of the mouth of your offspring, nor out of the mouth of your offspring's offspring," says the LORD, "from now on and forever."

60

1 "Arise, shine; for your light has come,
    and the LORD's glory has risen on you!
2 For behold, darkness will cover the earth,
    and thick darkness the peoples;
but the LORD will arise on you,
    and his glory shall be seen on you.
3 Nations will come to your light,
    and kings to the brightness of your rising.

4 "Lift up your eyes all around, and see:
    they all gather themselves together.
    They come to you.
Your sons will come from far away,
    and your daughters will be carried in arms.
5 Then you shall see and be radiant,
    and your heart will thrill and be enlarged;
because the abundance of the sea will be turned to you.
    The wealth of the nations will come to you.
6 A multitude of camels will cover you,
    the dromedaries of Midian and Ephah.
All from Sheba will come.
    They will bring gold and frankincense,
    and will proclaim the praises of the LORD.
7 All the flocks of Kedar will be gathered together to you.
    The rams of Nebaioth will serve you.
They will be accepted as offerings on my altar;
    and I will beautify my glorious house.

8 "Who are these who fly as a cloud,
    and as the doves to their windows?
9 Surely the islands will wait for me,

and the ships of Tarshish first,
to bring your sons from far away,
    their silver and their gold with them,
for the name of the LORD your God,
    and for the Holy One of Israel,
    because he has glorified you.

10 "Foreigners will build up your walls,
    and their kings will serve you;
for in my wrath I struck you,
    but in my favour I have had mercy on you.
11 Your gates also shall be open continually; they shall not be shut day nor night, that men may bring to you the wealth of the nations, and their kings led captive.
12 For that nation and kingdom that will not serve you shall perish; yes, those nations shall be utterly wasted.

13 "The glory of Lebanon shall come to you, the cypress tree, the pine, and the box tree together, to beautify the place of my sanctuary; and I will make the place of my feet glorious.
14 The sons of those who afflicted you will come bowing to you;
    and all those who despised you will bow themselves down at the soles of your feet.
They will call you the LORD's City,
    the Zion of the Holy One of Israel.

15 "Whereas you have been forsaken and hated,
    so that no one passed through you,
I will make you an eternal excellency,
    a joy of many generations.
16 You will also drink the milk of the nations,
    and will nurse from royal breasts.
Then you will know that I, the LORD, am your Saviour,
    your Redeemer,
    the Mighty One of Jacob.
17 For bronze I will bring gold;
    for iron I will bring silver;
    for wood, bronze,
    and for stones, iron.
I will also make peace your governor,
    and righteousness your ruler.
18 Violence shall no more be heard in your land,
    nor desolation or destruction within your borders;
but you will call your walls Salvation,
    and your gates Praise.
19 The sun will be no more your light by day,
    nor will the brightness of the moon give light to you,
but the LORD will be your everlasting light,
    and your God will be your glory.
20 Your sun will not go down any more,
    nor will your moon withdraw itself;
for the LORD will be your everlasting light,
    and the days of your mourning will end.
21 Then your people will all be righteous.
    They will inherit the land forever,
    the branch of my planting,
    the work of my hands,
    that I may be glorified.
22 The little one will become a thousand,
    and the small one a strong nation.
    I, the LORD, will do this quickly in its time."

61

1 The Lord GOD's Spirit is on me,
    because the LORD has anointed me to preach good news to the humble.
He has sent me to bind up the broken hearted,
    to proclaim liberty to the captives
    and release to those who are bound,[a]
2 to proclaim the year of the LORD's favour
    and the day of vengeance of our God,
    to comfort all who mourn,
3 to provide for those who mourn in Zion,
    to give to them a garland for ashes,
    the oil of joy for mourning,
    the garment of praise for the spirit of heaviness,
that they may be called trees of righteousness,
    the planting of the LORD,
    that he may be glorified.

4 They will rebuild the old ruins.
    They will raise up the former devastated places.
They will repair the ruined cities
    that have been devastated for many generations.
5 Strangers will stand and feed your flocks.
    Foreigners will work your fields and your vineyards.
6 But you will be called the LORD's priests.

---

a *61:1* LXX and DSS add: recovery of sight to the blind

Men will call you the servants of our God.
You will eat the wealth of the nations.
   You will boast in their glory.
7 Instead of your shame you will have double.
   Instead of dishonour, they will rejoice in their portion.
Therefore in their land they will possess double.
   Everlasting joy will be to them.
8 "For I, the LORD, love justice.
   I hate robbery and iniquity.
I will give them their reward in truth
   and I will make an everlasting covenant with them.
9 Their offspring will be known amongst the nations,
   and their offspring amongst the peoples.
All who see them will acknowledge them,
   that they are the offspring which the LORD has blessed."

10 I will greatly rejoice in the LORD!
   My soul will be joyful in my God,
for he has clothed me with the garments of salvation.
   He has covered me with the robe of righteousness,
   as a bridegroom decks himself with a garland
   and as a bride adorns herself with her jewels.
11 For as the earth produces its bud,
   and as the garden causes the things that are sown in it to spring up,
   so the Lord GOD will cause righteousness and praise to spring up
      before all the nations.

62

1 For Zion's sake I will not hold my peace,
   and for Jerusalem's sake I will not rest,
until her righteousness shines out like the dawn,
   and her salvation like a burning lamp.
2 The nations will see your righteousness,
   and all kings your glory.
You will be called by a new name,
   which the LORD's mouth will name.
3 You will also be a crown of beauty in the LORD's hand,
   and a royal diadem in your God's hand.
4 You will not be called Forsaken any more,
   nor will your land be called Desolate any more;
but you will be called Hephzibah,[a]
   and your land Beulah;[b]
for the LORD delights in you,
   and your land will be married.
5 For as a young man marries a virgin,
   so your sons will marry you.
As a bridegroom rejoices over his bride,
   so your God will rejoice over you.

6 I have set watchmen on your walls, Jerusalem.
   They will never be silent day nor night.
You who call on the LORD, take no rest,
   7 and give him no rest until he establishes,
   and until he makes Jerusalem a praise in the earth.

8 The LORD has sworn by his right hand,
   and by the arm of his strength,
"Surely I will no more give your grain to be food for your enemies,
   and foreigners will not drink your new wine, for which you have
      laboured,
9 but those who have harvested it will eat it, and praise the LORD.
   Those who have gathered it will drink it in the courts of my
      sanctuary."

10 Go through, go through the gates!
   Prepare the way of the people!
Build up, build up the highway!
   Gather out the stones!
   Lift up a banner for the peoples.
11 Behold, the LORD has proclaimed to the end of the earth:
   "Say to the daughter of Zion,
   'Behold, your salvation comes!
Behold, his reward is with him,
   and his recompense before him!'"
12 They will call them "The Holy People,
   The LORD's Redeemed".
You will be called "Sought Out,
   A City Not Forsaken".

63

1 Who is this who comes from Edom,
   with dyed garments from Bozrah?
Who is this who is glorious in his clothing,
   marching in the greatness of his strength?
"It is I who speak in righteousness,
   mighty to save."
2 Why is your clothing red,
   and your garments like him who treads in the wine vat?

3 "I have trodden the wine press alone.
   Of the peoples, no one was with me.
Yes, I trod them in my anger
   and trampled them in my wrath.
Their lifeblood is sprinkled on my garments,
   and I have stained all my clothing.
4 For the day of vengeance was in my heart,
   and the year of my redeemed has come.
5 I looked, and there was no one to help;
   and I wondered that there was no one to uphold.
Therefore my own arm brought salvation to me.
   My own wrath upheld me.
6 I trod down the peoples in my anger
   and made them drunk in my wrath.
   I poured their lifeblood out on the earth."

7 I will tell of the loving kindnesses of the LORD
   and the praises of the LORD,
   according to all that the LORD has given to us,
and the great goodness towards the house of Israel,
   which he has given to them according to his mercies,
   and according to the multitude of his loving kindnesses.
8 For he said, "Surely, they are my people,
   children who will not deal falsely;"
   so he became their Saviour.
9 In all their affliction he was afflicted,
   and the angel of his presence saved them.
In his love and in his pity he redeemed them.
   He bore them,
   and carried them all the days of old.

10 But they rebelled
   and grieved his Holy Spirit.
Therefore he turned and became their enemy,
   and he himself fought against them.

11 Then he remembered the days of old,
   Moses and his people, saying,
"Where is he who brought them up out of the sea with the shepherds of his
      flock?
   Where is he who put his Holy Spirit amongst them?"
12 Who caused his glorious arm to be at Moses' right hand?
   Who divided the waters before them, to make himself an everlasting
      name?
13 Who led them through the depths,
   like a horse in the wilderness,
   so that they didn't stumble?
14 As the livestock that go down into the valley,
   the LORD's Spirit caused them to rest.
   So you led your people to make yourself a glorious name.

15 Look down from heaven,
   and see from the habitation of your holiness and of your glory.
Where are your zeal and your mighty acts?
   The yearning of your heart and your compassion is restrained towards
      me.
16 For you are our Father,
   though Abraham doesn't know us,
   and Israel does not acknowledge us.
You, LORD, are our Father.
   Our Redeemer from everlasting is your name.
17 O LORD, why do you make us wander from your ways,
   and harden our heart from your fear?
Return for your servants' sake,
   the tribes of your inheritance.
18 Your holy people possessed it but a little while.
   Our adversaries have trodden down your sanctuary.
19 We have become like those over whom you never ruled,
   like those who were not called by your name.

64

1 Oh that you would tear the heavens,
   that you would come down,
   that the mountains might quake at your presence—
2 as when fire kindles the brushwood,
   and the fire causes the water to boil.
Make your name known to your adversaries,
   that the nations may tremble at your presence!
3 When you did awesome things which we didn't look for,
   you came down, and the mountains quaked at your presence.
4 For from of old men have not heard,
   nor perceived by the ear,
   nor has the eye seen a God besides you,
   who works for him who waits for him.
5 You meet him who rejoices and does righteousness,
   those who remember you in your ways.

---

a *62:4 Hephzibah means "I delight in her".*

| b *62:4 Beulah means "married"*

Behold, you were angry, and we sinned.
We have been in sin for a long time.
Shall we be saved?
6 For we have all become like one who is unclean,
and all our righteousness is like a polluted garment.
We all fade like a leaf;
and our iniquities, like the wind, take us away.
7 There is no one who calls on your name,
who stirs himself up to take hold of you;
for you have hidden your face from us,
and have consumed us by means of our iniquities.

8 But now, LORD, you are our Father.
We are the clay and you our potter.
We all are the work of your hand.
9 Don't be furious, LORD.
Don't remember iniquity forever.
Look and see, we beg you,
we are all your people.
10 Your holy cities have become a wilderness.
Zion has become a wilderness,
Jerusalem a desolation.
11 Our holy and our beautiful house where our fathers praised you
is burnt with fire.
All our pleasant places are laid waste.
12 Will you hold yourself back for these things, LORD?
Will you keep silent and punish us very severely?

65

1 "I am enquired of by those who didn't ask.
I am found by those who didn't seek me.
I said, 'See me, see me,' to a nation that was not called by my name.
2 I have spread out my hands all day to a rebellious people,
who walk in a way that is not good,
after their own thoughts;
3 a people who provoke me to my face continually,
sacrificing in gardens,
and burning incense on bricks;
4 who sit amongst the graves,
and spend nights in secret places;
who eat pig's meat,
and broth of abominable things is in their vessels;
5 who say, 'Stay by yourself,
don't come near to me,
for I am holier than you.'
These are smoke in my nose,
a fire that burns all day.

6 "Behold, it is written before me:
I will not keep silence,
but will repay,
yes, I will repay into their bosom
7 your own iniquities and the iniquities of your fathers together", says the LORD,
"who have burnt incense on the mountains,
and blasphemed me on the hills.
Therefore I will first measure their work into their bosom."

8 The LORD says,
"As the new wine is found in the cluster,
and one says, 'Don't destroy it, for a blessing is in it:'
so I will do for my servants' sake,
that I may not destroy them all.
9 I will bring offspring out of Jacob,
and out of Judah an inheritor of my mountains.
My chosen will inherit it,
and my servants will dwell there.
10 Sharon will be a fold of flocks,
and the valley of Achor a place for herds to lie down in,
for my people who have sought me.

11 "But you who forsake the LORD,
who forget my holy mountain,
who prepare a table for Fortune,
and who fill up mixed wine to Destiny;
12 I will destine you to the sword,
and you will all bow down to the slaughter;
because when I called, you didn't answer.
When I spoke, you didn't listen;
but you did that which was evil in my eyes,
and chose that in which I didn't delight."

13 Therefore the Lord GOD says,
"Behold, my servants will eat,
but you will be hungry;
behold, my servants will drink,
but you will be thirsty.
Behold, my servants will rejoice,
but you will be disappointed.
14 Behold, my servants will sing for joy of heart,

but you will cry for sorrow of heart,
and will wail for anguish of spirit.
15 You will leave your name for a curse to my chosen,
and the Lord GOD will kill you.
He will call his servants by another name,
16 so that he who blesses himself in the earth will bless himself in the God of truth;
and he who swears in the earth will swear by the God of truth;
because the former troubles are forgotten,
and because they are hidden from my eyes.

17 "For, behold, I create new heavens and a new earth;
and the former things will not be remembered,
nor come into mind.
18 But be glad and rejoice forever in that which I create;
for, behold, I create Jerusalem to be a delight,
and her people a joy.
19 I will rejoice in Jerusalem,
and delight in my people;
and the voice of weeping and the voice of crying
will be heard in her no more.

20 "No more will there be an infant who only lives a few days,
nor an old man who has not filled his days;
for the child will die one hundred years old,
and the sinner being one hundred years old will be accursed.
21 They will build houses and inhabit them.
They will plant vineyards and eat their fruit.
22 They will not build and another inhabit.
They will not plant and another eat;
for the days of my people will be like the days of a tree,
and my chosen will long enjoy the work of their hands.
23 They will not labour in vain
nor give birth for calamity;
for they are the offspring of the LORD's blessed
and their descendants with them.
24 It will happen that before they call, I will answer;
and while they are yet speaking, I will hear.
25 The wolf and the lamb will feed together.
The lion will eat straw like the ox.
Dust will be the serpent's food.
They will not hurt nor destroy in all my holy mountain,"
says the LORD.

66

1 The LORD says:
"Heaven is my throne, and the earth is my footstool.
What kind of house will you build to me?
Where will I rest?
2 For my hand has made all these things,
and so all these things came to be," says the LORD:
"but I will look to this man,
even to he who is poor and of a contrite spirit,
and who trembles at my word.
3 He who kills an ox is as he who kills a man;
he who sacrifices a lamb, as he who breaks a dog's neck;
he who offers an offering, as he who offers pig's blood;
he who burns frankincense, as he who blesses an idol.
Yes, they have chosen their own ways,
and their soul delights in their abominations.
4 I also will choose their delusions,
and will bring their fears on them;
because when I called, no one answered;
when I spoke, they didn't listen,
but they did that which was evil in my eyes,
and chose that in which I didn't delight."

5 Hear the LORD's word,
you who tremble at his word:
"Your brothers who hate you,
who cast you out for my name's sake, have said,
'Let the LORD be glorified,
that we may see your joy;'
but it is those who shall be disappointed.
6 A voice of tumult from the city,
a voice from the temple,
a voice of the LORD that repays his enemies what they deserve.

7 "Before she travailed, she gave birth.
Before her pain came, she delivered a son.
8 Who has heard of such a thing?
Who has seen such things?
Shall a land be born in one day?
Shall a nation be born at once?
For as soon as Zion travailed,
she gave birth to her children.
9 Shall I bring to the birth, and not cause to be delivered?" says the LORD.
"Shall I who cause to give birth shut the womb?" says your God.

10 "Rejoice with Jerusalem, and be glad for her, all you who love her.

Rejoice for joy with her, all you who mourn over her;
11 that you may nurse and be satisfied at the comforting breasts;
that you may drink deeply,
and be delighted with the abundance of her glory."

12 For the LORD says, "Behold, I will extend peace to her like a river,
and the glory of the nations like an overflowing stream,
and you will nurse.
You will be carried on her side,
and will be dandled on her knees.
13 As one whom his mother comforts,
so I will comfort you.
You will be comforted in Jerusalem."

14 You will see it, and your heart shall rejoice,
and your bones will flourish like the tender grass.
The LORD's hand will be known amongst his servants;
and he will have indignation against his enemies.

15 For, behold, the LORD will come with fire,
and his chariots will be like the whirlwind;
to render his anger with fierceness,
and his rebuke with flames of fire.
16 For the LORD will execute judgement by fire and by his sword on all
flesh;
and those slain by the LORD will be many.
17 "Those who sanctify themselves and purify themselves to go to the
gardens, following one in the middle, eating pig's meat, abominable things,
and the mouse, they shall come to an end together," says the LORD.
18 "For I know their works and their thoughts. The time comes that I
will gather all nations and languages, and they will come, and will see my
glory.
19 "I will set a sign amongst them, and I will send those who escape of
them to the nations, to Tarshish, Pul, and Lud, who draw the bow, to Tubal
and Javan, to far-away islands, who have not heard my fame, nor have seen
my glory; and they shall declare my glory amongst the nations. 20 They
shall bring all your brothers out of all the nations for an offering to the
LORD, on horses, in chariots, in litters, on mules, and on camels, to my
holy mountain Jerusalem, says the LORD, as the children of Israel bring
their offering in a clean vessel into the LORD's house. 21 Of them I will also
select priests and Levites," says the LORD.
22 "For as the new heavens and the new earth, which I will make, shall
remain before me," says the LORD, "so your offspring and your name shall
remain. 23 It shall happen that from one new moon to another, and from one
Sabbath to another, all flesh will come to worship before me," says the
LORD. 24 "They will go out, and look at the dead bodies of the men who
have transgressed against me; for their worm will not die, nor will their fire
be quenched, and they will be loathsome to all mankind."

The Book of Jeremiah

1

1 The words of Jeremiah the son of Hilkiah, one of the priests who were in Anathoth in the land of Benjamin. 2 The LORD's[a] word came to him in the days of Josiah the son of Amon, king of Judah, in the thirteenth year of his reign. 3 It came also in the days of Jehoiakim the son of Josiah, king of Judah, to the end of the eleventh year of Zedekiah, the son of Josiah, king of Judah, to the carrying away of Jerusalem captive in the fifth month.

4 Now the LORD's word came to me, saying,

5 "Before I formed you in the womb, I knew you.

Before you were born, I sanctified you.

I have appointed you a prophet to the nations."

6 Then I said, "Ah, Lord[b] GOD! Behold,[c] I don't know how to speak; for I am a child."

7 But the LORD said to me, "Don't say, 'I am a child;' for you must go to whomever I send you, and you must say whatever I command you. 8 Don't be afraid because of them, for I am with you to rescue you," says the LORD.

9 Then the LORD stretched out his hand and touched my mouth. Then the LORD said to me, "Behold, I have put my words in your mouth. 10 Behold, I have today set you over the nations and over the kingdoms, to uproot and to tear down, to destroy and to overthrow, to build and to plant."

11 Moreover the LORD's word came to me, saying, "Jeremiah, what do you see?"

I said, "I see a branch of an almond tree."

12 Then the LORD said to me, "You have seen well; for I watch over my word to perform it."

13 The LORD's word came to me the second time, saying, "What do you see?"

I said, "I see a boiling cauldron; and it is tipping away from the north."

14 Then the LORD said to me, "Out of the north, evil will break out on all the inhabitants of the land. 15 For behold, I will call all the families of the kingdoms of the north," says the LORD.

"They will come, and they will each set his throne at the entrance of the gates of Jerusalem,

and against all its walls all around, and against all the cities of Judah.

16 I will utter my judgements against them concerning all their wickedness,

in that they have forsaken me,

and have burnt incense to other gods,

and worshipped the works of their own hands.

17 "You therefore put your belt on your waist, arise, and say to them all that I command you. Don't be dismayed at them, lest I dismay you before them. 18 For behold, I have made you today a fortified city, an iron pillar, and bronze walls against the whole land—against the kings of Judah, against its princes, against its priests, and against the people of the land. 19 They will fight against you, but they will not prevail against you; for I am with you", says the LORD, "to rescue you."

2

1 The LORD's word came to me, saying, 2 "Go and proclaim in the ears of Jerusalem, saying, 'The LORD says,

"I remember for you the kindness of your youth,

your love as a bride,

how you went after me in the wilderness,

in a land that was not sown.

3 Israel was holiness to the LORD,

the first fruits of his increase.

All who devour him will be held guilty.

Evil will come on them,"' says the LORD."

4 Hear the LORD's word, O house of Jacob, and all the families of the house of Israel! 5 The LORD says,

"What unrighteousness have your fathers found in me,

that they have gone far from me,

and have walked after worthless vanity,

and have become worthless?

6 They didn't say, 'Where is the LORD who brought us up out of the land of Egypt,

who led us through the wilderness,

through a land of deserts and of pits,

through a land of drought and of the shadow of death,

through a land that no one passed through,

and where no man lived?'

7 I brought you into a plentiful land

to eat its fruit and its goodness;

but when you entered, you defiled my land,

and made my heritage an abomination.

8 The priests didn't say, 'Where is the LORD?'

and those who handle the law didn't know me.

The rulers also transgressed against me,

and the prophets prophesied by Baal

and followed things that do not profit.

9 "Therefore I will yet contend with you," says the LORD,

"and I will contend with your children's children.

10 For pass over to the islands of Kittim, and see.

Send to Kedar, and consider diligently,

and see if there has been such a thing.

11 Has a nation changed its gods,

which really are no gods?

But my people have changed their glory for that which doesn't profit.

12 "Be astonished, you heavens, at this

and be horribly afraid.

Be very desolate," says the LORD.

13 "For my people have committed two evils:

they have forsaken me, the spring of living waters,

and cut out cisterns for themselves: broken cisterns that can't hold water.

14 Is Israel a slave?

Is he born into slavery?

Why has he become a captive?

15 The young lions have roared at him and raised their voices.

They have made his land waste.

His cities are burnt up, without inhabitant.

16 The children also of Memphis and Tahpanhes have broken the crown of your head.

17 "Haven't you brought this on yourself,

in that you have forsaken the LORD your God,[d] when he led you by the way?

18 Now what do you gain by going to Egypt, to drink the waters of the Shihor?

Or why do you go on the way to Assyria, to drink the waters of the River?[e]

19 "Your own wickedness will correct you,

and your backsliding will rebuke you.

Know therefore and see that it is an evil and bitter thing,

that you have forsaken the LORD your God,

and that my fear is not in you," says the Lord, the LORD of Armies.

20 "For long ago I broke off your yoke,

and burst your bonds.

You said, 'I will not serve;'

for on every high hill and under every green tree you bowed yourself,

playing the prostitute.

21 Yet I had planted you a noble vine,

a pure and faithful seed.

How then have you turned into the degenerate branches of a foreign vine to me?

22 For though you wash yourself with lye,

and use much soap,

yet your iniquity is marked before me," says the Lord GOD.

23 "How can you say, 'I am not defiled.

I have not gone after the Baals'?

See your way in the valley.

Know what you have done.

You are a swift dromedary traversing her ways, 24 a wild donkey used to the wilderness, that sniffs the wind in her craving.

When she is in heat, who can turn her away?

All those who seek her will not weary themselves. In her month, they will find her.

25 "Keep your feet from being bare,

and your throat from thirst.

But you said, 'It is in vain.

No, for I have loved strangers,

and I will go after them.'

26 As the thief is ashamed when he is found,

so the house of Israel is ashamed—

they, their kings, their princes, their priests, and their prophets,

27 who tell wood, 'You are my father,'

and a stone, 'You have given birth to me,'

for they have turned their back to me,

and not their face,

but in the time of their trouble they will say, 'Arise, and save us!'

28 "But where are your gods that you have made for yourselves?

Let them arise, if they can save you in the time of your trouble,

for you have as many gods as you have towns, O Judah.

29 "Why will you contend with me?

You all have transgressed against me," says the LORD.

30 "I have struck your children in vain.

They received no correction.

Your own sword has devoured your prophets,

like a destroying lion.

31 Generation, consider the LORD's word.

Have I been a wilderness to Israel?

Or a land of thick darkness?

Why do my people say, 'We have broken loose.

We will come to you no more'?

32 "Can a virgin forget her ornaments,

---

a 1:2 When rendered in ALL CAPITAL LETTERS, "LORD" or "GOD" is the translation of God's Proper Name.

b 1:6 The word translated "Lord" is "Adonai."

c 1:6 "Behold", from "הִנֵּה", means look at, take notice, observe, see, or gaze at. It is often used as an interjection.

d 2:17 The Hebrew word rendered "God" is "אֱלֹהִים" (Elohim).

e 2:18 i.e., the Euphrates River

or a bride her attire?

Yet my people have forgotten me for days without number.

33 How well you prepare your way to seek love!

Therefore you have even taught the wicked women your ways.

34 Also the blood of the souls of the innocent poor is found in your skirts.

You didn't find them breaking in,

but it is because of all these things.

35 "Yet you said, 'I am innocent.

Surely his anger has turned away from me.'

"Behold, I will judge you,

because you say, 'I have not sinned.'

36 Why do you go about so much to change your ways?

You will be ashamed of Egypt also,

as you were ashamed of Assyria.

37 You will also leave that place with your hands on your head;

for the LORD has rejected those in whom you trust,

and you won't prosper with them.

3

1 "They say, 'If a man puts away his wife, and she goes from him, and becomes another man's, should he return to her again?' Wouldn't that land be greatly polluted? But you have played the prostitute with many lovers; yet return again to me," says the LORD.

2 "Lift up your eyes to the bare heights, and see! Where have you not been lain with? You have sat waiting for them by the road, as an Arabian in the wilderness. You have polluted the land with your prostitution and with your wickedness. 3 Therefore the showers have been withheld and there has been no latter rain; yet you have had a prostitute's forehead and you refused to be ashamed. 4 Will you not from this time cry to me, 'My Father, you are the guide of my youth!'?

5 "'Will he retain his anger forever? Will he keep it to the end?' Behold, you have spoken and have done evil things, and have had your way."

6 Moreover, the LORD said to me in the days of Josiah the king, "Have you seen that which backsliding Israel has done? She has gone up on every high mountain and under every green tree, and has played the prostitute there. 7 I said after she had done all these things, 'She will return to me;' but she didn't return, and her treacherous sister Judah saw it. 8 I saw when, for this very cause, that backsliding Israel had committed adultery, I had put her away and given her a certificate of divorce, yet treacherous Judah, her sister, had no fear, but she also went and played the prostitute. 9 Because she took her prostitution lightly, the land was polluted, and she committed adultery with stones and with wood. 10 Yet for all this her treacherous sister, Judah, has not returned to me with her whole heart, but only in pretence," says the LORD.

11 The LORD said to me, "Backsliding Israel has shown herself more righteous than treacherous Judah. 12 Go, and proclaim these words towards the north, and say, 'Return, you backsliding Israel,' says the LORD; 'I will not look in anger on you, for I am merciful,' says the LORD. 'I will not keep anger forever. 13 Only acknowledge your iniquity, that you have transgressed against the LORD your God, and have scattered your ways to the strangers under every green tree, and you have not obeyed my voice,'" says the LORD. 14 "Return, backsliding children," says the LORD, "for I am a husband to you. I will take one of you from a city, and two from a family, and I will bring you to Zion. 15 I will give you shepherds according to my heart, who will feed you with knowledge and understanding. 16 It will come to pass, when you are multiplied and increased in the land in those days," says the LORD, "they will no longer say, 'the ark of the LORD's covenant!' It will not come to mind. They won't remember it. They won't miss it, nor will another be made. 17 At that time they will call Jerusalem 'The LORD's Throne;' and all the nations will be gathered to it, to the LORD's name, to Jerusalem. They will no longer walk after the stubbornness of their evil heart. 18 In those days the house of Judah will walk with the house of Israel, and they will come together out of the land of the north to the land that I gave for an inheritance to your fathers.

19 "But I said, 'How I desire to put you amongst the children, and give you a pleasant land, a goodly heritage of the armies of the nations!' and I said, 'You shall call me "My Father", and shall not turn away from following me.'

20 "Surely as a wife treacherously departs from her husband, so you have dealt treacherously with me, house of Israel," says the LORD. 21 A voice is heard on the bare heights, the weeping and the petitions of the children of Israel; because they have perverted their way, they have forgotten the LORD their God. 22 Return, you backsliding children, and I will heal your backsliding.

"Behold, we have come to you; for you are the LORD our God. 23 Truly help from the hills, the tumult on the mountains, is in vain. Truly the salvation of Israel is in the LORD our God. 24 But the shameful thing has devoured the labour of our fathers from our youth, their flocks and their herds, their sons and their daughters. 25 Let us lie down in our shame, and let our confusion cover us; for we have sinned against the LORD our God, we and our fathers, from our youth even to this day. We have not obeyed the LORD our God's voice."

4

1 "If you will return, Israel," says the LORD, "if you will return to me, and if you will put away your abominations out of my sight; then you will not be removed; 2 and you will swear, 'As the LORD lives,' in truth, in justice, and in righteousness. The nations will bless themselves in him, and they will glory in him."

3 For the LORD says to the men of Judah and to Jerusalem, "Break up your fallow ground, and don't sow amongst thorns. 4 Circumcise yourselves to the LORD, and take away the foreskins of your heart, you men of Judah and inhabitants of Jerusalem; lest my wrath go out like fire, and burn so that no one can quench it, because of the evil of your doings. 5 Declare in Judah, and publish in Jerusalem; and say, 'Blow the trumpet in the land!' Cry aloud and say, 'Assemble yourselves! Let's go into the fortified cities!' 6 Set up a standard towards Zion. Flee for safety! Don't wait; for I will bring evil from the north, and a great destruction."

7 A lion has gone up from his thicket, and a destroyer of nations. He is on his way. He has gone out from his place, to make your land desolate, that your cities be laid waste, without inhabitant. 8 For this, clothe yourself with sackcloth, lament and wail; for the fierce anger of the LORD hasn't turned back from us. 9 "It will happen at that day," says the LORD, "that the heart of the king will perish, along with the heart of the princes. The priests will be astonished, and the prophets will wonder."

10 Then I said, "Ah, Lord GOD! Surely you have greatly deceived this people and Jerusalem, saying, 'You will have peace;' whereas the sword reaches to the heart."

11 At that time it will be said to this people and to Jerusalem, "A hot wind blows from the bare heights in the wilderness towards the daughter of my people, not to winnow, nor to cleanse. 12 A full wind from these will come for me. Now I will also utter judgements against them."

13 Behold, he will come up as clouds, and his chariots will be as the whirlwind. His horses are swifter than eagles. Woe to us! For we are ruined. 14 Jerusalem, wash your heart from wickedness, that you may be saved. How long will your evil thoughts lodge within you? 15 For a voice declares from Dan, and publishes evil from the hills of Ephraim: 16 "Tell the nations, behold, publish against Jerusalem, 'Watchers come from a far country, and raise their voice against the cities of Judah. 17 As keepers of a field, they are against her all around, because she has been rebellious against me,'" says the LORD. 18 "Your way and your doings have brought these things to you. This is your wickedness, for it is bitter, for it reaches to your heart."

19 My anguish, my anguish! I am pained at my very heart! My heart trembles within me. I can't hold my peace, because you have heard, O my soul, the sound of the trumpet, the alarm of war. 20 Destruction on destruction is decreed, for the whole land is laid waste. Suddenly my tents are destroyed, and my curtains gone in a moment. 21 How long will I see the standard and hear the sound of the trumpet?

22 "For my people are foolish. They don't know me. They are foolish children, and they have no understanding. They are skilful in doing evil, but they don't know how to do good." 23 I saw the earth and, behold, it was waste and void, and the heavens, and they had no light. 24 I saw the mountains, and behold, they trembled, and all the hills moved back and forth. 25 I saw, and behold, there was no man, and all the birds of the sky had fled. 26 I saw, and behold, the fruitful field was a wilderness, and all its cities were broken down at the presence of the LORD, before his fierce anger. 27 For the LORD says, "The whole land will be a desolation; yet I will not make a full end. 28 For this the earth will mourn, and the heavens above be black, because I have spoken it. I have planned it, and I have not repented, neither will I turn back from it."

29 Every city flees for the noise of the horsemen and archers. They go into the thickets and climb up on the rocks. Every city is forsaken, and not a man dwells therein. 30 You, when you are made desolate, what will you do? Though you clothe yourself with scarlet, though you deck yourself with ornaments of gold, though you enlarge your eyes with makeup, you make yourself beautiful in vain. Your lovers despise you. They seek your life. 31 For I have heard a voice as of a woman in travail, the anguish as of her who gives birth to her first child, the voice of the daughter of Zion, who gasps for breath, who spreads her hands, saying, "Woe is me now! For my soul faints before the murderers."

5

1 "Run back and forth through the streets of Jerusalem, and see now, and know, and seek in its wide places, if you can find a man, if there is anyone who does justly, who seeks truth; then I will pardon her. 2 Though they say, 'As the LORD lives,' surely they swear falsely."

3 O LORD, don't your eyes look on truth? You have stricken them, but they were not grieved. You have consumed them, but they have refused to receive correction. They have made their faces harder than a rock. They have refused to return.

4 Then I said, "Surely these are poor. They are foolish; for they don't know the LORD's way, nor the law of their God. 5 I will go to the great men and will speak to them, for they know the way of the LORD, and the law of their God." But these with one accord have broken the yoke, and burst the bonds. 6 Therefore a lion out of the forest will kill them. A wolf of the evenings will destroy them. A leopard will watch against their cities. Everyone who goes out there will be torn in pieces, because their transgressions are many and their backsliding has increased.

7 "How can I pardon you? Your children have forsaken me, and sworn by what are no gods. When I had fed them to the full, they committed adultery, and assembled themselves in troops at the prostitutes' houses. 8 They were as fed horses roaming at large. Everyone neighed after his neighbour's wife. 9 Shouldn't I punish them for these things?" says the LORD. "Shouldn't my soul be avenged on such a nation as this?

10 "Go up on her walls, and destroy, but don't make a full end. Take away her branches, for they are not the LORD's. 11 For the house of Israel and the house of Judah have dealt very treacherously against me," says the LORD.

12 They have denied the LORD, and said, "It is not he. Evil won't come on us. We won't see sword or famine. 13 The prophets will become wind, and the word is not in them. Thus it will be done to them."

14 Therefore the LORD, the God of Armies says, "Because you speak this word, behold, I will make my words in your mouth fire, and this people wood, and it will devour them. 15 Behold, I will bring a nation on you from far away, house of Israel," says the LORD. "It is a mighty nation. It is an ancient nation, a nation whose language you don't know and don't understand what they say. 16 Their quiver is an open tomb. They are all mighty men. 17 They will eat up your harvest and your bread, which your sons and your daughters should eat. They will eat up your flocks and your herds. They will eat up your vines and your fig trees. They will beat down your fortified cities in which you trust with the sword.

18 "But even in those days," says the LORD, "I will not make a full end of you. 19 It will happen when you say, 'Why has the LORD our God done all these things to us?' Then you shall say to them, 'Just as you have forsaken me and served foreign gods in your land, so you will serve strangers in a land that is not yours.'

20 "Declare this in the house of Jacob, and publish it in Judah, saying, 21 'Hear this now, foolish people without understanding, who have eyes, and don't see, who have ears, and don't hear: 22 Don't you fear me?' says the LORD; 'Won't you tremble at my presence, who have placed the sand for the bound of the sea by a perpetual decree, that it can't pass it? Though its waves toss themselves, yet they can't prevail. Though they roar, they still can't pass over it.'

23 "But this people has a revolting and a rebellious heart. They have revolted and gone. 24 They don't say in their heart, 'Let's now fear the LORD our God, who gives rain, both the former and the latter, in its season, who preserves to us the appointed weeks of the harvest.'

25 "Your iniquities have turned away these things, and your sins have withheld good from you. 26 For wicked men are found amongst my people. They watch, as fowlers lie in wait. They set a trap. They catch men. 27 As a cage is full of birds, so are their houses full of deceit. Therefore they have become great, and grew rich. 28 They have grown fat. They shine; yes, they excel in deeds of wickedness. They don't plead the cause, the cause of the fatherless, that they may prosper; and they don't defend the rights of the needy.

29 "Shouldn't I punish for these things?" says the LORD. "Shouldn't my soul be avenged on such a nation as this?

30 "An astonishing and horrible thing has happened in the land. 31 The prophets prophesy falsely, and the priests rule by their own authority; and my people love to have it so. What will you do in the end of it?

6

1 "Flee for safety, you children of Benjamin, out of the middle of Jerusalem! Blow the trumpet in Tekoa and raise up a signal on Beth Haccherem, for evil looks out from the north with a great destruction. 2 I will cut off the beautiful and delicate one, the daughter of Zion. 3 Shepherds with their flocks will come to her. They will pitch their tents against her all around. They will feed everyone in his place."

4 "Prepare war against her! Arise! Let's go up at noon. Woe to us! For the day declines, for the shadows of the evening are stretched out. 5 Arise! Let's go up by night, and let's destroy her palaces." 6 For the LORD of Armies said, "Cut down trees, and cast up a mound against Jerusalem. This is the city to be visited. She is filled with oppression within herself. 7 As a well produces its waters, so she produces her wickedness. Violence and destruction is heard in her. Sickness and wounds are continually before me. 8 Be instructed, Jerusalem, lest my soul be alienated from you, lest I make you a desolation, an uninhabited land."

9 The LORD of Armies says, "They will thoroughly glean the remnant of Israel like a vine. Turn again your hand as a grape gatherer into the baskets."

10 To whom should I speak and testify, that they may hear? Behold, their ear is uncircumcised, and they can't listen. Behold, the LORD's word has become a reproach to them. They have no delight in it. 11 Therefore I am full of the LORD's wrath. I am weary with holding it in.

"Pour it out on the children in the street,
and on the assembly of young men together;
for even the husband with the wife will be taken,
the aged with him who is full of days.
12 Their houses will be turned to others,
their fields and their wives together;
for I will stretch out my hand on the inhabitants of the land, says the
LORD."

13 "For from their least even to their greatest, everyone is given to covetousness.
From the prophet even to the priest, everyone deals falsely.
14 They have healed also the hurt of my people superficially,
saying, 'Peace, peace!' when there is no peace.
15 Were they ashamed when they had committed abomination?
No, they were not at all ashamed, neither could they blush.
Therefore they will fall amongst those who fall.
When I visit them, they will be cast down," says the LORD.

16 The LORD says, "Stand in the ways and see, and ask for the old paths, 'Where is the good way?' and walk in it, and you will find rest for your souls. But they said, 'We will not walk in it.' 17 I set watchmen over you, saying, 'Listen to the sound of the trumpet!' But they said, 'We will not

listen!' 18 Therefore hear, you nations, and know, congregation, what is amongst them. 19 Hear, earth! Behold, I will bring evil on this people, even the fruit of their thoughts, because they have not listened to my words; and as for my law, they have rejected it. 20 To what purpose does frankincense from Sheba come to me, and the sweet cane from a far country? Your burnt offerings are not acceptable, and your sacrifices are not pleasing to me."

21 Therefore The LORD says, "Behold, I will lay stumbling blocks before this people. The fathers and the sons together will stumble against them. The neighbour and his friend will perish." 22 The LORD says, "Behold, a people comes from the north country. A great nation will be stirred up from the uttermost parts of the earth. 23 They take hold of bow and spear. They are cruel, and have no mercy. Their voice roars like the sea, and they ride on horses, everyone set in array, as a man to the battle, against you, daughter of Zion."

24 We have heard its report. Our hands become feeble. Anguish has taken hold of us, and pains as of a woman in labour. 25 Don't go out into the field or walk by the way; for the sword of the enemy and terror are on every side. 26 Daughter of my people, clothe yourself with sackcloth, and wallow in ashes! Mourn, as for an only son, most bitter lamentation, for the destroyer will suddenly come on us.

27 "I have made you a tester of metals and a fortress amongst my people, that you may know and try their way. 28 They are all grievous rebels, going around to slander. They are bronze and iron. All of them deal corruptly. 29 The bellows blow fiercely. The lead is consumed in the fire. In vain they go on refining, for the wicked are not plucked away. 30 Men will call them rejected silver, because the LORD has rejected them."

7

1 The word that came to Jeremiah from the LORD, saying, 2 "Stand in the gate of the LORD's house, and proclaim this word there, and say, 'Hear the LORD's word, all you of Judah, who enter in at these gates to worship the LORD.'"

3 The LORD of Armies, the God of Israel says, "Amend your ways and your doings, and I will cause you to dwell in this place. 4 Don't trust in lying words, saying, 'The LORD's temple, the LORD's temple, the LORD's temple, are these.' 5 For if you thoroughly amend your ways and your doings, if you thoroughly execute justice between a man and his neighbour; 6 if you don't oppress the foreigner, the fatherless, and the widow, and don't shed innocent blood in this place, and don't walk after other gods to your own hurt, 7 then I will cause you to dwell in this place, in the land that I gave to your fathers, from of old even forever more. 8 Behold, you trust in lying words that can't profit. 9 Will you steal, murder, commit adultery, swear falsely, burn incense to Baal, and walk after other gods that you have not known, 10 then come and stand before me in this house, which is called by my name, and say, 'We are delivered,' that you may do all these abominations? 11 Has this house, which is called by my name, become a den of robbers in your eyes? Behold, I myself have seen it," says the LORD.

12 "But go now to my place which was in Shiloh, where I caused my name to dwell at the first, and see what I did to it for the wickedness of my people Israel. 13 Now, because you have done all these works," says the LORD, "and I spoke to you, rising up early and speaking, but you didn't hear; and I called you, but you didn't answer; 14 therefore I will do to the house which is called by my name, in which you trust, and to the place which I gave to you and to your fathers, as I did to Shiloh. 15 I will cast you out of my sight, as I have cast out all your brothers, even the whole offspring^a of Ephraim.

16 "Therefore don't pray for this people. Don't lift up a cry or prayer for them or make intercession to me; for I will not hear you. 17 Don't you see what they do in the cities of Judah and in the streets of Jerusalem? 18 The children gather wood, and the fathers kindle the fire, and the women knead the dough, to make cakes to the queen of the sky, and to pour out drink offerings to other gods, that they may provoke me to anger. 19 Do they provoke me to anger?" says the LORD. "Don't they provoke themselves, to the confusion of their own faces?"

20 Therefore the Lord GOD says: "Behold, my anger and my wrath will be poured out on this place, on man, on animal, on the trees of the field, and on the fruit of the ground; and it will burn and will not be quenched."

21 The LORD of Armies, the God of Israel says: "Add your burnt offerings to your sacrifices and eat meat. 22 For I didn't speak to your fathers or command them in the day that I brought them out of the land of Egypt concerning burnt offerings or sacrifices; 23 but this thing I commanded them, saying, 'Listen to my voice, and I will be your God, and you shall be my people. Walk in all the way that I command you, that it may be well with you.' 24 But they didn't listen or turn their ear, but walked in their own counsels and in the stubbornness of their evil heart, and went backward, and not forward. 25 Since the day that your fathers came out of the land of Egypt to this day, I have sent to you all my servants the prophets, daily rising up early and sending them. 26 Yet they didn't listen to me or incline their ear, but made their neck stiff. They did worse than their fathers.

27 "You shall speak all these words to them, but they will not listen to you. You shall also call to them, but they will not answer you. 28 You shall tell them, 'This is the nation that has not listened to the LORD their God's voice, nor received instruction. Truth has perished, and is cut off from their mouth.' 29 Cut off your hair, and throw it away, and take up a lamentation on the bare heights; for the LORD has rejected and forsaken the generation of his wrath.

---

a *7:15* or, seed

30 "For the children of Judah have done that which is evil in my sight," says the LORD. "They have set their abominations in the house which is called by my name, to defile it. 31 They have built the high places of Topheth, which is in the valley of the son of Hinnom, to burn their sons and their daughters in the fire, which I didn't command, nor did it come into my mind. 32 Therefore behold, the days come", says the LORD, "that it will no more be called 'Topheth' or 'The valley of the son of Hinnom', but 'The valley of Slaughter'; for they will bury in Topheth until there is no place to bury. 33 The dead bodies of this people will be food for the birds of the sky, and for the animals of the earth. No one will frighten them away. 34 Then I will cause to cease from the cities of Judah and from the streets of Jerusalem the voice of mirth and the voice of gladness, the voice of the bridegroom and the voice of the bride; for the land will become a waste."

8

1 "At that time," says the LORD, "they will bring the bones of the kings of Judah, the bones of his princes, the bones of the priests, the bones of the prophets, and the bones of the inhabitants of Jerusalem, out of their graves. 2 They will spread them before the sun, the moon, and all the army of the sky, which they have loved, which they have served, after which they have walked, which they have sought, and which they have worshipped. They will not be gathered or be buried. They will be like dung on the surface of the earth. 3 Death will be chosen rather than life by all the residue that remain of this evil family, that remain in all the places where I have driven them," says the LORD of Armies. 4 "Moreover you shall tell them, 'The LORD says:

"'Do men fall, and not rise up again?
    Does one turn away, and not return?
5 Why then have the people of Jerusalem fallen back by a perpetual
        backsliding?
    They cling to deceit.
    They refuse to return.
6 I listened and heard, but they didn't say what is right.
    No one repents of his wickedness, saying, "What have I done?"
Everyone turns to his course,
    as a horse that rushes headlong in the battle.
7 Yes, the stork in the sky knows her appointed times.
    The turtledove, the swallow, and the crane observe the time of their
        coming;
    but my people don't know the LORD's law.

8 "'How do you say, "We are wise, and the LORD's law is with us"?
    But, behold, the false pen of the scribes has made that a lie.
9 The wise men are disappointed.
    They are dismayed and trapped.
Behold, they have rejected the LORD's word.
    What kind of wisdom is in them?
10 Therefore I will give their wives to others
    and their fields to those who will possess them.
For everyone from the least even to the greatest is given to covetousness;
    from the prophet even to the priest everyone deals falsely.
11 They have healed the hurt of the daughter of my people slightly, saying,
    "Peace, peace," when there is no peace.
12 Were they ashamed when they had committed abomination?
    No, they were not at all ashamed.
    They couldn't blush.
Therefore they will fall amongst those who fall.
    In the time of their visitation they will be cast down, says the LORD.

13 "'I will utterly consume them, says the LORD.
    No grapes will be on the vine,
    no figs on the fig tree,
    and the leaf will fade.
The things that I have given them
    will pass away from them.'"

14 "Why do we sit still?
    Assemble yourselves!
    Let's enter into the fortified cities,
    and let's be silent there;
for the LORD our God has put us to silence,
    and given us poisoned water to drink,
    because we have sinned against the LORD.
15 We looked for peace, but no good came;
    and for a time of healing, and behold, dismay!
16 The snorting of his horses is heard from Dan.
    The whole land trembles at the sound of the neighing of his strong
        ones;
for they have come, and have devoured the land and all that is in it,
    the city and those who dwell therein."
17 "For, behold, I will send serpents,
    adders amongst you,
    which will not be charmed;
    and they will bite you," says the LORD.
18 Oh that I could comfort myself against sorrow!
    My heart is faint within me.
19 Behold, the voice of the cry of the daughter of my people from a land that
        is very far off:
    "Isn't the LORD in Zion?
    Isn't her King in her?"

"Why have they provoked me to anger with their engraved images,
    and with foreign idols?"
20 "The harvest is past.
    The summer has ended,
    and we are not saved."
21 For the hurt of the daughter of my people, I am hurt.
    I mourn.
    Dismay has taken hold of me.
22 Is there no balm in Gilead?
    Is there no physician there?
Why then isn't the health of the daughter of my people recovered?

9

1 Oh that my head were waters,
    and my eyes a spring of tears,
that I might weep day and night
    for the slain of the daughter of my people!
2 Oh that I had in the wilderness
    a lodging place of wayfaring men,
that I might leave my people
    and go from them!
For they are all adulterers,
    an assembly of treacherous men.
3 "They bend their tongue,
    as their bow, for falsehood.
They have grown strong in the land,
    but not for truth;
for they proceed from evil to evil,
    and they don't know me," says the LORD.
4 "Everyone beware of his neighbour,
    and don't trust in any brother;
for every brother will utterly supplant,
    and every neighbour will go around like a slanderer.
5 Friends deceive each other,
    and will not speak the truth.
They have taught their tongue to speak lies.
    They weary themselves committing iniquity.
6 Your habitation is in the middle of deceit.
    Through deceit, they refuse to know me," says the LORD.
7 Therefore the LORD of Armies says,
"Behold, I will melt them and test them;
    for how should I deal with the daughter of my people?
8 Their tongue is a deadly arrow.
    It speaks deceit.
One speaks peaceably to his neighbour with his mouth,
    but in his heart, he waits to ambush him.
9 Shouldn't I punish them for these things?" says the LORD.
    "Shouldn't my soul be avenged on a nation such as this?"
10 I will weep and wail for the mountains,
    and lament for the pastures of the wilderness,
because they are burnt up, so that no one passes through;
    Men can't hear the voice of the livestock.
Both the birds of the sky and the animals have fled.
    They are gone.

11 "I will make Jerusalem heaps,
    a dwelling place of jackals.
I will make the cities of Judah a desolation,
    without inhabitant."
12 Who is wise enough to understand this? Who is he to whom the mouth of the LORD has spoken, that he may declare it? Why has the land perished and burnt up like a wilderness, so that no one passes through?
13 The LORD says, "Because they have forsaken my law which I set before them, and have not obeyed my voice or walked in my ways, 14 but have walked after the stubbornness of their own heart and after the Baals, which their fathers taught them." 15 Therefore the LORD of Armies, the God of Israel, says, "Behold, I will feed them, even this people, with wormwood and give them poisoned water to drink. 16 I will scatter them also amongst the nations, whom neither they nor their fathers have known. I will send the sword after them, until I have consumed them."
17 The LORD of Armies says,
"Consider, and call for the mourning women, that they may come.
    Send for the skilful women, that they may come.
18 Let them make haste
    and take up a wailing for us,
that our eyes may run down with tears
    and our eyelids gush out with waters.
19 For a voice of wailing is heard out of Zion,
    'How we are ruined!
We are greatly confounded
    because we have forsaken the land,
    because they have cast down our dwellings.'"

20 Yet hear the LORD's word, you women.
    Let your ear receive the word of his mouth.
Teach your daughters wailing.
    Everyone teach her neighbour a lamentation.

21 For death has come up into our windows.
It has entered into our palaces
to cut off the children from outside,
and the young men from the streets.
22 Speak, "The LORD says,
"'The dead bodies of men will fall as dung on the open field,
and as the handful after the harvester.
No one will gather them.'"
23 The LORD says,
"Don't let the wise man glory in his wisdom.
Don't let the mighty man glory in his might.
Don't let the rich man glory in his riches.
24 But let him who glories glory in this,
that he has understanding, and knows me,
that I am the LORD who exercises loving kindness, justice, and
righteousness in the earth,
for I delight in these things," says the LORD.
25 "Behold, the days come," says the LORD, "that I will punish all those
who are circumcised only in their flesh: 26 Egypt, Judah, Edom, the children
of Ammon, Moab, and all who have the corners of their hair cut off, who
dwell in the wilderness, for all the nations are uncircumcised, and all the
house of Israel are uncircumcised in heart."

10

1 Hear the word which the LORD speaks to you, house of Israel! 2 The
LORD says,
"Don't learn the way of the nations,
and don't be dismayed at the signs of the sky;
for the nations are dismayed at them.
3 For the customs of the peoples are vanity;
for one cuts a tree out of the forest,
the work of the hands of the workman with the axe.
4 They deck it with silver and with gold.
They fasten it with nails and with hammers,
so that it can't move.
5 They are like a palm tree, of turned work,
and don't speak.
They must be carried,
because they can't move.
Don't be afraid of them;
for they can't do evil,
neither is it in them to do good."
6 There is no one like you, LORD.
You are great,
and your name is great in might.
7 Who shouldn't fear you,
King of the nations?
For it belongs to you.
Because amongst all the wise men of the nations,
and in all their royal estate,
there is no one like you.
8 But they are together brutish and foolish,
instructed by idols!
It is just wood.
9 There is silver beaten into plates, which is brought from Tarshish,
and gold from Uphaz,
the work of the engraver and of the hands of the goldsmith.
Their clothing is blue and purple.
They are all the work of skilful men.
10 But the LORD is the true God.
He is the living God,
and an everlasting King.
At his wrath, the earth trembles.
The nations aren't able to withstand his indignation.
11 "You shall say this to them: 'The gods that have not made the
heavens and the earth will perish from the earth, and from under the
heavens.'"
12 God has made the earth by his power.
He has established the world by his wisdom,
and by his understanding has he stretched out the heavens.
13 When he utters his voice,
the waters in the heavens roar,
and he causes the vapours to ascend from the ends of the earth.
He makes lightnings for the rain,
and brings the wind out of his treasuries.
14 Every man has become brutish and without knowledge.
Every goldsmith is disappointed by his engraved image;
for his molten image is falsehood,
and there is no breath in them.
15 They are vanity, a work of delusion.
In the time of their visitation they will perish.
16 The portion of Jacob is not like these;
for he is the maker of all things;
and Israel is the tribe of his inheritance.
The LORD of Armies is his name.
17 Gather up your wares out of the land,
you who live under siege.
18 For the LORD says,
"Behold, I will sling out the inhabitants of the land at this time,
and will distress them, that they may feel it."

19 Woe is me because of my injury!
My wound is serious;
but I said,
"Truly this is my grief, and I must bear it."
20 My tent has been destroyed,
and all my cords are broken.
My children have gone away from me, and they are no more.
There is no one to spread my tent any more,
to set up my curtains.
21 For the shepherds have become brutish,
and have not enquired of the LORD.
Therefore they have not prospered,
and all their flocks have scattered.
22 The voice of news, behold, it comes,
and a great commotion out of the north country,
to make the cities of Judah a desolation,
a dwelling place of jackals.
23 LORD, I know that the way of man is not in himself.
It is not in man who walks to direct his steps.
24 LORD, correct me, but gently;
not in your anger,
lest you reduce me to nothing.
25 Pour out your wrath on the nations that don't know you,
and on the families that don't call on your name;
for they have devoured Jacob.
Yes, they have devoured him, consumed him,
and have laid waste his habitation.

11

1 The word that came to Jeremiah from the LORD, saying, 2 "Hear the
words of this covenant, and speak to the men of Judah, and to the
inhabitants of Jerusalem; 3 and say to them, the LORD, the God of Israel
says: 'Cursed is the man who doesn't hear the words of this covenant, 4
which I commanded your fathers in the day that I brought them out of the
land of Egypt, out of the iron furnace,' saying, 'Obey my voice and do them,
according to all which I command you; so you shall be my people, and I will
be your God; 5 that I may establish the oath which I swore to your fathers,
to give them a land flowing with milk and honey,' as it is today."
Then I answered, and said, "Amen, LORD."
6 The LORD said to me, "Proclaim all these words in the cities of
Judah, and in the streets of Jerusalem, saying, 'Hear the words of this
covenant, and do them. 7 For I earnestly protested to your fathers in the
day that I brought them up out of the land of Egypt, even to this day, rising
early and protesting, saying, "Obey my voice." 8 Yet they didn't obey, nor
turn their ear, but everyone walked in the stubbornness of their evil heart.
Therefore I brought on them all the words of this covenant, which I
commanded them to do, but they didn't do them.'"
9 The LORD said to me, "A conspiracy is found amongst the men of
Judah, and amongst the inhabitants of Jerusalem. 10 They have turned back
to the iniquities of their forefathers, who refused to hear my words. They
have gone after other gods to serve them. The house of Israel and the
house of Judah have broken my covenant which I made with their fathers.
11 Therefore the LORD says, 'Behold, I will bring evil on them which they
will not be able to escape; and they will cry to me, but I will not listen to
them. 12 Then the cities of Judah and the inhabitants of Jerusalem will go
and cry to the gods to which they offer incense, but they will not save them
at all in the time of their trouble. 13 For according to the number of your
cities are your gods, Judah; and according to the number of the streets of
Jerusalem you have set up altars to the shameful thing, even altars to burn
incense to Baal.'
14 "Therefore don't pray for this people. Don't lift up cry or prayer for
them; for I will not hear them in the time that they cry to me because of their
trouble.
15 What has my beloved to do in my house,
since she has behaved lewdly with many,
and the holy flesh has passed from you?
When you do evil,
then you rejoice."

16 The LORD called your name, "A green olive tree,
beautiful with goodly fruit."
With the noise of a great roar he has kindled fire on it,
and its branches are broken.
17 For the LORD of Armies, who planted you, has pronounced evil against
you, because of the evil of the house of Israel and of the house of Judah,
which they have done to themselves in provoking me to anger by offering
incense to Baal.
18 The LORD gave me knowledge of it, and I knew it. Then you showed
me their doings. 19 But I was like a gentle lamb that is led to the slaughter. I
didn't know that they had devised plans against me, saying,
"Let's destroy the tree with its fruit,
and let's cut him off from the land of the living,
that his name may be no more remembered."
20 But, LORD of Armies, who judges righteously,
who tests the heart and the mind,
I will see your vengeance on them;
for to you I have revealed my cause.
21 "Therefore the LORD says concerning the men of Anathoth, who
seek your life, saying, 'You shall not prophesy in the LORD's name, that
you not die by our hand'— 22 therefore the LORD of Armies says, 'Behold, I

will punish them. The young men will die by the sword. Their sons and their daughters will die by famine. 23 There will be no remnant to them, for I will bring evil on the men of Anathoth, even the year of their visitation.'"

12

1 You are righteous, LORD,
　　when I contend with you;
yet I would like to plead a case with you.
　　Why does the way of the wicked prosper?
　　Why are they all at ease who deal very treacherously?
2 You have planted them. Yes, they have taken root.
　　They grow. Yes, they produce fruit.
You are near in their mouth,
　　and far from their heart.
3 But you, LORD, know me.
　　You see me, and test my heart towards you.
Pull them out like sheep for the slaughter,
　　and prepare them for the day of slaughter.
4 How long will the land mourn,
　　and the herbs of the whole country wither?
Because of the wickedness of those who dwell therein,
　　the animals and birds are consumed;
because they said,
　　"He won't see our latter end."
5 "If you have run with the footmen,
　　and they have wearied you,
　　then how can you contend with horses?
Though in a land of peace you are secure,
　　yet how will you do in the pride of the Jordan?
6 For even your brothers, and the house of your father,
　　even they have dealt treacherously with you!
　　Even they have cried aloud after you!
Don't believe them,
　　though they speak beautiful words to you.

7 "I have forsaken my house.
　　I have cast off my heritage.
　　I have given the dearly beloved of my soul into the hand of her enemies.
8 My heritage has become to me as a lion in the forest.
　　She has uttered her voice against me.
　　Therefore I have hated her.
9 Is my heritage to me as a speckled bird of prey?
　　Are the birds of prey against her all around?
Go, assemble all the animals of the field.
　　Bring them to devour.
10 Many shepherds have destroyed my vineyard.
　　They have trodden my portion under foot.
　　They have made my pleasant portion a desolate wilderness.
11 They have made it a desolation.
　　It mourns to me, being desolate.
The whole land is made desolate,
　　because no one cares.
12 Destroyers have come on all the bare heights in the wilderness;
　　for the sword of the LORD devours from the one end of the land even
　　　　to the other end of the land.
　　No flesh has peace.
13 They have sown wheat,
　　and have reaped thorns.
They have exhausted themselves,
　　and profit nothing.
You will be ashamed of your fruits,
　　because of the LORD's fierce anger."

14 The LORD says, "Concerning all my evil neighbours, who touch the inheritance which I have caused my people Israel to inherit: Behold, I will pluck them up from off their land, and will pluck up the house of Judah from amongst them. 15 It will happen that after I have plucked them up, I will return and have compassion on them. I will bring them again, every man to his heritage, and every man to his land. 16 It will happen, if they will diligently learn the ways of my people, to swear by my name, 'As the LORD lives;' even as they taught my people to swear by Baal, then they will be built up in the middle of my people. 17 But if they will not hear, then I will pluck up that nation, plucking up and destroying it," says the LORD.

13

1 The LORD said to me, "Go, and buy yourself a linen belt, and put it on your waist, and don't put it in water." 2 So I bought a belt according to the LORD's word, and put it on my waist. 3 The LORD's word came to me the second time, saying, 4 "Take the belt that you have bought, which is on your waist, and arise, go to the Euphrates, and hide it there in a cleft of the rock." 5 So I went and hid it by the Euphrates, as the LORD commanded me. 6 After many days, the LORD said to me, "Arise, go to the Euphrates, and take the belt from there, which I commanded you to hide there." 7 Then I went to the Euphrates, and dug, and took the belt from the place where I had hidden it; and behold, the belt was ruined. It was profitable for nothing.

8 Then the LORD's word came to me, saying, 9 "The LORD says, 'In this way I will ruin the pride of Judah, and the great pride of Jerusalem. 10 This evil people, who refuse to hear my words, who walk in the stubbornness of their heart, and have gone after other gods to serve them and to worship them, will even be as this belt, which is profitable for nothing. 11 For as the belt clings to the waist of a man, so I have caused the whole house of Israel and the whole house of Judah to cling to me,' says the LORD; 'that they may be to me for a people, for a name, for praise, and for glory; but they would not hear.'

12 "Therefore you shall speak to them this word: 'The LORD, the God of Israel says, "Every container should be filled with wine."' They will tell you, 'Do we not certainly know that every container should be filled with wine?' 13 Then tell them, 'The LORD says, "Behold, I will fill all the inhabitants of this land, even the kings who sit on David's throne, the priests, the prophets, and all the inhabitants of Jerusalem, with drunkenness. 14 I will dash them one against another, even the fathers and the sons together," says the LORD: "I will not pity, spare, or have compassion, that I should not destroy them."'"

15 Hear, and give ear.
　　Don't be proud,
　　for the LORD has spoken.
16 Give glory to the LORD your God,
　　before he causes darkness,
　　and before your feet stumble on the dark mountains,
and while you look for light,
　　he turns it into the shadow of death,
　　and makes it deep darkness.
17 But if you will not hear it,
　　my soul will weep in secret for your pride.
My eye will weep bitterly,
　　and run down with tears,
　　because the LORD's flock has been taken captive.
18 Say to the king and to the queen mother,
　　"Humble yourselves.
Sit down, for your crowns have come down,
　　even the crown of your glory.
19 The cities of the South are shut up,
　　and there is no one to open them.
Judah is carried away captive: all of them.
　　They are wholly carried away captive.
20 Lift up your eyes,
　　and see those who come from the north.
Where is the flock that was given to you,
　　your beautiful flock?
21 What will you say when he sets over you as head those whom you have
　　　　yourself taught to be friends to you?
　　Won't sorrows take hold of you, as of a woman in travail?
22 If you say in your heart,
　　"Why have these things come on me?"
Your skirts are uncovered because of the greatness of your iniquity,
　　and your heels suffer violence.
23 Can the Ethiopian change his skin,
　　or the leopard his spots?
Then may you also do good,
　　who are accustomed to do evil.

24 "Therefore I will scatter them
　　as the stubble that passes away
　　by the wind of the wilderness.
25 This is your lot,
　　the portion measured to you from me," says the LORD,
"because you have forgotten me,
　　and trusted in falsehood."
26 Therefore I will also uncover your skirts on your face,
　　and your shame will appear.
27 I have seen your abominations, even your adulteries
　　and your neighing, the lewdness of your prostitution,
　　on the hills in the field.
Woe to you, Jerusalem!
　　You will not be made clean.
　　How long will it yet be?"

14

1 This is the LORD's word that came to Jeremiah concerning the drought:
2 "Judah mourns,
　　and its gates languish.
They sit in black on the ground.
　　The cry of Jerusalem goes up.
3 Their nobles send their little ones to the waters.
　　They come to the cisterns,
　　and find no water.
They return with their vessels empty.
　　They are disappointed and confounded,
　　and cover their heads.
4 Because of the ground which is cracked,
　　because no rain has been in the land,
the ploughmen are disappointed.
　　They cover their heads.
5 Yes, the doe in the field also calves and forsakes her young,

because there is no grass.
6 The wild donkeys stand on the bare heights.
    They pant for air like jackals.
Their eyes fail,
    because there is no vegetation.
7 Though our iniquities testify against us,
    work for your name's sake, LORD;
for our rebellions are many.
    We have sinned against you.
8 You hope of Israel,
    its Saviour in the time of trouble,
why should you be as a foreigner in the land,
    and as a wayfaring man who turns aside to stay for a night?
9 Why should you be like a scared man,
    as a mighty man who can't save?
Yet you, LORD, are in the middle of us,
    and we are called by your name.
    Don't leave us.
10 The LORD says to this people:
"Even so they have loved to wander.
    They have not restrained their feet.
Therefore the LORD does not accept them.
    Now he will remember their iniquity,
    and punish them for their sins."

11 The LORD said to me, "Don't pray for this people for their good. 12 When they fast, I will not hear their cry; and when they offer burnt offering and meal offering, I will not accept them; but I will consume them by the sword, by famine, and by pestilence." 13 Then I said, "Ah, Lord GOD! Behold, the prophets tell them, 'You will not see the sword, neither will you have famine; but I will give you assured peace in this place.'"

14 Then the LORD said to me, "The prophets prophesy lies in my name. I didn't send them. I didn't command them. I didn't speak to them. They prophesy to you a lying vision, divination, and a thing of nothing, and the deceit of their own heart. 15 Therefore the LORD says concerning the prophets who prophesy in my name, but I didn't send them, yet they say, 'Sword and famine will not be in this land.' Those prophets will be consumed by sword and famine. 16 The people to whom they prophesy will be cast out in the streets of Jerusalem because of the famine and the sword. They will have no one to bury them—them, their wives, their sons, or their daughters, for I will pour their wickedness on them.

17 "You shall say this word to them:
"'Let my eyes run down with tears night and day,
    and let them not cease;
for the virgin daughter of my people is broken with a great breach,
    with a very grievous wound.
18 If I go out into the field,
    then behold, the slain with the sword!
If I enter into the city,
    then behold, those who are sick with famine!
For both the prophet and the priest go about in the land,
    and have no knowledge.'"

19 Have you utterly rejected Judah?
    Has your soul loathed Zion?
Why have you struck us, and there is no healing for us?
    We looked for peace, but no good came;
    and for a time of healing, and behold, dismay!
20 We acknowledge, LORD, our wickedness,
    and the iniquity of our fathers;
    for we have sinned against you.
21 Do not abhor us, for your name's sake.
    Do not disgrace the throne of your glory.
    Remember, and don't break your covenant with us.
22 Are there any amongst the vanities of the nations that can cause rain?
    Or can the sky give showers?
    Aren't you he, the LORD our God?
Therefore we will wait for you;
    for you have made all these things.

15

1 Then the LORD said to me, "Though Moses and Samuel stood before me, yet my mind would not turn towards this people. Cast them out of my sight, and let them go out! 2 It will happen when they ask you, 'Where shall we go out?' then you shall tell them, 'The LORD says:
"Such as are for death, to death;
such as are for the sword, to the sword;
such as are for the famine, to the famine;
and such as are for captivity, to captivity."'

3 "I will appoint over them four kinds," says the LORD: "the sword to kill, the dogs to tear, the birds of the sky, and the animals of the earth, to devour and to destroy. 4 I will cause them to be tossed back and forth amongst all the kingdoms of the earth, because of Manasseh, the son of Hezekiah, king of Judah, for that which he did in Jerusalem.

5 For who will have pity on you, Jerusalem?
    Who will mourn you?
    Who will come to ask of your welfare?
6 You have rejected me," says the LORD.
    "You have gone backward.
Therefore I have stretched out my hand against you

and destroyed you.
    I am weary of showing compassion.
7 I have winnowed them with a fan in the gates of the land.
    I have bereaved them of children.
I have destroyed my people.
    They didn't return from their ways.
8 Their widows are increased more than the sand of the seas.
    I have brought on them against the mother of the young men a
        destroyer at noonday.
    I have caused anguish and terrors to fall on her suddenly.
9 She who has borne seven languishes.
    She has given up the spirit.
Her sun has gone down while it was yet day.
    She has been disappointed and confounded.
    I will deliver their residue to the sword before their enemies," says the
        LORD.

10 Woe is me, my mother, that you have borne me, a man of strife,
    and a man of contention to the whole earth!
I have not lent, neither have men lent to me;
    yet every one of them curses me.
    11 The LORD said,
"Most certainly I will strengthen you for good.
    Most certainly I will cause the enemy to make supplication to you in
        the time of evil
    and in the time of affliction.
12 Can one break iron,
    even iron from the north, and bronze?
13 I will give your substance and your treasures for a plunder without price,
    and that for all your sins,
    even in all your borders.
14 I will make them to pass with your enemies into a land which you don't
        know;
    for a fire is kindled in my anger,
    which will burn on you."

15 LORD, you know.
    Remember me, visit me,
    and avenge me of my persecutors.
You are patient, so don't take me away.
    Know that for your sake I have suffered reproach.
16 Your words were found,
    and I ate them.
Your words were to me a joy and the rejoicing of my heart,
    for I am called by your name, LORD, God of Armies.
17 I didn't sit in the assembly of those who make merry and rejoice.
    I sat alone because of your hand,
    for you have filled me with indignation.
18 Why is my pain perpetual,
    and my wound incurable,
    which refuses to be healed?
Will you indeed be to me as a deceitful brook,
    like waters that fail?
    19 Therefore the LORD says,
"If you return, then I will bring you again,
    that you may stand before me;
and if you take out the precious from the vile,
    you will be as my mouth.
They will return to you,
    but you will not return to them.
20 I will make you to this people a fortified bronze wall.
    They will fight against you,
    but they will not prevail against you;
for I am with you to save you
    and to deliver you," says the LORD.
21 "I will deliver you out of the hand of the wicked,
    and I will redeem you out of the hand of the terrible."

16

1 Then The LORD's word came to me, saying, 2 "You shall not take a wife, neither shall you have sons or daughters, in this place." 3 For the LORD says concerning the sons and concerning the daughters who are born in this place, and concerning their mothers who bore them, and concerning their fathers who became their father in this land: 4 "They will die grievous deaths. They will not be lamented, neither will they be buried. They will be as dung on the surface of the ground. They will be consumed by the sword and by famine. Their dead bodies will be food for the birds of the sky and for the animals of the earth."

5 For the LORD says, "Don't enter into the house of mourning. Don't go to lament. Don't bemoan them, for I have taken away my peace from this people," says the LORD, "even loving kindness and tender mercies. 6 Both great and small will die in this land. They will not be buried. Men won't lament for them, cut themselves, or make themselves bald for them. 7 Men won't break bread for them in mourning, to comfort them for the dead. Men won't give them the cup of consolation to drink for their father or for their mother.

8 "You shall not go into the house of feasting to sit with them, to eat and to drink." 9 For the LORD of Armies, the God of Israel says: "Behold, I will cause to cease out of this place, before your eyes and in your days, the voice of mirth and the voice of gladness, the voice of the bridegroom and

the voice of the bride. 10 It will happen, when you tell this people all these words, and they ask you, 'Why has the LORD pronounced all this great evil against us?' or 'What is our iniquity?' or 'What is our sin that we have committed against the LORD our God?' 11 then you shall tell them, 'Because your fathers have forsaken me,' says the LORD, 'and have walked after other gods, have served them, have worshipped them, have forsaken me, and have not kept my law. 12 You have done evil more than your fathers, for behold, you each walk after the stubbornness of his evil heart, so that you don't listen to me. 13 Therefore I will cast you out of this land into the land that you have not known, neither you nor your fathers. There you will serve other gods day and night, for I will show you no favour.'

14 "Therefore behold, the days come," says the LORD, "that it will no more be said, 'As the LORD lives, who brought up the children of Israel out of the land of Egypt;' 15 but, 'As the LORD lives, who brought up the children of Israel from the land of the north, and from all the countries where he had driven them.' I will bring them again into their land that I gave to their fathers.

16 "Behold, I will send for many fishermen," says the LORD, "and they will fish them up. Afterward I will send for many hunters, and they will hunt them from every mountain, from every hill, and out of the clefts of the rocks. 17 For my eyes are on all their ways. They are not hidden from my face. Their iniquity isn't concealed from my eyes. 18 First I will recompense their iniquity and their sin double, because they have polluted my land with the carcasses of their detestable things, and have filled my inheritance with their abominations."

19 LORD, my strength, my stronghold,
    and my refuge in the day of affliction,
the nations will come to you from the ends of the earth,
    and will say,
"Our fathers have inherited nothing but lies,
    vanity and things in which there is no profit.
20 Should a man make to himself gods
    which yet are no gods?"

21 "Therefore behold, I will cause them to know,
    this once I will cause them to know my hand and my might.
Then they will know that my name is the LORD."

17

1 "The sin of Judah is written with a pen of iron,
    and with the point of a diamond.
It is engraved on the tablet of their heart,
    and on the horns of your altars.
2 Even their children remember their altars
    and their Asherah poles by the green trees on the high hills.
3 My mountain in the field,
    I will give your substance and all your treasures for a plunder,
    and your high places, because of sin, throughout all your borders.
4 You, even of yourself, will discontinue from your heritage that I gave you.
    I will cause you to serve your enemies in the land which you don't
        know,
    for you have kindled a fire in my anger which will burn forever."
5 The LORD says:
"Cursed is the man who trusts in man,
    relies on strength of flesh,
    and whose heart departs from the LORD.
6 For he will be like a bush in the desert,
    and will not see when good comes,
but will inhabit the parched places in the wilderness,
    an uninhabited salt land.

7 "Blessed is the man who trusts in the LORD,
    and whose confidence is in the LORD.
8 For he will be as a tree planted by the waters,
    who spreads out its roots by the river,
and will not fear when heat comes,
    but its leaf will be green,
and will not be concerned in the year of drought.
    It won't cease from yielding fruit.
9 The heart is deceitful above all things
    and it is exceedingly corrupt.
    Who can know it?

10 "I, the LORD, search the mind.
    I try the heart,
even to give every man according to his ways,
    according to the fruit of his doings."

11 As the partridge that sits on eggs which she has not laid,
    so is he who gets riches, and not by right.
In the middle of his days, they will leave him.
    At his end, he will be a fool.
12 A glorious throne, set on high from the beginning,
    is the place of our sanctuary.
13 LORD, the hope of Israel,
    all who forsake you will be disappointed.
Those who depart from me will be written in the earth,
    because they have forsaken the LORD,
    the spring of living waters.

14 Heal me, O LORD, and I will be healed.
    Save me, and I will be saved;
    for you are my praise.
15 Behold, they ask me,
    "Where is the LORD's word?
    Let it be fulfilled now."
16 As for me, I have not hurried from being a shepherd after you.
    I haven't desired the woeful day. You know.
    That which came out of my lips was before your face.
17 Don't be a terror to me.
    You are my refuge in the day of evil.
18 Let them be disappointed who persecute me,
    but don't let me be disappointed.
Let them be dismayed,
    but don't let me be dismayed.
Bring on them the day of evil,
    and destroy them with double destruction.

19 The LORD said this to me: "Go and stand in the gate of the children of the people, through which the kings of Judah come in and by which they go out, and in all the gates of Jerusalem. 20 Tell them, 'Hear the LORD's word, you kings of Judah, all Judah, and all the inhabitants of Jerusalem, that enter in by these gates: 21 The LORD says, "Be careful, and bear no burden on the Sabbath day, nor bring it in by the gates of Jerusalem. 22 Don't carry a burden out of your houses on the Sabbath day. Don't do any work, but make the Sabbath day holy, as I commanded your fathers. 23 But they didn't listen. They didn't turn their ear, but made their neck stiff, that they might not hear, and might not receive instruction. 24 It will happen, if you diligently listen to me," says the LORD, "to bring in no burden through the gates of this city on the Sabbath day, but to make the Sabbath day holy, to do no work therein; 25 then there will enter in by the gates of this city kings and princes sitting on David's throne, riding in chariots and on horses, they and their princes, the men of Judah and the inhabitants of Jerusalem; and this city will remain forever. 26 They will come from the cities of Judah, and from the places around Jerusalem, from the land of Benjamin, from the lowland, from the hill country, and from the South, bringing burnt offerings, sacrifices, meal offerings, and frankincense, and bringing sacrifices of thanksgiving to the LORD's house. 27 But if you will not listen to me to make the Sabbath day holy, and not to bear a burden and enter in at the gates of Jerusalem on the Sabbath day, then I will kindle a fire in its gates, and it will devour the palaces of Jerusalem. It will not be quenched."'"

18

1 The word which came to Jeremiah from the LORD, saying, 2 "Arise, and go down to the potter's house, and there I will cause you to hear my words."

3 Then I went down to the potter's house, and behold, he was making something on the wheels. 4 When the vessel that he made of the clay was marred in the hand of the potter, he made it again another vessel, as seemed good to the potter to make it.

5 Then the LORD's word came to me, saying, 6 "House of Israel, can't I do with you as this potter?" says the LORD. "Behold, as the clay in the potter's hand, so are you in my hand, house of Israel. 7 At the instant I speak concerning a nation, and concerning a kingdom, to pluck up and to break down and to destroy it, 8 if that nation, concerning which I have spoken, turns from their evil, I will repent of the evil that I thought to do to them. 9 At the instant I speak concerning a nation, and concerning a kingdom, to build and to plant it, 10 if they do that which is evil in my sight, that they not obey my voice, then I will repent of the good with which I said I would benefit them.

11 "Now therefore, speak to the men of Judah, and to the inhabitants of Jerusalem, saying, 'The LORD says: "Behold, I frame evil against you, and devise a plan against you. Everyone return from his evil way now, and amend your ways and your doings."'" 12 But they say, 'It is in vain; for we will walk after our own plans, and we will each follow the stubbornness of his evil heart.'"

13 Therefore the LORD says:
"Ask now amongst the nations,
    'Who has heard such things?'
The virgin of Israel has done a very horrible thing.
14 Will the snow of Lebanon fail from the rock of the field?
    Will the cold waters that flow down from afar be dried up?
15 For my people have forgotten me.
    They have burnt incense to false gods.
They have been made to stumble in their ways
    in the ancient paths,
    to walk in byways, in a way not built up,
16 to make their land an astonishment,
    and a perpetual hissing.
Everyone who passes by it will be astonished,
    and shake his head.
17 I will scatter them as with an east wind before the enemy.
    I will show them the back, and not the face,
    in the day of their calamity.

18 Then they said, "Come! Let's devise plans against Jeremiah; for the law won't perish from the priest, nor counsel from the wise, nor the word from the prophet. Come, and let's strike him with the tongue, and let's not give heed to any of his words."

19 Give heed to me, LORD,
    and listen to the voice of those who contend with me.

20 Should evil be recompensed for good?
  For they have dug a pit for my soul.
Remember how I stood before you to speak good for them,
  to turn away your wrath from them.
21 Therefore deliver up their children to the famine,
  and give them over to the power of the sword.
Let their wives become childless and widows.
  Let their men be killed
  and their young men struck by the sword in battle.
22 Let a cry be heard from their houses
  when you bring a troop suddenly on them;
for they have dug a pit to take me
  and hidden snares for my feet.
23 Yet, LORD, you know all their counsel against me to kill me.
  Don't forgive their iniquity.
  Don't blot out their sin from your sight,
Let them be overthrown before you.
  Deal with them in the time of your anger.

19

1 Thus said the LORD, "Go, and buy a potter's earthen container, and take some of the elders of the people and of the elders of the priests; 2 and go out to the valley of the son of Hinnom, which is by the entry of the gate Harsith, and proclaim there the words that I will tell you. 3 Say, 'Hear the LORD's word, kings of Judah and inhabitants of Jerusalem: The LORD of Armies, the God of Israel says, "Behold, I will bring evil on this place, which whoever hears, his ears will tingle. 4 Because they have forsaken me, and have defiled this place, and have burnt incense in it to other gods that they didn't know—they, their fathers, and the kings of Judah—and have filled this place with the blood of innocents, 5 and have built the high places of Baal to burn their children in the fire for burnt offerings to Baal, which I didn't command, nor speak, which didn't even enter into my mind. 6 Therefore, behold, the days come," says the LORD, "that this place will no more be called 'Topheth', nor 'The Valley of the son of Hinnom', but 'The valley of Slaughter'.

7 """I will make the counsel of Judah and Jerusalem void in this place. I will cause them to fall by the sword before their enemies, and by the hand of those who seek their life. I will give their dead bodies to be food for the birds of the sky and for the animals of the earth. 8 I will make this city an astonishment and a hissing. Everyone who passes by it will be astonished and hiss because of all its plagues. 9 I will cause them to eat the flesh of their sons and the flesh of their daughters. They will each eat the flesh of his friend in the siege and in the distress with which their enemies, and those who seek their life, will distress them.'"

10 "Then you shall break the container in the sight of the men who go with you, 11 and shall tell them, 'The LORD of Armies says: "Even so I will break this people and this city as one breaks a potter's vessel, that can't be made whole again. They will bury in Topheth until there is no place to bury. 12 This is what I will do to this place," says the LORD, "and to its inhabitants, even making this city as Topheth. 13 The houses of Jerusalem and the houses of the kings of Judah, which are defiled, will be as the place of Topheth, even all the houses on whose roofs they have burnt incense to all the army of the sky and have poured out drink offerings to other gods."'"

14 Then Jeremiah came from Topheth, where the LORD had sent him to prophesy, and he stood in the court of the LORD's house, and said to all the people: 15 "The LORD of Armies, the God of Israel says, 'Behold, I will bring on this city and on all its towns all the evil that I have pronounced against it, because they have made their neck stiff, that they may not hear my words.'"

20

1 Now Pashhur, the son of Immer the priest, who was chief officer in the LORD's house, heard Jeremiah prophesying these things. 2 Then Pashhur struck Jeremiah the prophet and put him in the stocks that were in the upper gate of Benjamin, which was in the LORD's house. 3 On the next day, Pashhur released Jeremiah out of the stocks. Then Jeremiah said to him, "The LORD has not called your name Pashhur, but Magormissabib.ᵃ 4 For the LORD says, 'Behold, I will make you a terror to yourself and to all your friends. They will fall by the sword of their enemies, and your eyes will see it. I will give all Judah into the hand of the king of Babylon, and he will carry them captive to Babylon, and will kill them with the sword. 5 Moreover I will give all the riches of this city, and all its gains, and all its precious things, yes, I will give all the treasures of the kings of Judah into the hand of their enemies. They will make them captives, take them, and carry them to Babylon. 6 You, Pashhur, and all who dwell in your house will go into captivity. You will come to Babylon, and there you will die, and there you will be buried, you, and all your friends, to whom you have prophesied falsely.'"

7 LORD, you have persuaded me, and I was persuaded.
  You are stronger than I, and have prevailed.
I have become a laughingstock all day.
  Everyone mocks me.
8 For as often as I speak, I cry out;
  I cry, "Violence and destruction!"
because the LORD's word has been made a reproach to me,
  and a derision, all day.
9 If I say that I will not make mention of him,

or speak any more in his name,
then there is in my heart as it were a burning fire shut up in my bones.
  I am weary with holding it in.
  I can't.
10 For I have heard the defaming of many:
  "Terror on every side!
  Denounce, and we will denounce him!"
say all my familiar friends,
  those who watch for my fall.
"Perhaps he will be persuaded,
  and we will prevail against him,
  and we will take our revenge on him."
11 But the LORD is with me as an awesome mighty one.
  Therefore my persecutors will stumble,
  and they won't prevail.
They will be utterly disappointed
  because they have not dealt wisely,
  even with an everlasting dishonour which will never be forgotten.
12 But the LORD of Armies, who tests the righteous,
  who sees the heart and the mind,
let me see your vengeance on them,
  for I have revealed my cause to you.
13 Sing to the LORD!
  Praise the LORD,
  for he has delivered the soul of the needy from the hand of evildoers.
14 Cursed is the day in which I was born.
  Don't let the day in which my mother bore me be blessed.
15 Cursed is the man who brought news to my father, saying,
  "A boy is born to you," making him very glad.
16 Let that man be as the cities which the LORD overthrew,
  and didn't repent.
Let him hear a cry in the morning,
  and shouting at noontime,
17 because he didn't kill me from the womb.
  So my mother would have been my grave,
  and her womb always great.
18 Why did I come out of the womb to see labour and sorrow,
  that my days should be consumed with shame?

21

1 The word which came to Jeremiah from the LORD, when King Zedekiah sent to him Pashhur the son of Malchijah, and Zephaniah the son of Maaseiah, the priest, saying, 2 "Please enquire of the LORD for us; for Nebuchadnezzar king of Babylon makes war against us. Perhaps the LORD will deal with us according to all his wondrous works, that he may withdraw from us."

3 Then Jeremiah said to them, "Tell Zedekiah: 4 'The LORD, the God of Israel says, "Behold, I will turn back the weapons of war that are in your hands, with which you fight against the king of Babylon, and against the Chaldeans who besiege you outside the walls; and I will gather them into the middle of this city. 5 I myself will fight against you with an outstretched hand and with a strong arm, even in anger, in wrath, and in great indignation. 6 I will strike the inhabitants of this city, both man and animal. They will die of a great pestilence. 7 Afterward," says the LORD, "I will deliver Zedekiah king of Judah, his servants, and the people, even those who are left in this city from the pestilence, from the sword, and from the famine, into the hand of Nebuchadnezzar king of Babylon, and into the hand of their enemies, and into the hand of those who seek their life. He will strike them with the edge of the sword. He will not spare them, have pity, or have mercy."'

8 "You shall say to this people, 'The LORD says: "Behold, I set before you the way of life and the way of death. 9 He who remains in this city will die by the sword, by the famine, and by the pestilence, but he who goes out and passes over to the Chaldeans who besiege you, he will live, and he will escape with his life. 10 For I have set my face on this city for evil, and not for good," says the LORD. "It will be given into the hand of the king of Babylon, and he will burn it with fire."'

11 "Concerning the house of the king of Judah, hear the LORD's word:
12 House of David, the LORD says,
'Execute justice in the morning,
  and deliver him who is robbed out of the hand of the oppressor,
lest my wrath go out like fire,
  and burn so that no one can quench it,
  because of the evil of your doings.
13 Behold, I am against you, O inhabitant of the valley,
  and of the rock of the plain,' says the LORD.
'You that say, "Who would come down against us?"
  or, "Who would enter into our homes?"
14 I will punish you according to the fruit of your doings,' says the LORD;
  'and I will kindle a fire in her forest,
  and it will devour all that is around her.'"

22

1 The LORD said, "Go down to the house of the king of Judah, and speak this word there: 2 'Hear the LORD's word, king of Judah, who sits on David's throne—you, your servants, and your people who enter in by these gates. 3 The LORD says: "Execute justice and righteousness, and deliver him who is robbed out of the hand of the oppressor. Do no wrong. Do no

---

ᵃ 20:3 "Magormissabib" means "surrounded by terror"

violence to the foreigner, the fatherless, or the widow. Don't shed innocent blood in this place. 4 For if you do this thing indeed, then kings sitting on David's throne will enter in by the gates of this house, riding in chariots and on horses—they, their servants, and their people. 5 But if you will not hear these words, I swear by myself," says the LORD, "that this house will become a desolation."'"

6 For the LORD says concerning the house of the king of Judah:
"You are Gilead to me,
    the head of Lebanon.
Yet surely I will make you a wilderness,
    cities which are not inhabited.
7 I will prepare destroyers against you,
    everyone with his weapons,
and they will cut down your choice cedars,
    and cast them into the fire.

8 "Many nations will pass by this city, and they will each ask his neighbour, 'Why has the LORD done this to this great city?' 9 Then they will answer, 'Because they abandoned the covenant of the LORD their God, worshipped other gods, and served them.'"

10 Don't weep for the dead.
    Don't bemoan him;
but weep bitterly for him who goes away,
    for he will return no more,
    and not see his native country.

11 For the LORD says touching Shallum the son of Josiah, king of Judah, who reigned instead of Josiah his father, and who went out of this place: "He won't return there any more. 12 But he will die in the place where they have led him captive. He will see this land no more."

13 "Woe to him who builds his house by unrighteousness,
    and his rooms by injustice;
who uses his neighbour's service without wages,
    and doesn't give him his hire;
14 who says, 'I will build myself a wide house and spacious rooms,'
    and cuts out windows for himself,
with a cedar ceiling,
    and painted with red.

15 "Should you reign because you strive to excel in cedar?
    Didn't your father eat and drink,
    and do justice and righteousness?
    Then it was well with him.
16 He judged the cause of the poor and needy;
    so then it was well.
Wasn't this to know me?"
    says the LORD.
17 But your eyes and your heart are only for your covetousness,
    for shedding innocent blood,
    for oppression, and for doing violence."

18 Therefore the LORD says concerning Jehoiakim the son of Josiah, king of Judah:
"They won't lament for him,
    saying, 'Ah my brother!' or, 'Ah sister!'
They won't lament for him,
    saying 'Ah lord!' or, 'Ah his glory!'
19 He will be buried with the burial of a donkey,
    drawn and cast out beyond the gates of Jerusalem."

20 "Go up to Lebanon, and cry out.
    Lift up your voice in Bashan,
and cry from Abarim;
    for all your lovers have been destroyed.
21 I spoke to you in your prosperity,
    but you said, 'I will not listen.'
This has been your way from your youth,
    that you didn't obey my voice.
22 The wind will feed all your shepherds,
    and your lovers will go into captivity.
Surely then you will be ashamed
    and confounded for all your wickedness.
23 Inhabitant of Lebanon,
    who makes your nest in the cedars,
how greatly to be pitied you will be when pangs come on you,
    the pain as of a woman in travail!

24 "As I live," says the LORD, "though Coniah the son of Jehoiakim king of Judah were the signet on my right hand, I would still pluck you from there. 25 I would give you into the hand of those who seek your life, and into the hand of them of whom you are afraid, even into the hand of Nebuchadnezzar king of Babylon, and into the hand of the Chaldeans. 26 I will cast you out with your mother who bore you into another country, where you were not born; and there you will die. 27 But to the land to which their soul longs to return, there they will not return."

28 Is this man Coniah a despised broken vessel?
    Is he a vessel in which no one delights?
Why are they cast out, he and his offspring,
    and cast into a land which they don't know?
29 O earth, earth, earth,
    hear the LORD's word!
30 The LORD says,
    "Record this man as childless,

a man who will not prosper in his days;
for no more will a man of his offspring prosper,
    sitting on David's throne
    and ruling in Judah."

23

1 "Woe to the shepherds who destroy and scatter the sheep of my pasture!" says the LORD. 2 Therefore the LORD, the God of Israel, says against the shepherds who feed my people: "You have scattered my flock, driven them away, and have not visited them. Behold, I will visit on you the evil of your doings," says the LORD. 3 "I will gather the remnant of my flock out of all the countries where I have driven them, and will bring them again to their folds; and they will be fruitful and multiply. 4 I will set up shepherds over them who will feed them. They will no longer be afraid or dismayed, neither will any be lacking," says the LORD.

5 "Behold, the days come," says the LORD,
    "that I will raise to David a righteous Branch;
and he will reign as king and deal wisely,
    and will execute justice and righteousness in the land.
6 In his days Judah will be saved,
    and Israel will dwell safely.
This is his name by which he will be called:
    The LORD our righteousness.

7 "Therefore, behold, the days come," says the LORD, "that they will no more say, 'As the LORD lives, who brought up the children of Israel out of the land of Egypt;' 8 but, 'As the LORD lives, who brought up and who led the offspring of the house of Israel out of the north country, and from all the countries where I had driven them.' Then they will dwell in their own land."

9 Concerning the prophets:
My heart within me is broken.
    All my bones shake.
I am like a drunken man,
    and like a man whom wine has overcome,
because of the LORD,
    and because of his holy words.
10 "For the land is full of adulterers;
    for because of the curse the land mourns.
The pastures of the wilderness have dried up.
    Their course is evil,
    and their might is not right;
11 for both prophet and priest are profane.
    Yes, in my house I have found their wickedness," says the LORD.
12 Therefore their way will be to them as slippery places in the darkness.
    They will be driven on,
    and fall therein;
for I will bring evil on them,
    even the year of their visitation," says the LORD.

13 "I have seen folly in the prophets of Samaria.
    They prophesied by Baal,
    and caused my people Israel to err.
14 In the prophets of Jerusalem I have also seen a horrible thing:
    they commit adultery and walk in lies.
They strengthen the hands of evildoers,
    so that no one returns from his wickedness.
They have all become to me as Sodom,
    and its inhabitants as Gomorrah.
15 Therefore the LORD of Armies says concerning the prophets:
"Behold, I will feed them with wormwood,
    and make them drink poisoned water;
    for from the prophets of Jerusalem ungodliness has gone out into all
        the land."
16 The LORD of Armies says,
"Don't listen to the words of the prophets who prophesy to you.
    They teach you vanity.
    They speak a vision of their own heart,
    and not out of the mouth of the LORD.
17 They say continually to those who despise me,
    'The LORD has said, "You will have peace;"'
and to everyone who walks in the stubbornness of his own heart they say,
    'No evil will come on you.'
18 For who has stood in the council of the LORD,
    that he should perceive and hear his word?
    Who has listened to my word, and heard it?
19 Behold, the LORD's storm, his wrath, has gone out.
    Yes, a whirling storm!
    It will burst on the head of the wicked.
20 The LORD's anger will not return until he has executed
    and performed the intents of his heart.
    In the latter days, you will understand it perfectly.
21 I didn't send these prophets, yet they ran.
    I didn't speak to them, yet they prophesied.
22 But if they had stood in my council,
    then they would have caused my people to hear my words,
and would have turned them from their evil way,
    and from the evil of their doings.

23 "Am I a God at hand," says the LORD,
    "and not a God afar off?
24 Can anyone hide himself in secret places

so that I can't see him?" says the LORD.

"Don't I fill heaven and earth?" says the LORD.

25 "I have heard what the prophets have said, who prophesy lies in my name, saying, 'I had a dream! I had a dream!' 26 How long will this be in the heart of the prophets who prophesy lies, even the prophets of the deceit of their own heart? 27 They intend to cause my people to forget my name by their dreams which they each tell his neighbour, as their fathers forgot my name because of Baal. 28 The prophet who has a dream, let him tell a dream; and he who has my word, let him speak my word faithfully. What is the straw to the wheat?" says the LORD. 29 "Isn't my word like fire?" says the LORD; "and like a hammer that breaks the rock in pieces?

30 "Therefore behold, I am against the prophets," says the LORD, "who each steal my words from his neighbour. 31 Behold, I am against the prophets," says the LORD, "who use their tongues, and say, 'He says.' 32 Behold, I am against those who prophesy lying dreams," says the LORD, "who tell them, and cause my people to err by their lies, and by their vain boasting; yet I didn't send them or command them. They don't profit this people at all," says the LORD.

33 "When this people, or the prophet, or a priest, asks you, saying, 'What is the message from the LORD?' Then you shall tell them, '"What message? I will cast you off," says the LORD.' 34 As for the prophet, the priest, and the people, who say, 'The message from the LORD,' I will even punish that man and his household. 35 You will say everyone to his neighbour, and everyone to his brother, 'What has the LORD answered?' and, 'What has the LORD said?' 36 You will mention the message from the LORD no more, for every man's own word has become his message; for you have perverted the words of the living God, of the LORD of Armies, our God. 37 You will say to the prophet, 'What has the LORD answered you?' and, 'What has the LORD spoken?' 38 Although you say, 'The message from the LORD,' therefore the LORD says: 'Because you say this word, "The message from the LORD," and I have sent to you, telling you not to say, "The message from the LORD," 39 therefore behold, I will utterly forget you, and I will cast you off with the city that I gave to you and to your fathers, away from my presence. 40 I will bring an everlasting reproach on you, and a perpetual shame, which will not be forgotten.'"

24

1 The LORD showed me, and behold, two baskets of figs were set before the LORD's temple, after Nebuchadnezzar king of Babylon had carried away captive Jeconiah the son of Jehoiakim, king of Judah, and the princes of Judah, with the craftsmen and smiths, from Jerusalem, and had brought them to Babylon. 2 One basket had very good figs, like the figs that are first-ripe; and the other basket had very bad figs, which could not be eaten, they were so bad.

3 Then the LORD asked me, "What do you see, Jeremiah?"

I said, "Figs. The good figs are very good, and the bad are very bad, so bad that they can't be eaten."

4 The LORD's word came to me, saying, 5 "The LORD, the God of Israel says: 'Like these good figs, so I will regard the captives of Judah, whom I have sent out of this place into the land of the Chaldeans, as good. 6 For I will set my eyes on them for good, and I will bring them again to this land. I will build them, and not pull them down. I will plant them, and not pluck them up. 7 I will give them a heart to know me, that I am the LORD. They will be my people, and I will be their God; for they will return to me with their whole heart.

8 "'As the bad figs, which can't be eaten, they are so bad,' surely the LORD says, 'So I will give up Zedekiah the king of Judah, and his princes, and the remnant of Jerusalem who remain in this land, and those who dwell in the land of Egypt. 9 I will even give them up to be tossed back and forth amongst all the kingdoms of the earth for evil, to be a reproach and a proverb, a taunt and a curse, in all places where I will drive them. 10 I will send the sword, the famine, and the pestilence amongst them, until they are consumed from off the land that I gave to them and to their fathers.'"

25

1 The word that came to Jeremiah concerning all the people of Judah, in the fourth year of Jehoiakim the son of Josiah, king of Judah (this was the first year of Nebuchadnezzar king of Babylon), 2 which Jeremiah the prophet spoke to all the people of Judah, and to all the inhabitants of Jerusalem: 3 From the thirteenth year of Josiah the son of Amon, king of Judah, even to this day, these twenty-three years, the LORD's word has come to me, and I have spoken to you, rising up early and speaking; but you have not listened.

4 The LORD has sent to you all his servants the prophets, rising up early and sending them (but you have not listened or inclined your ear to hear), 5 saying, "Return now everyone from his evil way, and from the evil of your doings, and dwell in the land that the LORD has given to you and to your fathers, from of old and even forever more. 6 Don't go after other gods to serve them or worship them, and don't provoke me to anger with the work of your hands; then I will do you no harm."

7 "Yet you have not listened to me," says the LORD, "that you may provoke me to anger with the work of your hands to your own hurt."

8 Therefore the LORD of Armies says: "Because you have not heard my words, 9 behold, I will send and take all the families of the north," says the LORD, "and I will send to Nebuchadnezzar the king of Babylon, my servant, and will bring them against this land, and against its inhabitants, and against all these nations around. I will utterly destroy them, and make them an astonishment, and a hissing, and perpetual desolations.

10 Moreover I will take from them the voice of mirth and the voice of gladness, the voice of the bridegroom and the voice of the bride, the sound

of the millstones, and the light of the lamp. 11 This whole land will be a desolation, and an astonishment; and these nations will serve the king of Babylon seventy years.

12 "It will happen, when seventy years are accomplished, that I will punish the king of Babylon and that nation," says the LORD, "for their iniquity. I will make the land of the Chaldeans desolate forever. 13 I will bring on that land all my words which I have pronounced against it, even all that is written in this book, which Jeremiah has prophesied against all the nations. 14 For many nations and great kings will make bondservants of them, even of them. I will recompense them according to their deeds, and according to the work of their hands."

15 For the LORD, the God of Israel, says to me: "Take this cup of the wine of wrath from my hand, and cause all the nations to whom I send you to drink it. 16 They will drink, and reel back and forth, and be insane, because of the sword that I will send amongst them."

17 Then I took the cup at the LORD's hand, and made all the nations to drink, to whom the LORD had sent me: 18 Jerusalem, and the cities of Judah, with its kings and its princes, to make them a desolation, an astonishment, a hissing, and a curse, as it is today; 19 Pharaoh king of Egypt, with his servants, his princes, and all his people; 20 and all the mixed people, and all the kings of the land of Uz, all the kings of the Philistines, Ashkelon, Gaza, Ekron, and the remnant of Ashdod; 21 Edom, Moab, and the children of Ammon; 22 and all the kings of Tyre, all the kings of Sidon, and the kings of the isle which is beyond the sea; 23 Dedan, Tema, Buz, and all who have the corners of their beard cut off; 24 and all the kings of Arabia, all the kings of the mixed people who dwell in the wilderness; 25 and all the kings of Zimri, all the kings of Elam, and all the kings of the Medes; 26 and all the kings of the north, far and near, one with another; and all the kingdoms of the world, which are on the surface of the earth. The king of Sheshach will drink after them.

27 "You shall tell them, 'The LORD of Armies, the God of Israel says: "Drink, and be drunk, vomit, fall, and rise no more, because of the sword which I will send amongst you."' 28 It shall be, if they refuse to take the cup at your hand to drink, then you shall tell them, 'The LORD of Armies says: "You shall surely drink. 29 For, behold, I begin to work evil at the city which is called by my name; and should you be utterly unpunished? You will not be unpunished; for I will call for a sword on all the inhabitants of the earth, says the LORD of Armies."'

30 "Therefore prophesy against them all these words, and tell them,
"'The LORD will roar from on high,
and utter his voice from his holy habitation.
He will mightily roar against his fold.
He will give a shout, as those who tread grapes,
against all the inhabitants of the earth.
31 A noise will come even to the end of the earth;
for the LORD has a controversy with the nations.
He will enter into judgement with all flesh.
As for the wicked, he will give them to the sword,'" says the LORD."
32 The LORD of Armies says,
"Behold, evil will go out from nation to nation,
and a great storm will be raised up from the uttermost parts of the earth."

33 The slain of the LORD will be at that day from one end of the earth even to the other end of the earth. They won't be lamented. They won't be gathered or buried. They will be dung on the surface of the ground.
34 Wail, you shepherds, and cry.
Wallow in dust, you leader of the flock;
for the days of your slaughter and of your dispersions have fully come,
and you will fall like fine pottery.
35 The shepherds will have no way to flee.
The leader of the flock will have no escape.
36 A voice of the cry of the shepherds,
and the wailing of the leader of the flock,
for the LORD destroys their pasture.
37 The peaceful folds are brought to silence
because of the fierce anger of the LORD.
38 He has left his covert, as the lion;
for their land has become an astonishment because of the fierceness
of the oppression,
and because of his fierce anger.

26

1 In the beginning of the reign of Jehoiakim the son of Josiah, king of Judah, this word came from the LORD: 2 "The LORD says: 'Stand in the court of the LORD's house, and speak to all the cities of Judah which come to worship in the LORD's house, all the words that I command you to speak to them. Don't omit a word. 3 It may be they will listen, and every man turn from his evil way, that I may relent from the evil which I intend to do to them because of the evil of their doings.'" 4 You shall tell them, "The LORD says: 'If you will not listen to me, to walk in my law which I have set before you, 5 to listen to the words of my servants the prophets whom I send to you, even rising up early and sending them—but you have not listened— 6 then I will make this house like Shiloh, and will make this city a curse to all the nations of the earth.'"

7 The priests and the prophets and all the people heard Jeremiah speaking these words in the LORD's house. 8 When Jeremiah had finished speaking all that the LORD had commanded him to speak to all the people, the priests and the prophets and all the people seized him, saying, "You shall surely die! 9 Why have you prophesied in the LORD's name, saying, 'This house will be like Shiloh, and this city will be desolate, without

inhabitant'?" All the people were crowded around Jeremiah in the LORD's house.

10 When the princes of Judah heard these things, they came up from the king's house to the LORD's house; and they sat in the entry of the new gate of the LORD's house. 11 Then the priests and the prophets spoke to the princes and to all the people, saying, "This man is worthy of death, for he has prophesied against this city, as you have heard with your ears."

12 Then Jeremiah spoke to all the princes and to all the people, saying, "The LORD sent me to prophesy against this house and against this city all the words that you have heard. 13 Now therefore amend your ways and your doings, and obey the LORD your God's voice; then the LORD will relent from the evil that he has pronounced against you. 14 But as for me, behold, I am in your hand. Do with me what is good and right in your eyes. 15 Only know for certain that if you put me to death, you will bring innocent blood on yourselves, on this city, and on its inhabitants; for in truth the LORD has sent me to you to speak all these words in your ears."

16 Then the princes and all the people said to the priests and to the prophets: "This man is not worthy of death; for he has spoken to us in the name of the LORD our God."

17 Then certain of the elders of the land rose up, and spoke to all the assembly of the people, saying, 18 "Micah the Morashtite prophesied in the days of Hezekiah king of Judah; and he spoke to all the people of Judah, saying, 'The LORD of Armies says:

"'Zion will be ploughed as a field,
    and Jerusalem will become heaps,
    and the mountain of the house as the high places of a forest.'

19 Did Hezekiah king of Judah and all Judah put him to death? Didn't he fear the LORD, and entreat the favour of the LORD, and the LORD relented of the disaster which he had pronounced against them? We would commit great evil against our own souls that way!"

20 There was also a man who prophesied in the LORD's name, Uriah the son of Shemaiah of Kiriath Jearim; and he prophesied against this city and against this land according to all the words of Jeremiah. 21 When Jehoiakim the king, with all his mighty men and all the princes heard his words, the king sought to put him to death; but when Uriah heard it, he was afraid, and fled, and went into Egypt. 22 Then Jehoiakim the king sent Elnathan the son of Achbor and certain men with him into Egypt. 23 They fetched Uriah out of Egypt and brought him to Jehoiakim the king, who killed him with the sword and cast his dead body into the graves of the common people.

24 But the hand of Ahikam the son of Shaphan was with Jeremiah, so that they didn't give him into the hand of the people to put him to death.

27

1 In the beginning of the reign of Jehoiakim the son of Josiah, king of Judah, this word came to Jeremiah from the LORD, saying, 2 the LORD says to me: "Make bonds and bars, and put them on your neck. 3 Then send them to the king of Edom, to the king of Moab, to the king of the children of Ammon, to the king of Tyre, and to the king of Sidon, by the hand of the messengers who come to Jerusalem to Zedekiah king of Judah. 4 Give them a command to their masters, saying, 'The LORD of Armies, the God of Israel says, "You shall tell your masters: 5 'I have made the earth, the men, and the animals that are on the surface of the earth by my great power and by my outstretched arm. I give it to whom it seems right to me. 6 Now I have given all these lands into the hand of Nebuchadnezzar the king of Babylon, my servant. I have also given the animals of the field to him to serve him. 7 All the nations will serve him, his son, and his son's son, until the time of his own land comes. Then many nations and great kings will make him their bondservant.

8 "'"It will happen that I will punish the nation and the kingdom which will not serve the same Nebuchadnezzar king of Babylon, and that will not put their neck under the yoke of the king of Babylon,' says the LORD, 'with the sword, with famine, and with pestilence, until I have consumed them by his hand. 9 But as for you, don't listen to your prophets, to your diviners, to your dreams, to your soothsayers, or to your sorcerers, who speak to you, saying, "You shall not serve the king of Babylon;" 10 for they prophesy a lie to you, to remove you far from your land, so that I would drive you out, and you would perish. 11 But the nation that brings their neck under the yoke of the king of Babylon and serves him, that nation I will let remain in their own land,' says the LORD; 'and they will till it and dwell in it.'"'"

12 I spoke to Zedekiah king of Judah according to all these words, saying, "Bring your necks under the yoke of the king of Babylon, and serve him and his people, and live. 13 Why will you die, you and your people, by the sword, by the famine, and by the pestilence, as the LORD has spoken concerning the nation that will not serve the king of Babylon? 14 Don't listen to the words of the prophets who speak to you, saying, 'You shall not serve the king of Babylon;' for they prophesy a lie to you. 15 For I have not sent them," says the LORD, "but they prophesy falsely in my name; that I may drive you out, and that you may perish, you, and the prophets who prophesy to you."

16 Also I spoke to the priests and to all this people, saying, the LORD says, "Don't listen to the words of your prophets who prophesy to you, saying, 'Behold, the vessels of the LORD's house will now shortly be brought again from Babylon;' for they prophesy a lie to you. 17 Don't listen to them. Serve the king of Babylon, and live. Why should this city become a desolation? 18 But if they are prophets, and if the LORD's word is with them, let them now make intercession to the LORD of Armies, that the vessels which are left in the LORD's house, in the house of the king of Judah, and at Jerusalem, don't go to Babylon. 19 For the LORD of Armies says concerning the pillars, concerning the sea, concerning the bases, and

concerning the rest of the vessels that are left in this city, 20 which Nebuchadnezzar king of Babylon didn't take when he carried away captive Jeconiah the son of Jehoiakim, king of Judah, from Jerusalem to Babylon, and all the nobles of Judah and Jerusalem— 21 yes, the LORD of Armies, the God of Israel, says concerning the vessels that are left in the LORD's house, and in the house of the king of Judah, and at Jerusalem: 22 'They will be carried to Babylon, and there they will be, until the day that I visit them,' says the LORD; 'then I will bring them up, and restore them to this place.'"

28

1 That same year, in the beginning of the reign of Zedekiah king of Judah, in the fourth year, in the fifth month, Hananiah the son of Azzur, the prophet, who was of Gibeon, spoke to me in the LORD's house, in the presence of the priests and of all the people, saying, 2 "The LORD of Armies, the God of Israel, says, 'I have broken the yoke of the king of Babylon. 3 Within two full years I will bring again into this place all the vessels of the LORD's house that Nebuchadnezzar king of Babylon took away from this place and carried to Babylon. 4 I will bring again to this place Jeconiah the son of Jehoiakim, king of Judah, with all the captives of Judah, who went to Babylon,' says the LORD; 'for I will break the yoke of the king of Babylon.'"

5 Then the prophet Jeremiah said to the prophet Hananiah in the presence of the priests, and in the presence of all the people who stood in the LORD's house, 6 even the prophet Jeremiah said, "Amen! May the LORD do so. May the LORD perform your words which you have prophesied, to bring again the vessels of the LORD's house, and all those who are captives, from Babylon to this place. 7 Nevertheless listen now to this word that I speak in your ears, and in the ears of all the people: 8 The prophets who have been before me and before you of old prophesied against many countries, and against great kingdoms, of war, of evil, and of pestilence. 9 As for the prophet who prophesies of peace, when the word of the prophet happens, then the prophet will be known, that the LORD has truly sent him."

10 Then Hananiah the prophet took the bar from off the prophet Jeremiah's neck, and broke it. 11 Hananiah spoke in the presence of all the people, saying, "The LORD says: 'Even so I will break the yoke of Nebuchadnezzar king of Babylon from off the neck of all the nations within two full years.'" Then the prophet Jeremiah went his way.

12 Then the LORD's word came to Jeremiah, after Hananiah the prophet had broken the bar from off the neck of the prophet Jeremiah, saying, 13 "Go, and tell Hananiah, saying, 'The LORD says, "You have broken the bars of wood, but you have made in their place bars of iron." 14 For the LORD of Armies, the God of Israel says, "I have put a yoke of iron on the neck of all these nations, that they may serve Nebuchadnezzar king of Babylon; and they will serve him. I have also given him the animals of the field."'"

15 Then the prophet Jeremiah said to Hananiah the prophet, "Listen, Hananiah! The LORD has not sent you, but you make this people trust in a lie. 16 Therefore the LORD says, 'Behold, I will send you away from off the surface of the earth. This year you will die, because you have spoken rebellion against the LORD.'"

17 So Hananiah the prophet died the same year in the seventh month.

29

1 Now these are the words of the letter that Jeremiah the prophet sent from Jerusalem to the residue of the elders of the captivity, and to the priests, to the prophets, and to all the people whom Nebuchadnezzar had carried away captive from Jerusalem to Babylon, 2 (after Jeconiah the king, the queen mother, the eunuchs, the princes of Judah and Jerusalem, the craftsmen, and the smiths had departed from Jerusalem), 3 by the hand of Elasah the son of Shaphan and Gemariah the son of Hilkiah, (whom Zedekiah king of Judah sent to Babylon to Nebuchadnezzar king of Babylon). It said:

4 The LORD of Armies, the God of Israel, says to all the captives whom I have caused to be carried away captive from Jerusalem to Babylon: 5 "Build houses and dwell in them. Plant gardens and eat their fruit. 6 Take wives and father sons and daughters. Take wives for your sons, and give your daughters to husbands, that they may bear sons and daughters. Multiply there, and don't be diminished. 7 Seek the peace of the city where I have caused you to be carried away captive, and pray to the LORD for it; for in its peace you will have peace." 8 For the LORD of Armies, the God of Israel says: "Don't let your prophets who are amongst you and your diviners deceive you. Don't listen to your dreams which you cause to be dreamt. 9 For they prophesy falsely to you in my name. I have not sent them," says the LORD. 10 For the LORD says, "After seventy years are accomplished for Babylon, I will visit you and perform my good word towards you, in causing you to return to this place. 11 For I know the thoughts that I think towards you," says the LORD, "thoughts of peace, and not of evil, to give you hope and a future. 12 You shall call on me, and you shall go and pray to me, and I will listen to you. 13 You shall seek me and find me, when you search for me with all your heart. 14 I will be found by you," says the LORD, "and I will turn again your captivity, and I will gather you from all the nations, and from all the places where I have driven you, says the LORD. I will bring you again to the place from where I caused you to be carried away captive."

15 Because you have said, "The LORD has raised us up prophets in Babylon," 16 the LORD says concerning the king who

sits on David's throne, and concerning all the people who dwell in this city, your brothers who haven't gone with you into captivity, 17 the LORD of Armies says: "Behold, I will send on them the sword, the famine, and the pestilence, and will make them like rotten figs that can't be eaten, they are so bad. 18 I will pursue after them with the sword, with the famine, and with the pestilence, and will deliver them to be tossed back and forth amongst all the kingdoms of the earth, to be an object of horror, an astonishment, a hissing, and a reproach amongst all the nations where I have driven them, 19 because they have not listened to my words," says the LORD, "with which I sent to them my servants the prophets, rising up early and sending them; but you would not hear," says the LORD.

20 Hear therefore the LORD's word, all you captives whom I have sent away from Jerusalem to Babylon. 21 The LORD of Armies, the God of Israel, says concerning Ahab the son of Kolaiah, and concerning Zedekiah the son of Maaseiah, who prophesy a lie to you in my name: "Behold, I will deliver them into the hand of Nebuchadnezzar king of Babylon; and he will kill them before your eyes. 22 A curse will be taken up about them by all the captives of Judah who are in Babylon, saying, 'The LORD make you like Zedekiah and like Ahab, whom the king of Babylon roasted in the fire;' 23 because they have done foolish things in Israel, and have committed adultery with their neighbours' wives, and have spoken words in my name falsely, which I didn't command them. I am he who knows, and am witness," says the LORD.

24 Concerning Shemaiah the Nehelamite you shall speak, saying, 25 "The LORD of Armies, the God of Israel, says, 'Because you have sent letters in your own name to all the people who are at Jerusalem, and to Zephaniah the son of Maaseiah, the priest, and to all the priests, saying, 26 "The LORD has made you priest in the place of Jehoiada the priest, that there may be officers in the LORD's house, for every man who is crazy and makes himself a prophet, that you should put him in the stocks and in shackles. 27 Now therefore, why have you not rebuked Jeremiah of Anathoth, who makes himself a prophet to you, 28 because he has sent to us in Babylon, saying, The captivity is long. Build houses, and dwell in them. Plant gardens, and eat their fruit?"'"

29 Zephaniah the priest read this letter in the hearing of Jeremiah the prophet. 30 Then the LORD's word came to Jeremiah, saying, 31 "Send to all of the captives, saying, 'The LORD says concerning Shemaiah the Nehelamite: "Because Shemaiah has prophesied to you, and I didn't send him, and he has caused you to trust in a lie," 32 therefore the LORD says, "Behold, I will punish Shemaiah the Nehelamite and his offspring. He will not have a man to dwell amongst this people. He won't see the good that I will do to my people," says the LORD, "because he has spoken rebellion against the LORD."'"

30

1 The word that came to Jeremiah from the LORD, saying, 2 "The LORD, the God of Israel, says, 'Write all the words that I have spoken to you in a book. 3 For, behold, the days come,' says the LORD, 'that I will reverse the captivity of my people Israel and Judah,' says the LORD. 'I will cause them to return to the land that I gave to their fathers, and they will possess it.'"

4 These are the words that the LORD spoke concerning Israel and concerning Judah. 5 For the LORD says:
"We have heard a voice of trembling;
 a voice of fear, and not of peace.
6 Ask now, and see whether a man travails with child.
 Why do I see every man with his hands on his waist, as a woman in travail,
 and all faces are turned pale?
7 Alas, for that day is great, so that none is like it!
 It is even the time of Jacob's trouble;
 but he will be saved out of it.
8 It will come to pass in that day, says the LORD of Armies, that I will break his yoke from off your neck,
 and will burst your bonds.
Strangers will no more make them their bondservants;
9 but they will serve the LORD their God,
 and David their king,
 whom I will raise up to them.
10 Therefore don't be afraid, O Jacob my servant, says the LORD.
 Don't be dismayed, Israel.
For, behold, I will save you from afar,
 and save your offspring from the land of their captivity.
Jacob will return,
 and will be quiet and at ease.
 No one will make him afraid.
11 For I am with you, says the LORD, to save you;
 for I will make a full end of all the nations where I have scattered you,
 but I will not make a full end of you;
but I will correct you in measure,
 and will in no way leave you unpunished."
12 For the LORD says,
"Your hurt is incurable.
 Your wound is grievous.
13 There is no one to plead your cause,
 that you may be bound up.

You have no healing medicines.
14 All your lovers have forgotten you.
 They don't seek you.
For I have wounded you with the wound of an enemy,
 with the chastisement of a cruel one,
for the greatness of your iniquity,
 because your sins were increased.
15 Why do you cry over your injury?
 Your pain is incurable.
For the greatness of your iniquity,
 because your sins have increased,
 I have done these things to you.
16 Therefore all those who devour you will be devoured.
 All your adversaries, everyone of them, will go into captivity.
Those who plunder you will be plunder.
 I will make all who prey on you become prey.
17 For I will restore health to you,
 and I will heal you of your wounds," says the LORD,
"because they have called you an outcast,
 saying, 'It is Zion, whom no man seeks after.'"
18 The LORD says:
"Behold, I will reverse the captivity of Jacob's tents,
 and have compassion on his dwelling places.
The city will be built on its own hill,
 and the palace will be inhabited in its own place.
19 Thanksgiving will proceed out of them
 with the voice of those who make merry.
I will multiply them,
 and they will not be few;
I will also glorify them,
 and they will not be small.
20 Their children also will be as before,
 and their congregation will be established before me.
 I will punish all who oppress them.
21 Their prince will be one of them,
 and their ruler will proceed from amongst them.
I will cause him to draw near,
 and he will approach me;
 for who is he who has had boldness to approach me?" says the LORD.
22 "You shall be my people,
 and I will be your God.
23 Behold, the LORD's storm, his wrath, has gone out,
 a sweeping storm;
 it will burst on the head of the wicked.
24 The fierce anger of the LORD will not return until he has accomplished,
 and until he has performed the intentions of his heart.
In the latter days you will understand it."

31

1 "At that time," says the LORD, "I will be the God of all the families of Israel, and they will be my people."

2 The LORD says, "The people who survive the sword found favour in the wilderness; even Israel, when I went to cause him to rest."

3 The LORD appeared of old to me, saying,
"Yes, I have loved you with an everlasting love.
 Therefore I have drawn you with loving kindness.
4 I will build you again,
 and you will be built, O virgin of Israel.
You will again be adorned with your tambourines,
 and will go out in the dances of those who make merry.
5 Again you will plant vineyards on the mountains of Samaria.
 The planters will plant,
 and will enjoy its fruit.
6 For there will be a day that the watchmen on the hills of Ephraim cry,
 'Arise! Let's go up to Zion to the LORD our God.'"
7 For the LORD says,
"Sing with gladness for Jacob,
 and shout for the chief of the nations.
Publish, praise, and say,
 'LORD, save your people,
 the remnant of Israel!'
8 Behold, I will bring them from the north country,
 and gather them from the uttermost parts of the earth,
along with the blind and the lame,
 the woman with child and her who travails with child together.
 They will return as a great company.
9 They will come with weeping.
 I will lead them with petitions.
I will cause them to walk by rivers of waters,
 in a straight way in which they won't stumble;
for I am a father to Israel.
 Ephraim is my firstborn.

10 "Hear the LORD's word, you nations,
 and declare it in the distant islands. Say,
'He who scattered Israel will gather him,
 and keep him, as a shepherd does his flock.'
11 For the LORD has ransomed Jacob,
 and redeemed him from the hand of him who was stronger than he.

12 They will come and sing in the height of Zion,
and will flow to the goodness of the LORD,
to the grain, to the new wine, to the oil,
and to the young of the flock and of the herd.
Their soul will be as a watered garden.
They will not sorrow any more at all.
13 Then the virgin will rejoice in the dance,
the young men and the old together;
for I will turn their mourning into joy,
and will comfort them, and make them rejoice from their sorrow.
14 I will satiate the soul of the priests with fatness,
and my people will be satisfied with my goodness," says the LORD.

15 The LORD says:
"A voice is heard in Ramah,
lamentation and bitter weeping,
Rachel weeping for her children.
She refuses to be comforted for her children,
because they are no more."
16 The LORD says:
"Refrain your voice from weeping,
and your eyes from tears,
for your work will be rewarded," says the LORD.
"They will come again from the land of the enemy.
17 There is hope for your latter end," says the LORD.
"Your children will come again to their own territory.

18 "I have surely heard Ephraim grieving thus,
'You have chastised me,
and I was chastised, as an untrained calf.
Turn me, and I will be turned,
for you are the LORD my God.
19 Surely after that I was turned.
I repented.
After that I was instructed.
I struck my thigh.
I was ashamed, yes, even confounded,
because I bore the reproach of my youth.'
20 Is Ephraim my dear son?
Is he a darling child?
For as often as I speak against him,
I still earnestly remember him.
Therefore my heart yearns for him.
I will surely have mercy on him," says the LORD.

21 "Set up road signs.
Make guideposts.
Set your heart towards the highway,
even the way by which you went.
Turn again, virgin of Israel.
Turn again to these your cities.
22 How long will you go here and there,
you backsliding daughter?
For the LORD has created a new thing in the earth:
a woman will encompass a man."

23 The LORD of Armies, the God of Israel, says: "Yet again they will use this speech in the land of Judah and in its cities, when I reverse their captivity: 'The LORD bless you, habitation of righteousness, mountain of holiness.' 24 Judah and all its cities will dwell therein together, the farmers, and those who go about with flocks. 25 For I have satiated the weary soul, and I have replenished every sorrowful soul."

26 On this I awakened, and saw; and my sleep was sweet to me.

27 "Behold, the days come," says the LORD, "that I will sow the house of Israel and the house of Judah with the seed of man and with the seed of animal. 28 It will happen that, like as I have watched over them to pluck up and to break down and to overthrow and to destroy and to afflict, so I will watch over them to build and to plant," says the LORD. 29 "In those days they will say no more,

"'The fathers have eaten sour grapes,
and the children's teeth are set on edge.'

30 But everyone will die for his own iniquity. Every man who eats the sour grapes, his teeth will be set on edge.

31 "Behold, the days come," says the LORD, "that I will make a new covenant with the house of Israel, and with the house of Judah, 32 not according to the covenant that I made with their fathers in the day that I took them by the hand to bring them out of the land of Egypt, which covenant of mine they broke, although I was a husband to them," says the LORD. 33 "But this is the covenant that I will make with the house of Israel after those days," says the LORD:

"I will put my law in their inward parts,
and I will write it in their heart.
I will be their God,
and they shall be my people.

34 They will no longer each teach his neighbour,
and every man teach his brother, saying, 'Know the LORD;'
for they will all know me,

from their least to their greatest," says the LORD,
"for I will forgive their iniquity,
and I will remember their sin no more."

35 The LORD, who gives the sun for a light by day,
and the ordinances of the moon and of the stars for a light by night,
who stirs up the sea, so that its waves roar—
the LORD of Armies is his name, says:
36 "If these ordinances depart from before me," says the LORD,
"then the offspring of Israel also will cease from being a nation before me forever."
37 The LORD says: "If heaven above can be measured,
and the foundations of the earth searched out beneath,
then I will also cast off all the offspring of Israel for all that they have done," says the LORD.

38 "Behold, the days come," says the LORD, "that the city will be built to the LORD from the tower of Hananel to the gate of the corner. 39 The measuring line will go out further straight onward to the hill Gareb, and will turn towards Goah. 40 The whole valley of the dead bodies and of the ashes, and all the fields to the brook Kidron, to the corner of the horse gate towards the east, will be holy to the LORD. It will not be plucked up or thrown down any more forever."

32

1 This is the word that came to Jeremiah from the LORD in the tenth year of Zedekiah king of Judah, which was the eighteenth year of Nebuchadnezzar. 2 Now at that time the king of Babylon's army was besieging Jerusalem. Jeremiah the prophet was shut up in the court of the guard, which was in the king of Judah's house.

3 For Zedekiah king of Judah had shut him up, saying, "Why do you prophesy, and say, 'The LORD says, "Behold, I will give this city into the hand of the king of Babylon, and he will take it; 4 and Zedekiah king of Judah won't escape out of the hand of the Chaldeans, but will surely be delivered into the hand of the king of Babylon, and will speak with him mouth to mouth, and his eyes will see his eyes; 5 and he will bring Zedekiah to Babylon, and he will be there until I visit him," says the LORD, "though you fight with the Chaldeans, you will not prosper"'?"

6 Jeremiah said, "The LORD's word came to me, saying, 7 'Behold, Hanamel the son of Shallum your uncle will come to you, saying, "Buy my field that is in Anathoth; for the right of redemption is yours to buy it."'"

8 "So Hanamel my uncle's son came to me in the court of the guard according to the LORD's word, and said to me, 'Please buy my field that is in Anathoth, which is in the land of Benjamin; for the right of inheritance is yours, and the redemption is yours. Buy it for yourself.'

"Then I knew that this was the LORD's word. 9 I bought the field that was in Anathoth of Hanamel my uncle's son, and weighed him the money, even seventeen shekels[a] of silver. 10 I signed the deed, sealed it, called witnesses, and weighed the money in the balances to him. 11 So I took the deed of the purchase, both that which was sealed, containing the terms and conditions, and that which was open; 12 and I delivered the deed of the purchase to Baruch the son of Neriah, the son of Mahseiah, in the presence of Hanamel my uncle's son, and in the presence of the witnesses who signed the deed of the purchase, before all the Jews who sat in the court of the guard.

13 "I commanded Baruch before them, saying, 14 the LORD of Armies, the God of Israel, says: 'Take these deeds, this deed of the purchase which is sealed, and this deed which is open, and put them in an earthen vessel, that they may last many days.' 15 For the LORD of Armies, the God of Israel says: 'Houses and fields and vineyards will yet again be bought in this land.'

16 Now after I had delivered the deed of the purchase to Baruch the son of Neriah, I prayed to the LORD, saying,

17 "Ah Lord GOD! Behold, you have made the heavens and the earth by your great power and by your outstretched arm. There is nothing too hard for you. 18 You show loving kindness to thousands, and repay the iniquity of the fathers into the bosom of their children after them. The great, the mighty God, the LORD of Armies is your name: 19 great in counsel, and mighty in work; whose eyes are open to all the ways of the children of men, to give everyone according to his ways, and according to the fruit of his doings; 20 who performed signs and wonders in the land of Egypt, even to this day, both in Israel and amongst other men; and made yourself a name, as it is today; 21 and brought your people Israel out of the land of Egypt with signs, with wonders, with a strong hand, with an outstretched arm, and with great terror; 22 and gave them this land, which you swore to their fathers to give them, a land flowing with milk and honey. 23 They came in and possessed it, but they didn't obey your voice and didn't walk in your law. They have done nothing of all that you commanded them to do. Therefore you have caused all this evil to come upon them.

24 "Behold, siege ramps have been built against the city to take it. The city is given into the hand of the Chaldeans who fight against it, because of the sword, of the famine, and of the pestilence. What you have spoken has happened. Behold, you see it. 25 You have said to me, Lord GOD, 'Buy the field for

---

a *32:9* A shekel is about 10 grams or about 0.35 ounces.

money, and call witnesses;' whereas the city is given into the hand of the Chaldeans."

26 Then the LORD's word came to Jeremiah, saying, 27 "Behold, I am the LORD, the God of all flesh. Is there anything too hard for me? 28 Therefore the LORD says: Behold, I will give this city into the hand of the Chaldeans, and into the hand of Nebuchadnezzar king of Babylon, and he will take it. 29 The Chaldeans, who fight against this city, will come and set this city on fire, and burn it with the houses on whose roofs they have offered incense to Baal, and poured out drink offerings to other gods, to provoke me to anger.

30 "For the children of Israel and the children of Judah have done only that which was evil in my sight from their youth; for the children of Israel have only provoked me to anger with the work of their hands, says the LORD. 31 For this city has been to me a provocation of my anger and of my wrath from the day that they built it even to this day, so that I should remove it from before my face, 32 because of all the evil of the children of Israel and of the children of Judah, which they have done to provoke me to anger—they, their kings, their princes, their priests, their prophets, the men of Judah, and the inhabitants of Jerusalem. 33 They have turned their backs to me, and not their faces. Although I taught them, rising up early and teaching them, yet they have not listened to receive instruction. 34 But they set their abominations in the house which is called by my name, to defile it. 35 They built the high places of Baal, which are in the valley of the son of Hinnom, to cause their sons and their daughters to pass through fire to Molech, which I didn't command them. It didn't even come into my mind, that they should do this abomination, to cause Judah to sin."

36 Now therefore the LORD, the God of Israel, says concerning this city, about which you say, "It is given into the hand of the king of Babylon by the sword, by the famine, and by the pestilence:" 37 "Behold, I will gather them out of all the countries where I have driven them in my anger, and in my wrath, and in great indignation; and I will bring them again to this place. I will cause them to dwell safely. 38 Then they will be my people, and I will be their God. 39 I will give them one heart and one way, that they may fear me forever, for their good and the good of their children after them. 40 I will make an everlasting covenant with them, that I will not turn away from following them, to do them good. I will put my fear in their hearts, that they may not depart from me. 41 Yes, I will rejoice over them to do them good, and I will plant them in this land assuredly with my whole heart and with my whole soul."

42 For the LORD says: "Just as I have brought all this great evil on this people, so I will bring on them all the good that I have promised them. 43 Fields will be bought in this land, about which you say, 'It is desolate, without man or animal. It is given into the hand of the Chaldeans.' 44 Men will buy fields for money, sign the deeds, seal them, and call witnesses, in the land of Benjamin, and in the places around Jerusalem, in the cities of Judah, in the cities of the hill country, in the cities of the lowland, and in the cities of the South; for I will cause their captivity to be reversed," says the LORD.

33

1 Moreover the LORD's word came to Jeremiah the second time, while he was still locked up in the court of the guard, saying, 2 "The LORD who does it, the LORD who forms it to establish it—the LORD is his name, says: 3 'Call to me, and I will answer you, and will show you great and difficult things, which you don't know.' 4 For the LORD, the God of Israel, says concerning the houses of this city and concerning the houses of the kings of Judah, which are broken down to make a defence against the mounds and against the sword: 5 'While men come to fight with the Chaldeans, and to fill them with the dead bodies of men, whom I have killed in my anger and in my wrath, and for all whose wickedness I have hidden my face from this city, 6 behold, I will bring it health and healing, and I will cure them; and I will reveal to them abundance of peace and truth. 7 I will restore the fortunes of Judah and Israel, and will build them as at the first. 8 I will cleanse them from all their iniquity by which they have sinned against me. I will pardon all their iniquities by which they have sinned against me and by which they have transgressed against me. 9 This city will be to me for a name of joy, for praise, and for glory, before all the nations of the earth, which will hear all the good that I do to them, and they will fear and tremble for all the good and for all the peace that I provide to it.'"

10 The LORD says: "Yet again there will be heard in this place, about which you say, 'It is waste, without man and without animal, even in the cities of Judah, and in the streets of Jerusalem, that are desolate, without man and without inhabitant and without animal,' 11 the voice of joy and the voice of gladness, the voice of the bridegroom and the voice of the bride, the voice of those who say, 'Give thanks to the LORD of Armies, for the LORD is good, for his loving kindness endures forever;' who bring thanksgiving into the LORD's house. For I will cause the captivity of the land to be reversed as at the first," says the LORD.

12 The LORD of Armies says: "Yet again there will be in this place, which is waste, without man and without animal, and in all its cities, a habitation of shepherds causing their flocks to lie down. 13 In the cities of the hill country, in the cities of the lowland, in the cities of the South, in the land of Benjamin, in the places around Jerusalem, and in the cities of Judah, the flocks will again pass under the hands of him who counts them," says the LORD.

14 "Behold, the days come," says the LORD, "that I will perform that good word which I have spoken concerning the house of Israel and concerning the house of Judah.

15 "In those days and at that time,
  I will cause a Branch of righteousness to grow up to David.

He will execute justice and righteousness in the land.
16 In those days Judah will be saved,
  and Jerusalem will dwell safely.
This is the name by which she will be called:
  The LORD our righteousness."

17 For the LORD says: "David will never lack a man to sit on the throne of the house of Israel. 18 The Levitical priests won't lack a man before me to offer burnt offerings, to burn meal offerings, and to do sacrifice continually."

19 The LORD's word came to Jeremiah, saying, 20 "The LORD says: 'If you can break my covenant of the day and my covenant of the night, so that there will not be day and night in their time, 21 then my covenant could also be broken with David my servant, that he won't have a son to reign on his throne; and with the Levitical priests, my ministers. 22 As the army of the sky can't be counted, and the sand of the sea can't be measured, so I will multiply the offspring of David my servant and the Levites who minister to me.'"

23 The LORD's word came to Jeremiah, saying, 24 "Don't consider what this people has spoken, saying, 'Has the LORD cast off the two families which he chose?' Thus they despise my people, that they should be no more a nation before them." 25 The LORD says: "If my covenant of day and night fails, if I have not appointed the ordinances of heaven and earth, 26 then I will also cast away the offspring of Jacob, and of David my servant, so that I will not take of his offspring to be rulers over the offspring of Abraham, Isaac, and Jacob; for I will cause their captivity to be reversed and will have mercy on them."

34

1 The word which came to Jeremiah from the LORD, when Nebuchadnezzar king of Babylon, with all his army, all the kingdoms of the earth that were under his dominion, and all the peoples, were fighting against Jerusalem and against all its cities, saying: 2 "The LORD, the God of Israel, says, 'Go, and speak to Zedekiah king of Judah, and tell him, the LORD says, "Behold, I will give this city into the hand of the king of Babylon and he will burn it with fire. 3 You won't escape out of his hand, but will surely be taken and delivered into his hand. Your eyes will see the eyes of the king of Babylon, and he will speak with you mouth to mouth. You will go to Babylon."'

4 "Yet hear the LORD's word, O Zedekiah king of Judah. The LORD says concerning you, 'You won't die by the sword. 5 You will die in peace; and with the burnings of your fathers, the former kings who were before you, so they will make a burning for you. They will lament you, saying, "Ah Lord!" for I have spoken the word,' says the LORD."

6 Then Jeremiah the prophet spoke all these words to Zedekiah king of Judah in Jerusalem, 7 when the king of Babylon's army was fighting against Jerusalem and against all the cities of Judah that were left, against Lachish and against Azekah; for these alone remained of the cities of Judah as fortified cities.

8 The word came to Jeremiah from the LORD, after King Zedekiah had made a covenant with all the people who were at Jerusalem, to proclaim liberty to them, 9 that every man should let his male servant, and every man his female servant, who is a Hebrew or a Hebrewess, go free, that no one should make bondservants of them, of a Jew his brother. 10 All the princes and all the people obeyed who had entered into the covenant, that everyone should let his male servant and everyone his female servant go free, that no one should make bondservants of them any more. They obeyed and let them go, 11 but afterwards they turned, and caused the servants and the handmaids whom they had let go free to return, and brought them into subjection for servants and for handmaids.

12 Therefore the LORD's word came to Jeremiah from the LORD, saying, 13 "The LORD, the God of Israel, says: 'I made a covenant with your fathers in the day that I brought them out of the land of Egypt, out of the house of bondage, saying: 14 At the end of seven years, every man of you shall release his brother who is a Hebrew, who has been sold to you, and has served you six years. You shall let him go free from you. But your fathers didn't listen to me, and didn't incline their ear. 15 You had now turned, and had done that which is right in my eyes, in every man proclaiming liberty to his neighbour. You had made a covenant before me in the house which is called by my name; 16 but you turned and profaned my name, and every man caused his servant and every man his handmaid, whom you had let go free at their pleasure, to return. You brought them into subjection, to be to you for servants and for handmaids.'"

17 Therefore the LORD says: "You have not listened to me, to proclaim liberty, every man to his brother, and every man to his neighbour. Behold, I proclaim to you a liberty," says the LORD, "to the sword, to the pestilence, and to the famine. I will make you to be tossed back and forth amongst all the kingdoms of the earth. 18 I will give the men who have transgressed my covenant, who have not performed the words of the covenant which they made before me when they cut the calf in two and passed between its parts: 19 the princes of Judah, the princes of Jerusalem, the eunuchs, the priests, and all the people of the land, who passed between the parts of the calf. 20 I will even give them into the hand of their enemies and into the hand of those who seek their life. Their dead bodies will be food for the birds of the sky and for the animals of the earth.

21 "I will give Zedekiah king of Judah and his princes into the hands of their enemies, into the hands of those who seek their life and into the hands of the king of Babylon's army, who has gone away from you. 22 Behold, I will command," says the LORD, "and cause them to return to this city. They will fight against it, take it, and burn it with fire. I will make the cities of Judah a desolation, without inhabitant."

35

1 The word which came to Jeremiah from the LORD in the days of Jehoiakim the son of Josiah, king of Judah, saying, 2 "Go to the house of the Rechabites, and speak to them, and bring them into the LORD's house, into one of the rooms, and give them wine to drink."

3 Then I took Jaazaniah the son of Jeremiah, the son of Habazziniah, with his brothers, all his sons, and the whole house of the Rechabites; 4 and I brought them into the LORD's house, into the room of the sons of Hanan the son of Igdaliah, the man of God, which was by the room of the princes, which was above the room of Maaseiah the son of Shallum, the keeper of the threshold. 5 I set before the sons of the house of the Rechabites bowls full of wine, and cups; and I said to them, "Drink wine!"

6 But they said, "We will drink no wine; for Jonadab the son of Rechab, our father, commanded us, saying, 'You shall drink no wine, neither you nor your children, forever. 7 You shall not build a house, sow seed, plant a vineyard, or have any; but all your days you shall dwell in tents, that you may live many days in the land in which you live as nomads.' 8 We have obeyed the voice of Jonadab the son of Rechab, our father, in all that he commanded us, to drink no wine all our days, we, our wives, our sons, or our daughters; 9 and not to build houses for ourselves to dwell in. We have no vineyard, field, or seed; 10 but we have lived in tents, and have obeyed, and done according to all that Jonadab our father commanded us. 11 But when Nebuchadnezzar king of Babylon came up into the land, we said, 'Come! Let's go to Jerusalem for fear of the army of the Chaldeans, and for fear of the army of the Syrians; so we will dwell at Jerusalem.'"

12 Then the LORD's word came to Jeremiah, saying, 13 "The LORD of Armies, the God of Israel, says: 'Go and tell the men of Judah and the inhabitants of Jerusalem, "Will you not receive instruction to listen to my words?" says the LORD. 14 "The words of Jonadab the son of Rechab that he commanded his sons, not to drink wine, are performed; and to this day they drink none, for they obey their father's commandment; but I have spoken to you, rising up early and speaking, and you have not listened to me. 15 I have sent also to you all my servants the prophets, rising up early and sending them, saying, 'Every one of you must return now from his evil way, amend your doings, and don't go after other gods to serve them. Then you will dwell in the land which I have given to you and to your fathers;' but you have not inclined your ear, nor listened to me. 16 The sons of Jonadab the son of Rechab have performed the commandment of their father which he commanded them, but this people has not listened to me.'"

17 "Therefore the LORD, the God of Armies, the God of Israel, says: 'Behold, I will bring on Judah and on all the inhabitants of Jerusalem all the evil that I have pronounced against them, because I have spoken to them, but they have not heard; and I have called to them, but they have not answered.'"

18 Jeremiah said to the house of the Rechabites, "The LORD of Armies, the God of Israel, says: 'Because you have obeyed the commandment of Jonadab your father, and kept all his precepts, and done according to all that he commanded you,' 19 therefore the LORD of Armies, the God of Israel, says: 'Jonadab the son of Rechab will not lack a man to stand before me forever.'"

36

1 In the fourth year of Jehoiakim the son of Josiah, king of Judah, this word came to Jeremiah from the LORD, saying, 2 "Take a scroll of a book, and write in it all the words that I have spoken to you against Israel, against Judah, and against all the nations, from the day I spoke to you, from the days of Josiah even to this day. 3 It may be that the house of Judah will hear all the evil which I intend to do to them, that they may each return from his evil way; that I may forgive their iniquity and their sin."

4 Then Jeremiah called Baruch the son of Neriah; and Baruch wrote from the mouth of Jeremiah all the LORD's words, which he had spoken to him, on a scroll of a book. 5 Jeremiah commanded Baruch, saying, "I am restricted. I can't go into the LORD's house. 6 Therefore you go, and read from the scroll which you have written from my mouth, the LORD's words, in the ears of the people in the LORD's house on the fast day. Also you shall read them in the ears of all Judah who come out of their cities. 7 It may be they will present their supplication before the LORD, and will each return from his evil way; for the LORD has pronounced great anger and wrath against this people."

8 Baruch the son of Neriah did according to all that Jeremiah the prophet commanded him, reading in the book the LORD's words in the LORD's house. 9 Now in the fifth year of Jehoiakim the son of Josiah, king of Judah, in the ninth month, all the people in Jerusalem and all the people who came from the cities of Judah to Jerusalem, proclaimed a fast before the LORD. 10 Then Baruch read the words of Jeremiah from the book in the LORD's house, in the room of Gemariah the son of Shaphan the scribe, in the upper court, at the entry of the new gate of the LORD's house, in the ears of all the people.

11 When Micaiah the son of Gemariah, the son of Shaphan, had heard out of the book all the LORD's words, 12 he went down into the king's house, into the scribe's room; and behold, all the princes were sitting there, Elishama the scribe, Delaiah the son of Shemaiah, Elnathan the son of Achbor, Gemariah the son of Shaphan, Zedekiah the son of Hananiah, and all the princes. 13 Then Micaiah declared to them all the words that he had heard, when Baruch read the book in the ears of the people. 14 Therefore all the princes sent Jehudi the son of Nethaniah, the son of Shelemiah, the son of Cushi, to Baruch, saying, "Take in your hand the scroll in which you have read in the ears of the people, and come."

So Baruch the son of Neriah took the scroll in his hand, and came to them. 15 They said to him, "Sit down now, and read it in our hearing."

So Baruch read it in their hearing.

16 Now when they had heard all the words, they turned in fear one towards another, and said to Baruch, "We will surely tell the king of all these words." 17 They asked Baruch, saying, "Tell us now, how did you write all these words at his mouth?"

18 Then Baruch answered them, "He dictated all these words to me with his mouth, and I wrote them with ink in the book."

19 Then the princes said to Baruch, "You and Jeremiah go hide. Don't let anyone know where you are."

20 They went in to the king into the court, but they had laid up the scroll in the room of Elishama the scribe. Then they told all the words in the hearing of the king. 21 So the king sent Jehudi to get the scroll, and he took it out of the room of Elishama the scribe. Jehudi read it in the hearing of the king, and in the hearing of all the princes who stood beside the king. 22 Now the king was sitting in the winter house in the ninth month, and there was a fire in the brazier burning before him. 23 When Jehudi had read three or four columns, the king cut it with the penknife, and cast it into the fire that was in the brazier, until all the scroll was consumed in the fire that was in the brazier. 24 The king and his servants who heard all these words were not afraid, and didn't tear their garments. 25 Moreover Elnathan and Delaiah and Gemariah had made intercession to the king that he would not burn the scroll; but he would not listen to them. 26 The king commanded Jerahmeel the king's son, and Seraiah the son of Azriel, and Shelemiah the son of Abdeel, to arrest Baruch the scribe and Jeremiah the prophet; but the LORD hid them.

27 Then the LORD's word came to Jeremiah, after the king had burnt the scroll, and the words which Baruch wrote at the mouth of Jeremiah, saying, 28 "Take again another scroll, and write in it all the former words that were in the first scroll, which Jehoiakim the king of Judah has burnt. 29 Concerning Jehoiakim king of Judah you shall say, 'The LORD says: "You have burnt this scroll, saying, 'Why have you written therein, saying, "The king of Babylon will certainly come and destroy this land, and will cause to cease from there man and animal"?'" 30 Therefore the LORD says concerning Jehoiakim king of Judah: "He will have no one to sit on David's throne. His dead body will be cast out in the day to the heat, and in the night to the frost. 31 I will punish him, his offspring, and his servants for their iniquity. I will bring on them, on the inhabitants of Jerusalem, and on the men of Judah, all the evil that I have pronounced against them, but they didn't listen."'"

32 Then Jeremiah took another scroll, and gave it to Baruch the scribe, the son of Neriah, who wrote therein from the mouth of Jeremiah all the words of the book which Jehoiakim king of Judah had burnt in the fire; and many similar words were added to them.

37

1 Zedekiah the son of Josiah reigned as king instead of Coniah the son of Jehoiakim, whom Nebuchadnezzar king of Babylon made king in the land of Judah. 2 But neither he, nor his servants, nor the people of the land, listened to the LORD's words, which he spoke by the prophet Jeremiah.

3 Zedekiah the king sent Jehucal the son of Shelemiah and Zephaniah the son of Maaseiah, the priest, to the prophet Jeremiah, saying, "Pray now to the LORD our God for us."

4 Now Jeremiah came in and went out amongst the people, for they had not put him into prison. 5 Pharaoh's army had come out of Egypt; and when the Chaldeans who were besieging Jerusalem heard news of them, they withdrew from Jerusalem.

6 Then the LORD's word came to the prophet Jeremiah, saying, 7 "The LORD, the God of Israel, says, 'You shall tell the king of Judah, who sent you to me to enquire of me: "Behold, Pharaoh's army, which has come out to help you, will return to Egypt into their own land. 8 The Chaldeans will come again, and fight against this city. They will take it and burn it with fire."'

9 "The LORD says, 'Don't deceive yourselves, saying, "The Chaldeans will surely depart from us;" for they will not depart. 10 For though you had struck the whole army of the Chaldeans who fight against you, and only wounded men remained amongst them, they would each rise up in his tent and burn this city with fire.'"

11 When the army of the Chaldeans had withdrawn from Jerusalem for fear of Pharaoh's army, 12 then Jeremiah went out of Jerusalem to go into the land of Benjamin, to receive his portion there, in the middle of the people. 13 When he was in Benjamin's gate, a captain of the guard was there, whose name was Irijah, the son of Shelemiah, the son of Hananiah; and he seized Jeremiah the prophet, saying, "You are defecting to the Chaldeans!"

14 Then Jeremiah said, "That is false! I am not defecting to the Chaldeans."

But he didn't listen to him; so Irijah seized Jeremiah, and brought him to the princes. 15 The princes were angry with Jeremiah, and struck him, and put him in prison in the house of Jonathan the scribe; for they had made that the prison.

16 When Jeremiah had come into the dungeon house and into the cells, and Jeremiah had remained there many days, 17 then Zedekiah the king sent and had him brought out. The king asked him secretly in his house, "Is there any word from the LORD?"

Jeremiah said, "There is." He also said, "You will be delivered into the hand of the king of Babylon."

18 Moreover Jeremiah said to King Zedekiah, "How have I sinned against you, against your servants, or against this people, that you have

put me in prison? 19 Now where are your prophets who prophesied to you, saying, 'The king of Babylon will not come against you, nor against this land'? 20 Now please hear, my lord the king: please let my supplication be presented before you, that you not cause me to return to the house of Jonathan the scribe, lest I die there."

21 Then Zedekiah the king commanded, and they committed Jeremiah into the court of the guard. They gave him daily a loaf of bread out of the bakers' street, until all the bread in the city was gone. Thus Jeremiah remained in the court of the guard.

38

1 Shephatiah the son of Mattan, Gedaliah the son of Pashhur, Jucal the son of Shelemiah, and Pashhur the son of Malchijah heard the words that Jeremiah spoke to all the people, saying, 2 "The LORD says, 'He who remains in this city will die by the sword, by the famine, and by the pestilence, but he who goes out to the Chaldeans will live. He will escape with his life and he will live.' 3 The LORD says, 'This city will surely be given into the hand of the army of the king of Babylon, and he will take it.'"

4 Then the princes said to the king, "Please let this man be put to death, because he weakens the hands of the men of war who remain in this city, and the hands of all the people, in speaking such words to them; for this man doesn't seek the welfare of this people, but harm."

5 Zedekiah the king said, "Behold, he is in your hand; for the king can't do anything to oppose you."

6 Then they took Jeremiah and threw him into the dungeon of Malchijah the king's son, that was in the court of the guard. They let down Jeremiah with cords. In the dungeon there was no water, but mire; and Jeremiah sank in the mire.

7 Now when Ebedmelech the Ethiopian, a eunuch, who was in the king's house, heard that they had put Jeremiah in the dungeon (the king was then sitting in Benjamin's gate), 8 Ebedmelech went out of the king's house, and spoke to the king, saying, 9 "My lord the king, these men have done evil in all that they have done to Jeremiah the prophet, whom they have cast into the dungeon. He is likely to die in the place where he is, because of the famine; for there is no more bread in the city."

10 Then the king commanded Ebedmelech the Ethiopian, saying, "Take from here thirty men with you, and take up Jeremiah the prophet out of the dungeon, before he dies."

11 So Ebedmelech took the men with him, and went into the house of the king under the treasury, and took from there rags and worn-out garments, and let them down by cords into the dungeon to Jeremiah. 12 Ebedmelech the Ethiopian said to Jeremiah, "Now put these rags and worn-out garments under your armpits under the cords." Jeremiah did so. 13 So they lifted Jeremiah up with the cords, and took him up out of the dungeon; and Jeremiah remained in the court of the guard.

14 Then Zedekiah the king sent and took Jeremiah the prophet to himself into the third entry that is in the LORD's house. Then the king said to Jeremiah, "I will ask you something. Hide nothing from me."

15 Then Jeremiah said to Zedekiah, "If I declare it to you, will you not surely put me to death? If I give you counsel, you will not listen to me."

16 So Zedekiah the king swore secretly to Jeremiah, saying, "As the LORD lives, who made our souls, I will not put you to death, neither will I give you into the hand of these men who seek your life."

17 Then Jeremiah said to Zedekiah, "The LORD, the God of Armies, the God of Israel, says: 'If you will go out to the king of Babylon's princes, then your soul will live, and this city will not be burnt with fire. You will live, along with your house. 18 But if you will not go out to the king of Babylon's princes, then this city will be given into the hand of the Chaldeans, and they will burn it with fire, and you won't escape out of their hand.'"

19 Zedekiah the king said to Jeremiah, "I am afraid of the Jews who have defected to the Chaldeans, lest they deliver me into their hand, and they mock me."

20 But Jeremiah said, "They won't deliver you. Obey, I beg you, the LORD's voice, in that which I speak to you; so it will be well with you, and your soul will live. 21 But if you refuse to go out, this is the word that the LORD has shown me: 22 'Behold, all the women who are left in the king of Judah's house will be brought out to the king of Babylon's princes, and those women will say,
"Your familiar friends have turned on you,
    and have prevailed over you.
Your feet are sunk in the mire,
    they have turned away from you.'"

23 They will bring out all your wives and your children to the Chaldeans. You won't escape out of their hand, but will be taken by the hand of the king of Babylon. You will cause this city to be burnt with fire.'"

24 Then Zedekiah said to Jeremiah, "Let no man know of these words, and you won't die. 25 But if the princes hear that I have talked with you, and they come to you, and tell you, 'Declare to us now what you have said to the king; don't hide it from us, and we will not put you to death; also tell us what the king said to you;' 26 then you shall tell them, 'I presented my supplication before the king, that he would not cause me to return to Jonathan's house, to die there.'"

27 Then all the princes came to Jeremiah, and asked him; and he told them according to all these words that the king had commanded. So they stopped speaking with him, for the matter was not perceived.

28 So Jeremiah stayed in the court of the guard until the day that Jerusalem was taken.

39

1 In the ninth year of Zedekiah king of Judah, in the tenth month, Nebuchadnezzar king of Babylon and all his army came against Jerusalem, and besieged it. 2 In the eleventh year of Zedekiah, in the fourth month, the ninth day of the month, a breach was made in the city. 3 All the princes of the king of Babylon came in, and sat in the middle gate: Nergal Sharezer, Samgarnebo, Sarsechim the Rabsaris, Nergal Sharezer the Rabmag, with all the rest of the princes of the king of Babylon. 4 When Zedekiah the king of Judah and all the men of war saw them, then they fled and went out of the city by night, by the way of the king's garden, through the gate between the two walls; and he went out towards the Arabah.

5 But the army of the Chaldeans pursued them, and overtook Zedekiah in the plains of Jericho. When they had taken him, they brought him up to Nebuchadnezzar king of Babylon to Riblah in the land of Hamath; and he pronounced judgement on him. 6 Then the king of Babylon killed Zedekiah's sons in Riblah before his eyes. The king of Babylon also killed all the nobles of Judah. 7 Moreover he put out Zedekiah's eyes and bound him in fetters, to carry him to Babylon.

8 The Chaldeans burnt the king's house and the people's houses with fire and broke down the walls of Jerusalem. 9 Then Nebuzaradan the captain of the guard carried away captive into Babylon the rest of the people who remained in the city, the deserters also who fell away to him, and the rest of the people who remained. 10 But Nebuzaradan the captain of the guard left of the poor of the people, who had nothing, in the land of Judah, and gave them vineyards and fields at the same time.

11 Now Nebuchadnezzar king of Babylon commanded Nebuzaradan the captain of the guard concerning Jeremiah, saying, 12 "Take him and take care of him. Do him no harm; but do to him even as he tells you."

13 So Nebuzaradan the captain of the guard, Nebushazban, Rabsaris, and Nergal Sharezer, Rabmag, and all the chief officers of the king of Babylon 14 sent and took Jeremiah out of the court of the guard, and committed him to Gedaliah the son of Ahikam, the son of Shaphan, that he should bring him home. So he lived amongst the people.

15 Now the LORD's word came to Jeremiah while he was shut up in the court of the guard, saying, 16 "Go, and speak to Ebedmelech the Ethiopian, saying, 'The LORD of Armies, the God of Israel, says: "Behold, I will bring my words on this city for evil, and not for good; and they will be accomplished before you in that day. 17 But I will deliver you in that day," says the LORD; "and you will not be given into the hand of the men of whom you are afraid. 18 For I will surely save you. You won't fall by the sword, but you will escape with your life, because you have put your trust in me," says the LORD.'"

40

1 The word which came to Jeremiah from the LORD, after Nebuzaradan the captain of the guard had let him go from Ramah, when he had taken him being bound in chains amongst all the captives of Jerusalem and Judah who were carried away captive to Babylon. 2 The captain of the guard took Jeremiah and said to him, "The LORD your God pronounced this evil on this place; 3 and the LORD has brought it, and done according as he spoke. Because you have sinned against the LORD, and have not obeyed his voice, therefore this thing has come on you. 4 Now, behold, I release you today from the chains which are on your hand. If it seems good to you to come with me into Babylon, come, and I will take care of you; but if it seems bad to you to come with me into Babylon, don't. Behold, all the land is before you. Where it seems good and right to you to go, go there." 5 Now while he had not yet gone back, "Go back then," he said, "to Gedaliah the son of Ahikam, the son of Shaphan, whom the king of Babylon has made governor over the cities of Judah, and dwell with him amongst the people; or go wherever it seems right to you to go."

So the captain of the guard gave him food and a present, and let him go. 6 Then Jeremiah went to Gedaliah the son of Ahikam to Mizpah, and lived with him amongst the people who were left in the land.

7 Now when all the captains of the forces who were in the fields, even they and their men, heard that the king of Babylon had made Gedaliah the son of Ahikam governor in the land, and had committed to him men, women, children, and of the poorest of the land, of those who were not carried away captive to Babylon, 8 then Ishmael the son of Nethaniah, and Johanan and Jonathan the sons of Kareah, and Seraiah the son of Tanhumeth, and the sons of Ephai the Netophathite, and Jezaniah the son of the Maacathite, they and their men came to Gedaliah to Mizpah. 9 Gedaliah the son of Ahikam the son of Shaphan swore to them and to their men, saying, "Don't be afraid to serve the Chaldeans. Dwell in the land, and serve the king of Babylon, and it will be well with you. 10 As for me, behold, I will dwell at Mizpah, to stand before the Chaldeans who will come to us; but you, gather wine and summer fruits and oil, and put them in your vessels, and dwell in your cities that you have taken."

11 Likewise when all the Jews who were in Moab, and amongst the children of Ammon, and in Edom, and who were in all the countries, heard that the king of Babylon had left a remnant of Judah, and that he had set over them Gedaliah the son of Ahikam, the son of Shaphan, 12 then all the Jews returned out of all places where they were driven, and came to the land of Judah, to Gedaliah, to Mizpah, and gathered very much wine and summer fruits.

13 Moreover Johanan the son of Kareah, and all the captains of the forces who were in the fields, came to Gedaliah to Mizpah, 14 and said to him, "Do you know that Baalis the king of the children of Ammon has sent Ishmael the son of Nethaniah to take your life?"

But Gedaliah the son of Ahikam didn't believe them.

15 Then Johanan the son of Kareah spoke to Gedaliah in Mizpah secretly, saying, "Please let me go, and I will kill Ishmael the son of Nethaniah, and no man will know it. Why should he take your life, that all the Jews who are gathered to you should be scattered, and the remnant of Judah perish?"

16 But Gedaliah the son of Ahikam said to Johanan the son of Kareah, "You shall not do this thing, for you speak falsely of Ishmael."

41

1 Now in the seventh month, Ishmael the son of Nethaniah, the son of Elishama, of the royal offspring and one of the chief officers of the king, and ten men with him, came to Gedaliah the son of Ahikam to Mizpah; and there they ate bread together in Mizpah. 2 Then Ishmael the son of Nethaniah arose, and the ten men who were with him, and struck Gedaliah the son of Ahikam the son of Shaphan with the sword and killed him, whom the king of Babylon had made governor over the land. 3 Ishmael also killed all the Jews who were with Gedaliah at Mizpah, and the Chaldean men of war who were found there.

4 The second day after he had killed Gedaliah, and no man knew it, 5 men came from Shechem, from Shiloh, and from Samaria, even eighty men, having their beards shaved and their clothes torn, and having cut themselves, with meal offerings and frankincense in their hand, to bring them to the LORD's house. 6 Ishmael the son of Nethaniah went out from Mizpah to meet them, weeping all along as he went, and as he met them, he said to them, "Come to Gedaliah the son of Ahikam." 7 It was so, when they came into the middle of the city, that Ishmael the son of Nethaniah killed them, and cast them into the middle of the pit, he, and the men who were with him. 8 But ten men were found amongst those who said to Ishmael, "Don't kill us; for we have stores hidden in the field, of wheat, and of barley, and of oil, and of honey."

So he stopped, and didn't kill them amongst their brothers. 9 Now the pit in which Ishmael cast all the dead bodies of the men whom he had killed, by the side of Gedaliah (this was that which Asa the king had made for fear of Baasha king of Israel), Ishmael the son of Nethaniah filled it with those who were killed.

10 Then Ishmael carried away captive all of the people who were left in Mizpah, even the king's daughters, and all the people who remained in Mizpah, whom Nebuzaradan the captain of the guard had committed to Gedaliah the son of Ahikam. Ishmael the son of Nethaniah carried them away captive, and departed to go over to the children of Ammon.

11 But when Johanan the son of Kareah, and all the captains of the forces who were with him, heard of all the evil that Ishmael the son of Nethaniah had done, 12 then they took all the men, and went to fight with Ishmael the son of Nethaniah, and found him by the great waters that are in Gibeon. 13 Now when all the people who were with Ishmael saw Johanan the son of Kareah, and all the captains of the forces who were with him, then they were glad. 14 So all the people who Ishmael had carried away captive from Mizpah turned about and came back, and went to Johanan the son of Kareah. 15 But Ishmael the son of Nethaniah escaped from Johanan with eight men, and went to the children of Ammon.

16 Then Johanan the son of Kareah and all the captains of the forces who were with him took all the remnant of the people whom he had recovered from Ishmael the son of Nethaniah, from Mizpah, after he had killed Gedaliah the son of Ahikam—the men of war, with the women, the children, and the eunuchs, whom he had brought back from Gibeon. 17 They departed and lived in Geruth Chimham, which is by Bethlehem, to go to enter into Egypt 18 because of the Chaldeans; for they were afraid of them, because Ishmael the son of Nethaniah had killed Gedaliah the son of Ahikam, whom the king of Babylon made governor over the land.

42

1 Then all the captains of the forces, and Johanan the son of Kareah, and Jezaniah the son of Hoshaiah, and all the people from the least even to the greatest, came near, 2 and said to Jeremiah the prophet, "Please let our supplication be presented before you, and pray for us to the LORD your God, even for all this remnant, for we are left but a few of many, as your eyes see us, 3 that the LORD your God may show us the way in which we should walk, and the things that we should do."

4 Then Jeremiah the prophet said to them, "I have heard you. Behold, I will pray to the LORD your God according to your words; and it will happen that whatever thing the LORD answers you, I will declare it to you. I will keep nothing back from you."

5 Then they said to Jeremiah, "May the LORD be a true and faithful witness amongst us, if we don't do according to all the word with which the LORD your God sends you to tell us. 6 Whether it is good, or whether it is bad, we will obey the voice of the LORD our God, to whom we send you; that it may be well with us, when we obey the voice of the LORD our God."

7 After ten days, the LORD's word came to Jeremiah. 8 Then he called Johanan the son of Kareah, and all the captains of the forces who were with him, and all the people from the least even to the greatest, 9 and said to them, "The LORD, the God of Israel, to whom you sent me to present your supplication before him, says: 10 'If you will still live in this land, then I will build you, and not pull you down, and I will plant you, and not pluck you up; for I grieve over the distress that I have brought on you. 11 Don't be afraid of the king of Babylon, of whom you are afraid. Don't be afraid of him,' says the LORD, 'for I am with you to save you, and to deliver you from his hand. 12 I will grant you mercy, that he may have mercy on you, and cause you to return to your own land.

13 "'But if you say, "We will not dwell in this land," so that you don't obey the LORD your God's voice, 14 saying, "No, but we will go into the

land of Egypt, where we will see no war, nor hear the sound of the trumpet, nor have hunger of bread; and there we will dwell;"' 15 now therefore hear the LORD's word, O remnant of Judah! The LORD of Armies, the God of Israel, says, 'If you indeed set your faces to enter into Egypt, and go to live there, 16 then it will happen that the sword, which you fear, will overtake you there in the land of Egypt; and the famine, about which you are afraid, will follow close behind you there in Egypt; and you will die there. 17 So will it be with all the men who set their faces to go into Egypt to live there. They will die by the sword, by the famine, and by the pestilence. None of them will remain or escape from the evil that I will bring on them.' 18 For the LORD of Armies, the God of Israel, says: 'As my anger and my wrath has been poured out on the inhabitants of Jerusalem, so my wrath will be poured out on you, when you enter into Egypt; and you will be an object of horror, an astonishment, a curse, and a reproach; and you will see this place no more.'

19 "The LORD has spoken concerning you, remnant of Judah, 'Don't go into Egypt!' Know certainly that I have testified to you today. 20 For you have dealt deceitfully against your own souls; for you sent me to the LORD your God, saying, 'Pray for us to the LORD our God; and according to all that the LORD our God says, so declare to us, and we will do it.' 21 I have declared it to you today; but you have not obeyed the LORD your God's voice in anything for which he has sent me to you. 22 Now therefore know certainly that you will die by the sword, by the famine, and by the pestilence in the place where you desire to go to live."

43

1 When Jeremiah had finished speaking to all the people all the words of the LORD their God, with which the LORD their God had sent him to them, even all these words, 2 then Azariah the son of Hoshaiah, Johanan the son of Kareah, and all the proud men spoke, saying to Jeremiah, "You speak falsely. The LORD our God has not sent you to say, 'You shall not go into Egypt to live there;' 3 but Baruch the son of Neriah has turned you against us, to deliver us into the hand of the Chaldeans, that they may put us to death or carry us away captive to Babylon."

4 So Johanan the son of Kareah, and all the captains of the forces, and all the people, didn't obey the LORD's voice, to dwell in the land of Judah. 5 But Johanan the son of Kareah and all the captains of the forces took all the remnant of Judah, who had returned from all the nations where they had been driven, to live in the land of Judah— 6 the men, the women, the children, the king's daughters, and every person who Nebuzaradan the captain of the guard had left with Gedaliah the son of Ahikam, the son of Shaphan; and Jeremiah the prophet, and Baruch the son of Neriah. 7 They came into the land of Egypt, for they didn't obey the LORD's voice; and they came to Tahpanhes.

8 Then the LORD's word came to Jeremiah in Tahpanhes, saying, 9 "Take great stones in your hand and hide them in mortar in the brick work which is at the entry of Pharaoh's house in Tahpanhes, in the sight of the men of Judah. 10 Tell them, the LORD of Armies, the God of Israel, says: 'Behold, I will send and take Nebuchadnezzar the king of Babylon, my servant, and will set his throne on these stones that I have hidden; and he will spread his royal pavilion over them. 11 He will come, and will strike the land of Egypt; such as are for death will be put to death, and such as are for captivity to captivity, and such as are for the sword to the sword. 12 I will kindle a fire in the houses of the gods of Egypt. He will burn them, and carry them away captive. He will array himself with the land of Egypt, as a shepherd puts on his garment; and he will go out from there in peace. 13 He will also break the pillars of Beth Shemesh that is in the land of Egypt; and he will burn the houses of the gods of Egypt with fire.'"

44

1 The word that came to Jeremiah concerning all the Jews who lived in the land of Egypt, who lived at Migdol, and at Tahpanhes, and at Memphis, and in the country of Pathros, saying, 2 "The LORD of Armies, the God of Israel, says: 'You have seen all the evil that I have brought on Jerusalem, and on all the cities of Judah. Behold, today they are a desolation, and no man dwells in them, 3 because of their wickedness which they have committed to provoke me to anger, in that they went to burn incense, to serve other gods that they didn't know, neither they, nor you, nor your fathers. 4 However I sent to you all my servants the prophets, rising up early and sending them, saying, "Oh, don't do this abominable thing that I hate." 5 But they didn't listen and didn't incline their ear. They didn't turn from their wickedness, to stop burning incense to other gods. 6 Therefore my wrath and my anger was poured out, and was kindled in the cities of Judah and in the streets of Jerusalem; and they are wasted and desolate, as it is today.'

7 "Therefore now the LORD, the God of Armies, the God of Israel, says: 'Why do you commit great evil against your own souls, to cut off from yourselves man and woman, infant and nursing child out of the middle of Judah, to leave yourselves no one remaining, 8 in that you provoke me to anger with the works of your hands, burning incense to other gods in the land of Egypt where you have gone to live, that you may be cut off, and that you may be a curse and a reproach amongst all the nations of the earth? 9 Have you forgotten the wickedness of your fathers, the wickedness of the kings of Judah, the wickedness of their wives, your own wickedness, and the wickedness of your wives which they committed in the land of Judah and in the streets of Jerusalem? 10 They are not humbled even to this day, neither have they feared, nor walked in my law, nor in my statutes, that I set before you and before your fathers.'

11 "Therefore the LORD of Armies, the God of Israel, says: 'Behold, I will set my face against you for evil, even to cut off all Judah. 12 I will take

the remnant of Judah that have set their faces to go into the land of Egypt to live there, and they will all be consumed. They will fall in the land of Egypt. They will be consumed by the sword and by the famine. They will die, from the least even to the greatest, by the sword and by the famine. They will be an object of horror, an astonishment, a curse, and a reproach. 13 For I will punish those who dwell in the land of Egypt, as I have punished Jerusalem, by the sword, by the famine, and by the pestilence; 14 so that none of the remnant of Judah, who have gone into the land of Egypt to live there, will escape or be left to return into the land of Judah, to which they have a desire to return to dwell there; for no one will return except those who will escape.'"

15 Then all the men who knew that their wives burnt incense to other gods, and all the women who stood by, a great assembly, even all the people who lived in the land of Egypt, in Pathros, answered Jeremiah, saying, 16 "As for the word that you have spoken to us in the LORD's name, we will not listen to you. 17 But we will certainly perform every word that has gone out of our mouth, to burn incense to the queen of the sky and to pour out drink offerings to her, as we have done, we and our fathers, our kings and our princes, in the cities of Judah and in the streets of Jerusalem; for then we had plenty of food, and were well, and saw no evil. 18 But since we stopped burning incense to the queen of the sky, and pouring out drink offerings to her, we have lacked all things, and have been consumed by the sword and by the famine."

19 The women said, "When we burnt incense to the queen of the sky and poured out drink offerings to her, did we make her cakes to worship her, and pour out drink offerings to her, without our husbands?"

20 Then Jeremiah said to all the people—to the men and to the women, even to all the people who had given him an answer, saying, 21 "The incense that you burnt in the cities of Judah, and in the streets of Jerusalem, you and your fathers, your kings and your princes, and the people of the land, didn't the LORD remember them, and didn't it come into his mind? 22 Thus the LORD could no longer bear it, because of the evil of your doings and because of the abominations which you have committed. Therefore your land has become a desolation, an astonishment, and a curse, without inhabitant, as it is today. 23 Because you have burnt incense and because you have sinned against the LORD, and have not obeyed the LORD's voice, nor walked in his law, nor in his statutes, nor in his testimonies; therefore this evil has happened to you, as it is today."

24 Moreover Jeremiah said to all the people, including all the women, "Hear the LORD's word, all Judah who are in the land of Egypt! 25 The LORD of Armies, the God of Israel, says, 'You and your wives have both spoken with your mouths, and with your hands have fulfilled it, saying, "We will surely perform our vows that we have vowed, to burn incense to the queen of the sky, and to pour out drink offerings to her."

"'Establish then your vows, and perform your vows.'

26 "Therefore hear the LORD's word, all Judah who dwell in the land of Egypt: 'Behold, I have sworn by my great name,' says the LORD, 'that my name will no more be named in the mouth of any man of Judah in all the land of Egypt, saying, "As the Lord GOD lives." 27 Behold, I watch over them for evil, and not for good; and all the men of Judah who are in the land of Egypt will be consumed by the sword and by the famine, until they are all gone. 28 Those who escape the sword will return out of the land of Egypt into the land of Judah few in number. All the remnant of Judah, who have gone into the land of Egypt to live there, will know whose word will stand, mine or theirs.

29 "'This will be the sign to you,' says the LORD, 'that I will punish you in this place, that you may know that my words will surely stand against you for evil.' 30 The LORD says, 'Behold, I will give Pharaoh Hophra king of Egypt into the hand of his enemies and into the hand of those who seek his life, just as I gave Zedekiah king of Judah into the hand of Nebuchadnezzar king of Babylon, who was his enemy and sought his life.'"

45

1 The message that Jeremiah the prophet spoke to Baruch the son of Neriah, when he wrote these words in a book at the mouth of Jeremiah, in the fourth year of Jehoiakim the son of Josiah, king of Judah, saying, 2 "The LORD, the God of Israel, says to you, Baruch: 3 'You said, "Woe is me now! For the LORD has added sorrow to my pain! I am weary with my groaning, and I find no rest."'

4 "You shall tell him, the LORD says: 'Behold, that which I have built, I will break down, and that which I have planted I will pluck up; and this in the whole land. 5 Do you seek great things for yourself? Don't seek them; for, behold, I will bring evil on all flesh,' says the LORD, 'but I will let you escape with your life wherever you go.'"

46

1 The LORD's word which came to Jeremiah the prophet concerning the nations.

2 Of Egypt: concerning the army of Pharaoh Necoh king of Egypt, which was by the river Euphrates in Carchemish, which Nebuchadnezzar king of Babylon struck in the fourth year of Jehoiakim the son of Josiah, king of Judah.

3 "Prepare the buckler and shield,
    and draw near to battle!
4 Harness the horses, and get up, you horsemen,
    and stand up with your helmets.
Polish the spears,
    put on the coats of mail.
5 Why have I seen it?
    They are dismayed and are turned backward.

Their mighty ones are beaten down,
    have fled in haste,
    and don't look back.
Terror is on every side,"
    says the LORD.
6 "Don't let the swift flee away,
    nor the mighty man escape.
In the north by the river Euphrates
    they have stumbled and fallen.

7 "Who is this who rises up like the Nile,
    like rivers whose waters surge?
8 Egypt rises up like the Nile,
    like rivers whose waters surge.
He says, 'I will rise up. I will cover the earth.
    I will destroy cities and its inhabitants.'
9 Go up, you horses!
    Rage, you chariots!
Let the mighty men go out:
    Cush and Put, who handle the shield;
    and the Ludim, who handle and bend the bow.
10 For that day is of the Lord, the LORD of Armies,
    a day of vengeance,
    that he may avenge himself of his adversaries.
The sword will devour and be satiated,
    and will drink its fill of their blood;
    for the Lord, the LORD of Armies, has a sacrifice in the north country
        by the river Euphrates.
11 Go up into Gilead, and take balm, virgin daughter of Egypt.
    You use many medicines in vain.
    There is no healing for you.
12 The nations have heard of your shame,
    and the earth is full of your cry;
    for the mighty man has stumbled against the mighty,
    they both fall together."

13 The word that the LORD spoke to Jeremiah the prophet, how that Nebuchadnezzar king of Babylon should come and strike the land of Egypt:
14 "Declare in Egypt,
    publish in Migdol,
    and publish in Memphis and in Tahpanhes;
say, 'Stand up, and prepare,
    for the sword has devoured around you.'
15 Why are your strong ones swept away?
    They didn't stand, because the LORD pushed them.
16 He made many to stumble.
    Yes, they fell on one another.
They said, 'Arise! Let's go again to our own people,
    and to the land of our birth,
    from the oppressing sword.'
17 They cried there, 'Pharaoh king of Egypt is but a noise;
    he has let the appointed time pass by.'

18 "As I live," says the King,
    whose name is the LORD of Armies,
"surely like Tabor amongst the mountains,
    and like Carmel by the sea,
    so he will come.
19 You daughter who dwells in Egypt,
    furnish yourself to go into captivity;
for Memphis will become a desolation,
    and will be burnt up,
    without inhabitant.

20 "Egypt is a very beautiful heifer;
    but destruction out of the north has come.
    It has come.
21 Also her hired men in the middle of her are like calves of the stall,
    for they also are turned back.
    They have fled away together.
They didn't stand,
    for the day of their calamity has come on them,
    the time of their visitation.
22 Its sound will go like the serpent,
    for they will march with an army,
    and come against her with axes, as wood cutters.
23 They will cut down her forest," says the LORD,
    "though it can't be searched;
because they are more than the locusts,
    and are innumerable.
24 The daughter of Egypt will be disappointed;
    she will be delivered into the hand of the people of the north."

25 The LORD of Armies, the God of Israel, says: "Behold, I will punish Amon of No, and Pharaoh, and Egypt, with her gods and her kings, even Pharaoh, and those who trust in him. 26 I will deliver them into the hand of those who seek their lives, and into the hand of Nebuchadnezzar king of Babylon, and into the hand of his servants. Afterwards it will be inhabited, as in the days of old," says the LORD.

27 "But don't you be afraid, Jacob my servant.

Don't be dismayed, Israel;
for, behold, I will save you from afar,
and your offspring from the land of their captivity.
Jacob will return,
and will be quiet and at ease.
No one will make him afraid.
28 Don't be afraid, O Jacob my servant," says the LORD,
"for I am with you;
for I will make a full end of all the nations where I have driven you,
but I will not make a full end of you,
but I will correct you in measure,
and will in no way leave you unpunished."

47

1 The LORD's word that came to Jeremiah the prophet concerning the Philistines, before Pharaoh struck Gaza.
2 The LORD says:
"Behold, waters rise up out of the north,
and will become an overflowing stream,
and will overflow the land and all that is therein,
the city and those who dwell therein.
The men will cry,
and all the inhabitants of the land will wail.
3 At the noise of the stamping of the hoofs of his strong ones,
at the rushing of his chariots,
at the rumbling of his wheels,
the fathers don't look back for their children
because their hands are so feeble,
4 because of the day that comes to destroy all the Philistines,
to cut off from Tyre and Sidon every helper who remains;
for the LORD will destroy the Philistines,
the remnant of the isle of Caphtor.
5 Baldness has come on Gaza;
Ashkelon is brought to nothing.
You remnant of their valley,
how long will you cut yourself?

6 "'You sword of the LORD, how long will it be before you are quiet?
Put yourself back into your scabbard;
rest, and be still.'

7 "How can you be quiet,
since the LORD has given you a command?
Against Ashkelon, and against the seashore,
there he has appointed it."

48

1 Of Moab. The LORD of Armies, the God of Israel, says:
"Woe to Nebo!
For it is laid waste.
Kiriathaim is disappointed.
It is taken.
Misgab[a] is put to shame
and broken down.
2 The praise of Moab is no more.
In Heshbon they have devised evil against her:
'Come! Let's cut her off from being a nation.'
You also, Madmen, will be brought to silence.
The sword will pursue you.
3 The sound of a cry from Horonaim,
desolation and great destruction!
4 Moab is destroyed.
Her little ones have caused a cry to be heard.
5 For they will go up by the ascent of Luhith with continual weeping.
For at the descent of Horonaim they have heard the distress of the cry
of destruction.
6 Flee! Save your lives!
Be like the juniper bush in the wilderness.
7 For, because you have trusted in your works and in your treasures,
you also will be taken.
Chemosh will go out into captivity,
his priests and his princes together.
8 The destroyer will come on every city,
and no city will escape;
the valley also will perish,
and the plain will be destroyed, as the LORD has spoken.
9 Give wings to Moab,
that she may fly and get herself away:
and her cities will become a desolation,
without anyone to dwell in them.

10 "Cursed is he who does the work of the LORD negligently;
and cursed is he who keeps back his sword from blood.

11 "Moab has been at ease from his youth,
and he has settled on his dregs,
and has not been emptied from vessel to vessel,
neither has he gone into captivity;

therefore his taste remains in him,
and his scent is not changed.
12 Therefore behold, the days come," says the LORD,
"that I will send to him those who pour off,
and they will pour him off;
and they will empty his vessels,
and break their containers in pieces.
13 Moab will be ashamed of Chemosh,
as the house of Israel was ashamed of Bethel, their confidence.

14 "How do you say, 'We are mighty men,
and valiant men for the war'?
15 Moab is laid waste,
and they have gone up into his cities,
and his chosen young men have gone down to the slaughter,"
says the King, whose name is the LORD of Armies.
16 "The calamity of Moab is near to come,
and his affliction hurries fast.
17 All you who are around him, bemoan him;
and all you who know his name, say,
'How the strong staff is broken,
the beautiful rod!'

18 "You daughter who dwells in Dibon,
come down from your glory,
and sit in thirst;
for the destroyer of Moab has come up against you.
He has destroyed your strongholds.
19 Inhabitant of Aroer, stand by the way and watch.
Ask him who flees, and her who escapes;
say, 'What has been done?'
20 Moab is disappointed;
for it is broken down.
Wail and cry!
Tell it by the Arnon, that Moab is laid waste.
21 Judgement has come on the plain country—
on Holon, on Jahzah, on Mephaath,
22 on Dibon, on Nebo, on Beth Diblathaim,
23 on Kiriathaim, on Beth Gamul, on Beth Meon,
24 on Kerioth, on Bozrah,
and on all the cities of the land of Moab, far or near.
25 The horn of Moab is cut off,
and his arm is broken," says the LORD.

26 "Make him drunk,
for he magnified himself against the LORD.
Moab will wallow in his vomit,
and he also will be in derision.
27 For wasn't Israel a derision to you?
Was he found amongst thieves?
For as often as you speak of him,
you shake your head.
28 You inhabitants of Moab, leave the cities, and dwell in the rock.
Be like the dove that makes her nest over the mouth of the abyss.

29 "We have heard of the pride of Moab.
He is very proud in his loftiness, his pride,
his arrogance, and the arrogance of his heart.
30 I know his wrath," says the LORD, "that it is nothing;
his boastings have done nothing.
31 Therefore I will wail for Moab.
Yes, I will cry out for all Moab.
They will mourn for the men of Kir Heres.
32 With more than the weeping of Jazer
I will weep for you, vine of Sibmah.
Your branches passed over the sea.
They reached even to the sea of Jazer.
The destroyer has fallen on your summer fruits
and on your vintage.
33 Gladness and joy is taken away from the fruitful field
and from the land of Moab.
I have caused wine to cease from the wine presses.
No one will tread with shouting.
The shouting will be no shouting.
34 From the cry of Heshbon even to Elealeh,
even to Jahaz they have uttered their voice,
from Zoar even to Horonaim, to Eglath Shelishiyah;
for the waters of Nimrim will also become desolate.
35 Moreover I will cause to cease in Moab," says the LORD,
"him who offers in the high place,
and him who burns incense to his gods.
36 Therefore my heart sounds for Moab like flutes,
and my heart sounds like flutes for the men of Kir Heres.
Therefore the abundance that he has gotten has perished.
37 For every head is bald,
and every beard clipped.
There are cuttings on all the hands,

---

a 48:1 or, The stronghold

and sackcloth on the waist.
38 On all the housetops of Moab,
and in its streets, there is lamentation everywhere;
for I have broken Moab like a vessel in which no one delights," says
the LORD.
39 "How it is broken down!
How they wail!
How Moab has turned the back with shame!
So will Moab become a derision
and a terror to all who are around him."
40 For the LORD says: "Behold, he will fly as an eagle,
and will spread out his wings against Moab.
41 Kerioth is taken,
and the strongholds are seized.
The heart of the mighty men of Moab at that day
will be as the heart of a woman in her pangs.
42 Moab will be destroyed from being a people,
because he has magnified himself against the LORD.
43 Terror, the pit, and the snare are on you,
inhabitant of Moab," says the LORD.
44 "He who flees from the terror will fall into the pit;
and he who gets up out of the pit will be taken in the snare,
for I will bring on him, even on Moab,
the year of their visitation," says the LORD.

45 "Those who fled stand without strength under the shadow of Heshbon;
for a fire has gone out of Heshbon,
and a flame from the middle of Sihon,
and has devoured the corner of Moab,
and the crown of the head of the tumultuous ones.
46 Woe to you, O Moab!
The people of Chemosh are undone;
for your sons are taken away captive,
and your daughters into captivity.

47 "Yet I will reverse the captivity of Moab in the latter days,"
says the LORD.
Thus far is the judgement of Moab.

49

1 Of the children of Ammon. The LORD says:
"Has Israel no sons?
Has he no heir?
Why then does Malcam possess Gad,
and his people dwell in its cities?
2 Therefore behold, the days come,"
says the LORD,
"that I will cause an alarm of war to be heard against Rabbah of the children
of Ammon,
and it will become a desolate heap,
and her daughters will be burnt with fire;
then Israel will possess those who possessed him,"
says the LORD.
3 "Wail, Heshbon, for Ai is laid waste!
Cry, you daughters of Rabbah!
Clothe yourself in sackcloth.
Lament, and run back and forth amongst the fences;
for Malcam will go into captivity,
his priests and his princes together.
4 Why do you boast in the valleys,
your flowing valley, backsliding daughter?
You trusted in her treasures,
saying, 'Who will come to me?'
5 Behold, I will bring a terror on you,"
says the Lord, the LORD of Armies,
"from all who are around you.
All of you will be driven completely out,
and there will be no one to gather together the fugitives.

6 "But afterward I will reverse the captivity of the children of Ammon,"
says the LORD.

7 Of Edom, the LORD of Armies says:
"Is wisdom no more in Teman?
Has counsel perished from the prudent?
Has their wisdom vanished?
8 Flee! Turn back!
Dwell in the depths, inhabitants of Dedan;
for I will bring the calamity of Esau on him when I visit him.
9 If grape gatherers came to you,
would they not leave some gleaning grapes?
If thieves came by night,
wouldn't they steal until they had enough?
10 But I have made Esau bare,
I have uncovered his secret places,
and he will not be able to hide himself.
His offspring is destroyed,
with his brothers and his neighbours;
and he is no more.
11 Leave your fatherless children.

I will preserve them alive.
Let your widows trust in me."
12 For the LORD says: "Behold, they to whom it didn't pertain to drink
of the cup will certainly drink; and are you he who will altogether go
unpunished? You won't go unpunished, but you will surely drink. 13 For I
have sworn by myself," says the LORD, "that Bozrah will become an
astonishment, a reproach, a waste, and a curse. All its cities will be
perpetual wastes."
14 I have heard news from the LORD,
and an ambassador is sent amongst the nations,
saying, "Gather yourselves together!
Come against her!
Rise up to the battle!"

15 "For, behold, I have made you small amongst the nations,
and despised amongst men.
16 As for your terror,
the pride of your heart has deceived you,
O you who dwell in the clefts of the rock,
who hold the height of the hill,
though you should make your nest as high as the eagle,
I will bring you down from there," says the LORD.
17 "Edom will become an astonishment.
Everyone who passes by it will be astonished,
and will hiss at all its plagues.
18 As in the overthrow of Sodom and Gomorrah and its neighbour cities,"
says the LORD,
"no man will dwell there,
neither will any son of man live therein.

19 "Behold, he will come up like a lion from the pride of the Jordan against
the strong habitation;
for I will suddenly make them run away from it,
and whoever is chosen,
I will appoint him over it.
For who is like me?
Who will appoint me a time?
Who is the shepherd who will stand before me?"
20 Therefore hear the counsel of the LORD, that he has taken against Edom,
and his purposes that he has purposed against the inhabitants of
Teman:
Surely they will drag them away,
the little ones of the flock.
Surely he will make their habitation desolate over them.
21 The earth trembles at the noise of their fall;
there is a cry, the noise which is heard in the Red Sea.
22 Behold, he will come up and fly as the eagle,
and spread out his wings against Bozrah.
The heart of the mighty men of Edom at that day will be as the heart of
a woman in her pangs.

23 Of Damascus:
"Hamath and Arpad are confounded,
for they have heard evil news.
They have melted away.
There is sorrow on the sea.
It can't be quiet.
24 Damascus has grown feeble,
she turns herself to flee,
and trembling has seized her.
Anguish and sorrows have taken hold of her,
as of a woman in travail.
25 How is the city of praise not forsaken,
the city of my joy?
26 Therefore her young men will fall in her streets,
and all the men of war will be brought to silence in that day,"
says the LORD of Armies.
27 "I will kindle a fire in the wall of Damascus,
and it will devour the palaces of Ben Hadad."

28 Of Kedar, and of the kingdoms of Hazor, which Nebuchadnezzar king of
Babylon struck, The LORD says:
"Arise, go up to Kedar,
and destroy the children of the east.
29 They will take their tents and their flocks.
they will carry away for themselves their curtains,
all their vessels, and their camels;
and they will cry to them, 'Terror on every side!'
30 Flee!
Wander far off!
Dwell in the depths, you inhabitants of Hazor," says the LORD;
"for Nebuchadnezzar king of Babylon has taken counsel against you,
and has conceived a purpose against you.
31 Arise! Go up to a nation that is at ease,
that dwells without care," says the LORD;
"that has neither gates nor bars,
that dwells alone.
32 Their camels will be a booty,
and the multitude of their livestock a plunder.

I will scatter to all winds those who have the corners of their beards cut off;
  and I will bring their calamity from every side of them,"
    says the LORD.

33 Hazor will be a dwelling place of jackals,
  a desolation forever.
No man will dwell there,
  neither will any son of man live therein."

34 The LORD's word that came to Jeremiah the prophet concerning Elam, in the beginning of the reign of Zedekiah king of Judah, saying,
35 "The LORD of Armies says:
'Behold, I will break the bow of Elam,
  the chief of their might.
36 I will bring on Elam the four winds from the four quarters of the sky,
  and will scatter them towards all those winds.
    There will be no nation where the outcasts of Elam will not come.
37 I will cause Elam to be dismayed before their enemies,
  and before those who seek their life.
I will bring evil on them, even my fierce anger,' says the LORD;
  'and I will send the sword after them,
    until I have consumed them.
38 I will set my throne in Elam,
  and will destroy from there king and princes,' says the LORD.
39 'But it will happen in the latter days
  that I will reverse the captivity of Elam,' says the LORD."

50

1 The word that the LORD spoke concerning Babylon, concerning the land of the Chaldeans, by Jeremiah the prophet.
2 "Declare amongst the nations and publish,
  and set up a standard;
    publish, and don't conceal;
say, 'Babylon has been taken,
  Bel is disappointed,
    Merodach is dismayed!
Her images are disappointed.
  Her idols are dismayed.'
3 For a nation comes up out of the north against her,
  which will make her land desolate,
    and no one will dwell in it.
They have fled.
  They are gone,
    both man and animal.

4 "In those days, and in that time," says the LORD,
  "the children of Israel will come,
    they and the children of Judah together;
they will go on their way weeping,
  and will seek the LORD their God.
5 They will enquire concerning Zion with their faces turned towards it,
  saying, 'Come, and join yourselves to the LORD in an everlasting covenant
    that will not be forgotten.'
6 My people have been lost sheep.
  Their shepherds have caused them to go astray.
They have turned them away on the mountains.
  They have gone from mountain to hill.
    They have forgotten their resting place.
7 All who found them have devoured them.
  Their adversaries said, 'We are not guilty,
because they have sinned against the LORD,
  the habitation of righteousness,
    even the LORD, the hope of their fathers.'

8 "Flee out of the middle of Babylon!
  Go out of the land of the Chaldeans,
    and be as the male goats before the flocks.
9 For, behold, I will stir up
  and cause to come up against Babylon a company of great nations
    from the north country;
  and they will set themselves in array against her.
She will be taken from there.
  Their arrows will be as of an expert mighty man.
    None of them will return in vain.
10 Chaldea will be a prey.
  All who prey on her will be satisfied," says the LORD.

11 "Because you are glad,
  because you rejoice,
O you who plunder my heritage,
  because you are wanton as a heifer that treads out the grain,
    and neigh as strong horses,
12 your mother will be utterly disappointed.
  She who bore you will be confounded.
Behold, she will be the least of the nations,
  a wilderness, a dry land, and a desert.
13 Because of the LORD's wrath she won't be inhabited,
  but she will be wholly desolate.
Everyone who goes by Babylon will be astonished,
  and hiss at all her plagues.

14 Set yourselves in array against Babylon all around,
  all you who bend the bow;
    shoot at her.
Spare no arrows,
  for she has sinned against the LORD.
15 Shout against her all around.
  She has submitted herself.
    Her bulwarks have fallen.
Her walls have been thrown down,
  for it is the vengeance of the LORD.
Take vengeance on her.
  As she has done, do to her.
16 Cut off the sower from Babylon,
  and him who handles the sickle in the time of harvest.
For fear of the oppressing sword,
  they will each return to their own people,
    and they will each flee to their own land.

17 "Israel is a hunted sheep.
  The lions have driven him away.
First, the king of Assyria devoured him,
  and now at last Nebuchadnezzar king of Babylon has broken his bones."
18 Therefore the LORD of Armies, the God of Israel, says:
"Behold, I will punish the king of Babylon and his land,
  as I have punished the king of Assyria.
19 I will bring Israel again to his pasture,
  and he will feed on Carmel and Bashan.
His soul will be satisfied on the hills of Ephraim and in Gilead.
20 In those days, and in that time," says the LORD,
  "the iniquity of Israel will be sought for,
    and there will be none,
also the sins of Judah,
  and they won't be found;
    for I will pardon them whom I leave as a remnant.

21 "Go up against the land of Merathaim,
  even against it, and against the inhabitants of Pekod.
Kill and utterly destroy after them," says the LORD,
  "and do according to all that I have commanded you.
22 A sound of battle is in the land,
  and of great destruction.
23 How the hammer of the whole earth is cut apart and broken!
  How Babylon has become a desolation amongst the nations!
24 I have laid a snare for you,
  and you are also taken, Babylon,
    and you weren't aware.
You are found,
  and also caught,
    because you have fought against the LORD.
25 The LORD has opened his armoury,
  and has brought out the weapons of his indignation;
    for the Lord, the LORD of Armies, has a work to do in the land of the Chaldeans.
26 Come against her from the farthest border.
  Open her storehouses.
    Cast her up as heaps.
Destroy her utterly.
  Let nothing of her be left.
27 Kill all her bulls.
  Let them go down to the slaughter.
Woe to them! For their day has come,
  the time of their visitation.
28 Listen to those who flee and escape out of the land of Babylon,
  to declare in Zion the vengeance of the LORD our God,
    the vengeance of his temple.

29 "Call together the archers against Babylon,
  all those who bend the bow.
Encamp against her all around.
  Let none of it escape.
Pay her back according to her work.
  According to all that she has done, do to her;
for she has been proud against the LORD,
  against the Holy One of Israel.
30 Therefore her young men will fall in her streets.
  All her men of war will be brought to silence in that day," says the LORD.
31 "Behold, I am against you, you proud one," says the Lord, the LORD of Armies;
  "for your day has come,
    the time that I will visit you.
32 The proud one will stumble and fall,
  and no one will raise him up.
I will kindle a fire in his cities,
  and it will devour all who are around him."
33 The LORD of Armies says: "The children of Israel and the children of Judah are oppressed together.
  All who took them captive hold them fast.

They refuse to let them go.
34 Their Redeemer is strong.
The LORD of Armies is his name.
He will thoroughly plead their cause,
that he may give rest to the earth,
and disquiet the inhabitants of Babylon.

35 "A sword is on the Chaldeans," says the LORD,
"and on the inhabitants of Babylon,
on her princes,
and on her wise men.
36 A sword is on the boasters,
and they will become fools.
A sword is on her mighty men,
and they will be dismayed.
37 A sword is on their horses,
on their chariots,
and on all the mixed people who are in the middle of her;
and they will become as women.
A sword is on her treasures,
and they will be robbed.
38 A drought is on her waters,
and they will be dried up;
for it is a land of engraved images,
and they are mad over idols.
39 Therefore the wild animals of the desert
with the wolves will dwell there.
The ostriches will dwell therein.
It will be inhabited no more forever,
neither will it be lived in from generation to generation.
40 As when God overthrew Sodom and Gomorrah and its neighbour cities,"
says the LORD,
"so no man will dwell there,
neither will any son of man live therein.

41 "Behold, a people comes from the north.
A great nation and many kings will be stirred up from the uttermost
parts of the earth.
42 They take up bow and spear.
They are cruel, and have no mercy.
Their voice roars like the sea.
They ride on horses,
everyone set in array,
as a man to the battle,
against you, daughter of Babylon.
43 The king of Babylon has heard the news of them,
and his hands become feeble.
Anguish has taken hold of him,
pains as of a woman in labour.
44 Behold, the enemy will come up like a lion
from the thickets of the Jordan against the strong habitation;
for I will suddenly make them run away from it.
Whoever is chosen,
I will appoint him over it,
for who is like me?
Who will appoint me a time?
Who is the shepherd who can stand before me?"
45 Therefore hear the counsel of the LORD
that he has taken against Babylon;
and his purposes
that he has purposed against the land of the Chaldeans:
Surely they will drag them away,
even the little ones of the flock.
Surely he will make their habitation desolate over them.
46 The earth trembles at the noise of the taking of Babylon.
The cry is heard amongst the nations.

51

1 The LORD says:
"Behold, I will raise up against Babylon,
and against those who dwell in Lebkamai, a destroying wind.
2 I will send to Babylon strangers, who will winnow her.
They will empty her land;
for in the day of trouble they will be against her all around.
3 Against him who bends, let the archer bend his bow,
also against him who lifts himself up in his coat of mail.
Don't spare her young men!
Utterly destroy all her army!
4 They will fall down slain in the land of the Chaldeans,
and thrust through in her streets.
5 For Israel is not forsaken, nor Judah, by his God,
by the LORD of Armies;
though their land is full of guilt against the Holy One of Israel.

6 "Flee out of the middle of Babylon!
Everyone save his own life!
Don't be cut off in her iniquity,
for it is the time of the LORD's vengeance.
He will render to her a recompense.
7 Babylon has been a golden cup in the LORD's hand,
who made all the earth drunk.
The nations have drunk of her wine;
therefore the nations have gone mad.
8 Babylon has suddenly fallen and been destroyed!
Wail for her!
Take balm for her pain.
Perhaps she may be healed.

9 "We would have healed Babylon,
but she is not healed.
Forsake her,
and let's each go into his own country;
for her judgement reaches to heaven,
and is lifted up even to the skies.
10 'The LORD has produced our righteousness.
Come, and let's declare in Zion the work of the LORD our God.'

11 "Make the arrows sharp!
Hold the shields firmly!
The LORD has stirred up the spirit of the kings of the Medes,
because his purpose is against Babylon, to destroy it;
for it is the vengeance of the LORD,
the vengeance of his temple.
12 Set up a standard against the walls of Babylon!
Make the watch strong!
Set the watchmen,
and prepare the ambushes;
for the LORD has both purposed and done
that which he spoke concerning the inhabitants of Babylon.
13 You who dwell on many waters, abundant in treasures,
your end has come, the measure of your covetousness.
14 The LORD of Armies has sworn by himself, saying,
'Surely I will fill you with men,
as with locusts,
and they will lift up a shout against you.'

15 "He has made the earth by his power.
He has established the world by his wisdom.
By his understanding he has stretched out the heavens.
16 When he utters his voice,
there is a roar of waters in the heavens,
and he causes the vapours to ascend from the ends of the earth.
He makes lightning for the rain,
and brings the wind out of his treasuries.

17 "Every man has become stupid and without knowledge.
Every goldsmith is disappointed by his image,
for his molten images are falsehood,
and there is no breath in them.
18 They are vanity,
a work of delusion.
In the time of their visitation, they will perish.
19 The portion of Jacob is not like these,
for he formed all things,
including the tribe of his inheritance.
The LORD of Armies is his name.

20 "You are my battle axe and weapons of war.
With you I will break the nations into pieces.
With you I will destroy kingdoms.
21 With you I will break in pieces
the horse and his rider.
22 With you I will break in pieces
the chariot and him who rides therein.
With you I will break in pieces
man and woman.
With you I will break in pieces
the old man and the youth.
With you I will break in pieces
the young man and the virgin.
23 With you I will break in pieces
the shepherd and his flock.
With you I will break in pieces
the farmer and his yoke.
With you I will break in pieces
governors and deputies.
24 "I will render to Babylon and to all the inhabitants of Chaldea all
their evil that they have done in Zion in your sight," says the LORD.
25 "Behold, I am against you, destroying mountain," says the LORD,
"which destroys all the earth.
I will stretch out my hand on you,
roll you down from the rocks,
and will make you a burnt mountain.
26 They won't take a cornerstone from you,
nor a stone for foundations;
but you will be desolate forever," says the LORD.

27 "Set up a standard in the land!
Blow the trumpet amongst the nations!

Prepare the nations against her!
    Call together against her the kingdoms of Ararat, Minni, and
        Ashkenaz!
Appoint a marshal against her!
    Cause the horses to come up as the swarming locusts!
28 Prepare against her the nations,
    the kings of the Medes, its governors, and all its deputies, and all the
        land of their dominion!
29 The land trembles and is in pain;
    for the purposes of the LORD against Babylon stand,
    to make the land of Babylon a desolation, without inhabitant.
30 The mighty men of Babylon have stopped fighting,
    they remain in their strongholds.
Their might has failed.
    They have become as women.
Her dwelling places are set on fire.
    Her bars are broken.
31 One runner will run to meet another,
    and one messenger to meet another,
    to show the king of Babylon that his city is taken on every quarter.
32 So the passages are seized.
    They have burnt the reeds with fire.
    The men of war are frightened."
        33 For the LORD of Armies, the God of Israel says:
"The daughter of Babylon is like a threshing floor at the time when it is
        trodden.
    Yet a little while, and the time of harvest comes for her."

34 "Nebuchadnezzar the king of Babylon has devoured me.
    He has crushed me.
    He has made me an empty vessel.
He has, like a monster, swallowed me up.
    He has filled his mouth with my delicacies.
    He has cast me out.
35 May the violence done to me and to my flesh be on Babylon!"
    the inhabitant of Zion will say; and,
"May my blood be on the inhabitants of Chaldea!"
    will Jerusalem say.

    36 Therefore the LORD says:
"Behold, I will plead your cause,
    and take vengeance for you.
I will dry up her sea,
    and make her fountain dry.
37 Babylon will become heaps,
    a dwelling place for jackals,
    an astonishment, and a hissing,
        without inhabitant.
38 They will roar together like young lions.
    They will growl as lions' cubs.
39 When they are inflamed, I will make their feast,
    and I will make them drunk,
that they may rejoice,
    and sleep a perpetual sleep,
    and not wake up," says the LORD.

40 "I will bring them down like lambs to the slaughter,
    like rams with male goats.

41 "How Sheshach is taken!
    How the praise of the whole earth is seized!
    How Babylon has become a desolation amongst the nations!
42 The sea has come up on Babylon.
    She is covered with the multitude of its waves.
43 Her cities have become a desolation,
    a dry land, and a desert,
    a land in which no man dwells.
    No son of man passes by it.
44 I will execute judgement on Bel in Babylon,
    and I will bring out of his mouth that which he has swallowed up.
The nations will not flow any more to him.
    Yes, the wall of Babylon will fall.

45 "My people, go away from the middle of her,
    and each of you save yourselves from the LORD's fierce anger.
46 Don't let your heart faint.
    Don't fear for the news that will be heard in the land.
For news will come one year,
    and after that in another year news will come,
    and violence in the land,
    ruler against ruler.
47 Therefore behold, the days come that I will execute judgement on the
        engraved images of Babylon;
    and her whole land will be confounded.
    All her slain will fall in the middle of her.
48 Then the heavens and the earth,
    and all that is therein,
will sing for joy over Babylon;
    for the destroyers will come to her from the north," says the LORD.

49 "As Babylon has caused the slain of Israel to fall,
    so the slain of all the land will fall at Babylon.
50 You who have escaped the sword, go!
    Don't stand still!
Remember the LORD from afar,
    and let Jerusalem come into your mind."

51 "We are confounded
    because we have heard reproach.
Confusion has covered our faces,
    for strangers have come into the sanctuaries of the LORD's house."

52 "Therefore behold, the days come," says the LORD,
    "that I will execute judgement on her engraved images;
    and through all her land the wounded will groan.
53 Though Babylon should mount up to the sky,
    and though she should fortify the height of her strength,
    yet destroyers will come to her from me," says the LORD.

54 "The sound of a cry comes from Babylon,
    and of great destruction from the land of the Chaldeans!
55 For the LORD lays Babylon waste,
    and destroys out of her the great voice!
Their waves roar like many waters.
    The noise of their voice is uttered.
56 For the destroyer has come on her,
    even on Babylon.
Her mighty men are taken.
    Their bows are broken in pieces,
for the LORD is a God of retribution.
    He will surely repay.
57 I will make her princes, her wise men,
    her governors, her deputies, and her mighty men drunk.
They will sleep a perpetual sleep,
    and not wake up,"
    says the King, whose name is the LORD of Armies.
58 The LORD of Armies says:
"The wide walls of Babylon will be utterly overthrown.
    Her high gates will be burnt with fire.
The peoples will labour for vanity,
    and the nations for the fire;
    and they will be weary."

59 The word which Jeremiah the prophet commanded Seraiah the son of Neriah, the son of Mahseiah, when he went with Zedekiah the king of Judah to Babylon in the fourth year of his reign. Now Seraiah was chief quartermaster. 60 Jeremiah wrote in a book all the evil that should come on Babylon, even all these words that are written concerning Babylon. 61 Jeremiah said to Seraiah, "When you come to Babylon, then see that you read all these words, 62 and say, 'LORD, you have spoken concerning this place, to cut it off, that no one will dwell in it, neither man nor animal, but that it will be desolate forever.' 63 It will be, when you have finished reading this book, that you shall bind a stone to it, and cast it into the middle of the Euphrates. 64 Then you shall say, 'Thus will Babylon sink, and will not rise again because of the evil that I will bring on her; and they will be weary.'"
    Thus far are the words of Jeremiah.

52

1 Zedekiah was twenty-one years old when he began to reign. He reigned eleven years in Jerusalem. His mother's name was Hamutal the daughter of Jeremiah of Libnah. 2 He did that which was evil in the LORD's sight, according to all that Jehoiakim had done. 3 For through the LORD's anger this happened in Jerusalem and Judah, until he had cast them out from his presence.

Zedekiah rebelled against the king of Babylon. 4 In the ninth year of his reign, in the tenth month, in the tenth day of the month, Nebuchadnezzar king of Babylon came, he and all his army, against Jerusalem, and encamped against it; and they built forts against it round about. 5 So the city was besieged to the eleventh year of King Zedekiah.

6 In the fourth month, in the ninth day of the month, the famine was severe in the city, so that there was no bread for the people of the land. 7 Then a breach was made in the city, and all the men of war fled, and went out of the city by night by the way of the gate between the two walls, which was by the king's garden. Now the Chaldeans were against the city all around. The men of war went towards the Arabah, 8 but the army of the Chaldeans pursued the king, and overtook Zedekiah in the plains of Jericho; and all his army was scattered from him. 9 Then they took the king, and carried him up to the king of Babylon to Riblah in the land of Hamath; and he pronounced judgement on him. 10 The king of Babylon killed the sons of Zedekiah before his eyes. He also killed all the princes of Judah in Riblah. 11 He put out the eyes of Zedekiah; and the king of Babylon bound him in fetters, and carried him to Babylon, and put him in prison until the day of his death.

12 Now in the fifth month, in the tenth day of the month, which was the nineteenth year of King Nebuchadnezzar, king of Babylon, Nebuzaradan the captain of the guard, who stood before the king of Babylon, came into Jerusalem. 13 He burnt the LORD's house, and the king's house; and all the houses of Jerusalem, even every great house, he burnt with fire. 14 All the army of the Chaldeans, who were with the captain of the guard, broke down all the walls of Jerusalem all around. 15 Then Nebuzaradan the captain of

the guard carried away captive of the poorest of the people, and the rest of the people who were left in the city, and those who fell away, who defected to the king of Babylon, and the rest of the multitude. ₁₆ But Nebuzaradan the captain of the guard left of the poorest of the land to be vineyard keepers and farmers.

₁₇ The Chaldeans broke the pillars of bronze that were in the LORD's house and the bases and the bronze sea that were in the LORD's house in pieces, and carried all of their bronze to Babylon. ₁₈ They also took away the pots, the shovels, the snuffers, the basins, the spoons, and all the vessels of bronze with which they ministered. ₁₉ The captain of the guard took away the cups, the fire pans, the basins, the pots, the lamp stands, the spoons, and the bowls; that which was of gold, as gold, and that which was of silver, as silver.

₂₀ They took the two pillars, the one sea, and the twelve bronze bulls that were under the bases, which King Solomon had made for the LORD's house. The bronze of all these vessels was without weight. ₂₁ As for the pillars, the height of the one pillar was eighteen cubits;[a] and a line of twelve cubits encircled it; and its thickness was four fingers. It was hollow. ₂₂ A capital of bronze was on it; and the height of the one capital was five cubits,[b] with network and pomegranates on the capital all around, all of bronze. The second pillar also had the same, with pomegranates. ₂₃ There were ninety-six pomegranates on the sides; all the pomegranates were one hundred on the network all around.

₂₄ The captain of the guard took Seraiah the chief priest, and Zephaniah the second priest, and the three keepers of the threshold, ₂₅ and out of the city he took an officer who was set over the men of war; and seven men of those who saw the king's face, who were found in the city; and the scribe of the captain of the army, who mustered the people of the land; and sixty men of the people of the land, who were found in the middle of the city. ₂₆ Nebuzaradan the captain of the guard took them, and brought them to the king of Babylon to Riblah. ₂₇ The king of Babylon struck them, and put them to death at Riblah in the land of Hamath.

So Judah was carried away captive out of his land. ₂₈ This is the number of the people whom Nebuchadnezzar carried away captive:
in the seventh year, three thousand and twenty-three Jews;
₂₉ in the eighteenth year of Nebuchadnezzar, he carried away captive from Jerusalem eight hundred and thirty-two persons;
₃₀ in the twenty-third year of Nebuchadnezzar, Nebuzaradan the captain of the guard carried away captive of the Jews seven hundred and forty-five people.
All the people numbered four thousand and six hundred.

₃₁ In the thirty-seventh year of the captivity of Jehoiachin king of Judah, in the twelfth month, in the twenty-fifth day of the month, Evilmerodach king of Babylon, in the first year of his reign, lifted up the head of Jehoiachin king of Judah, and released him from prison. ₃₂ He spoke kindly to him, and set his throne above the throne of the kings who were with him in Babylon, ₃₃ and changed his prison garments. Jehoiachin ate bread before him continually all the days of his life. ₃₄ For his allowance, there was a continual allowance given him by the king of Babylon, every day a portion until the day of his death, all the days of his life.

---

[a] *52:21* A cubit is the length from the tip of the middle finger to the elbow on a man's arm, or about 18 inches or 46 centimetres.

[b] *52:22* A cubit is the length from the tip of the middle finger to the elbow on a man's arm, or about 18 inches or 46 centimetres.

The Lamentations of Jeremiah

1

1 How the city sits solitary,
  that was full of people!
She has become as a widow,
  who was great amongst the nations!
She who was a princess amongst the provinces
  has become a slave!

2 She weeps bitterly in the night.
  Her tears are on her cheeks.
Amongst all her lovers
  she has no one to comfort her.
All her friends have dealt treacherously with her.
  They have become her enemies.

3 Judah has gone into captivity because of affliction
  and because of great servitude.
She dwells amongst the nations.
  She finds no rest.
  All her persecutors overtook her in her distress.

4 The roads to Zion mourn,
  because no one comes to the solemn assembly.
All her gates are desolate.
  Her priests sigh.
Her virgins are afflicted,
  and she herself is in bitterness.

5 Her adversaries have become the head.
  Her enemies prosper;
for the LORD[a] has afflicted her for the multitude of her transgressions.
  Her young children have gone into captivity before the adversary.

6 All majesty has departed from the daughter of Zion.
  Her princes have become like deer that find no pasture.
  They have gone without strength before the pursuer.

7 Jerusalem remembers in the days of her affliction and of her miseries
  all her pleasant things that were from the days of old;
when her people fell into the hand of the adversary,
  and no one helped her.
The adversaries saw her.
  They mocked at her desolations.

8 Jerusalem has grievously sinned.
  Therefore she has become unclean.
All who honoured her despise her,
  because they have seen her nakedness.
  Yes, she sighs and turns backward.

9 Her filthiness was in her skirts.
  She didn't remember her latter end.
Therefore she has come down astoundingly.
  She has no comforter.
"See, LORD, my affliction;
  for the enemy has magnified himself."

10 The adversary has spread out his hand on all her pleasant things;
  for she has seen that the nations have entered into her sanctuary,
  concerning whom you commanded that they should not enter into
    your assembly.

11 All her people sigh.
  They seek bread.
  They have given their pleasant things for food to refresh their soul.
"Look, LORD, and see,
  for I have become despised."

12 "Is it nothing to you, all you who pass by?
  Look, and see if there is any sorrow like my sorrow,
  which is brought on me,
  with which the LORD has afflicted me in the day of his fierce anger.

13 "From on high has he sent fire into my bones,
  and it prevails against them.
He has spread a net for my feet.
  He has turned me back.
  He has made me desolate and I faint all day long.

14 "The yoke of my transgressions is bound by his hand.
  They are knit together.
  They have come up on my neck.

He made my strength fail.
The Lord[b] has delivered me into their hands,
  against whom I am not able to stand.

15 "The Lord has set at nothing all my mighty men within me.
  He has called a solemn assembly against me to crush my young men.
  The Lord has trodden the virgin daughter of Judah as in a wine press.

16 "For these things I weep.
  My eye, my eye runs down with water,
  because the comforter who should refresh my soul is far from me.
My children are desolate,
  because the enemy has prevailed."

17 Zion spreads out her hands.
  There is no one to comfort her.
The LORD has commanded concerning Jacob,
  that those who are around him should be his adversaries.
  Jerusalem is amongst them as an unclean thing.

18 "The LORD is righteous,
  for I have rebelled against his commandment.
Please hear all you peoples,
  and see my sorrow.
  My virgins and my young men have gone into captivity.

19 "I called for my lovers,
  but they deceived me.
My priests and my elders gave up the spirit in the city,
  while they sought food for themselves to refresh their souls.

20 "Look, LORD; for I am in distress.
  My heart is troubled.
My heart turns over within me,
  for I have grievously rebelled.
Abroad, the sword bereaves.
  At home, it is like death.

21 "They have heard that I sigh.
  There is no one to comfort me.
All my enemies have heard of my trouble.
  They are glad that you have done it.
You will bring the day that you have proclaimed,
  and they will be like me.

22 "Let all their wickedness come before you.
  Do to them as you have done to me for all my transgressions.
For my sighs are many,
  and my heart is faint.

2

1 How has the Lord covered the daughter of Zion with a cloud in his anger!
  He has cast the beauty of Israel down from heaven to the earth,
  and hasn't remembered his footstool in the day of his anger.

2 The Lord has swallowed up all the dwellings of Jacob
  without pity.
He has thrown down in his wrath the strongholds of the daughter of Judah.
  He has brought them down to the ground.
  He has profaned the kingdom and its princes.

3 He has cut off all the horn of Israel in fierce anger.
  He has drawn back his right hand from before the enemy.
He has burnt up Jacob like a flaming fire,
  which devours all around.

4 He has bent his bow like an enemy.
  He has stood with his right hand as an adversary.
He has killed all that were pleasant to the eye.
  In the tent of the daughter of Zion, he has poured out his wrath like
    fire.

5 The Lord has become as an enemy.
  He has swallowed up Israel.
He has swallowed up all her palaces.
  He has destroyed his strongholds.
  He has multiplied mourning and lamentation in the daughter of Judah.

6 He has violently taken away his tabernacle,
  as if it were a garden.
He has destroyed his place of assembly.
  The LORD has caused solemn assembly and Sabbath to be forgotten
    in Zion.
  In the indignation of his anger, he has despised the king and the
    priest.

---

a 1:5 When rendered in ALL CAPITAL LETTERS, "LORD" or "GOD" is the translation of God's Proper Name.

b 1:14 The word translated "Lord" is "Adonai."

7 The Lord has cast off his altar.
  He has abhorred his sanctuary.
He has given the walls of her palaces into the hand of the enemy.
  They have made a noise in the LORD's house,
    as in the day of a solemn assembly.

8 The LORD has purposed to destroy the wall of the daughter of Zion.
  He has stretched out the line.
  He has not withdrawn his hand from destroying;
He has made the rampart and wall lament.
  They languish together.

9 Her gates have sunk into the ground.
  He has destroyed and broken her bars.
Her king and her princes are amongst the nations where the law is not.
  Yes, her prophets find no vision from the LORD.

10 The elders of the daughter of Zion sit on the ground.
  They keep silence.
They have cast up dust on their heads.
  They have clothed themselves with sackcloth.
  The virgins of Jerusalem hang down their heads to the ground.

11 My eyes fail with tears.
  My heart is troubled.
My bile is poured on the earth,
  because of the destruction of the daughter of my people,
  because the young children and the infants swoon in the streets of the city.

12 They ask their mothers,
  "Where is grain and wine?"
  when they swoon as the wounded in the streets of the city,
  when their soul is poured out into their mothers' bosom.

13 What shall I testify to you?
  What shall I liken to you, daughter of Jerusalem?
What shall I compare to you,
  that I may comfort you, virgin daughter of Zion?
For your breach is as big as the sea.
  Who can heal you?

14 Your prophets have seen false and foolish visions for you.
  They have not uncovered your iniquity,
  to reverse your captivity,
  but have seen for you false revelations and causes of banishment.

15 All that pass by clap their hands at you.
  They hiss and wag their head at the daughter of Jerusalem, saying,
"Is this the city that men called 'The perfection of beauty,
  the joy of the whole earth'?"

16 All your enemies have opened their mouth wide against you.
  They hiss and gnash their teeth.
  They say, "We have swallowed her up.
Certainly this is the day that we looked for.
  We have found it.
  We have seen it."

17 The LORD has done that which he planned.
  He has fulfilled his word that he commanded in the days of old.
He has thrown down,
  and has not pitied.
He has caused the enemy to rejoice over you.
  He has exalted the horn of your adversaries.

18 Their heart cried to the Lord.
  O wall of the daughter of Zion,
  let tears run down like a river day and night.
Give yourself no relief.
  Don't let your eyes rest.

19 Arise, cry out in the night,
  at the beginning of the watches!
Pour out your heart like water before the face of the Lord.
  Lift up your hands towards him for the life of your young children,
  who faint for hunger at the head of every street.

20 "Look, LORD, and see to whom you have done thus!
  Should the women eat their offspring,
  the children that they held and bounced on their knees?
  Should the priest and the prophet be killed in the sanctuary of the Lord?

21 "The youth and the old man lie on the ground in the streets.
  My virgins and my young men have fallen by the sword.
You have killed them in the day of your anger.
  You have slaughtered, and not pitied.

22 "You have called, as in the day of a solemn assembly, my terrors on every side.
  There was no one that escaped or remained in the day of the LORD's anger.
  My enemy has consumed those whom I have cared for and brought up.

3

1 I am the man who has seen affliction
  by the rod of his wrath.
2 He has led me and caused me to walk in darkness,
  and not in light.
3 Surely he turns his hand against me
  again and again all day long.

4 He has made my flesh and my skin old.
  He has broken my bones.
5 He has built against me,
  and surrounded me with bitterness and hardship.
6 He has made me dwell in dark places,
  as those who have been long dead.

7 He has walled me about, so that I can't go out.
  He has made my chain heavy.
8 Yes, when I cry, and call for help,
  he shuts out my prayer.
9 He has walled up my ways with cut stone.
  He has made my paths crooked.

10 He is to me as a bear lying in wait,
  as a lion in hiding.
11 He has turned away my path,
  and pulled me in pieces.
  He has made me desolate.
12 He has bent his bow,
  and set me as a mark for the arrow.

13 He has caused the shafts of his quiver to enter into my kidneys.
  14 I have become a derision to all my people,
  and their song all day long.
15 He has filled me with bitterness.
  He has stuffed me with wormwood.

16 He has also broken my teeth with gravel.
  He has covered me with ashes.
17 You have removed my soul far away from peace.
  I forgot prosperity.
18 I said, "My strength has perished,
  along with my expectation from the LORD."

19 Remember my affliction and my misery,
  the wormwood and the bitterness.
20 My soul still remembers them,
  and is bowed down within me.
21 This I recall to my mind;
  therefore I have hope.

22 It is because of The LORD's loving kindnesses that we are not consumed,
  because his mercies don't fail.
23 They are new every morning.
  Great is your faithfulness.
24 "The LORD is my portion," says my soul.
  "Therefore I will hope in him."

25 The LORD is good to those who wait for him,
  to the soul who seeks him.
26 It is good that a man should hope
  and quietly wait for the salvation of the LORD.
  27 It is good for a man that he bear the yoke in his youth.

28 Let him sit alone and keep silence,
  because he has laid it on him.
29 Let him put his mouth in the dust,
  if it is so that there may be hope.
30 Let him give his cheek to him who strikes him.
  Let him be filled full of reproach.

31 For the Lord will not cast off forever.
  32 For though he causes grief,
  yet he will have compassion according to the multitude of his loving kindnesses.
33 For he does not afflict willingly,
  nor grieve the children of men.

34 To crush under foot all the prisoners of the earth,
  35 to turn away the right of a man before the face of the Most High,
  36 to subvert a man in his cause, the Lord doesn't approve.

37 Who is he who says, and it comes to pass,
   when the Lord doesn't command it?
38 Doesn't evil and good come out of the mouth of the Most High?
   39 Why should a living man complain,
   a man for the punishment of his sins?

40 Let us search and try our ways,
   and turn again to the LORD.
41 Let's lift up our heart with our hands to God[a] in the heavens.
   42 "We have transgressed and have rebelled.
   You have not pardoned.

43 "You have covered us with anger and pursued us.
   You have killed.
   You have not pitied.
44 You have covered yourself with a cloud,
   so that no prayer can pass through.
45 You have made us an off-scouring and refuse
   in the middle of the peoples.

46 "All our enemies have opened their mouth wide against us.
   47 Terror and the pit have come on us,
   devastation and destruction."

48 My eye runs down with streams of water,
   for the destruction of the daughter of my people.
49 My eye pours down
   and doesn't cease,
   without any intermission,
50 until the LORD looks down,
   and sees from heaven.
51 My eye affects my soul,
   because of all the daughters of my city.

52 They have chased me relentlessly like a bird,
   those who are my enemies without cause.
53 They have cut off my life in the dungeon,
   and have cast a stone on me.
54 Waters flowed over my head.
   I said, "I am cut off."

55 I called on your name, LORD,
   out of the lowest dungeon.
56 You heard my voice:
   "Don't hide your ear from my sighing,
   and my cry."

57 You came near in the day that I called on you.
   You said, "Don't be afraid."

58 Lord, you have pleaded the causes of my soul.
   You have redeemed my life.
59 LORD, you have seen my wrong.
   Judge my cause.
60 You have seen all their vengeance
   and all their plans against me.

61 You have heard their reproach, LORD,
   and all their plans against me,
62 the lips of those that rose up against me,
   and their plots against me all day long.
63 You see their sitting down and their rising up.
   I am their song.

64 You will pay them back, LORD,
   according to the work of their hands.
65 You will give them hardness of heart,
   your curse to them.
66 You will pursue them in anger,
   and destroy them from under the heavens of the LORD.

4

1 How the gold has become dim!
   The most pure gold has changed!
   The stones of the sanctuary are poured out
   at the head of every street.

2 The precious sons of Zion,
   comparable to fine gold,
   how they are esteemed as earthen pitchers,
   the work of the hands of the potter!

3 Even the jackals offer their breast.
   They nurse their young ones.
   But the daughter of my people has become cruel,
   like the ostriches in the wilderness.

4 The tongue of the nursing child clings to the roof of his mouth for thirst.
   The young children ask for bread,
   and no one breaks it for them.

5 Those who ate delicacies are desolate in the streets.
   Those who were brought up in purple embrace dunghills.

6 For the iniquity of the daughter of my people is greater than the sin of
      Sodom,
   which was overthrown as in a moment.
   No hands were laid on her.

7 Her nobles were purer than snow.
   They were whiter than milk.
They were more ruddy in body than rubies.
   Their polishing was like sapphire.

8 Their appearance is blacker than a coal.
   They are not known in the streets.
Their skin clings to their bones.
   It is withered.
   It has become like wood.

9 Those who are killed with the sword are better than those who are killed
      with hunger;
   for these pine away, stricken through,
   for lack of the fruits of the field.

10 The hands of the pitiful women have boiled their own children.
   They were their food in the destruction of the daughter of my people.

11 The LORD has accomplished his wrath.
   He has poured out his fierce anger.
He has kindled a fire in Zion,
   which has devoured its foundations.

12 The kings of the earth didn't believe,
   neither did all the inhabitants of the world,
   that the adversary and the enemy would enter into the gates of
      Jerusalem.

13 It is because of the sins of her prophets
   and the iniquities of her priests,
   that have shed the blood of the just in the middle of her.

14 They wander as blind men in the streets.
   They are polluted with blood,
   So that men can't touch their garments.

15 "Go away!" they cried to them.
   "Unclean! Go away! Go away! Don't touch!"
When they fled away and wandered, men said amongst the nations,
   "They can't live here any more."

16 The LORD's anger has scattered them.
   He will not pay attention to them any more.
They didn't respect the persons of the priests.
   They didn't favour the elders.

17 Our eyes still fail,
   looking in vain for our help.
   In our watching we have watched for a nation that could not save.

18 They hunt our steps,
   so that we can't go in our streets.
Our end is near.
   Our days are fulfilled,
   for our end has come.

19 Our pursuers were swifter than the eagles of the sky.
   They chased us on the mountains.
   They set an ambush for us in the wilderness.

20 The breath of our nostrils,
   the anointed of the LORD,
   was taken in their pits;
of whom we said,
   under his shadow we will live amongst the nations.

21 Rejoice and be glad, daughter of Edom,
   who dwells in the land of Uz.
The cup will pass through to you also.
   You will be drunken,
   and will make yourself naked.

22 The punishment of your iniquity is accomplished, daughter of Zion.
   He will no more carry you away into captivity.

---

a *3:41* The Hebrew word rendered "God" is "אֱלֹהִים" (Elohim).

He will visit your iniquity, daughter of Edom.
  He will uncover your sins.

5

1 Remember, LORD, what has come on us.
  Look, and see our reproach.
2 Our inheritance has been turned over to strangers,
  our houses to aliens.
3 We are orphans and fatherless.
  Our mothers are as widows.
4 We must pay for water to drink.
  Our wood is sold to us.
5 Our pursuers are on our necks.
  We are weary, and have no rest.
6 We have given our hands to the Egyptians,
  and to the Assyrians, to be satisfied with bread.
7 Our fathers sinned, and are no more.
  We have borne their iniquities.
8 Servants rule over us.
  There is no one to deliver us out of their hand.
9 We get our bread at the peril of our lives,
  because of the sword in the wilderness.
10 Our skin is black like an oven,
  because of the burning heat of famine.
11 They ravished the women in Zion,
  the virgins in the cities of Judah.
12 Princes were hanged up by their hands.
  The faces of elders were not honoured.
13 The young men carry millstones.
  The children stumbled under loads of wood.
14 The elders have ceased from the gate,
  and the young men from their music.
15 The joy of our heart has ceased.
  Our dance is turned into mourning.
16 The crown has fallen from our head.
  Woe to us, for we have sinned!
17 For this our heart is faint.
  For these things our eyes are dim:
18 for the mountain of Zion, which is desolate.
  The foxes walk on it.

19 You, LORD, remain forever.
  Your throne is from generation to generation.
20 Why do you forget us forever,
  and forsake us for so long a time?
21 Turn us to yourself, LORD, and we will be turned.
  Renew our days as of old.
22 But you have utterly rejected us.
  You are very angry against us.

The Book of Ezekiel

1

1 Now in the thirtieth year, in the fourth month, in the fifth day of the month, as I was amongst the captives by the river Chebar, the heavens were opened, and I saw visions of God.[a]

2 In the fifth of the month, which was the fifth year of King Jehoiachin's captivity, 3 the LORD's[b] word came to Ezekiel the priest, the son of Buzi, in the land of the Chaldeans by the river Chebar; and the LORD's hand was there on him.

4 I looked, and behold,[c] a stormy wind came out of the north: a great cloud, with flashing lightning, and a brightness around it, and out of the middle of it as it were glowing metal, out of the middle of the fire. 5 Out of its centre came the likeness of four living creatures. This was their appearance: They had the likeness of a man. 6 Everyone had four faces, and each one of them had four wings. 7 Their feet were straight feet. The sole of their feet was like the sole of a calf's foot; and they sparkled like burnished bronze. 8 They had the hands of a man under their wings on their four sides. The four of them had their faces and their wings like this: 9 Their wings were joined to one another. They didn't turn when they went. Each one went straight forward.

10 As for the likeness of their faces, they had the face of a man. The four of them had the face of a lion on the right side. The four of them had the face of an ox on the left side. The four of them also had the face of an eagle. 11 Such were their faces. Their wings were spread out above. Two wings of each one touched another, and two covered their bodies. 12 Each one went straight forward. Where the spirit was to go, they went. They didn't turn when they went. 13 As for the likeness of the living creatures, their appearance was like burning coals of fire, like the appearance of torches. The fire went up and down amongst the living creatures. The fire was bright, and lightning went out of the fire. 14 The living creatures ran and returned as the appearance of a flash of lightning.

15 Now as I saw the living creatures, behold, there was one wheel on the earth beside the living creatures, for each of the four faces of it. 16 The appearance of the wheels and their work was like a beryl. The four of them had one likeness. Their appearance and their work was as it were a wheel within a wheel. 17 When they went, they went in their four directions. They didn't turn when they went. 18 As for their rims, they were high and dreadful; and the four of them had their rims full of eyes all around.

19 When the living creatures went, the wheels went beside them. When the living creatures were lifted up from the earth, the wheels were lifted up. 20 Wherever the spirit was to go, they went. The spirit was to go there. The wheels were lifted up beside them; for the spirit of the living creature was in the wheels. 21 When those went, these went. When those stood, these stood. When those were lifted up from the earth, the wheels were lifted up beside them; for the spirit of the living creature was in the wheels.

22 Over the head of the living creature there was the likeness of an expanse, like an awesome crystal to look at, stretched out over their heads above. 23 Under the expanse, their wings were straight, one towards the other. Each one had two which covered on this side, and each one had two which covered their bodies on that side. 24 When they went, I heard the noise of their wings like the noise of great waters, like the voice of the Almighty, a noise of tumult like the noise of an army. When they stood, they let down their wings.

25 There was a voice above the expanse that was over their heads. When they stood, they let down their wings. 26 Above the expanse that was over their heads was the likeness of a throne, as the appearance of a sapphire[d] stone. On the likeness of the throne was a likeness as the appearance of a man on it above. 27 I saw as it were glowing metal, as the appearance of fire within it all around, from the appearance of his waist and upward; and from the appearance of his waist and downward I saw as it were the appearance of fire, and there was brightness around him. 28 As the appearance of the rainbow that is in the cloud in the day of rain, so was the appearance of the brightness all around.

This was the appearance of the likeness of the LORD's glory. When I saw it, I fell on my face, and I heard a voice of one that spoke.

2

1 He said to me, "Son of man, stand on your feet, and I will speak with you." 2 The Spirit entered into me when he spoke to me, and set me on my feet; and I heard him who spoke to me.

3 He said to me, "Son of man, I send you to the children of Israel, to a nation of rebels who have rebelled against me. They and their fathers have transgressed against me even to this very day. 4 The children are impudent and stiff-hearted. I am sending you to them, and you shall tell them, 'This is what the Lord[e] GOD says.' 5 They, whether they will hear, or whether they will refuse—for they are a rebellious house—yet they will know that there has been a prophet amongst them. 6 You, son of man, don't be afraid of them, neither be afraid of their words, though briers and thorns are with you, and you dwell amongst scorpions. Don't be afraid of their words, nor be dismayed at their looks, though they are a rebellious house. 7 You shall

speak my words to them, whether they will hear or whether they will refuse; for they are most rebellious. 8 But you, son of man, hear what I tell you. Don't be rebellious like that rebellious house. Open your mouth, and eat that which I give you."

9 When I looked, behold, a hand was stretched out to me; and behold, a scroll of a book was in it. 10 He spread it before me. It was written within and without; and lamentations, mourning, and woe were written in it.

3

1 He said to me, "Son of man, eat what you find. Eat this scroll, and go, speak to the house of Israel."

2 So I opened my mouth, and he caused me to eat the scroll.

3 He said to me, "Son of man, eat this scroll that I give you and fill your belly and your bowels with it."

Then I ate it. It was as sweet as honey in my mouth.

4 He said to me, "Son of man, go to the house of Israel, and speak my words to them. 5 For you are not sent to a people of a strange speech and of a hard language, but to the house of Israel— 6 not to many peoples of a strange speech and of a hard language, whose words you can't understand. Surely, if I sent you to them, they would listen to you. 7 But the house of Israel will not listen to you, for they will not listen to me; for all the house of Israel are obstinate[f] and hard-hearted. 8 Behold, I have made your face hard against their faces, and your forehead hard against their foreheads. 9 I have made your forehead as a diamond, harder than flint. Don't be afraid of them, neither be dismayed at their looks, though they are a rebellious house."

10 Moreover he said to me, "Son of man, receive in your heart and hear with your ears all my words that I speak to you. 11 Go to them of the captivity, to the children of your people, and speak to them, and tell them, 'This is what the Lord GOD says,' whether they will hear, or whether they will refuse."

12 Then the Spirit lifted me up, and I heard behind me the voice of a great rushing, saying, "Blessed be the LORD's glory from his place." 13 I heard the noise of the wings of the living creatures as they touched one another, and the noise of the wheels beside them, even the noise of a great rushing. 14 So the Spirit lifted me up, and took me away; and I went in bitterness, in the heat of my spirit; and the LORD's hand was strong on me. 15 Then I came to them of the captivity at Tel Aviv who lived by the river Chebar, and to where they lived; and I sat there overwhelmed amongst them seven days.

16 At the end of seven days, the LORD's word came to me, saying, 17 "Son of man, I have made you a watchman to the house of Israel. Therefore hear the word from my mouth, and warn them from me. 18 When I tell the wicked, 'You will surely die;' and you give him no warning, nor speak to warn the wicked from his wicked way, to save his life, that wicked man will die in his iniquity; but I will require his blood at your hand. 19 Yet if you warn the wicked, and he doesn't turn from his wickedness, nor from his wicked way, he will die in his iniquity; but you have delivered your soul." 20 "Again, when a righteous man turns from his righteousness and commits iniquity, and I lay a stumbling block before him, he will die. Because you have not given him warning, he will die in his sin, and his righteous deeds which he has done will not be remembered; but I will require his blood at your hand. 21 Nevertheless if you warn the righteous man, that the righteous not sin, and he does not sin, he will surely live, because he took warning; and you have delivered your soul."

22 The LORD's hand was there on me; and he said to me, "Arise, go out into the plain, and I will talk with you there."

23 Then I arose, and went out into the plain, and behold, the LORD's glory stood there, like the glory which I saw by the river Chebar. Then I fell on my face.

24 Then the Spirit entered into me and set me on my feet. He spoke with me, and said to me, "Go, shut yourself inside your house. 25 But you, son of man, behold, they will put ropes on you, and will bind you with them, and you will not go out amongst them. 26 I will make your tongue stick to the roof of your mouth so that you will be mute and will not be able to correct them, for they are a rebellious house. 27 But when I speak with you, I will open your mouth, and you shall tell them, 'This is what the Lord GOD says.' He who hears, let him hear; and he who refuses, let him refuse; for they are a rebellious house."

4

1 "You also, son of man, take a tile, and lay it before yourself, and portray on it a city, even Jerusalem. 2 Lay siege against it, build forts against it, and cast up a mound against it. Also set camps against it and plant battering rams against it all around. 3 Take for yourself an iron pan and set it for a wall of iron between you and the city. Then set your face towards it. It will be besieged, and you shall lay siege against it. This shall be a sign to the house of Israel.

4 "Moreover lie on your left side, and lay the iniquity of the house of Israel on it. According to the number of the days that you shall lie on it, you shall bear their iniquity. 5 For I have appointed the years of their iniquity to be to you a number of days, even three hundred and ninety days. So you shall bear the iniquity of the house of Israel.

6 "Again, when you have accomplished these, you shall lie on your right side, and shall bear the iniquity of the house of Judah. I have

---

a *1:1* The Hebrew word rendered "God" is "אֱלֹהִים" (Elohim).

b *1:3* When rendered in ALL CAPITAL LETTERS, "LORD" or "GOD" is the translation of God's Proper Name.

c *1:4* "Behold", from "הִנֵּה", means look at, take notice, observe, see, or gaze at. It is often used as an interjection.

d *1:26* or, lapis lazuli

e *2:4* The word translated "Lord" is "Adonai."

f *3:7* Literally, have a hard forehead

appointed forty days, each day for a year, to you. 7 You shall set your face towards the siege of Jerusalem, with your arm uncovered; and you shall prophesy against it. 8 Behold, I put ropes on you, and you shall not turn yourself from one side to the other, until you have accomplished the days of your siege.

9 "Take for yourself also wheat, barley, beans, lentils, millet, and spelt, and put them in one vessel. Make bread of it. According to the number of the days that you will lie on your side, even three hundred and ninety days, you shall eat of it. 10 Your food which you shall eat shall be by weight, twenty shekels[a] a day. From time to time you shall eat it. 11 You shall drink water by measure, the sixth part of a hin.[b] From time to time you shall drink. 12 You shall eat it as barley cakes, and you shall bake it in their sight with dung that comes out of man." 13 The LORD said, "Even thus will the children of Israel eat their bread unclean, amongst the nations where I will drive them."

14 Then I said, "Ah Lord GOD! Behold, my soul has not been polluted; for from my youth up even until now I have not eaten of that which dies of itself, or is torn of animals. No abominable meat has come into my mouth!"

15 Then he said to me, "Behold, I have given you cow's dung for man's dung, and you shall prepare your bread on it."

16 Moreover he said to me, "Son of man, behold, I will break the staff of bread in Jerusalem. They will eat bread by weight, and with fearfulness. They will drink water by measure, and in dismay; 17 that they may lack bread and water, be dismayed one with another, and pine away in their iniquity.

5

1 "You, son of man, take a sharp sword. You shall take it as a barber's razor to yourself, and shall cause it to pass over your head and over your beard. Then take balances to weigh and divide the hair. 2 A third part you shall burn in the fire in the middle of the city, when the days of the siege are fulfilled. You shall take a third part, and strike with the sword around it. A third part you shall scatter to the wind, and I will draw out a sword after them. 3 You shall take a small number of these and bind them in the folds of your robe. 4 Of these again you shall take, and cast them into the middle of the fire, and burn them in the fire. From it a fire will come out into all the house of Israel.

5 "The Lord GOD says: 'This is Jerusalem. I have set her in the middle of the nations, and countries are around her. 6 She has rebelled against my ordinances in doing wickedness more than the nations, and against my statutes more than the countries that are around her; for they have rejected my ordinances, and as for my statutes, they have not walked in them.'

7 "Therefore the Lord GOD says: 'Because you are more turbulent than the nations that are around you, and have not walked in my statutes, neither have kept my ordinances, neither have followed the ordinances of the nations that are around you; 8 therefore the Lord GOD says: 'Behold, I, even I, am against you; and I will execute judgements amongst you in the sight of the nations. 9 I will do in you that which I have not done, and which I will not do anything like it any more, because of all your abominations. 10 Therefore the fathers will eat the sons within you, and the sons will eat their fathers. I will execute judgements on you; and I will scatter the whole remnant of you to all the winds. 11 Therefore as I live,' says the Lord GOD, 'surely, because you have defiled my sanctuary with all your detestable things, and with all your abominations, therefore I will also diminish you. My eye won't spare, and I will have no pity. 12 A third part of you will die with the pestilence, and they will be consumed with famine within you. A third part will fall by the sword around you. A third part I will scatter to all the winds, and will draw out a sword after them.

13 "'Thus my anger will be accomplished, and I will cause my wrath towards them to rest, and I will be comforted. They will know that I, the LORD, have spoken in my zeal, when I have accomplished my wrath on them.

14 "'Moreover I will make you a desolation and a reproach amongst the nations that are around you, in the sight of all that pass by. 15 So it will be a reproach and a taunt, an instruction and an astonishment, to the nations that are around you, when I execute judgements on you in anger and in wrath, and in wrathful rebukes—I, the LORD, have spoken it— 16 when I send on them the evil arrows of famine that are for destruction, which I will send to destroy you. I will increase the famine on you and will break your staff of bread. 17 I will send on you famine and evil animals, and they will bereave you. Pestilence and blood will pass through you. I will bring the sword on you. I, the LORD, have spoken it.'"

6

1 The LORD's word came to me, saying, 2 "Son of man, set your face towards the mountains of Israel, and prophesy to them, 3 and say, 'You mountains of Israel, hear the word of the Lord GOD! The Lord GOD says to the mountains and to the hills, to the watercourses and to the valleys: "Behold, I, even I, will bring a sword on you, and I will destroy your high places. 4 Your altars will become desolate, and your incense altars will be broken. I will cast down your slain men before your idols. 5 I will lay the dead bodies of the children of Israel before their idols. I will scatter your bones around your altars. 6 In all your dwelling places, the cities will be laid waste and the high places will be desolate, so that your altars may be laid waste and made desolate, and your idols may be broken and cease, and your incense altars may be cut down, and your works may be abolished. 7 The slain will fall amongst you, and you will know that I am the LORD.

8 "'Yet I will leave a remnant, in that you will have some that escape the sword amongst the nations, when you are scattered through the countries. 9 Those of you that escape will remember me amongst the nations where they are carried captive, how I have been broken with their lewd heart, which has departed from me, and with their eyes, which play the prostitute after their idols. Then they will loathe themselves in their own sight for the evils which they have committed in all their abominations. 10 They will know that I am the LORD. I have not said in vain that I would do this evil to them.'"

11 "The Lord GOD says: 'Strike with your hand, and stamp with your foot, and say, "Alas!", because of all the evil abominations of the house of Israel; for they will fall by the sword, by the famine, and by the pestilence. 12 He who is far off will die of the pestilence. He who is near will fall by the sword. He who remains and is besieged will die by the famine. Thus I will accomplish my wrath on them. 13 You will know that I am the LORD when their slain men are amongst their idols around their altars, on every high hill, on all the tops of the mountains, under every green tree, and under every thick oak—the places where they offered pleasant aroma to all their idols. 14 I will stretch out my hand on them and make the land desolate and waste, from the wilderness towards Diblah, throughout all their habitations. Then they will know that I am the LORD.'"

7

1 Moreover the LORD's word came to me, saying, 2 "You, son of man, the Lord GOD says to the land of Israel, 'An end! The end has come on the four corners of the land. 3 Now the end is on you, and I will send my anger on you, and will judge you according to your ways. I will bring on you all your abominations. 4 My eye will not spare you, neither will I have pity; but I will bring your ways on you, and your abominations will be amongst you. Then you will know that I am the LORD.'

5 "The Lord GOD says: 'A disaster! A unique disaster! Behold, it comes. 6 An end has come. The end has come! It awakes against you. Behold, it comes. 7 Your doom has come to you, inhabitant of the land! The time has come! The day is near, a day of tumult, and not of joyful shouting, on the mountains. 8 Now I will shortly pour out my wrath on you, and accomplish my anger against you, and will judge you according to your ways. I will bring on you all your abominations. 9 My eye won't spare, neither will I have pity. I will punish you according to your ways. Your abominations will be amongst you. Then you will know that I, the LORD, strike.

10 "'Behold, the day! Behold, it comes! Your doom has gone out. The rod has blossomed. Pride has budded. 11 Violence has risen up into a rod of wickedness. None of them will remain, nor of their multitude, nor of their wealth. There will be nothing of value amongst them. 12 The time has come! The day draws near. Don't let the buyer rejoice, nor the seller mourn; for wrath is on all its multitude. 13 For the seller won't return to that which is sold, although they are still alive; for the vision concerns the whole multitude of it. None will return. None will strengthen himself in the iniquity of his life. 14 They have blown the trumpet, and have made all ready; but no one goes to the battle, for my wrath is on all its multitude.

15 "'The sword is outside, and the pestilence and the famine within. He who is in the field will die by the sword. He who is in the city will be devoured by famine and pestilence. 16 But of those who escape, they will escape and will be on the mountains like doves of the valleys, all of them moaning, everyone in his iniquity. 17 All hands will be feeble, and all knees will be weak as water. 18 They will also clothe themselves with sackcloth, and horror will cover them. Shame will be on all faces, and baldness on all their heads. 19 They will cast their silver in the streets, and their gold will be as an unclean thing. Their silver and their gold won't be able to deliver them in the day of the LORD's wrath. They won't satisfy their souls or fill their bellies; because it has been the stumbling block of their iniquity. 20 As for the beauty of his ornament, he set it in majesty; but they made the images of their abominations and their detestable things therein. Therefore I have made it to them as an unclean thing. 21 I will give it into the hands of the strangers for a prey, and to the wicked of the earth for a plunder; and they will profane it. 22 I will also turn my face from them, and they will profane my secret place. Robbers will enter into it, and profane it.

23 "'Make chains, for the land is full of bloody crimes, and the city is full of violence. 24 Therefore I will bring the worst of the nations, and they will possess their houses. I will also make the pride of the strong to cease. Their holy places will be profaned. 25 Destruction comes! They will seek peace, and there will be none. 26 Mischief will come on mischief, and rumour will be on rumour. They will seek a vision of the prophet; but the law will perish from the priest, and counsel from the elders. 27 The king will mourn, and the prince will be clothed with desolation. The hands of the people of the land will be troubled. I will do to them after their way, and according to their own judgements I will judge them. Then they will know that I am the LORD.'"

8

1 In the sixth year, in the sixth month, in the fifth day of the month, as I sat in my house, and the elders of Judah sat before me, the Lord GOD's hand fell on me there. 2 Then I saw, and behold, a likeness as the appearance of fire—from the appearance of his waist and downward, fire, and from his waist and upward, as the appearance of brightness, as it were glowing metal. 3 He stretched out the form of a hand, and took me by a lock of my head; and the Spirit lifted me up between earth and the sky, and

---

[a] *4:10* A shekel is about 10 grams or about 0.35 ounces.

[b] *4:11* A hin is about 6.5 litres or 1.7 gallons.

brought me in the visions of God to Jerusalem, to the door of the gate of the inner court that looks towards the north, where there was the seat of the image of jealousy, which provokes to jealousy. ₄ Behold, the glory of the God of Israel was there, according to the appearance that I saw in the plain.

₅ Then he said to me, "Son of man, lift up your eyes now the way towards the north."

So I lifted up my eyes the way towards the north, and saw, northward of the gate of the altar this image of jealousy in the entry.

₆ He said to me, "Son of man, do you see what they do? Even the great abominations that the house of Israel commit here, that I should go far off from my sanctuary? But you will again see yet other great abominations."

₇ He brought me to the door of the court; and when I looked, behold, a hole in the wall. ₈ Then he said to me, "Son of man, dig now in the wall."

When I had dug in the wall, I saw a door.

₉ He said to me, "Go in, and see the wicked abominations that they do here."

₁₀ So I went in and looked, and saw every form of creeping things, abominable animals, and all the idols of the house of Israel, portrayed around on the wall. ₁₁ Seventy men of the elders of the house of Israel stood before them. In the middle of them Jaazaniah the son of Shaphan stood, every man with his censer in his hand; and the smell of the cloud of incense went up.

₁₂ Then he said to me, "Son of man, have you seen what the elders of the house of Israel do in the dark, every man in his rooms of imagery? For they say, 'The LORD doesn't see us. The LORD has forsaken the land.'" ₁₃ He said also to me, "You will again see more of the great abominations which they do."

₁₄ Then he brought me to the door of the gate of the LORD's house which was towards the north; and I saw the women sit there weeping for Tammuz. ₁₅ Then he said to me, "Have you seen this, son of man? You will again see yet greater abominations than these."

₁₆ He brought me into the inner court of the LORD's house; and I saw at the door of the LORD's temple, between the porch and the altar, there were about twenty-five men with their backs towards the LORD's temple and their faces towards the east. They were worshipping the sun towards the east.

₁₇ Then he said to me, "Have you seen this, son of man? Is it a light thing to the house of Judah that they commit the abominations which they commit here? For they have filled the land with violence, and have turned again to provoke me to anger. Behold, they put the branch to their nose. ₁₈ Therefore I will also deal in wrath. My eye won't spare, neither will I have pity. Though they cry in my ears with a loud voice, yet I will not hear them."

9

₁ Then he cried in my ears with a loud voice, saying, "Cause those who are in charge of the city to draw near, each man with his destroying weapon in his hand." ₂ Behold, six men came from the way of the upper gate, which lies towards the north, every man with his slaughter weapon in his hand. One man in the middle of them was clothed in linen, with a writer's inkhorn by his side. They went in, and stood beside the bronze altar.

₃ The glory of the God of Israel went up from the cherub, whereupon it was, to the threshold of the house; and he called to the man clothed in linen, who had the writer's inkhorn by his side. ₄ The LORD said to him, "Go through the middle of the city, through the middle of Jerusalem, and set a mark on the foreheads of the men that sigh and that cry over all the abominations that are done within it."

₅ To the others he said in my hearing, "Go through the city after him, and strike. Don't let your eye spare, neither have pity. ₆ Kill utterly the old man, the young man, the virgin, little children and women; but don't come near any man on whom is the mark. Begin at my sanctuary."

Then they began at the old men who were before the house.

₇ He said to them, "Defile the house, and fill the courts with the slain. Go out!"

They went out, and struck in the city.

₈ While they were killing, and I was left, I fell on my face, and cried, and said, "Ah Lord GOD! Will you destroy all the residue of Israel in your pouring out of your wrath on Jerusalem?"

₉ Then he said to me, "The iniquity of the house of Israel and Judah is exceedingly great, and the land is full of blood, and the city full of perversion; for they say, 'The LORD has forsaken the land, and the LORD doesn't see.' ₁₀ As for me also, my eye won't spare, neither will I have pity, but I will bring their way on their head."

₁₁ Behold, the man clothed in linen, who had the inkhorn by his side, reported the matter, saying, "I have done as you have commanded me."

10

₁ Then I looked, and see, in the expanse that was over the head of the cherubim there appeared above them as it were a sapphire[a] stone, as the appearance of the likeness of a throne. ₂ He spoke to the man clothed in linen, and said, "Go in between the whirling wheels, even under the cherub, and fill both your hands with coals of fire from between the cherubim, and scatter them over the city."

He went in as I watched. ₃ Now the cherubim stood on the right side of the house when the man went in; and the cloud filled the inner court. ₄ The LORD's glory mounted up from the cherub, and stood over the threshold of the house; and the house was filled with the cloud, and the court was full of

the brightness of the LORD's glory. ₅ The sound of the wings of the cherubim was heard even to the outer court, as the voice of God Almighty when he speaks.

₆ It came to pass, when he commanded the man clothed in linen, saying, "Take fire from between the whirling wheels, from between the cherubim," that he went in and stood beside a wheel. ₇ The cherub stretched out his hand from between the cherubim to the fire that was between the cherubim, and took some of it, and put it into the hands of him who was clothed in linen, who took it and went out. ₈ The form of a man's hand appeared here in the cherubim under their wings.

₉ I looked, and behold, there were four wheels beside the cherubim, one wheel beside one cherub, and another wheel beside another cherub. The appearance of the wheels was like a beryl stone. ₁₀ As for their appearance, the four of them had one likeness, like a wheel within a wheel. ₁₁ When they went, they went in their four directions. They didn't turn as they went, but to the place where the head looked they followed it. They didn't turn as they went. ₁₂ Their whole body, including their backs, their hands, their wings, and the wheels, were full of eyes all around, even the wheels that the four of them had. ₁₃ As for the wheels, they were called in my hearing, "the whirling wheels". ₁₄ Every one them had four faces. The first face was the face of the cherub. The second face was the face of a man. The third face was the face of a lion. The fourth was the face of an eagle.

₁₅ The cherubim mounted up. This is the living creature that I saw by the river Chebar. ₁₆ When the cherubim went, the wheels went beside them; and when the cherubim lifted up their wings to mount up from the earth, the wheels also didn't turn from beside them. ₁₇ When they stood, these stood. When they mounted up, these mounted up with them; for the spirit of the living creature was in them.

₁₈ The LORD's glory went out from over the threshold of the house and stood over the cherubim. ₁₉ The cherubim lifted up their wings and mounted up from the earth in my sight when they went out, with the wheels beside them. Then they stood at the door of the east gate of the LORD's house; and the glory of the God of Israel was over them above.

₂₀ This is the living creature that I saw under the God of Israel by the river Chebar; and I knew that they were cherubim. ₂₁ Every one had four faces, and every one four wings. The likeness of the hands of a man was under their wings. ₂₂ As for the likeness of their faces, they were the faces which I saw by the river Chebar, their appearances and themselves. They each went straight forward.

11

₁ Moreover the Spirit lifted me up and brought me to the east gate of the LORD's house, which looks eastward. Behold, twenty-five men were at the door of the gate; and I saw amongst them Jaazaniah the son of Azzur, and Pelatiah the son of Benaiah, princes of the people. ₂ He said to me, "Son of man, these are the men who devise iniquity, and who give wicked counsel in this city; ₃ who say, 'The time is not near to build houses. This is the cauldron, and we are the meat.' ₄ Therefore prophesy against them. Prophesy, son of man."

₅ The LORD's Spirit fell on me, and he said to me, "Speak, 'The LORD says: "Thus you have said, house of Israel; for I know the things that come into your mind. ₆ You have multiplied your slain in this city, and you have filled its streets with the slain."

₇ "'Therefore the Lord GOD says: "Your slain whom you have laid in the middle of it, they are the meat, and this is the cauldron; but you will be brought out of the middle of it. ₈ You have feared the sword; and I will bring the sword on you," says the Lord GOD. ₉ "I will bring you out of the middle of it, and deliver you into the hands of strangers, and will execute judgements amongst you. ₁₀ You will fall by the sword. I will judge you in the border of Israel. Then you will know that I am the LORD. ₁₁ This will not be your cauldron, neither will you be the meat in the middle of it. I will judge you in the border of Israel. ₁₂ You will know that I am the LORD, for you have not walked in my statutes. You have not executed my ordinances, but have done after the ordinances of the nations that are around you."'"

₁₃ When I prophesied, Pelatiah the son of Benaiah died. Then I fell down on my face, and cried with a loud voice, and said, "Ah Lord GOD! Will you make a full end of the remnant of Israel?"

₁₄ The LORD's word came to me, saying, ₁₅ "Son of man, your brothers, even your brothers, the men of your relatives, and all the house of Israel, all of them, are the ones to whom the inhabitants of Jerusalem have said, 'Go far away from the LORD. This land has been given to us for a possession.'

₁₆ "Therefore say, 'The Lord GOD says: "Whereas I have removed them far off amongst the nations, and whereas I have scattered them amongst the countries, yet I will be to them a sanctuary for a little while in the countries where they have come."'

₁₇ "Therefore say, 'The Lord GOD says: "I will gather you from the peoples, and assemble you out of the countries where you have been scattered, and I will give you the land of Israel."

₁₈ "'They will come there, and they will take away all its detestable things and all its abominations from there. ₁₉ I will give them one heart, and I will put a new spirit within them. I will take the stony heart out of their flesh, and will give them a heart of flesh, ₂₀ that they may walk in my statutes, and keep my ordinances, and do them. They will be my people, and I will be their God. ₂₁ But as for them whose heart walks after the heart

---

of their detestable things and their abominations, I will bring their way on their own heads,' says the Lord GOD."

22 Then the cherubim lifted up their wings, and the wheels were beside them. The glory of the God of Israel was over them above. 23 The LORD's glory went up from the middle of the city, and stood on the mountain which is on the east side of the city. 24 The Spirit lifted me up, and brought me in the vision by the Spirit of God into Chaldea, to the captives.

So the vision that I had seen went up from me. 25 Then I spoke to the captives all the things that the LORD had shown me.

12

1 The LORD's word also came to me, saying, 2 "Son of man, you dwell in the middle of the rebellious house, who have eyes to see, and don't see, who have ears to hear, and don't hear; for they are a rebellious house.

3 "Therefore, you son of man, prepare your baggage for moving, and move by day in their sight. You shall move from your place to another place in their sight. It may be they will consider, though they are a rebellious house. 4 You shall bring out your baggage by day in their sight, as baggage for moving. You shall go out yourself at evening in their sight, as when men go out into exile. 5 Dig through the wall in their sight, and carry your baggage out that way. 6 In their sight you shall bear it on your shoulder, and carry it out in the dark. You shall cover your face, so that you don't see the land, for I have set you for a sign to the house of Israel."

7 I did so as I was commanded. I brought out my baggage by day, as baggage for moving, and in the evening I dug through the wall with my hand. I brought it out in the dark, and bore it on my shoulder in their sight.

8 In the morning, the LORD's word came to me, saying, 9 "Son of man, hasn't the house of Israel, the rebellious house, said to you, 'What are you doing?'

10 "Say to them, 'The Lord GOD says: "This burden concerns the prince in Jerusalem, and all the house of Israel amongst whom they are."'

11 "Say, 'I am your sign. As I have done, so will it be done to them. They will go into exile, into captivity.

12 "'The prince who is amongst them will bear his baggage on his shoulder in the dark, and will go out. They will dig through the wall to carry things out that way. He will cover his face, because he will not see the land with his eyes. 13 I will also spread my net on him, and he will be taken in my snare. I will bring him to Babylon to the land of the Chaldeans; yet he will not see it, though he will die there. 14 I will scatter towards every wind all who are around him to help him, and all his bands. I will draw out the sword after them.

15 "'They will know that I am the LORD when I disperse them amongst the nations and scatter them through the countries. 16 But I will leave a few men of them from the sword, from the famine, and from the pestilence, that they may declare all their abominations amongst the nations where they come. Then they will know that I am the LORD.'"

17 Moreover the LORD's word came to me, saying, 18 "Son of man, eat your bread with quaking, and drink your water with trembling and with fearfulness. 19 Tell the people of the land, 'The Lord GOD says concerning the inhabitants of Jerusalem and the land of Israel: "They will eat their bread with fearfulness and drink their water in dismay, that her land may be desolate, and all that is therein, because of the violence of all those who dwell therein. 20 The cities that are inhabited will be laid waste, and the land will be a desolation. Then you will know that I am the LORD."'"

21 The LORD's word came to me, saying, 22 "Son of man, what is this proverb that you have in the land of Israel, saying, 'The days are prolonged, and every vision fails'? 23 Tell them therefore, 'The Lord GOD says: "I will make this proverb to cease, and they will no more use it as a proverb in Israel;"' but tell them, "'The days are at hand, and the fulfilment of every vision. 24 For there will be no more any false vision nor flattering divination within the house of Israel. 25 For I am the LORD. I will speak, and the word that I speak will be performed. It will be no more deferred; for in your days, rebellious house, I will speak the word and will perform it," says the Lord GOD.'"

26 Again the LORD's word came to me, saying, 27 "Son of man, behold, they of the house of Israel say, 'The vision that he sees is for many days to come, and he prophesies of times that are far off.'

28 "Therefore tell them, 'The Lord GOD says: "None of my words will be deferred any more, but the word which I speak will be performed," says the Lord GOD.'"

13

1 The LORD's word came to me, saying, 2 "Son of man, prophesy against the prophets of Israel who prophesy, and say to those who prophesy out of their own heart, 'Hear the LORD's word: 3 The Lord GOD says, "Woe to the foolish prophets, who follow their own spirit, and have seen nothing! 4 Israel, your prophets have been like foxes in the waste places. 5 You have not gone up into the gaps or built up the wall for the house of Israel, to stand in the battle in the LORD's day. 6 They have seen falsehood and lying divination, who say, 'The LORD says;' but the LORD has not sent them. They have made men to hope that the word would be confirmed. 7 Haven't you seen a false vision, and haven't you spoken a lying divination, in that you say, 'The LORD says;' but I have not spoken?"

8 "'Therefore the Lord GOD says: "Because you have spoken falsehood and seen lies, therefore, behold, I am against you," says the Lord GOD. 9 My hand will be against the prophets who see false visions and who utter lying divinations. They will not be in the council of my people, neither will they be written in the writing of the house of Israel, neither will they enter into the land of Israel. Then you will know that I am the Lord GOD."

10 "'Because, even because they have seduced my people, saying, "Peace;" and there is no peace. When one builds up a wall, behold, they plaster it with whitewash. 11 Tell those who plaster it with whitewash that it will fall. There will be an overflowing shower; and you, great hailstones, will fall. A stormy wind will tear it. 12 Behold, when the wall has fallen, won't it be said to you, "Where is the plaster with which you have plastered it?"

13 "'Therefore the Lord GOD says: "I will even tear it with a stormy wind in my wrath. There will be an overflowing shower in my anger, and great hailstones in wrath to consume it. 14 So I will break down the wall that you have plastered with whitewash, and bring it down to the ground, so that its foundation will be uncovered. It will fall, and you will be consumed in the middle of it. Then you will know that I am the LORD. 15 Thus I will accomplish my wrath on the wall, and on those who have plastered it with whitewash. I will tell you, 'The wall is no more, nor those who plastered it— 16 to wit, the prophets of Israel who prophesy concerning Jerusalem, and who see visions of peace for her, and there is no peace,'" says the Lord GOD.'"

17 You, son of man, set your face against the daughters of your people, who prophesy out of their own heart; and prophesy against them, 18 and say, "The Lord GOD says: 'Woe to the women who sew magic bands on all elbows and make veils for the head of persons of every stature to hunt souls! Will you hunt the souls of my people and save souls alive for yourselves? 19 You have profaned me amongst my people for handfuls of barley and for pieces of bread, to kill the souls who should not die and to save the souls alive who should not live, by your lying to my people who listen to lies.'

20 "Therefore the Lord GOD says: 'Behold, I am against your magic bands, with which you hunt the souls to make them fly, and I will tear them from your arms. I will let the souls fly free, even the souls whom you ensnare like birds. 21 I will also tear your veils and deliver my people out of your hand; and they will no longer be in your hand to be ensnared. Then you will know that I am the LORD. 22 Because with lies you have grieved the heart of the righteous, whom I have not made sad; and strengthened the hands of the wicked, that he should not return from his wicked way, and be saved alive. 23 Therefore you shall no more see false visions nor practise divination. I will deliver my people out of your hand. Then you will know that I am the LORD.'"

14

1 Then some of the elders of Israel came to me and sat before me. 2 The LORD's word came to me, saying, 3 "Son of man, these men have taken their idols into their heart, and put the stumbling block of their iniquity before their face. Should I be enquired of at all by them? 4 Therefore speak to them and tell them, 'The Lord GOD says: "Every man of the house of Israel who takes his idols into his heart and puts the stumbling block of his iniquity before his face then comes to the prophet, I the LORD will answer him there according to the multitude of his idols, 5 that I may take the house of Israel in their own heart, because they are all estranged from me through their idols."'

6 "Therefore tell the house of Israel, 'The Lord GOD says: "Return, and turn yourselves from your idols! Turn away your faces from all your abominations.

7 "'"For everyone of the house of Israel, or of the strangers who live in Israel, who separates himself from me and takes his idols into his heart, and puts the stumbling block of his iniquity before his face, and comes to the prophet to enquire for himself of me, I the LORD will answer him by myself. 8 I will set my face against that man and will make him an astonishment, for a sign and a proverb, and I will cut him off from amongst my people. Then you will know that I am the LORD.

9 "'"If the prophet is deceived and speaks a word, I, the LORD, have deceived that prophet, and I will stretch out my hand on him, and will destroy him from amongst my people Israel. 10 They will bear their iniquity. The iniquity of the prophet will be even as the iniquity of him who seeks him, 11 that the house of Israel may no more go astray from me, neither defile themselves any more with all their transgressions; but that they may be my people, and I may be their God," says the Lord GOD.'"

12 The LORD's word came to me, saying, 13 "Son of man, when a land sins against me by committing a trespass, and I stretch out my hand on it, and break the staff of its bread and send famine on it, and cut off from it man and animal— 14 though these three men, Noah, Daniel, and Job, were in it, they would deliver only their own souls by their righteousness," says the Lord GOD.

15 "If I cause evil animals to pass through the land, and they ravage it and it is made desolate, so that no man may pass through because of the animals— 16 though these three men were in it, as I live," says the Lord GOD, "they would deliver neither sons nor daughters. They only would be delivered, but the land would be desolate.

17 "Or if I bring a sword on that land, and say, 'Sword, go through the land, so that I cut off from it man and animal'— 18 though these three men were in it, as I live," says the Lord GOD, "they would deliver neither sons nor daughters, but they only would be delivered themselves.

19 "Or if I send a pestilence into that land, and pour out my wrath on it in blood, to cut off from it man and animal— 20 though Noah, Daniel, and Job, were in it, as I live," says the Lord GOD, "they would deliver neither son nor daughter; they would deliver only their own souls by their righteousness."

21 For the Lord GOD says: "How much more when I send my four severe judgements on Jerusalem—the sword, the famine, the evil animals, and the pestilence—to cut off from it man and animal! 22 Yet, behold, there will be left a remnant in it that will be carried out, both sons and daughters.

Behold, they will come out to you, and you will see their way and their doings. Then you will be comforted concerning the evil that I have brought on Jerusalem, even concerning all that I have brought on it. ₂₃ They will comfort you, when you see their way and their doings; then you will know that I have not done all that I have done in it without cause," says the Lord GOD.

15

₁ The LORD's word came to me, saying, ₂ "Son of man, what is the vine tree more than any tree, the vine branch which is amongst the trees of the forest? ₃ Will wood be taken of it to make anything? Will men take a pin of it to hang any vessel on it? ₄ Behold, it is cast into the fire for fuel; the fire has devoured both its ends, and the middle of it is burnt. Is it profitable for any work? ₅ Behold, when it was whole, it was suitable for no work. How much less, when the fire has devoured it, and it has been burnt, will it yet be suitable for any work?"

₆ Therefore the Lord GOD says: "As the vine wood amongst the trees of the forest, which I have given to the fire for fuel, so I will give the inhabitants of Jerusalem. ₇ I will set my face against them. They will go out from the fire, but the fire will still devour them. Then you will know that I am the LORD, when I set my face against them. ₈ I will make the land desolate, because they have acted unfaithfully," says the Lord GOD.

16

₁ Again the LORD's word came to me, saying, ₂ "Son of man, cause Jerusalem to know her abominations; ₃ and say, 'The Lord GOD says to Jerusalem: "Your origin and your birth is of the land of the Canaanite. An Amorite was your father, and your mother was a Hittite. ₄ As for your birth, in the day you were born your navel was not cut. You weren't washed in water to cleanse you. You weren't salted at all, nor wrapped in blankets at all. ₅ No eye pitied you, to do any of these things to you, to have compassion on you; but you were cast out in the open field, because you were abhorred in the day that you were born.

₆ """When I passed by you, and saw you wallowing in your blood, I said to you, 'Though you are in your blood, live!' Yes, I said to you, 'Though you are in your blood, live!' ₇ I caused you to multiply as that which grows in the field, and you increased and grew great, and you attained to excellent beauty. Your breasts were formed, and your hair grew; yet you were naked and bare.

₈ """Now when I passed by you, and looked at you, behold, your time was the time of love; and I spread my garment over you and covered your nakedness. Yes, I pledged myself to you and entered into a covenant with you," says the Lord GOD, "and you became mine.

₉ """Then I washed you with water. Yes, I thoroughly washed away your blood from you, and I anointed you with oil. ₁₀ I clothed you also with embroidered work and put leather sandals on you. I dressed you with fine linen and covered you with silk. ₁₁ I decked you with ornaments, put bracelets on your hands, and put a chain on your neck. ₁₂ I put a ring on your nose, earrings in your ears, and a beautiful crown on your head. ₁₃ Thus you were decked with gold and silver. Your clothing was of fine linen, silk, and embroidered work. You ate fine flour, honey, and oil. You were exceedingly beautiful, and you prospered to royal estate. ₁₄ Your renown went out amongst the nations for your beauty; for it was perfect, through my majesty which I had put on you," says the Lord GOD.

₁₅ """But you trusted in your beauty, and played the prostitute because of your renown, and poured out your prostitution on everyone who passed by. It was his. ₁₆ You took some of your garments, and made for yourselves high places decked with various colours, and played the prostitute on them. This shouldn't happen, neither shall it be. ₁₇ You also took your beautiful jewels of my gold and of my silver, which I had given you, and made for yourself images of men, and played the prostitute with them. ₁₈ You took your embroidered garments, covered them, and set my oil and my incense before them. ₁₉ My bread also which I gave you, fine flour, oil, and honey, with which I fed you, you even set it before them for a pleasant aroma; and so it was," says the Lord GOD.

₂₀ """Moreover you have taken your sons and your daughters, whom you have borne to me, and you have sacrificed these to them to be devoured. Was your prostitution a small matter, ₂₁ that you have slain my children and delivered them up, in causing them to pass through the fire to them? ₂₂ In all your abominations and your prostitution you have not remembered the days of your youth, when you were naked and bare, and were wallowing in your blood.

₂₃ """It has happened after all your wickedness—woe, woe to you!" says the Lord GOD— ₂₄ "that you have built for yourselves a vaulted place, and have made yourselves a lofty place in every street. ₂₅ You have built your lofty place at the head of every way, and have made your beauty an abomination, and have opened your feet to everyone who passed by, and multiplied your prostitution. ₂₆ You have also committed sexual immorality with the Egyptians, your neighbours, great of flesh; and have multiplied your prostitution, to provoke me to anger. ₂₇ See therefore, I have stretched out my hand over you, and have diminished your portion, and delivered you to the will of those who hate you, the daughters of the Philistines, who are ashamed of your lewd way. ₂₈ You have played the prostitute also with the Assyrians, because you were insatiable; yes, you have played the prostitute with them, and yet you weren't satisfied. ₂₉ You have moreover multiplied your prostitution to the land of merchants, to Chaldea; and yet you weren't satisfied with this.

₃₀ """How weak is your heart," says the Lord GOD, "since you do all these things, the work of an impudent prostitute; ₃₁ in that you build your vaulted place at the head of every way, and make your lofty place in every street, and have not been as a prostitute, in that you scorn pay.

₃₂ """Adulterous wife, who takes strangers instead of her husband! ₃₃ People give gifts to all prostitutes; but you give your gifts to all your lovers, and bribe them, that they may come to you on every side for your prostitution. ₃₄ You are different from other women in your prostitution, in that no one follows you to play the prostitute; and whereas you give hire, and no hire is given to you, therefore you are different.'"

₃₅ "Therefore, prostitute, hear the LORD's word: ₃₆ 'The Lord GOD says, "Because your filthiness was poured out, and your nakedness uncovered through your prostitution with your lovers; and because of all the idols of your abominations, and for the blood of your children, that you gave to them; ₃₇ therefore see, I will gather all your lovers, with whom you have taken pleasure, and all those whom you have loved, with all those whom you have hated. I will even gather them against you on every side, and will uncover your nakedness to them, that they may see all your nakedness. ₃₈ I will judge you as women who break wedlock and shed blood are judged; and I will bring on you the blood of wrath and jealousy. ₃₉ I will also give you into their hand, and they will throw down your vaulted place, and break down your lofty places. They will strip you of your clothes and take your beautiful jewels. They will leave you naked and bare. ₄₀ They will also bring up a company against you, and they will stone you with stones, and thrust you through with their swords. ₄₁ They will burn your houses with fire, and execute judgements on you in the sight of many women. I will cause you to cease from playing the prostitute, and you will also give no hire any more. ₄₂ So I will cause my wrath towards you to rest, and my jealousy will depart from you. I will be quiet, and will not be angry any more.

₄₃ """Because you have not remembered the days of your youth, but have raged against me in all these things; therefore, behold, I also will bring your way on your head," says the Lord GOD: "and you shall not commit this lewdness with all your abominations.

₄₄ """Behold, everyone who uses proverbs will use this proverb against you, saying, 'As is the mother, so is her daughter.' ₄₅ You are the daughter of your mother, who loathes her husband and her children; and you are the sister of your sisters, who loathed their husbands and their children. Your mother was a Hittite, and your father an Amorite. ₄₆ Your elder sister is Samaria, who dwells at your left hand, she and her daughters; and your younger sister, who dwells at your right hand, is Sodom with her daughters. ₄₇ Yet you have not walked in their ways, nor done their abominations; but soon you were more corrupt than they in all your ways. ₄₈ As I live," says the Lord GOD, "Sodom your sister has not done, she nor her daughters, as you have done, you and your daughters.

₄₉ """Behold, this was the iniquity of your sister Sodom: pride, fullness of bread, and prosperous ease was in her and in her daughters. She also didn't strengthen the hand of the poor and needy. ₅₀ They were arrogant and committed abomination before me. Therefore I took them away when I saw it. ₅₁ Samaria hasn't committed half of your sins; but you have multiplied your abominations more than they, and have justified your sisters by all your abominations which you have done. ₅₂ You also bear your own shame yourself, in that you have given judgement for your sisters; through your sins that you have committed more abominable than they, they are more righteous than you. Yes, be also confounded, and bear your shame, in that you have justified your sisters.

₅₃ """I will reverse their captivity, the captivity of Sodom and her daughters, and the captivity of Samaria and her daughters, and the captivity of your captives amongst them; ₅₄ that you may bear your own shame, and may be ashamed because of all that you have done, in that you are a comfort to them. ₅₅ Your sisters, Sodom and her daughters, will return to their former estate; and Samaria and her daughters will return to their former estate; and you and your daughters will return to your former estate. ₅₆ For your sister Sodom was not mentioned by your mouth in the day of your pride, ₅₇ before your wickedness was uncovered, as at the time of the reproach of the daughters of Syria, and of all who are around her, the daughters of the Philistines, who despise you all around. ₅₈ You have borne your lewdness and your abominations," says the LORD.

₅₉ "'For the Lord GOD says: "I will also deal with you as you have done, who have despised the oath in breaking the covenant. ₆₀ Nevertheless I will remember my covenant with you in the days of your youth, and I will establish an everlasting covenant with you. ₆₁ Then you will remember your ways and be ashamed when you receive your sisters, your elder sisters and your younger; and I will give them to you for daughters, but not by your covenant. ₆₂ I will establish my covenant with you. Then you will know that I am the LORD; ₆₃ that you may remember, and be confounded, and never open your mouth any more because of your shame, when I have forgiven you all that you have done," says the Lord GOD.'"

17

₁ The LORD's word came to me, saying, ₂ "Son of man, tell a riddle, and speak a parable to the house of Israel; ₃ and say, 'The Lord GOD says: "A great eagle with great wings and long feathers, full of feathers which had various colours, came to Lebanon and took the top of the cedar. ₄ He cropped off the topmost of its young twigs, and carried it to a land of traffic. He planted it in a city of merchants.

₅ """He also took some of the seed of the land and planted it in fruitful soil. He placed it beside many waters. He set it as a willow tree. ₆ It grew and became a spreading vine of low stature, whose branches turned towards him, and its roots were under him. So it became a vine, produced branches, and shot out sprigs.

7 "'"There was also another great eagle with great wings and many feathers. Behold, this vine bent its roots towards him, and shot out its branches towards him, from the ground where it was planted, that he might water it. 8 It was planted in a good soil by many waters, that it might produce branches and that it might bear fruit, that it might be a good vine."'

9 Say, 'The Lord GOD says: "Will it prosper? Won't he pull up its roots and cut off its fruit, that it may wither, that all its fresh springing leaves may wither? It can't be raised from its roots by a strong arm or many people. 10 Yes, behold, being planted, will it prosper? Won't it utterly wither when the east wind touches it? It will wither in the ground where it grew."'"

11 Moreover the LORD's word came to me, saying, 12 "Say now to the rebellious house, 'Don't you know what these things mean?' Tell them, 'Behold, the king of Babylon came to Jerusalem, and took its king, and its princes, and brought them to him to Babylon. 13 He took one of the royal offspring,[a] and made a covenant with him. He also brought him under an oath, and took away the mighty of the land, 14 that the kingdom might be brought low, that it might not lift itself up, but that by keeping his covenant it might stand. 15 But he rebelled against him in sending his ambassadors into Egypt, that they might give him horses and many people. Will he prosper? Will he who does such things escape? Will he break the covenant, and still escape?

16 "'As I live,' says the Lord GOD, 'surely in the place where the king dwells who made him king, whose oath he despised, and whose covenant he broke, even with him in the middle of Babylon he will die. 17 Pharaoh with his mighty army and great company won't help him in the war, when they cast up mounds and build forts to cut off many persons. 18 For he has despised the oath by breaking the covenant; and behold, he had given his hand, and yet has done all these things. He won't escape.

19 "Therefore the Lord GOD says: 'As I live, I will surely bring on his own head my oath that he has despised and my covenant that he has broken. 20 I will spread my net on him, and he will be taken in my snare. I will bring him to Babylon, and will enter into judgement with him there for his trespass that he has trespassed against me. 21 All his fugitives in all his bands will fall by the sword, and those who remain will be scattered towards every wind. Then you will know that I, the LORD, have spoken it.'

22 "The Lord GOD says: 'I will also take some of the lofty top of the cedar, and will plant it. I will crop off from the topmost of its young twigs a tender one, and I will plant it on a high and lofty mountain. 23 I will plant it in the mountain of the height of Israel; and it will produce boughs, and bear fruit, and be a good cedar. Birds of every kind will dwell in the shade of its branches. 24 All the trees of the field will know that I, the LORD, have brought down the high tree, have exalted the low tree, have dried up the green tree, and have made the dry tree flourish.

"'I, the LORD, have spoken and have done it.'"

18

1 The LORD's word came to me again, saying, 2 "What do you mean, that you use this proverb concerning the land of Israel, saying,
'The fathers have eaten sour grapes,
    and the children's teeth are set on edge'?

3 "As I live," says the Lord GOD, "you shall not use this proverb any more in Israel. 4 Behold, all souls are mine; as the soul of the father, so also the soul of the son is mine. The soul who sins, he shall die.

5 "But if a man is just,
    and does that which is lawful and right,
6 and has not eaten on the mountains,
    hasn't lifted up his eyes to the idols of the house of Israel,
hasn't defiled his neighbour's wife,
    hasn't come near a woman in her impurity,
7 and has not wronged any,
    but has restored to the debtor his pledge,
has taken nothing by robbery,
    has given his bread to the hungry,
    and has covered the naked with a garment;
8 he who hasn't lent to them with interest,
    hasn't taken any increase from them,
who has withdrawn his hand from iniquity,
    has executed true justice between man and man,
9 has walked in my statutes,
    and has kept my ordinances,
    to deal truly;
he is just,
    he shall surely live," says the Lord GOD.

10 "If he fathers a son who is a robber who sheds blood, and who does any one of these things, 11 or who does not do any of those things but has eaten at the mountain shrines
    and defiled his neighbour's wife,
12 has wronged the poor and needy,
    has taken by robbery,
has not restored the pledge,
    and has lifted up his eyes to the idols,
    has committed abomination,
13 has lent with interest,
    and has taken increase from the poor,

shall he then live? He shall not live. He has done all these abominations. He shall surely die. His blood will be on him.

14 "Now, behold, if he fathers a son who sees all his father's sins which he has done, and fears, and doesn't do likewise,
15 who hasn't eaten on the mountains,
    hasn't lifted up his eyes to the idols of the house of Israel,
    hasn't defiled his neighbour's wife,
16 hasn't wronged any,
    hasn't taken anything to pledge,
hasn't taken by robbery,
    but has given his bread to the hungry,
    and has covered the naked with a garment;
17 who has withdrawn his hand from the poor,
    who hasn't received interest or increase,
has executed my ordinances,
    has walked in my statutes;
he shall not die for the iniquity of his father. He shall surely live. 18 As for his father, because he cruelly oppressed, robbed his brother, and did that which is not good amongst his people, behold, he will die in his iniquity.

19 "Yet you say, 'Why doesn't the son bear the iniquity of the father?' When the son has done that which is lawful and right, and has kept all my statutes, and has done them, he will surely live. 20 The soul who sins, he shall die. The son shall not bear the iniquity of the father, neither shall the father bear the iniquity of the son. The righteousness of the righteous shall be on him, and the wickedness of the wicked shall be on him.

21 "But if the wicked turns from all his sins that he has committed, and keeps all my statutes, and does that which is lawful and right, he shall surely live. He shall not die. 22 None of his transgressions that he has committed will be remembered against him. In his righteousness that he has done, he shall live. 23 Have I any pleasure in the death of the wicked?" says the Lord GOD, "and not rather that he should return from his way, and live?

24 "But when the righteous turns away from his righteousness, and commits iniquity, and does according to all the abominations that the wicked man does, should he live? None of his righteous deeds that he has done will be remembered. In his trespass that he has trespassed, and in his sin that he has sinned, in them he shall die.

25 "Yet you say, 'The way of the Lord is not equal.' Hear now, house of Israel: Is my way not equal? Aren't your ways unequal? 26 When the righteous man turns away from his righteousness, and commits iniquity, and dies in it, then he dies in his iniquity that he has done. 27 Again, when the wicked man turns away from his wickedness that he has committed, and does that which is lawful and right, he will save his soul alive. 28 Because he considers, and turns away from all his transgressions that he has committed, he shall surely live. He shall not die. 29 Yet the house of Israel says, 'The way of the Lord is not fair.' House of Israel, aren't my ways fair? Aren't your ways unfair?

30 "Therefore I will judge you, house of Israel, everyone according to his ways," says the Lord GOD. "Return, and turn yourselves from all your transgressions, so iniquity will not be your ruin. 31 Cast away from you all your transgressions in which you have transgressed; and make yourself a new heart and a new spirit. For why will you die, house of Israel? 32 For I have no pleasure in the death of him who dies," says the Lord GOD. "Therefore turn yourselves, and live!

19

1 "Moreover, take up a lamentation for the princes of Israel, 2 and say,
'What was your mother?
    A lioness.
She couched amongst lions,
    in the middle of the young lions she nourished her cubs.
3 She brought up one of her cubs.
    He became a young lion.
He learnt to catch the prey.
    He devoured men.
4 The nations also heard of him.
    He was taken in their pit;
    and they brought him with hooks to the land of Egypt.

5 "'Now when she saw that she had waited,
    and her hope was lost,
then she took another of her cubs,
    and made him a young lion.
6 He went up and down amongst the lions.
    He became a young lion.
He learnt to catch the prey.
    He devoured men.
7 He knew their palaces,
    and laid waste their cities.
The land was desolate with its fullness,
    because of the noise of his roaring.
8 Then the nations attacked him on every side from the provinces.
    They spread their net over him.
    He was taken in their pit.
9 They put him in a cage with hooks,
    and brought him to the king of Babylon.
They brought him into strongholds,

---

so that his voice should no more be heard on the mountains of Israel.

10 "'Your mother was like a vine in your blood, planted by the waters.
It was fruitful and full of branches by reason of many waters.
11 It had strong branches for the sceptres of those who ruled.
Their stature was exalted amongst the thick boughs.
They were seen in their height
with the multitude of their branches.
12 But it was plucked up in fury.
It was cast down to the ground,
and the east wind dried up its fruit.
Its strong branches were broken off and withered.
The fire consumed them.
13 Now it is planted in the wilderness,
in a dry and thirsty land.
14 Fire has gone out of its branches.
It has devoured its fruit,
so that there is in it no strong branch to be a sceptre to rule.'
This is a lamentation, and shall be for a lamentation."

20

1 In the seventh year, in the fifth month, the tenth day of the month, some of the elders of Israel came to enquire of the LORD, and sat before me.

2 The LORD's word came to me, saying, 3 "Son of man, speak to the elders of Israel, and tell them, 'The Lord GOD says: "Is it to enquire of me that you have come? As I live," says the Lord GOD, "I will not be enquired of by you."'

4 "Will you judge them, son of man? Will you judge them? Cause them to know the abominations of their fathers. 5 Tell them, 'The Lord GOD says: "In the day when I chose Israel, and swore to the offspring of the house of Jacob, and made myself known to them in the land of Egypt, when I swore to them, saying, 'I am the LORD your God;' 6 in that day I swore to them to bring them out of the land of Egypt into a land that I had searched out for them, flowing with milk and honey, which is the glory of all lands. 7 I said to them, 'Each of you throw away the abominations of his eyes. Don't defile yourselves with the idols of Egypt. I am the LORD your God.'

8 "'"But they rebelled against me and wouldn't listen to me. They didn't all throw away the abominations of their eyes. They also didn't forsake the idols of Egypt. Then I said I would pour out my wrath on them, to accomplish my anger against them in the middle of the land of Egypt. 9 But I worked for my name's sake, that it should not be profaned in the sight of the nations amongst which they were, in whose sight I made myself known to them in bringing them out of the land of Egypt. 10 So I caused them to go out of the land of Egypt and brought them into the wilderness. 11 I gave them my statutes and showed them my ordinances, which if a man does, he will live in them. 12 Moreover also I gave them my Sabbaths, to be a sign between me and them, that they might know that I am the LORD who sanctifies them.

13 "'"But the house of Israel rebelled against me in the wilderness. They didn't walk in my statutes and they rejected my ordinances, which if a man keeps, he shall live in them. They greatly profaned my Sabbaths. Then I said I would pour out my wrath on them in the wilderness, to consume them. 14 But I worked for my name's sake, that it should not be profaned in the sight of the nations, in whose sight I brought them out. 15 Moreover also I swore to them in the wilderness that I would not bring them into the land which I had given them, flowing with milk and honey, which is the glory of all lands, 16 because they rejected my ordinances, and didn't walk in my statutes, and profaned my Sabbaths; for their heart went after their idols.

17 Nevertheless my eye spared them, and I didn't destroy them. I didn't make a full end of them in the wilderness. 18 I said to their children in the wilderness, 'Don't walk in the statutes of your fathers. Don't observe their ordinances or defile yourselves with their idols. 19 I am the LORD your God. Walk in my statutes, keep my ordinances, and do them. 20 Make my Sabbaths holy. They shall be a sign between me and you, that you may know that I am the LORD your God.'

21 "'"But the children rebelled against me. They didn't walk in my statutes, and didn't keep my ordinances to do them, which if a man does, he shall live in them. They profaned my Sabbaths. Then I said I would pour out my wrath on them, to accomplish my anger against them in the wilderness. 22 Nevertheless I withdrew my hand and worked for my name's sake, that it should not be profaned in the sight of the nations, in whose sight I brought them out. 23 Moreover I swore to them in the wilderness, that I would scatter them amongst the nations and disperse them through the countries, 24 because they had not executed my ordinances, but had rejected my statutes, and had profaned my Sabbaths, and their eyes were after their fathers' idols. 25 Moreover also I gave them statutes that were not good, and ordinances in which they couldn't live. 26 I polluted them in their own gifts, in that they caused all that opens the womb to pass through the fire, that I might make them desolate, to the end that they might know that I am the LORD."'

27 "Therefore, son of man, speak to the house of Israel, and tell them, 'The Lord GOD says: "Moreover, in this your fathers have blasphemed me, in that they have committed a trespass against me. 28 For when I had brought them into the land which I swore to give to them, then they saw every high hill and every thick tree, and they offered there their sacrifices, and there they presented the provocation of their offering. There they also

made their pleasant aroma, and there they poured out their drink offerings. 29 Then I said to them, 'What does the high place where you go mean?' So its name is called Bamah^a to this day."

30 "Therefore tell the house of Israel, 'The Lord GOD says: "Do you pollute yourselves in the way of your fathers? Do you play the prostitute after their abominations? 31 When you offer your gifts, when you make your sons pass through the fire, do you pollute yourselves with all your idols to this day? Should I be enquired of by you, house of Israel? As I live, says the Lord GOD, I will not be enquired of by you!

32 "'"That which comes into your mind will not be at all, in that you say, 'We will be as the nations, as the families of the countries, to serve wood and stone.' 33 As I live," says the Lord GOD, "surely with a mighty hand, with an outstretched arm, and with wrath poured out, I will be king over you. 34 I will bring you out from the peoples, and will gather you out of the countries in which you are scattered with a mighty hand, with an outstretched arm, and with wrath poured out. 35 I will bring you into the wilderness of the peoples, and there I will enter into judgement with you face to face. 36 Just as I entered into judgement with your fathers in the wilderness of the land of Egypt, so I will enter into judgement with you," says the Lord GOD. 37 "I will cause you to pass under the rod, and I will bring you into the bond of the covenant. 38 I will purge out from amongst you the rebels and those who disobey me. I will bring them out of the land where they live, but they shall not enter into the land of Israel. Then you will know that I am the LORD."

39 "'As for you, house of Israel, the Lord GOD says: "Go, everyone serve his idols, and hereafter also, if you will not listen to me; but you shall no more profane my holy name with your gifts and with your idols. 40 For in my holy mountain, in the mountain of the height of Israel," says the Lord GOD, "there all the house of Israel, all of them, shall serve me in the land. There I will accept them, and there I will require your offerings and the first fruits of your offerings, with all your holy things. 41 I will accept you as a pleasant aroma when I bring you out from the peoples and gather you out of the countries in which you have been scattered. I will be sanctified in you in the sight of the nations. 42 You will know that I am the LORD when I bring you into the land of Israel, into the country which I swore to give to your fathers. 43 There you will remember your ways, and all your deeds in which you have polluted yourselves. Then you will loathe yourselves in your own sight for all your evils that you have committed. 44 You will know that I am the LORD, when I have dealt with you for my name's sake, not according to your evil ways, nor according to your corrupt doings, you house of Israel," says the Lord GOD.'"

45 The LORD's word came to me, saying, 46 "Son of man, set your face towards the south, and preach towards the south, and prophesy against the forest of the field in the south. 47 Tell the forest of the south, 'Hear the LORD's word: The Lord GOD says, "Behold, I will kindle a fire in you, and it will devour every green tree in you, and every dry tree. The burning flame will not be quenched, and all faces from the south to the north will be burnt by it. 48 All flesh will see that I, the LORD, have kindled it. It will not be quenched."'"

49 Then I said, "Ah Lord GOD! They say of me, 'Isn't he a speaker of parables?'"

21

1 The LORD's word came to me, saying, 2 "Son of man, set your face towards Jerusalem, and preach towards the sanctuaries, and prophesy against the land of Israel. 3 Tell the land of Israel, 'The LORD says: "Behold, I am against you, and will draw my sword out of its sheath, and will cut off from you the righteous and the wicked. 4 Seeing then that I will cut off from you the righteous and the wicked, therefore my sword will go out of its sheath against all flesh from the south to the north. 5 All flesh will know that I, the LORD, have drawn my sword out of its sheath. It will not return any more."'

6 "Therefore sigh, you son of man. You shall sigh before their eyes with a broken heart^b and with bitterness. 7 It shall be, when they ask you, 'Why do you sigh?' that you shall say, 'Because of the news, for it comes! Every heart will melt, all hands will be feeble, every spirit will faint, and all knees will be weak as water. Behold, it comes, and it shall be done, says the Lord GOD.'"

8 The LORD's word came to me, saying, 9 "Son of man, prophesy, and say, 'The LORD says:
"A sword! A sword!
It is sharpened,
and also polished.
10 It is sharpened that it may make a slaughter.
It is polished that it may be as lightning.
Should we then make mirth?
The rod of my son condemns every tree.
11 It is given to be polished,
that it may be handled.
The sword is sharpened.
Yes, it is polished
to give it into the hand of the killer."'
12 Cry and wail, son of man;
for it is on my people.
It is on all the princes of Israel.
They are delivered over to the sword with my people.
Therefore beat your thigh.

---

a 20:29 "Bamah" means "High Place".

b 21:6 literally, the breaking of your thighs

13 "For there is a trial. What if even the rod that condemns will be no more?" says the Lord GOD.

14 "You therefore, son of man, prophesy,
   and strike your hands together.
Let the sword be doubled the third time,
   the sword of the fatally wounded.
It is the sword of the great one who is fatally wounded,
   which enters into their rooms.
15 I have set the threatening sword against all their gates,
   that their heart may melt,
   and their stumblings be multiplied.
Ah! It is made as lightning.
   It is pointed for slaughter.
16 Gather yourselves together.
   Go to the right.
Set yourselves in array.
   Go to the left,
   wherever your face is set.
17 I will also strike my hands together,
   and I will cause my wrath to rest.
   I, the LORD, have spoken it."

18 The LORD's word came to me again, saying, 19 "Also, you son of man, appoint two ways, that the sword of the king of Babylon may come. They both will come out of one land, and mark out a place. Mark it out at the head of the way to the city. 20 You shall appoint a way for the sword to come to Rabbah of the children of Ammon, and to Judah in Jerusalem the fortified. 21 For the king of Babylon stood at the parting of the way, at the head of the two ways, to use divination. He shook the arrows back and forth. He consulted the teraphim.ᵃ He looked in the liver. 22 In his right hand was the lot for Jerusalem, to set battering rams, to open the mouth in the slaughter, to lift up the voice with shouting, to set battering rams against the gates, to cast up mounds, and to build forts. 23 It will be to them as a false divination in their sight, who have sworn oaths to them; but he brings iniquity to memory, that they may be taken.

24 "Therefore the Lord GOD says: 'Because you have caused your iniquity to be remembered, in that your transgressions are uncovered, so that in all your doings your sins appear; because you have come to memory, you will be taken with the hand.

25 "'You, deadly wounded wicked one, the prince of Israel, whose day has come, in the time of the iniquity of the end, 26 the Lord GOD says: "Remove the turban, and take off the crown. This will not be as it was. Exalt that which is low, and humble that which is high. 27 I will overturn, overturn, overturn it. This also will be no more, until he comes whose right it is; and I will give it.'"

28 "You, son of man, prophesy and say, 'The Lord GOD says this concerning the children of Ammon, and concerning their reproach:
"A sword! A sword is drawn!
   It is polished for the slaughter,
to cause it to devour,
   that it may be as lightning;
29 while they see for you false visions,
   while they divine lies to you,
to lay you on the necks of the wicked who are deadly wounded,
   whose day has come in the time of the iniquity of the end.
30 Cause it to return into its sheath.
   In the place where you were created,
   in the land of your birth, I will judge you.
31 I will pour out my indignation on you.
   I will blow on you with the fire of my wrath.
I will deliver you into the hand of brutish men,
   skilful to destroy.
32 You will be for fuel to the fire.
   Your blood will be in the middle of the land.
You will be remembered no more;
   for I, the LORD, have spoken it.'"

22

1 Moreover the LORD's word came to me, saying, 2 "You, son of man, will you judge? Will you judge the bloody city? Then cause her to know all her abominations. 3 You shall say, 'The Lord GOD says: "A city that sheds blood within herself, that her time may come, and that makes idols against herself to defile her! 4 You have become guilty in your blood that you have shed, and are defiled in your idols which you have made! You have caused your days to draw near, and have come to the end of your years. Therefore I have made you a reproach to the nations, and a mocking to all the countries. 5 Those who are near and those who are far from you will mock you, you infamous one, full of tumult.

6 "'"Behold, the princes of Israel, everyone according to his power, have been in you to shed blood. 7 In you have they treated father and mother with contempt.ᵇ Amongst you they have oppressed the foreigner. In you have they wronged the fatherless and the widow. 8 You have despised my holy things, and have profaned my Sabbaths. 9 Slanderous men have been in you to shed blood. In you they have eaten on the mountains. They have committed lewdness amongst you. 10 In you have they uncovered their fathers' nakedness. In you have they humbled her who was unclean in

her impurity. 11 One has committed abomination with his neighbour's wife, and another has lewdly defiled his daughter-in-law. Another in you has humbled his sister, his father's daughter. 12 In you have they taken bribes to shed blood. You have taken interest and increase, and you have greedily gained of your neighbours by oppression, and have forgotten me," says the Lord GOD.

13 "'"Behold, therefore I have struck my hand at your dishonest gain which you have made, and at the blood which has been shed within you. 14 Can your heart endure, or can your hands be strong, in the days that I will deal with you? I, the LORD, have spoken it, and will do it. 15 I will scatter you amongst the nations, and disperse you through the countries. I will purge your filthiness out of you. 16 You will be profaned in yourself in the sight of the nations. Then you will know that I am the LORD."'"

17 The LORD's word came to me, saying, 18 "Son of man, the house of Israel has become dross to me. All of them are bronze, tin, iron, and lead in the middle of the furnace. They are the dross of silver. 19 Therefore the Lord GOD says: 'Because you have all become dross, therefore, behold, I will gather you into the middle of Jerusalem. 20 As they gather silver, bronze, iron, lead, and tin into the middle of the furnace, to blow the fire on it, to melt it, so I will gather you in my anger and in my wrath, and I will lay you there and melt you. 21 Yes, I will gather you, and blow on you with the fire of my wrath, and you will be melted in the middle of it. 22 As silver is melted in the middle of the furnace, so you will be melted in the middle of it; and you will know that I, the LORD, have poured out my wrath on you.'"

23 The LORD's word came to me, saying, 24 "Son of man, tell her, 'You are a land that is not cleansed nor rained on in the day of indignation.' 25 There is a conspiracy of her prophets within it, like a roaring lion ravening the prey. They have devoured souls. They take treasure and precious things. They have made many widows within it. 26 Her priests have done violence to my law and have profaned my holy things. They have made no distinction between the holy and the common, neither have they caused men to discern between the unclean and the clean, and have hidden their eyes from my Sabbaths. So I am profaned amongst them. 27 Her princes within it are like wolves ravening the prey, to shed blood and to destroy souls, that they may get dishonest gain. 28 Her prophets have plastered for them with whitewash, seeing false visions, and divining lies to them, saying, 'The Lord GOD says,' when the LORD has not spoken. 29 The people of the land have used oppression and exercised robbery. Yes, they have troubled the poor and needy, and have oppressed the foreigner wrongfully.

30 "I sought for a man amongst them who would build up the wall and stand in the gap before me for the land, that I would not destroy it; but I found no one. 31 Therefore I have poured out my indignation on them. I have consumed them with the fire of my wrath. I have brought their own way on their heads," says the Lord GOD.

23

1 The LORD's word came again to me, saying, 2 "Son of man, there were two women, the daughters of one mother. 3 They played the prostitute in Egypt. They played the prostitute in their youth. Their breasts were fondled there, and their youthful nipples were caressed there. 4 Their names were Oholah the elder, and Oholibah her sister. They became mine, and they bore sons and daughters. As for their names, Samaria is Oholah, and Jerusalem Oholibah.

5 "Oholah played the prostitute when she was mine. She doted on her lovers, on the Assyrians her neighbours, 6 who were clothed with blue—governors and rulers, all of them desirable young men, horsemen riding on horses. 7 She gave herself as a prostitute to them, all of them the choicest men of Assyria. She defiled herself with the idols of whoever she lusted after. 8 She hasn't left her prostitution since leaving Egypt; for in her youth they lay with her. They caressed her youthful nipples and they poured out their prostitution on her.

9 "Therefore I delivered her into the hand of her lovers, into the hand of the Assyrians on whom she doted. 10 These uncovered her nakedness. They took her sons and her daughters, and they killed her with the sword. She became a byword amongst women; for they executed judgements on her.

11 "Her sister Oholibah saw this, yet she was more corrupt in her lusting than she, and in her prostitution which was more depraved than the prostitution of her sister. 12 She lusted after the Assyrians, governors and rulers—her neighbours, clothed most gorgeously, horsemen riding on horses, all of them desirable young men. 13 I saw that she was defiled. They both went the same way.

14 "She increased her prostitution; for she saw men portrayed on the wall, the images of the Chaldeans portrayed with red, 15 dressed with belts on their waists, with flowing turbans on their heads, all of them looking like princes, after the likeness of the Babylonians in Chaldea, the land of their birth. 16 As soon as she saw them, she lusted after them and sent messengers to them into Chaldea. 17 The Babylonians came to her into the bed of love, and they defiled her with their prostitution. She was polluted with them, and her soul was alienated from them. 18 So she uncovered her prostitution and uncovered her nakedness. Then my soul was alienated from her, just like my soul was alienated from her sister. 19 Yet she multiplied her prostitution, remembering the days of her youth, in which she had played the prostitute in the land of Egypt. 20 She lusted after their lovers, whose flesh is as the flesh of donkeys, and whose issue is like the

---

ᵃ 21:21 teraphim were household idols that may have been associated with inheritance rights to the household property.

ᵇ 22:7 Literally, made light of father and mother.

issue of horses. 21 Thus you called to memory the lewdness of your youth, in the caressing of your nipples by the Egyptians because of your youthful breasts.

22 "Therefore, Oholibah, the Lord GOD says: 'Behold, I will raise up your lovers against you, from whom your soul is alienated, and I will bring them against you on every side: 23 the Babylonians and all the Chaldeans, Pekod, Shoa, Koa, and all the Assyrians with them; all of them desirable young men, governors and rulers, princes and men of renown, all of them riding on horses. 24 They will come against you with weapons, chariots, and wagons, and with a company of peoples. They will set themselves against you with buckler, shield, and helmet all around. I will commit the judgement to them, and they will judge you according to their judgements. 25 I will set my jealousy against you, and they will deal with you in fury. They will take away your nose and your ears. Your remnant will fall by the sword. They will take your sons and your daughters; and the rest of you will be devoured by the fire. 26 They will also strip you of your clothes and take away your beautiful jewels. 27 Thus I will make your lewdness to cease from you, and remove your prostitution from the land of Egypt, so that you will not lift up your eyes to them, nor remember Egypt any more.'

28 "For the Lord GOD says: 'Behold, I will deliver you into the hand of them whom you hate, into the hand of them from whom your soul is alienated. 29 They will deal with you in hatred, and will take away all your labour, and will leave you naked and bare. The nakedness of your prostitution will be uncovered, both your lewdness and your prostitution. 30 These things will be done to you because you have played the prostitute after the nations, and because you are polluted with their idols. 31 You have walked in the way of your sister; therefore I will give her cup into your hand.'

32 "The Lord GOD says:
'You will drink of your sister's cup,
    which is deep and large.
You will be ridiculed and held in derision.
    It contains much.
33 You will be filled with drunkenness and sorrow,
    with the cup of astonishment and desolation,
    with the cup of your sister Samaria.
34 You will even drink it and drain it out.
    You will gnaw the broken pieces of it,
    and will tear your breasts;
for I have spoken it,' says the Lord GOD.

35 "Therefore the Lord GOD says: 'Because you have forgotten me and cast me behind your back, therefore you also bear your lewdness and your prostitution.'"

36 The LORD said moreover to me: "Son of man, will you judge Oholah and Oholibah? Then declare to them their abominations. 37 For they have committed adultery, and blood is in their hands. They have committed adultery with their idols. They have also caused their sons, whom they bore to me, to pass through the fire to them to be devoured. 38 Moreover this they have done to me: they have defiled my sanctuary in the same day, and have profaned my Sabbaths. 39 For when they had slain their children to their idols, then they came the same day into my sanctuary to profane it; and behold, they have done this in the middle of my house.

40 "Furthermore you sisters have sent for men who come from far away, to whom a messenger was sent, and behold, they came; for whom you washed yourself, painted your eyes, decorated yourself with ornaments, 41 and sat on a stately bed, with a table prepared before it, whereupon you set my incense and my oil.

42 "The voice of a multitude being at ease was with her. With men of the common sort were brought drunkards from the wilderness; and they put bracelets on their hands, and beautiful crowns on their heads. 43 Then I said of her who was old in adulteries, 'Now they will play the prostitute with her, and she with them.' 44 They went in to her, as they go in to a prostitute. So they went in to Oholah and to Oholibah, the lewd women. 45 Righteous men will judge them with the judgement of adulteresses and with the judgement of women who shed blood, because they are adulteresses, and blood is in their hands.

46 "For the Lord GOD says: 'I will bring up a mob against them, and will give them to be tossed back and forth and robbed. 47 The company will stone them with stones and dispatch them with their swords. They will kill their sons and their daughters, and burn up their houses with fire.

48 "'Thus I will cause lewdness to cease out of the land, that all women may be taught not to be lewd like you. 49 They will recompense your lewdness on you, and you will bear the sins of your idols. Then you will know that I am the Lord GOD.'"

24

1 Again, in the ninth year, in the tenth month, in the tenth day of the month, the LORD's word came to me, saying, 2 "Son of man, write the name of the day, this same day. The king of Babylon drew close to Jerusalem this same day. 3 Utter a parable to the rebellious house, and tell them, 'The Lord GOD says,
"Put the cauldron on the fire.
    Put it on,
    and also pour water into it.
4 Gather its pieces into it,
    even every good piece:
    the thigh and the shoulder.
    Fill it with the choice bones.
5 Take the choice of the flock,
    and also a pile of wood for the bones under the cauldron.

Make it boil well.
    Yes, let its bones be boiled within it."
6 "'Therefore the Lord GOD says:
"Woe to the bloody city,
    to the cauldron whose rust is in it,
    and whose rust hasn't gone out of it!
Take out of it piece after piece
    without casting lots for it.

7 "'"For the blood she shed is in the middle of her.
    She set it on the bare rock.
She didn't pour it on the ground,
    to cover it with dust.
8 That it may cause wrath to come up to take vengeance,
    I have set her blood on the bare rock,
    that it should not be covered."
9 "'Therefore the Lord GOD says:
"Woe to the bloody city!
    I also will make the pile great.
10 Heap on the wood.
    Make the fire hot.
Boil the meat well.
    Make the broth thick,
    and let the bones be burnt.
11 Then set it empty on its coals,
    that it may be hot,
and its bronze may burn,
    and that its filthiness may be molten in it,
    that its rust may be consumed.
12 She is weary with toil;
    yet her great rust,
    rust by fire, doesn't leave her.
13 "'"In your filthiness is lewdness. Because I have cleansed you and you weren't cleansed, you won't be cleansed from your filthiness any more, until I have caused my wrath towards you to rest.

14 "'"I, the LORD, have spoken it. It will happen, and I will do it. I won't go back. I won't spare. I won't repent. According to your ways and according to your doings, they will judge you," says the Lord GOD.'"

15 Also the LORD's word came to me, saying, 16 "Son of man, behold, I will take away from you the desire of your eyes with one stroke; yet you shall neither mourn nor weep, neither shall your tears run down. 17 Sigh, but not aloud. Make no mourning for the dead. Bind your headdress on you, and put your sandals on your feet. Don't cover your lips, and don't eat mourner's bread."

18 So I spoke to the people in the morning, and at evening my wife died. So I did in the morning as I was commanded.

19 The people asked me, "Won't you tell us what these things mean to us, that you act like this?"

20 Then I said to them, "The LORD's word came to me, saying, 21 'Speak to the house of Israel, "The Lord GOD says: 'Behold, I will profane my sanctuary, the pride of your power, the desire of your eyes, and that which your soul pities; and your sons and your daughters whom you have left behind will fall by the sword. 22 You will do as I have done. You won't cover your lips or eat mourner's bread. 23 Your turbans will be on your heads, and your sandals on your feet. You won't mourn or weep; but you will pine away in your iniquities, and moan one towards another. 24 Thus Ezekiel will be a sign to you; according to all that he has done, you will do. When this comes, then you will know that I am the Lord GOD.'"'"

25 "You, son of man, shouldn't it be in the day when I take from them their strength, the joy of their glory, the desire of their eyes, and that whereupon they set their heart—their sons and their daughters— 26 that in that day he who escapes will come to you, to cause you to hear it with your ears? 27 In that day your mouth will be opened to him who has escaped, and you will speak and be no more mute. So you will be a sign to them. Then they will know that I am the LORD."

25

1 The LORD's word came to me, saying, 2 "Son of man, set your face towards the children of Ammon, and prophesy against them. 3 Tell the children of Ammon, 'Hear the word of the Lord GOD! The Lord GOD says, "Because you said, 'Aha!' against my sanctuary when it was profaned, and against the land of Israel when it was made desolate, and against the house of Judah when they went into captivity, 4 therefore, behold, I will deliver you to the children of the east for a possession. They will set their encampments in you and make their dwellings in you. They will eat your fruit and they will drink your milk. 5 I will make Rabbah a stable for camels and the children of Ammon a resting place for flocks. Then you will know that I am the LORD." 6 For the Lord GOD says: "Because you have clapped your hands, stamped with the feet, and rejoiced with all the contempt of your soul against the land of Israel, 7 therefore, behold, I have stretched out my hand on you, and will deliver you for a plunder to the nations. I will cut you off from the peoples, and I will cause you to perish out of the countries. I will destroy you. Then you will know that I am the LORD."

8 "'The Lord GOD says: "Because Moab and Seir say, 'Behold, the house of Judah is like all the nations,' 9 therefore, behold, I will open the side of Moab from the cities, from his cities which are on its frontiers, the glory of the country, Beth Jeshimoth, Baal Meon, and Kiriathaim, 10 to the children of the east, to go against the children of Ammon; and I will give them for a possession, that the children of Ammon may not be remembered

amongst the nations. ₁₁ I will execute judgements on Moab. Then they will know that I am the LORD."

₁₂ "'The Lord GOD says: "Because Edom has dealt against the house of Judah by taking vengeance, and has greatly offended, and taken revenge on them," ₁₃ therefore the Lord GOD says, "I will stretch out my hand on Edom, and will cut off man and animal from it; and I will make it desolate from Teman. They will fall by the sword even to Dedan. ₁₄ I will lay my vengeance on Edom by the hand of my people Israel. They will do in Edom according to my anger and according to my wrath. Then they will know my vengeance," says the Lord GOD.

₁₅ "'The Lord GOD says: "Because the Philistines have taken revenge, and have taken vengeance with contempt of soul to destroy with perpetual hostility," ₁₆ therefore the Lord GOD says, "Behold, I will stretch out my hand on the Philistines, and I will cut off the Cherethites, and destroy the remnant of the sea coast. ₁₇ I will execute great vengeance on them with wrathful rebukes. Then they will know that I am the LORD, when I lay my vengeance on them."'"

26

₁ In the eleventh year, in the first of the month, the LORD's word came to me, saying, ₂ "Son of man, because Tyre has said against Jerusalem, 'Aha! She is broken! She who was the gateway of the peoples has been returned to me. I will be replenished, now that she is laid waste;' ₃ therefore the Lord GOD says, 'Behold, I am against you, Tyre, and will cause many nations to come up against you, as the sea causes its waves to come up. ₄ They will destroy the walls of Tyre, and break down her towers. I will also scrape her dust from her, and make her a bare rock. ₅ She will be a place for the spreading of nets in the middle of the sea; for I have spoken it,' says the Lord GOD. 'She will become plunder for the nations. ₆ Her daughters who are in the field will be slain with the sword. Then they will know that I am the LORD.'

₇ "For the Lord GOD says: 'Behold, I will bring on Tyre Nebuchadnezzar king of Babylon, king of kings, from the north, with horses, with chariots, with horsemen, and an army with many people. ₈ He will kill your daughters in the field with the sword. He will make forts against you, cast up a mound against you, and raise up the buckler against you. ₉ He will set his battering engines against your walls, and with his axes he will break down your towers. ₁₀ By reason of the abundance of his horses, their dust will cover you. Your walls will shake at the noise of the horsemen, of the wagons, and of the chariots, when he enters into your gates, as men enter into a city which is broken open. ₁₁ He will tread down all your streets with the hoofs of his horses. He will kill your people with the sword. The pillars of your strength will go down to the ground. ₁₂ They will make a plunder of your riches and make a prey of your merchandise. They will break down your walls and destroy your pleasant houses. They will lay your stones, your timber, and your dust in the middle of the waters. ₁₃ I will cause the noise of your songs to cease. The sound of your harps won't be heard any more. ₁₄ I will make you a bare rock. You will be a place for the spreading of nets. You will be built no more; for I the LORD have spoken it,' says the Lord GOD.

₁₅ "The Lord GOD says to Tyre: 'Won't the islands shake at the sound of your fall, when the wounded groan, when the slaughter is made within you? ₁₆ Then all the princes of the sea will come down from their thrones, and lay aside their robes, and strip off their embroidered garments. They will clothe themselves with trembling. They will sit on the ground, and will tremble every moment, and be astonished at you. ₁₇ They will take up a lamentation over you, and tell you,
"How you are destroyed,
    who were inhabited by seafaring men,
the renowned city,
    who was strong in the sea,
she and her inhabitants,
    who caused their terror to be on all who lived there!"
₁₈ Now the islands will tremble in the day of your fall.
    Yes, the islands that are in the sea will be dismayed at your departure.'

₁₉ "For the Lord GOD says: 'When I make you a desolate city, like the cities that are not inhabited, when I bring up the deep on you, and the great waters cover you, ₂₀ then I will bring you down with those who descend into the pit, to the people of old time, and will make you dwell in the lower parts of the earth, in the places that are desolate of old, with those who go down to the pit, that you be not inhabited; and I will set glory in the land of the living. ₂₁ I will make you a terror, and you will no more have any being. Though you are sought for, yet you will never be found again,' says the Lord GOD."

27

₁ The LORD's word came again to me, saying, ₂ "You, son of man, take up a lamentation over Tyre; ₃ and tell Tyre, 'You who dwell at the entry of the sea, who are the merchant of the peoples to many islands, the Lord GOD says:
"You, Tyre, have said,
    'I am perfect in beauty.'
₄ Your borders are in the heart of the seas.
    Your builders have perfected your beauty.
₅ They have made all your planks of cypress trees from Senir.
    They have taken a cedar from Lebanon to make a mast for you.
₆ They have made your oars of the oaks of Bashan.
    They have made your benches of ivory inlaid in cypress wood from
        the islands of Kittim.
₇ Your sail was of fine linen with embroidered work from Egypt,

that it might be to you for a banner.
    Blue and purple from the islands of Elishah was your awning.
₈ The inhabitants of Sidon and Arvad were your rowers.
    Your wise men, Tyre, were in you.
    They were your pilots.
₉ The old men of Gebal
    and its wise men were your repairers of ship seams in you.
All the ships of the sea with their mariners were in you
    to deal in your merchandise.

₁₀ "'"Persia, Lud, and Put were in your army,
    your men of war.
They hung the shield and helmet in you.
    They showed your beauty.
₁₁ The men of Arvad with your army were on your walls all around,
    and valiant men were in your towers.
They hung their shields on your walls all around.
    They have perfected your beauty.
₁₂ "'"Tarshish was your merchant by reason of the multitude of all kinds of riches. They traded for your wares with silver, iron, tin, and lead.
₁₃ "'"Javan, Tubal, and Meshech were your traders. They traded the persons of men and vessels of bronze for your merchandise.
₁₄ "'"They of the house of Togarmah traded for your wares with horses, war horses, and mules.
₁₅ "'"The men of Dedan traded with you. Many islands were the market of your hand. They brought you horns of ivory and ebony in exchange.
₁₆ "'"Syria was your merchant by reason of the multitude of your handiworks. They traded for your wares with emeralds, purple, embroidered work, fine linen, coral, and rubies.
₁₇ "'"Judah and the land of Israel were your traders. They traded wheat of Minnith, confections, honey, oil, and balm for your merchandise.
₁₈ "'"Damascus was your merchant for the multitude of your handiworks by reason of the multitude of all kinds of riches, with the wine of Helbon, and white wool.
₁₉ "'"Vedan and Javan traded with yarn for your wares; wrought iron, cassia, and calamus were amongst your merchandise.
₂₀ "'"Dedan was your merchant in precious saddle blankets for riding.
₂₁ "'"Arabia and all the princes of Kedar were your favourite dealers in lambs, rams, and goats. In these, they were your merchants.
₂₂ "'"The traders of Sheba and Raamah were your traders. They traded for your wares with the best of all spices, all precious stones, and gold.
₂₃ "'"Haran, Canneh, Eden, the traders of Sheba, Asshur and Chilmad, were your traders. ₂₄ These were your traders in choice wares, in wrappings of blue and embroidered work, and in cedar chests of rich clothing bound with cords, amongst your merchandise.
₂₅ "'"The ships of Tarshish were your caravans for your merchandise.
    You were replenished
    and made very glorious in the heart of the seas.
₂₆ Your rowers have brought you into great waters.
    The east wind has broken you in the heart of the seas.
₂₇ Your riches, your wares, your merchandise,
    your mariners, your pilots, your repairers of ship seams,
the dealers in your merchandise,
    and all your men of war who are in you,
with all your company which is amongst you,
    will fall into the heart of the seas in the day of your ruin.
₂₈ At the sound of the cry of your pilots,
    the pasture lands will shake.
₂₉ All who handle the oars,
    the mariners and all the pilots of the sea,
    will come down from their ships.
They will stand on the land,
    ₃₀ and will cause their voice to be heard over you,
    and will cry bitterly.
They will cast up dust on their heads.
    They will wallow in the ashes.
₃₁ They will make themselves bald for you,
    and clothe themselves with sackcloth.
They will weep for you in bitterness of soul,
    with bitter mourning.
₃₂ In their wailing they will take up a lamentation for you,
    and lament over you, saying,
'Who is there like Tyre,
    like her who is brought to silence in the middle of the sea?'
₃₃ When your wares came from the seas,
    you filled many peoples.
You enriched the kings of the earth
    with the multitude of your riches and of your merchandise.
₃₄ In the time that you were broken by the seas,
    in the depths of the waters,
    your merchandise and all your company fell within you.
₃₅ All the inhabitants of the islands are astonished at you,
    and their kings are horribly afraid.
    They are troubled in their face.
₃₆ The merchants amongst the peoples hiss at you.
    You have come to a terrible end,
    and you will be no more."'"

28

1 The LORD's word came again to me, saying, 2 "Son of man, tell the prince of Tyre, 'The Lord GOD says:
"Because your heart is lifted up,
  and you have said, 'I am a god,
I sit in the seat of God,
  in the middle of the seas;'
yet you are man,
  and no god,
  though you set your heart as the heart of a god—
3 behold, you are wiser than Daniel.
  There is no secret that is hidden from you.
4 By your wisdom and by your understanding you have gotten yourself riches,
  and have gotten gold and silver into your treasuries.
5 By your great wisdom
  and by your trading you have increased your riches,
  and your heart is lifted up because of your riches—"
6 "'therefore the Lord GOD says:
"Because you have set your heart as the heart of God,
  7 therefore, behold, I will bring strangers on you,
  the terrible of the nations.
They will draw their swords against the beauty of your wisdom.
  They will defile your brightness.
8 They will bring you down to the pit.
  You will die the death of those who are slain
  in the heart of the seas.
9 Will you yet say before him who kills you, 'I am God'?
  But you are man, and not God,
  in the hand of him who wounds you.
10 You will die the death of the uncircumcised
  by the hand of strangers;
  for I have spoken it," says the Lord GOD.'"

11 Moreover the LORD's word came to me, saying, 12 "Son of man, take up a lamentation over the king of Tyre, and tell him, 'The Lord GOD says:
"You were the seal of full measure,
  full of wisdom,
  and perfect in beauty.
13 You were in Eden,
  the garden of God.
Every precious stone adorned you:
  ruby, topaz, emerald,
  chrysolite, onyx, jasper,
  sapphire,ª turquoise, and beryl.
Gold work of tambourines
  and of pipes was in you.
  They were prepared in the day that you were created.
14 You were the anointed cherub who covers.
  Then I set you up on the holy mountain of God.
  You have walked up and down in the middle of the stones of fire.
15 You were perfect in your ways from the day that you were created,
  until unrighteousness was found in you.
16 By the abundance of your commerce, your insides were filled with violence,
  and you have sinned.
Therefore I have cast you as profane out of God's mountain.
  I have destroyed you, covering cherub,
  from the middle of the stones of fire.
17 Your heart was lifted up because of your beauty.
  You have corrupted your wisdom by reason of your splendour.
I have cast you to the ground.
  I have laid you before kings,
  that they may see you.
18 By the multitude of your iniquities,
  in the unrighteousness of your commerce,
  you have profaned your sanctuaries.
Therefore I have brought out a fire from the middle of you.
  It has devoured you.
I have turned you to ashes on the earth
  in the sight of all those who see you.
19 All those who know you amongst the peoples will be astonished at you.
  You have become a terror,
  and you will exist no more."'"

20 The LORD's word came to me, saying, 21 "Son of man, set your face towards Sidon, and prophesy against it, 22 and say, 'The Lord GOD says:
"Behold, I am against you, Sidon.
  I will be glorified amongst you.
Then they will know that I am the LORD,
  when I have executed judgements in her,
  and am sanctified in her.
23 For I will send pestilence into her,
  and blood into her streets.
The wounded will fall within her,
  with the sword on her on every side.

Then they will know that I am the LORD.
24 "'"There will no longer be a pricking brier to the house of Israel, nor a hurting thorn of any that are around them that scorned them. Then they will know that I am the Lord GOD."
25 "'The Lord GOD says: "When I have gathered the house of Israel from the peoples amongst whom they are scattered, and am shown as holy amongst them in the sight of the nations, then they will dwell in their own land which I gave to my servant Jacob. 26 They will dwell in it securely. Yes, they will build houses, plant vineyards, and will dwell securely when I have executed judgements on all those around them who have treated them with contempt. Then they will know that I am the LORD their God."'"

29

1 In the tenth year, in the tenth month, on the twelfth day of the month, the LORD's word came to me, saying, 2 "Son of man, set your face against Pharaoh king of Egypt, and prophesy against him and against all Egypt. 3 Speak and say, 'The Lord GOD says:
"Behold, I am against you, Pharaoh king of Egypt,
  the great monster that lies in the middle of his rivers,
that has said, 'My river is my own,
  and I have made it for myself.'
4 I will put hooks in your jaws,
  and I will make the fish of your rivers stick to your scales.
I will bring you up out of the middle of your rivers,
  with all the fish of your rivers which stick to your scales.
5 I'll cast you out into the wilderness,
  you and all the fish of your rivers.
You'll fall on the open field.
  You won't be brought together or gathered.
I have given you for food to the animals of the earth
  and to the birds of the sky.
6 "'"All the inhabitants of Egypt will know that I am the LORD, because they have been a staff of reed to the house of Israel. 7 When they took hold of you by your hand, you broke and tore all their shoulders. When they leaned on you, you broke and paralysed all of their thighs."
8 "'Therefore the Lord GOD says: "Behold, I will bring a sword on you, and will cut off man and animal from you. 9 The land of Egypt will be a desolation and a waste. Then they will know that I am the LORD.
"'"Because he has said, 'The river is mine, and I have made it,' 10 therefore, behold, I am against you and against your rivers. I will make the land of Egypt an utter waste and desolation, from the tower of Seveneh even to the border of Ethiopia. 11 No foot of man will pass through it, nor will any animal foot pass through it. It won't be inhabited for forty years. 12 I will make the land of Egypt a desolation in the middle of the countries that are desolate. Her cities amongst the cities that are laid waste will be a desolation forty years. I will scatter the Egyptians amongst the nations, and will disperse them through the countries."
13 "'For the Lord GOD says: "At the end of forty years I will gather the Egyptians from the peoples where they were scattered. 14 I will reverse the captivity of Egypt, and will cause them to return into the land of Pathros, into the land of their birth. There they will be a lowly kingdom. 15 It will be the lowest of the kingdoms. It won't lift itself up above the nations any more. I will diminish them so that they will no longer rule over the nations. 16 It will no longer be the confidence of the house of Israel, bringing iniquity to memory, when they turn to look after them. Then they will know that I am the Lord GOD."'"

17 It came to pass in the twenty-seventh year, in the first month, in the first day of the month, the LORD's word came to me, saying, 18 "Son of man, Nebuchadnezzar king of Babylon caused his army to serve a great service against Tyre. Every head was made bald, and every shoulder was worn; yet he had no wages, nor did his army, from Tyre, for the service that he had served against it. 19 Therefore the Lord GOD says: 'Behold, I will give the land of Egypt to Nebuchadnezzar king of Babylon. He will carry off her multitude, take her plunder, and take her prey. That will be the wages for his army. 20 I have given him the land of Egypt as his payment for which he served, because they worked for me,' says the Lord GOD.
21 "In that day I will cause a horn to sprout for the house of Israel, and I will open your mouth amongst them. Then they will know that I am the LORD."

30

1 The LORD's word came again to me, saying, 2 "Son of man, prophesy, and say, 'The Lord GOD says:
"Wail, 'Alas for the day!'
  3 For the day is near,
  even the LORD's day is near.
It will be a day of clouds,
  a time of the nations.
4 A sword will come on Egypt,
  and anguish will be in Ethiopia,
  when the slain fall in Egypt.
They take away her multitude,
  and her foundations are broken down.
5 "'"Ethiopia, Put, Lud, all the mixed people, Cub, and the children of the land that is allied with them, will fall with them by the sword."
6 "'The LORD says:
"They also who uphold Egypt will fall.

ª 28:13 or, lapis lazuli

The pride of her power will come down.
They will fall by the sword in it from the tower of Seveneh,"
    says the Lord GOD.
7 "They will be desolate in the middle of the countries that are desolate.
    Her cities will be amongst the cities that are wasted.
8 They will know that I am the LORD
    when I have set a fire in Egypt,
    and all her helpers are destroyed.
9 "'In that day messengers will go out from before me in ships to make the careless Ethiopians afraid. There will be anguish on them, as in the day of Egypt; for, behold, it comes."
10 "'The Lord GOD says:
"I will also make the multitude of Egypt to cease,
    by the hand of Nebuchadnezzar king of Babylon.
11 He and his people with him,
    the terrible of the nations,
will be brought in to destroy the land.
    They will draw their swords against Egypt,
    and fill the land with the slain.
12 I will make the rivers dry,
    and will sell the land into the hand of evil men.
I will make the land desolate,
    and all that is therein,
    by the hand of foreigners.
    I, the LORD, have spoken it."
13 "'The Lord GOD says:
"I will also destroy the idols,
    and I will cause the images to cease from Memphis.
There will be no more a prince from the land of Egypt.
    I will put a fear in the land of Egypt.
14 I will make Pathros desolate,
    and will set a fire in Zoan,
    and will execute judgements on No.
15 I will pour my wrath on Sin,
    the stronghold of Egypt.
    I will cut off the multitude of No.
16 I will set a fire in Egypt
    Sin will be in great anguish.
No will be broken up.
    Memphis will have adversaries in the daytime.
17 The young men of Aven and of Pibeseth will fall by the sword.
    They will go into captivity.
18 At Tehaphnehes also the day will withdraw itself,
    when I break the yokes of Egypt there.
The pride of her power will cease in her.
    As for her, a cloud will cover her,
    and her daughters will go into captivity.
19 Thus I will execute judgements on Egypt.
    Then they will know that I am the LORD.'"'"

20 In the eleventh year, in the first month, in the seventh day of the month, the LORD's word came to me, saying, 21 "Son of man, I have broken the arm of Pharaoh king of Egypt. Behold, it has not been bound up, to apply medicines, to put a bandage to bind it, that it may become strong to hold the sword. 22 Therefore the Lord GOD says: 'Behold, I am against Pharaoh king of Egypt, and will break his arms, the strong arm, and that which was broken. I will cause the sword to fall out of his hand. 23 I will scatter the Egyptians amongst the nations, and will disperse them through the countries. 24 I will strengthen the arms of the king of Babylon, and put my sword in his hand; but I will break the arms of Pharaoh, and he will groan before the king of Babylon with the groaning of a mortally wounded man. 25 I will hold up the arms of the king of Babylon, but the arms of Pharaoh will fall down. Then they will know that I am the LORD when I put my sword into the hand of the king of Babylon, and he stretches it out on the land of Egypt. 26 I will scatter the Egyptians amongst the nations and disperse them through the countries. Then they will know that I am the LORD.'"

31

1 In the eleventh year, in the third month, in the first day of the month, the LORD's word came to me, saying, 2 "Son of man, tell Pharaoh king of Egypt and his multitude:
'Whom are you like in your greatness?
3 Behold, the Assyrian was a cedar in Lebanon
    with beautiful branches,
and with a forest-like shade,
    of high stature;
    and its top was amongst the thick boughs.
4 The waters nourished it.
    The deep made it to grow.
Its rivers ran all around its plantation.
    It sent out its channels to all the trees of the field.
5 Therefore its stature was exalted above all the trees of the field;
    and its boughs were multiplied.
Its branches became long by reason of many waters,
    when it spread them out.
6 All the birds of the sky made their nests in its boughs.

Under its branches, all the animals of the field gave birth to their
    young.
    All great nations lived under its shadow.
7 Thus it was beautiful in its greatness,
    in the length of its branches;
    for its root was by many waters.
8 The cedars in the garden of God could not hide it.
    The cypress trees were not like its branches.
The pine trees were not like its branches;
    nor was any tree in the garden of God like it in its beauty.
9 I made it beautiful by the multitude of its branches,
    so that all the trees of Eden,
    that were in the garden of God, envied it.'
10 "Therefore thus said the Lord GOD: 'Because he is exalted in stature, and he has set his top amongst the thick branches, and his heart is lifted up in his height, 11 I will deliver him into the hand of the mighty one of the nations. He will surely deal with him. I have driven him out for his wickedness. 12 Foreigners, the tyrants of the nations, have cut him off and have left him. His branches have fallen on the mountains and in all the valleys, and his boughs are broken by all the watercourses of the land. All the peoples of the earth have gone down from his shadow and have left him. 13 All the birds of the sky will dwell on his ruin, and all the animals of the field will be on his branches, 14 to the end that none of all the trees by the waters exalt themselves in their stature, and don't set their top amongst the thick boughs. Their mighty ones don't stand up on their height, even all who drink water; for they are all delivered to death, to the lower parts of the earth, amongst the children of men, with those who go down to the pit.'
15 "The Lord GOD says: 'In the day when he went down to Sheol,ᵃ I caused a mourning. I covered the deep for him, and I restrained its rivers. The great waters were stopped. I caused Lebanon to mourn for him, and all the trees of the field fainted for him. 16 I made the nations to shake at the sound of his fall, when I cast him down to Sheolᵇ with those who descend into the pit. All the trees of Eden, the choice and best of Lebanon, all that drink water, were comforted in the lower parts of the earth. 17 They also went down into Sheol with him to those who are slain by the sword; yes, those who were his arm, who lived under his shadow in the middle of the nations.
18 "'To whom are you thus like in glory and in greatness amongst the trees of Eden? Yet you will be brought down with the trees of Eden to the lower parts of the earth. You will lie in the middle of the uncircumcised, with those who are slain by the sword.
"'This is Pharaoh and all his multitude,' says the Lord GOD."

32

1 In the twelfth year, in the twelfth month, in the first day of the month, "the LORD's word came to me, saying, 2 'Son of man, take up a lamentation over Pharaoh king of Egypt, and tell him,
"You were likened to a young lion of the nations;
    yet you are as a monster in the seas.
You broke out with your rivers,
    and troubled the waters with your feet,
    and fouled their rivers."
3 The Lord GOD says:
    "I will spread out my net on you with a company of many peoples.
    They will bring you up in my net.
4 I will leave you on the land.
    I will cast you out on the open field,
and will cause all the birds of the sky to settle on you.
    I will satisfy the animals of the whole earth with you.
5 I will lay your flesh on the mountains,
    and fill the valleys with your height.
6 I will also water the land in which you swim with your blood,
    even to the mountains.
    The watercourses will be full of you.
7 When I extinguish you, I will cover the heavens
    and make its stars dark.
I will cover the sun with a cloud,
    and the moon won't give its light.
8 I will make all the bright lights of the sky dark over you,
    and set darkness on your land," says the Lord GOD.
9 "I will also trouble the hearts of many peoples,
    when I bring your destruction amongst the nations,
    into the countries which you have not known.
10 Yes, I will make many peoples amazed at you,
    and their kings will be horribly afraid for you,
when I brandish my sword before them.
    They will tremble at every moment,
every man for his own life,
    in the day of your fall."
11 For the Lord GOD says:
    "The sword of the king of Babylon will come on you.
12 I will cause your multitude to fall by the swords of the mighty.
    They are all the ruthless of the nations.
They will bring the pride of Egypt to nothing,
    and all its multitude will be destroyed.
13 I will destroy also all its animals from beside many waters.
    The foot of man won't trouble them any more,

ᵃ *31:15* Sheol is the place of the dead.

ᵇ *31:16* Sheol is the place of the dead.

nor will the hoofs of animals trouble them.
14 Then I will make their waters clear,
and cause their rivers to run like oil,"
says the Lord GOD.
15 "When I make the land of Egypt desolate and waste,
a land destitute of that of which it was full,
when I strike all those who dwell therein,
then they will know that I am the LORD.

16 "'"This is the lamentation with which they will lament. The daughters of the nations will lament with this. They will lament with it over Egypt, and over all her multitude," says the Lord GOD.'"

17 Also in the twelfth year, in the fifteenth day of the month, the LORD's word came to me, saying, 18 "Son of man, wail for the multitude of Egypt, and cast them down, even her and the daughters of the famous nations, to the lower parts of the earth, with those who go down into the pit. 19 Whom do you pass in beauty? Go down, and be laid with the uncircumcised. 20 They will fall amongst those who are slain by the sword. She is delivered to the sword. Draw her away with all her multitudes. 21 The strong amongst the mighty will speak to him out of the middle of Sheol[a] with those who help him. They have gone down. The uncircumcised lie still, slain by the sword.

22 "Asshur is there with all her company. Her graves are all around her. All of them are slain, fallen by the sword, 23 whose graves are set in the uttermost parts of the pit, and her company is around her grave, all of them slain, fallen by the sword, who caused terror in the land of the living.

24 "There is Elam and all her multitude around her grave; all of them slain, fallen by the sword, who have gone down uncircumcised into the lower parts of the earth, who caused their terror in the land of the living, and have borne their shame with those who go down to the pit. 25 They have made Elam a bed amongst the slain with all her multitude. Her graves are around her, all of them uncircumcised, slain by the sword; for their terror was caused in the land of the living, and they have borne their shame with those who go down to the pit. He is put amongst those who are slain.

26 "There is Meshech, Tubal, and all their multitude. Their graves are around them, all of them uncircumcised, slain by the sword; for they caused their terror in the land of the living. 27 They will not lie with the mighty who are fallen of the uncircumcised, who have gone down to Sheol with their weapons of war and have laid their swords under their heads. Their iniquities are on their bones; for they were the terror of the mighty in the land of the living.

28 "But you will be broken amongst the uncircumcised, and will lie with those who are slain by the sword.

29 "There is Edom, her kings, and all her princes, who in their might are laid with those who are slain by the sword. They will lie with the uncircumcised, and with those who go down to the pit.

30 "There are the princes of the north, all of them, and all the Sidonians, who have gone down with the slain. They are put to shame in the terror which they caused by their might. They lie uncircumcised with those who are slain by the sword, and bear their shame with those who go down to the pit.

31 "Pharaoh will see them and will be comforted over all his multitude, even Pharaoh and all his army, slain by the sword," says the Lord GOD. 32 "For I have put his terror in the land of the living. He will be laid amongst the uncircumcised, with those who are slain by the sword, even Pharaoh and all his multitude," says the Lord GOD.

33

1 The LORD's word came to me, saying, 2 "Son of man, speak to the children of your people, and tell them, 'When I bring the sword on a land, and the people of the land take a man from amongst them, and set him for their watchman, 3 if, when he sees the sword come on the land, he blows the trumpet and warns the people, 4 then whoever hears the sound of the trumpet and doesn't heed the warning, if the sword comes and takes him away, his blood will be on his own head. 5 He heard the sound of the trumpet and didn't take warning. His blood will be on him; whereas if he had heeded the warning, he would have delivered his soul. 6 But if the watchman sees the sword come and doesn't blow the trumpet, and the people aren't warned, and the sword comes and takes any person from amongst them, he is taken away in his iniquity, but his blood I will require at the watchman's hand.'

7 "So you, son of man, I have set you a watchman to the house of Israel. Therefore hear the word from my mouth, and give them warnings from me. 8 When I tell the wicked, 'O wicked man, you will surely die,' and you don't speak to warn the wicked from his way, that wicked man will die in his iniquity, but I will require his blood at your hand. 9 Nevertheless, if you warn the wicked of his way to turn from it, and he doesn't turn from his way; he will die in his iniquity, but you have delivered your soul.

10 "You, son of man, tell the house of Israel: 'You say this, "Our transgressions and our sins are on us, and we pine away in them. How then can we live?"' 11 Tell them, '"As I live," says the Lord GOD, "I have no pleasure in the death of the wicked, but that the wicked turn from his way and live. Turn, turn from your evil ways! For why will you die, house of Israel?"'

12 "You, son of man, tell the children of your people, 'The righteousness of the righteous will not deliver him in the day of his disobedience. And as for the wickedness of the wicked, he will not fall by it

in the day that he turns from his wickedness; neither will he who is righteous be able to live by it in the day that he sins. 13 When I tell the righteous that he will surely live, if he trusts in his righteousness and commits iniquity, none of his righteous deeds will be remembered; but he will die in his iniquity that he has committed. 14 Again, when I say to the wicked, "You will surely die," if he turns from his sin and does that which is lawful and right, 15 if the wicked restore the pledge, give again that which he had taken by robbery, walk in the statutes of life, committing no iniquity, he will surely live. He will not die. 16 None of his sins that he has committed will be remembered against him. He has done that which is lawful and right. He will surely live.

17 "'Yet the children of your people say, "The way of the Lord is not fair;" but as for them, their way is not fair. 18 When the righteous turns from his righteousness and commits iniquity, he will even die therein. 19 When the wicked turns from his wickedness and does that which is lawful and right, he will live by it. 20 Yet you say, "The way of the Lord is not fair." House of Israel, I will judge every one of you after his ways.'"

21 In the twelfth year of our captivity, in the tenth month, in the fifth day of the month, one who had escaped out of Jerusalem came to me, saying, "The city has been defeated!" 22 Now the LORD's hand had been on me in the evening, before he who had escaped came; and he had opened my mouth until he came to me in the morning; and my mouth was opened, and I was no longer mute.

23 The LORD's word came to me, saying, 24 "Son of man, those who inhabit the waste places in the land of Israel speak, saying, 'Abraham was one, and he inherited the land; but we are many. The land is given us for inheritance.' 25 Therefore tell them, 'The Lord GOD says: "You eat with the blood, and lift up your eyes to your idols, and shed blood. So should you possess the land? 26 You stand on your sword, you work abomination, and every one of you defiles his neighbour's wife. So should you possess the land?"'

27 "You shall tell them, 'The Lord GOD says: "As I live, surely those who are in the waste places will fall by the sword. I will give whoever is in the open field to the animals to be devoured, and those who are in the strongholds and in the caves will die of the pestilence. 28 I will make the land a desolation and an astonishment. The pride of her power will cease. The mountains of Israel will be desolate, so that no one will pass through. 29 Then they will know that I am the LORD, when I have made the land a desolation and an astonishment because of all their abominations which they have committed."'

30 "As for you, son of man, the children of your people talk about you by the walls and in the doors of the houses, and speak to one another, everyone to his brother, saying, 'Please come and hear what the word is that comes out from the LORD.' 31 They come to you as the people come, and they sit before you as my people, and they hear your words, but don't do them; for with their mouth they show much love, but their heart goes after their gain. 32 Behold, you are to them as a very lovely song of one who has a pleasant voice, and can play well on an instrument; for they hear your words, but they don't do them.

33 "When this comes to pass—behold, it comes—then they will know that a prophet has been amongst them."

34

1 The LORD's word came to me, saying, 2 "Son of man, prophesy against the shepherds of Israel. Prophesy, and tell them, even the shepherds, 'The Lord GOD says: "Woe to the shepherds of Israel who feed themselves! Shouldn't the shepherds feed the sheep? 3 You eat the fat. You clothe yourself with the wool. You kill the fatlings, but you don't feed the sheep. 4 You haven't strengthened the diseased. You haven't healed that which was sick. You haven't bound up that which was broken. You haven't brought back that which was driven away. You haven't sought that which was lost, but you have ruled over them with force and with rigor. 5 They were scattered, because there was no shepherd. They became food to all the animals of the field, and were scattered. 6 My sheep wandered through all the mountains and on every high hill. Yes, my sheep were scattered on all the surface of the earth. There was no one who searched or sought."

7 "'Therefore, you shepherds, hear the LORD's word: 8 "As I live," says the Lord GOD, "surely because my sheep became a prey, and my sheep became food to all the animals of the field, because there was no shepherd, and my shepherds didn't search for my sheep, but the shepherds fed themselves, and didn't feed my sheep, 9 therefore, you shepherds, hear the LORD's word!" 10 The Lord GOD says: "Behold, I am against the shepherds. I will require my sheep at their hand, and cause them to cease from feeding the sheep. The shepherds won't feed themselves any more. I will deliver my sheep from their mouth, that they may not be food for them."

11 "'For the Lord GOD says: "Behold, I myself, even I, will search for my sheep, and will seek them out. 12 As a shepherd seeks out his flock in the day that he is amongst his sheep that are scattered abroad, so I will seek out my sheep. I will deliver them out of all places where they have been scattered in the cloudy and dark day. 13 I will bring them out from the peoples, and gather them from the countries, and will bring them into their own land. I will feed them on the mountains of Israel, by the watercourses, and in all the inhabited places of the country. 14 I will feed them with good pasture, and their fold will be on the mountains of the height of Israel. There they will lie down in a good fold. They will feed on rich pasture on the

---

mountains of Israel. 15 I myself will be the shepherd of my sheep, and I will cause them to lie down," says the Lord GOD. 16 "I will seek that which was lost, and will bring back that which was driven away, and will bind up that which was broken, and will strengthen that which was sick; but I will destroy the fat and the strong. I will feed them in justice.'"

17 "As for you, O my flock, the Lord GOD says: 'Behold, I judge between sheep and sheep, the rams and the male goats. 18 Does it seem a small thing to you to have fed on the good pasture, but you must tread down with your feet the residue of your pasture? And to have drunk of the clear waters, but must you foul the residue with your feet? 19 As for my sheep, they eat that which you have trodden with your feet, and they drink that which you have fouled with your feet.'

20 "Therefore the Lord GOD says to them: 'Behold, I, even I, will judge between the fat sheep and the lean sheep. 21 Because you thrust with side and with shoulder, and push all the diseased with your horns, until you have scattered them abroad, 22 therefore I will save my flock, and they will no more be a prey. I will judge between sheep and sheep. 23 I will set up one shepherd over them, and he will feed them, even my servant David. He will feed them, and he will be their shepherd. 24 I, the LORD, will be their God, and my servant David prince amongst them. I, the LORD, have spoken it.

25 "'I will make with them a covenant of peace, and will cause evil animals to cease out of the land. They will dwell securely in the wilderness and sleep in the woods. 26 I will make them and the places around my hill a blessing. I will cause the shower to come down in its season. There will be showers of blessing. 27 The tree of the field will yield its fruit, and the earth will yield its increase, and they will be secure in their land. Then they will know that I am the LORD, when I have broken the bars of their yoke, and have delivered them out of the hand of those who made slaves of them. 28 They will no more be a prey to the nations, neither will the animals of the earth devour them; but they will dwell securely, and no one will make them afraid. 29 I will raise up to them a plantation for renown, and they will no more be consumed with famine in the land, and not bear the shame of the nations any more. 30 They will know that I, the LORD, their God am with them, and that they, the house of Israel, are my people, says the Lord GOD. 31 You my sheep, the sheep of my pasture, are men, and I am your God,' says the Lord GOD."

35

1 Moreover the LORD's word came to me, saying, 2 "Son of man, set your face against Mount Seir, and prophesy against it, 3 and tell it, 'The Lord GOD says: "Behold, I am against you, Mount Seir, and I will stretch out my hand against you. I will make you a desolation and an astonishment. 4 I will lay your cities waste, and you will be desolate. Then you will know that I am the LORD.

5 "'Because you have had a perpetual hostility, and have given over the children of Israel to the power of the sword in the time of their calamity, in the time of the iniquity of the end, 6 therefore, as I live," says the Lord GOD, "I will prepare you for blood, and blood will pursue you. Since you have not hated blood, therefore blood will pursue you. 7 Thus I will make Mount Seir an astonishment and a desolation. I will cut off from it him who passes through and him who returns. 8 I will fill its mountains with its slain. The slain with the sword will fall in your hills and in your valleys and in all your watercourses. 9 I will make you a perpetual desolation, and your cities will not be inhabited. Then you will know that I am the LORD.

10 "'Because you have said, 'These two nations and these two countries will be mine, and we will possess it,' although the LORD was there, 11 therefore, as I live," says the Lord GOD, "I will do according to your anger, and according to your envy which you have shown out of your hatred against them; and I will make myself known amongst them when I judge you. 12 You will know that I, the LORD, have heard all your insults which you have spoken against the mountains of Israel, saying, 'They have been laid desolate. They have been given to us to devour.' 13 You have magnified yourselves against me with your mouth, and have multiplied your words against me. I have heard it." 14 The Lord GOD says: "When the whole earth rejoices, I will make you desolate. 15 As you rejoiced over the inheritance of the house of Israel because it was desolate, so I will do to you. You will be desolate, Mount Seir, and all Edom, even all of it. Then they will know that I am the LORD.'"

36

1 You, son of man, prophesy to the mountains of Israel, and say, "You mountains of Israel, hear the LORD's word. 2 The Lord GOD says: 'Because the enemy has said against you, "Aha!" and, "The ancient high places are ours in possession!"' 3 therefore prophesy, and say, 'The Lord GOD says: "Because, even because they have made you desolate, and swallowed you up on every side, that you might be a possession to the residue of the nations, and you are taken up in the lips of talkers, and the evil report of the people;" 4 therefore, you mountains of Israel, hear the word of the Lord GOD: The Lord GOD says to the mountains and to the hills, to the watercourses and to the valleys, to the desolate wastes and to the cities that are forsaken, which have become a prey and derision to the residue of the nations that are all around; 5 therefore the Lord GOD says: "Surely in the fire of my jealousy I have spoken against the residue of the nations, and against all Edom, that have appointed my land to themselves for a possession with the joy of all their heart, with despite of soul, to cast it out for a prey.'" 6 Therefore prophesy concerning the land of Israel, and tell the mountains, the hills, the watercourses and the valleys, 'The Lord GOD says: "Behold, I have spoken in my jealousy and in my wrath, because you have borne the shame of the nations." 7 Therefore the Lord GOD says: "I have sworn, 'Surely the nations that are around you will bear their shame.'

8 "'But you, mountains of Israel, you shall shoot out your branches and yield your fruit to my people Israel; for they are at hand to come. 9 For, behold, I am for you, and I will come to you, and you will be tilled and sown. 10 I will multiply men on you, all the house of Israel, even all of it. The cities will be inhabited and the waste places will be built. 11 I will multiply man and animal on you. They will increase and be fruitful. I will cause you to be inhabited as you were before, and you will do better than at your beginnings. Then you will know that I am the LORD. 12 Yes, I will cause men to walk on you, even my people Israel. They will possess you, and you will be their inheritance, and you will never again bereave them of their children."

13 "'The Lord GOD says: "Because they say to you, 'You are a devourer of men, and have been a bereaver of your nation;' 14 therefore you shall devour men no more, and not bereave your nation any more," says the Lord GOD. 15 "I won't let you hear the shame of the nations any more. You won't bear the reproach of the peoples any more, and you won't cause your nation to stumble any more," says the Lord GOD.'"

16 Moreover the LORD's word came to me, saying, 17 "Son of man, when the house of Israel lived in their own land, they defiled it by their ways and by their deeds. Their way before me was as the uncleanness of a woman in her impurity. 18 Therefore I poured out my wrath on them for the blood which they had poured out on the land, and because they had defiled it with their idols. 19 I scattered them amongst the nations, and they were dispersed through the countries. I judged them according to their way and according to their deeds. 20 When they came to the nations where they went, they profaned my holy name, in that men said of them, 'These are the LORD's people, and have left his land.' 21 But I had respect for my holy name, which the house of Israel had profaned amongst the nations where they went.

22 "Therefore tell the house of Israel, 'The Lord GOD says: "I don't do this for your sake, house of Israel, but for my holy name, which you have profaned amongst the nations where you went. 23 I will sanctify my great name, which has been profaned amongst the nations, which you have profaned amongst them. Then the nations will know that I am the LORD," says the Lord GOD, "when I am proven holy in you before their eyes.

24 "'For I will take you from amongst the nations and gather you out of all the countries, and will bring you into your own land. 25 I will sprinkle clean water on you, and you will be clean. I will cleanse you from all your filthiness and from all your idols. 26 I will also give you a new heart, and I will put a new spirit within you. I will take away the stony heart out of your flesh, and I will give you a heart of flesh. 27 I will put my Spirit within you, and cause you to walk in my statutes. You will keep my ordinances and do them. 28 You will dwell in the land that I gave to your fathers. You will be my people, and I will be your God. 29 I will save you from all your uncleanness. I will call for the grain and will multiply it, and lay no famine on you. 30 I will multiply the fruit of the tree and the increase of the field, that you may receive no more the reproach of famine amongst the nations.

31 "'Then you will remember your evil ways, and your deeds that were not good; and you will loathe yourselves in your own sight for your iniquities and for your abominations. 32 I don't do this for your sake," says the Lord GOD. "Let it be known to you. Be ashamed and confounded for your ways, house of Israel."

33 "'The Lord GOD says: "In the day that I cleanse you from all your iniquities, I will cause the cities to be inhabited and the waste places will be built. 34 The land that was desolate will be tilled instead of being a desolation in the sight of all who passed by. 35 They will say, 'This land that was desolate has become like the garden of Eden. The waste, desolate, and ruined cities are fortified and inhabited.' 36 Then the nations that are left around you will know that I, the LORD, have built the ruined places and planted that which was desolate. I, the LORD, have spoken it, and I will do it."

37 "'The Lord GOD says: "For this, moreover, I will be enquired of by the house of Israel, to do it for them: I will increase them with men like a flock. 38 As the flock for sacrifice, as the flock of Jerusalem in her appointed feasts, so the waste cities will be filled with flocks of men. Then they will know that I am the LORD.'"

37

1 The LORD's hand was on me, and he brought me out in the LORD's Spirit, and set me down in the middle of the valley; and it was full of bones. 2 He caused me to pass by them all around; and behold, there were very many in the open valley, and behold, they were very dry. 3 He said to me, "Son of man, can these bones live?"

I answered, "Lord GOD, you know."

4 Again he said to me, "Prophesy over these bones, and tell them, 'You dry bones, hear the LORD's word. 5 The Lord GOD says to these bones: "Behold, I will cause breath to enter into you, and you will live. 6 I will lay sinews on you, and will bring up flesh on you, and cover you with skin, and put breath in you, and you will live. Then you will know that I am the LORD."'"

7 So I prophesied as I was commanded. As I prophesied, there was a noise, and behold, there was an earthquake. Then the bones came together, bone to its bone. 8 I saw, and, behold, there were sinews on them, and flesh came up, and skin covered them above; but there was no breath in them.

9 Then he said to me, "Prophesy to the wind, prophesy, son of man, and tell the wind, 'The Lord GOD says: "Come from the four winds, breath, and breathe on these slain, that they may live."'"

10 So I prophesied as he commanded me, and the breath came into them, and they lived, and stood up on their feet, an exceedingly great army.

11 Then he said to me, "Son of man, these bones are the whole house of Israel. Behold, they say, 'Our bones are dried up, and our hope is lost. We are completely cut off.' 12 Therefore prophesy, and tell them, 'The Lord GOD says: "Behold, I will open your graves, and cause you to come up out of your graves, my people; and I will bring you into the land of Israel. 13 You will know that I am the LORD, when I have opened your graves and caused you to come up out of your graves, my people. 14 I will put my Spirit in you, and you will live. Then I will place you in your own land; and you will know that I, the LORD, have spoken it and performed it," says the LORD.'"

15 The LORD's word came again to me, saying, 16 "You, son of man, take one stick and write on it, 'For Judah, and for the children of Israel his companions.' Then take another stick, and write on it, 'For Joseph, the stick of Ephraim, and for all the house of Israel his companions.' 17 Then join them for yourself to one another into one stick, that they may become one in your hand.

18 "When the children of your people speak to you, saying, 'Won't you show us what you mean by these?' 19 tell them, 'The Lord GOD says: "Behold, I will take the stick of Joseph, which is in the hand of Ephraim, and the tribes of Israel his companions; and I will put them with it, with the stick of Judah, and make them one stick, and they will be one in my hand. 20 The sticks on which you write will be in your hand before their eyes."' 21 Say to them, 'The Lord GOD says: "Behold, I will take the children of Israel from amongst the nations where they have gone, and will gather them on every side, and bring them into their own land. 22 I will make them one nation in the land, on the mountains of Israel. One king will be king to them all. They will no longer be two nations. They won't be divided into two kingdoms any more at all. 23 They won't defile themselves any more with their idols, nor with their detestable things, nor with any of their transgressions; but I will save them out of all their dwelling places in which they have sinned, and will cleanse them. So they will be my people, and I will be their God.

24 "'"My servant David will be king over them. They all will have one shepherd. They will also walk in my ordinances and observe my statutes, and do them. 25 They will dwell in the land that I have given to Jacob my servant, in which your fathers lived. They will dwell therein, they, and their children, and their children's children, forever. David my servant will be their prince forever. 26 Moreover I will make a covenant of peace with them. It will be an everlasting covenant with them. I will place them, multiply them, and will set my sanctuary amongst them forever more. 27 My tent also will be with them. I will be their God, and they will be my people. 28 The nations will know that I am the LORD who sanctifies Israel, when my sanctuary is amongst them forever more."'"

38

1 The LORD's word came to me, saying, 2 "Son of man, set your face towards Gog, of the land of Magog, the prince of Rosh, Meshech, and Tubal, and prophesy against him, 3 and say, 'The Lord GOD says: "Behold, I am against you, Gog, prince of Rosh, Meshech, and Tubal. 4 I will turn you around, and put hooks into your jaws, and I will bring you out, with all your army, horses and horsemen, all of them clothed in full armour, a great company with buckler and shield, all of them handling swords; 5 Persia, Cush, and Put with them, all of them with shield and helmet; 6 Gomer, and all his hordes; the house of Togarmah in the uttermost parts of the north, and all his hordes—even many peoples with you.

7 "'"Be prepared, yes, prepare yourself, you, and all your companies who are assembled to you, and be a guard to them. 8 After many days you will be visited. In the latter years you will come into the land that is brought back from the sword, that is gathered out of many peoples, on the mountains of Israel, which have been a continual waste; but it is brought out of the peoples and they will dwell securely, all of them. 9 You will ascend. You will come like a storm. You will be like a cloud to cover the land, you and all your hordes, and many peoples with you."

10 "'The Lord GOD says: "It will happen in that day that things will come into your mind, and you will devise an evil plan. 11 You will say, 'I will go up to the land of unwalled villages. I will go to those who are at rest, who dwell securely, all of them dwelling without walls, and having neither bars nor gates, 12 to take the plunder and to take prey; to turn your hand against the waste places that are inhabited, and against the people who are gathered out of the nations, who have gotten livestock and goods, who dwell in the middle of the earth.' 13 Sheba, Dedan, and the merchants of Tarshish, with all its young lions, will ask you, 'Have you come to take the plunder? Have you assembled your company to take the prey, to carry away silver and gold, to take away livestock and goods, to take great plunder?'"'

14 "Therefore, son of man, prophesy, and tell Gog, 'The Lord GOD says: "In that day when my people Israel dwells securely, will you not know it? 15 You will come from your place out of the uttermost parts of the north, you, and many peoples with you, all of them riding on horses, a great company and a mighty army. 16 You will come up against my people Israel as a cloud to cover the land. It will happen in the latter days that I will bring you against my land, that the nations may know me when I am sanctified in you, Gog, before their eyes."

17 "'The Lord GOD says: "Are you he of whom I spoke in old time by my servants the prophets of Israel, who prophesied in those days for years that I would bring you against them? 18 It will happen in that day, when Gog comes against the land of Israel," says the Lord GOD, "that my wrath will come up into my nostrils. 19 For in my jealousy and in the fire of my wrath I have spoken. Surely in that day there will be a great shaking in the land of Israel, 20 so that the fish of the sea, the birds of the sky, the animals of the field, all creeping things who creep on the earth, and all the men who are on the surface of the earth will shake at my presence. Then the mountains will be thrown down, the steep places will fall, and every wall will fall to the ground. 21 I will call for a sword against him to all my mountains," says the Lord GOD. "Every man's sword will be against his brother. 22 I will enter into judgement with him with pestilence and with blood. I will rain on him, on his hordes, and on the many peoples who are with him, torrential rains with great hailstones, fire, and sulphur. 23 I will magnify myself and sanctify myself, and I will make myself known in the eyes of many nations. Then they will know that I am the LORD."'"

39

1 "You, son of man, prophesy against Gog, and say, 'The Lord GOD says: "Behold, I am against you, Gog, prince of Rosh, Meshech, and Tubal. 2 I will turn you around, will lead you on, and will cause you to come up from the uttermost parts of the north; and I will bring you onto the mountains of Israel. 3 I will strike your bow out of your left hand, and will cause your arrows to fall out of your right hand. 4 You will fall on the mountains of Israel, you, and all your hordes, and the peoples who are with you. I will give you to the ravenous birds of every sort and to the animals of the field to be devoured. 5 You will fall on the open field, for I have spoken it," says the Lord GOD. 6 "I will send a fire on Magog and on those who dwell securely in the islands. Then they will know that I am the LORD.

7 "'"I will make my holy name known amongst my people Israel. I won't allow my holy name to be profaned any more. Then the nations will know that I am the LORD, the Holy One in Israel. 8 Behold, it comes, and it will be done," says the Lord GOD. "This is the day about which I have spoken.

9 "'"Those who dwell in the cities of Israel will go out and will make fires of the weapons and burn them, both the shields and the bucklers, the bows and the arrows, and the war clubs and the spears, and they will make fires with them for seven years; 10 so that they will take no wood out of the field, and not cut down any out of the forests; for they will make fires with the weapons. They will plunder those who plundered them, and rob those who robbed them," says the Lord GOD.

11 "'"It will happen in that day, that I will give to Gog a place for burial in Israel, the valley of those who pass through on the east of the sea; and it will stop those who pass through. They will bury Gog and all his multitude there, and they will call it 'The valley of Hamon Gog'.

12 "'"The house of Israel will be burying them for seven months, that they may cleanse the land. 13 Yes, all the people of the land will bury them; and they will become famous in the day that I will be glorified," says the Lord GOD.

14 "'"They will set apart men of continual employment who will pass through the land. Those who pass through will go with those who bury those who remain on the surface of the land, to cleanse it. After the end of seven months they will search. 15 Those who search through the land will pass through; and when anyone sees a man's bone, then he will set up a sign by it, until the undertakers have buried it in the valley of Hamon Gog. 16 Hamonah will also be the name of a city. Thus they will cleanse the land."'

17 "You, son of man, the Lord GOD says: 'Speak to the birds of every sort, and to every animal of the field, "Assemble yourselves, and come; gather yourselves on every side to my sacrifice that I sacrifice for you, even a great sacrifice on the mountains of Israel, that you may eat meat and drink blood. 18 You shall eat the flesh of the mighty, and drink the blood of the princes of the earth, of rams, of lambs, and of goats, of bulls, all of them fatlings of Bashan. 19 You shall eat fat until you are full, and drink blood until you are drunk, of my sacrifice which I have sacrificed for you. 20 You shall be filled at my table with horses and charioteers, with mighty men, and with all men of war," says the Lord GOD.'

21 "I will set my glory amongst the nations. Then all the nations will see my judgement that I have executed, and my hand that I have laid on them. 22 So the house of Israel will know that I am the LORD their God, from that day and forward. 23 The nations will know that the house of Israel went into captivity for their iniquity, because they trespassed against me, and I hid my face from them; so I gave them into the hand of their adversaries, and they all fell by the sword. 24 I did to them according to their uncleanness and according to their transgressions. I hid my face from them.

25 "Therefore the Lord GOD says: 'Now I will reverse the captivity of Jacob and have mercy on the whole house of Israel. I will be jealous for my holy name. 26 They will forget their shame and all their trespasses by which they have trespassed against me, when they dwell securely in their land. No one will make them afraid 27 when I have brought them back from the peoples, gathered them out of their enemies' lands, and am shown holy amongst them in the sight of many nations. 28 They will know that I am the LORD their God, in that I caused them to go into captivity amongst the nations, and have gathered them to their own land. Then I will leave none of them captive any more. 29 I won't hide my face from them any more, for I have poured out my Spirit on the house of Israel,' says the Lord GOD."

40

1 In the twenty-fifth year of our captivity, in the beginning of the year, in the tenth day of the month, in the fourteenth year after the city was struck, in the same day, the LORD's hand was on me, and he brought me there. 2 In the visions of God he brought me into the land of Israel, and set me down on a very high mountain, on which was something like the frame of a city to the south. 3 He brought me there; and, behold, there was a man whose appearance was like the appearance of bronze, with a line of flax in his hand and a measuring reed; and he stood in the gate. 4 The man said to me, "Son of man, see with your eyes, and hear with your ears, and set your

heart on all that I will show you; for you have been brought here so that I may show them to you. Declare all that you see to the house of Israel."

5 Behold, there was a wall on the outside of the house all around, and in the man's hand a measuring reed six cubits[a] long, of a cubit and a hand width each. So he measured the thickness of the building, one reed; and the height, one reed.

6 Then he came to the gate which looks towards the east, and went up its steps. He measured the threshold of the gate, one reed wide; and the other threshold, one reed wide. 7 Every lodge was one reed long and one reed wide. Between the lodges was five cubits. The threshold of the gate by the porch of the gate towards the house was one reed.

8 He measured also the porch of the gate towards the house, one reed. 9 Then he measured the porch of the gate, eight cubits; and its posts, two cubits; and the porch of the gate was towards the house.

10 The side rooms of the gate eastward were three on this side, and three on that side. The three of them were of one measure. The posts had one measure on this side and on that side. 11 He measured the width of the opening of the gate, ten cubits; and the length of the gate, thirteen cubits; 12 and a border before the lodges, one cubit on this side, and a border, one cubit on that side; and the side rooms, six cubits on this side, and six cubits on that side. 13 He measured the gate from the roof of the one side room to the roof of the other, a width of twenty-five cubits, door against door. 14 He also made posts, sixty cubits; and the court reached to the posts, around the gate. 15 From the forefront of the gate at the entrance to the forefront of the inner porch of the gate were fifty cubits. 16 There were closed windows to the side rooms, and to their posts within the gate all around, and likewise to the arches. Windows were around inward. Palm trees were on each post.

17 Then he brought me into the outer court. Behold, there were rooms and a pavement made for the court all around. Thirty rooms were on the pavement. 18 The pavement was by the side of the gates, corresponding to the length of the gates, even the lower pavement. 19 Then he measured the width from the forefront of the lower gate to the forefront of the inner court outside, one hundred cubits, both on the east and on the north.

20 He measured the length and width of the gate of the outer court which faces towards the north. 21 The lodges of it were three on this side and three on that side. Its posts and its arches were the same as the measure of the first gate: its length was fifty cubits, and the width twenty-five cubits. 22 Its windows, its arches, and its palm trees were the same as the measure of the gate which faces towards the east. They went up to it by seven steps. Its arches were before them. 23 There was a gate to the inner court facing the other gate, on the north and on the east. He measured one hundred cubits from gate to gate.

24 He led me towards the south; and behold, there was a gate towards the south. He measured its posts and its arches according to these measurements. 25 There were windows in it and in its arches all around, like the other windows: the length was fifty cubits, and the width twenty-five cubits. 26 There were seven steps to go up to it, and its arches were before them. It had palm trees, one on this side, and another on that side, on its posts. 27 There was a gate to the inner court towards the south. He measured one hundred cubits from gate to gate towards the south.

28 Then he brought me to the inner court by the south gate. He measured the south gate according to these measurements; 29 with its lodges, its posts, and its arches, according to these measurements. There were windows in it and in its arches all around. It was fifty cubits long, and twenty-five cubits wide. 30 There were arches all around, twenty-five cubits long and five cubits wide. 31 Its arches were towards the outer court. Palm trees were on its posts. The ascent to it had eight steps.

32 He brought me into the inner court towards the east. He measured the gate according to these measurements; 33 with its lodges, its posts, and its arches, according to these measurements. There were windows in it and in its arches all around. It was fifty cubits long, and twenty-five cubits wide. 34 Its arches were towards the outer court. Palm trees were on its posts on this side and on that side. The ascent to it had eight steps.

35 He brought me to the north gate, and he measured it according to these measurements— 36 its lodges, its posts, and its arches. There were windows in it all around. The length was fifty cubits and the width twenty-five cubits. 37 Its posts were towards the outer court. Palm trees were on its posts on this side and on that side. The ascent to it had eight steps.

38 A room with its door was by the posts at the gates. They washed the burnt offering there. 39 In the porch of the gate were two tables on this side and two tables on that side, on which to kill the burnt offering, the sin offering, and the trespass offering. 40 On the one side outside, as one goes up to the entry of the gate towards the north, were two tables; and on the other side, which belonged to the porch of the gate, were two tables. 41 Four tables were on this side, and four tables on that side, by the side of the gate: eight tables, on which they killed the sacrifices. 42 There were four cut stone tables for the burnt offering, a cubit and a half long, a cubit and a half wide, and one cubit high. They laid the instruments with which they killed the burnt offering and the sacrifice on them. 43 The hooks, a hand width long, were fastened within all around. The meat of the offering was on the tables.

44 Outside of the inner gate were rooms for the singers in the inner court, which was at the side of the north gate. They faced towards the south. One at the side of the east gate faced towards the north. 45 He said to me, "This room, which faces towards the south, is for the priests who perform the duty of the house. 46 The room which faces towards the north is for the priests who perform the duty of the altar. These are the sons of Zadok, who from amongst the sons of Levi come near to the LORD to minister to him." 47 He measured the court, one hundred cubits long and one hundred cubits wide, square. The altar was before the house.

48 Then he brought me to the porch of the house, and measured each post of the porch, five cubits on this side, and five cubits on that side. The width of the gate was three cubits on this side and three cubits on that side. 49 The length of the porch was twenty cubits and the width eleven cubits, even by the steps by which they went up to it. There were pillars by the posts, one on this side, and another on that side.

41

1 He brought me to the nave and measured the posts, six cubits wide on the one side and six cubits wide on the other side, which was the width of the tent. 2 The width of the entrance was ten cubits,[b] and the sides of the entrance were five cubits on the one side, and five cubits on the other side. He measured its length, forty cubits, and the width, twenty cubits.

3 Then he went inward and measured each post of the entrance, two cubits; and the entrance, six cubits; and the width of the entrance, seven cubits. 4 He measured its length, twenty cubits, and the width, twenty cubits, before the nave. He said to me, "This is the most holy place."

5 Then he measured the wall of the house, six cubits; and the width of every side room, four cubits, all around the house on every side. 6 The side rooms were in three storeys, one over another, and thirty in each story. They entered into the wall which belonged to the house for the side rooms all around, that they might be supported and not penetrate the wall of the house. 7 The side rooms were wider on the higher levels, because the walls were narrower at the higher levels. Therefore the width of the house increased upward; and so one went up from the lowest level to the highest through the middle level.

8 I saw also that the house had a raised base all around. The foundations of the side rooms were a full reed of six great cubits. 9 The thickness of the outer wall of the side rooms was five cubits. That which was left was the place of the side rooms that belonged to the house. 10 Between the rooms was a width of twenty cubits around the house on every side. 11 The doors of the side rooms were towards an open area that was left, one door towards the north, and another door towards the south. The width of the open area was five cubits all around.

12 The building that was before the separate place at the side towards the west was seventy cubits wide; and the wall of the building was five cubits thick all around, and its length ninety cubits.

13 So he measured the temple, one hundred cubits long; and the separate place, and the building, with its walls, one hundred cubits long; 14 also the width of the face of the temple, and of the separate place towards the east, one hundred cubits.

15 He measured the length of the building before the separate place which was at its back, and its galleries on the one side and on the other side, one hundred cubits from the inner temple, and the porches of the court, 16 the thresholds, and the closed windows, and the galleries around on their three storeys, opposite the threshold, with wood ceilings all around, and from the ground up to the windows, (now the windows were covered), 17 to the space above the door, even to the inner house, and outside, and by all the wall all around inside and outside, by measure. 18 It was made with cherubim and palm trees. A palm tree was between cherub and cherub, and every cherub had two faces, 19 so that there was the face of a man towards the palm tree on the one side, and the face of a young lion towards the palm tree on the other side. It was made like this through all the house all around. 20 Cherubim and palm trees were made from the ground to above the door. The wall of the temple was like this.

21 The door posts of the nave were squared. As for the face of the nave, its appearance was as the appearance of the temple. 22 The altar was of wood, three cubits high, and its length two cubits. Its corners, its base, and its walls were of wood. He said to me, "This is the table that is before the LORD." 23 The temple and the sanctuary had two doors. 24 The doors had two leaves each, two turning leaves: two for the one door, and two leaves for the other. 25 There were made on them, on the doors of the nave, cherubim and palm trees, like those made on the walls. There was a threshold of wood on the face of the porch outside. 26 There were closed windows and palm trees on the one side and on the other side, on the sides of the porch. This is how the side rooms of the temple and the thresholds were arranged.

42

1 Then he brought me out into the outer court, the way towards the north. Then he brought me into the room that was opposite the separate place, and which was opposite the building towards the north. 2 Facing the length of one hundred cubits[c] was the north door, and the width was fifty cubits. 3 Opposite the twenty cubits which belonged to the inner court, and opposite the pavement which belonged to the outer court, was gallery

---

a 40:5 A normal cubit is the length from the tip of the middle finger to the elbow on a man's arm, or about 18 inches or 46 centimetres. A handbreadth is about 4.3 inches or 11 centimetres, so the long cubit described here would be about 22.3 inches or 57 centimetres long. Thus, a 6 long cubit measuring reed would have been about 3 yards 26.6 inches or about 3.42 metres long.

b 41:2 A cubit is the length from the tip of the middle finger to the elbow on a man's arm, or about 18 inches or 46 centimetres.
c 42:2 A cubit is the length from the tip of the middle finger to the elbow on a man's arm, or about 18 inches or 46 centimetres.

against gallery in the three storeys. ₄ Before the rooms was a walk of ten cubits' width inward, a way of one cubit; and their doors were towards the north. ₅ Now the upper rooms were shorter; for the galleries took away from these more than from the lower and the middle in the building. ₆ For they were in three storeys, and they didn't have pillars as the pillars of the courts. Therefore the uppermost was set back more than the lowest and the middle from the ground. ₇ The wall that was outside by the side of the rooms, towards the outer court before the rooms, was fifty cubits long. ₈ For the length of the rooms that were in the outer court was fifty cubits. Behold, those facing the temple were one hundred cubits. ₉ From under these rooms was the entry on the east side, as one goes into them from the outer court.

₁₀ In the thickness of the wall of the court towards the east, before the separate place, and before the building, there were rooms. ₁₁ The way before them was like the appearance of the rooms which were towards the north. Their length and width were the same. All their exits had the same arrangement and doors. ₁₂ Like the doors of the rooms that were towards the south was a door at the head of the way, even the way directly before the wall towards the east, as one enters into them.

₁₃ Then he said to me, "The north rooms and the south rooms, which are opposite the separate place, are the holy rooms, where the priests who are near to the LORD shall eat the most holy things. There they shall lay the most holy things, with the meal offering, the sin offering, and the trespass offering; for the place is holy. ₁₄ When the priests enter in, then they shall not go out of the holy place into the outer court until they lay their garments in which they minister there; for they are holy. Then they shall put on other garments, and shall approach that which is for the people."

₁₅ Now when he had finished measuring the inner house, he brought me out by the way of the gate which faces towards the east, and measured it all around. ₁₆ He measured on the east side with the measuring reed five hundred reeds, with the measuring reed all around. ₁₇ He measured on the north side five hundred reeds with the measuring reed all around. ₁₈ He measured on the south side five hundred reeds with the measuring reed. ₁₉ He turned about to the west side, and measured five hundred reeds with the measuring reed. ₂₀ He measured it on the four sides. It had a wall around it, the length five hundred cubits, and the width five hundred cubits, to make a separation between that which was holy and that which was common.

43

₁ Afterward he brought me to the gate, even the gate that looks towards the east. ₂ Behold, the glory of the God of Israel came from the way of the east. His voice was like the sound of many waters; and the earth was illuminated with his glory. ₃ It was like the appearance of the vision which I saw, even according to the vision that I saw when I came to destroy the city; and the visions were like the vision that I saw by the river Chebar; and I fell on my face. ₄ The LORD's glory came into the house by the way of the gate which faces towards the east. ₅ The Spirit took me up and brought me into the inner court; and behold, the LORD's glory filled the house.

₆ I heard one speaking to me out of the house, and a man stood by me. ₇ He said to me, "Son of man, this is the place of my throne and the place of the soles of my feet, where I will dwell amongst the children of Israel forever. The house of Israel will no more defile my holy name, neither they nor their kings, by their prostitution and by the dead bodies of their kings in their high places; ₈ in their setting of their threshold by my threshold and their door post beside my door post. There was a wall between me and them; and they have defiled my holy name by their abominations which they have committed. Therefore I have consumed them in my anger. ₉ Now let them put away their prostitution, and the dead bodies of their kings far from me. Then I will dwell amongst them forever.

₁₀ "You, son of man, show the house to the house of Israel, that they may be ashamed of their iniquities; and let them measure the pattern. ₁₁ If they are ashamed of all that they have done, make known to them the form of the house, its fashion, its exits, its entrances, its structure, all its ordinances, all its forms, and all its laws; and write it in their sight, that they may keep the whole form of it, and all its ordinances, and do them.

₁₂ "This is the law of the house. On the top of the mountain the whole limit around it shall be most holy. Behold, this is the law of the house.

₁₃ "These are the measurements of the altar by cubits (the cubitª is a cubit and a hand width): the bottom shall be a cubit, and the width a cubit, and its border around its edge a span;ᵇ and this shall be the base of the altar. ₁₄ From the bottom on the ground to the lower ledge shall be two cubits, and the width one cubit; and from the lesser ledge to the greater ledge shall be four cubits, and the width a cubit. ₁₅ The upper altar shall be four cubits; and from the altar hearth and upward there shall be four horns. ₁₆ The altar hearth shall be twelve cubits long by twelve wide, square in its four sides. ₁₇ The ledge shall be fourteen cubits long by fourteen wide in its four sides; and the border about it shall be half a cubit; and its bottom shall be a cubit around; and its steps shall look towards the east."

₁₈ He said to me, "Son of man, the Lord GOD says: 'These are the ordinances of the altar in the day when they make it, to offer burnt offerings on it, and to sprinkle blood on it. ₁₉ You shall give to the Levitical priests who are of the offspring of Zadok, who are near to me, to minister to me,' says the Lord GOD, 'a young bull for a sin offering. ₂₀ You shall take of its blood and put it on its four horns, and on the four corners of the ledge, and on the border all around. You shall cleanse it and make atonement for it

that way. ₂₁ You shall also take the bull of the sin offering, and it shall be burnt in the appointed place of the house, outside of the sanctuary.

₂₂ "On the second day you shall offer a male goat without defect for a sin offering; and they shall cleanse the altar, as they cleansed it with the bull. ₂₃ When you have finished cleansing it, you shall offer a young bull without defect and a ram out of the flock without defect. ₂₄ You shall bring them near to the LORD, and the priests shall cast salt on them, and they shall offer them up for a burnt offering to the LORD.

₂₅ "Seven days you shall prepare every day a goat for a sin offering. They shall also prepare a young bull and a ram out of the flock, without defect. ₂₆ Seven days shall they make atonement for the altar and purify it. So shall they consecrate it. ₂₇ When they have accomplished the days, it shall be that on the eighth day and onward, the priests shall make your burnt offerings on the altar and your peace offerings. Then I will accept you,' says the Lord GOD."

44

₁ Then he brought me back by the way of the outer gate of the sanctuary, which looks towards the east; and it was shut. ₂ The LORD said to me, "This gate shall be shut. It shall not be opened, no man shall enter in by it; for the LORD, the God of Israel, has entered in by it. Therefore it shall be shut. ₃ As for the prince, he shall sit in it as prince to eat bread before the LORD. He shall enter by the way of the porch of the gate, and shall go out the same way."

₄ Then he brought me by the way of the north gate before the house; and I looked, and behold, the LORD's glory filled the LORD's house; so I fell on my face.

₅ The LORD said to me, "Son of man, mark well, and see with your eyes, and hear with your ears all that I tell you concerning all the ordinances of the LORD's house and all its laws; and mark well the entrance of the house, with every exit of the sanctuary. ₆ You shall tell the rebellious, even the house of Israel, 'The Lord GOD says: "You house of Israel, let that be enough of all your abominations, ₇ in that you have brought in foreigners, uncircumcised in heart and uncircumcised in flesh, to be in my sanctuary, to profane it, even my house, when you offer my bread, the fat and the blood; and they have broken my covenant, to add to all your abominations. ₈ You have not performed the duty of my holy things; but you have set performers of my duty in my sanctuary for yourselves." ₉ The Lord GOD says, "No foreigner, uncircumcised in heart and uncircumcised in flesh, shall enter into my sanctuary, of any foreigners who are amongst the children of Israel.

₁₀ "'"But the Levites who went far from me when Israel went astray, who went astray from me after their idols, they will bear their iniquity. ₁₁ Yet they shall be ministers in my sanctuary, having oversight at the gates of the house, and ministering in the house. They shall kill the burnt offering and the sacrifice for the people, and they shall stand before them to minister to them. ₁₂ Because they ministered to them before their idols, and became a stumbling block of iniquity to the house of Israel, therefore I have lifted up my hand against them," says the Lord GOD, "and they will bear their iniquity. ₁₃ They shall not come near to me, to execute the office of priest to me, nor to come near to any of my holy things, to the things that are most holy; but they will bear their shame and their abominations which they have committed. ₁₄ Yet I will make them performers of the duty of the house, for all its service and for all that will be done therein.

₁₅ "'"But the Levitical priests, the sons of Zadok, who performed the duty of my sanctuary when the children of Israel went astray from me, shall come near to me to minister to me. They shall stand before me to offer to me the fat and the blood," says the Lord GOD. ₁₆ "They shall enter into my sanctuary, and they shall come near to my table, to minister to me, and they shall keep my instruction.

₁₇ "'"It will be that when they enter in at the gates of the inner court, they shall be clothed with linen garments. No wool shall come on them while they minister in the gates of the inner court, and within. ₁₈ They shall have linen turbans on their heads, and shall have linen trousers on their waists. They shall not clothe themselves with anything that makes them sweat. ₁₉ When they go out into the outer court, even into the outer court to the people, they shall put off their garments in which they minister and lay them in the holy rooms. They shall put on other garments, that they not sanctify the people with their garments.

₂₀ "'"They shall not shave their heads, or allow their locks to grow long. They shall only cut off the hair of their heads. ₂₁ None of the priests shall drink wine when they enter into the inner court. ₂₂ They shall not take for their wives a widow, or her who is put away; but they shall take virgins of the offspring of the house of Israel, or a widow who is the widow of a priest. ₂₃ They shall teach my people the difference between the holy and the common, and cause them to discern between the unclean and the clean.

₂₄ "'"In a controversy they shall stand to judge. They shall judge it according to my ordinances. They shall keep my laws and my statutes in all my appointed feasts. They shall make my Sabbaths holy.

₂₅ "'"They shall go in to no dead person to defile themselves; but for father, or for mother, or for son, or for daughter, for brother, or for sister who has had no husband, they may defile themselves. ₂₆ After he is cleansed, they shall reckon to him seven days. ₂₇ In the day that he goes

---

ª *43:13* A normal cubit is the length from the tip of the middle finger to the elbow on a man's arm, or about 18 inches or 46 centimetres. A hand width is about 4.3 inches or 11 cm.

ᵇ *43:13* A span is the length from the tip of a man's thumb to the tip of his little finger when his hand is stretched out (about half a cubit, or 9 inches, or 22.8 cm.)

into the sanctuary, into the inner court, to minister in the sanctuary, he shall offer his sin offering," says the Lord GOD.

28 "'They shall have an inheritance: I am their inheritance; and you shall give them no possession in Israel. I am their possession. 29 They shall eat the meal offering, and the sin offering, and the trespass offering; and every devoted thing in Israel shall be theirs. 30 The first of all the first fruits of every thing, and every offering of everything, of all your offerings, shall be for the priest. You shall also give to the priests the first of your dough, to cause a blessing to rest on your house. 31 The priests shall not eat of anything that dies of itself or is torn, whether it is bird or animal.

45

1 "'"Moreover, when you divide by lot the land for inheritance, you shall offer an offering to the LORD, a holy portion of the land. The length shall be the length of twenty-five thousand reeds, and the width shall be ten thousand. It shall be holy in all its border all around. 2 Of this there shall be a five hundred by five hundred square for the holy place, and fifty cubits[a] for its pasture lands all around. 3 Of this measure you shall measure a length of twenty-five thousand, and a width of ten thousand. In it shall be the sanctuary, which is most holy. 4 It is a holy portion of the land; it shall be for the priests, the ministers of the sanctuary, who come near to minister to the LORD. It shall be a place for their houses and a holy place for the sanctuary. 5 Twenty-five thousand cubits in length and ten thousand in width shall be for the Levites, the ministers of the house, as a possession for themselves, for twenty rooms.

6 "'"You shall appoint the possession of the city five thousand cubits wide and twenty-five thousand long, side by side with the offering of the holy portion. It shall be for the whole house of Israel.

7 "'"What is for the prince shall be on the one side and on the other side of the holy allotment and of the possession of the city, in front of the holy allotment and in front of the possession of the city, on the west side westward, and on the east side eastward, and in length corresponding to one of the portions, from the west border to the east border. 8 In the land it shall be to him for a possession in Israel. My princes shall no more oppress my people, but they shall give the land to the house of Israel according to their tribes."

9 "'The Lord GOD says: "Enough you, princes of Israel! Remove violence and plunder, and execute justice and righteousness! Stop dispossessing my people!" says the Lord GOD. 10 "You shall have just balances, a just ephah,[b] and a just bath. 11 The ephah and the bath shall be of one measure, that the bath may contain one tenth of a homer,[c] and the ephah one tenth of a homer. Its measure shall be the same as the homer. 12 The shekel[d] shall be twenty gerahs.[e] Twenty shekels plus twenty-five shekels plus fifteen shekels shall be your mina.[f]

13 "'"This is the offering that you shall offer: the sixth part of an ephah from a homer of wheat, and you shall give the sixth part of an ephah from a homer of barley, 14 and the set portion of oil, of the bath of oil, one tenth of a bath out of the cor, which is ten baths, even a homer (for ten baths are a homer),[g] 15 and one lamb of the flock out of two hundred, from the well-watered pastures of Israel—for a meal offering, for a burnt offering, and for peace offerings, to make atonement for them," says the Lord GOD. 16 "All the people of the land shall give to this offering for the prince in Israel. 17 It shall be the prince's part to give the burnt offerings, the meal offerings, and the drink offerings, in the feasts, and on the new moons, and on the Sabbaths, in all the appointed feasts of the house of Israel. He shall prepare the sin offering, the meal offering, the burnt offering, and the peace offerings, to make atonement for the house of Israel."

18 "'The Lord GOD says: "In the first month, on the first day of the month, you shall take a young bull without defect, and you shall cleanse the sanctuary. 19 The priest shall take of the blood of the sin offering and put it on the door posts of the house, and on the four corners of the ledge of the altar, and on the posts of the gate of the inner court. 20 So you shall do on the seventh day of the month for everyone who errs, and for him who is simple. So you shall make atonement for the house.

21 "'"In the first month, on the fourteenth day of the month, you shall have the Passover, a feast of seven days; unleavened bread shall be eaten. 22 On that day the prince shall prepare for himself and for all the people of the land a bull for a sin offering. 23 The seven days of the feast he shall prepare a burnt offering to the LORD, seven bulls and seven rams without defect daily the seven days; and a male goat daily for a sin offering. 24 He shall prepare a meal offering, an ephah[h] for a bull, an ephah for a ram, and a hin[i] of oil to an ephah.

25 "'"In the seventh month, on the fifteenth day of the month, during the feast, he shall do like that for seven days. He shall make the same provision for sin offering, the burnt offering, the meal offering, and the oil."

46

1 "'The Lord GOD says: "The gate of the inner court that looks towards the east shall be shut the six working days; but on the Sabbath day it shall be opened, and on the day of the new moon it shall be opened. 2 The prince shall enter by the way of the porch of the gate outside, and shall stand by the post of the gate; and the priests shall prepare his burnt offering and his peace offerings, and he shall worship at the threshold of the gate. Then he shall go out, but the gate shall not be shut until the evening. 3 The people of the land shall worship at the door of that gate before the LORD on the Sabbaths and on the new moons. 4 The burnt offering that the prince shall offer to the LORD shall be on the Sabbath day, six lambs without defect and a ram without defect; 5 and the meal offering shall be an ephah for the ram, and the meal offering for the lambs as he is able to give, and a hin[j] of oil to an ephah.[k] 6 On the day of the new moon it shall be a young bull without defect, six lambs, and a ram. They shall be without defect. 7 He shall prepare a meal offering: an ephah for the bull, and an ephah for the ram, and for the lambs according as he is able, and a hin of oil to an ephah. 8 When the prince enters, he shall go in by the way of the porch of the gate, and he shall go out by its way.

9 "'"But when the people of the land come before the LORD in the appointed feasts, he who enters by the way of the north gate to worship shall go out by the way of the south gate; and he who enters by the way of the south gate shall go out by the way of the north gate. He shall not return by the way of the gate by which he came in, but shall go out straight before him. 10 The prince shall go in with them when they go in. When they go out, he shall go out.

11 "'"In the feasts and in the appointed holidays, the meal offering shall be an ephah[l] for a bull, and an ephah for a ram, and for the lambs as he is able to give, and a hin of oil to an ephah. 12 When the prince prepares a free will offering, a burnt offering or peace offerings as a free will offering to the LORD, one shall open for him the gate that looks towards the east; and he shall prepare his burnt offering and his peace offerings, as he does on the Sabbath day. Then he shall go out; and after his going out one shall shut the gate.

13 "'"You shall prepare a lamb a year old without defect for a burnt offering to the LORD daily. Morning by morning you shall prepare it. 14 You shall prepare a meal offering with it morning by morning, the sixth part of an ephah,[m] and the third part of a hin of oil to moisten the fine flour; a meal offering to the LORD continually by a perpetual ordinance. 15 Thus they shall prepare the lamb, the meal offering, and the oil, morning by morning, for a continual burnt offering."

16 "'The Lord GOD says: "If the prince gives a gift to any of his sons, it is his inheritance. It shall belong to his sons. It is their possession by inheritance. 17 But if he gives of his inheritance a gift to one of his servants, it shall be his to the year of liberty; then it shall return to the prince; but as for his inheritance, it shall be for his sons. 18 Moreover the prince shall not take of the people's inheritance, to thrust them out of their possession. He shall give inheritance to his sons out of his own possession, that my people not each be scattered from his possession."'"

19 Then he brought me through the entry, which was at the side of the gate, into the holy rooms for the priests, which looked towards the north. Behold, there was a place on the back part westward. 20 He said to me, "This is the place where the priests shall boil the trespass offering and the sin offering, and where they shall bake the meal offering, that they not bring them out into the outer court, to sanctify the people."

21 Then he brought me out into the outer court and caused me to pass by the four corners of the court; and behold, in every corner of the court there was a court. 22 In the four corners of the court there were courts enclosed, forty cubits[n] long and thirty wide. These four in the corners were the same size. 23 There was a wall around in them, around the four, and boiling places were made under the walls all around. 24 Then he said to me, "These are the boiling houses, where the ministers of the house shall boil the sacrifice of the people."

47

1 He brought me back to the door of the temple; and behold, waters flowed out from under the threshold of the temple eastward, for the front of the temple faced towards the east. The waters came down from underneath, from the right side of the temple, on the south of the altar. 2 Then he brought me out by the way of the gate northward, and led me around by the way outside to the outer gate, by the way of the gate that looks towards the east. Behold, waters ran out on the right side.

3 When the man went out eastward with the line in his hand, he measured one thousand cubits,[o] and he caused me to pass through the waters, waters that were to the ankles. 4 Again he measured one thousand, and caused me to pass through the waters, waters that were to the knees. Again he measured one thousand, and caused me to pass through waters that were to the waist. 5 Afterward he measured one thousand; and it was a river that I could not pass through, for the waters had risen, waters to swim in, a river that could not be walked through.

6 He said to me, "Son of man, have you seen this?"

---

a *45:2* A cubit is the length from the tip of the middle finger to the elbow on a man's arm, or about 18 inches or 46 centimetres.
b *45:10* 1 ephah is about 22 litres or about 2/3 of a bushel
c *45:11* 1 homer is about 220 litres or 6 bushels
d *45:12* A shekel is about 10 grams or about 0.35 ounces.
e *45:12* a gerah is about 0.5 grams or about 7.7 grains
f *45:12* A mina is about 600 grams or 1.3 U. S. pounds.
g *45:14* 1 cor is the same as 1 homer in volume, and is about 211 litres, 55.9 gallons, or 6 bushels. 1 bath is about 21.1 litres, 5.59 gallons, or 2.4 pecks.
h *45:24* 1 ephah is about 22 litres or about 2/3 of a bushel
i *45:24* A hin is about 6.5 litres or 1.7 gallons.
j *46:5* A hin is about 6.5 litres or 1.7 gallons.
k *46:5* 1 ephah is about 22 litres or about 2/3 of a bushel
l *46:11* 1 ephah is about 22 litres or about 2/3 of a bushel
m *46:14* 1 ephah is about 22 litres or about 2/3 of a bushel
n *46:22* A cubit is the length from the tip of the middle finger to the elbow on a man's arm, or about 18 inches or 46 centimetres.
o *47:3* A cubit is the length from the tip of the middle finger to the elbow on a man's arm, or about 18 inches or 46 centimetres.

Then he brought me and caused me to return to the bank of the river. 7 Now when I had returned, behold, on the bank of the river were very many trees on the one side and on the other. 8 Then he said to me, "These waters flow out towards the eastern region and will go down into the Arabah. Then they will go towards the sea and flow into the sea which will be made to flow out; and the waters will be healed. 9 It will happen that every living creature which swarms, in every place where the rivers come, will live. Then there will be a very great multitude of fish; for these waters have come there, and the waters of the sea will be healed, and everything will live wherever the river comes. 10 It will happen that fishermen will stand by it. From En Gedi even to En Eglaim will be a place for the spreading of nets. Their fish will be after their kinds, as the fish of the great sea, exceedingly many. 11 But its swamps and marshes will not be healed. They will be given up to salt. 12 By the river banks, on both sides, will grow every tree for food, whose leaf won't wither, neither will its fruit fail. It will produce new fruit every month, because its waters issue out of the sanctuary. Its fruit will be for food, and its leaf for healing."

13 The Lord GOD says: "This shall be the border by which you shall divide the land for inheritance according to the twelve tribes of Israel. Joseph shall have two portions. 14 You shall inherit it, one as well as another; for I swore to give it to your fathers. This land will fall to you for inheritance.

15 "This shall be the border of the land:

"On the north side, from the great sea, by the way of Hethlon, to the entrance of Zedad; 16 Hamath, Berothah, Sibraim (which is between the border of Damascus and the border of Hamath), to Hazer Hatticon, which is by the border of Hauran. 17 The border from the sea shall be Hazar Enon at the border of Damascus; and on the north northward is the border of Hamath. This is the north side.

18 "The east side, between Hauran, Damascus, Gilead, and the land of Israel, shall be the Jordan; from the north border to the east sea you shall measure. This is the east side.

19 "The south side southward shall be from Tamar as far as the waters of Meriboth Kadesh, to the brook, to the great sea. This is the south side southward.

20 "The west side shall be the great sea, from the south border as far as opposite the entrance of Hamath. This is the west side.

21 "So you shall divide this land to yourselves according to the tribes of Israel. 22 You shall divide it by lot for an inheritance to you and to the aliens who live amongst you, who will father children amongst you. Then they shall be to you as the native-born amongst the children of Israel. They shall have inheritance with you amongst the tribes of Israel. 23 In whatever tribe the stranger lives, there you shall give him his inheritance," says the Lord GOD.

48

1 "Now these are the names of the tribes: From the north end, beside the way of Hethlon to the entrance of Hamath, Hazar Enan at the border of Damascus, northward beside Hamath (and they shall have their sides east and west), Dan, one portion.

2 "By the border of Dan, from the east side to the west side, Asher, one portion.

3 "By the border of Asher, from the east side even to the west side, Naphtali, one portion.

4 "By the border of Naphtali, from the east side to the west side, Manasseh, one portion.

5 "By the border of Manasseh, from the east side to the west side, Ephraim, one portion.

6 "By the border of Ephraim, from the east side even to the west side, Reuben, one portion.

7 "By the border of Reuben, from the east side to the west side, Judah, one portion.

8 "By the border of Judah, from the east side to the west side, shall be the offering which you shall offer, twenty-five thousand reeds in width, and in length as one of the portions, from the east side to the west side; and the sanctuary shall be in the middle of it.

9 "The offering that you shall offer to the LORD shall be twenty-five thousand reeds in length, and ten thousand in width. 10 For these, even for the priests, shall be the holy offering: towards the north twenty-five thousand in length, and towards the west ten thousand in width, and towards the east ten thousand in width, and towards the south twenty-five thousand in length; and the sanctuary of the LORD shall be in the middle of it. 11 It shall be for the priests who are sanctified of the sons of Zadok, who have kept my instruction, who didn't go astray when the children of Israel went astray, as the Levites went astray. 12 It shall be to them an offering from the offering of the land, a most holy thing, by the border of the Levites.

13 "Alongside the border of the priests, the Levites shall have twenty-five thousand cubits in length and ten thousand in width. All the length shall be twenty-five thousand, and the width ten thousand. 14 They shall sell none of it, nor exchange it, nor shall the first fruits of the land be alienated, for it is holy to the LORD.

15 "The five thousand cubits that are left in the width, in front of the twenty-five thousand, shall be for common use, for the city, for dwelling and for pasture lands; and the city shall be in the middle of it. 16 These shall be its measurements: the north side four thousand and five hundred, and the south side four thousand and five hundred, and on the east side four thousand and five hundred, and the west side four thousand and five hundred. 17 The city shall have pasture lands: towards the north two hundred and fifty, and towards the south two hundred and fifty, and towards the east two hundred and fifty, and towards the west two hundred

and fifty. 18 The remainder of the length, alongside the holy offering, shall be ten thousand eastward and ten thousand westward; and it shall be alongside the holy offering. Its increase shall be for food to those who labour in the city. 19 Those who labour in the city, out of all the tribes of Israel, shall cultivate it. 20 All the offering shall be a square of twenty-five thousand by twenty-five thousand. You shall offer it as a holy offering, with the possession of the city.

21 "The remainder shall be for the prince, on the one side and on the other of the holy offering and of the possession of the city; in front of the twenty-five thousand of the offering towards the east border, and westward in front of the twenty-five thousand towards the west border, alongside the portions, it shall be for the prince. The holy offering and the sanctuary of the house shall be in the middle of it. 22 Moreover, from the possession of the Levites, and from the possession of the city, being in the middle of that which is the prince's, between the border of Judah and the border of Benjamin, shall be for the prince.

23 "As for the rest of the tribes: from the east side to the west side, Benjamin, one portion.

24 "By the border of Benjamin, from the east side to the west side, Simeon, one portion.

25 "By the border of Simeon, from the east side to the west side, Issachar, one portion.

26 "By the border of Issachar, from the east side to the west side, Zebulun, one portion.

27 "By the border of Zebulun, from the east side to the west side, Gad, one portion.

28 "By the border of Gad, at the south side southward, the border shall be even from Tamar to the waters of Meribath Kadesh, to the brook, to the great sea.

29 "This is the land which you shall divide by lot to the tribes of Israel for inheritance, and these are their several portions, says the Lord GOD.

30 "These are the exits of the city: On the north side four thousand and five hundred reeds by measure; 31 and the gates of the city shall be named after the tribes of Israel, three gates northward: the gate of Reuben, one; the gate of Judah, one; the gate of Levi, one.

32 "At the east side four thousand and five hundred reeds, and three gates: even the gate of Joseph, one; the gate of Benjamin, one; the gate of Dan, one.

33 "At the south side four thousand and five hundred reeds by measure, and three gates: the gate of Simeon, one; the gate of Issachar, one; the gate of Zebulun, one.

34 "At the west side four thousand and five hundred reeds, with their three gates: the gate of Gad, one; the gate of Asher, one; the gate of Naphtali, one.

35 "It shall be eighteen thousand reeds in circumference; and the name of the city from that day shall be, 'The LORD is there.'

The Book of Daniel

1

1 In the third year of the reign of Jehoiakim king of Judah, Nebuchadnezzar king of Babylon came to Jerusalem and besieged it. 2 The Lord[a] gave Jehoiakim king of Judah into his hand, with some of the vessels of the house of God;[b] and he carried them into the land of Shinar to the house of his god. He brought the vessels into the treasure house of his god.

3 The king spoke to Ashpenaz, the master of his eunuchs, that he should bring in some of the children of Israel, even of the royal offspring[c] and of the nobles: 4 youths in whom was no defect, but well-favoured, skilful in all wisdom, endowed with knowledge, understanding science, and who had the ability to stand in the king's palace; and that he should teach them the learning and the language of the Chaldeans. 5 The king appointed for them a daily portion of the king's delicacies and of the wine which he drank, and that they should be nourished three years, that at its end they should stand before the king.

6 Now amongst these of the children of Judah were Daniel, Hananiah, Mishael, and Azariah. 7 The prince of the eunuchs gave names to them: to Daniel he gave the name Belteshazzar; to Hananiah, Shadrach; to Mishael, Meshach; and to Azariah, Abednego.

8 But Daniel purposed in his heart that he would not defile himself with the king's delicacies, nor with the wine which he drank. Therefore he requested of the prince of the eunuchs that he might not defile himself. 9 Now God made Daniel find kindness and compassion in the sight of the prince of the eunuchs. 10 The prince of the eunuchs said to Daniel, "I fear my lord the king, who has appointed your food and your drink. For why should he see your faces worse looking than the youths who are of your own age? Then you would endanger my head with the king."

11 Then Daniel said to the steward whom the prince of the eunuchs had appointed over Daniel, Hananiah, Mishael, and Azariah: 12 "Test your servants, I beg you, ten days; and let them give us vegetables to eat and water to drink. 13 Then let our faces be examined before you, and the face of the youths who eat of the king's delicacies; and as you see, deal with your servants." 14 So he listened to them in this matter, and tested them for ten days.

15 At the end of ten days, their faces appeared fairer and they were fatter in flesh than all the youths who ate of the king's delicacies. 16 So the steward took away their delicacies and the wine that they were given to drink, and gave them vegetables.

17 Now as for these four youths, God gave them knowledge and skill in all learning and wisdom; and Daniel had understanding in all visions and dreams.

18 At the end of the days which the king had appointed for bringing them in, the prince of the eunuchs brought them in before Nebuchadnezzar. 19 The king talked with them; and amongst them all was found no one like Daniel, Hananiah, Mishael, and Azariah. Therefore stood they before the king. 20 In every matter of wisdom and understanding concerning which the king enquired of them, he found them ten times better than all the magicians and enchanters who were in all his realm.

21 Daniel continued even to the first year of King Cyrus.

2

1 In the second year of the reign of Nebuchadnezzar, Nebuchadnezzar dreamt dreams; and his spirit was troubled, and his sleep went from him. 2 Then the king commanded that the magicians, the enchanters, the sorcerers, and the Chaldeans be called to tell the king his dreams. So they came in and stood before the king. 3 The king said to them, "I have dreamt a dream, and my spirit is troubled to know the dream."

4 Then the Chaldeans spoke to the king in the Syrian language, "O king, live forever! Tell your servants the dream, and we will show the interpretation."

5 The king answered the Chaldeans, "The thing has gone from me. If you don't make known to me the dream and its interpretation, you will be cut in pieces, and your houses will be made a dunghill. 6 But if you show the dream and its interpretation, you will receive from me gifts, rewards, and great honour. Therefore show me the dream and its interpretation."

7 They answered the second time and said, "Let the king tell his servants the dream, and we will show the interpretation."

8 The king answered, "I know of a certainty that you are trying to gain time, because you see the thing has gone from me. 9 But if you don't make known to me the dream, there is but one law for you; for you have prepared lying and corrupt words to speak before me, until the situation changes. Therefore tell me the dream, and I will know that you can show me its interpretation."

10 The Chaldeans answered the king and said, "There is not a man on the earth who can show the king's matter, because no king, lord, or ruler has asked such a thing of any magician, enchanter, or Chaldean. 11 It is a rare thing that the king requires, and there is no other who can show it before the king except the gods, whose dwelling is not with flesh."

12 Because of this, the king was angry and very furious, and commanded that all the wise men of Babylon be destroyed. 13 So the decree went out, and the wise men were to be slain. They sought Daniel and his companions to be slain.

14 Then Daniel returned answer with counsel and prudence to Arioch the captain of the king's guard, who had gone out to kill the wise men of Babylon. 15 He answered Arioch the king's captain, "Why is the decree so urgent from the king?" Then Arioch made the thing known to Daniel. 16 Daniel went in, and desired of the king that he would appoint him a time, and he would show the king the interpretation.

17 Then Daniel went to his house and made the thing known to Hananiah, Mishael, and Azariah, his companions: 18 that they would desire mercies of the God of heaven concerning this secret, that Daniel and his companions would not perish with the rest of the wise men of Babylon. 19 Then the secret was revealed to Daniel in a vision of the night. Then Daniel blessed the God of heaven. 20 Daniel answered,

"Blessed be the name of God forever and ever;
    for wisdom and might are his.
21 He changes the times and the seasons.
    He removes kings and sets up kings.
He gives wisdom to the wise,
    and knowledge to those who have understanding.
22 He reveals the deep and secret things.
    He knows what is in the darkness,
    and the light dwells with him.
23 I thank you and praise you,
    O God of my fathers,
who have given me wisdom and might,
    and have now made known to me what we desired of you;
    for you have made known to us the king's matter."

24 Therefore Daniel went in to Arioch, whom the king had appointed to destroy the wise men of Babylon. He went and said this to him: "Don't destroy the wise men of Babylon. Bring me in before the king, and I will show to the king the interpretation."

25 Then Arioch brought in Daniel before the king in haste, and said this to him: "I have found a man of the children of the captivity of Judah who will make known to the king the interpretation."

26 The king answered Daniel, whose name was Belteshazzar, "Are you able to make known to me the dream which I have seen, and its interpretation?"

27 Daniel answered before the king, and said, "The secret which the king has demanded can't be shown to the king by wise men, enchanters, magicians, or soothsayers; 28 but there is a God in heaven who reveals secrets, and he has made known to King Nebuchadnezzar what will be in the latter days. Your dream and the visions of your head on your bed are these:

29 "As for you, O king, your thoughts came on your bed, what should happen hereafter; and he who reveals secrets has made known to you what will happen. 30 But as for me, this secret is not revealed to me for any wisdom that I have more than any living, but to the intent that the interpretation may be made known to the king, and that you may know the thoughts of your heart.

31 "You, O king, saw, and behold,[d] a great image. This image, which was mighty, and whose brightness was excellent, stood before you; and its appearance was terrifying. 32 As for this image, its head was of fine gold, its breast and its arms of silver, its belly and its thighs of bronze, 33 its legs of iron, its feet part of iron and part of clay. 34 You saw until a stone was cut out without hands, which struck the image on its feet that were of iron and clay, and broke them in pieces. 35 Then the iron, the clay, the bronze, the silver, and the gold were broken in pieces together, and became like the chaff of the summer threshing floors. The wind carried them away, so that no place was found for them. The stone that struck the image became a great mountain and filled the whole earth.

36 "This is the dream; and we will tell its interpretation before the king. 37 You, O king, are king of kings, to whom the God of heaven has given the kingdom, the power, the strength, and the glory. 38 Wherever the children of men dwell, he has given the animals of the field and the birds of the sky into your hand, and has made you rule over them all. You are the head of gold.

39 "After you, another kingdom will arise that is inferior to you; and another third kingdom of bronze, which will rule over all the earth. 40 The fourth kingdom will be strong as iron, because iron breaks in pieces and subdues all things; and as iron that crushes all these, it will break in pieces and crush. 41 Whereas you saw the feet and toes, part of potters' clay and part of iron, it will be a divided kingdom; but there will be in it of the strength of the iron, because you saw the iron mixed with miry clay. 42 As the toes of the feet were part of iron, and part of clay, so the kingdom will be partly strong and partly brittle. 43 Whereas you saw the iron mixed with miry clay, they will mingle themselves with the seed of men; but they won't cling to one another, even as iron does not mix with clay.

44 "In the days of those kings the God of heaven will set up a kingdom which will never be destroyed, nor will its sovereignty be left to another people; but it will break in pieces and consume all these kingdoms, and it will stand forever. 45 Because you saw that a stone was cut out of the mountain without hands, and that it broke in pieces the iron, the bronze, the clay, the silver, and the gold, the great God has made known to the king

---

what will happen hereafter. The dream is certain, and its interpretation sure."

₄₆ Then King Nebuchadnezzar fell on his face, worshipped Daniel, and commanded that they should offer an offering and sweet odours to him. ₄₇ The king answered to Daniel, and said, "Of a truth your God is the God of gods, and the Lord of kings, and a revealler of secrets, since you have been able to reveal this secret."

₄₈ Then the king made Daniel great and gave him many great gifts, and made him rule over the whole province of Babylon and to be chief governor over all the wise men of Babylon. ₄₉ Daniel requested of the king, and he appointed Shadrach, Meshach, and Abednego over the affairs of the province of Babylon, but Daniel was in the king's gate.

3

₁ Nebuchadnezzar the king made an image of gold, whose height was sixty cubits[a] and its width six cubits. He set it up in the plain of Dura, in the province of Babylon. ₂ Then Nebuchadnezzar the king sent to gather together the local governors, the deputies, and the governors, the judges, the treasurers, the counsellors, the sheriffs, and all the rulers of the provinces, to come to the dedication of the image which Nebuchadnezzar the king had set up. ₃ Then the local governors, the deputies, and the governors, the judges, the treasurers, the counsellors, the sheriffs, and all the rulers of the provinces were gathered together to the dedication of the image that Nebuchadnezzar the king had set up; and they stood before the image that Nebuchadnezzar had set up.

₄ Then the herald cried aloud, "To you it is commanded, peoples, nations, and languages, ₅ that whenever you hear the sound of the horn, flute, zither, lyre, harp, pipe, and all kinds of music, you fall down and worship the golden image that Nebuchadnezzar the king has set up. ₆ Whoever doesn't fall down and worship shall be cast into the middle of a burning fiery furnace the same hour."

₇ Therefore at that time, when all the peoples heard the sound of the horn, flute, zither, lyre, harp, pipe, and all kinds of music, all the peoples, the nations, and the languages fell down and worshipped the golden image that Nebuchadnezzar the king had set up.

₈ Therefore at that time certain Chaldeans came near and brought accusation against the Jews. ₉ They answered Nebuchadnezzar the king, "O king, live for ever! ₁₀ You, O king, have made a decree that every man who hears the sound of the horn, flute, zither, lyre, harp, pipe, and all kinds of music shall fall down and worship the golden image; ₁₁ and whoever doesn't fall down and worship shall be cast into the middle of a burning fiery furnace. ₁₂ There are certain Jews whom you have appointed over the affairs of the province of Babylon: Shadrach, Meshach, and Abednego. These men, O king, have not respected you. They don't serve your gods, and don't worship the golden image which you have set up."

₁₃ Then Nebuchadnezzar in rage and fury commanded that Shadrach, Meshach, and Abednego be brought. Then these men were brought before the king. ₁₄ Nebuchadnezzar answered them, "Is it true, Shadrach, Meshach, and Abednego, that you don't serve my gods and you don't worship the golden image which I have set up? ₁₅ Now if you are ready whenever you hear the sound of the horn, flute, zither, lyre, harp, pipe, and all kinds of music to fall down and worship the image which I have made, good; but if you don't worship, you shall be cast the same hour into the middle of a burning fiery furnace. Who is that god who will deliver you out of my hands?"

₁₆ Shadrach, Meshach, and Abednego answered the king, "Nebuchadnezzar, we have no need to answer you in this matter. ₁₇ If it happens, our God whom we serve is able to deliver us from the burning fiery furnace; and he will deliver us out of your hand, O king. ₁₈ But if not, let it be known to you, O king, that we will not serve your gods or worship the golden image which you have set up."

₁₉ Then Nebuchadnezzar was full of fury, and the form of his appearance was changed against Shadrach, Meshach, and Abednego. He spoke, and commanded that they should heat the furnace seven times more than it was usually heated. ₂₀ He commanded certain mighty men who were in his army to bind Shadrach, Meshach, and Abednego, and to cast them into the burning fiery furnace. ₂₁ Then these men were bound in their pants, their tunics, and their mantles, and their other clothes, and were cast into the middle of the burning fiery furnace. ₂₂ Therefore because the king's commandment was urgent and the furnace exceedingly hot, the flame of the fire killed those men who took up Shadrach, Meshach, and Abednego. ₂₃ These three men, Shadrach, Meshach, and Abednego, fell down bound into the middle of the burning fiery furnace.

₂₄ Then Nebuchadnezzar the king was astonished and rose up in haste. He spoke and said to his counsellors, "Didn't we cast three men bound into the middle of the fire?"

They answered the king, "True, O king."

₂₅ He answered, "Look, I see four men loose, walking in the middle of the fire, and they are unharmed. The appearance of the fourth is like a son of the gods.[b]"

₂₆ Then Nebuchadnezzar came near to the mouth of the burning fiery furnace. He spoke and said, "Shadrach, Meshach, and Abednego, you servants of the Most High God, come out, and come here!"

Then Shadrach, Meshach, and Abednego came out of the middle of the fire. ₂₇ The local governors, the deputies, and the governors, and the king's counsellors, being gathered together, saw these men, that the fire

had no power on their bodies. The hair of their head wasn't singed. Their pants weren't changed. The smell of fire wasn't even on them.

₂₈ Nebuchadnezzar spoke and said, "Blessed be the God of Shadrach, Meshach, and Abednego, who has sent his angel and delivered his servants who trusted in him, and have changed the king's word, and have yielded their bodies, that they might not serve nor worship any god except their own God. ₂₉ Therefore I make a decree that every people, nation, and language which speak anything evil against the God of Shadrach, Meshach, and Abednego shall be cut in pieces, and their houses shall be made a dunghill, because there is no other god who is able to deliver like this."

₃₀ Then the king promoted Shadrach, Meshach, and Abednego in the province of Babylon.

4

₁ Nebuchadnezzar the king,

to all the peoples, nations, and languages, who dwell in all the earth:

Peace be multiplied to you.

₂ It has seemed good to me to show the signs and wonders that the Most High God has worked towards me.

₃ How great are his signs!

How mighty are his wonders!

His kingdom is an everlasting kingdom.

His dominion is from generation to generation.

₄ I, Nebuchadnezzar, was at rest in my house, and flourishing in my palace. ₅ I saw a dream which made me afraid; and the thoughts on my bed and the visions of my head troubled me. ₆ Therefore I made a decree to bring in all the wise men of Babylon before me, that they might make known to me the interpretation of the dream. ₇ Then the magicians, the enchanters, the Chaldeans, and the soothsayers came in; and I told them the dream, but they didn't make known to me its interpretation. ₈ But at last, Daniel came in before me, whose name was Belteshazzar according to the name of my god, and in whom is the spirit of the holy gods. I told the dream before him, saying,

₉ "Belteshazzar, master of the magicians, because I know that the spirit of the holy gods is in you and no secret troubles you, tell me the visions of my dream that I have seen, and its interpretation. ₁₀ These were the visions of my head on my bed: I saw, and behold, a tree in the middle of the earth; and its height was great. ₁₁ The tree grew and was strong. Its height reached to the sky and its sight to the end of all the earth. ₁₂ Its leaves were beautiful, and it had much fruit, and in it was food for all. The animals of the field had shade under it, and the birds of the sky lived in its branches, and all flesh was fed from it.

₁₃ "I saw in the visions of my head on my bed, and behold, a holy watcher came down from the sky. ₁₄ He cried aloud and said this: 'Cut down the tree, and cut off its branches! Shake off its leaves and scatter its fruit! Let the animals get away from under it and the birds from its branches. ₁₅ Nevertheless leave the stump of its roots in the earth, even with a band of iron and bronze, in the tender grass of the field; and let it be wet with the dew of the sky. Let his portion be with the animals in the grass of the earth. ₁₆ Let his heart be changed from man's, and let an animal's heart be given to him. Then let seven times pass over him.

₁₇ "'The sentence is by the decree of the watchers and the demand by the word of the holy ones, to the intent that the living may know that the Most High rules in the kingdom of men, and gives it to whomever he will, and sets up over it the lowest of men.'

₁₈ "This dream I, King Nebuchadnezzar, have seen; and you, Belteshazzar, declare the interpretation, because all the wise men of my kingdom are not able to make known to me the interpretation; but you are able, for the spirit of the holy gods is in you."

₁₉ Then Daniel, whose name was Belteshazzar, was stricken mute for a while, and his thoughts troubled him. The king answered, "Belteshazzar, don't let the dream or the interpretation, trouble you."

Belteshazzar answered, "My lord, may the dream be for those who hate you, and its interpretation to your adversaries. ₂₀ The tree that you saw, which grew and was strong, whose height reached to the sky and its sight to all the earth; ₂₁ whose leaves were beautiful and its fruit plentiful, and in it was food for all; under which the animals of the field lived, and on whose branches the birds of the sky had their habitation— ₂₂ it is you, O king, that have grown and become strong; for your greatness has grown, and reaches to the sky, and your dominion to the end of the earth.

₂₃ "Whereas the king saw a holy watcher coming down from the sky and saying, 'Cut down the tree, and destroy it; nevertheless leave the stump of its roots in the earth, even with a band of iron and bronze, in the tender grass of the field, and let it be wet with the dew of the sky. Let his portion be with the animals of the field, until seven times pass over him.'

---

a *3:1* A cubit is the length from the tip of the middle finger to the elbow on a man's arm, or about 18 inches or 46 centimetres.

b *3:25* Or, the Son of God.

24 "This is the interpretation, O king, and it is the decree of the Most High, which has come on my lord the king: 25 You will be driven from men and your dwelling shall be with the animals of the field. You will be made to eat grass as oxen, and will be wet with the dew of the sky, and seven times shall pass over you, until you know that the Most High rules in the kingdom of men, and gives it to whomever he will. 26 Whereas it was commanded to leave the stump of the roots of the tree, your kingdom shall be sure to you after you know that Heaven rules. 27 Therefore, O king, let my counsel be acceptable to you, and break off your sins by righteousness, and your iniquities by showing mercy to the poor. Perhaps there may be a lengthening of your tranquillity."

28 All this came on the King Nebuchadnezzar. 29 At the end of twelve months he was walking in the royal palace of Babylon. 30 The king spoke and said, "Is not this great Babylon, which I have built for the royal dwelling place by the might of my power and for the glory of my majesty?"

31 While the word was in the king's mouth, a voice came from the sky, saying, "O King Nebuchadnezzar, to you it is spoken: 'The kingdom has departed from you. 32 You shall be driven from men, and your dwelling shall be with the animals of the field. You shall be made to eat grass like oxen. Seven times shall pass over you, until you know that the Most High rules in the kingdom of men, and gives it to whomever he will.'"

33 This was fulfilled the same hour on Nebuchadnezzar. He was driven from men and ate grass like oxen; and his body was wet with the dew of the sky until his hair had grown like eagles' feathers, and his nails like birds' claws.

34 At the end of the days I, Nebuchadnezzar, lifted up my eyes to heaven, and my understanding returned to me; and I blessed the Most High, and I praised and honoured him who lives forever,

for his dominion is an everlasting dominion,
and his kingdom from generation to generation.
35 All the inhabitants of the earth are reputed as nothing;
and he does according to his will in the army of heaven,
and amongst the inhabitants of the earth;
and no one can stop his hand,
or ask him, "What are you doing?"

36 At the same time my understanding returned to me; and for the glory of my kingdom, my majesty and brightness returned to me. My counsellors and my lords sought me; and I was established in my kingdom, and excellent greatness was added to me. 37 Now I, Nebuchadnezzar, praise and extol and honour the King of heaven; for all his works are truth, and his ways justice; and those who walk in pride he is able to abase.

5

1 Belshazzar the king made a great feast to a thousand of his lords, and drank wine before the thousand. 2 Belshazzar, while he tasted the wine, commanded that the golden and silver vessels which Nebuchadnezzar his father had taken out of the temple which was in Jerusalem be brought to him, that the king and his lords, his wives and his concubines, might drink from them. 3 Then they brought the golden vessels that were taken out of the temple of God's house which was at Jerusalem; and the king and his lords, his wives and his concubines, drank from them. 4 They drank wine, and praised the gods of gold, and of silver, of bronze, of iron, of wood, and of stone.

5 In the same hour, the fingers of a man's hand came out and wrote near the lamp stand on the plaster of the wall of the king's palace. The king saw the part of the hand that wrote. 6 Then the king's face was changed in him, and his thoughts troubled him; and the joints of his thighs were loosened, and his knees struck one against another.

7 The king cried aloud to bring in the enchanters, the Chaldeans, and the soothsayers. The king spoke and said to the wise men of Babylon, "Whoever reads this writing and shows me its interpretation shall be clothed with purple, and have a chain of gold about his neck, and shall be the third ruler in the kingdom."

8 Then all the king's wise men came in; but they could not read the writing, and couldn't make known to the king the interpretation. 9 Then King Belshazzar was greatly troubled, and his face was changed in him, and his lords were perplexed.

10 The queen by reason of the words of the king and his lords came into the banquet house. The queen spoke and said, "O king, live forever; don't let your thoughts trouble you, nor let your face be changed. 11 There is a man in your kingdom in whom is the spirit of the holy gods; and in the days of your father, light and understanding and wisdom, like the wisdom of the gods, were found in him. The king, Nebuchadnezzar, your father—yes, the king, your father—made him master of the magicians, enchanters, Chaldeans, and soothsayers, 12 because an excellent spirit, knowledge, understanding, interpreting of dreams, showing of dark sentences, and dissolving of doubts were found in the same Daniel, whom the king named Belteshazzar. Now let Daniel be called, and he will show the interpretation."

13 Then Daniel was brought in before the king. The king spoke and said to Daniel, "Are you that Daniel of the children of the captivity of Judah, whom the king my father brought out of Judah? 14 I have heard of you, that the spirit of the gods is in you and that light, understanding, and excellent wisdom are found in you. 15 Now the wise men, the enchanters, have been brought in before me, that they should read this writing, and make known to

me its interpretation; but they could not show the interpretation of the thing. 16 But I have heard of you, that you can give interpretations and dissolve doubts. Now if you can read the writing and make known to me its interpretation, you shall be clothed with purple, and have a chain of gold around your neck, and shall be the third ruler in the kingdom."

17 Then Daniel answered before the king, "Let your gifts be to yourself, and give your rewards to another. Nevertheless, I will read the writing to the king, and make known to him the interpretation.

18 "To you, king, the Most High God gave Nebuchadnezzar your father the kingdom, and greatness, and glory, and majesty. 19 Because of the greatness that he gave him, all the peoples, nations, and languages trembled and feared before him. He killed whom he wanted to, and he kept alive whom he wanted to. He raised up whom he wanted to, and he put down whom he wanted to. 20 But when his heart was lifted up, and his spirit was hardened so that he dealt proudly, he was deposed from his kingly throne, and they took his glory from him. 21 He was driven from the sons of men, and his heart was made like the animals', and his dwelling was with the wild donkeys. He was fed with grass like oxen, and his body was wet with the dew of the sky, until he knew that the Most High God rules in the kingdom of men, and that he sets up over it whomever he will.

22 "You, his son, Belshazzar, have not humbled your heart, though you knew all this, 23 but have lifted up yourself against the Lord of heaven; and they have brought the vessels of his house before you, and you and your lords, your wives, and your concubines, have drunk wine from them. You have praised the gods of silver and gold, of bronze, iron, wood, and stone, which don't see, or hear, or know; and you have not glorified the God in whose hand your breath is, and whose are all your ways. 24 Then the part of the hand was sent from before him, and this writing was inscribed.

25 "This is the writing that was inscribed: 'MENE, MENE, TEKEL, UPHARSIN.'

26 "This is the interpretation of the thing:
MENE: God has counted your kingdom, and brought it to an end.
27 TEKEL: you are weighed in the balances, and are found wanting.
28 PERES: your kingdom is divided, and given to the Medes and Persians."

29 Then Belshazzar commanded, and they clothed Daniel with purple, and put a chain of gold about his neck, and made proclamation concerning him, that he should be the third ruler in the kingdom.

30 In that night Belshazzar the Chaldean King was slain. 31 Darius the Mede received the kingdom, being about sixty-two years old.

6

1 It pleased Darius to set over the kingdom one hundred and twenty local governors, who should be throughout the whole kingdom; 2 and over them three presidents, of whom Daniel was one, that these local governors might give account to them, and that the king should suffer no loss. 3 Then this Daniel was distinguished above the presidents and the local governors, because an excellent spirit was in him; and the king thought to set him over the whole realm.

4 Then the presidents and the local governors sought to find occasion against Daniel as touching the kingdom; but they could find no occasion or fault, because he was faithful. There wasn't any error or fault found in him. 5 Then these men said, "We won't find any occasion against this Daniel, unless we find it against him concerning the law of his God."

6 Then these presidents and local governors assembled together to the king, and said this to him, "King Darius, live forever! 7 All the presidents of the kingdom, the deputies and the local governors, the counsellors and the governors, have consulted together to establish a royal statute and to make a strong decree, that whoever asks a petition of any god or man for thirty days, except of you, O king, he shall be cast into the den of lions. 8 Now, O king, establish the decree and sign the writing, that it not be changed, according to the law of the Medes and Persians, which doesn't alter." 9 Therefore King Darius signed the writing and the decree.

10 When Daniel knew that the writing was signed, he went into his house (now his windows were open in his room towards Jerusalem) and he knelt on his knees three times a day, and prayed, and gave thanks before his God, as he did before. 11 Then these men assembled together, and found Daniel making petition and supplication before his God. 12 Then they came near, and spoke before the king concerning the king's decree: "Haven't you signed a decree that every man who makes a petition to any god or man within thirty days, except to you, O king, shall be cast into the den of lions?"

The king answered, "This thing is true, according to the law of the Medes and Persians, which doesn't alter."

13 Then they answered and said before the king, "That Daniel, who is of the children of the captivity of Judah, doesn't respect you, O king, nor the decree that you have signed, but makes his petition three times a day." 14 Then the king, when he heard these words, was very displeased, and set his heart on Daniel to deliver him; and he laboured until the going down of the sun to rescue him.

15 Then these men assembled together to the king, and said to the king, "Know, O king, that it is a law of the Medes and Persians, that no decree nor statute which the king establishes may be changed."

16 Then the king commanded, and they brought Daniel and cast him into the den of lions. The king spoke and said to Daniel, "Your God whom you serve continually, he will deliver you."

17 A stone was brought, and laid on the mouth of the den; and the king sealed it with his own signet, and with the signet of his lords; that nothing might be changed concerning Daniel. 18 Then the king went to his palace, and passed the night fasting. No musical instruments were brought before him; and his sleep fled from him.

19 Then the king arose very early in the morning, and went in haste to the den of lions. 20 When he came near to the den to Daniel, he cried with a troubled voice. The king spoke and said to Daniel, "Daniel, servant of the living God, is your God, whom you serve continually, able to deliver you from the lions?"

21 Then Daniel said to the king, "O king, live forever! 22 My God has sent his angel, and has shut the lions' mouths, and they have not hurt me, because innocence was found in me before him; and also before you, O king, I have done no harm."

23 Then the king was exceedingly glad, and commanded that they should take Daniel up out of the den. So Daniel was taken up out of the den, and no kind of harm was found on him, because he had trusted in his God.

24 The king commanded, and they brought those men who had accused Daniel, and they cast them into the den of lions—them, their children, and their wives; and the lions mauled them, and broke all their bones in pieces before they came to the bottom of the den.

25 Then King Darius wrote to all the peoples, nations, and languages who dwell in all the earth:

"Peace be multiplied to you.

26 "I make a decree that in all the dominion of my kingdom men tremble and fear before the God of Daniel.

"For he is the living God,
    and steadfast forever.
His kingdom is that which will not be destroyed.
    His dominion will be even to the end.
27 He delivers and rescues.
    He works signs and wonders in heaven and in earth,
    who has delivered Daniel from the power of the lions."

28 So this Daniel prospered in the reign of Darius and in the reign of Cyrus the Persian.

7

1 In the first year of Belshazzar king of Babylon, Daniel had a dream and visions of his head while on his bed. Then he wrote the dream and told the sum of the matters.

2 Daniel spoke and said, "I saw in my vision by night, and, behold, the four winds of the sky broke out on the great sea. 3 Four great animals came up from the sea, different from one another.

4 "The first was like a lion, and had eagle's wings. I watched until its wings were plucked, and it was lifted up from the earth and made to stand on two feet as a man. A man's heart was given to it.

5 "Behold, there was another animal, a second, like a bear. It was raised up on one side, and three ribs were in its mouth between its teeth. They said this to it: 'Arise! Devour much flesh!'

6 "After this I saw, and behold, another, like a leopard, which had on its back four wings of a bird. The animal also had four heads; and dominion was given to it.

7 "After this I saw in the night visions, and, behold, there was a fourth animal, awesome, powerful, and exceedingly strong. It had great iron teeth. It devoured and broke in pieces, and stamped the residue with its feet. It was different from all the animals that were before it. It had ten horns.

8 "I considered the horns, and behold, there came up amongst them another horn, a little one, before which three of the first horns were plucked up by the roots; and behold, in this horn were eyes like the eyes of a man, and a mouth speaking arrogantly.

9 "I watched until thrones were placed,
    and one who was ancient of days sat.
His clothing was white as snow,
    and the hair of his head like pure wool.
His throne was fiery flames,
    and its wheels burning fire.
10 A fiery stream issued and came out from before him.
    Thousands of thousands ministered to him.
    Ten thousand times ten thousand stood before him.
The judgement was set.
    The books were opened.

11 "I watched at that time because of the voice of the arrogant words which the horn spoke. I watched even until the animal was slain, and its body destroyed, and it was given to be burnt with fire. 12 As for the rest of the animals, their dominion was taken away; yet their lives were prolonged for a season and a time.

13 "I saw in the night visions, and behold, there came with the clouds of the sky one like a son of man, and he came even to the Ancient of Days, and they brought him near before him. 14 Dominion was given him, and glory, and a kingdom, that all the peoples, nations, and languages should serve him. His dominion is an everlasting dominion, which will not pass away, and his kingdom one that will not be destroyed.

15 "As for me, Daniel, my spirit was grieved within my body, and the visions of my head troubled me. 16 I came near to one of those who stood by, and asked him the truth concerning all this.

"So he told me, and made me know the interpretation of the things. 17 'These great animals, which are four, are four kings, who will arise out of the earth. 18 But the saints of the Most High will receive the kingdom, and possess the kingdom forever, even forever and ever.'

19 "Then I desired to know the truth concerning the fourth animal, which was different from all of them, exceedingly terrible, whose teeth were of iron, and its nails of bronze; which devoured, broke in pieces, and stamped the residue with its feet; 20 and concerning the ten horns that were on its head and the other horn which came up, and before which three fell, even that horn that had eyes and a mouth that spoke arrogantly, whose look was more stout than its fellows. 21 I saw, and the same horn made war with the saints, and prevailed against them, 22 until the ancient of days came, and judgement was given to the saints of the Most High, and the time came that the saints possessed the kingdom.

23 "So he said, 'The fourth animal will be a fourth kingdom on earth, which will be different from all the kingdoms, and will devour the whole earth, and will tread it down and break it in pieces. 24 As for the ten horns, ten kings will arise out of this kingdom. Another will arise after them; and he will be different from the former, and he will put down three kings. 25 He will speak words against the Most High, and will wear out the saints of the Most High. He will plan to change the times and the law; and they will be given into his hand until a time and times and half a time.

26 "'But the judgement will be set, and they will take away his dominion, to consume and to destroy it to the end. 27 The kingdom and the dominion, and the greatness of the kingdoms under the whole sky, will be given to the people of the saints of the Most High. His kingdom is an everlasting kingdom, and all dominions will serve and obey him.'

28 "Here is the end of the matter. As for me, Daniel, my thoughts troubled me greatly, and my face was changed in me; but I kept the matter in my heart."

8

1 In the third year of the reign of King Belshazzar, a vision appeared to me, even to me, Daniel, after that which appeared to me at the first. 2 I saw the vision. Now it was so, that when I saw, I was in the citadel of Susa, which is in the province of Elam. I saw in the vision, and I was by the river Ulai. 3 Then I lifted up my eyes and saw, and behold, a ram which had two horns stood before the river. The two horns were high, but one was higher than the other, and the higher came up last. 4 I saw the ram pushing westward, northward, and southward. No animals could stand before him. There wasn't any who could deliver out of his hand, but he did according to his will, and magnified himself.

5 As I was considering, behold, a male goat came from the west over the surface of the whole earth, and didn't touch the ground. The goat had a notable horn between his eyes. 6 He came to the ram that had the two horns, which I saw standing before the river, and ran on him in the fury of his power. 7 I saw him come close to the ram, and he was moved with anger against him, and struck the ram, and broke his two horns. There was no power in the ram to stand before him; but he cast him down to the ground and trampled on him. There was no one who could deliver the ram out of his hand. 8 The male goat magnified himself exceedingly. When he was strong, the great horn was broken; and instead of it there came up four notable horns towards the four winds of the sky.

9 Out of one of them came out a little horn which grew exceedingly great—towards the south, and towards the east, and towards the glorious land. 10 It grew great, even to the army of the sky; and it cast down some of the army and of the stars to the ground and trampled on them. 11 Yes, it magnified itself, even to the prince of the army; and it took away from him the continual burnt offering, and the place of his sanctuary was cast down. 12 The army was given over to it together with the continual burnt offering through disobedience. It cast down truth to the ground, and it did its pleasure and prospered.

13 Then I heard a holy one speaking; and another holy one said to that certain one who spoke, "How long will the vision about the continual burnt offering, and the disobedience that makes desolate, to give both the sanctuary and the army to be trodden under foot be?"

14 He said to me, "To two thousand and three hundred evenings and mornings. Then the sanctuary will be cleansed."

15 When I, even I Daniel, had seen the vision, I sought to understand it. Then behold, there stood before me someone with the appearance of a man. 16 I heard a man's voice between the banks of the Ulai, which called and said, "Gabriel, make this man understand the vision."

17 So he came near where I stood; and when he came, I was frightened, and fell on my face; but he said to me, "Understand, son of man, for the vision belongs to the time of the end."

18 Now as he was speaking with me, I fell into a deep sleep with my face towards the ground; but he touched me and set me upright. 19 He said, "Behold, I will make you know what will be in the latter time of the indignation, for it belongs to the appointed time of the end. 20 The ram which you saw, that had the two horns, they are the kings of Media and Persia. 21 The rough male goat is the king of Greece. The great horn that is between his eyes is the first king. 22 As for that which was broken, in the place where four stood up, four kingdoms will stand up out of the nation, but not with his power.

23 "In the latter time of their kingdom, when the transgressors have come to the full, a king of fierce face, and understanding riddles, will stand up. 24 His power will be mighty, but not by his own power. He will destroy awesomely, and will prosper in what he does. He will destroy the mighty ones and the holy people. 25 Through his policy he will cause deceit to prosper in his hand. He will magnify himself in his heart, and he will destroy many in their security. He will also stand up against the prince of princes, but he will be broken without human hands.

26 "The vision of the evenings and mornings which has been told is true; but seal up the vision, for it belongs to many days to come."

27 I, Daniel, fainted, and was sick for some days. Then I rose up and did the king's business. I wondered at the vision, but no one understood it.

9

1 In the first year of Darius the son of Ahasuerus, of the offspring of the Medes, who was made king over the realm of the Chaldeans— 2 in the

first year of his reign I, Daniel, understood by the books the number of the years about which the LORD's[a] word came to Jeremiah the prophet for the accomplishing of the desolations of Jerusalem, even seventy years. ₃ I set my face to the Lord God, to seek by prayer and petitions, with fasting and sackcloth and ashes.

₄ I prayed to the LORD my God, and made confession, and said,

"Oh, Lord, the great and dreadful God, who keeps covenant and loving kindness with those who love him and keep his commandments, ₅ we have sinned, and have dealt perversely, and have done wickedly, and have rebelled, even turning aside from your precepts and from your ordinances. ₆ We haven't listened to your servants the prophets, who spoke in your name to our kings, our princes, and our fathers, and to all the people of the land.

₇ "Lord, righteousness belongs to you, but to us confusion of face, as it is today; to the men of Judah, and to the inhabitants of Jerusalem, and to all Israel, who are near and who are far off, through all the countries where you have driven them, because of their trespass that they have trespassed against you. ₈ Lord, to us belongs confusion of face, to our kings, to our princes, and to our fathers, because we have sinned against you. ₉ To the Lord our God belong mercies and forgiveness, for we have rebelled against him. ₁₀ We haven't obeyed the LORD our God's voice, to walk in his laws, which he set before us by his servants the prophets. ₁₁ Yes, all Israel have transgressed your law, turning aside, that they should not obey your voice.

"Therefore the curse and the oath written in the law of Moses the servant of God has been poured out on us, for we have sinned against him. ₁₂ He has confirmed his words, which he spoke against us and against our judges who judged us, by bringing on us a great evil; for under the whole sky, such has not been done as has been done to Jerusalem. ₁₃ As it is written in the law of Moses, all this evil has come on us. Yet we have not entreated the favour of the LORD our God, that we should turn from our iniquities and have discernment in your truth. ₁₄ Therefore the LORD has watched over the evil, and brought it on us; for the LORD our God is righteous in all his works which he does, and we have not obeyed his voice.

₁₅ "Now, Lord our God, who has brought your people out of the land of Egypt with a mighty hand, and have gotten yourself renown, as it is today, we have sinned. We have done wickedly. ₁₆ Lord, according to all your righteousness, please let your anger and your wrath be turned away from your city Jerusalem, your holy mountain; because for our sins and for the iniquities of our fathers, Jerusalem and your people have become a reproach to all who are around us.

₁₇ "Now therefore, our God, listen to the prayer of your servant and to his petitions, and cause your face to shine on your sanctuary that is desolate, for the Lord's sake. ₁₈ My God, turn your ear and hear. Open your eyes and see our desolations, and the city which is called by your name; for we do not present our petitions before you for our righteousness, but for your great mercies' sake. ₁₉ Lord, hear. Lord, forgive. Lord, listen and do. Don't defer, for your own sake, my God, because your city and your people are called by your name."

₂₀ While I was speaking, praying, and confessing my sin and the sin of my people Israel, and presenting my supplication before the LORD my God for the holy mountain of my God— ₂₁ yes, while I was speaking in prayer— the man Gabriel, whom I had seen in the vision at the beginning, being caused to fly swiftly, touched me about the time of the evening offering. ₂₂ He instructed me and talked with me, and said, "Daniel, I have now come to give you wisdom and understanding. ₂₃ At the beginning of your petitions the commandment went out, and I have come to tell you, for you are greatly beloved. Therefore consider the matter and understand the vision.

₂₄ "Seventy weeks are decreed on your people and on your holy city, to finish disobedience, to make an end of sins, to make reconciliation for iniquity, to bring in everlasting righteousness, to seal up vision and prophecy, and to anoint the most holy.

₂₅ "Know therefore and discern that from the going out of the commandment to restore and build Jerusalem to the Anointed One,[b] the prince, will be seven weeks and sixty-two weeks. It will be built again, with street and moat, even in troubled times. ₂₆ After the sixty-two weeks the Anointed One[c] will be cut off, and will have nothing. The people of the prince who come will destroy the city and the sanctuary. Its end will be with a flood, and war will be even to the end. Desolations are determined. ₂₇ He will make a firm covenant with many for one week. In the middle of the week he will cause the sacrifice and the offering to cease. On the wing of abominations will come one who makes desolate; and even to the decreed full end, wrath will be poured out on the desolate."

10

₁ In the third year of Cyrus king of Persia a message was revealed to Daniel, whose name was called Belteshazzar; and the message was true,

even a great warfare. He understood the message, and had understanding of the vision.

₂ In those days I, Daniel, was mourning three whole weeks. ₃ I ate no pleasant food. No meat or wine came into my mouth. I didn't anoint myself at all, until three whole weeks were fulfilled.

₄ In the twenty-fourth day of the first month, as I was by the side of the great river, which is Hiddekel,[d] ₅ I lifted up my eyes and looked, and behold, there was a man clothed in linen, whose waist was adorned with pure gold of Uphaz. ₆ His body also was like beryl, and his face as the appearance of lightning, and his eyes as flaming torches. His arms and his feet were like burnished bronze. The voice of his words was like the voice of a multitude.

₇ I, Daniel, alone saw the vision, for the men who were with me didn't see the vision, but a great quaking fell on them, and they fled to hide themselves. ₈ So I was left alone and saw this great vision. No strength remained in me; for my face grew deathly pale, and I retained no strength. ₉ Yet I heard the voice of his words. When I heard the voice of his words, then I fell into a deep sleep on my face, with my face towards the ground.

₁₀ Behold, a hand touched me, which set me on my knees and on the palms of my hands. ₁₁ He said to me, "Daniel, you greatly beloved man, understand the words that I speak to you, and stand upright, for I have been sent to you, now." When he had spoken this word to me, I stood trembling.

₁₂ Then he said to me, "Don't be afraid, Daniel; for from the first day that you set your heart to understand, and to humble yourself before your God, your words were heard. I have come for your words' sake. ₁₃ But the prince of the kingdom of Persia withstood me twenty-one days; but, behold, Michael, one of the chief princes, came to help me because I remained there with the kings of Persia. ₁₄ Now I have come to make you understand what will happen to your people in the latter days, for the vision is yet for many days."

₁₅ When he had spoken these words to me, I set my face towards the ground and was mute. ₁₆ Behold, one in the likeness of the sons of men touched my lips. Then I opened my mouth, and spoke and said to him who stood before me, "My lord, by reason of the vision my sorrows have overtaken me, and I retain no strength. ₁₇ For how can the servant of this my lord talk with this my lord? For as for me, immediately there remained no strength in me. There was no breath left in me."

₁₈ Then one like the appearance of a man touched me again, and he strengthened me. ₁₉ He said, "Greatly beloved man, don't be afraid. Peace be to you. Be strong. Yes, be strong."

When he spoke to me, I was strengthened, and said, "Let my lord speak, for you have strengthened me."

₂₀ Then he said, "Do you know why I have come to you? Now I will return to fight with the prince of Persia. When I go out, behold, the prince of Greece will come. ₂₁ But I will tell you that which is inscribed in the writing of truth. There is no one who holds with me against these but Michael your prince.

11

₁ "As for me, in the first year of Darius the Mede, I stood up to confirm and strengthen him.

₂ "Now I will show you the truth. Behold, three more kings will stand up in Persia. The fourth will be far richer than all of them. When he has grown strong through his riches, he will stir up all against the realm of Greece. ₃ A mighty king will stand up, who will rule with great dominion, and do according to his will. ₄ When he stands up, his kingdom will be broken and will be divided towards the four winds of the sky, but not to his posterity, nor according to his dominion with which he ruled; for his kingdom will be plucked up, even for others besides these.

₅ "The king of the south will be strong. One of his princes will become stronger than him, and have dominion. His dominion will be a great dominion. ₆ At the end of years they will join themselves together; and the daughter of the king of the south will come to the king of the north to make an agreement, but she will not retain the strength of her arm. He will also not stand, nor will his arm; but she will be given up, with those who brought her, and he who became the father of her, and he who strengthened her in those times.

₇ "But out of a shoot from her roots one will stand up in his place, who will come to the army and will enter into the fortress of the king of the north, and will deal against them and will prevail. ₈ He will also carry their gods with their molten images, and with their goodly vessels of silver and of gold, captive into Egypt. He will refrain some years from the king of the north. ₉ He will come into the realm of the king of the south, but he will return into his own land. ₁₀ His sons will wage war, and will assemble a multitude of great forces which will come on, and overflow, and pass through. They will return and wage war, even to his fortress.

₁₁ "The king of the south will be moved with anger and will come out and fight with him, even with the king of the north. He will send out a great multitude, and the multitude will be given into his hand. ₁₂ The multitude will be carried off, and his heart will be exalted. He will cast down tens of thousands, but he won't prevail. ₁₃ The king of the north will return, and will send out a multitude greater than the former. He will come on at the end of the times, even of years, with a great army and with abundant supplies.

₁₄ "In those times many will stand up against the king of the south. Also the children of the violent amongst your people will lift themselves up to establish the vision, but they will fall. ₁₅ So the king of the north will

---

a 9:2 When rendered in ALL CAPITAL LETTERS, "LORD" or "GOD" is the translation of God's Proper Name.
b 9:25 "Anointed One" can also be translated "Messiah" (same as "Christ").
c 9:26 "Anointed One" can also be translated "Messiah" (same as "Christ").
d 10:4 or, Tigris River

come and cast up a mound, and take a well-fortified city. The forces of the south won't stand, neither will his select troops, neither will there be any strength to stand. 16 But he who comes against him will do according to his own will, and no one will stand before him. He will stand in the glorious land, and destruction will be in his hand. 17 He will set his face to come with the strength of his whole kingdom, and with him equitable conditions. He will perform them. He will give him the daughter of women, to destroy the kingdom, but she will not stand, and won't be for him. 18 After this he will turn his face to the islands, and will take many, but a prince will cause the reproach offered by him to cease. Yes, moreover, he will cause his reproach to turn on him. 19 Then he will turn his face towards the fortresses of his own land; but he will stumble and fall, and won't be found.

20 "Then one who will cause a tax collector to pass through the kingdom to maintain its glory will stand up in his place; but within few days he shall be destroyed, not in anger, and not in battle.

21 "In his place a contemptible person will stand up, to whom they had not given the honour of the kingdom; but he will come in time of security, and will obtain the kingdom by flatteries. 22 The overwhelming forces will be overwhelmed from before him, and will be broken. Yes, also the prince of the covenant. 23 After the treaty made with him he will work deceitfully; for he will come up and will become strong with few people. 24 In time of security he will come even on the fattest places of the province. He will do that which his fathers have not done, nor his fathers' fathers. He will scatter amongst them prey, plunder, and wealth. Yes, he will devise his plans against the strongholds, but only for a time.

25 "He will stir up his power and his courage against the king of the south with a great army; and the king of the south will wage war in battle with an exceedingly great and mighty army, but he won't stand; for they will devise plans against him. 26 Yes, those who eat of his delicacies will destroy him, and his army will be swept away. Many will fall down slain. 27 As for both these kings, their hearts will be to do evil, and they will speak lies at one table; but it won't prosper, for the end will still be at the appointed time. 28 Then he will return into his land with great wealth. His heart will be against the holy covenant. He will take action, and return to his own land.

29 "He will return at the appointed time and come into the south; but it won't be in the latter time as it was in the former. 30 For ships of Kittim will come against him. Therefore he will be grieved, and will return, and have indignation against the holy covenant, and will take action. He will even return, and have regard to those who forsake the holy covenant.

31 "Forces from him will profane the sanctuary, even the fortress, and will take away the continual burnt offering. Then they will set up the abomination that makes desolate. 32 He will corrupt those who do wickedly against the covenant by flatteries; but the people who know their God will be strong and take action.

33 "Those who are wise amongst the people will instruct many; yet they will fall by the sword and by flame, by captivity and by plunder, many days. 34 Now when they fall, they will be helped with a little help; but many will join themselves to them with flatteries. 35 Some of those who are wise will fall—to refine them, and to purify, and to make them white, even to the time of the end, because it is yet for the time appointed.

36 "The king will do according to his will. He will exalt himself and magnify himself above every god, and will speak marvellous things against the God of gods. He will prosper until the indignation is accomplished, for that which is determined will be done. 37 He won't regard the gods of his fathers, or the desire of women, or regard any god; for he will magnify himself above all. 38 But in their place, he will honour the god of fortresses. He will honour a god whom his fathers didn't know with gold, silver, and with precious stones and pleasant things. 39 He will deal with the strongest fortresses by the help of a foreign god. He will increase with glory whoever acknowledges him. He will cause them to rule over many, and will divide the land for a price.

40 "At the time of the end the king of the south will contend with him; and the king of the north will come against him like a whirlwind, with chariots, with horsemen, and with many ships. He will enter into the countries, and will overflow and pass through. 41 He will enter also into the glorious land, and many countries will be overthrown; but these will be delivered out of his hand: Edom, Moab, and the chief of the children of Ammon. 42 He will also stretch out his hand on the countries. The land of Egypt won't escape. 43 But he will have power over the treasures of gold and of silver, and over all the precious things of Egypt. The Libyans and the Ethiopians will follow his steps. 44 But news out of the east and out of the north will trouble him; and he will go out with great fury to destroy and utterly to sweep away many. 45 He will plant the tents of his palace between the sea and the glorious holy mountain; yet he will come to his end, and no one will help him.

12

1 "At that time Michael will stand up, the great prince who stands for the children of your people; and there will be a time of trouble, such as never was since there was a nation even to that same time. At that time your people will be delivered, everyone who is found written in the book. 2 Many of those who sleep in the dust of the earth will awake, some to everlasting life, and some to shame and everlasting contempt. 3 Those who are wise will shine as the brightness of the expanse. Those who turn many to righteousness will shine as the stars forever and ever. 4 But you, Daniel, shut up the words and seal the book, even to the time of the end. Many will run back and forth, and knowledge will be increased."

5 Then I, Daniel, looked, and behold, two others stood, one on the river bank on this side, and the other on the river bank on that side. 6 One said to the man clothed in linen, who was above the waters of the river, "How long will it be to the end of these wonders?"

7 I heard the man clothed in linen, who was above the waters of the river, when he held up his right hand and his left hand to heaven, and swore by him who lives forever that it will be for a time, times, and a half; and when they have finished breaking in pieces the power of the holy people, all these things will be finished.

8 I heard, but I didn't understand. Then I said, "My lord, what will be the outcome of these things?"

9 He said, "Go your way, Daniel; for the words are shut up and sealed until the time of the end. 10 Many will purify themselves, and make themselves white, and be refined, but the wicked will do wickedly; and none of the wicked will understand, but those who are wise will understand.

11 "From the time that the continual burnt offering is taken away and the abomination that makes desolate set up, there will be one thousand and two hundred and ninety days. 12 Blessed is he who waits, and comes to the one thousand and three hundred and thirty-five days.

13 "But go your way until the end; for you will rest, and will stand in your inheritance at the end of the days."

The Book of Hosea

1

1 The LORD's[a] word that came to Hosea the son of Beeri, in the days of Uzziah, Jotham, Ahaz, and Hezekiah, kings of Judah, and in the days of Jeroboam the son of Joash, king of Israel.

2 When the LORD spoke at first by Hosea, the LORD said to Hosea, "Go, take for yourself a wife of prostitution and children of unfaithfulness; for the land commits great adultery, forsaking the LORD."

3 So he went and took Gomer the daughter of Diblaim; and she conceived, and bore him a son.

4 The LORD said to him, "Call his name Jezreel, for yet a little while, and I will avenge the blood of Jezreel on the house of Jehu, and will cause the kingdom of the house of Israel to cease. 5 It will happen in that day that I will break the bow of Israel in the valley of Jezreel."

6 She conceived again, and bore a daughter.

Then he said to him, "Call her name Lo-Ruhamah,[b] for I will no longer have mercy on the house of Israel, that I should in any way pardon them. 7 But I will have mercy on the house of Judah, and will save them by the LORD their God,[c] and will not save them by bow, sword, battle, horses, or horsemen."

8 Now when she had weaned Lo-Ruhamah, she conceived, and bore a son.

9 He said, "Call his name Lo-Ammi,[d] for you are not my people, and I will not be yours. 10 Yet the number of the children of Israel will be as the sand of the sea, which can't be measured or counted; and it will come to pass that, in the place where it was said to them, 'You are not my people,' they will be called 'sons of the living God.' 11 The children of Judah and the children of Israel will be gathered together, and they will appoint themselves one head, and will go up from the land; for great will be the day of Jezreel.

2

1 "Say to your brothers, 'My people!'[e]
    and to your sisters, 'My loved one!'[f]
2 Contend with your mother!
    Contend, for she is not my wife,
        neither am I her husband;
and let her put away her prostitution from her face,
    and her adulteries from between her breasts;
3 lest I strip her naked,
    and make her bare as in the day that she was born,
and make her like a wilderness,
    and set her like a dry land,
    and kill her with thirst.
4 Indeed, on her children I will have no mercy,
    for they are children of unfaithfulness.
5 For their mother has played the prostitute.
    She who conceived them has done shamefully;
for she said, 'I will go after my lovers,
    who give me my bread and my water,
    my wool and my flax,
    my oil and my drink.'
6 Therefore behold,[g] I will hedge up your way with thorns,
    and I will build a wall against her,
    that she can't find her way.
7 She will follow after her lovers,
    but she won't overtake them;
and she will seek them,
    but won't find them.
Then she will say, 'I will go and return to my first husband,
    for then it was better with me than now.'
8 For she didn't know that I gave her the grain, the new wine, and the oil,
    and multiplied her silver and gold, which they used for Baal.
9 Therefore I will take back my grain in its time,
    and my new wine in its season,
    and will pluck away my wool and my flax which should have covered her nakedness.
10 Now I will uncover her lewdness in the sight of her lovers,
    and no one will deliver her out of my hand.
11 I will also cause all her celebrations to cease:
    her feasts, her new moons, her Sabbaths, and all her solemn assemblies.
12 I will lay waste her vines and her fig trees,
    about which she has said, 'These are my wages that my lovers have given me,'
    and I will make them a forest,
    and the animals of the field shall eat them.
13 I will visit on her the days of the Baals,
    to which she burnt incense
when she decked herself with her earrings and her jewels,

and went after her lovers
    and forgot me," says the LORD.
14 "Therefore behold, I will allure her,
    and bring her into the wilderness,
    and speak tenderly to her.
15 I will give her vineyards from there,
    and the valley of Achor for a door of hope;
and she will respond there
    as in the days of her youth,
    and as in the day when she came up out of the land of Egypt.
16 It will be in that day," says the LORD,
    "that you will call me 'my husband,'
    and no longer call me 'my master.'
17 For I will take away the names of the Baals out of her mouth,
    and they will no longer be mentioned by name.
18 In that day I will make a covenant for them with the animals of the field,
    and with the birds of the sky,
    and with the creeping things of the ground.
I will break the bow, the sword, and the battle out of the land,
    and will make them lie down safely.
19 I will betroth you to me forever.
    Yes, I will betroth you to me in righteousness, in justice, in loving
        kindness, and in compassion.
20 I will even betroth you to me in faithfulness;
    and you shall know the LORD.
21 It will happen in that day, that I will respond," says the LORD.
    "I will respond to the heavens,
    and they will respond to the earth;
        22 and the earth will respond to the grain, and the new wine, and the
            oil;
    and they will respond to Jezreel.
23 I will sow her to me in the earth;
    and I will have mercy on her who had not obtained mercy;
    and I will tell those who were not my people, 'You are my people;'
    and they will say, 'You are My God!'"

3

1 The LORD said to me, "Go again, love a woman loved by another, and an adulteress, even as the LORD loves the children of Israel, though they turn to other gods, and love cakes of raisins."

2 So I bought her for myself for fifteen pieces of silver and a homer[h] and a half of barley. 3 I said to her, "You shall stay with me many days. You shall not play the prostitute, and you shall not be with any other man. I will also be so towards you."

4 For the children of Israel shall live many days without king, without prince, without sacrifice, without sacred stone, and without ephod or idols. 5 Afterward the children of Israel shall return and seek the LORD their God, and David their king, and shall come with trembling to the LORD and to his blessings in the last days.

4

1 Hear the LORD's word, you children of Israel,
    for the LORD has a charge against the inhabitants of the land:
"Indeed there is no truth, nor goodness,
    nor knowledge of God in the land.
2 There is cursing, lying, murder, stealing, and committing adultery;
    they break boundaries, and bloodshed causes bloodshed.
3 Therefore the land will mourn,
    and everyone who dwells in it will waste away,
with all living things in her,
    even the animals of the field and the birds of the sky;
    yes, the fish of the sea also die.

4 "Yet let no man bring a charge, neither let any man accuse;
    for your people are like those who bring charges against a priest.
5 You will stumble in the day,
    and the prophet will also stumble with you in the night;
    and I will destroy your mother.
6 My people are destroyed for lack of knowledge.
    Because you have rejected knowledge, I will also reject you,
    that you may be no priest to me.
Because you have forgotten your God's law,
    I will also forget your children.
7 As they were multiplied, so they sinned against me.
    I will change their glory into shame.
8 They feed on the sin of my people,
    and set their heart on their iniquity.
9 It will be like people, like priest;
    and I will punish them for their ways,
    and will repay them for their deeds.
10 They will eat, and not have enough.
    They will play the prostitute, and will not increase;
    because they have abandoned listening to the LORD.
11 Prostitution, wine, and new wine take away understanding.

---

a *1:1* When rendered in ALL CAPITAL LETTERS, "LORD" or "GOD" is the translation of God's Proper Name.
b *1:6* Lo-Ruhamah means "not loved".
c *1:7* The Hebrew word rendered "God" is "אֱלֹהִים" (Elohim).
d *1:9* Lo-Ammi means "not my people".

e *2:1* 'Ammi' in Hebrew
f *2:1* 'Ruhamah' in Hebrew
g *2:6* "Behold", from "הִנֵּה", means look at, take notice, observe, see, or gaze at. It is often used as an interjection.
h *3:2* 1 homer is about 220 litres or 6 bushels

12 My people consult with their wooden idol,
    and answer to a stick of wood.
Indeed the spirit of prostitution has led them astray,
    and they have been unfaithful to their God.
13 They sacrifice on the tops of the mountains,
    and burn incense on the hills, under oaks, poplars, and terebinths,
    because its shade is good.
Therefore your daughters play the prostitute,
    and your brides commit adultery.
14 I will not punish your daughters when they play the prostitute,
    nor your brides when they commit adultery;
because the men consort with prostitutes,
    and they sacrifice with the shrine prostitutes;
    so the people without understanding will come to ruin.

15 "Though you, Israel, play the prostitute,
    yet don't let Judah offend;
    and don't come to Gilgal,
    neither go up to Beth Aven,
    nor swear, 'As the LORD lives.'
16 For Israel has behaved extremely stubbornly, like a stubborn heifer.
    Then how will the LORD feed them like a lamb in a meadow?
17 Ephraim is joined to idols.
    Leave him alone!
18 Their drink has become sour.
    They play the prostitute continually.
    Her rulers dearly love their shameful way.
19 The wind has wrapped her up in its wings;
    and they shall be disappointed because of their sacrifices.

5

1 "Listen to this, you priests!
    Listen, house of Israel,
    and give ear, house of the king!
For the judgement is against you;
    for you have been a snare at Mizpah,
    and a net spread on Tabor.
2 The rebels are deep in slaughter,
    but I discipline all of them.
3 I know Ephraim,
    and Israel is not hidden from me;
for now, Ephraim, you have played the prostitute.
    Israel is defiled.
4 Their deeds won't allow them to turn to their God,
    for the spirit of prostitution is within them,
    and they don't know the LORD.
5 The pride of Israel testifies to his face.
    Therefore Israel and Ephraim will stumble in their iniquity.
    Judah also will stumble with them.
6 They will go with their flocks and with their herds to seek the LORD,
    but they won't find him.
    He has withdrawn himself from them.
7 They are unfaithful to the LORD;
    for they have borne illegitimate children.
    Now the new moon will devour them with their fields.

8 "Blow the cornet in Gibeah,
    and the trumpet in Ramah!
    Sound a battle cry at Beth Aven, behind you, Benjamin!
9 Ephraim will become a desolation in the day of rebuke.
    Amongst the tribes of Israel, I have made known that which will surely
    be.
10 The princes of Judah are like those who remove a landmark.
    I will pour out my wrath on them like water.
11 Ephraim is oppressed,
    he is crushed in judgement,
    because he is intent in his pursuit of idols.
12 Therefore I am to Ephraim like a moth,
    and to the house of Judah like rottenness.

13 "When Ephraim saw his sickness,
    and Judah his wound,
    then Ephraim went to Assyria,
    and sent to King Jareb:
but he is not able to heal you,
    neither will he cure you of your wound.
14 For I will be to Ephraim like a lion,
    and like a young lion to the house of Judah.
I myself will tear in pieces and go away.
    I will carry off, and there will be no one to deliver.
15 I will go and return to my place,
    until they acknowledge their offence,
    and seek my face.
    In their affliction they will seek me earnestly."

6

1 "Come! Let's return to the LORD;
    for he has torn us to pieces,

and he will heal us;
he has injured us,
    and he will bind up our wounds.
2 After two days he will revive us.
    On the third day he will raise us up,
    and we will live before him.
3 Let's acknowledge the LORD.
    Let's press on to know the LORD.
As surely as the sun rises,
    the LORD will appear.
He will come to us like the rain,
    like the spring rain that waters the earth."

4 "Ephraim, what shall I do to you?
    Judah, what shall I do to you?
    For your love is like a morning cloud,
    and like the dew that disappears early.
5 Therefore I have cut them to pieces with the prophets;
    I killed them with the words of my mouth.
    Your judgements are like a flash of lightning.
6 For I desire mercy, and not sacrifice;
    and the knowledge of God more than burnt offerings.
7 But they, like Adam, have broken the covenant.
    They were unfaithful to me there.
8 Gilead is a city of those who work iniquity;
    it is stained with blood.
9 As gangs of robbers wait to ambush a man,
    so the company of priests murder on the path towards Shechem,
    committing shameful crimes.
10 In the house of Israel I have seen a horrible thing.
    There is prostitution in Ephraim.
    Israel is defiled.

11 "Also, Judah, there is a harvest appointed for you,
    when I restore the fortunes of my people.

7

1 When I would heal Israel,
    then the iniquity of Ephraim is uncovered,
    also the wickedness of Samaria;
    for they commit falsehood,
    and the thief enters in,
    and the gang of robbers ravages outside.
2 They don't consider in their hearts that I remember all their wickedness.
    Now their own deeds have engulfed them.
    They are before my face.
3 They make the king glad with their wickedness,
    and the princes with their lies.
4 They are all adulterers.
    They are burning like an oven that the baker stops stirring,
    from the kneading of the dough, until it is leavened.
5 On the day of our king, the princes made themselves sick with the heat of
    wine.
    He joined his hand with mockers.
6 For they have prepared their heart like an oven,
    while they lie in wait.
    Their anger smoulders all night.
    In the morning it burns as a flaming fire.
7 They are all hot as an oven,
    and devour their judges.
All their kings have fallen.
    There is no one amongst them who calls to me.
8 Ephraim mixes himself amongst the nations.
    Ephraim is a pancake not turned over.
9 Strangers have devoured his strength,
    and he doesn't realise it.
Indeed, grey hairs are here and there on him,
    and he doesn't realise it.
10 The pride of Israel testifies to his face;
    yet they haven't returned to the LORD their God,
    nor sought him, for all this.

11 "Ephraim is like an easily deceived dove, without understanding.
    They call to Egypt.
    They go to Assyria.
12 When they go, I will spread my net on them.
    I will bring them down like the birds of the sky.
    I will chastise them, as their congregation has heard.
13 Woe to them!
    For they have wandered from me.
Destruction to them!
    For they have trespassed against me.
Though I would redeem them,
    yet they have spoken lies against me.
14 They haven't cried to me with their heart,
    but they howl on their beds.
They assemble themselves for grain and new wine.
    They turn away from me.
15 Though I have taught and strengthened their arms,
    yet they plot evil against me.

16 They return, but not to the Most High.
    They are like a faulty bow.
    Their princes will fall by the sword for the rage of their tongue.
    This will be their derision in the land of Egypt.

8

1 "Put the trumpet to your lips!
    Something like an eagle is over the LORD's house,
    because they have broken my covenant
    and rebelled against my law.
2 They cry to me, 'My God, we, Israel, acknowledge you!'
    3 Israel has cast off that which is good.
    The enemy will pursue him.
4 They have set up kings, but not by me.
    They have made princes, and I didn't approve.
    Of their silver and their gold they have made themselves idols,
    that they may be cut off.
5 Let Samaria throw out his calf idol!
    My anger burns against them!
    How long will it be until they are capable of purity?
6 For this is even from Israel!
    The workman made it, and it is no God;
    indeed, the calf of Samaria shall be broken in pieces.
7 For they sow the wind,
    and they will reap the whirlwind.
He has no standing grain.
    The stalk will yield no head.
    If it does yield, strangers will swallow it up.
8 Israel is swallowed up.
    Now they are amongst the nations like a worthless thing.
9 For they have gone up to Assyria,
    like a wild donkey wandering alone.
    Ephraim has hired lovers for himself.
10 But although they sold themselves amongst the nations,
    I will now gather them;
    and they begin to waste away because of the oppression of the king of
        mighty ones.
11 Because Ephraim has multiplied altars for sinning,
    they became for him altars for sinning.
12 I wrote for him the many things of my law,
    but they were regarded as a strange thing.
13 As for the sacrifices of my offerings,
    they sacrifice meat and eat it,
    but the LORD doesn't accept them.
Now he will remember their iniquity,
    and punish their sins.
    They will return to Egypt.
14 For Israel has forgotten his Maker and built palaces;
    and Judah has multiplied fortified cities;
    but I will send a fire on his cities,
    and it will devour its fortresses."

9

1 Don't rejoice, Israel, to jubilation like the nations;
    for you were unfaithful to your God.
    You love the wages of a prostitute at every grain threshing floor.
2 The threshing floor and the wine press won't feed them,
    and the new wine will fail her.
3 They won't dwell in the LORD's land;
    but Ephraim will return to Egypt,
    and they will eat unclean food in Assyria.
4 They won't pour out wine offerings to the LORD,
    neither will they be pleasing to him.
    Their sacrifices will be to them like the bread of mourners;
    all who eat of it will be polluted;
    for their bread will be for their appetite.
    It will not come into the LORD's house.
5 What will you do in the day of solemn assembly,
    and in the day of the feast of the LORD?
6 For, behold, when they flee destruction,
    Egypt will gather them up.
    Memphis will bury them.
    Nettles will possess their pleasant things of silver.
    Thorns will be in their tents.
7 The days of visitation have come.
    The days of reckoning have come.
Israel will consider the prophet to be a fool,
    and the man who is inspired to be insane,
    because of the abundance of your sins,
    and because your hostility is great.
8 A prophet watches over Ephraim with my God.
    A fowler's snare is on all of his paths,
    and hostility in the house of his God.
9 They have deeply corrupted themselves,
    as in the days of Gibeah.
    He will remember their iniquity.
    He will punish them for their sins.
10 I found Israel like grapes in the wilderness.

    I saw your fathers as the first ripe in the fig tree at its first season;
    but they came to Baal Peor, and consecrated themselves to the
        shameful thing,
    and became abominable like that which they loved.
11 As for Ephraim, their glory will fly away like a bird.
    There will be no birth, no one with child, and no conception.
12 Though they bring up their children,
    yet I will bereave them, so that not a man shall be left.
    Indeed, woe also to them when I depart from them!
13 I have seen Ephraim, like Tyre, planted in a pleasant place;
    but Ephraim will bring out his children to the murderer.
14 Give them—LORD what will you give?
    Give them a miscarrying womb and dry breasts.
15 "All their wickedness is in Gilgal;
    for there I hated them.
    Because of the wickedness of their deeds, I will drive them out of my
        house!
    I will love them no more.
    All their princes are rebels.
16 Ephraim is struck.
    Their root has dried up.
    They will bear no fruit.
    Even though they give birth, yet I will kill the beloved ones of their
        womb."
17 My God will cast them away, because they didn't listen to him;
    and they will be wanderers amongst the nations.

10

1 Israel is a luxuriant vine that produces his fruit.
    According to the abundance of his fruit he has multiplied his altars.
    As their land has prospered, they have adorned their sacred stones.
2 Their heart is divided.
    Now they will be found guilty.
    He will demolish their altars.
    He will destroy their sacred stones.
3 Surely now they will say, "We have no king; for we don't fear the LORD;
    and the king, what can he do for us?"
4 They make promises, swearing falsely in making covenants.
    Therefore judgement springs up like poisonous weeds in the furrows
        of the field.
5 The inhabitants of Samaria will be in terror for the calves of Beth Aven,
    for its people will mourn over it,
    along with its priests who rejoiced over it,
    for its glory, because it has departed from it.
6 It also will be carried to Assyria for a present to a great king.
    Ephraim will receive shame,
    and Israel will be ashamed of his own counsel.
7 Samaria and her king float away
    like a twig on the water.
8 The high places also of Aven, the sin of Israel, will be destroyed.
    The thorn and the thistle will come up on their altars.
    They will tell the mountains, "Cover us!" and the hills, "Fall on us!"

9 "Israel, you have sinned from the days of Gibeah.
    There they remained.
    The battle against the children of iniquity doesn't overtake them in
        Gibeah.
10 When it is my desire, I will chastise them;
    and the nations will be gathered against them
    when they are bound to their two transgressions.
11 Ephraim is a trained heifer that loves to thresh,
    so I will put a yoke on her beautiful neck.
    I will set a rider on Ephraim.
    Judah will plough.
    Jacob will break his clods.
12 Sow to yourselves in righteousness,
    reap according to kindness.
Break up your fallow ground,
    for it is time to seek the LORD,
    until he comes and rains righteousness on you.
13 You have ploughed wickedness.
    You have reaped iniquity.
    You have eaten the fruit of lies,
    for you trusted in your way, in the multitude of your mighty men.
14 Therefore a battle roar will arise amongst your people,
    and all your fortresses will be destroyed,
    as Shalman destroyed Beth Arbel in the day of battle.
    The mother was dashed in pieces with her children.
15 So Bethel will do to you because of your great wickedness.
    At daybreak the king of Israel will be destroyed.

11

1 "When Israel was a child, then I loved him,
    and called my son out of Egypt.
2 They called to them, so they went from them.
    They sacrificed to the Baals,
    and burnt incense to engraved images.

3 Yet I taught Ephraim to walk.
  I took them by their arms,
  but they didn't know that I healed them.
4 I drew them with cords of a man, with ties of love;
  and I was to them like those who lift up the yoke on their necks;
  and I bent down to him and I fed him.

5 "They won't return into the land of Egypt;
  but the Assyrian will be their king,
  because they refused to repent.
6 The sword will fall on their cities,
  and will destroy the bars of their gates,
  and will put an end to their plans.
7 My people are determined to turn from me.
  Though they call to the Most High,
  he certainly won't exalt them.

8 "How can I give you up, Ephraim?
  How can I hand you over, Israel?
  How can I make you like Admah?
  How can I make you like Zeboiim?
My heart is turned within me,
  my compassion is aroused.
9 I will not execute the fierceness of my anger.
  I will not return to destroy Ephraim,
  for I am God, and not man—the Holy One amongst you.
  I will not come in wrath.
10 They will walk after the LORD,
  who will roar like a lion;
  for he will roar, and the children will come trembling from the west.
11 They will come trembling like a bird out of Egypt,
  and like a dove out of the land of Assyria;
and I will settle them in their houses," says the LORD.

12 Ephraim surrounds me with falsehood,
  and the house of Israel with deceit.
  Judah still strays from God,
  and is unfaithful to the Holy One.

12

1 Ephraim feeds on wind,
  and chases the east wind.
  He continually multiplies lies and desolation.
  They make a covenant with Assyria,
  and oil is carried into Egypt.
2 The LORD also has a controversy with Judah,
  and will punish Jacob according to his ways;
  according to his deeds he will repay him.
3 In the womb he took his brother by the heel,
  and in his manhood he contended with God.
4 Indeed, he struggled with the angel, and prevailed;
  he wept, and made supplication to him.
  He found him at Bethel, and there he spoke with us—
  5 even the LORD, the God of Armies.
  The LORD is his name of renown!
6 Therefore turn to your God.
  Keep kindness and justice,
  and wait continually for your God.

7 A merchant has dishonest scales in his hand.
  He loves to defraud.
8 Ephraim said, "Surely I have become rich.
  I have found myself wealth.
  In all my wealth they won't find in me any iniquity that is sin."

9 "But I am the LORD your God from the land of Egypt.
  I will yet again make you dwell in tents,
  as in the days of the solemn feast.
10 I have also spoken to the prophets,
  and I have multiplied visions;
  and by the ministry of the prophets I have used parables.
11 If Gilead is wicked,
  surely they are worthless.
In Gilgal they sacrifice bulls.
  Indeed, their altars are like heaps in the furrows of the field.
12 Jacob fled into the country of Aram.
  Israel served to get a wife.
  For a wife he tended flocks and herds.
13 By a prophet the LORD brought Israel up out of Egypt,
  and by a prophet he was preserved.
14 Ephraim has bitterly provoked anger.
  Therefore his blood will be left on him,
  and his Lord[a] will repay his contempt.

13

1 When Ephraim spoke, there was trembling.
  He exalted himself in Israel,
  but when he became guilty through Baal, he died.

2 Now they sin more and more,
  and have made themselves molten images of their silver,
  even idols according to their own understanding,
  all of them the work of the craftsmen.
  They say of them, 'They offer human sacrifice and kiss the calves.'
3 Therefore they will be like the morning mist,
  like the dew that passes away early,
  like the chaff that is driven with the whirlwind out of the threshing floor,
  and like the smoke out of the chimney.

4 "Yet I am the LORD your God from the land of Egypt;
  and you shall acknowledge no god but me,
  and besides me there is no saviour.
5 I knew you in the wilderness,
  in the land of great drought.
6 According to their pasture, so were they filled;
  they were filled, and their heart was exalted.
  Therefore they have forgotten me.
7 Therefore I am like a lion to them.
  Like a leopard, I will lurk by the path.
8 I will meet them like a bear that is bereaved of her cubs,
  and will tear the covering of their heart.
  There I will devour them like a lioness.
  The wild animal will tear them.
9 You are destroyed, Israel, because you are against me,
  against your helper.
10 Where is your king now, that he may save you in all your cities?
  And your judges, of whom you said, 'Give me a king and princes'?
11 I have given you a king in my anger,
  and have taken him away in my wrath.
12 The guilt of Ephraim is stored up.
  His sin is stored up.
13 The sorrows of a travailing woman will come on him.
  He is an unwise son,
  for when it is time, he doesn't come to the opening of the womb.
14 I will ransom them from the power of Sheol.[b]
  I will redeem them from death!
  Death, where are your plagues?
  Sheol, where is your destruction?

"Compassion will be hidden from my eyes.
  15 Though he is fruitful amongst his brothers, an east wind will come,
  the breath of the LORD coming up from the wilderness;
  and his spring will become dry,
  and his fountain will be dried up.
  He will plunder the storehouse of treasure.
16 Samaria will bear her guilt,
  for she has rebelled against her God.
  They will fall by the sword.
  Their infants will be dashed in pieces,
  and their pregnant women will be ripped open."

14

1 Israel, return to the LORD your God;
  for you have fallen because of your sin.
2 Take words with you, and return to the LORD.
  Tell him, "Forgive all our sins,
  and accept that which is good;
  so we offer bulls as we vowed of our lips.
3 Assyria can't save us.
  We won't ride on horses;
  neither will we say any more to the work of our hands, 'Our gods!'
  for in you the fatherless finds mercy."

4 "I will heal their waywardness.
  I will love them freely;
  for my anger is turned away from them.
5 I will be like the dew to Israel.
  He will blossom like the lily,
  and send down his roots like Lebanon.
6 His branches will spread,
  and his beauty will be like the olive tree,
  and his fragrance like Lebanon.
7 Men will dwell in his shade.
  They will revive like the grain,
  and blossom like the vine.
  Their fragrance will be like the wine of Lebanon.
8 Ephraim, what have I to do any more with idols?
  I answer, and will take care of him.
  I am like a green cypress tree;
  from me your fruit is found."

9 Who is wise, that he may understand these things?
  Who is prudent, that he may know them?
  For the ways of the LORD are right,

---

a *12:14* The word translated "Lord" is "Adonai."

b *13:14* Sheol is the place of the dead.

and the righteous walk in them,
but the rebellious stumble in them.

The Book of Joel

1

1 The LORD's[a] word that came to Joel, the son of Pethuel.

2 Hear this, you elders,
  and listen, all you inhabitants of the land!
Has this ever happened in your days,
  or in the days of your fathers?

3 Tell your children about it,
  and have your children tell their children,
  and their children, another generation.

4 What the swarming locust has left, the great locust has eaten.
  What the great locust has left, the grasshopper has eaten.
  What the grasshopper has left, the caterpillar has eaten.

5 Wake up, you drunkards, and weep!
  Wail, all you drinkers of wine, because of the sweet wine,
  for it is cut off from your mouth.

6 For a nation has come up on my land, strong, and without number.
  His teeth are the teeth of a lion,
  and he has the fangs of a lioness.

7 He has laid my vine waste,
  and stripped my fig tree.
  He has stripped its bark, and thrown it away.
  Its branches are made white.

8 Mourn like a virgin dressed in sackcloth
  for the husband of her youth!

9 The meal offering and the drink offering are cut off from the LORD's
    house.
  The priests, the LORD's ministers, mourn.

10 The field is laid waste.
  The land mourns, for the grain is destroyed,
  The new wine has dried up,
  and the oil languishes.

11 Be confounded, you farmers!
  Wail, you vineyard keepers,
  for the wheat and for the barley;
  for the harvest of the field has perished.

12 The vine has dried up, and the fig tree withered—
  the pomegranate tree, the palm tree also, and the apple tree,
  even all of the trees of the field are withered;
  for joy has withered away from the sons of men.

13 Put on sackcloth and mourn, you priests!
  Wail, you ministers of the altar.
Come, lie all night in sackcloth, you ministers of my God,[b]
  for the meal offering and the drink offering are withheld from your
    God's house.

14 Sanctify a fast.
  Call a solemn assembly.
  Gather the elders and all the inhabitants of the land to the house of the
    LORD, your God,
  and cry to the LORD.

15 Alas for the day!
  For the day of the LORD is at hand,
  and it will come as destruction from the Almighty.

16 Isn't the food cut off before our eyes,
  joy and gladness from the house of our God?

17 The seeds rot under their clods.
  The granaries are laid desolate.
  The barns are broken down, for the grain has withered.

18 How the animals groan!
  The herds of livestock are perplexed, because they have no pasture.
  Yes, the flocks of sheep are made desolate.

19 LORD, I cry to you,
  for the fire has devoured the pastures of the wilderness,
  and the flame has burnt all the trees of the field.

20 Yes, the animals of the field pant to you,
  for the water brooks have dried up,
  and the fire has devoured the pastures of the wilderness.

2

1 Blow the trumpet in Zion,
  and sound an alarm in my holy mountain!
Let all the inhabitants of the land tremble,
  for the day of the LORD comes,
  for it is close at hand:

2 A day of darkness and gloominess,
  a day of clouds and thick darkness.
As the dawn spreading on the mountains,
  a great and strong people;
  there has never been the like,
  neither will there be any more after them,
  even to the years of many generations.

3 A fire devours before them,
  and behind them, a flame burns.
The land is as the garden of Eden before them,
  and behind them, a desolate wilderness.
Yes, and no one has escaped them.

4 Their appearance is as the appearance of horses,
  and they run as horsemen.

5 Like the noise of chariots on the tops of the mountains, they leap,
  like the noise of a flame of fire that devours the stubble,
  like a strong people set in battle array.

6 At their presence the peoples are in anguish.
  All faces have grown pale.

7 They run like mighty men.
  They climb the wall like warriors.
  They each march in his line, and they don't swerve off course.

8 One doesn't jostle another.
  They each march in their own path.
  They burst through the defences
  and don't break ranks.

9 They rush on the city.
  They run on the wall.
  They climb up into the houses.
  They enter in at the windows like thieves.

10 The earth quakes before them.
  The heavens tremble.
  The sun and the moon are darkened,
  and the stars withdraw their shining.

11 The LORD thunders his voice before his army,
  for his forces are very great;
  for he is strong who obeys his command;
  for the day of the LORD is great and very awesome,
  and who can endure it?

12 "Yet even now," says the LORD, "turn to me with all your heart,
  and with fasting, and with weeping, and with mourning."

13 Tear your heart and not your garments,
  and turn to the LORD, your God;
  for he is gracious and merciful,
  slow to anger, and abundant in loving kindness,
  and relents from sending calamity.

14 Who knows? He may turn and relent,
  and leave a blessing behind him,
  even a meal offering and a drink offering to the LORD, your God.

15 Blow the trumpet in Zion!
  Sanctify a fast.
  Call a solemn assembly.

16 Gather the people.
  Sanctify the assembly.
  Assemble the elders.
  Gather the children, and those who nurse from breasts.
Let the bridegroom go out of his room,
  and the bride out of her chamber.

17 Let the priests, the ministers of the LORD, weep between the porch and
    the altar,
  and let them say, "Spare your people, LORD,
  and don't give your heritage to reproach,
  that the nations should rule over them.
Why should they say amongst the peoples,
  'Where is their God?'"

18 Then the LORD was jealous for his land,
  and had pity on his people.

19 The LORD answered his people,
  "Behold,[c] I will send you grain, new wine, and oil,
  and you will be satisfied with them;
  and I will no more make you a reproach amongst the nations.

20 But I will remove the northern army far away from you,
  and will drive it into a barren and desolate land,
  its front into the eastern sea,
  and its back into the western sea;
  and its stench will come up,
  and its bad smell will rise."
Surely he has done great things.

21 Land, don't be afraid.
  Be glad and rejoice, for the LORD has done great things.

22 Don't be afraid, you animals of the field;
  for the pastures of the wilderness spring up,
  for the tree bears its fruit.
  The fig tree and the vine yield their strength.

23 "Be glad then, you children of Zion,
  and rejoice in the LORD, your God;
  for he gives you the early rain in just measure,
  and he causes the rain to come down for you,
  the early rain and the latter rain, as before.

24 The threshing floors will be full of wheat,
  and the vats will overflow with new wine and oil.

---

a 1:1 When rendered in ALL CAPITAL LETTERS, "LORD" or "GOD" is the translation of God's Proper Name.

b 1:13 The Hebrew word rendered "God" is "אֱלֹהִים" (Elohim).

c 2:19 "Behold", from "הִנֵּה", means look at, take notice, observe, see, or gaze at. It is often used as an interjection.

25 I will restore to you the years that the swarming locust has eaten,
    the great locust, the grasshopper, and the caterpillar,
    my great army, which I sent amongst you.
26 You will have plenty to eat and be satisfied,
    and will praise the name of the LORD, your God,
    who has dealt wondrously with you;
    and my people will never again be disappointed.
27 You will know that I am amongst Israel,
    and that I am the LORD, your God, and there is no one else;
    and my people will never again be disappointed.

28 "It will happen afterward, that I will pour out my Spirit on all flesh;
    and your sons and your daughters will prophesy.
    Your old men will dream dreams.
    Your young men will see visions.
29 And also on the servants and on the handmaids in those days,
    I will pour out my Spirit.
30 I will show wonders in the heavens and in the earth:
    blood, fire, and pillars of smoke.
31 The sun will be turned into darkness,
    and the moon into blood,
    before the great and terrible day of the LORD comes.
32 It will happen that whoever will call on the LORD's name shall be saved;
    for in Mount Zion and in Jerusalem there will be those who escape,
    as the LORD has said,
    and amongst the remnant, those whom the LORD calls.

3

1 "For, behold, in those days,
    and in that time,
    when I restore the fortunes of Judah and Jerusalem,
2 I will gather all nations,
    and will bring them down into the valley of Jehoshaphat;
    and I will execute judgement on them there for my people,
    and for my heritage, Israel, whom they have scattered amongst the
        nations.
    They have divided my land,
3 and have cast lots for my people,
    and have given a boy for a prostitute,
    and sold a girl for wine, that they may drink.

4 "Yes, and what are you to me, Tyre and Sidon,
    and all the regions of Philistia?
Will you repay me?
    And if you repay me,
    I will swiftly and speedily return your repayment on your own head.
5 Because you have taken my silver and my gold,
    and have carried my finest treasures into your temples,
6 and have sold the children of Judah and the children of Jerusalem to
        the sons of the Greeks,
    that you may remove them far from their border.
7 Behold, I will stir them up out of the place where you have sold them,
    and will return your repayment on your own head;
8 and I will sell your sons and your daughters into the hands of the children
        of Judah,
    and they will sell them to the men of Sheba,
    to a faraway nation,
    for the LORD has spoken it."

9 Proclaim this amongst the nations:
    "Prepare for war!
    Stir up the mighty men.
Let all the warriors draw near.
    Let them come up. 10 Beat your ploughshares into swords,
    and your pruning hooks into spears.
    Let the weak say, 'I am strong.'
11 Hurry and come, all you surrounding nations,
    and gather yourselves together."
Cause your mighty ones to come down there, LORD.
12 "Let the nations arouse themselves,
    and come up to the valley of Jehoshaphat;
    for there I will sit to judge all the surrounding nations.
13 Put in the sickle;
    for the harvest is ripe.
    Come, tread, for the wine press is full,
    the vats overflow, for their wickedness is great."
14 Multitudes, multitudes in the valley of decision!
    For the day of the LORD is near in the valley of decision.
15 The sun and the moon are darkened,
    and the stars withdraw their shining.
16 The LORD will roar from Zion,
    and thunder from Jerusalem;
    and the heavens and the earth will shake;
    but the LORD will be a refuge to his people,
    and a stronghold to the children of Israel.
17 "So you will know that I am the LORD, your God,
    dwelling in Zion, my holy mountain.
Then Jerusalem will be holy,
    and no strangers will pass through her any more.

18 It will happen in that day,
    that the mountains will drop down sweet wine,
    the hills will flow with milk,
    all the brooks of Judah will flow with waters;
    and a fountain will flow out from the LORD's house,
    and will water the valley of Shittim.
19 Egypt will be a desolation
    and Edom will be a desolate wilderness,
    for the violence done to the children of Judah,
    because they have shed innocent blood in their land.
20 But Judah will be inhabited forever,
    and Jerusalem from generation to generation.
21 I will cleanse their blood
    that I have not cleansed,
    for the LORD dwells in Zion."

The Book of Amos

1

1 The words of Amos, who was amongst the herdsmen of Tekoa, which he saw concerning Israel in the days of Uzziah king of Judah and in the days of Jeroboam the son of Joash, king of Israel, two years before the earthquake. 2 He said:

"The LORD[a] will roar from Zion,
and utter his voice from Jerusalem;
and the pastures of the shepherds will mourn,
and the top of Carmel will wither."

3 The LORD says:
"For three transgressions of Damascus, yes, for four,
I will not turn away its punishment,
because they have threshed Gilead with threshing instruments of iron;
4 but I will send a fire into the house of Hazael,
and it will devour the palaces of Ben Hadad.
5 I will break the bar of Damascus,
and cut off the inhabitant from the valley of Aven,
and him who holds the sceptre from the house of Eden;
and the people of Syria shall go into captivity to Kir,"
says the LORD.

6 The LORD says:
"For three transgressions of Gaza, yes, for four,
I will not turn away its punishment,
because they carried away captive the whole community,
to deliver them up to Edom;
7 but I will send a fire on the wall of Gaza,
and it will devour its palaces.
8 I will cut off the inhabitant from Ashdod,
and him who holds the sceptre from Ashkelon;
and I will turn my hand against Ekron;
and the remnant of the Philistines will perish,"
says the Lord[b] GOD.

9 The LORD says:
"For three transgressions of Tyre, yes, for four,
I will not turn away its punishment;
because they delivered up the whole community to Edom,
and didn't remember the brotherly covenant;
10 but I will send a fire on the wall of Tyre,
and it will devour its palaces."

11 The LORD says:
"For three transgressions of Edom, yes, for four,
I will not turn away its punishment,
because he pursued his brother with the sword
and cast off all pity,
and his anger raged continually,
and he kept his wrath forever;
12 but I will send a fire on Teman,
and it will devour the palaces of Bozrah."

13 The LORD says:
"For three transgressions of the children of Ammon, yes, for four,
I will not turn away its punishment,
because they have ripped open the pregnant women of Gilead,
that they may enlarge their border.
14 But I will kindle a fire in the wall of Rabbah,
and it will devour its palaces,
with shouting in the day of battle,
with a storm in the day of the whirlwind;
15 and their king will go into captivity,
he and his princes together,"
says the LORD.

2

1 The LORD says:
"For three transgressions of Moab, yes, for four,
I will not turn away its punishment,
because he burnt the bones of the king of Edom into lime;
2 but I will send a fire on Moab,
and it will devour the palaces of Kerioth;
and Moab will die with tumult, with shouting, and with the sound of the trumpet;
3 and I will cut off the judge from amongst them,
and will kill all its princes with him,"
says the LORD.

4 The LORD says:
"For three transgressions of Judah, yes, for four,
I will not turn away its punishment,
because they have rejected the LORD's law,
and have not kept his statutes,
and their lies have led them astray,
after which their fathers walked;
5 but I will send a fire on Judah,

and it will devour the palaces of Jerusalem."

6 The LORD says:
"For three transgressions of Israel, yes, for four,
I will not turn away its punishment,
because they have sold the righteous for silver,
and the needy for a pair of sandals;
7 They trample the heads of the poor into the dust of the earth
and deny justice to the oppressed.
A man and his father use the same maiden, to profane my holy name.
8 They lay themselves down beside every altar on clothes taken in pledge.
In the house of their God[c] they drink the wine of those who have been fined.
9 Yet I destroyed the Amorite before them,
whose height was like the height of the cedars,
and he was strong as the oaks;
yet I destroyed his fruit from above,
and his roots from beneath.
10 Also I brought you up out of the land of Egypt
and led you forty years in the wilderness,
to possess the land of the Amorite.
11 I raised up some of your sons for prophets,
and some of your young men for Nazirites.
Isn't this true,
you children of Israel?" says the LORD.
12 "But you gave the Nazirites wine to drink,
and commanded the prophets, saying, 'Don't prophesy!'
13 Behold,[d] I will crush you in your place,
as a cart crushes that is full of grain.
14 Flight will perish from the swift.
The strong won't strengthen his force.
The mighty won't deliver himself.
15 He who handles the bow won't stand.
He who is swift of foot won't escape.
He who rides the horse won't deliver himself.
16 He who is courageous amongst the mighty
will flee away naked on that day,"
says the LORD.

3

1 Hear this word that the LORD has spoken against you, children of Israel, against the whole family which I brought up out of the land of Egypt, saying:
2 "I have only chosen you of all the families of the earth.
Therefore I will punish you for all of your sins."
3 Do two walk together,
unless they have agreed?
4 Will a lion roar in the thicket,
when he has no prey?
Does a young lion cry out of his den,
if he has caught nothing?
5 Can a bird fall in a trap on the earth,
where no snare is set for him?
Does a snare spring up from the ground,
when there is nothing to catch?
6 Does the trumpet alarm sound in a city,
without the people being afraid?
Does evil happen to a city,
and the LORD hasn't done it?
7 Surely the Lord GOD will do nothing,
unless he reveals his secret to his servants the prophets.
8 The lion has roared.
Who will not fear?
The Lord GOD has spoken.
Who can but prophesy?
9 Proclaim in the palaces at Ashdod,
and in the palaces in the land of Egypt,
and say, "Assemble yourselves on the mountains of Samaria,
and see what unrest is in her,
and what oppression is amongst them."
10 "Indeed they don't know to do right," says the LORD,
"Who hoard plunder and loot in their palaces."
11 Therefore the Lord GOD says:
"An adversary will overrun the land;
and he will pull down your strongholds,
and your fortresses will be plundered."
12 The LORD says:
"As the shepherd rescues out of the mouth of the lion two legs,
or a piece of an ear,
so shall the children of Israel be rescued who sit in Samaria on the corner of a couch,
and on the silken cushions of a bed."
13 "Listen, and testify against the house of Jacob," says the Lord GOD, the God of Armies.
14 "For in the day that I visit the transgressions of Israel on him,

---

a 1:2 When rendered in ALL CAPITAL LETTERS, "LORD" or "GOD" is the translation of God's Proper Name.
b 1:8 The word translated "Lord" is "Adonai."

c 2:8 The Hebrew word rendered "God" is "אֱלֹהִים" (Elohim).
d 2:13 "Behold", from "הִנֵּה", means look at, take notice, observe, see, or gaze at. It is often used as an interjection.

I will also visit the altars of Bethel;
and the horns of the altar will be cut off,
and fall to the ground.
15 I will strike the winter house with the summer house;
and the houses of ivory will perish,
and the great houses will have an end,"
says the LORD.

4

1 Listen to this word, you cows of Bashan, who are on the mountain of Samaria, who oppress the poor, who crush the needy, who tell their husbands, "Bring us drinks!"
2 The Lord GOD has sworn by his holiness,
"Behold, the days shall come on you that they will take you away with hooks,
and the last of you with fish hooks.
3 You will go out at the breaks in the wall,
everyone straight before her;
and you will cast yourselves into Harmon," says the LORD.
4 "Go to Bethel, and sin;
to Gilgal, and sin more.
Bring your sacrifices every morning,
your tithes every three days,
5 offer a sacrifice of thanksgiving of that which is leavened,
and proclaim free will offerings and brag about them;
for this pleases you, you children of Israel," says the Lord GOD.
6 "I also have given you cleanness of teeth in all your cities,
and lack of bread in every town;
yet you haven't returned to me," says the LORD.
7 "I also have withheld the rain from you,
when there were yet three months to the harvest;
and I caused it to rain on one city,
and caused it not to rain on another city.
One field was rained on,
and the field where it didn't rain withered.
8 So two or three cities staggered to one city to drink water,
and were not satisfied;
yet you haven't returned to me," says the LORD.
9 "I struck you with blight and mildew many times in your gardens and your vineyards,
and the swarming locusts have devoured your fig trees and your olive trees;
yet you haven't returned to me," says the LORD.
10 "I sent plagues amongst you like I did Egypt.
I have slain your young men with the sword,
and have carried away your horses.
I filled your nostrils with the stench of your camp,
yet you haven't returned to me," says the LORD.
11 "I have overthrown some of you,
as when God overthrew Sodom and Gomorrah,
and you were like a burning stick plucked out of the fire;
yet you haven't returned to me," says the LORD.
12 "Therefore I will do this to you, Israel;
because I will do this to you,
prepare to meet your God, Israel.
13 For, behold, he who forms the mountains, creates the wind, declares to man what is his thought,
who makes the morning darkness, and treads on the high places of the earth:
The LORD, the God of Armies, is his name."

5

1 Listen to this word which I take up for a lamentation over you, O house of Israel:
2 "The virgin of Israel has fallen;
She shall rise no more.
She is cast down on her land;
there is no one to raise her up."
3 For the Lord GOD says:
"The city that went out a thousand shall have a hundred left,
and that which went out one hundred shall have ten left to the house of Israel."
4 For the LORD says to the house of Israel:
"Seek me, and you will live;
5 but don't seek Bethel,
nor enter into Gilgal,
and don't pass to Beersheba;
for Gilgal shall surely go into captivity,
and Bethel shall come to nothing.
6 Seek the LORD, and you will live,
lest he break out like fire in the house of Joseph,
and it devour, and there be no one to quench it in Bethel.
7 You who turn justice to wormwood,
and cast down righteousness to the earth!
8 Seek him who made the Pleiades and Orion,
and turns the shadow of death into the morning,
and makes the day dark with night;
who calls for the waters of the sea,
and pours them out on the surface of the earth, the LORD is his name,
9 who brings sudden destruction on the strong,

so that destruction comes on the fortress.
10 They hate him who reproves in the gate,
and they abhor him who speaks blamelessly.
11 Therefore, because you trample on the poor and take taxes from him of wheat,
you have built houses of cut stone, but you will not dwell in them.
You have planted pleasant vineyards,
but you shall not drink their wine.
12 For I know how many are your offences,
and how great are your sins—
you who afflict the just,
who take a bribe,
and who turn away the needy in the courts.
13 Therefore a prudent person keeps silent in such a time,
for it is an evil time.
14 Seek good, and not evil,
that you may live;
and so the LORD, the God of Armies, will be with you,
as you say.
15 Hate evil, love good,
and establish justice in the courts.
It may be that the LORD, the God of Armies, will be gracious to the remnant of Joseph."
16 Therefore the LORD, the God of Armies, the Lord, says:
"Wailing will be in all the wide ways.
They will say in all the streets, 'Alas! Alas!'
They will call the farmer to mourning,
and those who are skilful in lamentation to wailing.
17 In all vineyards there will be wailing,
for I will pass through the middle of you," says the LORD.
18 "Woe to you who desire the day of the LORD!
Why do you long for the day of the LORD?
It is darkness,
and not light.
19 As if a man fled from a lion,
and a bear met him;
or he went into the house and leaned his hand on the wall,
and a snake bit him.
20 Won't the day of the LORD be darkness, and not light?
Even very dark, and no brightness in it?
21 I hate, I despise your feasts,
and I can't stand your solemn assemblies.
22 Yes, though you offer me your burnt offerings and meal offerings,
I will not accept them;
neither will I regard the peace offerings of your fat animals.
23 Take away from me the noise of your songs!
I will not listen to the music of your harps.
24 But let justice roll on like rivers,
and righteousness like a mighty stream.
25 "Did you bring to me sacrifices and offerings in the wilderness forty years, house of Israel? 26 You also carried the tent of your king and the shrine of your images, the star of your god, which you made for yourselves.
27 Therefore I will cause you to go into captivity beyond Damascus," says the LORD, whose name is the God of Armies.

6

1 Woe to those who are at ease in Zion,
and to those who are secure on the mountain of Samaria,
the notable men of the chief of the nations,
to whom the house of Israel come!
2 Go to Calneh, and see.
From there go to Hamath the great.
Then go down to Gath of the Philistines.
Are they better than these kingdoms?
Is their border greater than your border?
3 Alas for you who put far away the evil day,
and cause the seat of violence to come near,
4 who lie on beds of ivory,
and stretch themselves on their couches,
and eat the lambs out of the flock,
and the calves out of the middle of the stall,
5 who strum on the strings of a harp,
who invent for themselves instruments of music, like David;
6 who drink wine in bowls,
and anoint themselves with the best oils,
but they are not grieved for the affliction of Joseph.
7 Therefore they will now go captive with the first who go captive.
The feasting and lounging will end.
8 "The Lord GOD has sworn by himself," says the LORD, the God of Armies:
"I abhor the pride of Jacob,
and detest his fortresses.
Therefore I will deliver up the city with all that is in it.
9 It will happen that if ten men remain in one house,
they will die.
10 "When a man's relative carries him, even he who burns him, to bring bodies out of the house, and asks him who is in the innermost parts of the house, 'Is there yet any with you?' And he says, 'No;' then he will say, 'Hush! Indeed we must not mention the LORD's name.'

11 "For, behold, the LORD commands, and the great house will be smashed to pieces,
    and the little house into bits.
12 Do horses run on the rocky crags?
    Does one plough there with oxen?
But you have turned justice into poison,
    and the fruit of righteousness into bitterness,
13 you who rejoice in a thing of nothing, who say,
    'Haven't we taken for ourselves horns by our own strength?'
14 For, behold, I will raise up against you a nation, house of Israel,"
    says the LORD, the God of Armies;
    "and they will afflict you from the entrance of Hamath to the brook of the Arabah."

7

1 Thus the Lord GOD showed me: behold, he formed locusts in the beginning of the shooting up of the latter growth; and behold, it was the latter growth after the king's harvest. 2 When they finished eating the grass of the land, then I said, "Lord GOD, forgive, I beg you! How could Jacob stand? For he is small."

3 The LORD relented concerning this. "It shall not be," says the LORD.

4 Thus the Lord GOD showed me, the Lord GOD called for judgement by fire; and it dried up the great deep, and would have devoured the land. 5 Then I said, "Lord GOD, stop, I beg you! How could Jacob stand? For he is small."

6 The LORD relented concerning this. "This also shall not be," says the Lord GOD.

7 Thus he showed me: behold, the Lord stood beside a wall made by a plumb line, with a plumb line in his hand. 8 The LORD said to me, "Amos, what do you see?"

I said, "A plumb line."

Then the Lord said, "Behold, I will set a plumb line in the middle of my people Israel. I will not again pass by them any more. 9 The high places of Isaac will be desolate, the sanctuaries of Israel will be laid waste; and I will rise against the house of Jeroboam with the sword."

10 Then Amaziah the priest of Bethel sent to Jeroboam king of Israel, saying, "Amos has conspired against you in the middle of the house of Israel. The land is not able to bear all his words. 11 For Amos says, 'Jeroboam will die by the sword, and Israel shall surely be led away captive out of his land.'"

12 Amaziah also said to Amos, "You seer, go, flee away into the land of Judah, and there eat bread, and prophesy there, 13 but don't prophesy again any more at Bethel; for it is the king's sanctuary, and it is a royal house!"

14 Then Amos answered Amaziah, "I was no prophet, neither was I a prophet's son; but I was a herdsman, and a farmer of sycamore figs; 15 and the LORD took me from following the flock, and the LORD said to me, 'Go, prophesy to my people Israel.' 16 Now therefore listen to the LORD's word: 'You say, Don't prophesy against Israel, and don't preach against the house of Isaac.' 17 Therefore the LORD says: 'Your wife shall be a prostitute in the city, and your sons and your daughters shall fall by the sword, and your land shall be divided by line; and you yourself shall die in a land that is unclean, and Israel shall surely be led away captive out of his land.'"

8

1 Thus the Lord GOD showed me: behold, a basket of summer fruit.
2 He said, "Amos, what do you see?"
I said, "A basket of summer fruit."
Then the LORD said to me,
"The end has come on my people Israel.
    I will not again pass by them any more.
3 The songs of the temple will be wailing in that day," says the Lord GOD.
    "The dead bodies will be many. In every place they will throw them out with silence.
4 Hear this, you who desire to swallow up the needy,
    and cause the poor of the land to fail,
5 saying, 'When will the new moon be gone, that we may sell grain?
And the Sabbath, that we may market wheat,
making the ephah[a] small, and the shekel[b] large,
    and dealing falsely with balances of deceit;
6 that we may buy the poor for silver,
    and the needy for a pair of sandals,
    and sell the sweepings with the wheat?'"
7 The LORD has sworn by the pride of Jacob,
    "Surely I will never forget any of their works.
8 Won't the land tremble for this,
    and everyone mourn who dwells in it?
Yes, it will rise up wholly like the River;
    and it will be stirred up and sink again, like the River of Egypt.
9 It will happen in that day," says the Lord GOD,
    "that I will cause the sun to go down at noon,
    and I will darken the earth in the clear day.
10 I will turn your feasts into mourning,
    and all your songs into lamentation;
and I will make you wear sackcloth on all your bodies,
    and baldness on every head.
I will make it like the mourning for an only son,

and its end like a bitter day.
11 Behold, the days come," says the Lord GOD,
    "that I will send a famine in the land,
    not a famine of bread,
    nor a thirst for water,
    but of hearing the LORD's words.
12 They will wander from sea to sea,
    and from the north even to the east;
    they will run back and forth to seek the LORD's word,
    and will not find it.
13 In that day the beautiful virgins
    and the young men will faint for thirst.
14 Those who swear by the sin of Samaria,
    and say, 'As your god, Dan, lives,'
    and, 'As the way of Beersheba lives,'
    they will fall, and never rise up again."

9

1 I saw the Lord standing beside the altar, and he said, "Strike the tops of the pillars, that the thresholds may shake. Break them in pieces on the head of all of them. I will kill the last of them with the sword. Not one of them will flee away. Not one of them will escape. 2 Though they dig into Sheol,[c] there my hand will take them; and though they climb up to heaven, there I will bring them down. 3 Though they hide themselves in the top of Carmel, I will search and take them out from there; and though they be hidden from my sight in the bottom of the sea, there I will command the serpent, and it will bite them. 4 Though they go into captivity before their enemies, there I will command the sword, and it will kill them. I will set my eyes on them for evil, and not for good. 5 For the Lord, the LORD of Armies, is he who touches the land and it melts, and all who dwell in it will mourn; and it will rise up wholly like the River, and will sink again, like the River of Egypt. 6 It is he who builds his rooms in the heavens, and has founded his vault on the earth; he who calls for the waters of the sea, and pours them out on the surface of the earth—the LORD is his name. 7 Are you not like the children of the Ethiopians to me, children of Israel?" says the LORD. "Haven't I brought up Israel out of the land of Egypt, and the Philistines from Caphtor, and the Syrians from Kir? 8 Behold, the eyes of the Lord GOD are on the sinful kingdom, and I will destroy it from off the surface of the earth, except that I will not utterly destroy the house of Jacob," says the LORD. 9 "For behold, I will command, and I will sift the house of Israel amongst all the nations as grain is sifted in a sieve, yet not the least kernel will fall on the earth. 10 All the sinners of my people will die by the sword, who say, 'Evil won't overtake nor meet us.' 11 In that day I will raise up the tent of David who is fallen and close up its breaches, and I will raise up its ruins, and I will build it as in the days of old, 12 that they may possess the remnant of Edom and all the nations who are called by my name," says the LORD who does this.

13 "Behold, the days come," says the LORD,
    "that the ploughman shall overtake the reaper,
    and the one treading grapes him who sows seed;
    and sweet wine will drip from the mountains,
    and flow from the hills.
14 I will bring my people Israel back from captivity,
    and they will rebuild the ruined cities, and inhabit them;
    and they will plant vineyards, and drink wine from them.
They shall also make gardens,
    and eat their fruit.
15 I will plant them on their land,
    and they will no more be plucked up out of their land which I have given them,"
    says the LORD your God.

---

a 8:5 1 ephah is about 22 litres or about 2/3 of a bushel
b 8:5 a normal shekel is about 10 grams or about 0.35 ounces.

c 9:2 Sheol is the place of the dead.

The Book of Obadiah

1

1 The vision of Obadiah. This is what the Lord[a] GOD[b] says about Edom. We have heard news from the LORD, and an ambassador is sent amongst the nations, saying, "Arise, and let's rise up against her in battle. 2 Behold,[c] I have made you small amongst the nations. You are greatly despised. 3 The pride of your heart has deceived you, you who dwell in the clefts of the rock, whose habitation is high, who says in his heart, 'Who will bring me down to the ground?' 4 Though you mount on high as the eagle, and though your nest is set amongst the stars, I will bring you down from there," says the LORD. 5 "If thieves came to you, if robbers by night—oh, what disaster awaits you—wouldn't they only steal until they had enough? If grape pickers came to you, wouldn't they leave some gleaning grapes? 6 How Esau will be ransacked! How his hidden treasures are sought out! 7 All the men of your alliance have brought you on your way, even to the border. The men who were at peace with you have deceived you, and prevailed against you. Friends who eat your bread lay a snare under you. There is no understanding in him."

8 "Won't I in that day", says the LORD, "destroy the wise men out of Edom, and understanding out of the mountain of Esau? 9 Your mighty men, Teman, will be dismayed, to the end that everyone may be cut off from the mountain of Esau by slaughter. 10 For the violence done to your brother Jacob, shame will cover you, and you will be cut off forever. 11 In the day that you stood on the other side, in the day that strangers carried away his substance and foreigners entered into his gates and cast lots for Jerusalem, even you were like one of them. 12 But don't look down on your brother in the day of his disaster, and don't rejoice over the children of Judah in the day of their destruction. Don't speak proudly in the day of distress. 13 Don't enter into the gate of my people in the day of their calamity. Don't look down on their affliction in the day of their calamity, neither seize their wealth on the day of their calamity. 14 Don't stand in the crossroads to cut off those of his who escape. Don't deliver up those of his who remain in the day of distress. 15 For the day of the LORD is near all the nations! As you have done, it will be done to you. Your deeds will return upon your own head. 16 For as you have drunk on my holy mountain, so all the nations will drink continually. Yes, they will drink, swallow down, and will be as though they had not been. 17 But in Mount Zion, there will be those who escape, and it will be holy. The house of Jacob will possess their possessions. 18 The house of Jacob will be a fire, the house of Joseph a flame, and the house of Esau for stubble. They will burn amongst them and devour them. There will not be any remaining to the house of Esau." Indeed, the LORD has spoken.

19 Those of the South will possess the mountain of Esau, and those of the lowland, the Philistines. They will possess the field of Ephraim, and the field of Samaria. Benjamin will possess Gilead. 20 The captives of this army of the children of Israel, who are amongst the Canaanites, will possess even to Zarephath; and the captives of Jerusalem, who are in Sepharad, will possess the cities of the Negev. 21 Saviours will go up on Mount Zion to judge the mountains of Esau, and the kingdom will be the LORD's.

---

[a] 1:1 The word translated "Lord" is "Adonai."
[b] 1:1 When rendered in ALL CAPITAL LETTERS, "LORD" or "GOD" is the translation of God's Proper Name.

[c] 1:2 "Behold", from "הִנֵּה", means look at, take notice, observe, see, or gaze at. It is often used as an interjection.

The Book of Jonah

1

1 Now the LORD's[a] word came to Jonah the son of Amittai, saying, 2 "Arise, go to Nineveh, that great city, and preach against it, for their wickedness has come up before me."

3 But Jonah rose up to flee to Tarshish from the presence of the LORD. He went down to Joppa, and found a ship going to Tarshish; so he paid its fare, and went down into it, to go with them to Tarshish from the presence of the LORD.

4 But the LORD sent out a great wind on the sea, and there was a mighty storm on the sea, so that the ship was likely to break up. 5 Then the mariners were afraid, and every man cried to his god. They threw the cargo that was in the ship into the sea to lighten the ship. But Jonah had gone down into the innermost parts of the ship and he was laying down, and was fast asleep. 6 So the ship master came to him, and said to him, "What do you mean, sleeper? Arise, call on your God![b] Maybe your God[c] will notice us, so that we won't perish."

7 They all said to each other, "Come! Let's cast lots, that we may know who is responsible for this evil that is on us." So they cast lots, and the lot fell on Jonah. 8 Then they asked him, "Tell us, please, for whose cause this evil is on us. What is your occupation? Where do you come from? What is your country? Of what people are you?"

9 He said to them, "I am a Hebrew, and I fear the LORD, the God[d] of heaven, who has made the sea and the dry land."

10 Then the men were exceedingly afraid, and said to him, "What have you done?" For the men knew that he was fleeing from the presence of the LORD, because he had told them. 11 Then they said to him, "What shall we do to you, that the sea may be calm to us?" For the sea grew more and more stormy.

12 He said to them, "Take me up, and throw me into the sea. Then the sea will be calm for you; for I know that because of me this great storm is on you."

13 Nevertheless the men rowed hard to get them back to the land; but they could not, for the sea grew more and more stormy against them. 14 Therefore they cried to the LORD, and said, "We beg you, LORD, we beg you, don't let us die for this man's life, and don't lay on us innocent blood; for you, LORD, have done as it pleased you." 15 So they took up Jonah and threw him into the sea; and the sea ceased its raging. 16 Then the men feared the LORD exceedingly; and they offered a sacrifice to the LORD and made vows.

17 The LORD prepared a huge fish to swallow up Jonah, and Jonah was in the belly of the fish three days and three nights.

2

1 Then Jonah prayed to the LORD, his God, out of the fish's belly. 2 He said,

"I called because of my affliction to the LORD.
   He answered me.
Out of the belly of Sheol[e] I cried.
   You heard my voice.
3 For you threw me into the depths,
   in the heart of the seas.
The flood was all around me.
   All your waves and your billows passed over me.
4 I said, 'I have been banished from your sight;
   yet I will look again towards your holy temple.'
5 The waters surrounded me,
   even to the soul.
The deep was around me.
   The weeds were wrapped around my head.
6 I went down to the bottoms of the mountains.
   The earth barred me in forever;
   yet you have brought my life up from the pit, LORD my God.

7 "When my soul fainted within me, I remembered the LORD.
   My prayer came in to you, into your holy temple.
8 Those who regard vain idols forsake their own mercy.
9 But I will sacrifice to you with the voice of thanksgiving.
   I will pay that which I have vowed.
Salvation belongs to the LORD."

10 Then the LORD spoke to the fish, and it vomited out Jonah on the dry land.

3

1 The LORD's word came to Jonah the second time, saying, 2 "Arise, go to Nineveh, that great city, and preach to it the message that I give you."

3 So Jonah arose, and went to Nineveh, according to the LORD's word. Now Nineveh was an exceedingly great city, three days' journey across. 4 Jonah began to enter into the city a day's journey, and he cried out, and said, "In forty days, Nineveh will be overthrown!"

5 The people of Nineveh believed God; and they proclaimed a fast and put on sackcloth, from their greatest even to their least. 6 The news reached the king of Nineveh, and he arose from his throne, took off his royal robe, covered himself with sackcloth, and sat in ashes. 7 He made a proclamation and published through Nineveh by the decree of the king and his nobles, saying, "Let neither man nor animal, herd nor flock, taste anything; let them not feed, nor drink water; 8 but let them be covered with sackcloth, both man and animal, and let them cry mightily to God. Yes, let them turn everyone from his evil way and from the violence that is in his hands. 9 Who knows whether God will not turn and relent, and turn away from his fierce anger, so that we might not perish?"

10 God saw their works, that they turned from their evil way. God relented of the disaster which he said he would do to them, and he didn't do it.

4

1 But it displeased Jonah exceedingly, and he was angry. 2 He prayed to the LORD, and said, "Please, LORD, wasn't this what I said when I was still in my own country? Therefore I hurried to flee to Tarshish, for I knew that you are a gracious God and merciful, slow to anger, and abundant in loving kindness, and you relent of doing harm. 3 Therefore now, LORD, take, I beg you, my life from me, for it is better for me to die than to live."

4 The LORD said, "Is it right for you to be angry?"

5 Then Jonah went out of the city and sat on the east side of the city, and there made himself a booth and sat under it in the shade, until he might see what would become of the city. 6 The LORD God prepared a vine and made it to come up over Jonah, that it might be a shade over his head to deliver him from his discomfort. So Jonah was exceedingly glad because of the vine. 7 But God prepared a worm at dawn the next day, and it chewed on the vine so that it withered. 8 When the sun arose, God prepared a sultry east wind; and the sun beat on Jonah's head, so that he was faint and requested for himself that he might die. He said, "It is better for me to die than to live."

9 God said to Jonah, "Is it right for you to be angry about the vine?"

He said, "I am right to be angry, even to death."

10 The LORD said, "You have been concerned for the vine, for which you have not laboured, neither made it grow; which came up in a night and perished in a night. 11 Shouldn't I be concerned for Nineveh, that great city, in which are more than one hundred and twenty thousand persons who can't discern between their right hand and their left hand, and also many animals?"

---

a *1:1* When rendered in ALL CAPITAL LETTERS, "LORD" or "GOD" is the translation of God's Proper Name.
b *1:6* or, gods
c *1:6* or, gods
d *1:9* The Hebrew word rendered "God" is "אֱלֹהִים" (Elohim).
e *2:2* Sheol is the place of the dead.

The Book of Micah

1

1 The LORD's[a] word that came to Micah of Morasheth in the days of Jotham, Ahaz, and Hezekiah, kings of Judah, which he saw concerning Samaria and Jerusalem.
2 Hear, you peoples, all of you!
　　Listen, O earth, and all that is therein.
Let the Lord[b] GOD be witness against you,
　　the Lord from his holy temple.
3 For behold,[c] the LORD comes out of his place,
　　and will come down and tread on the high places of the earth.
4 The mountains melt under him,
　　and the valleys split apart like wax before the fire,
　　like waters that are poured down a steep place.

5 "All this is for the disobedience of Jacob,
　　and for the sins of the house of Israel.
What is the disobedience of Jacob?
　　Isn't it Samaria?
And what are the high places of Judah?
　　Aren't they Jerusalem?
6 Therefore I will make Samaria like a rubble heap of the field,
　　like places for planting vineyards;
and I will pour down its stones into the valley,
　　and I will uncover its foundations.
7 All her idols will be beaten to pieces,
　　all her temple gifts will be burnt with fire,
　　and I will destroy all her images;
for of the hire of a prostitute has she gathered them,
　　and to the hire of a prostitute shall they return."

8 For this I will lament and wail.
　　I will go stripped and naked.
　　I will howl like the jackals
　　and mourn like the ostriches.
9 For her wounds are incurable;
　　for it has come even to Judah.
It reaches to the gate of my people,
　　even to Jerusalem.
10 Don't tell it in Gath.
　　Don't weep at all.
　　At Beth Ophrah[d] I have rolled myself in the dust.
11 Pass on, inhabitant of Shaphir, in nakedness and shame.
　　The inhabitant of Zaanan won't come out.
　　The wailing of Beth Ezel will take from you his protection.
12 For the inhabitant of Maroth waits anxiously for good,
　　because evil has come down from the LORD to the gate of Jerusalem.
13 Harness the chariot to the swift steed, inhabitant of Lachish.
　　She was the beginning of sin to the daughter of Zion;
　　for the transgressions of Israel were found in you.
14 Therefore you will give a parting gift to Moresheth Gath.
　　The houses of Achzib will be a deceitful thing to the kings of Israel.
15 I will yet bring a conqueror to you, inhabitants of Mareshah.
　　The glory of Israel will come to Adullam.
16 Shave your heads,
　　and cut off your hair for the children of your delight.
Enlarge your baldness like the vulture,
　　for they have gone into captivity from you!

2

1 Woe to those who devise iniquity
　　and work evil on their beds!
When the morning is light, they practise it,
　　because it is in the power of their hand.
2 They covet fields and seize them,
　　and houses, then take them away.
They oppress a man and his house,
　　even a man and his heritage.
3 Therefore the LORD says:
"Behold, I am planning against these people a disaster,
　　from which you will not remove your necks,
　　neither will you walk haughtily,
　　for it is an evil time.
4 In that day they will take up a parable against you,
　　and lament with a doleful lamentation, saying,
　　'We are utterly ruined!
　　My people's possession is divided up.
　　Indeed he takes it from me and assigns our fields to traitors!'"
5 Therefore you will have no one who divides the land by lot in the LORD's assembly.

6 "Don't prophesy!"—they prophesy—
　　"Don't prophesy about these things.
　　Disgrace won't overtake us."
7 Shall it be said, O house of Jacob,
　　"Is the LORD's Spirit angry?
　　Are these his doings?
　　Don't my words do good to him who walks blamelessly?"
8 But lately my people have risen up as an enemy.
　　You strip the robe and clothing from those who pass by without a care, returning from battle.
9 You drive the women of my people out from their pleasant houses;
　　from their young children you take away my blessing forever.
10 Arise, and depart!
　　For this is not your resting place,
　　because of uncleanness that destroys,
　　even with a grievous destruction.
11 If a man walking in a spirit of falsehood lies, saying,
　　"I will prophesy to you of wine and of strong drink,"
　　he would be the prophet of this people.
12 I will surely assemble all of you, Jacob.
　　I will surely gather the remnant of Israel.
I will put them together as the sheep of Bozrah,
　　as a flock in the middle of their pasture.
　　They will swarm with people.
13 He who breaks open the way goes up before them.
　　They break through the gate, and go out.
　　Their king passes on before them,
　　with the LORD at their head.

3

1 I said,
"Please listen, you heads of Jacob,
　　and rulers of the house of Israel:
　　Isn't it for you to know justice?
2 You who hate the good,
　　and love the evil;
　　who tear off their skin,
　　and their flesh from off their bones;
　　3 who also eat the flesh of my people,
　　and peel their skin from off them,
　　and break their bones,
　　and chop them in pieces, as for the pot,
　　and as meat within the cauldron.
4 Then they will cry to the LORD,
　　but he will not answer them.
Yes, he will hide his face from them at that time,
　　because they made their deeds evil."
5 The LORD says concerning the prophets who lead my people astray—for those who feed their teeth, they proclaim, "Peace!" and whoever doesn't provide for their mouths, they prepare war against him:
6 "Therefore night is over you, with no vision,
　　and it is dark to you, that you may not divine;
　　and the sun will go down on the prophets,
　　and the day will be black over them.
7 The seers shall be disappointed,
　　and the diviners confounded.
Yes, they shall all cover their lips,
　　for there is no answer from God."[e]
8 But as for me, I am full of power by the LORD's Spirit,
　　and of judgement, and of might,
　　to declare to Jacob his disobedience,
　　and to Israel his sin.
9 Please listen to this, you heads of the house of Jacob,
　　and rulers of the house of Israel,
　　who abhor justice,
　　and pervert all equity,
　　10 who build up Zion with blood,
　　and Jerusalem with iniquity.
11 Her leaders judge for bribes,
　　and her priests teach for a price,
　　and her prophets of it tell fortunes for money;
yet they lean on the LORD, and say,
　　"Isn't the LORD amongst us?
　　No disaster will come on us."
12 Therefore Zion for your sake will be ploughed like a field,
　　and Jerusalem will become heaps of rubble,
　　and the mountain of the temple like the high places of a forest.

4

1 But in the latter days,
　　it will happen that the mountain of the LORD's temple will be established on the top of the mountains,
　　and it will be exalted above the hills;
　　and peoples will stream to it.

---

[a] *1:1* When rendered in ALL CAPITAL LETTERS, "LORD" or "GOD" is the translation of God's Proper Name.
[b] *1:2* The word translated "Lord" is "Adonai."

[c] *1:3* "Behold", from "הִנֵּה", means look at, take notice, observe, see, or gaze at. It is often used as an interjection.
[d] *1:10* Beth Ophrah means literally "House of Dust."
[e] *3:7* The Hebrew word rendered "God" is "אֱלֹהִים" (Elohim).

2 Many nations will go and say,
    "Come! Let's go up to the mountain of the LORD,
        and to the house of the God of Jacob;
        and he will teach us of his ways,
        and we will walk in his paths."
For the law will go out of Zion,
    and the LORD's word from Jerusalem;
3 and he will judge between many peoples,
    and will decide concerning strong nations afar off.
    They will beat their swords into ploughshares,
    and their spears into pruning hooks.
Nation will not lift up sword against nation,
    neither will they learn war any more.
4 But every man will sit under his vine and under his fig tree.
    No one will make them afraid,
        for the mouth of the LORD of Armies has spoken. 5 Indeed all the
        nations may walk in the name of their gods,
    but we will walk in the name of the LORD our God forever and ever.
6 "In that day," says the LORD,
    "I will assemble that which is lame,
    and I will gather that which is driven away,
    and that which I have afflicted;
    7 and I will make that which was lame a remnant,
    and that which was cast far off a strong nation:
    and the LORD will reign over them on Mount Zion from then on, even
        forever."
8 You, tower of the flock, the hill of the daughter of Zion,
    to you it will come.
Yes, the former dominion will come,
    the kingdom of the daughter of Jerusalem.

9 Now why do you cry out aloud?
    Is there no king in you?
    Has your counsellor perished,
    that pains have taken hold of you as of a woman in travail?
10 Be in pain, and labour to give birth, daughter of Zion,
    like a woman in travail;
    for now you will go out of the city,
    and will dwell in the field,
    and will come even to Babylon.
There you will be rescued.
    There the LORD will redeem you from the hand of your enemies.

11 Now many nations have assembled against you, that say,
    "Let her be defiled,
    and let our eye gloat over Zion."
12 But they don't know the thoughts of the LORD,
    neither do they understand his counsel;
    for he has gathered them like the sheaves to the threshing floor.
13 Arise and thresh, daughter of Zion,
    for I will make your horn iron,
    and I will make your hoofs bronze.
You will beat in pieces many peoples.
I will devote their gain to the LORD,
    and their substance to the Lord of the whole earth.

5

1 Now you shall gather yourself in troops,
    daughter of troops.
He has laid siege against us.
    They will strike the judge of Israel with a rod on the cheek.
2 But you, Bethlehem Ephrathah,
    being small amongst the clans of Judah,
    out of you one will come out to me who is to be ruler in Israel;
    whose goings out are from of old, from ancient times.
3 Therefore he will abandon them until the time that she who is in labour
        gives birth.
    Then the rest of his brothers will return to the children of Israel.
4 He shall stand, and shall shepherd in the strength of the LORD,
    in the majesty of the name of the LORD his God.
    They will live, for then he will be great to the ends of the earth.
5 He will be our peace when Assyria invades our land
    and when he marches through our fortresses,
    then we will raise against him seven shepherds,
    and eight leaders of men.
6 They will rule the land of Assyria with the sword,
    and the land of Nimrod in its gates.
He will deliver us from the Assyrian,
    when he invades our land,
    and when he marches within our border.
7 The remnant of Jacob will be amongst many peoples
    like dew from the LORD,
    like showers on the grass,
    that don't wait for man

    nor wait for the sons of men.
8 The remnant of Jacob will be amongst the nations,
    amongst many peoples,
    like a lion amongst the animals of the forest,
    like a young lion amongst the flocks of sheep;
    who, if he goes through, treads down and tears in pieces,
    and there is no one to deliver.
9 Let your hand be lifted up above your adversaries,
    and let all of your enemies be cut off.
10 "It will happen in that day", says the LORD,
    "that I will cut off your horses from amongst you
    and will destroy your chariots.
11 I will cut off the cities of your land
    and will tear down all your strongholds.
12 I will destroy witchcraft from your hand.
    You shall have no soothsayers.
13 I will cut off your engraved images and your pillars from amongst you;
    and you shall no more worship the work of your hands.
14 I will uproot your Asherah poles from amongst you;
    and I will destroy your cities.
15 I will execute vengeance in anger
    and wrath on the nations that didn't listen."

6

1 Listen now to what the LORD says:
"Arise, plead your case before the mountains,
    and let the hills hear what you have to say.
2 Hear, you mountains, the LORD's indictment,
    and you enduring foundations of the earth;
    for the LORD has a case against his people,
    and he will contend with Israel.
3 My people, what have I done to you?
    How have I burdened you?
    Answer me!
4 For I brought you up out of the land of Egypt,
    and redeemed you out of the house of bondage.
    I sent before you Moses, Aaron, and Miriam.
5 My people, remember now what Balak king of Moab devised,
    and what Balaam the son of Beor answered him from Shittim to Gilgal,
    that you may know the righteous acts of the LORD."

6 How shall I come before the LORD,
    and bow myself before the exalted God?
Shall I come before him with burnt offerings,
    with calves a year old?
7 Will the LORD be pleased with thousands of rams?
    With tens of thousands of rivers of oil?
Shall I give my firstborn for my disobedience?
    The fruit of my body for the sin of my soul?
8 He has shown you, O man, what is good.
    What does the LORD require of you, but to act justly,
    to love mercy, and to walk humbly with your God?

9 The LORD's voice calls to the city—
    and wisdom fears your name—
"Listen to the rod,
    and he who appointed it.
10 Are there yet treasures of wickedness in the house of the wicked,
    and a short ephah[a] that is accursed?
11 Shall I tolerate dishonest scales,
    and a bag of deceitful weights?
12 Her rich men are full of violence,
    her inhabitants speak lies,
    and their tongue is deceitful in their speech.
13 Therefore I also have struck you with a grievous wound.
    I have made you desolate because of your sins.
14 You shall eat, but not be satisfied.
    Your hunger will be within you.
    You will store up, but not save,
    and that which you save I will give up to the sword.
15 You will sow, but won't reap.
    You will tread the olives, but won't anoint yourself with oil;
    and crush grapes, but won't drink the wine.
16 For the statutes of Omri are kept,
    and all the works of Ahab's house.
    You walk in their counsels,
    that I may make you a ruin,
    and your inhabitants a hissing.
    You will bear the reproach of my people."

7

1 Misery is mine!
    Indeed, I am like one who gathers the summer fruits, as gleanings of
        the vineyard.
    There is no cluster of grapes to eat.

---

a *6:10* An ephah is a measure of volume (about 22 litres or about 2/3 of a bushel), and a short ephah is made smaller than a full ephah for the purpose of cheating customers.

My soul desires to eat the early fig.

2 The godly man has perished out of the earth,
and there is no one upright amongst men.
They all lie in wait for blood;
every man hunts his brother with a net.

3 Their hands are on that which is evil to do it diligently.
The ruler and judge ask for a bribe.
The powerful man dictates the evil desire of his soul.
Thus they conspire together.

4 The best of them is like a brier.
The most upright is worse than a thorn hedge.
The day of your watchmen,
even your visitation, has come;
now is the time of their confusion.

5 Don't trust in a neighbour.
Don't put confidence in a friend.
With the woman lying in your embrace,
be careful of the words of your mouth!

6 For the son dishonours the father,
the daughter rises up against her mother,
the daughter-in-law against her mother-in-law;
a man's enemies are the men of his own house.

7 But as for me, I will look to the LORD.
I will wait for the God of my salvation.
My God will hear me.

8 Don't rejoice against me, my enemy.
When I fall, I will arise.
When I sit in darkness, the LORD will be a light to me.

9 I will bear the indignation of the LORD,
because I have sinned against him,
until he pleads my case and executes judgement for me.
He will bring me out to the light.
I will see his righteousness.

10 Then my enemy will see it,
and shame will cover her who said to me,
"Where is the LORD your God?"
My eyes will see her.
Now she will be trodden down like the mire of the streets.

11 A day to build your walls!
In that day, he will extend your boundary.

12 In that day they will come to you from Assyria and the cities of Egypt,
and from Egypt even to the River,
and from sea to sea,
and mountain to mountain.

13 Yet the land will be desolate because of those who dwell therein,
for the fruit of their doings.

14 Shepherd your people with your staff,
the flock of your heritage,
who dwell by themselves in a forest.
Let them feed in the middle of fertile pasture land,
in Bashan and Gilead, as in the days of old.

15 "As in the days of your coming out of the land of Egypt,
I will show them marvellous things."

16 The nations will see and be ashamed of all their might.
They will lay their hand on their mouth.
Their ears will be deaf.

17 They will lick the dust like a serpent.
Like crawling things of the earth, they will come trembling out of their
dens.
They will come with fear to the LORD our God,
and will be afraid because of you.

18 Who is a God like you, who pardons iniquity,
and passes over the disobedience of the remnant of his heritage?
He doesn't retain his anger forever,
because he delights in loving kindness.

19 He will again have compassion on us.
He will tread our iniquities under foot.
You will cast all their sins into the depths of the sea.

20 You will give truth to Jacob,
and mercy to Abraham,
as you have sworn to our fathers from the days of old.

1

1 A revelation about Nineveh. The book of the vision of Nahum the Elkoshite. 2 The LORD[a] is a jealous God[b] and avenges. The LORD avenges and is full of wrath. The LORD takes vengeance on his adversaries, and he maintains wrath against his enemies. 3 The LORD is slow to anger, and great in power, and will by no means leave the guilty unpunished. The LORD has his way in the whirlwind and in the storm, and the clouds are the dust of his feet. 4 He rebukes the sea and makes it dry, and dries up all the rivers. Bashan and Carmel languish. The flower of Lebanon languishes. 5 The mountains quake before him, and the hills melt away. The earth trembles at his presence, yes, the world, and all who dwell in it. 6 Who can stand before his indignation? Who can endure the fierceness of his anger? His wrath is poured out like fire, and the rocks are broken apart by him. 7 The LORD is good, a stronghold in the day of trouble; and he knows those who take refuge in him. 8 But with an overflowing flood, he will make a full end of her place, and will pursue his enemies into darkness. 9 What do you plot against the LORD? He will make a full end. Affliction won't rise up the second time. 10 For entangled like thorns, and drunken as with their drink, they are consumed utterly like dry stubble. 11 One has gone out of you who devises evil against the LORD, who counsels wickedness.

12 The LORD says: "Though they are in full strength and likewise many, even so they will be cut down and pass away. Though I have afflicted you, I will afflict you no more. 13 Now I will break his yoke from off you, and will burst your bonds apart."

14 The LORD has commanded concerning you: "No more descendants will bear your name. Out of the house of your gods, I will cut off the engraved image and the molten image. I will make your grave, for you are vile."

15 Behold,[c] on the mountains the feet of him who brings good news, who publishes peace! Keep your feasts, Judah! Perform your vows, for the wicked one will no more pass through you. He is utterly cut off.

2

1 He who dashes in pieces has come up against you. Keep the fortress! Watch the way! Strengthen your waist! Fortify your power mightily!

2 For the LORD restores the excellency of Jacob as the excellency of Israel, for the destroyers have destroyed them and ruined their vine branches.

3 The shield of his mighty men is made red. The valiant men are in scarlet. The chariots flash with steel in the day of his preparation, and the pine spears are brandished. 4 The chariots rage in the streets. They rush back and forth in the wide ways. Their appearance is like torches. They run like the lightnings. 5 He summons his picked troops. They stumble on their way. They dash to its wall, and the protective shield is put in place. 6 The gates of the rivers are opened, and the palace is dissolved. 7 It is decreed: she is uncovered, she is carried away; and her servants moan as with the voice of doves, beating on their breasts. 8 But Nineveh has been from of old like a pool of water, yet they flee away. "Stop! Stop!" they cry, but no one looks back. 9 Take the plunder of silver. Take the plunder of gold, for there is no end of treasure, an abundance of every precious thing. 10 She is empty, void, and waste. The heart melts, the knees knock together, their bodies and faces have grown pale. 11 Where is the den of the lions, and the feeding place of the young lions, where the lion and the lioness walked with the lion's cubs, and no one made them afraid? 12 The lion tore in pieces enough for his cubs, and strangled prey for his lionesses, and filled his caves with the kill and his dens with prey. 13 "Behold, I am against you," says the LORD of Armies, "and I will burn her chariots in the smoke, and the sword will devour your young lions; and I will cut off your prey from the earth, and the voice of your messengers will no longer be heard."

3

1 Woe to the bloody city! It is all full of lies and robbery—no end to the prey. 2 The noise of the whip, the noise of the rattling of wheels, prancing horses, and bounding chariots, 3 the horseman charging, and the flashing sword, the glittering spear, and a multitude of slain, and a great heap of corpses, and there is no end of the bodies. They stumble on their bodies 4 because of the multitude of the prostitution of the alluring prostitute, the mistress of witchcraft, who sells nations through her prostitution, and families through her witchcraft. 5 "Behold, I am against you," says the LORD of Armies, "and I will lift your skirts over your face. I will show the nations your nakedness, and the kingdoms your shame. 6 I will throw abominable filth on you and make you vile, and will make you a spectacle. 7 It will happen that all those who look at you will flee from you, and say, 'Nineveh is laid waste! Who will mourn for her?' Where will I seek comforters for you?"

8 Are you better than No-Amon,[d] who was situated amongst the rivers,[e] who had the waters around her, whose rampart was the sea, and her wall was of the sea? 9 Cush and Egypt were her boundless strength. Put and Libya were her helpers. 10 Yet was she carried away. She went into captivity. Her young children also were dashed in pieces at the head of all the streets, and they cast lots for her honourable men, and all her great men were bound in chains. 11 You also will be drunken. You will be hidden. You also will seek a stronghold because of the enemy. 12 All your fortresses

will be like fig trees with the first-ripe figs. If they are shaken, they fall into the mouth of the eater. 13 Behold, your troops amongst you are women. The gates of your land are set wide open to your enemies. The fire has devoured your bars.

14 Draw water for the siege. Strengthen your fortresses. Go into the clay, and tread the mortar. Make the brick kiln strong. 15 There the fire will devour you. The sword will cut you off. It will devour you like the grasshopper. Multiply like grasshoppers. Multiply like the locust. 16 You have increased your merchants more than the stars of the skies. The grasshopper strips and flees away. 17 Your guards are like the locusts, and your officials like the swarms of locusts, which settle on the walls on a cold day, but when the sun appears, they flee away, and their place is not known where they are.

18 Your shepherds slumber, king of Assyria. Your nobles lie down. Your people are scattered on the mountains, and there is no one to gather them. 19 There is no healing your wound, for your injury is fatal. All who hear the report of you clap their hands over you, for who hasn't felt your endless cruelty?

---

a *1:2* When rendered in ALL CAPITAL LETTERS, "LORD" or "GOD" is the translation of God's Proper Name.
b *1:2* The Hebrew word rendered "God" is "אֱלֹהִים" (Elohim).
c *1:15* "Behold", from "הִנֵּה", means look at, take notice, observe, or gaze at. It is often used as an interjection.
d *3:8* or, Thebes
e *3:8* or, Nile

The Book of Habakkuk

1

₁ The revelation which Habakkuk the prophet saw. ₂ LORD,[a] how long will I cry, and you will not hear? I cry out to you "Violence!" and will you not save? ₃ Why do you show me iniquity, and look at perversity? For destruction and violence are before me. There is strife, and contention rises up. ₄ Therefore the law is paralysed, and justice never prevails; for the wicked surround the righteous; therefore justice comes out perverted.

₅ "Look amongst the nations, watch, and wonder marvellously; for I am working a work in your days which you will not believe though it is told you. ₆ For, behold,[b] I am raising up the Chaldeans, that bitter and hasty nation who march through the width of the earth, to possess dwelling places that are not theirs. ₇ They are feared and dreaded. Their judgement and their dignity proceed from themselves. ₈ Their horses also are swifter than leopards, and are more fierce than the evening wolves. Their horsemen press proudly on. Yes, their horsemen come from afar. They fly as an eagle that hurries to devour. ₉ All of them come for violence. Their hordes face forward. They gather prisoners like sand. ₁₀ Yes, they scoff at kings, and princes are a derision to them. They laugh at every stronghold, for they build up an earthen ramp and take it. ₁₁ Then they sweep by like the wind and go on. They are indeed guilty, whose strength is their god."

₁₂ Aren't you from everlasting, LORD my God,[c] my Holy One? We will not die. LORD, you have appointed them for judgement. You, Rock, have established him to punish. ₁₃ You who have purer eyes than to see evil, and who cannot look on perversity, why do you tolerate those who deal treacherously and keep silent when the wicked swallows up the man who is more righteous than he, ₁₄ and make men like the fish of the sea, like the creeping things that have no ruler over them? ₁₅ He takes up all of them with the hook. He catches them in his net and gathers them in his dragnet. Therefore he rejoices and is glad. ₁₆ Therefore he sacrifices to his net and burns incense to his dragnet, because by them his life is luxurious and his food is good. ₁₇ Will he therefore continually empty his net, and kill the nations without mercy?

2

₁ I will stand at my watch and set myself on the ramparts, and will look out to see what he will say to me, and what I will answer concerning my complaint.

₂ The LORD answered me, "Write the vision, and make it plain on tablets, that he who runs may read it. ₃ For the vision is yet for the appointed time, and it hurries towards the end, and won't prove false. Though it takes time, wait for it, because it will surely come. It won't delay. ₄ Behold, his soul is puffed up. It is not upright in him, but the righteous will live by his faith. ₅ Yes, moreover, wine is treacherous: an arrogant man who doesn't stay at home, who enlarges his desire as Sheol;[d] he is like death and can't be satisfied, but gathers to himself all nations and heaps to himself all peoples.

₆ Won't all these take up a parable against him, and a taunting proverb against him, and say, 'Woe to him who increases that which is not his, and who enriches himself by extortion! How long?' ₇ Won't your debtors rise up suddenly, and wake up those who make you tremble, and you will be their victim? ₈ Because you have plundered many nations, all the remnant of the peoples will plunder you because of men's blood, and for the violence done to the land, to the city and to all who dwell in it.

₉ Woe to him who gets an evil gain for his house, that he may set his nest on high, that he may be delivered from the hand of evil! ₁₀ You have devised shame to your house by cutting off many peoples, and have sinned against your soul. ₁₁ For the stone will cry out of the wall, and the beam out of the woodwork will answer it.

₁₂ Woe to him who builds a town with blood, and establishes a city by iniquity! ₁₃ Behold, isn't it from the LORD of Armies that the peoples labour for the fire, and the nations weary themselves for vanity? ₁₄ For the earth will be filled with the knowledge of the LORD's glory, as the waters cover the sea.

₁₅ "Woe to him who gives his neighbour drink, pouring your inflaming wine until they are drunk, so that you may gaze at their naked bodies! ₁₆ You are filled with shame, and not glory. You will also drink and be exposed! The cup of the LORD's right hand will come around to you, and disgrace will cover your glory. ₁₇ For the violence done to Lebanon will overwhelm you, and the destruction of the animals will terrify you, because of men's blood and for the violence done to the land, to every city and to those who dwell in them.

₁₈ "What value does the engraved image have, that its maker has engraved it; the molten image, even the teacher of lies, that he who fashions its form trusts in it, to make mute idols? ₁₉ Woe to him who says to the wood, 'Awake!' or to the mute stone, 'Arise!' Shall this teach? Behold, it is overlaid with gold and silver, and there is no breath at all within it. ₂₀ But the LORD is in his holy temple. Let all the earth be silent before him!"

3

₁ A prayer of Habakkuk, the prophet, set to victorious music.

₂ LORD, I have heard of your fame.
  I stand in awe of your deeds, LORD.
Renew your work in the middle of the years.
  In the middle of the years make it known.
  In wrath, you remember mercy.
₃ God came from Teman,
  the Holy One from Mount Paran. Selah.

His glory covered the heavens,
  and his praise filled the earth.
₄ His splendour is like the sunrise.
  Rays shine from his hand, where his power is hidden.
₅ Plague went before him,
  and pestilence followed his feet.
₆ He stood, and shook the earth.
  He looked, and made the nations tremble.
  The ancient mountains were crumbled.
  The age-old hills collapsed.
  His ways are eternal.
₇ I saw the tents of Cushan in affliction.
  The dwellings of the land of Midian trembled.
₈ Was the LORD displeased with the rivers?
  Was your anger against the rivers,
  or your wrath against the sea,
  that you rode on your horses,
  on your chariots of salvation?
₉ You uncovered your bow.
  You called for your sworn arrows. Selah.
You split the earth with rivers.
₁₀ The mountains saw you, and were afraid.
  The storm of waters passed by.
  The deep roared and lifted up its hands on high.
₁₁ The sun and moon stood still in the sky
  at the light of your arrows as they went,
  at the shining of your glittering spear.
₁₂ You marched through the land in wrath.
  You threshed the nations in anger.
₁₃ You went out for the salvation of your people,
  for the salvation of your anointed.
You crushed the head of the land of wickedness.
  You stripped them head to foot. Selah.

₁₄ You pierced the heads of his warriors with their own spears.
  They came as a whirlwind to scatter me,
  gloating as if to devour the wretched in secret.
₁₅ You trampled the sea with your horses,
  churning mighty waters.
₁₆ I heard, and my body trembled.
  My lips quivered at the voice.
Rottenness enters into my bones, and I tremble in my place
  because I must wait quietly for the day of trouble,
  for the coming up of the people who invade us.
₁₇ For even though the fig tree doesn't flourish,
  nor fruit be in the vines,
  the labour of the olive fails,
  the fields yield no food,
  the flocks are cut off from the fold,
  and there is no herd in the stalls,
₁₈ yet I will rejoice in the LORD.
  I will be joyful in the God of my salvation!
₁₉ GOD, the Lord,[e] is my strength.
  He makes my feet like deer's feet,
  and enables me to go in high places.
  For the music director, on my stringed instruments.

ᵃ *1:2* When rendered in ALL CAPITAL LETTERS, "LORD" or "GOD" is the translation of God's Proper Name.

ᵇ *1:6* "Behold", from "הִנֵּה", means look at, take notice, observe, see, or gaze at. It is often used as an interjection.

ᶜ *1:12* The Hebrew word rendered "God" is "אֱלֹהִים" (Elohim).

ᵈ *2:5* Sheol is the place of the dead.

ᵉ *3:19* The word translated "Lord" is "Adonai."

The Book of Zephaniah

1

₁ The LORD's[a] word which came to Zephaniah, the son of Cushi, the son of Gedaliah, the son of Amariah, the son of Hezekiah, in the days of Josiah, the son of Amon, king of Judah.

₂ I will utterly sweep away everything from the surface of the earth, says the LORD. ₃ I will sweep away man and animal. I will sweep away the birds of the sky, the fish of the sea, and the heaps of rubble with the wicked. I will cut off man from the surface of the earth, says the LORD. ₄ I will stretch out my hand against Judah and against all the inhabitants of Jerusalem. I will cut off the remnant of Baal from this place—the name of the idolatrous and pagan priests, ₅ those who worship the army of the sky on the housetops, those who worship and swear by the LORD and also swear by Malcam, ₆ those who have turned back from following the LORD, and those who haven't sought the LORD nor enquired after him.

₇ Be silent at the presence of the Lord[b] GOD, for the day of the LORD is at hand. For the LORD has prepared a sacrifice. He has consecrated his guests. ₈ It will happen in the day of the LORD's sacrifice that I will punish the princes, the king's sons, and all those who are clothed with foreign clothing. ₉ In that day, I will punish all those who leap over the threshold, who fill their master's house with violence and deceit.

₁₀ In that day, says the LORD, there will be the noise of a cry from the fish gate, a wailing from the second quarter, and a great crashing from the hills. ₁₁ Wail, you inhabitants of Maktesh, for all the people of Canaan are undone! All those who were loaded with silver are cut off. ₁₂ It will happen at that time, that I will search Jerusalem with lamps, and I will punish the men who are settled on their dregs, who say in their heart, "The LORD will not do good, neither will he do evil." ₁₃ Their wealth will become a plunder, and their houses a desolation. Yes, they will build houses, but won't inhabit them. They will plant vineyards, but won't drink their wine.

₁₄ The great day of the LORD is near. It is near and hurries greatly, the voice of the day of the LORD. The mighty man cries there bitterly. ₁₅ That day is a day of wrath, a day of distress and anguish, a day of trouble and ruin, a day of darkness and gloom, a day of clouds and blackness, ₁₆ a day of the trumpet and alarm against the fortified cities and against the high battlements. ₁₇ I will bring such distress on men that they will walk like blind men because they have sinned against the LORD. Their blood will be poured out like dust and their flesh like dung. ₁₈ Neither their silver nor their gold will be able to deliver them in the day of the LORD's wrath, but the whole land will be devoured by the fire of his jealousy; for he will make an end, yes, a terrible end, of all those who dwell in the land.

2

₁ Gather yourselves together, yes, gather together, you nation that has no shame, ₂ before the appointed time when the day passes as the chaff, before the fierce anger of the LORD comes on you, before the day of the LORD's anger comes on you. ₃ Seek the LORD, all you humble of the land, who have kept his ordinances. Seek righteousness. Seek humility. It may be that you will be hidden in the day of the LORD's anger. ₄ For Gaza will be forsaken, and Ashkelon a desolation. They will drive out Ashdod at noonday, and Ekron will be rooted up. ₅ Woe to the inhabitants of the sea coast, the nation of the Cherethites! The LORD's word is against you, Canaan, the land of the Philistines. I will destroy you until there is no inhabitant. ₆ The sea coast will be pastures, with cottages for shepherds and folds for flocks. ₇ The coast will be for the remnant of the house of Judah. They will find pasture. In the houses of Ashkelon, they will lie down in the evening, for the LORD, their God,[c] will visit them and restore them. ₈ I have heard the reproach of Moab and the insults of the children of Ammon, with which they have reproached my people and magnified themselves against their border. ₉ Therefore, as I live, says the LORD of Armies, the God of Israel, surely Moab will be as Sodom, and the children of Ammon as Gomorrah, a possession of nettles and salt pits, and a perpetual desolation. The remnant of my people will plunder them, and the survivors of my nation will inherit them. ₁₀ This they will have for their pride, because they have reproached and magnified themselves against the people of the LORD of Armies. ₁₁ The LORD will be awesome to them, for he will famish all the gods of the land. Men will worship him, everyone from his place, even all the shores of the nations.

₁₂ You Cushites also, you will be killed by my sword.

₁₃ He will stretch out his hand against the north, destroy Assyria, and will make Nineveh a desolation, as dry as the wilderness. ₁₄ Herds will lie down in the middle of her, all kinds of animals. Both the pelican and the porcupine will lodge in its capitals. Their calls will echo through the windows. Desolation will be in the thresholds, for he has laid bare the cedar beams. ₁₅ This is the joyous city that lived carelessly, that said in her heart, "I am, and there is no one besides me." How she has become a desolation, a place for animals to lie down in! Everyone who passes by her will hiss and shake their fists.

3

₁ Woe to her who is rebellious and polluted, the oppressing city! ₂ She didn't obey the voice. She didn't receive correction. She didn't trust in the LORD. She didn't draw near to her God.

₃ Her princes within her are roaring lions. Her judges are evening wolves. They leave nothing until the next day. ₄ Her prophets are arrogant and treacherous people. Her priests have profaned the sanctuary. They have done violence to the law. ₅ The LORD, within her, is righteous. He will do no wrong. Every morning he brings his justice to light. He doesn't fail, but the unjust know no shame.

₆ I have cut off nations. Their battlements are desolate. I have made their streets waste, so that no one passes by. Their cities are destroyed, so that there is no man, so that there is no inhabitant. ₇ I said, "Just fear me. Receive correction," so that her dwelling won't be cut off, according to all that I have appointed concerning her. But they rose early and corrupted all their doings.

₈ "Therefore wait for me", says the LORD, "until the day that I rise up to the prey, for my determination is to gather the nations, that I may assemble the kingdoms to pour on them my indignation, even all my fierce anger, for all the earth will be devoured with the fire of my jealousy.

₉ For then I will purify the lips of the peoples, that they may all call on the LORD's name, to serve him shoulder to shoulder. ₁₀ From beyond the rivers of Cush, my worshippers, even the daughter of my dispersed people, will bring my offering. ₁₁ In that day you will not be disappointed for all your doings in which you have transgressed against me; for then I will take away out from amongst you your proudly exulting ones, and you will no more be arrogant in my holy mountain. ₁₂ But I will leave amongst you an afflicted and poor people, and they will take refuge in the LORD's name. ₁₃ The remnant of Israel will not do iniquity nor speak lies, neither will a deceitful tongue be found in their mouth, for they will feed and lie down, and no one will make them afraid."

₁₄ Sing, daughter of Zion! Shout, Israel! Be glad and rejoice with all your heart, daughter of Jerusalem. ₁₅ The LORD has taken away your judgements. He has thrown out your enemy. The King of Israel, the LORD, is amongst you. You will not be afraid of evil any more. ₁₆ In that day, it will be said to Jerusalem, "Don't be afraid, Zion. Don't let your hands be weak." ₁₇ The LORD, your God, is amongst you, a mighty one who will save. He will rejoice over you with joy. He will calm you in his love. He will rejoice over you with singing. ₁₈ I will remove those who grieve about the appointed feasts from you. They are a burden and a reproach to you. ₁₉ Behold,[d] at that time I will deal with all those who afflict you; and I will save those who are lame and gather those who were driven away. I will give them praise and honour, whose shame has been in all the earth. ₂₀ At that time I will bring you in, and at that time I will gather you; for I will give you honour and praise amongst all the peoples of the earth when I restore your fortunes before your eyes, says the LORD.

---

[a] *1:1* When rendered in ALL CAPITAL LETTERS, "LORD" or "GOD" is the translation of God's Proper Name.
[b] *1:7* The word translated "Lord" is "Adonai."
[c] *2:7* The Hebrew word rendered "God" is "אֱלֹהִים" (Elohim).
[d] *3:19* "Behold", from "הִנֵּה", means look at, take notice, observe, see, or gaze at. It is often used as an interjection.

The Book of Haggai

1

1 In the second year of Darius the king, in the sixth month, in the first day of the month, the LORD's[a] word came by Haggai the prophet, to Zerubbabel the son of Shealtiel, governor of Judah, and to Joshua the son of Jehozadak, the high priest, saying, 2 "This is what the LORD of Armies says: These people say, 'The time hasn't yet come, the time for the LORD's house to be built.'"

3 Then the LORD's word came by Haggai the prophet, saying, 4 "Is it a time for you yourselves to dwell in your panelled houses, while this house lies waste? 5 Now therefore this is what the LORD of Armies says: 'Consider your ways. 6 You have sown much, and bring in little. You eat, but you don't have enough. You drink, but you aren't filled with drink. You clothe yourselves, but no one is warm; and he who earns wages earns wages to put them into a bag with holes in it.'

7 "This is what the LORD of Armies says: 'Consider your ways. 8 Go up to the mountain, bring wood, and build the house. I will take pleasure in it, and I will be glorified," says the LORD. 9 "You looked for much, and, behold,[b] it came to little; and when you brought it home, I blew it away. Why?" says the LORD of Armies, "Because of my house that lies waste, while each of you is busy with his own house. 10 Therefore for your sake the heavens withhold the dew, and the earth withholds its fruit. 11 I called for a drought on the land, on the mountains, on the grain, on the new wine, on the oil, on that which the ground produces, on men, on livestock, and on all the labour of the hands."

12 Then Zerubbabel the son of Shealtiel and Joshua the son of Jehozadak, the high priest, with all the remnant of the people, obeyed the LORD their God's[c] voice, and the words of Haggai the prophet, as the LORD their God had sent him; and the people feared the LORD.

13 Then Haggai, the LORD's messenger, spoke the LORD's message to the people, saying, "I am with you," says the LORD.

14 The LORD stirred up the spirit of Zerubbabel the son of Shealtiel, governor of Judah, and the spirit of Joshua the son of Jehozadak, the high priest, and the spirit of all the remnant of the people; and they came and worked on the house of the LORD of Armies, their God, 15 in the twenty-fourth day of the month, in the sixth month, in the second year of Darius the king.

2

1 In the seventh month, in the twenty-first day of the month, the LORD's word came by Haggai the prophet, saying, 2 "Speak now to Zerubbabel the son of Shealtiel, governor of Judah, and to Joshua the son of Jehozadak, the high priest, and to the remnant of the people, saying, 3 'Who is left amongst you who saw this house in its former glory? How do you see it now? Isn't it in your eyes as nothing? 4 Yet now be strong, Zerubbabel,' says the LORD. 'Be strong, Joshua son of Jehozadak, the high priest. Be strong, all you people of the land,' says the LORD, 'and work, for I am with you,' says the LORD of Armies. 5 This is the word that I covenanted with you when you came out of Egypt, and my Spirit lived amongst you. 'Don't be afraid.' 6 For this is what the LORD of Armies says: 'Yet once more, it is a little while, and I will shake the heavens, the earth, the sea, and the dry land; 7 and I will shake all nations. The treasure of all nations will come, and I will fill this house with glory, says the LORD of Armies. 8 The silver is mine, and the gold is mine,' says the LORD of Armies. 9 'The latter glory of this house will be greater than the former,' says the LORD of Armies; 'and in this place I will give peace,' says the LORD of Armies."

10 In the twenty-fourth day of the ninth month, in the second year of Darius, the LORD's word came by Haggai the prophet, saying, 11 "The LORD of Armies says: Ask now the priests concerning the law, saying, 12 'If someone carries holy meat in the fold of his garment, and with his fold touches bread, stew, wine, oil, or any food, will it become holy?'"

The priests answered, "No."

13 Then Haggai said, "If one who is unclean by reason of a dead body touch any of these, will it be unclean?"

The priests answered, "It will be unclean."

14 Then Haggai answered, "'So is this people, and so is this nation before me,' says the LORD; 'and so is every work of their hands. That which they offer there is unclean. 15 Now, please consider from this day and backward, before a stone was laid on a stone in the LORD's temple. 16 Through all that time, when one came to a heap of twenty measures, there were only ten. When one came to the wine vat to draw out fifty, there were only twenty. 17 I struck you with blight, mildew, and hail in all the work of your hands; yet you didn't turn to me,' says the LORD. 18 'Consider, please, from this day and backward, from the twenty-fourth day of the ninth month, since the day that the foundation of the LORD's temple was laid, consider it. 19 Is the seed yet in the barn? Yes, the vine, the fig tree, the pomegranate, and the olive tree haven't produced. From today I will bless you.'"

20 The LORD's word came the second time to Haggai in the twenty-fourth day of the month, saying, 21 "Speak to Zerubbabel, governor of Judah, saying, 'I will shake the heavens and the earth. 22 I will overthrow the throne of kingdoms. I will destroy the strength of the kingdoms of the nations. I will overthrow the chariots and those who ride in them. The horses and their riders will come down, everyone by the sword of his brother. 23 In that day, says the LORD of Armies, I will take you, Zerubbabel my servant, the son of Shealtiel,' says the LORD, 'and will make you like a signet ring, for I have chosen you,' says the LORD of Armies."

---

a *1:1* When rendered in ALL CAPITAL LETTERS, "LORD" or "GOD" is the translation of God's Proper Name.

b *1:9* "Behold", from "הִנֵּה", means look at, take notice, observe, see, or gaze at. It is often used as an interjection.

c *1:12* The Hebrew word rendered "God" is "אֱלֹהִים" (Elohim).

The Book of Zechariah

1

1 In the eighth month, in the second year of Darius, the LORD's[a] word came to the prophet Zechariah the son of Berechiah, the son of Iddo, saying, 2 "The LORD was very displeased with your fathers. 3 Therefore tell them, the LORD of Armies says: 'Return to me,' says the LORD of Armies, 'and I will return to you,' says the LORD of Armies. 4 Don't you be like your fathers, to whom the former prophets proclaimed, saying: The LORD of Armies says, 'Return now from your evil ways and from your evil doings;' but they didn't hear nor listen to me, says the LORD. 5 Your fathers, where are they? And the prophets, do they live forever? 6 But my words and my decrees, which I commanded my servants the prophets, didn't they overtake your fathers?

"Then they repented and said, 'Just as the LORD of Armies determined to do to us, according to our ways and according to our practices, so he has dealt with us.'"

7 On the twenty-fourth day of the eleventh month, which is the month Shebat, in the second year of Darius, the LORD's word came to the prophet Zechariah the son of Berechiah, the son of Iddo, saying, 8 "I had a vision in the night, and behold,[b] a man riding on a red horse, and he stood amongst the myrtle trees that were in a ravine; and behind him there were red, brown, and white horses. 9 Then I asked, 'My lord, what are these?'"

The angel who talked with me said to me, "I will show you what these are."

10 The man who stood amongst the myrtle trees answered, "They are the ones the LORD has sent to go back and forth through the earth."

11 They reported to the LORD's angel who stood amongst the myrtle trees, and said, "We have walked back and forth through the earth, and behold, all the earth is at rest and in peace."

12 Then the LORD's angel replied, "O LORD of Armies, how long will you not have mercy on Jerusalem and on the cities of Judah, against which you have had indignation these seventy years?"

13 The LORD answered the angel who talked with me with kind and comforting words. 14 So the angel who talked with me said to me, "Proclaim, saying, 'The LORD of Armies says: "I am jealous for Jerusalem and for Zion with a great jealousy. 15 I am very angry with the nations that are at ease; for I was but a little displeased, but they added to the calamity." 16 Therefore the LORD says: "I have returned to Jerusalem with mercy. My house shall be built in it," says the LORD of Armies, "and a line shall be stretched out over Jerusalem."'

17 "Proclaim further, saying, 'The LORD of Armies says: "My cities will again overflow with prosperity, and the LORD will again comfort Zion, and will again choose Jerusalem."'"

18 I lifted up my eyes and saw, and behold, four horns. 19 I asked the angel who talked with me, "What are these?"

He answered me, "These are the horns which have scattered Judah, Israel, and Jerusalem."

20 The LORD showed me four craftsmen. 21 Then I asked, "What are these coming to do?"

He said, "These are the horns which scattered Judah, so that no man lifted up his head; but these have come to terrify them, to cast down the horns of the nations that lifted up their horn against the land of Judah to scatter it."

2

1 I lifted up my eyes, and saw, and behold, a man with a measuring line in his hand. 2 Then I asked, "Where are you going?"

He said to me, "To measure Jerusalem, to see what is its width and what is its length."

3 Behold, the angel who talked with me went out, and another angel went out to meet him, 4 and said to him, "Run, speak to this young man, saying, 'Jerusalem will be inhabited as villages without walls, because of the multitude of men and livestock in it. 5 For I,' says the LORD, 'will be to her a wall of fire around it, and I will be the glory in the middle of her.

6 Come! Come! Flee from the land of the north,' says the LORD; 'for I have spread you abroad as the four winds of the sky,' says the LORD. 7 'Come, Zion! Escape, you who dwell with the daughter of Babylon.' 8 For the LORD of Armies says: 'For honour he has sent me to the nations which plundered you; for he who touches you touches the apple of his eye. 9 For, behold, I will shake my hand over them, and they will be a plunder to those who served them; and you will know that the LORD of Armies has sent me. 10 Sing and rejoice, daughter of Zion! For behold, I come and I will dwell within you,' says the LORD. 11 Many nations shall join themselves to the LORD in that day, and shall be my people; and I will dwell amongst you, and you shall know that the LORD of Armies has sent me to you. 12 The LORD will inherit Judah as his portion in the holy land, and will again choose Jerusalem. 13 Be silent, all flesh, before the LORD; for he has roused himself from his holy habitation!"

3

1 He showed me Joshua the high priest standing before the LORD's angel, and Satan standing at his right hand to be his adversary. 2 The LORD said to Satan, "The LORD rebuke you, Satan! Yes, the LORD who has chosen Jerusalem rebuke you! Isn't this a burning stick plucked out of the fire?"

3 Now Joshua was clothed with filthy garments, and was standing before the angel. 4 He answered and spoke to those who stood before him, saying, "Take the filthy garments off him." To him he said, "Behold, I have caused your iniquity to pass from you, and I will clothe you with rich clothing."

5 I said, "Let them set a clean turban on his head."

So they set a clean turban on his head, and clothed him; and the LORD's angel was standing by.

6 The LORD's angel solemnly assured Joshua, saying, 7 "The LORD of Armies says: 'If you will walk in my ways, and if you will follow my instructions, then you also shall judge my house, and shall also keep my courts, and I will give you a place of access amongst these who stand by. 8 Hear now, Joshua the high priest, you and your fellows who sit before you, for they are men who are a sign; for, behold, I will bring out my servant, the Branch. 9 For, behold, the stone that I have set before Joshua: on one stone are seven eyes; behold, I will engrave its inscription,' says the LORD of Armies, 'and I will remove the iniquity of that land in one day. 10 In that day,' says the LORD of Armies, 'you will invite every man his neighbour under the vine and under the fig tree.'"

4

1 The angel who talked with me came again and wakened me, as a man who is wakened out of his sleep. 2 He said to me, "What do you see?"

I said, "I have seen, and behold, a lamp stand all of gold, with its bowl on the top of it, and its seven lamps on it; there are seven pipes to each of the lamps which are on the top of it; 3 and two olive trees by it, one on the right side of the bowl, and the other on the left side of it."

4 I answered and spoke to the angel who talked with me, saying, "What are these, my lord?"

5 Then the angel who talked with me answered me, "Don't you know what these are?"

I said, "No, my lord."

6 Then he answered and spoke to me, saying, "This is the LORD's word to Zerubbabel, saying, 'Not by might, nor by power, but by my Spirit,' says the LORD of Armies. 7 Who are you, great mountain? Before Zerubbabel you are a plain; and he will bring out the capstone with shouts of 'Grace, grace, to it!'"

8 Moreover the LORD's word came to me, saying, 9 "The hands of Zerubbabel have laid the foundation of this house. His hands shall also finish it; and you will know that the LORD of Armies has sent me to you. 10 Indeed, who despises the day of small things? For these seven shall rejoice, and shall see the plumb line in the hand of Zerubbabel. These are the LORD's eyes, which run back and forth through the whole earth."

11 Then I asked him, "What are these two olive trees on the right side of the lamp stand and on the left side of it?"

12 I asked him the second time, "What are these two olive branches, which are beside the two golden spouts that pour the golden oil out of themselves?"

13 He answered me, "Don't you know what these are?"

I said, "No, my lord."

14 Then he said, "These are the two anointed ones who stand by the Lord[c] of the whole earth."

5

1 Then again I lifted up my eyes and saw, and behold, a flying scroll. 2 He said to me, "What do you see?"

I answered, "I see a flying scroll; its length is twenty cubits,[d] and its width ten cubits."

3 Then he said to me, "This is the curse that goes out over the surface of the whole land, for everyone who steals shall be cut off according to it on the one side; and everyone who swears falsely shall be cut off according to it on the other side. 4 I will cause it to go out," says the LORD of Armies, "and it will enter into the house of the thief, and into the house of him who swears falsely by my name; and it will remain in the middle of his house, and will destroy it with its timber and its stones."

5 Then the angel who talked with me came forward and said to me, "Lift up now your eyes and see what this is that is appearing."

6 I said, "What is it?"

He said, "This is the ephah[e] basket that is appearing." He said moreover, "This is their appearance in all the land— 7 and behold, a lead cover weighing one talent[f] was lifted up—and there was a woman sitting in the middle of the ephah[g] basket." 8 He said, "This is Wickedness;" and he threw her down into the middle of the ephah basket; and he threw the lead weight on its mouth.

9 Then I lifted up my eyes and saw, and behold, there were two women; and the wind was in their wings. Now they had wings like the wings

---

a 1:1 When rendered in ALL CAPITAL LETTERS, "LORD" or "GOD" is the translation of God's Proper Name.

b 1:8 "Behold", from "הִנֵּה", means look at, take notice, observe, see, or gaze at. It is often used as an interjection.

c 4:14 The word translated "Lord" is "Adonai."

d 5:2 A cubit is the length from the tip of the middle finger to the elbow on a man's arm, or about 18 inches or 46 centimetres.

e 5:6 An ephah is a measure of volume of about 22 litres, 5.8 U. S. gallons, or about 2/3 of a bushel.

f 5:7 A talent is about 30 kilograms or 66 pounds.

g 5:7 1 ephah is about 22 litres or about 2/3 of a bushel

of a stork, and they lifted up the ephah basket between earth and the sky. 10 Then I said to the angel who talked with me, "Where are these carrying the ephah basket?"

11 He said to me, "To build her a house in the land of Shinar. When it is prepared, she will be set there in her own place."

6

1 Again I lifted up my eyes, and saw, and behold, four chariots came out from between two mountains; and the mountains were mountains of bronze. 2 In the first chariot were red horses. In the second chariot were black horses. 3 In the third chariot were white horses. In the fourth chariot were dappled horses, all of them powerful. 4 Then I asked the angel who talked with me, "What are these, my lord?"

5 The angel answered me, "These are the four winds of the sky, which go out from standing before the Lord of all the earth. 6 The one with the black horses goes out towards the north country; and the white went out after them; and the dappled went out towards the south country." 7 The strong went out, and sought to go that they might walk back and forth through the earth. He said, "Go around and through the earth!" So they walked back and forth through the earth.

8 Then he called to me, and spoke to me, saying, "Behold, those who go towards the north country have quieted my spirit in the north country."

9 The LORD's word came to me, saying, 10 "Take of them of the captivity, even of Heldai, of Tobijah, and of Jedaiah; and come the same day, and go into the house of Josiah the son of Zephaniah, where they have come from Babylon. 11 Yes, take silver and gold, and make crowns, and set them on the head of Joshua the son of Jehozadak, the high priest; 12 and speak to him, saying, 'The LORD of Armies says, "Behold, the man whose name is the Branch! He will grow up out of his place; and he will build the LORD's temple. 13 He will build the LORD's temple. He will bear the glory, and will sit and rule on his throne. He will be a priest on his throne. The counsel of peace will be between them both. 14 The crowns shall be to Helem, to Tobijah, to Jedaiah, and to Hen the son of Zephaniah, for a memorial in the LORD's temple.

15 Those who are far off shall come and build in the LORD's temple; and you shall know that the LORD of Armies has sent me to you. This will happen, if you will diligently obey the LORD your God's voice."""a

7

1 In the fourth year of King Darius, the LORD's word came to Zechariah in the fourth day of the ninth month, the month of Chislev. 2 The people of Bethel sent Sharezer and Regem Melech and their men to entreat the LORD's favour, 3 and to speak to the priests of the house of the LORD of Armies and to the prophets, saying, "Should I weep in the fifth month, separating myself, as I have done these so many years?"

4 Then the word of the LORD of Armies came to me, saying, 5 "Speak to all the people of the land and to the priests, saying, 'When you fasted and mourned in the fifth and in the seventh month for these seventy years, did you at all fast to me, really to me? 6 When you eat and when you drink, don't you eat for yourselves and drink for yourselves? 7 Aren't these the words which the LORD proclaimed by the former prophets when Jerusalem was inhabited and in prosperity, and its cities around her, and the South and the lowland were inhabited?'"

8 The LORD's word came to Zechariah, saying, 9 "Thus has the LORD of Armies spoken, saying, 'Execute true judgement, and show kindness and compassion every man to his brother. 10 Don't oppress the widow, the fatherless, the foreigner, nor the poor; and let none of you devise evil against his brother in your heart.' 11 But they refused to listen, and turned their backs, and stopped their ears, that they might not hear. 12 Yes, they made their hearts as hard as flint, lest they might hear the law and the words which the LORD of Armies had sent by his Spirit by the former prophets. Therefore great wrath came from the LORD of Armies. 13 It has come to pass that, as he called and they refused to listen, so they will call and I will not listen," said the LORD of Armies; 14 "but I will scatter them with a whirlwind amongst all the nations which they have not known. Thus the land was desolate after them, so that no man passed through nor returned; for they made the pleasant land desolate."

8

1 The word of the LORD of Armies came to me. 2 The LORD of Armies says: "I am jealous for Zion with great jealousy, and I am jealous for her with great wrath."

3 The LORD says: "I have returned to Zion, and will dwell in the middle of Jerusalem. Jerusalem shall be called 'The City of Truth;' and the mountain of the LORD of Armies, 'The Holy Mountain.'"

4 The LORD of Armies says: "Old men and old women will again dwell in the streets of Jerusalem, every man with his staff in his hand because of their old age. 5 The streets of the city will be full of boys and girls playing in its streets."

6 The LORD of Armies says: "If it is marvellous in the eyes of the remnant of this people in those days, should it also be marvellous in my eyes?" says the LORD of Armies.

7 The LORD of Armies says: "Behold, I will save my people from the east country and from the west country. 8 I will bring them, and they will dwell within Jerusalem. They will be my people, and I will be their God, in truth and in righteousness."

9 The LORD of Armies says: "Let your hands be strong, you who hear in these days these words from the mouth of the prophets who were in the day that the foundation of the house of the LORD of Armies was laid, even the temple, that it might be built. 10 For before those days there was no wages for man nor any wages for an animal, neither was there any peace to him who went out or came in, because of the adversary. For I set all men everyone against his neighbour. 11 But now I will not be to the remnant of this people as in the former days," says the LORD of Armies. 12 "For the seed of peace and the vine will yield its fruit, and the ground will give its increase, and the heavens will give their dew. I will cause the remnant of this people to inherit all these things. 13 It shall come to pass that, as you were a curse amongst the nations, house of Judah and house of Israel, so I will save you, and you shall be a blessing. Don't be afraid. Let your hands be strong."

14 For the LORD of Armies says: "As I thought to do evil to you when your fathers provoked me to wrath," says the LORD of Armies, "and I didn't repent, 15 so again I have thought in these days to do good to Jerusalem and to the house of Judah. Don't be afraid. 16 These are the things that you shall do: speak every man the truth with his neighbour. Execute the judgement of truth and peace in your gates, 17 and let none of you devise evil in your hearts against his neighbour, and love no false oath; for all these are things that I hate," says the LORD.

18 The word of the LORD of Armies came to me. 19 The LORD of Armies says: "The fasts of the fourth, fifth, seventh, and tenth months shall be for the house of Judah joy, gladness, and cheerful feasts. Therefore love truth and peace."

20 The LORD of Armies says: "Many peoples and the inhabitants of many cities will yet come. 21 The inhabitants of one will go to another, saying, 'Let's go speedily to entreat the favour of the LORD, and to seek the LORD of Armies. I will go also.' 22 Yes, many peoples and strong nations will come to seek the LORD of Armies in Jerusalem and to entreat the favour of the LORD." 23 The LORD of Armies says: "In those days, ten men out of all the languages of the nations will take hold of the skirt of him who is a Jew, saying, 'We will go with you, for we have heard that God is with you.'"

9

1 A revelation.

The LORD's word is against the land of Hadrach,
 and will rest upon Damascus—
for the eye of man
 and of all the tribes of Israel is towards the LORD—
2 and Hamath, also, which borders on it,
 Tyre and Sidon, because they are very wise.
3 Tyre built herself a stronghold,
 and heaped up silver like the dust,
 and fine gold like the mire of the streets.
4 Behold, the Lord will dispossess her,
 and he will strike her power in the sea;
 and she will be devoured with fire.

5 Ashkelon will see it, and fear;
 Gaza also, and will writhe in agony;
 as will Ekron, for her expectation will be disappointed;
 and the king will perish from Gaza,
 and Ashkelon will not be inhabited.
6 Foreigners will dwell in Ashdod,
 and I will cut off the pride of the Philistines.
7 I will take away his blood out of his mouth,
 and his abominations from between his teeth;
and he also will be a remnant for our God;
 and he will be as a chieftain in Judah,
 and Ekron as a Jebusite.
8 I will encamp around my house against the army,
 that no one pass through or return;
 and no oppressor will pass through them any more:
for now I have seen with my eyes.

9 Rejoice greatly, daughter of Zion!
 Shout, daughter of Jerusalem!
Behold, your King comes to you!
 He is righteous, and having salvation;
 lowly, and riding on a donkey,
 even on a colt, the foal of a donkey.
10 I will cut off the chariot from Ephraim
 and the horse from Jerusalem.
The battle bow will be cut off;
 and he will speak peace to the nations.
His dominion will be from sea to sea,
 and from the River to the ends of the earth.

11 As for you also,
 because of the blood of your covenant,
 I have set free your prisoners from the pit in which is no water.
12 Turn to the stronghold, you prisoners of hope!
 Even today I declare that I will restore double to you.
13 For indeed I bend Judah as a bow for me.
 I have loaded the bow with Ephraim.
I will stir up your sons, Zion,
 against your sons, Greece,

---

a *6:15* The Hebrew word rendered "God" is "אֱלֹהִים" (Elohim).

and will make you like the sword of a mighty man.

14 The LORD will be seen over them.
    His arrow will flash like lightning.
The Lord GOD will blow the trumpet,
    and will go with whirlwinds of the south.
15 The LORD of Armies will defend them.
    They will destroy and overcome with sling stones.
They will drink, and roar as through wine.
    They will be filled like bowls,
    like the corners of the altar.

16 The LORD their God will save them in that day as the flock of his people;
    for they are like the jewels of a crown,
    lifted on high over his land.
17 For how great is his goodness,
    and how great is his beauty!
Grain will make the young men flourish,
    and new wine the virgins.

10

1 Ask of the LORD rain in the spring time,
    the LORD who makes storm clouds,
    and he gives rain showers to everyone for the plants in the field.
2 For the teraphim[a] have spoken vanity,
    and the diviners have seen a lie;
    and they have told false dreams.
They comfort in vain.
    Therefore they go their way like sheep.
    They are oppressed, because there is no shepherd.

3 My anger is kindled against the shepherds,
    and I will punish the male goats,
for the LORD of Armies has visited his flock, the house of Judah,
    and will make them as his majestic horse in the battle.
4 From him will come the cornerstone,
    from him the tent peg,
    from him the battle bow,
    from him every ruler together.
5 They will be as mighty men,
    treading down muddy streets in the battle.
They will fight, because the LORD is with them.
    The riders on horses will be confounded.

6 "I will strengthen the house of Judah,
    and I will save the house of Joseph.
I will bring them back,
    for I have mercy on them.
They will be as though I had not cast them off,
    for I am the LORD their God, and I will hear them.
7 Ephraim will be like a mighty man,
    and their heart will rejoice as through wine.
Yes, their children will see it and rejoice.
    Their heart will be glad in the LORD.
8 I will signal for them and gather them,
    for I have redeemed them.
    They will increase as they were before.
9 I will sow them amongst the peoples.
    They will remember me in far countries.
    They will live with their children and will return.
10 I will bring them again also out of the land of Egypt,
    and gather them out of Assyria.
I will bring them into the land of Gilead and Lebanon;
    and there won't be room enough for them.
11 He will pass through the sea of affliction,
    and will strike the waves in the sea,
    and all the depths of the Nile will dry up;
    and the pride of Assyria will be brought down,
    and the sceptre of Egypt will depart.
12 I will strengthen them in the LORD.
    They will walk up and down in his name," says the LORD.

11

1 Open your doors, Lebanon,
    that the fire may devour your cedars.
2 Wail, cypress tree, for the cedar has fallen,
    because the stately ones are destroyed.
Wail, you oaks of Bashan,
    for the strong forest has come down.
3 A voice of the wailing of the shepherds!
    For their glory is destroyed—a voice of the roaring of young lions!
    For the pride of the Jordan is ruined.
4 The LORD my God says: "Feed the flock of slaughter. 5 Their buyers slaughter them and go unpunished. Those who sell them say, 'Blessed be the LORD, for I am rich;' and their own shepherds don't pity them. 6 For I will no more pity the inhabitants of the land," says the LORD; "but, behold, I will deliver every one of the men into his neighbour's hand and into the

hand of his king. They will strike the land, and out of their hand I will not deliver them."
7 So I fed the flock to be slaughtered, especially the oppressed of the flock. I took for myself two staffs. The one I called "Favour" and the other I called "Union", and I fed the flock. 8 I cut off the three shepherds in one month; for my soul was weary of them, and their soul also loathed me. 9 Then I said, "I will not feed you. That which dies, let it die; and that which is to be cut off, let it be cut off; and let those who are left eat each other's flesh." 10 I took my staff Favour and cut it apart, that I might break my covenant that I had made with all the peoples. 11 It was broken in that day; and thus the poor of the flock that listened to me knew that it was the LORD's word. 12 I said to them, "If you think it best, give me my wages; and if not, keep them." So they weighed for my wages thirty pieces of silver. 13 The LORD said to me, "Throw it to the potter—the handsome price that I was valued at by them!" I took the thirty pieces of silver and threw them to the potter in the LORD's house. 14 Then I cut apart my other staff, Union, that I might break the brotherhood between Judah and Israel.
15 The LORD said to me, "Take for yourself yet again the equipment of a foolish shepherd. 16 For, behold, I will raise up a shepherd in the land who will not visit those who are cut off, neither will seek those who are scattered, nor heal that which is broken, nor feed that which is sound; but he will eat the meat of the fat sheep, and will tear their hoofs in pieces. 17 Woe to the worthless shepherd who leaves the flock! The sword will strike his arm and his right eye. His arm will be completely withered, and his right eye will be totally blinded!"

12

1 A revelation of the LORD's word concerning Israel: The LORD, who stretches out the heavens and lays the foundation of the earth, and forms the spirit of man within him says: 2 "Behold, I will make Jerusalem a cup of reeling to all the surrounding peoples, and it will also be on Judah in the siege against Jerusalem. 3 It will happen in that day that I will make Jerusalem a burdensome stone for all the peoples. All who burden themselves with it will be severely wounded, and all the nations of the earth will be gathered together against it. 4 In that day," says the LORD, "I will strike every horse with terror and his rider with madness. I will open my eyes on the house of Judah, and will strike every horse of the peoples with blindness. 5 The chieftains of Judah will say in their heart, 'The inhabitants of Jerusalem are my strength in the LORD of Armies their God.'
6 In that day I will make the chieftains of Judah like a pan of fire amongst wood, and like a flaming torch amongst sheaves. They will devour all the surrounding peoples on the right hand and on the left; and Jerusalem will yet again dwell in their own place, even in Jerusalem.
7 The LORD also will save the tents of Judah first, that the glory of David's house and the glory of the inhabitants of Jerusalem not be magnified above Judah. 8 In that day the LORD will defend the inhabitants of Jerusalem. He who is feeble amongst them at that day will be like David, and David's house will be like God, like the LORD's angel before them. 9 It will happen in that day, that I will seek to destroy all the nations that come against Jerusalem.
10 I will pour on David's house and on the inhabitants of Jerusalem the spirit of grace and of supplication. They will look to me[b] whom they have pierced; and they shall mourn for him as one mourns for his only son, and will grieve bitterly for him as one grieves for his firstborn. 11 In that day there will be a great mourning in Jerusalem, like the mourning of Hadadrimmon in the valley of Megiddo. 12 The land will mourn, every family apart; the family of David's house apart, and their wives apart; the family of the house of Nathan apart, and their wives apart; 13 the family of the house of Levi apart, and their wives apart; the family of the Shimeites apart, and their wives apart; 14 all the families who remain, every family apart, and their wives apart.

13

1 "In that day there will be a fountain opened to David's house and to the inhabitants of Jerusalem, for sin and for uncleanness.
2 It will come to pass in that day, says the LORD of Armies, that I will cut off the names of the idols out of the land, and they will be remembered no more. I will also cause the prophets and the spirit of impurity to pass out of the land. 3 It will happen that when anyone still prophesies, then his father and his mother who bore him will tell him, 'You must die, because you speak lies in the LORD's name;' and his father and his mother who bore him will stab him when he prophesies. 4 It will happen in that day that the prophets will each be ashamed of his vision when he prophesies; they won't wear a hairy mantle to deceive, 5 but he will say, 'I am no prophet, I am a tiller of the ground; for I have been made a bondservant from my youth.' 6 One will say to him, 'What are these wounds between your arms?' Then he will answer, 'Those with which I was wounded in the house of my friends.'

7 "Awake, sword, against my shepherd,
    and against the man who is close to me," says the LORD of Armies.
"Strike the shepherd, and the sheep will be scattered;
    and I will turn my hand against the little ones.
8 It shall happen that in all the land," says the LORD,
    "two parts in it will be cut off and die;
    but the third will be left in it.
9 I will bring the third part into the fire,

---

a 10:2 teraphim were household idols that may have been associated with inheritance rights to the household property.

b 12:10 After "me", the Hebrew has the two letters "Aleph Tav" (the first and last letters of the Hebrew alphabet), not as a word, but as a grammatical marker.

and will refine them as silver is refined,
and will test them like gold is tested.
They will call on my name, and I will hear them.
I will say, 'It is my people;'
and they will say, 'The LORD is my God.'"

14

1 Behold, a day of the LORD comes, when your plunder will be divided within you. 2 For I will gather all nations against Jerusalem to battle; and the city will be taken, the houses rifled, and the women ravished. Half of the city will go out into captivity, and the rest of the people will not be cut off from the city. 3 Then the LORD will go out and fight against those nations, as when he fought in the day of battle. 4 His feet will stand in that day on the Mount of Olives, which is before Jerusalem on the east; and the Mount of Olives will be split in two from east to west, making a very great valley. Half of the mountain will move towards the north, and half of it towards the south. 5 You shall flee by the valley of my mountains, for the valley of the mountains shall reach to Azel. Yes, you shall flee, just like you fled from before the earthquake in the days of Uzziah king of Judah. The LORD my God will come, and all the holy ones with you.[a]

6 It will happen in that day that there will not be light, cold, or frost. 7 It will be a unique day which is known to the LORD—not day, and not night; but it will come to pass that at evening time there will be light.

8 It will happen in that day that living waters will go out from Jerusalem, half of them towards the eastern sea, and half of them towards the western sea. It will be so in summer and in winter.

9 The LORD will be King over all the earth. In that day the LORD will be one, and his name one.

10 All the land will be made like the Arabah, from Geba to Rimmon south of Jerusalem; and she will be lifted up and will dwell in her place, from Benjamin's gate to the place of the first gate, to the corner gate, and from the tower of Hananel to the king's wine presses. 11 Men will dwell therein, and there will be no more curse; but Jerusalem will dwell safely.

12 This will be the plague with which the LORD will strike all the peoples who have fought against Jerusalem: their flesh will consume away while they stand on their feet, and their eyes will consume away in their sockets, and their tongue will consume away in their mouth. 13 It will happen in that day that a great panic from the LORD will be amongst them; and they will each seize the hand of his neighbour, and his hand will rise up against the hand of his neighbour. 14 Judah also will fight at Jerusalem; and the wealth of all the surrounding nations will be gathered together: gold, silver, and clothing, in great abundance.

15 A plague like this will fall on the horse, on the mule, on the camel, on the donkey, and on all the animals that will be in those camps.

16 It will happen that everyone who is left of all the nations that came against Jerusalem will go up from year to year to worship the King, the LORD of Armies, and to keep the feast of booths. 17 It will be that whoever of all the families of the earth doesn't go up to Jerusalem to worship the King, the LORD of Armies, on them there will be no rain. 18 If the family of Egypt doesn't go up and doesn't come, neither will it rain on them. This will be the plague with which the LORD will strike the nations that don't go up to keep the feast of booths. 19 This will be the punishment of Egypt and the punishment of all the nations that don't go up to keep the feast of booths.

20 In that day there will be inscribed on the bells of the horses, "HOLY TO THE LORD"; and the pots in the LORD's house will be like the bowls before the altar. 21 Yes, every pot in Jerusalem and in Judah will be holy to the LORD of Armies; and all those who sacrifice will come and take of them, and cook in them. In that day there will no longer be a Canaanite[b] in the house of the LORD of Armies.

---

[a] *14:5* Septuagint reads "him" instead of "you".

[b] *14:21* or, merchant

The Book of Malachi

1

1 A revelation, the LORD's[a] word to Israel by Malachi.

2 "I have loved you," says the LORD.

Yet you say, "How have you loved us?"

"Wasn't Esau Jacob's brother?" says the LORD, "Yet I loved Jacob; 3 but Esau I hated, and made his mountains a desolation, and gave his heritage to the jackals of the wilderness." 4 Whereas Edom says, "We are beaten down, but we will return and build the waste places," the LORD of Armies says, "They shall build, but I will throw down; and men will call them 'The Wicked Land,' even the people against whom the LORD shows wrath forever."

5 Your eyes will see, and you will say, "The LORD is great—even beyond the border of Israel!"

6 "A son honours his father, and a servant his master. If I am a father, then where is my honour? And if I am a master, where is the respect due me?" says the LORD of Armies to you priests who despise my name. "You say, 'How have we despised your name?' 7 You offer polluted bread on my altar. You say, 'How have we polluted you?' In that you say, 'The LORD's table is contemptible.' 8 When you offer the blind for sacrifice, isn't that evil? And when you offer the lame and sick, isn't that evil? Present it now to your governor! Will he be pleased with you? Or will he accept your person?" says the LORD of Armies.

9 "Now, please entreat the favour of God,[b] that he may be gracious to us. With this, will he accept any of you?" says the LORD of Armies.

10 "Oh that there were one amongst you who would shut the doors, that you might not kindle fire on my altar in vain! I have no pleasure in you," says the LORD of Armies, "neither will I accept an offering at your hand. 11 For from the rising of the sun even to its going down, my name is great amongst the nations, and in every place incense will be offered to my name, and a pure offering; for my name is great amongst the nations," says the LORD of Armies. 12 "But you profane it when you say, 'The LORD's table is polluted, and its fruit, even its food, is contemptible.' 13 You say also, 'Behold,[c] what a weariness it is!' And you have sniffed at it", says the LORD of Armies; "and you have brought that which was taken by violence, the lame, and the sick; thus you bring the offering. Should I accept this at your hand?" says the LORD.

14 "But the deceiver is cursed who has in his flock a male, and vows and sacrifices to the Lord[d] a defective thing; for I am a great King," says the LORD of Armies, "and my name is awesome amongst the nations."

2

1 "Now, you priests, this commandment is for you. 2 If you will not listen, and if you will not take it to heart, to give glory to my name," says the LORD of Armies, "then I will send the curse on you, and I will curse your blessings. Indeed, I have cursed them already, because you do not take it to heart. 3 Behold, I will rebuke your offspring,[e] and will spread dung on your faces, even the dung of your feasts; and you will be taken away with it. 4 You will know that I have sent this commandment to you, that my covenant may be with Levi," says the LORD of Armies. 5 "My covenant was with him of life and peace; and I gave them to him that he might be reverent towards me; and he was reverent towards me, and stood in awe of my name. 6 The law of truth was in his mouth, and unrighteousness was not found in his lips. He walked with me in peace and uprightness, and turned many away from iniquity. 7 For the priest's lips should keep knowledge, and they should seek the law at his mouth; for he is the messenger of the LORD of Armies. 8 But you have turned away from the path. You have caused many to stumble in the law. You have corrupted the covenant of Levi," says the LORD of Armies. 9 "Therefore I have also made you contemptible and wicked before all the people, according to the way you have not kept my ways, but have had respect for persons in the law. 10 Don't we all have one father? Hasn't one God created us? Why do we deal treacherously every man against his brother, profaning the covenant of our fathers? 11 Judah has dealt treacherously, and an abomination is committed in Israel and in Jerusalem; for Judah has profaned the holiness of the LORD which he loves, and has married the daughter of a foreign god. 12 The LORD will cut off the man who does this, him who wakes and him who answers, out of the tents of Jacob and him who offers an offering to the LORD of Armies.

13 "This again you do: you cover the LORD's altar with tears, with weeping, and with sighing, because he doesn't regard the offering any more, neither receives it with good will at your hand. 14 Yet you say, 'Why?' Because the LORD has been witness between you and the wife of your youth, against whom you have dealt treacherously, though she is your companion and the wife of your covenant. 15 Did he not make you one, although he had the residue of the Spirit? Why one? He sought godly offspring. Therefore take heed to your spirit, and let no one deal treacherously against the wife of his youth. 16 One who hates and divorces", says the LORD, the God of Israel, "covers his garment with violence!" says the LORD of Armies. "Therefore pay attention to your spirit, that you don't be unfaithful.

17 You have wearied the LORD with your words. Yet you say, 'How have we wearied him?' In that you say, 'Everyone who does evil is good in the LORD's sight, and he delights in them;' or 'Where is the God of justice?'

3

1 "Behold, I send my messenger, and he will prepare the way before me! The Lord, whom you seek, will suddenly come to his temple. Behold, the messenger of the covenant, whom you desire, is coming!" says the LORD of Armies. 2 "But who can endure the day of his coming? And who will stand when he appears? For he is like a refiner's fire, and like launderers' soap; 3 and he will sit as a refiner and purifier of silver, and he will purify the sons of Levi, and refine them as gold and silver; and they shall offer to the LORD offerings in righteousness. 4 Then the offering of Judah and Jerusalem will be pleasant to the LORD as in the days of old and as in ancient years.

5 I will come near to you to judgement. I will be a swift witness against the sorcerers, against the adulterers, against the perjurers, and against those who oppress the hireling in his wages, the widow, and the fatherless, and who deprive the foreigner of justice, and don't fear me," says the LORD of Armies.

6 "For I, the LORD, don't change; therefore you, sons of Jacob, are not consumed. 7 From the days of your fathers you have turned away from my ordinances and have not kept them. Return to me, and I will return to you," says the LORD of Armies. "But you say, 'How shall we return?'

8 Will a man rob God? Yet you rob me! But you say, 'How have we robbed you?' In tithes and offerings. 9 You are cursed with the curse; for you rob me, even this whole nation. 10 Bring the whole tithe into the storehouse, that there may be food in my house, and test me now in this," says the LORD of Armies, "if I will not open you the windows of heaven, and pour you out a blessing, that there will not be enough room for. 11 I will rebuke the devourer for your sakes, and he shall not destroy the fruits of your ground; neither shall your vine cast its fruit before its time in the field," says the LORD of Armies. 12 "All nations shall call you blessed, for you will be a delightful land," says the LORD of Armies.

13 "Your words have been harsh against me," says the LORD. "Yet you say, 'What have we spoken against you?' 14 You have said, 'It is vain to serve God,' and 'What profit is it that we have followed his instructions and that we have walked mournfully before the LORD of Armies? 15 Now we call the proud happy; yes, those who work wickedness are built up; yes, they tempt God, and escape.'

16 Then those who feared the LORD spoke one with another; and the LORD listened and heard, and a book of memory was written before him for those who feared the LORD and who honoured his name. 17 They shall be mine," says the LORD of Armies, "my own possession in the day that I make. I will spare them, as a man spares his own son who serves him. 18 Then you shall return and discern between the righteous and the wicked, between him who serves God and him who doesn't serve him.

4

1 "For behold, the day comes, burning like a furnace, when all the proud and all who work wickedness will be stubble. The day that comes will burn them up," says the LORD of Armies, "so that it will leave them neither root nor branch. 2 But to you who fear my name shall the sun of righteousness arise with healing in its wings. You will go out and leap like calves of the stall. 3 You shall tread down the wicked; for they will be ashes under the soles of your feet in the day that I make," says the LORD of Armies.

4 "Remember the law of Moses my servant, which I commanded to him in Horeb for all Israel, even statutes and ordinances.

5 Behold, I will send you Elijah the prophet before the great and terrible day of the LORD comes. 6 He will turn the hearts of the fathers to the children and the hearts of the children to their fathers, lest I come and strike the earth with a curse."

---

a *1:1* When rendered in ALL CAPITAL LETTERS, "LORD" or "GOD" is the translation of God's Proper Name.

b *1:9* The Hebrew word rendered "God" is "אֱלֹהִים" (Elohim).

c *1:13* "Behold", from "הִנֵּה", means look at, take notice, observe, see, or gaze at. It is often used as an interjection.

d *1:14* The word translated "Lord" is "Adonai."

e *2:3* or, seed

Tobit

Tobit is recognised as Deuterocanonical Scripture by the Roman Catholic, Greek Orthodox, and Russian Orthodox Churches.

1

1 The book of the words of Tobit, the son of Tobiel, the son of Ananiel, the son of Aduel, the son of Gabael, of the seed of Asiel, of the tribe of Naphtali; 2 who in the days of Enemessar[a] king of the Assyrians was carried away captive out of Thisbe, which is on the right hand of Kedesh Naphtali in Galilee above Asher.

3 I, Tobit walked in the ways of truth and righteousness all the days of my life, and I did many alms deeds to my kindred and my nation, who went with me into the land of the Assyrians, to Nineveh. 4 When I was in my own country, in the land of Israel, while I was yet young, all the tribe of Naphtali my father fell away from the house of Jerusalem, which was chosen out of all the tribes of Israel, that all the tribes should sacrifice there, and the temple of the habitation of the Most High was hallowed and built therein for all ages. 5 All the tribes which fell away together sacrificed to the heifer Baal, and so did the house of Naphtali my father. 6 I alone went often to Jerusalem at the feasts, as it has been ordained to all Israel by an everlasting decree, having the first fruits and the tenths of my increase, and that which was first shorn; and I gave them at the altar to the priests the sons of Aaron. 7 I gave a tenth part of all my increase to the sons of Levi, who ministered at Jerusalem. A second tenth part I sold away, and went, and spent it each year at Jerusalem. 8 A third tenth I gave to them to whom it was appropriate, as Deborah my father's mother had commanded me, because I was left an orphan by my father. 9 When I became a man, I took as wife Anna of the seed of our own family. With her, I became the father of Tobias. 10 When I was carried away captive to Nineveh, all my kindred and my relatives ate of the bread of the Gentiles; 11 but I kept myself from eating, 12 because I remembered God with all my soul. 13 So the Most High gave me grace and favour[b] in the sight of Enemessar, and I was his purchasing agent. 14 And I went into Media, and left ten talents of silver in trust with Gabael, the brother of Gabrias, at Rages of Media.

15 And when Enemessar was dead, Sennacherib his son reigned in his place. In his time, the highways were troubled,[c] and I could no longer go into Media. 16 In the days of Enemessar, I did many alms deeds to my kindred: I gave my bread to the hungry, 17 and my garments to the naked. If I saw any of my race dead, and thrown out on[d] the wall of Nineveh, I buried him. 18 If Sennacherib the king killed any, when he came fleeing from Judea, I buried them privately; for in his wrath he killed many; and the bodies were sought for by the king, and were not found. 19 But one of the Ninevites went and showed to the king concerning me, how I buried them, and hid myself; and when I knew that I was sought for to be put to death, I withdrew myself for fear. 20 And all my goods were forcibly taken away, and there was nothing left to me, save my wife Anna and my son Tobias. 21 No more than fifty five days passed before two of his sons killed him, and they fled into the mountains of Ararat. And Sarchedonus[e] his son reigned in his place; and he appointed Achiacharus my brother Anael's son over all the accounts of his kingdom, and over all his affairs. 22 Achiacharus requested me, and I came to Nineveh. Now Achiacharus was cupbearer, keeper of the signet, steward, and overseer of the accounts. Sarchedonus appointed him next to himself, but he was my brother's son.

2

1 Now when I had come home again, and my wife Anna was restored to me, and my son Tobias, in the feast of Pentecost, which is the holy feast of the seven weeks, there was a good dinner prepared for me, and I sat down to eat. 2 I saw abundance of meat, and I said to my son, "Go and bring whatever poor man you find of our kindred, who is mindful of the Lord. Behold, I wait for you."

3 Then he came, and said, "Father, one of our race is strangled, and has been cast out in the marketplace." 4 Before I had tasted anything, I sprang up, and took him up into a chamber until the sun had set. 5 Then I returned, washed myself, ate my bread in heaviness, 6 and remembered the prophecy of Amos, as he said,
"'Your feasts will be turned into mourning,
and all your mirth into lamentation.'[**]

7 So I wept: and when the sun had set, I went and dug a grave, and buried him. 8 My neighbours mocked me, and said, "He is no longer afraid to be put to death for this matter; and yet he fled away. Behold, he buries the dead again." 9 The same night I returned from burying him, and slept by the wall of my courtyard, being polluted; and my face was uncovered. 10 I didn't know that there were sparrows in the wall. My eyes were open and the sparrows dropped warm dung into my eyes, and white films came over my eyes. I went to the physicians, and they didn't help me; but Achiacharus nourished me, until I went[f] into Elymais.

11 My wife Anna wove cloth in the women's chambers, 12 and sent the work back to the owners. They on their part paid her wages, and also gave her a kid. 13 But when it came to my house, it began to cry, and I said to her,

"Where did this kid come from? Is it stolen? Give it back to the owners; for it is not lawful to eat anything that is stolen." 14 But she said, "It has been given to me for a gift more than the wages."

I didn't believe her, and I asked her to return it to the owners; and I was ashamed of her.

But she answered and said to me, "Where are your alms and your righteous deeds? Behold, you and all your works are known.[g]"

3

1 I was grieved and wept, and prayed in sorrow, saying,

2 O Lord, you are righteous, and all your works and all your ways are mercy and truth, and you judge true and righteous judgement forever. 3 Remember me, and look at me. Don't take vengeance on me for my sins and my ignorances, and the sins of my fathers who sinned before you. 4 For they disobeyed your commandments. You gave us as plunder, for captivity, for death, and for a proverb of reproach to all the nations amongst whom we are dispersed. 5 Now your judgements are many and true, that you should deal with me according to my sins and the sins of my fathers, because we didn't keep your commandments, for we didn't walk in truth before you. 6 Now deal with me according to that which is pleasing in your sight. Command my spirit to be taken from me, that I may be released, and become earth. For it is more profitable for me to die rather than to live, because I have heard false reproaches, and there is much sorrow in me. Command that I be released from my distress, now, and go to the everlasting place. Don't turn your face away from me."

7 The same day it happened to Sarah the daughter of Raguel in Ecbatana of Media, that she also was reproached by her father's maidservants; 8 because that she had been given to seven husbands, and Asmodaeus the evil spirit[h] killed them, before they had lain with her. And they said to her, "Do you not know that you strangle your husbands? You have had already seven husbands, and you haven't borne the name of any one of them. 9 Why do you scourge us? If they are dead, go your ways with them. Let us never see either son or daughter from you." 10 When she heard these things, she was grieved exceedingly, so that she thought about hanging herself. Then she said, "I am the only daughter of my father. If I do this, it will be a reproach to him, and I will bring down his old age with sorrow to the grave." 11 Then she prayed by the window, and said, "Blessed are you, O Lord my God, and blessed is your holy and honourable name forever! Let all your works praise you forever! 12 And now, Lord, I have set my eyes and my face towards you. 13 Command that I be released from the earth, and that I no longer hear reproach. 14 You know, Lord, that I am pure from all sin with man, 15 and that I never polluted my name or the name of my father in the land of my captivity. I am the only daughter of my father, and he has no child that will be his heir, nor brother near him, nor son belonging to him, that I should keep myself for a wife to him. Seven husbands of mine are dead already. Why should I live? If it doesn't please you to kill me, command some regard to be had of me, and pity taken of me, and that I hear no more reproach."

16 The prayer of both was heard before the glory of the great God. 17 Raphael also was sent to heal them both, to scale away the white films from Tobit's eyes, and to give Sarah the daughter of Raguel for a wife to Tobias the son of Tobit; and to bind Asmodaeus the evil spirit[i]; because it belonged to Tobias that he should inherit her. At that very time, Tobit returned and entered into his house, and Sarah the daughter of Raguel came down from her upper chamber.

4

1 In that day Tobit remembered the money which he had left in trust with Gabael in Rages of Media, 2 and he said to himself, I have asked for death; why do I not call my son Tobias, that I may explain to him about the money before I die? 3 And he called him, and said,

"My child, if I die, bury me. Don't despise your mother. Honour her all the days of your life, and do that which is pleasing to her, and don't grieve her. 4 Remember, my child, that she has seen many dangers for you, when you were in her womb. When she is dead, bury her by me in one grave. 5 My child, be mindful of the Lord our God all your days, and don't let your will be set to sin and to transgress his commandments: do righteousness all the days of your life, and don't follow the ways of unrighteousness. 6 For if you do what is true, your deeds will prosperously succeed for you, and for all those who do righteousness. 7 Give alms from your possessions. When you give alms, don't let your eye be envious. Don't turn away your face from any poor man, and the face of God won't be turned away from you. 8 As your possessions are, give alms of it according to your abundance. If you have little, don't be afraid to give alms according to that little; 9 for you lay up a good treasure for yourself against the day of necessity; 10 because alms-giving delivers from death, and doesn't allow you to come into darkness. 11 Alms is a good gift in the sight of the Most High for all that give it. 12 Beware, my child, of all fornication, and take first a wife of the seed of your fathers. Don't take a strange wife, who is not of your father's tribe; for we are the descendants of the prophets. Remember, my child, that Noah, Abraham, Isaac, and Jacob, our fathers of old time, all took wives of their kindred, and were blessed in their children, and their seed will inherit the land. 13 And now, my child, love your kindred, and don't scorn your kindred

---

a *1:2* That is, Shalmaneser. Compare 2 Kings 17:3, 23.
b *1:13* Gr. beauty.
c *1:15* Gr. his highways were troubled.
d *1:17* Some ancient authorities read behind.
e *1:21* That is, Esar-haddon, and so in verse 22.
** 2:6 Amos 8:10

f *2:10* Some authorities read until he went.
g *2:14* Gr. all things are known with you.
h *3:8* Gr. demon.
i *3:10* Gr. Hades.
j *3:17* Gr. demon.

and the sons and the daughters of your people in your heart, to take a wife of them; for in scornfulness is destruction and much trouble, and in idleness is decay and great lack; for idleness is the mother of famine. 14 Don't let the wages of any man who works for you wait with you, but give it to him out of hand. If you serve God, you will be rewarded. Take heed to yourself, my child, in all your works, and be discreet in all your behaviour. 15 And what you yourself hate, do to no man. Don't drink wine to drunkenness, and don't let drunkenness go with you on your way. 16 Give of your bread to the hungry, and of your garments to those who are naked. Give alms from all your abundance. Don't let your eye be envious when you give alms. 17 Pour out your bread on the burial[a] of the just, and give nothing to sinners. 18 Ask counsel of every man who is wise, and don't despise any counsel that is profitable. 19 Bless the Lord your God at all times, and ask of him that your ways may be made straight, and that all your paths and counsels may prosper; for every nation has no counsel; but the Lord himself gives all good things, and he humbles whom he will, as he will. And now, my child, remember my commandments, and let them not be blotted out of your mind. 20 And now I explain to you about the ten talents of silver, which I left in trust with Gabael the son of Gabrias at Rages of Media. 21 And fear not, my child, because we are made poor. You have much wealth, if you fear God, and depart from all sin, and do that which is pleasing in his sight."

5

1 Then Tobias answered and said to him, "Father, I will do all things, whatever you have commanded me. 2 But how could I receive the money, since I don't know him?"

3 He gave him the handwriting, and said to him, "Seek a man who will go with you, and I will give him wages, while I still live; and go and receive the money."

4 He went to seek a man, and found Raphael who was an angel; 5 and he didn't know it. He said to him, "Can I go with you to Rages of Media? Do you know those places well?"

6 The angel said to him, "I will go with you. I know the way well. I have lodged with our brother Gabael."

7 Tobias said to him, "Wait for me, and I will tell my father."

8 He said to him, "Go, and don't wait. And he went in and said to his father, "Behold, I have found someone who will go with me."

But he said, "Call him to me, that I may know of what tribe he is, and whether he be a trustworthy man to go with you."

9 So he called him, and he came in, and they saluted one another. 10 And Tobit said to him, "Brother, of what tribe and of what family are you? Tell me."

11 He said to him, "Do you seek a tribe and a family, or a hired man which will go with your son?"

And Tobit said to him, "I want to know, brother, your kindred and your name."

12 And he said, "I am Azarias, the son of Ananias the great, of your kindred."

13 And he said to him, "Welcome, brother. Don't be angry with me, because I sought to know your tribe and family. You are my brother, of an honest and good lineage; for I knew Ananias and Jathan, the sons of Shemaiah the great, when we went together to Jerusalem to worship, and offered the firstborn, and the tenths of our increase; and they didn't go astray in the error of our kindred. My brother, you are of a great stock. 14 But tell me, what wages shall I give you? A drachma a day, and those things that be necessary for you, as to my son? 15 And moreover, if you both return safe and sound, I will add something to your wages."

16 And so they agreed. And he said to Tobias, "Prepare yourself for the journey. May God prosper you." So his son prepared what was needful for the journey, and his father said to him, "Go with this man; but God, who dwells in heaven, will prosper your journey. May his angel go with you."

Then they both departed, and the young man's dog went with them.

17 But Anna his mother wept, and said to Tobit, "Why have you sent away our child? Isn't he the staff of our hand, in going in and out before us? 18 Don't be greedy to add money to money; but let it be as refuse compared to our child. 19 For what the Lord has given us to live is enough for us."

20 Tobit said to her, "Don't worry, my sister. He will return safe and sound, and your eyes will see him. 21 For a good angel will go with him. His journey will be prospered, and he will return safe and sound."

22 So she stopped weeping.

6

1 Now as they went on their journey, they came at evening to the river Tigris, and they lodged there. 2 But the young man went down to wash himself, and a fish leapt out of the river, and would have swallowed up the young man. 3 But the angel said to him, "Grab the fish!"

So the young man grabbed the fish, and hauled it up onto the land.

4 And the angel said to him, "Cut the fish open, and take the heart, the liver, and the bile, and keep them with you." 5 And the young man did as the angel commanded him; but they roasted the fish, and ate it. And they both went on their way, till they drew near to Ecbatana.

6 The young man said to the angel, "Brother Azarias, of what use is the heart, the liver, and the bile of the fish?"

7 He said to him, "About the heart and the liver: If a demon or an evil spirit troubles anyone, we must burn those and make smoke of them before the man or the woman, and the affliction will flee. 8 But as for the bile, it is

good to anoint a man that has white films in his eyes, and he will be healed."

9 But when they drew near to Rages, 10 the angel said to the young man, "Brother, today we will lodge with Raguel. He is your kinsman. He has an only daughter named Sarah. I will speak about her, that she should be given to you for a wife. 11 For her inheritance belongs to you, and you only are of her kindred. 12 The maid is fair and wise. And now hear me, and I will speak to her father. When we return from Rages we will celebrate the marriage; for I know that Raguel may in no way marry her to another according to the law of Moses, or else he would be liable to death, because it belongs to you to take the inheritance, rather than any other."

13 Then the young man said to the angel, "Brother Azarias, I have heard that this maid has been given to seven men, and that they all perished in the bride-chamber. 14 Now I am the only son of my father, and I am afraid, lest I go in and die, even as those before me. For a demon loves her, which harms no man, but those which come to her. Now I fear lest I die, and bring my father's and my mother's life to the grave with sorrow because of me. They have no other son to bury them."

15 But the angel said to him, "Don't you remember the words which your father commanded you, that you should take a wife of your own kindred? Now hear me, brother; for she will be your wife. Don't worry about the demon; for this night she will be given you as wife. 16 And when[b] you come into the bride-chamber, you shall take the ashes of incense, and shall lay upon them some of the heart and liver of the fish, and shall make smoke with them. 17 The demon will smell it, and flee away, and never come again any more. But when you go near to her, both of you rise up, and cry to God who is merciful. He will save you, and have mercy on you. Don't be afraid, for she was prepared for you from the beginning; and you will save her, and she will go with you. And I suppose that you will have children with her."

When Tobias heard these things, he loved her, and his soul was strongly joined to her.

7

1 They came to Ecbatana, and arrived at the house of Raguel. But Sarah met them; and she greeted them, and they her. Then she brought them into the house. 2 Raguel said to Edna his wife, "This young man really resembles Tobit my cousin!" 3 And Raguel asked them, "Where are you two from, kindred?"

They said to him, "We are of the sons of Naphtali, who are captives in Nineveh."

4 He said to them, "Do you know Tobit our brother?"

They said, "We know him."

Then he said to them, "Is he in good health?"

5 They said, "He is both alive, and in good health." Tobias said, "He is my father."

6 And Raguel sprang up, and kissed him, wept, 7 blessed him, and said to him, "You are the son of an honest and good man." When he had heard that Tobit had lost his sight, he was grieved, and wept; 8 and Edna his wife and Sarah his daughter wept. They received them gladly; and they killed a ram of the flock, and served them meat.

But Tobias said to Raphael, "Brother Azarias, speak of those things of which you talked about in the way, and let the matter be finished."

9 So he communicated the thing to Raguel. Raguel said to Tobias, "Eat, drink, and make merry; 10 for it belongs to you to take my child. However I will tell you the truth. 11 I have given my child to seven men of our relatives, and whenever they came in to her, they died in the night. But for the present be merry."

And Tobias said, "I will taste nothing here, until you all make a covenant and enter into that covenant with me."

12 Raguel said, "Take her to yourself from now on according to custom. You are her relative, and she is yours. The merciful God will give all good success to you." 13 And he called his daughter Sarah, and took her by the hand, and gave her to be wife of Tobias, and said, "Behold, take her to yourself after the law of Moses, and lead her away to your father." And he blessed them. 14 He called Edna his wife, then took a book, wrote a contract, and sealed it. 15 Then they began to eat.

16 And Raguel called his wife Edna, and said to her, "Sister, prepare the other chamber, and bring her in there." 17 She did as he asked her, and brought her in there. She wept, and she received the tears of her daughter, and said to her, 18 "Be comforted, my child. May the Lord of heaven and earth give you favour[c] for this your sorrow. Be comforted, my daughter."

8

1 When they had finished their supper, they brought Tobias in to her. 2 But as he went, he remembered the words of Raphael, and took the ashes of the incense, and put the heart and the liver of the fish on them, and made smoke with them. 3 When the demon smelled that smell, it fled into the uppermost parts of Egypt, and the angel bound him. 4 But after they were both shut in together, Tobias rose up from the bed, and said, "Sister, arise, and let's pray that the Lord may have mercy on us." 5 And Tobias began to say, "Blessed are you, O God of our fathers, and blessed is your holy and glorious name forever. Let the heavens bless you, and all your creatures. 6 You made Adam, and gave him Eve his wife for a helper and support. From them came the seed of men. You said, it is not good that the man should be alone. Let's make him a helper like him. 7 And now, O Lord, I take not this my sister for lust, but in truth. Command that I may find mercy and grow old with her."

---

a *4:17* Or, tomb
b *6:16* Gr. if.

c *7:18* Many ancient authorities read joy.

8 She said with him, "Amen." And they both slept that night.

9 Raguel arose, and went and dug a grave, 10 saying, "Lest he also should die." 11 And Raguel came into his house, 12 and said to Edna his wife, "Send one of the maidservants, and let them see if he is alive. If not, we will bury him, and no man will know it."

13 So the maidservant opened the door, and went in, and found them both sleeping, 14 and came out, and told them that he was alive.

15 Then Raguel blessed God, saying, "Blessed are you, O God, with all pure and holy blessing! Let your saints bless you, and all your creatures! Let all your angels and your elect bless you forever! 16 Blessed are you, because you have made me glad; and it has not happened to me as I suspected; but you have dealt with us according to your great mercy. 17 Blessed are you, because you have had mercy on two that were the only begotten children of their parents. Show them mercy, O Lord. Fulfil their life in health with gladness and mercy.

18 He commanded his servants to fill the grave. 19 He kept the wedding feast for them fourteen days. 20 Before the days of the wedding feast were finished, Raguel sware to him, that he should not depart till the fourteen days of the wedding feast were fulfilled; 21 and that then he should take half of his goods, and go in safety to his father; and the rest, said he, when my wife and I die.

9

1 And Tobias called Raphael, and said to him, 2 "Brother Azarias, take with you a servant and two camels, and go to Rages of Media to Gabael, and receive the money for me, and bring him to the wedding feast, 3 because Raguel has sworn that I must not depart. 4 My father counts the days; and if I wait long, he will be very grieved. 5 So Raphael went on his way, and lodged with Gabael, and gave him the handwriting; so he brought forth the bags with their seals, and gave them to them. 6 Then they rose up early in the morning together, and came to the wedding feast. Tobias blessed his wife.

10

1 Tobit his father counted every day. When the days of the journey were expired, and they didn't come, 2 he said, "Is he perchance detained?[a] Or is Gabael perchance dead, and there is no one to give him the money?" 3 He was very grieved.

4 But his wife said to him, "The child has perished, seeing he waits long." She began to bewail him, and said, 5 "I care about nothing,[b] my child, since I have let you go, the light of my eyes." 6 Tobit said to her, "Hold your peace. Don't worry. He is in good health."

7 And she said to him, "Hold your peace. Don't deceive me. My child has perished." And she went out every day into the way by which they went, and ate no bread in the day-time, and didn't stop bewailing her son Tobias for whole nights, until the fourteen days of the wedding feast were expired, which Raguel had sworn that he should spend there.

Then Tobias said to Raguel, "Send me away, for my father and my mother look no more to see me." 8 But his father-in-law said to him, "Stay with me, and I will send to your father, and they will declare to him how things go with you." 9 Tobias said, "No. Send me away to my father."

10 Raguel arose, and gave him Sarah his wife, and half his goods, servants and cattle and money; 11 and he blessed them, and sent them away, saying, "The God of heaven will prosper you, my children, before I die." 12 And he said to his daughter, "Honour your father-in-law and your mother-in-law. They are now your parents. Let me hear a good report of you." Then he kissed her.

Edna said to Tobias, "May the Lord of heaven restore you, dear brother, and grant to me that I may see your children of my daughter Sarah, that I may rejoice before the Lord. Behold, I commit my daughter to you in special trust. Don't cause her grief."

11

1 After these things Tobias also went his way, blessing God because he had prospered his journey; and he blessed Raguel and Edna his wife. Then he went on his way until they drew near to Nineveh. 2 Raphael said to Tobias, "Don't you know, brother, how you left your father? 3 Let's run forward before your wife, and prepare the house. 4 But take in your hand the bile of the fish." So they went their way, and the dog went after them.

5 Anna sat looking around towards the path for her son. 6 She saw him coming, and said to his father, "Behold, your son is coming with the man that went with him!"

7 Raphael said, "I know, Tobias, that your father will open his eyes. 8 Therefore anoint his eyes with the bile, and being pricked with it, he will rub, and will make the white films fall away. Then he will see you."

9 Anna ran to him, and fell upon the neck of her son, and said to him, "I have seen you, my child! I am ready to die." They both wept.

10 Tobit went towards the door and stumbled; but his son ran to him, 11 and took hold of his father. He rubbed the bile on his father's eyes, saying, "Cheer up, my father." 12 When his eyes began to hurt, he rubbed them. 13 Then the white films peeled away from the corners of his eyes; and he saw his son, and fell upon his neck.

14 He wept, and said, "Blessed are you, O God, and blessed is your name forever! Blessed are all your holy angels! 15 For you scourged, and had mercy on me. Behold, I see my son Tobias." And his son went in rejoicing, and told his father the great things that had happened to him in Media.

16 Tobit went out to meet his daughter-in-law at the gate of Nineveh, rejoicing and blessing God. Those who saw him go marvelled, because he had received his sight. 17 Tobit gave thanks before them, because God had shown mercy on him. When Tobit came near to Sarah his daughter-in-law, he blessed her, saying, "Welcome, daughter! Blessed is God who has brought you to us, and blessed are your father and your mother." And there was joy amongst all his kindred who were at Nineveh. 18 Achiacharus and Nasbas his brother's son came. 19 Tobias' wedding feast was kept seven days with great gladness.

12

1 And Tobit called his son Tobias, and said to him, "See, my child, that the man which went with you have his wages, and you must give him more."

2 And he said to him, "Father, it is no harm to me to give him the half of those things which I have brought; 3 for he has led me for you in safety, and he cured my wife, and brought my money, and likewise cured you."

4 The old man said, "It is due to him."

5 And he called the angel, and said to him, "Take half of all that you have brought."

6 Then he called them both privately, and said to them, "Bless God, and give him thanks, and magnify him, and give him thanks in the sight of all that live, for the things which he has done with you. It is good to bless God and exalt his name, showing forth with honour the works of God. Don't be slack to give him thanks. 7 It is good to conceal the secret of a king, but to reveal gloriously the works of God. Do good, and evil won't find you. 8 Good is prayer with fasting, alms, and righteousness. A little with righteousness is better than much with unrighteousness. It is better to give alms than to lay up gold. 9 Alms delivers from death, and it purges away all sin. Those who give alms and do righteousness will be filled with life; 10 but those who sin are enemies to their own life. 11 Surely I will conceal nothing from you. I have said, 'It is good to conceal the secret of a king, but to reveal gloriously the works of God.' 12 And now, when you prayed, and Sarah your daughter-in-law, I brought the memorial of your prayer before the Holy One. When you buried the dead, I was with you likewise. 13 And when you didn't delay to rise up, and leave your dinner, that you might go and cover the dead, your good deed was not hidden from me. I was with you. 14 And now God sent me to heal you and Sarah your daughter-in-law. 15 I am Raphael, one of the seven holy angels which present the prayers of the saints and go in before the glory of the Holy One."

16 And they were both troubled, and fell upon their faces; for they were afraid. 17 And he said to them, "Don't be afraid. You will all have peace; but bless God forever. 18 For I came not of any favour of my own, but by the will of your God. Therefore bless him forever. 19 All these days I appeared to you. I didn't eat or drink, but you all saw a vision. 20 Now give God thanks, because I ascend to him who sent me. Write in a book all the things which have been done." 21 Then they rose up, and saw him no more. 22 They confessed the great and wonderful works of God, and how the angel of the Lord had appeared to them.

13

1 And Tobit wrote a prayer for rejoicing, and said,
"Blessed is God who lives forever!
    Blessed is his kingdom!
2 For he scourges, and shows mercy.
    He leads down to the grave,[c] and brings up again.
    There is no one who will escape his hand.
3 Give thanks to him before the Gentiles, all you children of Israel!
    For he has scattered us amongst them.
4 Declare his greatness, there.
    Extol him before all the living,
because he is our Lord,
    and God is our Father forever.
5 He will scourge us for our iniquities, and will again show mercy,
    and will gather us out of all the nations amongst whom you are all
        scattered.
6 If you turn to him with your whole heart and with your whole soul,
    to do truth before him,
then he will turn to you,
    and won't hide his face from you.
See what he will do with you.
    Give him thanks with your whole mouth.
Bless the Lord of righteousness.
    Exalt the everlasting King.
I give him thanks in the land of my captivity,
    and show his strength and majesty to a nation of sinners.
Turn, you sinners, and do righteousness before him.
    Who can tell if he will accept you and have mercy on you?
7 I exalt my God.
    My soul exalts the King of heaven,
    and rejoices in his greatness.
8 Let all men speak,
    and let them give him thanks in Jerusalem.
9 O Jerusalem, the holy city,
    he will scourge you for the works of your sons,
    and will again have mercy on the sons of the righteous.
10 Give thanks to the Lord with goodness,

a 10:2 Many ancient authorities read "Are they perchance put to shame?"

b 10:5 Some authorities read "Woe is me."
c 13:2 Gr. Hades.

and bless the everlasting King,
that his tabernacle may be built in you again with joy,
and that he may make glad in you those who are captives,
and love in you forever those who are miserable.
11 Many nations will come from afar to the name of the Lord God
with gifts in their hands, even gifts to the King of heaven.
Generations of generations will praise you,
and sing songs of rejoicing.
12 All those who hate you are cursed.
All those who love you forever will be blessed.
13 Rejoice and be exceedingly glad for the sons of the righteous;
for they will be gathered together and will bless the Lord of the
righteous.
14 Oh blessed are those who love you.
They will rejoice for your peace.
Blessed are all those who mourned for all your scourges;
because they will rejoice for you when they have seen all your glory.
They will be made glad forever.
15 Let my soul bless God the great King.
16 For Jerusalem will be built with sapphires, emeralds, and precious
stones;
your walls and towers and battlements with pure gold.
17 The streets of Jerusalem will be paved with beryl, carbuncle, and stones
of Ophir.
18 All her streets will say, "Hallelujah!"
and give praise, saying, "Blessed be God, who has exalted you
forever!"

14

1 Then Tobit finished giving thanks. 2 He was fifty-eight years old when he lost his sight. After eight years, he received it again. He gave alms and he feared the Lord God more and more, and gave thanks to him.

3 Now he grew very old; and he called his son with the six sons of his son, and said to him, "My child, take your sons. Behold, I have grown old, and am ready to depart out of this life. 4 Go into Media, my child, for I surely believe all the things which Jonah the prophet spoke of Nineveh, that it will be overthrown, but in Media there will rather be peace for a season. Our kindred will be scattered in the earth from the good land. Jerusalem will be desolate, and the house of God in it will be burnt up, and will be desolate for a time. 5 God will again have mercy on them, and bring them back into the land, and they will build the house, but not like to the former house, until the times of that age are fulfilled. Afterward they will return from the places of their captivity, and build up Jerusalem with honour. The house of God will be built in it forever with a glorious building, even as the prophets spoke concerning it. 6 And all the nations will turn to fear the Lord God truly, and will bury their idols. 7 All the nations will bless the Lord, and his people will give thanks to God, and the Lord will exalt his people; and all those who love the Lord God in truth and righteousness will rejoice, showing mercy to our kindred. 8 And now, my child, depart from Nineveh, because those things which the prophet Jonah spoke will surely come to pass. 9 But you must keep the law and the ordinances, and show yourself merciful and righteous, that it may be well with you. 10 Bury me decently, and your mother with me. Don't stay at Nineveh. See, my child, what Aman did to Achiacharus who nourished him, how out of light he brought him into darkness, and all the recompense that he made him. Achiacharus was saved, but the other had his recompense, and he went down into darkness. Manasses gave alms, and escaped the snare of death which he set for him; but Aman fell into the snare, and perished. 11 And now, my children, consider what alms does, and how righteousness delivers."

While he was saying these things, he gave up the ghost in the bed; but he was one hundred and fifty eight years old. Tobias buried him magnificently. 12 When Anna died, he buried her with his father. But Tobias departed with his wife and his sons to Ecbatana to Raguel his father-in-law, 13 and he grew old in honour, and he buried his father-in-law and mother-in-law magnificently, and he inherited their possessions, and his father Tobit's. 14 He died at Ecbatana of Media, being one hundred and twenty seven years old. 15 Before he died, he heard of the destruction of Nineveh, which Nebuchadnezzar and Ahasuerus took captive. Before his death, he rejoiced over Nineveh.

Judith

Judith is recognised as Deuterocanonical Scripture by the Roman Catholic, Greek Orthodox, and Russian Orthodox Churches.

1

₁In the twelfth year of the reign of Nebuchadnezzar, who reigned over the Assyrians in Nineveh, the great city, in the days of Arphaxad, who reigned over the Medes in Ecbatana, ₂and built around Ecbatana walls of hewn stones three cubits broad and six cubits long, and made the height of the wall seventy cubits, and its breadth fifty cubits, ₃and set its towers at its gates one hundred cubits high, and its breadth in the foundation was sixty cubits, ₄and made its gates, even gates that were raised to the height of seventy cubits, and their breadth forty cubits, for his mighty army to go out of, and the setting in array of his footmen— ₅in those days King Nebuchadnezzar made war with King Arphaxad in the great plain. This plain is on the borders of Ragau. ₆There came to meet him all that lived in the hill country, and all that lived by Euphrates, Tigris, and Hydaspes, and in the plain of Arioch the king of the Elymaeans. Many nations of the sons of Chelod assembled themselves to the battle.

₇And Nebuchadnezzar king of the Assyrians sent to all who lived in Persia, and to all who lived westward, to those who lived in Cilicia, Damascus, Libanus, Antilibanus, and to all who lived along the sea coast, ₈and to those amongst the nations that were of Carmel and Gilead, and to the higher Galilee and the great plain of Esdraelon, ₉and to all who were in Samaria and its cities, and beyond Jordan to Jerusalem, Betane, Chellus, Kadesh, the river of Egypt, Tahpanhes, Rameses, and all the land of Goshen, ₁₀until you come above Tanis and Memphis, and to all that lived in Egypt, until you come to the borders of Ethiopia. ₁₁All those who lived in all the land made light of the commandment of Nebuchadnezzar king of the Assyrians, and didn't go with him to the war; for they were not afraid of him, but he was before them as one man. They turned away his messengers from their presence without effect, and with disgrace.

₁₂And Nebuchadnezzar was exceedingly angry with all this land, and he swore by his throne and kingdom that he would surely be avenged upon all the coasts of Cilicia, Damascus, and Syria, that he would kill with his sword all the inhabitants of the land of Moab, the children of Ammon, all Judea, and all who were in Egypt, until you come to the borders of the two seas. ₁₃And he set the battle in array with his army against King Arphaxad in the seventeenth year; and he prevailed in his battle, and turned to flight all the army of Arphaxad, with all his horses and all his chariots. ₁₄He took possession of his cities. He came to Ecbatana and took the towers, plundered its streets, and turned its beauty into shame. ₁₅He took Arphaxad in the mountains of Ragau, struck him through with his darts, and utterly destroyed him to this day. ₁₆He returned with them to Nineveh, he and all his company of sundry nations—an exceedingly great multitude of men of war. There he took his ease and banqueted, he and his army, for one hundred and twenty days.

2

₁In the eighteenth year, the twenty-second day of the first month, there was talk in the house of Nebuchadnezzar king of the Assyrians that he should be avenged on all the land, even as he spoke. ₂He called together all his servants and all his great men, and communicated with them his secret counsel, and with his own mouth, recounted the wickedness of all the land. ₃They decreed to destroy all flesh which didn't follow the word of his mouth.

₄It came to pass, when he had ended his counsel, Nebuchadnezzar king of the Assyrians called Holofernes the chief captain of his army, who was second to himself, and said to him, ₅"The great king, the lord of all the earth, says: 'Behold, you shall go out from my presence, and take with you men who trust in their strength, to one hundred and twenty thousand footmen and twelve thousand horses with their riders. ₆And you shall go out against all the west country, because they disobeyed the commandment of my mouth. ₇You shall declare to them that they should prepare earth and water, because I will go out in my wrath against them, and will cover the whole face of the earth with the feet of my army, who will plunder them. ₈Their slain will fill their valleys and brooks, and the river will be filled with their dead until it overflows. ₉I will lead them as captives to the utmost parts of all the earth. ₁₀But you shall go forth, and take all their coasts for me first. If they will yield themselves to you,ᵃ then you must reserve them for me until the day of their reproof. ₁₁As for those who resist, your eye shall not spare; but you shall give them up to be slain and to be plundered in all your land. ₁₂For as I live, and by the power of my kingdom, I have spoken, and I will do this with my hand. ₁₃Moreover, you shall not transgress anything of the commandments of your lord, but you shall surely accomplish them, as I have commanded you. You shall not defer to do them.'"

₁₄So Holofernes went out from the presence of his lord, and called all the governors, the captains, and officers of the army of Asshur. ₁₅He counted chosen men for the battle, as his lord had commanded him, to one hundred and twenty thousand, with twelve thousand archers on horseback. ₁₆He arranged them as a great multitude is ordered for the war. ₁₇He took camels, donkeys, and mules for their baggage, an exceedingly great multitude, and sheep, oxen, and goats without number for their provision, ₁₈and a large supply of rations for every man, and a huge amount of gold

and silver out of the king's house. ₁₉He went out, he and all his army, on their journey, to go before King Nebuchadnezzar, and to cover all the face of the earth westward with their chariots, horsemen, and chosen footmen. ₂₀A great company of various nations went out with them like locusts and like the sand of the earth. For they could not be counted by reason of their multitude.

₂₁And they departed out of Nineveh three days' journey towards the plain of Bectileth, and encamped from Bectileth near the mountain which is at the left hand of the Upper Cilicia. ₂₂And he took all his army, his footmen, horsemen, and chariots, and went away from there into the hill country, ₂₃and destroyed Put and Lud, and plundered all the children of Rasses and the children of Ishmael, which were along the wilderness to the south of the land of the Chellians. ₂₄And he went over Euphrates, and went through Mesopotamia, and broke down all the high cities that were upon the river Arbonai, until you come to the sea. ₂₅And he took possession of the borders of Cilicia, and killed all who resisted him, and came to the borders of Japheth, which were towards the south, opposite Arabia. ₂₆He surrounded all the children of Midian, and set their tents on fire, and plundered their sheepfolds. ₂₇He went down into the plain of Damascus in the days of wheat harvest, and set all their fields on fire, and utterly destroyed their flocks and herds, plundered their cities, laid their plains waste, and struck all their young men with the edge of the sword.

₂₈And the fear and the dread of him fell upon those who lived on the sea coast, upon those who were in Sidon and Tyre, those who lived in Sur and Ocina, and all who lived in Jemnaan. Those who lived in Azotus and Ascalon feared him exceedingly.

3

₁And they sent to him messengers with words of peace, saying, ₂"Behold, we the servants of Nebuchadnezzar the great king lie before you. Use us as it is pleasing in your sight. ₃Behold, our dwellings, and all our country, and all our fields of wheat, and our flocks and herds, and all the sheepfolds of our tents, lie before your face. Use them as it may please you. ₄Behold, even our cities and those who dwell in them are your servants. Come and deal with them as it is good in your eyes."

₅So the men came to Holofernes, and declared to him according to these words.

₆He came down towards the sea coast, he and his army, and set garrisons in the high cities, and took out of them chosen men for allies. ₇They received him, they and all the country round about them, with garlands and dances and timbrels. ₈He cast down all their borders, and cut down their sacred groves. It had been given to him to destroy all the gods of the land, that all the nations would worship Nebuchadnezzar only, and that all their tongues and their tribes would call upon him as a god.

₉Then he came towards Esdraelon near to Dotaea, which is opposite the great ridge of Judea. ₁₀He encamped between Geba and Scythopolis. He was there a whole month, that he might gather together all the baggage of his army.

4

₁The children of Israel who lived in Judea heard all that Holofernes the chief captain of Nebuchadnezzar king of the Assyrians had done to the nations, and how he had plundered all their temples and destroyed them utterly. ₂They were exceedingly afraid at his approach, and were troubled for Jerusalem and for the temple of the Lord their God; ₃because they had newly come up from the captivity, and all the people of Judea were recently gathered together; and the vessels, the altar, and the house were sanctified after being profaned.

₄And they sent into every coast of Samaria, to Konae, to Beth-horon, Belmaim, Jericho, to Choba, Aesora, and to the valley of Salem; ₅and they occupied beforehand all the tops of the high mountains, fortified the villages that were in them, and stored supplies for the provision of war, for their fields were newly reaped. ₆Joakim the high priest, who was in those days at Jerusalem, wrote to those who lived in Bethulia and Betomesthaim, which is opposite Esdraelon towards the plain that is near to Dothaim, ₇charging them to seize upon the ascents of the hill country; because by them was the entrance into Judea, and it was easy to stop them from approaching, inasmuch as the approach was narrow, with space for two men at the most. ₈And the children of Israel did as Joakim the high priest had commanded them, as did the senate of all the people of Israel, which was in session at Jerusalem.

₉And every man of Israel cried to God with great earnestness, and with great earnestness they humbled their souls. ₁₀They, their wives, their children, their cattle, and every sojourner, hireling, and servant bought with their money put sackcloth on their loins. ₁₁Every man and woman of Israel, including the little children and the inhabitants of Jerusalem, fell prostrate before the temple, cast ashes upon their heads, and spread out their sackcloth before the Lord. They put sackcloth around the altar. ₁₂They cried to the God of Israel earnestly with one consent, that he would not give their children as prey, their wives as plunder, the cities of their inheritance to destruction, and the sanctuary to being profaned and being made a reproach, for the nations to rejoice at. ₁₃The Lord heard their voice, and looked at their affliction. The people continued fasting many days in all Judea and Jerusalem before the sanctuary of the Lord Almighty. ₁₄And Joakim the high priest, and all the priests who stood before the Lord, and those who ministered to the Lord, had their loins dressed in sackcloth and offered the continual burnt offering, the vows, and the free gifts of the

---

ᵃ *2:10* Gr. they will yield...and you shall reserve.

people. 15 They had ashes on their turbans. They cried to the Lord with all their power, that he would look upon all the house of Israel for good.

5

1 Holofernes, the chief captain of the army of Asshur, was told that the children of Israel had prepared for war, had shut up the passages of the hill country, had fortified all the tops of the high hills, and had set up barricades in the plains. 2 Then he was exceedingly angry, and he called all the princes of Moab, the captains of Ammon, and all the governors of the sea coast, 3 and he said to them, "Tell me now, you sons of Canaan, who are these people who dwell in the hill country? What are the cities that they inhabit? How large is their army? Where is their power and their strength? What king is set over them, to be the leader of their army? 4 Why have they turned their backs, that they should not come and meet me, more than all who dwell in the west?"

5 Then Achior, the leader of all the children of Ammon, said to him, "Let my lord now hear a word from the mouth of your servant, and I will tell you the truth concerning these people who dwell in this hill country, near to the place where you dwell. No lie will come out of the mouth of your servant. 6 These people are descended from the Chaldeans. 7 They sojourned before this in Mesopotamia, because they didn't want to follow the gods of their fathers, which were in the land of the Chaldeans. 8 They departed from the way of their parents, and worshipped the God of heaven, the God whom they knew. Their parents cast them out from the face of their gods, and they fled into Mesopotamia and sojourned there many days. 9 Then their God commanded them to depart from the place where they sojourned, and to go into the land of Canaan. They lived there, and prospered with gold and silver, and with exceedingly much cattle. 10 Then they went down into Egypt, for a famine covered all the land of Canaan. They sojourned there until they had grown up. They became a great multitude there, so that one could not count the population of their nation. 11 Then the king of Egypt rose up against them, and dealt subtly with them, and brought them low, making them labour in brick,[a] and made them slaves. 12 They cried to their God, and he struck all the land of Egypt with incurable plagues; so the Egyptians cast them out of their sight. 13 God dried up the Red sea before them, 14 and brought them into the way of Sinai Kadesh-Barnea and they cast out all that lived in the wilderness. 15 They lived in the land of the Amorites, and they destroyed by their strength everyone in Heshbon. Passing over Jordan, they possessed all the hill country. 16 They cast out before them the Canaanite, the Perizzite, the Jebusite, the Shechemite, and all the Girgashites, and they lived in that country many days.

17 And while they didn't sin before their God, they prospered, because God who hates iniquity was with them. 18 But when they departed from the way which he appointed them, they were destroyed in many severe battles, and were led captives into a land that was not theirs. The temple of their God was razed to the ground, and their cities were taken by their adversaries. 19 And now they have returned to their God, and have come up from the dispersion where they were dispersed, and have possessed Jerusalem, where their sanctuary is, and are settled in the hill country; for it was desolate.

20 And now, my lord and master, if there is any error in this people, and they sin against their God, we will find out what this thing is in which they stumble, and we will go up and overcome them. 21 But if there is no lawlessness in their nation, let my lord now pass by, lest their Lord defend them, and their God be for them, and we will be a reproach before all the earth."

22 It came to pass, when Achior had finished speaking these words, all the people standing around the tent complained. The great men of Holofernes, and all who lived by the sea side and in Moab, said that he should be cut to pieces. 23 For, they said, "We will not be afraid of the children of Israel, because, behold, they are a people that has no power nor might to make the battle strong. 24 Therefore now we will go up, and they will be a prey to be devoured by all your army, Lord Holofernes."

6

1 And when the disturbance of the men that were around the council had ceased, Holofernes the chief captain of the army of Asshur said to Achior and to all the children of Moab[b] before all the people of the foreigners:

2 "And who are you, Achior, and the mercenaries of Ephraim,[c] that you have prophesied amongst us as today, and have said that we should not make war with the race of Israel, because their God will defend them? And who is God but Nebuchadnezzar? 3 He will send forth his might, and will destroy them from the face of the earth, and their God will not deliver them; but we his servants will strike them as one man. They will not sustain the might of our cavalry. 4 For with them we will burn them up. Their mountains will be drunken with their blood. Their plains will be filled with their dead bodies. Their footsteps will not stand before us, but they will surely perish, says King Nebuchadnezzar, lord of all the earth; for he said, 'The words that I have spoken[d] will not be in vain.'

5 But you, Achior, hireling of Ammon, who have spoken these words in the day of your iniquity, will see my face no more from this day, until I am avenged of the race of those that came out of Egypt. 6 And then the sword of my army, and the multitude of those who serve me, will pass through your sides, and you will fall amongst their slain when I return. 7 Then my

servants will bring you back into the hill country, and will set you in one of the cities by the passes. 8 You will not perish until you are destroyed with them. 9 And if you hope in your heart that they will not be taken, don't let your countenance fall. I have spoken it, and none of my words will fall to the ground."

10 Then Holofernes commanded his servants who waited in his tent to take Achior, and bring him back to Bethulia, and deliver him into the hands of the children of Israel. 11 So his servants took him, and brought him out of the camp into the plain, and they moved from the midst of the plains into the hill country, and came to the springs that were under Bethulia. 12 When the men of the city saw them on the top of the hill, they took up their weapons, and went out of the city against them to the top of the hill. Every man that used a sling kept them from coming up, and threw stones at them. 13 They took cover under the hill, bound Achior, cast him down, left him at the foot of the hill, and went away to their lord.

14 But the children of Israel descended from their city, and came to him, untied him, led him away into Bethulia, and presented him to the rulers of their city, 15 which were in those days Ozias the son of Micah, of the tribe of Simeon, and Chabris the son of Gothoniel, and Charmis the son of Melchiel. 16 Then they called together all the elders of the city; and all their young men ran together, with their women, to the assembly. They set Achior in the midst of all their people. Then Ozias asked him what had happened. 17 He answered and declared to them the words of the council of Holofernes, and all the words that he had spoken in the midst of the princes of the children of Asshur, and all the great words that Holofernes had spoken against the house of Israel. 18 Then the people fell down and worshipped God, and cried, saying, 19 "O Lord God of heaven, behold their arrogance, and pity the low estate of our race. Look upon the face of those who are sanctified to you this day." 20 They comforted Achior, and praised him exceedingly. 21 Then Ozias took him out of the assembly into his house, and made a feast for the elders. They called on the God of Israel for help all that night.

7

1 The next day Holofernes commanded all his army and all the people who had come to be his allies, that they should move their camp towards Bethulia, seize the passes of the hill country, and make war against the children of Israel. 2 Every mighty man of them moved that day. The army of their men of war was one hundred and seventy thousand footmen, plus twelve thousand horsemen, besides the baggage and the men who were on foot amongst them—an exceedingly great multitude. 3 They encamped in the valley near Bethulia, by the fountain. They spread themselves in breadth over Dothaim even to Belmaim, and in length from Bethulia to Cyamon, which is near Esdraelon.

4 But the children of Israel, when they saw the multitude of them, were terrified, and everyone said to his neighbour, "Now these men will lick up the face of all the earth. Neither the high mountains, nor the valleys, nor the hills will be able to bear their weight. 5 Every man took up his weapons of war, and when they had kindled fires upon their towers, they remained and watched all that night.

6 But on the second day Holofernes led out all his cavalry in the sight of the children of Israel which were in Bethulia, 7 viewed the ascents to their city, and searched out the springs of the waters, seized upon them, and set garrisons of men of war over them. Then he departed back to his people.

8 All the rulers of the children of Esau, all the leaders of the people of Moab, and the captains of the sea coast came to him and said, 9 "Let our lord now hear a word, that there not be losses in your army. 10 For this people of the children of Israel do not trust in their spears, but in the height of the mountains wherein they dwell, for it is not easy to come up to the tops of their mountains. 11 And now, my lord, don't fight against them as men fight who join battle, and there will not so much as one man of your people perish. 12 Remain in your camp, and keep every man of your army safe. Let your servants get possession of the water spring, which flows from the foot of the mountain, 13 because all the inhabitants of Bethulia get their water from there. Then thirst will kill them, and they will give up their city. Then we and our people will go up to the tops of the mountains that are near, and will camp upon them, to watch that not one man gets out of the city. 14 They will be consumed with famine—they, their wives, and their children. Before the sword comes against them they will be laid low in the streets where they dwell. 15 And you will pay them back with evil, because they rebelled, and didn't meet your face in peace."

16 Their words were pleasing in the sight of Holofernes and in the sight of all his servants; and he ordered them to do as they had spoken. 17 And the army of the children of Ammon moved, and with them five thousand of the children of Asshur, and they encamped in the valley. They seized the waters and the springs of the waters of the children of Israel. 18 The children of Esau went up with the children of Ammon, and encamped in the hill country near Dothaim. They sent some of them towards the south, and towards the east, near Ekrebel, which is near Chusi, that is upon the brook Mochmur. The rest of the army of the Assyrians encamped in the plain, and covered all the face of the land. Their tents and baggage were pitched upon it in a great crowd. They were an exceedingly great multitude.

19 The children of Israel cried to the Lord their God, for their spirit fainted; for all their enemies had surrounded them. There was no way to escape out from amongst them. 20 All the army of Asshur remained around

---

[a] *5:11* Some authorities read and he brought them low with clay and brick, etc.

[b] *6:1* Some authorities read Ammon. Compare ver. 5.

[c] *6:2* Some authorities read Ammon. Compare ver. 5.

[d] *6:4* Gr. he has spoken.

them, their footmen and their chariots and their horsemen, for thirty-four days. All their vessels of water ran dry for all the inhabitants of Bethulia. ₂₁ The cisterns were emptied, and they had no water to drink their fill for one day; for they rationed drink by measure. ₂₂ Their young children were discouraged. The women and the young men fainted for thirst. They fell down in the streets of the city, and in the passages of the gates. There was no longer any strength in them.

₂₃ All the people, including the young men, the women, and the children, were gathered together against Ozias, and against the rulers of the city. They cried with a loud voice, and said before all the elders, ₂₄ "God be judge between all of you and us, because you have done us great wrong, in that you have not spoken words of peace with the children of Asshur. ₂₅ Now we have no helper; but God has sold us into their hands, that we should be laid low before them with thirst and great destruction. ₂₆ And now summon them, and deliver up the whole city as prey to the people of Holofernes, and to all his army. ₂₇ For it is better for us to be captured by them. For we will be servants, and our souls will live, and we will not see the death of our babies before our eyes, and our wives and our children fainting in death. ₂₈ We take to witness against you the heaven and the earth, and our God and the Lord of our fathers, who punishes us according to our sins and the sins of our fathers. Do what we have said today!"

₂₉ And there was great weeping of all with one consent in the midst of the assembly; and they cried to the Lord God with a loud voice. ₃₀ And Ozias said to them, "Brethren, be of good courage! Let us endure five more days, during which the Lord our God will turn his mercy towards us; for he will not forsake us utterly. ₃₁ But if these days pass, and no help comes to us, I will do what you say." ₃₂ Then he dispersed the people, every man to his own camp; and they went away to the walls and towers of their city. He sent the women and children into their houses. They were brought very low in the city.

8

₁ In those days Judith heard about this. She was the daughter of Merari, the son of Ox, the son of Joseph, the son of Oziel, the son of Elkiah, the son of Ananias, the son of Gideon, the son of Raphaim, the son of Ahitub, the son of Elihu, the son of Eliab, the son of Nathanael, the son of Salamiel, the son of Salasadai, the son of Israel. ₂ Her husband was Manasses, of her tribe and of her family. He died in the days of barley harvest. ₃ For he stood over those who bound sheaves in the field, and was overcome by the burning heat, and he fell on his bed, and died in his city Bethulia. So they buried him with his fathers in the field which is between Dothaim and Balamon. ₄ Judith was a widow in her house three years and four months. ₅ She made herself a tent upon the roof of her house, and put on sackcloth upon her loins. The garments of her widowhood were upon her. ₆ And she fasted all the days of her widowhood, except the eves of the Sabbaths, the Sabbaths, the eves of the new moons, the new moons, and the feasts and joyful days of the house of Israel. ₇ She was beautiful in appearance, and lovely to behold. Her husband Manasses had left her gold, silver, menservants, maidservants, cattle, and lands. She remained on those lands. ₈ No one said anything evil about her, for she feared God exceedingly.

₉ She heard the evil words of the people against the governor, because they fainted for lack of water; and Judith heard all the words that Ozias spoke to them, how he swore to them that he would deliver the city to the Assyrians after five days. ₁₀ So she sent her maid, who was over all things that she had, to summon Ozias, Chabris, and Charmis, the elders of her city. ₁₁ They came to her, and she said to them, "Hear me now, O you rulers of the inhabitants of Bethulia! For your word that you have spoken before the people this day is not right. You have set the oath which you have pronounced between God and you, and have promised to deliver the city to our enemies, unless within these days the Lord turns to help you. ₁₂ Now who are you that you have tested God this day, and stand in the place of God amongst the children of men? ₁₃ Now try the Lord Almighty, and you will never know anything. ₁₄ For you will not find the depth of the heart of man, and you will not perceive the things that he thinks. How will you search out God, who has made all these things, and know his mind, and comprehend his purpose? No, my kindred, don't provoke the Lord our God to anger! ₁₅ For if he has not decided to help us within these five days, he has power to defend us in such time as he will, or to destroy us before the face of our enemies. ₁₆ But don't you pledge the counsels of the Lord our God! For God is not like a human being, that he should be threatened, neither is he like a son of man, that he should be won over by pleading. ₁₇ Therefore let's wait for the salvation that comes from him, and call upon him to help us. He will hear our voice, if it pleases him. ₁₈ For there arose none in our age, neither is there any of us today, tribe, or kindred, or family, or city, which worship gods made with hands, as it was in the former days; ₁₉ for which cause our fathers were given to the sword, and for plunder, and fell with a great destruction before our enemies. ₂₀ But we know no other god beside him. Therefore we hope that he will not despise us, nor any of our race. ₂₁ For if we are captured, all Judea will be captured and our sanctuary will be plundered; and he will require our blood for profaning it. ₂₂ The slaughter of our kindred, the captivity of the land, and the desolation of our inheritance, he will bring on our heads amongst the Gentiles, wherever we will be in bondage. We will be an offence and a reproach to those who take us for a possession. ₂₃ For our bondage will not be ordered to favour; but the Lord our God will turn it to dishonour. ₂₄ And now,

kindred, let's show an example to our kindred, because their soul depends on us, and the sanctuary, the house, and the altar depend on us. ₂₅ Besides all this let's give thanks to the Lord our God, who tries us, even as he did our fathers also. ₂₆ Remember all the things which he did to Abraham, and all the things in which he tried Isaac, and all the things which happened to Jacob in Mesopotamia of Syria, when he kept the sheep of Laban his mother's brother. ₂₇ For he has not tried us in the fire, as he did them, to search out their hearts, neither has he taken vengeance on us; but the Lord scourges those who come near to him, to admonish them."

₂₈ And Ozias said to her, "All that you have spoken, you have spoken with a good heart. There is no one who will deny your words. ₂₉ For this is not the first day wherein your wisdom is manifested; but from the beginning of your days all the people have known your understanding, because the disposition of your heart is good. ₃₀ But the people were exceedingly thirsty, and compelled us to do as we spoke to them, and to bring an oath upon ourselves, which we will not break. ₃₁ And now pray for us, because you are a godly woman, and the Lord will send us rain to fill our cisterns, and we will faint no more."

₃₂ Then Judith said to them, "Hear me, and I will do a thing, which will go down to all generations amongst the children of our race. ₃₃ You shall all stand at the gate tonight. I will go out with my maid. Within the days after which you said that you would deliver the city to our enemies, the Lord will deliver Israel by my hand. ₃₄ But you shall not enquire of my act; for I will not tell you until the things are finished that I will do."

₃₅ Then Ozias and the rulers said to her, "Go in peace. May the Lord God be before you, to take vengeance on our enemies." ₃₆ So they returned from the tent, and went to their stations.

9

₁ But Judith fell upon her face, and put ashes upon her head, and uncovered the sackcloth with which she was clothed. The incense of that evening was now being offered at Jerusalem in the house of God, and Judith cried to the Lord with a loud voice, and said, ₂ "O Lord God of my father Simeon, into whose hand you gave a sword to take vengeance on the strangers who loosened the belt of a virgin to defile her, uncovered her thigh to her shame, and profaned her womb to her reproach; for you said, 'It shall not be so;' and they did so. ₃ Therefore you gave their rulers to be slain, and their bed, which was ashamed for her who was deceived,ᵃ to be dyed in blood, and struck the servants with their masters, and the masters upon their thrones; ₄ and gave their wives for a prey, and their daughters to be captives, and all their spoils to be divided amongst your dear children; which were moved with zeal for you, and abhorred the pollution of their blood, and called upon you for aid. O God, O my God, hear me also who am a widow. ₅ For you did the things that were before those things, and those things, and such as come after; and you planned the things which are now, and the things which are to come. The things which you planned came to pass. ₆ Yes, the things which you determined stood before you, and said, 'Behold, we are here; for all your ways are prepared, and your judgement is with foreknowledge.' ₇ For, behold, the Assyrians are multiplied in their power. They are exalted with horse and rider. They were proud of the strength of their footmen. They have trusted in shield, spear, bow, and sling. They don't know that you are the Lord who breaks the battles. 'The Lord' is your name. ₈ Break their strength in your power, and bring down their force in your wrath; for they intend to profane your sanctuary, and to defile the tabernacle where your glorious name rests, and to destroy the horn of your altar with the sword. ₉ Look at their pride, and send your wrath upon their heads. Give into my hand, which am a widow, the might that I have conceived. ₁₀ Strike by the deceit of my lips the servant with the prince, and the prince with his servant. Break down their arrogance by the hand of a woman. ₁₁ For your power stands not in numbers, nor your might in strong men, but you are a God of the afflicted. You are a helper of the oppressed, a helper of the weak, a protector of the forsaken, a saviour of those who are without hope. ₁₂ Please, please, God of my father, and God of the inheritance of Israel, Lord of the heavens and of the earth, Creator of the waters, King of all your creation, hear my prayer. ₁₃ Make my speech and deceit to be their wound and bruise, who intend hard things against your covenant, your holy house, the top of Zion, and the house of the possession of your children. ₁₄ Make every nation and tribe of yours to know that you are God, the God of all power and might, and that there is no other who protects the race of Israel but you."

10

₁ It came to pass, when she had ceased to cry to the God of Israel, and had finished saying all these words, ₂ that she rose up where she had fallen down, called her maid, and went down into the house that she lived on the Sabbath days and on her feast days. ₃ She pulled off the sackcloth which she had put on, took off the garments of her widowhood, washed her body all over with water, anointed herself with rich ointment, braided the hair of her head, and put a tiara upon it. She put on her garments of gladness, which she used to wear in the days of the life of Manasses her husband. ₄ She took sandals for her feet, and put on her anklet, bracelets, rings, earrings, and all her jewellery. She made herself very beautiful to deceive the eyes of all men who would see her. ₅ She gave her maid a leather container of wine and a flask of oil, and filled a bag with roasted grain, lumps of figs, and fine bread. She packed all her vessels together, and laid them upon her.

ᵃ *9:3* Some authorities read which was ashamed for their deceit that they practised.

₆They went out to the gate of the city of Bethulia, and found Ozias and the elders of the city, Chabris and Charmis standing by it. ₇But when they saw her, that her countenance was altered and her apparel was changed, they were greatly astonished by her beauty and said to her, ₈"May the God of our fathers give you favour, and accomplish your purposes to the glory of the children of Israel, and to the exaltation of Jerusalem."

Then she worshipped God, ₉and said to them, "Command that they open the gate of the city for me, and I will go out to accomplish the things you spoke with me about."

And they commanded the young men to open to her, as she had spoken; ₁₀and they did so.

Then Judith went out, she, and her handmaid with her. The men of the city watched her until she had gone down the mountain, until she had passed the valley, and they could see her no more. ₁₁They went straight onward in the valley. The watch of the Assyrians met her; ₁₂and they took her, and asked her, "Of what people are you? Where are you coming from? Where are you going?"

She said, "I am a daughter of the Hebrews. I am fleeing away from their presence, because they are about to be given you to be consumed. ₁₃I am coming into the presence of Holofernes the chief captain of your army, to declare words of truth. I will show him a way that he can go and win all the hill country, and there will not be lacking of his men one person, nor one life."

₁₄Now when the men heard her words, and considered her countenance, the beauty thereof was exceedingly marvellous in their eyes. They said to her, ₁₅"You have saved your life, in that you have hurried to come down to the presence of our master. Now come to his tent. Some of us will guide you until they deliver you into his hands. ₁₆But when[a] you stand before him, don't be afraid in your heart, but declare to him what you just said, and he will treat you well." ₁₇They chose out of them a hundred men, and appointed them to accompany her and her maid; and they brought them to the tent of Holofernes.

₁₈And there was great excitement throughout all the camp, for her coming was reported amongst the tents. They came and surrounded her as she stood outside Holofernes' tent, until they told him about her. ₁₉They marvelled at her beauty, and marvelled at the children of Israel because of her. Each one said to his neighbour, "Who would despise these people, who have amongst them such women? For it is not good that one man of them be left, seeing that, if they are let go, they will be able to deceive the whole earth."

₂₀Then the guards of Holofernes and all his servants came out and brought her into the tent. ₂₁And Holofernes was resting upon his bed under the canopy, which was woven with purple, gold, emeralds, and precious stones. ₂₂And they told him about her; and he came out into the space before his tent, with silver lamps going before him. ₂₃But when Judith had come before him and his servants, they all marvelled at the beauty of her countenance. She fell down upon her face and bowed down to him, but his servants raised her up.

11

₁Holofernes said to her, "Woman, take courage. Don't be afraid in your heart; for I never hurt anyone who has chosen to serve Nebuchadnezzar, the king of all the earth. ₂And now, if your people who dwell in the hill country had not slighted me, I would not have lifted up my spear against them; but they have done these things to themselves. ₃And now tell me why you fled from them and came to us; for you have come to save yourself. Take courage! You will live tonight, and hereafter; ₄for there is no one that will wrong you, but all will treat you well, as is done to the servants of King Nebuchadnezzar my lord."

₅And Judith said to him, "Receive the words of your servant, and let your handmaid speak in your presence, and I won't lie to my lord tonight. ₆If you will follow the words of your handmaid, God will bring the thing to pass perfectly with you; and my lord will not fail to accomplish his purposes. ₇As Nebuchadnezzar king of all the earth lives, and as his power lives, who has sent you for the preservation of every living thing, not only do men serve him by you, but also the beasts of the field, the cattle, and the birds of the sky will live through your strength, in the time of Nebuchadnezzar and of all his house. ₈For we have heard of your wisdom and the subtle plans of your soul. It has been reported in all the earth that you only are brave in all the kingdom, mighty in knowledge, and wonderful in feats of war. ₉And now as concerning the matter which Achior spoke in your council, we have heard his words; for the men of Bethulia saved him, and he declared to them all that he had spoken before you. ₁₀Therefore, O lord and master, don't neglect his word, but lay it up in your heart, for it is true; for our race will not be punished, neither will the sword prevail against them, unless they sin against their God. ₁₁And now, that my lord may not be defeated and frustrated in his purpose, and that death may fall upon them, their sin has overtaken them, wherewith they will provoke their God to anger, whenever they do wickedness. ₁₂Since their food failed them, and all their water was scant, they took counsel to kill their livestock, and determined to consume all those things which God charged them by his laws that they should not eat. ₁₃They are resolved to spend the first fruits of the grain and the tithes of the wine and the oil, which they had sanctified and reserved for the priests who stand before the face of our God in Jerusalem, which it is not fitting for any of the people so much as to touch with their hands. ₁₄They have sent some to Jerusalem, because they also that dwell there have done this thing, to bring them permission from the

council of elders. ₁₅When these instructions come to them and they do it, they will be given to you to be destroyed the same day. ₁₆Therefore I your servant, knowing all this, fled away from their presence. God sent me to work things with you, at which all the earth will be astonished, even as many as hear it. ₁₇For your servant is religious, and serves the God of heaven day and night. Now, my lord, I will stay with you; and your servant will go out by night into the valley. I will pray to God, and he will tell me when they have committed their sins. ₁₈Then I will come and tell you. Then you can go out with all your army, and there will be none of them that will resist you. ₁₉And I will lead you through the midst of Judea, until you come to Jerusalem. I will set your throne in the midst of it. You will drive them as sheep that have no shepherd, and a dog will not so much as open his mouth before you; for these things were told me according to my foreknowledge, and were declared to me, and I was sent to tell you."

₂₀Her words were pleasing in the sight of Holofernes and of all his servants. They marvelled at her wisdom, and said, ₂₁"There is not such a woman from one end of the earth to the other, for beauty of face and wisdom of words."

₂₂Holofernes said to her, "God did well to send you before the people, that might would be in our hands, and destruction amongst those who slighted my lord. ₂₃And now you are beautiful in your countenance, and wise in your words. If you will do as you have spoken, your God will be my God, and you will dwell in the palace of King Nebuchadnezzar, and will be renowned through the whole earth."

12

₁He commanded that she should be brought in where his silver vessels were set, and asked that his servants should prepare some of his own delicacies for her, and that she should drink from his own wine.

₂And Judith said, "I can't eat of it, lest there be an occasion of stumbling; but provision will be made for me from the things that have come with me."

₃And Holofernes said to her, "But if the things that are with you should run out, from where will we be able to give you more like it? For there is none of your race with us."

₄And Judith said to him, "As your soul lives, my lord, your servant will not use up those things that are with me until the Lord works by my hand the things that he has determined." ₅Then Holofernes' servants brought her into the tent, and she slept until midnight. Then she rose up towards the morning watch, ₆and sent to Holofernes, saying, "Let my lord now command that they allow your servant to go out to pray."

₇Holofernes commanded his guards that they should not stop her. She stayed in the camp three days, and went out every night into the valley of Bethulia and washed herself at the fountain of water in the camp. ₈And when she came up, she implored the Lord God of Israel to direct her way to the triumph of the children of his people. ₉She came in clean and remained in the tent until she ate her food towards evening.

₁₀It came to pass on the fourth day, that Holofernes made a feast for his own servants only, and called none of the officers to the banquet. ₁₁And he said to Bagoas the eunuch, who had charge over all that he had, "Go now, and persuade this Hebrew woman who is with you that she come to us, and eat and drink with us. ₁₂For behold, it would be a disgrace if we shall let such a woman go, not having had her company; for if we don't draw her to ourselves, she will laugh us to scorn."

₁₃Bagoas went from the presence of Holofernes, and came in to her, and said, "Let this fair lady not fear to come to my lord, and to be honoured in his presence, and to drink wine and be merry with us, and to be made this day as one of the daughters of the children of Asshur who serve in Nebuchadnezzar's palace."

₁₄Judith said to him, "Who am I, that I should contradict my lord? For whatever would be pleasing in his eyes, I will do speedily, and this will be my joy to the day of my death." ₁₅She arose, and decked herself with her apparel and all her woman's attire; and her servant went and laid fleeces on the ground for her next to Holofernes, which she had received from Bagoas for her daily use, that she might sit and eat upon them.

₁₆Judith came in and sat down, and Holofernes' heart was ravished with her. His passion was aroused, and he exceedingly desired her company. He was watching for a time to deceive her from the day that he had seen her. ₁₇Holofernes said to her, "Drink now, and be merry with us." ₁₈Judith said, "I will drink now, my lord, because my life is magnified in me this day more than all the days since I was born." ₁₉Then she took and ate and drank before him what her servant had prepared. ₂₀Holofernes took great delight in her, and drank exceedingly much wine, more than he had drunk at any time in one day since he was born.

13

₁But when the evening had come, his servants hurried to depart. Bagoas shut the tent outside, and dismissed those who waited from the presence of his lord. They went away to their beds; for they were all weary, because the feast had been long. ₂But Judith was left alone in the tent, with Holofernes lying along upon his bed; for he was drunk with wine. ₃Judith had said to her servant that she should stand outside her bedchamber, and wait for her to come out, as she did daily; for she said she would go out to her prayer. She spoke to Bagoas according to the same words. ₄All went away from her presence, and none was left in the bedchamber, small or great. Judith, standing by his bed, said in her heart, O Lord God of all power, look in this hour upon the works of my hands for the exaltation of Jerusalem. ₅For now is the time to help your inheritance, and to do the

―――――――――――――――――――――――――
[a] *10:16* Gr. if.

thing that I have purposed to the destruction of the enemies which have risen up against us. 6 She came to the bedpost which was at Holofernes' head, and took down his sword from there. 7 She drew near to the bed, took hold of the hair of his head, and said, "Strengthen me, O Lord God of Israel, this day." 8 She struck twice upon his neck with all her might and cut off his head, 9 tumbled his body down from the bed, and took down the canopy from the posts. After a little while she went out, and gave Holofernes' head to her maid; 10 and she put it in her bag of food. They both went out together to prayer, according to their custom. They passed through the camp, circled around that valley, and went up to the mountain of Bethulia, and came to its gates.

11 Judith said afar off to the watchmen at the gates, "Open, open the gate, now. God is with us, even our God, to show his power yet in Israel, and his might against the enemy, as he has done even this day."

12 It came to pass, when the men of her city heard her voice, they made haste to go down to the gate of their city, and they called together the elders of the city. 13 They all ran together, both small and great, for it seemed unbelievable to them that she had come. They opened the gate and received them, making a fire to give light, and surrounded them. 14 She said to them with a loud voice, "Praise God! Praise him! Praise God, who has not taken away his mercy from the house of Israel, but has destroyed our enemies by my hand tonight!"

15 Then she took the head out of the bag and showed it, and said to them, "Behold, the head of Holofernes, the chief captain of the army of Asshur, and behold, the canopy under which he laid in his drunkenness. The Lord struck him by the hand of a woman. 16 And as the Lord lives, who preserved me in my way that I went, my countenance deceived him to his destruction, and he didn't commit sin with me, to defile and shame me."

17 All the people were exceedingly amazed, and bowed themselves, and worshipped God, and said with one accord, "Blessed are you, O our God, who have this day humiliated the enemies of your people."

18 Ozias said to her, "Blessed are you, daughter, in the sight of the Most High God, above all the women upon the earth; and blessed is the Lord God, who created the heavens and the earth, who directed you to cut off the head of the prince of our enemies. 19 For your hope will not depart from the heart of men that remember the strength of God forever. 20 May God turn these things to you for a perpetual praise, to visit you with good things, because you didn't spare your life by reason of the affliction of our race, but prevented our ruin, walking a straight way before our God."

And all the people said, "Amen! Amen!"

14

1 Judith said to them, "Hear me now, my kindred, and take this head, and hang it upon the battlement of your wall. 2 It will be, so soon as the morning appears, and the sun comes up on the earth, you shall each take up his weapons of war, and every valiant man of you go out of the city. You shall set a captain over them, as though you would go down to the plain towards the watch of the children of Asshur; but you men shall not go down. 3 These will take up their full armour, and shall go into their camp and rouse up the captains of the army of Asshur. They will run together to Holofernes' tent. They won't find him. Fear will fall upon them, and they will flee before your face. 4 You men, and all that inhabit every border of Israel, shall pursue them and overthrow them as they go. 5 But before you do these things, summon Achior the Ammonite to me, that he may see and know him that despised the house of Israel, and that sent him to us, as it were to death."

6 And they called Achior out of the house of Ozias; but when he came, and saw the head of Holofernes in a man's hand in the assembly of the people, he fell upon his face, and his spirit failed. 7 But when they had recovered him,[a] he fell at Judith's feet, bowed down to her, and said, "Blessed are you in every tent of Judah! In every nation, those who hear your name will be troubled. 8 Now tell me all the things that you have done in these days."

And Judith declared to him in the midst of the people all the things that she had done, from the day that she went out until the time that she spoke to them. 9 But when she finished speaking, the people shouted with a loud voice, and made a joyful noise in their city. 10 But when Achior saw all the things that the God of Israel had done, he believed in God exceedingly, and circumcised the flesh of his foreskin, and was joined to the house of Israel, to this day.

11 But as soon as the morning arose, they hanged the head of Holofernes upon the wall, and every man took up his weapons, and they went forth by bands to the ascents of the mountain. 12 But when the children of Asshur saw them, they sent word to their leaders, and they went to their captains and tribunes, and to every one of their rulers. 13 They came to Holofernes' tent, and said to him that was over all that he had, "Wake our lord up, now, for the slaves have been bold to come down against us to battle, that they may be utterly destroyed."

14 Bagoas went in, and knocked at the outer door of the tent; for he supposed that Holofernes was sleeping with Judith. 15 But when no one answered, he opened it, went into the bedchamber, and found him cast upon the threshold dead; and his head had been taken from him. 16 He cried with a loud voice, with weeping, groaning, and shouting, and tore his garments. 17 He entered into the tent where Judith lodged, and he didn't find her. He leapt out to the people, and cried aloud, 18 "The slaves have dealt treacherously! One woman of the Hebrews has brought shame upon the house of King Nebuchadnezzar; for, behold, Holofernes lies upon the ground, and his head is not on him!"

19 But when the rulers of the army of Asshur heard this, they tore their tunics, and their souls were troubled exceedingly. There were cries and an exceedingly great noise in the midst of the camp.

15

1 When those who were in the tents heard, they were amazed at what happened. 2 Trembling and fear fell upon them, and no man dared stay any more in the sight of his neighbour, but rushing out with one accord, they fled into every way of the plain and of the hill country. 3 Those who had encamped in the hill country round about Bethulia fled away. And then the children of Israel, every one who was a warrior amongst them, rushed out upon them. 4 Ozias sent to Betomasthaim, Bebai, Chobai, and Chola, and to every border of Israel, to tell about the things that had been accomplished, and that all should rush upon their enemies to destroy them. 5 But when the children of Israel heard this, they all fell upon them with one accord, and struck them to Chobai. Yes, and in like manner also, people from Jerusalem and from all the hill country came (for men had told them about what happened in their enemies' camp), and those who were in Gilead and in Galilee fell upon their flank with a great slaughter, until they were past Damascus and its borders. 6 The rest of the people who lived at Bethulia fell upon the camp of Asshur, and plundered them, and were enriched exceedingly. 7 The children of Israel returned from the slaughter, and got possession of that which remained. The villages and the cities that were in the hill country and in the plain country took many spoils; for there was an exceedingly great supply.

8 Joakim the high priest, and the elders of the children of Israel who lived in Jerusalem, came to see the good things which the Lord had showed to Israel, and to see Judith and to greet her. 9 When they came to her, they all blessed her with one accord, and said to her, "You are the exaltation of Jerusalem! You are the great glory of Israel! You are the great rejoicing of our race! 10 You have done all these things by your hand. You have done with Israel the things that are good, and God is pleased with it. May you be blessed by the Almighty Lord forever!"

And all the people said, "Amen!"

11 And the people plundered the camp for thirty days; and they gave Holofernes' tent to Judith, along with all his silver cups, his beds, his bowls, and all his furniture. She took them, placed them on her mule, prepared her wagons, and piled them on it.

12 And all the women of Israel ran together to see her; and they blessed her, and made a dance amongst them for her. She took branches in her hand, and distributed them to the women who were with her.[b] 13 Then they made themselves garlands of olive, she and those who were with her, and she went before all the people in the dance, leading all the women. All the men of Israel followed in their armour with garlands, and with songs in their mouths.

16

1 And Judith began to sing this song of thanksgiving in all Israel, and all the people sang with loud voices this song of praise. 2 Judith said,
"Begin a song to my God with timbrels.
    Sing to my Lord with cymbals.
Make melody to him with psalm and praise.
    Exalt him, and call upon his name.
3 For the Lord is the God that crushes battles.
    For in his armies in the midst of the people,
        he delivered me out of the hand of those who persecuted me.
4 Asshur came out of the mountains from the north.
    He came with ten thousands of his army.
Its multitude stopped the torrents.
    Their horsemen covered the hills.
5 He said that he would burn up my borders,
    kill my young men with the sword,
    throw my nursing children to the ground,
    give my infants up as prey,
    and make my virgins a plunder.

6 "The Almighty Lord brought them to nothing by the hand of a woman.
    7 For their mighty one didn't fall by young men,
        neither did sons of the Titans strike him.
Tall giants didn't attack him,
    but Judith the daughter of Merari made him weak with the beauty of
        her countenance.

8 "For she put off the apparel of her widowhood
    for the exaltation of those who were distressed in Israel.
She anointed her face with ointment,
    bound her hair in a tiara,
    and took a linen garment to deceive him.
9 Her sandal ravished his eye.
    Her beauty took his soul prisoner.
    The sword passed through his neck.
10 "The Persians quaked at her daring.
    The Medes were daunted at her boldness.

11 "Then my lowly ones shouted aloud.
    My oppressed people were terrified and trembled for fear.

---

a 14:7 Many authorities read he had recovered himself.

b 15:12 Compare 2 Maccabees 10:7.

They lifted up their voices and the enemy fled.
12 The children of slave-girls pierced them through,
and wounded them as fugitives' children.
They perished by the army of my Lord.

13 "I will sing to my God a new song:
O Lord, you are great and glorious,
marvellous in strength, invincible.
14 Let all your creation serve you;
for you spoke, and they were made.
You sent out your spirit, and it built them.
There is no one who can resist your voice.
15 For the mountains will be moved from their foundations with the waters,
and the rocks will melt as wax at your presence:
But you are yet merciful to those who fear you.
16 For all sacrifice is little for a sweet savour,
and all the fat is very little for a whole burnt offering to you;
but he who fears the Lord is great continually.

17 "Woe to the nations who rise up against my race!
The Lord Almighty will take vengeance on them in the day of
judgement
and put fire and worms in their flesh;
and they will weep and feel their pain forever."

18 Now when they came to Jerusalem, they worshipped God. When the people were purified, they offered their whole burnt offerings, their free will offerings, and their gifts. 19 Judith dedicated all Holofernes' stuff, which the people had given her, and gave the canopy, which she had taken for herself out of his bedchamber, for a gift to the Lord.

20 And the people continued feasting in Jerusalem before the sanctuary for three months, and Judith remained with them.

21 After these days, everyone departed to his own inheritance. Judith went away to Bethulia, and remained in her own possession, and was honourable in her time in all the land. 22 Many desired her, but no man knew her all the days of her life from the day that Manasses her husband died and was gathered to his people. 23 She increased in greatness exceedingly; and she grew old in her husband's house, to one hundred and five years. She let her maid go free. Then she died in Bethulia. They buried her in the cave of her husband Manasses. 24 The house of Israel mourned for her seven days. She distributed her goods before she died to all those who were nearest of kin to Manasses her husband, and to those who were nearest of her own kindred. 25 There was no one who made the children of Israel afraid any more in the days of Judith, nor for a long time after her death.

Esther

translated from the Greek Septuagint

Introduction

The book of Esther in the Greek Septuagint contains 5 additions that the traditional Hebrew text doesn't have. These additions are recognised as Deuterocanonical Scripture by the Roman Catholic, Greek Orthodox, and Russian Orthodox Churches. Those additions are enclosed in [square brackets]. Because the additions by themselves make little sense without the broader context of the book, we present here a translation of the whole book of Esther from the Greek.

We have chosen not to distract the reader with confusing out-of-order chapter numbers that would result from using the KJV versification, but rather merge these 5 additions as extensions at the beginning of 1:1 and after 3:13, 4:17, 8:12, and 10:3. This makes some verses (1:1, 5:1, and 8:12) really long, but it also makes the verses line up with the same verse numbers in Esther as translated from the traditional Hebrew text. Some of the proper names in this book have been changed to the more familiar Hebrew form instead of the direct transliteration from the Greek.

1

1 [In the second year of the reign of Ahasuerus the great king, on the first day of Nisan, Mordecai the son of Jair, the son of Shimei, the son of Kish, of the tribe of Benjamin, a Jew dwelling in the city Susa, a great man, serving in the king's palace, saw a vision. Now he was one of the captives whom Nebuchadnezzar king of Babylon had carried captive from Jerusalem with Jeconiah the king of Judea. This was his dream: Behold, voices and a noise, thunders and earthquake, tumult upon the earth. And, behold, two great serpents came out, both ready for conflict. A great voice came from them. Every nation was prepared for battle by their voice, even to fight against the nation of the just. Behold, a day of darkness and blackness, suffering and anguish, affection and tumult upon the earth. And all the righteous nation was troubled, fearing their own afflictions. They prepared to die, and cried to God. Something like a great river from a little spring with much water, came from their cry. Light and the sun arose, and the lowly were exalted, and devoured the honourable.

Mordecai, who had seen this vision and what God desired to do, having arisen, kept it in his heart, and desired by all means to interpret it, even until night.

Mordecai rested quietly in the palace with Gabatha and Tharrha the king's two chamberlains, eunuchs who guarded the palace. He heard their conversation and searched out their plans. He learnt that they were preparing to lay hands on King Ahasuerus; and he informed the king concerning them. The king examined the two chamberlains. They confessed, and were led away and executed. The king wrote these things for a record. Mordecai also wrote concerning these matters. The king commanded Mordecai to serve in the palace, and gave gifts for this service. But Haman the son of Hammedatha the Bougean was honoured in the sight of the king, and he endeavored to harm Mordecai and his people, because of the king's two chamberlains.]

a And it came to pass after these things b in the days of Ahasuerus, — (this Ahasuerus ruled over one hundred and twenty-seven provinces from India)— 2 in those days, when King Ahasuerus was on the throne in the city of Susa, 3 in the third year of his reign, he made a feast for his friends, for people from the rest of the nations, for the nobles of the Persians and Medes, and for the chief of the local governors. 4 After this—after he had shown them the wealth of his kingdom and the abundant glory of his wealth during one hundred and eighty days— 5 when the days of the wedding feast were completed, the king made a banquet lasting six days for the people of the nations who were present in the city, in the court of the king's house, 6 which was adorned with fine linen and flax on cords of fine linen and purple, fastened to golden and silver studs on pillars of white marble and stone. There were golden and silver couches on a pavement of emerald stone, and of mother-of-pearl, and of white marble, with transparent coverings variously flowered, having roses arranged around it. 7 There were gold and silver cups, and a small cup of carbuncle set out, of the value of thirty thousand talents, with abundant and sweet wine, which the king himself drank. 8 This banquet was not according to the appointed law, but as the king desired to have it. He charged the stewards to perform his will and that of the company.

9 Also Vashti the queen made a banquet for the women in the palace where King Ahasuerus lived. 10 Now on the seventh day, the king, being merry, told Haman, Bazan, Tharrha, Baraze, Zatholtha, Abataza, and Tharaba, the seven chamberlains, servants of King Ahasuerus, 11 to bring in the queen to him, to c enthrone her, and crown her with the diadem, and to show her to the princes, and her beauty to the nations, for she was beautiful. 12 But queen Vashti refused to come with the chamberlains; so the king was grieved and angered. 13 And he said to his friends, "This is what Vashti said. Therefore pronounce your legal judgement on this case."

14 So Arkesaeus, Sarsathaeus, and Malisear, the princes of the Persians and Medes, who were near the king, who sat chief in rank by the king, drew near to him, 15 and reported to him according to the laws what it was proper to do to queen Vashti, because she had not done the things commanded by the king through the chamberlains. 16 And Memucan said to the king and to the princes, "Queen Vashti has not wronged the king only, but also all the king's rulers and princes; 17 for he has told them the words of the queen, and how she d disobeyed the king. As she then refused to obey King Ahasuerus, 18 so this day the other wives of the chiefs of the Persians and Medes, having heard what she said to the king, will dare in the same way to dishonour their husbands. 19 If then it seems good to the king, let him make a royal decree, and let it be written according to the laws of the Medes and Persians, and let him not alter it: 'Don't allow the queen to come in to him any more. Let the king give her royalty to a woman better than she.' 20 Let the law of the king which he will have made be widely proclaimed in his kingdom. Then all the women will give honour to their husbands, from the poor even to the rich." 21 This advice pleased the king and the princes; and the king did as Memucan had said, 22 and sent into all his kingdom through the several provinces, according to their language, so that men might be feared in their own houses.

2

1 After this, the king's anger was pacified, and he no more mentioned Vashti, bearing in mind what she had said, and how he had condemned her. 2 Then the servants of the king said, "Let chaste, beautiful young virgins be sought for the king. 3 Let the king appoint local governors in all the provinces of his kingdom, and let them select beautiful, chaste young ladies and bring them to the city Susa, into the women's apartment. Let them be consigned to the king's chamberlain, the keeper of the women. Then let things for purification and other needs be given to them. 4 Let the woman who pleases the king be queen instead of Vashti."

This thing pleased the king; and he did so.

5 Now there was a Jew in the city Susa, and his name was Mordecai, the son of Jairus, the son of Shimei, the son of Kish, of the tribe of Benjamin. 6 He had been brought as a prisoner from Jerusalem, whom Nebuchadnezzar king of Babylon had carried into captivity. 7 He had a foster child, daughter of Aminadab his father's brother. Her name was Esther. When her parents died, he brought her up to womanhood as his own. This lady was beautiful. 8 And because the king's ordinance was published, many ladies were gathered to the city of Susa under the hand of Hegai; and Esther was brought to Hegai, the keeper of the women. 9 The lady pleased him, and she found favour in his sight. He hurried to give her the things for purification, her portion, and the seven maidens appointed her out of the palace. He treated her and her maidens well in the women's apartment. 10 But Esther didn't reveal her family or her kindred, for Mordecai had charged her not to tell. 11 But Mordecai used to walk every day by the women's court, to see what would become of Esther.

12 Now this was the time for a virgin to go into the king, when she had completed twelve months; for so are the days of purification fulfilled, six months while they are anointing themselves with oil of myrrh, and six months with spices and women's purifications. 13 And then the lady goes in to the king. The officer that he commands to do so will bring her to come in with him from the women's apartment to the king's chamber. 14 She enters in the evening, and in the morning she departs to the second women's apartment, where Hegai the king's chamberlain is keeper of the women. She doesn't go in to the king again, unless she is called by name. 15 And when the time was fulfilled for Esther the daughter of Aminadab the brother of Mordecai's father to go in to the king, she neglected nothing which the chamberlain, the women's keeper, commanded; for Esther found grace in the sight of all who looked at her. 16 So Esther went in to King Ahasuerus in the twelfth month, which is Adar, in the seventh year of his reign. 17 The king loved Esther, and she found favour beyond all the other virgins. He put the queen's crown on her. 18 The king made a banquet for all his friends and great men for seven days, and he highly celebrated the marriage of Esther; and he granted a remission of taxes to those who were under his dominion.

19 Meanwhile, Mordecai served in the courtyard. 20 Now Esther had not revealed her country, for so Mordecai commanded her, to fear God, and perform his commandments, as when she was with him. Esther didn't change her manner of life.

21 Two chamberlains of the king, the chiefs of the body-guard, were grieved, because Mordecai was promoted; and they sought to kill King Ahasuerus. 22 And the matter was discovered by Mordecai, and he made it known to Esther, and she declared to the king the matter of the conspiracy. 23 And the king examined the two chamberlains and hanged them. Then the king gave orders to make a note for a memorial in the royal library of the goodwill shown by Mordecai, as a commendation.

3

1 After this, King Ahasuerus highly honoured Haman the son of Hammedatha, the Bugaean. He exalted him and set his seat above all his friends. 2 All in the palace bowed down to him, for so the king had given orders to do; but Mordecai didn't bow down to him. 3 And they in the king's palace said to Mordecai, "Mordecai, why do you transgress the commands of the king?" 4 They questioned him daily, but he didn't listen to them; so they reported to Haman that Mordecai resisted the commands of the king; and Mordecai had shown to them that he was a Jew. 5 When Haman understood that Mordecai didn't bow down to him, he was greatly enraged, 6 and plotted to utterly destroy all the Jews who were under the rule of Ahasuerus.

7 In the twelfth year of the reign of Ahasuerus, Haman made a decision by casting lots by day and month, to kill the race of Mordecai in one day. The lot fell on the fourteenth day of the month of Adar. 8 So he spoke to

---

a 1:1 Note: In the Hebrew and some copies of LXX, Esther begins here.
b 1:1 Greek words.
c 1:11 Greek to make her queen.
d 1:17 Greek contradicted.

King Ahasuerus, saying, "There is a nation scattered amongst the nations in all your kingdom, and their laws differ from all the other nations. They disobey the king's laws. It is not expedient for the king to tolerate them. ₉If it seem good to the king, let him make a decree to destroy them, and I will remit into the king's treasury ten thousand talents of silver."

₁₀So the king took off his ring, and gave it into the hands of Haman to seal the decrees against the Jews. ₁₁The king said to Haman, "Keep the silver, and treat the nation as you will." ₁₂So the king's recorders were called in the first month, on the thirteenth day, and they wrote as Haman commanded to the captains and governors in every province, from India even to Ethiopia, to one hundred and twenty-seven provinces; and to the rulers of the nations according to their languages, in the name of King Ahasuerus. ₁₃The message was sent by couriers throughout the kingdom of Ahasuerus, to utterly destroy the race of the Jews on the first day of the twelfth month, which is Adar, and to plunder their goods.ᵃ [The following is the copy of the letter. "From the great King Ahasuerus to the rulers and the governors under them of one hundred and twenty-seven provinces, from India even to Ethiopia, who hold authority under him:

"Ruling over many nations and having obtained dominion over the whole world, I was determined (not elated by the confidence of power, but ever conducting myself with great moderation and gentleness) to make the lives of my subjects continually tranquil, desiring both to maintain the kingdom quiet and orderly to its utmost limits, and to restore the peace desired by all men. When I had asked my counsellors how this should be brought to pass, Haman, who excels in soundness of judgement amongst us, and has been manifestly well inclined without wavering and with unshaken fidelity, and had obtained the second post in the kingdom, informed us that a certain ill-disposed people is scattered amongst all the tribes throughout the world, opposed in their law to every other nation, and continually neglecting the commands of the king, so that the united government blamelessly administered by us is not quietly established. Having then conceived that this nation is continually set in opposition to every man, introducing as a change a foreign code of laws, and injuriously plotting to accomplish the worst of evils against our interests, and against the happy establishment of the monarchy, we instruct you in the letter written by Haman, who is set over the public affairs and is our second governor, to destroy them all utterly with their wives and children by the swords of the enemies, without pitying or sparing any, on the fourteenth day of the twelfth month Adar, of the present year; that the people aforetime and now ill-disposed to us having been violently consigned to death in one day, may hereafter secure to us continually a well constituted and quiet state of affairs."] ₁₄Copies of the letters were published in every province; and an order was given to all the nations to be ready for that day. ₁₅This business was hastened also in Susa. The king and Haman began to drink, but the city was confused.

4

₁But Mordecai, having perceived what was done, tore his garments, put on sackcloth, and sprinkled dust upon himself. Having rushed forth through the open street of the city, he cried with a loud voice, "A nation that has done no wrong is going to be destroyed!" ₂He came to the king's gate, and stood; for it was not lawful for him to enter into the palace wearing sackcloth and ashes. ₃And in every province where the letters were published, there was crying, lamentation, and great mourning on the part of the Jews. They wore sackcloth and ashes. ₄The queen's maids and chamberlains went in and told her; and when she had heard what was done, she was deeply troubled. She sent clothes to Mordecai to replace his sackcloth, but he refused. ₅So Esther called for her chamberlain Hathach, who waited upon her; and she sent to learn the truth from Mordecai. ₇Mordecai showed him what was done, and the promise which Haman had made the king of ten thousand talents to be paid into the treasury, that he might destroy the Jews. ₈And he gave him the copy of what was published in Susa concerning their destruction to show to Esther; and told him to charge her to go in and entreat the king, and to beg him for the people. "Remember, he said, the days of your humble condition, how you were nursed by my hand; because Haman, who holds the next place to the king, has spoken against us to cause our death. Call upon the Lord, and speak to the king concerning us, to deliver us from death."

₉So Hathach went in and told her all these words. ₁₀Esther said to Hathach, "Go to Mordecai, and say, ₁₁'All the nations of the empire know than any man or woman who goes in to the king into the inner court without being called, that person must die, unless the king stretches out his golden sceptre; then he shall live. I haven't been called to go into the king for thirty days.'"

₁₂So Hathach reported to Mordecai all the words of Esther. ₁₃Then Mordecai said to Hathach, "Go, and say to her, 'Esther, don't say to yourself that you alone will escape in the kingdom, more than all the other Jews. ₁₄For if you keep quiet on this occasion, help and protection will come to the Jews from another place; but you and your father's house will perish. Who knows if you have been made queen for this occasion?'"

₁₅And Esther sent the messenger who came to her to Mordecai, saying, ₁₆"Go and assemble the Jews that are in Susa, and all of you fast for me. Don't eat or drink for three days, night and day. My maidens and I

will also fast. Then I will go in to the king contrary to the law, even if I must die."

₁₇So Mordecai went and did all that Esther commanded him.ᵇ ₁₈[He prayed to the Lord, making mention of all the works of the Lord. ₁₉He said, "Lordᶜ God, you are king ruling over all, for all things are in your power, and there is no one who can oppose you in your purpose to save Israel; ₂₀for you have made the heaven and the earth and every wonderful thing under heaven. ₂₁You are Lord of all, and there is no one who can resist you, Lord. ₂₂You know all things. You know, Lord, that it is not in insolence, nor arrogance, nor love of glory, that I have done this, to refuse to bow down to the arrogant Haman. ₂₃For I would gladly have kissed the soles of his feet for the safety of Israel. ₂₄But I have done this that I might not set the glory of man above the glory of God. I will not worship anyone except you, my Lord, and I will not do these things in arrogance. ₂₅And now, O Lord God, the King, the God of Abraham, spare your people, for our enemies are planning our destruction, and they have desired to destroy your ancient inheritance. ₂₆Do not overlook your people, whom you have redeemed for yourself out of the land of Egypt. ₂₇Listen to my prayer. Have mercy on your inheritance and turn our mourning into gladness, that we may live and sing praise to your name, O Lord. Don't utterly destroy the mouth of those who praise you, O Lord."

₂₈All Israel cried with all their might, for death was before their eyes. ₂₉And queen Esther took refuge in the Lord, being taken as it were in the agony of death. ₃₀Having taken off her glorious apparel, she put on garments of distress and mourning. Instead of grand perfumes she filled her head with ashes and dung. She greatly humbled her body, and she filled every place of her glad adorning with her tangled hair. ₃₁She implored the Lord God of Israel, and said, "O my Lord, you alone are our king. Help me. I am destitute, and have no helper but you, ₃₂for my danger is near at handᵈ. ₃₃I have heard from my birth in the tribe of my kindred that you, Lord, took Israel out of all the nations, and our fathers out of all their kindred for a perpetual inheritance, and have done for them all that you have said. ₃₄And now we have sinned before you, and you have delivered us into the hands of our enemies, ₃₅because we honoured their gods. You are righteous, O Lord. ₃₆But now they have not been content with the bitterness of our slavery, but have laid their hands on the hands of their idols ₃₇to abolish the decree of your mouth, and utterly to destroy your inheritance, and to stop the mouth of those who praise you, and to extinguish the glory of your house and your altar, ₃₈and to open the mouth of the Gentiles to speak theᵉ praises of vanities, and that a mortal king should be admired forever. ₃₉O Lord, don't surrender your sceptre to those who don't exist, and don't let them laugh at our fall, but turn their counsel against themselves, and make an example of him who has begun to injure us. ₄₀Remember us, O Lord! Manifest yourself in the time of our affliction. Encourage me, O King of gods, and ruler of all dominion! ₄₁Put harmonious speech into my mouth before the lion, and turn his heart to hate him who fights against us, to the utter destruction of those who agree with him. ₄₂But deliver us by your hand, and help me who am alone and have no one but you, O Lord. ₄₃You know all things, and know that I hate the glory of transgressors,ᶠ and that I abhor the bed of the uncircumcised and of every stranger. ₄₄You know my necessity, for I abhor the symbol of my proud station, which is upon my head in the days of myᵍ splendour. I abhor it as a menstruous cloth, and I don't wear it in the days of my tranquillity. ₄₅Your handmaid has not eaten at Haman's table, and I have not honoured the banquet of the king, neither have I drunk wine of libations. ₄₆Neither has your handmaid rejoiced since the day of my promotion until now, except in you, O Lord God of Abraham. ₄₇O god, who has power over all, listen to the voice of the desperate, and deliver us from the hand of those who devise mischief. Deliver me from my fear.]

5

₁ʰ It came to pass on the third day, when she had ceased praying, that she took off her servant's dress and put on her glorious apparel. Being splendidly dressed and having called upon God the Overseer and Preserver of all things, she took her two maids, and she leaned upon one, as a delicate female, and the other followed bearing her train. She was blooming in the perfection of her beauty. Her face was cheerful and looked lovely, but her heart was filled with fear. Having passed through all the doors, she stood before the king. He was sitting on his royal throne. He had put on all his glorious apparel, covered all over with gold and precious stones, and was very terrifying. And having raised his face resplendent with glory, he looked with intense anger. The queen fell, and changed her colour as she fainted. She bowed herself upon the head of the maid who went before her. But God changed the spirit of the king to gentleness, and in intense feeling, he sprang from off his throne, and took her into his arms, until she recovered. He comforted her with peaceful words, and said to her, "What is the matter, Esther? I am your relative. Cheer up! You shall not die, for our command is openly declared to you: 'Draw near.'"

₂And having raised the golden sceptre, he laid it upon her neck, and embraced her. He said, "Speak to me."

So she said to him, "I saw you, my lord, as an angel of God, and my heart was troubled for fear of your glory; for you, my lord, are to be

ᵃ 3:13 Note: The part in brackets is not in ᴴᵉᵇʳᵉʷ

ᵇ 4:17 Note: The part between brackets, ⁱ·ᵉ· to the end of chapter 5 is not in the Hebrew

ᶜ 4:19 See 3 Kings 8.53. Note.

ᵈ 4:32 Greek in my hand.

ᵉ 4:38 Greek virtues.

ᶠ 4:43 ᵒʳ· opinion.

ᵍ 4:44 Greek vision.

ʰ 5:1 From the first verse to the third, the Greek widely differs from the Hebrew wondered at, and your face is full of grace." While she was speaking, she fainted and fell.

Then the king was troubled, and all his servants comforted her. ₃The king said, "What do you desire, Esther? What is your request? Ask even to the half of my kingdom, and it shall be yours."

₄Esther said, "Today is a special day. So if it seems good to the king, let both him and Haman come to the feast which I will prepare this day."

₅The king said, "Hurry and bring Haman here, that we may do as Esther said." So they both came to the feast about which Esther had spoken. ₆At the banquet, the king said to Esther, "What is your request, queen Esther? You shall have all that you require."

₇She said, "My request and my petition is: ₈if I have found favour in the king's sight, let the king and Haman come again tomorrow to the feast which I shall prepare for them, and tomorrow I will do as I have done today."

₉So Haman went out from the king very glad and merry; but when Haman saw Mordecai the Jew in the court, he was greatly enraged. ₁₀Having gone into his own house, he called his friends, and his wife Zeresh. ₁₁He showed them his wealth and the glory with which the king had invested him, and how he had promoted him to be chief ruler in the kingdom. ₁₂Haman said, "The queen has called no one to the feast with the king but me, and I am invited tomorrow. ₁₃But these things don't please me while I see Mordecai the Jew in the court."

₁₄Then Zeresh his wife and his friends said to him, "Let a fifty cubit tallª gallows be made for you. In the morning you speak to the king, and let Mordecai be hanged on the gallows; but you go in to the feast with the king, and be merry."

The saying pleased Haman, and the gallows was prepared.

6

₁The Lord removed sleep from the king that night; so he told his servant to bring in theᵇ books, the registers of daily events, to read to him. ₂And he found theᶜ records written concerning Mordecai, how he had told the king about the king's two chamberlains, when they were keeping guard, and sought to lay hands on Ahasuerus. ₃The king said, "What honour or favour have we done for Mordecai?"

The king's servants said, "You haven't done anything for him."

₄And while the king was enquiring about the kindness of Mordecai, behold, Haman was in the court. The king said, "Who is in the court?" Now Haman had come in to speak to the king about hanging Mordecai on the gallows which he had prepared. ₅The king's servants said, "Behold, Haman stands in the court."

And the king said, "Call him!"

₆The king said to Haman, "What should I do for the man whom I wish to honour?"

Haman said within himself, "Whom would the king honour but myself?" ₇He said to the king, "As for the man whom the king wishes to honour, ₈let the king's servants bring the robe of fine linen which the king puts on, and the horse on which the king rides, ₉and let him give it to one of the king's noble friends, and let him dress the man whom the king loves. Let him mount him on the horse, and proclaim through theᵈ streets of the city, saying, "This is what will be done for every man whom the king honours!"

₁₀Then the king said to Haman, "You have spoken well. Do so for Mordecai the Jew, who waits in the palace, and let not a word of what you have spoken be neglected!"

₁₁So Haman took the robe and the horse, dressed Mordecai, mounted him on the horse, and went through the streets of the city, proclaiming, "This is what will be done for every man whom the king wishes to honour."

₁₂Then Mordecai returned to the palace; but Haman went home mourning, with his head covered.

₁₃Haman related the events that had happened to him to Zeresh his wife and to his friends. His friends and his wife said to him, "If Mordecai is of the race of the Jews, and you have begun to be humbled before him, you will assuredly fall; you will not be able to withstand him, for the living God is with him." ₁₄While they were still speaking, the chamberlains arrived to rush Haman to the banquet which Esther had prepared.

7

₁So the king and Haman went in to drink with the queen. ₂The king said to Esther at the banquet on the second day, "What is it, queen Esther? What is your request? What is your petition? It shall be done for you, up to half of my kingdom."

₃She answered and said, "If I have found favour in the sight of the king, let my life be granted as my petition, and my people as my request. ₄For both I and my people are sold for destruction, pillage, and genocide. If both we and our children were sold for male and female slaves, I would not have bothered you, for thisᵉ isn't worthy of the king's palace."

₅The king said, "Who has dared to do this thing?"

₆Esther said, "The enemy is Haman, this wicked man!"

Then Haman was terrified in the presence of the king and the queen.

₇The king rose up from the banquet to go into the garden. Haman began to

beg the queen for mercy, for he saw that he was in serious trouble. ₈The king returned from the garden; and Haman had fallen upon the couch, begging the queen for mercy. The king said, "Will you even assault my wife in my house?"

And when Haman heard it, he changed countenance. ₉And Bugathan, one of the chamberlains, said to the king, "Behold, Haman has also prepared a gallows for Mordecai, who spoke concerning the king, and a fifty cubit high gallows has been set up on Haman's property."

The king said, "Let him beᶠ hanged on it!" ₁₀So Haman was hanged on the gallows that had been prepared for Mordecai. Then the king's wrath was abated.

8

₁On that day, King Ahasuerus gave to Esther all that belonged to Haman the slanderer. The king called Mordecai, for Esther had told that he was related to her. ₂The king took the ring which he had taken away from Haman and gave it to Mordecai. Esther appointed Mordecai over all that had been Haman's. ₃She spoke yet again to the king, and fell at his feet, and implored him to undo Haman's mischief and all that he had done against the Jews. ₄Then the king extended the golden sceptre to Esther; and Esther arose to stand near the king. ₅Esther said, "If it seems good to you, and I have found favour in your sight, let an order be sent that the letters sent by Haman may be reversed—letters that were written for the destruction of the Jews who are in your kingdom. ₆For how could I see the affliction of my people, and how could I survive the destruction of myᵍ kindred?"

₇Then the king said to Esther, "If I have given and freely granted you all that was Haman's, and hanged him on a gallows because he laid his hands upon the Jews, what more do you seek? ₈Write in my name whatever seems good to you, and seal it with my ring; for whatever is written at the command of the king, and sealed with my ring, cannot be countermanded. ₉So the scribes were called in the first month, which is Nisan, on the twenty-third day of the same year; and orders were written to the Jews, whatever the king had commanded to theʰ local governors and chiefs of the local governors, from India even to Ethiopia—one hundred and twenty-seven local governors, according to the several provinces, in their own languages. ₁₀They were written by order of the king, sealed with his ring, and the letters were sent by the couriers. ₁₁In them, he charged them to use their own laws in every city, to help each other, and to treat their adversaries and those who attacked them as they pleased, ₁₂on one day in all the kingdom of Ahasuerus, on the thirteenth day of the twelfth month, which is Adar. ₁₃Let the copies be posted in conspicuous places throughout the kingdom. Let all the Jews be ready against this day, to fight against their enemies. The following is a copy of the letter containing orders:

ⁱ[The great King Ahasuerus sends greetings to the rulers of provinces in one hundred and twenty-seven local governance regions, from India to Ethiopia, even to those who are faithful to our interests. Many who have been frequently honoured by the most abundant kindness of theirʲ benefactors have conceived ambitious designs, and not only endeavour to hurt our subjects, but moreover, not being able to bear prosperity, they also endeavour to plot against their own benefactors. They not only would utterly abolish gratitude from amongst men, but also, elated by the boastings of men who are strangers to all that is good, they supposed that they would escape the sin-hating vengeance of the ever-seeing God. And oftentimes evil exhortation has made partakers of the guilt of shedding innocent blood, and has involved in irremediable calamities many of those who had been appointed to offices of authority, who had been entrusted with the management of their friends' affairs; while men, by the false sophistry of an evil disposition, have deceived the simple goodwill of the ruling powers. And it is possible to see this, not so much from more ancient traditional accounts, as it is immediately in your power to see it by examining what things have been wickedlyᵏ perpetrated by the baseness of men unworthily holding power. It is right to take heed with regard to the future, that we may maintain the government in undisturbed peace for all men, adopting needful changes, and ever judging those cases which come under our notice with truly equitable decisions. For whereas Haman, a Macedonian, the son of Hammedatha, in reality an alien from the blood of the Persians, and differing widely from our mild course of government, having been hospitably entertained by us, obtained so large a share of our universal kindness as to be called our father, and to continue the person next to the royal throne, reverenced of all; he however, overcome byˡ pride, endeavored to deprive us of our dominion, and our life;ᵐ having by various and subtle artifices demanded for destruction both Mordecai our deliverer and perpetual benefactor, and Esther the blameless consort of our kingdom, along with their whole nation. For by these methods he thought, having surprised us in a defenceless state, to transfer the dominion of the Persians to the Macedonians. But we find that the Jews, who have been consigned to destruction by theⁿ most abominable of men, are not malefactors, but living according to the most just laws, and being the sons

---

ª *5:14* ᴳʳᵉᵉᵏ a tree cut.

ᵇ *6:1* ᴳʳᵉᵉᵏ letters.

ᶜ *6:2* ᴳʳᵉᵉᵏ letters.

ᵈ *6:9* ᴼʳ, wide space.

ᵉ *7:4* see Hebrew: slanderer

ᶠ *7:9* ᴼʳ, impaled.

ᵍ *8:6* ᴳʳᵉᵉᵏ country.

ʰ *8:9* ᴳʳᵉᵉᵏ stewards.

ⁱ *8:13* the passages in brackets are not in the ᴴᵉᵇʳᵉʷ.

ʲ *8:13* perhaps rulers, see Luke 22. 25.

ᵏ *8:13* ᴳʳᵉᵉᵏ contrived.

ˡ *8:13* ᴳʳᵉᵉᵏ not having borne.

ᵐ *8:13* ᴳʳᵉᵉᵏ spirit.

ⁿ *8:13* ᴳʳᵉᵉᵏ thrice guilty.

of the living God, the most high and[a] mighty, who maintains the kingdom, to us as well as to our forefathers, in the most excellent order. You will therefore do well in refusing to obey the letter sent by Haman the son of Hammedatha, because he who has done these things has been hanged with his whole family at the gates of Susa, Almighty God having swiftly returned to him a worthy punishment. We enjoin you then, having openly published a copy of this letter in every place, to give the Jews permission to use their own lawful customs and to strengthen them, that on the thirteenth of the twelfth month Adar, on the self-same day, they may defend themselves against those who attack them in a time of affliction. For in the place of the destruction of the chosen race, Almighty God has granted them this time of gladness. Therefore you also, amongst your notable feasts, must keep a distinct day with all festivity, that both now and hereafter it may be a day of deliverance to us and who are well disposed towards the Persians, but to those that plotted against us a memorial of destruction. And every city and province collectively, which shall not do accordingly, shall be consumed with vengeance by spear and fire. It shall be made not only inaccessible to men, but most hateful to wild beasts and birds forever.] Let the copies be posted in conspicuous places throughout the kingdom and let all the Jews be ready against this day, to fight against their enemies. 14 So the horsemen went forth with haste to perform the king's commands. The ordinance was also published in Susa.

15 Mordecai went out robed in royal apparel, wearing a golden crown and a diadem of fine purple linen. The people in Susa saw it and rejoiced. 16 The Jews had light and gladness 17 in every city and province where the ordinance was published. Wherever the proclamation took place, the Jews had joy and gladness, feasting and mirth. Many of the Gentiles were circumcised and became Jews for fear of the Jews.

9

1 Now in the twelfth month, on the thirteenth day of the month, which is Adar, the letters written by the king arrived. 2 In that day, the adversaries of the Jews perished; for no one resisted, through fear of them. 3 For the chiefs of the local governors, and the princes and the royal scribes, honoured the Jews; for the fear of Mordecai was upon them. 4 For the order of the king was in force, that he should be celebrated in all the kingdom. 6 In the city Susa the Jews killed five hundred men, 7 including Pharsannes, Delphon, Phasga, 8 Pharadatha, Barea, Sarbaca, 9 Marmasima, Ruphaeus, Arsaeus, and Zabuthaeus, 10 the ten sons of Haman the son of Hammedatha the Bugaean, the enemy of the Jews; and they plundered their property on the same day. 11 The number of those who perished in Susa was reported to the king.

12 Then the king said to Esther, "The Jews have slain five hundred men in the city Susa. What do you think they have done in the rest of the country? What more do you ask, that it may be done for you?"

13 Esther said to the king, "Let it be granted to the Jews to do the same to them tomorrow. Also, hang the bodies of the ten sons of Haman."

14 He permitted it to be done; and he gave up to the Jews of the city the bodies of the sons of Haman to hang. 15 The Jews assembled in Susa on the fourteenth day of Adar and killed three hundred men, but plundered no property.

16 The rest of the Jews who were in the kingdom assembled, and helped one another, and obtained rest from their enemies; for they destroyed fifteen thousand of them on the thirteenth day of Adar, but took no spoil. 17 They rested on the fourteenth of the same month, and kept it as a day of rest with joy and gladness.

18 The Jews in the city of Susa assembled also on the fourteenth day and rested; and they also observed the fifteenth with joy and gladness. 19 On this account then, the Jews dispersed in every foreign land keep the fourteenth of Adar as a[b] holy day with joy, each sending gifts of food to his neighbour.

20 Mordecai wrote these things in a book and sent them to the Jews, as many as were in the kingdom of Ahasuerus, both those who were near and those who were far away, 21 to establish these as joyful days and to keep the fourteenth and fifteenth of Adar; 22 for on these days the Jews obtained rest from their enemies; and in that month, which was Adar, in which a change was made for them from mourning to joy, and from sorrow to a holiday, to spend the whole of it in good days of[c] feasting and gladness, sending portions to their friends and to the poor. 23 And the Jews consented to this as Mordecai wrote to them, 24 showing how Haman the son of Hammedatha the Macedonian fought against them, how he made a decree and cast[d] lots to destroy them utterly; 25 also how he went in to the king, telling him to hang Mordecai; but all the calamities he tried to bring upon the Jews came upon himself, and he was hanged, along with his children. 26 Therefore these days were called Purim, because of the lots (for in their language they are called Purim) because of the words of this letter, and because of all they suffered on this account, and all that happened to them. 27 Mordecai established it, and the Jews took upon themselves, upon their offspring, and upon those who were joined to them to observe it, neither would they on any account behave differently; but these days were to be a memorial kept in every generation, city, family, and province. 28 These days of Purim shall be kept forever, and their memorial shall not fail in any generation.

29 Queen Esther the daughter of Aminadab and Mordecai the Jew wrote all that they had done, and gave the confirmation of the letter about Purim. 31 Mordecai and Esther the queen established this decision on their own, pledging their own well-being to their plan. 32 And Esther established it by a command forever, and it was written for a memorial.

10

1 The king levied a tax upon his kingdom both by land and sea. 2 As for his strength and valour, and the wealth and glory of his kingdom, behold, they are written in the book of the Persians and Medes for a memorial.

3 Mordecai[e] was viceroy to King Ahasuerus, and was a great man in the kingdom, honoured by the Jews, and lived his life loved by all his nation.[f] 4 [Mordecai said, "These things have come from God. 5 For I remember the dream which I had concerning these matters; for not one detail of them has failed. 6 There was the little spring which became a river, and there was light, and the sun and much water. The river is Esther, whom the king married and made queen. 7 The two serpents are Haman and me. 8 The nations are those which combined to destroy the name of the Jews. 9 But as for my nation, this is Israel, even those who cried to God and were delivered; for the Lord delivered his people. The Lord rescued us out of all these calamities; and God worked such signs and great wonders as have not been done amongst the nations. 10 Therefore he ordained two lots. One for the people of God, and one for all the other nations. 11 And these two lots came for an appointed season, and for a day of judgement, before God, and for all the nations. 12 God remembered his people and vindicated his inheritance. 13 They shall observe these days in the month Adar, on the fourteenth and on the fifteenth day of the month, with an assembly, joy, and gladness before God, throughout the generations forever amongst his people Israel. 14 In the fourth year of the reign of Ptolemeus and Cleopatra, Dositheus, who said he was a priest and Levite, and Ptolemeus his son brought this letter of Purim, which they said was authentic, and that Lysimachus the son of Ptolemeus, who was in Jerusalem, had interpreted.]

---

a 8:13 Greek greatest.
b 9:19 Greek good day.
c 9:22 Greek weddings.
d 9:24 Greek lot.
e 10:3 Greek succeeded to Or, came into the place of.
f 10:3 the passages in brackets are not in the Hebrew.

The Wisdom of Solomon

The *Wisdom of Solomon* is recognised as Deuterocanonical Scripture by the Roman Catholic, Greek Orthodox, and Russian Orthodox Churches.

1

1 Love righteousness, all you who are judges of the earth.
Think of the Lord[a] with a good mind.
Seek him in singleness of heart,
2 because he is found by those who don't put him to the test,
and is manifested to those who trust him.
3 for crooked thoughts separate from God.
His Power convicts when it is tested,
and exposes the foolish;
4 because wisdom will not enter into a soul that devises evil,
nor dwell in a body that is enslaved by sin.
5 For a holy spirit of discipline will flee deceit,
and will depart from thoughts that are without understanding,
and will be ashamed when unrighteousness has come in.

6 For[b] wisdom is a spirit who loves man,
and she will not hold a[c] blasphemer guiltless for his lips,
because God is witness of his inmost self,
and is a true overseer of his heart,
and a hearer of his tongue.
7 Because the spirit of the Lord has filled[d] the world,
and that which holds all things together knows what is said.
8 Therefore no one who utters unrighteous things will be unseen;
neither will Justice, when it convicts, pass him by.
9 For in his counsels the ungodly will be searched out,
and the sound of his words will come to the Lord to bring his lawless deeds to conviction;
10 because a jealous ear listens to all things,
and the noise of murmurings is not hidden.
11 Beware then of unprofitable murmuring,
and keep your tongue from slander;
because no secret utterance will go on its way void,
and a lying mouth destroys a soul.
12 Don't court death in the error of your life.
Don't draw destruction upon yourselves by the works of your hands;
13 because God didn't make death,
neither does he delight when the living perish.
14 For he created all things that they might have being.
The generative powers of the world are wholesome,
and there is no poison of destruction in them,
nor has Hades[e] royal dominion upon earth;
15 for righteousness is immortal,
16 but ungodly men by their hands and their words summon death;
deeming him a friend they[f] pined away.
They made a covenant with him,
because they are worthy to belong with him.

2

1 For they said[g] within themselves, with unsound reasoning,
"Our life is short and sorrowful.
There is no healing when a man comes to his end,
and no one was ever known who[h] was released from Hades.
2 Because we were born by mere chance,
and hereafter we will be as though we had never been,
because the breath in our nostrils is smoke,
and reason is a spark kindled by the beating of our heart,
3 which being extinguished, the body will be turned into ashes,
and the spirit will be dispersed as thin air.
4 Our name will be forgotten in time.
No one will remember our works.
Our life will pass away as the traces of a cloud,
and will be scattered as is a mist,
when it is chased by the rays of the sun,
and[i] overcome by its heat.
5 For our allotted time is the passing of a shadow,
and our end doesn't retreat,
because it is securely sealed, and no one[j] turns it back.

6 "Come therefore and let's enjoy the good things that exist.
Let's use the creation earnestly as in our youth.
7 Let's fill ourselves with costly wine and perfumes,
and let no spring flower pass us by.
8 Let's crown ourselves with rosebuds before they wither.
9 Let none of us go without his share in our proud revelry.
Let's leave tokens of mirth everywhere,
because this is our portion, and this is our lot.

10 Let's oppress the righteous poor.
Let's not spare the widow,
nor regard the grey hair of the old man.
11 But let our strength be a law of righteousness;
for that which is weak is proven useless.
12 But let's lie in wait for the righteous man,
because he annoys us,
is contrary to our works,
reproaches us with sins against the law,
and charges us with sins against our training.
13 He professes to have knowledge of God,
and calls himself a child of the Lord.
14 He became to us a reproof of our thoughts.
15 He is grievous to us even to look at,
because his life is unlike other men's,
and his paths are strange.
16 We were regarded by him as something worthless,
and he abstains from our ways as from uncleanness.
He calls the latter end of the righteous happy.
He boasts that God is his father.
17 Let's see if his words are true.
Let's test what will happen at the end of his life.
18 For if the righteous man is God's son, he will uphold him,
and he will deliver him out of the hand of his adversaries.
19 Let's test him with insult and torture,
that we may find out how gentle he is,
and test his patience.
20 Let's condemn him to a shameful death,
for he will be protected, according to his words."

21 Thus they reasoned, and they were led astray;
for their wickedness blinded them,
22 and they didn't know the mysteries of God,
neither did they hope for wages of holiness,
nor did they discern that there is a prize for blameless souls.
23 Because God created man for incorruption,
and made him an image of his own everlastingness;
24 but death entered into the world by the envy of the devil,
and those who belong to him experience it.

3

1 But the souls of the righteous are in the hand of God,
and no torment will touch them.
2 In the eyes of the foolish they seemed to have died.
Their departure was considered a disaster,
3 and their travel away from us ruin,
but they are in peace.
4 For even if in the sight of men they are punished,
their hope is full of immortality.
5 Having borne a little chastening, they will receive great good;
because God tested them, and found them worthy of himself.
6 He tested them like gold in the furnace,
and he accepted them as a whole burnt offering.
7 In the time of their visitation they will shine.
They will run back and forth like sparks amongst stubble.
8 They will judge nations and have dominion over peoples.
The Lord will reign over them forever.
9 Those who trust him will understand truth.
The faithful will live with him in love,
because grace and mercy are with his chosen ones.

10 But the ungodly will be punished even as their reasoning deserves,
those who neglected righteousness and revolted from the Lord;
11 for he who despises wisdom and discipline is miserable.
Their hope is void and their toils unprofitable.
Their works are useless.
12 Their wives are foolish and their children are wicked.
13 Their descendants are cursed.
For the barren woman who is undefiled is happy,
she who has not conceived in transgression.
She will have fruit when God examines souls.
14 So is the eunuch which has done no lawless deed with his hands,
nor imagined wicked things against the Lord;
for a precious gift will be given to him for his faithfulness,
and a delightful inheritance in the Lord's sanctuary.
15 For good labours have fruit of great renown.
The root of understanding can't fail.
16 But children of adulterers will not come to maturity.
The seed of an unlawful union will vanish away.
17 For if they live long, they will not be esteemed,
and in the end, their old age will be without honour.
18 If they die young, they will have no hope,
nor consolation in the day of judgement.

---

a *1:1* Gr. in goodness.
b *1:6* Some authorities read the spirit of wisdom is loving to man.
c *1:6* Or, reviler
d *1:7* Gr. the inhabited earth.
e *1:14* Or, a royal house

f *1:16* Or, were consumed with love of him
g *2:1* Or, amongst
h *2:1* Or, returned out of Hades
i *2:4* Gr. weighed down.
j *2:5* Or, comes again

19 For the end of an unrighteous generation is always grievous.

4

1 It is better to be childless with virtue,
    for immortality is in the memory of virtue,
        because it is recognised both before God and before men.
2 When it is present, people imitate it.
    They long after it when it has departed.
Throughout all time it marches, crowned in triumph,
    victorious in the competition for the prizes that are undefiled.
3 But the multiplying brood of the ungodly will be of no profit,
    and their illegitimate offshoots won't take deep root,
        nor will they establish a sure hold.
4 For even if they grow branches and flourish for a season,
    standing unsure, they will be shaken by the wind.
    They will be uprooted by the violence of winds.
5 Their branches will be broken off before they come to maturity.
    Their fruit will be useless,
        never ripe to eat, and fit for nothing.
6 For unlawfully conceived children are witnesses of wickedness
    against parents when they are investigated.

7 But a righteous man, even if he dies before his time, will be at rest.
8 For honourable old age is not that which stands in length of time,
    nor is its measure given by number of years,
        9 but understanding is grey hair to men,
        and an unspotted life is ripe old age.

10 Being found well-pleasing to God, someone was loved.
    While living amongst sinners he was transported.
11 He was caught away, lest evil should change his understanding,
    or guile deceive his soul.
12 For the fascination of wickedness obscures the things which are good,
    and the whirl of desire perverts an innocent mind.
13 Being made perfect quickly,
    he filled a long time;
        14 for his soul was pleasing to the Lord.
    Therefore he hurried out of the midst of wickedness.
15 But the peoples saw and didn't understand,
    not considering this, that grace and mercy are with his chosen,
        and that he visits his holy ones;
16 but a righteous man who is dead will condemn the ungodly who are
        living,
    and youth who is quickly perfected will condemn the many years of an
        unrighteous man's old age.
17 For the ungodly will see a wise man's end,
    and won't understand what the Lord planned for him,
        and why he safely kept him.
18 They will see, and they will despise;
    but the Lord will laugh them to scorn.
After this, they will become a dishonoured carcass
    and a reproach amongst the dead forever;
19 because he will dash them speechless to the ground,
    and will shake them from the foundations.
They will lie utterly waste.
    They will be in anguish
        and their memory will perish.

20 They will come with coward fear when their sins are counted.
    Their lawless deeds will convict them to their face.

5

1 Then the righteous man will stand in great boldness
    before the face of those who afflicted him,
        and those who make his labours of no account.
2 When they see him, they will be troubled with terrible fear,
    and will be amazed at the marvel of salvation.
3 They will speak amongst themselves repenting,
    and for distress of spirit they will groan,
        "This was he whom we used to hold in derision,
        as a parable of reproach.
4 We fools considered his life madness,
    and his end without honour.
5 How was he counted amongst sons of God?
    How is his lot amongst saints?
6 Truly we went astray from the way of truth.
    The light of righteousness didn't shine for us.
    The sun didn't rise for us.
7 We[a] took our fill of the paths of lawlessness and destruction.
    We travelled through trackless deserts,
        but we didn't know the Lord's way.
8 What did our arrogance profit us?
    What good have riches and boasting brought us?

9 Those things all passed away as a shadow,
    like a rumour that runs by,

10 like a ship passing through the billowy water,
    which, when it has gone by, there is no trace to be found,
        no pathway of its keel in the waves.
11 Or it is like when a bird flies through the air,
    no evidence of its passage is found,
        but the light wind, lashed with the stroke of its pinions,
        and torn apart with the violent rush of the moving wings, is passed
            through.
    Afterwards no sign of its coming remains.
12 Or it is like when an arrow is shot at a mark,
    the air it divided closes up again immediately,
        so that men don't know where it passed through.
13 So we also, as soon as we were born, ceased to be;
    and we had no sign of virtue to show,
        but we were utterly consumed in our wickedness."
14 Because the hope of the ungodly man is like chaff carried by the wind,
    and[b] as[c] foam vanishing before a tempest;
    and is scattered like smoke by the wind,
        and passes by as the remembrance of a guest who stays just a day.

15 But the righteous live forever.
    Their reward is in the Lord,
        and the care for them with the Most High.
16 Therefore they will receive the crown of royal dignity
    and the diadem of beauty from the Lord's hand,
because he will cover them with his right hand,
    and he will shield them with his arm.
17 He will take his zeal as complete armour,
    and will make the whole creation his weapons to punish his enemies:
18 He will put on righteousness as a breastplate,
    and will wear impartial judgement as a helmet.
19 He will take holiness as an invincible shield.
    20 He will sharpen stern wrath for a sword.
    The universe will go with him to fight against his frenzied foes.
21 Shafts of lightning will fly with true aim.
    They will leap to the mark from the clouds, as from a well-drawn bow.
22 Hailstones full of wrath will be hurled as from a catapult.
    The water of the sea will be angered against them.
    Rivers will sternly overwhelm them.
23 A mighty wind will encounter them.
    It will winnow them away like a tempest.
So lawlessness will make all the land desolate.
    Their evil-doing will overturn the thrones of princes.

6

1 Hear therefore, you kings, and understand.
    Learn, you judges of the ends of the earth.
        2 Give ear, you rulers who have dominion over many people,
        and make your boast[d] in multitudes of nations,
3 because your dominion was given to you from the Lord,
    and your sovereignty from the Most High.
He will search out your works,
    and will enquire about your plans,
4 because being officers of his kingdom, you didn't judge rightly,
    nor did you keep the law,
        nor did you walk according to God's counsel.
5 He will come upon you awfully and swiftly,
    because a stern judgement comes on those who are in high places.
6 For the man of low estate may be pardoned in mercy,
    but mighty men will be mightily tested.
7 For the Sovereign Lord of all will not be impressed with anyone,
    neither will he show deference to greatness;
because it is he who made both small and great,
    and cares about them all;
8 but the scrutiny that comes upon the powerful is strict.
9 Therefore, my words are to you, O princes,
    that you may learn wisdom and not fall away.
10 For those who have kept the things that are holy in holiness will be made
        holy.
    Those who have been taught them will find what to say in defence.
11 Therefore set your desire on my words.
    Long for them, and you princes will be instructed.

12 Wisdom is radiant and doesn't fade away;
    and is easily seen by those who love her,
        and found by those who seek her.
13 She anticipates those who desire her, making herself known.
14 He who rises up early to seek her won't have difficulty,
    for he will find her sitting at his gates.
        15 For to think upon her is perfection of understanding,
        and he who watches for her will quickly be free from care;
16 because she herself goes around, seeking those who are worthy of her,
    and in their paths she appears to them graciously,
        and in every purpose she meets them.
17 For her true beginning is desire for instruction;

---

a 5:7 See Proverbs 14:14.
b 5:14 Gr. like foam chased to thinness: or, as thin foam chased.

c 5:14 Most Greek authorities read hoar frost: some authorities, perhaps rightly, a spider's web.
d 6:2 Or, in the multitudes of your nations

and desire for instruction is love.
18 And love is observance of her laws.
     To give heed to her laws confirms immortality.
19 Immortality brings closeness to God.
     20 So then desire for wisdom promotes to a kingdom.

21 If therefore you delight in thrones and sceptres, you princes of peoples,
     honour wisdom, that you may reign forever.
22 But what wisdom is, and how she came into being, I will declare.
     I won't hide mysteries from you;
     but I will explore from her first beginning,
     bring the knowledge of her into clear light,
     and I will not pass by the truth.
23 Indeed, I won't travel with consuming envy,
     because envy will have no fellowship with wisdom.
24 But a multitude of wise men is salvation to the world,
     and an understanding king is stability for his people.
25 Therefore be instructed by my words, and you will profit.

7

1 I myself am also[a] mortal, like everyone else,
     and am a descendant of one formed first and born of the earth.
2 I moulded into flesh in the time of ten months in my mother's womb,
     being compacted in blood from the seed of man and pleasure of
          marriage.
3 I also, when I was born, drew in the common air,
     and fell upon the kindred earth,
uttering, like all, for my first voice, the same cry.
4 I was nursed with care in swaddling clothes.
5 For no king had a different beginning,
     6 but all men have one entrance into life, and a common departure.

7 For this cause I prayed, and understanding was given to me.
     I asked, and a spirit of wisdom came to me.
8 I preferred her before sceptres and thrones.
     I considered riches nothing in comparison to her.
9 Neither did I liken to her any priceless gem,
     because all gold in her presence is a little sand,
     and silver will be considered as clay before her.
10 I loved her more than health and beauty,
     and I chose to have her rather than light,
     because her bright shining is never laid to sleep.
11 All good things came to me with her,
     and innumerable riches are in her hands.
12 And I rejoiced over them all because wisdom leads them;
     although I didn't know that she was their mother.
13 As I learnt without guile, I impart without grudging.
     I don't hide her riches.
14 For she is a treasure for men that doesn't fail,
     and those who use it obtain friendship with God,
     commended by the gifts which they present through discipline.

15 But may God grant that I may speak his judgement,
     and to conceive thoughts worthy of what has been given me;
     because he is one who guides even wisdom and who corrects the
          wise.
16 For both we and our words are in his hand,
     with all understanding and skill in various crafts.
17 For he himself gave me an unerring knowledge of the things that are,
     to know the structure of the universe and the operation of the
          elements;
     18 the beginning, end, and middle of times;
     the alternations of the solstices and the changes of seasons;
     19 the circuits of years and the positions of stars;
     20 the natures of living creatures and the raging of wild beasts;
     the violence of[b] winds and the thoughts of men;
     the diversities of plants and the virtues of roots.
21 All things that are either secret or manifest I learnt,
     22 for wisdom, that is the architect of all things, taught me.

For there is in her a spirit that is quick to understand, holy,
     unique, manifold, subtle, freely moving, clear in utterance, unpolluted,
     distinct, invulnerable, loving what is good, keen, unhindered,
     23 beneficent, loving towards man, steadfast, sure, free from care, all-
          powerful, all-surveying,
     and penetrating through all spirits that are quick to understand, pure,
          most subtle.
24 For wisdom is more mobile than any motion.
     Yes, she pervades and penetrates all things by reason of her purity.
25 For she is a breath of the power of God,
     and a pure emanation of the glory of the Almighty.
Therefore nothing defiled can find entrance into her.
26 For she is a reflection of everlasting light,
     an unspotted mirror of the working of God,
     and an image of his goodness.

27 Although she is one, she has power to do all things.
     Remaining in herself, she renews all things.
From generation to generation passing into holy souls,
     she makes friends of God and prophets.
     28 For God loves nothing as much as one who dwells with wisdom.
29 For she is fairer than the sun,
     and above all the constellations of the stars.
     She is better than light.
30 For daylight yields to night,
     but evil does not prevail against wisdom.

8

1 But she reaches from one end to the other with full strength,
     and orders all things well.

2 I loved her and sought her from my youth.
     I sought to take her for my bride.
     I became enamoured by her beauty.
3 She glorifies her noble birth by living with God.
     The Sovereign Lord of all loves her.
4 For she is initiated into the knowledge of God,
     and she chooses his works.
5 But if riches are a desired possession in life,
     what is richer than wisdom, which makes all things?
6 And if understanding is effective,
     who more than[c] wisdom is an architect of the things that exist?
7 If a man loves righteousness,
     the fruits of wisdom's labour[d] are virtues,
     for she teaches soberness, understanding, righteousness, and
          courage.
     There is nothing in life more profitable for people than these.
8 And if anyone longs for wide experience,
     she knows the things of old, and infers the things to come.
     She understands subtleties of speeches and interpretations of dark
          sayings.
     She foresees signs and wonders, and the issues of seasons and
          times.

9 Therefore I determined to take her to live with me,
     knowing that she is one who would give me good counsel,
     and encourage me in cares and grief.
10 Because of her, I will have glory amongst multitudes,
     and honour in the sight of elders, though I am young.
11 I will be found keen when I give judgement.
     I will be admired in the presence of rulers.
12 When I am silent, they will wait for me.
     When I open my lips, they will heed what I say.
     If I continue speaking, they will put their hands on their mouths.
13 Because of her, I will have immortality,
     and leave behind an eternal memory to those who come after me.
14 I will govern peoples.
     Nations will be subjected to me.
15 Dreaded monarchs will fear me when they hear of me.
     Amongst the people, I will show myself to be good, and courageous in
          war.
16 When I come into my house, I will find rest with her.
     For conversation with her has no bitterness,
     and living with her has no pain, but gladness and joy.
17 When I considered these things in myself,
     and thought in my heart how immortality is in kinship to wisdom,
18 and in her friendship is good delight,
     and in the labours of her hands is wealth that doesn't fail,
     and understanding is in her companionship,
     and great renown in having fellowship with her words,
     I went about seeking how to take her to myself.
19 Now I was a clever child, and received a good soul.
     20 Or rather, being good, I came into an undefiled body.
21 But perceiving that I could not otherwise possess wisdom unless God
          gave her to me—
     yes, and to know and understand by whom the grace is given—
     I pleaded with the Lord and implored him, and with my whole heart I
          said:

9

1 "O God of my ancestors and Lord of mercy,
     who made all things by your word;
2 and by your wisdom you formed man,
     that he should have dominion over the creatures that were made by
          you,
3 and rule the world in holiness and righteousness,
     and execute judgement in uprightness of soul,
     4 give me wisdom, her who sits by you on your thrones.
Don't reject me from amongst your[e] servants,
     5 because I am your servant and the son of your handmaid,
     a weak and short-lived man,
     with little power to understand judgement and laws.

---

a 7:1 Many authorities read a mortal man.
b 7:20 Or, spirits
c 8:6 Gr. she.

d 8:7 Gr. her labours
e 9:4 Or, children

6 For even if a man is perfect amongst the sons of men,
  if the wisdom that comes from you is not with him, he will count for nothing.
7 You chose me to be king of your people,
  and a judge for your sons and daughters.
8 You gave a command to build a sanctuary on your holy mountain,
  and[a] an altar in the city where you live,
  a copy of the holy tent which you prepared from the beginning.
9 Wisdom is with you and knows your works,
  and was present when you were making the world,
  and understands what is pleasing in your eyes,
  and what is right according to your commandments.
10 Send her from the holy heavens,
  and ask her to come from the throne of your glory,
  that being present with me she may work,
  and I may learn what pleases you well.
11 For she knows all things and understands,
  and she will guide me prudently in my actions.
  She will guard me in her glory.
12 So my works will be acceptable.
  I will judge your people righteously,
  and I will be worthy of my father's[b] throne.
13 For what man will know the counsel of God?
  Or who will conceive what the Lord wills?
14 For the thoughts of mortals are unstable,
  and our plans are prone to fail.
15 For a corruptible body weighs down the soul.
  The earthy tent burdens a mind that is full of cares.
16 We can hardly guess the things that are on earth,
  and we find the things that are close at hand with labour;
  but who has traced out the things that are in the heavens?
17 Who gained knowledge of your counsel, unless you gave wisdom,
  and sent your holy spirit from on high?
18 It was thus that the ways of those who are on earth were corrected,
  and men were taught the things that are pleasing to you.
  They were saved through wisdom."

10

1 Wisdom[c] guarded to the end the first formed father of the world, who was created alone,
  and delivered him out of his own transgression,
2 and gave him strength to rule over all things.
3 But when an unrighteous man fell away from her in his anger,
  he perished himself in the rage with which he killed his brother.
4 When for his cause the earth was drowning with a flood,
  wisdom again saved it,
  guiding the righteous man's course by a paltry piece of wood.

5 Moreover, when nations consenting together in wickedness had been confounded,
  wisdom[d] knew the righteous man, and preserved him blameless to God,
  and kept him strong when his heart yearned towards his child.

6 While the ungodly were perishing, wisdom[e] delivered a righteous man,
  when he fled from the fire that descended out of heaven on the five cities.
7 To whose wickedness a smoking waste still witnesses,
  and plants bearing fair fruit that doesn't ripen,
  a disbelieving soul has a memorial: a standing pillar of salt.
8 For having passed wisdom by,
  not only were they disabled from recognising the things which are good,
  but they also left behind them for their life a monument of their folly,
  to the end that where they stumbled, they might fail even to be unseen;
9 but wisdom delivered those who waited on her out of troubles.

10 When a righteous man was a fugitive from a brother's wrath,[f] wisdom guided him in straight paths.
  She showed him God's kingdom, and gave him knowledge of holy things.
  She prospered him in his toils, and multiplied the fruits of his labour.
11 When in their covetousness men dealt harshly with him,
  she stood by him and made him rich.
12 She guarded him from enemies,
  and she kept him safe from those who lay in wait.
  Over his severe conflict, she watched as judge,
  that he might know that godliness is more powerful than every one.

13 When a righteous man was sold,[g] wisdom didn't forsake him,
  but she delivered him from sin.

She went down with him into a dungeon,
14 and in bonds she didn't depart from him,
  until she brought him the sceptre of a kingdom,
  and authority over those that dealt like a tyrant with him.
  She also showed those who had mockingly accused him to be false,
  and gave him eternal glory.

15 Wisdom[h] delivered a holy people and a blameless seed from a nation of oppressors.
16 She entered into the soul of a servant of the Lord,
  and withstood terrible kings in wonders and signs.
17 She rendered to holy men a reward of their toils.
  She guided them along a marvellous way,
  and became to them a covering in the day-time,
  and a starry flame through the night.
18 She brought them over the Red sea,
  and led them through much water;
19 but she drowned their enemies,
  and she cast them up from the bottom of the deep.
20 Therefore the righteous plundered the ungodly,
  and they sang praise to your holy name, O Lord,
  and extolled with one accord your hand that fought for them,
21 because wisdom opened the mouth of the mute,
and made the tongues of babes to speak clearly.

11

1 Wisdom prospered their works in the hand of a holy prophet.

2 They travelled through a desert without inhabitant,
  and they pitched their tents in trackless regions.
3 They withstood enemies and repelled foes.
4 They thirsted, and they called upon you,
  and water was given to them out of the[i] flinty rock,
  and healing of their thirst out of the hard stone.
5 For by what things their foes were punished,
  by these they in their need were benefitted.
6 When enemies were troubled with clotted blood
  instead of a river's ever-flowing fountain,
7 to rebuke the decree for the slaying of babies,
  you gave them abundant water beyond all hope,
8 having shown by the thirst which they had suffered
  how you punished the adversaries.
9 For when they were tried, although chastened in mercy,
  they learnt how the ungodly were tormented, being judged with wrath.
10 For you tested these as a father admonishing them;
  but you searched out those as a stern king condemning them.
11 Yes and whether they were far off or near,
  they were equally distressed;
12 for a double grief seized them,
  and a groaning at the memory of things past.
13 For when they heard that through their own punishments the others benefitted,
  they recognised the Lord.
14 For him who long before was thrown out and exposed they stopped mocking.
  In the end of what happened, they marvelled,
  having thirsted in another manner than the righteous.

15 But in return for the senseless imaginings of their unrighteousness,
  wherein they were led astray to worship irrational reptiles and wretched vermin,
  you sent upon them a multitude of irrational creatures to punish them,
16 that they might learn that by what things a man sins, by these he is punished.
17 For your all-powerful hand
  that created the world out of formless matter
  didn't lack means to send upon them a multitude of bears, fierce lions,
18 or newly-created and unknown wild beasts, full of rage,
  either breathing out a blast of fiery breath,
  or belching out smoke,
  or flashing dreadful sparks from their eyes;
19 which had power not only to consume them by their violence,
  but to destroy them even by the terror of their sight.
20 Yes and without these they might have fallen by a single breath,
  being pursued by Justice, and scattered abroad by the breath of your power;
  but you arranged all things by measure, number, and weight.

21 For to be greatly strong is yours at all times.
  Who could withstand the might of your arm?
22 Because the whole world before you is as a grain in a balance,
  and as a drop of dew that comes down upon the earth in the morning.

---

a *9:8* Or, a place of sacrifice
b *9:12* Gr. thrones.
c *10:1* Gr. She.
d *10:5* Gr. she
e *10:6* Gr. she

f *10:10* Gr. she.
g *10:13* Gr. she.
h *10:15* Gr. she.
i *11:4* See Deuteronomy 8:15; Psalms 114:8.

23 But you have mercy on all men, because you have power to do all things,
 and you overlook the sins of men to the end that they may repent.
24 For you love all things that are,
 and abhor none of the things which you made;
 For you never would have formed anything if you hated it.
25 How would anything have endured unless you had willed it?
 Or that which was not called by you, how would it have been preserved?
26 But you spare all things, because they are yours,
 O Sovereign Lord, you who love the living.

12

1 For your incorruptible spirit is in all things.
2 Therefore you convict little by little those who fall from the right way,
 and, putting them in remembrance by the things wherein they sin, you admonish them,
 that escaping from their wickedness they may believe in you, O Lord.

3 For truly the old inhabitants of your holy land,
 4 hating them because they practised detestable works of enchantments and unholy rites—
 5 merciless slaughters of children
 and sacrificial banquets of men's flesh and of blood—
 6 allies in an impious fellowship,
 and murderers of their own helpless babes,
 it was your counsel to destroy by the hands of our fathers;
 7 that the land which in your sight is most precious of all
 might receive a worthy colony of God's servants.ᵃ
8 Nevertheless you even spared these as men,
 and you sent hornetsᵇ as forerunners of your army,
 to cause them to perish little by little.
9 Not that you were unable to subdue the ungodly under the hand of the righteous in battle,
 or by terrible beasts or by a stern word to make away with them at once,
10 but judging them little by little you gave them a chance to repent,
 not being ignorant that their nature by birth was evil,
 their wickedness inborn,
 and that their manner of thought would never be changed.
11 For they were a cursed seed from the beginning.
 It wasn't through fear of any that you left them unpunished for their sins.

12 For who will say, "What have you done?"
 Or "Who will withstand your judgement?"
Who will accuse you for the perishing of nations which you caused?
 Or who will come and stand before you as an avenger for unrighteous men?
13 For there isn't any God beside you that cares for all,
 that you might show that you didn't judge unrighteously.
14 No king or prince will be able to confront you
 about those whom you have punished.
15 But being righteous, you rule all things righteously,
 deeming it a thing alien from your power
 to condemn one who doesn't deserve to be punished.
16 For your strength is the source of righteousness,
 and your sovereignty over all makes you to forbear all.
17 For when men don't believe that you are perfect in power, you show your strength,
 and in dealing with those who think this, you confuse their boldness.
18 But you, being sovereign in strength, judge in gentleness,
 and with great forbearance you govern us;
 for the power is yours whenever you desire it.

19 But you taught your people by such works as these,
 how the righteous must be kind.
You made your sons to have good hope,
 because you give repentance when men have sinned.
20 For if on those who were enemies of your servantsᶜ and deserving of death,
 you took vengeance with so great deliberation and indulgence,
 giving them times and opportunities when they might escape from their wickedness,
21 with how great care you judged your sons,
 to whose fathers you gave oaths and covenants of good promises!
22 Therefore while you chasten us, you scourge our enemies ten thousand times more,
 to the intent that we may ponder your goodness when we judge,
 and when we are judged may look for mercy.

23 Therefore also the unrighteous that lived in a life of folly,
 you tormented through their own abominations.
24 For truly they went astray very far in the ways of error,
 Taking as gods those animalsᵈ which even amongst their enemies were held in dishonour,

deceived like foolish babes.
25 Therefore, as to unreasoning children, you sent your judgement to mock them.
26 But those who would not be admonished by mild correction
 will experience the deserved judgement of God.
27 For through the sufferings they were indignant of,
 being punished in these creatures which they supposed to be gods,
 they saw and recognised as the true God him whom they previously refused to know.
 Therefore also the result of extreme condemnation came upon them.

13

1 For truly all men who had no perception of God were foolish by nature,
 and didn't gain power to know him who exists from the good things that are seen.
 They didn't recognise the architect from his works.
2 But they thought that either fire, or wind, or swift air,
 or circling stars, or raging water, or luminaries of heaven
 were gods that rule the world.
3 If it was through delight in their beauty that they took them to be gods,
 let them know how much better their Sovereign Lord is than these,
 for the first author of beauty created them.
4 But if it was through astonishment at their power and influence,
 then let them understand from them how much more powerful he who formed them is.
5 For from the greatness of the beauty of created things,
 mankind forms the corresponding perception of their Maker.ᵉ
6 But yet for these men there is but small blame,
 for they too perhaps go astray
 while they are seeking God and desiring to find him.
7 For they diligently search while living amongst his works,
 and they trust their sight that the things that they look at are beautiful.
8 But again even they are not to be excused.
9 For if they had power to know so much,
 that they should be able to explore the world,
 how is it that they didn't find the Sovereign Lord sooner?

10 But they were miserable, and their hopes were in dead things,
 who called them gods which are works of men's hands,
 gold and silver, skilfully made, and likenesses of animals,
 or a useless stone, the work of an ancient hand.
11 Yes and someᶠ woodcutter might saw down a tree that is easily moved,
 skilfully strip away all its bark,
 and fashion it in attractive form, make a useful vessel to serve his life's needs.
12 Burning the scraps from his handiwork to cook his food,
 he eats his fill.
13 Taking a discarded scrap which served no purpose,
 a crooked piece of wood and full of knots,
 he carves it with the diligence of his idleness,
 and shapes it by the skill of his idleness.
He shapes it in the image of a man,
 14 or makes it like some worthless animal,
 smearing it with something red, painting it red,
 and smearing over every stain in it.
15 Having made a worthy chamber for it,
 he sets it in a wall, securing it with iron.
16 He plans for it that it may not fall down,
 knowing that it is unable to help itself
 (for truly it is an image, and needs help).
17 When he makes his prayer concerning goods and his marriage and children,
 he is not ashamed to speak to that which has no life.
18 Yes, for health, he calls upon that which is weak.
 For life, he implores that which is dead.
 For aid, he supplicates that which has no experience.
 For a good journey, he asks that which can't so much as move a step.
19 And for profit in business and good success of his hands,
 he asks ability from that which has hands with no ability.

14

1 Again, one preparing to sail, and about to journey over raging waves,
 calls upon a piece of wood more fragile than the vessel that carries him.
2 For the hunger for profit planned it,
 and wisdom was the craftsman who built it.
3 Your providence, O Father, guides it along,
 because even in the sea you gave a way,
 and in the waves a sure path,
4 showing that you can save out of every danger,
 that even a man without skill may put to sea.
5 It is your will that the works of your wisdom should not be ineffective.
 Therefore men also entrust their lives to a little piece of wood,
 and passing through the surge on a raft come safely to land.

ᵃ *12:7* Or, children
ᵇ *12:8* Or, wasps
ᶜ *12:20* Or, children

ᵈ *12:24* Gr. living creatures: and so elsewhere in this book.
ᵉ *13:5* Gr. is the first maker of them seen.
ᶠ *13:11* Gr. carpenter who is a woodcutter.

6 For[a] in the old time also, when proud giants were perishing,
    the hope of the world, taking refuge on a raft,
    your hand guided the seed of generations of the race of men.
7 For blessed is wood through which comes righteousness;
    8 but the idol made with hands is accursed, itself and he that made it;
    because his was the working, and the corruptible thing was called a god.
9 For both the ungodly and his ungodliness are alike hateful to God;
    10 for truly the deed will be punished together with him who committed it.
    11 Therefore also there will be a visitation amongst the idols of the nation,
    because, though formed of things which God created, they were made an abomination,
    stumbling blocks to the souls of men,
    and a snare to the feet of the foolish.

12 For the devising of idols was the beginning of fornication,
    and the invention of them the corruption of life.
13 For they didn't exist from the beginning, and they won't exist forever.
14 For by the boastfulness of men they entered into the world,
    and therefore a speedy end was planned for them.

15 For a father worn with untimely grief,
    making an image of the child quickly taken away,
    now honoured him as a god which was then a dead human being,
    and delivered to those that were under him mysteries and solemn rites.
16 Afterward the ungodly custom, in process of time grown strong, was kept as a law,
    and the engraved images received worship by the commandments of princes.
17 And when men could not honour them in presence because they lived far off,
    imagining the likeness from afar,
    they made a visible image of the king whom they honoured,
    that by their zeal they might flatter the absent as if present.

18 But worship was raised to a yet higher pitch, even by those who didn't know him,
    urged forward by the ambition of the architect;
19 for he, wishing perhaps to please his ruler,
    used his art to force the likeness towards a greater beauty.
20 So the multitude, allured by reason of the grace of his handiwork,
    now consider an object of devotion him that a little before was honoured as a man.
21 And this became an ambush,
    because men, in bondage either to calamity or to tyranny,
    invested stones and stocks with the Name that shouldn't be shared.

22 Afterward it was not enough for them to go astray concerning the knowledge of God,
    but also, while they live in a great war of ignorance, they call a multitude of evils peace.
23 For either slaughtering children in solemn rites, or celebrating secret mysteries,
    or holding frenzied revels of strange customs,
24 no longer do they guard either life or purity of marriage,
    but one brings upon another either death by treachery, or anguish by adultery.
25 And all things confusedly are filled with blood and murder, theft and deceit,
    corruption, faithlessness, tumult, perjury,
26 confusion about what is good, forgetfulness of favours,
    ingratitude for benefits,
    defiling of souls, confusion of sex,
    disorder in marriage, adultery and wantonness.
    27 For the worship of idols that may not be named *
    is a beginning and cause and end of every evil.
28 For their worshippers either make merry to madness, or prophesy lies,
    or live unrighteously, or lightly commit perjury.
29 For putting their trust in lifeless idols,
    when they have sworn a wicked oath, they expect not to suffer harm.
30 But on both counts, the just doom will pursue them,
    because they had evil thoughts of God by giving heed to idols,
    and swore unrighteously in deceit through contempt for holiness.
31 For it is not the power of things by which men swear,
    but it is the just penalty for those who sin
    that always visits the transgression of the unrighteous.

15

1 But you, our God, are gracious and true,
patient, and in mercy ordering all things.
2 For even if we sin, we are yours, knowing your dominion;
    but we will not sin, knowing that we have been accounted yours.
3 For to be acquainted with you is[b] perfect righteousness,
    and to know your dominion is the root of immortality.
4 For we weren't led astray by any evil plan of men's,
    nor yet by painters' fruitless labour,
    a form stained with varied colours,
5 the sight of which leads fools into[c] lust.
    Their desire is for the breathless form of a dead image.
6 Lovers of evil things, and worthy of such hopes,
    are those who make, desire, and worship them.

7 For a potter, kneading soft earth,
    laboriously moulds each article for our service.
He fashions out of the same clay
    both the vessels that minister to clean uses, and those of a contrary sort,
    all in like manner.
What shall be the use of each article of either sort,
    the potter is the judge.
8 Also, labouring to an evil end, he moulds a vain god out of the same clay,
    he who, having but a little before been made of earth,
    after a short space goes his way to the earth out of which he was taken,
    when he is required to render back the[d] soul which was lent him.
9 However he has anxious care,
    not because his powers must fail,
    nor because his span of life is short;
But he compares himself with goldsmiths and silversmiths,
    and he imitates molders in[e] brass,
    and considers it great that he moulds counterfeit gods.
10 His heart is ashes.
    His hope is of less value than earth.
    His life is of less honour than clay.
11 because he was ignorant of him who moulded him,
    and of him that inspired into him[f] an active[g] soul,
    and breathed into him a vital spirit.
12 But[h] he accounted our life to be a game,
    and our[i] lifetime a festival for profit;
for, he says, one must get gain however one can, even if it is by evil.
13 For this man, beyond all others, knows that he sins,
    out of earthy matter making brittle vessels and engraved images.
14 But most foolish and more miserable than a baby,
    are the enemies of your people, who oppressed them;
15 because they even considered all the idols of the nations to be gods,
    which have neither the use of eyes for seeing,
    nor nostrils for drawing breath,
    nor ears to hear,
    nor fingers for handling,
    and their feet are helpless for walking.
16 For a man made them,
    and one whose own spirit is borrowed moulded them;
    for no one has power as a man to mould a god like himself.
17 But, being mortal, he makes a dead thing by the work of lawless hands;
    for he is better than the objects of his worship,
    since he indeed had life, but they never did.

18 Yes, and they worship the creatures that are most hateful,
    for, being compared as to lack of sense, these are worse than all others;
19 Neither, as seen beside other creatures, are they beautiful, so that one should desire them,
    but they have escaped both the praise of God and his blessing.

16

1 For this cause, they were deservedly punished through creatures like those which they worship,
    and tormented through a multitude of vermin.
2 Instead of this punishment, you, giving benefits to your people,
    prepared quails for food,
a delicacy to satisfy the desire of their appetite,
3 to the end that your enemies, desiring food,
    might for the hideousness of the creatures sent amongst them,
    loathe even the necessary appetite;
but these, your people, having for a short time suffered lack,
    might even partake of delicacies.
4 For it was necessary that inescapable lack should come upon those oppressors,
    but that to these it should only be showed how their enemies were tormented.
5 For even when terrible raging of wild beasts came upon your people,
    and they were perishing by the bites of crooked serpents,

---

a *14:6* The Greek text here may be corrupt.
** *14:27* Exodus 23:13; Psalms 16:4; Hosea 2:17; Wisdom 14:21
b *15:3* Gr. entire.
c *15:5* Some authorities read reproach.
d *15:8* Or, life

e *15:9* Or, copper
f *15:11* Gr. a soul that moves to activity.
g *15:11* Or, life
h *15:12* Some authorities read they accounted.
i *15:12* Or, way of life

your wrath didn't continue to the uttermost;

6 but for admonition were they troubled for a short time,
    having a token of salvation
    to put them in remembrance of the commandment of your law;

7 for he who turned towards it was not saved because of that which was
        seen,
    but because of you, the Saviour of all.

8 Yes, and in this you persuaded our enemies
    that you are he who delivers out of every evil.

9 For the bites of locusts and flies truly killed them.
    No healing for their life was found,
    because they were worthy to be punished by such things.

10 But your children weren't overcome by the very fangs of venomous
        dragons,
    for your mercy passed by where they were and healed them.

11 For they were bitten to put them in remembrance of your oracles,
    and were quickly saved, lest, falling into deep forgetfulness,
    they should become unable to respond to your kindness.

12 For truly it was neither herb nor poultice that cured them,
    but your word, O Lord, which heals all people.

13 For you have authority over life and death,
    and you lead down to the gates of Hades, and lead up again.

14 But though a man kills by his wickedness,
    he can't retrieve the spirit that has departed
    or release the imprisoned soul.

15 But it is not possible to escape your hand;

16 for ungodly men, refusing to know you, were scourged in the strength of
        your arm,
    pursued with strange rains and hails and relentless storms,
    and utterly consumed with fire.

17 For, what was most marvellous,
    in the water which quenches all things, the fire burnt hotter;
    for the world fights for the righteous.

18 For at one time the flame was restrained,
    that it might not burn up the creatures sent against the ungodly,
    but that these themselves as they looked might see that they were
        chased by the judgement of God.

19 At another time even in the midst of water it burns more intensely than
        fire,
    that it may destroy the produce of an unrighteous land.

20 Instead of these things, you gave your people angels' food to eat,
    and you provided ready-to-eat bread for them from heaven without
        toil,
    having the virtue of every pleasant flavour,
    and agreeable to every taste.

21 For your nature showed your sweetness towards your children,
    while that bread, serving the desire of the eater,
    changed itself according to every man's choice.

22 But snow and ice endured fire, and didn't melt,
    that people might know that fire was destroying the fruits of the
        enemies,
    burning in the hail and flashing in the rains;

23 and that this fire, again, in order that righteous people may be nourished,
    has even forgotten its own power.

24 For the creation, ministering to you, its maker,
    strains its force against the unrighteous for punishment
    and in kindness, slackens it on behalf of those who trust in you.

25 Therefore at that time also, converting itself into all forms,
    it ministered to your all-nourishing bounty,
    according to the desire of those who had need,

26 that your children, whom you loved, O Lord, might learn
    that it is not the growth of crops that nourishes a man,
    but that your word preserves those who trust you.

27 For that which was not destroyed by fire,
    melted away when it was simply warmed by a faint sunbeam,

28 that it might be known that we must rise before the sun to give you
        thanks,
    and must pray to you at the dawning of the light;

29 for the hope of the unthankful will melt as the winter's hoar frost,
    and will flow away as water that has no use.

17

1 For your judgements are great, and hard to interpret;
    therefore undisciplined souls went astray.

2 For when lawless men had supposed that they held a holy nation in their
        power,
    they, prisoners of darkness, and bound in the fetters of a long night,
    kept close beneath their roofs,
    lay exiled from the eternal providence.

3 For while they thought that they were unseen in their secret sins,
    they were divided from one another by a dark curtain of forgetfulness,
    stricken with terrible awe, and very troubled by apparitions,

4 For neither did the dark recesses that held them guard them from fears,
    but terrifying sounds rang around them,
    and dismal phantoms appeared with unsmiling faces.

5 And no power of fire prevailed to give light,

neither were the brightest flames of the stars strong enough to
    illuminate that gloomy night;

6 but only the glimmering of a self-kindled fire appeared to them, full of fear.
    In terror, they considered the things which they saw
    to be worse than that sight, on which they could not gaze.

7 The mockeries of their magic arts were powerless, now,
    and a shameful rebuke of their boasted understanding:

8 For those who promised to drive away terrors and disorders from a sick
        soul,
    these were sick with a ludicrous fearfulness.

9 For even if no troubling thing frighted them,
    yet, scared with the creeping of vermin and hissing of serpents,

10 they perished trembling in fear,
    refusing even to look at the air, which could not be escaped on any
        side.

11 For wickedness, condemned by a witness within, is a coward thing,
    and, being pressed hard by conscience, always has added forecasts
        of the worst.

12 For fear is nothing else but a surrender of the help which reason
        offers;

13 and from within, the expectation of being less
    prefers ignorance of the cause that brings the torment.

14 But they, all through the night which was powerless indeed,
    and which came upon them out of the recesses of powerless Hades,
    sleeping the same sleep,

15 now were haunted by monstrous apparitions,
    and now were paralysed by their soul's surrendering;
    for sudden and unexpected fear came upon them.

16 So then whoever it might be, sinking down in his place,
    was kept captive, shut up in that prison which was not barred with
        iron;

17 for whether he was a farmer, or a shepherd,
    or a labourer whose toils were in the wilderness,
    he was overtaken, and endured that inescapable sentence;
    for they were all bound with one chain of darkness.

18 Whether there was a whistling wind,
    or a melodious sound of birds amongst the spreading branches,
    or a measured fall of water running violently,

19 or a harsh crashing of rocks hurled down,
    or the swift course of animals bounding along unseen,
    or the voice of wild beasts harshly roaring,
    or an echo rebounding from the hollows of the mountains,
    all these things paralysed them with terror.

20 For the whole world was illuminated with clear light,
    and was occupied with unhindered works,

21 while over them alone was spread a heavy night,
    an image of the darkness that should afterward receive them;
    but to themselves, they were heavier than darkness.

18

1 But for your holy ones there was great light.
    Their enemies, hearing their voice but not seeing their form,
    counted it a happy thing that they too had suffered,

2 yet for that they do not hurt them, though wronged by them before, they
        are thankful;
    and because they had been at variance with them, they begged for
        pardon.

3 Therefore you provided a burning pillar of fire,
    to be a guide for your people's unknown journey,
    and a harmless sun for their glorious exile.

4 For the Egyptians well deserved to be deprived of light and imprisoned by
        darkness,
    they who had imprisoned your children,
    through whom the incorruptible light of the law was to be given to the
        race of men.

5 After they had taken counsel to kill the babes of the holy ones,
    and when a single child had been abandoned and saved to convict
        them of their sin,
    you took away from them their multitude of children,
    and destroyed all their army together in a mighty flood.

6 Our fathers were made aware of that night beforehand,
    that, having sure knowledge, they might be cheered by the oaths
        which they had trusted.

7 Salvation of the righteous and destruction of the enemies was expected
        by your people.

8 For as you took vengeance on the adversaries,
    by the same means, calling us to yourself, you glorified us.

9 For holy children of good men offered sacrifice in secret,
    and with one consent they agreed to the covenant of the divine law,
    that they would partake alike in the same good things and the same
        perils,
    the fathers already leading the sacred songs of praise.

10 But the discordant cry of the enemies echoed back,
    and a pitiful voice of lamentation for children was spread abroad.

11 Both servant and master were punished with the same just doom,
    and the commoner suffering the same as king;

12 Yes, they all together, under one form of death,
    had corpses without number.
    For the living were not sufficient even to bury them,

Since at a single stroke, their most cherished offspring was
  consumed.
13 For while they were disbelieving all things by reason of the
  enchantments,
  upon the destruction of the firstborn they confessed the people to be
   God's children.
14 For while peaceful silence wrapped all things,
  and night in her own swiftness was half spent,
15 your all-powerful word leapt from heaven, from the royal throne,
  a stern warrior, into the midst of the doomed land,
16 bearing as a sharp sword your authentic commandment,
  and standing, it filled all things with death,
  and while it touched the heaven it stood upon the earth.
17 Then immediately apparitions in dreams terribly troubled them,
  and unexpected fears came upon them.
18 And each, one thrown here half dead, another there,
  made known why he was dying;
19 for the dreams, disturbing them, forewarned them of this,
  that they might not perish without knowing why they were afflicted.

20 The experience of death also touched the righteous,
  and a multitude were destroyed in the wilderness,
  but the wrath didn't last long.
21 For a blameless man hurried to be their champion,
  bringing the weapon of his own ministry,
  prayer, and the atoning sacrifice of incense.
He withstood the indignation and set an end to the calamity,
  showing that he was your servant.
22 And he overcame the anger,
  not by strength of body, not by force of weapons,
  but by his word, he subdued the avenger
  by bringing to remembrance oaths and covenants made with the
   fathers.
23 For when the dead had already fallen in heaps one upon another,
  he intervened and stopped the wrath,
  and cut off its way to the living.
24 For the whole world was pictured on his long robe,
  and the glories of the fathers were upon the engraving of the four
   rows of precious stones,
  and your majesty was upon the diadem on his head.
25 The destroyer yielded to these, and they feared;
  for it was enough only to test the wrath.

19

1 But indignation without mercy came upon the ungodly to the end;
  for God also foreknew their future,
2 how, having changed their minds to let your people go,
  and having sped them eagerly on their way,
  they would change their minds and pursue them.
3 For while they were yet in the midst of their mourning,
  and lamenting at the graves of the dead,
  they made another foolish decision,
  and pursued as fugitives those whom they had begged to leave and
   driven out.
4 For the doom which they deserved was drawing them to this end,
  and it made them forget the things that had happened to them,
  that they might fill up the punishment which was yet lacking from their
   torments,
  5 and that your people might journey on by a marvellous road,
  but they themselves might find a strange death.

6 For the whole creation, each part in its diverse kind, was made new again,
  complying with your commandments,
  that your servants might be kept unharmed.
7 Then the cloud that overshadowed the camp was seen,
  and dry land rising up out of what had been water,
  out of the Red sea an unhindered highway,
  and a grassy plain out of the violent surge,
  8 by which they passed over with all their army,
  these who were covered with your hand,
  having seen strange marvels.
9 For like horses they roamed at large,
  and they skipped about like lambs,
  praising you, O Lord, who was their deliverer.
10 For they still remembered the things that happened in the time of their
   sojourning,
  how instead of bearing cattle, the land brought forth lice,
  and instead of fish, the river spewed out a multitude of frogs.
11 But afterwards, they also saw a new kind of birds,
  when, led on by desire, they asked for luxurious dainties;
12 for, to comfort them, quails came up for them from the sea.

13 Punishments came upon the sinners,
  not without the signs that were given beforehand by the violence of
   the thunder,
  for they justly suffered through their own wickednesses,
  for the hatred which they practised towards guests was grievous
   indeed.
14 For while the others didn't receive the strangers when they came to them,
the Egyptians made slaves of guests who were their benefactors.
15 And not only so, but while punishment of some sort will come upon the
  former,
  since they received as enemies those who were aliens;
  16 because these first welcomed with feastings,
  and then afflicted with dreadful toils,
  those who had already shared with them in the same rights.
17 And moreover they were stricken with loss of sight
  (even as were those others at the righteous man's doors),
  when, being surrounded with yawning darkness,
  they each looked for the passage through his own door.

18 For as the notes of a lute vary the character of the rhythm,
  even so the elements, changing their order one with another,
  continuing always in its sound,
  as may clearly be conjectured from the sight of the things that have
   happened.
19 For creatures of the dry land were turned into creatures of the waters,
  and creatures that swim moved upon the land.
20 Fire kept the mastery of its own power in water,
  and water forgot its quenching nature.
21 On the contrary, flames didn't consume flesh of perishable creatures that
   walked amongst them,
  neither did they melt the crystalline grains of ambrosial food that were
   melted easily.

22 For in all things, O Lord, you magnified your people,
  and you glorified them and didn't lightly regard them,
  standing by their side in every time and place.

The Wisdom of Jesus the Son of Sirach, or Ecclesiaticus

The Wisdom of Jesus the Son of Sirach, also called *Ecclesiasticus*, is recognised as Deuterocanonical Scripture by the Roman Catholic, Greek Orthodox, and Russian Orthodox Churches.

The Prologue of the Wisdom of Jesus the Son of Sirach.

WHEREAS many and great things have been delivered to us by the law and the prophets, and by the others that have followed in their steps, for which we must give Israel the praise for instruction and wisdom; and since not only the readers need to become skilful themselves, but also those who love learning must be able to profit those who are outside, both by speaking and writing; my grandfather Jesus, having much given himself to the reading of the law, and the prophets, and the other books of our fathers, and having gained great familiarity with them, was also drawn on himself to write somewhat pertaining to instruction and wisdom, in order that those who love learning, and are devoted to these things, might make progress much more by living according to the law. You are entreated therefore to read with favour and attention, and to pardon us, if in any parts of what we have laboured to interpret, we may seem to fail in some of the phrases. For things originally spoken in Hebrew don't have the same force in them when they are translated into another language. Not only these, but the law itself, and the prophecies, and the rest of the books, have no small difference, when they are spoken in their original language. For having come into Egypt in the thirty-eighth year of Energetes the king, and having continued there some time, I found a copy giving no small instruction. I thought it therefore most necessary for me to apply some diligence and travail to translate this book, applying indeed much watchfulness and skill in that space of time to bring the book to an end and publish for them also, who in the land of their travels are desiring to learn, preparing their character in advance, so as to live according to the law.

1

1 All wisdom comes from the Lord,
   and is with him forever.
2 Who can count the sand of the seas,
   the drops of rain,
   and the days of eternity?
3 Who will search out the height of the sky,
   the breadth of the earth, the deep,
   and wisdom?
4 Wisdom has been created before all things,
   and the understanding of prudence from everlasting. 5 [a]
6 To whom has the root of wisdom been revealed?
   Who has known her shrewd counsels? 7 [b]
8 There is one wise, greatly to be feared,
   sitting upon his throne: the Lord.
9 He created her.
   He saw and measured her.
   He poured her out upon all his works.
10 She is with all flesh according to his gift.
   He gave her freely to those who love him.

11 The fear of the Lord is glory, exultation,
   gladness, and a crown of rejoicing.
12 The fear of the Lord will delight the heart,
   and will give gladness, joy, and length of days.
13 Whoever fears the Lord, it will go well with him at the last.
   He will be blessed in the day of his death.

14 To fear the Lord is the beginning of wisdom.
   It was created together with the faithful in the womb.
15 She[c] laid an eternal foundation with men.
   She will be trusted amongst their offspring.
16 To fear the Lord is the fullness of wisdom.
   She inebriates men with her fruits.
17 She will fill all her house with desirable things,
   and her storehouses with her produce.
18 The fear of the Lord is the crown of wisdom,
   making peace and[d] perfect health to flourish.[e]
19 He both saw and measured her.
   He rained down skill and knowledge of understanding,
   and exalted the honour of those who hold her fast.
20 To fear the Lord is the root of wisdom.
   Her branches are length of days. 21 [f]

22 Unjust wrath can never be justified,
   for his wrath tips the scale to his downfall.

23 A man that is patient will resist for a season,
   and afterward gladness will spring up to him.
24 He will hide his words until the right moment,
   and the lips of many will tell of his understanding.

25 A wise saying is in the treasures of wisdom;
   but godliness is an abomination to a sinner.
26 If you desire wisdom, keep the commandments
   and the Lord will give her to you freely;
27 for the fear of the Lord is wisdom and instruction.
   Faith and humility are his good pleasure.
28 Don't disobey the fear of the Lord.
   Don't come to him with a double heart.
29 Don't be a hypocrite in men's sight.
   Keep watch over your lips.
30 Don't exalt yourself,
   lest you fall and bring dishonour upon your soul.
The Lord will reveal your secrets
   and will cast you down in the midst of the congregation,
   because you didn't come to the fear of the Lord
   and your heart was full of deceit.

2

1 My son, if you come to serve the Lord,
   prepare your soul for temptation.
2 Set your heart aright, constantly endure,
   and don't make haste in time of calamity.
3 Cling to him, and don't depart,
   that you may be increased at your latter end.
4 Accept whatever is brought upon you,
   and be patient when you suffer humiliation.
5 For gold is tried in the fire,
   and acceptable men in the furnace of humiliation.
6 Put your trust in him, and he will help you.
   Make your ways straight, and set your hope on him.

7 All you who fear the Lord, wait for his mercy.
   Don't turn aside, lest you fall.
8 All you who fear the Lord, put your trust in him,
   and your reward will not fail.
9 All you who fear the Lord, hope for good things,
   and for eternal gladness and mercy.
10 Look at the generations of old, and see:
   Who ever put his trust in the Lord, and was ashamed?
   Or who remained in his fear, and was forsaken?
   Or who called upon him, and he neglected him?
11 For the Lord is full of compassion and mercy.
   He forgives sins and saves in time of affliction.

12 Woe to fearful hearts, to faint hands,
   and to the sinner who goes two ways!
13 Woe to the faint heart! For it doesn't believe.
   Therefore it won't be defended.
14 Woe to you who have lost your patience!
   And what will you all do when the Lord visits you?

15 Those who fear the Lord will not disobey his words.
   Those who love him will keep his ways.
16 Those who fear the Lord will seek his good pleasure.
   Those who love him will be filled with the law.
17 Those who fear the Lord will prepare their hearts,
   and will humble their souls in his sight.
18 We will fall into the hands of the Lord,
   and not into the hands of men;
for as his majesty is,
   so also is his mercy.

3

1 Hear me, your father, O my children,
   and do what you hear, that you all may be safe.
2 For the Lord honours the father over the children,
   and has confirmed the judgement of the mother over her sons.
3 He who honours his father will make atonement for sins.
   4 He who gives glory to his mother is as one who lays up treasure.
5 Whoever honours his father will have joy in his own children.
   He will be heard in the day of his prayer.
6 He who gives glory to his father will have length of days.
   He who listens to the Lord will bring rest to his mother,

---

[a] *1:5* Verse 5 is omitted by the best authorities: The source of wisdom is God's word in the highest heaven, and her ways are the eternal commandments.
[b] *1:7* Verse 7 is omitted by the best authorities: To whom was the knowledge of wisdom manifested? Who has understood her abundant experience?
[c] *1:15* Gr. nested.

[d] *1:18* Gr. health of cure.
[e] *1:18* The remainder of this verse is omitted by the best authorities: Both are gifts of God for peace; glory opens out for those who love him. He saw her and took her measure.
[f] *1:21* Verse 21 is omitted by the best authorities: The fear of the Lord drives away sins. Where it resides, it will turn away all anger.

7 [a] and will serve under his parents, as to masters.
8 Honour your father in deed and word,
  that a blessing may come upon you from him.
9 For the blessing of the father establishes the houses of children,
  but the curse of the mother roots out the foundations.

10 Don't glorify yourself in the dishonour of your father,
  for your father's dishonour is no glory to you.
11 For the glory of a man is from the honour of his father,
  and a mother in dishonour is a reproach to her children.
12 My son, help your father in his old age,
  and don't grieve him as long as he lives.
13 If he fails in understanding, have patience with him.
  Don't dishonour him in your full strength.
14 For the kindness to your father will not be forgotten.
  Instead of sins it will be added to build you up.
15 In the day of your affliction it will be remembered for you,
  as fair weather upon ice,
  so your sins will also melt away.
16 He who forsakes his father is as a blasphemer.
  He who provokes his mother is cursed by the Lord.

17 My son, go on with your business in humility;
  so you will be loved by an acceptable man.
18 The greater you are, humble yourself the more,
  and you will find favour before the Lord. 19 [b]
20 For the power of the Lord is great,
  and he is glorified by those who are lowly.
21 Don't seek things that are too hard for you,
  and don't search out things that are above your strength.
22 Think about the things that have been commanded you,
  for you have no need of the things that are secret.
23 Don't be overly busy in tasks that are beyond you,
  for more things are shown to you than men can understand.
24 For the conceit of many has led them astray.
  Evil opinion has caused their judgement to slip.
25 [c]There is no light without eyes.
  There is no wisdom without knowledge.

26 A stubborn heart will do badly at the end.
  He who loves danger will perish in it.
27 A stubborn heart will be burdened with troubles.
  The sinner will heap sin upon sins.
28 The calamity of the proud has no healing,
  for a weed of wickedness has taken root in him.
29 The heart of the prudent will understand a proverb.
  A wise man desires the ear of a listener.

30 Water will quench a flaming fire;
  almsgiving will make atonement for sins.
31 He who repays good turns is mindful of that which comes afterward.
  In the time of his falling he will find a support.

4

1 My son, don't deprive the poor of his living.
  Don't make the needy eyes wait long.
2 Don't make a hungry soul sorrowful,
  or provoke a man in his distress.
3 Don't add more trouble to a heart that is provoked.
  Don't put off giving to him who is in need.
4 Don't reject a suppliant in his affliction.
  Don't turn your face away from a poor man.
5 Don't turn your eye away from one who asks.
  Give no occasion to a man to curse you.
6 For if he curses you in the bitterness of his soul,
  he who made him will hear his supplication.

7 Endear yourself to the assembly.
  Bow your head to a great man.
8 Incline your ear to a poor man.
  Answer him with peaceful words in humility.
9 Deliver him who is wronged from the hand of him who wrongs him;
  Don't be hesitant in giving judgement.
10 Be as a father to the fatherless,
  and like a husband to their mother.
So you will be as a son of the Most High,
  and he will love you more than your mother does.

11 Wisdom exalts her sons,
  and takes hold of those who seek her.
12 He who loves her loves life.
  Those who seek her early will be filled with gladness.
13 He who holds her fast will inherit glory.

Where[d] he enters, the Lord will bless.
14 Those who serve her minister to the Holy One.
  The Lord loves those who love her.
15 He who listens to her will judge the nations.
  He who heeds her will dwell securely.
16 If he trusts her, he will inherit her,
  and his generations will possess her.
17 For at the first she will walk with him in crooked ways,
  and will bring fear and dread upon him,
  and torment him with her discipline,
  until she may trust his soul, and try him by her judgements.
18 Then she will return him again to the straight way,
  and will gladden him, and reveal to him her secrets.
19 If he goes astray, she will forsake him,
  and hand him over to his fall.

20 Watch for the opportunity, and beware of evil.
  Don't be ashamed of your soul.
21 For there is a shame that brings sin,
  and there is a shame that is glory and grace.
22 Don't show partiality, discrediting your soul.
  Don't revere any man to your falling.
23 Don't refrain from speaking when it is for safety.
  [e]Don't hide your wisdom for the sake of seeming fair.
24 For wisdom will be known by speech,
  and instruction by the word of the tongue.
25 Don't speak against the truth
  and be shamed for your ignorance.
26 Don't be ashamed to confess your sins.
  Don't fight the river's current.
27 Don't lay yourself down for a fool to tread upon.
  Don't be partial to one who is mighty.
28 Strive for the truth to death,
  and the Lord God will fight for you.

29 Don't be hasty with your tongue,
  or slack and negligent in your deeds.
30 Don't be like a lion in your house,
  or suspicious of your servants.
31 Don't let your hand be stretched out to receive,
  and closed when you should repay.

5

1 Don't set your heart upon your goods.
  Don't say, "They are sufficient for me."
2 Don't follow your own mind and your strength
  to walk in the desires of your heart.
3 Don't say, "Who will have dominion over me?"
  for the Lord will surely take vengeance on you.

4 Don't say, "I sinned, and what happened to me?"
  for the Lord is patient.
5 Don't be so confident of atonement
  that you add sin upon sins.
6 Don't say, "His compassion is great.
  He will be pacified for the multitude of my sins,"
  for mercy and wrath are with him,
  and his indignation will rest on sinners.
7 Don't wait to turn to the Lord.
  Don't put off from day to day;
  for suddenly the wrath of the Lord will come on you,
  and you will perish in the time of vengeance.

8 Don't set your heart upon unrighteous gains,
  for you will profit nothing in the day of calamity.
9 Don't winnow with every wind.
  Don't walk in every path.
  This is what the sinner who has a double tongue does.
10 Be steadfast in your understanding.
  Let your speech be consistent.

11 Be swift to hear
  and answer with patience.
12 If you have understanding, answer your neighbour;
  but if not, put your hand over your mouth.
13 Glory and dishonour is in talk.
  A man's tongue may be his downfall.
14 Don't be called a whisperer.
  Don't lie in wait with your tongue;
  for shame is on the thief,
  and an evil condemnation is on him who has a double tongue.
15 Don't be ignorant in a great or small matter.

6

1 Don't become an enemy instead of a friend;

---

a 3:7 Some manuscripts add those who fear the Lord honour their father,
b 3:19 Some manuscripts add Many are lofty and renowned, but he reveals his secrets to the humble.
c 3:25 Some manuscripts omit verse 25.
d 4:13 Or, she
e 4:23 Some manuscripts omit this line.

for an evil name will inherit shame and reproach.
So it is with the sinner who has a double tongue.

2 Don't exalt yourself in the counsel of your soul,
that your soul not be torn in pieces like a bull.
3 You will eat up your leaves, destroy your fruit,
and leave yourself like a dry tree.
4 A wicked soul will destroy him who has it,
and will make him a laughing stock to his enemies.

5 Sweet words will multiply a man's friends.
A gracious tongue will multiply courtesies.
6 Let those that are at peace with you be many,
but your advisers one of a thousand.
7 If you want to gain a friend, get him in a time of testing,
and don't be in a hurry to trust him.
8 For there is a friend just for an occasion.
He won't continue in the day of your affliction.
9 And there is a friend who turns into an enemy.
He will discover strife to your reproach.
10 And there is a friend who is a companion at the table,
but he won't continue in the day of your affliction.
11 In your prosperity he will be as yourself,
and will be bold over your servants.
12 If you are brought low, he will be against you,
and will hide himself from your face.
13 Separate yourself from your enemies,
and beware of your friends.

14 A faithful friend is a strong defence.
He who has found him has found a treasure.
15 There is nothing that can be taken in exchange for a faithful friend.
His excellency is beyond price.
16 A faithful friend is a life-saving medicine.
Those who fear the Lord will find him.
17 He who fears the Lord directs his friendship properly;
for as he is, so is his neighbour also.

18 My son, gather instruction from your youth up.
Even when you have grey hair you will find wisdom.
19 Come to her as one who ploughs and sows
and wait for her good fruit;
for your toil will be little in her cultivation,
and you will soon eat of her fruit.
20 How exceedingly harsh she is to the unlearned!
He who is without understanding will not remain in her.
21 She will rest upon him as a mighty stone of trial.
He won't hesitate to cast her from him.
22 For wisdom is according to her name.
She isn't manifest to many.

23 Give ear, my son, and accept my judgement.
Don't refuse my counsel.
24 Bring your feet into her fetters,
and your neck into her chain.
25 Put your shoulder under her and bear her.
Don't be grieved with her bonds.
26 Come to her with all your soul.
Keep her ways with your whole power.
27 Search and seek, and she will be made known to you.
When you get hold of her, don't let her go.
28 For at the last you will find her rest;
and she will be turned for you into gladness.
29 Her fetters will be to you for a covering of strength,
and her chains for a robe of glory.
30 For there is a golden ornament upon her,
and her bands are ˚ a purple cord.
31 You shall put her on as a robe of glory,
and shall put her on as a crown of rejoicing.

32 My son, if you are willing, you will be instructed.
If you will yield your soul, you will be prudent.
33 If you love to hear, you will receive.
If you incline your ear, you will be wise.
34 Stand in the multitude of the elders.
Attach yourself to whomever is wise.
35 Be willing to listen to every godly discourse.
Don't let the proverbs of understanding escape you.
36 If you see a man of understanding, get to him early.
Let your foot wear out the steps of his doors.
37 Let your mind dwell on the ordinances of the Lord
and meditate continually on his commandments.
He will establish your heart
and your desire for wisdom will be given to you.

1 Do no evil,
so no evil will overtake you.
2 Depart from wrong,
and it will turn away from you.
3 My son, don't sow upon the furrows of unrighteousness,
and you won't reap them sevenfold.

4 Don't seek preeminence from the Lord,
nor the seat of honour from the king.
5 Don't justify yourself in the presence of the Lord,
and don't display your wisdom before the king.
6 Don't seek to be a judge,
lest you not be able to take away iniquities,
lest perhaps you fear the person of a mighty man,
and lay a stumbling block in the way of your uprightness.

7 Don't sin against the multitude of the city.
Don't disgrace yourself in the crowd.

8 Don't commit a sin twice,
for even in one you will not be unpunished.
9 Don't say, "He will look upon the multitude of my gifts.
When I make an offering to the Most High God, he will accept it."
10 Don't be faint-hearted in your prayer.
Don't neglect to give alms.

11 Don't laugh a man to scorn when he is in the bitterness of his soul,
for there is one who humbles and exalts.
12 Don't devise\u1d43 a lie against your brother,
or do the same to a friend.
13 Refuse to utter a lie,
for that habit results in no good.
14 Don't babble in the assembly of elders.
Don't repeat your words in your prayer.

15 Don't hate hard labour
or farm work, which the Most High has created.
16 Don't number yourself amongst the multitude of sinners.
Remember that wrath will not wait.
17 Humble your soul greatly,
for the punishment of the ungodly man is fire and the worm.

18 Don't exchange a friend for something,
neither a true brother for the gold of Ophir.
19 Don't deprive yourself of a wise and good wife,
for her grace is worth more than gold.
20 Don't abuse a servant who works faithfully,
or a hireling who gives you his life.
21 Let your soul love a wise servant.
Don't defraud him of liberty.

22 Do you have cattle? Look after them.
If they are profitable to you, let them stay by you.
23 Do you have children? Correct them,
and make them obedient from their youth.
24 Do you have daughters? Take care of their bodies,
and don't be overly indulgent towards them.
25 Give your daughter in marriage, and you will have accomplished a great matter.
Give her to a man of understanding.

26 Do you have a wife who pleases you? Don't cast her out.
ᵇ But don't trust yourself to one who is hateful.

27 Honour your father with your whole heart,
and don't forget the birth pangs of your mother.
28 Remember that you were born of them.
What will you repay them for the things that they have done for you?

29 Fear the Lord with all your soul;
and revere his priests.
30 With all your strength love him who made you.
Don't forsake his ministers.
31 Fear the Lord and honour the priest.
Give him his portion, even as it is commanded you:
the first fruits, the trespass offering, the gift of the shoulders,
the sacrifice of sanctification, and the first fruits of holy things.

32 Also stretch out your hand to the poor man,
that your blessing may be complete.
33 A gift has grace in the sight of every living man.
Don't withhold grace for a dead man.
34 Don't avoid those who weep,
and mourn with those who mourn.

---

35 Don't be slow to visit a sick man,
    for by such things you will gain love.
36 In all your words, remember eternity,
    and you will never sin.

8

1 Don't contend with a mighty man,
    lest perhaps you fall into his hands.
2 Don't strive with a rich man, lest perhaps he overpower you;
    for gold has destroyed many,
    and turned away the hearts of kings.
3 Don't argue with a loudmouthed man.
    Don't heap wood upon his fire.

4 Don't make fun of a rude man,
    lest your ancestors be dishonoured.
5 Don't reproach a man when he turns from sin.
    Remember that we are all worthy of punishment.
6 Don't dishonour a man in his old age,
    for some of us are also growing old.
7 Don't rejoice over anyone's death.
    Remember that we all die.

8 Don't neglect the discourse of the wise.
    Be conversant with their proverbs;
    for from them you will learn discipline
    and how to serve great men.
9 Don't miss the discourse of the aged,
    for they also learnt from their parents,
    because from them you will learn understanding,
    and to give an answer in time of need.

10 Don't kindle the coals of a sinner,
    lest you be burnt with the flame of his fire.
11 Don't rise up from the presence of an insolent man,
    lest he lie in wait as an ambush for your mouth.
12 Don't lend to a man who is stronger than you;
    and if you lend, count it as a loss.
13 Don't be surety beyond your means.
    If you give surety, think as one who will have to pay.

14 Don't go to law with a judge;
    for according to his honour they will give judgement for him.
15 Don't travel with a reckless man,
    lest he be burdensome to you;
    for he will do as he pleases,
    and you will perish with his folly.
16 Don't fight with a wrathful man.
    Don't travel with him through the desert,
    for blood is as nothing in his sight.
    Where there is no help, he will overthrow you.
17 Don't consult with a fool,
    for he will not be able to keep a secret.
18 Do no secret thing before a stranger,
    for you don't know what it will cause.
19 Don't open your heart to every man.
    Don't let him return you a favour.

9

1 Don't be jealous over the wife of your bosom,
    and don't teach her an evil lesson against yourself.
2 Don't give your soul to a woman
    and let her trample down your strength.
3 Don't go to meet a woman who plays the prostitute,
    lest perhaps you fall into her snares.
4 Don't associate with a woman who is a singer,
    lest perhaps you be caught by her tricks.
5 Don't gaze at a virgin,
    lest perhaps you stumble and incur penalties for her.
6 Don't give your soul to prostitutes,
    that you not lose your inheritance.
7 Don't look around in the streets of the city.
    Don't wander in its deserted places.
8 Turn your eye away from a beautiful woman,
    and don't gaze at another's beauty.
Many have been led astray by the beauty of a woman;
    and with this, passion is kindled like a fire.
9 Don't dine at all with a woman who has a husband,
    or revel with her at wine,[a]
    lest perhaps your soul turn away to her,
    and with your spirit you slide into destruction.

10 Don't forsake an old friend;
    for a new one is not comparable to him.

A new friend is like new wine:
    if it becomes old, you will drink it with gladness.

11 Don't envy the success of a sinner;
    for you don't know what his end will be.
12 Don't delight in the delights of the ungodly.
    Remember they will not go unpunished to[b] the grave.

13 Keep yourself far from the man who has[c] power to kill,
    and you will not be troubled by the fear of death.
If you come to him, commit no fault,
    lest he take away your life.
Know surely that you go about in the midst of snares,
    and walk upon the battlements of a city.

14 As well as you can, aim to know your neighbours,
    and take counsel with the wise.
15 Let your conversation be with men of understanding.
    Let all your discourse be in the law of the Most High.
16 Let righteous people be companions at your table.
    Let your glorying be in the fear of the Lord.

17 A work is commended because of the skill of the artisan;
    so he who rules the people will be considered wise for his speech.
18 A loudmouthed man is dangerous in his city.
    He who is reckless in his speech will be hated.

10

1 A wise judge will instruct his people.
    The government of a man of understanding will be well ordered.
2 As is the judge of his people, so are his officials.
    As the city's ruler is, so are all those who dwell in it.
3 An undisciplined king will destroy his people.
    A city will be established through the understanding of the powerful.
4 The government of the earth is in the Lord's hand.
    In due time, he will raise up over it the right person at the right time.
5 A man's prosperity is in the Lord's hand.
    He will lay his honour upon the person of the scribe.

6 Don't be angry with your neighbour for every wrong.
    Do nothing by works of violence.
7 Pride is hateful before the Lord and men.
    Arrogance is abhorrent in the judgement of both.
8 Sovereignty is transferred from nation to nation
    because of injustice, violence, and greed for money.
9 Why are dirt and ashes proud?[d]
    Because in life, my body decays.
10 A long disease mocks the physician.
    The king of today will die tomorrow.
11 For when a man is dead,
    he will inherit maggots, vermin, and worms.
12 It is the beginning of pride when a man departs from the Lord.
    His heart has departed from him who made him.
13 For the beginning of pride is sin.
    He who keeps it will pour out abomination.
For this cause the Lord brought upon them strange calamities
    and utterly overthrew them.
14 The Lord cast down the thrones of rulers
    and set the lowly in their place.
15 The Lord plucked up the roots of nations
    and planted the lowly in their place.
16 The Lord overthrew the lands of nations
    and destroyed them to the foundations of the earth.
17 He took some of them away and destroyed them,
    and made their memory to cease from the earth.
18 Pride has not been created for men,
    nor wrathful anger for the offspring of women.

19 Whose offspring has honour?
    Human offspring who fear the Lord.
Whose offspring has no honour?
    Human offspring who break the commandments.
20 In the midst of kindred he who rules them has honour.
    Those who fear the Lord have honour in his eyes. 21 [e]
22 The rich man, the honourable, and the poor
    all glory in the fear of the Lord.
23 It is not right to dishonour a poor man who has understanding.
    It is not fitting to glorify a man who is a sinner.
24 The prince, the judge, and the mighty man will be honoured.
    There is not one of them greater than he who fears the Lord.
25 Free men will minister to a wise servant.
    A man who has knowledge will not complain.

26 Don't flaunt your wisdom in doing your work.

---

a *9:9* The preceding line of this verse is omitted by the best authorities.
b *9:12* Gr. Hades.
c *9:13* Or, authority

d *10:9* Two lines of this verse are here omitted by the best authorities.
e *10:21* Verse 21 is omitted by the best authorities: Fear of the Lord is the beginning of acceptance, but obstinance and pride are the beginning of rejection.

Don't boast in the time of your distress.

27 Better is he who labours and abounds in all things,
than he who boasts and lacks bread.

28 My son, glorify your soul in humility,
and ascribe to yourself honour according to your worthiness.

29 Who will justify him who sins against his own soul?
Who will honour him who dishonours his own life?

30 A poor man is honoured for his knowledge.
A rich man is honoured for his riches.

31 But he who is honoured in poverty, how much more in riches?
He who is dishonoured in riches, how much more in poverty?

11

1 The wisdom of the lowly will lift up his head,
and make him sit in the midst of great men.

2 Don't commend a man for his good looks.
Don't abhor a man for his outward appearance.

3 The bee is little amongst flying creatures,
but what it produces is the best of confections.

4 Don't boast about the clothes you wear,
and don't exalt yourself in the day of honour;
for the Lord's works are wonderful,
and his works are hidden amongst men.

5 Many[a] kings have sat down upon the ground,
but one who was never thought of has worn a crown.

6 Many mighty men have been greatly disgraced.
Men of renown have been delivered into other men's hands.

7 Don't blame before you investigate.
Understand first, and then rebuke.

8 Don't answer before you have heard.
Don't interrupt while someone else is speaking.

9 Don't argue about a matter that doesn't concern you.
Don't sit with sinners when they judge.

10 My son, don't be busy about many matters;
for if you meddle much, you will not be unpunished.
If you pursue, you will not overtake,
and you will not escape by fleeing.

11 There is one who toils, labours, and hurries,
and is even more behind.

12 There is one who is sluggish, and needs help,
lacking in strength, and who abounds in poverty,
but the Lord's eyes looked upon him for good,
and he raised him up from his low condition,

13 and lifted up his head
so that many marvelled at him.

14 Good things and bad, life and death,
poverty and riches, are from the Lord.   15-16 [b]

17 The Lord's gift remains with the godly.
His good pleasure will prosper forever.

18 One grows rich by his diligence and self-denial,
and this is the portion of his reward:

19 when he says, "I have found rest,
and now I will eat of my goods!"
he doesn't know how much time will pass
until he leaves them to others and dies.

20 Be steadfast in your covenant and be doing it,
and grow old in your work.

21 Don't marvel at the works of a sinner,
but trust the Lord and stay in your labour;
for it is an easy thing in the sight of the Lord
to swiftly and suddenly make a poor man rich.

22 The Lord's blessing is in the reward of the godly.
He makes his blessing flourish in an hour that comes swiftly.

23 Don't say, "What use is there of me?
What further good things can be mine?"

24 Don't say, "I have enough.
What harm could happen to me now?"

25 In the day of good things, bad things are forgotten.
In the day of bad things, a man will not remember things that are
good.

26 For it is an easy thing in the sight of the Lord
to reward a man in the day of death according to his ways.

27 The affliction of an hour causes delights to be forgotten.
In the end, a man's deeds are revealed.

28 Call no man happy before his death.
A man will be known in his children.

29 Don't bring every man into your house,
for many are the tricks of a deceitful man.

30 Like a decoy partridge in a cage, so is the heart of a proud man.
Like a spy, he looks for your weakness.

31 For he lies in wait to turn things that are good into evil,
and assigns blame in things that are praiseworthy.

32 From a spark of fire, a heap of many coals is kindled,
and a sinful man lies in wait to shed blood.

33 Take heed of an evil-doer, for he plans wicked things,
lest perhaps he ruin your reputation forever.

34 Receive a stranger into your house, and he will distract you with
arguments
and estrange you from your own family.

12

1 If you do good, know to whom you do it,
and your good deeds will have thanks.

2 Do good to a godly man, and you will find a reward—
if not from him, then from the Most High.

3 No good will come to him who continues to do evil,
nor to him who gives no alms.

4 Give to the godly man,
and don't help the sinner.

5 Do good to one who is lowly.
Don't give to an ungodly man.
Keep back his bread, and don't give it to him,
lest he subdue you with it;
for you would receive twice as much evil
for all the good you would have done to him.

6 For the Most High also hates sinners,
and will repay vengeance to the ungodly.[c]

7 Give to the good man,
and don't help the sinner.

8 A man's friend won't be[d] fully tried in prosperity.
His enemy won't be hidden in adversity.

9 In a man's prosperity, his enemies are grieved.
In his adversity, even his friend leaves.

10 Never trust your enemy,
for his wickedness is like corrosion in copper.

11 Though he humbles himself and walks bowed down,
still be careful and beware of him.
You will be to him as one who has wiped a mirror,
to be sure it doesn't completely tarnish.

12 Don't set him next to you,
lest he overthrow you and stand in your place.
Don't let him sit on your right hand,
lest he seek to take your seat,
and at the last you acknowledge my words,
and be pricked with my sayings.

13 Who will pity a charmer that is bitten by a snake,
or any who come near wild beasts?

14 Even so, who will pity him who goes to a sinner,
and is associated with him in his sins?

15 For a while he will stay with you,
and if you falter, he will not stay.

16 The enemy will speak sweetly with his lips,
and in his heart plan to throw you into a pit.
The enemy may weep with his eyes,
but if he finds opportunity, he will want more blood.

17 If adversity meets you, you will find him there before you.
Pretending to help you, he will trip you.

18 He will shake his head, clap his hands,
whisper much, and change his countenance.

13

1 He who touches pitch will be defiled.
He who has fellowship with a proud man will become like him.

2 Don't take up a burden above your strength.
Have no fellowship with one who is mightier and richer than yourself.
What fellowship would the earthen pot have with the kettle?
The kettle will strike, and the pot will be dashed in pieces.

3 The rich man does a wrong and threatens.
The poor is wronged and apologises.

4 If you are profitable, he will exploit you.
If you are in need, he will forsake you.

5 If you own something, he will live with you.
He will drain your resources and will not be sorry.

6 Does he need you? Then he will deceive you,
smile at you, and give you hope.
He will speak kindly to you and say, "What do you need?"

7 He will shame you by his delicacies
until he has made you bare twice or thrice,
and in the end he will laugh you to scorn.
Afterward he will see you, will forsake you,
and shake his head at you.

---

a *11:5* Gr. tyrants
b *11:15-16* Verses 15 and 16 are omitted by the best authorities.

c *12:6* The remainder of this verse is omitted by the best authorities.
d *12:8* Or, punished

8 Beware that you are not deceived
  and brought low in your enjoyment.
9 If a mighty man invites you, be reserved,
  and he will invite you more.
10 Don't press him, lest you be thrust back.
  Don't stand far off, lest you be forgotten.
11 Don't try to speak with him as an equal,
  and don't believe his many words;
for he will test you with much talk,
  and will examine you in a smiling manner.
12 He who doesn't keep secrets to himself is unmerciful.
  He won't hesitate to harm and to bind.
13 Keep them to yourself and be careful,
  for you walk^a in danger of falling. 14 ^b

15 Every living creature loves its own kind,
  and every man loves his neighbour.
16 All flesh associates with their own kind.
  A man will stick to people like himself.
17 What fellowship would the wolf have with the lamb?
  So is the sinner to the godly.
18 What peace is there between a hyena and a dog?
  What peace is there between a rich man and the poor?
19 Wild donkeys are the prey of lions in the wilderness;
  likewise poor men are feeding grounds for the rich.
20 Lowliness is an abomination to a proud man;
  likewise a poor man is an abomination to the rich.

21 When a rich man is shaken, he is supported by his friends,
  but when the humble is down, he is pushed away even by his friends.
22 When a rich man falls, there are many helpers.
  He speaks things not to be spoken, and men justify him.
A humble man falls, and men rebuke him.
  He utters wisdom, and is not listened to.
23 A rich man speaks, and all keep silence.
  They extol what he says to the clouds.
A poor man speaks, and they say, "Who is this?"
  If he stumbles, they will help to overthrow him.

24 Riches are good if they have no sin.
  Poverty is evil only in the opinion of the ungodly.

25 The heart of a man changes his countenance,
  whether it is for good or for evil.^c
26 A cheerful countenance is a sign of a prosperous heart.
  Devising proverbs takes strenuous thinking.

14

1 Blessed is the man who has not slipped with his mouth,
  and doesn't suffer from sorrow for sins.
2 Blessed is he whose soul does not condemn him,
  and who has not given up hope.

3 Riches are not appropriate for a stingy person.
  What would a miser do with money?
4 He who gathers by denying himself gathers for others.
  Others will revel in his goods.
5 If one is mean to himself, to whom will he be good?
  He won't enjoy his possessions.
6 There is none more evil than he who is grudging to himself.
  This is a punishment for his wickedness.
7 Even if he does good, he does it in forgetfulness.
  In the end, he reveals his wickedness.
8 A miser is evil.
  He turns away and disregards souls.
9 A covetous man's eye is not satisfied with his portion.
  Wicked injustice dries up his soul.
10 A miser begrudges bread,
  and it is lacking at his table.

11 My son, according to what you have, treat yourself well,
  and bring worthy offerings to the Lord.
12 Remember that death will not wait,
  and that the covenant of Hades hasn't been shown to you.
13 Do good to your friends before you die.
  According to your ability, reach out and give to them.
14 Don't deprive yourself of a good day.
  Don't let your share of a desired good pass you by.
15 Won't you leave your labours to another,
  and your toils be divided by lot?
16 Give, take, and treat yourself well,
  because there is no seeking of luxury in Hades.
17 All flesh grows old like a garment,
  for the covenant from the beginning is, "You must die!"

18 Like the leaves flourishing on a thick tree,
  some it sheds, and some grow,
so also are the generations of flesh and blood:
  one comes to an end and another is born.
19 Every work rots and falls away,
  and its builder will depart with it.

20 Blessed is the man who meditates on wisdom,
  and who reasons by his understanding.
21 He who considers her ways in his heart
  will also have knowledge of her secrets.
22 Go after her like a hunter,
  and lie in wait in her paths.
23 He who peers in at her windows
  will also listen at her doors.
24 He who lodges close to her house
  will also fasten a nail in her walls.
25 He will pitch his tent near at hand to her,
  and will lodge in a lodging where good things are.
26 He will set his children under her shelter,
  and will rest under her branches.
27 By her he will be covered from heat,
  and will lodge in her glory.

15

1 He who fears the Lord will do this.
  He who has possession of the law will obtain her.
2 She will meet him like a mother,
  and receive him like a wife married in her virginity.
3 She will feed him with bread of understanding
  and give him water of wisdom to drink.
4 He will be stayed upon her, and will not be moved.
  He will rely upon her, and will not be confounded.
5 She will exalt him above his neighbours.
  She will open his mouth in the midst of the congregation.
6 He will inherit joy, a crown of gladness,
  and an everlasting name.
7 Foolish men will not obtain her.
  Sinners will not see her.
8 She is far from pride.
  Liars will not remember her.
9 Praise is not attractive in the mouth of a sinner;
  for it was not sent to him from the Lord.
10 For praise will be spoken in wisdom;
  The Lord will prosper it.

11 Don't say, "It is through the Lord that I fell away;"
  for you shall not do the things that he hates.
12 Don't say, "It is he that caused me to err;"
  for he has no need of a sinful man.
13 The Lord hates every abomination;
  and those who fear him don't love them.
14 He himself made man from the beginning
  and left him in the hand of his own counsel.
15 If you choose, you can keep the commandments.
  To be faithful is a matter of your choice.
16 He has set fire and water before you.
  You will stretch forth your hand to whichever you desire.
17 Before man is life and death.
  Whichever he likes, it will be given to him.
18 For the wisdom of the Lord is great.
  He is mighty in power, and sees all things.
19 His eyes are upon those who fear him.
  He knows every act of man.
20 He has not commanded any man to be ungodly.
  He has not given any man license to sin.

16

1 Don't desire a multitude of unprofitable children,
  neither delight in ungodly sons.
2 If they multiply, don't delight in them
  unless the fear of the Lord is in them.
3 Don't trust in their life.
  Don't rely on their numbers;
  for one can be better than a thousand,
  and to die childless than to have ungodly children.
4 For from one who has understanding, a city will be populated,
  but a race of wicked men will be made desolate.
5 I have seen many such things with my eyes.
  My ear has heard mightier things than these.

6 In a congregation of sinners, a fire will be kindled.
  In a disobedient nation, wrath is kindled.
7 He was not pacified towards the giants of old time,
  who revolted in their strength.

---

a *13:13* Gr. along with.
b *13:14* The remainder of verse 13, and verse 14, are omitted by the best authorities.

c *13:25* The remainder of this verse is omitted by the best authorities.

8 He didn't spare Lot's neighbours,
  whom he abhorred for their pride.
9 He didn't pity the people of perdition
  who were taken away in their sins,
    10 or in like manner, the six hundred thousand footmen
  who were gathered together in the hardness of their hearts.
11 Even if there is one stiff-necked person,
  it is a marvel if he will be unpunished;
  for mercy and wrath are both with him who is mighty to forgive,
  and he pours out wrath.
12 As his mercy is great, so is his correction also.
  He judges a man according to his works.
13 The sinner will not escape with plunder.
  The perseverance of the godly will not be frustrated.
14 He will make room for every work of mercy.
  Each man will receive according to his works. 15-16 ᵃ

17 Don't say, "I will be hidden from the Lord,"
  and "Who will remember me from on high?"
I will not be known amongst so many people,
  for what is my soul in a boundless creation?
18 Behold, the heaven, the heaven of heavens,
  the deep, and the earth, will be moved when he visits.
19 The mountains and the foundations of the earth together
  are shaken with trembling when he looks at them.
20 No heart will think about these things.
  Who could comprehend his ways?
21 Like a tempest which no man can see,
  so, the majority of his works areᵇ hidden.
22 Who will declare his works of righteousness?
  Who will wait for them?
  For his covenant is afar off.ᶜ
23 He who is lacking inᵈ understanding thinks about these things.
  An unwise and erring man thinks foolishly.

24 My son, listen to me, learn knowledge,
  and heed my words with your heart.
25 I will impart instruction with precision,
  and declare knowledge exactly.

26 In the judgement of the Lord are his works from the beginning.
  From the making of them he determined their boundaries.
27 He arranged his works for all time,
  and their beginnings to their generations.
They aren't hungry or weary,
  and they don't cease from their works.
28 No one pushes aside his neighbour.
  They will never disobey his word.
29 After this also the Lord looked at the earth
  and filled it with his blessings.
30 All manner of living things covered its surface,
  and they return into it.

17

1 The Lord created mankind out of earth,
  and turned them back to it again.
2 He gave them days by number, and a set time,
  and gave them authority over the things that are on it.
3 He endowed them with strength proper to them,
  and made them according to his own image.
4 He put the fear of man upon all flesh,
  and gave him dominion over beasts and birds. 5 ᵉ
6 He gave them counsel, tongue, eyes,
  ears, and heart to have understanding.
7 He filled them with the knowledge of wisdom,
  and showed them good and evil.
8 He set his eye upon their hearts,
  to show them the majesty of his works. 9 ᶠ
10 And they will praise his holy name,
  ᵍ that they may declare the majesty of his works.
11 He added to them knowledge,
  and gave them a law of life for a heritage.
12 He made an everlasting covenant with them,
  and showed them his decrees.
13 Their eyes saw the majesty of his glory.
  Their ears heard the glory of his voice.
14 He said to them, "Beware of all unrighteousness."
  So he gave them commandment, each man concerning his neighbour.

15 Their ways are ever before him.
  They will not be hidden from his eyes. 16 ʰ
17 ⁱFor every nation he appointed a ruler,
  but Israel is the Lord's portion. 18 ʲ
19 All their works are as clear as the sun before him.
  His eyes are continually upon their ways.
20 Their iniquities are not hidden from him.
  All their sins are before the Lord. 21 ᵏ
22 With him the alms of a man is as a signet.
  He will keep a man's kindness as the pupil of the eye.ˡ
23 Afterwards he will rise up and repay them,
  and render their repayment upon their head.
24 However to those who repent he grants a return.
  He comforts those who are losing hope.

25 Return to the Lord, and forsake sins.
  Make your prayer before his face offend less.
26 Turn again to the Most High, and turn away from iniquity.ᵐ
  Greatly hate the abominable thing.
27 Who will give praise to the Most High in Hades,
  in place of the living who return thanks?
28 Thanksgiving perishes from the dead, as from one who doesn't exist.
  He who is in life and health will praise the Lord.
29 How great is the mercy of the Lord,
  and his forgiveness to those who turn to him!
30 For humans are not capable of everything,
  because the son of man is not immortal.
31 What is brighter than the sun? Yet even this can be eclipsed.
  So flesh and blood devise evil.
32 He looks upon the power of the height of heaven,
  while all men are earth and ashes.

18

1 He who lives forever created the whole universe.
2 The Lord alone is just. 3 ⁿ
4 He has given power to declare his works to no one.
  Who could trace out his mighty deeds?
5 Who could measure the strength of his majesty?
  Who could also proclaim his mercies?
6 As for the wondrous works of the Lord, it is not possible to take from them
      nor add to them,
  neither is it possible to explore them.
7 When a man has finished, then he is just at the beginning.
  When he stops, then he will be perplexed.
8 What is mankind, and what purpose do they serve?
  What is their good, and what is their evil?
9 The number of man's days at the most are a hundred years.
10 As a drop of water from the sea, and a pebble from the sand,
  so are a few years in the day of eternity.
11 For this cause the Lord was patient over them,
  and poured out his mercy upon them.
12 He saw and perceived their end, that it is evil.
  Therefore he multiplied his forgiveness.
13 The mercy of a man is on his neighbour;
  but the mercy of the Lord is on all flesh:
  reproving, chastening, teaching,
  and bringing back, as a shepherd does his flock.
14 He has mercy on those who accept chastening,
  and that diligently seek after his judgements.

15 My son, don't add reproach to your good deeds,
  and no harsh words in any of your giving.
16 Doesn't the dew relieve the scorching heat?
  So a word is better than a gift.
17 Behold, isn't a word better than a gift?
  Both are with a gracious person.
18 A fool is ungracious and abusive.
  The gift of a grudging person consumes the eyes.

19 Learn before you speak.
  Take care of your health before you get sick.
20 Before judgement, examine yourself,
  and in the hour of scrutiny you will find forgiveness.
21 Humble yourself before you get sick.
  In the time of sins, repent.
22 Let nothing hinder you to pay your vow in due time.
  Don't wait until death to be released.
23 Before you make a vow, prepare yourself.
  Don't be like a man who tests the Lord.

ᵃ 16:15-16 Verses 15 and 16 are omitted by the best authorities.
ᵇ 16:21 Gr. *amongst hidden things.*
ᶜ 16:22 The remainder of this verse is omitted by the best authorities.
ᵈ 16:23 Gr. *heart.*
ᵉ 17:5 Verse 5 is omitted by the best authorities.
ᶠ 17:9 Verse 9 is omitted by the best authorities.
ᵍ 17:10 This line is added by the best authorities.
ʰ 17:16 Verses 16, 18, and 21 are omitted by the best authorities.

ⁱ 17:17 The preceding part of this verse is omitted by the best authorities.
ʲ 17:18 Verses 16, 18, and 21 are omitted by the best authorities.
ᵏ 17:21 Verses 16, 18, and 21 are omitted by the best authorities.
ˡ 17:22 The remainder of this verse is omitted by the best authorities.
ᵐ 17:26 A line is here omitted by the best authorities.
ⁿ 18:3 The remainder of verse 2, and verse 3, are omitted by the best authorities.

24 Think about the wrath coming in the days of the end,
  and the time of vengeance, when he turns away his face.
25 In the days of fullness remember the time of hunger.
  Remember poverty and lack in the days of wealth.
26 From morning until evening, the time changes.
  All things are speedy before the Lord.
27 A wise man is cautious in everything.
  In days of sinning, he will beware of offence.ᵃ
28 Every man of understanding knows wisdom.
  He will give thanks to him who found her.
29 They who were of understanding in sayings also became wise themselves,
  and poured out apt proverbs.

30 Don't go after your lusts.
  Restrain your appetites.
31 If you give fully to your soul the delight of her desire,
  she will make youᵇ the laughing stock of your enemies.
32 Don't make merry in much luxury,
  and don't be tied to its expense.
33 Don't be made a beggar by banqueting with borrowed money
  when you have nothing in your purse.ᶜ

19

1 A worker who is a drunkard will not become rich.
  He who despises small things will fall little by little.
2 Wine and women will make men of understanding go astray.
  He who joins with prostitutes is reckless.
3 Decay and worms will have him as their heritage.
  A reckless soul will be taken away.

4 He who is hasty to trust is shallow-hearted.
  He who sins offends against his own soul.
5 He who rejoices in wickedness will be condemned.ᵈ
6 ᵉ He who hates gossip has less wickedness.
7 Never repeat what is told you,
  and you won't lose anything.
8 Whether it is of friend or foe, don't tell it.
  Unless it is a sin to you, don't reveal it.
9 For if he has heard you and observed you,
  when the time comes, he will hate you.
10 Have you heard something? Let it die with you.
  Be brave: it will not make you burst!
11 A fool will travail in pain with a word,
  as a woman in labour with a child.
12 As an arrow that sticks in the flesh of the thigh,
  so is gossip in a fool.

13 Question a friend; it may be he didn't do it.
  If he did something, it may be that he may do it no more.
14 Question your neighbour; it may be he didn't say it.
  If he has said it, it may be that he may not say it again.
15 Question a friend; for many times there is slander.
  Don't trust every word.
16 There is one who slips, and not from the heart.
  Who is he who hasn't sinned with his tongue?
17 Reprove your neighbour before you threaten him;
  and give place to the law of the Most High. 18-19 ᶠ

20 All wisdom is the fear of the Lord.
  In all wisdom is the doing of the law. 21 ᵍ
22 The knowledge of wickedness is not wisdom.
  The prudence of sinners is not counsel.
23 There is a wickedness, and it is an abomination.
There is a fool lacking in wisdom.
24 Better is one who has little understanding, and fears God,
  than one who has much intelligence and transgresses the law.
25 There is an exquisite subtlety, and it is unjust.
  And there is one who perverts favour to gain a judgement.ʰ
26 There is one who does wickedly, who hangs down his head with mourning;
  but inwardly he is full of deceit,
27 bowing down his face, and pretending to be deaf in one ear.
  Where he isn't known, he will take advantage of you.
28 And if for lack of power he is hindered from sinning,
  if he finds opportunity, he will do mischief.
29 A man will be known by his appearance.
  One who has understanding will be known by his face when you meet him.
30 A man's attire, grinning laughter,

and the way he walks show what he is.

20

1 There is a reproof that is not timely;
  and there is a person who is wise enough to keep silent.
2 How good is it to reprove, rather than to be angry.
  He who confesses will be kept back from harm. 3 ⁱ
4 As is the lust of a eunuch to deflower a virgin,
  so is he who executes judgements with violence.
5 There is one who keeps silent and is found wise;
  and there is one who is hated for his much talk.
6 There is one who keeps silent, for he has no answer to make;
  And there is one who keeps silent, knowing when to speak.
7 A wise man will be silent until his time has come,
  but the braggart and fool will miss his time.
8 He who uses many words will be abhorred.
  He who takes authority for himself will be hated in it.

9 There is a prosperity that a man finds in misfortunes;
  and there is a gain that turns to loss.
10 There is a gift that will not profit you;
  and there is a gift that pays back double.
11 There are losses because of glory;
  and there is one who has lifted up his head from a low estate.
12 There is one who buys much for a little,
  and pays for it again sevenfold.
13 He who is wise in words will make himself beloved;
  but the pleasantries of fools will be wasted.
14 The gift of a fool will not profit you,ʲ
  for he looks for repayment many times instead of one.
15 He will give little and insult much.
  He will open his mouth like a crier.
Today he will lend, and tomorrow he will ask for it back.
  Such a one is a hateful man.
16 The fool will say, "I have no friend,
  and I have no thanks for my good deeds.
  Those who eat my bread have an evil tongue."
17 How often, and of how many, will he be laughed to scorn!ᵏ

18 A slip on a pavement is better than a slip with the tongue.
  So the fall of the wicked will come speedily.
19 A man without grace is a tale out of season.
  It will be continually in the mouth of the ignorant.
20 A parable from a fool's mouth will be rejected;
  for he won't tell it at the proper time.

21 There is one who is hindered from sinning through lack.
  When he rests, he will not be troubled.
22 There is one who destroys his soul through bashfulness.
  By a foolish countenance, he will destroy it.
23 There is one who for bashfulness makes promises to his friend;
  and he makes him his enemy for nothing.

24 A lie is an ugly blot on a person.
  It will be continually in the mouth of the ignorant.
25 A thief is better than a man who is continually lying,
  but they both will inherit destruction.
26 The destination of a liar is dishonour.
  His shame is with him continually.

27 He who is wise in words will advance himself.
  And one who is prudent will please great men.
28 He who tills his land will raise his harvest high.
  He who pleases great men will get pardon for iniquity.
29 Favours and gifts blind the eyes of the wise,
  and as a muzzle on the mouth, turn away reproofs.
30 Wisdom that is hidden, and treasure that is out of sight—
  what profit is in either of them?
31 Better is a man who hides his folly
  than a man who hides his wisdom. 32 ˡ

21

1 My son, have you sinned?
  Do it no more;
  and ask forgiveness for your past sins.
2 Flee from sin as from the face of a snake;
  for if you go near, it will bite you.
Its teeth are like lion's teeth,
  slaying people's souls.
3 All iniquity is as a two-edged sword.

ᵃ *18:27* The remainder of this verse is omitted by the best authorities.
ᵇ *18:31* Or, a rejoicing to
ᶜ *18:33* The remainder of this verse is omitted by the best authorities.
ᵈ *19:5* The remainder of this verse is omitted by the best authorities.
ᵉ *19:6* The preceding part of this verse is omitted by the best authorities.
ᶠ *19:18-19* Verses 18 and 19 are omitted by the best authorities.

ᵍ *19:21* The remainder of verse 20 and verse 21 are omitted by the best authorities.
ʰ *19:25* The remainder of this verse is omitted by the best authorities.
ⁱ *20:3* Verse 3 is omitted by the best authorities.
ʲ *20:14* A line of this verse is here omitted by the best authorities.
ᵏ *20:17* The latter part of verse 17 is omitted by the best authorities.
ˡ *20:32* Verse 32 is omitted by the best authorities.

Its stroke has no healing.

4 Terror and violence will waste away riches.
    So the house of an arrogant man will be laid waste.
5 Supplication from a poor man's mouth reaches to the ears of[a] God,
    and his judgement comes speedily.
6 One who hates reproof is in the path of the sinner.
    He who fears the Lord will repent in his heart.
7 He who is mighty in tongue is known far away;
    but the man of understanding knows when he slips.

8 He who builds his house with other men's money
    is like one who gathers stones for his own tomb.
9 The congregation of wicked men is as a bundle of tow
    with a flame of fire at the end of them.
10 The way of sinners is paved with stones;
    and at the end of it is the pit of Hades.

11 He who keeps the law becomes master of its intent.
    The fulfilment of the fear of the Lord is wisdom.
12 He who is not clever will not be instructed.
    There is a cleverness which makes bitterness abound.
13 The knowledge of a wise man will be made to abound as a flood,
    and his counsel as a fountain of life.
14 The inward parts of a fool are like a broken vessel.
    He will hold no knowledge.

15 If a man of knowledge hears a wise word,
    he will commend it and add to it.
The wanton man hears it, and it displeases him,
    so he throws it away behind his back.
16 The chatter of a fool is like a burden in the way,
    but grace will be found on the lips of the wise.
17 The utterance of the prudent man will be sought for in the congregation.
    They will ponder his words in their heart.

18 As a house that is destroyed, so is wisdom to a fool.
    The knowledge of an unwise man is talk without sense.[b]
19 Instruction is as fetters on the feet of an unwise man,
    and as manacles on the right hand.
20 A fool lifts up his voice with laughter,
    but a clever man smiles quietly.
21 Instruction is to a prudent man as an ornament of gold,
    and as a bracelet upon his right arm.

22 The foot of a fool rushes into a house,
    but a man of experience will be ashamed of entering.
23 A foolish man peers into the door of a house,
    but a man who is instructed will stand outside.
24 It is rude for someone to listen at a door,
    but a prudent person will be grieved with the disgrace.
25 The lips of strangers will be grieved at these things,
    but the words of prudent men will be weighed in the balance.

26 The heart of fools is in their mouth,
    but the mouth of wise men is their heart.
27 When the ungodly curses an adversary,
    he curses his own soul.
28 A whisperer defiles his own soul,
    and will be hated wherever he travels.

22

1 A slothful man is compared to a stone that is defiled.
    Everyone will at hiss at him in his disgrace.
2 A slothful man is compared to the filth of a dunghill.
    Anyone who picks it up will shake it out of his hand.

3 An undisciplined child is a disgrace to his father,
    and a foolish daughter is born to his loss.
4 A prudent daughter will inherit a husband of her own.
    She who brings shame is the grief of her father.
5 She who is arrogant brings shame on father and husband.
    She will be despised by both of them.
6 Ill-timed conversation is like music in mourning,
    but stripes and correction are wisdom in every season.

7 He who teaches a fool is like one who glues potsherds together,
    even like one who wakes a sleeper out of a deep sleep.
8 He who teaches a fool is as one who teaches a man who slumbers.
    In the end he will say, "What is it?" 9-10 [c]
11 Weep for the dead, for he lacks light.
    Weep for a fool, for he lacks understanding.
Weep more sweetly for the dead, because he has found rest,

but the life of the fool is worse than death.
12 Mourning for the dead lasts seven days,
    but for a fool and an ungodly man, it lasts all the days of his life.

13 Don't talk much with a foolish man,
    and don't go to one who has no understanding.
Beware of him, lest you have trouble and be defiled in his onslaught.
    Turn away from him, and you will find rest,
    and you won't be wearied in his madness.
14 What would be heavier than lead?
    What is its name, but "Fool"?
15 Sand, salt, and a mass of iron is easier to bear
    than a man without understanding.

16 Timber girded and bound into a building will not be released with
        shaking.
    So a heart established in due season on well advised counsel will not
        be afraid.
17 A heart settled upon a thoughtful understanding
    is as an ornament of plaster on a polished wall.
18 Fences set on a high place will not stand against the wind;
    so a fearful heart in the imagination of a fool will not stand against any
        fear.

19 He who pricks the eye will make tears fall.
    He who pricks the heart makes it show feeling.
20 Whoever casts a stone at birds scares them away.
    He who insults a friend will dissolve friendship.
21 If you have drawn a sword against a friend, don't despair,
    for there may be a way back.
22 If you have opened your mouth against a friend, don't be afraid,
    for there may be reconciliation,
    unless it is for insulting, arrogance, disclosing of a secret, or a
        treacherous blow—
    for these things any friend will flee.

23 Gain trust with your neighbour in his poverty,
    that in his prosperity you may have gladness.
Stay steadfast to him in the time of his affliction,
    that you may be heir with him in his inheritance.[d]
24 Before fire is the vapour and smoke of a furnace,
    so insults precede bloodshed.
25 I won't be ashamed to shelter a friend.
    I won't hide myself from his face.
26 If any evil happens to me because of him,
    everyone who hears it will beware of him.

27 Who will set a watch over my mouth,
    and a seal of shrewdness upon my lips,
    that I may not fall from it, and that my tongue may not destroy me?

23

1 O Lord, Father and Master of my life,
    don't abandon me to their counsel.
    Don't let me fall because of them.
2 Who will set scourges over my thought,
    and a discipline of wisdom over my heart,
    that they spare me not for my errors,
    and not overlook their sins?
3 Otherwise my errors might be multiplied,
    and my sins abound,
    I fall before my adversaries,
    and my enemy rejoice over me.[e]
4 O Lord, Father and God of my life,
    don't give me a haughty eyes,[f]
        5 and turn away evil desire from me.[g]
6 Let neither gluttony nor lust overtake me.
    Don't give me over to a shameless mind.

7 Listen, my children, to the discipline of the mouth.
    He who keeps it will not be caught.
8 The sinner will be overpowered through his lips.
    By them, the insulter and the arrogant will stumble.
9 Don't accustom your mouth to an oath,
    and don't be accustomed to naming the Holy One,
10 for as a servant who is continually scourged will not lack bruises,
    so he also who swears and continually utters the Name will not be
        cleansed from sin.
11 A man of many oaths will be filled with iniquity.
    The scourge will not depart from his house.
If he offends, his sin will be upon him.
    If he disregards it, he has sinned doubly.
If he has sworn falsely, he will not be justified,
    for his house will be filled with calamities.

---

a 21:5 Gr. him.
b 21:18 Gr. unexamined words.
c 22:9-10 Verses 9 and 10 are omitted by the best authorities.
d 22:23 The remainder of this verse is omitted by the best authorities.

e 23:3 The remainder of this verse is omitted by the best authorities.
f 23:4 The remainder of this verse is omitted by the best authorities.
g 23:5 The remainder of this verse is omitted by the best authorities.

12 There is a manner of speech that is clothed with death.
   Let it not be found in the heritage of Jacob,
   for all these things will be far from the godly,
   and they will not wallow in sins.
13 Don't accustom your mouth to gross rudeness,
   for it involves sinful speech.
14 Remember your father and your mother,
   for you sit in the midst of great men,
   that you be not forgetful before them,
   and become a fool by your bad habit;
so you may wish that you had not been born,
   and curse the day of your birth.
15 A man who is accustomed to abusive language
   won't be corrected all the days of his life.

16 Two sorts of people multiply sins,
   and the third will bring wrath:
   a hot passion, like a burning fire, will not be quenched until it is
      consumed;
   a fornicator in the body of his flesh will never cease until he has burnt
      out the fire.
17 All bread is sweet to a fornicator.
   He will not cease until he dies.
18 A man who goes astray from his own marriage bed
   says in his heart, "Who sees me?
Darkness is around me, and the walls hide me.
   No one sees me. Of whom am I afraid?
   The Most High will not remember my sins."
19 The eyes of men are his terror.
   He doesn't know that the eyes of the Lord are ten thousand times
      brighter than the sun,
   seeing all the ways of men,
   and looking into secret places.
20 All things were known to him before they were created,
   and also after they were completed.
21 This man will be punished in the streets of the city.
   He will be seized where he least expects it.

22 So also is a wife who leaves her husband,
   and produces an heir by another man.
23 For first, she was disobedient in the law of the Most High.
   Second, she trespassed against her own husband.
   Third, she played the adulteress in fornication,
   and had children by another man.
24 She shall be brought out into the congregation.
   Her punishment will extend to her children.
25 Her children will not take root.
   Her branches will bear no fruit.
26 She will leave her memory for a curse.
   Her reproach won't be blotted out.
27 And those who are left behind will know that there is nothing better than
      the fear of the Lord,
   and nothing sweeter than to heed the commandments of the Lord. 28 [a]

24

1 Wisdom will praise her own soul,
   and will proclaim her glory in the midst of her people.
2 She will open her mouth in the congregation of the Most High,
   and proclaim her glory in the presence of his power.
3 "I came out of the mouth of the Most High,
   and covered the earth as a mist.
4 I lived in high places,
   and my throne is in the pillar of the cloud.
5 Alone I surrounded the circuit of heaven,
   and walked in the depth of the abyss.
6 In the waves of the sea, and in all the earth,
   and in every people and nation, I obtained a possession.
7 With all these I sought rest.
   In whose inheritance shall I lodge?
8 Then the Creator of all things gave me a command.
   He who created me made my tent to rest,
   and said, 'Let your dwelling be in Jacob,
   and your inheritance in Israel.'
9 He created me from the beginning, before the ages.
   For all ages, I will not cease to exist.
10 In the holy tabernacle, I ministered before him.
   So I was established in Zion.
11 In the beloved city, likewise he gave me rest.
   In Jerusalem was my domain.
12 I took root in a people that was honoured,
   even in the portion of the Lord's own inheritance.

13 I was exalted like a cedar in Lebanon,
   And like a cypress tree on the mountains of Hermon.

14 I was exalted like a palm tree on the sea shore,
   like rose bushes in Jericho,
   and like a fair olive tree in the plain.
   I was exalted like a plane tree.
15 Like cinnamon and aspalathus, I have given a scent to perfumes.
   Like choice myrrh, I spread abroad a pleasant fragrance,
   like[b] galbanum, onycha, stacte,
   and as the smell of frankincense in the tabernacle.
16 Like the terebinth, I stretched out my branches.
   My branches are glorious and graceful.
17 Like the vine, I put forth grace.
   My flowers are the fruit of glory and riches. 18 [c]

19 "Come to me, all you who desire me,
   and be filled with my fruits.
20 For my memory is sweeter than honey,
   and my inheritance than the honeycomb.
21 Those who eat me will be hungry for more.
   Those who drink me will be thirsty for more.
22 He who obeys me will not be ashamed.
   Those who work with me will not sin."

23 All these things are the book of the covenant of the Most High God,
   the law which Moses commanded us for an inheritance for the
      assemblies of Jacob. 24 [d]
25 It is he who makes wisdom abundant, as Pishon,
   and as Tigris in the days of first fruits.
26 He makes understanding full as the Euphrates,
   and as the Jordan in the days of harvest,
27 who makes instruction shine forth as the light,
   as Gihon in the days of vintage.
28 The first man didn't know her perfectly.
   In like manner, the last has not explored her.
29 For her thoughts are filled from the sea,
   and her counsels from the great deep.

30 I came out as a canal stream from a river,
   and as an irrigation ditch into a garden.
31 I said, "I will water my garden,
   and will drench my garden bed."
Behold, my stream became a river,
   and my river became a sea.
32 I will yet bring instruction to light as the morning,
   and will make these things clear from far away.
33 I will continue to pour out teaching like prophecy,
   and leave it to all generations.
34 See that I have not laboured for myself only,
   but for all those who diligently seek wisdom.

25

1 I enjoy three things,
   and they are beautiful before the Lord and men:
   the agreement of kindred,
   the friendship of neighbours,
   and a woman and her husband who walk together in agreement.
2 But my soul hates three sorts of people,
   and I am greatly offended at their life:
   a poor man who is arrogant,
   a rich man who is a liar,
   and an old fool who is an adulterer.

3 If you gathered nothing in your youth,
   how could you find anything in your old age?
4 How beautiful a thing is judgement in the grey-haired,
   and for elders to know good counsel!
5 How beautiful is the wisdom of old men,
   and understanding and counsel to men who are in honour!
6 Much experience is the crown of the aged.
   Their glory is the fear of the Lord.

7 There are nine things that I have thought of, and in my heart counted
      happy,
   and the tenth I will utter with my tongue:
   a man who has joy with his children,
   and a man who lives and sees the fall of his enemies.
8 Happy is he who dwells with a wife of understanding,
   he who has not slipped with his tongue,
   and he who has not served a man who is unworthy of him.
9 Happy is he who has found prudence,
   and he who speaks in the ears of those who listen.
10 How great is he who has found wisdom!
   Yet is there none above him who fears the Lord.
11 The fear of the Lord surpasses all things.
   To whom shall he who holds it be likened? 12 [e]

---

a *23:28* Verse 28 is omitted by the best authorities.
b *24:15* See Exodus 30:34.
c *24:18* Verse 18 is omitted by the best authorities.

d *24:24* Verse 24 is omitted by the best authorities.
e *25:12* Verse 12 is omitted by the best authorities.

13 Any wound but a wound of the heart!
　　Any wickedness but the wickedness of a woman!
14 Any calamity but a calamity from those who hate me!
　　Any vengeance but the vengeance of enemies!
15 There is no venom worse than a snake's venom.
　　There is no wrath worse than an enemy's wrath.

16 I would rather dwell with a lion and a dragon
　　than keep house with a wicked woman.
17 The wickedness of a woman changes her appearance,
　　and darkens her countenance like that of a bear.
18 Her husband will sit amongst his neighbours,
　　and when he hears it, he sighs bitterly.
19 All malice is small compared to the malice of a woman.
　　Let the portion of a sinner fall on her.
20 As walking up a sandy hill is to the feet of the aged,
　　so is a wife full of words to a quiet man.
21 Don't be ensnared by a woman's beauty.
　　Don't desire a woman for her beauty.
22 There is anger, impudence, and great reproach
　　if a woman supports her husband.
23 A wicked woman is abasement of heart,
　　sadness of countenance, and a wounded heart.
A woman who won't make her husband happy
　　is like hands that hang down, and weak knees.
24 The beginning of sin came from a woman.
　　Because of her, we all die.
25 Don't give water an outlet,
　　and don't give a wicked woman freedom of speech.
26 If she doesn't go as you direct,
　　cut her away from your flesh.[a]

26

1 Happy is the husband of a good wife.
　　The number of his days will be doubled.
2 A faithful wife gives joy to her husband.
　　He will fulfil his years in peace.
3 A good wife is a great gift.
　　She will be given to those who fear the Lord.
4 Whether a man is rich or poor,
　　a good heart makes a cheerful face at all times.

5 Of three things my heart was afraid,
　　and concerning the fourth[b] kind I made supplication:
　　The slander of a city, the assembly of a mob, and a false accusation.
　　All these are more grievous than death.
6 A grief of heart and sorrow is a woman who is jealous of another woman.
　　Her tongue-lashing makes it known to all.
7 A wicked woman is like a chafing yoke.
　　He who takes hold of her is like one who grasps a scorpion.
8 A drunken woman causes great wrath.
　　She will not cover her own shame.
9 The fornication of a woman is in the lifting up of her eyes;
　　it will be known by her eyelids.
10 Keep strict watch on a headstrong daughter,
　　lest she find liberty for herself, and use it.
11 Watch out for an impudent eye,
　　and don't be surprised if it sins against you.
12 She will open her mouth like a thirsty traveller,
　　and drink from every water that is near.
She will sit down at every post,
　　and open her quiver to any arrow.

13 The grace of a wife will delight her husband.
　　Her knowledge will strengthen[c] his bones.
14 A silent woman is a gift of the Lord.
　　There is nothing worth so much as a well-instructed soul.
15 A modest woman is grace upon grace.
　　There are no scales that can weigh the value of a self-controlled soul.
16 As the sun when it arises in the highest places of the Lord,
　　so is the beauty of a good wife in her well-organised home.
17 As the lamp that shines upon the holy lampstand,
　　so is the beauty of the face on a well-proportioned body.
18 As the golden pillars are upon a base of silver,
　　so are beautiful feet with the breasts of one who is steadfast. 19-27 [d]

28 For two things my heart is grieved,
　　and for the third anger comes upon me:
　　a warrior who suffers for poverty,
　　men of understanding who are counted as garbage,
　　and one who turns back from righteousness to sin—
　　the Lord will prepare him for the sword!

29 It is difficult for a merchant to keep himself from wrong doing,

and for a retailer to be acquitted of sin.

27

1 Many have sinned for profit.
　　He who seeks to multiply wealth will turn his eye away.
2 As a nail will stick fast between the joinings of stones,
　　so sin will thrust itself in between buying and selling.
3 Unless a person holds on diligently to the fear of the Lord,
　　his house will be overthrown quickly.

4 In the shaking of a sieve, the refuse remains,
　　so does the filth of man in his thoughts.
5 The furnace tests the potter's vessels;
　　so the test of a person is in his thoughts.
6 The fruit of a tree discloses its cultivation,
　　so is the utterance of the thought of a person's heart.
7 Praise no man before you hear his thoughts,
　　for this is how people are tested.

8 If you follow righteousness, you will obtain it,
and put it on like a long robe of glory.
9 Birds will return to their own kind,
　　so truth will return to those who practise it.
10 The lion lies in wait for prey.
　　So does sin for those who do evil.

11 The discourse of a godly man is always wise,
　　but the fool changes like the moon.
12 Limit your time amongst people void of understanding,
　　but persevere amongst the thoughtful.
13 The talk of fools is offensive.
　　Their laughter is wantonly sinful.
14 Their talk with much swearing makes hair stand upright.
　　Their strife makes others plug their ears.
15 The strife of the proud leads to bloodshed.
　　Their abuse of each other is a grievous thing to hear.

16 He who reveals secrets destroys trust,
　　and will not find a close friend.
17 Love a friend, and keep faith with him;
　　but if you reveal his secrets,
　　you shall not follow him;
18 for as a man has destroyed his enemy,
　　so you have destroyed the friendship of your neighbour.
19 As a bird which you have released out of your hand,
　　so you have let your neighbour go, and you will not catch him again.
20 Don't pursue him, for he has gone far away,
　　and has escaped like a gazelle out of the snare.
21 For a wound may be bound up, and after abuse there may be reconciliation;
　　but he who reveals secrets is without hope.

22 One who winks the eye contrives evil things;
　　and those who know him will keep their distance.
23 When you are present, he will speak sweetly,
　　and will admire your words;
　　but afterward he will twist his speech
　　and set a trap in your words.
24 I have hated many things, but nothing like him.
　　The Lord will hate him.

25 One who casts a stone straight up casts it on his own head.
　　A deceitful blow opens wounds.
26 He who digs a pit will fall into it.
　　He who sets a snare will be caught in it.
27 He who does evil things, they will roll back upon him,
　　and he will not know where they came from.
28 Mockery and reproach are from the arrogant.
　　Vengeance lies in wait for them like a lion.
29 Those who rejoice at the fall of the godly will be caught in a snare.
　　Anguish will consume them before they die.

30 Wrath and anger, these also are abominations.
　　A sinner will possess them.

28

1 He who takes vengeance will find vengeance from the Lord,
　　and he will surely make his sins firm.
2 Forgive your neighbour the hurt that he has done,
　　and then your sins will be pardoned when you pray.
3 Does anyone harbour anger against another
　　and expect healing from the Lord?
4 Upon a man like himself he has no mercy,
　　and does he make supplication for his own sins?
5 He himself, being flesh, nourishes wrath.
　　Who will make atonement for his sins?
6 Remember your last end, and stop enmity.

---

a 25:26 The remainder of this verse is omitted by the best authorities.
b 26:5 Gr. countenance.

c 26:13 or, fatten
d 26:19-27 Verses 19-27 are omitted by the best authorities.

Remember corruption and death, and be true to the commandments.
7 Remember the commandments, and don't be angry with your neighbour.
Remember the covenant of the Highest, and overlook ignorance.

8 Abstain from strife, and you will diminish your sins,
for a passionate man will kindle strife.
9 A man who is a sinner will trouble friends
and sow discord amongst those who are at peace.
10 As is the fuel of the fire, so it will burn;
and as the stoutness of the strife is, so it will burn.
As is the strength of the man, so will be his wrath;
and as is his wealth, so he will exalt his anger.
11 A contention begun in haste kindles a fire;
and hasty fighting sheds blood.

12 If you blow on a spark, it will burn;
and if you spit upon it, it will be quenched.
Both of these come out of your mouth.

13 Curse the whisperer and double-tongued,
for he has destroyed many who were at peace.
14 A slanderer has shaken many,
and dispersed them from nation to nation.
It has pulled down strong cities
and overthrown the houses of great men.
15 A slanderer has cast out brave women
and deprived them of their labours.
16 He who listens to it will not find rest,
nor will he live quietly.
17 The stroke of a whip makes a mark in the flesh,
but the stroke of a tongue will break bones.
18 Many have fallen by the edge of the sword,
yet not so many as those who have fallen because of the tongue.
19 Happy is he who is sheltered from it,
who has not passed through its wrath,
who has not drawn its yoke,
and has not been bound with its bands.
20 For its yoke is a yoke of iron,
and its bands are bands of brass.
21 Its death is an evil death,
and Hades is better than it.
22 It will not have rule over godly men.
They will not be burnt in its flame.
23 Those who forsake the Lord will fall into it.
It will burn amongst them, and won't be quenched.
It will be sent against them like a lion.
It will destroy them like a leopard.
24 As you hedge your possession about with thorns,
and secure your silver and your gold,
25 so make a balance and a weight for your words,
and make a door and a bar for your mouth.
26 Take heed lest you slip with it,
lest you fall before one who lies in wait.

29

1 He who shows mercy will lend to his neighbour.
He who strengthens him with his hand keeps the commandments.
2 Lend to your neighbour in time of his need.
Repay your neighbour on time.
3 Confirm your word, and keep faith with him;
and at all seasons you will find what you need.
4 Many have considered a loan to be a windfall,
and have given trouble to those who helped them.
5 Until he has received, he will kiss a man's hands.
For his neighbour's money he will speak submissively.
Then when payment is due, he will prolong the time,
return excuses, and complain about the season.
6 If he prevails, the creditor will hardly receive half;
and he will count it as a windfall.
If not, he has deprived him of his money,
and he has gotten him for an enemy without cause.
He will pay him with cursing and railing.
Instead of honour, he will pay him disgrace.
7 Many on account of fraud have turned away.
They are afraid of being defrauded for nothing.
8 However be patient with a man in poor estate.
Don't keep him waiting for your alms.
9 Help a poor man for the commandment's sake.
According to his need don't send him empty away.
10 Lose your money for a brother and a friend.
Don't let it rust under a stone and be lost.
11 Allocate your treasure according to the commandments of the Most High
and it will profit you more than gold.
12 Store up almsgiving in your store-chambers
and it will deliver you out of all affliction.

13 It will fight for you against your enemy
better than a mighty shield and a ponderous spear.

14 A good man will be surety for his neighbour.
He who has lost shame will fail him.
15 Don't forget the kindness of your guarantor,
for he has given his life for you.
16 A sinner will waste the property of his guarantor.
17 He who is thankless will fail him who delivered him.
18 Being surety has undone many who were prospering
and shaken them as a wave of the sea.
It has driven mighty men from their homes.
They wandered amongst foreign nations.
19 A sinner who falls into suretiship and undertakes contracts for work
will fall into lawsuits.
20 Help your neighbour according to your power,
and be careful not to fall yourself.

21 The essentials of life are water, bread,
a garment, and a house for privacy.
22 Better is the life of a poor man under a shelter of logs
than sumptuous fare in another man's house.
23 With little or with much, be well satisfied.ᵃ
24 It is a miserable life to go from house to house.
Where you are a guest, you dare not open your mouth.
25 You will entertain, serve drinks, and have no thanks.
In addition to this, you will hear bitter words.
26 "Come here, you sojourner, set a table,
and if you have anything in your hand, feed me with it."
27 "Leave, you sojourner, for an honoured guest is here.
My brother has come to be my guest. I need my house."
28 These things are grievous to a man of understanding:
The scolding about lodging and the insults of creditors.

30

1 He who loves his son will continue to lay stripes upon him,
that he may have joy from him in the end.
2 He who chastises his son will have profit from him,
and will brag about him amongst his acquaintances.
3 He who teaches his son will provoke his enemy to jealousy.
Before friends, he will rejoice in him.
4 His father dies, and is as though he had not died;
for he has left one behind him like himself.
5 In his life, he saw his son and rejoiced.
When he died, it was without regret.
6 He left behind him an avenger against his enemies,
and one to repay kindness to his friends.

7 He who makes too much of his son will bind up his wounds.
His heart will be troubled at every cry.
8 An unbroken horse becomes stubborn.
An unrestrained son becomes headstrong.
9 Pamper your child, and he will make you afraid.
Play with him, and he will grieve you.
10 Don't laugh with him, lest you have sorrow with him,
and you gnash your teeth in the end.
11 Give him no liberty in his youth,
and don't ignore his follies.ᵇ
12 ᶜBow down his neck in his youth,
and beat him on the sides while he is a child,
lest he become stubborn, and be disobedient to you,
and there be sorrow to your soul.ᵈ
13 Chastise your son, and give him work,
lest his shameless behaviour be an offence to you.

14 Better is a poor man who is healthy and fit,
than a rich man who is afflicted in his body.
15 Health and fitness are better than all gold,
and a strong body better than wealth without measure.
16 There is no wealth better than health of body.
There is no gladness above the joy of the heart.
17 Death is better than a bitter life,
and eternal rest than a continual sickness.

18 Good things poured out upon a mouth that is closed
are like food offerings laid upon a grave.
19 What does an offering profit an idol?
For it can't eat or smell.
So is he who is punished by the Lord,
20 seeing with his eyes and groaning,
like a eunuch embracing a virgin and groaning.

21 Don't give your soul to sorrow.
Don't afflict yourself deliberately.
22 Gladness of heart is the life of a man.

ᵃ *29:23* The remainder of this verse is omitted by the best authorities.
ᵇ *30:11* This line and the previous two lines are absent from some older MSS.
ᶜ *30:12* These three lines are absent from the oldest MSS.
ᵈ *30:12* These three lines are absent from the oldest MSS.

Cheerfulness of a man lengthens his days.
23 Love your own soul, and comfort your heart.
    Remove sorrow far from you,
        for sorrow has destroyed many,
        and there is no profit in it.
24 Envy and wrath shorten life.
    Anxiety brings old age before its time.
25 Those who are cheerful and merry
    will benefit from their food.

31

1 Wakefulness that comes from riches consumes the flesh,
    and anxiety about it takes away sleep.
2 Wakeful anxiety will crave slumber.
    In a severe disease, sleep will be broken.

3 A rich man toils in gathering money together.
    When he rests, he is filled with his good things.
4 A poor man toils in lack of substance.
    When he rests, he becomes needy.
5 He who loves gold won't be justified.
    He who follows destruction will himself have his fill of it.
6 Many have been given over to ruin for the sake of gold.
    Their destruction meets them face to face.
7 It is a stumbling block to those who sacrifice to it.
    Every fool will be taken by it.
8 Blessed is the rich person who is found blameless,
    and who doesn't go after gold.
9 Who is he, that we may call him blessed?
    For he has done wonderful things amongst his people.
10 Who has been tried by it, and found perfect?
    Then let him boast.
Who has had the power to transgress, and has not transgressed?
    And to do evil, and has not done it?
11 His prosperity will be made sure.
    The congregation will proclaim his alms.

12 Do you sit at a great table? Don't be greedy there.
    Don't say, "There is a lot of food on it!"
13 Remember that a greedy eye is a wicked thing.
    What has been created more greedy than an eye?
    Therefore it sheds tears from every face.
14 Don't stretch your hand wherever it looks.
    Don't thrust yourself with it into the dish.
15 Consider your neighbour's feelings by your own.
    Be discreet in every point.
16 Eat like a human being those things which are set before you.
    Don't eat greedily, lest you be hated.
17 Be first to stop for manners' sake.
    Don't be insatiable, lest you offend.
18 And if you sit amongst many,
    Don't reach out your hand before them.

19 How sufficient to a well-mannered man is a very little.
    He doesn't breathe heavily in his bed.
20 Healthy sleep comes from moderate eating.
    He rises early, and his wits are with him.
The pain of wakefulness, colic,
    and griping are with an insatiable man.
21 And if you have been forced to eat,
    rise up in the middle of it, and you shall have rest.
22 Hear me, my son, and don't despise me,
    and in the end you will appreciate my words.
In all your works be skilful,
    and no disease will come to you.

23 People bless him who is liberal with his food.
    The testimony of his excellence will be believed.
24 The city will murmur at him who is a stingy with his food.
    The testimony of his stinginess will be accurate.

25 Don't show yourself valiant in wine,
    for wine has destroyed many.
26 The furnace tests the temper of steel by dipping;
    so does wine test hearts in the quarrelling of the proud.
27 Wine is as good as life to men,
    if you drink it in moderation.
What life is there to a man who is without wine?
    It has been created to make men glad.
28 Wine drunk in season and in moderation
    is joy of heart and gladness of soul:
29 Wine drunk excessively is bitterness of soul,
    with provocation and conflict.
30 Drunkenness increases the rage of a fool to his hurt.
    It diminishes strength and adds wounds.

31 Don't rebuke your neighbour at a banquet of wine.
    Don't despise him in his mirth.
Don't speak a word of reproach to him.
    Don't distress him by making demands of him.

32

1 Have they made you ruler of a feast?
    Don't be lifted up.
    Be amongst them as one of them.
    Take care of them first, and then sit down.
2 And when you have done all your duties, take your place,
    that you may be gladdened on their account,
    and receive a wreath for your good service.

3 Speak, you who are older, for it's your right, but with sound knowledge;
    and don't interrupt the music.
4 Don't pour out talk where there is a performance of music.
    Don't display your wisdom at the wrong time.
5 As a ruby signet in a setting of gold,
    so is a music concert at a wine banquet.
6 As an emerald signet in a work of gold,
    so is musical melody with pleasant wine.

7 Speak, young man, if you are obliged to,
    but no more than twice, and only if asked.
8 Sum up your speech, many things in few words.
    Be as one who knows and yet holds his tongue.
9 When amongst great men, don't behave as their equal.
    When another is speaking, don't babble.

10 Lightning speeds before thunder.
    Approval goes before one who is modest.
11 Rise up in good time, and don't be last.
    Go home quickly and don't loiter
12 Amuse yourself there and do what is in your heart.
    Don't sin by proud speech.
13 For these things bless your Maker,
    who gives you to drink freely of his good things.

14 He who fears the Lord will receive discipline.
    Those who seek him early will find favour.
15 He who seeks the law shall be filled with it,
    but the hypocrite will stumble at it.
16 Those who fear the Lord will find true judgement,
    and will kindle righteous acts like a light.
17 A sinful man shuns reproof,
    and will find a judgement according to his will.

18 A sensible person won't neglect a thought.
    An insolent and proud man won't crouch in fear,
    even after he has done a thing by himself without counsel.
19 Do nothing without counsel,
    but when you have acted, don't regret it.
20 Don't go in a way of conflict.
    Don't stumble in stony places.
21 Don't be overconfident on a smooth road.
    22 Beware of your own children.
23 In every work guard your own soul,
    for this is the keeping of the commandments.

24 He who believes the law gives heed to the commandment.
    He who trusts in the Lord will suffer no loss.

33

1 No evil will happen to him who fears the Lord,
    but in trials once and again he will deliver him.
2 A wise man will not hate the law,
    but he who is a hypocrite about it is like a boat in a storm.
3 A man of understanding will put his trust in the law.
    And the law is faithful to him, as when one asks a divine oracle.

4 Prepare your speech, and so you will be heard.
    Bind up instruction, and make your answer.
5 The heart of a fool is like a cartwheel.
    His thoughts are like a rolling axle.
6 A stallion horse is like a mocking friend.
    He neighs under every one who sits upon him.

7 Why does one day excel another,
    when all the light of every day in the year is from the sun?
8 They were distinguished by the Lord's knowledge,
    and he varied seasons and feasts.
9 Some of them he exalted and hallowed,
    and some of them he has made ordinary days.
10 And all men are from the ground.
    Adam was created from dust.
11 In the abundance of his knowledge the Lord distinguished them,
    and made their ways different.
12 Some of them he blessed and exalted,
    and some of them he made holy and brought near to himself.
Some of them he cursed and brought low,
    and overthrew them from their place.
13 As the clay of the potter in his hand,
    all his ways are according to his good pleasure,

so men are in the hand of him who made them,
to render to them according to his judgement.

14 Good is the opposite of evil,
and life is the opposite of death;
so[a] the sinner is the opposite of the godly.
15 Look upon all the works of the Most High like this,
they come in pairs, one against another.

16 I was the last on watch,
like one who gleans after the grape gatherers.
17 By the Lord's blessing I arrived before them,
and filled my winepress like one who gathers grapes.
18 Consider that I laboured not for myself alone,
but for all those who seek instruction.
19 Hear me, you great men of the people,
and listen with your ears, you rulers of the congregation.

20 To son and wife, to brother and friend,
don't give power over yourself while you live,
and don't give your goods to another,
lest you regret it and must ask for them.
21 While you still live and breath is in you,
don't give yourself over to anybody.
22 For it is better that your children should ask from you
than that you should look to the hand of your children.
23 Excel in all your works.
Don't bring a stain on your honour.
24 In the day that you end the days of your life,
in the time of death, distribute your inheritance.

25 Fodder, a stick, and burdens are for a donkey.
Bread, discipline, and work are for a servant.
26 Set your slave to work, and you will find rest.
Leave his hands idle, and he will seek liberty.
27 Yoke and thong will bow the neck.
For an evil slave there are racks and tortures.
28 Send him to labour, that he not be idle,
for idleness teaches much mischief.
29 Set him to work, as is fit for him.
If he doesn't obey, make his fetters heavy.
30 Don't be excessive towards any.
Do nothing unjust.

31 If you have a slave, treat him like yourself,
because you have bought him with blood.
32 If you have a slave, treat him like yourself.
For like your own soul, you will need him.
If you treat him ill, and he departs and runs away,
33 which way will you go to seek him?

34

1 Vain and false hopes are for a man void of understanding.
Dreams give wings to fools.
2 As one who grasps at a shadow and follows after the wind,
so is he who sets his mind on dreams.
3 The vision of dreams is a reflection,
the likeness of a face near a face.
4 From an unclean thing what can be cleansed?
From that which is false what can be true?
5 Divinations, and soothsayings, and dreams, are vain.
The heart has fantasies like a woman in labour.
6 If they are not sent in a visitation from the Most High,
don't give your heart to them.
7 For dreams have led many astray.
They have failed by putting their hope in them.
8 Without lying the law will be fulfilled.
Wisdom is complete in a faithful mouth.

9 A well-instructed man knows many things.
He who has much experience will declare understanding.
10 He who has no experience knows few things.
But he who has travelled increases cleverness.
11 I have seen many things in my travels.
My understanding is more than my words.
12 I was often in danger even to death.
I was preserved because of these experiences.
13 The spirit of those who fear the Lord will live,
for their hope is in him who saves them.
14 Whoever fears the Lord won't be afraid, and won't be a coward,
for he is his hope.
15 Blessed is the soul of him who fears the Lord.
To whom does he give heed? Who is his support?
16 The eyes of the Lord are on those who love him,
a mighty protection and strong support,
a cover from the hot blast, a shade from the noonday sun,

a guard from stumbling, and a help from falling.
17 He raises up the soul, and enlightens the eyes.
He gives health, life, and blessing.

18 He who sacrifices a thing wrongfully gotten, his offering is made in mockery.
The mockeries of wicked men are not acceptable.
19 The Most High has no pleasure in the offerings of the ungodly,
Neither is he pacified for sins by the multitude of sacrifices.
20 Like one who kills a son before his father's eyes
is he who brings a sacrifice from the goods of the poor.
21 The bread of the needy is the life of the poor.
He who deprives him of it is a man of blood.
22 Like one who murders his neighbour is he who takes away his living.
Like a shedder of blood is he who deprives a hireling of his hire.

23 When one builds, and another pulls down,
what profit do they have but toil?
24 When one prays, and another curses,
whose voice will the Lord listen to?
25 He who washes himself after touching a dead body, and touches it again,
what does he gain by his washing?
26 Even so a man fasting for his sins,
and going again, and doing the same,
who will listen to his prayer?
What profit does he have in his humiliation?

35

1 He who keeps the law multiplies offerings.
He who heeds the commandments sacrifices a peace offering.
2 He who returns a kindness offers fine flour.
He who gives alms sacrifices a thank offering.
3 To depart from wickedness pleases the Lord.
To depart from unrighteousness is an atoning sacrifice.
4 See that you don't appear in the presence of the Lord empty.
5 For all these things are done because of the commandment.
6 The offering of the righteous enriches the altar.
The sweet fragrance of it is before the Most High.
7 The sacrifice of a righteous man is acceptable.
It won't be forgotten.
8 Glorify the Lord with generosity.
Don't reduce the first fruits of your hands.
9 In every gift show a cheerful countenance,
And dedicate your tithe with gladness.
10 Give to the Most High according as he has given.
As your hand has found, give generously.
11 For the Lord repays,
and he will repay you sevenfold.

12 Don't plan to bribe him with gifts, for he will not receive them.
Don't set your mind on an unrighteous sacrifice,
For the Lord is the judge,
and with him is no respect of persons.
13 He won't accept any person against a poor man.
He will listen to the prayer of him who is wronged.
14 He will in no way despise the supplication of the fatherless
or the widow, when she pours out her tale.
15 Don't the tears of the widow run down her cheek?
Isn't her cry against him who has caused them to fall?
16 He who serves God according to his good pleasure will be accepted.
His supplication will reach to the clouds.
17 The prayer of the humble pierces the clouds.
until it comes near, he will not be comforted.
He won't depart until the Most High visits
and he judges righteously and executes judgement.
18 And the Lord will not be slack, neither will he be patient towards them,
until he has crushed the loins of the unmerciful.
He will repay vengeance to the heathen
until he has taken away the multitude of the arrogant
and broken in pieces the sceptres of the unrighteous,
19 until he has rendered to every man according to his deeds,
and repaid the works of men according to their plans,
until he has judged the cause of his people,
and he will make them rejoice in his mercy.
20 Mercy is as welcome in the time of his affliction,
as clouds of rain in the time of drought.

36

1 Have mercy upon us, O Lord the God of all, and look at us with favour;
2 and send your fear upon all the nations.[b]
3 Lift up your hand against the foreign nations
and let them see your mighty power.
4 As you showed your holiness in us before them,
so be magnified in them before us.
5 Let them know you, as we also have known you,
that there is no God but only you, O God.

---

[a] *33:14* A line of this verse is here omitted by the best authorities.

[b] *36:2* The remainder of this verse is omitted by the best authorities.

6 Show new signs, and work various wonders.
  Glorify your hand and your right arm.[a]
7 Raise up indignation and pour out wrath.
  Take away the adversary and destroy the enemy.
8 Hasten the time and remember your oath.
  Let them declare your mighty works.
9 Let him who escapes be devoured by raging fire.
  May those who harm your people find destruction.
10 Crush the heads of the rulers of the enemies
  who say, "There is no one but ourselves."
11 Gather all the tribes of Jacob together,
  and[b] take them for your inheritance, as from the beginning.
12 O Lord, have mercy upon the people that is called by your name,
  and upon Israel, whom you likened to a firstborn.
13 Have compassion upon the city of your sanctuary,
  Jerusalem, the place of your rest.
14 Fill Zion. Exalt your oracles
  and fill your people with your glory.
15 Give testimony to those who were your creatures in the beginning,
  and fulfil the prophecies that have been spoken in your name.
16 Reward those who wait for you,
  and men will put their trust in your prophets.
17 Listen, O Lord, to the prayer of your servants,
  according to the blessing of Aaron concerning your people;
  and all those who are on the earth will know
  that you are the Lord, the[c] eternal God.

18 The belly will eat any food,
  but one food is better than another.
19 The mouth tastes meats taken in hunting,
  so does an understanding heart detect false speech.
20 A contrary heart will cause heaviness.
  A man of experience will pay him back.
21 A woman will receive any man,
  but one daughter is better than another.
22 The beauty of a woman cheers the countenance.
  A man desires nothing more.
23 If kindness and humility are on her tongue,
  her husband is not like other sons of men.
24 He who gets a wife gets his richest treasure,
  a help meet for him and a pillar of support.
25 Where no hedge is, the property will be plundered.
  He who has no wife will mourn as he wanders.
26 For who would trust a nimble robber who skips from city to city?
  Even so, who would trust a man who has no nest, and lodges
  wherever he finds himself at nightfall?

37

1 Every friend will say, "I also am his friend";
  but there is a friend which is only a friend in name.
2 Isn't there a grief in it even to death
  when a companion and friend is turned into an enemy?
3 O wicked imagination, why were you formed
  to cover the dry land with deceit?
4 There is a companion who rejoices in the gladness of a friend,
  but in time of affliction will be against him.
5 There is a companion who for the belly's sake labours with his friend,
  yet in the face of battle will carry his buckler.
6 Don't forget a friend in your soul.
  Don't be unmindful of him in your riches.

7 Every counsellor extols counsel,
  but some give counsel in their own interest.
8 Let your soul beware of a counsellor,
  and know in advance what is his interest
  (for he will take counsel for himself),
  lest he cast the lot against you,
  9 and say to you, "Your way is good."
  Then he will stand near you, to see what will happen to you.
10 Don't take counsel with one who looks askance at you.
  Hide your counsel from those who are jealous of you.
11 Don't consult with a woman about her rival,
  with a coward about war,
  with a merchant about business,
  with a buyer about selling,
  with an envious man about thankfulness,
  with an unmerciful man about kindliness,
  with a sluggard about any kind of work,
  with a hireling in your house about finishing his work,
  or with an idle servant about much business.
  Pay no attention to these in any matter of counsel.
12 But rather be continually with a godly man,
  whom you know to be a keeper of the commandments,
  who in his soul is as your own soul,

and who will grieve with you, if you fail.
13 Make the counsel of your heart stand,
  for there is no one more faithful to you than it.
14 For a man's soul is sometimes inclined to inform him
  better than seven watchmen who sit on high on a watch-tower.
15 Above all this ask the Most High
  that he may direct your way in truth.

16 Let reason be the beginning of every work.
  Let counsel go before every action.
17 As a token of the changing of the heart,
  18 four kinds of things rise up:
  good and evil, life and death.
  That which rules over them continually is the tongue.
19 There is one who is clever and the instructor of many,
  and yet is unprofitable to his own soul.
20 There is one who is subtle in words, and is hated.
  He will be destitute of all food.
21 For grace was not given to him from the Lord,
  because he is deprived of all wisdom.
22 There is one who is wise to his own soul;
  and the fruits of his understanding are trustworthy in the mouth.
23 A wise man will instruct his own people.
  The fruits of his understanding are trustworthy.
24 A wise man will be filled with blessing.
  All those who see him will call him happy.
25 The life of a man is counted by days.
  The days of Israel are innumerable.
26 The wise man will inherit confidence amongst his people.
  His name will live forever.

27 My son, test your soul in your life.
  See what is evil for it, and don't give in to it.
28 For not all things are profitable for all men.
  Not every soul has pleasure in everything.
29 Don't be insatiable in any luxury.
  Don't be greedy in the things that you eat.
30 For overeating brings disease,
  and gluttony causes nausea.
31 Because of gluttony, many have perished,
  but he who takes heed shall prolong his life.

38

1 Honour a physician according to your need with the honours due to him,
  for truly the Lord has created him.
2 For healing comes from the Most High,
  and he shall receive a gift from the king.
3 The skill of the physician will lift up his head.
  He will be admired in the sight of great men.
4 The Lord created medicines out of the earth.
  A prudent man will not despise them.
5 Wasn't water made sweet with wood,
  that its power might be known?
6 He gave men skill
  that he might be glorified in his marvellous works.
7 With them he heals
  and takes away pain.
8 With these, the pharmacist makes a mixture.
  God's works won't be brought to an end.
  From him, peace is upon the face of the earth.

9 My son, in your sickness don't be negligent,
  but pray to the Lord, and he will heal you.
10 Put away wrong doing, and direct your hands in righteousness.
  Cleanse your heart from all sin.
11 Give a sweet savour and a memorial of fine flour,
  and pour oil on your offering, according to your means.
12 Then give place to the physician, for truly the Lord has created him.
  Don't let him leave you, for you need him.
13 There is a time when in recovery is in their hands.
  14 For they also shall ask the Lord
  to prosper them in diagnosis and in healing for the maintenance of
    life.
15 He who sins before his Maker,
  let him fall into the hands of the physician.

16 My son, let your tears fall over the dead,
  and as one who suffers grievously, begin lamentation.
  Wind up his body with due honour.
  Don't neglect his burial.
17 Make bitter weeping and make passionate wailing.
  Let your mourning be according to his merit,
  for one day or two, lest you be spoken evil of;
  and so be comforted for your sorrow.

---

a *36:6* The remainder of this verse is omitted by the best authorities.
b *36:11* The ancient authorities read I took them for my inheritance:
but the Greek text is here very confused.

c *36:17* Gr. God of the ages.

18 For from sorrow comes death.
    Sorrow of heart saps one's strength.
19 In calamity, sorrow also remains.
    A poor man's life is grievous to the heart.
20 Don't give your heart to sorrow.
    Put it away, remembering the end.
21 Don't forget it, for there is no returning again.
    You do him no good, and you would harm yourself.
22 Remember his end, for so also will yours be:
    yesterday for me, and today for you.
23 When the dead is at rest, let his remembrance rest.
    Be comforted for him when his spirit departs from him.

24 The wisdom of the scribe comes by the opportunity of leisure.
    He who has little business can become wise.
25 How could he become wise who holds the plough,
    who glories in the shaft of the goad,
    who drives oxen and is occupied in their labours,
    and who mostly talks about bulls?
26 He will set his heart upon turning his furrows.
    His lack of sleep is to give his heifers their fodder.
27 So is every craftsman and master artisan
    who passes his time by night as by day,
    those who cut engravings of signets.
His diligence is to make great variety.
    He sets his heart to preserve likeness in his portraiture,
    and is careful to finish his work.
28 So too is the smith sitting by the anvil
    and considering the unwrought iron.
The smoke of the fire will waste his flesh.
    He toils in the heat of the furnace.
The noise of the hammer deafens his ear.
    His eyes are upon the pattern of the object.
He will set his heart upon perfecting his works.
    He will be careful to adorn them perfectly.
29 So is the potter sitting at his work
    and turning the wheel around with his feet,
    who is always anxiously set at his work.
    He produces his handiwork in quantity.
30 He will fashion the clay with his arm
    and will bend its strength in front of his feet.
He will apply his heart to finish the glazing.
    He will be careful to clean the kiln.

31 All these put their trust in their hands.
    Each becomes skilful in his own work.
32 Without these no city would be inhabited.
    Men wouldn't reside as foreigners or walk up and down there.
33 They won't be sought for in the council of the people.
    They won't mount on high in the assembly.
    They won't sit on the seat of the judge.
    They won't understand the covenant of judgement.
    Neither will they declare instruction and judgement.
    They won't be found where parables are.
34 But they will maintain the fabric of the age.
    Their prayer is in the handiwork of their craft.

39

1 Not so he who has applied his soul
    and meditates in the law of the Most High.
He will seek out the wisdom of all the ancients
    and will be occupied with prophecies.
2 He will keep the sayings of the men of renown
    and will enter in amidst the subtleties of parables.
3 He will seek out the hidden meaning of proverbs
    and be conversant in the dark sayings of parables.
4 He will serve amongst great men
    and appear before him who rules.
He will travel through the land of foreign nations,
    for he has learnt what is good and evil amongst men.
5 He will apply his heart to return early to the Lord who made him,
    and will make supplication before the Most High,
    and will open his mouth in prayer,
    and will ask for pardon for his sins.

6 If the great Lord wills,
    he will be filled with the spirit of understanding;
    he will pour forth the words of his wisdom
    and in prayer give thanks to the Lord.
7 He will direct his counsel and knowledge,
    and he will meditate in his secrets.
8 He will show the instruction which he has been taught
    and will glory in the law of the covenant of the Lord.
9 Many will commend his understanding.
    So long as the world endures, it won't be blotted out.
His memory won't depart.
    His name will live from generation to generation.
10 Nations will declare his wisdom.
    The congregation will proclaim his praise.

11 If he continues, he will leave a greater name than a thousand.
    If he finally rests, it is enough for him.

12 Yet more I will utter, which I have thought about.
    I am filled like the full moon.
13 Listen to me, you holy children,
    and bud forth like a rose growing by a brook of water.
14 Give a sweet fragrance like frankincense.
    Put forth flowers like a lily.
    Scatter a sweet smell and sing a song of praise.
    Bless the Lord for all his works!
15 Magnify his name
    and give utterance to his praise
    with the songs on your lips and with harps!
Say this when you utter his praise:

16 All the works of the Lord are exceedingly good,
    and every command will be done in its time.
17 No one can say, "What is this?" "Why is that?"
    for at the proper time they will all be sought out.
At his word, the waters stood as a heap,
    as did the reservoirs of water at the word of his mouth.
18 At his command all his good pleasure is fulfilled.
    There is no one who can hinder his salvation.
19 The works of all flesh are before him.
    It's impossible to be hidden from his eyes.
20 He sees from everlasting to everlasting.
    There is nothing too wonderful for him.
21 No one can say, "What is this?" "Why is that?"
    for all things are created for their own uses.

22 His blessing covered the dry land as a river
    and saturated it as a flood.
23 As he has made the waters salty,
    so the heathen will inherit his wrath.
24 His ways are plain to the holy.
    They are stumbling blocks to the wicked.
25 Good things are created from the beginning for the good.
    So are evil things for sinners.
26 The main things necessary for the life of man
    are water, fire, iron, salt,
    wheat flour, and honey, milk,
    the blood of the grape, oil, and clothing.
27 All these things are for good to the godly,
    but for sinners, they will be turned into evils.

28 There are winds that are created for vengeance,
    and in their fury they lay on their scourges heavily.
In the time of reckoning, they pour out their strength,
    and will appease the wrath of him who made them.
29 Fire, hail, famine, and death—
    all these are created for vengeance—
        30 wild beasts' teeth, scorpions, adders,
    and a sword punishing the ungodly to destruction.
31 They will rejoice in his commandment,
    and will be made ready upon earth when needed.
    In their seasons, they won't disobey his command.

32 Therefore from the beginning I was convinced,
    and I thought it through and left it in writing:
33 All the works of the Lord are good.
    He will supply every need in its time.
34 No one can say, "This is worse than that,"
    for they will all be well approved in their time.
35 Now with all your hearts and voices, sing praises
    and bless the Lord's name!

40

1 Great travail is created for every man.
    A heavy yoke is upon the sons of Adam,
    from the day of their coming forth from their mother's womb,
    until the day for their burial in the mother of all things.
2 The expectation of things to come, and the day of death,
    trouble their thoughts, and cause fear in their hearts.
3 From him who sits on a throne of glory,
    even to him who is humbled in earth and ashes,
4 from him who wears purple and a crown,
    even to him who is clothed in burlap,
5 there is wrath, jealousy, trouble, unrest,
    fear of death, anger, and strife.
In the time of rest upon his bed,
    his night sleep changes his knowledge.
6 He gets little or no rest,
    and afterward in his sleep, as in a day of keeping watch,
    he is troubled in the vision of his heart,
    as one who has escaped from the front of battle.
7 In the very time of his deliverance, he awakens,
    and marvels that the fear is nothing.

8 To all creatures, human and animal,
   and upon sinners sevenfold more,
   9 come death, bloodshed, strife, sword,
   calamities, famine, suffering, and plague.
10 All these things were created for the wicked,
   and because of them the flood came.
11 All things that are of the earth turn to the earth again.
   All things that are of the waters return into the sea.

12 All bribery and injustice will be blotted out.
   Good faith will stand forever.
13 The goods of the unjust will be dried up like a river,
   and like a great thunder in rain will go off in noise.
14 In opening his hands, a man will be made glad;
   so lawbreakers will utterly fail.
15 The children of the ungodly won't grow many branches,
   and are as unhealthy roots on a sheer rock.
16 The reeds by every water or river bank
   will be plucked up before all grass.
17 Kindness is like a garden of blessings.
   Almsgiving endures forever.

18 The life of one who labours and is content will be made sweet.
   He who finds a treasure is better than both.
19 Children and the building of a city establish a name.
   A blameless wife is better than both.
20 Wine and music rejoice the heart.
   The love of wisdom is better than both.
21 The pipe and the lute make pleasant melody.
   A pleasant tongue is better than both.
22 Your eye desires grace and beauty,
   but the green shoots of grain more than both.
23 A friend and a companion is always welcome,
   and a wife with her husband is better than both.
24 Relatives and helpers are for a time of affliction,
   but almsgiving rescues better than both.
25 Gold and silver will make the foot stand sure,
   and counsel is esteemed better than both.
26 Riches and strength will lift up the heart.
   The fear of the Lord is better than both.
There is nothing lacking in the fear of the Lord.
   In it, there is no need to seek help.
27 The fear of the Lord is like a garden of blessing
   and covers a man more than any glory.

28 My son, don't lead a beggar's life.
   It is better to die than to beg.
29 A man who looks to the table of another,
   his life is not to be considered a life.
He will pollute his soul with another person's food,
   but a wise and well-instructed person will beware of that.
30 Begging will be sweet in the mouth of the shameless,
   but it kindles a fire in his belly.

41

1 O death, how bitter is the memory of you to a man who is at peace in his
      possessions,
   to the man who has nothing to distract him and has prosperity in all
      things,
   and who still has strength to enjoy food!
2 O death, your sentence is acceptable to a man who is needy and who fails
      in strength,
   who is in extreme old age, is distracted about all things,
   is perverse, and has lost patience!
3 Don't be afraid of the sentence of death.
   Remember those who have been before you and who come after.
This is the sentence from the Lord over all flesh.
      4 And why do you refuse when it is the good pleasure of the Most
         High?
Whether life lasts ten, or a hundred, or a thousand years,
   there is no enquiry about life in Hades.[a]

5 The children of sinners are abominable children
   and they frequent the dwellings of the ungodly.
6 The inheritance of sinners' children will perish
   and with their posterity will be a perpetual disgrace.
7 Children will complain of an ungodly father,
   because they suffer disgrace because of him.
8 Woe to you, ungodly men,
   who have forsaken the law of the Most High God![b]
9 If you are born, you will be born to a curse.
   If you die, a curse will be your portion.
10 All things that are of the earth will go back to the earth;
   so the ungodly will go from a curse to perdition.

11 The mourning of men is about their bodies;

but the evil name of sinners will be blotted out.
12 Have regard for your name,
   for it continues with you longer than a thousand great treasures of
      gold.
13 A good life has its number of days,
   but a good name continues forever.

14 My children, follow instruction in peace.
   But wisdom that is hidden and a treasure that is not seen,
   what benefit is in them both?
15 Better is a man who hides his foolishness
   than a man who hides his wisdom.
16 Therefore show respect for my words;
   for it is not good to retain every kind of shame.
   Not everything is approved by all in good faith.

17 Be ashamed of sexual immorality before father and mother,
   of a lie before a prince and a mighty man,
      18 of an offence before a judge and ruler,
   of iniquity before the congregation and the people,
   of unjust dealing before a partner and friend,
      19 and of theft in the place where you sojourn.
Be ashamed in regard of the truth of God and his covenant,
   of leaning on your elbow at dinner,
   of contemptuous behaviour in the matter of giving and taking,
      20 of silence before those who greet you,
   of looking at a woman who is a prostitute,
      21 of turning away your face from a kinsman,
   of taking away a portion or a gift,
   of gazing at a woman who has a husband,
      22 of meddling with his maid—and don't come near her bed,
   of abusive speech to friends—and after you have given, don't insult,
      23 of repeating and speaking what you have heard,
   and of revealing secrets.
24 So you will be ashamed of the right things
   and find favour in the sight of every man.

42

1 Don't be ashamed of these things,
   and don't sin to save face:
      2 of the law of the Most High and his covenant,
   of judgement to do justice to the ungodly,
      3 of reckoning with a partner and with travellers,
   of a gift from the inheritance of friends,
      4 of exactness of scales and weights,
   of getting much or little,
      5 of bargaining dealing with merchants,
   of frequent correction of children,
   and of making the back of an evil slave to bleed.
6 A seal is good where an evil wife is.
   Where there are many hands, lock things up.
7 Whatever you hand over, let it be by number and weight.
   In giving and receiving, let all be in writing.
8 Don't be ashamed to instruct the unwise and foolish,
   and one of extreme old age who contends with those who are young.
So you will be well instructed indeed
   and approved in the sight of every living man.

9 A daughter is a secret cause of wakefulness to a father.
   Care for her takes away sleep—
   in her youth, lest she pass the flower of her age;
   when she is married, lest she should be hated;
      10 in her virginity, lest she should be defiled and be with child in her
         father's house;
   when she has a husband, lest she should transgress;
   and when she is married, lest she should be barren.
11 Keep a strict watch over a headstrong daughter,
   lest she make you a laughingstock to your enemies,
   a byword in the city and notorious amongst the people,
   and shame you in public.

12 Don't gaze at every beautiful body.
   Don't sit in the midst of women.
13 For from garments comes a moth,
   and from a woman comes a woman's wickedness.
14 Better is the wickedness of a man than a pleasant woman,
   a woman who puts you to shame and disgrace.

15 I will make mention now of the works of the Lord,
   and will declare the things that I have seen.
   The Lord's works are in his words.
16 The sun that gives light looks at all things.
   The Lord's work is full of his glory.
17 The Lord has not given power to the saints to declare all his marvellous
      works,
   which the Almighty Lord firmly settled,

_____

[a] *41:4* or, the place of the dead or, Sheol

[b] *41:8* The remainder of this verse is omitted by the best authorities.

that the universe might be established in his glory.
18 He searches out the deep and the heart.
　　He has understanding of their secrets.
For the Most High knows all knowledge.
　　He sees the signs of the world.
19 He declares the things that are past and the things that shall be,
　　and reveals the traces of hidden things.
20 No thought escapes him.
　　There is not a word hidden from him.
21 He has ordered the mighty works of his wisdom.
　　He is from everlasting to everlasting.
Nothing has been added to them, nor diminished from them.
　　He had no need of any counsellor.
22 How desirable are all his works!
　　One may see this even in a spark.
23 All these things live and remain forever in all manner of uses.
　　They are all obedient.
24 All things are in pairs, one opposite the other.
　　He has made nothing imperfect.
25 One thing establishes the good things of another.
　　Who could ever see enough of his glory?

43

1 The pride of the heavenly heights is the clear sky,
　　the appearance of heaven, in the spectacle of its glory.
2 The sun, when it appears, bringing tidings as it rises,
　　is a marvellous instrument, the work of the Most High.
3 At noon, it dries up the land.
　　Who can stand against its burning heat?
4 A man tending a furnace is in burning heat,
　　but the sun three times more, burning up the mountains,
　　breathing out fiery vapours,
　　and sending out bright beams, it blinds the eyes.
5 Great is the Lord who made it.
　　At his word, he hastens on its course.

6 The moon marks the changing seasons,
　　declares times, and is a sign for the world.
7 From the moon is the sign of feast days,
　　a light that wanes when it completes its course.
8 The month is called after its name,
　　increasing wonderfully in its changing—
　　an instrument of the army on high,
　　shining in the structure of heaven,
　　9 the beauty of heaven, the glory of the stars,
　　an ornament giving light in the highest places of the Lord.
10 At the word of the Holy One, they will stand in due order.
　　They won't faint in their watches.
11 Look at the rainbow, and praise him who made it.
　　It is exceedingly beautiful in its brightness.
12 It encircles the sky with its glorious circle.
　　The hands of the Most High have stretched it out.

13 By his commandment, he makes the snow fall
　　and swiftly sends the lightnings of his judgement.
14 Therefore the storehouses are opened,
　　and clouds fly out like birds.
15 By his mighty power, he makes the clouds strong
　　and the hailstones are broken in pieces.
16 At his appearing, the mountains will be shaken.
　　At his will, the south wind will blow.
17 The voice of his thunder rebukes the earth.
　　So does the northern storm and the whirlwind.
Like birds flying down, he sprinkles the snow.
　　It falls down like the lighting of locusts.
18 The eye is dazzled at the beauty of its whiteness.
　　The heart is amazed as it falls.
19 He also pours out frost on the earth like salt.
　　When it is freezes, it has points like thorns.

20 The cold north wind blows
　　and ice freezes on the water.
It settles on every pool of water.
　　The water puts it on like it was a breastplate.
21 It will devour the mountains, burn up the wilderness,
　　and consume the green grass like fire.
22 A mist coming speedily heals all things.
　　A dew coming after heat brings cheerfulness.

23 By his counsel, he has calmed the deep
　　and planted islands in it.
24 Those who sail on the sea tell of its dangers.
　　We marvel when we hear it with our ears.
25 There are also those strange and wondrous works in it—
　　variety of all that has life and the huge creatures of the sea.
26 Because of him, his messengers succeed.
　　By his word, all things hold together.

27 We may say many things, but couldn't say enough.

The summary of our words is, "He is everything!"
28 How could we have strength to glorify him?
　　For he is himself the greater than all his works.
29 The Lord is awesome and exceedingly great!
　　His power is marvellous!
30 Glorify the Lord and exalt him as much as you can!
　　For even yet, he will surpass that.
When you exalt him, summon your full strength.
　　Don't be weary, because you can't praise him enough.
31 Who has seen him, that he may describe him?
　　Who can magnify him as he is?
32 Many things greater than these are hidden,
　　for we have seen just a few of his works.
33 For the Lord made all things.
　　He gave wisdom to the godly.

44

1 Let us now praise famous men,
　　our ancestors in their generations.
2 The Lord created great glory in them—
　　his mighty power from the beginning.
3 Some ruled in their kingdoms
　　and were men renowned for their power,
　　giving counsel by their understanding.
Some have spoken in prophecies,
　　4 leaders of the people by their counsels,
　　and by their understanding, giving instruction for the people.
　　Their words in their instruction were wise.
5 Some composed musical tunes,
　　and set forth verses in writing,
　　6 rich men endowed with ability,
　　living peaceably in their homes.
7 All these were honoured in their generations,
　　and were outstanding in their days.
8 Some of them have left a name behind them,
　　so that others declare their praises.
9 But of others, there is no memory.
　　They perished as though they had not been.
　　They become as though they had not been born,
　　they and their children after them.
10 But these were men of mercy,
　　whose righteous deeds have not been forgotten.
11 A good inheritance remains with their offspring.
　　Their children are within the covenant.
12 Their offspring stand fast,
　　with their children, for their sakes.
13 Their offspring will remain forever.
　　Their glory won't be blotted out.
14 Their bodies were buried in peace.
　　Their name lives to all generations.
15 People will declare their wisdom.
　　The congregation proclaims their praise.

16 Enoch pleased the Lord, and was taken up,
　　an example of repentance to all generations.

17 Noah was found perfect and righteous.
　　In the season of wrath, he kept the race alive.
Therefore a remnant was left on the earth
　　when the flood came.
18 Everlasting covenants were made with him,
　　that all flesh should no more be blotted out by a flood.

19 Abraham was a great father of a multitude of nations.
　　There was none found like him in glory,
　　20 who kept the law of the Most High,
　　and was taken into covenant with him.
In his flesh he established the covenant.
　　When he was tested, he was found faithful.
21 Therefore he assured him by an oath
　　that the nations would be blessed through his offspring,
　　that he would multiply him like the dust of the earth,
　　exalt his offspring like the stars,
　　and cause them to inherit from sea to sea,
　　and from the Euphrates River to the utmost parts of the earth.

22 In Isaac also, he established the same assurance for Abraham his father's sake,
　　the blessing of all men, and the covenant.
23 He made it rest upon the head of Jacob.
　　He acknowledged him in his blessings,
　　gave to him by inheritance,
　　and divided his portions.
　　He distributed them amongst twelve tribes.

45

1 He brought out of him a man of mercy,
　　who found favour in the sight of all people,
　　a man loved by God and men, even Moses,

whose memory is blessed.

2 He made him equal to the glory of the saints,
    and magnified him in the fears of his enemies.
3 By his words he caused the wonders to cease.
    God glorified him in the sight of kings.
He gave him commandments for his people
    and showed him part of his glory.
4 He sanctified him in his faithfulness and meekness.
    He chose him out of all people.
5 He made him to hear his voice,
    led him into the thick darkness,
    and gave him commandments face to face,
    even the law of life and knowledge,
    that he might teach Jacob the covenant,
    and Israel his judgements.

6 He exalted Aaron, a holy man like Moses,
    even his brother, of the tribe of Levi.
7 He established an everlasting covenant with him,
    and gave him the priesthood of the people.
He blessed him with stateliness,
    and dressed him in a glorious robe.
8 He clothed him in perfect splendour,
    and strengthened him with symbols of authority:
    the linen trousers, the long robe, and the ephod.
9 He encircled him with pomegranates;
    with many golden bells around him,
    to make a sound as he went,
    to make a sound that might be heard in the temple,
    for a reminder for the children of his people;
      10 with a holy garment, with gold, blue, and purple, the work of the embroiderer;
    with an oracle of judgement—Urim and Thummim;
      11 with twisted scarlet, the work of the craftsman;
    with precious stones engraved like a signet, in a setting of gold, the work of the jeweller,
    for a reminder engraved in writing, after the number of the tribes of Israel;
      12 with a crown of gold upon the mitre, having engraved on it, as on a signet, "HOLINESS",
    an ornament of honour, the work of an expert,
    the desires of the eyes, goodly and beautiful.
13 Before him there never have been anything like it.
    No stranger put them on, but only his sons and his offspring perpetually.
14 His sacrifices shall be wholly burnt,
    twice every day continually.
15 Moses consecrated him,
    and anointed him with holy oil.
It was an everlasting covenant with him
    and to his offspring, all the days of heaven,
    to minister to the Lord, to serve as a priest,
    and to bless his people in his name.
16 He chose him out of all living
    to offer sacrifice to the Lord—
    incense, and a sweet fragrance, for a memorial,
    to make atonement for your people.
17 He gave to him in his commandments,
    authority in the covenants of judgements,
    to teach Jacob the testimonies,
    and to enlighten Israel in his law.
18 Strangers conspired against him
    and envied him in the wilderness:
    Dathan and Abiram with their company,
    and the congregation of Korah, with wrath and anger.
19 The Lord saw it, and it displeased him.
    In the wrath of his anger, they were destroyed.
He did wonders upon them,
    to consume them with flaming fire.
20 He added glory to Aaron,
    and gave him a heritage.
He divided to him the first fruits of the increase,
    and prepared bread of first fruits in abundance.
21 For they eat the sacrifices of the Lord,
    which he gave to him and to his offspring.
22 However, in the land of the people, he has no inheritance,
    and he has no portion amongst the people,
    for the Lord himself is your portion and inheritance.

23 Phinehas the son of Eleazar is the third in glory,
    in that he was zealous in the fear of the Lord,
    and stood fast when the people turned away,
    and he made atonement for Israel.
24 Therefore, a covenant of peace was established for him,
    that he should be leader of the sanctuary and of his people,
    that he and his offspring should have the dignity of the priesthood forever.

25 Also he made a covenant with David the son of Jesse, of the tribe of Judah.
    The inheritance of the king is his alone from son to son.
    So the inheritance of Aaron is also to his seed.

26 May God give you wisdom in your heart
    to judge his people in righteousness,
    that their good things may not be abolished,
    and that their glory may endure for all their generations.

46

1 Joshua the son of Nun was valiant in war,
    and was the successor of Moses in prophecies.
He was made great according to his name
    for the saving of[a] God's elect,
    to take vengeance on the enemies that rose up against them,
    that he might give Israel their inheritance.
2 How was he glorified in the lifting up his hands,
    and in stretching out his sword against the cities!
3 Who before him stood so firm?
    For the Lord himself brought his enemies to him.
4 Didn't the sun go back by his hand?
    Didn't one day become as two?
5 He called upon the Most High, the Mighty One,
    when his foes pressed in all around him,
    and the great Lord heard him.
6 With hailstones of mighty power,
    he caused war to break violently upon the nation,
    and[b] on the slope he destroyed those who resisted,
    so that the nations might know his armour,
    how he fought in the sight of the Lord;
    for he followed the Mighty One.
7 Also in the time of Moses, he did a work of mercy—
    he and Caleb the son of Jephunneh—
    in that they withstood the adversary,
    hindered the people from sin,
    and stilled their wicked complaining.
8 And of six hundred thousand people on foot, they two alone were preserved
    to bring them into their inheritance,
    into a land flowing with milk and honey.
9 The Lord gave strength to Caleb,
    and it remained with him to his old age,
    so that he entered the hill country,
    and his offspring obtained it for an inheritance,
      10 that all the children of Israel might see that it is good to follow the Lord.

11 Also the judges, every one by his name,
    all whose hearts didn't engage in immorality,
    and who didn't turn away from the Lord—
    may their memory be blessed!
12 May their bones flourish again out of their place.
    May the name of those who have been honoured be renewed in their children.

13 Samuel, the prophet of the Lord, loved by his Lord,
    established a kingdom and anointed princes over his people.
14 By the law of the Lord he judged the congregation,
    and the Lord watched over Jacob.
15 By his faithfulness he was proved to be a prophet.
    By his words he was known to be faithful in vision.
16 When his enemies pressed on him on every side,
    he called upon the Lord, the Mighty One,
    with the offering of the suckling lamb.
17 Then the Lord thundered from heaven.
    He made his voice heard with a mighty sound.
18 He utterly destroyed the rulers of the Tyrians
    and all the princes of the Philistines.
19 Before the time of his age-long sleep,
    he testified in the sight of the lord and his anointed,
    "I have not taken any man's goods, so much as a sandal;"
    and no one accused him.
20 Even after he fell asleep, he prophesied,
    and showed the king his end,
    and lifted up his voice from the earth in prophecy,
    to blot out the wickedness of the people.

47

1 After him, Nathan rose up
    to prophesy in the days of David.
2 As is the fat when it is separated from the peace offering,
    so was David separated from the children of Israel.
3 He played with lions as with kids,
    and with bears as with lambs of the flock.
4 In his youth didn't he kill a giant,

---

a 46:1 Gr. his.

b 46:6 See Joshua 10:11

and take away reproach from the people
    when he lifted up his hand with a sling stone,
    and beat down the boasting Goliath?
5 For he called upon the Most High Lord,
    and he gave him strength in his right hand
    to kill a man mighty in war,
    to exalt the horn of his people.
6 So they glorified him for his tens of thousands,
    and praised him for the blessings of the Lord,
    in that a glorious diadem was given to him.
7 For he destroyed the enemies on every side,
    and defeated the Philistines his adversaries.
He broke their horn in pieces to this day.
8 In every work of his he gave thanks to the Holy One Most High with words
    of glory.
He sang praise with his whole heart,
    and loved him who made him.
9 He set singers before the altar,
    to make sweet melody by their music.[a]
10 He gave beauty to the feasts,
    and set in order the seasons to completion
    while they praised his holy name,
    and the sanctuary resounded from early morning.
11 The Lord took away his sins,
    and exalted his horn forever.
He gave him a covenant of kings,
    and a glorious throne in Israel.

12 After him a wise son rose up,
    who because of him lived in security.
13 Solomon reigned in days of peace.
    God gave him rest all around,
    that he might set up a house for his name,
    and prepare a sanctuary forever.
14 How wise you were made in your youth,
    and filled as a river with understanding!
15 Your influence covered the earth,
    and you filled it with parables and riddles.
16 Your name reached to the far away islands,
    and you were loved for your peace.
17 For your songs, proverbs, parables,
    and interpretations, the countries marvelled at you.
18 By the name of the Lord God,
    who is called the God of Israel,
    you gathered gold like tin,
    and multiplied silver like lead.
19 You bowed your loins to women,
    and in your body you were brought into subjection.
20 You blemished your honour,
    and defiled your offspring,
    to bring wrath upon your children.
I was grieved for your folly,
    21 because the sovereignty was divided,
    and a disobedient kingdom ruled out of Ephraim.
22 But the Lord will never forsake his mercy.
He won't destroy any of his works,
    nor blot out the posterity of his elect.
He won't take away the offspring him who loved him.
He gave a remnant to Jacob,
    and to David a root from his own family.

23 So Solomon rested with his fathers.
    Of his offspring, he left behind him Rehoboam,
    the foolishness of the people, and one who lacked understanding,
    who made the people revolt by his counsel.
Also Jeroboam the son of Nebat,
    who made Israel to sin,
    and gave a way of sin to Ephraim.
24 Their sins were multiplied exceedingly,
    until they were removed from their land.
25 For they sought out all manner of wickedness,
    until vengeance came upon them.

48

1 Then Elijah arose, the prophet like fire.
    His word burnt like a torch.
2 He brought a famine upon them,
    and by his zeal made them few in number.
3 By the word of the Lord he shut up the heavens.
    He brought down fire three times.
4 How you were glorified, O Elijah, in your wondrous deeds!
    Whose glory is like yours?
5 You raised up a dead man from death,
    from Hades, by the word of the Most High.
6 You brought down kings to destruction,
    and honourable men from their sickbeds.

7 You heard rebuke in Sinai,
    and judgements of vengeance in Horeb.
8 You anointed kings for retribution,
    and prophets to succeed after you.
9 You were taken up in a tempest of fire,
    in a chariot of fiery horses.
10 You were recorded for reproofs in their seasons,
    to pacify anger, before it broke out into wrath,
    to turn the heart of the father to the son,
    and to restore the tribes of Jacob.
11 Blessed are those who saw you,
    and those who have been beautified with love;
    for we also shall surely live.

12 Elijah was wrapped in a whirlwind.
    Elisha was filled with his spirit.
    In his days he was not moved by the fear of any ruler,
    and no one brought him into subjection.
13 Nothing was too hard for him.
    When he was buried, his body prophesied.
14 As in his life he did wonders,
    so his works were also marvellous in death.
15 For all this the people didn't repent.
    They didn't depart from their sins,
    until they were carried away as a plunder from their land,
    and were scattered through all the earth.
The people were left very few in number,
    but with a ruler from the house of David.
16 Some of them did that which was right,
    but some multiplied sins.

17 Hezekiah fortified his city,
    and brought water into its midst.
He tunneled through rock with iron,
    and built cisterns for water.
18 In his days Sennacherib invaded,
    and sent Rabshakeh, and departed.
He lifted up his hand against Zion,
    and boasted great things in his arrogance.
19 Then their hearts and their hands were shaken,
    and they were in pain, as women in labour.
20 But they called upon the Lord who is merciful,
    spreading out their hands to him.
The Holy One quickly heard them out of Heaven,
    and delivered them by the hand of Isaiah.
21 He struck the camp of the Assyrians,
    and his angel utterly destroyed them.
22 For Hezekiah did that which was pleasing to the Lord,
    and was strong in the ways of his ancestor David,
    which Isaiah the prophet commanded,
    who was great and faithful in his vision.

23 In his days the sun went backward.
    He prolonged the life of the king.
24 He saw by an excellent spirit what would come to pass in the future;
    and he comforted those who mourned in Zion.
25 He showed the things that would happen through the end of time,
    and the hidden things before they came.

49

1 The memory of Josiah is like the composition of incense
    prepared by the work of the perfumer.
It will be sweet as honey in every mouth,
    and like music at a banquet of wine.
2 He did what was right in the reforming of the people,
    and took away the abominations of iniquity.
3 He set his heart right towards the Lord.
    In lawless days, he made godliness prevail.

4 Except David, Hezekiah, and Josiah,
    all were wicked,
    because they abandoned the law of the Most High.
    The kings of Judah came to an end.
5 They gave their power to others,
    and their glory to a foreign nation.
6 They set the chosen city of the sanctuary on fire
    and made her streets desolate, as it was written by the hand of
    Jeremiah.
7 For they mistreated him;
    yet he was sanctified in the womb to be a prophet,
    to root out, to afflict, to destroy
    and likewise to build and to plant.

8 Ezekiel saw the vision of glory,
    which God showed him on the chariot of the cherubim.
9 For truly he remembered the enemies in rainstorm,

---

[a] *47:9* The remainder of this verse is omitted by the best authorities.

and to do good to those who directed their ways aright.

10 Also of the twelve prophets,[a]
    may their bones flourish again out of their place.
He comforted the people of Jacob,
    and delivered them by confident hope.

11 How shall we magnify Zerubbabel?
    He was like a signet ring on the right hand.
12 So was Jesus the son of Josedek,
    who in their days built the house,
    and exalted a[b] people holy to the Lord,
    prepared for everlasting glory.
13 Also of Nehemiah the memory is great.
    He raised up for us fallen walls,
    set up the gates and bars,
    and rebuilt our houses.

14 No man was created upon the earth like Enoch,
    for he was taken up from the earth.
15 Nor was there a man born like Joseph,
    a leader of his kindred, a supporter of the people.
    Even his bones were cared for.
16 Shem and Seth were honoured amongst men,
    but above every living thing in the creation was Adam.

50

1 It was Simon, the son of Onias, the high priest,
    who in his life repaired the house,
    and in his days strengthened the temple.
2 The foundation was built by him to the height of the double walls,
    the lofty retaining walls of the temple enclosure.
3 In his days, a water cistern was dug,
    the brazen vessel like the sea in circumference.
4 He planned to save his people from ruin,
    and fortified the city against siege.
5 How glorious he was when the people gathered around him
    as he came out of the house of the veil!
6 He was like the morning star amongst clouds,
    like the full moon,
    7 like the sun shining on the temple of the Most High,
    like the rainbow shining in clouds of glory,
    8 like roses in the days of first fruits,
    like lilies by a water spring,
    like the shoot of the frankincense tree in summer time,
    9 like fire and incense in the censer,
    like a vessel of beaten gold adorned with all kinds of precious stones,
    10 like an olive tree loaded with fruit,
    and like a cypress growing high amongst the clouds.
11 When he put on his glorious robe,
    and clothed himself in perfect splendour,
    ascending to the holy altar,
    he made the court of the sanctuary glorious.

12 When he received the portions out of the priests' hands,
    as he stood by the hearth of the altar,
    with his kindred like a garland around him,
    he was like a young cedar in Lebanon
    surrounded by the trunks of palm trees.
13 All the sons of Aaron in their glory,
    held the Lord's offering in their hands before all the congregation of Israel.
14 Finishing the service at the altars,
    that he might arrange the offering of the Most High, the Almighty,
    15 he stretched out his hand to the cup of libation,
    and poured out the cup of the grape.
He poured it out at the foot of the altar,
    a sweet smelling fragrance to the Most High, the King of all.
16 Then the sons of Aaron shouted.
    They sounded the trumpets of beaten work.
They made a great fanfare to be heard,
    for a reminder before the Most High.
17 Then all the people together hurried,
    and fell down to the ground on their faces
    to worship their Lord, the Almighty, God Most High.

18 The singers also praised him with their voices.
    There was a sweet melody in the whole house.
19 And the people implored the Lord Most High,
    in prayer before him who is merciful,
    until the worship of the Lord was finished,
    and so they accomplished his service.
20 Then he went down, and lifted up his hands
    over the whole congregation of the children of Israel,
    to give blessing to the Lord with his lips,
    and to glory in his name.

21 He bowed himself down in worship the second time,
    to declare the blessing from the Most High.

22 Now bless the God of all,
    who everywhere does great things,
    who exalts our days from the womb,
    and deals with us according to his mercy.
23 May he grant us joyfulness of heart,
    and that peace may be in our days in Israel for the days of eternity,
    24 to entrust his mercy with us,
    and let him deliver us in his time!

25 With two nations my soul is vexed,
    and the third is no nation:
    26 Those who sit on the mountain of[c] Samaria, the Philistines,
    and the foolish people who live in Shechem.

27 I have written in this book the instruction of understanding and knowledge,
    I Jesus, the son of Sirach Eleazar, of Jerusalem,
    who out of his heart poured forth wisdom.
28 Blessed is he who will exercise these things.
    He who lays them up in his heart will become wise.
29 For if he does them, he will be strong in all things,
    for the light of the Lord is his guide.[d]

51

A Prayer of Jesus the son of Sirach.
1 I will give thanks to you, O Lord, O King,
    and will praise you, O God my Saviour.
I give thanks to your name,
    2 for you have been my protector and helper,
    and delivered my body out of destruction,
    and out of the snare of a slanderous tongue,
    from lips that fabricate lies.
You were my helper before those who stood by,
    3 and delivered me, according to the abundance of your mercy and of your name,
    from the gnashings of teeth ready to devour,
    out of the hand of those seeking my life,
    out of the many afflictions I endured,
    4 from the choking of a fire on every side,
    and out of the midst of fire that I hadn't kindled,
    5 out of the depth of the belly of Hades,
    from an unclean tongue,
    and from lying words—
    6 the slander of an unrighteous tongue to the king.
My soul drew near to death.
    My life was near to Hades.
7 They surrounded me on every side.
    There was no one to help me.
I was looking for human help,
    and there was none.
8 Then I remembered your mercy, O Lord,
    and your working which has been from everlasting,
    how you deliver those who wait for you,
    and save them out of the hand of their enemies.
9 I lifted up my prayer from the earth,
    and prayed for deliverance from death.
10 I called upon the Lord, the Father of my Lord,
    that he would not forsake me in the days of affliction,
    in the time when there was no help against the proud.
11 I will praise your name continually.
    I will sing praise with thanksgiving.
    My prayer was heard.
12 You saved me from destruction
    and delivered me from the evil time.
Therefore I will give thanks and praise to you,
    and bless the name of the Lord.

13 When I was yet young,
    before I went abroad,
    I sought wisdom openly in my prayer.
14 Before the temple I asked for her.
    I will seek her out even to the end.
15 From the first flower to the ripening grape my heart delighted in her.
    My foot walked in uprightness.
    From my youth I followed her steps.
16 I inclined my ear a little, and received her,
    and found for myself much instruction.
17 I profited in her.
    I will give glory to him who gives me wisdom.
18 For I determined to practise her.
    I was zealous for that which is good.
    I will never be put to shame.
19 My soul has wrestled with her.

---

a 49:10 The remainder of this line is omitted by the best authorities.
b 49:12 Some ancient authorities read temple.

c 50:26 According to some ancient versions, Seir.
d 50:29 The remainder of this verse is omitted by the best authorities.

In my conduct I was exact.
I spread out my hands to the heaven above,
   and bewailed my ignorances of her.
20 I directed my soul to her.
   In purity I found her.
I got myself a heart joined with her from the beginning.
   Therefore I won't be forsaken.
21 My belly also was troubled to seek her.
   Therefore I have gained a good possession.
22 The Lord gave me a tongue for my reward.
   I will praise him with it.

23 Draw near to me, all you who are uneducated,
   and live in the house of instruction.
24 Why therefore are you all lacking in these things,
   and your souls are very thirsty?
25 I opened my mouth and spoke,
   "Get her for yourselves without money."
26 Put your neck under the yoke,
   and let your soul receive instruction.
   She is near to find.

27 See with your eyes
   how that I laboured just a little
   and found for myself much rest.
28 Get instruction with a great sum of silver,
   and gain much gold by her.
29 May your soul rejoice in his mercy,
   and may you all not be put to shame in praising him.
30 Work your work before the time comes,
   and in his time he will give you your reward.

Baruch

The book of *Baruch* is recognised as Deuterocanonical Scripture by the Roman Catholic, Greek Orthodox, and Russian Orthodox Churches. In some Bibles, Baruch chapter 6 is listed as a separate book called *The Letter of Jeremiah*, reflecting its separation from Baruch in some copies of the Greek Septuagint.

1

1 These are the words of the book which Baruch the son of Nerias, the son of Maaseas, the son of Sedekias, the son of Asadias, the son of Helkias, wrote in Babylon, 2 in the fifth year, in the seventh day of the month, at the time when the Chaldeans took Jerusalem and burnt it with fire. 3 Baruch read the words of this book in the hearing of Jechonias the son of Joakim king of Judah, and in the hearing of all the people who came to hear the book, 4 and in the hearing of the mighty men, and of the kings' sons, and in the hearing of the elders, and in the hearing of all the people, from the least to the greatest, even of all those who lived at Babylon by the river Sud. 5 Then they wept, fasted,[a] and prayed before the Lord. 6 They also made a collection of money according to every man's ability; 7 and they sent it to Jerusalem to Joakim the high priest, the son of Helkias, the son of Salom, and to the priests and to all the people who were found with him at Jerusalem, 8 at the same time when he took the vessels of the house of the Lord, that had been carried out of the temple, to return them into the land of Judah, the tenth day of Sivan—silver vessels which Sedekias the son of Josias king of Judah had made, 9 after Nabuchodonosor king of Babylon had carried away Jechonias, the princes, the captives, the mighty men, and the people of the land from Jerusalem, and brought them to Babylon.

10 And they said: Behold, we have sent you money; therefore buy with the money burnt offerings, sin offerings, and incense, and prepare an oblation, and offer upon the altar of the Lord our God; 11 and pray for the life of Nabuchodonosor king of Babylon, and for the life of Baltasar his son, that their days may be[b] as the days of heaven above the earth. 12 The Lord will give us strength and light to our eyes. We will live under the shadow of Nabuchodonosor king of Babylon and under the shadow of Baltasar his son, and we shall serve them many days, and find favour in their sight. 13 Pray for us also to the Lord our God, for we have sinned against the Lord our God. To this day the wrath of the Lord and his indignation is not turned from us. 14 You shall read this book which we have sent to you, to make confession in the house of the Lord upon the day of the feast and on the days of the solemn assembly.

15 You shall say: To the Lord our God belongs righteousness, but to us confusion of face, as at this day—to the men of Judah, to the inhabitants of Jerusalem, 16 to our kings, to our princes, to our priests, to our prophets, and to our fathers, 17 because we have sinned before the Lord. 18 We have disobeyed him and have not listened to the voice of the Lord our God, to walk in the commandments of the Lord that he has set before us. 19 Since the day that the Lord brought our fathers out of the land of Egypt to this present day, we have been disobedient to the Lord our God, and we have been negligent in not listening to his voice. 20 Therefore the plagues have clung to us, along with the curse which the Lord declared through Moses his servant in the day that he brought our fathers out of the land of Egypt to give us a land that flows with milk and honey, as at this day. 21 Nevertheless we didn't listen to the voice of the Lord our God, according to all the words of the prophets whom he sent to us, 22 but we each walked in the imagination of his own wicked heart, to serve strange gods and to do what is evil in the sight of the Lord our God.

2

1 Therefore the Lord has made good his word which he pronounced against us, and against our judges who judged Israel, and against our kings, and against our princes, and against the men of Israel and Judah, 2 to bring upon us great plagues such as never happened before under the whole heaven,[c] as it came to pass in Jerusalem, according to the things that are written in the law of Moses, 3 that we should each eat the flesh of our own son, and each eat the flesh of our own daughter. 4 Moreover he has given them to be in subjection to all the kingdoms that are around us, to be a reproach and a desolation amongst all the people around us, where the Lord has scattered them. 5 Thus they were cast down and not exalted, because we sinned against the Lord our God in not listening to his voice. 6 To the Lord our God belongs righteousness, but to us and to our fathers confusion of face, as at this day. 7 All these plagues have come upon us which the Lord has pronounced against us. 8 Yet have we not entreated the favour of the Lord by everyone turning from the thoughts of his wicked heart. 9 Therefore the Lord has kept watch over the plagues. The Lord has brought them upon us, for the Lord is righteous in all his works which he has commanded us. 10 Yet we have not listened to his voice, to walk in the commandments of the Lord that he has set before us.

11 And now, O Lord, you God of Israel who have brought your people out of the land of Egypt with a mighty hand, with signs, with wonders, with great power, and with a high arm, and have gotten yourself a name, as at this day: 12 O Lord our God, we have sinned. We have been ungodly. We have done wrong in all your ordinances. 13 Let your wrath turn from us, for we are but a few left amongst the heathen where you have scattered us. 14 Hear our prayer, O Lord, and our petition, and deliver us for your own

sake. Give us favour in the sight of those who have led us away captive, 15 that all the earth may know that you are the Lord our God, because Israel and his posterity is called by your name. 16 O Lord, look down from your holy house and consider us. Incline your ear, O Lord, and hear. 17 Open your eyes, and see; for the dead that are in Hades, whose breath is taken from their bodies, will give to the Lord neither glory nor righteousness; 18 but the soul who is greatly vexed, who goes stooping and feeble, and the eyes that fail, and the hungry soul, will declare your glory and righteousness, O Lord.

19 For we do not present our supplication before you, O Lord our God, for the righteousness of our fathers and of our kings. 20 For you have sent your wrath and your indignation upon us, as you have spoken by your servants the prophets, saying, 21 "The Lord says, 'Bow your shoulders to serve the king of Babylon, and remain in the land that I gave to your fathers. 22 But if you won't hear the voice of the Lord to serve the king of Babylon, 23 I will cause to cease out of the cities of Judah and from the region near Jerusalem the voice of mirth, the voice of gladness, voice of the bridegroom, and the voice of the bride. The whole land will be desolate without inhabitant.'" 24 But we wouldn't listen to your voice, to serve the king of Babylon. Therefore you have made good your words that you spoke by your servants the prophets, that the bones of our kings and the bones of our fathers would be taken out of their places. 25 Behold, they are cast out to the heat by day and to the frost by night. They died in great miseries by famine, by sword, and by[d] pestilence. 26 You have made the house that is called by your name as it is today because of the wickedness of the house of Israel and the house of Judah.

27 Yet, O Lord our God, you have dealt with us after all your kindness and according to all your great mercy, 28 as you spoke by your servant Moses in the day when you commanded him to write your law in the presence of the children of Israel, saying, 29 "If you won't hear my voice, surely this very great multitude will be turned into a small number amongst the nations where I will scatter them. 30 For I know that they will not hear me, because they are a stiff-necked people; but in the land of their captivity they will take it to heart, 31 and will know that I am the Lord their God. I will give them a heart and ears to hear. 32 Then they will praise me in the land of their captivity, and think about my name, 33 and will return from their stiff neck and from their wicked deeds; for they will remember the way of their fathers who sinned before the Lord. 34 I will bring them again into the land which I promised to their fathers, to Abraham, to Isaac, and to Jacob, and they will rule over it. I will increase them, and they won't be diminished. 35 And I will make an everlasting covenant with them to be their God, and they will be my people. I will no more remove my people Israel out of the land that I have given them."

3

1 O Lord Almighty, you God of Israel, the soul in anguish and the troubled spirit cries to you. 2 Hear, O Lord, and have mercy; for you are a merciful God. Yes, have mercy upon us, because we have sinned before you. 3 For you are enthroned forever, and we keep perishing. 4 O Lord Almighty, you God of Israel, hear now the prayer of the dead Israelites, and of the children of those who were sinners before you, who didn't listen to the voice of you their God; because of this, these plagues cling to us. 5 Don't remember the iniquities of our fathers, but remember your power and your name at this time. 6 For you are the Lord our God, and we will praise you, O Lord. 7 For this cause, you have put your fear in our hearts, to the intent that we should call upon your name. We will praise you in our captivity, for we have called to mind all the iniquity of our fathers who sinned before you. 8 Behold, we are yet this day in our captivity where you have scattered us, for a reproach and a curse, and to be subject to penalty according to all the iniquities of our fathers who departed from the Lord our God.

9 Hear, O Israel, the commandments of life! Give ear to understand wisdom! 10 How is it, O Israel, that you are in your enemies' land, that you have become old in a strange country, that you are defiled with the dead, 11 that you are counted with those who are in Hades? 12 You have forsaken the fountain of wisdom. 13 If you had walked in the way of God, you would have dwelled in peace forever. 14 Learn where there is wisdom, where there is strength, and where there is understanding, that you may also know where there is length of days and life, where there is the light of the eyes and peace. 15 Who has found out her place? Who has come into her treasuries? 16 Where are the princes of the heathen, and those who ruled the beasts that are on the earth, 17 those who had their pastime with the fowls of the air, and those who hoarded up silver and gold, in which people trust, and of their getting there is no end? 18 For those who diligently sought silver, and were so anxious, and whose works are past finding out, 19 they have vanished and gone down to Hades, and others have come up in their place.

20 Younger men have seen the light and lived upon the earth, but they haven't known the way of knowledge, 21 nor understood its paths. Their children haven't embraced it. They are far off from their way. 22 It has not been heard of in Canaan, neither has it been seen in Teman. 23 The sons also of Agar who seek understanding, which are in the land, the merchants of Merran and Teman, and the authors of fables, and the searchers out of understanding—none of these have known the way of wisdom or remembered her paths.

24 O Israel, how great is the house of God! How large is the place of his possession! 25 It is great and has no end. It is high and unmeasurable.

---

[a] *1:5* Another reading is, and vowed vows.
[b] *1:11* See Deuteronomy 11:21.

[c] *2:2* Another reading is, even as he has done.
[d] *2:25* See Jeremiah 32:36.

26 Giants were born that were famous of old, great of stature, and expert in war. 27 God didn't choose these, nor did he give the way of knowledge to them, 28 so they perished, because they had no wisdom. They perished through their own foolishness. 29 Who has gone up into heaven, taken her, and brought her down from the clouds? 30 Who has gone over the sea, found her, and will bring her for choice gold? 31 There is no one who knows her way, nor any who comprehend her path. 32 But he that knows all things knows her, he found her out with his understanding. He who prepared the earth for all time has filled it with four-footed beasts. 33 It is he who sends forth the light, and it goes. He called it, and it obeyed him with fear. 34 The stars shone in their watches, and were glad. When he called them, they said, "Here we are." They shone with gladness to him who made them. 35 This is our God. No other can be compared to him. 36 He has found out all the way of knowledge, and has given it to Jacob his servant and to Israel who is loved by him. 37 Afterward she appeared upon earth, and lived with men.

4

1 This is the book of God's commandments and the law that endures forever. All those who hold it fast will live, but those who leave it will die. 2 Turn, O Jacob, and take hold of it. Walk towards the shining of its light. 3 Don't give your glory to another, nor the things that are to your advantage to a foreign nation. 4 O Israel, we are happy; for the things that are pleasing to God are made known to us.

5 Be of good cheer, my people, the memorial of Israel. 6 You were not sold to the nations for destruction, but because you moved God to wrath, you were delivered to your adversaries. 7 For you provoked him who made you by sacrificing to demons and not to God. 8 You forgot the everlasting God who brought you up. You also grieved Jerusalem, who nursed you. 9 For she saw the wrath that came upon you from God, and said, "Listen, you who dwell near Zion; for God has brought upon me great mourning. 10 For I have seen the captivity of my sons and daughters, which the Everlasting has brought upon them. 11 For with joy I nourished them, but sent them away with weeping and mourning. 12 Let no man rejoice over me, a widow and forsaken by many. For the sins of my children, I am left desolate, because they turned away from the law of God 13 and had no regard for his statutes. They didn't walk in the ways of God's commandments or tread in the paths of discipline in his righteousness. 14 Let those who dwell near Zion come and remember the captivity of my sons and daughters, which the Everlasting has brought upon them. 15 For he has brought a nation upon them from afar, a shameless nation with a strange language, who didn't respect old men or pity children. 16 They have carried away the dear beloved sons of the widow, and left her who was alone desolate of her daughters."

17 But I—how can I help you? 18 For he who brought these calamities upon you will deliver you from the hand of your enemies. 19 Go your way, O my children. Go your way, for I am left desolate. 20 I have put off the garment of peace, and put on the sackcloth of my petition. I will cry to the Everlasting as long as I live.

21 Take courage, my children. Cry to God, and he will deliver you from the power and hand of the enemies. 22 For I have trusted in the Everlasting, that he will save you; and joy has come to me from the Holy One, because of the mercy that will soon come to you from your Everlasting Saviour. 23 For I sent you out with mourning and weeping, but God will give you to me again with joy and gladness forever. 24 For as now those who dwell near Zion have seen your captivity, so they will shortly see your salvation from our God which will come upon you with great glory and brightness of the Everlasting. 25 My children, suffer patiently the wrath that has come upon you from God, for your enemy has persecuted you; but shortly you will see his destruction and will tread upon their necks. 26 My delicate ones have travelled rough roads. They were taken away like a flock carried off by enemies.

27 Take courage, my children, and cry to God; for you will be remembered by him who has brought this upon you. 28 For as it was your decision to go astray from God, return and seek him ten times more. 29 For he who brought these calamities upon you will bring you everlasting joy again with your salvation. 30 Take courage, O Jerusalem, for he who called you by name will comfort you. 31 Miserable are those who afflicted you and rejoiced at your fall. 32 Miserable are the cities which your children served. Miserable is she who received your sons. 33 For as she rejoiced at your fall and was glad of your ruin, so she will be grieved at her own desolation. 34 And I will take away her pride in her great multitude and her boasting will be turned into mourning. 35 For fire will come upon her from the Everlasting for many days; and she will be inhabited by demons for a long time.

36 O Jerusalem, look around you towards the east, and behold the joy that comes to you from God. 37 Behold, your sons come, whom you sent away. They come gathered together from the east to the west at the word of the Holy One, rejoicing in the glory of God.

5

1 Take off the garment of your mourning and affliction, O Jerusalem, and put on forever the beauty of the glory from God. 2 Put on the robe of the righteousness from God. Set on your head a diadem of the glory of the Everlasting. 3 For God will show your splendour everywhere under heaven. 4 For your name will be called by God forever "Righteous Peace, Godly Glory".

5 Arise, O Jerusalem, and stand upon the height. Look around you towards the east and see your children gathered from the going down of the sun to its rising at the word of the Holy One, rejoicing that God has remembered them. 6 For they went from you on foot, being led away by their enemies, but God brings them in to you carried on high with glory, on a royal throne. 7 For God has appointed that every high mountain and the everlasting hills should be made low, and the valleys filled up to make the ground level, that Israel may go safely in the glory of God. 8 Moreover the woods and every sweet smelling tree have shaded Israel by the commandment of God. 9 For God will lead Israel with joy in the light of his glory with the mercy and righteousness that come from him.

6

The Letter of Jeremy (Jeremiah)

1 A copy of a letter that Jeremy sent to those who were to be led captives into Babylon by the king of the Babylonians, to give them the message that God commanded him.

2 Because of the sins which you have committed before God, you will be led away captives to Babylon by Nabuchodonosor king of the Babylonians. 3 So when you come to Babylon, you will remain there many years, and for a long season, even for seven generations. After that, I will bring you out peacefully from there. 4 But now you will see in Babylon gods of silver, gold, wood carried on shoulders, which cause the nations to fear. 5 Beware therefore that you in no way become like these foreigners. Don't let fear take hold of you because of them when you see the multitude before them and behind them, worshipping them. 6 But say in your hearts, "O Lord, we must worship you." 7 For my angel is with you, and I myself care for your souls. 8 For their tongue is polished by the workman, and they themselves are overlaid with gold and with silver; yet they are only fake, and can't speak. 9 And taking gold, as if it were for a virgin who loves to be happy, they make crowns for the heads of their gods. 10 Sometimes also the priests take gold and silver from their gods, and spend it on themselves. 11 They will even give some of it to the common prostitutes. They dress them like men with garments, even the gods of silver, gods of gold, and gods of wood. 12 Yet these gods can't save themselves from rust and moths, even though they are covered with purple garments. 13 They wipe their faces because of the dust of the temple, which is thick upon them. 14 And he who can't put to death one who offends against him holds a sceptre, as though he were judge of a country. 15 He has also a dagger in his right hand, and an axe, but can't deliver himself from war and robbers. 16 By this they are known not to be gods. Therefore don't fear them. 17 For like a vessel that a man uses is worth nothing when it is broken, even so it is with their gods. When they are set up in the temples, their eyes are full of dust through the feet of those who come in. 18 As the courts are secured on every side upon him who offends the king, as being committed to suffer death, even so the priests secure their temples with doors, with locks, and bars, lest they be carried off by robbers. 19 They light candles for them, yes, more than for themselves, even though they can't see one. 20 They are like one of the beams of the temple. Men say their hearts are eaten out when things creeping out of the earth devour both them and their clothing. They don't feel it 21 when their faces are blackened through the smoke that comes out of the temple. 22 Bats, swallows, and birds land on their bodies and heads. So do the cats. 23 By this you may know that they are no gods. Therefore don't fear them. 24 Notwithstanding the gold with which they are covered to make them beautiful, unless someone wipes off the tarnish, they won't shine; for they didn't even feel it when they were molten. 25 Things in which there is no breath are bought at any cost. 26 Having no feet, they are carried upon shoulders. By this, they declare to men that they are worth nothing. 27 Those who serve them are also ashamed, for if they fall to the ground at any time, they can't rise up again by themselves. If they are bowed down, they can't make themselves straight; but the offerings are set before them, as if they were dead men. 28 And the things that are sacrificed to them, their priests sell and spend. In like manner, their wives also lay up part of it in salt; but to the poor and to the impotent they give none of it. 29 The menstruous woman and the woman in childbed touch their sacrifices, knowing therefore by these things that they are no gods. Don't fear them. 30 For how can they be called gods? Because women set food before the gods of silver, gold, and wood. 31 And in their temples the priests sit on seats, having their clothes torn and their heads and beards shaven, and nothing on their heads. 32 They roar and cry before their gods, as men do at the feast when one is dead. 33 The priests also take off garments from them and clothe their wives and children with them. 34 Whether it is evil or good what one does to them, they are not able to repay it. They can't set up a king or put him down. 35 In like manner, they can neither give riches nor money. Though a man make a vow to them and doesn't keep it, they will never exact it. 36 They can save no man from death. They can't deliver the weak from the mighty. 37 They can't restore a blind man to his sight, or deliver anyone who is in distress. 38 They can show no mercy to the widow, or do good to the fatherless. 39 They are like the stones that are cut out of the mountain, these gods of wood that are overlaid with gold and with silver. Those who minister to them will be confounded.

40 How could a man then think or say that they are gods, when even the Chaldeans themselves dishonour them? 41 If they shall see one mute who can't speak, they bring him and ask him to call upon Bel, as though he were able to understand. 42 Yet they can't perceive this themselves, and forsake them; for they have no understanding. 43 The women also with cords around them sit in the ways, burning bran for incense; but if any of them, drawn by someone who passes by, lies with him, she reproaches her fellow, that she was not thought as worthy as herself and her cord wasn't broken. 44 Whatever is done amongst them is false. How could a man then think or say that they are gods? 45 They are fashioned by carpenters and goldsmiths. They can be nothing else than what the workmen make them to be. 46 And they themselves who fashioned them can never continue long.

How then should the things that are fashioned by them? ₄₇ For they have left lies and reproaches to those who come after. ₄₈ For when there comes any war or plague upon them, the priests consult with themselves, where they may be hidden with them. ₄₉ How then can't men understand that they are no gods, which can't save themselves from war or from plague? ₅₀ For seeing they are only wood and overlaid with gold and silver, it will be known hereafter that they are false. ₅₁ It will be manifest to all nations and kings that they are no gods, but the works of men's hands, and that there is no work of God in them. ₅₂ Who then may not know that they are not gods?

₅₃ For they can't set up a king in a land or give rain to men. ₅₄ They can't judge their own cause, or redress a wrong, being unable; for they are like crows between heaven and earth. ₅₅ For even when fire falls upon the house of gods of wood overlaid with gold or with silver, their priests will flee away, and escape, but they themselves will be burnt apart like beams. ₅₆ Moreover they can't withstand any king or enemies. How could a man then admit or think that they are gods? ₅₇ Those gods of wood overlaid with silver or with gold aren't able to escape from thieves or robbers. ₅₈ The gold, silver, and garments with which they are clothed—those who are strong will take from them, and go away with them. They won't be able to help themselves. ₅₉ Therefore it is better to be a king who shows his manhood, or else a vessel in a house profitable for whatever the owner needs, than such false gods—or even a door in a house, to keep the things safe that are in it, than such false gods; or better to be a pillar of wood in a palace than such false gods.

₆₀ For sun, moon, and stars, being bright and sent to do their jobs, are obedient. ₆₁ Likewise also the lightning when it flashes is beautiful to see. In the same way, the wind also blows in every country. ₆₂ And when God commands the clouds to go over the whole world, they do as they are told. ₆₃ And the fire sent from above to consume mountains and woods does as it is commanded; but these are to be compared to them neither in show nor power. ₆₄ Therefore a man shouldn't think or say that they are gods, seeing they aren't able to judge causes or to do good to men. ₆₅ Knowing therefore that they are no gods, don't fear them. ₆₆ For they can neither curse nor bless kings. ₆₇ They can't show signs in the heavens amongst the nations, or shine as the sun, or give light as the moon. ₆₈ The beasts are better than they; for they can get under a covert, and help themselves. ₆₉ In no way then is it manifest to us that they are gods. Therefore don't fear them. ₇₀ For as a scarecrow in a garden of cucumbers that keeps nothing, so are their gods of wood overlaid with gold and silver. ₇₁ Likewise also their gods of wood overlaid with gold and with silver, are like a white thorn in an orchard that every bird sits upon. They are also like a dead body that is thrown out into the dark. ₇₂ You will know them to be no gods by the bright purple that rots upon them. They themselves will be consumed afterwards, and will be a reproach in the country. ₇₃ Better therefore is the just man who has no idols; for he will be far from reproach.

The First Book of the Maccabees

The First Book of the Maccabees is recognised as Deuterocanonical Scripture by the Roman Catholic, Greek Orthodox, and Russian Orthodox Churches.

1

₁ After Alexander the Macedonian, the son of Philip, who came out of the land of Chittim, and struck Darius king of the Persians and Medes, it came to pass, after he had struck him, that he reigned in his place, in former time, over[a] Greece. ₂ He fought many battles, won many strongholds, killed the kings of the earth, ₃ went through to the ends of the earth, and took spoils of a multitude of nations. The earth was quiet before him. He was exalted. His heart was lifted up. ₄ He gathered together an exceedingly strong army and ruled over countries, nations, and principalities, and they paid him tribute.

₅ After these things he fell sick, and perceived that he was going to die. ₆ He called his honourable servants, which had been brought up with him from his youth, and he divided to them his kingdom while he was still alive. ₇ Alexander reigned twelve years, then he died. ₈ Then his servants ruled, each one in his place. ₉ They all put crowns upon themselves after he was dead, and so did their sons after them many years; and they multiplied evils in the earth.

₁₀ There came out of them a sinful root, Antiochus Epiphanes, son of Antiochus the king, who had been a hostage at Rome, and he reigned in[b] the one hundred and thirty seventh year of the kingdom of the Greeks.

₁₁ In those days transgressors of the law came out of Israel and persuaded many, saying, let's go make a covenant with the[c] Gentiles around us; for since we were separated from them many evils have befallen us. ₁₂ That proposal was good in their eyes. ₁₃ Some of the people eagerly went to the king, and he authorised them to observe the ordinances of the[d] Gentiles. ₁₄ So[e] they built a gymnasium in Jerusalem according to the laws of the[f] Gentiles. ₁₅ They made themselves uncircumcised, forsook the holy covenant, joined themselves to the[g] Gentiles, and sold themselves to do evil.

₁₆ The kingdom was established in the sight of Antiochus, and he planned to reign over Egypt, that he might reign over both kingdoms. ₁₇ He entered into Egypt with a[h] great multitude, with chariots, with elephants, with cavalry, and with a great[i] navy. ₁₈ He made war against Ptolemy king of Egypt. Ptolemy was put to shame before him, and fled; and many fell wounded to death. ₁₉ They took possession of the strong cities in the land of Egypt, and he took the spoils of Egypt.

₂₀ Antiochus, after he had defeated Egypt, returned in[j] the one hundred and forty third year, and went up against Israel and Jerusalem with a[k] great multitude, ₂₁ and entered presumptuously into the sanctuary, and took the golden altar, the lampstand for the light, and all its utensils. ₂₂ He took the table of the show bread, the cups for the drink offerings, the bowls, the golden censers, the veil, the crowns, and the gold decoration on the front of the temple. He peeled it all off. ₂₃ He took the silver, the gold, and the precious vessels. He took the hidden treasures which he found. ₂₄ When he had taken all of these, he went away into his own land. He made a great slaughter, and spoke very arrogantly. ₂₅ Great mourning came upon Israel, in every place where they were. ₂₆ The rulers and elders groaned. The virgins and young men were made feeble. The beauty of the women was changed. ₂₇ Every bridegroom took up lamentation. She who sat in the marriage chamber was mourning. ₂₈ The land was moved for its inhabitants, and all the house of Jacob was clothed with shame.

₂₉ [l]After two full years, the king sent a chief collector of tribute to the cities of Judah, and he came to Jerusalem with a[m] great multitude. ₃₀ He spoke words of peace to them in subtlety, and they believed him. Then he fell upon the city suddenly, struck it very severely, and destroyed many people of Israel. ₃₁ He took the spoils of the city, set it on fire, and pulled down its houses and its walls on every side. ₃₂ They led captive the women and the children, and seized the livestock. ₃₃ Then they fortified the city of David with a large, strong wall and with strong towers, and it became their citadel. ₃₄ They put a sinful nation, transgressors of the law, there, and they strengthened themselves in it. ₃₅ They stored up weapons and food, and gathering together the spoils of Jerusalem, they stored them there, and they became a great menace. ₃₆ It became a place to lie in wait against the sanctuary, and an evil adversary to Israel continually. ₃₇ They shed innocent blood on every side of the sanctuary, and defiled the sanctuary. ₃₈ The inhabitants of Jerusalem fled because of them. She became a habitation of foreigners. She became foreign to those who were born in her, and her children forsook her. ₃₉ Her sanctuary was laid waste like a wilderness,[n] her

feasts were turned into mourning, her Sabbaths into reproach, and her honour into contempt. ₄₀ According to her glory, so was her dishonour multiplied, and her exaltation was turned into mourning.

₄₁ King Antiochus wrote to his whole kingdom that all should be one people, ₄₂ and that each should forsake his own laws. All the nations agreed according to the word of the king. ₄₃ Many of Israel consented to his worship, sacrificed to the idols, and profaned the Sabbath. ₄₄ The king sent letters by the hand of messengers to Jerusalem and the cities of Judah, that they should follow laws strange to the land, ₄₅ and should forbid whole burnt offerings and sacrifice and drink offerings in the sanctuary; and should profane the Sabbaths and feasts, ₄₆ and pollute the sanctuary and those who were holy; ₄₇ that they should build altars, and temples, and shrines for idols, and should sacrifice swine's flesh and unclean animals; ₄₈ and that they should leave their sons uncircumcised, that they should make their souls abominable with all manner of uncleanness and profanation; ₄₉ so that they might forget the law, and change all the ordinances. ₅₀ Whoever doesn't do according to the word of the king, he shall die. ₅₁ According to all these words wrote he to his whole kingdom. He appointed overseers over all the people, and he commanded the cities of Judah to sacrifice, city by city. ₅₂ From the people were gathered together to them many, everyone who had forsaken the law; and they did evil things in the land. ₅₃ They made Israel to hide themselves in every place of refuge which they had.

₅₄ On the fifteenth day of Chislev, in[o] the one hundred and forty fifth year, they built an abomination of desolation upon the altar,[p] and in the cities of Judah on every side they built idol altars.[q] ₅₅ At the doors of the houses and in the streets they burnt incense. ₅₆ They tore the books of the law which they found in pieces and set them on fire. ₅₇ Anyone who was found with any a book of the covenant, and if any consented to the law, the king's sentence delivered him to death. ₅₈ Thus did they in their might to Israel, to those who were found month by month in the cities. ₅₉ On the twenty-fifth day of the month they sacrificed upon the idol altar that was on top of the altar of burnt offering. ₆₀ [r]They put to death women who had circumcised their children, according to the commandment. ₆₁ They hung their babies around their necks, and their houses, and those who had circumcised them. ₆₂ Many in Israel were fully resolved and confirmed in themselves not to eat unclean things. ₆₃ [s]They chose to die, that they might not be defiled with the food, and that they might not profane the holy covenant; and they died. ₆₄ Exceedingly great wrath came upon Israel.

2

₁ In those days Mattathias the son of John, the son of Simeon, a priest of the sons of Joarib, from Jerusalem rose up; and he lived at Modin. ₂ And he had five sons:[t] John, who was surnamed Gaddis; ₃ Simon, who was called Thassi; ₄ Judas, who was called Maccabaeus; ₅ Eleazar, who was called Avaran; and Jonathan, who was called Apphus.

₆ He saw the blasphemies that were committed in Judah and in Jerusalem, ₇ and he said, "Woe is me! Why was I born to see the destruction of my people and the destruction of the holy city, and to dwell there when it was given into the hand of the enemy, the sanctuary into the hand of foreigners? ₈ Her temple has become like a man who was glorious. ₉ Her vessels of glory are carried away into captivity. Her infants are slain in her streets. Her young men are slain with the enemy's sword. ₁₀ What nation has not inherited her palaces and taken possession of her spoils? ₁₁ Her adornment has all been taken away. Instead of a free woman, she has become a slave. ₁₂ Behold, our holy things, our beauty, and our glory are laid waste. The Gentiles have profaned them. ₁₃ Why should we live any longer?"

₁₄ Mattathias and his sons tore their clothes, put on sackcloth, and mourned exceedingly.

₁₅ And the king's officers who were enforcing the apostasy came into the city Modin to sacrifice. ₁₆ Many of Israel came to them, and Mattathias and his sons were gathered together. ₁₇ The king's officers answered and spoke to Mattathias, saying, "You are a ruler and an honourable and great man in this city, and strengthened with sons and kindred. ₁₈ Now therefore come first and do the commandment of the king, as all the nations have done, including the men of Judah and those who remain in Jerusalem. You and your house will be numbered amongst the king's[u] friends, and you and your sons will be honoured with silver and gold and many gifts."

₁₉ And Mattathias answered and said with a loud voice, "If all the nations that are in the house of the king's dominion listen to him, to fall away each one from the worship of his fathers, and have made choice to follow his commandments, ₂₀ yet I and my sons and my kindred will walk in the covenant of our fathers. ₂₁ Far be it from us that we should forsake the

---

a *1:1* That is, the Greek Empire. Compare 1 Maccabees 1:10 and 1 Maccabees 6:2.

b *1:10* circa B.C. 176.

c *1:11* Or, nations: and so throughout this book.

d *1:13* Or, nations: and so throughout this book.

e *1:14* See 2 Maccabees 4:9, 12.

f *1:14* Or, nations: and so throughout this book.

g *1:15* Or, nations: and so throughout this book

h *1:17* Gr. heavy.

i *1:17* Or, armament

j *1:20* circa B.C. 170. See 2 Maccabees 5:11-16.

k *1:20* Gr. heavy.

l *1:29* See 2 Maccabees 5:24.

m *1:29* Gr. heavy.

n *1:39* See 2 Maccabees 6:6.

o *1:54* circa B.C. 168. See 2 Maccabees 5:11.

p *1:54* The two words rendered altar are different in the Greek: and so in 1 Maccabees 1:59.

q *1:54* The two words rendered altar are different in the Greek: and so in 1 Maccabees 1:59.

r *1:60* See 2 Maccabees 6:10.

s *1:63* See 2 Maccabees 6:19 and 7:1, etc.

t *2:2* Gr. Joannes.

u *2:18* See 1 Maccabees 3:38; 10:10, etc.; Compare 1 Maccabees 10:65; 11:27; 2 Maccabees 8:9.

law and the ordinances. 22 We will not listen to the king's words, to turn aside from our worship, to the right hand, or to the left."

23 When he had finished speaking these words, a Jew came in the sight of all to sacrifice on the altar which was at Modin, according to the king's commandment. 24 Mattathias saw it, so his zeal was kindled, and his guts trembled, and he vented his wrath according to judgement, and ran and killed him upon the altar. 25 He killed the king's officer, who compelled men to sacrifice, at the same time, and pulled down the altar. 26 He was zealous for the law, even as Phinehas did to Zimri the son of Salu.

27 Mattathias cried out in the city with a loud voice, saying, "Whoever is zealous for the law and maintains the covenant, let him follow me!" 28 He and his sons fled into the mountains, and left all that they had in the city.

29 Then many who sought justice and judgement went down into the wilderness to live there— 30 they, their children, their wives, and their livestock—because evils were multiplied upon them. 31 It was told the king's officers and the forces that were in Jerusalem, the city of David, that certain men who had broken the king's commandment had gone down into the secret places in the wilderness; 32 and many pursued after them, and having overtaken them, they encamped against them and set the battle in array against them on the Sabbath day. 33 They said to them, "Enough of this! Come out and do according to the word of the king, and you will all live!"

34 They said, "We won't come out. We won't do the word of the king, to profane the Sabbath day."

35 Then the enemy hurried to attack them.

36 They didn't answer them. They didn't cast a stone at them, or block their secret places, 37 saying, "Let's all die in our innocence. Heaven and earth testify for us, that you put us to death unjustly."

38 So they attacked them on the Sabbath, and they died—they, their wives, their children, and their livestock—in number a thousand souls of men.

39 When Mattathias and his friends found out about it, and they mourned over them exceedingly. 40 One said to another, "If we all do as our kindred have done, and don't fight against the Gentiles for our lives and our ordinances, they will quickly destroy us from off the earth." 41 So they decided that day, saying, "Whoever comes against us to battle on the Sabbath day, let's fight against him, and we will in no way all die, as our kindred died in the secret places."

42 Then a company of the Hasidaeans,[a] mighty men of Israel, everyone who offered himself willingly for the law, were gathered together to them. 43 All those who fled from the evils were added to them, and supported them. 44 They mustered an army, and struck sinners in their anger, and lawless men in their wrath. The rest fled to the Gentiles for safety. 45 And Mattathias and his friends went around and pulled down the altars. 46 They forcibly circumcised the boys who were uncircumcised, as many as they found in the coasts of Israel. 47 They pursued the arrogant, and the work prospered in their hand. 48 They rescued the law out of the hand of the Gentiles and out of the hand of the kings. They never allowed the sinner to triumph.

49 The days of Mattathias drew near that he should die, and he said to his sons, "Now pride and scorn have gained strength. It is a season of overthrow and indignant wrath. 50 Now, my children, be zealous for the law, and give your lives for the covenant of your fathers. 51 Call to remembrance the deeds of our fathers which they did in their generations; and receive great glory and an everlasting name. 52 Wasn't Abraham found faithful in temptation, and it was reckoned to him for righteousness? 53 Joseph in the time of his distress kept the commandment, and became lord of Egypt. 54 Phinehas our father, because he was exceedingly zealous, obtained the covenant of an everlasting priesthood. 55 Joshua became a judge in Israel for fulfilling the word. 56 Caleb obtained a heritage in the land for testifying in the congregation. 57 David inherited the throne of a kingdom forever and ever for being merciful. 58 Elijah was taken up into heaven because he was exceedingly zealous for the law. 59 Hananiah, Azariah, and Mishael believed, and were saved out of the flame. 60 Daniel was delivered from the mouth of lions for his innocence.

61 "Thus consider from generation to generation that no one who put their trust in him will lack for strength. 62 Don't be afraid of the words of a sinful man; for his glory will be dung and worms. 63 Today he will be lifted up, and tomorrow he will in no way be found, because he has returned to dust, and his thought has perished. 64 You, my children, be strong, and show yourselves men on behalf of the law; for in it you will obtain glory. 65 Behold, Simon your brother, whom I know to be a man of counsel. Always listen to him. He shall be a father to you. 66 Judas Maccabaeus has been strong and mighty from his youth. He shall be your captain and shall fight[b] the battle of the people. 67 Rally around all the doers of the law, and avenge the wrong done to your people. 68 Repay the Gentiles, and obey the commandments of the law."

69 He blessed them, and was gathered to his ancestors. 70 He died in[c] the one hundred and forty sixth year, and his sons buried him in the tombs of his ancestors at Modin. All Israel made great lamentation for him.

3

1 His son Judas, who was called Maccabaeus, rose up in his place. 2 All his kindred helped him, and so did all those who joined with his father, and they fought with gladness the battle of Israel. 3 He got his people great glory, and put on a breastplate like a giant, and bound his warlike harness around him, and set battles in array, protecting the army with his sword. 4 He was like a lion in his deeds, and like a lion's cub roaring for prey. 5 He hunted and pursued the lawless, and he burnt up those who troubled his people. 6 The lawless shrunk back for fear of him, and all the workers of lawlessness were very troubled, and deliverance prospered in his hand. 7 He angered many kings and made Jacob glad with his acts. His memory is blessed forever. 8 He went through the cities of Judah, destroyed the ungodly[d] out of the land, and turned away wrath from Israel. 9 He was renowned to the utmost part of the earth. He gathered together those who were ready to perish.

10 Apollonius gathered the Gentiles together with a great army from Samaria to fight against Israel. 11 Judas learnt of it, and he went out to meet him, struck him, and killed him. Many fell wounded to death, and the rest fled. 12 They took their spoils, and Judas took Apollonius' sword, and he fought with it all his days.

13 Seron, the commander of the army of Syria, heard that Judas had gathered a large company, including a body of faithful men who stayed with him, went out to war. 14 He said, "I will make myself a name and get myself glory in the kingdom. I will fight against Judas and those who are with him, who despise the king's command. 15 A mighty army of the ungodly went up with him to help him, to take vengeance on the children of Israel.

16 He came near to the ascent of Bethhoron, and Judas went out to meet him with a small company. 17 But when they saw the army coming to meet them, they said to Judas, "What? Shall we be able, being a small company, to fight against so great and strong a multitude? We for our part are faint, having tasted no food this day."

18 Judas said, "It is an easy thing for many to be hemmed in by the hands of a few. With[e] heaven it is all one, to save by many or by few; 19 for victory in battle stands not in the multitude of an army, but strength is from heaven. 20 They come to us in fullness of insolence and lawlessness, to destroy us and our wives and our children, and to plunder us, 21 but we fight for our lives and our laws. 22 He himself will crush them before our face; but as for you, don't be afraid of them."

23 Now when he had finished speaking, he rushed suddenly against Seron and his army, and they were defeated before him. 24 They pursued them down the descent of Bethhoron to the plain, and about eight hundred men of them fell; but the rest fled into the land of the Philistines.

25 The fear of Judas and his kindred, and the dread of them, began to fall on the nations around them. 26 His fame reached the king, and every nation told of the battles of Judas.

27 But when King Antiochus heard these words, he was full of indignation; and he sent and gathered together all the forces of his realm, an exceedingly strong army. 28 He opened his treasury and gave his forces pay for a year, and commanded them to be ready for every need. 29 He saw that the money was gone from his treasures, and that the tributes of the country were small, because of the dissension and disaster which he had brought upon the land, to the end that he might take away the laws which had been from the first days. 30 He was afraid that he wouldn't have enough as at other times for the charges and the gifts which he used to give with a liberal hand, more abundantly than the kings who were before him. 31 And he was exceedingly perplexed in his mind, and he determined to go into Persia, and to take the tributes of those countries, and to gather much money. 32 He left Lysias, an honourable man, and one of royal lineage, to be over the affairs of the king from the river Euphrates to the borders of Egypt, 33 and to bring up his son Antiochus, until he came again. 34 He delivered to Lysias half of his forces and the elephants, and gave him charge of all the things that he would have done, and concerning those who lived in Judea and in Jerusalem, 35 that he should send an army against them to root out and destroy the strength of Israel and the remnant of Jerusalem, and to take away their memory from the place, 36 and that he should make foreigners live in all their territory, and should divide their land to them by lot. 37 The king took the half that remained of the forces, and left Antioch, his royal city, in the one hundred and forty seventh year;[f] and he passed over the river Euphrates, and went through the upper countries.

38 Lysias chose Ptolemy the son of Dorymenes, Nicanor, and Gorgias, mighty men of the king's friends;[g] 39 and with them, he sent forty thousand infantry and seven thousand cavalry to go into the land of Judah and to destroy it, according to the word of the king. 40 They set out with all their army, and came and encamped near Emmaus in the plain country. 41 The merchants of the country heard of their fame, and took silver and gold in large quantities, and fetters,[h] and came into the camp to take the children of Israel for slaves. Forces of Syria and of the land of the Philistines[i] joined with them.

42 Judas and his kindred saw that evils were multiplied, and that the forces were encamping in their borders. They learnt about the king's words which he had commanded, to destroy the people and make an end of them. 43 Then they each said to his neighbour, "Let's repair the ruins of our people. Let's fight for our people and the holy place." 44 The congregation was gathered together, that they might be ready for battle, and that they might pray and ask for mercy and compassion. 45 Jerusalem was without inhabitant like a wilderness. There was none of her offspring who went in or

---

a 2:42 That is, Chasidim.

b 2:66 Some ancient authorities read you shall fight.

c 2:70 circa B.C. 167.

d 3:8 Gr. out of it.

e 3:18 Some ancient authorities read the God of heaven.

f 3:37 circa B.C. 166.

g 3:38 See 1 Maccabees 2:18.

h 3:41 Most of the authorities read servants.

i 3:41 Gr. foreigners.

went out. The sanctuary was trampled down. Children of foreigners were in the citadel. The Gentiles lived there. Joy was taken away from Jacob, and the pipe and the harp ceased. ₄₆ They gathered themselves together, and came to Mizpeh, near Jerusalem; for in Mizpeh there used to be a place of prayer for Israel. ₄₇ They fasted that day, put on sackcloth, put ashes on their heads, tore their clothes, ₄₈ and opened the book of the law, to learn about the things for which the Gentiles consulted the images of their idols. ₄₉ They brought the priests' garments, the first fruits, and the tithes. They stirred up the Nazarites, who had accomplished their days. ₅₀ They cried aloud towards heaven, saying, "What should we do with these men? Where should we carry them away? ₅₁ Your holy place is trampled down and profaned. Your priests mourn in humiliation. ₅₂ Behold, the Gentiles are assembled together against us to destroy us. You know what things they imagine against us. ₅₃ How will we be able to stand against them, unless you help us?" ₅₄ They sounded with the trumpets, and gave a loud shout.

₅₅ And after this Judas appointed leaders of the people: captains of thousands, captains of hundreds, captains of fifties, and captains of tens. ₅₆ He said to those who were building houses, were betrothing wives, were planting vineyards, and were fearful, that they should return, each man to his own house, according to the law. ₅₇ The army marched out and encamped upon the south side of Emmaus. ₅₈ Judas said, "Arm yourselves and be valiant men! Be ready in the morning to fight with these Gentiles who are assembled together against us to destroy us and our holy place. ₅₉ For it is better for us to die in battle than to see the calamities of our nation and the holy place. ₆₀ Nevertheless, as may be the will in heaven, so shall he do.

4

₁ Gorgias took five thousand infantry, a thousand chosen cavalry, and the army moved out at night, ₂ that it might fall upon the army of the Jews and strike them suddenly. The men of the citadel were his guides. ₃ Judas heard of this, and he and the valiant men moved, that he might strike the king's army which was at Emmaus ₄ while the forces were still dispersed from the camp. ₅ Gorgias came into the camp of Judas at night and found no man. He sought them in the mountains; for he said, "These men are running away from us."

₆ As soon as it was day, Judas appeared in the plain with three thousand men. However they didn't have the armour and swords they desired. ₇ They saw the camp of the Gentiles strong and fortified, with cavalry all around it; and these were expert in war. ₈ Judas said to the men who were with him, "Don't be afraid of their numbers, or when they charge. ₉ Remember how our fathers were saved in the Red sea, when Pharaoh pursued them with an army. ₁₀ Now let's cry to heaven, if he will have us, and will remember the covenant of our fathers, and destroy this army before our face today. ₁₁ Then all the Gentiles will know that there is one who redeems and saves Israel.

₁₂ The foreigners lifted up their eyes, and saw them coming near them. ₁₃ They went out of the camp to battle. Those who were with Judas sounded their trumpets ₁₄ and joined battle. The Gentiles were defeated, and fled into the plain. ₁₅ But all those in the rear fell by the sword. They pursued them to ͣ Gazara, and to the plains of Idumaea, Azotus, and Jamnia. About three thousand of those men fell. ₁₆ Then Judas and his army returned from pursuing them; ₁₇ and he said to the people, "Don't be greedy for the spoils, because there is a battle before us. ₁₈ Gorgias and his army are near us on the mountain. But stand now against our enemies and fight against them, and afterwards take the spoils with boldness." ₁₉ While Judas was finishing this speech, a part of them appeared looking out from the mountain. ₂₀ They saw that their army had been put to flight, and that the Jews were burning the camp; for the smoke that was seen declared what was done. ₂₁ But when they perceived these things, they were very afraid. Perceiving also the army of Judas in the plain ready for battle, ₂₂ they all fled into the land of the ᵇ Philistines. ₂₃ Judas returned to plunder the camp, and they took much gold, silver, blue, sea purple, and great riches. ₂₄ Then they returned home, and sang a song of thanksgiving, and gave praise to heaven, because he is good, because his mercy endures forever. ₂₅ Israel had a great deliverance that day.

₂₆ The foreigners who had escaped came and told Lysias all the things that had happened. ₂₇ When he heard of it, he was confounded and discouraged, because the things he desired had not been done to Israel, nor had such things happened as the king commanded him.

₂₈ In the next year, he gathered together sixty thousand chosen infantry and five thousand cavalry, that he might subdue them. ₂₉ They came into Idumaea and encamped at Bethsura. Judas met them with ten thousand men. ₃₀ He saw that the army was strong, and he prayed and said, "Blessed are you, O Saviour of Israel, who defeated the attack of the mighty warrior by the hand of your servant David, and delivered the army of the ͨ Philistines into the hands of Jonathan the son of Saul, and of his armour bearer. ₃₁ Hem in this army in the hand of your people Israel, and let them be ashamed for their army and their cavalry. ₃₂ Give them faintness of heart. Cause the boldness of their strength to melt away, and let them quake at their destruction. ₃₃ Strike them down with the sword of those who love you, and let all who know your name praise you with thanksgiving."

₃₄ They joined in battle; and about five thousand men of Lysias' army fell. They fell down near them. ₃₅ But when Lysias saw that his troops were put to flight, and the boldness that had come upon those who were with Judas, and how they were ready either to live or to die nobly, he withdrew to Antioch, and gathered together hired soldiers, that he might come again into Judea with an even greater army.

₃₆ But Judas and his kindred said, "Behold, our enemies are defeated. Let's go up to cleanse the holy place and to rededicate it." ₃₇ All the army was gathered together, and they went up to mount Zion. ₃₈ They saw the sanctuary laid desolate, the altar profaned, the gates burnt up, shrubs growing in the courts as in a forest or as on one of the mountains, and the priests' chambers pulled down; ₃₉ and they tore their clothes, made great lamentation, put ashes upon their heads, ₄₀ fell on their faces to the ground, ͩ blew with the solemn trumpets, ͤ and cried towards heaven. ₄₁ Then Judas appointed certain men to fight against those who were in the citadel until he had cleansed the holy place.

₄₂ He chose blameless priests who were devoted to the law; ₄₃ and they cleansed the holy place and carried the defiled stones out to an unclean place. ₄₄ They deliberated what to do with the altar of burnt offerings, which had been profaned. ₄₅ A good plan came into their mind, that they should pull it down, lest it would be a reproach to them, because the Gentiles had defiled it. So they pulled down the altar ₄₆ and laid up the stones on the temple hill in a convenient place, until a prophet would come to give an answer concerning them. ₄₇ They took whole stones according to the law, and built a new altar like the former. ₄₈ They built the holy place and the inner parts of the house; and they consecrated the courts. ₄₉ They made new holy vessels, and they brought the lampstand, the altar of incense, and the table into the temple. ₅₀ They burnt incense on the altar, and they lit the lamps that were upon the lampstand, and they gave light in the temple. ₅₁ They set loaves upon the table, hung up the curtains, and finished all the work which they had done.

₅₂ They rose up early in the morning, on the twenty-fifth day of the ninth month, which is the month Chislev, in ͬ the one hundred and forty eighth year, ₅₃ and offered sacrifice according to the law on the new altar of burnt offerings which they had made. ₅₄ At the time and day the Gentiles had profaned it, even then it was dedicated with songs, harps, lutes, and with cymbals. ₅₅ All the people fell on their faces, worshipped, and gave praise towards heaven, which had given them good success. ₅₆ They celebrated the dedication of the altar eight days, and offered burnt offerings with gladness, and sacrificed a sacrifice of deliverance and praise. ₅₇ They decorated the front of the temple with crowns of gold and small shields. They dedicated the gates and the priests' chambers, and made doors for them. ₅₈ There was exceedingly great gladness amongst the people, and the reproach of the Gentiles was turned away.

₅₉ Judas and his kindred and the whole congregation of Israel ordained that the days of the dedication of the altar should be kept in their seasons from year to year for eight days, from the twenty-fifth day of the month Chislev, with gladness and joy.

₆₀ At that time, they fortified mount Zion with high walls and strong towers around it, lest perhaps the Gentiles might come and trample them down, as they had done before. ₆₁ Judas stationed a garrison to guard it. They fortified Bethsura to keep it, that the people might have a stronghold near Idumaea.

5

₁ It came to pass, when the Gentiles all around heard that the altar had been rebuilt and the sanctuary dedicated as before, they were exceedingly angry. ₂ They took counsel to destroy the race of Jacob that was in the midst of them, and they began to kill and destroy amongst the people. ₃ Judas fought against the children of Esau in Idumaea at Akrabattine, because they besieged Israel. He struck them with a great slaughter, humbled them, and took their spoils. ₄ He remembered the wickedness of the children of ᵍ Baean, who were a snare and a stumbling block to the people, lying in wait for them on the highways. ₅ They were shut up by him in the towers. He encamped against them, and destroyed them utterly, and burnt with fire the towers of the place with all who were in them. ₆ He passed over to the children of Ammon, and found a mighty band and many people, with Timotheus for their leader. ₇ He fought many battles with them, and they were defeated before his face. He struck them, ₈ and took possession of Jazer and its villages, ʰ and returned again into Judea.

₉ The Gentiles who were in Gilead gathered themselves together against the Israelites who were on their borders, to destroy them. They fled to the stronghold of Dathema, ₁₀ and sent letters to Judas and his kindred, saying, "The Gentiles who are around us are gathered together against us to destroy us. ₁₁ They are preparing to come and get possession of the stronghold where we fled for refuge, and Timotheus is the leader of their army. ₁₂ Now therefore come and deliver us from their hand, for many of us have fallen. ₁₃ All our kindred who were in the land of ᶦ Tubias have been put to death. They have carried their wives, their children, and their stuff into captivity. They destroyed about a thousand men there."

₁₄ While the letters were still being read, behold, other messengers came from Galilee with their clothes torn, bringing a similar report,

---

ᵃ 4:15 Gr. Gazera.
ᵇ 4:22 Gr. foreigners.
ᶜ 4:30 Gr. foreigners.
ᵈ 4:40 Compare Numbers 31:6.
ᵉ 4:40 Gr. trumpets of signals.

ᶠ 4:52 circa B.C. 165.
ᵍ 5:4 Compare 2 Maccabees 10:18-23.
ʰ 5:8 Gr. daughters. Compare Numbers 21:25.
ᶦ 5:13 Compare 2 Maccabees 12:17.

15 saying, "People of Ptolemais, of Tyre, of Sidon, and all Galilee of the[a] Gentiles have gathered together to destroy us."

16 Now when Judas and the people heard these words, a great congregation assembled together to determine what they should do for their kindred who were in distress and under attack. 17 Judas said to Simon his brother, "Choose men and go deliver your kindred who are in Galilee, but Jonathan my brother and I will go into the land of Gilead." 18 He left Joseph the son of Zacharias, and Azarias, as leaders of the people, with the remnant of the army, in Judea, to guard it. 19 He commanded them, saying, "Take charge of this people, and fight no battle with the Gentiles until we return." 20 Then three thousand men were assigned to go into Galilee with Simon, but eight thousand men were assigned to Judas to go into the land of Gilead.

21 Simon went into Galilee and fought many battles with the Gentiles, and the Gentiles were defeated before him. 22 He pursued them to the gate of Ptolemais. About three thousand men of the Gentiles fell, and he took their spoils. 23 They took to them those who were in Galilee and in Arbatta, with their wives, their children, and all that they had, and brought them into Judea with great gladness. 24 Judas Maccabaeus and his brother Jonathan passed over the Jordan, and went three days' journey in the wilderness. 25 They met with the Nabathaeans, and these met them in a peaceful manner and told them all things that had happened to their kindred in the land of Gilead, 26 and how many of them were shut up in Bosora, Bosor, Alema,[b] Casphor, Maked, and[c] Carnaim—all these cities are strong and large— 27 and how they were shut up in the rest of the cities of the land of Gilead, and that tomorrow they planned to encamp against the strongholds, and to take them, and to destroy all these men in one day.

28 Judas and his army turned suddenly by the way of the wilderness to Bosora; and he took the city, and killed all the males with the edge of the sword, took all their spoils, and burnt the city with fire. 29 He left there at night, and went until he came to the stronghold. 30 When the morning came, they lifted up their eyes and saw many people who couldn't be counted, bearing ladders and engines of war, to take the stronghold; and they were fighting against them. 31 Judas saw that the battle had begun, and that the cry of the city went up to heaven, with trumpets and a great sound, 32 and he said to the men of his army, "Fight today for your kindred!" 33 Then he went out behind them in three companies. They sounded their trumpets and cried out in prayer. 34 And the army of Timotheus perceived that it was Maccabaeus, and they fled from before him. He struck them with a great slaughter. About eight thousand men of them fell on that day.

35 He turned away to Mizpeh and fought against it, took it, killed all its males, took its spoils, and burnt it with fire. 36 From there he marched and took[d] Casphor, Maked, Bosor, and the other cities of the land of Gilead.

37 Now after these things, Timotheus gathered another army and encamped near Raphon beyond the brook. 38 Judas sent men to spy on the army; and they brought him word, saying, "All the Gentiles who are around us are gathered together to them, an exceedingly great army. 39 They have hired Arabians to help them, and are encamped beyond the brook, ready to come against you to battle." So Judas went to meet them.

40 Timotheus said to the captains of his army when Judas and his army drew near to the brook of water, "If he crosses over to us first, we won't be able to withstand him, for he will certainly defeat us; 41 but if he is afraid, and encamps beyond the river, we will cross over to him, and defeat him." 42 Now when Judas came near to the water brook, he caused the scribes of the people to remain by the brook, and commanded them saying, "Allow no man to encamp, but let all come to the battle." 43 Then he crossed over the first against them, and all the people after him; and all the Gentiles were defeated before his face, and threw away their weapons, and fled to the temple at[e] Carnaim. 44 They took the city and burnt the temple with fire, together with all who were in it. Carnaim was subdued. They couldn't stand any longer before the face of Judas.

45 Judas gathered together all Israel, those who were in the land of Gilead, from the least to the greatest, with their wives, their children, and their stuff, an exceedingly great army, that they might come into the land of Judah. 46 They came as far as Ephron, and this same city was large and very strong. It was on the road where they were going. They couldn't turn away from it on the right hand or on the left, but needed to pass through the middle of it. 47 The people of the city shut them out and blocked the gates with stones. 48 Judas sent to them with words of peace, saying, "We will pass through your land to go into our own land, and no one will harm you. We will only pass by on our feet." But they wouldn't open to him. 49 Then Judas commanded proclamation to be made in the army, that each man should encamp in the place where he was. 50 So the men of the army encamped, and fought against the city all that day and all that night, and the city was delivered into his hands. 51 He destroyed all the males with the edge of the sword, razed the city, took its plunder, and passed through the city over those who were slain. 52 They went over the Jordan into the great plain near Bethshan. 53 And Judas gathered together those who lagged behind and encouraged the people all the way through, until he came into the land of Judah. 54 They went up to mount Zion with gladness and joy, and offered whole burnt offerings, because not so much as one of them was slain until they returned in peace.

55 In the days when Judas and Jonathan were in the land of Gilead, and Simon his brother in Galilee before Ptolemais, 56 Joseph the son of Zacharias, and Azarias, rulers of the army, heard of their exploits and of the war, and what things they had done. 57 They said, "Let's also get us a name, and let's go fight against the Gentiles who are around us." 58 So they gave orders to the men of the army that was with them, and went towards Jamnia. 59 Gorgias and his men came out of the city to meet them in battle. 60 Joseph and Azarias were put to flight, and were pursued to the borders of Judea. About two thousand men of Israel fell on that day. 61 There was a great overthrow amongst the people, because they didn't listen to Judas and his kindred, thinking to do some exploit. 62 But they were not of the family of those men by whose hand deliverance was given to Israel.

63 The man Judas and his kindred were glorified exceedingly in the sight of all Israel, and of all the Gentiles, wherever their name was heard of. 64 Men gathered together to them, acclaiming them.

65 Judas and his kindred went out and fought against the children of Esau in the land towards the south. He struck Hebron and its villages,[f] pulled down its strongholds, and burnt its towers all around. 66 He marched to go into the land of the[g] Philistines, and he went through[h] Samaria. 67 In that day certain priests, desiring to do exploits there, were slain in battle, when they went out to battle unadvisedly. 68 But Judas turned towards Azotus, to the land of the[i] Philistines, pulled down their altars, burnt the carved images of their gods with fire, took the plunder of their cities, and returned into the land of Judah.

6

1 King Antiochus was travelling through the upper countries; and he heard that in Elymais in Persia there was a city renowned for riches, for silver and gold, 2 and that the temple which was in it was exceedingly rich, and that in it were golden shields, breastplates, and weapons which Alexander, son of Philip, the Macedonian king, who reigned first amongst the Greeks, left behind there. 3 So he came and tried to take the city and to pillage it; and he was not able, because his plan was known to them of the city, 4 and they rose up against him in battle. He fled and returned to Babylon with great disappointment.

5 Then someone came into Persia bringing him news that the armies which went against the land of Judah had been put to flight, 6 and that Lysias went first with a strong army and was put to shame before them, and that they had grown strong because of weapons, power, and a supply of plunder which they took from the armies that they had cut off, 7 and that they had pulled down the abomination which he had built upon the altar that was in Jerusalem, and that they had surrounded the sanctuary with high walls, as before, and also Bethsura, his city.

8 It came to pass, when the king heard these words, he was astonished and moved exceedingly. He laid himself down on his bed, and fell sick for grief, because it had not turned out for him as he had planned. 9 He was there many days, because great grief continually gripped him, and he realised that he would die. 10 He called for all his[j] friends, and said to them, "Sleep departs from my eyes, and my heart fails because of worry. 11 I said in my heart, 'To what suffering I have come! How great a flood it is that I'm in, now! For I was gracious and loved in my power.' 12 But now I remember the evils which I did at Jerusalem, and that I took all the vessels of silver and gold that were in it, and sent out to destroy the inhabitants of Judah without a cause. 13 I perceive that it is because of this that these evils have come upon me. Behold, I am perishing through great grief in a strange land."

14 Then he called for Philip, one of his[k] friends, and set him over all his kingdom. 15 He gave him his crown, his robe, and his signet ring, so that he could guide Antiochus his son, and nourish him up that he might be king. 16 Then King Antiochus died there in the one hundred and forty-ninth year.[l] 17 When Lysias learnt that the king was dead, he set up Antiochus his son to reign, whom he had nourished up being young, and he called his name Eupator.

18 Those who were in the citadel kept hemming Israel in around the sanctuary, and always sought to harm them and to strengthen the Gentiles. 19 Judas planned to destroy them, and called all the people together to besiege them. 20 They were gathered together, and besieged them in[m] the one hundred fiftieth year, and he made mounds to shoot from, and engines of war. 21 Some of those who were hemmed in came out, and some of the ungodly men of Israel were joined to them. 22 They went to the king, and said, "How long will you not execute judgement, and avenge our kindred? 23 We were willing to serve your father and to live by his words, and to follow his commandments. 24 Because of this, the children of our people besieged the citadel[n] and were alienated from us; but as many of us as they could catch, they killed, and plundered our inheritances. 25 Not against us only did they stretch out their hand, but also against all their borders. 26 Behold, they are encamped this day against the citadel at Jerusalem to take it. They have fortified the sanctuary and Bethsura. 27 If you don't

---

a *5:15* Gr. foreigners.
b *5:26* Compare 2 Maccabees 12:13.
c *5:26* compare 2 Maccabees 12:21.
d *5:36* See 1 Maccabees 5:26
e *5:43* See 1 Maccabees 5:26.
f *5:65* Gr. daughters. Compare Numbers 21:25.
g *5:66* Gr. foreigners.

h *5:66* Or, Marisa See Josephus, Antiquities 12:8. 6, and 2 Maccabees 12:35.
i *5:68* Gr. foreigners.
j *6:10* See 1 Maccabees 2:18.
k *6:14* See 1 Maccabees 2:18.
l *6:16* Circa B.C. 164.
m *6:20* circa B.C. 163.
n *6:24* Gr. it.

quickly prevent them, they will do greater things than these, and you won't be able to control them.

₂₈ When the king heard this, he was angry, and gathered together all his[a] friends, the rulers of his army, and those who were over the cavalry. ₂₉ Bands of hired soldiers came to him from other kingdoms and from islands of the sea. ₃₀ The number of his forces was one hundred thousand infantry, and twenty thousand cavalry, and thirty-two elephants trained for war. ₃₁ They went through Idumaea, and encamped against Bethsura, and fought against it many days, and made engines of war. The Jews came out and burnt them with fire, and fought valiantly.

₃₂ Judas marched away from the citadel and encamped at Bethzacharias, near the king's camp. ₃₃ The king rose early in the morning, and marched his army[b] at full speed along the road to Bethzacharias. His forces made themselves ready to battle and sounded their trumpets. ₃₄ They offered the elephants the juice of grapes and mulberries, that they might prepare them for the battle. ₃₅ They distributed the animals amongst the phalanxes. They set by each elephant a thousand men armed with coats of mail and helmets of brass on their heads. Five hundred chosen cavalry were appointed for each elephant. ₃₆ These were ready beforehand, wherever the elephant was. Wherever the elephant went, they went with it. They didn't leave it. ₃₇ Strong, covered wooden towers were upon them, one upon each elephant, fastened upon it with secure harnesses. Upon each were four valiant men who fought upon them, beside his Indian driver. ₃₈ The rest of the cavalry he set on this side and that side on the two flanks of the army, striking terror into the enemy, and protected by the phalanxes. ₃₉ Now when the sun shone upon the shields of gold and brass, the mountains lit up, and blazed like flaming torches.

₄₀ A part of the king's army was spread upon the high hills and some on the low ground, and they went on firmly and in order. ₄₁ All who heard the noise of their multitude, the marching of the multitude, and the rattling of the weapons trembled; for the army was exceedingly great and strong. ₄₂ Judas and his army drew near for battle, and six hundred men of the king's army fell. ₄₃ Eleazar, who was called Avaran, saw one of the animals armed with royal breastplates, and it was taller than all the animals, and the king seemed to be on it. ₄₄ He gave his life to deliver his people, and to get himself an everlasting name. ₄₅ He ran upon him courageously into the midst of the phalanx, and killed on the right hand and on the left, and they parted away from him on this side and on that. ₄₆ He crept under the elephant, and stabbed it from beneath, and killed it. The elephant fell to the earth upon him, and he died there. ₄₇ They saw the strength of the kingdom and the fierce attack of the army, and turned away from them.

₄₈ But the soldiers of the king's army went up to Jerusalem to meet them, and the king encamped towards Judea and towards mount Zion. ₄₉ He made peace with the people of Bethsura. He came out of the city because they had no food there to endure the siege, because it was a Sabbath to the land. ₅₀ The king took Bethsura, and appointed a garrison there to keep it. ₅₁ He encamped against the sanctuary many days; and set there mounds to shoot from, and engines of war, and machines for throwing fire and stones, and weapons to throw darts, and slings. ₅₂ The Jews also made engines of war against their engines, and fought for many days. ₅₃ But there was no food in the sanctuary, because it was the seventh year, and those who fled for safety into Judea from amongst the Gentiles had eaten up the rest of the stores. ₅₄ There were only a few people left in the sanctuary, because the famine prevailed against them, and they were scattered, each man to his own place.

₅₅ Lysias heard that Philip, whom Antiochus the king, while he was yet alive, appointed to raise his son Antiochus to be king, ₅₆ had returned from Persia and Media, and with him the forces that went with the king, and that he was seeking to take control of the government. ₅₇ He made haste, and gave orders to depart. He said to the king and the leaders of the army and to the men, "We get weaker daily, our food is scant, the place where we encamp is strong, and the affairs of the kingdom lie upon us. ₅₈ Now therefore let's negotiate with these men, and make peace with them and with all their nation, ₅₉ and covenant with them, that they may walk after their own laws, as before; for because of their laws which we abolished they were angered, and did all these things."

₆₀ The speech pleased the king and the princes, and he sent to them to make peace; and they accepted it. ₆₁ The king and the princes swore to them. On these conditions, they came out from the stronghold. ₆₂ Then the king entered into mount Zion. He saw the strength of the place, and broke the oath which he had sworn, and gave orders to pull down the wall all around. ₆₃ Then he left in haste and returned to Antioch, and found Philip master of the city. He fought against him, and took the city by force.

7

₁ In the one hundred and fifty first year,[c] Demetrius the son of Seleucus came out of Rome, and went up with a few men to a city by the sea, and reigned there. ₂ It came to pass, when he would go into the house of the kingdom of his fathers, that the army laid hands on Antiochus and Lysias, to bring them to him. ₃ The thing became known to him, and he said, "Don't show me their faces!" ₄ So the army killed them. Then Demetrius sat upon the throne of his kingdom.

₅ All the lawless and ungodly men of Israel came to him. Alcimus was their leader, desiring to be high priest. ₆ They accused the people to the king, saying, "Judas and his kindred have destroyed all your friends, and have scattered us from our own land. ₇ Now therefore send a man whom you trust, and let him go and see all the destruction which he has brought on us and the king's country, and how he has punished them and all who helped them." ₈ So the king chose Bacchides, one of the king's[d] friends, who was ruler in the country beyond the river, and was a great man in the kingdom, and faithful to the king. ₉ He sent him and that ungodly Alcimus, whom he made the high priest; and he commanded him to take vengeance upon the children of Israel.

₁₀ They marched away and came with a great army into the land of Judah. He sent messengers to Judas and his kindred with words of peace deceitfully. ₁₁ They paid no attention to their words; for they saw that they had come with a great army. ₁₂ A group of scribes gathered together to Alcimus and Bacchides to seek just terms. ₁₃ The[e] Hasidaeans were the first amongst the children of Israel who sought peace from them, ₁₄ for they said, "One who is a priest of the seed of Aaron has come with the army, and he will do us no wrong." ₁₅ He spoke with them words of peace, and swore to them, saying, "We won't seek to harm you or your friends." ₁₆ They trusted him. Then he seized sixty men of them, and killed them in one day, according to the word which was written,

₁₇ [f] The flesh of your saints
  and their blood was shed all around Jerusalem,
  and there was no one to bury them.

₁₈ The fear and the dread of them fell upon all the people, for they said, "There is neither truth nor justice in them; for they have broken the covenant and the oath which they swore." ₁₉ Bacchides withdrew from Jerusalem, and encamped in Bezeth. He sent and seized many of the deserters who were with him, and some of the people, and he killed them, throwing them into a large pit. ₂₀ He placed Alcimus in charge of the country and left with him a force to aid him. Then Bacchides went away to the king.

₂₁ Alcimus struggled to maintain his high priesthood. ₂₂ All those who troubled their people joined him, and they took control of the land of Judah, and did great damage in Israel. ₂₃ Judas saw all the wrongs that Alcimus and his company had done amongst the children of Israel, even more than the Gentiles. ₂₄ He went out into all the borders of Judea and took vengeance on the men who had deserted from him, and they were restrained from going out into the country. ₂₅ But when Alcimus saw that Judas and his company had grown strong, and knew that he was not able to withstand them, he returned to the king, and brought evil accusations against them.

₂₆ [g] Then the king sent Nicanor, one of his honourable princes, a man who hated Israel and was their enemy, and commanded him to destroy the people. ₂₇ Nicanor came to Jerusalem with a great army. He sent to Judas and his kindred deceitfully with words of peace, saying, ₂₈ "Let there be no battle between me and you; I will come with a few men, that I may see your faces in peace." ₂₉ He came to Judas, and they saluted one another peaceably. The enemies were ready to seize Judas by violence. ₃₀ This was known to Judas, that he came to him with deceit, and he was very afraid of him, and would see his face no more. ₃₁ Nicanor found out that his plan was disclosed; and he went out to meet Judas in battle beside Capharsalama. ₃₂ About five hundred men of Nicanor's army fell, and the rest fled into the city of David.

₃₃ After these things, Nicanor went up to mount Zion. Some of the priests came out of the sanctuary, with some of the elders of the people, to salute him peaceably, and to show him the whole burnt sacrifice that was being offered for the king. ₃₄ He mocked them, laughed at them, derided them shamefully,[h] spoke arrogantly, ₃₅ and swore in a rage, saying, "Unless Judas and his army are now delivered into my hands, it shall be that, if I return safely, I will burn up this house!" And he went out in a great rage. ₃₆ The priests entered in, and stood before the altar and the temple; and they wept, and said, ₃₇ "You chose this house to be called by your name, to be a house of prayer and supplication for your people. ₃₈ Take vengeance on this man and his army, and let them fall by the sword. Remember their blasphemies, and don't allow them to live any longer."

₃₉ Then Nicanor went out from Jerusalem and encamped in Bethhoron, and there the Syrian army met him. ₄₀ Judas encamped in Adasa with three thousand men. Judas prayed and said, ₄₁ "When those who came from the king blasphemed, your angel went out, and struck amongst them one hundred and eighty-five thousand. ₄₂ Even so, crush this army before us today, and let all the rest know that he has spoken wickedly against your sanctuary. Judge him according to his wickedness." ₄₃ On the thirteenth day of the month Adar, the armies met in battle. Nicanor's army was defeated, and he himself was the first to fall in the battle. ₄₄ Now when his army saw that Nicanor had fallen, they threw away their weapons and fled. ₄₅ They pursued them a day's journey from Adasa until you come to[i] Gazara, and they sounded an alarm after them with the signal trumpets. ₄₆ Men came out of all the surrounding villages of Judea, and outflanked them. These turned them back on those, and they all fell by the sword. There wasn't one of them left. ₄₇ The Jews took the spoils and the booty, and they cut off Nicanor's head and his right hand, which he had stretched out so arrogantly, and brought them, and hung them up beside Jerusalem. ₄₈ The

---

a *6:28* See 1 Maccabees 2:18.
b *6:33* Or, itself eager for the fight
c *7:1* circa B.C. 162.
d *7:8* See 1 Maccabees 2:18.
e *7:13* That is, Chasidim.

f *7:17* Psalms 79:2, 3.
g *7:26* See 2 Maccabees 14:12.
h *7:34* Gr. polluted them.
i *7:45* Gr. Gazera.

people were exceedingly glad, and they kept that day as a day of great gladness. 49 aThey ordained to keep this day year by year on the thirteenth day of Adar. 50 So the land of Judah had rest a few days.

8

1 Judas heard of the fame of the Romans, that they are valiant men, and have pleasure in all who join themselves to them, and make friends with all who come to them, 2 and that they are valiant men. They told him of their wars and exploits which they do amongst the Gauls, and how they conquered them, and forced them to pay tribute; 3 and what things they did in the land of Spain, that they might take control of the silver and gold mines which were there; 4 and how by their policy and persistence they conquered all the place (and the place was exceedingly far from them), and the kings who came against them from the uttermost part of the earth, until they had defeated them, and struck them severely; and how the rest give them tribute year by year. 5 Philip, and Perseus, king of Chittim, and those who lifted up themselves against them, they defeated in battle, and conquered them. 6 Antiochus also, the great king of Asia, came against them to battle, having one hundred and twenty elephants, with cavalry, chariots, and an exceedingly great army, and he was defeated by them. 7 They took him alive, and decreed that both he and those who reigned after him should give them a great tribute, and should give hostages, and a parcel of land from the best of their provinces: 8 the countries of India, Media, and Lydia. They took them from him, and gave them to King Eumenes. 9 Judas heard how the Greeks planned to come and destroy them, 10 but this became known to them, and they sent against them a general who fought against them, and many of them fell down wounded to death, and they made captive their wives and their children, and plundered them, and conquered their land, and pulled down their strongholds, and plundered them, and brought them into bondage to this day. 11 The remaining kingdoms and islands, as many as rose up against them at any time, they destroyed and made them to be their servants; 12 but with their friends and those who relied on them they stayed friends. They conquered the kingdoms that were near and those that were far off, and all that heard of their fame were afraid of them. 13 Moreover, whoever they desired to help and to make kings, these they make kings; and whoever they desired, they depose. They are exalted exceedingly. 14 For all this, none of them ever put on a crown, neither did they clothe themselves with purple, as a display of grandeur. 15 Judas heard how they had made for themselves a senate house, and day by day, three hundred and twenty men sat in council, consulting always for the people, to the end they might be well governed, 16 and how they commit their government to one man year by year, that he should rule over them, and control all their country, and all are obedient to that one, and there is neither envy nor emulation amongst them.

17 So Judas chose Eupolemus the son of John, the son of Accos, and Jason the son of Eleazar, and sent them to Rome, to establish friendship and alliance with them, 18 and that they should free the yoke from themselves; for they saw that the kingdom of the Greeks kept Israel in bondage. 19 Then they went to Rome, a very long journey, and they entered into the senate house, and said, 20 "Judas, who is also called Maccabaeus, and his kindred, and the people of the Jews, have sent us to you, to make an alliance and peace with you, and that we might be registered as your allies and friends."

21 This thing was pleasing to them. 22 This is the copy of the writing which they wrote back again on tables of brass, and sent to Jerusalem, that it might be with them there for a memorial of peace and alliance:

23 "Good success be to the Romans, and to the nation of the Jews, by sea and by land forever. May the sword and the enemy be far from them. 24 But if war arises for Rome first, or any of their allies in all their dominion, 25 the nation of the Jews shall help them as allies, as the occasion shall indicate to them, with all their heart. 26 To those who make war upon them, they shall not give supplies, food, weapons, money, or ships, as it has seemed good to Rome, and they shall keep their ordinances without taking anything in return. 27 In the same way, moreover, if war comes first upon the nation of the Jews, the Romans shall willingly help them as allies, as the occasion shall indicate to them; 28 and to those who are fighting with them, there shall not be given food, weapons, money, or ships, as it has seemed good to Rome. They shall keep these ordinances, and that without deceit. 29 According to these terms, the Romans made a treaty with the Jewish people. 30 But if hereafter the one party and the other shall determine to add or diminish anything, they shall do it at their pleasure, and whatever they add or take away shall be ratified.

31 Concerning the evils which King Demetrius is doing to them, we have written to him, saying, 'Why have you made your yoke heavy on our friends and allies the Jews? 32 If therefore they plead any more against you, we will do them justice, and fight with you on sea and on land.'"

9

1 Demetrius heard that Nicanor had fallen with his forces in battle, and he sent Bacchides and Alcimus again into the land of Judah a second time, and the right wing of his army with them. 2 They went by the way that leads to Gilgal, and encamped against Mesaloth, which is in Arbela, and took possession of it, and killed many people. 3 The first month of the one hundred and fifty-second year, b they encamped against Jerusalem. 4 Then they marched away and went to Berea with twenty thousand infantry and two thousand cavalry. 5 Judas was encamped at Elasa with three thousand chosen men. 6 They saw the multitude of the forces, that they were many,

and they were terrified. Many slipped away out of the army. There were not left of them more than eight hundred men.

7 Judas saw that his army slipped away and that the battle pressed upon him, and he was very troubled in spirit, because he had no time to gather them together, and he became faint. 8 He said to those who were left, "Let's arise and go up against our adversaries, if perhaps we may be able to fight with them."

9 They tried to dissuade him, saying, "There is no way we are able; but let's rather save our lives now. Let's return again with our kindred, and fight against them; but we are too few."

10 Judas said, "Let it not be so that I should do this thing, to flee from them. If our time has come, let's die in a manly way for our kindred's sake, and not leave a cause of reproach against our honour."

11 The army marched out from the camp, and stood to encounter them. The cavalry was divided into two companies, and the slingers and the archers went before the army, and all the mighty men that fought in the front of the battle. 12 Bacchides was in the right wing. The phalanx advanced on the two parts, and they blew with their trumpets. 13 The men by Judas' side sounded with their trumpets, and the earth shook with the shout of the armies, and the battle was joined, and continued from morning until evening.

14 Judas saw that Bacchides and the strength of his army were on the right side, and all that were brave in heart went with him, 15 and the right wing was defeated by them, and he pursued after them to the mount Azotus. 16 Those who were on the left wing saw that the right wing was defeated, and they turned and followed in the footsteps of Judas and of those who were with him. 17 The battle became desperate, and many on both sides fell wounded to death. 18 Judas fell, and the rest fled.

19 Jonathan and Simon took Judas their brother, and buried him in the tomb of his ancestors at Modin. 20 They wept for him. All Israel made great lamentation for him, and mourned many days, and said, 21 "How is the mighty fallen, the saviour of Israel!" 22 The rest of the acts of Judas, and his wars, and the valiant deeds which he did, and his greatness, are not written; for they were exceedingly many.

23 It came to pass after the death of Judas, that the lawless emerged within all the borders of Israel. All those who did iniquity rose up. 24 In those days there was an exceedingly great famine, and the country went over to their side. 25 Bacchides chose the ungodly men and made them rulers of the country. 26 They enquired and searched for the friends of Judas, and brought them to Bacchides, and he took vengeance on them and used them despitefully. 27 There was great suffering in Israel, such as was not since the time prophets stopped appearing to them.

28 All the friends of Judas were gathered together, and they said to Jonathan, 29 "Since your brother Judas has died, we have no man like him to go out against our enemies and Bacchides, and amongst those of our nation who hate us. 30 Now therefore we have chosen you this day to be our prince and leader in his place, that you may fight our battles." 31 So Jonathan took the governance upon him at that time, and rose up in the place of his brother Judas.

32 When Bacchides found out, he tried to kill him. 33 Jonathan, and Simon his brother, and all who were with him, knew it; and they fled into the wilderness of Tekoah, and encamped by the water of the pool of Asphar. 34 Bacchides found this out on the Sabbath day, and came—he and all his army—over the Jordan.

35 Jonathan sent his brother, a leader of the multitude, and implored his friends the Nabathaeans, that they might store their baggage, which was much, with them. 36 The children of Jambri came out of Medaba, and seized John and all that he had, and went their way with it.

37 But after these things, they brought word to Jonathan and Simon his brother that the children of Jambri were celebrating a great wedding, and were bringing the bride, a daughter of one of the great nobles of Canaan, from Nadabath with a large escort. 38 They remembered John their brother, and went up, and hid themselves under the cover of the mountain. 39 They lifted up their eyes and looked, and saw a great procession with much baggage. The bridegroom came out with his friends and his kindred to meet them with timbrels, musicians, and many weapons. 40 They rose up against them from their ambush and killed them, and many fell wounded to death. The remnant fled into the mountain, and the Jews took all their spoils. 41 So the wedding was turned into mourning, and the voice of their musicians into lamentation. 42 They avenged fully the blood of their brother, and turned back to the marshes of the Jordan.

43 Bacchides heard it, and he came on the Sabbath day to the banks of Jordan with a great army. 44 Jonathan said to his company, "Let's stand up now and fight for our lives, for things are different today than they were yesterday and the day before. 45 For, behold, the battle is before us and behind us. Moreover the water of the Jordan is on this side and on that side, and marsh and thicket. There is no place to escape. 46 Now therefore cry to heaven, that you may be delivered out of the hand of your enemies." 47 So the battle was joined, and Jonathan stretched out his hand to strike Bacchides, and he turned away back from him. 48 Jonathan and those who were with him leapt into the Jordan, and swam over to the other side. The enemy didn't pass over the Jordan against them. 49 About a thousand men of Bacchides' company fell that day; 50 and he returned to Jerusalem. They built strong cities in Judea, the stronghold that was in Jericho, and Emmaus, Bethhoron, Bethel, Timnath, Pharathon, and Tephon, with high walls and gates and bars. 51 He set garrisons in them to harass Israel. 52 He fortified the city Bethsura, Gazara, and the citadel, and put troops and

_____

a *7:49* See 2 Maccabees 15:36.

b *9:3* circa B.C. 161.

stores of food in them. 53 He took the sons of the chief men of the country for hostages, and put them under guard in the citadel at Jerusalem.

54 And in the one hundred and fifty-third year,[a] in the second month, Alcimus gave orders to pull down the wall of the inner court of the sanctuary. He also pulled down the works of the prophets. 55 He began to pull down. At that time was Alcimus stricken, and his works were hindered; and his mouth was stopped, and he was taken with a palsy, and he could no more speak anything and give orders concerning his house. 56 Alcimus died at that time with great torment. 57 Bacchides saw that Alcimus was dead, and he returned to the king. Then the land of Judah had rest for two years.

58 Then all the lawless men took counsel, saying, "Behold, Jonathan and his men are dwelling at ease and in security. Now therefore we will bring Bacchides, and he will capture them all in one night. 59 They went and consulted with him. 60 He marched out and came with a great army, and sent letters secretly to all his allies who were in Judea, that they should seize Jonathan and those who were with him; but they couldn't, because their plan was known to them. 61 Jonathan's men seized about fifty of the men of the country who were authors of the wickedness, and he killed them. 62 Jonathan, Simon, and those who were with him, went away to Bethbasi, which is in the wilderness, and he built up that which had been pulled down, and they made it strong. 63 Bacchides found out about it, and he gathered together all his multitude, and sent orders to those who were of Judea. 64 He went and encamped against Bethbasi and fought against it many days, and made engines of war.

65 Jonathan left his brother Simon in the city, and went out into the country, and he went with a few men. 66 He struck Odomera and his kindred, and the children of Phasiron in their tents. 67 They began to strike them, and to go up with their forces. Then Simon and those who were with him went out of the city, and set the engines of war on fire, 68 and fought against Bacchides, and he was defeated by them. They afflicted him severely; for his counsel and expedition was in vain. 69 They were very angry with the lawless men who gave him counsel to come into the country, and they killed many of them. Then they decided to depart into his own land.

70 Jonathan learnt of this and sent ambassadors to him, to the end that they should make peace with him, and that he should restore to them the captives. 71 He accepted the thing, and did according to his words, and swore to him that he would not seek his harm all the days of his life. 72 He restored to him the captives which he had taken before out of the land of Judah, and he returned and departed into his own land, and didn't come any more into their borders. 73 Thus the sword ceased from Israel. Jonathan lived at Michmash. Jonathan began to judge the people; and he destroyed the ungodly out of Israel.

10

1 In the one hundred sixtieth year,[b] Alexander Epiphanes, the son of Antiochus, went up and took possession of Ptolemais. They received him, and he reigned there. 2 King Demetrius heard about this, and he gathered together exceedingly great forces, and went out to meet him in battle.

3 Demetrius sent a letter to Jonathan with words of peace, so as to honour him. 4 For he said, "Let's go beforehand to make peace with them, before he makes peace with Alexander against us; 5 for he will remember all the evils that we have done against him, and to his kindred and to his nation." 6 So he gave him authority to gather together forces, and to provide weapons, and that he should be his ally. He also commanded that they should release the hostages that were in the citadel to him.

7 Jonathan came to Jerusalem, and read the letter in the hearing of all the people, and of those who were in the citadel. 8 They were very afraid when they heard that the king had given him authority to gather together an army. 9 Those in the citadel released the hostages to Jonathan, and he restored them to their parents.

10 Jonathan lived in Jerusalem and began to build and renew the city. 11 He commanded those who did the work to build the walls and encircle Mount Zion with[c] square stones for defence; and they did so. 12 The foreigners who were in the strongholds which Bacchides had built fled away. 13 Each man left his place and departed into his own land. 14 Only at Bethsura, there were left some of those who had forsaken the law and the commandments, for it was a place of refuge to them.

15 King Alexander heard all the promises which Demetrius had sent to Jonathan. They told him of the battles and the valiant deeds which he and his kindred had done, and of the troubles which they had endured. 16 So he said, "Could we find another man like him? Now we will make him our[d] friend and ally." 17 He wrote a letter and sent it to him, in these words, saying, 18 "King Alexander to his brother Jonathan, greetings. 19 We have heard of you, that you are a mighty man of valour, and worthy to be our[e] friend. 20 Now we have appointed you this day to be high priest of your nation, and to be called the king's[f] friend, and to take our side, and to keep friendship with us." He also sent to him a purple robe and a golden crown.

21 And Jonathan put on the holy garments in the seventh month of the one hundred sixtieth year,[g] at the feast of tabernacles; and he gathered together forces and provided weapons in abundance.

22 When Demetrius heard these things, he was grieved and said, 23 "What is this that we have done, that Alexander has gotten ahead of us in

establishing friendship with the Jews to strengthen himself? 24 I also will write to them words of encouragement and of honour and of gifts, that they may be with me to aid me." 25 So he sent to them this message:

"King Demetrius to the nation of the Jews, greetings. 26 Since as you have kept your covenants with us, and continued in our friendship, and have not joined yourselves to our enemies, we have heard of this, and are glad. 27 Now continue still to keep faith with us, and we will repay you with good in return for your dealings with us. 28 We will grant you many immunities and give you gifts.

29 "Now I free you and release all the Jews from the tributes, from the salt tax, and from the crown levies. 30 Instead of the third part of the seed, and instead of half of the fruit of the trees, which falls to me to receive, I release it from this day and henceforth, so that I will not take it from the land of Judah, and from the three districts which are added to it from the country of Samaria and Galilee, from this day forth and for all time. 31 Let Jerusalem be holy and free, with her borders, tithes, and taxes. 32 I yield up also my authority over the citadel which is at Jerusalem, and give it to the high priest, that he may appoint in it men whom he chooses to keep it. 33 Every soul of the Jews who has been carried captive from the land of Judah into any part of my kingdom, I set at liberty without payment. Let all officials also cancel the taxes on their livestock.

34 "All the feasts, the Sabbaths, new moons, appointed days, three days before a feast, and three days after a feast, let them all be days of immunity and release for all the Jews who are in my kingdom. 35 No man shall have authority to exact anything from any of them, or to trouble them concerning any matter.

36 "Let there be enrolled amongst the king's forces about thirty thousand men of the Jews, and pay shall be given to them, as is due to all the king's forces. 37 Of them, some shall be placed in the king's great strongholds, and some of them shall be placed over the affairs of the kingdom, which are positions of trust. Let those who are over them and their rulers be of themselves, and let them walk after their own laws, even as the king has commanded in the land of Judah.

38 "The three districts that have been added to Judea from the country of Samaria, let them be annexed to Judea, that they may be reckoned to be under one ruler, that they may not obey any other authority than the high priest's. 39 As for Ptolemais and its land, I have given it as a gift to the sanctuary that is at Jerusalem, for the expenses of the sanctuary. 40 I also give every year fifteen thousand shekels of silver from the king's revenues from the places that are appropriate. 41 And all the additional funds which those who manage the king's affairs didn't pay as in the first years, they shall give from now on towards the works of the temple. 42 Besides this, the five thousand shekels of silver which they received from the uses of the sanctuary from the revenue year by year is also released, because it belongs to the priests who minister there. 43 Whoever flees to the temple that is at Jerusalem, and within all of its borders, whether one owe money to the king, or any other matter, let them go free, along with all that they have in my kingdom. 44 For the building and renewing of the structures of the sanctuary, the expense shall also be given out of the king's revenue. 45 For the building of the walls of Jerusalem and fortifying it all around, the expense shall also be given out of the king's revenue, also for the building of the walls in Judea."

46 Now when Jonathan and the people heard these words, they gave no credence to them, and didn't accept them, because they remembered the great evil which he had done in Israel, and that he had afflicted them very severely. 47 They were well pleased with Alexander, because he was the first who spoke words of peace to them, and they were allies with him always.

48 King Alexander gathered together great forces and encamped near Demetrius. 49 The two kings joined battle, and the army of Alexander fled; and Demetrius followed after him, and prevailed against them. 50 He strengthened the battle exceedingly until the sun went down; and Demetrius fell that day.

51 Alexander sent ambassadors to Ptolemy king of Egypt with this message: 52 "Since I have returned to my kingdom, and am seated on the throne of my fathers, and have established my dominion, and have overthrown Demetrius, and have taken possession of our country— 53 yes, I joined the battle with him, and he and his army were defeated by us, and we sat on the throne of his kingdom— 54 now also let's make friends with one another. Give me now your daughter as my wife. I will be joined with you, and will give both you and her gifts worthy of you."

55 Ptolemy the king answered, saying, "Happy is the day you returned to the land of your ancestors and sat on the throne of their kingdom. 56 Now I will do to you as you have written, but meet me at Ptolemais, that we may see one another; and I will join with you, even as you have said." 57 So Ptolemy went out of Egypt, himself and Cleopatra his daughter, and came to Ptolemais in the one hundred and sixty-second year.[h] 58 King Alexander met him, and he gave him his daughter Cleopatra, and celebrated her wedding at Ptolemais with great pomp, as kings do.

59 King Alexander wrote to Jonathan, that he should come to meet him. 60 He went with pomp to Ptolemais, and met the two kings. He gave them and their friends[i] silver and gold, and many gifts, and found favour in their sight. 61 Some malcontents out of Israel, men who were transgressors of the

---

a *9:54* circa B.C. 160.
b *10:1* circa B.C. 153.
c *10:11* So the versions and Josephus. Gr. four-foot stones.
d *10:16* See 1 Maccabees 2:18. Compare 1 Maccabees 10:65.
e *10:19* See 1 Maccabees 2:18. Compare 1 Maccabees 10:65.

f *10:20* See 1 Maccabees 2:18. Compare 1 Maccabees 10:65.
g *10:21* circa B.C. 153.
h *10:57* circa B.C. 151.
i *10:60* See 1 Maccabees 2:18. Compare 1 Maccabees 10:65.

law, gathered together against him to complain against him; but the king paid no attention to them. 62 The king commanded that they take off Jonathan's garments and clothe him in purple, and they did so. 63 The king made him sit with him, and said to his princes, "Go out with him into the midst of the city, and proclaim that no man may complain against him of any matter, and let no man trouble him for any reason." 64 It came to pass, when those who complained against him saw his honour according to the proclamation, and saw him clothed in purple, they all fled away. 65 The king gave him honour, and enrolled him amongst his chief friends,[a] and made him a captain and governor of a province. 66 Then Jonathan returned to Jerusalem with peace and gladness.

67 In the one hundred and sixty-fifth year,[b] Demetrius, son of Demetrius, came out of Crete into the land of his ancestors. 68 When King Alexander heard of it, he grieved exceedingly and returned to Antioch. 69 Demetrius appointed Apollonius, who was over Coelesyria, and he gathered together a great army, and encamped against Jamnia, and sent to Jonathan the high priest, saying,

70 "You alone lift up yourself against us, but I am ridiculed and in reproach because of you. Why do you assume authority against us in the mountains? 71 Now therefore, if you trust in your forces, come down to us into the plain, and let's match strength with each other there; for the power of the cities is with me. 72 Ask and learn who I am, and the rest who help us. They say, 'Your foot can't stand before our face; for your ancestors have been put to flight twice in their own land.' 73 Now you won't be able to withstand the cavalry and such an army as this in the plain, where is there is no stone or pebble, or place to flee."

74 Now when Jonathan heard the words of Apollonius, he was moved in his mind, and he chose ten thousand men, and went out from Jerusalem; and Simon his brother met him to help him. 75 Then he encamped against Joppa. The people of the city shut him out, because Apollonius had a garrison in Joppa. 76 So they fought against it. The people of the city were afraid, and opened to him; and Jonathan became master of Joppa.

77 Apollonius heard about that, and he gathered an army of three thousand cavalry, and a great army, and went to Azotus as though he were on a journey, and at the same time advanced onward into the plain, because he had a multitude of cavalry which he trusted. 78 He pursued him to Azotus, and the armies joined battle.[c] 79 Apollonius had secretly left a thousand cavalry behind them. 80 Jonathan learnt that there was an ambush behind him. They surrounded his army, and shot their arrows at the people, from morning until evening; 81 but the people stood fast, as Jonathan commanded them; and the enemy's horses grew tired.

82 Then Simon brought forward his army and joined battle with the phalanx (for the cavalry were exhausted), and they were defeated by him and fled. 83 The cavalry were scattered in the plain. They fled to Azotus and entered into Beth-dagon, their idol's temple, to save themselves. 84 Jonathan burnt Azotus and the cities around it and took their spoils. He burnt the temple of Dagon and those who fled into it with fire. 85 Those who had fallen by the sword plus those who were burnt were about eight thousand men.

86 From there, Jonathan left and encamped against Ascalon. The people of the city came out to meet him with great pomp. 87 Jonathan, with those who were on his side, returned to Jerusalem, having many spoils. 88 It came to pass, when King Alexander heard these things, he honoured Jonathan even more. 89 He sent him a gold buckle, as the custom is to give to the king's kindred. He gave him Ekron and all its land for a possession.

11

1 Then the king of Egypt gathered together great forces, as the sand which is by the sea shore, and many ships, and sought to make himself master of Alexander's kingdom by deceit, and to add it to his own kingdom. 2 He went out into Syria with words of peace, and the people of the cities opened their gates to him and met him; for King Alexander's command was that they should meet him, because he was his father-in-law. 3 Now as he entered into the cities of Ptolemais, he set his forces for a garrison in each city.

4 But when he came near to Azotus, they showed him the temple of Dagon burnt with fire, and Azotus and its pasture lands destroyed, and the bodies cast out, and those who had been burnt, whom he burnt in the war, for they had made heaps of them in his way. 5 They told the king what Jonathan had done, that they might cast blame on him; but the king kept silent. 6 Jonathan met the king with pomp at Joppa, and they greeted one another, and they slept there. 7 Jonathan went with the king as far as the river that is called Eleutherus, then returned to Jerusalem.

8 But King Ptolemy took control of the cities along the sea coast, to Selucia which is by the sea, and he devised evil plans concerning Alexander. 9 He sent ambassadors to King Demetrius, saying, "Come! Let's make a covenant with one another, and I will give you my daughter whom Alexander has, and you shall reign over your father's kingdom; 10 for I regret that I gave my daughter to him, for he tried to kill me. 11 He accused him, because he coveted his kingdom. 12 Taking his daughter from him, he gave her to Demetrius, and was estranged from Alexander, and their enmity was openly seen.

13 Ptolemy entered into Antioch, and put on himself the crown of Asia. He put two crowns upon his head, the crown of Egypt and that of Asia.

14 But King Alexander was in Cilicia at that time, because the people of that region were in revolt. 15 When Alexander heard of it, he came against him in war. Ptolemy marched out and met him with a strong force, and put him to flight. 16 Alexander fled into Arabia, that he might be sheltered there; but King Ptolemy was triumphant. 17 Zabdiel the Arabian took off Alexander's head, and sent it to Ptolemy. 18 King Ptolemy died the third day after, and those who were in his strongholds were slain by the inhabitants of the strongholds. 19 Demetrius became king in the one hundred and sixty-seventh year.[d]

20 In those days Jonathan gathered together the Judeans to take the citadel that was at Jerusalem. He made many engines of war to use against it. 21 Some lawless men who hated their own nation went to the king and reported to him that Jonathan was besieging the citadel. 22 He heard, and was angry, but when he heard it, he set out immediately, and came to Ptolemais, and wrote to Jonathan, that he should not besiege it, and that he should meet him and speak with him at Ptolemais with all speed.

23 But when Jonathan heard this, he gave orders to continue the siege. He chose some of the elders of Israel and of the priests, and put himself in peril 24 by taking silver, gold, clothing, and various other presents, and went to Ptolemais to the king. Then he found favour in his sight. 25 Some lawless men of those who were of the nation made complaints against him, 26 and the king did to him even as his predecessors had done to him, and exalted him in the sight of all his[e] friends, 27 and confirmed to him the high priesthood, and all the other honours that he had before, and gave him preeminence amongst his[f] chief friends. 28 And Jonathan requested of the king that he would make Judea free from tribute, along with the three[g] provinces and the country of Samaria, and promised him three hundred talents. 29 The king consented, and wrote letters to Jonathan concerning all these things as follows:

30 "King Demetrius to his brother Jonathan, and to the nation of the Jews, greetings. 31 The copy of the letter which we wrote to Lasthenes our kinsman concerning you, we have written also to you, that you may see it. 32 'King Demetrius to Lasthenes his father, greetings. 33 We have determined to do good to the nation of the Jews, who are our friends, and observe what is just towards us, because of their good will towards us. 34 We have confirmed therefore to them the borders of Judea, and also the three governments of Aphaerema, Lydda, and Ramathaim (these were added to Judea from the country of Samaria), and all their territory to them, for all who do sacrifice in Jerusalem, instead of the king's dues which the king received of them yearly before from the produce of the earth and the fruits of trees. 35 As for the other payments to us from henceforth, of the tithes and the taxes that pertain to us, and the salt pits, and the crown taxes due to us, all these we will give back to them. 36 Not one of these grants shall be annulled from this time forth and forever. 37 Now therefore be careful to make a copy of these things, and let it be given to Jonathan, and let it be set up on the holy mountain in a suitable and conspicuous place.'"

38 When King Demetrius saw that the land was quiet before him, and that no resistance was made to him, he sent away all his troops, each man to his own place, except the foreign troops, which he had raised from the islands of the Gentiles. So all the troops of his fathers hated him. 39 Now Tryphon was one of those who previously had been on Alexander's side, and he saw that all the forces murmured against Demetrius. So he went to Imalcue the Arabian, who was raising up Antiochus the young child of Alexander, 40 and urgently insisted to him that he should deliver him to him, that he might reign in his father's place. He told him all that Demetrius had done, and the hatred with which his forces hated him; and he stayed there many days.

41 Now Jonathan sent to King Demetrius, that he should remove the troops of the citadel from Jerusalem, and the troops who were in the strongholds; for they fought against Israel continually. 42 Demetrius sent to Jonathan, saying, "I will not only do this for you and your nation, but I will greatly honour you and your nation, if I find an opportunity. 43 Now therefore you shall do well if you send me men who will fight for me; for all my forces have revolted." 44 So Jonathan sent him three thousand valiant men to Antioch. They came to the king, and the king was glad at their coming. 45 The people of the city gathered themselves together into the midst of the city, to the number of one hundred and twenty thousand men, and they wanted to kill the king. 46 The king fled into the court of the palace, and the people of the city seized the main streets of the city and began to fight. 47 The king called the Jews to help him, and they were gathered together to him all at once, and they dispersed themselves in the city, and killed that day about one hundred thousand. 48 They set the city on fire, and seized many spoils that day, and saved the king. 49 The people of the city saw that the Jews had taken control of the city as they pleased, and they became faint in their hearts, and they cried out to the king with supplication, saying, 50 "Give us your right hand, and let the Jews cease from fighting against us and the city." 51 They threw away their weapons and made peace. The Jews were glorified in the sight of the king, and before all who were in his kingdom. Then they returned to Jerusalem, having much plunder. 52 So King Demetrius sat on the throne of his kingdom, and the land was quiet before him. 53 He lied in all that he spoke, and estranged himself from Jonathan, and didn't repay him according to the benefits with which he had repaid him, and treated him very harshly.

---

[a] 10:65 See 1 Maccabees 11:27; 2 Maccabees 8:9. Compare 1 Maccabees 2:18; 10:16, etc.

[b] 10:67 circa B.C. 148.

[c] 10:78 Most of the authorities here repeat after him.

[d] 11:19 circa B.C. 146.

[e] 11:26 See 1 Maccabees 2:18.

[f] 11:27 See 1 Maccabees 10:65.

[g] 11:28 Gr. toparchies

54 Now after this, Tryphon returned, and with him the young child Antiochus, who reigned and put on a crown. 55 All the forces which Demetrius had sent away with disgrace were gathered to him, and they fought against him, and he fled and was routed. 56 Tryphon took the elephants, and took control of Antioch. 57 The young Antiochus wrote to Jonathan, saying, "I confirm to you the high priesthood, and appoint you over the four districts, and to be one of the king's[a] friends." 58 He sent to him golden vessels and furniture for the table, and gave him permission to drink in golden vessels, and to be clothed in purple, and to have a golden buckle. 59 He made his brother Simon governor from the Ladder of Tyre to the borders of Egypt.

60 Jonathan went out and took his journey beyond the river and through the cities. All the forces of Syria gathered themselves to him to be his allies. He came to Ascalon, and the people of the city met him honourably. 61 He departed from there to Gaza, and the people of Gaza shut him out. So he besieged it and burnt its pasture lands with fire, and plundered them. 62 The people of Gaza pleaded with Jonathan, and he gave them his right hand, and took the sons of their princes for hostages, and sent them away to Jerusalem. Then he passed through the country as far as Damascus.

63 Then Jonathan heard that Demetrius' princes had come to Kedesh, which is in Galilee, with a great army, intending to remove him from his office. 64 He went to meet them, but he left Simon his brother in the country. 65 Simon encamped against Bethsura, and fought against it many days, and hemmed it in. 66 They asked him to give them his right hand, and he gave it to them. He removed them from there, took possession of the city, and set a garrison over it.

67 Jonathan and his army encamped at the water of Gennesareth, and early in the morning they marched to the plain of Hazor. 68 Behold, an army of foreigners met him in the plain. They laid an ambush for him in the mountains, but they themselves met him face to face. 69 But those who lay in ambush rose out of their places and joined battle. All those who were on Jonathan's side fled. 70 Not one of them was left, except Mattathias the son of Absalom, and Judas the son of Chalphi, captains of the forces. 71 Jonathan tore his clothes, put dirt on his head, and prayed. 72 He turned again to them in battle, and routed them, and they fled. 73 When the men on his side who had fled saw this, they returned to him and pursued with him to Kedesh to their camp, and they encamped there. 74 About three thousand men of the foreigners fell on that day. Then Jonathan returned to Jerusalem.

12

1 Jonathan saw that the time was favourable for him, so he chose men and sent them to Rome to confirm and renew the friendship that they had with them. 2 He also sent similar letters to the Spartans, and to other places. 3 They went to Rome, entered into the senate house, and said, "Jonathan the high priest and the nation of the Jews have sent us to renew for them the friendship and the alliance, as in former time." 4 They gave them letters to the men in every place, that they should provide safe conduct for them on their way to the land of Judah. 5 This is the copy of the letters which Jonathan wrote to the Spartans:

6 "Jonathan the high priest, and the senate of the nation, and the priests, and the rest of the people of the Jews, to their kindred the Spartans, greetings. 7 Even before this time letters were sent to Onias the high priest from Arius,[b] who was reigning amongst you, to signify that you are our kindred, as the copy written below shows. 8 Onias welcomed honourably the man who was sent and received the letters, wherein declaration was made of alliance and friendship. 9 Therefore we also, even though we need none of these things, having for our encouragement the holy books which are in our hands, 10 have undertaken to send that we might renew our brotherhood and friendship with you, to the end that we should not become estranged from you altogether; for a long time has passed since you sent your letter to us. 11 We therefore at all times without ceasing, both in our feasts, and on the other convenient days, remember you in the sacrifices which we offer, and in our prayers, as it is right and proper to be mindful of kindred. 12 Moreover, we are glad for your glory. 13 But as for ourselves, many afflictions and many wars have encompassed us, and the kings who are around us have fought against us. 14 We were unwilling to be troublesome to you, and to the rest of our allies and friends, in these wars; 15 for we have the help which is from heaven to help us, and we have been delivered from our enemies, and our enemies have been humbled. 16 We chose therefore Numenius the son of Antiochus and Antipater the son of Jason, and have sent them to the Romans, to renew the friendship that we had with them, and the former alliance. 17 We commanded them therefore to go also to you, and to salute you, and to deliver you our letters concerning the renewing of friendship and our brotherhood. 18 And now you will do well if you give us a reply."

19 And this is the copy of the letters which they sent to Onias:

20 "Arius king of the Spartans to Onias the chief priest, greetings. 21 It has been found in writing, concerning the Spartans and the Jews, that they are kindred, and that they are of the descendants of Abraham. 22 Now, since this has come to our knowledge, you will do well to write to us of your[c] prosperity. 23 We moreover write on our part to you, that your livestock and goods are ours, and ours are yours. We do command therefore that they make report to you accordingly."

24 Now Jonathan heard that Demetrius' princes had returned to fight against him with a greater army than before, 25 so he marched away from Jerusalem, and met them in the country of Hamath; for he gave them no opportunity to set foot in his country. 26 He sent spies into his camp, and they came again, and reported to him that they were preparing to attack them at night. 27 But as soon as the sun was down, Jonathan commanded his men to watch, and to be armed, that all the night long they might be ready for battle. He stationed sentinels around the camp. 28 The adversaries heard that Jonathan and his men were ready for battle, and they feared, and trembled in their hearts, and they kindled fires in their camp then withdrew. 29 But Jonathan and his men didn't know it until the morning; for they saw the fires burning. 30 Jonathan pursued after them, but didn't overtake them; for they had gone over the river Eleutherus. 31 Then Jonathan turned towards the Arabians, who are called Zabadaeans, and struck them, and took their spoils. 32 He came out from there, and came to Damascus, and took his journey through all the country.

33 Simon went out, and took his journey as far as Ascalon, and the strongholds that were near it. Then he turned towards Joppa and took possession of it; 34 for he had heard that they were planning to hand over the stronghold to Demetrius' men. He set a garrison there to guard it.

35 Then Jonathan returned and called the elders of the people together. He planned with them to build strongholds in Judea, 36 and to make the walls of Jerusalem higher, and to raise a great mound between the citadel and the city, to separate it from the city, that so it might be isolated, that its garrison might neither buy nor sell. 37 They were gathered together to build the city. Part of the wall of the brook that is on the east side fell down, and he repaired the section called Chaphenatha. 38 Simon also built Adida in the[d] plain country, made it strong, and set up gates and bars.

39 And Tryphon sought to reign over Asia and to crown himself, and to stretch out his hand against Antiochus the king. 40 He was afraid that Jonathan wouldn't allow him, and that he would fight against him; and he sought a way to seize him, that he might destroy him. So he marched out and came to Bethshan. 41 Jonathan came out to meet him with forty thousand men chosen for battle, and came to Bethshan. 42 Tryphon saw that he came with a great army, and he was afraid to stretch out his hand against him. 43 He received him honourably, and commended him to all his[e] friends, and gave him gifts, and commanded his forces to be obedient to him, as to himself. 44 He said to Jonathan, "Why have you put all this people to so much trouble, seeing there is no war between us? 45 Now send them away to their homes, but choose for yourself a few men who shall be with you, and come with me to Ptolemais, and I will give it to you, and the rest of the strongholds and the rest of the forces, and all the king's officers. Then I will turn around and depart; for this is why I came."

46 He put his trust in him, and did even as he said, and sent away his forces, and they departed into the land of Judah. 47 But he reserved to himself three thousand men, of whom he left two thousand in Galilee, but one thousand went with him. 48 Now as soon as Jonathan entered into Ptolemais, the people of Ptolemais shut the gates and seized him. They killed all those who came in with him with the sword.

49 Tryphon sent troops and cavalry into Galilee, and into the Great Plain, to destroy all Jonathan's men. 50 They perceived that he had been seized and had perished, along with those who were with him. They encouraged one another and went on their way close together, prepared to fight. 51 Those who followed them saw that they were ready to fight for their lives, and turned back again. 52 They all came in peace into the land of Judah, and they mourned for Jonathan and those who were with him, and they were very afraid. All Israel mourned with a great mourning. 53 And all the Gentiles who were around them sought to destroy them utterly; for they said, "They have no ruler nor anyone to help them. Now therefore let's fight against them, and take away their memory from amongst men."

13

1 Simon heard that Tryphon had gathered together a mighty army to come into the land of Judah and destroy it utterly. 2 He saw that the people were trembling in great fear. So he went up to Jerusalem and gathered the people together. 3 He encouraged them, and said to them, "You yourselves know all the things that I, my kindred, and my father's house have done for the laws and the sanctuary, and the battles and the distresses which we have seen. 4 Because of this, all my brothers have perished for Israel's sake, and I am left alone. 5 Now be it far from me, that I should spare my own life in any time of affliction, for I am not better than my kindred. 6 However, I will take vengeance for my nation, for the sanctuary, and for our wives and children, because all the Gentiles have gathered out of hatred to destroy us."

7 The spirit of the people revived as soon as they heard these words. 8 They answered with a loud voice, saying, "You are our leader in the place of Judas and Jonathan your brothers. 9 Fight our battles, and we will do all that you tell us to do."

10 He gathered together all the men of war, and hurried to finish the walls of Jerusalem. He fortified it all around. 11 He sent Jonathan the son of Absalom, and with him a great army, to Joppa. He threw out those who were in it, and lived there.

12 Tryphon left Ptolemais with a mighty army to enter into the land of Judah, and Jonathan was with him under guard. 13 But Simon encamped at Adida, near the plain. 14 Tryphon knew that Simon had risen up in the place

a 11:57 See 1 Maccabees 2:18.
b 12:7 So the old Latin versions and Josephus: compare also ver. 20. All the other authorities read Darius in this place.
c 12:22 Gr. peace
d 12:38 Gr. Sephela.
e 12:43 See 1 Maccabees 2:18.

of his brother Jonathan, and meant to join battle with him, so he sent ambassadors to him, saying, 15 "It is for money which Jonathan your brother owed to the king's treasury, by reason of the offices which he had, that we are detaining him. 16 Now send one hundred talents of silver and two of his sons for hostages, so that when he is released he may not revolt against us, and we will release him."

17 Simon knew that they spoke to him deceitfully, but he sent to get the money and the children, lest perhaps he would arouse great hostility amongst the people, 18 who might say, "Because I didn't send him the money and the children, he perished." 19 So he sent the children and the hundred talents, but Tryphon lied, and didn't release Jonathan.

20 After this, Tryphon came to invade the land and destroy it, and he went around by the way that leads to Adora. Simon and his army marched near him to every place, wherever he went. 21 Now the people of the citadel sent to Tryphon ambassadors, urging him to come to them through the wilderness, and to send them food. 22 So Tryphon prepared all his cavalry to come, but on that night a very heavy snow fell, and he didn't come because of the snow. He marched off and went into the land of Gilead. 23 When he came near to Bascama, he killed Jonathan, and he was buried there. 24 Then Tryphon turned back, and went away into his own land.

25 Simon sent, and took the bones of Jonathan his brother, and buried him at Modin, the city of his fathers. 26 All Israel made great lamentation over him, and mourned for him many days. 27 Simon built a monument on the tomb of his father and his kindred, and raised it high so that it could be seen, with polished stone on the front and back. 28 He also set up seven pyramids, one near another, for his father, his mother, and his four brothers. 29 For these, he made an elaborate setting, erecting great pillars around them, and upon the pillars he made suits of armour for a perpetual memorial, and beside the suits of armour, he carved ships, so that they could be seen by all who sail on the sea. 30 This is the tomb which he made at Modin. It remains to this day.

31 Now Tryphon deceived the young King Antiochus and killed him, 32 and reigned in his place. He put on himself the crown of Asia and brought a great calamity upon the land. 33 Simon built up the strongholds of Judea, and walled them all around with high towers, great walls, gates, and bars; and he stored food in the strongholds. 34 Simon chose men, and sent to King Demetrius with a request that he grant the country an immunity, because all that Tryphon did was to plunder. 35 King Demetrius sent to him according to these words, and answered him, and wrote a letter to him, as follows:

36 "King Demetrius to Simon the high priest and friend[a] of kings, and to the elders and nation of the Jews, greetings. 37 The golden crown and the palm branch, which you sent, we have received. We are ready to make a steadfast peace with you, yes, and to write to our officers to release you from tribute. 38 Whatever things we confirmed to you, they are confirmed. The strongholds, which you have built, let them be your own. 39 As for any oversights and faults committed to this day, we forgive them, and the crown tax which you owed us. If there were any other tax collected in Jerusalem, let it be collected no longer. 40 If any amongst you are qualified to be enrolled in our court, let them be enrolled, and let there be peace between us."

41 In the one hundred seventieth year,[b] the yoke of the Gentiles was taken away from Israel. 42 The people began to write in their instruments and contracts, "In the first year of Simon, the great high priest and captain and leader of the Jews."

43 In those days Simon encamped against[c] Gazara, and surrounded it with troops. He made a seige engine, and brought it up to the city, and struck a tower, and captured it. 44 Those who were in the engine leapt out into the city; and there was a great uproar in the city. 45 The people of the city tore their clothes, and went up on the walls with their wives and children, and cried with a loud voice, asking Simon to give them[d] his right hand. 46 They said, "Don't deal with us according to our wickednesses, but according to your mercy." 47 So Simon was reconciled to them, and didn't fight against them; but he expelled them from the city and cleansed the houses where the idols were, and then entered into it with singing and giving praise. 48 He removed all uncleanness out of it, and placed in it men who would keep the law, and made it stronger than it was before, and built a dwelling place for himself in it.

49 But the people of the citadel in Jerusalem were hindered from going out and from going into the country, and from buying and selling. So they were very hungry, and a great number of them perished from famine. 50 Then they cried out to Simon, that he should give them his right hand; and he gave it to them; but he expelled them from there, and he cleansed the citadel from its pollutions. 51 He entered into it on the twenty-third day of the second month, in the one hundred and seventy-first year,[e] with praise and palm branches, with harps, with cymbals, and with stringed instruments, with hymns, and with songs, because a great enemy had been destroyed out of Israel. 52 Simon ordained that they should keep that day every year with gladness. He made the hill of the temple that was by the citadel stronger than before, and he lived there with his men. 53 Simon saw

that his son John was a man, so he made him leader of all his forces; and he lived in Gazara.

14

1 In the one hundred and seventy-second year,[f] King Demetrius gathered his forces together, and went into Media to get help, that he might fight against Tryphon. 2 When Arsaces, the king of Persia and Media, heard that Demetrius had come into his borders, he sent one of his princes to take him alive. 3 He went and struck the army of Demetrius, and seized him and brought him to Arsaces, who put him under guard.

4 The land had rest all the days of Simon. He sought the good of his nation. His authority and his honour was pleasing to them all his days. 5 Amid all his honours, he took Joppa for a harbour, and made it an entrance for the islands of the sea. 6 He enlarged the borders of his nation and took possession of the country. 7 He gathered together a great number of captives, and took control of Gazara, Bethsura, and the citadel, and he removed its uncleannesses from it. There was no one who resisted him. 8 They tilled their land in peace, and the land gave her increase, and the trees of the plains gave their fruit. 9 The old men sat in the streets; they all conversed together about good things. The young men put on glorious and warlike apparel. 10 He provided food for the cities and furnished them with means of defence, until the glory of his name was known to the end of the earth. 11 He made peace in the land, and Israel rejoiced with great joy. 12 Each man sat under his vine and his fig tree, and there was no one to make them afraid. 13 No one was left in the land who fought against them. The kings were defeated in those days. 14 He strengthened all those of his people who were humble. He searched out the law, and every lawless and wicked person he took away. 15 He glorified the sanctuary, and added to the vessels of the temple.

16 It was heard at Rome that Jonathan was dead, and even in Sparta, and they were exceedingly grieved. 17 But as soon as they heard that his brother Simon was made high priest in his place, and ruled the country and the cities in it, 18 they wrote to him on brass tablets to renew with him the friendship and the alliance which they had confirmed with his brothers Judas and Jonathan. 19 These were read before the congregation at Jerusalem.

20 This is the copy of the letters which the Spartans sent:

"The rulers and the city of the Spartans, to Simon the high priest, to the elders, the priests, and the rest of the people of the Jews, our kindred, greetings. 21 The ambassadors who were sent to our people reported to us about your glory and honour. We were glad for their coming, 22 and we registered the things that were spoken by them in the public records[g] as follows: 'Numenius son of Antiochus, and Antipater son of Jason, the Jews' ambassadors, came to us to renew the friendship they had with us. 23 It pleased the people to entertain the men honourably, and to put the copy of their words in the public records,[h] to the end that the people of the Spartans might have a record of them. Moreover they wrote a copy of these things to Simon the high priest.'"

24 After this, Simon sent Numenius to Rome with a great shield of gold of weighing one thousand minas,[i] in order to confirm the alliance with them.

25 But when the people heard these things, they said, "What thanks shall we give to Simon and his sons? 26 For he and his brothers and the house of his father have made themselves strong, and have fought and chased away Israel's enemies, and confirmed liberty to Israel.[j]" 27 So they wrote on tablets of brass, and set them on pillars on mount Zion. This is the copy of the writing:

"On the eighteenth day of Elul, in the one hundred and seventy-second year,[k] which is the third year of Simon the high priest, 28 in Asaramel, in a great congregation of priests and people and princes of the nation, and of the elders of the country, it was proclaimed to us:[l] 29 'Since wars often occurred in the country, Simon the son of Mattathias, the son of the sons of Joarib, and his brothers, put themselves in jeopardy and withstood the enemies of their nation, that their sanctuary and the law might be established, and glorified their nation with great glory. 30 Jonathan rallied the nation, became their high priest, and was gathered to his people. 31 Their enemies planned to invade their country, that they might destroy their country utterly, and stretch out their hands against their sanctuary. 32 Then Simon rose up and fought for his nation. He spent much of his own money to arm the valiant men of his nation and give them wages. 33 He fortified the cities of Judea and Bethsura that lies on the borders of Judea, where the weapons of the enemies were had been stored, and there he placed a garrison of Jews. 34 He fortified Joppa which is upon the sea, and Gazara which is upon the borders of Azotus, where the enemies used to live, and placed Jews there, and set in there all things necessary for their restoration. 35 The people saw Simon's faith,[m] and the glory which he resolved to bring to his nation, and they made him their leader and high priest, because he had done all these things, and for the justice and the faith which he kept to his nation, and because he sought by all means to exalt his people. 36 In his days, things prospered in his hands, so that the Gentiles were taken away out of their country, and they also who were in

---

a 13:36 See 1 Maccabees 2:18.

b 13:41 circa B.C. 143.

c 13:43 See 1 Maccabees 13:53 (compare 1 Maccabees 13:48); 1 Maccabees 14:7, 34; 15:28; 16:1: also Josephus. All the authorities read Gaza in this verse.

d 13:45 Gr. right hands.

e 13:51 circa B.C. 142.

f 14:1 circa B.C. 141.

g 14:22 Gr. counsels of the people.

h 14:23 Gr. books that are appointed for the people.

i 14:24 1,000 minas is about 499 kg or 1,098 pounds.

j 14:26 Gr. him.

k 14:27 circa B.C. 141.

l 14:28 Gr. he made known.

m 14:35 Some authorities read acts.

the city of David, those who were in Jerusalem, who had made themselves a citadel, out of which they used to go, and polluted everything around the sanctuary, and did great damage to its purity. ₃₇ He placed Jews in it and fortified it for the safety of the country and the city, and made high the walls of Jerusalem. ₃₈ King Demetrius confirmed to him the high priesthood according to these things, ₃₉ and made him one of his friends,[a] and honoured him with great honour; ₄₀ for he had heard that the Jews had been called by the Romans friends, allies, and kindred, and that they had met the ambassadors of Simon honourably; ₄₁ and that the Jews and the priests were well pleased that Simon should be their leader and high priest forever, until there should arise a faithful prophet; ₄₂ and that he should be governor over them, and should take charge of the sanctuary, to set them over their works, and over the country, and over the weapons, and over the strongholds; and that he should take charge of the sanctuary, ₄₃ and that he should be obeyed by all, and that all contracts in the country should be written in his name, and that he should be clothed in purple, and wear gold; ₄₄ and that it should not be lawful for any of the people or of the priests to nullify any of these things, or to oppose the words that he should speak, or to gather an assembly in the country without him, or to be clothed in purple, or wear a buckle of gold; ₄₅ but whoever should do otherwise, or nullify any of these things, he will be liable to punishment.'" ₄₆ All the people consented to ordain for Simon that he should do according to these words. ₄₇ So Simon accepted this, and consented to be high priest, and to be captain and governor[b] of the Jews and of the priests, and to be protector of all.

₄₈ They commanded to put this writing on tablets of brass, and to set them up within the precinct of the sanctuary in a conspicuous place, ₄₉ and moreover to put copies of them in the treasury, so that Simon and his sons might have them.

15

₁ Antiochus son of Demetrius the king sent a letter from the islands of the sea to Simon the priest and[c] governor of the Jews, and to all the nation. ₂ Its contents follow:

"King Antiochus to Simon the chief priest and[d] governor, and to the nation of the Jews, greetings. ₃ Whereas certain troublemakers have made themselves masters of the kingdom of our fathers, but my purpose is to claim the kingdom, that I may restore it as it was before; and moreover I have raised a multitude of foreign soldiers, and have prepared warships; ₄ moreover I plan to land in the country, that I may punish those who have destroyed our country, and those who have made many cities in the kingdom desolate; ₅ now therefore I confirm to you all the tax remissions which the kings who were before me remitted to you, and whatever gifts besides they remitted to you, ₆ and I permit you to coin money for your country with your own stamp, ₇ but that Jerusalem and the sanctuary should be free. All the weapons that you have prepared, and the strongholds that you have built, which you have in your possession, let them remain yours. ₈ Every debt owed to the king, and the things that will be owed to the king from henceforth and for evermore, let them be remitted to you. ₉ Moreover, when we have established our kingdom, we will glorify you and your nation and the temple with great glory, so that your glory will be made manifest in all the earth.

₁₀ In the one hundred and seventy-fourth year,[e] Antiochus went into the land of his fathers; and all the forces came together to him, so that there were few men with Tryphon. ₁₁ King Antiochus pursued him, and he came, as he fled, to Dor, which is by the sea; ₁₂ for he knew that troubles had come upon him all at once, and that his forces had deserted him. ₁₃ Antiochus encamped against Dor, and with him one hundred and twenty thousand men of war and eight thousand cavalry. ₁₄ He surrounded the city, and the ships joined in the attack from the sea. He harassed the city by land and sea, and permitted no one to go out or in.

₁₅ Numenius and his company came from Rome, having letters to the kings and to the countries, in which were written these things: ₁₆ "Lucius, consul of the Romans, to King Ptolemy, greetings. ₁₇ The Jews' ambassadors came to us as our friends and allies, to renew the old friendship and alliance, being sent from Simon the high priest, and from the people of the Jews. ₁₈ Moreover they brought a shield of gold weighing one thousand minas.[f] ₁₉ It pleased us therefore to write to the kings and to the countries, that they should not seek their harm or fight against them, their cities, and their country, or be allies with those who fight against them. ₂₀ Moreover, it seemed good to us to receive the shield from them. ₂₁ If therefore any troublemakers have fled from their country to you, deliver them to Simon the high priest, that he may take vengeance on them according to their law."

₂₂ He wrote the same things to King Demetrius, to Attalus, to Arathes, to Arsaces, ₂₃ to all the countries, to[g] Sampsames, to the Spartans, to Delos, to Myndos, to Sicyon, to Caria, to Samos, to Pamphylia, to Lycia, to Halicarnassus, to Rhodes, to Phaselis, to Cos, to Side, to Aradus, Gortyna, Cnidus, Cyprus, and Cyrene. ₂₄ They also wrote this copy to Simon the high priest.

₂₅ But King Antiochus encamped against Dor the second day, bringing his forces up to it continually, and making engines of war; and he shut up

Tryphon from going in or out. ₂₆ Simon sent him two thousand chosen men to fight on his side, with silver, gold, and instruments of war in abundance. ₂₇ He would not receive them, but nullified all the covenants which he had made with him before, and was estranged from him. ₂₈ He sent to him Athenobius, one of his friends,[h] to confer with him, saying, "You hold possession of Joppa, Gazara, and the citadel that is in Jerusalem, cities of my kingdom. ₂₉ You have devastated their territory, and done great harm in the land, and control of many places in my kingdom. ₃₀ Now therefore hand over the cities which you have taken, and the tributes of the places which you have taken control of outside of the borders of Judea; ₃₁ or else give me for them five hundred talents of silver; and for the harm that you have done, and the tributes of the cities, another five hundred talents. Otherwise we will come and subdue you."

₃₂ Athenobius, the king's friend,[i] came to Jerusalem. When he saw the glory of Simon, the cupboard of gold and silver vessels, and his great attendance, he was amazed. He reported to him the king's words. ₃₃ Simon answered, and said to him, "We have not taken other men's land nor do we have possession of that which belongs to others, but of the inheritance of our fathers. However, it had been in possession of our enemies wrongfully for a while. ₃₄ But we, having opportunity, firmly hold the inheritance of our fathers. ₃₅ As for Joppa and Gazara, which you demand, they did great harm amongst the people throughout our country. We will give one hundred talents for them."

Athenobius didn't answer even one word, ₃₆ but returned in a rage to the king, and reported to him these words, and the glory of Simon, and all that he had seen; and the king was exceedingly angry. ₃₇ Meanwhile, Tryphon embarked on board a ship, and fled to Orthosia.

₃₈ The king appointed Cendebaeus chief captain of the sea coast, and gave him troops of infantry and cavalry. ₃₉ He commanded him to encamp against Judea, and he commanded him to build up Kidron, and to fortify the gates, and that he should fight against the people; but the king pursued Tryphon. ₄₀ So Cendebaeus came to Jamnia and began to provoke the people, and to invade Judea, and to take the people captive and kill them. ₄₁ He built Kidron and stationed cavalry and infantry there, to the end that going out they might make raids on the highways of Judea, as the king had commanded him.

16

₁ John went up from Gazara and told Simon his father what Cendebaeus was doing. ₂ Simon called his two oldest sons, Judas and John, and said to them, "I and my brothers and my father's house have fought the battles of Israel from our youth, even to this day; and things have prospered in our hands, that we have often delivered Israel. ₃ But now I am old, and you moreover, by his mercy, are of a sufficient age. Take the place of me and my brother, and go out and fight for our nation; and let the help which is from heaven be with you.

₄ He chose out of the country twenty thousand men of war and cavalry, and they went against Cendebaeus, and slept at Modin. ₅ Rising up in the morning, they went into the plain, and, behold, a great army of infantry and cavalry came to meet them. There was a brook between them. ₆ He encamped near them, he and his people. He saw that the people were afraid to pass over the brook, and he passed over first. When the men saw him, they passed over after him. ₇ He divided the people, and placed the calvary in the midst of the infantry; but the enemies' cavalry were exceedingly many. ₈ They sounded the trumpets; and Cendebaeus and his army were put to flight, and many of them fell wounded to death, but those who were left fled to the stronghold. ₉ At that time Judas, John's brother, was wounded; but John pursued after them until he came to Kidron, which Cendebaeus had built. ₁₀ They fled to the towers that are in the fields of Azotus; and he burnt it with fire. About two thousand men men of them fell. Then he returned into Judea in peace.

₁₁ Ptolemy the son of Abubus had been appointed governor over the plain of Jericho, and he had much silver and gold; ₁₂ for he was the high priest's son-in-law. ₁₃ His heart was lifted up, and he planned to make himself master of the country, and he made deceitful plans against Simon and his sons, to do away with them. ₁₄ Now Simon was visiting the cities that were in the country, and attending to their needs. He went down to Jericho—himself with Mattathias and Judas his sons—in the one hundred and seventy-seventh year,[j] in the eleventh month, which is the month Sebat. ₁₅ The son of Abubus received them deceitfully into the little stronghold that is called Dok, which he had built, and made them a great banquet, and hid men there. ₁₆ When Simon and his sons had drunk freely, Ptolemy and his men rose up, took their weapons, rushed in against Simon in the banqueting place, and killed him, his two sons, and some of his servants. ₁₇ He committed a great iniquity, and repaid evil for good.

₁₈ Ptolemy wrote these things and sent to the king, that he should send him forces to aid him, and should deliver them their country and the cities. ₁₉ He sent others to Gazara to do away with John. To the captains of thousands, he sent letters to come to him, that he might give them silver, gold, and gifts. ₂₀ He sent others to take possession of Jerusalem and the temple hill. ₂₁ One ran before to Gazara, and told John that his father and kindred had perished, and he has sent to kill you also. ₂₂ When he heard, he

---

[a] *14:39* See 1 Maccabees 2:18.
[b] *14:47* Gr. ethnarch.
[c] *15:1* Gr. ethnarch.
[d] *15:2* Gr. ethnarch.
[e] *15:10* circa B.C. 139
[f] *15:18* 1,000 minas is about 499 kg. or about 1,098 pounds.

[g] *15:23* Some authorities read Sampsaces: the Latin versions have Lampsacus.
[h] *15:28* See 1 Maccabees 2:18.
[i] *15:32* See 1 Maccabees 2:18.
[j] *16:14* circa B.C. 136.

was greatly shocked. He seized the men who came to destroy him and killed them; for he perceived that they were seeking to destroy him.

23 And the rest of the acts of John and of his wars and of his valiant deeds which he did, and of the building of the walls which he built, and of his achievements, 24 behold, they are written in the chronicles [a] of his high priesthood, from the time that he was made high priest after his father.

---

[a] *16:24* Gr. book of days.

The Second Book of the Maccabees

The Second Book of the Maccabees is recognised as Deuterocanonical Scripture by the Roman Catholic, Greek Orthodox, and Russian Orthodox Churches.

1

₁ The kindred, the Jews who are in Jerusalem and those who are in the country of Judea, send greetings and good peace to the kindred, the Jews who are throughout Egypt. ₂ May God do good to you, and remember his covenant with Abraham, Isaac, and Jacob, his faithful servants, ₃ and give you all a heart to worship him and do his will with a strong heart and a willing soul. ₄ May God open your heart to his law and his statutes, and make peace, ₅ and listen to your requests, and be reconciled with you, and not forsake you in an evil time. ₆ Now we are praying for you here.

₇ In the reign of Demetrius, in the one hundred and sixty-ninth year, we the Jews have already written to you in the suffering and in the distress that has come upon us in these years, from the time that Jason and his company revolted from the holy land and the kingdom, ₈ and set the gate on fire, and shed innocent blood. We prayed to the Lord, and were heard. We offered sacrifices and meal offerings. We lit the lamps. We set out the show bread.ᵃ ₉ Now see that you keep the days of the feast of tabernacles in the month Chislev in the one hundred and eighty-eighth year.

₁₀ The people of Jerusalem and those who are in Judea, with the senate and Judas, to Aristobulus, King Ptolemy's teacher, who is also of the stock of the anointed priests, and to the Jews who are in Egypt, we send greetings and health.

₁₁ Having been saved by God out of great perils, as men arrayed against a king, we thank him greatly. ₁₂ For he threw out into Persia those who fought against us in the holy city. ₁₃ For when the prince had come there, with an army that seemed irresistible, they were cut to pieces in the temple of Nanaea by the treachery of Nanaea's priests. ₁₄ For Antiochus, on the pretence that he would marry her, came into the place, he and his friends who were with him, that they might take a large part of the treasures as a dowry. ₁₅ And when the priests of Nanaea's temple had set the treasures out, and he had come there with a small company within the wall of the sacred precinct, they locked the temple when Antiochus had come in. ₁₆ Opening the secret door of the panelled ceiling, they threw stones and struck down the prince. They cut him and his company in pieces, and cut off their heads, and threw them to the people who were outside. ₁₇ Blessed be our God in all things, who handed over those who had committed impiety.

₁₈ Since we are now about to celebrate the purification of the temple in the month Chislev, on the twenty-fifth day, we thought it necessary to notify you, so that you may also keep a feast of tabernacles, and remember the fire which was given when Nehemiah offered sacrifices, after he had built both the temple and the altar.

₁₉ For indeed when our fathers were about to be led into the land of Persia, the godly priests of that time took some of the fire of the altar, and hid it secretly in the hollow of a well that was without water, where they made sure that the place was unknown to anyone. ₂₀ Now after many years, when it pleased God, Nehemiah, having received a charge from the king of Persia, sent in quest of the fire the descendants of the priests who hid it. When they declared to us that they had found no fire, but thick liquid, ₂₁ he commanded them to draw some of it out and bring it to him. When the sacrifices had been offered, Nehemiah commanded the priests to sprinkle with that liquid both the wood and the things laid on it. ₂₂ When that was done and some time had passed, and the sun shone out, which before was hidden with clouds, a great blaze was kindled, so that all men marvelled. ₂₃ The priests made a prayer while the sacrifice was being consumed—both the priests and all the others. Jonathan led and the rest responded, as Nehemiah did.

₂₄ The prayer was like this: "O Lord, Lord God, the Creator of all things, who are awesome, strong, righteous, and merciful, who alone are King and gracious, ₂₅ who alone supply every need, who alone are righteous, almighty, and eternal, you who save Israel out of all evil, who chose the ancestors and sanctified them, ₂₆ accept the sacrifice for all your people Israel, and preserve your own portion, and consecrate it. ₂₇ Gather together our scattered people, set at liberty those who are in bondage amongst the heathen, look upon those who are despised and abhorred, and let the heathen know that you are our God. ₂₈ Punish those who oppress us and in arrogance shamefully entreat us. ₂₉ Plant your people in your holy place, even as Moses said."

₃₀ Then the priests sang the hymns. ₃₁ As soon as the sacrifice was consumed, then Nehemiah commanded that the rest of the liquid be poured on large stones. ₃₂ When this was done, a flame was kindled; but when the light from the altar shone back, it went out. ₃₃ When the matter became known, and it was told the king of the Persians that, in the place where the priests who were led away had hid the fire, the liquid appeared which Nehemiah and those who were with him purified the sacrifice, ₃₄ then the king enclosed the place and made it sacred after he had investigated the matter. ₃₅ When the king would show favour to any, he would exchange many presents and give them some of this liquid. ₃₆ Nehemiah and those who were with him called this thing "Nephthar", which is by interpretation, "Cleansing"; but most men call it Nephthai.

2

₁ It is also found in the records that Jeremiah the prophet commanded those who were carried away to take some of the fire, as has been mentioned, ₂ and how that the prophet charged those who were carried away, having given them the law, that they should not forget the statutes of the Lord or be led astray in their minds when they saw images of gold and silver, and their adornment. ₃ With other such words exhorted he them, that the law should not depart from their hearts.

₄ It was in the writing that the prophet, being warned by God, commanded that the tabernacle and the ark should follow with him,ᵇ when he went out to the mountain where Moses had gone up and saw God's inheritance. ₅ Jeremiah came and found a cave, he brought the tabernacle, the ark, and the altar of incense into it; then he sealed the entrance. ₆ Some of those who followed with him came there that they might mark the way, and could not find it. ₇ But when Jeremiah learnt about that, he rebuked them, saying, "The place shall be unknown until God gathers the people together again and shows mercy. ₈ Then the Lord will disclose these things, and the glory of the Lord shall be seen with the cloud, as it was also shown to Moses, also as Solomon implored that the place might be consecrated greatly, ₉ and it was also declared that he, having wisdom, offered a sacrifice of dedication, and of the finishing of the temple. ₁₀ As Moses prayed to the Lord and fire came down out of heaven and consumed the sacrifice, even so Solomon also prayed, and the fire came down and consumed the burnt offerings. ₁₁ ᶜMoses said, 'Because the sin offering had not been eaten, it was consumed in like manner.' ₁₂ Likewise Solomon kept the eight days."

₁₃ The same things were reported both in the public archives and in Nehemiah's records, and also how he, founding a library, gathered together the books about the kings and prophets, and the writings of David, and letters of kings about sacred gifts. ₁₄ In like manner Judas also gathered together for us all those books that had been scattered by reason of the war, and they are still with us. ₁₅ If therefore you have need of them, send some people to bring them to you.

₁₆ Seeing then that we are about to celebrate the purification, we write to you. You will therefore do well if you celebrate the days. ₁₇ Now God, who saved all his people, and restored the heritage to all, with the kingdom, the priesthood, and the consecration, ₁₈ even as he promised through the law—in God have we hope, that he will soon have mercy upon us, and gather us together out of everywhere under heaven into his holy place; for he delivered us out of great evils, and purified the place.

———————

₁₉ Now the things concerning Judas Maccabaeus and his brothers, the purification of the greatest temple, the dedication of the altar, ₂₀ and further the wars against Antiochus Epiphanes and Eupator his son, ₂₁ and the manifestations that came from heaven to those who fought with one another in brave deeds for the religion of the Jews; so that, being but a few, they seized the whole country, chased the barbarous multitudes, ₂₂ recovered again the temple renowned all the world over, freed the city, and restored the laws which were about to be overthrown, seeing the Lord became gracious to them with all kindness. ₂₃ These things which have been declared by Jason of Cyrene in five books, we will attempt to abridge in one book. ₂₄ For having in view the confused mass of the numbers, and theᵈ difficulty which awaits those who would enter into the narratives of the history, by reason of the abundance of the matter, ₂₅ we were careful that those who choose to read may be attracted, and that those who wish us well may find it easy to recall, and that all readers may benefit. ₂₆ Although to us, who have taken upon ourselves the painful labour of the abridgement, the task is not easy, but a matter of sweat and sleeplessness, ₂₇ even as it is no light thing to him who prepares a banquet, and seeks the benefit of others. Nevertheless, for the sake of the gratitude of the many we will gladly endure the painful labour, ₂₈ leaving to the historian the exact handling of every particular, and again having no strength to fill in the outlines of our abridgement. ₂₉ For as the masterbuilder of a new house must care for the whole structure, and again he who undertakes to decorate and paint it must seek out the things fit for its adorning; even so I think it is also with us. ₃₀ To occupy the ground, and to indulge in long discussions, and to be curious in particulars, is fitting for the first author of the history; ₃₁ but to strive after brevity of expression, and to avoid a laboured fullness in the treatment, is to be granted to him who would bring a writing into a new form. ₃₂ Here then let's begin the narration, only adding this much to that which has already been said; for it is a foolish thing to make a long prologue to the history, and to abridge the history itself.

3

₁ When the holy city was inhabited with unbroken peace and the laws were kept very well because of the godliness of Onias the high priest and his hatred of wickedness, ₂ it came to pass that even the kings themselves honoured the place and glorified the temple with the noblest presents, ₃ so that even King Seleucus of Asia bore all the costs belonging to the services of the sacrifices out of his own revenues. ₄ But a man named Simon of the tribe of Benjamin, having been made guardian of the temple, disagreed with

---

ᵃ *1:8* Gr. loaves
ᵇ *2:4* Gr. and when. The Greek text here is probably corrupt.

ᶜ *2:11* See Leviticus 10:16 and 9:24.
ᵈ *2:24* Or, weariness

the high priest about the ruling of the market in the city. 5 When he couldn't overcome Onias, he went to Apollonius of ªTarsus, who at that time was governor of Coelesyria and Phoenicia. 6 He brought him word how that the treasury in Jerusalem was full of untold sums of money, so that the multitude of the funds was innumerable, and that they didn't pertain to the account of the sacrifices, but that it was possible that these should fall under the king's power. 7 When Apollonius met the king, he informed him of the money about which he had been told. So the king appointed Heliodorus, who was his chancellor, and sent him with a command to accomplish the removal of the reported money. 8 So Heliodorus set out on his journey at once, ostensibly to visit the cities of Coelesyria and Phoenicia, but in fact to execute the king's purpose.

9 When he had come to Jerusalem and had been courteously received by the high priest of the city, he told him about the information which had been given, and declared why he had come; and he enquired if in truth these things were so. 10 The high priest explained to him that there were in the treasury deposits of widows and orphans, 11 and moreover some money belonging to Hyrcanus the son of Tobias, a man in very high place, not as that impious Simon falsely alleged; and that in all there were four hundred talents of silver and two hundred of gold, 12 and that it was altogether impossible that wrong should be done to those who had put trust in the holiness of the place, and in the majesty and inviolable sanctity of the temple, honoured over all the world. 13 But Heliodorus, because of the king's command given him, said that in any case this money must be confiscated for the king's treasury.

14 So having appointed a day, he entered in to direct the enquiry concerning these matters; and there was no small distress throughout the whole city. 15 The priests, prostrating themselves before the altar in their priestly garments, and called towards heaven upon him who gave the law concerning deposits, that he should preserve these treasures safe for those who had deposited them. 16 Whoever saw the appearance of the high priest was wounded in mind; for his countenance and the change of his colour betrayed the distress of his soul. 17 For a terror and a shuddering of the body had come over the man, by which the pain that was in his heart was plainly shown to those who looked at him. 18 Those who were in the houses rushed out in crowds to make a universal supplication, because the place was about to come into dishonour. 19 The women, girded with sackcloth under their breasts, thronged the streets. The virgins who were kept indoors ran together, some to the gates, others to the walls, and some looked out through the windows. 20 All, stretching out their hands towards heaven, made their solemn supplication. 21 Then it was pitiful to see the multitude prostrating themselves all mixed together, and the anxiety of the high priest in his great distress.

22 While therefore they called upon the Almighty Lord to keep the things entrusted to them ᵇ safe and secure for those who had entrusted them, 23 Heliodorus went on to execute that which had been decreed. 24 But when he was already present there with his guards near the treasury, the Sovereign of spirits and of all authority caused a great manifestation, so that all who had presumed to come with him, stricken with dismay at the power of God, fainted in terror. 25 For they saw a horse with a frightening rider, adorned with beautiful trappings, and he rushed fiercely and struck at Heliodorus with his forefeet. It seemed like he who sat on the horse had complete armour of gold. 26 Two others also appeared to him, young men notable in their strength, and beautiful in their glory, and splendid in their apparel, who stood by him on either side, and scourged him unceasingly, inflicting on him many sore stripes. 27 When he had fallen suddenly to the ground, and great darkness had come over him, his guards picked him up and put him on a stretcher, 28 and carried him—this man who had just now entered with a great retinue and all his guard into the aforesaid treasury, himself now brought to utter helplessness, manifestly made to recognise the sovereignty of God. 29 So, while he, through the working of God, speechless and bereft of all hope and deliverance, lay prostrate, 30 they blessed the Lord who acted marvellously for his own place. The temple, which a little before was full of terror and alarm, was filled with joy and gladness after the Almighty Lord appeared.

31 But quickly some of Heliodorus's familiar friends implored Onias to call upon the Most High to grant life to him who lay quite at the last gasp. 32 The high priest, secretly fearing lest the king might come to think that some treachery towards Heliodorus had been perpetrated by the Jews, brought a sacrifice for the recovery of the man. 33 But as the high priest was making the atoning sacrifice, the same young men appeared again to Heliodorus, arrayed in the same garments. They stood and said, "Give Onias the high priest great thanks, for for his sake the Lord has granted you life. 34 See that you, since you have been scourged from heaven, proclaim to all men the sovereign majesty of God." When they had spoken these words, they vanished out of sight. 35 So Heliodorus, having offered a sacrifice to the Lord and vowed ᶜgreat vows to him who had saved his life, and having bidden Onias farewell, returned with his army to the king. 36 He testified to all men the works of the greatest God, which he had seen with his eyes.

37 When the king asked Heliodorus what sort of man was fit to be sent yet once again to Jerusalem, he said, 38 "If you have any enemy or conspirator against the state, send him there, and you will receive him back well scourged, if he even escapes with his life; because truly there is some power of God in that place. 39 For he who has his dwelling in heaven himself has his eyes on that place and helps it. Those who come to hurt it, he strikes and destroys."

40 This was the history of Heliodorus and the keeping of the treasury.

4

1 The previously mentioned Simon, who had given information about the money against his country, slandered Onias, saying that it was he who had incited Heliodorus and had been the real cause of these evils. 2 He dared to call him a conspirator against the state who was actually the benefactor of the city, the guardian of his fellow countrymen, and a zealot for the laws. 3 When his hatred grew so great that even murders were perpetrated through one of Simon's approved agents, 4 Onias, seeing the danger of the contention, and that ᵈApollonius the son of Menestheus, the governor of Coelesyria and Phoenicia, was increasing Simon's malice, 5 appealed to the king, not to be an accuser of his fellow-citizens, but looking to the good of all theᵉ people, both public and private; 6 for he saw that without the king's involvement it was impossible for the state to obtain peace any more, and that Simon would not cease from his madness.

7 When Seleucus was deceased, and Antiochus, who was called Epiphanes, succeeded to the kingdom, Jason the brother of Onias supplanted his brother in the high priesthood, 8 having promised to the king at an audience three hundred and sixty talents of silver, and out of another fund eighty talents. 9 In addition to this, he undertook to assign one hundred and fifty more, if it might be allowed him ᶠthrough the king's authority to set him up a gymnasium and a body of youths to be trained in it, and to register the inhabitants of Jerusalem as citizens of Antioch. 10 When the king had assented, and Jason had taken possession of the office, he immediately shifted those of his own race to the Greek way of life. 11 Setting aside the royal ordinances of special favour to the Jews, granted by the means of John the father of Eupolemus, who went on the mission to the Romans to establish friendship and alliance, and seeking to overthrow the lawful ways of living, he brought in new customs forbidden by the law. 12 For he eagerly established a gymnasium under the citadel itself, and caused the noblest of the young men to wear the Greek hat. 13 Thus there was an extreme of hellenization, and an advance of a foreign religion, by reason of the exceeding profaneness of Jason, who was an ungodly man and not a high priest; 14 so that the priests had no more any zeal for the services of the altar; but despising the sanctuary and neglecting the sacrifices, they hastened to enjoy that which was unlawfully provided in the wrestling arena, after the summons to the discus-throwing. 15 They despised the honours of their fathers, and valued the prestige of the Greeks best of all. 16 For this reason, severe calamity overtook them. The men whose ways of living they earnestly followed, and to whom they desired to be made like in all things, these became their enemies and punished them. 17 For it is not a light thing to show irreverence to God's laws, but later events will make this clear.

18 Now when certain games that came every fifth year were kept at Tyre, and the king was present, 19 the vile Jason sent sacred envoys,ᵍ as being Antiochians of Jerusalem, bearing three hundred drachmas of silver to the sacrifice of Hercules, which even the bearers thereof thought not right to use for any sacrifice, because it was not fit, but to spend it for another purpose. 20 Although the intended purpose of the sender this money was for the sacrifice of Hercules, yet on account of ʰpresent circumstances it went to the construction of trireme warships.

21 Now when Apollonius the son of Menestheus was sent into Egypt for the ⁱ enthronement of Philometor as king, Antiochus, learning that Philometor had shown himself hostile towards the government, took precautions for the security of his realm. Therefore, going to Joppa, he travelled on to Jerusalem. 22 Being magnificently received by Jason and the city, he was brought in with torches and shouting. Then he led his army down into Phoenicia.

23 Now after a space of three years, Jason sent Menelaus, the previously mentioned Simon's brother, to carry the money to the king, and to make reports concerning some necessary matters. 24 But he being commended to the king, and having been glorified by the display of his authority, secured the high priesthood for himself, outbidding Jason by three hundred talents of silver. 25 After receiving the royal mandates, he returned bringing nothing worthy of the high priesthood, but having the passion of a cruel tyrant and the rage of a savage animal. 26 So Jason, who had supplanted his own brother, was supplanted by another and driven as a fugitive into the country of the Ammonites, 27 Menelaus had possession of the office; but of the money that had been promised to the king nothing was regularly paid, even though Sostratus the governor of the citadel demanded it— 28 for his job was the gathering of the revenues—so they were both called by the king to his presence. 29 Menelaus left his own brother Lysimachus for hisʲ deputy in the high priesthood; and Sostratus left Crates, who was over the Cyprians.

30 Now while this was the state of things, it came to pass that the people of Tarsus and Mallus revolted because they were to be given as a

---

ª *3:5* Greek Thraseas
ᵇ *3:22* Gr. safe with all security.
ᶜ *3:35* Gr. greatest.
ᵈ *4:4* Compare 2 Maccabees 4:21. See also 2 Maccabees 3:5. The Greek as commonly read means Apollonius, as being the governor...Phoenicia, did rage, and increase etc.

ᵉ *4:5* Gr. multitude.
ᶠ *4:9* Gr. through his.
ᵍ *4:19* See ver. 9.
ʰ *4:20* Some authorities read the bearers.
ⁱ *4:21* The exact meaning of the Greek word is uncertain.
ʲ *4:29* Gr. successor.

present to Antiochis, the king's concubine. ₃₁ The king therefore quickly came to settle matters, leaving for his ªdeputy Andronicus, a man of high rank. ₃₂ Then Menelaus, supposing that he had gotten a favourable opportunity, presented to Andronicus certain vessels of gold belonging to the temple, which he had stolen. He had already sold others into Tyre and the neighbouring cities. ₃₃ When Onias had sure knowledge of this, he sharply reproved him, having withdrawn himself into a sanctuary at Daphne, that lies by Antioch. ₃₄ Therefore Menelaus, taking Andronicus aside, asked him to kill Onias. Coming to Onias, and being persuaded to use treachery, and being received as a friend, Andronicus gave him his right hand with oaths and, though he was suspicious, persuaded him to come out of the sanctuary. Then, with no regard for justice, he immediately put him to death. ₃₅ For this reason not only Jews, but many also of the other nations, had indignation and displeasure at the unjust murder of the man. ₃₆ And when the king had come back from the places in Cilicia, the Jews who were in the city appealed to him against Andronicus (the Greeks also joining with them in hatred of the wickedness), urging that Onias had been wrongfully slain. ₃₇ Antiochus therefore was heartily sorry, and was moved to pity, and wept, because of the sober and well ordered life of him who was dead. ₃₈ Being inflamed with anger, he immediately stripped off Andronicus's purple robe, and tore off his under garments, and when he had led him round through the whole city to that very place where he had committed the outrage against Onias, there he put the murderer out of the way, the Lord rendering to him the punishment he had deserved.

₃₉ Now when many sacrileges had been committed in the city by Lysimachus with the consent of Menelaus, and when the report of them had spread abroad outside, the people gathered themselves together against Lysimachus, after many vessels of gold had already been stolen. ₄₀ When the multitudes were rising against him and were filled with anger, Lysimachus armed about three thousand men, and with unrighteous violence began the attack under the leadership of Hauran, a man far gone in years and no less also in folly. ₄₁ But when they perceived the assault of Lysimachus, some caught up stones, others logs of wood, and some took handfuls of the ashes that lay near, and they flung them all in wild confusion at Lysimachus and those who were with him. ₄₂ As a result, they wounded many of them, they killed some, and they forced the rest of them to flee, but the author of the sacrilege himself they killed beside the treasury.

₄₃ But about these matters, there was an accusation laid against Menelaus. ₄₄ When the king had come to Tyre, the three men who were sent by the senate pleaded the cause before him. ₄₅ But Menelaus, seeing himself now defeated, promised much money to Ptolemy the son of Dorymenes, that he might win over the king. ₄₆ Therefore Ptolemy taking the king aside into a cloister, as if to get some fresh air, convinced him to change his mind. ₄₇ He who was the cause of all the evil, Menelaus, he discharged from the accusations; but these hapless men, who, if they had pleaded even before Scythians, would have been discharged uncondemned, them he sentenced to death. ₄₈ Those who were spokesmen for the city and the families of Israel and the holy vessels soon suffered that unrighteous penalty. ₄₉ Therefore even certain Tyrians, moved with hatred of the wickedness, provided magnificently for their burial. ₅₀ But Menelaus, through the covetous dealings of those who were in power, remained still in his office, growing in wickedness, established as a great conspirator against his fellow-citizens.

5

₁ Now about this time Antiochus made his second invasion into Egypt. ₂ It happened that throughout all the city, for almost forty days, cavalry appeared in the midst of the sky in swift motion, wearing robes woven with gold and carrying spears, equipped with troops for battle— ₃ drawing swords, squadrons of cavalry in array, encounters and pursuits of both armies, shaking shields, multitudes of lances, throwing of missiles, flashing of golden trappings, and putting on all sorts of armour. ₄ Therefore everyone prayed that the manifestation might have been given for good.

₅ When a false rumour had arisen that Antiochus was dead, Jason took not less than a thousand men, and suddenly made an assault upon the city. When those who were on the wall were being routed, and the city was at length nearly taken, Menelaus took refuge in the citadel. ₆ But Jason slaughtered his own citizens without mercy, not considering that good success against kinsmen is the greatest misfortune, but supposing himself to be setting up trophies over enemies, and not over fellow-countrymen. ₇ He didn't win control of the government, but receiving shame as the result of his conspiracy, he fled again as a fugitive into the country of the Ammonites. ₈ At last therefore he met with a miserable end. Having been imprisoned at the court of Aretas the prince of the Arabians, fleeing from city to city, pursued by all men, hated as an rebel against the laws, and abhorred as the executioner of his country and his fellow citizens, he was cast ashore in Egypt. ₉ He who had driven many from their own country into exile perished in exile, having crossed the sea to the Lacedaemonians, hoping to find shelter there because they wereᵇ near of kin. ₁₀ He who had thrown out a multitude unburied had none to mourn for him. He didn't have any funeral at all and no place in the tomb of his ancestors.

₁₁ Now when news came to the king concerning that which was done, he thought that Judea was in revolt. So, setting out from Egypt in a rage, he took the city by force of weapons, ₁₂ and commanded his soldiers to cut down without mercy those who came in their way, and to kill those who went into their houses. ₁₃ Then there was killing of young and old, destruction of boys, women, and children, and slaying of virgins and infants. ₁₄ In a total of three days, eighty thousand were destroyed, of which forty thousand were slain in close combat, and no fewer were sold into slavery than slain.

₁₅ Not content with this, he presumed to enter into the most holy temple of all the earth, having Menelaus for his guide (who had proved himself a traitor both to the laws and to his country), ₁₆ even taking the sacred vessels with his polluted hands, and dragging down with his profane hands the offerings that had been dedicated by other kings to enhance the glory and honour of the place. ₁₇ Antiochus was lifted up in mind, not seeing that because of the sins of those who lived in the city the Sovereign Lord had been provoked to anger a little while, and therefore his eye was turned away from the place. ₁₈ But had it not been so that they were already bound by many sins, this man, even as Heliodorus who was sent by King Seleucus to view the treasury, would, as soon as he came forward, have been scourged and turned back from his daring deed. ₁₉ However the Lord didn't choose the nation for the place's sake, but the place for the nation's sake. ₂₀ Therefore also the place itself, having shared in the calamities that happened to the nation, did afterward share in its benefits; and the place which was forsaken in the wrath of the Almighty was, at the reconciliation of the great Sovereign, restored again with all glory.

₂₁ As for Antiochus, when he had carried away out of the temple one thousand and eight hundred talents, he hurried away to Antioch, thinking in his arrogance that he could sail on land and walk on the sea, because his heart was lifted up. ₂₂ Moreover he left governors to afflict the race: at Jerusalem, Philip, by race a Phrygian, and in character more barbarous than him who set him there; ₂₃ and at Gerizim, Andronicus; and besides these, Menelaus, who worse than all the rest, exalted himself against his fellow-citizens. Having a malicious mindᶜ towards the Jewsᵈ whom he had made his citizens, ₂₄ he sent thatᵉ lord of pollutions Apollonius with an army of twenty-two thousand, commanding him to kill all those who were of full age, and to sell the women and the boys as slaves. ₂₅ He came to Jerusalem, and pretending to be a man of peace, waited till the holy day of the Sabbath, and finding the Jews at rest from work, he commanded his men to parade fully armed. ₂₆ He put to the sword all those who came out to the spectacle. Running into the city with the armed men, he killed great multitudes. ₂₇ But Judas, who is also called Maccabaeus, with about nine others, withdrew himself, and with his company kept himself alive in the mountains like wild animals do. They continued feeding on what grew wild, that they might not be partakers of the defilement.

6

₁ Not long after this, the king sent out ᶠan old man of Athens to compel the Jews to depart from the laws of their fathers and not to live by the laws of God, ₂ and also to pollute the sanctuary in Jerusalem and to call it by the name of Olympian Zeus, and to call the sanctuary in Gerizim by the name of Zeus the Protector of foreigners, even as the people who lived in that place did.

₃ The visitation of this evil was harsh and utterly grievous. ₄ For the temple was filled with debauchery and revelling by the heathen, who ᵍ dallied with prostitutes, and had intercourse with women within the sacred precincts, and moreover brought inside things that were not appropriate. ₅ The altar was filled with those abominable things which had been prohibited by the laws. ₆ A man could neither keep the Sabbath, nor observe the feasts of their ancestors, nor so much as confess himself to be a Jew.

₇ On the day of the king's birth every month, they were led along with bitter constraint to eat of the sacrifices. When the feast of Dionysia came, they were compelled to go in procession in honour of Dionysus, wearing wreaths of ivy. ₈ A decree went out to the neighbouring Greek cities, by the suggestion of Ptolemy, that they should observe the same conduct against the Jews, and should make them eat of the sacrifices, ₉ and that they should kill those who didn't choose to go over to the Greek rites. So the present misery was for all to see. ₁₀ For example, two women were brought in for having circumcised their children. These, when they had led them publicly around the city with the babes hung from their breasts, they threw down headlong from the wall. ₁₁ Others who had run together into the caves nearby to keep the seventh day secretly, were betrayed to Philip and were all burnt together, because their piety kept them from defending themselves, in view of the honour of that most solemn day.

₁₂ I urge those who read this book to not be discouraged because of the calamities, but recognise that these punishments were not for the destruction, but for the chastening of our race. ₁₃ For indeed it is a sign of great kindness that those who act impiously are not let alone for a long time, but immediately meet with retribution. ₁₄ For in the case of the other nations, the Sovereign Lord waits patiently to punish them until they have attained to the full measure of their sins; but not with us, ₁₅ that he may not take vengeance on us afterward,ʰ when we have come to theⁱ height of our sins. ₁₆ Therefore he never withdraws his mercy from us; but though he

---

ª *4:31* Gr. successor.
ᵇ *5:9* See 1 Maccabees 12:7.
ᶜ *5:23* Some authorities read towards the Jews, he sent. The Greek text of this sentence is uncertain.
ᵈ *5:23* Compare 2 Maccabees 4:9, 19; 9:19.

ᵉ *5:24* Gr. Μυσάρχην, which also may mean ruler of the Mysians.
ᶠ *6:1* Or, Geron an Athenian
ᵍ *6:4* Or, idled with their fellows
ʰ *6:15* Or, when our sins have come to their height
ⁱ *6:15* Gr. end.

chastens with calamity, he doesn't forsake his own people. 17 However let this that we have spoken suffice to remind you; but after a few words, we must come to the narrative.

18 Eleazar, one of the principal scribes, a man already well advanced in years, and of a noble countenance, was compelled to open his mouth to eat swine's flesh. 19 But he, welcoming death with honour rather than life with defilement, advanced of his own accord to the instrument of torture, but first spat out the flesh, 20 as men ought to come who are resolute to repel such things as not even for the natural love of life is it lawful to taste.

21 But those who had the charge of that forbidden sacrificial feast took the man aside, for the acquaintance which of old times they had with him, and privately implored him to bring flesh of his own providing, such as was proper for him to use, and to make as if he did eat of the flesh from the sacrifice, as had been commanded by the king; 22 that by so doing he might be delivered from death, and so his ancient friendship with them might be treated kindly. 23 But he, having formed a high resolve, and one that became his years, the dignity of old age, and the grey hairsᵃ which he had reached with honour, and his excellentᵇ education from a child, or rather the holy lawsᶜ of God's ordaining, declared his mind accordingly, bidding them to quickly send him to Hades.

24 "For it doesn't become our years to dissemble," he said, "that many of the young should suppose that Eleazar, the man of ninety years, had gone over to an alien religion; 25 and so they, by reason of my deception, and for the sake of this brief and momentary life, would be led astray because of me, and I defile and disgrace myself in my old age. 26 For even if for the present time I would remove from me the punishment of men, yet whether I live or die, I wouldn't escape the hands of the Almighty. 27 Therefore, by bravely parting with my life now, I will show myself worthy of my old age, 28 and ᵈleave behind a noble example to the young to die willingly and nobly a glorious death for the revered and holy laws."

When he had said these words, he went immediately to the instrument of torture. 29 ᵉ When they changed the good will they bore towards him a little before into ill because these words of his were, as they thought, sheer madness, 30 and when he was at the point to die with theᶠ blows, he groaned aloud and said, "To the Lord, who has the holy knowledge, it is manifest that, while I might have been delivered from death, I endure severe pains in my body by being scourged; but in soul I gladly suffer these things because of my fear of him."

31 So this man also died like this, leaving his death for an example of nobleness and a memorial of virtue, not only to the young but also to the great body of his nation.

7

1 It came to pass that seven brothers and their mother were at the king's command taken and shamefully handled with scourges and cords, to compel them to taste of the abominable swine's flesh. 2 One of them made himself the spokesman and said, "What would you ask and learn from us? For we are ready to die rather than transgress the laws of our ancestors."

3 The king fell into a rage, and commanded that pans and cauldrons be heated. 4 When these were immediately heated, he gave orders to cut out the tongue of him who had been their spokesman, and to scalp him, and to cut off his extremities, with the rest of his brothers and his mother looking on. 5 And when he was utterlyᵍ maimed, the king gave orders to bring him to the fire, being yet alive, and to fry him in the pan. And as the smoke from the pan spread far, they and their mother also exhorted one another to die nobly, saying this: 6 "The Lord God sees, and in truth isʰ entreated for us, as Moses declared in ⁱhis song, which witnesses against the people to their faces, saying, 'And he will have compassion on his servants.'"

7 And when the first had died like this, they brought the second to the mocking; and they pulled off the skin of his head with the hair and asked him, "Will you eat, before your body is punished in every limb?"

8 But he answered in the language of his ancestors and said to them, "No." Therefore he also underwent the next torture in succession, as the first had done. 9 When he was at the last gasp, he said, "You, miscreant, release us out of this present life, but the King of the world will raise us who have died for his laws up to an everlasting renewal of life."

10 After him, the third was made a victim of their mocking. When he was required, he quickly put out his tongue, and stretched out his hands courageously, 11 and nobly said, "I got these from heaven. For his laws' sake I treat these with contempt. From him, I hope to receive these back again." 12 As a result, the king himself and those who were with him were astonished at the young man's soul, for he regarded the pains as nothing.

13 When he too was dead, they shamefully handled and tortured the fourth in the same way. 14 Being near to death he said this: "It is good to die at the hands of men and look for the hope which is given by God, that we will be raised up again by him. For as for you, you will have no resurrection to life."

15 Next after him, they brought the fifth and shamefully handled him. 16 But he looked towards ʲthe king and said, "Because you have authority amongst men, though you are corruptible, you do what you please. But don't think that our race has been forsaken by God. 17 But hold on to your ways, and see how his sovereign majesty will torture you and your descendants!"

18 After him they brought the sixth. When he was about to die, he said, "Don't be vainly deceived, for we suffer these things for our own doings, as sinning against our own God. Astounding things have come to pass; 19 but don't think you that you will be unpunished, having tried to fight against God!"

20 But above all, the mother was marvellous and worthy of honourable memory; for when she watched seven sons perishing within the space of one day, she bore the sight with a good courage because of her hope in the Lord. 21 She exhorted each one of them in the language of their fathers, filled with a noble spirit and stirring up her woman's thoughts with manly courage, saying to them, 22 "I don't know how you came into my womb. It wasn't I who gave you your ᵏspirit and your life. It wasn't I who brought into order the first elements of each one of you. 23 Therefore the Creator of the world, who shaped the first origin of man and devised the first origin of all things, in mercy gives back to you again both your ˡspirit and your life, as you now treat yourselves with contempt for his laws' sake."

24 But Antiochus, thinking himself to be despised, and suspecting the reproachful voice, while the youngest was yet alive didn't only make his appeal to him by words, but also at the same time promised with oaths that he would enrich him andᵐ raise him to high honour if he would turn from the ways of his ancestors, and that he would take him for his ⁿfriend and entrust him with public affairs. 25 But when the young man would in no way listen, the king called to him his mother, and urged her to advise the youth to save himself. 26 When he had urged her with many words, she undertook to persuade her son. 27 But bending towards him, laughing the cruel tyrant to scorn, she spoke this in the language of her fathers: "My son, have pity upon me who carried you nine months in my womb, and nursed you three years, and nourished and brought you up to this age, and sustained you. 28 I beg you, my child, to lift your eyes to the sky and the earth, and to see all things that are in it, and thus to recognise that God made them not of things that were, and that the race of men in this way comes into being. 29 Don't be afraid of this butcher, but, proving yourself worthy of your brothers, accept your death, that in God's mercy I may receive you again with your brothers."

30 But before she had finished speaking, the young man said, "What are you all waiting for? I don't obey the commandment of the king, but I listen to the commandment of the law that was given to our fathers through Moses. 31 But you, who have devised all kinds of evil against the Hebrews, will in no way escape God's hands. 32 For we are suffering because of our own sins. 33 If for rebuke and chastening, our living Lord has been angered a little while, yet he will again be reconciled with his own servants. 34 But you, O unholy man and of all most vile, don't be vainly lifted up in your wild pride with uncertain hopes, raising your hand against the heavenly children. 35 For you have not yet escaped the judgement of the Almighty God who sees all things. 36 For these our brothers, having endured a ᵒ short pain that brings everlasting life, have now ᵖ died under God's covenant. But you, through God's judgement, will receive in just measure the penalties of your arrogance. 37 But I, as my brothers, give up both body and soul for the laws of our fathers, calling upon God that he may speedily become �qgracious to the nation, and that you, amidst trials and plagues, may confess that he alone is God, 38 and that in me and my brothers ʳ you may bring to an end the wrath of the Almighty which has been justly brought upon our whole race."

39 But the king, falling into a rage, handled him worse than all the rest, being exasperated at his mocking. 40 So he also died pure, putting his whole trust in the Lord.

41 Last of all, after her sons, the mother died.

42 Let it then suffice to have said thus much concerning the sacrificial feasts and the extreme tortures.

8

1 But Judas, who is also called Maccabaeus, and those who were with him, making their way secretly into the villages, called to them their kindred. Taking to them those who had continued in the Jews' religion, gathered together about six thousand. 2 They called upon the Lord to look at the people who were oppressed by all, and to have compassion on the sanctuary that had been profaned by the ungodly men, 3 and to have pity on the city that was suffering ruin and ready to be levelled to the ground, and to listen to the blood that cried out to him, 4 and to remember the lawless destruction of the innocent infants, and concerning the blasphemies that had been committed against his name, and to show his hatred of wickedness.

ᵃ *6:23* The Greek text appears to be corrupt.
ᵇ *6:23* Some authorities read manner of life.
ᶜ *6:23* Gr. legislation.
ᵈ *6:28* Gr. one that has left behind.
ᵉ *6:29* The Greek text of this verse is uncertain.
ᶠ *6:30* Or, blows
ᵍ *7:5* Gr. useless.
ʰ *7:6* Or, comforted in
ⁱ *7:6* See Deuteronomy 31:21 and 32:36.
ʲ *7:16* Gr. him.

ᵏ *7:22* Or, breath
ˡ *7:23* Or, breath
ᵐ *7:24* Gr. make him one that is counted happy.
ⁿ *7:24* See 2 Maccabees 8:9.
ᵒ *7:36* Gr. short pain of ever-flowing life.
ᵖ *7:36* Gr. fallen. By the omission of one Greek letter the words would signify having endured a short pain, have now drunk of ever-flowing life under God's covenant.
q *7:37* Gr. propitious.
ʳ *7:38* Some authorities read may be stayed.

₅When Maccabaeus had trained his men for service, the heathen at once found him irresistible, for the wrath of the Lord was turned into mercy. ₆ ᵃComing without warning, he set fire to cities and villages. And in winning back the most important positions, putting to flight no small number of the enemies, ₇he especially took advantage of the nights for such assaults. His courage was loudly talked of everywhere.

₈But when Philip saw the man gaining ground little by little, and increasing more and more in his success, he wrote to Ptolemy, the governor of Coelesyria and Phoenicia, that he should support the king's cause. ₉Ptolemy quickly appointed Nicanor the son of Patroclus, one of the king's ᵇ chief friends, and sent him, in command of no fewer than twenty thousand of all nations, to destroy the whole race of Judea. With him he joined Gorgias also, a captain and one who had experience in matters of war. ₁₀Nicanor resolved by the sale of the captive Jews to make up for the king the tribute of two thousand talents which he was to pay to the Romans. ₁₁Immediately he sent to the cities upon the sea coast, inviting them to buy Jewish ᶜslaves, promising to deliver seventy ᵈslaves for a talent, not expecting the judgement that was to overtake him from the Almighty.

₁₂News came to Judas concerning Nicanor's invasion. When he communicated to those who were with him the presence of the army, ₁₃those who were cowardly and distrustful of God's judgement ᵉran away and left the country. ₁₄Others sold all that they had left, and at the same time implored the Lord to deliver those who had been sold as slaves by the impious Nicanor before he ever met them, ₁₅if not for their own sakes, then for the covenants made with their ancestors, and because he had called them by his holy and glorious name. ₁₆So Maccabaeus gathered his men together, six thousand in number, and exhorted them not to be frightened by the enemy, nor to fear the great multitude of the heathen who came wrongfully against them, but to fight nobly, ₁₇setting before their eyes the outrage that had been lawlessly perpetrated upon the holy place, and the torture of the city that had been turned to mockery, and further the overthrow of the way of life received from their ancestors. ₁₈"For they," he said, "trust their weapons and daring deeds, but we trust in the almighty God, since he is able at a nod to cast down those who are coming against us, and even the whole world." ₁₉Moreover, he recounted to them the help given from time to time in the days of their ancestors, both in the days of Sennacherib, when one hundred and eighty-five thousand perished, ₂₀and in the land of Babylon, in the battle that was fought against the ᶠGauls, how they came to the battle with eight thousand in all, with four thousand Macedonians, and how, the Macedonians being hard pressed, the ᵍsix thousand destroyed the hundred and twenty thousand because of the help which they had from heaven, and took a great deal of plunder.

₂₁And when he had with these words filled them with courage and made them ready to die for the laws and their country, he divided his army into four parts. ₂₂He appointed his brothers, Simon, Joseph, and Jonathan, to be leaders of the divisions with him, giving each the command of one thousand and five hundred men. ₂₃Moreover Eleazer also, having read aloud the sacred book, and having given as watchword, "THE HELP OF GOD", leading the first band himself, joined battle with Nicanor.

₂₄Since the Almighty fought on their side, they killed more than nine thousand of the enemy, and wounded andʰ disabled most of Nicanor's army, and compelled them all to flee. ₂₅They took the money of those who had come there to buy them as slaves. After they had pursued them for some ⁱdistance, they returned, being constrained by the time of the day; ₂₆for it was the day before the Sabbath, and for this reason they made no effort to chase them far. ₂₇ ʲ When they had gathered ᵏthe weapons of the enemy together, and had stripped off their spoils, they kept the Sabbath, greatly blessing and thanking the Lord who had saved them to this day, because he had begun to show mercy to them. ₂₈After the Sabbath, when they had given some of the spoils to the ˡ maimed, and to the widows and orphans, they distributed the rest amongst themselves and their children. ₂₉When they had accomplished these things and had made a common supplication, they implored the merciful Lord to be wholly reconciled with his servants.

₃₀Having had an encounter with the forces of Timotheus and Bacchides, they killed more than twenty thousand of them, and made themselves masters of exceedingly high strongholds, and divided very much plunder, giving the ᵐmaimed, orphans, widows, and the aged an equal share with themselves. ₃₁ ⁿ When they had gathered the weapons ᵒ of the enemy together, they stored them all up carefully in the most strategic positions, and they carried the rest of the spoils to Jerusalem. ₃₂They killed the ᵖphylarch of Timotheus's forces, a most unholy man, and one who had done the Jews much harm. ₃₃ �q As they celebrated the feast of victory in the ʳ city of their fathers, they burnt those who had set the sacred ˢgates on fire, including Callisthenes, who had fled into ᵗa little house. So they received the proper reward for their impiety.

₃₄The thrice-accursed Nicanor, who had brought the thousand merchants to buy the Jews as slaves, ₃₅being through the help of the Lord humbled by them who in his eyes were held to be of least account, took off his glorious apparel, and passing through the country, ᵘshunning all company like a fugitive slave, arrived at Antioch, ᵛ having, as he thought, had the greatest possible good fortune, though his army was destroyed. ₃₆He who had taken upon himself to make tribute sure for the Romans by the captivity of the men of Jerusalem published abroad that the Jews had One who fought for them, and that ʷbecause this was so, the Jews were invulnerable, because they followed the laws ordained by him.

9

₁Now about that time, Antiochus retreated ˣin disorder from the region of Persia. ₂For he had entered into the city called Persepolis, and he attempted to rob ʸa temple and to control the city. Therefore the multitudes rushed in and the people of the country turned to defend themselves with weapons; and it came to pass that Antiochus was put to flight by the people of the country and broke his camp with disgrace. ₃While he was at Ecbatana, news was brought to him about what had happened to Nicanor and the forces of Timotheus. ₄Being overcome by his anger, he planned to make the Jews suffer for the evil deeds of those who had put him to flight. Therefore, with judgement from heaven even now accompanying him, he ordered his charioteer to drive without ceasing until he completed the journey; for he arrogantly said this: "I will make Jerusalem a common graveyard of Jews when I come there."

₅But the All-seeing Lord, the God of Israel, struck him with a ᶻfatal and invisible stroke. As soon as he had finished speaking this word, an incurable pain of the bowels seized him, with bitter torments of the inner parts— ₆and that most justly, for he had tormented other men's bowels with many and strange sufferings. ₇But he in no way ceased from his rude insolence. No, he was filled with even more arrogance, breathing fire in his passion against the Jews, and giving orders to hasten the journey. But it came to pass moreover that he fell from his chariot as it rushed along, and having a grievous fall was tortured in all of the members of his body. ₈He who had just supposed himself to have the waves of the sea at his bidding because he was so superhumanly arrogant, and who thought to weigh the heights of the mountains in a balance, was now brought to the ground and carried in a litter, ᵃᵃshowing to all that the power was obviously God's, ₉so that worms swarmed out of the impious man's body, and while he was still living in anguish and pains, his flesh fell off, and by reason of the stench all the army turned with loathing from his decay. ₁₀The man who a little before supposed himself to touch the stars of heaven, no one could endure to carry because of his intolerable stench. ₁₁Therefore he began in great part to cease from his arrogance, being broken in spirit, and to come to knowledge under the scourge of God, his pains increasing every moment. ₁₂When he himself could not stand his own smell, he said these words: "It is right to be subject to God, and that one who is mortal should not think they are equal to God."

₁₃The vile man vowed to the sovereign Lord, who now no more would have pity upon him, saying ₁₄that the holy city, to which he was going in haste to lay it even with the ground and to ᵇᵇmake it a common graveyard, he would declare free. ₁₅Concerning the Jews, whom he had decided not even to count worthy of burial, but to cast them out to the animals with their infants for the birds to devour, he would make them all equal to citizens of Athens. ₁₆The holy sanctuary, which before he had plundered, he would adorn with best offerings, and would restore all the sacred vessels many times multiplied, and out of his own revenues would defray the charges that were required for the sacrifices. ₁₇Beside all this, he said that he would become a Jew and would visit every inhabited place, proclaiming the power of God. ₁₈But when his sufferings did in no way cease, for the judgement of God had come upon him in righteousness, having given up all hope for himself, he wrote to the Jews the letter written below, having the nature of a supplication, to this effect:

₁₉"To the worthy Jewish citizens, Antiochus, king and general, wishes much joy and health and prosperity. ₂₀May you and your children fare well, and may your affairs be as you wish. Having my hope in heaven, ₂₁I remembered with affection your honour and good will. Returning out of the region of Persia, and being taken with an annoying sickness, I deemed it

---

ᵃ *8:6* The Greek text of verses 6 and 7 is uncertain.
ᵇ *8:9* See 1 Maccabees 10:65. Compare 2 Maccabees 1:14; 7:24; 10:13; 14:11; 1 Maccabees 2:18.
ᶜ *8:11* Gr. bodies.
ᵈ *8:11* Gr. bodies.
ᵉ *8:13* The Greek text here is uncertain.
ᶠ *8:20* Gr. Galatians.
ᵍ *8:20* Some authorities read eight.
ʰ *8:24* Gr. disabled in their limbs.
ⁱ *8:25* Or, while
ʲ *8:27* The exact meaning of this clause is uncertain.
ᵏ *8:27* Gr. their weapons...the spoils of the enemy.
ˡ *8:28* Or, wounded Gr. shamefully handled.
ᵐ *8:30* Or, wounded Gr. shamefully handled.
ⁿ *8:31* The exact meaning of this clause is uncertain.
ᵒ *8:31* Gr. of them.

ᵖ *8:32* That is, probably, the captain of an irregular auxiliary force. Some write Phylarches, as a proper name.
q *8:33* The Greek text here is perhaps corrupt.
ʳ *8:33* Or, country
ˢ *8:33* Or, porches
ᵗ *8:33* Or, a solitary hut
ᵘ *8:35* Gr. having made himself solitary.
ᵛ *8:35* Or, having won the greatest possible favour by reason of the destruction of his army
ʷ *8:36* Or, because of this their way of life Gr. because of this manner.
ˣ *9:1* Or, with dishonour
ʸ *9:2* Or, temples
ᶻ *9:5* Gr. remediless.
ᵃᵃ *9:8* Or, showing manifestly to all the power of God
ᵇᵇ *9:14* Gr. build.

necessary to take thought for the common safety of all, 22 not despairing of myself, but having great hope to escape from the sickness. 23 But considering that my father also, at the time he led an army into the upper country, appointed his successor, 24 to the end that, if anything fell out contrary to expectation, or if any unwelcome tidings were brought, the people in the country, knowing to whom the state had been left, might not be troubled, 25 and, moreover, observing how the princes who are along the borders and neighbours to my kingdom watch for opportunities and look for the future event, I have appointed my son Antiochus to be king, whom I often entrusted and commended to most of you when I was hurrying to the upper provinces. I have written to him what is written below. 26 I therefore urge you and beg you, having in your remembrance the benefits done to you in common and severally, to preserve your present good will, each of you, towards me and my son. 27 For I am persuaded that he in gentleness and kindness will follow my purpose and treat you with moderation and kindness.

28 So the murderer and blasphemer, having endured the most intense sufferings, even as he had dealt with other men, ended his life amongst the mountains by a most piteous fate in a strange land. 29 Philip his foster brother took the body home and then, fearing the son of Antiochus, he withdrew himself to Ptolemy Philometor in Egypt.

10

1 Then Maccabaeus and those who were with him, the Lord leading them on, recovered the temple and the city. 2 They pulled down the altars that had been built in the marketplace by the foreigners, and also the sacred enclosures. 3 Having cleansed the sanctuary, they made another altar of sacrifice. a Striking flint and starting a fire, they offered sacrifices after they had ceased for two years, burnt incense, lit lamps, and set out the show bread. 4 When they had done these things, they fell prostrate and implored the Lord that they might fall no more into such evils; but that, if they ever did sin, they might be chastened by him with forbearance, and not be delivered to blaspheming and barbarous heathen. 5 Now on the same day that the sanctuary was profaned by foreigners, upon that very day it came to pass that the sanctuary was cleansed, even on the twenty-fifth day of the same month, which is Chislev. 6 They observed eight days with gladness in the manner of the feast of tabernacles, remembering how b not long before, during the feast of tabernacles, they were wandering in the mountains and in the caves like wild animals. 7 Therefore carrying wands wreathed with leaves, and beautiful branches, and palm fronds also, they offered up hymns of thanksgiving to him who had successfully brought to pass the cleansing of his own place. 8 They ordained also with a public statute and decree, for all the nation of the Jews, that they should observe these days every year.

9 Such were the events of the end of Antiochus, who was called Epiphanes.

10 Now we will declare what came to pass under Antiochus c Eupator, who proved himself a son of that ungodly man, and will summarize the main evils of the wars. 11 For this man, when he succeeded to the kingdom, appointed one Lysias to be chancellor and supreme governor of Coelesyria and Phoenicia. 12 For Ptolemy who was called Macron, setting an example of observing justice towards the Jews because of the wrong that had been done to them, endeavored to deal with them on peaceful terms. 13 Whereupon being accused by the king's d friends before Eupator, and hearing himself called traitor at every turn because he had abandoned Cyprus which Philometor had entrusted to him, and had withdrawn himself to Antiochus Epiphanes, and e failing to uphold the honour of his office, he took poison and did away with himself.

14 But when Gorgias was made governor of the district, he maintained a force of mercenaries, and at every turn kept up war with the Jews. 15 Together with him the Idumaeans also, being masters of important strongholds, harassed the Jews; and received those who had taken refuge from Jerusalem, they endeavored to keep up the war. 16 But Maccabaeus and his men, having made solemn supplication and having implored God to fight on their side, rushed upon the strongholds of the Idumaeans. 17 Assaulting them vigorously, they took control of the positions, and kept off all who fought upon the wall, and killed those whom they encountered, killing no fewer than twenty thousand.

18 Because no fewer than nine thousand had fled into two very strong towers having everything needed for a seige, 19 Maccabaeus, having left Simon and Joseph, and also Zacchaeus and those who were with him, a force sufficient to besiege them, departed himself to places where he was most needed. 20 But Simon and those who were with him, yielding to covetousness, were bribed by some of those who were in the towers, and receiving seventy thousand drachmas, let some of them slip away. 21 But when word was brought to Maccabaeus of what was done, he gathered the leaders of the people together, and accused those men of having sold their kindred for money by setting their enemies free to fight against them. 22 So

he killed these men for having turned traitors, and immediately took possession of the two towers. 23 Prospering with his weapons in everything he undertook, he destroyed more than twenty thousand in the two strongholds.

24 Now Timotheus, who had been defeated by the Jews before, having gathered together foreign forces in great multitudes, and having collected the cavalry which belonged to Asia, not a few, came as though he would take Judea by force of weapons. 25 But as he drew near, Maccabaeus and his men sprinkled dirt on their heads and girded their loins with sackcloth, in supplication to God, 26 and falling down upon the step in front of the altar, implored him to become f gracious to them, and g be an enemy to their enemies and an adversary to their adversaries, as the law declares. 27 Rising from their prayer they took up their weapons, and advanced some distance from the city. When they had come near to their enemies, they h halted. 28 When the dawn was now breaking, the two armies joined in battle, the one part having this, beside virtue, for a pledge of success and victory, that they had fled to the Lord for refuge, the others making their passion their leader in the fight.

29 When the battle became strong, there appeared out of heaven to their adversaries five splendid men on horses with bridles of gold, i and two of them, leading on the Jews, 30 and taking Maccabaeus in the midst of them, and covering him with their own armour, guarded him from wounds, while they shot arrows and thunderbolts at the enemies. For this reason, they were blinded and thrown into confusion, and were cut to pieces, filled with bewilderment. 31 Twenty thousand and five hundred were slain, beside six hundred cavalry.

32 Timotheus himself fled into a stronghold called Gazara, a fortress of great strength, j where Chaereas was in command. 33 Then Maccabaeus and his men were glad and laid siege to the fortress for four days. 34 Those who were within, trusting in the strength of the place, blasphemed exceedingly, and hurled out impious words. 35 But at dawn of the fifth day, certain young men of Maccabaeus' company, inflamed with anger because of the blasphemies, assaulted the wall with masculine force and with k furious anger, and cut down whoever came in their way. 36 Others climbing up in the same way, while the enemies were distracted with those who had made their way within, set fire to the towers, and kindled fires that burnt the blasphemers alive, while others broke open the gates, and, having given entrance to the rest of the band, occupied the city. 37 They killed Timotheus, who was hidden in a cistern, and his brother Chaereas, and Apollophanes. 38 When they had accomplished these things, they blessed the Lord with hymns and thanksgiving, blessing him who provides great benefits to Israel and gives them the victory.

11

1 Now after a very little time, Lysias, the king's guardian, kinsman, and chancellor, being very displeased about the things that had happened, 2 collected about eighty thousand infantry and all his cavalry and came against the Jews, planing to make the city a home for Greeks, 3 and to levy tribute on the temple, as l on the other sacred places of the nations, and to put up the high priesthood for sale every year. 4 He took no account of God's power, but was puffed up with his ten thousands of infantry, his thousands of cavalry, and his eighty elephants. 5 Coming into Judea and approaching Bethsuron, which was a strong place and about five stadia m away from Jerusalem, he pressed it hard.

6 When Maccabaeus and his men learnt that he was besieging the strongholds, they and all the people with lamentations and tears made supplication to the Lord to send a good angel to save Israel. 7 Maccabaeus himself took up weapons first, and exhorted the others to put themselves in jeopardy together with him and help their kindred; and they went out with him very willingly. 8 As they were there, close to Jerusalem, a horseman appeared at their head in white apparel, brandishing n weapons of gold. 9 They all together praised the merciful God, and were yet more strengthened in heart, being ready to o assail not only men but the wildest animals and walls of iron, 10 they advanced in array, having him who is in heaven to fight on their side, for the Lord had mercy on them. 11 Hurling themselves like lions against the enemy, they killed eleven thousand infantry and one thousand and six hundred cavalry, and forced all the rest to flee. 12 Most of them escaped wounded and naked. Lysias himself also escaped by shameful flight. 13 But as he was a man not void of understanding, pondering the defeat which had befallen him, and considering that the Hebrews could not be overcome because the Almighty God fought on their side, he sent again 14 and persuaded them to come to terms on condition that all their rights were acknowledged, and p promised that he would also persuade the king to become their friend. 15 Maccabaeus gave consent upon all the conditions which Lysias proposed to him, being careful of the common good; for whatever requests Maccabaeus delivered in writing to Lysias concerning the Jews the king allowed.

16 The letter written to the Jews from Lysias was to this effect:

---

a *10:3* Gr. firing.
b *10:6* Or, not long before they kept the feast of tabernacles by wandering
c *10:10* That is, son of a good father.
d *10:13* See 2 Maccabees 8:9
e *10:13* The Greek text here is corrupt.
f *10:26* Gr. propitious.
g *10:26* See Exodus 23:22.
h *10:27* Gr. were by themselves.

i *10:29* Some authorities read and leading on the Jews; who also, taking.
j *10:32* See ver. 37.
k *10:35* Gr. passion as of wild animals.
l *11:3* Or, on all the sacred places of the heathen
m *11:5* One stadia was roughly 189 metres or 618 feet, so 5 stadia was about a little less than 1 km or a little more than half a mile.
n *11:8* Gr. a panoply.
o *11:9* Gr. wound.
p *11:14* The Greek text here is corrupt.

"Lysias to the [a]people of the Jews, greetings. [17]John and Absalom, who were sent from you, having delivered the document written below, made request concerning the things written therein. [18]Whatever things therefore needed to be brought before the king I declared to him, and what things were possible he allowed. [19]If then you will all preserve your good will towards the government, I will also endeavour in the future to contribute to your good. [20]Concerning this, I have given order in detail, both to these men and to those who are sent from me, to confer with you. [21]Farewell. Written in the one hundred and forty-eighth year, on the twenty-fourth day of the month [b]Dioscorinthius."

[22]And the king's letter contained these words:

"King Antiochus to his brother Lysias, greetings. [23]Seeing that our father passed to the gods having the wish that the subjects of his kingdom [c]should be undisturbed and give themselves to the care of their own affairs, [24]we, having heard that the Jews do not consent to our father's purpose to turn them to the customs of the Greeks, but choose rather their own way of living, and make request that the customs of their law be allowed to them— [25]choosing therefore that this nation also should be free from disturbance, we determine that their temple is to be restored to them, and that they live according to the customs that were in the days of their ancestors. [26]You will therefore do well to send messengers to them and give them the right hand of friendship, that they, knowing our mind, may be of good heart, and gladly occupy themselves with the conduct of their own affairs."

[27]And to the nation, the king's letter was as follows:

"King Antiochus to the senate of the Jews and to the other Jews, greetings. [28]If you are all well, it is as we desire. We ourselves also are in good health. [29]Menelaus informed us that your desire was to return home and follow your own business. [30]They therefore who depart home up to the thirtieth day of Xanthicus shall have our [d]friendship, with full permission [31]that the Jews use their own foods and observe their own laws, even as formerly. None of them shall be in any way molested for the things that have been done in ignorance. [32]Moreover I have sent Menelaus also, that he may encourage you. [33]Farewell. Written in the one hundred and forty-eighth year, on the fifteenth day of Xanthicus."

[34]The Romans also sent to them a letter in these words:

"Quintus Memmius and Titus Manius, ambassadors of the Romans, to the people of the Jews, greetings. [35]In regard to the things which Lysias the king's kinsman granted you, we also give consent. [36]But as for the things which he judged should be referred to the king, send someone promptly, after you have considered them, that we may publish such decrees as are appropriate for your case; for we are on our way to Antioch. [37]Therefore send someone with speed, that we also may learn what is your mind. [38][e]Farewell. Written in the one hundred and forty-eighth year, on the fifteenth day of Xanthicus.

12

[1]So when this agreement had been made, Lysias departed to the king, and the Jews went about their farming.

[2]But some of the governors of districts, Timotheus and Apollonius the son of Gennaeus, and also Hieronymus and Demophon, and beside them Nicanor the governor of Cyprus, would not allow them to enjoy tranquillity and live in peace. [3]Men of Joppa perpetrated this great impiety: they invited the Jews who lived amongst them to go with their wives and children into the boats which they had provided, as though they had no ill will towards them. [4]When[f] the Jews,[g] relying on the public vote of the city, accepted the invitation, as men desiring to live in peace and suspecting nothing, they took them out to sea and drowned not less than two hundred of them. [5]When Judas heard of the cruelty done to his fellow-countrymen, giving command to the men that were with him [6]and calling upon God the righteous Judge, he came against the murderers of his kindred, and set the harbour on fire at night, burnt the boats, and put to the sword those who had fled there. [7]But when the town gates were closed, he withdrew, intending to come again to root out the whole community of the men of Joppa. [8]But learning that the men of Jamnia intended to do the same thing to the Jews who lived amongst them, [9]he attacked the Jamnites at night, and set fire to the harbour together with the fleet, so that the glare of the light was seen at Jerusalem, two hundred and forty furlongs[h] distant.

[10]Now when they had drawn off nine furlongs[i] from there, as they marched against Timotheus, an army of Arabians attacked him, no fewer than five thousand infantry and five hundred cavalry. [11]And when a hard battle had been fought, and Judas and his company, by the help of God, had good success, the nomads being overcome implored Judas to grant them friendship, promising to give him livestock, and to help [j]his people in all other ways. [12]So Judas, thinking that they would indeed be profitable in many things, agreed to live in peace with them; and receiving pledges of friendship they departed to their tents.

[13]He also attacked a certain city, strong and fenced with earthworks and walls, and inhabited by a mixed multitude of various nations. It was named Caspin. [14]Those who were within, trusting in the strength of the walls and their store of provisions, behaved themselves rudely towards Judas and those who were with him, railing, and furthermore blaspheming and speaking impious words. [15]But Judas and his company, calling upon the great Sovereign of the world, who without rams and cunning engines of war hurled down Jericho in the times of Joshua, rushed wildly against the wall. [16]Having taken the city by the will of God, they made unspeakable slaughter, so much that the adjoining lake, which was two furlongs[k] broad, appeared to be filled with the deluge of blood.

[17]When they had gone seven hundred and fifty furlongs[l] from there, they made their way to Charax, to the Jews that are called [m]Tubieni. [18]They didn't find Timotheus in that district, for he had by then departed from the district without accomplishing anything, but had left behind a very strong garrison in one place. [19]But Dositheus and Sosipater, who were captains under Maccabaeus, went out and destroyed those who had been left by Timotheus in the stronghold, more than ten thousand men. [20]Maccabaeus, arranging his own army in divisions, set [n]these two over the bands, and marched in haste against Timotheus, who had with him one hundred and twenty thousand infantry and two thousand and five hundred cavalry. [21]When Timotheus heard of the approach of Judas, he at once sent away the women and the children with the baggage into the fortress called [o]Carnion; for the place was hard to besiege and difficult of access by reason of the narrowness of the approaches on all sides. [22]When the band of Judas, who led the first division, appeared in sight, and when terror and fear came upon the enemy, because the manifestation of him who sees all things came upon them, they fled in every direction, carried this way and that, so that they were often injured by their own men, and pierced with the points of their own swords. [23]Judas continued the pursuit more vigorously, putting the wicked wretches to the sword, and he destroyed as many as thirty thousand men.

[24]Timotheus himself, falling in with the company of Dositheus and Sosipater, implored them with much crafty guile to let him go with his life, because he had in his power the parents of many of them and the kindred of some. [p]"Otherwise, he said, little regard will [q]be shown to these." [25]So when he had with many words confirmed the agreement to restore them without harm, they let him go that they might save their kindred.

[26]Then Judas, marching against [r]Carnion and the temple of Atergatis, killed twenty-five thousand people. [27]After he had put these to flight and destroyed them, he marched against Ephron also, a strong city, [s]wherein were multitudes of people of all nations. Stalwart young men placed [t]on the walls made a vigorous defence. There were great stores of war engines and darts there. [28]But calling upon the Sovereign who with might shatters the [u]strength of [v]the enemy, they took the city into their hands, and killed as many as twenty-five thousand of those who were in it.

[29]Setting out from there, they marched in haste against Scythopolis, which is six hundred furlongs[w] away from Jerusalem. [30]But when the Jews who were settled there testified of the good will that the Scythopolitans had shown towards them, and of their kind treatment of them in the times of their misfortune, [31]they gave thanks, and further exhorted them to remain well disposed towards the race for the future. Then they went up to Jerusalem, the feast of weeks being close at hand.

[32]But after the feast called Pentecost, they marched in haste against Gorgias the governor of Idumaea. [33]He came out with three thousand infantry and four hundred cavalry. [34]When they had set themselves in array, it came to pass that a few of the Jews fell. [35]A certain Dositheus, one [x]of Bacenor's company, who was on horseback and was a strong man, pressed hard on Gorgias, and taking hold of his cloke dragged him along by main force. While he planned to take the accursed man alive, one of the Thracian cavalry bore down on him and disabled his shoulder, and so Gorgias escaped to [y]Marisa.

[36]When those who were with Esdris had been fighting long and were weary, Judas called upon the Lord to show himself, fighting on their side and leading in the battle. [37]Then in the language of his ancestors he raised the battle cry joined with hymns. Then he rushed against Gorgias' troops when they were not expecting it, and put them to flight.

---

[a] *11:16* Gr. multitude.

[b] *11:21* This month name is not found elsewhere, and is perhaps corrupt.

[c] *11:23* Or, should not be disquieted but

[d] *11:30* Gr. right hand.

[e] *11:38* Gr. Be in good health.

[f] *12:4* Gr. they also.

[g] *12:4* Gr. after.

[h] *12:9* a furlong is about 201 metres or 220 yards, so 240 furlongs is about 48 km. or 30 miles

[i] *12:10* a furlong is about 201 metres or 220 yards, so 9 furlongs is about 1.8 km. or 1 1/8 miles

[j] *12:11* Gr. them.

[k] *12:16* a furlong is about 201 metres or 220 yards, so 2 furlongs is about 402 metres or 1/4 mile

[l] *12:17* a furlong is about 201 metres or 220 yards, so 750 furlongs is about 151 km. or 94 miles

[m] *12:17* That is, men of Tob: see Judges 11:3, 2 Samuel 10:6, and compare 1 Maccabees 5:13.

[n] *12:20* Gr. them.

[o] *12:21* Compare Carnain,1 Maccabees 5:26, 43, 44.

[p] *12:24* Gr. and the result will be that these be disregarded. The Greek text here is perhaps corrupt.

[q] *12:24* Or, have been shown

[r] *12:26* Compare Carnain, 1 Maccabees 5:26, 43, 44.

[s] *12:27* The Greek text here is perhaps corrupt.

[t] *12:27* Gr. in front of.

[u] *12:28* Some authorities read weight.

[v] *12:28* Or, his enemies

[w] *12:29* a furlong is about 201 metres or 220 yards, so 600 furlongs is about 121 km. or 75 miles

[x] *12:35* The Greek text is uncertain.

[y] *12:35* Compare 1 Maccabees 5:65.

38 Judas gathered his army and came to the city of [a]Adullam. As the seventh day was coming on, they purified themselves according to the custom, and kept the Sabbath there.

39 On the following day, [b]when it had become necessary, Judas and his company came to take up the bodies of those who had fallen, [c]and in company with their kinsmen to bring them back to the sepulchres of their ancestors. 40 But under the garments of each one of the dead they found [d]consecrated tokens of the idols of Jamnia, which the law forbids the Jews to have anything to do with. It became clear to all that it was for this cause that they had fallen. 41 All therefore, blessing the ways of the Lord, the righteous Judge, who makes manifest the things that are hidden, 42 turned themselves to supplication, praying that the sin committed might be wholly blotted out. The noble Judas exhorted the multitude to keep themselves from sin, for they had seen with their own eyes what happened because of the sin of those who had fallen. 43 When he had made a collection man by man to the sum of two thousand drachmas of silver, he sent to Jerusalem to offer a sacrifice for sin, doing very well and honourably in this, in that he took thought for the resurrection. 44 For if he wasn't expecting that those who had fallen would rise again, it would be superfluous and idle to pray for the dead. 45 But if he was looking forward to an honourable memorial of gratitude laid up for those who [e]die [f]in godliness, then the thought was holy and godly. Therefore he made the atoning sacrifice for those who had died, that they might be released from their sin.

13

1 In the one hundred and forty-ninth year, news was brought to Judas and his company that Antiochus Eupator was coming with multitudes against Judea, 2 and with him Lysias his guardian and chancellor, each having a Greek force of one hundred and ten thousand infantry, five thousand and three hundred cavalry, twenty-two elephants, and three hundred chariots armed with scythes.

3 And Menelaus also joined himself with them, and with great hypocrisy encouraged Antiochus, not for the saving of his country, but because he thought that he would be set over the government. 4 But the King of kings stirred up the anger of Antiochus against the wicked wretch. When Lysias informed him that this man was the cause of all the evils, the king commanded to bring him to Beroea, and to put him to death in the way customary in that place. 5 Now there is in that place a tower that is fifty cubits high, full of ashes, and it had all around it a [g]circular rim sloping steeply on every side into the ashes. 6 Here one who is guilty of sacrilege or notorious for other crimes is pushed down to destruction. 7 By such a fate it happened that the breaker of the law, Menelaus, died, without obtaining so much as a grave in the earth, and that justly; 8 for inasmuch as he had perpetrated many sins [h]against the altar, whose fire and whose ashes were holy, he received his death in ashes.

9 Now the king,[i] infuriated in spirit, was coming with intent to inflict on the Jews the very worst of the sufferings that had been done in his father's time. 10 But when Judas heard of these things, he commanded the multitude to call upon the Lord day and night, if ever at any other time, so now to help those who were at the point of being deprived of the law, their country, and the holy temple, 11 and not to allow the people who had just begun to be revived to fall into the hands of those profane heathen. 12 So when they had all done the same thing together, [j] begging the merciful Lord with weeping and fastings and prostration for three days without ceasing, Judas exhorted them and commanded they should join him.

13 Having consulted privately with the elders, he resolved that before the king's army entered into Judea and made themselves masters of the city, they should go out and decide the matter by the help of [k]God. 14 And committing the decision to the [l]Lord of the world, and exhorting those who were with him to contend nobly for laws, temple, city, country, and way of life, he pitched his camp by Modin. 15 He gave out to his men the watchword, "VICTORY IS GOD'S", with a chosen force of the bravest young men he attacked by the king's pavilion by night, and killed of his army as many as two thousand men, and [m]brought down the leading elephant with him who was in the [n]tower on him. 16 At last they filled the [o]army with terror and alarm, and departed with good success. 17 This had been accomplished when the day was just dawning, because of the Lord's protection that gave [p]Judas help.

18 But the king, having had a taste of the exceeding boldness of the Jews, made strategic attacks on their positions, 19 and on a strong fortress of the Jews at Bethsura. He advanced, was turned back, failed, and was defeated. 20 Judas sent the things that were necessary to those who were within. 21 But Rhodocus, from the Jewish ranks, made secrets known to the enemy. He was sought out, arrested, and shut up in prison. 22 The king negotiated with them in Bethsura the second time, gave his hand, took theirs, departed, attacked the forces of Judas, was put to the worse, 23 heard that Philip who had been left as chancellor in Antioch had become reckless, was confounded, made to the Jews an overture of peace, submitted himself and swore to acknowledge all their rights, came to terms with them and offered sacrifice, honoured the sanctuary and the place, 24 showed kindness and graciously received Maccabaeus, left Hegemonides governor from Ptolemais even to the [q] Gerrenians, 25 and came to Ptolemais. The men of Ptolemais were displeased at the treaty, for they had exceedingly great indignation against the Jews. They desired to annul the articles of the agreement. 26 Lysias [r]came forward to speak, made the best defence that was possible, persuaded, pacified, gained their good will, and departed to Antioch. This was the issue of the attack and departure of the king.

14

1 Three years later, news was brought to Judas and his company that Demetrius the son of Seleucus, having sailed into the harbour of Tripolis with a mighty army and a fleet, 2 had taken possession of the country, having made away with Antiochus and his guardian Lysias.

3 But one Alcimus, who had formerly been high priest, and had wilfully polluted himself in the times when there was no mingling with the Gentiles, considering that there was no deliverance for him in any way, nor any more access to the holy altar, 4 came to King Demetrius in about the one hundred and fifty-first year, presenting to him a crown of gold and a palm, and beside these some of the festal olive boughs of the temple. For that day, he held his peace; 5 but having gotten opportunity to further his own madness, being called by Demetrius into a meeting of his council, and asked how the Jews stood affected and what they intended, he answered:

6 "Those of the Jews called [s]Hasidaeans, whose leader is Judas Maccabaeus, keep up war and are seditious, not allowing the kingdom to find tranquillity. 7 Therefore, having laid aside my ancestral glory—I mean the high priesthood—I have now come [t]here, 8 first for the genuine care I have for the things that concern the king, and secondly because I have regard also to my own fellow citizens. For through the unadvised dealing of those of whom I spoke before, our whole race is in no small misfortune. 9 O king, having informed yourself of these things, take thought both for our country and for our race, which is surrounded by enemies, according to the gracious kindness with which you receive all. 10 For as long as Judas remains alive, it is impossible for the government to find peace. 11 When he had spoken such words as these, at once [u]the rest of the king's [v]friends, having ill will against Judas, inflamed Demetrius yet more. 12 He immediately appointed Nicanor, who had been master of the elephants, and made him governor of Judea. He sent him out, 13 giving him written instructions to kill Judas himself and to scatter those who were with him, and to set up Alcimus as high priest of the [w]great temple. 14 Those in Judea who [x]had driven Judas into exile thronged to Nicanor in flocks, supposing that the misfortunes and calamities of the Jews would be successes to themselves.

15 But when the Jews heard of Nicanor's advance and the assault of the heathen, they sprinkled dirt on their heads and made solemn prayers to him who had established his own people for evermore, and who always, making manifest his presence, upholds those who are his own heritage. 16 [y]When the leader had given orders, he immediately set out from there and joined battle with them at a village called Lessau. 17 But Simon, the brother of Judas, had encountered Nicanor, yet not till late, having been delayed by reason of the sudden consternation caused by his adversaries.

18 Nevertheless Nicanor, hearing of the valour of those who were with Judas, and their courage in fighting for their country, shrank from bringing the matter to the decision of the sword. 19 Therefore he sent Posidonius, Theodotus, and Mattathias to give and receive pledges of friendship. 20 So when these proposals had been long considered, and the leader had made the [z]troops acquainted with them, and it appeared that they were all of like mind, they consented to the covenants. 21 They appointed a day on which to meet together by themselves. A chariot came forward from each army. They set up seats of honour. 22 Judas stationed armed men ready in convenient places, lest perhaps there should suddenly be treachery on the part of the enemy. They held a conference as was appropriate. 23 Nicanor waited in Jerusalem, and did nothing to cause disturbance, but dismissed the flocks of people that had gathered together. 24 He kept Judas always in his presence. He had gained a hearty affection for the man. 25 He urged him to marry and have children. He married, settled quietly, and took part in common life.

---

a 12:38 Gr. Odollam.
b 12:39 The Greek text here is uncertain.
c 12:39 Or, and to bring them back to be with their kinsmen in the sepulchres
d 12:40 Perhaps these were consecrated images of the idols.
e 12:45 Gr. fall asleep.
f 12:45 Or, on the side of godliness
g 13:5 Gr. contrivance or machine.
h 13:8 Gr. about.
i 13:9 Some authorities read indignant.
j 13:12 Gr. and implored.
k 13:13 Some authorities read the Lord.
l 13:14 Some authorities read Creator.
m 13:15 The Greek text here is probably corrupt.

n 13:15 Gr. house.
o 13:16 Gr. camp.
p 13:17 Gr. him.
q 13:24 The form of this word is uncertain. Compare Girzites (or Gizrites), 1 Samuel 27:8. One manuscript reads Gerarenes.
r 13:26 Gr. came forward to the tribune or judgement seat.
s 14:6 That is, Chasidim.
t 14:7 Some authorities read a second time.
u 14:11 Or, the king's friends likewise
v 14:11 See 2 Maccabees 8:9.
w 14:13 Gr. greatest.
x 14:14 See 2 Maccabees 5:27.
y 14:16 The Greek text of this verse and the next is corrupt.
z 14:20 Or, people Gr. multitudes.

26 But Alcimus, perceiving the good will that was between them, [a]and having taken possession of the covenants that had been made, came to Demetrius and told him that Nicanor was disloyal to the government, for he had appointed that conspirator against his kingdom, Judas, to be his successor. 27 The king, falling into a rage, and being exasperated by the false accusations of that most wicked man, wrote to Nicanor, signifying that he was displeased at the covenants, and commanding him to send Maccabaeus prisoner to Antioch in all haste. 28 When this message came to Nicanor, he was confounded, and was very troubled at the thought of annulling the articles that had been agreed upon, the man having done no wrong; 29 but because there was no opposing the king, he watched his time to execute this purpose by strategy. 30 But Maccabaeus, when he perceived that Nicanor was behaving more harshly in his dealings with him, and that he had become ruler in his customary bearing, understanding that this harshness came not of good, gathered together not a few of his men, and concealed himself from Nicanor.

31 But the other,[b] when he became aware that he had been bravely defeated by the strategy of Judas,[c] came to the great[d] and holy temple, while the priests were offering the usual sacrifices, and commanded them to hand over the man. 32 When they declared with oaths that they had no knowledge where the man was whom he sought, 33 he stretched out his right hand towards the sanctuary, and swore this oath: "If you won't deliver up to me Judas as a prisoner, I will level this [e]temple of God even with the ground, break down the altar, and I will erect here a temple to Dionysus for all to see.

34 And having said this, he departed. But the priests, stretching forth their hands towards heaven, called upon him who always fights for our nation, in these words: 35 "You, O Lord of the universe, who in yourself have need of nothing, were well pleased that a sanctuary of your habitation[f] should be set amongst us. 36 So now, O holy Lord of all holiness, keep undefiled forever this house that has been recently cleansed."

37 Now information was given to Nicanor against one Razis, an elder of Jerusalem, who was a lover of his countrymen and a man of very good report, and one called Father of the Jews for his good will. 38 For in the former times when there was no mingling with the Gentiles, he had been accused of following the Jews' religion, and had risked body and life with all earnestness for the religion of the Jews. 39 Nicanor, wishing to make evident the ill will that he bore against the Jews, sent above five hundred soldiers to seize him; 40 for he thought by seizing him to inflict an injury on them. 41 But when the [g]troops were at the point of taking the tower, and were forcing the door of the court, and asked for fire to burn the doors, he, being surrounded on every side, fell upon his sword, 42 choosing rather to die nobly than to fall into the hands of the wicked wretches, and suffer outrage unworthy of his own nobleness. 43 But since he missed his stroke through the excitement of the struggle, and the crowds were now rushing within the door, he ran bravely up to the wall and cast himself down bravely amongst the crowds. 44 But as they quickly gave back, a space was made, and he fell on the middle of [h]his side. 45 Still having breath within him, and being inflamed with anger, he rose up, and though his blood gushed out in streams and his wounds were grievous, he ran through the crowds, and standing upon a steep rock, 46 when as his blood was now well near spent, he drew forth his bowels through the wound, and taking them in both his hands he shook them at the crowds. Calling upon him who is Lord of life and spirit to restore him [i]these again, he died like this.

15

1 But Nicanor, hearing that Judas and his company were in the region of Samaria, resolved to attack them with complete safety on the day of rest. 2 When the Jews who were compelled to follow him said, "Don't destroy so savagely and barbarously, but give due glory to the day which he who sees all things has honoured and hallowed above other days."

3 Then the thrice-accursed wretch asked if there were a Sovereign in heaven who had commanded to keep the Sabbath day.

4 When they declared, "There is the Lord, living himself as Sovereign in heaven, who told us observe the seventh day."

5 He replied, "I also am a sovereign on the earth, who commands you to take up weapons and execute the king's business." Nevertheless he didn't prevail to execute his cruel plan.

6 And Nicanor, [j] in his utter boastfulness and arrogance, had determined to set up a monument of complete victory over Judas and all those who were with him. 7 But Maccabaeus still trusted unceasingly, with all hope that he should obtain help from the Lord. 8 He exhorted his company not to be fearful at the assault of the heathen, but keeping in mind the help which in former times they had often received from heaven, so now also to look for the victory which would come to them from the Almighty, 9 and encouraging them out of the law and the prophets, and reminding them of the conflicts that they had won, he made them more eager. 10 And when he had aroused their courage, he gave them orders, at the same time pointing out the faithlessness of the heathen and their breach of their oaths. 11 Arming each one of them, not so much with the sure defence of shields and spears as with the encouragement of good words, and moreover relating to them a dream worthy to be believed, he made them all exceedingly glad.

12 The vision of that dream was this: Onias, he who had been high priest, a noble and good man, modest in bearing, yet gentle in manner and well-spoken, and trained from a child in all points of virtue, with outstretched hands invoking blessings on the whole body of the Jews. 13 Then he saw a man appear, of venerable age and exceeding glory, and the dignity around him was wonderful and most majestic. 14 Onias answered and said, "This is the lover of the kindred, he who prays much for the people and the holy city: Jeremiah the prophet of God. 15 Jeremiah stretched out his right hand and delivered to Judas a gold sword, and in giving it addressed him thus: 16 "Take this holy sword, a gift from God, with which you shall strike down the adversaries."

17 Being encouraged by the words of Judas, which were noble and effective, and able to incite to virtue and to stir the souls of the young to manly courage, they determined not to carry on a campaign, but nobly to bear down upon the enemy, and fighting hand to hand with all courage bring the matter to a conclusion, because the city, the sanctuary, and the temple were in danger. 18 For their fear for wives and children, and furthermore for family and relatives, was less important to them; but greatest and first was their fear for the consecrated sanctuary. 19 Also those who were shut up in the city were in no light distress, being troubled because of the encounter in the open country.

20 When all were now waiting for the decision of the issue, and the enemy had already joined battle, and the army had been set in array, and the elephants[k] brought back to a convenient post,[l] and the cavalry deployed on the flanks, 21 Maccabaeus, perceiving the presence of the [m]troops, and the various weapons with which they were equipped, and the savageness of the [n]elephants, holding up his hands to heaven called upon the Lord who works wonders, knowing that success comes not by weapons, but that, according to how the Lord judges, he gains the victory for those who are worthy. 22 And calling upon God, he said this: "You, O Sovereign Lord, sent your angel in the time of King Hezekiah of Judea, and he killed of the [o]army of Sennacherib as many as one hundred and eighty-five thousand. 23 So now also, O Sovereign of the heavens, send a good angel before us to bring terror and trembling. 24 Through the greatness of your arm let them be stricken with dismay who with blasphemy have come here against your holy people." As he finished these words, 25 Nicanor and his company advanced with trumpets and victory songs; 26 but Judas and his company joined battle with the enemy with invocation and prayers. 27 Fighting with their hands and praying to God with their hearts, they killed no less than thirty-five thousand men, being made exceedingly glad by the manifestation of God.

28 When the engagement was over and they were returning again with joy, they recognised Nicanor lying dead in full armour. 29 Then there was shouting and noise, and they blessed the Sovereign Lord in the language of their ancestors. 30 He who in all things was in body and soul the foremost champion of his fellow-citizens, he who kept through life the good will of his youth towards his countrymen, ordered that Nicanor's head be cut off with his hand and arm, and that they be brought to Jerusalem. 31 When he had arrived there and had called his countrymen together and set the priests before the altar, he sent for those who were in the citadel.

32 Showing the head of the vile Nicanor and the hand of that profane man, which with proud brags he had stretched out against the holy house of the Almighty, 33 and cutting out the tongue of the impious Nicanor, he said that he would give it in pieces to the birds, and hang up these rewards of his folly near the sanctuary. 34 They all, looking up to heaven, blessed the Lord who had manifested himself, saying, "Blessed is he who has preserved his own place undefiled!" 35 He hung Nicanor's head and shoulder from the citadel, a clear sign evident to all of the help of the Lord. 36 They all ordained with a common decree to in no way let this day pass undistinguished, but to mark with honour the thirteenth day of the twelfth month (it is called Adar in the Syrian language), the day before the day of Mordecai.

37 This then having been the account of the attempt of Nicanor, and the city having from those times been held by the Hebrews, I also will here make an end of my book. 38 If I have written well and to the point in my story, this is what I myself desired; but if its poorly done and mediocre, this is the best I could do. 39 For as it is [p]distasteful to drink wine alone and likewise to drink water alone, [q]while the mingling of wine with water at once gives full pleasantness to the flavour; so also the fashioning of the language delights the ears of those who read the story.

Here is the end.

---

[a] 14:26 Or, and the covenants that had been made, took occasion and came
[b] 14:31 Or, though he was conscious that he had been nobly defeated by
[c] 14:31 Gr. the man
[d] 14:31 Gr. greatest.
[e] 14:33 Or, chapel Gr. enclosure.
[f] 14:35 Gr. tabernacling.
[g] 14:41 Or, people Gr. multitudes.
[h] 14:44 Or, the void place

[i] 14:46 Some authorities read the same.
[j] 15:6 Gr. carrying his neck high.
[k] 15:20 Gr. animals.
[l] 15:20 Or, stationed for convenient action
[m] 15:21 Gr. multitudes.
[n] 15:21 Gr. animals.
[o] 15:22 Gr. camp.
[p] 15:39 Or, hurtful
[q] 15:39 Gr. but even as.

The First Book of Esdras

The First Book of Esdras is recognised as Deuterocanonical Scripture by the Greek Orthodox and Russian Orthodox Churches. It is not recognised by the Roman Catholic Church, but 1 Esdras is placed as an appendix to the Latin Vulgate Bible.

1

1 *Josias held the Passover in Jerusalem to his Lord, and offered the Passover the fourteenth day of the first month, 2 having set the priests according to their daily courses, being arrayed in their vestments, in the Lord's temple. 3 He spoke to the Levites, *the temple servants of Israel, that they should make themselves holy to the Lord, to set the holy ark of the Lord in the house that King Solomon the son of David had built. 4 He said, "You no longer need to carry it on your shoulders. Now therefore serve the Lord your God, and minister to his people Israel, and prepare yourselves by your fathers' houses and kindred, 5 according to the writing of King David of Israel, and according to the magnificence of Solomon his son. Stand in the holy place according to the divisions of your Levite families who minister in the presence of your kindred the descendants of Israel. 6 Offer the Passover in order, prepare the sacrifices for your kindred, and keep the Passover according to the Lord's commandment, which was given to Moses.

7 To the people which were present, Josias gave thirty thousand lambs and kids, and three thousand calves. These things were given from the king's possessions, as he promised, to the people and to the priests and Levites. 8 Helkias, Zacharias, and aEsyelus, the rulers of the temple, gave to the priests for the Passover two thousand and six hundred sheep, and three hundred calves. 9 Jeconias, Samaias, Nathanael his brother, Sabias, Ochielus, and Joram, captains over thousands, gave to the Levites for the Passover five thousand sheep and seven hundred calves.

10 When these things were done, the priests and Levites, having the unleavened bread, stood in proper order according to the kindred, 11 and according to the several divisions by fathers' houses, before the people, to offer to the Lord as it is written in the book of Moses. They did this in the morning. 12 They roasted the Passover lamb with fire, as required. They boiled the sacrifices in the brazen vessels and cauldrons with a pleasing smell, 13 and set them before all the people. Afterward they prepared for themselves and for their kindred the priests, the sons of Aaron. 14 For the priests offered the fat until night. The Levites prepared for themselves and for their kindred the priests, the sons of Aaron. 15 The holy singers also, the sons of Asaph, were in their order, according to the appointment of David: Asaph, Zacharias, and Eddinus, who represented the king. 16 Moreover the gatekeepers were at every gate. No one needed to depart from his daily duties, for their kindred the Levites prepared for them.

17 So the things that belonged to the Lord's sacrifices were accomplished in that day, in holding the Passover, 18 and offering sacrifices on the altar of the Lord, according to the commandment of King Josias. 19 So the children of Israel which were present at that time held the Passover and the feast of unleavened bread seven days. 20 Such a Passover had not been held in Israel since the time of the prophet Samuel. 21 Indeed, none of the kings of Israel held such a Passover as Josias with the priests, the Levites, and the Jews, held with all Israel that were present in their dwelling place at Jerusalem. 22 This Passover was held in the eighteenth year of the reign of Josias. 23 The works of Josias were upright before his Lord with a heart full of godliness. 24 Moreover the things that came to pass in his days have been written in times past, concerning those who sinned and did wickedly against the Lord more than any other people or kingdom, and how they grieved him bexceedingly, so that the Lord's words were confirmed against Israel.

25 *Now after all these acts of Josias, it came to pass that Pharaoh the king of Egypt came to make war at Carchemish on the Euphrates; and Josias went out against him. 26 But the king of Egypt sent to him, saying, "What do I have to do with you, O king of Judea? 27 I wasn't sent out from the Lord God against you, for my war is against the Euphrates. Now the Lord is with me, yes, the Lord is with me hastening me forward. Depart from me, and don't be against the Lord."

28 However, Josias didn't turn back to his chariot, but tried to fight with him, not regarding the words of the prophet Jeremy from the Lord's mouth, 29 but joined battle with him in the plain of Megiddo, and the commanders came down against King Josias. 30 Then the king said to his servants, "Carry me away out of the battle, for I am very weak!" Immediately his servants carried him away out of the army. 31 Then he got into his second chariot. After he was brought back to Jerusalem he died, and was buried in the tomb of his ancestors. 32 All Judea mourned for Josias. Jeremy the prophet lamented for Josias, and the chief men with the women made lamentation for him to this day. This was given out for an ordinance to be done continually in all the nation of Israel. 33 These things are written in the book of the histories of the kings of Judea, and every one of the acts that Josias did, and his glory, and his understanding in the law of the Lord, and the things that he had done before, and the things now told, are reported in the book of the kings of Israel and Judah.

34 *The people took cJoachaz the son of Josias, and made him king instead of Josias his father, when he was twenty-three years old. 35 He reigned in Judah and Jerusalem for three months. Then the king of Egypt deposed him from reigning in Jerusalem. 36 He set a tax upon the people of one hundred talents of silver and one talent of gold. 37 The king of Egypt also made King Joakim his brother king of Judea and Jerusalem. 38 And Joakim imprisoned the nobles and apprehended his brother Zarakes, and brought him up out of Egypt.

39 *Joakim was twenty-five years old when he began to reign in Judea and Jerusalem. He did that which was evil in the sight of the Lord. 40 King Nabuchodonosor of Babylon came up against him, bound him with a chain of brass, and carried him to Babylon. 41 Nabuchodonosor also took some of the Lord's holy vessels, carried them away, and stored them in his own temple at Babylon. 42 But those things that are reported of him, and of his uncleanness and impiety, are written in the chronicles of the kings. 43 Then Joakim his son reigned in his place. When he was made king, he was eighteen years old. 44 He reigned three months and ten days in Jerusalem. He did that which was evil before the Lord.

45 So after a year Nabuchodonosor sent and caused him to be brought to Babylon with the holy vessels of the Lord, 46 and made Sedekias king of Judea and Jerusalem when he was twenty-one years old. He reigned eleven years. 47 He also did that which was evil in the sight of the Lord, and didn't heed the words that were spoken by Jeremy the prophet from the Lord's mouth. 48 After King Nabuchodonosor had made him to swear by the name of the Lord, he broke his oath and rebelled. Hardening his neck and his heart, he transgressed the laws of the Lord, the God of Israel. 49 Moreover the governors of the people and of the priests did many things wickedly, exceeding all the defilements of all nations, and defiled the temple of the Lord, which was sanctified in Jerusalem. 50 The God of their ancestors sent by his messenger to call them back, because he had compassion on them and on his dwelling place. 51 But they mocked his messengers. In the day when the Lord spoke, they scoffed at his prophets 52 until he, being angry with his people for their great ungodliness, commanded to bring up the kings of the Chaldeans against them. 53 They killed their young men with the sword around their holy temple, and spared neither young man or young woman, old man or child; but he delivered all of them into their hands. 54 They took all the holy vessels of the Lord, both great and small, with the treasure chests of the Lord's ark and the king's treasures, and carried them away to Babylon. 55 They burnt the Lord's house, broke down Jerusalem's walls, and burnt its towers with fire. 56 As for her glorious things, they didn't stop until they had brought them all to nothing. He carried the people who weren't slain with the sword to Babylon. 57 They were servants to him and to his children until the Persians reigned, to fulfil the word of the Lord by the mouth of Jeremy: 58 "Until the land has enjoyed its Sabbaths, the whole time of her desolation shall she keep Sabbath, to fulfil seventy years.

2

1 In the *first year of King Cyrus of the Persians, that the word of the Lord by the mouth of Jeremy might be accomplished, 2 the Lord stirred up the spirit of King Cyrus of the Persians, and he made a proclamation throughout all his kingdom, and also by writing, 3 saying, "Cyrus king of the Persians says: The Lord of Israel, the Most High Lord, has made me king of the whole world, 4 and commanded me to build him a house at Jerusalem that is in Judea. 5 If therefore there are any of you that are of his people, let the Lord, even his Lord, be with him, and let him go up to Jerusalem that is in Judea, and build the house of the Lord of Israel. He is the Lord who dwells in Jerusalem. 6 Therefore, of those who dwell in various places, let those who are in his own place help each one with gold, with silver, 7 with gifts, with horses, and cattle, beside the other things which have been added by vow for the temple of the Lord which is in Jerusalem."

8 Then the chief of the families of Judah and of the tribe of Benjamin stood up, with the priests, the Levites, and all whose spirit the Lord had stirred to go up, to build the house for the Lord which is in Jerusalem. 9 Those who lived around them helped them in all things with silver and gold, with horses and cattle, and with very many gifts that were vowed by a great number whose minds were so moved.

10 King Cyrus also brought out the holy vessels of the Lord, which Nabuchodonosor had carried away from Jerusalem and had stored in his temple of idols. 11 Now when King Cyrus of the Persians had brought them out, he delivered them to Mithradates his treasurer, 12 and by him they were delivered to dSanabassar the governor of Judea. 13 This was the number of them: one thousand gold cups, one thousand silver cups, twenty-nine silver censers, thirty gold bowls, two thousand and four hundred and ten silver bowls, and one thousand other vessels. 14 So all the vessels of gold and of silver were brought up, even five thousand and four hundred and seventy-nine, 15 and were carried back by Sanabassar, together with the returning exiles, from Babylon to Jerusalem.

16 *In the time of King Artaxerxes of the Persians, Belemus, Mithradates, Tabellius, eRathumus, Beeltethmus, and fSamellius the scribe,

---

** 1:1 2 Kings 23:21; 2 Chronicles 35:1
** 1:3 Numbers 3:9
a *1:8* Jehiel, 2 Chronicles 35:8.
b *1:24* Or, sensibly Judges 16:17.
** 1:25 2 Chronicles 35:20
** 1:34 2 Kings 23:30; 2 Chronicles 36:1
c *1:34* Another reading is, Jeconias.

** 1:39 2 Chronicles 36:4-5
** 2:1 2 Chronicles 36:22,23; Ezra 1:1
d *2:12* Another reading is, Simanassar.
** 2:16 Ezra 4:7
e *2:16* Rehum,
f *2:16* Shimshai.

with their other associates, dwelling in Samaria and other places, wrote to him against those who lived in Judea and Jerusalem the following letter:

17 "To King Artaxerxes our Lord, from your servants, Rathumus the recorder, Samellius the scribe, and the rest of their council, and the judges who are in Coelesyria and Phoenicia: 18 Let it now be known to our lord the king, that the Jews that have come up from you to us, having come to Jerusalem, are building that rebellious and wicked city, and are repairing its marketplaces and walls, and are laying the foundation of a temple. 19 Now if this city is built and its walls are finished, they will not only refuse to give tribute, but will even stand up against kings. 20 Since the things pertaining to the temple are now in hand, we think it appropriate not to neglect such a matter, 21 but to speak to our lord the king, to the intent that, if it is your pleasure, search may be made in the books of your ancestors. 22 You will find in the chronicles what is written concerning these things, and will understand that that city was rebellious, troubling both kings and cities, 23 and that the Jews were rebellious, and kept starting wars there in the past. For this cause, this city was laid waste. 24 Therefore now we do declare to you, O lord the king, that if this city is built again, and its walls set up again, you will from then on have no passage into Coelesyria and Phoenicia."

25 Then the king wrote back again to Rathumus the recorder, Beeltethmus, Samellius the scribe, and to the rest that of their associates who lived in Samaria, Syria, and Phoenicia, as follows:

26 "I have read the letter which you have sent to me. Therefore I commanded to make search, and it has been found that that city of old time has fought against kings, 27 and the men were given to rebellion and war in it, and that mighty and fierce kings were in Jerusalem, who reigned and exacted tribute in Coelesyria and Phoenicia. 28 Now therefore I have commanded to prevent those men from building the city, and heed to be taken that there be nothing done contrary to this order, 29 and that those wicked doings proceed no further to the annoyance of kings." 30 Then King Artaxerxes, his letters being read, Rathumus, and Samellius the scribe, and the rest of their associates, went in haste to Jerusalem with cavalry and a multitude of people in battle array, and began to hinder the builders. So the building of the temple in Jerusalem ceased until the second year of the reign of King Darius of the Persians.

3

1 Now King Darius made a great feast for all his subjects, for all who were born in his house, for all the princes of Media and of Persia, 2 and for all the local governors and captains and governors who were under him, from India to Ethiopia, in the one hundred and twenty seven provinces. 3 They ate and drank, and when they were satisfied went home. Then King Darius went into his bedchamber slept, but awakened out of his sleep.

4 Then the three young men of the bodyguard, who guarded the king, spoke one to another: 5 "Let every one of us state what one thing is strongest. King Darius will give him whose statement seems wiser than the others great gifts and great honours in token of victory. 6 He shall be clothed in purple, drink from gold cups, sleep on a gold bed, and have a chariot with bridles of gold, a fine linen turban, and a chain around his neck. 7 He shall sit next to Darius because of his wisdom, and shall be called cousin of Darius."

8 Then they each wrote his sentence, sealed them, and laid them under King Darius' pillow, 9 and said, "When the king wakes up, someone will give him the writing. Whoever the king and the three princes of Persia judge that his sentence is the wisest, to him shall the victory be given, as it is written." 10 The first wrote, "Wine is the strongest." 11 The second wrote, "The king is strongest." 12 The third wrote, "Women are strongest, but above all things Truth is the victor."

13 Now when the king woke up, they took the writing and gave it to him, so he read it. 14 Sending out, he called all the princes of Persia and of Media, the local governors, the captains, the governors, and the chief officers 15 and sat himself down in the royal seat of judgement; and the writing was read before them. 16 He said, "Call the young men, and they shall explain their own sentences. So they were called and came in. 17 They said to them, "Explain what you have written."

Then the first, who had spoken of the strength of wine, began 18 and said this: "O sirs, how exceedingly strong wine is! It causes all men who drink it to go astray. 19 It makes the mind of the king and of the fatherless child to be the same, likewise of the bondman and of the freeman, of the poor man and of the rich. 20 It also turns every thought into cheer and mirth, so that a man remembers neither sorrow nor debt. 21 It makes every heart rich, so that a man remembers neither king nor local governor. It makes people say things in large amounts. 22 When they are in their cups, they forget their love both to friends and kindred, and before long draw their swords. 23 But when they awake from their wine, they don't remember what they have done. 24 O sirs, isn't wine the strongest, seeing that it forces people to do this?" And when he had said this, he stopped speaking.

4

1 Then the second, who had spoken of the strength of the king, began to say, 2 "O sirs, don't men excel in strength who rule over the sea and land, and all things in them? 3 But yet the king is stronger. He is their lord and has dominion over them. In whatever he commands them, they obey. 4 If he tells them to make war the one against the other, they do it. If he sends them out against the enemies, they go, and conquer mountains, walls, and towers. 5 They kill and are killed, and don't disobey the king's commandment. If they win the victory, they bring everything to the king—all the plunder and everything else. 6 Likewise for those who are not soldiers, and don't have anything to do with wars, but farm, when they have reaped

again that which they had sown, they bring some to the king and compel one another to pay tribute to the king. 7 He is just one man! If he commands people to kill, they kill. If he commands them to spare, they spare. 8 If he commands them to strike, they strike. If he commands them to make desolate, they make desolate. If he commands to build, they build. 9 If he commands them to cut down, they cut down. If he commands them to plant, they plant. 10 So all his people and his armies obey him. Furthermore, he lies down, he eats and drinks, and takes his rest; 11 and these keep watch around him. None of them may depart and do his own business. They don't disobey him in anything. 12 O sirs, how could the king not be the strongest, seeing that he is obeyed like this?" Then he stopped talking.

13 Then the third, who had spoken of women, and of truth, (this was Zorobabel) began to speak: 14 "O sirs, isn't the king great, and men are many, and isn't wine strong? Who is it then who rules them, or has the lordship over them? Aren't they women? 15 Women have given birth to the king and all the people who rule over sea and land. 16 They came from women. Women nourished up those who planted the vineyards, from where the wine comes. 17 Women also make garments for men. These bring glory to men. Without women, men can't exist. 18 Yes, and if men have gathered together gold and silver and any other beautiful thing, and see a woman who is lovely in appearance and beauty, 19 they let all those things go and gape at her, and with open mouth stare at her. They all have more desire for her than for gold, or silver, or any other beautiful thing. 20 A man leaves his own father who brought him up, leaves his own country, and joins with his wife. 21 With his wife he ends his days, with no thought for his father, mother, or country. 22 By this also you must know that women have dominion over you. Don't you labour and toil, and bring it all to give to women? 23 Yes, a man takes his sword and goes out to travel, to rob, to steal, and to sail on the sea and on rivers. 24 He sees a lion and walks in the darkness. When he has stolen, plundered, and robbed, he brings it to the woman he loves. 25 Therefore a man loves his wife better than father or mother. 26 Yes, there are many who have lost their minds for women, and become slaves for their sakes. 27 Many also have perished, have stumbled, and sinned, for women. 28 Now don't you believe me? Isn't the king great in his power? Don't all regions fear to touch him? 29 Yet I saw him and Apame the king's concubine, the daughter of the illustrious Barticus, sitting at the right hand of the king, 30 and taking the crown from the king's head, and setting it upon her own head. Yes, she struck the king with her left hand. 31 At this, the king gaped and gazed at her with open mouth. If she smiles at him, he laughs. But if she takes any displeasure at him, he flatters her, that she might be reconciled to him again. 32 O sirs, how can it not be that women are strong, seeing they do this?"

33 Then the king and the nobles looked at one another. So he began to speak concerning truth. 34 "O sirs, aren't women strong? The earth is great. The sky is high. The sun is swift in its course, for it circles around the sky, and returns on its course again in one day. 35 Isn't he who makes these things great? Therefore the truth is great, and stronger than all things. 36 All the earth calls upon truth, and the sky blesses truth. All works shake and tremble, but with truth there is no unrighteous thing. 37 Wine is unrighteous. The king is unrighteous. Women are unrighteous. All the children of men are unrighteous, and all their works are unrighteous. There is no truth in them. They shall also perish in their unrighteousness. 38 But truth remains, and is strong forever. Truth lives and conquers forevermore. 39 With truth there is no partiality towards persons or rewards, but truth does the things that are just, instead of any unrighteous or wicked things. All men approve truth's works. 40 In truth's judgement is not any unrighteousness. Truth is the strength, the kingdom, the power, and the majesty of all ages. Blessed be the God of truth!"

41 With that, he stopped speaking. Then all the people shouted and said, "Great is truth, and strong above all things!"

42 Then the king said to him, "Ask what you wish, even more than is appointed in writing, and we will give it to you, because you are found wisest. You shall sit next me, and shall be called my cousin."

43 Then he said to the king, "Remember your vow, which you vowed to build Jerusalem, in the day when you came to your kingdom, 44 and to send back all the vessels that were taken out of Jerusalem, which Cyrus set apart when he vowed to destroy Babylon, and vowed to send them back there. 45 You also vowed to build the temple which the Edomites burnt when Judea was made desolate by the Chaldeans. 46 Now, O lord the king, this is what I request, and what I desire of you, and this is the princely generosity that may proceed from you: I ask therefore that you make good the vow, the performance of which you have vowed to the King of Heaven with your own mouth."

47 Then King Darius stood up, kissed him, and wrote letters for him to all the treasurers and governors and captains and local governors, that they should safely bring on their way both him, and all those who would go up with him to build Jerusalem. 48 He wrote letters also to all the governors who were in Coelesyria and Phoenicia, and to them in Libanus, that they should bring cedar wood from Libanus to Jerusalem, and that they should help him build the city. 49 Moreover he wrote for all the Jews who would go out of his realm up into Judea concerning their freedom, that no officer, no governor, no local governor, nor treasurer, should forcibly enter into their doors, 50 and that all the country which they occupied should be free to them without tribute, and that the Edomites should give up the villages of the Jews which they held at that time, 51 and that there should be given twenty talents yearly towards the building of the temple, until the time that it was built, 52 and another ten talents yearly for burnt offerings to be presented upon the altar every day, as they had a commandment to make seventeen offerings, 53 and that all those who would come from Babylonia

to build the city should have their freedom—they and their descendants, and all the priests that came. 54 He wrote also to give them their support and the priests' vestments in which they minister. 55 For the Levites he wrote that their support should be given them until the day that the house was finished and Jerusalem built up. 56 He commanded that land and wages should be given to all who guarded the city. 57 He also sent away all the vessels from Babylon that Cyrus had set apart, and all that Cyrus had given in commandment, he commanded also to be done and to be sent to Jerusalem.

58 Now when this young man had gone out, he lifted up his face to heaven towards Jerusalem, and praised the King of heaven, 59 and said, "From you comes victory. From you comes wisdom. Yours is the glory, and I am your servant. 60 Blessed are you, who have given me wisdom. I give thanks to you, O Lord of our fathers. 61 So he took the letters, went out, came to Babylon, and told it all his kindred. 62 They praised the God of their ancestors, because he had given them freedom and liberty 63 to go up and to build Jerusalem and the temple which is called by his name. They feasted with instruments of music and gladness seven days.

5

1 After this, the chiefs of fathers' houses were chosen to go up according to their tribes, with their wives, sons, and daughters, with their menservants and maidservants, and their livestock. 2 Darius sent with them one thousand cavalry to bring them back to Jerusalem with peace, with musical instruments, drums, and flutes. 3 All their kindred were making merry, and he made them go up together with them.

4 These are the names of the men who went up, according to their families amongst their tribes, after their several divisions. 5 The priests, the sons of Phinees, the sons of Aaron: Jesus the son of Josedek, the son of Saraias, and Joakim the son of Zorobabel, the son of Salathiel, of the house of David, of the lineage of Phares, of the tribe of Judah, 6 who spoke wise words before Darius the king of Persia in the second year of his reign, in the month Nisan, which is the first month.

7 *These are the names of the Judeans who came up from the captivity, where they lived as foreigners, whom Nabuchodonosor the king of Babylon had carried away to Babylon. 8 They returned to Jerusalem and to the other parts of Judea, every man to his own city, who came with Zorobabel, with Jesus, Nehemias, a Zaraias, Resaias,b Eneneus, Mardocheus, Beelsarus,c Aspharsus,d Reelias, Roimus, and Baana, their leaders.

9 The number of them of the nation and their leaders: the sons of Phoros, two thousand and one hundred and seventy two; the sons ofe Saphat, four hundred and seventy two; 10 the sons off Ares, seven hundred and fifty six; 11 the sons ofg Phaath Moab, of the sons of Jesus and Joab, two thousand and eight hundred and twelve; 12 the sons of Elam, one thousand and two hundred and fifty four; the sons ofh Zathui, nine hundred and forty five; the sons ofi Chorbe, seven hundred and five; the sons of Bani, six hundred and forty eight; 13 the sons of Bebai, six hundred and twenty three; the sons ofj Astad,k one thousand and three hundred and

twenty two; 14 the sons of Adonikam, six hundred and sixty seven; the sons ofl Bagoi, two thousand and sixty six; the sons ofm Adinu, four hundred and fifty four; 15 the sons ofn Ater, of Ezekias, ninety two; the sons of Kilan and Azetas, sixty seven; the sons ofo Azaru, four hundred and thirty two; 16 the sons ofp Annis, one hundred and one; the sons of Arom, the sons ofq Bassai, three hundred and twenty three; the sons of Arsiphurith, one hundred and twelve; 17 the sons of Baiterus, three thousand and five; the sons ofr Bethlomon, one hundred and twenty three; 18 those from Netophas, fifty five; those from Anathoth, one hundred and fifty eight; those froms Bethasmoth, forty two; 19 those from t Kariathiarius, twenty five: those from Caphira and Beroth, seven hundred and forty three; 20 the Chadiasai and Ammidioi, four hundred and twenty two; those fromu Kirama and vGabbe, six hundred and twenty one; 21 those fromw Macalon, one hundred and twenty two; those from xBetolion, fifty two; the sons of yNiphis, one hundred and fifty six; 22 the sons of zCalamolalus and aaOnus, seven hundred and twenty five; the sons of bb Jerechu, ccthree hundred and forty five; 23 and the sons of ddSanaas, three thousand and three hundred and thirty.

24 The priests: the sons of eeJeddu, the son of Jesus, amongst the sons of Sanasib, nine hundred and seventy two; the sons of ff Emmeruth, one thousand and fifty two; 25 the sons of ggPhassurus, one thousand and two hundred and forty seven; and the sons of hhCharme, one thousand and seventeen. 26 The Levites: the sons of Jesus, Kadmiel, Bannas, and Sudias, seventy four. 27 The holy singers: the sons of Asaph, one hundred and twenty eight. 28 The gatekeepers: the sons ofii Salum, the sons ofjj Atar, the sons of Tolman, the sons ofkk Dacubi, the sons ofll Ateta, the sonsofmm Sabi, in all one hundred and thirty nine.

29 The temple servants: the sons ofnn Esau, the sons ofoo Asipha, the sons of Tabaoth, the sons ofpp Keras, the sons ofqq Sua, the sons ofrr Phaleas, the sons of Labana, the sons ofss Aggaba. 30 the sons oftt Acud, the sons of Uta, the sons of Ketab, the sons ofuu Accaba, the sons ofvv Subai, the sons ofww Anan, the sons ofxx Cathua, the sons ofyy Geddur, 31 the sons ofzz Jairus, the sons ofaaa Daisan, the sons ofbbb Noeba, the sons of Chaseba, the sons ofccc Gazera, the sons ofddd Ozias, the sons ofeee Phinoe, the sons of Asara, the sons offff Basthai, the sons ofggg Asana, the sons ofhhh Maani, the sons ofiii Naphisi, the sons ofjjj Acub, the sons ofkkk Achipha, the sons oflll Asur, the sons of Pharakim, the sons ofmmm Basaloth, 32 the sons ofnnn Meedda, the sons of Cutha, the sons ofooo Charea, the sons ofppp Barchus, the sons ofqqq Serar, the sons ofrrr Thomei, the sons ofsss Nasi, the sons of Atipha.

33 The sons of the servants of Solomon: the sons ofttt Assaphioth, the sons ofuuu Pharida, the sons ofvvv Jeeli, the sons ofwww Lozon, the sons ofxxx Isdael, the sons ofyyy Saphuthi, 34 the sons ofzzz Agia, the sons ofaaaa Phacareth, the sons of Sabie, the sons of Sarothie, the sons ofbbbb Masias, the sons of Gas, the sons of Addus, the sons of Subas, the sons of Apherra, the sons of Barodis, the sons of Saphat, the sons of Allon.

35 All the temple-servants and the sons of the servants of Solomon were three hundred and seventy two. 36 These came up fromcccc Thermeleth,

---

** 5:7 Ezra 2:1
a *5:8* Seralah.
b *5:8* Or, Enenis.
c *5:8* Mispar.
d *5:8* Reclaiah
e *5:9* Shephatiah.
f *5:10* Arah.
g *5:11* Pahath-moab.
h *5:12* Zattu.
i *5:12* Zaccai.
j *5:13* Asgad.
k *5:13* According to other readings, 3622, or 3222.
l *5:14* Bigvai.
m *5:14* Adin.
n *5:15* Ater of Hezekiah.
o *5:15* Another reading is, Azuru.
p *5:16* Another reading is, Annias.
q *5:16* Bezai.
r *5:17* Bethlehem.
s *5:18* Azmaveth.
t *5:19* Kiriath-arim or Kiriath-jearim.
u *5:20* Rumah.
v *5:20* Geba.
w *5:21* Michmas.
x *5:21* Bethel.
y *5:21* Magbish
z *5:22* Lod, Hadid.
aa *5:22* Ono.
bb *5:22* Jericho.
cc *5:22* Another reading is, two
dd *5:23* Senaah.
ee *5:24* Jedaiah.
ff *5:24* Immer.
gg *5:25* Pashhur.
hh *5:25* Harim.
ii *5:28* Shallum.
jj *5:28* Ater.
kk *5:28* Akkub.
ll *5:28* Hatita.
mm *5:28* Shobai.
nn *5:29* Ziha.

oo *5:29* Hasupha.
pp *5:29* Keros.
qq *5:29* Siaha.
rr *5:29* Padon.
ss *5:29* Hagaba.
tt *5:30* Akkub.
uu *5:30* Hagab.
vv *5:30* Shamlai.
ww *5:30* Hanan.
xx *5:30* Giddel.
yy *5:30* Gahar
zz *5:31* Reaiah.
aaa *5:31* Rezin.
bbb *5:31* Nekoda.
ccc *5:31* Gazzam.
ddd *5:31* Uzza.
eee *5:31* Paseah.
fff *5:31* Besai.
ggg *5:31* Asnah.
hhh *5:31* Meunim.
iii *5:31* Nephisim.
jjj *5:31* Bakbuk. According to other readings, Acum, or Acuph.
kkk *5:31* Hakupha.
lll *5:31* Harhur.
mmm *5:31* Bazluth.
nnn *5:32* Mehida.
ooo *5:32* Harsha
ppp *5:32* Barkos.
qqq *5:32* Sisera.
rrr *5:32* Temah
sss *5:32* Neziah. Another reading is, Nasith.
ttt *5:33* Hussophereth.
uuu *5:33* Peruda.
vvv *5:33* Jaalah.
www *5:33* Darkon.
xxx *5:33* Giddel.
yyy *5:33* Shephatia.
zzz *5:34* Hattil.
aaaa *5:34* Pochereth-haz-zebaim, Ezra 2:57.
bbbb *5:34* Another reading is, Misaias.
cccc *5:36* Telmelah.

and[a] Thelersas,[b] Charaathalan leading them, and Allar; 37 and they could not show their families, nor their stock, how they were of Israel: the sons of[c] Dalan the son of[d] Ban, the sons of[e] Nekodan, six hundred and fifty two.

38 Of the priests, those who usurped the office of the priesthood and were not found: the sons of[f] Obdia, the sons of[g] Akkos, the sons of Jaddus, who married Augia one of the daughters of[h] Zorzelleus, and was called after his name. 39 When the description of the kindred of these men was sought in the register and was not found, they were removed from executing the office of the priesthood; 40 for Nehemias and Attharias told them that they should not be partakers of the holy things until a high priest wearing[i] Urim and Thummim should arise.

41 So all those of Israel, from twelve years old and upward, beside menservants and women servants, were in number forty two thousand and three hundred and sixty. 42 Their menservants and handmaids were seven thousand and three hundred and thirty and seven; the minstrels and singers, two hundred and forty five; 43 four hundred and thirty and five camels, seven thousand and thirty six horses, two hundred and forty five mules, and five thousand and five hundred and twenty five beasts of burden.

44 And some of the chief men of their families, when they came to the temple of God that is in Jerusalem, vowed to set up the house again in its own place according to their ability, 45 and to give into the holy treasury of the works one thousand minas[j] of gold, five thousand minas of silver, and one hundred priestly vestments.

46 The priests and the Levites and some of the people lived in Jerusalem and the country. The holy singers also and the gatekeepers and all Israel lived in their villages.

47 But when the seventh month was at hand, and when the children of Israel were each in their own place, they all came together with one purpose into the broad place before the first porch which is towards the east. 48 Then Jesus the son of Josedek, his kindred the priests, Zorobabel the son of Salathiel, and his kindred stood up and made the altar of the God of Israel ready 49 to offer burnt sacrifices upon it, in accordance with the express commands in the book of Moses the man of God. 50 Some people joined them out of the other nations of the land, and they erected the altar upon its own place, because all the nations of the land were hostile to them and oppressed them; and they offered sacrifices at the proper times and burnt offerings to the Lord both morning and evening. 51 They also held the feast of tabernacles, as it is commanded in the law, and offered sacrifices daily, as appropriate. 52 After that, they offered the continual oblations and the sacrifices of the Sabbaths, of the new moons, and of all the consecrated feasts. 53 All those who had made any vow to God began to offer sacrifices to God from the new moon of the seventh month, although the temple of God was not yet built. 54 They gave money, food, and drink to the masons and carpenters. 55 They also gave carts to the people of Sidon and Tyre, that they should bring cedar trees from Libanus, and convey them in rafts to the harbour of Joppa, according to the commandment which was written for them by Cyrus king of the Persians.

56 In the second year after his coming to the temple of God at Jerusalem, in the second month, Zorobabel the son of Salathiel, Jesus the son of Josedek, their kindred, the Levitical priests, and all those who had come to Jerusalem out of the captivity began work. 57 They laid the foundation of God's temple on the new moon of the second month, in the second year after they had come to Judea and Jerusalem. 58 ˙They appointed the Levites who were at least twenty years old over the Lord's works. Then Jesus, with his sons and kindred, Kadmiel his brother, the sons of Jesus, Emadabun, and the sons of Joda the son of Iliadun, and their sons and kindred, all the Levites, with one accord stood up and started the business, labouring to advance the works in the house of God. So the builders built the Lord's temple.

59 The priests stood arrayed in their vestments with musical instruments and trumpets, and the Levites the sons of Asaph with their cymbals, 60 singing songs of thanksgiving and praising the Lord, according to the directions of King David of Israel. 61 They sang aloud, praising the Lord in songs of thanksgiving, because his goodness and his glory are forever in all Israel. 62 All the people sounded trumpets and shouted with a loud voice, singing songs of thanksgiving to the Lord for the raising up of the Lord's house. 63 ˙Some of the Levitical priests and of the heads of their families, the elderly who had seen the former house came to the building of this one with lamentation and great weeping. 64 But many with trumpets and joy shouted with a loud voice, 65 so that the people couldn't hear the trumpets for the weeping of the people, for the multitude sounded loudly, so that it was heard far away.

66 ˙Therefore when the enemies of the tribe of Judah and Benjamin heard it, they came to know what that noise of trumpets meant. 67 They learnt that those who returned from captivity built the temple for the Lord, the God of Israel. 68 So they went to Zorobabel and Jesus, and to the chief men of the families, and said to them, "We will build together with you. 69 For we, just like you, obey your Lord, and sacrifice to him from the days of King[k] Asbasareth of the Assyrians, who brought us here."

70 Then Zorobabel, Jesus and the chief men of the families of Israel said to them, "It is not for you to build the house for the Lord our God. 71 We ourselves alone will build for the Lord of Israel, as King Cyrus of the Persians has commanded us." 72 But the heathen of the land pressed hard upon the inhabitants of Judea, cut off their supplies, and hindered their building. 73 By their secret plots, and popular persuasions and commotions, they hindered the finishing of the building all the time that King Cyrus lived. So they were hindered from building for two years, until the reign of Darius.

6

1 Now ˙in the second year of the reign of Darius, Aggaeus and Zacharius the son of[l] Addo, the prophets, prophesied to the Jews in Judea and Jerusalem in the name of the Lord, the God of Israel. 2 Then Zorobabel the son of Salathiel and Jesus the son of Josedek stood up and began to build the house of the Lord at Jerusalem, the prophets of the Lord being with them and helping them.

3 ˙At the same time [m]Sisinnes the governor of Syria and Phoenicia came to them, with [n]Sathrabuzanes and his companions, and said to them, 4 "By whose authority do you build this house and this roof, and perform all the other things? Who are the builders who do these things?" 5 Nevertheless, the elders of the Jews obtained favour, because the Lord had visited the captives; 6 and they were not hindered from building until such time as communication was made to Darius concerning them, and his answer received.

7 A copy of the letter which Sisinnes, governor of Syria and Phoenicia, and Sathrabuzanes, with their companions, the rulers in Syria and Phoenicia, wrote and sent to Darius:

8 "To King Darius, greetings. Let it be fully known to our lord the king, that having come into the country of Judea, and entered into the city of Jerusalem, we found in the city of Jerusalem the elders of the Jews that were of the captivity 9 building a great new house for the Lord of hewn and costly stones, with timber laid in the walls. 10 Those works are being done with great speed. The work goes on prosperously in their hands, and it is being accomplished with all glory and diligence. 11 Then asked we these elders, saying, 'By whose authority are you building this house and laying the foundations of these works?' 12 Therefore, to the intent that we might give knowledge to you by writing who were the leaders, we questioned them, and we required of them the names in writing of their principal men. 13 So they gave us this answer, 'We are the servants of the Lord who made heaven and earth. 14 As for this house, it was built many years ago by a great and strong king of Israel, and was finished. 15 But when our fathers sinned against the Lord of Israel who is in heaven, and provoked him to wrath, he gave them over into the hands of King Nabuchodonosor of Babylon, king of the Chaldeans. 16 They pulled down the house, burnt it, and carried away the people captive to Babylon. 17 But in the first year that Cyrus reigned over the country of Babylon, King Cyrus wrote that this house should be rebuilt. 18 The holy vessels of gold and of silver that Nabuchodonosor had carried away out of the house at Jerusalem and had set up in his own temple, those King Cyrus brought out of the temple in Babylonia, and they were delivered to Zorobabel and to [o]Sanabassarus the governor, 19 with commandment that he should carry away all these vessels, and put them in the temple at Jerusalem, and that the Lord's temple should be built on its site. 20 Then Sanabassarus, having come here, laid the foundations of the Lord's house which is in Jerusalem. From that time to this we are still building. It is not yet fully completed.' 21 Now therefore, if it seems good, O king, let a search be made amongst the royal archives of our lord the king that are in Babylon. 22 If it is found that the building of the house of the Lord which is in Jerusalem has been done with the consent of King Cyrus, and it seems good to our lord the king, let him send us directions concerning these things."

23 ˙Then King Darius commanded that a search be made amongst the archives that were laid up at Babylon. So at Ekbatana the palace, which is in the country of Media, a scroll was found where these things were recorded: 24 "In the first year of the reign of Cyrus, King Cyrus commanded to build up the house of the Lord which is in Jerusalem, where they sacrifice with continual fire. 25 Its height shall be sixty cubits, and the breadth sixty cubits, with three rows of hewn stones, and one row of new wood from that country. Its expenses are to be given out of the house of King Cyrus. 26 The holy vessels of the house of the Lord, both gold and silver, that Nabuchodonosor took out of the house at Jerusalem and carried away to Babylon, should be restored to the house at Jerusalem, and be set in the place where they were before." 27 Also he commanded that Sisinnes the governor of Syria and Phoenicia, and Sathrabuzanes, and their companions, and those who were appointed rulers in Syria and Phoenicia,

---

a *5:36* Telharsha.
b *5:36* Cherub. Addan.
c *5:37* Delaiah. Another reading is, Asan.
d *5:37* Tobiah Another reading is, Baenan.
e *5:37* Nekoda.
f *5:38* Habaiah, or Hobaiah.
g *5:38* Hakkoz.
h *5:38* Barzillai. Another reading is, Phaezeldaeus.
i *5:40* Gr. the manifestation and truth.
j *5:45* A mina is about 570 grams or 1.25 pounds.
** 5:58 Ezra 3:8-9

** 5:63 Ezra 3:12-13
** 5:66 Ezra 4:1
k *5:69* Another reading is, Asbacaphath.
** 6:1 Ezra 4:24; 5:1
l *6:1* Iddo. Another reading is, Eddin
** 6:3 Ezra 5:3
m *6:3* Tattenai.
n *6:3* Shetharbozenai
o *6:18* Another reading is, Sabunassarus.
** 6:23 Ezra 6:1

should be careful not to meddle with the place, but allow Zorobabel, the servant of the Lord, and governor of Judea, and the elders of the Jews, to build that house of the Lord in its place. ₂₈"I also command to have it built up whole again; and that they look diligently to help those who are of the captivity of Judea, until the house of the Lord is finished, ₂₉and that out of the tribute of Coelesyria and Phoenicia a portion shall be carefully given to these men for the sacrifices of the Lord, that is, to Zorobabel the governor for bulls, rams, and lambs, ₃₀and also corn, salt, wine and oil, and that continually every year without further question, according as the priests who are in Jerusalem may direct to be daily spent, ₃₁that drink offerings may be made to the Most High God for the king and his children, and that they may pray for their lives." ₃₂He commanded that whoever should transgress, yes, or neglect anything written here, a beam shall be taken out of his own house, and he shall be hanged on it, and all his goods seized for the king. ₃₃"Therefore may the Lord, whose name is called upon there, utterly destroy every king and nation that stretches out his hand to hinder or damage that house of the Lord in Jerusalem. ₃₄I, King Darius have ordained that these things be done with diligence."

7

₁Then ˙ Sisinnes the governor of Coelesyria and Phoenicia, and Sathrabuzanes, with their companions, following the commandments of King Darius, ₂very carefully supervised the holy work, assisting the elders of the Jews and rulers of the temple. ₃So the holy work prospered, while Aggaeus and Zacharias the prophets prophesied. ₄They finished these things by the commandment of the Lord, the God of Israel, and with the consent of Cyrus, Darius, and Artaxerxes, kings of the Persians. ₅So the holy house was finished by the twenty-third day of the month Adar, in the sixth year of King Darius. ₆The children of Israel, the priests, the Levites, and the others who returned from captivity who joined them did what was written in the book of Moses. ₇For the dedication of the Lord's temple, they offered one hundred bulls, two hundred rams, four hundred lambs, ₈ and twelve male goats for the sin of all Israel, according to the number of the twelve princes of the tribes of Israel. ₉The priests and the Levites stood arrayed in their vestments, according to their kindred, for the services of the Lord, the God of Israel, according to the book of Moses. The gatekeepers were at every gate.

₁₀The children of Israel who came out of captivity held the Passover the fourteenth day of the first month, when the priests and the Levites were sanctified together, ₁₁with all those who returned from captivity; for they were sanctified. For the Levites were all sanctified together, ₁₂and they offered the Passover for all who returned from captivity, for their kindred the priests, and for themselves. ₁₃The children of Israel who came out of the captivity ate, even all those who had separated themselves from the abominations of the heathen of the land, and sought the Lord. ₁₄They kept the feast of unleavened bread seven days, rejoicing before the Lord, ₁₅because he had turned the counsel of the king of Assyria towards them, to strengthen their hands in the works of the Lord, the God of Israel.

8

₁ ˙ After these things, when Artaxerxes the king of the Persians reigned, Esdras came, who was the son of Azaraias, the son of Zechrias, the son of Helkias, the son of Salem, ₂the son of Sadduk, the son of Ahitob, the son of Amarias, the son of Ozias,ᵃ the son of Memeroth, the son of Zaraias, the son of Savias, the son of Boccas, the son of Abisne, the son of Phinees, the son of Eleazar, the son of Aaron, the chief priest. ₃This Esdras went up from Babylon as a skilled scribe in the law of Moses, which was given by the God of Israel. ₄The king honoured him, for he found favour in his sight in all his requests. ₅There went up with him also some of the children of Israel, and of the priests, Levites, holy singers, gatekeepers, and temple servants to Jerusalem ₆in the seventh year of the reign of Artaxerxes, in the fifth month (this was the king's seventh year); for they left Babylon on the new moon of the first month and came to Jerusalem, by the prosperous journey which the Lord gave themᵇ for his sake. ₇For Esdras had very great skill, so that he omitted nothing of the law and commandments of the Lord, but taught all Israel the ordinances and judgements.

₈Now the commission, which was written from King Artaxerxes, came to Esdras the priest and reader of the law of the Lord, was as follows:

₉"King Artaxerxes to Esdras the priest and reader of the law of the Lord, greetings. ₁₀Having determined to deal graciously, I have given orders that those of the nation of the Jews, and of the priests and Levites, and of those within our realm who are willing and freely choose to, should go with you to Jerusalem. ₁₁As many therefore as are so disposed, let them depart with you, as it has seemed good both to me and my seven friends the counsellors, ₁₂that they may look to the affairs of Judea and Jerusalem, in accordance with what is in the Lord's law, ₁₃and carry the gifts to the Lord of Israel to Jerusalem, which I and my friends have vowed, and that all the gold and silver that can be found in the country of Babylonia for the Lord in Jerusalem, ₁₄with that also which is given of the people for the temple of

the Lord their God that is at Jerusalem, be collected: even the gold and silver for bulls, rams, and lambs, and what goes with them, ₁₅to the end that they may offer sacrifices to the Lord upon the altar of the Lord their God, which is in Jerusalem. ₁₆Whatever you and your kindred decide to do with gold and silver, do that according to the will of your God. ₁₇The holy vessels of the Lord, which are given you for the use of the temple of your God, which is in Jerusalem, ₁₈and whatever else you shall remember for the use of the temple of your God, you shall give it out of the king's treasury. ₁₉I, King Artaxerxes, have also commanded the keepers of the treasures in Syria and Phoenicia, that whatever Esdras the priest and reader of the law of the Most High God shall send for, they should give it to him with all diligence, ₂₀to the sum of one hundred talents of silver, likewise also of wheat even to one hundred corsᶜ, and one hundred firkinsᵈ of wine, andᵉ salt in abundance. ₂₁Let all things be performed after God's law diligently to the most high God, that wrath come not upon the kingdom of the king and his sons. ₂₂I command you also that no tax, nor any other imposition, be laid upon any of the priests, or Levites, or holy singers, or gatekeepers, or temple servants, or any that have employment in this temple, and that no man has authority to impose any tax on them. ₂₃You, Esdras, according to the wisdom of God, ordain judges and justices that they may judge in all Syria and Phoenicia all those who know the law of your God; and those who don't know it, you shall teach. ₂₄Whoever transgresses the law of your God and of the king shall be punished diligently, whether it be by death, or other punishment, by penalty of money, or by imprisonment."

₂₅Then Esdras the scribe said, "Blessed be the only Lord, the God of my fathers, who has put these things into the heart of the king, to glorify his house that is in Jerusalem, ₂₆and has honoured me in the sight of the king, his counsellors, and all his friends and nobles. ₂₇Therefore I was encouraged by the help of the Lord my God, and gathered together out of Israel men to go up with me.

₂₈These are the chief according to their families and their several divisions, who went up with me from Babylon in the reign of King Artaxerxes: ₂₉of the sons of Phinees, Gerson; of the sons of Ithamar, Gamael; of the sons of David,ᶠ Attusᵍ the son of Sechenias; ₃₀of the sons of Phoros, Zacharais; and with him were counted one hundred and fifty men; ₃₁of the sons of Phaath Moab, Eliaonias the son ofʰ Zaraias, and with him two hundred men; ₃₂ ⁱof the sons of Zathoes, Sechenias the son of Jezelus, and with him three hundred men; of the sons of Adin, Obeth the son of Jonathan, and with him two hundred and fifty men; ₃₃of the sons of Elam, Jesias son of Gotholias, and with him seventy men; ₃₄of the sons of Saphatias, Zaraias son of Michael, and with him seventy men; ₃₅of the sons of Joab, Abadias son of Jehiel. Jezelus, and with him two hundred and twelve men; ₃₆ ʲ of the sons of Banias, Salimoth son of Josaphias, and with him one hundred and sixty men; ₃₇of the sons of Babi, Zacharias son of Bebai, and with him twenty-eight men; ₃₈of the sons of Azgad: Astath, Joannes son of Hakkatan Akatan, and with him one hundred and ten men; ₃₉of the sons of Adonikam, the last, and these are the names of them, Eliphalat, Jeuel, and Samaias, and with them seventy men; ₄₀of the sons of Bago, Uthi the son of Istalcurus, and with him seventy men.

₄₁I gathered them together to the river called Theras. There we pitched our tents three days, and I inspected them. ₄₂When I had found there none of the priests and Levites, ₄₃then sent I to Eleazar, Iduel, Maasmas, ₄₄Elnathan, Samaias, Joribus, Nathan, Ennatan, Zacharias, and Mosollamus, principal men and men of understanding. ₄₅I asked them to go to Loddeus the captain, who was in the place of the treasury, ₄₆and commanded them that they should speak to Loddeus, to his kindred, and to the treasurers in that place, to send us such men as might execute the priests' office in our Lord's house. ₄₇By the mighty hand of our Lord, they brought to us men of understanding of the sons ofᵏ Mooli the son of Levi, the son of Israel,ˡ Asebebias, and his sons, and his kindred, who were eighteen, ₄₈andᵐ Asebias, Annuus, and Osaias his brother, of the sons of Chanuneus, and their sons were twenty men; ₄₉and of the temple servants whom David and the principal men had appointed for the servants of the Levites, two hundred and twenty temple servants. The list of all their names was reported.

₅₀There I vowed a fast for the young men before our Lord, to seek from him a prosperous journey both for us and for our children and livestock that were with us; ₅₁for I was ashamed to ask of the king infantry, cavalry, and an escort for protection against our adversaries. ₅₂For we had said to the king that the power of our Lord would be with those who seek him, to support them in all ways. ₅₃Again we prayed to our lord about these things, and found him to be merciful.

₅₄Then I set apart twelve men of the chiefs of the priests,ⁿ Eserebias, Assamias, and ten men of their kindred with them. ₅₅I weighed out to them the silver, the gold, and the holy vessels of the house of our Lord, which the king, his counsellors, the nobles, and all Israel had given. ₅₆When I had weighed it, I delivered to them six hundred and fifty talents of silver, silver vessels weighing one hundred talents, one hundred talents of gold, ₅₇twenty golden vessels, and twelve vessels of brass, even of fine brass,

** 7:1 Ezra 6:13
** 8:1 Ezra 7:1
ᵃ *8:2* The Vatican MS. omits the son of Memeroth, the son of Zaraias, the son of Savias.
ᵇ *8:6* Some MSS. omit for his sake.
ᶜ *8:20* a cor is about 230 litres, so 100 cors is about 23 kilolitres or 652 bushels
ᵈ *8:20* a firkin is about 41 litres or 11 gallons.
ᵉ *8:20* So some authorities. See Ezra 7:22. The common reading is, other things.

ᶠ *8:29* Hattush.
ᵍ *8:29* Ezra 8:3, of the sons of Shecaniah; of the sons of Parosh.
ʰ *8:31* Zerehiah.
ⁱ *8:32* Ezra 8:5, of the sons of Shecaniah; of the sons of Jahaziel.
ʲ *8:36* Ezra 8:10, of the sons of Shelomith, the son of Josiphiah.
ᵏ *8:47* Mahli.
ˡ *8:47* Sherebiah.
ᵐ *8:48* Hashabiah.
ⁿ *8:54* Sherebiah, Hashabiah.

glittering like gold. 58 I said to them, "You are holy to the Lord, the vessels are holy, and the gold and the silver are a vow to the Lord, the Lord of our fathers. 59 Watch and keep them until you deliver them to the chiefs of the priests and Levites, and to the principal men of the families of Israel in Jerusalem, in the chambers of our Lord's house. 60 So the priests and the Levites who received the silver, the gold, and the vessels which were in Jerusalem, brought them into the temple of the Lord.

61 We left the river Theras on the twelfth day of the first month. We came to Jerusalem by the mighty hand of our Lord which was upon us. The Lord delivered us from from every enemy on the way, and so we came to Jerusalem. 62 When we had been there three days, the silver and gold was weighed and delivered in our Lord's house on the fourth day to[a] Marmoth the priest the son of[b] Urias. 63 With him was Eleazar the son of Phinees, and with them were Josabdus the son of Jesus and[c] Moeth the son of Sabannus, the Levites. All was delivered to them by number and weight. 64 All the weight of them was recorded at the same hour. 65 Moreover those who had come out of captivity offered sacrifices to the Lord, the God of Israel, even twelve bulls for all Israel, ninety-six rams, 66 seventy-two lambs, and twelve goats for a peace offering—all of them a sacrifice to the Lord. 67 They delivered the king's commandments to the king's stewards and to the governors of Coelesyria and Phoenicia; and they honoured the people and the temple of the Lord.

68 Now when these things were done, the principal men came to me and said, 69 "The nation of Israel, the princes, the priests, and the Levites haven't put away from themselves the foreign people of the land nor the uncleannesses of the Gentiles—the Canaanites, Hittites, Pherezites, Jebusites, Moabites, Egyptians, and Edomites. 70 For both they and their sons have married with their daughters, and the holy seed is mixed with the foreign people of the land. From the beginning of this matter the rulers and the nobles have been partakers of this iniquity."

71 And as soon as I had heard these things, I tore my clothes and my holy garment, and plucked the hair from off my head and beard, and sat down sad and full of heaviness. 72 So all those who were moved at the word of the Lord, the God of Israel, assembled to me while I mourned for the iniquity, but I sat still full of heaviness until the evening sacrifice. 73 Then rising up from the fast with my clothes and my holy garment torn, and bowing my knees and stretching out my hands to the Lord, 74 I said, "O Lord, I am ashamed and confounded before your face, 75 for our sins are multiplied above our heads, and our errors have reached up to heaven 76 ever since the time of our fathers. We are in great sin, even to this day. 77 For our sins and our fathers' with our kindred, our kings, and our priests were given up to the kings of the earth, to the sword, and to captivity, and for a prey with shame, to this day. 78 Now in some measure mercy has been shown to us from you, O Lord, that there should be left us a root and a name in the place of your sanctuary, 79 and to uncover a light in the house of the Lord our God, and to give us food in the time of our servitude. 80 Yes, when we were in bondage, we were not forsaken by our Lord, but he gave us favour before the kings of Persia, so that they gave us food, 81 glorified the temple of our Lord, and raised up the desolate Zion, to give us a sure dwelling in Judea and Jerusalem.

82 "Now, O Lord, what shall we say, having these things? For we have transgressed your commandments which you gave by the hand of your servants the prophets, saying, 83 'The land, which you enter into to possess as an inheritance, is a land polluted with the pollutions of the foreigners of the land, and they have filled it with their uncleanness. 84 Therefore now you shall not join your daughters to their sons, neither shall you take their daughters for your sons. 85 You shall never seek to have peace with them, that you may be strong, and eat the good things of the land, and that you may leave it for an inheritance to your children for evermore.' 86 All that has happened is done to us for our wicked works and great sins, for you, O Lord, made our sins light, 87 and gave to us such a root; but we have turned back again to transgress your law in mingling ourselves with the uncleanness of the heathen of the land. 88 You weren't angry with us to destroy us until you had left us neither root, seed, nor name. 89 O Lord of Israel, you are true, for we are left a root this day. 90 Behold, now we are before you in our iniquities, for we can't stand any longer before you because of these things."

91 *As Esdras in his prayer made his confession, weeping, and lying flat on the ground before the temple, a very great throng of men, women, and children gathered to him from Jerusalem; for there was great weeping amongst the multitude. 92 Then Jechonias the son of Jeelus, one of the sons of Israel, called out, and said, "O Esdras, we have sinned against the Lord God, we have married foreign women of the heathen of the land, but there is still hope for Israel. 93 Let's make an oath to the Lord about this, that we will put away all our foreign wives with their children, 94 as seems good to you, and to as many as obey the Lord's Law. 95 Arise, and take action, for this is your task, and we will be with you to do valiantly." 96 So Esdras arose, and took an oath from the chief of the priests and Levites of all Israel to do these things; and they swore to it.

9

1 *Then Esdras rose up from the court of the temple and went to the chamber of Jonas the son of Eliasib, 2 and lodged there, and ate no bread and drank no water, mourning for the great iniquities of the multitude. 3 A proclamation was made in all Judea and Jerusalem to all those who returned from captivity, that they should be gathered together at Jerusalem, 4 and that whoever didn't meet there within two or three days, in accordance with the ruling of the elders, that their livestock would be seized for the use of the temple, and they would be expelled from the multitude of those who returned from captivity.

5 Within three days, all those of the tribe of Judah and Benjamin gathered together at Jerusalem. This was the ninth month, on the twentieth day of the month. 6 All the multitude sat together shivering in the broad place before the temple because of the present foul weather. 7 So Esdras arose up and said to them, "You have transgressed the law and married foreign wives, increasing the sins of Israel. 8 Now make confession and give glory to the Lord, the God of our fathers, 9 and do his will, and separate yourselves from the heathen of the land, and from the foreign women."

10 Then the whole multitude cried out, and said with a loud voice, "Just as you have spoken, so we will do. 11 But because the multitude is great, and it is foul weather, so that we can't stand outside, and this is not a work of one day or two, seeing our sin in these things has spread far, 12 therefore let the rulers of the multitude stay, and let all those of our settlements that have foreign wives come at the time appointed, 13 and with them the rulers and judges of every place, until we turn away the wrath of the Lord from us for this matter."

14 So Jonathan the son of Azael and[d] Ezekias the son of Thocanus took the matter on themselves. Mosollamus and Levis and Sabbateus were judges with them. 15 Those who returned from captivity did according to all these things.

16 Esdras the priest chose for himself principal men of their families, all by name. On the new moon of the tenth month they met together to examine the matter. 17 So their cases of men who had foreign wives was brought to an end by the new moon of the first month.

18 Of the priests who had come together and had foreign wives, there were found 19 of the sons of Jesus the son of Josedek, and his kindred,[e] Mathelas, Eleazar, and[f] Joribus, and[g] Joadanus. 20 They gave their hands to put away their wives, and to offer rams to make reconciliation for their error. 21 Of the sons of Emmer: Ananias, Zabdeus, [h]Manes, [i]Sameus, [j]Hiereel, and [k]Azarias. 22 Of the sons of [l]Phaisur: Elionas, Massias, Ishmael, Nathanael, [m]Ocidelus, and [n]Saloas.

23 Of the Levites: Jozabdus, Semeis, [o]Colius who was called [p]Calitas, [q]Patheus, Judas, and Jonas. 24 Of the holy singers: [r]Eliasibus and Bacchurus. 25 Of the gatekeepers: Sallumus and[s] Tolbanes.

26 Of Israel, of the sons of Phoros:[t] Hiermas,[u] Ieddias,[v] Melchias, Maelus,[w] Eleazar, Asibas, [x] and Banneas. 27 Of the sons of Ela: Matthanias, Zacharias, [y] Jezrielus, Oabdius, Hieremoth, and[z] Aedias. 28 Of the sons of [aa]Zamoth: [bb]Eliadas, [cc]Eliasimus, [dd]Othonias, Jarimoth, [ee]Sabathus, and[ff] Zardeus. 29 Of the sons of Bebai: Joannes, Ananias, [gg]Jozabdus, and [hh]Ematheis. 30 Of the sons of [ii] Mani: [jj]Olamus, [kk]Mamuchus, [ll]Jedeus, Jasubas, [mm] Jasaelus, and Hieremoth. 31 Of the sons of Addi: Naathus, Moossias, Laccunus, Naidus, Matthanias, Sesthel, Balnuus, and Manasseas. 32 Of the sons of Annas: Elionas, Aseas, Melchias, Sabbeus,

---

a *8:62* Meremoth.
b *8:62* Uriah.
c *8:63* Noadiah the son of Binnui.
** *8:91* Ezra 10:1
** *9:1* Ezra 10:6
d *9:14* Another reading is, Ezias.
e *9:19* Maaseiah.
f *9:19* Jarib.
g *9:19* Gedaliah
h *9:21* Harim
i *9:21* Maaseiah.
j *9:21* Jehiel.
k *9:21* Uzziah.
l *9:22* Pashhur.
m *9:22* Jozabad.
n *9:22* Elasah.
o *9:23* Kelaiah.
p *9:23* Kelita.
q *9:23* Pethahiah.
r *9:24* Eliashib.
s *9:25* Telem.

t *9:26* Parosh.
u *9:26* Ramiah
v *9:26* Izziah. Another reading is, Iezias
w *9:26* Mijamin.
x *9:26* Malchijah.
y *9:27* Jehiel.
z *9:27* Abdi.
aa *9:28* Zattu.
bb *9:28* Elioenai.
cc *9:28* Eliashib.
dd *9:28* Mattaniah.
ee *9:28* Zabad.
ff *9:28* Aziza.
gg *9:29* Zabbai.
hh *9:29* Athlai.
ii *9:30* Bani.
jj *9:30* Meshullam.
kk *9:30* Malluch.
ll *9:30* Adaiah.
mm *9:30* Sheal.

and Simon Chosameus. 33 Of the sons of Asom: [a]Maltanneus, [b]Mattathias, [c]Sabanneus, Eliphalat, Manasses, and Semei. 34 Of the sons of Baani: Jeremias, Momdis, Ismaerus, Juel, Mamdai, Pedias, Anos, Carabasion, Enasibus, Mamnitamenus, Eliasis, Bannus, Eliali, Someis, Selemias, and Nathanias. Of the sons of Ezora: Sesis, Ezril, Azaelus, Samatus, Zambri, and Josephus. 35 Of the sons of Nooma: Mazitias, Zabadeas, Edos, Juel, and Banaias. 36 All these had taken foreign wives, and they put them away with their children.

37 The priests and Levites, and those who were of Israel, lived in Jerusalem and in the country, on the new moon of the seventh month, and the children of Israel in their settlements.

38 [**]The whole multitude gathered together with one accord into the broad place before the porch of the temple towards the east. 39 They said to Esdras the priest and reader, "Bring the law of Moses that was given by the Lord, the God of Israel."

40 So Esdras the chief priest brought the law to the whole multitude both of men and women, and to all the priests, to hear the law on the new moon of the seventh month. 41 He read in the broad place before the porch of the temple from morning until midday, before both men and women; and all the multitude gave attention to the law. 42 Esdras the priest and reader of the law stood up upon the pulpit of wood which had been prepared. 43 Beside him stood Mattathias, Sammus, Ananias, Azarias, Urias, [d]Ezekias, and Baalsamus on the right hand, 44 and on his left hand, [e]Phaldeus, Misael, Melchias, [f]Lothasubus, Nabarias, and Zacharias. 45 Then Esdras took the book of the law before the multitude, and sat honourably in the first place before all. 46 When he opened the law, they all stood straight up. So Esdras blessed the Lord God Most High, the God of armies, the Almighty. 47 All the people answered, "Amen." Lifting up their hands, they fell to the ground and worshipped the Lord. 48 Also Jesus, Annus, Sarabias, Iadinus, Jacubus, Sabateus, [g]Auteas, Maiannas, Calitas, Azarias, Jozabdus, Ananias, and Phalias, the Levites, taught the law of the Lord, [h]and read to the multitude the law of the Lord, explaining what was read.

49 Then Attharates said to Esdras the chief priest and reader, and to the Levites who taught the multitude, even to all, 50 "This day is holy to the Lord—now they all wept when they heard the law— 51 go then, eat the fat, drink the sweet, and send portions to those who have nothing; 52 for the day is holy to the Lord. Don't be sorrowful, for the Lord will bring you to honour." 53 So the Levites commanded all things to the people, saying, "This day is holy. Don't be sorrowful." 54 Then they went their way, every one to eat, drink, enjoy themselves, to give portions to those who had nothing, and to rejoice greatly, 55 because they [i]understood the words they were instructed with, and for which they had been assembled.

a *9:33* Mattenai.
b *9:33* Mattattah.
c *9:33* Zabad.
** *9:38* Nehemiah 8:1
d *9:43* Hilkiah.

e *9:44* Pedaiah.
f *9:44* Hashuin.
g *9:48* Hodiah.
h *9:48* Some authorities omit and read...Lord.
i *9:55* Or, were inspired by

The Prayer of Manasses, King of Judah, When He Was Held Captive in Babylon

The Prayer of Manasses is recognised as Deuterocanonical Scripture by the Greek Orthodox and Russian Orthodox Churches. It is included in an appendix to the Latin Vulgate Bible.

1

1 O LORD Almighty in heaven, God of our fathers Abraham, Isaac, and Jacob, and of their righteous offspring, 2 you who have made heaven and earth, with all their order, 3 who have bound the sea by the word of your commandment, who have shut up the deep, and sealed it by your terrible and glorious name, 4 whom all things fear, yes, tremble before your power, 5 for the majesty of your glory can't be borne, and the anger of your threatening towards sinners is unbearable. 6 Your merciful promise is unmeasurable and unsearchable, 7 for you are the Lord Most High, of great compassion, patient and abundant in mercy, and relent at human suffering. 8 [a] You, O Lord, according to your great goodness have promised repentance and forgiveness to those who have sinned against you. Of your infinite mercies, you have appointed repentance to sinners, that they may be saved. You therefore, O Lord, who are the God of the just, have not appointed repentance to the just, to Abraham, Isaac, and Jacob, which have not sinned against you, but you have appointed repentance to me who am a sinner. 9 For I have sinned more than the number of the sands of the sea. My transgressions are multiplied,[b] O Lord, my transgressions are multiplied, and I am not worthy to behold and see the height of heaven for the multitude of my iniquities. 10 I am bowed down with many iron bands, so that I can't lift up my head by reason of my sins,[c] neither have I any relief; for I have provoked your wrath, and done that which is evil before you:[d] I didn't do your will, neither did I keep your commandments. I have set up abominations, and have multiplied detestable things. 11 Now therefore I bow the knee of my heart, asking you for grace. 12 I have sinned, O Lord, I have sinned, and I acknowledge my iniquities; 13 but, I humbly ask you, forgive me, O Lord, forgive me, and please don't destroy me with my iniquities. Don't be angry with me forever, by reserving evil for me. Don't condemn me into the lower parts of the earth. For you, O Lord, are the God of those who repent. 14 In me you will show all your goodness, for you will save me, who am unworthy, according to your great mercy. 15 Then I will praise you forever all the days of my life; for all the army of heaven sings your praise, and yours is the glory forever and ever. Amen.

---

[a] *1:8* The Alex. MS. omits You... saved.
[b] *1:9* The Alex. MS. omits O Lord... multiplied.

[c] *1:10* Some authorities omit by reason of my sins.
[d] *1:10* The Alex. MS. omits I did... commandments.

Psalm 151 is recognised as Deuterocanonical Scripture by the Greek Orthodox and Russian Orthodox Churches.

1

This Psalm is a genuine one of David, though extra,[a] composed when he fought in single combat with Goliath.

₁ I was small amongst my brothers,
    and youngest in my father's house.
    I tended my father's sheep.

₂ My hands formed a musical instrument,
    and my fingers tuned a lyre.

₃ Who shall tell my Lord?
    The Lord himself, he himself hears.

₄ He sent forth his angel and took me from my father's sheep,
    and he anointed me with his anointing oil.

₅ My brothers were handsome and tall;
    but the Lord didn't take pleasure in them.

₆ I went out to meet the Philistine,
    and he cursed me by his idols.

₇ But I drew his own sword and beheaded him,
    and removed reproach from the children of Israel.

---

[a] *1:0* or, supernumerary

The Third Book of the Maccabees

The Third Book of the Maccabees is recognised as Deuterocanonical Scripture by the Greek Orthodox and Russian Orthodox Churches. It is considered to be apocrypha by most other church traditions.

1

₁ Now Philopater, on learning from those who came back that Antiochus had made himself master of the places which belonged to himself, sent orders to all his infantry and cavalry, took with him his sister Arsinoe, and marched out as far as the parts of Raphia, where Antiochus and his forces encamped. ₂ And one Theodotus, intending to carry out his design, took with him the bravest of the armed men who had been before committed to his trust by Ptolemy, and got through at night to the tent of Ptolemy, to kill him on his own responsibility, and so to end the war. ₃ But Dositheus, called the son of Drimulus, by birth a Jew, afterward a renegade from the laws and observances of his country, conveyed Ptolemy away, and made an obscure person lie down in his stead in the tent. It turned out that this man received the fate which was meant for the other. ₄ A fierce battle then took place. The men of Antiochus were prevailing. Arsinoe continually went up and down the ranks, and with dishevelled hair, with tears and entreaties, begged the soldiers to fight bravely for themselves, their children, and wives, and promised that if they proved conquerors, she would give them each two minas of gold. ₅ It thus fell out that their enemies were defeated in hand-to-hand encounter, and that many of them were taken prisoners. ₆ Having vanquished this attempt, the king then decided to proceed to the neighbouring cities, and encourage them. ₇ By doing this, and by making donations to their temples, he inspired his subjects with confidence.

₈ The Jews sent some of their council and of their elders to him. The greetings, welcoming gifts, and congratulations of the past, given by them, filled him with the greater eagerness to visit their city. ₉ Having arrived at Jerusalem, sacrificed, and offered thank-offerings to the Greatest God, and done whatever else was suitable to the sanctity of the place, and entered the inner court, ₁₀ he was so impressed with the magnificence of the place, and so wondered at the orderly arrangements of the temple, that he considered entering the sanctuary itself. ₁₁ When they told him that this was not permissible, none of the nation, not even the priests in general, but only the supreme high priest of all, and he only once in a year, was allowed to go in, he would by no means give way. ₁₂ Then they read the law to him, but he persisted in intruding, exclaiming that he ought to be allowed. He said, "Even if they were deprived of this honour, I shouldn't be." ₁₃ He asked why, when he entered all the other temples, did none of the priests who were present forbid him. ₁₄ He was thoroughly answered by someone, that he did wrong to boast of this. ₁₅ "Well, since I have done this," said he, "be the cause what it may, shall I not enter with or without your consent?"

₁₆ When the priests fell down in their sacred vestments imploring the Greatest God to come and help in time of need, and to avert the violence of the fierce aggressor, and when they filled the temple with lamentations and tears, ₁₇ then those who had been left behind in the city were scared, and rushed out, uncertain of the event. ₁₈ Virgins, who had been shut up within their chambers, came out with their mothers, scattering dust and ashes on their heads, and filling the streets with outcries. ₁₉ Women who had recently been arrayed for marriage left their bridal chambers, left the reserve that befitted them, and ran around the city in a disorderly manner. ₂₀ New-born babes were deserted by the mothers or nurses who waited upon them— some here, some there, in houses, or in fields; these now, with an ardour which could not be checked, swarmed into the Most High temple. ₂₁ Various prayers were offered up by those who assembled in this place because of the unholy attempt of the king. ₂₂ Along with these there were some of the citizens who took courage and would not submit to his obstinacy and his intention of carrying out his purpose. ₂₃ Calling out to arms, and to die bravely in defence of the law of their fathers, they created a great uproar in the place, and were with difficulty brought back by the aged and the elders to the station of prayer which they had occupied before. ₂₄ During this time, the multitude kept on praying. ₂₅ The elders who surrounded the king tried in many ways to divert his arrogant mind from the design which he had formed. ₂₆ He, in his hardened mood, insensible to all persuasion, was going onward with the view of carrying out this design. ₂₇ Yet even his own officers, when they saw this, joined the Jews in an appeal to Him who has all power to aid in the present crisis, and not wink at such haughty lawlessness. ₂₈ Such was the frequency and the vehemence of the cry of the assembled crowd, that an indescribable noise ensued. ₂₉ Not the men only, but the very walls and floor seemed to sound out, all things preferring death rather than to see the place defiled.

2

₁ Now it was that the high priest Simon bowed his knees near the holy place, spread out his hands in reverent form, and uttered the following prayer: ₂ "O Lord, Lord, King of the heavens, and Ruler of the whole creation, Holy amongst the holy, sole Governor, Almighty, give ear to us who are oppressed by a wicked and profane one, who celebrates in his confidence and strength. ₃ It is you, the Creator of all, the Lord of the universe, who are a righteous Governor, and judge all who act with pride and insolence. ₄ It was you who destroyed the former workers of unrighteousness, amongst whom were the giants, who trusted in their strength and daring, by covering them with a measureless flood. ₅ It was you who made the Sodomites, those workers of exceedingly iniquity, men notorious for their vices, an example to later generations, when you covered them with fire and brimstone[a]. ₆ You made known your power when you caused the bold Pharaoh, the enslaver of your people, to pass through the ordeal of many and diverse inflictions. ₇ You rolled the depths of the sea over him when he pursued with chariots and with a multitude of followers, and gave a safe passage to those who put their trust in you, the Lord of the whole creation. ₈ These saw and felt the works of your hands, and praised you, the Almighty. ₉ You, O King, when you created the immeasurable and measureless earth, chose this city. You made this place sacred to your name, even though you need nothing. You glorified it with your illustrious presence, after constructing it to the glory of your great and honourable name. ₁₀ You promised, out of love for the people of Israel, that if we fall away from you, become afflicted, and then come to this house and pray, you would hear our prayer. ₁₁ Truly you are faithful and true. ₁₂ When you often aided our fathers when hard pressed and humiliated, and delivered them out of great dangers, ₁₃ see now, holy King, how through our many and great sins we are crushed and made subject to our enemies, and have become weak and powerless. ₁₄ In our low condition, this bold and profane man seeks to dishonour this your holy place, consecrated out of the earth to the name of your Majesty. ₁₅ Your dwelling place, the heaven of heavens, is indeed unapproachable to men. ₁₆ But since it seemed good to you to exhibit your glory amongst your people Israel, you sanctified this place. ₁₇ Don't punish us by means of the uncleanness of their men, and don't chastise us by means of their profanity, lest the lawless ones should boast in their rage, and exult in exuberant pride of speech, and say, ₁₈ 'We have trampled upon the holy house, as idolatrous houses are trampled upon.' ₁₉ Blot out our iniquities, do away with our errors, and show your compassion in this hour. ₂₀ Let your mercies quickly go before us. Grant us peace, that the downcast and broken hearted may praise you with their mouth."

₂₁ At that time God, who sees all things, who is beyond all Holy amongst the holy, heard that prayer, so suitable, and scourged the man who was greatly uplifted with scorn and insolence. ₂₂ Shaking him back and forth as a reed is shaken with the wind, he threw him down on the pavement, powerless, with limbs paralysed, and by a righteous judgement deprived of the ability to speak. ₂₃ His friends and bodyguards, seeing the swift recompense which had suddenly overtaken him, struck with exceeding terror, and fearing that he would die, speedily removed him. ₂₄ When in course of time he had come to himself, this severe punishment caused no repentance within him, but he departed with bitter threatenings.

₂₅ He proceeded to Egypt, grew worse in wickedness through his previously mentioned companions in wine, who were lost to all goodness, ₂₆ and not satisfied with countless acts of impiety, his audacity so increased that he raised evil reports there, and many of his friends, watching his purpose attentively, joined in furthering his will. ₂₇ His purpose was to inflict a public stigma upon our race. Therefore he erected a stone pillar in the courtyard, and caused the following inscription to be engraved upon it: ₂₈ "Entrance to this temple is to be refused to all those who would not sacrifice. All the Jews were to be registered amongst the slaves. Those who resisted are to be forcibly seized and put to death. ₂₉ Those who are thus registered are to be marked on their persons by the ivy-leaf symbol of Dionysus, and to be reduced to these limited rights." ₃₀ To do away with the appearance of hating them all, he had it written underneath, that if any of them should elect to enter the community of those initiated in the rites, these should have equal rights with the Alexandrians.

₃₁ Some of those who were over the city, therefore, abhorring any approach to the city of piety, unhesitatingly gave in to the king, and expected to derive some great honour from a future connection with him. ₃₂ A nobler spirit, however, prompted the majority to cling to their religious observances, and by paying money that they might live unmolested, these sought to escape the registration, ₃₃ cheerfully looking forward to future aid, they abhorred their own apostates, considering them to be national foes, and depriving them of common fellowship and mutual help.

3

₁ On discovering this, so incensed was the wicked king, that he no longer confined his rage to the Jews in Alexandria. Laying his hand more heavily upon those who lived in the country, he gave orders that they should be quickly collected into one place, and most cruelly deprived of their lives. ₂ While this was going on, a hostile rumour was uttered abroad by men who had banded together to injure the Jewish race. The pretext of their charge was that the Jews kept them away from the ordinances of the law. ₃ Now the Jews always maintained a feeling of unwavering loyalty towards the kings, ₄ yet, as they worshipped God and observed his law, they made certain distinctions, and avoided certain things. Hence they appeared hateful to some people, ₅ although, as they adorned their conversation with works of righteousness, they had established themselves in the good opinion of the world. ₆ What all the rest of mankind said was, however, disregarded by the foreigners, ₇ who said much of the exclusiveness of the Jews with regard to their worship and meats. They alleged that they were unsociable men, hostile to the king's interests, refusing to associate with him or his troops. By this way of speaking, they brought much hatred on them. ₈ This unexpected uproar and sudden gathering of people was observed by the Greeks who lived in the city, concerning men who had never harmed them. Yet to aid them was not in

---

[a] *2:5* or, sulphur

their power, since all was oppression around, but they encouraged them in their troubles, and expected a favourable turn of affairs. 9 He who knows all things will not, they said, disregard so great a people. 10 Some of the neighbours, friends, and business associates of the Jews even called them secretly to an interview, pledged them their assistance, and promised to do their very utmost for them.

11 Now the king, elated with his prosperous fortune, and not regarding the superior power of God, but thinking to persevere in his present purpose, wrote the following letter to the prejudice of the Jews: 12 "King Ptolemy Philopater, to the commanders and soldiers in Egypt, and in all places, health and happiness! 13 I am doing well, and so, too, are my affairs. 14 Since our Asiatic campaign, the particulars of which you know, and which by the aid of the gods, not lightly given, and by our own vigour, has been brought to a successful conclusion according to our expectation, 15 we resolved, not with strength of spear, but with gentleness and much humanity, as it were to nurse the inhabitants of Coele-Syria and Phoenicia, and to be their willing benefactors. 16 So, having bestowed considerable sums of money upon the temples of the several cities, we proceeded even as far as Jerusalem, and went up to honour the temple of these wretched beings who never cease from their folly. 17 To outward appearance they received us willingly, but belied that appearance by their deeds. When we were eager to enter their temple, and to honour it with the most beautiful and exquisite gifts, 18 they were so carried away by their old arrogance as to forbid us the entrance, while we, out of our forbearance towards all men, refrained from exercising our power upon them. 19 Thus, exhibiting their enmity against us, they alone amongst the nations lift up their heads against kings and benefactors, as men unwilling to submit to any reasonable thing. 20 We then, having endeavored to make allowance for the madness of these people, and on our victorious return treating all people in Egypt courteously, acted in a manner which was befitting. 21 Accordingly, bearing no ill will against their kinsmen, but rather remembering our connection with them, and the numerous matters with sincere heart from a remote period entrusted to them, we wished to venture a total alteration of their state, by giving them the rights of citizens of Alexandria, and to admit them to the everlasting rites of our solemnities. 22 All this, however, they have taken in a very different spirit. With their innate malignity, they have spurned the fair offer, and constantly inclining to evil, 23 have rejected the inestimable rights. Not only so, but by using speech, and by refraining from speech, they abhor the few amongst them who are heartily disposed towards us, ever deeming that their infamous way of life will force us to do away with our reform. 24 Having then received certain proofs that these Jews bear us every sort of ill will, we must look forward to the possibility of some sudden tumult amongst ourselves when these impious men may turn traitors and barbarous enemies. 25 Therefore, as soon as the contents of this letter become known to you, in that same hour we order those Jews who dwell amongst you, with wives and children, to be sent to us, vilified and abused, in chains of iron, to undergo a cruel and shameful death, suitable to enemies. 26 For by the punishment of them in one body we perceive that we have found the only means of establishing our affairs for the future on a firm and satisfactory basis. 27 Whoever protects a Jew, whether it be old man, child, or nursing baby, shall with his whole house be tortured to death. 28 Whoever informs against the Jews, besides receiving the property of the person charged, shall be presented with two thousand drachmas[a] from the royal treasury, shall be made free, and shall be crowned. 29 Whatever place shelters a Jew shall be made unapproachable and shall be put under the ban of fire, and be forever rendered useless to every living being for all time to come." 30 The king's letter was written in the above form.

4

1 Wherever this decree was received, the people kept up a revelry of joy and shouting, as if their long-pent-up, hardened hatred would now show itself openly. 2 The Jews suffered great throes of sorrow and wept much, while their hearts, all things around being lamentable, were set on fire as they bewailed the sudden destruction which was decreed against them. 3 What home, or city, or any inhabited place, or what streets were there, which their condition didn't fill with wailing and lamentation? 4 They were sent out unanimously by the generals in various cities, with such stern and pitiless feeling that the exceptional nature of the infliction moved even some of their enemies. These, influenced by sentiments of common humanity, and reflecting upon the uncertain issue of life, shed tears at their miserable expulsion. 5 A multitude of aged hoary-haired old men were driven along with halting bending feet, urged onward by the impulse of a violent, shameless force to quick speed. 6 Girls who had entered the bridal chamber quite lately, to enjoy the partnership of marriage, exchanged pleasure for misery; and with dust scattered upon their myrrh-anointed heads, were hurried along unveiled; and, in the midst of outlandish insults, set up with one accord a lamentable cry instead of the marriage hymn. 7 Bound and exposed to public gaze, they were hurried violently on board ship. 8 The husbands of these, in the prime of their youthful vigour, instead of crowns, wore ropes round their necks. Instead of feasting and youthful celebration, they spent the rest of their nuptial days in wailing, and saw only the grave at hand. 9 They were dragged along by unyielding chains, like wild animals. Of these, some had their necks thrust into the benches of the rowers, while the feet of others were enclosed in hard fetters. 10 The planks of the deck above them blocked out the light and shut out the day on every side, so that they might be treated like traitors during the whole voyage.

11 They were carried like this in this vessel, and at the end of it arrived at Schedia. The king had ordered them to be cast into the vast hippodrome, which was built in front of the city. This place was well adapted by its situation to expose them to the gaze of all comers into the city, and of those who went from the city into the country. Thus they could hold no communication with his forces. They weren't deemed worthy of any civilized accommodation. 12 When this was done, the king, hearing that their kindred in the city often went out and lamented the melancholy distress of these victims, 13 was full of rage, and commanded that they should be carefully subjected to the same—and not one bit milder—treatment. 14 The whole nation was now to be registered. Every individual was to be specified by name, not for that hard servitude of labour which we have a little before mentioned, but that he might expose them to the before-mentioned tortures; and finally, in the short space of a day, might exterminate them by his cruelties. 15 The registering of these men was carried on cruelly, zealously, assiduously, from the rising of the sun to its going down, and was not brought to an end in forty days. 16 The king was filled with great and constant joy, and celebrated banquets before the temple idols. His erring heart, far from the truth, and his profane mouth gave glory to idols, deaf and incapable of speaking or aiding, and uttered unworthy speech against the Greatest God. 17 At the end of the above-mentioned interval of time, the registrars brought word to the king that the multitude of the Jews was too great for registration, 18 inasmuch as there were many still left in the land, of whom some were in inhabited houses, and others were scattered about in various places, so that all the commanders in Egypt were insufficient for the work. 19 The king threatened them, and charged them with taking bribes, in order to contrive the escape of the Jews, but was clearly convinced of the truth of what had been said. 20 They said, and proved, that paper and pens had failed them for the carrying out of their purpose. 21 Now this was an active interference of the unconquerable Providence which assisted the Jews from heaven.

5

1 Then he called Hermon, who had charge of the elephants. Full of rage, altogether fixed in his furious design, 2 he commanded him, with a quantity of unmixed wine with handfuls of incense infused, to drug the elephants early on the following day. These five hundred elephants were, when infuriated by the copious drinks of frankincense, to be led up to the execution of death upon the Jews. 3 The king, after issuing these orders, went to his feasting, and gathered together all those of his friends and of the army who hated the Jews the most. 4 The master of the elephants, Hermon, fulfilled his commission punctually. 5 The servants appointed for the purpose went out about evening and bound the hands of the miserable victims, and took other precautions for their security at night, thinking that the whole race would perish together. 6 The heathen believed the Jews to be destitute of all protection, for chains bound them. 7 They invoked the Almighty Lord, and ceaselessly implored with tears their merciful God and Father, Ruler of all, Lord of every power, 8 to overthrow the evil purpose which had gone out against them, and to deliver them by extraordinary manifestation from that death which was in store for them. 9 Their earnest entreaty went up to heaven. 10 Then Hermon, who had filled his merciless elephants with copious drinks of mixed wine and frankincense, came early to the palace to report on these preparations. 11 He, however, who has sent his good creature sleep from all time by night or by day thus gratifying whom he wills, diffused a portion of it now upon the king. 12 By this sweet and profound influence of the Lord, he was held fast, and thus his unjust purpose was quite frustrated, and his unflinching resolve greatly falsified. 13 But the Jews, having escaped the hour which had been fixed, praised their holy God, and again prayed him who is easily reconciled to display the power of his powerful hand to the arrogant Gentiles. 14 The middle of the tenth hour had nearly arrived, when the person who sent invitations, seeing the guests who were invited present, came and shook the king. 15 He gained his attention with difficulty, and hinting that the mealtime was getting past, talked the matter over with him. 16 The king listened to this, and then turning aside to his drinking, commanded the guests to sit down before him. 17 This done, he asked them to enjoy themselves, and to indulge in mirth at this somewhat late hour of the banquet. 18 Conversation grew on, and the king sent for Hermon, and enquired of him, with fierce denunciations, why the Jews had been allowed to outlive that day. 19 Hermon explained that he had done his bidding over night; and in this he was confirmed by his friends. 20 The king, then, with a barbarity exceeding that of Phalaris, said, "They might thank his sleep of that day. Lose no time, and get ready the elephants against tomorrow, as you did before, for the destruction of these accursed Jews." 21 When the king said this, the company present were glad, and approved. Then each man went to his own home. 22 They didn't employ the night in sleep, but in contriving cruel mockeries for those deemed miserable. 23 The morning cock had just crowed, and Hermon, having harnessed the brutes, was stimulating them in the great colonnade. 24 The city crowds were collected together to see the hideous spectacle, and waited impatiently for the dawn. 25 The Jews, breathless with momentary suspense, stretched out their hands and prayed the Greatest God, in mournful strains, again to help them speedily. 26 The sun's rays were not yet shining, and the king was waiting for his friends when Hermon came to him, calling him out, and saying that his desires could now be realised. 27 The king, receiving him, was astonished at his unusual invitation. Overwhelmed with a spirit of oblivion about everything, enquired about the object of this earnest preparation. 28 But this was the working of that Almighty God who

---

had made him forget all his purpose. ₂₉Hermon and all his friends pointed out the preparation of the animals. They are ready, O king, according to your own strict injunction. ₃₀The king was filled with fierce anger at these words, for, by the Providence of God regarding these things, his mind had become entirely confused. He looked hard at Hermon, and threatened him as follows: ₃₁"Your parents, or your children, were they here, would have given a large meal to these wild animals, not these innocent Jews, who have loyally served me and my forefathers. ₃₂Had it not been for familiar friendship, and the claims of your office, your life should have gone for theirs."

₃₃Hermon, being threatened in this unexpected and alarming manner, was troubled in his eyes, and his face fell. ₃₄The friends, too, stole out one by one, and dismissed the assembled multitudes to their respective occupations. ₃₅The Jews, having heard of these events, praised the glorious God and King of kings, because they had obtained this help, too, from him. ₃₆Now the king arranged another banquet in the same way, and proclaimed an invitation to mirth. ₃₇He summoned Hermon to his presence, and said, with threats, "How often, O wretch, must I repeat my orders to you about these same persons? ₃₈Once more, arm the elephants for the extermination of the Jews tomorrow!" ₃₉His kinsmen, who were reclining with him, wondered at his instability, and thus expressed themselves: ₄₀"O king, how long do you test us, as of men bereft of reason? This is the third time that you have ordered their destruction. When the thing is to be done, you change your mind, and recall your instructions. ₄₁Because of this, the feeling of expectation causes tumult in the city. It swarms with factions, and is continually on the point of being plundered."

₄₂The king, just like another Phalaris, a prey to thoughtlessness, made no account of the changes which his own mind had undergone, issuing in the deliverance of the Jews. He swore a fruitless oath, and determined immediately to send them to hades, crushed by the knees and feet of the elephants. ₄₃He would also invade Judea, level its towns with fire and the sword, destroy that temple which the heathen might not enter, and prevent sacrifices ever after being offered up there. ₄₄Joyfully his friends broke up, together with his kinsmen; and, trusting in his determination, arranged their forces in guard at the most convenient places of the city. ₄₅The master of the elephants urged the animals into an almost maniacal state, drenched them with incense and wine, and decked them with frightful devices. ₄₆About early morning, when the city was filled with an immense number of people at the hippodrome, he entered the palace and called the king to the business in hand. ₄₇The king's heart teemed with impious rage; and he rushed forth with the mass, along with the elephants. With unsoftened feelings and pitiless eyes, he longed to gaze at the hard and wretched doom of the previously mentioned Jews. ₄₈But the Jews, when the elephants went out at the gate, followed by the armed force. When they saw the dust raised by the throng, and heard the loud cries of the crowd, ₄₉thought that they had come to the last moment of their lives, to the end of what they had tremblingly expected. They gave way, therefore, to lamentations and moans. They kissed each other. Those nearest of kin to each other hung around one another's necks—fathers hugging their sons and mothers their daughters. Other women held their infants to their breasts, which drew what seemed their last milk. ₅₀Nevertheless, when they reflected upon the help previously granted them from heaven, they prostrated themselves with one accord, removed even the sucking children from the breasts, and ₅₁sent up an exceedingly great cry asking the Lord of all power to reveal himself, and have mercy upon those who now lay at the gates of hades.

6

₁Then Eleazar, an illustrious priest of the country, who had attained to length of days, and whose life had been adorned with virtue, caused the elders who were around him to cease to cry out to the holy God, and prayed this: ₂"O king, mighty in power, most high, Almighty God, who regulates the whole creation with your tender mercy, ₃look at the seed of Abraham, at the children of the sanctified Jacob, your sanctified inheritance, O Father, now being wrongfully destroyed as foreigners in a foreign land. ₄You destroyed Pharaoh with his army of chariots when that lord of this same Egypt was uplifted with lawless daring and loud-sounding tongue. Shedding the beams of your mercy upon the race of Israel, you overwhelmed him and his proud army. ₅When Sennacherim, the grievous king of the Assyrians, exulting in his countless army, had subdued the whole land with his spear and was lifting himself against your holy city with boastings grievous to be endured, you, O Lord, demolished him and displayed your might to many nations. ₆When the three friends in the land of Babylon of their own will exposed their lives to the fire rather than serve vain things, you sent a moist coolness through the fiery furnace, and brought the fire on all their adversaries. ₇It was you who, when Daniel was hurled, through slander and envy, as a prey to lions down below, brought him back again unharmed to light. ₈When Jonah was pining away in the belly of the sea-born monster, you looked at him, O Father, and recovered him to the sight of his own. ₉Now, you who hate insolence, you who abound in mercy, you who are the protector of all things, appear quickly to those of the race of Israel, who are insulted by abhorred, lawless gentiles. ₁₀If our life during our exile has been stained with iniquity, deliver us from the hand of the enemy, and destroy us, O Lord, by the death which you prefer. ₁₁Don't let the vain-minded congratulate vain idols at the destruction of your beloved, saying, 'Their god didn't deliver them.' ₁₂You who are All-powerful and Almighty, O Eternal One, behold! Have mercy on us who are being withdrawn from life, like traitors, by the unreasoning insolence of lawless men. ₁₃Let the heathen cower before your invincible might today, O glorious One, who have all power to save the race of Jacob. ₁₄The whole

band of infants and their parents ask you with tears. ₁₅Let it be shown to all the nations that you are with us, O Lord, and have not turned your face away from us, but as you said that you would not forget them even in the land of their enemies, so fulfil this saying, O Lord."

₁₆Now, at the time that Eleazar had ended his prayer, the king came along to the hippodrome with the wild animals, and with his tumultuous power. ₁₇When the Jews saw this, they uttered a loud cry to heaven so that the adjacent valleys resounded and caused an irrepressible lamentation throughout the army. ₁₈Then the all-glorious, all-powerful, and true God, displayed his holy countenance, and opened the gates of heaven, from which two angels, dreadful of form, came down and were visible to all but the Jews. ₁₉They stood opposite, and filled the enemies' army with confusion and cowardice, and bound them with immoveable shackles. ₂₀A cold shudder came over the person of the king, and oblivion paralysed the vehemence of his spirit. ₂₁They turned back the animals on the armed forces who followed them; and the animals trampled them and destroyed them. ₂₂The king's wrath was converted into compassion; and he wept at the things he had devised. ₂₃For when he heard the cry, and saw them all on the verge of destruction, with tears he angrily threatened his friends, saying, ₂₄"You have governed badly, and have exceeded tyrants in cruelty. You have laboured to deprive me, your benefactor, at once of my dominion and my life, by secretly devising measures injurious to the kingdom. ₂₅Who has gathered here, unreasonably removing each from his home, those who, in fidelity to us, had held the fortresses of the country? ₂₆Who has consigned to unmerited punishments those who in good will towards us from the beginning have in all things surpassed all nations, and who often have engaged in the most dangerous undertakings? ₂₇Loose, loose the unjust bonds! Send them to their homes in peace, begging pardon for what has been done. ₂₈Release the sons of the almighty living God of heaven, who from our ancestors' times until now has granted a glorious and uninterrupted prosperity to our affairs." ₂₉He said these things and they, released the same moment, having now escaped death, praised God their holy Saviour.

₃₀The king then departed to the city, and called his financier to himself, and asked him provide a seven days' quantity of wine and other materials for feasting for the Jews. He decided that they should keep a cheerful festival of deliverance in the very place in which they expected to meet with their destruction. ₃₁Then they who were before despised and near to hades, yes, rather advanced into it, partook of the cup of salvation, instead of a grievous and lamentable death. Full of exultation, they apportioned the place intended for their fall and burial into banqueting booths. ₃₂Ceasing their miserable strain of woe, they took up the subject of their fatherland, singing in praise to God their wonder-working Saviour. All groans and all wailing were laid aside. They formed dances as a sign of peaceful joy. ₃₃So the king also collected a number of guests for the occasion, and returned unceasing thanks with much magnificence for the unexpected deliverance afforded him. ₃₄Those who had marked them out as for death and for carrion, and had registered them with joy, howled aloud, and were clothed with shame, and had the fire of their rage ingloriously put out. ₃₅But the Jews, as we just said, instituted a dance, and then gave themselves up to feasting, glad thanksgiving, and psalms. ₃₆They made a public ordinance to commemorate these things for generations to come, as long as they should be sojourners. They thus established these days as days of mirth, not for the purpose of drinking or luxury, but because God had saved them. ₃₇They requested the king to send them back to their homes. ₃₈They were being enrolled from the twenty-fifth of Pachon to the fourth of Epiphi, a period of forty days. The measures taken for their destruction lasted from the fifth of Epiphi till the seventh, that is, three days. ₃₉The Ruler over all during this time manifested his mercy gloriously, and delivered them all together unharmed. ₄₀They feasted upon the king's provision up to the fourteenth day, then asked to be sent away. ₄₁The king commended them, and wrote the following letter, of magnanimous import for them, to the commanders of every city:

7

₁"King Ptolemy Philopator to the commanders throughout Egypt, and to all who are set over affairs, joy and strength. ₂We, too, and our children are well. God has directed our affairs as we wish. ₃Certain of our friends out of malice vehemently urged us to punish the Jews of our realm in a body, with the infliction of a monstrous punishment. ₄They pretended that our affairs would never be in a good state till this took place. Such, they said, was the hatred borne by the Jews to all other people. ₅They brought them fettered in grievous chains as slaves, no, as traitors. Without enquiry or examination they endeavored to annihilate them. They buckled themselves with a savage cruelty, worse than Scythian custom. ₆For this cause we severely threatened them; yet, with the clemency which we usually extend to all men, we at length permitted them to live. Finding that the God of heaven cast a shield of protection over the Jews so as to preserve them, and that he fought for them as a father always fights for his sons, ₇and taking into consideration their constancy and fidelity towards us and towards our ancestors, we have, as we ought, acquitted them of every sort of charge. ₈We have dismissed them to their several homes, telling all men everywhere to do them no wrong, or unrighteously revile them about the past. ₉For know this, that should we conceive any evil design, or in any way aggrieve them, we shall ever have as our adversary, not man, but the highest God, the ruler of all might. From Him there will be no escape, as the avenger of such deeds. Farewell."

₁₀When they had received this letter, they didn't hurry to depart immediately. They petitioned the king to be allowed to inflict fitting punishment upon those of their race who had willingly transgressed the holy god, and the law of God. 11 They alleged that men who had for their bellies' sake transgressed the ordinances of God, would never be faithful to the interests of the king. 12 The king admitted the truth of this reasoning, and commended them. Full power was given them, without warrant or special commission, to destroy those who had transgressed the law of God boldly in every part of the king's dominions. 13 Their priests, then, as it was appropriate, saluted him with good wishes, and all the people echoed with the "Hallelujah!" Then they joyfully departed. 14 Then they punished and shamefully destroyed every polluted Jew that fell in their way, 15 slaying this way, in that day, more than three hundred men, and esteeming this destruction of the wicked a season of joy. 16 They themselves having held closely to their God to death, and having enjoyed a full deliverance, departed from the city garlanded with sweet-flowered wreaths of every kind. Uttering exclamations of joy, with songs of praise, and melodious hymns, they thanked the God of their fathers, the eternal Saviour of Israel. 17 Having arrived at Ptolemais, called from the specialty of that district "Rose-bearing", where the fleet, in accordance with the general wish, waited for them seven days, 18 they partook of a banquet of deliverance, for the king generously granted them all the means of securing a return home. 19 They were accordingly brought back in peace, while they gave utterance to appropriate thanks; and they determined to observe these days during their sojourn as days of joyfulness. 20 These they registered as sacred upon a pillar, when they had dedicated the place of their festivity to be one of prayer. They departed unharmed, free, abundant in joy, preserved by the king's command, by land, by sea, and by river, each to his own home. 21 They had more weight than before amongst their enemies, and were honoured and feared. No one in any way robbed them of their goods. 22 Every man received back his own, according to inventory, those who had obtained their goods, giving them up with the greatest terror. For the greatest God made perfect wonders for their salvation. 23 Blessed be the Redeemer of Israel forever! Amen.

The Second Book of Esdras

The Second Book of Esdras is included in the Slavonic Bible as *3 Esdras*, but is not found in the Greek Septuagint. It is included in the Appendix to the Latin Vulgate Bible as *4 Esdras*. It is considered to be Apocrypha by most church traditions. It is preserved here for its supplementary historical value.

1

1 The second book of the prophet Esdras, the son of Saraias, the son of Azaraias, the son of Helkias, the son of Salemas, the son of Sadoc, the son of Ahitob, 2 the son of Achias, the son of Phinees, the son of Heli, the son of Amarias, the son of Aziei, the son of Marimoth, the son of Arna, the son of Ozias, the son of Borith, the son of Abissei, the son of Phinees, the son of Eleazar, 3 the son of Aaron, of the tribe of Levi, who was captive in the land of the Medes, in the reign of Artaxerxes king of the Persians.

4 The Lord's word came to me, saying, 5 "Go your way and show my people their sinful deeds, and their children their wickedness which they have done against me, that they may tell their children's children, 6 because the sins of their fathers have increased in them, for they have forgotten me, and have offered sacrifices to foreign gods. 7 Didn't I bring them out of the land of Egypt, out of the house of bondage? But they have provoked me to wrath and have despised my counsels. 8 So pull out the hair of your head and cast all evils upon them, for they have not been obedient to my law, but they are a rebellious people. 9 How long shall I endure them, to whom I have done so much good? 10 I have overthrown many kings for their sakes. I have struck down Pharoah with his servants and all his army. 11 I have destroyed all the nations before them. In the east, I have scattered the people of two provinces, even of Tyre and Sidon, and have slain all their adversaries. 12 Speak therefore to them, saying:

13 "The Lord says, truly I brought you through the sea, and where there was no path I made highways for you. I gave you Moses for a leader and Aaron for a priest. 14 I gave you light in a pillar of fire. I have done great wonders amongst you, yet you have forgotten me, says the Lord.

15 "The Lord Almighty says: The quails were for a token to you. I gave you a camp for your protection, but you complained there. 16 You didn't celebrate in my name for the destruction of your enemies, but even to this day you still complain. 17 Where are the benefits that I have given you? When you were hungry and thirsty in the wilderness, didn't you cry to me, 18 saying, 'Why have you brought us into this wilderness to kill us? It would have been better for us to have served the Egyptians than to die in this wilderness.' 19 I had pity on your mourning and gave you manna for food. You ate angels' bread. 20 When you were thirsty, didn't I split the rock, and water flowed out in abundance? Because of the heat, I covered you with the leaves of the trees. 21 I divided fruitful lands amongst you. I drove out the Canaanites, the Pherezites, and the Philistines before you. What more shall I do for you?" says the Lord.

22 The Lord Almighty says, "When you were in the wilderness, at the bitter stream, being thirsty and blaspheming my name, 23 I gave you not fire for your blasphemies, but threw a tree in the water, and made the river sweet. 24 What shall I do to you, O Jacob? You, Judah, would not obey me. I will turn myself to other nations, and I will give my name to them, that they may keep my statutes. 25 Since you have forsaken me, I also will forsake you. When you ask me to be merciful to you, I will have no mercy upon you. 26 Whenever you call upon me, I will not hear you, for you have defiled your hands with blood, and your feet are swift to commit murder. 27 It is not as though you have forsaken me, but your own selves," says the Lord.

28 The Lord Almighty says, "Haven't I asked you as a father his sons, as a mother her daughters, and a nurse her young babies, 29 that you would be my people, and I would be your God, that you would be my children, and I would be your father? 30 I gathered you together, as a hen gathers her chicks under her wings. But now, what should I do to you? I will cast you out from my presence. 31 When you offer burnt sacrifices to me, I will turn my face from you, for I have rejected your solemn feast days, your new moons, and your circumcisions of the flesh. 32 I sent to you my servants the prophets, whom you have taken and slain, and torn their bodies in pieces, whose blood I will require from you," says the Lord.

33 The Lord Almighty says, "Your house is desolate. I will cast you out as the wind blows stubble. 34 Your children won't be fruitful, for they have neglected my commandment to you, and done that which is evil before me. 35 I will give your houses to a people that will come, which not having heard of me yet believe me. Those to whom I have shown no signs will do what I have commanded. 36 They have seen no prophets, yet they will remember their former condition. 37 I call to witness the gratitude of the people who will come, whose little ones rejoice with gladness. Although they see me not with bodily eyes, yet in spirit they will believe what I say."

38 And now, father, behold with glory, and see the people that come from the east: 39 to whom I will give for leaders, Abraham, Isaac, and Jacob, Oseas, Amos, and Micheas, Joel, Abdias, and Jonas, 40 Nahum, and Abacuc, Sophonias, Aggaeus, Zachary, and Malachy, who is also called the Lord's messenger.

2

1 The Lord says, "I brought this people out of bondage. I gave them my commandments by my servants the prophets, whom they would not listen to, but made my counsels void. 2 The mother who bore them says to them, 'Go your way, my children, for I am a widow and forsaken. 3 I brought you up with gladness, and I have lost you with sorrow and heaviness, for you have sinned before the Lord God, and done that which is evil before me. 4 But now what can I do for you? For I am a widow and forsaken. Go your way, my children, and ask for mercy from the Lord.' 5 As for me, O father, I call upon you for a witness in addition to the mother of these children, because they would not keep my covenant, 6 that you may bring them to confusion, and their mother to ruin, that they may have no offspring. 7 Let them be scattered abroad amongst the heathen. Let their names be blotted out of the earth, for they have despised my covenant. 8 Woe to you, Assur, you who hide the unrighteous with you! You wicked nation, remember what I did to Sodom and Gomorrah, 9 whose land lies in lumps of pitch and heaps of ashes. That is what I will also do to those who have not listened to me," says the Lord Almighty.

10 The Lord says to Esdras, "Tell my people that I will give them the kingdom of Jerusalem, which I would have given to Israel. 11 I will also take their glory back to myself, and give these the everlasting tabernacles which I had prepared for them. 12 They will have the tree of life for fragrant perfume. They will neither labour nor be weary. 13 Ask, and you will receive. Pray that your days may be few, that they may be shortened. The kingdom is already prepared for you. Watch! 14 Call heaven and earth to witness. Call them to witness, for I have left out evil, and created the good, for I live, says the Lord.

15 "Mother, embrace your children. I will bring them out with gladness like a dove does. Establish their feet, for I have chosen you, says the Lord. 16 I will raise those who are dead up again from their places, and bring them out from their tombs, for I recognise my name in them. 17 Don't be afraid, you mother of children, for I have chosen you, says the Lord. 18 For your help, I will send my servants Esaias and Jeremy, after whose counsel I have sanctified and prepared for you twelve trees laden with various fruits, 19 and as many springs flowing with milk and honey, and seven mighty mountains, on which roses and lilies grow, with which I will fill your children with joy. 20 Do right to the widow. Secure justice for the fatherless. Give to the poor. Defend the orphan. Clothe the naked. 21 Heal the broken and the weak. Don't laugh a lame man to scorn. Defend the maimed. Let the blind man have a vision of my glory. 22 Protect the old and young within your walls. 23 Wherever you find the dead, set a sign upon them and commit them to the grave, and I will give you the first place in my resurrection. 24 Stay still, my people, and take your rest, for your rest will come. 25 Nourish your children, good nurse, and establish their feet. 26 As for the servants whom I have given you, not one of them will perish, for I will require them from amongst your number. 27 Don't be anxious, for when the day of suffering and anguish comes, others will weep and be sorrowful, but you will rejoice and have abundance. 28 The nations will envy you, but they will be able to do nothing against you, says the Lord. 29 My hands will cover you, so that your children don't see Gehenna.[a] 30 Be joyful, mother, with your children, for I will deliver you, says the Lord. 31 Remember your children who sleep, for I will bring them out of the secret places of the earth and show mercy to them, for I am merciful, says the Lord Almighty. 32 Embrace your children until I come, and proclaim mercy to them, for my wells run over, and my grace won't fail."

33 I, Esdras, received a command from the Lord on Mount Horeb to go to Israel, but when I came to them, they rejected me and rejected the Lord's commandment. 34 Therefore I say to you, O nations that hear and understand, "Look for your shepherd. He will give you everlasting rest, for he is near at hand who will come at the end of the age. 35 Be ready for the rewards of the kingdom, for the everlasting light will shine on you forevermore. 36 Flee the shadow of this world, receive the joy of your glory. I call to witness my saviour openly. 37 Receive that which is given to you by the Lord, and be joyful, giving thanks to him who has called you to heavenly kingdoms. 38 Arise and stand up, and see the number of those who have been sealed at the Lord's feast. 39 Those who withdrew themselves from the shadow of the world have received glorious garments from the Lord. 40 Take again your full number, O Zion, and make up the reckoning of those of yours who are clothed in white, which have fulfilled the law of the Lord. 41 The number of your children, whom you long for, is fulfilled. Ask the power of the Lord, that your people, which have been called from the beginning, may be made holy."

42 I, Esdras, saw upon Mount Zion a great multitude, whom I could not number, and they all praised the Lord with songs. 43 In the midst of them, there was a young man of a high stature, taller than all the rest, and upon every one of their heads he set crowns, and he was more exalted than they were. I marvelled greatly at this. 44 So I asked the angel, and said, "What are these, my Lord?"

45 He answered and said to me, "These are those who have put off the mortal clothing, and put on the immortal, and have confessed the name of God. Now are they crowned, and receive palms."

46 Then said I to the angel, "Who is the young man who sets crowns on them, and gives them palms in their hands?"

47 So he answered and said to me, "He is the Son of God, whom they have confessed in the world."

Then I began to praise those who stood so valiantly for the name of the Lord.

48 Then the angel said to me, "Go your way, and tell my people what kind of things, and how great wonders of the Lord God you have seen."

---

a *2:29* or, Hell.

3

₁In the thirtieth year after the ruin of the city, I Salathiel, also called Esdras, was in Babylon, and lay troubled upon my bed, and my thoughts came up over my heart, ₂for I saw the desolation of Zion and the wealth of those who lived at Babylon. ₃My spirit was very agitated, so that I began to speak words full of fear to the Most High, and said, ₄"O sovereign Lord, didn't you speak at the beginning when you formed the earth—and that yourself alone—and commanded the dust ₅and it gave you Adam, a body without a soul? Yet it was the workmanship of your hands, and you breathed into him the breath of life, and he was made alive in your presence. ₆You led him into the garden which your right hand planted before the earth appeared. ₇You gave him your one commandment, which he transgressed, and immediately you appointed death for him and his descendants. From him were born nations, tribes, peoples, and kindred without number. ₈Every nation walked after their own will, did ungodly things in your sight, and despised your commandments, and you didn't hinder them. ₉Nevertheless, again in process of time, you brought the flood on those who lived in the world and destroyed them. ₁₀It came to pass that the same thing happened to them. Just as death came to Adam, so was the flood to these. ₁₁Nevertheless, you left one of them, Noah with his household, and all the righteous men who descended from him.

₁₂"It came to pass that when those who lived upon the earth began to multiply, they also multiplied children, peoples, and many nations, and began again to be more ungodly than their ancestors. ₁₃It came to pass, when they did wickedly before you, you chose one from amongst them, whose name was Abraham. ₁₄You loved, and to him only you showed the end of the times secretly by night, ₁₅and made an everlasting covenant with him, promising him that you would never forsake his descendants. To him, you gave Isaac, and to Isaac you gave Jacob and Esau. ₁₆You set apart Jacob for yourself, but rejected Esau. Jacob became a great multitude. ₁₇It came to pass that when you led his descendants out of Egypt, you brought them up to Mount Sinai. ₁₈You bowed the heavens also, shook the earth, moved the whole world, made the depths tremble, and troubled the age. ₁₉Your glory went through four gates, of fire, of earthquake, of wind, and of ice, that you might give the law to the descendants of Jacob, and the commandment to the descendants of Israel.

₂₀"Yet you didn't take away from them their wicked heart, that your law might produce fruit in them. ₂₁For the first Adam, burdened with a wicked heart transgressed and was overcome, as were all who are descended from him. ₂₂Thus disease was made permanent. The law was in the heart of the people along with the wickedness of the root. So the good departed away and that which was wicked remained. ₂₃So the times passed away, and the years were brought to an end. Then you raised up a servant, called David, ₂₄whom you commanded to build a city to your name, and to offer burnt offerings to you in it from what is yours. ₂₅When this was done many years, then those who inhabited the city did evil, ₂₆in all things doing as Adam and all his generations had done, for they also had a wicked heart. ₂₇So you gave your city over into the hands of your enemies.

₂₈"Then I said in my heart, 'Are their deeds of those who inhabit Babylon any better? Is that why it gained dominion over Zion?' ₂₉For it came to pass when I came here, that I also saw impieties without number, and my soul saw many sinners in this thirtieth year, so that my heart failed me. ₃₀For I have seen how you endure them sinning, and have spared those who act ungodly, and have destroyed your people, and have preserved your enemies; ₃₁and you have not shown how your way may be comprehended. Are the deeds of Babylon better than those of Zion? ₃₂Or is there any other nation that knows you beside Israel? Or what tribes have so believed your covenants as these tribes of Jacob? ₃₃Yet their reward doesn't appear, and their labour has no fruit, for I have gone here and there through the nations, and I see that they abound in wealth, and don't think about your commandments. ₃₄Weigh therefore our iniquities now in the balance, and theirs also who dwell in the world, and so will it be found which way the scale inclines. ₃₅Or when was it that they who dwell on the earth have not sinned in your sight? Or what nation has kept your commandments so well? ₃₆You will find some men by name who have kept your precepts, but you won't find nations."

4

₁The angel who was sent to me, whose name was Uriel, gave me an answer, ₂and said to me, "Your understanding has utterly failed you regarding this world. Do you think you can comprehend the way of the Most High?"

₃Then I said, "Yes, my Lord."

He answered me, and said, "I have been sent to show you three ways, and to set before you three problems. ₄If you can solve one for me, I also will show you the way that you desire to see, and I will teach you why the heart is wicked."

₅I said, "Say on, my Lord."

Then said he to me, "Go, weigh for me the weight of fire, or measure for me blast of wind, or call back for me the day that is past."

₆Then answered I and said, "Who of the sons of men is able to do this, that you should ask me about such things?"

₇He said to me, "If I had asked you, 'How many dwellings are there in the heart of the sea? Or how many springs are there at the fountain head of the deep? Or how many streams are above the firmament? Or which are the exits ªof hell? Or which are the entrances of paradise?' ₈perhaps you would say to me, 'I never went down into the deep, or as yet into hell, neither did I ever climb up into heaven.' ₉Nevertheless now I have only asked you about the fire, wind, and the day, things which you have experienced, and from which you can't be separated, and yet have you given me no answer about them."

₁₀He said moreover to me, "You can't understand your own things that you grew up with. ₁₁How then can your mind comprehend the way of the Most High? How can he who is already worn out with the corrupted world understand incorruption?"

ᵇWhen I heard these things, I fell on my face ₁₂and said to him, "It would have been better if we weren't here at all, than that we should come here and live in the midst of ungodliness, and suffer, and not know why."

₁₃He answered me, and said, ᶜ"A forest of the trees of the field went out, and took counsel together, ₁₄and said, 'Come! Let's go and make war against the sea, that it may depart away before us, and that we may make ourselves more forests.' ₁₅The waves of the sea also in like manner took counsel together, and said, 'Come! Let's go up and subdue the forest of the plain, that there also we may gain more territory.' ₁₆The counsel of the wood was in vain, for the fire came and consumed it. ₁₇Likewise also the counsel of the waves of the sea, for the sand stood up and stopped them. ₁₈If you were judge now between these two, which would you justify, or which would you condemn?"

₁₉I answered and said, "It is a foolish counsel that they both have taken, for the ground is given to the wood, and the place of the sea is given to bear its waves."

₂₀Then answered he me, and said, "You have given a right judgement. Why don't you judge your own case? ₂₁For just as the ground is given to the wood, and the sea to its waves, even so those who dwell upon the earth may understand nothing but what is upon the earth. Only he who dwells above the heavens understands the things that are above the height of the heavens."

₂₂Then answered I and said, "I beg you, O Lord, why has the power of understanding been given to me? ₂₃For it was not in my mind to be curious of the ways above, but of such things as pass by us daily, because Israel is given up as a reproach to the heathen. The people whom you have loved have been given over to ungodly nations. The law of our forefathers is made of no effect, and the written covenants are nowhere regarded. ₂₄We pass away out of the world like locusts. Our life is like a vapour, and we aren't worthy to obtain mercy. ₂₅What will he then do for his name by which we are called? I have asked about these things."

₂₆Then he answered me, and said, "If you are alive you will see, and if you live long, you will marvel, for the world hastens quickly to pass away. ₂₇For it is not able to bear the things that are promised to the righteous in the times to come; for this world is full of sadness and infirmities. ₂₈For the evilᵈ about which you asked me has been sown, but its harvest hasn't yet come. ₂₉If therefore that which is sown isn't reaped, and if the place where the evil is sown doesn't pass away, the field where the good is sown won't come. ₃₀For a grain of evil seed was sown in the heart of Adam from the beginning, and how much wickedness it has produced to this time! How much more it will yet produce until the time of threshing comes! ₃₁Ponder now by yourself, how much fruit of wickedness a grain of evil seed has produced. ₃₂When the grains which are without number are sown, how great a threshing floor they will fill!"

₃₃Then I answered and said, ᵉ"How long? When will these things come to pass? Why are our years few and evil?"

₃₄He answered me, and said, "Don't hurry faster than the Most High; for your haste isᶠ for your own self, but he who is above hurries on behalf of many. ₃₅Didn't the souls of the righteous ask question of these things in their chambers, saying, 'How long ᵍwill we be here? When does the fruit of the threshing floor come?' ₃₆To them, Jeremiel the archangel answered, 'When the number is fulfilled of those who are like you. For he has weighed the world in the balance. ₃₇By measure, he has measured the times. By number, he has counted the seasons. He won't ʰmove or stir them until that measure is fulfilled.'"

₃₈Then I answered, "O sovereign Lord, all of us are full of ungodliness. ₃₉Perhaps it is for our sakes that the threshing time of the righteous is kept back—because of the sins of those who dwell on the earth."

₄₀So he answered me, "Go your way to a woman with child, and ask of her when she has fulfilled her nine months, if her womb may keep the baby any longer within her."

₄₁Then I said, "No, Lord, that can it not."

He said to me, "In Hades, the chambers of souls are like the womb. ₄₂For just like a woman in labour hurries to escape the anguish of the labour pains, even so these places hurry to deliver those things that are committed to them from the beginning. ₄₃Then you will be shown those things which you desire to see."

₄₄Then I answered, "If I have found favour in your sight, and if it is possible, and if I am worthy, ₄₅show me this also, whether there is more to come than is past, or whether the greater part has gone over us. ₄₆For what is gone I know, but I don't know what is to come."

₄₇He said to me, "Stand up on my right side, and I will explain the parable to you."

ª *4:7* So the Syriac. The Latin omits of hell? or which are the paths.
ᵇ *4:11* So the Syriac and Aethiopic. The Latin is corrupt.
ᶜ *4:13* So the Oriental versions. The Latin is corrupt. See Judges 9:8.
ᵈ *4:28* so the Syriac and Aethiopic.

ᵉ *4:33* So the chief oriental versions.
ᶠ *4:34* So the Syriac. The Latin is corrupt.
ᵍ *4:35* So the Syriac. The Latin has shall I hope on this fashion?
ʰ *4:37* Syr. rest.

48 So I stood, looked, and saw a hot burning oven passed by before me. It happened that when the flame had gone by I looked, and saw that the smoke remained. 49 After this, a watery cloud passed in front of me, and sent down much rain with a storm. When the stormy rain was past, the drops still remained in it."

50 Then said he to me, "Consider with yourself; as the rain is more than the drops, and the fire is greater than the smoke, so the quantity which is past was far greater; but the drops and the smoke still remained."

51 Then I prayed, and said, "Do you think that I will live until that time? Or who will be alive in those days?"

52 He answered me, "As for the signs you asked me about, I may tell you of them in part; but I wasn't sent to tell you about your life, for I don't know.

5

1 "Nevertheless, concerning the signs, behold, the days will come when those who dwell on earth will be taken a with great amazement, and the way of truth will be hidden, and the land will be barren of faith. 2 Iniquity will be increased above what now you see, and beyond what you have heard long ago. 3 The land that you now see ruling will be a trackless waste, and men will see it desolate. 4 But if the Most High grants you to live, you will see what is after the third period will be troubled. The sun will suddenly shine in the night, and the moon in the day. 5 Blood will drop out of wood, and the stone will utter its voice. The peoples will be troubled, and the stars will fall. 6 He will rule whom those who dwell on the earth don't expect, and the birds will fly away together. 7 The Sodomite sea will cast out fish, and make a noise in the night, which many have not known; but all will hear its voice. 8 There will also be chaos in many places. Fires will break out often, and the wild animals will change their places, and women will bring forth monsters. 9 Salt waters will be found in the sweet, and all friends will destroy one another. Then reason will hide itself, and understanding withdraw itself into its chamber. 10 It will be sought by many, and won't be found. Unrighteousness and lack of restraint will be multiplied on earth. 11 One country will ask another, 'Has righteousness, or a man that does righteousness, gone through you?' And it will say, 'No.' 12 It will come to pass at that time that men will hope, but won't obtain. They will labour, but their ways won't prosper. 13 I am permitted to show you such signs. If you will pray again, and weep as now, and fast seven days, you will hear yet greater things than these."

14 Then I woke up, and an extreme trembling went through my body, and my mind was so troubled that it fainted. 15 So the angel who had come to talk with me held me, comforted me, and set me on my feet.

16 In the second night, it came to pass that b Phaltiel the captain of the people came to me, saying, "Where have you been? Why is your face sad? 17 Or don't you know that Israel is committed to you in the land of their captivity? 18 Get up then, and eat some bread, and don't forsake us, like a shepherd who leaves the flock in the power of cruel wolves."

19 Then said I to him, "Go away from me and don't come near me for seven days, and then you shall come to me." He heard what I said and left me.

20 So I fasted seven days, mourning and weeping, like Uriel the angel had commanded me. 21 After seven days, the thoughts of my heart were very grievous to me again, 22 and my soul recovered the spirit of understanding, and I began to speak words before the Most High again. 23 I said, "O sovereign Lord of all the woods of the earth, and of all the trees thereof, you have chosen one vine for yourself. 24 Of all the lands of the world you have chosen one c country for yourself. Of all the flowers of the world, you have chosen one lily for yourself. 25 Of all the depths of the sea, you have filled one river for yourself. Of all built cities, you have consecrated Zion for yourself. 26 Of all the birds that are created you have named for yourself one dove. Of all the livestock that have been made, you have provided for yourself one sheep. 27 Amongst all the multitudes of peoples you have gotten yourself one people. To this people, whom you loved, you gave a law that is approved by all. 28 Now, O Lord, why have you given this one people over to many, and d have dishonoured the one root above others, and have scattered your only one amongst many? 29 Those who opposed your promises have trampled down those who believed your covenants. 30 If you really do hate your people so much, they should be punished with your own hands."

31 Now when I had spoken these words, the angel that came to me the night before was sent to me, 32 and said to me, "Hear me, and I will instruct you. Listen to me, and I will tell you more."

33 I said, "Speak on, my Lord."

Then said he to me, "You are very troubled in mind for Israel's sake. Do you love that people more than he who made them?"

34 I said, "No, Lord; but I have spoken out of grief; for my heart is in agony every hour while I labour to comprehend the way of the Most High, and to seek out part of his judgement."

35 He said to me, "You can't."

And I said, "Why, Lord? Why was I born? Why wasn't my mother's womb my grave, that I might not have seen the travail of Jacob, and the wearisome toil of the people of Israel?"

36 He said to me, "Count for me those who haven't yet come. Gather together for me the drops that are scattered abroad, and make the withered flowers green again for me. 37 Open for me the chambers that are closed, and bring out the winds for me that are shut up in them. Or show me the image of a voice. Then I will declare to you the travail that you asked to see."

38 And I said, "O sovereign Lord, who may know these things except he who doesn't have his dwelling with men? 39 As for me, I lack wisdom. How can I then speak of these things you asked me about?"

40 Then said he to me, "Just as you can do none of these things that I have spoken of, even so you can't find out my judgement, or the end of the love that I have promised to my people."

41 I said, "But, behold, O Lord, you have made the promise to those who are alive at the end. What should they do who have been before us, or we ourselves, or those who will come after us?"

42 He said to me, "I will compare my judgement to a ring. Just as there is no slowness of those who are last, even so there is no swiftness of those who be first."

43 So I answered, "Couldn't you make them all at once that have been made, and that are now, and that are yet to come, that you might show your judgement sooner?"

44 Then he answered me, "The creature may not move faster than the creator, nor can the world hold them at once who will be created in it."

45 And I said, "How have you said to your servant, that e you will surely make alive at once the creature that you have created? f If therefore they will be alive at once, and the creation will sustain them, even so it might now also support them to be present at once."

46 And he said to me, "Ask the womb of a woman, and say to her, 'If you bear ten children, why do you it at different times? Ask her therefore to give birth to ten children at once."

47 I said, "She can't, but must do it each in their own time."

48 Then said he to me, "Even so, I have given the womb of the earth to those who are sown in it in their own times. 49 For just as a young child may not give birth, neither she who has grown old any more, even so have I organised the world which I created."

50 I asked, "Seeing that you have now shown me the way, I will speak before you. Is our mother, of whom you have told me, still young? Or does she now draw near to old age?"

51 He answered me, "Ask a woman who bears children, and she will tell you. 52 Say to her, 'Why aren't they whom you have now brought forth like those who were before, but smaller in stature?' 53 She also will answer you, 'Those who are born in the strength of youth are different from those who are born in the time of old age, when the womb fails.' 54 Consider therefore you also, how you are shorter than those who were before you. 55 So are those who come after you smaller than you, as born of the creature which now begins to be old, and is past the strength of youth."

56 Then I said, "Lord, I implore you, if I have found favour in your sight, show your servant by whom you visit your creation."

6

1 He said to me, "In the beginning, when the earth was made, before the portals of the world were fixed and before the gatherings of the winds blew, 2 before the voices of the thunder sounded and before the flashes of the lightning shone, before the foundations of paradise were laid, 3 before the fair flowers were seen, before the powers of the earthquake were established, before the innumerable army of angels were gathered together, 4 before the heights of the air were lifted up, before the measures of the firmament were named, before the footstool of Zion g was established, 5 before the present years were reckoned, before the imaginations of those who now sin were estranged, and before they were sealed who have gathered faith for a treasure— 6 then I considered these things, and they all were made through me alone, and not through another; just as by me also they will be ended, and not by another."

7 Then I answered, "What will be the dividing of the times? Or when will be the end of the first and the beginning of the age that follows?"

8 He said to me, "From Abraham to Isaac, because Jacob and Esau were born to him, for Jacob's hand held Esau's heel from the beginning. 9 For Esau is the end of this age, and Jacob is the beginning of the one that follows. 10 h The beginning of a man is his hand, and the end of a man is his heel. Seek nothing else between the heel and the hand, Esdras!"

11 Then I answered, "O sovereign Lord, if I have found favour in your sight, 12 I beg you, show your servant the end of your signs which you showed me part on a previous night."

13 So he answered, "Stand up upon your feet, and you will hear a mighty sounding voice. 14 If the place you stand on is greatly moved 15 when it speaks don't be afraid, for the word is of the end, and the foundations of the earth will understand 16 that the speech is about them. They will tremble and be moved, for they know that their end must be changed."

17 It happened that when I had heard it, I stood up on my feet, and listened, and, behold, there was a voice that spoke, and its sound was like the sound of many waters. 18 It said, "Behold, the days come when I draw near to visit those who dwell upon the earth, 19 and when I investigate those who have caused harm unjustly with their unrighteousness, and when the affliction of Zion is complete, 20 and when the seal will be set on the age that is to pass away, then I will show these signs: the books will be opened before the firmament, and all will see together. 21 The children a year old will

---

a *5:1* So the syriac.
b *5:16* The Syriac has Psaltiel.
c *5:24* After the Oriental versions. The Latin has pit.
d *5:28* After the Oriental versions. The Latin reads have prepared.

e *5:45* So the Syriac.
f *5:45* The Latin omits If...alive at once.
g *6:4* So the Syriac.
h *6:10* So the Syriac, etc. The Latin is defective.

speak with their voices. The women with child will deliver premature children at three or four months, and they will live and dance. 22 Suddenly the sown places will appear unsown. The full storehouses will suddenly be found empty. 23 The trumpet will give a sound which when every man hears, they will suddenly be afraid. 24 At that time friends will make war against one another like enemies. The earth will stand in fear with those who dwell in it. The springs of the fountains will stand still, so that for three hours they won't flow.

25 "It will be that whoever remains after all these things that I have told you of, he will be saved and will see my salvation, and the end of my world. 26 They will see the men who have been taken up, who have not tasted death from their birth. The heart of the inhabitants will be changed and turned into a different spirit. 27 For evil will be blotted out and deceit will be quenched. 28 Faith will flourish. Corruption will be overcome, and the truth, which has been so long without fruit, will be declared."

29 When he talked with me, behold, little by little, the place I stood on *rocked back and forth. 30 He said to me, "I came to show you these things *tonight. 31 If therefore you will pray yet again, and fast seven more days, I will *again tell you greater things than these. 32 For your voice has surely been heard before the Most High. For the Mighty has seen your righteousness. He has also seen your purity, which you have maintained ever since your youth. 33 Therefore he has sent me to show you all these things, and to say to you, 'Believe, and don't be afraid! 34 Don't be hasty to think vain things about the former times, that you may not hasten in the latter times.'"

35 It came to pass after this, that I wept again, and fasted seven days in like manner, that I might fulfil the three weeks which he told me. 36 On the eighth night, my heart was troubled within me again, and I began to speak in the presence of the Most High. 37 For my spirit was greatly aroused, and my soul was in distress. 38 I said, "O Lord, truly you spoke at the beginning of the creation, on the first day, and said this: 'Let heaven and earth be made,' and your word perfected the work. 39 Then the spirit was hovering, and darkness and silence were on every side. The sound of man's voice was not yet there.*d* 40 Then you commanded a ray of light to be brought out of your treasuries, that your works might then appear.

41 "On the second day, again you made the spirit of the firmament and commanded it to divide and to separate the waters, that the one part might go up, and the other remain beneath.

42 "On the third day, you commanded that the waters should be gathered together in the seventh part of the earth. You dried up six parts and kept them, to the intent that of these some being both planted and tilled might serve before you. 43 For as soon as your word went out, the work was done. 44 Immediately, great and innumerable fruit grew, with many pleasant tastes, and flowers of inimitable colour, and fragrances of most exquisite smell. This was done the third day.

45 "On the fourth day, you commanded that the sun should shine, the moon give its light, and the stars should be in their order; 46 and gave them a command to serve mankind, who was to be made.

47 "On the fifth day, you said to the seventh part, where the water was gathered together, that it should produce living creatures, fowls and fishes; and so it came to pass 48 that the mute and lifeless water produced living things as it was told, that the nations might therefore praise your wondrous works.

49 "Then you preserved two living creatures. The one you called Behemoth, and the other you called Leviathan. 50 You separated the one from the other; for the seventh part, namely, where the water was gathered together, might not hold them both. 51 To Behemoth, you gave one part, which was dried up on the third day, that he should dwell in it, in which are a thousand hills; 52 but to Leviathan you gave the seventh part, namely, the watery part. You have kept them to be devoured by whom you wish, when you wish.

53 "But on the sixth day, you commanded the earth to produce before you cattle, animals, and creeping things. 54 Over these, you ordained Adam as ruler over all the works that you have made. Of him came all of us, the people whom you have chosen.

55 "All this have I spoken before you, O Lord, because you have said that for our sakes you made *this world. 56 As for the other nations, which also come from Adam, you have said that they are nothing, and are like spittle. You have likened the abundance of them to a drop that falls from a bucket. 57 Now, O Lord, behold these nations, which are reputed as nothing, being rulers over us and devouring us. 58 But we your people, whom you have called your firstborn, your only children, and your fervent lover, are given into their hands. 59 Now if the world is made for our sakes, why don't we possess our world for an inheritance? How long will this endure?"

7

1 When I had finished speaking these words, the angel which had been sent to me the nights before was sent to me. 2 He said to me, "Rise, Esdras, and hear the words that I have come to tell you."

3 I said, "Speak on, my Lord."

Then he said to me, "There is a sea set in a wide place, that it might be *broad and vast, 4 but its entrance is set in a narrow place so as to be like a river. 5 Whoever desires to go into the sea to look at it, or to rule it, if he didn't go through the narrow entrance, how could he come into the broad part? 6 Another thing also: There is a city built and set in a plain country, and full of all good things, 7 but its entrance is narrow, and is set in a dangerous place to fall, having fire on the right hand, and deep water on the left. 8 There is one only path between them both, even between the fire and the water, so that only one person can go there at once. 9 If this city is now given to a man for an inheritance, if the heir doesn't pass the danger before him, how will he receive his inheritance?"

10 I said, "That is so, Lord."

Then said he to me, "Even so also is Israel's portion. 11 I made the world for their sakes. What is now done was decreed when Adam transgressed my statutes. 12 Then the entrances of this world were made narrow, sorrowful, and toilsome. They are but few and evil, full of perils, and involved in great toils. 13 For the entrances of the greater world are wide and safe, and produce fruit of immortality. 14 So if those who live don't enter these difficult and vain things, they can never receive those that are reserved for them. 15 Now therefore why are you disturbed, seeing you are but a corruptible man? Why are you moved, since you are mortal? 16 Why haven't you considered in your mind that which is to come, rather than that which is present?"

17 Then I answered and said, "O sovereign Lord, behold, you have ordained in your law that the righteous will inherit these things, but that the ungodly will perish. 18 The righteous therefore will suffer difficult things, and hope for easier things, but those who have done wickedly have suffered the difficult things, and yet will not see the easier things."

19 He said to me, "You are not a judge above God, neither do you have more understanding than the Most High. 20 Yes, let many perish who now live, rather than that the law of God which is set before them be despised. 21 For God strictly commanded those who came, even as they came, what they should do to live, and what they should observe to avoid punishment. 22 Nevertheless, they weren't obedient to him, but spoke against him and imagined for themselves vain things. 23 They made cunning plans of wickedness, and said moreover of the Most High that he doesn't exist, and they didn't know his ways. 24 They despised his law and denied his covenants. They haven't been faithful to his statutes, and haven't performed his works. 25 Therefore, Esdras, for the empty are empty things, and for the full are the full things. 26 For behold, the time will come, and it will be, when these signs of which I told you before will come to pass, that the bride will appear, even the city coming forth, and she will be seen who now is withdrawn from the earth. 27 Whoever is delivered from the foretold evils will see my wonders. 28 For my son Jesus will be revealed with those who are with him, and those who remain will rejoice four hundred years. 29 After these years my son Christ*g* will die, along with all of those who have the breath of life*h*. 30 Then the world will be turned into the old silence seven days, like as in the first beginning, so that no human will remain. 31 After seven days the world that is not yet awake will be raised up, and what is corruptible will die. 32 The earth will restore those who are asleep in it, and the dust those who dwell in it in silence, and the *secret places will deliver those souls that were committed to them. 33 The Most High will be revealed on the judgement seat, *j* and compassion will pass away, and patience will be withdrawn. 34 Only judgement will remain. Truth will stand. Faith will grow strong. 35 Recompense will follow. The reward will be shown. Good deeds will awake, and wicked deeds won't sleep.*k* 36 The *pit of torment will appear, and near it will be the place of rest. The furnace of hell*m* will be shown, and near it the paradise of delight. 37 Then the Most High will say to the nations that are raised from the dead, 'Look and understand whom you have denied, whom you haven't served, whose commandments you have despised. 38 Look on this side and on that. Here is delight and rest, and there fire and torments.' Thus *n*he will speak to them in the day of judgement. 39 This is a day that has neither sun, nor moon, nor stars, 40 neither cloud, nor thunder, nor lightning, neither wind, nor water, nor air, neither darkness, nor evening, nor morning, 41 neither summer, nor spring, nor heat, nor*o* winter, neither frost, nor cold, nor hail, nor rain, nor dew, 42 neither noon, nor night, nor dawn, neither shining, nor brightness, nor light, except only the splendour of the glory of the Most High, by which all will see the things that are set before them. 43 It will endure as though it were a week of years. 44 This is my judgement and its prescribed order; but I have only shown these things to you."

45 I answered, "I said then, O Lord, and I say now: Blessed are those who are now alive and keep your commandments! 46 But what about those for whom I prayed? For who is there of those who are alive who has not sinned, and who of the children of men hasn't transgressed your covenant? 47 Now I see that the world to come will bring delight to few, but torments to many. 48 For an evil heart has grown up in us, which has led us astray from these commandments and has brought us into corruption and into the ways of death. It has shown us the paths of perdition and removed us far from life—and that, not a few only, but nearly all who have been created."

---

a *6:29* After the Oriental versions. The Latin is corrupt.
b *6:30* So the Syriac. The Latin is corrupt.
c *6:31* The Latin has tell you by day.
d *6:39* The Latin adds from you.
e *6:55* So the Syriac. The Latin has the firstborn world.
f *7:3* So the chief Oriental versions. The Latin MSS. have deep.
g *7:29* "Christ" means "Anointed One".
h *7:29* Lat. man

i *7:32* Or, chambers See 2 Esdras 4:35.
j *7:33* The Syriac adds and the end will come.
k *7:35* The passage from verse [36] to verse [105], formerly missing, has been restored to the text. See Preface, page ix.
l *7:36* So the chief Oriental versions. The Latin MSS. have place.
m *7:36* Lat. Gehenna.
n *7:38* So the chief Oriental versions. The Latin has will you speak.
o *7:41* Or, storm

49 He answered me, "Listen to me, and I will instruct you. I will admonish you yet again. 50 For this reason, the Most High has not made one world, but two. 51 For because you have said that the just are not many, but few, and the ungodly abound, hear the explanation. 52 If you have just a few precious stones, will you add them to lead and clay?"

53 I said, "Lord, how could that be?"

54 He said to me, "Not only that, but ask the earth, and she will tell you. Defer to her, and she will declare it to you. 55 Say to her, 'You produce gold, silver, and brass, and also iron, lead, and clay; 56 but silver is more abundant than gold, and brass than silver, and iron than brass, and lead than iron, and clay than lead.' 57 Judge therefore which things are precious and to be desired, what is abundant or what is rare?"

58 I said, "O sovereign Lord, that which is plentiful is of less worth, for that which is more rare is more precious."

59 He answered me, "Weigh within yourself the things that you have thought, for he who has what is hard to get rejoices over him who has what is plentiful. 60 So also is the judgement which I have promised; for I will rejoice over the few that will be saved, because these are those who have made my glory to prevail now, and through them, my name is now honoured. 61 I won't grieve over the multitude of those who perish; for these are those who are now like mist, and have become like flame and smoke; they are set on fire and burn hotly, and are extinguished."

62 I answered, "O earth, why have you produced, if the mind is made out of dust, like all other created things? 63 For it would have been better that the dust itself had been unborn, so that the mind might not have been made from it. 64 But now the mind grows with us, and because of this we are tormented, because we perish and we know it. 65 Let the race of men lament and the animals of the field be glad. Let all who are born lament, but let the four-footed animals and the livestock rejoice. 66 For it is far better with them than with us; for they don't look forward to judgement, neither do they know of torments or of salvation promised to them after death. 67 For what does it profit us, that we will be preserved alive, but yet be afflicted with torment? 68 For all who are born are defiled with iniquities, and are full of sins and laden with transgressions. 69 If after death we were not to come into judgement, perhaps it would have been better for us."

70 He answered me, "When the Most High made the world and Adam and all those who came from him, he first prepared the judgement and the things that pertain to the judgement. 71 Now understand from your own words, for you have said that the mind grows with us. 72 They therefore who dwell on the earth will be tormented for this reason, that having understanding they have committed iniquity, and receiving commandments have not kept them, and having obtained a law they dealt unfaithfully with that which they received. 73 What then will they have to say in the judgement, or how will they answer in the last times? 74 For how long a time has the Most High been patient with those who inhabit the world, and not for their sakes, but because of the times which he has foreordained!"

75 I answered, "If I have found grace in your sight, O Lord, show this also to your servant, whether after death, even now when every one of us gives up his soul, we will be kept in rest until those times come, in which you renew the creation, or whether we will be tormented immediately."

76 He answered me, "I will show you this also; but don't join yourself with those who are scorners, nor count yourself with those who are tormented. 77 For you have a treasure of works laid up with the Most High, but it won't be shown you until the last times. 78 For concerning death the teaching is: When the decisive sentence has gone out from the Most High that a man shall die, as the spirit leaves the body to return again to him who gave it, it adores the glory of the Most High first of all. 79 And if it is one of those who have been scorners and have not kept the way of the Most High, and that have despised his law, and who hate those who fear God, 80 these spirits won't enter into habitations, but will wander and be in torments immediately, ever grieving and sad, in seven ways. 81 The first way, because they have despised the law of the Most High. 82 The second way, because they can't now make a good repentance that they may live. 83 The third way, they will see the reward laid up for those who have believed the covenants of the Most High. 84 The fourth way, they will consider the torment laid up for themselves in the last days. 85 The fifth way, they will see the dwelling places of the others guarded by angels, with great quietness. 86 The sixth way, they will see how immediately some of them will pass into torment. 87 The seventh way, which is more grievous than all the aforesaid ways, because they will pine away in confusion and be consumed with shame, and will be withered up by fears, seeing the glory of the Most High before whom they have sinned while living, and before whom they will be judged in the last times.

88 "Now this is the order of those who have kept the ways of the Most High, when they will be separated from their mortal body. 89 In the time that they lived in it, they painfully served the Most High, and were in jeopardy every hour, that they might keep the law of the lawgiver perfectly. 90 Therefore this is the teaching concerning them: 91 First of all they will see with great joy the glory of him who takes them up, for they will have rest in seven orders. 92 The first order, because they have laboured with great effort to overcome the evil thought which was fashioned together with them, that it might not lead them astray from life into death. 93 The second order, because they see the perplexity in which the souls of the ungodly wander, and the punishment that awaits them. 94 The third order, they see the testimony which he who fashioned them gives concerning them, that while they lived they kept the law which was given them in trust. 95 The

fourth order, they understand the rest which, being gathered in their chambers, they now enjoy with great quietness, guarded by angels, and the glory that awaits them in the last days. 96 The fifth order, they rejoice that they have now escaped from that which is corruptible, and that they will inherit that which is to come, while they see in addition the difficulty and the pain from which they have been delivered, and the spacious liberty which they will receive with joy and immortality. 97 The sixth order, when it is shown to them how their face will shine like the sun, and how they will be made like the light of the stars, being incorruptible from then on. 98 The seventh order, which is greater than all the previously mentioned orders, because they will rejoice with confidence, and because they will be bold without confusion, and will be glad without fear, for they hurry to see the face of him whom in their lifetime they served, and from whom they will receive their reward in glory. 99 This is the order of the souls of the just, as from henceforth is announced to them. Previously mentioned are the ways of torture which those who would not give heed will suffer from after this."

100 I answered, "Will time therefore be given to the souls after they are separated from the bodies, that they may see what you have described to me?"

101 He said, "Their freedom will be for seven days, that for seven days they may see the things you have been told, and afterwards they will be gathered together in their habitations."

102 I answered, "If I have found favour in your sight, show further to me your servant whether in the day of judgement the just will be able to intercede for the ungodly or to entreat the Most High for them, 103 whether fathers for children, or children for parents, or kindred for kindred, or kinsfolk for their next of kin, or friends for those who are most dear."

104 He answered me, "Since you have found favour in my sight, I will show you this also. The day of judgement is[a] a day of decision, and displays to all the seal of truth. Even as now a father doesn't send his son, or a son his father, or a master his slave, or a friend him that is most dear, that in his place he may understand, or sleep, or eat, or be healed, 105 so no one will ever pray for another in that day, neither will one lay a burden on another, for then everyone will each bear his own righteousness or unrighteousness."

106 I answered, "How do we now find that first Abraham prayed for the people of Sodom, and Moses for the ancestors who sinned in the wilderness, 107 and Joshua after him for Israel in the days of 'Achan, 108 and Samuel [b]in the days of Saul, and David for the plague, and Solomon for those who would worship in the sanctuary, 109 and Elijah for those that received rain, and for the dead, that he might live, 110 and Hezekiah for the people in the days of Sennacherib, and many others prayed for many? 111 If therefore now, when corruption has grown and unrighteousness increased, the righteous have prayed for the ungodly, why will it not be so then also?"

112 He answered me, "This present world is not the end. The full glory doesn't remain in it. Therefore those who were able prayed for the weak. 113 But the day of judgement will be the end of this age, and the beginning of the immortality to come, in which corruption has passed away, 114 intemperance is at an end, infidelity is cut off, but righteousness has grown, and truth has sprung up. 115 Then no one will be able to have mercy on him who is condemned in judgement, nor to harm someone who is victorious."

116 I answered then, "This is my first and last saying, that it would have been better if the earth had not produced Adam, or else, when it had produced him, to have restrained him from sinning. 117 For what profit is it for all who are in this present time to live in heaviness, and after death to look for punishment? 118 O Adam, what have you done? For though it was you who sinned, the evil hasn't fallen on you alone, but on all of us who come from you. 119 For what profit is it to us, if an immortal time is promised to us, but we have done deeds that bring death? 120 And that there is promised us an everlasting hope, but we have most miserably failed? 121 And that there are reserved habitations of health and safety, but we have lived wickedly? 122 And that the glory of the Most High will defend those who have led a pure life, but we have walked in the most wicked ways of all? 123 And that a paradise will be revealed, whose fruit endures without decay, in which is abundance and healing, but we won't enter into it, 124 for we have lived in perverse ways? 125 And that the faces of those who have practised self-control will shine more than the stars, but our faces will be blacker than darkness? 126 For while we lived and committed iniquity, we didn't consider what we would have to suffer after death."

127 Then he answered, "This is the significance of the battle which humans born on the earth will fight: 128 if they are overcome, they will suffer as you have said, but if they get the victory, they will receive the thing that I say. 129 For this is the way that Moses spoke to the people while he lived, saying, 'Choose life, that you may live!' 130 Nevertheless they didn't believe him or the prophets after him, not even me, who have spoken to them. 131 Therefore there won't be such heaviness in their destruction, as there will be joy over those who are assured of salvation."

132 Then I answered, "I know, Lord, that the Most High is now called merciful, in that he has mercy upon those who have not yet come into the world; 133 and compassionate, in that he has compassion upon those who turn to his law; 134 and patient, in that he is patient with those who have sinned, since they are his creatures; 135 and bountiful, in that he is ready to give rather than to take away; 136 and very merciful, in that he multiplies more and more mercies to those who are present, and who are past, and also to those who are to come— 137 for if he wasn't merciful, the world

_____

a 7:104 The Latin has a bold day
** 7:107 Joshua 7:1

b 7:108 So the Syriac and other versions. The Latin omits in the days of Saul.

wouldn't continue with those who dwell in it— 138 and one who forgives, for if he didn't forgive out of his goodness, that those who have committed iniquities might be relieved of them, not even one ten thousandth part of mankind would remain living; 139 and a judge, for if he didn't pardon those who were created by his word, and blot out the multitude of sins, 140 there would perhaps be very few left of an innumerable multitude."

8

1 He answered me, "The Most High has made this world for many, but the world to come for few. 2 Now I will tell you a parable, Esdras. Just as when you ask the earth, it will say to you that it gives very much clay from which earthen vessels are made, but little dust that gold comes from. Even so is the course of the present world. 3 Many have been created, but few will be saved."

4 I answered, "Drink your fill of understanding then, O my soul, and let my heart devour wisdom. 5 For you ᵃhave come here apart from your will, and depart against your will, for you have only been given a short time to live. 6 O Lord over us, grant to your servant that we may pray before you, and give us seed for our heart and cultivation for our understanding, that fruit may grow from it, by which everyone who is corrupt, who bears the ᵇlikeness of a man, may live. 7 For you alone exist, and we all one workmanship of your hands, just as you have said. 8 Because you give life to the body that is now fashioned in the womb, and give it members, your creature is preserved in fire and water, and your workmanship endures nine months as your creation which is created in it. 9 But that which keeps and that which is kept will both be kept ᶜby your keeping. When the womb gives up again what has grown in it, 10 you have commanded that out of the parts of the body, that is to say, out of the breasts, be given milk, which is the fruit of the breasts, 11 that the body that is fashioned may be nourished for a time, and afterwards you guide it in your mercy. 12 Yes, you have brought it up in your righteousness, nurtured it in your law, and corrected it with your judgement. 13 You put it to death as your creation, and make it live as your work. 14 If therefore you ᵈlightly and suddenly destroy him which with so great labour was fashioned by your commandment, to what purpose was he made? 15 Now therefore I will speak. About man in general, you know best, but about your people for whose sake I am sorry, 16 and for your inheritance, for whose cause I mourn, for Israel, for whom I am heavy, and for the seed of Jacob, for whose sake I am troubled, 17 therefore I will begin to pray before you for them; for I see the failings of us who dwell in the land; 18 but I have heard the swiftness of the judgement which is to come. 19 Therefore hear my voice, and understand my saying, and I will speak before you."

The beginning of the words of Esdras, before he was taken up. He said, 20 "O Lord, you who remain forever, whose eyes are exalted, and whose chambers are in the air, 21 whose throne is beyond measure, whose glory is beyond comprehension, before whom the army of angels stand with trembling, 22 ᵉ at whose bidding they are changed to wind and fire, whose word is sure, and sayings constant, whose ordinance is strong, and commandment fearful, 23 whose look dries up the depths, and whose indignation makes the mountains to melt away, and whose truth bears witness— 24 hear, O Lord, the prayer of your servant, and give ear to the petition of your handiwork. 25 Attend to my words, for as long as I live, I will speak, and as long as I have understanding, I will answer. 26 Don't look at the sins of your people, but on those who have served you in truth. 27 Don't regard the doings of those who act wickedly, but of those who have kept your covenants in affliction. 28 Don't think about those who have lived wickedly before you, but remember those who have willingly known your fear. 29 Let it not be your will to destroy those who have lived like cattle, but look at those who have ᶠclearly taught your law. 30 Don't be indignant at those who are deemed worse than animals, but love those who have always put their trust in your glory. 31 For we and our fathers have ᵍpassed our lives in ʰways that bring death, but you are called merciful because of us sinners. 32 For if you have a desire to have mercy upon us who have no works of righteousness, then you will be called merciful. 33 For the just, which have many good works laid up with you, will be rewarded for their own deeds. 34 For what is man, that you should take displeasure at him? Or what is a corruptible race, that you should be so bitter towards it? 35 For in truth, there is no man amongst those who are born who has not done wickedly, and amongst those who have lived, there is none which have not done wrong. 36 For in this, O Lord, your righteousness and your goodness will be declared, if you are merciful to those who have no store of good works."

37 Then he answered me, "Some things you have spoken rightly, and it will happen according to your words. 38 For indeed I will not think about the fashioning of those who have sinned, or about their death, their judgement, or their destruction; 39 but I will rejoice over the creation of the righteous and their pilgrimage, their salvation, and the reward that they will have. 40 Therefore as I have spoken, so it will be. 41 For as the farmer sows many seeds in the ground, and plants many trees, and yet not all that is sown will

ⁱcome up in due season, neither will all that is planted take root, even so those who are sown in the world will not all be saved."

42 Then I answered, "If I have found favour, let me speak before you. 43 If the farmer's seed doesn't come up because it hasn't received your rain in due season, or if it is ruined by too much rain and perishes, 44 likewise man, who is formed with your hands and is called your own image, because he is made like you, for whose sake you have formed all things, even him have you made like the farmer's seed. 45 Don't be angry with us, but spare your people and have mercy upon your inheritance, for you have mercy upon your own creation."

46 Then he answered me, "Things present are for those who live now, and things to come for those who will live hereafter. 47 For you come far short of being able to love my creature more than I. But you have compared yourself to the unrighteous. Don't do that! 48 Yet in this will you be admirable to the Most High, 49 in that you have humbled yourself, as it becomes you, and have not judged yourself amongst the righteous, so as to be much glorified. 50 For many grievous miseries will fall on those who dwell in the world in the last times, because they have walked in great pride. 51 But understand for yourself, and for those who enquire concerning the glory of those like you, 52 because paradise is opened to you. The tree of life is planted. The time to come is prepared. Plenteousness is made ready. A city is built. Rest is ʲallowed. Goodness is perfected, and wisdom is perfected beforehand. 53 The root of evil is sealed up from you. Weakness is done away from you, and ᵏdeath is hidden. Hell and corruption have fled into forgetfulness. 54 Sorrows have passed away, and in the end, the treasure of immortality is shown. 55 Therefore ask no more questions concerning the multitude of those who perish. 56 For when they had received liberty, they despised the Most High, scorned his law, and forsook his ways. 57 Moreover they have trodden down his righteous, 58 and said in their heart that there is no God—even knowing that they must die. 59 For as the things I have said will welcome you, so thirst and pain which are prepared for them. For the Most High didn't intend that men should be destroyed, 60 but those who are created have themselves defiled the name of him who made them, and were unthankful to him who prepared life for them. 61 Therefore my judgement is now at hand, 62 which I have not shown to all men, but to you, and a few like you."

Then I answered, 63 "Behold, O Lord, now you have shown me the multitude of the wonders which you will do in the last times, but you haven't shown me when."

9

1 He answered me, "Measure diligently within yourself. When you see that a certain part of the signs are past, which have been told you beforehand, 2 then will you understand that it is the very time in which the Most High will visit the world which was made by him. 3 When earthquakes, tumult of peoples, plans of nations, wavering of leaders, and confusion of princes are seen in the world, 4 then will you understand that the Most High spoke of these things from the days that were of old, from the beginning. 5 For just as with everything that is made in the world, the beginning ˡis evident and the end manifest, 6 so also are the times of the Most High: the beginnings are manifest in wonders and mighty works, and the end in effects and signs. 7 Everyone who will be saved, and will be able to escape by his works, or by faith by which they have believed, 8 will be preserved from the said perils, and will see my salvation in my land and within my borders, which I have sanctified for myself from the beginning. 9 Then those who now have abused my ways will be amazed. Those who have cast them away despitefully will live in torments. 10 For as many as in their life have received benefits, and yet have not known me, 11 and as many as have scorned my law, while they still had liberty and when an opportunity to repent was open to them, didn't understand, but despised ᵐ it, 12 must know ⁿit in torment after death. 13 Therefore don't be curious any longer how the ungodly will be punished, but enquire how the righteous will be saved, ᵒthose who the world belongs to, and for whom the world was created."

14 I answered, 15 "I have said before, and now speak, and will say it again hereafter, that there are more of those who perish than of those who will be saved, 16 like a wave is greater than a drop."

17 He answered me, "Just as the field is, so also the seed. As the flowers are, so are the colours. As the work is, so also is the ᵖjudgement on it. As is the farmer, so also is his threshing floor. For there was a time in the world 18 when I was preparing for those who now live, before the world was made for them to dwell in. Then no one spoke against me, 19 for ᑫno one existed. But now those who are created in this world that is prepared, both ʳwith a table that doesn't fail and a law which is unsearchable, are corrupted in their ways. 20 So I considered my world, and behold, it was destroyed, and my earth, and behold, it was in peril, because of the plans that had come into it. 21 I saw and spared them, but not greatly, and saved

---

ᵃ 8:5 So the Syriac. The Latin is incorrect.

ᵇ 8:6 So the Latin has place.

ᶜ 8:9 So the Syriac. The Latin is imperfect.

ᵈ 8:14 So the Syriac. The Latin is incorrect.

ᵉ 8:22 According to the chief Oriental versions. The Latin has, even they whose service takes the form of wind etc.

ᶠ 8:29 The Syriac has received the brightness of your law.

ᵍ 8:31 So the Syriac and Aethiopic versions.

ʰ 8:31 Lat. manners.

ⁱ 8:41 Lat. be saved.

ʲ 8:52 The Syriac has established.

ᵏ 8:53 After the chief Oriental versions.

ˡ 9:5 So the Syriac. The Latin is corrupt.

ᵐ 9:11 Or, me

ⁿ 9:12 Or, me

ᵒ 9:13 So the Syriac and other versions. The Latin has and whose... created, and when.

ᵖ 9:17 So the Aethiopic and Arabic. The Latin has creation.

ᑫ 9:19 So the Syriac.

ʳ 9:19 So the Syriac.

myself a grape out of a cluster, and a plant out of ᵃa great forest. ₂₂ Let the multitude perish then, which were born in vain. Let my grape be saved, and my plant, for I have made them perfect with great labour. ₂₃ Nevertheless, if you will wait seven more days—however don't fast in them, ₂₄ but go into a field of flowers, where no house is built, and eat only of the flowers of the field, and you shall taste no flesh, and shall drink no wine, but shall eat flowers only— ₂₅ and pray to the Most High continually, then I will come and talk with you."

₂₆ So I went my way, just as he commanded me, into the field which is called ᵇArdat. There I sat amongst the flowers, and ate of the herbs of the field, and this food satisfied me. ₂₇ It came to pass after seven days that I lay on the grass, and my heart was troubled again, like before. ₂₈ My mouth was opened, and I began to speak before the Lord Most High, and said, ₂₉ "O Lord, you showed yourself amongst us, to our fathers in the wilderness, when they went out of Egypt, and when they came into the wilderness, where no man treads and that bears no fruit. ₃₀ You said, 'Hear me, O Israel. Heed my words, O seed of Jacob. ₃₁ For behold, I sow my law in you, and it will bring forth fruit in you, and you will be glorified in it forever.' ₃₂ But our fathers, who received the law, didn't keep it, and didn't observe the statutes. The fruit of the law didn't perish, for it couldn't, because it was yours. ₃₃ Yet those who received it perished, because they didn't keep the thing that was sown in them. ₃₄ Behold, it is a custom that when the ground has received seed, or the sea a ship, or any vessel food or drink, and when it comes to pass that that which is sown, or that which is launched, ₃₅ or the things which have been received, should come to an end, these come to an end, but the receptacles remain. Yet with us, it doesn't happen that way. ₃₆ For we who have received the law will perish by sin, along with our heart which received it. ₃₇ Notwithstanding the law doesn't perish, but remains in its honour."

₃₈ When I spoke these things in my heart, I looked around me with my eyes, and on my right side I saw a woman, and behold, she mourned and wept with a loud voice, and was much grieved in mind. Her clothes were torn, and she had ashes on her head. ₃₉ Then let I my thoughts go in which I was occupied, and turned myself to her, ₄₀ and said to her, "Why are you weeping? Why are you grieved in your mind?"

₄₁ She said to me, "Leave me alone, my Lord, that I may weep for myself and add to my sorrow, for I am very troubled in my mind, and brought very low."

₄₂ I said to her, "What ails you? Tell me."

₄₃ She said to me, "I, your servant, was barren and had no child, though I had a husband thirty years. ₄₄ Every hour and every day these thirty years I made my prayer to the Most High day and night. ₄₅ It came to pass after thirty years that God heard me, your handmaid, and saw my low estate, and considered my trouble, and gave me a son. I rejoiced in him greatly, I and my husband, and all my ᶜneighbours. We gave great honour to the Mighty One. ₄₆ I nourished him with great care. ₄₇ So when he grew up, and I came to take him a wife, I made him a feast day.

10

₁ "So it came to pass that when my son was entered into his wedding chamber, he fell down and died. ₂ Then we all put out the lamps, and all my ᵈneighbours rose up to comfort me. I remained quiet until the second day at night. ₃ It came to pass, when they had all stopped consoling me, encouraging me to be quiet, then rose I up by night, and fled, and came here into this field, as you see. ₄ Now I don't intend to return into the city, but to stay here, and not eat or drink, but to continually mourn and fast until I die."

₅ Then I left the reflections I was engaged in, and answered her in anger, ₆ "You most foolish woman, don't you see our mourning, and what has happened to us? ₇ For Zion the mother of us all is full of sorrow, and much humbled. ₈ ᵉIt is right now to mourn deeply, since we all mourn, and to be sorrowful, since we are all in sorrow, but you are mourning for one son. ₉ Ask the earth, and she will tell you that it is she which ought to mourn for so many that grow upon her. ₁₀ For out of her, all had their beginnings, and others will come; and, behold, almost all of them walk into destruction, and the multitude of them is utterly doomed. ₁₁ Who then should mourn more, ᶠshe who has lost so great a multitude, or you, who are grieved but for one? ₁₂ But if you say to me, 'My lamentation is not like the earth's, for I have lost the fruit of my womb, which I brought forth with pains, and bare with sorrows;' ₁₃ but it is with the earth after the manner of the earth. The multitude present in it has gone as it came. ₁₄ Then say I to you, 'Just as you have brought forth with sorrow, even so the earth also has given her fruit, namely, people, ever since the beginning to him who made her.' ₁₅ Now therefore keep your sorrow to yourself, and bear with a good courage the adversities which have happened to you. ₁₆ For if you will acknowledge the decree of God to be just, you will both receive your son in time, and will be praised amongst women. ₁₇ Go your way then into the city to your husband."

₁₈ She said to me, "I won't do that. I will not go into the city, but I will die here."

₁₉ So I proceeded to speak further to her, and said, ₂₀ "Don't do so, but allow yourself to be persuaded by reason of the adversities of Zion; and be comforted by reason of the sorrow of Jerusalem. ₂₁ For you see that our

sanctuary has been laid waste, our altar broken down, our temple destroyed, ₂₂ our lute has been brought low, our song is put to silence, our rejoicing is at an end, the light of our candlestick is put out, the ark of our covenant is plundered, our holy things are defiled, and the name that we are called is profaned. Our free men are despitefully treated, our priests are burnt, our Levites have gone into captivity, our virgins are defiled and our wives ravished, our righteous men carried away, our little ones betrayed, our young men are brought into bondage, and our strong men have become weak. ₂₃ What is more than all, the seal of Zion has now lost the seal of her honour, and is delivered into the hands of those who hate us. ₂₄ Therefore shake off your great heaviness, and put away from yourself the multitude of sorrows, that the Mighty One may be merciful to you again, and the Most High may give you rest, even ease from your troubles."

₂₅ It came to pass while I was talking with her, behold, her face suddenly began to shine exceedingly, and her countenance glistered like lightning, so that I was very afraid of her, and wondered what this meant. ₂₆ Behold, suddenly she made a great and very fearful cry, so that the earth shook at the noise. ₂₇ I looked, and behold, the woman appeared to me no more, but there was a city built, and a place shown itself from large foundations. Then I was afraid, and cried with a loud voice, ₂₈ "Where is Uriel the angel, who came to me at the first? For he has caused me to fall into this great trance, and my end has turned into corruption, and my prayer a reproach!"

₂₉ As I was speaking these words, behold, the angel who had come to me at first came to me, and he looked at me. ₃₀ Behold, I lay as one who had been dead, and my understanding was taken from me. He took me by the right hand, and comforted me, and set me on my feet, and said to me, ₃₁ "What ails you? Why are you so troubled? Why is your understanding and the thoughts of your heart troubled?"

₃₂ I said, "Because you have forsaken me; yet I did according to your words, and went into the field, and, behold, I have seen, and still see, that which I am not able to explain."

₃₃ He said to me, "Stand up like a man, and I will instruct you."

₃₄ Then I said, "Speak on, my Lord; only don't forsake me, lest I die before my time. ₃₅ For I have seen what I didn't know, and hear what I don't know. ₃₆ Or is my sense deceived, or my soul in a dream? ₃₇ Now therefore I beg you to explain to your servant what this vision means."

₃₈ He answered me, "Listen to me, and I will inform you, and tell you about the things you are afraid of, for the Most High has revealed many secret things to you. ₃₉ He has seen that your way is righteous, because you are continually sorry for your people, and make great lamentation for Zion. ₄₀ This therefore is the meaning of the vision. ₄₁ The woman who appeared to you a little while ago, whom you saw mourning, and began to comfort her, ₄₂ but now you no longer see the likeness of the woman, but a city under construction appeared to you, ₄₃ and she told you of the death of her son, this is the interpretation: ₄₄ This woman, whom you saw, is Zion,ᵍ whom you now see as a city being built. ₄₅ She told you that she had been barren for thirty years because there were three thousand years in the world in which there was no offering as yet offered in her. ₄₆ And it came to pass after three thousand years that Solomon built the city and offered offerings. It was then that the barren bore a son. ₄₇ She told you that she nourished him with great care. That was the dwelling in Jerusalem. ₄₈ When she said to you, 'My son died when he entered into his marriage chamber, and that misfortune befell her,' this was the destruction that came to Jerusalem. ₄₉ Behold, you saw her likeness, how she mourned for her son, and you began to comfort her for what has happened to her. These were the things to be opened to you. ₅₀ For now the Most High, seeing that you are sincerely grieved and suffer from your whole heart for her, has shown you the brightness of her glory and the attractiveness of her beauty. ₅₁ Therefore I asked you to remain in the field where no house was built, ₅₂ for I knew that the Most High would show this to you. ₅₃ Therefore I commanded you to come into the field, where no foundation of any building was. ₅₄ For no human construction could stand in the place in which the city of the Most High was to be shown. ₅₅ Therefore don't be afraid nor let your heart be terrified, but go your way in and see the beauty and greatness of the building, as much as your eyes are able to see. ₅₆ Then will you hear as much as your ears may comprehend. ₅₇ For you are more blessed than many, and are called by name to be with the Most High, like only a few. ₅₈ But tomorrow at night you shall remain here, ₅₉ and so the Most High will show you those visions in dreams of what the Most High will do to those who live on the earth in the last days."

So I slept that night and another, as he commanded me.

11

₁ It came to pass the second night that I saw a dream, and behold, an eagle which had twelve feathered wings and three heads came up from the sea. ₂ I saw, and behold, she spread her wings over all the earth, and all the winds of heaven blew on her, ʰand the clouds were gathered together against her. ₃ I saw, and out of her wings there grew other wings near them; and they became little, tiny wings. ₄ But her heads were at rest. The head in the middle was larger than the other heads, yet rested it with them. ₅ Moreover I saw, and behold, the eagle flew with her wings to reign over the earth and over those who dwell therein. ₆ I saw how all things under

---

ᵃ *9:21* So the Syriac and other versions. The Latin has great tribes.

ᵇ *9:26* The Syriac and Aethiopic have Arphad.

ᶜ *9:45* Lat. townsmen.

ᵈ *10:2* Lat. townsmen.

ᵉ *10:8* See the Oriental versions. The Latin is corrupt.

ᶠ *10:11* So the Syriac.

ᵍ *10:44* So the Syriac and other versions. The Latin is incorrect.

ʰ *11:2* So the chief Oriental versions. The Latin has only and were gathered together.

heaven were subject to her, and no one spoke against her—no, not one creature on earth. 7 I saw, and behold, the eagle rose on her talons, and uttered her voice to her wings, saying, 8 "Don't all watch at the same time. Let each one sleep in his own place and watch in turn; 9 but let the heads be preserved for the last."

10 I saw, and behold, the voice didn't come out of her heads, but from the midst of her body. 11 I counted [a]her wings that were near the others, and behold, there were eight of them. 12 I saw, and behold, on the right side one wing arose and reigned over all the earth. 13 When it reigned, the end of it came, and it disappeared, so that its place appeared no more. The next wing rose up and reigned, and it ruled a long time. 14 It happened that when it reigned, its end came also, so that it disappeared, like the first. 15 Behold, a voice came to it, and said, 16 "Listen, you who have ruled over the earth all this time! I proclaim this to you, before you disappear, 17 none after you will rule as long as you, not even half as long."

18 Then the third arose, and ruled as the others before, and it also disappeared. 19 So it went with all the wings one after another, as every one ruled, and then disappeared. 20 I saw, and behold, in process of time the [b]wings that followed were set up on the [c]right side, that they might rule also. Some of them ruled, but in a while they disappeared. 21 Some of them also were set up, but didn't rule.

22 After this I saw, and behold, the twelve wings disappeared, along with two of the little wings. 23 There was no more left on the eagle's body, except the three heads that rested, and six little wings. 24 I saw, and behold, two little wings divided themselves from the six and remained under the head that was on the right side; but four remained in their place. 25 I saw, and behold, these [d]under wings planned to set themselves up and to rule. 26 I saw, and behold, there was one set up, but in a while it disappeared. 27 A second also did so, and it disappeared faster than the first. 28 I saw, and behold, the two that remained also planned between themselves to reign. 29 While they thought about it, behold, one of the heads that were at rest awakened, the one that was in the middle, for that was greater than the two other heads. 30 I saw how it joined the two other heads with it. 31 Behold, the head turned with those who were with it, and ate the two [e]under wings that planned to reign. 32 But this head held the whole earth in possession, and ruled over those who dwell in it with much oppression. It had stronger governance over the world than all the wings that had gone before.

33 After this I saw, and behold, the head also that was in the middle suddenly disappeared, like the wings. 34 But the two heads remained, which also reigned the same way over the earth and over those who dwell in it. 35 I saw, and behold, the head on the right side devoured the one that was on the left side.

36 Then I heard a voice, which said to me, "Look in front of you, and consider the thing that you see."

37 I saw, and behold, something like a lion roused out of the woods roaring. I heard how he sent out a man's voice to the eagle, and spoke, saying, 38 "Listen and I will talk with you. The Most High will say to you, 39 'Aren't you the one that remains of the four animals whom I made to reign in my world, that the end of my times might come through them? 40 The fourth came and overcame all the animals that were past, and ruled the world with great trembling, and the whole extent of the earth with grievous oppression. He lived on the earth such a long time with deceit. 41 You have judged the earth, but not with truth. 42 For you have afflicted the meek, you have hurt the peaceful, you have hated those who speak truth, you have loved liars, destroyed the dwellings of those who produced fruit, and threw down the walls of those who did you no harm. 43 Your insolence has come up to the Most High, and your pride to the Mighty. 44 The Most High also has looked at his times, and behold, they are ended, and his ages are fulfilled. 45 Therefore appear no more, you eagle, nor your horrible wings, nor your evil little wings, nor your cruel heads, nor your hurtful talons, nor all your worthless body, 46 that all the earth may be refreshed and relieved, being delivered from your violence, and that she may hope for the judgement and mercy of him who made her.'"

12

1 It came to pass, while the lion spoke these words to the eagle, I saw, 2 and behold, the head that remained disappeared, and [f]the two wings which went over to it arose and set themselves up to reign; and their kingdom was brief and full of uproar. 3 I saw, and behold, they disappeared, and the whole body of the eagle was burnt, so that the earth was in great fear.

Then I woke up because of great perplexity of mind and great fear, and said to my spirit, 4 "Behold, you have done this to me, because you search out the ways of the Most High. 5 Behold, I am still weary in my mind, and very weak in my spirit. There isn't even a little strength in me, because of the great fear with which I was frightened tonight. 6 Therefore I will now ask the Most High that he would strengthen me to the end."

7 Then I said, "O sovereign Lord, if I have found favour in your sight, and if I am justified with you more than many others, and if my prayer has indeed come up before your face, 8 strengthen me then, and show me, your

servant, the interpretation and plain meaning of this fearful vision, that you may fully comfort my soul. 9 For you have judged me worthy to show me the end of time and the last events of the times."

10 He said to me, "This is the interpretation of this vision which you saw: 11 The eagle, whom you saw come up from the sea, is the fourth kingdom which appeared in a vision to your brother Daniel. 12 But it was not explained to him, as I now explain it to you or have explained it. 13 Behold, the days come that a kingdom will rise up on earth, and it will be feared more than all the kingdoms that were before it. 14 Twelve kings will reign in it, one after another. 15 Of those, the second will begin to reign, and will reign a longer time than others of the twelve. 16 This is the interpretation of the twelve wings which you saw. 17 As for when you heard a voice which spoke, not going out from the heads, but from the midst of its body, this is the interpretation: 18 That [g]after the time of that kingdom, there will arise no small contentions, and it will stand in peril of falling. Nevertheless, it won't fall then, but will be restored again to its former power. 19 You saw the eight under wings sticking to her wings. This is the interpretation: 20 That in it eight kings will arise, whose times will be short and their years swift. 21 Two of them will perish when the middle time approaches. Four will be kept for a while until the time of the ending of it will approach; but two will be kept to the end. 22 You saw three heads resting. This is the interpretation: 23 In its last days, the Most High will raise up three [h]kingdoms and renew many things in them. They will rule over the earth, 24 and over those who dwell in it, with much oppression, more than all those who were before them. Therefore they are called the heads of the eagle. 25 For these are those who will accomplish her wickedness, and who will finish her last actions. 26 You saw that the great head disappeared. It signifies that one of them will die on his bed, and yet with pain. 27 But for the two that remained, the sword will devour them. 28 For the sword of the one will devour him that was with him, but he will also fall by the sword in the last days. 29 You saw two under wings passing [i]over to the head that is on the right side. 30 This is the interpretation: These are they whom the Most High has kept to his end. This is the brief reign that was full of trouble, as you saw.

31 "The lion, whom you saw rising up out of the forest, roaring, speaking to the eagle, and rebuking her for her unrighteousness, and all her words which you have heard, 32 this is the anointed one, whom the Most High has kept to the end [j][of days, who will spring up out of the seed of David, and he will come and speak] to them and reprove them for their wickedness and unrighteousness, and will[k] heap up before them their contemptuous dealings. 33 For at first he will set them alive in his judgement, and when he has reproved them, he will destroy them. 34 For he will deliver the rest of my people with mercy, those who have been preserved throughout my borders, and he will make them joyful until the coming of the end, even the day of judgement, about which I have spoken to you from the beginning. 35 This is the dream that you saw, and this is its interpretation. 36 Only you have been worthy to know the secret of the Most High. 37 Therefore write all these things that you have seen in a book, and put it in a secret place. 38 You shall teach them to the wise of your people, whose hearts you know are able to comprehend and keep these secrets. 39 But wait here yourself seven more days, that you may be shown whatever it pleases the Most High to show you." Then he departed from me.

40 It came to pass, when all the people [l]saw that the seven days were past, and I had not come again into the city, they all gathered together, from the least to the greatest, and came to me, and spoke to me, saying, 41 "How have we offended you? What evil have we done against you, that you have utterly forsaken us, and sit in this place? 42 For of all the prophets, only you are left to us, like a cluster of the vintage, and like a lamp in a dark place, and like a harbour for a ship saved from the tempest. 43 Aren't the evils which have come to us sufficient? 44 If you will forsake us, how much better had it been for us if we also had been consumed in the burning of Zion! 45 For we are not better than those who died there." Then they wept with a loud voice. I answered them, 46 "Take courage, O Israel! Don't be sorrowful, you house of Jacob; 47 for the Most High remembers you. The Mighty has not forgotten you [m]forever. 48 As for me, I have not forsaken you. I haven't departed from you; but I have come into this place to pray for the desolation of Zion, and that I might seek mercy for the humiliation of your sanctuary. 49 Now go your way, every man to his own house, and after these days I will come to you."

50 So the people went their way into the city, as I told them to do. 51 But I sat in the field seven days, as the angel commanded me. In those days, I ate only of the flowers of the field, and my food was from plants.

13

1 It came to pass after seven days, I dreamt a dream by night. 2 Behold, a wind arose from the sea that moved all its waves. 3 I saw, and behold, [n][this wind caused to come up from the midst of the sea something like the appearance of a man. I saw, and behold,] that man [o]flew with the clouds of heaven. When he turned his face to look, everything that he saw trembled. 4 Whenever the voice went out of his mouth, all who heard his voice melted, like the [p]wax melts when it feels the fire.

---

a 11:11 The Syriac has her little wings, and, etc.
b 11:20 The Syriac has little wings.
c 11:20 The Aethiopic has left.
d 11:25 The Syriac has little wings.
e 11:31 The Syriac has little wings.
f 12:2 So the chief Oriental versions.
g 12:18 The Oriental versions havein the midst of.
h 12:23 The Oriental versions have kings

i 12:29 So the Syriac. The Latin has over the head.
j 12:32 The words in brackets are added from the Syriac.
k 12:32 The Syriac has set in order.
l 12:40 So the Syriac. The Latin has heard.
m 12:47 So the Syriac.
n 13:3 The words in brackets are added from the Syriac.
o 13:3 So the Syriac. The Latin has grew strong
p 13:4 So the Syriac and other Oriental versions.

5 After this I saw, and behold, an innumerable multitude of people was gathered together from the four winds of heaven to make war against the man who came out of the sea. 6 I saw, and behold, he carved himself a great mountain, and flew up onto it. 7 I tried to see the region or place from which the mountain was carved, and I couldn't.

8 After this I saw, and behold, all those who were gathered together to fight against him were very afraid, and yet they dared to fight. 9 Behold, as he saw the assault of the multitude that came, he didn't lift up his hand, or hold a spear or any weapon of war; 10 but I saw only how he sent out of his mouth something like a flood of fire, and out of his lips a flaming breath, and out of his tongue he shot out a storm of sparks.[a] 11 These were all mixed together: the flood of fire, the flaming breath, and the great storm, and fell upon the assault of the multitude which was prepared to fight, and burnt up every one of them, so that all of a sudden an innumerable multitude was seen to be nothing but dust of ashes and smell of smoke. When I saw this, I was amazed.

12 Afterward, I saw the same man come down from the mountain, and call to himself another multitude which was peaceful. 13 Many people came to him. Some of them were glad. Some were sorry. Some of them were bound, and some others brought some of those as offerings. Then through great fear I woke up and prayed to the Most High, and said, 14 "You have shown your servant these wonders from the beginning, and have counted me worthy that you should receive my prayer. 15 Now show me also the interpretation of this dream. 16 For as I conceive in my understanding, woe to those who will be left in those days! Much more woe to those who are not left! 17 For those who were not left will be in heaviness, 18 understanding the things that are laid up in the latter days, but not attaining to them. 19 But woe to them also who are left, because they will see great perils and much distress, like these dreams declare. 20 Yet is it [b]better for one to be in peril and to come into [c]these things, than to pass away as a cloud out of the world, and not to see the things that [d]will happen in the last days."

He answered me, 21 "I will tell you the interpretation of the vision, and I will also open to you the things about which you mentioned. 22 You have spoken of those who are left behind. This is the interpretation: 23 He that will [e]endure the peril in that time will protect those who fall into danger, even those who have works and faith towards the Almighty. 24 Know therefore that those who are left behind are more blessed than those who are dead. 25 These are the interpretations of the vision: Whereas you saw a man coming up from the midst of the sea, 26 this is he whom the Most High has been keeping for many ages, who by his own self will deliver his creation. He will direct those who are left behind. 27 Whereas you saw that out of his mouth came wind, fire, and storm, 28 and whereas he held neither spear, nor any weapon of war, but destroyed the assault of that multitude which came to fight against him, this is the interpretation: 29 Behold, the days come when the Most High will begin to deliver those who are on the earth. 30 Astonishment of mind will come upon those who dwell on the earth. 31 One will plan to make war against another, city against city, place against place, people against people, and kingdom against kingdom. 32 It will be, when these things come to pass, and the signs happen which I showed you before, then my Son will be revealed, whom you saw as a man ascending. 33 It will be, when all the nations hear his voice, every man will leave his own land and the battle they have against one another. 34 An innumerable multitude will be gathered together, as you saw, desiring to come and to fight against him. 35 But he will stand on the top of Mount Zion. 36 Zion will come, and will be shown to all men, being prepared and built, like you saw the mountain carved without hands. 37 My Son will rebuke the nations which have come for their wickedness, with plagues that are like a storm, 38 and will rebuke them to their face with their evil thoughts, and the torments with which they will be tormented, which are like a flame. He will destroy them without labour by the law, which is like fire. 39 Whereas you saw that he gathered to himself another multitude that was peaceful, 40 these are the ten tribes which were led away out of their own land in the time of Osea the king, whom Salmananser the king of the Assyrians led away captive, and he carried them beyond the River, and they were taken into another land. 41 But they made this plan amongst themselves, that they would leave the multitude of the heathen, and go out into a more distant region, where mankind had never lived, 42 that there they might keep their statutes which they had not kept in their own land. 43 They entered by the narrow passages of the river Euphrates. 44 For the Most High then did signs for them, and stopped the springs of the River until they had passed over. 45 For through that country there was a long way to go, namely, of a year and a half. The same region is called [f]Arzareth. 46 Then they lived there until the latter time. Now when they begin to come again, 47 the Most High stops the springs of the River again, that they may go through. Therefore you saw the multitude gathered together with peace. 48 But those who are left behind of your people are those who are found within my holy border. 49 It will be therefore when he will destroy the multitude of the nations that are gathered together, he will defend the people who remain. 50 Then will he show them very many wonders."

51 Then I said, "O sovereign Lord, explain this to me: Why have I seen the man coming up from the midst of the sea?"

52 He said to me, as no one can explore or know what is in the depths of the sea, even so no man on earth can see my Son, or those who are with him, except in the time of [g]his day. 53 This is the interpretation of the dream which you saw, and for this only you are enlightened about this, 54 for you have forsaken your own ways, and applied your diligence to mine, and have searched out my law. 55 You have ordered your life in wisdom, and have called understanding your mother. 56 Therefore I have shown you this, for there is a reward laid up with the Most High. It will be, after another three days I will speak other things to you, and declare to you mighty and wondrous things."

57 Then I went out and passed into the field, giving praise and thanks greatly to the Most High because of his wonders, which he did from time to time, 58 and because he governs the time, and such things as happen in their seasons. So I sat there three days.

14

1 It came to pass upon the third day, I sat under an oak, and, behold, a voice came out of a bush near me, and said, "Esdras, Esdras!"

2 I said, "Here I am, Lord," and I stood up on my feet.

3 Then he said to me, "I revealed myself in a bush and talked with Moses when my people were in bondage in Egypt. 4 I sent him, and [h] he led my people out of Egypt. I brought him up to Mount Sinai, where I kept him with me for many days. 5 I told him many wondrous things, and showed him the secrets of the times and the end of the seasons. I commanded him, saying, 6 'You shall publish these openly, and these you shall hide.' 7 Now I say to you: 8 Lay up in your heart the signs that I have shown, the dreams that you have seen, and the interpretations which you have heard; 9 for you will be taken away from men, and from now on you will live with my Son and with those who are like you, until the times have ended. 10 For the world has lost its youth, and the times begin to grow old. 11 [i]For the age is divided into twelve parts, and ten parts of it are already gone, [j]even the half of the tenth part. 12 There remain of it two parts after the middle of the tenth part. 13 Now therefore set your house in order, reprove your people, comfort the lowly amongst them, [k] and instruct those of them who are wise, and now renounce the life that is corruptible, 14 and let go of the mortal thoughts, cast away from you the burdens of man, put off now your weak nature, 15 lay aside the thoughts that are most grievous to you, and hurry to escape from these times. 16 For worse evils than those which you have seen happen will be done after this. 17 For look how much the world will be weaker through age, so much that more evils will increase on those who dwell in it. 18 For the truth will withdraw itself further off, and falsehood will be near. For now [l]the eagle which you saw in vision hurries to come."

19 Then I answered and said, [m]"Let me speak in your presence, O Lord. 20 Behold, I will go, as you have commanded me, and reprove the people who now live, but who will warn those who will be born afterward? For the world is set in darkness, and those who dwell in it are without light. 21 For your law has been burnt, therefore no one knows the things that are done by you, or the works that will be done. 22 But if I have found favour before you, send the Holy Spirit to me, and I will write all that has been done in the world since the beginning, even the things that were written in your law, that men may be able to find the path, and that those who would live in the latter days may live."

23 He answered me and said, "Go your way, gather the people together, and tell them not to seek you for forty days. 24 But prepare for yourself many tablets, and take with you Sarea, Dabria, Selemia, Ethanus, and Asiel, these five, which are ready to write swiftly; 25 and come here, and I will light a lamp of understanding in your heart which will not be put out until the things have ended about which you will write. 26 When you are done, some things you shall publish openly, and some things you shall deliver in secret to the wise. Tomorrow at this hour you will begin to write."

27 Then went I out, as he commanded me, and gathered all the people together, and said, 28 "Hear these words, O Israel! 29 Our fathers at the beginning were foreigners in Egypt, and they were delivered from there, 30 and received the law of life, which they didn't keep, which you also have transgressed after them. 31 Then the land of Zion was given to you for a possession; but you yourselves and your ancestors have done unrighteousness, and have not kept the ways which the Most High commanded you. 32 Because he is a righteous judge, in due time, he took from you what he had given you. 33 Now you are here, and your kindred are amongst you. 34 Therefore if you will rule over your own understanding and instruct your hearts, you will be kept alive, and after death you will obtain mercy. 35 For after death the judgement will come, when we will live again. Then the names of the righteous will become manifest, and the works of the ungodly will be declared. 36 Let no one therefore come to me now, nor seek me for forty days."

37 So I took the five men, as he commanded me, and we went out into the field, and remained there. 38 It came to pass on the next day that, behold,

---

a *13:10* So the Syriac and Arabic.

b *13:20* Lat. easier.

c *13:20* So the Syriac.

d *13:20* So the Syriac.

e *13:23* So the Syriac.

f *13:45* That is, another land. See Deuteronomy 29:28.

g *13:52* So the Oriental versions. The Latin omits his.

h *14:4* Another reading is. I.

i *14:11* Verses 11, 12 are omitted in the Syriac. The Aethiopic has For the age is divided into ten parts, and is come to the tenth: and half of the tenth remains. Now etc.

j *14:11* Lat. and.

k *14:13* The Latin alone omits and...wise.

l *14:18* So the Oriental versions.

m *14:19* The Latin omits I will speak.

a voice called me, saying, "Esdras, open your mouth, and drink what I give you to drink."

39 Then opened I my mouth, and behold, a full cup was handed to me. It was full of something like water, but its colour was like fire. 40 I took it, and drank. When I had drunk it, my heart uttered understanding, and wisdom grew in my breast, for my spirit retained its memory. 41 My mouth was opened, and shut no more. 42 The Most High gave understanding to the five men, and they wrote by course the things that were told them, in ᵃcharacters which they didn't know, and they sat forty days. Now they wrote in the daytime, and at night they ate bread. 43 As for me, I spoke in the day, and by night I didn't hold my tongue. 44 So in forty days, ninety-four books were written.

45 It came to pass, when the forty days were fulfilled, that the Most High spoke to me, saying, "The first books that you have written, publish openly, and let the worthy and unworthy read them; 46 but keep the last seventy, that you may deliver them to those who are wise amongst your people; 47 for in them is the spring of understanding, the fountain of wisdom, and the stream of knowledge."

48 I did so.

15

1 "Behold, speak in the ears of my people the words of prophecy which I will put in your mouth," says the Lord. 2 "Cause them to be written on paper, for they are faithful and true. 3 Don't be afraid of their plots against you. Don't let the unbelief of those who speak against you trouble you. 4 For all the unbelievers will die in their unbelief.

5 "Behold," says the Lord, "I bring evils on the whole earth: sword, famine, death, and destruction. 6 For wickedness has prevailed over every land, and their hurtful works have reached their limit. 7 Therefore," says the Lord, 8 "I will hold my peace no more concerning their wickedness which they profanely commit, neither will I tolerate them in these things, which they wickedly practise. Behold, the innocent and righteous blood cries to me, and the souls of the righteous cry out continually. 9 I will surely avenge them," says the Lord, "and will receive to me all the innocent blood from amongst them. 10 Behold, my people is led like a flock to the slaughter. I will not allow them now to dwell in the land of Egypt, 11 but I will bring them out with a mighty hand and with a high arm, and will strike Egypt with plagues, as before, and will destroy all its land."

12 Let Egypt and its foundations mourn, for the plague of the chastisement and the punishment that God will bring upon it. 13 Let the farmers that till the ground mourn, for their seeds will fail and their trees will be ruined through the blight and hail, and a terrible tempest. 14 Woe to the world and those who dwell in it! 15 For the sword and their destruction draws near, and nation will rise up against nation to battle with weapons in their hands. 16 For there will be sedition amongst men, and growing strong against one another. In their might, they won't respect their king or the chief of their great ones. 17 For a man will desire to go into a city, and will not be able. 18 For because of their pride the cities will be troubled, the houses will be destroyed, and men will be afraid. 19 A man will have no pity on his neighbours, but will assault their houses with the sword and plunder their goods, because of the lack of bread, and for great suffering.

20 "Behold," says God, "I call together all the kings of the earth to stir up those who are from the rising of the sun, from the south, from the east, and Libanus, to turn themselves one against another, and repay the things that they have done to them. 21 Just as they do yet this day to my chosen, so I will do also, and repay into their bosom." The Lord God says: 22 "My right hand won't spare the sinners, and my sword won't cease over those who shed innocent blood on the earth. 23 A fire has gone out from his wrath and has consumed the foundations of the earth and the sinners, like burnt straw. 24 Woe to those who sin and don't keep my commandments!" says the Lord. 25 "I will not spare them. Go your way, you rebellious children! Don't defile my sanctuary!" 26 For the Lord knows all those who trespass against him, therefore he will deliver them to death and destruction. 27 For now evils have come upon the whole earth, and you will remain in them; for God will not deliver you, because you have sinned against him.

28 Behold, a horrible sight appearing from the east! 29 The nations of the dragons of Arabia will come out with many chariots. From the day that they set out, their hissing is carried over the earth, so that all those who will hear them may also fear and tremble. 30 Also the Carmonians, raging in wrath, will go out like the wild boars of the forest. They will come with great power and join battle with them, and will devastate a portion of the land of the Assyrians with their teeth. 31 Then the dragons will have the upper hand, remembering their nature. If they will turn themselves, conspiring together in great power to persecute them, 32 then these will be troubled, and keep silence through their power, and will turn and flee. 33 From the land of the Assyrians, an enemy in ambush will attack them and destroy one of them. Upon their army will be fear and trembling, and indecision upon their kings.

34 Behold, clouds from the east, and from the north to the south! They are very horrible to look at, full of wrath and storm. 35 They will clash against one another. They will pour out a heavy storm on the earth, even their own storm. There will be blood from the sword to the horse's belly, 36 and to the thigh of man, and to the camel's hock. 37 There will be fearfulness and great trembling upon earth. They who see that wrath will be afraid, and trembling will seize them. 38 After this, great storms will be stirred up from the south, from the north, and another part from the west. 39 Strong winds will arise from the east, and will shut it up, even the cloud which he raised up in wrath; and the storm that was to cause destruction by the east wind will be violently driven towards the south and west. 40 Great and mighty clouds, full of wrath, will be lifted up with the storm, that they may destroy all the earth and those who dwell in it. They will pour out over every high and lofty one a terrible storm, 41 fire, hail, flying swords, and many waters, that all plains may be full, and all rivers, with the abundance of those waters. 42 They will break down the cities and walls, mountains and hills, trees of the forest, and grass of the meadows, and their grain. 43 They will go on steadily to Babylon and destroy her. 44 They will come to it and surround it. They will pour out the storm and all wrath on her. Then the dust and smoke will go up to the sky, and all those who are around it will mourn for it. 45 Those who remain will serve those who have destroyed it.

46 You, Asia, who are partaker in the beauty of Babylon, and in the glory of her person— 47 woe to you, you wretch, because you have made yourself like her. You have decked out your daughters for prostitution, that they might please and glory in your lovers, which have always lusted after you! 48 You have followed her who is hateful in all her works and inventions. Therefore God says, 49 "I will send evils on you: widowhood, poverty, famine, sword, and pestilence, to lay waste your houses and bring you to destruction and death. 50 The glory of your power will be dried up like a flower when the heat rises that is sent over you. 51 You will be weakened like a poor woman who is beaten and wounded, so that you won't be able to receive your mighty ones and your lovers. 52 Would I have dealt with you with such jealousy," says the Lord, 53 "if you had not always slain my chosen, exalting and clapping of your hands, and saying over their dead, when you were drunk?

54 "Beautify your face! 55 The reward of a prostitute will be in your bosom, therefore you will be repaid. 56 Just as you will do to my chosen," says the Lord, "even so God will do to you, and will deliver you to your adversaries. 57 Your children will die of hunger. You will fall by the sword. Your cities will be broken down, and all your people in the field will perish by the sword. 58 Those who are in the mountains will die of hunger, eat their own flesh, and drink their own blood, because of hunger for bread and thirst for water. 59 You, unhappy above all others, will come and will again receive evils. 60 In the passage, they will rush on the hateful city and will destroy some portion of your land, and mar part of your glory, and will return again to Babylon that was destroyed. 61 You will be cast down by them as stubble, and they will be to you as fire. 62 They will devour you, your cities, your land, and your mountains. They will burn all your forests and your fruitful trees with fire. 63 They will carry your children away captive, and will plunder your wealth, and mar the glory of your face."

16

1 Woe to you, Babylon, and Asia! Woe to you, Egypt and Syria! 2 Put on sackcloth and garments of goats' hair, wail for your children and lament; for your destruction is at hand. 3 A sword has been sent upon you, and who is there to turn it back? 4 A fire has been sent upon you, and who is there to quench it? 5 Calamities are sent upon you, and who is there to drive them away? 6 Can one drive away a hungry lion in the forest? Can one quench a fire in stubble, once it has begun to burn? 7 Can one turn back an arrow that is shot by a strong archer? 8 The Lord God sends the calamities, and who will drive them away? 9 A fire will go out from his wrath, and who may quench it? 10 He will flash lightning, and who will not fear? He will thunder, and who wouldn't tremble? 11 The Lord will threaten, and who will not be utterly broken in pieces at his presence? 12 The earth and its foundations quake. The sea rises up with waves from the deep, and its waves will be troubled, along with the fish in them, at the presence of the Lord, and before the glory of his power. 13 For his right hand that bends the bow is strong, his arrows that he shoots are sharp, and will not miss when they begin to be shot into the ends of the world. 14 Behold, the calamities are sent out, and will not return again until they come upon the earth. 15 The fire is kindled and will not be put out until it consumes the foundations of the earth. 16 Just as an arrow which is shot by a mighty archer doesn't return backward, even so the calamities that are sent out upon earth won't return again. 17 Woe is me! Woe is me! Who will deliver me in those days?

18 The beginning of sorrows, when there will be great mourning; the beginning of famine, and many will perish; the beginning of wars, and the powers will stand in fear; the beginning of calamities, and all will tremble! What will they do when the calamities come? 19 Behold, famine and plague, suffering and anguish! They are sent as scourges for correction. 20 But for all these things they will not turn them from their wickedness, nor be always mindful of the scourges. 21 Behold, food will be so cheap on earth that they will think themselves to be in good condition, and even then calamities will grow on earth: sword, famine, and great confusion. 22 For many of those who dwell on earth will perish of famine; and others who escape the famine, the sword will destroy. 23 The dead will be cast out like dung, and there will be no one to comfort them; for the earth will be left desolate, and its cities will be cast down. 24 There will be no farmer left to cultivate the earth or to sow it. 25 The trees will give fruit, but who will gather it? 26 The grapes will ripen, but who will tread them? For in all places there will be a great solitude; 27 for one man will desire to see another, or to hear his voice. 28 For of a city there will be ten left, and two of the field, who have hidden themselves in the thick groves, and in the clefts of the rocks. 29 As in an orchard of olives upon every tree there may be left three or four olives, 30 or as when a vineyard is gathered, there are some clusters left by those who diligently search through the vineyard, 31 even so in those days, there will be three or four left by those who search their houses with the sword. 32 The earth will be left desolate, and its fields will be for briers, and its

roads and all her paths will grow thorns, because no sheep will pass along them. 33 The virgins will mourn, having no bridegrooms. The women will mourn, having no husbands. Their daughters will mourn, having no helpers. 34 Their bridegrooms will be destroyed in the wars, and their husbands will perish of famine.

35 Hear now these things, and understand them, you servants of the Lord. 36 Behold, the Lord's word: receive it. Don't doubt the things about which the Lord speaks. 37 Behold, the calamities draw near, and are not delayed. 38 Just as a woman with child in the ninth month, when the hour of her delivery draws near, within two or three hours great pains surround her womb, and when the child comes out from the womb, there will be no waiting for a moment, 39 even so the calamities won't delay coming upon the earth. The world will groan, and sorrows will seize it on every side.

40 "O my people, hear my word: prepare for battle, and in those calamities be like strangers on the earth. 41 He who sells, let him be as he who flees away, and he who buys, as one who will lose. 42 Let he who does business be as he who has no profit by it, and he who builds, as he who won't dwell in it, 43 and he who sows, as if he wouldn't reap, so also he who prunes the vines, as he who won't gather the grapes, 44 those who marry, as those who will have no children, and those who don't marry, as the widowed. 45 Because of this, those who labour, labour in vain; 46 for foreigners will reap their fruits, plunder their goods, overthrow their houses, and take their children captive, for in captivity and famine they will conceive their children. 47 Those who conduct business, do so only to be plundered. The more they adorn their cities, their houses, their possessions, and their own persons, 48 the more I will hate them for their sins," says the Lord. 49 Just as a respectable and virtuous woman hates a prostitute, 50 so will righteousness hate iniquity, when she adorns herself, and will accuse her to her face, when he comes who will defend him who diligently searches out every sin on earth.

51 Therefore don't be like her or her works. 52 For yet a little while, and iniquity will be taken away out of the earth, and righteousness will reign over us. 53 Don't let the sinner say that he has not sinned; for God will burn coals of fire on the head of one who says "I haven't sinned before God and his glory." 54 Behold, the Lord knows all the works of men, their imaginations, their thoughts, and their hearts. 55 He said, "Let the earth be made," and it was made, "Let the sky be made," and it was made. 56 At his word, the stars were established, and he knows the number of the stars. 57 He searches the deep and its treasures. He has measured the sea and what it contains. 58 He has shut the sea in the midst of the waters, and with his word, he hung the earth over the waters. 59 He has spread out the sky like a vault. He has founded it over the waters. 60 He has made springs of water in the desert and pools on the tops of the mountains to send out rivers from the heights to water the earth. 61 He formed man, and put a heart in the midst of the body, and gave him breath, life, and understanding, 62 yes, the spirit of God Almighty. He who made all things and searches out hidden things in hidden places, 63 surely he knows your imagination, and what you think in your hearts. Woe to those who sin, and try to hide their sin! 64 Because the Lord will exactly investigate all your works, and he will put you all to shame. 65 When your sins are brought out before men, you will be ashamed, and your own iniquities will stand as your accusers in that day. 66 What will you do? Or how will you hide your sins before God and his angels? 67 Behold, God is the judge. Fear him! Stop sinning, and forget your iniquities, to never again commit them. So will God lead you out, and deliver you from all suffering.

68 For, behold, the burning wrath of a great multitude is kindled over you, and they will take away some of you, and feed you with that which is sacrificed to idols. 69 Those who consent to them will be held in derision and in contempt, and be trodden under foot. 70 For there will be in various places, and in the next cities, a great insurrection against those who fear the Lord. 71 They will be like mad men, sparing none, but spoiling and destroying those who still fear the Lord. 72 For they will destroy and plunder their goods, and throw them out of their houses. 73 Then the trial of my elect will be made known, even as the gold that is tried in the fire. 74 Hear, my elect ones, says the Lord: "Behold, the days of suffering are at hand, and I will deliver you from them. 75 Don't be afraid, and don't doubt, for God is your guide. 76 You who keep my commandments and precepts," says the Lord God, "don't let your sins weigh you down, and don't let your iniquities lift themselves up." 77 Woe to those who are choked with their sins and covered with their iniquities, like a field is choked with bushes, and its path covered with thorns, that no one may travel through! 78 It is shut off and given up to be consumed by fire.

The Fourth Book of the Maccabees

The Fourth Book of the Maccabees appears in an appendix to the Greek Septuagint. It is considered to be apocrypha by most church traditions. It is preserved here for its supplementary historical value.

1

₁ As I am going to demonstrate a most philosophical proposition, namely, that religious reasoning is absolute master of the emotions, I would willingly advise you to give the utmost heed to philosophy. ₂ For reason is necessary to everyone as a step to science. In addition, it embraces the praise of self-control, the highest virtue. ₃ If, then, reasoning appears to hold the mastery over the emotions which stand in the way of temperance, such as gluttony and lust, ₄ it surely also and manifestly rules over the affections which are contrary to justice, such as malice, and of those which are hindrances to courage, such as wrath, pain, and fear. ₅ Perhaps some may ask, "How is it, then, that reasoning, if it rules the emotions, isn't also master of forgetfulness and ignorance?" They attempt a ridiculous argument. ₆ For reasoning does not rule over its own emotions, but over those that are contrary to justice, courage, temperance, and self-control; and yet over these, so as to withstand, without destroying them.

₇ I might prove to you from many other considerations, that religious reasoning is sole master of the emotions; ₈ but I will prove it with the greatest force from the fortitude of Eleazar, and seven kindred, and their mother, who suffered death in defence of virtue. ₉ For all these, treating pains with contempt even to death, by this contempt, demonstrated that reasoning has command over the emotions. ₁₀ For their virtues, then, it is right that I should commend those men who died with their mother at this time on behalf of nobility and goodness; and for their honours, I may count them blessed. ₁₁ For they, winning admiration not only from men in general, but even from the persecutors, for their courage and endurance, became the means of the destruction of the tyranny against their nation, having conquered the tyrant by their endurance, so that by them their country was purified. ₁₂ But we may now at once enter upon the question, having commenced, as is our custom, with laying down the doctrine, and so proceed to the account of these people, giving glory to the all-wise God.

₁₃ Therefore the question whether reasoning is absolute master of the emotions. ₁₄ Let's determine, then, what reasoning is and what emotion is, and how many forms of emotion there are, and whether reasoning rules over all of these. ₁₅ Reasoning is intellect accompanied by a life of righteousness, putting foremost the consideration of wisdom. ₁₆ Wisdom is a knowledge of divine and human things, and of their causes. ₁₇ This is contained in the education of the law, by means of which we learn divine things reverently and human things profitably. ₁₈ The forms of wisdom are self-control, justice, courage, and temperance. ₁₉ The leading one of these is self-control, by whose means, indeed, it is that reasoning rules over the emotions. ₂₀ Of the emotions, pleasure and pain are the two most comprehensive; and they also by nature refer to the soul. ₂₁ There are many attendant affections surrounding pleasure and pain. ₂₂ Before pleasure is lust; and after pleasure, joy. ₂₃ Before pain is fear; and after pain is sorrow. ₂₄ Wrath is an affection, common to pleasure and to pain, if any one will pay attention when it comes upon him. ₂₅ There exists in pleasure a malicious disposition, which is the most complex of all the affections. ₂₆ In the soul, it is arrogance, love of money, thirst for honour, contention, faithlessness, and the evil eye. ₂₇ In the body, it is greediness, indiscriminate eating, and solitary gluttony.

₂₈ As pleasure and pain are, therefore, two growths out of the body and the soul, so there are many offshoots of these emotions. ₂₉ Reasoning, the universal farmer, purging and pruning each of these, tying up, watering, and transplanting, in every way improves the materials of the morals and affections. ₃₀ For reasoning is the leader of the virtues, but it is the sole ruler of the emotions.

Observe then first, through the very things which stand in the way of temperance, that reasoning is absolute ruler of the emotions. ₃₁ Now temperance consists of a command over the lusts. ₃₂ But of the lusts, some belong to the soul and others to the body. Reasoning appears to rule over both. ₃₃ Otherwise, how is it that when urged on to forbidden meats, we reject the gratification which would come from them? Isn't it because reasoning is able to command the appetites? I believe so. ₃₄ Hence it is, then, that when craving seafood, birds, four-footed animals, and all kinds of food which are forbidden to us by the law, we withhold ourselves through the mastery of reasoning. ₃₅ For the affections of our appetites are resisted by the temperate understanding, and bent back again, and all the impulses of the body are reined in by reasoning.

2

₁ Is it any wonder? If the lusts of the soul, after participation with what is beautiful, are frustrated, ₂ on this ground, therefore, the temperate Joseph is praised in that by reasoning, he subdued, on reflection, the indulgence of the senses. ₃ For, although young, and ripe for sexual intercourse, he nullified by reasoning the stimulus of his emotions. ₄ It isn't merely the stimulus of sensual indulgence, but that of every desire, that reasoning is able to master. ₅ For instance, the law says, "You shall not covet your neighbour's wife, nor anything that belongs to your neighbour." ₆ Now, then, since it is the law which has forbidden us to desire, I shall much the more easily persuade you, that reasoning is able to govern our lusts, just as it does the affections which are impediments to justice. ₇ Since in what way is a solitary eater, a glutton, and a drunkard reclaimed, unless it is

clear that reasoning is lord of the emotions? ₈ Therefore, a man who regulates his course by the law, even if he is a lover of money, immediately puts pressure on his own disposition by lending to the needy without interest, and cancelling the debt on the seventh year. ₉ If a man is greedy, he is ruled by the law acting through reasoning, so that he doesn't glean his harvest crops or vintage. In reference to other points we may perceive that it is reasoning that conquers his emotions. ₁₀ For the law conquers even affection towards parents, not surrendering virtue on their account. ₁₁ It prevails over love for one's wife, rebuking her when she breaks the law. ₁₂ It lords it over the love of parents towards their children, for they punish them for vice. It domineers over the intimacy of friends, reproving them when wicked. ₁₃ Don't think it is a strange assertion that reasoning can on behalf of the law conquer even enmity. ₁₄ It doesn't allow cutting down the fruit trees of an enemy, but preserves them from the destroyers, and collects their fallen ruins. ₁₅ Reason appears to be master of the more violent emotions, like love of empire, empty boasting, and slander. ₁₆ For the temperate understanding repels all these malignant emotions, as it does wrath; for it masters even this. ₁₇ Thus Moses, when angered against Dathan and Abiram, did nothing to them in wrath, but regulated his anger by reasoning. ₁₈ For the temperate mind is able, as I said, to be superior to the emotions, and to correct some and destroy others. ₁₉ For why else did our most wise father Jacob blame Simeon and Levi for having irrationally slain the whole race of the Shechemites, saying, "Cursed be their anger!"? ₂₀ For if reasoning didn't possess the power of subduing angry affections, he would not have said this. ₂₁ For at the time when God created man, he implanted within him his emotions and moral nature. ₂₂ At that time he enthroned the mind above all as the holy leader, through the medium of the senses. ₂₃ He gave a law to this mind, by living according to which it will maintain a temperate, just, good, and courageous reign. ₂₄ How, then, a man may say, if reasoning is master of the emotions, has it no control over forgetfulness and ignorance?

3

₁ The argument is exceedingly ridiculous, for reasoning doesn't appear to rule over its own affections, but over those of the body, ₂ in such a way as that any one of you may not be able to root out desire, but reasoning will enable you to avoid being enslaved to it. ₃ One may not be able to root out anger from the soul, but it is possible to withstand anger. ₄ Any one of you may not be able to eradicate malice, but reasoning has force to work with you to prevent you yielding to malice. ₅ For reasoning is not an eradicator, but an antagonist of the emotions.

₆ This may be more clearly comprehended from the thirst of King David. ₇ For after David had been attacking the Philistines the whole day, he with the soldiers of his nation killed many of them; ₈ then when evening came, sweating and very weary, he came to the royal tent, around which the entire army of our ancestors was encamped. ₉ Now all the rest of them were at supper; ₁₀ but the king, being very much thirsty, although he had numerous springs, could not by their means quench his thirst; ₁₁ but a certain irrational longing for the water in the enemy's camp grew stronger and fiercer upon him, undid and consumed him. ₁₂ Therefore his bodyguards being troubled at this longing of the king, two valiant young soldiers, respecting the desire of the king, fully armed themselves, and taking a pitcher, got over the ramparts of the enemies. ₁₃ Unperceived by the guardians of the gate, they went throughout the whole camp of the enemy in quest. ₁₄ Having boldly discovered the fountain, they filled out of it the drink for the king. ₁₅ But he, though parched with thirst, reasoned that a drink regarded of equal value to blood would be terribly dangerous to his soul. ₁₆ Therefore, setting up reasoning in opposition to his desire, he poured out the drink to God. ₁₇ For the temperate mind has power to conquer the pressure of the emotions, to quench the fires of excitement, ₁₈ and to wrestle down the pains of the body, however excessive, and through the excellency of reasoning, to spurn all the assaults of the emotions. ₁₉ But the occasion now invites us to give an illustration of temperate reasoning from history. ₂₀ For at a time when our fathers were in possession of undisturbed peace through obedience to the law and were prosperous, so that Seleucus Nicanor, the king of Asia, both assigned them money for divine service, and accepted their form of government, ₂₁ then certain people, bringing in new things contrary to the public harmony, in various ways fell into calamities.

4

₁ For a certain man named Simon, who was in opposition to an honourable and good man who once held the high priesthood for life, named Onias. After slandering Onias in every way, Simon couldn't injure him with the people, so he went away as an exile, with the intention of betraying his country. ₂ When coming to Apollonius, the military governor of Syria, Phoenicia, and Cilicia, he said, ₃ "Having good will to the king's affairs, I have come to inform you that tens of thousands in private wealth is laid up in the treasuries of Jerusalem which do not belong to the temple, but belong to King Seleucus." ₄ Apollonius, acquainting himself with the particulars of this, praised Simon for his care of the king's interests, and going up to Seleucus informed him of the treasure. ₅ Getting authority about it, and quickly advancing into our country with the accursed Simon and a very heavy force, ₆ he said that he came with the commands of the king that he should take the private money of the treasury. ₇ The nation, indignant at this proclamation, and replying to the effect that it was extremely unfair that those who had committed deposits to the sacred treasury should be deprived of them, resisted as well as they could. ₈ But Appolonius went away with threats into the temple. ₉ The priests, with the women and children, asked God to throw his shield over the holy, despised place, ₁₀ and

Appolonius was going up with his armed force to seize the treasure, when angels from heaven appeared riding on horseback, all radiant in armour, filling them with much fear and trembling. 11 Apollonius fell half dead on the court which is open to all nations, and extended his hands to heaven, and implored the Hebrews, with tears, to pray for him, and take away the wrath of the heavenly army. 12 For he said that he had sinned, so as to be consequently worthy of death, and that if he were saved, he would proclaim to all people the blessedness of the holy place. 13 Onias the high priest, induced by these words, although for other reasons anxious that King Seleucus wouldn't suppose that Apollonius was slain by human device and not by Divine punishment, prayed for him; 14 and he being thus unexpectedly saved, departed to report to the king what had happened to him. 15 But on the death of Seleucus the king, his son Antiochus Epiphanes succeeded to the kingdom—a terrible man of arrogant pride.

16 He, having deposed Onias from the high priesthood, appointed his brother Jason to be high priest, 17 who had made a covenant, if he would give him this authority, to pay yearly three thousand and six hundred and sixty talents. 18 He committed to him the high priesthood and rulership over the nation. 19 He both changed the manner of living of the people, and perverted their civil customs into all lawlessness. 20 So that he not only erected a gymnasium on the very citadel of our country, but neglected the guardianship of the temple. 21 Because of that, Divine vengeance was grieved and instigated Antiochus himself against them. 22 For being at war with Ptolemy in Egypt, he heard that on a report of his death being spread abroad, the inhabitants of Jerusalem had exceedingly rejoiced, and he quickly marched against them. 23 Having subdued them, he established a decree that if any of them lived according to the ancestral laws, he should die. 24 When he could by no means destroy by his decrees the obedience to the law of the nation, but saw all his threats and punishments without effect, 25 for even women, because they continued to circumcise their children, were flung down a precipice along with them, knowing beforehand of the punishment. 26 When, therefore, his decrees were disregarded by the people, he himself compelled by means of tortures every one of this race, by tasting forbidden meats, to renounce the Jewish religion.

5

1 The tyrant Antiochus, therefore, sitting in public state with his assessors upon a certain lofty place, with his armed troops standing in a circle around him, 2 commanded his spearbearers to seize every one of the Hebrews, and to compel them to taste swine's flesh and things offered to idols. 3 Should any of them be unwilling to eat the accursed food, they were to be tortured on the wheel and so killed. 4 When many had been seized, a foremost man of the assembly, a Hebrew, by name Eleazar, a priest by family, by profession a lawyer, and advanced in years, and for this reason known to many of the king's followers, was brought near to him.

5 Antiochus, seeing him, said, 6 "I would counsel you, old man, before your tortures begin, to taste the swine's flesh, and save your life; for I feel respect for your age and hoary head, which since you have had so long, you appear to me to be no philosopher in retaining the superstition of the Jews. 7 For therefore, since nature has conferred upon you the most excellent flesh of this animal, do you loathe it? 8 It seems senseless not to enjoy what is pleasant, yet not disgraceful; and from notions of sinfulness, to reject the gifts of nature. 9 You will be acting, I think, still more senselessly, if you follow vain conceits about the truth. 10 You will, moreover, be despising me to your own punishment. 11 Won't you awake from your trifling philosophy, give up the folly of your notions, and regaining understanding worthy of your age, search into the truth of an expedient course? 12 Won't you respect my kindly admonition and have pity on your own years? 13 For bear in mind that if there is any power which watches over this religion of yours, it will pardon you for all transgressions of the law which you commit through compulsion."

14 While the tyrant incited him in this manner to the unlawful eating of meat, Eleazar begged permission to speak. 15 Having received permission to speak, he began to address the people as follows: 16 "We, O Antiochus, who are persuaded that we live under a divine law, consider no compulsion to be so forcible as obedience to that law. 17 Therefore we consider that we ought not to transgress the law in any way. 18 Indeed, were our law (as you suppose) not truly divine, and if we wrongly think it divine, we would have no right even in that case to destroy our sense of religion. 19 Don't think that eating unclean meat is a trifling offence. 20 For transgression of the law, whether in small or great matters, is of equal importance; 21 for in either case the law is equally slighted. 22 But you deride our philosophy, as though we lived in it irrationally. 23 Yet it instructs us in self-control, so that we are superior to all pleasures and lusts; and it trains us in courage, so that we cheerfully undergo every grievance. 24 It instructs us in justice, so that in all our dealings we render what is due. It teaches us piety, so that we properly worship the one and only God. 25 That is why we don't eat the unclean; for believing that the law was established by God, we are convinced that the Creator of the world, in giving his laws, sympathises with our nature. 26 Those things which are suitable for our souls, he has directed us to eat; but those which are not, he has forbidden. 27 But, tyrant-like, you not only force us to break the law, but also to eat, that you may ridicule us as we thus profanely eat. 28 But you won't have this cause of laughter against me, 29 nor will I transgress the sacred oaths of my forefathers to keep the law. 30 No, not if you pluck out my eyes, and consume my entrails. 31 I am not so old, and void of courage as to not be youthful in reason and in defence of my religion. 32 Now then, prepare your wheels, and kindle a fiercer flame. 33 I will not so pity my old age, as on my account to break the law of my country. 34 I will not play false to you, O law, my instructor, or forsake you, O beloved self-control! 35 I will not put you to shame, O philosopher Reason,

or deny you, O honoured priesthood and knowledge of the law. 36 Mouth! You shall not pollute my old age, nor the full stature of a perfect life. 37 My ancestors will receive me as pure, not having feared your compulsion, even to death. 38 For you will rule like a tyrant over the ungodly, but you will not lord it over my thoughts about religion, either by your arguments, or through deeds."

6

1 When Eleazar had in this manner answered the exhortations of the tyrant, the spearbearers came up, and rudely dragged Eleazar to the instruments of torture. 2 First, they stripped the old man, adorned as he was with the beauty of piety. 3 Then tying back his arms and hands, they disdainfully flogged him. 4 A herald opposite cried out, "Obey the commands of the king!"

5 But the high-minded and truly noble Eleazar, as one tortured in a dream, ignored it. 6 But raising his eyes on high to heaven, the old man's flesh was stripped off by the scourges, and his blood streamed down, and his sides were pierced through. 7 Falling on the ground from his body having no power to endure the pains, he still kept his reasoning upright and unbending. 8 Then one of the harsh spearbearers rushed at him and began to kick him in the side to force him to get up again after he fell. 9 But he endured the pains, despised the cruelty, and persevered through the indignities. 10 Like a noble athlete, the old man, when struck, vanquished his torturers. 11 His face sweating, and he panting for breath, he was admired even by the torturers for his courage.

12 Therefore, partly in pity for his old age, 13 partly from the sympathy of acquaintance, and partly in admiration of his endurance, some of the attendants of the king said, 14 "Why do you unreasonably destroy yourself, O Eleazar, with these miseries? 15 We will bring you some meat cooked by yourself, and you can save yourself by pretending that you have eaten swine's flesh."

16 Eleazar, as though the advice more painfully tortured him, cried out, 17 "Let us who are children of Abraham not be so evil advised as by giving way to make use of an unbecoming pretence. 18 For it would be irrational, if having lived up to old age in all truth, and having scrupulously guarded our character for it, we would now turn back 19 and ourselves become a pattern of impiety to the young, as being an example of eating pollution. 20 It would be disgraceful if we would live on some short time, and that scorned by all men for cowardice, 21 and be condemned by the tyrant for cowardice by not contending to the death for our divine law. 22 Therefore you, O children of Abraham, die nobly for your religion. 23 You spearbearers of the tyrant, why do you linger?"

24 Beholding him so high-minded against misery, and not changing at their pity, they led him to the fire. 25 Then with their wickedly contrived instruments they burnt him on the fire, and poured stinking fluids down into his nostrils. 26 He being at length burnt down to the bones, and about to expire, raised his eyes Godward, and said, 27 "You know, O God, that when I might have been saved, I am slain for the sake of the law by tortures of fire. 28 Be merciful to your people, and be satisfied with the punishment of me on their account. 29 Let my blood be a purification for them, and take my life in exchange for theirs." 30 Thus speaking, the holy man departed, noble in his torments, and even to the agonies of death resisted in his reasoning for the sake of the law. 31 Confessedly, therefore, religious reasoning is master of the emotions. 32 For had the emotions been superior to reasoning, I would have given them the witness of this mastery. 33 But now, since reasoning conquered the emotions, we befittingly award it the authority of first place. 34 It is only fair that we should allow that the power belongs to reasoning, since it masters external miseries. 35 It would be ridiculous if it weren't so. I prove that reasoning has not only mastered pains, but that it is also superior to the pleasures, and withstands them.

7

1 The reasoning of our father Eleazar, like a first-rate pilot, steering the vessel of piety in the sea of emotions, 2 and flouted by the threats of the tyrant, and overwhelmed with the breakers of torture, 3 in no way shifted the rudder of piety until it sailed into the harbour of victory over death. 4 No besieged city has ever held out against many and various war machines as that holy man did when his pious soul was tried with the fiery trial of tortures and rackings and moved his besiegers through the religious reasoning that shielded him. 5 For father Eleazar, projecting his disposition, broke the raging waves of the emotions as with a jutting cliff. 6 O priest worthy of the priesthood! You didn't pollute your sacred teeth, nor make your appetite, which had always embraced the clean and lawful, a partaker of profanity. 7 O harmonizer with the law, and sage devoted to a divine life! 8 Of such a character ought those to be who perform the duties of the law at the risk of their own blood, and defend it with generous sweat by sufferings even to death. 9 You, father, have gloriously established our right government by your endurance; and making of much account our past service, prevented its destruction, and by your deeds, have made credible the words of philosophy. 10 O aged man of more power than tortures, elder more vigorous than fire, greatest king over the emotions, Eleazar! 11 For as father Aaron, armed with a censer, hastening through the consuming fire, vanquished the flame-bearing angel, 12 so, Eleazar, the descendant of Aaron, wasted away by the fire, didn't give up his reasoning. 13 What is most wonderful is that though he was an old man, though the labours of his body were now spent, his muscles were relaxed, and his sinews worn out, he recovered youth. 14 By the spirit of reasoning, and the reasoning of Isaac, he rendered powerless the many-headed rack. 15 O blessed old age, and reverend hoar head, and life obedient to the law, which the faithful seal of

death perfected. 16 If, then, an old man, through religion, despised tortures even to death, then certainly religious reasoning is ruler of the emotions. 17 But perhaps some might say, "It is not all who conquer emotions, as not all possess wise reasoning." 18 But those who have meditated upon religion with their whole heart, these alone can master the emotions of the flesh: 19 they who believe that to God they don't die; for, as our forefathers, Abraham, Isaac, and Jacob, they live to God. 20 This circumstance, then, is by no means an objection, that some who have weak reasoning are governed by their emotions, 21 since what person, walking religiously by the whole rule of philosophy, and believing in God, 22 and knowing that it is a blessed thing to endure all kinds of hardships for virtue, would not, for the sake of religion, master his emotion? 23 For only the wise and brave man is lord over his emotions. 24 This is why even boys, trained with the philosophy of religious reasoning, have conquered still more bitter tortures; 25 for when the tyrant was manifestly vanquished in his first attempt, in being unable to force the old man to eat the unclean thing,

8

1 then, indeed, vehemently swayed with emotion, he commanded to bring others of the adult Hebrews, and if they would eat of the unclean thing, to let them go when they had eaten; but if they objected, to torment them more grievously. 2 The tyrant having given this charge, seven kindred were brought into his presence, along with their aged mother. They were handsome, modest, well-born, and altogether comely. 3 When the tyrant saw them encircling their mother as in a dance, he was pleased with them. Being struck with their becoming and innocent manner, smiled at them, and calling them near, said, 4 "O youths, with favourable feelings, I admire the beauty of each of you. Greatly honouring so numerous a band of kindred, I not only counsel you not to share the madness of the old man who has been tortured before, 5 but I beg you to yield, and to enjoy my friendship; for I possess the power, not only of punishing those who disobey my commands, but of doing good to those who obey them. 6 Put confidence in me, then, and you will receive places of authority in my government, if you forsake your national way of life, 7 and, conforming to the Greek way of life, alter your rule and revel in youth's delights. 8 For if you provoke me by your disobedience, you will compel me to destroy every one of you with terrible punishments by tortures. 9 Have mercy, then, upon your own selves, whom I, although an enemy, am compassionate for your age and attractive appearance. 10 Won't you consider this: that if you disobey, there will be nothing left for you but to die in torture?"

11 When he had said this, he ordered the instruments of torture to be brought forward, that fear might prevail upon them to eat unclean meat. 12 When the spearman brought forward the wheels, the racks, the hooks, racks, cauldrons, pans, finger-racks, iron hands and wedges, and bellows, the tyrant continued: 13 "Fear, young men, and the righteousness which you worship will be merciful to you if you transgress because of compulsion."

14 Now they having listened to these words of persuasion, and seeing the fearful instruments, not only were not afraid, but even answered the arguments of the tyrant, and through their good reasoning destroyed his power. 15 Now let's consider the matter. Had any of them been weak-spirited and cowardly amongst them, what reasoning would they have employed but these? 16 "O wretched that we are, and exceedingly senseless! When the king exhorts us, and calls us to his bounty, should we not obey him? 17 Why do we cheer ourselves with vain counsels, and venture upon a disobedience bringing death? 18 Shall we not fear, O kindred, the instruments of torture and weigh the threatenings of torment and shun this vain-glory and destructive pride? 19 Let's have compassion upon our age and relent over the years of our mother. 20 Let's bear in mind that we will be dying as rebels. 21 Divine Justice will pardon us if we fear the king through necessity. 22 Why withdraw ourselves from a most sweet life, and deprive ourselves of this pleasant world? 23 Let's not oppose necessity, nor seek vain-glory by our own torture. 24 The law itself wouldn't arbitrarily put us to death because we dread torture. 25 Why has such angry zeal taken root in us, and such fatal obstinacy approved itself to us, when we might live unmolested by the king?"

26 But the young men didn't say or think anything of this kind when about to be tortured. 27 For they were well aware of the sufferings, and masters of the pains. 28-29 So that as soon as the tyrant had ceased counselling them to eat the unclean, they all with one voice, as from the same heart said,

9

1 "Why do you delay, O tyrant? For we are more ready to die than to transgress the injunctions of our fathers. 2 We would be disgracing our fathers if we didn't obey the law, and take knowledge for our guide. 3 O tyrant, counsellor of law-breaking, do not, hating us as you do, pity us more than we pity ourselves. 4 For we consider your escape to be worse than death. 5 You try to scare us by threatening us with death by tortures, as though you had learnt nothing by the death of Eleazar. 6 But if aged men of the Hebrews have died in the cause of religion after enduring torture, more rightly should we younger men die, scorning your cruel tortures, which our aged instructor overcame. 7 Make the attempt, then, O tyrant. If you put us to death for our religion, don't think that you harm us by torturing us. 8 For we through this ill-treatment and endurance will gain the rewards of virtue. 9 But you, for the wicked and despotic slaughter of us, will, from the Divine vengeance, endure eternal torture by fire."

10 When they had said this, the tyrant was not only exasperated against them for being disobedient, but enraged with them for being ungrateful. 11 So, at his bidding, the torturers brought the oldest of them, and tearing through his tunic, bound his hands and arms on each side with thongs.

12 When they had laboured hard without effect in scourging him, they hurled him on the wheel. 13 The noble youth, extended upon this, became dislocated. 14 With every member disjointed, he denounced the tyrant, saying, 15 "O most accursed tyrant, and enemy of heavenly justice, and cruel-hearted, I am no murderer, nor sacrilegious man, whom you torture, but a defender of the Divine law."

16 And when the spearmen said, "Consent to eat, that you may be released from your tortures," 17 he answered, "Not so powerful, O accursed lackeys, is your wheel, as to stifle my reasoning. Cut my limbs, and burn my flesh, and twist my joints. 18 For through all my torments I will convince you that the children of the Hebrews are alone unconquered on behalf of virtue."

19 While he was saying this, they heaped up fuel, and setting fire to it, strained him on the wheel still more. 20 The wheel was defiled all over with blood. The hot ashes were quenched by the droppings of gore, and pieces of flesh were scattered about the axles of the machine. 21 Although the framework of his bones was now destroyed, the high-minded and Abrahamic youth didn't groan. 22 But, as though transformed by fire into immortality, he nobly endured the rackings, saying, 23 "Imitate me, O kindred. Never desert your station, nor renounce my brotherhood in courage. Fight the holy and honourable fight of religion, 24 by which means our just and paternal Providence, becoming merciful to the nation, will punish the pestilent tyrant." 25 Saying this, the revered youth abruptly closed his life.

26 When all admired his courageous soul, the spearmen brought forward him who was second oldest, and having put on iron gauntlets with sharp hooks, bound him to the rack. 27 When, on enquiring whether he would eat before he was tortured, they heard his noble sentiment. 28 After they with the iron gauntlets had violently dragged all the flesh from the neck to the chin, the panther-like animals tore off the very skin of his head, but he, bearing with firmness this misery, said, 29 "How sweet is every form of death for the religion of our fathers!" Then he said to the tyrant, 30 "Don't you think, most cruel of all tyrants, that you are now tortured more than I, finding your arrogant conception of tyranny conquered by our perseverance in behalf of our religion? 31 For I lighten my suffering by the pleasures which are connected with virtue. 32 But you are tortured with threatenings for impiety. You won't escape, most corrupt tyrant, the vengeance of Divine wrath."

10

1 Now this one endured this praiseworthy death. The third was brought along, and exhorted by many to taste and save his life. 2 But he cried out and said, "Don't you know that the father of those who are dead is my father also, and that the same mother bore me, and that I was brought up in the same way? 3 I don't renounce the noble relationship of my kindred. 4 Now then, whatever instrument of vengeance you have, apply it to my body, for you aren't able to touch my soul, even if you want to." 5 But they, highly incensed at his boldness of speech, dislocated his hands and feet with racking engines, and wrenching them from their sockets, dismembered him. 6 They dragged around his fingers, his arms, his legs, and his ankles. 7 Not being able by any means to strangle him, they tore off his skin, together with the extreme tips of his fingers, and then dragged him to the wheel, 8 around which his vertebral joints were loosened, and he saw his own flesh torn to shreds, and streams of blood flowing from his entrails. 9 When about to die, he said, 10 "We, O accursed tyrant, suffer this for the sake of Divine education and virtue. 11 But you, for your impiety and blood shedding, will endure unceasing torments."

12 Thus having died worthily of his kindred, they dragged forward the fourth, saying, 13 "Don't share the madness of your kindred, but respect the king and save yourself."

14 But he said to them, "You don't have a fire so scorching as to make me play the coward. 15 By the blessed death of my kindred, and the eternal punishment of the tyrant, and the glorious life of the pious, I will not repudiate the noble brotherhood. 16 Invent, O tyrant, tortures, that you may learn, even through them, that I am the brother of those tormented before."

17 When he had said this, the blood-thirsty, murderous, and unholy Antiochus ordered his tongue to be cut out. 18 But he said, "Even if you take away the organ of speech, God still hears the silent. 19 Behold, my tongue is extended, cut it off; for in spite of that you won't silence our reasoning. 20 We gladly lose our limbs on behalf of God. 21 But God will speedily find you, since you cut off the tongue, the instrument of divine melody."

11

1 When he had died, disfigured in his torments, the fifth leapt forward, and said, 2 "I don't intend, O tyrant, to get excused from the torment which is on behalf of virtue. 3 But I have come of my own accord, that by my death you may owe heavenly vengeance and punishment for more crimes. 4 O you hater of virtue and of men, what have we done that you thus revel in our blood? 5 Does it seem evil to you that we worship the Founder of all things, and live according to his surpassing law? 6 But this is worthy of honours, not torments, 7 if you had been capable of the higher feelings of men, and possessed the hope of salvation from God. 8 Behold now, being alien from God, you make war against those who are religious towards God."

9 As he said this, the spearbearers bound him and drew him to the rack, 10 to which binding him at his knees, and fastening them with iron fetters, they bent down his loins upon the wedge of the wheel; and his body was then dismembered, scorpion-fashion. 11 With his breath thus confined, and his body strangled, he said, 12 "A great favour you bestow upon us, O tyrant, by enabling us to manifest our adherence to the law by means of nobler sufferings."

13 He also being dead, the sixth, quite a youth, was brought out. On the tyrant asking him whether he would eat and be delivered, he said, 14 "I am indeed younger than my brothers, but in understanding I am as old; 15 for having been born and reared to the same end. We are bound to die also on behalf of the same cause. 16 So that if you think it is proper to torment us for not eating the unclean, then torment!"

17 As he said this, they brought him to the wheel. 18 Extended upon this, with limbs racked and dislocated, he was gradually roasted from beneath. 19 Having heated sharp spits, they approached them to his back; and having transfixed his sides, they burnt away his entrails. 20 He, while tormented, said, "O good and holy contest, in which for the sake of religion, we kindred have been called to the arena of pain, and have not been conquered. 21 For religious understanding, O tyrant, is unconquered. 22 Armed with upright virtue, I also will depart with my kindred. 23 I, too, bearing with me a great avenger, O inventor of tortures, and enemy of the truly pious. 24 We six youths have destroyed your tyranny. 25 For isn't your inability to overrule our reasoning, and to compel us to eat the unclean, your destruction? 26 Your fire is cold to us. Your racks are painless, and your violence harmless. 27 For the guards not of a tyrant but of a divine law are our defenders. Through this we keep our reasoning unconquered."

12

1 When he, too, had undergone blessed martyrdom, and died in the cauldron into which he had been thrown, the seventh, the youngest of all, came forward, 2 whom the tyrant pitying, though he had been dreadfully reproached by his kindred, 3 seeing him already encompassed with chains, had him brought nearer, and endeavored to counsel him, saying, 4 "You see the end of the madness of your kindred, for they have died in torture through disobedience. You, if disobedient, having been miserably tormented, will yourself perish prematurely. 5 But if you obey, you will be my friend, and have a charge over the affairs of the kingdom." 6 Having thus exhorted him, he sent for the boy's mother, that, by showing compassion to her for the loss of so many sons, he might incline her, through the hope of safety, to render the survivor obedient.

7 He, after his mother had urged him on in the Hebrew tongue, (as we will soon relate) said, 8 "Release me that I may speak to the king and all his friends." 9 They, rejoicing exceedingly at the promise of the youth, quickly let him go. 10 He, running up to the pans, said, 11 "Impious tyrant, and most blasphemous man, were you not ashamed, having received prosperity and a kingdom from God, to kill His servants, and to rack the doers of godliness? 12 Therefore the divine vengeance is reserving you for eternal fire and torments, which will cling to you for all time. 13 Weren't you ashamed, man as you are, yet most savage, to cut out the tongues of men of like feeling and origin, and having thus abused to torture them? 14 But they, bravely dying, fulfilled their religion towards God. 15 But you will groan as you deserve for having slain without cause the champions of virtue. 16 Therefore," he continued, "I myself, being about to die, 17 will not forsake my kindred. 18 I call upon the God of my fathers to be merciful to my race. 19 But you, both living and dead, he will punish." 20 Thus having prayed, he hurled himself into the pans; and so expired.

13

1 If then, the seven kindred despised troubles even to death, it is admitted on all sides that righteous reasoning is absolute master over the emotions. 2 For just as if they had eaten of the unholy as slaves to the emotions, we would have said that they had been conquered by them. 3 Now it is not so. But by means of the reasoning which is praised by God, they mastered their emotions. 4 It is impossible to overlook the leadership of reflection, for it gained the victory over both emotions and troubles. 5 How, then, can we avoid according to these men mastery of emotion through right reasoning, since they didn't withdraw from the pains of fire? 6 For just as by means of towers projecting in front of harbours men break the threatening waves, and thus assure a still course to vessels entering port, 7 so that seven-towered right-reasoning of the young men, securing the harbour of religion, conquered the tempest of emotions. 8 For having arranged a holy choir of piety, they encouraged one another, saying, 9 "Brothers, may we die brotherly for the law. Let us imitate the three young men in Assyria who despised the equally afflicting furnace. 10 Let's not be cowards in the manifestation of piety." 11 One said, "Courage, brother!" and another, "Nobly endure!" 12 Another said, "Remember of what stock you are;" and by the hand of our father Isaac endured to be slain for the sake of piety. 13 One and all, looking at each other serene and confident, said, "Let's sacrifice with all our heart our souls to God who gave them, and employ our bodies for the keeping of the law. 14 Let's not fear him who thinks he kills; 15 for great is the trial of soul and danger of eternal torment laid up for those who transgress the commandment of God. 16 Let's arm ourselves, therefore, in the self-control, which is divine reasoning. 17 If we suffer like this, Abraham, Isaac, and Jacob will receive us, and all the fathers will commend us. 18 As each one of the kindred was hauled away, the rest exclaimed, "Don't disgrace us, O brother, nor falsify those who died before you!"

19 Now you are not ignorant of the charm of brotherhood, which the Divine and all wise Providence has imparted through fathers to children, and has engendered through the mother's womb. 20 In which these brothers having remained an equal time, and having been formed for the same period, and been increased by the same blood, and having been perfected through the same principle of life, 21 and having been brought forth at equal intervals, and having sucked milk from the same springs, hence their brotherly souls are reared up lovingly together, 22 and increase the more powerfully by reason of this simultaneous rearing, and by daily companionship, and by other education, and exercise in the law of God.

23 Brotherly love being thus sympathetically constituted, the seven kindred had a more sympathetic mutual harmony. 24 For being educated in the same law, and practising the same virtues, and reared up in a just course of life, they increased this harmony with each other. 25 For the same ardour for what is right and honourable increased their goodwill and harmony towards each other. 26 For it acting along with religion, made their brotherly feeling more desirable to them. 27 And yet, although nature, companionship, and virtuous morals increased their brotherly love, those who were left endured to see their kindred, who were mistreated for their religion, tortured even to death.

14

1 More that this, they even urged them on to this mistreatment; so that they not only despised pains themselves, but they even got the better of their affections of brotherly love. 2 Reasoning is more royal than a king, and freer than freemen! 3 What a sacred and harmonious concert of the seven kindred as concerning piety! 4 None of the seven youths turned cowardly or shrank back from death. 5 But all of them, as though running the road to immortality, hastened on to death through tortures. 6 For just as hands and feet are moved sympathetically with the directions of the soul, so those holy youths agreed to death for religion's sake, as through the immortal soul of religion. 7 O holy seven of harmonious kindred! For as the seven days of creation, about religion, 8 so the youths, circling around the number seven, annulled the fear of torments. 9 We now shudder at the recital of the affliction of those young men; but they not only saw, and not only heard the immediate execution of the threat, but undergoing it, persevered; and that through the pains of fire. 10 What could be more painful? For the power of fire, being sharp and quick, speedily dissolved their bodies. 11 Don't think it wonderful that reasoning ruled over those men in their torments, when even a woman's mind despised more manifold pains. 12 For the mother of those seven youths endured the rackings of each of her children.

13 Consider how comprehensive is the love of offspring, which draws every one to sympathy of affection, 14 where irrational animals possess a similar sympathy and love for their offspring with men. 15 The tame birds frequenting the roofs of our houses defend their fledglings. 16 Others build their nests, and hatch their young, on the tops of mountains and in the precipices of valleys, and the holes and tops of trees, and keep away the intruder. 17 If not able to do this, they fly circling round them in agony of affection, calling out in their own note, and save their offspring in whatever manner they are able. 18 But why should we point attention to the sympathy towards children shown by irrational animals? 19 Even bees, at the season of honey-making, attack all who approach, and pierce with their sting, as with a sword, those who draw near their hive, and repel them even to death. 20 But sympathy with her children didn't turn away the mother of the young men, who had a spirit kindred with that of Abraham.

15

1 O reasoning of the sons, lord over the emotions, and religion more desirable to a mother than children! 2 The mother, when two things were set before her, religion and the safety of her seven sons for a time, on the conditional promise of a tyrant, 3 rather elected the religion which according to God preserves to eternal life. 4 In what way can I describe ethically the affections of parents towards their children, the resemblance of soul and of form impressed into the small type of a child in a wonderful manner, especially through the greater sympathy of mothers with the feelings of those born of them! 5 For by how much mothers are by nature weak in disposition and prolific in offspring, by so much the fonder they are of children. 6 Of all mothers, the mother of the seven was the fondest of children, who in seven childbirths had deeply engendered love towards them. 7 Through her many pains undergone in connection with each one, she was compelled to feel sympathy with them; 8 yet, through fear of God, she neglected the temporary salvation of her children. 9 Not only so, but on account of the excellent disposition to the law, her maternal affection towards them was increased. 10 For they were both just and temperate, and courageous, high-minded, fond of their kindred, and so fond of their mother that even to death they obeyed her by observing the law.

11 Yet, though there were so many circumstances connected with love of children to draw on a mother to sympathy, in the case of none of them were the various tortures able to pervert her principle. 12 But she inclined each one separately and all together to death for religion. 13 O holy nature and parental feeling, and reward of bringing up children, and unconquerable maternal affection! 14 At the racking and roasting of each one of them, the observant mother was prevented by religion from changing. 15 She saw her children's flesh dissolving around the fire, and their extremities quivering on the ground, and the flesh of their heads dropped forward down to their beards, like masks.

16 O you mother, who was tried at this time with bitterer pangs than those at birth! 17 O you only woman who have produced perfect holiness! 18 Your firstborn, expiring, didn't turn you, nor the second, looking miserable in his torments, nor the third, breathing out his soul. 19 You didn't weep when you saw each of their eyes looking sternly at their tortures, and their nostrils foreboding death! 20 When you saw children's flesh heaped upon children's flesh that had been torn off, heads decapitated upon heads, dead falling upon the dead, and a choir of children turned through torture into a burying ground, you didn't lament. 21 Not so do siren melodies or songs of swans attract the hearers to listening, O voices of children calling on your mother in the midst of torments! 22 With what and what manner of torments was the mother herself tortured, as her sons were undergoing the wheel and the fires! 23 But religious reasoning, having strengthened her

courage in the midst of sufferings, enabled her to forego, for the time, parental love.

24 Although seeing the destruction of seven children, the noble mother, after one embrace, stripped off her feelings through faith in God. 25 For just as in a council room, seeing in her own soul vehement counsellors, nature and parentage and love of her children, and the racking of her children, 26 she holding two votes, one for the death, the other for the preservation of her children, 27 didn't lean to that which would have saved her children for the safety of a brief space. 28 But this daughter of Abraham remembered his holy fortitude.

29 O holy mother of a nation, avenger of the law, defender of religion, and prime bearer in the battle of the affections! 30 O you nobler in endurance than males, and more courageous than men in perseverance! 31 For like Noah's ship, bearing the world in the world-filling flood, bore up against the waves, 32 so you, the guardian of the law, when surrounded on every side by the flood of emotions, and assaulted by violent storms which were the torments of your children, bore up nobly against the storms against religion.

16

1 If, then, even a woman, and that an aged one, and the mother of seven children, endured to see her children's torments even to death, it must be admitted that religious reasoning is master even of the emotions. 2 I have proved, then, that not only men have obtained the mastery of their emotions, but also that a woman despised the greatest torments. 3 The lions around Daniel were not so fierce, nor the furnace of Misael burning with most vehement fires as that natural love of children burnt within her, when she saw her seven sons tortured. 4 But with the reasoning of religion the mother quenched emotions so great and powerful. 5 For we must consider also this: that, had the woman been faint hearted, as being their mother, she would have lamented over them, and perhaps might have spoken thus: 6 "Ah! I am wretched and many times miserable, who having born seven sons, have become the mother of none. 7 O seven useless childbirths, and seven profitless periods of labour, and fruitless givings of suck, and miserable nursings at the breast. 8 Vainly, for your sakes, O sons, have I endured many pangs, and the more difficult anxieties of rearing. 9 Alas, of my children, some of you unmarried, and some who have married to no profit, I will not see your children, nor have the joy of being a grandmother. 10 Ah, that I who had many and fair children, should be a lone widow full of sorrows! 11 Nor, should I die, will I have a son to bury me." But with such a lament as this, the holy and God-fearing mother wept for none of them. 12 Nor did she divert any of them from death, nor grieve for them as for the dead. 13 But as one possessed with an adamant mind, and as one bringing forth again her full number of sons to immortality, she rather urged them to death on behalf of religion. 14 O woman, soldier of God for religion, you, aged and a female, have conquered through endurance even a tyrant; and even though weak, have been found more powerful in deeds and words. 15 For when you were seized along with your children, you stood looking at Eleazar in torture, and said to your sons in the Hebrew tongue, 16 "O sons, the contest is noble, to which you being called as a witness for the nation, strive zealously for the laws of your country. 17 For it would be disgraceful if this old man endured pains for the sake of righteousness, and that you who are younger would be afraid of the tortures. 18 Remember that through God, you obtained existence and have enjoyed it. 19 Therefore, you ought to bear every affliction because of God. 20 For him also our father Abraham was zealous to sacrifice Isaac our progenitor, and didn't shudder at the sight of his own paternal hand descending down with the sword upon him. 21 The righteous Daniel was cast to the lions; and Ananias, Azarias, and Misael were hurled into a fiery furnace, yet they endured through God. 22 You, then, having the same faith towards God, don't be troubled. 23 For it is unreasonable that they who know religion wouldn't stand up against troubles. 24 With these arguments, the mother of seven, exhorting each of her sons, encouraged and persuaded them not to transgress God's commandment. 25 They saw this, too, that those who die for God, live to God, like Abraham, Isaac, Jacob, and all the patriarchs.

17

1 Some of the spearbearers said that when she herself was about to be seized for the purpose of being put to death, she threw herself on the pile, rather than let them touch her body. 2 O you mother, who together with seven children destroyed the violence of the tyrant, and rendered void his wicked intentions, and exhibited the nobleness of faith! 3 For you, like a house bravely built on the pillar of your children, bore the shock of tortures without swaying. 4 Cheer up, therefore, O holy-minded mother! Hold the firm hope of your steadfastness with God. 5 Not so gracious does the moon appear with the stars in heaven, as you are established as honourable before God, and fixed in the sky with your sons whom you illuminated with religion to the stars. 6 For your bearing of children was after the manner of a child of Abraham.

7 If it were lawful for us to paint as on a tablet the religion of your story, the spectators wouldn't shudder at seeing the mother of seven children enduring for the sake of religion various tortures even to death. 8 It would have been a worthwhile thing to have inscribed on the tomb itself these words as a memorial to those of the nation, 9 "Here an aged priest, and an aged woman, and seven sons, are buried through the violence of a tyrant, who wished to destroy the society of the Hebrews. 10 These also avenged their nation, looking to God, and enduring torments to death."

11 For it was truly a divine contest which was carried through by them. 12 For at that time virtue presided over the contest, approving the victory through endurance, namely, immortality, eternal life. 13 Eleazar was the first to contend. The mother of the seven children entered the contest, and the kindred contended. 14 The tyrant was the antagonist; and the world and living men were the spectators. 15 Reverence for God conquered, and crowned her own athletes. 16 Who didn't admire those champions of true legislation? Who were not amazed? 17 The tyrant himself, and all their council, admired their endurance, 18 through which, they also now stand beside the divine throne and live a blessed life. 19 For Moses says, "All the saints are under your hands." 20 These, therefore, having been sanctified through God, have been honoured not only with this honour, but that also by the fact that because of them, the enemy didn't overcome our nation. 21 That tyrant was punished and their country purified. 22 For they became the ransom to the sin of the nation. The Divine Providence saved Israel, which was afflicted before, by the blood of those pious ones and the death that appeased wrath. 23 For the tyrant Antiochus, looking to their courageous virtue and to their endurance in torture, proclaimed that endurance as an example to his soldiers. 24 They proved to be to him noble and brave for land battles and for sieges; and he conquered and stormed the towns of all his enemies.

18

1 O Israelite children, descendants of the seed of Abraham, obey this law and in every way be religious, 2 knowing that religious reasoning is lord of the emotions, and those not only inward but outward.

3 Therefore those people who gave up their bodies to pains for the sake of religion were not only admired by men, but were deemed worthy of a divine portion. 4 The nation through them obtained peace, and having renewed the observance of the law in their country, drove the enemy out of the land. 5 The tyrant Antiochus was both punished on earth, and is punished now that he is dead; for when he was quite unable to compel the Israelites to adopt foreign customs, and to desert the manner of life of their fathers, 6 then, departing from Jerusalem, he made war against the Persians. 7 The righteous mother of the seven children spoke also as follows to her offspring: "I was a pure virgin, and didn't go beyond my father's house, but I took care of the rib from which woman was made. 8 No destroyer of the desert or ravisher of the plain injured me, nor did the destructive, deceitful snake make plunder of my chaste virginity. I remained with my husband during the time of my maturity. 9 When these, my children, arrived at maturity, their father died. He was blessed! For having sought out a life of fertility in children, he was not grieved with a period of loss of children. 10 He used to teach you, when yet with you, the law and the prophets. 11 He used to read to you about the slaying of Abel by Cain, the offering up of Isaac, and the imprisonment of Joseph. 12 He used to tell you of the zealous Phinehas, and informed you of Ananias, Azarias, and Misael in the fire. 13 He used to glorify Daniel, who was in the den of lions, and pronounce him blessed. 14 He used to remind you of the scripture of Esaias, which says, "Even if you pass through the fire, it won't burn you." 15 He chanted to you David, the hymn writer, who says, "Many are the afflictions of the just." 16 He declared the proverbs of Solomon, who says, "He is a tree of life to all those who do His will." 17 He used to confirm what Ezekiel said: "Will these dry bones live?" 18 For he didn't forget the song which Moses taught, proclaiming, "I will kill, and I will make alive." 19 This is our life and the length of our days.

20 O that bitter, and yet not bitter, day when the bitter tyrant of the Greeks, quenching fire with fire in his cruel cauldrons, brought with boiling rage the seven sons of the daughter of Abraham to the rack, and to all his torments! 21 He pierced the balls of their eyes, and cut out their tongues, and put them to death with varied tortures. 22 Therefore divine retribution pursued and will pursue the pestilent wretch. 23 But the children of Abraham, with their victorious mother, are assembled together to the choir of their father, having received pure and immortal souls from God. 24 To him be glory forever and ever. Amen.

1

1 In the third year of the reign of Jehoiakim king of Judah, Nebuchadnezzar king of Babylon came to Jerusalem and besieged it. 2 The Lord[a] gave Jehoiakim king of Judah into his hand, with part of the vessels of the house of God;[b] and he carried them into the land of Shinar to the house of his god. He brought the vessels into the treasure house of his god.

3 The king spoke to Ashpenaz the master of his eunuchs, that he should bring in some of the children of Israel, even of the royal offspring[c] and of the nobles— 4 youths in whom was no defect, but well-favoured, and skilful in all wisdom, and endowed with knowledge, and understanding science, and who had the ability to serve in the king's palace; and that he should teach them the learning and the language of the Chaldeans. 5 The king appointed for them a daily portion of the king's delicacies, and of the wine which he drank, and that they should be nourished three years; that at its end they should serve the king.

6 Now amongst these were of the children of Judah: Daniel, Hananiah, Mishael, and Azariah. 7 The prince of the eunuchs gave names to them: to Daniel he gave the name Belteshazzar; to Hananiah, Shadrach; to Mishael, Meshach; and to Azariah, Abednego.

8 But Daniel purposed in his heart that he would not defile himself with the king's delicacies, nor with the wine which he drank. Therefore he requested of the prince of the eunuchs that he might not defile himself. 9 Now God made Daniel find kindness and compassion in the sight of the prince of the eunuchs. 10 The prince of the eunuchs said to Daniel, "I fear my lord the king, who has appointed your food and your drink. For why should he see your faces worse looking than the youths who are of your own age? Then you would endanger my head with the king."

11 Then Daniel said to the steward whom the prince of the eunuchs had appointed over Daniel, Hananiah, Mishael, and Azariah: 12 "Test your servants, I beg you, ten days; and let them give us vegetables to eat and water to drink. 13 Then let our faces be examined before you, and the face of the youths who eat of the king's delicacies; and as you see, deal with your servants." 14 So he listened to them in this matter, and tested them for ten days.

15 At the end of ten days, their faces appeared fairer, and they were fatter in flesh, than all the youths who ate of the king's delicacies. 16 So the steward took away their delicacies, and the wine that they would drink, and gave them vegetables.

17 Now as for these four youths, God gave them knowledge and skill in all learning and wisdom; and Daniel had understanding in all visions and dreams.

18 At the end of the days which the king had appointed for bringing them in, the prince of the eunuchs brought them in before Nebuchadnezzar. 19 The king talked with them; and amongst them all was found no one like Daniel, Hananiah, Mishael, and Azariah. Therefore they served the king. 20 In every matter of wisdom and understanding concerning which the king enquired of them, he found them ten times better than all the magicians and enchanters who were in all his realm.

21 Daniel continued serving even to the first year of King Cyrus.

2

1 In the second year of the reign of Nebuchadnezzar, Nebuchadnezzar dreamed dreams; and his spirit was troubled, and his sleep went from him. 2 Then the king commanded that the magicians, the enchanters, the sorcerers, and the Chaldeans be called to tell the king his dreams. So they came in and stood before the king. 3 The king said to them, "I have dreamt a dream, and my spirit is troubled to know the dream."

4 Then the Chaldeans spoke to the king in the Syrian language, "O king, live forever! Tell your servants the dream, and we will show the interpretation."

5 The king answered the Chaldeans, "The thing has gone from me. If you don't make known to me the dream and its interpretation, you will be cut in pieces, and your houses will be made a dunghill. 6 But if you show the dream and its interpretation, you will receive from me gifts, rewards, and great honour. Therefore show me the dream and its interpretation."

7 They answered the second time and said, "Let the king tell his servants the dream, and we will show the interpretation."

8 The king answered, "I know of a certainty that you are trying to gain time, because you see the thing has gone from me. 9 But if you don't make known to me the dream, there is but one law for you; for you have prepared lying and corrupt words to speak before me, until the situation changes. Therefore tell me the dream, and I will know that you can show me its interpretation."

10 The Chaldeans answered before the king, and said, "There is not a man on the earth who can show the king's matter, because no king, lord, or ruler, has asked such a thing of any magician, enchanter, or Chaldean. 11 It is a rare thing that the king requires, and there is no other who can show it before the king, except the gods, whose dwelling is not with flesh."

12 Because of this, the king was angry and very furious, and commanded that all the wise men of Babylon be destroyed. 13 So the decree

went out, and the wise men were to be slain. They sought Daniel and his companions to be slain.

14 Then Daniel returned answer with counsel and prudence to Arioch the captain of the king's guard, who had gone out to kill the wise men of Babylon. 15 He answered Arioch the king's captain, "Why is the decree so urgent from the king?" Then Arioch made the thing known to Daniel. 16 Daniel went in, and desired of the king that he would appoint him a time, and he would show the king the interpretation.

17 Then Daniel went to his house and made the thing known to Hananiah, Mishael, and Azariah, his companions, 18 that they would desire mercies of the God of heaven concerning this secret, and that Daniel and his companions would not perish with the rest of the wise men of Babylon. 19 Then the secret was revealed to Daniel in a vision of the night. Then Daniel blessed the God of heaven. 20 Daniel answered,

"Blessed be the name of God forever and ever;
    for wisdom and might are his.
21 He changes the times and the seasons.
    He removes kings and sets up kings.
He gives wisdom to the wise,
    and knowledge to those who have understanding.
22 He reveals the deep and secret things.
    He knows what is in the darkness,
    and the light dwells with him.
23 I thank you and praise you,
    O God of my fathers,
who have given me wisdom and might,
    and have now made known to me what we desired of you;
    for you have made known to us the king's matter."

24 Therefore Daniel went in to Arioch, whom the king had appointed to destroy the wise men of Babylon. He went and said this to him: "Don't destroy the wise men of Babylon. Bring me in before the king, and I will show to the king the interpretation."

25 Then Arioch brought in Daniel before the king in haste, and said this to him: "I have found a man of the children of the captivity of Judah who will make known to the king the interpretation."

26 The king answered Daniel, whose name was Belteshazzar, "Are you able to make known to me the dream which I have seen, and its interpretation?"

27 Daniel answered before the king, and said, "The secret which the king has demanded can't be shown to the king by wise men, enchanters, magicians, or soothsayers; 28 but there is a God in heaven who reveals secrets, and he has made known to King Nebuchadnezzar what will be in the latter days. Your dream, and the visions of your head on your bed, are these:

29 "As for you, O king, your thoughts came on your bed, what should happen hereafter; and he who reveals secrets has made known to you what will happen. 30 But as for me, this secret is not revealed to me for any wisdom that I have more than any living, but to the intent that the interpretation may be made known to the king, and that you may know the thoughts of your heart.

31 "You, O king, saw, and behold,[d] a great image. This image, which was mighty, and whose brightness was excellent, stood before you; and its appearance was terrifying. 32 As for this image, its head was of fine gold, its breast and its arms of silver, its belly and its thighs of bronze, 33 its legs of iron, its feet part of iron, and part of clay. 34 You saw until a stone was cut out without hands, which struck the image on its feet that were of iron and clay, and broke them in pieces. 35 Then the iron, the clay, the bronze, the silver, and the gold were broken in pieces together, and became like the chaff of the summer threshing floors. The wind carried them away, so that no place was found for them. The stone that struck the image became a great mountain, and filled the whole earth.

36 "This is the dream; and we will tell its interpretation before the king. 37 You, O king, are king of kings, to whom the God of heaven has given the kingdom, the power, the strength, and the glory. 38 Wherever the children of men dwell, he has given the animals of the field and the birds of the sky into your hand, and has made you rule over them all. You are the head of gold.

39 "After you, another kingdom will arise that is inferior to you; and a third kingdom of bronze, which will rule over all the earth. 40 The fourth kingdom will be strong as iron, because iron breaks in pieces and subdues all things; and as iron that crushes all these, it will break in pieces and crush. 41 Whereas you saw the feet and toes, part of potters' clay, and part of iron, it will be a divided kingdom; but there will be in it of the strength of the iron, because you saw the iron mixed with miry clay. 42 As the toes of the feet were part of iron, and part of clay, so the kingdom will be partly strong, and partly brittle. 43 Whereas you saw the iron mixed with miry clay, they will mingle themselves with the seed of men; but they won't cling to one another, even as iron does not mix with clay.

44 "In the days of those kings the God of heaven will set up a kingdom which will never be destroyed, nor will its sovereignty be left to another people; but it will break in pieces and consume all these kingdoms, and it will stand forever. 45 Because you saw that a stone was cut out of the mountain without hands, and that it broke in pieces the iron, the bronze, the clay, the silver, and the gold. The great God has made known to the king

---

a *1:2* The word translated "Lord" is "Adonai."

b *1:2* The Hebrew word rendered "God" is "אֱלֹהִים" (Elohim).

c *1:3* or, seed

d *2:31* "Behold", from "הֵנֵּה", means look at, take notice, observe, see, or gaze at. It is often used as an interjection.

what will happen hereafter. The dream is certain, and its interpretation sure."

46 Then King Nebuchadnezzar fell on his face, worshipped Daniel, and commanded that they should offer an offering and sweet odours to him. 47 The king answered to Daniel, and said, "Of a truth your God is the God of gods, and the Lord of kings, and a revealler of secrets, since you have been able to reveal this secret."

48 Then the king made Daniel great, and gave him many great gifts, and made him rule over the whole province of Babylon, and to be chief governor over all the wise men of Babylon. 49 Daniel requested of the king, and he appointed Shadrach, Meshach, and Abednego over the affairs of the province of Babylon; but Daniel was in the king's gate.

3

1 Nebuchadnezzar the king made an image of gold, whose height was sixty cubits,[a] and its width six cubits. He set it up in the plain of Dura, in the province of Babylon. 2 Then Nebuchadnezzar the king sent to gather together the local governors, the deputies, and the governors, the judges, the treasurers, the counsellors, the sheriffs, and all the rulers of the provinces, to come to the dedication of the image which Nebuchadnezzar the king had set up. 3 Then the local governors, the deputies, and the governors, the judges, the treasurers, the counsellors, the sheriffs, and all the rulers of the provinces, were gathered together to the dedication of the image that Nebuchadnezzar the king had set up; and they stood before the image that Nebuchadnezzar had set up.

4 Then the herald cried aloud, "To you it is commanded, peoples, nations, and languages, 5 that whenever you hear the sound of the horn, flute, zither, lyre, harp, pipe, and all kinds of music, you fall down and worship the golden image that Nebuchadnezzar the king has set up. 6 Whoever doesn't fall down and worship shall be cast into the middle of a burning fiery furnace the same hour."

7 Therefore at that time, when all the peoples heard the sound of the horn, flute, zither, lyre, harp, pipe, and all kinds of music, all the peoples, the nations, and the languages, fell down and worshipped the golden image that Nebuchadnezzar the king had set up.

8 Therefore at that time certain Chaldeans came near, and brought accusation against the Jews. 9 They answered Nebuchadnezzar the king, "O king, live for ever! 10 You, O king, have made a decree that every man who hears the sound of the horn, flute, zither, lyre, harp, pipe, and all kinds of music shall fall down and worship the golden image; 11 and whoever doesn't fall down and worship shall be cast into the middle of a burning fiery furnace. 12 There are certain Jews whom you have appointed over the affairs of the province of Babylon: Shadrach, Meshach, and Abednego. These men, O king, have not respected you. They don't serve your gods, and don't worship the golden image which you have set up."

13 Then Nebuchadnezzar in rage and fury commanded that Shadrach, Meshach, and Abednego be brought. Then these men were brought before the king. 14 Nebuchadnezzar answered them, "Is it on purpose, Shadrach, Meshach, and Abednego, that you don't serve my god, nor worship the golden image which I have set up? 15 Now if you are ready whenever you hear the sound of the horn, flute, zither, lyre, harp, pipe, and all kinds of music to fall down and worship the image which I have made, good; but if you don't worship, you shall be cast the same hour into the middle of a burning fiery furnace. Who is that god who will deliver you out of my hands?"

16 Shadrach, Meshach, and Abednego answered the king, "Nebuchadnezzar, we have no need to answer you in this matter. 17 If it happens, our God whom we serve is able to deliver us from the burning fiery furnace; and he will deliver us out of your hand, O king. 18 But if not, let it be known to you, O king, that we will not serve your gods or worship the golden image which you have set up."

19 Then Nebuchadnezzar was full of fury, and the form of his appearance was changed against Shadrach, Meshach, and Abednego. He spoke, and commanded that they should heat the furnace seven times more than it was usually heated. 20 He commanded certain mighty men who were in his army to bind Shadrach, Meshach, and Abednego, and to cast them into the burning fiery furnace. 21 Then these men were bound in their pants, their tunics, their mantles, and their other clothes, and were cast into the middle of the burning fiery furnace. 22 Therefore because the king's commandment was urgent, and the furnace exceedingly hot, the flame of the fire killed those men who took up Shadrach, Meshach, and Abednego. 23 These three men, Shadrach, Meshach, and Abednego, fell down bound into the middle of the burning fiery furnace.

THE SONG OF THE THREE HOLY CHILDREN[b]

24 They walked in the midst of the fire, praising God, and blessing the Lord. 25 Then Azarias stood, and prayed like this. Opening his mouth in the midst of the fire he said, 26 "Blessed are you, O Lord, you God of our fathers! Your name is worthy to be praised and glorified for evermore; 27 for you are righteous in all the things that you have done. Yes, all your works are true. Your ways are right, and all your judgements are truth. 28 In all the things that you have brought upon us, and upon the holy city of our fathers, Jerusalem, you have executed true judgements. For according to truth and

justice you have brought all these things upon us because of our sins. 29 For we have sinned and committed iniquity in departing from you. 30 In all things we have trespassed, and not obeyed your commandments or kept them. We haven't done as you have commanded us, that it might go well with us. 31 Therefore all that you have brought upon us, and everything that you have done to us, you have done in true judgement. 32 You delivered us into the hands of lawless enemies, most hateful rebels, and to an unjust king who is the most wicked in all the world. 33 And now we can't open our mouth. Shame and reproach have come on your servants and those who worship you. 34 Don't utterly deliver us up, for your name's sake. Don't annul your covenant. 35 Don't cause your mercy to depart from us, for the sake of Abraham who is loved by you, and for the sake of Isaac your servant, and Israel your holy one, 36 to whom you promised that you would multiply their offspring as the stars of the sky, and as the sand that is on the sea shore. 37 For we, O Lord, have become less than any nation, and are brought low this day in all the world because of our sins. 38 There isn't at this time prince, or prophet, or leader, or burnt offering, or sacrifice, or oblation, or incense, or place to offer before you, and to find mercy. 39 Nevertheless in a contrite heart and a humble spirit let us be accepted, 40 like the burnt offerings of rams and bullocks, and like ten thousands of fat lambs. So let our sacrifice be in your sight this day, that we may wholly go after you, for they shall not be ashamed who put their trust in you. 41 And now we follow you with all our heart. We fear you, and seek your face. 42 Put us not to shame; but deal with us after your kindness, and according to the multitude of your mercy. 43 Deliver us also according to your marvellous works, and give glory to your name, O Lord. Let all those who harm your servants be confounded. 44 Let them be ashamed of all their power and might, and let their strength be broken. 45 Let them know that you are the Lord, the only God, and glorious over the whole world."

46 The king's servants who put them in didn't stop making the furnace hot with naphtha, pitch, tinder, and small wood, 47 so that the flame streamed out forty nine cubits above the furnace. 48 It spread and burnt those Chaldeans whom it found around the furnace. 49 But the angel of the Lord came down into the furnace together with Azarias and his fellows, and he struck the flame of the fire out of the furnace, 50 and made the midst of the furnace as it had been a moist whistling wind, so that the fire didn't touch them at all. It neither hurt nor troubled them.

51 Then the three, as out of one mouth, praised, glorified, and blessed God in the furnace, saying, 52 "Blessed are you, O Lord, you God of our fathers, to be praised and exalted above all forever! 53 Blessed is your glorious and holy name, to be praised and exalted above all forever! 54 Blessed are you in the temple of your holy glory, to be praised and glorified above all forever! 55 Blessed are you who see the depths and sit upon the cherubim, to be praised and exalted above all forever. 56 Blessed are you on the throne of your kingdom, to be praised and extolled above all forever! 57 Blessed are you in the firmament of heaven, to be praised and glorified forever!

58 O all you works of the Lord, bless the Lord! Praise and exalt him above all forever! 59 O you heavens, bless the Lord! Praise and exalt him above all for ever! 60 O you angels of the Lord, bless the Lord! Praise and exalt him above all forever! 61 O all you waters that are above the sky, bless the Lord! Praise and exalt him above all forever! 62 O all you powers of the Lord, bless the Lord! Praise and exalt him above all forever! 63 O you sun and moon, bless the Lord! Praise and exalt him above all forever! 64 O you stars of heaven, bless the Lord! Praise and exalt him above all forever! 65 O every shower and dew, bless the Lord! Praise and exalt him above all forever! 66 O all you winds, bless the Lord! Praise and exalt him above all forever! 67 O you fire and heat, bless the Lord! Praise and exalt him above all forever! 68 O you dews and storms of snow, bless the Lord! Praise and exalt him above all forever! 69 O you nights and days, bless the Lord! Praise and exalt him above all forever! 70 O you light and darkness, bless the Lord! Praise and exalt him above all forever! 71 O you cold and heat, bless the Lord! Praise and exalt him above all forever! 72 O you frost and snow, bless the Lord! Praise and exalt him above all forever! 73 O you lightnings and clouds, bless the Lord! Praise and exalt him above all forever! 74 O let the earth bless the Lord! Let it praise and exalt him above all forever! 75 O you mountains and hills, bless the Lord! Praise and exalt him above all forever! 76 O all you things that grow on the earth, bless the Lord! Praise and exalt him above all forever! 77 [c]O sea and rivers, bless the Lord! Praise and exalt him above all forever! 78 O you springs, bless the Lord! Praise and exalt him above all forever! 79 O you whales and all that move in the waters, bless the Lord! Praise and exalt him above all forever! 80 O all you birds of the air, bless the Lord! Praise and exalt him above all forever! 81 O all you beasts and cattle, bless the Lord! Praise and exalt him above all forever! 82 O you children of men, bless the Lord! Praise and exalt him above all forever! 83 O let Israel bless the Lord! Praise and exalt him above all forever. 84 O you priests of the Lord, bless the Lord! Praise and exalt him above all forever! 85 O you servants of the Lord, bless the Lord! Praise and exalt him above all forever! 86 O you spirits and souls of the righteous, bless the Lord! Praise and exalt him above all forever! 87 O you who are holy and humble of heart, bless the Lord! Praise and exalt him above all forever! 88 O Hananiah, Mishael, and Azariah, bless the Lord! Praise and exalt him above all forever;

---

a 3:1 A cubit is the length from the tip of the middle finger to the elbow on a man's arm, or about 18 inches or 46 centimetres.

b 3:24 The Song of the Three Holy Children is an addition to Daniel found in the Greek Septuagint but not found in the traditional Hebrew text of Daniel. This portion is recognised as Deuterocanonical Scripture by the Roman Catholic, Greek Orthodox, and Russian Orthodox Churches. It is found inserted between Daniel 3:23 and Daniel 3:24 of the traditional Hebrew Bible. Here, the verses after 23 from the Hebrew Bible are numbered starting at 91 to make room for these verses.

c 3:77 Some authorities transpose this verse and the next one.

for he has rescued us from Hades, and saved us from the hand of death! He has delivered us out of the midst of the furnace and burning flame. He has delivered us out of the midst of the fire. ₈₉ O give thanks to the Lord, for he is good; for his mercy is forever. ₉₀ O all you who worship the Lord, bless the God of gods, praise him, and give him thanks; for his mercy is forever!"

Deliverance from the Furnace

₉₁ ᵃ Then Nebuchadnezzar the king was astonished and rose up in haste. He spoke and said to his counsellors, "Didn't we cast three men bound into the middle of the fire?"

They answered the king, "True, O king."

₉₂ He answered, "Look, I see four men loose, walking in the middle of the fire, and they are unharmed. The appearance of the fourth is like a son of the gods."

₉₃ Then Nebuchadnezzar came near to the mouth of the burning fiery furnace. He spoke and said, "Shadrach, Meshach, and Abednego, you servants of the Most High God, come out, and come here!"

Then Shadrach, Meshach, and Abednego came out of the middle of the fire. ₉₄ The local governors, the deputies, and the governors, and the king's counsellors, being gathered together, saw these men, that the fire had no power on their bodies. The hair of their head wasn't singed. Their pants weren't changed. The smell of fire wasn't even on them.

₉₅ Nebuchadnezzar spoke and said, "Blessed be the God of Shadrach, Meshach, and Abednego, who has sent his angel and delivered his servants who trusted in him, and have changed the king's word, and have yielded their bodies, that they might not serve nor worship any god, except their own God. ₉₆ Therefore I make a decree, that every people, nation, and language, who speak anything evil against the God of Shadrach, Meshach, and Abednego, shall be cut in pieces, and their houses shall be made a dunghill, because there is no other god who is able to deliver like this."

₉₇ Then the king promoted Shadrach, Meshach, and Abednego in the province of Babylon.

4

₁ Nebuchadnezzar the king,

to all the peoples, nations, and languages, who dwell in all the earth:

Peace be multiplied to you.

₂ It has seemed good to me to show the signs and wonders that the Most High God has worked towards me.

₃ How great are his signs!

How mighty are his wonders!

His kingdom is an everlasting kingdom.

His dominion is from generation to generation.

₄ I, Nebuchadnezzar, was at rest in my house, and flourishing in my palace. ₅ I saw a dream which made me afraid; and the thoughts on my bed and the visions of my head troubled me. ₆ Therefore I made a decree to bring in all the wise men of Babylon before me, that they might make known to me the interpretation of the dream. ₇ Then the magicians, the enchanters, the Chaldeans, and the soothsayers came in; and I told the dream before them; but they didn't make known to me its interpretation. ₈ But at the last Daniel came in before me, whose name was Belteshazzar, according to the name of my god, and in whom is the spirit of the holy gods. I told the dream before him, saying,

₉ "Belteshazzar, master of the magicians, because I know that the spirit of the holy gods is in you, and no secret troubles you, tell me the visions of my dream that I have seen, and its interpretation. ₁₀ These were the visions of my head on my bed: I saw, and behold, a tree in the middle of the earth; and its height was great. ₁₁ The tree grew, and was strong, and its height reached to the sky, and its sight to the end of all the earth. ₁₂ Its leaves were beautiful, and it had much fruit, and in it was food for all. The animals of the field had shade under it, and the birds of the sky lived in its branches, and all flesh was fed from it.

₁₃ "I saw in the visions of my head on my bed, and behold, a watcher and a holy one came down from the sky. ₁₄ He cried aloud, and said this, 'Cut down the tree and cut off its branches! Shake off its leaves and scatter its fruit! Let the animals get away from under it, and the fowls from its branches. ₁₅ Nevertheless leave the stump of its roots in the earth, even with a band of iron and bronze, in the tender grass of the field; and let it be wet with the dew of the sky. Let his portion be with the animals in the grass of the earth. ₁₆ Let his heart be changed from man's, and let an animal's heart be given to him. Then let seven times pass over him.

₁₇ "'The sentence is by the decree of the watchers, and the demand by the word of the holy ones, to the intent that the living may know that the Most High rules in the kingdom of men, and gives it to whomever he will, and sets up over it the lowest of men.'

₁₈ "This dream I, King Nebuchadnezzar, have seen; and you, Belteshazzar, declare the interpretation, because all the wise men of my kingdom are not able to make known to me the interpretation; but you are able, for the spirit of the holy gods is in you."

₁₉ Then Daniel, whose name was Belteshazzar, was stricken mute for a while, and his thoughts troubled him. The king answered, "Belteshazzar, don't let the dream, or the interpretation, trouble you."

Belteshazzar answered, "My lord, may the dream be for those who hate you, and its interpretation to your adversaries. ₂₀ The tree that you saw, which grew and was strong, whose height reached to the sky, and its sight to all the earth; ₂₁ whose leaves were beautiful, and its fruit plentiful, and in it was food for all; under which the animals of the field lived, and on whose branches the birds of the sky had their habitation— ₂₂ it is you, O king, who have grown and become strong; for your greatness has grown, and reaches to the sky, and your dominion to the end of the earth.

₂₃ "Whereas the king saw a watcher and a holy one coming down from the sky, and saying, 'Cut down the tree, and destroy it; nevertheless leave the stump of its roots in the earth, even with a band of iron and bronze, in the tender grass of the field, and let it be wet with the dew of the sky. Let his portion be with the animals of the field, until seven times pass over him.'

₂₄ "This is the interpretation, O king, and it is the decree of the Most High, which has come on my lord the king: ₂₅ that you shall be driven from men, and your dwelling shall be with the animals of the field. You shall be made to eat grass as oxen, and shall be wet with the dew of the sky, and seven times shall pass over you; until you know that the Most High rules in the kingdom of men, and gives it to whomever he will. ₂₆ Their command to leave the stump of the roots of the tree means your kingdom will be sure to you, after you will have known that the heavens do rule. ₂₇ Therefore, O king, let my counsel be acceptable to you, and break off your sins by righteousness, and your iniquities by showing mercy to the poor. Perhaps there may be a lengthening of your tranquillity."

₂₈ All this came on the King Nebuchadnezzar. ₂₉ At the end of twelve months he was walking in the royal palace of Babylon. ₃₀ The king spoke and said, "Is not this great Babylon, which I have built for the royal dwelling place, by the might of my power and for the glory of my majesty?"

₃₁ While the word was in the king's mouth, a voice came from the sky, saying, "O King Nebuchadnezzar, to you it is spoken: 'The kingdom has departed from you. ₃₂ You shall be driven from men, and your dwelling shall be with the animals of the field. You shall be made to eat grass as oxen. Seven times shall pass over you, until you know that the Most High rules in the kingdom of men, and gives it to whomever he will.'"

₃₃ This was fulfilled the same hour on Nebuchadnezzar. He was driven from men, and ate grass as oxen, and his body was wet with the dew of the sky, until his hair had grown like eagles' feathers, and his nails like birds' claws.

₃₄ At the end of the days I, Nebuchadnezzar, lifted up my eyes to heaven, and my understanding returned to me, and I blessed the Most High, and I praised and honoured him who lives forever.

For his dominion is an everlasting dominion,

and his kingdom from generation to generation.

₃₅ All the inhabitants of the earth are reputed as nothing;

and he does according to his will in the army of heaven,

and amongst the inhabitants of the earth;

and no one can stop his hand,

or ask him, "What are you doing?"

₃₆ At the same time my understanding returned to me; and for the glory of my kingdom, my majesty and brightness returned to me. My counsellors and my lords sought me; and I was established in my kingdom, and excellent greatness was added to me. ₃₇ Now I, Nebuchadnezzar, praise and extol and honour the King of heaven; for all his works are right and his ways just; and those who walk in pride he is able to humble.

5

₁ Belshazzar the king made a great feast to a thousand of his lords, and drank wine before the thousand. ₂ Belshazzar, while he tasted the wine, commanded that the golden and silver vessels which Nebuchadnezzar his father had taken out of the temple which was in Jerusalem be brought to him, that the king and his lords, his wives and his concubines, might drink from them. ₃ Then they brought the golden vessels that were taken out of the temple of God's house which was at Jerusalem; and the king and his lords, his wives and his concubines, drank from them. ₄ They drank wine, and praised the gods of gold, and of silver, of bronze, of iron, of wood, and of stone.

₅ In the same hour, the fingers of a man's hand came out and wrote near the lamp stand on the plaster of the wall of the king's palace. The king saw the part of the hand that wrote. ₆ Then the king's face was changed in him, and his thoughts troubled him; and the joints of his thighs were loosened, and his knees struck one against another.

₇ The king cried aloud to bring in the enchanters, the Chaldeans, and the soothsayers. The king spoke and said to the wise men of Babylon,

---

ᵃ *3:91* Verses 91-97 were numbered 24-30 in the traditional Hebrew text of Daniel.

"Whoever reads this writing and shows me its interpretation shall be clothed with purple, and have a chain of gold about his neck, and shall be the third ruler in the kingdom."

8 Then all the king's wise men came in; but they could not read the writing and couldn't make known to the king the interpretation. 9 Then King Belshazzar was greatly troubled. His face was changed in him, and his lords were perplexed.

10 The queen by reason of the words of the king and his lords came into the banquet house. The queen spoke and said, "O king, live forever; don't let your thoughts trouble you, nor let your face be changed. 11 There is a man in your kingdom in whom is the spirit of the holy gods. In the days of your father, light, understanding, and wisdom like the wisdom of the gods were found in him. The king, Nebuchadnezzar, your father—yes, the king, your father—made him master of the magicians, enchanters, Chaldeans, and soothsayers 12 because an excellent spirit, knowledge, understanding, interpreting of dreams, showing of dark sentences, and dissolving of doubts were found in the same Daniel, whom the king named Belteshazzar. Now let Daniel be called, and he will show the interpretation."

13 Then Daniel was brought in before the king. The king spoke and said to Daniel, "Are you that Daniel of the children of the captivity of Judah, whom the king my father brought out of Judah? 14 I have heard of you, that the spirit of the gods is in you, and that light, understanding, and excellent wisdom are found in you. 15 Now the wise men, the enchanters, have been brought in before me to read this writing, and make known to me its interpretation; but they could not show the interpretation of the thing. 16 But I have heard of you, that you can give interpretations and dissolve doubts. Now if you can read the writing, and make known to me its interpretation, you shall be clothed with purple, and have a chain of gold around your neck, and shall be the third ruler in the kingdom."

17 Then Daniel answered the king, "Let your gifts be to yourself, and give your rewards to another. Nevertheless, I will read the writing to the king, and make known to him the interpretation.

18 "To you, king, the Most High God gave Nebuchadnezzar your father the kingdom, and greatness, and glory, and majesty. 19 Because of the greatness that he gave him, all the peoples, nations, and languages trembled and feared before him. He killed whom he wanted to, and he kept alive whom he wanted to. He raised up whom he wanted to, and he put down whom he wanted to. 20 But when his heart was lifted up, and his spirit was hardened so that he dealt proudly, he was deposed from his kingly throne, and they took his glory from him. 21 He was driven from the sons of men and his heart was made like the animals', and his dwelling was with the wild donkeys. He was fed with grass like oxen, and his body was wet with the dew of the sky, until he knew that the Most High God rules in the kingdom of men, and that he sets up over it whomever he will.

22 "You, his son, Belshazzar, have not humbled your heart, though you knew all this, 23 but have lifted up yourself against the Lord of heaven; and they have brought the vessels of his house before you, and you and your lords, your wives, and your concubines, have drunk wine from them. You have praised the gods of silver, gold, bronze, iron, wood, and stone, which don't see, hear, or know; and you have not glorified the God in whose hand is your breath and whose are all your ways. 24 Then the part of the hand was sent from before him, and this writing was inscribed.

25 "This is the writing that was inscribed: 'MENE, MENE, TEKEL, UPHARSIN.'

26 "This is the interpretation of the thing:
MENE: God has counted your kingdom, and brought it to an end.
27 TEKEL: you are weighed in the balances, and are found wanting.
28 PERES: your kingdom is divided, and given to the Medes and Persians."

29 Then Belshazzar commanded, and they clothed Daniel with purple, and put a chain of gold about his neck, and proclaimed that he should be the third highest ruler in the kingdom.

30 In that night Belshazzar the Chaldean King was slain. 31 Darius the Mede received the kingdom, being about sixty-two years old.

6

1 It pleased Darius to set over the kingdom one hundred and twenty local governors, who should be throughout the whole kingdom; 2 and over them three presidents, of whom Daniel was one; that these local governors might give account to them, and that the king should suffer no loss. 3 Then this Daniel was distinguished above the presidents and the local governors, because an excellent spirit was in him; and the king thought to set him over the whole realm.

4 Then the presidents and the local governors sought to find occasion against Daniel as touching the kingdom; but they could find no occasion or fault, because he was faithful. There wasn't any error or fault found in him. 5 Then these men said, "We won't find any occasion against this Daniel, unless we find it against him concerning the law of his God."

6 Then these presidents and local governors assembled together to the king, and said this to him, "King Darius, live forever! 7 All the presidents of the kingdom, the deputies and the local governors, the counsellors and the governors, have consulted together to establish a royal statute, and to make a strong decree, that whoever asks a petition of any god or man for thirty days, except of you, O king, he shall be cast into the den of lions. 8 Now, O king, establish the decree, and sign the writing, that it not be changed, according to the law of the Medes and Persians, which doesn't alter." 9 Therefore King Darius signed the writing and the decree.

10 When Daniel knew that the writing was signed, he went into his house (now his windows were open in his room towards Jerusalem) and he knelt on his knees three times a day, and prayed, and gave thanks before his God, as he did before. 11 Then these men assembled together, and found Daniel making petition and supplication before his God. 12 Then they came near, and spoke before the king concerning the king's decree: "Haven't you signed a decree that every man who makes a petition to any god or man within thirty days, except to you, O king, shall be cast into the den of lions?"

The king answered, "This thing is true, according to the law of the Medes and Persians, which doesn't alter."

13 Then they answered and said before the king, "That Daniel, who is of the children of the captivity of Judah, doesn't respect you, O king, nor the decree that you have signed, but makes his petition three times a day." 14 Then the king, when he heard these words, was very displeased, and set his heart on Daniel to deliver him; and he laboured until the going down of the sun to rescue him.

15 Then these men assembled together to the king, and said to the king, "Know, O king, that it is a law of the Medes and Persians, that no decree nor statute which the king establishes may be changed."

16 Then the king commanded, and they brought Daniel, and cast him into the den of lions. The king spoke and said to Daniel, "Your God whom you serve continually, he will deliver you."

17 A stone was brought, and laid on the mouth of the den; and the king sealed it with his own signet, and with the signet of his lords, that nothing might be changed concerning Daniel. 18 Then the king went to his palace, and passed the night fasting. No musical instruments were brought before him; and his sleep fled from him.

19 Then the king arose very early in the morning, and went in haste to the den of lions. 20 When he came near to the den to Daniel, he cried with a troubled voice. The king spoke and said to Daniel, "Daniel, servant of the living God, is your God, whom you serve continually, able to deliver you from the lions?"

21 Then Daniel said to the king, "O king, live forever! 22 My God has sent his angel, and has shut the lions' mouths, and they have not hurt me; because I am innocent in his sight. Also before you, O king, I have done no harm."

23 Then the king was exceedingly glad, and commanded that they should take Daniel up out of the den. So Daniel was taken up out of the den, and no kind of harm was found on him, because he had trusted in his God.

24 The king commanded, and they brought those men who had accused Daniel, and they cast them into the den of lions—them, their children, and their wives; and the lions mauled them and broke all their bones in pieces before they came to the bottom of the den.

25 Then King Darius wrote to all the peoples, nations, and languages, who dwell in all the earth:
"Peace be multiplied to you.
26 "I make a decree that in all the dominion of my kingdom men tremble and fear before the God of Daniel;
"for he is the living God,
    and steadfast forever.
His kingdom is that which will not be destroyed.
    His dominion will be even to the end.
27 He delivers and rescues.
    He works signs and wonders in heaven and in earth,
    who has delivered Daniel from the power of the lions."

28 So this Daniel prospered in the reign of Darius, and in the reign of Cyrus the Persian.

7

1 In the first year of Belshazzar king of Babylon, Daniel had a dream and visions of his head on his bed. Then he wrote the dream and told the sum of the matters.

2 Daniel spoke and said, "I saw in my vision by night and behold, the four winds of the sky broke out on the great sea. 3 Four great animals came up from the sea, different from one another.

4 "The first was like a lion, and had eagle's wings. I watched until its wings were plucked, and it was lifted up from the earth, and made to stand on two feet as a man. A man's heart was given to it.

5 "Behold, there was another animal, a second, like a bear. It was raised up on one side, and three ribs were in its mouth between its teeth. They said this to it: 'Arise! Devour much flesh!'

6 "After this I saw, and behold, another, like a leopard, which had on its back four wings of a bird. The animal also had four heads; and dominion was given to it.

7 "After this I saw in the night visions, and, behold, there was a fourth animal, awesome and powerful, and exceedingly strong. It had great iron teeth. It devoured and broke in pieces, and stamped the residue with its feet. It was different from all the animals that were before it. It had ten horns.

8 "I considered the horns, and behold, another horn came up amongst them, a little one, before which three of the first horns were plucked up by the roots: and behold, in this horn were eyes like the eyes of a man, and a mouth speaking great things.

9 "I watched until thrones were placed,
    and one who was ancient of days sat.
His clothing was white as snow,
    and the hair of his head like pure wool.
His throne was fiery flames,
    and its wheels burning fire.
10 A fiery stream issued and came out from before him.
    Thousands of thousands ministered to him.
    Ten thousand times ten thousand stood before him.
The judgement was set.

The books were opened.

11 "I watched at that time because of the voice of the great words which the horn spoke. I watched even until the animal was slain, its body destroyed, and it was given to be burnt with fire. 12 As for the rest of the animals, their dominion was taken away; yet their lives were prolonged for a season and a time.

13 "I saw in the night visions, and behold, one like a son of man came with the clouds, and he came to the ancient of days, and they brought him near before him. 14 Dominion was given him, with glory and a kingdom, that all the peoples, nations, and languages should serve him. His dominion is an everlasting dominion, which will not pass away, and his kingdom will not be destroyed.

15 "As for me, Daniel, my spirit was grieved within my body, and the visions of my head troubled me. 16 I came near to one of those who stood by, and asked him the truth concerning all this.

"So he told me, and made me know the interpretation of the things. 17 'These great animals, which are four, are four kings, who will arise out of the earth. 18 But the saints of the Most High will receive the kingdom, and possess the kingdom forever, even forever and ever.'

19 "Then I desired to know the truth concerning the fourth animal, which was different from all of them, exceedingly terrible, whose teeth were of iron, and its nails of bronze; which devoured, broke in pieces, and stamped the residue with its feet; 20 and concerning the ten horns that were on its head, and the other horn which came up, and before which three fell, even that horn that had eyes, and a mouth that spoke great things, whose look was more stout than its fellows. 21 I saw, and the same horn made war with the saints and prevailed against them 22 until the ancient of days came, and judgement was given to the saints of the Most High, and the time came that the saints possessed the kingdom.

23 "So he said, 'The fourth animal will be a fourth kingdom on earth, which will be different from all the kingdoms, and will devour the whole earth, and will tread it down, and break it in pieces. 24 As for the ten horns, ten kings will arise out of this kingdom. Another will arise after them; and he will be different from the former, and he will put down three kings. 25 He will speak words against the Most High, and will wear out the saints of the Most High. He will plan to change the times and the law; and they will be given into his hand until a time and times and half a time.

26 "'But the judgement will be set, and they will take away his dominion, to consume and to destroy it to the end. 27 The kingdom and the dominion, and the greatness of the kingdoms under the whole sky, will be given to the people of the saints of the Most High. His kingdom is an everlasting kingdom, and all dominions will serve and obey him.'

28 "Here is the end of the matter. As for me, Daniel, my thoughts troubled me greatly, and my face was changed in me; but I kept the matter in my heart."

8

1 In the third year of the reign of King Belshazzar, a vision appeared to me, even to me, Daniel, after that which appeared to me at the first. 2 I saw the vision. Now it was so, that when I saw, I was in the citadel of Susa, which is in the province of Elam. I saw in the vision, and I was by the river Ulai. 3 Then I lifted up my eyes, and saw, and behold, a ram which had two horns stood before the river. The two horns were high; but one was higher than the other, and the higher came up last. 4 I saw the ram pushing westward, northward, and southward. No animals could stand before him. There wasn't anyone who could deliver out of his hand; but he did according to his will, and magnified himself.

5 As I was considering, behold, a male goat came from the west over the surface of the whole earth, and didn't touch the ground. The goat had a notable horn between his eyes. 6 He came to the ram that had the two horns, which I saw standing before the river, and ran on him in the fury of his power. 7 I saw him come close to the ram, and he was moved with anger against him, and struck the ram, and broke his two horns. There was no power in the ram to stand before him; but he cast him down to the ground, and trampled on him. There was no one who could deliver the ram out of his hand. 8 The male goat magnified himself exceedingly. When he was strong, the great horn was broken; and instead of it there came up four notable horns towards the four winds of the sky.

9 Out of one of them came out a little horn, which grew exceedingly great, towards the south, and towards the east, and towards the glorious land. 10 It grew great, even to the army of the sky; and it cast down some of the army and of the stars to the ground, and trampled on them. 11 Yes, it magnified itself, even to the prince of the army; and it took away from him the continual burnt offering, and the place of his sanctuary was cast down. 12 The army was given over to it together with the continual burnt offering through disobedience. It cast down truth to the ground, and it did its pleasure and prospered.

13 Then I heard a holy one speaking; and another holy one said to that certain one who spoke, "How long will the vision about the continual burnt offering, and the disobedience that makes desolate, to give both the sanctuary and the army to be trodden under foot be?"

14 He said to me, "To two thousand and three hundred evenings and mornings. Then the sanctuary will be cleansed."

15 When I, even I Daniel, had seen the vision, I sought to understand it. Then behold, there stood before me something like the appearance of a man. 16 I heard a man's voice between the banks of the Ulai, which called, and said, "Gabriel, make this man understand the vision."

17 So he came near where I stood; and when he came, I was frightened, and fell on my face; but he said to me, "Understand, son of man; for the vision belongs to the time of the end."

18 Now as he was speaking with me, I fell into a deep sleep with my face towards the ground; but he touched me, and set me upright. 19 He said, "Behold, I will make you know what will be in the latter time of the indignation; for it belongs to the appointed time of the end. 20 The ram which you saw, that had the two horns, they are the kings of Media and Persia. 21 The rough male goat is the king of Greece. The great horn that is between his eyes is the first king. 22 As for that which was broken, in the place where four stood up, four kingdoms will stand up out of the nation, but not with his power.

23 "In the latter time of their kingdom, when the transgressors have come to the full, a king of fierce face, and understanding dark sentences, will stand up. 24 His power will be mighty, but not by his own power. He will destroy awesomely, and will prosper in what he does. He will destroy the mighty ones and the holy people. 25 Through his policy he will cause deceit to prosper in his hand. He will magnify himself in his heart, and he will destroy many in their security. He will also stand up against the prince of princes; but he will be broken without human power.

26 "The vision of the evenings and mornings which has been told is true; but seal up the vision, for it belongs to many days to come."

27 I, Daniel, fainted, and was sick for some days. Then I rose up, and did the king's business. I wondered at the vision, but no one understood it.

9

1 In the first year of Darius the son of Ahasuerus, of the offspring of the Medes, who was made king over the realm of the Chaldeans, 2 in the first year of his reign I, Daniel, understood by the books the number of the years about which the LORD's[a] word came to Jeremiah the prophet, for the accomplishing of the desolations of Jerusalem, even seventy years. 3 I set my face to the Lord God, to seek by prayer and petitions, with fasting in sackcloth and ashes.

4 I prayed to the LORD my God, and made confession, and said, "Oh, Lord, the great and dreadful God, who keeps covenant and loving kindness with those who love him and keep his commandments, 5 we have sinned, and have dealt perversely, and have done wickedly, and have rebelled, even turning aside from your precepts and from your ordinances. 6 We haven't listened to your servants the prophets, who spoke in your name to our kings, our princes, and our fathers, and to all the people of the land.

7 "Lord, righteousness belongs to you, but to us confusion of face, as it is today—to the men of Judah, and to the inhabitants of Jerusalem, and to all Israel, who are near, and who are far off, through all the countries where you have driven them, because of their trespass that they have trespassed against you. 8 Lord, to us belongs confusion of face, to our kings, to our princes, and to our fathers, because we have sinned against you. 9 To the Lord our God belong mercies and forgiveness; for we have rebelled against him. 10 We haven't obeyed the LORD our God's voice, to walk in his laws, which he set before us by his servants the prophets. 11 Yes, all Israel have transgressed your law, turning aside, that they wouldn't obey your voice.

"Therefore the curse and the oath written in the law of Moses the servant of God has been poured out on us; for we have sinned against him. 12 He has confirmed his words, which he spoke against us, and against our judges who judged us, by bringing on us a great evil; for under the whole sky, such has not been done as has been done to Jerusalem. 13 As it is written in the law of Moses, all this evil has come on us. Yet we have not entreated the favour of the LORD our God, that we should turn from our iniquities and have discernment in your truth. 14 Therefore the LORD has watched over the evil, and brought it on us; for the LORD our God is righteous in all his works which he does, and we have not obeyed his voice.

15 "Now, Lord our God, who has brought your people out of the land of Egypt with a mighty hand, and have gotten yourself renown, as it is today, we have sinned. We have done wickedly. 16 Lord, according to all your righteousness, please let your anger and your wrath be turned away from your city Jerusalem, your holy mountain, because for our sins, and for the iniquities of our fathers, Jerusalem and your people have become a reproach to all who are around us.

17 "Now therefore, our God, listen to the prayer of your servant, and to his petitions, and cause your face to shine on your sanctuary that is desolate, for the Lord's sake. 18 My God, turn your ear and hear. Open your eyes and see our desolations and the city which is called by your name; for we don't present our petitions before you for our righteousness, but for your great mercies' sake. 19 Lord, hear. Lord, forgive. Lord, listen and do. Don't defer, for your own sake, my God, because your city and your people are called by your name."

---

20 While I was speaking, praying, and confessing my sin and the sin of my people Israel, and presenting my supplication before the LORD my God for the holy mountain of my God— 21 yes, while I was speaking in prayer, the man Gabriel, whom I had seen in the vision at the beginning, being caused to fly swiftly, touched me about the time of the evening offering. 22 He instructed me and talked with me, and said, "Daniel, I have now come to give you wisdom and understanding. 23 At the beginning of your petitions the commandment went out and I have come to tell you, for you are greatly beloved. Therefore consider the matter and understand the vision.

24 "Seventy weeks are decreed on your people and on your holy city, to finish disobedience, to put an end to sin, to make reconciliation for iniquity, to bring in everlasting righteousness, to seal up vision and prophecy, and to anoint the most holy.

25 "Know therefore and discern that from the going out of the commandment to restore and to build Jerusalem to the Anointed One,[a] the prince, will be seven weeks and sixty-two weeks. It will be built again with street and moat, even in troubled times. 26 After the sixty-two weeks the Anointed One[b] will be cut off and will have nothing. The people of the prince who come will destroy the city and the sanctuary. Its end will be with a flood, and war will be even to the end. Desolations are determined. 27 He will make a firm covenant with many for one week. In the middle of the week he will cause the sacrifice and the offering to cease. On the wing of abominations will come one who makes desolate. Even to the full end that is decreed, wrath will be poured out on the desolate."

10

1 In the third year of Cyrus king of Persia a revelation was revealed to Daniel, whose name was called Belteshazzar. The revelation was true, even a great warfare. He understood the revelation, and had understanding of the vision.

2 In those days I, Daniel, was mourning three whole weeks. 3 I ate no pleasant bread. No meat or wine came into my mouth. I didn't anoint myself at all, until three whole weeks were fulfilled.

4 In the twenty-fourth day of the first month, as I was by the side of the great river, which is Hiddekel, 5 I lifted up my eyes and looked, and behold, there was a man clothed in linen, whose thighs were adorned with pure gold of Uphaz. 6 His body also was like beryl, and his face like the appearance of lightning, and his eyes like flaming torches. His arms and his feet were like burnished bronze. The voice of his words was like the voice of a multitude.

7 I, Daniel, alone saw the vision; for the men who were with me didn't see the vision; but a great quaking fell on them, and they fled to hide themselves. 8 So I was left alone, and saw this great vision. No strength remained in me; for my face grew deathly pale, and I retained no strength. 9 Yet I heard the voice of his words. When I heard the voice of his words, then I fell into a deep sleep on my face, with my face towards the ground.

10 Behold, a hand touched me, which set me on my knees and on the palms of my hands. 11 He said to me, "Daniel, you greatly beloved man, understand the words that I speak to you. Stand upright, for I have been sent to you, now." When he had spoken this word to me, I stood trembling.

12 Then he said to me, "Don't be afraid, Daniel; for from the first day that you set your heart to understand, and to humble yourself before your God, your words were heard. I have come for your words' sake. 13 But the prince of the kingdom of Persia withstood me twenty-one days; but, behold, Michael, one of the chief princes, came to help me because I remained there with the kings of Persia. 14 Now I have come to make you understand what will happen to your people in the latter days; for the vision is yet for many days."

15 When he had spoken these words to me, I set my face towards the ground, and was mute. 16 Behold, one in the likeness of the sons of men touched my lips. Then I opened my mouth, and spoke and said to him who stood before me, "My lord, by reason of the vision my sorrows have overtaken me, and I retain no strength. 17 For how can the servant of my lord talk with my lord? For as for me, immediately there remained no strength in me. There was no breath left in me."

18 Then one like the appearance of a man touched me again, and he strengthened me. 19 He said, "Greatly beloved man, don't be afraid. Peace be to you. Be strong. Yes, be strong."

When he spoke to me, I was strengthened, and said, "Let my lord speak; for you have strengthened me."

20 Then he said, "Do you know why I have come to you? Now I will return to fight with the prince of Persia. When I go out, behold, the prince of Greece will come. 21 But I will tell you what is inscribed in the writing of truth. There is no one who supports me against these except Michael, your prince.

11

1 "As for me, in the first year of Darius the Mede, I stood up to confirm and strengthen him.

2 "Now I will show you the truth. Behold, three more kings will stand up in Persia. The fourth will be far richer than all of them. When he has grown strong through his riches, he will stir up all against the realm of Greece. 3 A mighty king will stand up who will rule with great dominion, and do according to his will. 4 When he stands up, his kingdom will be broken, and will be divided towards the four winds of the sky, but not to his posterity, nor according to his dominion with which he ruled; for his kingdom will be plucked up, even for others besides these.

5 "The king of the south will be strong. One of his princes will become stronger than him and have dominion. His dominion will be a great dominion. 6 At the end of years they will join themselves together. The daughter of the king of the south will come to the king of the north to make an agreement, but she will not retain the strength of her arm. He will also not stand, nor will his arm; but she will be given up, with those who brought her and he who became her father, and he who strengthened her in those times.

7 "But out of a shoot from her roots one will stand up in his place who will come to the army and will enter into the fortress of the king of the north, and will deal against them and will prevail. 8 He will also carry their gods, with their molten images and their precious vessels of silver and of gold, captive into Egypt. He will refrain some years from the king of the north. 9 He will come into the realm of the king of the south, but he will return into his own land. 10 His sons will wage war and will assemble a multitude of great forces which will keep coming and overflow and pass through. They will return and wage war, even to his fortress.

11 "The king of the south will be moved with anger and will come out and fight with him, even with the king of the north. He will send out a great multitude, and the multitude will be given into his hand. 12 The multitude will be lifted up, and his heart will be exalted. He will cast down tens of thousands, but he won't prevail. 13 The king of the north will return, and will send out a multitude greater than the former. He will come on at the end of the times, even of years, with a great army and with abundant supplies.

14 "In those times many will stand up against the king of the south. Also the children of the violent amongst your people will lift themselves up to establish the vision; but they will fall. 15 So the king of the north will come and cast up a mound, and take a well-fortified city. The forces of the south won't stand, neither will his chosen people, neither will there be any strength to stand. 16 But he who comes against him will do according to his own will, and no one will stand before him. He will stand in the glorious land, and destruction will be in his hand. 17 He will set his face to come with the strength of his whole kingdom, and with him equitable conditions. He will perform them. He will give him the daughter of women to corrupt her; but she will not stand, and won't be for him. 18 After this he will turn his face to the islands, and will take many; but a prince will cause the reproach offered by him to cease. Yes, moreover, he will cause his reproach to turn on him. 19 Then he will turn his face towards the fortresses of his own land; but he will stumble and fall, and won't be found.

20 "Then one who will cause a tax collector to pass through the kingdom to maintain its glory will stand up in his place; but within few days he shall be destroyed, not in anger, and not in battle.

21 "In his place, a contemptible person will stand up, to whom they had not given the honour of the kingdom; but he will come in time of security, and will obtain the kingdom by flatteries. 22 The overwhelming forces will be overwhelmed from before him, and will be broken. Yes, also the prince of the covenant. 23 After the treaty is made with him, he will work deceitfully; for he will come up, and will become strong with a small people. 24 In time of security, he will come even on the fattest places of the province. He will do that which his fathers have not done, nor his fathers' fathers. He will scatter amongst them prey, plunder, and substance. Yes, he will devise his plans against the strongholds, even for a time.

25 "He will stir up his power and his courage against the king of the south with a great army; and the king of the south will wage war in battle with an exceedingly great and mighty army; but he won't stand, for they will devise plans against him. 26 Yes, those who eat of his delicacies will destroy him, and his army will be swept away. Many will fall down slain. 27 As for both these kings, their hearts will be to do mischief, and they will speak lies at one table; but it won't prosper, for the end will still be at the appointed time. 28 Then he will return into his land with great wealth. His heart will be against the holy covenant. He will take action and return to his own land.

29 "He will return at the appointed time and come into the south; but it won't be in the latter time as it was in the former. 30 For ships of Kittim will come against him. Therefore he will be grieved, and will return, and have indignation against the holy covenant, and will take action. He will even return, and have regard to those who forsake the holy covenant.

31 "Forces will stand on his part and they will profane the sanctuary, even the fortress, and will take away the continual burnt offering. Then they will set up the abomination that makes desolate. 32 He will corrupt those who do wickedly against the covenant by flatteries; but the people who know their God will be strong and take action.

33 "Those who are wise amongst the people will instruct many; yet they will fall by the sword and by flame, by captivity and by plunder, many days. 34 Now when they fall, they will be helped with a little help; but many will join themselves to them with flatteries. 35 Some of those who are wise will fall, to refine them, and to purify, and to make them white, even to the time of the end; because it is yet for the appointed time.

36 "The king will do according to his will. He will exalt himself, and magnify himself above every god, and will speak marvellous things against the God of gods. He will prosper until the indignation is accomplished; for what is determined will be done. 37 He won't regard the gods of his fathers, or the desire of women, or regard any god; for he will magnify himself above all. 38 But in his place he will honour the god of fortresses. He will honour a god whom his fathers didn't know with gold, silver, precious stones, and pleasant things. 39 He will deal with the strongest fortresses by the help of a foreign god. He will increase with glory whoever

---

[a] 9:25 "Anointed One" can also be translated "Messiah" (same as "Christ").   [b] 9:26 "Anointed One" can also be translated "Messiah" (same as "Christ").

Page | 451

acknowledges him. He will cause them to rule over many, and will divide the land for a price.

40 "At the time of the end, the king of the south will contend with him; and the king of the north will come against him like a whirlwind, with chariots, with horsemen, and with many ships. He will enter into the countries, and will overflow and pass through. 41 He will enter also into the glorious land, and many countries will be overthrown; but these will be delivered out of his hand: Edom, Moab, and the chief of the children of Ammon. 42 He will also stretch out his hand against the countries. The land of Egypt won't escape. 43 But he will have power over the treasures of gold and of silver, and over all the precious things of Egypt. The Libyans and the Ethiopians will be at his steps. 44 But news out of the east and out of the north will trouble him; and he will go out with great fury to destroy and utterly to sweep away many. 45 He will plant the tents of his palace between the sea and the glorious holy mountain; yet he will come to his end, and no one will help him.

12

1 "At that time Michael will stand up, the great prince who stands for the children of your people. There will be a time of trouble, such as never was since there was a nation even to that same time. At that time, your people will be delivered—everyone who is found written in the book. 2 Many of those who sleep in the dust of the earth will awake, some to everlasting life, and some to shame and everlasting contempt. 3 Those who are wise will shine as the brightness of the expanse. Those who turn many to righteousness will shine like the stars forever and ever. 4 But you, Daniel, shut up the words and seal the book, even to the time of the end. Many will run back and forth, and knowledge will be increased."

5 Then I, Daniel, looked, and behold, two others stood, one on the river bank on this side, and the other on the river bank on that side. 6 One said to the man clothed in linen, who was above the waters of the river, "How long will it be to the end of these wonders?"

7 I heard the man clothed in linen, who was above the waters of the river, when he held up his right hand and his left hand to heaven, and swore by him who lives forever that it will be for a time, times, and a half; and when they have finished breaking in pieces the power of the holy people, all these things will be finished.

8 I heard, but I didn't understand. Then I said, "My lord, what will be the outcome of these things?"

9 He said, "Go your way, Daniel; for the words are shut up and sealed until the time of the end. 10 Many will purify themselves, make themselves white, and be refined; but the wicked will do wickedly. None of the wicked will understand; but those who are wise will understand.

11 "From the time that the continual burnt offering is taken away and the abomination that makes desolate set up, there will be one thousand and two hundred and ninety days. 12 Blessed is he who waits and comes to the one thousand and three hundred and thirty-five days.

13 "But go your way until the end; for you will rest and will stand in your inheritance at the end of the days."

13

THE HISTORY OF SUSANNA

1 [a] A man lived in Babylon, and his name was Joakim. 2 He took a wife, whose name was Susanna, the daughter of Helkias, a very fair woman, and one who feared the Lord. 3 Her parents were also righteous, and taught their daughter according to the law of Moses. 4 Now Joakim was a great rich man, and had a beautiful garden next to his house. The Jews used to come to him, because he was more honourable than all others. 5 The same year, two of the elders of the people were appointed to be judges, such as the Lord spoke of, that wickedness came from Babylon from elders who were judges, who were supposed to govern the people. 6 These were often at Joakim's house. All that had any lawsuits came to them.

7 When the people departed away at noon, Susanna went into her husband's garden to walk. 8 The two elders saw her going in every day and walking; and they were inflamed with lust for her. 9 They perverted their own mind and turned away their eyes, that they might not look to heaven, nor remember just judgements. 10 And although they both were wounded with lust for her, yet dared not show the other his grief. 11 For they were ashamed to declare their lust, what they desired to do with her. 12 Yet they watched eagerly from day to day to see her. 13 The one said to the other, "Let's go home, now; for it is dinner time." 14 So when they had gone out, they parted company, and turning back again, they came to the same place. After they had asked one another the cause, they acknowledged their lust. Then they appointed a time both together, when they might find her alone.

15 It happened, as they watched on an opportune day, she went in as before with only two maids, and she desired to wash herself in the garden; for it was hot. 16 There was nobody there except the two elders who had hid themselves and watched her. 17 Then she said to her maids, "Bring me olive oil and ointment, and shut the garden doors, that I may wash myself." 18 They did as she asked them and shut the garden doors, and went out themselves at the side doors to fetch the things that she had commanded them. They didn't see the elders, because they were hidden.

19 Now when the maids had gone out, the two elders rose up and ran to her, saying, 20 "Behold, the garden doors are shut, that no man can see us, and we are in love with you. Therefore consent to us, and lie with us. 21 If

you will not, we will testify against you, that a young man was with you; therefore you sent your maids away from you."

22 Then Susanna sighed, and said, "I am trapped; for if I do this thing, it is death to me. If I don't do it, I can't escape your hands. 23 It is better for me to fall into your hands, and not do it, than to sin in the sight of the Lord." 24 With that Susanna cried with a loud voice; and the two elders cried out against her. 25 Then one of them ran and opened the garden doors.

26 So when the servants of the house heard the cry in the garden, they rushed in at the side door to see what had happened to her. 27 But when the elders had told their tale, the servants were greatly ashamed; for there was never such a report made of Susanna.

28 It came to pass on the next day, when the people assembled to her husband Joakim, the two elders came full of their wicked intent against Susanna to put her to death, 29 and said before the people, "Send for Susanna, the daughter of Helkias, Joakim's wife." So they sent; 30 and she came with her father and mother, her children, and all her kindred. 31 Now Susanna was a very delicate woman, and beautiful to behold. 32 These wicked men commanded her to be unveiled, for she was veiled, that they might be filled with her beauty. 33 Therefore her friends and all who saw her wept. 34 Then the two elders stood up in the midst of the people and laid their hands upon her head. 35 She, weeping, looked up towards heaven; for her heart trusted in the Lord.

36 The elders said, "As we walked in the garden alone, this woman came in with two maids, shut the garden doors, and sent the maids away. 37 Then a young man who was hidden there came to her and lay with her. 38 And we, being in a corner of the garden, saw this wickedness and ran to them. 39 And when we saw them together, we couldn't hold the man; for he was stronger than we, and opened the doors, and leapt out. 40 But having taken this woman, we asked who the young man was, but she would not tell us. We testify these things."

41 Then the assembly believed them, as those who were elders of the people and judges; so they condemned her to death.

42 Then Susanna cried out with a loud voice, and said, "O everlasting God, you know the secrets, and know all things before they happen. 43 You know that they have testified falsely against me. Behold, I must die, even though I never did such things as these men have maliciously invented against me."

44 The Lord heard her voice. 45 Therefore when she was led away to be put to death, God raised up the holy spirit of a young youth, whose name was Daniel. 46 He cried with a loud voice, "I am clear from the blood of this woman!"

47 Then all the people turned them towards him, and said, "What do these words that you have spoken mean?"

48 So he, standing in the midst of them, said, "Are you all such fools, you sons of Israel, that without examination or knowledge of the truth you have condemned a daughter of Israel? 49 Return again to the place of judgement; for these have testified falsely against her."

50 Therefore all the people turned again in haste, and the elders said to him, "Come, sit down amongst us, and show it to us, seeing God has given you the honour of an elder."

51 Then Daniel said to them, "Put them far apart from each another, and I will examine them." 52 So when they were put apart one from another, he called one of them, and said to him, "O you who have become old in wickedness, now your sins have returned which you have committed before, 53 in pronouncing unjust judgement, condemning the innocent, and letting the guilty go free; although the Lord says, 'You shall not kill the innocent and righteous.' 54 Now then, if you saw her, tell me, under which tree did you see them companying together?"

He answered, "Under a mastick tree."

55 And Daniel said, "You have certainly lied against your own head; for even now the angel of God has received the sentence of God and will cut you in two." 56 So he put him aside, and commanded to bring the other, and said to him, "O you seed of Canaan, and not of Judah, beauty has deceived you, and lust has perverted your heart. 57 Thus you have dealt with the daughters of Israel, and they for fear were intimate with you; but the daughter of Judah would not tolerate your wickedness. 58 Now therefore tell me, under which tree did you take them being intimate together?"

He answered, "Under an evergreen oak tree."

59 Then Daniel said to him, "You have also certainly lied against your own head; for the angel of God waits with the sword to cut you in two, that he may destroy you."

60 With that, all the assembly cried out with a loud voice, and blessed God, who saves those who hope in him. 61 Then they arose against the two elders, for Daniel had convicted them of false testimony out of their own mouth. 62 According to the law of Moses they did to them what they maliciously intended to do to their neighbour. They put them to death, and the innocent blood was saved the same day. 63 Therefore Helkias and his wife praised God for their daughter Susanna, with Joakim her husband, and all the kindred, because there was no dishonesty found in her. 64 And from that day forth, Daniel had a great reputation in the sight of the people.

14

Bel and the Dragon

---

a 13:1 *The History of Susanna* is translated from chapter 13 of *Daniel* in the Greek Septuagint. It is not found in the traditional Hebrew text of *Daniel. The History of Susanna* is recognised as Deuterocanonical Scripture by the Roman Catholic, Greek Orthodox, and Russian Orthodox Churches.

1 [a]King Astyages was gathered to his fathers, and Cyrus the Persian received his kingdom. 2 Daniel lived with the king, and was honoured above all his friends.

3 Now the Babylonians had an idol called Bel, and every day twelve great measures of fine flour, forty sheep, and six firkins [b] of wine were spent on it. 4 The king honoured it and went daily to worship it; but Daniel worshipped his own God. The king said to him, "Why don't you worship Bel?"

5 He said, "Because I may not honour idols made with hands, but only the living God, who has created the sky and the earth, and has sovereignty over all flesh."

6 Then the king said to him, "Don't you think that Bel is a living god? Don't you see how much he eats and drinks every day?"

7 Then Daniel laughed, and said, "O king, don't be deceived; for this is just clay inside, and brass outside, and never ate or drank anything."

8 So the king was angry, and called for his priests, and said to them, "If you don't tell me who this is who devours these expenses, you shall die. 9 But if you can show me that Bel devours them, then Daniel shall die; for he has spoken blasphemy against Bel."

Daniel said to the king, "Let it be according to your word."

10 Now there were seventy priests of Bel, besides their wives and children. The king went with Daniel into Bel's temple. 11 So Bel's priests said, "Behold, we will leave; but you, O king, set out the food, and mix the wine and set it out, shut the door securely, and seal it with your own signet. 12 When you come in the morning, if you don't find that Bel has eaten everything, we will suffer death, or else Daniel, who speaks falsely against us."

13 They weren't concerned, for under the table they had made a secret entrance, by which they entered in continually, and consumed those things. 14 It happened, when they had gone out, the king set the food before Bel. Now Daniel had commanded his servants to bring ashes, and they scattered them all over the temple in the presence of the king alone. Then they went out, shut the door, sealed it with the king's signet, and so departed.

15 Now in the night, the priests came with their wives and children, as they usually did, and ate and drank it all. 16 In the morning, the king arose, and Daniel with him. 17 The king said, "Daniel, are the seals whole?"

He said, "Yes, O king, they are whole."

18 And as soon as he had opened the door, the king looked at the table, and cried with a loud voice, "You are great, O Bel, and with you is no deceit at all!"

19 Then Daniel laughed, and held the king that he should not go in, and said, "Behold now the pavement, and mark well whose footsteps these are."

20 The king said, "I see the footsteps of men, women, and children." Then the king was angry, 21 and took the priests with their wives and children, who showed him the secret doors, where they came in and consumed the things that were on the table. 22 Therefore the king killed them, and delivered Bel into Daniel's power, who overthrew it and its temple.

23 In that same place there was a great dragon which the people of Babylon worshipped. 24 The king said to Daniel, "Will you also say that this is of brass? Behold, he lives, eats and drinks. You can't say that he is no living god. Therefore worship him."

25 Then Daniel said, "I will worship the Lord my God; for he is a living God. 26 But allow me, O king, and I will kill this dragon without sword or staff."

The king said, "I allow you."

27 Then Daniel took pitch, fat, and hair, and melted them together, and made lumps of them. He put these in the dragon's mouth, so the dragon ate and burst apart. Daniel said, "Behold, these are the gods you all worship."

28 When the people of Babylon heard that, they took great indignation, and conspired against the king, saying, "The king has become a Jew. He has pulled down Bel, slain the dragon, and put the priests to the sword."

29 So they came to the king, and said, "Deliver Daniel to us, or else we will destroy you and your house."

30 Now when the king saw that they trapped him, being constrained, the king delivered Daniel to them. 31 They cast him into the lion's den, where he was six days. 32 There were seven lions in the den, and they had been giving them two carcasses and two sheep every day, which then were not given to them, intending that they would devour Daniel.

33 Now there was in Jewry the prophet Habakkuk, [c] who had made stew, and had broken bread into a bowl. He was going into the field to bring it to the reapers.

34 But the angel of the Lord said to Habakkuk, "Go carry the dinner that you have into Babylon to Daniel, in the lions' den."

35 Habakkuk said, "Lord, I never saw Babylon. I don't know where the den is."

36 Then the angel of the Lord took him by the crown, and lifted him up by the hair of his head, and with the blast of his breath set him in Babylon over the den.

37 Habakkuk cried, saying, "O Daniel, Daniel, take the dinner which God has sent you.".

38 Daniel said, "You have remembered me, O God, and have not abandoned those who love you."

39 So Daniel got up and ate. And the angel of God immediately returned Habakkuk to his own place.

40 On the seventh day the king came to mourn for Daniel. When he came to the den he looked in, and there sat Daniel!

41 The king shouted with a loud voice, "You are great, O Lord, the God of Daniel, and there is no other besides you!"

42 Then he pulled Daniel[i] out and threw into the den those who had attempted his destruction, and they were instantly eaten before his eyes.

---

[a] 14:1 *Bel and the Dragon* is translated from chapter 14 of *Daniel* in the Greek Septuagint. It is not found in the traditional Hebrew text of *Daniel*. *Bel and the Dragon* is recognised as Deuterocanonical Scripture by the Roman Catholic, Greek Orthodox, and Russian Orthodox Churches.

[b] 14:3 a firkin is about 41 litres or 11 gallons.

[c] 14:33 Gr. Ambakoum.

The New Testament

#40 - Matthew: Written primarily for a Jewish audience, Matthew's Gospel emphasizes Jesus as the promised Messiah of the Old Testament prophecies. Throughout the narrative, the author of Matthew showcases Jesus' teachings, miracles, death, and resurrection, emphasizing the Kingdom of Heaven.

#41 - Mark: Believed to be the earliest Gospel, Mark provides a rapid and dynamic narrative of Jesus' life, focusing on His deeds and His role as the suffering servant. The emphasis is on action and Jesus' ultimate sacrifice for humanity.

#42 - Luke: Traditionally ascribed to Paul's companion, Luke's Gospel emphasizes Jesus' teachings, compassion towards the marginalized, and the role of the Holy Spirit, and is notable for its parables, such as the Good Samaritan and the Prodigal Son.

#43 - John: Distinct from the Synoptic Gospels, John delves into the deeper theological aspects of Jesus' nature and identity. It focuses on His divinity, presenting Jesus as the Word made flesh, the giver of eternal life, and the source of living water.

#44 - Acts: Acts of the Apostles narrates the early Christian community's development and spread, beginning with Jesus' ascension and focusing on the ministries of Peter and Paul. It describes the Pentecost, the growth of the church in Jerusalem, the conversion and missionary journeys of Paul, and his journey to Rome, emphasizing the spread of Christianity from Jerusalem to the Gentile world.

#45 - Romans: Paul's theological masterpiece, Romans delves deep into topics like sin, justification, sanctification, and the transformative power of the Gospel. It is a comprehensive explanation of Christian doctrine and the life of faith.

#46 - 1 Corinthians: Addressing issues in the Corinthian church, Paul tackles topics like divisions, morality, and spiritual gifts. The famous chapter on love (Chapter 13) emphasizes love's supreme importance in the Christian life.

#47 - 2 Corinthians: A personal letter where Paul defends his apostolic authority and offers insights into his hardships for the sake of the Gospel. Themes of reconciliation and the power of Christ in weakness are central.

#48 - Galatians: The Book of Galatians, a letter written by the Apostle Paul to the Christian communities in Galatia, is a passionate and emphatic message emphasizing the importance of faith in Jesus Christ over the observance of the Jewish Law for salvation. In this letter, Paul addresses the challenge posed by certain individuals who were insisting that Gentile Christians must follow Jewish customs, including circumcision. He asserts his apostolic authority, recounts his personal journey to faith, and argues fervently that justification comes by faith, not by works of the Law. Throughout the letter, Paul encourages the Galatians to live by the Spirit, exhibiting the fruits of love, joy, peace, and other virtues, as opposed to being enslaved by the Law or engaging in behaviors reflective of their former lives. Galatians stands as a pivotal text in Christian theology, highlighting themes of grace, freedom, and the transformative power of faith in Christ.

#49 - Ephesians: A profound exploration of the church's identity and mission, Ephesians delves into the believer's position in Christ, the importance of unity, and the armor of God.

#50 - Philippians: Penned from prison, this letter radiates joy in Christ. Paul encourages the Philippian believers to have the mind of Christ and rejoice regardless of circumstances.

#51 - Colossians: Traditionally attributed to Paul but regarded by many scholars as written by a later author, the Epistle to the Colossians addresses a Christian community in Colossae. It focuses on the supremacy of Christ over all principalities and powers and emphasizes the completeness of believers in Christ, countering local heresies that combined elements of paganism and Jewish traditions with Christianity.

#52 - 1 Thessalonians: One of Paul's earliest letters, it comforts and encourages the Thessalonian believers, addressing concerns about the Second Coming of Christ.

#53 - 2 Thessalonians: Further elaborates on Christ's return, correcting misunderstandings and urging steadfastness in the face of persecution.

#54 - 1 Timothy: Considered by the majority of scholars to be a pseudonymous work, 1 Timothy is a pastoral epistle. It offers guidance on church organization and conduct, addressing doctrinal issues, worship practices, and leadership roles, including qualifications for bishops and deacons.

#55 - 2 Timothy: Written by an unknown author at the end of the 1st century, 2 Timothy is framed as a personal letter offering guidance and encouragement to a young leader, Timothy. It emphasizes perseverance in faith and sound teaching in the face of false doctrines and hardships.

#56 - Titus: An unknown author identifying himself as Paul advises Titus on church leadership and Christian living, emphasizing good works as evidence of genuine faith.

#57 - Philemon: Paul's personal letter to Philemon, a slave owner, urging him to welcome back his runaway slave Onesimus as a brother in Christ.

#58 - Hebrews: This epistle presents Jesus as the ultimate revelation of God's love and mercy and is superior to all other mediators. Through deep theological exposition, the book demonstrates Christ's supremacy and His role as our high priest, encouraging believers to remain steadfast in their faith.

#59 - James: Written by Jesus' half-brother, The Epistle of James offers practical advice on living a genuine faith. It emphasizes the necessity of works accompanying faith, the power of the tongue, and the importance of patience.

#60 - 1 Peter: The author of 1 Peter encourages believers undergoing persecutions. He reminds them of their living hope through Christ's resurrection and calls for holy living as God's chosen people.

#61 - 2 Peter: The author of 2 Peter warns against false teachers and the dangers of apostasy. He reaffirms the promise of Christ's return and the importance of godly living.

#62 - 1 John: The author of 1 John writes to assure believers of their salvation and encourages them to remain faithful to the truth. The epistle emphasizes love as a hallmark of the Christian life.

#63 - 2 John: A short letter warning against deceivers and emphasizing the commandment to love one another.

#64 - 3 John: The author of 3 John writes in appreciation of Gaius for his faithfulness and addresses issues of hospitality in the early church.

#65 - Jude: The author of Jude delivers an urgent call to contend for the faith against false teachers. The letter highlights God's judgment on the ungodly.

#66 - Revelation: Written by a certain John of Patmos, Revelation is an apocalyptic text that uses vivid imagery and symbolism to convey a vision of cosmic conflict and the ultimate triumph of good over evil. It addresses the persecution of Christians and the hope of salvation, depicting the end of the world, the final judgment, and the establishment of a new heaven and earth. Revelation primarily reflects the challenges of early Christian communities under Roman rule.

The Good News According to Matthew

1

1 The book of the genealogy of Jesus Christ,[a] the son of David, the son of Abraham.

2 Abraham became the father of Isaac. Isaac became the father of Jacob. Jacob became the father of Judah and his brothers. 3 Judah became the father of Perez and Zerah by Tamar. Perez became the father of Hezron. Hezron became the father of Ram. 4 Ram became the father of Amminadab. Amminadab became the father of Nahshon. Nahshon became the father of Salmon. 5 Salmon became the father of Boaz by Rahab. Boaz became the father of Obed by Ruth. Obed became the father of Jesse. 6 Jesse became the father of King David. David the king[b] became the father of Solomon by her who had been Uriah's wife. 7 Solomon became the father of Rehoboam. Rehoboam became the father of Abijah. Abijah became the father of Asa. 8 Asa became the father of Jehoshaphat. Jehoshaphat became the father of Joram. Joram became the father of Uzziah. 9 Uzziah became the father of Jotham. Jotham became the father of Ahaz. Ahaz became the father of Hezekiah. 10 Hezekiah became the father of Manasseh. Manasseh became the father of Amon. Amon became the father of Josiah. 11 Josiah became the father of Jechoniah and his brothers at the time of the exile to Babylon.

12 After the exile to Babylon, Jechoniah became the father of Shealtiel. Shealtiel became the father of Zerubbabel. 13 Zerubbabel became the father of Abiud. Abiud became the father of Eliakim. Eliakim became the father of Azor. 14 Azor became the father of Zadok. Zadok became the father of Achim. Achim became the father of Eliud. 15 Eliud became the father of Eleazar. Eleazar became the father of Matthan. Matthan became the father of Jacob. 16 Jacob became the father of Joseph, the husband of Mary, from whom was born Jesus,[c] who is called Christ.

17 So all the generations from Abraham to David are fourteen generations; from David to the exile to Babylon fourteen generations; and from the carrying away to Babylon to the Christ, fourteen generations.

18 Now the birth of Jesus Christ was like this: After his mother, Mary, was engaged to Joseph, before they came together, she was found pregnant by the Holy Spirit. 19 Joseph, her husband, being a righteous man, and not willing to make her a public example, intended to put her away secretly. 20 But when he thought about these things, behold,[d] an angel of the Lord appeared to him in a dream, saying, "Joseph, son of David, don't be afraid to take to yourself Mary as your wife, for that which is conceived in her is of the Holy Spirit. 21 She shall give birth to a son. You shall name him Jesus,[e] for it is he who shall save his people from their sins."

22 Now all this has happened that it might be fulfilled which was spoken by the Lord through the prophet, saying,

23 "Behold, the virgin shall be with child,
    and shall give birth to a son.
They shall call his name Immanuel,"

which is, being interpreted, "God with us."[**]

24 Joseph arose from his sleep, and did as the angel of the Lord commanded him, and took his wife to himself; 25 and didn't know her sexually until she had given birth to her firstborn son. He named him Jesus.

2

1 Now when Jesus was born in Bethlehem of Judea in the days of King Herod, behold, wise men[f] from the east came to Jerusalem, saying, 2 "Where is he who is born King of the Jews? For we saw his star in the east, and have come to worship him." 3 When King Herod heard it, he was troubled, and all Jerusalem with him. 4 Gathering together all the chief priests and scribes of the people, he asked them where the Christ would be born. 5 They said to him, "In Bethlehem of Judea, for this is written through the prophet,

6 'You Bethlehem, land of Judah,
    are in no way least amongst the princes of Judah;
for out of you shall come a governor
    who shall shepherd my people, Israel.'"[**]

7 Then Herod secretly called the wise men, and learnt from them exactly what time the star appeared. 8 He sent them to Bethlehem, and said, "Go and search diligently for the young child. When you have found him, bring me word, so that I also may come and worship him."

9 They, having heard the king, went their way; and behold, the star, which they saw in the east, went before them until it came and stood over where the young child was. 10 When they saw the star, they rejoiced with exceedingly great joy. 11 They came into the house and saw the young child with Mary, his mother, and they fell down and worshipped him. Opening their treasures, they offered to him gifts: gold, frankincense, and myrrh. 12 Being warned in a dream not to return to Herod, they went back to their own country another way.

13 Now when they had departed, behold, an angel of the Lord appeared to Joseph in a dream, saying, "Arise and take the young child and his mother, and flee into Egypt, and stay there until I tell you, for Herod will seek the young child to destroy him."

14 He arose and took the young child and his mother by night and departed into Egypt, 15 and was there until the death of Herod, that it might be fulfilled which was spoken by the Lord through the prophet, saying, "Out of Egypt I called my son."[**]

16 Then Herod, when he saw that he was mocked by the wise men, was exceedingly angry, and sent out and killed all the male children who were in Bethlehem and in all the surrounding countryside, from two years old and under, according to the exact time which he had learnt from the wise men. 17 Then that which was spoken by Jeremiah the prophet was fulfilled, saying,

18 "A voice was heard in Ramah,
    lamentation, weeping and great mourning,
Rachel weeping for her children;
    she wouldn't be comforted,
        because they are no more."[**]

19 But when Herod was dead, behold, an angel of the Lord appeared in a dream to Joseph in Egypt, saying, 20 "Arise and take the young child and his mother, and go into the land of Israel, for those who sought the young child's life are dead."

21 He arose and took the young child and his mother, and came into the land of Israel. 22 But when he heard that Archelaus was reigning over Judea in the place of his father, Herod, he was afraid to go there. Being warned in a dream, he withdrew into the region of Galilee, 23 and came and lived in a city called Nazareth; that it might be fulfilled which was spoken through the prophets that he will be called a Nazarene.

3

1 In those days, John the Baptiser came, preaching in the wilderness of Judea, saying, 2 "Repent, for the Kingdom of Heaven is at hand!" 3 For this is he who was spoken of by Isaiah the prophet, saying,
"The voice of one crying in the wilderness,
    make the way of the Lord ready!
    Make his paths straight!"[**]

4 Now John himself wore clothing made of camel's hair with a leather belt around his waist. His food was locusts and wild honey. 5 Then people from Jerusalem, all of Judea, and all the region around the Jordan went out to him. 6 They were baptised by him in the Jordan, confessing their sins.

7 But when he saw many of the Pharisees and Sadducees coming for his baptism, he said to them, "You offspring of vipers, who warned you to flee from the wrath to come? 8 Therefore produce fruit worthy of repentance! 9 Don't think to yourselves, 'We have Abraham for our father,' for I tell you that God is able to raise up children to Abraham from these stones. 10 Even now the axe lies at the root of the trees. Therefore every tree that doesn't produce good fruit is cut down, and cast into the fire.

11 "I indeed baptise you in water for repentance, but he who comes after me is mightier than I, whose sandals I am not worthy to carry. He will baptise you in the Holy Spirit.[g] 12 His winnowing fork is in his hand, and he will thoroughly cleanse his threshing floor. He will gather his wheat into the barn, but the chaff he will burn up with unquenchable fire."

13 Then Jesus came from Galilee to the Jordan[h] to John, to be baptised by him. 14 But John would have hindered him, saying, "I need to be baptised by you, and you come to me?"

15 But Jesus, answering, said to him, "Allow it now, for this is the fitting way for us to fulfil all righteousness." Then he allowed him.

16 Jesus, when he was baptised, went up directly from the water: and behold, the heavens were opened to him. He saw the Spirit of God descending as a dove, and coming on him. 17 Behold, a voice out of the heavens said, "This is my beloved Son, with whom I am well pleased."

4

1 Then Jesus was led up by the Spirit into the wilderness to be tempted by the devil. 2 When he had fasted forty days and forty nights, he was hungry afterward. 3 The tempter came and said to him, "If you are the Son of God, command that these stones become bread."

4 But he answered, "It is written, 'Man shall not live by bread alone, but by every word that proceeds out of God's mouth.'"[**]

5 Then the devil took him into the holy city. He set him on the pinnacle of the temple, 6 and said to him, "If you are the Son of God, throw yourself down, for it is written,
'He will command his angels concerning you,' and,
'On their hands they will bear you up,
    so that you don't dash your foot against a stone.'"[**]

7 Jesus said to him, "Again, it is written, 'You shall not test the Lord, your God.'"[**]

---

[a] *1:1* Messiah (Hebrew) and Christ (Greek) both mean "Anointed One"

[b] *1:6* NU omits "the king".

[c] *1:16* "Jesus" means "Salvation".

[d] *1:20* "Behold," from "ἰδοὺ", means look at, take notice, observe, see, or gaze at. It is often used as an interjection.

[e] *1:21* "Jesus" means "Salvation".

[**] 1:23 Isaiah 7:14

[f] *2:1* The word for "wise men" (magoi) can also mean teachers, scientists, physicians, astrologers, seers, interpreters of dreams, or sorcerers.

[**] 2:6 Micah 5:2

[**] 2:15 Hosea 11:1

[**] 2:18 Jeremiah 31:15

[**] 3:3 Isaiah 40:3

[g] *3:11* TR and NU add "and with fire"

[h] *3:13* i.e., the Jordan River

[**] 4:4 Deuteronomy 8:3

[**] 4:6 Psalms 91:11-12

[**] 4:7 Deuteronomy 6:16

8 Again, the devil took him to an exceedingly high mountain, and showed him all the kingdoms of the world and their glory. 9 He said to him, "I will give you all of these things, if you will fall down and worship me."

10 Then Jesus said to him, "Get behind me,[a] Satan! For it is written, 'You shall worship the Lord your God, and you shall serve him only.'" *

11 Then the devil left him, and behold, angels came and served him.

12 Now when Jesus heard that John was delivered up, he withdrew into Galilee. 13 Leaving Nazareth, he came and lived in Capernaum, which is by the sea, in the region of Zebulun and Naphtali, 14 that it might be fulfilled which was spoken through Isaiah the prophet, saying,

15 "The land of Zebulun and the land of Naphtali,
    towards the sea, beyond the Jordan,
    Galilee of the Gentiles,
16 the people who sat in darkness saw a great light;
    to those who sat in the region and shadow of death,
    to them light has dawned."*

17 From that time, Jesus began to preach, and to say, "Repent! For the Kingdom of Heaven is at hand."

18 Walking by the sea of Galilee, he[b] saw two brothers: Simon, who is called Peter, and Andrew, his brother, casting a net into the sea; for they were fishermen. 19 He said to them, "Come after me, and I will make you fishers for men."

20 They immediately left their nets and followed him. 21 Going on from there, he saw two other brothers, James the son of Zebedee, and John his brother, in the boat with Zebedee their father, mending their nets. He called them. 22 They immediately left the boat and their father, and followed him.

23 Jesus went about in all Galilee, teaching in their synagogues, preaching the Good News of the Kingdom, and healing every disease and every sickness amongst the people. 24 The report about him went out into all Syria. They brought to him all who were sick, afflicted with various diseases and torments, possessed with demons, epileptics, and paralytics; and he healed them. 25 Great multitudes from Galilee, Decapolis, Jerusalem, Judea, and from beyond the Jordan followed him.

5

1 Seeing the multitudes, he went up onto the mountain. When he had sat down, his disciples came to him. 2 He opened his mouth and taught them, saying,

3 "Blessed are the poor in spirit,
    for theirs is the Kingdom of Heaven.*
4 Blessed are those who mourn,
    for they shall be comforted.*
5 Blessed are the gentle,
    for they shall inherit the earth.[c]*
6 Blessed are those who hunger and thirst for righteousness,
    for they shall be filled.
7 Blessed are the merciful,
    for they shall obtain mercy.
8 Blessed are the pure in heart,
    for they shall see God.
9 Blessed are the peacemakers,
    for they shall be called children of God.
10 Blessed are those who have been persecuted for righteousness' sake,
    for theirs is the Kingdom of Heaven.

11 "Blessed are you when people reproach you, persecute you, and say all kinds of evil against you falsely, for my sake. 12 Rejoice, and be exceedingly glad, for great is your reward in heaven. For that is how they persecuted the prophets who were before you.

13 "You are the salt of the earth, but if the salt has lost its flavour, with what will it be salted? It is then good for nothing, but to be cast out and trodden under the feet of men.

14 You are the light of the world. A city located on a hill can't be hidden. 15 Neither do you light a lamp and put it under a measuring basket, but on a stand; and it shines to all who are in the house. 16 Even so, let your light shine before men, that they may see your good works and glorify your Father who is in heaven.

17 "Don't think that I came to destroy the law or the prophets. I didn't come to destroy, but to fulfil. 18 For most certainly, I tell you, until heaven and earth pass away, not even one smallest letter[d] or one tiny pen stroke[e] shall in any way pass away from the law, until all things are accomplished. 19 Therefore, whoever shall break one of these least commandments and teach others to do so, shall be called least in the Kingdom of Heaven; but whoever shall do and teach them shall be called great in the Kingdom of Heaven. 20 For I tell you that unless your righteousness exceeds that of

the scribes and Pharisees, there is no way you will enter into the Kingdom of Heaven.

21 "You have heard that it was said to the ancient ones, 'You shall not murder;" and 'Whoever murders will be in danger of the judgement.' 22 But I tell you that everyone who is angry with his brother without a cause [f] will be in danger of the judgement. Whoever says to his brother, 'Raca!' [g] will be in danger of the council. Whoever says, 'You fool!' will be in danger of the fire of Gehenna.[h]

23 "If therefore you are offering your gift at the altar, and there remember that your brother has anything against you, 24 leave your gift there before the altar, and go your way. First be reconciled to your brother, and then come and offer your gift. 25 Agree with your adversary quickly while you are with him on the way; lest perhaps the prosecutor deliver you to the judge, and the judge deliver you to the officer, and you be cast into prison. 26 Most certainly I tell you, you shall by no means get out of there until you have paid the last penny.[i]

27 "You have heard that it was said, [j] 'You shall not commit adultery;" 28 but I tell you that everyone who gazes at a woman to lust after her has committed adultery with her already in his heart. 29 If your right eye causes you to stumble, pluck it out and throw it away from you. For it is more profitable for you that one of your members should perish than for your whole body to be cast into Gehenna.[k] 30 If your right hand causes you to stumble, cut it off, and throw it away from you. For it is more profitable for you that one of your members should perish, than for your whole body to be cast into Gehenna.[l]

31 "It was also said, 'Whoever shall put away his wife, let him give her a writing of divorce,' 32 but I tell you that whoever puts away his wife, except for the cause of sexual immorality, makes her an adulteress; and whoever marries her when she is put away commits adultery.

33 "Again you have heard that it was said to the ancient ones, 'You shall not make false vows, but shall perform to the Lord your vows,' 34 but I tell you, don't swear at all: neither by heaven, for it is the throne of God; 35 nor by the earth, for it is the footstool of his feet; nor by Jerusalem, for it is the city of the great King. 36 Neither shall you swear by your head, for you can't make one hair white or black. 37 But let your 'Yes' be 'Yes' and your 'No' be 'No.' Whatever is more than these is of the evil one.

38 "You have heard that it was said, 'An eye for an eye, and a tooth for a tooth.'" 39 But I tell you, don't resist him who is evil; but whoever strikes you on your right cheek, turn to him the other also. 40 If anyone sues you to take away your coat, let him have your cloak also. 41 Whoever compels you to go one mile, go with him two. 42 Give to him who asks you, and don't turn away him who desires to borrow from you.

43 "You have heard that it was said, 'You shall love your neighbour ' and hate your enemy.'[m] 44 But I tell you, love your enemies, bless those who curse you, do good to those who hate you, and pray for those who mistreat you and persecute you, 45 that you may be children of your Father who is in heaven. For he makes his sun to rise on the evil and the good, and sends rain on the just and the unjust. 46 For if you love those who love you, what reward do you have? Don't even the tax collectors do the same? 47 If you only greet your friends, what more do you do than others? Don't even the tax collectors[n] do the same? 48 Therefore you shall be perfect, just as your Father in heaven is perfect.

6

1 "Be careful that you don't do your charitable giving[o] before men, to be seen by them, or else you have no reward from your Father who is in heaven. 2 Therefore, when you do merciful deeds, don't sound a trumpet before yourself, as the hypocrites do in the synagogues and in the streets, that they may get glory from men. Most certainly I tell you, they have received their reward. 3 But when you do merciful deeds, don't let your left hand know what your right hand does, 4 so that your merciful deeds may be in secret, then your Father who sees in secret will reward you openly.

5 "When you pray, you shall not be as the hypocrites, for they love to stand and pray in the synagogues and in the corners of the streets, that they may be seen by men. Most certainly, I tell you, they have received their reward. 6 But you, when you pray, enter into your inner room, and having shut your door, pray to your Father who is in secret; and your Father who sees in secret will reward you openly. 7 In praying, don't use vain repetitions as the Gentiles do; for they think that they will be heard for their much speaking. 8 Therefore don't be like them, for your Father knows what things you need before you ask him. 9 Pray like this:
"'Our Father in heaven, may your name be kept holy.
10 Let your Kingdom come.
    Let your will be done on earth as it is in heaven.

---

a *4:10* TR and NU read "Go away" instead of "Get behind me"
** *4:10* Deuteronomy 6:13
** *4:16* Isaiah 9:1-2
b *4:18* TR reads "Jesus" instead of "he"
** *5:3* Isaiah 57:15; 66:2
** *5:4* Isaiah 61:2; 66:10,13
c *5:5* or, land.
** *5:5* Psalms 37:11
d *5:18* literally, iota
e *5:18* or, serif
** *5:21* Exodus 20:13
f *5:22* NU omits "without a cause".
g *5:22* "Raca" is an Aramaic insult, related to the word for "empty" and conveying the idea of empty-headedness.

h *5:22* or, Hell
i *5:26* literally, kodrantes. A kodrantes was a small copper coin worth about 2 lepta (widow's mites)—not enough to buy very much of anything.
j *5:27* TR adds "to the ancients".
** *5:27* Exodus 20:14
k *5:29* or, Hell
l *5:30* or, Hell
** *5:31* Deuteronomy 24:1
** *5:33* Numbers 30:2; Deuteronomy 23:21; Ecclesiastes 5:4
** *5:38* Exodus 21:24; Leviticus 24:20; Deuteronomy 19:21
** *5:43* Leviticus 19:18
m *5:43* not in the Bible, but see Qumran Manual of Discipline Ix, 21-26
n *5:47* NU reads "Gentiles" instead of "tax collectors".
o *6:1* NU reads "acts of righteousness" instead of "charitable giving"

11 Give us today our daily bread.
12 Forgive us our debts,
as we also forgive our debtors.
13 Bring us not into temptation,
but deliver us from the evil one.
For yours is the Kingdom, the power, and the glory forever. Amen.'ᵃ
14 "For if you forgive men their trespasses, your heavenly Father will also forgive you. 15 But if you don't forgive men their trespasses, neither will your Father forgive your trespasses.

16 "Moreover when you fast, don't be like the hypocrites, with sad faces. For they disfigure their faces that they may be seen by men to be fasting. Most certainly I tell you, they have received their reward. 17 But you, when you fast, anoint your head and wash your face, 18 so that you are not seen by men to be fasting, but by your Father who is in secret; and your Father, who sees in secret, will reward you.

19 "Don't lay up treasures for yourselves on the earth, where moth and rust consume, and where thieves break through and steal; 20 but lay up for yourselves treasures in heaven, where neither moth nor rust consume, and where thieves don't break through and steal; 21 for where your treasure is, there your heart will be also.

22 "The lamp of the body is the eye. If therefore your eye is sound, your whole body will be full of light. 23 But if your eye is evil, your whole body will be full of darkness. If therefore the light that is in you is darkness, how great is the darkness!

24 "No one can serve two masters, for either he will hate the one and love the other, or else he will be devoted to one and despise the other. You can't serve both God and Mammon. 25 Therefore I tell you, don't be anxious for your life: what you will eat, or what you will drink; nor yet for your body, what you will wear. Isn't life more than food, and the body more than clothing? 26 See the birds of the sky, that they don't sow, neither do they reap, nor gather into barns. Your heavenly Father feeds them. Aren't you of much more value than they?

27 "Which of you by being anxious, can add one momentᵇ to his lifespan? 28 Why are you anxious about clothing? Consider the lilies of the field, how they grow. They don't toil, neither do they spin, 29 yet I tell you that even Solomon in all his glory was not dressed like one of these. 30 But if God so clothes the grass of the field, which today exists and tomorrow is thrown into the oven, won't he much more clothe you, you of little faith?

31 "Therefore don't be anxious, saying, 'What will we eat?', 'What will we drink?' or, 'With what will we be clothed?' 32 For the Gentiles seek after all these things; for your heavenly Father knows that you need all these things. 33 But seek first God's Kingdom and his righteousness; and all these things will be given to you as well. 34 Therefore don't be anxious for tomorrow, for tomorrow will be anxious for itself. Each day's own evil is sufficient.

7

1 "Don't judge, so that you won't be judged. 2 For with whatever judgement you judge, you will be judged; and with whatever measure you measure, it will be measured to you. 3 Why do you see the speck that is in your brother's eye, but don't consider the beam that is in your own eye? 4 Or how will you tell your brother, 'Let me remove the speck from your eye,' and behold, the beam is in your own eye? 5 You hypocrite! First remove the beam out of your own eye, and then you can see clearly to remove the speck out of your brother's eye.

6 "Don't give that which is holy to the dogs, neither throw your pearls before the pigs, lest perhaps they trample them under their feet, and turn and tear you to pieces.

7 "Ask, and it will be given you. Seek, and you will find. Knock, and it will be opened for you. 8 For everyone who asks receives. He who seeks finds. To him who knocks it will be opened. 9 Or who is there amongst you who, if his son asks him for bread, will give him a stone? 10 Or if he asks for a fish, who will give him a serpent? 11 If you then, being evil, know how to give good gifts to your children, how much more will your Father who is in heaven give good things to those who ask him! 12 Therefore, whatever you desire for men to do to you, you shall also do to them; for this is the law and the prophets.

13 "Enter in by the narrow gate; for the gate is wide and the way is broad that leads to destruction, and there are many who enter in by it. 14 Howᶜ narrow is the gate and the way is restricted that leads to life! There are few who find it.

15 "Beware of false prophets, who come to you in sheep's clothing, but inwardly are ravening wolves. 16 By their fruits you will know them. Do you gather grapes from thorns or figs from thistles? 17 Even so, every good tree produces good fruit; but the corrupt tree produces evil fruit. 18 A good tree can't produce evil fruit, neither can a corrupt tree produce good fruit. 19 Every tree that doesn't grow good fruit is cut down and thrown into the fire. 20 Therefore by their fruits you will know them.

21 "Not everyone who says to me, 'Lord, Lord,' will enter into the Kingdom of Heaven, but he who does the will of my Father who is in heaven. 22 Many will tell me in that day, 'Lord, Lord, didn't we prophesy in your name, in your name cast out demons, and in your name do many mighty works?' 23 Then I will tell them, 'I never knew you. Depart from me, you who work iniquity.'

24 "Everyone therefore who hears these words of mine and does them, I will liken him to a wise man who built his house on a rock. 25 The rain came down, the floods came, and the winds blew and beat on that house; and it didn't fall, for it was founded on the rock. 26 Everyone who hears these words of mine and doesn't do them will be like a foolish man who built his house on the sand. 27 The rain came down, the floods came, and the winds blew and beat on that house; and it fell—and its fall was great."

28 When Jesus had finished saying these things, the multitudes were astonished at his teaching, 29 for he taught them with authority, and not like the scribes.

8

1 When he came down from the mountain, great multitudes followed him. 2 Behold, a leper came to him and worshipped him, saying, "Lord, if you want to, you can make me clean."

3 Jesus stretched out his hand and touched him, saying, "I want to. Be made clean." Immediately his leprosy was cleansed. 4 Jesus said to him, "See that you tell nobody; but go, show yourself to the priest, and offer the gift that Moses commanded, as a testimony to them."

5 When he came into Capernaum, a centurion came to him, asking him for help, 6 saying, "Lord, my servant lies in the house paralysed, grievously tormented."

7 Jesus said to him, "I will come and heal him."

8 The centurion answered, "Lord, I'm not worthy for you to come under my roof. Just say the word, and my servant will be healed. 9 For I am also a man under authority, having under myself soldiers. I tell this one, 'Go,' and he goes; and tell another, 'Come,' and he comes; and tell my servant, 'Do this,' and he does it."

10 When Jesus heard it, he marvelled and said to those who followed, "Most certainly I tell you, I haven't found so great a faith, not even in Israel. 11 I tell you that many will come from the east and the west, and will sit down with Abraham, Isaac, and Jacob in the Kingdom of Heaven, 12 but the children of the Kingdom will be thrown out into the outer darkness. There will be weeping and gnashing of teeth." 13 Jesus said to the centurion, "Go your way. Let it be done for you as you have believed." His servant was healed in that hour.

14 When Jesus came into Peter's house, he saw his wife's mother lying sick with a fever. 15 He touched her hand, and the fever left her. So she got up and served him.ᵈ 16 When evening came, they brought to him many possessed with demons. He cast out the spirits with a word, and healed all who were sick, 17 that it might be fulfilled which was spoken through Isaiah the prophet, saying, "He took our infirmities and bore our diseases."*

18 Now when Jesus saw great multitudes around him, he gave the order to depart to the other side.

19 A scribe came and said to him, "Teacher, I will follow you wherever you go."

20 Jesus said to him, "The foxes have holes and the birds of the sky have nests, but the Son of Man has nowhere to lay his head."

21 Another of his disciples said to him, "Lord, allow me first to go and bury my father."

22 But Jesus said to him, "Follow me, and leave the dead to bury their own dead."

23 When he got into a boat, his disciples followed him. 24 Behold, a violent storm came up on the sea, so much that the boat was covered with the waves; but he was asleep. 25 The disciples came to him and woke him up, saying, "Save us, Lord! We are dying!"

26 He said to them, "Why are you fearful, O you of little faith?" Then he got up, rebuked the wind and the sea, and there was a great calm.

27 The men marvelled, saying, "What kind of man is this, that even the wind and the sea obey him?"

28 When he came to the other side, into the country of the Gergesenes,ᵉ two people possessed by demons met him there, coming out of the tombs, exceedingly fierce, so that nobody could pass that way. 29 Behold, they cried out, saying, "What do we have to do with you, Jesus, Son of God? Have you come here to torment us before the time?" 30 Now there was a herd of many pigs feeding far away from them. 31 The demons begged him, saying, "If you cast us out, permit us to go away into the herd of pigs."

32 He said to them, "Go!"

They came out and went into the herd of pigs; and behold, the whole herd of pigs rushed down the cliff into the sea and died in the water. 33 Those who fed them fled and went away into the city and told everything, including what happened to those who were possessed with demons. 34 Behold, all the city came out to meet Jesus. When they saw him, they begged that he would depart from their borders.

9

1 He entered into a boat and crossed over, and came into his own city. 2 Behold, they brought to him a man who was paralysed, lying on a bed. Jesus, seeing their faith, said to the paralytic, "Son, cheer up! Your sins are forgiven you."

3 Behold, some of the scribes said to themselves, "This man blasphemes."

ᵃ 6:13 NU omits "For yours is the Kingdom, the power, and the glory forever. Amen."

ᵇ 6:27 literally, cubit

ᶜ 7:14 TR reads "Because" instead of "How"

ᵈ 8:15 TR reads "them" instead of "him"

** 8:17 Isaiah 53:4

ᵉ 8:28 NU reads "Gadarenes"

₄ Jesus, knowing their thoughts, said, "Why do you think evil in your hearts? ₅ For which is easier, to say, 'Your sins are forgiven;' or to say, 'Get up, and walk'? ₆ But that you may know that the Son of Man has authority on earth to forgive sins—" (then he said to the paralytic), "Get up, and take up your mat, and go to your house."

₇ He arose and departed to his house. ₈ But when the multitudes saw it, they marvelled and glorified God, who had given such authority to men.

₉ As Jesus passed by from there, he saw a man called Matthew sitting at the tax collection office. He said to him, "Follow me." He got up and followed him. ₁₀ As he sat in the house, behold, many tax collectors and sinners came and sat down with Jesus and his disciples. ₁₁ When the Pharisees saw it, they said to his disciples, "Why does your teacher eat with tax collectors and sinners?"

₁₂ When Jesus heard it, he said to them, "Those who are healthy have no need for a physician, but those who are sick do. ₁₃ But you go and learn what this means: 'I desire mercy, and not sacrifice,'" for I came not to call the righteous, but sinners to repentance."ᵃ

₁₄ Then John's disciples came to him, saying, "Why do we and the Pharisees fast often, but your disciples don't fast?"

₁₅ Jesus said to them, "Can the friends of the bridegroom mourn as long as the bridegroom is with them? But the days will come when the bridegroom will be taken away from them, and then they will fast. ₁₆ No one puts a piece of unshrunk cloth on an old garment; for the patch would tear away from the garment, and a worse hole is made. ₁₇ Neither do people put new wine into old wine skins, or else the skins would burst, and the wine be spilled, and the skins ruined. No, they put new wine into fresh wine skins, and both are preserved."

₁₈ While he told these things to them, behold, a ruler came and worshipped him, saying, "My daughter has just died, but come and lay your hand on her, and she will live."

₁₉ Jesus got up and followed him, as did his disciples. ₂₀ Behold, a woman who had a discharge of blood for twelve years came behind him, and touched the fringeᵇ of his garment; ₂₁ for she said within herself, "If I just touch his garment, I will be made well."

₂₂ But Jesus, turning around and seeing her, said, "Daughter, cheer up! Your faith has made you well." And the woman was made well from that hour.

₂₃ When Jesus came into the ruler's house and saw the flute players and the crowd in noisy disorder, ₂₄ he said to them, "Make room, because the girl isn't dead, but sleeping."

They were ridiculing him. ₂₅ But when the crowd was sent out, he entered in, took her by the hand, and the girl arose. ₂₆ The report of this went out into all that land.

₂₇ As Jesus passed by from there, two blind men followed him, calling out and saying, "Have mercy on us, son of David!" ₂₈ When he had come into the house, the blind men came to him. Jesus said to them, "Do you believe that I am able to do this?"

They told him, "Yes, Lord."

₂₉ Then he touched their eyes, saying, "According to your faith be it done to you." ₃₀ Then their eyes were opened. Jesus strictly commanded them, saying, "See that no one knows about this." ₃₁ But they went out and spread abroad his fame in all that land.

₃₂ As they went out, behold, a mute man who was demon possessed was brought to him. ₃₃ When the demon was cast out, the mute man spoke. The multitudes marvelled, saying, "Nothing like this has ever been seen in Israel!"

₃₄ But the Pharisees said, "By the prince of the demons, he casts out demons."

₃₅ Jesus went about all the cities and the villages, teaching in their synagogues and preaching the Good News of the Kingdom, and healing every disease and every sickness amongst the people. ₃₆ But when he saw the multitudes, he was moved with compassion for them because they were harassedᶜ and scattered, like sheep without a shepherd. ₃₇ Then he said to his disciples, "The harvest indeed is plentiful, but the labourers are few. ₃₈ Pray therefore that the Lord of the harvest will send out labourers into his harvest."

10

₁ He called to himself his twelve disciples, and gave them authority over unclean spirits, to cast them out, and to heal every disease and every sickness. ₂ Now the names of the twelve apostles are these. The first, Simon, who is called Peter; Andrew, his brother; James the son of Zebedee; John, his brother; ₃ Philip; Bartholomew; Thomas; Matthew the tax collector; James the son of Alphaeus; Lebbaeus, who was also calledᵈ Thaddaeus; ₄ Simon the Zealot; and Judas Iscariot, who also betrayed him.

₅ Jesus sent these twelve out and commanded them, saying, "Don't go amongst the Gentiles, and don't enter into any city of the Samaritans. ₆ Rather, go to the lost sheep of the house of Israel. ₇ As you go, preach, saying, 'The Kingdom of Heaven is at hand!' ₈ Heal the sick, cleanse the lepers,ᵉ and cast out demons. Freely you received, so freely give. ₉ Don't

take any gold, silver, or brass in your money belts. ₁₀ Take no bag for your journey, neither two coats, nor sandals, nor staff: for the labourer is worthy of his food. ₁₁ Into whatever city or village you enter, find out who in it is worthy, and stay there until you go on. ₁₂ As you enter into the household, greet it. ₁₃ If the household is worthy, let your peace come on it, but if it isn't worthy, let your peace return to you. ₁₄ Whoever doesn't receive you or hear your words, as you go out of that house or that city, shake the dust off your feet. ₁₅ Most certainly I tell you, it will be more tolerable for the land of Sodom and Gomorrah in the day of judgement than for that city.

₁₆ "Behold, I send you out as sheep amongst wolves. Therefore be wise as serpents and harmless as doves. ₁₇ But beware of men, for they will deliver you up to councils, and in their synagogues they will scourge you. ₁₈ Yes, and you will be brought before governors and kings for my sake, for a testimony to them and to the nations. ₁₉ But when they deliver you up, don't be anxious how or what you will say, for it will be given you in that hour what you will say. ₂₀ For it is not you who speak, but the Spirit of your Father who speaks in you.

₂₁ "Brother will deliver up brother to death, and the father his child. Children will rise up against parents and cause them to be put to death. ₂₂ You will be hated by all men for my name's sake, but he who endures to the end will be saved. ₂₃ But when they persecute you in this city, flee into the next, for most certainly I tell you, you will not have gone through the cities of Israel until the Son of Man has come.

₂₄ "A disciple is not above his teacher, nor a servant above his lord. ₂₅ It is enough for the disciple that he be like his teacher, and the servant like his lord. If they have called the master of the house Beelzebul,ᶠ how much more those of his household! ₂₆ Therefore don't be afraid of them, for there is nothing covered that will not be revealed, or hidden that will not be known. ₂₇ What I tell you in the darkness, speak in the light; and what you hear whispered in the ear, proclaim on the housetops. ₂₈ Don't be afraid of those who kill the body, but are not able to kill the soul. Rather, fear him who is able to destroy both soul and body in Gehenna.ᵍ

₂₉ "Aren't two sparrows sold for an assarion coin?ʰ Not one of them falls to the ground apart from your Father's will. ₃₀ But the very hairs of your head are all numbered. ₃₁ Therefore don't be afraid. You are of more value than many sparrows. ₃₂ Everyone therefore who confesses me before men, I will also confess him before my Father who is in heaven. ₃₃ But whoever denies me before men, I will also deny him before my Father who is in heaven.

₃₄ "Don't think that I came to send peace on the earth. I didn't come to send peace, but a sword. ₃₅ For I came to set a man at odds against his father, and a daughter against her mother, and a daughter-in-law against her mother-in-law. ₃₆ A man's foes will be those of his own household. ₃₇ He who loves father or mother more than me is not worthy of me; and he who loves son or daughter more than me isn't worthy of me. ₃₈ He who doesn't take his cross and follow after me isn't worthy of me. ₃₉ He who seeks his life will lose it; and he who loses his life for my sake will find it.

₄₀ "He who receives you receives me, and he who receives me receives him who sent me. ₄₁ He who receives a prophet in the name of a prophet will receive a prophet's reward. He who receives a righteous man in the name of a righteous man will receive a righteous man's reward. ₄₂ Whoever gives one of these little ones just a cup of cold water to drink in the name of a disciple, most certainly I tell you, he will in no way lose his reward."

11

₁ When Jesus had finished directing his twelve disciples, he departed from there to teach and preach in their cities.

₂ Now when John heard in the prison the works of Christ, he sent two of his disciples ₃ and said to him, "Are you he who comes, or should we look for another?"

₄ Jesus answered them, "Go and tell John the things which you hear and see: ₅ the blind receive their sight, the lame walk, the lepers are cleansed, the deaf hear, the dead are raised up, and the poor have good news preached to them. ₆ Blessed is he who finds no occasion for stumbling in me."

₇ As these went their way, Jesus began to say to the multitudes concerning John, "What did you go out into the wilderness to see? A reed shaken by the wind? ₈ But what did you go out to see? A man in soft clothing? Behold, those who wear soft clothing are in kings' houses. ₉ But why did you go out? To see a prophet? Yes, I tell you, and much more than a prophet. ₁₀ For this is he, of whom it is written, 'Behold, I send my messenger before your face, who will prepare your way before you.'" ₁₁ Most certainly I tell you, amongst those who are born of women there has not arisen anyone greater than John the Baptiser; yet he who is least in the Kingdom of Heaven is greater than he. ₁₂ From the days of John the Baptiser until now, the Kingdom of Heaven suffers violence, and the violent take it by force.ⁱ ₁₃ For all the prophets and the law prophesied until John. ₁₄ If you are willing to receive it, this is Elijah, who is to come. ₁₅ He who has ears to hear, let him hear.

** 9:13 Hosea 6:6
ᵃ 9:13 NU omits "to repentance".
ᵇ 9:20 or, tassel
ᶜ 9:36 TR reads "weary" instead of "harassed"
ᵈ 10:3 NU omits "Lebbaeus, who was also called"
ᵉ 10:8 TR adds "raise the dead,"
ᶠ 10:25 Literally, Lord of the Flies, or the devil
ᵍ 10:28 or, Hell.

ʰ 10:29 An assarion is a small coin worth one tenth of a drachma or a sixteenth of a denarius. An assarion is approximately the wages of one half hour of agricultural labour.
** 10:36 Micah 7:6
** 11:5 Isaiah 35:5
** 11:5 Isaiah 61:1-4
** 11:10 Malachi 3:1
ⁱ 11:12 or, plunder it.

16 "But to what shall I compare this generation? It is like children sitting in the marketplaces, who call to their companions 17 and say, 'We played the flute for you, and you didn't dance. We mourned for you, and you didn't lament.' 18 For John came neither eating nor drinking, and they say, 'He has a demon.' 19 The Son of Man came eating and drinking, and they say, 'Behold, a gluttonous man and a drunkard, a friend of tax collectors and sinners!' But wisdom is justified by her children."ᵃ

20 Then he began to denounce the cities in which most of his mighty works had been done, because they didn't repent. 21 "Woe to you, Chorazin! Woe to you, Bethsaida! For if the mighty works had been done in Tyre and Sidon which were done in you, they would have repented long ago in sackcloth and ashes. 22 But I tell you, it will be more tolerable for Tyre and Sidon on the day of judgement than for you. 23 You, Capernaum, who are exalted to heaven, you will go down to Hades. ᵇ For if the mighty works had been done in Sodom which were done in you, it would have remained until today. 24 But I tell you that it will be more tolerable for the land of Sodom on the day of judgement, than for you."

25 At that time, Jesus answered, "I thank you, Father, Lord of heaven and earth, that you hid these things from the wise and understanding, and revealed them to infants. 26 Yes, Father, for so it was well-pleasing in your sight. 27 All things have been delivered to me by my Father. No one knows the Son, except the Father; neither does anyone know the Father, except the Son and he to whom the Son desires to reveal him.

28 "Come to me, all you who labour and are heavily burdened, and I will give you rest. 29 Take my yoke upon you and learn from me, for I am gentle and humble in heart; and you will find rest for your souls. 30 For my yoke is easy, and my burden is light."

12

1 At that time, Jesus went on the Sabbath day through the grain fields. His disciples were hungry and began to pluck heads of grain and to eat. 2 But the Pharisees, when they saw it, said to him, "Behold, your disciples do what is not lawful to do on the Sabbath."

3 But he said to them, "Haven't you read what David did when he was hungry, and those who were with him: 4 how he entered into God's house and ate the show bread, which was not lawful for him to eat, nor for those who were with him, but only for the priests?* 5 Or have you not read in the law that on the Sabbath day the priests in the temple profane the Sabbath and are guiltless? 6 But I tell you that one greater than the temple is here. 7 But if you had known what this means, 'I desire mercy, and not sacrifice,'* you wouldn't have condemned the guiltless. 8 For the Son of Man is Lord of the Sabbath."

9 He departed from there and went into their synagogue. 10 And behold, there was a man with a withered hand. They asked him, "Is it lawful to heal on the Sabbath day?" so that they might accuse him.

11 He said to them, "What man is there amongst you who has one sheep, and if this one falls into a pit on the Sabbath day, won't he grab on to it and lift it out? 12 Of how much more value then is a man than a sheep! Therefore it is lawful to do good on the Sabbath day." 13 Then he told the man, "Stretch out your hand." He stretched it out; and it was restored whole, just like the other. 14 But the Pharisees went out and conspired against him, how they might destroy him.

15 Jesus, perceiving that, withdrew from there. Great multitudes followed him; and he healed them all, 16 and commanded them that they should not make him known, 17 that it might be fulfilled which was spoken through Isaiah the prophet, saying,

18 "Behold, my servant whom I have chosen,
my beloved in whom my soul is well pleased.
I will put my Spirit on him.
He will proclaim justice to the nations.
19 He will not strive, nor shout,
neither will anyone hear his voice in the streets.
20 He won't break a bruised reed.
He won't quench a smoking flax,
until he leads justice to victory.
21 In his name, the nations will hope."*

22 Then one possessed by a demon, blind and mute, was brought to him; and he healed him, so that the blind and mute man both spoke and saw. 23 All the multitudes were amazed, and said, "Can this be the son of David?" 24 But when the Pharisees heard it, they said, "This man does not cast out demons except by Beelzebul, the prince of the demons."

25 Knowing their thoughts, Jesus said to them, "Every kingdom divided against itself is brought to desolation, and every city or house divided against itself will not stand. 26 If Satan casts out Satan, he is divided against himself. How then will his kingdom stand? 27 If I by Beelzebul cast out demons, by whom do your children cast them out? Therefore they will be your judges. 28 But if I by the Spirit of God cast out demons, then God's Kingdom has come upon you. 29 Or how can one enter into the house of the strong man and plunder his goods, unless he first bind the strong man? Then he will plunder his house.

30 "He who is not with me is against me, and he who doesn't gather with me, scatters. 31 Therefore I tell you, every sin and blasphemy will be forgiven men, but the blasphemy against the Spirit will not be forgiven men. 32 Whoever speaks a word against the Son of Man, it will be forgiven him;

but whoever speaks against the Holy Spirit, it will not be forgiven him, either in this age, or in that which is to come.

33 "Either make the tree good and its fruit good, or make the tree corrupt and its fruit corrupt; for the tree is known by its fruit. 34 You offspring of vipers, how can you, being evil, speak good things? For out of the abundance of the heart, the mouth speaks. 35 The good man out of his good treasureᶜ brings out good things, and the evil man out of his evil treasure brings out evil things. 36 I tell you that every idle word that men speak, they will give account of it in the day of judgement. 37 For by your words you will be justified, and by your words you will be condemned."

38 Then certain of the scribes and Pharisees answered, "Teacher, we want to see a sign from you."

39 But he answered them, "An evil and adulterous generation seeks after a sign, but no sign will be given to it but the sign of Jonah the prophet. 40 For as Jonah was three days and three nights in the belly of the huge fish, so will the Son of Man be three days and three nights in the heart of the earth. 41 The men of Nineveh will stand up in the judgement with this generation and will condemn it, for they repented at the preaching of Jonah; and behold, someone greater than Jonah is here. 42 The Queen of the South will rise up in the judgement with this generation and will condemn it, for she came from the ends of the earth to hear the wisdom of Solomon; and behold, someone greater than Solomon is here.

43 "When an unclean spirit has gone out of a man, he passes through waterless places seeking rest, and doesn't find it. 44 Then he says, 'I will return into my house from which I came;' and when he has come back, he finds it empty, swept, and put in order. 45 Then he goes and takes with himself seven other spirits more evil than he is, and they enter in and dwell there. The last state of that man becomes worse than the first. Even so will it be also to this evil generation."

46 While he was yet speaking to the multitudes, behold, his mother and his brothers stood outside, seeking to speak to him. 47 One said to him, "Behold, your mother and your brothers stand outside, seeking to speak to you."

48 But he answered him who spoke to him, "Who is my mother? Who are my brothers?" 49 He stretched out his hand towards his disciples, and said, "Behold, my mother and my brothers! 50 For whoever does the will of my Father who is in heaven, he is my brother, and sister, and mother."

13

1 On that day Jesus went out of the house and sat by the seaside. 2 Great multitudes gathered to him, so that he entered into a boat and sat; and all the multitude stood on the beach. 3 He spoke to them many things in parables, saying, "Behold, a farmer went out to sow. 4 As he sowed, some seeds fell by the roadside, and the birds came and devoured them. 5 Others fell on rocky ground, where they didn't have much soil, and immediately they sprang up, because they had no depth of earth. 6 When the sun had risen, they were scorched. Because they had no root, they withered away. 7 Others fell amongst thorns. The thorns grew up and choked them. 8 Others fell on good soil and yielded fruit: some one hundred times as much, some sixty, and some thirty. 9 He who has ears to hear, let him hear."

10 The disciples came, and said to him, "Why do you speak to them in parables?"

11 He answered them, "To you it is given to know the mysteries of the Kingdom of Heaven, but it is not given to them. 12 For whoever has, to him will be given, and he will have abundance; but whoever doesn't have, from him will be taken away even that which he has. 13 Therefore I speak to them in parables, because seeing they don't see, and hearing, they don't hear, neither do they understand. 14 In them the prophecy of Isaiah is fulfilled, which says,

'By hearing you will hear,
and will in no way understand;
Seeing you will see,
and will in no way perceive;
15 for this people's heart has grown callous,
their ears are dull of hearing,
and they have closed their eyes;
or else perhaps they might perceive with their eyes,
hear with their ears,
understand with their heart,
and would turn again,
and I would heal them.'*

16 "But blessed are your eyes, for they see; and your ears, for they hear. 17 For most certainly I tell you that many prophets and righteous men desired to see the things which you see, and didn't see them; and to hear the things which you hear, and didn't hear them.

18 "Hear, then, the parable of the farmer. 19 When anyone hears the word of the Kingdom and doesn't understand it, the evil one comes and snatches away that which has been sown in his heart. This is what was sown by the roadside. 20 What was sown on the rocky places, this is he who hears the word and immediately with joy receives it; 21 yet he has no root in himself, but endures for a while. When oppression or persecution arises because of the word, immediately he stumbles. 22 What was sown amongst the thorns, this is he who hears the word, but the cares of this age

---

ᵃ *11:19* NU reads "actions" instead of "children"
ᵇ *11:23* or, Hell
** 12:4 1 Samuel 21:3-6
** 12:7 Hosea 6:6

** 12:21 Isaiah 42:1-4
ᶜ *12:35* TR adds "of the heart"
** 13:15 Isaiah 6:9-10

and the deceitfulness of riches choke the word, and he becomes unfruitful. 23 What was sown on the good ground, this is he who hears the word and understands it, who most certainly bears fruit and produces, some one hundred times as much, some sixty, and some thirty."

24 He set another parable before them, saying, "The Kingdom of Heaven is like a man who sowed good seed in his field, 25 but while people slept, his enemy came and sowed darnel weeds[a] also amongst the wheat, and went away. 26 But when the blade sprang up and produced grain, then the darnel weeds appeared also. 27 The servants of the householder came and said to him, 'Sir, didn't you sow good seed in your field? Where did these darnel weeds come from?'

28 "He said to them, 'An enemy has done this.'

"The servants asked him, 'Do you want us to go and gather them up?'

29 "But he said, 'No, lest perhaps while you gather up the darnel weeds, you root up the wheat with them. 30 Let both grow together until the harvest, and in the harvest time I will tell the reapers, "First, gather up the darnel weeds, and bind them in bundles to burn them; but gather the wheat into my barn."'"

31 He set another parable before them, saying, "The Kingdom of Heaven is like a grain of mustard seed which a man took, and sowed in his field, 32 which indeed is smaller than all seeds. But when it is grown, it is greater than the herbs and becomes a tree, so that the birds of the air come and lodge in its branches."

33 He spoke another parable to them. "The Kingdom of Heaven is like yeast which a woman took and hid in three measures[b] of meal, until it was all leavened."

34 Jesus spoke all these things in parables to the multitudes; and without a parable, he didn't speak to them, 35 that it might be fulfilled which was spoken through the prophet, saying,
"I will open my mouth in parables;
I will utter things hidden from the foundation of the world."[*]

36 Then Jesus sent the multitudes away, and went into the house. His disciples came to him, saying, "Explain to us the parable of the darnel weeds of the field."

37 He answered them, "He who sows the good seed is the Son of Man, 38 the field is the world, the good seeds are the children of the Kingdom, and the darnel weeds are the children of the evil one. 39 The enemy who sowed them is the devil. The harvest is the end of the age, and the reapers are angels. 40 As therefore the darnel weeds are gathered up and burnt with fire; so will it be at the end of this age. 41 The Son of Man will send out his angels, and they will gather out of his Kingdom all things that cause stumbling and those who do iniquity, 42 and will cast them into the furnace of fire. There will be weeping and gnashing of teeth. 43 Then the righteous will shine like the sun in the Kingdom of their Father. He who has ears to hear, let him hear.

44 "Again, the Kingdom of Heaven is like treasure hidden in the field, which a man found and hid. In his joy, he goes and sells all that he has and buys that field.

45 "Again, the Kingdom of Heaven is like a man who is a merchant seeking fine pearls, 46 who having found one pearl of great price, he went and sold all that he had and bought it.

47 "Again, the Kingdom of Heaven is like a dragnet that was cast into the sea and gathered some fish of every kind, 48 which, when it was filled, fishermen drew up on the beach. They sat down and gathered the good into containers, but the bad they threw away. 49 So it will be in the end of the world.[c] The angels will come and separate the wicked from amongst the righteous, 50 and will cast them into the furnace of fire. There will be weeping and gnashing of teeth." 51 Jesus said to them, "Have you understood all these things?"

They answered him, "Yes, Lord."

52 He said to them, "Therefore every scribe who has been made a disciple in the Kingdom of Heaven is like a man who is a householder, who brings out of his treasure new and old things."

53 When Jesus had finished these parables, he departed from there. 54 Coming into his own country, he taught them in their synagogue, so that they were astonished and said, "Where did this man get this wisdom and these mighty works? 55 Isn't this the carpenter's son? Isn't his mother called Mary, and his brothers James, Joses, Simon, and Judas?[d] 56 Aren't all of his sisters with us? Where then did this man get all of these things?" 57 They were offended by him.

But Jesus said to them, "A prophet is not without honour, except in his own country and in his own house." 58 He didn't do many mighty works there because of their unbelief.

14

1 At that time, Herod the tetrarch heard the report concerning Jesus, 2 and said to his servants, "This is John the Baptiser. He is risen from the dead. That is why these powers work in him." 3 For Herod had arrested John, bound him, and put him in prison for the sake of Herodias, his brother Philip's wife. 4 For John said to him, "It is not lawful for you to have her." 5 When he would have put him to death, he feared the multitude, because they counted him as a prophet. 6 But when Herod's birthday came, the daughter of Herodias danced amongst them and pleased Herod. 7 Therefore he promised with an oath to give her whatever she should ask. 8 She, being prompted by her mother, said, "Give me here on a platter the head of John the Baptiser."

9 The king was grieved, but for the sake of his oaths and of those who sat at the table with him, he commanded it to be given, 10 and he sent and beheaded John in the prison. 11 His head was brought on a platter and given to the young lady; and she brought it to her mother. 12 His disciples came, took the body, and buried it. Then they went and told Jesus. 13 Now when Jesus heard this, he withdrew from there in a boat to a deserted place apart. When the multitudes heard it, they followed him on foot from the cities.

14 Jesus went out, and he saw a great multitude. He had compassion on them and healed their sick. 15 When evening had come, his disciples came to him, saying, "This place is deserted, and the hour is already late. Send the multitudes away, that they may go into the villages, and buy themselves food."

16 But Jesus said to them, "They don't need to go away. You give them something to eat."

17 They told him, "We only have here five loaves and two fish."

18 He said, "Bring them here to me." 19 He commanded the multitudes to sit down on the grass; and he took the five loaves and the two fish, and looking up to heaven, he blessed, broke and gave the loaves to the disciples; and the disciples gave to the multitudes. 20 They all ate and were filled. They took up twelve baskets full of that which remained left over from the broken pieces. 21 Those who ate were about five thousand men, in addition to women and children.

22 Immediately Jesus made the disciples get into the boat and go ahead of him to the other side, while he sent the multitudes away. 23 After he had sent the multitudes away, he went up into the mountain by himself to pray. When evening had come, he was there alone. 24 But the boat was now in the middle of the sea, distressed by the waves, for the wind was contrary. 25 In the fourth watch of the night,[e] Jesus came to them, walking on the sea.[*] 26 When the disciples saw him walking on the sea, they were troubled, saying, "It's a ghost!" and they cried out for fear. 27 But immediately Jesus spoke to them, saying, "Cheer up! It is I! [f] Don't be afraid."

28 Peter answered him and said, "Lord, if it is you, command me to come to you on the waters."

29 He said, "Come!"

Peter stepped down from the boat and walked on the waters to come to Jesus. 30 But when he saw that the wind was strong, he was afraid, and beginning to sink, he cried out, saying, "Lord, save me!"

31 Immediately Jesus stretched out his hand, took hold of him, and said to him, "You of little faith, why did you doubt?" 32 When they got up into the boat, the wind ceased. 33 Those who were in the boat came and worshipped him, saying, "You are truly the Son of God!"

34 When they had crossed over, they came to the land of Gennesaret. 35 When the people of that place recognised him, they sent into all that surrounding region and brought to him all who were sick; 36 and they begged him that they might just touch the fringe[g] of his garment. As many as touched it were made whole.

15

1 Then Pharisees and scribes came to Jesus from Jerusalem, saying, 2 "Why do your disciples disobey the tradition of the elders? For they don't wash their hands when they eat bread."

3 He answered them, "Why do you also disobey the commandment of God because of your tradition? 4 For God commanded, 'Honour your father and your mother,'[*] and, 'He who speaks evil of father or mother, let him be put to death.'[*] 5 But you say, 'Whoever may tell his father or his mother, "Whatever help you might otherwise have gotten from me is a gift devoted to God," 6 he shall not honour his father or mother.' You have made the commandment of God void because of your tradition. 7 You hypocrites! Well did Isaiah prophesy of you, saying,
8 'These people draw near to me with their mouth,
   and honour me with their lips;
   but their heart is far from me.
9 And they worship me in vain,
   teaching as doctrine rules made by men.'"[*]

10 He summoned the multitude, and said to them, "Hear, and understand. 11 That which enters into the mouth doesn't defile the man; but that which proceeds out of the mouth, this defiles the man."

12 Then the disciples came and said to him, "Do you know that the Pharisees were offended when they heard this saying?"

13 But he answered, "Every plant which my heavenly Father didn't plant will be uprooted. 14 Leave them alone. They are blind guides of the blind. If the blind guide the blind, both will fall into a pit."

---

a 13:25 darnel is a weed grass (probably bearded darnel or lolium temulentum) that looks very much like wheat until it is mature, when the difference becomes very apparent.
b 13:33 literally, three sata. Three sata is about 39 litres or a bit more than a bushel
** 13:35 Psalms 78:2
c 13:49 or, end of the age.
d 13:55 or, Judah

e 14:25 The night was equally divided into four watches, so the fourth watch is approximately 3:00 a.m. to sunrise.
** 14:25 See Job 9:8
f 14:27 or, I AM!
g 14:36 or, tassel
** 15:4 Exodus 20:12; Deuteronomy 5:16
** 15:4 Exodus 21:17; Leviticus 20:9
** 15:9 Isaiah 29:13

₁₅ Peter answered him, "Explain the parable to us."

₁₆ So Jesus said, "Do you also still not understand? ₁₇ Don't you understand that whatever goes into the mouth passes into the belly and then out of the body? ₁₈ But the things which proceed out of the mouth come out of the heart, and they defile the man. ₁₉ For out of the heart come evil thoughts, murders, adulteries, sexual sins, thefts, false testimony, and blasphemies. ₂₀ These are the things which defile the man; but to eat with unwashed hands doesn't defile the man."

₂₁ Jesus went out from there and withdrew into the region of Tyre and Sidon. ₂₂ Behold, a Canaanite woman came out from those borders and cried, saying, "Have mercy on me, Lord, you son of David! My daughter is severely possessed by a demon!"

₂₃ But he answered her not a word.

His disciples came and begged him, saying, "Send her away; for she cries after us."

₂₄ But he answered, "I wasn't sent to anyone but the lost sheep of the house of Israel."

₂₅ But she came and worshipped him, saying, "Lord, help me."

₂₆ But he answered, "It is not appropriate to take the children's bread and throw it to the dogs."

₂₇ But she said, "Yes, Lord, but even the dogs eat the crumbs which fall from their masters' table."

₂₈ Then Jesus answered her, "Woman, great is your faith! Be it done to you even as you desire." And her daughter was healed from that hour.

₂₉ Jesus departed from there and came near to the sea of Galilee; and he went up on the mountain and sat there. ₃₀ Great multitudes came to him, having with them the lame, blind, mute, maimed, and many others, and they put them down at his feet. He healed them, ₃₁ so that the multitude wondered when they saw the mute speaking, the injured healed, the lame walking, and the blind seeing—and they glorified the God of Israel.

₃₂ Jesus summoned his disciples and said, "I have compassion on the multitude, because they have continued with me now three days and have nothing to eat. I don't want to send them away fasting, or they might faint on the way."

₃₃ The disciples said to him, "Where could we get so many loaves in a deserted place as to satisfy so great a multitude?"

₃₄ Jesus said to them, "How many loaves do you have?"

They said, "Seven, and a few small fish."

₃₅ He commanded the multitude to sit down on the ground; ₃₆ and he took the seven loaves and the fish. He gave thanks and broke them, and gave to the disciples, and the disciples to the multitudes. ₃₇ They all ate and were filled. They took up seven baskets full of the broken pieces that were left over. ₃₈ Those who ate were four thousand men, in addition to women and children. ₃₉ Then he sent away the multitudes, got into the boat, and came into the borders of Magdala.

16

₁ The Pharisees and Sadducees came, and testing him, asked him to show them a sign from heaven. ₂ But he answered them, "When it is evening, you say, 'It will be fair weather, for the sky is red.' ₃ In the morning, 'It will be foul weather today, for the sky is red and threatening.' Hypocrites! You know how to discern the appearance of the sky, but you can't discern the signs of the times! ₄ An evil and adulterous generation seeks after a sign, and there will be no sign given to it, except the sign of the prophet Jonah."

He left them and departed. ₅ The disciples came to the other side and had forgotten to take bread. ₆ Jesus said to them, "Take heed and beware of the yeast of the Pharisees and Sadducees."

₇ They reasoned amongst themselves, saying, "We brought no bread."

₈ Jesus, perceiving it, said, "Why do you reason amongst yourselves, you of little faith, because you have brought no bread? ₉ Don't you yet perceive or remember the five loaves for the five thousand, and how many baskets you took up, ₁₀ or the seven loaves for the four thousand, and how many baskets you took up? ₁₁ How is it that you don't perceive that I didn't speak to you concerning bread? But beware of the yeast of the Pharisees and Sadducees."

₁₂ Then they understood that he didn't tell them to beware of the yeast of bread, but of the teaching of the Pharisees and Sadducees.

₁₃ Now when Jesus came into the parts of Caesarea Philippi, he asked his disciples, saying, "Who do men say that I, the Son of Man, am?"

₁₄ They said, "Some say John the Baptiser, some, Elijah, and others, Jeremiah or one of the prophets."

₁₅ He said to them, "But who do you say that I am?"

₁₆ Simon Peter answered, "You are the Christ, the Son of the living God."

₁₇ Jesus answered him, "Blessed are you, Simon Bar Jonah, for flesh and blood has not revealed this to you, but my Father who is in heaven. ₁₈ I also tell you that you are Peter,ᵃ and on this rock ᵇ I will build my assembly, and the gates of Hadesᶜ will not prevail against it. ₁₉ I will give to you the keys of the Kingdom of Heaven, and whatever you bind on earth will have been bound in heaven; and whatever you release on earth will have been released in heaven." ₂₀ Then he commanded the disciples that they should tell no one that he was Jesus the Christ.

₂₁ From that time, Jesus began to show his disciples that he must go to Jerusalem and suffer many things from the elders, chief priests, and scribes, and be killed, and the third day be raised up.

₂₂ Peter took him aside and began to rebuke him, saying, "Far be it from you, Lord! This will never be done to you."

₂₃ But he turned and said to Peter, "Get behind me, Satan! You are a stumbling block to me, for you are not setting your mind on the things of God, but on the things of men."

₂₄ Then Jesus said to his disciples, "If anyone desires to come after me, let him deny himself, take up his cross, and follow me. ₂₅ For whoever desires to save his life will lose it, and whoever will lose his life for my sake will find it. ₂₆ For what will it profit a man if he gains the whole world and forfeits his life? Or what will a man give in exchange for his life? ₂₇ For the Son of Man will come in the glory of his Father with his angels, and then he will render to everyone according to his deeds. ₂₈ Most certainly I tell you, there are some standing here who will in no way taste of death until they see the Son of Man coming in his Kingdom."

17

₁ After six days, Jesus took with him Peter, James, and John his brother, and brought them up into a high mountain by themselves. ₂ He was changedᵈ before them. His face shone like the sun, and his garments became as white as the light. ₃ Behold, Moses and Elijah appeared to them talking with him.

₄ Peter answered and said to Jesus, "Lord, it is good for us to be here. If you want, let's make three tents here: one for you, one for Moses, and one for Elijah."

₅ While he was still speaking, behold, a bright cloud overshadowed them. Behold, a voice came out of the cloud, saying, "This is my beloved Son, in whom I am well pleased. Listen to him."

₆ When the disciples heard it, they fell on their faces, and were very afraid. ₇ Jesus came and touched them and said, "Get up, and don't be afraid." ₈ Lifting up their eyes, they saw no one, except Jesus alone.

₉ As they were coming down from the mountain, Jesus commanded them, saying, "Don't tell anyone what you saw, until the Son of Man has risen from the dead."

₁₀ His disciples asked him, saying, "Then why do the scribes say that Elijah must come first?"

₁₁ Jesus answered them, "Elijah indeed comes first, and will restore all things; ₁₂ but I tell you that Elijah has come already, and they didn't recognise him, but did to him whatever they wanted to. Even so the Son of Man will also suffer by them." ₁₃ Then the disciples understood that he spoke to them of John the Baptiser.

₁₄ When they came to the multitude, a man came to him, kneeling down to him and saying, ₁₅"Lord, have mercy on my son, for he is epileptic and suffers grievously; for he often falls into the fire, and often into the water. ₁₆ So I brought him to your disciples, and they could not cure him."

₁₇ Jesus answered, "Faithless and perverse generation! How long will I be with you? How long will I bear with you? Bring him here to me." ₁₈ Jesus rebuked the demon, and it went out of him, and the boy was cured from that hour.

₁₉ Then the disciples came to Jesus privately, and said, "Why weren't we able to cast it out?"

₂₀ He said to them, "Because of your unbelief. For most certainly I tell you, if you have faith as a grain of mustard seed, you will tell this mountain, 'Move from here to there,' and it will move; and nothing will be impossible for you. ₂₁ But this kind doesn't go out except by prayer and fasting." ᵉ

₂₂ While they were staying in Galilee, Jesus said to them, "The Son of Man is about to be delivered up into the hands of men, ₂₃ and they will kill him, and the third day he will be raised up."

They were exceedingly sorry.

₂₄ When they had come to Capernaum, those who collected the didrachma coinsᶠ came to Peter, and said, "Doesn't your teacher pay the didrachma?" ₂₅ He said, "Yes."

When he came into the house, Jesus anticipated him, saying, "What do you think, Simon? From whom do the kings of the earth receive toll or tribute? From their children, or from strangers?"

₂₆Peter said to him, "From strangers."

Jesus said to him, "Therefore the children are exempt. ₂₇ But, lest we cause them to stumble, go to the sea, cast a hook, and take up the first fish that comes up. When you have opened its mouth, you will find a stater coin.ᵍ Take that, and give it to them for me and you."

18

₁ In that hour the disciples came to Jesus, saying, "Who then is greatest in the Kingdom of Heaven?"

₂ Jesus called a little child to himself, and set him in the middle of them ₃ and said, "Most certainly I tell you, unless you turn and become as little children, you will in no way enter into the Kingdom of Heaven. ₄

ᵃ 16:18 Peter's name, Petros in Greek, is the word for a specific rock or stone.
ᵇ 16:18 Greek, petra, a rock mass or bedrock.
ᶜ 16:18 or, Hell
ᵈ 17:2 or, transfigured
ᵉ 17:21 NU omits verse 21.
ᶠ 17:24 A didrachma is a Greek silver coin worth 2 drachmas, about as much as 2 Roman denarii, or about 2 days' wages. It was commonly used to pay the half-shekel temple tax, because 2 drachmas were worth one half shekel of silver. A shekel is about 10 grams or about 0.35 ounces.

ᵍ 17:27 A stater is a silver coin equivalent to four Attic or two Alexandrian drachmas, or a Jewish shekel: just exactly enough to cover the half-shekel temple tax for two people. A shekel is about 10 grams or about 0.35 ounces, usually in the form of a silver coin.

Whoever therefore humbles himself as this little child is the greatest in the Kingdom of Heaven. 5 Whoever receives one such little child in my name receives me, 6 but whoever causes one of these little ones who believe in me to stumble, it would be better for him if a huge millstone were hung around his neck and that he were sunk in the depths of the sea.

7 "Woe to the world because of occasions of stumbling! For it must be that the occasions come, but woe to that person through whom the occasion comes! 8 If your hand or your foot causes you to stumble, cut it off and cast it from you. It is better for you to enter into life maimed or crippled, rather than having two hands or two feet to be cast into the eternal fire. 9 If your eye causes you to stumble, pluck it out and cast it from you. It is better for you to enter into life with one eye, rather than having two eyes to be cast into the Gehenna[a] of fire. 10 See that you don't despise one of these little ones, for I tell you that in heaven their angels always see the face of my Father who is in heaven. 11 For the Son of Man came to save that which was lost.[b]

12 "What do you think? If a man has one hundred sheep, and one of them goes astray, doesn't he leave the ninety-nine, go to the mountains, and seek that which has gone astray? 13 If he finds it, most certainly I tell you, he rejoices over it more than over the ninety-nine which have not gone astray. 14 Even so it is not the will of your Father who is in heaven that one of these little ones should perish.

15 "If your brother sins against you, go, show him his fault between you and him alone. If he listens to you, you have gained back your brother. 16 But if he doesn't listen, take one or two more with you, that at the mouth of two or three witnesses every word may be established.* 17 If he refuses to listen to them, tell it to the assembly. If he refuses to hear the assembly also, let him be to you as a Gentile or a tax collector. 18 Most certainly I tell you, whatever things you bind on earth will have been bound in heaven, and whatever things you release on earth will have been released in heaven. 19 Again, assuredly I tell you, that if two of you will agree on earth concerning anything that they will ask, it will be done for them by my Father who is in heaven. 20 For where two or three are gathered together in my name, there I am in the middle of them."

21 Then Peter came and said to him, "Lord, how often shall my brother sin against me, and I forgive him? Until seven times?"

22 Jesus said to him, "I don't tell you until seven times, but, until seventy times seven. 23 Therefore the Kingdom of Heaven is like a certain king who wanted to settle accounts with his servants. 24 When he had begun to settle, one was brought to him who owed him ten thousand talents.[c] 25 But because he couldn't pay, his lord commanded him to be sold, with his wife, his children, and all that he had, and payment to be made. 26 The servant therefore fell down and knelt before him, saying, 'Lord, have patience with me, and I will repay you all!' 27 The lord of that servant, being moved with compassion, released him and forgave him the debt.

28 "But that servant went out and found one of his fellow servants who owed him one hundred denarii,[d] and he grabbed him and took him by the throat, saying, 'Pay me what you owe!'

29 "So his fellow servant fell down at his feet and begged him, saying, 'Have patience with me, and I will repay you!' 30 He would not, but went and cast him into prison until he should pay back that which was due. 31 So when his fellow servants saw what was done, they were exceedingly sorry, and came and told their lord all that was done. 32 Then his lord called him in and said to him, 'You wicked servant! I forgave you all that debt because you begged me. 33 Shouldn't you also have had mercy on your fellow servant, even as I had mercy on you?' 34 His lord was angry, and delivered him to the tormentors until he should pay all that was due to him. 35 So my heavenly Father will also do to you, if you don't each forgive your brother from your hearts for his misdeeds."

19

1 When Jesus had finished these words, he departed from Galilee and came into the borders of Judea beyond the Jordan. 2 Great multitudes followed him, and he healed them there.

3 Pharisees came to him, testing him and saying, "Is it lawful for a man to divorce his wife for any reason?"

4 He answered, "Haven't you read that he who made them from the beginning made them male and female,* 5 and said, 'For this cause a man shall leave his father and mother, and shall be joined to his wife; and the two shall become one flesh'?* 6 So that they are no more two, but one flesh. What therefore God has joined together, don't let man tear apart."

7 They asked him, "Why then did Moses command us to give her a certificate of divorce and divorce her?"

8 He said to them, "Moses, because of the hardness of your hearts, allowed you to divorce your wives, but from the beginning it has not been so. 9 I tell you that whoever divorces his wife, except for sexual

immorality, and marries another, commits adultery; and he who marries her when she is divorced commits adultery."

10 His disciples said to him, "If this is the case of the man with his wife, it is not expedient to marry."

11 But he said to them, "Not all men can receive this saying, but those to whom it is given. 12 For there are eunuchs who were born that way from their mother's womb, and there are eunuchs who were made eunuchs by men; and there are eunuchs who made themselves eunuchs for the Kingdom of Heaven's sake. He who is able to receive it, let him receive it."

13 Then little children were brought to him that he should lay his hands on them and pray; and the disciples rebuked them. 14 But Jesus said, "Allow the little children, and don't forbid them to come to me; for the Kingdom of Heaven belongs to ones like these." 15 He laid his hands on them, and departed from there.

16 Behold, one came to him and said, "Good teacher, what good thing shall I do, that I may have eternal life?"

17 He said to him, "Why do you call me good?[e] No one is good but one, that is, God. But if you want to enter into life, keep the commandments."

18 He said to him, "Which ones?"

Jesus said, "'You shall not murder.' 'You shall not commit adultery.' 'You shall not steal.' 'You shall not offer false testimony.' 19 'Honour your father and your mother.'* And, 'You shall love your neighbour as yourself.'"*

20 The young man said to him, "All these things I have observed from my youth. What do I still lack?"

21 Jesus said to him, "If you want to be perfect, go, sell what you have, and give to the poor, and you will have treasure in heaven; and come, follow me." 22 But when the young man heard this, he went away sad, for he was one who had great possessions.

23 Jesus said to his disciples, "Most certainly I say to you, a rich man will enter into the Kingdom of Heaven with difficulty. 24 Again I tell you, it is easier for a camel to go through a needle's eye than for a rich man to enter into God's Kingdom."

25 When the disciples heard it, they were exceedingly astonished, saying, "Who then can be saved?"

26 Looking at them, Jesus said, "With men this is impossible, but with God all things are possible."

27 Then Peter answered, "Behold, we have left everything and followed you. What then will we have?"

28 Jesus said to them, "Most certainly I tell you that you who have followed me, in the regeneration when the Son of Man will sit on the throne of his glory, you also will sit on twelve thrones, judging the twelve tribes of Israel. 29 Everyone who has left houses, or brothers, or sisters, or father, or mother, or wife, or children, or lands, for my name's sake, will receive one hundred times, and will inherit eternal life. 30 But many will be last who are first, and first who are last.

20

1 "For the Kingdom of Heaven is like a man who was the master of a household, who went out early in the morning to hire labourers for his vineyard. 2 When he had agreed with the labourers for a denarius[f] a day, he sent them into his vineyard. 3 He went out about the third hour,[g] and saw others standing idle in the marketplace. 4 He said to them, 'You also go into the vineyard, and whatever is right I will give you.' So they went their way. 5 Again he went out about the sixth and the ninth hour,[h] and did likewise. 6 About the eleventh hour[i] he went out and found others standing idle. He said to them, 'Why do you stand here all day idle?'

7 "They said to him, 'Because no one has hired us.'

"He said to them, 'You also go into the vineyard, and you will receive whatever is right.'

8 "When evening had come, the lord of the vineyard said to his manager, 'Call the labourers and pay them their wages, beginning from the last to the first.' 9 "When those who were hired at about the eleventh hour came, they each received a denarius. 10 When the first came, they supposed that they would receive more; and they likewise each received a denarius. 11 When they received it, they murmured against the master of the household, 12 saying, 'These last have spent one hour, and you have made them equal to us who have borne the burden of the day and the scorching heat!'

13 "But he answered one of them, 'Friend, I am doing you no wrong. Didn't you agree with me for a denarius? 14 Take that which is yours, and go your way. It is my desire to give to this last just as much as to you. 15 Isn't it lawful for me to do what I want to with what I own? Or is your eye evil, because I am good?' 16 So the last will be first, and the first last. For many are called, but few are chosen."

17 As Jesus was going up to Jerusalem, he took the twelve disciples aside, and on the way he said to them, 18 "Behold, we are going up to

---

a *18:9* or, Hell

b *18:11* NU omits verse 11.

** 18:16 Deuteronomy 19:15

c *18:24* Ten thousand talents (about 300 metric tonnes of silver) represents an extremely large sum of money, equivalent to about 60,000,000 denarii, where one denarius was typical of one day's wages for agricultural labour.

d *18:28* 100 denarii was about one sixtieth of a talent, or about 500 grams (1.1 pounds) of silver.

** 19:4 Genesis 1:27

** 19:5 Genesis 2:24

e *19:17* So MT and TR. NU reads "Why do you ask me about what is good?"

** 19:19 Exodus 20:12-16; Deuteronomy 5:16-20

** 19:19 Leviticus 19:18

f *20:2* A denarius is a silver Roman coin worth 1/25th of a Roman aureus. This was a common wage for a day of farm labour.

g *20:3* Time was measured from sunrise to sunset, so the third hour would be about 9:00 a.m.

h *20:5* noon and 3:00 p.m.

i *20:6* 5:00 p.m.

Jerusalem, and the Son of Man will be delivered to the chief priests and scribes, and they will condemn him to death, ₁₉ and will hand him over to the Gentiles to mock, to scourge, and to crucify; and the third day he will be raised up."

₂₀ Then the mother of the sons of Zebedee came to him with her sons, kneeling and asking a certain thing of him. ₂₁ He said to her, "What do you want?"

She said to him, "Command that these, my two sons, may sit, one on your right hand and one on your left hand, in your Kingdom."

₂₂ But Jesus answered, "You don't know what you are asking. Are you able to drink the cup that I am about to drink, and be baptised with the baptism that I am baptised with?"

They said to him, "We are able."

₂₃ He said to them, "You will indeed drink my cup, and be baptised with the baptism that I am baptised with; but to sit on my right hand and on my left hand is not mine to give, but it is for whom it has been prepared by my Father."

₂₄ When the ten heard it, they were indignant with the two brothers. ₂₅ But Jesus summoned them, and said, "You know that the rulers of the nations lord it over them, and their great ones exercise authority over them. ₂₆ It shall not be so amongst you; but whoever desires to become great amongst you shall be[a] your servant. ₂₇ Whoever desires to be first amongst you shall be your bondservant, ₂₈ even as the Son of Man came not to be served, but to serve, and to give his life as a ransom for many."

₂₉ As they went out from Jericho, a great multitude followed him. ₃₀ Behold, two blind men sitting by the road, when they heard that Jesus was passing by, cried out, "Lord, have mercy on us, you son of David!" ₃₁ The multitude rebuked them, telling them that they should be quiet, but they cried out even more, "Lord, have mercy on us, you son of David!"

₃₂ Jesus stood still and called them, and asked, "What do you want me to do for you?"

₃₃ They told him, "Lord, that our eyes may be opened."

₃₄ Jesus, being moved with compassion, touched their eyes; and immediately their eyes received their sight, and they followed him.

21

₁ When they came near to Jerusalem and came to Bethsphage,[b] to the Mount of Olives, then Jesus sent two disciples, ₂ saying to them, "Go into the village that is opposite you, and immediately you will find a donkey tied, and a colt with her. Untie them and bring them to me. ₃ If anyone says anything to you, you shall say, 'The Lord needs them,' and immediately he will send them."

₄ All this was done that it might be fulfilled which was spoken through the prophet, saying,

₅ "Tell the daughter of Zion,
behold, your King comes to you,
humble, and riding on a donkey,
on a colt, the foal of a donkey.'"

₆ The disciples went and did just as Jesus commanded them, ₇ and brought the donkey and the colt and laid their clothes on them; and he sat on them. ₈ A very great multitude spread their clothes on the road. Others cut branches from the trees and spread them on the road. ₉ The multitudes who went in front of him, and those who followed, kept shouting, "Hosanna[c] to the son of David! Blessed is he who comes in the name of the Lord! Hosanna in the highest!" *

₁₀ When he had come into Jerusalem, all the city was stirred up, saying, "Who is this?"

₁₁ The multitudes said, "This is the prophet, Jesus, from Nazareth of Galilee."

₁₂ Jesus entered into the temple of God and drove out all of those who sold and bought in the temple, and overthrew the money changers' tables and the seats of those who sold the doves. ₁₃ He said to them, "It is written, 'My house shall be called a house of prayer,' * but you have made it a den of robbers!" *

₁₄ The lame and the blind came to him in the temple, and he healed them. ₁₅ But when the chief priests and the scribes saw the wonderful things that he did, and the children who were crying in the temple and saying, "Hosanna to the son of David!" they were indignant, ₁₆ and said to him, "Do you hear what these are saying?"

Jesus said to them, "Yes. Did you never read, 'Out of the mouth of children and nursing babies, you have perfected praise'?" *

₁₇ He left them and went out of the city to Bethany, and camped there.

₁₈ Now in the morning, as he returned to the city, he was hungry. ₁₉ Seeing a fig tree by the road, he came to it and found nothing on it but leaves. He said to it, "Let there be no fruit from you forever!"

Immediately the fig tree withered away.

₂₀ When the disciples saw it, they marvelled, saying, "How did the fig tree immediately wither away?"

₂₁ Jesus answered them, "Most certainly I tell you, if you have faith and don't doubt, you will not only do what was done to the fig tree, but even if you told this mountain, 'Be taken up and cast into the sea,' it would be done. ₂₂ All things, whatever you ask in prayer, believing, you will receive."

₂₃ When he had come into the temple, the chief priests and the elders of the people came to him as he was teaching, and said, "By what authority do you do these things? Who gave you this authority?"

₂₄ Jesus answered them, "I also will ask you one question, which if you tell me, I likewise will tell you by what authority I do these things. ₂₅ The baptism of John, where was it from? From heaven or from men?"

They reasoned with themselves, saying, "If we say, 'From heaven,' he will ask us, 'Why then did you not believe him?' ₂₆ But if we say, 'From men,' we fear the multitude, for all hold John as a prophet." ₂₇ They answered Jesus, and said, "We don't know."

He also said to them, "Neither will I tell you by what authority I do these things. ₂₈ But what do you think? A man had two sons, and he came to the first, and said, 'Son, go work today in my vineyard.' ₂₉ He answered, 'I will not,' but afterward he changed his mind, and went. ₃₀ He came to the second, and said the same thing. He answered, 'I'm going, sir,' but he didn't go. ₃₁ Which of the two did the will of his father?"

They said to him, "The first."

Jesus said to them, "Most certainly I tell you that the tax collectors and the prostitutes are entering into God's Kingdom before you. ₃₂ For John came to you in the way of righteousness, and you didn't believe him; but the tax collectors and the prostitutes believed him. When you saw it, you didn't even repent afterward, that you might believe him.

₃₃ "Hear another parable. There was a man who was a master of a household who planted a vineyard, set a hedge about it, dug a wine press in it, built a tower, leased it out to farmers, and went into another country. ₃₄ When the season for the fruit came near, he sent his servants to the farmers to receive his fruit. ₃₅ The farmers took his servants, beat one, killed another, and stoned another. ₃₆ Again, he sent other servants more than the first; and they treated them the same way. ₃₇ But afterward he sent to them his son, saying, 'They will respect my son.' ₃₈ But the farmers, when they saw the son, said amongst themselves, 'This is the heir. Come, let's kill him and seize his inheritance.' ₃₉ So they took him and threw him out of the vineyard, then killed him. ₄₀ When therefore the lord of the vineyard comes, what will he do to those farmers?"

₄₁ They told him, "He will miserably destroy those miserable men, and will lease out the vineyard to other farmers who will give him the fruit in its season."

₄₂ Jesus said to them, "Did you never read in the Scriptures,
'The stone which the builders rejected
was made the head of the corner.
This was from the Lord.
It is marvellous in our eyes'? *

₄₃ "Therefore I tell you, God's Kingdom will be taken away from you and will be given to a nation producing its fruit. ₄₄ He who falls on this stone will be broken to pieces, but on whomever it will fall, it will scatter him as dust."

₄₅ When the chief priests and the Pharisees heard his parables, they perceived that he spoke about them. ₄₆ When they sought to seize him, they feared the multitudes, because they considered him to be a prophet.

22

₁ Jesus answered and spoke to them again in parables, saying, ₂ "The Kingdom of Heaven is like a certain king, who made a wedding feast for his son, ₃ and sent out his servants to call those who were invited to the wedding feast, but they would not come. ₄ Again he sent out other servants, saying, 'Tell those who are invited, "Behold, I have prepared my dinner. My cattle and my fatlings are killed, and all things are ready. Come to the wedding feast!"' ₅ But they made light of it, and went their ways, one to his own farm, another to his merchandise; ₆ and the rest grabbed his servants, treated them shamefully, and killed them. ₇ When the king heard that, he was angry, and sent his armies, destroyed those murderers, and burnt their city.

₈ "Then he said to his servants, 'The wedding is ready, but those who were invited weren't worthy. ₉ Go therefore to the intersections of the highways, and as many as you may find, invite to the wedding feast.' ₁₀ Those servants went out into the highways and gathered together as many as they found, both bad and good. The wedding was filled with guests.

₁₁ "But when the king came in to see the guests, he saw there a man who didn't have on wedding clothing, ₁₂ and he said to him, 'Friend, how did you come in here not wearing wedding clothing?' He was speechless. ₁₃ Then the king said to the servants, 'Bind him hand and foot, take him away, and throw him into the outer darkness. That is where the weeping and grinding of teeth will be.' ₁₄ For many are called, but few chosen."

₁₅ Then the Pharisees went and took counsel how they might entrap him in his talk. ₁₆ They sent their disciples to him, along with the Herodians, saying, "Teacher, we know that you are honest, and teach the way of God in truth, no matter whom you teach; for you aren't partial to anyone. ₁₇ Tell us therefore, what do you think? Is it lawful to pay taxes to Caesar, or not?"

₁₈ But Jesus perceived their wickedness, and said, "Why do you test me, you hypocrites? ₁₉ Show me the tax money."

They brought to him a denarius.

₂₀ He asked them, "Whose is this image and inscription?"

₂₁ They said to him, "Caesar's."

---

a *20:26* TR reads "let him be" instead of "shall be"

b *21:1* TR & NU read "Bethphage" instead of "Bethsphage"

** 21:5 Zechariah 9:9

c *21:9* "Hosanna" means "save us" or "help us, we pray".

** 21:9 Psalms 118:26

** 21:13 Isaiah 56:7

** 21:13 Jeremiah 7:11

** 21:16 Psalms 8:2

** 21:42 Psalms 118:22-23

Then he said to them, "Give therefore to Caesar the things that are Caesar's, and to God the things that are God's."

22 When they heard it, they marvelled, and left him and went away.

23 On that day Sadducees (those who say that there is no resurrection) came to him. They asked him, 24 saying, "Teacher, Moses said, 'If a man dies, having no children, his brother shall marry his wife and raise up offspringa for his brother.' 25 Now there were with us seven brothers. The first married and died, and having no offspring left his wife to his brother. 26 In the same way, the second also, and the third, to the seventh. 27 After them all, the woman died. 28 In the resurrection therefore, whose wife will she be of the seven? For they all had her."

29 But Jesus answered them, "You are mistaken, not knowing the Scriptures, nor the power of God. 30 For in the resurrection they neither marry nor are given in marriage, but are like God's angels in heaven. 31 But concerning the resurrection of the dead, haven't you read that which was spoken to you by God, saying, 32 'I am the God of Abraham, and the God of Isaac, and the God of Jacob'?' God is not the God of the dead, but of the living."

33 When the multitudes heard it, they were astonished at his teaching.

34 But the Pharisees, when they heard that he had silenced the Sadducees, gathered themselves together. 35 One of them, a lawyer, asked him a question, testing him. 36 "Teacher, which is the greatest commandment in the law?"

37 Jesus said to him, "'You shall love the Lord your God with all your heart, with all your soul, and with all your mind.'' 38 This is the first and great commandment. 39 A second likewise is this, 'You shall love your neighbour as yourself.'' 40 The whole law and the prophets depend on these two commandments."

41 Now while the Pharisees were gathered together, Jesus asked them a question, 42 saying, "What do you think of the Christ? Whose son is he?"

They said to him, "Of David."

43 He said to them, "How then does David in the Spirit call him Lord, saying,

44 'The Lord said to my Lord,
sit on my right hand,
until I make your enemies a footstool for your feet'?'

45 "If then David calls him Lord, how is he his son?"

46 No one was able to answer him a word, neither did any man dare ask him any more questions from that day forward.

23

1 Then Jesus spoke to the multitudes and to his disciples, 2 saying, "The scribes and the Pharisees sit on Moses' seat. 3 All things therefore whatever they tell you to observe, observe and do, but don't do their works; for they say, and don't do. 4 For they bind heavy burdens that are grievous to be borne, and lay them on men's shoulders; but they themselves will not lift a finger to help them. 5 But they do all their works to be seen by men. They make their phylacteriesb broad and enlarge the fringesc of their garments, 6 and love the place of honour at feasts, the best seats in the synagogues, 7 the salutations in the marketplaces, and to be called 'Rabbi, Rabbi'd by men. 8 But you are not to be called 'Rabbi', for one is your teacher, the Christ, and all of you are brothers. 9 Call no man on the earth your father, for one is your Father, he who is in heaven. 10 Neither be called masters, for one is your master, the Christ. 11 But he who is greatest amongst you will be your servant. 12 Whoever exalts himself will be humbled, and whoever humbles himself will be exalted.

13 "Woe to you, scribes and Pharisees, hypocrites! For you devour widows' houses, and as a pretence you make long prayers. Therefore you will receive greater condemnation.

14 "But woe to you, scribes and Pharisees, hypocrites! Because you shut up the Kingdom of Heaven against men; for you don't enter in yourselves, neither do you allow those who are entering in to enter.e 15 Woe to you, scribes and Pharisees, hypocrites! For you travel around by sea and land to make one proselyte; and when he becomes one, you make him twice as much a son of Gehennaf as yourselves.

16 "Woe to you, you blind guides, who say, 'Whoever swears by the temple, it is nothing; but whoever swears by the gold of the temple, he is obligated.' 17 You blind fools! For which is greater, the gold or the temple that sanctifies the gold? 18 And, 'Whoever swears by the altar, it is nothing; but whoever swears by the gift that is on it, he is obligated.' 19 You blind fools! For which is greater, the gift, or the altar that sanctifies the gift? 20 He therefore who swears by the altar, swears by it and by everything on it. 21 He who swears by the temple, swears by it and by him who has been livingg in it. 22 He who swears by heaven, swears by the throne of God and by him who sits on it.

23 "Woe to you, scribes and Pharisees, hypocrites! For you tithe mint, dill, and cumin,h and have left undone the weightier matters of the law:

justice, mercy, and faith. But you ought to have done these, and not to have left the other undone. 24 You blind guides, who strain out a gnat, and swallow a camel!

25 "Woe to you, scribes and Pharisees, hypocrites! For you clean the outside of the cup and of the platter, but within they are full of extortion and unrighteousness.i 26 You blind Pharisee, first clean the inside of the cup and of the platter, that its outside may become clean also.

27 "Woe to you, scribes and Pharisees, hypocrites! For you are like whitened tombs, which outwardly appear beautiful, but inwardly are full of dead men's bones and of all uncleanness. 28 Even so you also outwardly appear righteous to men, but inwardly you are full of hypocrisy and iniquity.

29 "Woe to you, scribes and Pharisees, hypocrites! For you build the tombs of the prophets and decorate the tombs of the righteous, 30 and say, 'If we had lived in the days of our fathers, we wouldn't have been partakers with them in the blood of the prophets.' 31 Therefore you testify to yourselves that you are children of those who killed the prophets. 32 Fill up, then, the measure of your fathers. 33 You serpents, you offspring of vipers, how will you escape the judgement of Gehenna?j 34 Therefore, behold, I send to you prophets, wise men, and scribes. Some of them you will kill and crucify; and some of them you will scourge in your synagogues and persecute from city to city, 35 that on you may come all the righteous blood shed on the earth, from the blood of righteous Abel to the blood of Zachariah son of Barachiah, whom you killed between the sanctuary and the altar. 36 Most certainly I tell you, all these things will come upon this generation.

37 "Jerusalem, Jerusalem, who kills the prophets and stones those who are sent to her! How often I would have gathered your children together, even as a hen gathers her chicks under her wings, and you would not! 38 Behold, your house is left to you desolate. 39 For I tell you, you will not see me from now on, until you say, 'Blessed is he who comes in the name of the Lord!''

24

1 Jesus went out from the temple, and was going on his way. His disciples came to him to show him the buildings of the temple. 2 But he answered them, "You see all of these things, don't you? Most certainly I tell you, there will not be left here one stone on another, that will not be thrown down."

3 As he sat on the Mount of Olives, the disciples came to him privately, saying, "Tell us, when will these things be? What is the sign of your coming, and of the end of the age?"

4 Jesus answered them, "Be careful that no one leads you astray. 5 For many will come in my name, saying, 'I am the Christ,' and will lead many astray. 6 You will hear of wars and rumours of wars. See that you aren't troubled, for all this must happen, but the end is not yet. 7 For nation will rise against nation, and kingdom against kingdom; and there will be famines, plagues, and earthquakes in various places. 8 But all these things are the beginning of birth pains.

9 "Then they will deliver you up to oppression and will kill you. You will be hated by all of the nations for my name's sake. 10 Then many will stumble, and will deliver up one another, and will hate one another. 11 Many false prophets will arise and will lead many astray. 12 Because iniquity will be multiplied, the love of many will grow cold. 13 But he who endures to the end will be saved. 14 This Good News of the Kingdom will be preached in the whole world for a testimony to all the nations, and then the end will come.

15 "When, therefore, you see the abomination of desolation,' which was spoken of through Daniel the prophet, standing in the holy place (let the reader understand), 16 then let those who are in Judea flee to the mountains. 17 Let him who is on the housetop not go down to take out the things that are in his house. 18 Let him who is in the field not return back to get his clothes. 19 But woe to those who are with child and to nursing mothers in those days! 20 Pray that your flight will not be in the winter nor on a Sabbath, 21 for then there will be great suffering,k such as has not been from the beginning of the world until now, no, nor ever will be. 22 Unless those days had been shortened, no flesh would have been saved. But for the sake of the chosen ones, those days will be shortened.

23 "Then if any man tells you, 'Behold, here is the Christ!' or, 'There!' don't believe it. 24 For false christs and false prophets will arise, and they will show great signs and wonders, so as to lead astray, if possible, even the chosen ones.

25 "Behold, I have told you beforehand.

26 "If therefore they tell you, 'Behold, he is in the wilderness,' don't go out; or 'Behold, he is in the inner rooms,' don't believe it. 27 For as the lightning flashes from the east, and is seen even to the west, so will the

---

a 22:24 or, seed
** 22:32 Exodus 3:6
** 22:37 Deuteronomy 6:5
** 22:39 Leviticus 19:18
** 22:44 Psalms 110:1
b 23:5 phylacteries (tefillin in Hebrew) are small leather pouches that some Jewish men wear on their forehead and arm in prayer. They are used to carry a small scroll with some Scripture in it. See Deuteronomy 6:8.
c 23:5 or, tassels
d 23:7 NU omits the second "Rabbi".

e 23:14 Some Greek texts reverse the order of verses 13 and 14, and some omit verse 13, numbering verse 14 as 13. NU omits verse 14.
f 23:15 or, Hell
g 23:21 NU reads "lives"
h 23:23 cumin is an aromatic seed from Cuminum cyminum, resembling caraway in flavour and appearance. It is used as a spice.
i 23:25 TR reads "self-indulgence" instead of "unrighteousness"
j 23:33 or, Hell
** 23:39 Psalms 118:26
** 24:15 Daniel 9:27; 11:31; 12:11
k 24:21 or, oppression

coming of the Son of Man be. 28 For wherever the carcass is, that is where the vultures[a] gather together.

29 "But immediately after the suffering[b] of those days, the sun will be darkened, the moon will not give its light, the stars will fall from the sky, and the powers of the heavens will be shaken;[*] 30 and then the sign of the Son of Man will appear in the sky. Then all the tribes of the earth will mourn, and they will see the Son of Man coming on the clouds of the sky with power and great glory. 31 He will send out his angels with a great sound of a trumpet, and they will gather together his chosen ones from the four winds, from one end of the sky to the other.

32 "Now from the fig tree learn this parable: When its branch has now become tender and produces its leaves, you know that the summer is near. 33 Even so you also, when you see all these things, know that he is near, even at the doors. 34 Most certainly I tell you, this generation[c] will not pass away until all these things are accomplished. 35 Heaven and earth will pass away, but my words will not pass away.

36 "But no one knows of that day and hour, not even the angels of heaven,[d] but my Father only. 37 As the days of Noah were, so will the coming of the Son of Man be. 38 For as in those days which were before the flood they were eating and drinking, marrying and giving in marriage, until the day that Noah entered into the ship, 39 and they didn't know until the flood came and took them all away, so will the coming of the Son of Man be. 40 Then two men will be in the field: one will be taken and one will be left. 41 Two women will be grinding at the mill: one will be taken and one will be left. 42 Watch therefore, for you don't know in what hour your Lord comes. 43 But know this, that if the master of the house had known in what watch of the night the thief was coming, he would have watched, and would not have allowed his house to be broken into. 44 Therefore also be ready, for in an hour that you don't expect, the Son of Man will come.

45 "Who then is the faithful and wise servant, whom his lord has set over his household, to give them their food in due season? 46 Blessed is that servant whom his lord finds doing so when he comes. 47 Most certainly I tell you that he will set him over all that he has. 48 But if that evil servant should say in his heart, 'My lord is delaying his coming,' 49 and begins to beat his fellow servants, and eat and drink with the drunkards, 50 the lord of that servant will come in a day when he doesn't expect it and in an hour when he doesn't know it, 51 and will cut him in pieces and appoint his portion with the hypocrites. That is where the weeping and grinding of teeth will be.

25

1 "Then the Kingdom of Heaven will be like ten virgins who took their lamps and went out to meet the bridegroom. 2 Five of them were foolish, and five were wise. 3 Those who were foolish, when they took their lamps, took no oil with them, 4 but the wise took oil in their vessels with their lamps. 5 Now while the bridegroom delayed, they all slumbered and slept. 6 But at midnight there was a cry, 'Behold! The bridegroom is coming! Come out to meet him!' 7 Then all those virgins arose, and trimmed their lamps.[e] 8 The foolish said to the wise, 'Give us some of your oil, for our lamps are going out.' 9 But the wise answered, saying, 'What if there isn't enough for us and you? You go rather to those who sell, and buy for yourselves.' 10 While they went away to buy, the bridegroom came, and those who were ready went in with him to the wedding feast, and the door was shut. 11 Afterward the other virgins also came, saying, 'Lord, Lord, open to us.' 12 But he answered, 'Most certainly I tell you, I don't know you.' 13 Watch therefore, for you don't know the day nor the hour in which the Son of Man is coming.

14 "For it is like a man going into another country, who called his own servants and entrusted his goods to them. 15 To one he gave five talents,[f] to another two, to another one, to each according to his own ability. Then he went on his journey. 16 Immediately he who received the five talents went and traded with them, and made another five talents. 17 In the same way, he also who got the two gained another two. 18 But he who received the one talent went away and dug in the earth and hid his lord's money. 19 "Now after a long time the lord of those servants came, and settled accounts with them. 20 He who received the five talents came and brought another five talents, saying, 'Lord, you delivered to me five talents. Behold, I have gained another five talents in addition to them.'

21 "His lord said to him, 'Well done, good and faithful servant. You have been faithful over a few things, I will set you over many things. Enter into the joy of your lord.'

22 "He also who got the two talents came and said, 'Lord, you delivered to me two talents. Behold, I have gained another two talents in addition to them.'

23 "His lord said to him, 'Well done, good and faithful servant. You have been faithful over a few things. I will set you over many things. Enter into the joy of your lord.'

24 "He also who had received the one talent came and said, 'Lord, I knew you that you are a hard man, reaping where you didn't sow, and gathering where you didn't scatter. 25 I was afraid, and went away and hid your talent in the earth. Behold, you have what is yours.'

26 "But his lord answered him, 'You wicked and slothful servant. You knew that I reap where I didn't sow, and gather where I didn't scatter. 27 You ought therefore to have deposited my money with the bankers, and at my coming I should have received back my own with interest. 28 Take away therefore the talent from him and give it to him who has the ten talents. 29 For to everyone who has will be given, and he will have abundance, but from him who doesn't have, even that which he has will be taken away. 30 Throw out the unprofitable servant into the outer darkness, where there will be weeping and gnashing of teeth.'

31 "But when the Son of Man comes in his glory, and all the holy angels with him, then he will sit on the throne of his glory. 32 Before him all the nations will be gathered, and he will separate them one from another, as a shepherd separates the sheep from the goats. 33 He will set the sheep on his right hand, but the goats on the left. 34 Then the King will tell those on his right hand, 'Come, blessed of my Father, inherit the Kingdom prepared for you from the foundation of the world; 35 for I was hungry and you gave me food to eat. I was thirsty and you gave me drink. I was a stranger and you took me in. 36 I was naked and you clothed me. I was sick and you visited me. I was in prison and you came to me.'

37 "Then the righteous will answer him, saying, 'Lord, when did we see you hungry and feed you, or thirsty and give you a drink? 38 When did we see you as a stranger and take you in, or naked and clothe you? 39 When did we see you sick or in prison and come to you?'

40 "The King will answer them, 'Most certainly I tell you, because you did it to one of the least of these my brothers,[g] you did it to me.' 41 Then he will say also to those on the left hand, 'Depart from me, you cursed, into the eternal fire which is prepared for the devil and his angels; 42 for I was hungry, and you didn't give me food to eat; I was thirsty, and you gave me no drink; 43 I was a stranger, and you didn't take me in; naked, and you didn't clothe me; sick, and in prison, and you didn't visit me.'

44 "Then they will also answer, saying, 'Lord, when did we see you hungry, or thirsty, or a stranger, or naked, or sick, or in prison, and didn't help you?'

45 "Then he will answer them, saying, 'Most certainly I tell you, because you didn't do it to one of the least of these, you didn't do it to me.' 46 These will go away into eternal punishment, but the righteous into eternal life."

26

1 When Jesus had finished all these words, he said to his disciples, 2 "You know that after two days the Passover is coming, and the Son of Man will be delivered up to be crucified."

3 Then the chief priests, the scribes, and the elders of the people were gathered together in the court of the high priest, who was called Caiaphas. 4 They took counsel together that they might take Jesus by deceit and kill him. 5 But they said, "Not during the feast, lest a riot occur amongst the people."

6 Now when Jesus was in Bethany, in the house of Simon the leper, 7 a woman came to him having an alabaster jar of very expensive ointment, and she poured it on his head as he sat at the table. 8 But when his disciples saw this, they were indignant, saying, "Why this waste? 9 For this ointment might have been sold for much and given to the poor."

10 However, knowing this, Jesus said to them, "Why do you trouble the woman? She has done a good work for me. 11 For you always have the poor with you, but you don't always have me. 12 For in pouring this ointment on my body, she did it to prepare me for burial. 13 Most certainly I tell you, wherever this Good News is preached in the whole world, what this woman has done will also be spoken of as a memorial of her."

14 Then one of the twelve, who was called Judas Iscariot, went to the chief priests 15 and said, "What are you willing to give me if I deliver him to you?" So they weighed out for him thirty pieces of silver. 16 From that time he sought opportunity to betray him.

17 Now on the first day of unleavened bread, the disciples came to Jesus, saying to him, "Where do you want us to prepare for you to eat the Passover?"

18 He said, "Go into the city to a certain person, and tell him, 'The Teacher says, "My time is at hand. I will keep the Passover at your house with my disciples."'"

19 The disciples did as Jesus commanded them, and they prepared the Passover.

20 Now when evening had come, he was reclining at the table with the twelve disciples. 21 As they were eating, he said, "Most certainly I tell you that one of you will betray me."

22 They were exceedingly sorrowful, and each began to ask him, "It isn't me, is it, Lord?"

23 He answered, "He who dipped his hand with me in the dish will betray me. 24 The Son of Man goes even as it is written of him, but woe to that man through whom the Son of Man is betrayed! It would be better for that man if he had not been born."

25 Judas, who betrayed him, answered, "It isn't me, is it, Rabbi?"
He said to him, "You said it."

---

a 24:28 or, eagles
b 24:29 or, oppression
** 24:29 Isaiah 13:10; 34:4
c 24:34 The word for "generation" (genea) can also be translated as "race."
d 24:36 NU adds "nor the son"
e 25:7 The end of the wick of an oil lamp needs to be cut off periodically to avoid having it become clogged with carbon deposits. The wick height is also adjusted so that the flame burns evenly and gives good light without producing a lot of smoke.
f 25:15 A talent is about 30 kilograms or 66 pounds (usually used to weigh silver unless otherwise specified)
g 25:40 The word for "brothers" here may be also correctly translated "brothers and sisters" or "siblings."

26 As they were eating, Jesus took bread, gave thanks for[a] it, and broke it. He gave to the disciples and said, "Take, eat; this is my body." 27 He took the cup, gave thanks, and gave to them, saying, "All of you drink it, 28 for this is my blood of the new covenant, which is poured out for many for the remission of sins. 29 But I tell you that I will not drink of this fruit of the vine from now on, until that day when I drink it anew with you in my Father's Kingdom."

30 When they had sung a hymn, they went out to the Mount of Olives.

31 Then Jesus said to them, "All of you will be made to stumble because of me tonight, for it is written, 'I will strike the shepherd, and the sheep of the flock will be scattered.'[*] 32 But after I am raised up, I will go before you into Galilee."

33 But Peter answered him, "Even if all will be made to stumble because of you, I will never be made to stumble."

34 Jesus said to him, "Most certainly I tell you that tonight, before the rooster crows, you will deny me three times."

35 Peter said to him, "Even if I must die with you, I will not deny you." All of the disciples also said likewise. Then Jesus came with them to a place called Gethsemane, and said to his disciples, "Sit here, while I go there and pray." 37 He took with him Peter and the two sons of Zebedee, and began to be sorrowful and severely troubled. 38 Then he said to them, "My soul is exceedingly sorrowful, even to death. Stay here and watch with me."

39 He went forward a little, fell on his face, and prayed, saying, "My Father, if it is possible, let this cup pass away from me; nevertheless, not what I desire, but what you desire."

40 He came to the disciples and found them sleeping, and said to Peter, "What, couldn't you watch with me for one hour? 41 Watch and pray, that you don't enter into temptation. The spirit indeed is willing, but the flesh is weak."

42 Again, a second time he went away and prayed, saying, "My Father, if this cup can't pass away from me unless I drink it, your desire be done."

43 He came again and found them sleeping, for their eyes were heavy. 44 He left them again, went away, and prayed a third time, saying the same words. 45 Then he came to his disciples and said to them, "Are you still sleeping and resting? Behold, the hour is at hand, and the Son of Man is betrayed into the hands of sinners. 46 Arise, let's be going. Behold, he who betrays me is at hand."

47 While he was still speaking, behold, Judas, one of the twelve, came, and with him a great multitude with swords and clubs, from the chief priests and elders of the people. 48 Now he who betrayed him had given them a sign, saying, "Whoever I kiss, he is the one. Seize him." 49 Immediately he came to Jesus, and said, "Greetings, Rabbi!" and kissed him.

50 Jesus said to him, "Friend, why are you here?"

Then they came and laid hands on Jesus, and took him. 51 Behold, one of those who were with Jesus stretched out his hand and drew his sword, and struck the servant of the high priest, and cut off his ear.

52 Then Jesus said to him, "Put your sword back into its place, for all those who take the sword will die by the sword. 53 Or do you think that I couldn't ask my Father, and he would even now send me more than twelve legions of angels? 54 How then would the Scriptures be fulfilled that it must be so?"

55 In that hour Jesus said to the multitudes, "Have you come out as against a robber with swords and clubs to seize me? I sat daily in the temple teaching, and you didn't arrest me. 56 But all this has happened that the Scriptures of the prophets might be fulfilled."

Then all the disciples left him and fled.

57 Those who had taken Jesus led him away to Caiaphas the high priest, where the scribes and the elders were gathered together. 58 But Peter followed him from a distance to the court of the high priest, and entered in and sat with the officers, to see the end.

59 Now the chief priests, the elders, and the whole council sought false testimony against Jesus, that they might put him to death, 60 and they found none. Even though many false witnesses came forward, they found none. But at last two false witnesses came forward 61 and said, "This man said, 'I am able to destroy the temple of God, and to build it in three days.'"

62 The high priest stood up and said to him, "Have you no answer? What is this that these testify against you?" 63 But Jesus stayed silent. The high priest answered him, "I adjure you by the living God that you tell us whether you are the Christ, the Son of God."

64 Jesus said to him, "You have said so. Nevertheless, I tell you, after this you will see the Son of Man sitting at the right hand of Power, and coming on the clouds of the sky."

65 Then the high priest tore his clothing, saying, "He has spoken blasphemy! Why do we need any more witnesses? Behold, now you have heard his blasphemy. 66 What do you think?"

They answered, "He is worthy of death!" 67 Then they spat in his face and beat him with their fists, and some slapped him, 68 saying, "Prophesy to us, you Christ! Who hit you?"

69 Now Peter was sitting outside in the court, and a maid came to him, saying, "You were also with Jesus, the Galilean!"

70 But he denied it before them all, saying, "I don't know what you are talking about."

71 When he had gone out onto the porch, someone else saw him and said to those who were there, "This man also was with Jesus of Nazareth."

72 Again he denied it with an oath, "I don't know the man."

73 After a little while those who stood by came and said to Peter, "Surely you are also one of them, for your speech makes you known."

74 Then he began to curse and to swear, "I don't know the man!" Immediately the rooster crowed. 75 Peter remembered the word which Jesus had said to him, "Before the rooster crows, you will deny me three times." Then he went out and wept bitterly.

27

1 Now when morning had come, all the chief priests and the elders of the people took counsel against Jesus to put him to death. 2 They bound him, led him away, and delivered him up to Pontius Pilate, the governor.

3 Then Judas, who betrayed him, when he saw that Jesus was condemned, felt remorse, and brought back the thirty pieces of silver to the chief priests and elders, 4 saying, "I have sinned in that I betrayed innocent blood."

But they said, "What is that to us? You see to it."

5 He threw down the pieces of silver in the sanctuary and departed. Then he went away and hanged himself.

6 The chief priests took the pieces of silver and said, "It's not lawful to put them into the treasury, since it is the price of blood." 7 They took counsel, and bought the potter's field with them to bury strangers in. 8 Therefore that field has been called "The Field of Blood" to this day. 9 Then that which was spoken through Jeremiah[b] the prophet was fulfilled, saying, "They took the thirty pieces of silver,
the price of him upon whom a price had been set,
whom some of the children of Israel priced,
10 and they gave them for the potter's field,
as the Lord commanded me."[*]

11 Now Jesus stood before the governor; and the governor asked him, saying, "Are you the King of the Jews?"

Jesus said to him, "So you say."

12 When he was accused by the chief priests and elders, he answered nothing. 13 Then Pilate said to him, "Don't you hear how many things they testify against you?"

14 He gave him no answer, not even one word, so that the governor marvelled greatly.

15 Now at the feast the governor was accustomed to release to the multitude one prisoner whom they desired. 16 They had then a notable prisoner called Barabbas. 17 When therefore they were gathered together, Pilate said to them, "Whom do you want me to release to you? Barabbas, or Jesus who is called Christ?" 18 For he knew that because of envy they had delivered him up.

19 While he was sitting on the judgement seat, his wife sent to him, saying, "Have nothing to do with that righteous man, for I have suffered many things today in a dream because of him."

20 Now the chief priests and the elders persuaded the multitudes to ask for Barabbas and destroy Jesus. 21 But the governor answered them, "Which of the two do you want me to release to you?"

They said, "Barabbas!"

22 Pilate said to them, "What then shall I do to Jesus who is called Christ?"

They all said to him, "Let him be crucified!"

23 But the governor said, "Why? What evil has he done?"

But they cried out exceedingly, saying, "Let him be crucified!"

24 So when Pilate saw that nothing was being gained, but rather that a disturbance was starting, he took water and washed his hands before the multitude, saying, "I am innocent of the blood of this righteous person. You see to it."

25 All the people answered, "May his blood be on us and on our children!"

26 Then he released Barabbas to them, but Jesus he flogged and delivered to be crucified.

27 Then the governor's soldiers took Jesus into the Praetorium, and gathered the whole garrison together against him. 28 They stripped him and put a scarlet robe on him. 29 They braided a crown of thorns and put it on his head, and a reed in his right hand; and they knelt down before him and mocked him, saying, "Hail, King of the Jews!" 30 They spat on him, and took the reed and struck him on the head. 31 When they had mocked him, they took the robe off him, and put his clothes on him, and led him away to crucify him.

32 As they came out, they found a man of Cyrene, Simon by name, and they compelled him to go with them, that he might carry his cross. 33 When they came to a place called "Golgotha", that is to say, "The place of a skull," 34 they gave him sour wine[c] to drink mixed with gall.[d] When he had tasted it, he would not drink. 35 When they had crucified him, they divided his clothing amongst them, casting lots,[e] 36 and they sat and watched him there. 37 They set up over his head the accusation against him written, "THIS IS JESUS, THE KING OF THE JEWS."

---

a 26:26 TR reads "blessed" instead of "gave thanks for"
** 26:31 Zechariah 13:7
b 27:9 some manuscripts omit "Jeremiah"
** 27:10 Zechariah 11:12-13; Jeremiah 19:1-13; 32:6-9
c 27:34 or, vinegar

d 27:34 Gall is a bitter-tasting, dark green oil from a wormwood plant that is alcoholic in its effect.
e 27:35 TR adds "that it might be fulfilled which was spoken by the prophet: 'They divided my garments amongst them, and for my clothing they cast lots;'" [see Psalms 22:18 and John 19:24]

38 Then there were two robbers crucified with him, one on his right hand and one on the left.

39 Those who passed by blasphemed him, wagging their heads 40 and saying, "You who destroy the temple and build it in three days, save yourself! If you are the Son of God, come down from the cross!"

41 Likewise the chief priests also mocking with the scribes, the Pharisees,[a] and the elders, said, 42 "He saved others, but he can't save himself. If he is the King of Israel, let him come down from the cross now, and we will believe in him. 43 He trusts in God. Let God deliver him now, if he wants him; for he said, 'I am the Son of God.'" 44 The robbers also who were crucified with him cast on him the same reproach.

45 Now from the sixth hour[b] there was darkness over all the land until the ninth hour.[c] 46 About the ninth hour Jesus cried with a loud voice, saying, "Eli, Eli, lima[d] sabachthani?" That is, "My God, my God, why have you forsaken me?"[**]

47 Some of them who stood there, when they heard it, said, "This man is calling Elijah."

48 Immediately one of them ran and took a sponge, filled it with vinegar, put it on a reed, and gave him a drink. 49 The rest said, "Let him be. Let's see whether Elijah comes to save him."

50 Jesus cried again with a loud voice, and yielded up his spirit.

51 Behold, the veil of the temple was torn in two from the top to the bottom. The earth quaked and the rocks were split. 52 The tombs were opened, and many bodies of the saints who had fallen asleep were raised; 53 and coming out of the tombs after his resurrection, they entered into the holy city and appeared to many.

54 Now the centurion and those who were with him watching Jesus, when they saw the earthquake and the things that were done, were terrified, saying, "Truly this was the Son of God!"

55 Many women were there watching from afar, who had followed Jesus from Galilee, serving him. 56 Amongst them were Mary Magdalene, Mary the mother of James and Joses, and the mother of the sons of Zebedee.

57 When evening had come, a rich man from Arimathaea named Joseph, who himself was also Jesus' disciple, came. 58 This man went to Pilate and asked for Jesus' body. Then Pilate commanded the body to be given up. 59 Joseph took the body and wrapped it in a clean linen cloth 60 and laid it in his own new tomb, which he had cut out in the rock. Then he rolled a large stone against the door of the tomb, and departed. 61 Mary Magdalene was there, and the other Mary, sitting opposite the tomb.

62 Now on the next day, which was the day after the Preparation Day, the chief priests and the Pharisees were gathered together to Pilate, 63 saying, "Sir, we remember what that deceiver said while he was still alive: 'After three days I will rise again.' 64 Command therefore that the tomb be made secure until the third day, lest perhaps his disciples come at night and steal him away, and tell the people, 'He is risen from the dead;' and the last deception will be worse than the first."

65 Pilate said to them, "You have a guard. Go, make it as secure as you can." 66 So they went with the guard and made the tomb secure, sealing the stone.

28

1 Now after the Sabbath, as it began to dawn on the first day of the week, Mary Magdalene and the other Mary came to see the tomb. 2 Behold, there was a great earthquake, for an angel of the Lord descended from the sky and came and rolled away the stone from the door and sat on it. 3 His appearance was like lightning, and his clothing white as snow. 4 For fear of him, the guards shook, and became like dead men. 5 The angel answered the women, "Don't be afraid, for I know that you seek Jesus, who has been crucified. 6 He is not here, for he has risen, just like he said. Come, see the place where the Lord was lying. 7 Go quickly and tell his disciples, 'He has risen from the dead, and behold, he goes before you into Galilee; there you will see him.' Behold, I have told you."

8 They departed quickly from the tomb with fear and great joy, and ran to bring his disciples word. 9 As they went to tell his disciples, behold, Jesus met them, saying, "Rejoice!"

They came and took hold of his feet, and worshipped him.

10 Then Jesus said to them, "Don't be afraid. Go tell my brothers[e] that they should go into Galilee, and there they will see me."

11 Now while they were going, behold, some of the guards came into the city and told the chief priests all the things that had happened. 12 When they were assembled with the elders and had taken counsel, they gave a large amount of silver to the soldiers, 13 saying, "Say that his disciples came by night and stole him away while we slept. 14 If this comes to the governor's ears, we will persuade him and make you free of worry." 15 So they took the money and did as they were told. This saying was spread abroad amongst the Jews, and continues until today.

16 But the eleven disciples went into Galilee, to the mountain where Jesus had sent them. 17 When they saw him, they bowed down to him; but some doubted. 18 Jesus came to them and spoke to them, saying, "All authority has been given to me in heaven and on earth. 19 Go[f] and make disciples of all nations, baptising them in the name of the Father and of the Son and of the Holy Spirit, 20 teaching them to observe all things that I commanded you. Behold, I am with you always, even to the end of the age." Amen.

---

a 27:41 TR omits "the Pharisees"

b 27:45 noon

c 27:45 3:00 p.m.

d 27:46 TR reads "lama" instead of "lima"

** 27:46 Psalms 22:1

e 28:10 The word for "brothers" here may be also correctly translated "brothers and sisters" or "siblings."

f 28:19 TR and NU add "therefore"

The Good News According to Mark

1

1 The beginning of the Good News of Jesus Christ, the Son of God.

2 As it is written in the prophets,

"Behold,[a] I send my messenger before your face,
who will prepare your way before you:ʼ

3 the voice of one crying in the wilderness,
'Make ready the way of the Lord!
Make his paths straight!'"ʼ

4 John came baptising[b] in the wilderness and preaching the baptism of repentance for forgiveness of sins. 5 All the country of Judea and all those of Jerusalem went out to him. They were baptised by him in the Jordan river, confessing their sins. 6 John was clothed with camel's hair and a leather belt around his waist. He ate locusts and wild honey. 7 He preached, saying, "After me comes he who is mightier than I, the thong of whose sandals I am not worthy to stoop down and loosen. 8 I baptised you in[c] water, but he will baptise you in the Holy Spirit."

9 In those days, Jesus came from Nazareth of Galilee, and was baptised by John in the Jordan. 10 Immediately coming up from the water, he saw the heavens parting and the Spirit descending on him like a dove. 11 A voice came out of the sky, "You are my beloved Son, in whom I am well pleased."

12 Immediately the Spirit drove him out into the wilderness. 13 He was there in the wilderness forty days, tempted by Satan. He was with the wild animals; and the angels were serving him.

14 Now after John was taken into custody, Jesus came into Galilee, preaching the Good News of God's Kingdom, 15 and saying, "The time is fulfilled, and God's Kingdom is at hand! Repent, and believe in the Good News."

16 Passing along by the sea of Galilee, he saw Simon and Andrew, the brother of Simon, casting a net into the sea, for they were fishermen. 17 Jesus said to them, "Come after me, and I will make you into fishers for men."

18 Immediately they left their nets, and followed him.

19 Going on a little further from there, he saw James the son of Zebedee, and John his brother, who were also in the boat mending the nets. 20 Immediately he called them, and they left their father, Zebedee, in the boat with the hired servants, and went after him.

21 They went into Capernaum, and immediately on the Sabbath day he entered into the synagogue and taught. 22 They were astonished at his teaching, for he taught them as having authority, and not as the scribes. 23 Immediately there was in their synagogue a man with an unclean spirit, and he cried out, 24 saying, "Ha! What do we have to do with you, Jesus, you Nazarene? Have you come to destroy us? I know who you are: the Holy One of God!"

25 Jesus rebuked him, saying, "Be quiet, and come out of him!"

26 The unclean spirit, convulsing him and crying with a loud voice, came out of him. 27 They were all amazed, so that they questioned amongst themselves, saying, "What is this? A new teaching? For with authority he commands even the unclean spirits, and they obey him!" 28 The report of him went out immediately everywhere into all the region of Galilee and its surrounding area.

29 Immediately, when they had come out of the synagogue, they came into the house of Simon and Andrew, with James and John. 30 Now Simon's wife's mother lay sick with a fever, and immediately they told him about her. 31 He came and took her by the hand and raised her up. The fever left her immediately,[d] and she served them.

32 At evening, when the sun had set, they brought to him all who were sick and those who were possessed by demons. 33 All the city was gathered together at the door. 34 He healed many who were sick with various diseases and cast out many demons. He didn't allow the demons to speak, because they knew him.

35 Early in the morning, while it was still dark, he rose up and went out, and departed into a deserted place, and prayed there. 36 Simon and those who were with him searched for him. 37 They found him and told him, "Everyone is looking for you."

38 He said to them, "Let's go elsewhere into the next towns, that I may preach there also, because I came out for this reason." 39 He went into their synagogues throughout all Galilee, preaching and casting out demons.

40 A leper came to him, begging him, kneeling down to him, and saying to him, "If you want to, you can make me clean."

41 Being moved with compassion, he stretched out his hand, and touched him, and said to him, "I want to. Be made clean." 42 When he had said this, immediately the leprosy departed from him and he was made clean. 43 He strictly warned him and immediately sent him out, 44 and said to him, "See that you say nothing to anybody, but go show yourself to the priest and offer for your cleansing the things which Moses commanded, for a testimony to them."

45 But he went out, and began to proclaim it much, and to spread about the matter, so that Jesus could no more openly enter into a city, but was outside in desert places. People came to him from everywhere.

2

1 When he entered again into Capernaum after some days, it was heard that he was at home. 2 Immediately many were gathered together, so that there was no more room, not even around the door; and he spoke the word to them. 3 Four people came, carrying a paralytic to him. 4 When they could not come near to him for the crowd, they removed the roof where he was. When they had broken it up, they let down the mat that the paralytic was lying on. 5 Jesus, seeing their faith, said to the paralytic, "Son, your sins are forgiven you."

6 But there were some of the scribes sitting there and reasoning in their hearts, 7 "Why does this man speak blasphemies like that? Who can forgive sins but God alone?"

8 Immediately Jesus, perceiving in his spirit that they so reasoned within themselves, said to them, "Why do you reason these things in your hearts? 9 Which is easier, to tell the paralytic, 'Your sins are forgiven;' or to say, 'Arise, and take up your bed, and walk'? 10 But that you may know that the Son of Man has authority on earth to forgive sins"—he said to the paralytic— 11 "I tell you, arise, take up your mat, and go to your house."

12 He arose, and immediately took up the mat and went out in front of them all, so that they were all amazed and glorified God, saying, "We never saw anything like this!"

13 He went out again by the seaside. All the multitude came to him, and he taught them. 14 As he passed by, he saw Levi the son of Alphaeus sitting at the tax office. He said to him, "Follow me." And he arose and followed him.

15 He was reclining at the table in his house, and many tax collectors and sinners sat down with Jesus and his disciples, for there were many, and they followed him. 16 The scribes and the Pharisees, when they saw that he was eating with the sinners and tax collectors, said to his disciples, "Why is it that he eats and drinks with tax collectors and sinners?"

17 When Jesus heard it, he said to them, "Those who are healthy have no need for a physician, but those who are sick. I came not to call the righteous, but sinners to repentance."

18 John's disciples and the Pharisees were fasting, and they came and asked him, "Why do John's disciples and the disciples of the Pharisees fast, but your disciples don't fast?"

19 Jesus said to them, "Can the groomsmen fast while the bridegroom is with them? As long as they have the bridegroom with them, they can't fast. 20 But the days will come when the bridegroom will be taken away from them, and then they will fast in that day. 21 No one sews a piece of unshrunk cloth on an old garment, or else the patch shrinks and the new tears away from the old, and a worse hole is made. 22 No one puts new wine into old wineskins; or else the new wine will burst the skins, and the wine pours out, and the skins will be destroyed; but they put new wine into fresh wineskins."

23 He was going on the Sabbath day through the grain fields; and his disciples began, as they went, to pluck the ears of grain. 24 The Pharisees said to him, "Behold, why do they do that which is not lawful on the Sabbath day?"

25 He said to them, "Did you never read what David did when he had need and was hungry—he, and those who were with him? 26 How he entered into God's house at the time of Abiathar the high priest, and ate the show bread, which is not lawful to eat except for the priests, and gave also to those who were with him?"

27 He said to them, "The Sabbath was made for man, not man for the Sabbath. 28 Therefore the Son of Man is lord even of the Sabbath."

3

1 He entered again into the synagogue, and there was a man there whose hand was withered. 2 They watched him, whether he would heal him on the Sabbath day, that they might accuse him. 3 He said to the man whose hand was withered, "Stand up." 4 He said to them, "Is it lawful on the Sabbath day to do good or to do harm? To save a life or to kill?" But they were silent. 5 When he had looked around at them with anger, being grieved at the hardening of their hearts, he said to the man, "Stretch out your hand." He stretched it out, and his hand was restored as healthy as the other. 6 The Pharisees went out, and immediately conspired with the Herodians against him, how they might destroy him.

7 Jesus withdrew to the sea with his disciples; and a great multitude followed him from Galilee, from Judea, 8 from Jerusalem, from Idumaea, beyond the Jordan, and those from around Tyre and Sidon. A great multitude, hearing what great things he did, came to him. 9 He spoke to his disciples that a little boat should stay near him because of the crowd, so that they wouldn't press on him. 10 For he had healed many, so that as many as had diseases pressed on him that they might touch him. 11 The unclean spirits, whenever they saw him, fell down before him and cried, "You are the Son of God!" 12 He sternly warned them that they should not make him known.

13 He went up into the mountain and called to himself those whom he wanted, and they went to him. 14 He appointed twelve, that they might be with him, and that he might send them out to preach 15 and to have authority to heal sicknesses and to cast out demons: 16 Simon (to whom he gave the name Peter); 17 James the son of Zebedee; and John, the brother of James, (whom he called Boanerges, which means, Sons of Thunder);

---

a *1:2* "Behold", from "ἰδοὺ", means look at, take notice, observe, see, or gaze at. It is often used as an interjection.

** 1:2 Malachi 3:1

** 1:3 Isaiah 40:3

b *1:4* or, immersing

c *1:8* The Greek word (en) translated here as "in" could also be translated as "with" in some contexts.

d *1:31* NU omits "immediately".

18 Andrew; Philip; Bartholomew; Matthew; Thomas; James, the son of Alphaeus; Thaddaeus; Simon the Zealot; 19 and Judas Iscariot, who also betrayed him.

Then he came into a house. 20 The multitude came together again, so that they could not so much as eat bread. 21 When his friends heard it, they went out to seize him; for they said, "He is insane." 22 The scribes who came down from Jerusalem said, "He has Beelzebul," and, "By the prince of the demons he casts out the demons."

23 He summoned them and said to them in parables, "How can Satan cast out Satan? 24 If a kingdom is divided against itself, that kingdom cannot stand. 25 If a house is divided against itself, that house cannot stand. 26 If Satan has risen up against himself, and is divided, he can't stand, but has an end. 27 But no one can enter into the house of the strong man to plunder unless he first binds the strong man; then he will plunder his house.

28 "Most certainly I tell you, all sins of the descendants of man will be forgiven, including their blasphemies with which they may blaspheme; 29 but whoever may blaspheme against the Holy Spirit never has forgiveness, but is subject to eternal condemnation."ᵃ 30 —because they said, "He has an unclean spirit."

31 His mother and his brothers came, and standing outside, they sent to him, calling him. 32 A multitude was sitting around him, and they told him, "Behold, your mother, your brothers, and your sistersᵇ are outside looking for you."

33 He answered them, "Who are my mother and my brothers?" 34 Looking around at those who sat around him, he said, "Behold, my mother and my brothers! 35 For whoever does the will of God is my brother, my sister, and mother."

4

1 Again he began to teach by the seaside. A great multitude was gathered to him, so that he entered into a boat in the sea and sat down. All the multitude were on the land by the sea. 2 He taught them many things in parables, and told them in his teaching, 3 "Listen! Behold, the farmer went out to sow. 4 As he sowed, some seed fell by the road, and the birdsᶜ came and devoured it. 5 Others fell on the rocky ground, where it had little soil, and immediately it sprang up, because it had no depth of soil. 6 When the sun had risen, it was scorched; and because it had no root, it withered away. 7 Others fell amongst the thorns, and the thorns grew up and choked it, and it yielded no fruit. 8 Others fell into the good ground and yielded fruit, growing up and increasing. Some produced thirty times, some sixty times, and some one hundred times as much." 9 He said, "Whoever has ears to hear, let him hear."

10 When he was alone, those who were around him with the twelve asked him about the parables. 11 He said to them, "To you is given the mystery of God's Kingdom, but to those who are outside, all things are done in parables, 12 that 'seeing they may see and not perceive, and hearing they may hear and not understand, lest perhaps they should turn again, and their sins should be forgiven them.'"**

13 He said to them, "Don't you understand this parable? How will you understand all of the parables? 14 The farmer sows the word. 15 The ones by the road are the ones where the word is sown; and when they have heard, immediately Satan comes and takes away the word which has been sown in them. 16 These in the same way are those who are sown on the rocky places, who, when they have heard the word, immediately receive it with joy. 17 They have no root in themselves, but are short-lived. When oppression or persecution arises because of the word, immediately they stumble. 18 Others are those who are sown amongst the thorns. These are those who have heard the word, 19 and the cares of this age, and the deceitfulness of riches, and the lusts of other things entering in choke the word, and it becomes unfruitful. 20 Those which were sown on the good ground are those who hear the word, accept it, and bear fruit, some thirty times, some sixty times, and some one hundred times."

21 He said to them, "Is a lamp brought to be put under a basket ᵈ or under a bed? Isn't it put on a stand? 22 For there is nothing hidden except that it should be made known, neither was anything made secret but that it should come to light. 23 If any man has ears to hear, let him hear."

24 He said to them, "Take heed what you hear. With whatever measure you measure, it will be measured to you; and more will be given to you who hear. 25 For whoever has, to him more will be given; and he who doesn't have, even that which he has will be taken away from him."

26 He said, "God's Kingdom is as if a man should cast seed on the earth, 27 and should sleep and rise night and day, and the seed should spring up and grow, though he doesn't know how. 28 For the earth bears fruit by itself: first the blade, then the ear, then the full grain in the ear. 29 But when the fruit is ripe, immediately he puts in the sickle, because the harvest has come."

30 He said, "How will we liken God's Kingdom? Or with what parable will we illustrate it? 31 It's like a grain of mustard seed, which, when it is sown in the earth, though it is less than all the seeds that are on the earth, 32 yet when it is sown, grows up and becomes greater than all the herbs, and puts out great branches, so that the birds of the sky can lodge under its shadow."

33 With many such parables he spoke the word to them, as they were able to hear it. 34 Without a parable he didn't speak to them; but privately to his own disciples he explained everything.

35 On that day, when evening had come, he said to them, "Let's go over to the other side." 36 Leaving the multitude, they took him with them, even as he was, in the boat. Other small boats were also with him. 37 A big wind storm arose, and the waves beat into the boat, so much that the boat was already filled. 38 He himself was in the stern, asleep on the cushion; and they woke him up and asked him, "Teacher, don't you care that we are dying?"

39 He awoke and rebuked the wind, and said to the sea, "Peace! Be still!" The wind ceased and there was a great calm. 40 He said to them, "Why are you so afraid? How is it that you have no faith?"

41 They were greatly afraid and said to one another, "Who then is this, that even the wind and the sea obey him?"

5

1 They came to the other side of the sea, into the country of the Gadarenes. 2 When he had come out of the boat, immediately a man with an unclean spirit met him out of the tombs. 3 He lived in the tombs. Nobody could bind him any more, not even with chains, 4 because he had been often bound with fetters and chains, and the chains had been torn apart by him, and the fetters broken in pieces. Nobody had the strength to tame him. 5 Always, night and day, in the tombs and in the mountains, he was crying out, and cutting himself with stones. 6 When he saw Jesus from afar, he ran and bowed down to him, 7 and crying out with a loud voice, he said, "What have I to do with you, Jesus, you Son of the Most High God? I adjure you by God, don't torment me." 8 For he said to him, "Come out of the man, you unclean spirit!"

9 He asked him, "What is your name?"

He said to him, "My name is Legion, for we are many." 10 He begged him much that he would not send them away out of the country. 11 Now on the mountainside there was a great herd of pigs feeding. 12 All the demons begged him, saying, "Send us into the pigs, that we may enter into them."

13 At once Jesus gave them permission. The unclean spirits came out and entered into the pigs. The herd of about two thousand rushed down the steep bank into the sea, and they were drowned in the sea. 14 Those who fed the pigs fled, and told it in the city and in the country.

The people came to see what it was that had happened. 15 They came to Jesus, and saw him who had been possessed by demons sitting, clothed, and in his right mind, even him who had the legion; and they were afraid. 16 Those who saw it declared to them what happened to him who was possessed by demons, and about the pigs. 17 They began to beg him to depart from their region.

18 As he was entering into the boat, he who had been possessed by demons begged him that he might be with him. 19 He didn't allow him, but said to him, "Go to your house, to your friends, and tell them what great things the Lord has done for you and how he had mercy on you."

20 He went his way, and began to proclaim in Decapolis how Jesus had done great things for him, and everyone marvelled.

21 When Jesus had crossed back over in the boat to the other side, a great multitude was gathered to him; and he was by the sea. 22 Behold, one of the rulers of the synagogue, Jairus by name, came; and seeing him, he fell at his feet 23 and begged him much, saying, "My little daughter is at the point of death. Please come and lay your hands on her, that she may be made healthy, and live."

24 He went with him, and a great multitude followed him, and they pressed upon him on all sides. 25 A certain woman who had a discharge of blood for twelve years, 26 and had suffered many things by many physicians, and had spent all that she had, and was no better, but rather grew worse, 27 having heard the things concerning Jesus, came up behind him in the crowd and touched his clothes. 28 For she said, "If I just touch his clothes, I will be made well." 29 Immediately the flow of her blood was dried up, and she felt in her body that she was healed of her affliction.

30 Immediately Jesus, perceiving in himself that the power had gone out from him, turned around in the crowd and asked, "Who touched my clothes?"

31 His disciples said to him, "You see the multitude pressing against you, and you say, 'Who touched me?'"

32 He looked around to see her who had done this thing. 33 But the woman, fearing and trembling, knowing what had been done to her, came and fell down before him, and told him all the truth.

34 He said to her, "Daughter, your faith has made you well. Go in peace, and be cured of your disease."

35 While he was still speaking, people came from the synagogue ruler's house, saying, "Your daughter is dead. Why bother the Teacher any more?"

36 But Jesus, when he heard the message spoken, immediately said to the ruler of the synagogue, "Don't be afraid, only believe." 37 He allowed no one to follow him except Peter, James, and John the brother of James. 38 He came to the synagogue ruler's house, and he saw an uproar, weeping, and great wailing. 39 When he had entered in, he said to them, "Why do you make an uproar and weep? The child is not dead, but is asleep."

40 They ridiculed him. But he, having put them all out, took the father of the child, her mother, and those who were with him, and went in where

---

ᵃ *3:29* NU reads, guilty of an eternal sin.
ᵇ *3:32* TR omits "your sisters"
ᶜ *4:4* TR adds "of the air"

** *4:12* Isaiah 6:9-10
ᵈ *4:21* literally, a modion, a dry measuring basket containing about a peck (about 9 litres)

the child was lying. 41 Taking the child by the hand, he said to her, "Talitha cumi!" which means, being interpreted, "Girl, I tell you, get up!" 42 Immediately the girl rose up and walked, for she was twelve years old. They were amazed with great amazement. 43 He strictly ordered them that no one should know this, and commanded that something should be given to her to eat.

6

1 He went out from there. He came into his own country, and his disciples followed him. 2 When the Sabbath had come, he began to teach in the synagogue, and many hearing him were astonished, saying, "Where did this man get these things?" and, "What is the wisdom that is given to this man, that such mighty works come about by his hands? 3 Isn't this the carpenter, the son of Mary and brother of James, Joses, Judah, and Simon? Aren't his sisters here with us?" So they were offended at him.

4 Jesus said to them, "A prophet is not without honour, except in his own country, and amongst his own relatives, and in his own house." 5 He could do no mighty work there, except that he laid his hands on a few sick people and healed them. 6 He marvelled because of their unbelief.

He went around the villages teaching. 7 He called to himself the twelve, and began to send them out two by two; and he gave them authority over the unclean spirits. 8 He commanded them that they should take nothing for their journey, except a staff only: no bread, no wallet, no money in their purse, 9 but to wear sandals, and not put on two tunics. 10 He said to them, "Wherever you enter into a house, stay there until you depart from there. 11 Whoever will not receive nor hear you, as you depart from there, shake off the dust that is under your feet for a testimony against them. Assuredly, I tell you, it will be more tolerable for Sodom and Gomorrah in the day of judgement than for that city!"

12 They went out and preached that people should repent. 13 They cast out many demons, and anointed many with oil who were sick and healed them. 14 King Herod heard this, for his name had become known, and he said, "John the Baptiser has risen from the dead, and therefore these powers are at work in him." 15 But others said, "He is Elijah." Others said, "He is a prophet, or like one of the prophets." 16 But Herod, when he heard this, said, "This is John, whom I beheaded. He has risen from the dead." 17 For Herod himself had sent out and arrested John and bound him in prison for the sake of Herodias, his brother Philip's wife, for he had married her. 18 For John had said to Herod, "It is not lawful for you to have your brother's wife." 19 Herodias set herself against him and desired to kill him, but she couldn't, 20 for Herod feared John, knowing that he was a righteous and holy man, and kept him safe. When he heard him, he did many things, and he heard him gladly.

21 Then a convenient day came when Herod on his birthday made a supper for his nobles, the high officers, and the chief men of Galilee. 22 When the daughter of Herodias herself came in and danced, she pleased Herod and those sitting with him. The king said to the young lady, "Ask me whatever you want, and I will give it to you." 23 He swore to her, "Whatever you ask of me, I will give you, up to half of my kingdom."

24 She went out and said to her mother, "What shall I ask?"

She said, "The head of John the Baptiser."

25 She came in immediately with haste to the king and requested, "I want you to give me right now the head of John the Baptiser on a platter."

26 The king was exceedingly sorry, but for the sake of his oaths and of his dinner guests, he didn't wish to refuse her. 27 Immediately the king sent out a soldier of his guard and commanded to bring John's head; and he went and beheaded him in the prison, 28 and brought his head on a platter, and gave it to the young lady; and the young lady gave it to her mother.

29 When his disciples heard this, they came and took up his corpse and laid it in a tomb.

30 The apostles gathered themselves together to Jesus, and they told him all things, whatever they had done, and whatever they had taught. 31 He said to them, "Come away into a deserted place, and rest awhile." For there were many coming and going, and they had no leisure so much as to eat. 32 They went away in the boat to a deserted place by themselves. 33 They[a] saw them going, and many recognised him and ran there on foot from all the cities. They arrived before them and came together to him. 34 Jesus came out, saw a great multitude, and he had compassion on them because they were like sheep without a shepherd; and he began to teach them many things. 35 When it was late in the day, his disciples came to him and said, "This place is deserted, and it is late in the day. 36 Send them away, that they may go into the surrounding country and villages and buy themselves bread, for they have nothing to eat."

37 But he answered them, "You give them something to eat."

They asked him, "Shall we go and buy two hundred denarii[b] worth of bread and give them something to eat?"

38 He said to them, "How many loaves do you have? Go see."

When they knew, they said, "Five, and two fish."

39 He commanded them that everyone should sit down in groups on the green grass. 40 They sat down in ranks, by hundreds and by fifties. 41 He took the five loaves and the two fish; and looking up to heaven, he blessed and broke the loaves, and he gave to his disciples to set before them, and he divided the two fish amongst them all. 42 They all ate and were filled. 43 They took up twelve baskets full of broken pieces and also of the fish. 44 Those who ate the loaves were[c] five thousand men.

45 Immediately he made his disciples get into the boat and go ahead to the other side, to Bethsaida, while he himself sent the multitude away. 46 After he had taken leave of them, he went up the mountain to pray.

47 When evening had come, the boat was in the middle of the sea, and he was alone on the land. 48 Seeing them distressed in rowing, for the wind was contrary to them, about the fourth watch of the night he came to them, walking on the sea; * and he would have passed by them, 49 but they, when they saw him walking on the sea, supposed that it was a ghost, and cried out; 50 for they all saw him and were troubled. But he immediately spoke with them and said to them, "Cheer up! It is I![d] Don't be afraid." 51 He got into the boat with them; and the wind ceased, and they were very amazed amongst themselves, and marvelled; 52 for they hadn't understood about the loaves, but their hearts were hardened.

53 When they had crossed over, they came to land at Gennesaret and moored to the shore. 54 When they had come out of the boat, immediately the people recognised him, 55 and ran around that whole region, and began to bring those who were sick on their mats to where they heard he was. 56 Wherever he entered—into villages, or into cities, or into the country—they laid the sick in the marketplaces and begged him that they might just touch the fringe[e] of his garment; and as many as touched him were made well.

7

1 Then the Pharisees and some of the scribes gathered together to him, having come from Jerusalem. 2 Now when they saw some of his disciples eating bread with defiled, that is unwashed, hands, they found fault. 3 (For the Pharisees and all the Jews don't eat unless they wash their hands and forearms, holding to the tradition of the elders. 4 They don't eat when they come from the marketplace unless they bathe themselves, and there are many other things which they have received to hold to: washings of cups, pitchers, bronze vessels, and couches.) 5 The Pharisees and the scribes asked him, "Why don't your disciples walk according to the tradition of the elders, but eat their bread with unwashed hands?"

6 He answered them, "Well did Isaiah prophesy of you hypocrites, as it is written,

'This people honours me with their lips,
   but their heart is far from me.
7 They worship me in vain,
   teaching as doctrines the commandments of men.'*

8 "For you set aside the commandment of God, and hold tightly to the tradition of men—the washing of pitchers and cups, and you do many other such things." 9 He said to them, "Full well do you reject the commandment of God, that you may keep your tradition. 10 For Moses said, 'Honour your father and your mother;'* and, 'He who speaks evil of father or mother, let him be put to death.'* 11 But you say, 'If a man tells his father or his mother, "Whatever profit you might have received from me is Corban,"'[f] that is to say, given to God, 12 "then you no longer allow him to do anything for his father or his mother, 13 making void the word of God by your tradition which you have handed down. You do many things like this."

14 He called all the multitude to himself and said to them, "Hear me, all of you, and understand. 15 There is nothing from outside of the man that going into him can defile him; but the things which proceed out of the man are those that defile the man. 16 If anyone has ears to hear, let him hear!"[g]

17 When he had entered into a house away from the multitude, his disciples asked him about the parable. 18 He said to them, "Are you also without understanding? Don't you perceive that whatever goes into the man from outside can't defile him, 19 because it doesn't go into his heart, but into his stomach, then into the latrine, making all foods clean?"[h] 20 He said, "That which proceeds out of the man, that defiles the man. 21 For from within, out of the hearts of men, proceed evil thoughts, adulteries, sexual sins, murders, thefts, 22 covetings, wickedness, deceit, lustful desires, an evil eye, blasphemy, pride, and foolishness. 23 All these evil things come from within and defile the man."

24 From there he arose and went away into the borders of Tyre and Sidon. He entered into a house and didn't want anyone to know it, but he couldn't escape notice. 25 For a woman whose little daughter had an unclean spirit, having heard of him, came and fell down at his feet. 26 Now the woman was a Greek, a Syrophoenician by race. She begged him that he would cast the demon out of her daughter. 27 But Jesus said to her, "Let the children be filled first, for it is not appropriate to take the children's bread and throw it to the dogs."

28 But she answered him, "Yes, Lord. Yet even the dogs under the table eat the children's crumbs."

29 He said to her, "For this saying, go your way. The demon has gone out of your daughter."

30 She went away to her house, and found the child having been laid on the bed, with the demon gone out.

---

a *6:33* TR reads "The multitudes" instead of "They"
b *6:37* 200 denarii was about 7 or 8 months wages for an agricultural labourer.
c *6:44* TR adds "about"
** 6:48 See Job 9:8
d *6:50* or, "I AM!"
e *6:56* or, tassel
** 7:7 Isaiah 29:13

** 7:10 Exodus 20:12; Deuteronomy 5:16
** 7:10 Exodus 21:17; Leviticus 20:9
f *7:11* Corban is a Hebrew word for an offering devoted to God.
g *7:16* NU omits verse 16.
h *7:19* NU ends Jesus' direct quote and question after "latrine", ending the verse with "Thus he declared all foods clean.

31 Again he departed from the borders of Tyre and Sidon, and came to the sea of Galilee through the middle of the region of Decapolis. 32 They brought to him one who was deaf and had an impediment in his speech. They begged him to lay his hand on him. 33 He took him aside from the multitude privately and put his fingers into his ears; and he spat and touched his tongue. 34 Looking up to heaven, he sighed, and said to him, "Ephphatha!" that is, "Be opened!" 35 Immediately his ears were opened, and the impediment of his tongue was released, and he spoke clearly. 36 He commanded them that they should tell no one, but the more he commanded them, so much the more widely they proclaimed it. 37 They were astonished beyond measure, saying, "He has done all things well. He makes even the deaf hear and the mute speak!"

8

1 In those days, when there was a very great multitude, and they had nothing to eat, Jesus called his disciples to himself and said to them, 2 "I have compassion on the multitude, because they have stayed with me now three days and have nothing to eat. 3 If I send them away fasting to their home, they will faint on the way, for some of them have come a long way."

4 His disciples answered him, "From where could one satisfy these people with bread here in a deserted place?"

5 He asked them, "How many loaves do you have?"

They said, "Seven."

6 He commanded the multitude to sit down on the ground, and he took the seven loaves. Having given thanks, he broke them and gave them to his disciples to serve, and they served the multitude. 7 They also had a few small fish. Having blessed them, he said to serve these also. 8 They ate and were filled. They took up seven baskets of broken pieces that were left over. 9 Those who had eaten were about four thousand. Then he sent them away.

10 Immediately he entered into the boat with his disciples and came into the region of Dalmanutha. 11 The Pharisees came out and began to question him, seeking from him a sign from heaven and testing him. 12 He sighed deeply in his spirit and said, "Why does this generation[a] seek a sign? Most certainly I tell you, no sign will be given to this generation."

13 He left them, and again entering into the boat, departed to the other side. 14 They forgot to take bread; and they didn't have more than one loaf in the boat with them. 15 He warned them, saying, "Take heed: beware of the yeast of the Pharisees and the yeast of Herod."

16 They reasoned with one another, saying, "It's because we have no bread."

17 Jesus, perceiving it, said to them, "Why do you reason that it's because you have no bread? Don't you perceive yet or understand? Is your heart still hardened? 18 Having eyes, don't you see? Having ears, don't you hear? Don't you remember? 19 When I broke the five loaves amongst the five thousand, how many baskets full of broken pieces did you take up?"

They told him, "Twelve."

20 "When the seven loaves fed the four thousand, how many baskets full of broken pieces did you take up?"

They told him, "Seven."

21 He asked them, "Don't you understand yet?"

22 He came to Bethsaida. They brought a blind man to him and begged him to touch him. 23 He took hold of the blind man by the hand, and brought him out of the village. When he had spat on his eyes, and laid his hands on him, he asked him if he saw anything.

24 He looked up, and said, "I see men; but I see them like walking trees."

25 Then again he laid his hands on his eyes. He looked intently, and was restored, and saw everyone clearly. 26 He sent him away to his house, saying, "Don't enter into the village, nor tell anyone in the village."

27 Jesus went out, with his disciples, into the villages of Caesarea Philippi. On the way he asked his disciples, "Who do men say that I am?"

28 They told him, "John the Baptiser, and others say Elijah, but others, one of the prophets."

29 He said to them, "But who do you say that I am?"

Peter answered, "You are the Christ."

30 He commanded them that they should tell no one about him. 31 He began to teach them that the Son of Man must suffer many things, and be rejected by the elders, the chief priests, and the scribes, and be killed, and after three days rise again. 32 He spoke to them openly. Peter took him and began to rebuke him. 33 But he, turning around and seeing his disciples, rebuked Peter, and said, "Get behind me, Satan! For you have in mind not the things of God, but the things of men."

34 He called the multitude to himself with his disciples and said to them, "Whoever wants to come after me, let him deny himself, and take up his cross, and follow me. 35 For whoever wants to save his life will lose it; and whoever will lose his life for my sake and the sake of the Good News will save it. 36 For what does it profit a man to gain the whole world and forfeit his life? 37 For what will a man give in exchange for his life? 38 For whoever will be ashamed of me and of my words in this adulterous and sinful generation, the Son of Man also will be ashamed of him when he comes in his Father's glory with the holy angels."

9

1 He said to them, "Most certainly I tell you, there are some standing here who will in no way taste death until they see God's Kingdom come with power."

2 After six days Jesus took with him Peter, James, and John, and brought them up onto a high mountain privately by themselves, and he was changed into another form in front of them. 3 His clothing became glistening, exceedingly white, like snow, such as no launderer on earth can whiten them. 4 Elijah and Moses appeared to them, and they were talking with Jesus.

5 Peter answered Jesus, "Rabbi, it is good for us to be here. Let's make three tents: one for you, one for Moses, and one for Elijah." 6 For he didn't know what to say, for they were very afraid.

7 A cloud came, overshadowing them, and a voice came out of the cloud, "This is my beloved Son. Listen to him."

8 Suddenly looking around, they saw no one with them any more, except Jesus only.

9 As they were coming down from the mountain, he commanded them that they should tell no one what things they had seen, until after the Son of Man had risen from the dead. 10 They kept this saying to themselves, questioning what the "rising from the dead" meant.

11 They asked him, saying, "Why do the scribes say that Elijah must come first?"

12 He said to them, "Elijah indeed comes first, and restores all things. How is it written about the Son of Man, that he should suffer many things and be despised? 13 But I tell you that Elijah has come, and they have also done to him whatever they wanted to, even as it is written about him."

14 Coming to the disciples, he saw a great multitude around them, and scribes questioning them. 15 Immediately all the multitude, when they saw him, were greatly amazed, and running to him, greeted him. 16 He asked the scribes, "What are you asking them?"

17 One of the multitude answered, "Teacher, I brought to you my son, who has a mute spirit; 18 and wherever it seizes him, it throws him down; and he foams at the mouth, grinds his teeth, and becomes rigid. I asked your disciples to cast it out, and they weren't able."

19 He answered him, "Unbelieving generation, how long shall I be with you? How long shall I bear with you? Bring him to me."

20 They brought him to him, and when he saw him, immediately the spirit convulsed him and he fell on the ground, wallowing and foaming at the mouth.

21 He asked his father, "How long has it been since this has been happening to him?"

He said, "From childhood. 22 Often it has cast him both into the fire and into the water to destroy him. But if you can do anything, have compassion on us and help us."

23 Jesus said to him, "If you can believe, all things are possible to him who believes."

24 Immediately the father of the child cried out with tears, "I believe. Help my unbelief!"

25 When Jesus saw that a multitude came running together, he rebuked the unclean spirit, saying to him, "You mute and deaf spirit, I command you, come out of him, and never enter him again!"

26 After crying out and convulsing him greatly, it came out of him. The boy became like one dead, so much that most of them said, "He is dead." 27 But Jesus took him by the hand and raised him up; and he arose.

28 When he had come into the house, his disciples asked him privately, "Why couldn't we cast it out?"

29 He said to them, "This kind can come out by nothing but by prayer and fasting."

30 They went out from there and passed through Galilee. He didn't want anyone to know it, 31 for he was teaching his disciples, and said to them, "The Son of Man is being handed over to the hands of men, and they will kill him; and when he is killed, on the third day he will rise again."

32 But they didn't understand the saying, and were afraid to ask him.

33 He came to Capernaum, and when he was in the house he asked them, "What were you arguing amongst yourselves on the way?"

34 But they were silent, for they had disputed with one another on the way about who was the greatest.

35 He sat down and called the twelve; and he said to them, "If any man wants to be first, he shall be last of all, and servant of all." 36 He took a little child and set him in the middle of them. Taking him in his arms, he said to them, 37 "Whoever receives one such little child in my name receives me; and whoever receives me, doesn't receive me, but him who sent me."

38 John said to him, "Teacher, we saw someone who doesn't follow us casting out demons in your name; and we forbade him, because he doesn't follow us."

39 But Jesus said, "Don't forbid him, for there is no one who will do a mighty work in my name and be able quickly to speak evil of me. 40 For whoever is not against us is on our side. 41 For whoever will give you a cup of water to drink in my name because you are Christ's, most certainly I tell you, he will in no way lose his reward.

42 "Whoever will cause one of these little ones who believe in me to stumble, it would be better for him if he were thrown into the sea with a millstone hung around his neck. 43 If your hand causes you to stumble, cut it off. It is better for you to enter into life maimed, rather than having your two hands to go into Gehenna,[b] into the unquenchable fire, 44 'where their

---

a 8:12 The word translated "generation" here (genea) could also be translated "people", "race", or "family".

b 9:43 or, Hell

worm doesn't die, and the fire is not quenched.' *ᵃ ₄₅ If your foot causes you to stumble, cut it off. It is better for you to enter into life lame, rather than having your two feet to be cast into Gehenna, ᵇ into the fire that will never be quenched— ₄₆ 'where their worm doesn't die, and the fire is not quenched.' ᶜ ₄₇ If your eye causes you to stumble, throw it out. It is better for you to enter into God's Kingdom with one eye, rather than having two eyes to be cast into the Gehenna ᵈ of fire, ₄₈ 'where their worm doesn't die, and the fire is not quenched.' * ₄₉ For everyone will be salted with fire, and every sacrifice will be seasoned with salt. ₅₀ Salt is good, but if the salt has lost its saltiness, with what will you season it? Have salt in yourselves, and be at peace with one another."

10

₁ He arose from there and came into the borders of Judea and beyond the Jordan. Multitudes came together to him again. As he usually did, he was again teaching them.

₂ Pharisees came to him testing him, and asked him, "Is it lawful for a man to divorce his wife?"

₃ He answered, "What did Moses command you?"

₄ They said, "Moses allowed a certificate of divorce to be written, and to divorce her."

₅ But Jesus said to them, "For your hardness of heart, he wrote you this commandment. ₆ But from the beginning of the creation, God made them male and female.* ₇ For this cause a man will leave his father and mother, and will join to his wife, ₈ and the two will become one flesh,* so that they are no longer two, but one flesh. ₉ What therefore God has joined together, let no man separate."

₁₀ In the house, his disciples asked him again about the same matter. ₁₁ He said to them, "Whoever divorces his wife and marries another commits adultery against her. ₁₂ If a woman herself divorces her husband and marries another, she commits adultery."

₁₃ They were bringing to him little children, that he should touch them, but the disciples rebuked those who were bringing them. ₁₄ But when Jesus saw it, he was moved with indignation and said to them, "Allow the little children to come to me! Don't forbid them, for God's Kingdom belongs to such as these. ₁₅ Most certainly I tell you, whoever will not receive God's Kingdom like a little child, he will in no way enter into it." ₁₆ He took them in his arms and blessed them, laying his hands on them.

₁₇ As he was going out into the way, one ran to him, knelt before him, and asked him, "Good Teacher, what shall I do that I may inherit eternal life?"

₁₈ Jesus said to him, "Why do you call me good? No one is good except one—God. ₁₉ You know the commandments: 'Do not murder,' 'Do not commit adultery,' 'Do not steal,' 'Do not give false testimony,' 'Do not defraud,' 'Honour your father and mother.'"*

₂₀ He said to him, "Teacher, I have observed all these things from my youth."

₂₁ Jesus looking at him loved him, and said to him, "One thing you lack. Go, sell whatever you have and give to the poor, and you will have treasure in heaven; and come, follow me, taking up the cross."

₂₂ But his face fell at that saying, and he went away sorrowful, for he was one who had great possessions.

₂₃ Jesus looked around and said to his disciples, "How difficult it is for those who have riches to enter into God's Kingdom!"

₂₄ The disciples were amazed at his words. But Jesus answered again, "Children, how hard it is for those who trust in riches to enter into God's Kingdom! ₂₅ It is easier for a camel to go through a needle's eye than for a rich man to enter into God's Kingdom."

₂₆ They were exceedingly astonished, saying to him, "Then who can be saved?"

₂₇ Jesus, looking at them, said, "With men it is impossible, but not with God, for all things are possible with God."

₂₈ Peter began to tell him, "Behold, we have left all and have followed you."

₂₉ Jesus said, "Most certainly I tell you, there is no one who has left house, or brothers, or sisters, or father, or mother, or wife, or children, or land, for my sake, and for the sake of the Good News, ₃₀ but he will receive one hundred times more now in this time: houses, brothers, sisters, mothers, children, and land, with persecutions; and in the age to come eternal life. ₃₁ But many who are first will be last, and the last first."

₃₂ They were on the way, going up to Jerusalem; and Jesus was going in front of them, and they were amazed; and those who followed were afraid. He again took the twelve, and began to tell them the things that were going to happen to him. ₃₃ "Behold, we are going up to Jerusalem. The Son of Man will be delivered to the chief priests and the scribes. They will condemn him to death, and will deliver him to the Gentiles. ₃₄ They will mock him, spit on him, scourge him, and kill him. On the third day he will rise again."

₃₅ James and John, the sons of Zebedee, came near to him, saying, "Teacher, we want you to do for us whatever we will ask."

₃₆ He said to them, "What do you want me to do for you?"

₃₇ They said to him, "Grant to us that we may sit, one at your right hand and one at your left hand, in your glory."

₃₈ But Jesus said to them, "You don't know what you are asking. Are you able to drink the cup that I drink, and to be baptised with the baptism that I am baptised with?"

₃₉ They said to him, "We are able."

Jesus said to them, "You shall indeed drink the cup that I drink, and you shall be baptised with the baptism that I am baptised with; ₄₀ but to sit at my right hand and at my left hand is not mine to give, but for whom it has been prepared."

₄₁ When the ten heard it, they began to be indignant towards James and John.

₄₂ Jesus summoned them and said to them, "You know that they who are recognised as rulers over the nations lord it over them, and their great ones exercise authority over them. ₄₃ But it shall not be so amongst you, but whoever wants to become great amongst you shall be your servant. ₄₄ Whoever of you wants to become first amongst you shall be bondservant of all. ₄₅ For the Son of Man also came not to be served but to serve, and to give his life as a ransom for many."

₄₆ They came to Jericho. As he went out from Jericho with his disciples and a great multitude, the son of Timaeus, Bartimaeus, a blind beggar, was sitting by the road. ₄₇ When he heard that it was Jesus the Nazarene, he began to cry out and say, "Jesus, you son of David, have mercy on me!" ₄₈ Many rebuked him, that he should be quiet, but he cried out much more, "You son of David, have mercy on me!"

₄₉ Jesus stood still and said, "Call him."

They called the blind man, saying to him, "Cheer up! Get up. He is calling you!"

₅₀ He, casting away his cloak, sprang up, and came to Jesus.

₅₁ Jesus asked him, "What do you want me to do for you?"

The blind man said to him, "Rabboni,ᵉ that I may see again."

₅₂ Jesus said to him, "Go your way. Your faith has made you well." Immediately he received his sight and followed Jesus on the way.

11

₁ When they came near to Jerusalem, to Bethsphageᶠ and Bethany, at the Mount of Olives, he sent two of his disciples ₂ and said to them, "Go your way into the village that is opposite you. Immediately as you enter into it, you will find a young donkey tied, on which no one has sat. Untie him and bring him. ₃ If anyone asks you, 'Why are you doing this?' say, 'The Lord needs him;' and immediately he will send him back here."

₄ They went away, and found a young donkey tied at the door outside in the open street, and they untied him. ₅ Some of those who stood there asked them, "What are you doing, untying the young donkey?" ₆ They said to them just as Jesus had said, and they let them go.

₇ They brought the young donkey to Jesus and threw their garments on it, and Jesus sat on it. ₈ Many spread their garments on the way, and others were cutting down branches from the trees and spreading them on the road. ₉ Those who went in front and those who followed cried out, "Hosanna!ᵍ Blessed is he who comes in the name of the Lord!* ₁₀ Blessed is the kingdom of our father David that is coming in the name of the Lord! Hosanna in the highest!"

₁₁ Jesus entered into the temple in Jerusalem. When he had looked around at everything, it being now evening, he went out to Bethany with the twelve.

₁₂ The next day, when they had come out from Bethany, he was hungry. ₁₃ Seeing a fig tree afar off having leaves, he came to see if perhaps he might find anything on it. When he came to it, he found nothing but leaves, for it was not the season for figs. ₁₄ Jesus told it, "May no one ever eat fruit from you again!" and his disciples heard it.

₁₅ They came to Jerusalem, and Jesus entered into the temple and began to throw out those who sold and those who bought in the temple, and overthrew the money changers' tables and the seats of those who sold the doves. ₁₆ He would not allow anyone to carry a container through the temple. ₁₇ He taught, saying to them, "Isn't it written, 'My house will be called a house of prayer for all the nations'?* But you have made it a den of robbers!"*

₁₈ The chief priests and the scribes heard it, and sought how they might destroy him. For they feared him, because all the multitude was astonished at his teaching.

₁₉ When evening came, he went out of the city. ₂₀ As they passed by in the morning, they saw the fig tree withered away from the roots. ₂₁ Peter, remembering, said to him, "Rabbi, look! The fig tree which you cursed has withered away."

₂₂ Jesus answered them, "Have faith in God. ₂₃ For most certainly I tell you, whoever may tell this mountain, 'Be taken up and cast into the sea,' and doesn't doubt in his heart, but believes that what he says is happening, he shall have whatever he says. ₂₄ Therefore I tell you, all things whatever you pray and ask for, believe that you have received them,

---

** 9:44 Isaiah 66:24
ᵃ 9:44 NU omits verse 44.
ᵇ 9:45 or, Hell
ᶜ 9:46 NU omits verse 46.
ᵈ 9:47 or, Hell
** 9:48 Isaiah 66:24
** 10:6 Genesis 1:27
** 10:8 Genesis 2:24

** 10:19 Exodus 20:12-16; Deuteronomy 5:16-20
ᵉ 10:51 Rabboni is a transliteration of the Hebrew word for "great teacher."
ᶠ 11:1 TR & NU read "Bethphage" instead of "Bethsphage"
ᵍ 11:9 "Hosanna" means "save us" or "help us, we pray".
** 11:9 Psalms 118:25-26
** 11:17 Isaiah 56:7
** 11:17 Jeremiah 7:11

and you shall have them. 25 Whenever you stand praying, forgive, if you have anything against anyone; so that your Father, who is in heaven, may also forgive you your transgressions. 26 But if you do not forgive, neither will your Father in heaven forgive your transgressions."a

27 They came again to Jerusalem, and as he was walking in the temple, the chief priests, the scribes, and the elders came to him, 28 and they began saying to him, "By what authority do you do these things? Or who gave you this authority to do these things?"

29 Jesus said to them, "I will ask you one question. Answer me, and I will tell you by what authority I do these things. 30 The baptism of John—was it from heaven, or from men? Answer me."

31 They reasoned with themselves, saying, "If we should say, 'From heaven;' he will say, 'Why then did you not believe him?' 32 If we should say, 'From men'"—they feared the people, for all held John to really be a prophet. 33 They answered Jesus, "We don't know."

Jesus said to them, "Neither will I tell you by what authority I do these things."

12

1 He began to speak to them in parables. "A man planted a vineyard, put a hedge around it, dug a pit for the wine press, built a tower, rented it out to a farmer, and went into another country. 2 When it was time, he sent a servant to the farmer to get from the farmer his share of the fruit of the vineyard. 3 They took him, beat him, and sent him away empty. 4 Again, he sent another servant to them; and they threw stones at him, wounded him in the head, and sent him away shamefully treated. 5 Again he sent another, and they killed him, and many others, beating some, and killing some. 6 Therefore still having one, his beloved son, he sent him last to them, saying, 'They will respect my son.' 7 But those farmers said amongst themselves, 'This is the heir. Come, let's kill him, and the inheritance will be ours.' 8 They took him, killed him, and cast him out of the vineyard. 9 What therefore will the lord of the vineyard do? He will come and destroy the farmers, and will give the vineyard to others. 10 Haven't you even read this Scripture:
'The stone which the builders rejected
    was made the head of the corner.
11 This was from the Lord.
    It is marvellous in our eyes'?"**

12 They tried to seize him, but they feared the multitude; for they perceived that he spoke the parable against them. They left him and went away. 13 They sent some of the Pharisees and the Herodians to him, that they might trap him with words. 14 When they had come, they asked him, "Teacher, we know that you are honest, and don't defer to anyone; for you aren't partial to anyone, but truly teach the way of God. Is it lawful to pay taxes to Caesar, or not? 15 Shall we give, or shall we not give?"

But he, knowing their hypocrisy, said to them, "Why do you test me? Bring me a denarius, that I may see it."

16 They brought it.

He said to them, "Whose is this image and inscription?"

They said to him, "Caesar's."

17 Jesus answered them, "Render to Caesar the things that are Caesar's, and to God the things that are God's."

They marvelled greatly at him.

18 Some Sadducees, who say that there is no resurrection, came to him. They asked him, saying, 19 "Teacher, Moses wrote to us, 'If a man's brother dies and leaves a wife behind him, and leaves no children, that his brother should take his wife and raise up offspring for his brother.' 20 There were seven brothers. The first took a wife, and dying left no offspring. 21 The second took her, and died, leaving no children behind him. The third likewise; 22 and the seven took her and left no children. Last of all the woman also died. 23 In the resurrection, when they rise, whose wife will she be of them? For the seven had her as a wife."

24 Jesus answered them, "Isn't this because you are mistaken, not knowing the Scriptures nor the power of God? 25 For when they will rise from the dead, they neither marry nor are given in marriage, but are like angels in heaven. 26 But about the dead, that they are raised, haven't you read in the book of Moses about the Bush, how God spoke to him, saying, 'I am the God of Abraham, the God of Isaac, and the God of Jacob'?* 27 He is not the God of the dead, but of the living. You are therefore badly mistaken."

28 One of the scribes came and heard them questioning together, and knowing that he had answered them well, asked him, "Which commandment is the greatest of all?"

29 Jesus answered, "The greatest is: 'Hear, Israel, the Lord our God, the Lord is one. 30 You shall love the Lord your God with all your heart, with all your soul, with all your mind, and with all your strength.'* This is the first commandment. 31 The second is like this: 'You shall love your neighbour as yourself.'* There is no other commandment greater than these."

32 The scribe said to him, "Truly, teacher, you have said well that he is one, and there is none other but he; 33 and to love him with all the heart, with all the understanding, all the soul, and with all the strength, and to love his neighbour as himself, is more important than all whole burnt offerings and sacrifices."

34 When Jesus saw that he answered wisely, he said to him, "You are not far from God's Kingdom."

No one dared ask him any question after that. 35 Jesus responded, as he taught in the temple, "How is it that the scribes say that the Christ is the son of David? 36 For David himself said in the Holy Spirit,
'The Lord said to my Lord,
    "Sit at my right hand,
        until I make your enemies the footstool of your feet."'*
37 Therefore David himself calls him Lord, so how can he be his son?"

The common people heard him gladly. 38 In his teaching he said to them, "Beware of the scribes, who like to walk in long robes, and to get greetings in the marketplaces, 39 and to get the best seats in the synagogues and the best places at feasts, 40 those who devour widows' houses, and for a pretence make long prayers. These will receive greater condemnation."

41 Jesus sat down opposite the treasury and saw how the multitude cast money into the treasury. Many who were rich cast in much. 42 A poor widow came and she cast in two small brass coins,b which equal a quadrans coin.c 43 He called his disciples to himself and said to them, "Most certainly I tell you, this poor widow gave more than all those who are giving into the treasury, 44 for they all gave out of their abundance, but she, out of her poverty, gave all that she had to live on."

13

1 As he went out of the temple, one of his disciples said to him, "Teacher, see what kind of stones and what kind of buildings!"

2 Jesus said to him, "Do you see these great buildings? There will not be left here one stone on another, which will not be thrown down."

3 As he sat on the Mount of Olives opposite the temple, Peter, James, John, and Andrew asked him privately, 4 "Tell us, when will these things be? What is the sign that these things are all about to be fulfilled?"

5 Jesus, answering, began to tell them, "Be careful that no one leads you astray. 6 For many will come in my name, saying, 'I am he!'d and will lead many astray.

7 "When you hear of wars and rumours of wars, don't be troubled. For those must happen, but the end is not yet. 8 For nation will rise against nation, and kingdom against kingdom. There will be earthquakes in various places. There will be famines and troubles. These things are the beginning of birth pains.

9 "But watch yourselves, for they will deliver you up to councils. You will be beaten in synagogues. You will stand before rulers and kings for my sake, for a testimony to them. 10 The Good News must first be preached to all the nations. 11 When they lead you away and deliver you up, don't be anxious beforehand or premeditate what you will say, but say whatever will be given you in that hour. For it is not you who speak, but the Holy Spirit.

12 "Brother will deliver up brother to death, and the father his child. Children will rise up against parents and cause them to be put to death. 13 You will be hated by all men for my name's sake, but he who endures to the end will be saved.

14 "But when you see the abomination of desolation,* spoken of by Daniel the prophet, standing where it ought not" (let the reader understand), "then let those who are in Judea flee to the mountains, 15 and let him who is on the housetop not go down, nor enter in, to take anything out of his house. 16 Let him who is in the field not return back to take his cloak. 17 But woe to those who are with child and to those who nurse babies in those days! 18 Pray that your flight won't be in the winter. 19 For in those days there will be oppression, such as there has not been the like from the beginning of the creation which God created until now, and never will be. 20 Unless the Lord had shortened the days, no flesh would have been saved; but for the sake of the chosen ones, whom he picked out, he shortened the days. 21 Then if anyone tells you, 'Look, here is the Christ!' or, 'Look, there!' don't believe it. 22 For false christs and false prophets will arise and will show signs and wonders, that they may lead astray, if possible, even the chosen ones. 23 But you watch.

"Behold, I have told you all things beforehand. 24 But in those days, after that oppression, the sun will be darkened, and the moon will not give its light, 25 the stars will be falling from the sky, and the powers that are in the heavens will be shaken.' 26 Then they will see the Son of Man coming in clouds with great power and glory. 27 Then he will send out his angels, and will gather together his chosen ones from the four winds, from the ends of the earth to the ends of the sky.

28 "Now from the fig tree, learn this parable. When the branch has now become tender and produces its leaves, you know that the summer is near; 29 even so you also, when you see these things coming to pass, know that

a 11:26 NU omits verse 26.
** 12:11 Psalms 118:22-23
** 12:26 Exodus 3:6
** 12:30 Deuteronomy 6:4-5
** 12:31 Leviticus 19:18
** 12:36 Psalms 110:1

b 12:42 literally, lepta (or widow's mites). Lepta are very small brass coins worth half a quadrans each, which is a quarter of the copper assarion. Lepta are worth less than 1% of an agricultural worker's daily wages.
c 12:42 A quadrans is a coin worth about 1/64 of a denarius. A denarius is about one day's wages for an agricultural labourer.
d 13:6 or, "I AM!"
** 13:14 Daniel 9:17; 11:31; 12:11
** 13:25 Isaiah 13:10; 34:4

it is near, at the doors. 30 Most certainly I say to you, this generation[a] will not pass away until all these things happen. 31 Heaven and earth will pass away, but my words will not pass away.

32 "But of that day or that hour no one knows—not even the angels in heaven, nor the Son, but only the Father. 33 Watch, keep alert, and pray; for you don't know when the time is.

34 "It is like a man travelling to another country, having left his house and given authority to his servants, and to each one his work, and also commanded the doorkeeper to keep watch. 35 Watch therefore, for you don't know when the lord of the house is coming—whether at evening, or at midnight, or when the rooster crows, or in the morning; 36 lest, coming suddenly, he might find you sleeping. 37 What I tell you, I tell all: Watch!"

14

1 It was now two days before the Passover and the Feast of Unleavened Bread, and the chief priests and the scribes sought how they might seize him by deception and kill him. 2 For they said, "Not during the feast, because there might be a riot amongst the people."

3 While he was at Bethany, in the house of Simon the leper, as he sat at the table, a woman came having an alabaster jar of ointment of pure nard—very costly. She broke the jar and poured it over his head. 4 But there were some who were indignant amongst themselves, saying, "Why has this ointment been wasted? 5 For this might have been sold for more than three hundred denarii[b] and given to the poor." So they grumbled against her.

6 But Jesus said, "Leave her alone. Why do you trouble her? She has done a good work for me. 7 For you always have the poor with you, and whenever you want to, you can do them good; but you will not always have me. 8 She has done what she could. She has anointed my body beforehand for the burying. 9 Most certainly I tell you, wherever this Good News may be preached throughout the whole world, that which this woman has done will also be spoken of for a memorial of her."

10 Judas Iscariot, who was one of the twelve, went away to the chief priests, that he might deliver him to them. 11 They, when they heard it, were glad, and promised to give him money. He sought how he might conveniently deliver him.

12 On the first day of unleavened bread, when they sacrificed the Passover, his disciples asked him, "Where do you want us to go and prepare that you may eat the Passover?"

13 He sent two of his disciples and said to them, "Go into the city, and there a man carrying a pitcher of water will meet you. Follow him, 14 and wherever he enters in, tell the master of the house, 'The Teacher says, "Where is the guest room, where I may eat the Passover with my disciples?"' 15 He will himself show you a large upper room furnished and ready. Get ready for us there."

16 His disciples went out, and came into the city, and found things as he had said to them, and they prepared the Passover.

17 When it was evening he came with the twelve. 18 As they sat and were eating, Jesus said, "Most certainly I tell you, one of you will betray me—he who eats with me."

19 They began to be sorrowful, and to ask him one by one, "Surely not I?" And another said, "Surely not I?"

20 He answered them, "It is one of the twelve, he who dips with me in the dish. 21 For the Son of Man goes as it is written about him, but woe to that man by whom the Son of Man is betrayed! It would be better for that man if he had not been born."

22 As they were eating, Jesus took bread, and when he had blessed it, he broke it and gave to them, and said, "Take, eat. This is my body."

23 He took the cup, and when he had given thanks, he gave to them. They all drank of it. 24 He said to them, "This is my blood of the new covenant, which is poured out for many. 25 Most certainly I tell you, I will no more drink of the fruit of the vine until that day when I drink it anew in God's Kingdom." 26 When they had sung a hymn, they went out to the Mount of Olives.

27 Jesus said to them, "All of you will be made to stumble because of me tonight, for it is written, 'I will strike the shepherd, and the sheep will be scattered.' 28 However, after I am raised up, I will go before you into Galilee."

29 But Peter said to him, "Although all will be offended, yet I will not."

30 Jesus said to him, "Most certainly I tell you that you today, even this night, before the rooster crows twice, you will deny me three times."

31 But he spoke all the more, "If I must die with you, I will not deny you." They all said the same thing.

32 They came to a place which was named Gethsemane. He said to his disciples, "Sit here while I pray." 33 He took with him Peter, James, and John, and began to be greatly troubled and distressed. 34 He said to them, "My soul is exceedingly sorrowful, even to death. Stay here and watch."

35 He went forward a little, and fell on the ground, and prayed that if it were possible, the hour might pass away from him. 36 He said, "Abba,[c] Father, all things are possible to you. Please remove this cup from me. However, not what I desire, but what you desire."

37 He came and found them sleeping, and said to Peter, "Simon, are you sleeping? Couldn't you watch one hour? 38 Watch and pray, that you may not enter into temptation. The spirit indeed is willing, but the flesh is weak."

39 Again he went away and prayed, saying the same words. 40 Again he returned and found them sleeping, for their eyes were very heavy; and they didn't know what to answer him. 41 He came the third time and said to them, "Sleep on now, and take your rest. It is enough. The hour has come. Behold, the Son of Man is betrayed into the hands of sinners. 42 Arise! Let's get going. Behold, he who betrays me is at hand."

43 Immediately, while he was still speaking, Judas, one of the twelve, came—and with him a multitude with swords and clubs, from the chief priests, the scribes, and the elders. 44 Now he who betrayed him had given them a sign, saying, "Whomever I will kiss, that is he. Seize him, and lead him away safely." 45 When he had come, immediately he came to him and said, "Rabbi! Rabbi!" and kissed him. 46 They laid their hands on him and seized him. 47 But a certain one of those who stood by drew his sword and struck the servant of the high priest, and cut off his ear.

48 Jesus answered them, "Have you come out, as against a robber, with swords and clubs to seize me? 49 I was daily with you in the temple teaching, and you didn't arrest me. But this is so that the Scriptures might be fulfilled."

50 They all left him, and fled. 51 A certain young man followed him, having a linen cloth thrown around himself over his naked body. The young men grabbed him, 52 but he left the linen cloth and fled from them naked. 53 They led Jesus away to the high priest. All the chief priests, the elders, and the scribes came together with him.

54 Peter had followed him from a distance, until he came into the court of the high priest. He was sitting with the officers, and warming himself in the light of the fire. 55 Now the chief priests and the whole council sought witnesses against Jesus to put him to death, and found none. 56 For many gave false testimony against him, and their testimony didn't agree with each other. 57 Some stood up and gave false testimony against him, saying, 58 "We heard him say, 'I will destroy this temple that is made with hands, and in three days I will build another made without hands.'" 59 Even so, their testimony didn't agree.

60 The high priest stood up in the middle, and asked Jesus, "Have you no answer? What is it which these testify against you?" 61 But he stayed quiet, and answered nothing. Again the high priest asked him, "Are you the Christ, the Son of the Blessed?"

62 Jesus said, "I am. You will see the Son of Man sitting at the right hand of Power, and coming with the clouds of the sky."

63 The high priest tore his clothes and said, "What further need have we of witnesses? 64 You have heard the blasphemy! What do you think?" They all condemned him to be worthy of death. 65 Some began to spit on him, and to cover his face, and to beat him with fists, and to tell him, "Prophesy!" The officers struck him with the palms of their hands.

66 As Peter was in the courtyard below, one of the maids of the high priest came, 67 and seeing Peter warming himself, she looked at him and said, "You were also with the Nazarene, Jesus!"

68 But he denied it, saying, "I neither know nor understand what you are saying." He went out on the porch, and the rooster crowed.

69 The maid saw him and began again to tell those who stood by, "This is one of them." 70 But he again denied it. After a little while again those who stood by said to Peter, "You truly are one of them, for you are a Galilean, and your speech shows it." 71 But he began to curse and to swear, "I don't know this man of whom you speak!"

72 The rooster crowed the second time. Peter remembered the words that Jesus said to him, "Before the rooster crows twice, you will deny me three times." When he thought about that, he wept.

15

1 Immediately in the morning the chief priests, with the elders, scribes, and the whole council, held a consultation, bound Jesus, carried him away, and delivered him up to Pilate. 2 Pilate asked him, "Are you the King of the Jews?"

He answered, "So you say."

3 The chief priests accused him of many things. 4 Pilate again asked him, "Have you no answer? See how many things they testify against you!"

5 But Jesus made no further answer, so that Pilate marvelled.

6 Now at the feast he used to release to them one prisoner, whomever they asked of him. 7 There was one called Barabbas, bound with his fellow insurgents, men who in the insurrection had committed murder. 8 The multitude, crying aloud, began to ask him to do as he always did for them. 9 Pilate answered them, saying, "Do you want me to release to you the King of the Jews?" 10 For he perceived that for envy the chief priests had delivered him up. 11 But the chief priests stirred up the multitude, that he should release Barabbas to them instead. 12 Pilate again asked them, "What then should I do to him whom you call the King of the Jews?"

13 They cried out again, "Crucify him!"

14 Pilate said to them, "Why, what evil has he done?"

But they cried out exceedingly, "Crucify him!"

15 Pilate, wishing to please the multitude, released Barabbas to them, and handed over Jesus, when he had flogged him, to be crucified.

16 The soldiers led him away within the court, which is the Praetorium; and they called together the whole cohort. 17 They clothed him with purple; and weaving a crown of thorns, they put it on him. 18 They began to salute him, "Hail, King of the Jews!" 19 They struck his head with a reed and spat on him, and bowing their knees, did homage to him. 20 When they had

---

a *13:30* The word translated "generation" (genea) could also be translated "race", "family", or "people".

b *14:5* 300 denarii was about a year's wages for an agricultural labourer.

** 14:27 Zechariah 13:7

c *14:36* Abba is a Greek spelling for the Aramaic word for "Father" or "Daddy" used in a familiar, respectful, and loving way.

mocked him, they took the purple cloak off him, and put his own garments on him. They led him out to crucify him.

₂₁ They compelled one passing by, coming from the country, Simon of Cyrene, the father of Alexander and Rufus, to go with them that he might bear his cross. ₂₂ They brought him to the place called Golgotha, which is, being interpreted, "The place of a skull." ₂₃ They offered him wine mixed with myrrh to drink, but he didn't take it.

₂₄ Crucifying him, they parted his garments amongst them, casting lots on them, what each should take. ₂₅ It was the third hour[a] when they crucified him. ₂₆ The superscription of his accusation was written over him: "THE KING OF THE JEWS." ₂₇ With him they crucified two robbers, one on his right hand, and one on his left. ₂₈ The Scripture was fulfilled which says, "He was counted with transgressors."[b]

₂₉ Those who passed by blasphemed him, wagging their heads and saying, "Ha! You who destroy the temple and build it in three days, ₃₀ save yourself, and come down from the cross!"

₃₁ Likewise, also the chief priests mocking amongst themselves with the scribes said, "He saved others. He can't save himself. ₃₂ Let the Christ, the King of Israel, now come down from the cross, that we may see and believe him."[c] Those who were crucified with him also insulted him.

₃₃ When the sixth hour[d] had come, there was darkness over the whole land until the ninth hour.[e] ₃₄ At the ninth hour Jesus cried with a loud voice, saying, "Eloi, Eloi, lama sabachthani?" which is, being interpreted, "My God, my God, why have you forsaken me?" *

₃₅ Some of those who stood by, when they heard it, said, "Behold, he is calling Elijah."

₃₆ One ran, and filling a sponge full of vinegar, put it on a reed and gave it to him to drink, saying, "Let him be. Let's see whether Elijah comes to take him down."

₃₇ Jesus cried out with a loud voice, and gave up the spirit. ₃₈ The veil of the temple was torn in two from the top to the bottom. ₃₉ When the centurion, who stood by opposite him, saw that he cried out like this and breathed his last, he said, "Truly this man was the Son of God!"

₄₀ There were also women watching from afar, amongst whom were both Mary Magdalene and Mary the mother of James the less and of Joses, and Salome; ₄₁ who, when he was in Galilee, followed him and served him; and many other women who came up with him to Jerusalem.

₄₂ When evening had now come, because it was the Preparation Day, that is, the day before the Sabbath, ₄₃ Joseph of Arimathaea, a prominent council member who also himself was looking for God's Kingdom, came. He boldly went in to Pilate, and asked for Jesus' body. ₄₄ Pilate was surprised to hear that he was already dead; and summoning the centurion, he asked him whether he had been dead long. ₄₅ When he found out from the centurion, he granted the body to Joseph. ₄₆ He bought a linen cloth, and taking him down, wound him in the linen cloth and laid him in a tomb which had been cut out of a rock. He rolled a stone against the door of the tomb. ₄₇ Mary Magdalene and Mary the mother of Joses, saw where he was laid.

16

₁ When the Sabbath was past, Mary Magdalene, and Mary the mother of James, and Salome bought spices, that they might come and anoint him. ₂ Very early on the first day of the week, they came to the tomb when the sun had risen. ₃ They were saying amongst themselves, "Who will roll away the stone from the door of the tomb for us?" ₄ for it was very big. Looking up, they saw that the stone was rolled back.

₅ Entering into the tomb, they saw a young man sitting on the right side, dressed in a white robe; and they were amazed. ₆ He said to them, "Don't be amazed. You seek Jesus, the Nazarene, who has been crucified. He has risen! He is not here. See the place where they laid him! ₇ But go, tell his disciples and Peter, 'He goes before you into Galilee. There you will see him, as he said to you.'"

₈ They went out,[f] and fled from the tomb, for trembling and astonishment had come on them. They said nothing to anyone; for they were afraid.[g]

₉ [h]Now when he had risen early on the first day of the week, he appeared first to Mary Magdalene, from whom he had cast out seven demons. ₁₀ She went and told those who had been with him, as they mourned and wept. ₁₁ When they heard that he was alive and had been seen by her, they disbelieved.

₁₂ After these things he was revealed in another form to two of them as they walked, on their way into the country. ₁₃ They went away and told it to the rest. They didn't believe them, either.

₁₄ Afterward he was revealed to the eleven themselves as they sat at the table; and he rebuked them for their unbelief and hardness of heart, because they didn't believe those who had seen him after he had risen. ₁₅ He said to them, "Go into all the world and preach the Good News to the whole creation. ₁₆ He who believes and is baptised will be saved; but he who disbelieves will be condemned. ₁₇ These signs will accompany those who believe: in my name they will cast out demons; they will speak with new languages; ₁₈ they will take up serpents; and if they drink any deadly thing, it will in no way hurt them; they will lay hands on the sick, and they will recover."

₁₉ So then the Lord,[i] after he had spoken to them, was received up into heaven and sat down at the right hand of God. ₂₀ They went out and preached everywhere, the Lord working with them and confirming the word by the signs that followed. Amen.

---

a *15:25* 9:00 a.m.

b *15:28* NU omits verse 28.

c *15:32* TR omits "him"

d *15:33* or, noon

e *15:33* 3:00 p.m.

** *15:34* Psalms 22:1

f *16:8* TR adds "quickly"

g *16:8* One isolated manuscript omits verses 9-20 but adds this "short ending of Mark" to the end of verse 8: They told all that had been commanded them briefly to those around Peter. After that, Jesus himself sent them out, from east to west, with the sacred and imperishable proclamation of eternal salvation.

h *16:9* NU includes the text of verses 9-20, but mentions in a footnote that a few manuscripts omitted it. The translators of the International English Bible regard Mark 16:9-20 as reliable based on an overwhelming majority of textual evidence, including not only the authoritative Greek Majority Text New Testament, but also the TR and many of the manuscripts cited in the NU text.

i *16:19* NU adds "Jesus"

The Good News According to Luke

1

1 Since many have undertaken to set in order a narrative concerning those matters which have been fulfilled amongst us, 2 even as those who from the beginning were eyewitnesses and servants of the word delivered them to us, 3 it seemed good to me also, having traced the course of all things accurately from the first, to write to you in order, most excellent Theophilus; 4 that you might know the certainty concerning the things in which you were instructed.

5 There was in the days of Herod, the king of Judea, a certain priest named Zacharias, of the priestly division of Abijah. He had a wife of the daughters of Aaron, and her name was Elizabeth. 6 They were both righteous before God, walking blamelessly in all the commandments and ordinances of the Lord. 7 But they had no child, because Elizabeth was barren, and they both were well advanced in years.

8 Now while he executed the priest's office before God in the order of his division 9 according to the custom of the priest's office, his lot was to enter into the temple of the Lord and burn incense. 10 The whole multitude of the people were praying outside at the hour of incense.

11 An angel of the Lord appeared to him, standing on the right side of the altar of incense. 12 Zacharias was troubled when he saw him, and fear fell upon him. 13 But the angel said to him, "Don't be afraid, Zacharias, because your request has been heard. Your wife, Elizabeth, will bear you a son, and you shall call his name John. 14 You will have joy and gladness, and many will rejoice at his birth. 15 For he will be great in the sight of the Lord, and he will drink no wine nor strong drink. He will be filled with the Holy Spirit, even from his mother's womb. 16 He will turn many of the children of Israel to the Lord their God. 17 He will go before him in the spirit and power of Elijah, 'to turn the hearts of the fathers to the children,'' and the disobedient to the wisdom of the just; to prepare a people prepared for the Lord."

18 Zacharias said to the angel, "How can I be sure of this? For I am an old man, and my wife is well advanced in years."

19 The angel answered him, "I am Gabriel, who stands in the presence of God. I was sent to speak to you and to bring you this good news. 20 Behold,[a] you will be silent and not able to speak until the day that these things will happen, because you didn't believe my words, which will be fulfilled in their proper time."

21 The people were waiting for Zacharias, and they marvelled that he delayed in the temple. 22 When he came out, he could not speak to them. They perceived that he had seen a vision in the temple. He continued making signs to them, and remained mute. 23 When the days of his service were fulfilled, he departed to his house. 24 After these days Elizabeth his wife conceived, and she hid herself five months, saying, 25 "Thus has the Lord done to me in the days in which he looked at me, to take away my reproach amongst men."

26 Now in the sixth month, the angel Gabriel was sent from God to a city of Galilee named Nazareth, 27 to a virgin pledged to be married to a man whose name was Joseph, of David's house. The virgin's name was Mary. 28 Having come in, the angel said to her, "Rejoice, you highly favoured one! The Lord is with you. Blessed are you amongst women!"

29 But when she saw him, she was greatly troubled at the saying, and considered what kind of salutation this might be. 30 The angel said to her, "Don't be afraid, Mary, for you have found favour with God. 31 Behold, you will conceive in your womb and give birth to a son, and shall name him 'Jesus.' 32 He will be great and will be called the Son of the Most High. The Lord God will give him the throne of his father David, 33 and he will reign over the house of Jacob forever. There will be no end to his Kingdom."

34 Mary said to the angel, "How can this be, seeing I am a virgin?"

35 The angel answered her, "The Holy Spirit will come on you, and the power of the Most High will overshadow you. Therefore also the holy one who is born from you will be called the Son of God. 36 Behold, Elizabeth your relative also has conceived a son in her old age; and this is the sixth month with her who was called barren. 37 For nothing spoken by God is impossible."[b]

38 Mary said, "Behold, the servant of the Lord; let it be done to me according to your word."

Then the angel departed from her.

39 Mary arose in those days and went into the hill country with haste, into a city of Judah, 40 and entered into the house of Zacharias and greeted Elizabeth. 41 When Elizabeth heard Mary's greeting, the baby leapt in her womb; and Elizabeth was filled with the Holy Spirit. 42 She called out with a loud voice and said, "Blessed are you amongst women, and blessed is the fruit of your womb! 43 Why am I so favoured, that the mother of my Lord should come to me? 44 For behold, when the voice of your greeting came into my ears, the baby leapt in my womb for joy! 45 Blessed is she who believed, for there will be a fulfilment of the things which have been spoken to her from the Lord!"

46 Mary said,
"My soul magnifies the Lord.

47 My spirit has rejoiced in God my Saviour,

48 for he has looked at the humble state of his servant.

For behold, from now on, all generations will call me blessed.

49 For he who is mighty has done great things for me.
Holy is his name.

50 His mercy is for generations and generations on those who fear him.

51 He has shown strength with his arm.
He has scattered the proud in the imagination of their hearts.

52 He has put down princes from their thrones,
and has exalted the lowly.

53 He has filled the hungry with good things.
He has sent the rich away empty.

54 He has given help to Israel, his servant, that he might remember mercy,

55 as he spoke to our fathers,
to Abraham and his offspring[c] forever."

56 Mary stayed with her about three months, and then returned to her house.

57 Now the time that Elizabeth should give birth was fulfilled, and she gave birth to a son. 58 Her neighbours and her relatives heard that the Lord had magnified his mercy towards her, and they rejoiced with her. 59 On the eighth day, they came to circumcise the child; and they would have called him Zacharias, after the name of his father. 60 His mother answered, "Not so; but he will be called John."

61 They said to her, "There is no one amongst your relatives who is called by this name." 62 They made signs to his father, what he would have him called.

63 He asked for a writing tablet, and wrote, "His name is John."

They all marvelled. 64 His mouth was opened immediately and his tongue freed, and he spoke, blessing God. 65 Fear came on all who lived around them, and all these sayings were talked about throughout all the hill country of Judea. 66 All who heard them laid them up in their heart, saying, "What then will this child be?" The hand of the Lord was with him.

67 His father Zacharias was filled with the Holy Spirit, and prophesied, saying,

68 "Blessed be the Lord, the God of Israel,
for he has visited and redeemed his people;

69 and has raised up a horn of salvation for us in the house of his servant David

70 (as he spoke by the mouth of his holy prophets who have been from of old),

71 salvation from our enemies and from the hand of all who hate us;

72 to show mercy towards our fathers,
to remember his holy covenant,

73 the oath which he swore to Abraham our father,

74 to grant to us that we, being delivered out of the hand of our enemies,
should serve him without fear,

75 in holiness and righteousness before him all the days of our life.

76 And you, child, will be called a prophet of the Most High;
for you will go before the face of the Lord to prepare his ways,

77 to give knowledge of salvation to his people by the remission of their sins,

78 because of the tender mercy of our God,
by which the dawn from on high will visit us,

79 to shine on those who sit in darkness and the shadow of death;
to guide our feet into the way of peace."

80 The child was growing and becoming strong in spirit, and was in the desert until the day of his public appearance to Israel.

2

1 Now in those days, a decree went out from Caesar Augustus that all the world should be enrolled. 2 This was the first enrolment made when Quirinius was governor of Syria. 3 All went to enrol themselves, everyone to his own city. 4 Joseph also went up from Galilee, out of the city of Nazareth, into Judea, to David's city, which is called Bethlehem, because he was of the house and family of David, 5 to enrol himself with Mary, who was pledged to be married to him as wife, being pregnant.

6 While they were there, the day had come for her to give birth. 7 She gave birth to her firstborn son. She wrapped him in bands of cloth and laid him in a feeding trough, because there was no room for them in the inn.

8 There were shepherds in the same country staying in the field, and keeping watch by night over their flock. 9 Behold, an angel of the Lord stood by them, and the glory of the Lord shone around them, and they were terrified. 10 The angel said to them, "Don't be afraid, for behold, I bring you good news of great joy which will be to all the people. 11 For there is born to you today, in David's city, a Saviour, who is Christ[d] the Lord. 12 This is the sign to you: you will find a baby wrapped in strips of cloth, lying in a feeding trough." 13 Suddenly, there was with the angel a multitude of the heavenly army praising God and saying,

14 "Glory to God in the highest,
on earth peace, good will towards men."

15 When the angels went away from them into the sky, the shepherds said to one another, "Let's go to Bethlehem, now, and see this thing that has happened, which the Lord has made known to us." 16 They came with haste and found both Mary and Joseph, and the baby was lying in the feeding trough. 17 When they saw it, they publicised widely the saying

---

** 1:17 Malachi 4:6

a *1:20* "Behold", from "ἰδοὺ", means look at, take notice, observe, see, or gaze at. It is often used as an interjection.

b *1:37* or, "For everything spoken by God is possible."

c *1:55* or, seed

d *2:11* "Christ" means "Anointed One".

which was spoken to them about this child. 18 All who heard it wondered at the things which were spoken to them by the shepherds. 19 But Mary kept all these sayings, pondering them in her heart. 20 The shepherds returned, glorifying and praising God for all the things that they had heard and seen, just as it was told them.

21 When eight days were fulfilled for the circumcision of the child, his name was called Jesus, which was given by the angel before he was conceived in the womb.

22 When the days of their purification according to the law of Moses were fulfilled, they brought him up to Jerusalem to present him to the Lord 23 (as it is written in the law of the Lord, "Every male who opens the womb shall be called holy to the Lord"),* 24 and to offer a sacrifice according to that which is said in the law of the Lord, "A pair of turtledoves, or two young pigeons."*

25 Behold, there was a man in Jerusalem whose name was Simeon. This man was righteous and devout, looking for the consolation of Israel, and the Holy Spirit was on him. 26 It had been revealed to him by the Holy Spirit that he should not see death before he had seen the Lord's Christ.ᵃ 27 He came in the Spirit into the temple. When the parents brought in the child, Jesus, that they might do concerning him according to the custom of the law, 28 then he received him into his arms and blessed God, and said,

29 "Now you are releasing your servant, Master,
    according to your word, in peace;
30 for my eyes have seen your salvation,
31 which you have prepared before the face of all peoples;
32 a light for revelation to the nations,
    and the glory of your people Israel."

33 Joseph and his mother were marvelling at the things which were spoken concerning him. 34 Simeon blessed them, and said to Mary, his mother, "Behold, this child is appointed for the falling and the rising of many in Israel, and for a sign which is spoken against. 35 Yes, a sword will pierce through your own soul, that the thoughts of many hearts may be revealed."

36 There was one Anna, a prophetess, the daughter of Phanuel, of the tribe of Asher (she was of a great age, having lived with a husband seven years from her virginity, 37 and she had been a widow for about eighty-four years), who didn't depart from the temple, worshipping with fastings and petitions night and day. 38 Coming up at that very hour, she gave thanks to the Lord, and spoke of him to all those who were looking for redemption in Jerusalem.

39 When they had accomplished all things that were according to the law of the Lord, they returned into Galilee, to their own city, Nazareth. 40 The child was growing, and was becoming strong in spirit, being filled with wisdom, and the grace of God was upon him.

41 His parents went every year to Jerusalem at the feast of the Passover. 42 When he was twelve years old, they went up to Jerusalem according to the custom of the feast; 43 and when they had fulfilled the days, as they were returning, the boy Jesus stayed behind in Jerusalem. Joseph and his mother didn't know it, 44 but supposing him to be in the company, they went a day's journey; and they looked for him amongst their relatives and acquaintances. 45 When they didn't find him, they returned to Jerusalem, looking for him. 46 After three days they found him in the temple, sitting in the middle of the teachers, both listening to them and asking them questions. 47 All who heard him were amazed at his understanding and his answers. 48 When they saw him, they were astonished; and his mother said to him, "Son, why have you treated us this way? Behold, your father and I were anxiously looking for you."

49 He said to them, "Why were you looking for me? Didn't you know that I must be in my Father's house?" 50 They didn't understand the saying which he spoke to them. 51 And he went down with them and came to Nazareth. He was subject to them, and his mother kept all these sayings in her heart. 52 And Jesus increased in wisdom and stature, and in favour with God and men.

3

1 Now in the fifteenth year of the reign of Tiberius Caesar, Pontius Pilate being governor of Judea, and Herod being tetrarch of Galilee, and his brother Philip tetrarch of the region of Ituraea and Trachonitis, and Lysanias tetrarch of Abilene, 2 during the high priesthood of Annas and Caiaphas, the word of God came to John, the son of Zacharias, in the wilderness. 3 He came into all the region around the Jordan, preaching the baptism of repentance for remission of sins. 4 As it is written in the book of the words of Isaiah the prophet,
"The voice of one crying in the wilderness,
    'Make ready the way of the Lord.
Make his paths straight.
5 Every valley will be filled.
Every mountain and hill will be brought low.
    The crooked will become straight,
    and the rough ways smooth.
6 All flesh will see God's salvation."'*

7 He said therefore to the multitudes who went out to be baptised by him, "You offspring of vipers, who warned you to flee from the wrath to come? 8 Therefore produce fruits worthy of repentance, and don't begin to say amongst yourselves, 'We have Abraham for our father;' for I tell you that God is able to raise up children to Abraham from these stones! 9 Even now the axe also lies at the root of the trees. Every tree therefore that doesn't produce good fruit is cut down and thrown into the fire."

10 The multitudes asked him, "What then must we do?"

11 He answered them, "He who has two coats, let him give to him who has none. He who has food, let him do likewise."

12 Tax collectors also came to be baptised, and they said to him, "Teacher, what must we do?"

13 He said to them, "Collect no more than that which is appointed to you."

14 Soldiers also asked him, saying, "What about us? What must we do?"

He said to them, "Extort from no one by violence, neither accuse anyone wrongfully. Be content with your wages."

15 As the people were in expectation, and all men reasoned in their hearts concerning John, whether perhaps he was the Christ, 16 John answered them all, "I indeed baptise you with water, but he comes who is mightier than I, the strap of whose sandals I am not worthy to loosen. He will baptise you in the Holy Spirit and fire. 17 His winnowing fan is in his hand, and he will thoroughly cleanse his threshing floor, and will gather the wheat into his barn; but he will burn up the chaff with unquenchable fire."

18 Then with many other exhortations he preached good news to the people, 19 but Herod the tetrarch,ᵇ being reproved by him for Herodias, his brother'sᶜ wife, and for all the evil things which Herod had done, 20 added this also to them all, that he shut up John in prison.

21 Now when all the people were baptised, Jesus also had been baptised and was praying. The sky was opened, 22 and the Holy Spirit descended in a bodily form like a dove on him; and a voice came out of the sky, saying "You are my beloved Son. In you I am well pleased."

23 Jesus himself, when he began to teach, was about thirty years old, being the son (as was supposed) of Joseph, the son of Heli, 24 the son of Matthat, the son of Levi, the son of Melchi, the son of Jannai, the son of Joseph, 25 the son of Mattathias, the son of Amos, the son of Nahum, the son of Esli, the son of Naggai, 26 the son of Maath, the son of Mattathias, the son of Semein, the son of Joseph, the son of Judah, 27 the son of Joanan, the son of Rhesa, the son of Zerubbabel, the son of Shealtiel, the son of Neri, 28 the son of Melchi, the son of Addi, the son of Cosam, the son of Elmodam, the son of Er, 29 the son of Jose, the son of Eliezer, the son of Jorim, the son of Matthat, the son of Levi, 30 the son of Simeon, the son of Judah, the son of Joseph, the son of Jonan, the son of Eliakim, 31 the son of Melea, the son of Menan, the son of Mattatha, the son of Nathan, the son of David, 32 the son of Jesse, the son of Obed, the son of Boaz, the son of Salmon, the son of Nahshon, 33 the son of Amminadab, the son of Aram,ᵈ the son of Hezron, the son of Perez, the son of Judah, 34 the son of Jacob, the son of Isaac, the son of Abraham, the son of Terah, the son of Nahor, 35 the son of Serug, the son of Reu, the son of Peleg, the son of Eber, the son of Shelah, 36 the son of Cainan, the son of Arphaxad, the son of Shem, the son of Noah, the son of Lamech, 37 the son of Methuselah, the son of Enoch, the son of Jared, the son of Mahalaleel, the son of Cainan, 38 the son of Enos, the son of Seth, the son of Adam, the son of God.

4

1 Jesus, full of the Holy Spirit, returned from the Jordan and was led by the Spirit into the wilderness 2 for forty days, being tempted by the devil. He ate nothing in those days. Afterward, when they were completed, he was hungry.

3 The devil said to him, "If you are the Son of God, command this stone to become bread."

4 Jesus answered him, saying, "It is written, 'Man shall not live by bread alone, but by every word of God.'"*

5 The devil, leading him up on a high mountain, showed him all the kingdoms of the world in a moment of time. 6 The devil said to him, "I will give you all this authority and their glory, for it has been delivered to me, and I give it to whomever I want. 7 If you therefore will worship before me, it will all be yours."

8 Jesus answered him, "Get behind me, Satan! For it is written, 'You shall worship the Lord your God, and you shall serve him only.'"*

9 He led him to Jerusalem and set him on the pinnacle of the temple, and said to him, "If you are the Son of God, cast yourself down from here, 10 for it is written,
'He will put his angels in charge of you, to guard you;'
11 and,
'On their hands they will bear you up,
    lest perhaps you dash your foot against a stone.'"*

12 Jesus answering, said to him, "It has been said, 'You shall not tempt the Lord your God.'"*

13 When the devil had completed every temptation, he departed from him until another time.

** 2:23 Exodus 13:2,12
** 2:24 Leviticus 12:8
ᵃ 2:26 "Christ" (Greek) and "Messiah" (Hebrew) both mean "Anointed One"
** 3:6 Isaiah 40:3-5
ᵇ 3:19 a tetrarch is one of four governors of a province
ᶜ 3:19 TR reads "brother Philip's" instead of "brother's"

ᵈ 3:33 NU reads "Admin, the son of Arni" instead of "Aram"
** 4:4 Deuteronomy 8:3
** 4:8 Deuteronomy 6:13
** 4:11 Psalms 91:11-12
** 4:12 Deuteronomy 6:16

14 Jesus returned in the power of the Spirit into Galilee, and news about him spread through all the surrounding area. 15 He taught in their synagogues, being glorified by all.

16 He came to Nazareth, where he had been brought up. He entered, as was his custom, into the synagogue on the Sabbath day, and stood up to read. 17 The book of the prophet Isaiah was handed to him. He opened the book, and found the place where it was written,

18 "The Spirit of the Lord is on me,
    because he has anointed me to preach good news to the poor.
He has sent me to heal the broken hearted,[a]
    to proclaim release to the captives,
    recovering of sight to the blind,
    to deliver those who are crushed,
19 and to proclaim the acceptable year of the Lord."*

20 He closed the book, gave it back to the attendant, and sat down. The eyes of all in the synagogue were fastened on him. 21 He began to tell them, "Today, this Scripture has been fulfilled in your hearing."

22 All testified about him and wondered at the gracious words which proceeded out of his mouth; and they said, "Isn't this Joseph's son?"

23 He said to them, "Doubtless you will tell me this proverb, 'Physician, heal yourself! Whatever we have heard done at Capernaum, do also here in your hometown.'" 24 He said, "Most certainly I tell you, no prophet is acceptable in his hometown. 25 But truly I tell you, there were many widows in Israel in the days of Elijah, when the sky was shut up three years and six months, when a great famine came over all the land. 26 Elijah was sent to none of them, except to Zarephath, in the land of Sidon, to a woman who was a widow. 27 There were many lepers in Israel in the time of Elisha the prophet, yet not one of them was cleansed, except Naaman, the Syrian."

28 They were all filled with wrath in the synagogue as they heard these things. 29 They rose up, threw him out of the city, and led him to the brow of the hill that their city was built on, that they might throw him off the cliff. 30 But he, passing through the middle of them, went his way.

31 He came down to Capernaum, a city of Galilee. He was teaching them on the Sabbath day, 32 and they were astonished at his teaching, for his word was with authority. 33 In the synagogue there was a man who had a spirit of an unclean demon; and he cried out with a loud voice, 34 saying, "Ah! what have we to do with you, Jesus of Nazareth? Have you come to destroy us? I know who you are: the Holy One of God!"

35 Jesus rebuked him, saying, "Be silent and come out of him!" When the demon had thrown him down in the middle of them, he came out of him, having done him no harm.

36 Amazement came on all and they spoke together, one with another, saying, "What is this word? For with authority and power he commands the unclean spirits, and they come out!" 37 News about him went out into every place of the surrounding region.

38 He rose up from the synagogue and entered into Simon's house. Simon's mother-in-law was afflicted with a great fever, and they begged him to help her. 39 He stood over her and rebuked the fever, and it left her. Immediately she rose up and served them. 40 When the sun was setting, all those who had any sick with various diseases brought them to him; and he laid his hands on every one of them, and healed them. 41 Demons also came out of many, crying out and saying, "You are the Christ, the Son of God!" Rebuking them, he didn't allow them to speak, because they knew that he was the Christ.

42 When it was day, he departed and went into an uninhabited place and the multitudes looked for him, and came to him, and held on to him, so that he wouldn't go away from them. 43 But he said to them, "I must preach the good news of God's Kingdom to the other cities also. For this reason I have been sent." 44 He was preaching in the synagogues of Galilee.

5

1 Now while the multitude pressed on him and heard the word of God, he was standing by the lake of Gennesaret. 2 He saw two boats standing by the lake, but the fishermen had gone out of them and were washing their nets. 3 He entered into one of the boats, which was Simon's, and asked him to put out a little from the land. He sat down and taught the multitudes from the boat.

4 When he had finished speaking, he said to Simon, "Put out into the deep and let down your nets for a catch."

5 Simon answered him, "Master, we worked all night and caught nothing; but at your word I will let down the net." 6 When they had done this, they caught a great multitude of fish, and their net was breaking. 7 They beckoned to their partners in the other boat, that they should come and help them. They came and filled both boats, so that they began to sink. 8 But Simon Peter, when he saw it, fell down at Jesus' knees, saying, "Depart from me, for I am a sinful man, Lord." 9 For he was amazed, and all who were with him, at the catch of fish which they had caught; 10 and so also were James and John, sons of Zebedee, who were partners with Simon.

Jesus said to Simon, "Don't be afraid. From now on you will be catching people alive."

11 When they had brought their boats to land, they left everything, and followed him.

12 While he was in one of the cities, behold, there was a man full of leprosy. When he saw Jesus, he fell on his face and begged him, saying, "Lord, if you want to, you can make me clean."

13 He stretched out his hand and touched him, saying, "I want to. Be made clean."

Immediately the leprosy left him. 14 He commanded him to tell no one, "But go your way and show yourself to the priest, and offer for your cleansing according to what Moses commanded, for a testimony to them."

15 But the report concerning him spread much more, and great multitudes came together to hear and to be healed by him of their infirmities. 16 But he withdrew himself into the desert and prayed.

17 On one of those days, he was teaching; and there were Pharisees and teachers of the law sitting by who had come out of every village of Galilee, Judea, and Jerusalem. The power of the Lord was with him to heal them. 18 Behold, men brought a paralysed man on a cot, and they sought to bring him in to lay before Jesus. 19 Not finding a way to bring him in because of the multitude, they went up to the housetop and let him down through the tiles with his cot into the middle before Jesus. 20 Seeing their faith, he said to him, "Man, your sins are forgiven you."

21 The scribes and the Pharisees began to reason, saying, "Who is this who speaks blasphemies? Who can forgive sins, but God alone?"

22 But Jesus, perceiving their thoughts, answered them, "Why are you reasoning so in your hearts? 23 Which is easier to say, 'Your sins are forgiven you,' or to say, 'Arise and walk'? 24 But that you may know that the Son of Man has authority on earth to forgive sins," he said to the paralysed man, "I tell you, arise, take up your cot, and go to your house."

25 Immediately he rose up before them, and took up that which he was laying on, and departed to his house, glorifying God. 26 Amazement took hold on all, and they glorified God. They were filled with fear, saying, "We have seen strange things today."

27 After these things he went out and saw a tax collector named Levi sitting at the tax office, and said to him, "Follow me!"

28 He left everything, and rose up and followed him. 29 Levi made a great feast for him in his house. There was a great crowd of tax collectors and others who were reclining with them. 30 Their scribes and the Pharisees murmured against his disciples, saying, "Why do you eat and drink with the tax collectors and sinners?"

31 Jesus answered them, "Those who are healthy have no need for a physician, but those who are sick do. 32 I have not come to call the righteous, but sinners, to repentance."

33 They said to him, "Why do John's disciples often fast and pray, likewise also the disciples of the Pharisees, but yours eat and drink?"

34 He said to them, "Can you make the friends of the bridegroom fast while the bridegroom is with them? 35 But the days will come when the bridegroom will be taken away from them. Then they will fast in those days."

36 He also told a parable to them. "No one puts a piece from a new garment on an old garment, or else he will tear the new, and also the piece from the new will not match the old. 37 No one puts new wine into old wine skins, or else the new wine will burst the skins, and it will be spilled and the skins will be destroyed. 38 But new wine must be put into fresh wine skins, and both are preserved. 39 No man having drunk old wine immediately desires new, for he says, 'The old is better.'"

6

1 Now on the second Sabbath after the first, he was going through the grain fields. His disciples plucked the heads of grain and ate, rubbing them in their hands. 2 But some of the Pharisees said to them, "Why do you do that which is not lawful to do on the Sabbath day?"

3 Jesus, answering them, said, "Haven't you read what David did when he was hungry, he and those who were with him, 4 how he entered into God's house, and took and ate the show bread, and gave also to those who were with him, which is not lawful to eat except for the priests alone?" 5 He said to them, "The Son of Man is lord of the Sabbath."

6 It also happened on another Sabbath that he entered into the synagogue and taught. There was a man there, and his right hand was withered. 7 The scribes and the Pharisees watched him, to see whether he would heal on the Sabbath, that they might find an accusation against him. 8 But he knew their thoughts; and he said to the man who had the withered hand, "Rise up and stand in the middle." He arose and stood. 9 Then Jesus said to them, "I will ask you something: Is it lawful on the Sabbath to do good, or to do harm? To save a life, or to kill?" 10 He looked around at them all, and said to the man, "Stretch out your hand." He did, and his hand was restored as sound as the other. 11 But they were filled with rage, and talked with one another about what they might do to Jesus.

12 In these days, he went out to the mountain to pray, and he continued all night in prayer to God. 13 When it was day, he called his disciples, and from them he chose twelve, whom he also named apostles: 14 Simon, whom he also named Peter; Andrew, his brother; James; John; Philip; Bartholomew; 15 Matthew; Thomas; James the son of Alphaeus; Simon who was called the Zealot; 16 Judas the son of James; and Judas Iscariot, who also became a traitor.

17 He came down with them and stood on a level place, with a crowd of his disciples and a great number of the people from all Judea and Jerusalem and the sea coast of Tyre and Sidon, who came to hear him and to be healed of their diseases, 18 as well as those who were troubled by unclean spirits; and they were being healed. 19 All the multitude sought to touch him, for power came out of him and healed them all.

20 He lifted up his eyes to his disciples, and said:
"Blessed are you who are poor,

---

a *4:18* NU omits "to heal the broken hearted"

** 4:19 Isaiah 61:1-2

for God's Kingdom is yours.

21 Blessed are you who hunger now,
for you will be filled.
Blessed are you who weep now,
for you will laugh.

22 Blessed are you when men hate you, and when they exclude and mock you, and throw out your name as evil, for the Son of Man's sake. 23 Rejoice in that day and leap for joy, for behold, your reward is great in heaven, for their fathers did the same thing to the prophets.

24 "But woe to you who are rich!
For you have received your consolation.

25 Woe to you, you who are full now,
for you will be hungry.
Woe to you who laugh now,
for you will mourn and weep.

26 Woe,[a] when[b] men speak well of you,
for their fathers did the same thing to the false prophets.

27 "But I tell you who hear: love your enemies, do good to those who hate you, 28 bless those who curse you, and pray for those who mistreat you. 29 To him who strikes you on the cheek, offer also the other; and from him who takes away your cloak, don't withhold your coat also. 30 Give to everyone who asks you, and don't ask him who takes away your goods to give them back again.

31 "As you would like people to do to you, do exactly so to them.

32 "If you love those who love you, what credit is that to you? For even sinners love those who love them. 33 If you do good to those who do good to you, what credit is that to you? For even sinners do the same. 34 If you lend to those from whom you hope to receive, what credit is that to you? Even sinners lend to sinners, to receive back as much. 35 But love your enemies, and do good, and lend, expecting nothing back; and your reward will be great, and you will be children of the Most High; for he is kind towards the unthankful and evil.

36 "Therefore be merciful,
even as your Father is also merciful.

37 Don't judge,
and you won't be judged.
Don't condemn,
and you won't be condemned.
Set free,
and you will be set free.

38 "Give, and it will be given to you: good measure, pressed down, shaken together, and running over, will be given to you.[c] For with the same measure you measure it will be measured back to you."

39 He spoke a parable to them. "Can the blind guide the blind? Won't they both fall into a pit? 40 A disciple is not above his teacher, but everyone when he is fully trained will be like his teacher. 41 Why do you see the speck of chaff that is in your brother's eye, but don't consider the beam that is in your own eye? 42 Or how can you tell your brother, 'Brother, let me remove the speck of chaff that is in your eye,' when you yourself don't see the beam that is in your own eye? You hypocrite! First remove the beam from your own eye, and then you can see clearly to remove the speck of chaff that is in your brother's eye.

43 "For there is no good tree that produces rotten fruit, nor again a rotten tree that produces good fruit. 44 For each tree is known by its own fruit. For people don't gather figs from thorns, nor do they gather grapes from a bramble bush. 45 The good man out of the good treasure of his heart brings out that which is good, and the evil man out of the evil treasure of his heart brings out that which is evil, for out of the abundance of the heart, his mouth speaks.

46 "Why do you call me, 'Lord, Lord,' and don't do the things which I say? 47 Everyone who comes to me, and hears my words and does them, I will show you who he is like. 48 He is like a man building a house, who dug and went deep and laid a foundation on the rock. When a flood arose, the stream broke against that house, and could not shake it, because it was founded on the rock. 49 But he who hears and doesn't do, is like a man who built a house on the earth without a foundation, against which the stream broke, and immediately it fell; and the ruin of that house was great."

7

1 After he had finished speaking in the hearing of the people, he entered into Capernaum. 2 A certain centurion's servant, who was dear to him, was sick and at the point of death. 3 When he heard about Jesus, he sent to him elders of the Jews, asking him to come and save his servant. 4 When they came to Jesus, they begged him earnestly, saying, "He is worthy for you to do this for him, 5 for he loves our nation, and he built our synagogue for us." 6 Jesus went with them. When he was now not far from the house, the centurion sent friends to him, saying to him, "Lord, don't trouble yourself, for I am not worthy for you to come under my roof. 7 Therefore I didn't even think myself worthy to come to you; but say the word, and my servant will be healed. 8 For I also am a man placed under authority, having under myself soldiers. I tell this one, 'Go!' and he goes;

and to another, 'Come!' and he comes; and to my servant, 'Do this,' and he does it."

9 When Jesus heard these things, he marvelled at him, and turned and said to the multitude who followed him, "I tell you, I have not found such great faith, no, not in Israel." 10 Those who were sent, returning to the house, found that the servant who had been sick was well.

11 Soon afterwards, he went to a city called Nain. Many of his disciples, along with a great multitude, went with him. 12 Now when he came near to the gate of the city, behold, one who was dead was carried out, the only born[d] son of his mother, and she was a widow. Many people of the city were with her. 13 When the Lord saw her, he had compassion on her and said to her, "Don't cry." 14 He came near and touched the coffin, and the bearers stood still. He said, "Young man, I tell you, arise!" 15 He who was dead sat up and began to speak. Then he gave him to his mother.

16 Fear took hold of all, and they glorified God, saying, "A great prophet has arisen amongst us!" and, "God has visited his people!" 17 This report went out concerning him in the whole of Judea and in all the surrounding region.

18 The disciples of John told him about all these things. 19 John, calling to himself two of his disciples, sent them to Jesus, saying, "Are you the one who is coming, or should we look for another?" 20 When the men had come to him, they said, "John the Baptiser has sent us to you, saying, 'Are you he who comes, or should we look for another?'"

21 In that hour he cured many of diseases and plagues and evil spirits; and to many who were blind he gave sight. 22 Jesus answered them, "Go and tell John the things which you have seen and heard: that the blind receive their sight, the lame walk, the lepers are cleansed, the deaf hear, the dead are raised up, and the poor have good news preached to them. 23 Blessed is he who finds no occasion for stumbling in me."

24 When John's messengers had departed, he began to tell the multitudes about John, "What did you go out into the wilderness to see? A reed shaken by the wind? 25 But what did you go out to see? A man clothed in soft clothing? Behold, those who are gorgeously dressed and live delicately are in kings' courts. 26 But what did you go out to see? A prophet? Yes, I tell you, and much more than a prophet. 27 This is he of whom it is written,
'Behold, I send my messenger before your face,
who will prepare your way before you.'

28 "For I tell you, amongst those who are born of women there is not a greater prophet than John the Baptiser; yet he who is least in God's Kingdom is greater than he."

29 When all the people and the tax collectors heard this, they declared God to be just, having been baptised with John's baptism. 30 But the Pharisees and the lawyers rejected the counsel of God, not being baptised by him themselves.

31 [e] "To what then should I compare the people of this generation? What are they like? 32 They are like children who sit in the marketplace and call to one another, saying, 'We piped to you, and you didn't dance. We mourned, and you didn't weep.' 33 For John the Baptiser came neither eating bread nor drinking wine, and you say, 'He has a demon.' 34 The Son of Man has come eating and drinking, and you say, 'Behold, a glutton and a drunkard, a friend of tax collectors and sinners!' 35 Wisdom is justified by all her children."

36 One of the Pharisees invited him to eat with him. He entered into the Pharisee's house and sat at the table. 37 Behold, a woman in the city who was a sinner, when she knew that he was reclining in the Pharisee's house, brought an alabaster jar of ointment. 38 Standing behind at his feet weeping, she began to wet his feet with her tears, and she wiped them with the hair of her head, kissed his feet, and anointed them with the ointment. 39 Now when the Pharisee who had invited him saw it, he said to himself, "This man, if he were a prophet, would have perceived who and what kind of woman this is who touches him, that she is a sinner."

40 Jesus answered him, "Simon, I have something to tell you."
He said, "Teacher, say on."

41 "A certain lender had two debtors. The one owed five hundred denarii, and the other fifty. 42 When they couldn't pay, he forgave them both. Which of them therefore will love him most?"

43 Simon answered, "He, I suppose, to whom he forgave the most."
He said to him, "You have judged correctly." 44 Turning to the woman, he said to Simon, "Do you see this woman? I entered into your house, and you gave me no water for my feet, but she has wet my feet with her tears, and wiped them with the hair of her head. 45 You gave me no kiss, but she, since the time I came in, has not ceased to kiss my feet. 46 You didn't anoint my head with oil, but she has anointed my feet with ointment. 47 Therefore I tell you, her sins, which are many, are forgiven, for she loved much. But one to whom little is forgiven, loves little." 48 He said to her, "Your sins are forgiven."

49 Those who sat at the table with him began to say to themselves, "Who is this who even forgives sins?"

50 He said to the woman, "Your faith has saved you. Go in peace."

8

1 Soon afterwards, he went about through cities and villages, preaching and bringing the good news of God's Kingdom. With him were

---

a 6:26 TR adds "to you"
b 6:26 TR adds "all"
c 6:38 literally, into your bosom.

d 7:12 The phrase "only born" is from the Greek word "μονογενη", which is sometimes translated "only begotten" or "one and only".
** 7:27 Malachi 3:1
e 7:31 TR adds "But the Lord said,"

the twelve, 2 and certain women who had been healed of evil spirits and infirmities: Mary who was called Magdalene, from whom seven demons had gone out; 3 and Joanna, the wife of Chuzas, Herod's steward; Susanna; and many others who served them[a] from their possessions. 4 When a great multitude came together and people from every city were coming to him, he spoke by a parable: 5 "The farmer went out to sow his seed. As he sowed, some fell along the road, and it was trampled under foot, and the birds of the sky devoured it. 6 Other seed fell on the rock, and as soon as it grew, it withered away, because it had no moisture. 7 Other fell amid the thorns, and the thorns grew with it and choked it. 8 Other fell into the good ground and grew and produced one hundred times as much fruit." As he said these things, he called out, "He who has ears to hear, let him hear!"

9 Then his disciples asked him, "What does this parable mean?"

10 He said, "To you it is given to know the mysteries of God's Kingdom, but to the rest it is given in parables, that 'seeing they may not see, and hearing they may not understand.'"

11 "Now the parable is this: The seed is the word of God. 12 Those along the road are those who hear; then the devil comes and takes away the word from their heart, that they may not believe and be saved. 13 Those on the rock are they who, when they hear, receive the word with joy; but these have no root. They believe for a while, then fall away in time of temptation. 14 What fell amongst the thorns, these are those who have heard, and as they go on their way they are choked with cares, riches, and pleasures of life; and they bring no fruit to maturity. 15 Those in the good ground, these are those who with an honest and good heart, having heard the word, hold it tightly, and produce fruit with perseverance.

16 "No one, when he has lit a lamp, covers it with a container or puts it under a bed; but puts it on a stand, that those who enter in may see the light. 17 For nothing is hidden that will not be revealed, nor anything secret that will not be known and come to light. 18 Be careful therefore how you hear. For whoever has, to him will be given; and whoever doesn't have, from him will be taken away even that which he thinks he has."

19 His mother and brothers came to him, and they could not come near him for the crowd. 20 Some people told him, "Your mother and your brothers stand outside, desiring to see you."

21 But he answered them, "My mother and my brothers are these who hear the word of God and do it."

22 Now on one of those days, he entered into a boat, himself and his disciples, and he said to them, "Let's go over to the other side of the lake." So they launched out. 23 But as they sailed, he fell asleep. A wind storm came down on the lake, and they were taking on dangerous amounts of water. 24 They came to him and awoke him, saying, "Master, Master, we are dying!" He awoke and rebuked the wind and the raging of the water; then they ceased, and it was calm.* 25 He said to them, "Where is your faith?" Being afraid, they marvelled, saying to one another, "Who is this then, that he commands even the winds and the water, and they obey him?"

26 Then they arrived at the country of the Gadarenes, which is opposite Galilee. 27 When Jesus stepped ashore, a certain man out of the city who had demons for a long time met him. He wore no clothes, and didn't live in a house, but in the tombs. 28 When he saw Jesus, he cried out and fell down before him, and with a loud voice said, "What do I have to do with you, Jesus, you Son of the Most High God? I beg you, don't torment me!" 29 For Jesus was commanding the unclean spirit to come out of the man. For the unclean spirit had often seized the man. He was kept under guard and bound with chains and fetters. Breaking the bonds apart, he was driven by the demon into the desert.

30 Jesus asked him, "What is your name?"

He said, "Legion," for many demons had entered into him. 31 They begged him that he would not command them to go into the abyss.

32 Now there was there a herd of many pigs feeding on the mountain, and they begged him that he would allow them to enter into those. Then he allowed them. 33 The demons came out of the man and entered into the pigs, and the herd rushed down the steep bank into the lake and were drowned.

34 When those who fed them saw what had happened, they fled and told it in the city and in the country. 35 People went out to see what had happened. They came to Jesus and found the man from whom the demons had gone out, sitting at Jesus' feet, clothed and in his right mind; and they were afraid. 36 Those who saw it told them how he who had been possessed by demons was healed. 37 All the people of the surrounding country of the Gadarenes asked him to depart from them, for they were very much afraid. Then he entered into the boat and returned. 38 But the man from whom the demons had gone out begged him that he might go with him, but Jesus sent him away, saying, 39 "Return to your house, and declare what great things God has done for you." He went his way, proclaiming throughout the whole city what great things Jesus had done for him.

40 When Jesus returned, the multitude welcomed him, for they were all waiting for him. 41 Behold, a man named Jairus came. He was a ruler of the synagogue. He fell down at Jesus' feet and begged him to come into his house, 42 for he had an only born[b] daughter, about twelve years of age, and she was dying. But as he went, the multitudes pressed against him. 43 A woman who had a flow of blood for twelve years, who had spent all her living on physicians and could not be healed by any, 44 came behind him and touched the fringe[c] of his cloak. Immediately the flow of her blood stopped.

45 Jesus said, "Who touched me?"

When all denied it, Peter and those with him said, "Master, the multitudes press and jostle you, and you say, 'Who touched me?'"

46 But Jesus said, "Someone did touch me, for I perceived that power has gone out of me." 47 When the woman saw that she was not hidden, she came trembling; and falling down before him declared to him in the presence of all the people the reason why she had touched him, and how she was healed immediately. 48 He said to her, "Daughter, cheer up. Your faith has made you well. Go in peace."

49 While he still spoke, one from the ruler of the synagogue's house came, saying to him, "Your daughter is dead. Don't trouble the Teacher."

50 But Jesus hearing it, answered him, "Don't be afraid. Only believe, and she will be healed."

51 When he came to the house, he didn't allow anyone to enter in, except Peter, John, James, the father of the child, and her mother. 52 All were weeping and mourning her, but he said, "Don't weep. She isn't dead, but sleeping."

53 They were ridiculing him, knowing that she was dead. 54 But he put them all outside, and taking her by the hand, he called, saying, "Child, arise!" 55 Her spirit returned, and she rose up immediately. He commanded that something be given to her to eat. 56 Her parents were amazed, but he commanded them to tell no one what had been done.

9

1 He called the twelve[d] together and gave them power and authority over all demons, and to cure diseases. 2 He sent them out to preach God's Kingdom and to heal the sick. 3 He said to them, "Take nothing for your journey—no staffs, nor wallet, nor bread, nor money. Don't have two tunics each. 4 Into whatever house you enter, stay there, and depart from there. 5 As many as don't receive you, when you depart from that city, shake off even the dust from your feet for a testimony against them."

6 They departed and went throughout the villages, preaching the Good News and healing everywhere.

7 Now Herod the tetrarch heard of all that was done by him; and he was very perplexed, because it was said by some that John had risen from the dead, 8 and by some that Elijah had appeared, and by others that one of the old prophets had risen again. 9 Herod said, "I beheaded John, but who is this about whom I hear such things?" He sought to see him.

10 The apostles, when they had returned, told him what things they had done.

He took them and withdrew apart to a desert region of[e] a city called Bethsaida. 11 But the multitudes, perceiving it, followed him. He welcomed them, spoke to them of God's Kingdom, and he cured those who needed healing. 12 The day began to wear away; and the twelve came and said to him, "Send the multitude away, that they may go into the surrounding villages and farms and lodge and get food, for we are here in a deserted place."

13 But he said to them, "You give them something to eat."

They said, "We have no more than five loaves and two fish, unless we should go and buy food for all these people." 14 For they were about five thousand men.

He said to his disciples, "Make them sit down in groups of about fifty each." 15 They did so, and made them all sit down. 16 He took the five loaves and the two fish, and looking up to the sky, he blessed them, broke them, and gave them to the disciples to set before the multitude. 17 They ate and were all filled. They gathered up twelve baskets of broken pieces that were left over.

18 As he was praying alone, the disciples were near him, and he asked them, "Who do the multitudes say that I am?"

19 They answered, "'John the Baptiser,' but others say, 'Elijah,' and others, that one of the old prophets has risen again."

20 He said to them, "But who do you say that I am?"

Peter answered, "The Christ of God."

21 But he warned them and commanded them to tell this to no one, 22 saying, "The Son of Man must suffer many things, and be rejected by the elders, chief priests, and scribes, and be killed, and the third day be raised up."

23 He said to all, "If anyone desires to come after me, let him deny himself, take up his cross,[f] and follow me. 24 For whoever desires to save his life will lose it, but whoever will lose his life for my sake will save it. 25 For what does it profit a man if he gains the whole world, and loses or forfeits his own self? 26 For whoever will be ashamed of me and of my words, of him will the Son of Man be ashamed when he comes in his glory, and the glory of the Father, and of the holy angels. 27 But I tell you the truth: There are some of those who stand here who will in no way taste of death until they see God's Kingdom."

28 About eight days after these sayings, he took with him Peter, John, and James, and went up onto the mountain to pray. 29 As he was praying, the appearance of his face was altered, and his clothing became white and dazzling. 30 Behold, two men were talking with him, who were Moses and

---

a 8:3 TR reads "him" instead of "them"
** 8:10 Isaiah 6:9
** 8:24 See Psalms 107:29
b 8:42 The phrase "only born" is from the Greek word "μονογενη", which is sometimes translated "only begotten" or "one and only".

c 8:44 or, tassel
d 9:1 TR reads "his twelve disciples" instead of "the twelve"
e 9:10 NU omits "a desert region of".
f 9:23 TR, NU add "daily"

Elijah, 31 who appeared in glory and spoke of his departure,[a] which he was about to accomplish at Jerusalem.

32 Now Peter and those who were with him were heavy with sleep, but when they were fully awake, they saw his glory, and the two men who stood with him. 33 As they were parting from him, Peter said to Jesus, "Master, it is good for us to be here. Let's make three tents: one for you, one for Moses, and one for Elijah," not knowing what he said.

34 While he said these things, a cloud came and overshadowed them, and they were afraid as they entered into the cloud. 35 A voice came out of the cloud, saying, "This is my beloved Son. Listen to him!" 36 When the voice came, Jesus was found alone. They were silent, and told no one in those days any of the things which they had seen.

37 On the next day, when they had come down from the mountain, a great multitude met him. 38 Behold, a man from the crowd called out, saying, "Teacher, I beg you to look at my son, for he is my only born[b] child. 39 Behold, a spirit takes him, he suddenly cries out, and it convulses him so that he foams; and it hardly departs from him, bruising him severely. 40 I begged your disciples to cast it out, and they couldn't."

41 Jesus answered, "Faithless and perverse generation, how long shall I be with you and bear with you? Bring your son here."

42 While he was still coming, the demon threw him down and convulsed him violently. But Jesus rebuked the unclean spirit, healed the boy, and gave him back to his father. 43 They were all astonished at the majesty of God.

But while all were marvelling at all the things which Jesus did, he said to his disciples, 44 "Let these words sink into your ears, for the Son of Man will be delivered up into the hands of men." 45 But they didn't understand this saying. It was concealed from them, that they should not perceive it, and they were afraid to ask him about this saying.

46 An argument arose amongst them about which of them was the greatest. 47 Jesus, perceiving the reasoning of their hearts, took a little child, and set him by his side, 48 and said to them, "Whoever receives this little child in my name receives me. Whoever receives me receives him who sent me. For whoever is least amongst you all, this one will be great."

49 John answered, "Master, we saw someone casting out demons in your name, and we forbade him, because he doesn't follow with us."

50 Jesus said to him, "Don't forbid him, for he who is not against us is for us."

51 It came to pass, when the days were near that he should be taken up, he intently set his face to go to Jerusalem 52 and sent messengers before his face. They went and entered into a village of the Samaritans, so as to prepare for him. 53 They didn't receive him, because he was travelling with his face set towards Jerusalem. 54 When his disciples, James and John, saw this, they said, "Lord, do you want us to command fire to come down from the sky and destroy them, just as Elijah did?"

55 But he turned and rebuked them, "You don't know of what kind of spirit you are. 56 For the Son of Man didn't come to destroy men's lives, but to save them."

They went to another village. 57 As they went on the way, a certain man said to him, "I want to follow you wherever you go, Lord."

58 Jesus said to him, "The foxes have holes and the birds of the sky have nests, but the Son of Man has no place to lay his head."

59 He said to another, "Follow me!"

But he said, "Lord, allow me first to go and bury my father."

60 But Jesus said to him, "Leave the dead to bury their own dead, but you go and announce God's Kingdom."

61 Another also said, "I want to follow you, Lord, but first allow me to say good-bye to those who are at my house."

62 But Jesus said to him, "No one, having put his hand to the plough and looking back, is fit for God's Kingdom."

10

1 Now after these things, the Lord also appointed seventy others, and sent them two by two ahead of him[c] into every city and place where he was about to come. 2 Then he said to them, "The harvest is indeed plentiful, but the labourers are few. Pray therefore to the Lord of the harvest, that he may send out labourers into his harvest. 3 Go your ways. Behold, I send you out as lambs amongst wolves. 4 Carry no purse, nor wallet, nor sandals. Greet no one on the way. 5 Into whatever house you enter, first say, 'Peace be to this house.' 6 If a son of peace is there, your peace will rest on him; but if not, it will return to you. 7 Remain in that same house, eating and drinking the things they give, for the labourer is worthy of his wages. Don't go from house to house. 8 Into whatever city you enter and they receive you, eat the things that are set before you. 9 Heal the sick who are there and tell them, 'God's Kingdom has come near to you.' 10 But into whatever city you enter and they don't receive you, go out into its streets and say, 11 'Even the dust from your city that clings to us, we wipe off against you. Nevertheless know this, that God's Kingdom has come near to you.' 12 I tell you, it will be more tolerable in that day for Sodom than for that city.

13 "Woe to you, Chorazin! Woe to you, Bethsaida! For if the mighty works had been done in Tyre and Sidon which were done in you, they would have repented long ago, sitting in sackcloth and ashes. 14 But it will be more tolerable for Tyre and Sidon in the judgement than for you. 15

You, Capernaum, who are exalted to heaven, will be brought down to Hades.[d] 16 Whoever listens to you listens to me, and whoever rejects you rejects me. Whoever rejects me rejects him who sent me."

17 The seventy returned with joy, saying, "Lord, even the demons are subject to us in your name!"

18 He said to them, "I saw Satan having fallen like lightning from heaven. 19 Behold, I give you authority to tread on serpents and scorpions, and over all the power of the enemy. Nothing will in any way hurt you. 20 Nevertheless, don't rejoice in this, that the spirits are subject to you, but rejoice that your names are written in heaven."

21 In that same hour, Jesus rejoiced in the Holy Spirit, and said, "I thank you, O Father, Lord of heaven and earth, that you have hidden these things from the wise and understanding, and revealed them to little children. Yes, Father, for so it was well-pleasing in your sight."

22 Turning to the disciples, he said, "All things have been delivered to me by my Father. No one knows who the Son is, except the Father, and who the Father is, except the Son, and he to whomever the Son desires to reveal him."

23 Turning to the disciples, he said privately, "Blessed are the eyes which see the things that you see, 24 for I tell you that many prophets and kings desired to see the things which you see, and didn't see them, and to hear the things which you hear, and didn't hear them."

25 Behold, a certain lawyer stood up and tested him, saying, "Teacher, what shall I do to inherit eternal life?"

26 He said to him, "What is written in the law? How do you read it?"

27 He answered, "You shall love the Lord your God with all your heart, with all your soul, with all your strength, and with all your mind;* and your neighbour as yourself."*

28 He said to him, "You have answered correctly. Do this, and you will live."

29 But he, desiring to justify himself, asked Jesus, "Who is my neighbour?"

30 Jesus answered, "A certain man was going down from Jerusalem to Jericho, and he fell amongst robbers, who both stripped him and beat him, and departed, leaving him half dead. 31 By chance a certain priest was going down that way. When he saw him, he passed by on the other side. 32 In the same way a Levite also, when he came to the place and saw him, passed by on the other side. 33 But a certain Samaritan, as he travelled, came where he was. When he saw him, he was moved with compassion, 34 came to him, and bound up his wounds, pouring on oil and wine. He set him on his own animal, brought him to an inn, and took care of him. 35 On the next day, when he departed, he took out two denarii, gave them to the host, and said to him, 'Take care of him. Whatever you spend beyond that, I will repay you when I return.' 36 Now which of these three do you think seemed to be a neighbour to him who fell amongst the robbers?"

37 He said, "He who showed mercy on him."

Then Jesus said to him, "Go and do likewise."

38 As they went on their way, he entered into a certain village, and a certain woman named Martha received him into her house. 39 She had a sister called Mary, who also sat at Jesus' feet and heard his word. 40 But Martha was distracted with much serving, and she came up to him, and said, "Lord, don't you care that my sister left me to serve alone? Ask her therefore to help me."

41 Jesus answered her, "Martha, Martha, you are anxious and troubled about many things, 42 but one thing is needed. Mary has chosen the good part, which will not be taken away from her."

11

1 When he finished praying in a certain place, one of his disciples said to him, "Lord, teach us to pray, just as John also taught his disciples."

2 He said to them, "When you pray, say,
'Our Father in heaven,
　may your name be kept holy.
May your Kingdom come.
　May your will be done on earth, as it is in heaven.
3 Give us day by day our daily bread.
4 Forgive us our sins,
　for we ourselves also forgive everyone who is indebted to us.
Bring us not into temptation,
　but deliver us from the evil one.'"

5 He said to them, "Which of you, if you go to a friend at midnight and tell him, 'Friend, lend me three loaves of bread, 6 for a friend of mine has come to me from a journey, and I have nothing to set before him,' 7 and he from within will answer and say, 'Don't bother me. The door is now shut, and my children are with me in bed. I can't get up and give it to you'? 8 I tell you, although he will not rise and give it to him because he is his friend, yet because of his persistence, he will get up and give him as many as he needs.

9 "I tell you, keep asking, and it will be given you. Keep seeking, and you will find. Keep knocking, and it will be opened to you. 10 For everyone who asks receives. He who seeks finds. To him who knocks it will be opened.

11 "Which of you fathers, if your son asks for bread, will give him a stone? Or if he asks for a fish, he won't give him a snake instead of a fish,

---

a 9:31 literally, "exodus"

b 9:38 The phrase "only born" is from the Greek word "μονογενη", which is sometimes translated "only begotten" or "one and only".

c 10:1 literally, "before his face"

d 10:15 Hades is the lower realm of the dead, or Hell.

** 10:27 Deuteronomy 6:5

** 10:27 Leviticus 19:18

will he? 12 Or if he asks for an egg, he won't give him a scorpion, will he? 13 If you then, being evil, know how to give good gifts to your children, how much more will your heavenly Father give the Holy Spirit to those who ask him?"

14 He was casting out a demon, and it was mute. When the demon had gone out, the mute man spoke; and the multitudes marvelled. 15 But some of them said, "He casts out demons by Beelzebul, the prince of the demons." 16 Others, testing him, sought from him a sign from heaven. 17 But he, knowing their thoughts, said to them, "Every kingdom divided against itself is brought to desolation. A house divided against itself falls. 18 If Satan also is divided against himself, how will his kingdom stand? For you say that I cast out demons by Beelzebul. 19 But if I cast out demons by Beelzebul, by whom do your children cast them out? Therefore they will be your judges. 20 But if I by God's finger cast out demons, then God's Kingdom has come to you.

21 "When the strong man, fully armed, guards his own dwelling, his goods are safe. 22 But when someone stronger attacks him and overcomes him, he takes from him his whole armour in which he trusted, and divides his plunder.

23 "He who is not with me is against me. He who doesn't gather with me scatters.

24 The unclean spirit, when he has gone out of the man, passes through dry places, seeking rest; and finding none, he says, 'I will turn back to my house from which I came out.' 25 When he returns, he finds it swept and put in order. 26 Then he goes and takes seven other spirits more evil than himself, and they enter in and dwell there. The last state of that man becomes worse than the first."

27 It came to pass, as he said these things, a certain woman out of the multitude lifted up her voice and said to him, "Blessed is the womb that bore you, and the breasts which nursed you!"

28 But he said, "On the contrary, blessed are those who hear the word of God, and keep it."

29 When the multitudes were gathering together to him, he began to say, "This is an evil generation. It seeks after a sign. No sign will be given to it but the sign of Jonah the prophet. 30 For even as Jonah became a sign to the Ninevites, so the Son of Man will also be to this generation. 31 The Queen of the South will rise up in the judgement with the men of this generation and will condemn them, for she came from the ends of the earth to hear the wisdom of Solomon; and behold, one greater than Solomon is here. 32 The men of Nineveh will stand up in the judgement with this generation, and will condemn it, for they repented at the preaching of Jonah; and behold, one greater than Jonah is here.

33 "No one, when he has lit a lamp, puts it in a cellar or under a basket, but on a stand, that those who come in may see the light. 34 The lamp of the body is the eye. Therefore when your eye is good, your whole body is also full of light; but when it is evil, your body also is full of darkness. 35 Therefore see whether the light that is in you isn't darkness. 36 If therefore your whole body is full of light, having no part dark, it will be wholly full of light, as when the lamp with its bright shining gives you light."

37 Now as he spoke, a certain Pharisee asked him to dine with him. He went in and sat at the table. 38 When the Pharisee saw it, he marvelled that he had not first washed himself before dinner. 39 The Lord said to him, "Now you Pharisees cleanse the outside of the cup and of the platter, but your inward part is full of extortion and wickedness. 40 You foolish ones, didn't he who made the outside make the inside also? 41 But give for gifts to the needy those things which are within, and behold, all things will be clean to you. 42 But woe to you Pharisees! For you tithe mint and rue and every herb, but you bypass justice and God's love. You ought to have done these, and not to have left the other undone. 43 Woe to you Pharisees! For you love the best seats in the synagogues and the greetings in the marketplaces. 44 Woe to you, scribes and Pharisees, hypocrites! For you are like hidden graves, and the men who walk over them don't know it."

45 One of the lawyers answered him, "Teacher, in saying this you insult us also."

46 He said, "Woe to you lawyers also! For you load men with burdens that are difficult to carry, and you yourselves won't even lift one finger to help carry those burdens. 47 Woe to you! For you build the tombs of the prophets, and your fathers killed them. 48 So you testify and consent to the works of your fathers. For they killed them, and you build their tombs. 49 Therefore also the wisdom of God said, 'I will send to them prophets and apostles; and some of them they will kill and persecute, 50 that the blood of all the prophets, which was shed from the foundation of the world, may be required of this generation, 51 from the blood of Abel to the blood of Zachariah, who perished between the altar and the sanctuary.' Yes, I tell you, it will be required of this generation. 52 Woe to you lawyers! For you took away the key of knowledge. You didn't enter in yourselves, and those who were entering in, you hindered."

53 As he said these things to them, the scribes and the Pharisees began to be terribly angry, and to draw many things out of him, 54 lying in wait for him, and seeking to catch him in something he might say, that they might accuse him.

12

1 Meanwhile, when a multitude of many thousands had gathered together, so much so that they trampled on each other, he began to tell his disciples first of all, "Beware of the yeast of the Pharisees, which is hypocrisy. 2 But there is nothing covered up that will not be revealed, nor hidden that will not be known. 3 Therefore whatever you have said in the darkness will be heard in the light. What you have spoken in the ear in the inner rooms will be proclaimed on the housetops.

4 "I tell you, my friends, don't be afraid of those who kill the body, and after that have no more that they can do. 5 But I will warn you whom you should fear. Fear him who after he has killed, has power to cast into Gehenna.[a] Yes, I tell you, fear him.

6 "Aren't five sparrows sold for two assaria coins[b]? Not one of them is forgotten by God. 7 But the very hairs of your head are all counted. Therefore don't be afraid. You are of more value than many sparrows.

8 "I tell you, everyone who confesses me before men, the Son of Man will also confess before the angels of God; 9 but he who denies me in the presence of men will be denied in the presence of God's angels. 10 Everyone who speaks a word against the Son of Man will be forgiven, but those who blaspheme against the Holy Spirit will not be forgiven. 11 When they bring you before the synagogues, the rulers, and the authorities, don't be anxious how or what you will answer or what you will say; 12 for the Holy Spirit will teach you in that same hour what you must say."

13 One of the multitude said to him, "Teacher, tell my brother to divide the inheritance with me."

14 But he said to him, "Man, who made me a judge or an arbitrator over you?" 15 He said to them, "Beware! Keep yourselves from covetousness, for a man's life doesn't consist of the abundance of the things which he possesses."

16 He spoke a parable to them, saying, "The ground of a certain rich man produced abundantly. 17 He reasoned within himself, saying, 'What will I do, because I don't have room to store my crops?' 18 He said, 'This is what I will do. I will pull down my barns, build bigger ones, and there I will store all my grain and my goods. 19 I will tell my soul, "Soul, you have many goods laid up for many years. Take your ease, eat, drink, and be merry."'

20 "But God said to him, 'You foolish one, tonight your soul is required of you. The things which you have prepared—whose will they be?' 21 So is he who lays up treasure for himself, and is not rich towards God."

22 He said to his disciples, "Therefore I tell you, don't be anxious for your life, what you will eat, nor yet for your body, what you will wear. 23 Life is more than food, and the body is more than clothing. 24 Consider the ravens: they don't sow, they don't reap, they have no warehouse or barn, and God feeds them. How much more valuable are you than birds! 25 Which of you by being anxious can add a cubit[c] to his height? 26 If then you aren't able to do even the least things, why are you anxious about the rest? 27 Consider the lilies, how they grow. They don't toil, neither do they spin; yet I tell you, even Solomon in all his glory was not arrayed like one of these. 28 But if this is how God clothes the grass in the field, which today exists and tomorrow is cast into the oven, how much more will he clothe you, O you of little faith?

29 "Don't seek what you will eat or what you will drink; neither be anxious. 30 For the nations of the world seek after all of these things, but your Father knows that you need these things. 31 But seek God's Kingdom, and all these things will be added to you.

32 "Don't be afraid, little flock, for it is your Father's good pleasure to give you the Kingdom. 33 Sell what you have and give gifts to the needy. Make for yourselves purses which don't grow old, a treasure in the heavens that doesn't fail, where no thief approaches and no moth destroys. 34 For where your treasure is, there will your heart be also.

35 "Let your waist be dressed and your lamps burning. 36 Be like men watching for their lord when he returns from the wedding feast, that when he comes and knocks, they may immediately open to him. 37 Blessed are those servants whom the lord will find watching when he comes. Most certainly I tell you that he will dress himself, make them recline, and will come and serve them. 38 They will be blessed if he comes in the second or third watch and finds them so. 39 But know this, that if the master of the house had known in what hour the thief was coming, he would have watched and not allowed his house to be broken into. 40 Therefore be ready also, for the Son of Man is coming in an hour that you don't expect him."

41 Peter said to him, "Lord, are you telling this parable to us, or to everybody?"

42 The Lord said, "Who then is the faithful and wise steward, whom his lord will set over his household, to give them their portion of food at the right times? 43 Blessed is that servant whom his lord will find doing so when he comes. 44 Truly I tell you that he will set him over all that he has. 45 But if that servant says in his heart, 'My lord delays his coming,' and begins to beat the menservants and the maidservants, and to eat and drink and to be drunken, 46 then the lord of that servant will come in a day when he isn't expecting him and in an hour that he doesn't know, and will cut him in two, and place his portion with the unfaithful. 47 That servant who knew his lord's will, and didn't prepare nor do what he wanted, will be beaten with many stripes, 48 but he who didn't know, and did things worthy of stripes, will be beaten with few stripes. To whomever much is given, of him will much be required; and to whom much was entrusted, of him more will be asked.

---

[a] 12:5 or, Hell
[b] 12:6 An assarion was a small copper coin worth about an hour's wages for an agricultural labourer.

[c] 12:25 A cubit is the length from the tip of the middle finger to the elbow on a man's arm, or about 18 inches or 46 centimetres.

49 "I came to throw fire on the earth. I wish it were already kindled. 50 But I have a baptism to be baptised with, and how distressed I am until it is accomplished! 51 Do you think that I have come to give peace in the earth? I tell you, no, but rather division. 52 For from now on, there will be five in one house divided, three against two, and two against three. 53 They will be divided, father against son, and son against father; mother against daughter, and daughter against her mother; mother-in-law against her daughter-in-law, and daughter-in-law against her mother-in-law." *

54 He said to the multitudes also, "When you see a cloud rising from the west, immediately you say, 'A shower is coming,' and so it happens. 55 When a south wind blows, you say, 'There will be a scorching heat,' and it happens. 56 You hypocrites! You know how to interpret the appearance of the earth and the sky, but how is it that you don't interpret this time?

57 "Why don't you judge for yourselves what is right? 58 For when you are going with your adversary before the magistrate, try diligently on the way to be released from him, lest perhaps he drag you to the judge, and the judge deliver you to the officer, and the officer throw you into prison. 59 I tell you, you will by no means get out of there until you have paid the very last penny.ª"

13

1 Now there were some present at the same time who told him about the Galileans whose blood Pilate had mixed with their sacrifices. 2 Jesus answered them, "Do you think that these Galileans were worse sinners than all the other Galileans, because they suffered such things? 3 I tell you, no, but unless you repent, you will all perish in the same way. 4 Or those eighteen on whom the tower in Siloam fell and killed them—do you think that they were worse offenders than all the men who dwell in Jerusalem? 5 I tell you, no, but, unless you repent, you will all perish in the same way."

6 He spoke this parable. "A certain man had a fig tree planted in his vineyard, and he came seeking fruit on it and found none. 7 He said to the vine dresser, 'Behold, these three years I have come looking for fruit on this fig tree, and found none. Cut it down! Why does it waste the soil?' 8 He answered, 'Lord, leave it alone this year also, until I dig around it and fertilise it. 9 If it bears fruit, fine; but if not, after that, you can cut it down.'"

10 He was teaching in one of the synagogues on the Sabbath day. 11 Behold, there was a woman who had a spirit of infirmity eighteen years. She was bent over and could in no way straighten herself up. 12 When Jesus saw her, he called her and said to her, "Woman, you are freed from your infirmity." 13 He laid his hands on her, and immediately she stood up straight and glorified God.

14 The ruler of the synagogue, being indignant because Jesus had healed on the Sabbath, said to the multitude, "There are six days in which men ought to work. Therefore come on those days and be healed, and not on the Sabbath day!"

15 Therefore the Lord answered him, "You hypocrites! Doesn't each one of you free his ox or his donkey from the stall on the Sabbath and lead him away to water? 16 Ought not this woman, being a daughter of Abraham whom Satan had bound eighteen long years, be freed from this bondage on the Sabbath day?"

17 As he said these things, all his adversaries were disappointed; and all the multitude rejoiced for all the glorious things that were done by him.

18 He said, "What is God's Kingdom like? To what shall I compare it? 19 It is like a grain of mustard seed which a man took and put in his own garden. It grew and became a large tree, and the birds of the sky live in its branches."

20 Again he said, "To what shall I compare God's Kingdom? 21 It is like yeast, which a woman took and hid in three measures ᵇ of flour, until it was all leavened."

22 He went on his way through cities and villages, teaching, and travelling on to Jerusalem. 23 One said to him, "Lord, are they few who are saved?"

He said to them, 24 "Strive to enter in by the narrow door, for many, I tell you, will seek to enter in and will not be able. 25 When once the master of the house has risen up and has shut the door, and you begin to stand outside and to knock at the door, saying, 'Lord, Lord, open to us!' then he will answer and tell you, 'I don't know you or where you come from.' 26 Then you will begin to say, 'We ate and drank in your presence, and you taught in our streets.' 27 He will say, 'I tell you, I don't know where you come from. Depart from me, all you workers of iniquity.' 28 There will be weeping and gnashing of teeth when you see Abraham, Isaac, Jacob, and all the prophets in God's Kingdom, and yourselves being thrown outside. 29 They will come from the east, west, north, and south, and will sit down in God's Kingdom. 30 Behold, there are some who are last who will be first, and there are some who are first who will be last."

31 On that same day, some Pharisees came, saying to him, "Get out of here and go away, for Herod wants to kill you."

32 He said to them, "Go and tell that fox, 'Behold, I cast out demons and perform cures today and tomorrow, and the third day I complete my mission. 33 Nevertheless I must go on my way today and tomorrow and the next day, for it can't be that a prophet should perish outside of Jerusalem.'

34 "Jerusalem, Jerusalem, you who kills the prophets and stones those who are sent to her! How often I wanted to gather your children together, like a hen gathers her own brood under her wings, and you

refused! 35 Behold, your house is left to you desolate. I tell you, you will not see me until you say, 'Blessed is he who comes in the name of the Lord!'" *

14

1 When he went into the house of one of the rulers of the Pharisees on a Sabbath to eat bread, they were watching him. 2 Behold, a certain man who had dropsy was in front of him. 3 Jesus, answering, spoke to the lawyers and Pharisees, saying, "Is it lawful to heal on the Sabbath?"

4 But they were silent.

He took him, and healed him, and let him go. 5 He answered them, "Which of you, if your sonᶜ or an ox fell into a well, wouldn't immediately pull him out on a Sabbath day?"

6 They couldn't answer him regarding these things.

7 He spoke a parable to those who were invited, when he noticed how they chose the best seats, and said to them, 8 "When you are invited by anyone to a wedding feast, don't sit in the best seat, since perhaps someone more honourable than you might be invited by him, 9 and he who invited both of you would come and tell you, 'Make room for this person.' Then you would begin, with shame, to take the lowest place. 10 But when you are invited, go and sit in the lowest place, so that when he who invited you comes, he may tell you, 'Friend, move up higher.' Then you will be honoured in the presence of all who sit at the table with you. 11 For everyone who exalts himself will be humbled, and whoever humbles himself will be exalted."

12 He also said to the one who had invited him, "When you make a dinner or a supper, don't call your friends, nor your brothers, nor your kinsmen, nor rich neighbours, or perhaps they might also return the favour, and pay you back. 13 But when you make a feast, ask the poor, the maimed, the lame, or the blind; 14 and you will be blessed, because they don't have the resources to repay you. For you will be repaid in the resurrection of the righteous."

15 When one of those who sat at the table with him heard these things, he said to him, "Blessed is he who will feast in God's Kingdom!"

16 But he said to him, "A certain man made a great supper, and he invited many people. 17 He sent out his servant at supper time to tell those who were invited, 'Come, for everything is ready now.' 18 They all as one began to make excuses.

"The first said to him, 'I have bought a field, and I must go and see it. Please have me excused.'

19 "Another said, 'I have bought five yoke of oxen, and I must go try them out. Please have me excused.'

20 "Another said, 'I have married a wife, and therefore I can't come.'

21 "That servant came, and told his lord these things. Then the master of the house, being angry, said to his servant, 'Go out quickly into the streets and lanes of the city, and bring in the poor, maimed, blind, and lame.'

22 "The servant said, 'Lord, it is done as you commanded, and there is still room.'

23 "The lord said to the servant, 'Go out into the highways and hedges, and compel them to come in, that my house may be filled. 24 For I tell you that none of those men who were invited will taste of my supper.'"

25 Now great multitudes were going with him. He turned and said to them, 26 "If anyone comes to me, and doesn't disregardᵈ his own father, mother, wife, children, brothers, and sisters, yes, and his own life also, he can't be my disciple. 27 Whoever doesn't bear his own cross and come after me, can't be my disciple. 28 For which of you, desiring to build a tower, doesn't first sit down and count the cost, to see if he has enough to complete it? 29 Or perhaps, when he has laid a foundation and isn't able to finish, everyone who sees begins to mock him, 30 saying, 'This man began to build and wasn't able to finish.' 31 Or what king, as he goes to encounter another king in war, will not sit down first and consider whether he is able with ten thousand to meet him who comes against him with twenty thousand? 32 Or else, while the other is yet a great way off, he sends an envoy and asks for conditions of peace. 33 So therefore, whoever of you who doesn't renounce all that he has, he can't be my disciple.

34 "Salt is good, but if the salt becomes flat and tasteless, with what do you season it? 35 It is fit neither for the soil nor for the manure pile. It is thrown out. He who has ears to hear, let him hear."

15

1 Now all the tax collectors and sinners were coming close to him to hear him. 2 The Pharisees and the scribes murmured, saying, "This man welcomes sinners, and eats with them."

3 He told them this parable: 4 "Which of you men, if you had one hundred sheep and lost one of them, wouldn't leave the ninety-nine in the wilderness and go after the one that was lost, until he found it? 5 When he has found it, he carries it on his shoulders, rejoicing. 6 When he comes home, he calls together his friends and his neighbours, saying to them, 'Rejoice with me, for I have found my sheep which was lost!' 7 I tell you that even so there will be more joy in heaven over one sinner who repents, than over ninety-nine righteous people who need no repentance.

** 12:53 Micah 7:6
ª 12:59 literally, lepton. A lepton is a very small brass Jewish coin worth half a Roman quadrans each, which is worth a quarter of the copper assarion. Lepta are worth less than 1% of an agricultural worker's daily wages.

ᵇ 13:21 literally, three sata. 3 sata is about 39 litres or a bit more than a bushel.
** 13:35 Psalms 118:26
ᶜ 14:5 TR reads "donkey" instead of "son"
ᵈ 14:26 or, hate

8 "Or what woman, if she had ten drachma[a] coins, if she lost one drachma coin, wouldn't light a lamp, sweep the house, and seek diligently until she found it? 9 When she has found it, she calls together her friends and neighbours, saying, 'Rejoice with me, for I have found the drachma which I had lost!' 10 Even so, I tell you, there is joy in the presence of the angels of God over one sinner repenting."

11 **He said,** "A certain man had two sons. 12 The younger of them said to his father, 'Father, give me my share of your property.' So he divided his livelihood between them. 13 Not many days after, the younger son gathered all of this together and travelled into a far country. There he wasted his property with riotous living. 14 When he had spent all of it, there arose a severe famine in that country, and he began to be in need. 15 He went and joined himself to one of the citizens of that country, and he sent him into his fields to feed pigs. 16 He wanted to fill his belly with the pods that the pigs ate, but no one gave him any. 17 But when he came to himself, he said, 'How many hired servants of my father's have bread enough to spare, and I'm dying with hunger! 18 I will get up and go to my father, and will tell him, "Father, I have sinned against heaven and in your sight. 19 I am no more worthy to be called your son. Make me as one of your hired servants."'

20 "He arose and came to his father. But while he was still far off, his father saw him and was moved with compassion, and ran, fell on his neck, and kissed him. 21 The son said to him, 'Father, I have sinned against heaven and in your sight. I am no longer worthy to be called your son.'

22 "But the father said to his servants, 'Bring out the best robe and put it on him. Put a ring on his hand and sandals on his feet. 23 Bring the fattened calf, kill it, and let's eat and celebrate; 24 for this, my son, was dead and is alive again. He was lost and is found.' Then they began to celebrate.

25 "Now his elder son was in the field. As he came near to the house, he heard music and dancing. 26 He called one of the servants to him and asked what was going on. 27 He said to him, 'Your brother has come, and your father has killed the fattened calf, because he has received him back safe and healthy.' 28 But he was angry and would not go in. Therefore his father came out and begged him. 29 But he answered his father, 'Behold, these many years I have served you, and I never disobeyed a commandment of yours, but you never gave me a goat, that I might celebrate with my friends. 30 But when this your son came, who has devoured your living with prostitutes, you killed the fattened calf for him.'

31 "He said to him, 'Son, you are always with me, and all that is mine is yours. 32 But it was appropriate to celebrate and be glad, for this, your brother, was dead, and is alive again. He was lost, and is found.'"

16

1 He also said to his disciples, "There was a certain rich man who had a manager. An accusation was made to him that this man was wasting his possessions. 2 He called him, and said to him, 'What is this that I hear about you? Give an accounting of your management, for you can no longer be manager.'

3 "The manager said within himself, 'What will I do, seeing that my lord is taking away the management position from me? I don't have strength to dig. I am ashamed to beg. 4 I know what I will do, so that when I am removed from management, they may receive me into their houses.' 5 Calling each one of his lord's debtors to him, he said to the first, 'How much do you owe to my lord?' 6 He said, 'A hundred batos[b] of oil.' He said to him, 'Take your bill, and sit down quickly and write fifty.' 7 Then he said to another, 'How much do you owe?' He said, 'A hundred cors[c] of wheat.' He said to him, 'Take your bill, and write eighty.'

8 "His lord commended the dishonest manager because he had done wisely, for the children of this world are, in their own generation, wiser than the children of the light. 9 I tell you, make for yourselves friends by means of unrighteous mammon, so that when you fail, they may receive you into the eternal tents. 10 He who is faithful in a very little is faithful also in much. He who is dishonest in a very little is also dishonest in much. 11 If therefore you have not been faithful in the unrighteous mammon, who will commit to your trust the true riches? 12 If you have not been faithful in that which is another's, who will give you that which is your own? 13 No servant can serve two masters, for either he will hate the one and love the other; or else he will hold to one and despise the other. You aren't able to serve God and Mammon."[d]

14 **The Pharisees, who were lovers of money, also heard all these things, and they scoffed at him.** 15 He said to them, "You are those who justify yourselves in the sight of men, but God knows your hearts. For that which is exalted amongst men is an abomination in the sight of God.

16 "The law and the prophets were until John. From that time the Good News of God's Kingdom is preached, and everyone is forcing his way into it. 17 But it is easier for heaven and earth to pass away than for one tiny stroke of a pen in the law to fall.

18 "Everyone who divorces his wife and marries another commits adultery. He who marries one who is divorced from a husband commits adultery.

19 "Now there was a certain rich man, and he was clothed in purple and fine linen, living in luxury every day. 20 A certain beggar, named Lazarus, was taken to his gate, full of sores, 21 and desiring to be fed with the crumbs that fell from the rich man's table. Yes, even the dogs came and licked his sores. 22 The beggar died, and he was carried away by the angels to Abraham's bosom. The rich man also died and was buried. 23 In Hades,[e] he lifted up his eyes, being in torment, and saw Abraham far off, and Lazarus at his bosom. 24 He cried and said, 'Father Abraham, have mercy on me, and send Lazarus, that he may dip the tip of his finger in water and cool my tongue! For I am in anguish in this flame.'

25 "But Abraham said, 'Son, remember that you, in your lifetime, received your good things, and Lazarus, in the same way, bad things. But here he is now comforted and you are in anguish. 26 Besides all this, between us and you there is a great gulf fixed, that those who want to pass from here to you are not able, and that no one may cross over from there to us.'

27 "He said, 'I ask you therefore, father, that you would send him to my father's house— 28 for I have five brothers—that he may testify to them, so they won't also come into this place of torment.'

29 "But Abraham said to him, 'They have Moses and the prophets. Let them listen to them.'

30 "He said, 'No, father Abraham, but if one goes to them from the dead, they will repent.'

31 "He said to him, 'If they don't listen to Moses and the prophets, neither will they be persuaded if one rises from the dead.'"

17

1 **He said to the disciples,** "It is impossible that no occasions of stumbling should come, but woe to him through whom they come! 2 It would be better for him if a millstone were hung around his neck, and he were thrown into the sea, rather than that he should cause one of these little ones to stumble. 3 Be careful. If your brother sins against you, rebuke him. If he repents, forgive him. 4 If he sins against you seven times in the day, and seven times returns, saying, 'I repent,' you shall forgive him."

5 **The apostles said to the Lord, "Increase our faith."**

6 **The Lord said,** "If you had faith like a grain of mustard seed, you would tell this sycamore tree, 'Be uprooted and be planted in the sea,' and it would obey you. 7 But who is there amongst you, having a servant ploughing or keeping sheep, that will say when he comes in from the field, 'Come immediately and sit down at the table'? 8 Wouldn't he rather tell him, 'Prepare my supper, clothe yourself properly, and serve me while I eat and drink. Afterward you shall eat and drink'? 9 Does he thank that servant because he did the things that were commanded? I think not. 10 Even so you also, when you have done all the things that are commanded you, say, 'We are unworthy servants. We have done our duty.'"

11 **As he was on his way to Jerusalem, he was passing along the borders of Samaria and Galilee. 12 As he entered into a certain village, ten men who were lepers met him, who stood at a distance. 13 They lifted up their voices, saying, "Jesus, Master, have mercy on us!"**

14 **When he saw them, he said to them,** "Go and show yourselves to the priests." As they went, they were cleansed. 15 One of them, when he saw that he was healed, turned back, glorifying God with a loud voice. 16 He fell on his face at Jesus' feet, giving him thanks; and he was a Samaritan.

17 **Jesus answered,** "Weren't the ten cleansed? But where are the nine? 18 Were there none found who returned to give glory to God, except this foreigner?" 19 **Then he said to him,** "Get up, and go your way. Your faith has healed you."

20 **Being asked by the Pharisees when God's Kingdom would come, he answered them,** "God's Kingdom doesn't come with observation; 21 neither will they say, 'Look, here!' or, 'Look, there!' for behold, God's Kingdom is within you."

22 **He said to the disciples,** "The days will come when you will desire to see one of the days of the Son of Man, and you will not see it. 23 They will tell you, 'Look, here!' or 'Look, there!' Don't go away or follow after them, 24 for as the lightning, when it flashes out of one part under the sky, shines to another part under the sky, so will the Son of Man be in his day. 25 But first, he must suffer many things and be rejected by this generation. 26 As it was in the days of Noah, even so it will also be in the days of the Son of Man. 27 They ate, they drank, they married, and they were given in marriage until the day that Noah entered into the ship, and the flood came and destroyed them all. 28 Likewise, even as it was in the days of Lot: they ate, they drank, they bought, they sold, they planted, they built; 29 but in the day that Lot went out from Sodom, it rained fire and sulphur from the sky and destroyed them all. 30 It will be the same way in the day that the Son of Man is revealed. 31 In that day, he who will be on the housetop and his goods in the house, let him not go down to take them away. Let him who is in the field likewise not turn back. 32 Remember Lot's wife! 33 Whoever seeks to save his life loses it, but whoever loses his life preserves it. 34 I tell you, in that night there will be two people in one bed. One will be taken and the other will be left. 35 There will be two grinding grain together. One will be taken and the other will be left." 36 [f]

37 **They, answering, asked him, "Where, Lord?"**

He said to them, "Where the body is, there the vultures will also be gathered together."

---

a *15:8* A drachma coin was worth about 2 days wages for an agricultural labourer.
b *16:6* 100 batos is about 395 litres or 104 U. S. gallons.
c *16:7* 100 cors = about 2,110 litres or 600 bushels.
d *16:13* "Mammon" refers to riches or a false god of wealth.
e *16:23* or, Hell
f *17:36* Some Greek manuscripts add: "Two will be in the field: the one taken, and the other left."

18

1 He also spoke a parable to them that they must always pray and not give up, 2 saying, "There was a judge in a certain city who didn't fear God and didn't respect man. 3 A widow was in that city, and she often came to him, saying, 'Defend me from my adversary!' 4 He wouldn't for a while; but afterward he said to himself, 'Though I neither fear God nor respect man, 5 yet because this widow bothers me, I will defend her, or else she will wear me out by her continual coming.'"

6 The Lord said, "Listen to what the unrighteous judge says. 7 Won't God avenge his chosen ones who are crying out to him day and night, and yet he exercises patience with them? 8 I tell you that he will avenge them quickly. Nevertheless, when the Son of Man comes, will he find faith on the earth?"

9 He also spoke this parable to certain people who were convinced of their own righteousness, and who despised all others: 10 "Two men went up into the temple to pray; one was a Pharisee, and the other was a tax collector. 11 The Pharisee stood and prayed by himself like this: 'God, I thank you that I am not like the rest of men: extortionists, unrighteous, adulterers, or even like this tax collector. 12 I fast twice a week. I give tithes of all that I get.' 13 But the tax collector, standing far away, wouldn't even lift up his eyes to heaven, but beat his breast, saying, 'God, be merciful to me, a sinner!' 14 I tell you, this man went down to his house justified rather than the other; for everyone who exalts himself will be humbled, but he who humbles himself will be exalted."

15 They were also bringing their babies to him, that he might touch them. But when the disciples saw it, they rebuked them. 16 Jesus summoned them, saying, "Allow the little children to come to me, and don't hinder them, for God's Kingdom belongs to such as these. 17 Most certainly, I tell you, whoever doesn't receive God's Kingdom like a little child, he will in no way enter into it."

18 A certain ruler asked him, saying, "Good Teacher, what shall I do to inherit eternal life?"

19 Jesus asked him, "Why do you call me good? No one is good, except one: God. 20 You know the commandments: 'Don't commit adultery,' 'Don't murder,' 'Don't steal,' 'Don't give false testimony,' 'Honour your father and your mother.'"*

21 He said, "I have observed all these things from my youth up."

22 When Jesus heard these things, he said to him, "You still lack one thing. Sell all that you have and distribute it to the poor. Then you will have treasure in heaven; then come, follow me."

23 But when he heard these things, he became very sad, for he was very rich.

24 Jesus, seeing that he became very sad, said, "How hard it is for those who have riches to enter into God's Kingdom! 25 For it is easier for a camel to enter in through a needle's eye than for a rich man to enter into God's Kingdom."

26 Those who heard it said, "Then who can be saved?"

27 But he said, "The things which are impossible with men are possible with God."

28 Peter said, "Look, we have left everything and followed you."

29 He said to them, "Most certainly I tell you, there is no one who has left house, or wife, or brothers, or parents, or children, for God's Kingdom's sake, 30 who will not receive many times more in this time, and in the world to come, eternal life."

31 He took the twelve aside and said to them, "Behold, we are going up to Jerusalem, and all the things that are written through the prophets concerning the Son of Man will be completed. 32 For he will be delivered up to the Gentiles, will be mocked, treated shamefully, and spit on. 33 They will scourge and kill him. On the third day, he will rise again."

34 They understood none of these things. This saying was hidden from them, and they didn't understand the things that were said.

35 As he came near Jericho, a certain blind man sat by the road, begging. 36 Hearing a multitude going by, he asked what this meant. 37 They told him that Jesus of Nazareth was passing by. 38 He cried out, "Jesus, you son of David, have mercy on me!" 39 Those who led the way rebuked him, that he should be quiet; but he cried out all the more, "You son of David, have mercy on me!"

40 Standing still, Jesus commanded him to be brought to him. When he had come near, he asked him, 41 "What do you want me to do?"

He said, "Lord, that I may see again."

42 Jesus said to him, "Receive your sight. Your faith has healed you."

43 Immediately he received his sight and followed him, glorifying God. All the people, when they saw it, praised God.

19

1 He entered and was passing through Jericho. 2 There was a man named Zacchaeus. He was a chief tax collector, and he was rich. 3 He was trying to see who Jesus was, and couldn't because of the crowd, because he was short. 4 He ran on ahead and climbed up into a sycamore tree to see him, for he was going to pass that way. 5 When Jesus came to the place, he looked up and saw him, and said to him, "Zacchaeus, hurry and come down, for today I must stay at your house." 6 He hurried, came down, and received him joyfully. 7 When they saw it, they all murmured, saying, "He has gone in to lodge with a man who is a sinner."

8 Zacchaeus stood and said to the Lord, "Behold, Lord, half of my goods I give to the poor. If I have wrongfully exacted anything of anyone, I restore four times as much."

9 Jesus said to him, "Today, salvation has come to this house, because he also is a son of Abraham. 10 For the Son of Man came to seek and to save that which was lost."

11 As they heard these things, he went on and told a parable, because he was near Jerusalem, and they supposed that God's Kingdom would be revealed immediately. 12 He said therefore, "A certain nobleman went into a far country to receive for himself a kingdom and to return. 13 He called ten servants of his and gave them ten mina coins, [a] and told them, 'Conduct business until I come.' 14 But his citizens hated him, and sent an envoy after him, saying, 'We don't want this man to reign over us.'

15 "When he had come back again, having received the kingdom, he commanded these servants, to whom he had given the money, to be called to him, that he might know what they had gained by conducting business. 16 The first came before him, saying, 'Lord, your mina has made ten more minas.'

17 "He said to him, 'Well done, you good servant! Because you were found faithful with very little, you shall have authority over ten cities.'

18 "The second came, saying, 'Your mina, Lord, has made five minas.'

19 "So he said to him, 'And you are to be over five cities.'

20 Another came, saying, 'Lord, behold, your mina, which I kept laid away in a handkerchief, 21 for I feared you, because you are an exacting man. You take up that which you didn't lay down, and reap that which you didn't sow.'

22 "He said to him, 'Out of your own mouth I will judge you, you wicked servant! You knew that I am an exacting man, taking up that which I didn't lay down and reaping that which I didn't sow. 23 Then why didn't you deposit my money in the bank, and at my coming, I might have earned interest on it?' 24 He said to those who stood by, 'Take the mina away from him and give it to him who has the ten minas.'

25 "They said to him, 'Lord, he has ten minas!' 26 'For I tell you that to everyone who has, will more be given; but from him who doesn't have, even that which he has will be taken away from him. 27 But bring those enemies of mine who didn't want me to reign over them here, and kill them before me.'" 28 Having said these things, he went on ahead, going up to Jerusalem.

29 When he came near to Bethsphage[b] and Bethany, at the mountain that is called Olivet, he sent two of his disciples, 30 saying, "Go your way into the village on the other side, in which, as you enter, you will find a colt tied, which no man has ever sat upon. Untie it and bring it. 31 If anyone asks you, 'Why are you untying it?' say to him: 'The Lord needs it.'"

32 Those who were sent went away and found things just as he had told them. 33 As they were untying the colt, its owners said to them, "Why are you untying the colt?" 34 They said, "The Lord needs it." 35 Then they brought it to Jesus. They threw their cloaks on the colt and sat Jesus on them. 36 As he went, they spread their cloaks on the road.

37 As he was now getting near, at the descent of the Mount of Olives, the whole multitude of the disciples began to rejoice and praise God with a loud voice for all the mighty works which they had seen, 38 saying, "Blessed is the King who comes in the name of the Lord!* Peace in heaven, and glory in the highest!"

39 Some of the Pharisees from the multitude said to him, "Teacher, rebuke your disciples!"

40 He answered them, "I tell you that if these were silent, the stones would cry out."

41 When he came near, he saw the city and wept over it, 42 saying, "If you, even you, had known today the things which belong to your peace! But now, they are hidden from your eyes. 43 For the days will come on you when your enemies will throw up a barricade against you, surround you, hem you in on every side, 44 and will dash you and your children within you to the ground. They will not leave in you one stone on another, because you didn't know the time of your visitation."

45 He entered into the temple and began to drive out those who bought and sold in it, 46 saying to them, "It is written, 'My house is a house of prayer,'* but you have made it a 'den of robbers'!"*

47 He was teaching daily in the temple, but the chief priests, the scribes, and the leading men amongst the people sought to destroy him. 48 They couldn't find what they might do, for all the people hung on to every word that he said.

20

1 On one of those days, as he was teaching the people in the temple and preaching the Good News, the[c] priests and scribes came to him with the elders. 2 They asked him, "Tell us: by what authority do you do these things? Or who is giving you this authority?"

3 He answered them, "I also will ask you one question. Tell me: 4 the baptism of John, was it from heaven, or from men?"

5 They reasoned with themselves, saying, "If we say, 'From heaven,' he will say, 'Why didn't you believe him?' 6 But if we say, 'From men,' all the people will stone us, for they are persuaded that John was a prophet." 7 They answered that they didn't know where it was from.

** 18:20 Exodus 20:12-16; Deuteronomy 5:16-20
a *19:13* 10 minas was more than 3 years' wages for an agricultural labourer.
b *19:29* TR, NU read "Bethpage" instead of "Bethsphage"
** 19:38 Psalms 118:26

** 19:46 Isaiah 56:7
** 19:46 Jeremiah 7:11
c *20:1* TR adds "chief"

8 Jesus said to them, "Neither will I tell you by what authority I do these things."

9 He began to tell the people this parable: "A a man planted a vineyard and rented it out to some farmers, and went into another country for a long time. 10 At the proper season, he sent a servant to the farmers to collect his share of the fruit of the vineyard. But the farmers beat him and sent him away empty. 11 He sent yet another servant, and they also beat him and treated him shamefully, and sent him away empty. 12 He sent yet a third, and they also wounded him and threw him out. 13 The lord of the vineyard said, 'What shall I do? I will send my beloved son. It may be that seeing him, they will respect him.'

14 "But when the farmers saw him, they reasoned amongst themselves, saying, 'This is the heir. Come, let's kill him, that the inheritance may be ours.' 15 Then they threw him out of the vineyard and killed him. What therefore will the lord of the vineyard do to them? 16 He will come and destroy these farmers, and will give the vineyard to others."

When they heard that, they said, "May that never be!"

17 But he looked at them and said, "Then what is this that is written,
'The stone which the builders rejected
    was made the chief cornerstone'?*
18 Everyone who falls on that stone will be broken to pieces,
    but it will crush whomever it falls on to dust."

19 The chief priests and the scribes sought to lay hands on him that very hour, but they feared the people—for they knew he had spoken this parable against them. 20 They watched him and sent out spies, who pretended to be righteous, that they might trap him in something he said, so as to deliver him up to the power and authority of the governor. 21 They asked him, "Teacher, we know that you say and teach what is right, and aren't partial to anyone, but truly teach the way of God. 22 Is it lawful for us to pay taxes to Caesar, or not?"

23 But he perceived their craftiness, and said to them, "Why do you test me? 24 Show me a denarius. Whose image and inscription are on it?"

They answered, "Caesar's."

25 He said to them, "Then give to Caesar the things that are Caesar's, and to God the things that are God's."

26 They weren't able to trap him in his words before the people. They marvelled at his answer and were silent. 27 Some of the Sadducees came to him, those who deny that there is a resurrection. 28 They asked him, "Teacher, Moses wrote to us that if a man's brother dies having a wife, and he is childless, his brother should take the wife and raise up children for his brother. 29 There were therefore seven brothers. The first took a wife, and died childless. 30 The second took her as wife, and he died childless. 31 The third took her, and likewise the seven all left no children, and died. 32 Afterward the woman also died. 33 Therefore in the resurrection whose wife of them will she be? For the seven had her as a wife."

34 Jesus said to them, "The children of this age marry and are given in marriage. 35 But those who are considered worthy to attain to that age and the resurrection from the dead neither marry nor are given in marriage. 36 For they can't die any more, for they are like the angels and are children of God, being children of the resurrection. 37 But that the dead are raised, even Moses showed at the bush, when he called the Lord 'The God of Abraham, the God of Isaac, and the God of Jacob.' * 38 Now he is not the God of the dead, but of the living, for all are alive to him."

39 Some of the scribes answered, "Teacher, you speak well." 40 They didn't dare to ask him any more questions.

41 He said to them, "Why do they say that the Christ is David's son? 42 David himself says in the book of Psalms,
'The Lord said to my Lord,
    "Sit at my right hand,
43   until I make your enemies the footstool of your feet."' *
44 "David therefore calls him Lord, so how is he his son?"

45 In the hearing of all the people, he said to his disciples, 46 "Beware of those scribes who like to walk in long robes, and love greetings in the marketplaces, the best seats in the synagogues, and the best places at feasts; 47 who devour widows' houses, and for a pretence make long prayers. These will receive greater condemnation."

21

1 He looked up and saw the rich people who were putting their gifts into the treasury. 2 He saw a certain poor widow casting in two small brass coins.b 3 He said, "Truly I tell you, this poor widow put in more than all of them, 4 for all these put in gifts for God from their abundance, but she, out of her poverty, put in all that she had to live on."

5 As some were talking about the temple and how it was decorated with beautiful stones and gifts, he said, 6 "As for these things which you see, the days will come in which there will not be left here one stone on another that will not be thrown down."

7 They asked him, "Teacher, so when will these things be? What is the sign that these things are about to happen?"

8 He said, "Watch out that you don't get led astray, for many will come in my name, saying, 'I am hec,' and, 'The time is at hand.' Therefore don't follow them. 9 When you hear of wars and disturbances, don't be terrified, for these things must happen first, but the end won't come immediately."

10 Then he said to them, "Nation will rise against nation, and kingdom against kingdom. 11 There will be great earthquakes, famines, and plagues in various places. There will be terrors and great signs from heaven. 12 But before all these things, they will lay their hands on you and will persecute you, delivering you up to synagogues and prisons, bringing you before kings and governors for my name's sake. 13 It will turn out as a testimony for you. 14 Settle it therefore in your hearts not to meditate beforehand how to answer, 15 for I will give you a mouth and wisdom which all your adversaries will not be able to withstand or to contradict. 16 You will be handed over even by parents, brothers, relatives, and friends. They will cause some of you to be put to death. 17 You will be hated by all men for my name's sake. 18 And not a hair of your head will perish.

19 "By your endurance you will win your lives.

20 "But when you see Jerusalem surrounded by armies, then know that its desolation is at hand. 21 Then let those who are in Judea flee to the mountains. Let those who are in the middle of her depart. Let those who are in the country not enter therein. 22 For these are days of vengeance, that all things which are written may be fulfilled. 23 Woe to those who are pregnant and to those who nurse infants in those days! For there will be great distress in the land and wrath to this people. 24 They will fall by the edge of the sword, and will be led captive into all the nations. Jerusalem will be trampled down by the Gentiles until the times of the Gentiles are fulfilled.

25 "There will be signs in the sun, moon, and stars; and on the earth anxiety of nations, in perplexity for the roaring of the sea and the waves; 26 men fainting for fear and for expectation of the things which are coming on the world, for the powers of the heavens will be shaken. 27 Then they will see the Son of Man coming in a cloud with power and great glory. 28 But when these things begin to happen, look up and lift up your heads, because your redemption is near."

29 He told them a parable. "See the fig tree and all the trees. 30 When they are already budding, you see it and know by your own selves that the summer is already near. 31 Even so you also, when you see these things happening, know that God's Kingdom is near. 32 Most certainly I tell you, this generation will not pass away until all things are accomplished. 33 Heaven and earth will pass away, but my words will by no means pass away.

34 "So be careful, or your hearts will be loaded down with carousing, drunkenness, and cares of this life, and that day will come on you suddenly. 35 For it will come like a snare on all those who dwell on the surface of all the earth. 36 Therefore be watchful all the time, praying that you may be counted worthy to escape all these things that will happen, and to stand before the Son of Man."

37 Every day Jesus was teaching in the temple, and every night he would go out and spend the night on the mountain that is called Olivet. 38 All the people came early in the morning to him in the temple to hear him.

22

1 Now the feast of unleavened bread, which is called the Passover, was approaching. 2 The chief priests and the scribes sought how they might put him to death, for they feared the people.

3 Satan entered into Judas, who was also called Iscariot, who was counted with the twelve. 4 He went away and talked with the chief priests and captains about how he might deliver him to them. 5 They were glad, and agreed to give him money. 6 He consented and sought an opportunity to deliver him to them in the absence of the multitude.

7 The day of unleavened bread came, on which the Passover must be sacrificed. 8 Jesus sent Peter and John, saying, "Go and prepare the Passover for us, that we may eat."

9 They said to him, "Where do you want us to prepare?"

10 He said to them, "Behold, when you have entered into the city, a man carrying a pitcher of water will meet you. Follow him into the house which he enters. 11 Tell the master of the house, 'The Teacher says to you, "Where is the guest room, where I may eat the Passover with my disciples?"' 12 He will show you a large, furnished upper room. Make preparations there."

13 They went, found things as Jesus had told them, and they prepared the Passover.

14 When the hour had come, he sat down with the twelve apostles. 15 He said to them, "I have earnestly desired to eat this Passover with you before I suffer, 16 for I tell you, I will no longer by any means eat of it until it is fulfilled in God's Kingdom." 17 He received a cup, and when he had given thanks, he said, "Take this and share it amongst yourselves, 18 for I tell you, I will not drink at all again from the fruit of the vine, until God's Kingdom comes."

19 He took bread, and when he had given thanks, he broke and gave it to them, saying, "This is my body which is given for you. Do this in memory of me." 20 Likewise, he took the cup after supper, saying, "This cup is the new covenant in my blood, which is poured out for you. 21 But behold, the hand of him who betrays me is with me on the table. 22 The Son of Man indeed goes as it has been determined, but woe to that man through whom he is betrayed!"

23 They began to question amongst themselves which of them it was who would do this thing.

---

a 20:9 NU (in brackets) and TR add "certain"
** 20:17 Psalms 118:22
** 20:37 Exodus 3:6
** 20:43 Psalms 110:1

b 21:2 literally, "two lepta." 2 lepta was about 1% of a day's wages for an agricultural labourer.
c 21:8 or, I AM

₂₄ A dispute also arose amongst them, which of them was considered to be greatest. ₂₅ He said to them, "The kings of the nations lord it over them, and those who have authority over them are called 'benefactors.' ₂₆ But not so with you. Rather, the one who is greater amongst you, let him become as the younger, and one who is governing, as one who serves. ₂₇ For who is greater, one who sits at the table, or one who serves? Isn't it he who sits at the table? But I am amongst you as one who serves.

₂₈ "But you are those who have continued with me in my trials. ₂₉ I confer on you a kingdom, even as my Father conferred on me, ₃₀ that you may eat and drink at my table in my Kingdom. You will sit on thrones, judging the twelve tribes of Israel."

₃₁ The Lord said, "Simon, Simon, behold, Satan asked to have all of you, that he might sift you as wheat, ₃₂ but I prayed for you, that your faith wouldn't fail. You, when once you have turned again, establish your brothers."ᵃ

₃₃ He said to him, "Lord, I am ready to go with you both to prison and to death!"

₃₄ He said, "I tell you, Peter, the rooster will by no means crow today until you deny that you know me three times."

₃₅ He said to them, "When I sent you out without purse, bag, and sandals, did you lack anything?"

They said, "Nothing."

₃₆ Then he said to them, "But now, whoever has a purse, let him take it, and likewise a bag. Whoever has none, let him sell his cloak, and buy a sword. ₃₇ For I tell you that this which is written must still be fulfilled in me: 'He was counted with transgressors.' For that which concerns me is being fulfilled."

₃₈ They said, "Lord, behold, here are two swords."

He said to them, "That is enough."

₃₉ He came out and went, as his custom was, to the Mount of Olives. His disciples also followed him. ₄₀ When he was at the place, he said to them, "Pray that you don't enter into temptation."

₄₁ He was withdrawn from them about a stone's throw, and he knelt down and prayed, ₄₂ saying, "Father, if you are willing, remove this cup from me. Nevertheless, not my will, but yours, be done."

₄₃ An angel from heaven appeared to him, strengthening him. ₄₄ Being in agony, he prayed more earnestly. His sweat became like great drops of blood falling down on the ground.

₄₅ When he rose up from his prayer, he came to the disciples and found them sleeping because of grief, ₄₆ and said to them, "Why do you sleep? Rise and pray that you may not enter into temptation."

₄₇ While he was still speaking, a crowd appeared. He who was called Judas, one of the twelve, was leading them. He came near to Jesus to kiss him. ₄₈ But Jesus said to him, "Judas, do you betray the Son of Man with a kiss?"

₄₉ When those who were around him saw what was about to happen, they said to him, "Lord, shall we strike with the sword?" ₅₀ A certain one of them struck the servant of the high priest, and cut off his right ear.

₅₁ But Jesus answered, "Let me at least do this"—and he touched his ear and healed him. ₅₂ Jesus said to the chief priests, captains of the temple, and elders, who had come against him, "Have you come out as against a robber, with swords and clubs? ₅₃ When I was with you in the temple daily, you didn't stretch out your hands against me. But this is your hour, and the power of darkness."

₅₄ They seized him and led him away, and brought him into the high priest's house. But Peter followed from a distance. ₅₅ When they had kindled a fire in the middle of the courtyard and had sat down together, Peter sat amongst them. ₅₆ A certain servant girl saw him as he sat in the light, and looking intently at him, said, "This man also was with him."

₅₇ He denied Jesus, saying, "Woman, I don't know him."

₅₈ After a little while someone else saw him and said, "You also are one of them!"

But Peter answered, "Man, I am not!"

₅₉ After about one hour passed, another confidently affirmed, saying, "Truly this man also was with him, for he is a Galilean!"

₆₀ But Peter said, "Man, I don't know what you are talking about!" Immediately, while he was still speaking, a rooster crowed. ₆₁ The Lord turned and looked at Peter. Then Peter remembered the Lord's word, how he said to him, "Before the rooster crows you will deny me three times." ₆₂ He went out, and wept bitterly.

₆₃ The men who held Jesus mocked him and beat him. ₆₄ Having blindfolded him, they struck him on the face and asked him, "Prophesy! Who is the one who struck you?" ₆₅ They spoke many other things against him, insulting him.

₆₆ As soon as it was day, the assembly of the elders of the people were gathered together, both chief priests and scribes, and they led him away into their council, saying, ₆₇ "If you are the Christ, tell us."

But he said to them, "If I tell you, you won't believe, ₆₈ and if I ask, you will in no way answer me or let me go. ₆₉ From now on, the Son of Man will be seated at the right hand of the power of God."

₇₀ They all said, "Are you then the Son of God?"

He said to them, "You say it, because I am."

₇₁ They said, "Why do we need any more witness? For we ourselves have heard from his own mouth!"

23

₁ The whole company of them rose up and brought him before Pilate. ₂ They began to accuse him, saying, "We found this man perverting the nation, forbidding paying taxes to Caesar, and saying that he himself is Christ, a king."

₃ Pilate asked him, "Are you the King of the Jews?"

He answered him, "So you say."

₄ Pilate said to the chief priests and the multitudes, "I find no basis for a charge against this man."

₅ But they insisted, saying, "He stirs up the people, teaching throughout all Judea, beginning from Galilee even to this place."

₆ But when Pilate heard Galilee mentioned, he asked if the man was a Galilean. ₇ When he found out that he was in Herod's jurisdiction, he sent him to Herod, who was also in Jerusalem during those days.

₈ Now when Herod saw Jesus, he was exceedingly glad, for he had wanted to see him for a long time, because he had heard many things about him. He hoped to see some miracle done by him. ₉ He questioned him with many words, but he gave no answers. ₁₀ The chief priests and the scribes stood, vehemently accusing him. ₁₁ Herod with his soldiers humiliated him and mocked him. Dressing him in luxurious clothing, they sent him back to Pilate. ₁₂ Herod and Pilate became friends with each other that very day, for before that they were enemies with each other.

₁₃ Pilate called together the chief priests, the rulers, and the people, ₁₄ and said to them, "You brought this man to me as one that perverts the people, and behold, having examined him before you, I found no basis for a charge against this man concerning those things of which you accuse him. ₁₅ Neither has Herod, for I sent you to him, and see, nothing worthy of death has been done by him. ₁₆ I will therefore chastise him and release him."

₁₇ Now he had to release one prisoner to them at the feast.ᵇ ₁₈ But they all cried out together, saying, "Away with this man! Release to us Barabbas!"— ₁₉ one who was thrown into prison for a certain revolt in the city, and for murder.

₂₀ Then Pilate spoke to them again, wanting to release Jesus, ₂₁ but they shouted, saying, "Crucify! Crucify him!"

₂₂ He said to them the third time, "Why? What evil has this man done? I have found no capital crime in him. I will therefore chastise him and release him." ₂₃ But they were urgent with loud voices, asking that he might be crucified. Their voices and the voices of the chief priests prevailed. ₂₄ Pilate decreed that what they asked for should be done. ₂₅ He released him who had been thrown into prison for insurrection and murder, for whom they asked, but he delivered Jesus up to their will.

₂₆ When they led him away, they grabbed one Simon of Cyrene, coming from the country, and laid the cross on him to carry it after Jesus. ₂₇ A great multitude of the people followed him, including women who also mourned and lamented him. ₂₈ But Jesus, turning to them, said, "Daughters of Jerusalem, don't weep for me, but weep for yourselves and for your children. ₂₉ For behold, the days are coming in which they will say, 'Blessed are the barren, the wombs that never bore, and the breasts that never nursed.' ₃₀ Then they will begin to tell the mountains, 'Fall on us!' and tell the hills, 'Cover us.'* ₃₁ For if they do these things in the green tree, what will be done in the dry?"

₃₂ There were also others, two criminals, led with him to be put to death. ₃₃ When they came to the place that is called "The Skull", they crucified him there with the criminals, one on the right and the other on the left.

₃₄ Jesus said, "Father, forgive them, for they don't know what they are doing."

Dividing his garments amongst them, they cast lots. ₃₅ The people stood watching. The rulers with them also scoffed at him, saying, "He saved others. Let him save himself, if this is the Christ of God, his chosen one!"

₃₆ The soldiers also mocked him, coming to him and offering him vinegar, ₃₇ and saying, "If you are the King of the Jews, save yourself!"

₃₈ An inscription was also written over him in letters of Greek, Latin, and Hebrew: "THIS IS THE KING OF THE JEWS."

₃₉ One of the criminals who was hanged insulted him, saying, "If you are the Christ, save yourself and us!"

₄₀ But the other answered, and rebuking him said, "Don't you even fear God, seeing you are under the same condemnation? ₄₁ And we indeed justly, for we receive the due reward for our deeds, but this man has done nothing wrong." ₄₂ He said to Jesus, "Lord, remember me when you come into your Kingdom."

₄₃ Jesus said to him, "Assuredly I tell you, today you will be with me in Paradise."

₄₄ It was now about the sixth hour,ᶜ and darkness came over the whole land until the ninth hour.ᵈ ₄₅ The sun was darkened, and the veil of the temple was torn in two. ₄₆ Jesus, crying with a loud voice, said, "Father, into your hands I commit my spirit!" Having said this, he breathed his last.

₄₇ When the centurion saw what was done, he glorified God, saying, "Certainly this was a righteous man." ₄₈ All the multitudes that came together to see this, when they saw the things that were done, returned home beating their breasts. ₄₉ All his acquaintances and the women who followed with him from Galilee stood at a distance, watching these things.

ᵃ *22:32* The word for "brothers" here may be also correctly translated "brothers and sisters" or "siblings."
** *22:37* Isaiah 53:12
ᵇ *23:17* NU omits verse 17.

** *23:30* Hosea 10:8
ᶜ *23:44* Time was counted from sunrise, so the sixth hour was about noon.
ᵈ *23:44* 3:00 p.m.

50 Behold, there was a man named Joseph, who was a member of the council, a good and righteous man 51 (he had not consented to their counsel and deed), from Arimathaea, a city of the Jews, who was also waiting for God's Kingdom. 52 This man went to Pilate, and asked for Jesus' body. 53 He took it down and wrapped it in a linen cloth, and laid him in a tomb that was cut in stone, where no one had ever been laid. 54 It was the day of the Preparation, and the Sabbath was drawing near. 55 The women who had come with him out of Galilee followed after, and saw the tomb and how his body was laid. 56 They returned and prepared spices and ointments. On the Sabbath they rested according to the commandment.

24

1 But on the first day of the week, at early dawn, they and some others came to the tomb, bringing the spices which they had prepared. 2 They found the stone rolled away from the tomb. 3 They entered in, and didn't find the Lord Jesus' body. 4 While they were greatly perplexed about this, behold, two men stood by them in dazzling clothing. 5 Becoming terrified, they bowed their faces down to the earth.

The men said to them, "Why do you seek the living amongst the dead? 6 He isn't here, but is risen. Remember what he told you when he was still in Galilee, 7 saying that the Son of Man must be delivered up into the hands of sinful men and be crucified, and the third day rise again?"

8 They remembered his words, 9 returned from the tomb, and told all these things to the eleven and to all the rest. 10 Now they were Mary Magdalene, Joanna, and Mary the mother of James. The other women with them told these things to the apostles. 11 These words seemed to them to be nonsense, and they didn't believe them. 12 But Peter got up and ran to the tomb. Stooping and looking in, he saw the strips of linen lying by themselves, and he departed to his home, wondering what had happened.

13 Behold, two of them were going that very day to a village named Emmaus, which was sixty stadia[a] from Jerusalem. 14 They talked with each other about all of these things which had happened. 15 While they talked and questioned together, Jesus himself came near, and went with them. 16 But their eyes were kept from recognising him. 17 He said to them, "What are you talking about as you walk, and are sad?"

18 One of them, named Cleopas, answered him, "Are you the only stranger in Jerusalem who doesn't know the things which have happened there in these days?"

19 He said to them, "What things?"

They said to him, "The things concerning Jesus the Nazarene, who was a prophet mighty in deed and word before God and all the people; 20 and how the chief priests and our rulers delivered him up to be condemned to death, and crucified him. 21 But we were hoping that it was he who would redeem Israel. Yes, and besides all this, it is now the third day since these things happened. 22 Also, certain women of our company amazed us, having arrived early at the tomb; 23 and when they didn't find his body, they came saying that they had also seen a vision of angels, who said that he was alive. 24 Some of us went to the tomb and found it just like the women had said, but they didn't see him."

25 He said to them, "Foolish people, and slow of heart to believe in all that the prophets have spoken! 26 Didn't the Christ have to suffer these things and to enter into his glory?" 27 Beginning from Moses and from all the prophets, he explained to them in all the Scriptures the things concerning himself.

28 They came near to the village where they were going, and he acted like he would go further.

29 They urged him, saying, "Stay with us, for it is almost evening, and the day is almost over."

He went in to stay with them. 30 When he had sat down at the table with them, he took the bread and gave thanks. Breaking it, he gave it to them. 31 Their eyes were opened and they recognised him; then he vanished out of their sight. 32 They said to one another, "Weren't our hearts burning within us while he spoke to us along the way, and while he opened the Scriptures to us?" 33 They rose up that very hour, returned to Jerusalem, and found the eleven gathered together, and those who were with them, 34 saying, "The Lord is risen indeed, and has appeared to Simon!" 35 They related the things that happened along the way, and how he was recognised by them in the breaking of the bread.

36 As they said these things, Jesus himself stood amongst them, and said to them, "Peace be to you."

37 But they were terrified and filled with fear, and supposed that they had seen a spirit.

38 He said to them, "Why are you troubled? Why do doubts arise in your hearts? 39 See my hands and my feet, that it is truly me. Touch me and see, for a spirit doesn't have flesh and bones, as you see that I have." 40 When he had said this, he showed them his hands and his feet. 41 While they still didn't believe for joy, and wondered, he said to them, "Do you have anything here to eat?"

42 They gave him a piece of a broiled fish and some honeycomb. 43 He took them, and ate in front of them. 44 He said to them, "This is what I told you while I was still with you, that all things which are written in the law of Moses, the prophets, and the psalms concerning me must be fulfilled."

45 Then he opened their minds, that they might understand the Scriptures. 46 He said to them, "Thus it is written, and thus it was necessary for the Christ to suffer and to rise from the dead the third day, 47 and that repentance and remission of sins should be preached in his name to all the nations, beginning at Jerusalem. 48 You are witnesses of these things. 49 Behold, I send out the promise of my Father on you. But wait in the city of Jerusalem until you are clothed with power from on high."

50 He led them out as far as Bethany, and he lifted up his hands and blessed them. 51 While he blessed them, he withdrew from them and was carried up into heaven. 52 They worshipped him and returned to Jerusalem with great joy, 53 and were continually in the temple, praising and blessing God. Amen.

---

[a] 24:13 60 stadia = about 11 kilometres or about 7 miles.

The Good News According to John

1

1 In the beginning was the Word, and the Word was with God, and the Word was God. 2 The same was in the beginning with God. 3 All things were made through him. Without him, nothing was made that has been made. 4 In him was life, and the life was the light of men. 5 The light shines in the darkness, and the darkness hasn't overcome[a] it.

6 There came a man sent from God, whose name was John. 7 The same came as a witness, that he might testify about the light, that all might believe through him. 8 He was not the light, but was sent that he might testify about the light. 9 The true light that enlightens everyone was coming into the world.

10 He was in the world, and the world was made through him, and the world didn't recognise him. 11 He came to his own, and those who were his own didn't receive him. 12 But as many as received him, to them he gave the right to become God's children, to those who believe in his name: 13 who were born, not of blood, nor of the will of the flesh, nor of the will of man, but of God.

14 The Word became flesh and lived amongst us. We saw his glory, such glory as of the only born[b] Son of the Father, full of grace and truth. 15 John testified about him. He cried out, saying, "This was he of whom I said, 'He who comes after me has surpassed me, for he was before me.'" 16 From his fullness we all received grace upon grace. 17 For the law was given through Moses. Grace and truth were realised through Jesus Christ.[c] 18 No one has seen God at any time. The only born[d] Son,[e] who is in the bosom of the Father, has declared him.

19 This is John's testimony, when the Jews sent priests and Levites from Jerusalem to ask him, "Who are you?"

20 He declared, and didn't deny, but he declared, "I am not the Christ."

21 They asked him, "What then? Are you Elijah?"

He said, "I am not."

"Are you the prophet?"

He answered, "No."

22 They said therefore to him, "Who are you? Give us an answer to take back to those who sent us. What do you say about yourself?"

23 He said, "I am the voice of one crying in the wilderness, 'Make straight the way of the Lord,'" as Isaiah the prophet said.

24 The ones who had been sent were from the Pharisees. 25 They asked him, "Why then do you baptise if you are not the Christ, nor Elijah, nor the prophet?"

26 John answered them, "I baptise in water, but amongst you stands one whom you don't know. 27 He is the one who comes after me, who is preferred before me, whose sandal strap I'm not worthy to loosen." 28 These things were done in Bethany beyond the Jordan, where John was baptising.

29 The next day, he saw Jesus coming to him, and said, "Behold,[f] the Lamb of God, who takes away the sin of the world! 30 This is he of whom I said, 'After me comes a man who is preferred before me, for he was before me.' 31 I didn't know him, but for this reason I came baptising in water, that he would be revealed to Israel." 32 John testified, saying, "I have seen the Spirit descending like a dove out of heaven, and it remained on him. 33 I didn't recognise him, but he who sent me to baptise in water said to me, 'On whomever you will see the Spirit descending and remaining on him is he who baptises in the Holy Spirit.' 34 I have seen and have testified that this is the Son of God."

35 Again, the next day, John was standing with two of his disciples, 36 and he looked at Jesus as he walked, and said, "Behold, the Lamb of God!" 37 The two disciples heard him speak, and they followed Jesus. 38 Jesus turned and saw them following, and said to them, "What are you looking for?"

They said to him, "Rabbi" (which is to say, being interpreted, Teacher), "where are you staying?"

39 He said to them, "Come and see."

They came and saw where he was staying, and they stayed with him that day. It was about the tenth hour.[g] 40 One of the two who heard John and followed him was Andrew, Simon Peter's brother. 41 He first found his own brother, Simon, and said to him, "We have found the Messiah!" (which is, being interpreted, Christ[h]). 42 He brought him to Jesus. Jesus looked at him and said, "You are Simon the son of Jonah. You shall be called Cephas" (which is by interpretation, Peter).[i]

43 On the next day, he was determined to go out into Galilee, and he found Philip. Jesus said to him, "Follow me." 44 Now Philip was from Bethsaida, the city of Andrew and Peter. 45 Philip found Nathanael, and said to him, "We have found him of whom Moses in the law and also the prophets, wrote: Jesus of Nazareth, the son of Joseph."

46 Nathanael said to him, "Can any good thing come out of Nazareth?" Philip said to him, "Come and see."

47 Jesus saw Nathanael coming to him, and said about him, "Behold, an Israelite indeed, in whom is no deceit!"

48 Nathanael said to him, "How do you know me?"

Jesus answered him, "Before Philip called you, when you were under the fig tree, I saw you."

49 Nathanael answered him, "Rabbi, you are the Son of God! You are King of Israel!"

50 Jesus answered him, "Because I told you, 'I saw you underneath the fig tree,' do you believe? You will see greater things than these!" 51 He said to him, "Most certainly, I tell you all, hereafter you will see heaven opened, and the angels of God ascending and descending on the Son of Man."

2

1 The third day, there was a wedding in Cana of Galilee. Jesus' mother was there. 2 Jesus also was invited, with his disciples, to the wedding. 3 When the wine ran out, Jesus' mother said to him, "They have no wine."

4 Jesus said to her, "Woman, what does that have to do with you and me? My hour has not yet come."

5 His mother said to the servants, "Whatever he says to you, do it."

6 Now there were six water pots of stone set there after the Jews' way of purifying, containing two or three metretes[j] apiece. 7 Jesus said to them, "Fill the water pots with water." So they filled them up to the brim. 8 He said to them, "Now draw some out, and take it to the ruler of the feast." So they took it. 9 When the ruler of the feast tasted the water now become wine, and didn't know where it came from (but the servants who had drawn the water knew), the ruler of the feast called the bridegroom 10 and said to him, "Everyone serves the good wine first, and when the guests have drunk freely, then that which is worse. You have kept the good wine until now!" 11 This beginning of his signs Jesus did in Cana of Galilee, and revealed his glory; and his disciples believed in him.

12 After this, he went down to Capernaum, he, and his mother, his brothers, and his disciples; and they stayed there a few days.

13 The Passover of the Jews was at hand, and Jesus went up to Jerusalem. 14 He found in the temple those who sold oxen, sheep, and doves, and the changers of money sitting. 15 He made a whip of cords and drove all out of the temple, both the sheep and the oxen; and he poured out the changers' money and overthrew their tables. 16 To those who sold the doves, he said, "Take these things out of here! Don't make my Father's house a marketplace!" 17 His disciples remembered that it was written, "Zeal for your house will eat me up."*

18 The Jews therefore answered him, "What sign do you show us, seeing that you do these things?"

19 Jesus answered them, "Destroy this temple, and in three days I will raise it up."

20 The Jews therefore said, "It took forty-six years to build this temple! Will you raise it up in three days?" 21 But he spoke of the temple of his body. 22 When therefore he was raised from the dead, his disciples remembered that he said this, and they believed the Scripture and the word which Jesus had said.

23 Now when he was in Jerusalem at the Passover, during the feast, many believed in his name, observing his signs which he did. 24 But Jesus didn't entrust himself to them, because he knew everyone, 25 and because he didn't need for anyone to testify concerning man; for he himself knew what was in man.

3

1 Now there was a man of the Pharisees named Nicodemus, a ruler of the Jews. 2 He came to Jesus by night and said to him, "Rabbi, we know that you are a teacher come from God, for no one can do these signs that you do, unless God is with him."

3 Jesus answered him, "Most certainly I tell you, unless one is born anew,[k] he can't see God's Kingdom."

4 Nicodemus said to him, "How can a man be born when he is old? Can he enter a second time into his mother's womb and be born?"

5 Jesus answered, "Most certainly I tell you, unless one is born of water and Spirit, he can't enter into God's Kingdom. 6 That which is born of the flesh is flesh. That which is born of the Spirit is spirit. 7 Don't marvel that I said to you, 'You must be born anew.' 8 The wind[l] blows where it wants to, and you hear its sound, but don't know where it comes from and where it is going. So is everyone who is born of the Spirit."

9 Nicodemus answered him, "How can these things be?"

10 Jesus answered him, "Are you the teacher of Israel, and don't understand these things? 11 Most certainly I tell you, we speak that which we know and testify of that which we have seen, and you don't receive our witness. 12 If I told you earthly things and you don't believe, how will you believe if I tell you heavenly things? 13 No one has ascended into heaven but he who descended out of heaven, the Son of Man, who is in heaven. 14

---

a 1:5 The word translated "overcome" (κατέλαβεν) can also be translated "comprehended." It refers to getting a grip on an enemy to defeat him.

b 1:14 The phrase "only born" is from the Greek word "μονογενους", which is sometimes translated "only begotten" or "one and only".

c 1:17 "Christ" means "Anointed One".

d 1:18 The phrase "only born" is from the Greek word "μονογενη", which is sometimes translated "only begotten" or "one and only".

e 1:18 NU reads "God"

** 1:23 Isaiah 40:3

f 1:29 "Behold", from "ἰδοὺ", means look at, take notice, observe, see, or gaze at. It is often used as an interjection.

g 1:39 4:00 p.m.

h 1:41 "Messiah" (Hebrew) and "Christ" (Greek) both mean "Anointed One".

i 1:42 "Cephas" (Aramaic) and "Peter" (Greek) both mean "Rock".

j 2:6 2 to 3 metretes is about 20 to 30 U. S. Gallons, or 75 to 115 litres.

** 2:17 Psalms 69:9

k 3:3 The word translated "anew" here and in John 3:7 (ἄνωθεν) also means "again" and "from above".

l 3:8 The same Greek word (πνεῦμα) means wind, breath, and spirit.

As Moses lifted up the serpent in the wilderness, even so must the Son of Man be lifted up, ₁₅ that whoever believes in him should not perish, but have eternal life. ₁₆ For God so loved the world, that he gave his only born[a] Son, that whoever believes in him should not perish, but have eternal life. ₁₇ For God didn't send his Son into the world to judge the world, but that the world should be saved through him. ₁₈ He who believes in him is not judged. He who doesn't believe has been judged already, because he has not believed in the name of the only born Son of God. ₁₉ This is the judgement, that the light has come into the world, and men loved the darkness rather than the light, for their works were evil. ₂₀ For everyone who does evil hates the light and doesn't come to the light, lest his works would be exposed. ₂₁ But he who does the truth comes to the light, that his works may be revealed, that they have been done in God."

₂₂ After these things, Jesus came with his disciples into the land of Judea. He stayed there with them and baptised. ₂₃ John also was baptising in Enon near Salim, because there was much water there. They came and were baptised; ₂₄ for John was not yet thrown into prison. ₂₅ Therefore a dispute arose on the part of John's disciples with some Jews about purification. ₂₆ They came to John and said to him, "Rabbi, he who was with you beyond the Jordan, to whom you have testified, behold, he baptises, and everyone is coming to him."

₂₇ John answered, "A man can receive nothing unless it has been given him from heaven. ₂₈ You yourselves testify that I said, 'I am not the Christ,' but, 'I have been sent before him.' ₂₉ He who has the bride is the bridegroom; but the friend of the bridegroom, who stands and hears him, rejoices greatly because of the bridegroom's voice. Therefore my joy is made full. ₃₀ He must increase, but I must decrease.

₃₁ "He who comes from above is above all. He who is from the earth belongs to the earth and speaks of the earth. He who comes from heaven is above all. ₃₂ What he has seen and heard, of that he testifies; and no one receives his witness. ₃₃ He who has received his witness has set his seal to this, that God is true. ₃₄ For he whom God has sent speaks the words of God; for God gives the Spirit without measure. ₃₅ The Father loves the Son, and has given all things into his hand. ₃₆ One who believes in the Son has eternal life, but one who disobeys[b] the Son won't see life, but the wrath of God remains on him."

4

₁ Therefore when the Lord knew that the Pharisees had heard that Jesus was making and baptising more disciples than John ₂ (although Jesus himself didn't baptise, but his disciples), ₃ he left Judea and departed into Galilee. ₄ He needed to pass through Samaria. ₅ So he came to a city of Samaria called Sychar, near the parcel of ground that Jacob gave to his son Joseph. ₆ Jacob's well was there. Jesus therefore, being tired from his journey, sat down by the well. It was about the sixth hour.[c]

₇ A woman of Samaria came to draw water. Jesus said to her, "Give me a drink." ₈ For his disciples had gone away into the city to buy food.

₉ The Samaritan woman therefore said to him, "How is it that you, being a Jew, ask for a drink from me, a Samaritan woman?" (For Jews have no dealings with Samaritans.)

₁₀ Jesus answered her, "If you knew the gift of God, and who it is who says to you, 'Give me a drink,' you would have asked him, and he would have given you living water."

₁₁ The woman said to him, "Sir, you have nothing to draw with, and the well is deep. So where do you get that living water? ₁₂ Are you greater than our father Jacob, who gave us the well and drank from it himself, as did his children and his livestock?"

₁₃ Jesus answered her, "Everyone who drinks of this water will thirst again, ₁₄ but whoever drinks of the water that I will give him will never thirst again; but the water that I will give him will become in him a well of water springing up to eternal life."

₁₅ The woman said to him, "Sir, give me this water, so that I don't get thirsty, neither come all the way here to draw."

₁₆ Jesus said to her, "Go, call your husband, and come here."

₁₇ The woman answered, "I have no husband."

Jesus said to her, "You said well, 'I have no husband,' ₁₈ for you have had five husbands; and he whom you now have is not your husband. This you have said truly."

₁₉ The woman said to him, "Sir, I perceive that you are a prophet. ₂₀ Our fathers worshipped in this mountain, and you Jews say that in Jerusalem is the place where people ought to worship."

₂₁ Jesus said to her, "Woman, believe me, the hour is coming when neither in this mountain nor in Jerusalem will you worship the Father. ₂₂ You worship that which you don't know. We worship that which we know; for salvation is from the Jews. ₂₃ But the hour comes, and now is, when the true worshippers will worship the Father in spirit and truth, for the Father seeks such to be his worshippers. ₂₄ God is spirit, and those who worship him must worship in spirit and truth."

₂₅ The woman said to him, "I know that Messiah is coming, he who is called Christ.[d] When he has come, he will declare to us all things."

₂₆ Jesus said to her, "I am he, the one who speaks to you."

₂₇ Just then, his disciples came. They marvelled that he was speaking with a woman; yet no one said, "What are you looking for?" or, "Why do you speak with her?" ₂₈ So the woman left her water pot, went away into the city, and said to the people, ₂₉ "Come, see a man who told me everything that I have done. Can this be the Christ?" ₃₀ They went out of the city, and were coming to him.

₃₁ In the meanwhile, the disciples urged him, saying, "Rabbi, eat."

₃₂ But he said to them, "I have food to eat that you don't know about."

₃₃ The disciples therefore said to one another, "Has anyone brought him something to eat?"

₃₄ Jesus said to them, "My food is to do the will of him who sent me and to accomplish his work. ₃₅ Don't you say, 'There are yet four months until the harvest'? Behold, I tell you, lift up your eyes and look at the fields, that they are white for harvest already. ₃₆ He who reaps receives wages and gathers fruit to eternal life, that both he who sows and he who reaps may rejoice together. ₃₇ For in this the saying is true, 'One sows, and another reaps.' ₃₈ I sent you to reap that for which you haven't laboured. Others have laboured, and you have entered into their labour."

₃₉ From that city many of the Samaritans believed in him because of the word of the woman, who testified, "He told me everything that I have done." ₄₀ So when the Samaritans came to him, they begged him to stay with them. He stayed there two days. ₄₁ Many more believed because of his word. ₄₂ They said to the woman, "Now we believe, not because of your speaking; for we have heard for ourselves, and know that this is indeed the Christ, the Saviour of the world."

₄₃ After the two days he went out from there and went into Galilee. ₄₄ For Jesus himself testified that a prophet has no honour in his own country. ₄₅ So when he came into Galilee, the Galileans received him, having seen all the things that he did in Jerusalem at the feast, for they also went to the feast. ₄₆ Jesus came therefore again to Cana of Galilee, where he made the water into wine. There was a certain nobleman whose son was sick at Capernaum. ₄₇ When he heard that Jesus had come out of Judea into Galilee, he went to him and begged him that he would come down and heal his son, for he was at the point of death. ₄₈ Jesus therefore said to him, "Unless you see signs and wonders, you will in no way believe."

₄₉ The nobleman said to him, "Sir, come down before my child dies."

₅₀ Jesus said to him, "Go your way. Your son lives." The man believed the word that Jesus spoke to him, and he went his way. ₅₁ As he was going down, his servants met him and reported, saying "Your child lives!" ₅₂ So he enquired of them the hour when he began to get better. They said therefore to him, "Yesterday at the seventh hour,[e] the fever left him." ₅₃ So the father knew that it was at that hour in which Jesus said to him, "Your son lives." He believed, as did his whole house. ₅₄ This is again the second sign that Jesus did, having come out of Judea into Galilee.

5

₁ After these things, there was a feast of the Jews, and Jesus went up to Jerusalem. ₂ Now in Jerusalem by the sheep gate, there is a pool, which is called in Hebrew, "Bethesda", having five porches. ₃ In these lay a great multitude of those who were sick, blind, lame, or paralysed, waiting for the moving of the water; ₄ for an angel went down at certain times into the pool and stirred up the water. Whoever stepped in first after the stirring of the water was healed of whatever disease he had.[f] ₅ A certain man was there who had been sick for thirty-eight years. ₆ When Jesus saw him lying there, and knew that he had been sick for a long time, he asked him, "Do you want to be made well?"

₇ The sick man answered him, "Sir, I have no one to put me into the pool when the water is stirred up, but while I'm coming, another steps down before me."

₈ Jesus said to him, "Arise, take up your mat, and walk."

₉ Immediately, the man was made well, and took up his mat and walked.

Now that day was a Sabbath. ₁₀ So the Jews said to him who was cured, "It is the Sabbath. It is not lawful for you to carry the mat."

₁₁ He answered them, "He who made me well said to me, 'Take up your mat and walk.' "

₁₂ Then they asked him, "Who is the man who said to you, 'Take up your mat and walk'?"

₁₃ But he who was healed didn't know who it was, for Jesus had withdrawn, a crowd being in the place.

₁₄ Afterward Jesus found him in the temple and said to him, "Behold, you are made well. Sin no more, so that nothing worse happens to you."

₁₅ The man went away, and told the Jews that it was Jesus who had made him well. ₁₆ For this cause the Jews persecuted Jesus and sought to kill him, because he did these things on the Sabbath. ₁₇ But Jesus answered them, "My Father is still working, so I am working, too."

₁₈ For this cause therefore the Jews sought all the more to kill him, because he not only broke the Sabbath, but also called God his own Father, making himself equal with God. ₁₉ Jesus therefore answered them, "Most certainly, I tell you, the Son can do nothing of himself, but what he sees the Father doing. For whatever things he does, these the Son also does likewise. ₂₀ For the Father has affection for the Son, and shows him all things that he himself does. He will show him greater works than these, that you may marvel. ₂₁ For as the Father raises the dead and gives them life, even so the Son also gives life to whom he desires. ₂₂ For the Father judges no one, but he has given all judgement to the Son, ₂₃ that all may

---

[a] *3:16* The phrase "only born" is from the Greek word "μονογενη", which is sometimes translated "only begotten" or "one and only".
[b] *3:36* The same word can be translated "disobeys" or "disbelieves" in this context.
[c] *4:6* noon
[d] *4:25* "Messiah" (Hebrew) and "Christ" (Greek) both mean "Anointed One".
[e] *4:52* 1:00 p.m.
[f] *5:4* NU omits from "waiting" in verse 3 to the end of verse 4.

honour the Son, even as they honour the Father. He who doesn't honour the Son doesn't honour the Father who sent him.

24 "Most certainly I tell you, he who hears my word and believes him who sent me has eternal life, and doesn't come into judgement, but has passed out of death into life. 25 Most certainly I tell you, the hour comes, and now is, when the dead will hear the Son of God's voice; and those who hear will live. 26 For as the Father has life in himself, even so he gave to the Son also to have life in himself. 27 He also gave him authority to execute judgement, because he is a son of man. 28 Don't marvel at this, for the hour comes in which all who are in the tombs will hear his voice 29 and will come out; those who have done good, to the resurrection of life; and those who have done evil, to the resurrection of judgement. 30 I can of myself do nothing. As I hear, I judge; and my judgement is righteous, because I don't seek my own will, but the will of my Father who sent me.

31 "If I testify about myself, my witness is not valid. 32 It is another who testifies about me. I know that the testimony which he testifies about me is true. 33 You have sent to John, and he has testified to the truth. 34 But the testimony which I receive is not from man. However, I say these things that you may be saved. 35 He was the burning and shining lamp, and you were willing to rejoice for a while in his light. 36 But the testimony which I have is greater than that of John; for the works which the Father gave me to accomplish, the very works that I do, testify about me, that the Father has sent me. 37 The Father himself, who sent me, has testified about me. You have neither heard his voice at any time, nor seen his form. 38 You don't have his word living in you, because you don't believe him whom he sent.

39 "You search the Scriptures, because you think that in them you have eternal life; and these are they which testify about me. 40 Yet you will not come to me, that you may have life. 41 I don't receive glory from men. 42 But I know you, that you don't have God's love in yourselves. 43 I have come in my Father's name, and you don't receive me. If another comes in his own name, you will receive him. 44 How can you believe, who receive glory from one another, and you don't seek the glory that comes from the only God?

45 "Don't think that I will accuse you to the Father. There is one who accuses you, even Moses, on whom you have set your hope. 46 For if you believed Moses, you would believe me; for he wrote about me. 47 But if you don't believe his writings, how will you believe my words?"

6

1 After these things, Jesus went away to the other side of the sea of Galilee, which is also called the Sea of Tiberias. 2 A great multitude followed him, because they saw his signs which he did on those who were sick. 3 Jesus went up into the mountain, and he sat there with his disciples. 4 Now the Passover, the feast of the Jews, was at hand. 5 Jesus therefore, lifting up his eyes and seeing that a great multitude was coming to him, said to Philip, "Where are we to buy bread, that these may eat?" 6 He said this to test him, for he himself knew what he would do.

7 Philip answered him, "Two hundred denarii[a] worth of bread is not sufficient for them, that every one of them may receive a little."

8 One of his disciples, Andrew, Simon Peter's brother, said to him, 9 "There is a boy here who has five barley loaves and two fish, but what are these amongst so many?"

10 Jesus said, "Have the people sit down." Now there was much grass in that place. So the men sat down, in number about five thousand. 11 Jesus took the loaves, and having given thanks, he distributed to the disciples, and the disciples to those who were sitting down, likewise also of the fish as much as they desired. 12 When they were filled, he said to his disciples, "Gather up the broken pieces which are left over, that nothing be lost." 13 So they gathered them up, and filled twelve baskets with broken pieces from the five barley loaves, which were left over by those who had eaten. 14 When therefore the people saw the sign which Jesus did, they said, "This is truly the prophet who comes into the world." 15 Jesus therefore, perceiving that they were about to come and take him by force to make him king, withdrew again to the mountain by himself.

16 When evening came, his disciples went down to the sea. 17 They entered into the boat, and were going over the sea to Capernaum. It was now dark, and Jesus had not come to them. 18 The sea was tossed by a great wind blowing. 19 When therefore they had rowed about twenty-five or thirty stadia,[b] they saw Jesus walking on the sea* and drawing near to the boat; and they were afraid. 20 But he said to them, "It is I.[c] Don't be afraid." 21 They were willing therefore to receive him into the boat. Immediately the boat was at the land where they were going.

22 On the next day, the multitude that stood on the other side of the sea saw that there was no other boat there, except the one in which his disciples had embarked, and that Jesus hadn't entered with his disciples into the boat, but his disciples had gone away alone. 23 However, boats from Tiberias came near to the place where they ate the bread after the Lord had given thanks. 24 When the multitude therefore saw that Jesus wasn't there, nor his disciples, they themselves got into the boats and came to Capernaum, seeking Jesus. 25 When they found him on the other side of the sea, they asked him, "Rabbi, when did you come here?"

26 Jesus answered them, "Most certainly I tell you, you seek me, not because you saw signs, but because you ate of the loaves and were filled. 27 Don't work for the food which perishes, but for the food which remains to eternal life, which the Son of Man will give to you. For God the Father has sealed him."

28 They said therefore to him, "What must we do, that we may work the works of God?"

29 Jesus answered them, "This is the work of God, that you believe in him whom he has sent."

30 They said therefore to him, "What then do you do for a sign, that we may see and believe you? What work do you do? 31 Our fathers ate the manna in the wilderness. As it is written, 'He gave them bread out of heaven[d] to eat.'"

32 Jesus therefore said to them, "Most certainly, I tell you, it wasn't Moses who gave you the bread out of heaven, but my Father gives you the true bread out of heaven. 33 For the bread of God is that which comes down out of heaven and gives life to the world."

34 They said therefore to him, "Lord, always give us this bread."

35 Jesus said to them, "I am the bread of life. Whoever comes to me will not be hungry, and whoever believes in me will never be thirsty. 36 But I told you that you have seen me, and yet you don't believe. 37 All those whom the Father gives me will come to me. He who comes to me I will in no way throw out. 38 For I have come down from heaven, not to do my own will, but the will of him who sent me. 39 This is the will of my Father who sent me, that of all he has given to me I should lose nothing, but should raise him up at the last day. 40 This is the will of the one who sent me, that everyone who sees the Son and believes in him should have eternal life; and I will raise him up at the last day."

41 The Jews therefore murmured concerning him, because he said, "I am the bread which came down out of heaven." 42 They said, "Isn't this Jesus, the son of Joseph, whose father and mother we know? How then does he say, 'I have come down out of heaven'?"

43 Therefore Jesus answered them, "Don't murmur amongst yourselves. 44 No one can come to me unless the Father who sent me draws him; and I will raise him up in the last day. 45 It is written in the prophets, 'They will all be taught by God.' ' Therefore everyone who hears from the Father and has learnt, comes to me. 46 Not that anyone has seen the Father, except he who is from God. He has seen the Father. 47 Most certainly, I tell you, he who believes in me has eternal life. 48 I am the bread of life. 49 Your fathers ate the manna in the wilderness and they died. 50 This is the bread which comes down out of heaven, that anyone may eat of it and not die. 51 I am the living bread which came down out of heaven. If anyone eats of this bread, he will live forever. Yes, the bread which I will give for the life of the world is my flesh."

52 The Jews therefore contended with one another, saying, "How can this man give us his flesh to eat?"

53 Jesus therefore said to them, "Most certainly I tell you, unless you eat the flesh of the Son of Man and drink his blood, you don't have life in yourselves. 54 He who eats my flesh and drinks my blood has eternal life, and I will raise him up at the last day. 55 For my flesh is food indeed, and my blood is drink indeed. 56 He who eats my flesh and drinks my blood lives in me, and I in him. 57 As the living Father sent me, and I live because of the Father, so he who feeds on me will also live because of me. 58 This is the bread which came down out of heaven—not as our fathers ate the manna and died. He who eats this bread will live forever." 59 He said these things in the synagogue, as he taught in Capernaum.

60 Therefore many of his disciples, when they heard this, said, "This is a hard saying! Who can listen to it?"

61 But Jesus knowing in himself that his disciples murmured at this, said to them, "Does this cause you to stumble? 62 Then what if you would see the Son of Man ascending to where he was before? 63 It is the spirit who gives life. The flesh profits nothing. The words that I speak to you are spirit, and are life. 64 But there are some of you who don't believe." For Jesus knew from the beginning who they were who didn't believe, and who it was who would betray him. 65 He said, "For this cause I have said to you that no one can come to me, unless it is given to him by my Father."

66 At this, many of his disciples went back and walked no more with him. 67 Jesus said therefore to the twelve, "You don't also want to go away, do you?"

68 Simon Peter answered him, "Lord, to whom would we go? You have the words of eternal life. 69 We have come to believe and know that you are the Christ, the Son of the living God."

70 Jesus answered them, "Didn't I choose you, the twelve, and one of you is a devil?" 71 Now he spoke of Judas, the son of Simon Iscariot, for it was he who would betray him, being one of the twelve.

7

1 After these things, Jesus was walking in Galilee, for he wouldn't walk in Judea, because the Jews sought to kill him. 2 Now the feast of the Jews, the Feast of Booths, was at hand. 3 His brothers therefore said to him, "Depart from here and go into Judea, that your disciples also may see your works which you do. 4 For no one does anything in secret while he

---

a 6:7 A denarius was a silver coin worth about a day's wages for an agricultural labourer, so 200 denarii would be between 6 and 7 month's pay.
b 6:19 25 to 30 stadia is about 5 to 6 kilometres or about 3 to 4 miles
** 6:19 See Job 9:8
c 6:20 or, I AM

d 6:31 Greek and Hebrew use the same word for "heaven", "the heavens", "the sky", and "the air".
** 6:31 Exodus 16:4; Nehemiah 9:15; Psalms 78:24-25
** 6:45 Isaiah 54:13

seeks to be known openly. If you do these things, reveal yourself to the world." 5 For even his brothers didn't believe in him.

6 Jesus therefore said to them, "My time has not yet come, but your time is always ready. 7 The world can't hate you, but it hates me, because I testify about it, that its works are evil. 8 You go up to the feast. I am not yet going up to this feast, because my time is not yet fulfilled."

9 Having said these things to them, he stayed in Galilee. 10 But when his brothers had gone up to the feast, then he also went up, not publicly, but as it were in secret. 11 The Jews therefore sought him at the feast, and said, "Where is he?" 12 There was much murmuring amongst the multitudes concerning him. Some said, "He is a good man." Others said, "Not so, but he leads the multitude astray." 13 Yet no one spoke openly of him for fear of the Jews. 14 But when it was now the middle of the feast, Jesus went up into the temple and taught. 15 The Jews therefore marvelled, saying, "How does this man know letters, having never been educated?"

16 Jesus therefore answered them, "My teaching is not mine, but his who sent me. 17 If anyone desires to do his will, he will know about the teaching, whether it is from God or if I am speaking from myself. 18 He who speaks from himself seeks his own glory, but he who seeks the glory of him who sent him is true, and no unrighteousness is in him. 19 Didn't Moses give you the law, and yet none of you keeps the law? Why do you seek to kill me?"

20 The multitude answered, "You have a demon! Who seeks to kill you?"

21 Jesus answered them, "I did one work and you all marvel because of it. 22 Moses has given you circumcision (not that it is of Moses, but of the fathers), and on the Sabbath you circumcise a boy. 23 If a boy receives circumcision on the Sabbath, that the law of Moses may not be broken, are you angry with me because I made a man completely healthy on the Sabbath? 24 Don't judge according to appearance, but judge righteous judgement."

25 Therefore some of them of Jerusalem said, "Isn't this he whom they seek to kill? 26 Behold, he speaks openly, and they say nothing to him. Can it be that the rulers indeed know that this is truly the Christ? 27 However, we know where this man comes from, but when the Christ comes, no one will know where he comes from."

28 Jesus therefore cried out in the temple, teaching and saying, "You both know me, and know where I am from. I have not come of myself, but he who sent me is true, whom you don't know. 29 I know him, because I am from him, and he sent me."

30 They sought therefore to take him; but no one laid a hand on him, because his hour had not yet come. 31 But of the multitude, many believed in him. They said, "When the Christ comes, he won't do more signs than those which this man has done, will he?" 32 The Pharisees heard the multitude murmuring these things concerning him, and the chief priests and the Pharisees sent officers to arrest him.

33 Then Jesus said, "I will be with you a little while longer, then I go to him who sent me. 34 You will seek me and won't find me. You can't come where I am."

35 The Jews therefore said amongst themselves, "Where will this man go that we won't find him? Will he go to the Dispersion amongst the Greeks and teach the Greeks? 36 What is this word that he said, 'You will seek me, and won't find me;' and 'Where I am, you can't come'?"

37 Now on the last and greatest day of the feast, Jesus stood and cried out, "If anyone is thirsty, let him come to me and drink! 38 He who believes in me, as the Scripture has said, from within him will flow rivers of living water." 39 But he said this about the Spirit, which those believing in him were to receive. For the Holy Spirit was not yet given, because Jesus wasn't yet glorified.

40 Many of the multitude therefore, when they heard these words, said, "This is truly the prophet." 41 Others said, "This is the Christ." But some said, "What, does the Christ come out of Galilee? 42 Hasn't the Scripture said that the Christ comes of the offspring[a] of David, ' and from Bethlehem, ' the village where David was?" 43 So a division arose in the multitude because of him. 44 Some of them would have arrested him, but no one laid hands on him. 45 The officers therefore came to the chief priests and Pharisees; and they said to them, "Why didn't you bring him?"

46 The officers answered, "No man ever spoke like this man!"

47 The Pharisees therefore answered them, "You aren't also led astray, are you? 48 Have any of the rulers or any of the Pharisees believed in him? 49 But this multitude that doesn't know the law is cursed."

50 Nicodemus (he who came to him by night, being one of them) said to them, 51 "Does our law judge a man unless it first hears from him personally and knows what he does?"

52 They answered him, "Are you also from Galilee? Search and see that no prophet has arisen out of Galilee." '

53 Everyone went to his own house,

8

1 but Jesus went to the Mount of Olives.

2 Now very early in the morning, he came again into the temple, and all the people came to him. He sat down and taught them. 3 The scribes and

the Pharisees brought a woman taken in adultery. Having set her in the middle, 4 they told him, "Teacher, we found this woman in adultery, in the very act. 5 Now in our law, Moses commanded us to stone such women.' What then do you say about her?" 6 They said this testing him, that they might have something to accuse him of.

But Jesus stooped down and wrote on the ground with his finger. 7 But when they continued asking him, he looked up and said to them, "He who is without sin amongst you, let him throw the first stone at her." 8 Again he stooped down and wrote on the ground with his finger.

9 They, when they heard it, being convicted by their conscience, went out one by one, beginning from the oldest, even to the last. Jesus was left alone with the woman where she was, in the middle. 10 Jesus, standing up, saw her and said, "Woman, where are your accusers? Did no one condemn you?"

11 She said, "No one, Lord."

Jesus said, "Neither do I condemn you. Go your way. From now on, sin no more."[b]

12 Again, therefore, Jesus spoke to them, saying, "I am the light of the world.' He who follows me will not walk in the darkness, but will have the light of life."

13 The Pharisees therefore said to him, "You testify about yourself. Your testimony is not valid."

14 Jesus answered them, "Even if I testify about myself, my testimony is true, for I know where I came from, and where I am going; but you don't know where I came from, or where I am going. 15 You judge according to the flesh. I judge no one. 16 Even if I do judge, my judgement is true, for I am not alone, but I am with the Father who sent me. 17 It's also written in your law that the testimony of two people is valid.' 18 I am one who testifies about myself, and the Father who sent me testifies about me."

19 They said therefore to him, "Where is your Father?"

Jesus answered, "You know neither me nor my Father. If you knew me, you would know my Father also." 20 Jesus spoke these words in the treasury, as he taught in the temple. Yet no one arrested him, because his hour had not yet come. 21 Jesus said therefore again to them, "I am going away, and you will seek me, and you will die in your sins. Where I go, you can't come."

22 The Jews therefore said, "Will he kill himself, because he says, 'Where I am going, you can't come'?"

23 He said to them, "You are from beneath. I am from above. You are of this world. I am not of this world. 24 I said therefore to you that you will die in your sins; for unless you believe that I am[c] he, you will die in your sins."

25 They said therefore to him, "Who are you?"

Jesus said to them, "Just what I have been saying to you from the beginning. 26 I have many things to speak and to judge concerning you. However, he who sent me is true; and the things which I heard from him, these I say to the world."

27 They didn't understand that he spoke to them about the Father. 28 Jesus therefore said to them, "When you have lifted up the Son of Man, then you will know that I am he, and I do nothing of myself, but as my Father taught me, I say these things. 29 He who sent me is with me. The Father hasn't left me alone, for I always do the things that are pleasing to him."

30 As he spoke these things, many believed in him. 31 Jesus therefore said to those Jews who had believed him, "If you remain in my word, then you are truly my disciples. 32 You will know the truth, and the truth will make you free." '

33 They answered him, "We are Abraham's offspring, and have never been in bondage to anyone. How do you say, 'You will be made free'?"

34 Jesus answered them, "Most certainly I tell you, everyone who commits sin is the bondservant of sin. 35 A bondservant doesn't live in the house forever. A son remains forever. 36 If therefore the Son makes you free, you will be free indeed. 37 I know that you are Abraham's offspring, yet you seek to kill me, because my word finds no place in you. 38 I say the things which I have seen with my Father; and you also do the things which you have seen with your father."

39 They answered him, "Our father is Abraham."

Jesus said to them, "If you were Abraham's children, you would do the works of Abraham. 40 But now you seek to kill me, a man who has told you the truth which I heard from God. Abraham didn't do this. 41 You do the works of your father."

They said to him, "We were not born of sexual immorality. We have one Father, God."

42 Therefore Jesus said to them, "If God were your father, you would love me, for I came out and have come from God. For I haven't come of myself, but he sent me. 43 Why don't you understand my speech? Because you can't hear my word. 44 You are of your father the devil, and you want to do the desires of your father. He was a murderer from the beginning, and doesn't stand in the truth, because there is no truth in him. When he speaks a lie, he speaks on his own; for he is a liar, and the father of lies. 45 But because I tell the truth, you don't believe me. 46 Which of you convicts me of sin? If I tell the truth, why do you not believe me? 47 He who is of God

---

a 7:42 or, seed
** 7:42 2 Samuel 7:12
** 7:42 Micah 5:2
** 7:52 See Isaiah 9:1; Matthew 4:13-16
** 8:5 Leviticus 20:10; Deuteronomy 22:22

b 8:11 NU includes John 7:53–John 8:11, but puts brackets around it to indicate that the textual critics had less confidence that this was original.
** 8:12 Isaiah 60:1
** 8:17 Deuteronomy 17:6; 19:15
c 8:24 or, I AM
** 8:32 Psalms 119:45

hears the words of God. For this cause you don't hear, because you are not of God."

48 Then the Jews answered him, "Don't we say well that you are a Samaritan, and have a demon?"

49 Jesus answered, "I don't have a demon, but I honour my Father and you dishonour me. 50 But I don't seek my own glory. There is one who seeks and judges. 51 Most certainly, I tell you, if a person keeps my word, he will never see death."

52 Then the Jews said to him, "Now we know that you have a demon. Abraham died, as did the prophets; and you say, 'If a man keeps my word, he will never taste of death.' 53 Are you greater than our father Abraham, who died? The prophets died. Who do you make yourself out to be?"

54 Jesus answered, "If I glorify myself, my glory is nothing. It is my Father who glorifies me, of whom you say that he is our God. 55 You have not known him, but I know him. If I said, 'I don't know him,' I would be like you, a liar. But I know him and keep his word. 56 Your father Abraham rejoiced to see my day. He saw it and was glad."

57 The Jews therefore said to him, "You are not yet fifty years old! Have you seen Abraham?"

58 Jesus said to them, "Most certainly, I tell you, before Abraham came into existence, I AM.''"

59 Therefore they took up stones to throw at him, but Jesus hid himself and went out of the temple, having gone through the middle of them, and so passed by.

9

1 As he passed by, he saw a man blind from birth. 2 His disciples asked him, "Rabbi, who sinned, this man or his parents, that he was born blind?"

3 Jesus answered, "This man didn't sin, nor did his parents, but that the works of God might be revealed in him. 4 I must work the works of him who sent me while it is day. The night is coming, when no one can work. 5 While I am in the world, I am the light of the world." 6 When he had said this, he spat on the ground, made mud with the saliva, anointed the blind man's eyes with the mud, 7 and said to him, "Go, wash in the pool of Siloam" (which means "Sent"). So he went away, washed, and came back seeing.

8 Therefore the neighbours and those who saw that he was blind before said, "Isn't this he who sat and begged?" 9 Others were saying, "It is he." Still others were saying, "He looks like him."

He said, "I am he."

10 They therefore were asking him, "How were your eyes opened?"

11 He answered, "A man called Jesus made mud, anointed my eyes, and said to me, 'Go to the pool of Siloam and wash.' So I went away and washed, and I received sight."

12 Then they asked him, "Where is he?"

He said, "I don't know."

13 They brought him who had been blind to the Pharisees. 14 It was a Sabbath when Jesus made the mud and opened his eyes. 15 Again therefore the Pharisees also asked him how he received his sight. He said to them, "He put mud on my eyes, I washed, and I see."

16 Some therefore of the Pharisees said, "This man is not from God, because he doesn't keep the Sabbath."

Others said, "How can a man who is a sinner do such signs?" So there was division amongst them.

17 Therefore they asked the blind man again, "What do you say about him, because he opened your eyes?"

He said, "He is a prophet."

18 The Jews therefore didn't believe concerning him, that he had been blind and had received his sight, until they called the parents of him who had received his sight, 19 and asked them, "Is this your son, whom you say was born blind? How then does he now see?"

20 His parents answered them, "We know that this is our son, and that he was born blind; 21 but how he now sees, we don't know; or who opened his eyes, we don't know. He is of age. Ask him. He will speak for himself." 22 His parents said these things because they feared the Jews; for the Jews had already agreed that if any man would confess him as Christ, he would be put out of the synagogue. 23 Therefore his parents said, "He is of age. Ask him."

24 So they called the man who was blind a second time, and said to him, "Give glory to God. We know that this man is a sinner."

25 He therefore answered, "I don't know if he is a sinner. One thing I do know: that though I was blind, now I see."

26 They said to him again, "What did he do to you? How did he open your eyes?"

27 He answered them, "I told you already, and you didn't listen. Why do you want to hear it again? You don't also want to become his disciples, do you?"

28 They insulted him and said, "You are his disciple, but we are disciples of Moses. 29 We know that God has spoken to Moses. But as for this man, we don't know where he comes from."

30 The man answered them, "How amazing! You don't know where he comes from, yet he opened my eyes. 31 We know that God doesn't listen to

sinners, but if anyone is a worshipper of God and does his will, he listens to him.' 32 Since the world began it has never been heard of that anyone opened the eyes of someone born blind. 33 If this man were not from God, he could do nothing."

34 They answered him, "You were altogether born in sins, and do you teach us?" Then they threw him out.

35 Jesus heard that they had thrown him out, and finding him, he said, "Do you believe in the Son of God?"

36 He answered, "Who is he, Lord, that I may believe in him?"

37 Jesus said to him, "You have both seen him, and it is he who speaks with you."

38 He said, "Lord, I believe!" and he worshipped him.

39 Jesus said, "I came into this world for judgement, that those who don't see may see; and that those who see may become blind."

40 Those of the Pharisees who were with him heard these things, and said to him, "Are we also blind?"

41 Jesus said to them, "If you were blind, you would have no sin; but now you say, 'We see.' Therefore your sin remains.

10

1 "Most certainly, I tell you, one who doesn't enter by the door into the sheep fold, but climbs up some other way, is a thief and a robber. 2 But one who enters in by the door is the shepherd of the sheep. 3 The gatekeeper opens the gate for him, and the sheep listen to his voice. He calls his own sheep by name and leads them out. 4 Whenever he brings out his own sheep, he goes before them; and the sheep follow him, for they know his voice. 5 They will by no means follow a stranger, but will flee from him; for they don't know the voice of strangers." 6 Jesus spoke this parable to them, but they didn't understand what he was telling them.

7 Jesus therefore said to them again, "Most certainly, I tell you, I am the sheep's door. 8 All who came before me are thieves and robbers, but the sheep didn't listen to them. 9 I am the door. If anyone enters in by me, he will be saved, and will go in and go out and will find pasture. 10 The thief only comes to steal, kill, and destroy. I came that they may have life, and may have it abundantly.

11 "I am the good shepherd.' The good shepherd lays down his life for the sheep. 12 He who is a hired hand, and not a shepherd, who doesn't own the sheep, sees the wolf coming, leaves the sheep, and flees. The wolf snatches the sheep and scatters them. 13 The hired hand flees because he is a hired hand and doesn't care for the sheep. 14 I am the good shepherd. I know my own, and I'm known by my own; 15 even as the Father knows me, and I know the Father. I lay down my life for the sheep. 16 I have other sheep which are not of this fold.' I must bring them also, and they will hear my voice. They will become one flock with one shepherd. 17 Therefore the Father loves me, because I lay down my life, ' that I may take it again. 18 No one takes it away from me, but I lay it down by myself. I have power to lay it down, and I have power to take it again. I received this commandment from my Father."

19 Therefore a division arose again amongst the Jews because of these words. 20 Many of them said, "He has a demon and is insane! Why do you listen to him?" 21 Others said, "These are not the sayings of one possessed by a demon. It isn't possible for a demon to open the eyes of the blind, is it?"

22 It was the Feast of the Dedication[a] at Jerusalem. 23 It was winter, and Jesus was walking in the temple, in Solomon's porch. 24 The Jews therefore came around him and said to him, "How long will you hold us in suspense? If you are the Christ, tell us plainly."

25 Jesus answered them, "I told you, and you don't believe. The works that I do in my Father's name, these testify about me. 26 But you don't believe, because you are not of my sheep, as I told you. 27 My sheep hear my voice, and I know them, and they follow me. 28 I give eternal life to them. They will never perish, and no one will snatch them out of my hand. 29 My Father who has given them to me is greater than all. No one is able to snatch them out of my Father's hand. 30 I and the Father are one."

31 Therefore the Jews took up stones again to stone him. 32 Jesus answered them, "I have shown you many good works from my Father. For which of those works do you stone me?"

33 The Jews answered him, "We don't stone you for a good work, but for blasphemy, because you, being a man, make yourself God."

34 Jesus answered them, "Isn't it written in your law, 'I said, you are gods'?' 35 If he called them gods, to whom the word of God came (and the Scripture can't be broken), 36 do you say of him whom the Father sanctified and sent into the world, 'You blaspheme,' because I said, 'I am the Son of God'? 37 If I don't do the works of my Father, don't believe me. 38 But if I do them, though you don't believe me, believe the works, that you may know and believe that the Father is in me, and I in the Father."

39 They sought again to seize him, and he went out of their hand. 40 He went away beyond the Jordan into the place where John was baptising at first, and he stayed there. 41 Many came to him. They said, "John indeed did no sign, but everything that John said about this man is true." 42 Many believed in him there.

** 8:58 Exodus 3:14
** 9:31 Psalms 66:18; Proverbs 15:29; 28:9
** 10:11 Isaiah 40:11; Ezekiel 34:11-12,15,22
** 10:16 Isaiah 56:8
** 10:17 Isaiah 53:7-8

** 10:21 Exodus 4:11
a 10:22 The "Feast of the Dedication" is the Greek name for "Hanukkah", a celebration of the rededication of the Temple.
** 10:34 Psalms 82:6

11

1 Now a certain man was sick, Lazarus from Bethany, of the village of Mary and her sister, Martha. 2 It was that Mary who had anointed the Lord with ointment and wiped his feet with her hair, whose brother Lazarus was sick. 3 The sisters therefore sent to him, saying, "Lord, behold, he for whom you have great affection is sick."

4 But when Jesus heard it, he said, "This sickness is not to death, but for the glory of God, that God's Son may be glorified by it." 5 Now Jesus loved Martha, and her sister, and Lazarus. 6 When therefore he heard that he was sick, he stayed two days in the place where he was. 7 Then after this he said to the disciples, "Let's go into Judea again."

8 The disciples asked him, "Rabbi, the Jews were just trying to stone you. Are you going there again?"

9 Jesus answered, "Aren't there twelve hours of daylight? If a man walks in the day, he doesn't stumble, because he sees the light of this world. 10 But if a man walks in the night, he stumbles, because the light isn't in him." 11 He said these things, and after that, he said to them, "Our friend Lazarus has fallen asleep, but I am going so that I may awake him out of sleep."

12 The disciples therefore said, "Lord, if he has fallen asleep, he will recover."

13 Now Jesus had spoken of his death, but they thought that he spoke of taking rest in sleep. 14 So Jesus said to them plainly then, "Lazarus is dead. 15 I am glad for your sakes that I was not there, so that you may believe. Nevertheless, let's go to him."

16 Thomas therefore, who is called Didymus,[a] said to his fellow disciples, "Let's also go, that we may die with him."

17 So when Jesus came, he found that he had been in the tomb four days already. 18 Now Bethany was near Jerusalem, about fifteen stadia[b] away. 19 Many of the Jews had joined the women around Martha and Mary, to console them concerning their brother. 20 Then when Martha heard that Jesus was coming, she went and met him, but Mary stayed in the house. 21 Therefore Martha said to Jesus, "Lord, if you would have been here, my brother wouldn't have died. 22 Even now I know that whatever you ask of God, God will give you."

23 Jesus said to her, "Your brother will rise again."

24 Martha said to him, "I know that he will rise again in the resurrection at the last day."

25 Jesus said to her, "I am the resurrection and the life. He who believes in me will still live, even if he dies. 26 Whoever lives and believes in me will never die. Do you believe this?"

27 She said to him, "Yes, Lord. I have come to believe that you are the Christ, God's Son, he who comes into the world."

28 When she had said this, she went away and called Mary, her sister, secretly, saying, "The Teacher is here and is calling you."

29 When she heard this, she arose quickly and went to him. 30 Now Jesus had not yet come into the village, but was in the place where Martha met him. 31 Then the Jews who were with her in the house and were consoling her, when they saw Mary, that she rose up quickly and went out, followed her, saying, "She is going to the tomb to weep there."

32 Therefore when Mary came to where Jesus was and saw him, she fell down at his feet, saying to him, "Lord, if you would have been here, my brother wouldn't have died."

33 When Jesus therefore saw her weeping, and the Jews weeping who came with her, he groaned in the spirit and was troubled, 34 and said, "Where have you laid him?"

They told him, "Lord, come and see."

35 Jesus wept.

36 The Jews therefore said, "See how much affection he had for him!" 37 Some of them said, "Couldn't this man, who opened the eyes of him who was blind, have also kept this man from dying?"

38 Jesus therefore, again groaning in himself, came to the tomb. Now it was a cave, and a stone lay against it. 39 Jesus said, "Take away the stone."

Martha, the sister of him who was dead, said to him, "Lord, by this time there is a stench, for he has been dead four days."

40 Jesus said to her, "Didn't I tell you that if you believed, you would see God's glory?"

41 So they took away the stone from the place where the dead man was lying.[c] Jesus lifted up his eyes and said, "Father, I thank you that you listened to me. 42 I know that you always listen to me, but because of the multitude standing around I said this, that they may believe that you sent me." 43 When he had said this, he cried with a loud voice, "Lazarus, come out!"

44 He who was dead came out, bound hand and foot with wrappings, and his face was wrapped around with a cloth.

Jesus said to them, "Free him, and let him go."

45 Therefore many of the Jews who came to Mary and saw what Jesus did believed in him. 46 But some of them went away to the Pharisees and told them the things which Jesus had done. 47 The chief priests therefore and the Pharisees gathered a council, and said, "What are we doing? For this man does many signs. 48 If we leave him alone like this, everyone will

believe in him, and the Romans will come and take away both our place and our nation."

49 But a certain one of them, Caiaphas, being high priest that year, said to them, "You know nothing at all, 50 nor do you consider that it is advantageous for us that one man should die for the people, and that the whole nation not perish." 51 Now he didn't say this of himself, but being high priest that year, he prophesied that Jesus would die for the nation, 52 and not for the nation only, but that he might also gather together into one the children of God who are scattered abroad. 53 So from that day forward they took counsel that they might put him to death. 54 Jesus therefore walked no more openly amongst the Jews, but departed from there into the country near the wilderness, to a city called Ephraim. He stayed there with his disciples.

55 Now the Passover of the Jews was at hand. Many went up from the country to Jerusalem before the Passover, to purify themselves. 56 Then they sought for Jesus and spoke with one another as they stood in the temple, "What do you think—that he isn't coming to the feast at all?" 57 Now the chief priests and the Pharisees had commanded that if anyone knew where he was, he should report it, that they might seize him.

12

1 Then, six days before the Passover, Jesus came to Bethany, where Lazarus was, who had been dead, whom he raised from the dead. 2 So they made him a supper there. Martha served, but Lazarus was one of those who sat at the table with him. 3 Therefore Mary took a pound[d] of ointment of pure nard, very precious, and anointed Jesus' feet and wiped his feet with her hair. The house was filled with the fragrance of the ointment.

4 Then Judas Iscariot, Simon's son, one of his disciples, who would betray him, said, 5 "Why wasn't this ointment sold for three hundred denarii[e] and given to the poor?" 6 Now he said this, not because he cared for the poor, but because he was a thief, and having the money box, used to steal what was put into it.

7 But Jesus said, "Leave her alone. She has kept this for the day of my burial. 8 For you always have the poor with you, but you don't always have me."

9 A large crowd therefore of the Jews learnt that he was there; and they came, not for Jesus' sake only, but that they might see Lazarus also, whom he had raised from the dead. 10 But the chief priests conspired to put Lazarus to death also, 11 because on account of him many of the Jews went away and believed in Jesus.

12 On the next day a great multitude had come to the feast. When they heard that Jesus was coming to Jerusalem, 13 they took the branches of the palm trees and went out to meet him, and cried out, "Hosanna![f] Blessed is he who comes in the name of the Lord,* the King of Israel!"

14 Jesus, having found a young donkey, sat on it. As it is written, 15 "Don't be afraid, daughter of Zion. Behold, your King comes, sitting on a donkey's colt."* 16 His disciples didn't understand these things at first, but when Jesus was glorified, then they remembered that these things were written about him, and that they had done these things to him. 17 The multitude therefore that was with him when he called Lazarus out of the tomb and raised him from the dead was testifying about it. 18 For this cause also the multitude went and met him, because they heard that he had done this sign. 19 The Pharisees therefore said amongst themselves, "See how you accomplish nothing. Behold, the world has gone after him."

20 Now there were certain Greeks amongst those who went up to worship at the feast. 21 Therefore, these came to Philip, who was from Bethsaida of Galilee, and asked him, saying, "Sir, we want to see Jesus." 22 Philip came and told Andrew, and in turn, Andrew came with Philip, and they told Jesus.

23 Jesus answered them, "The time has come for the Son of Man to be glorified. 24 Most certainly I tell you, unless a grain of wheat falls into the earth and dies, it remains by itself alone. But if it dies, it bears much fruit. 25 He who loves his life will lose it. He who hates his life in this world will keep it to eternal life. 26 If anyone serves me, let him follow me. Where I am, there my servant will also be. If anyone serves me, the Father will honour him.

27 "Now my soul is troubled. What shall I say? 'Father, save me from this time'? But I came to this time for this cause. 28 Father, glorify your name!"

Then a voice came out of the sky, saying, "I have both glorified it and will glorify it again."

29 Therefore the multitude who stood by and heard it said that it had thundered. Others said, "An angel has spoken to him."

30 Jesus answered, "This voice hasn't come for my sake, but for your sakes. 31 Now is the judgement of this world. Now the prince of this world will be cast out. 32 And I, if I am lifted up from the earth, will draw all people to myself." 33 But he said this, signifying by what kind of death he should die.

34 The multitude answered him, "We have heard out of the law that the Christ remains forever.* How do you say, 'The Son of Man must be lifted up'? Who is this Son of Man?"

35 Jesus therefore said to them, "Yet a little while the light is with you. Walk while you have the light, that darkness doesn't overtake you. He who

---

a 11:16 "Didymus" means "Twin".
b 11:18 15 stadia is about 2.8 kilometres or 1.7 miles
c 11:41 NU omits "from the place where the dead man was lying."
d 12:3 a Roman pound of 12 ounces, or about 340 grams
e 12:5 300 denarii was about a year's wages for an agricultural labourer.

f 12:13 "Hosanna" means "save us" or "help us, we pray".
** 12:13 Psalms 118:25-26
** 12:15 Zechariah 9:9
** 12:34 Isaiah 9:7; Daniel 2:44; See Isaiah 53:8

walks in the darkness doesn't know where he is going. ₃₆ While you have the light, believe in the light, that you may become children of light." Jesus said these things, and he departed and hid himself from them. ₃₇ But though he had done so many signs before them, yet they didn't believe in him, ₃₈ that the word of Isaiah the prophet might be fulfilled, which he spoke:

"Lord, who has believed our report?
　　To whom has the arm of the Lord been revealed?"*

₃₉ For this cause they couldn't believe, for Isaiah said again:

₄₀ "He has blinded their eyes and he hardened their heart,
　　lest they should see with their eyes,
　　and perceive with their heart,
　　and would turn,
　　and I would heal them."*

₄₁ Isaiah said these things when he saw his glory, and spoke of him. ` ₄₂ Nevertheless, even many of the rulers believed in him, but because of the Pharisees they didn't confess it, so that they wouldn't be put out of the synagogue, ₄₃ for they loved men's praise more than God's praise.

₄₄ Jesus cried out and said, "Whoever believes in me, believes not in me, but in him who sent me. ₄₅ He who sees me sees him who sent me. ₄₆ I have come as a light into the world, that whoever believes in me may not remain in the darkness. ₄₇ If anyone listens to my sayings and doesn't believe, I don't judge him. For I came not to judge the world, but to save the world. ₄₈ He who rejects me, and doesn't receive my sayings, has one who judges him. The word that I spoke will judge him in the last day. ₄₉ For I spoke not from myself, but the Father who sent me gave me a commandment, what I should say and what I should speak. ₅₀ I know that his commandment is eternal life. The things therefore which I speak, even as the Father has said to me, so I speak."

13

₁ Now before the feast of the Passover, Jesus, knowing that his time had come that he would depart from this world to the Father, having loved his own who were in the world, he loved them to the end. ₂ During supper, the devil having already put into the heart of Judas Iscariot, Simon's son, to betray him, ₃ Jesus, knowing that the Father had given all things into his hands, and that he came from God and was going to God, ₄ arose from supper, and laid aside his outer garments. He took a towel and wrapped a towel around his waist. ₅ Then he poured water into the basin, and began to wash the disciples' feet and to wipe them with the towel that was wrapped around him. ₆ Then he came to Simon Peter. He said to him, "Lord, do you wash my feet?"

₇ Jesus answered him, "You don't know what I am doing now, but you will understand later."

₈ Peter said to him, "You will never wash my feet!"

Jesus answered him, "If I don't wash you, you have no part with me."

₉ Simon Peter said to him, "Lord, not my feet only, but also my hands and my head!"

₁₀ Jesus said to him, "Someone who has bathed only needs to have his feet washed, but is completely clean. You are clean, but not all of you." ₁₁ For he knew him who would betray him; therefore he said, "You are not all clean." ₁₂ So when he had washed their feet, put his outer garment back on, and sat down again, he said to them, "Do you know what I have done to you? ₁₃ You call me, 'Teacher' and 'Lord.' You say so correctly, for so I am. ₁₄ If I then, the Lord and the Teacher, have washed your feet, you also ought to wash one another's feet. ₁₅ For I have given you an example, that you should also do as I have done to you. ₁₆ Most certainly I tell you, a servant is not greater than his lord, neither is one who is sent greater than he who sent him. ₁₇ If you know these things, blessed are you if you do them. ₁₈ I don't speak concerning all of you. I know whom I have chosen; but that the Scripture may be fulfilled, 'He who eats bread with me has lifted up his heel against me.'* ₁₉ From now on, I tell you before it happens, that when it happens, you may believe that I am he. ₂₀ Most certainly I tell you, he who receives whomever I send, receives me; and he who receives me, receives him who sent me."

₂₁ When Jesus had said this, he was troubled in spirit, and testified, "Most certainly I tell you that one of you will betray me."

₂₂ The disciples looked at one another, perplexed about whom he spoke. ₂₃ One of his disciples, whom Jesus loved, was at the table, leaning against Jesus' breast. ₂₄ Simon Peter therefore beckoned to him, and said to him, "Tell us who it is of whom he speaks."

₂₅ He, leaning back, as he was, on Jesus' breast, asked him, "Lord, who is it?"

₂₆ Jesus therefore answered, "It is he to whom I will give this piece of bread when I have dipped it." So when he had dipped the piece of bread, he gave it to Judas, the son of Simon Iscariot. ₂₇ After the piece of bread, then Satan entered into him.

Then Jesus said to him, "What you do, do quickly."

₂₈ Now nobody at the table knew why he said this to him. ₂₉ For some thought, because Judas had the money box, that Jesus said to him, "Buy what things we need for the feast," or that he should give something to the poor. ₃₀ Therefore having received that morsel, he went out immediately. It was night.

₃₁ When he had gone out, Jesus said, "Now the Son of Man has been glorified, and God has been glorified in him. ₃₂ If God has been glorified in him, God will also glorify him in himself, and he will glorify him immediately. ₃₃ Little children, I will be with you a little while longer. You will seek me, and as I said to the Jews, 'Where I am going, you can't come,' so now I tell you. ₃₄ A new commandment I give to you, that you love one another. Just as I have loved you, you also love one another. ₃₅ By this everyone will know that you are my disciples, if you have love for one another."

₃₆ Simon Peter said to him, "Lord, where are you going?"

Jesus answered, "Where I am going, you can't follow now, but you will follow afterwards."

₃₇ Peter said to him, "Lord, why can't I follow you now? I will lay down my life for you."

₃₈ Jesus answered him, "Will you lay down your life for me? Most certainly I tell you, the rooster won't crow until you have denied me three times.

14

₁ "Don't let your heart be troubled. Believe in God. Believe also in me. ₂ In my Father's house are many homes. If it weren't so, I would have told you. I am going to prepare a place for you. ₃ If I go and prepare a place for you, I will come again and will receive you to myself; that where I am, you may be there also. ₄ You know where I go, and you know the way."

₅ Thomas said to him, "Lord, we don't know where you are going. How can we know the way?"

₆ Jesus said to him, "I am the way, the truth, and the life. No one comes to the Father, except through me. ₇ If you had known me, you would have known my Father also. From now on, you know him and have seen him."

₈ Philip said to him, "Lord, show us the Father, and that will be enough for us."

₉ Jesus said to him, "Have I been with you such a long time, and do you not know me, Philip? He who has seen me has seen the Father. How do you say, 'Show us the Father'? ₁₀ Don't you believe that I am in the Father, and the Father in me? The words that I tell you, I speak not from myself; but the Father who lives in me does his works. ₁₁ Believe me that I am in the Father, and the Father in me; or else believe me for the very works' sake. ₁₂ Most certainly I tell you, he who believes in me, the works that I do, he will do also; and he will do greater works than these, because I am going to my Father. ₁₃ Whatever you will ask in my name, I will do it, that the Father may be glorified in the Son. ₁₄ If you will ask anything in my name, I will do it. ₁₅ If you love me, keep my commandments. ₁₆ I will pray to the Father, and he will give you another Counsellor, ᵃ that he may be with you forever: ₁₇ the Spirit of truth, whom the world can't receive, for it doesn't see him and doesn't know him. You know him, for he lives with you and will be in you. ₁₈ I will not leave you orphans. I will come to you. ₁₉ Yet a little while, and the world will see me no more; but you will see me. Because I live, you will live also. ₂₀ In that day you will know that I am in my Father, and you in me, and I in you. ₂₁ One who has my commandments and keeps them, that person is one who loves me. One who loves me will be loved by my Father, and I will love him, and will reveal myself to him."

₂₂ Judas (not Iscariot) said to him, "Lord, what has happened that you are about to reveal yourself to us, and not to the world?"

₂₃ Jesus answered him, "If a man loves me, he will keep my word. My Father will love him, and we will come to him and make our home with him. ₂₄ He who doesn't love me doesn't keep my words. The word which you hear isn't mine, but the Father's who sent me.

₂₅ "I have said these things to you while still living with you. ₂₆ But the Counsellor, the Holy Spirit, whom the Father will send in my name, will teach you all things, and will remind you of all that I said to you. ₂₇ Peace I leave with you. My peace I give to you; not as the world gives, I give to you. Don't let your heart be troubled, neither let it be fearful. ₂₈ You heard how I told you, 'I am going away, and I will come back to you.' If you loved me, you would have rejoiced because I said 'I am going to my Father;' for the Father is greater than I. ₂₉ Now I have told you before it happens so that when it happens, you may believe. ₃₀ I will no more speak much with you, for the prince of the world comes, and he has nothing in me. ₃₁ But that the world may know that I love the Father, and as the Father commanded me, even so I do. Arise, let's go from here.

15

₁ "I am the true vine, and my Father is the farmer. ₂ Every branch in me that doesn't bear fruit, he takes away. Every branch that bears fruit, he prunes, that it may bear more fruit. ₃ You are already pruned clean because of the word which I have spoken to you. ₄ Remain in me, and I in you. As the branch can't bear fruit by itself unless it remains in the vine, so neither can you, unless you remain in me. ₅ I am the vine. You are the branches. He who remains in me and I in him bears much fruit, for apart from me you can do nothing. ₆ If a man doesn't remain in me, he is thrown out as a branch and is withered; and they gather them, throw them into the fire, and they are burnt. ₇ If you remain in me, and my words remain in you, you will ask whatever you desire, and it will be done for you.

₈ "In this my Father is glorified, that you bear much fruit; and so you will be my disciples. ₉ Even as the Father has loved me, I also have loved you. Remain in my love. ₁₀ If you keep my commandments, you will remain in my love, even as I have kept my Father's commandments and remain in

---

** 12:38 Isaiah 53:1
** 12:40 Isaiah 6:10
** 12:41 Isaiah 6:1

** 13:18 Psalms 41:9
ᵃ *14:16* Greek παράκλητος: Counsellor, Helper, Intercessor, Advocate, and Comforter.

his love. 11 I have spoken these things to you, that my joy may remain in you, and that your joy may be made full.

12 "This is my commandment, that you love one another, even as I have loved you. 13 Greater love has no one than this, that someone lay down his life for his friends. 14 You are my friends if you do whatever I command you. 15 No longer do I call you servants, for the servant doesn't know what his lord does. But I have called you friends, for everything that I heard from my Father, I have made known to you. 16 You didn't choose me, but I chose you and appointed you, that you should go and bear fruit, and that your fruit should remain; that whatever you will ask of the Father in my name, he may give it to you.

17 "I command these things to you, that you may love one another. 18 If the world hates you, you know that it has hated me before it hated you. 19 If you were of the world, the world would love its own. But because you are not of the world, since I chose you out of the world, therefore the world hates you. 20 Remember the word that I said to you: 'A servant is not greater than his lord.' If they persecuted me, they will also persecute you. If they kept my word, they will also keep yours. 21 But they will do all these things to you for my name's sake, because they don't know him who sent me. 22 If I had not come and spoken to them, they would not have had sin; but now they have no excuse for their sin. 23 He who hates me, hates my Father also. 24 If I hadn't done amongst them the works which no one else did, they wouldn't have had sin. But now they have seen and also hated both me and my Father. 25 But this happened so that the word may be fulfilled which was written in their law, 'They hated me without a cause.'*

26 "When the Counsellor[a] has come, whom I will send to you from the Father, the Spirit of truth, who proceeds from the Father, he will testify about me. 27 You will also testify, because you have been with me from the beginning.

16

1 "I have said these things to you so that you wouldn't be caused to stumble. 2 They will put you out of the synagogues. Yes, the time is coming that whoever kills you will think that he offers service to God. 3 They will do these things[b] because they have not known the Father nor me. 4 But I have told you these things so that when the time comes, you may remember that I told you about them. I didn't tell you these things from the beginning, because I was with you. 5 But now I am going to him who sent me, and none of you asks me, 'Where are you going?' 6 But because I have told you these things, sorrow has filled your heart. 7 Nevertheless I tell you the truth: It is to your advantage that I go away; for if I don't go away, the Counsellor won't come to you. But if I go, I will send him to you. 8 When he has come, he will convict the world about sin, about righteousness, and about judgement; 9 about sin, because they don't believe in me; 10 about righteousness, because I am going to my Father, and you won't see me any more; 11 about judgement, because the prince of this world has been judged.

12 "I still have many things to tell you, but you can't bear them now. 13 However, when he, the Spirit of truth, has come, he will guide you into all truth, for he will not speak from himself; but whatever he hears, he will speak. He will declare to you things that are coming. 14 He will glorify me, for he will take from what is mine and will declare it to you. 15 All things that the Father has are mine; therefore I said that he takes[c] of mine and will declare it to you.

16 "A little while, and you will not see me. Again a little while, and you will see me."

17 Some of his disciples therefore said to one another, "What is this that he says to us, 'A little while, and you won't see me, and again a little while, and you will see me;' and, 'Because I go to the Father'?" 18 They said therefore, "What is this that he says, 'A little while'? We don't know what he is saying."

19 Therefore Jesus perceived that they wanted to ask him, and he said to them, "Do you enquire amongst yourselves concerning this, that I said, 'A little while, and you won't see me, and again a little while, and you will see me'? 20 Most certainly I tell you that you will weep and lament, but the world will rejoice. You will be sorrowful, but your sorrow will be turned into joy. 21 A woman, when she gives birth, has sorrow because her time has come. But when she has delivered the child, she doesn't remember the anguish any more, for the joy that a human being is born into the world. 22 Therefore you now have sorrow, but I will see you again, and your heart will rejoice, and no one will take your joy away from you.

23 "In that day you will ask me no questions. Most certainly I tell you, whatever you may ask of the Father in my name, he will give it to you. 24 Until now, you have asked nothing in my name. Ask, and you will receive, that your joy may be made full.

25 "I have spoken these things to you in figures of speech. But the time is coming when I will no more speak to you in figures of speech, but will tell you plainly about the Father. 26 In that day you will ask in my name; and I don't say to you that I will pray to the Father for you, 27 for the Father himself loves you, because you have loved me, and have believed that I came from God. 28 I came from the Father and have come into the world. Again, I leave the world and go to the Father."

29 His disciples said to him, "Behold, now you are speaking plainly, and using no figures of speech. 30 Now we know that you know all things,

and don't need for anyone to question you. By this we believe that you came from God."

31 Jesus answered them, "Do you now believe? 32 Behold, the time is coming, yes, and has now come, that you will be scattered, everyone to his own place, and you will leave me alone. Yet I am not alone, because the Father is with me. 33 I have told you these things, that in me you may have peace. In the world you have trouble; but cheer up! I have overcome the world."

17

1 Jesus said these things, then lifting up his eyes to heaven, he said, "Father, the time has come. Glorify your Son, that your Son may also glorify you; 2 even as you gave him authority over all flesh, so he will give eternal life to all whom you have given him. 3 This is eternal life, that they should know you, the only true God, and him whom you sent, Jesus Christ. 4 I glorified you on the earth. I have accomplished the work which you have given me to do. 5 Now, Father, glorify me with your own self with the glory which I had with you before the world existed.

6 "I revealed your name to the people whom you have given me out of the world. They were yours, and you have given them to me. They have kept your word. 7 Now they have known that all things whatever you have given me are from you, 8 for the words which you have given me I have given to them; and they received them, and knew for sure that I came from you. They have believed that you sent me. 9 I pray for them. I don't pray for the world, but for those whom you have given me, for they are yours. 10 All things that are mine are yours, and yours are mine, and I am glorified in them. 11 I am no more in the world, but these are in the world, and I am coming to you. Holy Father, keep them through your name which you have given me, that they may be one, even as we are. 12 While I was with them in the world, I kept them in your name. I have kept those whom you have given me. None of them is lost except the son of destruction, that the Scripture might be fulfilled. 13 But now I come to you, and I say these things in the world, that they may have my joy made full in themselves. 14 I have given them your word. The world hated them because they are not of the world, even as I am not of the world. 15 I pray not that you would take them from the world, but that you would keep them from the evil one. 16 They are not of the world, even as I am not of the world. 17 Sanctify them in your truth. Your word is truth.* 18 As you sent me into the world, even so I have sent them into the world. 19 For their sakes I sanctify myself, that they themselves also may be sanctified in truth.

20 "Not for these only do I pray, but for those also who will believe in me through their word, 21 that they may all be one; even as you, Father, are in me, and I in you, that they also may be one in us; that the world may believe that you sent me. 22 The glory which you have given me, I have given to them, that they may be one, even as we are one, 23 I in them, and you in me, that they may be perfected into one, that the world may know that you sent me and loved them, even as you loved me. 24 Father, I desire that they also whom you have given me be with me where I am, that they may see my glory which you have given me, for you loved me before the foundation of the world. 25 Righteous Father, the world hasn't known you, but I knew you; and these knew that you sent me. 26 I made known to them your name, and will make it known; that the love with which you loved me may be in them, and I in them."

18

1 When Jesus had spoken these words, he went out with his disciples over the brook Kidron, where there was a garden, into which he and his disciples entered. 2 Now Judas, who betrayed him, also knew the place, for Jesus often met there with his disciples. 3 Judas then, having taken a detachment of soldiers and officers from the chief priests and the Pharisees, came there with lanterns, torches, and weapons. 4 Jesus therefore, knowing all the things that were happening to him, went out and said to them, "Who are you looking for?"

5 They answered him, "Jesus of Nazareth."

Jesus said to them, "I am he."

Judas also, who betrayed him, was standing with them. 6 When therefore he said to them, "I am he," they went backward and fell to the ground.

7 Again therefore he asked them, "Who are you looking for?"

They said, "Jesus of Nazareth."

8 Jesus answered, "I told you that I am he. If therefore you seek me, let these go their way," 9 that the word might be fulfilled which he spoke, "Of those whom you have given me, I have lost none."*

10 Simon Peter therefore, having a sword, drew it, struck the high priest's servant, and cut off his right ear. The servant's name was Malchus. 11 Jesus therefore said to Peter, "Put the sword into its sheath. The cup which the Father has given me, shall I not surely drink it?"

12 So the detachment, the commanding officer, and the officers of the Jews seized Jesus and bound him, 13 and led him to Annas first, for he was father-in-law to Caiaphas, who was high priest that year. 14 Now it was Caiaphas who advised the Jews that it was expedient that one man should perish for the people.

15 Simon Peter followed Jesus, as did another disciple. Now that disciple was known to the high priest, and entered in with Jesus into the court of the high priest; 16 but Peter was standing at the door outside. So

---

** 15:20 John 13:16
** 15:25 Psalms 35:19; 69:4
a 15:26 Greek Parakletos: Counsellor, Helper, Advocate, Intercessor, and Comforter.

b 16:3 TR adds "to you"
c 16:15 TR reads "will take" instead of "takes"
** 17:17 Psalms 119:142
** 18:9 John 6:39

the other disciple, who was known to the high priest, went out and spoke to her who kept the door, and brought in Peter. 17 Then the maid who kept the door said to Peter, "Are you also one of this man's disciples?"

He said, "I am not."

18 Now the servants and the officers were standing there, having made a fire of coals, for it was cold. They were warming themselves. Peter was with them, standing and warming himself.

19 The high priest therefore asked Jesus about his disciples and about his teaching.

20 Jesus answered him, "I spoke openly to the world. I always taught in synagogues and in the temple, where the Jews always meet. I said nothing in secret. 21 Why do you ask me? Ask those who have heard me what I said to them. Behold, they know the things which I said."

22 When he had said this, one of the officers standing by slapped Jesus with his hand, saying, "Do you answer the high priest like that?"

23 Jesus answered him, "If I have spoken evil, testify of the evil; but if well, why do you beat me?"

24 Annas sent him bound to Caiaphas, the high priest.

25 Now Simon Peter was standing and warming himself. They said therefore to him, "You aren't also one of his disciples, are you?"

He denied it and said, "I am not."

26 One of the servants of the high priest, being a relative of him whose ear Peter had cut off, said, "Didn't I see you in the garden with him?"

27 Peter therefore denied it again, and immediately the rooster crowed.

28 They led Jesus therefore from Caiaphas into the Praetorium. It was early, and they themselves didn't enter into the Praetorium, that they might not be defiled, but might eat the Passover. 29 Pilate therefore went out to them and said, "What accusation do you bring against this man?"

30 They answered him, "If this man weren't an evildoer, we wouldn't have delivered him up to you."

31 Pilate therefore said to them, "Take him yourselves, and judge him according to your law."

Therefore the Jews said to him, "It is illegal for us to put anyone to death," 32 that the word of Jesus might be fulfilled, which he spoke, signifying by what kind of death he should die.

33 Pilate therefore entered again into the Praetorium, called Jesus, and said to him, "Are you the King of the Jews?"

34 Jesus answered him, "Do you say this by yourself, or did others tell you about me?"

35 Pilate answered, "I'm not a Jew, am I? Your own nation and the chief priests delivered you to me. What have you done?"

36 Jesus answered, "My Kingdom is not of this world. If my Kingdom were of this world, then my servants would fight, that I wouldn't be delivered to the Jews. But now my Kingdom is not from here."

37 Pilate therefore said to him, "Are you a king then?"

Jesus answered, "You say that I am a king. For this reason I have been born, and for this reason I have come into the world, that I should testify to the truth. Everyone who is of the truth listens to my voice."

38 Pilate said to him, "What is truth?"

When he had said this, he went out again to the Jews, and said to them, "I find no basis for a charge against him. 39 But you have a custom that I should release someone to you at the Passover. Therefore, do you want me to release to you the King of the Jews?"

40 Then they all shouted again, saying, "Not this man, but Barabbas!" Now Barabbas was a robber.

19

1 So Pilate then took Jesus and flogged him. 2 The soldiers twisted thorns into a crown and put it on his head, and dressed him in a purple garment. 3 They kept saying, "Hail, King of the Jews!" and they kept slapping him.

4 Then Pilate went out again, and said to them, "Behold, I bring him out to you, that you may know that I find no basis for a charge against him."

5 Jesus therefore came out, wearing the crown of thorns and the purple garment. Pilate said to them, "Behold, the man!"

6 When therefore the chief priests and the officers saw him, they shouted, saying, "Crucify! Crucify!"

Pilate said to them, "Take him yourselves and crucify him, for I find no basis for a charge against him."

7 The Jews answered him, "We have a law, and by our law he ought to die, because he made himself the Son of God."

8 When therefore Pilate heard this saying, he was more afraid. 9 He entered into the Praetorium again, and said to Jesus, "Where are you from?" But Jesus gave him no answer. 10 Pilate therefore said to him, "Aren't you speaking to me? Don't you know that I have power to release you and have power to crucify you?"

11 Jesus answered, "You would have no power at all against me, unless it were given to you from above. Therefore he who delivered me to you has greater sin."

12 At this, Pilate was seeking to release him, but the Jews cried out, saying, "If you release this man, you aren't Caesar's friend! Everyone who makes himself a king speaks against Caesar!"

13 When Pilate therefore heard these words, he brought Jesus out and sat down on the judgement seat at a place called "The Pavement", but in

Hebrew, "Gabbatha." 14 Now it was the Preparation Day of the Passover, at about the sixth hour.ᵃ He said to the Jews, "Behold, your King!"

15 They cried out, "Away with him! Away with him! Crucify him!"

Pilate said to them, "Shall I crucify your King?"

The chief priests answered, "We have no king but Caesar!"

16 So then he delivered him to them to be crucified. So they took Jesus and led him away. 17 He went out, bearing his cross, to the place called "The Place of a Skull", which is called in Hebrew, "Golgotha", 18 where they crucified him, and with him two others, on either side one, and Jesus in the middle. 19 Pilate wrote a title also, and put it on the cross. There was written, "JESUS OF NAZARETH, THE KING OF THE JEWS." 20 Therefore many of the Jews read this title, for the place where Jesus was crucified was near the city; and it was written in Hebrew, in Latin, and in Greek. 21 The chief priests of the Jews therefore said to Pilate, "Don't write, 'The King of the Jews,' but, 'he said, I am King of the Jews.'"

22 Pilate answered, "What I have written, I have written."

23 Then the soldiers, when they had crucified Jesus, took his garments and made four parts, to every soldier a part; and also the tunic. Now the tunic was without seam, woven from the top throughout. 24 Then they said to one another, "Let's not tear it, but cast lots for it to decide whose it will be," that the Scripture might be fulfilled, which says,

"They parted my garments amongst them.
They cast lots for my clothing."ᵇ
Therefore the soldiers did these things.

25 But standing by Jesus' cross were his mother, his mother's sister, Mary the wife of Clopas, and Mary Magdalene. 26 Therefore when Jesus saw his mother, and the disciple whom he loved standing there, he said to his mother, "Woman, behold, your son!" 27 Then he said to the disciple, "Behold, your mother!" From that hour, the disciple took her to his own home.

28 After this, Jesus, seeingᵇ that all things were now finished, that the Scripture might be fulfilled, said, "I am thirsty!" 29 Now a vessel full of vinegar was set there; so they put a sponge full of the vinegar on hyssop, and held it at his mouth. 30 When Jesus therefore had received the vinegar, he said, "It is finished!" Then he bowed his head and gave up his spirit.

31 Therefore the Jews, because it was the Preparation Day, so that the bodies wouldn't remain on the cross on the Sabbath (for that Sabbath was a special one), asked of Pilate that their legs might be broken and that they might be taken away. 32 Therefore the soldiers came and broke the legs of the first and of the other who was crucified with him; 33 but when they came to Jesus and saw that he was already dead, they didn't break his legs. 34 However, one of the soldiers pierced his side with a spear, and immediately blood and water came out. 35 He who has seen has testified, and his testimony is true. He knows that he tells the truth, that you may believe. 36 For these things happened that the Scripture might be fulfilled, "A bone of him will not be broken."ᵇ 37 Again another Scripture says, "They will look on him whom they pierced."ᵇ

38 After these things, Joseph of Arimathaea, being a disciple of Jesus, but secretly for fear of the Jews, asked of Pilate that he might take away Jesus' body. Pilate gave him permission. He came therefore and took away his body. 39 Nicodemus, who at first came to Jesus by night, also came bringing a mixture of myrrh and aloes, about a hundred Roman pounds.ᶜ 40 So they took Jesus' body, and bound it in linen cloths with the spices, as the custom of the Jews is to bury. 41 Now in the place where he was crucified there was a garden. In the garden was a new tomb in which no man had ever yet been laid. 42 Then, because of the Jews' Preparation Day (for the tomb was near at hand), they laid Jesus there.

20

1 Now on the first day of the week, Mary Magdalene went early, while it was still dark, to the tomb, and saw that the stone had been taken away from the tomb. 2 Therefore she ran and came to Simon Peter and to the other disciple whom Jesus loved, and said to them, "They have taken away the Lord out of the tomb, and we don't know where they have laid him!"

3 Therefore Peter and the other disciple went out, and they went towards the tomb. 4 They both ran together. The other disciple outran Peter and came to the tomb first. 5 Stooping and looking in, he saw the linen cloths lying there; yet he didn't enter in. 6 Then Simon Peter came, following him, and entered into the tomb. He saw the linen cloths lying, 7 and the cloth that had been on his head, not lying with the linen cloths, but rolled up in a place by itself. 8 So then the other disciple who came first to the tomb also entered in, and he saw and believed. 9 For as yet they didn't know the Scripture, that he must rise from the dead. 10 So the disciples went away again to their own homes.

11 But Mary was standing outside at the tomb weeping. So as she wept, she stooped and looked into the tomb, 12 and she saw two angels in white sitting, one at the head and one at the feet, where the body of Jesus had lain. 13 They asked her, "Woman, why are you weeping?"

She said to them, "Because they have taken away my Lord, and I don't know where they have laid him." 14 When she had said this, she turned around and saw Jesus standing, and didn't know that it was Jesus.

15 Jesus said to her, "Woman, why are you weeping? Who are you looking for?"

ᵃ 19:14 "the sixth hour" would have been 6:00 a.m. according to the Roman timekeeping system, or noon for the Jewish timekeeping system in use, then.
** 19:24 Psalms 22:18
ᵇ 19:28 NU, TR read "knowing" instead of "seeing"

** 19:36 Exodus 12:46; Numbers 9:12; Psalms 34:20
** 19:37 Zechariah 12:10
ᶜ 19:39 100 Roman pounds of 12 ounces each, or about 72 pounds, or 33 Kilograms.

She, supposing him to be the gardener, said to him, "Sir, if you have carried him away, tell me where you have laid him, and I will take him away."

16 Jesus said to her, "Mary."

She turned and said to him, "Rabboni!"a which is to say, "Teacher!"b

17 Jesus said to her, "Don't hold me, for I haven't yet ascended to my Father; but go to my brothers and tell them, 'I am ascending to my Father and your Father, to my God and your God.'"

18 Mary Magdalene came and told the disciples that she had seen the Lord, and that he had said these things to her. 19 When therefore it was evening on that day, the first day of the week, and when the doors were locked where the disciples were assembled, for fear of the Jews, Jesus came and stood in the middle and said to them, "Peace be to you."

20 When he had said this, he showed them his hands and his side. The disciples therefore were glad when they saw the Lord. 21 Jesus therefore said to them again, "Peace be to you. As the Father has sent me, even so I send you." 22 When he had said this, he breathed on them, and said to them, "Receive the Holy Spirit! 23 If you forgive anyone's sins, they have been forgiven them. If you retain anyone's sins, they have been retained."

24 But Thomas, one of the twelve, called Didymus,c wasn't with them when Jesus came. 25 The other disciples therefore said to him, "We have seen the Lord!"

But he said to them, "Unless I see in his hands the print of the nails, put my finger into the print of the nails, and put my hand into his side, I will not believe."

26 After eight days, again his disciples were inside and Thomas was with them. Jesus came, the doors being locked, and stood in the middle, and said, "Peace be to you." 27 Then he said to Thomas, "Reach here your finger, and see my hands. Reach here your hand, and put it into my side. Don't be unbelieving, but believing."

28 Thomas answered him, "My Lord and my God!"

29 Jesus said to him, "Because you have seen me,d you have believed. Blessed are those who have not seen and have believed."

30 Therefore Jesus did many other signs in the presence of his disciples, which are not written in this book; 31 but these are written that you may believe that Jesus is the Christ, the Son of God, and that believing you may have life in his name.

21

1 After these things, Jesus revealed himself again to the disciples at the sea of Tiberias. He revealed himself this way. 2 Simon Peter, Thomas called Didymus,e Nathanael of Cana in Galilee, and the sons of Zebedee, and two others of his disciples were together. 3 Simon Peter said to them, "I'm going fishing."

They told him, "We are also coming with you." They immediately went out and entered into the boat. That night, they caught nothing. 4 But when day had already come, Jesus stood on the beach; yet the disciples didn't know that it was Jesus. 5 Jesus therefore said to them, "Children, have you anything to eat?"

They answered him, "No."

6 He said to them, "Cast the net on the right side of the boat, and you will find some."

They cast it therefore, and now they weren't able to draw it in for the multitude of fish. 7 That disciple therefore whom Jesus loved said to Peter, "It's the Lord!"

So when Simon Peter heard that it was the Lord, he wrapped his coat around himself (for he was naked), and threw himself into the sea. 8 But the other disciples came in the little boat (for they were not far from the land, but about two hundred cubitsf away), dragging the net full of fish. 9 So when they got out on the land, they saw a fire of coals there, with fish and bread laid on it. 10 Jesus said to them, "Bring some of the fish which you have just caught."

11 Simon Peter went up, and drew the net to land, full of one hundred and fifty-three great fish. Even though there were so many, the net wasn't torn.

12 Jesus said to them, "Come and eat breakfast!"

None of the disciples dared enquire of him, "Who are you?" knowing that it was the Lord.

13 Then Jesus came and took the bread, gave it to them, and the fish likewise. 14 This is now the third time that Jesus was revealed to his disciples after he had risen from the dead. 15 So when they had eaten their breakfast, Jesus said to Simon Peter, "Simon, son of Jonah, do you love me more than these?"

He said to him, "Yes, Lord; you know that I have affection for you."

He said to him, "Feed my lambs." 16 He said to him again a second time, "Simon, son of Jonah, do you love me?"

He said to him, "Yes, Lord; you know that I have affection for you."

He said to him, "Tend my sheep." 17 He said to him the third time, "Simon, son of Jonah, do you have affection for me?"

Peter was grieved because he asked him the third time, "Do you have affection for me?" He said to him, "Lord, you know everything. You know that I have affection for you."

Jesus said to him, "Feed my sheep. 18 Most certainly I tell you, when you were young, you dressed yourself and walked where you wanted to.

But when you are old, you will stretch out your hands, and another will dress you and carry you where you don't want to go."

19 Now he said this, signifying by what kind of death he would glorify God. When he had said this, he said to him, "Follow me."

20 Then Peter, turning around, saw a disciple following. This was the disciple whom Jesus loved, the one who had also leaned on Jesus' breast at the supper and asked, "Lord, who is going to betray you?" 21 Peter, seeing him, said to Jesus, "Lord, what about this man?"

22 Jesus said to him, "If I desire that he stay until I come, what is that to you? You follow me." 23 This saying therefore went out amongst the brothersg that this disciple wouldn't die. Yet Jesus didn't say to him that he wouldn't die, but, "If I desire that he stay until I come, what is that to you?"

24 This is the disciple who testifies about these things, and wrote these things. We know that his witness is true. 25 There are also many other things which Jesus did, which if they would all be written, I suppose that even the world itself wouldn't have room for the books that would be written.

---

a 20:16 Rabboni is a transliteration of the Hebrew word for "great teacher."
b 20:16 or, Master
c 20:24 or, Twin
d 20:29 TR adds "Thomas,"
e 21:2 or, Twin
f 21:8 200 cubits is about 100 yards or about 91 metres
g 21:23 The word for "brothers" here may be also correctly translated "brothers and sisters" or "siblings."

The Acts of the Apostles

1

1 The first book I wrote, Theophilus, concerned all that Jesus began both to do and to teach, 2 until the day in which he was received up, after he had given commandment through the Holy Spirit to the apostles whom he had chosen. 3 To these he also showed himself alive after he suffered, by many proofs, appearing to them over a period of forty days and speaking about God's Kingdom. 4 Being assembled together with them, he commanded them, "Don't depart from Jerusalem, but wait for the promise of the Father, which you heard from me. 5 For John indeed baptised in water, but you will be baptised in the Holy Spirit not many days from now."

6 Therefore, when they had come together, they asked him, "Lord, are you now restoring the kingdom to Israel?"

7 He said to them, "It isn't for you to know times or seasons which the Father has set within his own authority. 8 But you will receive power when the Holy Spirit has come upon you. You will be witnesses to me in Jerusalem, in all Judea and Samaria, and to the uttermost parts of the earth."

9 When he had said these things, as they were looking, he was taken up, and a cloud received him out of their sight. 10 While they were looking steadfastly into the sky as he went, behold,[a] two men stood by them in white clothing, 11 who also said, "You men of Galilee, why do you stand looking into the sky? This Jesus, who was received up from you into the sky, will come back in the same way as you saw him going into the sky."

12 Then they returned to Jerusalem from the mountain called Olivet, which is near Jerusalem, a Sabbath day's journey away. 13 When they had come in, they went up into the upper room where they were staying, that is Peter, John, James, Andrew, Philip, Thomas, Bartholomew, Matthew, James the son of Alphaeus, Simon the Zealot, and Judas the son of James. 14 All these with one accord continued steadfastly in prayer and supplication, along with the women and Mary the mother of Jesus, and with his brothers.

15 In these days, Peter stood up in the middle of the disciples (and the number of names was about one hundred and twenty), and said, 16 "Brothers, it was necessary that this Scripture should be fulfilled, which the Holy Spirit spoke before by the mouth of David concerning Judas, who was guide to those who took Jesus. 17 For he was counted with us, and received his portion in this ministry. 18 Now this man obtained a field with the reward for his wickedness; and falling headlong, his body burst open and all his intestines gushed out. 19 It became known to everyone who lived in Jerusalem that in their language that field was called 'Akeldama,' that is, 'The field of blood.' 20 For it is written in the book of Psalms,

'Let his habitation be made desolate.

Let no one dwell in it;"

and,

'Let another take his office."

21 "Of the men therefore who have accompanied us all the time that the Lord Jesus went in and out amongst us, 22 beginning from the baptism of John to the day that he was received up from us, of these one must become a witness with us of his resurrection."

23 They put forward two: Joseph called Barsabbas, who was also called Justus, and Matthias. 24 They prayed and said, "You, Lord, who know the hearts of all men, show which one of these two you have chosen 25 to take part in this ministry and apostleship from which Judas fell away, that he might go to his own place." 26 They drew lots for them, and the lot fell on Matthias; and he was counted with the eleven apostles.

2

1 Now when the day of Pentecost had come, they were all with one accord in one place. 2 Suddenly there came from the sky a sound like the rushing of a mighty wind, and it filled all the house where they were sitting. 3 Tongues like fire appeared and were distributed to them, and one sat on each of them. 4 They were all filled with the Holy Spirit and began to speak with other languages, as the Spirit gave them the ability to speak.

5 Now there were dwelling in Jerusalem Jews, devout men, from every nation under the sky. 6 When this sound was heard, the multitude came together and were bewildered, because everyone heard them speaking in his own language. 7 They were all amazed and marvelled, saying to one another, "Behold, aren't all these who speak Galileans? 8 How do we hear, everyone in our own native language? 9 Parthians, Medes, Elamites, and people from Mesopotamia, Judea, Cappadocia, Pontus, Asia, 10 Phrygia, Pamphylia, Egypt, the parts of Libya around Cyrene, visitors from Rome, both Jews and proselytes, 11 Cretans and Arabians—we hear them speaking in our languages the mighty works of God!" 12 They were all amazed and were perplexed, saying to one another, "What does this mean?" 13 Others, mocking, said, "They are filled with new wine."

14 But Peter, standing up with the eleven, lifted up his voice and spoke out to them, "You men of Judea and all you who dwell at Jerusalem, let this be known to you, and listen to my words. 15 For these aren't drunken, as you suppose, seeing it is only the third hour of the day.[b] 16 But this is what has been spoken through the prophet Joel:

17 'It will be in the last days, says God,
   that I will pour out my Spirit on all flesh.
Your sons and your daughters will prophesy.
   Your young men will see visions.
   Your old men will dream dreams.
18 Yes, and on my servants and on my handmaidens in those days,
   I will pour out my Spirit, and they will prophesy.
19 I will show wonders in the sky above,
   and signs on the earth beneath:
   blood, and fire, and billows of smoke.
20 The sun will be turned into darkness,
   and the moon into blood,
   before the great and glorious day of the Lord comes.
21 It will be that whoever will call on the name of the Lord will be saved."

22 "Men of Israel, hear these words! Jesus of Nazareth, a man approved by God to you by mighty works and wonders and signs which God did by him amongst you, even as you yourselves know, 23 him, being delivered up by the determined counsel and foreknowledge of God, you have taken by the hand of lawless men, crucified and killed; 24 whom God raised up, having freed him from the agony of death, because it was not possible that he should be held by it. 25 For David says concerning him,

'I saw the Lord always before my face,
   for he is on my right hand, that I should not be moved.
26 Therefore my heart was glad, and my tongue rejoiced.
   Moreover my flesh also will dwell in hope,
27 because you will not leave my soul in Hades,[c]
   neither will you allow your Holy One to see decay.
28 You made known to me the ways of life.
   You will make me full of gladness with your presence."

29 "Brothers, I may tell you freely of the patriarch David, that he both died and was buried, and his tomb is with us to this day. 30 Therefore, being a prophet, and knowing that God had sworn with an oath to him that of the fruit of his body, according to the flesh, he would raise up the Christ[d] to sit on his throne, 31 he foreseeing this, spoke about the resurrection of the Christ, that his soul wasn't left in Hades,[e] and his flesh didn't see decay. 32 This Jesus God raised up, to which we all are witnesses. 33 Being therefore exalted by the right hand of God, and having received from the Father the promise of the Holy Spirit, he has poured out this which you now see and hear. 34 For David didn't ascend into the heavens, but he says himself, 'The Lord said to my Lord, "Sit by my right hand
35 until I make your enemies a footstool for your feet."'"

36 "Let all the house of Israel therefore know certainly that God has made him both Lord and Christ, this Jesus whom you crucified."

37 Now when they heard this, they were cut to the heart, and said to Peter and the rest of the apostles, "Brothers, what shall we do?"

38 Peter said to them, "Repent and be baptised, every one of you, in the name of Jesus Christ for the forgiveness of sins, and you will receive the gift of the Holy Spirit. 39 For the promise is to you and to your children, and to all who are far off, even as many as the Lord our God will call to himself." 40 With many other words he testified and exhorted them, saying, "Save yourselves from this crooked generation!"

41 Then those who gladly received his word were baptised. There were added that day about three thousand souls. 42 They continued steadfastly in the apostles' teaching and fellowship, in the breaking of bread, and prayer. 43 Fear came on every soul, and many wonders and signs were done through the apostles. 44 All who believed were together, and had all things in common. 45 They sold their possessions and goods, and distributed them to all, according as anyone had need. 46 Day by day, continuing steadfastly with one accord in the temple, and breaking bread at home, they took their food with gladness and singleness of heart, 47 praising God and having favour with all the people. The Lord added to the assembly day by day those who were being saved.

3

1 Peter and John were going up into the temple at the hour of prayer, the ninth hour.[f] 2 A certain man who was lame from his mother's womb was being carried, whom they laid daily at the door of the temple which is called Beautiful, to ask gifts for the needy of those who entered into the temple. 3 Seeing Peter and John about to go into the temple, he asked to receive gifts for the needy. 4 Peter, fastening his eyes on him, with John, said, "Look at us." 5 He listened to them, expecting to receive something from them. 6 But Peter said, "I have no silver or gold, but what I have, that I give you. In the name of Jesus Christ of Nazareth, get up and walk!" 7 He took him by the right hand and raised him up. Immediately his feet and his ankle bones received strength. 8 Leaping up, he stood and began to walk. He entered with them into the temple, walking, leaping, and praising God. 9 All the people saw him walking and praising God. 10 They recognised him, that it was he who used to sit begging for gifts for the needy at the Beautiful Gate of the temple. They were filled with wonder and amazement at what had happened to him. 11 As the lame man who was healed held on to Peter and

---

[a] 1:10 "Behold", from "ἰδοὺ", means look at, take notice, observe, see, or gaze at. It is often used as an interjection.
** 1:20 Psalms 69:25
** 1:20 Psalms 109:8
[b] 2:15 about 9:00 a.m.
** 2:21 Joel 2:28-32

[c] 2:27 or, Hell
** 2:28 Psalms 16:8-11
[d] 2:30 "Christ" means "Anointed One".
[e] 2:31 or, Hell
** 2:35 Psalms 110:1
[f] 3:1 3:00 p.m.

John, all the people ran together to them in the porch that is called Solomon's, greatly wondering.

12 When Peter saw it, he responded to the people, "You men of Israel, why do you marvel at this man? Why do you fasten your eyes on us, as though by our own power or godliness we had made him walk? 13 The God of Abraham, Isaac, and Jacob, the God of our fathers, has glorified his Servant Jesus, whom you delivered up and denied in the presence of Pilate, when he had determined to release him. 14 But you denied the Holy and Righteous One and asked for a murderer to be granted to you, 15 and killed the Prince of life, whom God raised from the dead, to which we are witnesses. 16 By faith in his name, his name has made this man strong, whom you see and know. Yes, the faith which is through him has given him this perfect soundness in the presence of you all.

17 "Now, brothers,[a] I know that you did this in ignorance, as did also your rulers. 18 But the things which God announced by the mouth of all his prophets, that Christ should suffer, he thus fulfilled.

19 "Repent therefore, and turn again, that your sins may be blotted out, so that there may come times of refreshing from the presence of the Lord, 20 and that he may send Christ Jesus, who was ordained for you before, 21 whom heaven must receive until the times of restoration of all things, which God spoke long ago by the mouth of his holy prophets. 22 For Moses indeed said to the fathers, 'The Lord God will raise up a prophet for you from amongst your brothers, like me. You shall listen to him in all things whatever he says to you. 23 It will be that every soul that will not listen to that prophet will be utterly destroyed from amongst the people.'** 24 Yes, and all the prophets from Samuel and those who followed after, as many as have spoken, also told of these days. 25 You are the children of the prophets, and of the covenant which God made with our fathers, saying to Abraham, 'All the families of the earth will be blessed through your offspring.'[b]** 26 God, having raised up his servant Jesus, sent him to you first to bless you, in turning away every one of you from your wickedness."

4

1 As they spoke to the people, the priests and the captain of the temple and the Sadducees came to them, 2 being upset because they taught the people and proclaimed in Jesus the resurrection from the dead. 3 They laid hands on them, and put them in custody until the next day, for it was now evening. 4 But many of those who heard the word believed, and the number of the men came to be about five thousand.

5 In the morning, their rulers, elders, and scribes were gathered together in Jerusalem. 6 Annas the high priest was there, with Caiaphas, John, Alexander, and as many as were relatives of the high priest. 7 When they had stood Peter and John in the middle of them, they enquired, "By what power, or in what name, have you done this?"

8 Then Peter, filled with the Holy Spirit, said to them, "You rulers of the people and elders of Israel, 9 if we are examined today concerning a good deed done to a crippled man, by what means this man has been healed, 10 may it be known to you all, and to all the people of Israel, that in the name of Jesus Christ of Nazareth, whom you crucified, whom God raised from the dead, this man stands here before you whole in him. 11 He is 'the stone which was regarded as worthless by you, the builders, which has become the head of the corner.'** 12 There is salvation in no one else, for there is no other name under heaven that is given amongst men, by which we must be saved!"

13 Now when they saw the boldness of Peter and John, and had perceived that they were unlearned and ignorant men, they marvelled. They recognised that they had been with Jesus. 14 Seeing the man who was healed standing with them, they could say nothing against it. 15 But when they had commanded them to go aside out of the council, they conferred amongst themselves, 16 saying, "What shall we do to these men? Because indeed a notable miracle has been done through them, as can be plainly seen by all who dwell in Jerusalem, and we can't deny it. 17 But so that this spreads no further amongst the people, let's threaten them, that from now on they don't speak to anyone in this name." 18 They called them, and commanded them not to speak at all nor teach in the name of Jesus.

19 But Peter and John answered them, "Whether it is right in the sight of God to listen to you rather than to God, judge for yourselves, 20 for we can't help telling the things which we saw and heard."

21 When they had further threatened them, they let them go, finding no way to punish them, because of the people; for everyone glorified God for that which was done. 22 For the man on whom this miracle of healing was performed was more than forty years old.

23 Being let go, they came to their own company and reported all that the chief priests and the elders had said to them. 24 When they heard it, they lifted up their voice to God with one accord and said, "O Lord, you are God, who made the heaven, the earth, the sea, and all that is in them; 25 who by the mouth of your servant David, said,
'Why do the nations rage,
      and the peoples plot a vain thing?
26 The kings of the earth take a stand,
      and the rulers plot together,
      against the Lord, and against his Christ.'[c]**

27 "For truly,[d] both Herod and Pontius Pilate, with the Gentiles and the people of Israel, were gathered together against your holy servant Jesus, whom you anointed, 28 to do whatever your hand and your counsel foreordained to happen. 29 Now, Lord, look at their threats, and grant to your servants to speak your word with all boldness, 30 while you stretch out your hand to heal; and that signs and wonders may be done through the name of your holy Servant Jesus."

31 When they had prayed, the place was shaken where they were gathered together. They were all filled with the Holy Spirit, and they spoke the word of God with boldness.

32 The multitude of those who believed were of one heart and soul. Not one of them claimed that anything of the things which he possessed was his own, but they had all things in common. 33 With great power, the apostles gave their testimony of the resurrection of the Lord Jesus. Great grace was on them all. 34 For neither was there amongst them any who lacked, for as many as were owners of lands or houses sold them, and brought the proceeds of the things that were sold, 35 and laid them at the apostles' feet; and distribution was made to each, according as anyone had need.

36 Joses, who by the apostles was also called Barnabas (which is, being interpreted, Son of Encouragement), a Levite, a man of Cyprus by race, 37 having a field, sold it and brought the money and laid it at the apostles' feet.

5

1 But a certain man named Ananias, with Sapphira his wife, sold a possession, 2 and kept back part of the price, his wife also being aware of it, then brought a certain part and laid it at the apostles' feet. 3 But Peter said, "Ananias, why has Satan filled your heart to lie to the Holy Spirit and to keep back part of the price of the land? 4 While you kept it, didn't it remain your own? After it was sold, wasn't it in your power? How is it that you have conceived this thing in your heart? You haven't lied to men, but to God."

5 Ananias, hearing these words, fell down and died. Great fear came on all who heard these things. 6 The young men arose and wrapped him up, and they carried him out and buried him. 7 About three hours later, his wife, not knowing what had happened, came in. 8 Peter answered her, "Tell me whether you sold the land for so much."

She said, "Yes, for so much."

9 But Peter asked her, "How is it that you have agreed together to tempt the Spirit of the Lord? Behold, the feet of those who have buried your husband are at the door, and they will carry you out."

10 She fell down immediately at his feet and died. The young men came in and found her dead, and they carried her out and buried her by her husband. 11 Great fear came on the whole assembly, and on all who heard these things.

12 By the hands of the apostles many signs and wonders were done amongst the people. They were all with one accord in Solomon's porch. 13 None of the rest dared to join them; however, the people honoured them. 14 More believers were added to the Lord, multitudes of both men and women. 15 They even carried out the sick into the streets and laid them on cots and mattresses, so that as Peter came by, at least his shadow might overshadow some of them. 16 The multitude also came together from the cities around Jerusalem, bringing sick people and those who were tormented by unclean spirits; and they were all healed.

17 But the high priest rose up, and all those who were with him (which is the sect of the Sadducees), and they were filled with jealousy 18 and laid hands on the apostles, then put them in public custody. 19 But an angel of the Lord opened the prison doors by night, and brought them out and said, 20 "Go stand and speak in the temple to the people all the words of this life."

21 When they heard this, they entered into the temple about daybreak and taught. But the high priest and those who were with him came and called the council together, with all the senate of the children of Israel, and sent to the prison to have them brought. 22 But the officers who came didn't find them in the prison. They returned and reported, 23 "We found the prison shut and locked, and the guards standing before the doors, but when we opened them, we found no one inside!"

24 Now when the high priest, the captain of the temple, and the chief priests heard these words, they were very perplexed about them and what might become of this. 25 One came and told them, "Behold, the men whom you put in prison are in the temple, standing and teaching the people." 26 Then the captain went with the officers, and brought them without violence, for they were afraid that the people might stone them.

27 When they had brought them, they set them before the council. The high priest questioned them, 28 saying, "Didn't we strictly command you not to teach in this name? Behold, you have filled Jerusalem with your teaching, and intend to bring this man's blood on us."

29 But Peter and the apostles answered, "We must obey God rather than men. 30 The God of our fathers raised up Jesus, whom you killed, hanging him on a tree. 31 God exalted him with his right hand to be a Prince and a Saviour, to give repentance to Israel, and remission of sins. 32 We are his witnesses of these things; and so also is the Holy Spirit, whom God has given to those who obey him."

---

a *3:17* The word for "brothers" here may be also correctly translated "brothers and sisters" or "siblings."
** 3:23 Deuteronomy 18:15,18-19
b *3:25* or, seed
** 3:25 Genesis 22:18; 26:4

** 4:11 Psalms 118:22
c *4:26* Christ (Greek) and Messiah (Hebrew) both mean Anointed One.
** 4:26 Psalms 2:1-2
d *4:27* nu adds "in this city,"

33 But they, when they heard this, were cut to the heart, and were determined to kill them. 34 But one stood up in the council, a Pharisee named Gamaliel, a teacher of the law, honoured by all the people, and commanded to put the apostles out for a little while. 35 He said to them, "You men of Israel, be careful concerning these men, what you are about to do. 36 For before these days Theudas rose up, making himself out to be somebody; to whom a number of men, about four hundred, joined themselves. He was slain; and all, as many as obeyed him, were dispersed and came to nothing. 37 After this man, Judas of Galilee rose up in the days of the enrolment, and drew away some people after him. He also perished, and all, as many as obeyed him, were scattered abroad. 38 Now I tell you, withdraw from these men and leave them alone. For if this counsel or this work is of men, it will be overthrown. 39 But if it is of God, you will not be able to overthrow it, and you would be found even to be fighting against God!"

40 They agreed with him. Summoning the apostles, they beat them and commanded them not to speak in the name of Jesus, and let them go. 41 They therefore departed from the presence of the council, rejoicing that they were counted worthy to suffer dishonour for Jesus' name.

42 Every day, in the temple and at home, they never stopped teaching and preaching Jesus, the Christ.

6

1 Now in those days, when the number of the disciples was multiplying, a complaint arose from the Hellenists[a] against the Hebrews, because their widows were neglected in the daily service. 2 The twelve summoned the multitude of the disciples and said, "It is not appropriate for us to forsake the word of God and serve tables. 3 Therefore, select from amongst you, brothers, seven men of good report, full of the Holy Spirit and of wisdom, whom we may appoint over this business. 4 But we will continue steadfastly in prayer and in the ministry of the word."

5 These words pleased the whole multitude. They chose Stephen, a man full of faith and of the Holy Spirit, Philip, Prochorus, Nicanor, Timon, Parmenas, and Nicolaus, a proselyte of Antioch, 6 whom they set before the apostles. When they had prayed, they laid their hands on them.

7 The word of God increased and the number of the disciples greatly multiplied in Jerusalem. A great company of the priests were obedient to the faith.

8 Stephen, full of faith and power, performed great wonders and signs amongst the people. 9 But some of those who were of the synagogue called "The Libertines", and of the Cyrenians, of the Alexandrians, and of those of Cilicia and Asia arose, disputing with Stephen. 10 They weren't able to withstand the wisdom and the Spirit by which he spoke. 11 Then they secretly induced men to say, "We have heard him speak blasphemous words against Moses and God." 12 They stirred up the people, the elders, and the scribes, and came against him and seized him, then brought him in to the council, 13 and set up false witnesses who said, "This man never stops speaking blasphemous words against this holy place and the law. 14 For we have heard him say that this Jesus of Nazareth will destroy this place, and will change the customs which Moses delivered to us." 15 All who sat in the council, fastening their eyes on him, saw his face like it was the face of an angel.

7

1 The high priest said, "Are these things so?"

2 He said, "Brothers and fathers, listen. The God of glory appeared to our father Abraham when he was in Mesopotamia, before he lived in Haran, 3 and said to him, 'Get out of your land and away from your relatives, and come into a land which I will show you.' 4 Then he came out of the land of the Chaldaeans and lived in Haran. From there, when his father was dead, God moved him into this land where you are now living. 5 He gave him no inheritance in it, no, not so much as to set his foot on. He promised that he would give it to him for a possession, and to his offspring after him, when he still had no child. 6 God spoke in this way: that his offspring would live as aliens in a strange land, and that they would be enslaved and mistreated for four hundred years. 7 'I will judge the nation to which they will be in bondage,' said God, 'and after that they will come out and serve me in this place.' 8 He gave him the covenant of circumcision. So Abraham became the father of Isaac, and circumcised him the eighth day. Isaac became the father of Jacob, and Jacob became the father of the twelve patriarchs.

9 "The patriarchs, moved with jealousy against Joseph, sold him into Egypt. God was with him 10 and delivered him out of all his afflictions, and gave him favour and wisdom before Pharaoh, king of Egypt. He made him governor over Egypt and all his house. 11 Now a famine came over all the land of Egypt and Canaan, and great affliction. Our fathers found no food. 12 But when Jacob heard that there was grain in Egypt, he sent out our fathers the first time. 13 On the second time Joseph was made known to his brothers, and Joseph's family was revealed to Pharaoh. 14 Joseph sent and summoned Jacob his father and all his relatives, seventy-five souls. 15 Jacob went down into Egypt and he died, himself and our fathers; 16 and

they were brought back to Shechem and laid in the tomb that Abraham bought for a price in silver from the children of Hamor of Shechem.

17 "But as the time of the promise came close which God had sworn to Abraham, the people grew and multiplied in Egypt, 18 until there arose a different king who didn't know Joseph. 19 The same took advantage of our race and mistreated our fathers, and forced them to abandon their babies, so that they wouldn't stay alive. 20 At that time Moses was born, and was exceedingly handsome to God. He was nourished three months in his father's house. 21 When he was abandoned, Pharaoh's daughter took him up and reared him as her own son. 22 Moses was instructed in all the wisdom of the Egyptians. He was mighty in his words and works. 23 But when he was forty years old, it came into his heart to visit his brothers,[b] the children of Israel. 24 Seeing one of them suffer wrong, he defended him and avenged him who was oppressed, striking the Egyptian. 25 He supposed that his brothers understood that God, by his hand, was giving them deliverance; but they didn't understand.

26 "The day following, he appeared to them as they fought, and urged them to be at peace again, saying, 'Sirs, you are brothers. Why do you wrong one another?' 27 But he who did his neighbour wrong pushed him away, saying, 'Who made you a ruler and a judge over us? 28 Do you want to kill me as you killed the Egyptian yesterday?' 29 Moses fled at this saying, and became a stranger in the land of Midian, where he became the father of two sons.

30 "When forty years were fulfilled, an angel of the Lord appeared to him in the wilderness of Mount Sinai, in a flame of fire in a bush. 31 When Moses saw it, he wondered at the sight. As he came close to see, the voice of the Lord came to him, 32 'I am the God of your fathers: the God of Abraham, the God of Isaac, and the God of Jacob." Moses trembled and dared not look. 33 The Lord said to him, 'Take off your sandals, for the place where you stand is holy ground. 34 I have surely seen the affliction of my people who are in Egypt, and have heard their groaning. I have come down to deliver them. Now come, I will send you into Egypt.'

35 "This Moses whom they refused, saying, 'Who made you a ruler and a judge?'—God has sent him as both a ruler and a deliverer by the hand of the angel who appeared to him in the bush. 36 This man led them out, having worked wonders and signs in Egypt, in the Red Sea, and in the wilderness for forty years. 37 This is that Moses who said to the children of Israel, 'The Lord our God will raise up a prophet for you from amongst your brothers, like me.'[c] 38 This is he who was in the assembly in the wilderness with the angel that spoke to him on Mount Sinai, and with our fathers, who received living revelations to give to us, 39 to whom our fathers wouldn't be obedient, but rejected him and turned back in their hearts to Egypt, 40 saying to Aaron, 'Make us gods that will go before us, for as for this Moses who led us out of the land of Egypt, we don't know what has become of him." 41 They made a calf in those days, and brought a sacrifice to the idol, and rejoiced in the works of their hands. 42 But God turned away and gave them up to serve the army of the sky,[d] as it is written in the book of the prophets,

'Did you offer to me slain animals and sacrifices
 forty years in the wilderness, O house of Israel?
43 You took up the tabernacle of Moloch,
 the star of your god Rephan,
the figures which you made to worship,
 so I will carry you away' beyond Babylon.'

44 "Our fathers had the tabernacle of the testimony in the wilderness, even as he who spoke to Moses commanded him to make it according to the pattern that he had seen; 45 which also our fathers, in their turn, brought in with Joshua when they entered into the possession of the nations whom God drove out before the face of our fathers to the days of David, 46 who found favour in the sight of God, and asked to find a habitation for the God of Jacob. 47 But Solomon built him a house. 48 However, the Most High doesn't dwell in temples made with hands, as the prophet says,
49 'heaven is my throne,
 and the earth a footstool for my feet.
What kind of house will you build me?' says the Lord.
 'Or what is the place of my rest?
50 Didn't my hand make all these things?'

51 "You stiff-necked and uncircumcised in heart and ears, you always resist the Holy Spirit! As your fathers did, so you do. 52 Which of the prophets didn't your fathers persecute? They killed those who foretold the coming of the Righteous One, of whom you have now become betrayers and murderers. 53 You received the law as it was ordained by angels, and didn't keep it!"

54 Now when they heard these things, they were cut to the heart, and they gnashed at him with their teeth. 55 But he, being full of the Holy Spirit, looked up steadfastly into heaven and saw the glory of God, and Jesus standing on the right hand of God, 56 and said, "Behold, I see the heavens opened and the Son of Man standing at the right hand of God!"

57 But they cried out with a loud voice and stopped their ears, then rushed at him with one accord. 58 They threw him out of the city and stoned

---

a *6:1* The Hellenists used Greek language and culture, even though they were also of Hebrew descent.
** 7:3 Genesis 12:1
** 7:7 Genesis 15:13-14
b *7:23* The word for "brothers" here and where the context allows may be also correctly translated "brothers and sisters" or "siblings."
** 7:28 Exodus 2:14
** 7:32 Exodus 3:6

** 7:34 Exodus 3:5,7-8,10
c *7:37* TR adds "You shall listen to him."
** 7:37 Deuteronomy 18:15
** 7:40 Exodus 32:1
d *7:42* This idiom could also be translated "host of heaven", or "angelic beings", or "heavenly bodies."
** 7:43 Amos 5:25-27
** 7:50 Isaiah 66:1-2

him. The witnesses placed their garments at the feet of a young man named Saul. 59 They stoned Stephen as he called out, saying, "Lord Jesus, receive my spirit!" 60 He knelt down and cried with a loud voice, "Lord, don't hold this sin against them!" When he had said this, he fell asleep.

8

1 Saul was consenting to his death. A great persecution arose against the assembly which was in Jerusalem in that day. They were all scattered abroad throughout the regions of Judea and Samaria, except for the apostles. 2 Devout men buried Stephen and lamented greatly over him. 3 But Saul ravaged the assembly, entering into every house and dragged both men and women off to prison. 4 Therefore those who were scattered abroad went around preaching the word. 5 Philip went down to the city of Samaria and proclaimed to them the Christ. 6 The multitudes listened with one accord to the things that were spoken by Philip when they heard and saw the signs which he did. 7 For unclean spirits came out of many of those who had them. They came out, crying with a loud voice. Many who had been paralysed and lame were healed. 8 There was great joy in that city.

9 But there was a certain man, Simon by name, who used to practise sorcery in the city and amazed the people of Samaria, making himself out to be some great one, 10 to whom they all listened, from the least to the greatest, saying, "This man is that great power of God." 11 They listened to him because for a long time he had amazed them with his sorceries. 12 But when they believed Philip preaching good news concerning God's Kingdom and the name of Jesus Christ, they were baptised, both men and women. 13 Simon himself also believed. Being baptised, he continued with Philip. Seeing signs and great miracles occurring, he was amazed.

14 Now when the apostles who were at Jerusalem heard that Samaria had received the word of God, they sent Peter and John to them, 15 who, when they had come down, prayed for them, that they might receive the Holy Spirit; 16 for as yet he had fallen on none of them. They had only been baptised in the name of Christ Jesus. 17 Then they laid their hands on them, and they received the Holy Spirit. 18 Now when Simon saw that the Holy Spirit was given through the laying on of the apostles' hands, he offered them money, 19 saying, "Give me also this power, that whomever I lay my hands on may receive the Holy Spirit." 20 But Peter said to him, "May your silver perish with you, because you thought you could obtain the gift of God with money! 21 You have neither part nor lot in this matter, for your heart isn't right before God. 22 Repent therefore of this, your wickedness, and ask God if perhaps the thought of your heart may be forgiven you. 23 For I see that you are in the poison of bitterness and in the bondage of iniquity."

24 Simon answered, "Pray for me to the Lord, that none of the things which you have spoken happen to me."

25 They therefore, when they had testified and spoken the word of the Lord, returned to Jerusalem, and preached the Good News to many villages of the Samaritans.

26 Then an angel of the Lord spoke to Philip, saying, "Arise, and go towards the south to the way that goes down from Jerusalem to Gaza. This is a desert."

27 He arose and went; and behold, there was a man of Ethiopia, a eunuch of great authority under Candace, queen of the Ethiopians, who was over all her treasure, who had come to Jerusalem to worship. 28 He was returning and sitting in his chariot, and was reading the prophet Isaiah.

29 The Spirit said to Philip, "Go near, and join yourself to this chariot."

30 Philip ran to him, and heard him reading Isaiah the prophet, and said, "Do you understand what you are reading?"

31 He said, "How can I, unless someone explains it to me?" He begged Philip to come up and sit with him. 32 Now the passage of the Scripture which he was reading was this,
"He was led as a sheep to the slaughter.
    As a lamb before his shearer is silent,
    so he doesn't open his mouth.
33 In his humiliation, his judgement was taken away.
    Who will declare His generation?
    For his life is taken from the earth.'"*

34 The eunuch answered Philip, "Who is the prophet talking about? About himself, or about someone else?"

35 Philip opened his mouth, and beginning from this Scripture, preached to him about Jesus. 36 As they went on the way, they came to some water; and the eunuch said, "Behold, here is water. What is keeping me from being baptised?"

37 a 38 He commanded the chariot to stand still, and they both went down into the water, both Philip and the eunuch, and he baptised him.

39 When they came up out of the water, the Spirit of the Lord caught Philip away, and the eunuch didn't see him any more, for he went on his way rejoicing. 40 But Philip was found at Azotus. Passing through, he preached the Good News to all the cities until he came to Caesarea.

9

1 But Saul, still breathing threats and slaughter against the disciples of the Lord, went to the high priest 2 and asked for letters from him to the synagogues of Damascus, that if he found any who were of the Way, whether men or women, he might bring them bound to Jerusalem. 3 As he travelled, he got close to Damascus, and suddenly a light from the sky shone around him. 4 He fell on the earth, and heard a voice saying to him, "Saul, Saul, why do you persecute me?"

5 He said, "Who are you, Lord?"

The Lord said, "I am Jesus, whom you are persecuting.b 6 Butc rise up and enter into the city, then you will be told what you must do."

7 The men who travelled with him stood speechless, hearing the sound, but seeing no one. 8 Saul arose from the ground, and when his eyes were opened, he saw no one. They led him by the hand and brought him into Damascus. 9 He was without sight for three days, and neither ate nor drank.

10 Now there was a certain disciple at Damascus named Ananias. The Lord said to him in a vision, "Ananias!"

He said, "Behold, it's me, Lord."

11 The Lord said to him, "Arise and go to the street which is called Straight, and enquire in the house of Judahd for one named Saul, a man of Tarsus. For behold, he is praying, 12 and in a vision he has seen a man named Ananias coming in and laying his hands on him, that he might receive his sight."

13 But Ananias answered, "Lord, I have heard from many about this man, how much evil he did to your saints at Jerusalem. 14 Here he has authority from the chief priests to bind all who call on your name."

15 But the Lord said to him, "Go your way, for he is my chosen vessel to bear my name before the nations and kings, and the children of Israel. 16 For I will show him how many things he must suffer for my name's sake."

17 Ananias departed and entered into the house. Laying his hands on him, he said, "Brother Saul, the Lord, who appeared to you on the road by which you came, has sent me that you may receive your sight and be filled with the Holy Spirit." 18 Immediately something like scales fell from his eyes, and he received his sight. He arose and was baptised. 19 He took food and was strengthened.

Saul stayed several days with the disciples who were at Damascus. 20 Immediately in the synagogues he proclaimed the Christ, that he is the Son of God. 21 All who heard him were amazed, and said, "Isn't this he who in Jerusalem made havoc of those who called on this name? And he had come here intending to bring them bound before the chief priests!"

22 But Saul increased more in strength, and confounded the Jews who lived at Damascus, proving that this is the Christ. 23 When many days were fulfilled, the Jews conspired together to kill him, 24 but their plot became known to Saul. They watched the gates both day and night that they might kill him, 25 but his disciples took him by night and let him down through the wall, lowering him in a basket.

26 When Saul had come to Jerusalem, he tried to join himself to the disciples; but they were all afraid of him, not believing that he was a disciple. 27 But Barnabas took him and brought him to the apostles, and declared to them how he had seen the Lord on the way, and that he had spoken to him, and how at Damascus he had preached boldly in the name of Jesus. 28 He was with them entering intoe Jerusalem, 29 preaching boldly in the name of the Lord Jesus.f He spoke and disputed against the Hellenists,g but they were seeking to kill him. 30 When the brothersh knew it, they brought him down to Caesarea and sent him off to Tarsus.

31 So the assemblies throughout all Judea, Galilee, and Samaria had peace and were built up. They were multiplied, walking in the fear of the Lord and in the comfort of the Holy Spirit.

32 As Peter went throughout all those parts, he came down also to the saints who lived at Lydda. 33 There he found a certain man named Aeneas, who had been bedridden for eight years because he was paralysed. 34 Peter said to him, "Aeneas, Jesus Christ heals you. Get up and make your bed!" Immediately he arose. 35 All who lived at Lydda and in Sharon saw him, and they turned to the Lord.

36 Now there was at Joppa a certain disciple named Tabitha, which when translated means Dorcas.i This woman was full of good works and acts of mercy which she did. 37 In those days, she became sick and died. When they had washed her, they laid her in an upper room. 38 As Lydda was near Joppa, the disciples, hearing that Peter was there, sent two menj to him, imploring him not to delay in coming to them. 39 Peter got up and went with them. When he had come, they brought him into the upper room. All the widows stood by him weeping, and showing the tunics and other garments which Dorcas had made while she was with them. 40 Peter sent them all out, and knelt down and prayed. Turning to the body, he said, "Tabitha, get up!" She opened her eyes, and when she saw Peter, she sat up. 41 He gave her his hand and raised her up. Calling the saints and widows, he presented her alive. 42 This became known throughout all Joppa, and many believed in the Lord. 43 He stayed many days in Joppa with a tanner named Simon.

10

1 Now there was a certain man in Caesarea, Cornelius by name, a centurion of what was called the Italian Regiment, 2 a devout man, and one

---

** 8:33 Isaiah 53:7,8
a 8:37 TR adds Philip said, "If you believe with all your heart, you may." He answered, "I believe that Jesus Christ is the Son of God."
b 9:5 TR adds "It's hard for you to kick against the cattle prods."
c 9:6 TR omits "But"
d 9:11 or, Judas

e 9:28 TR and NU add "and going out"
f 9:29 TR and NU omit "Jesus" and reverse the order of verses 28 & 29.
g 9:29 The Hellenists were Hebrews who used Greek language and culture.
h 9:30 The word for "brothers" here and where the context allows may also be correctly translated "brothers and sisters" or "siblings."
i 9:36 "Dorcas" is Greek for "Gazelle."
j 9:38 Reading from NU, TR; MT omits "two men"

who feared God with all his house, who gave gifts for the needy generously to the people, and always prayed to God. 3 At about the ninth hour of the day,[a] he clearly saw in a vision an angel of God coming to him and saying to him, "Cornelius!"

4 He, fastening his eyes on him and being frightened, said, "What is it, Lord?"

He said to him, "Your prayers and your gifts to the needy have gone up for a memorial before God. 5 Now send men to Joppa, and get Simon, who is also called Peter. 6 He is staying with a tanner named Simon, whose house is by the seaside.[b]

7 When the angel who spoke to him had departed, Cornelius called two of his household servants and a devout soldier of those who waited on him continually. 8 Having explained everything to them, he sent them to Joppa.

9 Now on the next day as they were on their journey and got close to the city, Peter went up on the housetop to pray at about noon. 10 He became hungry and desired to eat, but while they were preparing, he fell into a trance. 11 He saw heaven opened and a certain container descending to him, like a great sheet let down by four corners on the earth, 12 in which were all kinds of four-footed animals of the earth, wild animals, reptiles, and birds of the sky. 13 A voice came to him, "Rise, Peter, kill and eat!"

14 But Peter said, "Not so, Lord; for I have never eaten anything that is common or unclean."

15 A voice came to him again the second time, "What God has cleansed, you must not call unclean." 16 This was done three times, and immediately the thing was received up into heaven.

17 Now while Peter was very perplexed in himself what the vision which he had seen might mean, behold, the men who were sent by Cornelius, having made enquiry for Simon's house, stood before the gate, 18 and called and asked whether Simon, who was also called Peter, was lodging there. 19 While Peter was pondering the vision, the Spirit said to him, "Behold, three[c] men seek you. 20 But arise, get down, and go with them, doubting nothing; for I have sent them."

21 Peter went down to the men, and said, "Behold, I am he whom you seek. Why have you come?"

22 They said, "Cornelius, a centurion, a righteous man and one who fears God, and well spoken of by all the nation of the Jews, was directed by a holy angel to invite you to his house, and to listen to what you say." 23 So he called them in and provided a place to stay.

On the next day Peter arose and went out with them, and some of the brothers from Joppa accompanied him. 24 On the next day they entered into Caesarea. Cornelius was waiting for them, having called together his relatives and his near friends. 25 When Peter entered, Cornelius met him, fell down at his feet, and worshipped him. 26 But Peter raised him up, saying, "Stand up! I myself am also a man." 27 As he talked with him, he went in and found many gathered together. 28 He said to them, "You yourselves know how it is an unlawful thing for a man who is a Jew to join himself or come to one of another nation, but God has shown me that I shouldn't call any man unholy or unclean. 29 Therefore I also came without complaint when I was sent for. I ask therefore, why did you send for me?"

30 Cornelius said, "Four days ago, I was fasting until this hour; and at the ninth hour,[d] I prayed in my house, and behold, a man stood before me in bright clothing 31 and said, 'Cornelius, your prayer is heard, and your gifts to the needy are remembered in the sight of God. 32 Send therefore to Joppa and summon Simon, who is also called Peter. He is staying in the house of a tanner named Simon, by the seaside. When he comes, he will speak to you.' 33 Therefore I sent to you at once, and it was good of you to come. Now therefore we are all here present in the sight of God to hear all things that have been commanded you by God."

34 Peter opened his mouth and said, "Truly I perceive that God doesn't show favouritism; 35 but in every nation he who fears him and works righteousness is acceptable to him. 36 The word which he sent to the children of Israel, preaching good news of peace by Jesus Christ—he is Lord of all— 37 you yourselves know what happened, which was proclaimed throughout all Judea, beginning from Galilee, after the baptism which John preached; 38 how God anointed Jesus of Nazareth with the Holy Spirit and with power, who went about doing good and healing all who were oppressed by the devil, for God was with him. 39 We are witnesses of everything he did both in the country of the Jews and in Jerusalem; whom they also[e] killed, hanging him on a tree. 40 God raised him up the third day and gave him to be revealed, 41 not to all the people, but to witnesses who were chosen before by God, to us, who ate and drank with him after he rose from the dead. 42 He commanded us to preach to the people and to testify that this is he who is appointed by God as the Judge of the living and the dead. 43 All the prophets testify about him, that through his name everyone who believes in him will receive remission of sins."

44 While Peter was still speaking these words, the Holy Spirit fell on all those who heard the word. 45 They of the circumcision who believed were amazed, as many as came with Peter, because the gift of the Holy Spirit was also poured out on the Gentiles. 46 For they heard them speaking in other languages and magnifying God.

Then Peter answered, 47 "Can anyone forbid these people from being baptised with water? They have received the Holy Spirit just like us." 48 He commanded them to be baptised in the name of Jesus Christ. Then they asked him to stay some days.

11

1 Now the apostles and the brothers[f] who were in Judea heard that the Gentiles had also received the word of God. 2 When Peter had come up to Jerusalem, those who were of the circumcision contended with him, 3 saying, "You went in to uncircumcised men and ate with them!"

4 But Peter began, and explained to them in order, saying, 5 "I was in the city of Joppa praying, and in a trance I saw a vision: a certain container descending, like it was a great sheet let down from heaven by four corners. It came as far as me. 6 When I had looked intently at it, I considered, and saw the four-footed animals of the earth, wild animals, creeping things, and birds of the sky. 7 I also heard a voice saying to me, 'Rise, Peter, kill and eat!' 8 But I said, 'Not so, Lord, for nothing unholy or unclean has ever entered into my mouth.' 9 But a voice answered me the second time out of heaven, 'What God has cleansed, don't you call unclean.' 10 This was done three times, and all were drawn up again into heaven. 11 Behold, immediately three men stood before the house where I was, having been sent from Caesarea to me. 12 The Spirit told me to go with them without discriminating. These six brothers also accompanied me, and we entered into the man's house. 13 He told us how he had seen the angel standing in his house and saying to him, 'Send to Joppa and get Simon, who is called Peter, 14 who will speak to you words by which you will be saved, you and all your house.' 15 As I began to speak, the Holy Spirit fell on them, even as on us at the beginning. 16 I remembered the word of the Lord, how he said, 'John indeed baptised in water, but you will be baptised in the Holy Spirit.' 17 If then God gave to them the same gift as us when we believed in the Lord Jesus Christ, who was I, that I could withstand God?"

18 When they heard these things, they held their peace and glorified God, saying, "Then God has also granted to the Gentiles repentance to life!"

19 They therefore who were scattered abroad by the oppression that arose about Stephen travelled as far as Phoenicia, Cyprus, and Antioch, speaking the word to no one except to Jews only. 20 But there were some of them, men of Cyprus and Cyrene, who, when they had come to Antioch, spoke to the Hellenists,[g] preaching the Lord Jesus. 21 The hand of the Lord was with them, and a great number believed and turned to the Lord. 22 The report concerning them came to the ears of the assembly which was in Jerusalem. They sent out Barnabas to go as far as Antioch, 23 who, when he had come, and had seen the grace of God, was glad. He exhorted them all, that with purpose of heart they should remain near to the Lord. 24 For he was a good man, and full of the Holy Spirit and of faith, and many people were added to the Lord.

25 Barnabas went out to Tarsus to look for Saul. 26 When he had found him, he brought him to Antioch. For a whole year they were gathered together with the assembly, and taught many people. The disciples were first called Christians in Antioch.

27 Now in these days, prophets came down from Jerusalem to Antioch. 28 One of them named Agabus stood up and indicated by the Spirit that there should be a great famine all over the world, which also happened in the days of Claudius. 29 As any of the disciples had plenty, each determined to send relief to the brothers who lived in Judea; 30 which they also did, sending it to the elders by the hands of Barnabas and Saul.

12

1 Now about that time, King Herod stretched out his hands to oppress some of the assembly. 2 He killed James, the brother of John, with the sword. 3 When he saw that it pleased the Jews, he proceeded to seize Peter also. This was during the days of unleavened bread. 4 When he had arrested him, he put him in prison and delivered him to four squads of four soldiers each to guard him, intending to bring him out to the people after the Passover. 5 Peter therefore was kept in the prison, but constant prayer was made by the assembly to God for him. 6 The same night when Herod was about to bring him out, Peter was sleeping between two soldiers, bound with two chains. Guards in front of the door kept the prison.

7 And behold, an angel of the Lord stood by him, and a light shone in the cell. He struck Peter on the side and woke him up, saying, "Stand up quickly!" His chains fell off his hands. 8 The angel said to him, "Get dressed and put on your sandals." He did so. He said to him, "Put on your cloak and follow me." 9 And he went out and followed him. He didn't know that what was being done by the angel was real, but thought he saw a vision. 10 When they were past the first and the second guard, they came to the iron gate that leads into the city, which opened to them by itself. They went out and went down one street, and immediately the angel departed from him.

11 When Peter had come to himself, he said, "Now I truly know that the Lord has sent out his angel and delivered me out of the hand of Herod, and from everything the Jewish people were expecting." 12 Thinking about that, he came to the house of Mary, the mother of John who was called Mark, where many were gathered together and were praying. 13 When Peter knocked at the door of the gate, a servant girl named Rhoda came to answer. 14 When she recognised Peter's voice, she didn't open the gate for joy, but ran in and reported that Peter was standing in front of the gate.

---

a 10:3 3:00 p.m.
b 10:6 TR adds "This one will tell you what it is necessary for you to do."
c 10:19 Reading from TR and NU. MT omits "three"
d 10:30 3:00 p.m.

e 10:39 TR omits "also"
f 11:1 The word for "brothers" here and where context allows may also be correctly translated "brothers and sisters" or "siblings."
g 11:20 A Hellenist is someone who keeps Greek customs and culture.

15 They said to her, "You are crazy!" But she insisted that it was so. They said, "It is his angel." 16 But Peter continued knocking. When they had opened, they saw him and were amazed. 17 But he, beckoning to them with his hand to be silent, declared to them how the Lord had brought him out of the prison. He said, "Tell these things to James and to the brothers." Then he departed and went to another place.

18 Now as soon as it was day, there was no small stir amongst the soldiers about what had become of Peter. 19 When Herod had sought for him and didn't find him, he examined the guards, then commanded that they should be put to death. He went down from Judea to Caesarea, and stayed there.

20 Now Herod was very angry with the people of Tyre and Sidon. They came with one accord to him and, having made Blastus, the king's personal aide, their friend, they asked for peace, because their country depended on the king's country for food. 21 On an appointed day, Herod dressed himself in royal clothing, sat on the throne, and gave a speech to them. 22 The people shouted, "The voice of a god, and not of a man!" 23 Immediately an angel of the Lord struck him, because he didn't give God the glory. Then he was eaten by worms and died.

24 But the word of God grew and multiplied. 25 Barnabas and Saul returned to^a Jerusalem when they had fulfilled their service, also taking with them John who was called Mark.

13

1 Now in the assembly that was at Antioch there were some prophets and teachers: Barnabas, Simeon who was called Niger, Lucius of Cyrene, Manaen the foster brother of Herod the tetrarch, and Saul. 2 As they served the Lord and fasted, the Holy Spirit said, "Separate Barnabas and Saul for me, for the work to which I have called them."

3 Then, when they had fasted and prayed and laid their hands on them, they sent them away. 4 So, being sent out by the Holy Spirit, they went down to Seleucia. From there they sailed to Cyprus. 5 When they were at Salamis, they proclaimed God's word in the Jewish synagogues. They also had John as their attendant. 6 When they had gone through the island to Paphos, they found a certain sorcerer, a false prophet, a Jew whose name was Bar Jesus, 7 who was with the proconsul, Sergius Paulus, a man of understanding. This man summoned Barnabas and Saul, and sought to hear the word of God. 8 But Elymas the sorcerer (for so is his name by interpretation) withstood them, seeking to turn the proconsul away from the faith. 9 But Saul, who is also called Paul, filled with the Holy Spirit, fastened his eyes on him 10 and said, "You son of the devil, full of all deceit and all cunning, you enemy of all righteousness, will you not cease to pervert the right ways of the Lord? 11 Now, behold, the hand of the Lord is on you, and you will be blind, not seeing the sun for a season!"

Immediately a mist and darkness fell on him. He went around seeking someone to lead him by the hand. 12 Then the proconsul, when he saw what was done, believed, being astonished at the teaching of the Lord.

13 Now Paul and his company set sail from Paphos and came to Perga in Pamphylia. John departed from them and returned to Jerusalem. 14 But they, passing on from Perga, came to Antioch of Pisidia. They went into the synagogue on the Sabbath day and sat down. 15 After the reading of the law and the prophets, the rulers of the synagogue sent to them, saying, "Brothers, if you have any word of exhortation for the people, speak."

16 Paul stood up, and gesturing with his hand said, "Men of Israel, and you who fear God, listen. 17 The God of this people^b chose our fathers, and exalted the people when they stayed as aliens in the land of Egypt, and with an uplifted arm, he led them out of it. 18 For a period of about forty years he put up with them in the wilderness. 19 When he had destroyed seven nations in the land of Canaan, he gave them their land for an inheritance for about four hundred and fifty years. 20 After these things, he gave them judges until Samuel the prophet. 21 Afterward they asked for a king, and God gave to them Saul the son of Kish, a man of the tribe of Benjamin, for forty years. 22 When he had removed him, he raised up David to be their king, to whom he also testified, 'I have found David the son of Jesse, a man after my heart, who will do all my will.' 23 From this man's offspring, God has brought salvation^c to Israel according to his promise, 24 before his coming, when John had first preached the baptism of repentance to Israel.^d 25 As John was fulfilling his course, he said, 'What do you suppose that I am? I am not he. But behold, one comes after me, the sandals of whose feet I am not worthy to untie.'

26 "Brothers, children of the stock of Abraham, and those amongst you who fear God, the word of this salvation is sent out to you. 27 For those who dwell in Jerusalem, and their rulers, because they didn't know him, nor the voices of the prophets which are read every Sabbath, fulfilled them by condemning him. 28 Though they found no cause for death, they still asked Pilate to have him killed. 29 When they had fulfilled all things that were written about him, they took him down from the tree and laid him in a tomb. 30 But God raised him from the dead, 31 and he was seen for many days by those who came up with him from Galilee to Jerusalem, who are his witnesses to the people. 32 We bring you good news of the promise made to the fathers, 33 that God has fulfilled this to us, their children, in that he raised up Jesus. As it is also written in the second psalm,
'You are my Son.
    Today I have become your father.'

34 "Concerning that he raised him up from the dead, now no more to return to corruption, he has spoken thus: 'I will give you the holy and sure blessings of David.' 35 Therefore he says also in another psalm, 'You will not allow your Holy One to see decay.' 36 For David, after he had in his own generation served the counsel of God, fell asleep, was laid with his fathers, and saw decay. 37 But he whom God raised up saw no decay. 38 Be it known to you therefore, brothers,^e that through this man is proclaimed to you remission of sins; 39 and by him everyone who believes is justified from all things, from which you could not be justified by the law of Moses. 40 Beware therefore, lest that come on you which is spoken in the prophets:
41 'Behold, you scoffers!
    Wonder and perish,
    for I work a work in your days,
    a work which you will in no way believe, if one declares it to you.'" *

42 So when the Jews went out of the synagogue, the Gentiles begged that these words might be preached to them the next Sabbath. 43 Now when the synagogue broke up, many of the Jews and of the devout proselytes followed Paul and Barnabas; who, speaking to them, urged them to continue in the grace of God.

44 The next Sabbath, almost the whole city was gathered together to hear the word of God. 45 But when the Jews saw the multitudes, they were filled with jealousy, and contradicted the things which were spoken by Paul, and blasphemed.

46 Paul and Barnabas spoke out boldly, and said, "It was necessary that God's word should be spoken to you first. Since indeed you thrust it from yourselves, and judge yourselves unworthy of eternal life, behold, we turn to the Gentiles. 47 For so has the Lord commanded us, saying,
'I have set you as a light for the Gentiles,
    that you should bring salvation to the uttermost parts of the earth.'" *

48 As the Gentiles heard this, they were glad and glorified the word of God. As many as were appointed to eternal life believed. 49 The Lord's word was spread abroad throughout all the region. 50 But the Jews stirred up the devout and prominent women and the chief men of the city, and stirred up a persecution against Paul and Barnabas, and threw them out of their borders. 51 But they shook off the dust of their feet against them, and came to Iconium. 52 The disciples were filled with joy and with the Holy Spirit.

14

1 In Iconium, they entered together into the synagogue of the Jews, and so spoke that a great multitude both of Jews and of Greeks believed. 2 But the disbelieving^f Jews stirred up and embittered the souls of the Gentiles against the brothers. 3 Therefore they stayed there a long time, speaking boldly in the Lord, who testified to the word of his grace, granting signs and wonders to be done by their hands. 4 But the multitude of the city was divided. Part sided with the Jews and part with the apostles. 5 When some of both the Gentiles and the Jews, with their rulers, made a violent attempt to mistreat and stone them, 6 they became aware of it and fled to the cities of Lycaonia, Lystra, Derbe, and the surrounding region. 7 There they preached the Good News.

8 At Lystra a certain man sat, impotent in his feet, a cripple from his mother's womb, who never had walked. 9 He was listening to Paul speaking, who, fastening eyes on him and seeing that he had faith to be made whole, 10 said with a loud voice, "Stand upright on your feet!" He leapt up and walked. 11 When the multitude saw what Paul had done, they lifted up their voice, saying in the language of Lycaonia, "The gods have come down to us in the likeness of men!" 12 They called Barnabas "Jupiter", and Paul "Mercury", because he was the chief speaker. 13 The priest of Jupiter, whose temple was in front of their city, brought oxen and garlands to the gates, and would have made a sacrifice along with the multitudes.

14 But when the apostles, Barnabas and Paul, heard of it, they tore their clothes and sprang into the multitude, crying out, 15 "Men, why are you doing these things? We also are men of the same nature as you, and bring you good news, that you should turn from these vain things to the living God, who made the sky, the earth, the sea, and all that is in them; 16 who in the generations gone by allowed all the nations to walk in their own ways. 17 Yet he didn't leave himself without witness, in that he did good and gave you^g rains from the sky and fruitful seasons, filling our hearts with food and gladness."

18 Even saying these things, they hardly stopped the multitudes from making a sacrifice to them. 19 But some Jews from Antioch and Iconium came there, and having persuaded the multitudes, they stoned Paul and dragged him out of the city, supposing that he was dead. 20 But as the disciples stood around him, he rose up, and entered into the city. On the next day he went out with Barnabas to Derbe.

21 When they had preached the Good News to that city and had made many disciples, they returned to Lystra, Iconium, and Antioch, 22

---

a *12:25* TR reads "from" instead of "to"

b *13:17* TR, NU add "Israel"

c *13:23* TR, NU read "a Saviour, Jesus" instead of "salvation"

d *13:24* TR, NU read "to all the people of Israel" instead of "to Israel"

** 13:33 Psalms 2:7

** 13:34 Isaiah 55:3

** 13:35 Psalms 16:10

e *13:38* The word for "brothers" here and where the context allows may also be correctly translated "brothers and sisters" or "siblings."

** 13:41 Habakkuk 1:5

** 13:47 Isaiah 49:6

f *14:2* or, disobedient

g *14:17* TR reads "us" instead of "you"

strengthening the souls of the disciples, exhorting them to continue in the faith, and that through many afflictions we must enter into God's Kingdom. 23 When they had appointed elders for them in every assembly, and had prayed with fasting, they commended them to the Lord on whom they had believed.

24 They passed through Pisidia and came to Pamphylia. 25 When they had spoken the word in Perga, they went down to Attalia. 26 From there they sailed to Antioch, from where they had been committed to the grace of God for the work which they had fulfilled. 27 When they had arrived and had gathered the assembly together, they reported all the things that God had done with them, and that he had opened a door of faith to the nations. 28 They stayed there with the disciples for a long time.

15

1 Some men came down from Judea and taught the brothers,ª "Unless you are circumcised after the custom of Moses, you can't be saved." 2 Therefore when Paul and Barnabas had no small discord and discussion with them, they appointed Paul, Barnabas, and some others of them to go up to Jerusalem to the apostles and elders about this question. 3 They, being sent on their way by the assembly, passed through both Phoenicia and Samaria, declaring the conversion of the Gentiles. They caused great joy to all the brothers. 4 When they had come to Jerusalem, they were received by the assembly and the apostles and the elders, and they reported everything that God had done with them.

5 But some of the sect of the Pharisees who believed rose up, saying, "It is necessary to circumcise them, and to command them to keep the law of Moses."

6 The apostles and the elders were gathered together to see about this matter. 7 When there had been much discussion, Peter rose up and said to them, "Brothers, you know that a good while ago God made a choice amongst you that by my mouth the nations should hear the word of the Good News and believe. 8 God, who knows the heart, testified about them, giving them the Holy Spirit, just like he did to us. 9 He made no distinction between us and them, cleansing their hearts by faith. 10 Now therefore why do you tempt God, that you should put a yoke on the neck of the disciples which neither our fathers nor we were able to bear? 11 But we believe that we are saved through the grace of the Lord Jesus,ᵇ just as they are."

12 All the multitude kept silence, and they listened to Barnabas and Paul reporting what signs and wonders God had done amongst the nations through them. 13 After they were silent, James answered, "Brothers, listen to me. 14 Simeon has reported how God first visited the nations to take out of them a people for his name. 15 This agrees with the words of the prophets. As it is written,

16 'After these things I will return.
I will again build the tabernacle of David, which has fallen.
I will again build its ruins.
I will set it up 17 that the rest of men may seek after the Lord:
all the Gentiles who are called by my name,
says the Lord, who does all these things.'

18 "All of God's works are known to him from eternity. 19 Therefore my judgement is that we don't trouble those from amongst the Gentiles who turn to God, 20 but that we write to them that they abstain from the pollution of idols, from sexual immorality, from what is strangled, and from blood. 21 For Moses from generations of old has in every city those who preach him, being read in the synagogues every Sabbath."

22 Then it seemed good to the apostles and the elders, with the whole assembly, to choose men out of their company, and send them to Antioch with Paul and Barnabas: Judas called Barsabbas, and Silas, chief men amongst the brothers.ᶜ 23 They wrote these things by their hand:

"The apostles, the elders, and the brothers, to the brothers who are of the Gentiles in Antioch, Syria, and Cilicia: greetings. 24 Because we have heard that some who went out from us have troubled you with words, unsettling your souls, saying, 'You must be circumcised and keep the law,' to whom we gave no commandment; 25 it seemed good to us, having come to one accord, to choose out men and send them to you with our beloved Barnabas and Paul, 26 men who have risked their lives for the name of our Lord Jesus Christ. 27 We have sent therefore Judas and Silas, who themselves will also tell you the same things by word of mouth. 28 For it seemed good to the Holy Spirit, and to us, to lay no greater burden on you than these necessary things: 29 that you abstain from things sacrificed to idols, from blood, from things strangled, and from sexual immorality, from which if you keep yourselves, it will be well with you. Farewell."

30 So, when they were sent off, they came to Antioch. Having gathered the multitude together, they delivered the letter. 31 When they had read it, they rejoiced over the encouragement. 32 Judas and Silas, also being prophets themselves, encouraged the brothers with many words and strengthened them. 33 After they had spent some time there, they were dismissed in peace from the brothers to the apostles. 34 ᵈ 35 But Paul and Barnabas stayed in Antioch, teaching and preaching the word of the Lord, with many others also.

36 After some days Paul said to Barnabas, "Let's return now and visit our brothers in every city in which we proclaimed the word of the Lord, to see how they are doing." 37 Barnabas planned to take John, who was called Mark, with them also. 38 But Paul didn't think that it was a good idea to take with them someone who had withdrawn from them in Pamphylia, and didn't go with them to do the work. 39 Then the contention grew so sharp that they separated from each other. Barnabas took Mark with him and sailed away to Cyprus, 40 but Paul chose Silas and went out, being commended by the brothers to the grace of God. 41 He went through Syria and Cilicia, strengthening the assemblies.

16

1 He came to Derbe and Lystra; and behold, a certain disciple was there, named Timothy, the son of a Jewess who believed, but his father was a Greek. 2 The brothers who were at Lystra and Iconium gave a good testimony about him. 3 Paul wanted to have him go out with him, and he took and circumcised him because of the Jews who were in those parts, for they all knew that his father was a Greek. 4 As they went on their way through the cities, they delivered the decrees to them to keep which had been ordained by the apostles and elders who were at Jerusalem. 5 So the assemblies were strengthened in the faith, and increased in number daily.

6 When they had gone through the region of Phrygia and Galatia, they were forbidden by the Holy Spirit to speak the word in Asia. 7 When they had come opposite Mysia, they tried to go into Bithynia, but the Spirit didn't allow them. 8 Passing by Mysia, they came down to Troas. 9 A vision appeared to Paul in the night. There was a man of Macedonia standing, begging him and saying, "Come over into Macedonia and help us." 10 When he had seen the vision, immediately we sought to go out to Macedonia, concluding that the Lord had called us to preach the Good News to them.

11 Setting sail therefore from Troas, we made a straight course to Samothrace, and the day following to Neapolis; 12 and from there to Philippi, which is a city of Macedonia, the foremost of the district, a Roman colony. We were staying some days in this city.

13 On the Sabbath day we went outside of the city by a riverside, where we supposed there was a place of prayer, and we sat down and spoke to the women who had come together. 14 A certain woman named Lydia, a seller of purple, of the city of Thyatira, one who worshipped God, heard us. The Lord opened her heart to listen to the things which were spoken by Paul. 15 When she and her household were baptised, she begged us, saying, "If you have judged me to be faithful to the Lord, come into my house and stay." So she persuaded us.

16 As we were going to prayer, a certain girl having a spirit of divination met us, who brought her masters much gain by fortune telling. 17 Following Paul and us, she cried out, "These men are servants of the Most High God, who proclaim to us a way of salvation!" 18 She was doing this for many days.

But Paul, becoming greatly annoyed, turned and said to the spirit, "I command you in the name of Jesus Christ to come out of her!" It came out that very hour. 19 But when her masters saw that the hope of their gain was gone, they seized Paul and Silas and dragged them into the marketplace before the rulers. 20 When they had brought them to the magistrates, they said, "These men, being Jews, are agitating our city 21 and advocate customs which it is not lawful for us to accept or to observe, being Romans."

22 The multitude rose up together against them and the magistrates tore their clothes from them, then commanded them to be beaten with rods. 23 When they had laid many stripes on them, they threw them into prison, charging the jailer to keep them safely. 24 Having received such a command, he threw them into the inner prison and secured their feet in the stocks.

25 But about midnight Paul and Silas were praying and singing hymns to God, and the prisoners were listening to them. 26 Suddenly there was a great earthquake, so that the foundations of the prison were shaken; and immediately all the doors were opened, and everyone's bonds were loosened. 27 The jailer, being roused out of sleep and seeing the prison doors open, drew his sword and was about to kill himself, supposing that the prisoners had escaped. 28 But Paul cried with a loud voice, saying, "Don't harm yourself, for we are all here!"

29 He called for lights, sprang in, fell down trembling before Paul and Silas, 30 brought them out, and said, "Sirs, what must I do to be saved?"

31 They said, "Believe in the Lord Jesus Christ, and you will be saved, you and your household." 32 They spoke the word of the Lord to him, and to all who were in his house.

33 He took them the same hour of the night and washed their stripes, and was immediately baptised, he and all his household. 34 He brought them up into his house and set food before them, and rejoiced greatly with all his household, having believed in God.

35 But when it was day, the magistrates sent the sergeants, saying, "Let those men go."

36 The jailer reported these words to Paul, saying, "The magistrates have sent to let you go; now therefore come out and go in peace."

37 But Paul said to them, "They have beaten us publicly without a trial, men who are Romans, and have cast us into prison! Do they now release us secretly? No, most certainly, but let them come themselves and bring us out!"

38 The sergeants reported these words to the magistrates, and they were afraid when they heard that they were Romans, 39 and they came and begged them. When they had brought them out, they asked them to depart

---

ª *15:1* The word for "brothers" here and where the context allows may also be correctly translated "brothers and sisters" or "siblings."
ᵇ *15:11* TR adds "Christ"
** 15:17 Amos 9:11-12

ᶜ *15:22* The word for "brothers" here and where the context allows may also be correctly translated "brothers and sisters" or "siblings."
ᵈ *15:34* Some manuscripts add: But it seemed good to Silas to stay there.

from the city. 40 They went out of the prison and entered into Lydia's house. When they had seen the brothers, they encouraged them, then departed.

17

1 Now when they had passed through Amphipolis and Apollonia, they came to Thessalonica, where there was a Jewish synagogue. 2 Paul, as was his custom, went in to them; and for three Sabbath days reasoned with them from the Scriptures, 3 explaining and demonstrating that the Christ had to suffer and rise again from the dead, and saying, "This Jesus, whom I proclaim to you, is the Christ."

4 Some of them were persuaded and joined Paul and Silas: of the devout Greeks a great multitude, and not a few of the chief women. 5 But the unpersuaded Jews took along[a] some wicked men from the marketplace and gathering a crowd, set the city in an uproar. Assaulting the house of Jason, they sought to bring them out to the people. 6 When they didn't find them, they dragged Jason and certain brothers[b] before the rulers of the city, crying, "These who have turned the world upside down have come here also, 7 whom Jason has received. These all act contrary to the decrees of Caesar, saying that there is another king, Jesus!" 8 The multitude and the rulers of the city were troubled when they heard these things. 9 When they had taken security from Jason and the rest, they let them go.

10 The brothers immediately sent Paul and Silas away by night to Beroea. When they arrived, they went into the Jewish synagogue. 11 Now these were more noble than those in Thessalonica, in that they received the word with all readiness of mind, examining the Scriptures daily to see whether these things were so. 12 Many of them therefore believed; also of the prominent Greek women, and not a few men. 13 But when the Jews of Thessalonica had knowledge that the word of God was proclaimed by Paul at Beroea also, they came there likewise, agitating the multitudes. 14 Then the brothers immediately sent out Paul to go as far as to the sea, and Silas and Timothy still stayed there. 15 But those who escorted Paul brought him as far as Athens. Receiving a commandment to Silas and Timothy that they should come to him very quickly, they departed.

16 Now while Paul waited for them at Athens, his spirit was provoked within him as he saw the city full of idols. 17 So he reasoned in the synagogue with the Jews and the devout persons, and in the marketplace every day with those who met him. 18 Some of the Epicurean and Stoic philosophers also[c] were conversing with him. Some said, "What does this babbler want to say?"

Others said, "He seems to be advocating foreign deities," because he preached Jesus and the resurrection.

19 They took hold of him and brought him to the Areopagus, saying, "May we know what this new teaching is, which you are speaking about? 20 For you bring certain strange things to our ears. We want to know therefore what these things mean." 21 Now all the Athenians and the strangers living there spent their time in nothing else, but either to tell or to hear some new thing.

22 Paul stood in the middle of the Areopagus and said, "You men of Athens, I perceive that you are very religious in all things. 23 For as I passed along and observed the objects of your worship, I also found an altar with this inscription: 'TO AN UNKNOWN GOD.' What therefore you worship in ignorance, I announce to you. 24 The God who made the world and all things in it, he, being Lord of heaven and earth, doesn't dwell in temples made with hands. 25 He isn't served by men's hands, as though he needed anything, seeing he himself gives to all life and breath and all things. 26 He made from one blood every nation of men to dwell on all the surface of the earth, having determined appointed seasons and the boundaries of their dwellings, 27 that they should seek the Lord, if perhaps they might reach out for him and find him, though he is not far from each one of us. 28 'For in him we live, move, and have our being.' As some of your own poets have said, 'For we are also his offspring.' 29 Being then the offspring of God, we ought not to think that the Divine Nature is like gold, or silver, or stone, engraved by art and design of man. 30 The times of ignorance therefore God overlooked. But now he commands that all people everywhere should repent, 31 because he has appointed a day in which he will judge the world in righteousness by the man whom he has ordained; of which he has given assurance to all men, in that he has raised him from the dead."

32 Now when they heard of the resurrection of the dead, some mocked; but others said, "We want to hear you again concerning this." 33 Thus Paul went out from amongst them. 34 But certain men joined with him and believed, including Dionysius the Areopagite, and a woman named Damaris, and others with them.

18

1 After these things Paul departed from Athens and came to Corinth. 2 He found a certain Jew named Aquila, a man of Pontus by race, who had recently come from Italy with his wife Priscilla, because Claudius had commanded all the Jews to depart from Rome. He came to them, 3 and because he practised the same trade, he lived with them and worked, for by trade they were tent makers. 4 He reasoned in the synagogue every Sabbath and persuaded Jews and Greeks.

5 When Silas and Timothy came down from Macedonia, Paul was compelled by the Spirit, testifying to the Jews that Jesus was the Christ. 6 When they opposed him and blasphemed, he shook out his clothing and said to them, "Your blood be on your own heads! I am clean. From now on, I will go to the Gentiles!"

7 He departed there and went into the house of a certain man named Justus, one who worshipped God, whose house was next door to the synagogue. 8 Crispus, the ruler of the synagogue, believed in the Lord with all his house. Many of the Corinthians, when they heard, believed and were baptised. 9 The Lord said to Paul in the night by a vision, "Don't be afraid, but speak and don't be silent; 10 for I am with you, and no one will attack you to harm you, for I have many people in this city."

11 He lived there a year and six months, teaching the word of God amongst them. 12 But when Gallio was proconsul of Achaia, the Jews with one accord rose up against Paul and brought him before the judgement seat, 13 saying, "This man persuades men to worship God contrary to the law."

14 But when Paul was about to open his mouth, Gallio said to the Jews, "If indeed it were a matter of wrong or of wicked crime, you Jews, it would be reasonable that I should bear with you; 15 but if they are questions about words and names and your own law, look to it yourselves. For I don't want to be a judge of these matters." 16 So he drove them from the judgement seat.

17 Then all the Greeks seized Sosthenes, the ruler of the synagogue, and beat him before the judgement seat. Gallio didn't care about any of these things.

18 Paul, having stayed after this many more days, took his leave of the brothers,[d] and sailed from there for Syria, together with Priscilla and Aquila. He shaved his head in Cenchreae, for he had a vow. 19 He came to Ephesus, and he left them there; but he himself entered into the synagogue and reasoned with the Jews. 20 When they asked him to stay with them a longer time, he declined; 21 but taking his leave of them, he said, "I must by all means keep this coming feast in Jerusalem, but I will return again to you if God wills." Then he set sail from Ephesus.

22 When he had landed at Caesarea, he went up and greeted the assembly, and went down to Antioch. 23 Having spent some time there, he departed and went through the region of Galatia and Phrygia, in order, establishing all the disciples. 24 Now a certain Jew named Apollos, an Alexandrian by race, an eloquent man, came to Ephesus. He was mighty in the Scriptures. 25 This man had been instructed in the way of the Lord; and being fervent in spirit, he spoke and taught accurately the things concerning Jesus, although he knew only the baptism of John. 26 He began to speak boldly in the synagogue. But when Priscilla and Aquila heard him, they took him aside, and explained to him the way of God more accurately. 27 When he had determined to pass over into Achaia, the brothers encouraged him; and wrote to the disciples to receive him. When he had come, he greatly helped those who had believed through grace; 28 for he powerfully refuted the Jews, publicly showing by the Scriptures that Jesus was the Christ.

19

1 While Apollos was at Corinth, Paul, having passed through the upper country, came to Ephesus and found certain disciples. 2 He said to them, "Did you receive the Holy Spirit when you believed?"

They said to him, "No, we haven't even heard that there is a Holy Spirit."

3 He said, "Into what then were you baptised?"

They said, "Into John's baptism."

4 Paul said, "John indeed baptised with the baptism of repentance, saying to the people that they should believe in the one who would come after him, that is, in Christ Jesus."[e]

5 When they heard this, they were baptised in the name of the Lord Jesus. 6 When Paul had laid his hands on them, the Holy Spirit came on them and they spoke with other languages and prophesied. 7 They were about twelve men in all.

8 He entered into the synagogue and spoke boldly for a period of three months, reasoning and persuading about the things concerning God's Kingdom.

9 But when some were hardened and disobedient, speaking evil of the Way before the multitude, he departed from them and separated the disciples, reasoning daily in the school of Tyrannus. 10 This continued for two years, so that all those who lived in Asia heard the word of the Lord Jesus, both Jews and Greeks.

11 God worked special miracles by the hands of Paul, 12 so that even handkerchiefs or aprons were carried away from his body to the sick, and the diseases departed from them, and the evil spirits went out. 13 But some of the itinerant Jews, exorcists, took on themselves to invoke over those who had the evil spirits the name of the Lord Jesus, saying, "We adjure you by Jesus whom Paul preaches." 14 There were seven sons of one Sceva, a Jewish chief priest, who did this.

15 The evil spirit answered, "Jesus I know, and Paul I know, but who are you?" 16 The man in whom the evil spirit was leapt on them, overpowered them, and prevailed against them, so that they fled out of that house naked and wounded. 17 This became known to all, both Jews and Greeks, who lived at Ephesus. Fear fell on them all, and the name of the Lord Jesus was magnified. 18 Many also of those who had believed came, confessing and declaring their deeds. 19 Many of those who practised

---

a *17:5* TR reads "And the Jews who were unpersuaded, becoming envious and taking along" instead of "But the unpersuaded Jews took along"
b *17:6* The word for "brothers" here and where the context allows may be also correctly translated "brothers and sisters" or "siblings."
c *17:18* TR omits "also"
d *18:18* The word for "brothers" here and where the context allows may be correctly translated "brothers and sisters" or "siblings."
e *19:4* NU omits Christ.

magical arts brought their books together and burnt them in the sight of all. They counted their price, and found it to be fifty thousand pieces of silver.[a] 20 So the word of the Lord was growing and becoming mighty.

21 Now after these things had ended, Paul determined in the Spirit, when he had passed through Macedonia and Achaia, to go to Jerusalem, saying, "After I have been there, I must also see Rome." 22 Having sent into Macedonia two of those who served him, Timothy and Erastus, he himself stayed in Asia for a while. 23 About that time there arose no small disturbance concerning the Way. 24 For a certain man named Demetrius, a silversmith who made silver shrines of Artemis, brought no little business to the craftsmen, 25 whom he gathered together with the workmen of like occupation, and said, "Sirs, you know that by this business we have our wealth. 26 You see and hear that not at Ephesus alone, but almost throughout all Asia, this Paul has persuaded and turned away many people, saying that they are no gods that are made with hands. 27 Not only is there danger that this our trade come into disrepute, but also that the temple of the great goddess Artemis will be counted as nothing and her majesty destroyed, whom all Asia and the world worships."

28 When they heard this they were filled with anger, and cried out, saying, "Great is Artemis of the Ephesians!" 29 The whole city was filled with confusion, and they rushed with one accord into the theatre, having seized Gaius and Aristarchus, men of Macedonia, Paul's companions in travel. 30 When Paul wanted to enter in to the people, the disciples didn't allow him. 31 Certain also of the Asiarchs, being his friends, sent to him and begged him not to venture into the theatre. 32 Some therefore cried one thing, and some another, for the assembly was in confusion. Most of them didn't know why they had come together. 33 They brought Alexander out of the multitude, the Jews putting him forward. Alexander beckoned with his hand, and would have made a defence to the people. 34 But when they perceived that he was a Jew, all with one voice for a time of about two hours cried out, "Great is Artemis of the Ephesians!"

35 When the town clerk had quieted the multitude, he said, "You men of Ephesus, what man is there who doesn't know that the city of the Ephesians is temple keeper of the great goddess Artemis, and of the image which fell down from Zeus? 36 Seeing then that these things can't be denied, you ought to be quiet and to do nothing rash. 37 For you have brought these men here, who are neither robbers of temples nor blasphemers of your goddess. 38 If therefore Demetrius and the craftsmen who are with him have a matter against anyone, the courts are open and there are proconsuls. Let them press charges against one another. 39 But if you seek anything about other matters, it will be settled in the regular assembly. 40 For indeed we are in danger of being accused concerning today's riot, there being no cause. Concerning it, we wouldn't be able to give an account of this commotion." 41 When he had thus spoken, he dismissed the assembly.

20

1 After the uproar had ceased, Paul sent for the disciples, took leave of them, and departed to go into Macedonia. 2 When he had gone through those parts and had encouraged them with many words, he came into Greece. 3 When he had spent three months there, and a plot was made against him by Jews as he was about to set sail for Syria, he determined to return through Macedonia. 4 These accompanied him as far as Asia: Sopater of Beroea, Aristarchus and Secundus of the Thessalonians, Gaius of Derbe, Timothy, and Tychicus and Trophimus of Asia. 5 But these had gone ahead, and were waiting for us at Troas. 6 We sailed away from Philippi after the days of Unleavened Bread, and came to them at Troas in five days, where we stayed seven days.

7 On the first day of the week, when the disciples were gathered together to break bread, Paul talked with them, intending to depart on the next day; and continued his speech until midnight. 8 There were many lights in the upper room where we[b] were gathered together. 9 A certain young man named Eutychus sat in the window, weighed down with deep sleep. As Paul spoke still longer, being weighed down by his sleep, he fell down from the third floor and was taken up dead. 10 Paul went down and fell upon him, and embracing him said, "Don't be troubled, for his life is in him."

11 When he had gone up, had broken bread and eaten, and had talked with them a long while, even until break of day, he departed. 12 They brought the boy in alive, and were greatly comforted.

13 But we, going ahead to the ship, set sail for Assos, intending to take Paul aboard there; for he had so arranged, intending himself to go by land. 14 When he met us at Assos, we took him aboard and came to Mitylene. 15 Sailing from there, we came the following day opposite Chios. The next day we touched at Samos and stayed at Trogyllium, and the day after we came to Miletus. 16 For Paul had determined to sail past Ephesus, that he might not have to spend time in Asia; for he was hastening, if it were possible for him, to be in Jerusalem on the day of Pentecost.

17 From Miletus he sent to Ephesus and called to himself the elders of the assembly. 18 When they had come to him, he said to them, "You yourselves know, from the first day that I set foot in Asia, how I was with you all the time, 19 serving the Lord with all humility, with many tears, and with trials which happened to me by the plots of the Jews; 20 how I didn't shrink from declaring to you anything that was profitable, teaching you publicly and from house to house, 21 testifying both to Jews and to Greeks

repentance towards God and faith towards our Lord Jesus.[c] 22 Now, behold, I go bound by the Spirit to Jerusalem, not knowing what will happen to me there; 23 except that the Holy Spirit testifies in every city, saying that bonds and afflictions wait for me. 24 But these things don't count; nor do I hold my life dear to myself, so that I may finish my race with joy, and the ministry which I received from the Lord Jesus, to fully testify to the Good News of the grace of God.

25 "Now, behold, I know that you all, amongst whom I went about preaching God's Kingdom, will see my face no more. 26 Therefore I testify to you today that I am clean from the blood of all men, 27 for I didn't shrink from declaring to you the whole counsel of God. 28 Take heed, therefore, to yourselves and to all the flock, in which the Holy Spirit has made you overseers, to shepherd the assembly of the Lord and[d] God which he purchased with his own blood. 29 For I know that after my departure, vicious wolves will enter in amongst you, not sparing the flock. 30 Men will arise from amongst your own selves, speaking perverse things, to draw away the disciples after them. 31 Therefore watch, remembering that for a period of three years I didn't cease to admonish everyone night and day with tears. 32 Now, brothers,[e] I entrust you to God and to the word of his grace, which is able to build up and to give you the inheritance amongst all those who are sanctified. 33 I coveted no one's silver, gold, or clothing. 34 You yourselves know that these hands served my necessities, and those who were with me. 35 In all things I gave you an example, that so labouring you ought to help the weak, and to remember the words of the Lord Jesus, that he himself said, 'It is more blessed to give than to receive.' "

36 When he had spoken these things, he knelt down and prayed with them all. 37 They all wept freely, and fell on Paul's neck and kissed him, 38 sorrowing most of all because of the word which he had spoken, that they should see his face no more. Then they accompanied him to the ship.

21

1 When we had departed from them and had set sail, we came with a straight course to Cos, and the next day to Rhodes, and from there to Patara. 2 Having found a ship crossing over to Phoenicia, we went aboard and set sail. 3 When we had come in sight of Cyprus, leaving it on the left hand, we sailed to Syria and landed at Tyre, for the ship was there to unload her cargo. 4 Having found disciples, we stayed there seven days. These said to Paul through the Spirit that he should not go up to Jerusalem. 5 When those days were over, we departed and went on our journey. They all, with wives and children, brought us on our way until we were out of the city. Kneeling down on the beach, we prayed. 6 After saying goodbye to each other, we went on board the ship, and they returned home again.

7 When we had finished the voyage from Tyre, we arrived at Ptolemais. We greeted the brothers and stayed with them one day. 8 On the next day, we who were Paul's companions departed and came to Caesarea. We entered into the house of Philip the evangelist, who was one of the seven, and stayed with him. 9 Now this man had four virgin daughters who prophesied. 10 As we stayed there some days, a certain prophet named Agabus came down from Judea. 11 Coming to us and taking Paul's belt, he bound his own feet and hands, and said, "The Holy Spirit says: 'So the Jews at Jerusalem will bind the man who owns this belt, and will deliver him into the hands of the Gentiles.'"

12 When we heard these things, both we and the people of that place begged him not to go up to Jerusalem. 13 Then Paul answered, "What are you doing, weeping and breaking my heart? For I am ready not only to be bound, but also to die at Jerusalem for the name of the Lord Jesus."

14 When he would not be persuaded, we ceased, saying, "The Lord's will be done."

15 After these days we took up our baggage and went up to Jerusalem. 16 Some of the disciples from Caesarea also went with us, bringing one Mnason of Cyprus, an early disciple, with whom we would stay.

17 When we had come to Jerusalem, the brothers received us gladly. 18 The day following, Paul went in with us to James; and all the elders were present. 19 When he had greeted them, he reported one by one the things which God had worked amongst the Gentiles through his ministry. 20 They, when they heard it, glorified God. They said to him, "You see, brother, how many thousands there are amongst the Jews of those who have believed, and they are all zealous for the law. 21 They have been informed about you, that you teach all the Jews who are amongst the Gentiles to forsake Moses, telling them not to circumcise their children and not to walk after the customs. 22 What then? The assembly must certainly meet, for they will hear that you have come. 23 Therefore do what we tell you. We have four men who have taken a vow. 24 Take them and purify yourself with them, and pay their expenses for them, that they may shave their heads. Then all will know that there is no truth in the things that they have been informed about you, but that you yourself also walk keeping the law. 25 But concerning the Gentiles who believe, we have written our decision that they should observe no such thing, except that they should keep themselves from food offered to idols, from blood, from strangled things, and from sexual immorality."

26 Then Paul took the men, and the next day purified himself and went with them into the temple, declaring the fulfilment of the days of purification, until the offering was offered for every one of them. 27 When the seven days were almost completed, the Jews from Asia, when they saw

---

[a] *19:19* The 50,000 pieces of silver here probably referred to 50,000 drachmas. If so, the value of the burnt books was equivalent to about 160 man-years of wages for agricultural labourers
[b] *20:8* TR reads "they" instead of "we"
[c] *20:21* TR adds "Christ"
[d] *20:28* TR, NU omit "the Lord and"
[e] *20:32* The word for "brothers" here and where the context allows may also be correctly translated "brothers and sisters" or "siblings."

him in the temple, stirred up all the multitude and laid hands on him, 28 crying out, "Men of Israel, help! This is the man who teaches all men everywhere against the people, and the law, and this place. Moreover, he also brought Greeks into the temple and has defiled this holy place!" 29 For they had seen Trophimus the Ephesian, with him in the city, and they supposed that Paul had brought him into the temple.

30 All the city was moved and the people ran together. They seized Paul and dragged him out of the temple. Immediately the doors were shut. 31 As they were trying to kill him, news came up to the commanding officer of the regiment that all Jerusalem was in an uproar. 32 Immediately he took soldiers and centurions and ran down to them. They, when they saw the chief captain and the soldiers, stopped beating Paul. 33 Then the commanding officer came near, arrested him, commanded him to be bound with two chains, and enquired who he was and what he had done. 34 Some shouted one thing and some another, amongst the crowd. When he couldn't find out the truth because of the noise, he commanded him to be brought into the barracks.

35 When he came to the stairs, he was carried by the soldiers because of the violence of the crowd; 36 for the multitude of the people followed after, crying out, "Away with him!" 37 As Paul was about to be brought into the barracks, he asked the commanding officer, "May I speak to you?"

He said, "Do you know Greek? 38 Aren't you then the Egyptian who before these days stirred up to sedition and led out into the wilderness the four thousand men of the Assassins?"

39 But Paul said, "I am a Jew from Tarsus in Cilicia, a citizen of no insignificant city. I beg you, allow me to speak to the people."

40 When he had given him permission, Paul, standing on the stairs, beckoned with his hand to the people. When there was a great silence, he spoke to them in the Hebrew language, saying,

22

1 "Brothers and fathers, listen to the defence which I now make to you."

2 When they heard that he spoke to them in the Hebrew language, they were even more quiet.

He said, 3 "I am indeed a Jew, born in Tarsus of Cilicia, but brought up in this city at the feet of Gamaliel, instructed according to the strict tradition of the law of our fathers, being zealous for God, even as you all are today. 4 I persecuted this Way to the death, binding and delivering into prisons both men and women, 5 as also the high priest and all the council of the elders testify, from whom also I received letters to the brothers, and travelled to Damascus to bring them also who were there to Jerusalem in bonds to be punished.

6 "As I made my journey and came close to Damascus, about noon suddenly a great light shone around me from the sky. 7 I fell to the ground and heard a voice saying to me, 'Saul, Saul, why are you persecuting me?' 8 I answered, 'Who are you, Lord?' He said to me, 'I am Jesus of Nazareth, whom you persecute.'

9 "Those who were with me indeed saw the light and were afraid, but they didn't understand the voice of him who spoke to me. 10 I said, 'What shall I do, Lord?' The Lord said to me, 'Arise, and go into Damascus. There you will be told about all things which are appointed for you to do.' 11 When I couldn't see for the glory of that light, being led by the hand of those who were with me, I came into Damascus.

12 "One Ananias, a devout man according to the law, well reported of by all the Jews who lived in Damascus, 13 came to me, and standing by me said to me, 'Brother Saul, receive your sight!' In that very hour I looked up at him. 14 He said, 'The God of our fathers has appointed you to know his will, and to see the Righteous One, and to hear a voice from his mouth. 15 For you will be a witness for him to all men of what you have seen and heard. 16 Now why do you wait? Arise, be baptised, and wash away your sins, calling on the name of the Lord.'

17 "When I had returned to Jerusalem and while I prayed in the temple, I fell into a trance 18 and saw him saying to me, 'Hurry and get out of Jerusalem quickly, because they will not receive testimony concerning me from you.' 19 I said, 'Lord, they themselves know that I imprisoned and beat in every synagogue those who believed in you. 20 When the blood of Stephen, your witness, was shed, I also was standing by, consenting to his death, and guarding the cloaks of those who killed him.'

21 "He said to me, 'Depart, for I will send you out far from here to the Gentiles.' "

22 They listened to him until he said that; then they lifted up their voice and said, "Rid the earth of this fellow, for he isn't fit to live!"

23 As they cried out, threw off their cloaks, and threw dust into the air, 24 the commanding officer commanded him to be brought into the barracks, ordering him to be examined by scourging, that he might know for what crime they shouted against him like that. 25 When they had tied him up with thongs, Paul asked the centurion who stood by, "Is it lawful for you to scourge a man who is a Roman, and not found guilty?"

26 When the centurion heard it, he went to the commanding officer and told him, "Watch what you are about to do, for this man is a Roman!"

27 The commanding officer came and asked him, "Tell me, are you a Roman?"

He said, "Yes."

28 The commanding officer answered, "I bought my citizenship for a great price."

Paul said, "But I was born a Roman."

29 Immediately those who were about to examine him departed from him, and the commanding officer also was afraid when he realised that he was a Roman, because he had bound him. 30 But on the next day, desiring to know the truth about why he was accused by the Jews, he freed him from the bonds and commanded the chief priests and all the council to come together, and brought Paul down and set him before them.

23

1 Paul, looking steadfastly at the council, said, "Brothers, I have lived before God in all good conscience until today."

2 The high priest, Ananias, commanded those who stood by him to strike him on the mouth.

3 Then Paul said to him, "God will strike you, you whitewashed wall! Do you sit to judge me according to the law, and command me to be struck contrary to the law?"

4 Those who stood by said, "Do you malign God's high priest?"

5 Paul said, "I didn't know, brothers, that he was high priest. For it is written, 'You shall not speak evil of a ruler of your people.'"*

6 But when Paul perceived that the one part were Sadducees and the other Pharisees, he cried out in the council, "Men and brothers, I am a Pharisee, a son of Pharisees. Concerning the hope and resurrection of the dead I am being judged!"

7 When he had said this, an argument arose between the Pharisees and Sadducees, and the crowd was divided. 8 For the Sadducees say that there is no resurrection, nor angel, nor spirit; but the Pharisees confess all of these. 9 A great clamour arose, and some of the scribes of the Pharisees' part stood up, and contended, saying, "We find no evil in this man. But if a spirit or angel has spoken to him, let's not fight against God!"

10 When a great argument arose, the commanding officer, fearing that Paul would be torn in pieces by them, commanded the soldiers to go down and take him by force from amongst them and bring him into the barracks.

11 The following night, the Lord stood by him and said, "Cheer up, Paul, for as you have testified about me at Jerusalem, so you must testify also at Rome."

12 When it was day, some of the Jews banded together and bound themselves under a curse, saying that they would neither eat nor drink until they had killed Paul. 13 There were more than forty people who had made this conspiracy. 14 They came to the chief priests and the elders, and said, "We have bound ourselves under a great curse to taste nothing until we have killed Paul. 15 Now therefore, you with the council inform the commanding officer that he should bring him down to you tomorrow, as though you were going to judge his case more exactly. We are ready to kill him before he comes near."

16 But Paul's sister's son heard they were lying in wait, and he came and entered into the barracks and told Paul. 17 Paul summoned one of the centurions and said, "Bring this young man to the commanding officer, for he has something to tell him."

18 So he took him and brought him to the commanding officer and said, "Paul, the prisoner, summoned me and asked me to bring this young man to you. He has something to tell you."

19 The commanding officer took him by the hand, and going aside, asked him privately, "What is it that you have to tell me?"

20 He said, "The Jews have agreed to ask you to bring Paul down to the council tomorrow, as though intending to enquire somewhat more accurately concerning him. 21 Therefore don't yield to them, for more than forty men lie in wait for him, who have bound themselves under a curse to neither eat nor drink until they have killed him. Now they are ready, looking for the promise from you."

22 So the commanding officer let the young man go, charging him, "Tell no one that you have revealed these things to me."

23 He called to himself two of the centurions, and said, "Prepare two hundred soldiers to go as far as Caesarea, with seventy horsemen and two hundred men armed with spears, at the third hour of the night."ᵃ 24 He asked them to provide mounts, that they might set Paul on one, and bring him safely to Felix the governor. 25 He wrote a letter like this:

26 "Claudius Lysias to the most excellent governor Felix: Greetings.

27 "This man was seized by the Jews, and was about to be killed by them when I came with the soldiers and rescued him, having learnt that he was a Roman. 28 Desiring to know the cause why they accused him, I brought him down to their council. 29 I found him to be accused about questions of their law, but not to be charged with anything worthy of death or of imprisonment. 30 When I was told that the Jews lay in wait for the man, I sent him to you immediately, charging his accusers also to bring their accusations against him before you. Farewell."

31 So the soldiers, carrying out their orders, took Paul and brought him by night to Antipatris. 32 But on the next day they left the horsemen to go with him, and returned to the barracks. 33 When they came to Caesarea and delivered the letter to the governor, they also presented Paul to him. 34 When the governor had read it, he asked what province he was from. When he understood that he was from Cilicia, he said, 35 "I will hear you fully when your accusers also arrive." He commanded that he be kept in Herod's palace.

24

1 After five days, the high priest, Ananias, came down with certain elders and an orator, one Tertullus. They informed the governor against Paul. 2 When he was called, Tertullus began to accuse him, saying, "Seeing that by you we enjoy much peace, and that prosperity is coming to this

---

** 23:5 Exodus 22:28

ᵃ 23:23 about 9:00 p.m.

nation by your foresight, ₃ we accept it in all ways and in all places, most excellent Felix, with all thankfulness. ₄ But that I don't delay you, I entreat you to bear with us and hear a few words. ₅ For we have found this man to be a plague, an instigator of insurrections amongst all the Jews throughout the world, and a ringleader of the sect of the Nazarenes. ₆ He even tried to profane the temple, and we arrested him.ᵃ ₇ ᵇ ₈ ᶜBy examining him yourself you may ascertain all these things of which we accuse him."

₉ The Jews also joined in the attack, affirming that these things were so.

₁₀ When the governor had beckoned to him to speak, Paul answered, "Because I know that you have been a judge of this nation for many years, I cheerfully make my defence, ₁₁ seeing that you can verify that it is not more than twelve days since I went up to worship at Jerusalem. ₁₂ In the temple they didn't find me disputing with anyone or stirring up a crowd, either in the synagogues or in the city. ₁₃ Nor can they prove to you the things of which they now accuse me. ₁₄ But this I confess to you, that according to the Way, which they call a sect, so I serve the God of our fathers, believing all things which are according to the law, and which are written in the prophets; ₁₅ having hope towards God, which these also themselves look for, that there will be a resurrection of the dead, both of the just and unjust. ₁₆ In this I also practise always having a conscience void of offence towards God and men. ₁₇ Now after some years, I came to bring gifts for the needy to my nation, and offerings; ₁₈ amid which certain Jews from Asia found me purified in the temple, not with a mob, nor with turmoil. ₁₉ They ought to have been here before you and to make accusation if they had anything against me. ₂₀ Or else let these men themselves say what injustice they found in me when I stood before the council, ₂₁ unless it is for this one thing that I cried standing amongst them, 'Concerning the resurrection of the dead I am being judged before you today!'"

₂₂ But Felix, having more exact knowledge concerning the Way, deferred them, saying, "When Lysias, the commanding officer, comes down, I will decide your case." ₂₃ He ordered the centurion that Paul should be kept in custody and should have some privileges, and not to forbid any of his friends to serve him or to visit him.

₂₄ After some days, Felix came with Drusilla his wife, who was a Jewess, and sent for Paul and heard him concerning the faith in Christ Jesus. ₂₅ As he reasoned about righteousness, self-control, and the judgement to come, Felix was terrified, and answered, "Go your way for this time, and when it is convenient for me, I will summon you." ₂₆ Meanwhile, he also hoped that money would be given to him by Paul, that he might release him. Therefore also he sent for him more often and talked with him. ₂₇ But when two years were fulfilled, Felix was succeeded by Porcius Festus, and desiring to gain favour with the Jews, Felix left Paul in bonds.

25

₁ Festus therefore, having come into the province, after three days went up to Jerusalem from Caesarea. ₂ Then the high priest and the principal men of the Jews informed him against Paul, and they begged him, ₃ asking a favour against him, that he would summon him to Jerusalem, plotting to kill him on the way. ₄ However Festus answered that Paul should be kept in custody at Caesarea, and that he himself was about to depart shortly. ₅ "Let them therefore", he said, "that are in power amongst you go down with me, and if there is anything wrong in the man, let them accuse him."

₆ When he had stayed amongst them more than ten days, he went down to Caesarea, and on the next day he sat on the judgement seat, and commanded Paul to be brought. ₇ When he had come, the Jews who had come down from Jerusalem stood around him, bringing against him many and grievous charges which they could not prove, ₈ while he said in his defence, "Neither against the law of the Jews, nor against the temple, nor against Caesar, have I sinned at all."

₉ But Festus, desiring to gain favour with the Jews, answered Paul and said, "Are you willing to go up to Jerusalem and be judged by me there concerning these things?"

₁₀ But Paul said, "I am standing before Caesar's judgement seat, where I ought to be tried. I have done no wrong to the Jews, as you also know very well. ₁₁ For if I have done wrong and have committed anything worthy of death, I don't refuse to die; but if none of those things is true that they accuse me of, no one can give me up to them. I appeal to Caesar!"

₁₂ Then Festus, when he had conferred with the council, answered, "You have appealed to Caesar. To Caesar you shall go."

₁₃ Now when some days had passed, King Agrippa and Bernice arrived at Caesarea and greeted Festus. ₁₄ As he stayed there many days, Festus laid Paul's case before the king, saying, "There is a certain man left a prisoner by Felix; ₁₅ about whom, when I was at Jerusalem, the chief priests and the elders of the Jews informed me, asking for a sentence against him. ₁₆ I answered them that it is not the custom of the Romans to give up any man to destruction before the accused has met the accusers face to face and has had opportunity to make his defence concerning the matter laid against him. ₁₇ When therefore they had come together here, I didn't delay, but on the next day sat on the judgement seat and commanded the man to be brought. ₁₈ When the accusers stood up, they brought no charges against him of such things as I supposed; ₁₉ but had certain questions against him about their own religion and about one Jesus, who was dead, whom Paul affirmed to be alive. ₂₀ Being perplexed how to

enquire concerning these things, I asked whether he was willing to go to Jerusalem and there be judged concerning these matters. ₂₁ But when Paul had appealed to be kept for the decision of the emperor, I commanded him to be kept until I could send him to Caesar."

₂₂ Agrippa said to Festus, "I also would like to hear the man myself." "Tomorrow," he said, "you shall hear him."

₂₃ So on the next day, when Agrippa and Bernice had come with great pomp, and they had entered into the place of hearing with the commanding officers and the principal men of the city, at the command of Festus, Paul was brought in. ₂₄ Festus said, "King Agrippa, and all men who are here present with us, you see this man about whom all the multitude of the Jews petitioned me, both at Jerusalem and here, crying that he ought not to live any longer. ₂₅ But when I found that he had committed nothing worthy of death, and as he himself appealed to the emperor, I determined to send him, ₂₆ of whom I have no certain thing to write to my lord. Therefore I have brought him out before you, and especially before you, King Agrippa, that, after examination I may have something to write. ₂₇ For it seems to me unreasonable, in sending a prisoner, not to also specify the charges against him."

26

₁ Agrippa said to Paul, "You may speak for yourself."

Then Paul stretched out his hand, and made his defence. ₂ "I think myself happy, King Agrippa, that I am to make my defence before you today concerning all the things that I am accused by the Jews, ₃ especially because you are expert in all customs and questions which are amongst the Jews. Therefore I beg you to hear me patiently.

₄ "Indeed, all the Jews know my way of life from my youth up, which was from the beginning amongst my own nation and at Jerusalem; ₅ having known me from the first, if they are willing to testify, that after the strictest sect of our religion I lived a Pharisee. ₆ Now I stand here to be judged for the hope of the promise made by God to our fathers, ₇ which our twelve tribes, earnestly serving night and day, hope to attain. Concerning this hope I am accused by the Jews, King Agrippa! ₈ Why is it judged incredible with you if God does raise the dead?

₉ "I myself most certainly thought that I ought to do many things contrary to the name of Jesus of Nazareth. ₁₀ I also did this in Jerusalem. I both shut up many of the saints in prisons, having received authority from the chief priests; and when they were put to death I gave my vote against them. ₁₁ Punishing them often in all the synagogues, I tried to make them blaspheme. Being exceedingly enraged against them, I persecuted them even to foreign cities.

₁₂ "Whereupon as I travelled to Damascus with the authority and commission from the chief priests, ₁₃ at noon, O king, I saw on the way a light from the sky, brighter than the sun, shining around me and those who travelled with me. ₁₄ When we had all fallen to the earth, I heard a voice saying to me in the Hebrew language, 'Saul, Saul, why are you persecuting me? It is hard for you to kick against the goads.'

₁₅ "I said, 'Who are you, Lord?'

"He said, 'I am Jesus, whom you are persecuting. ₁₆ But arise, and stand on your feet, for I have appeared to you for this purpose: to appoint you a servant and a witness both of the things which you have seen and of the things which I will reveal to you; ₁₇ delivering you from the people and from the Gentiles, to whom I send you, ₁₈ to open their eyes, that they may turn from darkness to light and from the power of Satan to God, that they may receive remission of sins and an inheritance amongst those who are sanctified by faith in me.'

₁₉ "Therefore, King Agrippa, I was not disobedient to the heavenly vision, ₂₀ but declared first to them of Damascus, at Jerusalem, and throughout all the country of Judea, and also to the Gentiles, that they should repent and turn to God, doing works worthy of repentance. ₂₁ For this reason the Jews seized me in the temple and tried to kill me. ₂₂ Having therefore obtained the help that is from God, I stand to this day testifying both to small and great, saying nothing but what the prophets and Moses said would happen, ₂₃ how the Christ must suffer, and how, by the resurrection of the dead, he would be first to proclaim light both to these people and to the Gentiles."

₂₄ As he thus made his defence, Festus said with a loud voice, "Paul, you are crazy! Your great learning is driving you insane!"

₂₅ But he said, "I am not crazy, most excellent Festus, but boldly declare words of truth and reasonableness. ₂₆ For the king knows of these things, to whom also I speak freely. For I am persuaded that none of these things is hidden from him, for this has not been done in a corner. ₂₇ King Agrippa, do you believe the prophets? I know that you believe."

₂₈ Agrippa said to Paul, "With a little persuasion are you trying to make me a Christian?"

₂₉ Paul said, "I pray to God, that whether with little or with much, not only you, but also all that hear me today, might become such as I am, except for these bonds."

₃₀ The king rose up with the governor and Bernice, and those who sat with them. ₃₁ When they had withdrawn, they spoke to one another, saying, "This man does nothing worthy of death or of bonds." ₃₂ Agrippa said to Festus, "This man might have been set free if he had not appealed to Caesar."

ᵃ *24:6* TR adds "We wanted to judge him according to our law,"
ᵇ *24:7* TR adds "but the commanding officer, Lysias, came by and with great violence took him out of our hands,"

ᶜ *24:8* TR adds "commanding his accusers to come to you."

27

1 When it was determined that we should sail for Italy, they delivered Paul and certain other prisoners to a centurion named Julius, of the Augustan band. 2 Embarking in a ship of Adramyttium, which was about to sail to places on the coast of Asia, we put to sea, Aristarchus, a Macedonian of Thessalonica being with us. 3 The next day, we touched at Sidon. Julius treated Paul kindly and gave him permission to go to his friends and refresh himself. 4 Putting to sea from there, we sailed under the lee of Cyprus, because the winds were contrary. 5 When we had sailed across the sea which is off Cilicia and Pamphylia, we came to Myra, a city of Lycia. 6 There the centurion found a ship of Alexandria sailing for Italy, and he put us on board. 7 When we had sailed slowly many days, and had come with difficulty opposite Cnidus, the wind not allowing us further, we sailed under the lee of Crete, opposite Salmone. 8 With difficulty sailing along it we came to a certain place called Fair Havens, near the city of Lasea.

9 When much time had passed and the voyage was now dangerous because the Fast had now already gone by, Paul admonished them 10 and said to them, "Sirs, I perceive that the voyage will be with injury and much loss, not only of the cargo and the ship, but also of our lives." 11 But the centurion gave more heed to the master and to the owner of the ship than to those things which were spoken by Paul. 12 Because the haven was not suitable to winter in, the majority advised going to sea from there, if by any means they could reach Phoenix and winter there, which is a port of Crete, looking southwest and northwest.

13 When the south wind blew softly, supposing that they had obtained their purpose, they weighed anchor and sailed along Crete, close to shore. 14 But before long, a stormy wind beat down from shore, which is called Euroclydon.[a] 15 When the ship was caught and couldn't face the wind, we gave way to it and were driven along. 16 Running under the lee of a small island called Clauda, we were able, with difficulty, to secure the boat. 17 After they had hoisted it up, they used cables to help reinforce the ship. Fearing that they would run aground on the Syrtis sand bars, they lowered the sea anchor, and so were driven along. 18 As we laboured exceedingly with the storm, the next day they began to throw things overboard. 19 On the third day, they threw out the ship's tackle with their own hands. 20 When neither sun nor stars shone on us for many days, and no small storm pressed on us, all hope that we would be saved was now taken away.

21 When they had been long without food, Paul stood up in the middle of them and said, "Sirs, you should have listened to me, and not have set sail from Crete and have gotten this injury and loss. 22 Now I exhort you to cheer up, for there will be no loss of life amongst you, but only of the ship. 23 For there stood by me this night an angel, belonging to the God whose I am and whom I serve, 24 saying, 'Don't be afraid, Paul. You must stand before Caesar. Behold, God has granted you all those who sail with you.' 25 Therefore, sirs, cheer up! For I believe God, that it will be just as it has been spoken to me. 26 But we must run aground on a certain island."

27 But when the fourteenth night had come, as we were driven back and forth in the Adriatic Sea, about midnight the sailors surmised that they were drawing near to some land. 28 They took soundings and found twenty fathoms.[b] After a little while, they took soundings again, and found fifteen fathoms.[c] 29 Fearing that we would run aground on rocky ground, they let go four anchors from the stern, and wished for daylight. 30 As the sailors were trying to flee out of the ship and had lowered the boat into the sea, pretending that they would lay out anchors from the bow, 31 Paul said to the centurion and to the soldiers, "Unless these stay in the ship, you can't be saved." 32 Then the soldiers cut away the ropes of the boat and let it fall off.

33 While the day was coming on, Paul begged them all to take some food, saying, "Today is the fourteenth day that you wait and continue fasting, having taken nothing. 34 Therefore I beg you to take some food, for this is for your safety; for not a hair will perish from any of your heads." 35 When he had said this and had taken bread, he gave thanks to God in the presence of all; then he broke it and began to eat. 36 Then they all cheered up, and they also took food. 37 In all, we were two hundred and seventy-six souls on the ship. 38 When they had eaten enough, they lightened the ship, throwing out the wheat into the sea. 39 When it was day, they didn't recognise the land, but they noticed a certain bay with a beach, and they decided to try to drive the ship onto it. 40 Casting off the anchors, they left them in the sea, at the same time untying the rudder ropes. Hoisting up the foresail to the wind, they made for the beach. 41 But coming to a place where two seas met, they ran the vessel aground. The bow struck and remained immovable, but the stern began to break up by the violence of the waves.

42 The soldiers' counsel was to kill the prisoners, so that none of them would swim out and escape. 43 But the centurion, desiring to save Paul, stopped them from their purpose, and commanded that those who could swim should throw themselves overboard first to go towards the land; 44 and the rest should follow, some on planks and some on other things from the ship. So they all escaped safely to the land.

28

1 When we had escaped, then they[d] learnt that the island was called Malta. 2 The natives showed us uncommon kindness; for they kindled a fire and received us all, because of the present rain and because of the cold. 3 But when Paul had gathered a bundle of sticks and laid them on the fire, a viper came out because of the heat and fastened on his hand. 4 When the natives saw the creature hanging from his hand, they said to one another, "No doubt this man is a murderer, whom, though he has escaped from the sea, yet Justice has not allowed to live." 5 However he shook off the creature into the fire, and wasn't harmed. 6 But they expected that he would have swollen or fallen down dead suddenly, but when they watched for a long time and saw nothing bad happen to him, they changed their minds and said that he was a god.

7 Now in the neighbourhood of that place were lands belonging to the chief man of the island, named Publius, who received us and courteously entertained us for three days. 8 The father of Publius lay sick of fever and dysentery. Paul entered in to him, prayed, and laying his hands on him, healed him. 9 Then when this was done, the rest also who had diseases in the island came and were cured. 10 They also honoured us with many honours; and when we sailed, they put on board the things that we needed.

11 After three months, we set sail in a ship of Alexandria which had wintered in the island, whose figurehead was "The Twin Brothers." 12 Touching at Syracuse, we stayed there three days. 13 From there we circled around and arrived at Rhegium. After one day, a south wind sprang up, and on the second day we came to Puteoli, 14 where we found brothers,[e] and were entreated to stay with them for seven days. So we came to Rome. 15 From there the brothers, when they heard of us, came to meet us as far as The Market of Appius and The Three Taverns. When Paul saw them, he thanked God and took courage. 16 When we entered into Rome, the centurion delivered the prisoners to the captain of the guard, but Paul was allowed to stay by himself with the soldier who guarded him.

17 After three days Paul called together those who were the leaders of the Jews. When they had come together, he said to them, "I, brothers, though I had done nothing against the people or the customs of our fathers, still was delivered prisoner from Jerusalem into the hands of the Romans, 18 who, when they had examined me, desired to set me free, because there was no cause of death in me. 19 But when the Jews spoke against it, I was constrained to appeal to Caesar, not that I had anything about which to accuse my nation. 20 For this cause therefore I asked to see you and to speak with you. For because of the hope of Israel I am bound with this chain."

21 They said to him, "We neither received letters from Judea concerning you, nor did any of the brothers come here and report or speak any evil of you. 22 But we desire to hear from you what you think. For, as concerning this sect, it is known to us that everywhere it is spoken against."

23 When they had appointed him a day, many people came to him at his lodging. He explained to them, testifying about God's Kingdom, and persuading them concerning Jesus, both from the law of Moses and from the prophets, from morning until evening. 24 Some believed the things which were spoken, and some disbelieved. 25 When they didn't agree amongst themselves, they departed after Paul had spoken one message: "The Holy Spirit spoke rightly through Isaiah the prophet to our fathers, 26 saying,

'Go to this people and say,
in hearing, you will hear,
    but will in no way understand.
In seeing, you will see,
    but will in no way perceive.
27 For this people's heart has grown callous.
    Their ears are dull of hearing.
    Their eyes they have closed.
Lest they should see with their eyes,
    hear with their ears,
    understand with their heart,
    and would turn again,
    then I would heal them.'"

28 "Be it known therefore to you that the salvation of God is sent to the nations, and they will listen."

29 When he had said these words, the Jews departed, having a great dispute amongst themselves.[f]

30 Paul stayed two whole years in his own rented house and received all who were coming to him, 31 preaching God's Kingdom and teaching the things concerning the Lord Jesus Christ with all boldness, without hindrance.

---

a *27:14* Or, "a northeaster".
b *27:28* 20 fathoms = 120 feet = 36.6 metres
c *27:28* 15 fathoms = 90 feet = 27.4 metres
d *28:1* NU reads "we"
e *28:14* The word for "brothers" here and where context allows may also be correctly translated "brothers and sisters" or "siblings."
** 28:27 Isaiah 6:9-10
f *28:29* NU omits verse 29.

Paul's Letter to the Romans

1

1 Paul, a servant of Jesus Christ,[a] called to be an apostle, set apart for the Good News of God, 2 which he promised before through his prophets in the holy Scriptures, 3 concerning his Son, who was born of the offspring[b] of David according to the flesh, 4 who was declared to be the Son of God with power according to the Spirit of holiness, by the resurrection from the dead, Jesus Christ our Lord, 5 through whom we received grace and apostleship for obedience of faith amongst all the nations for his name's sake; 6 amongst whom you are also called to belong to Jesus Christ; 7 to all who are in Rome, beloved of God, called to be saints: Grace to you and peace from God our Father and the Lord Jesus Christ.

8 First, I thank my God through Jesus Christ for all of you, that your faith is proclaimed throughout the whole world. 9 For God is my witness, whom I serve in my spirit in the Good News of his Son, how unceasingly I make mention of you always in my prayers, 10 requesting, if by any means now at last I may be prospered by the will of God to come to you. 11 For I long to see you, that I may impart to you some spiritual gift, to the end that you may be established; 12 that is, that I with you may be encouraged in you, each of us by the other's faith, both yours and mine.

13 Now I don't desire to have you unaware, brothers, that I often planned to come to you (and was hindered so far), that I might have some fruit amongst you also, even as amongst the rest of the Gentiles. 14 I am debtor both to Greeks and to foreigners, both to the wise and to the foolish. 15 So as much as is in me, I am eager to preach the Good News to you also who are in Rome.

16 For I am not ashamed of the Good News of Christ, because it is the power of God for salvation for everyone who believes, for the Jew first, and also for the Greek. 17 For in it is revealed God's righteousness from faith to faith. As it is written, "But the righteous shall live by faith."[*]

18 For the wrath of God is revealed from heaven against all ungodliness and unrighteousness of men who suppress the truth in unrighteousness, 19 because that which is known of God is revealed in them, for God revealed it to them. 20 For the invisible things of him since the creation of the world are clearly seen, being perceived through the things that are made, even his everlasting power and divinity, that they may be without excuse. 21 Because knowing God, they didn't glorify him as God, and didn't give thanks, but became vain in their reasoning, and their senseless heart was darkened.

22 Professing themselves to be wise, they became fools, 23 and traded the glory of the incorruptible God for the likeness of an image of corruptible man, and of birds, four-footed animals, and creeping things. 24 Therefore God also gave them up in the lusts of their hearts to uncleanness, that their bodies should be dishonoured amongst themselves; 25 who exchanged the truth of God for a lie, and worshipped and served the creature rather than the Creator, who is blessed forever. Amen.

26 For this reason, God gave them up to vile passions. For their women changed the natural function into that which is against nature. 27 Likewise also the men, leaving the natural function of the woman, burnt in their lust towards one another, men doing what is inappropriate with men, and receiving in themselves the due penalty of their error. 28 Even as they refused to have God in their knowledge, God gave them up to a reprobate mind, to do those things which are not fitting; 29 being filled with all unrighteousness, sexual immorality, wickedness, covetousness, malice; full of envy, murder, strife, deceit, evil habits, secret slanderers, 30 backbiters, hateful to God, insolent, arrogant, boastful, inventors of evil things, disobedient to parents, 31 without understanding, covenant breakers, without natural affection, unforgiving, unmerciful; 32 who, knowing the ordinance of God, that those who practise such things are worthy of death, not only do the same, but also approve of those who practise them.

2

1 Therefore you are without excuse, O man, whoever you are who judge. For in that which you judge another, you condemn yourself. For you who judge practise the same things. 2 We know that the judgement of God is according to truth against those who practise such things. 3 Do you think this, O man who judges those who practise such things, and do the same, that you will escape the judgement of God? 4 Or do you despise the riches of his goodness, forbearance, and patience, not knowing that the goodness of God leads you to repentance? 5 But according to your hardness and unrepentant heart you are treasuring up for yourself wrath in the day of wrath, revelation, and of the righteous judgement of God, 6 who "will pay back to everyone according to their works:"[*] 7 to those who by perseverance in well-doing seek for glory, honour, and incorruptibility, eternal life; 8 but to those who are self-seeking and don't obey the truth, but obey unrighteousness, will be wrath, indignation, 9 oppression, and anguish on every soul of man who does evil, to the Jew first, and also to the Greek.

10 But glory, honour, and peace go to every man who does good, to the Jew first, and also to the Greek. 11 For there is no partiality with God. 12 For as many as have sinned without the law will also perish without the law. As many as have sinned under the law will be judged by the law. 13 For it isn't the hearers of the law who are righteous before God, but the doers of the law will be justified 14 (for when Gentiles who don't have the law do by nature the things of the law, these, not having the law, are a law to themselves, 15 in that they show the work of the law written in their hearts, their conscience testifying with them, and their thoughts amongst themselves accusing or else excusing them) 16 in the day when God will judge the secrets of men, according to my Good News, by Jesus Christ.

17 Indeed you bear the name of a Jew, rest on the law, glory in God, 18 know his will, and approve the things that are excellent, being instructed out of the law, 19 and are confident that you yourself are a guide of the blind, a light to those who are in darkness, 20 a corrector of the foolish, a teacher of babies, having in the law the form of knowledge and of the truth. 21 You therefore who teach another, don't you teach yourself? You who preach that a man shouldn't steal, do you steal? 22 You who say a man shouldn't commit adultery, do you commit adultery? You who abhor idols, do you rob temples? 23 You who glory in the law, do you dishonour God by disobeying the law? 24 For "the name of God is blasphemed amongst the Gentiles because of you," [*] just as it is written. 25 For circumcision indeed profits, if you are a doer of the law, but if you are a transgressor of the law, your circumcision has become uncircumcision. 26 If therefore the uncircumcised keep the ordinances of the law, won't his uncircumcision be accounted as circumcision? 27 Won't those who are physically uncircumcised, but fulfil the law, judge you, who with the letter and circumcision are a transgressor of the law? 28 For he is not a Jew who is one outwardly, neither is that circumcision which is outward in the flesh; 29 but he is a Jew who is one inwardly, and circumcision is that of the heart, in the spirit, not in the letter; whose praise is not from men, but from God.

3

1 Then what advantage does the Jew have? Or what is the profit of circumcision? 2 Much in every way! Because first of all, they were entrusted with the revelations of God. 3 For what if some were without faith? Will their lack of faith nullify the faithfulness of God? 4 May it never be! Yes, let God be found true, but every man a liar. As it is written,
"that you might be justified in your words,
    and might prevail when you come into judgement."[*]

5 But if our unrighteousness commends the righteousness of God, what will we say? Is God unrighteous who inflicts wrath? I speak like men do. 6 May it never be! For then how will God judge the world? 7 For if the truth of God through my lie abounded to his glory, why am I also still judged as a sinner? 8 Why not (as we are slanderously reported, and as some affirm that we say), "Let's do evil, that good may come?" Those who say so are justly condemned.

9 What then? Are we better than they? No, in no way. For we previously warned both Jews and Greeks that they are all under sin. 10 As it is written,
"There is no one righteous;
    no, not one.
11 There is no one who understands.
    There is no one who seeks after God.
12 They have all turned away.
    They have together become unprofitable.
There is no one who does good,
    no, not so much as one."[*]
13 "Their throat is an open tomb.
    With their tongues they have used deceit."[*]
"The poison of vipers is under their lips."[*]
14 "Their mouth is full of cursing and bitterness."[*]
15 "Their feet are swift to shed blood.
    16 Destruction and misery are in their ways.
    17 The way of peace, they haven't known."[*]
18 "There is no fear of God before their eyes."[*]

19 Now we know that whatever things the law says, it speaks to those who are under the law, that every mouth may be closed, and all the world may be brought under the judgement of God. 20 Because by the works of the law, no flesh will be justified in his sight; for through the law comes the knowledge of sin.

21 But now apart from the law, a righteousness of God has been revealed, being testified by the law and the prophets; 22 even the righteousness of God through faith in Jesus Christ to all and on all those who believe. For there is no distinction, 23 for all have sinned, and fall short of the glory of God; 24 being justified freely by his grace through the redemption that is in Christ Jesus, 25 whom God sent to be an atoning sacrifice[c] through faith in his blood, for a demonstration of his righteousness through the passing over of prior sins, in God's forbearance; 26 to demonstrate his righteousness at this present time, that he might himself be just and the justifier of him who has faith in Jesus.

_____

a *1:1* "Christ" means "Anointed One".
b *1:3* or, seed
** 1:17 Habakkuk 2:4
** 2:6 Psalms 62:12; Proverbs 24:12
** 2:24 Isaiah 52:5; Ezekiel 36:22
** 3:4 Psalms 51:4
** 3:12 Psalms 14:1-3; 53:1-3; Ecclesiastes 7:20

** 3:13 Psalms 5:9
** 3:13 Psalms 140:3
** 3:14 Psalms 10:7
** 3:17 Isaiah 59:7-8
** 3:18 Psalms 36:1
c *3:25* or, a propitiation

27 Where then is the boasting? It is excluded. By what kind of law? Of works? No, but by a law of faith. 28 We maintain therefore that a man is justified by faith apart from the works of the law. 29 Or is God the God of Jews only? Isn't he the God of Gentiles also? Yes, of Gentiles also, 30 since indeed there is one God who will justify the circumcised by faith and the uncircumcised through faith.

31 Do we then nullify the law through faith? May it never be! No, we establish the law.

4

1 What then will we say that Abraham, our forefather, has found according to the flesh? 2 For if Abraham was justified by works, he has something to boast about, but not towards God. 3 For what does the Scripture say? "Abraham believed God, and it was accounted to him for righteousness."* 4 Now to him who works, the reward is not counted as grace, but as something owed. 5 But to him who doesn't work, but believes in him who justifies the ungodly, his faith is accounted for righteousness. 6 Even as David also pronounces blessing on the man to whom God counts righteousness apart from works:

7 "Blessed are they whose iniquities are forgiven,

whose sins are covered.

8 Blessed is the man whom the Lord will by no means charge with sin." *

9 Is this blessing then pronounced only on the circumcised, or on the uncircumcised also? For we say that faith was accounted to Abraham for righteousness. 10 How then was it counted? When he was in circumcision, or in uncircumcision? Not in circumcision, but in uncircumcision. 11 He received the sign of circumcision, a seal of the righteousness of the faith which he had while he was in uncircumcision, that he might be the father of all those who believe, though they might be in uncircumcision, that righteousness might also be accounted to them. 12 He is the father of circumcision to those who not only are of the circumcision, but who also walk in the steps of that faith of our father Abraham, which he had in uncircumcision.

13 For the promise to Abraham and to his offspring that he would be heir of the world wasn't through the law, but through the righteousness of faith. 14 For if those who are of the law are heirs, faith is made void, and the promise is made of no effect. 15 For the law produces wrath; for where there is no law, neither is there disobedience.

16 For this cause it is of faith, that it may be according to grace, to the end that the promise may be sure to all the offspring, not to that only which is of the law, but to that also which is of the faith of Abraham, who is the father of us all. 17 As it is written, "I have made you a father of many nations."* This is in the presence of him whom he believed: God, who gives life to the dead, and calls the things that are not, as though they were. 18 Against hope, Abraham in hope believed, to the end that he might become a father of many nations, according to that which had been spoken, "So will your offspring be."* 19 Without being weakened in faith, he didn't consider his own body, already having been worn out, (he being about a hundred years old), and the deadness of Sarah's womb. 20 Yet, looking to the promise of God, he didn't waver through unbelief, but grew strong through faith, giving glory to God, 21 and being fully assured that what he had promised, he was also able to perform. 22 Therefore it also was "credited to him for righteousness."* 23 Now it was not written that it was accounted to him for his sake alone, 24 but for our sake also, to whom it will be accounted, who believe in him who raised Jesus our Lord from the dead, 25 who was delivered up for our trespasses, and was raised for our justification.

5

1 Being therefore justified by faith, we have peace with God through our Lord Jesus Christ; 2 through whom we also have our access by faith into this grace in which we stand. We rejoice in hope of the glory of God. 3 Not only this, but we also rejoice in our sufferings, knowing that suffering produces perseverance; 4 and perseverance, proven character; and proven character, hope; 5 and hope doesn't disappoint us, because God's love has been poured into our hearts through the Holy Spirit who was given to us.

6 For while we were yet weak, at the right time Christ died for the ungodly. 7 For one will hardly die for a righteous man. Yet perhaps for a good person someone would even dare to die. 8 But God commends his own love towards us, in that while we were yet sinners, Christ died for us.

9 Much more then, being now justified by his blood, we will be saved from God's wrath through him. 10 For if while we were enemies, we were reconciled to God through the death of his Son, much more, being reconciled, we will be saved by his life.

11 Not only so, but we also rejoice in God through our Lord Jesus Christ, through whom we have now received the reconciliation. 12 Therefore, as sin entered into the world through one man, and death through sin, so death passed to all men because all sinned. 13 For until the law, sin was in the world; but sin is not charged when there is no law. 14 Nevertheless death reigned from Adam until Moses, even over those whose sins weren't like Adam's disobedience, who is a foreshadowing of him who was to come.

15 But the free gift isn't like the trespass. For if by the trespass of the one the many died, much more did the grace of God and the gift by the grace of the one man, Jesus Christ, abound to the many. 16 The gift is not as through one who sinned; for the judgement came by one to condemnation, but the free gift followed many trespasses to justification. 17 For if by the trespass of the one, death reigned through the one; so much more will those who receive the abundance of grace and of the gift of righteousness reign in life through the one, Jesus Christ.

18 So then as through one trespass, all men were condemned; even so through one act of righteousness, all men were justified to life. 19 For as through the one man's disobedience many were made sinners, even so through the obedience of the one, many will be made righteous. 20 The law came in that the trespass might abound; but where sin abounded, grace abounded more exceedingly, 21 that as sin reigned in death, even so grace might reign through righteousness to eternal life through Jesus Christ our Lord.

6

1 What shall we say then? Shall we continue in sin, that grace may abound? 2 May it never be! We who died to sin, how could we live in it any longer? 3 Or don't you know that all of us who were baptised into Christ Jesus were baptised into his death? 4 We were buried therefore with him through baptism into death, that just as Christ was raised from the dead through the glory of the Father, so we also might walk in newness of life.

5 For if we have become united with him in the likeness of his death, we will also be part of his resurrection; 6 knowing this, that our old man was crucified with him, that the body of sin might be done away with, so that we would no longer be in bondage to sin. 7 For he who has died has been freed from sin. 8 But if we died with Christ, we believe that we will also live with him, 9 knowing that Christ, being raised from the dead, dies no more. Death no longer has dominion over him! 10 For the death that he died, he died to sin one time; but the life that he lives, he lives to God. 11 Thus consider yourselves also to be dead to sin, but alive to God in Christ Jesus our Lord.

12 Therefore don't let sin reign in your mortal body, that you should obey it in its lusts. 13 Also, do not present your members to sin as instruments of unrighteousness, but present yourselves to God as alive from the dead, and your members as instruments of righteousness to God. 14 For sin will not have dominion over you, for you are not under law, but under grace.

15 What then? Shall we sin because we are not under law but under grace? May it never be! 16 Don't you know that when you present yourselves as servants and obey someone, you are the servants of whomever you obey, whether of sin to death, or of obedience to righteousness? 17 But thanks be to God that, whereas you were bondservants of sin, you became obedient from the heart to that form of teaching to which you were delivered. 18 Being made free from sin, you became bondservants of righteousness.

19 I speak in human terms because of the weakness of your flesh; for as you presented your members as servants to uncleanness and to wickedness upon wickedness, even so now present your members as servants to righteousness for sanctification. 20 For when you were servants of sin, you were free from righteousness. 21 What fruit then did you have at that time in the things of which you are now ashamed? For the end of those things is death. 22 But now, being made free from sin and having become servants of God, you have your fruit of sanctification and the result of eternal life. 23 For the wages of sin is death, but the free gift of God is eternal life in Christ Jesus our Lord.

7

1 Or don't you know, brothers[a] (for I speak to men who know the law), that the law has dominion over a man for as long as he lives? 2 For the woman that has a husband is bound by law to the husband while he lives, but if the husband dies, she is discharged from the law of the husband. 3 So then if, while the husband lives, she is joined to another man, she would be called an adulteress. But if the husband dies, she is free from the law, so that she is no adulteress, though she is joined to another man. 4 Therefore, my brothers, you also were made dead to the law through the body of Christ, that you would be joined to another, to him who was raised from the dead, that we might produce fruit to God. 5 For when we were in the flesh, the sinful passions which were through the law worked in our members to bring out fruit to death. 6 But now we have been discharged from the law, having died to that in which we were held; so that we serve in newness of the spirit, and not in oldness of the letter.

7 What shall we say then? Is the law sin? May it never be! However, I wouldn't have known sin except through the law. For I wouldn't have known coveting unless the law had said, "You shall not covet."* 8 But sin, finding occasion through the commandment, produced in me all kinds of coveting. For apart from the law, sin is dead. 9 I was alive apart from the law once, but when the commandment came, sin revived and I died. 10 The commandment which was for life, this I found to be for death; 11 for sin, finding occasion through the commandment, deceived me, and through it killed me. 12 Therefore the law indeed is holy, and the commandment holy, righteous, and good.

13 Did then that which is good become death to me? May it never be! But sin, that it might be shown to be sin, was producing death in me through that which is good; that through the commandment sin might become exceedingly sinful. 14 For we know that the law is spiritual, but I am

---

** 4:3 Genesis 15:6
** 4:8 Psalms 32:1-2
** 4:17 Genesis 17:5
** 4:18 Genesis 15:5

** 4:22 Genesis 15:6
a 7:1 The word for "brothers" here and where context allows may also be correctly translated "brothers and sisters" or "siblings."
** 7:7 Exodus 20:17; Deuteronomy 5:21

fleshly, sold under sin. ₁₅ For I don't understand what I am doing. For I don't practise what I desire to do; but what I hate, that I do. ₁₆ But if what I don't desire, that I do, I consent to the law that it is good. ₁₇ So now it is no more I that do it, but sin which dwells in me. ₁₈ For I know that in me, that is, in my flesh, dwells no good thing. For desire is present with me, but I don't find it doing that which is good. ₁₉ For the good which I desire, I don't do; but the evil which I don't desire, that I practise. ₂₀ But if what I don't desire, that I do, it is no more I that do it, but sin which dwells in me. ₂₁ I find then the law that, while I desire to do good, evil is present. ₂₂ For I delight in God's law after the inward person, ₂₃ but I see a different law in my members, warring against the law of my mind, and bringing me into captivity under the law of sin which is in my members. ₂₄ What a wretched man I am! Who will deliver me out of the body of this death? ₂₅ I thank God through Jesus Christ, our Lord! So then with the mind, I myself serve God's law, but with the flesh, sin's law.

8

₁ There is therefore now no condemnation to those who are in Christ Jesus, who don't walk according to the flesh, but according to the Spirit.ᵃ ₂ For the law of the Spirit of life in Christ Jesus made me free from the law of sin and of death. ₃ For what the law couldn't do, in that it was weak through the flesh, God did, sending his own Son in the likeness of sinful flesh and for sin, he condemned sin in the flesh, ₄ that the ordinance of the law might be fulfilled in us who don't walk according to the flesh, but according to the Spirit. ₅ For those who live according to the flesh set their minds on the things of the flesh, but those who live according to the Spirit, the things of the Spirit. ₆ For the mind of the flesh is death, but the mind of the Spirit is life and peace; ₇ because the mind of the flesh is hostile towards God, for it is not subject to God's law, neither indeed can it be. ₈ Those who are in the flesh can't please God.

₉ But you are not in the flesh but in the Spirit, if it is so that the Spirit of God dwells in you. But if any man doesn't have the Spirit of Christ, he is not his. ₁₀ If Christ is in you, the body is dead because of sin, but the spirit is alive because of righteousness. ₁₁ But if the Spirit of him who raised up Jesus from the dead dwells in you, he who raised up Christ Jesus from the dead will also give life to your mortal bodies through his Spirit who dwells in you.

₁₂ So then, brothers, we are debtors, not to the flesh, to live after the flesh. ₁₃ For if you live after the flesh, you must die; but if by the Spirit you put to death the deeds of the body, you will live. ₁₄ For as many as are led by the Spirit of God, these are children of God. ₁₅ For you didn't receive the spirit of bondage again to fear, but you received the Spirit of adoption, by whom we cry, "Abba!ᵇ Father!"

₁₆ The Spirit himself testifies with our spirit that we are children of God; ₁₇ and if children, then heirs—heirs of God and joint heirs with Christ, if indeed we suffer with him, that we may also be glorified with him.

₁₈ For I consider that the sufferings of this present time are not worthy to be compared with the glory which will be revealed towards us. ₁₉ For the creation waits with eager expectation for the children of God to be revealed. ₂₀ For the creation was subjected to vanity, not of its own will, but because of him who subjected it, in hope ₂₁ that the creation itself also will be delivered from the bondage of decay into the liberty of the glory of the children of God. ₂₂ For we know that the whole creation groans and travails in pain together until now. ₂₃ Not only so, but ourselves also, who have the first fruits of the Spirit, even we ourselves groan within ourselves, waiting for adoption, the redemption of our body. ₂₄ For we were saved in hope, but hope that is seen is not hope. For who hopes for that which he sees? ₂₅ But if we hope for that which we don't see, we wait for it with patience.

₂₆ In the same way, the Spirit also helps our weaknesses, for we don't know how to pray as we ought. But the Spirit himself makes intercession for us with groanings which can't be uttered. ₂₇ He who searches the hearts knows what is on the Spirit's mind, because he makes intercession for the saints according to God.

₂₈ We know that all things work together for good for those who love God, for those who are called according to his purpose. ₂₉ For whom he foreknew, he also predestined to be conformed to the image of his Son, that he might be the firstborn amongst many brothers.ᶜ ₃₀ Whom he predestined, those he also called. Whom he called, those he also justified. Whom he justified, those he also glorified.

₃₁ What then shall we say about these things? If God is for us, who can be against us? ₃₂ He who didn't spare his own Son, but delivered him up for us all, how would he not also with him freely give us all things? ₃₃ Who could bring a charge against God's chosen ones? It is God who justifies. ₃₄ Who is he who condemns? It is Christ who died, yes rather, who was raised from the dead, who is at the right hand of God, who also makes intercession for us.

₃₅ Who shall separate us from the love of Christ? Could oppression, or anguish, or persecution, or famine, or nakedness, or peril, or sword? ₃₆ Even as it is written,

"For your sake we are killed all day long.
We were accounted as sheep for the slaughter."*

₃₇ No, in all these things we are more than conquerors through him who loved us. ₃₈ For I am persuaded that neither death, nor life, nor angels, nor principalities, nor things present, nor things to come, nor powers, ₃₉ nor height, nor depth, nor any other created thing will be able to separate us from God's love which is in Christ Jesus our Lord.

9

₁ I tell the truth in Christ. I am not lying, my conscience testifying with me in the Holy Spirit ₂ that I have great sorrow and unceasing pain in my heart. ₃ For I could wish that I myself were accursed from Christ for my brothers' sake, my relatives according to the flesh ₄ who are Israelites; whose is the adoption, the glory, the covenants, the giving of the law, the service, and the promises; ₅ of whom are the fathers, and from whom is Christ as concerning the flesh, who is over all, God, blessed forever. Amen.

₆ But it is not as though the word of God has come to nothing. For they are not all Israel that are of Israel. ₇ Neither, because they are Abraham's offspring, are they all children. But, "your offspring will be accounted as from Isaac."* ₈ That is, it is not the children of the flesh who are children of God, but the children of the promise are counted as heirs. ₉ For this is a word of promise: "At the appointed time I will come, and Sarah will have a son."* ₁₀ Not only so, but Rebekah also conceived by one, by our father Isaac. ₁₁ For being not yet born, neither having done anything good or bad, that the purpose of God according to election might stand, not of works, but of him who calls,ᵈ ₁₂ it was said to her, "The elder will serve the younger."* ₁₃ Even as it is written, "Jacob I loved, but Esau I hated."*

₁₄ What shall we say then? Is there unrighteousness with God? May it never be! ₁₅ For he said to Moses, "I will have mercy on whom I have mercy, and I will have compassion on whom I have compassion."* ₁₆ So then it is not of him who wills, nor of him who runs, but of God who has mercy. ₁₇ For the Scripture says to Pharaoh, "For this very purpose I caused you to be raised up, that I might show in you my power, and that my name might be proclaimed in all the earth."* ₁₈ So then, he has mercy on whom he desires, and he hardens whom he desires.

₁₉ You will say then to me, "Why does he still find fault? For who withstands his will?" ₂₀ But indeed, O man, who are you to reply against God? Will the thing formed ask him who formed it, "Why did you make me like this?"* ₂₁ Or hasn't the potter a right over the clay, from the same lump to make one part a vessel for honour, and another for dishonour? ₂₂ What if God, willing to show his wrath and to make his power known, endured with much patience vessels of wrath prepared for destruction, ₂₃ and that he might make known the riches of his glory on vessels of mercy, which he prepared beforehand for glory— ₂₄ us, whom he also called, not from the Jews only, but also from the Gentiles? ₂₅ As he says also in Hosea,
"I will call them 'my people,' which were not my people;
    and her 'beloved,' who was not beloved."*
₂₆ "It will be that in the place where it was said to them, 'You are not my people,'
    there they will be called 'children of the living God.'"*
₂₇ Isaiah cries concerning Israel,
"If the number of the children of Israel are as the sand of the sea,
    it is the remnant who will be saved;
₂₈ for he will finish the work and cut it short in righteousness,
    because the Lord will make a short work upon the earth."*
₂₉ As Isaiah has said before,
"Unless the Lord of Armiesᵉ had left us a seed,
    we would have become like Sodom,
    and would have been made like Gomorrah."*

₃₀ What shall we say then? That the Gentiles, who didn't follow after righteousness, attained to righteousness, even the righteousness which is of faith; ₃₁ but Israel, following after a law of righteousness, didn't arrive at the law of righteousness. ₃₂ Why? Because they didn't seek it by faith, but as it were by works of the law. They stumbled over the stumbling stone, ₃₃ even as it is written,
"Behold,ᶠ I lay in Zion a stumbling stone and a rock of offence;
    and no one who believes in him will be disappointed."*

10

₁ Brothers, my heart's desire and my prayer to God is for Israel, that they may be saved. ₂ For I testify about them that they have a zeal for God, but not according to knowledge. ₃ For being ignorant of God's righteousness, and seeking to establish their own righteousness, they

---

ᵃ *8:1* NU omits "who don't walk according to the flesh, but according to the Spirit"
ᵇ *8:15* Abba is an Aramaic word for "Father" or "Daddy," which can be used affectionately and respectfully in prayer to our Father in heaven.
ᶜ *8:29* The word for "brothers" here and where context allows may also be correctly translated "brothers and sisters" or "siblings."
** 8:36 Psalms 44:22
** 9:7 Genesis 21:12
** 9:9 Genesis 18:10,14
ᵈ *9:11* NU puts the phrase "not of works, but of him who calls" at the beginning of verse 12 instead of the end of verse 11.
** 9:12 Genesis 25:23
** 9:13 Malachi 1:2-3

** 9:15 Exodus 33:19
** 9:17 Exodus 9:16
** 9:20 Isaiah 29:16; 45:9
** 9:25 Hosea 2:23
** 9:26 Hosea 1:10
** 9:28 Isaiah 10:22-23
ᵉ *9:29* Greek: Sabaoth (or Hebrew: Tze'va'ot)
** 9:29 Isaiah 1:9
ᶠ *9:33* "Behold", from "ἰδοὺ", means look at, take notice, observe, see, or gaze at. It is often used as an interjection.
** 9:33 Isaiah 8:14; 28:16

didn't subject themselves to the righteousness of God. 4 For Christ is the fulfilment[a] of the law for righteousness to everyone who believes.

5 For Moses writes about the righteousness of the law, "The one who does them will live by them."* 6 But the righteousness which is of faith says this, "Don't say in your heart, 'Who will ascend into heaven?'" (that is, to bring Christ down); 7 or, 'Who will descend into the abyss?'" (that is, to bring Christ up from the dead.)"* 8 But what does it say? "The word is near you, in your mouth and in your heart;"* that is, the word of faith which we preach: 9 that if you will confess with your mouth that Jesus is Lord and believe in your heart that God raised him from the dead, you will be saved. 10 For with the heart one believes resulting in righteousness; and with the mouth confession is made resulting in salvation. 11 For the Scripture says, "Whoever believes in him will not be disappointed."*

12 For there is no distinction between Jew and Greek; for the same Lord is Lord of all, and is rich to all who call on him. 13 For, "Whoever will call on the name of the Lord will be saved."* 14 How then will they call on him in whom they have not believed? How will they believe in him whom they have not heard? How will they hear without a preacher? 15 And how will they preach unless they are sent? As it is written, "How beautiful are the feet of those who preach the Good News of peace, who bring glad tidings of good things!"*

16 But they didn't all listen to the glad news. For Isaiah says, "Lord, who has believed our report?"* 17 So faith comes by hearing, and hearing by the word of God. 18 But I say, didn't they hear? Yes, most certainly, "Their sound went out into all the earth, their words to the ends of the world."*

19 But I ask, didn't Israel know? First Moses says, "I will provoke you to jealousy with that which is no nation. I will make you angry with a nation void of understanding."*

20 Isaiah is very bold and says, "I was found by those who didn't seek me. I was revealed to those who didn't ask for me."*

21 But about Israel he says, "All day long I stretched out my hands to a disobedient and contrary people."*

11

1 I ask then, did God reject his people? May it never be! For I also am an Israelite, a descendant of Abraham, of the tribe of Benjamin. 2 God didn't reject his people, whom he foreknew. Or don't you know what the Scripture says about Elijah? How he pleads with God against Israel: 3 "Lord, they have killed your prophets. They have broken down your altars. I am left alone, and they seek my life."* 4 But how does God answer him? "I have reserved for myself seven thousand men who have not bowed the knee to Baal."* 5 Even so too at this present time also there is a remnant according to the election of grace. 6 And if by grace, then it is no longer of works; otherwise grace is no longer grace. But if it is of works, it is no longer grace; otherwise work is no longer work.

7 What then? That which Israel seeks for, that he didn't obtain, but the chosen ones obtained it, and the rest were hardened. 8 According as it is written, "God gave them a spirit of stupor, eyes that they should not see, and ears that they should not hear, to this very day." *

9 David says, "Let their table be made a snare, a trap, a stumbling block, and a retribution to them.

10 Let their eyes be darkened, that they may not see. Always keep their backs bent."*

11 I ask then, did they stumble that they might fall? May it never be! But by their fall salvation has come to the Gentiles, to provoke them to jealousy. 12 Now if their fall is the riches of the world, and their loss the riches of the Gentiles, how much more their fullness!

13 For I speak to you who are Gentiles. Since then as I am an apostle to Gentiles, I glorify my ministry, 14 if by any means I may provoke to jealousy those who are my flesh, and may save some of them. 15 For if the rejection of them is the reconciling of the world, what would their acceptance be, but life from the dead?

16 If the first fruit is holy, so is the lump. If the root is holy, so are the branches. 17 But if some of the branches were broken off, and you, being a wild olive, were grafted in amongst them and became partaker with them of the root and of the richness of the olive tree, 18 don't boast over the branches. But if you boast, remember that it is not you who support the root, but the root supports you. 19 You will say then, "Branches were broken off, that I might be grafted in." 20 True; by their unbelief they were broken off, and you stand by your faith. Don't be conceited, but fear; 21 for if God didn't spare the natural branches, neither will he spare you. 22 See then the goodness and severity of God. Towards those who fell, severity; but towards you, goodness, if you continue in his goodness; otherwise you

also will be cut off. 23 They also, if they don't continue in their unbelief, will be grafted in, for God is able to graft them in again. 24 For if you were cut out of that which is by nature a wild olive tree, and were grafted contrary to nature into a good olive tree, how much more will these, which are the natural branches, be grafted into their own olive tree?

25 For I don't desire you to be ignorant, brothers,[b] of this mystery, so that you won't be wise in your own conceits, that a partial hardening has happened to Israel, until the fullness of the Gentiles has come in, 26 and so all Israel will be saved. Even as it is written, "There will come out of Zion the Deliverer, and he will turn away ungodliness from Jacob.

27 This is my covenant with them, when I will take away their sins."*

28 Concerning the Good News, they are enemies for your sake. But concerning the election, they are beloved for the fathers' sake. 29 For the gifts and the calling of God are irrevocable. 30 For as you in time past were disobedient to God, but now have obtained mercy by their disobedience, 31 even so these also have now been disobedient, that by the mercy shown to you they may also obtain mercy. 32 For God has bound all to disobedience, that he might have mercy on all.

33 Oh the depth of the riches both of the wisdom and the knowledge of God! How unsearchable are his judgements, and his ways past tracing out! 34 "For who has known the mind of the Lord? Or who has been his counsellor?"*

35 "Or who has first given to him, and it will be repaid to him again?"*

36 For of him and through him and to him are all things. To him be the glory for ever! Amen.

12

1 Therefore I urge you, brothers, by the mercies of God, to present your bodies a living sacrifice, holy, acceptable to God, which is your spiritual service. 2 Don't be conformed to this world, but be transformed by the renewing of your mind, so that you may prove what is the good, well-pleasing, and perfect will of God.

3 For I say through the grace that was given me, to everyone who is amongst you, not to think of yourself more highly than you ought to think; but to think reasonably, as God has apportioned to each person a measure of faith. 4 For even as we have many members in one body, and all the members don't have the same function, 5 so we, who are many, are one body in Christ, and individually members of one another, 6 having gifts differing according to the grace that was given to us: if prophecy, let's prophesy according to the proportion of our faith; 7 or service, let's give ourselves to service; or he who teaches, to his teaching; 8 or he who exhorts, to his exhorting; he who gives, let him do it with generosity; he who rules, with diligence; he who shows mercy, with cheerfulness.

9 Let love be without hypocrisy. Abhor that which is evil. Cling to that which is good. 10 In love of the brothers be tenderly affectionate to one another; in honour prefer one another, 11 not lagging in diligence, fervent in spirit, serving the Lord, 12 rejoicing in hope, enduring in troubles, continuing steadfastly in prayer, 13 contributing to the needs of the saints, and given to hospitality.

14 Bless those who persecute you; bless, and don't curse. 15 Rejoice with those who rejoice. Weep with those who weep. 16 Be of the same mind one towards another. Don't set your mind on high things, but associate with the humble. Don't be wise in your own conceits. 17 Repay no one evil for evil. Respect what is honourable in the sight of all men. 18 If it is possible, as much as it is up to you, be at peace with all men. 19 Don't seek revenge yourselves, beloved, but give place to God's wrath. For it is written, "Vengeance belongs to me; I will repay, says the Lord." * 20 Therefore "If your enemy is hungry, feed him. If he is thirsty, give him a drink; for in doing so, you will heap coals of fire on his head."*

21 Don't be overcome by evil, but overcome evil with good.

13

1 Let every soul be in subjection to the higher authorities, for there is no authority except from God, and those who exist are ordained by God. 2 Therefore he who resists the authority withstands the ordinance of God; and those who withstand will receive to themselves judgement. 3 For rulers are not a terror to the good work, but to the evil. Do you desire to have no fear of the authority? Do that which is good, and you will have praise from the authority, 4 for he is a servant of God to you for good. But if you do that which is evil, be afraid, for he doesn't bear the sword in vain; for he is a servant of God, an avenger for wrath to him who does evil. 5 Therefore you need to be in subjection, not only because of the wrath, but also for conscience' sake. 6 For this reason you also pay taxes, for they are

a *10:4* or, completion, or end
** 10:5 Leviticus 18:5
** 10:6 Deuteronomy 30:12
** 10:7 Deuteronomy 30:13
** 10:8 Deuteronomy 30:14
** 10:11 Isaiah 28:16
** 10:13 Joel 2:32
** 10:15 Isaiah 52:7
** 10:16 Isaiah 53:1
** 10:18 Psalms 19:4
** 10:19 Deuteronomy 32:21
** 10:20 Isaiah 65:1

** 10:21 Isaiah 65:2
** 11:3 1 Kings 19:10,14
** 11:4 1 Kings 19:18
** 11:8 Deuteronomy 29:4; Isaiah 29:10
** 11:10 Psalms 69:22,23
b *11:25* The word for "brothers" here and where context allows may also be correctly translated "brothers and sisters" or "siblings."
** 11:27 Isaiah 59:20-21; 27:9; Jeremiah 31:33-34
** 11:34 Isaiah 40:13
** 11:35 Job 41:11
** 12:19 Deuteronomy 32:35
** 12:20 Proverbs 25:21-22

servants of God's service, continually doing this very thing. 7 Therefore give everyone what you owe: if you owe taxes, pay taxes; if customs, then customs; if respect, then respect; if honour, then honour.

8 Owe no one anything, except to love one another; for he who loves his neighbour has fulfilled the law. 9 For the commandments, "You shall not commit adultery," "You shall not murder," "You shall not steal,"[a] "You shall not covet," * and whatever other commandments there are, are all summed up in this saying, namely, "You shall love your neighbour as yourself."* 10 Love doesn't harm a neighbour. Love therefore is the fulfilment of the law.

11 Do this, knowing the time, that it is already time for you to awaken out of sleep, for salvation is now nearer to us than when we first believed. 12 The night is far gone, and the day is near. Let's therefore throw off the deeds of darkness, and let's put on the armour of light. 13 Let's walk properly, as in the day; not in revelling and drunkenness, not in sexual promiscuity and lustful acts, and not in strife and jealousy. 14 But put on the Lord Jesus Christ, and make no provision for the flesh, for its lusts.

14

1 Now accept one who is weak in faith, but not for disputes over opinions. 2 One man has faith to eat all things, but he who is weak eats only vegetables. 3 Don't let him who eats despise him who doesn't eat. Don't let him who doesn't eat judge him who eats, for God has accepted him. 4 Who are you who judge another's servant? To his own lord he stands or falls. Yes, he will be made to stand, for God has power to make him stand.

5 One man esteems one day as more important. Another esteems every day alike. Let each man be fully assured in his own mind. 6 He who observes the day, observes it to the Lord; and he who does not observe the day, to the Lord he does not observe it. He who eats, eats to the Lord, for he gives God thanks. He who doesn't eat, to the Lord he doesn't eat, and gives God thanks. 7 For none of us lives to himself, and none dies to himself. 8 For if we live, we live to the Lord. Or if we die, we die to the Lord. If therefore we live or die, we are the Lord's. 9 For to this end Christ died, rose, and lived again, that he might be Lord of both the dead and the living.

10 But you, why do you judge your brother? Or you again, why do you despise your brother? For we will all stand before the judgement seat of Christ. 11 For it is written,

"'As I live,' says the Lord, 'to me every knee will bow.
Every tongue will confess to God.'"*

12 So then each one of us will give account of himself to God.

13 Therefore let's not judge one another any more, but judge this rather, that no man put a stumbling block in his brother's way, or an occasion for falling. 14 I know and am persuaded in the Lord Jesus that nothing is unclean of itself; except that to him who considers anything to be unclean, to him it is unclean. 15 Yet if because of food your brother is grieved, you walk no longer in love. Don't destroy with your food him for whom Christ died. 16 Then don't let your good be slandered, 17 for God's Kingdom is not eating and drinking, but righteousness, peace, and joy in the Holy Spirit. 18 For he who serves Christ in these things is acceptable to God and approved by men. 19 So then, let's follow after things which make for peace, and things by which we may build one another up. 20 Don't overthrow God's work for food's sake. All things indeed are clean, however it is evil for that man who creates a stumbling block by eating. 21 It is good to not eat meat, drink wine, nor do anything by which your brother stumbles, is offended, or is made weak.

22 Do you have faith? Have it to yourself before God. Happy is he who doesn't judge himself in that which he approves. 23 But he who doubts is condemned if he eats, because it isn't of faith; and whatever is not of faith is sin.

24 Now to him who is able to establish you according to my Good News and the preaching of Jesus Christ, according to the revelation of the mystery which has been kept secret through long ages, 25 but now is revealed, and by the Scriptures of the prophets, according to the commandment of the eternal God, is made known for obedience of faith to all the nations; 26 to the only wise God, through Jesus Christ, to whom be the glory forever! Amen. [b]

15

1 Now we who are strong ought to bear the weaknesses of the weak, and not to please ourselves. 2 Let each one of us please his neighbour for that which is good, to be building him up. 3 For even Christ didn't please himself. But, as it is written, "The reproaches of those who reproached you fell on me."* 4 For whatever things were written before were written for our learning, that through perseverance and through encouragement of the Scriptures we might have hope. 5 Now the God of perseverance and of encouragement grant you to be of the same mind with one another according to Christ Jesus, 6 that with one accord you may with one mouth glorify the God and Father of our Lord Jesus Christ.

7 Therefore accept one another, even as Christ also accepted you,[c] to the glory of God. 8 Now I say that Christ has been made a servant of the circumcision for the truth of God, that he might confirm the promises given to the fathers, 9 and that the Gentiles might glorify God for his mercy. As it is written,

"Therefore I will give praise to you amongst the Gentiles
and sing to your name."*

10 Again he says,

"Rejoice, you Gentiles, with his people."*

11 Again,

"Praise the Lord, all you Gentiles!
Let all the peoples praise him."*

12 Again, Isaiah says,

"There will be the root of Jesse,
he who arises to rule over the Gentiles;
in him the Gentiles will hope."*

13 Now may the God of hope fill you with all joy and peace in believing, that you may abound in hope in the power of the Holy Spirit.

14 I myself am also persuaded about you, my brothers,[d] that you yourselves are full of goodness, filled with all knowledge, able also to admonish others. 15 But I write the more boldly to you in part as reminding you, because of the grace that was given to me by God, 16 that I should be a servant of Christ Jesus to the Gentiles, serving as a priest of the Good News of God, that the offering up of the Gentiles might be made acceptable, sanctified by the Holy Spirit. 17 I have therefore my boasting in Christ Jesus in things pertaining to God. 18 For I will not dare to speak of any things except those which Christ worked through me for the obedience of the Gentiles, by word and deed, 19 in the power of signs and wonders, in the power of God's Spirit; so that from Jerusalem and around as far as to Illyricum, I have fully preached the Good News of Christ; 20 yes, making it my aim to preach the Good News, not where Christ was already named, that I might not build on another's foundation. 21 But, as it is written,

"They will see, to whom no news of him came.
They who haven't heard will understand."*

22 Therefore also I was hindered these many times from coming to you, 23 but now, no longer having any place in these regions, and having these many years a longing to come to you, 24 whenever I travel to Spain, I will come to you. For I hope to see you on my journey, and to be helped on my way there by you, if first I may enjoy your company for a while. 25 But now, I say, I am going to Jerusalem, serving the saints. 26 For it has been the good pleasure of Macedonia and Achaia to make a certain contribution for the poor amongst the saints who are at Jerusalem. 27 Yes, it has been their good pleasure, and they are their debtors. For if the Gentiles have been made partakers of their spiritual things, they owe it to them also to serve them in material things. 28 When therefore I have accomplished this, and have sealed to them this fruit, I will go on by way of you to Spain. 29 I know that when I come to you, I will come in the fullness of the blessing of the Good News of Christ.

30 Now I beg you, brothers, by our Lord Jesus Christ and by the love of the Spirit, that you strive together with me in your prayers to God for me, 31 that I may be delivered from those who are disobedient in Judea, and that my service which I have for Jerusalem may be acceptable to the saints, 32 that I may come to you in joy through the will of God, and together with you, find rest. 33 Now the God of peace be with you all. Amen.

16

1 I commend to you Phoebe, our sister, who is a servant[e] of the assembly that is at Cenchreae, 2 that you receive her in the Lord in a way worthy of the saints, and that you assist her in whatever matter she may need from you, for she herself also has been a helper of many, and of my own self.

3 Greet Prisca and Aquila, my fellow workers in Christ Jesus, 4 who risked their own necks for my life, to whom not only I give thanks, but also all the assemblies of the Gentiles. 5 Greet the assembly that is in their house. Greet Epaenetus, my beloved, who is the first fruits of Achaia to Christ. 6 Greet Mary, who laboured much for us. 7 Greet Andronicus and Junia, my relatives and my fellow prisoners, who are notable amongst the apostles, who were also in Christ before me. 8 Greet Amplias, my beloved in the Lord. 9 Greet Urbanus, our fellow worker in Christ, and Stachys, my beloved. 10 Greet Apelles, the approved in Christ. Greet those who are of the household of Aristobulus. 11 Greet Herodion, my kinsman. Greet them of the household of Narcissus, who are in the Lord. 12 Greet Tryphaena and Tryphosa, who labour in the Lord. Greet Persis, the beloved, who laboured much in the Lord. 13 Greet Rufus, the chosen in the Lord, and his mother and mine. 14 Greet Asyncritus, Phlegon, Hermes, Patrobas, Hermas, and the brothers[f] who are with them. 15 Greet Philologus and Julia, Nereus and his sister, and Olympas, and all the saints who are with them. 16 Greet one another with a holy kiss. The assemblies of Christ greet you.

---

a 13:9 TR adds "You shall not give false testimony,"
** 13:9 Exodus 20:13-15,17; Deuteronomy 5:17-19,21
** 13:9 Leviticus 19:18
** 14:11 Isaiah 45:23
b 14:26 TR places verses 24-26 after Romans 16:24 as verses 25-27.
** 15:3 Psalms 69:9
c 15:7 TR reads "us" instead of "you"
** 15:9 2 Samuel 22:50; Psalms 18:49
** 15:10 Deuteronomy 32:43

** 15:11 Psalms 117:1
** 15:12 Isaiah 11:10
d 15:14 The word for "brothers" here and where context allows may also be correctly translated "brothers and sisters" or "siblings."
** 15:21 Isaiah 52:15
e 16:1 or, deacon
f 16:14 The word for "brothers" here and where context allows may also be correctly translated "brothers and sisters" or "siblings."

17 Now I beg you, brothers, look out for those who are causing the divisions and occasions of stumbling, contrary to the doctrine which you learnt, and turn away from them. 18 For those who are such don't serve our Lord Jesus Christ, but their own belly; and by their smooth and flattering speech they deceive the hearts of the innocent. 19 For your obedience has become known to all. I rejoice therefore over you. But I desire to have you wise in that which is good, but innocent in that which is evil. 20 And the God of peace will quickly crush Satan under your feet.

The grace of our Lord Jesus Christ be with you.

21 Timothy, my fellow worker, greets you, as do Lucius, Jason, and Sosipater, my relatives. 22 I, Tertius, who write the letter, greet you in the Lord. 23 Gaius, my host and host of the whole assembly, greets you. Erastus, the treasurer of the city, greets you, as does Quartus, the brother. 24 The grace of our Lord Jesus Christ be with you all! Amen. 25 a

---

a *16:25* TR places Romans 14:24-26 at the end of Romans instead of at the end of chapter 14, and numbers these verses 16:25-27.

Paul's First Letter to the Corinthians

1

1 Paul, called to be an apostle of Jesus Christ[a] through the will of God, and our brother Sosthenes, 2 to the assembly of God which is at Corinth—those who are sanctified in Christ Jesus, called saints, with all who call on the name of our Lord Jesus Christ in every place, both theirs and ours: 3 Grace to you and peace from God our Father and the Lord Jesus Christ.

4 I always thank my God concerning you for the grace of God which was given you in Christ Jesus, 5 that in everything you were enriched in him, in all speech and all knowledge— 6 even as the testimony of Christ was confirmed in you— 7 so that you come behind in no gift, waiting for the revelation of our Lord Jesus Christ, 8 who will also confirm you until the end, blameless in the day of our Lord Jesus Christ. 9 God is faithful, through whom you were called into the fellowship of his Son, Jesus Christ our Lord.

10 Now I beg you, brothers,[b] through the name of our Lord, Jesus Christ, that you all speak the same thing, and that there be no divisions amongst you, but that you be perfected together in the same mind and in the same judgement. 11 For it has been reported to me concerning you, my brothers, by those who are from Chloe's household, that there are contentions amongst you. 12 Now I mean this, that each one of you says, "I follow Paul," "I follow Apollos," "I follow Cephas," and, "I follow Christ." 13 Is Christ divided? Was Paul crucified for you? Or were you baptised into the name of Paul? 14 I thank God that I baptised none of you except Crispus and Gaius, 15 so that no one should say that I had baptised you into my own name. 16 (I also baptised the household of Stephanas; besides them, I don't know whether I baptised any other.) 17 For Christ sent me not to baptise, but to preach the Good News—not in wisdom of words, so that the cross of Christ wouldn't be made void. 18 For the word of the cross is foolishness to those who are dying, but to us who are being saved it is the power of God. 19 For it is written,

"I will destroy the wisdom of the wise.

I will bring the discernment of the discerning to nothing."[*]

20 Where is the wise? Where is the scribe? Where is the debater of this age? Hasn't God made foolish the wisdom of this world? 21 For seeing that in the wisdom of God, the world through its wisdom didn't know God, it was God's good pleasure through the foolishness of the preaching to save those who believe. 22 For Jews ask for signs, Greeks seek after wisdom, 23 but we preach Christ crucified, a stumbling block to Jews and foolishness to Greeks, 24 but to those who are called, both Jews and Greeks, Christ is the power of God and the wisdom of God; 25 because the foolishness of God is wiser than men, and the weakness of God is stronger than men.

26 For you see your calling, brothers, that not many are wise according to the flesh, not many mighty, and not many noble; 27 but God chose the foolish things of the world that he might put to shame those who are wise. God chose the weak things of the world that he might put to shame the things that are strong. 28 God chose the lowly things of the world, and the things that are despised, and the things that don't exist, that he might bring to nothing the things that exist, 29 that no flesh should boast before God. 30 Because of him, you are in Christ Jesus, who was made to us wisdom from God, and righteousness and sanctification, and redemption, 31 that, as it is written, "He who boasts, let him boast in the Lord."[*]

2

1 When I came to you, brothers, I didn't come with excellence of speech or of wisdom, proclaiming to you the testimony of God. 2 For I determined not to know anything amongst you except Jesus Christ and him crucified. 3 I was with you in weakness, in fear, and in much trembling. 4 My speech and my preaching were not in persuasive words of human wisdom, but in demonstration of the Spirit and of power, 5 that your faith wouldn't stand in the wisdom of men, but in the power of God.

6 We speak wisdom, however, amongst those who are full grown, yet a wisdom not of this world nor of the rulers of this world who are coming to nothing. 7 But we speak God's wisdom in a mystery, the wisdom that has been hidden, which God foreordained before the worlds for our glory, 8 which none of the rulers of this world has known. For had they known it, they wouldn't have crucified the Lord of glory. 9 But as it is written, "Things which an eye didn't see, and an ear didn't hear,

which didn't enter into the heart of man,

these God has prepared for those who love him."[*]

10 But to us, God revealed them through the Spirit. For the Spirit searches all things, yes, the deep things of God. 11 For who amongst men knows the things of a man except the spirit of the man which is in him? Even so, no one knows the things of God except God's Spirit. 12 But we received not the spirit of the world, but the Spirit which is from God, that we might know the things that were freely given to us by God. 13 We also speak these things, not in words which man's wisdom teaches but which the Holy Spirit teaches, comparing spiritual things with spiritual things. 14 Now the natural man doesn't receive the things of God's Spirit, for they are foolishness to him; and he can't know them, because they are spiritually

discerned. 15 But he who is spiritual discerns all things, and he himself is to be judged by no one. 16 "For who has known the mind of the Lord that he should instruct him?"[*] But we have Christ's mind.

3

1 Brothers, I couldn't speak to you as to spiritual, but as to fleshly, as to babies in Christ. 2 I fed you with milk, not with solid food, for you weren't yet ready. Indeed, you aren't ready even now, 3 for you are still fleshly. For insofar as there is jealousy, strife, and factions amongst you, aren't you fleshly, and don't you walk in the ways of men? 4 For when one says, "I follow Paul," and another, "I follow Apollos," aren't you fleshly?

5 Who then is Apollos, and who is Paul, but servants through whom you believed, and each as the Lord gave to him? 6 I planted. Apollos watered. But God gave the increase. 7 So then neither he who plants is anything, nor he who waters, but God who gives the increase. 8 Now he who plants and he who waters are the same, but each will receive his own reward according to his own labour. 9 For we are God's fellow workers. You are God's farming, God's building.

10 According to the grace of God which was given to me, as a wise master builder I laid a foundation, and another builds on it. But let each man be careful how he builds on it. 11 For no one can lay any other foundation than that which has been laid, which is Jesus Christ. 12 But if anyone builds on the foundation with gold, silver, costly stones, wood, hay, or straw, 13 each man's work will be revealed. For the Day will declare it, because it is revealed in fire; and the fire itself will test what sort of work each man's work is. 14 If any man's work remains which he built on it, he will receive a reward. 15 If any man's work is burnt, he will suffer loss, but he himself will be saved, but as through fire.

16 Don't you know that you are God's temple and that God's Spirit lives in you? 17 If anyone destroys God's temple, God will destroy him; for God's temple is holy, which you are.

18 Let no one deceive himself. If anyone thinks that he is wise amongst you in this world, let him become a fool that he may become wise. 19 For the wisdom of this world is foolishness with God. For it is written, "He has taken the wise in their craftiness."[*] 20 And again, "The Lord knows the reasoning of the wise, that it is worthless."[*] 21 Therefore let no one boast in men. For all things are yours, 22 whether Paul, or Apollos, or Cephas, or the world, or life, or death, or things present, or things to come. All are yours, 23 and you are Christ's, and Christ is God's.

4

1 So let a man think of us as Christ's servants and stewards of God's mysteries. 2 Here, moreover, it is required of stewards that they be found faithful. 3 But with me it is a very small thing that I should be judged by you, or by a human court. Yes, I don't even judge my own self. 4 For I know nothing against myself. Yet I am not justified by this, but he who judges me is the Lord. 5 Therefore judge nothing before the time, until the Lord comes, who will both bring to light the hidden things of darkness and reveal the counsels of the hearts. Then each man will get his praise from God.

6 Now these things, brothers, I have in a figure transferred to myself and Apollos for your sakes, that in us you might learn not to think beyond the things which are written, that none of you be puffed up against one another. 7 For who makes you different? And what do you have that you didn't receive? But if you did receive it, why do you boast as if you had not received it?

8 You are already filled. You have already become rich. You have come to reign without us. Yes, and I wish that you did reign, that we also might reign with you! 9 For I think that God has displayed us, the apostles, last of all, like men sentenced to death. For we are made a spectacle to the world, both to angels and men. 10 We are fools for Christ's sake, but you are wise in Christ. We are weak, but you are strong. You have honour, but we have dishonour. 11 Even to this present hour we hunger, thirst, are naked, are beaten, and have no certain dwelling place. 12 We toil, working with our own hands. When people curse us, we bless. Being persecuted, we endure. 13 Being defamed, we entreat. We are made as the filth of the world, the dirt wiped off by all, even until now.

14 I don't write these things to shame you, but to admonish you as my beloved children. 15 For though you have ten thousand tutors in Christ, you don't have many fathers. For in Christ Jesus, I became your father through the Good News. 16 I beg you therefore, be imitators of me. 17 Because of this I have sent Timothy to you, who is my beloved and faithful child in the Lord, who will remind you of my ways which are in Christ, even as I teach everywhere in every assembly. 18 Now some are puffed up, as though I were not coming to you. 19 But I will come to you shortly, if the Lord is willing. And I will know, not the word of those who are puffed up, but the power. 20 For God's Kingdom is not in word, but in power. 21 What do you want? Shall I come to you with a rod, or in love and a spirit of gentleness?

5

1 It is actually reported that there is sexual immorality amongst you, and such sexual immorality as is not even named amongst the Gentiles, that one has his father's wife. 2 You are arrogant, and didn't mourn instead, that he who had done this deed might be removed from amongst you. 3 For I most certainly, as being absent in body but present in spirit, have already,

a 1:1 "Christ" means "Anointed One".
b 1:10 The word for "brothers" here and where context allows may also be correctly translated "brothers and sisters" or "siblings."
** 1:19 Isaiah 29:14
** 1:31 Jeremiah 9:24

** 2:9 Isaiah 64:4
** 2:16 Isaiah 40:13
** 3:19 Job 5:13
** 3:20 Psalms 94:11

as though I were present, judged him who has done this thing. 4 In the name of our Lord Jesus Christ, when you are gathered together with my spirit with the power of our Lord Jesus Christ, 5 you are to deliver such a one to Satan for the destruction of the flesh, that the spirit may be saved in the day of the Lord Jesus.

6 Your boasting is not good. Don't you know that a little yeast leavens the whole lump? 7 Purge out the old yeast, that you may be a new lump, even as you are unleavened. For indeed Christ, our Passover, has been sacrificed in our place. 8 Therefore let's keep the feast, not with old yeast, neither with the yeast of malice and wickedness, but with the unleavened bread of sincerity and truth.

9 I wrote to you in my letter to have no company with sexual sinners; 10 yet not at all meaning with the sexual sinners of this world, or with the covetous and extortionists, or with idolaters, for then you would have to leave the world. 11 But as it is, I wrote to you not to associate with anyone who is called a brother who is a sexual sinner, or covetous, or an idolater, or a slanderer, or a drunkard, or an extortionist. Don't even eat with such a person. 12 For what do I have to do with also judging those who are outside? Don't you judge those who are within? 13 But those who are outside, God judges. "Put away the wicked man from amongst yourselves."*

6

1 Dare any of you, having a matter against his neighbour, go to law before the unrighteous, and not before the saints? 2 Don't you know that the saints will judge the world? And if the world is judged by you, are you unworthy to judge the smallest matters? 3 Don't you know that we will judge angels? How much more, things that pertain to this life? 4 If then you have to judge things pertaining to this life, do you set them to judge who are of no account in the assembly? 5 I say this to move you to shame. Isn't there even one wise man amongst you who would be able to decide between his brothers? 6 But brother goes to law with brother, and that before unbelievers! 7 Therefore it is already altogether a defect in you that you have lawsuits one with another. Why not rather be wronged? Why not rather be defrauded? 8 No, but you yourselves do wrong and defraud, and that against your brothers.

9 Or don't you know that the unrighteous will not inherit God's Kingdom? Don't be deceived. Neither the sexually immoral, nor idolaters, nor adulterers, nor male prostitutes, nor homosexuals, 10 nor thieves, nor covetous, nor drunkards, nor slanderers, nor extortionists, will inherit God's Kingdom. 11 Some of you were such, but you were washed. You were sanctified. You were justified in the name of the Lord Jesus, and in the Spirit of our God.

12 "All things are lawful for me," but not all things are expedient. "All things are lawful for me," but I will not be brought under the power of anything. 13 "Foods for the belly, and the belly for foods," but God will bring to nothing both it and them. But the body is not for sexual immorality, but for the Lord, and the Lord for the body. 14 Now God raised up the Lord, and will also raise us up by his power. 15 Don't you know that your bodies are members of Christ? Shall I then take the members of Christ and make them members of a prostitute? May it never be! 16 Or don't you know that he who is joined to a prostitute is one body? For, "The two", he says, "will become one flesh."* 17 But he who is joined to the Lord is one spirit. 18 Flee sexual immorality! "Every sin that a man does is outside the body," but he who commits sexual immorality sins against his own body. 19 Or don't you know that your body is a temple of the Holy Spirit who is in you, whom you have from God? You are not your own, 20 for you were bought with a price. Therefore glorify God in your body and in your spirit, which are God's.

7

1 Now concerning the things about which you wrote to me: it is good for a man not to touch a woman. 2 But, because of sexual immoralities, let each man have his own wife, and let each woman have her own husband. 3 Let the husband give his wife the affection owed her,[a] and likewise also the wife her husband. 4 The wife doesn't have authority over her own body, but the husband does. Likewise also the husband doesn't have authority over his own body, but the wife does. 5 Don't deprive one another, unless it is by consent for a season, that you may give yourselves to fasting and prayer, and may be together again, that Satan doesn't tempt you because of your lack of self-control.

6 But this I say by way of concession, not of commandment. 7 Yet I wish that all men were like me. However, each man has his own gift from God, one of this kind, and another of that kind. 8 But I say to the unmarried and to widows, it is good for them if they remain even as I am. 9 But if they don't have self-control, let them marry. For it's better to marry than to burn with passion. 10 But to the married I command—not I, but the Lord—that the wife not leave her husband 11 (but if she departs, let her remain unmarried, or else be reconciled to her husband), and that the husband not leave his wife.

12 But to the rest I—not the Lord—say, if any brother has an unbelieving wife, and she is content to live with him, let him not leave her. 13 The woman who has an unbelieving husband, and he is content to live with her, let her not leave her husband. 14 For the unbelieving husband is sanctified in the wife, and the unbelieving wife is sanctified in the husband. Otherwise your children would be unclean, but now they are holy. 15 Yet if the unbeliever departs, let there be separation. The brother or the sister is not under bondage in such cases, but God has called us in peace. 16 For

how do you know, wife, whether you will save your husband? Or how do you know, husband, whether you will save your wife?

17 Only, as the Lord has distributed to each man, as God has called each, so let him walk. So I command in all the assemblies.

18 Was anyone called having been circumcised? Let him not become uncircumcised. Has anyone been called in uncircumcision? Let him not be circumcised. 19 Circumcision is nothing, and uncircumcision is nothing, but what matters is keeping God's commandments. 20 Let each man stay in that calling in which he was called. 21 Were you called being a bondservant? Don't let that bother you, but if you get an opportunity to become free, use it. 22 For he who was called in the Lord being a bondservant is the Lord's free man. Likewise he who was called being free is Christ's bondservant. 23 You were bought with a price. Don't become bondservants of men. 24 Brothers, let each man, in whatever condition he was called, stay in that condition with God.

25 Now concerning virgins, I have no commandment from the Lord, but I give my judgement as one who has obtained mercy from the Lord to be trustworthy. 26 Therefore I think that because of the distress that is on us, it's good for a man to remain as he is. 27 Are you bound to a wife? Don't seek to be freed. Are you free from a wife? Don't seek a wife. 28 But if you marry, you have not sinned. If a virgin marries, she has not sinned. Yet such will have oppression in the flesh, and I want to spare you. 29 But I say this, brothers: the time is short. From now on, both those who have wives may be as though they had none; 30 and those who weep, as though they didn't weep; and those who rejoice, as though they didn't rejoice; and those who buy, as though they didn't possess; 31 and those who use the world, as not using it to the fullest. For the mode of this world passes away.

32 But I desire to have you to be free from cares. He who is unmarried is concerned for the things of the Lord, how he may please the Lord; 33 but he who is married is concerned about the things of the world, how he may please his wife. 34 There is also a difference between a wife and a virgin. The unmarried woman cares about the things of the Lord, that she may be holy both in body and in spirit. But she who is married cares about the things of the world—how she may please her husband. 35 This I say for your own benefit, not that I may ensnare you, but for that which is appropriate, and that you may attend to the Lord without distraction.

36 But if any man thinks that he is behaving inappropriately towards his virgin, if she is past the flower of her age, and if need so requires, let him do what he desires. He doesn't sin. Let them marry. 37 But he who stands steadfast in his heart, having no urgency, but has power over his own will, and has determined in his own heart to keep his own virgin, does well. 38 So then both he who gives his own virgin in marriage does well, and he who doesn't give her in marriage does better.

39 A wife is bound by law for as long as her husband lives; but if the husband is dead, she is free to be married to whomever she desires, only in the Lord. 40 But she is happier if she stays as she is, in my judgement, and I think that I also have God's Spirit.

8

1 Now concerning things sacrificed to idols: We know that we all have knowledge. Knowledge puffs up, but love builds up. 2 But if anyone thinks that he knows anything, he doesn't yet know as he ought to know. 3 But anyone who loves God is known by him.

4 Therefore concerning the eating of things sacrificed to idols, we know that no idol is anything in the world, and that there is no other God but one. 5 For though there are things that are called "gods", whether in the heavens or on earth—as there are many "gods" and many "lords"— 6 yet to us there is one God, the Father, of whom are all things, and we for him; and one Lord, Jesus Christ, through whom are all things, and we live through him.

7 However, that knowledge isn't in all men. But some, with consciousness of an idol until now, eat as of a thing sacrificed to an idol, and their conscience, being weak, is defiled. 8 But food will not commend us to God. For neither, if we don't eat are we the worse, nor if we eat are we the better. 9 But be careful that by no means does this liberty of yours become a stumbling block to the weak. 10 For if a man sees you who have knowledge sitting in an idol's temple, won't his conscience, if he is weak, be emboldened to eat things sacrificed to idols? 11 And through your knowledge, he who is weak perishes, the brother for whose sake Christ died. 12 Thus, sinning against the brothers, and wounding their conscience when it is weak, you sin against Christ. 13 Therefore, if food causes my brother to stumble, I will eat no meat forever more, that I don't cause my brother to stumble.

9

1 Am I not free? Am I not an apostle? Haven't I seen Jesus Christ, our Lord? Aren't you my work in the Lord? 2 If to others I am not an apostle, yet at least I am to you; for you are the seal of my apostleship in the Lord.

3 My defence to those who examine me is this: 4 Have we no right to eat and to drink? 5 Have we no right to take along a wife who is a believer, even as the rest of the apostles, and the brothers of the Lord, and Cephas? 6 Or have only Barnabas and I no right to not work? 7 What soldier ever serves at his own expense? Who plants a vineyard, and doesn't eat of its fruit? Or who feeds a flock, and doesn't drink from the flock's milk? 8 Do I speak these things according to the ways of men? Or doesn't the law also say the same thing? 9 For it is written in the law of Moses, "You shall not muzzle an ox while it treads out the grain."* Is it for the oxen

---

** 5:13 Deuteronomy 17:7; 19:19; 21:21; 22:21; 24:7
** 6:16 Genesis 2:24

a 7:3 NU and TR have "what is owed her" instead of "the affection owed her".
** 9:9 Deuteronomy 25:4

that God cares, 10 or does he say it assuredly for our sake? Yes, it was written for our sake, because he who ploughs ought to plough in hope, and he who threshes in hope should partake of his hope. 11 If we sowed to you spiritual things, is it a great thing if we reap your fleshly things? 12 If others partake of this right over you, don't we yet more?

Nevertheless we didn't use this right, but we bear all things, that we may cause no hindrance to the Good News of Christ. 13 Don't you know that those who serve around sacred things eat from the things of the temple, and those who wait on the altar have their portion with the altar? 14 Even so the Lord ordained that those who proclaim the Good News should live from the Good News.

15 But I have used none of these things, and I don't write these things that it may be done so in my case; for I would rather die, than that anyone should make my boasting void. 16 For if I preach the Good News, I have nothing to boast about, for necessity is laid on me; but woe is to me if I don't preach the Good News. 17 For if I do this of my own will, I have a reward. But if not of my own will, I have a stewardship entrusted to me. 18 What then is my reward? That when I preach the Good News, I may present the Good News of Christ without charge, so as not to abuse my authority in the Good News.

19 For though I was free from all, I brought myself under bondage to all, that I might gain the more. 20 To the Jews I became as a Jew, that I might gain Jews; to those who are under the law, as under the law,[a] that I might gain those who are under the law; 21 to those who are without law, as without law (not being without law towards God, but under law towards Christ), that I might win those who are without law. 22 To the weak I became as weak, that I might gain the weak. I have become all things to all men, that I may by all means save some. 23 Now I do this for the sake of the Good News, that I may be a joint partaker of it. 24 Don't you know that those who run in a race all run, but one receives the prize? Run like that, so that you may win. 25 Every man who strives in the games exercises self-control in all things. Now they do it to receive a corruptible crown, but we an incorruptible. 26 I therefore run like that, not aimlessly. I fight like that, not beating the air, 27 but I beat my body and bring it into submission, lest by any means, after I have preached to others, I myself should be disqualified.

10

1 Now I would not have you ignorant, brothers, that our fathers were all under the cloud, and all passed through the sea; 2 and were all baptised into Moses in the cloud and in the sea; 3 and all ate the same spiritual food; 4 and all drank the same spiritual drink. For they drank of a spiritual rock that followed them, and the rock was Christ. 5 However with most of them, God was not well pleased, for they were overthrown in the wilderness.

6 Now these things were our examples, to the intent we should not lust after evil things as they also lusted. 7 Don't be idolaters, as some of them were. As it is written, "The people sat down to eat and drink, and rose up to play."* 8 Let's not commit sexual immorality, as some of them committed, and in one day twenty-three thousand fell. 9 Let's not test Christ,[b] as some of them tested, and perished by the serpents. 10 Don't grumble, as some of them also grumbled, and perished by the destroyer. 11 Now all these things happened to them by way of example, and they were written for our admonition, on whom the ends of the ages have come. 12 Therefore let him who thinks he stands be careful that he doesn't fall.

13 No temptation has taken you except what is common to man. God is faithful, who will not allow you to be tempted above what you are able, but will with the temptation also make the way of escape, that you may be able to endure it.

14 Therefore, my beloved, flee from idolatry. 15 I speak as to wise men. Judge what I say. 16 The cup of blessing which we bless, isn't it a sharing of the blood of Christ? The bread which we break, isn't it a sharing of the body of Christ? 17 Because there is one loaf of bread, we, who are many, are one body; for we all partake of the one loaf of bread. 18 Consider Israel according to the flesh. Don't those who eat the sacrifices participate in the altar?

19 What am I saying then? That a thing sacrificed to idols is anything, or that an idol is anything? 20 But I say that the things which the Gentiles sacrifice, they sacrifice to demons and not to God, and I don't desire that you would have fellowship with demons. 21 You can't both drink the cup of the Lord and the cup of demons. You can't both partake of the table of the Lord and of the table of demons. 22 Or do we provoke the Lord to jealousy? Are we stronger than he?

23 "All things are lawful for me," but not all things are profitable. "All things are lawful for me," but not all things build up. 24 Let no one seek his own, but each one his neighbour's good. 25 Whatever is sold in the butcher shop, eat, asking no question for the sake of conscience, 26 for "the earth is the Lord's, and its fullness."* 27 But if one of those who don't believe invites you to a meal, and you are inclined to go, eat whatever is set before you, asking no questions for the sake of conscience. 28 But if anyone says to you, "This was offered to idols," don't eat it for the sake of the one who told you, and for the sake of conscience. For "the earth is the Lord's, with all its fullness." 29 Conscience, I say, not your own, but the other's conscience. For why is my liberty judged by another conscience? 30 If I partake with thankfulness, why am I denounced for something I give thanks for?

31 Whether therefore you eat or drink, or whatever you do, do all to the glory of God. 32 Give no occasion for stumbling, whether to Jews, to Greeks, or to the assembly of God; 33 even as I also please all men in all things, not seeking my own profit, but the profit of the many, that they may be saved.

11

1 Be imitators of me, even as I also am of Christ.

2 Now I praise you, brothers, that you remember me in all things, and hold firm the traditions, even as I delivered them to you. 3 But I would have you know that the head[c] of every man is Christ, and the head[d] of the woman is man, and the head[e] of Christ is God. 4 Every man praying or prophesying, having his head covered, dishonours his head. 5 But every woman praying or prophesying with her head uncovered dishonours her head. For it is one and the same thing as if she were shaved. 6 For if a woman is not covered, let her hair also be cut off. But if it is shameful for a woman to have her hair cut off or be shaved, let her be covered. 7 For a man indeed ought not to have his head covered, because he is the image and glory of God, but the woman is the glory of the man. 8 For man is not from woman, but woman from man; 9 for man wasn't created for the woman, but woman for the man. 10 For this cause the woman ought to have authority over her own head, because of the angels.

11 Nevertheless, neither is the woman independent of the man, nor the man independent of the woman, in the Lord. 12 For as woman came from man, so a man also comes through a woman; but all things are from God. 13 Judge for yourselves. Is it appropriate that a woman pray to God unveiled? 14 Doesn't even nature itself teach you that if a man has long hair, it is a dishonour to him? 15 But if a woman has long hair, it is a glory to her, for her hair is given to her for a covering. 16 But if any man seems to be contentious, we have no such custom, neither do God's assemblies.

17 But in giving you this command I don't praise you, because you come together not for the better but for the worse. 18 For first of all, when you come together in the assembly, I hear that divisions exist amongst you, and I partly believe it. 19 For there also must be factions amongst you, that those who are approved may be revealed amongst you. 20 When therefore you assemble yourselves together, it is not the Lord's supper that you eat. 21 For in your eating each one takes his own supper first. One is hungry, and another is drunken. 22 What, don't you have houses to eat and to drink in? Or do you despise God's assembly and put them to shame who don't have enough? What shall I tell you? Shall I praise you? In this I don't praise you.

23 For I received from the Lord that which also I delivered to you, that the Lord Jesus on the night in which he was betrayed took bread. 24 When he had given thanks, he broke it and said, "Take, eat. This is my body, which is broken for you. Do this in memory of me." 25 In the same way he also took the cup after supper, saying, "This cup is the new covenant in my blood. Do this, as often as you drink, in memory of me." 26 For as often as you eat this bread and drink this cup, you proclaim the Lord's death until he comes.

27 Therefore whoever eats this bread or drinks the Lord's cup in a way unworthy of the Lord will be guilty of the body and the blood of the Lord. 28 But let a man examine himself, and so let him eat of the bread and drink of the cup. 29 For he who eats and drinks in an unworthy way eats and drinks judgement to himself if he doesn't discern the Lord's body. 30 For this cause many amongst you are weak and sickly, and not a few sleep. 31 For if we discerned ourselves, we wouldn't be judged. 32 But when we are judged, we are disciplined by the Lord, that we may not be condemned with the world. 33 Therefore, my brothers, when you come together to eat, wait for one another. 34 But if anyone is hungry, let him eat at home, lest your coming together be for judgement. The rest I will set in order whenever I come.

12

1 Now concerning spiritual things, brothers, I don't want you to be ignorant. 2 You know that when you were heathen,[f] you were led away to those mute idols, however you might be led. 3 Therefore I make known to you that no man speaking by God's Spirit says, "Jesus is accursed." No one can say, "Jesus is Lord," but by the Holy Spirit.

4 Now there are various kinds of gifts, but the same Spirit. 5 There are various kinds of service, and the same Lord. 6 There are various kinds of workings, but the same God who works all things in all. 7 But to each one is given the manifestation of the Spirit for the profit of all. 8 For to one is given through the Spirit the word of wisdom, and to another the word of knowledge according to the same Spirit, 9 to another faith by the same Spirit, and to another gifts of healings by the same Spirit, 10 and to another workings of miracles, and to another prophecy, and to another discerning of spirits, to another different kinds of languages, and to another the interpretation of languages. 11 But the one and the same Spirit produces all of these, distributing to each one separately as he desires.

12 For as the body is one and has many members, and all the members of the body, being many, are one body; so also is Christ. 13 For in one Spirit we were all baptised into one body, whether Jews or Greeks, whether bond or free; and were all given to drink into one Spirit.

14 For the body is not one member, but many. 15 If the foot would say, "Because I'm not the hand, I'm not part of the body," it is not therefore not

---

a 9:20 NU adds: though I myself am not under the law
** 10:7 Exodus 32:6
b 10:9 NU reads "the Lord" instead of "Christ".
** 10:26 Psalms 24:1

c 11:3 or, origin
d 11:3 or, origin
e 11:3 or, origin
f 12:2 or Gentiles

part of the body. 16 If the ear would say, "Because I'm not the eye, I'm not part of the body," it's not therefore not part of the body. 17 If the whole body were an eye, where would the hearing be? If the whole were hearing, where would the smelling be? 18 But now God has set the members, each one of them, in the body, just as he desired. 19 If they were all one member, where would the body be? 20 But now they are many members, but one body. 21 The eye can't tell the hand, "I have no need for you," or again the head to the feet, "I have no need for you." 22 No, much rather, those members of the body which seem to be weaker are necessary. 23 Those parts of the body which we think to be less honourable, on those we bestow more abundant honour; and our unpresentable parts have more abundant modesty, 24 while our presentable parts have no such need. But God composed the body together, giving more abundant honour to the inferior part, 25 that there should be no division in the body, but that the members should have the same care for one another. 26 When one member suffers, all the members suffer with it. When one member is honoured, all the members rejoice with it.

27 Now you are the body of Christ, and members individually. 28 God has set some in the assembly: first apostles, second prophets, third teachers, then miracle workers, then gifts of healings, helps, governments, and various kinds of languages. 29 Are all apostles? Are all prophets? Are all teachers? Are all miracle workers? 30 Do all have gifts of healings? Do all speak with various languages? Do all interpret? 31 But earnestly desire the best gifts. Moreover, I show a most excellent way to you.

13

1 If I speak with the languages of men and of angels, but don't have love, I have become sounding brass or a clanging cymbal. 2 If I have the gift of prophecy, and know all mysteries and all knowledge, and if I have all faith, so as to remove mountains, but don't have love, I am nothing. 3 If I give away all my goods to feed the poor, and if I give my body to be burnt, but don't have love, it profits me nothing.

4 Love is patient and is kind. Love doesn't envy. Love doesn't brag, is not proud, 5 doesn't behave itself inappropriately, doesn't seek its own way, is not provoked, takes no account of evil; 6 doesn't rejoice in unrighteousness, but rejoices with the truth; 7 bears all things, believes all things, hopes all things, endures all things.

8 Love never fails. But where there are prophecies, they will be done away with. Where there are various languages, they will cease. Where there is knowledge, it will be done away with. 9 For we know in part and we prophesy in part; 10 but when that which is complete has come, then that which is partial will be done away with. 11 When I was a child, I spoke as a child, I felt as a child, I thought as a child. Now that I have become a man, I have put away childish things. 12 For now we see in a mirror, dimly, but then face to face. Now I know in part, but then I will know fully, even as I was also fully known. 13 But now faith, hope, and love remain—these three. The greatest of these is love.

14

1 Follow after love and earnestly desire spiritual gifts, but especially that you may prophesy. 2 For he who speaks in another language speaks not to men, but to God, for no one understands; but in the Spirit he speaks mysteries. 3 But he who prophesies speaks to men for their edification, exhortation, and consolation. 4 He who speaks in another language edifies himself, but he who prophesies edifies the assembly. 5 Now I desire to have you all speak with other languages, but even more that you would prophesy. For he is greater who prophesies than he who speaks with other languages, unless he interprets, that the assembly may be built up.

6 But now, brothers,ᵃ if I come to you speaking with other languages, what would I profit you unless I speak to you either by way of revelation, or of knowledge, or of prophesying, or of teaching? 7 Even lifeless things that make a sound, whether pipe or harp, if they didn't give a distinction in the sounds, how would it be known what is piped or harped? 8 For if the trumpet gave an uncertain sound, who would prepare himself for war? 9 So also you, unless you uttered by the tongue words easy to understand, how would it be known what is spoken? For you would be speaking into the air. 10 There are, it may be, so many kinds of languages in the world, and none of them is without meaning. 11 If then I don't know the meaning of the language, I would be to him who speaks a foreigner, and he who speaks would be a foreigner to me. 12 So also you, since you are zealous for spiritual gifts, seek that you may abound to the building up of the assembly.

13 Therefore let him who speaks in another language pray that he may interpret. 14 For if I pray in another language, my spirit prays, but my understanding is unfruitful. 15 What should I do? I will pray with the spirit, and I will pray with the understanding also. I will sing with the spirit, and I will sing with the understanding also. 16 Otherwise, if you bless with the spirit, how will he who fills the place of the unlearned say the "Amen" at your giving of thanks, seeing he doesn't know what you say? 17 For you most certainly give thanks well, but the other person is not built up. 18 I thank my God, I speak with other languages more than you all. 19 However, in the assembly I would rather speak five words with my understanding, that I might instruct others also, than ten thousand words in another language.

20 Brothers, don't be children in thoughts, yet in malice be babies, but in thoughts be mature. 21 In the law it is written, "By men of strange languages and by the lips of strangers I will speak to this people. They won't even listen to me that way, says the Lord."* 22 Therefore other languages are for a sign, not to those who believe, but to the unbelieving; but prophesying is for a sign, not to the unbelieving, but to those who believe. 23 If therefore the whole assembly is assembled together and all speak with other languages, and unlearned or unbelieving people come in, won't they say that you are crazy? 24 But if all prophesy, and someone unbelieving or unlearned comes in, he is reproved by all, and he is judged by all. 25 And thus the secrets of his heart are revealed. So he will fall down on his face and worship God, declaring that God is amongst you indeed.

26 What is it then, brothers? When you come together, each one of you has a psalm, has a teaching, has a revelation, has another language, or has an interpretation. Let all things be done to build each other up. 27 If any man speaks in another language, let there be two, or at the most three, and in turn; and let one interpret. 28 But if there is no interpreter, let him keep silent in the assembly, and let him speak to himself and to God. 29 Let two or three of the prophets speak, and let the others discern. 30 But if a revelation is made to another sitting by, let the first keep silent. 31 For you all can prophesy one by one, that all may learn and all may be exhorted. 32 The spirits of the prophets are subject to the prophets, 33 for God is not a God of confusion but of peace, as in all the assemblies of the saints. 34 Let the wives be quiet in the assemblies, for it has not been permitted for them to be talking except in submission, as the law also says,* 35 if they desire to learn anything. "Let them ask their own husbands at home, for it is shameful for a wife to be talking in the assembly." 36 What!? Was it from you that the word of God went out? Or did it come to you alone?

37 If any man thinks himself to be a prophet or spiritual, let him recognise the things which I write to you, that they are the commandment of the Lord. 38 But if anyone is ignorant, let him be ignorant.

39 Therefore, brothers, desire earnestly to prophesy, and don't forbid speaking with other languages. 40 Let all things be done decently and in order.

15

1 Now I declare to you, brothers, the Good News which I preached to you, which also you received, in which you also stand, 2 by which also you are saved, if you hold firmly the word which I preached to you—unless you believed in vain.

3 For I delivered to you first of all that which I also received: that Christ died for our sins according to the Scriptures, 4 that he was buried, that he was raised on the third day according to the Scriptures, 5 and that he appeared to Cephas, then to the twelve. 6 Then he appeared to over five hundred brothers at once, most of whom remain until now, but some have also fallen asleep. 7 Then he appeared to James, then to all the apostles, 8 and last of all, as to the child born at the wrong time, he appeared to me also. 9 For I am the least of the apostles, who is not worthy to be called an apostle, because I persecuted the assembly of God. 10 But by the grace of God I am what I am. His grace which was given to me was not futile, but I worked more than all of them; yet not I, but the grace of God which was with me. 11 Whether then it is I or they, so we preach, and so you believed.

12 Now if Christ is preached, that he has been raised from the dead, how do some amongst you say that there is no resurrection of the dead? 13 But if there is no resurrection of the dead, neither has Christ been raised. 14 If Christ has not been raised, then our preaching is in vain and your faith also is in vain. 15 Yes, we are also found false witnesses of God, because we testified about God that he raised up Christ, whom he didn't raise up if it is true that the dead are not raised. 16 For if the dead aren't raised, neither has Christ been raised. 17 If Christ has not been raised, your faith is vain; you are still in your sins. 18 Then they also who are fallen asleep in Christ have perished. 19 If we have only hoped in Christ in this life, we are of all men most pitiable.

20 But now Christ has been raised from the dead. He became the first fruit of those who are asleep. 21 For since death came by man, the resurrection of the dead also came by man. 22 For as in Adam all die, so also in Christ all will be made alive. 23 But each in his own order: Christ the first fruits, then those who are Christ's at his coming. 24 Then the end comes, when he will deliver up the Kingdom to God the Father, when he will have abolished all rule and all authority and power. 25 For he must reign until he has put all his enemies under his feet. 26 The last enemy that will be abolished is death. 27 For, "He put all things in subjection under his feet."* But when he says, "All things are put in subjection", it is evident that he is excepted who subjected all things to him. 28 When all things have been subjected to him, then the Son will also himself be subjected to him who subjected all things to him, that God may be all in all.

29 Or else what will they do who are baptised for the dead? If the dead aren't raised at all, why then are they baptised for the dead? 30 Why do we also stand in jeopardy every hour? 31 I affirm, by the boasting in you which I have in Christ Jesus our Lord, I die daily. 32 If I fought with animals at Ephesus for human purposes, what does it profit me? If the dead are not raised, then "let's eat and drink, for tomorrow we die."* 33 Don't be deceived! "Evil companionships corrupt good morals." 34 Wake up righteously and don't sin, for some have no knowledge of God. I say this to your shame.

35 But someone will say, "How are the dead raised?" and, "With what kind of body do they come?" 36 You foolish one, that which you yourself sow is not made alive unless it dies. 37 That which you sow, you don't sow

a 14:6 The word for "brothers" here and where context allows may also be correctly translated "brothers and sisters" or "siblings."
** 14:21 Isaiah 28:11-12

** 14:34 Deuteronomy 27:9
** 15:27 Psalms 8:6
** 15:32 Isaiah 22:13

the body that will be, but a bare grain, maybe of wheat, or of some other kind. 38 But God gives it a body even as it pleased him, and to each seed a body of its own. 39 All flesh is not the same flesh, but there is one flesh of men, another flesh of animals, another of fish, and another of birds. 40 There are also celestial bodies and terrestrial bodies; but the glory of the celestial differs from that of the terrestrial. 41 There is one glory of the sun, another glory of the moon, and another glory of the stars; for one star differs from another star in glory.

42 So also is the resurrection of the dead. The body is sown perishable; it is raised imperishable. 43 It is sown in dishonour; it is raised in glory. It is sown in weakness; it is raised in power. 44 It is sown a natural body; it is raised a spiritual body. There is a natural body and there is also a spiritual body.

45 So also it is written, "The first man Adam became a living soul." * The last Adam became a life-giving spirit. 46 However, that which is spiritual isn't first, but that which is natural, then that which is spiritual. 47 The first man is of the earth, made of dust. The second man is the Lord from heaven. 48 As is the one made of dust, such are those who are also made of dust; and as is the heavenly, such are they also that are heavenly. 49 As we have borne the image of those made of dust, let's[a] also bear the image of the heavenly. 50 Now I say this, brothers,[b] that flesh and blood can't inherit God's Kingdom; neither does the perishable inherit imperishable.

51 Behold,[c] I tell you a mystery. We will not all sleep, but we will all be changed, 52 in a moment, in the twinkling of an eye, at the last trumpet. For the trumpet will sound and the dead will be raised incorruptible, and we will be changed. 53 For this perishable body must become imperishable, and this mortal must put on immortality. 54 But when this perishable body will have become imperishable, and this mortal will have put on immortality, then what is written will happen: "Death is swallowed up in victory." *
55 "Death, where is your sting?

Hades,[d] where is your victory?" *

56 The sting of death is sin, and the power of sin is the law. 57 But thanks be to God, who gives us the victory through our Lord Jesus Christ. 58 Therefore, my beloved brothers, be steadfast, immovable, always abounding in the Lord's work, because you know that your labour is not in vain in the Lord.

16

1 Now concerning the collection for the saints: as I commanded the assemblies of Galatia, you do likewise. 2 On the first day of every week, let each one of you save as he may prosper, that no collections are made when I come. 3 When I arrive, I will send whoever you approve with letters to carry your gracious gift to Jerusalem. 4 If it is appropriate for me to go also, they will go with me.

5 I will come to you when I have passed through Macedonia, for I am passing through Macedonia. 6 But with you it may be that I will stay with you, or even winter with you, that you may send me on my journey wherever I go. 7 For I do not wish to see you now in passing, but I hope to stay a while with you, if the Lord permits. 8 But I will stay at Ephesus until Pentecost, 9 for a great and effective door has opened to me, and there are many adversaries.

10 Now if Timothy comes, see that he is with you without fear, for he does the work of the Lord, as I also do. 11 Therefore let no one despise him. But set him forward on his journey in peace, that he may come to me; for I expect him with the brothers.

12 Now concerning Apollos the brother, I strongly urged him to come to you with the brothers, but it was not at all his desire to come now; but he will come when he has an opportunity.

13 Watch! Stand firm in the faith! Be courageous! Be strong! 14 Let all that you do be done in love.

15 Now I beg you, brothers—you know the house of Stephanas, that it is the first fruits of Achaia, and that they have set themselves to serve the saints— 16 that you also be in subjection to such, and to everyone who helps in the work and labours. 17 I rejoice at the coming of Stephanas, Fortunatus, and Achaicus; for that which was lacking on your part, they supplied. 18 For they refreshed my spirit and yours. Therefore acknowledge those who are like that.

19 The assemblies of Asia greet you. Aquila and Priscilla greet you warmly in the Lord, together with the assembly that is in their house. 20 All the brothers greet you. Greet one another with a holy kiss.

21 This greeting is by me, Paul, with my own hand. 22 If any man doesn't love the Lord Jesus Christ, let him be cursed.[e] Come, Lord![f] 23 The grace of the Lord Jesus Christ be with you. 24 My love to all of you in Christ Jesus. Amen.

** 15:45 Genesis 2:7
a 15:49 NU, TR read "we will" instead of "let's"
b 15:50 The word for "brothers" here and where context allows may also be correctly translated "brothers and sisters" or "siblings."
c 15:51 "Behold", from "ἰδοὺ", means look at, take notice, observe, see, or gaze at. It is often used as an interjection.

** 15:54 Isaiah 25:8
d 15:55 or, Hell
** 15:55 See Hosea 13:14
e 16:22 Greek: anathema.
f 16:22 Aramaic: Maranatha!

Paul's Second Letter to the Corinthians

1

1 Paul, an apostle of Christ[a] Jesus through the will of God, and Timothy our brother, to the assembly of God which is at Corinth, with all the saints who are in the whole of Achaia: 2 Grace to you and peace from God our Father and the Lord Jesus Christ.

3 Blessed be the God and Father of our Lord Jesus Christ, the Father of mercies and God of all comfort, 4 who comforts us in all our affliction, that we may be able to comfort those who are in any affliction, through the comfort with which we ourselves are comforted by God. 5 For as the sufferings of Christ abound to us, even so our comfort also abounds through Christ. 6 But if we are afflicted, it is for your comfort and salvation. If we are comforted, it is for your comfort, which produces in you the patient enduring of the same sufferings which we also suffer. 7 Our hope for you is steadfast, knowing that, since you are partakers of the sufferings, so you are also of the comfort.

8 For we don't desire to have you uninformed, brothers,[b] concerning our affliction which happened to us in Asia: that we were weighed down exceedingly, beyond our power, so much that we despaired even of life. 9 Yes, we ourselves have had the sentence of death within ourselves, that we should not trust in ourselves, but in God who raises the dead, 10 who delivered us out of so great a death, and does deliver, on whom we have set our hope that he will also still deliver us, 11 you also helping together on our behalf by your supplication; that, for the gift given to us by means of many, thanks may be given by many persons on your behalf.

12 For our boasting is this: the testimony of our conscience that in holiness and sincerity of God, not in fleshly wisdom but in the grace of God, we behaved ourselves in the world, and more abundantly towards you. 13 For we write no other things to you than what you read or even acknowledge, and I hope you will acknowledge to the end— 14 as also you acknowledged us in part—that we are your boasting, even as you also are ours, in the day of our Lord Jesus.

15 In this confidence, I was determined to come first to you, that you might have a second benefit, 16 and by you to pass into Macedonia, and again from Macedonia to come to you, and to be sent forward by you on my journey to Judea. 17 When I therefore planned this, did I show fickleness? Or the things that I plan, do I plan according to the flesh, that with me there should be the "Yes, yes" and the "No, no?" 18 But as God is faithful, our word towards you was not "Yes and no." 19 For the Son of God, Jesus Christ, who was preached amongst you by us—by me, Silvanus, and Timothy—was not "Yes and no," but in him is "Yes." 20 For however many are the promises of God, in him is the "Yes." Therefore also through him is the "Amen", to the glory of God through us.

21 Now he who establishes us with you in Christ and anointed us is God, 22 who also sealed us and gave us the down payment of the Spirit in our hearts.

23 But I call God for a witness to my soul, that to spare you, I didn't come to Corinth. 24 We don't control your faith, but are fellow workers with you for your joy. For you stand firm in faith.

2

1 But I determined this for myself, that I would not come to you again in sorrow. 2 For if I make you grieve, then who will make me glad but he who is made to grieve by me? 3 And I wrote this very thing to you, so that when I came, I wouldn't have sorrow from them of whom I ought to rejoice; having confidence in you all that my joy would be shared by all of you. 4 For out of much affliction and anguish of heart I wrote to you with many tears, not that you should be made to grieve, but that you might know the love that I have so abundantly for you.

5 But if any has caused sorrow, he has caused sorrow not to me, but in part (that I not press too heavily) to you all. 6 This punishment which was inflicted by the many is sufficient for such a one; 7 so that, on the contrary, you should rather forgive him and comfort him, lest by any means such a one should be swallowed up with his excessive sorrow. 8 Therefore I beg you to confirm your love towards him. 9 For to this end I also wrote, that I might know the proof of you, whether you are obedient in all things. 10 Now I also forgive whomever you forgive anything. For if indeed I have forgiven anything, I have forgiven that one for your sakes in the presence of Christ, 11 that no advantage may be gained over us by Satan, for we are not ignorant of his schemes.

12 Now when I came to Troas for the Good News of Christ, and when a door was opened to me in the Lord, 13 I had no relief for my spirit, because I didn't find Titus my brother, but taking my leave of them, I went out into Macedonia.

14 Now thanks be to God who always leads us in triumph in Christ, and reveals through us the sweet aroma of his knowledge in every place. 15 For we are a sweet aroma of Christ to God in those who are saved and in those who perish: 16 to the one a stench from death to death, to the other a sweet aroma from life to life. Who is sufficient for these things? 17 For we are not as so many, peddling the word of God. But as of sincerity, but as of God, in the sight of God, we speak in Christ.

3

1 Are we beginning again to commend ourselves? Or do we need, as do some, letters of commendation to you or from you? 2 You are our letter, written in our hearts, known and read by all men, 3 being revealed that you are a letter of Christ, served by us, written not with ink, but with the Spirit of the living God; not in tablets of stone, but in tablets that are hearts of flesh.

4 Such confidence we have through Christ towards God, 5 not that we are sufficient of ourselves to account anything as from ourselves; but our sufficiency is from God, 6 who also made us sufficient as servants of a new covenant, not of the letter but of the Spirit. For the letter kills, but the Spirit gives life.

7 But if the service of death, written engraved on stones, came with glory, so that the children of Israel could not look steadfastly on the face of Moses for the glory of his face, which was passing away, 8 won't service of the Spirit be with much more glory? 9 For if the service of condemnation has glory, the service of righteousness exceeds much more in glory. 10 For most certainly that which has been made glorious has not been made glorious in this respect, by reason of the glory that surpasses. 11 For if that which passes away was with glory, much more that which remains is in glory.

12 Having therefore such a hope, we use great boldness of speech, 13 and not as Moses, who put a veil on his face so that the children of Israel wouldn't look steadfastly on the end of that which was passing away. 14 But their minds were hardened, for until this very day at the reading of the old covenant the same veil remains, because in Christ it passes away. 15 But to this day, when Moses is read, a veil lies on their heart. 16 But whenever someone turns to the Lord, the veil is taken away. 17 Now the Lord is the Spirit; and where the Spirit of the Lord is, there is liberty. 18 But we all, with unveiled face seeing the glory of the Lord as in a mirror, are transformed into the same image from glory to glory, even as from the Lord, the Spirit.

4

1 Therefore, seeing we have this ministry, even as we obtained mercy, we don't faint. 2 But we have renounced the hidden things of shame, not walking in craftiness nor handling the word of God deceitfully, but by the manifestation of the truth commending ourselves to every man's conscience in the sight of God. 3 Even if our Good News is veiled, it is veiled in those who are dying, 4 in whom the god of this world has blinded the minds of the unbelieving, that the light of the Good News of the glory of Christ, who is the image of God, should not dawn on them. 5 For we don't preach ourselves, but Christ Jesus as Lord, and ourselves as your servants for Jesus' sake, 6 seeing it is God who said, "Light will shine out of darkness,"[*] who has shone in our hearts to give the light of the knowledge of the glory of God in the face of Jesus Christ.

7 But we have this treasure in clay vessels, that the exceeding greatness of the power may be of God and not from ourselves. 8 We are pressed on every side, yet not crushed; perplexed, yet not to despair; 9 pursued, yet not forsaken; struck down, yet not destroyed; 10 always carrying in the body the putting to death of the Lord Jesus, that the life of Jesus may also be revealed in our body. 11 For we who live are always delivered to death for Jesus' sake, that the life also of Jesus may be revealed in our mortal flesh. 12 So then death works in us, but life in you.

13 But having the same spirit of faith, according to that which is written, "I believed, and therefore I spoke."[*] We also believe, and therefore we also speak, 14 knowing that he who raised the Lord Jesus will raise us also with Jesus, and will present us with you. 15 For all things are for your sakes, that the grace, being multiplied through the many, may cause the thanksgiving to abound to the glory of God.

16 Therefore we don't faint, but though our outward person is decaying, yet our inward person is renewed day by day. 17 For our light affliction, which is for the moment, works for us more and more exceedingly an eternal weight of glory, 18 while we don't look at the things which are seen, but at the things which are not seen. For the things which are seen are temporal, but the things which are not seen are eternal.

5

1 For we know that if the earthly house of our tent is dissolved, we have a building from God, a house not made with hands, eternal, in the heavens. 2 For most certainly in this we groan, longing to be clothed with our habitation which is from heaven, 3 if indeed being clothed, we will not be found naked. 4 For indeed we who are in this tent do groan, being burdened, not that we desire to be unclothed, but that we desire to be clothed, that what is mortal may be swallowed up by life. 5 Now he who made us for this very thing is God, who also gave to us the down payment of the Spirit.

6 Therefore we are always confident and know that while we are at home in the body, we are absent from the Lord; 7 for we walk by faith, not by sight. 8 We are courageous, I say, and are willing rather to be absent from the body and to be at home with the Lord. 9 Therefore also we make it our aim, whether at home or absent, to be well pleasing to him. 10 For we must all be revealed before the judgement seat of Christ that each one may receive the things in the body according to what he has done, whether good or bad.

11 Knowing therefore the fear of the Lord, we persuade men, but we are revealed to God, and I hope that we are revealed also in your

---

[a] 1:1 "Christ" means "Anointed One".
[b] 1:8 The word for "brothers" here and where context allows may also be correctly translated "brothers and sisters" or "siblings."

[*] 4:6 Genesis 1:3
[*] 4:13 Psalms 116:10

consciences. 12 For we are not commending ourselves to you again, but speak as giving you occasion of boasting on our behalf, that you may have something to answer those who boast in appearance and not in heart. 13 For if we are beside ourselves, it is for God. Or if we are of sober mind, it is for you. 14 For the love of Christ compels us; because we judge thus: that one died for all, therefore all died. 15 He died for all, that those who live should no longer live to themselves, but to him who for their sakes died and rose again.

16 Therefore we know no one according to the flesh from now on. Even though we have known Christ according to the flesh, yet now we know him so no more. 17 Therefore if anyone is in Christ, he is a new creation. The old things have passed away. Behold,[a] all things have become new. 18 But all things are of God, who reconciled us to himself through Jesus Christ, and gave to us the ministry of reconciliation; 19 namely, that God was in Christ reconciling the world to himself, not reckoning to them their trespasses, and having committed to us the word of reconciliation.

20 We are therefore ambassadors on behalf of Christ, as though God were entreating by us: we beg you on behalf of Christ, be reconciled to God. 21 For him who knew no sin he made to be sin on our behalf, so that in him we might become the righteousness of God.

6

1 Working together, we entreat also that you do not receive the grace of God in vain. 2 For he says,
"At an acceptable time I listened to you.
In a day of salvation I helped you."**

Behold, now is the acceptable time. Behold, now is the day of salvation. 3 We give no occasion of stumbling in anything, that our service may not be blamed, 4 but in everything commending ourselves as servants of God: in great endurance, in afflictions, in hardships, in distresses, 5 in beatings, in imprisonments, in riots, in labours, in watchings, in fastings, 6 in pureness, in knowledge, in perseverance, in kindness, in the Holy Spirit, in sincere love, 7 in the word of truth, in the power of God, by the armour of righteousness on the right hand and on the left, 8 by glory and dishonour, by evil report and good report, as deceivers and yet true, 9 as unknown and yet well known, as dying and behold—we live, as punished and not killed, 10 as sorrowful yet always rejoicing, as poor yet making many rich, as having nothing and yet possessing all things.

11 Our mouth is open to you, Corinthians. Our heart is enlarged. 12 You are not restricted by us, but you are restricted by your own affections. 13 Now in return—I speak as to my children—you also open your hearts.

14 Don't be unequally yoked with unbelievers, for what fellowship do righteousness and iniquity have? Or what fellowship does light have with darkness? 15 What agreement does Christ have with Belial? Or what portion does a believer have with an unbeliever? 16 What agreement does a temple of God have with idols? For you are a temple of the living God. Even as God said, "I will dwell in them and walk in them. I will be their God and they will be my people."** 17 Therefore
"'Come out from amongst them,
    and be separate,' says the Lord.
'Touch no unclean thing.
    I will receive you.'
18 I will be to you a Father.
    You will be to me sons and daughters,'
    says the Lord Almighty."**

7

1 Having therefore these promises, beloved, let's cleanse ourselves from all defilement of flesh and spirit, perfecting holiness in the fear of God.
2 Open your hearts to us. We wronged no one. We corrupted no one. We took advantage of no one. 3 I say this not to condemn you, for I have said before that you are in our hearts to die together and live together. 4 Great is my boldness of speech towards you. Great is my boasting on your behalf. I am filled with comfort. I overflow with joy in all our affliction.

5 For even when we had come into Macedonia, our flesh had no relief, but we were afflicted on every side. Fightings were outside. Fear was inside. 6 Nevertheless, he who comforts the lowly, God, comforted us by the coming of Titus, 7 and not by his coming only, but also by the comfort with which he was comforted in you while he told us of your longing, your mourning, and your zeal for me, so that I rejoiced still more.

8 For though I grieved you with my letter, I do not regret it, though I did regret it. For I see that my letter made you grieve, though just for a while. 9 I now rejoice, not that you were grieved, but that you were grieved to repentance. For you were grieved in a godly way, that you might suffer loss by us in nothing. 10 For godly sorrow produces repentance leading to salvation, which brings no regret. But the sorrow of the world produces death. 11 For behold, this same thing, that you were grieved in a godly way, what earnest care it worked in you. Yes, what defence, indignation, fear, longing, zeal, and vindication! In everything you demonstrated yourselves to be pure in the matter. 12 So although I wrote to you, I wrote not for his cause that did the wrong, nor for his cause that suffered the wrong, but that your earnest care for us might be revealed in you in the sight of God. 13 Therefore we have been comforted. In our comfort we rejoiced the more exceedingly for the joy of Titus, because his spirit has been refreshed by you all. 14 For if in anything I have boasted to him on your behalf, I was not

disappointed. But as we spoke all things to you in truth, so our glorying also which I made before Titus was found to be truth. 15 His affection is more abundantly towards you, while he remembers all of your obedience, how with fear and trembling you received him. 16 I rejoice that in everything I am confident concerning you.

8

1 Moreover, brothers, we make known to you the grace of God which has been given in the assemblies of Macedonia, 2 how in a severe ordeal of affliction, the abundance of their joy and their deep poverty abounded to the riches of their generosity. 3 For according to their power, I testify, yes and beyond their power, they gave of their own accord, 4 begging us with much entreaty to receive this grace and the fellowship in the service to the saints. 5 This was not as we had expected, but first they gave their own selves to the Lord, and to us through the will of God. 6 So we urged Titus, that as he had made a beginning before, so he would also complete in you this grace. 7 But as you abound in everything—in faith, utterance, knowledge, all earnestness, and in your love to us—see that you also abound in this grace.

8 I speak not by way of commandment, but as proving through the earnestness of others the sincerity also of your love. 9 For you know the grace of our Lord Jesus Christ, that though he was rich, yet for your sakes he became poor, that you through his poverty might become rich. 10 I give advice in this: it is expedient for you who were the first to start a year ago, not only to do, but also to be willing. 11 But now complete the doing also, that as there was the readiness to be willing, so there may be the completion also out of your ability. 12 For if the readiness is there, it is acceptable according to what you have, not according to what you don't have. 13 For this is not that others may be eased and you distressed, 14 but for equality. Your abundance at this present time supplies their lack, that their abundance also may become a supply for your lack, that there may be equality. 15 As it is written, "He who gathered much had nothing left over, and he who gathered little had no lack."**

16 But thanks be to God, who puts the same earnest care for you into the heart of Titus. 17 For he indeed accepted our exhortation, but being himself very earnest, he went out to you of his own accord. 18 We have sent together with him the brother whose praise in the Good News is known throughout all the assemblies. 19 Not only so, but he was also appointed by the assemblies to travel with us in this grace, which is served by us to the glory of the Lord himself, and to show our readiness. 20 We are avoiding this, that any man should blame us concerning this abundance which is administered by us. 21 Having regard for honourable things, not only in the sight of the Lord, but also in the sight of men. 22 We have sent with them our brother whom we have many times proved earnest in many things, but now much more earnest, by reason of the great confidence which he has in you. 23 As for Titus, he is my partner and fellow worker for you. As for our brothers, they are the apostles of the assemblies, the glory of Christ. 24 Therefore show the proof of your love to them before the assemblies, and of our boasting on your behalf.

9

1 It is indeed unnecessary for me to write to you concerning the service to the saints, 2 for I know your readiness, of which I boast on your behalf to those of Macedonia, that Achaia has been prepared for the past year. Your zeal has stirred up very many of them. 3 But I have sent the brothers so that our boasting on your behalf may not be in vain in this respect, that, just as I said, you may be prepared, 4 lest by any means, if anyone from Macedonia comes there with me and finds you unprepared, we (to say nothing of you) would be disappointed in this confident boasting. 5 I thought it necessary therefore to entreat the brothers that they would go before to you and arrange ahead of time the generous gift that you promised before, that the same might be ready as a matter of generosity, and not of greediness.

6 Remember this: he who sows sparingly will also reap sparingly. He who sows bountifully will also reap bountifully. 7 Let each man give according as he has determined in his heart, not grudgingly or under compulsion, for God loves a cheerful giver. 8 And God is able to make all grace abound to you, that you, always having all sufficiency in everything, may abound to every good work. 9 As it is written,
"He has scattered abroad. He has given to the poor.
    His righteousness remains forever."**

10 Now may he who supplies seed to the sower and bread for food, supply and multiply your seed for sowing, and increase the fruits of your righteousness, 11 you being enriched in everything for all generosity, which produces thanksgiving to God through us. 12 For this service of giving that you perform not only makes up for lack amongst the saints, but abounds also through much giving of thanks to God, 13 seeing that through the proof given by this service, they glorify God for the obedience of your confession to the Good News of Christ and for the generosity of your contribution to them and to all, 14 while they themselves also, with supplication on your behalf, yearn for you by reason of the exceeding grace of God in you. 15 Now thanks be to God for his unspeakable gift!

---

a 5:17 "Behold", from "ἰδοὺ", means look at, take notice, observe, see, or gaze at. It is often used as an interjection.
** 6:2 Isaiah 49:8
** 6:16 Leviticus 26:12; Jeremiah 32:38; Ezekiel 37:27
** 6:17 Isaiah 52:11; Ezekiel 20:34,41
** 6:18 2 Samuel 7:14; 7:8
** 8:15 Exodus 16:18
** 9:9 Psalms 112:9

10

1 Now I Paul, myself, entreat you by the humility and gentleness of Christ, I who in your presence am lowly amongst you, but being absent am bold towards you. 2 Yes, I beg you that I may not, when present, show courage with the confidence with which I intend to be bold against some, who consider us to be walking according to the flesh. 3 For though we walk in the flesh, we don't wage war according to the flesh; 4 for the weapons of our warfare are not of the flesh, but mighty before God to the throwing down of strongholds, 5 throwing down imaginations and every high thing that is exalted against the knowledge of God and bringing every thought into captivity to the obedience of Christ, 6 and being in readiness to avenge all disobedience when your obedience is made full.

7 Do you look at things only as they appear in front of your face? If anyone trusts in himself that he is Christ's, let him consider this again with himself, that even as he is Christ's, so we also are Christ's. 8 For even if I boast somewhat abundantly concerning our authority, which the Lord gave for building you up and not for casting you down, I will not be ashamed, 9 that I may not seem as if I desire to terrify you by my letters. 10 For, "His letters", they say, "are weighty and strong, but his bodily presence is weak, and his speech is despised." 11 Let such a person consider this, that what we are in word by letters when we are absent, such are we also in deed when we are present.

12 For we are not bold to number or compare ourselves with some of those who commend themselves. But they themselves, measuring themselves by themselves, and comparing themselves with themselves, are without understanding. 13 But we will not boast beyond proper limits, but within the boundaries with which God appointed to us, which reach even to you. 14 For we don't stretch ourselves too much, as though we didn't reach to you. For we came even as far as to you with the Good News of Christ, 15 not boasting beyond proper limits in other men's labours, but having hope that as your faith grows, we will be abundantly enlarged by you in our sphere of influence, 16 so as to preach the Good News even to the parts beyond you, not to boast in what someone else has already done. 17 But "he who boasts, let him boast in the Lord."* 18 For it isn't he who commends himself who is approved, but whom the Lord commends.

11

1 I wish that you would bear with me in a little foolishness, but indeed you do bear with me. 2 For I am jealous over you with a godly jealousy. For I promised you in marriage to one husband, that I might present you as a pure virgin to Christ. 3 But I am afraid that somehow, as the serpent deceived Eve in his craftiness, so your minds might be corrupted from the simplicity that is in Christ. 4 For if he who comes preaches another Jesus whom we didn't preach, or if you receive a different spirit which you didn't receive, or a different "good news" which you didn't accept, you put up with that well enough. 5 For I reckon that I am not at all behind the very best apostles. 6 But though I am unskilled in speech, yet I am not unskilled in knowledge. No, in every way we have been revealed to you in all things.

7 Or did I commit a sin in humbling myself that you might be exalted, because I preached to you God's Good News free of charge? 8 I robbed other assemblies, taking wages from them that I might serve you. 9 When I was present with you and was in need, I wasn't a burden on anyone, for the brothers, when they came from Macedonia, supplied the measure of my need. In everything I kept myself from being burdensome to you, and I will continue to do so. 10 As the truth of Christ is in me, no one will stop me from this boasting in the regions of Achaia. 11 Why? Because I don't love you? God knows.

12 But what I do, that I will continue to do, that I may cut off opportunity from those who desire an opportunity, that in which they boast, they may be recognised just like us. 13 For such men are false apostles, deceitful workers, masquerading as Christ's apostles. 14 And no wonder, for even Satan masquerades as an angel of light. 15 It is no great thing therefore if his servants also masquerade as servants of righteousness, whose end will be according to their works.

16 I say again, let no one think me foolish. But if so, yet receive me as foolish, that I also may boast a little. 17 That which I speak, I don't speak according to the Lord, but as in foolishness, in this confidence of boasting. 18 Seeing that many boast after the flesh, I will also boast. 19 For you bear with the foolish gladly, being wise. 20 For you bear with a man if he brings you into bondage, if he devours you, if he takes you captive, if he exalts himself, or if he strikes you on the face. 21 To my shame, I speak as though we had been weak. Yet in whatever way anyone is bold (I speak in foolishness), I am bold also. 22 Are they Hebrews? So am I. Are they Israelites? So am I. Are they the offspring[a] of Abraham? So am I. 23 Are they servants of Christ? (I speak as one beside himself.) I am more so: in labours more abundantly, in prisons more abundantly, in stripes above measure, and in deaths often. 24 Five times I received forty stripes minus one from the Jews. 25 Three times I was beaten with rods. Once I was stoned. Three times I suffered shipwreck. I have been a night and a day in the deep. 26 I have been in travels often, perils of rivers, perils of robbers, perils from my countrymen, perils from the Gentiles, perils in the city, perils in the wilderness, perils in the sea, perils amongst false brothers; 27 in labour and travail, in watchings often, in hunger and thirst, in fastings often, and in cold and nakedness.

28 Besides those things that are outside, there is that which presses on me daily: anxiety for all the assemblies. 29 Who is weak, and I am not weak? Who is caused to stumble, and I don't burn with indignation?

30 If I must boast, I will boast of the things that concern my weakness. 31 The God and Father of the Lord Jesus Christ, he who is blessed forever more, knows that I don't lie. 32 In Damascus the governor under King Aretas guarded the Damascenes' city, desiring to arrest me. 33 I was let down in a basket through a window by the wall, and escaped his hands.

12

1 It is doubtless not profitable for me to boast, but I will come to visions and revelations of the Lord. 2 I know a man in Christ who was caught up into the third heaven fourteen years ago—whether in the body, I don't know, or whether out of the body, I don't know; God knows. 3 I know such a man (whether in the body, or outside of the body, I don't know; God knows), 4 how he was caught up into Paradise and heard unspeakable words, which it is not lawful for a man to utter. 5 On behalf of such a one I will boast, but on my own behalf I will not boast, except in my weaknesses. 6 For if I would desire to boast, I will not be foolish; for I will speak the truth. But I refrain, so that no man may think more of me than that which he sees in me or hears from me. 7 By reason of the exceeding greatness of the revelations, that I should not be exalted excessively, a thorn in the flesh was given to me: a messenger of Satan to torment me, that I should not be exalted excessively. 8 Concerning this thing, I begged the Lord three times that it might depart from me. 9 He has said to me, "My grace is sufficient for you, for my power is made perfect in weakness." Most gladly therefore I will rather glory in my weaknesses, that the power of Christ may rest on me. 10 Therefore I take pleasure in weaknesses, in injuries, in necessities, in persecutions, and in distresses, for Christ's sake. For when I am weak, then am I strong. 11 I have become foolish in boasting. You compelled me, for I ought to have been commended by you, for I am in no way inferior to the very best apostles, though I am nothing. 12 Truly the signs of an apostle were worked amongst you in all perseverance, in signs and wonders and mighty works. 13 For what is there in which you were made inferior to the rest of the assemblies, unless it is that I myself was not a burden to you? Forgive me this wrong!

14 Behold, this is the third time I am ready to come to you, and I will not be a burden to you; for I seek not your possessions, but you. For the children ought not to save up for the parents, but the parents for the children. 15 I will most gladly spend and be spent for your souls. If I love you more abundantly, am I loved the less? 16 Even so, I myself didn't burden you. But you might say that being crafty, I caught you with deception. 17 Did I take advantage of you by anyone of those whom I have sent to you? 18 I exhorted Titus, and I sent the brother with him. Did Titus take any advantage of you? Didn't we walk in the same spirit? Didn't we walk in the same steps?

19 Again, do you think that we are excusing ourselves to you? In the sight of God we speak in Christ. But all things, beloved, are for your edifying. 20 For I am afraid that perhaps when I come, I might find you not the way I want to, and that I might be found by you as you don't desire, that perhaps there would be strife, jealousy, outbursts of anger, factions, slander, whisperings, proud thoughts, or riots, 21 that again when I come my God would humble me before you, and I would mourn for many of those who have sinned before now, and not repented of the uncleanness, sexual immorality, and lustfulness which they committed.

13

1 This is the third time I am coming to you. "At the mouth of two or three witnesses shall every word be established."* 2 I have warned previously, and I warn again, as when I was present the second time, so now, being absent, I write to those who have sinned before now and to all the rest that if I come again, I will not spare, 3 seeing that you seek a proof of Christ who speaks in me who is not weak, but is powerful in you. 4 For he was crucified through weakness, yet he lives through the power of God. For we also are weak in him, but we will live with him through the power of God towards you.

5 Examine your own selves, whether you are in the faith. Test your own selves. Or don't you know about your own selves, that Jesus Christ is in you?—unless indeed you are disqualified. 6 But I hope that you will know that we aren't disqualified.

7 Now I pray to God that you do no evil; not that we may appear approved, but that you may do that which is honourable, though we may seem to have failed. 8 For we can do nothing against the truth, but for the truth. 9 For we rejoice when we are weak and you are strong. We also pray for this: your becoming perfect. 10 For this cause I write these things while absent, that I may not deal sharply when present, according to the authority which the Lord gave me for building up and not for tearing down.

11 Finally, brothers, rejoice! Be perfected. Be comforted. Be of the same mind. Live in peace, and the God of love and peace will be with you. 12 Greet one another with a holy kiss.

13 All the saints greet you.

14 The grace of the Lord Jesus Christ, God's love, and the fellowship of the Holy Spirit be with you all. Amen.

** 10:17 Jeremiah 9:24
a 11:22 or, seed

** 13:1 Deuteronomy 19:15

Paul's Letter to the Galatians

1

1 Paul, an apostle—not from men, nor through man, but through Jesus Christ,[a] and God the Father, who raised him from the dead— 2 and all the brothers[b] who are with me, to the assemblies of Galatia: 3 Grace to you and peace from God the Father and our Lord Jesus Christ, 4 who gave himself for our sins, that he might deliver us out of this present evil age, according to the will of our God and Father— 5 to whom be the glory forever and ever. Amen.

6 I marvel that you are so quickly deserting him who called you in the grace of Christ to a different "good news", 7 but there isn't another "good news." Only there are some who trouble you and want to pervert the Good News of Christ. 8 But even though we, or an angel from heaven, should preach to you any "good news" other than that which we preached to you, let him be cursed. 9 As we have said before, so I now say again: if any man preaches to you any "good news" other than that which you received, let him be cursed.

10 For am I now seeking the favour of men, or of God? Or am I striving to please men? For if I were still pleasing men, I wouldn't be a servant of Christ.

11 But I make known to you, brothers, concerning the Good News which was preached by me, that it is not according to man. 12 For I didn't receive it from man, nor was I taught it, but it came to me through revelation of Jesus Christ. 13 For you have heard of my way of living in time past in the Jews' religion, how that beyond measure I persecuted the assembly of God and ravaged it. 14 I advanced in the Jews' religion beyond many of my own age amongst my countrymen, being more exceedingly zealous for the traditions of my fathers. 15 But when it was the good pleasure of God, who separated me from my mother's womb and called me through his grace, 16 to reveal his Son in me, that I might preach him amongst the Gentiles, I didn't immediately confer with flesh and blood, 17 nor did I go up to Jerusalem to those who were apostles before me, but I went away into Arabia. Then I returned to Damascus.

18 Then after three years I went up to Jerusalem to visit Peter, and stayed with him fifteen days. 19 But of the other apostles I saw no one except James, the Lord's brother. 20 Now about the things which I write to you, behold,[c] before God, I'm not lying. 21 Then I came to the regions of Syria and Cilicia. 22 I was still unknown by face to the assemblies of Judea which were in Christ, 23 but they only heard, "He who once persecuted us now preaches the faith that he once tried to destroy." 24 So they glorified God in me.

2

1 Then after a period of fourteen years I went up again to Jerusalem with Barnabas, taking Titus also with me. 2 I went up by revelation, and I laid before them the Good News which I preach amongst the Gentiles, but privately before those who were respected, for fear that I might be running, or had run, in vain. 3 But not even Titus, who was with me, being a Greek, was compelled to be circumcised. 4 This was because of the false brothers secretly brought in, who stole in to spy out our liberty which we have in Christ Jesus, that they might bring us into bondage, 5 to whom we gave no place in the way of subjection, not for an hour, that the truth of the Good News might continue with you. 6 But from those who were reputed to be important—whatever they were, it makes no difference to me; God doesn't show partiality to man—they, I say, who were respected imparted nothing to me, 7 but to the contrary, when they saw that I had been entrusted with the Good News for the uncircumcised, even as Peter with the Good News for the circumcised— 8 for he who worked through Peter in the apostleship with the circumcised also worked through me with the Gentiles— 9 and when they perceived the grace that was given to me, James and Cephas and John, those who were reputed to be pillars, gave to Barnabas and me the right hand of fellowship, that we should go to the Gentiles, and they to the circumcision. 10 They only asked us to remember the poor—which very thing I was also zealous to do.

11 But when Peter came to Antioch, I resisted him to his face, because he stood condemned. 12 For before some people came from James, he ate with the Gentiles. But when they came, he drew back and separated himself, fearing those who were of the circumcision. 13 And the rest of the Jews joined him in his hypocrisy, so that even Barnabas was carried away with their hypocrisy. 14 But when I saw that they didn't walk uprightly according to the truth of the Good News, I said to Peter before them all, "If you, being a Jew, live as the Gentiles do, and not as the Jews do, why do you compel the Gentiles to live as the Jews do?

15 "We, being Jews by nature and not Gentile sinners, 16 yet knowing that a man is not justified by the works of the law but through faith in Jesus Christ, even we believed in Christ Jesus, that we might be justified by faith in Christ and not by the works of the law, because no flesh will be justified by the works of the law. 17 But if while we sought to be justified in Christ, we ourselves also were found sinners, is Christ a servant of sin? Certainly not! 18 For if I build up again those things which I destroyed, I prove myself a law-breaker. 19 For I through the law died to the law, that I might live to God. 20 I have been crucified with Christ, and it is no longer I who live, but Christ lives in me. That life which I now live in the flesh, I live by faith in the Son of God, who loved me and gave himself up for me. 21 I don't reject the grace of God. For if righteousness is through the law, then Christ died for nothing!"

3

1 Foolish Galatians, who has bewitched you not to obey the truth, before whose eyes Jesus Christ was openly portrayed amongst you as crucified? 2 I just want to learn this from you: Did you receive the Spirit by the works of the law, or by hearing of faith? 3 Are you so foolish? Having begun in the Spirit, are you now completed in the flesh? 4 Did you suffer so many things in vain, if it is indeed in vain? 5 He therefore who supplies the Spirit to you and does miracles amongst you, does he do it by the works of the law, or by hearing of faith? 6 Even so, Abraham "believed God, and it was counted to him for righteousness."[*] 7 Know therefore that those who are of faith are children of Abraham. 8 The Scripture, foreseeing that God would justify the Gentiles by faith, preached the Good News beforehand to Abraham, saying, "In you all the nations will be blessed."[*] 9 So then, those who are of faith are blessed with the faithful Abraham.

10 For as many as are of the works of the law are under a curse. For it is written, "Cursed is everyone who doesn't continue in all things that are written in the book of the law, to do them."[*] 11 Now that no man is justified by the law before God is evident, for, "The righteous will live by faith."[*] 12 The law is not of faith, but, "The man who does them will live by them."[*]

13 Christ redeemed us from the curse of the law, having become a curse for us. For it is written, "Cursed is everyone who hangs on a tree,"[*] 14 that the blessing of Abraham might come on the Gentiles through Christ Jesus, that we might receive the promise of the Spirit through faith.

15 Brothers, speaking of human terms, though it is only a man's covenant, yet when it has been confirmed, no one makes it void or adds to it. 16 Now the promises were spoken to Abraham and to his offspring.[d] He doesn't say, "To descendants[e]", as of many, but as of one, "To your offspring",[*] which is Christ. 17 Now I say this: A covenant confirmed beforehand by God in Christ, the law, which came four hundred and thirty years after, does not annul, so as to make the promise of no effect. 18 For if the inheritance is of the law, it is no more of promise; but God has granted it to Abraham by promise.

19 Then why is there the law? It was added because of transgressions, until the offspring should come to whom the promise has been made. It was ordained through angels by the hand of a mediator. 20 Now a mediator is not between one, but God is one.

21 Is the law then against the promises of God? Certainly not! For if there had been a law given which could make alive, most certainly righteousness would have been of the law. 22 But the Scripture imprisoned all things under sin, that the promise by faith in Jesus Christ might be given to those who believe.

23 But before faith came, we were kept in custody under the law, confined for the faith which should afterwards be revealed. 24 So that the law has become our tutor to bring us to Christ, that we might be justified by faith. 25 But now that faith has come, we are no longer under a tutor. 26 For you are all children of God, through faith in Christ Jesus. 27 For as many of you as were baptised into Christ have put on Christ. 28 There is neither Jew nor Greek, there is neither slave nor free man, there is neither male nor female; for you are all one in Christ Jesus. 29 If you are Christ's, then you are Abraham's offspring and heirs according to promise.

4

1 But I say that so long as the heir is a child, he is no different from a bondservant, though he is lord of all, 2 but is under guardians and stewards until the day appointed by the father. 3 So we also, when we were children, were held in bondage under the elemental principles of the world. 4 But when the fullness of the time came, God sent out his Son, born to a woman, born under the law, 5 that he might redeem those who were under the law, that we might receive the adoption as children. 6 And because you are children, God sent out the Spirit of his Son into your hearts, crying, "Abba,[f] Father!" 7 So you are no longer a bondservant, but a son; and if a son, then an heir of God through Christ.

8 However at that time, not knowing God, you were in bondage to those who by nature are not gods. 9 But now that you have come to know God, or rather to be known by God, why do you turn back again to the weak and miserable elemental principles, to which you desire to be in bondage all over again? 10 You observe days, months, seasons, and years. 11 I am afraid for you, that I might have wasted my labour for you.

12 I beg you, brothers, become as I am, for I also have become as you are. You did me no wrong, 13 but you know that because of weakness in the flesh I preached the Good News to you the first time. 14 That which was a

---

a *1:1* "Christ" means "Anointed One".

b *1:2* The word for "brothers" here and where context allows may also be correctly translated "brothers and sisters" or "siblings."

c *1:20* "Behold", from "ἰδού", means look at, take notice, observe, see, or gaze at. It is often used as an interjection.

** 3:6 Genesis 15:6

** 3:8 Genesis 12:3; 18:18; 22:18

** 3:10 Deuteronomy 27:26

** 3:11 Habakkuk 2:4

** 3:12 Leviticus 18:5

** 3:13 Deuteronomy 21:23

d *3:16* or, seed

e *3:16* or, seeds

** 3:16 Genesis 12:7; 13:15; 24:7

f *4:6* Abba is a Greek spelling for the Aramaic word for "Father" or "Daddy" used in a familiar, respectful, and loving way.

temptation to you in my flesh, you didn't despise nor reject; but you received me as an angel of God, even as Christ Jesus.

15 What was the blessing you enjoyed? For I testify to you that, if possible, you would have plucked out your eyes and given them to me. 16 So then, have I become your enemy by telling you the truth? 17 They zealously seek you in no good way. No, they desire to alienate you, that you may seek them. 18 But it is always good to be zealous in a good cause, and not only when I am present with you.

19 My little children, of whom I am again in travail until Christ is formed in you— 20 but I could wish to be present with you now, and to change my tone, for I am perplexed about you.

21 Tell me, you that desire to be under the law, don't you listen to the law? 22 For it is written that Abraham had two sons, one by the servant, and one by the free woman. 23 However, the son by the servant was born according to the flesh, but the son by the free woman was born through promise. 24 These things contain an allegory, for these are two covenants. One is from Mount Sinai, bearing children to bondage, which is Hagar. 25 For this Hagar is Mount Sinai in Arabia, and answers to the Jerusalem that exists now, for she is in bondage with her children. 26 But the Jerusalem that is above is free, which is the mother of us all. 27 For it is written,
"Rejoice, you barren who don't bear.

Break out and shout, you who don't travail.
For the desolate women have more children than her who has a husband." *

28 Now we, brothers, as Isaac was, are children of promise. 29 But as then, he who was born according to the flesh persecuted him who was born according to the Spirit, so also it is now. 30 However, what does the Scripture say? "Throw out the servant and her son, for the son of the servant will not inherit with the son of the free woman."* 31 So then, brothers, we are not children of a servant, but of the free woman.

5

1 Stand firm therefore in the liberty by which Christ has made us free, and don't be entangled again with a yoke of bondage.

2 Behold, I, Paul, tell you that if you receive circumcision, Christ will profit you nothing. 3 Yes, I testify again to every man who receives circumcision that he is a debtor to do the whole law. 4 You are alienated from Christ, you who desire to be justified by the law. You have fallen away from grace. 5 For we through the Spirit, by faith wait for the hope of righteousness. 6 For in Christ Jesus neither circumcision nor uncircumcision amounts to anything, but faith working through love.

7 You were running well! Who interfered with you that you should not obey the truth? 8 This persuasion is not from him who calls you. 9 A little yeast grows through the whole lump. 10 I have confidence towards you in the Lord that you will think no other way. But he who troubles you will bear his judgement, whoever he is.

11 But I, brothers, if I still preach circumcision, why am I still persecuted? Then the stumbling block of the cross has been removed. 12 I wish that those who disturb you would cut themselves off.

13 For you, brothers, were called for freedom. Only don't use your freedom as an opportunity for the flesh, but through love be servants to one another. 14 For the whole law is fulfilled in one word, in this: "You shall love your neighbour as yourself."* 15 But if you bite and devour one another, be careful that you don't consume one another.

16 But I say, walk by the Spirit, and you won't fulfil the lust of the flesh. 17 For the flesh lusts against the Spirit, and the Spirit against the flesh; and these are contrary to one another, that you may not do the things that you desire. 18 But if you are led by the Spirit, you are not under the law. 19 Now the deeds of the flesh are obvious, which are: adultery, sexual immorality, uncleanness, lustfulness, 20 idolatry, sorcery, hatred, strife, jealousies, outbursts of anger, rivalries, divisions, heresies, 21 envy, murders, drunkenness, orgies, and things like these; of which I forewarn you, even as I also forewarned you, that those who practise such things will not inherit God's Kingdom.

22 But the fruit of the Spirit is love, joy, peace, patience, kindness, goodness, faith,[a] 23 gentleness, and self-control. Against such things there is no law. 24 Those who belong to Christ have crucified the flesh with its passions and lusts.

25 If we live by the Spirit, let's also walk by the Spirit. 26 Let's not become conceited, provoking one another, and envying one another.

6

1 Brothers, even if a man is caught in some fault, you who are spiritual must restore such a one in a spirit of gentleness, looking to yourself so that you also aren't tempted. 2 Bear one another's burdens, and so fulfil the law of Christ. 3 For if a man thinks himself to be something when he is nothing, he deceives himself. 4 But let each man examine his own work, and then he will have reason to boast in himself, and not in someone else. 5 For each man will bear his own burden.

6 But let him who is taught in the word share all good things with him who teaches.

7 Don't be deceived. God is not mocked, for whatever a man sows, that he will also reap. 8 For he who sows to his own flesh will from the flesh reap corruption. But he who sows to the Spirit will from the Spirit reap eternal life. 9 Let's not be weary in doing good, for we will reap in due season if we don't give up. 10 So then, as we have opportunity, let's do what is good towards all men, and especially towards those who are of the household of the faith.

11 See with what large letters I write to you with my own hand. 12 As many as desire to make a good impression in the flesh compel you to be circumcised, just so they may not be persecuted for the cross of Christ. 13 For even they who receive circumcision don't keep the law themselves, but they desire to have you circumcised, so that they may boast in your flesh. 14 But far be it from me to boast except in the cross of our Lord Jesus Christ, through which the world has been crucified to me, and I to the world. 15 For in Christ Jesus neither is circumcision anything, nor uncircumcision, but a new creation. 16 As many as walk by this rule, peace and mercy be on them, and on God's Israel.

17 From now on, let no one cause me any trouble, for I bear the marks of the Lord Jesus branded on my body.

18 The grace of our Lord Jesus Christ be with your spirit, brothers. Amen.

** 4:27 Isaiah 54:1
** 4:30 Genesis 21:10

** 5:14 Leviticus 19:18
a 5:22 or, faithfulness

Paul's Letter to the Ephesians

1

1 Paul, an apostle of Christ[a] Jesus through the will of God, to the saints who are at Ephesus, and the faithful in Christ Jesus: 2 Grace to you and peace from God our Father and the Lord Jesus Christ.

3 Blessed be the God and Father of our Lord Jesus Christ, who has blessed us with every spiritual blessing in the heavenly places in Christ, 4 even as he chose us in him before the foundation of the world, that we would be holy and without defect before him in love, 5 having predestined us for adoption as children through Jesus Christ to himself, according to the good pleasure of his desire, 6 to the praise of the glory of his grace, by which he freely gave us favour in the Beloved. 7 In him we have our redemption through his blood, the forgiveness of our trespasses, according to the riches of his grace 8 which he made to abound towards us in all wisdom and prudence, 9 making known to us the mystery of his will, according to his good pleasure which he purposed in him 10 to an administration of the fullness of the times, to sum up all things in Christ, the things in the heavens and the things on the earth, in him. 11 We were also assigned an inheritance in him, having been foreordained according to the purpose of him who does all things after the counsel of his will, 12 to the end that we should be to the praise of his glory, we who had before hoped in Christ. 13 In him you also, having heard the word of the truth, the Good News of your salvation—in whom, having also believed, you were sealed with the promised Holy Spirit, 14 who is a pledge of our inheritance, to the redemption of God's own possession, to the praise of his glory.

15 For this cause I also, having heard of the faith in the Lord Jesus which is amongst you and the love which you have towards all the saints, 16 don't cease to give thanks for you, making mention of you in my prayers, 17 that the God of our Lord Jesus Christ, the Father of glory, may give to you a spirit of wisdom and revelation in the knowledge of him, 18 having the eyes of your hearts[b] enlightened, that you may know what is the hope of his calling, and what are the riches of the glory of his inheritance in the saints, 19 and what is the exceeding greatness of his power towards us who believe, according to that working of the strength of his might 20 which he worked in Christ when he raised him from the dead and made him to sit at his right hand in the heavenly places, 21 far above all rule, authority, power, dominion, and every name that is named, not only in this age, but also in that which is to come. 22 He put all things in subjection under his feet, and gave him to be head over all things for the assembly, 23 which is his body, the fullness of him who fills all in all.

2

1 You were made alive when you were dead in transgressions and sins, 2 in which you once walked according to the course of this world, according to the prince of the power of the air, the spirit who now works in the children of disobedience. 3 We also all once lived amongst them in the lusts of our flesh, doing the desires of the flesh and of the mind, and were by nature children of wrath, even as the rest. 4 But God, being rich in mercy, for his great love with which he loved us, 5 even when we were dead through our trespasses, made us alive together with Christ—by grace you have been saved— 6 and raised us up with him, and made us to sit with him in the heavenly places in Christ Jesus, 7 that in the ages to come he might show the exceeding riches of his grace in kindness towards us in Christ Jesus; 8 for by grace you have been saved through faith, and that not of yourselves; it is the gift of God, 9 not of works, that no one would boast. 10 For we are his workmanship, created in Christ Jesus for good works, which God prepared before that we would walk in them.

11 Therefore remember that once you, the Gentiles in the flesh, who are called "uncircumcision" by that which is called "circumcision" (in the flesh, made by hands), 12 that you were at that time separate from Christ, alienated from the commonwealth of Israel, and strangers from the covenants of the promise, having no hope and without God in the world. 13 But now in Christ Jesus you who once were far off are made near in the blood of Christ. 14 For he is our peace, who made both one, and broke down the middle wall of separation, 15 having abolished in his flesh the hostility, the law of commandments contained in ordinances, that he might create in himself one new man of the two, making peace, 16 and might reconcile them both in one body to God through the cross, having killed the hostility through it. 17 He came and preached peace to you who were far off and to those who were near. 18 For through him we both have our access in one Spirit to the Father. 19 So then you are no longer strangers and foreigners, but you are fellow citizens with the saints and of the household of God, 20 being built on the foundation of the apostles and prophets, Christ Jesus himself being the chief cornerstone; 21 in whom the whole building, fitted together, grows into a holy temple in the Lord; 22 in whom you also are built together for a habitation of God in the Spirit.

3

1 For this cause I, Paul, am the prisoner of Christ Jesus on behalf of you Gentiles, 2 if it is so that you have heard of the administration of that grace of God which was given me towards you, 3 how that by revelation the mystery was made known to me, as I wrote before in few words, 4 by which,

when you read, you can perceive my understanding in the mystery of Christ, 5 which in other generations was not made known to the children of men, as it has now been revealed to his holy apostles and prophets in the Spirit, 6 that the Gentiles are fellow heirs and fellow members of the body, and fellow partakers of his promise in Christ Jesus through the Good News, 7 of which I was made a servant according to the gift of that grace of God which was given me according to the working of his power. 8 To me, the very least of all saints, was this grace given, to preach to the Gentiles the unsearchable riches of Christ, 9 and to make all men see what is the administration[c] of the mystery which for ages has been hidden in God, who created all things through Jesus Christ, 10 to the intent that now through the assembly the manifold wisdom of God might be made known to the principalities and the powers in the heavenly places, 11 according to the eternal purpose which he accomplished in Christ Jesus our Lord. 12 In him we have boldness and access in confidence through our faith in him. 13 Therefore I ask that you may not lose heart at my troubles for you, which are your glory.

14 For this cause, I bow my knees to the Father of our Lord Jesus Christ, 15 from whom every family in heaven and on earth is named, 16 that he would grant you, according to the riches of his glory, that you may be strengthened with power through his Spirit in the inner person, 17 that Christ may dwell in your hearts through faith, to the end that you, being rooted and grounded in love, 18 may be strengthened to comprehend with all the saints what is the width and length and height and depth, 19 and to know Christ's love which surpasses knowledge, that you may be filled with all the fullness of God.

20 Now to him who is able to do exceedingly abundantly above all that we ask or think, according to the power that works in us, 21 to him be the glory in the assembly and in Christ Jesus to all generations, forever and ever. Amen.

4

1 I therefore, the prisoner in the Lord, beg you to walk worthily of the calling with which you were called, 2 with all lowliness and humility, with patience, bearing with one another in love, 3 being eager to keep the unity of the Spirit in the bond of peace. 4 There is one body and one Spirit, even as you also were called in one hope of your calling, 5 one Lord, one faith, one baptism, 6 one God and Father of all, who is over all and through all and in us all. 7 But to each one of us, the grace was given according to the measure of the gift of Christ. 8 Therefore he says,
"When he ascended on high,
    he led captivity captive,
    and gave gifts to people."[**]
9 Now this, "He ascended", what is it but that he also first descended into the lower parts of the earth? 10 He who descended is the one who also ascended far above all the heavens, that he might fill all things.

11 He gave some to be apostles; and some, prophets; and some, evangelists; and some, shepherds[d] and teachers; 12 for the perfecting of the saints, to the work of serving, to the building up of the body of Christ, 13 until we all attain to the unity of the faith and of the knowledge of the Son of God, to a full grown man, to the measure of the stature of the fullness of Christ, 14 that we may no longer be children, tossed back and forth and carried about with every wind of doctrine, by the trickery of men, in craftiness, after the wiles of error; 15 but speaking truth in love, we may grow up in all things into him who is the head, Christ, 16 from whom all the body, being fitted and knit together through that which every joint supplies, according to the working in measure of each individual part, makes the body increase to the building up of itself in love.

17 This I say therefore, and testify in the Lord, that you no longer walk as the rest of the Gentiles also walk, in the futility of their mind, 18 being darkened in their understanding, alienated from the life of God because of the ignorance that is in them, because of the hardening of their hearts. 19 They, having become callous, gave themselves up to lust, to work all uncleanness with greediness. 20 But you didn't learn Christ that way, 21 if indeed you heard him and were taught in him, even as truth is in Jesus: 22 that you put away, as concerning your former way of life, the old man that grows corrupt after the lusts of deceit, 23 and that you be renewed in the spirit of your mind, 24 and put on the new man, who in the likeness of God has been created in righteousness and holiness of truth.

25 Therefore, putting away falsehood, speak truth each one with his neighbour, for we are members of one another. 26 "Be angry, and don't sin."[**] Don't let the sun go down on your wrath, 27 and don't give place[e] to the devil. 28 Let him who stole steal no more; but rather let him labour, producing with his hands something that is good, that he may have something to give to him who has need. 29 Let no corrupt speech proceed out of your mouth, but only what is good for building others up as the need may be, that it may give grace to those who hear. 30 Don't grieve the Holy Spirit of God, in whom you were sealed for the day of redemption. 31 Let all bitterness, wrath, anger, outcry, and slander be put away from you, with all malice. 32 And be kind to one another, tender hearted, forgiving each other, just as God also in Christ forgave you.

---

a 1:1 "Christ" means "Anointed One".
b 1:18 TR reads "understanding" instead of "hearts"
c 3:9 TR reads "fellowship" instead of "administration"
** 4:8 Psalms 68:18

d 4:11 or, pastors
** 4:26 Psalms 4:4
e 4:27 or, opportunity

5

1 Be therefore imitators of God, as beloved children. 2 Walk in love, even as Christ also loved us and gave himself up for us, an offering and a sacrifice to God for a sweet-smelling fragrance.

3 But sexual immorality, and all uncleanness or covetousness, let it not even be mentioned amongst you, as becomes saints; 4 nor filthiness, nor foolish talking, nor jesting, which are not appropriate, but rather giving of thanks.

5 Know this for sure, that no sexually immoral person, nor unclean person, nor covetous man (who is an idolater), has any inheritance in the Kingdom of Christ and God.

6 Let no one deceive you with empty words, for because of these things the wrath of God comes on the children of disobedience. 7 Therefore don't be partakers with them. 8 For you were once darkness, but are now light in the Lord. Walk as children of light, 9 for the fruit of the Spirit is in all goodness and righteousness and truth, 10 proving what is well pleasing to the Lord. 11 Have no fellowship with the unfruitful deeds of darkness, but rather even reprove them. 12 For it is a shame even to speak of the things which are done by them in secret. 13 But all things, when they are reproved, are revealed by the light, for everything that reveals is light. 14 Therefore he says, "Awake, you who sleep, and arise from the dead, and Christ will shine on you."

15 Therefore watch carefully how you walk, not as unwise, but as wise, 16 redeeming the time, because the days are evil. 17 Therefore, don't be foolish, but understand what the will of the Lord is. 18 Don't be drunken with wine, in which is dissipation, but be filled with the Spirit, 19 speaking to one another in psalms, hymns, and spiritual songs; singing and making melody in your heart to the Lord; 20 giving thanks always concerning all things in the name of our Lord Jesus Christ to God, even the Father; 21 subjecting yourselves to one another in the fear of Christ.

22 Wives, be subject to your own husbands, as to the Lord. 23 For the husband is the head of the wife, as Christ also is the head of the assembly, being himself the saviour of the body. 24 But as the assembly is subject to Christ, so let the wives also be to their own husbands in everything.

25 Husbands, love your wives, even as Christ also loved the assembly and gave himself up for her, 26 that he might sanctify her, having cleansed her by the washing of water with the word, 27 that he might present the assembly to himself gloriously, not having spot or wrinkle or any such thing, but that she should be holy and without defect. 28 Even so husbands also ought to love their own wives as their own bodies. He who loves his own wife loves himself. 29 For no man ever hated his own flesh, but nourishes and cherishes it, even as the Lord also does the assembly, 30 because we are members of his body, of his flesh and bones. 31 "For this cause a man will leave his father and mother and will be joined to his wife. Then the two will become one flesh."* 32 This mystery is great, but I speak concerning Christ and the assembly. 33 Nevertheless each of you must also love his own wife even as himself; and let the wife see that she respects her husband.

6

1 Children, obey your parents in the Lord, for this is right. 2 "Honour your father and mother," which is the first commandment with a promise: 3 "that it may be well with you, and you may live long on the earth." *

4 You fathers, don't provoke your children to wrath, but nurture them in the discipline and instruction of the Lord.

5 Servants, be obedient to those who according to the flesh are your masters, with fear and trembling, in singleness of your heart, as to Christ, 6 not in the way of service only when eyes are on you, as men pleasers, but as servants of Christ, doing the will of God from the heart, 7 with good will doing service as to the Lord and not to men, 8 knowing that whatever good thing each one does, he will receive the same good again from the Lord, whether he is bound or free.

9 You masters, do the same things to them, and give up threatening, knowing that he who is both their Master and yours is in heaven, and there is no partiality with him.

10 Finally, be strong in the Lord and in the strength of his might. 11 Put on the whole armour of God, that you may be able to stand against the wiles of the devil. 12 For our wrestling is not against flesh and blood, but against the principalities, against the powers, against the world's rulers of the darkness of this age, and against the spiritual forces of wickedness in the heavenly places. 13 Therefore put on the whole armour of God, that you may be able to withstand in the evil day, and having done all, to stand. 14 Stand therefore, having the utility belt of truth buckled around your waist, and having put on the breastplate of righteousness, 15 and having fitted your feet with the preparation of the Good News of peace, 16 above all, taking up the shield of faith, with which you will be able to quench all the fiery darts of the evil one. 17 And take the helmet of salvation, and the sword of the Spirit, which is the word[a] of God; 18 with all prayer and requests, praying at all times in the Spirit, and being watchful to this end in all perseverance and requests for all the saints. 19 Pray for me, that utterance may be given to me in opening my mouth, to make known with boldness the mystery of the Good News, 20 for which I am an ambassador in chains; that in it I may speak boldly, as I ought to speak.

21 But that you also may know my affairs, how I am doing, Tychicus, the beloved brother and faithful servant in the Lord, will make known to you all things. 22 I have sent him to you for this very purpose, that you may know our state and that he may comfort your hearts.

23 Peace be to the brothers, and love with faith, from God the Father and the Lord Jesus Christ. 24 Grace be with all those who love our Lord Jesus Christ with incorruptible love. Amen.

** 5:31 Genesis 2:24
** 6:3 Deuteronomy 5:16

a *6:17* from the Greek "ῥῆμα" (rhema), which means "spoken word"

Paul's Letter to the Philippians

1

1 Paul and Timothy, servants of Jesus Christ,[a] to all the saints in Christ Jesus who are at Philippi, with the overseers[b] and servants:[c] 2 Grace to you and peace from God our Father and the Lord Jesus Christ.

3 I thank my God whenever I remember you, 4 always in every request of mine on behalf of you all, making my requests with joy, 5 for your partnership[d] in furtherance of the Good News from the first day until now; 6 being confident of this very thing, that he who began a good work in you will complete it until the day of Jesus Christ. 7 It is even right for me to think this way on behalf of all of you, because I have you in my heart, because both in my bonds and in the defence and confirmation of the Good News, you all are partakers with me of grace. 8 For God is my witness, how I long after all of you in the tender mercies of Christ Jesus.

9 This I pray, that your love may abound yet more and more in knowledge and all discernment, 10 so that you may approve the things that are excellent, that you may be sincere and without offence to the day of Christ, 11 being filled with the fruits of righteousness which are through Jesus Christ, to the glory and praise of God.

12 Now I desire to have you know, brothers,[e] that the things which happened to me have turned out rather to the progress of the Good News, 13 so that it became evident to the whole palace[f] guard, and to all the rest, that my bonds are in Christ, 14 and that most of the brothers in the Lord, being confident through my bonds, are more abundantly bold to speak the word of God without fear. 15 Some indeed preach Christ even out of envy and strife, and some also out of good will. 16 The former insincerely preach Christ from selfish ambition, thinking that they add affliction to my chains; 17 but the latter out of love, knowing that I am appointed for the defence of the Good News.

18 What does it matter? Only that in every way, whether in pretence or in truth, Christ is proclaimed. I rejoice in this, yes, and will rejoice. 19 For I know that this will turn out to my salvation through your prayers and the supply of the Spirit of Jesus Christ, 20 according to my earnest expectation and hope, that I will in no way be disappointed, but with all boldness, as always, now also Christ will be magnified in my body, whether by life or by death. 21 For to me to live is Christ, and to die is gain. 22 But if I live on in the flesh, this will bring fruit from my work; yet I don't know what I will choose. 23 But I am hard pressed between the two, having the desire to depart and be with Christ, which is far better. 24 Yet to remain in the flesh is more needful for your sake. 25 Having this confidence, I know that I will remain, yes, and remain with you all for your progress and joy in the faith, 26 that your boasting[g] may abound in Christ Jesus in me through my presence with you again.

27 Only let your way of life be worthy of the Good News of Christ, that whether I come and see you or am absent, I may hear of your state, that you stand firm in one spirit, with one soul striving for the faith of the Good News; 28 and in nothing frightened by the adversaries, which is for them a proof of destruction, but to you of salvation, and that from God. 29 Because it has been granted to you on behalf of Christ, not only to believe in him, but also to suffer on his behalf, 30 having the same conflict which you saw in me and now hear is in me.

2

1 If therefore there is any exhortation in Christ, if any consolation of love, if any fellowship of the Spirit, if any tender mercies and compassion, 2 make my joy full by being like-minded, having the same love, being of one accord, of one mind; 3 doing nothing through rivalry or through conceit, but in humility, each counting others better than himself; 4 each of you not just looking to his own things, but each of you also to the things of others.

5 Have this in your mind, which was also in Christ Jesus, 6 who, existing in the form of God, didn't consider equality with God a thing to be grasped, 7 but emptied himself, taking the form of a servant, being made in the likeness of men. 8 And being found in human form, he humbled himself, becoming obedient to the point of death, yes, the death of the cross. 9 Therefore God also highly exalted him, and gave to him the name which is above every name, 10 that at the name of Jesus every knee should bow, of those in heaven, those on earth, and those under the earth, 11 and that every tongue should confess that Jesus Christ is Lord, to the glory of God the Father.

12 So then, my beloved, even as you have always obeyed, not only in my presence, but now much more in my absence, work out your own salvation with fear and trembling. 13 For it is God who works in you both to will and to work for his good pleasure.

14 Do all things without complaining and arguing, 15 that you may become blameless and harmless, children of God without defect in the middle of a crooked and perverse generation, amongst whom you are seen as lights in the world, 16 holding up the word of life, that I may have something to boast in the day of Christ that I didn't run in vain nor labour in vain. 17 Yes, and if I am poured out on the sacrifice and service of your faith, I am glad and rejoice with you all. 18 In the same way, you also should be glad and rejoice with me.

19 But I hope in the Lord Jesus to send Timothy to you soon, that I also may be cheered up when I know how you are doing. 20 For I have no one else like-minded, who will truly care about you. 21 For they all seek their own, not the things of Jesus Christ. 22 But you know that he has proved himself. As a child serves a father, so he served with me in furtherance of the Good News. 23 Therefore I hope to send him at once, as soon as I see how it will go with me. 24 But I trust in the Lord that I myself also will come shortly.

25 But I thought it necessary to send to you Epaphroditus, my brother, fellow worker, fellow soldier, and your apostle and servant of my need, 26 since he longed for you all, and was very troubled because you had heard that he was sick. 27 For indeed he was sick nearly to death, but God had mercy on him, and not on him only, but on me also, that I might not have sorrow on sorrow. 28 I have sent him therefore the more diligently, that when you see him again, you may rejoice, and that I may be the less sorrowful. 29 Receive him therefore in the Lord with all joy, and hold such people in honour, 30 because for the work of Christ he came near to death, risking his life to supply that which was lacking in your service towards me.

3

1 Finally, my brothers, rejoice in the Lord! To write the same things to you, to me indeed is not tiresome, but for you it is safe.

2 Beware of the dogs; beware of the evil workers; beware of the false circumcision. 3 For we are the circumcision, who worship God in the Spirit, and rejoice in Christ Jesus, and have no confidence in the flesh; 4 though I myself might have confidence even in the flesh. If any other man thinks that he has confidence in the flesh, I yet more: 5 circumcised the eighth day, of the stock of Israel, of the tribe of Benjamin, a Hebrew of Hebrews; concerning the law, a Pharisee; 6 concerning zeal, persecuting the assembly; concerning the righteousness which is in the law, found blameless.

7 However, I consider those things that were gain to me as a loss for Christ. 8 Yes most certainly, and I count all things to be a loss for the excellency of the knowledge of Christ Jesus, my Lord, for whom I suffered the loss of all things, and count them nothing but refuse, that I may gain Christ 9 and be found in him, not having a righteousness of my own, that which is of the law, but that which is through faith in Christ, the righteousness which is from God by faith, 10 that I may know him and the power of his resurrection, and the fellowship of his sufferings, becoming conformed to his death, 11 if by any means I may attain to the resurrection from the dead. 12 Not that I have already obtained, or am already made perfect; but I press on, that I may take hold of that for which also I was taken hold of by Christ Jesus.

13 Brothers, I don't regard myself as yet having taken hold, but one thing I do: forgetting the things which are behind and stretching forward to the things which are before, 14 I press on towards the goal for the prize of the high calling of God in Christ Jesus. 15 Let us therefore, as many as are perfect, think this way. If in anything you think otherwise, God will also reveal that to you. 16 Nevertheless, to the extent that we have already attained, let's walk by the same rule. Let's be of the same mind.

17 Brothers, be imitators together of me, and note those who walk this way, even as you have us for an example. 18 For many walk, of whom I told you often, and now tell you even weeping, as the enemies of the cross of Christ, 19 whose end is destruction, whose god is the belly, and whose glory is in their shame, who think about earthly things. 20 For our citizenship is in heaven, from where we also wait for a Saviour, the Lord Jesus Christ, 21 who will change the body of our humiliation to be conformed to the body of his glory, according to the working by which he is able even to subject all things to himself.

4

1 Therefore, my brothers, beloved and longed for, my joy and crown, stand firm in the Lord in this way, my beloved.

2 I exhort Euodia, and I exhort Syntyche, to think the same way in the Lord. 3 Yes, I beg you also, true partner, help these women, for they laboured with me in the Good News with Clement also, and the rest of my fellow workers, whose names are in the book of life.

4 Rejoice in the Lord always! Again I will say, "Rejoice!" 5 Let your gentleness be known to all men. The Lord is at hand. 6 In nothing be anxious, but in everything, by prayer and petition with thanksgiving, let your requests be made known to God. 7 And the peace of God, which surpasses all understanding, will guard your hearts and your thoughts in Christ Jesus.

8 Finally, brothers, whatever things are true, whatever things are honourable, whatever things are just, whatever things are pure, whatever things are lovely, whatever things are of good report: if there is any virtue and if there is anything worthy of praise, think about these things. 9 Do the things which you learnt, received, heard, and saw in me, and the God of peace will be with you.

10 But I rejoice in the Lord greatly that now at length you have revived your thought for me; in which you did indeed take thought, but you lacked opportunity. 11 Not that I speak because of lack, for I have learnt in whatever state I am, to be content in it. 12 I know how to be humbled, and I also know how to abound. In any and all circumstances I have learnt the

---

a 1:1 "Christ" means "Anointed One".

b 1:1 or, superintendents, or bishops

c 1:1 Or, deacons

d 1:5 The word translated "partnership" (κοινωνία) also means "fellowship" and "sharing".

e 1:12 The word for "brothers" here and where context allows may also be correctly translated "brothers and sisters" or "siblings."

f 1:13 or, praetorian

g 1:26 or, rejoicing

secret both to be filled and to be hungry, both to abound and to be in need. 13 I can do all things through Christ who strengthens me. 14 However you did well that you shared in my affliction. 15 You yourselves also know, you Philippians, that in the beginning of the Good News, when I departed from Macedonia, no assembly shared with me in the matter of giving and receiving but you only. 16 For even in Thessalonica you sent once and again to my need. 17 Not that I seek for the gift, but I seek for the fruit that increases to your account. 18 But I have all things and abound. I am filled, having received from Epaphroditus the things that came from you, a sweet-smelling fragrance, an acceptable and well-pleasing sacrifice to God. 19 My God will supply every need of yours according to his riches in glory in Christ Jesus. 20 Now to our God and Father be the glory forever and ever! Amen.

21 Greet every saint in Christ Jesus. The brothers who are with me greet you. 22 All the saints greet you, especially those who are of Caesar's household.

23 The grace of the Lord Jesus Christ be with you all. Amen.

Paul's Letter to the Colossians

1

1 Paul, an apostle of Christ[a] Jesus through the will of God, and Timothy our brother, 2 to the saints and faithful brothers[b] in Christ at Colossae: Grace to you and peace from God our Father and the Lord Jesus Christ.

3 We give thanks to God the Father of our Lord Jesus Christ, praying always for you, 4 having heard of your faith in Christ Jesus and of the love which you have towards all the saints, 5 because of the hope which is laid up for you in the heavens, of which you heard before in the word of the truth of the Good News 6 which has come to you, even as it is in all the world and is bearing fruit and growing, as it does in you also, since the day you heard and knew the grace of God in truth, 7 even as you learnt from Epaphras our beloved fellow servant, who is a faithful servant of Christ on your[c] behalf, 8 who also declared to us your love in the Spirit.

9 For this cause, we also, since the day we heard this, don't cease praying and making requests for you, that you may be filled with the knowledge of his will in all spiritual wisdom and understanding, 10 that you may walk worthily of the Lord, to please him in all respects, bearing fruit in every good work and increasing in the knowledge of God, 11 strengthened with all power, according to the might of his glory, for all endurance and perseverance with joy, 12 giving thanks to the Father, who made us fit to be partakers of the inheritance of the saints in light, 13 who delivered us out of the power of darkness, and translated us into the Kingdom of the Son of his love, 14 in whom we have our redemption,[d] the forgiveness of our sins.

15 He is the image of the invisible God, the firstborn of all creation. 16 For by him all things were created in the heavens and on the earth, visible things and invisible things, whether thrones or dominions or principalities or powers. All things have been created through him and for him. 17 He is before all things, and in him all things are held together. 18 He is the head of the body, the assembly, who is the beginning, the firstborn from the dead, that in all things he might have the preeminence. 19 For all the fullness was pleased to dwell in him, 20 and through him to reconcile all things to himself by him, whether things on the earth or things in the heavens, having made peace through the blood of his cross.

21 You, being in past times alienated and enemies in your mind in your evil deeds, 22 yet now he has reconciled in the body of his flesh through death, to present you holy and without defect and blameless before him, 23 if it is so that you continue in the faith, grounded and steadfast, and not moved away from the hope of the Good News which you heard, which is being proclaimed in all creation under heaven, of which I, Paul, was made a servant.

24 Now I rejoice in my sufferings for your sake, and fill up on my part that which is lacking of the afflictions of Christ in my flesh for his body's sake, which is the assembly, 25 of which I was made a servant according to the stewardship of God which was given me towards you to fulfil the word of God, 26 the mystery which has been hidden for ages and generations. But now it has been revealed to his saints, 27 to whom God was pleased to make known what are the riches of the glory of this mystery amongst the Gentiles, which is Christ in you, the hope of glory. 28 We proclaim him, admonishing every man and teaching every man in all wisdom, that we may present every man perfect in Christ Jesus; 29 for which I also labour, striving according to his working, which works in me mightily.

2

1 For I desire to have you know how greatly I struggle for you and for those at Laodicea, and for as many as have not seen my face in the flesh; 2 that their hearts may be comforted, they being knit together in love, and gaining all riches of the full assurance of understanding, that they may know the mystery of God, both of the Father and of Christ, 3 in whom all the treasures of wisdom and knowledge are hidden. 4 Now I say this that no one may delude you with persuasiveness of speech. 5 For though I am absent in the flesh, yet I am with you in the spirit, rejoicing and seeing your order, and the steadfastness of your faith in Christ.

6 As therefore you received Christ Jesus the Lord, walk in him, 7 rooted and built up in him and established in the faith, even as you were taught, abounding in it in thanksgiving.

8 Be careful that you don't let anyone rob you through his philosophy and vain deceit, after the tradition of men, after the elemental spirits of the world, and not after Christ. 9 For in him all the fullness of the Deity dwells bodily, 10 and in him you are made full, who is the head of all principality and power. 11 In him you were also circumcised with a circumcision not made with hands, in the putting off of the body of the sins of the flesh, in the circumcision of Christ, 12 having been buried with him in baptism, in which you were also raised with him through faith in the working of God, who raised him from the dead. 13 You were dead through your trespasses and the uncircumcision of your flesh. He made you alive together with him, having forgiven us all our trespasses, 14 wiping out the handwriting in ordinances which was against us. He has taken it out of the way, nailing it to the cross. 15 Having stripped the principalities and the powers, he made a show of them openly, triumphing over them in it.

16 Let no one therefore judge you in eating or drinking, or with respect to a feast day or a new moon or a Sabbath day, 17 which are a shadow of the things to come; but the body is Christ's. 18 Let no one rob you of your prize by self-abasement and worshipping of the angels, dwelling in the things which he has not seen, vainly puffed up by his fleshly mind, 19 and not holding firmly to the Head, from whom all the body, being supplied and knit together through the joints and ligaments, grows with God's growth.

20 If you died with Christ from the elemental spirits of the world, why, as though living in the world, do you subject yourselves to ordinances, 21 "Don't handle, nor taste, nor touch" 22 (all of which perish with use), according to the precepts and doctrines of men? 23 These things indeed appear like wisdom in self-imposed worship, humility, and severity to the body, but aren't of any value against the indulgence of the flesh.

3

1 If then you were raised together with Christ, seek the things that are above, where Christ is, seated on the right hand of God. 2 Set your mind on the things that are above, not on the things that are on the earth. 3 For you died, and your life is hidden with Christ in God. 4 When Christ, our life, is revealed, then you will also be revealed with him in glory.

5 Put to death therefore your members which are on the earth: sexual immorality, uncleanness, depraved passion, evil desire, and covetousness, which is idolatry. 6 For these things' sake the wrath of God comes on the children of disobedience. 7 You also once walked in those, when you lived in them, 8 but now you must put them all away: anger, wrath, malice, slander, and shameful speaking out of your mouth. 9 Don't lie to one another, seeing that you have put off the old man with his doings, 10 and have put on the new man, who is being renewed in knowledge after the image of his Creator, 11 where there can't be Greek and Jew, circumcision and uncircumcision, barbarian, Scythian, bondservant, or free person; but Christ is all, and in all.

12 Put on therefore, as God's chosen ones, holy and beloved, a heart of compassion, kindness, lowliness, humility, and perseverance; 13 bearing with one another, and forgiving each other, if any man has a complaint against any; even as Christ forgave you, so you also do.

14 Above all these things, walk in love, which is the bond of perfection. 15 And let the peace of God rule in your hearts, to which also you were called in one body, and be thankful. 16 Let the word of Christ dwell in you richly; in all wisdom teaching and admonishing one another with psalms, hymns, and spiritual songs, singing with grace in your heart to the Lord.

17 Whatever you do, in word or in deed, do all in the name of the Lord Jesus, giving thanks to God the Father through him.

18 Wives, be in subjection to your husbands, as is fitting in the Lord.

19 Husbands, love your wives, and don't be bitter against them.

20 Children, obey your parents in all things, for this pleases the Lord. 21 Fathers, don't provoke your children, so that they won't be discouraged.

22 Servants, obey in all things those who are your masters according to the flesh, not just when they are looking, as men pleasers, but in singleness of heart, fearing God. 23 And whatever you do, work heartily, as for the Lord and not for men, 24 knowing that from the Lord you will receive the reward of the inheritance; for you serve the Lord Christ. 25 But he who does wrong will receive again for the wrong that he has done, and there is no partiality.

4

1 Masters, give to your servants that which is just and equal, knowing that you also have a Master in heaven.

2 Continue steadfastly in prayer, watching in it with thanksgiving, 3 praying together for us also, that God may open to us a door for the word, to speak the mystery of Christ, for which I am also in bonds, 4 that I may reveal it as I ought to speak.

5 Walk in wisdom towards those who are outside, redeeming the time. 6 Let your speech always be with grace, seasoned with salt, that you may know how you ought to answer each one.

7 All my affairs will be made known to you by Tychicus, the beloved brother, faithful servant, and fellow bondservant in the Lord. 8 I am sending him to you for this very purpose, that he may know your circumstances and comfort your hearts, 9 together with Onesimus, the faithful and beloved brother, who is one of you. They will make known to you everything that is going on here.

10 Aristarchus, my fellow prisoner, greets you, and Mark the cousin of Barnabas (concerning whom you received instructions, "if he comes to you, receive him"), 11 and Jesus who is called Justus. These are my only fellow workers for God's Kingdom who are of the circumcision, men who have been a comfort to me.

12 Epaphras, who is one of you, a servant of Christ, salutes you, always striving for you in his prayers, that you may stand perfect and complete in all the will of God. 13 For I testify about him that he has great zeal for you, and for those in Laodicea, and for those in Hierapolis. 14 Luke the beloved physician and Demas greet you. 15 Greet the brothers who are in Laodicea, with Nymphas and the assembly that is in his house. 16 When this letter has been read amongst you, cause it to be read also in the assembly of the Laodiceans, and that you also read the letter from Laodicea. 17 Tell Archippus, "Take heed to the ministry which you have received in the Lord, that you fulfil it."

---

a 1:1 "Christ" means "Anointed One".
b 1:2 The word for "brothers" here and where context allows may also be correctly translated "brothers and sisters" or "siblings."

c 1:7 NU reads our
d 1:14 TR adds "through his blood,"

[18] I, Paul, write this greeting with my own hand. Remember my chains. Grace be with you. Amen.

Paul's First Letter to the Thessalonians

1

₁ Paul, Silvanus, and Timothy, to the assembly of the Thessalonians in God the Father and the Lord Jesus Christ:[a] Grace to you and peace from God our Father and the Lord Jesus Christ.

₂ We always give thanks to God for all of you, mentioning you in our prayers, ₃ remembering without ceasing your work of faith and labour of love and perseverance of hope in our Lord Jesus Christ, before our God and Father. ₄ We know, brothers[b] loved by God, that you are chosen, ₅ and that our Good News came to you not in word only, but also in power, and in the Holy Spirit and with much assurance. You know what kind of men we showed ourselves to be amongst you for your sake. ₆ You became imitators of us and of the Lord, having received the word in much affliction, with joy of the Holy Spirit, ₇ so that you became an example to all who believe in Macedonia and in Achaia. ₈ For from you the word of the Lord has been declared, not only in Macedonia and Achaia, but also in every place your faith towards God has gone out, so that we need not to say anything. ₉ For they themselves report concerning us what kind of a reception we had from you, and how you turned to God from idols to serve a living and true God, ₁₀ and to wait for his Son from heaven, whom he raised from the dead: Jesus, who delivers us from the wrath to come.

2

₁ For you yourselves know, brothers, our visit to you wasn't in vain, ₂ but having suffered before and been shamefully treated, as you know, at Philippi, we grew bold in our God to tell you the Good News of God in much conflict. ₃ For our exhortation is not of error, nor of uncleanness, nor in deception. ₄ But even as we have been approved by God to be entrusted with the Good News, so we speak—not as pleasing men, but God, who tests our hearts. ₅ For neither were we at any time found using words of flattery, as you know, nor a cloak of covetousness (God is witness), ₆ nor seeking glory from men (neither from you nor from others), when we might have claimed authority as apostles of Christ. ₇ But we were gentle amongst you, like a nursing mother cherishes her own children.

₈ Even so, affectionately longing for you, we were well pleased to impart to you not the Good News of God only, but also our own souls, because you had become very dear to us. ₉ For you remember, brothers, our labour and travail; for working night and day, that we might not burden any of you, we preached to you the Good News of God. ₁₀ You are witnesses with God how holy, righteously, and blamelessly we behaved ourselves towards you who believe. ₁₁ As you know, we exhorted, comforted, and implored every one of you, as a father does his own children, ₁₂ to the end that you should walk worthily of God, who calls you into his own Kingdom and glory.

₁₃ For this cause we also thank God without ceasing that when you received from us the word of the message of God, you accepted it not as the word of men, but as it is in truth, God's word, which also works in you who believe. ₁₄ For you, brothers, became imitators of the assemblies of God which are in Judea in Christ Jesus; for you also suffered the same things from your own countrymen, even as they did from the Jews ₁₅ who killed both the Lord Jesus and their own prophets, and drove us out, and don't please God, and are contrary to all men, ₁₆ forbidding us to speak to the Gentiles that they may be saved, to fill up their sins always. But wrath has come on them to the uttermost.

₁₇ But we, brothers, being bereaved of you for a short season in presence, not in heart, tried even harder to see your face with great desire, ₁₈ because we wanted to come to you—indeed, I, Paul, once and again—but Satan hindered us. ₁₉ For what is our hope, or joy, or crown of rejoicing? Isn't it even you, before our Lord Jesus[c] at his coming? ₂₀ For you are our glory and our joy.

3

₁ Therefore when we couldn't stand it any longer, we thought it good to be left behind at Athens alone, ₂ and sent Timothy, our brother and God's servant in the Good News of Christ, to establish you and to comfort you concerning your faith, ₃ that no one would be moved by these afflictions. For you know that we are appointed to this task. ₄ For most certainly, when we were with you, we told you beforehand that we are to suffer affliction, even as it happened, and you know. ₅ For this cause I also, when I couldn't stand it any longer, sent that I might know your faith, for fear that by any means the tempter had tempted you, and our labour would have been in vain.

₆ But Timothy has just now come to us from you, and brought us glad news of your faith and love, and that you have good memories of us always, longing to see us, even as we also long to see you. ₇ For this cause, brothers, we were comforted over you in all our distress and affliction through your faith. ₈ For now we live, if you stand fast in the Lord. ₉ For what thanksgiving can we render again to God for you, for all the joy with which we rejoice for your sakes before our God, ₁₀ night and day praying exceedingly that we may see your face and may perfect that which is lacking in your faith?

₁₁ Now may our God and Father himself, and our Lord Jesus Christ, direct our way to you. ₁₂ May the Lord make you to increase and abound in love towards one another and towards all men, even as we also do towards you, ₁₃ to the end he may establish your hearts blameless in holiness before our God and Father at the coming of our Lord Jesus with all his saints.

4

₁ Finally then, brothers, we beg and exhort you in the Lord Jesus, that as you received from us how you ought to walk and to please God, that you abound more and more. ₂ For you know what instructions we gave you through the Lord Jesus. ₃ For this is the will of God: your sanctification, that you abstain from sexual immorality, ₄ that each one of you know how to control his own body[d] in sanctification and honour, ₅ not in the passion of lust, even as the Gentiles who don't know God, ₆ that no one should take advantage of and wrong a brother or sister in this matter; because the Lord is an avenger in all these things, as also we forewarned you and testified. ₇ For God called us not for uncleanness, but in sanctification. ₈ Therefore he who rejects this doesn't reject man, but God, who has also given his Holy Spirit to you.

₉ But concerning brotherly love, you have no need that one write to you. For you yourselves are taught by God to love one another, ₁₀ for indeed you do it towards all the brothers who are in all Macedonia. But we exhort you, brothers, that you abound more and more; ₁₁ and that you make it your ambition to lead a quiet life, and to do your own business, and to work with your own hands, even as we instructed you, ₁₂ that you may walk properly towards those who are outside, and may have need of nothing.

₁₃ But we don't want you to be ignorant, brothers, concerning those who have fallen asleep, so that you don't grieve like the rest, who have no hope. ₁₄ For if we believe that Jesus died and rose again, even so God will bring with him those who have fallen asleep in Jesus. ₁₅ For this we tell you by the word of the Lord, that we who are alive, who are left until the coming of the Lord, will in no way precede those who have fallen asleep. ₁₆ For the Lord himself will descend from heaven with a shout, with the voice of the archangel and with God's trumpet. The dead in Christ will rise first, ₁₇ then we who are alive, who are left, will be caught up together with them in the clouds to meet the Lord in the air. So we will be with the Lord forever. ₁₈ Therefore comfort one another with these words.

5

₁ But concerning the times and the seasons, brothers, you have no need that anything be written to you. ₂ For you yourselves know well that the day of the Lord comes like a thief in the night. ₃ For when they are saying, "Peace and safety," then sudden destruction will come on them, like birth pains on a pregnant woman. Then they will in no way escape. ₄ But you, brothers, aren't in darkness, that the day should overtake you like a thief. ₅ You are all children of light and children of the day. We don't belong to the night, nor to darkness, ₆ so then let's not sleep, as the rest do, but let's watch and be sober. ₇ For those who sleep, sleep in the night; and those who are drunk are drunk in the night. ₈ But since we belong to the day, let's be sober, putting on the breastplate of faith and love, and for a helmet, the hope of salvation. ₉ For God didn't appoint us to wrath, but to the obtaining of salvation through our Lord Jesus Christ, ₁₀ who died for us, that, whether we wake or sleep, we should live together with him. ₁₁ Therefore exhort one another, and build each other up, even as you also do.

₁₂ But we beg you, brothers, to know those who labour amongst you, and are over you in the Lord and admonish you, ₁₃ and to respect and honour them in love for their work's sake.

Be at peace amongst yourselves. ₁₄ We exhort you, brothers: Admonish the disorderly; encourage the faint-hearted; support the weak; be patient towards all. ₁₅ See that no one returns evil for evil to anyone, but always follow after that which is good for one another and for all.

₁₆ Always rejoice. ₁₇ Pray without ceasing. ₁₈ In everything give thanks, for this is the will of God in Christ Jesus towards you. ₁₉ Don't quench the Spirit. ₂₀ Don't despise prophecies. ₂₁ Test all things, and hold firmly that which is good. ₂₂ Abstain from every form of evil.

₂₃ May the God of peace himself sanctify you completely. May your whole spirit, soul, and body be preserved blameless at the coming of our Lord Jesus Christ.

₂₄ He who calls you is faithful, who will also do it.

₂₅ Brothers, pray for us.

₂₆ Greet all the brothers with a holy kiss. ₂₇ I solemnly command you by the Lord that this letter be read to all the holy brothers.

₂₈ The grace of our Lord Jesus Christ be with you. Amen.

Paul's Second Letter to the Thessalonians

1

1 Paul, Silvanus, and Timothy, to the assembly of the Thessalonians in God our Father and the Lord Jesus Christ: 2 Grace to you and peace from God our Father and the Lord Jesus Christ.

3 We are bound to always give thanks to God for you, brothers,[a] even as it is appropriate, because your faith grows exceedingly, and the love of each and every one of you towards one another abounds, 4 so that we ourselves boast about you in the assemblies of God for your perseverance and faith in all your persecutions and in the afflictions which you endure. 5 This is an obvious sign of the righteous judgement of God, to the end that you may be counted worthy of God's Kingdom, for which you also suffer. 6 For it is a righteous thing with God to repay affliction to those who afflict you, 7 and to give relief to you who are afflicted with us when the Lord Jesus is revealed from heaven with his mighty angels in flaming fire, 8 punishing those who don't know God, and to those who don't obey the Good News of our Lord Jesus, 9 who will pay the penalty: eternal destruction from the face of the Lord and from the glory of his might, 10 when he comes in that day to be glorified in his saints and to be admired amongst all those who have believed, because our testimony to you was believed.

11 To this end we also pray always for you that our God may count you worthy of your calling, and fulfil every desire of goodness and work of faith with power, 12 that the name of our Lord Jesus[b] may be glorified in you, and you in him, according to the grace of our God and the Lord Jesus Christ.

2

1 Now, brothers, concerning the coming of our Lord Jesus Christ and our gathering together to him, we ask you 2 not to be quickly shaken in your mind or troubled, either by spirit or by word or by letter as if from us, saying that the day of Christ has already come. 3 Let no one deceive you in any way. For it will not be unless the rebellion[c] comes first, and the man of sin is revealed, the son of destruction. 4 He opposes and exalts himself against all that is called God or that is worshipped, so that he sits as God in the temple of God, setting himself up as God. 5 Don't you remember that when I was still with you, I told you these things? 6 Now you know what is restraining him, to the end that he may be revealed in his own season. 7 For the mystery of lawlessness already works. Only there is one who restrains now, until he is taken out of the way. 8 Then the lawless one will be revealed, whom the Lord will kill with the breath of his mouth and destroy by the manifestation of his coming; 9 even he whose coming is according to the working of Satan with all power and signs and lying wonders, 10 and with all deception of wickedness for those who are being lost, because they didn't receive the love of the truth, that they might be saved. 11 Because of this, God sends them a powerful delusion, that they should believe a lie, 12 that they all might be judged who didn't believe the truth, but had pleasure in unrighteousness.

13 But we are bound to always give thanks to God for you, brothers loved by the Lord, because God chose you from the beginning for salvation through sanctification of the Spirit and belief in the truth, 14 to which he called you through our Good News, for the obtaining of the glory of our Lord Jesus Christ. 15 So then, brothers, stand firm and hold the traditions which you were taught by us, whether by word or by letter.

16 Now our Lord Jesus Christ himself, and God our Father, who loved us and gave us eternal comfort and good hope through grace, 17 comfort your hearts and establish you in every good work and word.

3

1 Finally, brothers, pray for us, that the word of the Lord may spread rapidly and be glorified, even as also with you, 2 and that we may be delivered from unreasonable and evil men; for not all have faith. 3 But the Lord is faithful, who will establish you and guard you from the evil one. 4 We have confidence in the Lord concerning you, that you both do and will do the things we command. 5 May the Lord direct your hearts into God's love and into the perseverance of Christ.

6 Now we command you, brothers, in the name of our Lord Jesus Christ, that you withdraw yourselves from every brother who walks in rebellion and not after the tradition which they received from us. 7 For you know how you ought to imitate us. For we didn't behave ourselves rebelliously amongst you, 8 neither did we eat bread from anyone's hand without paying for it, but in labour and travail worked night and day, that we might not burden any of you. 9 This was not because we don't have the right, but to make ourselves an example to you, that you should imitate us. 10 For even when we were with you, we commanded you this: "If anyone is not willing to work, don't let him eat." 11 For we hear of some who walk amongst you in rebellion, who don't work at all, but are busybodies. 12 Now those who are that way, we command and exhort in the Lord Jesus Christ, that they work with quietness and eat their own bread.

13 But you, brothers, don't be weary in doing what is right. 14 If any man doesn't obey our word in this letter, note that man and have no company with him, to the end that he may be ashamed. 15 Don't count him as an enemy, but admonish him as a brother.

16 Now may the Lord of peace himself give you peace at all times in all ways. The Lord be with you all.

17 I, Paul, write this greeting with my own hand, which is the sign in every letter. This is how I write. 18 The grace of our Lord Jesus Christ be with you all. Amen.

---

a 1:3 The word for "brothers" here and where context allows may also be correctly translated "brothers and sisters" or "siblings."

b 1:12 TR adds "Christ"

c 2:3 or, falling away, or, defection

Paul's First Letter to Timothy

1

1 Paul, an apostle of Jesus Christ according to the commandment of God our Saviour and the Lord Jesus Christ[a] our hope, 2 to Timothy, my true child in faith: Grace, mercy, and peace from God our Father and Christ Jesus our Lord.

3 As I urged you when I was going into Macedonia, stay at Ephesus that you might command certain men not to teach a different doctrine, 4 and not to pay attention to myths and endless genealogies, which cause disputes rather than God's stewardship, which is in faith. 5 But the goal of this command is love from a pure heart, a good conscience, and sincere faith, 6 from which things some, having missed the mark, have turned away to vain talking, 7 desiring to be teachers of the law, though they understand neither what they say nor about what they strongly affirm.

8 But we know that the law is good if a person uses it lawfully, 9 as knowing this, that law is not made for a righteous person, but for the lawless and insubordinate, for the ungodly and sinners, for the unholy and profane, for murderers of fathers and murderers of mothers, for manslayers, 10 for the sexually immoral, for homosexuals, for slave-traders, for liars, for perjurers, and for any other thing contrary to the sound doctrine, 11 according to the Good News of the glory of the blessed God, which was committed to my trust.

12 I thank him who enabled me, Christ Jesus our Lord, because he counted me faithful, appointing me to service, 13 although I used to be a blasphemer, a persecutor, and insolent. However, I obtained mercy because I did it ignorantly in unbelief. 14 The grace of our Lord abounded exceedingly with faith and love which is in Christ Jesus. 15 The saying is faithful and worthy of all acceptance, that Christ Jesus came into the world to save sinners, of whom I am chief. 16 However, for this cause I obtained mercy, that in me first, Jesus Christ might display all his patience for an example of those who were going to believe in him for eternal life. 17 Now to the King eternal, immortal, invisible, to God who alone is wise, be honour and glory forever and ever. Amen.

18 I commit this instruction to you, my child Timothy, according to the prophecies which were given to you before, that by them you may wage the good warfare, 19 holding faith and a good conscience, which some having thrust away made a shipwreck concerning the faith, 20 of whom are Hymenaeus and Alexander, whom I delivered to Satan that they might be taught not to blaspheme.

2

1 I exhort therefore, first of all, that petitions, prayers, intercessions, and givings of thanks be made for all men, 2 for kings and all who are in high places, that we may lead a tranquil and quiet life in all godliness and reverence. 3 For this is good and acceptable in the sight of God our Saviour, 4 who desires all people to be saved and come to full knowledge of the truth. 5 For there is one God and one mediator between God and men, the man Christ Jesus, 6 who gave himself as a ransom for all, the testimony at the proper time, 7 to which I was appointed a preacher and an apostle—I am telling the truth in Christ, not lying—a teacher of the Gentiles in faith and truth.

8 I desire therefore that the men in every place pray, lifting up holy hands without anger and doubting. 9 In the same way, that women also adorn themselves in decent clothing, with modesty and propriety, not[b] with braided hair, gold, pearls, or expensive clothing, 10 but with good works, which is appropriate for women professing godliness. 11 Let a woman learn in quietness with full submission. 12 But I don't permit a woman to teach, nor to exercise authority over a man, but to be in quietness. 13 For Adam was formed first, then Eve. 14 Adam wasn't deceived, but the woman, being deceived, has fallen into disobedience; 15 but she will be saved through her childbearing, if they continue in faith, love, and holiness with sobriety.

3

1 This is a faithful saying: someone who seeks to be an overseer[c] desires a good work. 2 The overseer therefore must be without reproach, the husband of one wife, temperate, sensible, modest, hospitable, good at teaching; 3 not a drinker, not violent, not greedy for money, but gentle, not quarrelsome, not covetous; 4 one who rules his own house well, having children in subjection with all reverence; 5 (for how could someone who doesn't know how to rule his own house take care of God's assembly?) 6 not a new convert, lest being puffed up he fall into the same condemnation as the devil. 7 Moreover he must have good testimony from those who are outside, to avoid falling into reproach and the snare of the devil.

8 Servants,[d] in the same way, must be reverent, not double-tongued, not addicted to much wine, not greedy for money, 9 holding the mystery of the faith in a pure conscience. 10 Let them also first be tested; then let them serve[e] if they are blameless. 11 Their wives in the same way must be reverent, not slanderers, temperate, and faithful in all things. 12 Let servants[f] be husbands of one wife, ruling their children and their own

houses well. 13 For those who have served well[g] gain for themselves a good standing and great boldness in the faith which is in Christ Jesus.

14 These things I write to you, hoping to come to you shortly, 15 but if I wait long, that you may know how men ought to behave themselves in God's house, which is the assembly of the living God, the pillar and ground of the truth. 16 Without controversy, the mystery of godliness is great:
God[h] was revealed in the flesh,
justified in the spirit,
seen by angels,
preached amongst the nations,
believed on in the world,
and received up in glory.

4

1 But the Spirit says expressly that in later times some will fall away from the faith, paying attention to seducing spirits and doctrines of demons, 2 through the hypocrisy of men who speak lies, branded in their own conscience as with a hot iron, 3 forbidding marriage and commanding to abstain from foods which God created to be received with thanksgiving by those who believe and know the truth. 4 For every creature of God is good, and nothing is to be rejected if it is received with thanksgiving. 5 For it is sanctified through the word of God and prayer.

6 If you instruct the brothers of these things, you will be a good servant of Christ Jesus, nourished in the words of the faith and of the good doctrine which you have followed. 7 But refuse profane and old wives' fables. Exercise yourself towards godliness. 8 For bodily exercise has some value, but godliness has value in all things, having the promise of the life which is now and of that which is to come. 9 This saying is faithful and worthy of all acceptance. 10 For to this end we both labour and suffer reproach, because we have set our trust in the living God, who is the Saviour of all men, especially of those who believe. 11 Command and teach these things.

12 Let no man despise your youth; but be an example to those who believe, in word, in your way of life, in love, in spirit, in faith, and in purity. 13 Until I come, pay attention to reading, to exhortation, and to teaching. 14 Don't neglect the gift that is in you, which was given to you by prophecy with the laying on of the hands of the elders. 15 Be diligent in these things. Give yourself wholly to them, that your progress may be revealed to all. 16 Pay attention to yourself and to your teaching. Continue in these things, for in doing this you will save both yourself and those who hear you.

5

1 Don't rebuke an older man, but exhort him as a father; the younger men as brothers; 2 the elder women as mothers; the younger as sisters, in all purity.

3 Honour widows who are widows indeed. 4 But if any widow has children or grandchildren, let them learn first to show piety towards their own family and to repay their parents, for this is[i] acceptable in the sight of God. 5 Now she who is a widow indeed and desolate, has her hope set on God and continues in petitions and prayers night and day. 6 But she who gives herself to pleasure is dead while she lives. 7 Also command these things, that they may be without reproach. 8 But if anyone doesn't provide for his own, and especially his own household, he has denied the faith and is worse than an unbeliever.

9 Let no one be enrolled as a widow under sixty years old, having been the wife of one man, 10 being approved by good works, if she has brought up children, if she has been hospitable to strangers, if she has washed the saints' feet, if she has relieved the afflicted, and if she has diligently followed every good work.

11 But refuse younger widows, for when they have grown wanton against Christ, they desire to marry, 12 having condemnation, because they have rejected their first pledge. 13 Besides, they also learn to be idle, going about from house to house. Not only idle, but also gossips and busybodies, saying things which they ought not. 14 I desire therefore that the younger widows marry, bear children, rule the household, and give no occasion to the adversary for insulting. 15 For already some have turned away after Satan. 16 If any man or woman who believes has widows, let them relieve them, and don't let the assembly be burdened, that it might relieve those who are widows indeed.

17 Let the elders who rule well be counted worthy of double honour, especially those who labour in the word and in teaching. 18 For the Scripture says, "You shall not muzzle the ox when it treads out the grain."[**] And, "The labourer is worthy of his wages."[**]

19 Don't receive an accusation against an elder except at the word of two or three witnesses. 20 Those who sin, reprove in the sight of all, that the rest also may be in fear. 21 I command you in the sight of God, and the Lord Jesus Christ, and the chosen angels, that you observe these things without prejudice, doing nothing by partiality. 22 Lay hands hastily on no one. Don't be a participant in other people's sins. Keep yourself pure.

23 Be no longer a drinker of water only, but use a little wine for your stomach's sake and your frequent infirmities.

---

a *1:1* NU reads Christ Jesus and omits the Lord.
b *2:9* The word for "not" is the negative particle "μη" which denies an expected idea, as opposed to the usual word for "not" (ου) which denies a fact. Thus "μη" in this context is denying an expected idea (that women can be properly dressed without good works).
c *3:1* or, superintendent, or bishop
d *3:8* or, Deacons.
e *3:10* or, serve as deacons
f *3:12* or, deacons
g *3:13* or, served well as deacons
h *3:16* NU replaces "God" with "who"
i *5:4* TR adds "good and"
** 5:18 Deuteronomy 25:4
** 5:18 Luke 10:7; Leviticus 19:13

₂₄ Some men's sins are evident, preceding them to judgement, and some also follow later. ₂₅ In the same way also there are good works that are obvious, and those that are otherwise can't be hidden.

6

₁ Let as many as are bondservants under the yoke count their own masters worthy of all honour, that the name of God and the doctrine not be blasphemed. ₂ Those who have believing masters, let them not despise them because they are brothers, but rather let them serve them, because those who partake of the benefit are believing and beloved. Teach and exhort these things.

₃ If anyone teaches a different doctrine and doesn't consent to sound words, the words of our Lord Jesus Christ, and to the doctrine which is according to godliness, ₄ he is conceited, knowing nothing, but obsessed with arguments, disputes, and word battles, from which come envy, strife, insulting, evil suspicions, ₅ constant friction of people of corrupt minds and destitute of the truth, who suppose that godliness is a means of gain. Withdraw yourself from such.[a]

₆ But godliness with contentment is great gain. ₇ For we brought nothing into the world, and we certainly can't carry anything out. ₈ But having food and clothing, we will be content with that. ₉ But those who are determined to be rich fall into a temptation, a snare, and many foolish and harmful lusts, such as drown men in ruin and destruction. ₁₀ For the love of money is a root of all kinds of evil. Some have been led astray from the faith in their greed, and have pierced themselves through with many sorrows.

₁₁ But you, man of God, flee these things, and follow after righteousness, godliness, faith, love, perseverance, and gentleness. ₁₂ Fight the good fight of faith. Take hold of the eternal life to which you were called, and you confessed the good confession in the sight of many witnesses. ₁₃ I command you before God who gives life to all things, and before Christ Jesus who before Pontius Pilate testified the good confession, ₁₄ that you keep the commandment without spot, blameless until the appearing of our Lord Jesus Christ, ₁₅ which at the right time he will show, who is the blessed and only Ruler, the King of kings and Lord of lords. ₁₆ He alone has immortality, dwelling in unapproachable light, whom no man has seen nor can see, to whom be honour and eternal power. Amen.

₁₇ Charge those who are rich in this present age that they not be arrogant, nor have their hope set on the uncertainty of riches, but on the living God, who richly provides us with everything to enjoy; ₁₈ that they do good, that they be rich in good works, that they be ready to distribute, willing to share; ₁₉ laying up in store for themselves a good foundation against the time to come, that they may lay hold of eternal life.

₂₀ Timothy, guard that which is committed to you, turning away from the empty chatter and oppositions of what is falsely called knowledge, ₂₁ which some profess, and thus have wandered from the faith.

Grace be with you. Amen.

---

[a] 6:5 NU omits "Withdraw yourself from such."

Paul's Second Letter to Timothy

1

1 Paul, an apostle of Jesus Christ[a] through the will of God, according to the promise of the life which is in Christ Jesus, 2 to Timothy, my beloved child: Grace, mercy, and peace, from God the Father and Christ Jesus our Lord.

3 I thank God, whom I serve as my forefathers did, with a pure conscience. How unceasing is my memory of you in my petitions, night and day 4 longing to see you, remembering your tears, that I may be filled with joy; 5 having been reminded of the sincere faith that is in you, which lived first in your grandmother Lois and your mother Eunice and, I am persuaded, in you also.

6 For this cause, I remind you that you should stir up the gift of God which is in you through the laying on of my hands. 7 For God didn't give us a spirit of fear, but of power, love, and self-control. 8 Therefore don't be ashamed of the testimony of our Lord, nor of me his prisoner; but endure hardship for the Good News according to the power of God, 9 who saved us and called us with a holy calling, not according to our works, but according to his own purpose and grace, which was given to us in Christ Jesus before times eternal, 10 but has now been revealed by the appearing of our Saviour, Christ Jesus, who abolished death, and brought life and immortality to light through the Good News. 11 For this I was appointed as a preacher, an apostle, and a teacher of the Gentiles. 12 For this cause I also suffer these things.

Yet I am not ashamed, for I know him whom I have believed, and I am persuaded that he is able to guard that which I have committed to him against that day.

13 Hold the pattern of sound words which you have heard from me, in faith and love which is in Christ Jesus. 14 That good thing which was committed to you, guard through the Holy Spirit who dwells in us.

15 This you know, that all who are in Asia turned away from me, of whom are Phygelus and Hermogenes. 16 May the Lord grant mercy to the house of Onesiphorus, for he often refreshed me, and was not ashamed of my chain, 17 but when he was in Rome, he sought me diligently and found me 18 (the Lord grant to him to find the Lord's mercy in that day); and in how many things he served at Ephesus, you know very well.

2

1 You therefore, my child, be strengthened in the grace that is in Christ Jesus. 2 The things which you have heard from me amongst many witnesses, commit the same things to faithful men who will be able to teach others also. 3 You therefore must endure hardship as a good soldier of Christ Jesus. 4 No soldier on duty entangles himself in the affairs of life, that he may please him who enrolled him as a soldier. 5 Also, if anyone competes in athletics, he isn't crowned unless he has competed by the rules. 6 The farmer who labours must be the first to get a share of the crops. 7 Consider what I say, and may the Lord give you understanding in all things.

8 Remember Jesus Christ, risen from the dead, of the offspring[b] of David, according to my Good News, 9 in which I suffer hardship to the point of chains as a criminal. But God's word isn't chained. 10 Therefore I endure all things for the chosen ones' sake, that they also may obtain the salvation which is in Christ Jesus with eternal glory. 11 This saying is trustworthy:
"For if we died with him,
we will also live with him.
12 If we endure,
we will also reign with him.
If we deny him,
he also will deny us.
13 If we are faithless,
he remains faithful;
for he can't deny himself."

14 Remind them of these things, charging them in the sight of the Lord that they don't argue about words to no profit, to the subverting of those who hear.

15 Give diligence to present yourself approved by God, a workman who doesn't need to be ashamed, properly handling the Word of Truth. 16 But shun empty chatter, for it will go further in ungodliness, 17 and those words will consume like gangrene, of whom is Hymenaeus and Philetus: 18 men who have erred concerning the truth, saying that the resurrection is already past, and overthrowing the faith of some. 19 However, God's firm foundation stands, having this seal: "The Lord knows those who are his,"* and, "Let every one who names the name of the Lord[c] depart from unrighteousness."

20 Now in a large house there are not only vessels of gold and of silver, but also of wood and of clay. Some are for honour and some for dishonour. 21 If anyone therefore purges himself from these, he will be a vessel for honour, sanctified, and suitable for the master's use, prepared for every good work.

22 Flee from youthful lusts; but pursue righteousness, faith, love, and peace with those who call on the Lord out of a pure heart. 23 But refuse foolish and ignorant questionings, knowing that they generate strife. 24 The Lord's servant must not quarrel, but be gentle towards all, able to teach, patient, 25 in gentleness correcting those who oppose him. Perhaps God may give them repentance leading to a full knowledge of the truth, 26 and they may recover themselves out of the devil's snare, having been taken captive by him to do his will.

3

1 But know this: that in the last days, grievous times will come. 2 For men will be lovers of self, lovers of money, boastful, arrogant, blasphemers, disobedient to parents, unthankful, unholy, 3 without natural affection, unforgiving, slanderers, without self-control, fierce, not lovers of good, 4 traitors, headstrong, conceited, lovers of pleasure rather than lovers of God, 5 holding a form of godliness but having denied its power. Turn away from these, also. 6 For some of these are people who creep into houses and take captive gullible women loaded down with sins, led away by various lusts, 7 always learning and never able to come to the knowledge of the truth. 8 Even as Jannes and Jambres opposed Moses, so these also oppose the truth, men corrupted in mind, who concerning the faith are rejected. 9 But they will proceed no further. For their folly will be evident to all men, as theirs also came to be.

10 But you followed my teaching, conduct, purpose, faith, patience, love, steadfastness, 11 persecutions, and sufferings—those things that happened to me at Antioch, Iconium, and Lystra. I endured those persecutions. The Lord delivered me out of them all. 12 Yes, and all who desire to live godly in Christ Jesus will suffer persecution. 13 But evil men and impostors will grow worse and worse, deceiving and being deceived. 14 But you remain in the things which you have learnt and have been assured of, knowing from whom you have learnt them. 15 From infancy, you have known the holy Scriptures which are able to make you wise for salvation through faith which is in Christ Jesus. 16 Every Scripture is God-breathed and[d] profitable for teaching, for reproof, for correction, and for instruction in righteousness, 17 that each person who belongs to God may be complete, thoroughly equipped for every good work.

4

1 I command you therefore before God and the Lord Jesus Christ, who will judge the living and the dead at his appearing and his Kingdom: 2 preach the word; be urgent in season and out of season; reprove, rebuke, and exhort with all patience and teaching. 3 For the time will come when they will not listen to the sound doctrine, but having itching ears, will heap up for themselves teachers after their own lusts, 4 and will turn away their ears from the truth, and turn away to fables. 5 But you be sober in all things, suffer hardship, do the work of an evangelist, and fulfil your ministry.

6 For I am already being offered, and the time of my departure has come. 7 I have fought the good fight. I have finished the course. I have kept the faith. 8 From now on, the crown of righteousness is stored up for me, which the Lord, the righteous judge, will give to me on that day; and not to me only, but also to all those who have loved his appearing.

9 Be diligent to come to me soon, 10 for Demas left me, having loved this present world, and went to Thessalonica; Crescens to Galatia; and Titus to Dalmatia. 11 Only Luke is with me. Take Mark and bring him with you, for he is useful to me for service. 12 But I sent Tychicus to Ephesus. 13 Bring the cloak that I left at Troas with Carpus when you come—and the books, especially the parchments. 14 Alexander the coppersmith did much evil to me. The Lord will repay him according to his deeds. 15 Beware of him, for he greatly opposed our words.

16 At my first defence, no one came to help me, but all left me. May it not be held against them. 17 But the Lord stood by me and strengthened me, that through me the message might be fully proclaimed, and that all the Gentiles might hear. So I was delivered out of the mouth of the lion. 18 And the Lord will deliver me from every evil work and will preserve me for his heavenly Kingdom. To him be the glory forever and ever. Amen.

19 Greet Prisca and Aquila, and the house of Onesiphorus. 20 Erastus remained at Corinth, but I left Trophimus at Miletus sick. 21 Be diligent to come before winter. Eubulus salutes you, as do Pudens, Linus, Claudia, and all the brothers.

22 The Lord Jesus Christ be with your spirit. Grace be with you. Amen.

---

a *1:1* "Christ" means "Anointed One".
b *2:8* or, seed
** *2:19* Numbers 16:5

c *2:19* TR reads "Christ" instead of "the Lord"
d *3:16* or, Every writing inspired by God is

Paul's Letter to Titus

1

₁ Paul, a servant of God and an apostle of Jesus Christ,[a] according to the faith of God's chosen ones and the knowledge of the truth which is according to godliness, ₂ in hope of eternal life, which God, who can't lie, promised before time began; ₃ but in his own time revealed his word in the message with which I was entrusted according to the commandment of God our Saviour, ₄ to Titus, my true child according to a common faith: Grace, mercy, and peace from God the Father and the Lord Jesus Christ our Saviour.

₅ I left you in Crete for this reason, that you would set in order the things that were lacking and appoint elders in every city, as I directed you— ₆ if anyone is blameless, the husband of one wife, having children who believe, who are not accused of loose or unruly behaviour. ₇ For the overseer must be blameless, as God's steward, not self-pleasing, not easily angered, not given to wine, not violent, not greedy for dishonest gain; ₈ but given to hospitality, a lover of good, sober minded, fair, holy, self-controlled, ₉ holding to the faithful word which is according to the teaching, that he may be able to exhort in the sound doctrine, and to convict those who contradict him.

₁₀ For there are also many unruly men, vain talkers and deceivers, especially those of the circumcision, ₁₁ whose mouths must be stopped: men who overthrow whole houses, teaching things which they ought not, for dishonest gain's sake. ₁₂ One of them, a prophet of their own, said, "Cretans are always liars, evil beasts, and idle gluttons." ₁₃ This testimony is true. For this cause, reprove them sharply, that they may be sound in the faith, ₁₄ not paying attention to Jewish fables and commandments of men who turn away from the truth. ₁₅ To the pure, all things are pure, but to those who are defiled and unbelieving, nothing is pure; but both their mind and their conscience are defiled. ₁₆ They profess that they know God, but by their deeds they deny him, being abominable, disobedient, and unfit for any good work.

2

₁ But say the things which fit sound doctrine, ₂ that older men should be temperate, sensible, sober minded, sound in faith, in love, and in perseverance, ₃ and that older women likewise be reverent in behaviour, not slanderers nor enslaved to much wine, teachers of that which is good, ₄ that they may train the young wives to love their husbands, to love their children, ₅ to be sober minded, chaste, workers at home, kind, being in subjection to their own husbands, that God's word may not be blasphemed.

₆ Likewise, exhort the younger men to be sober minded. ₇ In all things show yourself an example of good works. In your teaching, show integrity, seriousness, incorruptibility, ₈ and soundness of speech that can't be condemned, that he who opposes you may be ashamed, having no evil thing to say about us.

₉ Exhort servants to be in subjection to their own masters and to be well-pleasing in all things, not contradicting, ₁₀ not stealing, but showing all good fidelity, that they may adorn the doctrine of God, our Saviour, in all things. ₁₁ For the grace of God has appeared, bringing salvation to all men, ₁₂ instructing us to the intent that, denying ungodliness and worldly lusts, we would live soberly, righteously, and godly in this present age; ₁₃ looking for the blessed hope and appearing of the glory of our great God and Saviour, Jesus Christ, ₁₄ who gave himself for us, that he might redeem us from all iniquity and purify for himself a people for his own possession, zealous for good works.

₁₅ Say these things and exhort and reprove with all authority. Let no one despise you.

3

₁ Remind them to be in subjection to rulers and to authorities, to be obedient, to be ready for every good work, ₂ to speak evil of no one, not to be contentious, to be gentle, showing all humility towards all men. ₃ For we were also once foolish, disobedient, deceived, serving various lusts and pleasures, living in malice and envy, hateful, and hating one another. ₄ But when the kindness of God our Saviour and his love towards mankind appeared, ₅ not by works of righteousness which we did ourselves, but according to his mercy, he saved us through the washing of regeneration and renewing by the Holy Spirit, ₆ whom he poured out on us richly through Jesus Christ our Saviour; ₇ that being justified by his grace, we might be made heirs according to the hope of eternal life. ₈ This saying is faithful, and concerning these things I desire that you insist confidently, so that those who have believed God may be careful to maintain good works. These things are good and profitable to men; ₉ but shun foolish questionings, genealogies, strife, and disputes about the law; for they are unprofitable and vain. ₁₀ Avoid a factious man after a first and second warning, ₁₁ knowing that such a one is perverted and sinful, being self-condemned.

₁₂ When I send Artemas to you, or Tychicus, be diligent to come to me to Nicopolis, for I have determined to winter there. ₁₃ Send Zenas the lawyer and Apollos on their journey speedily, that nothing may be lacking for them. ₁₄ Let our people also learn to maintain good works to meet necessary needs, that they may not be unfruitful.

₁₅ All who are with me greet you. Greet those who love us in faith. Grace be with you all. Amen.

---

[a] *1:1* "Christ" means "Anointed One".

Paul's Letter to Philemon

1

1 Paul, a prisoner of Christ[a] Jesus, and Timothy our brother, to Philemon, our beloved fellow worker, 2 to the beloved Apphia, to Archippus our fellow soldier, and to the assembly in your house: 3 Grace to you and peace from God our Father and the Lord Jesus Christ.

4 I thank my God always, making mention of you in my prayers, 5 hearing of your love and of the faith which you have towards the Lord Jesus and towards all the saints, 6 that the fellowship of your faith may become effective in the knowledge of every good thing which is in us in Christ Jesus. 7 For we have much joy and comfort in your love, because the hearts of the saints have been refreshed through you, brother.

8 Therefore though I have all boldness in Christ to command you that which is appropriate, 9 yet for love's sake I rather appeal to you, being such a one as Paul, the aged, but also a prisoner of Jesus Christ. 10 I appeal to you for my child Onesimus, whom I have become the father of in my chains,[b] 11 who once was useless to you, but now is useful to you and to me. 12 I am sending him back. Therefore receive him, that is, my own heart, 13 whom I desired to keep with me, that on your behalf he might serve me in my chains for the Good News. 14 But I was willing to do nothing without your consent, that your goodness would not be as of necessity, but of free will. 15 For perhaps he was therefore separated from you for a while that you would have him forever, 16 no longer as a slave, but more than a slave, a beloved brother—especially to me, but how much rather to you, both in the flesh and in the Lord.

17 If then you count me a partner, receive him as you would receive me. 18 But if he has wronged you at all or owes you anything, put that to my account. 19 I, Paul, write this with my own hand: I will repay it (not to mention to you that you owe to me even your own self besides). 20 Yes, brother, let me have joy from you in the Lord. Refresh my heart in the Lord.

21 Having confidence in your obedience, I write to you, knowing that you will do even beyond what I say.

22 Also, prepare a guest room for me, for I hope that through your prayers I will be restored to you.

23 Epaphras, my fellow prisoner in Christ Jesus, greets you, 24 as do Mark, Aristarchus, Demas, and Luke, my fellow workers.

25 The grace of our Lord Jesus Christ be with your spirit. Amen.

---

[a] 1:1 "Christ" means "Anointed One".

[b] 1:10 Onesimus means "useful".

The Letter to the Hebrews

1

1 God, having in the past spoken to the fathers through the prophets at many times and in various ways, 2 has at the end of these days spoken to us by his Son, whom he appointed heir of all things, through whom also he made the worlds. 3 His Son is the radiance of his glory, the very image of his substance, and upholding all things by the word of his power, who, when he had by himself purified us of our sins, sat down on the right hand of the Majesty on high, 4 having become as much better than the angels as the more excellent name he has inherited is better than theirs. 5 For to which of the angels did he say at any time,

"You are my Son.
　Today I have become your father?"*

and again,

"I will be to him a Father,
　and he will be to me a Son?"*

6 When he again brings in the firstborn into the world he says, "Let all the angels of God worship him."* 7 Of the angels he says,

"He makes his angels winds,
　and his servants a flame of fire."*

8 But of the Son he says,

"Your throne, O God, is forever and ever.
　The sceptre of uprightness is the sceptre of your Kingdom.
9 You have loved righteousness and hated iniquity;
　therefore God, your God, has anointed you with the oil of gladness
　　above your fellows."*

10 And,

"You, Lord, in the beginning, laid the foundation of the earth.
　The heavens are the works of your hands.
11 They will perish, but you continue.
　They all will grow old like a garment does.
12 You will roll them up like a mantle,
　and they will be changed;
　but you are the same.
　Your years won't fail."*

13 But which of the angels has he told at any time,

"Sit at my right hand,
　until I make your enemies the footstool of your feet?"*

14 Aren't they all serving spirits, sent out to do service for the sake of those who will inherit salvation?

2

1 Therefore we ought to pay greater attention to the things that were heard, lest perhaps we drift away. 2 For if the word spoken through angels proved steadfast, and every transgression and disobedience received a just penalty, 3 how will we escape if we neglect so great a salvation—which at the first having been spoken through the Lord, was confirmed to us by those who heard, 4 God also testifying with them, both by signs and wonders, by various works of power, and by gifts of the Holy Spirit, according to his own will?

5 For he didn't subject the world to come, of which we speak, to angels. 6 But one has somewhere testified, saying,

"What is man, that you think of him?
　Or the son of man, that you care for him?
7 You made him a little lower than the angels.
　You crowned him with glory and honour.[a]
8 You have put all things in subjection under his feet."*

For in that he subjected all things to him, he left nothing that is not subject to him. But now we don't yet see all things subjected to him. 9 But we see him who has been made a little lower than the angels, Jesus, because of the suffering of death crowned with glory and honour, that by the grace of God he should taste of death for everyone.

10 For it became him, for whom are all things and through whom are all things, in bringing many children to glory, to make the author of their salvation perfect through sufferings. 11 For both he who sanctifies and those who are sanctified are all from one, for which cause he is not ashamed to call them brothers,[b] 12 saying,

"I will declare your name to my brothers.
　Amongst the congregation I will sing your praise."*

13 Again, "I will put my trust in him." Again, "Behold, here I am with the children whom God has given me."* 14 Since then the children have shared in flesh and blood, he also himself in the same way partook of the same, that through death he might bring to nothing him who had the power of death, that is, the devil, 15 and might deliver all of them who through fear of death were all their lifetime subject to bondage. 16 For most certainly, he doesn't give help to angels, but he gives help to the offspring[c] of Abraham. 17 Therefore he was obligated in all things to be made like his brothers, that he might become a merciful and faithful high priest in things pertaining to God, to make atonement for the sins of the people. 18 For in that he himself has suffered being tempted, he is able to help those who are tempted.

3

1 Therefore, holy brothers, partakers of a heavenly calling, consider the Apostle and High Priest of our confession: Jesus, 2 who was faithful to him who appointed him, as also Moses was in all his house. 3 For he has been counted worthy of more glory than Moses, because he who built the house has more honour than the house. 4 For every house is built by someone; but he who built all things is God. 5 Moses indeed was faithful in all his house as a servant, for a testimony of those things which were afterward to be spoken, 6 but Christ[d] is faithful as a Son over his house. We are his house, if we hold fast our confidence and the glorying of our hope firm to the end. 7 Therefore, even as the Holy Spirit says,

"Today if you will hear his voice,
8 don't harden your hearts as in the rebellion,
　in the day of the trial in the wilderness,
9 where your fathers tested me and tried me,
　and saw my deeds for forty years.
10 Therefore I was displeased with that generation,
　and said, 'They always err in their heart,
　but they didn't know my ways.'
11 As I swore in my wrath,
　'They will not enter into my rest.'"*

12 Beware, brothers, lest perhaps there might be in any one of you an evil heart of unbelief, in falling away from the living God; 13 but exhort one another day by day, so long as it is called "today", lest any one of you be hardened by the deceitfulness of sin. 14 For we have become partakers of Christ, if we hold the beginning of our confidence firm to the end, 15 while it is said,

"Today if you will hear his voice,
　don't harden your hearts, as in the rebellion."*

16 For who, when they heard, rebelled? Wasn't it all those who came out of Egypt led by Moses? 17 With whom was he displeased forty years? Wasn't it with those who sinned, whose bodies fell in the wilderness? 18 To whom did he swear that they wouldn't enter into his rest, but to those who were disobedient? 19 We see that they weren't able to enter in because of unbelief.

4

1 Let's fear therefore, lest perhaps anyone of you should seem to have come short of a promise of entering into his rest. 2 For indeed we have had good news preached to us, even as they also did, but the word they heard didn't profit them, because it wasn't mixed with faith by those who heard. 3 For we who have believed do enter into that rest, even as he has said, "As I swore in my wrath, they will not enter into my rest;"* although the works were finished from the foundation of the world. 4 For he has said this somewhere about the seventh day, "God rested on the seventh day from all his works;"* 5 and in this place again, "They will not enter into my rest."*

6 Seeing therefore it remains that some should enter into it, and they to whom the good news was preached before failed to enter in because of disobedience, 7 he again defines a certain day, "today", saying through David so long a time afterward (just as has been said),

"Today if you will hear his voice,
　don't harden your hearts."*

8 For if Joshua had given them rest, he would not have spoken afterward of another day. 9 There remains therefore a Sabbath rest for the people of God. 10 For he who has entered into his rest has himself also rested from his works, as God did from his. 11 Let's therefore give diligence to enter into that rest, lest anyone fall after the same example of disobedience. 12 For the word of God is living and active, and sharper than any two-edged sword, piercing even to the dividing of soul and spirit, of both joints and marrow, and is able to discern the thoughts and intentions of the heart. 13 There is no creature that is hidden from his sight, but all things are naked and laid open before the eyes of him to whom we must give an account.

14 Having then a great high priest who has passed through the heavens, Jesus, the Son of God, let's hold tightly to our confession. 15 For we don't have a high priest who can't be touched with the feeling of our infirmities, but one who has been in all points tempted like we are, yet without sin. 16 Let's therefore draw near with boldness to the throne of grace, that we may receive mercy and may find grace for help in time of need.

** 1:5 Psalms 2:7
** 1:5 2 Samuel 7:14; 1 Chronicles 17:13
** 1:6 Deuteronomy 32:43 LXX
** 1:7 Psalms 104:4
** 1:9 Psalms 45:6-7
** 1:12 Psalms 102:25-27
** 1:13 Psalms 110:1
a 2:7 TR adds "and set him over the works of your hands"
** 2:8 Psalms 8:4-6
b 2:11 The word for "brothers" here and where context allows may also be correctly translated "brothers and sisters" or "siblings."

** 2:12 Psalms 22:22
** 2:13 Isaiah 8:18
c 2:16 or, seed
d 3:6 "Christ" means "Anointed One".
** 3:11 Psalms 95:7-11
** 3:15 Psalms 95:7-8
** 4:3 Psalms 95:11
** 4:4 Genesis 2:2
** 4:5 Psalms 95:11
** 4:7 Psalms 95:7-8

5

1 For every high priest, being taken from amongst men, is appointed for men in things pertaining to God, that he may offer both gifts and sacrifices for sins. 2 The high priest can deal gently with those who are ignorant and going astray, because he himself is also surrounded with weakness. 3 Because of this, he must offer sacrifices for sins for the people, as well as for himself. 4 Nobody takes this honour on himself, but he is called by God, just like Aaron was. 5 So also Christ didn't glorify himself to be made a high priest, but it was he who said to him,

"You are my Son.
Today I have become your father."*

6 As he says also in another place,

"You are a priest forever,
after the order of Melchizedek."*

7 He, in the days of his flesh, having offered up prayers and petitions with strong crying and tears to him who was able to save him from death, and having been heard for his godly fear, 8 though he was a Son, yet learnt obedience by the things which he suffered. 9 Having been made perfect, he became to all of those who obey him the author of eternal salvation, 10 named by God a high priest after the order of Melchizedek.

11 About him we have many words to say, and hard to interpret, seeing you have become dull of hearing. 12 For although by this time you should be teachers, you again need to have someone teach you the rudiments of the first principles of the revelations of God. You have come to need milk, and not solid food. 13 For everyone who lives on milk is not experienced in the word of righteousness, for he is a baby. 14 But solid food is for those who are full grown, who by reason of use have their senses exercised to discern good and evil.

6

1 Therefore leaving the teaching of the first principles of Christ, let's press on to perfection—not laying again a foundation of repentance from dead works, of faith towards God, 2 of the teaching of baptisms, of laying on of hands, of resurrection of the dead, and of eternal judgement. 3 This will we do, if God permits. 4 For concerning those who were once enlightened and tasted of the heavenly gift, and were made partakers of the Holy Spirit, 5 and tasted the good word of God and the powers of the age to come, 6 and then fell away, it is impossible to renew them again to repentance; seeing they crucify the Son of God for themselves again, and put him to open shame. 7 For the land which has drunk the rain that comes often on it and produces a crop suitable for them for whose sake it is also tilled, receives blessing from God; 8 but if it bears thorns and thistles, it is rejected and near being cursed, whose end is to be burnt.

9 But, beloved, we are persuaded of better things for you, and things that accompany salvation, even though we speak like this. 10 For God is not unrighteous, so as to forget your work and the labour of love which you showed towards his name, in that you served the saints, and still do serve them. 11 We desire that each one of you may show the same diligence to the fullness of hope even to the end, 12 that you won't be sluggish, but imitators of those who through faith and perseverance inherited the promises.

13 For when God made a promise to Abraham, since he could swear by no one greater, he swore by himself, 14 saying, "Surely blessing I will bless you, and multiplying I will multiply you."* 15 Thus, having patiently endured, he obtained the promise. 16 For men indeed swear by a greater one, and in every dispute of theirs the oath is final for confirmation. 17 In this way God, being determined to show more abundantly to the heirs of the promise the immutability of his counsel, interposed with an oath, 18 that by two immutable things, in which it is impossible for God to lie, we may have a strong encouragement, who have fled for refuge to take hold of the hope set before us. 19 This hope we have as an anchor of the soul, a hope both sure and steadfast and entering into that which is within the veil, 20 where as a forerunner Jesus entered for us, having become a high priest forever after the order of Melchizedek.

7

1 For this Melchizedek, king of Salem, priest of God Most High, who met Abraham returning from the slaughter of the kings and blessed him, 2 to whom also Abraham divided a tenth part of all (being first, by interpretation, "king of righteousness", and then also "king of Salem", which means "king of peace", 3 without father, without mother, without genealogy, having neither beginning of days nor end of life, but made like the Son of God), remains a priest continually.

4 Now consider how great this man was, to whom even Abraham the patriarch gave a tenth out of the best plunder. 5 They indeed of the sons of Levi who receive the priest's office have a commandment to take tithes from the people according to the law, that is, of their brothers, though these have come out of the body of Abraham, 6 but he whose genealogy is not counted from them has accepted tithes from Abraham, and has blessed him who has the promises. 7 But without any dispute the lesser is blessed by the greater. 8 Here people who die receive tithes, but there one receives tithes of whom it is testified that he lives. 9 We can say that through

Abraham even Levi, who receives tithes, has paid tithes, 10 for he was yet in the body of his father when Melchizedek met him.

11 Now if perfection was through the Levitical priesthood (for under it the people have received the law), what further need was there for another priest to arise after the order of Melchizedek, and not be called after the order of Aaron? 12 For the priesthood being changed, there is of necessity a change made also in the law. 13 For he of whom these things are said belongs to another tribe, from which no one has officiated at the altar. 14 For it is evident that our Lord has sprung out of Judah, about which tribe Moses spoke nothing concerning priesthood. 15 This is yet more abundantly evident, if after the likeness of Melchizedek there arises another priest, 16 who has been made, not after the law of a fleshly commandment, but after the power of an endless life; 17 for it is testified,

"You are a priest forever,
according to the order of Melchizedek."*

18 For there is an annulling of a foregoing commandment because of its weakness and uselessness 19 (for the law made nothing perfect), and a bringing in of a better hope, through which we draw near to God. 20 Inasmuch as he was not made priest without the taking of an oath 21 (for they indeed have been made priests without an oath), but he with an oath by him that says of him,

"The Lord swore and will not change his mind,
'You are a priest forever,
according to the order of Melchizedek.'"*

22 By so much, Jesus has become the guarantee of a better covenant. 23 Many, indeed, have been made priests, because they are hindered from continuing by death. 24 But he, because he lives forever, has his priesthood unchangeable. 25 Therefore he is also able to save to the uttermost those who draw near to God through him, seeing that he lives forever to make intercession for them.

26 For such a high priest was fitting for us: holy, guiltless, undefiled, separated from sinners, and made higher than the heavens; 27 who doesn't need, like those high priests, to offer up sacrifices daily, first for his own sins, and then for the sins of the people. For he did this once for all, when he offered up himself. 28 For the law appoints men as high priests who have weakness, but the word of the oath, which came after the law, appoints a Son forever who has been perfected.

8

1 Now in the things which we are saying, the main point is this: we have such a high priest, who sat down on the right hand of the throne of the Majesty in the heavens, 2 a servant of the sanctuary and of the true tabernacle which the Lord pitched, not man. 3 For every high priest is appointed to offer both gifts and sacrifices. Therefore it is necessary that this high priest also have something to offer. 4 For if he were on earth, he would not be a priest at all, seeing there are priests who offer the gifts according to the law, 5 who serve a copy and shadow of the heavenly things, even as Moses was warned by God when he was about to make the tabernacle, for he said, "See, you shall make everything according to the pattern that was shown to you on the mountain."* 6 But now he has obtained a more excellent ministry, by as much as he is also the mediator of a better covenant, which on better promises has been given as law.

7 For if that first covenant had been faultless, then no place would have been sought for a second. 8 For finding fault with them, he said, "Behold,[a] the days are coming," says the Lord,

"that I will make a new covenant with the house of Israel and with the
house of Judah;

9 not according to the covenant that I made with their fathers
in the day that I took them by the hand to lead them out of the land of
Egypt;
for they didn't continue in my covenant,
and I disregarded them," says the Lord.

10 "For this is the covenant that I will make with the house of Israel
after those days," says the Lord;
"I will put my laws into their mind;
I will also write them on their heart.
I will be their God,
and they will be my people.

11 They will not teach every man his fellow citizen[b]
and every man his brother, saying, 'Know the Lord,'
for all will know me,
from their least to their greatest.

12 For I will be merciful to their unrighteousness.
I will remember their sins and lawless deeds no more."*

13 In that he says, "A new covenant", he has made the first obsolete. But that which is becoming obsolete and grows aged is near to vanishing away.

9

1 Now indeed even the first[c] covenant had ordinances of divine service and an earthly sanctuary. 2 For a tabernacle was prepared. In the first part were the lamp stand, the table, and the show bread, which is called the Holy Place. 3 After the second veil was the tabernacle which is

---

** 5:5 Psalms 2:7
** 5:6 Psalms 110:4
** 6:14 Genesis 22:17
** 7:17 Psalms 110:4
** 7:21 Psalms 110:4
** 8:5 Exodus 25:40

a 8:8 "Behold", from "ἰδοὺ", means look at, take notice, observe, see, or gaze at. It is often used as an interjection.
b 8:11 TR reads "neighbour" instead of "fellow citizen"
** 8:12 Jeremiah 31:31-34
c 9:1 TR adds "tabernacle"

called the Holy of Holies, 4 having a golden altar of incense and the ark of the covenant overlaid on all sides with gold, in which was a golden pot holding the manna, Aaron's rod that budded, and the tablets of the covenant; 5 and above it cherubim of glory overshadowing the mercy seat, of which things we can't speak now in detail.

6 Now these things having been thus prepared, the priests go in continually into the first tabernacle, accomplishing the services, 7 but into the second the high priest alone, once in the year, not without blood, which he offers for himself and for the errors of the people. 8 The Holy Spirit is indicating this, that the way into the Holy Place wasn't yet revealed while the first tabernacle was still standing. 9 This is a symbol of the present age, where gifts and sacrifices are offered that are incapable, concerning the conscience, of making the worshipper perfect, 10 being only (with foods and drinks and various washings) fleshly ordinances, imposed until a time of reformation.

11 But Christ having come as a high priest of the coming good things, through the greater and more perfect tabernacle, not made with hands, that is to say, not of this creation, 12 nor yet through the blood of goats and calves, but through his own blood, entered in once for all into the Holy Place, having obtained eternal redemption. 13 For if the blood of goats and bulls, and the ashes of a heifer sprinkling those who have been defiled, sanctify to the cleanness of the flesh, 14 how much more will the blood of Christ, who through the eternal Spirit offered himself without defect to God, cleanse your conscience from dead works to serve the living God? 15 For this reason he is the mediator of a new covenant, since a death has occurred for the redemption of the transgressions that were under the first covenant, that those who have been called may receive the promise of the eternal inheritance. 16 For where a last will and testament is, there must of necessity be the death of him who made it. 17 For a will is in force where there has been death, for it is never in force while he who made it lives. 18 Therefore even the first covenant has not been dedicated without blood. 19 For when every commandment had been spoken by Moses to all the people according to the law, he took the blood of the calves and the goats, with water and scarlet wool and hyssop, and sprinkled both the book itself and all the people, 20 saying, "This is the blood of the covenant which God has commanded you."*

21 He sprinkled the tabernacle and all the vessels of the ministry in the same way with the blood. 22 According to the law, nearly everything is cleansed with blood, and apart from shedding of blood there is no remission.

23 It was necessary therefore that the copies of the things in the heavens should be cleansed with these, but the heavenly things themselves with better sacrifices than these. 24 For Christ hasn't entered into holy places made with hands, which are representations of the true, but into heaven itself, now to appear in the presence of God for us; 25 nor yet that he should offer himself often, as the high priest enters into the holy place year by year with blood not his own, 26 or else he must have suffered often since the foundation of the world. But now once at the end of the ages, he has been revealed to put away sin by the sacrifice of himself. 27 Inasmuch as it is appointed for men to die once, and after this, judgement, 28 so Christ also, having been offered once to bear the sins of many, will appear a second time, not to deal with sin, but to save those who are eagerly waiting for him.

10

1 For the law, having a shadow of the good to come, not the very image of the things, can never with the same sacrifices year by year, which they offer continually, make perfect those who draw near. 2 Or else wouldn't they have ceased to be offered, because the worshippers, having been once cleansed, would have had no more consciousness of sins? 3 But in those sacrifices there is a yearly reminder of sins. 4 For it is impossible that the blood of bulls and goats should take away sins. 5 Therefore when he comes into the world, he says,
"You didn't desire sacrifice and offering,
but you prepared a body for me.
6 You had no pleasure in whole burnt offerings and sacrifices for sin.
7 Then I said, 'Behold, I have come (in the scroll of the book it is
written of me)
to do your will, O God.'"*
8 Previously saying, "Sacrifices and offerings and whole burnt offerings and sacrifices for sin you didn't desire, neither had pleasure in them" (those which are offered according to the law), 9 then he has said, "Behold, I have come to do your will." He takes away the first, that he may establish the second, 10 by which will we have been sanctified through the offering of the body of Jesus Christ once for all.

11 Every priest indeed stands day by day serving and offering often the same sacrifices, which can never take away sins, 12 but he, when he had offered one sacrifice for sins forever, sat down on the right hand of God, 13 from that time waiting until his enemies are made the footstool of his feet. 14 For by one offering he has perfected forever those who are being sanctified. 15 The Holy Spirit also testifies to us, for after saying,
16 "This is the covenant that I will make with them
after those days," says the Lord,

"I will put my laws on their heart,
I will also write them on their mind;"*
then he says,
17 "I will remember their sins and their iniquities no more."*
18 Now where remission of these is, there is no more offering for sin.

19 Having therefore, brothers, boldness to enter into the holy place by the blood of Jesus, 20 by the way which he dedicated for us, a new and living way, through the veil, that is to say, his flesh, 21 and having a great priest over God's house, 22 let's draw near with a true heart in fullness of faith, having our hearts sprinkled from an evil conscience and having our body washed with pure water, 23 let's hold fast the confession of our hope without wavering; for he who promised is faithful.

24 Let's consider how to provoke one another to love and good works, 25 not forsaking our own assembling together, as the custom of some is, but exhorting one another, and so much the more as you see the Day approaching.

26 For if we sin wilfully after we have received the knowledge of the truth, there remains no more a sacrifice for sins, 27 but a certain fearful expectation of judgement, and a fierceness of fire which will devour the adversaries. 28 A man who disregards Moses' law dies without compassion on the word of two or three witnesses. 29 How much worse punishment do you think he will be judged worthy of who has trodden under foot the Son of God, and has counted the blood of the covenant with which he was sanctified an unholy thing, and has insulted the Spirit of grace? 30 For we know him who said, "Vengeance belongs to me. I will repay," says the Lord.* Again, "The Lord will judge his people."* 31 It is a fearful thing to fall into the hands of the living God.

32 But remember the former days, in which, after you were enlightened, you endured a great struggle with sufferings: 33 partly, being exposed to both reproaches and oppressions, and partly, becoming partakers with those who were treated so. 34 For you both had compassion on me in my chains and joyfully accepted the plundering of your possessions, knowing that you have for yourselves a better possession and an enduring one in the heavens. 35 Therefore don't throw away your boldness, which has a great reward. 36 For you need endurance so that, having done the will of God, you may receive the promise.
37 "In a very little while,
he who comes will come and will not wait.
38 But the righteous one will live by faith.
If he shrinks back, my soul has no pleasure in him."*
39 But we are not of those who shrink back to destruction, but of those who have faith to the saving of the soul.

11

1 Now faith is assurance of things hoped for, proof of things not seen. 2 For by this, the elders obtained approval. 3 By faith we understand that the universe has been framed by the word of God, so that what is seen has not been made out of things which are visible.

4 By faith Abel offered to God a more excellent sacrifice than Cain, through which he had testimony given to him that he was righteous, God testifying with respect to his gifts; and through it he, being dead, still speaks.

5 By faith Enoch was taken away, so that he wouldn't see death, and he was not found, because God translated him. For he has had testimony given to him that before his translation he had been well pleasing to God. 6 Without faith it is impossible to be well pleasing to him, for he who comes to God must believe that he exists, and that he is a rewarder of those who seek him.

7 By faith Noah, being warned about things not yet seen, moved with godly fear,[a] prepared a ship for the saving of his house, through which he condemned the world and became heir of the righteousness which is according to faith.

8 By faith Abraham, when he was called, obeyed to go out to the place which he was to receive for an inheritance. He went out, not knowing where he went. 9 By faith he lived as an alien in the land of promise, as in a land not his own, dwelling in tents with Isaac and Jacob, the heirs with him of the same promise. 10 For he was looking for the city which has foundations, whose builder and maker is God.

11 By faith even Sarah herself received power to conceive, and she bore a child when she was past age, since she counted him faithful who had promised. 12 Therefore as many as the stars of the sky in multitude, and as innumerable as the sand which is by the sea shore, were fathered by one man, and him as good as dead.

13 These all died in faith, not having received the promises, but having seen[b] them and embraced them from afar, and having confessed that they were strangers and pilgrims on the earth. 14 For those who say such things make it clear that they are seeking a country of their own. 15 If indeed they had been thinking of that country from which they went out, they would have had enough time to return. 16 But now they desire a better country, that is, a heavenly one. Therefore God is not ashamed of them, to be called their God, for he has prepared a city for them.

** 9:20 Exodus 24:8
** 10:7 Psalms 40:6-8
** 10:16 Jeremiah 31:33
** 10:17 Jeremiah 31:34
** 10:30 Deuteronomy 32:35

** 10:30 Deuteronomy 32:36; Psalms 135:14
** 10:38 Habakkuk 2:3-4
a 11:7 or, reverence
b 11:13 TR adds "and being convinced of"

17 By faith, Abraham, being tested, offered up Isaac. Yes, he who had gladly received the promises was offering up his only born[a] son, 18 to whom it was said, "Your offspring will be accounted as from Isaac," * 19 concluding that God is able to raise up even from the dead. Figuratively speaking, he also did receive him back from the dead.

20 By faith Isaac blessed Jacob and Esau, even concerning things to come.

21 By faith Jacob, when he was dying, blessed each of the sons of Joseph, and worshipped, leaning on the top of his staff.

22 By faith Joseph, when his end was near, made mention of the departure of the children of Israel, and gave instructions concerning his bones.

23 By faith Moses, when he was born, was hidden for three months by his parents, because they saw that he was a beautiful child; and they were not afraid of the king's commandment.

24 By faith Moses, when he had grown up, refused to be called the son of Pharaoh's daughter, 25 choosing rather to share ill treatment with God's people than to enjoy the pleasures of sin for a time, 26 considering the reproach of Christ greater riches than the treasures of Egypt; for he looked to the reward. 27 By faith he left Egypt, not fearing the wrath of the king; for he endured, as seeing him who is invisible. 28 By faith he kept the Passover and the sprinkling of the blood, that the destroyer of the firstborn should not touch them.

29 By faith they passed through the Red Sea as on dry land. When the Egyptians tried to do so, they were swallowed up.

30 By faith the walls of Jericho fell down after they had been encircled for seven days.

31 By faith Rahab the prostitute didn't perish with those who were disobedient, having received the spies in peace.

32 What more shall I say? For the time would fail me if I told of Gideon, Barak, Samson, Jephthah, David, Samuel, and the prophets— 33 who through faith subdued kingdoms, worked out righteousness, obtained promises, stopped the mouths of lions,* 34 quenched the power of fire,* escaped the edge of the sword,* from weakness were made strong, grew mighty in war, and caused foreign armies to flee. 35 Women received their dead by resurrection.* Others were tortured, not accepting their deliverance, that they might obtain a better resurrection. 36 Others were tried by mocking and scourging, yes, moreover by bonds and imprisonment. 37 They were stoned.* They were sawn apart. They were tempted. They were slain with the sword.* They went around in sheep skins and in goat skins; being destitute, afflicted, ill-treated— 38 of whom the world was not worthy—wandering in deserts, mountains, caves, and the holes of the earth.

39 These all, having been commended for their faith, didn't receive the promise, 40 God having provided some better thing concerning us, so that apart from us they should not be made perfect.

12

1 Therefore let's also, seeing we are surrounded by so great a cloud of witnesses, lay aside every weight and the sin which so easily entangles us, and let's run with perseverance the race that is set before us, 2 looking to Jesus, the author and perfecter of faith, who for the joy that was set before him endured the cross, despising its shame, and has sat down at the right hand of the throne of God.

3 For consider him who has endured such contradiction of sinners against himself, that you don't grow weary, fainting in your souls. 4 You have not yet resisted to blood, striving against sin. 5 You have forgotten the exhortation which reasons with you as with children,
"My son, don't take lightly the chastening of the Lord,
nor faint when you are reproved by him;
6 for whom the Lord loves, he disciplines,
and chastises every son whom he receives."*
7 It is for discipline that you endure. God deals with you as with children, for what son is there whom his father doesn't discipline? 8 But if you are without discipline, of which all have been made partakers, then you are illegitimate, and not children. 9 Furthermore, we had the fathers of our flesh to chasten us, and we paid them respect. Shall we not much rather be in subjection to the Father of spirits and live? 10 For they indeed for a few days disciplined us as seemed good to them, but he for our profit, that we may be partakers of his holiness. 11 All chastening seems for the present to be not joyous but grievous; yet afterward it yields the peaceful fruit of righteousness to those who have been trained by it. 12 Therefore lift up the hands that hang down and the feeble knees, * 13 and make straight paths for your feet,* so what is lame may not be dislocated, but rather be healed.

14 Follow after peace with all men, and the sanctification without which no man will see the Lord, 15 looking carefully lest there be any man who falls short of the grace of God, lest any root of bitterness springing up

trouble you and many be defiled by it, 16 lest there be any sexually immoral person or profane person, like Esau, who sold his birthright for one meal. 17 For you know that even when he afterward desired to inherit the blessing, he was rejected, for he found no place for a change of mind though he sought it diligently with tears.

18 For you have not come to a mountain that might be touched and that burnt with fire, and to blackness, darkness, storm, 19 the sound of a trumpet, and the voice of words; which those who heard it begged that not one more word should be spoken to them, 20 for they could not stand that which was commanded, "If even an animal touches the mountain, it shall be stoned".[b]* 21 So fearful was the appearance that Moses said, "I am terrified and trembling."*

22 But you have come to Mount Zion and to the city of the living God, the heavenly Jerusalem, and to innumerable multitudes of angels, 23 to the festal gathering and assembly of the firstborn who are enrolled in heaven, to God the Judge of all, to the spirits of just men made perfect, 24 to Jesus, the mediator of a new covenant,* and to the blood of sprinkling that speaks better than that of Abel.

25 See that you don't refuse him who speaks. For if they didn't escape when they refused him who warned on the earth, how much more will we not escape who turn away from him who warns from heaven, 26 whose voice shook the earth then, but now he has promised, saying, "Yet once more I will shake not only the earth, but also the heavens."* 27 This phrase, "Yet once more" signifies the removing of those things that are shaken, as of things that have been made, that those things which are not shaken may remain. 28 Therefore, receiving a Kingdom that can't be shaken, let's have grace, through which we serve God acceptably, with reverence and awe, 29 for our God is a consuming fire.*

13

1 Let brotherly love continue. 2 Don't forget to show hospitality to strangers, for in doing so, some have entertained angels without knowing it. 3 Remember those who are in bonds, as bound with them, and those who are ill-treated, since you are also in the body. 4 Let marriage be held in honour amongst all, and let the bed be undefiled; but God will judge the sexually immoral and adulterers.

5 Be free from the love of money, content with such things as you have, for he has said, "I will in no way leave you, neither will I in any way forsake you."* 6 So that with good courage we say,
"The Lord is my helper. I will not fear.
What can man do to me?"*
7 Remember your leaders, men who spoke to you the word of God, and considering the results of their conduct, imitate their faith. 8 Jesus Christ is the same yesterday, today, and forever. 9 Don't be carried away by various and strange teachings, for it is good that the heart be established by grace, not by foods, through which those who were so occupied were not benefitted.

10 We have an altar from which those who serve the holy tabernacle have no right to eat. 11 For the bodies of those animals, whose blood is brought into the holy place by the high priest as an offering for sin, are burnt outside of the camp.* 12 Therefore Jesus also, that he might sanctify the people through his own blood, suffered outside of the gate. 13 Let's therefore go out to him outside of the camp, bearing his reproach. 14 For we don't have here an enduring city, but we seek that which is to come. 15 Through him, then, let's offer up a sacrifice of praise to God * continually, that is, the fruit of lips which proclaim allegiance to his name. 16 But don't forget to be doing good and sharing, for with such sacrifices God is well pleased.

17 Obey your leaders and submit to them, for they watch on behalf of your souls, as those who will give account, that they may do this with joy and not with groaning, for that would be unprofitable for you.

18 Pray for us, for we are persuaded that we have a good conscience, desiring to live honourably in all things. 19 I strongly urge you to do this, that I may be restored to you sooner.

20 Now may the God of peace, who brought again from the dead the great shepherd of the sheep with the blood of an eternal covenant, our Lord Jesus, 21 make you complete in every good work to do his will, working in you that which is well pleasing in his sight, through Jesus Christ, to whom be the glory forever and ever. Amen.

22 But I exhort you, brothers, endure the word of exhortation, for I have written to you in few words. 23 Know that our brother Timothy has been freed, with whom, if he comes shortly, I will see you.

24 Greet all of your leaders and all the saints. The Italians greet you.

25 Grace be with you all. Amen.

a *11:17* The phrase "only born" is from the Greek word "μονογενη", which is sometimes translated "only begotten" or "one and only".
** 11:18 Genesis 21:12
** 11:33 Daniel 6:22-23
** 11:34 Daniel 3:1-30
** 11:34 1 Kings 19:1-3; 2 Kings 6:31—7:20
** 11:35 1 Kings 17:17-23; 2 Kings 4:32-37
** 11:37 2 Chronicles 24:20-21
** 11:37 Jeremiah 26:20-23; 1 Kings 19:10
** 12:6 Proverbs 3:11-12
** 12:12 Isaiah 35:3

** 12:13 Proverbs 4:26
b *12:20* TR adds "or shot with an arrow"
** 12:20 Exodus 19:12-13
** 12:21 Deuteronomy 9:19
** 12:24 Jeremiah 31:31
** 12:26 Haggai 2:6
** 12:29 Deuteronomy 4:24
** 13:5 Deuteronomy 31:6
** 13:6 Psalms 118:6-7
** 13:11 Leviticus 16:27
** 13:15 Psalms 50:23

The Letter from James

1

1 James, a servant of God and of the Lord Jesus Christ,[a] to the twelve tribes which are in the Dispersion: Greetings.

2 Count it all joy, my brothers,[b] when you fall into various temptations, 3 knowing that the testing of your faith produces endurance. 4 Let endurance have its perfect work, that you may be perfect and complete, lacking in nothing.

5 But if any of you lacks wisdom, let him ask of God, who gives to all liberally and without reproach, and it will be given to him. 6 But let him ask in faith, without any doubting, for he who doubts is like a wave of the sea, driven by the wind and tossed. 7 For that man shouldn't think that he will receive anything from the Lord. 8 He is a double-minded man, unstable in all his ways.

9 Let the brother in humble circumstances glory in his high position; 10 and the rich, in that he is made humble, because like the flower in the grass, he will pass away. 11 For the sun arises with the scorching wind and withers the grass; and the flower in it falls, and the beauty of its appearance perishes. So the rich man will also fade away in his pursuits.

12 Blessed is a person who endures temptation, for when he has been approved, he will receive the crown of life which the Lord promised to those who love him.

13 Let no man say when he is tempted, "I am tempted by God," for God can't be tempted by evil, and he himself tempts no one. 14 But each one is tempted when he is drawn away by his own lust and enticed. 15 Then the lust, when it has conceived, bears sin. The sin, when it is full grown, produces death. 16 Don't be deceived, my beloved brothers. 17 Every good gift and every perfect gift is from above, coming down from the Father of lights, with whom can be no variation nor turning shadow. 18 Of his own will he gave birth to us by the word of truth, that we should be a kind of first fruits of his creatures.

19 So, then, my beloved brothers, let every man be swift to hear, slow to speak, and slow to anger; 20 for the anger of man doesn't produce the righteousness of God. 21 Therefore, putting away all filthiness and overflowing of wickedness, receive with humility the implanted word, which is able to save your souls.[c]

22 But be doers of the word, and not only hearers, deluding your own selves. 23 For if anyone is a hearer of the word and not a doer, he is like a man looking at his natural face in a mirror; 24 for he sees himself, and goes away, and immediately forgets what kind of man he was. 25 But he who looks into the perfect law of freedom and continues, not being a hearer who forgets but a doer of the work, this man will be blessed in what he does.

26 If anyone amongst you thinks himself to be religious while he doesn't bridle his tongue, but deceives his heart, this man's religion is worthless. 27 Pure religion and undefiled before our God and Father is this: to visit the fatherless and widows in their affliction, and to keep oneself unstained by the world.

2

1 My brothers, don't hold the faith of our glorious Lord Jesus Christ with partiality. 2 For if a man with a gold ring, in fine clothing, comes into your synagogue,[d] and a poor man in filthy clothing also comes in, 3 and you pay special attention to him who wears the fine clothing and say, "Sit here in a good place;" and you tell the poor man, "Stand there," or "Sit by my footstool" 4 haven't you shown partiality amongst yourselves, and become judges with evil thoughts? 5 Listen, my beloved brothers. Didn't God choose those who are poor in this world to be rich in faith and heirs of the Kingdom which he promised to those who love him? 6 But you have dishonoured the poor man. Don't the rich oppress you and personally drag you before the courts? 7 Don't they blaspheme the honourable name by which you are called?

8 However, if you fulfil the royal law according to the Scripture, "You shall love your neighbour as yourself,"[**] you do well. 9 But if you show partiality, you commit sin, being convicted by the law as transgressors. 10 For whoever keeps the whole law, and yet stumbles in one point, he has become guilty of all. 11 For he who said, "Do not commit adultery,"[**] also said, "Do not commit murder."[**] Now if you do not commit adultery but do murder, you have become a transgressor of the law. 12 So speak and so do as men who are to be judged by the law of freedom. 13 For judgement is without mercy to him who has shown no mercy. Mercy triumphs over judgement.

14 What good is it, my brothers, if a man says he has faith, but has no works? Can faith save him? 15 And if a brother or sister is naked and in lack of daily food, 16 and one of you tells them, "Go in peace. Be warmed and filled;" yet you didn't give them the things the body needs, what good is it? 17 Even so faith, if it has no works, is dead in itself. 18 Yes, a man will say, "You have faith, and I have works." Show me your faith without works, and I will show you my faith by my works.

19 You believe that God is one. You do well. The demons also believe—and shudder. 20 But do you want to know, vain man, that faith apart from works is dead? 21 Wasn't Abraham our father justified by works, in that he offered up Isaac his son on the altar? 22 You see that faith worked with his works, and by works faith was perfected. 23 So the Scripture was fulfilled which says, "Abraham believed God, and it was accounted to him as righteousness,"[**] and he was called the friend of God. 24 You see then that by works a man is justified, and not only by faith. 25 In the same way, wasn't Rahab the prostitute also justified by works when she received the messengers and sent them out another way? 26 For as the body apart from the spirit is dead, even so faith apart from works is dead.

3

1 Let not many of you be teachers, my brothers, knowing that we will receive heavier judgement. 2 For we all stumble in many things. Anyone who doesn't stumble in word is a perfect person, able to bridle the whole body also. 3 Indeed, we put bits into the horses' mouths so that they may obey us, and we guide their whole body. 4 Behold,[e] the ships also, though they are so big and are driven by fierce winds, are yet guided by a very small rudder, wherever the pilot desires. 5 So the tongue is also a little member, and boasts great things. See how a small fire can spread to a large forest! 6 And the tongue is a fire. The world of iniquity amongst our members is the tongue, which defiles the whole body, and sets on fire the course of nature, and is set on fire by Gehenna.[f] 7 For every kind of animal, bird, creeping thing, and sea creature is tamed, and has been tamed by mankind; 8 but nobody can tame the tongue. It is a restless evil, full of deadly poison. 9 With it we bless our God and Father, and with it we curse men who are made in the image of God. 10 Out of the same mouth comes blessing and cursing. My brothers, these things ought not to be so. 11 Does a spring send out from the same opening fresh and bitter water? 12 Can a fig tree, my brothers, yield olives, or a vine figs? Thus no spring yields both salt water and fresh water.

13 Who is wise and understanding amongst you? Let him show by his good conduct that his deeds are done in gentleness of wisdom. 14 But if you have bitter jealousy and selfish ambition in your heart, don't boast and don't lie against the truth. 15 This wisdom is not that which comes down from above, but is earthly, sensual, and demonic. 16 For where jealousy and selfish ambition are, there is confusion and every evil deed. 17 But the wisdom that is from above is first pure, then peaceful, gentle, reasonable, full of mercy and good fruits, without partiality, and without hypocrisy. 18 Now the fruit of righteousness is sown in peace by those who make peace.

4

1 Where do wars and fightings amongst you come from? Don't they come from your pleasures that war in your members? 2 You lust, and don't have. You murder and covet, and can't obtain. You fight and make war. You don't have, because you don't ask. 3 You ask, and don't receive, because you ask with wrong motives, so that you may spend it on your pleasures. 4 You adulterers and adulteresses, don't you know that friendship with the world is hostility towards God? Whoever therefore wants to be a friend of the world makes himself an enemy of God. 5 Or do you think that the Scripture says in vain, "The Spirit who lives in us yearns jealously"? 6 But he gives more grace. Therefore it says, "God resists the proud, but gives grace to the humble."[**] 7 Be subject therefore to God. Resist the devil, and he will flee from you. 8 Draw near to God, and he will draw near to you. Cleanse your hands, you sinners. Purify your hearts, you double-minded. 9 Lament, mourn, and weep. Let your laughter be turned to mourning and your joy to gloom. 10 Humble yourselves in the sight of the Lord, and he will exalt you.

11 Don't speak against one another, brothers. He who speaks against a brother and judges his brother, speaks against the law and judges the law. But if you judge the law, you are not a doer of the law but a judge. 12 Only one is the lawgiver, who is able to save and to destroy. But who are you to judge another?

13 Come now, you who say, "Today or tomorrow let's go into this city and spend a year there, trade, and make a profit." 14 Yet you don't know what your life will be like tomorrow. For what is your life? For you are a vapour that appears for a little time and then vanishes away. 15 For you ought to say, "If the Lord wills, we will both live, and do this or that." 16 But now you glory in your boasting. All such boasting is evil. 17 To him therefore who knows to do good and doesn't do it, to him it is sin.

5

1 Come now, you rich, weep and howl for your miseries that are coming on you. 2 Your riches are corrupted and your garments are moth-eaten. 3 Your gold and your silver are corroded, and their corrosion will be for a testimony against you and will eat your flesh like fire. You have laid up your treasure in the last days. 4 Behold, the wages of the labourers who mowed your fields, which you have kept back by fraud, cry out; and the cries of those who reaped have entered into the ears of the Lord of Armies.[g] 5 You have lived in luxury on the earth, and taken your pleasure. You have

---

a *1:1* "Christ" means "Anointed One".
b *1:2* The word for "brothers" here and where context allows may also be correctly translated "brothers and sisters" or "siblings."
c *1:21* or, preserve your life.
d *2:2* or, meeting
** 2:8 Leviticus 19:18
** 2:11 Exodus 20:14; Deuteronomy 5:18

** 2:11 Exodus 20:13; Deuteronomy 5:17
** 2:23 Genesis 15:6
e *3:4* "Behold", from "ἰδού", means look at, take notice, observe, see, or gaze at. It is often used as an interjection.
f *3:6* or, Hell
** 4:6 Proverbs 3:34
g *5:4* Greek: Sabaoth (or Hebrew: Tze'va'ot)

nourished your hearts as in a day of slaughter. 6 You have condemned and you have murdered the righteous one. He doesn't resist you.

7 Be patient therefore, brothers, until the coming of the Lord. Behold, the farmer waits for the precious fruit of the earth, being patient over it, until it receives the early and late rain. 8 You also be patient. Establish your hearts, for the coming of the Lord is at hand.

9 Don't grumble, brothers, against one another, so that you won't be judged. Behold, the judge stands at the door. 10 Take, brothers, for an example of suffering and of perseverance, the prophets who spoke in the name of the Lord. 11 Behold, we call them blessed who endured. You have heard of the perseverance of Job and have seen the Lord in the outcome, and how the Lord is full of compassion and mercy.

12 But above all things, my brothers, don't swear— not by heaven, or by the earth, or by any other oath; but let your "yes" be "yes", and your "no", "no", so that you don't fall into hypocrisy.[a]

13 Is any amongst you suffering? Let him pray. Is any cheerful? Let him sing praises. 14 Is any amongst you sick? Let him call for the elders of the assembly, and let them pray over him, anointing him with oil in the name of the Lord; 15 and the prayer of faith will heal him who is sick, and the Lord will raise him up. If he has committed sins, he will be forgiven. 16 Confess your sins to one another and pray for one another, that you may be healed. The insistent prayer of a righteous person is powerfully effective. 17 Elijah was a man with a nature like ours, and he prayed earnestly that it might not rain, and it didn't rain on the earth for three years and six months. 18 He prayed again, and the sky gave rain, and the earth produced its fruit.

19 Brothers, if any amongst you wanders from the truth and someone turns him back, 20 let him know that he who turns a sinner from the error of his way will save a soul from death and will cover a multitude of sins.

---

a *5:12* TR reads "under judgement" instead of "into hypocrisy"

Peter's First Letter

1

₁ Peter, an apostle of Jesus Christ,[a] to the chosen ones who are living as foreigners in the Dispersion in Pontus, Galatia, Cappadocia, Asia, and Bithynia, ₂ according to the foreknowledge of God the Father, in sanctification of the Spirit, that you may obey Jesus Christ and be sprinkled with his blood: Grace to you and peace be multiplied.

₃ Blessed be the God and Father of our Lord Jesus Christ, who according to his great mercy caused us to be born again to a living hope through the resurrection of Jesus Christ from the dead, ₄ to an incorruptible and undefiled inheritance that doesn't fade away, reserved in Heaven for you, ₅ who by the power of God are guarded through faith for a salvation ready to be revealed in the last time. ₆ In this you greatly rejoice, though now for a little while, if need be, you have been grieved in various trials, ₇ that the proof of your faith, which is more precious than gold that perishes, even though it is tested by fire, may be found to result in praise, glory, and honour at the revelation of Jesus Christ— ₈ whom, not having known, you love. In him, though now you don't see him, yet believing, you rejoice greatly with joy that is unspeakable and full of glory, ₉ receiving the result of your faith, the salvation of your souls.

₁₀ Concerning this salvation, the prophets sought and searched diligently. They prophesied of the grace that would come to you, ₁₁ searching for who or what kind of time the Spirit of Christ which was in them pointed to when he predicted the sufferings of Christ and the glories that would follow them. ₁₂ To them it was revealed that they served not themselves, but you, in these things, which now have been announced to you through those who preached the Good News to you by the Holy Spirit sent out from heaven; which things angels desire to look into.

₁₃ Therefore prepare your minds for action.[b] Be sober, and set your hope fully on the grace that will be brought to you at the revelation of Jesus Christ— ₁₄ as children of obedience, not conforming yourselves according to your former lusts as in your ignorance, ₁₅ but just as he who called you is holy, you yourselves also be holy in all of your behaviour, ₁₆ because it is written, "You shall be holy, for I am holy."[*]

₁₇ If you call on him as Father, who without respect of persons judges according to each man's work, pass the time of your living as foreigners here in reverent fear, ₁₈ knowing that you were redeemed, not with corruptible things like silver or gold, from the useless way of life handed down from your fathers, ₁₉ but with precious blood, as of a lamb without blemish or spot, the blood of Christ, ₂₀ who was foreknown indeed before the foundation of the world, but was revealed in this last age for your sake, ₂₁ who through him are believers in God, who raised him from the dead and gave him glory, so that your faith and hope might be in God.

₂₂ Seeing you have purified your souls in your obedience to the truth through the Spirit in sincere brotherly affection, love one another from the heart fervently, ₂₃ having been born again, not of corruptible seed, but of incorruptible, through the word of God, which lives and remains forever. ₂₄ For,

"All flesh is like grass,
    and all of man's glory like the flower in the grass.
The grass withers, and its flower falls;
₂₅ but the Lord's word endures forever."[*]
This is the word of Good News which was preached to you.

2

₁ Putting away therefore all wickedness, all deceit, hypocrisies, envies, and all evil speaking, ₂ as newborn babies, long for the pure spiritual milk, that with it you may grow, ₃ if indeed you have tasted that the Lord is gracious. ₄ Come to him, a living stone, rejected indeed by men, but chosen by God, precious. ₅ You also as living stones are built up as a spiritual house, to be a holy priesthood, to offer up spiritual sacrifices, acceptable to God through Jesus Christ. ₆ Because it is contained in Scripture,

"Behold,[c] I lay in Zion a chief cornerstone, chosen and precious.
    He who believes in him will not be disappointed."[*]

₇ For you who believe therefore is the honour, but for those who are disobedient,
"The stone which the builders rejected
    has become the chief cornerstone,"[*]
₈ and,
"a stumbling stone and a rock of offence."[*]

For they stumble at the word, being disobedient, to which also they were appointed. ₉ But you are a chosen race, a royal priesthood, a holy nation, a people for God's own possession, that you may proclaim the excellence of him who called you out of darkness into his marvellous light.

₁₀ In the past, you were not a people, but now are God's people, who had not obtained mercy, but now have obtained mercy.

₁₁ Beloved, I beg you as foreigners and pilgrims to abstain from fleshly lusts which war against the soul, ₁₂ having good behaviour amongst the nations, so in that of which they speak against you as evildoers, they may see your good works and glorify God in the day of visitation.

₁₃ Therefore subject yourselves to every ordinance of man for the Lord's sake: whether to the king, as supreme, ₁₄ or to governors, as sent by him for vengeance on evildoers and for praise to those who do well. ₁₅ For this is the will of God, that by well-doing you should put to silence the ignorance of foolish men. ₁₆ Live as free people, yet not using your freedom for a cloak of wickedness, but as bondservants of God.

₁₇ Honour all men. Love the brotherhood. Fear God. Honour the king.

₁₈ Servants, be in subjection to your masters with all respect, not only to the good and gentle, but also to the wicked. ₁₉ For it is commendable if someone endures pain, suffering unjustly, because of conscience towards God. ₂₀ For what glory is it if, when you sin, you patiently endure beating? But if when you do well, you patiently endure suffering, this is commendable with God. ₂₁ For you were called to this, because Christ also suffered for us, leaving you[d] an example, that you should follow his steps, ₂₂ who didn't sin, "neither was deceit found in his mouth."[*] ₂₃ When he was cursed, he didn't curse back. When he suffered, he didn't threaten, but committed himself to him who judges righteously. ₂₄ He himself bore our sins in his body on the tree, that we, having died to sins, might live to righteousness. You were healed by his wounds.[e] ₂₅ For you were going astray like sheep; but now you have returned to the Shepherd and Overseer[f] of your souls.

3

₁ In the same way, wives, be in subjection to your own husbands, so that, even if any don't obey the Word, they may be won by the behaviour of their wives without a word, ₂ seeing your pure behaviour in fear. ₃ Let your beauty come not from the outward adorning of braiding your hair, and of wearing gold ornaments or of putting on fine clothing, ₄ but from the hidden person of the heart, in the incorruptible adornment of a gentle and quiet spirit, which is very precious in God's sight. ₅ For this is how in the past the holy women who hoped in God also adorned themselves, being in subjection to their own husbands. ₆ So Sarah obeyed Abraham, calling him lord, whose children you now are if you do well and are not put in fear by any terror.

₇ You husbands, in the same way, live with your wives according to knowledge, giving honour to the woman as to the weaker vessel, as also being joint heirs of the grace of life, that your prayers may not be hindered.

₈ Finally, all of you be like-minded, compassionate, loving as brothers, tenderhearted, courteous, ₉ not rendering evil for evil or insult for insult; but instead blessing, knowing that you were called to this, that you may inherit a blessing. ₁₀ For,
"He who would love life
    and see good days,
let him keep his tongue from evil
    and his lips from speaking deceit.
₁₁ Let him turn away from evil and do good.
    Let him seek peace and pursue it.
₁₂ For the eyes of the Lord are on the righteous,
    and his ears open to their prayer;
    but the face of the Lord is against those who do evil."[*]

₁₃ Now who will harm you if you become imitators of that which is good? ₁₄ But even if you should suffer for righteousness' sake, you are blessed. "Don't fear what they fear, neither be troubled."[*] ₁₅ But sanctify the Lord God in your hearts. Always be ready to give an answer to everyone who asks you a reason concerning the hope that is in you, with humility and fear, ₁₆ having a good conscience. Thus, while you are spoken against as evildoers, they may be disappointed who curse your good way of life in Christ. ₁₇ For it is better, if it is God's will, that you suffer for doing what is right than for doing evil. ₁₈ Because Christ also suffered for sins once, the righteous for the unrighteous, that he might bring you to God, being put to death in the flesh, but made alive in the Spirit, ₁₉ in whom he also went and preached to the spirits in prison, ₂₀ who before were disobedient when God waited patiently in the days of Noah while the ship was being built. In it, few, that is, eight souls, were saved through water. ₂₁ This is a symbol of baptism, which now saves you—not the putting away of the filth of the flesh, but the answer of a good conscience towards God—through the resurrection of Jesus Christ, ₂₂ who is at the right hand of God, having gone into heaven, angels and authorities and powers being made subject to him.

4

₁ Therefore, since Christ suffered for us in the flesh, arm yourselves also with the same mind; for he who has suffered in the flesh has ceased from sin, ₂ that you no longer should live the rest of your time in the flesh

---

a *1:1* "Christ" means "Anointed One".

b *1:13* literally, "gird up the waist of your mind" or "put on the belt of the waist of your mind"

** 1:16 Leviticus 11:44-45

** 1:25 Isaiah 40:6-8

c *2:6* "Behold", from "הִנֵּה" or "ἰδοὺ", means look at, take notice, observe, see, or gaze at. It is often used as an interjection.

** 2:6 Isaiah 28:16

** 2:7 Psalms 118:22

** 2:8 Isaiah 8:14

d *2:21* TR reads "us" instead of "you"

** 2:22 Isaiah 53:9

e *2:24* or, stripes

f *2:25* "Overseer" is from the Greek ἐπίσκοπον, which can mean overseer, curator, guardian, or superintendent.

** 3:12 Psalms 34:12-16

** 3:14 Isaiah 8:12

for the lusts of men, but for the will of God. ₃ For we have spent enough of our past time doing the desire of the Gentiles, and having walked in lewdness, lusts, drunken binges, orgies, carousings, and abominable idolatries. ₄ They think it is strange that you don't run with them into the same excess of riot, speaking evil of you. ₅ They will give account to him who is ready to judge the living and the dead. ₆ For to this end the Good News was preached even to the dead, that they might be judged indeed as men in the flesh, but live as to God in the spirit.

₇ But the end of all things is near. Therefore be of sound mind, self-controlled, and sober in prayer. ₈ And above all things be earnest in your love amongst yourselves, for love covers a multitude of sins. ₉ Be hospitable to one another without grumbling. ₁₀ As each has received a gift, employ it in serving one another, as good managers of the grace of God in its various forms. ₁₁ If anyone speaks, let it be as it were the very words of God. If anyone serves, let it be as of the strength which God supplies, that in all things God may be glorified through Jesus Christ, to whom belong the glory and the dominion forever and ever. Amen.

₁₂ Beloved, don't be astonished at the fiery trial which has come upon you to test you, as though a strange thing happened to you. ₁₃ But because you are partakers of Christ's sufferings, rejoice, that at the revelation of his glory you also may rejoice with exceeding joy. ₁₄ If you are insulted for the name of Christ, you are blessed, because the Spirit of glory and of God rests on you. On their part he is blasphemed, but on your part he is glorified. ₁₅ But let none of you suffer as a murderer, or a thief, or an evil doer, or a meddler in other men's matters. ₁₆ But if one of you suffers for being a Christian, let him not be ashamed; but let him glorify God in this matter. ₁₇ For the time has come for judgement to begin with the household of God. If it begins first with us, what will happen to those who don't obey the Good News of God? ₁₈ "If it is hard for the righteous to be saved, what will happen to the ungodly and the sinner?"* ₁₉ Therefore let them also who suffer according to the will of God in doing good entrust their souls to him, as to a faithful Creator.

5

₁ Therefore I exhort the elders amongst you, as a fellow elder and a witness of the sufferings of Christ, and who will also share in the glory that will be revealed: ₂ shepherd the flock of God which is amongst you, exercising the oversight, not under compulsion, but voluntarily; not for dishonest gain, but willingly; ₃ not as lording it over those entrusted to you, but making yourselves examples to the flock. ₄ When the chief Shepherd is revealed, you will receive the crown of glory that doesn't fade away.

₅ Likewise, you younger ones, be subject to the elder. Yes, all of you clothe yourselves with humility and subject yourselves to one another; for "God resists the proud, but gives grace to the humble."* ₆ Humble yourselves therefore under the mighty hand of God, that he may exalt you in due time, ₇ casting all your worries on him, because he cares for you.

₈ Be sober and self-controlled. Be watchful. Your adversary, the devil, walks around like a roaring lion, seeking whom he may devour. ₉ Withstand him steadfast in your faith, knowing that your brothers who are in the world are undergoing the same sufferings. ₁₀ But may the God of all grace, who called you to his eternal glory by Christ Jesus, after you have suffered a little while, perfect, establish, strengthen, and settle you. ₁₁ To him be the glory and the power forever and ever. Amen.

₁₂ Through Silvanus, our faithful brother, as I consider him, I have written to you briefly, exhorting and testifying that this is the true grace of God in which you stand. ₁₃ She who is in Babylon, chosen together with you, greets you. So does Mark, my son. ₁₄ Greet one another with a kiss of love.

Peace be to all of you who are in Christ Jesus. Amen.

** 4:18 Proverbs 11:31 | ** 5:5 Proverbs 3:34

Peter's Second Letter

1

1 Simon Peter, a servant and apostle of Jesus Christ,[a] to those who have obtained a like precious faith with us in the righteousness of our God and Saviour, Jesus Christ: 2 Grace to you and peace be multiplied in the knowledge of God and of Jesus our Lord, 3 seeing that his divine power has granted to us all things that pertain to life and godliness, through the knowledge of him who called us by his own glory and virtue, 4 by which he has granted to us his precious and exceedingly great promises; that through these you may become partakers of the divine nature, having escaped from the corruption that is in the world by lust. 5 Yes, and for this very cause adding on your part all diligence, in your faith supply moral excellence; and in moral excellence, knowledge; 6 and in knowledge, self-control; and in self-control, perseverance; and in perseverance, godliness; 7 and in godliness, brotherly affection; and in brotherly affection, love. 8 For if these things are yours and abound, they make you to not be idle or unfruitful in the knowledge of our Lord Jesus Christ. 9 For he who lacks these things is blind, seeing only what is near, having forgotten the cleansing from his old sins. 10 Therefore, brothers,[b] be more diligent to make your calling and election sure. For if you do these things, you will never stumble. 11 For thus you will be richly supplied with the entrance into the eternal Kingdom of our Lord and Saviour, Jesus Christ.

12 Therefore I will not be negligent to remind you of these things, though you know them and are established in the present truth. 13 I think it right, as long as I am in this tent, to stir you up by reminding you, 14 knowing that the putting off of my tent comes swiftly, even as our Lord Jesus Christ made clear to me. 15 Yes, I will make every effort that you may always be able to remember these things even after my departure.

16 For we didn't follow cunningly devised fables when we made known to you the power and coming of our Lord Jesus Christ, but we were eyewitnesses of his majesty. 17 For he received from God the Father honour and glory when the voice came to him from the Majestic Glory, "This is my beloved Son, in whom I am well pleased."[*] 18 We heard this voice come out of heaven when we were with him on the holy mountain.

19 We have the more sure word of prophecy; and you do well that you heed it as to a lamp shining in a dark place, until the day dawns and the morning star arises in your hearts, 20 knowing this first, that no prophecy of Scripture is of private interpretation. 21 For no prophecy ever came by the will of man, but holy men of God spoke, being moved by the Holy Spirit.

2

1 But false prophets also arose amongst the people, as false teachers will also be amongst you, who will secretly bring in destructive heresies, denying even the Master who bought them, bringing on themselves swift destruction. 2 Many will follow their immoral[c] ways, and as a result, the way of the truth will be maligned. 3 In covetousness they will exploit you with deceptive words: whose sentence now from of old doesn't linger, and their destruction will not slumber.

4 For if God didn't spare angels when they sinned, but cast them down to Tartarus,[d] and committed them to pits of darkness to be reserved for judgement; 5 and didn't spare the ancient world, but preserved Noah with seven others, a preacher of righteousness, when he brought a flood on the world of the ungodly, 6 and turning the cities of Sodom and Gomorrah into ashes, condemned them to destruction, having made them an example to those who would live in an ungodly way, 7 and delivered righteous Lot, who was very distressed by the lustful life of the wicked 8 (for that righteous man dwelling amongst them was tormented in his righteous soul from day to day with seeing and hearing lawless deeds), 9 then the Lord knows how to deliver the godly out of temptation and to keep the unrighteous under punishment for the day of judgement, 10 but chiefly those who walk after the flesh in the lust of defilement and despise authority. Daring, self-willed, they are not afraid to speak evil of dignitaries, 11 whereas angels, though greater in might and power, don't bring a slanderous judgement against them before the Lord. 12 But these, as unreasoning creatures, born natural animals to be taken and destroyed, speaking evil in matters about which they are ignorant, will in their destroying surely be destroyed, 13 receiving the wages of unrighteousness; people who count it pleasure to revel in the daytime, spots and defects, revelling in their deceit while they feast with you; 14 having eyes full of adultery, and who can't cease from sin, enticing unsettled souls, having a heart trained in greed, accursed children! 15 Forsaking the right way, they went astray, having followed the way of Balaam the son of Beor, who loved the wages of wrongdoing; 16 but he was rebuked for his own disobedience. A speechless donkey spoke with a man's voice and stopped the madness of the prophet.

17 These are wells without water, clouds driven by a storm, for whom the blackness of darkness has been reserved forever. 18 For, uttering great swelling words of emptiness, they entice in the lusts of the flesh, by licentiousness, those who are indeed escaping from those who live in error; 19 promising them liberty, while they themselves are bondservants of corruption; for a man is brought into bondage by whoever overcomes him.

20 For if, after they have escaped the defilement of the world through the knowledge of the Lord and Saviour Jesus Christ, they are again entangled in it and overcome, the last state has become worse for them than the first. 21 For it would be better for them not to have known the way of righteousness, than after knowing it, to turn back from the holy commandment delivered to them. 22 But it has happened to them according to the true proverb, "The dog turns to his own vomit again,"[*] and "the sow that has washed to wallowing in the mire."

3

1 This is now, beloved, the second letter that I have written to you; and in both of them I stir up your sincere mind by reminding you 2 that you should remember the words which were spoken before by the holy prophets and the commandment of us, the apostles of the Lord and Saviour, 3 knowing this first, that in the last days mockers will come, walking after their own lusts 4 and saying, "Where is the promise of his coming? For, from the day that the fathers fell asleep, all things continue as they were from the beginning of the creation." 5 For they wilfully forget that there were heavens from of old, and an earth formed out of water and amid water by the word of God, 6 by which means the world that existed then, being overflowed with water, perished. 7 But the heavens that exist now and the earth, by the same word have been stored up for fire, being reserved against the day of judgement and destruction of ungodly men.

8 But don't forget this one thing, beloved, that one day is with the Lord as a thousand years, and a thousand years as one day. 9 The Lord is not slow concerning his promise, as some count slowness; but he is patient with us, not wishing that anyone should perish, but that all should come to repentance. 10 But the day of the Lord will come as a thief in the night, in which the heavens will pass away with a great noise, and the elements will be dissolved with fervent heat; and the earth and the works that are in it will be burnt up. 11 Therefore, since all these things will be destroyed like this, what kind of people ought you to be in holy living and godliness, 12 looking for and earnestly desiring the coming of the day of God, which will cause the burning heavens to be dissolved, and the elements will melt with fervent heat? 13 But, according to his promise, we look for new heavens and a new earth, in which righteousness dwells.

14 Therefore, beloved, seeing that you look for these things, be diligent to be found in peace, without defect and blameless in his sight. 15 Regard the patience of our Lord as salvation; even as our beloved brother Paul also, according to the wisdom given to him, wrote to you, 16 as also in all of his letters, speaking in them of these things. In those, there are some things that are hard to understand, which the ignorant and unsettled twist, as they also do to the other Scriptures, to their own destruction. 17 You therefore, beloved, knowing these things beforehand, beware, lest being carried away with the error of the wicked, you fall from your own steadfastness. 18 But grow in the grace and knowledge of our Lord and Saviour Jesus Christ. To him be the glory both now and forever. Amen.

---

a *1:1* "Christ" means "Anointed One".
b *1:10* The word for "brothers" here and where context allows may also be correctly translated "brothers and sisters" or "siblings."
** 1:17 Matthew 17:5; Mark 9:7; Luke 9:35

c *2:2* TR reads "destructive" instead of "immoral"
d *2:4* Tartarus is another name for Hell
** 2:22 Proverbs 26:11

John's First Letter

1

1 That which was from the beginning, that which we have heard, that which we have seen with our eyes, that which we saw, and our hands touched, concerning the Word of life 2 (and the life was revealed, and we have seen, and testify, and declare to you the life, the eternal life, which was with the Father, and was revealed to us); 3 that which we have seen and heard we declare to you, that you also may have fellowship with us. Yes, and our fellowship is with the Father and with his Son, Jesus Christ.[a] 4 And we write these things to you, that our joy may be fulfilled.

5 This is the message which we have heard from him and announce to you, that God is light, and in him is no darkness at all. 6 If we say that we have fellowship with him and walk in the darkness, we lie and don't tell the truth. 7 But if we walk in the light as he is in the light, we have fellowship with one another, and the blood of Jesus Christ his Son, cleanses us from all sin. 8 If we say that we have no sin, we deceive ourselves, and the truth is not in us. 9 If we confess our sins, he is faithful and righteous to forgive us the sins and to cleanse us from all unrighteousness. 10 If we say that we haven't sinned, we make him a liar, and his word is not in us.

2

1 My little children, I write these things to you so that you may not sin. If anyone sins, we have a Counsellor[b] with the Father, Jesus Christ, the righteous. 2 And he is the atoning sacrifice[c] for our sins, and not for ours only, but also for the whole world. 3 This is how we know that we know him: if we keep his commandments. 4 One who says, "I know him," and doesn't keep his commandments, is a liar, and the truth isn't in him. 5 But God's love has most certainly been perfected in whoever keeps his word. This is how we know that we are in him: 6 he who says he remains in him ought himself also to walk just like he walked.

7 Brothers, I write no new commandment to you, but an old commandment which you had from the beginning. The old commandment is the word which you heard from the beginning. 8 Again, I write a new commandment to you, which is true in him and in you, because the darkness is passing away and the true light already shines. 9 He who says he is in the light and hates his brother is in the darkness even until now. 10 He who loves his brother remains in the light, and there is no occasion for stumbling in him. 11 But he who hates his brother is in the darkness, and walks in the darkness, and doesn't know where he is going, because the darkness has blinded his eyes.

12 I write to you, little children, because your sins are forgiven you for his name's sake.

13 I write to you, fathers, because you know him who is from the beginning.

I write to you, young men, because you have overcome the evil one.

I write to you, little children, because you know the Father.

14 I have written to you, fathers, because you know him who is from the beginning.

I have written to you, young men, because you are strong, and the word of God remains in you, and you have overcome the evil one.

15 Don't love the world or the things that are in the world. If anyone loves the world, the Father's love isn't in him. 16 For all that is in the world—the lust of the flesh, the lust of the eyes, and the pride of life—isn't the Father's, but is the world's. 17 The world is passing away with its lusts, but he who does God's will remains forever.

18 Little children, these are the end times, and as you heard that the Antichrist is coming, even now many antichrists have arisen. By this we know that it is the final hour. 19 They went out from us, but they didn't belong to us; for if they had belonged to us, they would have continued with us. But they left, that they might be revealed that none of them belong to us. 20 You have an anointing from the Holy One, and you all have knowledge.[d] 21 I have not written to you because you don't know the truth, but because you know it, and because no lie is of the truth. 22 Who is the liar but he who denies that Jesus is the Christ? This is the Antichrist, he who denies the Father and the Son. 23 Whoever denies the Son doesn't have the Father. He who confesses the Son has the Father also.

24 Therefore, as for you, let that remain in you which you heard from the beginning. If that which you heard from the beginning remains in you, you also will remain in the Son, and in the Father. 25 This is the promise which he promised us, the eternal life.

26 These things I have written to you concerning those who would lead you astray. 27 As for you, the anointing which you received from him remains in you, and you don't need for anyone to teach you. But as his anointing teaches you concerning all things, and is true, and is no lie, and even as it taught you, you will remain in him.

28 Now, little children, remain in him, that when he appears, we may have boldness and not be ashamed before him at his coming. 29 If you know that he is righteous, you know that everyone who practices righteousness has been born of him.

3

1 See how great a love the Father has given to us, that we should be called children of God! For this cause the world doesn't know us, because it didn't know him. 2 Beloved, now we are children of God. It is not yet revealed what we will be; but we know that when he is revealed, we will be like him, for we will see him just as he is. 3 Everyone who has this hope set on him purifies himself, even as he is pure.

4 Everyone who sins also commits lawlessness. Sin is lawlessness. 5 You know that he was revealed to take away our sins, and no sin is in him. 6 Whoever remains in him doesn't sin. Whoever sins hasn't seen him and doesn't know him.

7 Little children, let no one lead you astray. He who does righteousness is righteous, even as he is righteous. 8 He who sins is of the devil, for the devil has been sinning from the beginning. To this end the Son of God was revealed: that he might destroy the works of the devil. 9 Whoever is born of God doesn't commit sin, because his seed remains in him, and he can't sin, because he is born of God. 10 In this the children of God are revealed, and the children of the devil. Whoever doesn't do righteousness is not of God, neither is he who doesn't love his brother. 11 For this is the message which you heard from the beginning, that we should love one another— 12 unlike Cain, who was of the evil one and killed his brother. Why did he kill him? Because his deeds were evil, and his brother's righteous.

13 Don't be surprised, my brothers, if the world hates you. 14 We know that we have passed out of death into life, because we love the brothers. He who doesn't love his brother remains in death. 15 Whoever hates his brother is a murderer, and you know that no murderer has eternal life remaining in him.

16 By this we know love, because he laid down his life for us. And we ought to lay down our lives for the brothers. 17 But whoever has the world's goods and sees his brother in need, then closes his heart of compassion against him, how does God's love remain in him?

18 My little children, let's not love in word only, or with the tongue only, but in deed and truth. 19 And by this we know that we are of the truth and persuade our hearts before him, 20 because if our heart condemns us, God is greater than our heart, and knows all things. 21 Beloved, if our hearts don't condemn us, we have boldness towards God; 22 so whatever we ask, we receive from him, because we keep his commandments and do the things that are pleasing in his sight. 23 This is his commandment, that we should believe in the name of his Son, Jesus Christ, and love one another, even as he commanded. 24 He who keeps his commandments remains in him, and he in him. By this we know that he remains in us, by the Spirit which he gave us.

4

1 Beloved, don't believe every spirit, but test the spirits, whether they are of God, because many false prophets have gone out into the world. 2 By this you know the Spirit of God: every spirit who confesses that Jesus Christ has come in the flesh is of God, 3 and every spirit who doesn't confess that Jesus Christ has come in the flesh is not of God; and this is the spirit of the Antichrist, of whom you have heard that it comes. Now it is in the world already. 4 You are of God, little children, and have overcome them, because greater is he who is in you than he who is in the world. 5 They are of the world. Therefore they speak of the world, and the world hears them. 6 We are of God. He who knows God listens to us. He who is not of God doesn't listen to us. By this we know the spirit of truth, and the spirit of error.

7 Beloved, let's love one another, for love is of God; and everyone who loves has been born of God and knows God. 8 He who doesn't love doesn't know God, for God is love. 9 By this God's love was revealed in us, that God has sent his only born[e] Son into the world that we might live through him. 10 In this is love, not that we loved God, but that he loved us, and sent his Son as the atoning sacrifice[f] for our sins. 11 Beloved, if God loved us in this way, we also ought to love one another. 12 No one has seen God at any time. If we love one another, God remains in us, and his love has been perfected in us.

13 By this we know that we remain in him and he in us, because he has given us of his Spirit. 14 We have seen and testify that the Father has sent the Son as the Saviour of the world. 15 Whoever confesses that Jesus is the Son of God, God remains in him, and he in God. 16 We know and have believed the love which God has for us. God is love, and he who remains in love remains in God, and God remains in him. 17 In this, love has been made perfect amongst us, that we may have boldness in the day of judgement, because as he is, even so we are in this world. 18 There is no fear in love; but perfect love casts out fear, because fear has punishment. He who fears is not made perfect in love. 19 We love him,[g] because he first loved us. 20 If a man says, "I love God," and hates his brother, he is a liar; for he who doesn't love his brother whom he has seen, how can he love

---

[a] 1:3 "Christ" means "Anointed One".

[b] 2:1 Greek παρακλητον: Counsellor, Helper, Intercessor, Advocate, and Comforter.

[c] 2:2 "atoning sacrifice" is from the Greek "ιλασμος", an appeasing, propitiating, or the means of appeasement or propitiation—the sacrifice that turns away God's wrath because of our sin.

[d] 2:20 Or, "know what is true", or, "know all things"

[e] 4:9 The phrase "only born" is from the Greek word "μονογενη", which is sometimes translated "only begotten" or "one and only".

[f] 4:10 "atoning sacrifice" is from the Greek "ιλασμος", an appeasing, propitiating, or the means of appeasement or propitiation—the sacrifice that turns away God's wrath because of our sin.

[g] 4:19 NU omits "him".

God whom he has not seen? 21 This commandment we have from him, that he who loves God should also love his brother.

5

1 Whoever believes that Jesus is the Christ has been born of God. Whoever loves the Father also loves the child who is born of him. 2 By this we know that we love the children of God, when we love God and keep his commandments. 3 For this is loving God, that we keep his commandments. His commandments are not grievous. 4 For whatever is born of God overcomes the world. This is the victory that has overcome the world: your faith. 5 Who is he who overcomes the world, but he who believes that Jesus is the Son of God?

6 This is he who came by water and blood, Jesus Christ; not with the water only, but with the water and the blood. It is the Spirit who testifies, because the Spirit is the truth. 7 For there are three who testify:[a] 8 the Spirit, the water, and the blood; and the three agree as one. 9 If we receive the witness of men, the witness of God is greater; for this is God's testimony which he has testified concerning his Son. 10 He who believes in the Son of God has the testimony in himself. He who doesn't believe God has made him a liar, because he has not believed in the testimony that God has given concerning his Son. 11 The testimony is this: that God gave to us eternal life, and this life is in his Son. 12 He who has the Son has the life. He who doesn't have God's Son doesn't have the life.

13 These things I have written to you who believe in the name of the Son of God, that you may know that you have eternal life, and that you may continue to believe in the name of the Son of God.

14 This is the boldness which we have towards him, that if we ask anything according to his will, he listens to us. 15 And if we know that he listens to us, whatever we ask, we know that we have the petitions which we have asked of him.

16 If anyone sees his brother sinning a sin not leading to death, he shall ask, and God will give him life for those who sin not leading to death. There is sin leading to death. I don't say that he should make a request concerning this. 17 All unrighteousness is sin, and there is sin not leading to death.

18 We know that whoever is born of God doesn't sin, but he who was born of God keeps himself, and the evil one doesn't touch him. 19 We know that we are of God, and the whole world lies in the power of the evil one. 20 We know that the Son of God has come and has given us an understanding, that we know him who is true; and we are in him who is true, in his Son Jesus Christ. This is the true God and eternal life.

21 Little children, keep yourselves from idols.

---

[a] 5:7 Only a few recent manuscripts add "in heaven: the Father, the Word, and the Holy Spirit; and these three are one. And there are three that testify on earth:"

John's Second Letter

1

1 The elder, to the chosen lady and her children, whom I love in truth, and not I only, but also all those who know the truth, 2 for the truth's sake, which remains in us, and it will be with us forever: 3 Grace, mercy, and peace will be with us, from God the Father and from the Lord Jesus Christ,[a] the Son of the Father, in truth and love.

4 I rejoice greatly that I have found some of your children walking in truth, even as we have been commanded by the Father. 5 Now I beg you, dear lady, not as though I wrote to you a new commandment, but that which we had from the beginning, that we love one another. 6 This is love, that we should walk according to his commandments. This is the commandment, even as you heard from the beginning, that you should walk in it.

7 For many deceivers have gone out into the world, those who don't confess that Jesus Christ came in the flesh. This is the deceiver and the Antichrist. 8 Watch yourselves, that we don't lose the things which we have accomplished, but that we receive a full reward. 9 Whoever transgresses and doesn't remain in the teaching of Christ doesn't have God. He who remains in the teaching has both the Father and the Son. 10 If anyone comes to you and doesn't bring this teaching, don't receive him into your house, and don't welcome him, 11 for he who welcomes him participates in his evil deeds.

12 Having many things to write to you, I don't want to do so with paper and ink, but I hope to come to you and to speak face to face, that our joy may be made full. 13 The children of your chosen sister greet you. Amen.

---

[a] 1:3 "Christ" means "Anointed One".

John's Third Letter

1

1 The elder to Gaius the beloved, whom I love in truth.

2 Beloved, I pray that you may prosper in all things and be healthy, even as your soul prospers. 3 For I rejoiced greatly when brothers came and testified about your truth, even as you walk in truth. 4 I have no greater joy than this: to hear about my children walking in truth.

5 Beloved, you do a faithful work in whatever you accomplish for those who are brothers and strangers. 6 They have testified about your love before the assembly. You will do well to send them forward on their journey in a way worthy of God, 7 because for the sake of the Name they went out, taking nothing from the Gentiles. 8 We therefore ought to receive such, that we may be fellow workers for the truth.

9 I wrote to the assembly, but Diotrephes, who loves to be first amongst them, doesn't accept what we say. 10 Therefore, if I come, I will call attention to his deeds which he does, unjustly accusing us with wicked words. Not content with this, he doesn't receive the brothers himself, and those who would, he forbids and throws out of the assembly.

11 Beloved, don't imitate that which is evil, but that which is good. He who does good is of God. He who does evil hasn't seen God. 12 Demetrius has the testimony of all, and of the truth itself; yes, we also testify, and you know that our testimony is true.

13 I had many things to write to you, but I am unwilling to write to you with ink and pen; 14 but I hope to see you soon. Then we will speak face to face.

Peace be to you. The friends greet you. Greet the friends by name.

The Letter from Jude

1

1 Jude,[a] a servant of Jesus Christ,[b] and brother of James, to those who are called, sanctified by God the Father, and kept for Jesus Christ: 2 May mercy, peace, and love be multiplied to you.

3 Beloved, while I was very eager to write to you about our common salvation, I was constrained to write to you exhorting you to contend earnestly for the faith which was once for all delivered to the saints. 4 For there are certain men who crept in secretly, even those who were long ago written about for this condemnation: ungodly men, turning the grace of our God into indecency, and denying our only Master, God, and Lord, Jesus Christ.

5 Now I desire to remind you, though you already know this, that the Lord, having saved a people out of the land of Egypt, afterward destroyed those who didn't believe. 6 Angels who didn't keep their first domain, but deserted their own dwelling place, he has kept in everlasting bonds under darkness for the judgement of the great day. 7 Even as Sodom and Gomorrah and the cities around them, having in the same way as these given themselves over to sexual immorality and gone after strange flesh, are shown as an example, suffering the punishment of eternal fire. 8 Yet in the same way, these also in their dreaming defile the flesh, despise authority, and slander celestial beings. 9 But Michael, the archangel, when contending with the devil and arguing about the body of Moses, dared not bring against him an abusive condemnation, but said, "May the Lord rebuke you!" 10 But these speak evil of whatever things they don't know. They are destroyed in these things that they understand naturally, like the creatures without reason. 11 Woe to them! For they went in the way of Cain, and ran riotously in the error of Balaam for hire, and perished in Korah's rebellion. 12 These are hidden rocky reefs in your love feasts when they feast with you, shepherds who without fear feed themselves; clouds without water, carried along by winds; autumn trees without fruit, twice dead, plucked up by the roots; 13 wild waves of the sea, foaming out their own shame; wandering stars, for whom the blackness of darkness has been reserved forever. 14 About these also Enoch, the seventh from Adam, prophesied, saying, "Behold,[c] the Lord came with ten thousands of his holy ones, 15 to execute judgement on all, and to convict all the ungodly of all their works of ungodliness which they have done in an ungodly way, and of all the hard things which ungodly sinners have spoken against him." 16 These are murmurers and complainers, walking after their lusts—and their mouth speaks proud things—showing respect of persons to gain advantage.

17 But you, beloved, remember the words which have been spoken before by the apostles of our Lord Jesus Christ. 18 They said to you, "In the last time there will be mockers, walking after their own ungodly lusts." 19 These are those who cause divisions and are sensual, not having the Spirit.

20 But you, beloved, keep building up yourselves on your most holy faith, praying in the Holy Spirit. 21 Keep yourselves in God's love, looking for the mercy of our Lord Jesus Christ to eternal life. 22 On some have compassion, making a distinction, 23 and some save, snatching them out of the fire with fear, hating even the clothing stained by the flesh.

24 Now to him who is able to keep them[d] from stumbling, and to present you faultless before the presence of his glory in great joy, 25 to God our Saviour, who alone is wise, be glory and majesty, dominion and power, both now and forever. Amen.

---

a *1:1* or, Judah
b *1:1* "Christ" means "Anointed One".

c *1:14* "Behold", from "ἰδού", means look at, take notice, observe, see, or gaze at. It is often used as an interjection.
d *1:24* TR and NU read "you"

The Revelation to John

1

1 This is the Revelation of Jesus Christ,[a] which God gave him to show to his servants the things which must happen soon, which he sent and made known by his angel[b] to his servant, John, 2 who testified to God's word and of the testimony of Jesus Christ, about everything that he saw.

3 Blessed is he who reads and those who hear the words of the prophecy, and keep the things that are written in it, for the time is near.

4 John, to the seven assemblies that are in Asia: Grace to you and peace from God, who is and who was and who is to come; and from the seven Spirits who are before his throne; 5 and from Jesus Christ, the faithful witness, the firstborn of the dead, and the ruler of the kings of the earth. To him who loves us, and washed us from our sins by his blood— 6 and he made us to be a Kingdom, priests' to his God and Father—to him be the glory and the dominion forever and ever. Amen.

7 Behold,[c] he is coming with the clouds, and every eye will see him, including those who pierced him. All the tribes of the earth will mourn over him. Even so, Amen.

8 "I am the Alpha and the Omega,[d]" says the Lord God,[e] "who is and who was and who is to come, the Almighty."

9 I John, your brother and partner with you in the oppression, Kingdom, and perseverance in Christ Jesus, was on the isle that is called Patmos because of God's Word and the testimony of Jesus Christ. 10 I was in the Spirit on the Lord's day, and I heard behind me a loud voice, like a trumpet 11 saying,[f] "What you see, write in a book and send to the seven assemblies:[g] to Ephesus, Smyrna, Pergamum, Thyatira, Sardis, Philadelphia, and to Laodicea."

12 I turned to see the voice that spoke with me. Having turned, I saw seven golden lamp stands. 13 And amongst the lamp stands was one like a son of man,' clothed with a robe reaching down to his feet, and with a golden sash around his chest. 14 His head and his hair were white as white wool, like snow. His eyes were like a flame of fire. 15 His feet were like burnished brass, as if it had been refined in a furnace. His voice was like the voice of many waters. 16 He had seven stars in his right hand. Out of his mouth proceeded a sharp two-edged sword. His face was like the sun shining at its brightest. 17 When I saw him, I fell at his feet like a dead man.

He laid his right hand on me, saying, "Don't be afraid. I am the first and the last, 18 and the Living one. I was dead, and behold, I am alive forever and ever. Amen. I have the keys of Death and of Hades.[h] 19 Write therefore the things which you have seen, and the things which are, and the things which will happen hereafter. 20 The mystery of the seven stars which you saw in my right hand, and the seven golden lamp stands is this: The seven stars are the angels[i] of the seven assemblies. The seven lamp stands are seven assemblies.

2

1 "To the angel of the assembly in Ephesus write:

"He who holds the seven stars in his right hand, he who walks amongst the seven golden lamp stands says these things:

2 "I know your works, and your toil and perseverance, and that you can't tolerate evil men, and have tested those who call themselves apostles, and they are not, and found them false. 3 You have perseverance and have endured for my name's sake, and have [j] not grown weary. 4 But I have this against you, that you left your first love. 5 Remember therefore from where you have fallen, and repent and do the first works; or else I am coming to you swiftly, and will move your lamp stand out of its place, unless you repent. 6 But this you have, that you hate the works of the Nicolaitans, which I also hate. 7 He who has an ear, let him hear what the Spirit says to the assemblies. To him who overcomes I will give to eat from the tree of life, which is in the Paradise of my God.

8 "To the angel of the assembly in Smyrna write:

"The first and the last, who was dead, and has come to life says these things:

9 "I know your works, oppression, and your poverty (but you are rich), and the blasphemy of those who say they are Jews, and they are not, but are a synagogue of Satan. 10 Don't be afraid of the things which you are about to suffer. Behold, the devil is about to throw some of you into prison, that you may be tested; and you will have oppression for ten days. Be faithful to death, and I will give you the crown of life. 11 He who has an ear, let him hear what the Spirit says to the assemblies. He who overcomes won't be harmed by the second death.

12 "To the angel of the assembly in Pergamum write:

"He who has the sharp two-edged sword says these things:

13 "I know your works and where you dwell, where Satan's throne is. You hold firmly to my name, and didn't deny my faith in the days of Antipas my witness, my faithful one, who was killed amongst you, where Satan dwells. 14 But I have a few things against you, because you have there some who hold the teaching of Balaam, who taught Balak to throw a stumbling block before the children of Israel, to eat things sacrificed to idols, and to commit sexual immorality. 15 So also you likewise have some who hold to the teaching of the Nicolaitans.[k] 16 Repent therefore, or else I am coming to you quickly and I will make war against them with the sword of my mouth. 17 He who has an ear, let him hear what the Spirit says to the assemblies. To him who overcomes, to him I will give of the hidden manna, [l] and I will give him a white stone, and on the stone a new name written which no one knows but he who receives it.

18 "To the angel of the assembly in Thyatira write:

"The Son of God, who has his eyes like a flame of fire, and his feet are like burnished brass, says these things:

19 "I know your works, your love, faith, service, patient endurance, and that your last works are more than the first. 20 But I have this against you, that you tolerate your[m] woman Jezebel, who calls herself a prophetess. She teaches and seduces my servants to commit sexual immorality and to eat things sacrificed to idols. 21 I gave her time to repent, but she refuses to repent of her sexual immorality. 22 Behold, I will throw her and those who commit adultery with her into a bed of great oppression, unless they repent of her works. 23 I will kill her children with Death, and all the assemblies will know that I am he who searches the minds and hearts. I will give to each one of you according to your deeds. 24 But to you I say, to the rest who are in Thyatira—as many as don't have this teaching, who don't know what some call 'the deep things of Satan'—to you I say, I am not putting any other burden on you. 25 Nevertheless, hold that which you have firmly until I come. 26 He who overcomes, and he who keeps my works to the end, to him I will give authority over the nations. 27 He will rule them with a rod of iron, shattering them like clay pots,' as I also have received of my Father; 28 and I will give him the morning star. 29 He who has an ear, let him hear what the Spirit says to the assemblies.

3

1 "And to the angel of the assembly in Sardis write:

"He who has the seven Spirits of God and the seven stars says these things:

"I know your works, that you have a reputation of being alive, but you are dead. 2 Wake up and strengthen the things that remain, which you were about to throw away,[n] for I have found no works of yours perfected before my God. 3 Remember therefore how you have received and heard. Keep it and repent. If therefore you won't watch, I will come as a thief, and you won't know what hour I will come upon you. 4 Nevertheless you have a few names in Sardis that didn't defile their garments. They will walk with me in white, for they are worthy. 5 He who overcomes will be arrayed in white garments, and I will in no way blot his name out of the book of life, and I will confess his name before my Father, and before his angels. 6 He who has an ear, let him hear what the Spirit says to the assemblies.

7 "To the angel of the assembly in Philadelphia write:

"He who is holy, he who is true, he who has the key of David, he who opens and no one can shut, and who shuts and no one opens, says these things:

8 "I know your works (behold, I have set before you an open door, which no one can shut), that you have a little power, and kept my word, and didn't deny my name. 9 Behold, I make some of the synagogue of Satan, of those who say they are Jews, and they are not, but lie—behold, I will make them to come and worship before your feet, and to know that I have loved you. 10 Because you kept my command to endure, I also will keep you from the hour of testing which is to come on the whole world, to test those who dwell on the earth. 11 I am coming quickly! Hold firmly that which you have, so that no one takes your crown. 12 He who overcomes, I will make him a pillar in the temple of my God, and he will go out from there no more. I will write on him the name of my God and the name of the city of my God, the new Jerusalem, which comes down out of heaven from my God, and my own new name. 13 He who has an ear, let him hear what the Spirit says to the assemblies.

14 "To the angel of the assembly in Laodicea write:

"The Amen, the Faithful and True Witness, the Beginning[o] of God's creation, says these things:

15 "I know your works, that you are neither cold nor hot. I wish you were cold or hot. 16 So, because you are lukewarm, and neither hot nor cold, I will vomit you out of my mouth. 17 Because you say, 'I am rich, and have gotten riches, and have need of nothing,' and don't know that you are the wretched one, miserable, poor, blind, and naked; 18 I counsel you to buy from me gold refined by fire, that you may become rich; and white

---

a *1:1* "Christ" means "Anointed One".

b *1:1* or, messenger (here and wherever angel is mentioned)

** 1:6 Exodus 19:6; Isaiah 61:6

c *1:7* "Behold", from "ἰδοὺ", means look at, take notice, observe, see, or gaze at. It is often used as an interjection.

d *1:8* TR adds "the Beginning and the End"

e *1:8* TR omits "God"

f *1:11* TR adds "I am the Alpha and the Omega, the First and the Last."

g *1:11* TR adds "which are in Asia"

** 1:13 Daniel 7:13

h *1:18* or, Hell

i *1:20* or, messengers (here and wherever angels are mentioned)

j *2:3* TR adds "have laboured and"

k *2:15* TR reads "which I hate" instead of "likewise"

l *2:17* Manna is supernatural food, named after the Hebrew for "What is it?". See Exodus 11:7-9.

m *2:20* TR, NU read "that" instead of "your"

** 2:27 Psalms 2:9

n *3:2* NU & TR read "which were about to die" instead of "which you were about to throw away".

o *3:14* or, Source, or Head

garments, that you may clothe yourself, and that the shame of your nakedness may not be revealed; and eye salve to anoint your eyes, that you may see. ₁₉ As many as I love, I reprove and chasten. Be zealous therefore, and repent. ₂₀ Behold, I stand at the door and knock. If anyone hears my voice and opens the door, then I will come in to him and will dine with him, and he with me. ₂₁ He who overcomes, I will give to him to sit down with me on my throne, as I also overcame and sat down with my Father on his throne. ₂₂ He who has an ear, let him hear what the Spirit says to the assemblies."

4

₁ After these things I looked and saw a door opened in heaven; and the first voice that I heard, like a trumpet speaking with me, was one saying, "Come up here, and I will show you the things which must happen after this."

₂ Immediately I was in the Spirit. Behold, there was a throne set in heaven, and one sitting on the throne ₃ that looked like a jasper stone and a sardius. There was a rainbow around the throne, like an emerald to look at. ₄ Around the throne were twenty-four thrones. On the thrones were twenty-four elders sitting, dressed in white garments, with crowns of gold on their heads. ₅ Out of the throne proceed lightnings, sounds, and thunders. There were seven lamps of fire burning before his throne, which are the seven Spirits of God. ₆ Before the throne was something like a sea of glass, similar to crystal. In the middle of the throne, and around the throne were four living creatures full of eyes before and behind. ₇ The first creature was like a lion, the second creature like a calf, the third creature had a face like a man, and the fourth was like a flying eagle. ₈ The four living creatures, each one of them having six wings, are full of eyes around and within. They have no rest day and night, saying, "Holy, holy, holyᵃ is the Lord God, the Almighty, who was and who is and who is to come!"

₉ When the living creatures give glory, honour, and thanks to him who sits on the throne, to him who lives forever and ever, ₁₀ the twenty-four elders fall down before him who sits on the throne and worship him who lives forever and ever, and throw their crowns before the throne, saying, ₁₁ "Worthy are you, our Lord and God, the Holy One,ᵇ to receive the glory, the honour, and the power, for you created all things, and because of your desire they existed and were created!"

5

₁ I saw, in the right hand of him who sat on the throne, a book written inside and outside, sealed shut with seven seals. ₂ I saw a mighty angel proclaiming with a loud voice, "Who is worthy to open the book, and to break its seals?" ₃ No one in heaven above, or on the earth, or under the earth, was able to open the book or to look in it. ₄ Then I wept much, because no one was found worthy to open the book or to look in it. ₅ One of the elders said to me, "Don't weep. Behold, the Lion who is of the tribe of Judah, the Root of David, has overcome: he who opens the book and its seven seals."

₆ I saw in the middle of the throne and of the four living creatures, and in the middle of the elders, a Lamb standing, as though it had been slain, having seven horns and seven eyes, which are the seven Spirits of God, sent out into all the earth. ₇ Then he came, and he took it out of the right hand of him who sat on the throne. ₈ Now when he had taken the book, the four living creatures and the twenty-four elders fell down before the Lamb, each one having a harp, and golden bowls full of incense, which are the prayers of the saints. ₉ They sang a new song, saying,
"You are worthy to take the book
    and to open its seals,
for you were killed,
    and bought us for God with your blood
    out of every tribe, language, people, and nation,
₁₀ and made us kings and priests to our God;
    and we will reign on the earth."

₁₁ I looked, and I heard something like a voice of many angels around the throne, the living creatures, and the elders. The number of them was ten thousands of ten thousands, and thousands of thousands, ₁₂ saying with a loud voice, "Worthy is the Lamb who has been killed to receive the power, wealth, wisdom, strength, honour, glory, and blessing!"

₁₃ I heard every created thing which is in heaven, on the earth, under the earth, on the sea, and everything in them, saying, "To him who sits on the throne and to the Lamb be the blessing, the honour, the glory, and the dominion, forever and ever! Amen!"ᶜ

₁₄ The four living creatures said, "Amen!" Then theᵈ elders fell down and worshipped.ᵉ

6

₁ I saw that the Lamb opened one of the seven seals, and I heard one of the four living creatures saying, as with a voice of thunder, "Come and see!" ₂ Then a white horse appeared, and he who sat on it had a bow. A crown was given to him, and he came out conquering, and to conquer.

₃ When he opened the second seal, I heard the second living creature saying, "Come!" ₄ Another came out, a red horse. To him who sat on it was given power to take peace from the earth, and that they should kill one another. There was given to him a great sword.

₅ When he opened the third seal, I heard the third living creature saying, "Come and see!" And behold, a black horse, and he who sat on it had a balance in his hand. ₆ I heard a voice in the middle of the four living creatures saying, "A choenixᶠ of wheat for a denarius, and three choenix of barley for a denarius! Don't damage the oil and the wine!"

₇ When he opened the fourth seal, I heard the fourth living creature saying, "Come and see!" ₈ And behold, a pale horse, and the name of he who sat on it was Death. Hadesᵍ followed with him. Authority over one fourth of the earth, to kill with the sword, with famine, with death, and by the wild animals of the earth was given to him.

₉ When he opened the fifth seal, I saw underneath the altar the souls of those who had been killed for the Word of God, and for the testimony of the Lamb which they had. ₁₀ They cried with a loud voice, saying, "How long, Master, the holy and true, until you judge and avenge our blood on those who dwell on the earth?" ₁₁ A long white robe was given to each of them. They were told that they should rest yet for a while, until their fellow servants and their brothers,ʰ who would also be killed even as they were, should complete their course.

₁₂ I saw when he opened the sixth seal, and there was a great earthquake. The sun became black as sackcloth made of hair, and the whole moon became as blood. ₁₃ The stars of the sky fell to the earth, like a fig tree dropping its unripe figs when it is shaken by a great wind. ₁₄ The sky was removed like a scroll when it is rolled up. Every mountain and island was moved out of its place. ₁₅ The kings of the earth, the princes, the commanding officers, the rich, the strong, and every slave and free person, hid themselves in the caves and in the rocks of the mountains. ₁₆ They told the mountains and the rocks, "Fall on us, and hide us from the face of him who sits on the throne, and from the wrath of the Lamb, ₁₇ for the great day of his wrath has come, and who is able to stand?"

7

₁ After this, I saw four angels standing at the four corners of the earth, holding the four winds of the earth, so that no wind would blow on the earth, or on the sea, or on any tree. ₂ I saw another angel ascend from the sunrise, having the seal of the living God. He cried with a loud voice to the four angels to whom it was given to harm the earth and the sea, ₃ saying, "Don't harm the earth, the sea, or the trees, until we have sealed the bondservants of our God on their foreheads!" ₄ I heard the number of those who were sealed, one hundred and forty-four thousand, sealed out of every tribe of the children of Israel:

₅ of the tribe of Judah twelve thousand were sealed,
of the tribe of Reuben twelve thousand,
of the tribe of Gad twelve thousand,
₆ of the tribe of Asher twelve thousand,
of the tribe of Naphtali twelve thousand,
of the tribe of Manasseh twelve thousand,
₇ of the tribe of Simeon twelve thousand,
of the tribe of Levi twelve thousand,
of the tribe of Issachar twelve thousand,
₈ of the tribe of Zebulun twelve thousand,
of the tribe of Joseph twelve thousand, and
of the tribe of Benjamin twelve thousand were sealed.

₉ After these things I looked, and behold, a great multitude which no man could count, out of every nation and of all tribes, peoples, and languages, standing before the throne and before the Lamb, dressed in white robes, with palm branches in their hands. ₁₀ They cried with a loud voice, saying, "Salvation be to our God, who sits on the throne, and to the Lamb!"

₁₁ All the angels were standing around the throne, the elders, and the four living creatures; and they fell on their faces before his throne, and worshipped God, ₁₂ saying, "Amen! Blessing, glory, wisdom, thanksgiving, honour, power, and might, be to our God forever and ever! Amen."

₁₃ One of the elders answered, saying to me, "These who are arrayed in the white robes, who are they, and where did they come from?"

₁₄ I told him, "My lord, you know."

He said to me, "These are those who came out of the great suffering.ⁱ They washed their robes and made them white in the Lamb's blood. ₁₅ Therefore they are before the throne of God, and they serve him day and night in his temple. He who sits on the throne will spread his tabernacle over them. ₁₆ They will never be hungry or thirsty any more. The sun won't beat on them, nor any heat; ₁₇ for the Lamb who is in the middle of the throne shepherds them and leads them to springs of life-giving waters. And God will wipe away every tear from their eyes."

8

₁ When he opened the seventh seal, there was silence in heaven for about half an hour. ₂ I saw the seven angels who stand before God, and seven trumpets were given to them.

₃ Another angel came and stood over the altar, having a golden censer. Much incense was given to him, that he should add it to the prayers of all the saints on the golden altar which was before the throne. ₄ The

---

ᵃ *4:8* Hodges/Farstad MT reads "holy" 9 times instead of 3.
ᵇ *4:11* TR omits "and God, the Holy One,"
ᶜ *5:13* TR omits "Amen!"
ᵈ *5:14* TR adds "twenty-four"
ᵉ *5:14* TR adds "the one living forever and ever"

ᶠ *6:6* A choenix is a dry volume measure that is a little more than a litre (a little more than a quart).
ᵍ *6:8* or, Hell
ʰ *6:11* The word for "brothers" here and where context allows may also be correctly translated "brothers and sisters" or "siblings."
ⁱ *7:14* or, oppression

smoke of the incense, with the prayers of the saints, went up before God out of the angel's hand. 5 The angel took the censer, and he filled it with the fire of the altar, then threw it on the earth. Thunders, sounds, lightnings, and an earthquake followed.

6 The seven angels who had the seven trumpets prepared themselves to sound.

7 The first sounded, and there followed hail and fire, mixed with blood, and they were thrown to the earth. One third of the earth was burnt up,[a] and one third of the trees were burnt up, and all green grass was burnt up.

8 The second angel sounded, and something like a great burning mountain was thrown into the sea. One third of the sea became blood, 9 and one third of the living creatures which were in the sea died. One third of the ships were destroyed.

10 The third angel sounded, and a great star fell from the sky, burning like a torch, and it fell on one third of the rivers, and on the springs of water. 11 The name of the star is "Wormwood." One third of the waters became wormwood. Many people died from the waters, because they were made bitter.

12 The fourth angel sounded, and one third of the sun was struck, and one third of the moon, and one third of the stars, so that one third of them would be darkened; and the day wouldn't shine for one third of it, and the night in the same way. 13 I saw, and I heard an eagle,[b] flying in mid heaven, saying with a loud voice, "Woe! Woe! Woe to those who dwell on the earth, because of the other blasts of the trumpets of the three angels, who are yet to sound!"

9

1 The fifth angel sounded, and I saw a star from the sky which had fallen to the earth. The key to the pit of the abyss was given to him. 2 He opened the pit of the abyss, and smoke went up out of the pit, like the smoke from a[c] burning furnace. The sun and the air were darkened because of the smoke from the pit. 3 Then out of the smoke came locusts on the earth, and power was given to them, as the scorpions of the earth have power. 4 They were told that they should not hurt the grass of the earth, neither any green thing, neither any tree, but only those people who don't have God's seal on their foreheads. 5 They were given power, not to kill them, but to torment them for five months. Their torment was like the torment of a scorpion when it strikes a person. 6 In those days people will seek death, and will in no way find it. They will desire to die, and death will flee from them.

7 The shapes of the locusts were like horses prepared for war. On their heads were something like golden crowns, and their faces were like people's faces. 8 They had hair like women's hair, and their teeth were like those of lions. 9 They had breastplates like breastplates of iron. The sound of their wings was like the sound of many chariots and horses rushing to war. 10 They have tails like those of scorpions, with stingers. In their tails they have power to harm men for five months. 11 They have over them as king the angel of the abyss. His name in Hebrew is "Abaddon",[d] but in Greek, he has the name "Apollyon".[e]

12 The first woe is past. Behold, there are still two woes coming after this.

13 The sixth angel sounded. I heard a voice from the horns of the golden altar which is before God, 14 saying to the sixth angel who had the trumpet, "Free the four angels who are bound at the great river Euphrates!"

15 The four angels were freed who had been prepared for that hour and day and month and year, so that they might kill one third of mankind. 16 The number of the armies of the horsemen was two hundred million.[f] I heard the number of them. 17 Thus I saw the horses in the vision and those who sat on them, having breastplates of fiery red, hyacinth blue, and sulphur yellow; and the horses' heads resembled lions' heads. Out of their mouths proceed fire, smoke, and sulphur. 18 By these three plagues, one third of mankind was killed: by the fire, the smoke, and the sulphur, which proceeded out of their mouths. 19 For the power of the horses is in their mouths and in their tails. For their tails are like serpents, and have heads; and with them they harm.

20 The rest of mankind, who were not killed with these plagues, didn't repent of the works of their hands, that they wouldn't worship demons, and the idols of gold, and of silver, and of brass, and of stone, and of wood, which can't see, hear, or walk. 21 They didn't repent of their murders, their sorceries,[g] their sexual immorality, or their thefts.

10

1 I saw a mighty angel coming down out of the sky, clothed with a cloud. A rainbow was on his head. His face was like the sun, and his feet like pillars of fire. 2 He had in his hand a little open book. He set his right foot on the sea, and his left on the land. 3 He cried with a loud voice, as a lion roars. When he cried, the seven thunders uttered their voices. 4 When the seven thunders sounded, I was about to write; but I heard a voice from the sky saying, "Seal up the things which the seven thunders said, and don't write them."

5 The angel whom I saw standing on the sea and on the land lifted up his right hand to the sky 6 and swore by him who lives forever and ever, who created heaven and the things that are in it, the earth and the things

that are in it, and the sea and the things that are in it, that there will no longer be delay, 7 but in the days of the voice of the seventh angel, when he is about to sound, then the mystery of God is finished, as he declared to his servants the prophets.

8 The voice which I heard from heaven, again speaking with me, said, "Go, take the book which is open in the hand of the angel who stands on the sea and on the land."

9 I went to the angel, telling him to give me the little book.

He said to me, "Take it and eat it. It will make your stomach bitter, but in your mouth it will be as sweet as honey."

10 I took the little book out of the angel's hand, and ate it. It was as sweet as honey in my mouth. When I had eaten it, my stomach was made bitter. 11 They[h] told me, "You must prophesy again over many peoples, nations, languages, and kings."

11

1 A reed like a rod was given to me. Someone said, "Rise and measure God's temple, and the altar, and those who worship in it. 2 Leave out the court which is outside of the temple, and don't measure it, for it has been given to the nations. They will tread the holy city under foot for forty-two months. 3 I will give power to my two witnesses, and they will prophesy one thousand and two hundred and sixty days, clothed in sackcloth."

4 These are the two olive trees and the two lamp stands, standing before the Lord of the earth. 5 If anyone desires to harm them, fire proceeds out of their mouth and devours their enemies. If anyone desires to harm them, he must be killed in this way. 6 These have the power to shut up the sky, that it may not rain during the days of their prophecy. They have power over the waters, to turn them into blood, and to strike the earth with every plague, as often as they desire.

7 When they have finished their testimony, the beast that comes up out of the abyss will make war with them, and overcome them, and kill them. 8 Their dead bodies will be in the street of the great city, which spiritually is called Sodom and Egypt, where also their Lord was crucified. 9 From amongst the peoples, tribes, languages, and nations, people will look at their dead bodies for three and a half days, and will not allow their dead bodies to be laid in a tomb. 10 Those who dwell on the earth will rejoice over them, and they will be glad. They will give gifts to one another, because these two prophets tormented those who dwell on the earth.

11 After the three and a half days, the breath of life from God entered into them, and they stood on their feet. Great fear fell on those who saw them. 12 I heard a loud voice from heaven saying to them, "Come up here!" They went up into heaven in a cloud, and their enemies saw them. 13 In that day there was a great earthquake, and a tenth of the city fell. Seven thousand people were killed in the earthquake, and the rest were terrified and gave glory to the God of heaven.

14 The second woe is past. Behold, the third woe comes quickly.

15 The seventh angel sounded, and great voices in heaven followed, saying, "The kingdom of the world has become the Kingdom of our Lord and of his Christ. He will reign forever and ever!"

16 The twenty-four elders, who sit on their thrones before God's throne, fell on their faces and worshipped God, 17 saying: "We give you thanks, Lord God, the Almighty, the one who is and who was,[i] because you have taken your great power and reigned. 18 The nations were angry, and your wrath came, as did the time for the dead to be judged, and to give your bondservants the prophets, their reward, as well as to the saints and those who fear your name, to the small and the great, and to destroy those who destroy the earth."

19 God's temple that is in heaven was opened, and the ark of the Lord's covenant was seen in his temple. Lightnings, sounds, thunders, an earthquake, and great hail followed.

12

1 A great sign was seen in heaven: a woman clothed with the sun, and the moon under her feet, and on her head a crown of twelve stars. 2 She was with child. She cried out in pain, labouring to give birth.

3 Another sign was seen in heaven. Behold, a great red dragon, having seven heads and ten horns, and on his heads seven crowns. 4 His tail drew one third of the stars of the sky, and threw them to the earth. The dragon stood before the woman who was about to give birth, so that when she gave birth he might devour her child. 5 She gave birth to a son, a male child, who is to rule all the nations with a rod of iron. Her child was caught up to God and to his throne. 6 The woman fled into the wilderness, where she has a place prepared by God, that there they may nourish her one thousand and two hundred and sixty days.

7 There was war in the sky. Michael and his angels made war on the dragon. The dragon and his angels made war. 8 They didn't prevail. No place was found for them any more in heaven. 9 The great dragon was thrown down, the old serpent, he who is called the devil and Satan, the deceiver of the whole world. He was thrown down to the earth, and his angels were thrown down with him.

10 I heard a loud voice in heaven, saying, "Now the salvation, the power, and the Kingdom of our God, and the authority of his Christ has come; for the accuser of our brothers has been thrown down, who accuses

---

[a] *8:7* TR omits "One third of the earth was burnt up"

[b] *8:13* TR reads "angel" instead of "eagle"

[c] *9:2* TR adds "great"

[d] *9:11* "Abaddon" is a Hebrew word that means "ruin", "destruction", or "the place of destruction"

[e] *9:11* "Apollyon" means "Destroyer".

[f] *9:16* literally, "ten thousands of ten thousands"

[g] *9:21* The word for "sorceries" (pharmakeia) also implies the use of potions, poisons, and drugs

[h] *10:11* TR reads "He" instead of "They"

[i] *11:17* TR adds "and who is coming"

them before our God day and night. 11 They overcame him because of the Lamb's blood, and because of the word of their testimony. They didn't love their life, even to death. 12 Therefore rejoice, heavens, and you who dwell in them. Woe to the earth and to the sea, because the devil has gone down to you, having great wrath, knowing that he has but a short time."

13 When the dragon saw that he was thrown down to the earth, he persecuted the woman who gave birth to the male child. 14 Two wings of the great eagle were given to the woman, that she might fly into the wilderness to her place, so that she might be nourished for a time, times, and half a time, from the face of the serpent. 15 The serpent spewed water out of his mouth after the woman like a river, that he might cause her to be carried away by the stream. 16 The earth helped the woman, and the earth opened its mouth and swallowed up the river which the dragon spewed out of his mouth. 17 The dragon grew angry with the woman, and went away to make war with the rest of her offspring,[a] who keep God's commandments and hold Jesus' testimony.

13

1 Then I stood[b] on the sand of the sea. I saw a beast coming up out of the sea, having ten horns and seven heads. On his horns were ten crowns, and on his heads, blasphemous names. 2 The beast which I saw was like a leopard, and his feet were like those of a bear, and his mouth like the mouth of a lion. The dragon gave him his power, his throne, and great authority. 3 One of his heads looked like it had been wounded fatally. His fatal wound was healed, and the whole earth marvelled at the beast. 4 They worshipped the dragon because he gave his authority to the beast; and they worshipped the beast, saying, "Who is like the beast? Who is able to make war with him?"

5 A mouth speaking great things and blasphemy was given to him. Authority to make war for forty-two months was given to him. 6 He opened his mouth for blasphemy against God, to blaspheme his name, his dwelling, and those who dwell in heaven. 7 It was given to him to make war with the saints and to overcome them. Authority over every tribe, people, language, and nation was given to him. 8 All who dwell on the earth will worship him, everyone whose name has not been written from the foundation of the world in the book of life of the Lamb who has been killed. 9 If anyone has an ear, let him hear. 10 If anyone is to go into captivity, he will go into captivity. If anyone is to be killed with the sword, he must be killed.[c] Here is the endurance and the faith of the saints.

11 I saw another beast coming up out of the earth. He had two horns like a lamb and it spoke like a dragon. 12 He exercises all the authority of the first beast in his presence. He makes the earth and those who dwell in it to worship the first beast, whose fatal wound was healed. 13 He performs great signs, even making fire come down out of the sky to the earth in the sight of people. 14 He deceives my own[d] people who dwell on the earth because of the signs he was granted to do in front of the beast, saying to those who dwell on the earth that they should make an image to the beast who had the sword wound and lived. 15 It was given to him to give breath to the image of the beast, that the image of the beast should both speak, and cause as many as wouldn't worship the image of the beast to be killed. 16 He causes all, the small and the great, the rich and the poor, and the free and the slave, to be given marks on their right hands or on their foreheads; 17 and that no one would be able to buy or to sell unless he has that mark, which is the name of the beast or the number of his name. 18 Here is wisdom. He who has understanding, let him calculate the number of the beast, for it is the number of a man. His number is six hundred and sixty-six.

14

1 I saw, and behold, the Lamb standing on Mount Zion, and with him a number, one hundred and forty-four thousand, having his name and the name of his Father written on their foreheads. 2 I heard a sound from heaven like the sound of many waters and like the sound of a great thunder. The sound which I heard was like that of harpists playing on their harps. 3 They sing a new song before the throne and before the four living creatures and the elders. No one could learn the song except the one hundred and forty-four thousand, those who had been redeemed out of the earth. 4 These are those who were not defiled with women, for they are virgins. These are those who follow the Lamb wherever he goes. These were redeemed by Jesus from amongst men, the first fruits to God and to the Lamb. 5 In their mouth was found no lie, for they are blameless.[e]

6 I saw an angel flying in mid heaven, having an eternal Good News to proclaim to those who dwell on the earth—to every nation, tribe, language, and people. 7 He said with a loud voice, "Fear the Lord, and give him glory, for the hour of his judgement has come. Worship him who made the heaven, the earth, the sea, and the springs of waters!"

8 Another, a second angel, followed, saying, "Babylon the great has fallen, which has made all the nations to drink of the wine of the wrath of her sexual immorality."

9 Another angel, a third, followed them, saying with a great voice, "If anyone worships the beast and his image, and receives a mark on his forehead or on his hand, 10 he also will drink of the wine of the wrath of God, which is prepared unmixed in the cup of his anger. He will be

tormented with fire and sulphur in the presence of the holy angels and in the presence of the Lamb. 11 The smoke of their torment goes up forever and ever. They have no rest day and night, those who worship the beast and his image, and whoever receives the mark of his name.

12 Here is the perseverance of the saints, those who keep the commandments of God and the faith of Jesus."

13 I heard a voice from heaven saying, "Write, 'Blessed are the dead who die in the Lord from now on.'"

"Yes," says the Spirit, "that they may rest from their labours, for their works follow with them."

14 I looked, and saw a white cloud, and on the cloud one sitting like a son of man,' having on his head a golden crown, and in his hand a sharp sickle. 15 Another angel came out of the temple, crying with a loud voice to him who sat on the cloud, "Send your sickle and reap, for the hour to reap has come; for the harvest of the earth is ripe!" 16 He who sat on the cloud thrust his sickle on the earth, and the earth was reaped.

17 Another angel came out of the temple which is in heaven. He also had a sharp sickle. 18 Another angel came out from the altar, he who has power over fire, and he called with a great voice to him who had the sharp sickle, saying, "Send your sharp sickle and gather the clusters of the vine of the earth, for the earth's grapes are fully ripe!" 19 The angel thrust his sickle into the earth, and gathered the vintage of the earth and threw it into the great wine press of the wrath of God. 20 The wine press was trodden outside of the city, and blood came out of the wine press, up to the bridles of the horses, as far as one thousand and six hundred stadia.[f]

15

1 I saw another great and marvellous sign in the sky: seven angels having the seven last plagues, for in them God's wrath is finished.

2 I saw something like a sea of glass mixed with fire, and those who overcame the beast, his image,[g] and the number of his name, standing on the sea of glass, having harps of God. 3 They sang the song of Moses, the servant of God, and the song of the Lamb, saying,

"Great and marvellous are your works, Lord God, the Almighty!
Righteous and true are your ways, you King of the nations.
4 Who wouldn't fear you, Lord,
    and glorify your name?
For you only are holy.
For all the nations will come and worship before you.
For your righteous acts have been revealed."

5 After these things I looked, and the temple of the tabernacle of the testimony in heaven was opened. 6 The seven angels who had the seven plagues came out, clothed with pure, bright linen, and wearing golden sashes around their chests.

7 One of the four living creatures gave to the seven angels seven golden bowls full of the wrath of God, who lives forever and ever. 8 The temple was filled with smoke from the glory of God and from his power. No one was able to enter into the temple until the seven plagues of the seven angels would be finished.

16

1 I heard a loud voice out of the temple, saying to the seven angels, "Go and pour out the seven bowls of the wrath of God on the earth!"

2 The first went, and poured out his bowl into the earth, and it became a harmful and painful sore on the people who had the mark of the beast, and who worshipped his image.

3 The second angel poured out his bowl into the sea, and it became blood as of a dead man. Every living thing in the sea died.

4 The third poured out his bowl into the rivers and springs of water, and they became blood. 5 I heard the angel of the waters saying, "You are righteous, who are and who were, O Holy One, because you have judged these things. 6 For they poured out the blood of saints and prophets, and you have given them blood to drink. They deserve this."

7 I heard the altar saying, "Yes, Lord God, the Almighty, true and righteous are your judgements."

8 The fourth poured out his bowl on the sun, and it was given to him to scorch men with fire. 9 People were scorched with great heat, and people blasphemed the name of God who has the power over these plagues. They didn't repent and give him glory.

10 The fifth poured out his bowl on the throne of the beast, and his kingdom was darkened. They gnawed their tongues because of the pain, 11 and they blasphemed the God of heaven because of their pains and their sores. They still didn't repent of their works.

12 The sixth poured out his bowl on the great river, the Euphrates. Its water was dried up, that the way might be prepared for the kings that come from the sunrise.[h] 13 I saw coming out of the mouth of the dragon, and out of the mouth of the beast, and out of the mouth of the false prophet, three unclean spirits, something like frogs; 14 for they are spirits of demons, performing signs, which go out to the kings of the whole inhabited earth, to gather them together for the war of that great day of God the Almighty.

15 "Behold, I come like a thief. Blessed is he who watches, and keeps his clothes, so that he doesn't walk naked, and they see his shame." 16 He

---

a 12:17 or, seed

b 13:1 NU reads he stood

c 13:10 TR reads "If anyone leads into captivity, into captivity he goes. If anyone will kill with the sword, he must be killed with a sword." instead of "If anyone is to go into captivity, he will go into captivity. If anyone is to be killed with the sword, he must be killed."

d 13:14 NU omits "my own"

e 14:5 TR adds "before the throne of God"

** 14:14 Daniel 7:13

f 14:20 1600 stadia = 296 kilometres or 184 miles

g 15:2 TR adds "his mark,"

h 16:12 or, east

gathered them together into the place which is called in Hebrew, "Harmagedon".

17 The seventh poured out his bowl into the air. A loud voice came out of the temple of heaven, from the throne, saying, "It is done!" 18 There were lightnings, sounds, and thunders; and there was a great earthquake such as has not happened since there were men on the earth—so great an earthquake and so mighty. 19 The great city was divided into three parts, and the cities of the nations fell. Babylon the great was remembered in the sight of God, to give to her the cup of the wine of the fierceness of his wrath. 20 Every island fled away, and the mountains were not found. 21 Great hailstones, about the weight of a talent,[a] came down out of the sky on people. People blasphemed God because of the plague of the hail, for this plague was exceedingly severe.

17

1 One of the seven angels who had the seven bowls came and spoke with me, saying, "Come here. I will show you the judgement of the great prostitute who sits on many waters, 2 with whom the kings of the earth committed sexual immorality. Those who dwell in the earth were made drunken with the wine of her sexual immorality." 3 He carried me away in the Spirit into a wilderness. I saw a woman sitting on a scarlet-coloured beast, full of blasphemous names, having seven heads and ten horns. 4 The woman was dressed in purple and scarlet, and decked with gold and precious stones and pearls, having in her hand a golden cup full of abominations and the impurities of the sexual immorality of the earth. 5 And on her forehead a name was written, "MYSTERY, BABYLON THE GREAT, THE MOTHER OF THE PROSTITUTES AND OF THE ABOMINATIONS OF THE EARTH." 6 I saw the woman drunken with the blood of the saints and with the blood of the martyrs of Jesus. When I saw her, I wondered with great amazement.

7 The angel said to me, "Why do you wonder? I will tell you the mystery of the woman and of the beast that carries her, which has the seven heads and the ten horns. 8 The beast that you saw was, and is not; and is about to come up out of the abyss and to go into destruction. Those who dwell on the earth and whose names have not been written in the book of life from the foundation of the world will marvel when they see that the beast was, and is not, and shall be present.[b]

9 Here is the mind that has wisdom. The seven heads are seven mountains on which the woman sits. 10 They are seven kings. Five have fallen, the one is, and the other has not yet come. When he comes, he must continue a little while. 11 The beast that was, and is not, is himself also an eighth, and is of the seven; and he goes to destruction. 12 The ten horns that you saw are ten kings who have received no kingdom as yet, but they receive authority as kings with the beast for one hour. 13 These have one mind, and they give their power and authority to the beast. 14 These will war against the Lamb, and the Lamb will overcome them, for he is Lord of lords and King of kings; and those who are with him are called, chosen, and faithful." 15 He said to me, "The waters which you saw, where the prostitute sits, are peoples, multitudes, nations, and languages. 16 The ten horns which you saw, they and the beast will hate the prostitute, will make her desolate, will strip her naked, will eat her flesh, and will burn her utterly with fire. 17 For God has put in their hearts to do what he has in mind, to be of one mind, and to give their kingdom to the beast, until the words of God should be accomplished. 18 The woman whom you saw is the great city which reigns over the kings of the earth."

18

1 After these things, I saw another angel coming down out of the sky, having great authority. The earth was illuminated with his glory. 2 He cried with a mighty voice, saying, "Fallen, fallen is Babylon the great, and she has become a habitation of demons, a prison of every unclean spirit, and a prison of every unclean and hated bird! 3 For all the nations have drunk of the wine of the wrath of her sexual immorality, the kings of the earth committed sexual immorality with her, and the merchants of the earth grew rich from the abundance of her luxury."

4 I heard another voice from heaven, saying, "Come out of her, my people, that you have no participation in her sins, and that you don't receive of her plagues, 5 for her sins have reached to the sky, and God has remembered her iniquities. 6 Return to her just as she returned, and repay her double as she did, and according to her works. In the cup which she mixed, mix to her double. 7 However much she glorified herself and grew wanton, so much give her of torment and mourning. For she says in her heart, 'I sit a queen, and am no widow, and will in no way see mourning.' 8 Therefore in one day her plagues will come: death, mourning, and famine; and she will be utterly burnt with fire, for the Lord God who has judged her is strong.

9 The kings of the earth who committed sexual immorality and lived wantonly with her will weep and wail over her, when they look at the smoke of her burning, 10 standing far away for the fear of her torment, saying, 'Woe, woe, the great city, Babylon, the strong city! For your judgement has come in one hour.' 11 The merchants of the earth weep and mourn over her, for no one buys their merchandise any more: 12 merchandise of gold, silver, precious stones, pearls, fine linen, purple, silk, scarlet, all expensive wood, every vessel of ivory, every vessel made of most precious wood, and of brass, and iron, and marble; 13 and cinnamon, incense, perfume, frankincense, wine, olive oil, fine flour, wheat, cattle, sheep, horses,

chariots, and people's bodies and souls. 14 The fruits which your soul lusted after have been lost to you. All things that were dainty and sumptuous have perished from you, and you will find them no more at all. 15 The merchants of these things, who were made rich by her, will stand far away for the fear of her torment, weeping and mourning, 16 saying, 'Woe, woe, the great city, she who was dressed in fine linen, purple, and scarlet, and decked with gold and precious stones and pearls! 17 For in an hour such great riches are made desolate.' Every ship master, and everyone who sails anywhere, and mariners, and as many as gain their living by sea, stood far away, 18 and cried out as they looked at the smoke of her burning, saying, 'What is like the great city?' 19 They cast dust on their heads, and cried, weeping and mourning, saying, 'Woe, woe, the great city, in which all who had their ships in the sea were made rich by reason of her great wealth!' For she is made desolate in one hour.

20 "Rejoice over her, O heaven, you saints, apostles, and prophets, for God has judged your judgement on her."

21 A mighty angel took up a stone like a great millstone and cast it into the sea, saying, "Thus with violence will Babylon, the great city, be thrown down, and will be found no more at all. 22 The voice of harpists, minstrels, flute players, and trumpeters will be heard no more at all in you. No craftsman of whatever craft will be found any more at all in you. The sound of a mill will be heard no more at all in you. 23 The light of a lamp will shine no more at all in you. The voice of the bridegroom and of the bride will be heard no more at all in you, for your merchants were the princes of the earth; for with your sorcery all the nations were deceived. 24 In her was found the blood of prophets and of saints, and of all who have been slain on the earth."

19

1 After these things I heard something like a loud voice of a great multitude in heaven, saying, "Hallelujah! Salvation, power, and glory belong to our God; 2 for his judgements are true and righteous. For he has judged the great prostitute who corrupted the earth with her sexual immorality, and he has avenged the blood of his servants at her hand."

3 A second said, "Hallelujah! Her smoke goes up forever and ever." 4 The twenty-four elders and the four living creatures fell down and worshipped God who sits on the throne, saying, "Amen! Hallelujah!"

5 A voice came from the throne, saying, "Give praise to our God, all you his servants, you who fear him, the small and the great!"

6 I heard something like the voice of a great multitude, and like the voice of many waters, and like the voice of mighty thunders, saying, "Hallelujah! For the Lord our God, the Almighty, reigns! 7 Let's rejoice and be exceedingly glad, and let's give the glory to him. For the wedding of the Lamb has come, and his wife has made herself ready." 8 It was given to her that she would array herself in bright, pure, fine linen, for the fine linen is the righteous acts of the saints.

9 He said to me, "Write, 'Blessed are those who are invited to the wedding supper of the Lamb.'" He said to me, "These are true words of God."

10 I fell down before his feet to worship him. He said to me, "Look! Don't do it! I am a fellow bondservant with you and with your brothers who hold the testimony of Jesus. Worship God, for the testimony of Jesus is the Spirit of Prophecy."

11 I saw the heaven opened, and behold, a white horse, and he who sat on it is called Faithful and True. In righteousness he judges and makes war. 12 His eyes are a flame of fire, and on his head are many crowns. He has names written and a name written which no one knows but he himself. 13 He is clothed in a garment sprinkled with blood. His name is called "The Word of God." 14 The armies which are in heaven, clothed in white, pure, fine linen, followed him on white horses. 15 Out of his mouth proceeds a sharp, double-edged sword that with it he should strike the nations. He will rule them with an iron rod.* He treads the wine press of the fierceness of the wrath of God, the Almighty. 16 He has on his garment and on his thigh a name written, "KING OF KINGS AND LORD OF LORDS."

17 I saw an angel standing in the sun. He cried with a loud voice, saying to all the birds that fly in the sky, "Come! Be gathered together to the great supper of God,[c] 18 that you may eat the flesh of kings, the flesh of captains, the flesh of mighty men, and the flesh of horses and of those who sit on them, and the flesh of all men, both free and slave, small and great." 19 I saw the beast, the kings of the earth, and their armies, gathered together to make war against him who sat on the horse and against his army. 20 The beast was taken, and with him the false prophet who worked the signs in his sight, with which he deceived those who had received the mark of the beast and those who worshipped his image. These two were thrown alive into the lake of fire that burns with sulphur. 21 The rest were killed with the sword of him who sat on the horse, the sword which came out of his mouth. So all the birds were filled with their flesh.

20

1 I saw an angel coming down out of heaven, having the key of the abyss and a great chain in his hand. 2 He seized the dragon, the old serpent, who is the devil and Satan, who deceives the whole inhabited earth,[d] and bound him for a thousand years, 3 and cast him into the abyss, and shut it and sealed it over him, that he should deceive the nations no more until the thousand years were finished. After this, he must be freed for a short time.

---

a *16:21* A talent is about 30 kilograms or 66 pounds.
b *17:8* TR reads "yet is" instead of "shall be present"
** *19:15* Psalms 2:9

c *19:17* TR reads "supper of the great God" instead of "great supper of God"
d *20:2* TR and NU omit "who deceives the whole inhabited earth".

4 I saw thrones, and they sat on them, and judgement was given to them. I saw the souls of those who had been beheaded for the testimony of Jesus and for the word of God, and such as didn't worship the beast nor his image, and didn't receive the mark on their forehead and on their hand. They lived and reigned with Christ for a thousand years. 5 The rest of the dead didn't live until the thousand years were finished. This is the first resurrection. 6 Blessed and holy is he who has part in the first resurrection. Over these, the second death has no power, but they will be priests of God and of Christ, and will reign with him one thousand years.

7 And after the thousand years, Satan will be released from his prison 8 and he will come out to deceive the nations which are in the four corners of the earth, Gog and Magog, to gather them together to the war, whose number is as the sand of the sea. 9 They went up over the width of the earth and surrounded the camp of the saints and the beloved city. Fire came down out of heaven from God and devoured them. 10 The devil who deceived them was thrown into the lake of fire and sulphur, where the beast and the false prophet are also. They will be tormented day and night forever and ever.

11 I saw a great white throne and him who sat on it, from whose face the earth and the heaven fled away. There was found no place for them. 12 I saw the dead, the great and the small, standing before the throne, and they opened books. Another book was opened, which is the book of life. The dead were judged out of the things which were written in the books, according to their works. 13 The sea gave up the dead who were in it. Death and Hades^a gave up the dead who were in them. They were judged, each one according to his works. 14 Death and Hades^b were thrown into the lake of fire. This is the second death, the lake of fire. 15 If anyone was not found written in the book of life, he was cast into the lake of fire.

21

1 I saw a new heaven and a new earth, for the first heaven and the first earth have passed away, and the sea is no more. 2 I saw the holy city, New Jerusalem, coming down out of heaven from God, prepared like a bride adorned for her husband. 3 I heard a loud voice out of heaven saying, "Behold, God's dwelling is with people; and he will dwell with them, and they will be his people, and God himself will be with them as their God. 4 He will wipe away every tear from their eyes. Death will be no more; neither will there be mourning, nor crying, nor pain any more. The first things have passed away."

5 He who sits on the throne said, "Behold, I am making all things new." He said, "Write, for these words of God are faithful and true." 6 He said to me, "I am the Alpha and the Omega, the Beginning and the End. I will give freely to him who is thirsty from the spring of the water of life. 7 He who overcomes, I will give him these things. I will be his God, and he will be my son. 8 But for the cowardly, unbelieving, sinners,^c abominable, murderers, sexually immoral, sorcerers,^d idolaters, and all liars, their part is in the lake that burns with fire and sulphur, which is the second death."

9 One of the seven angels who had the seven bowls which were loaded with the seven last plagues came, and he spoke with me, saying, "Come here. I will show you the bride, the Lamb's wife." 10 He carried me away in the Spirit to a great and high mountain, and showed me the holy city, Jerusalem, coming down out of heaven from God, 11 having the glory of God. Her light was like a most precious stone, like a jasper stone, clear as crystal; 12 having a great and high wall with twelve gates, and at the gates twelve angels, and names written on them, which are the names of the twelve tribes of the children of Israel. 13 On the east were three gates, and on the north three gates, and on the south three gates, and on the west three gates. 14 The wall of the city had twelve foundations, and on them twelve names of the twelve Apostles of the Lamb.

15 He who spoke with me had for a measure a golden reed to measure the city, its gates, and its walls. 16 The city is square. Its length is as great as its width. He measured the city with the reed: twelve thousand and twelve stadia.^e Its length, width, and height are equal. 17 Its wall is one hundred and forty-four cubits,^f by the measure of a man, that is, of an angel. 18 The construction of its wall was jasper. The city was pure gold, like pure glass. 19 The foundations of the city's wall were adorned with all kinds of precious stones. The first foundation was jasper, the second sapphire;^g the third chalcedony, the fourth emerald, 20 the fifth sardonyx, the sixth sardius, the seventh chrysolite, the eighth beryl, the ninth topaz, the tenth chrysoprase, the eleventh jacinth, and the twelfth amethyst. 21 The twelve gates were twelve pearls. Each one of the gates was made of one pearl. The street of the city was pure gold, like transparent glass.

22 I saw no temple in it, for the Lord God the Almighty and the Lamb are its temple. 23 The city has no need for the sun or moon to shine, for the very glory of God illuminated it and its lamp is the Lamb. 24 The nations will walk in its light. The kings of the earth bring the glory and honour of the nations into it. 25 Its gates will in no way be shut by day (for there will be no night there), 26 and they shall bring the glory and the honour of the nations into it so that they may enter. 27 There will in no way enter into it anything profane, or one who causes an abomination or a lie, but only those who are written in the Lamb's book of life.

22

1 He showed me a^h river of water of life, clear as crystal, proceeding out of the throne of God and of the Lamb, 2 in the middle of its street. On this side of the river and on that was the tree of life, bearing twelve kinds of fruits, yielding its fruit every month. The leaves of the tree were for the healing of the nations. 3 There will be no curse any more. The throne of God and of the Lamb will be in it, and his servants will serve him. 4 They will see his face, and his name will be on their foreheads. 5 There will be no night, and they need no lamp light or sun light; for the Lord God will illuminate them. They will reign forever and ever.

6 He said to me, "These words are faithful and true. The Lord God of the spirits of the prophets sent his angel to show to his bondservants the things which must happen soon."

7 "Behold, I am coming soon! Blessed is he who keeps the words of the prophecy of this book."

8 Now I, John, am the one who heard and saw these things. When I heard and saw, I fell down to worship before the feet of the angel who had shown me these things. 9 He said to me, "You must not do that! I am a fellow bondservant with you and with your brothers, the prophets, and with those who keep the words of this book. Worship God." 10 He said to me, "Don't seal up the words of the prophecy of this book, for the time is at hand. 11 He who acts unjustly, let him act unjustly still. He who is filthy, let him be filthy still. He who is righteous, let him do righteousness still. He who is holy, let him be holy still."

12 "Behold, I am coming soon! My reward is with me, to repay to each man according to his work. 13 I am the Alpha and the Omega, the First and the Last, the Beginning and the End. 14 Blessed are those who do his commandments,ⁱ that they may have the right to the tree of life, and may enter in by the gates into the city. 15 Outside are the dogs, the sorcerers, the sexually immoral, the murderers, the idolaters, and everyone who loves and practices falsehood. 16 I, Jesus, have sent my angel to testify these things to you for the assemblies. I am the root and the offspring of David, the Bright and Morning Star."

17 The Spirit and the bride say, "Come!" He who hears, let him say, "Come!" He who is thirsty, let him come. He who desires, let him take the water of life freely.

18 I testify to everyone who hears the words of the prophecy of this book: if anyone adds to them, God will add to him the plagues which are written in this book. 19 If anyone takes away from the words of the book of this prophecy, God will take away his part from the tree^j of life, and out of the holy city, which are written in this book. 20 He who testifies these things says, "Yes, I am coming soon."

Amen! Yes, come, Lord Jesus!

21 The grace of the Lord Jesus Christ be with all the saints. Amen.

---

^a *20:13* or, Hell
^b *20:14* or, Hell
^c *21:8* TR and NU omit "sinners"
^d *21:8* The word for "sorcerers" here also includes users of potions and drugs.
^e *21:16* 12,012 stadia = 2,221 kilometres or 1,380 miles. TR reads 12,000 stadia instead of 12,012 stadia.
^f *21:17* 144 cubits is about 65.8 metres or 216 feet
^g *21:19* or, lapis lazuli
^h *22:1* TR adds "pure"
ⁱ *22:14* NU reads "wash their robes" instead of "do his commandments".
^j *22:19* TR reads "Book" instead of "tree"

International English Bible Glossary

The following words used in the International English Bible (IEB) are not very common, either because they refer to ancient weights, measures, or money, or because they are in some way unique to the Bible.

Abaddon Abaddon is Hebrew for destruction.

Abba Abba is a Chaldee word for father, used in a respectful, affectionate, and familiar way, like papa, dad, or daddy. Often used in prayer to refer to our Father in Heaven.

adultery Adultery is having sexual intercourse with someone besides your own husband or wife. In the Bible, the only legitimate sexual intercourse is between a man and a woman who are married to each other.

alpha Alpha is the first letter of the Greek alphabet. It is sometimes used to mean the beginning or the first.

amen Amen means "So be it" or "I believe it is certainly so."

angel "Angel" literally means "messenger" or "envoy," and is usually used to refer to spiritual beings who normally are invisible to us, but can also appear as exceedingly strong creatures or as humans.

Apollyon Apollyon is Greek for destroyer.

apostle "Apostle" means a delegate, messenger, or one sent forth with orders. This term is applied in the New Testament in both a general sense connected with a ministry of establishing and strengthening church fellowships, as well as in a specific sense to "The 12 Apostles of the Lamb" (Revelation 21:14). The former category applies to a specific ministry that continues in the Church (Ephesians 4:11-13) and which includes many more than 12 people, while the latter refers to the apostles named in Matthew 10:2-4, except with Judas Iscariot replaced by Matthias (Acts 1:26).

Armageddon See Har-magedon.

assarion An assarion is a small Roman copper coin worth one tenth of a drachma, or about an hour's wages for an agricultural labourer.

aureus An aureus is a Roman gold coin, worth 25 silver denarii. An aureus weighed from 115 to 126.3 grains (7.45 to 8.18 grams).

baptise Baptise means to immerse in, or wash with something, usually water. Baptism in the Holy Spirit, fire, the Body of Christ, and suffering are also mentioned in the New Testament, along with baptism in water. Baptism is not just to cleanse the body, but as an outward sign of an inward spiritual cleansing and commitment. Baptism is a sign of repentance, as practised by John the Baptiser, and of faith in Jesus Christ, as practised by Jesus' disciples.

bath A bath is a liquid measure of about 22 litres, 5.8 U. S. gallons, or 4.8 imperial gallons.

batos A batos is a liquid measure of about 39.5 litres, 10.4 U. S. gallons, or 8.7 imperial gallons.

Beelzebul literally, lord of the flies. A name used for the devil.

Beersheba Beersheba is Hebrew for "well of the oath" or "well of the seven." A city in Israel.

behold Look! See! Wow! Notice this! Lo!

cherub A cherub is a kind of angel with wings and hands that is associated with the throne room of God and guardian duty. See Ezekiel 10.

cherubim Cherubim means more than one cherub or a mighty cherub.

phoenix A choenix is a dry volume measure that is a little more than a litre (which is a little more than a quart). A choenix was the daily ration of grain for a soldier in some armies.

concubine a woman who is united to a man for the purpose of providing him with sexual pleasure and children, but not being honoured as a full partner in marriage; a second-class wife. In Old Testament times (and in some places now), it was the custom of middle-eastern kings, chiefs, and wealthy men to marry multiple wives and concubines, but God commanded the Kings of Israel not to do so (Deuteronomy 17:17) and Jesus encouraged people to either remain single or marry as God originally intended: one man married to one woman (Matthew 19:3-12; 1 Corinthians 7:1-13).

cor A cor is a dry measure of about 391 litres, 103 U. S. gallons, or 86 imperial gallons.

corban Corban is a Hebrew word for an offering devoted to God.

crucify Crucify means to execute someone by nailing them to a cross with metal spikes. Their hands are stretched out on the crossbeam with spikes driven through their wrists or hands. Their feet or ankles are attached to a cross with a metal spike. The weight of the victim's body tends to force the air out of his lungs. To rise up to breathe, the victim has to put weight on the wounds, and use a lot of strength. The victim is nailed to the cross while the cross is on the ground, then the cross is raised up and dropped into a hole, thus jarring the wounds. Before crucifixion, the victim was usually whipped with a Roman cat of nine tails, which had bits of glass and metal tied to its ends. This caused chunks of flesh to be removed and open wounds to be placed against the raw wood of the cross. The victim was made to carry the heavy crossbeam of his cross from the place of judgement to the place of crucifixion, but often was physically unable after the scourging, so another person would be pressed into involuntary service to carry the cross for him. Roman crucifixion was generally done totally naked to maximize both shame and discomfort. Eventually, the pain, weakness, dehydration, and exhaustion of the muscles needed to breathe make breathing impossible, and the victim suffocates.

cubit A cubit is a unit of linear measure, from the elbow to the tip of the longest finger of a man. This unit is commonly converted to 0.46 metres or 18 inches, although that varies with height of the man doing the measurement. There is also a "long" cubit that is longer than a regular cubit by a handbreadth. (Ezekiel 43:13)

cummin Cummin is an aromatic seed from Cuminum cyminum, resembling caraway in flavour and appearance. It is used as a spice.

darnel Darnel is a weed grass (probably bearded darnel or Lolium temulentum) that looks very much like wheat until it is mature, when the seeds reveal a great difference. Darnel seeds aren't good for much except as chicken feed or to burn to prevent the spread of this weed.

denarii denarii: plural form of denarius, a silver Roman coin worth about a day's wages for a labourer.

denarius A denarius is a silver Roman coin worth about a day's wages for an agricultural labourer. A denarius was worth 1/25th of a Roman aureus.

devil The word "devil" comes from the Greek "diabolos," which means "one prone to slander; a liar." "Devil" is used to refer to a fallen angel, also called "Satan," who works to steal, kill, destroy, and do evil. The devil's doom is certain, and it is only a matter of time before he is thrown into the Lake of Fire, never to escape.

didrachma A didrachma is a Greek silver coin worth 2 drachmas, about as much as 2 Roman denari, or about 2 days wages. It was commonly used to pay the half-shekel temple tax.

disciple a student who follows a teacher to learn both by precept and example.

distaff part of a spinning wheel used for twisting threads.

drachma A drachma is a Greek silver coin worth about one Roman denarius, or about a day's wages for an agricultural labourer.

El-Elohe-Israel El-Elohe-Israel means "God, the God of Israel" or "The God of Israel is mighty."

ephah An ephah is a measure of volume of about 22 litres, 5.8 U. S. gallons, 4.8 imperial gallons, or a bit more than half a bushel.

Gehenna Gehenna is one word used for Hell. It comes from the Hebrew Gey-Hinnom, literally "valley of Hinnom." This word originated as the name for a place south of the old city of Jerusalem where the city's rubbish was burnt. At one time, live babies were thrown crying into the fire under the arms of the idol, Moloch, to die there. This place was so despised by the people after the righteous King Josiah abolished this hideous practise that it was made into a garbage heap. Bodies of diseased animals and executed criminals were thrown there and burnt.

gittith Gittith is a musical term possibly meaning "an instrument of Gath."

goad a sharp, pointed prodding device used to motivate reluctant animals (such as oxen and mules) to move in the right direction.

gospel Gospel means "good news" or "glad tidings," specifically the Good News of Jesus' life, death, and resurrection for our salvation, healing, and provision; and the hope of eternal life that Jesus made available to us by God's grace.

Hades Hades: The nether realm of the disembodied spirits. Also known as "hell." See also "Sheol".

Har-magedon Har-magedon, also called Armegeddon, is most likely a reference to hill ("har") of Megiddo, near the Carmel Range in Israel. This area has a large valley plain with plenty of room for armies to maneuver.

hin A hin is a measure of volume of about 6.5 litres or 1.7 gallons.

homer One homer is about 220 litres, 6.2 U. S. bushels, 6.1 imperial bushels, 58 U. S. gallons, or 48.4 imperial gallons.

hypocrite a stage actor; someone who pretends to be someone other than who they really are; a pretender; a dissembler

Ishmael Ishmael is the son of Abraham and Hagar. Ishmael literally means, "God hears."

Jehovah See "Yahweh."

Jesus "Jesus" is Greek for the Hebrew name "Yeshua," which is a short version of "Yehoshua," which comes from "Yoshia," which means "He will save."

kodrantes A kodrantes is a small coin worth one half of an Attic chalcus or two lepta. It is worth less than 2% of a day's wages for an agricultural labourer.

lepta Lepta are very small, brass, Jewish coins worth half a Roman quadrans each, which is worth a quarter of the copper assarion. Lepta are worth less than 1% of an agricultural worker's daily wages.

leviathan Leviathan is a poetic name for a large aquatic creature, possibly a crocodile or a dinosaur.

mahalath Mahalath is the name of a tune or a musical term.

manna Name for the food that God miraculously provided to the Israelites while they were wandering in the wilderness between Egypt and the promised land. From Hebrew man-hu (What is that?) or manan (to allot). See Exodus 16:14-35.

marriage the union of a husband and a wife for the purpose of cohabitation, procreation, and to enjoy each other's company. God's plan for marriage is between one man and one woman (Mark 10:6-9; 1 Corinthians 7). Although there are many cases of a man marrying more than one woman in the Old Testament, being married to one wife is a requirement to serve in certain church leadership positions (1 Timothy 3:2,12; Titus 1:5-6).

maschil Maschil is a musical and literary term for "contemplation" or "meditative psalm."

michtam A michtam is a poem.

mina A mina is a Greek coin worth 100 Greek drachmas (or 100 Roman denarii), or about 100 day's wages for an agricultural labourer.

myrrh Myrrh is the fragrant substance that oozes out of the stems and branches of the low, shrubby tree commiphora myrrha or commiphora kataf native to the Arabian deserts and parts of Africa. The fragrant gum drops to the ground and hardens into an oily yellowish-brown resin. Myrrh was highly valued as a perfume, and as an ingredient in medicinal and ceremonial ointments.

Nicolaitans Nicolaitans were most likely Gnostics who taught the detestable lie that the physical and spiritual realms were entirely separate and that immorality in the physical realm wouldn't harm your spiritual health.

omega Omega is the last letter of the Greek alphabet. It is sometimes used to mean the last or the end.

Peniel Peniel is Hebrew for "face of God."

phylactery a leather container for holding a small scroll containing important Scripture passages that is worn on the arm or forehead in prayer. These phylacteries (tefillin in Hebrew) are still used by orthodox Jewish men. See Deuteronomy 6:8.

Praetorium Praetorium: the Roman governor's residence and office building, and those who work there.

quadrans A quadrans is a Roman coin worth about 1/64 of a denarius. A denarius is about one day's wages for an agricultural labourer.

rabbi Rabbi is a transliteration of the Hebrew word for "my teacher," used as a title of respect for Jewish teachers.

Rahab Rahab is either (1) The prostitute who hid Joshua's 2 spies in Jericho (Joshua 2,6) and later became an ancestor of Jesus (Matthew 1:5) and an example of faith (Hebrews 11:31; James 2:25); or (2) Literally, "pride" or "arrogance" — possibly a reference to a large aquatic creature (Job 9:13; 26:12; Isaiah 51:9) or symbolically referring to Egypt (Psalms 87:4; 89:10; Isaiah 30:7).

repent to change one's mind; turn away from sin and turn towards God; to abhor one's past sins and determine to follow God.

Rhabboni Rhabboni: a transliteration of the Hebrew word for "great teacher."

Sabbath The seventh day of the week, set aside by God for man to rest.

saints The Greek word for "saints" literally means "holy ones." Saints are people set apart for service to God as holy and separate, living in righteousness. Used in the Bible to refer to all Christians and to all of those who worship Yahweh in Old Testament times.

Samaritan A Samaritan is a resident of Samaria. The Samaritans and the Jews generally detested each other during the time that Jesus walked amongst us.

sanctify To declare or set apart something as holy. To purify and separate a person from sin.

sata A sata is a dry measure of capacity approximately equal to 13 litres or 1.5 pecks.

Satan Satan means "accuser." This is one name for the devil, an enemy of God and God's people.

scribe A scribe is one who copies God's law. They were often respected as teachers and authorities on God's law.

selah Selah is a musical term indicating a pause or instrumental interlude for reflection.

seraphim Seraphim are 6-winged angels. See Isaiah 6:2-6.

sexual immorality The term "sexual immorality" in the New Testament comes from the Greek "porneia," which refers to any sexual activity besides that between a husband and his wife. In other words, prostitution (male or female), bestiality, homosexual activity, any sexual intercourse outside of marriage, and the production and consumption of pornography all are included in this term.

shekel A measure of weight, and when referring to that weight in gold, silver, or brass, of money. A shekel is approximately 16 grams, about a half an ounce, or 20 gerahs (Ezekiel 45:12).

Sheol Sheol is the place of the dead. See also "Hades".

Shibah Shibah is Hebrew for "oath" or "seven." See Beersheba.

shigionoth Victorious music.

soul "Soul" refers to the emotions and intellect of a living person, as well as that person's very life. It is distinguished in the Bible from a person's spirit and body. (1 Thessalonians 5:23, Hebrews 4:12)

span A span is the length from the tip of a man's thumb to the tip of his little finger when his hand is stretched out (about half a cubit, or 9 inches, or 22.8 cm.)

spirit Spirit, breath, and wind all derive from the same Hebrew and Greek words. A person's spirit is the very essence of that person's life, which comes from God, who is a Spirit being (John 4:24, Genesis 1:2; 2:7). The Bible distinguishes between a person's spirit, soul, and body (1 Thessalonians 5:23, Hebrews 4:12). Some beings may exist as spirits without necessarily having a visible body, such as angels and demons (Luke 9:39, 1 John 4:1-3).

stadia Stadia is plural for "stadion," a linear measure of about 184.9 metres or 606.6 feet (the length of the race course at Olympia).

stater A stater is a Greek silver coin equivalent to four Attic or two Alexandrian drachmas, or a Jewish shekel: just exactly enough to cover the half-shekel Temple Tax for two people.

tabernacle a dwelling place or place of worship, usually a tent.

talent A measure of weight or mass of 3000 shekels.

Tartarus Tartarus is the Greek name for an underworld for the wicked dead; another name for Gehenna or Hell.

teraphim Teraphim are household idols that may have been associated with inheritance rights to the household property.

Yah "Yah" is a shortened form of "Yahweh," which is God's proper name. This form is used occasionally in the Old Testament, mostly in the Psalms. See "Yahweh."

Yahweh "Yahweh" is God's proper name. In Hebrew, the four consonants roughly equivalent to YHWH were considered too holy to pronounce, so the Hebrew word for "Lord" (Adonai) was substituted when reading it aloud. When vowel points were added to the Hebrew Old Testament, the vowel points for "Adonai" were mixed with the consonants for "Yahweh," which if you pronounced it literally as written, would be pronounced "Yehovah" or "Jehovah." When the Old Testament was translated to Greek, the tradition of substituting "Lord" for God's proper name continued in the translation of God's name to "Lord" (Kurios). Some English Bibles translate God's proper name to "LORD" or "GOD" (usually with small capital letters), based on that same tradition. This can get really confusing, since two other words ("Adonai" and "Elohim") translate to "Lord" and "God," and they are sometimes used together. The ASV of 1901 (and some other translations) render YHWH as "Jehovah." The most probable pronunciation of God's proper name is "Yahweh." In Hebrew, the name "Yahweh" is related to the active declaration "I AM." See Exodus 3:13-14. Since Hebrew has no tenses, the declaration "I AM" can also be interpreted as "I WAS" and "I WILL BE." Compare Revelation 1:8.

Zion Zion is a name which originally referred one of the mountains of Jerusalem. It became a term synonymous with Jerusalem itself. The term "Heavenly Zion" is also used to refer the future dwelling place of God's people.

This companion glossary to the International English Bible is in the Public Domain. You may not copyright it or claim authorship over it, but you are free to use, sell, distribute, or copy it.

The Bible

The word "Bible" comes from the Greek word *Biblia, which means "Books."* *So the Bible is really a collection or library of many books. These books are divided into two main parts, the Old Testament and the New Testament.*

The Old Testement

The Old Testament tells the history of the people of Israel. This history is based on their faith in the God of Israel and on their religious life as the people of God. The authors of these books wrote about what God had done for them as a people and how they were to worship and obey God in return. The following chart shows the different groups of books that make up the Old Testament.

The Torah, The Law or "Books of Moses"

Genesis (50 Chapters)
Exodus (40 Chapters)
Leviticus (27 Chapters)
Numbers (36 Chapters)
Deuteronomy (34 Chapters)

Historical books

Joshua (24 Chapters)
Judges (21 Chapters)
Ruth (4 chapters)
1 Samuel (31 Chapters)
2 Samuel (24 Chapters)
1 Kings (22 Chapters)
2 Kings (25 Chapters)
1 Chronicles (29 Chapters)
2 Chronicles (36 Chapters)
Ezra (10 Chapters)
Nehemiah (13 Chapters)
Esther (10 Chapters)

Poetry & Wisdom books

Job (42 Chapters)
Psalms (150 Chapters)
Proverbs (31 Chapters)
Ecclesiastes (12 Chapters)
Song of Solomon (8 Chapters)

Major prophets

Isaiah (66 Chapters)
Jeremiah (52 Chapters)
Lamentations (5 Chapters)
Ezekiel (48 Chapters)
Daniel (12 Chapters)

Minor prophets

Hosea (14 Chapters)
Joel (3 Chapters)
Amos (9 Chapters)
Obadiah (1 Chapter)
Jonah (4 Chapters)
Micah (7 Chapters)
Nahum (3 Chapters)
Habakkuk (3 Chapters)
Zephaniah (3 Chapters)
Haggai (2 Chapters)
Zechariah (14 Chapters)
Malachi (4 Chapters)

Apocryphal/Deuterocanonical Books

The Apocryphal/Deuterocanonical books form part of the ancient Greek translation of the Old Testament known as the Septuagint. They. were located at various places- among the other books of the Old Testament. They cover the period in between-the Old 'Testament and New Testament and provide significant knowledge of developments during this period.
In order to serve the widest readership, the IEB includes several books that have been part of the 3 ancient Greek Septuagint (3 and D Maccabees and Psalm 151), but have never been recognized as Deuterocanonical by Roman Catholics nor considered part of the Apocrypha by Protestants These works, however, have been recognized as authoritative in Eastern Orthodox Churches.

History

1 Esdras
Additions to Esther
1 Maccabees
2 Maccabees
3 Maccabees
4 Maccabees

Letters

Baruch
Letter of Jeremiah

Wisdom

Wisdom of Solomon
Sirach

Devotional

Prayer of Azariah/ Song of Three Jews
Prayer of Manasseh
Psalm 151

Teaching Stories

Tobit
Judith
Susanna
Bel and the Dragon

Prophecy

2 Esdras

New Testament

The books of the New Testament were written by the followers of Jesus Christ. These followers wanted others to know the Good News about Jesus Christ and the possibility of a "new" life available to them through his death and resurrection. The following shows the different groups of books that make up the New Testament. Although scholarly opinion has varied, Paul has traditionally been identified as the author of the letters indicated below.

The Gospels

Matthew
Mark
Luke
John

History

Acts

Paul's Letters

Romans
1 Corinthians
2 Corinthians
Galatians
Ephesians
Philippians
Colossians
1 Thessalonians
2 Thessalonians
1 Timothy
2 Timothy
Titus
Philemon

General Letters

Hebrews
James
1 Peter
2 Peter
1 John
2 John
3 John
Jude

Prophecy

Revelation

'Our Father in heaven,
may your name be kept holy.
Let your Kingdom come.
Let your will be done on earth as it is in heaven.
Give us today our daily bread.
Forgive us our debts,
as we also forgive our debtors.
Bring us not into temptation,
but deliver us from the evil one.
For yours is the Kingdom, the power,
and the glory forever.
Amen.'

Behold, I stand at the door and knock. If anyone hears my voice and opens the door, then I will come in to him, and will dine with him, and he with me. **Revelation 3:20**

The grace of our Lord Jesus Christ *be* with you all. Amen.

Made in the USA
Middletown, DE
18 July 2025